ALL-NEW LAROUSSE FRENCH-ENGLISH ENGLISH-FRENCH DICTIONARY

DICTIONNAIRE LAROUSSE FRANÇAIS-ANGLAIS ANGLAIS-FRANÇAIS

POCKET BOOKS

New York   London   Toronto   Sydney

This POCKET BOOKS edition may not be sold in Spanish-speaking countries except by Larousse

 POCKET BOOKS, a division of Simon & Schuster, Inc.
1230 Avenue of the Americas, New York, NY 10020

Copyright © 1996 by Larousse

ISBN-13: 978-0-671-53407-3
ISBN-10:   0-671-53407-6
ISBN-13: 978-0-671-00277-0 (Canadian edition)
ISBN-10:   0-671-00277-5 (Canadian edition)

First Pocket Books printing of this revised edition June 1996

50 49 48 47 46 45 44 43

POCKET and colophon are registered trademarks of
Simon & Schuster, Inc.

Manufactured in the United States of America

For information regarding special discounts for bulk purchases, please
contact Simon & Schuster Special Sales at 1-800-456-6798
or business@simonandschuster.com

PREFACE

LAROUSSE'S FRENCH-ENGLISH ENGLISH-FRENCH DICTIONARY is the natural choice for tourists, students, teachers, business people and all those interested in modern languages.

Over 50,000 vocabulary entries provide a rich source of translations, and a wealth of illustrative examples and idiomatic expressions explain and contextualize difficult phrases. Americanisms and Anglicisms are clearly distinguished. A strong selection of neologisms and colloquialisms enrich the standard vocabulary, and the text features a large number of important and useful abbreviations. Clear typography allows the reader to distinguish headwords, compounds and other derivatives quickly and easily, and the careful use of indicators in square brackets helps to pinpoint exact meanings and contexts, steering the user clear of many of the common pitfalls in translation. Accurate pronunciation is assured through use of the International Phonetic Alphabet throughout.

Supplementary to the main text are verb tables and practical guides to expressing numbers and dates and telling the time. Combined with the above features, they make this dictionary an essential reference work at home or in the office, in schools and colleges, and while traveling abroad on holiday or on business.

PRÉFACE

LE DICTIONNAIRE LAROUSSE FRANÇAIS-ANGLAIS ANGLAIS-FRANÇAIS s'impose tout naturellement comme le compagnon idéal du touriste aussi bien que de l'enseignant, de l'homme d'affaires comme de l'élève ou de l'étudiant.

Tous ceux qui s'intéressent aux langues vivantes y trouveront en effet plus de 50 000 mots et expressions, assortis d'une foule d'exemples et de tournures idiomatiques, qui les guideront vers la traduction appropriée tout en illustrant et éclairant les points les plus délicats. Les variantes américaine et britannique de l'anglais sont signalées sans risque de confusion, et le vocabulaire de base s'enrichit de nombreux néologismes, exemples de langue parlée et abréviations. Grâce à une typographie claire, l'utilisateur distinguera rapidement et aisément les libellés de leurs dérivés - mots composés notamment. Le choix minutieux des indicateurs entre crochets répond au même souci d'efficacité : en délimitant aussi précisément que possible le sens ou contexte désiré, ils permettront d'éviter les pièges classiques de la traduction. La prononciation pouvant elle aussi se révéler problématique, nous avons eu recours tout au long de cet ouvrage à la transcription en alphabet phonétique international. Et, pour être tout à fait complets, nous avons ajouté au corps du texte des tableaux de conjugaison ainsi qu'un guide d'usage portant sur les chiffres, les dates et l'heure.

Au bureau ou chez soi, en contexte scolaire, en vacances ou en voyage d'affaires, toutes ces particularités font de cet ouvrage un outil linguistique indispensable.

ABBREVIATIONS _____ ABRÉVIATIONS

abbreviation	*abbr/abr*	abréviation
adjective	*adj*	adjectif
administration, administrative	ADMIN	administration
adverb	*adv*	adverbe
aeronautics, aviation	AERON/AÉRON	aéronautique
agriculture, farming	AGR(IC)	agriculture
American English	*Am*	anglais américain
anatomy	ANAT	anatomie
archaeology	ARCHAEOL/ ARCHÉOL	archéologie
architecture	ARCHIT	architecture
slang	*arg*	argot
article	*art*	article
astrology	ASTROL	astrologie
astronomy	ASTRON	astronomie
automobile, cars	AUT(OM)	automobile
auxiliary	*aux*	auxiliaire
before noun	*avant n*	avant le nom
Belgian French	*Belg*	belgicisme
biology	BIOL	biologie
botany	BOT	botanique
British English	*Br*	anglais britannique
Canadian English/French	*Can*	canadianisme
chemistry	CHEM/CHIM	chimie
cinema, film-making	CIN(EMA)	cinéma
commerce, business	COMM	commerce
compound	*comp*	nom anglais utilisé en apposition
comparative	*compar*	comparatif
computers, computer science	COMPUT	informatique
conjunction	*conj*	conjonction
construction, building trade	CONSTR	construction, bâtiment
continuous	*cont*	progressif
sewing	COUT	couture
culinary, cooking	CULIN	cuisine, art culinaire
definite	*def/déf*	défini
demonstrative	*dem/dém*	démonstratif
ecology	ÉCOL	écologie
economics	ECON/ÉCON	économie
electricity	ELEC/ÉLECTR	électricité
electronics	ELECTRON/ ÉLECTRON	électronique
especially	*esp*	particulièrement
exclamation	*excl*	interjection
feminine	*f*	féminin
informal	*fam*	familier
figurative	*fig*	figuré
finance, financial	FIN	finances
formal	*fml*	soutenu
soccer	FTBL	football

inseparable	*fus*	non séparable
generally, in most cases	*gen/gén*	généralement
geography, geographical	GEOGR/GÉOGR	géographie
geology, geological	GEOL/GÉOL	géologie
geometry	GEOM/GÉOM	géométrie
grammar	GRAM(M)	grammaire
Swiss French	*Helv*	helvétisme
history	HIST	histoire
humorous	*hum*	humoristique
industry	IND	industrie
indefinite	*indef/indéf*	indéfini
informal	*inf*	familier
infinitive	*infin*	infinitif
computers, computer science	INFORM	informatique
exclamation	*interj*	interjection
interrogative	*interr*	interrogatif
invariable	*inv*	invariable
ironic	*iro/iron*	ironique
juridical, legal	JUR	juridique
linguistics	LING	linguistique
literal	*lit/litt*	littéral
phrase(s)	*loc*	locution(s)
adjectival phrase	*loc adj*	locution adjectivale
adverbial phrase	*loc adv*	locution adverbiale
conjunctival phrase	*loc conj*	locution conjonctive
prepositional phrase	*loc prép*	locution prépositionnelle
masculine	*m*	masculin
mathematics	MATH(S)	mathématiques
medicine	MED/MÉD	médecine
weather, meteorology	METEOR/ MÉTÉOR	météorologie
military	MIL	domaine militaire
music	MUS	musique
mythology	MYTH	mythologie
noun	*n*	nom
nautical, maritime	NAUT/NAVIG	navigation
numeral	*num*	numéral
oneself	*o.s.*	
pejorative	*pej/péj*	péjoratif
personal	*pers*	personnel
pharmacology, pharmaceutics	PHARM	pharmacologie, pharmacie
philosophy	PHILO	philosophie
photography	PHOT	photographie
phrase(s)	*phr*	locution(s)
physics	PHYS	physique
plural	*pl*	pluriel
politics	POL(IT)	politique
possessive	*poss*	possessif
past participle	*pp*	participe passé
present participle	*ppr*	participe présent

preposition	prep/prép	préposition
pronoun	pron	pronom
psychology, psychiatry	PSYCH(OL)	psychologie, psychiatrie
past tense	pt	passé
	qqch	quelque chose
	qqn	quelqu'un
registered trademark	®	nom déposé
railways	RAIL	rail
relative	rel	relatif
religion	RELIG	religion
someone, somebody	sb	
school	SCH/SCOL	scolarité
Scottish English	Scot	anglais écossais
separable	sep	séparable
singular	sg	singulier
slang	sl	argot
sociology	SOCIOL	sociologie
formal	sout	soutenu
stock exchange	ST EX	Bourse
something	sthg	
subject	subj/suj	sujet
superlative	superl	superlatif
technology, technical	TECH(NOL)	domaine technique et technologique
telecommunications	TELEC/TÉLÉCOM	télécommunications
very informal	tfam	très familier
television	TV/TÉLÉ	télévision
printing, typography	TYPO	typographie
uncountable noun	U	substantif non comptable
university	UNIV	université
usually	usu	habituellement
link verb followed by a predicative adjective or noun	v attr	verbe suivi d'un attribut
verb	vb/v	verbe
veterinary science	VETER	médecine vétérinaire
intransitive verb	vi	verbe intransitif
impersonal verb	v impers	verbe impersonnel
very informal	v inf	très familier
pronominal verb	vp	verbe pronominal
transitive verb	vt	verbe transitif
vulgar	vulg	vulgaire
zoology	ZOOL	zoologie
cultural equivalent	≃	équivalence culturelle
indicates a new sense division	‖	indique une nouvelle catégorie sémantique
introduces a sub-entry, such as a plural form with its own specific meaning or a set phrase containing the headword (e.g. a phrasal or adverbial phrase)	○	introduit une sous-entrée, par exemple une forme plurielle ayant un sens propre, ou une locution (locution adverbiale, verbe verbe pronominal, etc.)

PHONETIC TRANSCRIPTION _____ TRANSCRIPTION PHONÉTIQUE

English Vowels

[ɪ]	pit, big, rid
[e]	pet, tend
[æ]	pat, bag, mad
[ʌ]	putt, cut
[ɒ]	pot, log
[ʊ]	put, full
[ə]	mother, suppose
[i:]	bean, weed
[ɑ:]	barn, car, laugh
[ɔ:]	born, lawn
[u:]	loop, loose
[ɜ:]	burn, learn, bird

Voyelles françaises

[i]	fille, île
[e]	pays, année
[ɛ]	bec, aime
[a]	lac, papillon
[ɑ]	tas, âme
[o]	drôle, aube
[ɔ]	hotte
[u]	outil, goût
[y]	usage, lune
[ø]	aveu, jeu
[œ]	peuple, bœuf
[ə]	le, je

English Diphthongs

[eɪ]	bay, late, great
[aɪ]	buy, light, aisle
[ɔɪ]	boy, foil
[əʊ]	no, road, blow
[aʊ]	now, shout, town
[ɪə]	peer, fierce, idea
[eə]	pair, bear, share
[ʊə]	poor, sure, tour

Nasales françaises

[ɛ̃]	limbe, main
[ɑ̃]	champ, ennui
[ɔ̃]	ongle, mon
[œ̃]	parfum, brun

Semi-vowels

you, spaniel	[j]	yeux, lieu
wet, why, twin	[w]	ouest, oui
	[ɥ]	lui, nuit

Semi-voyelles

Consonants / Consonnes

pop, people	[p]	prendre, grippe
bottle, bib	[b]	bateau, rosbif
train, tip	[t]	théâtre, temps
dog, did	[d]	dalle, ronde
come, kitchen	[k]	coq, quatre
gag, great	[g]	garder, épilogue
chain, wretched	[tʃ]	
jig, fridge	[dʒ]	
fib, physical	[f]	physique, fort
vine, livid	[v]	voir, rive
think, fifth	[θ]	
this, with	[ð]	
seal, peace	[s]	cela, savant
zip, his	[z]	fraise, zéro
sheep, machine	[ʃ]	charrue, schéma
usual, measure	[ʒ]	rouge, jabot
how, perhaps	[h]	
metal, comb	[m]	mât, drame
night, dinner	[n]	nager, trône
sung, parking	[ŋ]	

	[ɲ]	**agn**eau, **peigner**
little, he**l**p	[l]	**halle**, **lit**
right, ca**rr**y	[r]	**arracher**, sab**re**
lo**ch**	[x]	

Represents French "h aspiré", e.g. **hachis** ['aʃi].   [']   Représente le "h aspiré" français, p. ex. **hachis** ['aʃi]

Indicates that the following syllable carries primary stress.   [ˈ]   Indique un accent primaire sur la syllabe suivante.

Indicates that the following syllable carries secondary stress.   [ˌ]   Indique un accent secondaire sur la syllabe suivante.

Indicates that the final "r" is pronounced only when followed by a word beginning with a vowel; nearly always pronounced in American English.   [ʳ]   Indique que le "r" final d'un mot anglais ne se prononce que lorsqu'il forme une liaison avec la voyelle du mot suivant; presque toujours prononcé en anglais américain.

TRADEMARKS

Words considered to be trademarks have been designated in this dictionary by the symbol ®. However, neither the presence nor the absence of such designation should be regarded as affecting the legal status of any trademark.

NOMS DE MARQUE

Les noms de marque sont désignés dans ce dictionnaire par le symbole ®. Néanmoins, ni ce symbole ni son absence éventuelle ne peuvent être considérés comme susceptibles d'avoir une incidence quelconque sur le statut légal d'une marque.

CONJUGAISONS

Légende: *ppr* = participe présent, *pp* = participe passé, *pr ind* = présent de l'indicatif, *imp* = imparfait, *fut* = futur, *cond* = conditionnel, *pr subj* = présent du subjonctif

acquérir: *pp* acquis, *pr ind* acquiers, acquérons, acquièrent, *imp* acquérais, *fut* acquerrai, *pr subj* acquière

aller: *pp* allé, *pr ind* vais, vas, va, allons, allez, vont, *imp* allais, *fut* irai, *cond* irais, *pr subj* aille

asseoir: *ppr* asseyant, *pp* assis, *pr ind* assieds, asseyons, *imp* asseyais, *fut* assiérai, *pr subj* asseye

atteindre: *ppr* atteignant, *pp* atteint, *pr ind* atteins, atteignons, *imp* atteignais, *pr subj* atteigne

avoir: *ppr* ayant, *pp* eu, *pr ind* ai, as, a, avons, avez, ont, *imp* avais, *fut* aurai, *cond* aurais, *pr subj* aie, aies, ait, ayons, ayez, aient

boire: *ppr* buvant, *pp* bu, *pr ind* bois, buvons, boivent, *imp* buvais, *pr subj* boive

conduire: *ppr* conduisant, *pp* conduit, *pr ind* conduis, conduisons, *imp* conduisais, *pr subj* conduise

connaître: *ppr* connaissant, *pp* connu, *pr ind* connais, connaît, connaissons, *imp* connaissais, *pr subj* connaisse

coudre: *ppr* cousant, *pp* cousu, *pr ind* couds, cousons, *imp* cousais, *pr subj* couse

courir: *pp* couru, *pr ind* cours, courons, *imp* courais, *fut* courrai, *pr subj* coure

couvrir: *pp* couvert, *pr ind* couvre, couvrons, *imp* couvrais, *pr subj* couvre

craindre: *ppr* craignant, *pp* craint, *pr ind* crains, craignons, *imp* craignais, *pr subj* craigne

croire: *ppr* croyant, *pp* cru, *pr ind* crois, croyons, croient, *imp* croyais, *pr subj* croie

cueillir: *pp* cueilli, *pr ind* cueille, cueillons, *imp* cueillais, *fut* cueillerai, *pr subj* cueille

devoir: *pp* dû, due, *pr ind* dois, devons, doivent, *imp* devais, *fut* devrai, *pr subj* doive

dire: *ppr* disant, *pp* dit, *pr ind* dis, disons, dites, disent, *imp* disais, *pr subj* dise

dormir: *pp* dormi, *pr ind* dors, dormons, *imp* dormais, *pr subj* dorme

écrire: *ppr* écrivant, *pp* écrit, *pr ind* écris, écrivons, *imp* écrivais, *pr subj* écrive

essuyer: *pp* essuyé, *pr ind* essuie, essuyons, essuient, *imp* essuyais, *fut* essuierai, *pr subj* essuie

être: *ppr* étant, *pp* été, *pr ind* suis, es, est, sommes, êtes, sont, *imp* étais, *fut* serai, *cond* serais, *pr subj* sois, sois, soit, soyons, soyez, soient

faire: *ppr* faisant, *pp* fait, *pr ind* fais, fais, fait, faisons, faites, font, *imp* faisais, *fut* ferai, *cond* ferais, *pr subj* fasse

falloir: *pp* fallu, *pr ind* faut, *imp* fallait, *fut* faudra, *pr subj* faille

FINIR: *ppr* finissant, *pp* fini, *pr ind* finis, finis, finit, finissons, finissez, finissent, *imp* finissais, finissais, finissait, finissions, finissiez, finissaient, *fut* finirai, finiras, finira, finirons, finirez, finiront, *cond* finirais, finirais, finirait, finirions, finiriez, finiraient, *pr subj* finisse, finisses, **finisse, finissions,** finissiez, finissent

fuir: *ppr* fuyant, *pp* fui, *pr ind* fuis, fuyons, fuient, *imp* fuyais, *pr subj* **fuie**

haïr: *ppr* haïssant, *pp* haï, *pr ind* hais, haïssons, *imp* haïssais, *pr subj* haïsse

joindre: *comme* **atteindre**

lire: *ppr* lisant, *pp* lu, *pr ind* lis, lisons, *imp* lisais, *pr subj* lise

mentir: *pp* menti, *pr ind* mens, mentons, *imp* mentais, *pr subj* mente

mettre: *ppr* mettant, *pp* mis, *pr ind* mets, mettons, *imp* mettais, *pr subj* mette

mourir: *pp* mort, *pr ind* meurs, mourons, meurent, *imp* mourais, *fut* mourrai, *pr subj* meure

naître: *ppr* naissant, *pp* né, *pr ind* nais, naît, naissons, *imp* naissais, *pr subj* naisse

offrir: *pp* offert, *pr ind* offre, offrons, *imp* offrais, *pr subj* offre

paraître: *comme* **connaître**

PARLER: *ppr* parlant, *pp* parlé, *pr ind* parle, parles, parle, parlons, parlez, parlent, *imp* parlais, parlais, parlait, parlions, parliez, **parlaient,** *fut* parlerai, parleras, parlera, parlerons, parlerez, parleront, *cond* parlerais, parlerais, parlerait, parlerions, parleriez, parleraient, *pr subj* parle, **parles,** parle, parlions, parliez, parlent

partir: *pp* parti, *pr ind* pars, partons, *imp* partais, *pr subj* parte

plaire: *ppr* plaisant, *pp* plu, *pr ind* plais, plaît, plaisons, *imp* plaisais, *pr subj* plaise

pleuvoir: *pp* plu, *pr ind* pleut, *imp* pleuvait, *fut* pleuvra, *pr subj* pleuve

pouvoir: *pp* pu, *pr ind* peux, peux, peut, pouvons, pouvez, peuvent, *imp* pouvais, *fut* pourrai, *pr subj* puisse

prendre: *ppr* prenant, *pp* pris, *pr ind* prends, prenons, prennent, *imp* prenais, *pr subj* prenne

prévoir: *ppr* prévoyant, *pp* prévu, *pr ind* prévois, prévoyons, prévoient, *imp* prévoyais, *fut* prévoirai, *pr subj* prévoie

recevoir: *pp* reçu, *pr ind* reçois, recevons, reçoivent, *imp* recevais, *fut* recevrai, *pr subj* reçoive

RENDRE: *ppr* rendant, *pp* rendu, *pr ind* rends, rends, rend, rendons, rendez, rendent, *imp* rendais, rendais, rendait, rendions, rendiez, rendaient, *fut* rendrai, rendras, rendra, rendrons, rendrez, rendront, *cond* rendrais, rendrais, rendrait, rendrions, rendriez, rendraient, *pr subj* rende, **rendes,** rende, rendions, rendiez, rendent

résoudre: *ppr* résolvant, *pp* résolu, *pr ind* résous, résolvons, *imp* résolvais, *pr subj* résolve

rire: *ppr* riant, *pp* ri, *pr ind* ris, rions, *imp* riais, *pr subj* rie

savoir: *ppr* sachant, *pp* su, *pr ind* sais, savons, *imp* savais, *fut* saurai, *pr subj* sache

servir: *pp* servi, *pr ind* sers, servons, *imp* servais, *pr subj* serve

sortir: *comme* **partir**

suffire: *ppr* suffisant, *pp* suffi, *pr ind* suffis, suffisons, *imp* suffisais, *pr subj* suffise

suivre: *ppr* suivant, *pp* suivi, *pr ind* suis, suivons, *imp* suivais, *pr subj* suive

taire: *ppr* taisant, *pp* tu, *pr ind* tais, taisons, *imp* taisais, *pr subj* taise

tenir: *pp* tenu, *pr ind* tiens, tenons, tiennent, *imp* tenais, *fut* tiendrai, *pr subj* tienne

vaincre: *ppr* vainquant, *pp* vaincu, *pr ind* vaincs, vainc, vainquons, *imp* vainquais, *pr subj* vainque

valoir: *pp* valu, *pr ind* vaux, valons, *imp* valais, *fut* vaudrai, *pr subj* vaille

venir: *comme* **tenir**

vivre: *ppr* vivant, *pp* vécu, *pr ind* vis, vivons, *imp* vivais, *pr subj* vive

voir: *ppr* voyant, *pp* vu, *pr ind* vois, voyons, voient, *imp* voyais, *fut* verrai, *pr subj* voie

vouloir: *pp* voulu, *pr ind* veux, veux, veut, voulons, voulez, veulent, *imp* voulais, *fut* voudrai, *pr subj* veuille

NUMBERS

Cardinal numbers are used for counting. The most important ones are:

0 zéro	16 seize	80 quatre-vingts
1 un (ƒ une)	17 dix-sept	81 quatre-vingt-un (ƒ une)
2 deux	18 dix-huit	82 quatre-vingt-deux
3 trois	19 dix-neuf	90 quatre-vingt-dix
4 quatre	20 vingt	91 quatre-vingt-onze
5 cinq	21 vingt et un (ƒ une)	92 quatre-vingt-douze
6 six	22 vingt-deux	93 quatre-vingt-treize
7 sept	23 vingt-trois	100 cent
8 huit	30 trente	101 cent un (ƒ une)
9 neuf	40 quarante	102 cent deux
10 dix	50 cinquante	110 cent dix
11 onze	60 soixante	120 cent vingt
12 douze	70 soixante-dix	121 cent vingt et un (ƒ une)
13 treize	71 soixante et onze	200 deux cents
14 quatorze	72 soixante-douze	300 trois cents
15 quinze	73 soixante-treize	900 neuf cents

1 000 mille	2 000 deux mille
1 001 mille un (ƒ une)	3 000 trois mille
1 002 mille deux	1 000 000 un million
1 100 mille cent, onze cents	2 000 000 deux millions
1 200 mille deux cents, douze cents	1 000 000 000 un milliard
1 900 mille neuf cents, dix-neuf cents	

NOTES:

– **mille** never adds an -s in the plural.

– **quatre-vingt** takes an -s when it comes at the end of a number: **quatre-vingts**, **deux cent quatre-vingts**. Cent also adds an -s if it refers to two hundred or more and comes at the end of a number: **cinq cents**, **trois mille sept cents**. However, when **cent** and **vingt** do not come at the end of the number, they do not take -s in the plural: **trois cent vingt-cinq**, **quatre-vingt-huit**.

– both **million** and **milliard** are always followed by **de** if they are used with another noun. Unlike their English equivalents, they also add an -s when they are preceded by a plural number: **deux millions de chômeurs**, **trois milliards de francs**.

Ordinal numbers (first, second, third etc.) are used for putting things in order. They are formed by adding **-ième** to the end of the cardinal number, e.g. **deuxième**, **dixième**. If the cardinal number ends in **-e**, this is dropped, e.g. **onzième**, **seizième**. There are minor spelling changes with **cinq** and **neuf**: **cinquième**, **neuvième**. The French for first is **premier** (ƒ **première**). Twenty-first, thirty-first etc. are translated as **vingt et unième**, **trente et unième** etc.

Contrary to English, French uses a comma to mark the decimal part of a number: **6,5** (**six virgule cinq** = six point five); **8,34** (**huit virgule trente-quatre** = eight point three four). Numbers of four digits and above (**2 000**, **10 321**) are normally written with a space before the last three digits.

For more information on numbers, look at the entries for **six** and **sixième** on the French-English side of your dictionary, and at **six** and **sixth** on the English-French side.

DATES

The most usual ways of asking the date are: **quelle date sommes nous?** or **quelle est la date aujourd'hui?** The reply will normally start with **c'est ...** or **nous sommes ...**

Remember that the cardinal numbers are used in dates in French: **le dix janvier**, **le vingt-cinq février**, **le premier septembre**.

To say the year in French: 1995 can be pronounced as either mille neuf cent quatre-vingt-cinq or dix-neuf cent quatre-vingt-cinq.

The days of the week are:

Monday	**lundi**
Tuesday	**mardi**
Wednesday	**mercredi**
Thursday	**jeudi**
Friday	**vendredi**
Saturday	**samedi**
Sunday	**dimanche**

The months of the year are:

January	**janvier**
February	**février**
March	**mars**
April	**avril**
May	**mai**
June	**juin**
July	**juillet**
August	**août**
September	**septembre**
October	**octobre**
November	**novembre**
December	**décembre**

Note that the days of the week and the months of the year start with a small letter in French.

For more information on days and months, look at the entries for **samedi** and **septembre** on the French-English side of your dictionary, and at **Saturday** and **September** on the English-French side.

ENGLISH IRREGULAR VERBS

Infinitive	Past Tense	Past Participle	Infinitive	Past Tense	Past Participle
arise	arose	arisen	fly	flew	flown
awake	awoke	awoken	forget	forgot	forgotten
be	was, were	been	forsake	forsook	forsaken
bear	bore	born(e)	freeze	froze	frozen
beat	beat	beaten	get	got	got (*Am* gotten)
befall	befell	befallen	give	gave	given
begin	began	begun	go	went	gone
behold	beheld	beheld	grind	ground	ground
bend	bent	bent	grow	grew	grown
beseech	besought	besought	hang	hung	hung
beset	beset	beset		(hanged)	(hanged)
bet	bet (betted)	bet (betted)	have	had	had
bid	bid (bade)	bid (bidden)	hear	heard	heard
bind	bound	bound	hide	hid	hidden
bite	bit	bitten	hit	hit	hit
bleed	bled	bled	hold	held	held
blow	blew	blown	hurt	hurt	hurt
break	broke	broken	keep	kept	kept
breed	bred	bred	kneel	knelt	knelt
bring	brought	brought		(kneeled)	(kneeled)
build	built	built	know	knew	known
burn	burnt	burnt	lay	laid	laid
	(burned)	(burned)	lead	led	led
burst	burst	burst	lean	leant	leant
buy	bought	bought		(leaned)	(leaned)
can	could	–	leap	leapt	leapt
cast	cast	cast		(leaped)	(leaped)
catch	caught	caught	learn	learnt	learnt
choose	chose	chosen		(learned)	(learned)
cling	clung	clung	leave	left	left
come	came	come	lend	lent	lent
cost	cost	cost	let	let	let
creep	crept	crept	lie	lay	lain
cut	cut	cut	light	lit	lit
deal	dealt	dealt		(lighted)	(lighted)
dig	dug	dug	lose	lost	lost
do	did	done	make	made	made
draw	drew	drawn	may	might	–
dream	dreamed	dreamed	mean	meant	meant
	(dreamt)	(dreamt)	meet	met	met
drink	drank	drunk	mow	mowed	mown
drive	drove	driven			(mowed)
dwell	dwelt	dwelt	pay	paid	paid
eat	ate	eaten	put	put	put
fall	fell	fallen	quit	quit	quit
feed	fed	fed		(quitted)	(quitted)
feel	felt	felt	read	read	read
fight	fought	fought	rend	rent	rent
find	found	found	rid	rid	rid
flee	fled	fled	ride	rode	ridden
fling	flung	flung	ring	rang	rung

INFINITIVE	PAST TENSE	PAST PARTICIPLE	INFINITIVE	PAST TENSE	PAST PARTICIPLE
rise	rose	risen	**spit**	spat	spat
run	ran	run	**split**	split	split
saw	sawed	sawn	**spoil**	spoiled	spoiled
say	said	said		(spoilt)	(spoilt)
see	saw	seen	**spread**	spread	spread
seek	sought	sought	**spring**	sprang	sprung
sell	sold	sold	**stand**	stood	stood
send	sent	sent	**steal**	stole	stolen
set	set	set	**stick**	stuck	stuck
shake	shook	shaken	**sting**	stung	stung
shall	should	–	**stink**	stank	stunk
shear	sheared	shorn	**stride**	strode	stridden
		(sheared)	**strike**	struck	struck
shed	shed	shed			(stricken)
shine	shone	shone	**strive**	strove	striven
shoot	shot	shot	**swear**	swore	sworn
show	showed	shown	**sweep**	swept	swept
shrink	shrank	shrunk	**swell**	swelled	swollen
shut	shut	shut			(swelled)
sing	sang	sung	**swim**	swam	swum
sink	sank	sunk	**swing**	swung	swung
sit	sat	sat	**take**	took	taken
slay	slew	slain	**teach**	taught	taught
sleep	slept	slept	**tear**	tore	torn
slide	slid	slid	**tell**	told	told
sling	slung	slung	**think**	thought	thought
slit	slit	slit	**throw**	threw	thrown
smell	smelt	smelt	**thrust**	thrust	thrust
	(smelled)	(smelled)	**tread**	trod	trodden
sow	sowed	sown	**wake**	woke	woken
		(sowed)		(waked)	(waked)
speak	spoke	spoken	**wear**	wore	worn
speed	sped	sped	**weave**	wove	woven
	(speeded)	(speeded)		(weaved)	(weaved)
spell	spelt	spelt	**wed**	wedded	wedded
	(spelled)	(spelled)	**weep**	wept	wept
spend	spent	spent	**win**	won	won
spill	spilt	spilt	**wind**	wound	wound
	(spilled)	(spilled)	**wring**	wrung	wrung
spin	spun	spun	**write**	wrote	written

THE TIME

The most usual way of asking the time is: **quelle heure est-il?** Here are some possible answers:

il est cinq heures (du matin/du soir)

il est cinq heures cinq

il est cinq heures et quart

il est cinq heures et demie

il est six heures moins vingt-cinq

il est six heures moins le quart

il est midi (= midday)/**il est minuit** (= midnight)

In French you may find times expressed using the twenty-four hour clock: a train departing at **dix-huit heures**, for example, would leave at six o'clock in the evening.

FRANÇAIS–ANGLAIS
FRENCH–ENGLISH

a¹, A [a] *nm inv* a, A; **de A à Z** from beginning to end. ○ **A** (*abr de* **ampère**) A, amp. ‖ (*abr de* **autoroute**) M.

a² → **avoir**.

à [a] *prép (contraction de à + le =* **au**, *contraction de à + les =* **aux**) [introduisant un complément d'objet indirect] to; **donner qqch à qqn** to give sthg to sb, to give sb sthg. ‖ [introduisant un complément de lieu - situation] at, in; [- direction] to; **être à la maison/au bureau** to be at home/at the office; **il habite à Paris/à la campagne** he lives in Paris/in the country; **aller à Paris/à la campagne/au Pérou** to go to Paris/to the country/to Peru. ‖ [introduisant un complément de temps]: **à onze heures** at eleven o'clock; **au mois de février** in the month of February. ‖ [introduisant un complément de manière, de moyen]: **à haute voix** out loud, aloud; **rire aux éclats** to roar with laughter; **à pied/cheval** on foot/horseback. ‖ [indiquant une caractéristique] with; **une fille aux cheveux longs** a girl with long hair. ‖ [introduisant un chiffre]: **ils sont venus à dix** ten of them came; **un livre à 30 francs** a 30-franc book, a book costing 30 francs; **deux à deux** two by two. ‖ [marque l'appartenance]: **c'est à moi/toi/lui/elle** it's mine/yours/his/hers; **ce vélo est à ma sœur** this bike is my sister's OU belongs to my sister; **une amie à moi** a friend of mine. ‖ [introduit le but]: **coupe à champagne** champagne goblet; **appartement à vendre/louer** flat for sale/to let.

AB (*abr de* **assez bien**) fair grade (as assessment of schoolwork).

abaisser [abese] *vt* [rideau, voile] to lower; [levier, manette] to push OU pull down. ‖ [diminuer] to reduce, to lower. ○ **s'abaisser** *vp* [descendre - rideau] to fall, to come down; [- terrain] to fall away. ‖ [s'humilier] to demean o.s.; **s'~ à faire qqch** to lower o.s. to do sthg.

abandon [abãdɔ̃] *nm* [désertion, délaissement] desertion; **à l'~** [jardin, maison] neglected, in a state of neglect. ‖ [renonciation] abandoning, giving up. ‖ [nonchalance, confiance] abandon.

abandonner [abãdɔne] *vt* [quitter - femme, enfants] to abandon, to desert; [- voiture, propriété] to abandon. ‖ [renoncer à] to give up, to abandon. ‖ [se retirer de - course, concours] to withdraw from. ‖ [céder]: **~ qqch à qqn** to leave sthg to sb, to leave sb sthg.

abasourdi, -e [abazurdi] *adj* stunned.

abat-jour [abaʒur] *nm inv* lampshade.

abats [aba] *nmpl* [d'animal] offal (*U*); [de volaille] giblets.

abattement [abatmã] *nm* [faiblesse physique] weakness. ‖ [désespoir] dejection. ‖ [déduction] reduction; **~ fiscal** tax allowance.

abattis [abati] *nmpl* giblets.

abattoir [abatwar] *nm* abattoir, slaughterhouse.

abattre [abatr] *vt* [faire tomber - mur] to knock down; [- arbre] to cut down, to fell; [- avion] to bring down. ‖ [tuer - gén] to kill; [- dans un abattoir] to slaughter. ‖ [épuiser] to wear out; [démoraliser] to demoralize.

abbaye [abei] *nf* abbey.

abbé [abe] *nm* [prêtre] priest.

abc *nm* basics (*pl*).

abcès [apsɛ] *nm* abscess.

abdiquer [abdike] *vi* [roi] to abdicate.

abdomen [abdɔmɛn] *nm* abdomen.

abdominaux [abdɔmino] *nmpl* [muscles] abdominal or stomach muscles. || [exercices]: **faire des abdominaux** to do exercises for the stomach muscles.

abeille [abɛj] *nf* bee.

aberrant, -e [abɛʀɑ̃, ɑ̃t] *adj* absurd.

abîme [abim] *nm* abyss, gulf.

abîmer [abime] *vt* [détériorer - objet] to damage; [- partie du corps, vue] to ruin. ○ **s'abîmer** *vp* [gén] to be damaged; [- fruits] to go bad.

abject, -e [abʒɛkt] *adj* despicable, contemptible.

aboiement [abwamɑ̃] *nm* bark, barking (*U*).

abolir [abɔliʀ] *vt* to abolish.

abominable [abɔminabl] *adj* appalling, awful.

abondance [abɔ̃dɑ̃s] *nf* [profusion] abundance. || [opulence] affluence.

abondant, -e [abɔ̃dɑ̃, ɑ̃t] *adj* [gén] plentiful; [végétation, chevelure] luxuriant; [pluie] heavy.

abonder [abɔ̃de] *vi* to abound, to be abundant; ~ **en qqch** to be rich in sthg; ~ **dans le sens de qqn** to be entirely of sb's opinion.

abonné, -e [abɔne] *nm, f* [à un journal, à une chaîne de télé] subscriber; [à un théâtre] season-ticket holder. || [à un service public] consumer.

abonnement [abɔnmɑ̃] *nm* [à un journal, à une chaîne de télé] subscription; [à un théâtre] season ticket. || [au téléphone] rental; [au gaz, à l'électricité] standing charge.

abonner [abɔne] ○ **s'abonner** *vp*: **s'~ à qqch** [journal, chaîne de télé] to take out a subscription to sthg; [service public] to get connected to sthg; [théâtre] to buy a season ticket for sthg.

abord [abɔʀ] *nm*: **être d'un ~ facile/ difficile** to be very/not very approachable. ○ **abords** *nmpl* [gén] surrounding area (*sg*); [de ville] outskirts. ○ **d'abord** *loc adv* [en premier lieu] first. || [avant tout]: **(tout) d'~** first (of all), in the first place.

abordable [abɔʀdabl] *adj* [lieu] accessible; [de prix modéré] affordable.

aborder [abɔʀde] **1** *vi* to land. **2** *vt* [personne, lieu] to approach. || [question] to tackle.

aborigène [abɔʀiʒɛn] *adj* aboriginal. ○ **Aborigène** *nmf* (Australian) aborigine.

aboutir [abutiʀ] *vi* [chemin]: ~ **à/dans** to end at/in. || [négociation] to be successful; ~ **à qqch** to result in sthg.

aboyer [abwaje] *vi* to bark.

abrasif, -ive [abʀazif, iv] *adj* abrasive.

abrégé, -e [abʀeʒe] *adj* abridged.

abréger [abʀeʒe] *vt* [visite, réunion] to cut short; [discours] to shorten; [mot] to abbreviate.

abreuvoir [abʀœvwaʀ] *nm* [lieu] watering place; [installation] drinking trough.

abréviation [abʀevjasjɔ̃] *nf* abbreviation.

abri [abʀi] *nm* shelter; **à l'~ de** sheltered from; *fig* safe from.

abricot [abʀiko] *nm & adj inv* apricot.

abriter [abʀite] *vt* [protéger]: ~ **qqn/ qqch (de)** to shelter sb/sthg (from). ○ **s'abriter** *vp*: **s'~ (de)** to shelter (from).

abroger [abʀɔʒe] *vt* to repeal.

abrupt, -e [abʀypt] *adj* [raide] steep. || [rude] abrupt, brusque.

abruti, -e [abʀyti] *fam nm, f* moron.

abrutir [abʀytiʀ] *vt* [abêtir]: ~ **qqn** to deaden sb's mind. || [accabler]: ~ **qqn de travail** to work sb silly.

abrutissant, -e [abʀytisɑ̃, ɑ̃t] *adj* [bruit, travail] stupefying. || [jeu, feuilleton] moronic.

absence [apsɑ̃s] *nf* [de personne] absence. || [carence] lack.

absent, -e [apsɑ̃, ɑ̃t] **1** *adj* [personne]: ~ **(de)** [gén] away (from); [pour maladie] absent (from). || [regard, air] vacant, absent. **2** *nm, f* absentee.

absenter [apsɑ̃te] ○ **s'absenter** *vp*: **s'~ (de la pièce)** to leave (the room).

absinthe [apsɛ̃t] *nf* [boisson] absinth.

absolu, -e [apsɔly] *adj* [gén] absolute; [décision, jugement] uncompromising.

absolument [apsɔlymɑ̃] *adv* absolutely.

absorbant, -e [apsɔʀbɑ̃, ɑ̃t] *adj* [matière] absorbent. || [occupation] absorbing.

absorber [apsɔʀbe] *vt* [gén] to absorb. || [manger] to take.

abstenir [apstəniʀ] ○ **s'abstenir** *vp* [ne rien faire]: **s'~ (de qqch/de faire qqch)** to refrain (from sthg/from doing sthg). || [ne pas voter] to abstain.

abstention [apstɑ̃sjɔ̃] *nf* abstention.

abstentionnisme [apstɑ̃sjɔnism] *nm* abstaining.

abstinence [apstinɑ̃s] *nf* abstinence.

abstraction [apstraksjɔ̃] *nf* abstraction; **faire ~ de** to disregard.

abstrait, -e [apstrɛ, ɛt] *adj* abstract.

absurde [apsyrd] *adj* absurd.

absurdité [apsyrdite] *nf* absurdity; **dire des ~s** to talk nonsense (*U*).

abus [aby] *nm* abuse; **~ de confiance** breach of trust; **~ de pouvoir** abuse of power.

abuser [abyze] *vi* [dépasser les bornes] to go too far. || [user]: **~ de** [autorité, pouvoir] to overstep the bounds of; [temps] to take up too much of.

abusif, -ive [abyzif, iv] *adj* [excessif] excessive. || [fautif] improper.

acabit [akabi] *nm:* **du même ~** *péj* of the same type.

acacia [akasja] *nm* acacia.

académicien, -ienne [akademisjɛ̃, jɛn] *nm, f* academician; [de l'Académie française] member of the French Academy.

académie [akademi] *nf* SCOL & UNIV ≃ school district *Am.* || [institut] academy; **l'Académie française** the French Academy (*learned society of leading men and women of letters*).

acajou [akaʒu] *nm & adj inv* mahogany.

acariâtre [akarjatr] *adj* bad-tempered, cantankerous.

accablant, -e [akablɑ̃, ɑ̃t] *adj* [soleil, chaleur] oppressive. || [preuve, témoignage] overwhelming.

accabler [akable] *vt* [surcharger]: **~ qqn de** [travail] to overwhelm sb with; **~ qqn d'injures** to shower sb with abuse.

accalmie [akalmi] *nf litt & fig* lull.

accéder [aksede] ○ **accéder à** *vt* [pénétrer dans] to reach, to get to. || [parvenir à] to attain. || [consentir à] to comply with.

accélérateur [akseleratœr] *nm* accelerator.

accélération [akselerasjɔ̃] *nf* [de voiture, machine] acceleration.

accélérer [akselere] **1** *vt* to accelerate, to speed up. **2** *vi* AUTOM to accelerate.

accent [aksɑ̃] *nm* [gén] accent; **~ aigu/grave/circonflexe** acute/grave/circumflex (accent). || [intonation] tone; **mettre l' ~ sur** to stress, to emphasize.

accentuation [aksɑ̃tɥasjɔ̃] *nf* [à l'écrit] accenting; [en parlant] stress.

accentuer [aksɑ̃tɥe] *vt* [insister sur, souligner] to emphasize, to accentuate. || [in-

tensifier] to intensify. || [à l'écrit] to put the accents on; [en parlant] to stress. ○ **s'accentuer** *vp* to become more pronounced.

acceptable [aksɛptabl] *adj* satisfactory, acceptable.

acceptation [aksɛptasjɔ̃] *nf* acceptance.

accepter [aksɛpte] *vt* to accept; **~ de faire qqch** to agree to do sthg; **~ que** (+ *subjonctif*): **~ que qqn fasse qqch** to agree to sb doing sthg.

acception [aksɛpsjɔ̃] *nf* sense.

accès [aksɛ] *nm* [entrée] entry; **avoir/donner ~ à** to have/to give access to; **«~ interdit»** "no entry". || [voie d'entrée] entrance. || [crise] bout; **~ de colère** fit of anger.

accessible [aksesibl] *adj* [lieu, livre] accessible; [prix, équipement] affordable.

accession [aksesjɔ̃] *nf:* **~ à** [trône, présidence] accession to; [indépendance] attainment of.

accessoire [akseswar] **1** *nm* [gén] accessory. || [de théâtre, cinéma] prop. **2** *adj* secondary.

accident [aksidɑ̃] *nm* accident; **par ~** by chance, by accident; **~ de la route/de voiture/du travail** road/car/industrial accident.

accidenté, -e [aksidɑ̃te] **1** *adj* [terrain, surface] uneven. || [voiture] damaged. **2** *nm, f* (*gén pl*): **~ de la route** accident victim.

accidentel, -elle [aksidɑ̃tɛl] *adj* accidental.

acclamation [aklamasjɔ̃] *nf* (*gén pl*) cheers (*pl*), cheering (*U*).

acclamer [aklame] *vt* to cheer.

acclimatation [aklimatasjɔ̃] *nf* acclimatization.

acclimater [aklimate] *vt* to acclimatize.

accolade [akɔlad] *nf* TYPO brace. || [embrassade] embrace.

accommodant, -e [akɔmɔdɑ̃, ɑ̃t] *adj* obliging.

accommoder [akɔmɔde] *vt* CULIN to prepare.

accompagnateur, -trice [akɔ̃paɲatœr, tris] *nm, f* MUS accompanist. || [guide] guide.

accompagnement [akɔ̃paɲmɑ̃] *nm* MUS accompaniment.

accompagner [akɔ̃paɲe] *vt* [personne] to go with, to accompany. || [agrémenter]: **~ qqch de** to accompany sthg with. || MUS to accompany.

accompli, -e [akɔ̃pli] *adj* accomplished.

accomplir [akɔ̃plir] *vt* to carry out. ○ **s'accomplir** *vp* to come about.

accomplissement [akɔ̃plismɑ̃] *nm* [de travail] fulfilment.

accord [akɔr] *nm* [gén & LING] agreement. || MUS chord. || [acceptation] approval; **donner son ~ à qqch** to approve sthg. ○ **d'accord** 1 *loc adv* OK, all right. **2** *loc adj*: **être d'~ (avec)** to agree (with); **tomber** *ou* **se mettre d'~** to come to an agreement, to agree.

accordéon [akɔrdeɔ̃] *nm* accordion.

accorder [akɔrde] *vt* [donner]: **~ qqch à qqn** to grant sb sthg. || [attribuer]: **~ de l'importance à** to attach importance to. || [harmoniser] to match. || GRAM: **~ qqch avec qqch** to make sthg agree with sthg. || MUS to tune. ○ **s'accorder** *vp* [gén]: **s'~ (pour faire qqch)** to agree (to do sthg); **s'~ à faire qqch** to be unanimous in doing sthg. || [être assorti] to match. || GRAM to agree.

accoster [akɔste] 1 *vt* NAVIG to come alongside. || [personne] to accost. **2** *vi* NAVIG to dock.

accotement [akɔtmɑ̃] *nm* [de route] shoulder; **~ non stabilisé** soft verge *Br*, soft shoulder *Am*.

accouchement [akuʃmɑ̃] *nm* childbirth; **~ sans douleur** natural childbirth.

accoucher [akuʃe] *vi*: **~ (de)** to give birth (to).

accouder [akude] ○ **s'accouder** *vp*: **s'~ à** to lean one's elbows on.

accoudoir [akudwar] *nm* armrest.

accouplement [akupləmɑ̃] *nm* mating, coupling.

accourir [akurir] *vi* to run up, to rush up.

accouru, -e [akury] *pp* → **accourir**.

accoutré, -e [akutre] *adj péj*: **être bizarrement ~** to be oddly got up.

accoutrement [akutrəmɑ̃] *nm péj* get-up.

accoutumer [akutyme] *vt*: **~ qqn à qqn/qqch** to get sb used to sb/sthg; **~ qqn à faire qqch** to get sb used to doing sthg. ○ **s'accoutumer** *vp*: **s'~ à qqn/qqch** to get used to sb/sthg; **s'~ à faire qqch** to get used to doing sthg.

accréditer [akredite] *vt* [rumeur] to substantiate.

accro [akro] *fam adj*: **~ à** hooked on.

accroc [akro] *nm* [déchirure] tear. || [incident] hitch.

accrochage [akrɔʃaʒ] *nm* [accident] collision. || *fam* [dispute] row.

accrocher [akrɔʃe] *vt* [suspendre]: **~ qqch (à)** to hang sthg up (on). || [déchirer]: **~ qqch (à)** to catch sthg (on). || [attacher]: **~ qqch (à)** to hitch sthg (to). ○ **s'accrocher** *vp* [s'agripper]: **s'~ (à)** to hang on (to). || *fam* [se disputer] to row, to have a row. || *fam* [persévérer] to stick at it.

accroissement [akrwasmɑ̃] *nm* increase, growth.

accroître [akrwatr] *vt* to increase. ○ **s'accroître** *vp* to increase, to grow.

accroupir [akrupir] ○ **s'accroupir** *vp* to squat.

accru, -e [akry] *pp* → **accroître**.

accueil [akœj] *nm* [lieu] reception. || [action] welcome, reception.

accueillant, -e [akœjã, ɑ̃t] *adj* welcoming, friendly.

accueillir [akœjir] *vt* [gén] to welcome. || [loger] to accommodate.

accumulateur [akymylatœr] *nm* accumulator, battery.

accumulation [akymylasjɔ̃] *nf* accumulation.

accumuler [akymyle] *vt* to accumulate. ○ **s'accumuler** *vp* to pile up.

accusateur, -trice [akyzatœr, tris] 1 *adj* accusing. **2** *nm, f* accuser.

accusation [akyzasjɔ̃] *nf* [reproche] accusation. || JUR charge; **mettre en ~** to indict; **l'~** the prosecution.

accusé, -e [akyze] *nm, f* accused, defendant. ○ **accusé de réception** *nm* acknowledgment (of receipt).

accuser [akyze] *vt* [porter une accusation contre]: **~ qqn (de qqch)** to accuse sb (of sthg). || JUR: **~ qqn de qqch** to charge sb with sthg.

acerbe [asɛrb] *adj* acerbic.

acéré, -e [asere] *adj* sharp.

acharné, -e [aʃarne] *adj* [combat] fierce; [travail] unremitting.

acharnement [aʃarnəmɑ̃] *nm* relentlessness.

acharner [aʃarne] ○ **s'acharner** *vp* [combattre]: **s'~ contre** *ou* **après** *ou* **sur qqn** [ennemi, victime] to hound sb; [suj: malheur] to dog sb. || [s'obstiner]: **s'~ (à faire qqch)** to persist (in doing sthg).

achat [aʃa] *nm* purchase; **faire des ~s** to go shopping.

acheminer [aʃmine] *vt* to dispatch. ○ **s'acheminer** *vp*: **s'~ vers** [lieu, désastre] to head for; [solution, paix] to move towards.

acheter [aʃte] *vt litt & fig* to buy; ~ qqch à oᵤ **pour qqn** to buy sth for sb, to buy sb sth.

acheteur, -euse [aʃtœr, øz] *nm, f* buyer, purchaser.

achevé, -e [aʃve] *adj sout*: **d'un ridicule** ~ utterly ridiculous.

achèvement [aʃɛvmã] *nm* completion.

achever [aʃve] *vt* [terminer] to complete, to finish (off). || [tuer, accabler] to finish off. ○ **s'achever** *vp* to end, to come to an end.

achoppement [aʃɔpmã] → **pierre**.

acide [asid] **1** *adj* [saveur] sour. || [propos] sharp, acid. || CHIM acid. **2** *nm* CHIM acid.

acidité [asidite] *nf* CHIM acidity. || [saveur] sourness. || [de propos] sharpness.

acidulé, -e [asidyle] *adj* slightly acid.

acier [asje] *nm* steel; ~ **inoxydable** stainless steel.

aciérie [asjeri] *nf* steelworks (*sg*).

acné [akne] *nf* acne.

acolyte [akɔlit] *nm péj* henchman.

acompte [akɔ̃t] *nm* deposit.

à-côté [akote] (*pl* **à-côtés**) *nm* [gain d'appoint] extra.

à-coup [aku] (*pl* **à-coups**) *nm* jerk; **par** ~**s** in fits and starts.

acoustique [akustik] *nf* [d'une salle] acoustics (*pl*).

acquéreur [akerœr] *nm* buyer.

acquérir [akerir] *vt* [gén] to acquire.

acquiescer [akjese] *vi* to acquiesce; ~ **à** to agree to.

acquis, -e [aki, iz] **1** *pp* → **acquérir**. **2** *adj* [droit, avantage] established. ○ **acquis** *nmpl* [connaissances] knowledge (*U*).

acquisition [akizisjɔ̃] *nf* acquisition.

acquit [aki] *nm* receipt; **pour** ~ COMM received; **faire qqch par** ~ **de conscience** *fig* to do sth to set one's mind at rest.

acquittement [akitmã] *nm* JUR acquittal.

acquitter [akite] *vt* JUR to acquit. || [régler] to pay.

âcre [akr] *adj* [saveur] bitter. || [fumée] acrid.

acrobate [akrɔbat] *nmf* acrobat.

acrobatie [akrɔbasi] *nf* acrobatics (*U*).

acrylique [akrilik] *adj & nm* acrylic.

acte [akt] *nm* [action] act, action; **faire** ~ **de candidature** to submit an application. || THÉÂTRE act. || JUR deed; ~

d'accusation charge; ~ **de naissance/de mariage** birth/marriage certificate; ~ **de vente** bill of sale. || *loc*: **faire** ~ **de présence** to put in an appearance; **prendre** ~ **de** to note, to take note of. ○ **actes** *nmpl* [de colloque] proceedings.

acteur, -trice [aktœr, tris] *nm, f* actor (*f* actress).

actif, -ive [aktif, iv] *adj* [gén] active; **la population active** the working population. ○ **actif** *nm* FIN assets (*pl*). || *loc*: **avoir qqch à son** ~ to have sth to one's credit.

action [aksjɔ̃] *nf* [gén] action; **sous l'**~ **de** under the effect of. || [acte] action, act; **bonne/mauvaise** ~ good/bad deed. || JUR action, lawsuit. || FIN share.

actionnaire [aksjɔner] *nmf* FIN shareholder.

actionner [aksjɔne] *vt* to work, to activate.

activement [aktivmã] *adv* actively.

activer [aktive] *vt* to speed up. ○ **s'activer** *vp* to bustle about.

activiste [aktivist] *adj & nmf* activist.

activité [aktivite] *nf* [gén] activity; **en** ~ [volcan] active.

actualiser [aktɥalize] *vt* to bring up to date.

actualité [aktɥalite] *nf* [d'un sujet] topicality. || [événements]: **l'**~ **sportive/politique/littéraire** the current sports/political/literary scene. ○ **actualités** *nfpl*: **les** ~**s** the news (*sg*).

actuel, -elle [aktɥel] *adj* [contemporain, présent] current, present; **à l'heure** ~**le** at the present time.

actuellement [aktɥelmã] *adv* at present, currently.

acuité [akɥite] *nf* acuteness.

acupuncture, acuponcture [akypɔ̃ktyr] *nf* acupuncture.

adage [adaʒ] *nm* adage, saying.

adaptateur, -trice [adaptatœr, tris] *nm, f* adapter. ○ **adaptateur** *nm* ÉLECTR adapter.

adaptation [adaptasjɔ̃] *nf* adaptation.

adapter [adapte] *vt* [gén] to adapt. || [fixer] to fit. ○ **s'adapter** *vp*: **s'**~ **(à)** to adapt (to).

additif [aditif] *nm* [supplément] rider, additional clause. || [substance] additive.

addition [adisjɔ̃] *nf* [ajout, calcul] addition. || [note] bill *Br*, check *Am*.

additionner [adisjɔne] *vt* [ajouter]: ~ **une poudre d'eau** to add water to a powder. || [calculer] to add up.

adepte [adɛpt] *nmf* follower.

adéquat, -e [adekwa, at] *adj* suitable, appropriate.

adhérence [aderɑ̃s] *nf* [de pneu] grip.

adhérent, -e [aderɑ̃, ɑ̃t] *nm, f*: ~ **(de)** member (of).

adhérer [adere] *vi* [coller] to stick, to adhere; ~ **à** [se fixer sur] to stick or adhere to; [être d'accord avec] *fig* to support, to adhere to. || [être membre]: ~ **à** to become a member of, to join.

adhésif, -ive [adezif, iv] *adj* sticky, adhesive. ○ **adhésif** *nm* adhesive.

adhésion [adezjɔ̃] *nf* [à idée]: ~ **(à)** support (for). || [à parti]: ~ **(à)** membership (of).

adieu [adjø] **1** *interj* goodbye!, farewell! **2** *nm* (*gén pl*) farewell; **faire ses ~x à qqn** to say one's farewells to sb.

adjectif [adʒɛktif] *nm* GRAM adjective.

adjoint, -e [adʒwɛ̃, ɛ̃t] **1** *adj* deputy (*avant n*), assistant (*avant n*). **2** *nm, f* deputy, assistant; ~ **au maire** deputy mayor.

adjonction [adʒɔ̃ksjɔ̃] *nf* addition.

adjudant [adʒydɑ̃] *nm* [dans la marine] warrant officer; [dans l'armée] company sergeant major.

adjuger [adʒyʒe] *vt*: ~ **qqch (à qqn)** [aux enchères] to auction sthg (to sb); **adjugé!** sold!

admettre [admɛtr] *vt* [tolérer, accepter] to allow, to accept. || [autoriser] to allow. || [accueillir, reconnaître] to admit.

administrateur, -trice [administratœr, tris] *nm, f* [gérant] administrator.

administratif, -ive [administratif, iv] *adj* administrative.

administration [administrasjɔ̃] *nf* [service public]: **l'Administration** ≃ the Civil Service. || [gestion] administration.

administrer [administre] *vt* [gérer] to manage, to administer. || [médicament, sacrement] to administer.

admirable [admirabl] *adj* [personne, comportement] admirable. || [paysage, spectacle] wonderful.

admiratif, -ive [admiratif, iv] *adj* admiring.

admiration [admirasjɔ̃] *nf* admiration.

admirer [admire] *vt* to admire.

admis, -e [admi, iz] *pp* → **admettre**.

admissible [admisibl] *adj* [attitude] acceptable. || SCOL eligible.

admission [admisjɔ̃] *nf* admission.

ADN (*abr de* **acide désoxyribonucléique**) *nm* DNA.

ado [ado] (*abr de* **adolescent**) *nmf fam* teenager.

adolescence [adɔlesɑ̃s] *nf* adolescence.

adolescent, -e [adɔlesɑ̃, ɑ̃t] *nm, f* adolescent, teenager.

adonner [adɔne] ○ **s'adonner** *vp*: **s'~ à** [sport, activité] to devote o.s. to; [vice] to take to.

adopter [adɔpte] *vt* [gén] to adopt. || [loi] to pass.

adoptif, -ive [adɔptif, iv] *adj* [famille] adoptive; [pays, enfant] adopted.

adoption [adɔpsjɔ̃] *nf* adoption; **d'~** [pays, ville] adopted; [famille] adoptive.

adorable [adɔrabl] *adj* adorable, delightful.

adoration [adɔrasjɔ̃] *nf* [amour] adoration. || RELIG worship.

adorer [adɔre] *vt* [personne, chose] to adore. || RELIG to worship.

adosser [adose] ○ **s'adosser** *vp*: **s'~ à** ou **contre qqch** to lean against sthg.

adoucir [adusir] *vt* [gén] to soften. || [chagrin, peine] to ease, to soothe. ○ **s'adoucir** *vp* [temps] to become ou get milder. || [personne] to mellow.

adoucissant, -e [adusisɑ̃, ɑ̃t] *adj* soothing. ○ **adoucissant** *nm* softener.

adoucisseur [adusisœr] *nm*: ~ **d'eau** water softener.

adresse [adrɛs] *nf* [gén & INFORM] address. || [habileté] skill.

adresser [adrese] *vt* [faire parvenir]: ~ **qqch à qqn** to address sthg to sb. || [envoyer]: ~ **qqn à qqn** to refer sb to sb. ○ **s'adresser** *vp*: **s'~ à** [parler à] to speak to; [être destiné à] to be aimed at, to be intended for.

adroit, -e [adrwa, at] *adj* skilful.

adulte [adylt] *nmf & adj* adult.

adultère [adylter] **1** *nm* [acte] adultery. **2** *adj* adulterous.

advenir [advənir] *v impers* to happen; **qu'est-il advenu de ...?** what has happened to ou become of ...?

advenu [advəny] *pp* → **advenir**.

adverbe [advɛrb] *nm* adverb.

adversaire [adversɛr] *nmf* adversary, opponent.

adverse [advers] *adj* [opposé] opposing; → **parti**.

adversité [adversite] *nf* adversity.

aération [aerasjɔ̃] *nf* [circulation d'air] ventilation; [action] airing.

aérer [aere] *vt* [pièce, chose] to air. || *fig* [présentation, mise en page] to lighten.

aérien, -ienne [aerjɛ̃, jɛn] *adj* [câble] overhead (*avant n*). ‖ [transports, attaque] air (*avant n*).

aérobic [aerɔbik] *nm* aerobics (*U*).

aérodrome [aerɔdrom] *nm* aerodrome.

aérodynamique [aerɔdinamik] *adj* streamlined, aerodynamic.

aérogare [aerɔgar] *nf* [aéroport] airport. ‖ [gare] air terminal.

aéroglisseur [aerɔglisœr] *nm* hovercraft.

aéronautique [aerɔnotik] *nf* aeronautics (*U*).

aéronaval, -e, -als [aerɔnaval] *adj* air and sea (*avant n*).

aérophagie [aerɔfaʒi] *nf* abdominal wind.

aéroport [aerɔpɔr] *nm* airport.

aérosol [aerɔsɔl] *nm & adj inv* aerosol.

aérospatial, -e, -iaux [aerɔspasjal, jo] *adj* aerospace (*avant n*). ○ **aérospatiale** *nf* aerospace industry.

affable [afabl] *adj* [personne] affable, agreeable. ‖ [parole] kind.

affaiblir [afeblir] *vt litt & fig* to weaken. ○ **s'affaiblir** *vp litt & fig* to weaken, to become weaker.

affaire [afɛr] *nf* [question] matter. ‖ [situation, polémique] affair. ‖ [marché] deal; **faire une ~** to get a bargain oı a good deal. ‖ [entreprise] business. ‖ [procès] case. ‖ *loc:* **avoir ~ à qqn** to deal with sb; **faire l'~** to do nicely. ○ **affaires** *nfpl* COMM business (*U*). ‖ [objets personnels] things, belongings. ‖ [activités] affairs; **les Affaires étrangères** ≃ the Foreign Office (*sg*).

affairé, -e [afere] *adj* busy.

affairer [afere] ○ **s'affairer** *vp* to bustle about.

affaisser [afese] ○ **s'affaisser** *vp* [se creuser] to subside, to sink. ‖ [tomber] to collapse.

affaler [afale] ○ **s'affaler** *vp* to collapse.

affamé, -e [afame] *adj* starving.

affecter [afɛkte] *vt* [consacrer]: **~ qqch à** to allocate sthg to. ‖ [nommer]: **~ qqn à** to appoint sb to. ‖ [feindre] to feign. ‖ [émouvoir] to affect, to move.

affectif, -ive [afɛktif, iv] *adj* emotional.

affection [afɛksjɔ̃] *nf* [sentiment] affection; **avoir de l'~ pour** to be fond of.

affectionner [afɛksjɔne] *vt* to be fond of.

affectueusement [afɛktɥøzmɑ̃] *adv* affectionately.

affectueux, -euse [afɛktɥø, øz] *adj* affectionate.

affichage [afiʃaʒ] *nm* [d'affiche] putting up, displaying. ‖ ÉLECTRON: **~ à cristaux liquides** LCD, liquid crystal display; **~ numérique** digital display.

affiche [afiʃ] *nf* [gén] poster; [officielle] notice.

afficher [afiʃe] *vt* [liste, affiche] to put up; [vente, réglementation] to put up a notice about. ‖ [laisser transparaître] to display, to exhibit.

affilée [afile] ○ **d'affilée** *loc adv:* **trois jours d'~** three days running.

affiler [afile] *vt* to sharpen.

affiner [afine] *vt litt & fig* to refine.

affinité [afinite] *nf* affinity.

affirmatif, -ive [afirmatif, iv] *adj* [réponse] affirmative. ‖ [personne] positive. ○ **affirmative** *nf:* **dans l'affirmative** if yes, if the answer is yes; **répondre par l'affirmative** to reply in the affirmative.

affirmation [afirmasjɔ̃] *nf* assertion.

affirmer [afirme] *vt* [certifier] to maintain, to claim. ‖ [exprimer] to assert.

affligeant, -e [afliʒɑ̃, ɑ̃t] *adj* [désolant] saddening, distressing. ‖ [lamentable] appalling.

affliger [afliʒe] *vt sout* [attrister] to sadden, to distress. ‖ [de défaut, de maladie]: **être affligé de** to be afflicted with.

affluent [aflyɑ̃] *nm* tributary.

affluer [aflye] *vi* [choses] to pour in, to flood in. ‖ [personnes] to flock. ‖ [sang]: **~ (à)** to rush (to).

afflux [afly] *nm* [de liquide, dons, capitaux] flow. ‖ [de personnes] flood.

affolement [afɔlmɑ̃] *nm* panic.

affoler [afɔle] *vt* [inquiéter] to terrify. ○ **s'affoler** *vp* [paniquer] to panic.

affranchir [afrɑ̃ʃir] *vt* [lettre - avec timbre] to stamp; [- à la machine] to frank.

affreux, -euse [afrø, øz] *adj* [repoussant] horrible. ‖ [effrayant] terrifying. ‖ [détestable] awful, dreadful.

affriolant, -e [afrijɔlɑ̃, ɑ̃t] *adj* enticing.

affront [afrɔ̃] *nm* insult, affront.

affrontement [afrɔ̃tmɑ̃] *nm* confrontation.

affronter [afrɔ̃te] *vt* to confront.

affubler [afyble] *vt péj:* **être affublé de** to be got up in.

affût [afy] *nm:* **être à l'~ (de)** to be lying in wait (for); *fig* to be on the lookout (for).

affûter [afyte] *vt* to sharpen.

Afghanistan [afganistɑ̃] *nm*: l'~ Afghanistan.

afin [afɛ̃] ○ **afin de** *loc prép* in order to. ○ **afin que** *loc conj* (+ *subjonctif*) so that.

a fortiori [afɔrsjɔri] *adv* all the more.

africain, -e [afrikɛ̃, ɛn] *adj* African. ○ **Africain, -e** *nm, f* African.

Afrique [afrik] *nf*: l'~ Africa; l'~ du Nord North Africa; l'~ du Sud South Africa.

agacer [agase] *vt* to irritate.

âge [aʒ] *nm* age; **quel ~ as-tu?** how old are you?; **prendre de l'~** to age; l'~ **adulte** adulthood; **le troisième ~** [personnes] the over-sixties.

âgé, -e [aʒe] *adj* old, elderly; **être ~ de 20 ans** to be 20 years old or of age; **un enfant ~ de 3 ans** a 3-year-old child.

agence [aʒɑ̃s] *nf* agency; ~ **immobilière** estate agent's *Br*, real estate agent's *Am*; **Agence nationale pour l'emploi** ≃ job centre; ~ **de publicité** advertising agency; ~ **de voyages** travel agent's travel agency.

agencer [aʒɑ̃se] *vt* to arrange.

agenda [aʒɛ̃da] *nm* diary.

agenouiller [aʒnuje] ○ **s'agenouiller** *vp* to kneel.

agent [aʒɑ̃] *nm* agent; ~ **de change** stockbroker; ~ **de police** police officer; ~ **secret** secret agent.

agglomération [aglɔmerasjɔ̃] *nf* [ville] conurbation.

aggloméré [aglɔmere] *nm* chipboard.

agglomérer [aglɔmere] *vt* to mix together.

agglutiner [aglytine] ○ **s'agglutiner** *vp* [foule] to gather, to congregate.

aggraver [agrave] *vt* to make worse. ○ **s'aggraver** *vp* to get worse, to worsen.

agile [aʒil] *adj* agile, nimble.

agilité [aʒilite] *nf litt & fig* agility.

agios [aʒjo] *nmpl* FIN bank charges.

agir [aʒir] *vi* [faire, être efficace] to act. || [se comporter] to behave. || [influer]: ~ **sur** to have an effect on. ○ **s'agir** *v impers*: **il s'agit de ...** it's a matter of ...; **de quoi s'agit-il?** what's it about?

agissements [aʒismɑ̃] *nmpl péj* schemes, intrigues.

agitateur, -trice [aʒitatœr, tris] *nm, f* POLIT agitator.

agitation [aʒitasjɔ̃] *nf* agitation; [politique, sociale] unrest.

agité, -e [aʒite] *adj* [gén] restless; [enfant, classe] restless, fidgety; [journée, atmosphère] hectic. || [mer] rough.

agiter [aʒite] *vt* [remuer - flacon, objet] to shake; [- drapeau, bras] to wave. ○ **s'agiter** *vp* [personne] to move about, to fidget; [population] to get restless.

agneau [aɲo] *nm* [animal, viande] lamb. || [cuir] lambskin.

agonie [agɔni] *nf* [de personne] mortal agony; *fig* death throes (*pl*).

agoniser [agɔnize] *vi* [personne] to be dying; *fig* to be on its last legs.

agrafe [agraf] *nf* [de bureau] staple. || MÉD clip.

agrafer [agrafe] *vt* [attacher] to fasten.

agrafeuse [agraføz] *nf* stapler.

agraire [agrɛr] *adj* agrarian.

agrandir [agrɑ̃dir] *vt* [élargir - gén & PHOT] to enlarge; [- rue, écart] to widen. || *fig* [développer] to expand. ○ **s'agrandir** *vp* [s'étendre] to grow. || *fig* [se développer] to expand.

agrandissement [agrɑ̃dismɑ̃] *nm* [gén & PHOT] enlargement.

agréable [agreabl] *adj* pleasant, nice.

agréé, -e [agree] *adj* [concessionnaire, appareil] authorized.

agréer [agree] *vt sout* [accepter]: **veuillez ~ mes salutations distinguées** ou **l'expression de mes sentiments distingués** yours faithfully.

agrégation [agregasjɔ̃] *nf competitive examination for secondary school and university teachers.*

agrégé, -e [agreʒe] *nm, f holder of the agrégation.*

agrément [agremɑ̃] *nm* [approbation] consent, approval.

agrès [agrɛ] *nmpl* SPORT gym apparatus (*U*).

agresser [agrese] *vt* [suj: personne] to attack.

agresseur [agresœr] *nm* attacker.

agressif, -ive [agresif, iv] *adj* aggressive.

agression [agresjɔ̃] *nf* attack; MIL & PSYCHOL aggression.

agricole [agrikɔl] *adj* agricultural.

agriculteur, -trice [agrikyltœr, tris] *nm, f* farmer.

agriculture [agrikyltyr] *nf* agriculture, farming.

agripper [agripe] *vt* [personne] to cling ou hang on to. || [objet] to grip, to clutch.

agronomie [agrɔnɔmi] *nf* agronomy.

agrume [agrym] *nm* citrus fruit.

aguets [agɛ] ○ **aux aguets** *loc adv*: être/rester aux ~ to be ou keep on the lookout.

ahuri, -e [ayri] *adj*: être ~ (par qqch) to be taken aback (by sthg).

ahurissant, -e [ayrisɑ̃, ɑ̃t] *adj* astounding.

ai → **avoir**.

aide [ɛd] *nf* [gén] help; **appeler (qqn) à l'~** to call (to sb) for help; **venir en ~ à qqn** to come to sb's aid, to help sb. || [secours financier] aid; **~ sociale** social security *Br*, welfare *Am*. ○ **à l'aide de** *loc prép* with the help ou aid of.

aide-mémoire [ɛdmemwar] *nm inv* aide-mémoire; [pour examen] revision notes (*pl*).

aider [ede] *vt* to help; **~ qqn à faire qqch** to help sb to do sthg. ○ **s'aider** *vp* [s'assister mutuellement] to help each other. || [avoir recours]: **s'~ de** to use, to make use of.

aide-soignant, -e [ɛdswaɲɑ̃, ɑ̃t] *nm, f* nursing auxiliary *Br*, nurse's aide *Am*.

aie, aies *etc* → **avoir**.

aïe [aj] *interj* [exprime la douleur] ow!, ouch!

aïeul, -e [ajœl] *nm, f sout* grandparent, grandfather (*f* grandmother).

aïeux [ajø] *nmpl* ancestors.

aigle [ɛgl] *nm* eagle.

aigre [ɛgr] *adj* [gén] sour. || [propos] harsh.

aigre-doux, -douce [ɛgrədu, dus] *adj* CULIN sweet-and-sour.

aigreur [ɛgrœr] *nf* [d'un aliment] sourness. || [d'un propos] harshness. ○ **aigreurs d'estomac** *nfpl* heartburn (*U*).

aigri, -e [egri] *adj* embittered.

aigu, -uë [egy] *adj* [son] high-pitched. || [objet, lame] sharp; [angle] acute. || [douleur] sharp, acute. || [intelligence, sens] acute, keen. ○ **aigu** *nm* high note.

aiguillage [egɥijaʒ] *nm* [RAIL - manœuvre] switching *Am*; [- dispositif] switch *Am*.

aiguille [egɥij] *nf* [gén] needle; **~ à tricoter** knitting needle; **~ de pin** pine needle. || [de pendule] hand.

aiguiller [egɥije] *vt* RAIL to switch *Am*. || [personne, conversation] to steer, to direct.

aiguilleur [egɥijœr] *nm* RAIL switchman *Am*. || AÉRON: **~ du ciel** air traffic controller.

aiguiser [egize] *vt litt & fig* to sharpen.

ail [aj] (*pl* **ails** OU **aulx** [o]) *nm* garlic (*U*).

aile [ɛl] *nf* [gén] wing.

aileron [ɛlrɔ̃] *nm* [de requin] fin. || [d'avion] aileron.

ailier [elje] *nm* winger.

aille, ailles *etc* → **aller**.

ailleurs [ajœr] *adv* elsewhere, somewhere else; **nulle part/partout ~** nowhere/everywhere else. ○ **d'ailleurs** *loc adv* moreover, besides.

aimable [ɛmabl] *adj* kind, nice.

aimablement [ɛmabləmɑ̃] *adv* kindly.

aimant¹ [ɛmɑ̃, ɑ̃t] *adj* loving.

aimant² [ɛmɑ̃] *nm* magnet.

aimer [eme] *vt* [gén] to like; **~ bien qqch/qqn** to like sthg/sb, to be fond of sthg/sb; **~ bien faire qqch** to (really) like doing sthg; **~ (à) faire qqch** to like to do sthg, to like doing sthg; **je n'aime pas que tu rentres seule le soir** I don't like you coming home alone at night; **j'aimerais (bien) que tu viennes avec moi** I'd like you to come with me; **~ mieux qqch** to prefer sthg; **~ mieux faire qqch** to prefer doing ou to do sthg. || [d'amour] to love. ○ **s'aimer** *vp* (*emploi réciproque*) to love each other; **s'~ bien** to like each other.

aine [ɛn] *nf* groin.

aîné, -e [ene] **1** *adj* [plus âgé] elder, older; [le plus âgé] eldest, oldest. **2** *nm, f* [plus âgé] older ou elder one; [le plus âgé] oldest, eldest; **elle est mon ~e de deux ans** she is two years older than me.

ainsi [ɛ̃si] *adv* [manière] in this way, like this. || [valeur conclusive] thus; **et ~ de suite** and so on, and so forth; **pour ~ dire** so to speak. ○ **ainsi que** *loc conj* [et] as well as.

air [ɛr] *nm* [gén] air; **en plein ~** (out) in the open air, outside; **en l'~** [projet] (up) in the air; *fig* [paroles] empty; **~ conditionné** air-conditioning. || [apparence, mine] air, look; **il a l'~ triste** he looks sad; **il a l'~ de faire beau** it looks like being a nice day. || MUS tune.

aire [ɛr] *nf* [gén] area; **~ d'atterrissage** landing strip; **~ de jeu** playground; **~ de repos** lay-by; **~ de stationnement** parking area.

aisance [ɛzɑ̃s] *nf* [facilité] ease. || [richesse]: **il vit dans l'~** he has an affluent lifestyle.

aise [ɛz] *nf*: être à l'~ OU à son ~ [confortable] to feel comfortable; [financièrement] to be comfortably off; **mettez-vous à l'~** make yourself comfortable; **mettre qqn mal à l'~** to make sb feel ill at ease or uneasy. ○ **aises** *nfpl*: **aimer ses ~s** to like one's (home) comforts; **prendre ses ~s** to make o.s. comfortable.

aisé, -e [eze] *adj* [facile] easy. ‖ [riche] well-off.

aisselle [esel] *nf* armpit.

ajourner [aʒurne] *vt* [reporter - décision etc] to postpone; [- réunion, procès] to adjourn. ‖ [candidat] to refer.

ajout [aʒu] *nm* addition.

ajouter [aʒute] *vt* to add. ○ **s'ajouter** *vp*: **s'~ à qqch** to be in addition to sthg.

ajuster [aʒyste] *vt* [régler] to adjust. ‖ [vêtement] to alter. ‖ [tir, coup] to aim.

alarme [alarm] *nf* alarm; **donner l'~** to give or raise the alarm.

alarmer [alarme] *vt* to alarm. ○ **s'alarmer** *vp* to get or become alarmed.

albâtre [albatr] *nm* alabaster.

albatros [albatros] *nm* albatross.

albinos [albinos] *nmf* & *adj inv* albino.

album [albɔm] *nm* album; **~ (de) photo** photo album.

alcool [alkɔl] *nm* alcohol; **~ à brûler** methylated spirits (*pl*); **~ à 90 degrés** surgical spirit.

alcoolique [alkɔlik] *nmf* & *adj* alcoholic.

alcoolisé, -e [alkɔlize] *adj* alcoholic.

alcoolisme [alkɔlism] *nm* alcoholism.

Alc(o)otest® [alkɔtest] *nm* Breathalyser®.

alcôve [alkov] *nf* recess.

aléatoire [aleatwar] *adj* [avenir] uncertain. ‖ [choix] random.

alentour [alɑ̃tur] *adv* around, round about. ○ **alentours** *nmpl* surroundings; **aux ~s de** [spatial] in the vicinity of; [temporel] around.

alerte [alert] **1** *adj* [personne, esprit] agile, alert. ‖ [style, pas] lively. **2** *nf* alarm, alert; **donner l'~** to sound or give the alert; **~ à la bombe** bomb scare.

alerter [alerte] *vt* to warn, to alert.

algèbre [alʒebr] *nf* algebra.

Algérie [alʒeri] *nf*: **l'~** Algeria.

algérien, -ienne [alʒerjɛ̃, jen] *adj* Algerian. ○ **Algérien, -ienne** *nm, f* Algerian.

algue [alg] *nf* seaweed (*U*).

alibi [alibi] *nm* alibi.

aliénation [aljenasjɔ̃] *nf* alienation; **~ mentale** insanity.

aliéné, -e [aljene] **1** *adj* MÉD insane. ‖ JUR alienated. **2** *nm, f* MÉD insane person.

aliéner [aljene] *vt* to alienate.

alignement [aliɲmɑ̃] *nm* alignment, lining up.

aligner [aliɲe] *vt* [disposer en ligne] to line up, to align. ‖ [adapter]: **~ qqch sur** to align sthg with, to bring sthg into line with. ○ **s'aligner** *vp* to line up; **s'~ sur** POLIT to align o.s. with.

aliment [alimɑ̃] *nm* [nourriture] food (*U*).

alimentaire [alimɑ̃ter] *adj* [gén] food (*avant n*). ‖ JUR maintenance (*avant n*).

alimentation [alimɑ̃tasjɔ̃] *nf* [nourriture] diet; **magasin d'~** food store. ‖ [approvisionnement]: **~ (en)** supply or supplying (*U*) (of).

alimenter [alimɑ̃te] *vt* [nourrir] to feed. ‖ [approvisionner]: **~ qqch en** to supply sthg with.

alinéa [alinea] *nm* [retrait de ligne] indent. ‖ [dans document officiel] paragraph.

aliter [alite] *vt*: **être alité** to be bedridden. ○ **s'aliter** *vp* to take to one's bed.

allaitement [aletmɑ̃] *nm* [d'enfant] breast-feeding; [d'animal] suckling.

allaiter [alete] *vt* [enfant] to breast-feed; [animal] to suckle.

alléchant, -e [aleʃɑ̃, ɑ̃t] *adj* mouth-watering, tempting.

allécher [aleʃe] *vt*: **il a été alléché par l'odeur/la perspective** the smell/prospect made his mouth water.

allée [ale] *nf* [dans un jardin] path; [dans une ville] avenue. ‖ [trajet]: **~s et venues** comings and goings.

allégé, -e [aleʒe] *adj* [régime, produit] low-fat.

alléger [aleʒe] *vt* [fardeau] to lighten.

allégorie [alegɔri] *nf* allegory.

allègre [alegr] *adj* [ton] cheerful. ‖ [démarche] jaunty.

allégresse [alegres] *nf* elation.

alléguer [alege] *vt*: **~ une excuse** to put forward an excuse; **~ que** to plead (that).

Allemagne [almaɲ] *nf*: **l'~** Germany; **l'(ex-)~ de l'Est** (former) East Germany; **l'(ex-)~ de l'Ouest** (former) West Germany.

allemand, -e [almɑ̃, ɑ̃d] *adj* German. ○ **allemand** *nm* [langue] German. ○ **Allemand, -e** *nm, f* German; **un Allemand de l'Est/l'Ouest** an East/a West German.

aller [ale] 1 *nm* [trajet] outward journey. || [billet] one-way ticket *Am*. 2 *vi* [gén] to go; **allez!** come on!; **vas-y!** go on!; **allons-y!** let's go! || (+ *infinitif*): ~ **faire qqch** to go and do sthg; ~ **travailler/se promener** to go to work/for a walk. || [indiquant un état]: **comment vas-tu?** how are you?; **je vais bien** I'm very well, I'm fine; **comment ça va?** — **ça va** [santé] how are you? — fine ou all right; [situation] how are things? — fine ou all right. || [convenir]: **ce type de clou ne va pas pour ce travail** this kind of nail won't do ou isn't suitable for this job; ~ **avec** to go with; ~ **à qqn** to suit sb; [suj: vêtement, taille] to fit sb; **ces couleurs ne vont pas ensemble** these colours don't go well together. || *loc*: **cela va de soi, cela va sans dire** that goes without saying; **il en va de même pour lui** the same goes for him. 3 *v aux* (+ *infinitif*) [exprime le futur proche] to be going to, will; **je vais arriver en retard** I'll arrive late, I'll arrive late. ○ **s'en aller** *vp* [partir] to go, to be off; **allez-vous-en!** go away! || [disparaître] to go away.

allergie [alɛrʒi] *nf* allergy.

allergique [alɛrʒik] *adj*: ~ (à) allergic (to).

aller-retour [alerətur] *nm* return (ticket).

alliage [aljaʒ] *nm* alloy.

alliance [aljɑ̃s] *nf* [union - stratégique] alliance; [- par le mariage] union, marriage; **cousin par** ~ cousin by marriage. || [bague] wedding ring.

allié, -e [alje] 1 *adj*: ~ (à) allied (to). 2 *nm, f* ally.

allier [alje] *vt* [associer] to combine. ○ **s'allier** *vp* to become allies; **s'** ~ **qqn** to win sb over as an ally; **s'** ~ **à qqn** to ally with sb.

alligator [aligatɔr] *nm* alligator.

allô [alo] *interj* hello!

allocation [alɔkasjɔ̃] *nf* [attribution] allocation. || [aide financière]: ~ **chômage** unemployment benefit (*U*); ~ **logement** housing benefit (*U*); ~**s familiales** child benefit (*U*).

allocution [alɔkysjɔ̃] *nf* short speech.

allongé, -e [alɔ̃ʒe] *adj* [position]: **être** ~ to be lying down ou stretched out. || [forme] elongated.

allonger [alɔ̃ʒe] *vt* [gén] to lengthen, to make longer. || [jambe, bras] to stretch (out). || [personne] to lay down.

○ **s'allonger** *vp* [gén] to get longer. || [se coucher] to lie down.

allumage [alymaʒ] *nm* [de feu] lighting. || [d'appareil électrique] switching ou turning on. || [de moteur] ignition.

allume-cigares [alymsigar] *nm inv* cigar lighter.

allume-gaz [alymgaz] *nm inv* gas lighter.

allumer [alyme] *vt* [lampe, radio, télévision] to turn ou switch on; **allume dans la cuisine** turn the kitchen light on. || [gaz] to light; [cigarette] to light (up). || *fam* [personne] to turn on.

allumette [alymɛt] *nf* match.

allure [alyr] *nf* [vitesse] speed; **à toute** ~ at top ou full speed. || [prestance] presence; **avoir de l'** ~ to have style. || [apparence générale] appearance.

allusion [alyzjɔ̃] *nf* allusion; **faire** ~ **à** to refer ou allude to.

almanach [almana] *nm* almanac.

aloi [alwa] *nm*: **de bon** ~ [mesure] of real worth; **de mauvais** ~ [gaîté] not genuine; [plaisanterie] in bad taste.

alors [alɔr] *adv* [jadis] then, at that time. || [à ce moment-là] then. || [exprimant la conséquence] then, so; **il va se mettre en colère** — **et** ~? he'll be angry — so what? || [emploi expressif] well (then); ~, **qu'est-ce qu'on fait?** well, what are we doing?; **ça** ~! well fancy that! ○ **alors que** *loc conj* [exprimant le temps] while, when. || [exprimant l'opposition] even though; **elle est sortie** ~ **que c'était interdit** she went out even though it was forbidden; **ils aiment le café** ~ **que nous, nous buvons du thé** they like coffee whereas we drink tea.

alouette [alwɛt] *nf* lark.

alourdir [alurdir] *vt* [gén] to weigh down, to make heavy. || *fig* [impôts] to increase.

aloyau [alwajo] *nm* sirloin.

Alpes [alp] *nfpl*: **les** ~ the Alps.

alphabet [alfabɛ] *nm* alphabet.

alphabétique [alfabetik] *adj* alphabetical.

alphabétiser [alfabetize] *vt*: ~ **qqn** to teach sb (how) to read and write.

alpin, -e [alpɛ̃, in] *adj* alpine.

alpinisme [alpinism] *nm* mountaineering.

alter ego [alterego] *nm inv* alter ego.

altérer [altere] *vt* [détériorer] to spoil. || [santé] to harm, to affect; [vérité, récit] to distort. ○ **s'altérer** *vp* [matière - métal] to deteriorate; [- aliment] to go off, to spoil. || [santé] to deteriorate.

alternance [altɛrnɑ̃s] *nf* [succession] alternation; **en ~** alternately. || POLIT change of government party.

alternatif, -ive [altɛrnatif, iv] *adj* [périodique] alternating. || [parallèle] alternative. ○ **alternative** *nf* alternative.

alternativement [altɛrnativmɑ̃] *adv* alternately.

alterner [altɛrne] *vi* [se succéder]: **~ (avec)** to alternate (with).

altitude [altityd] *nf* altitude, height; **en ~** at (high) altitude.

alto [alto] *nm* [MUS - voix] alto; [- instrument] viola.

aluminium [alyminjɔm] *nm* aluminium *Br*, aluminum *Am*.

alvéole [alveɔl] *nf* [cavité] cavity. || [de ruche, poumon] alveolus.

amabilité [amabilite] *nf* kindness; **avoir l'~ de faire qqch** to be so kind as to do sthg.

amadouer [amadwe] *vt* [adoucir] to tame, to pacify; [persuader] to coax.

amaigrir [amegrir] *vt* to make thin or thinner.

amaigrissant, -e [amegrisɑ̃, ɑ̃t] *adj* reducing (*avant n*) *Am*.

amaigrissement [amegrismɑ̃] *nm* loss of weight.

amalgame [amalgam] *nm* TECHNOL amalgam. || [de styles] mixture. || [d'idées, de notions]: **il ne faut pas faire l'~ entre ces deux questions** the two issues must not be confused.

amalgamer [amalgame] *vt* to combine.

amande [amɑ̃d] *nf* almond.

amandier [amɑ̃dje] *nm* almond tree.

amant [amɑ̃] *nm* lover.

amarre [amar] *nf* rope, cable.

amarrer [amare] *vt* NAVIG to moor.

amas [ama] *nm* pile.

amasser [amase] *vt* [objets] to pile up. || [argent] to accumulate.

amateur [amatœr] *nm* [connaisseur - d'art, de bon café]: **~ de** lover of. || [non-professionnel] amateur; **faire qqch en ~** to do sthg as a hobby. || *péj* [dilettante] amateur.

amazone [amazon] *nf* horsewoman; **monter en ~** to ride sidesaddle.

Amazonie [amazoni] *nf*: **l'~** the Amazon (Basin).

amazonien, -ienne [amazonjɛ̃, jɛn] *adj* Amazonian; **la forêt ~ne** the Amazon rain forest.

ambassade [ɑ̃basad] *nf* embassy.

ambassadeur, -drice [ɑ̃basadœr, dris] *nm, f* ambassador.

ambiance [ɑ̃bjɑ̃s] *nf* atmosphere.

ambiant, -e [ɑ̃bjɑ̃, ɑ̃t] *adj*: **température ~e** room temperature.

ambidextre [ɑ̃bidɛkstr] *adj* ambidextrous.

ambigu, -uë [ɑ̃bigy] *adj* ambiguous.

ambiguïté [ɑ̃biguite] *nf* ambiguity.

ambitieux, -ieuse [ɑ̃bisjø, jøz] *adj* ambitious.

ambition [ɑ̃bisjɔ̃] *nf péj* [arrivisme] ambitiousness. || [désir] ambition; **avoir l'~ de faire qqch** to have an ambition to do sthg.

ambivalent, -e [ɑ̃bivalɑ̃, ɑ̃t] *adj* ambivalent.

ambre [ɑ̃br] *nm* [couleur] amber. || [matière]: **~ (gris)** ambergris.

ambré, -e [ɑ̃bre] *adj* [couleur] amber.

ambulance [ɑ̃bylɑ̃s] *nf* ambulance.

ambulancier, -ière [ɑ̃bylɑ̃sje, jɛr] *nm, f* ambulanceman (*f* ambulancewoman).

ambulant, -e [ɑ̃bylɑ̃, ɑ̃t] *adj* travelling (*avant n*).

âme [ɑm] *nf* [gén] soul; **~ sœur** soulmate. || [caractère] spirit, soul.

amélioration [ameljɔrasjɔ̃] *nf* improvement.

améliorer [ameljɔre] *vt* to improve. ○ **s'améliorer** *vp* to improve.

aménagement [amenaʒmɑ̃] *nm* [de lieu] fitting out.

aménager [amenaʒe] *vt* [pièce] to fit out. || [programme] to plan, to organize.

amende [amɑ̃d] *nf* fine.

amendement [amɑ̃dmɑ̃] *nm* POLIT amendment.

amender [amɑ̃de] *vt* POLIT to amend. || AGRIC to enrich. ○ **s'amender** *vp* to mend one's ways.

amener [amne] *vt* [mener] to bring. || [inciter]: **~ qqn à faire qqch** [suj: circonstances] to lead sb to do sthg; [suj: personne] to get sb to do sthg. || [occasionner, préparer] to bring about.

amenuiser [amənɥize] *vt* [réduire] to diminish, to reduce. ○ **s'amenuiser** *vp* to dwindle, to diminish.

amer, -ère [amɛr] *adj* bitter.

américain, -e [amerikɛ̃, ɛn] *adj* American. ○ **américain** *nm* [langue] American English. ○ **Américain, -e** *nm, f* American.

américanisme [amerikanism] *nm* Americanism.

Amérique [amerik] *nf*: l'~ America; l'~ **centrale** Central America; l'~ **du Nord** North America; l'~ **du Sud** South America; l'~ **latine** Latin America.

amertume [amɛrtym] *nf* bitterness.

améthyste [ametist] *nf* amethyst.

ameublement [amœbləmɑ̃] *nm* [meubles] furniture; [action de meubler] furnishing.

ami, -e [ami] **1** *adj* friendly. **2** *nm, f* [camarade] friend; **petit ~** boyfriend; **petite ~e** girlfriend.

amiable [amjabl] *adj* [accord] friendly, informal. ○ **à l'amiable** *loc adv & loc adj* out of court.

amiante [amjɑ̃t] *nm* asbestos.

amical, -e, -aux [amikal, o] *adj* friendly. ○ **amicale** *nf* association, club (*for people with a shared interest*).

amicalement [amikalmɑ̃] *adv* de façon amicale) amicably, in a friendly way. || [dans une lettre] yours (ever), (with) best wishes.

amidon [amidɔ̃] *nm* starch.

amidonner [amidɔne] *vt* to starch.

amincissant, -e [amɛ̃sisɑ̃, ɑ̃t] *adj* slimming.

amiral, -aux [amiral, o] *nm* admiral.

amitié [amitje] *nf* [affection] affection; **prendre qqn en ~** to befriend sb. || [rapports amicaux] friendship; **faire ses ~s à qqn** to give sb one's good or best wishes.

ammoniac, -iaque [amɔnjak] *adj* CHIM ammoniac. ○ **ammoniac** *nm* ammonia. ○ **ammoniaque** *nf* ammonia (water).

amnésie [amnezi] *nf* amnesia.

amniocentèse [amnjɔsɛtɛz] *nf* amniocentesis.

amnistie [amnisti] *nf* amnesty.

amnistier [amnistje] *vt* to amnesty.

amoindrir [amwɛ̃drir] *vt* to diminish.

amonceler [amɔ̃sle] *vt* to accumulate.

amont [amɔ̃] *nm* upstream (water); **en ~ de** [rivière] upriver or upstream from; *fig* prior to.

amoral, -e, -aux [amɔral, o] *adj* [qui ignore la morale] amoral.

amorce [amɔrs] *nf* [d'explosif] priming; [de cartouche, d'obus] cap. || PÊCHE bait. || *fig* [commencement] beginnings (*pl*), germ.

amorcer [amɔrse] *vt* [explosif] to prime. || PÊCHE to bait. || *fig* [commencer] to begin, to initiate.

amorphe [amɔrf] *adj* [personne] lifeless.

amortir [amɔrtir] *vt* [atténuer - choc] to absorb; [- bruit] to deaden, to muffle. || [dette] to pay off. || [achat] to write off.

amour [amur] *nm* [gén] love; **faire l'~** to make love. ○ **amours** *nfpl* [vie sentimentale] love-life.

amoureux, -euse [amurø, øz] **1** *adj* [personne] in love; **être/tomber ~ (de)** to be/fall in love (with). || [regard, geste] loving. **2** *nm, f* [prétendant] suitor.

amour-propre [amurprɔpr] *nm* pride, self-respect.

amovible [amɔvibl] *adj* [déplaçable] detachable, removable.

ampère [ɑ̃pɛr] *nm* amp, ampere.

amphétamine [ɑ̃fetamin] *nf* amphetamine.

amphithéâtre [ɑ̃fiteatr] *nm* HIST amphitheatre. || [d'université] lecture hall or theatre.

ample [ɑ̃pl] *adj* [vêtement - gén] loose-fitting; [- jupe] full. || [projet] extensive; **pour de plus ~s informations** for further details. || [geste] broad, sweeping.

amplement [ɑ̃pləmɑ̃] *adv* [largement] fully, amply.

ampleur [ɑ̃plœr] *nf* [de vêtement] fullness. || [d'événement, de dégâts] extent.

ampli [ɑ̃pli] *nm* amp.

amplificateur, -trice [ɑ̃plifikatœr, tris] *adj* ÉLECTR amplifying. ○ **amplificateur** *nm* [gén] amplifier.

amplifier [ɑ̃plifje] *vt* [mouvement, son] to amplify; [image] to magnify, to enlarge. || [scandale] to increase; [événement, problème] to highlight.

amplitude [ɑ̃plityd] *nf* [de geste] fullness. || [d'onde] amplitude. || [de température] range.

ampoule [ɑ̃pul] *nf* [de lampe] bulb. || [sur la peau] blister. || [médicament] ampoule, phial.

amputation [ɑ̃pytasjɔ̃] *nf* MÉD amputation.

amputer [ɑ̃pyte] *vt* MÉD to amputate; *fig* [couper] to cut (back or down).

amulette [amylɛt] *nf* amulet.

amusant, -e [amyzɑ̃, ɑ̃t] *adj* [drôle] funny; [distrayant] amusing; **c'est très ~** it's great fun.

amuse-gueule [amyzgœl] *nm inv fam* cocktail snack, (party) nibble.

amusement [amyzmɑ̃] *nm* amusement (*U*).

amuser [amyze] *vt* to amuse, to entertain. ○ **s'amuser** *vp* to have fun, to have a good time; **s'~ à faire qqch** to amuse o.s. (by) doing sthg.

amygdale [amidal] *nf* tonsil.

an [ā] *nm* year; **avoir sept ~s** to be seven (years old); **en l'~ 2000** in the year 2000; **le nouvel ~** the New Year.

anachronique [anakrɔnik] *adj* anachronistic.

anagramme [anagram] *nf* anagram.

anal, -e, -aux [anal, o] *adj* anal.

analgésique [analʒezik] *nm & adj* analgesic.

analogie [analɔʒi] *nf* analogy.

analogique [analɔʒik] *adj* analogue.

analogue [analɔg] *adj* analogous, comparable.

analphabète [analfabɛt] *nmf & adj* illiterate.

analyse [analiz] *nf* [étude] analysis. || CHIM & MÉD test, analysis. || [psychanalyse] analysis (*U*).

analyser [analize] *vt* [étudier, psychanalyser] to analyse. || CHIM & MÉD to test, to analyse.

analyste [analist] *nmf* analyst.

analyste-programmeur, -euse [analistprɔgramœr, øz] *nm, f* systems analyst.

analytique [analitik] *adj* analytical.

ananas [anana(s)] *nm* pineapple.

anarchie [anarʃi] *nf* POLIT anarchy. || [désordre] chaos, anarchy.

anarchique [anarʃik] *adj* anarchic.

anarchiste [anarʃist] *nmf & adj* anarchist.

anatomie [anatɔmi] *nf* anatomy.

anatomique [anatɔmik] *adj* anatomical.

ancestral, -e, -aux [āsɛstral, o] *adj* ancestral.

ancêtre [āsɛtr] *nmf* [aïeul] ancestor; *fig* [forme première] forerunner, ancestor.

anchois [āʃwa] *nm* anchovy.

ancien, -ienne [āsjē, jɛn] *adj* [gén] old. || (*avant n*) [précédent] former, old. || [du passé] ancient.

anciennement [āsjɛnmā] *adv* formerly, previously.

ancienneté [āsjɛnte] *nf* [d'une tradition] oldness. || [d'un employé] seniority.

ancre [ākr] *nf* NAVIG anchor; **jeter l'~** to drop anchor; **lever l'~** to weigh anchor; *fam* [partir] to make tracks.

ancrer [ākre] *vt* [bateau] to anchor; *fig* [idée, habitude] to root.

Andes [ād] *nfpl*: **les ~** the Andes.

andouille [āduj] *nf* [charcuterie] *type of sausage made of chitterlings (pig's intestines)*. || *fam* [imbécile] prat, twit.

âne [an] *nm* ZOOL ass, donkey. || *fam* [imbécile] ass.

anéantir [aneātir] *vt* [détruire] to annihilate; *fig* to ruin, to wreck. || [démoraliser] to crush, to overwhelm.

anecdote [anɛkdɔt] *nf* anecdote.

anecdotique [anɛkdɔtik] *adj* anecdotal.

anémie [anemi] *nf* MÉD anaemia; *fig* enfeeblement.

anémié, -e [anemje] *adj* anaemic.

anémique [anemik] *adj* anaemic.

anémone [anemɔn] *nf* anemone.

ânerie [anri] *nf fam* [parole, acte]: **dire/faire une ~** to say/do something stupid.

ânesse [anɛs] *nf* she-ass, she-donkey.

anesthésie [anɛstezi] *nf* anaesthesia; **~ locale/générale** local/general anaesthetic.

anesthésier [anɛstezje] *vt* to anaesthetize.

anesthésique [anɛstezik] *nm & adj* anaesthetic.

anesthésiste [anɛstezist] *nmf* anaesthetist.

ange [āʒ] *nm* angel; **~ gardien** guardian angel; **être aux ~s** *fig* to be in one's seventh heaven.

angélique [āʒelik] *adj* angelic.

angélus [āʒelys] *nm* [sonnerie] angelus (bell).

angine [āʒin] *nf* [pharyngite] pharyngitis; [amygdalite] tonsillitis.

anglais, -e [āglɛ, ɛz] *adj* English. ○ **anglais** *nm* [langue] English. ○ **Anglais, -e** *nm, f* Englishman (*f* Englishwoman); **les Anglais** the English. ○ **anglaises** *nfpl* ringlets.

angle [āgl] *nm* [coin] corner. || MATHS angle; **~ droit/aigu/obtus** right/acute/obtuse angle.

Angleterre [āglətɛr] *nf*: **l'~** England.

anglican, -e [āglikā, an] *adj & nm, f* Anglican.

anglophone [āglɔfɔn] **1** *nmf* English-speaker. **2** *adj* English-speaking, anglophone.

anglo-saxon, -onne [āglosaksɔ̃, ɔn] *adj* Anglo-Saxon. ○ **Anglo-Saxon, -onne** *nm, f* Anglo-Saxon.

angoisse [āgwas] *nf* anguish.

angoisser [āgwase] *vt* [effrayer] to

cause anxiety to. ○ **s'angoisser** *vp* [être anxieux] to be overcome with anxiety.

anguille [ãgij] *nf* eel.

anguleux, -euse [ãgylø, øz] *adj* angular.

anicroche [anikrɔʃ] *nf* hitch.

animal, -e, -aux [animal, o] *adj* [propre à l'animal] animal (*avant n*). ‖ [instinctif] instinctive. ○ **animal** *nm* [bête] animal; ~ **sauvage/domestique** wild/domestic animal.

animateur, -trice [animatœr, tris] *nm, f* RADIO & TÉLÉ presenter. ‖ [socioculturel, sportif] activities organizer.

animation [animasjɔ̃] *nf* [de rue] activity, life; [de conversation, visage] animation. ‖ [activités] activities (*pl*). ‖ CIN animation.

animé, -e [anime] *adj* [rue] lively; [conversation, visage] animated; [objet] animate.

animer [anime] *vt* [mettre de l'entrain dans] to animate, to liven up. ‖ [présenter] to present. ‖ [organiser des activités pour] to organize activities for. ○ **s'animer** *vp* [visage] to light up. ‖ [rue] to come to life, to liven up.

animosité [animozite] *nf* animosity.

anis [ani(s)] *nm* BOT anise; CULIN aniseed.

ankylosé, -e [ãkiloze] *adj* [paralysé] stiff; [engourdi] numb.

annales [anal] *nfpl* [d'examen] past papers.

anneau, -x [ano] *nm* [gén] ring. ‖ [maillon] link.

année [ane] *nf* year; **souhaiter la bonne ~ à qqn** to wish sb a Happy New Year; ~ **bissextile** leap year; ~**lumière** light year; ~ **scolaire** school year.

annexe [anɛks] **1** *nf* [de dossier] appendix, annexe. ‖ [de bâtiment] annexe. **2** *adj* related, associated.

annexer [anekse] *vt* [incorporer]: ~ **qqch (à qqch)** to append ou annex sthg (to sthg). ‖ [pays] to annex.

annexion [aneksjɔ̃] *nf* annexation.

annihiler [aniile] *vt* [réduire à néant] to destroy, to wreck.

anniversaire [aniversɛr] *nm* [de mariage, mort, événement] anniversary; [de naissance] birthday; **bon** ou **joyeux ~!** happy birthday!

annonce [anɔ̃s] *nf* [déclaration] announcement; *fig* sign, indication. ‖ [texte] advertisement; **petite ~** classified advertisement, small ad.

annoncer [anɔ̃se] *vt* [faire savoir] to announce. ‖ [prédire] to predict.

annoter [anɔte] *vt* to annotate.

annuaire [anɥɛr] *nm* annual, yearbook; ~ **téléphonique** telephone directory, phone book.

annuel, -elle [anɥɛl] *adj* [tous les ans] annual, yearly. ‖ [d'une année] annual.

annuité [anɥite] *nf* [paiement] annual payment ou instalment. ‖ [année de service] year (of service).

annulaire [anɥlɛr] *nm* ring finger.

annulation [anylasjɔ̃] *nf* [de rendez-vous, réservation] cancellation. ‖ [de mariage] annulment.

annuler [anyle] *vt* [rendez-vous, réservation] to cancel. ‖ [mariage] to annul.

anoblir [anɔblir] *vt* to ennoble.

anodin, -e [anɔdɛ̃, in] *adj* [blessure] minor. ‖ [propos] harmless. ‖ [détail, personne] insignificant.

anomalie [anɔmali] *nf* anomaly.

ânonner [anɔne] *vt & vi* to recite in a drone.

anonymat [anɔnima] *nm* anonymity.

anonyme [anɔnim] *adj* anonymous.

anorak [anɔrak] *nm* anorak.

anorexie [anɔrɛksi] *nf* anorexia.

anormal, -e, -aux [anɔrmal, o] **1** *adj* [inhabituel] abnormal, not normal. ‖ [intolérable, injuste] wrong, not right. ‖ [arriéré] (mentally) subnormal. **2** *nm, f* mental defective.

ANPE (*abr de* **Agence nationale pour l'emploi**) *nf French national employment agency*; ≃ job centre *Br*.

anse [ãs] *nf* [d'ustensile] handle. ‖ GÉOGR cove.

antagoniste [ãtagɔnist] *adj* antagonistic.

antarctique [ãtarktik] *adj* Antarctic; **le cercle polaire ~** the Antarctic Circle. ○ **Antarctique** *nm* [continent]: **l'~** Antarctica. ‖ [océan]: **l'~** the Antarctic (Ocean).

antécédent [ãtesedã] *nm* (*gén pl*) [passé] history (*sg*).

antenne [ãtɛn] *nf* [d'insecte] antenna, feeler. ‖ [de télévision, de radio] aerial *Br*, antenna. ‖ [succursale] branch, office.

antérieur, -e [ãterjœr] *adj* [dans le temps] earlier, previous; ~ **à** previous ou prior to. ‖ [dans l'espace] front (*avant n*).

antérieurement [ãterjœrmã] *adv* earlier, previously; ~ **à** prior to.

anthologie [ãtɔlɔʒi] *nf* anthology.

anthracite [ɑ̃trasit] **1** nm anthracite. **2** adj inv charcoal (grey).

anthropologie [ɑ̃trɔpɔlɔʒi] nf anthropology.

anthropophage [ɑ̃trɔpɔfaʒ] nmf cannibal.

antibiotique [ɑ̃tibjɔtik] nm & adj antibiotic.

antibrouillard [ɑ̃tibrujar] nm & adj inv: (phare ou feu) ~ fog lamp Br, foglight Am.

antichambre [ɑ̃tiʃɑ̃br] nf antechamber.

anticipation [ɑ̃tisipasjɔ̃] nf LITTÉRATURE: roman d'~ science fiction novel.

anticipé, -e [ɑ̃tisipe] adj early.

anticiper [ɑ̃tisipe] **1** vt to anticipate. **2** vi: ~ (sur qqch) to anticipate (sth).

anticonformiste [ɑ̃tikɔ̃fɔrmist] adj & nmf non-conformist.

anticorps [ɑ̃tikɔr] nm antibody.

anticyclone [ɑ̃tisiklon] nm anticyclone.

antidater [ɑ̃tidate] vt to backdate.

antidépresseur [ɑ̃tidepresœr] nm & adj m antidepressant.

antidote [ɑ̃tidɔt] nm antidote.

antigel [ɑ̃tiʒɛl] nm inv & adj inv antifreeze.

antillais, -e [ɑ̃tijɛ, ɛz] adj West Indian. ○ **Antillais, -e** nm, f West Indian.

Antilles [ɑ̃tij] nfpl: les ~ the West Indies.

antilope [ɑ̃tilɔp] nf antelope.

antimilitariste [ɑ̃timilitarist] nmf & adj antimilitarist.

antimite [ɑ̃timit] adj inv: boule ~ mothball.

antipathie [ɑ̃tipati] nf antipathy, hostility.

antipathique [ɑ̃tipatik] adj unpleasant; elle m'est ~ I dislike her, I don't like her.

antipelliculaire [ɑ̃tipelikylɛr] adj: shampooing ~ anti-dandruff shampoo.

antiphrase [ɑ̃tifraz] nf antiphrasis.

antiquaire [ɑ̃tikɛr] nmf antique dealer.

antique [ɑ̃tik] adj [de l'antiquité - civilisation] ancient; [- vase, objet] antique. || [vieux] antiquated, ancient.

antiquité [ɑ̃tikite] nf [époque]: l'Antiquité antiquity. || [objet] antique.

antirides [ɑ̃tirid] adj inv anti-wrinkle.

antirouille [ɑ̃tiruj] adj inv [traitement] rust (avant n); [revêtement, peinture] rustproof.

antisèche [ɑ̃tisɛʃ] nm & nf arg scol crib Br, cheat sheet Am.

antisémite [ɑ̃tisemit] **1** nmf anti-Semite. **2** adj anti-Semitic.

antiseptique [ɑ̃tisɛptik] nm & adj antiseptic.

antisismique [ɑ̃tisismik] adj earthquake-proof.

antithèse [ɑ̃titɛz] nf antithesis.

antiviral, -aux [ɑ̃tiviral, o] nm antivirus.

antivol [ɑ̃tivɔl] nm inv anti-theft device.

antre [ɑ̃tr] nm den, lair.

anus [anys] nm anus.

anxiété [ɑ̃ksjete] nf anxiety.

anxieux, -ieuse [ɑ̃ksjø, jøz] **1** adj anxious, worried; être ~ de faire qqch to be anxious to do sthg. **2** nm, f worrier.

aorte [aɔrt] nf aorta.

août [u(t)] nm August; voir aussi septembre.

apaisement [apɛzmɑ̃] nm [moral] comfort. || [de douleur] alleviation. || [de tension, de crise] calming.

apaiser [apeze] vt [personne] to calm down, to pacify. || [conscience] to salve; [douleur] to soothe; [soif] to slake, to quench; [faim] to assuage. ○ **s'apaiser** vp [personne] to calm down. || [besoin] to be assuaged; [tempête] to subside, to abate; [douleur] to die down.

apanage [apanaʒ] nm sout privilege; être l'~ de qqn/qqch to be the prerogative of sb/sthg.

aparté [aparte] nm THÉÂTRE aside. || [conversation] private conversation; prendre qqn en ~ to take sb aside.

apartheid [aparted] nm apartheid.

apathie [apati] nf apathy.

apathique [apatik] adj apathetic.

apatride [apatrid] nmf stateless person.

apercevoir [apɛrsəvwar] vt [voir] to see, to catch sight of. ○ **s'apercevoir** vp: s'~ de qqch to notice sthg; s'~ que to notice (that).

aperçu, -e [apɛrsy] pp → apercevoir. ○ **aperçu** nm general idea.

apéritif [aperitif] nm aperitif; prendre l'~ to have an aperitif, to have drinks (before a meal).

apesanteur [apəzɑ̃tœr] nf weightlessness.

à-peu-près [apøprɛ] nm inv approximation.

aphone [afɔn] adj voiceless.

aphrodisiaque [afrɔdizjak] nm & adj aphrodisiac.

aphte [aft] nm mouth ulcer.

apitoyer [apitwaje] *vt* to move to pity. ○ **s'apitoyer** *vp* to feel pity; **s'~ sur** to feel sorry for.

ap. J.-C. (*abr de* après Jésus-Christ) AD.

aplanir [aplanir] *vt* [aplatir] to level. ‖ *fig* [difficulté, obstacle] to smooth away, to iron out.

aplatir [aplatir] *vt* [gén] to flatten; [couture] to press flat; [cheveux] to smooth down.

aplomb [apl5] *nm* [stabilité] balance. ‖ [audace] nerve, cheek. ○ **d'aplomb** *loc adv* steady.

apocalypse [apɔkalips] *nf* apocalypse.

apogée [apɔʒe] *nm* ASTRON apogee; *fig* peak.

apolitique [apɔlitik] *adj* apolitical, unpolitical.

apologie [apɔlɔʒi] *nf* justification, apology.

apoplexie [apɔplɛksi] *nf* apoplexy.

apostrophe [apɔstrɔf] *nf* [signe graphique] apostrophe.

apostropher [apɔstrɔfe] *vt*: ~ **qqn** to speak rudely to sb.

apothéose [apɔteoz] *nf* [point culminant - d'un spectacle] grand finale; [- d'une carrière] crowning glory.

apôtre [apotr] *nm* apostle, disciple.

apparaître [aparɛtr] *vi* [gén] to appear. ‖ [se dévoiler] to come to light.

apparat [apara] *nm* pomp; **d'~** [dîner, habit] ceremonial.

appareil [aparɛj] *nm* [gén] device; [électrique] appliance. ‖ [téléphone] phone, telephone; **qui est à l'~?** who's speaking? ‖ [avion] aircraft. ○ **appareil digestif** *nm* digestive system. ○ **appareil photo** *nm* camera.

appareillage [aparɛjaʒ] *nm* [équipement] equipment. ‖ NAVIG getting under way.

appareiller [apareje] **1** *vt* [assortir] to match up. **2** *vi* NAVIG to get under way.

apparemment [aparamɑ̃] *adv* apparently.

apparence [aparɑ̃s] *nf* appearance. ○ **en apparence** *loc adv* seemingly, apparently.

apparent, -e [aparɑ̃, ɑ̃t] *adj* [superficiel, illusoire] apparent. ‖ [visible] visible.

apparenté, -e [aparɑ̃te] *adj*: ~ **à** [personne] related to; *fig* [ressemblant] similar to.

apparition [aparisjɔ̃] *nf* [gén] appear-

ance. ‖ [vision - RELIG] vision; [- de fantôme] apparition.

appart [apart] (*abr de* appartement) *nm fam* flat *Br*, apartment *Am*.

appartement [apartəmɑ̃] *nm* flat *Br*, apartment *Am*.

appartenir [apartənir] *vi* [être la propriété de]: ~ **à qqn** to belong to sb. ‖ [faire partie de]: ~ **à qqch** to belong to sthg, to be a member of sthg.

appartenu [apartəny] *pp inv* → appartenir.

apparu, -e [apary] *pp* → apparaître.

appâter [apate] *vt litt & fig* to lure.

appauvrir [apovrir] *vt* to impoverish. ○ **s'appauvrir** *vp* to grow poorer, to become impoverished.

appel [apɛl] *nm* [gén] call; **faire ~ à qqn** to appeal to sb; **faire ~ à qqch** [avoir recours à] to call on sthg; ~ **(téléphonique)** (phone) call. ‖ JUR appeal; **faire ~** JUR to appeal. ‖ [pour vérifier - gén] roll-call; [- SCOL] registration. ‖ COMM: ~ **d'offre** invitation to tender. ‖ [signe]: **faire un ~ de phares** to flash one's headlights.

appelé [aple] *nm* conscript.

appeler [aple] *vt* [gén] to call. ‖ [téléphoner] to ring, to call. ‖ [exiger] to call for. ○ **s'appeler** *vp* [se nommer] to be called; **il s'appelle Patrick** his name is Patrick, he's called Patrick. ‖ [se téléphoner]: **on s'appelle demain?** shall we talk tomorrow?

appendice [apɛ̃dis] *nm* appendix.

appendicite [apɛ̃disit] *nf* appendicitis.

appentis [apɑ̃ti] *nm* lean-to.

appesantir [apəzɑ̃tir] ○ **s'appesantir** *vp* [s'alourdir] to become heavy. ‖ [insister]: **s'~ sur qqch** to dwell on sthg.

appétissant, -e [apetisɑ̃, ɑ̃t] *adj* [nourriture] appetizing.

appétit [apeti] *nm* appetite; **bon ~!** enjoy your meal!

applaudir [aplodir] **1** *vt* to applaud. **2** *vi* to clap, to applaud; ~ **à qqch** *fig* to applaud sthg; ~ **à tout rompre** *fig* to bring the house down.

applaudissements [aplodismɑ̃] *nmpl* applause (U), clapping (U).

application [aplikasjɔ̃] *nf* [gén & INFORM] application.

applique [aplik] *nf* wall lamp.

appliquer [aplike] *vt* [gén] to apply; [loi] to enforce. ○ **s'appliquer** *vp* [s'étaler, se poser]: **cette peinture s'applique facilement** this paint goes on easily.

|| [se concentrer]: **s'~ (à faire qqch)** to apply o.s. (to doing sthg).

appoint [apwɛ̃] *nm* [monnaie] change; **faire l'~** to give the right money; **d'~** [salaire, chauffage] extra.

appointements [apwɛ̃tmɑ̃] *nmpl* salary (*sg*).

apport [apɔr] *nm* [gén & FIN] contribution. || [de chaleur] input.

apporter [apɔrte] *rt* [gén] to bring. || [raison, preuve] to provide, to give. || [mettre - soin] to exercise; [- attention] to give.

apposer [apoze] *rt* [affiche] to put up. || [signature] to append.

apposition [apozisjɔ̃] *nf* GRAM apposition.

appréciable [apresjabl] *adj* [notable] appreciable. || [précieux]: **un grand jardin, c'est ~!** I/we really appreciate having a big garden.

appréciation [apresjasjɔ̃] *nf* [de valeur] valuation; [de distance, poids] estimation. || [jugement] judgment. || SCOL assessment.

apprécier [apresje] *rt* [gén] to appreciate. || [évaluer] to estimate, to assess.

appréhender [apreɑ̃de] *rt* [arrêter] to arrest. || [craindre]: **~ qqch/de faire qqch** to dread sthg/doing sthg.

appréhension [apreɑ̃sjɔ̃] *nf* apprehension.

apprendre [aprɑ̃dr] *rt* [étudier] to learn; **~ à faire qqch** to learn (how) to do sthg. || [enseigner] to teach; **~ qqch à qqn** to teach sb sthg; **~ à qqn à faire qqch** to teach sb (how) to do sthg. || [nouvelle] to hear of, to learn of; **~ que** to hear that, to learn that; **~ qqch à qqn** to tell sb of sthg.

apprenti, -e [aprɑ̃ti] *nm, f* [élève] apprentice; *fig* beginner.

apprentissage [aprɑ̃tisaʒ] *nm* [de métier] apprenticeship. || [formation] learning.

apprêter [aprete] *rt* to prepare. ○ **s'apprêter** *rp* [être sur le point]: **s'~ à faire qqch** to get ready to do sthg.

appris, -e [apri, iz] *pp* → apprendre.

apprivoiser [aprivwaze] *rt* to tame.

approbateur, -trice [aprobatœr, tris] *adj* approving.

approbation [aprobasjɔ̃] *nf* approval.

approchant, -e [aproʃɑ̃, ɑ̃t] *adj* similar.

approche [aproʃ] *nf* [arrivée] approach;

à l'~ **des fêtes** as the Christmas holidays draw near.

approcher [aproʃe] **1** *rt* [mettre plus près] to move near, to bring near; **~ qqch de qqn/qqch** to move sthg near (to) sthg. || [aborder] to go up to, to approach. **2** *vi* to approach, to go/come near; **n'approchez pas!** keep oʊ stay away!; **~ de** [moment, fin] to approach. ○ **s'approcher** *rp* to come/go near, to approach; **s'~ de qqn/qqch** to approach sb/sthg.

approfondir [aprofɔ̃dir] *rt* [creuser] to make deeper. || [développer] to go further into.

approprié, -e [aproprije] *adj* : **~ (à)** appropriate (to).

approprier [aproprije] *rt* [adapter] to adapt. || *Belg* to clean. ○ **s'approprier** *rp* [s'adjuger] to appropriate.

approuver [apruve] *rt* [gén] to approve of.

approvisionnement [aprovizjɔnmɑ̃] *nm* supplies (*pl*), stocks (*pl*).

approvisionner [aprovizjɔne] *rt* [compte en banque] to pay money into. || [magasin, pays] to supply.

approximatif, -ive [aproksimatif, iv] *adj* approximate, rough.

approximation [aproksimasjɔ̃] *nf* approximation.

approximativement [aproksimativmɑ̃] *adr* approximately, roughly.

appt *abr de* **appartement**.

appui [apɥi] *nm* [soutien] support.

appui-tête [apɥitet] (*pl* **appuis-tête**) *nm* headrest.

appuyer [apɥije] **1** *rt* [poser]: **~ qqch sur/contre qqch** to lean sthg on/against sthg, to rest sthg on/against sthg. || [presser]: **~ qqch sur/contre** to press sthg on/against. || *fig* [soutenir] to support. **2** *vi* [reposer]: **~ sur** to lean oʊ rest on. || [presser] to push; **~ sur** [bouton] to press. || *fig* [insister]: **~ sur** to stress. ○ **s'appuyer** *rp* [se tenir]: **s'~ contre/sur** to lean against/on, to rest against/on. || [se baser]: **s'~ sur** to rely on.

âpre [apr] *adj* [goût, discussion, combat] bitter. || [ton, épreuve, critique] harsh. || [concurrence] fierce.

après [apre] **1** *prép* [gén] after; **~ avoir mangé, ils ...** after having eaten oʊ after they had eaten, they ...; **~ quoi** after which. || [indiquant l'attirance, l'attachement, l'hostilité]: **aboyer ~ qqn** to bark at sb. **2** *adr* [temps] afterwards; **un**

mois ~ one month later; **le mois d'~** the following or next month. || [lieu, dans un ordre, dans un rang]: **la rue d'~** the next street; **c'est ma sœur qui vient** ~ my sister's next. ○ **après coup** *loc adv* afterwards, after the event. ○ **après que** *loc conj* (+ *indicatif*) after; **je le verrai** ~ **qu'il aura fini** I'll see him after or when he's finished. ○ **après tout** *loc adv* after all. ○ **d'après** *loc prép* according to; **d'~ moi** in my opinion. ○ **et après** *loc adv* [questionnement sur la suite] and then what? || [exprime l'indifférence] so what?

après-demain [apʁɛdmɛ̃] *adv* the day after tomorrow.

après-guerre [apʁɛgɛʁ] *nm* post-war years (*pl*); **d'~** post-war.

après-midi [apʁɛmidi] *nm inv ou nf inv* afternoon.

après-rasage [apʁɛʁazaʒ] *nm & adj inv* aftershave.

après-ski [apʁɛski] *nm* [chaussure] snow-boot.

après-soleil [apʁɛsɔlɛj] *adj inv* aftersun (*avant n*).

après-vente [apʁɛvɑ̃t] → **service**.

à-propos [apʁopo] *nm inv* [de remarque] aptness; **faire preuve d'~** to show presence of mind.

apte [apt] *adj*: ~ **à qqch/à faire qqch** capable of sthg/of doing sthg; ~ **(au service)** MIL fit (for service).

aquarelle [akwaʁɛl] *nf* watercolour.

aquarium [akwaʁjɔm] *nm* aquarium.

aquatique [akwatik] *adj* [plante, animal] aquatic; [milieu, paysage] watery, marshy.

aqueduc [akdyk] *nm* aqueduct.

aqueux, -euse [akø, øz] *adj* watery.

aquilin [akilɛ̃] → **nez**.

arabe [aʁab] **1** *adj* [peuple] Arab. **2** *nm* [langue] Arabic. ○ **Arabe** *nmf* Arab.

arabesque [aʁabɛsk] *nf* [ornement] arabesque. || [ligne sinueuse] flourish.

Arabie [aʁabi] *nf*: **l'~** Arabia; **l'~ Saoudite** Saudi Arabia.

arachide [aʁaʃid] *nf* [plante] groundnut. || [graine] peanut, groundnut.

araignée [aʁɛɲe] *nf* spider. ○ **araignée de mer** *nf* spider crab.

arbalète [aʁbalɛt] *nf* crossbow.

arbitrage [aʁbitʁaʒ] *nm* [SPORT - gén] refereeing; [- au tennis, cricket] umpiring. || JUR arbitration.

arbitraire [aʁbitʁɛʁ] *adj* arbitrary.

arbitre [aʁbitʁ] *nm* [SPORT - gén] referee; [- au tennis, cricket] umpire. || [conciliateur] arbitrator.

arbitrer [aʁbitʁe] *vt* [SPORT - gén] to referee; [- au tennis, cricket] to umpire. || [conflit] to arbitrate.

arbre [aʁbʁ] *nm* BOT & *fig* tree; ~ **fruitier** fruit tree; ~ **généalogique** family tree. || [axe] shaft.

arbuste [aʁbyst] *nm* shrub.

arc [aʁk] *nm* [arme] bow. || [courbe] arc; ~ **de cercle** arc of a circle. || ARCHIT arch.

arcade [aʁkad] *nf* ARCHIT arch; ~**s** arcade (*sg*). || ANAT: ~ **sourcilière** arch of the eyebrows.

arc-bouter [aʁkbute] ○ **s'arc-bouter** *vp* to brace o.s.

arceau, -x [aʁso] *nm* ARCHIT arch. || [objet métallique] hoop.

arc-en-ciel [aʁkɑ̃sjɛl] (*pl* **arcs-en-ciel**) *nm* rainbow.

archaïque [aʁkaik] *adj* archaic.

arche [aʁʃ] *nf* ARCHIT arch.

archéologie [aʁkeɔlɔʒi] *nf* archaeology.

archéologique [aʁkeɔlɔʒik] *adj* archaeological.

archéologue [aʁkeɔlɔg] *nmf* archaeologist.

archet [aʁʃɛ] *nm* MUS bow.

archevêque [aʁʃəvɛk] *nm* archbishop.

archipel [aʁʃipɛl] *nm* archipelago.

architecte [aʁʃitɛkt] *nmf* architect.

architecture [aʁʃitɛktyʁ] *nf* architecture; *fig* structure.

archives [aʁʃiv] *nfpl* [de bureau] records; [de musée] archives.

archiviste [aʁʃivist] *nmf* archivist.

arctique [aʁktik] *adj* Arctic; **le cercle polaire** ~ the Arctic Circle. ○ **Arctique** *nm*: **l'~** the Arctic.

ardemment [aʁdamɑ̃] *adv* fervently, passionately.

ardent, -e [aʁdɑ̃, ɑ̃t] *adj* [soleil] blazing. || [soif, fièvre] raging; [passion] burning.

ardeur [aʁdœʁ] *nf* [vigueur] fervour, enthusiasm. || [chaleur] blazing heat.

ardoise [aʁdwaz] *nf* slate.

ardu, -e [aʁdy] *adj* [travail] arduous; [problème] difficult.

are [aʁ] *nm 100 square metres.*

arène [aʁɛn] *nf* arena. ○ **arènes** *nfpl* [romaines] amphitheatre (*sg*).

arête [aʁɛt] *nf* [de poisson] bone. || [du nez] bridge.

argent [aʁʒɑ̃] *nm* [métal, couleur] silver. || [monnaie] money; ~ **liquide** (ready) cash; ~ **de poche** pocket money.

argenté, -e [arʒɑ̃te] *adj* silvery, silver.
argenterie [arʒɑ̃tri] *nf* silverware.
Argentine [arʒɑ̃tin] *nf:* **l'~** Argentina.
argile [arʒil] *nf* clay.
argileux, -euse [arʒilø, øz] *adj* clayey.
argot [argo] *nm* slang.
argotique [argɔtik] *adj* slang (*avant n*), slangy.
argument [argymɑ̃] *nm* argument.
argumentation [argymɑ̃tasjɔ̃] *nf* argumentation.
argus [argys] *nm:* **coté à l'~** *rated in the guide to secondhand car prices.*
aride [arid] *adj litt & fig* arid.
aristocrate [aristɔkrat] *nmf* aristocrat.
aristocratie [aristɔkrasi] *nf* aristocracy.
arithmétique [aritmetik] *nf* arithmetic.
armateur [armatœr] *nm* ship owner.
armature [armatyr] *nf* CONSTR & *fig* framework. || [de parapluie] frame; [de soutien-gorge] underwiring.
arme [arm] *nf litt & fig* weapon; **~ blanche** blade; **~ à feu** firearm. ○ **armes** *nfpl* [blason] coat of arms (*sg*).
armée [arme] *nf* army; **l'~ de l'air** the air force; **l'~ de terre** the army. ○ **Armée du salut** *nf:* **l'Armée du salut** the Salvation Army.
armement [arməmɑ̃] *nm* [MIL - de personne] arming; [- de pays] armament; [- ensemble d'armes] arms (*pl*); **la course aux ~s** the arms race.
armer [arme] *vt* [pourvoir en armes] to arm; **être armé pour qqch/pour faire qqch** *fig* [préparé] to be equipped for sthg/to do sthg. || [fusil] to cock. || [appareil photo] to wind on. || [navire] to fit out.
armistice [armistis] *nm* armistice.
armoire [armwar] *nf* [gén] closet *Am*; [garde-robe] wardrobe; **c'est une ~ à glace!** *fam fig* he's built like a tank!; **~ à pharmacie** medicine cabinet.
armoiries [armwari] *nfpl* coat of arms (*sg*).
armure [armyr] *nf* armour.
armurier [armyrje] *nm* [d'armes à feu] gunsmith; [d'armes blanches] armourer.
arnaque [arnak] *nf fam* rip-off.
arnaquer [arnake] *vt fam* to do *Br*, to swindle; **se faire ~** to be had.
aromate [arɔmat] *nm* [épice] spice; [fine herbe] herb.
arôme [arom] *nm* [gén] aroma; [de fleur, parfum] fragrance. || [goût] flavour.

arpège [arpeʒ] *nm* arpeggio.
arpenter [arpɑ̃te] *vt* [marcher] to pace up and down.
arqué, -e [arke] *adj* [jambe] bow (*avant n*), bandy; [sourcil] arched.
arr. *abr de* **arrondissement.**
arrache-pied [araʃpje] ○ **d'arrache-pied** *loc adv:* **travailler d'~** to work away furiously.
arracher [araʃe] *vt* [extraire - plante] to pull up ou out; [- dent] to extract. || [déchirer - page] to tear off ou out; [- chemise, bras] to tear off. || [prendre]: **~ qqch à qqn** to snatch sthg from sb. || [soustraire]: **~ qqn à** [milieu, lieu] to drag sb away from; [lit, sommeil] to drag sb from.
arrangeant, -e [arɑ̃ʒɑ̃, ɑ̃t] *adj* obliging.
arrangement [arɑ̃ʒmɑ̃] *nm* [gén] arrangement. || [accord] agreement, arrangement.
arranger [arɑ̃ʒe] *vt* [gén] to arrange. || [convenir à] to suit. || [régler] to settle. || [améliorer] to sort out. || [réparer] to fix. ○ **s'arranger** *vp* to come to an agreement; **s'~ pour faire qqch** to manage to do sthg; **cela va s'~** things will work out.
arrdt. *abr de* **arrondissement.**
arrestation [arɛstasjɔ̃] *nf* arrest; **être en état d'~** to be under arrest.
arrêt [arɛ] *nm* [d'un mouvement] stopping; **à l'~** [véhicule] stationary; [machine] (switched) off. || [interruption] interruption; **sans ~** [sans interruption] non-stop; [sans relâche] constantly, continually; **être en ~ maladie** to be on sick leave. || [station]: **~ (d'autobus)** (bus) stop. || JUR decision, judgment.
arrêté [arete] *nm* ADMIN order, decree.
arrêter [arete] **1** *vt* [gén] to stop. || [cesser]: **~ de faire qqch** to stop doing sthg; **~ de fumer** to stop smoking. || [voleur] to arrest. **2** *vi* to stop. ○ **s'arrêter** *vp* to stop; **s'~ de faire** to stop doing.
arrhes [ar] *nfpl* deposit (*sg*).
arrière [arjer] **1** *adj inv* back, rear; **marche ~** reverse gear. **2** *nm* [partie postérieure] back; **à l'~** at the back *Br*, in back *Am*. || SPORT back. ○ **en arrière** *loc adv* [dans la direction opposée] back, backwards. || [derrière, à la traîne] behind; **rester en ~** to lag behind.
arriéré, -e [arjere] *adj* [mentalité, pays] backward. ○ **arriéré** *nm* arrears (*pl*).
arrière-boutique [arjerbutik] (*pl* **arrière-boutiques**) *nf* back shop.

arrière-garde [arjɛrgard] (*pl* arrière-gardes) *nf* rearguard.

arrière-goût [arjɛrgu] (*pl* arrière-goûts) *nm* aftertaste.

arrière-grand-mère [arjɛrgrɑ̃mɛr] (*pl* arrière-grands-mères) *nf* great-grandmother.

arrière-grand-père [arjɛrgrɑ̃pɛr] (*pl* arrière-grands-pères) *nm* great-grandfather.

arrière-pays [arjɛrpei] *nm inv* hinterland.

arrière-pensée [arjɛrpɑ̃se] (*pl* arrière-pensées) *nf* [raison intéressée] ulterior motive.

arrière-plan [arjɛrplɑ̃] (*pl* arrière-plans) *nm* background.

arrière-saison [arjɛrsɛzɔ̃] (*pl* arrière-saisons) *nf* late autumn.

arrière-train [arjɛrtrɛ̃] (*pl* arrière-trains) *nm* hindquarters (*pl*).

arrimer [arime] *vt* [attacher] to secure. || NAVIG to stow.

arrivage [arivaʒ] *nm* [de marchandises] consignment, delivery.

arrivée [arive] *nf* [venue] arrival. || TECHNOL inlet.

arriver [arive] **1** *vi* [venir] to arrive; **j'arrive!** (I'm) coming!; **~ à Paris** to arrive in ou reach Paris; **l'eau m'arrivait aux genoux** the water came up to my knees. || [parvenir]: **~ à faire qqch** to manage to do sthg, to succeed in doing sthg. **2** *v impers* to happen; **il arrive que** (+ *subjonctif*): **il arrive qu'il soit en retard** he is sometimes late; **il arrive à tout le monde de se tromper** anyone can make a mistake; **il lui arrive d'oublier quel jour on est** he sometimes forgets what day it is; **quoi qu'il arrive** whatever happens.

arrivisme [arivism] *nm péj* ambition.

arrogance [arɔgɑ̃s] *nf* arrogance.

arrogant, -e [arɔgɑ̃, ɑ̃t] *adj* arrogant.

arroger [arɔʒe] ○ **s'arroger** *vp*: **s'~ le droit de faire qqch** to take it upon o.s. to do sthg.

arrondir [arɔ̃dir] *vt* [forme] to make round. || [chiffre en haut] to round up; [- en bas] to round down.

arrondissement [arɔ̃dismɑ̃] *nm* ADMIN arrondissement (*administrative division of a département or city*).

arroser [arɔze] *vt* [jardin] to water, to spray. || *fam* [célébrer] to celebrate.

arrosoir [arɔzwar] *nm* watering can.

arsenal, -aux [arsənal, o] *nm* [de navires] naval dockyard. || [d'armes] arsenal.

arsenic [arsənik] *nm* arsenic.

art [ar] *nm* art; **le septième ~** cinema; **~s et métiers** *state-funded institution offering vocational courses by correspondence or evening classes.*

art. *abr de* article.

artère [artɛr] *nf* ANAT artery. || [rue] arterial road.

artériel, -ielle [arterjɛl] *adj* arterial.

artériosclérose [arterjɔskleroz] *nf* arteriosclerosis.

arthrite [artrit] *nf* arthritis.

arthrose [artroz] *nf* osteoarthritis.

artichaut [artiʃo] *nm* artichoke.

article [artikl] *nm* [gén] article. || *loc*: **à l'~ de la mort** at death's door.

articulation [artikylasjɔ̃] *nf* ANAT & TECHNOL joint. || [prononciation] articulation.

articuler [artikyle] *vt* [prononcer] to articulate. || ANAT & TECHNOL to articulate, to joint.

artifice [artifis] *nm* [moyen astucieux] clever device ou trick. || [tromperie] trick.

artificiel, -ielle [artifisjɛl] *adj* artificial.

artillerie [artijri] *nf* MIL artillery.

artisan, -e [artizɑ̃, an] *nm, f* craftsman (*f* craftswoman).

artisanal, -e, -aux [artizanal, o] *adj* craft (*avant n*).

artisanat [artizana] *nm* [métier] craft; [classe] craftsmen.

artiste [artist] *nmf* [créateur] artist; **~ peintre** painter. || [interprète] performer.

artistique [artistik] *adj* artistic.

as¹ [a] → avoir.

as² [as] *nm* [carte] ace. || [champion] star, ace.

ascendant, -e [asɑ̃dɑ̃, ɑ̃t] *adj* rising. ○ **ascendant** *nm* [influence] influence, power. || ASTROL ascendant.

ascenseur [asɑ̃sœr] *nm* lift *Br*, elevator *Am*.

ascension [asɑ̃sjɔ̃] *nf* [de montagne] ascent. || [progression] rise. ○ **Ascension** *nf*: **l'Ascension** Ascension (Day).

ascète [asɛt] *nmf* ascetic.

asiatique [azjatik] *adj* [de l'Asie en général] Asian. || [d'Extrême-Orient] oriental. ○ **Asiatique** *nmf* Asian.

Asie [azi] *nf*: **l'~** Asia; **l'~ du Sud-Est** Southeast Asia.

asile [azil] *nm* [refuge] refuge. || POLIT: **demander/accorder l'~ politique** to seek/to grant political asylum. || *vieilli* [psychiatrique] asylum.

asocial, -e, -iaux [asɔsjal, jo] **1** *adj* antisocial. **2** *nm, f* social misfit.

aspect [aspɛ] *nm* [apparence] appearance; **d'~ agréable** nice-looking. || [angle & LING] aspect.

asperge [aspɛrʒ] *nf* [légume] asparagus.

asperger [aspɛrʒe] *vt*: **~ qqch de qqch** to spray sthg with sthg; **~ qqn de qqch** [arroser] to spray sb with sthg; [éclabousser] to splash sb with sthg.

aspérité [asperite] *nf* [du sol] bump.

asphalte [asfalt] *nm* asphalt.

asphyxier [asfiksje] *vt* MÉD to asphyxiate, to suffocate.

aspic [aspik] *nm* [vipère] asp.

aspirant, -e [aspirã, ãt] *adj*: **hotte ~e** cooker hood *Br*, cooker range *Am*; **pompe ~e** suction pump. ○ **aspirant** *nm* [armée] ≃ officer cadet; [marine] ≃ midshipman.

aspirateur [aspiratœr] *nm* Hoover® *Br*, vacuum cleaner; **passer l'~** to do the vacuuming ou hoovering.

aspiration [aspirasjɔ̃] *nf* [souffle] inhalation. || TECHNOL suction. ○ **aspirations** *nfpl* aspirations.

aspirer [aspire] *vt* [air] to inhale; [liquide] to suck up. || TECHNOL to suck up, to draw up. || [désirer]: **~ à qqch/à faire qqch** to aspire to sthg/to do sthg.

aspirine [aspirin] *nf* aspirin.

assagir [asaʒir] *vt* to quieten down. ○ **s'assagir** *vp* to quieten down.

assaillant, -e [asajã, ãt] *nm, f* assailant, attacker.

assaillir [asajir] *vt* to attack, to assault; **~ qqn de qqch** *fig* to assail ou bombard sb with sthg.

assainir [asenir] *vt* [logement] to clean up. || ÉCON to rectify, to stabilize.

assaisonnement [asezɔnmã] *nm* [sauce] dressing.

assaisonner [asezɔne] *vt* [salade] to dress; [viande, plat] to season.

assassin, -e [asasɛ̃, in] *adj* provocative. ○ **assassin** *nm* [gén] murderer; POLIT assassin.

assassinat [asasina] *nm* [gén] murder; POLIT assassination.

assassiner [asasine] *vt* [tuer - gén] to murder; [- POLIT] to assassinate.

assaut [aso] *nm* [attaque] assault, attack; **prendre d'~** [lieu] to storm.

assécher [aseʃe] *vt* to drain.

ASSEDIC, Assedic [asedik] (*abr de* **Associations pour l'emploi dans l'industrie et le commerce**) *nfpl* French unemployment insurance scheme; **toucher les ~** to get unemployment benefit *Br* ou welfare *Am*.

assemblage [asãblaʒ] *nm* [gén] assembly.

assemblée [asãble] *nf* [réunion] meeting. || [public] gathering. || ADMIN & POLIT assembly; **l'Assemblée nationale** *lower house of the French parliament*.

assembler [asãble] *vt* [monter] to put together. || [réunir - objets] to gather (together). || [personnes - gén] to bring together, to assemble. ○ **s'assembler** *vp* to gather.

assener [asəne], **asséner** [asene] *vt*: **~ un coup à qqn** [frapper] to strike sb, to deal sb a blow.

assentiment [asãtimã] *nm* assent.

asseoir [aswar] *vt* [sur un siège] to put; **faire ~ qqn** to seat sb, to ask sb to take a seat. || *fig* [réputation] to establish. ○ **s'asseoir** *vp* to sit (down).

assermenté, -e [asɛrmãte] *adj* [fonctionnaire, expert] sworn.

assertion [asɛrsjɔ̃] *nf* assertion.

assez [ase] *adv* [suffisamment] enough; **~ de** enough; **~ de lait/chaises** enough milk/chairs; **en avoir ~ de qqn/qqch** to have had enough of sb/sthg, to be fed up with sb/sthg. || [plutôt] quite, rather.

assidu, -e [asidy] *adj* [élève] diligent. || [travail] painstaking. || [empressé]: **~ (auprès de qqn)** attentive (to sb).

assiduité [asidyite] *nf* [zèle] diligence. || [fréquence]: **avec ~** regularly. ○ **assiduités** *nfpl péj & sout* attentions.

assiéger [asjeʒe] *vt litt & fig* to besiege.

assiette [asjɛt] *nf* [vaisselle] plate; **~ creuse** ou **à soupe** soup plate; **~ à dessert** dessert plate; **~ plate** dinner plate. || [d'impôt] base. || CULIN: **~ anglaise** assorted cold meats (*pl*) *Br*, cold cuts (*pl*) *Am*.

assigner [asiɲe] *vt* JUR: **~ qqn en justice** to issue a writ against sb.

assimiler [asimile] *vt* [aliment, connaissances] to assimilate. || [confondre]: **~ qqch (à qqch)** to liken sthg (to sthg); **~ qqn à qqn** to compare sb to ou with sb.

assis, -e [asi, iz] **1** *pp* → **asseoir**. **2** *adj* sitting, seated; **place ~e** seat. ○ **assises** *nfpl* JUR ≃ Circuit court *Am*. || [congrès] conference (*sg*).

assistance [asistɑ̃s] *nf* [aide] assistance; **l'Assistance publique** *French authority which manages the social services and state-owned hospitals.* || [auditoire] audience.

assistant, -e [asistɑ̃, ɑ̃t] *nm, f* [auxiliaire] assistant; **~e sociale** social worker. || UNIV assistant lecturer.

assister [asiste] **1** *vi*: **~ à qqch** to be at sthg, to attend sthg. **2** *vt* to assist.

association [asɔsjasjɔ̃] *nf* [gén] association. || [union] society, association; **~ sportive** sports club. || COMM partnership.

associé, -e [asɔsje] **1** *adj* associated. **2** *nm, f* [actionnaire] partner.

associer [asɔsje] *vt* [idées] to associate. || [faire participer]: **~ qqn à qqch** [inclure] to bring sb in on sthg. ○ **s'associer** *vp* [prendre part]: **s'~ à qqch** [participer] to join ou participate in sthg; [partager] to share sthg. || [collaborer]: **s'~ à** ou **avec qqn** to join forces with sb.

assoiffé, -e [aswafe] *adj* thirsty; **~ de pouvoir** *fig* power-hungry.

assombrir [asɔ̃bʀiʀ] *vt* [plonger dans l'obscurité] to darken. || *fig* [attrister] to cast a shadow over. ○ **s'assombrir** *vp* [devenir sombre] to grow dark. || *fig* [s'attrister] to darken.

assommer [asɔme] *vt* [frapper] to knock out. || [ennuyer] to bore stiff.

Assomption [asɔ̃psjɔ̃] *nf*: **l'~** the Assumption.

assorti, -e [asɔʀti] *adj* [accordé]: **bien ~** well-matched; **mal ~** ill-matched; **une cravate ~e au costume** a tie which matches the suit.

assortiment [asɔʀtimɑ̃] *nm* assortment, selection.

assortir [asɔʀtiʀ] *vt* [objets]: **~ qqch à qqch** to match sthg to ou with sthg.

assoupi, -e [asupi] *adj* [endormi] dozing.

assoupir [asupiʀ] ○ **s'assoupir** *vp* [s'endormir] to doze off.

assouplir [asupliʀ] *vt* [corps] to make supple. || [matière] to soften. || [règlement] to relax.

assourdir [asuʀdiʀ] *vt* [rendre sourd] to deafen. || [amortir] to deaden, to muffle.

assouvir [asuviʀ] *vt* to satisfy.

assujettir [asyʒetiʀ] *vt* [peuple] to subjugate. || [soumettre]: **~ qqn à qqch** to subject sb to sthg.

assumer [asyme] *vt* [fonction - exercer] to carry out. || [risque, responsabilité] to accept. || [condition] to come to terms with. || [frais] to meet.

assurance [asyʀɑ̃s] *nf* [gén] assurance. || [contrat] insurance; **~ maladie** health insurance; **~ tous risques** AUTOM comprehensive insurance; **~-vie** life assurance.

assuré, -e [asyʀe] *nm, f* policy holder.

assurément [asyʀemɑ̃] *adv sout* certainly.

assurer [asyʀe] *vt* [promettre]: **~ à qqn que** to assure sb (that); **~ qqn de qqch** to assure sb of sthg. || [permanence, liaison] to provide. || [voiture] to insure. ○ **s'assurer** *vp* [vérifier]: **s'~ que** to make sure (that); **s'~ de qqch** to ensure sthg, to make sure of sthg. || COMM: **s'~ (contre qqch)** to insure o.s. (against sthg). || [obtenir]: **s'~ qqch** to secure sthg.

astérisque [asteʀisk] *nm* asterisk.

asthme [asm] *nm* MÉD asthma.

asticot [astiko] *nm* maggot.

astiquer [astike] *vt* to polish.

astre [astʀ] *nm* star.

astreignant, -e [astʀɛɲɑ̃, ɑ̃t] *adj* demanding.

astreindre [astʀɛ̃dʀ] *vt*: **~ qqn à qqch** to subject sb to sthg; **~ qqn à faire qqch** to compel sb to do sthg.

astreint, -e [astʀɛ̃, ɛ̃t] *pp* → **astreindre**.

astringent, -e [astʀɛ̃ʒɑ̃, ɑ̃t] *adj* astringent.

astrologie [astʀɔlɔʒi] *nf* astrology.

astrologue [astʀɔlɔg] *nm* astrologer.

astronaute [astʀɔnot] *nmf* astronaut.

astronomie [astʀɔnɔmi] *nf* astronomy.

astronomique [astʀɔnɔmik] *adj* astronomical.

astuce [astys] *nf* [ruse] (clever) trick. || [ingéniosité] shrewdness (*U*).

astucieux, -ieuse [astysjø, jøz] *adj* [idée] clever. || [personne] shrewd.

asymétrique [asimetʀik] *adj* asymmetric, asymmetrical.

atelier [atəlje] *nm* [d'artisan] workshop. || [de peintre] studio.

athée [ate] *nmf* atheist.

Athènes [atɛn] *n* Athens.

athlète [atlɛt] *nmf* athlete.

athlétisme [atletism] *nm* athletics (*U*).

atlantique [atlɑ̃tik] *adj* Atlantic. ○ **Atlantique** *nm*: **l'Atlantique** the Atlantic (Ocean).

atlas [atlas] *nm* atlas.

atmosphère [atmɔsfɛʀ] *nf* atmosphere.

atome [atom] *nm* atom.

atomique [atɔmik] *adj* [gén] nuclear. || CHIM & PHYS atomic.

atomiseur [atɔmizœr] *nm* spray.

atout [atu] *nm* [carte] trump; ~ cœur/ pique/trèfle/carreau hearts/spades/ clubs/diamonds are trumps. || *fig* [ressource] asset, advantage.

atroce [atrɔs] *adj* [crime] atrocious, dreadful. || [souffrance] horrific, atrocious.

atrocité [atrɔsite] *nf* [horreur] atrocity.

atrophier [atrɔfje] ○ **s'atrophier** *vp* to atrophy.

attabler [atable] ○ **s'attabler** *vp* to sit down (at the table).

attachant, -e [ataʃɑ̃, ɑ̃t] *adj* lovable.

attache [ataʃ] *nf* [lien] fastening. ○ **attaches** *nfpl* links, connections.

attaché, -e [ataʃe] *nm, f* attaché; ~ de presse [diplomatique] press attaché; [d'organisme, d'entreprise] press officer.

attaché-case [ataʃekez] (*pl* **attachés-cases**) *nm* attaché case.

attachement [ataʃmɑ̃] *nm* attachment.

attacher [ataʃe] **1** *vt* [lier]: ~ qqch (à) to fasten or tie sthg (to). || [paquet] to tie up. || [lacet] to do up; [ceinture de sécurité] to fasten. **2** *vi* CULIN: ~ (à) to stick (to). ○ **s'attacher** *vp* [émotionnellement]: s'~ à qqn/qqch to become attached to sb/sthg. || [se fermer] to fasten. || [s'appliquer]: s'~ à qqch/à faire qqch to devote o.s. to sthg/to doing sthg, to apply o.s. to sthg/to doing sthg.

attaquant, -e [atakɑ̃, ɑ̃t] *nm, f* attacker.

attaque [atak] *nf* [gén & MÉD] attack; ~ contre qqn/qqch attack on sb/sthg.

attaquer [atake] *vt* [gén] to attack. || [JUR - personne] to take to court; [- jugement] to contest. || *fam* [plat] to tuck into. ○ **s'attaquer** *vp* [combattre]: s'~ à qqn to attack sb. || *fig*: s'~ à qqch [tâche] to tackle sthg.

attardé, -e [atarde] *adj* [idées] outdated. || [enfant] backward.

attarder [atarde] ○ **s'attarder** *vp*: s'~ sur qqch to dwell on sthg; s'~ à faire qqch to stay on to do sthg, to stay behind to do sthg.

atteindre [atɛdr] *vt* [gén] to reach. || [toucher] to hit. || [affecter] to affect.

atteint, -e [atɛ̃, ɛ̃t] **1** *pp* → **atteindre**. **2** *adj* [malade]: être ~ de to be suffering from. ○ **atteinte** *nf* [préjudice]: porter ~e à to undermine; hors d'~e [hors de portée] out of reach; [inattaquable] beyond reach. || [effet] effect.

attelage [atlaʒ] *nm* [chevaux] team.

atteler [atle] *vt* [animaux, véhicules] to hitch up; [wagons] to couple.

attelle [atɛl] *nf* splint.

attenant, -e [atnɑ̃, ɑ̃t] *adj*: ~ (à qqch) adjoining (sthg).

attendre [atɑ̃dr] **1** *vt* [gén] to wait for; ~ que (+ *subjonctif*): ~ que la pluie s'arrête to wait for the rain to stop; **faire** ~ qqn [personne] to keep sb waiting. || [espérer]: ~ qqch (de qqn/qqch) to expect sthg (from sb/sthg). || [suj: surprise, épreuve] to be in store for. **2** *vi* to wait; **attends!** hang on! ○ **s'attendre** *vp*: s'~ à to expect. ○ **en attendant** *loc adv* [pendant ce temps] meanwhile, in the meantime. || [quand même] all the same.

attendrir [atɑ̃drir] *vt* [viande] to tenderize. || [personne] to move. ○ **s'attendrir** *vp*: s'~ (sur qqn/qqch) to be moved (by sb/sthg).

attendrissant, -e [atɑ̃drisɑ̃, ɑ̃t] *adj* moving, touching.

attendu, -e [atɑ̃dy] *pp* → **attendre**. ○ **attendu que** *loc conj* since, considering that.

attentat [atɑ̃ta] *nm* attack; ~ à la bombe bomb attack, bombing.

attente [atɑ̃t] *nf* [station] wait; **en** ~ in abeyance. || [espoir] expectation.

attenter [atɑ̃te] *vi*: ~ à [liberté, droit] to violate; ~ à ses jours to attempt suicide.

attentif, -ive [atɑ̃tif, iv] *adj* [auditoire]: ~ (à qqch) attentive (to sthg).

attention [atɑ̃sjɔ̃] **1** *nf* attention; à l'~ de for the attention of; **faire** ~ à [prudence] to be careful of; [concentration] to pay attention to. **2** *interj* watch out!, be careful!

attentionné, -e [atɑ̃sjone] *adj* thoughtful.

attentivement [atɑ̃tivmɑ̃] *adv* attentively, carefully.

atténuer [atenye] *vt* [douleur] to ease; [propos, ton] to tone down; [lumière] to dim, to subdue; [bruit] to quieten. ○ **s'atténuer** *vp* [lumière] to dim, to fade; [bruit] to fade; [douleur] to ease.

atterrer [atere] *vt* to stagger.

atterrir [aterir] *vi* to land.

atterrissage [aterisaʒ] *nm* landing.

attestation [atɛstasjɔ̃] *nf* [certificat] certificate.

attester [atɛste] *vt* [confirmer] to vouch for, to testify to. || [certifier] to attest.

auditeur

attirail [atiraj] *nm fam* [équipement] gear.

attirance [atirɑ̃s] *nf* attraction.

attirant, -e [atirɑ̃, ɑ̃t] *adj* attractive.

attirer [atire] *vt* [gén] to attract. || [amener vers soi]: ~ **qqn à/vers soi** to draw sb to/towards one. || [provoquer]: ~ **des ennuis à qqn** to cause trouble for sb. ○ **s'attirer** *vp*: **s'~ qqch** to bring sthg on o.s.

attiser [atize] *vt* [feu] to poke. || *fig* [haine] to stir up.

attitré, -e [atitre] *adj* [habituel] usual. || [titulaire - fournisseur] by appointment; [- représentant] accredited.

attitude [atityd] *nf* [comportement, approche] attitude. || [posture] posture.

attouchement [atuʃmɑ̃] *nm* caress.

attraction [atraksjɔ̃] *nf* [gén] attraction. || [force]: ~ **magnétique** magnetic force. ○ **attractions** *nfpl* [jeux] amusements. || [spectacle] attractions.

attrait [atrɛ] *nm* [séduction] appeal. || [intérêt] attraction.

attrape-nigaud [atrapnigo] (*pl* attrape-nigauds) *nm* con.

attraper [atrape] *vt* [gén] to catch. || *fam* [gronder] to tell off.

attrayant, -e [atrɛjɑ̃, ɑ̃t] *adj* attractive.

attribuer [atribɥe] *vt* [tâche, part]: ~ **qqch à qqn** to assign ou allocate sthg to sb, to assign ou allocate sb sthg; [récompense] to award sthg to sb, to award sb sthg. || [faute]: ~ **qqch à qqn** to attribute sthg to sb, to put sthg down to sb. ○ **s'attribuer** *vp* [s'approprier] to appropriate (for o.s.). || [revendiquer] to claim (for o.s.).

attribut [atriby] *nm* [gén] attribute. || GRAM complement.

attribution [atribysjɔ̃] *nf* [de prix] awarding, award. || [de part, tâche] allocation, assignment. || [d'avantage] bestowing. ○ **attributions** *nfpl* [fonctions] duties.

attrister [atriste] *vt* to sadden. ○ **s'attrister** *vp* to be saddened.

attroupement [atrupmɑ̃] *nm* crowd.

attrouper [atrupe] ○ **s'attrouper** *vp* to form a crowd, to gather.

au [o] → **à**.

aubade [obad] *nf* dawn serenade.

aubaine [obɛn] *nf* piece of good fortune.

aube [ob] *nf* [aurore] dawn, daybreak; **à l'~** at dawn.

aubépine [obepin] *nf* hawthorn.

auberge [obɛrʒ] *nf* [hôtel] inn; ~ **de jeunesse** youth hostel.

aubergine [obɛrʒin] *nf* BOT aubergine *Br*, eggplant *Am*. || *péj* [contractuelle] traffic warden *Br*, meter maid *Am*.

aubergiste [obɛrʒist] *nmf* innkeeper.

aucun, -e [okœ̃, yn] **1** *adj* [sens négatif]: **ne ... ~ no**; **il n'y a ~e voiture dans la rue** there aren't any cars in the street, there are no cars in the street. || [sens positif] any; **il lit plus qu'~ autre enfant** he reads more than any other child. **2** *pron* [sens négatif] none; ~ **des enfants** none of the children; ~ **(des deux)** neither (of them). || [sens positif]: **plus qu'~ de nous** more than any of us.

aucunement [okynmɑ̃] *adv* not at all, in no way.

audace [odas] *nf* [hardiesse] daring, boldness. || [insolence] audacity.

audacieux, -ieuse [odasjø, jøz] *adj* [projet] daring, bold. || [personne, geste] bold.

au-dedans [odədɑ̃] *loc adv* inside. ○ **au-dedans de** *loc prép* inside.

au-dehors [odəɔr] *loc adv* outside. ○ **au-dehors de** *loc prép* outside.

au-delà [odəla] **1** *loc adv* [plus loin] beyond. || [davantage, plus] more. **2** *nm*: **l'~** RELIG the beyond, the afterlife. ○ **au-delà de** *loc prép* beyond.

au-dessous [odəsu] *loc adv* below, underneath. ○ **au-dessous de** *loc prép* below, under.

au-dessus [odəsy] *loc adv* above. ○ **au-dessus de** *loc prép* above, over.

au-devant [odəvɑ̃] *loc adv* ahead. ○ **au-devant de** *loc prép*: **aller ~ de** to go to meet; **aller ~ du danger** to court danger.

audible [odibl] *adj* audible.

audience [odjɑ̃s] *nf* [public, entretien] audience. || JUR hearing.

Audimat® [odimat] *nm* audience rating.

audionumérique [odjonymerik] *adj* digital audio.

audiovisuel, -elle [odjovizɥɛl] *adj* audio-visual. ○ **audiovisuel** *nm* TV and radio.

audit [odit] *nm* audit.

auditeur, -trice [oditœr, tris] *nm, f* listener. ○ **auditeur** *nm* UNIV: ~ **libre** *person allowed to attend lectures without being registered*, auditor *Am*. || FIN auditor.

audition [odisjɔ̃] nf [fait d'entendre] hearing. || THÉÂTRE audition.

auditionner [odisjɔne] vt & vi to audition.

auditoire [oditwar] nm [public] audience.

auditorium [oditɔrjɔm] nm [de concert] auditorium; [d'enregistrement] studio.

auge [oʒ] nf [pour animaux] trough.

augmentation [ogmɑ̃tasjɔ̃] nf: ~ (de) increase (in); ~ (de salaire) rise (in salary).

augmenter [ogmɑ̃te] 1 vt to increase; [prix, salaire] to raise; [personne] to give a rise Br ou raise Am to. 2 vi to increase, to rise; **la douleur augmente** the pain is getting worse.

augure [ogyr] nm [présage] omen; **être de bon/mauvais ~** to be a good/bad sign.

aujourd'hui [oʒurdɥi] adv today.

aulx → ail.

aumône [omon] nf: **faire l'~ à qqn** to give alms to sb.

auparavant [oparavɑ̃] adv [tout d'abord] first (of all). || [avant] before, previously.

auprès [oprɛ] ○ **auprès de** loc prép [à côté de] beside, next to. || [comparé à] compared with. || [en s'adressant à] to.

auquel [okɛl] → lequel.

aurai, auras etc → avoir.

auréole [oreɔl] nf ASTRON & RELIG halo. || [trace] ring.

auriculaire [orikyler] nm little finger.

aurore [orɔr] nf dawn.

ausculter [oskylte] vt MÉD to sound.

auspice [ospis] nm (gén pl) sign, auspice; **sous les ~s de qqn** under the auspices of sb.

aussi [osi] adv [pareillement, en plus] also, too; **moi ~** me too; **j'y vais ~** I'm going too ou as well. || [dans une comparaison]: ~ ... que as ... as; **il n'est pas ~ intelligent que son frère** he's not as clever as his brother; **je n'ai jamais rien vu d'~ beau** I've never seen anything so beautiful; **~ incroyable que cela paraisse** incredible though ou as it may seem. ○ **(tout) aussi bien** loc adv just as easily, just as well; **j'aurais pu (tout) ~ bien refuser** I could just as easily have said no.

aussitôt [osito] adv immediately. ○ **aussitôt que** loc conj as soon as.

austère [ostɛr] adj [personne, vie] austere. || [vêtement] severe; [paysage] harsh.

austérité [osterite] nf [de personne, vie] austerity. || [de vêtement] severeness; [de paysage] harshness.

austral, -e [ostral] (pl australs OU austraux [ostro]) adj southern.

Australie [ostrali] nf: l'~ Australia.

australien, -ienne [ostraljɛ̃, jɛn] adj Australian. ○ **Australien, -ienne** nm, f Australian.

autant [otɑ̃] adv [comparatif]: ~ que as much as; **ce livre coûte ~ que l'autre** this book costs as much as the other one; ~ de (... que) [quantité] as much (... as); [nombre] as many (... as); **il a dépensé ~ d'argent que moi** he spent as much money as I did. || [à un tel point, en si grande quantité] so much; [en si grand nombre] so many; **il ne peut pas en dire ~** he can't say the same; **en faire ~** to do likewise. || [il vaut mieux]: ~ **dire la vérité** we/you etc may as well tell the truth. ○ **autant que** loc conj: (**pour**) ~ **que je sache** as far as I know. ○ **d'autant** loc adv accordingly, in proportion. ○ **d'autant que** loc conj: **d'~ (plus) que** all the more so since. ○ **pour autant** loc adv for all that.

autel [otɛl] nm altar.

auteur [otœr] nm [d'œuvre] author. || [responsable] perpetrator.

authentique [otɑ̃tik] adj authentic, genuine.

autiste [otist] adj autistic.

auto [oto] nf car.

autobiographie [otobjɔgrafi] nf autobiography.

autobronzant, -e [otobrɔ̃zɑ̃, ɑ̃t] adj self-tanning.

autobus [otobys] nm bus.

autocar [otokar] nm coach.

autochtone [otoktɔn] nmf & adj native.

autocollant, -e [otokɔlɑ̃, ɑ̃t] adj self-adhesive, sticky. ○ **autocollant** nm sticker.

auto-couchettes [otokuʃet] adj inv: **train ~** ≈ Motorail® train.

autocritique [otokritik] nf self-criticism.

autocuiseur [otokɥizœr] nm pressure cooker.

autodéfense [otodefɑ̃s] nf self-defence.

autodétruire [otodetrɥir] ○ **s'autodétruire** vp [machine] to self-destruct.

autodidacte [otodidakt] nmf self-taught person.

auto-école [otoekol] (pl **auto-écoles**) nf driving school.

autofinancement [otofinãsmã] nm self-financing.

autofocus [otofokys] nm & adj inv autofocus.

autographe [otograf] nm autograph.

automate [otomat] nm [robot] automaton.

automatique [otomatik] 1 nm [pistolet] automatic. 2 adj automatic.

automatisation [otomatizasjɔ̃] nf automation.

automatisme [otomatism] nm [réflexe] automatic reaction, automatism.

automne [oton] nm autumn, fall Am; **en ~** in autumn, in the fall Am.

automobile [otomobil] 1 nf car, automobile Am. 2 adj [industrie, accessoires] car (avant n), automobile (avant n) Am.

automobiliste [otomobilist] nmf motorist.

autonettoyant, -e [otonetwajã, ãt] adj self-cleaning.

autonome [otonom] adj [gén] autonomous, independent. || [appareil] self-contained.

autonomie [otonomi] nf [indépendance] autonomy, independence. || AUTOM & AVIAT range. || POLIT autonomy, self-government.

autonomiste [otonomist] nmf & adj separatist.

autoportrait [otoportrɛ] nm self-portrait.

autopsie [otopsi] nf post-mortem, autopsy.

autoradio [otoradjo] nm car radio.

autorisation [otorizasjɔ̃] nf [permission] permission, authorization; **avoir l'~ de faire qqch** to be allowed to do sthg. || [attestation] pass, permit.

autorisé, -e [otorize] adj [personne] in authority; **milieux ~s** official circles.

autoriser [otorize] vt to authorize, to permit; **~ qqn à faire qqch** [permission] to give sb permission to do sthg; [possibilité] to permit ou allow sb to do sthg.

autoritaire [otoritɛr] adj authoritarian.

autorité [otorite] nf authority; **faire ~** [ouvrage] to be authoritative; [personne] to be an authority.

autoroute [otorut] nf motorway Br, highway Am, freeway Am.

auto-stop [otostop] nm hitchhiking; **faire de l'~** to hitchhike, to hitch.

auto-stoppeur, -euse [otostopœr, øz] nm, f hitchhiker, hitcher.

autour [otur] adv round, around.
○ **autour de** loc prép [sens spatial] round, around. || [sens temporel] about, around.

autre [otr] 1 adj indéf [distinct, différent] other, different; **l'un et l'~ projets** both projects; **~ chose** something else. || [supplémentaire] other; **tu veux une ~ tasse de café?** would you like another cup of coffee? || [qui reste] other, remaining; **les ~s passagers ont été rapatriés en autobus** the other ou remaining passengers were bussed home. 2 pron indéf: **l'~** the other (one); **un ~** another (one); **d'une semaine à l'~** from one week to the next; **quelqu'un d'~** somebody else, someone else; **rien d'~** nothing else; **l'un et l'~ sont venus** they both came, both of them came; **l'un ou l'~ ira** one or other (of them) will go; **ni l'un ni l'~ n'est venu** neither (of them) came. ○ **entre autres** loc adv among other things.

autrefois [otrəfwa] adv in the past, formerly.

autrement [otrəmã] adv [différemment] otherwise, differently; **je n'ai pas pu faire ~ que d'y aller** I had no choice but to go; **~ dit** in other words. || [sinon] otherwise.

Autriche [otriʃ] nf: **l'~** Austria.

autrichien, -ienne [otriʃjɛ̃, jɛn] adj Austrian. ○ **Autrichien, -ienne** nm, f Austrian.

autruche [otryʃ] nf ostrich.

autrui [otrɥi] pron others, other people.

auvent [ovã] nm canopy.

aux [o] → à.

auxiliaire [oksiljɛr] 1 nmf [assistant] assistant. 2 nm GRAM auxiliary (verb). 3 adj [secondaire] auxiliary. || ADMIN assistant (avant n).

auxquels, auxquelles [okɛl] → lequel.

av. abr de avenue.

avachi, -e [avaʃi] adj [gén] misshapen. || [personne] listless; **il était ~ dans un fauteuil** he was slumped in an armchair.

aval, -als [aval] nm backing (U), endorsement. ○ **en aval** loc adv litt & fig downstream.

avalanche [avalãʃ] nf litt & fig avalanche.

avaler [avale] vt [gén] to swallow. || fig [supporter] to take; **dur à ~** difficult to swallow.

avance [avɑ̃s] *nf* [progression, somme d'argent] advance. ‖ [distance, temps] lead; **le train a dix minutes d'~** the train is ten minutes early; **prendre de l'~ (dans qqch)** to get ahead (in sthg). ○ **avances** *nfpl*: **faire des ~s à qqn** to make advances towards sb. ○ **à l'avance** *loc adv* in advance. ○ **d'avance** *loc adv* in advance. ○ **en avance** *loc adv*: **être en ~** to be early; **être en ~ sur qqch** to be ahead of sthg. ○ **par avance** *loc adv* in advance.

avancement [avɑ̃smɑ̃] *nm* [développement] progress. ‖ [promotion] promotion.

avancer [avɑ̃se] **1** *vt* [objet, tête] to move forward; [date, départ] to bring forward; [main] to hold out. ‖ [montre, horloge] to put forward. ‖ [argent]: **~ qqch à qqn** to advance sb sthg. **2** *vi* [approcher] to move forward. ‖ [progresser] to advance. ‖ [faire saillie]: **~ (dans/sur)** to jut out (into/over), to project (into/over). ‖ [montre, horloge]: **ma montre avance de dix minutes** my watch is ten minutes fast. ‖ [servir]: **ça n'avance à rien** that won't get us/you anywhere. ○ **s'avancer** *vp* [s'approcher] to move forward; **s'~ vers qqn/qqch** to move towards sb/sthg. ‖ [s'engager] to commit o.s.

avant [avɑ̃] **1** *prép* before. **2** *adv* before; **tu connais le cinéma? ma maison se situe un peu ~** you know the cinema? my house is just this side of it. **3** *adj inv* front; **les roues ~** the front wheels. **4** *nm* [partie antérieure] front. ‖ SPORT forward. ○ **avant de** *loc prép*: **~ de faire qqch** before doing sthg. ○ **avant que** *loc conj* (+ *subjonctif*): **je dois te parler ~ que tu partes** I must speak to you before you leave. ○ **avant tout** *loc adv* above all; **sa carrière passe ~ tout** his career comes first. ○ **en avant** *loc adv* forward, forwards.

avantage [avɑ̃taʒ] *nm* [gén & TENNIS] advantage; **se montrer à son ~** to look one's best.

avantager [avɑ̃taʒe] *vt* [favoriser] to favour. ‖ [mettre en valeur] to flatter.

avantageux, -euse [avɑ̃taʒø, øz] *adj* [profitable] profitable, lucrative.

avant-bras [avɑ̃bra] *nm inv* forearm.

avant-centre [avɑ̃sɑ̃tr] (*pl* **avants-centres**) *nm* centre forward.

avant-coureur [avɑ̃kurœr] → **signe**.

avant-dernier, -ière [avɑ̃dɛrnje, jɛr] (*mpl* **avant-derniers**, *fpl* **avant-dernières**) *adj* second to last, penultimate.

avant-garde [avɑ̃gard] (*pl* **avant-gardes**) *nf* MIL. vanguard. ‖ [idées] avant-garde.

avant-goût [avɑ̃gu] (*pl* **avant-goûts**) *nm* foretaste.

avant-hier [avɑ̃tjɛr] *adv* the day before yesterday.

avant-première [avɑ̃prəmjɛr] (*pl* **avant-premières**) *nf* preview.

avant-projet [avɑ̃prɔʒɛ] (*pl* **avant-projets**) *nm* draft.

avant-propos [avɑ̃prɔpo] *nm inv* foreword.

avant-veille [avɑ̃vɛj] (*pl* **avant-veilles**) *nf*: **l'~** two days earlier.

avare [avar] **1** *nmf* miser. **2** *adj* miserly; **être ~ de qqch** *fig* to be sparing with sthg.

avarice [avaris] *nf* avarice.

avarie [avari] *nf* damage (*U*).

avarié, -e [avarje] *adj* rotting, bad.

avatar [avatar] *nm* [transformation] metamorphosis. ○ **avatars** *nmpl* [mésaventures] misfortunes.

avec [avɛk] *prép* [gén] with; **~ respect** with respect, respectfully; **et ~ ça?** *fam* [dans un magasin] anything else? ‖ [vis-à-vis de] to, towards.

avenant, -e [avnɑ̃] *adj* pleasant. ○ **avenant** *nm* JUR additional clause. ○ **à l'avenant** *loc adv* in the same vein.

avènement [avɛnmɑ̃] *nm* [d'un roi] accession. ‖ *fig* [début] advent.

avenir [avnir] *nm* future; **avoir de l'~** to have a future; **d'~** [profession, concept] with a future, with prospects. ○ **à l'avenir** *loc adv* in future.

Avent [avɑ̃] *nm*: **l'~** Advent.

aventure [avɑ̃tyr] *nf* [gén] adventure. ‖ [liaison amoureuse] affair.

aventurer [avɑ̃tyre] *vt* [risquer] to risk. ○ **s'aventurer** *vp* to venture (out); **s'~ à faire qqch** *fig* to venture to do sthg.

aventureux, -euse [avɑ̃tyrø, øz] *adj* [personne, vie] adventurous. ‖ [projet] risky.

aventurier, -ière [avɑ̃tyrje, jɛr] *nm, f* adventurer.

avenu [avny] *adj m*: **nul et non ~** JUR null and void.

avenue [avny] *nf* avenue.

avérer [avere] ○ **s'avérer** *vp*: **il s'est**

axe

avéré (être) à la hauteur he proved (to be) up to it.

averse [avɛrs] *nf* downpour.

averti, -e [avɛrti] *adj* [expérimenté] experienced. || [initié]: ~ **(de)** informed or well-informed (about).

avertir [avɛrtir] *vt* [mettre en garde] to warn. || [prévenir] to inform; **avertissez-moi dès que possible** let me know as soon as possible.

avertissement [avɛrtismɑ̃] *nm* [gén] warning. || [avis] notice, notification.

avertisseur [avɛrtisœr] *nm* [Klaxon®] horn. || [d'incendie] alarm.

aveu, -x [avø] *nm* confession.

aveugle [avœgl] **1** *nmf* blind person; **les ~s** the blind. **2** *adj litt & fig* blind.

aveuglement [avœgləmɑ̃] *nm* blindness.

aveuglément [avœglemɑ̃] *adv* blindly.

aveugler [avœgle] *vt litt & fig* [priver de la vue] to blind.

aveuglette [avœglɛt] ○ **à l'aveuglette** *loc adv*: **marcher à l'~** to grope one's way; **avancer à l'~** *fig* to be in the dark.

aviateur, -trice [avjatœr, tris] *nm, f* aviator.

aviation [avjasjɔ̃] *nf* [transport aérien] aviation. || MIL airforce.

avide [avid] *adj* [vorace, cupide] greedy. || [désireux]: ~ **(de qqch/de faire qqch)** eager (for sthg/to do sthg).

avidité [avidite] *nf* [voracité, cupidité] greed. || [passion] eagerness.

avilir [avilir] *vt* [personne] to degrade. ○ **s'avilir** *vp* [personne] to demean o.s.

aviné, -e [avine] *adj* [personne] inebriated. || [haleine] smelling of alcohol.

avion [avjɔ̃] *nm* plane, aeroplane, airplane *Am*; **en ~** by plane, by air; **par ~** [courrier] airmail; ~ **à réaction** jet (plane).

aviron [avirɔ̃] *nm* [rame] oar. || SPORT: **l'~** rowing.

avis [avi] *nm* [opinion] opinion; **changer d'~** to change one's mind; **à mon ~** in my opinion. || [conseil] advice (*U*). || [notification] notification, notice.

avisé, -e [avize] *adj* [sensé] sensible; **être bien/mal ~ de faire qqch** to be well-advised/ill-advised to do sthg.

aviser [avize] **1** *vt* [informer]: ~ **qqn de qqch** to inform sb of sthg. **2** *vi* to reassess the situation. ○ **s'aviser** *vp sout* [s'apercevoir]: **s'~ de qqch** to notice sthg.

|| [oser]: **ne t'avise pas de répondre!** don't you dare answer me back!

av. J.-C. (*abr de* avant Jésus-Christ) BC.

avocat, -e [avɔka, at] *nm, f* JUR lawyer; ~ **de la défense** counsel for the defence *Br*, defense counsel *Am*; ~ **général** ≃ counsel for the prosecution *Br*, prosecuting attorney *Am*. ○ **avocat** *nm* [fruit] avocado.

avoine [avwan] *nf* oats (*pl*).

avoir [avwar] **1** *nm* [biens] assets (*pl*). || [document] credit note. **2** *vt* [posséder] to have; **j'ai fini** I have finished; **il a attendu pendant deux heures** he waited for two hours. **3** *vt* [posséder] to have (got). || [être âgé de]: **il a 20 ans** he is 20 (years old); **il a deux ans de plus que son frère** he is two years older than his brother. || [obtenir] to get. || [éprouver] to have; *voir aussi* **faim, peur, soif** *etc*. || *loc*: **se faire ~** *fam* to be had or conned; **j'en ai pour cinq minutes** it'll take me five minutes. ○ **avoir à** *vi* + *prép* [devoir]: ~ **à faire qqch** to have to do sthg; **tu n'avais pas à lui parler sur ce ton** you had no need to speak to him like that, you shouldn't have spoken to him like that; **tu n'avais qu'à me demander** you only had to ask me; **tu n'as qu'à y aller toi-même** just go (there) yourself, why don't you just go (there) yourself? ○ **il y a** *v impers* [présentatif] there is/are; **il y a un problème** there's a problem; **il y a des problèmes** there are (some) problems; **qu'est-ce qu'il y a?** what's the matter?, what is it?; **il n'y a qu'à en finir** we'll/you'll *etc* just have to have done (with it). || [temporel]: **il y a trois ans** three years ago; **il y a longtemps qu'il est parti** he left a long time ago.

avoisinant, -e [avwazinɑ̃, ɑ̃t] *adj* [lieu, maison] neighbouring. || [sens, couleur] similar.

avortement [avɔrtəmɑ̃] *nm* MÉD abortion.

avorter [avɔrte] *vi* MÉD: (**se faire**) ~ to have an abortion. || [échouer] to fail.

avorton [avɔrtɔ̃] *nm péj* [nabot] runt.

avouer [avwe] *vt* [confesser] to confess (to). || [reconnaître] to admit.

avril [avril] *nm* April; *voir aussi* **septembre.**

axe [aks] *nm* GÉOM & PHYS axis. || [de roue] axle. || [prolongement]: **dans l'~** directly in line with.

axer [akse] *vt*: ~ qqch sur/autour de qqch to centre sth on/around sth.

ayant [ɛjɑ̃] *ppr* → avoir.

azalée [azale] *nf* azalea.

azimut [azimyt] ○ **tous azimuts** *loc adj* [défense, offensive] all-out.

azote [azɔt] *nm* nitrogen.

azur [azyr] *nm littéraire* [couleur] azure. || [ciel] skies (*pl*).

b, B [be] *nm inv* b, B. ○ **B** (*abr de* **bien**), good grade (*as assessment on schoolwork*), ≃ B.

BA (*abr de* **bonne action**) *nf fam* good deed.

babines [babin] *nfpl* chops.

bâbord [babɔr] *nm* port; **à ~** to port, on the port side.

babouin [babwɛ̃] *nm* baboon.

baby-sitter [bebisitœr] (*pl* **baby-sitters**) *nmf* baby-sitter.

baby-sitting [bebisitiŋ] *nm*: **faire du ~** to baby-sit.

bac [bak] *nm* → **baccalauréat**. || [bateau] ferry. || [de réfrigérateur]: **~ à glace** ice tray; **~ à légumes** vegetable drawer.

baccalauréat [bakalɔrea] *nm* school-leaving examinations leading to university entrance qualification.

bâche [baʃ] *nf* [toile] tarpaulin.

bachelier, -ière [baʃəlje, jɛr] *nm, f* holder of the baccalauréat.

bacille [basil] *nm* bacillus.

bâcler [bakle] *vt* to botch.

bactérie [bakteri] *nf* bacterium.

badaud [bado] *nm* gawper.

badge [badʒ] *nm* badge.

badigeonner [badiʒɔne] *vt* [mur] to whitewash.

badiner [badine] *vi sout* to joke; **ne pas ~ avec qqch** not to treat sth lightly.

badminton [badmintɔn] *nm* badminton.

baffe [baf] *nf fam* slap.

baffle [bafl] *nm* speaker.

bafouiller [bafuje] *vi & vt* to mumble.

bagage [bagaʒ] *nm* (*gén pl*) [valises, sacs] luggage (*U*), baggage (*U*); **faire ses ~s** to pack; **~s à main** hand luggage. || [connaissances] (fund of) knowledge; **~ intellectuel/culturel** intellectual/cultural baggage.

bagagiste [bagaʒist] *nmf* [à l'hôtel etc] porter.

bagarre [bagar] *nf* brawl, fight.

bagarrer [bagare] *vi* to fight. ○ **se bagarrer** *vp* to fight.

bagatelle [bagatɛl] *nf* [objet] trinket. || [somme d'argent]: **acheter qqch pour une ~** to buy sth for next to nothing; **la ~ de X francs** *iron* a mere X francs. || [chose futile] trifle.

bagnard [baɲar] *nm* convict.

bagne [baɲ] *nm* [prison] labour camp.

bagnole [baɲɔl] *nf fam* car.

bague [bag] *nf* [bijou, anneau] ring; **~ de fiançailles** engagement ring. || TECH: **~ de serrage** clip.

baguer [bage] *vt* [oiseau, arbre] to ring.

baguette [bagɛt] *nf* [pain] French stick. || [petit bâton] stick; **~ magique** magic wand; **~ de tambour** drumstick; **mener qqn à la ~** to rule sb with a rod of iron. || [pour manger] chopstick. || [de chef d'orchestre] baton.

bahut [bay] *nm* [buffet] sideboard.

baie [bɛ] *nf* [fruit] berry. || GÉOGR bay. || [fenêtre]: **~ vitrée** picture window.

baignade [beɲad] *nf* [action] bathing (*U*) *Br*, swimming (*U*); **«~ interdite»** "no bathing/swimming".

baigner [beɲe] **1** *vt* [donner un bain à] to bath. || [tremper, remplir] to bathe; **baigné de soleil** bathed in sunlight. **2** *vi*: **~ dans son sang** to lie in a pool of blood; **les tomates baignaient dans l'huile** the tomatoes were swimming in oil. ○ **se baigner** *vp* [dans la mer] to go swimming, to swim. || [dans une baignoire] to have a bath.

baigneur, -euse [beɲœr, øz] *nm, f* bather *Br*, swimmer. ○ **baigneur** *nm* [poupée] baby doll.

baignoire [beɲwar] *nf* bath.

bail [baj] (*pl* **baux** [bo]) *nm* JUR lease.

bâillement [bajmɑ̃] *nm* yawning (*U*), yawn.

bâiller [baje] *vi* [personne] to yawn. || [vêtement] to gape.

bailleur, -eresse [bajœr, bajrɛs] *nm, f* lessor; **~ de fonds** backer.

bâillon [bajɔ̃] *nm* gag.

bâillonner [bajɔne] *vt* to gag.

bain [bɛ̃] *nm* [gén] bath; **prendre un ~** to have ou take a bath; **~ moussant** foaming bath oil. || [dans mer, piscine] swim; **~ de mer** sea bathing *Br* ou swimming. || *loc*: **prendre un ~ de soleil** to sunbathe.

bain-marie [bɛ̃mari] (*pl* **bains-marie**) *nm*: **au ~** in a bain-marie.

baïonnette [bajɔnɛt] *nf* [arme] bayonet. || ÉLECTR bayonet fitting.

baiser [beze] *nm* kiss.

baisse [bɛs] *nf* [gén]: **~ (de)** drop (in), fall (in); **en ~** falling; **la tendance est à la ~** there is a downward trend.

baisser [bese] **1** *vt* [gén] to lower; [radio] to turn down. **2** *vi* [descendre] to go down; **le jour baisse** it's getting dark. || [santé, vue] to fail. || [prix] to fall. ○ **se baisser** *vp* to bend down.

bajoues [baʒu] *nfpl* jowls.

bal [bal] *nm* ball; **~ masqué/costumé** masked/fancy-dress ball; **~ populaire** ou **musette** popular old-fashioned dance accompanied by accordion.

balade [balad] *nf fam* stroll.

balader [balade] *vt fam* [traîner avec soi] to trail around. || [emmener en promenade] to take for a walk. ○ **se balader** *vp fam* [se promener - à pied] to go for a walk; [- en voiture] to go for a drive.

baladeur, -euse [baladœr, øz] *adj* wandering. ○ **baladeur** *nm* personal stereo.

balafre [balafr] *nf* [blessure] gash. || [cicatrice] scar.

balafré, -e [balafre] *adj* scarred.

balai [balɛ] *nm* [de nettoyage] broom, brush. || *fam* [an]: **il a 50 ~s** he's 50 years old.

balai-brosse [balɛbrɔs] *nm* (long-handled) scrubbing brush.

balance [balɑ̃s] *nf* [instrument] scales (*pl*). || COMM & POLIT balance. ○ **Balance** *nf* ASTROL Libra.

balancer [balɑ̃se] *vt* [bouger] to swing. || *fam* [lancer] to chuck. || *fam* [jeter] to chuck out. ○ **se balancer** *vp* [sur une chaise] to rock backwards and forwards. || [sur une balançoire] to swing. || *fam*: **se ~ de qqch** not to give a damn about sthg.

balancier [balɑ̃sje] *nm* [de pendule] pendulum. || [de funambule] pole.

balançoire [balɑ̃swar] *nf* [suspendue] swing; [bascule] see-saw.

balayage [balɛjaʒ] *nm* [gén] sweeping; TECHNOL scanning.

balayer [baleje] *vt* [nettoyer] to sweep. || [chasser] to sweep away. || [suj: radar] to scan; [suj: projecteurs] to sweep (across).

balayette [balɛjɛt] *nf* small brush.

balayeur, -euse [balɛjœr, øz] *nm, f* roadsweeper *Br*, streetsweeper *Am*. ○ **balayeuse** *nf* [machine] roadsweeper.

balbutier [balbysje] **1** *vi* [bafouiller] to stammer. **2** *vt* [bafouiller] to stammer (out).

balcon [balkɔ̃] *nm* [de maison - terrasse] balcony; [- balustrade] parapet. || [de théâtre, de cinéma] circle.

balconnet [balkɔnɛ] *nm*: **soutien-gorge à ~** half-cup bra.

baldaquin [baldakɛ̃] *nm* → **lit**.

baleine [balɛn] *nf* [mammifère] whale. || [de parapluie] rib.

balise [baliz] *nf* NAVIG marker (buoy). AÉRON runway light. || AUTOM road sign. || INFORM tag.

baliser [balize] *vt* to mark out.

balivernes [balivɛrn] *nfpl* nonsense (U).

Balkans [balkɑ̃] *nmpl*: **les ~** the Balkans.

ballade [balad] *nf* ballad.

ballant, -e [balɑ̃, ɑ̃t] *adj*: **les bras ~s** arms dangling.

ballast [balast] *nm* [chemin de fer] ballast. || NAVIG ballast tank.

balle [bal] *nf* [d'arme à feu] bullet; **~ perdue** stray bullet. || [de jeu] ball. || [de marchandises] bale. || *fam* [argent] franc.

ballerine [balrin] *nf* [danseuse] ballerina. || [chaussure] ballet shoe.

ballet [balɛ] *nm* [gén] ballet.

ballon [balɔ̃] *nm* JEU & SPORT ball; **~ de football** football. || [montgolfière, de fête] balloon.

ballonné, -e [balɔne] *adj*: **avoir le ventre ~, être ~** to be bloated.

ballot [balo] *nm* [de marchandises] bundle. || *vieilli* [imbécile] twit.

ballottage [balɔtaʒ] *nm* POLIT second ballot; **en ~** standing for a second ballot.

ballotter [balɔte] **1** *vt* to toss about. **2** *vi* [chose] to roll around.

ball-trap [baltrap] *nm* clay pigeon shooting.

balluchon = **baluchon**.

balnéaire [balneɛr] *adj*: **station ~** seaside resort.

balourd, -e [balur, urd] *adj* clumsy.

balte [balt] *adj* Baltic. ○ **Balte** *nmf* native of the Baltic states.

Baltique [baltik] *nf*: **la ~** the Baltic (Sea).

baluchon, balluchon [balyʃɔ̃] *nm*
bundle; **faire son ~** *fam* to pack one's
bags (and leave).

balustrade [balystrad] *nf* [de terrasse]
balustrade. || [rambarde] guardrail.

bambin [bɑ̃bɛ̃] *nm* kiddie.

bambou [bɑ̃bu] *nm* [plante] bamboo.

ban [bɑ̃] *nm* [de mariage]: **publier** ou
afficher les ~s to publish ou display the
banns.

banal, -e, -als [banal] *adj* commonplace, banal.

banaliser [banalize] *vt*: **voiture banali-
sée** unmarked police car.

banalité [banalite] *nf* [caractère banal]
banality. || [cliché] commonplace.

banane [banan] *nf* [fruit] banana. ||
[sac] bum-bag. || [coiffure] quiff.

bananier, -ière [bananje, jɛr] *adj* banana (*avant n*). ○ **bananier** *nm* [arbre]
banana tree. || [cargo] banana boat.

banc [bɑ̃] *nm* [siège] bench; **le ~ des ac-
cusés** JUR the dock; **~ d'essai** test-bed; **~
de sable** sandbank.

bancaire [bɑ̃kɛr] *adj* bank (*avant n*),
banking (*avant n*).

bancal, -e, -als [bɑ̃kal] *adj* [meuble]
wobbly. || [théorie, idée] unsound.

bandage [bɑ̃daʒ] *nm* [de blessé] bandage.

bande [bɑ̃d] *nf* [de tissu, de papier] strip;
~ dessinée comic strip. || [bandage]
bandage. || [de billard] cushion. ||
[groupe] band; **en ~** in a group. || [pelli-
cule de film] film. || [d'enregistrement]
tape; **~ magnétique** (magnetic) tape; **~
originale** CIN original soundtrack. ||
[voie]: **~ d'arrêt d'urgence** hard shoul-
der. || RADIO: **~ de fréquence** waveband. ||
NAVIG: **donner de la ~** to list.

bande-annonce [bɑ̃danɔ̃s] *nf* trailer.

bandeau [bɑ̃do] *nm* [sur les yeux] blind-
fold. || [dans les cheveux] headband.

bandelette [bɑ̃dlɛt] *nf* strip (of cloth).

bander [bɑ̃de] **1** *vt* MÉD to bandage; **~
les yeux de qqn** to blindfold sb. || [arc] to
draw back. || [muscle] to flex. **2** *vi vulg* to
have a hard-on.

banderole [bɑ̃drɔl] *nf* streamer.

bande-son [bɑ̃dsɔ̃] (*pl* bandes-son) *nf*
soundtrack.

bandit [bɑ̃di] *nm* [voleur] bandit.

banditisme [bɑ̃ditism] *nm* serious
crime.

bandoulière [bɑ̃duljɛr] *nf* bandolier;
en ~ across the shoulder.

banlieue [bɑ̃ljø] *nf* suburbs (*pl*).

banlieusard, -e [bɑ̃ljøzar, ard] *nm, f*
person living in the suburbs.

bannière [banjɛr] *nf* [étendard] banner.

bannir [banir] *vt*: **~ qqn/qqch (de)** to
banish sb/sthg (from).

banque [bɑ̃k] *nf* [activité] banking. ||
[établissement, au jeu] bank. || INFORM: **~
de données** data bank. || MÉD: **~
d'organes/du sang/du sperme** organ/
blood/sperm bank.

banqueroute [bɑ̃krut] *nf* bankruptcy;
faire ~ to go bankrupt.

banquet [bɑ̃kɛ] *nm* (celebration) dinner; [de gala] banquet.

banquette [bɑ̃kɛt] *nf* seat.

banquier, -ière [bɑ̃kje, jɛr] *nm, f*
banker.

banquise [bɑ̃kiz] *nf* ice field.

baptême [batɛm] *nm* RELIG baptism,
christening. || [première fois]: **~ de l'air**
maiden flight.

baptiser [batize] *vt* to baptize, to
christen.

baquet [bakɛ] *nm* [cuve] tub.

bar [bar] *nm* [café, unité de pression] bar.
|| [poisson] bass.

baraque [barak] *nf* [cabane] hut. || *fam*
[maison] house. || [de forain] stall, stand.

baraqué, -e [barake] *adj fam* well-
built.

baraquement [barakmɑ̃] *nm* camp (*of
huts for refugees, workers etc*).

baratin [baratɛ̃] *nm fam* smooth talk;
faire du ~ à qqn to sweet-talk sb.

baratiner [baratine] *fam* **1** *vt* [femme]
to chat up; [client] to give one's sales
pitch to. **2** *vi* to be a smooth talker.

barbare [barbar] **1** *nm* barbarian. **2** *adj
péj* [non civilisé] barbarous. || [cruel] bar-
baric.

barbe [barb] *nf* beard; **~ à papa** candy
floss *Br*, cotton candy *Am*; **quelle** ou **la ~!**
fam what a drag!

barbelé, -e [barbəle] *adj* barbed.
○ **barbelé** *nm* barbed wire (*U*).

barbiche [barbiʃ] *nf* goatee (beard).

barbiturique [barbityrik] *nm* barbiturate.

barboter [barbɔte] *vi* to paddle.

barboteuse [barbɔtøz] *nf* romper-suit.

barbouillé, -e [barbuje] *adj*: **être ~,
avoir l'estomac ~** to feel sick.

barbouiller [barbuje] *vt* [salir]: **~ qqch
(de)** to smear sthg (with).

barbu, -e [barby] *adj* bearded.
○ **barbu** *nm* bearded man.

bardé, -e [barde] *adj*: **il est ~ de diplômes** he's got heaps of diplomas.

barder [barde] **1** *vt* CULIN to bard. **2** *vi fam*: **ça va ~** there'll be trouble.

barème [barɛm] *nm* [de référence] table; [de salaires] scale.

baril [baril] *nm* barrel.

bariolé, -e [barjɔle] *adj* multicoloured.

barjo(t) [barʒo] *adj inv fam* nuts.

barmaid [barmɛd] *nf* barmaid.

barman [barman] (*pl* **barmans** OU **barmen** [barmɛn]) *nm* barman.

baromètre [barɔmɛtr] *nm* barometer.

baron, -onne [barɔ̃, ɔn] *nm, f* baron (*f* baroness).

baroque [barɔk] *adj* [style] baroque. || [bizarre] weird.

barque [bark] *nf* small boat.

barquette [barkɛt] *nf* [tartelette] pastry boat. || [récipient - de fruits] punnet; [- de crème glacée] tub.

barrage [baraʒ] *nm* [de rue] roadblock. || CONSTR dam.

barre [bar] *nf* [gén & JUR] bar; **~ d'espacement** [sur machine à écrire] space bar; **~ fixe** GYM high bar; **~ des témoins** JUR witness box *Br* OU stand *Am*. || NAVIG helm. || [trait] stroke.

barreau [baro] *nm* bar; **le ~** JUR the Bar.

barrer [bare] *vt* [rue, route] to block. || [mot, phrase] to cross out. || [bateau] to steer. ○ **se barrer** *vp fam* to clear off.

barrette [barɛt] *nf* [pince à cheveux] (hair) slide *Br*, barrette *Am*.

barreur, -euse [barœr, øz] *nm, f* NAVIG helmsman; [à l'aviron] cox.

barricade [barikad] *nf* barricade.

barrière [barjɛr] *nf litt & fig* barrier.

barrique [barik] *nf* barrel.

baryton [baritɔ̃] *nm* baritone.

bas, basse [ba, baz *devant nm commençant par voyelle ou h muet*, bas] *adj* [gén] low. || *péj* [vil] base, low. || MUS bass. ○ **bas 1** *nm* [partie inférieure] bottom, lower part. || [vêtement] stocking. **2** *adv* low; **à ~ ...!** down with ...!; **parler ~** to speak in a low voice, to speak softly; **mettre ~** [animal] to give birth. ○ **en bas** *loc adv* at the bottom; [dans une maison] downstairs. ○ **en bas de** *loc prép* at the bottom of; **attendre qqn en ~ de chez lui** to wait for sb downstairs. ○ **bas de gamme** *adj* downmarket.

basalte [bazalt] *nm* basalt.

basané, -e [bazane] *adj* tanned.

bas-côté [bakote] *nm* [de route] verge.

bascule [baskyl] *nf* [balançoire] seesaw.

basculer [baskyle] **1** *vi* to fall over, to overbalance; [benne] to tip up; **~ dans qqch** *fig* to tip over into sthg. **2** *vt* to tip up, to tilt.

base [baz] *nf* [partie inférieure] base. || [principe fondamental] basis; **de ~** basic; **une boisson à ~ d'orange** an orange-based drink; **sur la ~ de** on the basis of. || INFORM: **~ de données** database.

baser [baze] *vt* to base. ○ **se baser** *vp*: **sur quoi vous basez-vous pour affirmer cela?** what are you basing this statement on?

bas-fond [bafɔ̃] *nm* [de l'océan] shallow. ○ **bas-fonds** *nmpl fig* [de la société] dregs. || [quartiers pauvres] slums.

basilic [bazilik] *nm* [plante] basil.

basilique [bazilik] *nf* basilica.

basique [bazik] *adj* basic.

basket [baskɛt] **1** *nm* = **basket-ball**. **2** *nf* [chaussure] trainer *Br*, sneaker *Am*; **lâche-moi les ~s!** *fam fig* get off my back!

basket-ball [basketbol] *nm* basketball.

basque [bask] **1** *adj* Basque; **le Pays ~** the Basque country. **2** *nm* [langue] Basque. **3** *nf* [vêtement] tail (*of coat*); **être toujours pendu aux ~s de qqn** *fam fig* to be always tagging along after sb. ○ **Basque** *nmf* Basque.

bas-relief [barəljɛf] *nm* bas-relief.

basse [bas] **1** *adj* → **bas**. **2** *nf* MUS bass.

basse-cour [baskur] *nf* [volaille] poultry. || [partie de ferme] farmyard.

bassement [basmɑ̃] *adv* despicably.

basset [basɛ] *nm* basset hound.

bassin [basɛ̃] *nm* [cuvette] bowl. || [pièce d'eau] (ornamental) pond. || [de piscine] **petit/grand ~** children's/main pool. || ANAT pelvis. || GÉOL basin; **le Bassin parisien** the Paris basin.

bassine [basin] *nf* bowl, basin.

bassiste [basist] *nmf* bass player.

basson [basɔ̃] *nm* [instrument] bassoon; [personne] bassoonist.

bastide [bastid] *nf traditional farmhouse or country house in southern France; walled town (in south-west France).*

bastingage [bastɛ̃gaʒ] *nm* (ship's) rail.

bastion [bastjɔ̃] *nm litt & fig* bastion.

bas-ventre [bavɑ̃tr] *nm* stomach.

bataille [bataj] *nf* MIL battle. || [bagarre] fight. || [jeu de cartes] ≃ beggar-my-neighbour. || *loc*: **en ~** [cheveux] dishevelled.

bataillon [batajɔ̃] *nm* MIL battalion; *fig* horde.

bâtard, -e [batar, ard] **1** *adj* [enfant] illegitimate. || *péj* [style, solution] hybrid. **2** *nm, f* illegitimate child. ○ **bâtard** *nm* [pain] ≃ Vienna loaf. || [chien] mongrel.

batavia [batavja] *nf* Webb lettuce.

bateau [bato] *nm* [embarcation - gén] boat; [- plus grand] ship; ~ à voile/moteur sailing/motor boat; ~ de pêche fishing boat; **mener qqn en** ~ *fig* to take sb for a ride. || [de trottoir] driveway entrance (*low kerb*). || (*en apposition inv*) [sujet. thème] well-worn.

bâti, -e [bati] *adj* [terrain] developed. || [personne]: **bien** ~ well-built.

batifoler [batifɔle] *vi* to frolic.

bâtiment [batimɑ̃] *nm* [édifice] building. || IND: **le** ~ the building trade. || NAVIG ship, vessel.

bâtir [batir] *vt* CONSTR to build. || *fig* [réputation, fortune] to build (up); [théorie, phrase] to construct. || COUTURE to tack.

bâtisse [batis] *nf souvent péj* house.

bâton [batɔ̃] *nm* [gén] stick; ~ de ski ski pole. || *fam fig* 10 000 francs. || *loc*: **mettre des** ~s **dans les roues à qqn** to put a spoke in sb's wheel; **parler à** ~s **rompus** to talk of this and that.

bâtonnet [batɔnɛ] *nm* rod.

batracien [batrasjɛ̃] *nm* amphibian.

battage [bataʒ] *nm*: ~ (**publicitaire** ou **médiatique**) (media) hype.

battant, -e [batɑ̃, ɑ̃t] **1** *adj*: **sous une pluie** ~e in the pouring ou driving rain; **le cœur** ~ with beating heart. **2** *nm, f* fighter. ○ **battant** *nm* [de porte] door (*of double doors*); [de fenêtre] half (*of double window*). || [de cloche] clapper.

battement [batmɑ̃] *nm* [mouvement - d'ailes] flap, beating (*U*); [- de cœur, pouls] beat, beating (*U*); [- de cils, paupières] flutter, fluttering (*U*). || [intervalle de temps] break; **une heure de** ~ an hour free.

batterie [batri] *nf* ÉLECTR & MIL battery; **recharger ses** ~s *fig* to recharge one's batteries. || [attirail]: ~ **de cuisine** kitchen utensils (*pl*). || MUS drums (*pl*).

batteur [batœr] *nm* MUS drummer. || CULIN beater, whisk. || [SPORT - de cricket] batsman; [- de base-ball] batter.

battre [batr] **1** *vt* [gén] to beat; ~ **en neige** [blancs d'œufs] to beat until stiff. || [cartes] to shuffle. **2** *vi* [gén] to beat; ~ **des cils** to blink; ~ **des mains** to clap (one's hands). ○ **se battre** *vp* to fight; **se** ~ **contre qqn** to fight sb.

battu, -e [baty] **1** *pp* → **battre**. **2** *adj* [tassé] hard-packed; **jouer sur terre** ~e TENNIS to play on clay. ○ **battue** *nf* [chasse] beat.

baume [bom] *nm litt & fig* balm; **mettre du** ~ **au cœur de qqn** to comfort sb.

baux → **bail**.

bavard, -e [bavar, ard] *adj* talkative.

bavardage [bavardaʒ] *nm* [papotage] chattering. || (*gén pl*) [racontar] gossip (*U*).

bavarder [bavarde] *vi* to chatter; *péj* to gossip.

bave [bav] *nf* [salive] dribble. || [d'animal] slaver. || [de limace] slime.

baver [bave] *vi* [personne] to dribble. || [animal] to slaver. || [stylo] to leak. || *loc*: **en** ~ *fam* to have a hard ou rough time of it.

bavette [bavɛt] *nf* [bavoir, de tablier] bib. || [viande] flank. || *loc*: **tailler une** ~ (**avec qqn**) *fam* to have a chinwag (with sb).

baveux, -euse [bavø, øz] *adj* [bébé] dribbling. || [omelette] runny.

bavoir [bavwar] *nm* bib.

bavure [bavyr] *nf* [tache] smudge. || [erreur] blunder.

bayer [baje] *vi*: ~ **aux corneilles** to stand gazing into space.

bazar [bazar] *nm* [boutique] general store. || *fam* [désordre] jumble, clutter.

BCBG (*abr de* **bon chic bon genre**) *nmf & adj term used to describe an upper-class lifestyle reflected especially in expensive but conservative clothes.*

bd *abr de* **boulevard**.

BD, bédé [bede] (*abr de* **bande dessinée**) *nf*: **une** ~ a comic strip.

béant, -e [beɑ̃, ɑ̃t] *adj* [plaie, gouffre] gaping; [yeux] wide open.

béat, -e [bea, at] *adj* [heureux] blissful.

beau, belle, beaux [bo, bɛl] *adj* (*bel devant voyelle ou h muet*) [joli - femme] beautiful, good-looking; [- homme] handsome, good-looking; [- chose] beautiful. || [temps] fine, good. || (*toujours avant le nom*) [important] fine, excellent; **une belle somme** a tidy sum (of money). || *iron* [mauvais]: **une belle grippe** a nasty dose of the flu; **un** ~ **travail** a fine piece of work. || (*sens intensif*): **un** ~ **jour** one fine day. ○ **beau 1** *adv*: **il fait** ~ the weather is good ou fine; **j'ai** ~ **essayer ... however hard I try ...., try as I may ... 2** *nm*: **être au** ~ **fixe** to be set fair; **avoir le moral au** ~ **fixe** *fig* to have a sunny disposition; **faire le ~** [chien] to sit up and beg. O **belle** *nf* [dans un jeu] decider. O **de plus belle** *loc adv* more than ever.

beaucoup [boku] **1** *adv* [un grand nombre]: **~ de** a lot of, many. || [une grande quantité]: **~ de** a lot of; **il n'a pas ~ de temps** he hasn't a lot of ou much time. || (*modifiant un verbe*) a lot. **c'est ~ dire** that's saying a lot. || (*modifiant un adjectif comparatif*) much, a lot; **c'est mieux** it's much ou a lot better. **2** *pron inv* many; **nous sommes ~ à penser que ...** many of us think that .... O **de beaucoup** *loc adv* by far.

beauf [bof] *nm péj* stereotype of average French man with narrow views. || *fam* [beau-frère] brother-in-law.

beau-fils [bofis] *nm* [gendre] son-in-law. || [de remariage] stepson.

beau-frère [bofrɛr] *nm* brother-in-law.

beau-père [bopɛr] *nm* [père du conjoint] father-in-law. || [de remariage] stepfather.

beauté [bote] *nf* beauty; **de toute ~** absolutely beautiful; **en ~** [magnifiquement] in great style.

beaux-arts [bozar] *nmpl* fine art (*sg*). O **Beaux-Arts** *nmpl*: **les Beaux-Arts** French national art school.

beaux-parents [boparɑ̃] *nmpl* [de l'homme] husband's parents, in-laws. || [de la femme] wife's parents, in-laws.

bébé [bebe] *nm* baby.

bébé-éprouvette [bebeepruvɛt] (*pl* bébés-éprouvette) *nm* test-tube baby.

bébête [bebɛt] *adj* silly.

bec [bɛk] *nm* [d'oiseau] beak. || [d'instrument de musique] mouthpiece. || [de casserole etc] lip; **~ de gaz** [réverbère] gaslamp (*in street*); **~ verseur** spout. || *fam* [bouche] mouth; **clouer le ~ à qqn** to shut sb up.

bécane [bekan] *nf fam* [moto, vélo] bike. || [ordinateur etc] machine.

bécasse [bekas] *nf* [oiseau] woodcock. || *fam* [femme sotte] silly goose.

bec-de-lièvre [bɛkdəljevr] (*pl* becs-de-lièvre) *nm* harelip.

bêche [bɛʃ] *nf* spade.

bêcher [beʃe] *vt* to dig.

bécoter [bekɔte] *vt fam* to snog *Br* ou smooch with. O **se bécoter** *vp* to snog *Br*, to smooch.

becquée [beke] *nf*: **donner la ~ à** to feed.

becqueter, béqueter [bɛkte] *vt* to peck at.

bedaine [bədɛn] *nf* potbelly.

bédé = BD.

bedonnant, -e [bədɔnɑ̃, ɑ̃t] *adj* potbellied.

bée [be] *adj*: **bouche ~** open-mouthed.

bégayer [begeje] **1** *vi* to have a stutter ou stammer. **2** *vt* to stammer (out).

bégonia [begɔnja] *nm* begonia.

bègue [bɛg] **1** *adj*: **être ~** to have a stutter ou stammer. **2** *nmf* stutterer, stammerer.

béguin [begɛ̃] *nm fam*: **avoir le ~ pour qqn** to have a crush on sb.

beige [bɛʒ] *adj & nm* beige.

beignet [bɛɲe] *nm* fritter.

bel [bɛl] → **beau**.

bêler [bele] *vi* to bleat.

belette [bəlɛt] *nf* weasel.

belge [bɛlʒ] *adj* Belgian. O **Belge** *nmf* Belgian.

Belgique [bɛlʒik] *nf*: **la ~** Belgium.

bélier [belje] *nm* [animal] ram. || [poutre] battering ram. O **Bélier** *nm* ASTROL Aries.

belle [bɛl] *adj & nf* → **beau**.

belle-famille [bɛlfamij] *nf* [de l'homme] husband's family, in-laws (*pl*). || [de la femme] wife's family, in-laws (*pl*).

belle-fille [bɛlfij] *nf* [épouse du fils] daughter-in-law. || [de remariage] stepdaughter.

belle-mère [bɛlmɛr] *nf* [mère du conjoint] mother-in-law. || [de remariage] stepmother.

belle-sœur [bɛlsœr] *nf* sister-in-law.

belligérant, -e [beliʒerɑ̃, ɑ̃t] *adj & nm, f* belligerent.

belliqueux, -euse [belikø, øz] *adj* [peuple] warlike; [humeur, tempérament] aggressive.

belvédère [belvedɛr] *nm* [construction] belvedere. || [terrasse] viewpoint.

bémol [bemɔl] *adj & nm* MUS flat.

bénédiction [benediksjɔ̃] *nf* blessing.

bénéfice [benefis] *nm* [avantage] advantage, benefit; **au ~ de** in aid of. || [profit] profit.

bénéficiaire [benefisjɛr] **1** *nmf* [gén] beneficiary; [de chèque] payee. **2** *adj* [marge] profit (*avant n*); [résultat, société] profit-making.

bénéficier [benefisje] *vi*: **~ de** [profiter de] to benefit from; [jouir de] to enjoy; [obtenir] to have, to get.

bénéfique [benefik] *adj* beneficial.

Bénélux [benelyks] *nm*: **le ~** Benelux.

bénévole [benevɔl] **1** *adj* voluntary. **2** *nmf* volunteer, voluntary worker.

bénin, -igne [benɛ̃, iɲ] *adj* [maladie, accident] minor; [tumeur] benign.

bénir [benir] *vt* [gén] to bless. || [se réjouir de] to thank God for.

bénitier [benitje] *nm* holy water font.

benjamin, -e [bɛ̃ʒamɛ̃, in] *nm, f* [de famille] youngest child; [de groupe] youngest member.

benne [bɛn] *nf* [de camion] tipper. || [de téléphérique] car. || [pour déchets] skip.

benzine [bɛ̃zin] *nf* benzine.

BEP, Bep (*abr de* **brevet d'études professionnelles**) *nm* school-leaver's diploma *(taken at age 18)*.

BEPC, Bepc (*abr de* **brevet d'études du premier cycle**) *nm* former school certificate *(taken at age 16)*.

béquille [bekij] *nf* [pour marcher] crutch. || [d'un deux-roues] stand.

berceau, -x [bɛrso] *nm* cradle.

bercer [bɛrse] *vt* [bébé, bateau] to rock.

berceuse [bɛrsøz] *nf* [chanson] lullaby. || *Can* [fauteuil] rocking chair.

béret [berɛ] *nm* beret.

berge [bɛrʒ] *nf* [bord] bank. || *fam* [an]: **il a plus de 50 ~s** he's over 50.

berger, -ère [bɛrʒe, ɛr] *nm, f* shepherd (*f* shepherdess). ○ **berger allemand** *nm* alsatian *Br*, German shepherd.

bergerie [bɛrʒəri] *nf* sheepfold.

Berlin [bɛrlɛ̃] *n* Berlin.

berline [bɛrlin] *nf* saloon (car) *Br*, sedan *Am*.

berlingot [bɛrlɛ̃go] *nm* [de lait] carton. || [bonbon] boiled sweet.

berlue [bɛrly] *nf*: **j'ai la ~!** I must be seeing things!

bermuda [bɛrmyda] *nm* bermuda shorts (*pl*).

berne [bɛrn] *nf*: **en ~ ≃** at half-mast.

berner [bɛrne] *vt* to fool.

besogne [bəzɔɲ] *nf* job, work (*U*).

besoin [bəzwɛ̃] *nm* need; **avoir ~ de qqch/de faire qqch** to need sthg/to do sthg; **au ~** if necessary, if need *ou* needs be. ○ **besoins** *nmpl* [exigences] needs. || *loc*: **faire ses ~s** to relieve o.s.

bestial, -e, -iaux [bɛstjal, jo] *adj* bestial, brutish.

bestiole [bɛstjɔl] *nf* (little) creature.

bétail [betaj] *nm* cattle (*pl*).

bête [bɛt] **1** *nf* [animal] animal; [insecte] insect; **~ de somme** beast of burden. **2** *adj* [stupide] stupid.

bêtise [betiz] *nf* [stupidité] stupidity. || [action, remarque] stupid thing; **faire/dire une ~** to do/say something stupid.

béton [betɔ̃] *nm* [matériau] concrete; **~ armé** reinforced concrete.

bétonnière [betɔnjɛr] *nf* cement mixer.

betterave [betrav] *nf* beetroot *Br*, beet *Am*; **~ sucrière** *ou* **à sucre** sugar beet.

beugler [bøgle] *vi* [bovin] to moo, to low.

beurre [bœr] *nm* [aliment] butter.

beurrer [bœre] *vt* to butter.

beurrier [bœrje] *nm* butter dish.

beuverie [bœvri] *nf* drinking session.

bévue [bevy] *nf* blunder.

biais [bjɛ] *nm* [ligne oblique] slant; **en ~** *ou* **de ~** [de travers] at an angle. || [moyen détourné] expedient; **par le ~ de** by means of.

biaiser [bjeze] *vi fig* to dodge the issue.

bibelot [biblo] *nm* trinket, curio.

biberon [bibrɔ̃] *nm* baby's bottle.

bible [bibl] *nf* bible.

bibliographie [biblijɔgrafi] *nf* bibliography.

bibliophile [biblijɔfil] *nmf* book lover.

bibliothécaire [biblijɔtekɛr] *nmf* librarian.

bibliothèque [biblijɔtɛk] *nf* [meuble] bookcase. || [édifice, collection] library.

biblique [biblik] *adj* biblical.

bicarbonate [bikarbɔnat] *nm*: **~ (de soude)** bicarbonate of soda.

biceps [bisɛps] *nm* biceps.

biche [biʃ] *nf* ZOOL hind, doe.

bicolore [bikɔlɔr] *adj* two-coloured.

bicoque [bikɔk] *nf péj* house.

bicorne [bikɔrn] *nm* cocked hat.

bicyclette [bisiklɛt] *nf* bicycle; **rouler à ~** to cycle.

bide [bid] *nm fam* [ventre] belly. || [échec] flop.

bidet [bidɛ] *nm* [sanitaire] bidet.

bidon [bidɔ̃] *nm* [récipient] can. || *fam* [ventre] belly. || (*en apposition inv*) *fam* [faux] phoney.

bidonville [bidɔ̃vil] *nm* shantytown.

bielle [bjɛl] *nf* connecting rod.

bien [bjɛ̃] (*compar & superl* **mieux**) **1** *adj inv* [satisfaisant] good; **il est ~ comme prof** he's a good teacher. || [en bonne santé] well. || [joli] good-looking; **tu ne trouves pas qu'elle est ~ comme ça?** don't you think she looks good *ou* nice like that? || [à l'aise] comfortable. || [convenable] respectable. **2** *nm* [sens moral]: **le ~ et le mal** good and evil. ‖ [intérêt] good; **je te dis ça pour ton ~** I'm telling you this for your own good. ‖ [richesse, propriété] property, possession; **~s de consommation** consumer goods. ‖ *loc:* **faire du ~ à qqn** to do sb good; **dire du ~ de qqn/qqch** to speak well of sb/sthg; **mener à ~** to bring to fruition, to complete. **3** *adv* [de manière satisfaisante] well; **tu as ~ fait** you did the right thing; **tu ferais ~ d'y aller** you would be wise to go; **c'est ~ fait!** it serves him/her *etc* right! ‖ [sens intensif] quite, really; **~ souvent** quite often; **j'espère ~ que ... I** DO hope that ...; **on a ~ ri** we had a good laugh; **il y a ~ trois heures que j'attends** I've been waiting for at least three hours. ‖ [renforçant un comparatif]: **il est parti ~ plus tard** he left much later. ‖ [servant à conclure ou à introduire]: **~, je t'écoute** well, I'm listening. ‖ [en effet]: **c'est ~ lui** it really IS him; **c'est ~ ce que je disais** that's just what I said. **4** *interj:* **eh ~!** oh well!; **eh ~, qu'en penses-tu?** well, what do you think? ○ **biens** *nmpl* property (*U*). ○ **bien de, bien des** *loc adj:* **~ des gens sont venus** quite a lot of people came; **il a ~ de la chance** he's very ou really lucky. ○ **bien entendu** *loc adv* of course. ○ **bien que** *loc conj* (+ *subjonctif*) although, though. ○ **bien sûr** *loc adv* of course, certainly.

bien-aimé, -e [bjɛ̃neme] (*mpl* **bien-aimés,** *fpl* **bien-aimées**) *adj & nm, f* beloved.

bien-être [bjɛ̃nɛtr] *nm inv* [physique] wellbeing.

bienfaisance [bjɛ̃fəzɑ̃s] *nf* charity.

bienfaisant, -e [bjɛ̃fəzɑ̃, ɑ̃t] *adj* beneficial.

bienfait [bjɛ̃fɛ] *nm* [effet bénéfique] benefit. ‖ [faveur] kindness.

bienfaiteur, -trice [bjɛ̃fɛtœr, tris] *nm, f* benefactor.

bien-fondé [bjɛ̃fɔ̃de] (*pl* **bien-fondés**) *nm* validity.

bienheureux, -euse [bjɛ̃nœrø, øz] *adj* RELIG blessed. ‖ [heureux] happy.

bientôt [bjɛ̃to] *adv* soon; **à ~!** see you soon!

bienveillance [bjɛ̃vejɑ̃s] *nf* kindness.

bienveillant, -e [bjɛ̃vejɑ̃, ɑ̃t] *adj* kindly.

bienvenu, -e [bjɛ̃vəny] **1** *adj* [qui arrive à propos] welcome. **2** *nm, f:* **être le ~/la ~e** to be welcome; **soyez le ~!** welcome!

○ **bienvenue** *nf* welcome; **souhaiter la ~ à qqn** to welcome sb.

bière [bjɛr] *nf* [boisson] beer; **~ blonde** lager; **~ brune** brown ale; **~ pression** draught beer. ‖ [cercueil] coffin.

bifteck [biftɛk] *nm* steak.

bifurcation [bifyrkasjɔ̃] *nf* [embranchement] fork; *fig* new direction.

bifurquer [bifyrke] *vi* [route, voie ferrée] to fork. ‖ [voiture] to turn off.

bigamie [bigami] *nf* bigamy.

bigoudi [bigudi] *nm* curler.

bijou, -x [biʒu] *nm* [joyau] jewel. ‖ *fig* [chef d'œuvre] gem.

bijouterie [biʒutri] *nf* [magasin] jeweler's (shop).

bijoutier, -ière [biʒutje, jɛr] *nm, f* jeweller.

Bikini® [bikini] *nm vieilli* bikini.

bilan [bilɑ̃] *nm* FIN balance sheet; **déposer son ~** to declare bankruptcy; **faire d'une situation** state of affairs; **faire le ~ (de)** to take stock (of); **~ de santé** check-up.

bilatéral, -e, -aux [bilateral, o] *adj* [stationnement] on both sides (of the road). ‖ [contrat, accord] bilateral.

bile [bil] *nf* bile; **se faire de la ~** *fam* to worry.

biliaire [biljɛr] *adj* biliary; **calcul ~** gallstone; **vésicule ~** gall bladder.

bilingue [bilɛ̃g] *adj* bilingual.

billard [bijar] *nm* [jeu] billiards (*U*). ‖ [table de jeu] billiard table.

bille [bij] *nf* [d'enfant] marble. ‖ [de bois] block of wood.

billet [bijɛ] *nm* [lettre] note. ‖ [argent]: **~ (de banque)** (bank) note; **un ~ de 100 francs** a 100-franc note. ‖ [ticket] ticket.

billetterie [bijɛtri] *nf* [à l'aéroport] ticket desk; [à la gare] booking office ou hall. ‖ BANQUE cash dispenser.

billion [biljɔ̃] *nm* billion *Br*, trillion *Am*.

bimensuel, -elle [bimɑ̃sɥɛl] *adj* twice-monthly. ○ **bimensuel** *nm* semi-monthly *Am*.

bimoteur [bimɔtœr] *nm* twin-engined plane.

binaire [binɛr] *adj* binary.

biner [bine] *vt* to hoe.

binocle [binɔkl] *nm* pince-nez. ○ **binocles** *nmpl fam vieilli* specs.

biochimie [bjoʃimi] *nf* biochemistry.

biodégradable [bjɔdegradabl] *adj* biodegradable.

biographie [bjɔgrafi] *nf* biography.

biologie [bjɔlɔʒi] *nf* biology.

biologique [bjɔlɔʒik] *adj* SCIENCE biological. || [naturel] organic.

biopsie [bjɔpsi] *nf* biopsy.

biréacteur [bireaktœr] *nm* twin-engined jet.

bis¹, -e [bi, biz] *adj* greyish-brown; **pain** ~ brown bread.

bis² [bis] *adv* [dans adresse]: 5 ~ 5a. || [à la fin d'un spectacle] encore.

bisannuel, -elle [bizanɥɛl] *adj* biennial.

biscornu, -e [biskɔrny] *adj* [difforme] irregularly shaped. || [bizarre] weird.

biscotte [biskɔt] *nf* toasted bread sold in packets and often eaten for breakfast.

biscuit [biskɥi] *nm* [sec] biscuit *Br*, cookie *Am*; [salé] cracker. || [gâteau] sponge.

bise [biz] *nf* [vent] north wind. || *fam* [baiser] kiss; **grosses ~s** love and kisses.

biseau, -x [bizo] *nm* bevel; **en ~** bevelled.

bison [bizɔ̃] *nm* bison.

bisou [bizu] *nm fam* kiss.

bissextile [bisɛkstil] → **année**.

bistouri [bisturi] *nm* lancet.

bistro(t) [bistro] *nm fam* cafe, bar.

bit [bit] *nm* INFORM bit.

bivouac [bivwak] *nm* bivouac.

bivouaquer [bivwake] *vi* to bivouac.

bizarre [bizar] *adj* strange, odd.

bizutage [bizytaʒ] *nm* practical jokes played on new arrivals in a school or college.

black-out [blakawt] *nm* blackout.

blafard, -e [blafar, ard] *adj* pale.

blague [blag] *nf* [plaisanterie] joke.

blaguer [blage] *fam vi* to joke.

blagueur, -euse [blagœr, øz] *fam* **1** *adj* jokey. **2** *nm, f* joker.

blaireau, -x [blɛro] *nm* [animal] badger. || [de rasage] shaving brush.

blâme [blam] *nm* [désapprobation] disapproval. || [sanction] reprimand.

blâmer [blame] *vt* [désapprouver] to blame. || [sanctionner] to reprimand.

blanc, blanche [blɑ̃, blɑ̃ʃ] *adj* [gén] white. || [non écrit] blank. || [pâle] pale. ○ **blanc** *nm* [couleur] white. || [personne] white (man). || [linge de maison]: **le ~ the** (household) linen. || [sur page] blank (space); **en ~** [chèque] blank. || [de volaille] white meat. || [vin] white (wine). || *loc*: **chauffé à ~** white-hot. ○ **blanche** *nf* [personne] white (woman). || MUS minim. ○ **blanc d'œuf** *nm* egg white.

blancheur [blɑ̃ʃœr] *nf* whiteness.

blanchir [blɑ̃ʃir] **1** *vt* [mur] to whitewash. || [linge, argent] to launder. || [légumes] to blanch. **2** *vi*: ~ (**de**) to go white (with).

blanchissage [blɑ̃ʃisaʒ] *nm* [de linge] laundering.

blanchisserie [blɑ̃ʃisri] *nf* laundry.

blasé, -e [blaze] *adj* blasé.

blason [blazɔ̃] *nm* coat of arms.

blasphème [blasfɛm] *nm* blasphemy.

blasphémer [blasfeme] *vt & vi* to blaspheme.

blatte [blat] *nf* cockroach.

blazer [blazɛr] *nm* blazer.

blé [ble] *nm* [céréale] wheat, corn. || *fam* [argent] dough.

blême [blɛm] *adj*: ~ (**de**) pale (with).

blennorragie [blenɔraʒi] *nf* gonorrhoea.

blessant, -e [blɛsɑ̃, ɑ̃t] *adj* hurtful.

blessé, -e [blese] *nm, f* wounded ou injured person.

blesser [blese] *vt* [physiquement - accidentellement] to injure, to hurt; [- par arme] to wound. || [moralement] to hurt. ○ **se blesser** *vp* to injure o.s., to hurt o.s.

blessure [blesyr] *nf litt & fig* wound.

bleu, -e [blø] *adj* [couleur] blue. || [viande] very rare. ○ **bleu** *nm* [couleur] blue. || [meurtrissure] bruise. || [fromage] blue cheese. || [vêtement]: ~ **de travail** overalls (*pl*).

bleuet [bløɛ] *nm* cornflower.

bleuir [bløir] *vt & vi* to turn blue.

bleuté, -e [bløte] *adj* bluish.

blindé, -e [blɛ̃de] *adj* [véhicule] armoured; [porte, coffre] armour-plated. ○ **blindé** *nm* armoured car.

blinder [blɛ̃de] *vt* [véhicule] to armour; [porte, coffre] to armour-plate.

blizzard [blizar] *nm* blizzard.

bloc [blɔk] *nm* [gén] block; **en ~** wholesale. || [assemblage] unit; ~ **opératoire** operating theatre.

blocage [blɔkaʒ] *nm* ÉCON freeze, freezing (*U*). || PSYCHOL (mental) block.

blockhaus [blɔkos] *nm* blockhouse.

bloc-notes [blɔknɔt] *nm* notepad.

blocus [blɔkys] *nm* blockade.

blond, -e [blɔ̃, blɔ̃d] **1** *adj* fair, blond. **2** *nm, f* fair-haired ou blond man (*f* fair-haired ou blonde woman). ○ **blond** *nm*: ~ **cendré/vénitien/platine** ash/strawberry/platinum blond. ○ **blonde** *nf* *nf* [cigarette] Virginia cigarette. ‖ [bière] lager.

blondeur [blɔ̃dœr] *nf* blondness, fairness.

bloquer [blɔke] *vt* [porte, freins] to jam; [roues] to lock. ‖ [route, chemin] to block; [personne]: **être bloqué** to be stuck. ‖ [prix, salaires, crédit] to freeze. ○ **se bloquer** *vp* [se coincer] to jam.

blottir [blɔtir] ○ **se blottir** *vp*: se ~ (contre) to snuggle up (to).

blouse [bluz] *nf* [de travail, d'écolier] smock.

blouson [bluzɔ̃] *nm* bomber jacket, blouson.

blue-jean [bludʒin] (*pl* **blue-jeans** [bludʒins]) *nm* jeans (*pl*).

blues [bluz] *nm inv* blues.

bluffer [blœfe] *fam vi & vt* to bluff.

blush [blœʃ] *nm* blusher.

boa [bɔa] *nm* boa.

bobard [bɔbar] *nm fam* fib.

bobine [bɔbin] *nf* [cylindre] reel, spool. ‖ ÉLECTR coil.

bobsleigh [bɔbslɛg] *nm* bobsleigh.

bocage [bɔkaʒ] *nm* GÉOGR bocage.

bocal, -aux [bɔkal, o] *nm* jar.

body-building [bɔdibildiŋ] *nm*: **le ~** body building (*U*).

bœuf [bœf, *pl* bø] *nm* [animal] ox. ‖ [viande] beef.

bof [bɔf] *interj fam* [exprime la lassitude] I don't really care.

bohème [bɔɛm] *adj* bohemian.

bohémien, -ienne [bɔemjɛ̃, jɛn] *nm, f* [tsigane] gipsy.

boire [bwar] **1** *vt* [s'abreuver] to drink. ‖ [absorber] to soak up, to absorb. **2** *vi* to drink.

bois [bwa] **1** *nm* wood; **en ~** wooden. **2** *nmpl* MUS woodwind (*U*). ‖ [cornes] antlers.

boisé, -e [bwaze] *adj* wooded.

boiserie [bwazri] *nf* panelling (*U*).

boisson [bwasɔ̃] *nf* [breuvage] drink.

boîte [bwat] *nf* [récipient] box; **en ~** tinned *Br*, canned; **~ de conserve** tin *Br*, can; **~ à gants** glove compartment; **~ aux lettres** [pour la réception] letterbox; [pour l'envoi] postbox *Br*, mailbox *Am*; **~ postale** post office box; **~ de vitesses** gearbox. ‖ *fam* [entreprise] company, firm; [lycée] school. ‖ *fam* [discothèque]: **~ (de nuit)** nightclub, club.

boiter [bwate] *vi* [personne] to limp.

boiteux, -euse [bwatø, øz] *adj* [per-

sonne] lame. ‖ [meuble] wobbly. ‖ *fig* [raisonnement] shaky.

boîtier [bwatje] *nm* [boîte] case. ‖ TECHNOL casing.

bol [bɔl] *nm* [récipient] bowl. ‖ [contenu] bowl, bowlful. ‖ *loc*: **prendre un ~ d'air** to get some fresh air.

bolet [bɔlɛ] *nm* boletus.

bolide [bɔlid] *nm* [véhicule] racing car.

Bolivie [bɔlivi] *nf*: **la ~** Bolivia.

bombance [bɔ̃bɑ̃s] *nf*: **faire ~** *fam* to have a feast.

bombardement [bɔ̃bardəmɑ̃] *nm* bombardment, bombing (*U*).

bombarder [bɔ̃barde] *vt* MIL to bomb. ‖ [assaillir]: **~ qqn/qqch de** to bombard sb/sthg.

bombardier [bɔ̃bardje] *nm* [avion] bomber. ‖ [aviateur] bombardier.

bombe [bɔ̃b] *nf* [projectile] bomb; *fig* bombshell; **~ atomique** atomic bomb; **~ à retardement** time bomb. ‖ [casquette] riding hat. ‖ [atomiseur] spray, aerosol.

bombé, -e [bɔ̃be] *adj* bulging, rounded.

bon, bonne [bɔ̃, bɔn] (*compar & superl* **meilleur**) *adj* [gén] good. ‖ [généreux] good, kind. ‖ [utilisable - billet, carte] valid. ‖ [correct] right. ‖ [dans l'expression d'un souhait]: **bonne année!** Happy New Year!; **bonne chance!** good luck!; **bonnes vacances!** have a nice holiday! ‖ *loc*: **tu es ~ pour une contravention** you'll end up with or you'll get a parking ticket; **~ à** (+ *infinitif*) fit to; **c'est ~ à savoir** that's worth knowing. ○ **bon 1** *adv*: **il fait ~** the weather's fine, it's fine; **sentir ~** to smell good. **2** *interj* [marque de satisfaction] good! ‖ [marque de surprise]: **ah ~!** really? **3** *nm* [constatant un droit] voucher; **~ de commande** order form; **~ du Trésor** FIN Treasury bill or bond. ○ **pour de bon** *loc adv* seriously, really.

bonbon [bɔ̃bɔ̃] *nm* [friandise] piece of candy *Am*. ‖ *Belg* [gâteau] biscuit.

bonbonne [bɔ̃bɔn] *nf* demijohn.

bonbonnière [bɔ̃bɔnjɛr] *nf* [boîte] sweet-box *Br*, candy box *Am*.

bond [bɔ̃] *nm* [d'animal, de personne] leap, bound; [de balle] bounce; **faire un ~** to leap (forward).

bonde [bɔ̃d] *nf* [d'évier] plug. ‖ [trou] bunghole. ‖ [bouchon] bung.

bondé, -e [bɔ̃de] *adj* packed.

bondir [bɔ̃dir] *vi* [sauter] to leap, to bound; **~ sur qqn/qqch** to pounce on sb/sthg. ‖ [s'élancer] to leap forward.

bonheur [bɔnœr] *nm* [félicité] happiness. || [chance] (good) luck, good fortune; **par ~** happily, fortunately; **porter ~** to be lucky, to bring good luck.

bonhomme [bɔnɔm] (*pl* **bonshommes** [bɔ̃zɔm]) *nm fam péj* [homme] fellow. || [représentation] man; **~ de neige** snowman.

bonification [bɔnifikasjɔ̃] *nf* SPORT bonus points (*pl*).

bonjour [bɔ̃ʒur] *nm* hello; [avant midi] good morning; [après midi] good afternoon.

bonne [bɔn] **1** *nf* maid. **2** *adj* → **bon**.

bonnet [bɔnɛ] *nm* [coiffure] (woolly) hat; **~ de bain** swimming cap. || [de soutien-gorge] cup.

bonneterie [bɔnɛtri] *nf* [commerce] hosiery (business ou trade).

bonsoir [bɔ̃swar] *nm* [en arrivant] hello, good evening; [en partant] goodbye, good evening; [en se couchant] good night.

bonté [bɔ̃te] *nf* [qualité] goodness, kindness; **avoir la ~ de faire qqch** *sout* to be so good ou kind as to do sthg.

bonus [bɔnys] *nm* [prime d'assurance] no-claims bonus.

bord [bɔr] *nm* [de table, de vêtement] edge; [de verre, de chapeau] rim; **à ras ~s** to the brim. || [de rivière] bank; [de lac] edge, shore; **au ~ de la mer** at the seaside. || [de bois, jardin] edge; [de route] edge, side. || [d'un moyen de transport]: **passer par-dessus ~** to fall overboard. ○ **à bord de** *loc prép*: **à ~ de qqch** on board sthg. ○ **au bord de** *loc prép* at the edge of; *fig* on the verge of.

bordeaux [bɔrdo] **1** *nm* [vin] Bordeaux. || [couleur] claret. **2** *adj inv* claret.

bordel [bɔrdɛl] *nm vulg* [maison close] brothel. || [désordre] shambles (*sg*).

border [bɔrde] *vt* [vêtement]: **~ qqch de** to edge sthg with. || [être en bordure de] to line. || [couverture, personne] to tuck in.

bordereau, -x [bɔrdəro] *nm* [relevé] slip.

bordure [bɔrdyr] *nf* [bord] edge; **en ~ de** on the edge of. || [de fleurs] border.

borgne [bɔrɲ] *adj* [personne] one-eyed.

borne [bɔrn] *nf* [marque] boundary marker. || *fam* [kilomètre] milestone. || [limite] limit, bounds (*pl*); **dépasser les ~s** to go too far. || ÉLECTR terminal.

borné, -e [bɔrne] *adj* [personne] narrow-minded; [esprit] narrow.

borner [bɔrne] ○ **se borner** *vp*: **se ~ à qqch/à faire qqch** [suj: personne] to confine o.s. to sthg/to doing sthg.

Bosnie [bɔsni] *nf*: **la ~** Bosnia.

bosniaque [bɔsnjak] *adj* Bosnian. ○ **Bosniaque** *nmf* Bosnian.

bosquet [bɔskɛ] *nm* copse.

bosse [bɔs] *nf* [sur tête, sur route] bump. || [de bossu, chameau] hump.

bosser [bɔse] *vi fam* to work hard.

bossu, -e [bɔsy] **1** *adj* hunchbacked. **2** *nm, f* hunchback.

botanique [bɔtanik] **1** *adj* botanical. **2** *nf*: **la ~** botany.

botte [bɔt] *nf* [chaussure] boot. || [de légumes] bunch. || [en escrime] thrust, lunge.

botter [bɔte] *vt* [chausser]: **être botté de cuir** to be wearing leather boots. || *fam* [donner un coup de pied à]: **ça me botte I** dig it.

bottier [bɔtje] *nm* [de bottes] bootmaker; [de chaussures] shoemaker.

Bottin ® [bɔtɛ̃] *nm* phone book.

bottine [bɔtin] *nf* (ankle) boot.

bouc [buk] *nm* [animal] (billy) goat; **~ émissaire** *fig* scapegoat. || [barbe] goatee.

boucan [bukã] *nm fam* row, racket.

bouche [buʃ] *nf* [gén] mouth; **~ d'incendie** fire hydrant; **~ de métro** metro entrance ou exit.

bouché, -e [buʃe] *adj* [en bouteille] bottled. || *fam* [personne] thick *Br*, dumb.

bouche-à-bouche [buʃabuʃ] *nm inv*: **faire du ~ à qqn** to give sb mouth-to-mouth resuscitation.

bouchée [buʃe] *nf* mouthful.

boucher[1] [buʃe] *vt* [fermer - bouteille] to cork; [- trou] to fill (in ou up). || [passage, vue] to block.

boucher[2], -ère [buʃe, ɛr] *nm, f* butcher.

boucherie [buʃri] *nf* [magasin] butcher's (shop). || *fig* [carnage] slaughter.

bouche-trou [buʃtru] (*pl* **bouche-trous**) *nm* [personne]: **servir de ~** to make up (the) numbers. || [objet] stopgap.

bouchon [buʃɔ̃] *nm* [pour obturer - gén] top; [- de réservoir] cap; [- de bouteille] cork. || [de canne à pêche] float. || [embouteillage] traffic jam.

boucle [bukl] *nf* [de ceinture, soulier] buckle. || [bijou]: **~ d'oreille** earring. ||

bourgeonner

[de cheveux] curl. || [de fleuve, d'avion & INFORM] loop.

boucle, **-e** [bukle] adj [cheveux] curly; [personne] curly-haired.

boucler [bukle] vt [attacher] to buckle; [ceinture de sécurité] to fasten. || [fermer] to shut. || fam [enfermer - voleur] to lock up; [- malade] to shut away. || [encercler] to seal off. || [terminer] to finish.

bouclier [buklije] nm litt & fig shield.

bouddhiste [budist] nmf & adj Buddhist.

bouder [bude] **1** vi to sulk. **2** vt [chose] to dislike; [personne] to shun.

boudeur, **-euse** [budœr, øz] adj sulky.

boudin [budɛ̃] nm CULIN blood pudding.

boue [bu] nf mud.

bouée [bwe] nf [balise] buoy. || [pour flotter] rubber ring; ~ **de sauvetage** lifebelt.

boueux, **-euse** [buø, øz] adj muddy.

bouffe [buf] nf fam grub.

bouffée [bufe] nf [de fumée] puff; [de parfum] whiff; [d'air] breath.

bouffer [bufe] vt fam [manger] to eat.

bouffi, **-e** [bufi] adj: ~ (**de**) swollen (with).

bouffon, **-onne** [bufɔ̃, ɔn] adj farcical. ○ **bouffon** nm HIST jester. || [pitre] clown.

bouge [buʒ] nm péj [taudis] hovel. || [café] dive.

bougeoir [buʒwar] nm candlestick.

bougeotte [buʒɔt] nf: **avoir la** ~ to have itchy feet.

bouger [buʒe] **1** vt [déplacer] to move. **2** vi [remuer] to move. || [changer] to change.

bougie [buʒi] nf [chandelle] candle. || [de moteur] spark plug, sparking plug.

bougon, **-onne** [bugɔ̃, ɔn] adj grumpy.

bougonner [bugɔne] vt & vi to grumble.

bouillant, **-e** [bujɑ̃, ɑ̃t] adj [qui bout] boiling. || [très chaud] boiling hot.

bouillie [buji] nf baby's cereal; **réduire en** ~ [légumes] to puree; [personne] to reduce to a pulp.

bouillir [bujir] vi [aliments] to boil; **faire** ~ to boil.

bouilloire [bujwar] nf kettle.

bouillon [bujɔ̃] nm [soupe] stock. || [bouillonnement] bubble; **faire bouillir à gros** ~**s** to bring to a rolling boil.

bouillonner [bujɔne] vi [liquide] to bubble. || fig [personne] to seethe.

bouillotte [bujɔt] nf hot-water bottle.

boul. abr de **boulevard**.

boulanger, **-ère** [bulɑ̃ʒe, ɛr] nm, f baker.

boulangerie [bulɑ̃ʒri] nf [magasin] baker's (shop). || [commerce] bakery trade.

boule [bul] nf [gén] ball; [de loto] counter; [de pétanque] bowl; ~ **de neige** snowball.

bouleau [bulo] nm silver birch.

bouledogue [buldɔg] nm bulldog.

boulet [bulɛ] nm [munition]: ~ **de canon** cannonball. || [de forçat] ball and chain. || fig [fardeau] millstone (round one's neck).

boulette [bulɛt] nf [petite boule] pellet. || [de viande] meatball.

boulevard [bulvar] nm [rue] boulevard. || THÉÂTRE light comedy (U).

bouleversant, **-e** [bulvɛrsɑ̃, ɑ̃t] adj distressing.

bouleversement [bulvɛrsəmɑ̃] nm disruption.

bouleverser [bulvɛrse] vt [objets] to turn upside down. || [modifier] to disrupt. || [émouvoir] to distress.

boulier [bulje] nm abacus.

boulimie [bulimi] nf bulimia.

boulon [bulɔ̃] nm bolt.

boulonner [bulɔne] **1** vt to bolt. **2** vi fam to slog (away).

boulot [bulo] nm fam [travail] work. || [emploi] job.

boum [bum] nf fam vieilli party.

bouquet [bukɛ] nm [de fleurs - gén] bunch (of flowers). || [de vin] bouquet. || [de feu d'artifice] crowning piece.

bouquin [bukɛ̃] nm fam book.

bouquiner [bukine] vi & vt fam to read.

bouquiniste [bukinist] nmf secondhand bookseller.

bourbier [burbje] nm [lieu] quagmire, mire; fig mess.

bourde [burd] nf fam [erreur] blunder.

bourdon [burdɔ̃] nm [insecte] bumblebee.

bourdonnement [burdɔnmɑ̃] nm [d'insecte, de voix] buzz (U).

bourdonner [burdɔne] vi [insecte, machine] to buzz. || [oreille] to ring.

bourgeois, **-e** [burʒwa, az] **1** adj [valeur] middle-class. || [cuisine] plain. || péj [personne] bourgeois. **2** nm, f bourgeois.

bourgeoisie [burʒwazi] nf ≃ middle classes (pl).

bourgeon [burʒɔ̃] nm bud.

bourgeonner [burʒɔne] vi to bud.

Bourgogne [burgɔɲ] *nf*: la ~ Burgundy.

bourlinguer [burlɛge] *vi fam* [voyager] to bum around the world.

bourrade [burad] *nf* thump.

bourrage [buraʒ] *nm* [de coussin] stuffing. ○ **bourrage de crâne** *nm* [propagande] brainwashing.

bourrasque [burask] *nf* gust of wind.

bourratif, -ive [buratif, iv] *adj* stodgy.

bourreau, -x [buro] *nm* HIST executioner.

bourrelet [burlɛ] *nm* [de graisse] roll of fat.

bourrer [bure] *vt* [remplir - coussin] to stuff; [- sac, armoire]: ~ qqch (de) to cram sthg full (with). || *fam* [gaver]: ~ qqn (de) to stuff sb (with).

bourrique [burik] *nf* [ânesse] she-ass. || *fam* [personne] pigheaded person.

bourru, -e [bury] *adj* [peu aimable] surly.

bourse [burs] *nf* [porte-monnaie] purse. || [d'études] grant. ○ **Bourse** *nf* [lieu] ≃ Wall Street *Am*. || [opérations]: **Bourse des valeurs** stock market, stock exchange; **Bourse de commerce** commodity market.

boursier, -ière [bursje, jɛr] *adj* [élève] on a grant. || FIN stock-market (*avant n*).

boursouflé, -e [bursufle] *adj* [enflé] swollen.

bousculade [buskylad] *nf* [cohue] crush. || [agitation] rush.

bousculer [buskyle] *vt* [faire tomber] to knock over. || [presser] to rush. || [modifier] to overturn.

bouse [buz] *nf*: ~ **de vache** cow dung.

bousiller [buzije] *vt fam* [abîmer] to ruin, to knacker *Br*.

boussole [busɔl] *nf* compass.

bout [bu] *nm* [extrémité, fin] end; **au ~ de** [temps] after; [espace] at the end of; **d'un ~ à l'autre** [de ville etc] from one end to the other; [de livre] from beginning to end. || [morceau] bit. || *loc*: **être à ~** to be exhausted; **à ~ portant** at point-blank range; **pousser qqn à ~** to drive sb to distraction; **venir à ~ de** [personne] to get the better of; [difficulté] to overcome.

boutade [butad] *nf* [plaisanterie] jest.

boute-en-train [butɑ̃trɛ̃] *nm inv* live wire; **il était le ~ de la soirée** he was the life and soul of the party.

bouteille [butɛj] *nf* bottle.

boutique [butik] *nf* [gén] shop; [de mode] boutique.

bouton [butɔ̃] *nm* COUTURE button; ~ **de manchette** cuff link. || [sur la peau] spot. || [de porte] knob. || [commutateur] switch. || [bourgeon] bud.

bouton-d'or [butɔ̃dɔr] (*pl* **boutons-d'or**) *nm* buttercup.

boutonner [butɔne] *vt* to button (up).

boutonneux, -euse [butɔnø, øz] *adj* spotty.

boutonnière [butɔnjɛr] *nf* [de vêtement] buttonhole.

bouton-pression [butɔ̃presjɔ̃] (*pl* **boutons-pression**) *nm* snap fastener *Am*.

bouture [butyr] *nf* cutting.

bovin, -e [bɔvɛ̃, in] *adj* bovine. ○ **bovins** *nmpl* cattle.

bowling [buliŋ] *nm* [jeu] bowling. || [lieu] bowling alley.

box [bɔks] (*pl* **boxes**) *nm* [d'écurie] loose box. || [compartiment] cubicle; **le ~ des accusés** the dock. || [parking] lock-up garage.

boxe [bɔks] *nf* boxing.

boxer[1] [bɔkse] *vi* to box.

boxer[2] [bɔksɛr] *nm* [chien] boxer.

boxeur [bɔksœr] *nm* SPORT boxer.

boyau [bwajo] *nm* [chambre à air] inner tube. ○ **boyaux** *nmpl* [intestins] guts.

boycotter [bɔjkɔte] *vt* to boycott.

BP (*abr de* **boîte postale**) *nf* PO Box.

bracelet [braslɛ] *nm* [bijou] bracelet. || [de montre] strap.

bracelet-montre [braslɛmɔ̃tr] *nm* wristwatch.

braconner [brakɔne] *vi* to go poaching, to poach.

braconnier [brakɔnje] *nm* poacher.

brader [brade] *vt* [solder] to sell off; [vendre à bas prix] to sell for next to nothing.

braderie [bradri] *nf* clearance sale.

braguette [bragɛt] *nf* flies (*pl*).

braille [braj] *nm* Braille.

brailler [braje] *vi* to bawl.

braire [brer] *vi* [âne] to bray.

braise [brez] *nf* embers (*pl*).

bramer [brame] *vi* [cerf] to bell.

brancard [brɑ̃kar] *nm* [civière] stretcher. || [de charrette] shaft.

brancardier, -ière [brɑ̃kardje, jɛr] *nm, f* stretcher-bearer.

branchage [brɑ̃ʃaʒ] *nm* branches (*pl*).

branche [brɑ̃ʃ] *nf* [gén] branch. || [de lunettes] arm.

branché, -e [brɑ̃ʃe] *adj* ÉLECTR plugged in, connected. || *fam* [à la mode] trendy.

branchement [brɑ̃ʃmɑ̃] *nm* [raccordement] connection, plugging in.

brancher [brɑ̃ʃe] *vt* [raccorder & INFORM] to connect; ~ **qqch sur** ÉLECTR to plug sthg into. || *fam* [orienter] to steer; ~ **qqn sur qqch** to start sb off on sthg. || *fam* [plaire] to appeal to.

branchies [brɑ̃ʃi] *nfpl* [de poisson] gills.

brandir [brɑ̃dir] *vt* to wave.

branlant, -e [brɑ̃lɑ̃, ɑ̃t] *adj* [escalier, mur] shaky; [meuble, dent] wobbly.

branle-bas [brɑ̃lba] *nm inv* pandemonium (*U*).

braquer [brake] **1** *vt* [diriger]: ~ **qqch sur** [arme] to aim sthg at; [regard] to fix sthg on. || *fam* [attaquer] to hold up. **2** *vi* to turn (the wheel). ○ **se braquer** *vp* [personne] to take a stand.

bras [brɑ] *nm* [gén] arm; ~ **droit** right-hand man ou woman; ~ **de fer** [jeu] arm wrestling; *fig* trial of strength; **avoir le ~ long** [avoir de l'influence] to have pull. || [de cours d'eau] branch; ~ **de mer** arm of the sea.

brasier [brazje] *nm* [incendie] blaze, inferno.

bras-le-corps [brɑlkɔr] ○ **à bras-le-corps** *loc adv* bodily.

brassage [brasaʒ] *nm* [de bière] brewing. || *fig* [mélange] mixing.

brassard [brasar] *nm* armband.

brasse [bras] *nf* [nage] breaststroke; ~ **papillon** butterfly (stroke).

brassée [brase] *nf* armful.

brasser [brase] *vt* [bière] to brew. || [mélanger] to mix. || *fig* [manier] to handle.

brasserie [brasri] *nf* [usine] brewery. || [café-restaurant] brasserie.

brassière [brasjɛr] *nf* [de bébé] (baby's) vest *Br* ou undershirt *Am*. || *Can* [soutien-gorge] bra.

brave [brav] *adj* (*après n*) [courageux] brave. || (*avant n*) [honnête] decent. || [naïf et gentil] nice.

braver [brave] *vt* [parents, règlement] to defy. || [mépriser] to brave.

bravo [bravo] *interj* bravo! ○ **bravos** *nmpl* cheers.

bravoure [bravur] *nf* bravery.

break [brɛk] *nm* [voiture] estate (car) *Br*, station wagon *Am*. || [pause] break.

brebis [brəbi] *nf* ewe; ~ **galeuse** black sheep.

brèche [brɛʃ] *nf* [de mur] gap. || MIL breach.

bredouiller [brəduje] *vi* to stammer.

bref, brève [bref, brɛv] *adj* [gén] short, brief; **soyez ~!** make it brief! || LING short. ○ **bref** *adv* in short, in a word. ○ **brève** *nf* PRESSE brief news item.

brelan [brəlɑ̃] *nm*: **un ~** three of a kind; **un ~ de valets** three jacks.

Brésil [brezil] *nm*: **le ~** Brazil.

Bretagne [brətaɲ] *nf*: **la ~** Brittany.

bretelle [brətɛl] *nf* [d'autoroute] access road. || [de pantalon]: ~**s** braces *Br*, suspenders *Am*. || [de bustier] strap.

breuvage [brœvaʒ] *nm* [boisson] beverage.

brève → bref.

brevet [brəvɛ] *nm* [certificat] certificate. || [diplôme] diploma. || [d'invention] patent.

breveter [brəvte] *vt* to patent.

bréviaire [brevjɛr] *nm* breviary.

bribe [brib] *nf* [fragment] scrap, bit; *fig* snippet; ~**s de conversation** snatches of conversation.

bric [brik] ○ **de bric et de broc** *loc adv* any old how.

bric-à-brac [brikabrak] *nm inv* bric-a-brac.

bricolage [brikolaʒ] *nm* [travaux] do-it-yourself, DIY. || [réparation provisoire] patching up.

bricole [brikɔl] *nf* [babiole] trinket. || [chose insignifiante] trivial matter.

bricoler [brikɔle] **1** *vi* to do odd jobs (around the house). **2** *vt* [réparer] to fix, to mend. || [fabriquer] to make.

bricoleur, -euse [brikɔlœr, øz] *nm, f* home handyman (*f* handywoman).

bride [brid] *nf* [de cheval] bridle.

bridé [bride] → œil.

brider [bride] *vt* [cheval] to bridle; *fig* to rein (in).

bridge [bridʒ] *nm* bridge.

brièvement [brijɛvmɑ̃] *adv* briefly.

brièveté [brijɛvte] *nf* brevity, briefness.

brigade [brigad] *nf* [d'ouvriers, de soldats] brigade. || [détachement] squad; ~ **volante** flying squad.

brigand [brigɑ̃] *nm* [bandit] bandit.

brillamment [brijamɑ̃] *adv* [gén] brilliantly; [réussir un examen] with flying colours.

brillant, -e [brijɑ̃, ɑ̃t] *adj* [qui brille - gén] sparkling; [- cheveux] glossy; [- yeux] bright. || [remarquable] brilliant. ○ **brillant** *nm* [diamant] brilliant.

briller [brije] *vi* to shine.

brimer [brime] *vt* to victimize, to bully.

brin [brɛ̃] *nm* [tige] twig; ~ **d'herbe** blade of grass. || [fil] strand. || [petite quantité]: **un ~ (de)** a bit (of).

brindille [brɛ̃dij] *nf* twig.

bringuebaler, brinquebaler [brɛ̃gbale] *vi* [voiture] to jolt along.

brio [brijo] *nm* [talent]: **avec ~** brilliantly.

brioche [brijɔʃ] *nf* [pâtisserie] brioche. || *fam* [ventre] paunch.

brioché, -e [brijɔʃe] *adj* [pain] brioche-style.

brique [brik] *nf* [pierre] brick. || [emballage] carton. || *fam* [argent] **10,000 francs.**

briquer [brike] *vt* to scrub.

briquet [brike] *nm* (cigarette) lighter.

brisant [brizɑ̃] *nm* [écueil] reef. ○ **brisants** *nmpl* [récif] breakers.

brise [briz] *nf* breeze.

brise-lames [brizlam] *nm inv* breakwater.

briser [brize] *vt* [gén] to break. || *fig* [carrière] to ruin; [espérances] to shatter. ○ **se briser** *vp* [gén] to break. || *fig* [espoir] to be dashed.

bristol [bristɔl] *nm* [papier] Bristol board.

britannique [britanik] *adj* British. ○ **Britannique** *nmf* British person, Briton; **les Britanniques** the British.

broc [bro] *nm* jug.

brocante [brɔkɑ̃t] *nf* [commerce] secondhand trade. || [objets] secondhand goods (*pl*).

brocanteur, -euse [brɔkɑ̃tœr, øz] *nm, f* dealer in secondhand goods.

broche [brɔʃ] *nf* [bijou] brooch. || CULIN spit; **cuire à la ~** to spit-roast. || ÉLECTR & MÉD pin.

broché, -e [brɔʃe] *adj* [tissu] brocade (*avant n*), brocaded. || TYPO: **livre ~** paperback (book).

brochet [brɔʃɛ] *nm* pike.

brochette [brɔʃɛt] *nf* [ustensile] skewer. || [plat] kebab.

brochure [brɔʃyr] *nf* [imprimé] brochure, booklet.

broder [brɔde] *vt & vi* to embroider.

broderie [brɔdri] *nf* [art] embroidery. || [ouvrage] (piece of) embroidery.

bromure [brɔmyr] *nm* bromide.

bronche [brɔ̃ʃ] *nf* bronchus; **j'ai des problèmes de ~s** I've got chest problems.

broncher [brɔ̃ʃe] *vi*: **sans ~** without complaining, uncomplainingly.

bronchite [brɔ̃ʃit] *nf* bronchitis (*U*).

bronzage [brɔ̃zaʒ] *nm* [de peau] tan, suntan.

bronze [brɔ̃z] *nm* bronze.

bronzé, -e [brɔ̃ze] *adj* tanned, suntanned.

bronzer [brɔ̃ze] *vi* [peau] to tan; [personne] to get a tan.

brosse [brɔs] *nf* brush; **~ à cheveux** hairbrush; **~ à dents** toothbrush; **avoir les cheveux en ~** to have a crew cut.

brosser [brɔse] *vt* [habits, cheveux] to brush. || [paysage, portrait] to paint. ○ **se brosser** *vp*: **se ~ les cheveux/les dents** to brush one's hair/teeth.

brouette [bruɛt] *nf* wheelbarrow.

brouhaha [bruaa] *nm* hubbub.

brouillard [brujar] *nm* [léger] mist; [dense] fog; **~ givrant** freezing fog.

brouille [bruj] *nf* quarrel.

brouillé, -e [bruje] *adj* [fâché]: **être ~ avec qqn** to be on bad terms with sb; **être ~ avec qqch** *fig* to be hopeless or useless at sthg. || [teint] muddy. || → **œuf.**

brouiller [bruje] *vt* [vue] to blur. || RADIO to cause interference to; [- délibérément] to jam. || [rendre confus] to muddle (up). ○ **se brouiller** *vp* [se fâcher] to fall out; **se ~ avec qqn (pour qqch)** to fall out with sb (over sthg). || [se troubler] to become blurred.

brouillon, -onne [brujɔ̃, ɔn] *adj* careless, untidy. ○ **brouillon** *nm* rough copy, draft.

broussaille [brusaj] *nf*: **les ~s** the undergrowth; **en ~** *fig* [cheveux] untidy; [sourcils] bushy.

brousse [brus] *nf* GÉOGR scrubland, bush.

brouter [brute] **1** *vt* to graze on. **2** *vi* [animal] to graze. || TECHNOL to judder.

broutille [brutij] *nf* trifle.

broyer [brwaje] *vt* to grind, to crush.

bru [bry] *nf* *sout* daughter-in-law.

brugnon [bryɲɔ̃] *nm* nectarine.

bruine [bryin] *nf* drizzle.

bruissement [bryismɑ̃] *nm* [de feuilles, d'étoffe] rustle, rustling (*U*).

bruit [bryi] *nm* [son] noise, sound; **~ de fond** background noise. || [vacarme & TECHNOL] noise; **faire du ~** to make a noise; **sans ~** silently, noiselessly. || [rumeur] rumour. || [retentissement] fuss; **faire du ~** to cause a stir.

bruitage [bryitaʒ] *nm* sound-effects (*pl*).

brûlant, -e [brylɑ̃, ɑ̃t] *adj* [gén] burning (hot); [liquide] boiling (hot); [plat] piping hot.

brûle-pourpoint [brylpurpwɛ̃] ○ **à brûle-pourpoint** *loc adv* point-blank, straight out.

brûler [bryle] **1** *vt* [gén] to burn; [suj: eau bouillante] to scald; **la fumée me brûle les yeux** the smoke is making my eyes sting. ‖ [feu rouge] to drive through; [étape] to miss out, to skip. **2** *vi* [gén] to burn; [maison, forêt] to be on fire. ‖ [être brûlant] to be burning (hot); **~ de fièvre** to be running a high temperature. ○ **se brûler** *vp* to burn o.s.

brûlure [brylyr] *nf* [lésion] burn; **~ au premier/troisième degré** first-degree/third-degree burn. ‖ [sensation] burning (sensation); **avoir des ~s d'estomac** to have heartburn.

brume [brym] *nf* mist.

brumeux, -euse [brymø, øz] *adj* misty; *fig* hazy.

brun, -e [brœ̃, bryn] **1** *adj* brown; [cheveux] dark. **2** *nm, f* dark-haired man (*f* woman). ○ **brun** *nm* [couleur] brown. ○ **brune** *nf* [cigarette] *cigarette made of dark tobacco.* ‖ [bière] brown ale.

brunir [brynir] *vi* [personne] to get a tan; [peau] to tan.

brushing [brœʃiŋ] *nm*: **faire un ~ à qqn** to give sb a blow-dry, to blow-dry sb's hair.

brusque [brysk] *adj* abrupt.

brusquement [bryskəmɑ̃] *adv* abruptly.

brusquer [bryske] *vt* to rush; [élève] to push.

brusquerie [bryskəri] *nf* abruptness.

brut, -e [bryt] *adj* [pierre précieuse, bois] rough; [sucre] unrefined; [métal, soie] raw; [champagne] extra dry; (**pétrole**) **~** crude (oil). ‖ *fig* [fait, idées] crude, raw. ‖ ÉCON gross. ○ **brute** *nf* brute.

brutal, -e, -aux [brytal, o] *adj* [violent] violent, brutal. ‖ [soudain] sudden. ‖ [manière] blunt.

brutaliser [brytalize] *vt* to mistreat.

brutalité [brytalite] *nf* [violence] violence, brutality. ‖ [caractère soudain] suddenness.

Bruxelles [bry(k)sɛl] *n* Brussels.

bruyamment [bryijamɑ̃] *adv* noisily.

bruyant, -e [bryijɑ̃, ɑ̃t] *adj* noisy.

bruyère [bryjɛr] *nf* [plante] heather.

BT *nm* (*abr de* **brevet de technicien**) *vo-cational training certificate (taken at age 18).*

BTS (*abr de* **brevet de technicien supérieur**) *nm advanced vocational training certificate (taken at the end of a 2-year higher education course).*

bu, -e [by] *pp* → **boire**.

buanderie [byɑ̃dri] *nf* laundry.

buccal, -e, -aux [bykal, o] *adj* buccal.

bûche [byʃ] *nf* [bois] log; **~ de Noël** Yule log.

bûcher[1] [byʃe] *nm* [supplice]: **le ~** the stake. ‖ [funéraire] pyre.

bûcher[2] [byʃe] **1** *vi* to swot. **2** *vt* to swot up.

bûcheron, -onne [byʃrɔ̃, ɔn] *nm, f* forestry worker.

bûcheur, -euse [byʃœr, øz] **1** *adj* hard-working. **2** *nm, f fam* swot.

bucolique [bykɔlik] *adj* pastoral.

budget [bydʒɛ] *nm* budget.

budgétaire [bydʒeter] *adj* budgetary; **année ~** financial year.

buée [bye] *nf* [sur vitre] condensation.

buffet [byfɛ] *nm* [meuble] sideboard. ‖ [repas] buffet. ‖ [café-restaurant]: **~ de gare** station buffet.

buis [bɥi] *nm* box(wood).

buisson [bɥisɔ̃] *nm* bush.

buissonnière [bɥisɔnjɛr] → **école**.

bulbe [bylb] *nm* bulb.

bulgare [bylgar] *adj* Bulgarian. ○ **bulgare** *nm* [langue] Bulgarian. ○ **Bulgare** *nmf* Bulgarian.

Bulgarie [bylgari] *nf*: **la ~** Bulgaria.

bulldozer [byldozer] *nm* bulldozer.

bulle [byl] *nf* [gén] bubble; **~ de savon** soap bubble. ‖ [de bande dessinée] speech balloon.

bulletin [byltɛ̃] *nm* [communiqué] bulletin; **~ (de la) météo** weather forecast; **~ de santé** medical bulletin. ‖ [imprimé] form; **~ de vote** ballot paper. ‖ SCOL report. ‖ [certificat] certificate; **~ de salaire** ou **de paye** pay slip.

bulletin-réponse [byltɛ̃repɔ̃s] (*pl* **bulletins-réponse**) *nm* reply form.

buraliste [byralist] *nmf* [d'un bureau de tabac] tobacconist.

bureau [byro] *nm* [gén] office; **~ de change** bureau de change; **~ d'études** design office; **~ de poste** post office; **~ de tabac** tobacconist's; **~ de vote** polling station. ‖ [meuble] desk.

bureaucrate [byrokrat] *nmf* bureaucrat.

bureaucratie [byrokrasi] *nf* bureaucracy.

bureautique [byrotik] *nf* office automation.

burette [byrɛt] *nf* [de mécanicien] oil-can.

burin [byrɛ̃] *nm* [outil] chisel.

buriné, -e [byrine] *adj* engraved; [visage, traits] lined.

burlesque [byrlɛsk] *adj* [comique] funny. || [ridicule] ludicrous, absurd. || THÉÂTRE burlesque.

bus [bys] *nm* bus.

busqué [byske] → **nez.**

buste [byst] *nm* [torse] chest; [poitrine de femme, sculpture] bust.

bustier [bystje] *nm* [corsage] strapless top; [soutien-gorge] longline bra.

but [byt] *nm* [point visé] target. || [objectif] goal, aim, purpose; **à ~ non lucratif** JUR non-profit-making *Br*, non-profit *Am*; **aller droit au ~** to go straight to the point; **dans le ~ de faire qqch** with the aim ou intention of doing sthg. || SPORT goal. || *loc*: **de ~ en blanc** point-blank, straight out.

butane [bytan] *nm*: **(gaz) ~** butane; [domestique] Calor gas® *Br*, butane.

buté, -e [byte] *adj* stubborn.

buter [byte] **1** *vi* [se heurter]: **~ sur/contre qqch** to stumble on/over sthg, to trip on/over sthg. **2** *vt tfam* [tuer] to do in, to bump off. ○ **se buter** *vp* to dig one's heels in.

butin [bytɛ̃] *nm* [de guerre] booty; [de vol] loot; [de recherche] finds (*pl*).

butiner [bytine] *vi* to collect nectar.

butte [byt] *nf* [colline] mound, rise; **être en ~ à** *fig* to be exposed to.

buvard [byvar] *nm* [papier] blotting-paper; [sous-main] blotter.

buvette [byvɛt] *nf* [café] refreshment room, buffet.

buveur, -euse [byvœr, øz] *nm, f* drinker.

c¹, C [se] *nm inv* c, C. ○ **C** (*abr de* **celsius, centigrade**) C.

c² *abr de* **centime.**

c' → **ce.**

CA *nm abr de* **chiffre d'affaires.**

ça [sa] *pron dém* [pour désigner] that; [- plus près] this. || [sujet indéterminé] it, that; **~ ira comme ~** that will be fine; **~ y est** that's it; **c'est ~** that's right. || [renforcement expressif]: **où ~?** where?; **qui ~?** who?

çà *adv*: **~ et là** here and there.

caban [kabɑ̃] *nm* reefer (jacket).

cabane [kaban] *nf* [abri] cabin, hut; [remise] shed; **~ à lapins** hutch.

cabanon [kabanɔ̃] *nm* [à la campagne] cottage. || [sur la plage] chalet. || [de rangement] shed.

cabaret [kabarɛ] *nm* cabaret.

cabas [kaba] *nm* shopping-bag.

cabillaud [kabijo] *nm* (fresh) cod.

cabine [kabin] *nf* [de navire, d'avion, de véhicule] cabin. || [compartiment, petit local] cubicle; **~ d'essayage** fitting room; **~ téléphonique** phone box.

cabinet [kabinɛ] *nm* [pièce]: **~ de toilette** ≃ bathroom. || [local professionnel] office; **~ dentaire/médical** dentist's/doctor's surgery *Br*, dentist's/doctor's office *Am*. || [de ministre] advisers (*pl*). ○ **cabinets** *nmpl* toilet (*sg*).

câble [kabl] *nm* cable; **télévision par ~** cable television.

câblé, -e [kable] *adj* TÉLÉ equipped with cable TV.

cabosser [kabose] *vt* to dent.

cabotage [kabɔtaʒ] *nm* coastal navigation.

cabrer [kabre] ○ **se cabrer** *vp* [cheval] to rear (up).

cabri [kabri] *nm* kid.

cabriole [kabrijɔl] *nf* [bond] caper; [pirouette] somersault.

cabriolet [kabrijɔlɛ] *nm* convertible.

caillouteux

CAC, **Cac** [kak] (abr de **Compagnie des agents de change**) nf: **l'indice ~-40** the French stock exchange shares index.

caca [kaka] nm fam pooh; **faire ~** to do a pooh; **~ d'oie** greeny-yellow.

cacahouète, **cacahuète** [kakawɛt] nf peanut.

cacao [kakao] nm [poudre] cocoa (powder). || [boisson] cocoa.

cachalot [kaʃalo] nm sperm whale.

cache [kaʃ] **1** nf [cachette] hiding place. **2** nm [masque] card (for masking text etc).

cache-cache [kaʃkaʃ] nm inv: **jouer à ~** to play hide and seek.

cachemire [kaʃmir] nm [laine] cashmere. || [dessin] paisley.

cache-nez [kaʃne] nm inv scarf.

cache-pot [kaʃpo] nm inv flowerpot-holder.

cacher [kaʃe] vt [gén] to hide; **je ne vous cache pas que ...** to be honest, ... || [vue] to mask. ○ **se cacher** vp: **se ~ (de qqn)** to hide (from sb).

cachet [kaʃɛ] nm [comprimé] tablet, pill. || [marque] postmark. || [style] style, character. || [rétribution] fee.

cacheter [kaʃte] vt to seal.

cachette [kaʃet] nf hiding place; **en ~** secretly.

cachot [kaʃo] nm [cellule] cell.

cachotterie [kaʃotri] nf little secret; **faire des ~s (à qqn)** to hide things (from sb).

cachottier, -ière [kaʃotje, ɛr] nm, f secretive person.

cactus [kaktys] nm cactus.

cadastre [kadastr] nm [registre] ≃ land register; [service] ≃ land office Am.

cadavérique [kadaverik] adj deathly.

cadavre [kadavr] nm corpse, (dead) body.

cadeau, -x [kado] **1** nm present, gift; **faire ~ de qqch à qqn** to give sthg to sb (as a present). **2** adj inv: **idée ~** gift idea.

cadenas [kadna] nm padlock.

cadenasser [kadnase] vt to padlock.

cadence [kadɑ̃s] nf [rythme musical] rhythm; **en ~ in** time. || [de travail] rate.

cadencé, -e [kadɑ̃se] adj rhythmical.

cadet, -ette [kadɛ, ɛt] nm, f [de deux enfants] younger; [de plusieurs enfants] youngest; **il est mon ~ de deux ans** he's two years younger than me. || SPORT junior.

cadran [kadrɑ̃] nm dial; **~ solaire** sundial.

cadre [kadr] nm [de tableau, de porte] frame. || [contexte] context. || [décor, milieu] surroundings (pl). || [responsable]: **~ moyen/supérieur** middle/senior manager. || [sur formulaire] box.

cadrer [kadre] **1** vi to agree, to tally. **2** vt CIN, PHOT & TÉLÉ to frame.

caduc, caduque [kadyk] adj [feuille] deciduous. || [qui n'est plus valide] obsolete.

cafard [kafar] nm [insecte] cockroach. || fig [mélancolie]: **avoir le ~** to feel low or down.

café [kafe] nm [plante, boisson] coffee; **~ crème** coffee with frothy milk; **~ en grains** coffee beans; **~ au lait** white coffee (with hot milk); **~ moulu** ground coffee; **~ noir** black coffee; **~ en poudre** or **soluble** instant coffee. || [lieu] bar, cafe.

caféine [kafein] nf caffeine.

cafétéria [kafeterja] nf cafeteria.

café-théâtre [kafeteatr] nm ≃ cabaret.

cafetière [kaftjer] nf [récipient] coffee-pot. || [électrique] coffee-maker; [italienne] percolator.

cafouiller [kafuje] vi fam [s'embrouiller] to get into a mess. || [moteur] to misfire; TÉLÉ to be on the blink.

cage [kaʒ] nf [pour animaux] cage. || [dans une maison]: **~ d'escalier** stairwell. || ANAT: **~ thoracique** rib cage.

cageot [kaʒo] nm [caisse] crate.

cagibi [kaʒibi] nm storage room Am.

cagneux, -euse [kaɲø, øz] adj: **avoir les genoux ~** to be knock-kneed.

cagnotte [kaɲɔt] nf [caisse commune] kitty. || [économies] savings (pl).

cagoule [kagul] nf [passe-montagne] balaclava. || [de voleur, de pénitent] hood.

cahier [kaje] nm [de notes] exercise book, notebook; **~ de brouillon** rough book; **~ de textes** homework book. || COMM: **~ des charges** specification.

cahin-caha [kaɛ̃kaa] adv: **aller ~** to be jogging along.

cahot [kao] nm bump, jolt.

cahoter [kaote] vi to jolt around.

cahute [kayt] nf shack.

caille [kaj] nf quail.

caillé, -e [kaje] adj [lait] curdled; [sang] clotted.

caillot [kajo] nm clot.

caillou, -x [kaju] nm [pierre] stone, pebble. || fam [crâne] head.

caillouteux, -euse [kajutø, øz] adj stony.

caïman [kaimɑ̃] *nm* cayman.

Caire [kɛr] *n*: Le ~ Cairo.

caisse [kɛs] *nf* [boîte] crate, box; ~ à outils toolbox. || [guichet] cash desk, till; [de supermarché] checkout, till; ~ enregistreuse cash register. || [organisme]: ~ d'épargne [fonds] savings fund; [établissement] savings bank; ~ de retraite pension fund.

caissier, -ière [kesje, jɛr] *nm, f* cashier.

cajoler [kaʒɔle] *vt* to make a fuss of, to cuddle.

cajou [kaʒu] → **noix**.

cake [kɛk] *nm* fruit-cake.

cal [kal] *nm* callus.

calamar [kalamar], **calmar** [kalmar] *nm* squid.

calamité [kalamite] *nf* disaster.

calandre [kalɑ̃dr] *nf* [de voiture] radiator grille. || [machine] calender.

calanque [kalɑ̃k] *nf* rocky inlet.

calcaire [kalkɛr] 1 *adj* [eau] hard; [sol] chalky; [roche] limestone (*avant n*). 2 *nm* limestone.

calciner [kalsine] *vt* to burn to a cinder.

calcium [kalsjɔm] *nm* calcium.

calcul [kalkyl] *nm* [opération]: le ~ arithmetic; ~ **mental** mental arithmetic. || [compte] calculation. || *fig* [plan] plan. || MÉD: ~ (**rénal**) kidney stone.

calculateur, -trice [kalkylatœr, tris] *adj péj* calculating. ○ **calculateur** *nm* computer. ○ **calculatrice** *nf* calculator.

calculer [kalkyle] 1 *vt* [déterminer] to calculate, to work out. || [prévoir] to plan.

calculette [kalkylɛt] *nf* pocket calculator.

cale [kal] *nf* [de navire] hold; ~ sèche dry dock. || [pour immobiliser] wedge.

calé, -e [kale] *adj fam* [personne] clever, brainy; être ~ **en** to be good at.

calèche [kalɛʃ] *nf* (horse-drawn) carriage.

caleçon [kalsɔ̃] *nm* [sous-vêtement masculin] boxer shorts (*pl*), pair of boxer shorts. || [vêtement féminin] leggings (*pl*), pair of leggings.

calembour [kalɑ̃bur] *nm* pun, play on words.

calendrier [kalɑ̃drije] *nm* [système, agenda, d'un festival] calendar. || [emploi du temps] timetable.

cale-pied [kalpje] (*pl* **cale-pieds**) *nm* toe-clip.

calepin [kalpɛ̃] *nm* notebook.

caler [kale] 1 *vt* [avec cale] to wedge. || [stabiliser, appuyer] to prop up. || *fam* [remplir]: ça cale (l'estomac) it's filling. 2 *vi* [moteur, véhicule] to stall. || *fam* [personne] to give up.

calfeutrer [kalføtre] *vt* to draughtproof. ○ **se calfeutrer** *vp* to shut o.s. up ou away.

calibre [kalibr] *nm* [de tuyau] diameter, bore; [de fusil] calibre; [de fruit, d'œuf] size. || *fam fig* [envergure] calibre.

Californie [kalifɔrni] *nf*: la ~ California.

califourchon [kalifurʃɔ̃] ○ **à califourchon** *loc adv* astride; être (assis) à ~ **sur** qqch to sit astride sthg.

câlin, -e [kalɛ̃, in] *adj* affectionate. ○ **câlin** *nm* cuddle.

câliner [kaline] *vt* to cuddle.

calleux, -euse [kalø, øz] *adj* calloused.

calligraphie [kaligrafi] *nf* calligraphy.

calmant, -e [kalmɑ̃, ɑ̃t] *adj* soothing. ○ **calmant** *nm* [pour la douleur] painkiller; [pour l'anxiété] tranquillizer, sedative.

calmar → **calamar**.

calme [kalm] 1 *adj* quiet, calm. 2 *nm* [gén] calm, calmness. || [absence de bruit] peace (and quiet).

calmer [kalme] *vt* [apaiser] to calm (down). || [réduire - douleur] to soothe; [- inquiétude] to allay. ○ **se calmer** *vp* [s'apaiser - personne, discussion] to calm down; [- tempête] to abate; [- mer] to become calm. || [diminuer - douleur] to ease; [- fièvre, inquiétude, désir] to subside.

calomnie [kalɔmni] *nf* [écrits] libel; [paroles] slander.

calorie [kalɔri] *nf* calorie.

calorique [kalɔrik] *adj* calorific.

calotte [kalɔt] *nf* [bonnet] skullcap. || GÉOGR: ~ **glaciaire** ice cap.

calque [kalk] *nm* [dessin] tracing. || [papier]: (**papier**) ~ tracing paper. || *fig* [imitation] (exact) copy.

calquer [kalke] *vt* [carte] to trace. || [imiter] to copy exactly; ~ qqch **sur** qqch to model sthg on sthg.

calvaire [kalvɛr] *nm* [croix] wayside cross. || *fig* [épreuve] ordeal.

calvitie [kalvisi] *nf* baldness.

camaïeu [kamajø] *nm* monochrome.

camarade [kamarad] *nmf* [compagnon, ami] friend; ~ **de classe** classmate; ~ **d'école** schoolfriend. || POLIT comrade.

camaraderie [kamaradri] *nf* [familiarité, entente] friendship.

Cambodge [kãbɔdʒ] *nm*: le ~ Cambodia.

cambouis [kãbwi] *nm* dirty grease.

cambré, -e [kãbre] *adj* arched.

cambriolage [kãbrijɔlaʒ] *nm* burglary.

cambrioler [kãbrijɔle] *vt* to burgle *Br*, to burglarize *Am*.

cambrioleur, -euse [kãbrijɔlœr, øz] *nm, f* burglar.

camée [kame] *nm* cameo.

caméléon [kameleɔ̃] *nm litt & fig* chameleon.

camélia [kamelja] *nm* camellia.

camelote [kamlɔt] *nf* [marchandise de mauvaise qualité] rubbish.

caméra [kamera] *nf* CIN & TÉLÉ camera. || [d'amateur] cinecamera.

cameraman [kameraman] (*pl* **cameramen** [kameramɛn] OU **cameramans**) *nm* cameraman.

Caméscope® [kameskɔp] *nm* camcorder.

camion [kamjɔ̃] *nm* lorry *Br*, truck *Am*.

camion-citerne [kamjɔ̃sitɛrn] *nm* tanker *Br*, tanker truck *Am*.

camionnette [kamjɔnɛt] *nf* van.

camionneur [kamjɔnœr] *nm* [conducteur] truck-driver *Am*. || [entrepreneur] trucker *Am*.

camisole [kamizɔl] O **camisole de force** *nf* straitjacket.

camouflage [kamuflaʒ] *nm* [déguisement] camouflage.

camoufler [kamufle] *vt* [déguiser] to camouflage; *fig* [dissimuler] to conceal, to cover up.

camp [kã] *nm* [gén] camp; ~ **de concentration** concentration camp. || SPORT half (of the field). || [parti] side.

campagnard, -e [kãpaɲar, ard] *adj* [de la campagne] country (*avant n*). || [rustique] rustic.

campagne [kãpaɲ] *nf* [régions rurales] country; **à la ~** in the country. || MIL, POLIT & PUBLICITÉ campaign; **faire ~ pour/contre** to campaign for/against; ~ **électorale** election campaign; ~ **de presse** press campaign; ~ **publicitaire** advertising campaign.

campement [kãpmã] *nm* camp, encampment.

camper [kãpe] *vi* to camp.

campeur, -euse [kãpœr, øz] *nm, f* camper.

camphre [kãfr] *nm* camphor.

camping [kãpiŋ] *nm* [activité] camping;

faire du ~ to go camping. || [terrain] campsite.

Canada [kanada] *nm*: le ~ Canada.

canadien, -ienne [kanadjɛ̃, jɛn] *adj* Canadian. O **canadienne** *nf* [veste] sheepskin jacket. O **Canadien, -ienne** *nm, f* Canadian.

canaille [kanaj] *nf* [scélérat] scoundrel.

canal, -aux [kanal, o] *nm* [gén] channel. || [voie d'eau] canal. || ANAT canal, duct. O **Canal** *nm*: **Canal+** *French TV pay channel*.

canalisation [kanalizasjɔ̃] *nf* [conduit] pipe.

canaliser [kanalize] *vt* [cours d'eau] to canalize. || *fig* [orienter] to channel.

canapé [kanape] *nm* [siège] sofa.

canapé-lit [kanapeli] *nm* sofa bed.

canard [kanar] *nm* [oiseau] duck. || [fausse note] wrong note. || *fam* [journal] rag.

canari [kanari] *nm* canary.

cancan [kãkã] *nm* [ragot] piece of gossip. || [danse] cancan.

cancer [kãser] *nm* MÉD cancer. O **Cancer** *nm* ASTROL Cancer.

cancéreux, -euse [kãserø, øz] **1** *adj* [tumeur] cancerous. **2** *nm, f* [personne] cancer sufferer.

cancérigène [kãseriʒɛn] *adj* carcinogenic.

cancre [kãkr] *nm fam* dunce.

cancrelat [kãkrəla] *nm* cockroach.

candélabre [kãdelabr] *nm* candelabra.

candeur [kãdœr] *nf* ingenuousness.

candi [kãdi] *adj*: **sucre ~** (sugar) candy.

candidat, -e [kãdida, at] *nm, f*: ~ **(à)** candidate (for).

candidature [kãdidatyr] *nf* [à un poste] application; **poser sa ~ pour qqch** to apply for sthg. || [à une élection] candidature.

candide [kãdid] *adj* ingenuous.

cane [kan] *nf* (female) duck.

caneton [kantɔ̃] *nm* (male) duckling.

canette [kanɛt] *nf* [de fil] spool. || [petite cane] (female) duckling. || [de boisson - bouteille] bottle; [- boîte] can.

canevas [kanva] *nm* COUTURE canvas.

caniche [kaniʃ] *nm* poodle.

canicule [kanikyl] *nf* heatwave.

canif [kanif] *nm* penknife.

canin, -e [kanɛ̃, in] *adj* canine; **exposition ~e** dog show. O **canine** *nf* canine (tooth).

caniveau [kanivo] *nm* gutter.

canne [kan] nf [bâton] walking stick; ~ à pêche fishing rod. || fam [jambe] pin. ○ **canne à sucre** nf sugar cane.

cannelle [kanel] nf [aromate] cinnamon.

cannibale [kanibal] nmf & adj cannibal.

canoë [kanɔe] nm canoe.

canoë-kayak [kanɔekajak] nm kayak.

canon [kanɔ̃] nm [arme] gun; HIST cannon. || [tube d'arme] barrel. || MUS: **chanter en** ~ to sing in canon.

canot [kano] nm dinghy; ~ **pneumatique** inflatable dinghy; ~ **de sauvetage** lifeboat.

cantatrice [kɑ̃tatris] nf prima donna.

cantine [kɑ̃tin] nf [réfectoire] canteen. || [malle] trunk.

cantique [kɑ̃tik] nm hymn.

canton [kɑ̃tɔ̃] nm [en France] ≃ district. || [en Suisse] canton.

cantonade [kɑ̃tɔnad] ○ **à la cantonade** loc adv: **parler à la** ~ to speak to everyone (in general).

cantonais, -e [kɑ̃tɔnɛ, ɛz] adj Cantonese; **riz** ~ egg fried rice. ○ **cantonais** nm [langue] Cantonese.

cantonner [kɑ̃tɔne] vt MIL to quarter, to billet Br. || [maintenir] to confine; ~ **qqn à** ou **dans** to confine sb to.

cantonnier [kɑ̃tɔnje] nm roadman.

canular [kanylar] nm fam hoax.

caoutchouc [kautʃu] nm [substance] rubber. || [plante] rubber plant.

caoutchouteux, -euse [kautʃutø, øz] adj rubbery.

cap [kap] nm GÉOGR cape; **le** ~ **de Bonne-Espérance** the Cape of Good Hope; **le** ~ **Horn** Cape Horn; **passer le** ~ **de qqch** fig to get through sthg. || [direction] course; **changer de** ~ to change course; **mettre le** ~ **sur** to head for. ○ **Cap** nm: **Le Cap** Cape Town.

CAP (abr de certificat d'aptitude professionnelle) nm vocational training certificate (taken at secondary school).

capable [kapabl] adj [apte]: ~ **(de qqch/de faire qqch)** capable (of sthg/of doing sthg). || [à même]: ~ **de faire qqch** likely to do sthg.

capacité [kapasite] nf [de récipient] capacity. || [de personne] ability.

cape [kap] nf [vêtement] cloak; **rire sous** ~ fig to laugh up one's sleeve.

CAPES, Capes [kapɛs] (abr de certificat d'aptitude au professorat de l'enseignement du second degré) nm secondary school teaching certificate.

capharnaüm [kafarnaɔm] nm mess.

capillaire [kapilɛr] adj [lotion] hair (avant n). || ANAT & BOT capillary.

capitaine [kapitɛn] nm captain.

capitainerie [kapitɛnri] nf harbour master's office.

capital, -e, -aux [kapital, o] adj [décision, événement] major. || JUR capital. ○ **capital** nm FIN capital; ~ **social** authorized ou share capital. ○ **capitale** nf [ville, lettre] capital. ○ **capitaux** nmpl capital (U).

capitalisme [kapitalism] nm capitalism.

capitaliste [kapitalist] nmf & adj capitalist.

capiteux, -euse [kapitø, øz] adj [vin] intoxicating; [parfum] heady.

capitonné, -e [kapitɔne] adj padded.

capituler [kapityle] vi to surrender; ~ **devant qqn/qqch** to surrender to sb/sthg.

caporal, -aux [kapɔral, o] nm MIL lance-corporal. || [tabac] caporal.

capot [kapo] nm [de voiture] hood Am. || [de machine] (protective) cover.

capote [kapɔt] nf [de voiture] top Am. || fam [préservatif]: ~ **(anglaise)** condom.

câpre [kapr] nf caper.

caprice [kapris] nm whim.

capricieux, -ieuse [kaprisjø, jøz] adj [changeant] capricious; [coléreux] temperamental.

capricorne [kaprikɔrn] nm ZOOL capricorn beetle. ○ **Capricorne** nm ASTROL Capricorn.

capsule [kapsyl] nf [de bouteille] cap. || ASTRON, BOT & MÉD capsule.

capter [kapte] vt [recevoir sur émetteur] to pick up. || [source, rivière] to harness. || fig [attention, confiance] to gain, to win.

captif, -ive [kaptif, iv] **1** adj captive. **2** nm, f prisoner.

captivant, -e [kaptivɑ̃, ɑ̃t] adj [livre, film] enthralling; [personne] captivating.

captiver [kaptive] vt to captivate.

captivité [kaptivite] nf captivity.

capture [kaptyr] nf [action] capture. || [prise] catch.

capturer [kaptyre] vt to catch, to capture.

capuche [kapyʃ] nf (detachable) hood.

capuchon [kapyʃɔ̃] nm [bonnet - d'imperméable] hood. || [bouchon] cap, top.

capucine [kapysin] nf [fleur] nasturtium.

caquet [kakɛ] *nm péj* [bavardage]: **rabattre le ~ à** OU **de qqn** to shut sb up.

caqueter [kakte] *vi* [poule] to cackle.

car¹ [kar] *nm* coach *Br*, bus *Am*.

car² [kar] *conj* for, because.

carabine [karabin] *nf* rifle.

caractère [karaktɛr] *nm* [gén] character; **avoir du ~** to have character; **avoir mauvais ~** to be bad-tempered; **en petits/gros ~s** in small/large print; **~s d'imprimerie** block capitals.

caractériel, -ielle [karakterjɛl] *adj* [troubles] emotional; [personne] emotionally disturbed.

caractériser [karakterize] *vt* to be characteristic of. ○ **se caractériser** *vp*: **se ~ par qqch** to be characterized by sthg.

caractéristique [karakteristik] **1** *nf* characteristic, feature. **2** *adj*: **~ (de)** characteristic (of).

carafe [karaf] *nf* [pour vin, eau] carafe; [pour alcool] decanter.

Caraïbes [karaib] *nfpl*: **les ~** the Caribbean.

carambolage [karɑ̃bɔlaʒ] *nm* pile-up.

caramel [karamɛl] *nm* CULIN caramel. ‖ [bonbon - dur] toffee, caramel; [- mou] fudge.

carapace [karapas] *nf* shell; *fig* protection, shield.

carapater [karapate] ○ **se carapater** *vp fam* to scarper, to hop it.

carat [kara] *nm* carat; **or à 9 ~s** 9-carat gold.

caravane [karavan] *nf* [de camping, de désert] caravan.

caravaning [karavaniŋ] *nm* caravanning.

carbone [karbɔn] *nm* carbon; **(papier) ~** carbon paper.

carbonique [karbɔnik] *adj*: **gaz ~** carbon dioxide; **neige ~** dry ice.

carboniser [karbɔnize] *vt* to burn to a cinder.

carburant [karbyrɑ̃] *nm* fuel.

carburateur [karbyratœr] *nm* carburettor.

carcan [karkɑ̃] *nm* HIST iron collar; *fig* yoke.

carcasse [karkas] *nf* [d'animal] carcass. ‖ [de bâtiment, navire] framework. ‖ [de véhicule] shell.

cardiaque [kardjak] *adj* cardiac; **être ~** to have a heart condition; **crise ~** heart attack.

cardigan [kardigɑ̃] *nm* cardigan.

cardinal, -e, -aux [kardinal, o] *adj* cardinal. ○ **cardinal** *nm* RELIG cardinal.

cardiologue [kardjɔlɔg] *nmf* heart specialist, cardiologist.

cardio-vasculaire [kardjovaskylɛr] (*pl* **cardio-vasculaires**) *adj* cardiovascular.

Carême [karɛm] *nm*: **le ~** Lent.

carence [karɑ̃s] *nf* [manque]: **~ (en)** deficiency (in).

carène [karɛn] *nf* NAVIG hull.

caressant, -e [karɛsɑ̃, ɑ̃t] *adj* affectionate.

caresse [karɛs] *nf* caress.

caresser [karese] *vt* [personne] to caress; [animal, objet] to stroke. ‖ *fig* [espoir] to cherish.

cargaison [kargɛzɔ̃] *nf* TRANSPORT cargo.

cargo [kargo] *nm* [navire] freighter. ‖ [avion] cargo plane.

caricature [karikatyr] *nf* [gén] caricature. ‖ *péj* [personne] sight.

carie [kari] *nf* MÉD caries.

carillon [karijɔ̃] *nm* [cloches] bells (*pl*). ‖ [d'horloge, de porte] chime.

carlingue [karlɛ̃g] *nf* [d'avion] cabin.

carnage [karnaʒ] *nm* slaughter, carnage.

carnassier [karnasje] *nm* carnivore.

carnaval [karnaval] *nm* carnival.

carnet [karnɛ] *nm* [petit cahier] notebook; **~ d'adresses** address book; **~ de notes** SCOL report card. ‖ [bloc de feuilles] book; **~ de chèques** cheque book; **~ de tickets** book of tickets.

carnivore [karnivɔr] **1** *adj* carnivorous. **2** *nm* carnivore.

carotte [karɔt] *nf* carrot.

carpe [karp] *nf* carp.

carpette [karpɛt] *nf* [petit tapis] rug. ‖ *fam péj* [personne] doormat.

carquois [karkwa] *nm* quiver.

carré, -e [kare] *adj* [gén] square; **20 mètres ~s** 20 square metres. ○ **carré** *nm* [quadrilatère] square. ‖ CARTES: **un ~ d'as** four aces. ‖ [petit terrain] patch, plot.

carreau [karo] *nm* [carrelage] tile. ‖ [vitre] window pane. ‖ [motif carré] check; **à ~x** [tissu] checked; [papier] squared. ‖ CARTES diamond.

carrefour [karfur] *nm* [de routes, de la vie] crossroads (*sg*).

carrelage [karlaʒ] *nm* [surface] tiles (*pl*).

carrément [karemɑ̃] *adv* [franchement]

bluntly. || [complètement] completely, quite. || [sans hésiter] straight.

carrière [karjɛr] *nf* [profession] career; **faire ~ dans qqch** to make a career (for o.s.) in sthg. || [gisement] quarry.

carriériste [karjerist] *nmf péj* careerist.

carriole [karjɔl] *nf* [petite charrette] cart. || *Can* [traîneau] sleigh.

carrossable [karɔsabl] *adj* suitable for vehicles.

carrosse [karɔs] *nm* (horse-drawn) coach.

carrosserie [karɔsri] *nf* [de voiture] bodywork, body.

carrossier [karɔsje] *nm* coachbuilder.

carrure [karyr] *nf* [de personne] build; *fig* stature.

cartable [kartabl] *nm* schoolbag.

carte [kart] *nf* [gén] card; **~ bancaire** cash card *Br*; **~ de crédit** credit card; **~ d'étudiant** student card; **~ grise** ≈ car registration papers *Am*, ≈ logbook *Br*; **~ d'identité** identity card; **Carte Orange** season ticket (*for use on public transport in Paris*); **~ postale** postcard; **~ à puce** smart card; **~ de séjour** residence permit; **Carte Vermeil** *card entitling senior citizens to reduced rates in cinemas, on public transport etc*; **~ de visite** visiting card *Br*, calling card *Am*; **donner ~ blanche à qqn** *fig* to give sb a free hand. || [de jeu]: **~ (à jouer)** (playing) card. || GÉOGR map; **~ routière** road map. || [au restaurant] menu; **à la ~** [menu] à la carte; [horaires] flexible; **~ des vins** wine list.

cartilage [kartilaʒ] *nm* cartilage.

cartomancien, -ienne [kartɔmɑ̃sjɛ̃, jɛn] *nm, f* fortune-teller (*using cards*).

carton [kartɔ̃] *nm* [matière] cardboard. || [emballage] cardboard box; **~ à dessin** portfolio.

cartonné, -e [kartɔne] *adj* [livre] hardback.

carton-pâte [kartɔ̃pat] *nm* pasteboard.

cartouche [kartuʃ] *nf* [gén & INFORM] cartridge. || [de cigarettes] carton.

cas [ka] *nm* case; **au ~ où** in case; **en aucun ~** under no circumstances; **en tout ~** in any case, anyway; **en ~ de** in case of; **en ~ de besoin** if need be; **le ~ échéant** if the need arises, if need be.

casanier, -ière [kazanje, jɛr] *adj & nm, f* stay-at-home.

casaque [kazak] *nf* [veste] overblouse. || HIPPISME blouse.

cascade [kaskad] *nf* [chute d'eau] waterfall; *fig* stream, torrent. || CIN stunt.

cascadeur, -euse [kaskadœr, øz] *nm, f* CIN stuntman (*f* stuntwoman).

cascher = **kas(e)her**.

case [kaz] *nf* [habitation] hut. || [de boîte, tiroir] compartment; [d'échiquier] square; [sur un formulaire] box.

caser [kaze] *vt fam* [trouver un emploi pour] to get a job for. || *fam* [marier] to marry off. || [placer] to put. ○ **se caser** *vp fam* [trouver un emploi] to get (o.s.) a job. || [se marier] to get hitched.

caserne [kazɛrn] *nf* barracks.

cash [kaʃ] *nm* cash; **payer ~** to pay (in) cash.

casier [kazje] *nm* [compartiment] compartment; [pour le courrier] pigeonhole. || [meuble - à bouteilles] rack; [- à courrier] set of pigeonholes. || PÊCHE lobster pot. ○ **casier judiciaire** *nm* police record.

casino [kazino] *nm* casino.

casque [kask] *nm* [de protection] helmet. || [à écouteurs] headphones (*pl*). ○ **Casques bleus** *nmpl*: **les Casques bleus** the UN peace-keeping force.

casquette [kaskɛt] *nf* cap.

cassant, -e [kasɑ̃, ɑ̃t] *adj* [fragile - verre] fragile; [- cheveux] brittle. || [dur] brusque.

cassation [kasasjɔ̃] → **cour.**

casse [kas] **1** *nf fam* [violence] aggro. || [de voitures] scrapyard. **2** *nm fam* [cambriolage] break-in.

casse-cou [kasku] *nmf inv* [personne] daredevil.

casse-croûte [kaskrut] *nm inv* snack.

casse-noisettes [kasnwazɛt], **casse-noix** [kasnwa] *nm inv* nutcrackers (*pl*).

casse-pieds [kaspje] **1** *adj inv fam* annoying. **2** *nmf inv* pain (in the neck).

casser [kase] **1** *vt* [briser] to break. || JUR to quash. || COMM: **les prix** to slash prices. **2** *vi* to break. ○ **se casser** *vp* [se briser] to break. || [membre]: **se ~ un bras** to break one's arm.

casserole [kasrɔl] *nf* [ustensile] saucepan.

casse-tête [kastɛt] *nm inv fig* [problème] headache. || [jeu] puzzle.

cassette [kasɛt] *nf* [coffret] casket. || [de musique, vidéo] cassette.

cassis [kasis] *nm* [fruit] blackcurrant; [arbuste] blackcurrant bush; [liqueur] blackcurrant liqueur. || [sur la route] dip.

cassure [kasyr] *nf* break.

caste [kast] *nf* caste.

casting [kastiŋ] *nm* [acteurs] cast; **aller à un ~** to go to an audition.

castor [kastɔr] *nm* beaver.

castrer [kastre] *vt* to castrate; [chat] to neuter; [chatte] to spay.

cataclysme [kataklism] *nm* cataclysm.

catadioptre [katadjɔptr], **Cataphote®** [katafɔt] *nm* [sur la route] cat's eye. || [de véhicule] reflector.

catalogue [katalɔg] *nm* catalogue.

cataloguer [katalɔge] *vt* [classer] to catalogue. || *péj* [juger] to label.

catalytique [katalitik] → **pot**.

catamaran [katamarɑ̃] *nm* [voilier] catamaran.

Cataphote® = **catadioptre**.

cataplasme [kataplasm] *nm* poultice.

catapulter [katapylte] *vt* to catapult.

cataracte [katarakt] *nf* cataract.

catastrophe [katastrɔf] *nf* disaster, catastrophe.

catastrophé, -e [katastrɔfe] *adj* shocked, upset.

catastrophique [katastrɔfik] *adj* disastrous, catastrophic.

catch [katʃ] *nm* wrestling.

catéchisme [kateʃism] *nm* catechism.

catégorie [kategɔri] *nf* [gén] category; [de personnel] grade; [de viande, fruits] quality; **~ socio-professionnelle** ÉCON socio-economic group.

catégorique [kategɔrik] *adj* categorical.

cathédrale [katedral] *nf* cathedral.

cathodique [katɔdik] → **tube**.

catholicisme [katɔlisism] *nm* Catholicism.

catholique [katɔlik] *adj* Catholic.

catimini [katimini] ○ **en catimini** *loc adv* secretly.

cauchemar [koʃmar] *nm litt & fig* nightmare.

cauchemardesque [koʃmardɛsk] *adj* nightmarish.

cause [koz] *nf* [gén] cause; **à ~ de** because of; **pour ~ de** on account of, because of. || JUR case. || *loc*: **être en ~** [intérêts] to be at stake; [honnêteté] to be in doubt or in question; **remettre en ~** to challenge, to question.

causer [koze] **1** *vt*: **~ qqch à qqn** to cause sb sthg. **2** *vi* [bavarder]: **~ (de)** to chat (about).

causerie [kozri] *nf* talk.

caustique [kostik] *adj & nm* caustic.

cautériser [koterize] *vt* to cauterize.

caution [kosjɔ̃] *nf* [somme d'argent] guarantee. || [personne] guarantor; **se porter ~ pour qqn** to act as guarantor for sb.

cautionner [kosjone] *vt* [se porter garant de] to guarantee. || *fig* [appuyer] to support, to back.

cavalcade [kavalkad] *nf* [de cavaliers] cavalcade. || [d'enfants] stampede.

cavalerie [kavalri] *nf* MIL cavalry.

cavalier, -ière [kavalje, jɛr] *nm, f* [à cheval] rider. || [partenaire] partner. ○ **cavalier** *nm* [aux échecs] knight.

cavalièrement [kavaljermɑ̃] *adv* in an offhand manner.

cave [kav] *nf* [sous-sol] cellar. || [de vins] (wine) cellar.

caveau [kavo] *nm* [petite cave] small cellar. || [sépulture] vault.

caverne [kavɛrn] *nf* cave.

caviar [kavjar] *nm* caviar.

cavité [kavite] *nf* cavity.

CCP (*abr de* **compte chèque postal**, **compte courant postal**) *nm* post office account; ≃ Giro *Br*.

CD *nm* (*abr de* **compact disc**) CD.

CDI *nm* (*abr de* **centre de documentation et d'information**) school library.

ce [sə] **1** *adj dém* (**cet** [sɛt] *devant voyelle ou h muet, f* **cette** [sɛt], *pl* **ces** [se]) [proche] this, these (*pl*); [éloigné] that, those (*pl*); **cette année, cette année-là** that year. **2** *pron dém* (**c'** *devant voyelle*): **c'est** it is, it's; **~ sont** they are, they're; **c'est à Paris** it's in Paris; **qui est-~?** who is it?; **~ qui, ~ que** what; **ils ont eu ~ qui leur revenait** they got what they deserved; ..., **~ qui est étonnant** ..., which is surprising; **vous savez bien ~ à quoi je pense** you know exactly what I'm thinking about. ○ **n'est-ce pas?** *loc adv* isn't it?/aren't you? *etc*; **~ café est bon, n'est-~ pas?** this coffee's good, isn't it?; **tu connais Pierre, n'est-~ pas?** you know Pierre, don't you?

CE 1 *nm* (*abr de* **cours élémentaire**) **~1** second year of primary school; **~2** third year of primary school. **2** *nf* (*abr de* **Communauté européenne**) EC.

ceci [səsi] *pron dém* this; **à ~ près que** with the exception that, except that.

cécité [sesite] *nf* blindness.

céder [sede] **1** *vt* [donner] to give up. || [revendre] to sell. **2** *vi* [personne]: **~ (à)** to give in (to), to yield (to). || [chaise, plancher] to give way.

CEDEX, Cedex [sedɛks] (*abr de courrier d'entreprise à distribution exceptionnelle*) *nm* accelerated postal service for bulk users.

cédille [sedij] *nf* cedilla.

cèdre [sɛdr] *nm* cedar.

CEE (*abr de* **Communauté économique européenne**) *nf* EEC.

CEI (*abr de* **Communauté d'États Indépendants**) *nf* CIS.

ceinture [sɛtyr] *nf* [gén] belt; **~ de sécurité** safety ou seat belt. || ANAT waist.

ceinturon [sɛtyrɔ̃] *nm* belt.

cela [səla] *pron dém* that; **~ ne vous regarde pas** it's ou that's none of your business; **il y a des années de ~** that was many years ago; **c'est ~** that's right; **~ dit** ... having said that ....

célèbre [selɛbr] *adj* famous.

célébrer [selebre] *vt* [gén] to celebrate. || [faire la louange de] to praise.

célébrité [selebrite] *nf* [renommée] fame. || [personne] celebrity.

céleri [sɛlri] *nm* celery.

céleste [selɛst] *adj* heavenly.

célibat [seliba] *nm* celibacy.

célibataire [selibatɛr] **1** *adj* single, unmarried. **2** *nmf* single person, single man (*f* woman).

celle → celui.

celle-ci → celui-ci.

celle-là → celui-là.

celles → celui.

celles-ci → celui-ci.

celles-là → celui-là.

cellier [selje] *nm* storeroom.

Cellophane® [selɔfan] *nf* Cellophane®.

cellulaire [selylɛr] *adj* BIOL & TÉLÉCOM cellular.

cellule [selyl] *nf* [gén & INFORM] cell. || [groupe] unit; [réunion] emergency committee meeting.

cellulite [selylit] *nf* cellulite.

celte [sɛlt] *adj* Celtic. ○ **Celte** *nmf* Celt.

celui [səlɥi] (*f* **celle** [sɛl], *mpl* **ceux** [sø], *fpl* **celles** [sɛl]) *pron dém* [suivi d'un complément prépositionnel] the one; **celle de devant** the one in front; **ceux d'entre vous qui ...** those of you who .... || [suivi d'un pronom relatif] **~ qui** [objet] the one which ou that; [personne] the one who; **ceux que je connais** those I know.

celui-ci [səlɥisi] (*f* **celle-ci** [sɛlsi], *mpl* **ceux-ci** [søsi], *fpl* **celles-ci** [sɛlsi]) *pron dém* this one, these ones (*pl*).

celui-là [səlɥila] (*f* **celle-là** [sɛlla], *mpl* **ceux-là** [søla], *fpl* **celles-là** [sɛlla]) *pron dém* that one, those ones (*pl*); **~ ... celui-ci** the former ... the latter.

cendre [sɑ̃dr] *nf* ash.

cendré, -e [sɑ̃dre] *adj* [chevelure]: **blond ~** ash blond.

cendrier [sɑ̃drije] *nm* [de fumeur] ashtray. || [de poêle] ashpan.

cène [sɛn] *nf* (Holy) Communion. ○ **Cène** *nf*: **la Cène** the Last Supper.

censé, -e [sɑ̃se] *adj*: **être ~ faire qqch** to be supposed to do sthg.

censeur [sɑ̃sœr] *nm* SCOL ≃ vice-principal *Am*. || CIN & PRESSE censor.

censure [sɑ̃syr] *nf* [CIN & PRESSE - contrôle] censorship; [- censeurs] censors (*pl*). || POLIT censure. || PSYCHOL censor.

censurer [sɑ̃syre] *vt* CIN, PRESSE & PSYCHOL to censor. || [juger] to censure.

cent [sɑ̃] **1** *adj num* one hundred, a hundred. **2** *nm* [nombre] a hundred; *voir aussi* **six**. || [mesure de proportion]: **pour ~** per cent.

centaine [sɑ̃tɛn] *nf* [cent unités] hundred. || [un grand nombre]: **une ~ de** about a hundred; **des ~s (de)** hundreds (of); **plusieurs ~s de** several hundred; **par ~s** in hundreds.

centenaire [sɑ̃tnɛr] **1** *adj* hundred-year-old (*avant n*); **être ~** to be a hundred years old. **2** *nmf* centenarian. **3** *nm* [anniversaire] centenary.

centième [sɑ̃tjɛm] *adj num, nm & nmf* hundredth; *voir aussi* **sixième**.

centigrade [sɑ̃tigrad] → **degré**.

centilitre [sɑ̃tilitr] *nm* centilitre.

centime [sɑ̃tim] *nm* centime.

centimètre [sɑ̃timɛtr] *nm* [mesure] centimetre. || [ruban, règle] tape measure.

central, -e, -aux [sɑ̃tral, o] *adj* central. ○ **central** *nm* [de réseau]: **~ téléphonique** telephone exchange. ○ **centrale** *nf* [usine] power plant ou station; **~e hydroélectrique** hydroelectric power station; **~e nucléaire** nuclear power plant ou station. || COMM: **~e d'achat** buying group.

centraliser [sɑ̃tralize] *vt* to centralize.

centre [sɑ̃tr] *nm* [gén] centre; **~ aéré** outdoor centre; **~ commercial** shopping centre; **~ culturel** arts centre; **~ de gravité** centre of gravity.

centrer [sɑ̃tre] *vt* to centre.

centre-ville [sɑ̃trəvil] *nm* city centre, town centre.

centrifuge [sɑ̃trify3] → **force**.

centrifugeuse [sɑ̃trifyʒøz] *nf* TECHNOL centrifuge. ‖ CULIN juice extractor.

centuple [sɑ̃typl] *nm*: être le ~ de qqch to be a hundred times sthg; **au ~ a** hundredfold.

cep [sɛp] *nm* stock.

cèpe [sɛp] *nm* cep.

cependant [səpɑ̃dɑ̃] *conj* however, yet.

céramique [seramik] *nf* [matière, objet] ceramic.

cerceau [sɛrso] *nm* hoop.

cercle [sɛrkl] *nm* circle; ~ **vicieux** vicious circle.

cercueil [sɛrkœj] *nm* coffin.

céréale [sereal] *nf* cereal.

cérémonial, -als [seremɔnjal] *nm* ceremonial.

cérémonie [seremɔni] *nf* ceremony.

cérémonieux, -ieuse [seremɔnjø, jøz] *adj* ceremonious.

cerf [sɛr] *nm* stag.

cerf-volant [sɛrvɔlɑ̃] *nm* [jouet] kite.

cerise [səriz] *nf & adj inv* cherry.

cerisier [sərizje] *nm* [arbre] cherry (tree); [bois] cherry (wood).

cerne [sɛrn] *nm* ring.

cerné [sɛrne] → **œil**.

cerner [sɛrne] *vt* [encercler] to surround. ‖ *fig* [sujet] to define.

certain, -e [sɛrtɛ̃, ɛn] **1** *adj* certain; être ~ de qqch to be certain or sure of sthg; je suis pourtant ~ d'avoir mis mes clés là but I'm certain or sure I left my keys there. **2** *adj indéf* (*avant n*) certain; **il a un ~ talent** he has some talent or a certain talent; **c'est un monsieur d'un ~ âge** he's getting on a bit; **un ~ M. Lebrun** a Mr Lebrun. ○ **certains** (*fpl* **certaines**) *pron indéf pl* some.

certainement [sɛrtɛnmɑ̃] *adv* certainly.

certes [sɛrt] *adv* of course.

certificat [sɛrtifika] *nm* [attestation, diplôme] certificate; ~ **médical** medical certificate.

certifié, -e [sɛrtifje] *adj*: **professeur ~** qualified teacher.

certifier [sɛrtifje] *vt* [assurer]: ~ qqch à qqn to assure sb of sthg. ‖ [authentifier] to certify.

certitude [sɛrtityd] *nf* certainty.

cerveau [sɛrvo] *nm* brain.

cervelle [sɛrvɛl] *nf* ANAT brain. ‖ [facultés mentales, aliment] brains (*pl*).

cervical, -e, -aux [sɛrvikal, o] *adj* cervical.

ces → **ce**.

CES (*abr de* **collège d'enseignement secondaire**) *nm* former secondary school.

césarienne [sezarjɛn] *nf* caesarean (section).

cesse [sɛs] *nf*: **n'avoir de ~ que** (+ *subjonctif*) *sout* not to rest until. ○ **sans cesse** *loc adv* continually, constantly.

cesser [sese] **1** *vi* to stop, to cease. **2** *vt* to stop; ~ **de faire qqch** to stop doing sthg.

cessez-le-feu [seselfø] *nm inv* ceasefire.

cession [sesjɔ̃] *nf* transfer.

c'est-à-dire [setadir] *conj* [en d'autres termes]: ~ **(que)** that is (to say). ‖ [introduit une restriction, précision, réponse]: ~ **que well ..., actually ....**

cet → **ce**.

cétacé [setase] *nm* cetacean.

cette → **ce**.

ceux → **celui**.

ceux-ci → **celui-ci**.

ceux-là → **celui-là**.

cf. (*abr de* **confer**) cf.

CFC (*abr de* **chlorofluorocarbone**) *nm* CFC.

chacun, -e [ʃakœ̃, yn] *pron indéf* each (one); [tout le monde] everyone, everybody; ~ **de nous/de vous/d'eux** each of us/you/them.

chagrin, -e [ʃagrɛ̃, in] *adj* [caractère, humeur] morose. ○ **chagrin** *nm* grief; **avoir du ~** to grieve.

chagriner [ʃagrine] *vt* [peiner] to grieve, to distress. ‖ [contrarier] to upset.

chahut [ʃay] *nm* uproar.

chahuter [ʃayte] **1** *vi* to cause an uproar. **2** *vt* [importuner - professeur] to rag, to tease; [- orateur] to heckle. ‖ [bousculer] to jostle.

chaîne [ʃɛn] *nf* [gén] chain; ~ **de montagnes** mountain range. ‖ IND: ~ **de fabrication/de montage** production/assembly line; **travail à la ~** production-line work. ‖ TÉLÉ channel. ‖ [appareil] stereo (system); ~ **hi-fi** hi-fi system.

chaînon [ʃɛnɔ̃] *nm litt & fig* link.

chair [ʃɛr] *nf* flesh; **avoir la ~ de poule** *fig* to have goosebumps *Am*.

chaire [ʃɛr] *nf* [estrade - de prédicateur] pulpit; [- de professeur] rostrum. ‖ UNIV chair.

chaise [ʃɛz] *nf* chair; ~ **longue** deckchair.

châle [ʃal] *nm* shawl.

chalet [ʃalɛ] *nm* [de montagne] chalet. ‖ *Can* [maison de campagne] (holiday) cottage.

chaleur [ʃalœr] *nf* heat; [agréable] warmth.

chaleureux, -euse [ʃalœrø, øz] *adj* warm.

challenge [ʃalɑʒ] *nm* SPORT tournament.

chaloupe [ʃalup] *nf* rowing boat *Br*, rowboat *Am*.

chalumeau [ʃalymo] *nm* TECHNOL blowlamp *Br*, blowtorch *Am*.

chalutier [ʃalytje] *nm* [bateau] trawler.

chamailler [ʃamaje] ○ **se chamailler** *vp fam* to squabble.

chambranle [ʃɑ̃brɑ̃l] *nm* [de porte, fenêtre] frame; [de cheminée] mantelpiece.

chambre [ʃɑ̃br] *nf* [où l'on dort]: ~ (à coucher) bedroom; ~ à un lit, ~ pour une personne single room; ~ pour deux personnes double room; ~ d'amis spare room. ‖ [local] room; ~ forte strongroom; ~ froide cold store; ~ noire darkroom. ‖ JUR division; ~ d'accusation court of criminal appeal. ‖ POLIT chamber, house; **Chambre des députés** ≃ House of Commons *Br*, ≃ House of Representatives *Am*. ‖ TECHNOL chamber; ~ à air [de pneu] inner tube.

chambrer [ʃɑ̃bre] *vt* [vin] to bring to room temperature. ‖ *fam* [se moquer]: ~ **qqn** to pull sb's leg.

chameau, -x [ʃamo] *nm* [mammifère] camel.

chamois [ʃamwa] *nm* chamois; [peau] chamois (leather).

champ [ʃɑ̃] *nm* [gén & INFORM] field; ~ **de bataille** battlefield; ~ **de courses** racecourse. ‖ [étendue] area.

champagne [ʃɑ̃paɲ] *nm* champagne.

champêtre [ʃɑ̃pɛtr] *adj* rural.

champignon [ʃɑ̃piɲɔ̃] *nm* BOT & MÉD fungus; [comestible] mushroom; ~ **vénéneux** toadstool.

champion, -ionne [ʃɑ̃pjɔ̃, jɔn] 1 *nm, f* champion. 2 *adj fam* brilliant.

championnat [ʃɑ̃pjɔna] *nm* championship.

chance [ʃɑ̃s] *nf* [bonheur] luck (*U*); **avoir de la ~** to be lucky; **ne pas avoir de ~** to be unlucky; **porter ~** to bring good luck. ‖ [probabilité, possibilité] chance, opportunity; **avoir des ~s de faire qqch** to have a chance of doing sthg.

chanceler [ʃɑ̃sle] *vi* [personne, gouvernement] to totter; [meuble] to wobble.

chancelier [ʃɑ̃səlje] *nm* [premier ministre] chancellor. ‖ [de consulat, d'ambassade] secretary.

chanceux, -euse [ʃɑ̃sø, øz] *adj* lucky.

chandail [ʃɑ̃daj] *nm* (thick) sweater.

Chandeleur [ʃɑ̃dlœr] *nf* Candlemas.

chandelier [ʃɑ̃dəlje] *nm* [pour une bougie] candlestick; [à plusieurs branches] candelabra.

chandelle [ʃɑ̃dɛl] *nf* [bougie] candle.

change [ʃɑ̃ʒ] *nm* [troc & FIN] exchange. ‖ [couche de bébé] diaper *Am*.

changeant, -e [ʃɑ̃ʒɑ̃, ɑ̃t] *adj* [temps, humeur] changeable.

changement [ʃɑ̃ʒmɑ̃] *nm* change.

changer [ʃɑ̃ʒe] 1 *vt* [gén] to change; ~ **qqn en** to change sb into; ~ **des francs en livres** to change francs into pounds, to exchange francs for pounds. ‖ [modifier] to change, to alter; **ça me/te changera** that will be a (nice) change for me/you. 2 *vi* [gén] to change; ~ **de train** (à) to change trains (at); ~ **d'avis** to change one's mind; **ça changera!** that'll make a change!; ~ **de direction** to change direction; ~ **de place** (avec qqn) to change places (with sb); **pour ~** for a change.

chanson [ʃɑ̃sɔ̃] *nf* song; **c'est toujours la même** ~ *fig* it's the same old story.

chansonnier, -ière [ʃɑ̃sɔnje, jɛr] *nm, f* cabaret singer-songwriter.

chant [ʃɑ̃] *nm* [chanson] song, singing (*U*); [sacré] hymn. ‖ [art] singing.

chantage [ʃɑ̃taʒ] *nm litt & fig* blackmail; **faire du** ~ **à qqn** to blackmail sb.

chanter [ʃɑ̃te] 1 *vt* [chanson] to sing. ‖ *littéraire* [célébrer] to sing of, to tell of; ~ **les louanges de qqn** to sing sb's praises. 2 *vi* [gén] to sing. ‖ *loc*: **faire** ~ **qqn** to blackmail sb; **si ça vous chante!** *fam* if you feel like or fancy it!

chanteur, -euse [ʃɑ̃tœr, øz] *nm, f* singer.

chantier [ʃɑ̃tje] *nm* CONSTR (building) site; [sur la route] roadworks (*pl*); ~ **naval** shipyard, dockyard. ‖ *fig* [désordre] shambles (*sg*), mess.

chantonner [ʃɑ̃tɔne] *vt & vi* to hum.

chaos [kao] *nm* chaos.

chap. (*abr de* **chapitre**) ch.

chaparder [ʃaparde] *vt* to steal.

chapeau, -x [ʃapo] *nm* [coiffure] hat.

chapeauter [ʃapote] *vt* [service] to head; [personnes] to supervise.

chapelet [ʃaplɛ] *nm* RELIG rosary. ‖ *fig* [d'injures] string, torrent.

chapelle [ʃapɛl] *nf* [petite église] chapel; [partie d'église] choir.

chapelure [ʃaplyr] *nf* (dried) bread-crumbs (*pl*).

chapiteau [ʃapito] *nm* [de cirque] big top.

chapitre [ʃapitr] *nm* [de livre & RELIG] chapter.

chaque [ʃak] *adj indéf* each, every; **j'ai payé ces livres 100 francs ~** I paid 100 francs each for these books.

char [ʃar] *nm* MIL: **~ (d'assaut)** tank. || [de carnaval] float. || *Can* [voiture] car.

charabia [ʃarabja] *nm* gibberish.

charade [ʃarad] *nf* charade.

charbon [ʃarbɔ̃] *nm* [combustible] coal; **~ de bois** charcoal.

charcuter [ʃarkyte] *vt fam péj* to butcher.

charcuterie [ʃarkytri] *nf* [magasin] pork butcher's. || [produits] pork meat products.

charcutier, -ière [ʃarkytje, jɛr] *nm, f* [commerçant] pork butcher.

chardon [ʃardɔ̃] *nm* [plante] thistle.

charge [ʃarʒ] *nf* [fardeau] load. || [fonction] office. || [responsabilité] responsibility; **être à la ~** [personne] to be dependent on; **les travaux sont à la ~ du propriétaire** the owner is liable for the cost of the work; **prendre qqch en ~** [s'occuper de] to take charge of sthg. || ÉLECTR, JUR & MIL charge. ○ **charges** *nfpl* [d'appartement] service charge. || ÉCON expenses, costs; **~s sociales** ≃ employer's contributions.

chargé, -e [ʃarʒe] *vt* **1** *adj* [véhicule, personne]: **~ (de)** loaded (with). || [responsable]: **~ (de)** responsible (for). || [occupé] full, busy. **2** *nm, f*: **~ d'affaires** chargé d'affaires; **~ de mission** head of mission.

chargement [ʃarʒəmɑ̃] *nm* [action] loading. || [marchandises] load.

charger [ʃarʒe] *vt* [gén & INFORM] to load. || ÉLECTR, JUR & MIL to charge. || [donner une mission à]: **~ qqn de faire qqch** to put sb in charge of doing sthg. ○ **se charger** *vp*: **se ~ de qqn/qqch** to take care of sb/sthg, to take charge of sb/sthg; **se ~ de faire qqch** to undertake to do sthg.

chargeur [ʃarʒœr] *nm* ÉLECTR charger. || [d'arme] magazine.

chariot [ʃarjo] *nm* [charrette] handcart. || [à bagages, dans un hôpital] wagon *Am*. || [de machine à écrire] carriage.

charisme [karism] *nm* charisma.

charitable [ʃaritabl] *adj* charitable.

charité [ʃarite] *nf* [aumône & RELIG] charity. || [bonté] kindness.

charlatan [ʃarlatɑ̃] *nm péj* charlatan.

charmant, -e [ʃarmɑ̃, ɑ̃t] *adj* charming.

charme [ʃarm] *nm* [séduction] charm. || [enchantement] spell. || [arbre] ironwood, hornbeam.

charmer [ʃarme] *vt* to charm; **être charmé de faire qqch** to be delighted to do sthg.

charmeur, -euse [ʃarmœr, øz] *adj* charming.

charnel, -elle [ʃarnɛl] *adj* carnal.

charnier [ʃarnje] *nm* mass grave.

charnière [ʃarnjɛr] **1** *nf* hinge; *fig* turning point. **2** *adj* [période] transitional.

charnu, -e [ʃarny] *adj* fleshy.

charogne [ʃarɔɲ] *nf* [d'animal] carrion (*U*).

charpente [ʃarpɑ̃t] *nf* [de bâtiment, de roman] framework. || [ossature] frame.

charpentier [ʃarpɑ̃tje] *nm* carpenter.

charretier, -ière [ʃartje, jɛr] *nm, f* carter.

charrette [ʃarɛt] *nf* cart.

charrier [ʃarje] **1** *vt* to carry. || *fam* [se moquer de]: **~ qqn** to take sb for a ride. **2** *vi fam* [exagérer] to go too far.

charrue [ʃary] *nf* plough, plow *Am*.

charte [ʃart] *nf* charter.

charter [ʃarter] *nm* chartered plane.

chas [ʃa] *nm* eye (*of needle*).

chasse [ʃas] *nf* [action] hunting; **~ à courre** hunting (*on horseback with hounds*). || [période]: **la ~ est ouverte/fermée** it's the open/close season. || [poursuite] chase; **prendre qqn/qqch en ~** to give chase to sb/sthg. || [des cabinets]: **~ (d'eau)** flush; **tirer la ~** to flush the toilet.

chassé-croisé [ʃasekrwaze] *nm* toing and froing.

chasse-neige [ʃasnɛʒ] *nm inv* snow-plough.

chasser [ʃase] *vt* [animal] to hunt. || [faire partir - personne] to drive ou chase away; [- odeur, souci] to dispel.

chasseur, -euse [ʃasœr, øz] *nm, f* hunter. ○ **chasseur** *nm* [d'hôtel] page, messenger. || MIL: **~ alpin** *soldier specially trained for operations in mountainous terrain*. || [avion] fighter.

châssis [ʃasi] *nm* [de fenêtre, de porte, de machine] frame. || [de véhicule] chassis.

chaste [ʃast] *adj* chaste.

chasteté [ʃastəte] *nf* chastity.

chasuble [ʃazybl] *nf* chasuble.

chat, chatte [ʃa, ʃat] *nm, f* cat.

châtaigne [ʃatɛɲ] *nf* [fruit] chestnut. || *fam* [coup] clout.

châtaignier [ʃatɛɲe] *nm* [arbre] chestnut (tree); [bois] chestnut.

châtain [ʃatɛ̃] *adj & nm* chestnut, chestnut-brown.

château, -x [ʃato] *nm* [forteresse]: ~ (fort) castle. || [résidence - seigneuriale] mansion; [- de monarque, d'évêque] palace; ~ de sable sandcastle. || [réservoir]: ~ d'eau water tower.

châtiment [ʃatimã] *nm* punishment.

chaton [ʃatɔ̃] *nm* [petit chat] kitten. || BOT catkin.

chatouiller [ʃatuje] *vt* [faire des chatouilles à] to tickle. || *fig* [titiller] to titillate.

chatoyant, -e [ʃatwajã, ãt] *adj* [reflet, étoffe] shimmering; [bijou] sparkling.

châtrer [ʃatre] *vt* to castrate; [chat] to neuter; [chatte] to spay.

chatte → chat.

chaud, -e [ʃo, ʃod] *adj* [gén] warm; [de température très élevée, sensuel] hot. || *fig* [enthousiaste]: **être ~ pour qqch/pour faire qqch** to be keen on sthg/on doing sthg. ○ **chaud 1** *adv*: **avoir ~** to be warm ou hot; **il fait ~** it's warm ou hot. **2** *nm* heat; **rester au ~** to stay in the warm.

chaudement [ʃodmã] *adv* warmly.

chaudière [ʃodjɛr] *nf* boiler.

chaudron [ʃodrɔ̃] *nm* cauldron.

chauffage [ʃofaʒ] *nm* [appareil] heating (system); ~ **central** central heating.

chauffant, -e [ʃofã, ãt] *adj* heating; **plaque ~e** hotplate.

chauffard [ʃofar] *nm péj* reckless driver.

chauffe-eau [ʃofo] *nm inv* water-heater.

chauffer [ʃofe] **1** *vt* [rendre chaud] to heat (up). **2** *vi* [devenir chaud] to heat up. || [moteur] to overheat. || *fam* [barder]: **ça va ~** there's going to be trouble.

chauffeur [ʃofœr] *nm* AUTOM driver.

chaume [ʃom] *nm* [paille] thatch.

chaumière [ʃomjɛr] *nf* cottage.

chaussée [ʃose] *nf* road, roadway; «~ déformée» "uneven road surface".

chausse-pied [ʃospje] (*pl* **chausse-pieds**) *nm* shoehorn.

chausser [ʃose] **1** *vt* [chaussures, lunettes, skis] to put on. **2** *vi*: **~ du 39** to take

size 39 (shoes). ○ **se chausser** *vp* to put one's shoes on.

chaussette [ʃosɛt] *nf* sock.

chausson [ʃosɔ̃] *nm* [pantoufle] slipper. || [de danse] ballet shoe. || [de bébé] bootee. || CULIN turnover; ~ **aux pommes** apple turnover.

chaussure [ʃosyr] *nf* [soulier] shoe; ~ **de marche** [de randonnée] hiking ou walking boot; [confortable] walking shoe; ~ **de ski** ski boot. || [industrie] footwear industry.

chauve [ʃov] *adj* [sans cheveux] bald.

chauve-souris [ʃovsuri] *nf* bat.

chauvin, -e [ʃovɛ̃, in] *adj* chauvinistic.

chaux [ʃo] *nf* lime; **blanchi à la ~** whitewashed.

chavirer [ʃavire] *vi* [bateau] to capsize. || *fig* [tourner] to spin.

chef [ʃef] *nm* [d'un groupe] head, leader; [au travail] boss; **en ~** in chief; ~ **d'entreprise** company head; ~ **de famille** head of the family; ~ **de gare** stationmaster; ~ **d'orchestre** conductor; ~ **de service** ADMIN departmental manager. || [cuisinier] chef.

chef-d'œuvre [ʃedœvr] (*pl* **chefs-d'œuvre**) *nm* masterpiece.

chef-lieu [ʃefljø] *nm* ≃ county town.

chemin [ʃəmɛ̃] *nm* [voie] path; ~ **de fer** railway; ~ **vicinal** byroad, minor road. || [parcours] way; *fig* road; **en ~** on the way.

cheminée [ʃəmine] *nf* [foyer] fireplace. || [conduit d'usine] chimney. || [encadrement] mantelpiece. || [de paquebot, locomotive] funnel.

cheminement [ʃəminmã] *nm* [progression] advance; *fig* [d'idée] development.

cheminer [ʃəmine] *vi* [avancer] to make one's way; *fig* [idée] to develop.

cheminot [ʃəmino] *nm* railroad man *Am*.

chemise [ʃəmiz] *nf* [d'homme] shirt; ~ **de nuit** [de femme] nightdress. || [dossier] folder.

chemisette [ʃəmizɛt] *nf* [d'homme] short-sleeved shirt; [de femme] short-sleeved blouse.

chemisier [ʃəmizje] *nm* [vêtement] blouse.

chenal, -aux [ʃənal, o] *nm* [canal] channel.

chêne [ʃɛn] *nm* [arbre] oak (tree); [bois] oak.

chenet [ʃəne] *nm* firedog.

chenil [ʃənil] *nm* [pour chiens] kennel.

chenille [ʃənij] *nf* [insecte] caterpillar. || [courroie] caterpillar track.

chèque [ʃɛk] nm cheque; **faire/toucher un ~** to write/cash a cheque; **~ (bancaire)** (bank) cheque; **~ barré** crossed cheque; **~ postal** post office cheque; **~ sans provision** bad cheque; **~ de voyage** traveller's cheque.

chèque-cadeau [ʃɛkkado] nm gift token.

chèque-repas [ʃɛkrəpa] (pl chèques-repas), **chèque-restaurant** [ʃɛkrɛstɔrɑ̃] (pl chèques-restaurant) nm luncheon voucher.

chéquier [ʃekje] nm chequebook.

cher, chère [ʃɛr] 1 adj [aimé] **~ (à qqn)** dear (to sb); **Cher Monsieur** [au début d'une lettre] Dear Sir. || [produit, vie, commerçant] expensive. 2 nm, f hum: **mon ~** dear. ○ **cher** adv: **valoir ~, coûter ~** to be expensive, to cost a lot; **payer ~** to pay a lot.

chercher [ʃɛrʃe] 1 vt [gén] to look for. || [prendre]: **aller/venir ~ qqn** [à un rendez-vous] to (go/come and) meet sb; [en voiture] to (go/come and) pick sb up; **aller/venir ~ qqch** to (go/come and) get sthg. 2 vi: **~ à faire qqch** to try to do sthg.

chercheur, -euse [ʃɛrʃœr, øz] nm, f [scientifique] researcher.

chéri, -e [ʃeri] 1 adj dear. 2 nm, f darling.

chétif, -ive [ʃetif, iv] adj [malingre] sickly, weak.

cheval, -aux [ʃəval, o] nm [animal] horse; **être à ~ sur qqch** [être assis] to be sitting astride sthg; fig [siècles] to straddle sthg; fig [tenir à] to be a stickler for sthg; **~ d'arçons** horse (in gymnastics). || [équitation] riding, horse-riding; **faire du ~** to ride. || AUTOM: **~, ~-vapeur** horsepower.

chevalerie [ʃəvalri] nf [qualité] chivalry. || HIST knighthood.

chevalet [ʃəvalɛ] nm [de peintre] easel.

chevalier [ʃəvalje] nm knight.

chevalière [ʃəvaljɛr] nf [bague] signet ring.

chevauchée [ʃəvoʃe] nf [course] ride, horse-ride.

chevaucher [ʃəvoʃe] vt [être assis] to sit ou be astride. ○ **se chevaucher** vp to overlap.

chevelu, -e [ʃəvly] adj hairy.

chevelure [ʃəvlyr] nf [cheveux] hair.

chevet [ʃəvɛ] nm head (of bed); **être au ~ de qqn** to be at sb's bedside.

cheveu, -x [ʃəvø] nm [chevelure] hair;

se faire couper les ~x to have one's hair cut.

cheville [ʃəvij] nf ANAT ankle. || [pour fixer une vis] Rawlplug®.

chèvre [ʃɛvr] 1 nf [animal] goat. 2 nm [fromage] goat's cheese.

chevreau, -x [ʃəvro] nm kid.

chèvrefeuille [ʃɛvrəfœj] nm honeysuckle.

chevreuil [ʃəvrœj] nm [animal] roe deer. || CULIN venison.

chevronné, -e [ʃəvrɔne] adj [expérimenté] experienced.

chevrotant, -e [ʃəvrɔtɑ̃, ɑ̃t] adj tremulous.

chevrotine [ʃəvrɔtin] nf buckshot.

chewing-gum [ʃwiŋgɔm] (pl chewing-gums) nm chewing gum (U).

chez [ʃe] prép [dans la maison de]: **il est ~ lui** he's at home; **il rentre ~ lui** he's going home; **aller ~ le médecin/coiffeur** to go to the doctor's/hairdresser's; **il va venir ~ nous** he is going to come to our place ou house. || [en ce qui concerne]: **~ les jeunes** among young people; **~ les Anglais** in England. || [dans les œuvres de]: **~ Proust** in (the works of) Proust. || [dans le caractère de]: **ce que j'apprécie ~ lui, c'est sa gentillesse** what I like about him is his kindness.

chic [ʃik] adj (inv en genre) [élégant] smart, chic. || vieilli [serviable] nice.

chicorée [ʃikɔre] nf [salade] endive; [à café] chicory.

chien [ʃjɛ̃] nm [animal] dog; **~ de chasse** [d'arrêt] gundog; **~ de garde** guard dog. || [d'arme] hammer. || loc: **avoir un mal de ~ à faire qqch** to have a lot of trouble doing sthg; **en ~ de fusil** curled up.

chiendent [ʃjɛ̃dɑ̃] nm couch grass.

chien-loup [ʃjɛ̃lu] nm Alsatian (dog).

chienne [ʃjɛn] nf (female) dog, bitch.

chiffon [ʃifɔ̃] nm [linge] rag.

chiffonner [ʃifɔne] vt [froisser - faire des plis] to crumple, to crease; [- déformer] to crumple. || fam fig [contrarier] to bother.

chiffre [ʃifr] nm [caractère] figure, number; **~ arabe/romain** Arabic/Roman numeral. || [montant] sum; **~ d'affaires** COMM turnover Br, net revenue Am; **~ rond** round number.

chiffrer [ʃifre] vt [évaluer] to calculate, to assess. || [coder] to encode.

chignole [ʃiɲɔl] nf drill.

chignon [ʃiɲɔ̃] *nm* bun (*in hair*); **se crêper le ~** *fig* to scratch each other's eyes out.

Chili [ʃili] *nm*: **le ~** Chile.

chimie [ʃimi] *nf* chemistry.

chimiothérapie [ʃimjɔterapi] *nf* chemotherapy.

chimique [ʃimik] *adj* chemical.

chimiste [ʃimist] *nmf* chemist.

chimpanzé [ʃɛ̃pɑ̃ze] *nm* chimpanzee.

Chine [ʃin] *nf*: **la ~** China.

chiné, -e [ʃine] *adj* mottled.

chiner [ʃine] *vi* to look for bargains.

chinois, -e [ʃinwa, waz] *adj* Chinese. ○ **chinois** *nm* [langue] Chinese. || [passoire] conical sieve. ○ **Chinois, -e** *nm, f* Chinese person; **les Chinois** the Chinese.

chiot [ʃjo] *nm* puppy.

chipie [ʃipi] *nf* vixen *péj*.

chips [ʃips] *nfpl*: **(pommes) ~** (potato) crisps *Br*, (potato) chips *Am*.

chiquenaude [ʃiknod] *nf* flick.

chiquer [ʃike] **1** *vt* to chew. **2** *vi* to chew tobacco.

chirurgical, -e, -aux [ʃiryrʒikal, o] *adj* surgical.

chirurgie [ʃiryrʒi] *nf* surgery.

chirurgien [ʃiryrʒjɛ̃] *nm* surgeon.

chiure [ʃjyr] *nf*: **~ (de mouche)** flyspecks (*pl*).

chlore [klɔr] *nm* chlorine.

chloroforme [klɔrɔfɔrm] *nm* chloroform.

chlorophylle [klɔrɔfil] *nf* chlorophyll.

choc [ʃɔk] *nm* [heurt, coup] impact. || [conflit] clash. || [émotion] shock. || (*en apposition*): **images-~s** shock pictures; **prix-~** amazing bargain.

chocolat [ʃɔkɔla] **1** *nm* chocolate; **~ au lait/noir** milk/plain chocolate; **~ à cuire/à croquer** cooking/eating chocolate. **2** *adj inv* chocolate (brown).

chœur [kœr] *nm* [chorale] choir; [d'opéra & *fig*] chorus; **en ~** *fig* all together. || [d'église] choir, chancel.

choisi, -e [ʃwazi] *adj* selected; [termes, langage] carefully chosen.

choisir [ʃwazir] **1** *vt*: **~ (de faire qqch)** to choose (to do sthg). **2** *vi* to choose.

choix [ʃwa] *nm* [gén] choice; **le livre de ton ~** any book you like; **au ~** as you prefer; **avoir le ~** to have the choice. || [qualité]: **de premier ~** grade ou class one; **articles de second ~** seconds.

choléra [kɔlera] *nm* cholera.

cholestérol [kɔlɛsterɔl] *nm* cholesterol.

chômage [ʃomaʒ] *nm* unemployment; **en ~, au ~** unemployed; **être mis au ~ technique** to be laid off.

chômeur, -euse [ʃomœr, øz] *nm, f*: **les ~s** the unemployed.

chope [ʃɔp] *nf* tankard.

choper [ʃɔpe] *vt fam* [voler, arrêter] to nick *Br*, to pinch. || [attraper] to catch.

choquant, -e [ʃɔkɑ̃, ɑ̃t] *adj* shocking.

choquer [ʃɔke] *vt* [scandaliser] to shock. || [traumatiser] to shake (up).

choral, -e, -als OU **-aux** [kɔral, o] *adj* choral. ○ **chorale** *nf* [groupe] choir.

chorégraphie [kɔregrafi] *nf* choreography.

choriste [kɔrist] *nmf* chorister.

chose [ʃoz] *nf* thing; **c'est (bien) peu de ~** it's nothing really; **c'est la moindre des ~s** it's the least I/we can do; **de deux ~s l'une** (it's got to be) one thing or the other; **parler de ~s et d'autres** to talk of this and that.

chou, -x [ʃu] *nm* [légume] cabbage. || [pâtisserie] choux bun.

chouchou, -oute [ʃuʃu, ut] *nm, f* favourite; [élève] teacher's pet.

choucroute [ʃukrut] *nf* sauerkraut.

chouette [ʃwɛt] **1** *nf* [oiseau] owl. **2** *adj fam vieilli* smashing *Br*, great. **3** *interj*: **~ (alors)!** great!

chou-fleur [ʃuflœr] *nm* cauliflower.

chrétien, -ienne [kretjɛ̃, jɛn] *adj & nm, f* Christian.

Christ [krist] *nm* Christ.

christianisme [kristjanism] *nm* Christianity.

chrome [krom] *nm* CHIM chromium.

chromé, -e [krome] *adj* chrome-plated; **acier ~** chrome steel.

chromosome [krɔmozom] *nm* chromosome.

chronique [krɔnik] **1** *nf* [annales] chronicle. || PRESSE: **~ sportive** sports section. **2** *adj* chronic.

chronologie [krɔnɔlɔʒi] *nf* chronology.

chronologique [krɔnɔlɔʒik] *adj* chronological.

chronomètre [krɔnɔmɛtr] *nm* SPORT stopwatch.

chronométrer [krɔnɔmetre] *vt* to time.

chrysanthème [krizɑ̃tɛm] *nm* chrysanthemum.

chuchotement [ʃyʃɔtmɑ̃] *nm* whisper.

chuchoter [ʃyʃɔte] *vt & vi* to whisper.

chut [ʃyt] *interj* sh!, hush!

chute [ʃyt] *nf* [gén] fall; ~ **d'eau** waterfall; ~ **de neige** snowfall. ‖ [de tissu] scrap.

ci [si] *adv* (*après n*): **ce livre-~** this book; **ces jours-~** these days.

ci-après [siaprɛ] *adv* below.

cible [sibl] *nf litt & fig* target.

cicatrice [sikatris] *nf* scar.

cicatriser [sikatrize] *vt litt & fig* to heal.

ci-contre [sikɔ̃tr] *adv* opposite.

ci-dessous [sidəsu] *adv* below.

ci-dessus [sidəsy] *adv* above.

cidre [sidr] *nm* cider.

Cie (*abr de* **compagnie**) Co.

ciel [sjɛl] (*pl sens 1* **ciels**, *pl sens 2* **cieux**) *nm* [firmament] sky; **à ~ ouvert** open-air. ‖ [paradis, providence] heaven.

○ **cieux** *nmpl* heaven (*sg*).

cierge [sjɛrʒ] *nm* RELIG (votive) candle.

cigale [sigal] *nf* cicada.

cigare [sigar] *nm* cigar.

cigarette [sigarɛt] *nf* cigarette.

cigogne [sigɔɲ] *nf* stork.

ci-inclus, -e [siɛ̃kly, yz] *adj* enclosed.

○ **ci-inclus** *adv* enclosed.

ci-joint, -e [siʒwɛ̃, ɛ̃t] *adj* enclosed.

○ **ci-joint** *adv*: **veuillez trouver ~ ...** please find enclosed ....

cil [sil] *nm* ANAT eyelash, lash.

ciller [sije] *vi* to blink (one's eyes).

cime [sim] *nf* [d'arbre, de montagne] top.

ciment [simɑ̃] *nm* cement.

cimenter [simɑ̃te] *vt* to cement.

cimetière [simtjɛr] *nm* cemetery.

ciné [sine] *nm fam* cinema.

cinéaste [sineast] *nmf* film-maker.

ciné-club [sineklœb] (*pl* **ciné-clubs**) *nm* film club.

cinéma [sinema] *nm* [salle, industrie] cinema. ‖ [art] cinema, film.

cinémathèque [sinematɛk] *nf* film archive.

cinématographique [sinematɔgrafik] *adj* cinematographic.

cinéphile [sinefil] *nmf* film buff.

cinglé, -e [sɛ̃gle] *fam adj* nuts, nutty.

cingler [sɛ̃gle] *vt* to lash.

cinq [sɛ̃k] **1** *adj num* five. **2** *nm* five; *voir aussi* **six**.

cinquantaine [sɛ̃kɑ̃tɛn] *nf* [nombre]: **une ~ de** about fifty. ‖ [âge]: **avoir la ~** to be in one's fifties.

cinquante [sɛ̃kɑ̃t] *adj num & nm* fifty; *voir aussi* **six**.

cinquantième [sɛ̃kɑ̃tjɛm] *adj num, nm & nmf* fiftieth; *voir aussi* **sixième**.

cinquième [sɛ̃kjɛm] **1** *adj num, nm & nmf* fifth. **2** *nf* second year (*of secondary school*); *voir aussi* **sixième**.

cintre [sɛ̃tr] *nm* [pour vêtements] coat hanger.

cintré, -e [sɛ̃tre] *adj* COUTURE waisted.

cirage [siraʒ] *nm* [produit] shoe polish.

circoncision [sirkɔ̃sizjɔ̃] *nf* circumcision.

circonférence [sirkɔ̃ferɑ̃s] *nf* GÉOM circumference. ‖ [pourtour] boundary.

circonflexe [sirkɔ̃flɛks] → **accent**.

circonscription [sirkɔ̃skripsjɔ̃] *nf* district.

circonscrire [sirkɔ̃skrir] *vt* [incendie, épidémie] to contain. ‖ *fig* [sujet] to define.

circonstance [sirkɔ̃stɑ̃s] *nf* [occasion] occasion. ‖ (*gén pl*) [contexte, conjoncture] circumstance; **~s atténuantes** JUR mitigating circumstances.

circonstancié, -e [sirkɔ̃stɑ̃sje] *adj* detailed.

circonstanciel, -ielle [sirkɔ̃stɑ̃sjɛl] *adj* GRAM adverbial.

circuit [sirkɥi] *nm* [chemin] route. ‖ [parcours touristique] tour. ‖ SPORT & TECHNOL circuit.

circulaire [sirkylɛr] *nf & adj* circular.

circulation [sirkylasjɔ̃] *nf* [mouvement] circulation; **mettre en ~** to circulate; **~ (du sang)** circulation. ‖ [trafic] traffic.

circuler [sirkyle] *vi* [sang, air, argent] to circulate; **faire ~ qqch** to circulate sthg. ‖ [aller et venir] to move (along); **on circule mal en ville** the traffic is bad in town. ‖ [train, bus] to run. ‖ *fig* [rumeur, nouvelle] to spread.

cire [sir] *nf* [matière] wax. ‖ [encaustique] polish.

ciré, -e [sire] *adj* [parquet] polished. ‖ → **toile**. ○ **ciré** *nm* oilskin.

cirer [sire] *vt* to polish.

cirque [sirk] *nm* [gén] circus. ‖ GÉOL cirque. ‖ *fam fig* [désordre, chahut] chaos (*U*).

cirrhose [siroz] *nf* cirrhosis (*U*).

cisaille [sizaj] *nf* shears (*pl*).

cisailler [sizaje] *vt* [métal] to cut; [branches] to prune.

ciseau, -x [sizo] *nm* chisel. ○ **ciseaux** *nmpl* scissors.

ciseler [sizle] *vt* [pierre, métal] to chisel. ‖ [bijou] to engrave.

Cisjordanie [sizʒɔrdani] *nf*: **la ~** the West Bank.

citadelle [sitadɛl] *nf litt & fig* citadel.

citadin, -e [sitadɛ̃, in] **1** *adj* city (*avant n*), urban. **2** *nm, f* city dweller.

citation [sitasjɔ̃] *nf* JUR summons (*sg*). || [extrait] quote, quotation.

cité [site] *nf* [ville] city. || [lotissement] housing estate; **~ universitaire** halls (*pl*) of residence.

citer [site] *vt* [exemple, propos, auteur] to quote. || JUR [convoquer] to summon.

citerne [sitɛrn] *nf* [d'eau] water tank. || [cuve] tank.

cité U [sitey] *nf fam abr de* **cité universitaire.**

citoyen, -enne [sitwajɛ̃, ɛn] *nm, f* citizen.

citoyenneté [sitwajɛnte] *nf* citizenship.

citron [sitrɔ̃] *nm* lemon; **~ pressé** fresh lemon juice; **~ vert** lime.

citronnade [sitrɔnad] *nf* (still) lemonade.

citronnier [sitrɔnje] *nm* lemon tree.

citrouille [sitruj] *nf* pumpkin.

civet [sive] *nm* stew; **~ de lièvre** jugged hare.

civière [sivjɛr] *nf* stretcher.

civil, -e [sivil] **1** *adj* [gén] civil. || [non militaire] civilian. **2** *nm, f* civilian; **dans le ~** in civilian life; **policier en ~** plainclothes policeman (*f* policewoman).

civilement [sivilmɑ̃] *adv*: **se marier ~** to get married at a registry office.

civilisation [sivilizasjɔ̃] *nf* civilization.

civilisé, -e [sivilize] *adj* civilized.

civique [sivik] *adj* civic; **instruction ~** civics (*U*).

civisme [sivism] *nm* sense of civic responsibility.

cl (*abr de* **centilitre**) cl.

clair, -e [klɛr] *adj* [gén] clear; **c'est ~ et net** there's no two ways about it. || [lumineux] bright. || [pâle - couleur, teint] light; [- tissu, cheveux] light-coloured. ○ **clair** *nm*: **mettre** OU **tirer qqch au ~** to shed light upon sthg. ○ **clair de lune** (*pl* **clairs de lune**) *nm* moonlight (*U*).

clairement [klɛrmɑ̃] *adv* clearly.

claire-voie [klɛrvwa] ○ **à claire-voie** *loc adv* openwork (*avant n*).

clairière [klɛrjɛr] *nf* clearing.

clairon [klɛrɔ̃] *nm* bugle.

claironner [klɛrɔne] *vt fig* [crier]: **~ qqch** to shout sthg from the rooftops.

clairsemé, -e [klɛrsəme] *adj* [cheveux] thin; [arbres] scattered; [population] sparse.

clairvoyant, -e [klɛrvwajɑ̃, ɑ̃t] *adj* perceptive.

clamer [klame] *vt* to proclaim.

clan [klɑ̃] *nm* clan.

clandestin, -e [klɑ̃dɛstɛ̃, in] **1** *adj* [journal, commerce] clandestine; [activité] covert. **2** *nm, f* [étranger] illegal immigrant OU alien; [voyageur] stowaway.

clapier [klapje] *nm* [à lapins] hutch.

clapoter [klapote] *vi* [vagues] to lap.

claquage [klakaʒ] *nm* MÉD strain; **se faire un ~** to pull OU to strain a muscle.

claque [klak] *nf* [gifle] slap.

claquer [klake] **1** *vt* [fermer] to slam. || **faire ~** [langue] to click; [doigts] to snap; [fouet] to crack. || *fam* [dépenser] to blow. **2** *vi* [porte, volet] to bang.

claquettes [klaket] *nfpl* [danse] tap dancing (*U*).

clarifier [klarifje] *vt litt & fig* to clarify.

clarinette [klarinɛt] *nf* [instrument] clarinet.

clarté [klarte] *nf* [lumière] brightness. || [netteté] clarity.

classe [klas] *nf* [gén] class; **~ touriste** economy class. || SCOL: **aller en ~** to go to school; **~ de neige** skiing trip (*with school*); **~ verte** field trip (*with school*). || MIL rank. || *loc*: **faire ses ~s** MIL to do one's training.

classé, -e [klase] *adj* [monument] listed.

classement [klasmɑ̃] *nm* [rangement] filing. || [classification] classification. || [rang - SCOL] position; [- SPORT] placing.

classer [klase] *vt* [ranger] to file. || [plantes, animaux] to classify. || [cataloguer]: **~ qqn (parmi)** to label sb (as). || [attribuer un rang à] to rank. ○ **se classer** *vp* to be classed, to rank; **se ~ troisième** to come third.

classeur [klasœr] *nm* [meuble] filing cabinet. || [d'écolier] ring binder.

classification [klasifikasjɔ̃] *nf* classification.

classique [klasik] **1** *nm* [auteur] classical author. || [œuvre] classic. **2** *adj* ART & MUS classical. || [sobre] classic. || [habituel] classic.

clause [kloz] *nf* clause.

claustrophobie [klostrɔfɔbi] *nf* claustrophobia.

clavecin [klavsɛ̃] *nm* harpsichord.

clavicule [klavikyl] *nf* collarbone.

clavier [klavje] *nm* keyboard.

clé, clef [kle] **1** *nf* [gén] key; **mettre qqn/qqch sous ~** to lock sb/sthg up; **~ de contact** AUTOM ignition key. || [outil]: **~**

anglaise ou à **molette** adjustable spanner *Br* ou wrench *Am*; monkey wrench. ‖ MUS [signe] clef; **~ de sol/fa** treble/bass clef. **2** *adj*: **industrie/rôle ~** key industry/role.

clémence [klemɑ̃s] *nf sout* [indulgence] clemency. ‖ *fig* [douceur] mildness.

clément, -e [klemɑ̃, ɑ̃t] *adj* [indulgent] lenient. ‖ *fig* [température] mild.

clémentine [klemɑ̃tin] *nf* clementine.

cleptomane → **kleptomane**.

clerc [klɛr] *nm* [assistant] clerk.

clergé [klɛrʒe] *nm* clergy.

cliché [kliʃe] *nm* PHOT negative. ‖ [banalité] cliché.

client, -e [kliɑ̃, ɑ̃t] *nm, f* [de notaire, d'agence] client; [de médecin] patient. ‖ [acheteur] customer.

clientèle [kliɑ̃tɛl] *nf* [ensemble des clients] customers (*pl*); [de profession libérale] clientele.

cligner [kliɲe] *vi*: **~ de l'œil** to wink; **~ des yeux** to blink.

clignotant, -e [kliɲɔtɑ̃, ɑ̃t] *adj* [lumière] flickering. ○ **clignotant** *nm* AUTOM indicator.

clignoter [kliɲɔte] *vi* [yeux] to blink. ‖ [lumière] to flicker.

climat [klima] *nm litt & fig* climate.

climatisation [klimatizasjɔ̃] *nf* airconditioning.

climatisé, -e [klimatize] *adj* airconditioned.

clin [klɛ̃] ○ **clin d'œil** *nm*: **faire un ~ d'œil (à)** to wink (at); **en un ~ d'œil** in a flash.

clinique [klinik] **1** *nf* clinic. **2** *adj* clinical.

clip [klip] *nm* [vidéo] pop video. ‖ [boucle d'oreilles] clip-on earring.

cliquer [klike] *vi* INFORM to click.

cliqueter [klikte] *vi* [pièces, clés, chaînes] to jingle, to jangle. ‖ [verres] to clink.

clivage [klivaʒ] *nm fig* [division] division.

clochard, -e [klɔʃar, ard] *nm, f* tramp.

cloche [klɔʃ] **1** *nf* [d'église] bell. ‖ *fam* [idiot] idiot. **2** *adj fam*: **ce qu'elle peut être ~, celle-là!** she can be a right idiot!

cloche-pied [klɔʃpje] ○ **à cloche-pied** *loc adv* hopping; **sauter à ~** to hop.

clocher [klɔʃe] *nm* [d'église] church tower.

clochette [klɔʃɛt] *nf* [petite cloche] (little) bell. ‖ [de fleur] bell.

clodo [klɔdo] *nmf fam* tramp.

cloison [klwazɔ̃] *nf* [mur] partition.

cloisonner [klwazɔne] *vt* [pièce, maison] to partition (off); *fig* to compartmentalize.

cloître [klwatr] *nm* cloister.

cloporte [klɔpɔrt] *nm* woodlouse.

cloque [klɔk] *nf* blister.

clore [klɔr] *vt* to close; [négociations] to conclude.

clos, -e [klo, kloz] **1** *pp* → **clore**. **2** *adj* closed.

clôture [klotyr] *nf* [haie] hedge; [de fil de fer] fence. ‖ [fermeture] closing, closure. ‖ [fin] end, conclusion.

clôturer [klotyre] *vt* [terrain] to enclose.

clou [klu] *nm* [pointe] nail; **~ de girofle** CULIN clove. ‖ [attraction] highlight.

clouer [klue] *vt* [fixer - couvercle, planche] to nail (down); [- tableau, caisse] to nail (up); *fig* [immobiliser]: **rester cloué sur place** to be rooted to the spot.

clouté, -e [klute] *adj* [vêtement] studded.

clown [klun] *nm* clown; **faire le ~** to clown around, to act the fool.

club [klœb] *nm* club.

cm (*abr de* **centimètre**) cm.

CM *nm* (*abr de* **cours moyen**): **~1** fourth year of primary school; **~2** fifth year of primary school.

CNRS (*abr de* **Centre national de la recherche scientifique**) *nm national scientific research organization.*

coaguler [kɔagyle] *vi* [sang] to clot. ‖ [lait] to curdle.

coalition [kɔalisjɔ̃] *nf* coalition.

coasser [kɔase] *vi* [grenouille] to croak.

cobaye [kɔbaj] *nm litt & fig* guinea pig.

cobra [kɔbra] *nm* cobra.

Coca® [kɔka] *nm* [boisson] Coke®.

cocaïne [kɔkain] *nf* cocaine.

cocarde [kɔkard] *nf* [insigne] roundel. ‖ [distinction] rosette.

cocasse [kɔkas] *adj* funny.

coccinelle [kɔksinɛl] *nf* [insecte] ladybird *Br*, ladybug *Am*. ‖ [voiture] Beetle.

coccyx [kɔksis] *nm* coccyx.

cocher[1] [kɔʃe] *nm* coachman.

cocher[2] [kɔʃe] *vt* to check (off) *Am*.

cochon, -onne [kɔʃɔ̃, ɔn] **1** *adj* dirty, smutty. **2** *nm, f fam péj* pig; **un tour de ~** a dirty trick. ○ **cochon** *nm* pig.

cochonnerie [kɔʃɔnri] *nf fam* [nourriture] muck (U). ‖ [chose] rubbish (U). ‖ [saleté] mess (U). ‖ [obscénité] dirty joke, smut (U).

cochonnet [kɔʃɔnɛ] *nm* JEU jack.

cocktail [kɔktɛl] *nm* [réception] cocktail party. || [boisson] cocktail. -|| *fig* [mélange] mixture.

coco [kɔko] *nm* → **noix**. || *péj* [communiste] commie.

cocon [kɔkɔ̃] *nm* ZOOL & *fig* cocoon.

cocorico [kɔkoriko] *nm* [du coq] cock-a-doodle-doo.

cocotier [kɔkɔtje] *nm* coconut tree.

cocotte [kɔkɔt] *nf* [marmite] casserole (dish). || [poule] hen. || *péj* [courtisane] tart.

Cocotte-Minute® [kɔkɔtminyt] *nf* pressure cooker.

cocu, -e [kɔky] *nm, f & adj fam* cuckold.

code [kɔd] *nm* [gén] code; **~ barres** bar code; **~ pénal** penal code; **~ postal** post-code *Br*, zip code *Am*; **~ de la route** highway code. || [phares] dipped headlights (*pl*).

coder [kɔde] *vt* to code.

coefficient [kɔefisjɑ̃] *nm* coefficient.

coéquipier, -ière [kɔekipje, jɛr] *nm, f* teammate.

cœur [kœr] *nm* heart; **de bon ~** willingly; **de tout son ~** with all one's heart; **apprendre par ~** to learn by heart; **avoir bon ~** to be kind-hearted; **avoir mal au ~** to feel sick; **s'en donner à ~ joie** [prendre beaucoup de plaisir] to have a whale of a time.

coexister [kɔɛgziste] *vi* to coexist.

coffre [kɔfr] *nm* [meuble] chest. || [de voiture] trunk *Am*. || [coffre-fort] safe.

coffre-fort [kɔfrəfɔr] *nm* safe.

coffret [kɔfrɛ] *nm* [petit coffre] casket; **~ à bijoux** jewellery box. || [de disques] boxed set.

cogner [kɔɲe] *vi* [heurter] to bang. || [soleil] to beat down. ○ **se cogner** *vp* [se heurter] to bump o.s.; **se ~ à** ou **contre qqch** to bump into sthg; **se ~ la tête/le genou** to hit one's head/knee.

cohabiter [kɔabite] *vi* [habiter ensemble] to live together. || POLIT to cohabit.

cohérence [kɔerɑ̃s] *nf* consistency, coherence.

cohérent, -e [kɔerɑ̃, ɑ̃t] *adj* [logique] consistent, coherent. || [unifié] coherent.

cohésion [kɔezjɔ̃] *nf* cohesion.

cohorte [kɔɔrt] *nf* [groupe] troop.

cohue [kɔy] *nf* [foule] crowd. || [bousculade] crush.

coi, coite [kwa, kwat] *adj*: **rester ~** *sout* to remain silent.

coiffe [kwaf] *nf* headdress.

coiffé, -e [kwafe] *adj*: **être bien/mal ~** to have tidy/untidy hair; **être ~ d'une casquette** to be wearing a cap.

coiffer [kwafe] *vt* [mettre sur la tête]: **qqn de qqch** to put sthg on sb's head. || [les cheveux]: **~ qqn** to do sb's hair. ○ **se coiffer** *vp* [les cheveux] to do one's hair. || [mettre sur sa tête]: **se ~ de** to wear, to put on.

coiffeur, -euse [kwafœr, øz] *nm, f* hairdresser. ○ **coiffeuse** *nf* [meuble] dressing table.

coiffure [kwafyr] *nf* [chapeau] hat. || [cheveux] hairstyle.

coin [kwɛ̃] *nm* [angle] corner; **au ~ du feu** by the fireside. || [parcelle, endroit] place, spot; **dans le ~** in the area; **~ cuisine** kitchen area. || [outil] wedge.

coincer [kwɛ̃se] *vt* [bloquer] to jam. || *fam* [prendre] to nab; *fig* to catch out. || [acculer] to corner, to trap.

coïncidence [kɔɛ̃sidɑ̃s] *nf* coincidence.

coïncider [kɔɛ̃side] *vi* to coincide.

coing [kwɛ̃] *nm* [fruit] quince.

col [kɔl] *nm* [de vêtement] collar; **~ roulé** polo neck *Br*, turtleneck *Am*. || [partie étroite] neck. || ANAT: **~ du fémur** neck of the thighbone ou femur; **~ de l'utérus** cervix, neck of the womb. || GÉOGR pass.

coléoptère [kɔleɔptɛr] *nm* beetle.

colère [kɔlɛr] *nf* [irritation] anger; **être/se mettre en ~** to be/get angry; **piquer une ~** to fly into a rage. || [accès d'humeur] fit of anger ou rage.

coléreux, -euse [kɔlerø, øz], **colérique** [kɔlerik] *adj* [tempérament] fiery; [personne] quick-tempered.

colimaçon [kɔlimasɔ̃] ○ **en colimaçon** *loc adv* spiral.

colique [kɔlik] *nf* (*gén pl*) [douleur] colic (U). || [diarrhée] diarrhoea.

colis [kɔli] *nm* parcel.

collaborateur, -trice [kɔlabɔratœr, tris] *nm, f* [employé] colleague. || HIST collaborator.

collaboration [kɔlabɔrasjɔ̃] *nf* collaboration.

collaborer [kɔlabɔre] *vi* [coopérer, sous l'Occupation] to collaborate. || [participer]: **~ à** to contribute to.

collant, -e [kɔlɑ̃, ɑ̃t] *adj* [substance] sticky. || *fam* [personne] clinging, clingy. ○ **collant** *nm* panty hose (U) *Am*.

colle [kɔl] *nf* [substance] glue. || [question] poser. || [SCOL - interrogation] test; [- retenue] detention.

collecte [kɔlɛkt] nf collection.

collectif, -ive [kɔlɛktif, iv] adj [responsabilité, travail] collective. || [billet, voyage] group (avant n).

collection [kɔlɛksjɔ̃] nf [d'objets, de livres, de vêtements] collection; **faire la ~ de** to collect. || COMM line.

collectionner [kɔlɛksjɔne] vt litt & fig to collect.

collectionneur, -euse [kɔlɛksjɔnœr, øz] nm, f collector.

collectivité [kɔlɛktivite] nf community; **les ~s locales** ADMIN the local communities.

collège [kɔlɛʒ] nm SCOL ≃ secondary school. || [de personnes] college.

collégien, -ienne [kɔleʒjɛ̃, jɛn] nm, f schoolboy (f schoolgirl).

collègue [kɔlɛg] nmf colleague.

coller [kɔle] **1** vt [fixer - affiche] to stick (up); [- timbre] to stick. || [appuyer] to press. || fam [mettre] to stick, to dump. || SCOL to give (a) detention to, to keep behind. **2** vi [adhérer] to stick. || [être adapté]: **~ à qqch** [vêtement] to cling to sthg. ○ **se coller** vp [se plaquer]: **se ~ contre qqn/qqch** to press o.s. against sb/sthg.

collerette [kɔlrɛt] nf [de vêtement] ruff.

collet [kɔlɛ] nm [de vêtement] collar; **être ~ monté** [affecté, guindé] to be strait-laced. || [piège] snare.

collier [kɔlje] nm [bijou] necklace. || [d'animal] collar. || [barbe] fringe of beard along the jawline.

colline [kɔlin] nf hill.

collision [kɔlizjɔ̃] nf [choc] collision, crash; **entrer en ~ avec** to collide with.

colloque [kɔlɔk] nm colloquium.

colmater [kɔlmate] vt [fuite] to plug, to seal off. || [brèche] to fill, to seal.

colombe [kɔlɔ̃b] nf dove.

Colombie [kɔlɔ̃bi] nf: **la ~** Colombia.

colon [kɔlɔ̃] nm settler.

côlon [kolɔ̃] nm colon.

colonel [kɔlɔnɛl] nm colonel.

colonial, -e, -iaux [kɔlɔnjal, jo] adj colonial.

colonialisme [kɔlɔnjalism] nm colonialism.

colonie [kɔlɔni] nf [territoire] colony. || [d'expatriés] community; **~ de vacances** holiday Br ou vacation Am camp (for children).

colonisation [kɔlɔnizasjɔ̃] nf colonization.

coloniser [kɔlɔnize] vt litt & fig to colonize.

colonne [kɔlɔn] nf column. ○ **colonne vertébrale** nf spine, spinal column.

colorant, -e [kɔlɔrɑ̃, ɑ̃t] adj colouring. ○ **colorant** nm colouring.

colorer [kɔlɔre] vt [teindre] to colour.

colorier [kɔlɔrje] vt to colour in.

coloris [kɔlɔri] nm shade.

coloriser [kɔlɔrize] vt CIN to colourize.

colossal, -e, -aux [kɔlɔsal, o] adj colossal, huge.

colporter [kɔlpɔrte] vt [marchandise] to hawk; [information] to spread.

coma [kɔma] nm coma; **être dans le ~** to be in a coma.

comateux, -euse [kɔmatø, øz] adj comatose.

combat [kɔ̃ba] nm [bataille] battle, fight. || fig [lutte] struggle. || SPORT fight.

combatif, -ive [kɔ̃batif, iv] adj [humeur] fighting (avant n).

combattant, -e [kɔ̃batɑ̃, ɑ̃t] nm, f [en guerre] combatant; [dans bagarre] fighter; **ancien ~** veteran.

combattre [kɔ̃batr] **1** vt litt & fig to fight (against). **2** vi to fight.

combattu, -e [kɔ̃baty] pp → **combattre**.

combien [kɔ̃bjɛ̃] **1** conj how much; **~ de** [nombre] how many; [quantité] how much; **~ de temps?** how long?; **ça fait ~?** [prix] how much is that?; [longueur, hauteur etc] how long/high etc is it? **2** adv how (much). **3** nm inv: **le ~ sommes-nous?** what date is it?; **tous les ~?** how often?

combinaison [kɔ̃binɛzɔ̃] nf [d'éléments] combination. || [de femme] slip. || [vêtement - de mécanicien] overall Am; [- de ski] ski suit. || [de coffre] combination.

combine [kɔ̃bin] nf fam trick.

combiné [kɔ̃bine] nm receiver.

combiner [kɔ̃bine] vt [arranger] to combine. || [organiser] to devise.

comble [kɔ̃bl] **1** nm height; **c'est un** ou **le ~!** that beats everything! **2** adj packed. ○ **combles** nmpl attic (sg), loft (sg).

combler [kɔ̃ble] vt [gâter]: **~ qqn de** to shower sb with. || [boucher] to fill in. || [déficit] to make good; [lacune] to fill.

combustible [kɔ̃bystibl] **1** nm fuel. **2** adj combustible.

combustion [kɔ̃bystjɔ̃] nf combustion.

comédie [kɔmedi] nf CIN & THÉÂTRE

comedy; ~ **musicale** musical. || [complication] palaver.

comédien, **-ienne** [kɔmedjɛ̃, jɛn] *nm, f* [acteur] actor (*f* actress); *fig & péj* sham.

comestible [kɔmɛstibl] *adj* edible.

comète [kɔmɛt] *nf* comet.

comique [kɔmik] **1** *nm* THÉÂTRE comic actor. **2** *adj* [style] comic. || [drôle] comical, funny.

comité [kɔmite] *nm* committee; ~ **d'entreprise** works council (*also organizing leisure activities*).

commandant [kɔmɑ̃dɑ̃] *nm* commander.

commande [kɔmɑ̃d] *nf* [de marchandises] order; **passer une** ~ to place an order; **sur** ~ to order; **disponible sur** ~ available on request. || TECHNOL control. || INFORM command.

commander [kɔmɑ̃de] **1** *vt* MIL. to command. || [contrôler] to operate, to control. || COMM to order. **2** *vi* to be in charge; ~ **à qqn de faire qqch** to order sb to do sthg.

commanditer [kɔmɑ̃dite] *vt* [entreprise] to finance. || [meurtre] to put up the money for.

commando [kɔmɑ̃do] *nm* commando (unit).

comme [kɔm] **1** *conj* [introduisant une comparaison] like. || [exprimant la manière] as; **fais** ~ **il te plaira** do as you wish; ~ **prévu/convenu** as planned/ agreed. || [tel que] like, such as. || [en tant que] as. || [ainsi que]: **les filles** ~ **les garçons iront jouer au foot** both girls and boys will play football. || [introduisant une cause] as, since; ~ **il pleuvait nous sommes rentrés** as it was raining we went back. **2** *adv* [marquant l'intensité] how; ~ **tu as grandi!** how you've grown!; ~ **c'est difficile!** it's so difficult!

commémoration [kɔmemɔrasjɔ̃] *nf* commemoration.

commémorer [kɔmemɔre] *vt* to commemorate.

commencement [kɔmɑ̃smɑ̃] *nm* beginning, start.

commencer [kɔmɑ̃se] **1** *vt* [entreprendre] to begin, to start; [être au début de] to begin. **2** *vi* to start, to begin; ~ **à faire qqch** to begin ou start to do sthg. to begin ou start doing sthg; ~ **par faire qqch** to begin ou start by doing sthg.

comment [kɔmɑ̃] **1** *adv* how; ~? what?; ~ **ça va?** how are you?; ~ **cela?** how come? **2** *nm inv* → **pourquoi.**

commentaire [kɔmɑ̃tɛr] *nm* [explication] commentary. || [observation] comment.

commentateur, **-trice** [kɔmɑ̃tatœr, tris] *nm, f* RADIO & TÉLÉ commentator.

commenter [kɔmɑ̃te] *vt* to comment on.

commérage [kɔmeraʒ] *nm péj* gossip (*U*).

commerçant, **-e** [kɔmɛrsɑ̃, ɑ̃t] **1** *adj* [rue] shopping (*avant n*); [quartier] commercial; [personne] business-minded. **2** *nm, f* shopkeeper.

commerce [kɔmɛrs] *nm* [achat et vente] commerce, trade; ~ **de gros/détail** wholesale/retail trade; ~ **extérieur** foreign trade. || [magasin] business; **le petit** ~ small shopkeepers (*pl*).

commercial, **-e**, **-iaux** [kɔmɛrsjal, jo] **1** *adj* [entreprise, valeur] commercial; [politique] trade (*avant n*). **2** *nm, f* marketing man (*f* woman).

commercialiser [kɔmɛrsjalize] *vt* to market.

commère [kɔmɛr] *nf péj* gossip.

commettre [kɔmɛtr] *vt* to commit.

commis, **-e** [kɔmi, iz] *pp* → **commettre.**
○ **commis** *nm* assistant; ~ **voyageur** commercial traveller.

commisération [kɔmizerasjɔ̃] *nf sout* commiseration.

commissaire [kɔmisɛr] *nm* commissioner; ~ **de police** (police) captain *Am*.

commissaire-priseur [kɔmisɛrprizœr] *nm* auctioneer.

commissariat [kɔmisarja] *nm*: ~ **de police** police station.

commission [kɔmisjɔ̃] *nf* [délégation] commission, committee. || [message] message. || [rémunération] commission.
○ **commissions** *nfpl* shopping (*U*); **faire les** ~**s** to do the shopping.

commissure [kɔmisyr] *nf*: **la** ~ **des lèvres** the corner of the mouth.

commode [kɔmɔd] **1** *nf* chest of drawers. **2** *adj* [pratique - système] convenient; [- outil] handy. || [aimable]: **pas** ~ awkward.

commodité [kɔmɔdite] *nf* convenience.

commotion [kɔmɔsjɔ̃] *nf* MÉD shock; ~ **cérébrale** concussion.

commun, **-e** [kɔmœ̃, yn] *adj* [gén] common; [- décision, effort] joint; [- salle] shared; **avoir qqch en** ~ to have sthg in common. || [courant] usual, common.
○ **commune** *nf* town.

communal, -e, -aux [kɔmynal, o] *adj*
[école] local; [bâtiments] council (*avant n*).

communauté [kɔmynote] *nf* [groupe]
community. ‖ [de sentiments, d'idées]
identity. ○ **Communauté euro-**
péenne *nf*: **la Communauté euro-**
péenne the European Community.

commune → **commun.**

communément [kɔmynemã] *adv* commonly.

communication [kɔmynikasjɔ̃] *nf*
[gén] communication. ‖ TÉLÉCOM: **~ (té-**
léphonique) (phone) call; **être en ~ avec**
qqn to be talking to sb; **obtenir la ~** to
get through.

communier [kɔmynje] *vi* RELIG to take
communion.

communion [kɔmynjɔ̃] *nf* RELIG communion.

communiqué [kɔmynike] *nm* communiqué; **~ de presse** press release.

communiquer [kɔmynike] *vt*: **~ qqch à**
[information, sentiment] to pass on ou
communicate sthg to; [chaleur] to transmit sthg to.

communisme [kɔmynism] *nm* communism.

communiste [kɔmynist] *nmf* & *adj*
communist.

commutateur [kɔmytatœr] *nm* switch.

compact, -e [kɔpakt] *adj* [épais, dense]
dense. ‖ [petit] compact. ○ **compact**
nm [disque laser] compact disc, CD.

compagne → **compagnon.**

compagnie [kɔpaɲi] *nf* [gén & COMM]
company; **tenir ~ à qqn** to keep sb company; **en ~ de** in the company of. ‖ [as-
semblée] gathering.

compagnon [kɔpaɲɔ̃], **compagne**
[kɔpaɲ] *nm, f* companion.

comparable [kɔparabl] *adj* comparable.

comparaison [kɔparɛzɔ̃] *nf* [parallèle]
comparison; **en ~ de, par ~ avec** com-
pared with, in ou by comparison with.

comparaître [kɔparɛtr] *vi* JUR: **~ (de-**
vant) to appear (before).

comparatif, -ive [kɔparatif, iv] *adj*
comparative.

comparé, -e [kɔpare] *adj* comparative;
[mérites] relative.

comparer [kɔpare] *vt* [confronter]: **~**
(avec) to compare (with). ‖ [assimiler]: **~**
qqch à to compare ou liken sthg to.

compartiment [kɔpartimã] *nm* compartment.

comparu, -e [kɔpary] *pp* → **comparaî-**
tre.

comparution [kɔparysjɔ̃] *nf* JUR appearance.

compas [kɔpa] *nm* [de dessin] pair of
compasses, compasses (*pl*). ‖ NAVIG compass.

compassion [kɔpasjɔ̃] *nf* sout compassion.

compatible [kɔpatibl] *adj*: **~ (avec)**
compatible (with).

compatir [kɔpatir] *vi*: **~ (à)** to sympathize (with).

compatriote [kɔpatrijɔt] *nmf* compat-
riot, fellow countryman (*f* country-
woman).

compensation [kɔpɑ̃sasjɔ̃] *nf* [dédom-
magement] compensation.

compensé, -e [kɔpɑ̃se] *adj* built-up.

compenser [kɔpɑ̃se] *vt* to compensate
ou make up for.

compétence [kɔpetɑ̃s] *nf* [qualification]
skill, ability. ‖ JUR competence; **cela**
n'entre pas dans mes ~s that's outside
my scope.

compétent, -e [kɔpetɑ̃, ɑ̃t] *adj* [capa-
ble] capable, competent. ‖ ADMIN & JUR
competent; **les autorités ~es** the relevant
authorities.

compétitif, -ive [kɔpetitif, iv] *adj*
competitive.

compétition [kɔpetisjɔ̃] *nf* competi-
tion; **faire de la ~** to go in for competitive
sport.

complaisant, -e [kɔplɛzɑ̃, ɑ̃t] *adj* [ai-
mable] obliging, kind. ‖ [indulgent] indulgent.

complément [kɔplemɑ̃] *nm* [gén &
GRAM] complement. ‖ [reste] remainder.

complémentaire [kɔplemɑ̃tɛr] *adj*
[supplémentaire] supplementary. ‖ [ca-
ractères, couleurs] complementary.

complet, -ète [kɔplɛ, ɛt] *adj* [gén]
complete. ‖ [plein] full. ○ **complet**
(-veston) *nm* suit.

complètement [kɔplɛtmɑ̃] *adv* [vrai-
ment] absolutely, totally. ‖ [entièrement]
completely.

compléter [kɔplete] *vt* [gén] to complete, to complement; [somme d'argent]
to make up.

complexe [kɔplɛks] **1** *nm* PSYCHOL complex; **~ d'infériorité/de supériorité**
inferiority/superiority complex. ‖ [en-
semble] complex. **2** *adj* complex, complicated.

complexé, -e [kɔ̃plɛkse] *adj* hung up, mixed up.

complexité [kɔ̃plɛksite] *nf* complexity.

complication [kɔ̃plikasjɔ̃] *nf* intricacy, complexity. ○ **complications** *nfpl* complications.

complice [kɔ̃plis] 1 *nmf* accomplice. 2 *adj* [sourire, regard, air] knowing.

complicité [kɔ̃plisite] *nf* complicity.

compliment [kɔ̃plimɑ̃] *nm* compliment.

complimenter [kɔ̃plimɑ̃te] *vt* to compliment.

compliqué, -e [kɔ̃plike] *adj* [problème] complex, complicated; [personne] complicated.

compliquer [kɔ̃plike] *vt* to complicate.

complot [kɔ̃plo] *nm* plot.

comploter [kɔ̃plɔte] *vt & vi litt & fig* to plot.

comportement [kɔ̃pɔrtəmɑ̃] *nm* behaviour.

comporter [kɔ̃pɔrte] *vt* [contenir] to include, to contain. || [être composé de] to consist of, to be made up of. ○ **se comporter** *vp* to behave.

composant [kɔ̃pozɑ̃] *nm* component.

composante [kɔ̃pozɑ̃t] *nf* component.

composé, -e [kɔ̃poze] *adj* compound. ○ **composé** *nm* [mélange] combination. || CHIM & LING compound.

composer [kɔ̃poze] 1 *vt* [constituer] to make up, to form. || [créer - musique] to compose, to write. || [numéro de téléphone] to dial. 2 *vi* to compromise. ○ **se composer** *vp* [être constitué]: **se ~ de** to be composed of, to be made up of.

composite [kɔ̃pozit] *adj* [disparate - mobilier] assorted, of various types; [- foule] heterogeneous. || [matériau] composite.

compositeur, -trice [kɔ̃pozitœr, tris] *nm, f* MUS composer. || TYPO typesetter.

composition [kɔ̃pozisjɔ̃] *nf* [gén] composition; [de roman] writing, composition. || SCOL test. || [caractère]: **être de bonne ~** to be good-natured.

composter [kɔ̃pɔste] *vt* [ticket, billet] to date-stamp.

compote [kɔ̃pɔt] *nf* compote; **~ de pommes** stewed apple.

compréhensible [kɔ̃preɑ̃sibl] *adj* [texte, parole] comprehensible; *fig* [réaction] understandable.

compréhensif, -ive [kɔ̃preɑ̃sif, iv] *adj* understanding.

compréhension [kɔ̃preɑ̃sjɔ̃] *nf* [de texte] comprehension, understanding. || [indulgence] understanding.

comprendre [kɔ̃prɑ̃dr] *vt* [gén] to understand; **je comprends!** I see!; **se faire ~** to make o.s. understood; **mal ~** to misunderstand. || [comporter] to comprise, to consist of. || [inclure] to include.

compresse [kɔ̃prɛs] *nf* compress.

compresseur [kɔ̃presœr] → **rouleau**.

compression [kɔ̃presjɔ̃] *nf* [de gaz] compression; *fig* cutback, reduction.

comprimé, -e [kɔ̃prime] *adj* compressed. ○ **comprimé** *nm* tablet.

comprimer [kɔ̃prime] *vt* [gaz, vapeur] to compress. || [personnes]: **être comprimés dans** to be packed into.

compris, -e [kɔ̃pri, iz] 1 *pp* → **comprendre**. 2 *adj* [inclus]: **charges (non) ~es** (not) including bills, bills (not) included; **tout ~** all inclusive, all in; **y ~** including.

compromettre [kɔ̃prɔmɛtr] *vt* to compromise.

compromis, -e [kɔ̃prɔmi, iz] *pp* → **compromettre**. ○ **compromis** *nm* compromise.

compromission [kɔ̃prɔmisjɔ̃] *nf péj* base action.

comptabilité [kɔ̃tabilite] *nf* [comptes] accounts (*pl*); [service]: **la ~** accounts, the accounts department.

comptable [kɔ̃tabl] *nmf* accountant.

comptant [kɔ̃tɑ̃] *adv*: **payer** ou **régler ~** to pay cash. ○ **au comptant** *loc adv*: **payer au ~** to pay cash.

compte [kɔ̃t] *nm* [action] count, counting (*U*); [total] number; **~ à rebours** countdown. || BANQUE, COMM & COMPTABILITÉ account; **~ bancaire** ou **en banque** bank account; **~ courant** current account, checking account *Am*; **~ d'épargne** savings account; **~ postal** post office account. || *loc*: **être/se mettre à son ~** to be/become self-employed; **prendre qqch en ~, tenir ~ de qqch** to take sthg into account; **se rendre ~ de qqch** to realize sthg; **tout ~ fait** all things considered. ○ **comptes** *nmpl* accounts; **faire ses ~s** to do one's accounts.

compte chèques, compte-chèques [kɔ̃tʃɛk] *nm* current account, checking account *Am*.

compte-gouttes [kɔ̃tgut] *nm inv* dropper.

compter [kɔ̃te] 1 *vt* [dénombrer] to count. || [avoir l'intention de]: **~ faire**

qqch to intend to do sthg, to plan to do sthg. **2** *vi* [calculer] to count. || [être important] to count, to matter. || **~ sur** [se fier à] to rely or count on.

compte rendu, compte-rendu [kɔ̃trɑ̃dy] *nm* report, account.

compteur [kɔ̃tœr] *nm* meter.

comptine [kɔ̃tin] *nf* nursery rhyme.

comptoir [kɔ̃twar] *nm* [de bar] bar; [de magasin] counter. || HIST trading post. || *Helv* [foire] trade fair.

compulser [kɔ̃pylse] *vt* to consult.

comte [kɔ̃t] *nm* count.

comtesse [kɔ̃tɛs] *nf* countess.

con, conne [kɔ̃, kɔn] *tfam* **1** *adj* bloody *Br* or damned stupid. **2** *nm, f* stupid bastard (*f* bitch).

concave [kɔ̃kav] *adj* concave.

concéder [kɔ̃sede] *vt*: **~ qqch à** [droit, terrain] to grant sthg to; [point, victoire] to concede sthg to; **~ que** to admit (that), to concede (that).

concentration [kɔ̃sɑ̃trasjɔ̃] *nf* concentration.

concentré, -e [kɔ̃sɑ̃tre] *adj* [gén] concentrated. || [personne]: **elle était très ~** she was concentrating hard. || → **lait**. ○ **concentré** *nm* concentrate.

concentrer [kɔ̃sɑ̃tre] *vt* to concentrate. ○ **se concentrer** *vp* [se rassembler] to be concentrated. || [personne] to concentrate.

concentrique [kɔ̃sɑ̃trik] *adj* concentric.

concept [kɔ̃sɛpt] *nm* concept.

conception [kɔ̃sɛpsjɔ̃] *nf* [gén] conception. || [d'un produit, d'une campagne] design, designing (*U*).

concernant [kɔ̃sɛrnɑ̃] *prép* regarding, concerning.

concerner [kɔ̃sɛrne] *vt* to concern; **être/se sentir concerné par qqch** to feel concerned by sthg; **en ce qui me concerne** as far as I'm concerned.

concert [kɔ̃sɛr] *nm* MUS concert.

concertation [kɔ̃sɛrtasjɔ̃] *nf* consultation.

concerter [kɔ̃sɛrte] ○ **se concerter** *vp* to consult (each other).

concerto [kɔ̃sɛrto] *nm* concerto.

concession [kɔ̃sesjɔ̃] *nf* [compromis & GRAM] concession. || [autorisation] rights (*pl*).

concessionnaire [kɔ̃sesjɔnɛr] *nmf* [automobile] (car) dealer.

concevable [kɔ̃səvabl] *adj* conceivable.

concevoir [kɔ̃səvwar] *vt* [enfant, projet] to conceive. || [comprendre] to conceive of; **je ne peux pas ~ comment/pourquoi** I cannot conceive how/why.

concierge [kɔ̃sjɛrʒ] *nmf* caretaker, concierge.

conciliation [kɔ̃siljasjɔ̃] *nf* [accord & JUR] conciliation.

concilier [kɔ̃silje] *vt* [mettre d'accord, allier] to reconcile; **~ qqch et** or **avec qqch** to reconcile sthg with sthg.

concis, -e [kɔ̃si, iz] *adj* [style, discours] concise; [personne] terse.

concision [kɔ̃sizjɔ̃] *nf* conciseness, concision.

concitoyen, -yenne [kɔ̃sitwajɛ̃, jɛn] *nm, f* fellow citizen.

conclu, -e [kɔ̃kly] *pp* → **conclure**.

concluant, -e [kɔ̃klyɑ̃, ɑ̃t] *adj* [convaincant] conclusive.

conclure [kɔ̃klyr] **1** *vt* to conclude; **en ~ que** to deduce (that). **2** *vi*: **les experts ont conclu à la folie** the experts concluded he/she was mad.

conclusion [kɔ̃klyzjɔ̃] *nf* [gén] conclusion. || [partie finale] close.

concombre [kɔ̃kɔ̃br] *nm* cucumber.

concordance [kɔ̃kɔrdɑ̃s] *nf* [conformité] agreement; **~ des temps** GRAM sequence of tenses.

concorder [kɔ̃kɔrde] *vi* [coïncider] to agree, to coincide. || [être en accord]: **~ (avec)** to be in accordance (with).

concourir [kɔ̃kurir] *vi* [contribuer]: **~ à** to work towards. || [participer à un concours] to compete.

concours [kɔ̃kur] *nm* [examen] competitive examination. || [compétition] competition, contest. || [coïncidence]: **~ de circonstances** combination of circumstances.

concret, -ète [kɔ̃krɛ, ɛt] *adj* concrete.

concrétiser [kɔ̃kretize] *vt* [projet] to give shape to; [rêve, espoir] to give solid form to. ○ **se concrétiser** *vp* [projet] to take shape; [rêve, espoir] to materialize.

conçu, -e [kɔ̃sy] *pp* → **concevoir**.

concubinage [kɔ̃kybinaʒ] *nm* living together, cohabitation.

concurrence [kɔ̃kyrɑ̃s] *nf* [rivalité] rivalry. || ÉCON competition.

concurrent, -e [kɔ̃kyrɑ̃, ɑ̃t] **1** *adj* rival, competing. **2** *nm, f* competitor.

concurrentiel, -ielle [kɔ̃kyrɑ̃sjɛl] *adj* competitive.

condamnation [kɔ̃danasjɔ̃] *nf* JUR sentence. || [dénonciation] condemnation.

condamné, -e [kɔ̃dane] *nm, f* convict, prisoner.

condamner [kɔ̃dane] *vt* JUR: ~ **qqn (à)** to sentence sb (to). || *fig* [obliger]: ~ **qqn à qqch** to condemn sb to sthg. || [malade]: **être condamné** to be terminally ill. || [interdire] to forbid. || [blâmer] to condemn. || [fermer] to fill in, to block up.

condensation [kɔ̃dɑ̃sasjɔ̃] *nf* condensation.

condensé [kɔ̃dɑ̃se] 1 *nm* summary. 2 *adj* → **lait**.

condenser [kɔ̃dɑ̃se] *vt* to condense.

condescendant, -e [kɔ̃desɑ̃dɑ̃, ɑ̃t] *adj* condescending.

condiment [kɔ̃dimɑ̃] *nm* condiment.

condisciple [kɔ̃disipl] *nm* fellow student.

condition [kɔ̃disjɔ̃] *nf* [gén] condition; **se mettre en ~** [physiquement] to get into shape. || [place sociale] station. ○ **conditions** *nfpl* [circonstances] conditions; **~s de vie** living conditions. || [de paiement] terms. ○ **à condition de** *loc prép* providing ou provided (that). ○ **à condition que** *loc conj* (+ *subjonctif*) providing ou provided (that).

conditionné, -e [kɔ̃disjɔne] *adj* [emballé]: ~ **sous vide** vacuum-packed. || → **air**.

conditionnel, -elle [kɔ̃disjɔnɛl] *adj* conditional. ○ **conditionnel** *nm* GRAM conditional.

conditionnement [kɔ̃disjɔnmɑ̃] *nm* [action d'emballer] packaging, packing. || [emballage] package. || PSYCHOL & TECHNOL conditioning.

conditionner [kɔ̃disjɔne] *vt* [déterminer] to govern. || PSYCHOL & TECHNOL to condition. || [emballer] to pack.

condoléances [kɔ̃dɔleɑ̃s] *nfpl* condolences.

conducteur, -trice [kɔ̃dyktœr, tris] 1 *adj* conductive. 2 *nm, f* [de véhicule] driver. ○ **conducteur** *nm* ÉLECTR conductor.

conduire [kɔ̃dyir] 1 *vt* [voiture, personne] to drive. || [transmettre] to conduct. || *fig* [diriger] to manage. || *fig* [à la ruine, au désespoir]: ~ **qqn à qqch** to drive sb to sthg. 2 *vi* AUTOM to drive. || [mener]: ~ **à** to lead to. ○ **se conduire** *vp* to behave.

conduit, -e [kɔ̃dyi, it] *pp* → **conduire**. ○ **conduit** *nm* [tuyau] conduit, pipe. || ANAT duct, canal. ○ **conduite** *nf* [pilotage d'un véhicule] driving; **~e à droite/**gauche right-hand/left-hand drive. || [comportement] behaviour (U). || [canalisation]: **~e de gaz/d'eau** gas/water main, gas/water pipe.

cône [kon] *nm* GÉOM cone.

confection [kɔ̃fɛksjɔ̃] *nf* [réalisation] making. || [industrie] clothing industry.

confectionner [kɔ̃fɛksjɔne] *vt* to make.

confédération [kɔ̃federasjɔ̃] *nf* [d'états] confederacy. || [d'associations] confederation.

conférence [kɔ̃ferɑ̃s] *nf* [exposé] lecture. || [réunion] conference; **~ de presse** press conference.

conférencier, -ière [kɔ̃ferɑ̃sje, jɛr] *nm, f* lecturer.

conférer [kɔ̃fere] *vt* [accorder]: ~ **qqch à qqn** to confer sthg on sb.

confesser [kɔ̃fese] *vt* [avouer] to confess. ○ **se confesser** *vp* to go to confession.

confession [kɔ̃fesjɔ̃] *nf* confession.

confessionnal, -aux [kɔ̃fesjɔnal, o] *nm* confessional.

confetti [kɔ̃feti] *nm* confetti (U).

confiance [kɔ̃fjɑ̃s] *nf* confidence; **avoir ~ en** to have confidence ou faith in; **avoir ~ en soi** to be self-confident; **en toute ~** with complete confidence; **de ~** trustworthy; **faire ~ à qqn/qqch** to trust sb/sthg.

confiant, -e [kɔ̃fjɑ̃, ɑ̃t] *adj* [sans méfiance] trusting.

confidence [kɔ̃fidɑ̃s] *nf* confidence.

confident, -e [kɔ̃fidɑ̃, ɑ̃t] *nm, f* confidant (f confidante).

confidentiel, -ielle [kɔ̃fidɑ̃sjɛl] *adj* confidential.

confier [kɔ̃fje] *vt* [donner]: ~ **qqn/qqch à qqn** to entrust sb/sthg to sb. || [dire]: ~ **qqch à qqn** to confide sthg to sb. ○ **se confier** *vp*: **se ~ à qqn** to confide in sb.

confiné, -e [kɔ̃fine] *adj* [air] stale; [atmosphère] enclosed. || [enfermé] shut away.

confins [kɔ̃fɛ̃] ○ **aux confins de** *loc prép* on the borders of.

confirmation [kɔ̃firmasjɔ̃] *nf* confirmation.

confirmer [kɔ̃firme] *vt* [certifier] to confirm. ○ **se confirmer** *vp* to be confirmed.

confiscation [kɔ̃fiskasjɔ̃] *nf* confiscation.

confiserie [kɔ̃fizri] *nf* [magasin] candy

store *Am*, confectioner's. ‖ [sucreries] candy (*U*) *Am*, confectionery (*U*).

confiseur, -euse [kɔ̃fizœr, øz] *nm, f* confectioner.

confisquer [kɔ̃fiske] *vt* to confiscate.

confiture [kɔ̃fityr] *nf* jam.

conflit [kɔ̃fli] *nm* [situation tendue] clash, conflict. ‖ [entre États] conflict.

confondre [kɔ̃fɔ̃dr] *vt* [ne pas distinguer] to confuse. ‖ [accusé] to confound. ‖ [stupéfier] to astound.

confondu, -e [kɔ̃fɔ̃dy] *pp* → **confondre**.

conformation [kɔ̃fɔrmasjɔ̃] *nf* structure.

conforme [kɔ̃fɔrm] *adj*: ~ à in accordance with.

conformément [kɔ̃fɔrmemɑ̃]
○ **conformément à** *loc prép* in accordance with.

conformer [kɔ̃fɔrme] *vt*: ~ qqch à to shape sthg according to. ○ **se conformer** *vp*: se ~ à [s'adapter] to conform to; [obéir] to comply with.

conformiste [kɔ̃fɔrmist] **1** *nmf* conformist. **2** *adj* [traditionaliste] conformist.

conformité [kɔ̃fɔrmite] *nf* [accord]: être en ~ avec to be in accordance with.

confort [kɔ̃fɔr] *nm* comfort; **tout ~** with all modern conveniences *Am*.

confortable [kɔ̃fɔrtabl] *adj* comfortable.

confrère [kɔ̃frɛr], **consœur** [kɔ̃sœr] *nm, f* colleague.

confrontation [kɔ̃frɔ̃tasjɔ̃] *nf* [face à face] confrontation.

confronter [kɔ̃frɔ̃te] *vt* [mettre face à face] to confront; *fig*: être **confronté à** to be confronted α faced with.

confus, -e [kɔ̃fy, yz] *adj* [indistinct, embrouillé] confused. ‖ [gêné] embarrassed.

confusion [kɔ̃fyzjɔ̃] *nf* [gén] confusion. ‖ [embarras] confusion, embarrassment.

congé [kɔ̃ʒe] *nm* [arrêt de travail] leave (*U*); ~ **(de) maladie** sick leave; ~ **de maternité** maternity leave. ‖ [vacances] holiday *Br*, vacation *Am*; **en** ~ on holiday; **une journée/semaine de** ~ a day/week off. ‖ [renvoi] notice; **donner son** ~ **à qqn** to give sb his/her notice; **prendre** ~ **(de qqn)** *sout* to take one's leave (of sb).

congédier [kɔ̃ʒedje] *vt* to dismiss.

congélateur [kɔ̃ʒelatœr] *nm* freezer.

congeler [kɔ̃ʒle] *vt* to freeze.

congénital, -e, -aux [kɔ̃ʒenital, o] *adj* congenital.

congère [kɔ̃ʒɛr] *nf* snowdrift.

congestion [kɔ̃ʒɛstjɔ̃] *nf* congestion; ~ **pulmonaire** pulmonary congestion.

Congo [kɔ̃go] *nm*: **le** ~ the Congo.

congratuler [kɔ̃gratyle] *vt* to congratulate.

congrès [kɔ̃grɛ] *nm* [colloque] assembly.

conifère [kɔnifɛr] *nm* conifer.

conjecture [kɔ̃ʒɛktyr] *nf* conjecture.

conjecturer [kɔ̃ʒɛktyre] *vt* & *vi* to conjecture.

conjoint, -e [kɔ̃ʒwɛ̃, ɛ̃t] **1** *adj* joint. **2** *nm, f* spouse.

conjonction [kɔ̃ʒɔ̃ksjɔ̃] *nf* conjunction.

conjonctivite [kɔ̃ʒɔ̃ktivit] *nf* conjunctivitis (*U*).

conjoncture [kɔ̃ʒɔ̃ktyr] *nf* ÉCON situation, circumstances (*pl*).

conjugaison [kɔ̃ʒygɛzɔ̃] *nf* [union] uniting. ‖ GRAM conjugation.

conjugal, -e, -aux [kɔ̃ʒygal, o] *adj* conjugal.

conjuguer [kɔ̃ʒyge] *vt* [unir] to combine. ‖ GRAM to conjugate.

conjuration [kɔ̃ʒyrasjɔ̃] *nf* [conspiration] conspiracy. ‖ [exorcisme] exorcism.

connaissance [kɔnɛsɑ̃s] *nf* [savoir] knowledge (*U*); **à ma** ~ to (the best of) my knowledge; **en** ~ **de cause** with full knowledge of the facts; **prendre** ~ **de qqch** to study sthg, to examine sthg. ‖ [personne] acquaintance; **faire** ~ **(avec qqn)** to become acquainted (with sb); **faire la** ~ **de** to meet. ‖ [conscience]: **perdre/reprendre** ~ to lose/regain consciousness.

connaisseur, -euse [kɔnɛsœr, øz] **1** *adj* expert (*avant n*). **2** *nm, f* connoisseur.

connaître [kɔnɛtr] *vt* [gén] to know; ~ **qqn de nom/de vue** to know sb by name/sight. ‖ [éprouver] to experience. ○ **se connaître** *vp* s'y ~ **en** [être expert] to know about. ‖ [soi-même] to know o.s. ‖ [se rencontrer] to meet (each other).

connecter [kɔnɛkte] *vt* to connect.

connexion [kɔnɛksjɔ̃] *nf* connection.

connu, -e [kɔny] **1** *pp* → **connaître**. **2** *adj* [célèbre] well-known, famous.

conquérant, -e [kɔ̃kerɑ̃, ɑ̃t] **1** *adj* conquering. **2** *nm, f* conqueror.

conquérir [kɔ̃kerir] *vt* to conquer.

conquête [kɔ̃kɛt] *nf* conquest.

conquis, -e [kɔ̃ki, iz] *pp* → **conquérir**.

consacrer [kɔ̃sakre] *vt* RELIG to consecrate. ‖ [employer]: ~ **qqch à** to devote sthg to. ○ **se consacrer** *vp*: se ~ à to dedicate o.s. to, to devote o.s. to.

conscience [kɔ̃sjɑ̃s] *nf* [connaissance & PSYCHOL] consciousness; **avoir ~ de qqch** to be aware of sthg. ‖ [morale] conscience; **bonne/mauvaise ~** clear/guilty conscience; **~ professionnelle** professional integrity, conscientiousness.

consciencieux, -ieuse [kɔ̃sjɑ̃sjø, jøz] *adj* conscientious.

conscient, -e [kɔ̃sjɑ̃, ɑ̃t] *adj* conscious; **être ~ de qqch** [connaître] to be conscious of sthg.

conscrit [kɔ̃skri] *nm* conscript, recruit, draftee *Am*.

consécration [kɔ̃sekrasjɔ̃] *nf* [reconnaissance] recognition; [de droit, coutume] establishment. ‖ RELIG consecration.

consécutif, -ive [kɔ̃sekytif, iv] *adj* [successif & GRAM] consecutive. ‖ [résultant]: ~ à resulting from.

conseil [kɔ̃sɛj] *nm* [avis] piece of advice, advice (*U*). ‖ [assemblée] council; **~ d'administration** board of directors; **~ de classe** staff meeting.

conseiller¹ [kɔ̃seje] 1 *vt* [recommander] to advise; **~ qqch à qqn** to recommend sthg to sb. ‖ [guider] to advise, to counsel. 2 *vi* [donner un conseil]: **~ à qqn de faire qqch** to advise sb to do sthg.

conseiller², -ère [kɔ̃seje, ɛr] *nm, f* [guide] counsellor. ‖ [d'un conseil] councillor; **~ municipal** town councillor *Br*, city councilman (*f* -woman) *Am*.

consentement [kɔ̃sɑ̃tmɑ̃] *nm* consent.

consentir [kɔ̃sɑ̃tir] *vi*: **~ à qqch** to consent to sthg.

conséquence [kɔ̃sekɑ̃s] *nf* consequence, result; **ne pas tirer à ~** to be of no consequence.

conséquent, -e [kɔ̃sekɑ̃, ɑ̃t] *adj* [cohérent] consistent. ‖ [important] sizeable, considerable. ○ **par conséquent** *loc adv* therefore, consequently.

conservateur, -trice [kɔ̃sɛrvatœr, tris] 1 *adj* conservative. 2 *nm, f* POLIT conservative. ‖ [administrateur] curator. ○ **conservateur** *nm* preservative.

conservation [kɔ̃sɛrvasjɔ̃] *nf* [état, entretien] preservation. ‖ [d'aliment] preserving.

conservatoire [kɔ̃sɛrvatwar] *nm* academy; **~ de musique** music college.

conserve [kɔ̃sɛrv] *nf* tinned *Br* ou canned food; **en ~** [en boîte] tinned, canned; [en bocal] preserved, bottled.

conserver [kɔ̃sɛrve] *vt* [garder, entretenir] to keep.

considérable [kɔ̃siderabl] *adj* considerable.

considération [kɔ̃siderasjɔ̃] *nf* [réflexion, motivation] consideration; **prendre qqch en ~** to take sthg into consideration. ‖ [estime] respect.

considérer [kɔ̃sidere] *vt* to consider; **tout bien considéré** all things considered.

consigne [kɔ̃siɲ] *nf* (*gén pl*) [instruction] instructions (*pl*). ‖ [entrepôt de bagages] checkroom *Am*, baggage room *Am*; **~ automatique** lockers (*pl*).

consigné, -e [kɔ̃siɲe] *adj* returnable.

consistance [kɔ̃sistɑ̃s] *nf* [solidité] consistency; *fig* substance.

consistant, -e [kɔ̃sistɑ̃, ɑ̃t] *adj* [épais] thick. ‖ [nourrissant] substantial.

consister [kɔ̃siste] *vi*: **~ en** to consist of; **~ à faire qqch** to consist in doing sthg.

consœur → **confrère**.

consolation [kɔ̃sɔlasjɔ̃] *nf* consolation.

console [kɔ̃sɔl] *nf* [table] console (table). ‖ INFORM: **~ de visualisation** VDU, visual display unit.

consoler [kɔ̃sɔle] *vt* [réconforter]: **~ qqn (de qqch)** to comfort sb (in sthg).

consolider [kɔ̃sɔlide] *vt litt & fig* to strengthen.

consommateur, -trice [kɔ̃sɔmatœr, tris] *nm, f* [acheteur] consumer; [d'un bar] customer.

consommation [kɔ̃sɔmasjɔ̃] *nf* [utilisation] consumption; **faire une grande** ou **grosse ~ de** to use (up) a lot of. ‖ [boisson] drink.

consommé, -e [kɔ̃sɔme] *adj sout* consummate. ○ **consommé** *nm* consommé.

consommer [kɔ̃sɔme] 1 *vt* [utiliser] to use (up). ‖ [manger] to eat. ‖ [énergie] to consume, to use. 2 *vi* [boire] to drink. ‖ [voiture]: **cette voiture consomme beaucoup** this car uses a lot of fuel.

consonance [kɔ̃sɔnɑ̃s] *nf* consonance.

consonne [kɔ̃sɔn] *nf* consonant.

conspiration [kɔ̃spirasjɔ̃] *nf* conspiracy.

conspirer [kɔ̃spire] *vi* to conspire.

constamment [kɔ̃stamɑ̃] *adv* constantly.

constant, -e [kɔ̃stɑ̃, ɑ̃t] *adj* constant.

constat [kɔ̃sta] *nm* [procès-verbal] report. ‖ [constatation] established fact.

constatation [kɔ̃statasjɔ̃] *nf* [révélation] observation. || [fait retenu] finding.

constater [kɔ̃state] *vt* [se rendre compte de] to see, to note. || [consigner - fait, infraction] to record; [- décès, authenticité] to certify.

constellation [kɔ̃stelasjɔ̃] *nf* ASTRON constellation.

consternation [kɔ̃stɛrnasjɔ̃] *nf* dismay.

consterner [kɔ̃stɛrne] *vt* to dismay.

constipation [kɔ̃stipasjɔ̃] *nf* constipation.

constipé, -e [kɔ̃stipe] *adj* MÉD constipated. || *fam fig* [manière, air] ill at ease.

constituer [kɔ̃stitɥe] *vt* [élaborer] to set up. || [composer] to make up. || [représenter] to constitute.

constitution [kɔ̃stitysjɔ̃] *nf* [création] setting up. || [de pays, de corps] constitution.

constructeur [kɔ̃stryktœr] *nm* [fabricant] manufacturer; [de navire] shipbuilder. || [bâtisseur] builder.

construction [kɔ̃stryksjɔ̃] *nf* IND building, construction; ~ **navale** shipbuilding. || [édifice] structure, building. || GRAM & *fig* construction.

construire [kɔ̃strɥir] *vt* [bâtir, fabriquer] to build. || [théorie, phrase] to construct.

construit, -e [kɔ̃strɥi, it] *pp* → **construire**.

consulat [kɔ̃syla] *nm* [résidence] consulate.

consultation [kɔ̃syltasjɔ̃] *nf* MÉD & POLIT consultation.

consulter [kɔ̃sylte] 1 *vt* [compulser] to consult. || [interroger, demander conseil à] to consult, to ask. || [spécialiste] to consult, to see. 2 *vi* [médecin] to take ou hold surgery; [avocat] to be available for consultation. ○ **se consulter** *vp* to confer.

contact [kɔ̃takt] *nm* [gén] contact; **prendre ~ avec** to make contact with; **rester en ~ (avec)** to stay in touch (with); **au ~ de** on contact with. || AUTOM ignition; **mettre/couper le ~** to switch on/off the ignition.

contacter [kɔ̃takte] *vt* to contact.

contagieux, -ieuse [kɔ̃taʒjø, jøz] *adj* MÉD contagious; *fig* infectious.

contagion [kɔ̃taʒjɔ̃] *nf* MÉD contagion.

contaminer [kɔ̃tamine] *vt* [infecter] to contaminate.

conte [kɔ̃t] *nm* story; ~ **de fées** fairy tale.

contemplation [kɔ̃tɑ̃plasjɔ̃] *nf* contemplation.

contempler [kɔ̃tɑ̃ple] *vt* to contemplate.

contemporain, -e [kɔ̃tɑ̃pɔrɛ̃, ɛn] *nm, f* contemporary.

contenance [kɔ̃tnɑ̃s] *nf* [capacité volumique] capacity. || [attitude]: **se donner une ~** to give an impression of composure; **perdre ~** to lose one's composure.

contenir [kɔ̃tnir] *vt* to contain, to hold, to take. ○ **se contenir** *vp* to contain o.s., to control o.s.

content, -e [kɔ̃tɑ̃, ɑ̃t] *adj* [satisfait]: ~ **(de qqn/qqch)** happy (with sb/sthg), content (with sth/sthg); ~ **de faire qqch** happy to do sthg.

contenter [kɔ̃tɑ̃te] *vt* to satisfy. ○ **se contenter** *vp*: **se ~ de qqch/de faire qqch** to content o.s. with sthg/with doing sthg.

contentieux [kɔ̃tɑ̃sjø] *nm* [litige] dispute; [service] legal department.

contenu, -e [kɔ̃tny] *pp* → **contenir**. ○ **contenu** *nm* [de récipient] contents (*pl*). || [de texte, discours] content.

conter [kɔ̃te] *vt* to tell.

contestable [kɔ̃tɛstabl] *adj* questionable.

contestation [kɔ̃tɛstasjɔ̃] *nf* [protestation] protest, dispute. || POLIT **la ~** anti-establishment activity.

conteste [kɔ̃tɛst] ○ **sans conteste** *loc adv* unquestionably.

contester [kɔ̃tɛste] 1 *vt* to dispute, to contest. 2 *vi* to protest.

conteur, -euse [kɔ̃tœr, øz] *nm, f* storyteller.

contexte [kɔ̃tɛkst] *nm* context.

contigu, -uë [kɔ̃tigy] *adj*: ~ **(à)** adjacent (to).

continent [kɔ̃tinɑ̃] *nm* continent.

continental, -e, -aux [kɔ̃tinɑ̃tal, o] *adj* continental.

contingent [kɔ̃tɛ̃ʒɑ̃] *nm* MIL draft *Am*. || COMM quota.

continu, -e [kɔ̃tiny] *adj* continuous.

continuation [kɔ̃tinɥasjɔ̃] *nf* continuation.

continuel, -elle [kɔ̃tinɥɛl] *adj* [continu] continuous. || [répété] continual.

continuellement [kɔ̃tinɥɛlmɑ̃] *adv* continually.

continuer [kɔ̃tinɥe] 1 *vt* [poursuivre] to carry on with, to continue (with). 2 *vi* to continue, to go on; ~ **à** ou **de faire qqch** to continue to do ou doing sthg.

continuité [kɔ̃tinɥite] *nf* continuity.

contorsionner [kɔ̃tɔrsjɔne] ○ **se contorsionner** *vp* to contort (o.s.), to writhe.

contour [kɔ̃tur] *nm* [limite] outline. || (*gén pl*) [courbe] bend.

contourner [kɔ̃turne] *vt litt & fig* to bypass, to get round.

contraceptif, -ive [kɔ̃traseptif, iv] *adj* contraceptive. ○ **contraceptif** *nm* contraceptive.

contraception [kɔ̃trasepsjɔ̃] *nf* contraception.

contracter [kɔ̃trakte] *vt* [muscle] to contract, to tense. || [maladie] to contract, to catch. || [engagement] to contract; [assurance] to take out.

contraction [kɔ̃traksjɔ̃] *nf* contraction; [état de muscle] tenseness.

contractuel, -elle [kɔ̃traktɥel] *nm, f* traffic policeman (*f* policewoman) *Am*.

contradiction [kɔ̃tradiksjɔ̃] *nf* contradiction.

contradictoire [kɔ̃tradiktwar] *adj* contradictory; **débat ~** open debate.

contraignant, -e [kɔ̃trɛɲɑ̃, ɑ̃t] *adj* restricting.

contraindre [kɔ̃trɛ̃dr] *vt*: **~ qqn à faire qqch** to compel oʊ force sb to do sthg; **être contraint de faire qqch** to be compelled oʊ forced to do sthg.

contraire [kɔ̃trɛr] **1** *nm*: **le ~** the opposite; **je n'ai jamais dit le ~** I have never denied it. **2** *adj* opposite; **~ à** [non conforme à] contrary to. ○ **au contraire** *loc adv* on the contrary.

contrairement [kɔ̃trɛrmɑ̃] ○ **contrairement à** *loc prép* contrary to.

contrarier [kɔ̃trarje] *vt* [contrecarrer] to thwart, to frustrate. || [irriter] to annoy.

contrariété [kɔ̃trarjete] *nf* annoyance.

contraste [kɔ̃trast] *nm* contrast.

contraster [kɔ̃traste] *vt & vi* to contrast.

contrat [kɔ̃tra] *nm* contract, agreement; **~ à durée déterminée/indéterminée** fixed-term/permanent contract.

contravention [kɔ̃travɑ̃sjɔ̃] *nf* [amende] fine; **~ pour stationnement interdit** parking ticket; **dresser une ~ à qqn** to fine sb.

contre [kɔ̃tr] *prép* [juxtaposition, opposition] against. || [proportion, comparaison]: **élu à 15 voix ~ 9** elected by 15 votes to 9. || [échange] (in exchange) for. ○ **par contre** *loc adv* on the other hand.

contre-attaque [kɔ̃tratak] (*pl* **contre-attaques**) *nf* counterattack.

contrebalancer [kɔ̃trəbalɑ̃se] *vt* to counterbalance, to offset.

contrebande [kɔ̃trəbɑ̃d] *nf* [activité] smuggling; [marchandises] contraband.

contrebandier, -ière [kɔ̃trəbɑ̃dje, jɛr] *nm, f* smuggler.

contrebas [kɔ̃trəba] ○ **en contrebas** *loc adv* (down) below.

contrebasse [kɔ̃trəbas] *nf* [instrument] (double) bass.

contrecarrer [kɔ̃trəkare] *vt* to thwart, to frustrate.

contrecœur [kɔ̃trəkœr] ○ **à contrecœur** *loc adv* grudgingly.

contrecoup [kɔ̃trəku] *nm* consequence.

contre-courant [kɔ̃trəkurɑ̃] ○ **à contre-courant** *loc adv* against the current.

contredire [kɔ̃trədir] *vt* to contradict. ○ **se contredire** *vp* [emploi réciproque] to contradict (each other). || [emploi réfléchi] to contradict o.s.

contredit, -e [kɔ̃trədi] *pp* → **contredire**.

contrée [kɔ̃tre] *nf* [pays] land; [région] region.

contre-espionnage [kɔ̃trɛspjɔnaʒ] *nm* counterespionage.

contre-exemple [kɔ̃trɛgzɑ̃pl] (*pl* **contre-exemples**) *nm* example to the contrary.

contre-expertise [kɔ̃trɛkspertiz] (*pl* **contre-expertises**) *nf* second (expert) opinion.

contrefaçon [kɔ̃trəfasɔ̃] *nf* [activité] counterfeiting; [produit] forgery.

contrefaire [kɔ̃trəfɛr] *vt* [signature, monnaie] to counterfeit, to forge. || [voix] to disguise.

contrefort [kɔ̃trəfɔr] *nm* [pilier] buttress. || [de chaussure] back. ○ **contreforts** *nmpl* foothills.

contre-indication [kɔ̃trɛ̃dikasjɔ̃] (*pl* **contre-indications**) *nf* contraindication.

contre-jour [kɔ̃trəʒur] ○ **à contre-jour** *loc adv* against the light.

contremaître, -esse [kɔ̃trəmetr, ɛs] *nm, f* foreman (*f* forewoman).

contremarque [kɛ̃trəmark] *nf* [pour sortir d'un spectacle] pass-out ticket.

contre-offensive [kɔ̃trɔfɑ̃siv] (*pl* **contre-offensives**) *nf* counteroffensive.

contre-ordre = contrordre.

contrepartie [kɔ̃trəparti] *nf* [compensation] compensation. ○ **en contrepartie** *loc adv* in return.

contrepèterie [kɔ̃trəpetri] *nf* spoonerism.

contre-pied [kɔ̃trəpje] *nm*: prendre le ~ de to do the opposite of.

contreplaqué, contre-plaqué [kɔ̃trəplake] *nm* plywood.

contrepoids [kɔ̃trəpwa] *nm litt* & *fig* counterbalance, counterweight.

contre-pouvoir [kɔ̃trəpuvwar] (*pl* **contre-pouvoirs**) *nm* counterbalance.

contrer [kɔ̃tre] *vt* [s'opposer à] to counter. || CARTES to double.

contresens [kɔ̃trəsɑ̃s] *nm* [erreur - de traduction] mistranslation; [- d'interprétation] misinterpretation. || [absurdité] nonsense (*U*). ○ **à contresens** *loc adv litt* & *fig* the wrong way.

contretemps [kɔ̃trətɑ̃] *nm* hitch, mishap. ○ **à contretemps** *loc adv* MUS out of time; *fig* at the wrong moment.

contribuable [kɔ̃tribɥabl] *nmf* taxpayer.

contribuer [kɔ̃tribɥe] *vi*: ~ à to contribute to ou towards.

contribution [kɔ̃tribysjɔ̃] *nf*: ~ (à) contribution (to); **mettre qqn à** ~ to call on sb's services. ○ **contributions** *nfpl* taxes.

contrit, -e [kɔ̃tri, it] *adj* contrite.

contrôle [kɔ̃trol] *nm* [vérification - de déclaration] check, checking (*U*); [- de documents, billets] inspection; ~ **d'identité** identity check. || [maîtrise, commande] control; **perdre le ~ de qqch** to lose control of sthg. || SCOL test.

contrôler [kɔ̃trole] *vt* [vérifier - documents, billets] to inspect; [- déclaration] to check; [- connaissances] to test. || [maîtriser, diriger] to control. || TECHNOL to monitor, to control.

contrôleur, -euse [kɔ̃trolœr, øz] *nm, f* [de train] ticket inspector; [d'autobus] (bus) conductor (*f* conductress); ~ **aérien** air traffic controller.

contrordre, contre-ordre (*pl* **contre-ordres**) [kɔ̃trɔrdr] *nm* countermand; **sauf** ~ unless otherwise instructed.

controverse [kɔ̃trɔvɛrs] *nf* controversy.

controversé, -e [kɔ̃trɔvɛrse] *adj* [personne, décision] controversial.

contumace [kɔ̃tymas] *nf* JUR: **condamné par** ~ sentenced in absentia.

contusion [kɔ̃tyzjɔ̃] *nf* bruise, contusion.

convaincant, -e [kɔ̃vɛ̃kɑ̃, ɑ̃t] *adj* convincing.

convaincre [kɔ̃vɛ̃kr] *vt* [persuader]: ~ **qqn (de qqch)** to convince sb (of sthg); ~ **qqn (de faire qqch)** to persuade sb (to do sthg). || JUR: ~ **qqn de** to find sb guilty of, to convict sb of.

convaincu, -e [kɔ̃vɛ̃ky] 1 *pp* → convaincre. 2 *adj* [partisan] committed; **d'un ton** ~, **d'un air** ~ with conviction.

convainquant [kɔ̃vɛ̃kɑ̃] *ppr* → convaincre.

convalescence [kɔ̃valesɑ̃s] *nf* convalescence; **être en** ~ to be convalescing ou recovering.

convalescent, -e [kɔ̃valesɑ̃, ɑ̃t] *adj* & *nm, f* convalescent.

convenable [kɔ̃vnabl] *adj* [manières, comportement] polite; [tenue, personne] decent, respectable. || [acceptable] adequate, acceptable.

convenance [kɔ̃vnɑ̃s] *nf*: **à ma/votre** ~ to my/your convenience. ○ **convenances** *nfpl* proprieties.

convenir [kɔ̃vnir] *vi* [décider]: ~ **de qqch/de faire qqch** to agree on sthg/to do sthg. || [plaire]: ~ **à qqn** to suit sb, to be convenient for sb. || [être approprié]: ~ **à ou pour** to be suitable for. || *sout* [admettre]: ~ **de qqch** to admit to sthg; ~ **que** to admit (that).

convention [kɔ̃vɑ̃sjɔ̃] *nf* [règle, assemblée] convention. || [accord] agreement.

conventionnel, -elle [kɔ̃vɑ̃sjɔnɛl] *adj* conventional.

convenu, -e [kɔ̃vny] 1 *pp* → convenir. 2 *adj* [décidé]: **comme** ~ as agreed.

convergent, -e [kɔ̃vɛrʒɑ̃, ɑ̃t] *adj* convergent.

converger [kɔ̃vɛrʒe] *vi*: ~ **(vers)** to converge (on).

conversation [kɔ̃vɛrsasjɔ̃] *nf* conversation.

conversion [kɔ̃vɛrsjɔ̃] *nf* [gén]: ~ **(à/en)** conversion (to/into).

convertible [kɔ̃vɛrtibl] *nm* [canapé-lit] sofa-bed.

convertir [kɔ̃vɛrtir] *vt*: ~ **qqn (à)** to convert sb (to); ~ **qqch (en)** to convert sthg (into). ○ **se convertir** *vp*: se ~ **(à)** to be converted (to).

convexe [kɔ̃vɛks] adj convex.

conviction [kɔ̃viksjɔ̃] nf conviction.

convier [kɔ̃vje] vt: ~ qqn à to invite sb to.

convive [kɔ̃viv] nmf guest (at a meal).

convivial, -e, -iaux [kɔ̃vivjal, jo] adj [réunion] convivial. || INFORM user-friendly.

convocation [kɔ̃vɔkasjɔ̃] nf [avis écrit] summons (sg), notification to attend.

convoi [kɔ̃vwa] nm [de véhicules] convoy. || [train] train.

convoiter [kɔ̃vwate] vt to covet.

convoitise [kɔ̃vwatiz] nf covetousness.

convoquer [kɔ̃vɔke] vt [assemblée] to convene. || [pour un entretien] to invite. || [subalterne, témoin] to summon. || [à un examen]: ~ qqn to ask sb to attend.

convoyer [kɔ̃vwaje] vt to escort.

convoyeur, -euse [kɔ̃vwajœr, øz] nm, f escort; ~ de fonds security guard.

convulsion [kɔ̃vylsjɔ̃] nf convulsion.

coopération [kɔɔperasjɔ̃] nf [collaboration] cooperation. || [aide]: la ~ ≃ overseas development.

coopérer [kɔɔpere] vi: ~ (à) to cooperate (in).

coordination [kɔɔrdinasjɔ̃] nf coordination.

coordonnée [kɔɔrdɔne] nf MATHS coordinate. ○ **coordonnées** nfpl GÉOGR coordinates. || [adresse] address and phone number, details.

coordonner [kɔɔrdɔne] vt to coordinate.

copain, -ine [kɔpɛ̃, in] 1 adj matey; être très ~s to be great pals. 2 nm, f friend, mate.

copeau, -x [kɔpo] nm [de bois] (wood) shaving.

Copenhague [kɔpenag] n Copenhagen.

copie [kɔpi] nf [double, reproduction] copy. || [SCOL - de devoir] fair copy; [- d'examen] paper, script.

copier [kɔpje] 1 vt to copy. 2 vi: ~ sur qqn to copy from sb.

copieux, -ieuse [kɔpjø, jøz] adj copious.

copilote [kɔpilɔt] nmf copilot.

copine → copain.

coproduction [kɔprɔdyksjɔ̃] nf coproduction.

copropriété [kɔprɔprijete] nf co-ownership, joint ownership.

coq [kɔk] nm cock, cockerel; sauter ou passer du ~ à l'âne to jump from one subject to another.

coque [kɔk] nf [de noix] shell. || [de navire] hull.

coquelicot [kɔkliko] nm poppy.

coqueluche [kɔklyʃ] nf whooping cough.

coquet, -ette [kɔkɛ, ɛt] adj [vêtements] smart, stylish; [ville, jeune fille] pretty. || (avant n) hum [important]: la ~te somme de 100 livres the tidy sum of £100. ○ **coquette** nf flirt.

coquetier [kɔktje] nm eggcup.

coquetterie [kɔketri] nf [désir de plaire] coquettishness.

coquillage [kɔkijaʒ] nm [mollusque] shellfish. || [coquille] shell.

coquille [kɔkij] nf [de mollusque, noix, œuf] shell. || TYPO misprint.

coquillettes [kɔkijɛt] nfpl pasta shells.

coquin, -e [kɔkɛ̃, in] 1 adj [sous-vêtement] sexy, naughty; [regard, histoire] saucy. 2 nm, f rascal.

cor [kɔr] nm [instrument] horn. || [au pied] corn. ○ **à cor et à cri** loc adv: réclamer qqch à ~ et à cri to clamour for sthg.

corail, -aux [kɔraj, o] nm [gén] coral. || RAIL: train ~ ≃ express train.

Coran [kɔrɑ̃] nm: le ~ the Koran.

corbeau, -x [kɔrbo] nm [oiseau] crow.

corbeille [kɔrbɛj] nf [panier] basket; ~ à papier waste paper basket. || THÉÂTRE (dress) circle.

corbillard [kɔrbijar] nm hearse.

cordage [kɔrdaʒ] nm [de bateau] rigging (U). || [de raquette] strings (pl).

corde [kɔrd] nf [filin] rope; ~ à linge washing ou clothes line; ~ à sauter skipping rope. || [d'instrument, arc] string. || ANAT: ~ vocale vocal cord. || HIPPISME rails (pl); ATHLÉTISME inside (lane).

cordial, -e, -iaux [kɔrdjal, jo] adj warm, cordial.

cordon [kɔrdɔ̃] nm string, cord; ~ ombilical umbilical cord; ~ de police police cordon.

cordon-bleu [kɔrdɔ̃blø] nm cordon bleu cook.

cordonnerie [kɔrdɔnri] nf [magasin] shoe repairer's, cobbler's.

cordonnier, -ière [kɔrdɔnje, jɛr] nm, f shoe repairer, cobbler.

Corée [kɔre] nf Korea.

coriace [kɔrjas] adj litt & fig tough.

cormoran [kɔrmɔrɑ̃] nm cormorant.

corne [kɔrn] nf [gén] horn; [de cerf] antler. || [callosité] hard skin (U), callus.

cornée [kɔrne] nf cornea.

côté

corneille [kɔrnɛj] *nf* crow.

cornemuse [kɔrnəmyz] *nf* bagpipes (*pl*).

corner¹ [kɔrne] *vt* [page] to turn down the corner of.

corner² [kɔrnɛr] *nm* FOOTBALL corner (kick).

cornet [kɔrnɛ] *nm* [d'aliment] cornet, cone. || [de jeu] (dice) shaker.

corniche [kɔrniʃ] *nf* [route] cliff road. || [moulure] cornice.

cornichon [kɔrniʃɔ̃] *nm* [condiment] gherkin. || *fam* [imbécile] twit.

Cornouailles [kɔrnwaj] *nf*: **la ~** Cornwall.

corolle [kɔrɔl] *nf* corolla.

coron [kɔrɔ̃] *nm* [village] mining village.

corporation [kɔrpɔrasjɔ̃] *nf* corporate body.

corporel, -elle [kɔrpɔrɛl] *adj* [physique - besoin] bodily; [- châtiment] corporal.

corps [kɔr] *nm* [gén] body. || [groupe]: **~ d'armée** (army) corps; **~ enseignant** [profession] teaching profession; [d'école] teaching staff.

corpulent, -e [kɔrpylɑ̃, ɑ̃t] *adj* corpulent, stout.

correct, -e [kɔrɛkt] *adj* [exact] correct, right. || [honnête] correct, proper. || [acceptable] decent; [travail] fair.

correcteur, -trice [kɔrɛktœr, tris] *nm*, *f* [d'examen] examiner, marker *Br*, grader *Am*. || TYPO proofreader.

correction [kɔrɛksjɔ̃] *nf* [d'erreur] correction. || [punition] punishment. || TYPO proofreading. || [notation] marking. || [bienséance] propriety.

corrélation [kɔrelasjɔ̃] *nf* correlation.

correspondance [kɔrɛspɔ̃dɑ̃s] *nf* [gén] correspondence; **cours par ~** correspondence course. || TRANSPORT connection; **assurer la ~ avec** to connect with.

correspondant, -e [kɔrɛspɔ̃dɑ̃, ɑ̃t] **1** *adj* corresponding. **2** *nm*, *f* [par lettres] penfriend, correspondent. || [par téléphone]: **je vous passe votre ~** I'll put you through. || PRESSE correspondent.

correspondre [kɔrɛspɔ̃dr] *vi* [être conforme]: **~ à** to correspond to. || [par lettres]: **~ avec** to correspond with.

corridor [kɔridɔr] *nm* corridor.

corrigé [kɔriʒe] *nm* correct version.

corriger [kɔriʒe] *vt* TYPO to correct, to proofread. || [noter] to mark. || [modifier] to correct. || [punir] to give sb a good hiding. ○ **se corriger** *vp* [d'un défaut]: **se ~ de** to cure o.s. of.

corroborer [kɔrɔbɔre] *vt* to corroborate.

corroder [kɔrode] *vt* [ronger] to corrode; *fig* to erode.

corrompre [kɔrɔ̃pr] *vt* [soudoyer] to bribe. || [dépraver] to corrupt.

corrosion [kɔrozjɔ̃] *nf* corrosion.

corruption [kɔrypsjɔ̃] *nf* [subornation] bribery. || [dépravation] corruption.

corsage [kɔrsaʒ] *nm* [chemisier] blouse. || [de robe] bodice.

corsaire [kɔrsɛr] *nm* [navire, marin] corsair, privateer. || [pantalon] pedal-pushers (*pl*).

corse [kɔrs] **1** *adj* Corsican. **2** *nm* [langue] Corsican. ○ **Corse 1** *nmf* Corsican. **2** *nf*: **la Corse** Corsica.

corsé, -e [kɔrse] *adj* [café] strong; [vin] full-bodied; [plat, histoire] spicy.

corset [kɔrsɛ] *nm* corset.

cortège [kɔrtɛʒ] *nm* procession.

corvée [kɔrve] *nf* MIL fatigue (duty). || [activité pénible] chore.

cosmétique [kɔsmetik] *nm & adj* cosmetic.

cosmique [kɔsmik] *adj* cosmic.

cosmonaute [kɔsmɔnot] *nmf* cosmonaut.

cosmopolite [kɔsmɔpɔlit] *adj* cosmopolitan.

cosmos [kɔsmos] *nm* [univers] cosmos. || [espace] outer space.

cossu, -e [kɔsy] *adj* [maison] opulent.

Costa Rica [kɔstarika] *nm*: **le ~** Costa Rica.

costaud (*f* **costaud** OU **-e**) [kɔsto, od] *adj* sturdily built.

costume [kɔstym] *nm* [folklorique, de théâtre] costume. || [vêtement d'homme] suit.

costumé, -e [kɔstyme] *adj* fancy-dress (*avant n*).

costumier, -ière [kɔstymje, jɛr] *nm*, *f* THÉÂTRE wardrobe master (*f* mistress).

cote [kɔt] *nf* [marque de classement] classification mark; [marque numérale] serial number. || FIN quotation. || [niveau] level; **~ d'alerte** [de cours d'eau] danger level; *fig* crisis point.

côte [kot] *nf* [ANAT, BOT & de bœuf] rib; [de porc, mouton, agneau] chop; **~ à ~** side by side. || [pente] hill. || [littoral] coast.

côté [kote] *nm* [gén] side; **être aux ~s de qqn** *fig* to be by sb's side; **d'un ~ ..., de l'autre ~ ...** on the one hand ..., on the other hand ... || [endroit, direction] direction, way; **de quel ~ est-il parti?** which way did he go?; **de l'autre ~ de** on the other side of; **du ~ de** [près de] near. ○ **à côté** *loc adv* [lieu - gén] nearby; [- dans la maison adjacente] next door. ○ **à côté de** *loc prép* [proximité] beside, next to. || [en comparaison avec] beside, compared to. ○ **de côté** *loc adv* [se placer, marcher] sideways. || [en réserve] aside.

coteau [kɔto] *nm* [colline] hill. || [versant] slope.

Côte-d'Ivoire [kotdivwar] *nf*: **la ~** the Ivory Coast.

côtelé, -e [kotle] *adj* ribbed; **velours ~** corduroy.

côtelette [kotlɛt] *nf* [de porc, mouton, d'agneau] chop; [de veau] cutlet.

côtier, -ière [kotje, jɛr] *adj* coastal.

cotisation [kɔtizasjɔ̃] *nf* [à club, parti] subscription; [à la Sécurité sociale] contribution.

cotiser [kɔtize] *vi* [à un club, un parti] to subscribe; [à la Sécurité sociale] to contribute. ○ **se cotiser** *vp* to club together.

coton [kɔtɔ̃] *nm* cotton; **~ (hydrophile)** cotton wool.

Coton-Tige® [kɔtɔ̃tiʒ] *nm* cotton bud.

côtoyer [kotwaje] *vt fig* [fréquenter] to mix with.

cou [ku] *nm* [de personne, bouteille] neck.

couchant [kuʃɑ̃] **1** *adj* → **soleil**. **2** *nm* west.

couche [kuʃ] *nf* [de peinture, de vernis] coat, layer; [de poussière] film, layer. || [épaisseur] layer; **~ d'ozone** ozone layer. || [de bébé] nappy *Br*, diaper *Am*. || [classe sociale] stratum. ○ **fausse couche** *nf* miscarriage.

couché, -e [kuʃe] *adj*: **être ~** [étendu] to be lying down; [au lit] to be in bed.

couche-culotte [kuʃkylɔt] *nf* disposable nappy *Br* ou diaper *Am*.

coucher¹ [kuʃe] **1** *vt* [enfant] to put to bed. || [objet, blessé] to lay down. **2** *vi* [passer la nuit] to spend the night. || *fam* [avoir des rapports sexuels]: **~ avec** to sleep with. ○ **se coucher** *vp* [s'allonger] to lie down. || [se mettre au lit] to go to bed. || [astre] to set.

coucher² [kuʃe] *nm* [d'astre] setting; **au ~ du soleil** at sunset.

couchette [kuʃɛt] *nf* [de train] couchette. || [de navire] berth.

coucou [kuku] **1** *nm* [oiseau] cuckoo. || [pendule] cuckoo clock. || *péj* [avion] crate. **2** *interj* peekaboo!

coude [kud] *nm* [de personne, de vêtement] elbow. || [courbe] bend.

cou-de-pied [kudpje] (*pl* **cous-de-pied**) *nm* instep.

coudre [kudr] *vt* [bouton] to sew on.

couette [kwɛt] *nf* [édredon] duvet. || [coiffure] bunches (*pl*).

couffin [kufɛ̃] *nm* [berceau] Moses basket.

couiner [kwine] *vi* [animal] to squeal. || [pleurnicher] to whine.

coulée [kule] *nf* [de matière liquide]: **~ de lave** lava flow; **~ de boue** mudslide. || [de métal] casting.

couler [kule] **1** *vi* [liquide] to flow. || [beurre, fromage, nez] to run. || [navire, entreprise] to sink. **2** *vt* [navire] to sink. || [métal, bronze] to cast.

couleur [kulœr] **1** *nf* [teinte, caractère] colour. || [linge] coloureds (*pl*). || CARTES suit. **2** *adj inv* [télévision, pellicule] colour (*avant n*).

couleuvre [kulœvr] *nf* grass snake.

coulisse [kulis] *nf* [glissière]: **fenêtre/ porte à ~** sliding window/door. ○ **coulisses** *nfpl* THÉÂTRE wings.

coulisser [kulise] *vi* to slide.

couloir [kulwar] *nm* [corridor] corridor. || GÉOGR gully. || SPORT & TRANSPORT lane.

coup [ku] *nm* [choc - physique, moral] blow; **~ de couteau** stab (*with a knife*); **un ~ dur** *fig* a heavy blow; **~ de pied** kick; **~ de poing** punch. || [action nuisible] trick. || [SPORT - au tennis] stroke; [- en boxe] blow, punch; [- au football] kick; **~ franc** free kick. || [d'éponge, de chiffon] wipe; **un ~ de crayon** a pencil stroke. || [bruit] noise; **~ de feu** shot, gunshot; **~ de tonnerre** thunderclap. || [action spectaculaire]: **~ d'état** coup (d'état); **~ de théâtre** *fig* dramatic turn of events. || *fam* [fois] time. || *loc*: **boire un ~** to have a drink; **donner un ~ de main à qqn** to give sb a helping hand; **jeter un ~ d'œil à** to glance at; **tenir le ~** to hold out; **valoir le ~** to be well worth it. ○ **coup de fil** *nm* phone call. ○ **coup de foudre** *nm* love at first sight. ○ **coup de soleil** *nm* sunburn (*U*). ○ **coup de téléphone** *nm* telephone ou phone call; **donner** ou **passer un ~ de téléphone à qqn** to telephone ou phone sb. ○ **coup de vent** *nm* gust of wind; **partir en ~ de vent** to rush off. ○ **coup sûr** *loc adv* definitely. ○ **après coup** *loc adv* afterwards. ○ **coup sur coup** *loc adv* one after the other. ○ **du coup**

loc adv as a result. ○ **tout à coup** *loc adv* suddenly. ○ **sous le coup de** *loc prép* [sous l'effet de] in the grip of.

coupable [kupabl] **1** *adj* [personne, pensée] guilty. || [action, dessein] culpable, reprehensible; [négligence, oubli] sinful. **2** *nmf* guilty person ou party.

coupant, -e [kupɑ̃, ɑ̃t] *adj* [tranchant] cutting. || *fig* [sec] sharp.

coupe [kup] *nf* [verre] glass. || [à fruits] dish. || SPORT cup. || [de vêtement, aux cartes] cut. || [plan, surface] (cross) section.

coupe-ongles [kupɔ̃gl] *nm inv* nail clippers.

coupe-papier [kuppapje] (*pl inv* OU **coupe-papiers**) *nm* paper knife.

couper [kupe] **1** *vt* [matériau, cheveux, blé] to cut. || [interrompre, trancher] to cut off. || [traverser] to cut across. || [pain, au tennis] to slice; [rôti] to carve. || [mélanger] to dilute. || [CARTES - avec atout] to trump; [- paquet] to cut. || [envie, appétit] to take away. **2** *vi* [gén] to cut. ○ **se couper** *vp* [se blesser] to cut o.s. || [se croiser] to cross. || [s'isoler]: **se ~ de** to cut o.s. off from.

couperet [kuprɛ] *nm* [de boucher] cleaver. || [de guillotine] blade.

couperosé, -e [kuproze] *adj* blotchy.

couple [kupl] *nm* [de personnes] couple.

coupler [kuple] *vt* [objets] to couple.

couplet [kuplɛ] *nm* verse.

coupole [kupɔl] *nf* ARCHIT dome, cupola.

coupon [kupɔ̃] *nm* [d'étoffe] remnant. || [billet] ticket.

coupon-réponse [kupɔ̃repɔ̃s] (*pl* **coupons-réponse**) *nm* reply coupon.

coupure [kupyr] *nf* [gén] cut; [billet de banque]: **petite ~** small denomination note; **~ de courant** ÉLECTR power cut; IN-FORM blackout. || *fig* [rupture] break.

cour [kur] *nf* [espace] courtyard. || [du roi, tribunal] court; *fig & hum* following; **Cour de cassation** Court of Appeal.

courage [kuraʒ] *nm* courage; **bon ~!** good luck!; **je n'ai pas le ~ de faire mes devoirs** I can't bring myself to do my homework.

courageux, -euse [kuraʒø, øz] *adj* [brave] brave. || [audacieux] bold.

couramment [kuramɑ̃] *adv* [parler une langue] fluently. || [communément] commonly.

courant, -e [kurɑ̃, ɑ̃t] *adj* [habituel] everyday (*avant n*). || [en cours] present. ○ **courant** *nm* [marin, atmosphérique, électrique] current; **~ d'air** draught. ||

[d'idées] current. || [laps de temps]: **dans le ~ du mois/de l'année** in the course of the month/the year. ○ **au courant** *loc adv*: **être au ~** to know (about it); **mettre qqn au ~ (de)** to tell sb (about); **tenir qqn au ~ (de)** to keep sb informed (about); **se mettre/se tenir au ~ (de)** to get/keep up to date (with).

courbature [kurbatyr] *nf* ache.

courbaturé, -e [kurbatyre] *adj* aching.

courbe [kurb] **1** *nf* curve; **~ de niveau** [sur une carte] contour (line). **2** *adj* curved.

courber [kurbe] **1** *vt* [tige] to bend. || [tête] to bow. **2** *vi* to bow. ○ **se courber** *vp* [chose] to bend. || [personne] to bow, to bend down.

courbette [kurbɛt] *nf* [révérence] bow; **faire des ~s** *fig* to bow and scrape.

coureur, -euse [kurœr, øz] *nm, f* SPORT runner; **~ cycliste** racing cyclist.

courge [kurʒ] *nf* [légume] marrow *Br*, squash *Am*. || *fam* [imbécile] dimwit.

courgette [kurʒɛt] *nf* zucchini *Am*.

courir [kurir] **1** *vi* [aller rapidement] to run. || SPORT to race. || [se précipiter, rivière] to rush. || [se propager]: **le bruit court que ...** rumour has it that ...; **faire ~ un bruit** to spread a rumour. **2** *vt* SPORT to run in. || [parcourir] to roam (through). || [fréquenter - bals, musées] to do the rounds of.

couronne [kurɔn] *nf* [ornement, autorité] crown. || [de fleurs] wreath.

couronnement [kurɔnmɑ̃] *nm* [de monarque] coronation. || *fig* [apogée] crowning achievement.

couronner [kurɔne] *vt* [monarque] to crown. || [récompenser] to give a prize to.

courre [kur] → **chasse**.

courrier [kurje] *nm* mail, letters (*pl*); **~ du cœur** agony column.

courroie [kurwa] *nf* TECHNOL belt; [attache] strap; **~ de transmission** driving belt; **~ de ventilateur** fanbelt.

cours [kur] *nm* [écoulement] flow; **~ d'eau** waterway; **donner** OU **laisser libre ~ à** *fig* to give free rein to. || [déroulement] course; **au ~ de** during, in the course of; [année, dossier] current; [affaires] in hand; **en ~ de route** on the way. || FIN price; **avoir ~** [monnaie] to be legal tender. || [leçon] class, lesson; **donner des ~ (à qqn)** to teach (sb). || [classe]: **~ élémentaire** years two and three of primary school; **~ moyen** last two years *of primary school*; ~ **préparatoire** ≃ nursery school *Am*.

course [kurs] *nf* [action] running (*U*); **au pas de ~** at a run. || [compétition] race. || [en taxi] journey. || [commission] errand; **faire des ~s** to go shopping.

coursier, -ière [kursje, jɛr] *nm, f* messenger.

court, -e [kur, kurt] *adj* short. ○ **court 1** *adv*: **être à ~ d'argent/d'idées/d'arguments** to be short of money/ideas/arguments; **prendre qqn de ~** to catch sb unawares; **tourner ~** to stop suddenly. **2** *nm*: **~ de tennis** tennis court.

court-bouillon [kurbujɔ̃] *nm* court-bouillon.

court-circuit [kursirkɥi] *nm* short circuit.

courtier, -ière [kurtje, jɛr] *nm, f* broker.

courtisan, -e [kurtizɑ̃, an] *nm, f* HIST courtier.

courtiser [kurtize] *vt* [femme] to woo, to court. || *péj* [flatter] to flatter.

court-métrage [kurmetraʒ] *nm* short (film).

courtois, -e [kurtwa, az] *adj* courteous.

courtoisie [kurtwazi] *nf* courtesy.

couru, -e [kury] *pp* → **courir**.

cousin, -e [kuzɛ̃, in] *nm, f* cousin; ~ **germain** first cousin.

coussin [kusɛ̃] *nm* [de siège] cushion.

cousu, -e [kuzy] *pp* → **coudre**.

coût [ku] *nm* cost.

couteau, -x [kuto] *nm* [gén] knife; ~ **à cran d'arrêt** flick knife.

coûter [kute] **1** *vi* [valoir] to cost; **ça coûte combien?** how much is it?; ~ **cher à qqn** to cost sb a lot; *fig* to cost sb dear ou dearly. || *fig* [être pénible] to be difficult. **2** *vt* *fig* to cost. ○ **coûte que coûte** *loc adv* at all costs.

coûteux, -euse [kutø, øz] *adj* costly, expensive.

coutume [kutym] *nf* [gén & JUR] custom.

couture [kutyr] *nf* [action] sewing. || [points] seam. || [activité] dressmaking.

couturier, -ière [kutyrje, jɛr] *nm, f* couturier.

couvée [kuve] *nf* [d'œufs] clutch; [de poussins] brood.

couvent [kuvɑ̃] *nm* [de sœurs] convent; [de moines] monastery.

couver [kuve] **1** *vt* [œufs] to sit on. || [dorloter] to mollycoddle. || [maladie] to be sickening for. **2** *vi* [poule] to brood; *fig* [complot] to hatch.

couvercle [kuvɛrkl] *nm* [de casserole, boîte] lid, cover.

couvert, -e [kuvɛr, ɛrt] **1** *pp* → **couvrir**. **2** *adj* [submergé] covered; ~ **de** covered with. || [habillé] dressed; **être bien ~** to be well wrapped up. || [nuageux] overcast. ○ **couvert** *nm* [abri]: **se mettre à ~** to take shelter. || [place à table] place (setting); **mettre** ou **dresser le ~** to set ou lay the table. ○ **couverts** *nmpl* cutlery (*U*).

couverture [kuvɛrtyr] *nf* [gén] cover. || [de lit] blanket; ~ **chauffante** electric blanket. || [toit] roofing (*U*).

couveuse [kuvøz] *nf* [machine] incubator.

couvre-feu [kuvrəfø] (*pl* couvre-feux) *nm* curfew.

couvrir [kuvrir] *vt* [gén] to cover; ~ **qqn/qqch de** *litt & fig* to cover sb/sthg with. || [protéger] to shield. ○ **se couvrir** *vp* [se vêtir] to wrap up. || [se recouvrir]: **se ~ de feuilles/de fleurs** to come into leaf/blossom. || [ciel] to cloud over. || [se protéger] to cover o.s.

CP *nm abr de* **cours préparatoire**.

crabe [krab] *nm* crab.

crachat [kraʃa] *nm* spit (*U*).

cracher [kraʃe] **1** *vi* [personne] to spit. **2** *vt* [sang] to spit (up); [lave, injures] to spit (out).

crachin [kraʃɛ̃] *nm* drizzle.

craie [krɛ] *nf* chalk.

craindre [krɛdr] *vt* [redouter] to fear, to be afraid of; ~ **de faire qqch** to be afraid of doing sthg; **je crains d'avoir oublié mes papiers** I'm afraid I've forgotten my papers; ~ **que** (+ *subjonctif*) to be afraid (that); **je crains qu'il oublie** ou **n'oublie** I'm afraid he may forget. || [être sensible à] to be susceptible to.

craint, -e [krɛ̃, ɛ̃t] *pp* → **craindre**.

crainte [krɛ̃t] *nf* fear; **de ~ de faire qqch** for fear of doing sthg; **de ~ que** (+ *subjonctif*) for fear that; **il a fui de ~ qu'on ne le voie** he fled for fear that he might be seen ou for fear of being seen.

craintif, -ive [krɛ̃tif, iv] *adj* timid.

cramoisi, -e [kramwazi] *adj* crimson.

crampe [krɑ̃p] *nf* cramp.

crampon [krɑ̃pɔ̃] *nm* [crochet - gén] clamp; [- pour alpinisme] crampon.

cramponner [krɑ̃pɔne] ○ **se cramponner** *vp* [s'agripper] to hang on; **se ~ à qqn/qqch** *litt & fig* to cling to sb/sthg.

cran [krɑ̃] nm [entaille, degré] notch, cut. || (U) [audace] guts (pl).

crâne [kran] nm skull.

crâner [krane] vi fam to show off.

crânien, -ienne [kranjɛ̃, jɛn] adj: **boîte ~ne** skull; **traumatisme ~** head injury.

crapaud [krapo] nm toad.

crapule [krapyl] nf scum (U).

craquelure [kraklyr] nf crack.

craquement [krakmɑ̃] nm crack, cracking (U).

craquer [krake] 1 vi [produire un bruit] to crack; [plancher, chaussure] to creak. || [se déchirer] to split. || [s'effondrer - personne] to crack up. || [être séduit par]: **~ pour** to fall for. 2 vt [allumette] to strike.

crasse [kras] nf [saleté] dirt, filth. || fam [mauvais tour] dirty trick.

crasseux, -euse [krasø, øz] adj filthy.

cratère [kratɛr] nm crater.

cravache [kravaʃ] nf riding crop.

cravate [kravat] nf tie.

crawl [krol] nm crawl.

crayon [krɛjɔ̃] nm [gén] pencil; **~ à bille** ballpoint (pen); **~ de couleur** crayon. || TECHNOL pen; **~ optique** light pen.

créancier, -ière [kreɑ̃sje, jɛr] nm, f creditor.

créateur, -trice [kreatœr, tris] 1 adj creative. 2 nm, f creator.

créatif, -ive [kreatif, iv] adj creative.

création [kreasjɔ̃] nf creation.

créativité [kreativite] nf creativity.

créature [kreatyr] nf creature.

crécelle [kresɛl] nf rattle.

crèche [krɛʃ] nf [de Noël] crib. || [garderie] crèche.

crédible [kredibl] adj credible.

crédit [kredi] nm [gén] credit; **faire ~ à qqn** to give sb credit; **acheter/vendre qqch à ~** to buy/sell sthg on credit.

crédit-bail [kredibaj] (pl **crédits-bails**) nm leasing.

créditeur, -trice [kreditœr, tris] 1 adj in credit. 2 nm, f creditor.

crédule [kredyl] adj credulous.

crédulité [kredylite] nf credulity.

créer [kree] vt [RELIG & inventer] to create. || [fonder] to found, to start up.

crémaillère [kremajɛr] nf [de cheminée] trammel; **pendre la ~** fig to have a housewarming (party). || TECHNOL rack.

crémation [kremasjɔ̃] nf cremation.

crématoire [krematwar] → **four**.

crème [krɛm] 1 nf [gén] cream; **~ fouettée/fraîche/glacée** whipped/fresh/

ice cream; **~ anglaise** custard; **~ hydratante** moisturizer. 2 adj inv cream.

crémerie [krɛmri] nf dairy.

crémier, -ière [kremje, jɛr] nm, f dairyman (f dairywoman).

créneau, -x [kreno] nm [de fortification] crenel. || [pour se garer]: **faire un ~** to reverse into a parking space. || [de marché] niche. || [horaire] window, gap.

créole [kreɔl] adj & nm creole.

crêpe [krɛp] 1 nf CULIN pancake. 2 nm [tissu] crepe.

crêperie [krɛpri] nf pancake restaurant.

crépi [krepi] nm roughcast.

crépir [krepir] vt to roughcast.

crépiter [krepite] vi [feu, flammes] to crackle; [pluie] to patter.

crépon [krepɔ̃] adj → **papier**.

crépu, -e [krepy] adj frizzy.

crépuscule [krepyskyl] nm [du jour] dusk, twilight; fig twilight.

crescendo [kreʃɛndo, kreʃɛ̃do] 1 adv crescendo; **aller ~** fig [bruit] to get ou grow louder and louder. 2 nm inv MUS & fig crescendo.

cresson [kresɔ̃] nm watercress.

crête [krɛt] nf [de coq] comb. || [de montagne, vague, oiseau] crest.

crétin, -e [kretɛ̃, in] fam 1 adj cretinous, idiotic. 2 nm, f cretin, idiot.

creuser [krøze] vt [trou] to dig. || [objet] to hollow out. || fig [approfondir] to go into deeply.

creux, creuse [krø, krøz] adj [vide, concave] hollow. || [période - d'activité réduite] slack; [- à tarif réduit] off-peak. || [paroles] empty. ○ **creux** nm [concavité] hollow. || [période] lull.

crevaison [krəvɛzɔ̃] nf puncture.

crevant, -e [krəvɑ̃, ɑ̃t] adj fam [fatigant] exhausting.

crevasse [krəvas] nf [de mur] crevice, crack; [de glacier] crevasse.

crevé, -e [krəve] adj [pneu] burst, punctured. || fam [fatigué] dead, shattered Br.

crever [krəve] 1 vi [éclater] to burst. || tfam [mourir] to die; **~ de** fig [jalousie, orgueil] to be bursting with. 2 vt [percer] to burst. || fam [épuiser] to wear out.

crevette [krəvɛt] nf: **~ (grise)** shrimp; **~ (rose)** prawn.

cri [kri] nm [de personne] cry, shout; [perçant] scream; [d'animal] cry; **pousser un ~** to cry (out), to shout; **pousser un ~**

de douleur to cry out in pain. ‖ [appel] cry; **le dernier ~** *fig* the latest thing.

criant, -e [krijɑ̃, ɑ̃t] *adj* [injustice] blatant.

criard, -e [krijar, ard] *adj* [voix] strident, piercing. ‖ [couleur] loud.

crible [kribl] *nm* [instrument] sieve; **passer qqch au ~** *fig* to examine sthg closely.

criblé, -e [krible] *adj* riddled; **être ~ de dettes** to be up to one's eyes in debt.

cric [krik] *nm* jack.

cricket [krikɛt] *nm* cricket.

crier [crije] **1** *vi* [pousser un cri] to shout (out), to yell. ‖ [parler fort] to shout. ‖ [protester]: **~ contre** *ou* **après qqn** to nag sb, to go on at sb. **2** *vt* to shout (out).

crime [krim] *nm* [délit] crime. ‖ [meurtre] murder.

criminalité [kriminalite] *nf* criminality.

criminel, -elle [kriminel] **1** *adj* criminal. **2** *nm, f* criminal; **~ de guerre** war criminal.

crin [krɛ̃] *nm* [d'animal] hair.

crinière [krinjer] *nf* mane.

crique [krik] *nf* creek.

criquet [krikɛ] *nm* locust; [sauterelle] grasshopper.

crise [kriz] *nf* MÉD attack; **~ cardiaque** heart attack; **~ de foie** bilious attack. ‖ [accès] fit; **~ de nerfs** attack of nerves. ‖ [phase critique] crisis.

crispation [krispasjɔ̃] *nf* [contraction] contraction. ‖ [agacement] irritation.

crispé, -e [krispe] *adj* tense, on edge.

crisper [krispe] *vt* [contracter - visage] to tense; [- poing] to clench. ‖ [agacer] to irritate. ○ **se crisper** *vp* [se contracter] to tense (up). ‖ [s'irriter] to get irritated.

crisser [krise] *vi* [pneu] to screech.

cristal, -aux [kristal, o] *nm* crystal; **~ de roche** quartz.

cristallin, -e [kristalɛ̃, in] *adj* [limpide] crystal clear, crystalline. ‖ [roche] crystalline. ○ **cristallin** *nm* crystalline lens.

critère [kriter] *nm* criterion.

critique [kritik] **1** *adj* critical. **2** *nmf* critic. **3** *nf* criticism.

critiquer [kritike] *vt* to criticize.

croasser [krɔase] *vi* to croak, to caw.

croate [krɔat] *adj* Croat, Croatian. ○ **Croate** *nmf* Croat, Croatian.

Croatie [krɔasi] *nf*: **la ~** Croatia.

croc [kro] *nm* [de chien] fang.

croche [krɔʃ] *nf* eighth (note) *Am*.

croche-pied [krɔʃpje] (*pl* **croche-pieds**) *nm*: **faire un ~ à qqn** to trip sb up.

crochet [krɔʃɛ] *nm* [de métal] hook; **vivre aux ~s de qqn** to live off sb. ‖ TRICOT crochet hook. ‖ TYPO square bracket. ‖ BOXE: **~ du gauche/du droit** left/right hook.

crochu, -e [krɔʃy] *adj* [doigts] claw-like; [nez] hooked.

crocodile [krɔkɔdil] *nm* crocodile.

croire [krwar] **1** *vt* [chose, personne] to believe. ‖ [penser] to think; **tu crois?** do you think so?; **il te croyait parti** he thought you'd left; **~ que** to think (that). **2** *vi*: **~ à** to believe in; **~ en** to believe in, to have faith in.

croisade [krwazad] *nf* HIST & *fig* crusade.

croisé, -e [krwaze] *adj* [veste] double-breasted. ○ **croisé** *nm* HIST crusader.

croisement [krwazmɑ̃] *nm* [intersection] junction, intersection. ‖ BIOL cross-breeding.

croiser [krwaze] **1** *vt* [jambes] to cross; [bras] to fold. ‖ [passer à côté de] to pass. ‖ [chemin] to cross, to cut across. ‖ [métisser] to interbreed. **2** *vi* NAVIG to cruise. ○ **se croiser** *vp* [chemins] to cross, to intersect; [personnes] to pass; [lettres] to cross; [regards] to meet.

croisière [krwazjer] *nf* cruise.

croisillon [krwazijɔ̃] *nm*: **à ~s** lattice (*avant n*).

croissance [krwasɑ̃s] *nf* growth, development.

croissant, -e [krwasɑ̃, ɑ̃t] *adj* increasing, growing. ○ **croissant** *nm* [de lune] crescent. ‖ CULIN croissant.

croître [krwatr] *vi* [grandir] to grow. ‖ [augmenter] to increase.

croix [krwa] *nf* cross; **en ~** in the shape of a cross; **~ gammée** swastika; **la Croix-Rouge** the Red Cross.

croquant, -e [krɔkɑ̃, ɑ̃t] *adj* crisp, crunchy.

croque-monsieur [krɔkməsjø] *nm inv* toasted cheese and ham sandwich.

croquer [krɔke] **1** *vt* [manger] to crunch. ‖ [dessiner] to sketch. **2** *vi* to be crunchy.

croquette [krɔkɛt] *nf* croquette.

croquis [krɔki] *nm* sketch.

cross [krɔs] *nm* [exercice] cross-country (running); [course] cross-country race.

crotte [krɔt] *nf* [de lapin etc] droppings (*pl*); [de chien] dirt.

crottin [krɔtɛ̃] *nm* [de cheval] (horse) manure.

crouler [krule] *vi* to crumble; **~ sous** *litt* & *fig* to collapse under.

croupe [krup] *nf* rump.

croupier [krupje] *nm* croupier.

croupir [krupir] *vi litt* & *fig* to stagnate.

croustillant, -e [krustijã, ãt] *adj* [croquant - pain] crusty; [- biscuit] crunchy.

croûte [krut] *nf* [du pain, terrestre] crust. || [de fromage] rind. || [de plaie] scab. || *fam péj* [tableau] daub.

croûton [krutɔ̃] *nm* [bout du pain] crust. || [pain frit] crouton.

croyance [krwajãs] *nf* belief.

croyant, -e [krwajã, ãt] **1** *adj* : **être ~** to be a believer. **2** *nm, f* believer.

CRS (*abr de* **Compagnie républicaine de sécurité**) *nm* member of the French riot police.

cru, -e [kry] **1** *pp* → **croire**. **2** *adj* [non cuit] raw. || [violent] harsh. || [direct] blunt. || [grivois] crude.

crû [kry] *pp* → **croître**.

cruauté [kryote] *nf* cruelty.

cruche [kryʃ] *nf* [objet] jug. || *fam péj* [personne niaise] twit.

crucial, -e, -iaux [krysjal, jo] *adj* crucial.

crucifix [krysifi] *nm* crucifix.

crudité [krydite] *nf* crudeness. ○ **crudités** *nfpl* crudités.

crue [kry] *nf* rise in the water level.

cruel, -elle [kryεl] *adj* cruel.

crustacé [krystase] *nm* shellfish, crustacean; **~s** shellfish (*U*).

Cuba [kyba] *n* Cuba.

cubain, -aine [kybɛ̃, εn] *adj* Cuban. ○ **Cubain, -aine** *nm, f* Cuban.

cube [kyb] *nm* cube.

cueillette [kœjεt] *nf* picking, harvesting.

cueillir [kœjir] *vt* [fruits, fleurs] to pick.

cuillère, cuiller [kɥijεr] *nf* spoon; **~ à café** coffee spoon; CULIN teaspoon; **~ à dessert** dessertspoon; **~ à soupe** soup spoon; CULIN tablespoon; **petite ~** teaspoon.

cuillerée [kɥijere] *nf* spoonful; **~ à café** CULIN teaspoonful; **~ à soupe** CULIN tablespoonful.

cuir [kɥir] *nm* leather; [non tanné] hide; **~ chevelu** ANAT scalp.

cuirasse [kɥiras] *nf* [de chevalier] breastplate; *fig* armour.

cuirassé [kɥirase] *nm* battleship.

cuire [kɥir] **1** *vt* [viande, œuf] to cook; [tarte, gâteau] to bake; **faire ~ qqch** to cook/bake sthg. **2** *vi* [viande, œuf] to cook; [tarte, gâteau] to bake.

cuisine [kɥizin] *nf* [pièce] kitchen. || [art] cooking, cookery; **faire la ~** to do the cooking, to cook.

cuisiné, -e [kɥizine] *adj* : **plat ~** ready-cooked meal.

cuisiner [kɥizine] **1** *vt* [aliment] to cook. || *fam* [personne] to grill. **2** *vi* to cook; **bien/mal ~** to be a good/bad cook.

cuisinier, -ière [kɥizinje, jεr] *nm, f* cook. ○ **cuisinière** *nf* cooker; **cuisinière électrique/à gaz** electric/gas cooker.

cuisse [kɥis] *nf* ANAT thigh. || CULIN leg.

cuisson [kɥisɔ̃] *nf* cooking.

cuit, -e [kɥi, kɥit] **1** *pp* → **cuire**. **2** *adj* : **bien ~** [steak] well-done.

cuivre [kɥivr] *nm* [métal] : **~ (rouge)** copper; **~ jaune** brass. ○ **cuivres** *nmpl* : **les ~s** MUS the brass.

cuivré, -e [kɥivre] *adj* [couleur, reflet] coppery; [teint] bronzed.

cul [ky] *nm tfam* [postérieur] bum. || [de bouteille] bottom.

culbute [kylbyt] *nf* [saut] somersault. || [chute] tumble, fall.

cul-de-sac [kydsak] (*pl* **culs-de-sac**) *nm* dead end.

culinaire [kyliner] *adj* culinary.

culminant [kylminã] → **point**.

culot [kylo] *nm fam* [toupet] cheek, nerve.

culotte [kylɔt] *nf* [sous-vêtement féminin] knickers (*pl*), panties (*pl*), pair of knickers ou panties.

culotté, -e [kylɔte] *adj* [effronté] : **elle est ~e** she's got a nerve.

culpabilité [kylpabilite] *nf* guilt.

culte [kylt] *nm* [vénération, amour] worship. || [religion] religion.

cultivateur, -trice [kyltivatœr, tris] *nm, f* farmer.

cultivé, -e [kyltive] *adj* [personne] educated, cultured.

cultiver [kyltive] *vt* [terre, goût, relation] to cultivate. || [plante] to grow.

culture [kyltyr] *nf* AGRIC cultivation, farming; **les ~s** cultivated land. || [savoir] culture, knowledge; **~ physique** physical training. || [civilisation] culture.

culturel, -elle [kyltyrεl] *adj* cultural.

culturisme [kyltyrism] *nm* bodybuilding.

cumin [kymɛ̃] *nm* cumin.

cumuler [kymyle] *vt* [fonctions, titres] to hold simultaneously.

cupide [kypid] *adj* greedy.

cure [kyr] *nf* (course of) treatment; **faire une ~ de fruits** to go on a fruit-based diet; **~ de désintoxication** [d'alcool] drying-out treatment; [de drogue] detoxification treatment; **~ de sommeil** sleep therapy; **faire une ~ thermale** to take the waters.

curé [kyre] *nm* parish priest.

cure-dents [kyrdɑ̃] *nm inv* toothpick.

curer [kyre] *vt* to clean out.

curieux, -ieuse [kyrjø, jøz] **1** *adj* [intéressé] curious. || [indiscret] inquisitive. || [étrange] strange, curious. **2** *nm, f* busybody.

curiosité [kyrjozite] *nf* curiosity.

curriculum vitae [kyrikylɔmvite] *nm inv* curriculum vitae.

curry [kyri], **carry** [kari], **cari** [kari] *nm* [épice] curry powder. || [plat] curry.

curseur [kyrsœr] *nm* cursor.

cutané, -e [kytane] *adj* cutaneous, skin (*avant n*).

cuve [kyv] *nf* [citerne] tank. || [à vin] vat.

cuvée [kyve] *nf* [récolte] vintage.

cuvette [kyvɛt] *nf* [récipient] basin, bowl. || [de lavabo] basin; [de W.-C.] bowl. || GÉOGR basin.

CV *nm* (*abr de* **curriculum vitae**) CV. || (*abr de* **cheval-vapeur**) hp; [puissance fiscale] *classification for scaling of car tax.*

cyanure [sjanyr] *nm* cyanide.

cyclable [siklabl] → **piste.**

cycle [sikl] *nm* cycle; **premier ~** UNIV ≃ first and second year; SCOL middle school *Br*, junior high school *Am*; **second ~** UNIV ≃ final year *Br*, ≃ senior year *Am*; SCOL upper school *Br*, high school *Am*; **troisième ~** UNIV ≃ postgraduate year ou years.

cyclique [siklik] *adj* cyclic, cyclical.

cyclisme [siklism] *nm* cycling.

cycliste [siklist] *nmf* cyclist.

cyclone [siklon] *nm* cyclone.

cygne [siɲ] *nm* swan.

cylindre [silɛ̃dr] *nm* AUTOM & GÉOM cylinder. || [rouleau] roller.

cymbale [sɛ̃bal] *nf* cymbal.

cynique [sinik] *adj* cynical.

cynisme [sinism] *nm* cynicism.

cyprès [siprɛ] *nm* cypress.

d, D [de] *nm inv* d, D.

d' → **de.**

d'abord [dabɔr] → **abord.**

d'accord [dakɔr] *loc adv*: **~!** all right!, OK!; **être ~ avec** to agree with.

dactylo [daktilo] *nf* [personne] typist; [procédé] typing.

dactylographier [daktilɔgrafje] *vt* to type.

dada [dada] *nm fam* [occupation] hobby. || *fam* [idée] hobbyhorse.

dahlia [dalja] *nm* dahlia.

daigner [deɲe] *vi* to deign.

daim [dɛ̃] *nm* [animal] fallow deer. || [peau] suede.

dallage [dalaʒ] *nm* [action] paving; [dalles] pavement.

dalle [dal] *nf* [de pierre] slab; [de lino] tile.

dalmatien, -ienne [dalmasjɛ̃, jɛn] *nm, f* dalmatian.

daltonien, -ienne [daltɔnjɛ̃, jɛn] *adj* colour-blind.

dame [dam] *nf* [femme] lady. || CARTES & ÉCHECS queen. ○ **dames** *nfpl* checkers *Am.*

damier [damje] *nm* [de jeu] checkerboard *Am.* || [motif]: **à ~** checked.

damné, -e [dane] *adj fam* damned.

dancing [dɑ̃siŋ] *nm* dance hall.

dandiner [dɑ̃dine] ○ **se dandiner** *vp* to waddle.

Danemark [danmark] *nm*: **le ~** Denmark.

danger [dɑ̃ʒe] *nm* danger; **en ~** in danger; **courir un ~** to run a risk.

dangereux, -euse [dɑ̃ʒrø, øz] *adj* dangerous.

danois, -e [danwa, az] *adj* Danish. ○ **danois** *nm* [langue] Danish. || [chien] Great Dane. ○ **Danois, -e** *nm, f* Dane.

dans [dɑ̃] *prép* [dans le temps] in; **je reviens ~ un mois** I'll be back in a month ou in a month's time. || [dans l'espace] in. || [avec mouvement] into. || [indiquant état, manière] in; **vivre ~ la misère** to live in poverty; **il est ~ le commerce** he's in business. || [environ]: **~ les ... about ....**

dansant, -e [dɑ̄sɑ̄, ɑ̄t] *adj litt & fig* dancing; **soirée ~e** dance; **thé ~** tea dance.

danse [dɑ̄s] *nf* [art] dancing. || [musique] dance.

danser [dɑ̄se] **1** *vi* [personne] to dance. **2** *vt* to dance.

danseur, -euse [dɑ̄sœr, øz] *nm, f* dancer.

dard [dar] *nm* [d'animal] sting.

date [dat] *nf* [jour+mois+année] date; **~ de naissance** date of birth. || [moment] event.

dater [date] **1** *vt* to date. **2** *vi* [marquer] to be or mark a milestone. || *fam* [être démodé] to be dated. ○ **à dater de** *loc prép* as of or from.

datte [dat] *nf* date.

dattier [datje] *nm* date palm.

dauphin [dofɛ̄] *nm* [mammifère] dolphin. || HIST heir apparent.

daurade, dorade [dɔrad] *nf* sea bream.

davantage [davɑ̄taʒ] *adv* [plus] more; **~ de** more. || [plus longtemps] (any) longer.

de [də] *(contraction de de + le = du* [dy], *de + les = des* [de]) **1** *prép* [provenance] from; **revenir ~ Paris** to come back or return from Paris; **il est sorti ~ la maison** he left the house, he went out of the house. || [avec à]: **~ ... à** from ... to; **~ dix heures à midi** from ten o'clock to or till midday; **il y avait ~ quinze à vingt mille spectateurs** there were between fifteen and twenty thousand spectators. || [appartenance] of; **la porte du salon** the door of the sitting room, the sitting-room door; **le frère ~ Pierre** Pierre's brother. || [indique la détermination, la qualité]: **un verre d'eau** a glass of water; **un peignoir ~ soie** a silk dressing gown; **un bébé ~ trois jours** a three-day-old baby; **le train ~ 9 h 30** the 9.30 train. **2** *article partitif* [dans une phrase affirmative] some; **je voudrais du vin/du lait** I'd like (some) wine/(some) milk; **acheter des légumes** to buy some vegetables. || [dans une interrogation ou une négation] any; **ils n'ont pas d'enfants** they don't have any children, they have no children; **voulez-vous du thé?** would you like some tea?

dé [de] *nm* [à jouer] dice, die. || COUTURE: **~ (à coudre)** thimble.

DEA (*abr de* **diplôme d'études approfondies**) *nm* postgraduate diploma.

dealer[1] [dile] *vt* to deal.

dealer[2] [dilœr] *nm fam* dealer.

déambuler [deɑ̄byle] *vi* to stroll (around).

débâcle [debakl] *nf* [débandade] rout; *fig* collapse.

déballer [debale] *vt* to unpack; *fam fig* to pour out.

débandade [debɑ̄dad] *nf* dispersal.

débarbouiller [debarbuje] *vt*: **~ qqn** to wash sb's face. ○ **se débarbouiller** *vp* to wash one's face.

débarcadère [debarkadɛr] *nm* landing stage.

débardeur [debardœr] *nm* [ouvrier] docker. || [vêtement] slipover.

débarquer [debarke] **1** *vt* [marchandises] to unload; [passagers & MIL] to land. **2** *vi* [d'un bateau] to disembark. || MIL to land. || *fam* [arriver à l'improviste] to turn up; *fig* to know nothing.

débarras [debara] *nm* junk room; **bon ~!** *fig* good riddance!

débarrasser [debarase] *vt* [pièce] to clear up; [table] to clear. || [ôter]: **~ qqn de qqch** to take sthg from sb. ○ **se débarrasser** *vp*: **se ~ de** to get rid of.

débat [deba] *nm* debate.

débattre [debatr] *vt* to debate, to discuss. ○ **se débattre** *vp* to struggle.

débattu, -e [debaty] *pp* → **débattre**.

débauche [deboʃ] *nf* debauchery.

débaucher [deboʃe] *vt* [corrompre] to debauch, to corrupt. || [licencier] to make redundant.

débile [debil] **1** *nmf* [attardé] retarded person; **~ mental** mentally retarded person. || *fam* [idiot] moron. **2** *adj fam* stupid.

débit [debi] *nm* [de liquide] (rate of) flow. || FIN debit; **avoir un ~ de 500 francs** to be 500 francs overdrawn.

débiter [debite] *vt* [arbre] to saw up; [viande] to cut up. || *fam fig* [prononcer] to spout. || FIN to debit.

débiteur, -trice [debitœr, tris] **1** *adj* [personne] debtor (*avant n*). || FIN debit (*avant n*), in the red. **2** *nm, f* debtor.

déblayer [debleje] *vt* [dégager] to clear; **~ le terrain** *fig* to clear the ground.

débloquer [debloke] **1** *vt* [machine] to get going again. || [crédit] to release. ||

[compte, salaires, prix] to unfreeze. **2** *vi fam* to talk rubbish.

déboires [debwar] *nmpl* [déceptions] disappointments. || [échecs] setbacks.

déboiser [debwaze] *vt* [région] to deforest; [terrain] to clear (of trees).

déboîter [debwate] **1** *vt* [objet] to dislodge. || [membre] to dislocate. **2** *vi* AUTOM to pull out. ○ **se déboîter** *vp* [se démonter] to come apart. || [membre] to dislocate.

débonnaire [deboner] *adj* good-natured, easy-going.

déborder [deborde] *vi* [fleuve, liquide] to overflow; *fig* to flood; ~ **de** [vie, joie] to be bubbling with.

débouché [debuʃe] *nm* [issue] end. || (*gén pl*) COMM outlet. || [de carrière] prospect, opening.

déboucher [debuʃe] **1** *vt* [bouteille] to open. || [conduite, nez] to unblock. **2** *vi*: ~ **sur** [arriver] to open out into; *fig* to lead to, to achieve.

débourser [deburse] *vt* to pay out.

debout [dəbu] *adv* [gén]: **être** ~ [sur ses pieds] to be standing (up); [réveillé] to be up; [objet] to be standing up or upright; **mettre qqch** ~ to stand sthg up; **se mettre** ~ to stand up; ~**!** get up!, on your feet! || *loc*: **tenir** ~ [bâtiment] to remain standing; [argument] to stand up.

déboutonner [debutone] *vt* to unbutton, to undo.

débraillé, **-e** [debraje] *adj* dishevelled.

débrayer [debreje] *vi* AUTOM to disengage the clutch, to declutch.

débris [debri] *nm* piece, fragment.

débrouillard, **-e** [debrujar, ard] *fam adj* resourceful.

débrouiller [debruje] *vt* [démêler] to untangle. || *fig* [résoudre] to unravel, to solve. ○ **se débrouiller** *vp*: **se** ~ (**pour faire qqch**) to manage (to do sthg); **se** ~ **en anglais/math** to get by in English/maths; **débrouille-toi!** you'll have to sort it out (by) yourself!

débroussailler [debrusaje] *vt* [terrain] to clear; *fig* to do the groundwork for.

début [deby] *nm* beginning, start; **au** ~ **de** at the beginning of; **dès le** ~ (right) from the start.

débutant, **-e** [debytɑ̃, ɑ̃t] *nm, f* beginner.

débuter [debyte] *vi* [commencer]: ~ (**par**) to begin (with), to start (with). || [faire ses débuts] to start out.

deçà [dəsa] ○ **en deçà de** *loc prép* [de ce côté-ci de] on this side of. || [en dessous de] short of.

décacheter [dekaʃte] *vt* to open.

décadence [dekadɑ̃s] *nf* [déclin] decline. || [débauche] decadence.

décadent, **-e** [dekadɑ̃, ɑ̃t] *adj* decadent.

décaféiné, **-e** [dekafeine] *adj* decaffeinated. ○ **décaféiné** *nm* decaffeinated coffee.

décalage [dekalaʒ] *nm* gap; *fig* gulf, discrepancy; ~ **horaire** [entre zones] time difference; [après un vol] jet lag.

décaler [dekale] *vt* [dans le temps - avancer] to bring forward; [- retarder] to put back. || [dans l'espace] to move, to shift.

décalquer [dekalke] *vt* to trace.

décamper [dekɑ̃pe] *vi fam* to clear off.

décapant, **-e** [dekapɑ̃, ɑ̃t] *adj* [nettoyant] stripping. ○ **décapant** *nm* (paint) stripper.

décaper [dekape] *vt* to strip, to sand.

décapiter [dekapite] *vt* [personne] to behead; [- accidentellement] to decapitate.

décapotable [dekapɔtabl] *nf & adj* convertible.

décapsuler [dekapsyle] *vt* to take the top off, to open.

décapsuleur [dekapsylœr] *nm* bottle opener.

décédé, **-e** [desede] *adj* deceased.

décéder [desede] *vi* to die.

déceler [desle] *vt* [repérer] to detect.

décembre [desɑ̃br] *nm* December; *voir aussi* **septembre**.

décemment [desamɑ̃] *adv* [convenablement] properly. || [raisonnablement] reasonably.

décence [desɑ̃s] *nf* decency.

décennie [deseni] *nf* decade.

décent, **-e** [desɑ̃, ɑ̃t] *adj* decent.

décentralisation [desɑ̃tralizasjɔ̃] *nf* decentralization.

déception [desɛpsjɔ̃] *nf* disappointment.

décerner [deserne] *vt*: ~ **qqch à** to award sthg to.

décès [dese] *nm* death.

décevant, **-e** [desəvɑ̃, ɑ̃t] *adj* disappointing.

décevoir [desəvwar] *vt* to disappoint.

déchaîné, **-e** [deʃene] *adj* [vent, mer] stormy, wild. || [personne] wild.

déchaîner [deʃene] *vt* [passion] to unleash; [rires] to cause an outburst of.

○ **se déchaîner** *vp* [éléments naturels] to erupt. || [personne] to fly into a rage.

déchanter [deʃɑ̃te] *vi* to become disillusioned.

décharge [deʃaʀʒ] *nf* JUR discharge. || ÉLECTR discharge; ~ **électrique** electric shock. || [dépotoir] garbage dump *Am*.

déchargement [deʃaʀʒəmɑ̃] *nm* unloading.

décharger [deʃaʀʒe] *vt* [véhicule, marchandises] to unload. || [arme - tirer] to fire, to discharge; [- enlever la charge] to unload. || [soulager - conscience] to salve; [- colère] to vent. || [libérer]: ~ **qqn de** to release sb from.

décharné, -e [deʃaʀne] *adj* [maigre] emaciated.

déchausser [deʃose] *vt*: ~ **qqn** to take sb's shoes off. ○ **se déchausser** *vp* [personne] to take one's shoes off. || [dent] to come loose.

déchéance [deʃeɑ̃s] *nf* [déclin] degeneration, decline.

déchet [deʃɛ] *nm* [de matériau] scrap. ○ **déchets** *nmpl* refuse (*U*), waste (*U*).

déchiffrer [deʃifʀe] *vt* [inscription, hiéroglyphes] to decipher; [énigme] to unravel. || MUS to sight-read.

déchiqueter [deʃikte] *vt* to tear to shreds.

déchirant, -e [deʃiʀɑ̃, ɑ̃t] *adj* heartrending.

déchirement [deʃiʀmɑ̃] *nm* [souffrance morale] heartbreak, distress.

déchirer [deʃiʀe] *vt* [papier, tissu] to tear up, to rip up. ○ **se déchirer** *vp* [matériau, muscle] to tear.

déchirure [deʃiʀyʀ] *nf* tear; *fig* wrench; ~ **musculaire** MÉD torn muscle.

déchu, -e [deʃy] *adj* [homme, ange] fallen; [souverain] deposed. || JUR: **être ~ de** to be deprived of.

décibel [desibɛl] *nm* decibel.

décidé, -e [deside] *adj* [résolu] determined. || [arrêté] settled.

décidément [desidemɑ̃] *adv* really.

décider [deside] *vt* [prendre une décision]: ~ **(de faire qqch)** to decide (to do sthg). || [convaincre]: ~ **qqn à faire qqch** to persuade sb to do sthg. ○ **se décider** *vp* [personne]: **se ~ (à faire qqch)** to make up one's mind (to do sthg). || [choisir]: **se ~ pour** to decide on, to settle on.

décilitre [desilitʀ] *nm* decilitre.

décimal, -e, -aux [desimal, o] *adj* decimal. ○ **décimale** *nf* decimal.

décimer [desime] *vt* to decimate.

décimètre [desimɛtʀ] *nm* [dixième de mètre] decimetre. || [règle] ruler; **double ~ ≃ foot** rule.

décisif, -ive [desizif, iv] *adj* decisive.

décision [desizjɔ̃] *nf* decision.

déclamer [deklame] *vt* to declaim.

déclaration [deklaʀasjɔ̃] *nf* [orale] declaration, announcement. || [écrite] report, declaration; [d'assurance] claim; ~ **d'impôts** tax return; ~ **de revenus** statement of income.

déclarer [deklaʀe] *vt* [annoncer] to declare. || [signaler] to report; **rien à ~** nothing to declare; ~ **une naissance** to register a birth. ○ **se déclarer** *vp* [se prononcer]: **se ~ pour/contre qqch** to come out in favour of/against sthg. || [se manifester] to break out.

déclenchement [deklɑ̃ʃmɑ̃] *nm* [de mécanisme] activating, setting off.

déclencher [deklɑ̃ʃe] *vt* [mécanisme] to activate, to set off; *fig* to launch. ○ **se déclencher** *vp* [mécanisme] to go off, to be activated; *fig* to be triggered off.

déclic [deklik] *nm* [bruit] click.

déclin [deklɛ̃] *nm* [de civilisation, population, santé] decline. || [fin] close.

déclinaison [deklinɛzɔ̃] *nf* GRAM declension.

décliner [dekline] **1** *vi* [santé, population, popularité] to decline. **2** *vt* [offre, honneur] to decline. || GRAM to decline.

décoder [dekode] *vt* to decode.

décoiffer [dekwafe] *vt* [cheveux] to mess up.

décoincer [dekwɛse] *vt* [chose] to loosen; [mécanisme] to unjam. || *fam* [personne] to loosen up.

décollage [dekolaʒ] *nm litt & fig* take-off.

décoller [dekole] **1** *vt* [étiquette, timbre] to unstick; [papier peint] to strip (off). **2** *vi litt & fig* to take off.

décolleté, -e [dekolte] *adj* [vêtement] low-cut. ○ **décolleté** *nm* [de personne] neck and shoulders (*pl*). || [de vêtement] neckline, neck.

décolonisation [dekolonizasjɔ̃] *nf* decolonization.

décolorer [dekolɔʀe] *vt* [par décolorant] to bleach, to lighten; [par usure] to fade.

décombres [dekɔ̃bʀ] *nmpl* debris (*U*).

décommander [dekomɑ̃de] *vt* to cancel.

décomposé, -e [dekɔ̃poze] *adj* [pourri] decomposed. || [visage] haggard; [personne] in shock.

décomposer [dekɔ̃poze] *vt* [gén]: ~ (en) to break down (into). ○ **se décomposer** *vp* [se putréfier] to rot, to decompose. || [se diviser]: **se ~ en** to be broken down into.

décomposition [dekɔ̃pozisjɔ̃] *nf* [putréfaction] decomposition.

décompresser [dekɔ̃prese] **1** *vt* TECHNOL to decompress. **2** *vi* to unwind.

décompte [dekɔ̃t] *nm* [calcul] breakdown (of an amount).

déconcentrer [dekɔ̃sɑ̃tre] *vt* [distraire] to distract. ○ **se déconcentrer** *vp* to be distracted.

déconcerter [dekɔ̃sɛrte] *vt* to disconcert.

déconfiture [dekɔ̃fityr] *nf* collapse, ruin.

décongeler [dekɔ̃ʒle] *vt* to defrost.

décongestionner [dekɔ̃ʒɛstjɔne] *vt* to relieve congestion in.

déconnecter [dekɔnɛkte] *vt* to disconnect.

déconseillé, -e [dekɔ̃seje] *adj*: **c'est fortement ~** it's extremely inadvisable.

déconseiller [dekɔ̃seje] *vt*: **~ qqch à qqn** to advise sb against sthg; **~ à qqn de faire qqch** to advise sb against doing sthg.

déconsidérer [dekɔ̃sidere] *vt* to discredit.

décontaminer [dekɔ̃tamine] *vt* to decontaminate.

décontenancer [dekɔ̃tnɑ̃se] *vt* to put out.

décontracté, -e [dekɔ̃trakte] *adj* [détendu] casual, laid-back.

décontracter [dekɔ̃trakte] *vt* to relax. ○ **se décontracter** *vp* to relax.

décor [dekɔr] *nm* [cadre] scenery. || THÉÂTRE scenery (*U*); CIN sets (*pl*), décor.

décorateur, -trice [dekɔratœr, tris] *nm*, *f* CIN & THÉÂTRE designer; **~ d'intérieur** interior decorator.

décoratif, -ive [dekɔratif, iv] *adj* decorative.

décoration [dekɔrasjɔ̃] *nf* decoration.

décorer [dekɔre] *vt* to decorate.

décortiquer [dekɔrtike] *vt* [noix] to shell; [graine] to husk; *fig* to analyse in minute detail.

découcher [dekuʃe] *vi* to stay out all night.

découdre [dekudr] *vt* COUTURE to unpick.

découler [dekule] *vi*: **~ de** to follow from.

découpage [dekupaʒ] *nm* [action] cutting out; [résultat] paper cutout.

découper [dekupe] *vt* [couper] to cut up. || *fig* [diviser] to cut out.

découragement [dekuraʒmɑ̃] *nm* discouragement.

décourager [dekuraʒe] *vt* to discourage; **~ qqn de qqch** to put sb off sthg; **~ qqn de faire qqch** to discourage sb from doing sthg. ○ **se décourager** *vp* to lose heart.

décousu, -e [dekuzy] **1** *pp* → découdre. **2** *adj fig* [conversation] disjointed.

découvert, -e [dekuvɛr, ɛrt] **1** *pp* → découvrir. **2** *adj* [tête] bare; [terrain] exposed. ○ **découvert** *nm* BANQUE overdraft; **être à ~ (de 6 000 francs)** to be (6,000 francs) overdrawn. ○ **découverte** *nf* discovery; **aller à la ~e de** to explore.

découvrir [dekuvrir] *vt* [trouver, surprendre] to discover. || [ôter ce qui couvre, mettre à jour] to uncover.

décrasser [dekrase] *vt* to scrub.

décret [dekrɛ] *nm* decree.

décréter [dekrete] *vt* [décider]: **~ que** to decide that.

décrire [dekrir] *vt* to describe.

décrit, -e [dekri, it] *pp* → décrire.

décrocher [dekrɔʃe] **1** *vt* [enlever] to take down. || [téléphone] to pick up. || *fam* [obtenir] to land. **2** *vi fam* [abandonner] to drop out.

décroître [dekrwatr] *vi* to decrease, to diminish; [jours] to get shorter.

décrypter [dekripte] *vt* to decipher.

déçu, -e [desy] **1** *pp* → décevoir. **2** *adj* disappointed.

dédaigner [dedeɲe] *vt* [mépriser - personne] to despise; [- conseils, injures] to scorn.

dédaigneux, -euse [dedɛɲø, øz] *adj* disdainful.

dédain [dedɛ̃] *nm* disdain, contempt.

dédale [dedal] *nm litt & fig* maze.

dedans [dədɑ̃] *adv & nm* inside. ○ **en dedans** *loc adv* inside, within. ○ **en dedans de** *loc prép* inside, within; *voir aussi* là-dedans.

dédicace [dedikas] *nf* dedication.

dédicacer [dedikase] *vt*: **~ qqch (à qqn)** to sign ou autograph sthg (for sb).

dédier [dedje] *vt*: **~ qqch (à qqn/à qqch)** to dedicate sthg (to sb/to sthg).

dédire [dedir] ○ **se dédire** *vp sout* to go back on one's word.

dédommagement [dedɔmaʒmɑ̃] *nm* compensation.

dédommager [dedɔmaʒe] *vt* [indemniser] to compensate. || *fig* [remercier] to repay.

dédouaner [dedwane] *vt* [marchandises] to clear through customs.

dédoubler [deduble] *vt* to halve, to split; [fil] to separate.

déduction [dedyksjɔ̃] *nf* deduction.

déduire [dedɥir] *vt*: ~ qqch (de) [ôter] to deduct sthg (from); [conclure] to deduce sthg (from).

déduit, -e [dedɥi, ɥit] *pp* → **déduire**.

déesse [deɛs] *nf* goddess.

défaillance [defajɑ̃s] *nf* [incapacité - de machine] failure; [- de personne, organisation] weakness. || [malaise] blackout, fainting fit.

défaillant, e [defajɑ̃, ɑ̃t] *adj* [faible] failing.

défaillir [defajir] *vi* [s'évanouir] to faint.

défaire [defɛr] *vt* [détacher] to undo; [valise] to unpack; [lit] to strip. ○ **se défaire** *vp* [ne pas tenir] to come undone. || *sout* [se séparer]: **se ~ de** to get rid of.

défait, -e [defɛ, ɛt] 1 *pp* → **défaire**. 2 *adj fig* [épuisé] haggard. ○ **défaite** *nf* defeat.

défaitiste [defetist] *nmf & adj* defeatist.

défaut [defo] *nm* [imperfection] flaw; [- de personne] fault, shortcoming; ~ de fabrication manufacturing fault. || [manque] lack; à ~ de for lack of want of; l'eau fait (cruellement) ~ there is a (serious) water shortage.

défavorable [defavɔrabl] *adj* unfavourable.

défavoriser [defavɔrize] *vt* to handicap, to penalize.

défection [defɛksjɔ̃] *nf* [absence] absence. || [abandon] defection.

défectueux, -euse [defɛktɥø, øz] *adj* faulty, defective.

défendeur, -eresse [defɑ̃dœr, rɛs] *nm, f* défendant.

défendre [defɑ̃dr] *vt* [personne, opinion, client] to defend. || [interdire] to forbid; ~ qqch à qqn to forbid sb sthg; ~ à qqn de faire qqch to forbid sb to do sthg; ~ que qqn fasse qqch to forbid sb to do sthg. ○ **se défendre** *vp* [se battre, se justifier] to defend o.s. || [nier] to deny doing sthg. || [thèse] to stand up.

défendu, -e [defɑ̃dy] 1 *pp* → **défendre**.

2 *adj*: «il est ~ de jouer au ballon» "no ball games".

défense [defɑ̃s] *nf* [d'éléphant] tusk. || [interdiction] prohibition, ban; «~ de fumer/de stationner/d'entrer» "no smoking/parking/entry"; «~ d'afficher» "stick no bills". || [protection] defence; prendre la ~ de to stand up for; légitime ~ JUR self-defence.

défenseur [defɑ̃sœr] *nm* [partisan] champion.

défensif, -ive [defɑ̃sif, iv] *adj* defensive. ○ **défensive** *nf*: être sur la défensive to be on the defensive.

déférence [deferɑ̃s] *nf* deference.

déferlement [defɛrləmɑ̃] *nm* [de vagues] breaking; *fig* surge, upsurge.

déferler [defɛrle] *vi* [vagues] to break; *fig* to surge.

défi [defi] *nm* challenge.

défiance [defjɑ̃s] *nf* distrust, mistrust.

déficience [defisjɑ̃s] *nf* deficiency.

déficit [defisit] *nm* FIN deficit.

déficitaire [defisiter] *adj* in deficit.

défier [defje] *vt* [braver]: ~ qqn de faire qqch to defy sb to do sthg.

défigurer [defigyre] *vt* [blesser] to disfigure. || [enlaidir] to deface.

défilé [defile] *nm* [parade] parade. || [couloir] defile, narrow pass.

défiler [defile] *vi* [dans une parade] to march past. || [se succéder] to pass. ○ **se défiler** *vp fam* to back out.

défini, -e [defini] *adj* [précis] clear, precise. || GRAM definite.

définir [definir] *vt* to define.

définitif, -ive [definitif, iv] *adj* definitive, final. ○ **en définitive** *loc adv* in the end.

définition [definisjɔ̃] *nf* definition.

définitivement [definitivmɑ̃] *adv* for good, permanently.

défoncer [defɔ̃se] *vt* [caisse, porte] to smash in; [route] to break up; [mur] to smash down; [chaise] to break.

déformation [defɔrmasjɔ̃] *nf* [d'objet, de théorie] distortion. || MÉD deformity; ~ professionnelle *mental conditioning caused by one's job*.

déformer [defɔrme] *vt* to distort. ○ **se déformer** *vp* [changer de forme] to be distorted, to be deformed; [se courber] to bend.

défouler [defule] *vt fam* to unwind. ○ **se défouler** *vp fam* to let off steam, to unwind.

défricher [defriʃe] vt [terrain] to clear; fig [question] to do the groundwork for.

défunt, -e [defœ̃, œ̃t] **1** adj [décédé] late. **2** nm, f deceased.

dégagé, -e [degaʒe] adj [ciel, vue] clear; [partie du corps] bare. || [désinvolte] casual, airy. || [libre]: ~ **de** free from.

dégager [degaʒe] **1** vt [odeur] to produce, to give off. || [délivrer - blessé] to free, to extricate. || [pièce] to clear. || [libérer]: ~ **qqn de** to release sb from. **2** vi fam [partir] to clear off. ○ **se dégager** vp [se délivrer]: **se ~ de qqch** to free o.s. from sthg; fig to get out of sthg. || [émaner] to be given off. || [émerger] to emerge.

dégarnir [degarnir] vt to strip, to clear. ○ **se dégarnir** vp [vitrine] to be cleared; [arbre] to lose its leaves; **il se dégarnit** he's going bald.

dégât [dega] nm litt & fig damage (U); **faire des ~s** to cause damage.

dégel [deʒɛl] nm [fonte des glaces] thaw.

dégeler [deʒle] **1** vt [produit surgelé] to thaw. **2** vi to thaw.

dégénéré, -e [deʒenere] adj & nm, f degenerate.

dégénérer [deʒenere] vi to degenerate; ~ **en** to degenerate into.

dégivrer [deʒivre] vt [pare-brise] to de-ice; [réfrigérateur] to defrost.

dégonfler [degɔ̃fle] **1** vt to deflate, to let down. **2** vi to go down. ○ **se dégonfler** vp [objet] to go down. || fam [personne] to chicken out.

dégouliner [deguline] vi to trickle.

dégourdi, -e [degurdi] adj clever.

dégourdir [degurdir] vt [membres - ankylosés] to restore the circulation to. || fig [déniaiser]: ~ **qqn** to teach sb a thing or two. ○ **se dégourdir** vp [membres]: **se ~ les jambes** to stretch one's legs. || fig [acquérir de l'aisance] to learn a thing or two.

dégoût [degu] nm disgust, distaste.

dégoûtant, -e [degutã, ãt] adj [sale] filthy, disgusting. || [révoltant, grossier] disgusting.

dégoûter [degute] vt to disgust.

dégradé, -e [degrade] adj [couleur] shading off. ○ **dégradé** nm gradation; **un ~ de bleu** a blue shading. ○ **en dégradé** loc adv [cheveux] layered.

dégrader [degrade] vt [officier] to degrade. || [abîmer] to damage. || fig [avilir] to degrade, to debase. ○ **se dégrader**

vp [bâtiment, santé] to deteriorate. || fig [personne] to degrade o.s.

dégrafer [degrafe] vt to undo, to unfasten.

degré [dəgre] nm [gén] degree; ~**s centigrades** ou **Celsius** degrees centigrade ou Celsius; **prendre qqn/qqch au premier ~** to take sb/sthg at face value.

dégressif, -ive [degresif, iv] adj: **tarif** ~ decreasing price scale.

dégringoler [degrɛ̃gɔle] fam vi [tomber] to tumble; fig to crash.

déguerpir [degɛrpir] vi to clear off.

dégueulasse [degœlas] tfam **1** adj [très sale, grossier] filthy. || [révoltant] dirty, rotten. **2** nmf scum (U).

dégueuler [degœle] vi fam to throw up.

déguisement [degizmã] nm disguise; [pour bal masqué] fancy dress.

déguiser [degize] vt to disguise. ○ **se déguiser** vp: **se ~ en** [pour tromper] to disguise o.s. as; [pour s'amuser] to dress up as.

dégustation [degystasjɔ̃] nf tasting, sampling; ~ **de vin** wine tasting.

déguster [degyste] **1** vt [savourer] to taste, to sample. **2** vi fam [subir]: **il va ~!** he'll be for it!

déhancher [deãʃe] ○ **se déhancher** vp [en marchant] to swing one's hips.

dehors [dəɔr] **1** adv outside; **aller ~** to go outside; **dormir ~** to sleep out of doors, to sleep out; **jeter** ou **mettre qqn ~** to throw sb out. **2** nm outside. **3** nmpl: **les ~** [les apparences] appearances. ○ **en dehors** loc adv outside, outwards. ○ **en dehors de** loc prép [excepté] apart from.

déjà [deʒa] adv [dès cet instant] already. || [précédemment] already, before. || [au fait]: **quel est ton nom ~?** what did you say your name was? || [renforce une affirmation]: **ce n'est ~ pas si mal** that's not bad at all.

déjeuner [deʒœne] **1** vi [le matin] to have breakfast. || [à midi] to have lunch. **2** nm [repas de midi] lunch. || Can [dîner] dinner.

déjouer [deʒwe] vt to frustrate; ~ **la surveillance de qqn** to elude sb's surveillance.

delà [dəla] ○ **au-delà de** loc prép beyond.

délabré, -e [delabre] adj ruined.

délacer [delase] vt to unlace, to undo.

délai [delɛ] nm [temps accordé] period; **sans ~** immediately, without delay; ~ **de**

livraison delivery time, lead time. || [sursis] extension (of deadline).

délaisser [delese] vt [abandonner] to leave. || [négliger] to neglect.

délasser [delase] vt to refresh. ○ **se délasser** vp to relax.

délation [delasjɔ̃] nf informing.

délavé, -e [delave] adj faded.

délayer [deleje] vt [diluer]: ~ **qqch dans qqch** to mix sthg with sthg.

délecter [delɛkte] ○ **se délecter** vp: **se ~ de qqch/à faire qqch** to delight in sthg/in doing sthg.

délégation [delegasjɔ̃] nf delegation.

délégué, -e [delege] **1** adj [personne] delegated. **2** nm, f [représentant]: **~ (à)** delegate (to).

déléguer [delege] vt: **~ qqn (à qqch)** to delegate sb (to sthg).

délester [delɛste] vt [circulation routière] to set up a diversion on, to divert.

délibération [deliberasjɔ̃] nf deliberation.

délibéré, -e [delibere] adj [intentionnel] deliberate. || [résolu] determined.

délibérer [delibere] vi: **~ (de ou sur)** to deliberate (on ou over).

délicat, -e [delika, at] adj [gén] delicate. || [exigeant] fussy, difficult.

délicatement [delikatmɑ̃] adv delicately.

délicatesse [delikatɛs] nf [gén] delicacy. || [tact] delicacy, tact.

délice [delis] nm delight.

délicieux, -ieuse [delisjø, jøz] adj [savoureux] delicious. || [agréable] delightful.

délié, -e [delje] adj [doigts] nimble.

délier [delje] vt to untie.

délimiter [delimite] vt [frontière] to fix; fig [question, domaine] to define, to demarcate.

délinquance [delɛ̃kɑ̃s] nf delinquency.

délinquant, -e [delɛ̃kɑ̃, ɑ̃t] nm, f delinquent.

délirant, -e [delirɑ̃, ɑ̃t] adj MÉD delirious. || [extravagant] frenzied. || fam [extraordinaire] crazy.

délire [delir] nm MÉD delirium.

délirer [delire] vi MÉD to be ou become delirious; fam fig to rave.

délit [deli] nm crime, offence; **en flagrant ~** red-handed, in the act.

délivrance [delivrɑ̃s] nf [soulagement] relief. || [accouchement] delivery.

délivrer [delivre] vt [prisonnier] to free, to release. || [pays] to deliver, to free; **~**

de to free from; fig to relieve from. || [remettre]: **~ qqch (à qqn)** to issue sthg (to sb). || [marchandise] to deliver.

déloger [delɔʒe] vt: **~ (de)** to dislodge (from).

déloyal, -e, -aux [delwajal, o] adj [infidèle] disloyal. || [malhonnête] unfair.

delta [dɛlta] nm delta.

deltaplane, delta-plane (pl **deltaplanes**) [dɛltaplan] nm hang glider.

déluge [delyʒ] nm RELIG: **le Déluge** the Flood. || [pluie] downpour, deluge; **un ~ de** fig a flood of.

déluré, -e [delyre] adj [malin] quick-witted; péj [dévergondé] saucy.

démagogie [demagɔʒi] nf pandering to public opinion, demagogy.

demain [dəmɛ̃] **1** adv [le jour suivant] tomorrow; **~ matin** tomorrow morning. || fig [plus tard] in the future. **2** nm tomorrow; **à ~!** see you tomorrow!

demande [dəmɑ̃d] nf [souhait] request. || [démarche] proposal; **~ en mariage** proposal of marriage. || [candidature] application; **~ d'emploi** job application; **«~s d'emploi»** "situations wanted". || ÉCON demand.

demandé, -e [dəmɑ̃de] adj in demand.

demander [dəmɑ̃de] **1** vt [réclamer, s'enquérir] to ask for; **~ qqch à qqn** to ask sb for sthg. || [appeler] to call; **on vous demande à la réception/au téléphone** you're wanted at reception/on the telephone. || [désirer] to ask, to want. || [exiger]: **tu m'en demandes trop** you're asking too much of me. || [nécessiter] to require. **2** vi [réclamer]: **~ à qqn de faire qqch** to ask sb to do sthg; **ne ~ qu'à ...** to be ready to .... || [nécessiter]: **ce projet demande à être étudié** this project requires investigation ou needs investigating. ○ **se demander** vp: **se ~ (si)** to wonder (if ou whether).

demandeur, -euse [dəmɑ̃dœr, øz] nm, f [solliciteur]: **~ d'emploi** job-seeker.

démangeaison [demɑ̃ʒɛzɔ̃] nf [irritation] itch, itching (U); fam fig urge.

démanger [demɑ̃ʒe] vi [gratter] to itch; **ça me démange de ...** fig I'm itching ou dying to ....

démanteler [demɑ̃tle] vt [construction] to demolish; fig to break up.

démaquillant, -e [demakijɑ̃, ɑ̃t] adj make-up-removing (avant n). ○ **démaquillant** nm make-up remover.

démaquiller [demakije] *vt* to remove make-up from. ○ **se démaquiller** *vp* to remove one's make-up.

démarche [demarʃ] *nf* [manière de marcher] gait, walk. || [raisonnement] approach, method. || [requête] step; **faire les ~s pour faire qqch** to take the necessary steps to do sthg.

démarcheur, -euse [demarʃœr, øz] *nm, f* [représentant] door-to-door salesman (*f* saleswoman).

démarquer [demarke] *vt* [solder] to mark down. ○ **se démarquer** *vp fig* [se distinguer]: **se ~ (de)** to distinguish o.s. (from).

démarrage [demaraʒ] *nm* starting, start; **~ en côte** hill start.

démarrer [demare] **1** *vi* [véhicule] to start (up); [conducteur] to drive off. || *fig* [affaire, projet] to get off the ground. **2** *vt* [véhicule] to start (up). || *fam fig* [commencer]: **~ qqch** to get sthg going.

démarreur [demarœr] *nm* starter.

démasquer [demaske] *vt* [personne] to unmask. || *fig* [complot, plan] to unveil.

démêlant, -e [demɛlɑ̃, ɑ̃t] *adj* conditioning (*avant n*). ○ **démêlant** *nm* conditioner.

démêlé [demɛle] *nm* quarrel; **avoir des ~s avec la justice** to get into trouble with the law.

démêler [demɛle] *vt* [cheveux, fil] to untangle; *fig* to unravel. ○ **se démêler** *vp*: **se ~ de** *fig* to extricate o.s. from.

déménagement [demenaʒmɑ̃] *nm* removal.

déménager [demenaʒe] **1** *vt* to move. **2** *vi* to move (house).

déménageur [demenaʒœr] *nm* mover *Am*.

démence [demɑ̃s] *nf* MÉD dementia; [bêtise] madness.

démener [demne] ○ **se démener** *vp litt & fig* to struggle.

dément, -e [demɑ̃, ɑ̃t] **1** *adj* MÉD demented; *fam* [extraordinaire, extravagant] crazy. **2** *nm, f* demented person.

démenti [demɑ̃ti] *nm* denial.

démentiel, -ielle [demɑ̃sjɛl] *adj* MÉD demented; *fam* [incroyable] crazy.

démentir [demɑ̃tir] *vt* [réfuter] to deny. || [contredire] to contradict.

démesure [deməzyr] *nf* excess, immoderation.

démettre [demɛtr] *vt* MÉD to put out (of joint). || [congédier]: **~ qqn de** to dismiss sb from. ○ **se démettre** *vp* MÉD: **se ~**

l'épaule to put one's shoulder out (of joint).

demeurant [dəmœrɑ̃] ○ **au demeurant** *loc adv* all things considered.

demeure [dəmœr] *nf sout* [domicile, habitation] residence. ○ **à demeure** *loc adv* permanently.

demeuré, -e [dəmœre] **1** *adj* simple, half-witted. **2** *nm, f* half-wit.

demeurer [dəmœre] *vi* (*aux: avoir*) [habiter] to live. || (*aux: être*) [rester] to remain.

demi, -e [dəmi] *adj* half; **un kilo et ~** one and a half kilos; **il est une heure et ~e** it's half past one; **à ~** half; **ouvrir à ~** to half-open; **faire les choses à ~** to do things by halves. ○ **demi** *nm* [bière] beer. || FOOTBALL midfielder.

demi-cercle [dəmisɛrkl] (*pl* **demi-cercles**) *nm* semicircle.

demi-douzaine [dəmiduzɛn] (*pl* **demi-douzaines**) *nf* half-dozen; **une ~ (de)** half a dozen.

demi-finale [dəmifinal] (*pl* **demi-finales**) *nf* semifinal.

demi-frère [dəmifrɛr] (*pl* **demi-frères**) *nm* half-brother.

demi-heure [dəmijœr] (*pl* **demi-heures**) *nf* half an hour, half-hour.

demi-journée [dəmiʒurne] (*pl* **demi-journées**) *nf* half a day, half-day.

demi-litre [dəmilitr] (*pl* **demi-litres**) *nm* half a litre, half-litre.

demi-mot [dəmimo] ○ **à demi-mot** *loc adv*: **comprendre à ~** to understand without things having to be spelled out.

déminer [demine] *vt* to clear of mines.

demi-pension [dəmipɑ̃sjɔ̃] (*pl* **demi-pensions**) *nf* [d'hôtel] half-board. || [d'école]: **être en ~** to take school dinners (*pl*).

démis, -e [demi, iz] *pp* → **démettre**.

demi-sœur [dəmisœr] (*pl* **demi-sœurs**) *nf* half-sister.

démission [demisjɔ̃] *nf* resignation.

démissionner [demisjɔne] *vi* [d'un emploi] to resign; *fig* to give up.

demi-tarif [dəmitarif] (*pl* **demi-tarifs**) **1** *adj* half-price. **2** *nm* [tarification] half-fare. || [billet] half-price ticket.

demi-tour [dəmitur] (*pl* **demi-tours**) *nm* [gén] half-turn; **faire ~** to turn back.

démocrate [demɔkrat] *nmf* democrat.

démocratie [demɔkrasi] *nf* democracy.

démocratique [demɔkratik] *adj* democratic.

démocratiser [demɔkratize] *vt* to democratize.

démodé, -e [demɔde] *adj* old-fashioned.

démographique [demɔgrafik] *adj* demographic.

demoiselle [dəmwazɛl] *nf* [jeune fille] maid; ~ **d'honneur** bridesmaid.

démolir [demɔlir] *vt* [gén] to demolish.

démolition [demɔlisjɔ̃] *nf* demolition.

démon [demɔ̃] *nm* [diable, personne] devil, demon; **le ~** RELIG the Devil.

démoniaque [demɔnjak] *adj* [diabolique] diabolical.

démonstratif, -ive [demɔ̃stratif, iv] *adj* [personne & GRAM] demonstrative. ○ **démonstratif** *nm* GRAM demonstrative.

démonstration [demɔ̃strasjɔ̃] *nf* [gén] demonstration.

démonter [demɔ̃te] *vt* [appareil] to dismantle, to take apart. || [troubler]: ~ **qqn** to put sb out. ○ **se démonter** *vp fam* to be put out.

démontrer [demɔ̃tre] *vt* [prouver] to prove, to demonstrate. || [témoigner de] to show, to demonstrate.

démoralisant, -e [demɔralizɑ̃, ɑ̃t] *adj* demoralizing.

démoraliser [demɔralize] *vt* to demoralize. ○ **se démoraliser** *vp* to lose heart.

démordre [demɔrdr] *vt*: **ne pas ~ de** to stick to.

démotiver [demɔtive] *vt* to demotivate.

démouler [demule] *vt* to turn out of a mould, to remove from a mould.

démunir [demynir] *vt* to deprive.

dénaturer [denatyre] *vt* [goût] to impair, to mar. || [déformer] to distort.

dénégation [denegasjɔ̃] *nf* denial.

dénicher [deniʃe] *vt fig* [personne] to flush out. || *fam* [objet] to unearth.

dénigrer [denigre] *vt* to denigrate, to run down.

dénivelé [denivle] *nm* difference in level or height.

dénivellation [denivɛlasjɔ̃] *nf* [différence de niveau] difference in height or level. || [pente] slope.

dénombrer [denɔ̃bre] *vt* [compter] to count; [énumérer] to enumerate.

dénominateur [denɔminatœr] *nm* denominator.

dénomination [denɔminasjɔ̃] *nf* name.

dénommé, -e [denɔme] *adj*: **un ~ Robert** someone by the name of Robert.

dénoncer [denɔ̃se] *vt* [gén] to denounce; ~ **qqn à qqn** to denounce sb to sb, to inform on sb. || *fig* [trahir] to betray.

dénonciation [denɔ̃sjasjɔ̃] *nf* denunciation.

dénoter [denɔte] *vt* to show, to indicate.

dénouement [denumɑ̃] *nm* [issue] outcome. || CIN & THÉÂTRE denouement.

dénouer [denwe] *vt* [nœud] to untie, to undo; *fig* to unravel.

dénoyauter [denwajote] *vt* [fruit] to stone.

denrée [dɑ̃re] *nf* [produit] produce (*U*); ~**s alimentaires** foodstuffs.

dense [dɑ̃s] *adj* [gén] dense. || [style] condensed.

densité [dɑ̃site] *nf* density.

dent [dɑ̃] *nf* [de personne, d'objet] tooth; ~ **de lait/de sagesse** milk/wisdom tooth.

dentaire [dɑ̃tɛr] *adj* dental.

dentelé, -e [dɑ̃tle] *adj* serrated, jagged.

dentelle [dɑ̃tɛl] *nf* lace (*U*).

dentier [dɑ̃tje] *nm* [dents] dentures (*pl*).

dentifrice [dɑ̃tifris] *nm* toothpaste.

dentiste [dɑ̃tist] *nmf* dentist.

dentition [dɑ̃tisjɔ̃] *nf* teeth (*pl*), dentition.

dénuder [denyde] *vt* to leave bare; [fil électrique] to strip.

dénué, -e [denɥe] *adj sout*: ~ **de** devoid of.

dénuement [denymɑ̃] *nm* destitution (*U*).

déodorant, -e [deɔdɔrɑ̃, ɑ̃t] *adj* deodorant. ○ **déodorant** *nm* deodorant.

déontologie [deɔ̃tɔlɔʒi] *nf* professional ethics (*pl*).

dépannage [depanaʒ] *nm* repair.

dépanner [depane] *vt* [réparer] to repair, to fix. || *fam* [aider] to bail out.

dépanneur, -euse [depanœr, øz] *nm, f* repairman (*f* repairwoman). ○ **dépanneuse** *nf* [véhicule] (breakdown) recovery vehicle.

dépareillé, -e [depareje] *adj* [ensemble] non-matching; [paire] odd.

départ [depar] *nm* [de personne] departure, leaving; [de véhicule] departure. || SPORT & *fig* start. ○ **au départ** *loc adv* to start with.

départager [departaʒe] *vt* [concurrents, opinions] to decide between.

département [departəmɑ̃] *nm* [territoire] *territorial and administrative division of France.* || [service] department.

départemental, -e, -aux [departəmɑ̃tal, o] *adj* of a French département. ○ **départementale** *nf* ≃ secondary road.

dépassé, -e [depase] *adj* [périmé] old-fashioned. || *fam* [déconcerté]: ~ **par** overwhelmed by.

dépassement [depasmɑ̃] *nm* [en voiture] overtaking.

dépasser [depase] **1** *vt* [doubler] to overtake. || [être plus grand que] to be taller than. || [excéder] to exceed, to be more than. || [aller au-delà de] to exceed. || [franchir] to pass. **2** *vi*: ~ **(de)** to stick out (from).

dépayser [depeize] *vt* [désorienter] to disorient *Am.* || [changer agréablement] to make a change of scene for.

dépecer [depase] *vt* [découper] to chop up. || [déchiqueter] to tear apart.

dépêche [depɛʃ] *nf* dispatch.

dépêcher [depeʃe] *vt sout* [envoyer] to dispatch. ○ **se dépêcher** *vp* to hurry up; se ~ **de faire qqch** to hurry to do sthg.

dépeindre [depɛ̃dr] *vt* to depict, to describe.

dépeint, -e [depɛ̃, ɛt] *pp* → **dépeindre**.

dépendance [depɑ̃dɑ̃s] *nf* [de personne] dependence. || [à la drogue] dependency. || [de bâtiment] outbuilding.

dépendre [depɑ̃dr] *vt* [être soumis]: ~ **de** to depend on; **ça dépend** it depends. || [appartenir]: ~ **de** to belong to.

dépens [depɑ̃] *nmpl* JUR costs; aux ~ **de qqn** at sb's expense; **je l'ai appris à mes** ~ I learned that to my cost.

dépense [depɑ̃s] *nf* [frais] expense. || FIN & *fig* expenditure (*U*); **les** ~s **publiques** public spending (*U*).

dépenser [depɑ̃se] *vt* [argent] to spend. || *fig* [énergie] to expend. ○ **se dépenser** *vp litt & fig* to exert o.s.

dépensier, -ière [depɑ̃sje, jɛr] *adj* extravagant.

déperdition [deperdisjɔ̃] *nf* loss.

dépérir [deperir] *vi* [personne] to waste away. || [plante] to wither.

dépeupler [depœple] *vt* [pays] to depopulate. || [étang, rivière, forêt] to drive the wildlife from.

déphasé, -e [defaze] *adj* ÉLECTR out of phase; *fam fig* out of touch.

dépilatoire [depilatwar] *adj*: **crème/lotion** ~ depilatory cream/lotion.

dépistage [depistaʒ] *nm* [de maladie] screening; ~ **du SIDA** AIDS testing.

dépister [depiste] *vt* [gibier, voleur] to track down. || [maladie] to screen for.

dépit [depi] *nm* pique, spite. ○ **en dépit de** *loc prép* in spite of.

déplacé, -e [deplase] *adj* [propos, attitude, présence] out of place.

déplacement [deplasmɑ̃] *nm* [d'objet] moving. || [voyage] travelling (*U*).

déplacer [deplase] *vt* [objet] to move, to shift. || [muter] to transfer. ○ **se déplacer** *vp* [se mouvoir - animal] to move (around); [- personne] to walk. || [voyager] to travel. || MÉD: se ~ **une vertèbre** to slip a disc.

déplaire [depler] *vt* [ne pas plaire]: **cela me déplaît** I don't like it.

déplaisant, -e [deplezɑ̃, ɑ̃t] *adj sout* unpleasant.

dépliant [deplijɑ̃] *nm* leaflet; ~ **touristique** tourist brochure.

déplier [deplije] *vt* to unfold.

déploiement [deplwamɑ̃] *nm* MIL deployment. || [d'ailes] spreading. || *fig* [d'efforts] display.

déplorer [deplɔre] *vt* [regretter] to deplore.

déployer [deplwaje] *vt* [déplier - gén] to unfold; [- plan, journal] to open; [ailes] to spread. || MIL to deploy. || [mettre en œuvre] to expend.

déplu [deply] *pp inv* → **déplaire**.

déportation [depɔrtasjɔ̃] *nf* [internement] transportation to a concentration camp.

déporté, -e [depɔrte] *nm, f* [interné] prisoner (*in a concentration camp*).

déporter [depɔrte] *vt* [dévier] to carry off course. || [interner] to send to a concentration camp.

déposer [depoze] **1** *vt* [poser] to put down. || [personne, paquet] to drop. || [argent, sédiment] to deposit. || JUR to file; ~ **son bilan** FIN to go into liquidation. **2** *vi* JUR to testify, to give evidence. ○ **se déposer** *vp* to settle.

dépositaire [depoziter] *nmf* COMM agent. || [d'objet] bailee; ~ **de** *fig* person entrusted with.

déposition [depozisjɔ̃] *nf* deposition.

déposséder [deposede] *vt*: ~ **qqn de** to dispossess sb of.

dépôt [depo] *nm* [d'objet, d'argent, de sédiment] deposit, depositing (*U*); **verser**

un ~ **(de garantie)** to put down a deposit; ~ **d'ordures** (rubbish) dump *Br*, garbage dump *Am*. ‖ [garage] depot. ‖ [entrepôt] store, warehouse. ‖ [prison] ≃ police cells (*pl*).

dépotoir [depɔtwar] *nm* [décharge] garbage dump *Am*; *fam fig* dump, tip.

dépouille [depuj] *nf* [peau] hide, skin. ‖ [humaine] remains (*pl*).

dépouillement [depujmɑ̃] *nm* [sobriété] austerity, sobriety.

dépouiller [depuje] *vt* [priver]: ~ **qqn (de)** to strip sb (of). ‖ [examiner] to peruse; ~ **un scrutin** to count the votes.

dépourvu, -e [depurvy] *adj*: ~ **de** without, lacking in. ○ **au dépourvu** *loc adv*: **prendre qqn au** ~ to catch sb unawares.

dépoussiérer [depusjere] *vt* to dust (off).

dépravé, -e [deprave] **1** *adj* depraved. **2** *nm, f* degenerate.

dépréciation [depresjasjɔ̃] *nf* depreciation.

déprécier [depresje] *vt* [marchandise] to reduce the value of. ‖ [œuvre] to disparage. ○ **se déprécier** *vp* [marchandise] to depreciate. ‖ [personne] to put o.s. down.

dépressif, -ive [depresif, iv] *adj* depressive.

dépression [depresjɔ̃] *nf* depression; ~ **nerveuse** nervous breakdown.

déprimant, -e [deprimɑ̃, ɑ̃t] *adj* depressing.

déprime [deprim] *nf fam*: **faire une** ~ to be (feeling) down.

déprimé, -e [deprime] *adj* depressed.

déprimer [deprime] **1** *vt* to depress. **2** *vi fam* to be (feeling) down.

déprogrammer [deprɔgrame] *vt* to remove from the schedule; TÉLÉ to take off the air.

depuis [dəpɥi] **1** *prép* [à partir d'une date ou d'un moment précis] since; **il est parti** ~ **hier** he's been away since yesterday; ~ **le début jusqu'à la fin** from beginning to end. ‖ [exprimant une durée] for; **il est malade** ~ **une semaine** he has been ill for a week; ~ **10 ans/longtemps** for 10 years/a long time. ‖ [dans l'espace] from; ~ **la route, on pouvait voir la mer** you could see the sea from the road. **2** *adv* since (then); ~, **nous ne l'avons pas revu** we haven't seen him since (then). ○ **depuis que** *loc conj* since.

député [depyte] *nm* [au parlement] representative *Am*.

déraciner [derasine] *vt litt & fig* to uproot.

déraillement [derajmɑ̃] *nm* derailment.

dérailler [deraje] *vi* [train] to leave the rails, to be derailed. ‖ *fam fig* [personne] to go to pieces.

dérailleur [derajœr] *nm* [de bicyclette] derailleur.

déraisonnable [derezɔnabl] *adj* unreasonable.

dérangement [derɑ̃ʒmɑ̃] *nm* trouble; **en** ~ out of order.

déranger [derɑ̃ʒe] **1** *vt* [personne] to disturb, to bother; **ça vous dérange si je fume?** do you mind if I smoke? ‖ [plan] to disrupt. ‖ [maison, pièce] to disarrange, to make untidy. **2** *vi* to be disturbing. ○ **se déranger** *vp* [se déplacer] to move. ‖ [se gêner] to put o.s. out.

dérapage [derapaʒ] *nm* [glissement] skid; *fig* excess.

déraper [derape] *vi* [glisser] to skid; *fig* to get out of hand.

déréglementer [dereglǝmɑ̃te] *vt* to deregulate.

dérégler [deregle] *vt* [mécanisme] to put out of order; *fig* to upset. ○ **se dérégler** *vp* [mécanisme] to go wrong.

dérider [deride] *vt fig*: ~ **qqn** to cheer sb up.

dérision [derizjɔ̃] *nf* derision; **tourner qqch en** ~ to hold sthg up to ridicule.

dérisoire [derizwar] *adj* derisory.

dérivatif, -ive [derivatif, iv] *adj* derivative. ○ **dérivatif** *nm* distraction.

dérive [deriv] *nf* [mouvement] drift, drifting (*U*); **aller** ou **partir à la** ~ *fig* to fall apart.

dérivé [derive] *nm* derivative.

dériver [derive] **1** *vt* [détourner] to divert. **2** *vi* [aller à la dérive] to drift. ‖ *fig* [découler]: ~ **de** to derive from.

dermatologie [dɛrmatɔlɔʒi] *nf* dermatology.

dermatologue [dɛrmatɔlɔg] *nmf* dermatologist.

dernier, -ière [dɛrnje, jɛr] **1** *adj* [gén] last; **l'année dernière** last year. ‖ [ultime] last, final. ‖ [plus récent] latest. **2** *nm, f* last; **ce** ~ the latter. ○ **en dernier** *loc adv* last.

dernièrement [dɛrnjɛrmɑ̃] *adv* recently, lately.

dernier-né, dernière-née [dɛrnjene, dɛrnjɛrne] *nm, f* [bébé] youngest (child).

dérobade [derɔbad] *nf* evasion, shirking (U).

dérobé, -e [derobe] *adj* [caché] hidden. ○ **à la dérobée** *loc adv* surreptitiously.

dérober [derobe] *vt sout* to steal. ○ **se dérober** *vp* [se soustraire]: **se ~ à qqch** to shirk sthg. || [s'effondrer] to give way.

dérogation [derɔgasjɔ̃] *nf* [action] dispensation; [résultat] exception.

déroulement [derulmɑ̃] *nm* [de bobine] unwinding. || *fig* [d'événement] development.

dérouler [derule] *vt* [fil] to unwind; [papier, tissu] to unroll. ○ **se dérouler** *vp* to take place.

déroute [derut] *nf* MIL rout; *fig* collapse.

dérouter [derute] *vt* [déconcerter] to disconcert, to put out. || [dévier] to divert.

derrière [dɛrjɛr] **1** *prép & adv* behind. **2** *nm* [partie arrière] back; **la porte de ~** the back door. || [partie du corps] bottom, behind.

des [de] **1** *art indéf* → **un. 2** *prép* → **de.**

dès [dɛ] *prép* from; **~ son arrivée** the minute he arrives/arrived, as soon as he arrives/arrived; **~ l'enfance** since childhood; **~ 1900** as far back as 1900, as early as 1900; **~ maintenant** from now on. ○ **dès que** *loc conj* as soon as.

désabusé, -e [dezabyze] *adj* disillusioned.

désaccord [dezakɔr] *nm* disagreement.

désaccordé, -e [dezakɔrde] *adj* out of tune.

désaffecté, -e [dezafɛkte] *adj* disused.

désagréable [dezagreabl] *adj* unpleasant.

désagréger [dezagreʒe] *vt* to break up. ○ **se désagréger** *vp* to break up.

désagrément [dezagremɑ̃] *nm* annoyance.

désaltérant, -e [dezalterɑ̃, ɑ̃t] *adj* thirst-quenching.

désaltérer [dezaltere] ○ **se désaltérer** *vp* to quench one's thirst.

désamorcer [dezamɔrse] *vt* [arme] to remove the primer from; [bombe] to defuse; *fig* [complot] to nip in the bud.

désappointer [dezapwɛ̃te] *vt* to disappoint.

désapprobation [dezaprɔbasjɔ̃] *nf* disapproval.

désapprouver [dezapruve] **1** *vt* to disapprove of. **2** *vi* to be disapproving.

désarmement [dezarmǝmɑ̃] *nm* disarmament.

désarmer [dezarme] *vt* to disarm; [fusil] to unload.

désarroi [dezarwa] *nm* confusion.

désastre [dezastr] *nm* disaster.

désastreux, -euse [dezastrø, øz] *adj* disastrous.

désavantage [dezavɑ̃taʒ] *nm* disadvantage.

désavantager [dezavɑ̃taʒe] *vt* to disadvantage.

désavantageux, -euse [dezavɑ̃taʒø, øz] *adj* unfavourable.

désavouer [dezavwe] *vt* to disown.

désaxé, -e [dezakse] *adj* [mentalement] disordered, unhinged.

descendance [desɑ̃dɑ̃s] *nf* [progéniture] descendants (*pl*).

descendant, -e [desɑ̃dɑ̃, ɑ̃t] *nm, f* [héritier] descendant.

descendre [desɑ̃dr] **1** *vt* (*aux: avoir*) [escalier, pente] to go/come down. || [rideau, tableau] to lower. || [apporter] to bring/take down. || *fam* [personne, avion] to shoot down. **2** *vi* (*aux: être*) [gén] to go/come down; [température, niveau] to fall. || [passager] to get off; **~ d'un bus** to get off a bus; **~ d'une voiture** to get out of a car. || [être issu]: **~ de** to be descended from. || [marée] to go out.

descendu, -e [desɑ̃dy] *pp* → **descendre.**

descente [desɑ̃t] *nf* [action] descent. || [pente] downhill slope ou stretch. || [irruption] raid. || [tapis]: **~ de lit** bedside rug.

descriptif, -ive [dɛskriptif, iv] *adj* descriptive. ○ **descriptif** *nm* [de lieu] particulars (*pl*); [d'appareil] specification.

description [dɛskripsjɔ̃] *nf* description.

désemparé, -e [dezɑ̃pare] *adj* [personne] helpless; [avion, navire] disabled.

désenfler [dezɑ̃fle] *vi* to go down, to become less swollen.

déséquilibre [dezekilibr] *nm* imbalance.

déséquilibré, -e [dezekilibre] *nm, f* unbalanced person.

déséquilibrer [dezekilibre] *vt* [physiquement]: **~ qqn** to throw sb off balance. || [perturber] to unbalance.

désert, -e [dezer, ert] *adj* [désertique - île] desert (*avant n*); [peu fréquenté] deserted. ○ **désert** *nm* desert.

déserter [dezɛrte] *vt & vi* to desert.

déserteur [dezɛrtœr] *nm* MIL deserter.

désertion [dezɛrsjɔ̃] *nf* desertion.

désertique [dezɛrtik] *adj* desert (*avant n*).

désespéré, -e [dezɛspere] *adj* [regard] desperate. || [situation] hopeless.

désespérément [dezɛsperemɑ̃] *adv* [avec acharnement] desperately.

désespérer [dezɛspere] 1 *vt* [décourager]: ~ qqn to drive sb to despair. 2 *vi*: ~ (de) to despair (of). ○ **se désespérer** *vp* to despair.

désespoir [dezɛspwar] *nm* despair; en ~ de cause as a last resort.

déshabillé [dezabije] *nm* negligee.

déshabiller [dezabije] *vt* to undress. ○ **se déshabiller** *vp* to undress, to get undressed.

désherbant, -e [dezɛrbɑ̃, ɑ̃t] *adj* weed-killing. ○ **désherbant** *nm* weed-killer.

déshérité, -e [dezerite] *nm, f* [pauvre] deprived person.

déshériter [dezerite] *vt* to disinherit.

déshonneur [dezɔnœr] *nm* disgrace.

déshonorer [dezɔnɔre] *vt* to disgrace, to bring disgrace on.

déshydrater [dezidrate] *vt* to dehydrate. ○ **se déshydrater** *vp* to become dehydrated.

désigner [dezine] *vt* [choisir] to appoint. || [signaler] to point out. || [nommer] to designate.

désillusion [dezilyzjɔ̃] *nf* disillusion.

désinfectant, -e [dezɛ̃fɛktɑ̃, ɑ̃t] *adj* disinfectant. ○ **désinfectant** *nm* disinfectant.

désinfecter [dezɛ̃fɛkte] *vt* to disinfect.

désinflation [dezɛ̃flasjɔ̃] *nf* disinflation.

désintégrer [dezɛ̃tegre] *vt* to break up. ○ **se désintégrer** *vp* to disintegrate, to break up.

désintéressé, -e [dezɛ̃terese] *adj* disinterested.

désintéresser [dezɛ̃terese] ○ **se désintéresser** *vp*: se ~ de to lose interest in.

désintoxication [dezɛ̃tɔksikasjɔ̃] *nf* detoxification.

désinvolte [dezɛ̃vɔlt] *adj* [à l'aise] casual. || *péj* [sans-gêne] offhand.

désinvolture [dezɛ̃vɔltyr] *nf* [légèreté] casualness. || *péj* [sans-gêne] offhandedness.

désir [dezir] *nm* [souhait] desire, wish. || [charnel] desire.

désirable [dezirabl] *adj* desirable.

désirer [dezire] *vt sout* [chose]: ~ faire qqch to wish to do sthg; **vous désirez?** [dans un magasin] can I help you?; [dans un café] what can I get you? || [sexuellement] to desire.

désistement [dezistǝmɑ̃] *nm*: ~ (de) withdrawal (from).

désister [deziste] ○ **se désister** *vp* [se retirer] to withdraw, to stand down.

désobéir [dezɔbeir] *vi*: ~ (à qqn) to disobey (sb).

désobéissant, -e [dezɔbeisɑ̃, ɑ̃t] *adj* disobedient.

désobligeant, -e [dezɔbliʒɑ̃, ɑ̃t] *adj sout* offensive.

désodorisant, -e [dezɔdɔrizɑ̃, ɑ̃t] *adj* deodorant. ○ **désodorisant** *nm* air freshener.

désœuvré, -e [dezœvre] *adj* idle.

désolation [dezɔlasjɔ̃] *nf* [destruction] desolation. || [affliction] distress.

désolé, -e [dezɔle] *adj* [ravagé] desolate. || [contrarié] very sorry.

désoler [dezɔle] *vt* [affliger] to sadden. || [contrarier] to upset, to make sorry. ○ **se désoler** *vp* [être contrarié] to be upset.

désolidariser [desɔlidarize] ○ **se désolidariser** *vp*: se ~ de to dissociate o.s. from.

désopilant, -e [dezɔpilɑ̃, ɑ̃t] *adj* hilarious.

désordonné, -e [dezɔrdɔne] *adj* [maison, personne] untidy.

désordre [dezɔrdr] *nm* [fouillis] untidiness; en ~ untidy. || [agitation] disturbances (*pl*), disorder (*U*).

désorganiser [dezɔrganize] *vt* to disrupt.

désorienté, -e [dezɔrjɑ̃te] *adj* disoriented, disorientated.

désormais [dezɔrmɛ] *adv* from now on, in future.

désosser [dezɔse] *vt* to bone.

despote [dɛspɔt] *nm* [chef d'État] despot; *fig* & *péj* tyrant.

despotisme [dɛspɔtism] *nm* [gouvernement] despotism; *fig* & *péj* tyranny.

desquels, desquelles [dekɛl] → lequel.

DESS (*abr de* diplôme d'études supérieures spécialisées) *nm postgraduate diploma*.

dessécher [deseʃe] *vt* [peau] to dry (out). ○ **se dessécher** *vp* [peau, terre] to dry out; [plante] to wither.

desserrer [desere] *vt* to loosen; [poing, dents] to unclench; [frein] to release.

dessert [desɛr] *nm* dessert.

desserte [desɛrt] *nf* [meuble] side-board.

desservir [desɛrvir] *vt* TRANSPORT to serve. || [table] to clear. || [désavantager] to do a disservice to.

dessin [desɛ̃] *nm* [graphique] drawing; ~ animé cartoon (*film*); ~ humoristique cartoon (*drawing*). || *fig* [contour] outline.

dessinateur, -trice [desinatœr, tris] *nm, f* artist, draughtsman (*f* draughtswoman).

dessiner [desine] **1** *vt* [représenter] to draw; *fig* to outline. **2** *vi* to draw.

dessous [dəsu] **1** *adv* underneath. **2** *nm* [partie inférieure - gén] underside; [- d'un tissu] wrong side. **3** *nmpl* [sous-vêtements féminins] underwear (*U*). ○ **en dessous** *loc adv* underneath; [plus bas] below.

dessous-de-plat [dəsudpla] *nm inv* tablemat.

dessus [dəsy] **1** *adv* on top; **faites attention à ne pas marcher ~** be careful not to walk on it. **2** *nm* [partie supérieure] top. || [étage supérieur] upstairs; **les voisins du ~** the upstairs neighbours. || *loc*: **avoir le ~** to have the upper hand. ○ **en dessus** *loc adv* on top.

dessus-de-lit [dəsydli] *nm inv* bedspread.

déstabiliser [destabilize] *vt* to destabilize.

destin [destɛ̃] *nm* fate.

destinataire [dɛstinatɛr] *nmf* addressee.

destination [dɛstinasjɔ̃] *nf* [direction] destination; **un avion à ~ de Paris** a plane to or for Paris. || [rôle] purpose.

destinée [dɛstine] *nf* destiny.

destiner [dɛstine] *vt* [consacrer]: ~ qqch à to intend sthg for, to mean sthg for. || [vouer]: ~ qqn à qqch/à faire qqch [à un métier] to destine sb for sthg/to do sthg.

destituer [dɛstitɥe] *vt* to dismiss.

destructeur, -trice [dɛstryktœr, tris] **1** *adj* destructive. **2** *nm, f* destroyer.

destruction [dɛstryksjɔ̃] *nf* destruction.

désuet, -ète [dezɥɛ, ɛt] *adj* [expression, coutume] obsolete; [style, tableau] outmoded.

désuni, -e [dezyni] *adj* divided.

détachable [detaʃabl] *adj* detachable, removable.

détachant, -e [detaʃɑ̃, ɑ̃t] *adj* stain-removing. ○ **détachant** *nm* stain remover.

détaché, -e [detaʃe] *adj* detached.

détachement [detaʃmɑ̃] *nm* [d'esprit] detachment. || [de fonctionnaire] secondment. || MIL detachment.

détacher [detaʃe] *vt* [enlever]: ~ qqch (de) [objet] to detach sthg (from). || [nettoyer] to remove stains from, to clean. || [délier] to undo; [cheveux] to untie. || ADMIN: ~ qqn auprès de to second sb to. ○ **se détacher** *vp* [tomber]: se ~ (de) to come off. || [se défaire] to come undone. || [ressortir]: se ~ sur to stand out on. || [se désintéresser]: se ~ de qqn to drift apart from sb.

détail [detaj] *nm* [précision] detail. || COMM: **le ~** retail. ○ **au détail** *loc adj* & *loc adv* retail. ○ **en détail** *loc adv* in detail.

détaillant, -e [detajɑ̃, ɑ̃t] *nm, f* retailer.

détaillé, -e [detaje] *adj* detailed.

détailler [detaje] *vt* [expliquer] to give details of. || [vendre] to retail.

détaler [detale] *vi* [personne] to clear out. || [animal] to bolt.

détartrant, -e [detartrɑ̃, ɑ̃t] *adj* descaling. ○ **détartrant** *nm* descaling agent.

détaxe [detaks] *nf*: ~ (sur) [suppression] removal of tax (from); [réduction] reduction in tax (on).

détecter [detɛkte] *vt* to detect.

détecteur, -trice [detɛktœr, tris] *adj* detecting, detector (*avant n*). ○ **détecteur** *nm* detector.

détection [detɛksjɔ̃] *nf* detection.

détective [detɛktiv] *nm* detective; ~ privé private detective.

déteindre [detɛ̃dr] *vi* to fade.

déteint, -e [detɛ̃, ɛ̃t] *pp* → déteindre.

dételer [detle] *vt* [cheval] to unharness.

détendre [detɑ̃dr] *vt* [corde] to loosen, to slacken. || [personne] to relax. ○ **se détendre** *vp* [se relâcher] to slacken; [atmosphère] to become more relaxed. || [se reposer] to relax.

détendu, -e [detɑ̃dy] **1** *pp* → détendre. **2** *adj* [personne] relaxed.

détenir [detnir] *vt* [objet] to have, to hold. || [personne] to detain, to hold.

détente [detɑ̃t] *nf* [de ressort] release. || [d'une arme] trigger. || [repos] relaxation.

détenteur, -trice [detɑ̃tœr, tris] *nm, f* [d'objet, de secret] possessor; [de prix, record] holder.

détention [detãsjɔ̃] *nf* [possession] possession. || [emprisonnement] detention.

détenu, -e [detny] 1 *pp* → détenir. 2 *adj* detained. 3 *nm, f* prisoner.

détergent, -e [detɛrʒã, ãt] *adj* detergent (*avant n*). ○ **détergent** *nm* detergent.

détérioration [deterjɔrasjɔ̃] *nf* [de bâtiment] deterioration; [de situation] worsening.

détériorer [deterjɔre] *vt* [abîmer] to damage. || [altérer] to ruin. ○ **se détériorer** *vp* [bâtiment] to deteriorate; [situation] to worsen.

déterminant, -e [detɛrminã, ãt] *adj* decisive, determining. ○ **déterminant** *nm* LING determiner.

détermination [detɛrminasjɔ̃] *nf* [résolution] decision.

déterminé, -e [detɛrmine] *adj* [quantité] given (*avant n*). || [expression] determined.

déterminer [detɛrmine] *vt* [préciser] to determine, to specify. || [provoquer] to bring about.

déterrer [detere] *vt* to dig up.

détestable [detɛstabl] *adj* dreadful.

détester [detɛste] *vt* to detest.

détonateur [detɔnatœr] *nm* TECHNOL detonator; *fig* trigger.

détoner [detɔne] *vi* to detonate.

détonner [detɔne] *vi* MUS to be out of tune; [couleur] to clash; [personne] to be out of place.

détour [detur] *nm* [crochet] detour. || [méandre] bend; **sans ~** *fig* directly.

détourné, -e [deturne] *adj* [dévié] indirect; *fig* roundabout (*avant n*).

détournement [deturnəmã] *nm* diversion; **~ d'avion** hijacking; **~ de fonds** embezzlement; **~ de mineur** corruption of a minor.

détourner [deturne] *vt* [dévier - gén] to divert; [- avion] to hijack. || [écarter]: **~ qqn de** to distract sb from; to divert sb from. || [tourner ailleurs] to turn away. || [argent] to embezzle. ○ **se détourner** *vp* to turn away; **se ~ de** *fig* to move away from.

détraquer [detrake] *vt fam* [dérégler] to break; *fig* to upset. ○ **se détraquer** *vp fam* [se dérégler] to go wrong; *fig* to become unsettled.

détresse [detrɛs] *nf* distress.

détriment [detrimã] ○ **au détriment de** *loc prép* to the detriment of.

détritus [detrity(s)] *nm* detritus.

détroit [detrwa] *nm* strait.

détromper [detrɔpe] *vt* to disabuse.

détrôner [detrone] *vt* [souverain] to dethrone; *fig* to oust.

détruire [detrɥir] *vt* [démolir, éliminer] to destroy. || *fig* [anéantir] to ruin.

détruit, -e [detrɥi, ɥit] *pp* → détruire.

dette [dɛt] *nf* debt.

DEUG, Deug [dœg] (*abr de* **diplôme d'études universitaires générales**) *nm university diploma taken after 2 years of arts courses.*

deuil [dœj] *nm* [douleur, mort] bereavement; [vêtements, période] mourning (*U*); **porter le ~** to be in OU wear mourning.

deux [dø] 1 *adj num* two; **ses ~ fils** both his sons, his two sons. 2 *nm* two; **les ~** both; **par ~** in pairs; *voir aussi* **six**.

deuxième [døzjɛm] *adj num, nm & nmf* second; *voir aussi* **sixième**.

deux-pièces [døpjɛs] *nm inv* [appartement] two-room flat *Br* OU apartment *Am*. || [bikini] two-piece (swimming costume).

deux-points [døpwɛ̃] *nm inv* colon.

deux-roues [døru] *nm inv* two-wheeled vehicle.

dévaler [devale] *vt* to run down.

dévaliser [devalize] *vt* [cambrioler - maison] to ransack; [- personne] to rob.

dévaloriser [devalɔrize] *vt* [monnaie] to devalue. || [personne] to run OU put down. ○ **se dévaloriser** *vp* [monnaie] to fall in value. || [personne] *fig* to run OU put o.s. down.

dévaluation [devalɥasjɔ̃] *nf* devaluation.

dévaluer [devalɥe] *vt* to devalue. ○ **se dévaluer** *vp* to devalue.

devancer [dəvãse] *vt* [précéder] to arrive before. || [anticiper] to anticipate.

devant [dəvã] 1 *prép* [en face de] in front of. || [en avant de, ahead of, in front of. || [en présence de, face à] in the face of. 2 *adv* [en face] in front. || [en avant] in front, ahead. 3 *nm* front; **prendre les ~s** to make the first move. ○ **de devant** *loc adj* [pattes, roues] front (*avant n*).

devanture [dəvãtyr] *nf* shop window.

dévaster [devaste] *vt* to devastate.

développement [devlɔpmã] *nm* [gén] development. || PHOT developing.

développer [devlɔpe] *vt* to develop; [industrie, commerce] to expand. ○ **se développer** *vp* [s'épanouir] to spread. || ÉCON to grow, to expand.

devenir 100

devenir [dəvnir] *vi* to become; **que devenez-vous?** *fig* how are you doing?

devenu, -e [dəvny] *pp* → devenir.

dévergondé, -e [devergɔ̃de] 1 *adj* shameless, wild. 2 *nm, f* shameless person.

déverser [deverse] *vt* [liquide] to pour out. || [ordures] to tip (out).

déviation [devjasjɔ̃] *nf* [gén] deviation. || [d'itinéraire] diversion.

dévier [devje] 1 *vi*: ~ de to deviate from. 2 *vt* to divert.

devin, devineresse [dəvɛ̃, dəvinrɛs] *nm, f*: **je ne suis pas ~!** I'm not psychic!

deviner [dəvine] *vt* to guess.

devinette [dəvinɛt] *nf* riddle.

devis [dəvi] *nm* estimate; **faire un ~** to (give an) estimate.

dévisager [devizaʒe] *vt* to stare at.

devise [dəviz] *nf* [formule] motto. || [monnaie] currency. ○ **devises** *nfpl* [argent] currency (*U*).

dévisser [devise] *vt* to unscrew.

dévoiler [devwale] *vt* to unveil; *fig* to reveal.

devoir [dəvwar] 1 *nm* [obligation] duty. || SCOL homework (*U*); **faire ses ~s** to do one's homework. 2 *vt* [argent, respect]: ~ **qqch (à qqn)** to owe (sb) sthg. || [marque l'obligation]: ~ **faire qqch** to have to do sthg; **je dois partir à l'heure ce soir** I have to or must leave on time tonight; **tu devrais faire attention** you should be or ought to be careful. || [marque la probabilité]: **il doit faire chaud là-bas** it must be hot over there. || [marque le futur, l'intention]: ~ **faire qqch** to be (due) to do sthg, to be going to do sthg; **elle doit arriver à 6 heures** she's due to arrive at 6 o'clock; **je dois voir mes parents ce week-end** I'm seeing or going to see my parents this weekend. || [être destiné à]: **cela devait arriver** it had to happen, it was bound to happen. ○ **se devoir** *vp*: **se ~ de faire qqch** to be duty-bound to do sthg; **comme il se doit** as is proper.

dévolu, -e [devɔly] *adj sout*: ~ **à** allotted to. ○ **dévolu** *nm*: **jeter son ~ sur** to set one's sights on.

dévorer [devɔre] *vt* to devour.

dévotion [devɔsjɔ̃] *nf* devotion; **avec ~** [prier] devoutly; [soigner, aimer] devotedly.

dévoué, -e [devwe] *adj* devoted.

dévouement [devumɑ̃] *nm* devotion.

dévouer [devwe] ○ **se dévouer** *vp* [se consacrer]: **se ~ à** to devote o.s. to. || *fig*

[se sacrifier]: **se ~ pour qqch/pour faire qqch** to sacrifice o.s. for sthg/to do sthg.

devrai, devras *etc* → devoir.

dextérité [deksterite] *nf* dexterity, skill.

diabète [djabɛt] *nm* diabetes (*U*).

diabétique [djabetik] *nmf & adj* diabetic.

diable [djabl] *nm* devil.

diabolique [djabɔlik] *adj* diabolical.

diabolo [djabɔlo] *nm* [boisson] fruit cordial and lemonade; ~ **menthe** mint (cordial) and lemonade.

diadème [djadɛm] *nm* diadem.

diagnostic [djagnɔstik] *nm* MÉD & *fig* diagnosis.

diagnostiquer [djagnɔstike] *vt* MÉD & *fig* to diagnose.

diagonale [djagɔnal] *nf* diagonal.

dialecte [djalɛkt] *nm* dialect.

dialogue [djalɔg] *nm* discussion.

dialoguer [djalɔge] *vi* [converser] to converse. || INFORM to interact.

diamant [djamɑ̃] *nm* [pierre] diamond.

diamètre [djametr] *nm* diameter.

diapason [djapazɔ̃] *nm* [instrument] tuning fork.

diapositive [djapozitiv] *nf* slide.

diarrhée [djare] *nf* diarrhea.

dictateur [diktatœr] *nm* dictator.

dictature [diktatyr] *nf* dictatorship.

dictée [dikte] *nf* dictation.

dicter [dikte] *vt* to dictate.

diction [diksjɔ̃] *nf* diction.

dictionnaire [diksjɔnɛr] *nm* dictionary.

dicton [diktɔ̃] *nm* saying, dictum.

dièse [djez] 1 *adj* sharp; **do/fa ~** C/F sharp. 2 *nm* sharp.

diesel [djezɛl] *adj inv* diesel.

diète [djɛt] *nf* diet.

diététicien, -ienne [djetetisjɛ̃, jɛn] *nm, f* dietician.

diététique [djetetik] 1 *nf* dietetics (*U*). 2 *adj* [produit, magasin] health (*avant n*).

dieu, -x [djø] *nm* god. ○ **Dieu** *nm* God; **mon Dieu!** my God!

diffamation [difamasjɔ̃] *nf* [écrite] libel; [orale] slander.

différé, -e [difere] *adj* recorded. ○ **différé** *nm*: **en ~** TÉLÉ recorded.

différence [diferɑ̃s] *nf* difference.

différencier [diferɑ̃sje] *vt*: ~ **qqch de qqch** to differentiate sthg from sthg. ○ **se différencier** *vp*: **se ~ de** to be different from.

différend [diferã] nm [désaccord] difference of opinion.

différent, -e [diferã, ãt] adj: ~ (de) different (from).

différer [difere] 1 vt [retarder] to postpone. 2 vi: ~ de to differ from, to be different from.

difficile [difisil] adj difficult.

difficilement [difisilmã] adv with difficulty.

difficulté [difikylte] nf [complexité, peine] difficulty. || [obstacle] problem.

difforme [difɔrm] adj deformed.

diffuser [difyze] vt [lumière] to diffuse. || [émission] to broadcast. || [livres] to distribute.

diffuseur [difyzœr] nm [appareil] diffuser. || [de livres] distributor.

diffusion [difyzjɔ̃] nf [d'émission, d'onde] broadcast. || [de livres] distribution.

digérer [diʒere] 1 vi to digest. 2 vt [repas, connaissance] to digest. || fam fig [désagrément] to put up with.

digestif, -ive [diʒestif, iv] adj digestive. ○ **digestif** nm liqueur.

digestion [diʒestjɔ̃] nf digestion.

digital, -e, -aux [diʒital, o] adj TECHNOL digital. || → **empreinte**.

digne [diɲ] adj [honorable] dignified. || [méritant]: ~ de worthy of.

dignité [diɲite] nf dignity.

digression [digresjɔ̃] nf digression.

digue [dig] nf dike.

dilapider [dilapide] vt to squander.

dilater [dilate] vt to dilate.

dilemme [dilɛm] nm dilemma.

diligence [diliʒɑ̃s] nf HIST & sout diligence.

diluant [dilɥɑ̃] nm thinner.

diluer [dilɥe] vt to dilute.

diluvien, -ienne [dilyvjɛ̃, jɛn] adj torrential.

dimanche [dimɑ̃ʃ] nm Sunday; voir aussi **samedi**.

dimension [dimɑ̃sjɔ̃] nf [mesure] dimension. || [taille] dimensions (pl), size. || fig [importance] magnitude.

diminuer [diminɥe] 1 vt [réduire] to diminish, to reduce. 2 vi [intensité] to diminish, to decrease.

diminutif, -ive [diminytif, iv] adj diminutive. ○ **diminutif** nm diminutive.

diminution [diminysjɔ̃] nf diminution.

dinde [dɛ̃d] nf [animal] turkey. || péj [femme] stupid woman.

dindon [dɛ̃dɔ̃] nm turkey; être le ~ de la farce fig to be made a fool of.

dîner [dine] 1 vi to dine. 2 nm dinner.

dingue [dɛ̃g] fam 1 adj [personne] crazy. || [histoire] incredible. 2 nmf loony.

dinosaure [dinozɔr] nm dinosaur.

diplomate [diplɔmat] 1 nmf [ambassadeur] diplomat. 2 adj diplomatic.

diplomatie [diplɔmasi] nf diplomacy.

diplomatique [diplɔmatik] adj diplomatic.

diplôme [diplom] nm diploma.

diplômé, -e [diplome] 1 adj: être ~ de/en to be a graduate of/in. 2 nm, f graduate.

dire [dir] vt: ~ qqch (à qqn) [parole] to say sthg (to sb); [vérité, mensonge, secret] to tell (sb) sthg; ~ à qqn de faire qqch to tell sb to do sthg; il m'a dit que ... he told me (that) ...; ~ du bien/du mal (de) to speak well/ill (of); que dirais-tu de ...? what would you say to ...?; qu'en dis-tu? what do you think (of it)?; on dirait que ... it looks as if ...; on dirait de la soie it looks like silk, you'd think it was silk; ça ne me dit rien [pas envie] I don't fancy that; [jamais entendu] I've never heard of it. ○ **se dire** vp [penser] to think (to o.s.). || [s'employer]: **ça ne se dit pas** [par décence] you mustn't say that; [par usage] people don't say that, nobody says that. || [se traduire]: «chat» se dit «gato» en espagnol the Spanish for "cat" is "gato". ○ **cela dit** loc adv having said that. ○ **dis donc** loc adv fam so; [au fait] by the way; [à qqn qui exagère] look here!

direct, -e [dirɛkt] adj direct. ○ **direct** nm BOXE jab. || [train] direct train. || RADIO & TÉLÉ: **en** ~ live.

directement [dirɛktəmã] adv directly.

directeur, -trice [dirɛktœr, tris] nm, f director, manager; ~ **général** general manager, managing director Br, chief executive officer Am.

direction [dirɛksjɔ̃] nf [gestion, ensemble des cadres] management. || [orientation] direction; **en** ou **dans la** ~ **de** in the direction of. || AUTOM steering.

directive [dirɛktiv] nf directive.

directrice → **directeur**.

dirigeable [diriʒabl] nm: (**ballon**) ~ airship.

dirigeant, -e [diriʒã, ãt] 1 adj ruling. 2 nm, f [de pays] leader; [d'entreprise] manager.

diriger [diriʒe] *vt* [mener - entreprise] to run, to manage; [- orchestre] to conduct; [- film, acteurs] to direct; [- recherches, projet] to supervise. || [conduire] to steer. || [orienter]: ~ qqch sur/vers to aim sthg at/towards. ○ **se diriger** *vp*: se ~ vers to go ou head towards.

discernement [disɛrnəmɑ̃] *nm* [jugement] discernment.

discerner [disɛrne] *vt* [distinguer]: ~ qqch de to distinguish sthg from. || [deviner] to discern.

disciple [disipl] *nmf* disciple.

disciplinaire [disipliner] *adj* disciplinary.

discipline [disiplin] *nf* discipline.

discipliner [disipline] *vt* [personne] to discipline; [cheveux] to control.

disco [disko] *nm* disco (music).

discontinu, -e [diskɔ̃tiny] *adj* [ligne] broken; [bruit, effort] intermittent.

discordant, -e [diskɔrdɑ̃, ɑ̃t] *adj* discordant.

discorde [diskɔrd] *nf* discord.

discothèque [diskɔtɛk] *nf* [boîte de nuit] discothèque. || [de prêt] record library.

discourir [diskurir] *vi* to talk at length.

discours [diskur] *nm* [allocution] speech.

discréditer [diskredite] *vt* to discredit.

discret, -ète [diskrɛ, ɛt] *adj* [gén] discreet; [réservé] reserved.

discrètement [diskrɛtmɑ̃] *adv* discreetly.

discrétion [diskresjɔ̃] *nf* [réserve, tact, silence] discretion.

discrimination [diskriminasjɔ̃] *nf* discrimination; sans ~ indiscriminately.

discriminatoire [diskriminatwar] *adj* discriminatory.

disculper [diskylpe] *vt* to exonerate. ○ **se disculper** *vp* to exonerate o.s.

discussion [diskysjɔ̃] *nf* [conversation, examen] discussion. || [contestation, altercation] argument.

discutable [diskytabl] *adj* [contestable] questionable.

discuter [diskyte] 1 *vt* [débattre]: ~ (de) qqch to discuss sthg. || [contester] to dispute. 2 *vi* [parlementer] to discuss. || [converser] to talk. || [contester] to argue.

diseur, -euse [dizœr, øz] *nm, f*: ~ de bonne aventure fortune-teller.

disgracieux, -ieuse [disgrasjø, jøz] *adj* [laid] plain.

disjoncteur [disʒɔ̃ktœr] *nm* trip switch, circuit breaker.

disloquer [dislɔke] *vt* MÉD to dislocate. || [machine, empire] to dismantle. ○ **se disloquer** *vp* [machine] to fall apart ou to pieces; *fig* [empire] to break up.

disparaître [disparɛtr] *vi* [gén] to disappear, to vanish. || [mourir] to die.

disparité [disparite] *nf* [différence - d'éléments] disparity; [- de couleurs] mismatch.

disparition [disparisjɔ̃] *nf* [gén] disappearance; [d'espèce] extinction; en voie de ~ endangered. || [mort] passing.

disparu, -e [dispary] 1 *pp* → disparaître. 2 *nm, f* dead person, deceased.

dispensaire [dispɑ̃ser] *nm* community clinic *Br*, free clinic *Am*.

dispense [dispɑ̃s] *nf* [exemption] exemption.

dispenser [dispɑ̃se] *vt* [distribuer] to dispense. || [exempter]: ~ qqn de qqch [corvée] to excuse sb sthg, to let sb off sthg.

disperser [disperse] *vt* to scatter (about ou around); [collection, brume, foule] to break up; *fig* [efforts, forces] to dissipate, to waste. ○ **se disperser** *vp* [feuilles, cendres] to scatter; [brume, foule] to break up, to clear. || [personne] to take on too much at once, to spread o.s. too thin.

disponibilité [disponibilite] *nf* [de choses] availability. || [de fonctionnaire] leave of absence. || [d'esprit] alertness, receptiveness.

disponible [disponibl] *adj* [place, personne] available, free.

disposé, -e [dispoze] *adj*: être ~ à faire qqch to be prepared ou willing to do sthg; être bien ~ envers qqn to be well-disposed towards ou to sb.

disposer [dispoze] 1 *vt* [arranger] to arrange. 2 *vi*: ~ de [moyens, argent] to have available (to one), to have at one's disposal; [chose] to have the use of; [temps] to have free ou available.

dispositif [dispozitif] *nm* [mécanisme] device, mechanism.

disposition [dispozisjɔ̃] *nf* [arrangement] arrangement. || [disponibilité]: à la ~ de at the disposal of, available to. ○ **dispositions** *nfpl* [mesures] arrangements, measures. || [dons]: avoir des ~s pour to have a gift for.

disproportionné, -e [disprɔpɔrsjɔne] *adj* out of proportion.

dispute [dispyt] *nf* argument, quarrel.

disputer [dispyte] *vt* [SPORT - course] to run; [- match] to play. ○ **se disputer** *vp* [se quereller] to quarrel, to fight. || [lutter pour] to fight over or for.

disquaire [disker] *nm* record dealer.

disqualifier [diskalifje] *vt* to disqualify.

disque [disk] *nm* MUS record; [vidéo] video disc; ~ **compact** or **laser** compact disc. || ANAT disc. || INFORM disk; ~ **dur** hard disk. || SPORT discus.

disquette [disket] *nf* diskette, floppy disk; ~ **système** system diskette.

dissection [diseksjɔ̃] *nf* dissection.

dissemblable [disɑ̃blabl] *adj* dissimilar.

disséminer [disemine] *vt* [graines, maisons] to scatter, to spread (out).

disséquer [diseke] *vt* litt & fig to dissect.

dissertation [disɛrtasjɔ̃] *nf* essay.

dissident, -e [disidɑ̃, ɑ̃t] *adj & nm, f* dissident.

dissimulation [disimylasjɔ̃] *nf* [hypocrisie] duplicity.

dissimuler [disimyle] *vt* to conceal. ○ **se dissimuler** *vp* [se cacher] to conceal o.s., to hide.

dissipation [disipasjɔ̃] *nf* [indiscipline] indiscipline, misbehaviour.

dissiper [disipe] *vt* [chasser] to break up, to clear; fig to dispel. || [distraire] to lead astray. ○ **se dissiper** *vp* [brouillard, fumée] to clear. || [élève] to misbehave. || fig [malaise, fatigue] to go away; [doute] to be dispelled.

dissocier [disɔsje] *vt* [séparer] to separate, to distinguish.

dissolution [disɔlysjɔ̃] *nf* JUR dissolution. || [mélange] dissolving.

dissolvant, -e [disɔlvɑ̃, ɑ̃t] *adj* solvent. ○ **dissolvant** *nm* [solvant] solvent; [pour vernis à ongles] nail varnish remover.

dissoudre [disudr] *vt*: (faire) ~ to dissolve. ○ **se dissoudre** *vp* [substance] to dissolve.

dissous, -oute [disu, ut] *pp* → dissoudre.

dissuader [disɥade] *vt* to dissuade.

dissuasion [disɥazjɔ̃] *nf* dissuasion; **force de** ~ deterrent (effect).

distance [distɑ̃s] *nf* [éloignement] distance; **à** ~ at a distance; [télécommander] by remote control; **à une** ~ **de 300 mètres** 300 metres away. || [intervalle] interval. || [écart] gap.

distancer [distɑ̃se] *vt* to outstrip.

distant, -e [distɑ̃, ɑ̃t] *adj* [éloigné]: **des villes** ~**es de 10 km** towns 10 km apart. || [froid] distant.

distendre [distɑ̃dr] *vt* [ressort, corde] to stretch. ○ **se distendre** *vp* to distend.

distendu, -e [distɑ̃dy] *pp* → distendre.

distiller [distile] *vt* [alcool] to distil; [pétrole] to refine.

distinct, -e [distɛ̃, ɛkt] *adj* distinct.

distinctement [distɛ̃ktəmɑ̃] *adv* distinctly, clearly.

distinctif, -ive [distɛ̃ktif, iv] *adj* distinctive.

distinction [distɛ̃ksjɔ̃] *nf* distinction.

distingué, -e [distɛ̃ge] *adj* distinguished.

distinguer [distɛ̃ge] *vt* [différencier] to tell apart, to distinguish. || [percevoir] to make out, to distinguish. || [rendre différent]: ~ **de** to distinguish from, to set apart from. ○ **se distinguer** *vp* [se différencier]: **se** ~ (**de**) to stand out (from). || [s'illustrer] to distinguish o.s.

distraction [distraksjɔ̃] *nf* [inattention] inattention, absent-mindedness. || [passe-temps] leisure activity.

distraire [distrɛr] *vt* [déranger] to distract. || [divertir] to amuse, to entertain. ○ **se distraire** *vp* to amuse o.s.

distrait, -e [distrɛ, ɛt] **1** *pp* → distraire. **2** *adj* absent-minded.

distribuer [distribɥe] *vt* to distribute; [courrier] to deliver; [ordres] to give out; [cartes] to deal.

distributeur, -trice [distribytœr, tris] *nm, f* distributor. ○ **distributeur** *nm* AUTOM & COMM distributor. || [machine]: ~ (**automatique**) **de billets** BANQUE cash machine, cash dispenser; TRANSPORT ticket machine; ~ **de boissons** drinks machine.

distribution [distribysjɔ̃] *nf* [répartition, diffusion, disposition] distribution; ~ **des prix** SCOL prize-giving. || CIN & THÉÂTRE cast.

dit, dite [di, dit] **1** *pp* → dire. **2** *adj* [appelé] known as. || JUR said, above. || [fixé]: **à l'heure** ~**e** at the appointed time.

divagation [divagasjɔ̃] *nf* wandering.

divaguer [divage] *vi* to ramble.

divan [divɑ̃] *nm* divan (seat).

divergence [divɛrʒɑ̃s] *nf* divergence, difference; [d'opinions] difference.

diverger [divɛrʒe] *vi* to diverge; [opinions] to differ.

divers, -e [diver, ɛrs] *adj* [différent] different, various. || [disparate] diverse. || (*avant n*) [plusieurs] various, several.

diversifier [diversifje] *vt* to vary, to diversify. ○ **se diversifier** *vp* to diversify.

diversion [diversjɔ̃] *nf* diversion.

diversité [diversite] *nf* diversity.

divertir [divertir] *vt* [distraire] to entertain, to amuse. ○ **se divertir** *vp* to amuse o.s., to entertain o.s.

divertissement [divertismɑ̃] *nm* [passe-temps] form of relaxation.

divin, -e [divɛ̃, in] *adj* divine.

divinité [divinite] *nf* divinity.

diviser [divize] *vt* [gén] to divide, to split up. || MATHS to divide; ~ **8 par 4** to divide 8 by 4.

division [divizjɔ̃] *nf* division.

divorce [divɔrs] *nm* JUR divorce.

divorcé, -e [divɔrse] **1** *adj* divorced. **2** *nm, f* divorcee, divorced person.

divorcer [divɔrse] *vi* to divorce.

divulguer [divylge] *vt* to divulge.

dix [dis] *adj num & nm* ten; *voir aussi* **six**.

dix-huit [dizɥit] *adj num & nm* eighteen; *voir aussi* **six**.

dix-huitième [dizɥitjem] *adj num, nm & nmf* eighteenth; *voir aussi* **sixième**.

dixième [dizjem] *adj num, nm & nmf* tenth; *voir aussi* **sixième**.

dix-neuf [diznœf] *adj num & nm* nineteen; *voir aussi* **six**.

dix-neuvième [diznœvjem] *adj num, nm & nmf* nineteenth; *voir aussi* **sixième**.

dix-sept [diset] *adj num & nm* seventeen; *voir aussi* **six**.

dix-septième [disetjem] *adj num, nm & nmf* seventeenth; *voir aussi* **sixième**.

dizaine [dizen] *nf* [environ dix]: **une ~ de** about ten.

do [do] *nm inv* MUS C; [chanté] doh.

doc [dɔk] (*abr de* **documentation**) *nf* literature, brochures (*pl*).

docile [dɔsil] *adj* [obéissant] docile.

dock [dɔk] *nm* [bassin] dock. || [hangar] warehouse.

docker [dɔker] *nm* docker.

docteur [dɔktœr] *nm* [médecin] doctor. || UNIV: ~ **ès lettres/sciences** ≃ PhD.

doctorat [dɔktɔra] *nm* [grade] doctorate.

doctrine [dɔktrin] *nf* doctrine.

document [dɔkymɑ̃] *nm* document.

documentaire [dɔkymɑ̃ter] *nm & adj* documentary.

documentaliste [dɔkymɑ̃talist] *nmf* [d'archives] archivist; PRESSE & TÉLÉ researcher.

documentation [dɔkymɑ̃tasjɔ̃] *nf* [travail] research. || [brochures] documentation.

documenter [dɔkymɑ̃te] ○ **se documenter** *vp* to do some research.

dodo [dodo] *nm fam* beddy-byes; **faire ~** to sleep.

dodu, -e [dody] *adj fam* [enfant, joue, bras] chubby; [animal] plump.

dogme [dɔgm] *nm* dogma.

dogue [dɔg] *nm* mastiff.

doigt [dwa] *nm* finger; **un ~ de** (just) a drop ou finger of; **montrer qqch du ~ to** point at sthg; ~ **de pied** toe.

dois → **devoir**.

doive → **devoir**.

dollar [dɔlar] *nm* dollar.

domaine [dɔmen] *nm* [propriété] estate. || [secteur, champ d'activité] field, domain.

dôme [dom] *nm* ARCHIT dome.

domestique [dɔmestik] **1** *nmf* (domestic) servant. **2** *adj* family (*avant n*); [travaux] household (*avant n*).

domestiquer [dɔmestike] *vt* [animal] to domesticate.

domicile [dɔmisil] *nm* [gén] (place of) residence; **travailler à** ~ to work from ou at home; **ils livrent à** ~ they do deliveries.

dominant, -e [dɔminɑ̃, ɑ̃t] *adj* [qui prévaut] dominant.

domination [dɔminasjɔ̃] *nf* [autorité] domination, dominion.

dominer [dɔmine] **1** *vt* [surplomber, avoir de l'autorité sur] to dominate. || [surpasser] to outclass. || [maîtriser] to control, to master. || *fig* [connaître] to master. **2** *vi* [prédominer] to predominate. || [triompher] to be on top, to hold sway. ○ **se dominer** *vp* to control o.s.

Dominique [dɔminik] *nf*: **la ~** Dominica.

domino [dɔmino] *nm* domino.

dommage [dɔmaʒ] *nm* [préjudice] harm (*U*); ~**s et intérêts**, ~**s-intérêts** damages; **c'est ~ que** + *subjonctif*) it's a pity ou shame (that). || [dégâts] damage (*U*).

dompter [dɔ̃te] *vt* [animal, fauve] to tame.

dompteur, -euse [dɔ̃tœr, øz] *nm, f* [de fauves] tamer.

DOM-TOM [dɔmtɔm] (*abr de* **départements d'outre-mer/territoires d'outre-**

mer) nmpl French overseas départements and territories.

don [dɔ̃] nm [cadeau] gift. || [aptitude] knack.

donateur, -trice [dɔnatœr, tris] nm, f donor.

donation [dɔnasjɔ̃] nf settlement.

donc [dɔ̃k] conj so; **je disais ~ ...** so as I was saying ...; **allons ~!** come on!; **tais-toi ~!** will you be quiet!

donjon [dɔ̃ʒɔ̃] nm keep.

donné, -e [dɔne] adj given; **étant ~ que** given that, considering (that). ○ **donnée** nf INFORM & MATHS datum, piece of data; **~es numériques** numerical data. || [élément] fact, particular.

donner [dɔne] 1 vt [gén] to give; [se débarrasser de] to give away; **~ qqch à qqn** to give sb sthg, to give sthg to sb; **~ sa voiture à réparer** to leave one's car to be repaired; **quel âge lui donnes-tu?** how old do you think he/she is? 2 vi [s'ouvrir]: **~ sur** to look out onto. || [produire] to produce, to yield.

donneur, -euse [dɔnœr, øz] nm, f MÉD donor. || CARTES dealer.

dont [dɔ̃] pron rel [complément de verbe ou d'adjectif]: **la personne ~ tu parles** the person you're speaking about, the person about whom you are speaking; **l'accident ~ il est responsable** the accident for which he is responsible. || [complément de nom ou de pronom - relatif à l'objet] of which, whose; [- relatif à personne] whose; **la boîte ~ le couvercle est jaune** the box whose lid is yellow, the box with the yellow lid; **celui ~ les parents sont divorcés** the one whose parents are divorced. || [indiquant la partie d'un tout]: **plusieurs personnes ont téléphoné, ~ ton frère** several people phoned, one of which was your brother ou among them was your brother.

dopage [dɔpaʒ] nm doping.

doper [dɔpe] vt to dope. ○ **se doper** vp to take stimulants.

dorade [dɔrad] = **daurade**.

doré, -e [dɔre] adj [couvert de dorure] gilded, gilt. || [couleur] golden.

dorénavant [dɔrenavɑ̃] adv from now on, in future.

dorer [dɔre] vt [couvrir d'or] to gild. || [peau] to tan. || CULIN to glaze.

dorloter [dɔrlɔte] vt to pamper, to cosset.

dormir [dɔrmir] vi [sommeiller] to sleep. || [rester inactif - personne] to slack, to

stand around (doing nothing); [- capitaux] to lie idle.

dortoir [dɔrtwar] nm dormitory.

dos [do] nm back; **de ~** from behind; **«voir au ~»** "see over"; **~ crawlé** backstroke.

DOS, Dos [dɔs] (abr de **Disk Operating System**) nm DOS.

dosage [dozaʒ] nm [de médicament] dose; [d'ingrédient] amount.

dos-d'âne [dodan] nm bump.

dose [doz] nf [quantité de médicament] dose. || [quantité] share; **forcer la ~** fam fig to overdo it.

doser [doze] vt [médicament, ingrédient] to measure out; fig to weigh up.

dossard [dosar] nm number (on competitor's back).

dossier [dosje] nm [de fauteuil] back. || [documents] file, dossier. || [classeur] file, folder. || fig [question] question.

dot [dɔt] nf dowry.

doter [dɔte] vt [pourvoir]: **~ de** [talent] to endow with; [machine] to equip with.

douane [dwan] nf [service, lieu] customs (pl); **passer la ~** to go through customs.

douanier, -ière [dwanje, jɛr] 1 adj customs (avant n). 2 nm, f customs officer.

doublage [dublaʒ] nm [renforcement] lining. || [de film] dubbing.

double [dubl] 1 adj double. 2 adv double. 3 nm [quantité]: **le ~** double. || [copie] copy; **en ~** in duplicate. || TENNIS doubles (pl).

doublement [dubləmɑ̃] adv doubly.

doubler [duble] 1 vt [multiplier] to double. || [renforcer]: **~ (de)** to line (with). || [dépasser] to overtake. || [film, acteur] to dub. 2 vi [véhicule] to overtake. || [augmenter] to double.

doublure [dublyr] nf [renforcement] lining. || CIN stand-in.

douce → **doux**.

doucement [dusmɑ̃] adv [descendre] carefully; [frapper] gently. || [parler] softly.

douceur [dusœr] nf [de saveur, parfum] sweetness. || [d'éclairage, de peau, de musique] softness. || [de climat] mildness. || [de caractère] gentleness. ○ **douceurs** nfpl [friandises] sweets.

douche [duʃ] nf [appareil, action] shower. || fam fig [déception] letdown.

doucher [duʃe] vt [donner une douche à]: **~ qqn** to give sb a shower. ○ **se dou-**

cher *vp* to take or have a shower, to shower.

doué, -e [dwe] *adj* talented; être ~ pour to have a gift for.

douillet, -ette [dujɛ, ɛt] *adj* [confortable] snug, cosy. || [sensible] soft.

douloureux, -euse [dulurø, øz] *adj* [physiquement] painful. || [moralement] distressing. || [regard, air] sorrowful.

doute [dut] *nm* doubt. ○ **sans doute** *loc adv* no doubt; **sans aucun ~** without (a) doubt.

douter [dute] 1 *vt* [ne pas croire]: ~ que (+ subjonctif) to doubt (that). 2 *vi* [ne pas avoir confiance]: ~ de qqn/de qqch to doubt sb/sthg, to have doubts about sb/sthg. ○ **se douter** *vp*: se ~ de qqch to suspect sthg.

douteux, -euse [dutø, øz] *adj* [incertain] doubtful. || [contestable] questionable. || *péj* [mœurs] dubious; [personne] dubious-looking.

doux, douce [du, dus] *adj* [éclairage, peau, musique] soft. || [saveur, parfum] sweet. || [climat, condiment] mild. || [pente, regard, caractère] gentle.

douzaine [duzɛn] *nf* [douze] dozen. || [environ douze]: **une ~ de** about twelve.

douze [duz] *adj num & nm* twelve; *voir aussi* **six**.

douzième [duzjɛm] *adj num, nm & nmf* twelfth; *voir aussi* **sixième**.

doyen, -enne [dwajɛ̃, ɛn] *nm, f* [le plus ancien] most senior member.

Dr (*abr de* **Docteur**) Dr.

draconien, -ienne [drakɔnjɛ̃, jɛn] *adj* draconian.

dragée [draʒe] *nf* [confiserie] sugared almond. || [comprimé] pill.

dragon [dragɔ̃] *nm* [monstre, personne autoritaire] dragon. || [soldat] dragoon.

draguer [drage] *vt* [nettoyer] to dredge. || *fam* [personne] to chat up, to get off with.

dragueur, -euse [dragœr, øz] *nm, f* *fam* [homme] womanizer; **quelle dragueuse!** she's always chasing after men!

drainage [drɛnaʒ] *nm* draining.

drainer [drene] *vt* [terrain, plaie] to drain. || *fig* [attirer] to drain off.

dramatique [dramatik] 1 *nf* play. 2 *adj* THÉÂTRE dramatic. || [grave] tragic.

dramatiser [dramatize] *vt* [exagérer] to dramatize.

drame [dram] *nm* [catastrophe] tragedy; **faire un ~ de qqch** *fig* to make a drama of sthg. || LITTÉRATURE drama.

drap [dra] *nm* [de lit] sheet. || [tissu] woollen cloth.

drapeau, -x [drapo] *nm* flag; être sous les ~x *fig* to be doing military service.

draper [drape] *vt* to drape.

draperie [drapri] *nf* [tenture] drapery.

dresser [drese] *vt* [lever] to raise. || [faire tenir] to put up. || *sout* [construire] to erect. || [acte, liste, carte] to draw up; [procès-verbal] to make out. || [dompter] to train. || *fig* [opposer]: ~ qqn contre qqn to set sb against sb. ○ **se dresser** *vp* [se lever] to stand up. || [s'élever] to rise (up); *fig* to stand; se ~ contre qqch to rise up against sthg.

dresseur, -euse [dresœr, øz] *nm, f* trainer.

dribbler [drible] SPORT *vi* to dribble.

drogue [drɔg] *nf* [stupéfiant & *fig*] drug; **la ~** drugs (*pl*).

drogué, -e [drɔge] 1 *adj* drugged. 2 *nm, f* drug addict.

droguer [drɔge] *vt* [victime] to drug. ○ **se droguer** *vp* [de stupéfiants] to take drugs.

droguerie [drɔgri] *nf* hardware shop.

droit, -e [drwa, drwat] *adj* [du côté droit] right. || [rectiligne, vertical, honnête] straight. ○ **droit** 1 *adv* straight; **tout ~** straight ahead. 2 *nm* JUR law. || [prérogative] right; **avoir ~ à** to be entitled to; **avoir le ~ de faire qqch** to be allowed to do sthg; **être en ~ de faire qqch** to have a right to do sthg; **~ de vote** right to vote; **~s de l'homme** human rights. ○ **droite** *nf* [gén] right, right-hand side; **à ~e** on the right; **à ~e de** to the right of. || POLIT: **la ~e** the right (wing); **de ~e** right-wing.

droitier, -ière [drwatje, jɛr] 1 *adj* right-handed. 2 *nm, f* right-handed person, right-hander.

drôle [drol] *adj* [amusant] funny. || **~ de** [bizarre] funny; *fam* [remarquable] amazing.

dromadaire [drɔmadɛr] *nm* dromedary.

dru, -e [dry] *adj* thick.

du → de.

dû, due [dy] 1 *pp → devoir*. 2 *adj* due, owing. ○ **dû** *nm* due.

Dublin [dyblɛ̃] *n* Dublin.

duc [dyk] *nm* duke.

duchesse [dyʃɛs] *nf* duchess.

duel [dɥɛl] *nm* duel.

dûment [dymɑ̃] *adv* duly.

dune [dyn] *nf* dune.

duo [dyo] *nm* MUS duet. || [couple] duo.

dupe [dyp] **1** *nf* dupe. **2** *adj* gullible.

duper [dype] *vt sout* to dupe, to take sb in.

duplex [dyplɛks] *nm* [appartement] duplex *Am*. ‖ RADIO & TÉLÉ link-up.

duplicata [dyplikata] *nm inv* duplicate.

dupliquer [dyplike] *vt* [document] to duplicate.

duquel [dykɛl] → **lequel**.

dur, -e [dyr] **1** *adj* [matière, personne, travail] hard; [carton] stiff. ‖ [viande] tough. ‖ [climat, punition, loi] harsh. **2** *nm, f fam*: ~ (à cuire) tough nut. ○ **dur** *adv* hard.

durable [dyrabl] *adj* lasting.

durant [dyrã] *prép* [pendant] for. ‖ [au cours de] during.

durcir [dyrsir] **1** *vt litt & fig* to harden. **2** *vi* to harden, to become hard.

durée [dyre] *nf* length.

durement [dyrmã] *adv* [violemment] hard, vigorously. ‖ [péniblement] severely. ‖ [méchamment] harshly.

durer [dyre] *vi* to last.

dureté [dyrte] *nf* [de matériau, de l'eau] hardness. ‖ [d'époque, de climat, de personne] harshness. ‖ [de punition] severity.

dus, dut *etc* → **devoir**.

DUT (*abr de* **diplôme universitaire de technologie**) *nm university diploma in technology*.

duvet [dyvɛ] *nm* [plumes, poils fins] down. ‖ [sac de couchage] sleeping bag.

dynamique [dinamik] *adj* dynamic.

dynamisme [dinamism] *nm* dynamism.

dynamite [dinamit] *nf* dynamite.

dynastie [dinasti] *nf* dynasty.

dyslexique [dislɛksik] *adj* dyslexic.

e, E [ə] *nm inv* e, E. ○ **E** (*abr de* **est**) E.

eau, -x [o] *nf* water; ~ **douce/salée/de mer** fresh/salt/sea water; ~ **gazeuse/plate** fizzy/still water; ~ **courante** running water; ~ **minérale** mineral water; ~ **oxygénée** hydrogen peroxide; ~ **de toilette** toilet water; **tomber à l'**~ *fig* to fall through.

eau-de-vie [odvi] (*pl* **eaux-de-vie**) *nf* brandy.

ébahi, -e [ebai] *adj* staggered, astounded.

ébauche [eboʃ] *nf* [esquisse] sketch; *fig* outline; **l'**~ **d'un sourire** the ghost of a smile.

ébaucher [eboʃe] *vt* [esquisser] to rough out. ‖ *fig* [commencer]: ~ **un geste** to start to make a gesture.

ébène [ebɛn] *nf* ebony.

ébéniste [ebenist] *nm* cabinet-maker.

éberlué, -e [eberlɥe] *adj* flabbergasted.

éblouir [ebluir] *vt* to dazzle.

éblouissement [ebluismã] *nm* [aveuglement] glare, dazzle. ‖ [vertige] dizziness. ‖ [émerveillement] amazement.

éborgner [eborɲe] *vt*: ~ **qqn** to put sb's eye out.

éboueur [ebwœr] *nm* garbage collector *Am*.

ébouillanter [ebujãte] *vt* to scald.

éboulement [ebulmã] *nm* caving in, fall.

éboulis [ebuli] *nm* mass of fallen rocks.

ébouriffer [eburife] *vt* [cheveux] to ruffle.

ébranler [ebrãle] *vt* [bâtiment, opinion] to shake. ○ **s'ébranler** *vp* [train] to move off.

ébrécher [ebreʃe] *vt* [assiette, verre] to chip; *fam fig* to break into.

ébriété [ebrijete] *nf* drunkenness.

ébrouer [ebrue] ○ **s'ébrouer** *vp* [animal] to shake o.s.

ébruiter [ebrɥite] *vt* to spread.

ébullition [ebylisjɔ̃] *nf* [de liquide] boiling point. || [effervescence]: **en ~** *fig* in a state of agitation.

écaille [ekaj] *nf* [de poisson, reptile] scale; [de tortue] shell. || [de plâtre, peinture, vernis] flake. || [matière] tortoiseshell; **en ~** [lunettes] horn-rimmed.

écailler [ekaje] *vt* [poisson] to scale. || [huîtres] to open. ○ **s'écailler** *vp* to flake or peel off.

écarlate [ekarlat] *adj* & *nf* scarlet.

écarquiller [ekarkije] *vt*: **~ les yeux** to stare wide-eyed.

écart [ekar] *nm* [espace] space. || [temps] gap. || [différence] difference. || [déviation] deviation: **faire un ~** [personne] to step aside; [cheval] to shy; **être à l'~** to be in the background.

écarteler [ekartəle] *vt* *fig* to tear apart.

écartement [ekartəmɑ̃] *nm*: **~ entre** space between.

écarter [ekarte] *vt* [bras, jambes] to open, to spread; **~ qqch de** to move sthg away from. || [obstacle, danger] to brush aside. || [foule, rideaux] to push aside; [solution] to dismiss; **~ qqn de** to exclude sb from. ○ **s'écarter** *vp* [se séparer] to part. || [se détourner]: **s'~ de** to deviate from.

ecchymose [ekimoz] *nf* bruise.

ecclésiastique [eklezjastik] **1** *nm* clergyman. **2** *adj* ecclesiastical.

écervelé, -e [esεrvəle] **1** *adj* scatty, scatterbrained. **2** *nm, f* scatterbrain.

échafaud [eʃafo] *nm* scaffold.

échafaudage [eʃafodaʒ] *nm* CONSTR scaffolding. || [amas] pile.

échalote [eʃalɔt] *nf* shallot.

échancrure [eʃɑ̃kryr] *nf* [de robe] low neckline. || [de côte] indentation.

échange [eʃɑ̃ʒ] *nm* [de choses] exchange; **en ~ (de)** in exchange (for).

échanger [eʃɑ̃ʒe] *vt* [troquer] to swap, to exchange. || [marchandise]: **~ qqch (contre)** to change sthg (for). || [communiquer] to exchange.

échantillon [eʃɑ̃tijɔ̃] *nm* [de produit, de population] sample; *fig* example.

échappatoire [eʃapatwar] *nf* way out.

échappement [eʃapmɑ̃] *nm* AUTOM exhaust; → **pot**.

échapper [eʃape] *vi*: **~ à** [personne, situation] to escape from; [danger, mort] to escape; [suj: détail, parole, sens] to escape. || [glisser]: **laisser ~** to let slip. ○ **s'échapper** *vp*: **~ (de)** to escape (from).

écharde [eʃard] *nf* splinter.

écharpe [eʃarp] *nf* scarf; **en ~** in a sling.

écharper [eʃarpe] *vt* to rip to pieces or shreds.

échasse [eʃas] *nf* [de berger, oiseau] stilt.

échassier [eʃasje] *nm* wader.

échauffement [eʃofmɑ̃] *nm* SPORT warm-up.

échauffer [eʃofe] *vt* [chauffer] to overheat. || [exciter] to excite. || [énerver] to irritate. ○ **s'échauffer** *vp* SPORT to warm up. || *fig* [s'animer] to become heated.

échéance [eʃeɑ̃s] *nf* [délai] expiry; **à longue ~** in the long term. || [date] payment date; **arriver à ~** to fall due.

échéant [eʃeɑ̃] *adj*: **le cas ~** if necessary, if need be.

échec [eʃεk] *nm* failure; **~ et mat** checkmate. ○ **échecs** *nmpl* chess (U).

échelle [eʃεl] *nf* [objet] ladder. || [ordre de grandeur] scale.

échelon [eʃlɔ̃] *nm* [barreau] rung. || *fig* [niveau] level.

échelonner [eʃlɔne] *vt* [espacer] to spread out.

échevelé, -e [eʃəvle] *adj* [ébouriffé] dishevelled. || [frénétique] wild.

échine [eʃin] *nf* ANAT spine.

échiquier [eʃikje] *nm* JEU chessboard.

écho [eko] *nm* echo.

échographie [ekɔgrafi] *nf* [examen] ultrasound (scan).

échoir [eʃwar] *vi* [être dévolu]: **~ à** to fall to. || [expirer] to fall due.

échouer [eʃwe] *vi* [ne pas réussir] to fail; **~ à un examen** to fail an exam. ○ **s'échouer** *vp* [navire] to run aground.

échu, -e [eʃy] *pp* → **échoir**.

éclabousser [eklabuse] *vt* [suj: liquide] to spatter.

éclair [eklεr] **1** *nm* [de lumière] flash of lightning. || *fig* [instant]: **~ de** flash of. **2** *adj inv*: **visite ~** flying visit; **guerre ~** blitzkrieg.

éclairage [eklεraʒ] *nm* [lumière] lighting. || *fig* [point de vue] light.

éclaircie [eklεrsi] *nf* bright interval, sunny spell.

éclaircir [eklεrsir] *vt* [rendre plus clair] to lighten. || [rendre moins épais] to thin. || *fig* [clarifier] to clarify. ○ **s'éclaircir** *vp* [devenir plus clair] to clear. || [devenir moins épais] to thin. || [se clarifier] to become clearer.

éclaircissement [eklɛrsismɑ̃] *nm* [explication] explanation.

éclairer [eklere] *vt* [de lumière] to light up. || [expliquer] to clarify. ○ **s'éclairer** *vp* [de lumière] to light one's way. || [regard, visage] to light up. || [rue, ville] to light up.

éclaireur [eklɛrœr] *nm* scout.

éclat [ekla] *nm* [de verre, d'os] splinter; [de pierre] chip. || [de lumière] brilliance. || [de couleur] vividness. || [faste] splendour. || [bruit] burst; ~ **de rire** burst of laughter; ~**s de voix** shouts. || *loc*: **rire aux ~s** to roar ou shriek with laughter.

éclater [eklate] *vi* [exploser - pneu] to burst; [- verre] to shatter; [- obus] to explode; **faire ~** [ballon] to burst; [pétard] to let off. || [incendie, rires] to break out. || *fig* [nouvelles, scandale] to break. ○ **s'éclater** *vp fam* to have a great time.

éclectique [eklɛktik] *adj* eclectic.

éclipse [eklips] *nf* ASTRON eclipse; ~ **de lune/soleil** eclipse of the moon/sun.

éclipser [eklipse] *vt* to eclipse. ○ **s'éclipser** *vp* ASTRON to go into eclipse. || *fam* [s'esquiver] to slip away.

éclopé, -e [eklɔpe] **1** *adj* lame. **2** *nm, f* lame person.

éclore [eklɔr] *vi* [s'ouvrir - fleur] to open out, to blossom; [- œuf] to hatch.

éclos, -e [eklo, oz] *pp* → **éclore**.

écluse [eklyz] *nf* lock.

écœurant, -e [ekœrɑ̃, ɑ̃t] *adj* [gén] disgusting. || [démoralisant] sickening.

écœurer [ekœre] *vt* [dégoûter] to sicken, to disgust. || *fig* [indigner] to sicken. || [décourager] to discourage.

école [ekɔl] *nf* [gén] school; ~ **maternelle** nursery school; ~ **normale** ≃ teacher training college *Br*, ≃ teachers college *Am*; ~ **primaire/secondaire** primary/secondary school *Br*, grade/high school *Am*; **grande** ~ *specialist training establishment, entered by competitive exam and highly prestigious*; **faire l'~ buissonnière** to play truant *Br* ou hooky *Am*; **faire ~** to be accepted. || [éducation] schooling; **l'~ privée** private education.

écolier, -ière [ekɔlje, jɛr] *nm, f* [élève] pupil.

écolo [ekɔlo] *nmf fam* ecologist; **les ~s** the Greens.

écologie [ekɔlɔʒi] *nf* ecology.

écologiste [ekɔlɔʒist] *nmf* ecologist.

éconduire [ekɔ̃dɥir] *vt* [repousser - demande] to dismiss; [- visiteur, soupirant] to show to the door.

économe [ekɔnɔm] **1** *nmf* bursar. **2** *adj* careful, thrifty.

économie [ekɔnɔmi] *nf* [science] economics (*U*). || POLIT economy; ~ **de marché** market economy. || [parcimonie] economy, thrift. || (*gén pl*) [pécule] savings (*pl*); **faire des ~s** to save up.

économique [ekɔnɔmik] *adj* ÉCON economic. || [avantageux] economical.

économiser [ekɔnɔmize] *vt litt & fig* to save.

économiste [ekɔnɔmist] *nmf* economist.

écoper [ekɔpe] *vt* NAVIG to bale out. *fam* [sanction]: ~ **(de) qqch** to get sthg.

écorce [ekɔrs] *nf* [d'arbre] bark. || [d'agrume] peel. || GÉOL crust.

écorcher [ekɔrʃe] *vt* [lapin] to skin. || [bras, jambe] to scratch. || *fig* [langue, nom] to mispronounce.

écorchure [ekɔrʃyr] *nf* graze, scratch.

écossais, -e [ekɔsɛ, ɛz] *adj* [de l'Écosse] Scottish; [whisky] Scotch. || [tissu] tartan. ○ **Écossais, -e** *nm, f* Scot, Scotsman (*f* Scotswoman).

Écosse [ekɔs] *nf*: **l'~** Scotland, *f*.

écosser [ekɔse] *vt* to shell.

écouler [ekule] *vt* to sell. ○ **s'écouler** *vp* [eau] to flow. || [temps] to pass.

écourter [ekurte] *vt* to shorten.

écouter [ekute] *vt* to listen to.

écouteur [ekutœr] *nm* [de téléphone] earpiece. ○ **écouteurs** *nmpl* [de radio] headphones.

écoutille [ekutij] *nf* hatchway.

écran [ekrɑ̃] *nm* [de protection] shield. || CIN & INFORM screen; **le petit ~** television.

écrasant, -e [ekrazɑ̃, ɑ̃t] *adj fig* [accablant] overwhelming.

écraser [ekraze] *vt* [comprimer - cigarette] to stub out; [- pied] to tread on; [- insecte, raisin] to crush. || [vaincre] to crush. || [renverser] to run over. ○ **s'écraser** *vp* [avion, automobile]: **s'~ (contre)** to crash (into).

écrémer [ekreme] *vt* [lait] to skim.

écrevisse [ekrəvis] *nf* crayfish.

écrier [ekrije] ○ **s'écrier** *vp* to cry out.

écrin [ekrɛ̃] *nm* case.

écrire [ekrir] *vt* [phrase, livre] to write. || [orthographier] to spell.

écrit, -e [ekri, it] **1** *pp* → **écrire**. **2** *adj* written. ○ **écrit** *nm* [ouvrage] writing. || [examen] written exam. ○ **par écrit** *loc adv* in writing.

écriteau, -x [ekrito] *nm* notice.

écriture [ekrityr] *nf* [gén] writing. || (*gén pl*) COMM [comptes] books (*pl*).

écrivain [ekrivɛ̃] *nm* writer, author.

écrou [ekru] *nm* TECHNOL nut.

écrouer [ekrue] *vt* to imprison.

écrouler [ekrule] ○ **s'écrouler** *vp litt* & *fig* to collapse.

écru, -e [ekry] *adj* [naturel] unbleached.

ECU [eky] (*abr de* **European Currency Unit**) *nm* ECU.

écu [eky] *nm* [bouclier, armoiries] shield. || [monnaie ancienne] crown. || = ECU.

écueil [ekœj] *nm* [rocher] reef. || *fig* [obstacle] stumbling block.

écuelle [ekɥɛl] *nf* [objet] bowl.

éculé, -e [ekyle] *adj* [chaussure] down-at-heel. || *fig* [plaisanterie] hackneyed.

écume [ekym] *nf* [mousse, bave] foam.

écumoire [ekymwar] *nf* skimmer.

écureuil [ekyrœj] *nm* squirrel.

écurie [ekyri] *nf* [pour chevaux & SPORT] stable. || *fig* [local sale] pigsty.

écusson [ekysɔ̃] *nm* [d'armoiries] coat-of-arms. || MIL badge.

écuyer, -ère [ekɥije, jɛr] *nm, f* [de cirque] rider. ○ **écuyer** *nm* [de chevalier] squire.

eczéma [ɛgzema] *nm* eczema.

édenté, -e [edɑ̃te] *adj* toothless.

EDF, Edf (*abr de* **Électricité de France**) *nf* French national electricity company.

édifice [edifis] *nm* [construction] building.

édifier [edifje] *vt* [ville, église] to build. || *fig* [théorie] to construct. || [personne] to edify; *iron* to enlighten.

Édimbourg [edɛ̃bur] *n* Edinburgh.

éditer [edite] *vt* to publish.

éditeur, -trice [editœr, tris] *nm, f* publisher.

édition [edisjɔ̃] *nf* [profession] publishing. || [de journal, livre] edition.

éditorial, -iaux [editɔrjal, jo] *nm* leader, editorial.

édredon [edrədɔ̃] *nm* eiderdown.

éducateur, -trice [edykatœr, tris] *nm, f* teacher; **~ spécialisé** teacher of children with special educational needs.

éducatif, -ive [edykatif, iv] *adj* educational.

éducation [edykasjɔ̃] *nf* [apprentissage] education; **l'Éducation nationale** ≃ the Department of Education *Am*, ≃ the Department for Education *Br*. || [parentale] upbringing. || [savoir-vivre] breeding.

édulcorant [edylkɔrɑ̃] *nm*: **~ (de synthèse)** (artificial) sweetener.

éduquer [edyke] *vt* to educate.

effacé, -e [efase] *adj* [teinte] faded. || [modeste - rôle] unobtrusive; [- personne] self-effacing.

effacer [efase] *vt* [mot] to erase, to rub out; INFORM to delete. || [souvenir] to erase. ○ **s'effacer** *vp* [s'estomper] to fade (away). || *sout* [s'écarter] to move aside. || *fig* [s'incliner] to give way.

effarant, -e [efarɑ̃, ɑ̃t] *adj* frightening.

effarer [efare] *vt* to frighten, to scare.

effaroucher [efaruʃe] *vt* [effrayer] to scare off. || [intimider] to overawe.

effectif, -ive [efektif, iv] *adj* [aide] positive. ○ **effectif** *nm* MIL strength. || [de groupe] total number.

effectivement [efektivmɑ̃] *adv* [réellement] effectively. || [confirmation] in fact.

effectuer [efektɥe] *vt* [réaliser - manœuvre] to carry out; [- trajet, paiement] to make.

efféminé, -e [efemine] *adj* effeminate.

effervescent, -e [efɛrvesɑ̃, ɑ̃t] *adj* [boisson] effervescent.

effet [efɛ] *nm* [gén] effect; **sous l'~ de** under the effects of; **~ de serre** greenhouse effect. || [impression recherchée] impression. || COMM [titre] bill. ○ **en effet** *loc adv* in fact, indeed.

effeuiller [efœje] *vt* [arbre] to remove the leaves from; [fleur] to remove the petals from.

efficace [efikas] *adj* [remède, mesure] effective. || [personne, machine] efficient.

effigie [efiʒi] *nf* effigy.

effiler [efile] *vt* [tissu] to fray. || [lame] to sharpen. || [cheveux] to thin.

effilocher [efilɔʃe] *vt* to fray. ○ **s'effilocher** *vp* to fray.

efflanqué, -e [eflɑ̃ke] *adj* emaciated.

effleurer [eflœre] *vt* [visage, bras] to brush (against). || *fig* [problème, thème] to touch on. || *fig* [suj: pensée, idée]: **~ qqn** to cross sb's mind.

effluve [eflyv] *nm* exhalation.

effondrement [efɔ̃drəmɑ̃] *nm* collapse.

effondrer [efɔ̃dre] ○ **s'effondrer** *vp litt* & *fig* to collapse.

efforcer [efɔrse] ○ **s'efforcer** *vp*: **s'~ de faire qqch** to make an effort to do sthg.

effort [efɔr] *nm* [de personne] effort.

effraction [efraksjɔ̃] *nf* breaking in; **entrer par ~ dans** to break into.

effrayer [efreje] *vt* to frighten, to scare.

effréné, -e [efrene] *adj* [course] frantic.

effriter [efrite] *vt* to cause to crumble. ○ **s'effriter** *vp* [mur] to crumble.

effroi [efrwa] *nm* fear, dread.

effronté, -e [efrɔ̃te] **1** *adj* insolent. **2** *nm, f* insolent person.

effronterie [efrɔ̃tri] *nf* insolence.

effroyable [efrwajabl] *adj* [catastrophe, misère] appalling. || [laideur] hideous.

effusion [efyzjɔ̃] *nf* [de liquide] effusion. || [de sentiments] effusiveness.

égal, -e, -aux [egal, o] **1** *adj* [équivalent] equal. || [régulier] even. || [indifférent] **ça m'est ~** I don't mind. **2** *nm, f* equal.

également [egalmɑ̃] *adv* [avec égalité] equally. || [aussi] as well, too.

égaler [egale] *vt* MATHS to equal. || [beauté] to match, to compare with.

égaliser [egalize] **1** *vt* [haie, cheveux] to trim. **2** *vi* SPORT to equalize *Br*, to tie *Am*.

égalitaire [egaliter] *adj* egalitarian.

égalité [egalite] *nf* [gén] equality. || [d'humeur] evenness. || SPORT: **être à ~** to be level.

égard [egar] *nm* consideration; **à cet ~** in this respect. ○ **à l'égard de** *loc prép* with regard to, towards.

égarer [egare] *vt* [objet] to mislay, to lose. ○ **s'égarer** *vp* [lettre] to get lost, to go astray; [personne] to get lost, to lose one's way. || *fig & sout* [personne] to stray from the point.

égayer [egeje] *vt* [personne] to cheer up. || [pièce] to brighten up.

égide [eʒid] *nf* protection; **sous l'~ de** *littéraire* under the aegis of.

église [egliz] *nf* church.

égocentrique [egɔsɑ̃trik] *adj* selfcentred, egocentric.

égoïsme [egɔism] *nm* selfishness, egoism.

égoïste [egɔist] **1** *nmf* selfish person. **2** *adj* selfish, egoistic.

égorger [egɔrʒe] *vt* [animal, personne] to cut the throat of.

égosiller [egɔzije] ○ **s'égosiller** *vp fam* [crier] to bawl, to shout. || [chanter] to sing one's head off.

égout [egu] *nm* sewer.

égoutter [egute] *vt* [vaisselle] to leave to drain. || [légumes, fromage] to drain. ○ **s'égoutter** *vp* to drip, to drain.

égouttoir [egutwar] *nm* [à légumes] colander, strainer. || [à vaisselle] rack (*for washing-up*).

égratigner [egratiɲe] *vt* to scratch; *fig* to have a go or dig at. ○ **s'égratigner** *vp*: **s'~ la main** to scratch one's hand.

égratignure [egratiɲyr] *nf* scratch, graze; *fig* dig.

égrener [egrəne] *vt* [détacher les grains de - épi, cosse] to shell; [- grappe] to pick grapes from. || [chapelet] to tell.

égrillard, -e [egrijar, ard] *adj* ribald, bawdy.

Égypte [eʒipt] *nf*: **l'~** Egypt.

égyptien, -ienne [eʒipsjɛ̃, jɛn] *adj* Egyptian. ○ **Égyptien, -ienne** *nm, f* Egyptian.

eh [e] *interj* hey!; **~ bien** well.

éhonté, -e [eɔ̃te] *adj* shameless.

Eiffel [efɛl] *n*: **la tour ~** the Eiffel Tower.

éjaculation [eʒakylasjɔ̃] *nf* ejaculation.

éjectable [eʒɛktabl] *adj*: **siège ~** ejector seat.

éjecter [eʒɛkte] *vt* [douille] to eject. || *fam* [personne] to kick out.

élaboration [elabɔrasjɔ̃] *nf* [de plan, système] working out, development.

élaboré, -e [elabɔre] *adj* elaborate.

élaborer [elabɔre] *vt* [plan, système] to work out, to develop.

élaguer [elage] *vt litt & fig* to prune.

élan [elɑ̃] *nm* ZOOL elk. || SPORT run-up; **prendre son ~** to take a run-up, to gather speed. || *fig* [de joie] outburst.

élancé, -e [elɑ̃se] *adj* slender.

élancer [elɑ̃se] *vi* MÉD to give shooting pains. ○ **s'élancer** *vp* [se précipiter] to rush, to dash. || SPORT to take a run-up.

élargir [elarʒir] *vt* to widen; [vêtement] to let out; *fig* to expand. ○ **s'élargir** *vp* [s'agrandir] to widen; [vêtement] to stretch; *fig* to expand.

élasticité [elastisite] *nf* PHYS elasticity.

élastique [elastik] **1** *nm* [pour attacher] elastic band. || [matière] elastic. **2** *adj* PHYS elastic. || [corps] flexible.

électeur, -trice [elɛktœr, tris] *nm, f* voter, elector.

élection [elɛksjɔ̃] *nf* [vote] election; **~ présidentielle** presidential election; **~s municipales** local elections.

électoral, -e, -aux [elɛktɔral, o] *adj* [campagne, réunion] election (*avant n*).

électricien, -ienne [elɛktrisjɛ̃, jɛn] *nm, f* electrician.

électricité [elɛktrisite] *nf* electricity.

électrifier [elɛktrifje] *vt* to electrify.

électrique [elɛktrik] *adj litt & fig* electric.

électrocardiogramme [elεktrɔkardjɔgram] *nm* electrocardiogram.

électrochoc [elεktrɔʃɔk] *nm* electric shock treatment.

électrocuter [elεktrɔkyte] *vt* to electrocute.

électrode [elεktrɔd] *nf* electrode.

électroencéphalogramme [elεktrɔãsefalɔgram] *nm* electroencephalogram.

électrogène [elεktrɔʒεn] *adj*: **groupe** ~ generating unit.

électrolyse [elεktrɔliz] *nf* electrolysis.

électromagnétique [elεktrɔmaɲetik] *adj* electromagnetic.

électroménager [elεktrɔmenaʒe] *nm* household electrical appliances (*pl*).

électron [elεktrɔ̃] *nm* electron.

électronicien, -ienne [elεktrɔnisjε̃, jεn] *nm, f* electronics specialist.

électronique [elεktrɔnik] **1** *nf* SCIENCE electronics (*U*). **2** *adj* electronic.

électrophone [elεktrɔfɔn] *nm* record player.

élégance [elegãs] *nf* [de personne, style] elegance.

élégant, -e [elegã, ãt] *adj* [personne, style] elegant.

élément [elemã] *nm* [gén] element; **être dans son** ~ to be in one's element. || [de machine] component.

élémentaire [elemãtεr] *adj* [gén] elementary. || [installation, besoin] basic.

éléphant [elefã] *nm* elephant.

élevage [εlvaʒ] *nm* breeding, rearing; [installation] farm.

élevé, -e [εlve] *adj* [haut] high. || [enfant]: **bien/mal** ~ well/badly brought up.

élève [εlεv] *nmf* [écolier, disciple] pupil.

élever [εlve] *vt* [gén] to raise. || [statue] to put up, to erect. || [à un rang supérieur] to elevate. || [esprit] to improve. || [enfant] to bring up. || [poulets] to rear, to breed. ○ **s'élever** *vp* [gén] to rise. || [montant]: **s'~ à** to add up to. || [protester]: **s'~ contre qqn/qqch** to protest against sb/sthg.

éleveur, -euse [εlvœr, øz] *nm, f* breeder.

éligible [eliʒibl] *adj* eligible.

élimé, -e [elime] *adj* threadbare.

élimination [eliminasjɔ̃] *nf* elimination.

éliminatoire [eliminatwar] **1** *nf* (*gén pl*) SPORT qualifying heat ou round. **2** *adj* qualifying (*avant n*).

éliminer [elimine] *vt* to eliminate.

élire [elir] *vt* to elect.

élite [elit] *nf* elite; **d'~** choice, select.

élitiste [elitist] *nmf & adj* elitist.

elle [εl] *pron pers* [sujet - personne] she; [- animal] it, she; [- chose] it. || [complément - personne] her; [- animal] it, her; [- chose] it. || **elles** *pron pers pl* [sujet] they. || [complément] them. ○ **elle-même** *pron pers* [personne] herself; [animal] itself, herself; [chose] itself. ○ **elles-mêmes** *pron pers pl* themselves.

ellipse [elips] *nf* GÉOM ellipse. || LING ellipsis.

élocution [elɔkysjɔ̃] *nf* delivery; **défaut d'~** speech defect.

éloge [elɔʒ] *nm* [louange] praise; **faire l'~ de qqn/qqch** [louer] to speak highly of sb/sthg.

élogieux, -ieuse [elɔʒjø, jøz] *adj* laudatory.

éloignement [elwaɲmã] *nm* [mise à l'écart] removal. || [séparation] absence. || [dans l'espace, le temps] distance.

éloigner [elwaɲe] *vt* [écarter] to move away; ~ **qqch de** to move sthg away from. || [détourner] to turn away. ○ **s'éloigner** *vp* [partir] to move ou go away. || *fig* [du sujet] to stray from the point. || [se détacher] to distance o.s.

éloquence [elɔkãs] *nf* [d'orateur, d'expression] eloquence.

éloquent, -e [elɔkã, ãt] *adj* [avocat, silence] eloquent. || [données] significant.

élu, -e [ely] **1** *pp* → élire. **2** *adj* POLIT elected. **3** *nm, f* POLIT elected representative.

élucider [elyside] *vt* to clear up.

éluder [elyde] *vt* to evade.

Elysée [elize] *nm*: **l'~** *the official residence of the French President and, by extension, the President himself.*

émacié, -e [emasje] *adj littéraire* emaciated.

émail, -aux [emaj, emo] *nm* enamel; **en** ~ enamel, enamelled.

émanation [emanasjɔ̃] *nf* emanation; **être l'~ de** *fig* to emanate from.

émanciper [emãsipe] *vt* to emancipate. ○ **s'émanciper** *vp* [se libérer] to become free ou liberated.

émaner [emane] *vi*: ~ **de** to emanate from.

émarger [emarʒe] *vt* [signer] to sign.

emballage [ãbalaʒ] *nm* packaging.

emballer [ãbale] *vt* [objet] to pack (up), to wrap (up). || *fam* [plaire] to thrill. ○ **s'emballer** *vp* [moteur] to race. || [cheval] to bolt. || *fam* [personne -

s'enthousiasmer] to get carried away; [- s'emporter] to lose one's temper.

embarcadère [ɑ̃barkadɛr] *nm* landing stage.

embarcation [ɑ̃barkasjɔ̃] *nf* small boat.

embardée [ɑ̃barde] *nf* swerve; **faire une ~** to swerve.

embargo [ɑ̃bargo] *nm* embargo.

embarquement [ɑ̃barkəmɑ̃] *nm* [de marchandises] loading. || [de passagers] boarding.

embarquer [ɑ̃barke] **1** *vt* [marchandises] to load. || [passagers] to (take on) board. || *fam* [arrêter] to pick up. || *fam fig* [engager]: **~ qqn dans** to involve sb in. || *fam* [emmener] to cart off. **2** *vi* : **~ (pour)** to sail (for). ○ **s'embarquer** *vp* [sur un bateau] to (set) sail. || *fam fig* [s'engager]: **s'~ dans** to get involved in.

embarras [ɑ̃bara] *nm* [incertitude] (state of) uncertainty; **avoir l' ~ du choix** to be spoilt for choice. || [situation difficile] predicament; **mettre qqn dans l'~** to place sb in an awkward position. || [gêne] embarrassment.

embarrassé, -e [ɑ̃barase] *adj* [encombré - pièce, bureau] cluttered; **avoir les mains ~es** to have one's hands full. || [gêné] embarrassed. || [confus] confused.

embarrasser [ɑ̃barase] *vt* [encombrer - pièce] to clutter up; [- personne] to hamper. || [gêner] to put in an awkward position. ○ **s'embarrasser** *vp* [se charger]: **s'~ de qqch** to burden o.s. with sthg; *fig* to bother about sthg.

embauche [ɑ̃boʃ] *nf*, **embauchage** [ɑ̃boʃaʒ] *nm* hiring, employment.

embaucher [ɑ̃boʃe] *vt* [employer] to employ, to take on.

embaumer [ɑ̃bome] **1** *vt* [cadavre] to embalm. || [parfumer] to scent. **2** *vi* to be fragrant.

embellir [ɑ̃belir] **1** *vt* [agrémenter] to brighten up. || *fig* [enjoliver] to embellish. **2** *vi* [devenir plus beau] to become more attractive.

embêtant, -e [ɑ̃bɛtɑ̃, ɑ̃t] *adj fam* annoying.

embêtement [ɑ̃bɛtmɑ̃] *nm fam* trouble.

embêter [ɑ̃bɛte] *vt fam* [contrarier, importuner] to annoy. ○ **s'embêter** *vp fam* [s'ennuyer] to be bored.

emblée [ɑ̃ble] ○ **d'emblée** *loc adv* right away.

emblème [ɑ̃blɛm] *nm* emblem.

emboîter [ɑ̃bwate] *vt*: **~ qqch dans qqch** to fit sthg into sthg. ○ **s'emboîter** *vp* to fit together.

embonpoint [ɑ̃bɔ̃pwɛ̃] *nm* stoutness.

embouchure [ɑ̃buʃyr] *nf* [de fleuve] mouth.

embourber [ɑ̃burbe] ○ **s'embourber** *vp* [s'enliser] to get stuck in the mud; *fig* to get bogged down.

embourgeoiser [ɑ̃burʒwaze] ○ **s'embourgeoiser** *vp* [personne] to adopt middle-class values; [quartier] to become gentrified.

embout [ɑ̃bu] *nm* [protection] tip; [extrémité d'un tube] nozzle.

embouteillage [ɑ̃butɛjaʒ] *nm* [circulation] traffic jam.

emboutir [ɑ̃butir] *vt fam* [voiture] to crash into. || TECHNOL to stamp.

embranchement [ɑ̃brɑ̃ʃmɑ̃] *nm* [carrefour] junction.

embraser [ɑ̃braze] *vt* [incendier, éclairer] to set ablaze. ○ **s'embraser** *vp* [prendre feu, s'éclairer] to be ablaze.

embrassade [ɑ̃brasad] *nf* embrace.

embrasser [ɑ̃brase] *vt* [donner un baiser à] to kiss. || [étreindre] to embrace. || *fig* [du regard] to take in. ○ **s'embrasser** *vp* to kiss (each other).

embrasure [ɑ̃brazyr] *nf*: **dans l'~ de la fenêtre** in the window.

embrayage [ɑ̃brɛjaʒ] *nm* [mécanisme] clutch.

embrayer [ɑ̃brɛje] *vi* AUTOM to engage the clutch.

embrocher [ɑ̃brɔʃe] *vt* to skewer.

embrouillamini [ɑ̃brujamini] *nm fam* muddle.

embrouiller [ɑ̃bruje] *vt* [mélanger] to mix (up), to muddle (up). || *fig* [compliquer] to confuse.

embruns [ɑ̃brœ̃] *nmpl* spray (*U*).

embryon [ɑ̃brijɔ̃] *nm litt* & *fig* embryo.

embûche [ɑ̃byʃ] *nf* pitfall.

embuer [ɑ̃bɥe] *vt* [de vapeur] to steam up. || [de larmes] to mist (over).

embuscade [ɑ̃byskad] *nf* ambush.

éméché, -e [emeʃe] *adj fam* tipsy.

émeraude [emrod] *nf* emerald.

émerger [emɛrʒe] *vi* [gén] to emerge. || NAVIG & *fig* to surface.

émeri [emri] *nm*: **papier** OU **toile ~** emery paper.

émerveiller [emɛrveje] *vt* to fill with wonder.

émetteur, -trice [emetœr, tris] *adj* transmitting; **poste ~** transmitter. ○ **émetteur** *nm* [appareil] transmitter.

émettre [emɛtr] *vt* [produire] to emit. || [diffuser] to transmit, to broadcast. || [mettre en circulation] to issue. || [exprimer] to express.

émeute [emøt] *nf* riot.

émietter [emjete] *vt* [du pain] to crumble. || [morceler] to divide up.

émigrant, -e [emigrã, ɑ̃t] *adj & nm, f* emigrant.

émigré, -e [emigre] **1** *adj* migrant. **2** *nm, f* emigrant.

émigrer [emigre] *vi* [personnes] to emigrate. || [animaux] to migrate.

émincé, -e [emɛ̃se] *adj* sliced thinly. ○ **émincé** *nm* thin slices of meat served in a sauce.

éminemment [eminamɑ̃] *adv* eminently.

éminent, -e [eminɑ̃, ɑ̃t] *adj* eminent, distinguished.

émir [emir] *nm* emir.

émirat [emira] *nm* emirate. ○ **Émirat** *nm*: **les Émirats arabes unis** the United Arab Emirates.

émis, -e [emi, iz] *pp* → **émettre**.

émissaire [emisɛr] **1** *nm* [envoyé] emissary, envoy. **2** *adj* → **bouc**.

émission [emisjɔ̃] *nf* [de gaz, de son etc] emission. || [RADIO & TÉLÉ - transmission] transmission, broadcasting; [- programme] programme *Br*, program *Am*. || [mise en circulation] issue.

emmagasiner [ɑ̃magazine] *vt* [stocker] to store. || *fig* [accumuler] to store up.

emmanchure [ɑ̃mɑ̃ʃyr] *nf* armhole.

emmêler [ɑ̃mele] *vt* [fils] to tangle up. || *fig* [idées] to muddle up, to confuse. ○ **s'emmêler** *vp* [fils] to get into a tangle. || *fig* [personne] to get mixed up.

emménagement [ɑ̃menaʒmɑ̃] *nm* moving in.

emménager [ɑ̃menaʒe] *vi* to move in.

emmener [ɑ̃mne] *vt* to take.

emmerder [ɑ̃mɛrde] *vt tfam* to piss off. ○ **s'emmerder** *vp tfam* [s'embêter] to be bored stiff.

emmitoufler [ɑ̃mitufle] *vt* to wrap up. ○ **s'emmitoufler** *vp* to wrap o.s. up.

émoi [emwa] *nm sout* [émotion] emotion.

émotif, -ive [emotif, iv] *adj* emotional.

émotion [emosjɔ̃] *nf* [sentiment] emotion. || [peur] fright, shock.

émotionnel, -elle [emosjɔnel] *adj* emotional.

émousser [emuse] *vt litt & fig* to blunt.

émouvant, -e [emuvɑ̃, ɑ̃t] *adj* moving.

émouvoir [emuvwar] *vt* [troubler] to disturb, to upset. || [susciter la sympathie de] to move, to touch. ○ **s'émouvoir** *vp* to show emotion, to be upset.

empailler [ɑ̃paje] *vt* [animal] to stuff. || [chaise] to upholster (with straw).

empaqueter [ɑ̃pakte] *vt* to pack (up), to wrap (up).

empâter [ɑ̃pate] *vt* [visage, traits] to fatten out. ○ **s'empâter** *vp* to put on weight.

empêchement [ɑ̃pɛʃmɑ̃] *nm* obstacle; **j'ai un ~** something has come up.

empêcher [ɑ̃peʃe] *vt* to prevent; **~ qqn/qqch de faire qqch** to prevent sb/sthg from doing sthg; **(il) n'empêche que** nevertheless, all the same.

empereur [ɑ̃prœr] *nm* emperor.

empesé, -e [ɑ̃pəze] *adj* [linge] starched. || *fig* [style] stiff.

empester [ɑ̃peste] *vi* to stink.

empêtrer [ɑ̃petre] *vt*: **être empêtré dans** to be tangled up in. ○ **s'empêtrer** *vp*: **s'~ (dans)** to get tangled up (in.)

emphase [ɑ̃faz] *nf péj* pomposity.

empiéter [ɑ̃pjete] *vi*: **~ sur** to encroach on.

empiffrer [ɑ̃pifre] ○ **s'empiffrer** *vp fam* to stuff o.s.

empiler [ɑ̃pile] *vt* [entasser] to pile up, to stack up.

empire [ɑ̃pir] *nm* HIST & *fig* empire.

empirer [ɑ̃pire] *vi & vt* to worsen.

empirique [ɑ̃pirik] *adj* empirical.

emplacement [ɑ̃plasmɑ̃] *nm* site, location.

emplette [ɑ̃plɛt] *nf* (*gén pl*) purchase.

emplir [ɑ̃plir] *vt sout*: **~ (de)** to fill (with). ○ **s'emplir** *vp*: **s'~ (de)** to fill (with).

emploi [ɑ̃plwa] *nm* [utilisation] use; **~ du temps** timetable. || [travail] job.

employé, -e [ɑ̃plwaje] *nm, f* employee; **~ de bureau** office employee *ou* worker.

employer [ɑ̃plwaje] *vt* [utiliser] to use. || [salarier] to employ.

employeur, -euse [ɑ̃plwajœr, øz] *nm, f* employer.

empocher [ɑ̃pɔʃe] *vt fam* to pocket.

empoignade [ɑ̃pwaɲad] *nf* row.

empoigner [ɑ̃pwaɲe] *vt* [saisir] to

grasp. ○ **s'empoigner** *vp fig* to come to blows.

empoisonnement [ɑ̃pwazɔnmɑ̃] *nm* [intoxication] poisoning.

empoisonner [ɑ̃pwazɔne] *vt* [gén] to poison. || *fam* [ennuyer] to annoy, to bug.

emporté, -e [ɑ̃pɔrte] *adj* short-tempered.

emportement [ɑ̃pɔrtəmɑ̃] *nm* anger.

emporter [ɑ̃pɔrte] *vt* [emmener] to take (away); **à ~** [plats] to take away, to go *Am.* || [entraîner] to carry along. || [arracher] to tear off, to blow off. || [faire mourir] to carry off. || [surpasser]: **l'~ sur** to get the better of. ○ **s'emporter** *vp* to get angry, to lose one's temper.

empoté, -e [ɑ̃pɔte] *fam* **1** *adj* clumsy. **2** *nm, f* clumsy person.

empreinte [ɑ̃prɛ̃t] *nf* [trace] print; *fig* mark, trace; **~s digitales** fingerprints.

empressement [ɑ̃presmɑ̃] *nm* [zèle] attentiveness. || [enthousiasme] eagerness.

empresser [ɑ̃prese] ○ **s'empresser** *vp*: **s'~ de faire qqch** to hurry to do sthg.

emprise [ɑ̃priz] *nf* [ascendant] influence.

emprisonnement [ɑ̃prizɔnmɑ̃] *nm* imprisonment.

emprisonner [ɑ̃prizɔne] *vt* [voleur] to imprison.

emprunt [ɑ̃prœ̃] *nm* FIN loan. || LING & *fig* borrowing.

emprunté, -e [ɑ̃prœ̃te] *adj* awkward, self-conscious.

emprunter [ɑ̃prœ̃te] *vt* [gén] to borrow; **~ qqch à** to borrow sthg from. || [route] to take.

ému, -e [emy] **1** *pp* → **émouvoir. 2** *adj* [personne] moved, touched; [regard, sourire] emotional.

émulation [emylasjɔ̃] *nf* [concurrence] rivalry. || [imitation] emulation.

émule [emyl] *nmf* [imitateur] emulator.

émulsion [emylsjɔ̃] *nf* emulsion.

en [ɑ̃] **1** *prép* [temps] in; **~ 1994** in 1994; **~ hiver/septembre** in winter/September. || [lieu] in; [direction] to. || [matière] made of; **c'est ~ métal** it's (made of) metal; **une théière ~ argent** a silver teapot. || [état, forme, manière]: **les arbres sont ~ fleurs** the trees are in blossom; **du sucre ~ morceaux** sugar cubes; **je l'ai eu ~ cadeau** I was given it as a present; **dire qqch ~ anglais** to say sthg in English; **~ vacances** on holiday. || [moyen] by; **~ avion/bateau/train** by plane/boat/train. || [mesure] in; **vous l'avez ~ 38?** do you

have it in a 38? || [devant un participe présent]: **~ arrivant à Paris** on arriving in Paris, as he/she *etc* arrived in Paris; **elle répondit ~ souriant** she replied with a smile. **2** *pron adv* [complément de verbe, de nom, d'adjectif]: **il s'~ est souvenu** he remembered it; **nous ~ avons déjà parlé** we've already spoken about it. || [avec un indéfini, exprimant une quantité]: **j'ai du chocolat, tu ~ veux?** I've got some chocolate, do you want some?; **il y ~ a plusieurs** there are several (of them). || [provenance] from there.

ENA, Ena [ena] (*abr de* **École nationale d'administration**) *nf prestigious grande école training future government officials.*

encadrement [ɑ̃kadrəmɑ̃] *nm* [de tableau, porte] frame. || [dans une entreprise] managerial staff; [à l'armée] officers (*pl*); [à l'école] staff.

encadrer [ɑ̃kadre] *vt* [photo, visage] to frame. || [employés] to supervise; [soldats] to be in command of; [élèves] to teach.

encaissé, -e [ɑ̃kese] *adj* [vallée] deep and narrow; [rivière] steep-banked.

encaisser [ɑ̃kese] *vt* [argent, coups, insultes] to take. || [chèque] to cash.

encart [ɑ̃kar] *nm* insert.

encastrer [ɑ̃kastre] *vt* to fit. ○ **s'encastrer** *vp* to fit (exactly).

encaustique [ɑ̃kostik] *nf* [cire] polish.

enceinte [ɑ̃sɛ̃t] **1** *adj f* pregnant; **~ de 4 mois** 4 months pregnant. **2** *nf* [muraille] wall. || [espace]: **dans l'~ de** within (the confines of). || [baffle]: **~ (acoustique)** speaker.

encens [ɑ̃sɑ̃] *nm* incense.

encenser [ɑ̃sɑ̃se] *vt fig* [louer] to flatter.

encensoir [ɑ̃sɑ̃swar] *nm* censer.

encercler [ɑ̃serkle] *vt* [cerner, environner] to surround. || [entourer] to circle.

enchaînement [ɑ̃ʃɛnmɑ̃] *nm* [succession] series. || [liaison] link.

enchaîner [ɑ̃ʃene] **1** *vt* [attacher] to chain up. || [coordonner] to link. **2** *vi*: **~ (sur)** to move on (to). ○ **s'enchaîner** *vp* [se suivre] to follow on from each other.

enchanté, -e [ɑ̃ʃɑ̃te] *adj* [ravi] delighted; **~ de faire votre connaissance** pleased to meet you. || [ensorcelé] enchanted.

enchantement [ɑ̃ʃɑ̃tmɑ̃] *nm* [sortilège] magic spell; **comme par ~** as if by magic. || [merveille] wonder.

enchanter [ɑ̃ʃɑ̃te] *vt* [ensorceler, charmer] to enchant. || [ravir] to delight.

enchâsser [ɑ̃ʃase] *vt* [sertir] to set.

enchère [ɑ̃ʃɛr] *nf* bid; **vendre qqch aux ~s** to sell sthg at or by auction.

enchevêtrer [ɑ̃ʃəvɛtre] *rt* [emmêler] to tangle up; *fig* to muddle, to confuse.

enclave [ɑ̃klav] *nf* enclave.

enclencher [ɑ̃klɑ̃ʃe] *rt* [mécanisme] to engage. ○ **s'enclencher** *rp* TECHNOL to engage. || *fig* [commencer] to begin.

enclin, -e [ɑ̃klɛ̃, in] *adj*: **~ à qqch/à faire qqch** inclined to sthg/to do sthg.

enclore [ɑ̃klɔr] *vt* to fence in, to enclose.

enclos, -e [ɑ̃klo, oz] *pp* → **enclore**.
○ **enclos** *nm* enclosure.

enclume [ɑ̃klym] *nf* anvil.

encoche [ɑ̃kɔʃ] *nf* notch.

encoignure [ɑ̃kwaɲyr, ɑ̃kɔɲyr] *nf* [coin] corner.

encolure [ɑ̃kɔlyr] *nf* neck.

encombrant, -e [ɑ̃kɔ̃brɑ̃, ɑ̃t] cumbersome; *fig* [personne] undesirable.

encombre [ɑ̃kɔ̃br] ○ **sans encombre** *loc adv* without a hitch.

encombré, -e [ɑ̃kɔ̃bre] *adj* [lieu] busy, congested; *fig* saturated.

encombrement [ɑ̃kɔ̃brəmɑ̃] *nm* [d'une pièce] clutter. || [d'un objet] overall dimensions (*pl*). || [embouteillage] traffic jam. || INFORM footprint.

encombrer [ɑ̃kɔ̃bre] *rt* to clutter (up).

encontre [ɑ̃kɔ̃tr] ○ **à l'encontre de** *loc prép*: **aller à l'~ de** to go against, to oppose.

encore [ɑ̃kɔr] *adv* [toujours] still; **~ un mois** one more month; **pas ~** not yet. || [de nouveau] again; **il m'a ~ menti** he's lied to me again; **l'ascenseur est en panne - ~!** the lift's out of order - not again! || [marque le renforcement] even; **~ mieux/pire** even better/worse. ○ **et encore** *loc adv*: **j'ai eu le temps de prendre un sandwich, et ~!** I had time for a sandwich, but only just!

encouragement [ɑ̃kuraʒmɑ̃] *nm* [parole] (word of) encouragement.

encourager [ɑ̃kuraʒe] *rt* to encourage; **~ qqn à faire qqch** to encourage sb to do sthg.

encourir [ɑ̃kurir] *rt sout* to incur.

encouru, -e [ɑ̃kury] *pp* → **encourir**.

encrasser [ɑ̃krase] *rt* TECHNOL to clog up. ○ **s'encrasser** *rp* TECHNOL to clog up.

encre [ɑ̃kr] *nf* ink.

encrer [ɑ̃kre] *rt* to ink.

encrier [ɑ̃krije] *nm* inkwell.

encroûter [ɑ̃krute] ○ **s'encroûter** *rp fam* to get into a rut.

encyclopédie [ɑ̃siklɔpedi] *nf* encyclopedia.

encyclopédique [ɑ̃siklɔpedik] *adj* encyclopedic.

endetter [ɑ̃dete] ○ **s'endetter** *rp* to get into debt.

endeuiller [ɑ̃dœje] *vt* to plunge into mourning.

endiablé, -e [ɑ̃djable] *adj* [frénétique] frantic, frenzied.

endiguer [ɑ̃dige] *rt* [fleuve] to dam. || *fig* [réprimer] to stem.

endimanché, -e [ɑ̃dimɑ̃ʃe] *adj* in one's Sunday best.

endive [ɑ̃div] *nf* chicory (*U*).

endoctriner [ɑ̃dɔktrine] *rt* to indoctrinate.

endommager [ɑ̃dɔmaʒe] *rt* to damage.

endormi, -e [ɑ̃dɔrmi] *adj* [personne] sleeping, asleep. || *fig* [village] sleepy; [jambe] numb; *fam* [apathique] sluggish.

endormir [ɑ̃dɔrmir] *rt* [assoupir, ennuyer] to send to sleep. || [anesthésier - patient] to anaesthetize; [- douleur] to ease. || *fig* [tromper] to allay. ○ **s'endormir** *rp* [s'assoupir] to fall asleep.

endosser [ɑ̃dose] *rt* [vêtement] to put on. || FIN & JUR to endorse. || *fig* [responsabilité] to take on.

endroit [ɑ̃drwa] *nm* [lieu, point] place; **à quel ~?** where? || [passage] part. || [côté] right side; **à l'~** the right way round.

enduire [ɑ̃dɥir] *rt*: **~ qqch (de)** to coat sthg (with).

enduit, -e [ɑ̃dɥi, ɥit] *pp* → **enduire**.
○ **enduit** *nm* coating.

endurance [ɑ̃dyrɑ̃s] *nf* endurance.

endurcir [ɑ̃dyrsir] *vt* to harden. ○ **s'endurcir** *rp*: **s'~ à** to become hardened to.

endurer [ɑ̃dyre] *rt* to endure.

énergétique [enɛrʒetik] *adj* [aliment] energy-giving.

énergie [enɛrʒi] *nf* energy.

énergique [enɛrʒik] *adj* [gén] energetic; [remède] powerful; [mesure] drastic.

énergumène [enɛrgymɛn] *nmf* rowdy character.

énerver [enɛrve] *vt* to irritate, to annoy. ○ **s'énerver** *rp* to get annoyed.

enfance [ɑ̃fɑ̃s] *nf* [âge] childhood.

enfant [ɑ̃fɑ̃] *nmf* [gén] child; **attendre un ~** to be expecting a baby.

enfanter [ɑ̃fɑ̃te] *vt littéraire* to give birth to.

enfantillage [ɑ̃fɑ̃tijaʒ] *nm* childishness (*U*).

enfantin, -e [ɑ̃fɑ̃tɛ̃, in] *adj* [propre à l'enfance] childlike; *péj* childish; [jeu, chanson] children's (*avant n*). || [facile] childishly simple.

enfer [ɑ̃fɛr] *nm* RELIG & *fig* hell.

enfermer [ɑ̃fɛrme] *vt* [séquestrer, ranger] to shut away. ○ **s'enfermer** *vp* to shut o.s. away ou up; **s'~ dans** *fig* to retreat into.

enfilade [ɑ̃filad] *nf* row.

enfiler [ɑ̃file] *vt* [aiguille, sur un fil] to thread. || [vêtements] to slip on.

enfin [ɑ̃fɛ̃] *adv* [en dernier lieu] finally, at last; [dans une liste] lastly. || [introduit une rectification] that is, well. || [introduit une concession] anyway.

enflammer [ɑ̃flame] *vt* [bois] to set fire to. ○ **s'enflammer** *vp* [bois] to catch fire. || *fig* [s'exalter] to flare up.

enflé, -e [ɑ̃fle] *adj* [style] turgid.

enfler [ɑ̃fle] *vi* to swell (up).

enfoncer [ɑ̃fɔ̃se] *vt* [faire pénétrer] to drive in; **~ qqch dans qqch** to drive sthg into sthg. || [enfouir]: **~ ses mains dans ses poches** to thrust one's hands into one's pockets. || [défoncer] to break down. ○ **s'enfoncer** *vp* **s'~ dans** [eau, boue] to sink into; [bois, ville] to disappear into. || [céder] to give way.

enfouir [ɑ̃fwir] *vt* [cacher] to hide. || [ensevelir] to bury.

enfourcher [ɑ̃furʃe] *vt* to mount.

enfourner [ɑ̃furne] *vt* [pain] to put in the oven. || *fam* [avaler] to gobble up.

enfreindre [ɑ̃frɛ̃dr] *vt* to infringe.

enfreint, -e [ɑ̃frɛ̃, ɛ̃t] *pp* → enfreindre.

enfuir [ɑ̃fɥir] ○ **s'enfuir** *vp* [fuir] to run away.

enfumer [ɑ̃fyme] *vt* to fill with smoke.

engagé, -e [ɑ̃ɡaʒe] *adj* [auteur, chanteur] politically committed.

engageant, -e [ɑ̃ɡaʒɑ̃, ɑ̃t] *adj* engaging.

engagement [ɑ̃ɡaʒmɑ̃] *nm* [promesse] commitment. || FOOTBALL & RUGBY kick-off.

engager [ɑ̃ɡaʒe] *vt* [lier] to commit. || [embaucher] to take on, to engage. || [faire entrer]: **~ qqch dans** to insert sthg into. || [commencer] to start. || [impliquer] to involve. || [encourager]: **~ qqn à faire qqch** to urge sb to do sthg. ○ **s'engager** *vp* [promettre]: **s'~ à qqch/à faire qqch** to commit o.s. to sthg/to doing sthg. ||

MIL: **s'~ (dans)** to enlist (in). || [pénétrer]: **s'~ dans** to enter.

engelure [ɑ̃ʒlyr] *nf* chilblain.

engendrer [ɑ̃ʒɑ̃dre] *vt* *littéraire* to father. || *fig* [produire] to cause, to give rise to; [sentiment] to engender.

engin [ɑ̃ʒɛ̃] *nm* [machine] machine. || MIL missile. || *fam péj* [objet] thing.

englober [ɑ̃ɡlɔbe] *vt* to include.

engloutir [ɑ̃ɡlutir] *vt* [dévorer] to gobble up. || [faire disparaître] to engulf. || *fig* [dilapider] to squander.

engorger [ɑ̃ɡɔrʒe] *vt* [obstruer] to block, to obstruct. || MÉD to engorge. ○ **s'engorger** *vp* to become blocked.

engouement [ɑ̃ɡumɑ̃] *nm* [enthousiasme] infatuation.

engouffrer [ɑ̃ɡufre] *vt* *fam* [dévorer] to wolf down. ○ **s'engouffrer** *vp*: **s'~ dans** to rush into.

engourdi, -e [ɑ̃ɡurdi] *adj* numb.

engourdir [ɑ̃ɡurdir] *vt* to numb; *fig* to dull. ○ **s'engourdir** *vp* to go numb.

engrais [ɑ̃ɡrɛ] *nm* fertilizer.

engraisser [ɑ̃ɡrese] **1** *vt* [animal] to fatten. || [terre] to fertilize. **2** *vi* to put on weight.

engrenage [ɑ̃ɡrənaʒ] *nm* TECHNOL gears (*pl*). || *fig* [circonstances]: **être pris dans l'~** to be caught up in the system.

engueuler [ɑ̃ɡœle] *vt* *fam*: **~ qqn** to bawl sb out. ○ **s'engueuler** *vp* *fam* to have a row.

enhardir [ɑ̃ardir] ○ **s'enhardir** *vp* to pluck up one's courage.

énième [enjɛm] *adj* *fam*: **la ~ fois** the nth time.

énigmatique [enigmatik] *adj* enigmatic.

énigme [eniɡm] *nf* [mystère] enigma. || [jeu] riddle.

enivrant, -e [ɑ̃nivrɑ̃, ɑ̃t] *adj* *litt* & *fig* intoxicating.

enivrer [ɑ̃nivre] *vt* *litt* to get drunk; *fig* to intoxicate. ○ **s'enivrer** *vp*: **s'~ (de)** to get drunk (on).

enjambée [ɑ̃ʒɑ̃be] *nf* stride.

enjamber [ɑ̃ʒɑ̃be] *vt* [obstacle] to step over. || [cours d'eau] to straddle.

enjeu [ɑ̃ʒø] *nm* [mise] stake.

enjoindre [ɑ̃ʒwɛ̃dr] *vt* *littéraire*: **~ à qqn de faire qqch** to enjoin sb to do sthg.

enjoint [ɑ̃ʒwɛ̃] *pp inv* → enjoindre.

enjôler [ɑ̃ʒole] *vt* to coax.

enjoliver [ɑ̃ʒolive] *vt* to embellish.

enjoliveur [ɑ̃ʒɔlivœr] *nm* [de roue] hub-cap; [de calandre] badge.

enjoué, -e [ɑ̃ʒwe] *adj* cheerful.

enlacer [ɑ̃lase] *vt* [prendre dans ses bras] to embrace, to hug. ○ **s'enlacer** *vp* [s'embrasser] to embrace, to hug.

enlaidir [ɑ̃ledir] **1** *vt* to make ugly. **2** *vi* to become ugly.

enlèvement [ɑ̃lɛvmɑ̃] *nm* [action d'enlever] removal. || [rapt] abduction.

enlever [ɑ̃lve] *vt* [gén] to remove; [vêtement] to take off. || [prendre]: ~ **qqch à qqn** to take sthg away from sb. || [kidnapper] to abduct.

enliser [ɑ̃lize] ○ **s'enliser** *vp* [s'embourber] to sink, to get stuck. || *fig* [piétiner]: **s'~ dans qqch** to get bogged down in sthg.

enluminure [ɑ̃lyminyr] *nf* illumination.

enneigé, -e [ɑ̃neʒe] *adj* snow-covered.

ennemi, -e [ɛnmi] **1** *adj* enemy (*avant n*). **2** *nm, f* enemy.

ennui [ɑ̃nɥi] *nm* [lassitude] boredom. || [problème] trouble (*U*).

ennuyer [ɑ̃nɥije] *vt* [agacer, contrarier] to annoy; **cela t'ennuierait de venir me chercher?** would you mind picking me up? || [lasser] to bore. || [inquiéter] to bother. ○ **s'ennuyer** *vp* [se morfondre] to be bored. || [déplorer l'absence]: **s'~ de qqn/qqch** to miss sb/sthg.

ennuyeux, -euse [ɑ̃nɥijø, øz] *adj* [lassant] boring. || [contrariant] annoying.

énoncé [enɔse] *nm* [libellé] wording.

énoncer [enɔse] *vt* [libeller] to word. || [exposer] to expound.

énorme [enɔrm] *adj litt & fig* [immense] enormous. || *fam fig* [incroyable] far-fetched.

énormément [enɔrmemɑ̃] *adv* enormously; ~ **de** a great deal of.

enquête [ɑ̃kɛt] *nf* [de police, recherches] investigation. || [sondage] survey.

enquêter [ɑ̃kete] *vi* [police, chercheur] to investigate. || [sonder] to conduct a survey.

enragé, -e [ɑ̃raʒe] *adj* [chien] rabid, with rabies. || *fig* [invétéré] keen.

enrager [ɑ̃raʒe] *vi* to be furious; **faire ~ qqn** to infuriate sb.

enrayer [ɑ̃reje] *vt* [épidémie] to check, to stop. || [mécanisme] to jam. ○ **s'enrayer** *vp* [mécanisme] to jam.

enregistrement [ɑ̃rəʒistrəmɑ̃] *nm* [de son, d'images, d'informations] recording. || [inscription] registration. || [à

l'aéroport] check-in; ~ **des bagages** baggage registration.

enregistrer [ɑ̃rəʒistre] *vt* [son, images, informations] to record. || INFORM to store. || [inscrire] to register. || [à l'aéroport] to check in. || *fam* [mémoriser] to make a mental note of.

enrhumé, -e [ɑ̃ryme] *adj*: **je suis ~** I have a cold.

enrhumer [ɑ̃ryme] ○ **s'enrhumer** *vp* to catch (a) cold.

enrichir [ɑ̃riʃir] *vt* [financièrement] to make rich. || [terre & *fig*] to enrich. ○ **s'enrichir** *vp* [financièrement] to grow rich. || [sol & *fig*] to become enriched.

enrobé, -e [ɑ̃robe] *adj* [recouvert]: ~ **de** coated with. || *fam* [grassouillet] plump.

enrober [ɑ̃robe] *vt* [recouvrir]: ~ **qqch de** to coat sthg with. || *fig* [requête, nouvelle] to wrap up.

enrôler [ɑ̃role] *vt* to enrol; MIL to enlist. ○ **s'enrôler** *vp* to enrol; MIL to enlist.

enroué, -e [ɑ̃rwe] *adj* hoarse.

enrouler [ɑ̃rule] *vt* to roll up; ~ **qqch autour de qqch** to wind sthg round sthg. ○ **s'enrouler** *vp* [entourer]: **s'~ sur** ou **autour de qqch** to wind around sthg. || [se pelotonner]: **s'~ dans qqch** to wrap o.s. up in sthg.

ensabler [ɑ̃sable] *vt* to silt up. ○ **s'ensabler** *vp* to silt up.

enseignant, -e [ɑ̃seɲɑ̃, ɑ̃t] **1** *adj* teaching (*avant n*). **2** *nm, f* teacher.

enseigne [ɑ̃seɲ] *nf* [de commerce] sign.

enseignement [ɑ̃seɲmɑ̃] *nm* [gén] teaching; ~ **primaire/secondaire** primary/secondary education.

enseigner [ɑ̃seɲe] *vt litt & fig* to teach; ~ **qqch à qqn** to teach sb sthg, to teach sthg to sb.

ensemble [ɑ̃sɑ̃bl] **1** *adv* together. **2** *nm* [totalité] whole; **idée d'~** general idea; **dans l'~** on the whole. || [harmonie] unity. || [vêtement] outfit. || [série] collection. || MATHS set. || MUS ensemble.

ensemencer [ɑ̃səmɑ̃se] *vt* [terre] to sow. || [rivière] to stock.

enserrer [ɑ̃sere] *vt* [entourer] to encircle; *fig* to imprison.

ensevelir [ɑ̃səvlir] *vt litt & fig* to bury.

ensoleillé, -e [ɑ̃sɔleje] *adj* sunny.

ensoleillement [ɑ̃sɔlɛjmɑ̃] *nm* sunshine.

ensorceler [ɑ̃sɔrsəle] *vt* to bewitch.

ensuite [ɑ̃sɥit] *adv* [après, plus tard] after, afterwards, later. || [puis] then, next, after that.

ensuivre [ɑ̃sɥivr] ○ **s'ensuivre** *rp* to follow; **il s'ensuit que** it follows that.

entaille [ɑ̃taj] *nf* cut.

entailler [ɑ̃taje] *vt* to cut.

entamer [ɑ̃tame] *vt* [commencer] to start (on); [- bouteille] to start, to open. || [capital] to dip into. || [cuir, réputation] to damage. || [courage] to shake.

entartrer [ɑ̃tartre] *vt* to fur up. ○ **s'entartrer** *vp* to fur up.

entasser [ɑ̃tase] *vt* [accumuler, multiplier] to pile up. || [serrer] to squeeze. ○ **s'entasser** *vp* [objets] to pile up. || [personnes]: **s'~ dans** to squeeze into.

entendre [ɑ̃tɑ̃dr] *vt* [percevoir, écouter] to hear; **~ parler de qqch** to hear of or about sthg. || *sout* [comprendre] to understand; **laisser ~ que** to imply that. || *sout* [vouloir]: **~ faire qqch** to intend to do sthg. || [vouloir dire] to mean. ○ **s'entendre** *vp* [sympathiser]: **s'~ avec qqn** to get on with sb. || [s'accorder] to agree.

entendu, -e [ɑ̃tɑ̃dy] **1** *pp* → **entendre. 2** *adj* [compris] agreed, understood. || [complice] knowing.

entente [ɑ̃tɑ̃t] *nf* [harmonie] understanding. || [accord] agreement.

enterrement [ɑ̃tɛrmɑ̃] *nm* burial.

enterrer [ɑ̃tere] *vt litt & fig* to bury.

en-tête [ɑ̃tɛt] (*pl* **en-têtes**) *nm* heading.

entêté, -e [ɑ̃tete] *adj* stubborn.

entêter [ɑ̃tete] ○ **s'entêter** *vp* to persist; **s'~ à faire qqch** to persist in doing sthg.

enthousiasme [ɑ̃tuzjasm] *nm* enthusiasm.

enthousiasmer [ɑ̃tuzjasme] *vt* to fill with enthusiasm. ○ **s'enthousiasmer** *vp*: **s'~ pour** to be enthusiastic about.

enticher [ɑ̃tiʃe] ○ **s'enticher** *vp*: **s'~ de qqn/qqch** to become obsessed with sb/sthg.

entier, -ière [ɑ̃tje, jɛr] *adj* whole, entire. ○ **en entier** *loc adv* in its entirety.

entièrement [ɑ̃tjɛrmɑ̃] *adv* [complètement] fully. || [pleinement] wholly, entirely.

entité [ɑ̃tite] *nf* entity.

entonner [ɑ̃tɔne] *vt* [chant] to strike up.

entonnoir [ɑ̃tɔnwar] *nm* [instrument] funnel. || [cavité] crater.

entorse [ɑ̃tɔrs] *nf* MÉD sprain; **se faire**

une **~ à la cheville/au poignet** to sprain one's ankle/wrist.

entortiller [ɑ̃tɔrtije] *vt* [entrelacer] to twist. || [envelopper]: **~ qqch autour de qqch** to wrap sthg round sthg. || *fam fig* [personne] to sweet-talk.

entourage [ɑ̃turaʒ] *nm* [milieu] entourage.

entourer [ɑ̃ture] *vt* [enclore, encercler]: **~ (de)** to surround (with). || *fig* [soutenir] to rally round.

entracte [ɑ̃trakt] *nm* interval; *fig* interlude.

entraide [ɑ̃trɛd] *nf* mutual assistance.

entrailles [ɑ̃traj] *nfpl* [intestins] entrails. || *sout* [profondeurs] depths.

entrain [ɑ̃trɛ̃] *nm* drive.

entraînement [ɑ̃trɛnmɑ̃] *nm* [préparation] practice; SPORT training.

entraîner [ɑ̃trene] *vt* TECHNOL to drive. || [tirer] to pull. || [susciter] to lead to. || SPORT to coach. || [emmener] to take along. ○ **s'entraîner** *vp* to practise; SPORT to train; **s'~ à faire qqch** to practise doing sthg.

entraîneur, -euse [ɑ̃trenœr, øz] *nm, f* trainer, coach.

entrave [ɑ̃trav] *nf* hobble; *fig* obstruction.

entraver [ɑ̃trave] *vt* to hobble; *fig* to hinder.

entre [ɑ̃tr] *prép* [gén] between; **~ nous** between you and me, between ourselves. || [parmi] among; **l'un d'~ nous ira** one of us will go; **généralement ils restent ~ eux** they tend to keep themselves to themselves; **ils se battent ~ eux** they're fighting among or amongst themselves.

entrebâiller [ɑ̃trəbaje] *vt* to open slightly.

entrechoquer [ɑ̃trəʃɔke] *vt* to bang together. ○ **s'entrechoquer** *vp* to bang into each other.

entrecôte [ɑ̃trəkot] *nf* entrecôte.

entrecouper [ɑ̃trəkupe] *vt* to intersperse.

entrecroiser [ɑ̃trəkrwaze] *vt* to interlace. ○ **s'entrecroiser** *vp* to intersect.

entrée [ɑ̃tre] *nf* [arrivée, accès] entry, entrance; **«~ interdite»** "no admittance"; **«~ libre»** [dans musée] "admission free"; [dans boutique] "browsers welcome". || [porte] entrance. || [vestibule] (entrance) hall. || [billet] ticket. || [plat] starter, first course.

entrefaites [ɑ̃trəfɛt] *nfpl*: **sur ces ~** just at that moment.

entrefilet [ãtrəfilɛ] *nm* paragraph.

entrejambe, entre-jambes [ãtrəʒãb] *nm* crotch.

entrelacer [ãtrəlase] *vt* to intertwine.

entremêler [ãtrəmele] *vt* to mix; ~ **de** to mix with.

entremets [ãtrəmɛ] *nm* dessert.

entremettre [ãtrəmɛtr] ○ **s'entremettre** *vp*: **s'~ (dans)** to mediate (in).

entremise [ãtrəmiz] *nf* intervention; **par l'~ de** through.

entrepont [ãtrəpõ] *nm* steerage.

entreposer [ãtrəpoze] *vt* to store.

entrepôt [ãtrəpo] *nm* warehouse.

entreprendre [ãtrəprãdr] *vt* to undertake; [commencer] to start; **~ de faire qqch** to undertake to do sthg.

entrepreneur, -euse [ãtrəprənœr, øz] *nm, f* [de services & CONSTR] contractor.

entrepris, -e [ãtrəpri, iz] *pp* → **entreprendre**.

entreprise [ãtrəpriz] *nf* [travail, initiative] enterprise. || [société] company.

entrer [ãtre] 1 *vi* (*aux*: être) [pénétrer] to enter, to go/come in; **~ dans** [gén] to enter; [pièce] to go/come into; [bain, voiture] to get into; *fig* [sujet] to go into; **faire ~ qqn** to show sb in. || [faire partie]: **~ dans** to go into, to be part of. || [être admis, devenir membre]: **~ à** [club, parti] to join; **~ dans** [les affaires, l'enseignement] to go into; [la police, l'armée] to join; **~ à l'université** to enter university; **~ à l'hôpital** to go into hospital. 2 *vt* (*aux*: avoir) [gén] to bring in. || INFORM to enter, to input.

entresol [ãtrəsɔl] *nm* mezzanine.

entre-temps [ãtrətã] *adv* meanwhile.

entretenir [ãtrətnir] *vt* [faire durer] to keep alive. || [cultiver] to maintain. || [soigner] to look after. || [personne, famille] to support. || [parler à]: **~ qqn de qqch** to speak to sb about sthg. ○ **s'entretenir** *vp* [se parler]: **s'~ (de)** to talk (about).

entretien [ãtrətjẽ] *nm* [de voiture, jardin] maintenance, upkeep. || [conversation] discussion; [colloque] debate.

entre-tuer [ãtrətɥe] ○ **s'entre-tuer** *vp* to kill each other.

entrevoir [ãtrəvwar] *vt* [distinguer] to make out. || [voir rapidement] to see briefly. || *fig* [deviner] to glimpse.

entrevu, -e [ãtrəvy] *pp* → **entrevoir**.

entrevue [ãtrəvy] *nf* meeting.

entrouvert, -e [ãtruvɛr, ɛrt] 1 *pp* → **entrouvrir**. 2 *adj* half-open.

entrouvrir [ãtruvrir] *vt* to open partly. ○ **s'entrouvrir** *vp* to open partly.

énumération [enymerasjõ] *nf* enumeration.

énumérer [enymere] *vt* to enumerate.

envahir [ãvair] *vt* [gén & MIL] to invade. || *fig* [suj: sommeil, doute] to overcome. || *fig* [déranger] to intrude on.

envahissant, -e [ãvaisã, ãt] *adj* [herbes] invasive. || [personne] intrusive.

envahisseur [ãvaisœr] *nm* invader.

enveloppe [ãvlɔp] *nf* [de lettre] envelope. || [d'emballage] covering. || [membrane] membrane; [de graine] husk.

envelopper [ãvlɔpe] *vt* [emballer] to wrap (up). || [suj: brouillard] to envelop. || [déguiser] to mask. ○ **s'envelopper** *vp*: **s'~ dans** to wrap o.s. up in.

envenimer [ãvnime] *vt* [blessure] to infect. || *fig* [querelle] to poison. ○ **s'envenimer** *vp* [s'infecter] to become infected. || *fig* [se détériorer] to become poisoned.

envergure [ãvɛrgyr] *nf* [largeur] span; [d'oiseau, d'avion] wingspan. || *fig* [qualité] calibre. || *fig* [importance] scope; **prendre de l'~** to expand.

envers[1] [ãvɛr] *prép* towards.

envers[2] [ãvɛr] *nm* [de tissu] wrong side; [de feuillet etc] back; [de médaille] reverse. || [face cachée] other side. ○ **à l'envers** *loc adv* [vêtement] inside out; [portrait, feuille] upside down; *fig* the wrong way.

envie [ãvi] *nf* [désir] desire; **avoir ~ de qqch/de faire qqch** to feel like sthg/like doing sthg, to want sthg/to do sthg. || [convoitise] envy; **ce tailleur me fait ~** I covet that suit.

envier [ãvje] *vt* to envy.

envieux, -ieuse [ãvjø, jøz] 1 *adj* envious. || *nm, f* envious person; **faire des ~** to make other people envious.

environ [ãvirõ] *adv* [à peu près] about.

environnement [ãvirɔnmã] *nm* environment.

environs [ãvirõ] *nmpl* (surrounding) area (*sg*); **aux ~ de** [lieu] near; [époque] round about, around.

envisager [ãvizaʒe] *vt* to consider; **~ de faire qqch** to be considering doing sthg.

envoi [ãvwa] *nm* [action] sending, dispatch. || [colis] parcel.

envol [ãvɔl] *nm* takeoff.

envolée [ãvɔle] *nf* [d'oiseaux & *fig*] flight. || [augmentation]: **l'~ du dollar** the rapid rise in the value of the dollar.

envoler [ɑ̃vɔle] ○ **s'envoler** *vp* [oiseau] to fly away. || [avion] to take off. || [disparaître] to disappear into thin air.

envoûter [ɑ̃vute] *vt* to bewitch.

envoyé, -e [ɑ̃vwaje] *nm, f* envoy.

envoyer [ɑ̃vwaje] *vt* to send; ~ qqch à qqn [expédier] to send sb sthg, to send sthg to sb; [jeter] to throw sb sthg, to throw sthg to sb; ~ qqn faire qqch to send sb to do sthg; ~ chercher qqn/qqch to send for sb/sthg.

épagneul [epaɲœl] *nm* spaniel.

épais, -aisse [epɛ, ɛs] *adj* [large, dense] thick. || [grossier] crude.

épaisseur [epɛsœr] *nf* [largeur, densité] thickness. || *fig* [consistance] depth.

épaissir [epesir] *vt* & *vi* to thicken. ○ **s'épaissir** *vp* [liquide] to thicken. || *fig* [mystère] to deepen.

épanchement [epɑ̃ʃmɑ̃] *nm* [effusion] outpouring. || MÉD effusion.

épancher [epɑ̃ʃe] ○ **s'épancher** *vp* [se confier] to pour one's heart out.

épanoui, -e [epanwi] *adj* [fleur] in full bloom. || [expression] radiant.

épanouir [epanwir] *vt* [personne] to make happy. ○ **s'épanouir** *vp* [fleur] to open. || [visage] to light up. || [corps] to fill out. || [personnalité] to blossom.

épanouissement [epanwismɑ̃] *nm* [de fleur] blooming, opening. || [de personnalité] flowering.

épargnant, -e [eparɲɑ̃, ɑ̃t] *nm, f* saver.

épargne [eparɲ] *nf* [action, vertu] saving. || [somme] savings (*pl*); ~ logement savings account (*to buy property*).

épargner [eparɲe] *vt* [gén] to spare; ~ qqch à qqn to spare sb sthg. || [économiser] to save.

éparpiller [eparpije] *vt* [choses, personnes] to scatter. ○ **s'éparpiller** *vp* [se disperser] to scatter.

épars, -e [epar, ars] *adj* sout [objets] scattered; [végétation, cheveux] sparse.

épatant, -e [epatɑ̃, ɑ̃t] *adj fam* great.

épaté, -e [epate] *adj* [nez] flat. || *fam* [étonné] amazed.

épaule [epol] *nf* shoulder.

épauler [epole] *vt* to support, to back up.

épaulette [epolɛt] *nf* MIL epaulet. || [rembourrage] shoulder pad.

épave [epav] *nf* wreck.

épée [epe] *nf* sword.

épeler [eple] *vt* to spell.

éperdu, -e [epɛrdy] *adj* [sentiment] passionate; ~ de [personne] overcome with.

éperon [eprɔ̃] *nm* [de cavalier, de montagne] spur; [de navire] ram.

éperonner [eprɔne] *vt* to spur on.

épervier [epɛrvje] *nm* sparrowhawk.

éphémère [efemɛr] **1** *adj* [bref] ephemeral, fleeting. **2** *nm* ZOOL mayfly.

éphéméride [efemerid] *nf* tear-off calendar.

épi [epi] *nm* [de céréale] ear. || [cheveux] tuft.

épice [epis] *nf* spice.

épicéa [episea] *nm* spruce.

épicer [epise] *vt* [plat] to spice.

épicerie [episri] *nf* [magasin] grocer's (shop). || [denrées] groceries (*pl*).

épicier, -ière [episje, jɛr] *nm, f* grocer.

épidémie [epidemi] *nf* epidemic.

épiderme [epidɛrm] *nm* epidermis.

épier [epje] *vt* [espionner] to spy on. || [observer] to look for.

épilation [epilasjɔ̃] *nf* hair removal.

épilepsie [epilɛpsi] *nf* epilepsy.

épiler [epile] *vt* [jambes] to remove hair from; [sourcils] to pluck. ○ **s'épiler** *vp*: s'~ les jambes to remove the hair from one's legs; s'~ les sourcils to pluck one's eyebrows.

épilogue [epilɔg] *nm* [de roman] epilogue. || [d'affaire] outcome.

épinards [epinar] *nmpl* spinach (*U*).

épine [epin] *nf* [piquant - de rosier] thorn; [- de hérisson] spine.

épineux, -euse [epinø, øz] *adj* thorny.

épingle [epɛ̃gl] *nf* [instrument] pin.

épingler [epɛ̃gle] *vt* [fixer] to pin (up). || *fam fig* [arrêter] to nab.

épinière [epinjɛr] → **moelle**.

Épiphanie [epifani] *nf* Epiphany.

épique [epik] *adj* epic.

épisode [epizɔd] *nm* episode.

épisodique [epizɔdik] *adj* [occasionnel] occasional. || [secondaire] minor.

épitaphe [epitaf] *nf* epitaph.

épithète [epitɛt] **1** *nf* GRAM attribute. || [qualificatif] term. **2** *adj* attributive.

éploré, -e [eplɔre] *adj* [personne] in tears; [visage, air] tearful.

épluche-légumes [eplyʃlegym] *nm inv* potato peeler.

éplucher [eplyʃe] *vt* [légumes] to peel. || [textes] to dissect; [comptes] to scrutinize.

épluchure [eplyʃyr] *nf* peelings (*pl*).

éponge [epɔ̃ʒ] *nf* sponge.

éponger [epɔ̃ʒe] *vt* [liquide, déficit] to mop up. || [visage] to mop, to wipe.

épopée [epɔpe] *nf* epic.

époque [epɔk] *nf* [de l'année] time. || [de l'histoire] period.

époumoner [epumɔne] ○ **s'époumoner** *vp* to shout o.s. hoarse.

épouse → **époux**.

épouser [epuze] *vt* [personne] to marry. || [forme] to hug. || *fig* [idée, principe] to espouse.

épousseter [epuste] *vt* to dust.

époustouflant, -e [epustuflɑ̃, ɑ̃t] *adj fam* amazing.

épouvantable [epuvɑ̃tabl] *adj* dreadful.

épouvantail [epuvɑ̃taj] *nm* [à moineaux] scarecrow; *fig* bogeyman.

épouvanter [epuvɑ̃te] *vt* to terrify.

époux, épouse [epu, epuz] *nm, f* spouse.

éprendre [eprɑ̃dr] ○ **s'éprendre** *vp sout*: s'~ de to fall in love with.

épreuve [eprœv] *nf* [essai, examen] test; à l'~ du feu fireproof; ~ de force *fig* trial of strength. || [malheur] ordeal. || SPORT event. || TYPO proof. || PHOT print.

épris, -e [epri, iz] **1** *pp* → **éprendre**. **2** *adj sout*: ~ de in love with.

éprouver [epruve] *vt* [tester] to test. || [ressentir] to feel. || [faire souffrir] to distress. || [difficultés, problèmes] to experience.

éprouvette [epruvɛt] *nf* [tube à essai] test tube. || [échantillon] sample.

EPS (*abr de* **éducation physique et sportive**) *nf* PE.

épuisé, -e [epɥize] *adj* [personne, corps] exhausted. || [marchandise] sold out, out of stock; [livre] out of print.

épuisement [epɥizmɑ̃] *nm* exhaustion.

épuiser [epɥize] *vt* to exhaust.

épuisette [epɥizɛt] *nf* landing net.

épurer [epyre] *vt* [eau, huile] to purify. || POLIT to purge.

équarrir [ekarir] *vt* [animal] to cut up. || [poutre] to square.

équateur [ekwatœr] *nm* equator.

Équateur [ekwatœr] *nm*: l'~ Ecuador.

équation [ekwasjɔ̃] *nf* equation.

équatorial, -e, -iaux [ekwatɔrjal, jo] *adj* equatorial.

équerre [eker] *nf* [instrument] set square; [en T] T-square.

équestre [ekɛstr] *adj* equestrian.

équilatéral, -e, -aux [ekɥilateral, o] *adj* equilateral.

équilibre [ekilibr] *nm* [gén] balance. || [psychique] stability.

équilibré, -e [ekilibre] *adj* [personne] well-balanced. || [vie] stable. || ARCHIT: aux proportions ~es well-proportioned.

équilibrer [ekilibre] *vt* to balance. ○ **s'équilibrer** *vp* to balance each other out.

équilibriste [ekilibrist] *nmf* tightrope walker.

équipage [ekipaʒ] *nm* crew.

équipe [ekip] *nf* team.

équipement [ekipmɑ̃] *nm* [matériel] equipment. || [aménagement] facilities (*pl*).

équiper [ekipe] *vt* [navire, armée] to equip. || [personne, local] to equip, to fit out; ~ qqn/qqch de to equip sb/sthg with, to fit sb/sthg out with. ○ **s'équiper** *vp*: s'~ (de) to equip o.s. (with).

équipier, -ière [ekipje, jɛr] *nm, f* team member.

équitable [ekitabl] *adj* fair.

équitation [ekitasjɔ̃] *nf* riding, horse-riding.

équité [ekite] *nf* fairness.

équivalent, -e [ekivalɑ̃, ɑ̃t] *adj* equivalent. ○ **équivalent** *nm* equivalent.

équivaloir [ekivalwar] *vi*: ~ à to be equivalent to.

équivoque [ekivɔk] **1** *adj* [ambigu] ambiguous. || [mystérieux] dubious. **2** *nf* ambiguity; **sans** ~ unequivocal (*adj*), unequivocally (*adv*).

érable [erabl] *nm* maple.

éradiquer [eradike] *vt* to eradicate.

érafler [erafle] *vt* [peau] to scratch. || [mur, voiture] to scrape.

éraflure [eraflyr] *nf* [de peau] scratch. || [de mur, voiture] scrape.

éraillé, -e [eraje] *adj* [voix] hoarse.

ère [ɛr] *nf* era.

érection [erɛksjɔ̃] *nf* erection.

éreintant, -e [erɛ̃tɑ̃, ɑ̃t] *adj* exhausting.

éreinter [erɛ̃te] *vt* [fatiguer] to exhaust. || [critiquer] to pull to pieces.

ergonomique [ɛrgɔnɔmik] *adj* ergonomic.

ériger [eriʒe] *vt* [monument] to erect. || [tribunal] to set up. || *fig* [transformer]: ~ qqn en to set sb up as.

ermite [ɛrmit] *nm* hermit.

éroder [erɔde] *vt* to erode.

érogène [erɔʒɛn] *adj* erogenous.

érosion [erozjɔ̃] *nf* erosion.

érotique [erɔtik] *adj* erotic.

érotisme [erɔtism] *nm* eroticism.

errance [erɑ̃s] *nf* wandering.

errer [ere] *vi* to wander.

erreur [erœr] *nf* mistake; **par ~** by mistake.

erroné, -e [erɔne] *adj sout* wrong.

éructer [erykte] *vi* to belch.

érudit, -e [erydi, it] **1** *adj* erudite, learned. **2** *nm, f* learned person.

éruption [erypsjɔ̃] *nf* MÉD rash. || [de volcan] eruption.

es → être.

escabeau, -x [eskabo] *nm* [échelle] stepladder. || *vieilli* [tabouret] stool.

escadre [eskadr] *nf* [navires] fleet. || [avions] wing.

escadrille [eskadrij] *nf* [navires] flotilla. || [avions] flight.

escadron [eskadrɔ̃] *nm* squadron.

escalade [eskalad] *nf* [de montagne, grille] climbing. || [des prix, de violence] escalation.

escalader [eskalade] *vt* to climb.

escale [eskal] *nf* [lieu - pour navire] port of call; [- pour avion] stopover. || [arrêt - de navire] call; [- d'avion] stopover, stop; **faire ~ à** [navire] to put in at, to call at; [avion] to stop over at.

escalier [eskalje] *nm* stairs (*pl*); **descendre/monter l'~** to go downstairs/upstairs; **~ roulant** OU **mécanique** escalator.

escalope [eskalɔp] *nf* escalope.

escamotable [eskamɔtabl] *adj* [train d'atterrissage] retractable; [antenne] telescopic. || [table] folding.

escamoter [eskamɔte] *vt* [faire disparaître] to make disappear. || [voler] to lift. || [rentrer] to retract.

escapade [eskapad] *nf* [voyage] outing. || [fugue] escapade.

escargot [eskargo] *nm* snail.

escarmouche [eskarmuʃ] *nf* skirmish.

escarpé, -e [eskarpe] *adj* steep.

escarpement [eskarpəmɑ̃] *nm* [de pente] steep slope. || GÉOGR escarpment.

escarpin [eskarpɛ̃] *nm* court shoe *Br*.

escarre [eskar] *nf* bedsore, pressure sore.

escient [esjɑ̃] *nm*: **à bon ~** advisedly; **à mauvais ~** ill-advisedly.

esclaffer [esklafe] ○ **s'esclaffer** *vp* to burst out laughing.

esclandre [esklɑ̃dr] *nm sout* scene.

esclavage [esklavaʒ] *nm* slavery.

esclave [esklav] **1** *nmf* slave. **2** *adj*: **être ~ de** to be a slave to.

escompte [eskɔ̃t] *nm* discount.

escompter [eskɔ̃te] *vt* [prévoir] to count on. || FIN to discount.

escorte [eskɔrt] *nf* escort.

escorter [eskɔrte] *vt* to escort.

escrime [eskrim] *nf* fencing.

escrimer [eskrime] ○ **s'escrimer** *vp*: **s'~ à faire qqch** to work (away) at doing sthg.

escroc [eskro] *nm* swindler.

escroquer [eskrɔke] *vt* to swindle; **~ qqch à qqn** to swindle sb out of sthg.

escroquerie [eskrɔkri] *nf* swindle, swindling (*U*).

eskimo, Eskimo → esquimau.

espace [espas] *nm* space; **~ vert** green space, green area.

espacer [espase] *vt* [dans l'espace] to space out. || [dans le temps - visites] to space out; [- paiements] to spread out.

espadon [espadɔ̃] *nm* [poisson] swordfish.

espadrille [espadrij] *nf* espadrille.

Espagne [espaɲ] *nf*: **l'~** Spain.

espagnol, -e [espaɲɔl] *adj* Spanish. ○ **espagnol** *nm* [langue] Spanish. ○ **Espagnol, -e** *nm, f* Spaniard; **les Espagnols** the Spanish.

espèce [espes] *nf* BIOL, BOT & ZOOL species. || [sorte] kind, sort; **~ d'idiot!** you stupid fool! ○ **espèces** *nfpl* cash; **payer en ~s** to pay (in) cash.

espérance [esperɑ̃s] *nf* hope; **~ de vie** life expectancy.

espérer [espere] **1** *vt* to hope for; **~ que** to hope (that); **~ faire qqch** to hope to do sthg. **2** *vi* to hope.

espiègle [espjegl] *adj* mischievous.

espion, -ionne [espjɔ̃, jɔn] *nm, f* spy.

espionnage [espjɔnaʒ] *nm* spying; **~ industriel** industrial espionage.

espionner [espjɔne] *vt* to spy on.

esplanade [esplanad] *nf* esplanade.

espoir [espwar] *nm* hope.

esprit [espri] *nm* [entendement, personne, pensée] mind; **reprendre ses ~s** to recover. || [attitude] spirit; **~ de compétition** competitive spirit; **~ critique** critical acumen. || [humour] wit. || [fantôme] spirit, ghost.

esquimau, -aude, -aux, eskimo [eskimo, od] *adj* Eskimo. ○ **Esquimau, -aude** *nm, f*, **Eskimo** *nmf* Eskimo.

esquinter [eskɛ̃te] *vt fam* [abîmer] to ruin. || [critiquer] to slate *Br*, to pan.

esquiver [ɛskive] *vt* to dodge. ○ **s'esquiver** *vp* to slip away.

essai [esɛ] *nm* [vérification] test, testing (*U*); **à l'~** on trial. || [tentative] attempt. || RUGBY try.

essaim [esɛ̃] *nm litt & fig* swarm.

essayage [esɛjaʒ] *nm* fitting.

essayer [eseje] *vt* to try; **~ de faire qqch** to try to do sthg.

essence [esɑ̃s] *nf* [fondement, de plante] essence. || [carburant] gas *Am*. || [d'arbre] species.

essentiel, -ielle [esɑ̃sjɛl] *adj* [indispensable] essential. || [fondamental] basic. ○ **essentiel** *nm* [point]: **l'~** [le principal] the essential ou main thing. || [quantité]: **l'~ de** the essential ou greater part of.

essentiellement [esɑ̃sjɛlmɑ̃] *adv* [avant tout] above all. || [par essence] essentially.

esseulé, -e [esœle] *adj littéraire* forsaken.

essieu, -x [esjø] *nm* axle.

essor [esɔr] *nm* flight, expansion, boom; **prendre son ~** to take flight; *fig* to take off.

essorer [esɔre] *vt* [à la main, à rouleaux] to wring out; [à la machine] to spin-dry; [salade] to spin, to dry.

essoreuse [esɔrøz] *nf* [à rouleaux] mangle; [électrique] spin-dryer; [à salade] salad spinner.

essouffler [esufle] *vt* to make breathless. ○ **s'essouffler** *vp* to be breathless ou out of breath; *fig* to run out of steam.

essuie-glace [esɥiglas] (*pl* **essuie-glaces**) *nm* windshield wiper *Am*.

essuie-mains [esɥimɛ̃] *nm inv* hand towel.

essuie-tout [esɥitu] *nm inv* kitchen roll.

essuyer [esɥije] *vt* [sécher] to dry. || [nettoyer] to dust. || *fig* [subir] to suffer. ○ **s'essuyer** *vp* to dry o.s.

est¹ [ɛst] 1 *nm* east; **un vent d'~** an easterly wind; **à l'~** in the east; **à l'~ (de)** to the east (of). 2 *adj inv* [gén] east; [province, région] eastern.

est² [ɛ] → **être**.

estafette [ɛstafɛt] *nf* dispatch-rider.

estafilade [ɛstafilad] *nf* slash, gash.

est-allemand, -e [ɛstalmɑ̃, ɑ̃d] *adj* East German.

estampe [ɛstɑ̃p] *nf* print.

est-ce que [ɛskə] *adv interr*: **est-ce qu'il fait beau?** is the weather good?; **~**

vous aimez l'accordéon? do you like the accordion?; **où ~ tu es?** where are you?

esthétique [ɛstetik] *adj* [relatif à la beauté] aesthetic. || [harmonieux] attractive.

estimation [ɛstimasjɔ̃] *nf* estimate, estimation.

estime [ɛstim] *nf* respect, esteem.

estimer [ɛstime] *vt* [expertiser] to value. || [évaluer] to estimate. || [respecter] to respect. || [penser]: **~ que** to feel (that).

estivant, -e [ɛstivɑ̃, ɑ̃t] *nm, f* (summer) holiday-maker *Br* ou vacationer *Am*.

estomac [ɛstɔma] *nm* ANAT stomach.

estomper [ɛstɔ̃pe] *vt* to blur; *fig* [douleur] to lessen. ○ **s'estomper** *vp* to be/become blurred; *fig* [douleur] to lessen.

Estonie [ɛstɔni] *nf*: **l'~** Estonia.

estrade [ɛstrad] *nf* dais.

estragon [ɛstragɔ̃] *nm* tarragon.

estropié, -e [ɛstrɔpje] 1 *adj* crippled. 2 *nm, f* cripple.

estuaire [ɛstɥɛr] *nm* estuary.

esturgeon [ɛstyrʒɔ̃] *nm* sturgeon.

et [e] *conj* [gén] and; **~ moi?** what about me?? || [dans les fractions et les nombres composés]: **vingt ~ un** twenty-one; **il y a deux ans ~ demi** two and a half years ago.

ét. (*abr de* **étage**) fl.

étable [etabl] *nf* cowshed.

établi [etabli] *nm* workbench.

établir [etablir] *vt* [gén] to establish; [record] to set. || [dresser] to draw up. ○ **s'établir** *vp* [s'installer] to settle. || [s'instaurer] to become established.

établissement [etablismɑ̃] *nm* establishment; **~ hospitalier** hospital; **~ scolaire** educational establishment.

étage [etaʒ] *nm* [de bâtiment] storey, floor; **un immeuble à quatre ~s** a four-storey block of flats; **au premier ~** on the first floor *Br*, on the second floor *Am*. || [de fusée] stage.

étagère [etaʒɛr] *nf* [rayon] shelf. || [meuble] shelves (*pl*), set of shelves.

étain [etɛ̃] *nm* [métal] tin; [alliage] pewter.

étais, était *etc* → **être**.

étal [etal] (*pl* **-s** ou **étaux** [eto]) *nm* [éventaire] stall. || [de boucher] butcher's block.

étalage [etalaʒ] *nm* [action, ensemble d'objets] display; **faire ~ de** *fig* to flaunt. || [devanture] window display.

étalagiste [etalaʒist] *nmf* [décorateur] window-dresser.

étaler [etale] *vt* [exposer] to display. || [étendre] to spread out. || [dans le temps] to stagger. || [mettre une couche de] to spread. || [exhiber] to parade. ○ **s'étaler** *vp* [s'étendre] to spread. || [dans le temps]: **s'~ (sur)** to be spread (over). || *fam* [tomber] to fall flat on one's face.

étalon [etalɔ̃] *nm* [cheval] stallion. || [mesure] standard.

étanche [etɑ̃ʃ] *adj* watertight; [montre] waterproof.

étancher [etɑ̃ʃe] *vt* [sang, larmes] to stem (the flow of). || [assouvir] to quench.

étang [etɑ̃] *nm* pond.

étant *ppr* → être.

étape [etap] *nf* [gén] stage. || [halte] stop; **faire ~ à** to break one's journey at.

état [eta] *nm* [manière d'être] state; **être en ~/hors d'~ de faire qqch** to be in a/in no fit state to do sthg; **en bon/mauvais ~** in good/poor condition; **en ~ de marche** in working order; **~ d'âme** mood; **~ d'esprit** state of mind; **~ de santé** (state of) health; **être dans tous ses ~s** *fig* to be in a state. || [métier, statut] status; **~ civil** ADMIN ≃ marital status. || [inventaire - gén] inventory; [- de dépenses] statement; **~ des lieux** *inventory and inspection of rented property.* ○ **État** *nm* [nation] state.

état-major [etamaʒɔr] *nm* ADMIN & MIL staff; [de parti] leadership. || [lieu] headquarters (*pl*).

États-Unis [etazyni] *nmpl*: **les ~ (d'Amérique)** the United States (of America).

étau, -x [eto] *nm* vice.

étayer [eteje] *vt* to prop up; *fig* to back up.

etc. (*abr de et cætera*) etc.

été [ete] **1** *pp inv* → être. **2** *nm* summer; **en ~** in (the) summer.

éteindre [etɛ̃dr] *vt* [incendie, bougie, cigarette] to put out; [radio, chauffage, lampe] to turn off, to switch off. ○ **s'éteindre** *vp* [feu, lampe] to go out. || *fig & littéraire* [personne] to pass away. || [race] to die out.

étendard [etɑ̃dar] *nm* standard.

étendre [etɑ̃dr] *vt* [déployer] to stretch; [journal, linge] to spread (out). || [coucher] to lay. || [appliquer] to spread. || [accroître] to extend. || [diluer] to dilute. ○ **s'étendre** *vp* [se coucher] to lie down. || [s'étaler au loin]: **s'~ (de/jusqu'à)** to

stretch (from/as far as). || [croître] to spread. || [s'attarder]: **s'~ sur** to elaborate on.

étendu, -e [etɑ̃dy] **1** *pp* → étendre. **2** *adj* [bras, main] outstretched. || [plaine, connaissances] extensive. ○ **étendue** *nf* [surface] area, expanse. || [importance] extent.

éternel, -elle [etɛrnɛl] *adj* eternal; **ce ne sera pas ~** this won't last for ever.

éterniser [etɛrnize] ○ **s'éterniser** *vp* [se prolonger] to drag out. || *fam* [rester] to stay for ever.

éternité [etɛrnite] *nf* eternity.

éternuer [etɛrnɥe] *vi* to sneeze.

êtes → être.

éther [etɛr] *nm* ether.

Éthiopie [etjɔpi] *nf*: **l'~** Ethiopia.

éthique [etik] **1** *nf* ethics (*U or pl*). **2** *adj* ethical.

ethnie [ɛtni] *nf* ethnic group.

ethnique [ɛtnik] *adj* ethnic.

ethnologie [ɛtnɔlɔʒi] *nf* ethnology.

éthylisme [etilism] *nm* alcoholism.

étiez, étions *etc* → être.

étincelant, -e [etɛ̃slɑ̃, ɑ̃t] *adj* sparkling.

étinceler [etɛ̃sle] *vi* to sparkle.

étincelle [etɛ̃sɛl] *nf* spark.

étioler [etjɔle] ○ **s'étioler** *vp* [plante] to wilt; [personne] to weaken.

étiqueter [etikte] *vt litt & fig* to label.

étiquette [etikɛt] *nf* [marque & fig] label. || [protocole] etiquette.

étirer [etire] *vt* to stretch. ○ **s'étirer** *vp* to stretch.

étoffe [etɔf] *nf* fabric, material.

étoile [etwal] *nf* star; **~ filante** shooting star; **à la belle ~** *fig* under the stars. ○ **étoile de mer** *nf* starfish.

étoilé, -e [etwale] *adj* [ciel, nuit] starry; **la bannière ~e** the Star-Spangled Banner. || [vitre, pare-brise] shattered.

étole [etɔl] *nf* stole.

étonnant, -e [etɔnɑ̃, ɑ̃t] *adj* astonishing.

étonnement [etɔnmɑ̃] *nm* astonishment, surprise.

étonner [etɔne] *vt* to surprise, to astonish. ○ **s'étonner** *vp*: **s'~ (de)** to be surprised (by); **s'~ que** (+ *subjonctif*) to be surprised (that).

étouffant, -e [etufɑ̃, ɑ̃t] *adj* stifling.

étouffée [etufe] ○ **à l'étouffée** *loc adv* steamed; [viande] braised.

étouffer [etufe] **1** *vt* [gén] to stifle. || [asphyxier] to suffocate. || [feu] to smother. || [scandale, révolte] to suppress. **2** *vi* to suffocate. ○ **s'étouffer** *vp* [s'étrangler] to choke.

étourderie [eturdəri] *nf* [distraction] thoughtlessness. || [bévue] careless mistake; [acte irréfléchi] thoughtless act.

étourdi, -e [eturdi] **1** *adj* scatterbrained. **2** *nm, f* scatterbrain.

étourdir [eturdir] *vt* [assommer] to daze.

étourdissement [eturdismã] *nm* dizzy spell.

étourneau, -x [eturno] *nm* starling.

étrange [etrãʒ] *adj* strange.

étranger, -ère [etrãʒe, ɛr] **1** *adj* [gén] foreign. || [différent, isolé] unknown, unfamiliar; **être ~ à qqn** to be unknown to sb. **2** *nm, f* [de nationalité différente] foreigner. || [inconnu] stranger. || [exclu] outsider. ○ **étranger** *nm*: **à l'~** abroad.

étranglement [etrãgləmã] *nm* [strangulation] strangulation. || [rétrécissement] constriction.

étrangler [etrãgle] *vt* [gén] to choke. || [stranguler] to strangle. || [réprimer] to stifle. || [serrer] to constrict. ○ **s'étrangler** *vp* [s'étouffer] to choke.

étrave [etrav] *nf* stem.

être [etr] **1** *nm* being; **les ~s vivants/humains** living/human beings. **2** *v aux* [pour les temps composés] to have/to be; **il est parti hier** he left yesterday; **il est déjà arrivé** he has already arrived; **il est né en 1952** he was born in 1952. || [pour le passif] to be; **la maison a été vendue** the house has been ou was sold. **3** *v attr* [état] to be; **la maison est blanche** the house is white; **il est médecin** he's a doctor. || [possession] **~ à qqn** to be sb's, to belong to sb; **c'est à vous, cette voiture?** is this your car?, is this car yours? **4** *v impers* [exprimant le temps]: **quelle heure est-il?** what time is it?, what's the time?; **il est dix heures dix** it's ten past *Br* ou after *Am* ten. || [suivi d'un adjectif]: **il est ... it is ...**; **il est inutile de** it's useless to. **5** *vi* [exister] to be. || [indique une situation, un état] to be; **il est à Paris** he's in Paris; **nous sommes au printemps/en été** it's spring/summer. || [indiquant une origine]: **il est de Paris** he's from Paris. ○ **être à** *v + prép* [indiquant une obligation]: **c'est à vérifier** it needs to be checked.

étreindre [etrɛ̃dr] *vt* [embrasser] to

hug, to embrace. ○ **s'étreindre** *vp* to embrace each other.

étreinte [etrɛ̃t] *nf* [enlacement] embrace. || [pression] stranglehold.

étrenner [etrene] *vt* to use for the first time.

étrennes [etrɛn] *nfpl* Christmas box (*sg*).

étrier [etrije] *nm* stirrup.

étriper [etripe] *vt* [animal] to disembowel. || *fam fig* [tuer] to kill. ○ **s'étriper** *vp fam* to tear each other to pieces.

étriqué, -e [etrike] *adj* [vêtement] tight. || [mesquin] narrow.

étroit, -e [etrwa, at] *adj* [gén] narrow. || [intime] close. || [serré] tight. ○ **à l'étroit** *loc adj*: **être à l'~** to be cramped.

étroitesse [etrwatɛs] *nf* narrowness.

étude [etyd] *nf* [gén] study; **à l'~** under consideration; **~ de marché** market research (*U*). || [de notaire - local] office; [- charge] practice. || MUS étude. ○ **études** *nfpl* studies; **faire des ~s** to study.

étudiant, -e [etydjã, ãt] *nm, f* student.

étudié, -e [etydje] *adj* studied.

étudier [etydje] *vt* to study.

étui [etɥi] *nm* case; **~ à cigarettes/lunettes** cigarette/glasses case.

étuve [etyv] *nf* [local] steam room; *fig* oven. || [appareil] sterilizer.

étuvée [etyve] ○ **à l'étuvée** *loc adv* braised.

étymologie [etimɔlɔʒi] *nf* etymology.

eu, -e [y] *pp* → **avoir**.

E-U, E-U A (*abr de* États-Unis (d'Amérique)) *nmpl* US, USA.

eucalyptus [økaliptys] *nm* eucalyptus.

euh [ø] *interj* er.

eunuque [ønyk] *nm* eunuch.

euphémisme [øfemism] *nm* euphemism.

euphorie [øfɔri] *nf* euphoria.

euphorisant, -e [øfɔrizã, ãt] *adj* exhilarating. ○ **euphorisant** *nm* antidepressant.

eurent → **avoir**.

Europe [ørɔp] *nf*: **l'~** Europe.

européen, -enne [ørɔpeɛ̃, ɛn] *adj* European. ○ **Européen, -enne** *nm, f* European.

eus, eut *etc* → **avoir**.

eût → **avoir**.

euthanasie [øtanazi] *nf* euthanasia.

eux [ø] *pron pers* [sujet] they; **ce sont ~ qui me l'ont dit** they're the ones who

told me. || [complément] them. ○ **eux-
mêmes** *pron pers* themselves.

évacuer [evakɥe] *vt* [gén] to evacuate. ||
[liquide] to drain.

évadé, -e [evade] *nm, f* escaped prisoner.

évader [evade] ○ **s'évader** *vp*: s'~ **(de)**
to escape (from).

évaluation [evalɥasjɔ̃] *nf* [action]
valuation; [résultat] estimate.

évaluer [evalɥe] *vt* [distance] to estimate; [tableau] to value; [risque] to
assess.

évangélique [evɑ̃ʒelik] *adj* evangelical.

évangile [evɑ̃ʒil] *nm* gospel.

évanouir [evanwir] ○ **s'évanouir** *vp*
[défaillir] to faint. || [disparaître] to fade.

évanouissement [evanwismɑ̃] *nm*
[syncope] fainting fit.

évaporer [evapɔre] ○ **s'évaporer** *vp*
to evaporate.

évasé, -e [evaze] *adj* flared.

évasif, -ive [evazif, iv] *adj* evasive.

évasion [evazjɔ̃] *nf* escape.

évêché [eveʃe] *nm* [territoire] diocese.

éveil [evɛj] *nm* awakening; **en ~** on the
alert.

éveillé, -e [eveje] *adj* [qui ne dort pas]
wide awake. || [vif, alerte] alert.

éveiller [eveje] *vt* to arouse; [intelli-
gence, dormeur] to awaken. ○ **s'éveiller**
vp [dormeur] to wake, to awaken. || [cu-
riosité] to be aroused. || [esprit, intelli-
gence] to be awakened.

événement [evɛnmɑ̃] *nm* event.

éventail [evɑ̃taj] *nm* [objet] fan; **en ~**
fan-shaped. || [choix] range.

éventaire [evɑ̃tɛr] *nm* [étalage] stall,
stand. || [corbeille] tray.

éventer [evɑ̃te] *vt* [rafraîchir] to fan. ||
[divulguer] to give away. ○ **s'éventer**
vp [se rafraîchir] to fan o.s. || [parfum,
vin] to go stale.

éventrer [evɑ̃tre] *vt* [étriper] to disem-
bowel. || [fendre] to rip open.

éventualité [evɑ̃tɥalite] *nf* [possibilité]
possibility. || [circonstance] eventuality;
dans l'~ de in the event of.

éventuel, -elle [evɑ̃tɥɛl] *adj* possible.

éventuellement [evɑ̃tɥɛlmɑ̃] *adv* pos-
sibly.

évêque [evɛk] *nm* bishop.

évertuer [evɛrtɥe] ○ **s'évertuer** *vp*:
s'~ **à faire qqch** to strive to do sthg.

évidemment [evidamɑ̃] *adv* obviously.

évidence [evidɑ̃s] *nf* [caractère] evi-

dence; [fait] obvious fact; **mettre en ~** to
emphasize, to highlight.

évident, -e [evidɑ̃, ɑ̃t] *adj* obvious.

évider [evide] *vt* to hollow out.

évier [evje] *nm* sink.

évincer [evɛ̃se] *vt*: ~ **qqn (de)** to oust sb
(from).

éviter [evite] *vt* [esquiver] to avoid. ||
[s'abstenir] : ~ **de faire qqch** to avoid
doing sthg. || [épargner] : ~ **qqch à qqn** to
save sb sthg.

évocateur, -trice [evɔkatœr, tris] *adj*
[geste, regard] meaningful.

évocation [evɔkasjɔ̃] *nf* evocation.

évolué, -e [evɔlɥe] *adj* [développé] de-
veloped. || [libéral, progressiste] broad-
minded.

évoluer [evɔlɥe] *vi* [changer] to evolve;
[personne] to change. || [se mouvoir] to
move about.

évolution [evɔlysjɔ̃] *nf* [transformation]
development. || BIOL evolution. || MÉD
progress.

évoquer [evɔke] *vt* [souvenir] to evoke.
|| [problème] to refer to.

exacerber [ɛgzasɛrbe] *vt* to heighten.

exact, -e [ɛgzakt] *adj* [calcul] correct. ||
[récit, copie] exact. || [ponctuel] punctual.

exactement [ɛgzaktəmɑ̃] *adv* exactly.

exaction [ɛgzaksjɔ̃] *nf* extortion.

exactitude [ɛgzaktityd] *nf* [de calcul,
montre] accuracy. || [ponctualité] punc-
tuality.

ex æquo [ɛgzeko] **1** *adj inv* & *nmf inv*
equal. **2** *adv* equal; **troisième ~** third
equal.

exagération [ɛgzaʒerasjɔ̃] *nf* exaggeration.

exagéré, -e [ɛgzaʒere] *adj* exaggerated.

exagérer [ɛgzaʒere] *vt* & *vi* to exaggerate.

exalté, -e [ɛgzalte] **1** *adj* [sentiment]
elated; [tempérament] over-excited;
[imagination] vivid. **2** *nm, f* fanatic.

exalter [ɛgzalte] *vt* to excite.
○ **s'exalter** *vp* to get carried away.

examen [ɛgzamɛ̃] *nm* examination;
SCOL exam, examination; ~ **médical**
medical (examination).

examinateur, -trice [ɛgzaminatœr,
tris] *nm, f* examiner.

examiner [ɛgzamine] *vt* to examine.

exaspération [ɛgzasperasjɔ̃] *nf* exasperation.

exaspérer [ɛgzaspere] *vt* to exasperate.

exaucer [ɛgzose] *vt* to grant.

excédent [ɛksedɑ̃] *nm* surplus; en ~ surplus (*avant n*).

excéder [ɛksede] *vt* [gén] to exceed. || [exaspérer] to exasperate.

excellence [ɛkselɑ̃s] *nf* excellence; par ~ par excellence.

excellent, -e [ɛkselɑ̃, ɑ̃t] *adj* excellent.

exceller [ɛksele] *vi*: ~ en oʊ dans qqch to excel at oʊ in sthg; ~ à faire qqch to excel at doing sthg.

excentré, -e [ɛksɑ̃tre] *adj*: c'est très ~ it's quite a long way out.

excentrique [ɛksɑ̃trik] 1 *nmf* eccentric. 2 *adj* [gén] eccentric. || [quartier] outlying.

excepté, -e [ɛksepte] *adj*: tous sont venus, lui ~ everyone came except (for) him. ○ **excepté** *prép* apart from, except.

exception [ɛksepsjɔ̃] *nf* exception; à l'~ de except for.

exceptionnel, -elle [ɛksepsjɔnɛl] *adj* exceptional.

excès [ɛksɛ] *nm* excess.

excessif, -ive [ɛksesif, iv] *adj* [démesuré] excessive. || [extrême] extreme.

excitant, -e [ɛksitɑ̃, ɑ̃t] *adj* [stimulant, passionnant] exciting. ○ **excitant** *nm* stimulant.

excitation [ɛksitasjɔ̃] *nf* [énervement] excitement. || MÉD stimulation.

excité, -e [ɛksite] 1 *adj* [énervé] excited. 2 *nm, f* hothead.

exciter [ɛksite] *vt* [gén] to excite. || MÉD to stimulate.

exclamation [ɛksklamasjɔ̃] *nf* exclamation.

exclamer [ɛksklame] ○ **s'exclamer** *vp*: s'~ (devant) to exclaim (at oʊ over).

exclu, -e [ɛkskly] 1 *pp* → exclure. 2 *adj* excluded. 3 *nm, f* outsider.

exclure [ɛksklyr] *vt* to exclude; [expulser] to expel.

exclusion [ɛksklyzjɔ̃] *nf* expulsion; à l'~ de to the exclusion of.

exclusivement [ɛksklyzivmɑ̃] *adv* [uniquement] exclusively.

exclusivité [ɛksklyzivite] *nf* COMM exclusive rights (*pl*). || CIN sole screening rights (*pl*); en ~ exclusively. || [de sentiment] exclusiveness.

excrément [ɛkskremɑ̃] *nm* (*gén pl*) excrement (*U*).

excroissance [ɛkskrwasɑ̃s] *nf* excrescence.

excursion [ɛkskyrsjɔ̃] *nf* excursion.

excursionniste [ɛkskyrsjɔnist] *nmf* vacationer *Am*.

excuse [ɛkskyz] *nf* excuse.

excuser [ɛkskyze] *vt* to excuse; excusez-moi [pour réparer] I'm sorry; [pour demander] excuse me. ○ **s'excuser** *vp* [demander pardon] to apologize; s'~ de qqch/de faire qqch to apologize for sthg/for doing sthg.

exécrable [ɛgzekrabl] *adj* atrocious.

exécutant, -e [ɛgzekytɑ̃, ɑ̃t] *nm, f* [personne] underling. || MUS performer.

exécuter [ɛgzekyte] *vt* [réaliser] to carry out; [tableau] to paint. || MUS to play, to perform. || [mettre à mort] to execute. ○ **s'exécuter** *vp* to comply.

exécutif, -ive [ɛgzekytif, iv] *adj* executive. ○ **exécutif** *nm*: l'~ the executive.

exécution [ɛgzekysjɔ̃] *nf* [réalisation] carrying out; [de tableau] painting. || MUS performance. || [mise à mort] execution.

exemplaire [ɛgzɑ̃plɛr] 1 *nm* copy. 2 *adj* exemplary.

exemple [ɛgzɑ̃pl] *nm* example; par ~ for example, for instance.

exempté, -e [ɛgzɑ̃te] *adj*: ~ (de) exempt (from).

exercer [ɛgzerse] *vt* [entraîner, mettre en usage] to exercise; [autorité, influence] to exert. || [métier] to carry on; [médecine] to practise. ○ **s'exercer** *vp* [s'entraîner] to practise; s'~ à qqch/à faire qqch to practise sthg/doing sthg.

exercice [ɛgzersis] *nm* [gén] exercise. || [de métier, fonction] carrying out.

exhaler [ɛgzale] *vt littéraire* [odeur] to give off. || [plainte, soupir] to utter.

exhaustif, -ive [ɛgzostif, iv] *adj* exhaustive.

exhiber [ɛgzibe] *vt* [présenter] to show; [faire étalage de] to show off. ○ **s'exhiber** *vp* to make an exhibition of o.s.

exhibitionniste [ɛgzibisjɔnist] *nmf* exhibitionist.

exhorter [ɛgzɔrte] *vt*: ~ qqn à qqch/à faire qqch to urge sb to sthg/to do sthg.

exhumer [ɛgzyme] *vt* to exhume; *fig* to unearth, to dig up.

exigeant, -e [ɛgziʒɑ̃, ɑ̃t] *adj* demanding.

exigence [ɛgziʒɑ̃s] *nf* demand.

exiger [ɛgziʒe] *vt* [demander] to demand; ~ que (+ *subjonctif*) to demand that; ~ qqch de qqn to demand sthg from sb. || [nécessiter] to require.

exigible [ɛgziʒibl] *adj* payable.

exigu, -ë [ɛgzigy] *adj* cramped.

exil [ɛgzil] *nm* exile; **en ~** exiled.

exilé, -e [ɛgzile] *nm, f* exile.

exiler [ɛgzile] *vt* to exile. ○ **s'exiler** *vp* POLIT to go into exile.

existence [ɛgzistɑ̃s] *nf* existence.

exister [ɛgziste] *vi* to exist.

exode [ɛgzɔd] *nm* exodus.

exonération [ɛgzɔnerasjɔ̃] *nf* exemption; **~ d'impôts** tax exemption.

exorbitant, -e [ɛgzɔrbitɑ̃, ɑ̃t] *adj* exorbitant.

exorbité, -e [ɛgzɔrbite] → **œil**.

exotique [ɛgzɔtik] *adj* exotic.

exotisme [ɛgzɔtism] *nm* exoticism.

expansif, -ive [ɛkspɑ̃sif, iv] *adj* expansive.

expansion [ɛkspɑ̃sjɔ̃] *nf* expansion.

expansionniste [ɛkspɑ̃sjɔnist] *nmf & adj* expansionist.

expatrié, -e [ɛkspatrije] *adj & nm, f* expatriate.

expatrier [ɛkspatrije] *vt* to expatriate. ○ **s'expatrier** *vp* to leave one's country.

expédier [ɛkspedje] *vt* [lettre, marchandise] to send, to dispatch. || [question] to dispose of. || [travail] to dash off.

expéditeur, -trice [ɛkspeditœr, tris] *nm, f* sender.

expéditif, -ive [ɛkspeditif, iv] *adj* quick, expeditious.

expédition [ɛkspedisjɔ̃] *nf* [envoi] sending. || [voyage, campagne militaire] expedition.

expérience [ɛksperjɑ̃s] *nf* [pratique] experience; **avoir de l'~** to have experience, to be experienced. || [essai] experiment.

expérimental, -e, -aux [ɛksperimɑ̃tal, o] *adj* experimental.

expérimenté, -e [ɛksperimɑ̃te] *adj* experienced.

expert, -e [ɛksper, ɛrt] *adj* expert. ○ **expert** *nm* expert.

expert-comptable [ɛksperkɔ̃tabl] *nm* certified public accountant *Am*.

expertise [ɛkspertiz] *nf* [examen] expert appraisal; [estimation] (expert) valuation. || [compétence] expertise.

expertiser [ɛkspertize] *vt* to value; [dégâts] to assess.

expier [ɛkspje] *vt* to pay for.

expiration [ɛkspirasjɔ̃] *nf* [d'air] exhalation. || [de contrat] expiry.

expirer [ɛkspire] **1** *vt* to breathe out. **2** *vi* [contrat] to expire.

explicatif, -ive [ɛksplikatif, iv] *adj* explanatory.

explication [ɛksplikasjɔ̃] *nf* explanation; **~ de texte** (literary) criticism.

explicite [ɛksplisit] *adj* explicit.

expliciter [ɛksplisite] *vt* to make explicit.

expliquer [ɛksplike] *vt* [gén] to explain. || [texte] to criticize. ○ **s'expliquer** *vp* [se justifier] to explain o.s. || [comprendre] to understand. || [discuter] to have it out. || [devenir compréhensible] to be explained, to become clear.

exploit [ɛksplwa] *nm* exploit, feat.

exploitant, -e [ɛksplwatɑ̃, ɑ̃t] *nm, f* farmer.

exploitation [ɛksplwatasjɔ̃] *nf* [mise en valeur] running; [de mine] working. || [entreprise] operation, concern; **~ agricole** farm. || [d'une personne] exploitation.

exploiter [ɛksplwate] *vt* [gén] to exploit. || [entreprise] to operate, to run.

explorateur, -trice [ɛksplɔratœr, tris] *nm, f* explorer.

explorer [ɛksplɔre] *vt* to explore.

exploser [ɛksploze] *vi* to explode.

explosif, -ive [ɛksplozif, iv] *adj* explosive. ○ **explosif** *nm* explosive.

explosion [ɛksplozjɔ̃] *nf* explosion; [de colère, joie] outburst.

exportateur, -trice [ɛkspɔrtatœr, tris] **1** *adj* exporting. **2** *nm, f* exporter.

exportation [ɛkspɔrtasjɔ̃] *nf* export.

exporter [ɛkspɔrte] *vt* to export.

exposé, -e [ɛkspoze] *adj* [orienté]: **bien ~** facing the sun. || [vulnérable] exposed. ○ **exposé** *nm* account; SCOL talk.

exposer [ɛkspoze] *vt* [orienter, mettre en danger] to expose. || [présenter] to display; [- tableaux] to show, to exhibit. || [expliquer] to explain, to set out. ○ **s'exposer** *vp*: **s'~ à qqch** to expose o.s. to sthg.

exposition [ɛkspozisjɔ̃] *nf* [présentation] exhibition. || [orientation] aspect.

exprès¹, -esse [ɛksprɛs] *adj* [formel] formal, express. || (*inv*) [urgent] express.

exprès² [ɛksprɛ] *adv* on purpose; **faire ~ de faire qqch** to do sthg deliberately or on purpose.

express [ɛksprɛs] **1** *nm inv* [train] express. || [café] espresso. **2** *adj inv* express.

expressément [ɛkspresemɑ̃] *adv* expressly.

expressif, -ive [ɛkspresif, iv] *adj* expressive.

expression [ɛksprɛsjɔ̃] *nf* expression.

exprimer [ɛksprime] *vt* [pensées. sentiments] to express. ○ **s'exprimer** *vp* to express o.s.

expropriation [ɛkspropriasjɔ̃] *nf* expropriation.

exproprier [ɛksproprije] *vt* to expropriate.

expulser [ɛkspylse] *vt*: ~ (de) to expel (from); [locataire] to evict (from).

expulsion [ɛkspylsjɔ̃] *nf* expulsion; [de locataire] eviction.

exquis, -e [ɛkski, iz] *adj* [délicieux] exquisite. || [distingué. agréable] delightful.

extase [ɛkstaz] *nf* ecstasy.

extasier [ɛkstazje] ○ **s'extasier** *vp*: s'~ **devant** to go into ecstasies over.

extensible [ɛkstɑ̃sibl] *adj* stretchable.

extension [ɛkstɑ̃sjɔ̃] *nf* [étirement] stretching. || [élargissement] extension.

exténuer [ɛkstenɥe] *vt* to exhaust.

extérieur, -e [ɛksterjœr] *adj* [au dehors] outside; [étranger] external; [apparent] outward. ○ **extérieur** *nm* [dehors] outside; [de maison] exterior; **à l'~ de qqch** outside sthg.

extérieurement [ɛksterjœrmɑ̃] *adv* [à l'extérieur] on the outside, externally. || [en apparence] outwardly.

extérioriser [ɛksterjɔrize] *vt* to show.

exterminer [ɛkstɛrmine] *vt* to exterminate.

externat [ɛkstɛrna] *nm* SCOL day school.

externe [ɛkstɛrn] **1** *nmf* SCOL day pupil. || MÉD ≃ extern *Am*. **2** *adj* outer, external.

extincteur [ɛkstɛ̃ktœr] *nm* (fire) extinguisher.

extinction [ɛkstɛ̃ksjɔ̃] *nf* [action d'éteindre] putting out, extinguishing. || *fig* [disparition] extinction; ~ **de voix** loss of one's voice.

extirper [ɛkstirpe] *vt*: ~ (de) [épine, réponse, secret] to drag (out of).

extorquer [ɛkstɔrke] *vt*: ~ **qqch à qqn** to extort sthg from sb.

extra [ɛkstra] **1** *nm inv* [employé] extra help (*U*). **2** *adj inv* [de qualité] top-quality. || *fam* [génial] great, fantastic.

extraction [ɛkstraksjɔ̃] *nf* extraction.

extrader [ɛkstrade] *vt* to extradite.

extraire [ɛkstrɛr] *vt*: ~ (de) to extract (from).

extrait, -e [ɛkstrɛ, ɛt] *pp* → **extraire**. ○ **extrait** *nm* extract; ~ **de naissance** birth certificate.

extraordinaire [ɛkstraɔrdinɛr] *adj* extraordinary.

extrapoler [ɛkstrapɔle] *vt* & *vi* to extrapolate.

extraterrestre [ɛkstratɛrɛstr] *nmf* & *adj* extraterrestrial.

extravagance [ɛkstravagɑ̃s] *nf* extravagance.

extravagant, -e [ɛkstravagɑ̃, ɑ̃t] *adj* extravagant; [idée, propos] wild.

extraverti, -e [ɛkstravɛrti] *nm, f* & *adj* extrovert.

extrême [ɛkstrɛm] **1** *nm* extreme; **d'un ~ à l'autre** from one extreme to the other. **2** *adj* extreme; [limite] furthest.

extrêmement [ɛkstrɛmmɑ̃] *adv* extremely.

Extrême-Orient [ɛkstrɛmɔrjɑ̃] *nm*: l'~ the Far East.

extrémiste [ɛkstremist] *nmf* & *adj* extremist.

extrémité [ɛkstremite] *nf* [bout] end. || [situation critique] straights (*pl*).

exubérant, -e [ɛgzyberɑ̃, ɑ̃t] *adj* [personne] exuberant.

exulter [ɛgzylte] *vi* to exult.

f, F [ɛf] *nm inv* f, F; **F3** three-room flat *Br* ou apartment *Am*. ○ **F** (*abr de* **Fahrenheit**) F. || (*abr de* **franc**) F, Fr.

fa [fa] *nm inv* F; [chanté] fa.

fable [fabl] *nf* fable.

fabricant, -e [fabrikɑ̃, ɑ̃t] *nm, f* manufacturer.

fabrication [fabrikasjɔ̃] *nf* manufacture, manufacturing.

fabrique [fabrik] *nf* [usine] factory.

fabriquer [fabrike] *vt* [confectionner] to manufacture, to make. || *fam* [faire]: **qu'est-ce que tu fabriques?** what are you up to? || [inventer] to fabricate.

fabuleux, -euse [fabylø, øz] *adj* fabulous.

fac [fak] *nf fam* college, uni *Br*.

façade [fasad] *nf litt* & *fig* facade.

face [fas] *nf* [visage] face. || [côté] side;
faire ~ à qqch [maison] to face sthg, to be
opposite sthg; *fig* [affronter] to face up to
sthg; **de ~** from the front; **en ~ de qqn/
qqch** opposite sb/sthg.

face-à-face [fasafas] *nm inv* debate.

facétie [fasesi] *nf* practical joke.

facette [faset] *nf litt & fig* facet.

fâché, -e [faʃe] *adj* [en colère] angry. ||
[brouillé] on bad terms.

fâcher [faʃe] *vt* [mettre en colère] to anger, to make angry. ○ **se fâcher** *vp* [se
mettre en colère]: **se ~ (contre qqn)** to get
angry (with sb). || [se brouiller]: **se ~
(avec qqn)** to fall out (with sb).

fâcheux, -euse [faʃø, øz] *adj* unfortunate.

facile [fasil] *adj* [aisé] easy; **~ à faire/
prononcer** easy to do/pronounce. || [peu
subtil] facile. || [conciliant] easy-going.

facilement [fasilmã] *adv* easily.

facilité [fasilite] *nf* [de tâche, problème]
easiness. || [capacité] ease. || [dispositions]
aptitude. || COMM: **~s de paiement** easy
(payment) terms.

faciliter [fasilite] *vt* to make easier.

façon [fasɔ̃] *nf* [manière] way. || [imita-
tion]: **~ cuir** imitation leather. ○ **de façon à** *loc prép* so as to. ○ **de façon
que** *loc conj* (+ *subjonctif*) so that. ○
de toute façon *loc adv* anyway, in
any case.

fac-similé [faksimile] (*pl* **fac-similés**)
nm facsimile.

facteur, -trice [faktœr, tris] *nm, f* [des
postes] mailman (*f* mailwoman) *Am.*
○ **facteur** *nm* [élément & MATHS] factor.

factice [faktis] *adj* artificial.

faction [faksjɔ̃] *nf* [groupe] faction.

facture [faktyr] *nf* [de gaz, d'électricité] bill. || ART technique.

facturer [faktyre] *vt* COMM to invoice.

facultatif, -ive [fakyltatif, iv] *adj* optional.

faculté [fakylte] *nf* [don & UNIV] faculty;
~ de lettres/de droit/de médecine
Faculty of Arts/Law/Medicine. || [possi-
bilité] freedom. || [pouvoir] power.
○ **facultés** *nfpl* (mental) faculties.

fade [fad] *adj* [sans saveur] bland. ||
[sans intérêt] insipid.

fagot [fago] *nm* bundle of sticks.

faible [fɛbl] 1 *adj* [gén] weak; **être ~ en
maths** to be not very good at maths. ||
[petit - montant, proportion] small;
[- revenu] low. || [lueur, bruit] faint. 2 *nm*
weakness.

faiblement [fɛbləmã] *adv* [mollement]
weakly, feebly. || [imperceptiblement]
faintly. || [peu] slightly.

faiblesse [fɛbles] *nf* [gén] weakness. ||
[petitesse] smallness.

faiblir [fɛblir] *vi* [personne, monnaie] to
weaken. || [forces] to diminish, to fail. ||
[tempête, vent] to die down.

faïence [fajãs] *nf* earthenware.

faignant, -e = fainéant.

faille [faj] 1 → **falloir**. 2 *nf* GÉOL fault. ||
[défaut] flaw.

faillir [fajir] *vi* [être sur le point de]: **~
faire qqch** to nearly *ou* almost do sthg.

faillite [fajit] *nf* FIN bankruptcy; **faire ~**
to go bankrupt; **en ~** bankrupt.

faim [fɛ̃] *nf* hunger; **avoir ~** to be hun-
gry.

fainéant, -e [feneã, ãt], **feignant, -e**,
faignant, -e [fɛɲã, ãt] 1 *adj* lazy, idle. 2
nm, f lazybones.

faire [fɛr] 1 *vt* [fabriquer, préparer] to
make; **~ une tarte/du café/un film** to
make a tart/coffee/a film; **~ qqch de
qqch** [transformer] to make sthg into
sthg. || [s'occuper à, entreprendre q. ch]:
qu'est-ce qu'il fait dans la vie? what
does he do (for a living)?; **que fais-tu dimanche?** what are you doing on Sun-
day? || [étudier] to do; **~ de l'anglais/des
maths/du droit** to do English/maths/
law. || [sport, musique] to play; **~ du
football/de la clarinette** to play
football/the clarinet. || [effectuer] to do;
~ la cuisine to cook, to do the cooking. ||
[occasionner]: **~ de la peine à qqn** to hurt
sb; **~ du bruit** to make a noise; **ça ne fait
rien** it doesn't matter. || [imiter]: **~ le
sourd/l'innocent** to act deaf/(the) inno-
cent. || [calcul, mesure]: **un et un font
deux** one and one are *ou* make two; **ça
fait combien (de kilomètres) jusqu'à la
mer?** how far is it to the sea?; **la table
fait 2 mètres de long** the table is 2
metres long. || [dire]: «**tiens**», **fit-elle**
"really", she said. || **ne ~ que** [faire sans
cesse] to do nothing but; **elle ne fait que
bavarder** she does nothing but gossip,
she's always gossiping; **je ne fais que
passer** I've just popped in. 2 *vi* [agir] to
do, to act; **tu ferais bien d'aller voir ce
qui se passe** you ought to *ou* you'd better
go and see what's happening. 3 *v attr*
[avoir l'air] to look; **~ démodé/joli** to
look old-fashioned/pretty. 4 *v substitut*
to do; **je lui ai dit de prendre une
échelle mais il ne l'a pas fait** I told him

to use a ladder but he didn't. **5** *v impers*
[climat. temps]: **il fait beau/froid** it's
fine/cold; **il fait 20 degrés** it's 20 de-
grees. || [exprime la durée, la distance]: **ça
fait six mois que je ne l'ai pas vu** it's six
months since I last saw him; **ça fait six
mois que je fais du portugais** I've been
going to Portuguese classes for six
months. **6** *v auxiliaire* [à l'actif] to make;
~ démarrer une voiture to start a car;
~ tomber qqch to make sth fall; **~ tra-
vailler qqn** to make sb work. || [au pas-
sif]: **~ faire qqch (par qqn)** to have sth
done (by sb); **~ réparer sa voiture/
nettoyer ses vitres** to have one's car
repaired/one's windows cleaned. ○ **se
faire** *rp* [être convenable]: **ça ne se fait
pas (de faire qqch)** it's not done (to do
sthg). || [devenir]: **se ~ (+ adjectif)** to
get, to become; **il se fait tard** it's getting
late; **se ~ beau** to make o.s. beautiful. ||
[causer] **(+ nom)**: **se ~ mal** to hurt o.s.;
se ~ des amis to make friends. || **(+ in-
finitif)**: **se ~ écraser** to get run over; **se ~
opérer** to have an operation; **se ~ faire
un costume** to have a suit made (for
o.s.). || *loc*: **comment se fait-il que ...?**
how is it that ...?, how come ...? ○ **se
faire à** *rp + prép* to get used to.

faire-part [fɛrpar] *nm inv* announcement.

fais, fait *etc* → **faire**.

faisable [fəzabl] *adj* feasible.

faisan, -e [fəzɑ̃, an] *nm, f* pheasant.

faisandé, -e [fəzɑ̃de] *adj* CULIN high.

faisceau, -x [fɛso] *nm* [rayon] beam.

faisons → **faire**.

fait, faite [fɛ, fɛt] **1** *pp* → **faire**. **2** *adj*
[fabriqué] made; **il n'est pas ~ pour me-
ner cette vie** he's not cut out for this kind
of life. || [physique]: **bien ~** well-built. ||
[fromage] ripe. || *loc*: **c'est bien ~ pour
lui** (it) serves him right. ○ **fait** *nm* [acte]
act; **mettre qqn devant le ~ accompli** to
present sb with a fait accompli; **prendre
qqn sur le ~** to catch sb in the act; **~s et
gestes** doings, actions. || [événement]
event; **~s divers** news in brief. || [réalité]
fact. ○ **au fait** *loc adv* by the way. ○ **en
fait** *loc adv* in (actual) fact. ○ **en fait
de** *loc prép* by way of.

faîte [fɛt] *nm* [de toit] ridge. || [d'arbre]
top. || *fig* [sommet] pinnacle.

faites → **faire**.

fait-tout (*pl inv*), **faitout** (*pl fai-
touts*) [fɛtu] *nm* stewpan.

falaise [falɛz] *nf* cliff.

fallacieux, -ieuse [falasjø, jøz] *adj*
[promesse] false. || [argument] fallacious.

falloir [falwar] *v impers*: **il me faut du
temps** I need (some) time; **il faut que tu
partes** you must go or leave, you'll have
to go or leave; **il faut faire attention** we/
you *etc* must be careful, we'll/you'll *etc*
have to be careful; **s'il le faut** if necessary. ○ **s'en falloir** *v impers*: **il s'en faut
de beaucoup pour qu'il ait l'examen** it'll
take a lot for him to pass the exam; **peu
s'en est fallu qu'il démissionne** he very
nearly resigned, he came close to resign-
ing.

fallu [faly] *pp inv* → **falloir**.

falot, -e [falo, ɔt] *adj* dull.

falsifier [falsifje] *vt* [document, signature, faits] to falsify.

famé, -e [fame] *adj*: **mal ~** with a (bad)
reputation.

famélique [famelik] *adj* half-starved.

fameux, -euse [famø, øz] *adj* [célèbre]
famous. || *fam* [remarquable] great.

familial, -e, -iaux [familjal, jo] *adj*
family (*avant n*).

familiariser [familjarize] *vt*: **~ qqn
avec** to familiarize sb with.

familiarité [familjarite] *nf* familiarity.
○ **familiarités** *nfpl* liberties.

familier, -ière [familje, jɛr] *adj* familiar. ○ **familier** *nm* regular (customer).

famille [famij] *nf* family; [ensemble des
parents] relatives, relations.

famine [famin] *nf* famine.

fan [fan] *nmf* *fam* fan.

fanal, -aux [fanal, o] *nm* [de phare] bea-
con. || [lanterne] lantern.

fanatique [fanatik] **1** *nmf* fanatic. **2** *adj*
fanatical.

fanatisme [fanatism] *nm* fanaticism.

faner [fane] **1** *vt* [altérer] to fade. **2** *vi*
[fleur] to wither. || [beauté, couleur] to
fade. ○ **se faner** *rp* [fleur] to wither. ||
[beauté, couleur] to fade.

fanfare [fɑ̃far] *nf* [orchestre] brass
band. || [musique] fanfare.

fanfaron, -onne [fɑ̃farɔ̃, ɔn] **1** *adj*
boastful. **2** *nm, f* braggart.

fanion [fanjɔ̃] *nm* pennant.

fantaisie [fɑ̃tezi] **1** *nf* [caprice] whim. ||
(*U*) [goût] fancy. || [imagination] imagi-
nation. **2** *adj inv*: **chapeau ~** fancy hat;
bijoux ~ fake jewellery.

fantaisiste [fɑ̃tezist] **1** *nmf* entertainer.
2 *adj* [bizarre] fanciful.

fantasme [fɑ̃tasm] *nm* fantasy.

fantasque [fɑ̃task] *adj* [personne] whimsical. || [humeur] capricious.

fantassin [fɑ̃tasɛ̃] *nm* infantryman.

fantastique [fɑ̃tastik] 1 *adj* fantastic. 2 *nm*: **le ~** the fantastic.

fantoche [fɑ̃tɔʃ] 1 *adj* puppet (*avant n*). 2 *nm* puppet.

fantôme [fɑ̃tom] 1 *nm* ghost. 2 *adj* [inexistant] phantom.

faon [fɑ̃] *nm* fawn.

farandole [farɑ̃dɔl] *nf* farandole.

farce [fars] *nf* CULIN stuffing. || [blague] (practical) joke; **~s et attrapes** jokes and novelties.

farceur, -euse [farscer, øz] *nm, f* (practical) joker.

farcir [farsir] *vt* CULIN to stuff. || [remplir]: **~ qqch de** to stuff or cram sthg with.

fard [far] *nm* make-up.

fardeau, -x [fardo] *nm* [poids] load; *fig* burden.

farder [farde] *vt* [maquiller] to make up. ○ **se farder** *vp* to make o.s. up, to put on one's make-up.

farfelu, -e [farfəly] *fam* 1 *adj* weird. 2 *nm, f* weirdo.

farfouiller [farfuje] *vi fam* to rummage.

farine [farin] *nf* flour.

farouche [faruʃ] *adj* [animal] wild, not tame; [personne] shy, withdrawn. || [sentiment] fierce.

fart [far(t)] *nm* (ski) wax.

fascicule [fasikyl] *nm* part, instalment.

fascination [fasinasjɔ̃] *nf* fascination.

fasciner [fasine] *vt* to fascinate.

fascisme [faʃism] *nm* fascism.

fasse, fassions *etc* → **faire**.

faste [fast] 1 *nm* splendour. 2 *adj* [favorable] lucky.

fastidieux, -ieuse [fastidjø, jøz] *adj* boring.

fastueux, -euse [fastɥø, øz] *adj* luxurious.

fatal, -e [fatal] *adj* [mortel, funeste] fatal. || [inévitable] inevitable.

fataliste [fatalist] *adj* fatalistic.

fatalité [fatalite] *nf* [destin] fate. || [inéluctabilité] inevitability.

fatigant, -e [fatigɑ̃, ɑ̃t] *adj* [épuisant] tiring. || [ennuyeux] tiresome.

fatiguant [fatigɑ̃] *ppr* → **fatiguer**.

fatigue [fatig] *nf* tiredness.

fatigué, -e [fatige] *adj* tired; [cœur, yeux] strained.

fatiguer [fatige] 1 *vt* [épuiser, affecter] to tire; [- cœur, yeux] to strain. || [ennuyer] to wear out. 2 *vi* [personne] to grow tired. || [moteur] to strain. ○ **se fatiguer** *vp* to get tired; **se ~ de qqch** to get tired of sthg; **se ~ à faire qqch** to wear o.s. out doing sthg.

fatras [fatra] *nm* jumble.

faubourg [fobur] *nm* suburb.

fauché, -e [foʃe] *adj fam* broke, hard-up.

faucher [foʃe] *vt* [couper - herbe, blé] to cut. || *fam* [voler]: **~ qqch à qqn** to pinch sthg from sb. || [piéton] to run over.

faucille [fosij] *nf* sickle.

faucon [fokɔ̃] *nm* hawk.

faudra → **falloir**.

faufiler [fofile] *vt* to tack, to baste. ○ **se faufiler** *vp*: **se ~ dans** to slip into; **se ~ entre** to thread one's way between.

faune [fon] *nf* [animaux] fauna. || *péj* [personnes]: **la ~ qui fréquente ce bar** the sort of people who hang round this bar.

faussaire [foser] *nmf* forger.

faussement [fosmɑ̃] *adv* [à tort] wrongly. || [prétendument] falsely.

fausser [fose] *vt* [déformer] to bend. || [rendre faux] to distort.

fausseté [foste] *nf* [hypocrisie] duplicity. || [de jugement, d'idée] falsity.

faut → **falloir**.

faute [fot] *nf* [erreur] mistake, error; **~ de frappe** [à la machine à écrire] typing error; [à l'ordinateur] keying error; **~ d'orthographe** spelling mistake. || [méfait, infraction] offence; **prendre qqn en ~** to catch sb out; **~ professionnelle** professional misdemeanour. || TENNIS fault; FOOTBALL foul. || [responsabilité] fault; **de ma/ta** *etc* **~** my/your *etc* fault; **par la ~ de qqn** because of sb. ○ **faute de** *loc prép* for want or lack of; **~ de mieux** for want or lack of anything better. ○ **sans faute** *loc adv* without fail.

fauteuil [fotœj] *nm* [siège] armchair; **~ roulant** wheelchair. || [de théâtre] seat.

fautif, -ive [fotif, iv] 1 *adj* [coupable] guilty. || [défectueux] faulty. 2 *nm, f* guilty party.

fauve [fov] 1 *nm* [animal] big cat. || [couleur] fawn. || ART Fauve. 2 *adj* [animal] wild. || [cuir, cheveux] tawny. || ART Fauvist.

faux, fausse [fo, fos] *adj* [incorrect] wrong. || [postiche, mensonger, hypocrite] false; **~ témoignage** JUR perjury. || [monnaie, papiers] forged, fake; [bijou, marbre] imitation, fake. || [injustifié]: **fausse alerte** false alarm. O **faux 1** *nm* [document, tableau] forgery, fake. **2** *nf* scythe. **3** *adv*: **chanter/jouer ~** MUS to sing/play out of tune; **sonner ~** *fig* not to ring true.

faux-filet, **faux filet** [fofilɛ] *nm* sirloin.

faux-fuyant [fofɥijɑ̃] *nm* excuse.

faux-monnayeur [fomɔnɛjœr] *nm* counterfeiter.

faux-sens [fosɑ̃s] *nm inv* mistranslation.

faveur [favœr] *nf* favour. O **en faveur de** *loc prép* in favour of.

favorable [favɔrabl] *adj*: **~ (à)** favourable (to).

favori, -ite [favɔri, it] *adj & nm, f* favourite.

favoriser [favɔrize] *vt* [avantager] to favour. || [contribuer à] to promote.

fax [faks] *nm* [appareil] fax machine; [document] fax.

faxer [fakse] *vt* to fax.

fayot [fajo] *nm fam* [personne] creep, crawler.

fébrile [febril] *adj* feverish.

fécond, -e [fekɔ̃, ɔ̃d] *adj* [femelle, terre, esprit] fertile. || [écrivain] prolific.

fécondation [fekɔ̃dasjɔ̃] *nf* fertilization; **~ in vitro** in vitro fertilization.

féconder [fekɔ̃de] *vt* [ovule] to fertilize. || [femme, femelle] to impregnate.

fécondité [fekɔ̃dite] *nf* [gén] fertility. || [d'écrivain] productiveness.

fécule [fekyl] *nf* starch.

féculent, -e [fekylɑ̃, ɑ̃t] *adj* starchy. O **féculent** *nm* starchy food.

fédéral, -e, -aux [federal, o] *adj* federal.

fédération [federasjɔ̃] *nf* federation.

fée [fe] *nf* fairy.

féerique [fe(e)rik] *adj* [enchanteur] enchanting.

feignant, -e = **fainéant**.

feindre [fɛ̃dr] **1** *vt* to feign; **~ de faire qqch** to pretend to do sthg. **2** *vi* to pretend.

feint, -e [fɛ̃, fɛ̃t] *pp* → **feindre**.

feinte [fɛ̃t] *nf* [ruse] ruse. || FOOTBALL dummy; BOXE feint.

fêlé, -e [fele] *adj* [assiette] cracked. || *fam* [personne] cracked, loony.

fêler [fele] *vt* to crack.

félicitations [felisitasjɔ̃] *nfpl* congratulations.

féliciter [felisite] *vt* to congratulate. O **se féliciter** *vp*: **se ~ de** to congratulate o.s. on.

félin, -e [felɛ̃, in] *adj* feline. O **félin** *nm* big cat.

fêlure [felyr] *nf* crack.

femelle [fəmɛl] *nf & adj* female.

féminin, -e [feminɛ̃, in] *adj* [gén] feminine. || [revue, équipe] women's (*avant n*). O **féminin** *nm* GRAM feminine.

féminisme [feminism] *nm* feminism.

féminité [feminite] *nf* femininity.

femme [fam] *nf* [personne de sexe féminin] woman; **~ de chambre** chambermaid; **~ de ménage** cleaning woman. || [épouse] wife.

fémur [femyr] *nm* femur.

fendre [fɑ̃dr] *vt* [bois] to split. || [foule, flots] to cut through. O **se fendre** *vp* [se crevasser] to crack.

fendu, -e [fɑ̃dy] *pp* → **fendre**.

fenêtre [fənɛtr] *nf* [gén & INFORM] window.

fenouil [fənuj] *nm* fennel.

fente [fɑ̃t] *nf* [fissure] crack. || [interstice, de vêtement] slit.

féodal, -e, -aux [feodal, o] *adj* feudal.

fer [fɛr] *nm* iron; **~ à cheval** horseshoe; **~ forgé** wrought iron; **~ à repasser** iron; **~ à souder** soldering iron.

ferai, feras *etc* → **faire**.

fer-blanc [fɛrblɑ̃] *nm* tinplate, tin.

férié, -e [ferje] → **jour**.

férir [ferir] *vt*: **sans coup ~** without meeting any resistance ou obstacle.

ferme¹ [fɛrm] *nf* farm.

ferme² [fɛrm] **1** *adj* firm; **être ~ sur ses jambes** to be steady on one's feet. **2** *adv* [beaucoup] a lot.

fermement [fɛrməmɑ̃] *adv* firmly.

ferment [fɛrmɑ̃] *nm* [levure] ferment. || *fig* [germe] seed, seeds (*pl*).

fermentation [fɛrmɑ̃tasjɔ̃] *nf* CHIM fermentation; *fig* ferment.

fermer [fɛrme] **1** *vt* [porte, tiroir, yeux] to close, to shut; [rideaux] to close, to draw; [store] to pull down; [enveloppe] to seal. || [bloquer] to close; **~ son esprit à qqch** to close one's mind to sthg. || [gaz, lumière] to turn off. || [vêtement] to do up. || [entreprise] to close down. **2** *vi* [gén] to shut, to close. || [vêtement] to do up. || [entreprise] to close down. O **se fermer** *vp* [porte] to close, to shut. || [plaie] to close up. || [vêtement] to do up.

fermeté [fɛrməte] *nf* firmness.

fermeture [fɛrmətyr] *nf* [de porte] closing. || [de vêtement, sac] fastening; **~ Éclair®** zip *Br*, zipper *Am*. || [d'établissement - temporaire] closing;

fictif

[- définitive] closure; ~ **hebdomadaire/
annuelle** weekly/annual closing.

fermier, -ière [fɛrmje, jɛr] *nm, f*
farmer.

fermoir [fɛrmwar] *nm* clasp.

féroce [ferɔs] *adj* [animal, appétit] ferocious; [personne, désir] fierce.

ferraille [fɛraj] *nf* [vieux fer] scrap iron
(U). || *fam* [monnaie] loose change.

ferroviaire [fɛrɔvjɛr] *adj* rail (*avant
n*).

ferry-boat [fɛribot] (*pl* **ferry-boats**)
nm ferry.

fertile [fɛrtil] *adj litt & fig* fertile; ~ **en**
fig filled with, full of.

fertiliser [fɛrtilize] *vt* to fertilize.

fertilité [fɛrtilite] *nf* fertility.

féru, -e [fery] *adj sout* [passionné]: être
~ **de qqch** to have a passion for sthg.

fervent, -e [fɛrvɑ̃, ɑ̃t] *adj* [chrétien] fervent; [amoureux, démocrate] ardent.

ferveur [fɛrvœr] *nf* [dévotion] fervour.

fesse [fɛs] *nf* buttock.

fessée [fese] *nf* spanking, smack (on the
bottom).

festin [fɛstɛ̃] *nm* banquet, feast.

festival, -als [fɛstival] *nm* festival.

festivités [fɛstivite] *nfpl* festivities.

feston [fɛstɔ̃] *nm* COUTURE scallop.

festoyer [fɛstwaje] *vi* to feast.

fêtard, -e [fɛtar, ard] *nm, f* fun-loving
person.

fête [fɛt] *nf* [congé] holiday; **les ~s (de
fin d'année)** the Christmas holidays; ~
nationale national holiday. || [réunion,
réception] celebration. || [kermesse] fair;
~ **foraine** funfair. || [jour de célébration
- de personne] saint's day; [- de saint] feast
(day). || [soirée] party. || *loc*: **faire la ~** to
have a good time.

fêter [fete] *vt* [événement] to celebrate;
[personne] to have a party for.

fétiche [fetiʃ] *nm* [objet de culte] fetish.
|| [mascotte] mascot.

fétichisme [fetiʃism] *nm* [culte, perver-
sion] fetishism.

fétide [fetid] *adj* fetid.

fétu [fety] *nm*: ~ **(de paille)** wisp (of
straw).

feu, -e [fø] *adj*: ~ **M. X** the late Mr X; ~
mon mari my late husband. ○ **feu,** ~ *x*
nm [flamme, incendie] fire; **au ~!** fire!; **en
~** *litt & fig* on fire; **avez-vous du ~?** have
you got a light?; **faire ~** MIL to fire; **mettre le ~ à qqch** to set fire to sthg, to set
sthg on fire; **prendre ~** to catch fire; ~ **de
camp** camp fire; ~ **de cheminée** chimney

fire. || [signal] light; ~ **rouge/vert** red/
green light; ~ **x de croisement** dipped
headlights; ~ **x de position** sidelights; ~ **x
de route** headlights on full beam. || CULIN
burner *Am*; **à** ~ **doux/vif** on a low/high
flame. || CIN & THÉÂTRE light (U). ○ **feu
d'artifice** *nm* firework.

feuillage [fœjaʒ] *nm* foliage.

feuille [fœj] *nf* [d'arbre] leaf; ~ **morte**
dead leaf; ~ **de vigne** BOT vine leaf. ||
[page] sheet. || [document] form.

feuillet [fœjɛ] *nm* page.

feuilleter [fœjte] *vt* to flick through.

feuilleton [fœjtɔ̃] *nm* serial.

feutre [føtr] *nm* [étoffe] felt. || [chapeau]
felt hat. || [crayon] felt-tip pen.

feutré, -e [føtre] *adj* [garni de feutre]
trimmed with felt; [qui a l'aspect du feu-
tre] felted. || [bruit, cri] muffled.

feutrine [føtrin] *nf* lightweight felt.

fève [fɛv] *nf* broad bean.

février [fevrije] *nm* February; *voir aussi* **septembre**.

fg *abr de* **faubourg**.

fiable [fjabl] *adj* reliable.

fiacre [fjakr] *nm* hackney carriage.

fiançailles [fjɑ̃saj] *nfpl* engagement
(*sg*).

fiancé, -e [fjɑ̃se] *nm, f* fiancé (*f* fiancée).

fiancer [fjɑ̃se] ○ **se fiancer** *vp*: **se ~
(avec)** to get engaged (to).

fibre [fibr] *nf* ANAT, BIOL & TECHNOL fibre;
~ **de verre** fibreglass, glass fibre.

ficeler [fisle] *vt* [lier] to tie up.

ficelle [fisɛl] *nf* [fil] string. || [pain] *thin
French stick*. || (*gén pl*) [truc] trick.

fiche [fiʃ] *nf* [document] card; ~ **de paie**
pay slip. || ÉLECTR & TECHNOL pin.

ficher [fiʃe] (*pp vt sens 1 & 2* **fiché,** *pp
vt sens 3 & 4* **fichu**) *vt* [enfoncer]: ~ **qqch
dans** to stick sthg into. || [inscrire] to put
on file. || *fam* [faire]: **qu'est-ce qu'il
fiche?** what's he doing? || *fam* [mettre] to
put; ~ **qqch par terre** *fig* to mess or muck
sthg up. ○ **se ficher** *vp* [s'enfoncer - suj:
clou, pique]: **se ~ dans** to go into. || *fam*
[se moquer]: **se ~ de** to make fun of. ||
fam [ne pas tenir compte]: **se ~ de** not to
give a damn about.

fichier [fiʃje] *nm* file.

fichu, -e [fiʃy] *adj fam* [cassé, fini] done
for. || (*avant n*) [désagréable] nasty. ||
loc: **être mal ~** *fam* [personne] to feel rotten. ○ **fichu** *nm* scarf.

fictif, -ive [fiktif, iv] *adj* [imaginaire]
imaginary. || [faux] false.

fiction [fiksjɔ̃] *nf* LITTÉRATURE fiction. ||
[monde imaginaire] dream world.

fidèle [fidɛl] 1 *nmf* RELIG believer. ||
[adepte] fan. 2 *adj* [loyal, exact, sem-
blable] : ~ à (à) faithful (to); ~ à la réalité
accurate. || [habitué] regular.

fidélité [fidelite] *nf* faithfulness.

fief [fjɛf] *nm* fief; *fig* stronghold.

fiel [fjɛl] *nm litt & fig* gall.

fier¹, fière [fjɛr] *adj* [gén] proud; ~ de
qqn/qqch proud of sb/sthg; ~ de faire
qqch proud to be doing sthg. || [noble]
noble.

fier² [fje] ○ **se fier** *vp* : se ~ à to trust,
to rely on.

fierté [fjɛrte] *nf* [satisfaction, dignité]
pride. || [arrogance] arrogance.

fièvre [fjɛvr] *nf* MÉD fever; avoir 40 de ~
to have a temperature of 105 (degrees).

fiévreux, -euse [fjevrø, øz] *adj litt &
fig* feverish.

fig. *abr de* figure.

figer [fiʒe] *vt* to paralyse. ○ **se figer** *vp*
[s'immobiliser] to freeze. || [se solidifier] to
congeal.

fignoler [fiɲɔle] *vt* to put the finishing
touches to.

figue [fig] *nf* fig.

figuier [figje] *nm* fig-tree.

figurant, -e [figyrɑ̃, ɑ̃t] *nm, f* extra.

figuratif, -ive [figyratif, iv] *adj* figurative.

figure [figyr] *nf* [gén] figure; faire ~ de
to look like. || [visage] face.

figuré, -e [figyre] *adj* [sens] figurative.
○ **figuré** *nm* : au ~ in the figurative
sense.

figurer [figyre] 1 *vt* to represent. 2 *vi* : ~
dans/parmi to figure in/among.

figurine [figyrin] *nf* figurine.

fil [fil] *nm* [brin] thread; perdre le ~ (de
qqch) *fig* to lose the thread (of sthg). ||
[câble] wire; ~ de fer wire. || [cours]
course; au ~ de in the course of. || [tissu]
linen. || [tranchant] edge.

filament [filamɑ̃] *nm* ANAT & ÉLECTR fila-
ment. || [végétal] fibre. || [de colle, bave]
thread.

filandreux, -euse [filɑ̃drø, øz] *adj*
[viande] stringy.

filature [filatyr] *nf* [usine] mill; [fabri-
cation] spinning. || [poursuite] tailing.

file [fil] *nf* line; à la ~ in a line; se garer
en double ~ to double-park; ~ d'attente
queue *Br*, line *Am*.

filer [file] 1 *vt* [soie, coton] to spin. ||
[personne] to tail. || *fam* [donner] : ~ qqch

à qqn to slip sthg to sb, to slip sb sthg. 2
vi [bas] to run *Am*. || [aller vite - temps,
véhicule] to fly (by). || *fam* [partir] to
dash off. || *loc* : ~ doux to behave nicely.

filet [filɛ] *nm* [à mailles] net; ~ de pêche
fishing net; ~ à provisions string bag. ||
CULIN fillet. || [de liquide] drop, dash; [de
lumière] shaft.

filial, -e, -iaux [filjal, jo] *adj* filial.
○ **filiale** *nf* ÉCON subsidiary.

filiation [filjasjɔ̃] *nf* [lien de parenté]
line.

filière [filjɛr] *nf* [voie] : suivre la ~ hié-
rarchique to go through the right chan-
nels. || [réseau] network.

filiforme [filiform] *adj* skinny.

filigrane [filigran] *nm* [dessin] water-
mark; en ~ *fig* between the lines.

filin [filɛ̃] *nm* rope.

fille [fij] *nf* [enfant] daughter. || [femme]
girl; jeune ~ girl; vieille ~ *péj* spinster.

fillette [fijɛt] *nf* little girl.

filleul, -e [fijœl] *nm, f* godchild.

film [film] *nm* [gén] film; ~ catastrophe
disaster movie; ~ d'épouvante horror
film; ~ policier detective film.

filmer [filme] *vt* to film.

filmographie [filmɔgrafi] *nf* filmog-
raphy, films (*pl*).

filon [filɔ̃] *nm* [de mine] vein. || *fam fig*
[possibilité] cushy number.

fils [fis] *nm* son.

filtrant, -e [filtrɑ̃, ɑ̃t] *adj* [verre] tinted.

filtre [filtr] *nm* filter; ~ à café coffee
filter.

filtrer [filtre] 1 *vt* to filter; *fig* to screen.
2 *vi* to filter; *fig* to filter through.

fin, fine [fɛ̃, fin] 1 *adj* [gén] fine. || [par-
tie du corps] slender; [couche, papier]
thin. || [subtil] shrewd. || [ouïe, vue] keen.
2 *adv* finely; ~ prêt quite ready. ○ **fin** *nf*
end; ~ mars at the end of March; mettre
~ à to put a stop ou an end to; prendre ~
to come to an end; arriver ou parvenir à
ses ~s to achieve one's ends ou aims.
○ **fin de série** *nf* oddment. ○ **à la fin**
loc adv : tu vas m'écouter, à la ~? will
you listen to me? ○ **à la fin de** *loc prép*
at the end of. ○ **sans fin** *loc adj* endless.

final, -e [final] (*pl* **finals** OU **finaux**) *adj*
final. ○ **finale** *nf* SPORT final.

finalement [finalmɑ̃] *adv* finally.

finaliste [finalist] *nmf & adj* finalist.

finalité [finalite] *nf sout* [fonction] purpose.

finance [finɑ̃s] *nf* finance.

financer [finɑ̃se] *vt* to finance, to fund.

financier, -ière [finãsje, jɛr] *adj* financial. ○ **financier** *nm* financier.

finaud, -e [fino, od] *adj* wily, crafty.

finesse [fines] *nf* [gén] fineness. || [minceur] slenderness. || [perspicacité] shrewdness. || [subtilité] subtlety.

fini, -e [fini] *adj péj* [fieffé]: **un crétin ~** a complete idiot. || [limité] finite. ○ **fini** *nm* [d'objet] finish.

finir [finir] **1** *vt* [gén] to finish, to end. || [vider] to empty. **2** *vi* [gén] to finish, to end; **~ par faire qqch** to do sthg eventually; **mal ~** to end badly. || [arrêter]: **~ de faire qqch** to stop doing sthg; **en ~ (avec)** to finish (with).

finition [finisjɔ̃] *nf* [d'objet] finish.

finlandais, -e [fɛ̃lɑ̃dɛ, ɛz] *adj* Finnish. ○ **Finlandais, -e** *nm, f* Finn.

Finlande [fɛ̃lɑ̃d] *nf*: **la ~** Finland.

finnois, -e [finwa, az] *adj* Finnish. ○ **finnois** *nm* [langue] Finnish. ○ **Finnois, -e** *nm, f* Finn.

fiole [fjɔl] *nf* flask.

floriture [fjɔrityr] *nf* flourish.

floul = fuel.

firmament [firmamɑ̃] *nm* firmament.

firme [firm] *nf* firm.

fis, fit *etc* → **faire**.

fisc [fisk] *nm* ≃ Internal Revenue *Am*.

fiscal, -e, -aux [fiskal, o] *adj* tax (*avant n*), fiscal.

fiscalité [fiskalite] *nf* tax system.

fissure [fisyr] *nf litt & fig* crack.

fissurer [fisyre] *vt* [fendre] to crack; *fig* to split. ○ **se fissurer** *vp* to crack.

fiston [fistɔ̃] *nm fam* son.

FIV (*abr de* **fécondation in vitro**) *nf* IVF.

fixation [fiksasjɔ̃] *nf* [action de fixer] fixing. || [attache] fastening, fastener; [de ski] binding. || PSYCHOL fixation.

fixe [fiks] *adj* fixed; [encre] permanent. ○ **fixe** *nm* fixed salary.

fixement [fiksəmɑ̃] *adv* fixedly.

fixer [fikse] *vt* [gén] to fix; [règle] to set; **~ son choix sur** to decide on. || [monter] to hang. || [regarder] to stare at. || [renseigner]: **être fixé sur qqch** to know all about sthg. ○ **se fixer** *vp* to settle; **se ~ sur** [suj: choix, personne] to settle on; [suj: regard] to rest on.

fjord [fjɔrd] *nm* fjord.

flacon [flakɔ̃] *nm* small bottle.

flageller [flaʒele] *vt* [fouetter] to flagellate.

flageoler [flaʒɔle] *vi* to tremble.

flageolet [flaʒɔlɛ] *nm* [haricot] flageolet bean. || MUS flageolet.

flagrant, -e [flagrɑ̃, ɑ̃t] *adj* flagrant; → **délit**.

flair [flɛr] *nm* sense of smell; *fig* intuition.

flairer [flɛre] *vt* to sniff, to smell; *fig* to scent.

flamand, -e [flamɑ̃, ɑ̃d] *adj* Flemish.

flamant [flamɑ̃] *nm* flamingo; **~ rose** pink flamingo.

flambeau, -x [flɑ̃bo] *nm* torch; *fig* flame.

flamber [flɑ̃be] **1** *vi* [brûler] to blaze. || *fam* JEU to play for high stakes. **2** *vt* [crêpe] to flambé. || [volaille] to singe.

flamboyant, -e [flɑ̃bwajɑ̃, ɑ̃t] *adj* [ciel, regard] blazing; [couleur] flaming.

flamboyer [flɑ̃bwaje] *vi* to blaze.

flamme [flam] *nf* flame; *fig* fervour, fire.

flan [flɑ̃] *nm* baked custard.

flanc [flɑ̃] *nm* [de personne, navire, montagne] side; [d'animal, d'armée] flank.

flancher [flɑ̃ʃe] *vi fam* to give up.

flanelle [flanɛl] *nf* flannel.

flâner [flɑne] *vi* [se promener] to stroll.

flanquer [flɑ̃ke] *vt fam* [jeter]: **~ qqch par terre** to fling sthg to the ground; **~ qqn dehors** ou **à la porte** to chuck ou fling sb out. || *fam* [donner]: **~ une gifle à qqn** to clout sb round the ear; **~ la frousse à qqn** to put the wind up sb. || [accompagner]: **être flanqué de** to be flanked by.

flapi, -e [flapi] *adj fam* dead beat.

flaque [flak] *nf* pool.

flash [flaʃ] *nm* PHOT flash. || RADIO & TÉLÉ: **~ (d'information)** newsflash; **~ publicitaire** commercial.

flash-back [flaʃbak] (*pl inv* OU **flash-backs**) *nm* CIN flashback.

flasher [flaʃe] *vi fam*: **~ sur qqn/qqch** to be turned on by sb/sthg.

flasque [flask] **1** *nf* flask. **2** *adj* flabby, limp.

flatter [flate] *vt* [louer] to flatter. || [caresser] to stroke. ○ **se flatter** *vp* to flatter o.s.; **je me flatte de le convaincre** I flatter myself that I can convince him.

flatterie [flatri] *nf* flattery.

flatteur, -euse [flatœr, øz] **1** *adj* flattering. **2** *nm, f* flatterer.

fléau, -x [fleo] *nm litt & fig* [calamité] scourge. || [instrument] flail.

flèche [flɛʃ] *nf* [gén] arrow. || [d'église] spire. || *fig* [critique] shaft.

fléchette [fleʃɛt] *nf* dart.

fléchir [fleʃir] 1 *vt* to bend, to flex; *fig* to sway. 2 *ri* to bend; *fig* to weaken.

fléchissement [fleʃismɑ̃] *nm* flexing, bending; *fig* weakening.

flegmatique [flɛgmatik] *adj* phlegmatic.

flegme [flɛgm] *nm* composure.

flemmard, -e [flɛmar, ard] *fam* 1 *adj* lazy. 2 *nm, f* lazybones (*sg*), idler.

flemme [flɛm] *nf fam* laziness; **j'ai la ~ (de sortir)** I can't be bothered (to go out).

flétrir [fletrir] *vt* [fleur, visage] to wither. ○ **se flétrir** *vp* to wither.

fleur [flœr] *nf* BOT & *fig* flower; **en ~, en ~s** [arbre] in flower, in blossom; **à ~s** [motif] flowered.

fleuret [flœrɛ] *nm* foil.

fleuri, -e [flœri] *adj* [jardin, pré] in flower; [tissu] flowered; [table, appartement] decorated with flowers. || *fig* [style] flowery.

fleurir [flœrir] 1 *ri* to blossom; *fig* to flourish. 2 *vt* [maison] to decorate with flowers; [tombe] to lay flowers on.

fleuriste [flœrist] *nmf* florist.

fleuron [flœrɔ̃] *nm fig* jewel.

fleuve [flœv] *nm* [cours d'eau] river. || (*en apposition*) [interminable] lengthy, interminable.

flexible [flɛksibl] *adj* flexible.

flexion [flɛksjɔ̃] *nf* [de genou, de poutre] bending. || LING inflexion.

flic [flik] *nm fam* cop.

flinguer [flɛ̃ge] *vt fam* to gun down. ○ **se flinguer** *vp fam* to blow one's brains out.

flipper [flipœr] *nm* pin-ball machine.

flirter [flœrte] *vi*: **~ (avec qqn)** to flirt (with sb).

flocon [flɔkɔ̃] *nm* flake; **~ de neige** snowflake.

flonflon [flɔ̃flɔ̃] *nm* (*gén pl*) blare.

flop [flɔp] *nm* [échec] flop, failure.

floraison [flɔrɛzɔ̃] *nf litt & fig* flowering, blossoming.

floral, -e, -aux [flɔral, o] *adj* floral.

flore [flɔr] *nf* flora.

Floride [flɔrid] *nf*: **la ~** Florida.

florissant, -e [flɔrisɑ̃, ɑ̃t] *adj* [santé] blooming; [économie] flourishing.

flot [flo] *nm* flood, stream; **être à ~** [navire] to be afloat; *fig* to be back to normal. ○ **flots** *nmpl littéraire* waves.

flottaison [flɔtɛzɔ̃] *nf* floating.

flottant, -e [flɔtɑ̃, ɑ̃t] *adj* [gén] floating. || [robe] loose-fitting.

flotte [flɔt] *nf* AÉRON & NAVIG fleet. || *fam* [eau] water. || *fam* [pluie] rain.

flottement [flɔtmɑ̃] *nm* [indécision] hesitation, wavering. || [de monnaie] floating.

flotter [flɔte] 1 *ri* [sur l'eau] to float. || [drapeau] to flap; [brume, odeur] to drift. || [dans un vêtement]: **tu flottes dedans** it's baggy on you. 2 *v impers fam*: **il flotte** it's raining.

flotteur [flɔtœr] *nm* [de ligne de pêche, d'hydravion] float; [de chasse d'eau] ballcock.

flou, -e [flu] *adj* [couleur, coiffure] soft. || [photo] blurred, fuzzy. || [pensée] vague, woolly. ○ **flou** *nm* [de photo] fuzziness; [de décision] vagueness.

flouer [flue] *vt fam* to do, to swindle.

fluctuer [flyktɥe] *ri* to fluctuate.

fluet, -ette [flɥɛ, ɛt] *adj* [personne] thin, slender; [voix] thin.

fluide [flɥid] 1 *nm* [matière] fluid. 2 *adj* [matière] fluid; [circulation] flowing freely.

fluidifier [flɥidifje] *vt* [trafic] to improve the flow of.

fluidité [flɥidite] *nf* [gén] fluidity; [de circulation] easy flow.

fluor [flyɔr] *nm* fluorine.

fluorescent, -e [flyɔrɛsɑ̃, ɑ̃t] *adj* fluorescent.

flûte [flyt] 1 *nf* MUS flute. || [verre] flute (glass). 2 *interj fam* bother!

flûtiste [flytist] *nmf* flautist.

fluvial, -e, -iaux [flyvjal, jo] *adj* [eaux, pêche] river (*avant n*); [alluvions] fluvial.

flux [fly] *nm* [écoulement] flow. || [marée] flood tide. || PHYS flux.

FM (*abr de* **frequency modulation**) *nf* FM.

FMI (*abr de* **Fonds monétaire international**) *nm* IMF.

FN (*abr de* **Front national**) *nm* extreme right-wing French political party.

foc [fɔk] *nm* jib.

focal, -e, -aux [fɔkal, o] *adj* focal.

fœtal, -e, -aux [fetal, o] *adj* foetal.

fœtus [fetys] *nm* foetus.

foi [fwa] *nf* RELIG faith. || [confiance] trust; **avoir ~ en qqn/qqch** to trust sb/sthg, to have faith in sb/sthg. || *loc*: **être de bonne/mauvaise ~** to be in good/bad faith.

foie [fwa] *nm* ANAT & CULIN liver.

foin [fwɛ̃] *nm* hay.

foire [fwar] *nf* [fête] funfair. || [exposition, salon] trade fair.

fois [fwa] *nf* time; **une ~** once; **deux ~** twice; **trois/quatre ~** three/four times; **deux ~ plus long** twice as long; **neuf ~ sur dix** nine times out of ten; **deux ~ trois** two times three; **cette ~** this time; **il était une ~ ...** once upon a time there was ...; **une (bonne) ~ pour toutes** once and for all. ○ **à la fois** *loc adv* at the same time, at once. ○ **des fois** *loc adv* [parfois] sometimes. ○ **une fois que** *loc conj* once.

foison [fwazɔ̃] ○ **à foison** *loc adv* in abundance.

foisonner [fwazɔne] *vi* to abound.

folâtre [fɔlatr] *adj* playful.

folâtrer [fɔlatre] *vi* to romp (about).

folie [fɔli] *nf litt & fig* madness.

folklore [fɔlklɔr] *nm* [de pays] folklore.

folklorique [fɔlklɔrik] *adj* [danse] folk. || *fig* [situation, personne] bizarre, quaint.

folle → **fou**.

follement [fɔlmɑ̃] *adv* madly, wildly.

fomenter [fɔmɑ̃te] *vt* to foment.

foncé, -e [fɔ̃se] *adj* dark.

foncer [fɔ̃se] *vi* [teinte] to darken. || [se ruer]: **~ sur** to rush at. || *fam* [se dépêcher] to get a move on.

foncier, -ière [fɔ̃sje, jɛr] *adj* [impôt] land (*avant n*); **propriétaire ~** landowner. || [fondamental] basic, fundamental.

foncièrement [fɔ̃sjɛrmɑ̃] *adv* basically.

fonction [fɔ̃ksjɔ̃] *nf* [gén] function; **faire ~ de** to act as. || [profession] post; **entrer en ~** to take up one's post ou duties. ○ **en fonction de** *loc prép* according to.

fonctionnaire [fɔ̃ksjɔner] *nmf* [de l'État] state employee; [dans l'administration] civil servant.

fonctionnel, -elle [fɔ̃ksjɔnɛl] *adj* functional.

fonctionnement [fɔ̃ksjɔnmɑ̃] *nm* working, functioning.

fonctionner [fɔ̃ksjɔne] *vi* to work, to function.

fond [fɔ̃] *nm* [de récipient, puits, mer] bottom; [de pièce] back; **sans ~** bottomless. || [substance] heart, root; **le ~ de ma pensée** what I really think; **le ~ et la forme** content and form. || [arrière-plan] background. ○ **fond de teint** *nm* foundation. ○ **à fond** *loc adv* [entièrement] thoroughly; **se donner à ~** to give one's all. || [très vite] at top speed. ○ **au fond,**

dans le fond *loc adv* basically. ○ **au fond de** *loc prép*: **au ~ de moi-même/lui-même** *etc* at heart, deep down.

fondamental, -e, -aux [fɔ̃damɑ̃tal, o] *adj* fundamental.

fondant, -e [fɔ̃dɑ̃, ɑ̃t] *adj* [neige, glace] melting; [aliment] which melts in the mouth.

fondateur, -trice [fɔ̃datœr, tris] *nm, f* founder.

fondation [fɔ̃dasjɔ̃] *nf* foundation. ○ **fondations** *nfpl* CONSTR foundations.

fondé, -e [fɔ̃de] *adj* [craintes, reproches] justified, well-founded.

fondement [fɔ̃dmɑ̃] *nm* [base, motif] foundation; **sans ~** groundless, without foundation.

fonder [fɔ̃de] *vt* [créer] to found. || [baser]: **~ qqch sur** to base sthg on. ○ **se fonder** *vp*: **se ~ sur** [suj: personne] to base o.s. on; [suj: argument] to be based on.

fonderie [fɔ̃dri] *nf* [usine] foundry.

fondre [fɔ̃dr] **1** *vt* [beurre, neige] to melt; [sucre, sel] to dissolve; [métal] to melt down. || [mouler] to cast. **2** *vi* [beurre, neige] to melt; [sucre, sel] to dissolve; *fig* to melt away. || [maigrir] to lose weight. || [se ruer]: **~ sur** to swoop down on.

fonds [fɔ̃] **1** *nm* [ressources] fund; **le Fonds monétaire international** the International Monetary Fund. || [bien immobilier]: **~ (de commerce)** business. **2** *nmpl* funds.

fondu, -e [fɔ̃dy] *pp* → **fondre**. ○ **fondue** *nf* fondue.

font → **faire**.

fontaine [fɔ̃tɛn] *nf* [naturelle] spring; [publique] fountain.

fonte [fɔ̃t] *nf* [de glace, beurre] melting; [de métal] melting down. || [alliage] cast iron.

foot [fut] = **football**.

football [futbol] *nm* soccer.

footballeur, -euse [futbolœr, øz] *nm, f* soccer player.

footing [futiŋ] *nm* jogging.

for [fɔr] *nm*: **dans son ~ intérieur** in his/her heart of hearts.

forage [fɔraʒ] *nm* drilling.

forain, -e [fɔrɛ̃, ɛn] *adj* → **fête**. ○ **forain** *nm* stallholder.

forçat [fɔrsa] *nm* convict.

force [fɔrs] *nf* [vigueur] strength. || [violence, puissance, MIL & PHYS] force; **faire faire qqch à qqn de ~** to force sb to do sthg; **~ centrifuge** PHYS centrifugal force.

○ **forces** *nfpl* [physique] strength (*sg*); **de toutes ses ~s** with all his/her strength. ○ **à force de** *loc prép* by dint of.

forcément [fɔrsemɑ̃] *adv* inevitably.

forcené, -e [fɔrsəne] *nm, f* maniac.

forceps [fɔrsɛps] *nm* forceps (*pl*).

forcer [fɔrse] **1** *vt* [gén] to force; **~ qqn à qqch/à faire qqch** to force sb into sthg/ to do sthg. || [admiration, respect] to compel, to command. || [talent, voix] to strain. **2** *vi*: **ça ne sert à rien de ~, ça ne passe pas** there's no point in forcing it, it won't go through; **~ sur qqch** to overdo sthg. ○ **se forcer** *vp* [s'obliger]: **se ~ à faire qqch** to force o.s. to do sthg.

forcir [fɔrsir] *vi* to put on weight.

forer [fɔre] *vt* to drill.

forestier, -ière [fɔrɛstje, jɛr] *adj* forest (*avant n*).

forêt [fɔrɛ] *nf* forest.

forfait [fɔrfɛ] *nm* [prix fixe] fixed price. || SPORT: **déclarer ~** [abandonner] to withdraw; *fig* to give up. || *littéraire* [crime] heinous crime.

forfaitaire [fɔrfɛtɛr] *adj* inclusive.

forge [fɔrʒ] *nf* forge.

forger [fɔrʒe] *vt* [métal] to forge. || *fig* [caractère] to form.

forgeron [fɔrʒərɔ̃] *nm* blacksmith.

formaliser [fɔrmalize] ○ **se formaliser** *vp*: **se ~ (de)** to take offence (at).

formalisme [fɔrmalism] *nm* formality.

formaliste [fɔrmalist] **1** *nmf* formalist. **2** *adj* [milieu] conventional; [personne]: **être ~** to be a stickler for the rules.

formalité [fɔrmalite] *nf* formality.

format [fɔrma] *nm* [dimension] size.

formatage [fɔrmataʒ] *nm* INFORM formatting.

formater [fɔrmate] *vt* INFORM to format.

formateur, -trice [fɔrmatœr, tris] **1** *adj* formative. **2** *nm, f* trainer.

formation [fɔrmasjɔ̃] *nf* [gén] formation. || [apprentissage] training.

forme [fɔrm] *nf* [aspect] shape, form; **en ~ de** in the shape of. || [état] form; **être en (pleine) ~** to be in (great) shape, to be on (top) form. ○ **formes** *nfpl* figure (*sg*).

formel, -elle [fɔrmɛl] *adj* [définitif, ferme] positive, definite. || [poli] formal.

former [fɔrme] *vt* [gén] to form. || [personnel, élèves] to train. || [goût, sensibilité] to develop. ○ **se former** *vp* [se constituer] to form. || [s'instruire] to train o.s.

Formica® [fɔrmika] *nm inv* Formica®.

formidable [fɔrmidabl] *adj* [épatant] great, tremendous. || [incroyable] incredible.

formol [fɔrmɔl] *nm* formalin.

formulaire [fɔrmyler] *nm* form; **remplir un ~** to fill in a form.

formule [fɔrmyl] *nf* [expression] expression; **~ de politesse** [orale] polite phrase; [épistolaire] letter ending. || CHIM & MATHS formula. || [méthode] way, method.

formuler [fɔrmyle] *vt* to formulate, to express.

fort, -e [fɔr, fɔrt] **1** *adj* [gén] strong; **et le plus ~, c'est que ...** and the most amazing thing about it is ...; **c'est plus ~ que moi!** I can't help it. || [corpulent] heavy, big. || [doué] gifted; **être ~ en qqch** to be good at sthg. || [puissant - voix] loud; [- vent, lumière, accent] strong. || [considérable] large; **il y a de ~es chances qu'il gagne** there's a good chance he'll win. **2** *adv* [frapper, battre] hard; [sonner, parler] loud, loudly. || *sout* [très] very. **3** *nm* [château] fort. || [spécialité]: **ce n'est pas mon ~** it's not my forte or strong point.

forteresse [fɔrtərɛs] *nf* fortress.

fortifiant, -e [fɔrtifjɑ̃, ɑ̃t] *adj* fortifying. ○ **fortifiant** *nm* tonic.

fortification [fɔrtifikasjɔ̃] *nf* fortification.

fortifier [fɔrtifje] *vt* [personne, ville] to fortify.

fortuit, -e [fɔrtɥi, it] *adj* chance (*avant n*), fortuitous.

fortune [fɔrtyn] *nf* [richesse] fortune. || [hasard] luck, fortune.

fortuné, -e [fɔrtyne] *adj* [riche] wealthy. || [chanceux] fortunate, lucky.

forum [fɔrɔm] *nm* forum.

fosse [fos] *nf* [trou] pit. || [tombe] grave.

fossé [fose] *nm* ditch; *fig* gap.

fossette [fɔsɛt] *nf* dimple.

fossile [fɔsil] *nm* [de plante, d'animal] fossil. || *fig & péj* [personne] fossil, fogy.

fossoyeur, -euse [foswajœr, øz] *nm, f* gravedigger.

fou, folle [fu, fɔl] **1** *adj* (*fol devant voyelle ou h muet*) mad, insane; [prodigieux] tremendous. **2** *nm, f* madman (*f* madwoman).

foudre [fudr] *nf* lightning.

foudroyant, -e [fudrwajɑ̃, ɑ̃t] *adj* [progrès, vitesse] lightning (*avant n*); [succès] stunning. || [regard] withering.

foudroyer [fudrwaje] *vt* [suj: foudre] to strike; **l'arbre a été foudroyé** the tree was struck by lightning. || *fig* [abattre] to strike down, to kill; ~ **qqn du regard** to glare at sb.

fouet [fwɛ] *nm* [en cuir] whip. || CULIN whisk.

fouetter [fwete] *vt* [gén] to whip; [suj: pluie] to lash (against).

fougère [fuʒɛr] *nf* fern.

fougue [fug] *nf* ardour.

fougueux, -euse [fugø, øz] *adj* ardent, spirited.

fouille [fuj] *nf* [de personne, maison] search. || [du sol] dig, excavation.

fouiller [fuje] **1** *vt* [gén] to search. || *fig* [approfondir] to examine closely. **2** *vi*: ~ **dans** to go through.

fouillis [fuji] *nm* jumble, muddle.

fouine [fwin] *nf* stone-marten.

fouiner [fwine] *vi* to ferret about.

foulard [fular] *nm* scarf.

foule [ful] *nf* [de gens] crowd.

foulée [fule] *nf* [de coureur] stride.

fouler [fule] *vt* [raisin] to press; [sol] to walk on. ○ **se fouler** *vp* MÉD: **se ~ le poignet/la cheville** to sprain one's wrist/ankle.

foulure [fulyr] *nf* sprain.

four [fur] *nm* [de cuisson] oven; ~ **électrique/à micro-ondes** electric/microwave oven; ~ **crématoire** HIST oven.

fourbe [furb] *adj* treacherous, deceitful.

fourbu, -e [furby] *adj* tired out, exhausted.

fourche [furʃ] *nf* [outil] pitchfork. || [de vélo, route] fork. || *Belg* SCOL free period.

fourchette [furʃet] *nf* [couvert] fork. || [écart] range, bracket.

fourgon [furgɔ̃] *nm* [camionnette] van; ~ **cellulaire** police van *Br*, patrol wagon *Am*. || [ferroviaire]: ~ **à bestiaux** cattle truck; ~ **postal** mail van.

fourgonnette [furgɔnɛt] *nf* small van.

fourmi [furmi] *nf* [insecte] ant.

fourmilière [furmiljɛr] *nf* anthill.

fourmiller [furmije] *vi* [pulluler] to swarm; ~ **de** *fig* to be swarming with.

fournaise [furnɛz] *nf* furnace.

fourneau, -x [furno] *nm* [cuisinière, poêle] stove. || [de fonderie] furnace.

fournée [furne] *nf* batch.

fourni, -e [furni] *adj* [barbe, cheveux] thick.

fournir [furnir] *vt* [procurer]: ~ **qqch à qqn** to supply ou provide sb with sthg. || [produire]: ~ **un effort** to make an effort.

|| [approvisionner]: ~ **qqn (en)** to supply sb (with).

fournisseur, -euse [furnisœr, øz] *nm, f* supplier.

fourniture [furnityr] *nf* supply, supplying (*U*). ○ **fournitures** *nfpl*: ~**s de bureau** office supplies; ~**s scolaires** school supplies.

fourrage [furaʒ] *nm* fodder.

fourré [fure] *nm* thicket.

fourreau, -x [furo] *nm* [d'épée] sheath; [de parapluie] cover. || [robe] sheath dress.

fourrer [fure] *vt* CULIN to stuff, to fill. || *fam* [mettre]: ~ **qqch (dans)** to stuff sthg (into). ○ **se fourrer** *vp*: **se ~ une idée dans la tête** to get an idea into one's head; **je ne savais plus où me ~** I didn't know where to put myself.

fourre-tout [furtu] *nm inv* [sac] holdall.

fourreur [furœr] *nm* furrier.

fourrière [furjɛr] *nf* pound.

fourrure [furyr] *nf* fur.

fourvoyer [furvwaje] ○ **se fourvoyer** *vp sout* [se tromper] to go off on the wrong track.

foutre [futr] *vt* tfam [mettre] to shove, to stick; ~ **qqn dehors** ou **à la porte** to chuck sb out. || [donner]: ~ **la trouille à qqn** to put the wind up sb; **il lui a foutu une baffe** he thumped him one. || [faire] to do; **j'en ai rien à** ~ I don't give a toss. ○ **se foutre** *vp* tfam [se mettre]: **se ~ dans** [situation] to get o.s. into. || [se moquer]: **se ~ de (la gueule de) qqn** to laugh at sb. || [ne pas s'intéresser]: **je m'en fous** I don't give a damn about it.

foyer [fwaje] *nm* [maison] home. || [résidence] home, hostel. || [de lunettes] focus; **verres à double ~** bifocals.

fracas [fraka] *nm* roar.

fracasser [frakase] *vt* to smash, to shatter.

fraction [fraksjɔ̃] *nf* fraction.

fractionner [fraksjone] *vt* to divide (up), to split up.

fracture [fraktyr] *nf* MÉD fracture.

fracturer [fraktyre] *vt* MÉD to fracture. || [coffre, serrure] to break open.

fragile [fraʒil] *adj* [gén] fragile; [peau, santé] delicate.

fragiliser [fraʒilize] *vt* to weaken.

fragilité [fraʒilite] *nf* fragility.

fragment [fragmɑ̃] *nm* [morceau] fragment. || [extrait - d'œuvre] extract; [- de conversation] snatch.

fragmenter [fragmãte] *vt* to fragment, to break up.

fraîche → frais.

fraîcheur [freʃœr] *nf* [d'air, d'accueil] coolness. || [de teint, d'aliment] freshness.

frais, fraîche [fre, freʃ] *adj* [air, accueil] cool. || [récent - trace] fresh; [- encre] wet. || [teint] fresh, clear. ○ **frais 1** *nm*: **mettre qqch au ~** to put sthg in a cool place. **2** *nmpl* [dépenses] expenses, costs; **faire des ~** to spend a lot of money. **3** *adv*: **il fait ~** it's cool.

fraise [frez] *nf* [fruit] strawberry. || [de dentiste] drill; [de menuisier] bit.

fraiseuse [frezøz] *nf* milling machine.

fraisier [frezje] *nm* [plante] strawberry plant. || [gâteau] strawberry sponge.

framboise [frãbwaz] *nf* [fruit] raspberry. || [liqueur] raspberry liqueur.

franc, franche [frã, frãʃ] *adj* [sincère] frank. || [net] clear, definite. ○ **franc** *nm* franc.

français, -e [frãse, ɛz] *adj* French. ○ **français** *nm* [langue] French. ○ **Français, -e** *nm, f* Frenchman (*f* Frenchwoman); **les Français** the French.

France [frãs] *nf*: **la ~** France; **~ 2, ~ 3** TÉLÉ *French state-owned television channels.*

franche → franc.

franchement [frãʃmã] *adv* [sincèrement] frankly. || [nettement] clearly. || [tout à fait] completely, downright.

franchir [frãʃir] *vt* [obstacle] to get over. || [porte] to go through; [seuil] to cross.

franchise [frãʃiz] *nf* [sincérité] frankness. || COMM franchise. || [d'assurance] excess. || [détaxe] exemption.

franc-jeu [frãʒø] *nm*: **jouer ~** to play fair.

franc-maçon, -onne [frãmasɔ̃, ɔn] (*mpl* **francs-maçons,** *fpl* **franc-maçonnes**) *adj* masonic. ○ **franc-maçon** *nm* freemason.

franco [frãko] *adv* COMM: **~ de port** carriage paid.

francophone [frãkɔfɔn] **1** *adj* French-speaking. **2** *nmf* French speaker.

francophonie [frãkɔfɔni] *nf*: **la ~** French-speaking nations (*pl*).

franc-parler [frãparle] *nm*: **avoir son ~** to speak one's mind.

franc-tireur [frãtirœr] *nm* MIL irregular.

frange [frãʒ] *nf* fringe.

frangipane [frãʒipan] *nf* almond paste.

Franglais [frãglɛ] *nm* Franglais.

franquette [frãkɛt] ○ **à la bonne franquette** *loc adv* informally, without any ceremony.

frappant, -e [frapã, ãt] *adj* striking.

frapper [frape] **1** *vt* [gén] to strike. || [boisson] to chill. **2** *vi* to knock.

frasques [frask] *nfpl* pranks, escapades.

fraternel, -elle [fraternel] *adj* fraternal, brotherly.

fraterniser [fraternize] *vi* to fraternize.

fraternité [fraternite] *nf* brotherhood.

fraude [frod] *nf* fraud.

frauder [frode] *vt & vi* to cheat.

frauduleux, -euse [frodylø, øz] *adj* fraudulent.

frayer [freje] ○ **se frayer** *vp*: **se ~ un chemin (à travers une foule)** to force one's way through (a crowd).

frayeur [frejœr] *nf* fright, fear.

fredaines [frəden] *nfpl* pranks.

fredonner [frədɔne] *vt & vi* to hum.

freezer [frizœr] *nm* freezer compartment.

frégate [fregat] *nf* [bateau] frigate.

frein [frɛ̃] *nm* AUTOM brake. || *fig* [obstacle] brake, check.

freinage [frɛnaʒ] *nm* braking.

freiner [frene] **1** *vt* [mouvement, véhicule] to slow down; [inflation, dépenses] to curb. || [personne] to restrain. **2** *vi* to brake.

frelaté, -e [frəlate] *adj* [vin] adulterated; *fig* corrupt.

frêle [frel] *adj* [enfant, voix] frail.

frelon [frəlɔ̃] *nm* hornet.

frémir [fremir] *vi* [corps, personne] to tremble. || [eau] to simmer.

frémissement [fremismã] *nm* [de corps, personne] shiver, trembling (*U*). || [d'eau] simmering.

frêne [fren] *nm* ash.

frénésie [frenezi] *nf* frenzy.

frénétique [frenetik] *adj* frenzied.

fréquence [frekãs] *nf* frequency.

fréquent, -e [frekã, ãt] *adj* frequent.

fréquentation [frekãtasjɔ̃] *nf* [d'endroit] frequenting. || [de personne] association. ○ **fréquentations** *nfpl* company (*U*).

fréquenté, -e [frekãte] *adj*: **très ~** busy; **c'est très bien/mal ~** the right/wrong sort of people go there.

fréquenter [frekãte] *vt* [endroit] to frequent. || [personne] to associate with; [petit ami] to go out with, to see.

frère [frɛr] *nm* brother.

fresque [frɛsk] *nf* fresco.

fret [frɛ] *nm* freight.

frétiller [fretije] *vi* [poisson, personne] to wriggle.

fretin [frətɛ̃] *nm*: **le menu ~** the small fry.

friable [frijabl] *adj* crumbly.

friand, -e [frijɑ̃, ɑ̃d] *adj*: **être ~ de** to be partial to.

friandise [frijɑ̃diz] *nf* delicacy.

fric [frik] *nm fam* cash.

friche [friʃ] *nf* fallow land; **en ~** fallow.

friction [friksjɔ̃] *nf* [massage] massage. || *fig* [désaccord] friction.

frictionner [friksjɔne] *vt* to rub.

Frigidaire® [friʒidɛr] *nm* fridge, refrigerator.

frigide [friʒid] *adj* frigid.

frigo [frigo] *nm fam* fridge.

frigorifié, -e [frigɔrifje] *adj fam* frozen.

frileux, -euse [frilø, øz] *adj* [craignant le froid] sensitive to the cold.

frimer [frime] *vi fam* [bluffer] to pretend; [se mettre en valeur] to show off.

frimousse [frimus] *nf fam* dear little face.

fringale [frɛ̃gal] *nf fam*: **avoir la ~** to be starving.

fringant, -e [frɛ̃gɑ̃, ɑ̃t] *adj* highspirited.

fripe [frip] *nf*: **les ~s** secondhand clothes.

fripon, -onne [fripɔ̃, ɔn] **1** *nm, f fam vieilli* rogue, rascal. **2** *adj* mischievous, cheeky.

fripouille [fripuj] *nf fam* scoundrel.

frire [frir] **1** *vt* to fry. **2** *vi* to fry.

frise [friz] *nf* ARCHIT frieze.

frisé, -e [frize] *adj* [cheveux] curly; [personne] curly-haired.

friser [frize] **1** *vt* [cheveux] to curl. || *fig* [ressembler à] to border on. **2** *vi* to curl.

frisquet [friskɛ] *adj m*: **il fait ~** it's chilly.

frisson [frisɔ̃] *nm* [gén] shiver; [de dégoût] shudder.

frissonner [frisɔne] *vi* [trembler] to shiver; [de dégoût] to shudder.

frit, -e [fri, frit] *pp* → **frire**.

frite [frit] *nf* chip *Br*, (French) fry *Am*.

friteuse [fritøz] *nf* deep fat fryer.

friture [frityr] *nf* [poisson] fried fish. || *fam* RADIO crackle.

frivole [frivɔl] *adj* frivolous.

frivolité [frivɔlite] *nf* frivolity.

froid, froide [frwa, frwad] *adj litt & fig* cold. ○ **froid 1** *nm* [température] cold; **prendre ~** to catch (a) cold. || [tension] coolness. **2** *adv*: **il fait ~** it's cold; **avoir ~** to be cold.

froidement [frwadmɑ̃] *adv* [accueillir] coldly. || [écouter, parler] coolly. || [tuer] cold-bloodedly.

froisser [frwase] *vt* [tissu, papier] to crumple, to crease. || *fig* [offenser] to offend. ○ **se froisser** *vp* [tissu] to crumple, to crease. || MÉD: **se ~ un muscle** to strain a muscle. || [se vexer] to take offence.

frôler [frole] *vt* to brush against; *fig* to have a brush with, to come close to.

fromage [frɔmaʒ] *nm* cheese.

fromagerie [frɔmaʒri] *nf* cheese-dairy.

froment [frɔmɑ̃] *nm* wheat.

froncer [frɔ̃se] *vt* COUTURE to gather. || [plisser]: **~ les sourcils** to frown.

frondaison [frɔ̃dɛzɔ̃] *nf* [phénomène] foliation. || [feuillage] foliage.

fronde [frɔ̃d] *nf* [arme] sling; [jouet] slingshot *Am*. || [révolte] rebellion.

front [frɔ̃] *nm* ANAT forehead. || *fig* [audace] cheek. || [avant] front; **~ de mer** (sea) front. || MÉTÉOR, MIL & POLIT front.

frontal, -e, -aux [frɔ̃tal, o] *adj* ANAT frontal. || [collision, attaque] head-on.

frontalier, -ière [frɔ̃talje, jɛr] **1** *adj* frontier (*avant n*); **travailleur ~** person who lives on one side of the border and works on the other. **2** *nm, f* inhabitant of border area.

frontière [frɔ̃tjɛr] **1** *adj* border (*avant n*). **2** *nf* frontier, border; *fig* frontier.

fronton [frɔ̃tɔ̃] *nm* ARCHIT pediment.

frottement [frɔtmɑ̃] *nm* [action] rubbing. || [contact, difficulté] friction.

frotter [frɔte] **1** *vt* to rub; [parquet] to scrub. **2** *vi* to rub, to scrape.

frottis [frɔti] *nm* smear.

fructifier [fryktifje] *vi* [investissement] to give ou yield a profit. || [terre] to be productive. || [arbre, idée] to bear fruit.

fructueux, -euse [fryktɥø, øz] *adj* fruitful, profitable.

frugal, -e, -aux [frygal, o] *adj* frugal.

fruit [frɥi] *nm litt & fig* fruit (*U*); **~s de mer** seafood (*U*).

fruité, -e [frɥite] *adj* fruity.

fruitier, -ière [frɥitje, jɛr] **1** *adj* [arbre] fruit (*avant n*). **2** *nm, f* fruiterer.

fruste [fryst] *adj* uncouth.

frustration [frystrasjɔ̃] *nf* frustration.

frustrer [frystre] *vt* [priver]: ~ qqn de to deprive sb of. || [décevoir] to frustrate.

fuchsia [fyʃja] *nm* fuchsia.

fuel, fioul [fjul] *nm* [de chauffage] fuel. || [carburant] fuel oil.

fugace [fygas] *adj* fleeting.

fugitif, -ive [fyʒitif, iv] **1** *adj* fleeting. **2** *nm, f* fugitive.

fugue [fyg] *nf* [de personne] flight; **faire une ~** to run away. || MUS fugue.

fui [fɥi] *pp inv* → fuir.

fuir [fɥir] **1** *vi* [détaler] to flee. || [tuyau] to leak. **2** *vt* [éviter] to avoid, to shun.

fuite [fɥit] *nf* [de personne] escape, flight. || [écoulement, d'information] leak.

fulgurant, -e [fylgyrɑ̃, ɑ̃t] *adj* [découverte] dazzling. || [vitesse] lightning (*avant n*). || [douleur] searing.

fulminer [fylmine] *vi* [personne]: ~ (contre) to fulminate (against).

fumé, -e [fyme] *adj* CULIN smoked. || [verres] tinted.

fumée [fyme] *nf* [de combustion] smoke.

fumer [fyme] **1** *vi* [personne, cheminée] to smoke. || [bouilloire, plat] to steam. **2** *vt* [cigarette, aliment] to smoke.

fumeur, -euse [fymœr, øz] *nm, f* smoker.

fumier [fymje] *nm* AGRIC dung, manure.

fumiste [fymist] *nmf péj* shirker.

fumisterie [fymistəri] *nf fam* shirking.

fumoir [fymwar] *nm* [pour aliments] smokehouse. || [pièce] smoking room.

funambule [fynɑ̃byl] *nmf* tightrope walker.

funèbre [fynɛbr] *adj* [de funérailles] funeral (*avant n*). || [lugubre] funereal; [sentiments] dismal.

funérailles [fyneraj] *nfpl* funeral (*sg*).

funéraire [fynerɛr] *adj* funeral (*avant n*).

funeste [fynɛst] *adj* [accident] fatal. || [initiative, erreur] disastrous. || [présage] of doom.

funiculaire [fynikylɛr] *nm* funicular railway.

fur [fyr] ○ **au fur et à mesure** *loc adv* as I/you *etc* go along; **au ~ et à mesure des besoins** as (and when) needed. ○ **au fur et à mesure que** *loc conj* as (and when).

furet [fyrɛ] *nm* [animal] ferret.

fureter [fyrte] *vi* [fouiller] to ferret around.

fureur [fyrœr] *nf* [colère] fury.

furibond, -e [fyribɔ̃, ɔ̃d] *adj* furious.

furie [fyri] *nf* [colère, agitation] fury; **en ~** [personne] infuriated; [éléments] raging. || *fig* [femme] shrew.

furieux, -ieuse [fyrjø, jøz] *adj* [personne] furious. || [énorme] tremendous.

furoncle [fyrɔ̃kl] *nm* boil.

furtif, -ive [fyrtif, iv] *adj* furtive.

fus, fut *etc* → être.

fusain [fyzɛ̃] *nm* [crayon] charcoal. || [dessin] charcoal drawing.

fuseau, -x [fyzo] *nm* [outil] spindle. || [pantalon] ski-pants (*pl*). ○ **fuseau horaire** *nm* time zone.

fusée [fyze] *nf* [pièce d'artifice & AÉRON] rocket.

fuselage [fyzlaʒ] *nm* fuselage.

fuselé, -e [fyzle] *adj* [doigts] tapering; [jambes] slender.

fuser [fyze] *vi* [cri, rire] to burst forth ou out.

fusible [fyzibl] *nm* fuse.

fusil [fyzi] *nm* [arme] gun.

fusillade [fyzijad] *nf* [combat] gunfire (*U*), fusillade.

fusiller [fyzije] *vt* [exécuter] to shoot.

fusion [fyzjɔ̃] *nf* [gén] fusion. || [fonte] smelting. || ÉCON & POLIT merger.

fusionner [fyzjɔne] *vt & vi* to merge.

fustiger [fystiʒe] *vt* to castigate.

fut → être.

fût [fy] *nm* [d'arbre] trunk. || [tonneau] barrel, cask. || [d'arme] stock.

futile [fytil] *adj* [insignifiant] futile. || [frivole] frivolous.

futur, -e [fytyr] *adj* future (*avant n*). ○ **futur** *nm* future.

futuriste [fytyrist] *adj* futuristic.

fuyant, -e [fɥijɑ̃, ɑ̃t] *adj* [perspective, front] receding (*avant n*). || [regard] evasive.

fuyard, -e [fɥijar, ard] *nm, f* runaway.

G

g, G [ʒe] *nm inv* g, G.

gabardine [gabardin] *nf* gabardine.

gabarit [gabari] *nm* [dimension] size.

gâcher [gaʃe] *vt* [gaspiller] to waste. || [gâter] to spoil. || CONSTR to mix.

gâchette [gaʃɛt] *nf* trigger.

gâchis [gaʃi] *nm* [gaspillage] waste (*U*).

gadget [gadʒɛt] *nm* gadget.

gadoue [gadu] *nf fam* [boue] mud.

gaélique [gaelik] 1 *adj* Gaelic. 2 *nm* Gaelic.

gaffe [gaf] *nf fam* [maladresse] clanger. || [outil] boat hook.

gaffer [gafe] *vi fam* to put one's foot in it.

gag [gag] *nm* gag.

gage [gaʒ] *nm* [assurance, preuve] proof. || [dans jeu] forfeit.

gager [gaʒe] *vt*: ~ **que** to bet (that).

gageure [gaʒyr] *nf* challenge.

gagnant, -e [gaɲɑ̃, ɑ̃t] 1 *adj* winning (*avant n*). 2 *nm, f* winner.

gagne-pain [gaɲpɛ̃] *nm inv* livelihood.

gagner [gaɲe] 1 *vt* [salaire, argent, repos] to earn. || [course, prix, affection] to win. || [obtenir, économiser] to gain. || [atteindre] to reach; [- suj: feu, engourdissement] to spread to; [- suj: sommeil, froid] to overcome. 2 *vi* [être vainqueur] to win. || [bénéficier] to gain; ~ **à faire qqch** to be better off doing sthg; **qu'est-ce que j'y gagne?** what do I get out of it? || [s'améliorer]: ~ **en** to increase in.

gai, -e [gɛ] *adj* [joyeux] cheerful, happy. || [vif, plaisant] bright.

gaieté [gete] *nf* [joie] cheerfulness. || [vivacité] brightness.

gaillard, -e [gajar, ard] *nm, f* strapping individual.

gain [gɛ̃] *nm* [profit] gain, profit. || [économie] saving. ○ **gains** *nmpl* earnings.

gaine [gɛn] *nf* [étui, enveloppe] sheath. || [sous-vêtement] girdle, corset.

gainer [gene] *vt* to sheathe.

gala [gala] *nm* gala, reception.

galant, -e [galɑ̃, ɑ̃t] *adj* [courtois] gallant.

galanterie [galɑ̃tri] *nf* [courtoisie] gallantry, politeness. || [flatterie] compliment.

galaxie [galaksi] *nf* galaxy.

galbe [galb] *nm* curve.

gale [gal] *nf* MÉD scabies (*U*).

galère [galɛr] *nf* NAVIG galley; **quelle ~!** *fig* what a hassle!, what a drag!

galérer [galere] *vi fam* to have a hard time.

galerie [galri] *nf* [gén] gallery. || THÉÂTRE circle. || [porte-bagages] roof rack.

galet [galɛ] *nm* [caillou] pebble.

galette [galɛt] *nf* CULIN pancake.

galipette [galipɛt] *nf fam* somersault.

Galles [gal] → **pays**.

gallicisme [galisism] *nm* [expression] French idiom; [dans une langue étrangère] gallicism.

gallois, -e [galwa, az] *adj* Welsh. ○ **gallois** *nm* [langue] Welsh. ○ **Gallois, -e** *nm, f* [Welshman (*f* Welshwoman)]; **les Gallois** the Welsh.

galon [galɔ̃] *nm* COUTURE braid (*U*). || MIL stripe.

galop [galo] *nm* [allure] gallop; **au ~** [cheval] at a gallop; *fig* at the double.

galoper [galɔpe] *vi* [cheval] to gallop. || [personne] to run about.

galopin [galɔpɛ̃] *nm fam* brat.

galvaniser [galvanize] *vt litt & fig* to galvanize.

galvauder [galvode] *vt* [ternir] to tarnish.

gambader [gɑ̃bade] *vi* [sautiller] to leap about; [agneau] to gambol.

gamelle [gamɛl] *nf* [plat] kit *Am*.

gamin, -e [gamɛ̃, in] 1 *adj* [puéril] childish. 2 *nm, f fam* [enfant] kid.

gamme [gam] *nf* [série] range; ~ **de produits** product range. || MUS scale.

ganglion [gɑ̃glijɔ̃] *nm* ganglion.

gangrène [gɑ̃grɛn] *nf* gangrene; *fig* corruption, canker.

gangue [gɑ̃g] *nf* [de minerai] gangue. || *fig* [carcan] straitjacket.

gant [gɑ̃] *nm* glove; ~ **de toilette** face cloth, flannel *Br*.

garage [garaʒ] *nm* garage.

garagiste [garaʒist] *nmf* [propriétaire] garage owner; [réparateur] garage mechanic.

garant, -e [garɑ̃, ɑ̃t] *nm, f* [responsable] guarantor; **se porter ~ de** to vouch for.

garantie [garɑ̃ti] *nf* [gén] guarantee.

garantir [garãtir] *rt* [assurer & COMM] to guarantee; ~ **à qqn que** to assure ou guarantee sb that.

garçon [garsɔ̃] *nm* [enfant] boy. || [célibataire]: **vieux ~** confirmed bachelor. || [serveur]: ~ **(de café)** waiter.

garçonnet [garsɔnɛ] *nm* little boy.

garçonnière [garsɔnjɛr] *nf* bachelor flat *Br* ou apartment *Am*.

garde [gard] **1** *nf* [surveillance] protection. || [veille]: **pharmacie de ~** duty chemist. || MIL. guard; **monter la ~** to go on guard. || *loc*: **être/se tenir sur ses ~s** to be/stay on one's guard; **mettre qqn en ~ contre qqch** to put sb on their guard about sthg. **2** *nmf* keeper; ~ **du corps** bodyguard.

garde-à-vous [gardavu] *nm inv* attention; **se mettre au ~** to stand to attention.

garde-boue [gardəbu] *nm inv* mudguard *Br*, fender *Am*.

garde-chasse [gardəʃas] (*pl* **gardeschasse** ou **gardes-chasses**) *nm* gamekeeper.

garde-fou [gardəfu] (*pl* **garde-fous**) *nm* railing, parapet.

garde-malade [gardəmalad] (*pl* **gardes-malades**) *nmf* nurse.

garde-manger [gardəmãʒe] *nm inv* [pièce] pantry, larder; [armoire] meat safe *Br*, cooler *Am*.

garde-pêche [gardəpɛʃ] (*pl* **gardespêche**) *nm* [personne] fishwarden *Am*.

garder [garde] *rt* [gén] to keep; [vêtement] to keep on. || [surveiller] to mind, to look after; [défendre] to guard. ○ **se garder** *rp* [se conserver] to keep. || [s'abstenir]: **se ~ de faire qqch** to take care not to do sthg.

garderie [gardəri] *nf* crèche *Br*, day nursery *Br*, day-care center *Am*.

garde-robe [gardərɔb] (*pl* **garderobes**) *nf* wardrobe.

gardien, -ienne [gardjɛ̃, jɛn] *nm, f* [surveillant] guard, keeper; ~ **de but** goalkeeper; ~ **de nuit** night watchman. || *fig* [défenseur] protector, guardian. || [agent]: ~ **de la paix** policeman.

gare [gar] *nf* station; ~ **routière** [de marchandises] road haulage depot; [pour passagers] bus station.

garer [gare] *rt* [ranger] to park. ○ **se garer** *rp* [stationner] to park. || [se ranger] to pull over.

gargariser [gargarize] ○ **se gargariser** *rp* [se rincer] to gargle. || *péj* [se délecter]: **se ~ de** to delight ou revel in.

gargouiller [garguje] *ri* [eau] to gurgle. || [intestins] to rumble.

garnement [garnəmã] *nm* rascal, pest.

garni [garni] *nm vieilli* furnished accommodation (*U*).

garnir [garnir] *rt* [équiper] to fit out, to furnish. || [remplir] to fill. || [orner]: **qqch de** to decorate sthg with.

garnison [garnizɔ̃] *nf* garrison.

garniture [garnityr] *nf* [ornement] trimming; [de lit] bed linen. || [CULIN - pour accompagner] garnish *Br*, fixings (*pl*) *Am*; [- pour remplir] filling.

garrigue [garig] *nf* scrub.

garrot [garo] *nm* [de cheval] withers (*pl*). || MÉD tourniquet.

gars [ga] *nm fam* [garçon, homme] lad. || [type] guy, bloke *Br*.

gas-oil [gazɔjl, gazwal], **gazole** [gazɔl] *nm* diesel oil.

gaspillage [gaspijaʒ] *nm* waste.

gaspiller [gaspije] *rt* to waste.

gastrique [gastrik] *adj* gastric.

gastro-entérite [gastrɔãterit] (*pl* **gastro-entérites**) *nf* gastroenteritis (*U*).

gastronome [gastrɔnɔm] *nmf* gourmet.

gastronomie [gastrɔnɔmi] *nf* gastronomy.

gâteau, -x [gato] *nm* cake; ~ **sec** biscuit *Br*, cookie *Am*.

gâter [gate] *rt* [gén] to spoil; [vacances, affaires] to ruin, to spoil. || *iron* [combler] to be too good to. ○ **se gâter** *rp* [temps] to change for the worse. || [situation] to take a turn for the worse.

gâteux, -euse [gatø, øz] *adj* senile.

gauche [goʃ] **1** *nf* [côté] left, left-hand side; **à ~ (de)** on the left (of). || POLIT: **la ~** the left (wing); **de ~** left-wing. **2** *adj* [côté] left. || [personne] clumsy.

gaucher, -ère [goʃe, ɛr] **1** *adj* left-handed. **2** *nm, f* left-handed person.

gauchiste [goʃist] *nmf* leftist.

gaufre [gofr] *nf* waffle.

gaufrer [gofre] *rt* to emboss.

gaufrette [gofrɛt] *nf* wafer.

gaule [gol] *nf* [perche] pole. || [canne à pêche] fishing rod.

gauler [gole] *rt* to bring ou shake down.

gaulliste [golist] *nmf & adj* Gaullist.

gaver [gave] *rt* [animal] to force-feed. || [personne]: ~ **qqn de** to feed sb full of.

gay [gɛ] *adj inv & nm* gay.

gaz [gaz] *nm inv* gas.

gaze [gaz] *nf* gauze.

gazelle [gazɛl] *nf* gazelle.

gazer [gaze] *rt* to gas.

gazette [gazɛt] *nf* newspaper, gazette.

gazeux, -euse [gazø, øz] *adj* CHIM gaseous. || [boisson] fizzy.

gazoduc [gazɔdyk] *nm* gas pipeline.

gazole → **gas-oil**.

gazon [gazɔ̃] *nm* [herbe] grass; [terrain] lawn.

gazouiller [gazuje] *vi* [oiseau] to chirp, to twitter. || [bébé] to gurgle.

GB, G-B (*abr de* **Grande-Bretagne**) *nf* GB.

gd *abr de* **grand**.

GDF, Gdf (*abr de* **Gaz de France**) *French national gas company.*

geai [ʒɛ] *nm* jay.

géant, -e [ʒeɑ̃, ɑ̃t] **1** *adj* gigantic, giant. **2** *nm, f* giant.

geindre [ʒɛ̃dr] *vi* [gémir] to moan. || *fam* [pleurnicher] to whine.

gel [ʒɛl] *nm* MÉTÉOR frost. || [d'eau] freezing. || [cosmétique] gel.

gélatine [ʒelatin] *nf* gelatine.

gelée [ʒəle] *nf* MÉTÉOR frost. || CULIN jelly.

geler [ʒəle] *vt & vi* [gén] to freeze. || [projet] to halt.

gélule [ʒelyl] *nf* capsule.

Gémeaux [ʒemo] *nmpl* ASTROL Gemini.

gémir [ʒemir] *vi* [gén] to moan.

gémissement [ʒemismɑ̃] *nm* [gén] moan; [du vent] moaning (*U*).

gemme [ʒɛm] *nf* gem, precious stone.

gênant, -e [ʒɛnɑ̃, ɑ̃t] *adj* [encombrant] in the way. || [embarrassant] awkward, embarrassing. || [énervant]: **être ~** to be a nuisance.

gencive [ʒɑ̃siv] *nf* gum.

gendarme [ʒɑ̃darm] *nm* policeman.

gendarmerie [ʒɑ̃darməri] *nf* [corps] police force. || [lieu] police station.

gendre [ʒɑ̃dr] *nm* son-in-law.

gène [ʒɛn] *nm* gene.

gêne [ʒɛn] *nf* [physique] difficulty. || [psychologique] embarrassment. || [financière] difficulty.

généalogie [ʒenealɔʒi] *nf* genealogy.

généalogique [ʒenealɔʒik] *adj* genealogical; **arbre ~** family tree.

gêner [ʒene] *vt* [physiquement - gén] to be too tight for; [- suj: chaussures] to pinch. || [moralement] to embarrass. || [incommoder] to bother. || [encombrer] to hamper.

général, -e, -aux [ʒeneral, o] *adj* general; **en ~** generally, in general; **répétition -e** dress rehearsal. ○ **général** *nm* MIL. general.

généralement [ʒeneralmɑ̃] *adv* generally.

généralisation [ʒeneralizasjɔ̃] *nf* generalization.

généraliser [ʒeneralize] *vt & vi* to generalize. ○ **se généraliser** *vp* to become general ou widespread.

généraliste [ʒeneralist] **1** *nmf* CP *Br*, family doctor. **2** *adj* general.

généralité [ʒeneralite] *nf* [idée] generality.

générateur, -trice [ʒeneratœr, tris] *adj* generating. ○ **générateur** *nm* TECHNOL generator.

génération [ʒenerasjɔ̃] *nf* generation.

générer [ʒenere] *vt* to generate.

généreux, -euse [ʒenerø, øz] *adj* generous; [terre] fertile.

générique [ʒenerik] **1** *adj* generic. **2** *nm* credits (*pl*).

générosité [ʒenerozite] *nf* generosity.

genèse [ʒənɛz] *nf* [création] genesis.

genêt [ʒəne] *nm* broom.

génétique [ʒenetik] **1** *adj* genetic. **2** *nf* genetics (*U*).

Genève [ʒənɛv] *n* Geneva.

génial, -e, -iaux [ʒenjal, jo] *adj* [personne] of genius. || [idée, invention] inspired. || *fam* [formidable]: **c'est ~!** that's great!, that's terrific!

génie [ʒeni] *nm* [personne, aptitude] genius. || TECHNOL engineering.

genièvre [ʒənjɛvr] *nm* juniper.

génisse [ʒenis] *nf* heifer.

génital, -e, -aux [ʒenital, o] *adj* genital.

génitif [ʒenitif] *nm* genitive (case).

génocide [ʒenɔsid] *nm* genocide.

genou, -x [ʒənu] *nm* knee; **à ~x** on one's knees, kneeling.

genouillère [ʒənujɛr] *nf* [bandage] knee bandage. || SPORT kneepad.

genre [ʒɑ̃r] *nm* [type] type, kind. || LITTÉRATURE genre. || [style de personne] style. || GRAM gender.

gens [ʒɑ̃] *nmpl* people.

gentiane [ʒɑ̃sjan] *nf* gentian.

gentil, -ille [ʒɑ̃ti, ij] *adj* [agréable] nice. || [aimable] kind, nice.

gentillesse [ʒɑ̃tijes] *nf* kindness.

gentiment [ʒɑ̃timɑ̃] *adv* [sagement] nicely. || [aimablement] kindly, nicely. || *Helv* [tranquillement] calmly, quietly.

génuflexion [ʒenyflɛksjɔ̃] *nf* genuflexion.

géographie [ʒeɔgrafi] *nf* geography.

géologie [ʒeɔlɔʒi] *nf* geology.

géologue [ʒeɔlɔg] *nmf* geologist.

géomètre [ʒeɔmɛtr] *nmf* [spécialiste] geometer, geometrician. || [technicien] surveyor.

géométrie [ʒeɔmetri] *nf* geometry.

gérance [ʒerɑ̃s] *nf* management.

géranium [ʒeranjɔm] *nm* geranium.

gérant, -e [ʒerɑ̃, ɑ̃t] *nm, f* manager.

gerbe [ʒɛrb] *nf* [de blé] sheaf; [de fleurs] spray. || [d'étincelles, d'eau] shower.

gercé, -e [ʒɛrse] *adj* chapped.

gérer [ʒere] *vt* to manage.

germain, -e [ʒɛrmɛ̃, ɛn] → **cousin**.

germanique [ʒɛrmanik] *adj* Germanic.

germe [ʒɛrm] *nm* BOT & MÉD germ; [de pomme de terre] eye. || *fig* [origine] seed, cause.

germer [ʒɛrme] *vi* to germinate.

gésier [ʒezje] *nm* gizzard.

gésir [ʒezir] *vi littéraire* to lie.

gestation [ʒɛstasjɔ̃] *nf* gestation.

geste [ʒɛst] *nm* [mouvement] gesture. || [acte] act, deed.

gesticuler [ʒɛstikyle] *vi* to gesticulate.

gestion [ʒɛstjɔ̃] *nf* management; ~ **de fichiers** INFORM file management.

ghetto [ɡeto] *nm litt & fig* ghetto.

gibet [ʒibɛ] *nm* gallows (*sg*), gibbet.

gibier [ʒibje] *nm* game.

giboulée [ʒibule] *nf* sudden shower.

gicler [ʒikle] *vi* to squirt, to spurt.

gifle [ʒifl] *nf* slap.

gifler [ʒifle] *vt* to slap; *fig* [suj: vent, pluie] to whip, to lash.

gigantesque [ʒiɡɑ̃tɛsk] *adj* gigantic.

gigolo [ʒiɡɔlo] *nm* gigolo.

gigot [ʒiɡo] *nm* CULIN leg.

gigoter [ʒiɡɔte] *vi* to squirm, to wriggle.

gilet [ʒile] *nm* [cardigan] cardigan. || [sans manches] waistcoat *Br*, vest *Am*.

gin [dʒin] *nm* gin.

gingembre [ʒɛ̃ʒɑ̃br] *nm* ginger.

girafe [ʒiraf] *nf* giraffe.

giratoire [ʒiratwar] *adj* gyrating; **sens** ~ roundabout *Br*, traffic circle *Am*.

girofle [ʒirɔfl] → **clou**.

girouette [ʒirwɛt] *nf* weathercock.

gisement [ʒizmɑ̃] *nm* deposit.

gît → **gésir**.

gitan, -e [ʒitɑ̃, an] *adj* Gipsy (*avant n*). ○ **Gitan, -e** *nm, f* Gipsy.

gîte [ʒit] *nm* [logement]: ~ (**rural**) gîte, *self-catering accommodation in the country*. || [du bœuf] shin *Br*, shank *Am*.

givre [ʒivr] *nm* frost.

glabre [ɡlabr] *adj* hairless.

glace [ɡlas] *nf* [eau congelée] ice. || [crème glacée] ice cream. || [vitre] pane; [- de voiture] window. || [miroir] mirror.

glacé, -e [ɡlase] *adj* [gelé] frozen. || [très froid] freezing. || *fig* [hostile] cold.

glacer [ɡlase] *vt* [geler, paralyser] to chill. || [étoffe, papier] to glaze. || [gâteau] to ice *Br*, to frost *Am*.

glacial, -e, -iaux [ɡlasjal, jo] *adj litt & fig* icy.

glacier [ɡlasje] *nm* GÉOGR glacier. || [marchand] ice cream seller ou man.

glaçon [ɡlasɔ̃] *nm* [dans boisson] ice cube.

glaïeul [ɡlajœl] *nm* gladiolus.

glaire [ɡlɛr] *nf* MÉD phlegm.

glaise [ɡlɛz] *nf* clay.

gland [ɡlɑ̃] *nm* [de chêne] acorn. || [ornement] tassel. || ANAT glans.

glande [ɡlɑ̃d] *nf* gland.

glaner [ɡlane] *vt* to glean.

glapir [ɡlapir] *vi* to yelp, to yap.

glas [ɡla] *nm* knell.

glauque [ɡlok] *adj* [couleur] bluey-green. || *fam* [lugubre] gloomy. || *fam* [sordide] sordid.

glissade [ɡlisad] *nf* slip.

glissant, -e [ɡlisɑ̃, ɑ̃t] *adj* slippery.

glissement [ɡlismɑ̃] *nm* [action de glisser] gliding, sliding.

glisser [ɡlise] **1** *vi* [se déplacer]: ~ (**sur**) to glide (over), to slide (over). || [déraper]: ~ (**sur**) to slip (on). || *fig* [passer rapidement]: ~ **sur** to skate over. || [surface] to be slippery. || [progresser] to slip; ~ **dans/vers** to slip into/towards. **2** *vt* to slip; ~ **un regard à qqn** *fig* to give sb a sidelong glance. ○ **se glisser** *vp* to slip; **se** ~ **dans** [lit] to slip ou slide into; *fig* to slip ou creep into.

glissière [ɡlisjɛr] *nf* runner.

global, -e, -aux [ɡlɔbal, o] *adj* global.

globalement [ɡlɔbalmɑ̃] *adv* on the whole.

globe [ɡlɔb] *nm* [sphère, terre] globe. || [de verre] glass cover.

globule [ɡlɔbyl] *nm* globule; ~ **blanc/rouge** white/red corpuscle.

globuleux [ɡlɔbylø] → **œil**.

gloire [ɡlwar] *nf* [renommée] glory; [de vedette] fame, stardom. || [mérite] credit.

glorieux, -ieuse [ɡlɔrjø, jøz] *adj* [mort, combat] glorious; [héros, soldat] renowned.

glossaire [ɡlɔsɛr] *nm* glossary.

glousser [ɡluse] *vi* [poule] to cluck. || *fam* [personne] to chortle, to chuckle.

glouton, -onne [glutɔ̃, -ɔn] **1** *adj* greedy. **2** *nm, f* glutton.

glu [gly] *nf* [colle] glue.

gluant, -e [glyɑ̃, ɑ̃t] *adj* sticky.

glucide [glysid] *nm* glucide.

glycine [glisin] *nf* wisteria.

go [go] ○ **tout de go** *loc adv* straight.

GO (*abr de* **grandes ondes**) *nfpl* LW.

goal [gol] *nm* goalkeeper.

gobelet [gɔblɛ] *nm* beaker, tumbler.

gober [gɔbe] *vt* [avaler] to gulp down. || *fam* [croire] to swallow.

godet [gɔdɛ] *nm* [récipient] jar, pot.

godiller [gɔdije] *vi* [rameur] to scull. || [skieur] to wedeln.

goéland [gɔelɑ̃] *nm* gull, seagull.

goélette [gɔelɛt] *nf* schooner.

goguenard, -e [gɔɡnar, ard] *adj* mocking.

goinfre [gwɛ̃fr] *nmf fam* pig.

goitre [gwatr] *nm* goitre.

golf [gɔlf] *nm* [sport] golf; [terrain] golf course.

golfe [gɔlf] *nm* gulf, bay; **le ~ de Gascogne** the Bay of Biscay; **le ~ Persique** the (Persian) Gulf.

gomme [gɔm] *nf* [substance, bonbon] gum. || [pour effacer] eraser.

gommer [gɔme] *vt* to rub out, to erase; *fig* to erase.

gond [gɔ̃] *nm* hinge.

gondole [gɔ̃dɔl] *nf* gondola.

gondoler [gɔ̃dɔle] *vi* [bois] to warp; [carton] to curl.

gonfler [gɔ̃fle] **1** *vt* [ballon, pneu] to blow up, to inflate; [rivière, poitrine, yeux] to swell; [joues] to blow out. || *fig* [grossir] to exaggerate. **2** *vi* to swell.

gong [gɔ̃g] *nm* gong.

gorge [gɔrʒ] *nf* [gosier, cou] throat. || (*gén pl*) [vallée] gorge.

gorgée [gɔrʒe] *nf* mouthful.

gorger [gɔrʒe] *vt*: **~ qqn de qqch** [gaver] to stuff sb with sthg.

gorille [gɔrij] *nm* [animal] gorilla.

gosier [gozje] *nm* throat, gullet.

gosse [gɔs] *nmf fam* kid.

gothique [gɔtik] *adj* ARCHIT Gothic.

gouache [gwaʃ] *nf* gouache.

goudron [gudrɔ̃] *nm* tar.

goudronner [gudrɔne] *vt* to tar.

gouffre [gufr] *nm* abyss.

goujat [guʒa] *nm* boor.

goulet [gulɛ] *nm* narrows (*pl*).

goulot [gulo] *nm* neck.

goulu, -e [guly] *adj* greedy, gluttonous.

goupillon [gupijɔ̃] *nm* RELIG (holy water) sprinkler. || [à bouteille] bottle brush.

gourd, -e [gur, gurd] *adj* numb.

gourde [gurd] **1** *nf* [récipient] flask, waterbottle. || *fam* [personne] idiot. **2** *adj fam* thick.

gourdin [gurdɛ̃] *nm* club.

gourmand, -e [gurmɑ̃, ɑ̃d] **1** *adj* greedy. **2** *nm, f* glutton.

gourmandise [gurmɑ̃diz] *nf* [caractère] greed, greediness. || [sucrerie] sweet thing.

gourmette [gurmɛt] *nf* chain bracelet.

gousse [gus] *nf* pod.

goût [gu] *nm* taste; **de mauvais ~** tasteless, in bad taste.

goûter [gute] **1** *vt* [déguster] to taste. || [savourer] to enjoy. **2** *vi* to have an afternoon snack; **~ à** to taste. **3** *nm afternoon snack for children, typically consisting of bread, butter, chocolate and a drink.*

goutte [gut] *nf* [de pluie, d'eau] drop. || MÉD [maladie] gout. ○ **gouttes** *nfpl* MÉD drops.

goutte-à-goutte [gutagut] *nm inv* (intravenous) drip *Br*, IV *Am*.

gouttelette [gutlɛt] *nf* droplet.

gouttière [gutjɛr] *nf* [CONSTR - horizontale] gutter; [- verticale] drainpipe. || MÉD splint.

gouvernail [guvɛrnaj] *nm* rudder.

gouvernante [guvɛrnɑ̃t] *nf* [d'enfants] governess. || [de maison] housekeeper.

gouvernement [guvɛrnəmɑ̃] *nm* government.

gouverner [guvɛrne] *vt* to govern.

gouverneur [guvɛrnœr] *nm* governor.

grâce [gras] *nf* [charme] grace; **de bonne ~** with good grace, willingly; **de mauvaise ~** with bad grace, reluctantly. || [faveur] favour. || [miséricorde] mercy. ○ **grâce à** *loc prép* thanks to.

gracier [grasje] *vt* to pardon.

gracieusement [grasjøzmɑ̃] *adv* [avec grâce] graciously. || [gratuitement] free (of charge).

gracieux, -ieuse [grasjø, jøz] *adj* [charmant] graceful. || [gratuit] free.

gradation [gradasjɔ̃] *nf* gradation.

grade [grad] *nm* [échelon] rank; [universitaire] qualification.

gradé, -e [grade] **1** *adj* noncommissioned. **2** *nm, f* noncommissioned officer, NCO.

gradin [gradɛ̃] *nm* [de stade, de théâtre] tier; [de terrain] terrace.

graduation [graduasjɔ̃] *nf* graduation.

graduel, -elle [graduɛl] *adj* gradual.

graduer [gradue] *vt* [récipient, règle] to graduate.

graffiti [grafiti] *nm inv* graffiti (*U*).

grain [grɛ̃] *nm* [gén] grain; [de moutarde] seed; [de café] bean; **~ de raisin** grape. || [point]: **~ de beauté** beauty spot.

graine [grɛn] *nf* BOT seed.

graisse [grɛs] *nf* ANAT & CULIN fat. || [pour lubrifier] grease.

graisser [grese] *vt* [machine] to grease, to lubricate.

grammaire [gramɛr] *nf* grammar.

grammatical, -e, -aux [gramatikal, o] *adj* grammatical.

gramme [gram] *nm* gram, gramme.

grand, -e [grɑ̃, grɑ̃d] **1** *adj* [en hauteur] tall; [en dimensions] big, large; [en quantité, nombre] large, great; **un ~ nombre de** a large ou great number of; **en ~** [dimension] full-size. || [âgé] grown-up; **les ~es personnes** grown-ups; **~ frère** big ou older brother. || [important, remarquable] great; **un ~ homme** a great man. || [intense]: **un ~ buveur/fumeur** a heavy drinker/smoker. **2** *nm, f* (*gén pl*) [personnage] great man (*f* woman). || [enfant] older ou bigger boy (*f* girl).

grand-angle [grɑ̃tɑ̃gl] *nm* wide-angle lens.

grand-chose [grɑ̃ʃoz] ○ **pas grand-chose** *pron indéf* not much.

Grande-Bretagne [grɑ̃dbrətaɲ] *nf*: **la ~** Great Britain.

grandeur [grɑ̃dœr] *nf* [taille] size. || [apogée & *fig*] greatness; **~ d'âme** *fig* magnanimity.

grandir [grɑ̃dir] **1** *vt*: **~ qqn** [suj: chaussures] to make sb look taller; *fig* to increase sb's standing. **2** *vi* [personne, plante] to grow; [obscurité, bruit] to increase, to grow.

grand-mère [grɑ̃mɛr] *nf* grandmother.

grand-père [grɑ̃pɛr] *nm* grandfather.

grands-parents [grɑ̃parɑ̃] *nmpl* grandparents.

grange [grɑ̃ʒ] *nf* barn.

granit(e) [granit] *nm* granite.

granulé, -e [granyle] *adj* [surface] granular. ○ **granulé** *nm* tablet.

granuleux, -euse [granylø, øz] *adj* granular.

graphique [grafik] **1** *nm* diagram; [graphe] graph. **2** *adj* graphic.

graphisme [grafism] *nm* [écriture] handwriting. || ART style of drawing.

graphologie [grafɔlɔʒi] *nf* graphology.

grappe [grap] *nf* [de fruits] bunch; [de fleurs] stem. || *fig* [de gens] knot.

grappiller [grapije] *vt litt & fig* to gather, to pick up.

grappin [grapɛ̃] *nm* [ancre] grapnel.

gras, grasse [gra, gras] *adj* [personne, animal] fat. || [plat, aliment] fatty. || [cheveux, mains] greasy. || [crayon] soft. || *fig* [rire] throaty; [toux] phlegmy. ○ **gras 1** *nm* [du jambon] fat. || TYPO bold (type). **2** *adv*: **manger ~** to eat fatty foods.

grassement [grasmɑ̃] *adv* [rire] coarsely. || [payer] a lot.

gratifier [gratifje] *vt* [accorder]: **~ qqn de qqch** to present sb with sthg, to present sthg to sb; *fig* to reward sb with sthg. || [stimuler] to gratify.

gratin [gratɛ̃] *nm* CULIN dish sprinkled with breadcrumbs or cheese and browned. || *fam fig* [haute société] upper crust.

gratiné, -e [gratine] *adj* CULIN sprinkled with breadcrumbs or cheese and browned. || *fam fig* [ardu] stiff.

gratis [gratis] *adv* free.

gratitude [gratityd] *nf*: **~ (envers)** gratitude (to ou towards).

gratte-ciel [gratsjɛl] *nm inv* skyscraper.

grattement [gratmɑ̃] *nm* scratching.

gratter [grate] **1** *vt* [gén] to scratch; [pour enlever] to scrape off. **2** *vi* [démanger] to itch, to be itchy. || *fam* [écrire] to scribble. ○ **se gratter** *vp* to scratch.

gratuit, -e [gratɥi, it] *adj* [entrée] free. || [violence] gratuitous.

gratuitement [gratɥitmɑ̃] *adv* [sans payer] free, for nothing. || [sans raison] gratuitously.

gravats [grava] *nmpl* rubble (*U*).

grave [grav] *adj* [attitude, faute, maladie] serious, grave; **ce n'est pas ~** [ce n'est rien] don't worry about it. || [voix] deep.

gravement [gravmɑ̃] *adv* gravely, seriously.

graver [grave] *vt* [gén] to engrave. || [bois] to carve. || [disque] to cut.

gravier [gravje] *nm* gravel (*U*).

gravillon [gravijɔ̃] *nm* fine gravel (*U*).

gravir [gravir] *vt* to climb.

gravité [gravite] *nf* [importance] seriousness, gravity. || PHYS gravity.

graviter [gravite] *vi* [astre] to revolve. || *fig* [évoluer] to gravitate.

gravure [gravyr] *nf* [technique]: **~ (sur)**

engraving (on). || [reproduction] print; [dans livre] plate.

gré [gre] *nm* [goût]: **à mon/son ~** for my/his taste, for my/his liking. || [volonté]: **bon ~ mal ~** willy nilly; **de ~ ou de force** *fig* whether you/they *etc* like it or not; **de mon/son plein ~** of my/his own free will.

grec, grecque [grɛk] *adj* Greek. ○ **grec** *nm* [langue] Greek. ○ **Grec, Grecque** *nm, f* Greek.

Grèce [grɛs] *nf*: **la ~** Greece.

gréement [gremã] *nm* rigging.

greffe [grɛf] *nf* MÉD transplant; [de peau] graft. || BOT graft.

greffer [grefe] *vt* MÉD to transplant; [peau] to graft; **~ un rein/un cœur à qqn** to give sb a kidney/heart transplant. || BOT to graft.

greffier [grefje] *nm* clerk of the court.

grêle [grɛl] **1** *nf* hail. **2** *adj* [jambes] spindly. || [son] shrill.

grêler [grele] *v impers* to hail; **il grêle** it's hailing.

grêlon [grelɔ̃] *nm* hailstone.

grelot [grəlo] *nm* bell.

grelotter [grəlɔte] *vi*: **~ (de)** to shiver (with).

grenade [grənad] *nf* [fruit] pomegranate. || MIL grenade.

grenat [grəna] *adj inv* dark red.

grenier [grənje] *nm* [de maison] attic. || [à foin] loft.

grenouille [grənuj] *nf* frog.

grès [grɛ] *nm* [roche] sandstone. || [poterie] stoneware.

grésiller [grezije] *vi* [friture] to sizzle; [feu] to crackle. || [radio] to crackle.

grève [grɛv] *nf* [arrêt du travail] strike; **faire ~** to strike, to go on strike. || [rivage] shore.

grever [grəve] *vt* to burden; [budget] to put a strain on.

gréviste [grevist] *nmf* striker.

gribouiller [gribuje] *vt & vi* [écrire] to scrawl. || [dessiner] to doodle.

grief [grijɛf] *nm* grievance; **faire ~ de qqch à qqn** to hold sthg against sb.

grièvement [grijɛvmã] *adv* seriously.

griffe [grif] *nf* [d'animal] claw. || Belg [éraflure] scratch.

griffer [grife] *vt* [suj: chat etc] to claw.

grignoter [griɲɔte] **1** *vt* [manger] to nibble. || *fam fig* [réduire - capital] to eat away (at). **2** *vi* [manger] to nibble. || *fam fig* [prendre]: **~ sur** to nibble away at.

gril [gril] *nm* grill.

grillade [grijad] *nf* CULIN grilled meat.

grillage [grijaʒ] *nm* [de porte, de fenêtre] wire netting. || [clôture] wire fence.

grille [grij] *nf* [portail] gate. || [d'orifice, de guichet] grille; [de fenêtre] bars (*pl*). || [de mots croisés, de loto] grid. || [tableau] table.

grille-pain [grijpɛ̃] *nm inv* toaster.

griller [grije] **1** *vt* [viande] to broil *Am*; [pain] to toast; [café, marrons] to roast. || *fig* [au soleil - personne] to burn; [- végétation] to shrivel. || *fam fig* [dépasser - concurrents] to outstrip; **~ un feu rouge** to jump the lights. || *fig* [compromettre] to ruin. **2** *vi* [ampoule] to blow.

grillon [grijɔ̃] *nm* [insecte] cricket.

grimace [grimas] *nf* grimace.

grimer [grime] *vt* CIN & THÉÂTRE to make up.

grimper [grɛ̃pe] **1** *vt* to climb. **2** *vi* to climb; **~ à un arbre/une échelle** to climb a tree/a ladder.

grincement [grɛ̃smã] *nm* [de charnière] squeaking; [de porte, plancher] creaking.

grincer [grɛ̃se] *vi* [charnière] to squeak; [porte, plancher] to creak.

grincheux, -euse [grɛ̃ʃø, øz] **1** *adj* grumpy. **2** *nm, f* moaner, grumbler.

grippe [grip] *nf* MÉD flu (*U*).

grippé, -e [gripe] *adj* [malade]: **être ~** to have flu.

gripper [gripe] *vi* [mécanisme] to jam.

gris, -e [gri, griz] *adj* [couleur] grey. || *fig* [morne] dismal. ○ **gris** *nm* [couleur] grey.

grisaille [grizaj] *nf* [de ciel] greyness. || *fig* [de vie] dullness.

grisant, -e [grizã, ãt] *adj* intoxicating.

griser [grize] *vt* to intoxicate.

grisonner [grizɔne] *vi* to turn grey.

grisou [grizu] *nm* firedamp.

grive [griv] *nf* thrush.

grivois, -e [grivwa, az] *adj* ribald.

Groenland [grɔenlãd] *nm*: **le ~** Greenland.

grog [grɔg] *nm* (hot) toddy.

grognement [grɔɲmã] *nm* [son] grunt; [d'ours, de chien] growl.

grogner [grɔɲe] *vi* [émettre un son] to grunt; [ours, chien] to growl.

groin [grwɛ̃] *nm* snout.

grommeler [grɔmle] *vt & vi* to mutter.

grondement [grɔ̃dmã] *nm* [d'animal] growl; [de tonnerre, de train] rumble; [de torrent] roar.

gronder [grɔ̃de] **1** *vi* [animal] to growl; [tonnerre] to rumble. **2** *vt* to scold.

gros, grosse [gro, gros] *adj* (*gén avant n*) [gén] large, big; *péj* big. || (*avant ou après n*) [corpulent] fat. || [important, grave - ennuis] serious; [- dépense] major. ○ **gros 1** *adv* [beaucoup] a lot. **2** *nm* [partie]: **le (plus) ~ (de qqch)** the main part (of sthg). ○ **en gros** *loc adv & loc adj* COMM wholesale. || [en grands caractères] in large letters. || [grosso modo] roughly.

groseille [grozɛj] *nf* currant.

grosse [gros] *adj* → **gros**.

grossesse [grosɛs] *nf* pregnancy.

grosseur [grosœr] *nf* [dimension, taille] size. || MÉD lump.

grossier, -ière [grosje, jɛr] *adj* [matière] coarse. || [sommaire] rough. || [insolent] rude. || [vulgaire] crude. || [erreur] crass.

grossièrement [grosjɛrmɑ̃] *adv* [sommairement] roughly. || [vulgairement] crudely.

grossir [grosir] **1** *vi* [prendre du poids] to put on weight. || [s'intensifier] to increase. **2** *vt* [suj: microscope, verre] to magnify. || [suj: vêtement]: **~ qqn** to make sb look fatter. || [exagérer] to exaggerate.

grossiste [grosist] *nmf* wholesaler.

grosso modo [grosomɔdo] *adv* roughly.

grotte [grɔt] *nf* cave.

grouiller [gruje] *vi*: **~ (de)** to swarm (with).

groupe [grup] *nm* group. ○ **groupe sanguin** *nm* blood group.

groupement [grupmɑ̃] *nm* [action] grouping. || [groupe] group.

grouper [grupe] *vt* to group. ○ **se grouper** *vp* to come together.

grue [gry] *nf* TECHNOL & ZOOL crane.

grumeau, -x [grymo] *nm* lump.

Guatemala [gwatemala] *nm*: **le ~** Guatemala.

gué [ge] *nm* ford; **traverser à ~** to ford.

guenilles [gənij] *nfpl* rags.

guenon [gənɔ̃] *nf* female monkey.

guépard [gepar] *nm* cheetah.

guêpe [gɛp] *nf* wasp.

guêpier [gepje] *nm* wasp's nest; *fig* hornet's nest.

guère [gɛr] *adv* [peu] hardly; **il ne l'aime ~** he doesn't like him/her very much.

guéridon [geridɔ̃] *nm* pedestal table.

guérilla [gerija] *nf* guerrilla warfare.

guérir [gerir] **1** *vt* to cure. **2** *vi* to recover, to get better.

guérison [gerizɔ̃] *nf* [de malade] recovery. || [de maladie] cure.

guerre [gɛr] *nf* MIL & *fig* war; **faire la ~ à un pays** to make *ou* wage war on a country; **Première/Seconde Guerre mondiale** First/Second World War.

guerrier, -ière [gɛrje, jɛr] *adj* [de guerre] war (*avant n*). || [peuple] warlike. ○ **guerrier** *nm* warrior.

guet-apens [gɛtapɑ̃] *nm* ambush; *fig* trap.

guêtre [gɛtr] *nf* gaiter.

guetter [gete] *vt* [épier] to lie in wait for. || [attendre] to be on the look-out for, to watch for. || [menacer] to threaten.

gueule [gœl] *nf* [d'animal, ouverture] mouth. || *tfam* [bouche de l'homme] yap *Am*. || *fam* [visage] face.

gueuleton [gœltɔ̃] *nm fam* blow-out.

gui [gi] *nm* mistletoe.

guichet [giʃɛ] *nm* counter; [de gare, de théâtre] ticket office.

guide [gid] *nm* [gén] guide. || [livre] guidebook.

guider [gide] *vt* to guide.

guidon [gidɔ̃] *nm* handlebars (*pl*).

guignol [giɲɔl] *nm* [théâtre] ≃ Punch and Judy show.

guillemet [gijmɛ] *nm* inverted comma, quotation mark.

guilleret, -ette [gijrɛ, ɛt] *adj* perky.

guillotine [gijɔtin] *nf* [instrument] guillotine. || [de fenêtre] sash.

guindé, -e [gɛ̃de] *adj* stiff.

guirlande [girlɑ̃d] *nf* [de fleurs] garland. || [de papier] chain; [de Noël] tinsel (*U*).

guise [giz] *nf*: **à ma ~** as I please *ou* like; **en ~ de** by way of.

guitare [gitar] *nf* guitar.

guitariste [gitarist] *nmf* guitarist.

guttural, -e, -aux [gytyral, o] *adj* guttural.

gymnastique [ʒimnastik] *nf* SPORT & *fig* gymnastics (*U*).

gynécologue [ʒinekɔlɔg] *nmf* gynaecologist.

h¹, H [aʃ] *nm inv* h, H.

h² (*abr de* **heure**) hr.

ha (*abr de* **hectare**) ha.

hab. *abr de* **habitant**.

habile [abil] *adj* skilful; [démarche] clever.

habileté [abilte] *nf* skill.

habiller [abije] *vt* [vêtir]: ~ **qqn (de)** to dress sb (in). ‖ [recouvrir] to cover. ○ **s'habiller** *vp* [se vêtir] to dress, to get dressed. ‖ [se vêtir élégamment] to dress up.

habit [abi] *nm* [costume] suit. ‖ RELIG habit. ○ **habits** *nmpl* [vêtements] clothes.

habitacle [abitakl] *nm* [d'avion] cockpit; [de voiture] passenger compartment.

habitant, -e [abitɑ̃, ɑ̃t] *nm, f* [de pays] inhabitant. ‖ [d'immeuble] occupant. ‖ *Can* [paysan] farmer.

habitation [abitasjɔ̃] *nf* [fait d'habiter] housing. ‖ [résidence] house, home.

habiter [abite] **1** *vt* [résider] to live in. **2** *vi* to live; ~ **à** to live in.

habitude [abityd] *nf* [façon de faire] habit; **avoir l'~ de faire qqch** to be in the habit of doing sthg; **d'~** usually.

habituel, -elle [abityɛl] *adj* [coutumier] usual, customary.

habituer [abitye] *vt*: ~ **qqn à qqch/à faire qqch** to get sb used to sthg/to doing sthg. ○ **s'habituer** *vp*: **s'~ à qqch/à faire qqch** to get used to sthg/to doing sthg.

hache [aʃ] *nf* axe.

hacher [aʃe] *vt* [couper - gén] to chop finely; [- viande] to mince *Br*, to grind *Am*.

hachisch = **haschisch**.

hachoir [aʃwar] *nm* [couteau] chopper. ‖ [appareil] mincer *Br*, grinder *Am*.

hachure [aʃyr] *nf* hatching.

hagard, -e [agar, ard] *adj* haggard.

haie [ɛ] *nf* [d'arbustes] hedge. ‖ [de personnes] row. ‖ SPORT hurdle.

haillons [ˈajɔ] *nmpl* rags.

haine [ˈɛn] *nf* hatred.

haïr [ˈair] *vt* to hate.

Haïti [aiti] *n* Haiti.

hâle [ˈal] *nm* tan.

hâlé, -e [ˈale] *adj* tanned.

haleine [alɛn] *nf* breath.

haleter [ˈalte] *vi* to pant.

hall [ˈol] *nm* [vestibule, entrée] foyer, lobby. ‖ [salle publique] concourse.

halle [ˈal] *nf* covered market.

hallucination [alysinasjɔ̃] *nf* hallucination.

halo [ˈalo] *nm* [cercle lumineux] halo.

halogène [alɔʒɛn] *nm & adj* halogen.

halte [ˈalt] **1** *nf* stop. **2** *interj* stop!

haltère [altɛr] *nm* dumbbell.

haltérophilie [alterɔfili] *nf* weightlifting.

hamac [ˈamak] *nm* hammock.

hamburger [ˈɑ̃burgœr] *nm* hamburger.

hameau, -x [ˈamo] *nm* hamlet.

hameçon [amsɔ̃] *nm* fish-hook.

hamster [ˈamstɛr] *nm* hamster.

hanche [ˈɑ̃ʃ] *nf* hip.

handball [ˈɑ̃dbal] *nm* handball.

handicap [ˈɑ̃dikap] *nm* handicap.

handicapé, -e [ˈɑ̃dikape] **1** *adj* handicapped. **2** *nm, f* handicapped person.

handicaper [ˈɑ̃dikape] *vt* to handicap.

hangar [ˈɑ̃gar] *nm* shed; AÉRON hangar.

hanneton [ˈantɔ̃] *nm* cockchafer.

hanter [ˈɑ̃te] *vt* to haunt.

hantise [ˈɑ̃tiz] *nf* obsession.

happer [ˈape] *vt* [attraper] to snap up.

haranguer [ˈarɑ̃ge] *vt* to harangue.

haras [ˈara] *nm* stud (farm).

harassant, -e [ˈarasɑ̃, ɑ̃t] *adj* exhausting.

harceler [ˈarsəle] *vt* [relancer] to harass. ‖ MIL to harry. ‖ [importuner]: ~ **qqn (de)** to pester sb (with).

hardes [ˈard] *nfpl* old clothes.

hardi, -e [ˈardi] *adj* bold, daring.

hareng [ˈarɑ̃] *nm* herring.

hargne [ˈarɲ] *nf* spite (*U*), bad temper.

haricot [ˈariko] *nm* bean; ~**s verts/blancs/rouges** green/haricot/kidney beans.

harmonica [armɔnika] *nm* harmonica, mouth organ.

harmonie [armɔni] *nf* [gén] harmony.

harmonieux, -ieuse [armɔnjø, jøz] *adj* [gén] harmonious. ‖ [voix] melodious. ‖ [traits, silhouette] regular.

harmoniser [armɔnize] *vt* MUS & *fig* to harmonize; [salaires] to bring into line.

harnacher ['arnaʃe] *vt* [cheval] to harness.

harnais ['arnɛ] *nm* [de cheval, de parachutiste] harness. || TECHNOL train.

harpe ['arp] *nf* harp.

harpon ['arpɔ̃] *nm* harpoon.

harponner ['arpɔne] *vt* [poisson] to harpoon. || *fam* [personne] to waylay.

hasard ['azar] *nm* chance; **au ~** at random; **par ~** by accident, by chance.

hasarder ['azarde] *vt* [tenter] to venture. ○ **se hasarder** *vp*: **se ~ à faire qqch** to risk doing sthg.

haschisch, haschich, hachisch ['aʃiʃ] *nm* hashish.

hâte ['at] *nf* haste.

hâter ['ate] *vt* [avancer] to bring forward. ○ **se hâter** *vp* to hurry.

hausse ['os] *nf* [augmentation] rise, increase.

hausser ['ose] *vt* to raise.

haut, -e [o, ot] *adj* [gén] high; **~ de 20 m** 20 m high. || [classe sociale, pays, région] upper. || [responsable] senior. ○ **haut 1** *adv* [gén] high; [placé] highly. || [fort] loudly. **2** *nm* [hauteur] height; **faire 2 m de ~** to be 2 m high or in height. || [sommet, vêtement] top. || *loc*: **avoir** or **connaître des ~s et des bas** to have one's ups and downs. ○ **de haut en bas** *loc adv* from top to bottom. ○ **du haut de** *loc prép* from the top of. ○ **en haut de** *loc prép* at the top of.

hautain, -e ['otɛ̃, ɛn] *adj* haughty.

hautbois ['obwa] *nm* oboe.

haut de gamme [odgam] *adj* upmarket.

haute-fidélité [otfidelite] *nf* high fidelity, hi-fi.

hauteur ['otœr] *nf* height.

haut-fourneau ['ofurno] *nm* blast furnace.

haut-parleur ['oparlœr] (*pl* **haut-parleurs**) *nm* loudspeaker.

havre ['avr] *nm* [refuge] haven.

Haye ['ɛ] *n*: **La ~** the Hague.

hayon ['ajɔ̃] *nm* hatchback.

hebdomadaire [ɛbdɔmadɛr] *nm & adj* weekly.

héberger [ebɛrʒe] *vt* [loger] to put up. || [suj: hôtel] to take in.

hébété, -e [ebete] *adj* dazed.

hébraïque [ebraik] *adj* Hebrew.

hébreu, -x [ebrø] *adj* Hebrew. ○ **hébreu** *nm* [langue] Hebrew. ○ **Hébreu, -x** *nm* Hebrew.

hécatombe [ekatɔ̃b] *nf litt & fig* slaughter.

hectare [ɛktar] *nm* hectare.

hégémonie [eʒemɔni] *nf* hegemony.

hein ['ɛ̃] *interj fam* eh?, what?; **tu m'en veux, ~?** you're cross with me, aren't you?

hélas [elas] *interj* unfortunately, alas.

héler ['ele] *vt sout* to hail.

hélice [elis] *nf* [d'avion, de bateau] propeller. || MATHS helix.

hélicoptère [elikɔptɛr] *nm* helicopter.

hélium [eljɔm] *nm* helium.

hématome [ematom] *nm* MÉD haematoma.

hémicycle [emisikl] *nm* POLIT: **l'~** the Assemblée Nationale.

hémisphère [emisfɛr] *nm* hemisphere.

hémophile [emɔfil] **1** *nmf* haemophiliac. **2** *adj* haemophilic.

hémorragie [emɔraʒi] *nf* MÉD haemorrhage. || *fig* [perte, fuite] loss.

hémorroïdes [emɔrɔid] *nfpl* haemorrhoids, piles.

hennir ['enir] *vi* to neigh, to whinny.

hépatite [epatit] *nf* MÉD hepatitis.

herbe [ɛrb] *nf* BOT grass. || CULIN & MÉD herb. || *fam* [marijuana] grass.

herbicide [ɛrbisid] *nm* weedkiller, herbicide.

héréditaire [eredite r] *adj* hereditary.

hérédité [eredite] *nf* [génétique] heredity.

hérésie [erezi] *nf* heresy.

hérisson ['erisɔ̃] *nm* ZOOL hedgehog.

héritage [eritaʒ] *nm* [de biens] inheritance. || [culturel] heritage.

hériter [erite] **1** *vi* to inherit; **~ de qqch** to inherit sthg. **2** *vt*: **~ qqch de qqn** *litt & fig* to inherit sthg from sb.

héritier, -ière [eritje, jɛr] *nm, f* heir (*f* heiress).

hermétique [ɛrmetik] *adj* [étanche] hermetic. || [incompréhensible] inaccessible, impossible to understand. || [impénétrable] impenetrable.

hermine [ɛrmin] *nf* [animal] stoat. || [fourrure] ermine.

hernie ['ɛrni] *nf* hernia.

héroïne [erɔin] *nf* [personne] heroine. || [drogue] heroin.

héroïque [erɔik] *adj* heroic.

héroïsme [erɔism] *nm* heroism.

héron ['erɔ̃] *nm* heron.

héros ['ero] *nm* hero.

hertz ['ɛrts] *nm inv* hertz.

hésitant, -e [ezitɑ̃, ɑ̃t] *adj* hesitant.

hésitation [ezitasjɔ̃] nf hesitation.

hésiter [ezite] vi to hesitate; ~ **entre/sur** to hesitate between/over; ~ **à faire qqch** to hesitate to do sthg.

hétéroclite [eteroklit] adj motley.

hétérogène [eterɔʒɛn] adj heterogeneous.

hétérosexuel, -elle [eterɔsɛksyɛl] adj & nm, f heterosexual.

hêtre ['ɛtr] nm beech.

heure [œr] nf [unité de temps] hour; **250 km à l'**~ 250 km per ou an hour; **faire des** ~s **supplémentaires** to work overtime. || [moment du jour] time; **il est deux** ~ it's two o'clock; **quelle** ~ **est-il?** what time is it?; **être à l'**~ to be on time; ~ **de pointe** rush hour; ~s **de bureau** office hours. || SCOL class, period. || loc: **c'est l'**~ **(de faire qqch)** it's time (to do sthg); **de bonne** ~ early.

heureusement [œrøzmɑ̃] adv [par chance] luckily, fortunately.

heureux, -euse [œrø, øz] adj [gén] happy; [favorable] fortunate.

heurt ['œr] nm [choc] collision, impact. || [désaccord] clash.

heurter ['œrte] vt [rentrer dans - gén] to hit; [- suj: personne] to bump into. || [offenser - personne, sensibilité] to offend. ○ **se heurter** vp [gén]: **se** ~ **(contre)** to collide (with). || [rencontrer]: **se** ~ **à qqch** to come up against sthg.

hexagonal, -e, -aux [ɛgzagɔnal, o] adj GÉOM hexagonal. || [français] French.

hexagone [ɛgzagɔn] nm GÉOM hexagon.

hiatus [jatys] nm inv hiatus.

hiberner [iberne] vi to hibernate.

hibou, -x ['ibu] nm owl.

hideux, -euse ['idø, øz] adj hideous.

hier [ijɛr] adv yesterday.

hiérarchie ['jerarʃi] nf hierarchy.

hiéroglyphe [jerɔglif] nm hieroglyph, hieroglyphic.

hilare [ilar] adj beaming.

hilarité [ilarite] nf hilarity.

Himalaya [imalaja] nm: **l'**~ the Himalayas (pl).

hindou, -e [ɛ̃du] adj Hindu. ○ **Hindou, -e,** nm, f Hindu.

hippie, hippy ['ipi] (pl **hippies**) nmf & adj hippy.

hippique [ipik] adj horse (avant n).

hippodrome [ipɔdrom] nm racecourse.

hippopotame [ipopotam] nm hippopotamus.

hirondelle [irɔ̃dɛl] nf swallow.

hirsute [irsyt] adj [chevelure, barbe] shaggy.

hispanique [ispanik] adj [gén] Hispanic.

hisser ['ise] vt [voile, drapeau] to hoist. || [charge] to heave, to haul. ○ **se hisser** vp [grimper]: **se** ~ **(sur)** to heave ou haul o.s. up (onto).

histoire [istwar] nf [science] history. || [récit, mensonge] story. || [aventure] funny ou strange thing. || (gén pl) [ennui] trouble (U).

historique [istɔrik] adj [roman, recherches] historical. || [monument, événement] historic.

hiver [iver] nm winter; **en** ~ in (the) winter.

HLM (abr de **habitation à loyer modéré**) nm ou nf low-rent, state-owned housing.

hocher ['ɔʃe] vt: ~ **la tête** [affirmativement] to nod (one's head); [négativement] to shake one's head.

hochet ['ɔʃɛ] nm rattle.

hockey ['ɔkɛ] nm hockey.

holding ['ɔldiŋ] nm ou nf holding company.

hold-up ['ɔldœp] nm inv hold-up.

hollandais, -e ['ɔlɑ̃dɛ, ɛz] adj Dutch. ○ **hollandais** nm [langue] Dutch. ○ **Hollandais, -e** nm, f Dutchman (f Dutchwoman).

Hollande ['ɔlɑ̃d] nf: **la** ~ Holland.

holocauste [ɔlɔkost] nm holocaust.

homard ['ɔmar] nm lobster.

homéopathie [ɔmeɔpati] nf homeopathy.

homicide [ɔmisid] nm [meurtre] murder.

hommage [ɔmaʒ] nm [témoignage d'estime] tribute; **rendre** ~ **à qqn/qqch** to pay tribute to sb/sthg.

homme [ɔm] nm man; ~ **d'affaires** businessman; ~ **d'État** statesman; ~ **politique** politician.

homogène [ɔmɔʒɛn] adj homogeneous.

homologue [ɔmɔlɔg] nm counterpart, opposite number.

homonyme [ɔmɔnim] nm LING homonym. || [personne, ville] namesake.

homosexualité [ɔmɔsɛksyalite] nf homosexuality.

homosexuel, -elle [ɔmɔsɛksyɛl] adj & nm, f homosexual.

Honduras ['ɔ̃dyras] nm: **le** ~ Honduras.

Hongrie ['ɔ̃gri] nf: **la** ~ Hungary.

hongrois, -e ['ɔ̃grwa, az] *adj* Hungarian. ○ **hongrois** *nm* [langue] Hungarian. ○ **Hongrois, -e** *nm, f* Hungarian.

honnête [ɔnɛt] *adj* [intègre] honest. || [convenable - travail, résultat] reasonable.

honnêtement [ɔnɛtmɑ̃] *adv* [de façon intègre, franchement] honestly.

honnêteté [ɔnɛtte] *nf* honesty.

honneur [ɔnœr] *nm* honour; **faire ~ à qqn/à qqch** to be a credit to sb/to sthg; **faire ~ à un repas** *fig* to do justice to a meal.

honorable [ɔnɔrabl] *adj* [digne] honourable. || [convenable] respectable.

honoraire [ɔnɔrɛr] *adj* honorary. ○ **honoraires** *nmpl* fee (*sg*), fees.

honorer [ɔnɔre] *vt* [faire honneur à] to be a credit to. || [payer] to honour.

honte ['ɔ̃t] *nf* [sentiment] shame; **avoir ~ de qqn/qqch** to be ashamed of sb/sthg; **avoir ~ de faire qqch** to be ashamed of doing sthg.

honteux, -euse ['ɔ̃tø, øz] *adj* shameful; [personne] ashamed.

hôpital, -aux [ɔpital, o] *nm* hospital.

hoquet ['ɔkɛ] *nm* hiccup.

horaire [ɔrɛr] **1** *nm* [de départ, d'arrivée] timetable. || [de travail] hours (*pl*) (of work). **2** *adj* hourly.

horizon [ɔrizɔ̃] *nm* [ligne, perspective] horizon. || [panorama] view.

horizontal, -e, -aux [ɔrizɔ̃tal, o] *adj* horizontal.

horloge [ɔrlɔʒ] *nf* clock.

hormis ['ɔrmi] *prép* save.

hormone [ɔrmɔn] *nf* hormone.

horodateur [ɔrɔdatœr] *nm* [à l'usine] clock; [au parking] ticket machine.

horoscope [ɔrɔskɔp] *nm* horoscope.

horreur [ɔrœr] *nf* horror; **avoir ~ de qqn/qqch** to hate sb/sthg; **avoir ~ de faire qqch** to hate doing sthg; **quelle ~!** how dreadful!, how awful!

horrible [ɔribl] *adj* [affreux] horrible. || *fig* [terrible] terrible, dreadful.

horrifier [ɔrifje] *vt* to horrify.

horripiler [ɔripile] *vt* to exasperate.

hors ['ɔr] ○ **hors de** *loc prép* outside.

hors-bord ['ɔrbɔr] *nm inv* speedboat.

hors-d'œuvre ['ɔrdœvr] *nm inv* hors d'oeuvre, starter.

hors-jeu ['ɔrʒø] *nm inv & adj inv* offside.

hors-la-loi ['ɔrlalwa] *nm inv* outlaw.

hors-piste ['ɔrpist] *nm inv* off-piste skiing.

hortensia [ɔrtɑ̃sja] *nm* hydrangea.

horticulture [ɔrtikyltyr] *nf* horticulture.

hospice [ɔspis] *nm* home.

hospitalier, -ière [ɔspitalje, jɛr] *adj* [accueillant] hospitable. || [relatif aux hôpitaux] hospital (*avant n*).

hospitaliser [ɔspitalize] *vt* to hospitalize.

hospitalité [ɔspitalite] *nf* hospitality.

hostie [ɔsti] *nf* host.

hostile [ɔstil] *adj*: ~ (**à**) hostile (to).

hostilité [ɔstilite] *nf* hostility.

hôte, hôtesse [ot, otɛs] *nm, f* host (*f* hostess); **hôtesse de l'air** air hostess. ○ **hôte** *nm* [invité] guest.

hôtel [otɛl] *nm* [d'hébergement] hotel. || [établissement public]: ~ **de ville** town hall.

hotte ['ɔt] *nf* [panier] basket. || [d'aération] hood.

houblon ['ublɔ̃] *nm* BOT hop. || [de la bière] hops (*pl*).

houille ['uj] *nf* coal.

houiller, -ère ['uje, ɛr] *adj* coal (*avant n*). ○ **houillère** *nf* coalmine.

houle ['ul] *nf* swell.

houlette [ulɛt] *nf* *sout*: **sous la ~ de qqn** under the guidance of sb.

houppe ['up] *nf* [à poudre] powder puff. || [de cheveux] tuft.

hourra, hurrah ['ura] *interj* hurrah!

houspiller ['uspije] *vt* to tell off.

housse ['us] *nf* cover.

houx ['u] *nm* holly.

hublot ['yblo] *nm* [de bateau] porthole.

huer ['ye] *vt* [siffler] to boo.

huile [ɥil] *nf* [gén] oil; ~ **d'arachide/ d'olive** groundnut/olive oil. || [peinture] oil painting. || *fam* [personnalité] bigwig.

huis [ɥi] *nm littéraire* door; **à ~ clos** JUR in camera.

huissier [ɥisje] *nm* JUR bailiff.

huit [ɥit] **1** *adj num* eight. **2** *nm* eight; **lundi en ~** a week on *Br*, from *Am* Monday, Monday week *Br*; *voir aussi* **six**.

huitième ['ɥitjɛm] **1** *adj num & nmf* eighth. **2** *nm* eighth. || [championnat]: **le ~ de finale** round before the quarter-final; *voir aussi* **sixième**.

huître [ɥitr] *nf* oyster.

humain, -e [ymɛ̃, ɛn] *adj* [gén] human. || [sensible] humane. ○ **humain** *nm* [être humain] human (being).

humanitaire [ymaniter] *adj* humanitarian.

humanité [ymanite] *nf* humanity.
❍ **humanités** *nfpl Belg* humanities.
humble [œbl] *adj* humble.
humecter [ymɛkte] *vt* to moisten.
humer ['yme] *vt* to smell.
humérus [ymerys] *nm* humerus.
humeur [ymœr] *nf* [disposition] mood;
être de bonne/mauvaise ~ to be in a
good/bad mood. || [caractère] nature.
humide [ymid] *adj* [air, climat] humid;
[terre, herbe, mur] wet, damp; [saison]
rainy; [front, yeux] moist.
humidité [ymidite] *nf* [de climat, d'air]
humidity; [de terre, mur] dampness.
humiliation [ymiljasjɔ̃] *nf* humiliation.
humilier [ymilje] *vt* to humiliate.
humilité [ymilite] *nf* humility.
humoristique [ymɔristik] *adj* humorous.
humour [ymur] *nm* humour.
humus [ymys] *nm* humus.
huppé, -e ['ype] *adj fam* [société]
upper-crust. || [oiseau] crested.
hurlement ['yrləmɑ̃] *nm* howl.
hurler ['yrle] *vi* [gén] to howl.
hurrah = **hourra**.
hutte ['yt] *nf* hut.
hybride [ibrid] *nm & adj* hybrid.
hydratant, -e [idratɑ̃, ɑ̃t] *adj* moistur-
izing.
hydrater [idrate] *vt* [peau] to moistur-
ize.
hydraulique [idrolik] *adj* hydraulic.
hydravion [idravjɔ̃] *nm* seaplane,
hydroplane.
hydrocarbure [idrɔkarbyr] *nm* hydro-
carbon.
hydrocution [idrɔkysjɔ̃] *nf* immersion
syncope.
hydroélectrique [idroelɛktrik] *adj*
hydroelectric.
hydrogène [idrɔʒɛn] *nm* hydrogen.
hydroglisseur [idrɔglisœr] *nm* jetfoil,
hydroplane.
hydrophile [idrɔfil] *adj* → **coton**.
hyène [jɛn] *nf* hyena.
hygiène [iʒjɛn] *nf* hygiene.
hygiénique [iʒjenik] *adj* [sanitaire] hy-
gienic. || [bon pour la santé] healthy.
hymne [imn] *nm* hymn.
hypermarché [ipɛrmarʃe] *nm* hypermarket.
hypermétrope [ipɛrmetrɔp] **1** *nmf*
longsighted person. **2** *adj* longsighted.
hypertension [ipɛrtɑ̃sjɔ̃] *nf* high blood
pressure, hypertension.

hypertrophié [ipɛrtrɔfje] *adj* hyper-
trophic; *fig* exaggerated.
hypnotiser [ipnotize] *vt* to hypnotize.
hypocondriaque [ipɔkɔ̃drijak] *nmf &
adj* hypochondriac.
hypocrisie [ipɔkrizi] *nf* hypocrisy.
hypocrite [ipɔkrit] **1** *nmf* hypocrite. **2**
adj hypocritical.
hypoglycémie [ipɔglisemi] *nf* hypo-
glycaemia.
hypotension [ipɔtɑ̃sjɔ̃] *nf* low blood
pressure.
hypothèque [ipɔtɛk] *nf* mortgage.
hypothèse [ipɔtɛz] *nf* hypothesis.
hystérie [isteri] *nf* hysteria.
hystérique [isterik] *adj* hysterical.

i, I [i] *nm inv* i, I; **mettre les points sur les
i** to dot the i's and cross the t's.
ibérique [iberik] *adj*: **la péninsule ~** the
Iberian Peninsula.
iceberg [ajsbɛrg] *nm* iceberg.
ici [isi] *adv* [lieu] here; **par ~** [direction]
this way; [alentour] around here. ||
[temps] now; **d'~ là** by then.
icône [ikon] *nf* INFORM & RELIG icon.
idéal, -e [ideal] (*pl* **idéals** OU **idéaux**
[ideo]) *adj* ideal. ❍ **idéal** *nm* ideal.
idéaliste [idealist] **1** *nmf* idealist. **2** *adj*
idealistic.
idée [ide] *nf* idea; **à l'~ de/que** at the
idea of/that; **se faire des ~s** to imagine
things; **cela ne m'est jamais venu à l'~** it
never occurred to me.
identification [idɑ̃tifikasjɔ̃] *nf*: **~ (à)**
identification (with).
identifier [idɑ̃tifje] *vt* to identify.
❍ **s'identifier** *vp*: **s'~ à qqn/qqch** to
identify with sb/sthg.
identique [idɑ̃tik] *adj*: **~ (à)** identical
(to).
identité [idɑ̃tite] *nf* identity.
idéologie [ideɔlɔʒi] *nf* ideology.
idiomatique [idjɔmatik] *adj* idiomatic.
idiot, -e [idjo, ɔt] **1** *adj* idiotic; MÉD idiot
(*avant n*). **2** *nm, f* idiot.

idiotie [idjɔsi] *nf* [stupidité] idiocy. ‖ [action, parole] idiotic thing.

idole [idɔl] *nf* idol.

idylle [idil] *nf* [amour] romance.

idyllique [idilik] *adj* [idéal] idyllic.

igloo, iglou [iglu] *nm* igloo.

ignare [iɲar] *nmf* ignoramus.

ignoble [iɲɔbl] *adj* [abject] base. ‖ [hideux] vile.

ignominie [iɲɔmini] *nf* [état] disgrace. ‖ [action] disgraceful act.

ignorance [iɲɔrɑ̃s] *nf* ignorance.

ignorant, -e [iɲɔrɑ̃, ɑ̃t] **1** *adj* ignorant. **2** *nm, f* ignoramus.

ignorer [iɲɔre] *vt* [ne pas savoir] not to know, to be unaware of. ‖ [ne pas tenir compte de] to ignore.

il [il] *pron pers* [sujet - personne] he; [- animal] it, he; [- chose] it. ‖ [sujet d'un verbe impersonnel] it; **~ pleut** it's raining. ○ **ils** *pron pers pl* they.

île [il] *nf* island; **les ~s Anglo-Normandes** the Channel Islands; **les ~s Baléares** the Balearic Islands; **les ~s Britanniques** the British Isles; **les ~s Canaries** the Canary Islands; **les ~s Malouines** the Falkland Islands.

illégal, -e, -aux [ilegal, o] *adj* illegal.

illégitime [ileʒitim] *adj* [enfant] illegitimate; [union] unlawful. ‖ [non justifié] unwarranted.

illettré, -e [iletre] *adj & nm, f* illiterate.

illicite [ilisit] *adj* illicit.

illimité, -e [ilimite] *adj* [sans limites] unlimited. ‖ [indéterminé] indefinite.

illisible [ilizibl] *adj* [indéchiffrable] illegible. ‖ [incompréhensible & INFORM] unreadable.

illogique [ilɔʒik] *adj* illogical.

illumination [ilyminasjɔ̃] *nf* [éclairage] lighting. ‖ [idée soudaine] inspiration.

illuminer [ilymine] *vt* to light up; [bâtiment, rue] to illuminate.

illusion [ilyzjɔ̃] *nf* illusion.

illustration [ilystrasjɔ̃] *nf* illustration.

illustre [ilystr] *adj* illustrious.

illustré, -e [ilystre] *adj* illustrated. ○ **illustré** *nm* illustrated magazine.

illustrer [ilystre] *vt* [gén] to illustrate. ○ **s'illustrer** *vp* to distinguish o.s.

îlot *nm* [île] small island, islet. ‖ *fig* [de résistance] pocket.

ils → il.

image [imaʒ] *nf* [vision mentale, comparaison, ressemblance] image. ‖ [dessin] picture.

imaginaire [imaʒinɛr] *adj* imaginary.

imagination [imaʒinasjɔ̃] *nf* imagination; **avoir de l'~** to be imaginative.

imaginer [imaʒine] *vt* [supposer, croire] to imagine. ‖ [trouver] to think of. ○ **s'imaginer** *vp* [se voir] to see o.s. ‖ [croire] to imagine.

imbattable [ɛ̃batabl] *adj* unbeatable.

imbécile [ɛ̃besil] *nmf* imbecile.

imberbe [ɛ̃bɛrb] *adj* beardless.

imbiber [ɛ̃bibe] *vt*: **~ qqch de qqch** to soak sthg with ou in sthg.

imbriqué, -e [ɛ̃brike] *adj* overlapping.

imbroglio [ɛ̃brɔljo] *nm* imbroglio.

imbu, -e [ɛ̃by] *adj*: **être ~ de** to be full of.

imbuvable [ɛ̃byvabl] *adj* [eau] undrinkable. ‖ *fam* [personne] unbearable.

imitateur, -trice [imitatœr, tris] *nm, f* [comique] impersonator. ‖ *péj* [copieur] imitator.

imitation [imitasjɔ̃] *nf* imitation.

imiter [imite] *vt* [s'inspirer de, contrefaire] to imitate. ‖ [reproduire l'aspect de] to look (just) like.

immaculé, -e [imakyle] *adj* immaculate.

immangeable [ɛ̃mɑ̃ʒabl] *adj* inedible.

immanquable [ɛ̃mɑ̃kabl] *adj* impossible to miss; [sort, échec] inevitable.

immatriculation [imatrikylasjɔ̃] *nf* registration.

immédiat, -e [imedja, at] *adj* immediate.

immédiatement [imedjatmɑ̃] *adv* immediately.

immense [imɑ̃s] *adj* immense.

immerger [imɛrʒe] *vt* to submerge. ○ **s'immerger** *vp* to submerge o.s.

immeuble [imœbl] *nm* building.

immigration [imigrasjɔ̃] *nf* immigration.

immigré, -e [imigre] *adj & nm, f* immigrant.

immigrer [imigre] *vi* to immigrate.

imminent, -e [iminɑ̃, ɑ̃t] *adj* imminent.

immiscer [imise] ○ **s'immiscer** *vp*: **s'~ dans** to interfere in ou with.

immobile [imɔbil] *adj* [personne, visage] motionless. ‖ [mécanisme] fixed, stationary. ‖ *fig* [figé] immovable.

immobilier, -ière [imɔbilje, jɛr] *adj*: **biens ~s** property *Br*, real estate (*U*) *Am*.

immobiliser [imɔbilize] *vt* to immobilize. ○ **s'immobiliser** *vp* to stop.

immobilité [imɔbilite] *nf* immobility.

immodéré, -e [imɔdere] *adj* inordinate.

immonde [imɔ̃d] *adj* [sale] foul. || [abject] vile.

immondices [imɔ̃dis] *nfpl* waste (U), refuse (U).

immoral, -e, -aux [imɔral, o] *adj* immoral.

immortaliser [imɔrtalize] *vt* to immortalize.

immortel, -elle [imɔrtɛl] *adj* immortal.

immuable [imɥabl] *adj* [éternel - loi] immutable. || [constant] unchanging.

immuniser [imynize] *vt* [vacciner] to immunize. || *fig* [garantir]: ~ qqn contre qqch to make sb immune to sthg.

immunité [imynite] *nf* immunity.

impact [ɛ̃pakt] *nm* impact; avoir de l'~ sur to have an impact on.

impair, -e [ɛ̃pɛr] *adj* odd. ○ **impair** *nm* [faux-pas] gaffe.

imparable [ɛ̃parabl] *adj* [coup] unstoppable. || [argument] unanswerable.

impardonnable [ɛ̃pardɔnabl] *adj* unforgivable.

imparfait, -e [ɛ̃parfɛ, ɛt] *adj* [défectueux] imperfect. || [inachevé] incomplete. ○ **imparfait** *nm* GRAM imperfect (tense).

impartial, -e, -iaux [ɛ̃parsjal, jo] *adj* impartial.

impasse [ɛ̃pas] *nf* [rue] dead end. || *fig* [difficulté] impasse, deadlock.

impassible [ɛ̃pasibl] *adj* impassive.

impatience [ɛ̃pasjɑ̃s] *nf* impatience.

impatient, -e [ɛ̃pasjɑ̃, ɑ̃t] *adj* impatient.

impatienter [ɛ̃pasjɑ̃te] *vt* to annoy. ○ **s'impatienter** *vp*: s'~ (de/contre) to get impatient (at/with).

impayé, -e [ɛ̃peje] *adj* unpaid, outstanding. ○ **impayé** *nm* outstanding payment.

impeccable [ɛ̃pekabl] *adj* [parfait] impeccable, faultless. || [propre] spotless, immaculate.

impénétrable [ɛ̃penetrabl] *adj* impenetrable.

impénitent, -e [ɛ̃penitɑ̃, ɑ̃t] *adj* unrepentant.

impensable [ɛ̃pɑ̃sabl] *adj* unthinkable.

impératif, -ive [ɛ̃peratif, iv] *adj* [ton, air] imperious. || [besoin] imperative, essential. ○ **impératif** *nm* GRAM imperative.

impératrice [ɛ̃peratris] *nf* empress.

imperceptible [ɛ̃pɛrsɛptibl] *adj* imperceptible.

imperfection [ɛ̃pɛrfɛksjɔ̃] *nf* imperfection.

impérialisme [ɛ̃perjalism] *nm* POLIT imperialism; *fig* dominance.

impérieux, -ieuse [ɛ̃perjø, jøz] *adj* [ton, air] imperious. || [nécessité] urgent.

impérissable [ɛ̃perisabl] *adj* undying.

imperméabiliser [ɛ̃pɛrmeabilize] *vt* to waterproof.

imperméable [ɛ̃pɛrmeabl] **1** *adj* waterproof. **2** *nm* raincoat.

impersonnel, -elle [ɛ̃pɛrsɔnɛl] *adj* impersonal.

impertinence [ɛ̃pɛrtinɑ̃s] *nf* impertinence (U).

impertinent, -e [ɛ̃pɛrtinɑ̃, ɑ̃t] **1** *adj* impertinent. **2** *nm, f* impertinent person.

imperturbable [ɛ̃pɛrtyrbabl] *adj* imperturbable.

impétueux, -euse [ɛ̃petɥø, øz] *adj* [personne, caractère] impetuous.

impitoyable [ɛ̃pitwajabl] *adj* merciless, pitiless.

implacable [ɛ̃plakabl] *adj* implacable.

implanter [ɛ̃plɑ̃te] *vt* [entreprise, système] to establish. || *fig* [préjugé] to implant. ○ **s'implanter** *vp* [entreprise] to set up; [coutume] to become established.

implication [ɛ̃plikasjɔ̃] *nf* [participation]: ~ (dans) involvement (in). || (gén pl) [conséquence] implication.

implicite [ɛ̃plisit] *adj* implicit.

impliquer [ɛ̃plike] *vt* [compromettre]: ~ qqn dans to implicate sb in. || [requérir, entraîner] to imply. ○ **s'impliquer** *vp*: s'~ dans to become involved in.

implorer [ɛ̃plɔre] *vt* to beseech.

implosion [ɛ̃plozjɔ̃] *nf* implosion.

impoli, -e [ɛ̃pɔli] *adj* rude, impolite.

impopulaire [ɛ̃pɔpylɛr] *adj* unpopular.

importance [ɛ̃pɔrtɑ̃s] *nf* [gén] importance; [de problème, montant] magnitude. || [de dommages] extent. || [de ville] size.

important, -e [ɛ̃pɔrtɑ̃, ɑ̃t] *adj* [gén] important. || [considérable] considerable, sizeable; [- dommages] extensive.

importation [ɛ̃pɔrtasjɔ̃] *nf* COMM & *fig* import.

importer [ɛ̃pɔrte] **1** *vt* to import. **2** *v impers*: ~ (à) to matter (to); il importe de/que it is important to/that; qu'importe!, peu importe! it doesn't matter!; n'importe qui anyone (at all); n'importe quoi anything (at all); n'importe où anywhere (at all); n'importe quand at any time (at all).

import-export [ɛpɔrɛkspɔr] *nm*
import-export.

importuner [ɛpɔrtyne] *vt* to irk.

imposable [ɛpozabl] *adj* taxable.

imposant, -e [ɛpozã, ãt] *adj* imposing.

imposer [ɛpoze] *vt* [gén] : ~ qqch/qqn à
qqn to impose sthg/sb on sb. || [impressionner]: en ~ à qqn to impress sb. || [taxer] to tax. ○ **s'imposer** *vp* [être nécessaire] to be essential ou imperative. ||
[forcer le respect] to stand out.

impossibilité [ɛpɔsibilite] *nf* impossibility; être dans l'~ de faire qqch to
find it impossible ou to be unable to do
sthg.

impossible [ɛpɔsibl] 1 *adj* impossible. 2
nm: tenter l'~ to attempt the impossible.

imposteur [ɛpɔstœr] *nm* impostor.

impôt [ɛpo] *nm* tax; ~s locaux council
tax *Br*, local tax *Am*; ~ sur le revenu income tax.

impotent, -e [ɛpotã, ãt] *adj* disabled.

impraticable [ɛpratikabl] *adj* [inaccessible] impassable.

imprécis, -e [ɛpresi, iz] *adj* imprecise.

imprégner [ɛpreɲe] *vt* [imbiber]: ~
qqch de qqch to soak sthg in sthg.
○ **s'imprégner** *vp*: s'~ de qqch
[s'imbiber] to soak sthg up; *fig* to soak
sthg up, to steep o.s. in sthg.

imprenable [ɛprənabl] *adj* [forteresse]
impregnable. || [vue] unimpeded.

imprésario, impresario [ɛpresarjo]
nm impresario.

impression [ɛpresjɔ̃] *nf* [gén] impression; avoir l'~ que to have the impression ou feeling that. || [de livre, tissu]
printing. || PHOT print.

impressionner [ɛpresjɔne] *vt* [frapper]
to impress. || [choquer] to shock, to upset. || [intimider] to frighten. || PHOT to expose.

impressionniste [ɛpresjɔnist] *nmf* &
adj impressionist.

imprévisible [ɛprevizibl] *adj* unforeseeable.

imprévu, -e [ɛprevy] *adj* unforeseen.
○ **imprévu** *nm* unforeseen situation.

imprimante [ɛprimãt] *nf* printer.

imprimé, -e [ɛprime] *adj* printed.
○ **imprimé** *nm* POSTES printed matter
(*U*). || [formulaire] printed form. || [sur
tissu] print.

imprimer [ɛprime] *vt* [texte, tissu] to
print. || [mouvement] to impart.

imprimerie [ɛprimri] *nf* [technique]
printing. || [usine] printing works (*sg*).

improbable [ɛprɔbabl] *adj* improbable.

improductif, -ive [ɛprɔdyktif, iv] *adj*
unproductive.

impromptu, -e [ɛprɔ̃pty] *adj* impromptu.

impropre [ɛprɔpr] *adj* GRAM incorrect. ||
[inadapté]: ~ à unfit for.

improviser [ɛprɔvize] *vt* to improvise.
○ **s'improviser** *vp* [devenir]: s'~ metteur en scène to act as director.

improviste [ɛprɔvist] ○ **à l'improviste** *loc adv* unexpectedly, without
warning.

imprudence [ɛprydãs] *nf* [de personne,
d'acte] rashness. || [acte] rash act.

imprudent, -e [ɛprydã, ãt] 1 *adj* rash.
2 *nm, f* rash person.

impudent, -e [ɛpydã, ãt] 1 *adj* impudent. 2 *nm, f* impudent person.

impudique [ɛpydik] *adj* shameless.

impuissant, -e [ɛpyisã, ãt] *adj* [incapable]: ~ à faire qqch powerless to do
sthg. || [homme, fureur] impotent.

impulsif, -ive [ɛpylsif, iv] 1 *adj* impulsive. 2 *nm, f* impulsive person.

impulsion [ɛpylsjɔ̃] *nf* [poussée, essor]
impetus. || [instinct] impulse, instinct. ||
fig: sous l'~ de qqn [influence] at the
prompting ou instigation of sb; sous l'~
de qqch [effet] impelled by sthg.

impunément [ɛpynemã] *adv* with impunity.

impunité [ɛpynite] *nf* impunity; en
toute ~ with impunity.

impur, -e [ɛpyr] *adj* impure.

impureté [ɛpyrte] *nf* impurity.

imputer [ɛpyte] *vt*: ~ qqch à qqn/à
qqch to attribute sthg to sb/to sthg; ~
qqch à qqch FIN to charge sthg to sthg.

imputrescible [ɛpytresibl] *adj* [bois]
rotproof; [déchets] non-degradable.

inabordable [inabɔrdabl] *adj* [prix]
prohibitive. || [personne] unapproachable.

inacceptable [inakseptabl] *adj* unacceptable.

inaccessible [inaksesibl] *adj* [destination, domaine, poste, personne] inaccessible;
[objectif, poste] unattainable.

inaccoutumé, -e [inakutyme] *adj* unaccustomed.

inachevé, -e [inaʃve] *adj* unfinished,
uncompleted.

inactif, -ive [inaktif, iv] *adj* [sans occupation, non utilisé] idle. || [sans emploi]
non-working.

inaction [inaksjɔ̃] *nf* inaction.

inadapté, -e [inadapte] *adj* [non adapté]: ~ (à) unsuitable (for), unsuited (to). || [asocial] maladjusted.

inadmissible [inadmisibl] *adj* [conduite] unacceptable.

inadvertance [inadvɛrtɑ̃s] *nf* littéraire oversight; **par ~** inadvertently.

inaltérable [inalterabl] *adj* [matériau] stable. || [sentiment] unfailing.

inamovible [inamɔvibl] *adj* fixed.

inanimé, -e [inanime] *adj* [sans vie] inanimate. || [inerte, évanoui] senseless.

inanition [inanisjɔ̃] *nf*: **tomber/mourir d'~** to faint with/die of hunger.

inaperçu, -e [inapɛrsy] *adj* unnoticed.

inappréciable [inapresjabl] *adj* [précieux] invaluable.

inapprochable [inaprɔʃabl] *adj*: **il est vraiment ~ en ce moment** you can't say anything to him at the moment.

inapte [inapt] *adj* [incapable]: ~ à qqch/à faire qqch incapable of sthg/of doing sthg. || MIL unfit.

inattaquable [inatakabl] *adj* [irréprochable] irreproachable, beyond reproach. || [irréfutable] irrefutable.

inattendu, -e [inatɑ̃dy] *adj* unexpected.

inattention [inatɑ̃sjɔ̃] *nf* inattention; **faute d'~** careless mistake.

inaudible [inodibl] *adj* [impossible à entendre] inaudible.

inauguration [inogyrasjɔ̃] *nf* [cérémonie] inauguration, opening (ceremony).

inaugurer [inogyre] *vt* [monument] to unveil; [installation, route] to open; [procédé, édifice] to inaugurate.

inavouable [inavwabl] *adj* unmentionable.

incalculable [ɛ̃kalkylabl] *adj* incalculable.

incandescence [ɛ̃kɑ̃desɑ̃s] *nf* incandescence.

incantation [ɛ̃kɑ̃tasjɔ̃] *nf* incantation.

incapable [ɛ̃kapabl] **1** *nmf* [raté] incompetent. **2** *adj*: ~ **de faire qqch** [inapte à] incapable of doing sthg; [dans l'impossibilité de] unable to do sthg.

incapacité [ɛ̃kapasite] *nf* [impossibilité]: ~ **à** OU **de faire qqch** inability to do sthg. || [invalidité] disability.

incarcération [ɛ̃karserasjɔ̃] *nf* incarceration.

incarner [ɛ̃karne] *vt* [personnifier] to be the incarnation of. || CIN & THÉÂTRE to play.

incassable [ɛ̃kasabl] *adj* unbreakable.

incendie [ɛ̃sɑ̃di] *nm* fire; *fig* flames (*pl*).

incendier [ɛ̃sɑ̃dje] *vt* [mettre le feu à] to set alight, to set fire to.

incertain, -e [ɛ̃sɛrtɛ̃, ɛn] *adj* [gén] uncertain; [temps] unsettled.

incertitude [ɛ̃sɛrtityd] *nf* uncertainty.

incessamment [ɛ̃sesamɑ̃] *adv* at any moment, any moment now.

incessant, -e [ɛ̃sesɑ̃, ɑ̃t] *adj* incessant.

inceste [ɛ̃sɛst] *nm* incest.

inchangé, -e [ɛ̃ʃɑ̃ʒe] *adj* unchanged.

incidence [ɛ̃sidɑ̃s] *nf* [conséquence] effect, impact (*U*).

incident, -e [ɛ̃sidɑ̃, ɑ̃t] *adj* [accessoire] incidental. ○ **incident** *nm* [gén] incident; [ennui] hitch.

incinérer [ɛ̃sinere] *vt* [corps] to cremate. || [ordures] to incinerate.

inciser [ɛ̃size] *vt* to incise, to make an incision in.

incisif, -ive [ɛ̃sizif, iv] *adj* incisive. ○ **incisive** *nf* incisor.

inciter [ɛ̃site] *vt* [provoquer]: ~ **qqn à qqch/à faire qqch** to incite sb to sthg/to do sthg. || [encourager]: ~ **qqn à faire qqch** to encourage sb to do sthg.

inclassable [ɛ̃klasabl] *adj* unclassifiable.

inclinable [ɛ̃klinabl] *adj* reclinable, reclining.

inclinaison [ɛ̃klinɛzɔ̃] *nf* [pente] incline. || [de tête, chapeau] angle, tilt.

incliner [ɛ̃kline] *vt* [pencher] to tilt, to lean. ○ **s'incliner** *vp* [se pencher] to tilt, to lean. || [céder]: s'~ **(devant)** to give in (to), to yield (to).

inclure [ɛ̃klyr] *vt* [mettre dedans]: ~ **qqch dans qqch** to include sthg in sthg; [joindre] to enclose sthg with sthg.

inclus, -e [ɛ̃kly, yz] **1** *pp* → **inclure**. **2** *adj* [compris - taxe, frais] included; [- joint - lettre] enclosed; [y compris]: **jusqu'à la page 10 ~e** up to and including page 10.

incognito [ɛ̃kɔɲito] *adv* incognito.

incohérent, -e [ɛ̃kɔerɑ̃, ɑ̃t] *adj* [paroles] incoherent; [actes] inconsistent.

incollable [ɛ̃kɔlabl] *adj* [riz] nonstick. || *fam* [imbattable] unbeatable.

incolore [ɛ̃kɔlɔr] *adj* colourless.

incomber [ɛ̃kɔbe] *vi*: ~ **à qqn** to be sb's responsibility; **il incombe à qqn de faire qqch** (*emploi impersonnel*) it falls to sb OU it is incumbent on sb to do sthg.

incommoder [ɛ̃kɔmɔde] *vt* sout to trouble.

incomparable [ɛ̃kɔ̃parabl] *adj* [sans pareil] incomparable.

incompatible [ɛ̃kɔ̃patibl] *adj* incompatible.

incompétent, -e [ɛ̃kɔ̃petɑ̃, ɑ̃t] *adj* [incapable] incompetent.

incomplet, -ète [ɛ̃kɔ̃plɛ, ɛt] *adj* incomplete.

incompréhensible [ɛ̃kɔ̃preɑ̃sibl] *adj* incomprehensible.

incompris, -e [ɛ̃kɔ̃pri, iz] *nm, f* misunderstood person.

inconcevable [ɛ̃kɔ̃svabl] *adj* unimaginable.

inconciliable [ɛ̃kɔ̃siljabl] *adj* irreconcilable.

inconditionnel, -elle [ɛ̃kɔ̃disjɔnɛl] **1** *adj* [total] unconditional. || [fervent] ardent. **2** *nm, f* ardent supporter ou admirer.

inconfortable [ɛ̃kɔ̃fɔrtabl] *adj* uncomfortable.

incongru, -e [ɛ̃kɔ̃gry] *adj* [malséant] unseemly, inappropriate. || [bizarre] incongruous.

inconnu, -e [ɛ̃kɔny] **1** *adj* unknown. **2** *nm, f* stranger.

inconsciemment [ɛ̃kɔ̃sjamɑ̃] *adv* [sans en avoir conscience] unconsciously, unwittingly. || [à la légère] thoughtlessly.

inconscient, -e [ɛ̃kɔ̃sjɑ̃, ɑ̃t] *adj* [évanoui, machinal] unconscious. || [irresponsable] thoughtless. ○ **inconscient** *nm*: l'~ the unconscious.

inconsidéré, -e [ɛ̃kɔ̃sidere] *adj* ill-considered, thoughtless.

inconsistant, -e [ɛ̃kɔ̃sistɑ̃, ɑ̃t] *adj* [caractère] frivolous.

inconsolable [ɛ̃kɔ̃sɔlabl] *adj* inconsolable.

incontestable [ɛ̃kɔ̃tɛstabl] *adj* unquestionable, indisputable.

incontinent, -e [ɛ̃kɔ̃tinɑ̃, ɑ̃t] *adj* MÉD incontinent.

incontournable [ɛ̃kɔ̃turnabl] *adj* unavoidable.

inconvenant, -e [ɛ̃kɔ̃vnɑ̃, ɑ̃t] *adj* improper, unseemly.

inconvénient [ɛ̃kɔ̃venjɑ̃] *nm* [obstacle] problem. || [désavantage] disadvantage, drawback. || [risque] risk.

incorporé, -e [ɛ̃kɔrpɔre] *adj* [intégré] built-in.

incorporer [ɛ̃kɔrpɔre] *vt* [gén] to incorporate; ~ qqch dans to incorporate sthg into; ~ qqch à CULIN to mix ou blend sthg into. || MIL to enlist.

incorrect, -e [ɛ̃kɔrɛkt] *adj* [faux] incorrect. || [inconvenant] inappropriate; [impoli] rude. || [déloyal] unfair.

incorrection [ɛ̃kɔrɛksjɔ̃] *nf* [impolitesse] impropriety. || [de langage] grammatical mistake.

incorrigible [ɛ̃kɔriʒibl] *adj* incorrigible.

incorruptible [ɛ̃kɔryptibl] *adj* incorruptible.

incrédule [ɛ̃kredyl] *adj* [sceptique] incredulous, sceptical. || RELIG unbelieving.

increvable [ɛ̃krəvabl] *adj* [ballon, pneu] puncture-proof. || *fam fig* [personne] tireless; [machine] that will withstand rough treatment.

incriminer [ɛ̃krimine] *vt* [personne] to incriminate. || [conduite] to condemn.

incroyable [ɛ̃krwajabl] *adj* incredible, unbelievable.

incroyant, -e [ɛ̃krwajɑ̃, ɑ̃t] *nm, f* unbeliever.

incruster [ɛ̃kryste] *vt* [insérer]: ~ qqch dans qqch to inlay sthg into sthg. || [décorer]: ~ qqch de qqch to inlay sthg with sthg. ○ **s'incruster** *vp* [s'insérer]: s'~ dans qqch to become embedded in sthg.

incubation [ɛ̃kybasjɔ̃] *nf* [d'œuf, de maladie] incubation; *fig* hatching.

inculpation [ɛ̃kylpasjɔ̃] *nf* charge.

inculper [ɛ̃kylpe] *vt* to charge; ~ qqn de to charge sb with.

inculquer [ɛ̃kylke] *vt*: ~ qqch à qqn to instil sthg in sb.

inculte [ɛ̃kylt] *adj* [terre] uncultivated. || *péj* [personne] uneducated.

incurable [ɛ̃kyrabl] *adj* incurable.

incursion [ɛ̃kyrsjɔ̃] *nf* incursion, foray.

Inde [ɛ̃d] *nf*: l'~ India.

indécent, -e [ɛ̃desɑ̃, ɑ̃t] *adj* [impudique] indecent. || [immoral] scandalous.

indéchiffrable [ɛ̃deʃifrabl] *adj* [texte, écriture] indecipherable. || *fig* [regard] inscrutable, impenetrable.

indécis, -e [ɛ̃desi, iz] *adj* [personne - sur le moment] undecided; [- de nature] indecisive. || [sourire] vague.

indécision [ɛ̃desizjɔ̃] *nf* indecision; [perpétuelle] indecisiveness.

indécrottable [ɛ̃dekrɔtabl] *adj fam* [incorrigible] hopeless.

indéfendable [ɛ̃defɑ̃dabl] *adj* indefensible.

indéfini, -e [ɛ̃defini] *adj* [quantité, pronom] indefinite.

indéfinissable [ɛ̃definisabl] *adj* indefinable.

indéformable [ɛdeformabl] *adj* that retains its shape.

indélébile [ɛdelebil] *adj* indelible.

indélicat, -e [ɛdelika, at] *adj* [mufle] indelicate. || [malhonnête] dishonest.

indemne [ɛdɛmn] *adj* unscathed, unharmed.

indemniser [ɛdɛmnize] *vt*: ~ qqn de qqch [perte, préjudice] to compensate sb for sthg.

indemnité [ɛdɛmnite] *nf* [de perte, préjudice] compensation. || [de frais] allowance.

indémodable [ɛdemodabl] *adj*: ce style est ~ this style doesn't date.

indéniable [ɛdenjabl] *adj* undeniable.

indépendance [ɛdepɑ̃dɑ̃s] *nf* independence.

indépendant, -e [ɛdepɑ̃dɑ̃, ɑ̃t] *adj* [gén] independent; [entrée] separate; ~ de ma volonté beyond my control. || [travailleur] self-employed.

indéracinable [ɛderasinabl] *adj* [arbre] impossible to uproot; *fig* ineradicable.

indescriptible [ɛdɛskriptibl] *adj* indescribable.

indestructible [ɛdɛstryktibl] *adj* indestructible.

indéterminé, -e [ɛdetɛrmine] *adj* [indéfini] indeterminate, indefinite.

index [ɛdɛks] *nm* [doigt] index finger. || [registre] index.

indexer [ɛdɛkse] *vt* ÉCON: ~ qqch sur qqch to index sthg to sthg. || [livre] to index.

indicateur, -trice [ɛdikatœr, tris] *adj*: poteau ~ signpost; panneau ~ road sign. O **indicateur** *nm* [guide] directory, guide; ~ des chemins de fer railway timetable. || TECHNOL gauge. || ÉCON indicator. || [de police] informer.

indicatif, -ive [ɛdikatif, iv] *adj* indicative. O **indicatif** *nm* RADIO & TÉLÉ signature tune. || [code]: ~ (téléphonique) dialling code *Br*, dial code *Am*. || GRAM: l'~ the indicative.

indication [ɛdikasjɔ̃] *nf* [mention] indication. || [renseignement] information (*U*). || [directive] instruction; sauf ~ contraire unless otherwise instructed.

indice [ɛdis] *nm* [signe] sign. || [dans une enquête] clue. || [taux] rating; ~ du coût de la vie ÉCON cost-of-living index. || MATHS index.

indicible [ɛdisibl] *adj* inexpressible.

indien, -ienne [ɛdjɛ̃, jɛn] *adj* [d'Inde] Indian. || [d'Amérique] American Indian,

Native American. O **Indien, -ienne** *nm, f* [d'Inde] Indian. || [d'Amérique] American Indian, Native American.

indifféremment [ɛdiferamɑ̃] *adv* indifferently.

indifférent, -e [ɛdiferɑ̃, ɑ̃t] *adj* [gén]: ~ à indifferent to.

indigène [ɛdiʒɛn] **1** *nmf* native. **2** *adj* [peuple] native; [faune, flore] indigenous.

indigent, -e [ɛdiʒɑ̃, ɑ̃t] *adj* [pauvre] destitute, poverty-stricken; *fig* [intellectuellement] impoverished.

indigeste [ɛdiʒɛst] *adj* indigestible.

indigestion [ɛdiʒɛstjɔ̃] *nf* [alimentaire] indigestion. || *fig* [saturation] surfeit.

indignation [ɛdiɲasjɔ̃] *nf* indignation.

indigné, -e [ɛdiɲe] *adj* indignant.

indigner [ɛdiɲe] *vt* to make indignant. O **s'indigner** *vp*: s'~ de OU contre qqch to get indignant about sthg.

indigo [ɛdigo] **1** *nm* indigo. **2** *adj inv* indigo (blue).

indiquer [ɛdike] *vt* [désigner] to indicate, to point out. || [afficher, montrer - suj: carte, pendule, aiguille] to show, to indicate. || [recommander]: ~ qqn/qqch à qqn to tell sb of sb/sthg, to suggest sb/sthg to sb. || [dire, renseigner sur] to tell. || [fixer - heure, date, lieu] to name, to indicate.

indirect, -e [ɛdirɛkt] *adj* [gén] indirect; [itinéraire] roundabout.

indiscipliné, -e [ɛdisipline] *adj* [écolier, esprit] undisciplined, unruly. || *fig* [mèches de cheveux] unmanageable.

indiscret, -ète [ɛdiskrɛ, ɛt] **1** *adj* indiscreet; [curieux] inquisitive. **2** *nm, f* indiscreet person.

indiscrétion [ɛdiskresjɔ̃] *nf* indiscretion; [curiosité] curiosity.

indiscutable [ɛdiskytabl] *adj* unquestionable, indisputable.

indispensable [ɛdispɑ̃sabl] *adj* indispensable, essential; ~ à indispensable to, essential to; il est ~ de faire qqch it is essential OU vital to do sthg.

indisposer [ɛdispoze] *vt sout* [rendre malade] to indispose.

indistinct, -e [ɛdistɛ̃(kt), ɛkt] *adj* indistinct; [souvenir] hazy.

individu [ɛdividy] *nm* individual.

individuel, -elle [ɛdividɥɛl] *adj* individual.

indivisible [ɛdivizibl] *adj* indivisible.

Indochine [ɛdoʃin] *nf*: l'~ Indochina.

indolent, -e [ɛdolɑ̃, ɑ̃t] *adj* [personne] indolent, lethargic.

indolore [ɛ̃dɔlɔr] *adj* painless.

indomptable [ɛ̃dɔ̃tabl] *adj* [animal] untamable. || [personne] indomitable.

Indonésie [ɛ̃dɔnezi] *nf:* l'~ Indonesia.

indu, -e [ɛ̃dy] *adj* [heure] ungodly, unearthly.

indubitable [ɛ̃dybitabl] *adj* indubitable, undoubted; **il est ~ que** it is indisputable·ot beyond doubt that.

induire [ɛ̃dɥir] *rt* to induce; **~ qqn à faire qqch** to induce sb to do sthg; **~ qqn en erreur** to mislead sb.

indulgence [ɛ̃dylʒɑ̃s] *nf* [de juge] leniency; [de parent] indulgence.

indulgent, -e [ɛ̃dylʒɑ̃, ɑ̃t] *adj* [juge] lenient; [parent] indulgent.

indûment [ɛ̃dymɑ̃] *adr* unduly.

industrialiser [ɛ̃dystrijalize] *rt* to industrialize. ○ **s'industrialiser** *rp* to become industrialized.

industrie [ɛ̃dystri] *nf* industry.

industriel, -ielle [ɛ̃dystrijɛl] *adj* industrial. ○ **industriel** *nm* industrialist.

inébranlable [inebrɑ̃labl] *adj* *fig* [conviction] unshakeable.

inédit, -e [inedi, it] *adj* [texte] unpublished. || [trouvaille] novel, original.

ineffaçable [inefasabl] *adj* indelible.

inefficace [inefikas] *adj* [personne, machine] inefficient. || [solution, remède, mesure] ineffective.

inefficacité [inefikasite] *nf* [de personne, machine] inefficiency. || [de solution, remède, mesure] ineffectiveness.

inégal, -e, -aux [inegal, o] *adj* [différent, disproportionné] unequal. || [irrégulier] uneven.

inégalé, -e [inegale] *adj* unequalled.

inégalité [inegalite] *nf* [injustice, disproportion] inequality. || [différence] difference, disparity. || [irrégularité] unevenness. || [d'humeur] changeability.

inélégant, -e [inelegɑ̃, ɑ̃t] *adj* [dans l'habillement] inelegant. || *fig* [indélicat] discourteous.

inéligible [ineliʒibl] *adj* ineligible.

inéluctable [inelyktabl] *adj* inescapable.

inepte [inɛpt] *adj* inept.

ineptie [inɛpsi] *nf* [bêtise] ineptitude. || [chose idiote] nonsense (*U*).

inépuisable [inepɥizabl] *adj* inexhaustible.

inerte [inɛrt] *adj* [corps, membre] lifeless. || [personne] passive, inert.

inertie [inɛrsi] *nf* [manque de réaction] apathy, inertia.

inespéré, -e [inɛspere] *adj* unexpected, unhoped-for.

inestimable [inɛstimabl] *adj*: **d'une valeur ~** priceless; *fig* invaluable.

inévitable [inevitabl] *adj* [obstacle] unavoidable; [conséquence] inevitable.

inexact, -e [inɛgza(kt), akt] *adj* [faux, incomplet] inaccurate, inexact. || [en retard] unpunctual.

inexactitude [inɛgzaktityd] *nf* [erreur, imprécision] inaccuracy.

inexcusable [inɛkskyzabl] *adj* unforgivable, inexcusable.

inexistant, -e [inɛgzistɑ̃, ɑ̃t] *adj* nonexistent.

inexorable [inɛgzɔrabl] *adj* inexorable.

inexpérience [inɛksperjɑ̃s] *nf* lack of experience, inexperience.

inexplicable [inɛksplikabl] *adj* inexplicable, unexplainable.

inexpliqué, -e [inɛksplike] *adj* unexplained.

inexpressif, -ive [inɛkspresif, iv] *adj* inexpressive.

inexprimable [inɛksprimabl] *adj* inexpressible.

in extremis [inɛkstremis] *adr* at the last minute.

inextricable [inɛkstrikabl] *adj* [fouillis] inextricable. || *fig* [affaire, mystère] that cannot be unravelled.

infaillible [ɛ̃fajibl] *adj* [personne, méthode] infallible; [instinct] unerring.

infâme [ɛ̃fam] *adj* [ignoble] despicable. || *hum ou littéraire* [dégoûtant] vile.

infanterie [ɛ̃fɑ̃tri] *nf* infantry.

infanticide [ɛ̃fɑ̃tisid] **1** *nmf* infanticide, child-killer. **2** *adj* infanticidal.

infantile [ɛ̃fɑ̃til] *adj* [maladie] childhood (*avant n*). || [médecine] for children. || [comportement] infantile.

infarctus [ɛ̃farktys] *nm* infarction, infarct; **~ du myocarde** coronary thrombosis, myocardial infarction.

infatigable [ɛ̃fatigabl] *adj* [personne] tireless. || [attitude] untiring.

infect, -e [ɛ̃fɛkt] *adj* [dégoûtant] vile.

infecter [ɛ̃fɛkte] *rt* [plaie] to infect. ○ **s'infecter** *rp* to become infected, to turn septic.

infectieux, -ieuse [ɛ̃fɛksjø, jøz] *adj* infectious.

infection [ɛ̃fɛksjɔ̃] *nf* MÉD infection. || *fig & péj* [puanteur] stench.

inférieur, -e [ɛ̃ferjœr] **1** *adj* [qui est en bas] lower. || [dans une hiérarchie] inferior; ~ à [qualité] inferior to; [quantité] less than. **2** *nm, f* inferior.

infériorité [ɛ̃ferjɔrite] *nf* inferiority.

infernal, -e, -aux [ɛ̃fɛrnal, o] *adj* [enfant] unbearable. ‖ *fig* [bruit, chaleur, rythme] infernal.

infester [ɛ̃feste] *vt* to infest; **être infesté de** [rats, moustiques] to be infested with.

infidèle [ɛ̃fidɛl] *adj* [mari, femme, ami]: ~ (à) unfaithful (to).

infidélité [ɛ̃fidelite] *nf* [trahison] infidelity.

infiltration [ɛ̃filtrasjɔ̃] *nf* infiltration.

infiltrer [ɛ̃filtre] *vt* to infiltrate. ○ **s'infiltrer** *vp* [pluie, lumière]: **s'~ par/dans** to filter through/into.

infime [ɛ̃fim] *adj* minute, infinitesimal.

infini, -e [ɛ̃fini] *adj* [sans bornes] infinite, boundless. ‖ *fig* [interminable] endless, interminable. ○ **infini** *nm* infinity.

infiniment [ɛ̃finimɑ̃] *adv* extremely, immensely.

infinité [ɛ̃finite] *nf* infinity, infinite number.

infinitif, -ive [ɛ̃finitif, iv] *adj* infinitive. ○ **infinitif** *nm* infinitive.

infirme [ɛ̃firm] **1** *adj* [handicapé] disabled; [avec l'âge] infirm. **2** *nmf* disabled person.

infirmerie [ɛ̃firməri] *nf* infirmary.

infirmier, -ière [ɛ̃firmje, jɛr] *nm, f* nurse.

infirmité [ɛ̃firmite] *nf* [handicap] disability; [de vieillesse] infirmity.

inflammable [ɛ̃flamabl] *adj* inflammable, flammable.

inflammation [ɛ̃flamasjɔ̃] *nf* inflammation.

inflation [ɛ̃flasjɔ̃] *nf* ÉCON inflation.

inflationniste [ɛ̃flasjɔnist] *adj & nmf* inflationist.

infléchir [ɛ̃fleʃir] *vt fig* [politique] to modify.

inflexible [ɛ̃flɛksibl] *adj* inflexible.

inflexion [ɛ̃flɛksjɔ̃] *nf* [de tête] nod. ‖ [de voix] inflection.

infliger [ɛ̃fliʒe] *vt*: ~ **qqch à qqn** to inflict sthg on sb; [amende] to impose sthg on sb.

influençable [ɛ̃flyɑ̃sabl] *adj* easily influenced.

influence [ɛ̃flyɑ̃s] *nf* influence.

influencer [ɛ̃flyɑ̃se] *vt* to influence.

influer [ɛ̃flye] *vi*: ~ **sur qqch** to influence sthg, to have an effect on sthg.

informaticien, -ienne [ɛ̃fɔrmatisjɛ̃, jɛn] *nm, f* computer scientist.

information [ɛ̃fɔrmasjɔ̃] *nf* [renseignement] piece of information. ‖ [renseignements & INFORM] information (*U*). ‖ [nouvelle] piece of news. ○ **informations** *nfpl* MÉDIA news (*sg*).

informatique [ɛ̃fɔrmatik] **1** *nf* [technique] data-processing. ‖ [science] computer science. **2** *adj* data-processing (*avant n*), computer (*avant n*).

informatiser [ɛ̃fɔrmatize] *vt* to computerize.

informe [ɛ̃fɔrm] *adj* [masse, vêtement, silhouette] shapeless.

informel, -elle [ɛ̃fɔrmɛl] *adj* informal.

informer [ɛ̃fɔrme] *vt* to inform; ~ **qqn sur** ou **de qqch** to inform sb about sthg. ○ **s'informer** *vp* to inform o.s.; **s'~ sur qqch** to find out about sthg.

infortune [ɛ̃fɔrtyn] *nf* misfortune.

infos [ɛ̃fo] (*abr de* **informations**) *nfpl fam*: **les ~** the news (*sg*).

infraction [ɛ̃fraksjɔ̃] *nf*: **être en ~** to be in breach of the law.

infranchissable [ɛ̃frɑ̃ʃisabl] *adj* insurmountable.

infrarouge [ɛ̃fraruʒ] *nm & adj* infrared.

infrastructure [ɛ̃frastryktyr] *nf* infrastructure.

infroissable [ɛ̃frwasabl] *adj* crease-resistant.

infructueux, -euse [ɛ̃fryktɥø, øz] *adj* fruitless.

infuser [ɛ̃fyze] *vi* [tisane] to infuse; [thé] to brew.

infusion [ɛ̃fyzjɔ̃] *nf* infusion.

ingénier [ɛ̃ʒenje] ○ **s'ingénier** *vp*: **s'~ à faire qqch** to try hard to do sthg.

ingénieur [ɛ̃ʒenjœr] *nm* engineer.

ingénieux, -ieuse [ɛ̃ʒenjø, jøz] *adj* ingenious.

ingéniosité [ɛ̃ʒenjozite] *nf* ingenuity.

ingénu, -e [ɛ̃ʒeny] *adj hum & péj* [trop candide] naïve.

ingérable [ɛ̃ʒerabl] *adj* unmanageable.

ingérer [ɛ̃ʒere] *vt* to ingest. ○ **s'ingérer** *vp*: **s'~ dans** to interfere in.

ingrat, -e [ɛ̃gra, at] **1** *adj* [personne] ungrateful. ‖ [métier] thankless, unrewarding. ‖ [sol] barren. ‖ [physique] unattractive. **2** *nm, f* ungrateful wretch.

ingratitude [ɛ̃gratityd] *nf* ingratitude.

ingrédient [ɛ̃gredjɑ̃] *nm* ingredient.

inguérissable [ɛ̃gerisabl] *adj* incurable.

ingurgiter [ɛ̃gyrʒite] *vt* [avaler] to swallow. || *fig* [connaissances] to absorb.

inhabitable [inabitabl] *adj* uninhabitable.

inhabité, -e [inabite] *adj* uninhabited.

inhabituel, -elle [inabituɛl] *adj* unusual.

inhalateur, -trice [inalatœr, tris] *adj*: appareil ~ inhaler. ○ **inhalateur** *nm* inhaler.

inhalation [inalasjɔ̃] *nf* inhalation.

inhérent, -e [inerɑ̃, ɑ̃t] *adj*: ~ à inherent in.

inhibition [inibisjɔ̃] *nf* inhibition.

inhospitalier, -ière [inɔspitalje, jɛr] *adj* inhospitable.

inhumain, -e [inymɛ̃, ɛn] *adj* inhuman.

inhumation [inymasjɔ̃] *nf* burial.

inhumer [inyme] *vt* to bury.

inimaginable [inimaʒinabl] *adj* incredible, unimaginable.

inimitable [inimitabl] *adj* inimitable.

ininflammable [inɛ̃flamabl] *adj* non-flammable.

inintelligible [inɛ̃teliʒibl] *adj* unintelligible.

inintéressant, -e [inɛ̃teresɑ̃, ɑ̃t] *adj* uninteresting.

ininterrompu, -e [inɛ̃tɛrɔ̃py] *adj* [file, vacarme] uninterrupted; [ligne, suite] unbroken; [travail, effort] continuous.

initial, -e, -iaux [inisjal, jo] *adj* [lettre] initial. ○ **initiale** *nf* initial.

initiateur, -trice [inisjatœr, tris] *nm, f* [précurseur] innovator.

initiation [inisjasjɔ̃] *nf*: ~ (à) [discipline] introduction (to); [rituel] initiation (into).

initiative [inisjativ] *nf* initiative; prendre l'~ de qqch/de faire qqch to take the initiative for sthg/in doing sthg.

initié, -e [inisje] *nm, f* initiate.

initier [inisje] *vt*: ~ qqn à to initiate sb into.

injecté, -e [ɛ̃ʒɛkte] *adj*: yeux ~s de sang bloodshot eyes.

injecter [ɛ̃ʒɛkte] *vt* to inject.

injection [ɛ̃ʒɛksjɔ̃] *nf* injection.

injoignable [ɛ̃jwaɲabl] *adj*: j'ai essayé de lui téléphoner mais il est ~ I tried to phone him but I couldn't get through to him ou reach him ou get hold of him.

injonction [ɛ̃ʒɔ̃ksjɔ̃] *nf* injunction.

injure [ɛ̃ʒyr] *nf* insult.

injurier [ɛ̃ʒyrje] *vt* to insult.

injurieux, -ieuse [ɛ̃ʒyrjø, jøz] *adj* abusive, insulting.

injuste [ɛ̃ʒyst] *adj* unjust, unfair.

injustice [ɛ̃ʒystis] *nf* injustice.

inlassable [ɛ̃lasabl] *adj* tireless.

inlassablement [ɛ̃lasabləmɑ̃] *adv* tirelessly.

inné, -e [ine] *adj* innate.

innocence [inɔsɑ̃s] *nf* innocence.

innocent, -e [inɔsɑ̃, ɑ̃t] **1** *adj* innocent. **2** *nm, f* JUR innocent person. || [inoffensif, candide] innocent. || *vieilli* [idiot] simpleton.

innocenter [inɔsɑ̃te] *vt* JUR to clear.

innombrable [inɔ̃brabl] *adj* innumerable; [foule] vast.

innover [inɔve] *vi* to innovate.

inoccupé, -e [inɔkype] *adj* [lieu] empty, unoccupied.

inoculer [inɔkyle] *vt* MÉD: ~ qqch à qqn [volontairement] to inoculate sb with sthg.

inodore [inɔdɔr] *adj* odourless.

inoffensif, -ive [inɔfɑ̃sif, iv] *adj* harmless.

inondation [inɔ̃dasjɔ̃] *nf* [action] flooding. || [résultat] flood.

inonder [inɔ̃de] *vt* to flood; ~ de *fig* to flood with.

inopérable [inɔperabl] *adj* inoperable.

inopérant, -e [inɔperɑ̃, ɑ̃t] *adj* ineffective.

inopiné, -e [inɔpine] *adj* unexpected.

inopportun, -e [inɔpɔrtœ̃, yn] *adj* inopportune.

inoubliable [inublijabl] *adj* unforgettable.

inouï, -e [inwi] *adj* incredible, extraordinary.

Inox® [inɔks] *nm inv & adj inv* stainless steel.

inoxydable [inɔksidabl] *adj* stainless; [casserole] stainless steel (*avant n*).

inqualifiable [ɛ̃kalifjabl] *adj* unspeakable.

inquiet, -iète [ɛ̃kjɛ, jɛt] *adj* [gén] anxious. || [tourmenté] feverish.

inquiéter [ɛ̃kjete] *vt* [donner du souci à] to worry. ○ **s'inquiéter** *vp* [s'alarmer] to be worried. || [se préoccuper]: s'~ de [s'enquérir de] to enquire about; [se soucier de] to worry about.

inquiétude [ɛ̃kjetyd] *nf* anxiety, worry.

insaisissable [ɛ̃sezisabl] *adj* [personne] elusive. || *fig* [nuance] imperceptible.

insalubre [ɛ̃salybr] *adj* unhealthy.

insatiable [ɛ̃sasjabl] *adj* insatiable.

insatisfait, -e [ɛsatisfɛ, ɛt] **1** *adj* [personne] dissatisfied. **2** *nm, f* malcontent.

inscription [ɛskripsjɔ̃] *nf* [action, écrit] inscription. || [enregistrement] enrolment, registration.

inscrire [ɛskrir] *vt* [écrire] to write down; [- sur la pierre, le métal] to inscribe. || [personne]: **~ qqn à qqch** to enrol ou register sb for sthg; **~ qqn sur qqch** to put sb's name down on sthg. ○ **s'inscrire** *vp* [personne]: **s'~ à qqch** to enrol ou register for sthg; **s'~ sur qqch** to put one's name down on sthg.

inscrit, -e [ɛskri, it] **1** *pp* → **inscrire**. **2** *adj* [sur liste] registered; **être ~ sur une liste** to have one's name on a list.

insecte [ɛsɛkt] *nm* insect.

insecticide [ɛsɛktisid] *nm & adj* insecticide.

insécurité [ɛsekyrite] *nf* insecurity.

insémination [ɛseminasjɔ̃] *nf* insemination; **~ artificielle** artificial insemination.

insensé, -e [ɛsɑ̃se] *adj* [déraisonnable] insane. || [incroyable, excentrique] extraordinary.

insensibiliser [ɛsɑ̃sibilize] *vt* to anaesthetize.

insensible [ɛsɑ̃sibl] *adj* [gén]: **~ (à)** insensitive (to). || [imperceptible] imperceptible.

insensiblement [ɛsɑ̃sibləmɑ̃] *adv* imperceptibly.

inséparable [ɛseparabl] *adj*: **~ (de)** inseparable (from).

insérer [ɛsere] *vt* to insert; **~ une annonce dans un journal** to put an advertisement in a newspaper. ○ **s'insérer** *vp* [s'intégrer]: **s'~ dans** to fit into.

insidieux, -ieuse [ɛsidjø, jøz] *adj* insidious.

insigne [ɛsiɲ] **1** *nm* badge. **2** *adj* littéraire [honneur] distinguished. || hum [maladresse] remarkable.

insignifiant, -e [ɛsiɲifjɑ̃, ɑ̃t] *adj* insignificant.

insinuation [ɛsinɥasjɔ̃] *nf* insinuation, innuendo.

insinuer [ɛsinɥe] *vt* to insinuate, to imply. ○ **s'insinuer** *vp*: **s'~ dans** [eau, humidité, odeur] to seep into; *fig* [personne] to insinuate o.s. into.

insipide [ɛsipid] *adj* [aliment] insipid, tasteless; *fig* insipid.

insistance [ɛsistɑ̃s] *nf* insistence.

insister [ɛsiste] *vi* to insist; **~ sur** to insist on; **~ pour faire qqch** to insist on doing sthg.

insolation [ɛsɔlasjɔ̃] *nf* [malaise] sunstroke (*U*).

insolence [ɛsɔlɑ̃s] *nf* insolence (*U*).

insolent, -e [ɛsɔlɑ̃, ɑ̃t] **1** *adj* [personne, acte] insolent. **2** *nm, f* insolent person.

insolite [ɛsɔlit] *adj* unusual.

insoluble [ɛsɔlybl] *adj* insoluble.

insolvable [ɛsɔlvabl] *adj* insolvent.

insomnie [ɛsɔmni] *nf* insomnia (*U*).

insondable [ɛsɔ̃dabl] *adj* [gouffre, mystère] unfathomable; [bêtise] abysmal.

insonoriser [ɛsɔnɔrize] *vt* to soundproof.

insouciance [ɛsusjɑ̃s] *nf* [légèreté] carefree attitude.

insouciant, -e [ɛsusjɑ̃, ɑ̃t] *adj* [sans-souci] carefree.

insoumis, -e [ɛsumi, iz] *adj* [caractère] rebellious. || [soldat] deserting.

insoupçonné, -e [ɛsupsɔne] *adj* unsuspected.

insoutenable [ɛsutnabl] *adj* [rythme] unsustainable. || [scène, violence] unbearable. || [théorie] untenable.

inspecter [ɛspɛkte] *vt* to inspect.

inspecteur, -trice [ɛspɛktœr, tris] *nm, f* inspector.

inspection [ɛspɛksjɔ̃] *nf* [contrôle] inspection. || [fonction] inspectorate.

inspiration [ɛspirasjɔ̃] *nf* [gén] inspiration; [idée] bright idea, brainwave; **avoir de l'~** to be inspired. || [d'air] breathing in.

inspirer [ɛspire] *vt* [gén] to inspire; **~ qqch à qqn** to inspire sb with sthg. || [air] to breathe in, to inhale. ○ **s'inspirer** *vp* [prendre modèle sur]: **s'~ de qqn/qqch** to be inspired by sb/sthg.

instable [ɛstabl] *adj* [gén] unstable. || [vie, temps] unsettled.

installation [ɛstalasjɔ̃] *nf* [de gaz, eau, électricité] installation. || [de personne - comme médecin, artisan] setting up; [- dans appartement] settling in. || (*gén pl*) [équipement] installations (*pl*); fittings (*pl*); [industrielle] plant (*U*); [de loisirs] facilities (*pl*); **~ électrique** wiring.

installer [ɛstale] *vt* [gaz, eau, électricité] to install, to put in. || [rideaux, étagères] to put up; [meubles] to put in. || [personne]: **~ qqn** to get sb settled, to install sb. ○ **s'installer** *vp* [comme médecin, artisan etc] to set (o.s.) up. || [emménager] to settle in; **s'~ chez qqn** to move in with sb. || [dans fauteuil] to settle down. || *fig* [maladie, routine] to set in.

instamment [ɛ̃stamɑ̃] *adv* insistently.

instance [ɛ̃stɑ̃s] *nf* [autorité] authority. || JUR proceedings (*pl*). ○ **en instance** *loc adj* pending. ○ **en instance de** *loc adv* on the point of.

instant [ɛ̃stɑ̃] *nm* instant; **à l'~** [il y a peu de temps] a moment ago; [immédiatement] this minute; **à tout ~** [en permanence] at all times; **pour l'~** for the moment.

instantané, -e [ɛ̃stɑ̃tane] *adj* [immédiat] instantaneous. || [soluble] instant. ○ **instantané** *nm* snapshot.

instar [ɛ̃star] ○ **à l'instar de** *loc prép* following the example of.

instaurer [ɛ̃store] *vt* [instituer] to establish; *fig* [peur, confiance] to instil.

instigateur, -trice [ɛ̃stigatœr, tris] *nm, f* instigator.

instigation [ɛ̃stigasjɔ̃] *nf* ○ **à l'instigation de, sur l'instigation de** *loc prép* at the instigation of.

instinct [ɛ̃stɛ̃] *nm* instinct.

instinctif, -ive [ɛ̃stɛ̃ktif, iv] **1** *adj* instinctive. **2** *nm, f* instinctive person.

instituer [ɛ̃stitɥe] *vt* [pratique] to institute. || JUR [personne] to appoint.

institut [ɛ̃stity] *nm* [gén] institute. || [de soins]: **~ de beauté** beauty salon.

instituteur, -trice [ɛ̃stitytœr, tris] *nm, f* primary *Br* ou grade *Am* school teacher.

institution [ɛ̃stitysjɔ̃] *nf* [gén] institution. || [école privée] private school. ○ **institutions** *nfpl* POLIT institutions.

instructif, -ive [ɛ̃stryktif, iv] *adj* instructive, educational.

instruction [ɛ̃stryksjɔ̃] *nf* [enseignement, savoir] education. || [directive] order. || JUR (pre-trial) investigation. ○ **instructions** *nfpl* instructions.

instruit, -e [ɛ̃strɥi, ɥit] *adj* educated.

instrument [ɛ̃strymɑ̃] *nm* instrument; **~ de musique** musical instrument.

insu [ɛ̃sy] ○ **à l'insu de** *loc prép*: **à l'~ de qqn** without sb knowing; **ils ont tout organisé à mon ~** they organized it all without my knowing.

insubmersible [ɛ̃sybmɛrsibl] *adj* unsinkable.

insubordination [ɛ̃sybɔrdinasjɔ̃] *nf* insubordination.

insuccès [ɛ̃syksɛ] *nm* failure.

insuffisance [ɛ̃syfizɑ̃s] *nf* [manque] insufficiency. || MÉD deficiency. ○ **insuffisances** *nfpl* [faiblesses] shortcomings.

insuffisant, -e [ɛ̃syfizɑ̃, ɑ̃t] *adj* [en quantité] insufficient. || [en qualité] inadequate, unsatisfactory.

insulaire [ɛ̃syler] **1** *nmf* islander. **2** *adj* GÉOGR island (*avant n*).

insuline [ɛ̃sylin] *nf* insulin.

insulte [ɛ̃sylt] *nf* insult.

insulter [ɛ̃sylte] *vt* to insult.

insupportable [ɛ̃syportabl] *adj* unbearable.

insurgé, -e [ɛ̃syrʒe] *adj & nm, f* insurgent, rebel.

insurger [ɛ̃syrʒe] ○ **s'insurger** *vp* to rebel, to revolt; **s'~ contre qqch** to be outraged by sthg.

insurmontable [ɛ̃syrmɔ̃tabl] *adj* [difficulté] insurmountable; [dégoût] uncontrollable.

insurrection [ɛ̃syrɛksjɔ̃] *nf* insurrection.

intact, -e [ɛ̃takt] *adj* intact.

intarissable [ɛ̃tarisabl] *adj* inexhaustible; **il est ~** he could go on talking for ever.

intégral, -e, -aux [ɛ̃tegral, o] *adj* [paiement] in full; [texte] unabridged, complete. || MATHS: **calcul ~** integral calculus.

intégralement [ɛ̃tegralmɑ̃] *adv* fully, in full.

intégrant, -e [ɛ̃tegrɑ̃, ɑ̃t] → **parti**.

intègre [ɛ̃tegr] *adj* honest, of integrity.

intégré, -e [ɛ̃tegre] *adj* [élément] built-in.

intégrer [ɛ̃tegre] *vt* [assimiler]: **~ (dans)** to integrate (into). ○ **s'intégrer** *vp* [s'incorporer]: **s'~ dans** ou **à** to fit into. || [s'adapter] to integrate.

intégrisme [ɛ̃tegrism] *nm* fundamentalism.

intégrité [ɛ̃tegrite] *nf* [totalité] entirety. || [honnêteté] integrity.

intellectuel, -elle [ɛ̃telɛktɥel] *adj & nm, f* intellectual.

intelligence [ɛ̃teliʒɑ̃s] *nf* [facultés mentales] intelligence; **~ artificielle** artificial intelligence.

intelligent, -e [ɛ̃teliʒɑ̃, ɑ̃t] *adj* intelligent.

intelligible [ɛ̃teliʒibl] *adj* [voix] clear. || [concept, texte] intelligible.

intello [ɛ̃telo] *adj inv & nmf péj* highbrow.

intempéries [ɛ̃tɑ̃peri] *nfpl* bad weather (*U*).

intempestif, -ive [ɛ̃tɑ̃pɛstif, iv] *adj* untimely.

intenable [ɛ̃tənabl] *adj* [chaleur, personne] unbearable. || [position] untenable, indefensible.

intendance [ɛ̃tɑ̃dɑ̃s] *nf* MIL. commissariat; SCOL & UNIV bursar's office.

intendant, -e [ɛ̃tɑ̃dɑ̃, ɑ̃t] *nm, f* SCOL & UNIV bursar.

intense [ɛ̃tɑ̃s] *adj* [gén] intense.

intensif, -ive [ɛ̃tɑ̃sif, iv] *adj* intensive.

intensité [ɛ̃tɑ̃site] *nf* intensity.

intenter [ɛ̃tɑ̃te] *vt* JUR: ~ qqch contre ou à qqn to bring sthg against sb.

intention [ɛ̃tɑ̃sjɔ̃] *nf* intention; **avoir l'~ de faire qqch** to intend to do sthg. ○ **à l'intention de** *loc prép* for.

intentionné, -e [ɛ̃tɑ̃sjɔne] *adj*: **bien ~** well-meaning; **mal ~** ill-disposed.

intentionnel, -elle [ɛ̃tɑ̃sjɔnɛl] *adj* intentional.

interactif, -ive [ɛ̃tɛraktif, iv] *adj* interactive.

intercalaire [ɛ̃tɛrkaler] **1** *nm* insert. **2** *adj*: **feuillet ~** insert.

intercaler [ɛ̃tɛrkale] *vt*: ~ qqch dans qqch [feuillet, citation] to insert sthg in sthg; [dans le temps] to fit sthg into sthg.

intercéder [ɛ̃tɛrsede] *vi*: ~ pour ou en faveur de qqn auprès de qqn to intercede with sb on behalf of sb.

intercepter [ɛ̃tɛrsɛpte] *vt* [lettre, ballon] to intercept. || [chaleur] to block.

interchangeable [ɛ̃tɛrʃɑ̃ʒabl] *adj* interchangeable.

interclasse [ɛ̃tɛrklas] *nm* break.

interdiction [ɛ̃tɛrdiksjɔ̃] *nf* [défense]: «~ de stationner» "strictly no parking". || [prohibition, suspension]: ~ (de) ban (on), banning (of); ~ de séjour *order banning released prisoner from living in certain areas.*

interdire [ɛ̃tɛrdir] *vt* [prohiber]: ~ qqch à qqn to forbid sb sthg; ~ à qqn de faire qqch to forbid sb to do sthg. || [empêcher] to prevent; ~ à qqn de faire qqch to prevent sb from doing sthg. || [bloquer] to block.

interdit, -e [ɛ̃tɛrdi, it] **1** *pp* → **interdire. 2** *adj* [défendu] forbidden; **il est ~ de fumer** you're not allowed to smoke. || [ébahi]: **rester ~** to be stunned.

intéressant, -e [ɛ̃teresɑ̃, ɑ̃t] *adj* [captivant] interesting. || [avantageux] advantageous, good.

intéressé, -e [ɛ̃terese] *adj* [concerné]

concerned, involved; *péj* [motivé] self-interested.

intéresser [ɛ̃terese] *vt* [captiver] to interest. || COMM [faire participer]: ~ **les employés (aux bénéfices)** to give one's employees a share in the profits. || [concerner] to concern. ○ **s'intéresser** *vp*: **s'~ à qqn/qqch** to take an interest in sb/sthg, to be interested in sb/sthg.

intérêt [ɛ̃terɛ] *nm* [gén] interest; ~ **pour** interest in; **tu as ~ à réserver** you would be well advised to book. || [importance] significance. ○ **intérêts** *nmpl* FIN interest (*sg*). || COMM: **avoir des ~s dans** to have a stake in.

interface [ɛ̃tɛrfas] *nf* INFORM interface; ~ **graphique** graphic interface.

interférer [ɛ̃tɛrfere] *vi* PHYS to interfere. || *fig* [s'immiscer]: ~ **dans qqch** to interfere in sthg.

intérieur, -e [ɛ̃terjœr] *adj* [gén] inner. || [de pays] domestic. ○ **intérieur** *nm* [gén] inside; **à l'~ (de qqch)** inside (sthg). || [de pays] interior.

intérim [ɛ̃terim] *nm* [période] interim period; **par ~** acting. || [travail temporaire] temporary ou casual work; [dans bureau] temping. .

intérimaire [ɛ̃terimɛr] **1** *adj* [ministre, directeur] acting (*avant n*). || [employé, fonctions] temporary. **2** *nmf* [employé] temp.

intérioriser [ɛ̃terjɔrize] *vt* to internalize.

interjection [ɛ̃tɛrʒɛksjɔ̃] *nf* LING interjection.

interligne [ɛ̃tɛrliɲ] *nm* (line) spacing.

interlocuteur, -trice [ɛ̃tɛrlɔkytœr, tris] *nm, f* [dans conversation] speaker; **mon ~** the person to whom I am/was speaking. || [dans négociation] negotiator.

interloquer [ɛ̃tɛrlɔke] *vt* to disconcert.

interlude [ɛ̃tɛrlyd] *nm* interlude.

intermède [ɛ̃tɛrmɛd] *nm* interlude.

intermédiaire [ɛ̃tɛrmedjɛr] **1** *nm* intermediary, go-between; **par l'~ de qqn/qqch** through sb/sthg. **2** *adj* intermediate.

interminable [ɛ̃tɛrminabl] *adj* never-ending, interminable.

intermittence [ɛ̃tɛrmitɑ̃s] *nf* [discontinuité]: **par ~** intermittently, off and on.

intermittent, -e [ɛ̃tɛrmitɑ̃, ɑ̃t] *adj* intermittent.

internat [ɛ̃terna] *nm* [SCOL - établissement] boarding school; [- système] boarding.

international, -e, -aux [ɛ̃tɛrnasjɔnal, o] *adj* international.

interne [ɛ̃tɛrn] **1** *nmf* [élève] boarder. ‖ MÉD & UNIV intern *Am.* **2** *adj* ANAT internal; [oreille] inner. ‖ [du pays] domestic.

interner [ɛ̃tɛrne] *vt* POLIT to intern. ‖ MÉD to confine (*to psychiatric hospital*).

interpeller [ɛ̃tɛrpəle] *vt* [apostropher] to call or shout out to. ‖ [interroger] to take in for questioning.

interphone® [ɛ̃tɛrfɔn] *nm* intercom; [d'un immeuble] entry phone.

interposer [ɛ̃tɛrpoze] ○ **s'interposer** *vp*: **s'~ entre qqn et qqn** to intervene or come between sb and sb.

interprète [ɛ̃tɛrprɛt] *nmf* [gén] interpreter. ‖ CIN, MUS & THÉÂTRE performer.

interpréter [ɛ̃tɛrprete] *vt* to interpret.

interrogateur, -trice [ɛ̃tɛrɔgatœr, tris] *adj* inquiring (*avant n*).

interrogatif, -ive [ɛ̃tɛrɔgatif, iv] *adj* GRAM interrogative.

interrogation [ɛ̃tɛrɔgasjɔ̃] *nf* [de prisonnier] interrogation; [de témoin] questioning. ‖ [question] question. ‖ SCOL test.

interrogatoire [ɛ̃tɛrɔgatwar] *nm* [de police, juge] questioning.

interrogeable [ɛ̃tɛrɔʒabl] *adj*: **répondeur ~ à distance** answerphone with remote playback facility.

interroger [ɛ̃tɛrɔʒe] *vt* [questionner] to question; [accusé, base de données] to interrogate; **~ qqn (sur qqch)** to question sb (about sthg). ○ **s'interroger** *vp*: **s'~ sur** to wonder about.

interrompre [ɛ̃tɛrɔ̃pr] *vt* to interrupt. ○ **s'interrompre** *vp* to stop.

interrompu, -e [ɛ̃tɛrɔ̃py] *pp* → interrompre.

interrupteur [ɛ̃tɛryptœr] *nm* switch.

interruption [ɛ̃tɛrypsjɔ̃] *nf* [arrêt] break. ‖ [action] interruption.

intersection [ɛ̃tɛrsɛksjɔ̃] *nf* intersection.

interstice [ɛ̃tɛrstis] *nm* chink, crack.

interurbain, -e [ɛ̃tɛryrbɛ̃, ɛn] *adj* long-distance.

intervalle [ɛ̃tɛrval] *nm* [spatial] space, gap. ‖ [temporel] interval, period (of time); **à 6 jours d'~** after 6 days. ‖ MUS interval.

intervenant, -e [ɛ̃tɛrvənɑ̃, ɑ̃t] *nm, f* [orateur] speaker.

intervenir [ɛ̃tɛrvənir] *vi* [personne] to intervene; **~ auprès de qqn** to intervene with sb; **faire ~ qqn** to bring or call in sb. ‖ [événement] to take place.

intervention [ɛ̃tɛrvɑ̃sjɔ̃] *nf* [gén] intervention. ‖ MÉD operation; **subir une ~ chirurgicale** to have an operation, to have surgery. ‖ [discours] speech.

intervenu, -e [ɛ̃tɛrvəny] *pp* → intervenir.

intervertir [ɛ̃tɛrvertir] *vt* to reverse, to invert.

interview [ɛ̃tɛrvju] *nf* interview.

interviewer [ɛ̃tɛrvjuve] *vt* to interview.

intestin [ɛ̃tɛstɛ̃] *nm* intestine.

intestinal, -e, -aux [ɛ̃tɛstinal, o] *adj* intestinal.

intime [ɛ̃tim] **1** *nmf* close friend. **2** *adj* [gén] intimate; [vie, journal] private.

intimider [ɛ̃timide] *vt* to intimidate.

intimité [ɛ̃timite] *nf* [familiarité, confort] intimacy. ‖ [vie privée] privacy.

intitulé [ɛ̃tityle] *nm* [titre] title; [de paragraphe] heading.

intituler [ɛ̃tityle] *vt* to call, to entitle. ○ **s'intituler** *vp* [ouvrage] to be called or entitled.

intolérable [ɛ̃tɔlerabl] *adj* intolerable.

intolérance [ɛ̃tɔlerɑ̃s] *nf* [religieuse, politique] intolerance.

intolérant, -e [ɛ̃tɔlerɑ̃, ɑ̃t] *adj* intolerant.

intonation [ɛ̃tɔnasjɔ̃] *nf* intonation.

intouchable [ɛ̃tuʃabl] *nmf* & *adj* untouchable.

intoxication [ɛ̃tɔksikasjɔ̃] *nf* [empoisonnement] poisoning.

intoxiquer [ɛ̃tɔksike] *vt*: **~ qqn par** [empoisonner] to poison sb with.

intraduisible [ɛ̃tradɥizibl] *adj* [texte] untranslatable.

intraitable [ɛ̃trɛtabl] *adj*: **~ (sur)** inflexible (about).

intransigeant, -e [ɛ̃trɑ̃ziʒɑ̃, ɑ̃t] *adj* intransigent.

intransitif, -ive [ɛ̃trɑ̃zitif, iv] *adj* intransitive.

intransportable [ɛ̃trɑ̃spɔrtabl] *adj*: **il est ~** he/it cannot be moved.

intraveineux, -euse [ɛ̃travɛnø, øz] *adj* intravenous.

intrépide [ɛ̃trepid] *adj* bold, intrepid.

intrigue [ɛ̃trig] *nf* [manœuvre] intrigue. ‖ CIN, LITTÉRATURE & THÉÂTRE plot.

intriguer [ɛ̃trige] **1** *vt* to intrigue. **2** *vi* to scheme, to intrigue.

introduction [ɛ̃trɔdyksjɔ̃] *nf* [gén]: **~ (à)** introduction (to). ‖ [insertion] insertion.

introduire [ɛ̃trɔdɥir] *vt* [gén] to introduce. || [faire entrer] to show in. || [insérer] to insert. ○ **s'introduire** *vp* [pénétrer] to enter.

introduit, -e [ɛ̃trɔdɥi, it] *pp* → **introduire.**

introspection [ɛ̃trɔspɛksjɔ̃] *nf* introspection.

introuvable [ɛ̃truvabl] *adj* nowhere to be found.

introverti, -e [ɛ̃trɔverti] **1** *adj* introverted. **2** *nm, f* introvert.

intrus, -e [ɛ̃try, yz] *nm, f* intruder.

intrusion [ɛ̃tryzjɔ̃] *nf* [gén & GÉOL] intrusion. || [ingérence] interference.

intuitif, -ive [ɛ̃tɥitif, iv] *adj* intuitive.

intuition [ɛ̃tɥisjɔ̃] *nf* intuition.

inusable [inyzabl] *adj* hardwearing.

inusité, -e [inyzite] *adj* unusual, uncommon.

inutile [inytil] *adj* [objet, personne] useless; [effort, démarche] pointless.

inutilisable [inytilizabl] *adj* unusable.

inutilité [inytilite] *nf* [de personne, d'objet] uselessness; [de démarche, d'effort] pointlessness.

invaincu, -e [ɛ̃vɛ̃ky] *adj* SPORT unbeaten.

invalide [ɛ̃valid] **1** *nmf* disabled person. **2** *adj* disabled.

invalidité [ɛ̃validite] *nf* MÉD disability.

invariable [ɛ̃varjabl] *adj* [immuable] unchanging. || GRAM invariable.

invasion [ɛ̃vazjɔ̃] *nf* invasion.

invendable [ɛ̃vɑ̃dabl] *adj* unsaleable, unsellable.

invendu, -e [ɛ̃vɑ̃dy] *adj* unsold. ○ **invendu** *nm* (*gén pl*) remainder.

inventaire [ɛ̃vɑ̃ter] *nm* [gén] inventory. || [COMM - activité] stocktaking *Br*, inventory *Am*; [- liste] list.

inventer [ɛ̃vɑ̃te] *vt* to invent.

inventeur [ɛ̃vɑ̃tœr] *nm* [de machine] inventor.

invention [ɛ̃vɑ̃sjɔ̃] *nf* [découverte, mensonge] invention. || [imagination] inventiveness.

inventorier [ɛ̃vɑ̃tɔrje] *vt* to make an inventory of.

inverse [ɛ̃vɛrs] **1** *nm* opposite, reverse. **2** *adj* [sens] opposite; [ordre] reverse; **en sens ~ (de)** in the opposite direction (to).

inversement [ɛ̃vɛrsəmɑ̃] *adv* MATHS inversely. || [au contraire] on the other hand. || [vice versa] vice versa.

inverser [ɛ̃vɛrse] *vt* to reverse.

investigation [ɛ̃vɛstigasjɔ̃] *nf* investigation.

investir [ɛ̃vɛstir] *vt* to invest.

investissement [ɛ̃vɛstismɑ̃] *nm* investment.

investisseur, -euse [ɛ̃vɛstisœr, øz] *nm, f* investor.

investiture [ɛ̃vɛstityr] *nf* investiture.

invétéré, -e [ɛ̃vetere] *adj* péj inveterate.

invincible [ɛ̃vɛ̃sibl] *adj* [gén] invincible.

inviolable [ɛ̃vjɔlabl] *adj* JUR inviolable. || [coffre] impregnable.

invisible [ɛ̃vizibl] *adj* invisible.

invitation [ɛ̃vitasjɔ̃] *nf*: **~ (à)** invitation (to); **sur ~** by invitation.

invité, -e [ɛ̃vite] *nm, f* guest.

inviter [ɛ̃vite] *vt* to invite; **~ qqn à faire qqch** to invite sb to do sthg.

in vitro [invitro] → **fécondation.**

invivable [ɛ̃vivabl] *adj* unbearable.

involontaire [ɛ̃vɔlɔ̃ter] *adj* [acte] involuntary.

invoquer [ɛ̃vɔke] *vt* [alléguer] to put forward. || [citer, appeler à l'aide] to invoke; [paix] to call for.

invraisemblable [ɛ̃vrɛsɑ̃blabl] *adj* [incroyable] unlikely, improbable. || [extravagant] incredible.

invulnérable [ɛ̃vylnerabl] *adj* invulnerable.

iode [jɔd] *nm* iodine.

ion [jɔ̃] *nm* ion.

IRA [ira] (*abr de* **Irish Republican Army**) *nf* IRA.

irai, iras *etc* → **aller.**

Irak, Iraq [irak] *nm*: **l'~** Iraq.

irakien, -ienne, iraqien, -ienne [irakjɛ̃, jɛn] *adj* Iraqi. ○ **Irakien, -ienne, Iraqien, -ienne** *nm, f* Iraqi.

Iran [irɑ̃] *nm*: **l'~** Iran.

iranien, -ienne [iranjɛ̃, jɛn] *adj* Iranian. ○ **iranien** *nm* [langue] Iranian. ○ **Iranien, -ienne** *nm, f* Iranian.

Iraq = Irak.

iraqien = irakien.

irascible [irasibl] *adj* irascible.

iris [iris] *nm* ANAT & BOT iris.

irisé, -e [irize] *adj* iridescent.

irlandais, -e [irlɑ̃de, ɛz] *adj* Irish. ○ **irlandais** *nm* [langue] Irish. ○ **Irlandais, -e** *nm, f* Irishman (*f* Irishwoman).

Irlande [irlɑ̃d] *nf*: **l'~** Ireland; **l'~ du Nord/Sud** Northern/Southern Ireland.

ironie [irɔni] *nf* irony.

ironique [irɔnik] *adj* ironic.

ironiser [irɔnize] *vi* to speak ironically.

irradier [iradje] **1** *vi* to radiate. **2** *vt* to irradiate.

irraisonné, -e [irɛzɔne] *adj* irrational.

irrationnel, -elle [irasjɔnɛl] *adj* irrational.

irréalisable [irealizabl] *adj* unrealizable.

irrécupérable [irekyperabl] *adj* [irréparable] beyond repair. || *fam* [personne] beyond hope.

irréductible [iredyktibl] **1** *nmf* diehard. **2** *adj* CHIM, MATHS & MÉD irreducible. || *fig* [volonté] indomitable; [personne] implacable; [communiste] diehard (*avant n*).

irréel, -elle [ireel] *adj* unreal.

irréfléchi, -e [irefleʃi] *adj* unthinking.

irréfutable [irefytabl] *adj* irrefutable.

irrégularité [iregylarite] *nf* [gén] irregularity. || [de terrain, performance] unevenness.

irrégulier, -ière [iregylje, jɛr] *adj* [gén] irregular. || [terrain, surface] uneven, irregular. || [employé, athlète] erratic.

irrémédiable [iremedjabl] *adj* [irréparable] irreparable.

irremplaçable [irɑ̃plasabl] *adj* irreplaceable.

irréparable [ireparabl] *adj* [objet] beyond repair. || *fig* [perte, erreur] irreparable.

irrépressible [irepresibl] *adj* irrepressible.

irréprochable [ireprɔʃabl] *adj* irreproachable.

irrésistible [irezistibl] *adj* [tentation, femme] irresistible. || [amusant] entertaining.

irrésolu, -e [irezɔly] *adj* [indécis] irresolute. || [sans solution] unresolved.

irrespirable [irespirabl] *adj* [air] unbreathable. || *fig* [oppressant] oppressive.

irresponsable [irɛspɔ̃sabl] **1** *nmf* irresponsible person. **2** *adj* irresponsible.

irréversible [ireversibl] *adj* irreversible.

irrévocable [irevɔkabl] *adj* irrevocable.

irrigation [irigasjɔ̃] *nf* irrigation.

irriguer [irige] *vt* to irrigate.

irritable [iritabl] *adj* irritable.

irritation [iritasjɔ̃] *nf* irritation.

irriter [irite] *vt* [exaspérer] to irritate, to annoy. || MÉD to irritate. ○ **s'irriter** *vp*

to get irritated; **s'~ contre qqn/de qqch** to get irritated with sb/at sthg.

irruption [irypsjɔ̃] *nf* [invasion] invasion. || [entrée brusque] irruption.

islam [islam] *nm* Islam.

islamique [islamik] *adj* Islamic.

islandais, -e [islɑ̃dɛ, ɛz] *adj* Icelandic.

Islande [islɑ̃d] *nf*: **l'~** Iceland.

isolant, -e [izɔlɑ̃, ɑ̃t] *adj* insulating. ○ **isolant** *nm* insulator, insulating material.

isolation [izɔlasjɔ̃] *nf* insulation.

isolé, -e [izɔle] *adj* isolated.

isoler [izɔle] *vt* [séparer] to isolate. || CONSTR & ÉLECTR to insulate; **~ qqch du froid** to insulate sthg (against the cold); **~ qqch du bruit** to soundproof sthg. ○ **s'isoler** *vp*: **s'~ (de)** to isolate o.s. (from).

isoloir [izɔlwar] *nm* polling booth.

isotherme [izɔtɛrm] *adj* isothermal.

Israël [israɛl] *n* Israel.

israélien, -ienne [israeljɛ̃, jɛn] *adj* Israeli. ○ **Israélien, -ienne** *nm, f* Israeli.

israélite [israelit] *adj* Jewish. ○ **Israélite** *nmf* Jew.

issu, -e [isy] *adj*: **~ de** [résultant de] emerging ou stemming from. ○ **issue** *nf* [sortie] exit; **~e de secours** emergency exit. || *fig* [solution] way out, solution. || [terme] outcome.

isthme [ism] *nm* isthmus.

Italie [itali] *nf*: **l'~** Italy.

italien, -ienne [italjɛ̃, jɛn] *adj* Italian. ○ **italien** *nm* [langue] Italian. ○ **Italien, -ienne** *nm, f* Italian.

italique [italik] *nm* TYPO italics (*pl*).

itinéraire [itinerɛr] *nm* itinerary, route.

itinérant, -e [itinerɑ̃, ɑ̃t] *adj* [spectacle, troupe] itinerant.

IUT (*abr de* **institut universitaire de technologie**) *nm* ≃ technical college.

IVG (*abr de* **interruption volontaire de grossesse**) *nf* abortion.

ivoire [ivwar] *nm* ivory.

ivre [ivr] *adj* drunk.

ivresse [ivrɛs] *nf* drunkenness.

ivrogne [ivrɔɲ] *nmf* drunkard.

J, J [ʒi] *nm inv* j, J.

j' → je.

jabot [ʒabo] *nm* [d'oiseau] crop. || [de chemise] frill.

jacasser [ʒakase] *vi péj* to chatter, to jabber.

jacinthe [ʒasɛ̃t] *nf* hyacinth.

Jacuzzi® [ʒakuzi] *nm* Jacuzzi®.

jade [ʒad] *nm* jade.

jadis [ʒadis] *adv* formerly, in former times.

jaguar [ʒagwar] *nm* jaguar.

jaillir [ʒajir] *vi* [liquide] to gush; [flammes] to leap. || [cri] to ring out. || [personne] to spring out.

jais [ʒɛ] *nm* jet.

jalon [ʒalɔ̃] *nm* marker pole.

jalonner [ʒalɔne] *vt* to mark (out).

jalousie [ʒaluzi] *nf* [envie] jealousy. || [store] blind.

jaloux, -ouse [ʒalu, uz] *adj:* ~ (de) jealous (of).

Jamaïque [ʒamaik] *nf:* la ~ Jamaica.

jamais [ʒamɛ] *adv* [sens négatif] never; **je ne reviendrai ~, ~ je ne reviendrai** I'll never come back; **je ne viendrai ~ plus, plus ~ je ne viendrai** I'll never come here again. || [sens positif]: **plus que ~** more than ever; **il est plus triste que ~** he's sadder than ever; **si ~ tu le vois** if you should happen to see him, should you happen to see him. ○ **à jamais** *loc adv* for ever.

jambe [ʒɑ̃b] *nf* leg.

jambières [ʒɑ̃bjɛr] *nfpl* [de football] shin pads; [de cricket] pads.

jambon [ʒɑ̃bɔ̃] *nm* ham.

jante [ʒɑ̃t] *nf* (wheel) rim.

janvier [ʒɑ̃vje] *nm* January; *voir aussi* septembre.

Japon [ʒapɔ̃] *nm:* le ~ Japan.

japonais, -e [ʒapɔnɛ, ɛz] *adj* Japanese. ○ **japonais** *nm* [langue] Japanese. ○ **Japonais, -e** *nm, f* Japanese (person); **les Japonais** the Japanese.

japper [ʒape] *vi* to yap.

jaquette [ʒakɛt] *nf* [vêtement] jacket. || [de livre] (dust) jacket.

jardin [ʒardɛ̃] *nm* garden; ~ **public** park.

jardinage [ʒardinaʒ] *nm* gardening.

jardinier, -ière [ʒardinje, jɛr] *nm, f* gardener. ○ **jardinière** *nf* [bac à fleurs] window box.

jargon [ʒargɔ̃] *nm* [langage spécialisé] jargon. || *fam* [charabia] gibberish.

jarret [ʒarɛ] *nm* ANAT back of the knee. || CULIN knuckle of veal.

jarretelle [ʒartɛl] *nf* garter Am.

jarretière [ʒartjɛr] *nf* garter.

jaser [ʒaze] *vi* [bavarder] to gossip.

jasmin [ʒasmɛ̃] *nm* jasmine.

jatte [ʒat] *nf* bowl.

jauge [ʒoʒ] *nf* [instrument] gauge.

jauger [ʒoʒe] *vt* to gauge.

jaunâtre [ʒonatr] *adj* yellowish.

jaune [ʒon] 1 *nm* [couleur] yellow. 2 *adj* yellow. ○ **jaune d'œuf** *nm* (egg) yolk.

jaunir [ʒonir] *vt & vi* to turn yellow.

jaunisse [ʒonis] *nf* MÉD jaundice.

java [ʒava] *nf* type of popular dance.

Javel [ʒavɛl] *nf:* (eau de) ~ bleach.

javelot [ʒavlo] *nm* javelin.

jazz [dʒaz] *nm* jazz.

J.-C. (*abr de* Jésus-Christ) J.C.

je [ʒə], **j'** (*devant voyelle et h muet*) *pron pers* I.

jean [dʒin], **jeans** [dʒins] *nm* jeans (*pl*), pair of jeans.

Jeep® [dʒip] *nf* Jeep®.

jerrycan, jerricane [ʒerikan] *nm* jerry can.

jersey [ʒɛrzɛ] *nm* jersey.

jésuite [ʒezɥit] *nm* Jesuit.

Jésus-Christ [ʒezykri] *nm* Jesus Christ.

jet¹ [ʒɛ] *nm* [action de jeter] throw. || [de liquide] jet.

jet² [dʒɛt] *nm* [avion] jet.

jetable [ʒətabl] *adj* disposable.

jetée [ʒəte] *nf* jetty.

jeter [ʒəte] *vt* to throw; [se débarrasser de] to throw away; ~ **qqch à qqn** [lancer] to throw sthg to sb, to throw sb sthg; [pour faire mal] to throw sthg at sb. ○ **se jeter** *vp:* **se ~ sur** to pounce on; **se ~ dans** [suj: rivière] to flow into.

jeton [ʒətɔ̃] *nm* [de jeu] counter; [de téléphone] token.

jeu, -x [ʒø] *nm* [divertissement] play (U), playing (U); ~ **de mots** play on words, pun. || [régi par des règles] game; ~ **de société** parlour game. || [d'argent]: **le ~**

gambling. || [d'échecs, de clés] set; ~ de **cartes** pack of cards. || [manière de jouer - MUS] playing; [- THÉÂTRE] acting; [- SPORT] game. || [TECHNOL] play. || *loc:* **cacher son ~** to play one's cards close to one's chest. ○ **Jeux Olympiques** *nmpl:* **les Jeux Olympiques** the Olympic Games.

jeudi [ʒødi] *nm* Thursday; *voir aussi* **samedi**.

jeun [ʒœ̃] ○ **à jeun** *loc adv* on an empty stomach.

jeune [ʒœn] **1** *adj* young; [style, apparence] youthful; **~ homme/femme** young man/woman. **2** *nm* young person; **les ~s** young people.

jeûne [ʒøn] *nm* fast.

jeunesse [ʒœnɛs] *nf* [âge] youth; [de style, apparence] youthfulness. || [jeunes gens] young people (*pl*).

JO *nmpl* (*abr de* **Jeux Olympiques**) *Olympic Games.*

joaillier, -ère [ʒɔaje, jɛr] *nm, f* jeweller.

job [dʒɔb] *nm fam* job.

jockey [ʒɔkɛ] *nm* jockey.

jogging [dʒɔgiŋ] *nm* [activité] jogging. || [vêtement] tracksuit, jogging suit.

joie [ʒwa] *nf* joy.

joindre [ʒwɛ̃dr] *vt* [rapprocher] to join; [mains] to put together. || [ajouter]: **~ qqch (à)** to attach sthg (to); [adjoindre] to enclose sthg (with). || [par téléphone] to contact, to reach. ○ **se joindre** *vp:* **se ~ à qqn** to join sb; **se ~ à qqch** to join in sthg.

joint, -e [ʒwɛ̃, ɛ̃t] *pp* → **joindre.** ○ **joint** *nm* [d'étanchéité] seal. || *fam* [drogue] joint.

joli, -e [ʒɔli] *adj* [femme, chose] pretty, attractive. || [somme, situation] nice.

joliment [ʒɔlimɑ̃] *adv* [bien] prettily, attractively; *iron* nicely. || *fam* [beaucoup] really.

jonc [ʒɔ̃] *nm* rush, bulrush.

joncher [ʒɔ̃ʃe] *vt* to strew; **être jonché de** to be strewn with.

jonction [ʒɔ̃ksjɔ̃] *nf* [de routes] junction.

jongler [ʒɔ̃gle] *vi* to juggle.

jongleur, -euse [ʒɔ̃glœr, øz] *nm, f* juggler.

jonquille [ʒɔ̃kij] *nf* daffodil.

Jordanie [ʒɔrdani] *nf:* **la ~** Jordan.

joue [ʒu] *nf* cheek; **tenir** ou **mettre qqn en ~** *fig* to take aim at sb.

jouer [ʒwe] **1** *vi* [gén] to play; **~ à qqch** [jeu, sport] to play sthg; **~ de** MUS to play. || CIN & THÉÂTRE to act. || [parier] to gamble. **2** *vt* [carte, partie] to play. || [somme d'argent] to bet, to wager; *fig* to gamble with. || [THÉÂTRE - personnage, rôle] to play; [- pièce] to put on, to perform. || CIN to show. || MUS to perform, to play.

jouet [ʒwɛ] *nm* toy.

joueur, -euse [ʒwœr, øz] *nm, f* SPORT player; **~ de football** footballer, football player. || [au casino] gambler.

joufflu, -e [ʒufly] *adj* [personne] chubby-cheeked.

joug [ʒu] *nm* yoke.

jouir [ʒwir] *vi* [profiter]: **~ de** to enjoy. || [sexuellement] to have an orgasm.

jouissance [ʒwisɑ̃s] *nf* JUR [d'un bien] use. || [sexuelle] orgasm.

joujou, -x [ʒuʒu] *nm* toy.

jour [ʒur] *nm* [unité de temps] day; **huit ~s** a week; **quinze ~s** a fortnight *Br*, two weeks; **de ~ en ~** day by day; **au ~ le ~** from day to day; **le ~ de l'an** New Year's Day; **~ de congé** day off; **~ férié** public holiday; **~ ouvrable** working day. || [lumière] daylight; **de ~** in the daytime, by day. || *loc:* **mettre qqch à ~** to update sthg, to bring sthg up to date; **de nos ~s** these days, nowadays.

journal, -aux [ʒurnal, o] *nm* [publication] newspaper, paper. || TÉLÉ: **~ télévisé** television news. || [écrit]: **~ (intime)** diary, journal.

journalier, -ière [ʒurnalje, jɛr] *adj* daily.

journalisme [ʒurnalism] *nm* journalism.

journaliste [ʒurnalist] *nmf* journalist, reporter.

journée [ʒurne] *nf* day.

joute [ʒut] *nf* joust; *fig* duel.

jovial, -e, -iaux [ʒɔvjal, jo] *adj* jovial, jolly.

joyau, -x [ʒwajo] *nm* jewel.

joyeux, -euse [ʒwajø, øz] *adj* joyful, happy; **~ Noël!** Merry Christmas!

jubiler [ʒybile] *vi fam* to be jubilant.

jucher [ʒyʃe] *vt:* **~ qqn sur qqch** to perch sb on sthg.

judaïque [ʒydaik] *adj* [loi] Judaic; [tradition, religion] Jewish.

judaïsme [ʒydaism] *nm* Judaism.

judas [ʒyda] *nm* [ouverture] peephole.

judiciaire [ʒydisjɛr] *adj* judicial.

judicieux, -ieuse [ʒydisjø, jøz] *adj* judicious.

judo [ʒydo] *nm* judo.

juge [ʒyʒ] *nm* judge; ~ **d'instruction** examining magistrate.

jugé [ʒyʒe] ○ **au jugé** *loc adv* by guesswork; **tirer au** ~ to fire blind.

jugement [ʒyʒmã] *nm* judgment.

jugeote [ʒyʒɔt] *nf fam* common sense.

juger [ʒyʒe] **1** *vt* to judge; [accusé] to try; ~ **que** to judge (that), to consider (that); ~ **qqn/qqch inutile** to consider sb/sthg useless. **2** *vi* to judge; ~ **de qqch** to judge sthg; **si j'en juge d'après mon expérience** judging from my experience.

juif, -ive [ʒyif, iv] *adj* Jewish. ○ **Juif, -ive** *nm, f* Jew.

juillet [ʒyijɛ] *nm* July; **la fête du 14 Juillet** *national holiday to mark the anniversary of the storming of the Bastille*; *voir aussi* **septembre**.

juin [ʒyɛ̃] *nm* June; *voir aussi* **septembre**.

juke-box [dʒukbɔks] *nm inv* jukebox.

jumeau, -elle, -x [ʒymo, ɛl, o] **1** *adj* twin (*avant n*). **2** *nm, f* twin. ○ **jumelles** *nfpl* OPTIQUE binoculars.

jumelé, -e [ʒymle] *adj* [villes] twinned; [maisons] semidetached.

jumeler [ʒymle] *vt* to twin.

jumelle → **jumeau**.

jument [ʒymã] *nf* mare.

jungle [ʒœ̃gl] *nf* jungle.

junior [ʒynjɔr] *adj & nmf* SPORT junior.

junte [ʒœ̃t] *nf* junta.

jupe [ʒyp] *nf* skirt.

jupe-culotte [ʒypkylɔt] *nf* culottes (*pl*).

jupon [ʒypɔ̃] *nm* petticoat, slip.

juré [ʒyre] *nm* JUR juror.

jurer [ʒyre] **1** *vt*: ~ **qqch à qqn** to swear ou pledge sthg to sb; ~ **(à qqn) que ...** to swear (to sb) that ...; ~ **de faire qqch** to swear ou vow to do sthg. **2** *vi* [blasphémer] to swear, to curse. ‖ [ne pas aller ensemble]: ~ **(avec)** to clash (with).

juridiction [ʒyridiksjɔ̃] *nf* jurisdiction.

juridique [ʒyridik] *adj* legal.

jurisprudence [ʒyrisprydãs] *nf* jurisprudence.

juriste [ʒyrist] *nmf* lawyer.

juron [ʒyrɔ̃] *nm* swearword, oath.

jury [ʒyri] *nm* JUR jury. ‖ [SCOL - d'examen] examining board; [- de concours] admissions board.

jus [ʒy] *nm* [de fruits, légumes] juice. ‖ [de viande] gravy.

jusque, jusqu' [ʒysk(ə)] ○ **jusqu'à** *loc prép* [sens temporel] until, till; **jusqu'à**

présent up until now, so far. ‖ [sens spatial] as far as; **jusqu'au bout** to the end. ‖ [même] even. ○ **jusqu'à ce que** *loc conj* until, till. ○ **jusqu'en** *loc prép* up until. ○ **jusqu'ici** *loc adv* [lieu] up to here; [temps] up until now, so far. ○ **jusque-là** *loc adv* [lieu] up to there; [temps] up until then.

justaucorps [ʒystokɔr] *nm* [maillot] leotard.

juste [ʒyst] **1** *adj* [équitable] fair. ‖ [exact] right, correct. ‖ [trop petit] tight. **2** *adv* [bien] correctly, right. ‖ [exactement, seulement] just.

justement [ʒystəmã] *adv* [avec raison] rightly. ‖ [précisément] exactly, precisely.

justesse [ʒystɛs] *nf* [de remarque] aptness; [de raisonnement] soundness. ○ **de justesse** *loc adv* only just.

justice [ʒystis] *nf* JUR justice; **passer en** ~ to stand trial. ‖ [équité] fairness.

justicier, -ière [ʒystisje, jɛr] *nm, f* righter of wrongs.

justifiable [ʒystifjabl] *adj* justifiable.

justificatif, -ive [ʒystifikatif, iv] *adj* supporting. ○ **justificatif** *nm* written proof (*U*).

justification [ʒystifikasjɔ̃] *nf* justification.

justifier [ʒystifje] *vt* [gén] to justify. ○ **se justifier** *vp* to justify o.s.

jute [ʒyt] *nm* jute.

juteux, -euse [ʒytø, øz] *adj* juicy.

juvénile [ʒyvenil] *adj* youthful.

juxtaposer [ʒykstapoze] *vt* to juxtapose.

k, K [ka] *nm inv* k, K.

K7 [kaset] (*abr de* **cassette**) *nf* cassette.

kaki [kaki] **1** *nm* [couleur] khaki. ‖ [fruit] persimmon. **2** *adj inv* khaki.

kaléidoscope [kaleidɔskɔp] *nm* kaleidoscope.

kamikaze [kamikaz] *nm* kamikaze pilot.

kangourou [kãguru] *nm* kangaroo.

karaoké [karaɔke] *nm* karaoke.

karaté [karate] *nm* karate.

karting [kartiŋ] *nm* go-karting.

kas(c)her, **cascher** [kaʃɛr] *adj inv* kosher.

kayak [kajak] *nm* kayak.

Kenya [kenja] *nm*: le ~ Kenya.

képi [kepi] *nm* kepi.

kermesse [kɛrmɛs] *nf* [foire] fair. ‖ [fête de bienfaisance] fête.

kérosène [kerɔzɛn] *nm* kerosene.

ketchup [kɛtʃœp] *nm* ketchup.

kg (*abr de* **kilogramme**) kg.

kibboutz [kibutz] *nm inv* kibbutz.

kidnapper [kidnape] *vt* to kidnap.

kidnappeur, -euse [kidnapœr, øz] *nm, f* kidnapper.

kilo [kilo] *nm* kilo.

kilogramme [kilɔgram] *nm* kilogram.

kilométrage [kilɔmetraʒ] *nm* [de voiture] ≃ mileage. ‖ [distance] distance.

kilomètre [kilɔmɛtr] *nm* kilometre.

kilo-octet [kilookte] *nm* INFORM kilobyte.

kilowatt [kilɔwat] *nm* kilowatt.

kilt [kilt] *nm* kilt.

kimono [kimɔno] *nm* kimono.

kinésithérapeute [kineziterapøt] *nmf* physiotherapist.

kiosque [kjɔsk] *nm* [de vente] kiosk. ‖ [pavillon] pavilion.

kirsch [kirʃ] *nm* cherry brandy.

kitchenette [kitʃənɛt] *nf* kitchenette.

kitsch [kitʃ] *adj inv* kitsch.

kiwi [kiwi] *nm* [oiseau] kiwi. ‖ [fruit] kiwi, kiwi fruit (*U*).

Klaxon® [klaksɔ] *nm* horn.

klaxonner [klaksɔne] *vi* to hoot.

kleptomane, **cleptomane** [klɛptɔman] *nmf* kleptomaniac.

km (*abr de* **kilomètre**) km.

km/h (*abr de* **kilomètre par heure**) kph.

Ko (*abr de* **kilo-octet**) K.

K.-O. [kao] *nm*: mettre qqn ~ to knock sb out.

Koweït [kɔwɛt] *nm*: le ~ Kuwait.

krach [krak] *nm* crash; ~ boursier stock market crash.

kurde [kyrd] **1** *adj* Kurdish. **2** *nm* [langue] Kurdish. ○ **Kurde** *nmf* Kurd.

kyrielle [kirjɛl] *nf fam* stream.

kyste [kist] *nm* cyst.

l, L [ɛl] **1** *nm inv* l, L. **2** (*abr de* **litre**) l.

la¹ [la] *art déf & pron déf* → **le**.

la² [la] *nm inv* MUS A; [chanté] la.

là [la] *adv* [lieu] there; passe par ~ go that way; c'est ~ que je travaille that's where I work; je suis ~ I'm here. ‖ [temps] then; à quelques jours de ~ a few days later, a few days after that. ‖ [avec une proposition relative]: ~ où [lieu] where; [temps] when; *voir aussi* ce, là-bas, là-dedans *etc*.

là-bas [laba] *adv* (over) there.

label [label] *nm* [étiquette]: ~ de qualité label guaranteeing quality. ‖ [commerce] label, brand name.

labeur [labœr] *nm sout* labour.

labo [labo] (*abr de* **laboratoire**) *nm fam* lab.

laborantin, -e [labɔrãtɛ̃, in] *nm, f* laboratory assistant.

laboratoire [labɔratwar] *nm* laboratory.

laborieux, -ieuse [labɔrjø, jøz] *adj* [difficile] laborious.

labourer [labure] *vt* AGRIC to plough.

laboureur [laburœr] *nm* ploughman.

labyrinthe [labirɛ̃t] *nm* labyrinth.

lac [lak] *nm* lake; les Grands Lacs the Great Lakes; le ~ Léman Lake Geneva.

lacer [lase] *vt* to tie.

lacérer [lasere] *vt* [déchirer] to shred. || [blesser, griffer] to slash.

lacet [lase] *nm* [cordon] lace. || [de route] bend. || [piège] snare.

lâche [laʃ] **1** *nmf* coward. **2** *adj* [nœud] loose. || [personne, comportement] cowardly.

lâcher [laʃe] **1** *vt* [libérer - bras, objet] to let go of; [- animal] to let go, to release; *fig* [- mot] to let slip. || [laisser tomber]: ~ qqch to drop stng. **2** *vi* to give way.

lâcheté [laʃte] *nf* [couardise] cowardice.

laconique [lakɔnik] *adj* laconic.

lacrymogène [lakrimɔʒɛn] *adj* tear (*avant n*).

lacune [lakyn] *nf* [manque] gap.

là-dedans [ladədɑ̃] *adv* inside, in there; **il y a quelque chose qui m'intrigue ~** there's something in that which intrigues me.

là-dessous [ladsu] *adv* underneath, under there; *fig* behind that.

là-dessus [ladsy] *adv* on that; **~, il partit** at that point ou with that, he left; **je suis d'accord ~** I agree about that.

lagon [lagɔ̃] *nm*, **lagune** [lagyn] *nf* lagoon.

là-haut [lao] *adv* up there.

laïc (*f* **laïque**), **laïque** [laik] *adj* lay (*avant n*); [école] state (*avant n*).

laid, -e [lɛ, lɛd] *adj* [esthétiquement] ugly. || [moralement] wicked.

laideron [lɛdrɔ̃] *nm* ugly woman.

laideur [lɛdœr] *nf* [physique] ugliness.

lainage [lɛnaʒ] *nm* [étoffe] woollen material; [vêtement] woolly ou woollen garment.

laine [lɛn] *nf* wool.

laineux, -euse [lɛnø, øz] *adj* woolly.

laïque → **laïc**.

laisse [lɛs] *nf* [corde] lead, leash; **tenir en ~** [chien] to keep on a lead ou leash.

laisser [lese] **1** *v aux* (+*infinitif*): ~ **qqn faire qqch** to let sb do ou stng; **laisse-le faire** leave him alone, don't interfere; ~ **tomber qqch** *litt & fig* to drop stng. **2** *vt* [gén] to leave. || [céder]: ~ **qqch à qqn** to let sb have stng. ○ **se laisser** *vp*: **se ~ faire** to let o.s. be persuaded; **se ~ aller** to relax; [dans son apparence] to let o.s. go.

laisser-aller [leseale] *nm inv* carelessness.

laissez-passer [lesepase] *nm inv* pass.

lait [lɛ] *nm* [gén] milk; ~ **entier/écrémé** whole/skimmed milk; ~ **concentré** ou **condensé** [sucré] condensed milk; [non sucré] evaporated milk. || [cosmétique]: ~ **démaquillant** cleansing milk ou lotion.

laitage [lɛtaʒ] *nm* milk product.

laiterie [lɛtri] *nf* dairy.

laitier, -ière [lɛtje, jɛr] **1** *adj* dairy (*avant n*). **2** *nm, f* milkman (*f* milkwoman).

laiton [lɛtɔ̃] *nm* brass.

laitue [lety] *nf* lettuce.

laïus [lajys] *nm* long speech.

lambeau, -x [lɑ̃bo] *nm* [morceau] shred.

lambris [lɑ̃bri] *nm* panelling.

lame [lam] *nf* [fer] blade; ~ **de rasoir** razor blade. || [lamelle] strip. || [vague] wave.

lamé, -e [lame] *adj* lamé. ○ **lamé** *nm* lamé.

lamelle [lamɛl] *nf* [de champignon] gill. || [tranche] thin slice. || [de verre] slide.

lamentable [lamɑ̃tabl] *adj* [résultats, sort] appalling. || [ton] plaintive.

lamentation [lamɑ̃tasjɔ̃] *nf* [plainte] lamentation. || (*gén pl*) [jérémiade] moaning (*U*).

lamenter [lamɑ̃te] ○ **se lamenter** *vp* to complain.

laminer [lamine] *vt* IND to laminate; *fig* [personne, revenus] to eat away at.

lampadaire [lɑ̃pader] *nm* [dans maison] standard lamp *Br*, floor lamp *Am*; [de rue] street lamp ou light.

lampe [lɑ̃p] *nf* lamp, light; ~ **de chevet** bedside lamp; ~ **halogène** halogen light; ~ **de poche** torch *Br*, flashlight *Am*.

lampion [lɑ̃pjɔ̃] *nm* Chinese lantern.

lance [lɑ̃s] *nf* [arme] spear. || [de tuyau] nozzle; ~ **d'incendie** fire hose.

lance-flammes [lɑ̃sflam] *nm inv* flame-thrower.

lancement [lɑ̃smɑ̃] *nm* [d'entreprise, produit, navire] launching.

lance-pierres [lɑ̃spjɛr] *nm inv* catapult.

lancer [lɑ̃se] **1** *vt* [pierre, javelot] to throw; ~ **qqch sur qqn** to throw stng at sb. || [fusée, produit, style] to launch. || [cri] to let out; [injures] to hurl. || [moteur] to start up. || [INFORM - programme] to start; [- système] to boot (up). || *fig* [sur un sujet]: ~ **qqn sur qqch** to get sb started on stng. **2** *nm* PÊCHE casting. || SPORT throwing; ~ **du poids** shotput. ○ **se lancer** *vp* [s'engager]: **se ~ dans** [dépenses, explication, lecture] to embark on.

lancinant, -e [lɑ̃sinɑ̃, ɑ̃t] *adj* [douleur] shooting. || *fig* [obsédant] haunting.

landau [lɑ̃do] *nm* [d'enfant] pram.

lande [lɑ̃d] *nf* moor.

langage [lɑ̃gaʒ] *nm* language.

lange [lɑ̃ʒ] *nm* nappy *Br*, diaper *Am*.

langer [lɑ̃ʒe] *vt* to change.

langoureux, -euse [lɑ̃gurø, øz] *adj* languorous.

langouste [lɑ̃gust] *nf* crayfish.

langoustine [lɑ̃gustin] *nf* langoustine.

langue [lɑ̃g] *nf* ANAT & *fig* tongue. || LING language; ~ **maternelle** mother tongue; ~ **morte/vivante** dead/modern language.

languette [lɑ̃gɛt] *nf* tongue.

langueur [lɑ̃gœr] *nf* [apathie] apathy.

languir [lɑ̃gir] *vi sout* [attendre] to wait; **faire ~ qqn** to keep sb waiting.

lanière [lanjɛr] *nf* strip.

lanterne [lɑ̃tɛrn] *nf* [éclairage] lantern. || [phare] light.

laper [lape] *vt* & *vi* to lap.

lapider [lapide] *vt* [tuer] to stone.

lapin, -e [lapɛ̃, in] *nm, f* CULIN & ZOOL rabbit. || [fourrure] rabbit fur.

laps [laps] *nm:* **(dans) un ~ de temps** (in) a while.

lapsus [lapsys] *nm* slip (of the tongue/pen).

laque [lak] *nf* [vernis, peinture] lacquer. || [pour cheveux] hair spray, lacquer.

laqué, -e [lake] *adj* lacquered.

laquelle → **lequel**.

larcin [larsɛ̃] *nm* [vol] larceny, theft.

lard [lar] *nm* [graisse de porc] lard. || [viande] bacon.

lardon [lardɔ̃] *nm* CULIN *cube or strip of bacon*. || *fam* [enfant] kid.

large [larʒ] **1** *adj* [étendu, grand] wide; ~ **de 5 mètres** 5 metres wide. || [important, considérable] large, big. || [esprit, sourire] broad. || [généreux - personne] generous. **2** *nm* [largeur]: **5 mètres de ~** 5 metres wide. || [mer]: **le ~** the open sea; **au ~ de la côte française** off the French coast.

largement [larʒəmɑ̃] *adv* [diffuser, répandre] widely. || [dépasser] considerably; [récompenser] amply; **avoir ~ le temps** to have plenty of time. || [au moins] easily.

largeur [larʒœr] *nf* [d'avenue, de cercle] width. || *fig* [d'idées, d'esprit] breadth.

larguer [large] *vt* [voile] to unfurl. || [bombe, parachutiste] to drop. || *fam fig* [abandonner] to chuck.

larme [larm] *nf* [pleur] tear; **être en ~s** to be in tears.

larmoyant, -e [larmwajɑ̃, ɑ̃t] *adj* [yeux, personne] tearful. || *péj* [histoire] tearjerking.

larve [larv] *nf* ZOOL larva. || *péj* [personne] wimp.

laryngite [larɛ̃ʒit] *nf* laryngitis (*U*).

larynx [larɛ̃ks] *nm* larynx.

las, lasse [la, las] *adj littéraire* [fatigué] weary.

lascif, -ive [lasif, iv] *adj* lascivious.

laser [lazɛr] **1** *nm* laser. **2** *adj inv* laser (*avant n*).

lasser [lase] *vt sout* [personne] to weary. ○ **se lasser** *vp* to weary.

lassitude [lasityd] *nf* lassitude.

lasso [laso] *nm* lasso.

latent, -e [latɑ̃, ɑ̃t] *adj* latent.

latéral, -e, -aux [lateral, o] *adj* lateral.

latex [latɛks] *nm inv* latex.

latin, -e [latɛ̃, in] *adj* Latin. ○ **latin** *nm* [langue] Latin.

latiniste [latinist] *nmf* [spécialiste] Latinist; [étudiant] Latin student.

latino-américain, -e [latinoamerikɛ̃, ɛn] (*mpl* **latino-américains**, *fpl* **latino-américaines**) *adj* Latin-American, Hispanic.

latitude [latityd] *nf litt* & *fig* latitude.

latrines [latrin] *nfpl* latrines.

latte [lat] *nf* lath, slat.

lauréat, -e [lɔrea, at] *nm, f* prize-winner, winner.

laurier [lɔrje] *nm* BOT laurel.

lavable [lavabl] *adj* washable.

lavabo [lavabo] *nm* [cuvette] basin. || (*gén pl*) [local] toilet.

lavage [lavaʒ] *nm* washing.

lavande [lavɑ̃d] *nf* BOT lavender.

lave [lav] *nf* lava.

lave-glace [lavglas] (*pl* **lave-glaces**) *nm* windshield washer *Am*.

lave-linge [lavlɛ̃ʒ] *nm inv* washing machine.

laver [lave] *vt* [nettoyer] to wash. || *fig* [disculper]: ~ **qqn de qqch** to clear sb of sthg. ○ **se laver** *vp* [se nettoyer] to wash o.s., to have a wash; **se ~ les mains/les cheveux** to wash one's hands/hair.

laverie [lavri] *nf* [commerce] laundry; ~ **automatique** laundderette.

lavette [lavɛt] *nf* [en tissu] dishcloth. || *fam* [homme] drip.

laveur, -euse [lavœr, øz] *nm, f* washer; ~ **de carreaux** window cleaner (*person*).

lave-vaisselle [lavvesɛl] *nm inv* dishwasher.

lavoir [lavwar] *nm* [lieu] laundry.

lesbienne

laxatif, -ive [laksatif, iv] *adj* laxative.
○ **laxatif** *nm* laxative.

laxisme [laksism] *nm* laxity.

laxiste [laksist] *adj* lax.

layette [lɛjɛt] *nf* layette.

le [lə], **l'** *(devant voyelle ou h muet)* (*f* **la** [la], *pl* **les** [le]) **1** *art déf* [gén] the. || [devant les noms abstraits]: **l'amour** love; **la liberté** freedom. || [temps]: **~ 15 janvier 1993** 15th January 1993; **je suis arrivé ~ 15 janvier 1993** I arrived on the 15th of January 1993; **~ lundi** [habituellement] on Mondays; [jour précis] on (the) Monday. || [possession]: **se laver les mains** to wash one's hands; **avoir les cheveux blonds** to have fair hair. || [distributif] per, a; **10 francs ~ mètre** 10 francs per ou a metre. **2** *pron pers* [personne] him (*f* her), (*pl*) them; [chose] it, (*pl*) them; [animal] it, him (*f* her), (*pl*) them; **tu dois avoir la clé, donne-la moi** you must have the key, give it to me. || [représente une proposition]: **je ~ sais bien** I know, I'm well aware (of it).

LEA *(abr de langues étrangères appliquées) nfpl* applied modern languages.

leader [lidœr] *nm* [de parti, course] leader.

lécher [leʃe] *vt* [passer la langue sur, effleurer] to lick; [suj: vague] to wash against. || *fam* [fignoler] to polish (up).

lèche-vitrines [lɛʃvitrin] *nm inv* window-shopping; **faire du ~** to go window-shopping.

leçon [ləsɔ̃] *nf* [gén] lesson; **~s de conduite** driving lessons; **~s particulières** private lessons ou classes. || [conseil] advice (*U*); **faire la ~ à qqn** to lecture sb.

lecteur, -trice [lɛktœr, tris] *nm, f* [de livres] reader. || UNIV foreign language assistant. ○ **lecteur** *nm* [gén] head; **~ de cassettes/CD** cassette/CD player. || INFORM reader.

lecture [lɛktyr] *nf* reading.

légal, -e, -aux [legal, o] *adj* legal.

légalement [legalmɑ̃] *adv* legally.

légaliser [legalize] *vt* [rendre légal] to legalize.

légalité [legalite] *nf* [de contrat, d'acte] legality, lawfulness. || [loi] law.

légataire [legatɛr] *nmf* legatee.

légendaire [leʒɑ̃dɛr] *adj* legendary.

légende [leʒɑ̃d] *nf* [fable] legend. || [de carte, de schéma] key; [de photo] caption.

léger, -ère [leʒe, ɛr] *adj* [objet, étoffe, repas] light. || [bruit, différence, odeur] slight. || [alcool, tabac] low-strength. ||

[insouciant - ton] light-hearted; [- réfléchi] thoughtless. ○ **à la légère** *loc adv* lightly, thoughtlessly.

légèrement [leʒɛrmɑ̃] *adv* [s'habiller, poser] lightly. || [agir] thoughtlessly. || [blesser, remuer] slightly.

légèreté [leʒɛrte] *nf* [d'objet, de repas, de punition] lightness. || [de style] gracefulness. || [de conduite] thoughtlessness.

légiférer [leʒifere] *vi* to legislate.

légion [leʒjɔ̃] *nf* MIL legion.

légionnaire [leʒjɔnɛr] *nm* legionary.

législatif, -ive [leʒislatif, iv] *adj* legislative. ○ **législatives** *nfpl*: **les législatives** the legislative elections.

législation [leʒislasjɔ̃] *nf* legislation.

légiste [leʒist] *adj* [juriste] jurist. || → **médecin**.

légitime [leʒitim] *adj* legitimate.

légitimer [leʒitime] *vt* [reconnaître] to recognize; [enfant] to legitimize. || [justifier] to justify.

legs [leg] *nm* legacy.

léguer [lege] *vt*: **~ qqch à qqn** JUR to bequeath sthg to sb; *fig* to pass sthg on to sb.

légume [legym] *nm* vegetable.

leitmotiv [lajtmɔtif, lɛtmɔtif] *nm* leitmotif.

Léman [lemɑ̃] → **lac**.

lendemain [lɑ̃dmɛ̃] *nm* [jour] day after; **le ~ matin** the next morning; **au ~ de** after, in the days following.

lent, -e [lɑ̃, lɑ̃t] *adj* slow.

lente [lɑ̃t] *nf* nit.

lentement [lɑ̃tmɑ̃] *adv* slowly.

lenteur [lɑ̃tœr] *nf* slowness (*U*).

lentille [lɑ̃tij] *nf* BOT & CULIN lentil. || [d'optique] lens; **~s de contact** contact lenses.

léopard [leɔpar] *nm* leopard.

LEP, Lep *(abr de lycée d'enseignement professionnel) nm former secondary school for vocational training*.

lèpre [lɛpr] *nf* MÉD leprosy.

lequel [ləkɛl] (*f* **laquelle** [lakɛl], *mpl* **lesquels** [lekɛl], *fpl* **lesquelles** [lekɛl]) (*contraction de à + lequel* = **auquel**, *de + lequel* = **duquel**, *à + lesquels/lesquelles* = **auxquels/auxquelles**, *de + lesquels/lesquelles* = **desquels/desquelles**) **1** *pron rel* [complément - personne] whom; [- chose] which. || [sujet - personne] who; [- chose] which. **2** *pron interr*: **~?** which (one)?

les → **le**.

lesbienne [lɛsbjɛn] *nf* lesbian.

léser [leze] *vt* [frustrer] to wrong.

lésiner [lezine] *vi* to skimp; **ne pas ~ sur** not to skimp on.

lésion [lezjɔ̃] *nf* lesion.

lesquels, lesquelles → lequel.

lessive [lesiv] *nf* [nettoyage, linge] washing. || [produit] washing powder.

lest [lɛst] *nm* ballast.

leste [lɛst] *adj* [agile] nimble, agile. || [licencieux] crude.

lester [lɛste] *vt* [garnir de lest] to ballast.

léthargie [letaʁʒi] *nf litt & fig* lethargy.

Lettonie [lɛtɔni] *nf*: **la ~** Latvia.

lettre [lɛtʁ] *nf* [gén] letter; **en toutes ~s** in words, in full. || [sens des mots]: **à la ~** to the letter. ○ **lettres** *nfpl* [culture littéraire] letters. || UNIV arts; **~s classiques** classics; **~s modernes** French language and literature.

leucémie [løsemi] *nf* leukemia.

leur [lœʁ] *pron pers inv* (to) them; **je voudrais ~ parler** I'd like to speak to them; **je ~ ai donné la lettre** I gave them the letter, I gave the letter to them. ○ **leur** (*pl* **leurs**) *adj poss* their. ○ **le leur** (*f* **la leur**, *pl* **les leurs**) *pron poss* theirs.

leurrer [lœʁe] *vt* to deceive. ○ **se leurrer** *vp* to deceive o.s.

levain [ləvɛ̃] *nm* CULIN: **pain au ~/sans ~** leavened/unleavened bread.

levant [ləvɑ̃] **1** *nm* east. **2** *adj* → **soleil**.

lever [ləve] **1** *vt* [objet, blocus, interdiction] to lift. || [main, tête, armée] to raise. || [séance] to close, to end. || [enfant, malade]: **~ qqn** to get sb up. **2** *vi* [pâte] to rise. **3** *nm* [d'astre] rising, rise; **~ du jour** daybreak; **~ du soleil** sunrise. || [de personne]: **il est toujours de mauvaise humeur au ~** he's always in a bad mood when he gets up. ○ **se lever** *vp* [personne] to get up, to rise; [vent] to get up. || [soleil, lune] to rise; [jour] to break. || [temps] to clear.

lève-tard [lɛvtaʁ] *nmf inv* late riser.

lève-tôt [lɛvto] *nmf inv* early riser.

levier [ləvje] *nm litt & fig* lever; **~ de vitesses** gear lever *Br*, gear shift *Am*.

lévitation [levitasjɔ̃] *nf* levitation.

lèvre [lɛvʁ] *nf* ANAT lip; [de vulve] labium.

lévrier, levrette [levʁije, ləvʁɛt] *nm, f* greyhound.

levure [ləvyʁ] *nf* yeast; **~ chimique** baking powder.

lexique [lɛksik] *nm* [dictionnaire] glossary. || [vocabulaire] vocabulary.

lézard [lezaʁ] *nm* [animal] lizard.

lézarder [lezaʁde] **1** *vt* to crack. **2** *vi fam* [paresser] to bask. ○ **se lézarder** *vp* to crack.

liaison [ljezɔ̃] *nf* [jonction, enchaînement] connection. || CULIN & LING liaison. || [contact, relation] contact; **avoir une ~** to have an affair. || TRANSPORT link.

liane [ljan] *nf* creeper.

liant, -e [ljɑ̃, ɑ̃t] *adj* sociable. ○ **liant** *nm* [substance] binder.

liasse [ljas] *nf* bundle; [de billets de banque] wad.

Liban [libɑ̃] *nm*: **le ~** Lebanon.

libanais, -e [libanɛ, ɛz] *adj* Lebanese. ○ **Libanais, -e** *nm, f* Lebanese (person); **les Libanais** the Lebanese.

libeller [libele] *vt* [chèque] to make out. || [lettre] to word.

libellule [libelyl] *nf* dragonfly.

libéral, -e, -aux [liberal, o] **1** *adj* [attitude, idée, parti] liberal. **2** *nm, f* POLIT liberal.

libéraliser [liberalize] *vt* to liberalize.

libéralisme [liberalism] *nm* liberalism.

libération [liberasjɔ̃] *nf* [de prisonnier] release, freeing. || [de pays, de la femme] liberation. || [d'énergie] release.

libérer [libere] *vt* [prisonnier, fonds] to release, to free. || [pays, la femme] to liberate; **~ qqn de qqch** to free sb from sthg. || [passage] to clear. || [énergie] to release. ○ **se libérer** *vp* [se rendre disponible] to get away. || [se dégager]: **se ~ de** [lien] to free o.s. from; [engagement] to get out of.

liberté [libɛʁte] *nf* [gén] freedom; **en ~** free; **parler en toute ~** to speak freely; **~ d'expression** freedom of expression; **~ d'opinion** freedom of thought. || JUR release. || [loisir] free time.

libertin, -e [libɛʁtɛ̃, in] *nm, f* libertine.

libidineux, -euse [libidinø, øz] *adj* lecherous.

libido [libido] *nf* libido.

libraire [libʁɛʁ] *nmf* bookseller.

librairie [libʁeʁi] *nf* [magasin] bookshop.

libre [libʁ] *adj* [gén] free; **~ de qqch** free from sthg; **être ~ de faire qqch** to be free to do sthg. || [école, secteur] private. || [passage] clear.

libre-échange [libʁeʃɑ̃ʒ] *nm* free trade (U).

librement [libʁəmɑ̃] *adv* freely.

libre-service [libʁəsɛʁvis] *nm* [magasin] self-service store or shop; [restaurant] self-service restaurant.

Libye [libi] *nf*: la ~ Libya.

libyen, -yenne [libjɛ̃, jɛn] *adj* Libyan. ○ **Libyen, -yenne** *nm, f* Libyan.

licence [lisɑ̃s] *nf* [permis] permit; COMM licence. || UNIV (first) degree; ~ ès lettres/en droit ≃ Bachelor of Arts/Law degree. || littéraire [liberté] licence.

licencié, -e [lisɑ̃sje] **1** *adj* UNIV graduate (*avant n*). **2** *nm, f* UNIV graduate.

licenciement [lisɑ̃simɑ̃] *nm* dismissal; [économique] layoff.

licencier [lisɑ̃sje] *vt* to dismiss; [pour cause économique] to lay off.

lichen [likɛn] *nm* lichen.

licite [lisit] *adj* lawful, legal.

licorne [likɔrn] *nf* unicorn.

lie [li] *nf* [dépôt] dregs (*pl*), sediment. ○ **lie-de-vin** *adj inv* burgundy, wine-coloured.

lié, -e [lje] *adj* [mains] bound. || [amis]: être très ~ avec to be great friends with.

liège [ljɛʒ] *nm* cork.

lien [ljɛ̃] *nm* [sangle] bond. || [relation, affinité] bond, tie; **avoir des ~s de parenté avec** to be related to. || *fig* [enchaînement] connection, link.

lier [lje] *vt* [attacher] to tie (up); ~ **qqn/qqch à** to tie sb/sthg to. || [suj: contrat, promesse] to bind. || [relier par la logique] to link, to connect; ~ **qqch à** to link sthg to, to connect sthg with. || [commencer]: ~ **connaissance/conversation avec** to strike up an acquaintance/a conversation with. || [suj: sentiment, intérêt] to unite. || CULIN to thicken. ○ **se lier** *vp* [s'attacher]: **se ~ (d'amitié) avec qqn** to make friends with sb.

lierre [ljɛr] *nm* ivy.

liesse [ljɛs] *nf* jubilation.

lieu, -x [ljø] *nm* [endroit] place; **en ~ sûr** in a safe place; ~ **de naissance** birthplace. || *loc*: **avoir ~** to take place. ○ **lieux** *nmpl* [scène] scene (*sg*); **sur les ~x (d'un crime/d'un accident)** at the scene (of a crime/an accident). || [domicile] premises. ○ **lieu commun** *nm* commonplace. ○ **lieu-dit** *nm* locality, place. ○ **au lieu de** *loc prép*: **au ~ de qqch/de faire qqch** instead of sthg/of doing sthg. ○ **en dernier lieu** *loc adv* lastly. ○ **en premier lieu** *loc adv* in the first place.

lieue [ljø] *nf* league.

lieutenant [ljøtnɑ̃] *nm* lieutenant.

lièvre [ljɛvr] *nm* hare.

lifter [lifte] *vt* TENNIS to spin, to put a spin on.

lifting [liftiŋ] *nm* face-lift.

ligament [ligamɑ̃] *nm* ligament.

ligaturer [ligatyre] *vt* MÉD to ligature, to ligate.

ligne [liɲ] *nf* [gén] line; **à la ~** new line or paragraph; **en ~** [personnes] in a line; ~ **de départ/d'arrivée** starting/finishing line; ~ **aérienne** airline. || [forme - de voiture, meuble] lines (*pl*); [- silhouette]: **garder la ~** to keep one's figure; **surveiller sa ~** to watch one's waistline. || [de pêche] fishing line; **pêcher à la ~** to go angling. || *loc*: **dans les grandes ~s** in outline; **entrer en ~ de compte** to be taken into account.

lignée [liɲe] *nf* [famille] descendants (*pl*); **dans la ~ de** *fig* [d'écrivains, d'artistes] in the tradition of.

ligoter [ligɔte] *vt* [attacher] to tie up; ~ **qqn à qqch** to tie sb to sthg.

ligue [lig] *nf* league.

liguer [lige] ○ **se liguer** *vp* to form a league; **se ~ contre** to conspire against.

lilas [lila] *nm & adj inv* lilac.

limace [limas] *nf* ZOOL slug.

limaille [limaj] *nf* filings (*pl*).

limande [limɑ̃d] *nf* dab.

lime [lim] *nf* [outil] file; ~ **à ongles** nail file. || BOT lime.

limer [lime] *vt* [ongles] to file; [aspérités] to file down; [barreau] to file through.

limier [limje] *nm* [chien] bloodhound. || [détective] sleuth.

limitation [limitasjɔ̃] *nf* limitation; [de naissances] control; ~ **de vitesse** speed limit.

limite [limit] **1** *nf* [gén] limit; **à la ~** [au pire] at worst. || [terme, échéance] deadline; ~ **d'âge** age limit. **2** *adj* [extrême] maximum (*avant n*); **cas ~** borderline case; **date ~** deadline; **date ~ de vente/consommation** sell-by/use-by date.

limiter [limite] *vt* [borner] to border, to bound. || [restreindre] to limit. ○ **se limiter** *vp* [se restreindre]: **se ~ à qqch/à faire qqch** to limit o.s. to sthg/to doing sthg. || [se borner]: **se ~ à** to be limited to.

limitrophe [limitrɔf] *adj* [frontalier] border (*avant n*). || [voisin] adjacent.

limoger [limɔʒe] *vt* to dismiss.

limon [limɔ̃] *nm* GÉOL alluvium, silt.

limonade [limɔnad] *nf* lemonade.

limpide [lɛ̃pid] *adj* [eau] limpid. || [ciel, regard] clear. || [explication, style] clear, lucid.

lin [lɛ̃] *nm* BOT flax. || [tissu] linen.

linceul [lɛ̃sœl] *nm* shroud.

linéaire [lineɛr] *adj* [mesure, perspective] linear.

linge [lɛ̃ʒ] *nm* [lessive] washing. || [de lit, de table] linen. || [sous-vêtements] underwear. || [morceau de tissu] cloth.

lingerie [lɛ̃ʒri] *nf* [local] linen room. || [sous-vêtements] lingerie.

lingot [lɛ̃go] *nm* ingot.

linguistique [lɛ̃gɥistik] **1** *nf* linguistics (*U*). **2** *adj* linguistic.

linoléum [linɔleɔm] *nm* lino, linoleum.

lion, lionne [ljɔ̃, ljɔn] *nm, f* lion (*f* lioness). ○ **Lion** *nm* ASTROL Leo.

lionceau, -x [ljɔ̃so] *nm* lion cub.

lipide [lipid] *nm* lipid.

liquéfier [likefje] *vt* to liquefy. ○ **se liquéfier** *vp* [matière] to liquefy. || *fig* [personne] to turn to jelly.

liqueur [likœr] *nf* liqueur.

liquidation [likidasjɔ̃] *nf* [de compte & BOURSE] settlement. || [de société, stock] liquidation.

liquide [likid] **1** *nm* [substance] liquid. || [argent] cash; **en ~** in cash. **2** *adj* [corps & LING] liquid.

liquider [likide] *vt* [compte & BOURSE] to settle. || [société, stock] to liquidate. || *arg crime* [témoin] to liquidate, to eliminate; *fig* [problème] to eliminate, to get rid of.

lire¹ [lir] *vt* to read.

lire² [lir] *nf* lira.

lis, lys [lis] *nm* lily.

Lisbonne [lizbɔn] *n* Lisbon.

liséré [lizre], **liséré** [lizere] *nm* [ruban] binding. || [bande] border, edging.

liseron [lizrɔ̃] *nm* bindweed.

liseuse [lizøz] *nf* [vêtement] bedjacket. || [lampe] reading light.

lisible [lizibl] *adj* [écriture] legible.

lisière [lizjɛr] *nf* [limite] edge.

lisse [lis] *adj* [surface, peau] smooth.

lisser [lise] *vt* [papier, vêtements] to smooth (out). || [moustache, cheveux] to smooth (down). || [plumes] to preen.

liste [list] *nf* list; **~ d'attente** waiting list; **~ électorale** electoral roll; **~ de mariage** wedding present list; **être sur la ~ rouge** to be ex-directory.

lister [liste] *vt* to list.

listing [listiŋ] *nm* listing.

lit [li] *nm* [gén] bed; **faire son ~** to make one's bed; **garder le ~** to stay in bed; **se mettre au ~** to go to bed; **~ à baldaquin** four-poster bed; **~ de camp** camp bed.

litanie [litani] *nf* litany.

literie [litri] *nf* bedding.

lithographie [litɔgrafi] *nf* [procédé] lithography. || [image] lithograph.

litière [litjɛr] *nf* litter.

litige [litiʒ] *nm* JUR lawsuit. || [désaccord] dispute.

litigieux, -euse [litiʒjø, jøz] *adj* JUR litigious. || [douteux] disputed.

litre [litr] *nm* [mesure, quantité] litre. || [récipient] litre bottle.

littéraire [literɛr] *adj* literary.

littéral, -e, -aux [literal, o] *adj* [gén] literal. || [écrit] written.

littérature [literatyr] *nf* [gén] literature.

littoral, -e, -aux [litɔral, o] *adj* coastal. ○ **littoral** *nm* coast, coastline.

Lituanie [litɥani] *nf*: **la ~** Lithuania.

liturgie [lityrʒi] *nf* liturgy.

livide [livid] *adj* [blême] pallid.

livraison [livrɛzɔ̃] *nf* [de marchandise] delivery; **~ à domicile** home delivery.

livre [livr] **1** *nm* [gén] book; **~ de cuisine** cookery book; **~ de poche** paperback. **2** *nf* pound; **~ sterling** pound sterling.

livrée [livre] *nf* [uniforme] livery.

livrer [livre] *vt* COMM to deliver. || [coupable, complice]: **~ qqn à qqn** to hand sb over to sb. || [abandonner]: **~ qqn à lui-même** to leave sb to his own devices. ○ **se livrer** *vp* [se rendre]: **se ~ à** [police, ennemi] to give o.s. up to. || [se confier]: **se ~ à** [ami] to open up to, to confide in. || [se consacrer]: **se ~ à** [occupation] to devote o.s. to; [excès] to indulge in.

livret [livre] *nm* [carnet] booklet; **~ de caisse d'épargne** passbook, bankbook; **~ de famille** *official family record book, given by registrar to newlyweds*; **~ scolaire** ≃ school report.

livreur, -euse [livrœr, øz] *nm, f* delivery man (*f* woman).

lobby [lɔbi] (*pl* **lobbies**) *nm* lobby.

lobe [lɔb] *nm* ANAT & BOT lobe.

lober [lɔbe] *vt* to lob.

local, -e, -aux [lɔkal, o] *adj* local; [douleur] localized. ○ **local** *nm* room, premises (*pl*). ○ **locaux** *nmpl* premises, offices.

localiser [lɔkalize] *vt* [avion, bruit] to locate. || [épidémie, conflit] to localize.

localité [lɔkalite] *nf* (small) town.

locataire [lɔkatɛr] *nmf* tenant.

location [lɔkasjɔ̃] *nf* [de propriété - par propriétaire] letting *Br*, renting *Am*; [- par locataire] renting; [de machine] leasing. || [bail] lease. || [maison, appartement] rented property.

location-vente [lɔkasjɔ̃vɑ̃t] *nf* ≃ hire purchase *Br*, ≃ installment plan *Am*.

locomotion [lɔkɔmɔsjɔ̃] *nf* locomotion.

locomotive [lɔkɔmɔtiv] *nf* [machine] locomotive. || *fig* [leader] moving force.

locution [lɔkysjɔ̃] *nf* expression, phrase.

loft [lɔft] *nm* (converted) loft.

logarithme [lɔgaritm] *nm* logarithm.

loge [lɔʒ] *nf* [de concierge, de francs-maçons] lodge. || [d'acteur] dressing room.

logement [lɔʒmɑ̃] *nm* [hébergement] accommodation. || [appartement] flat *Br*, apartment *Am*; ~ **de fonction** company flat *Br* ou apartment *Am*.

loger [lɔʒe] **1** *vi* [habiter] to live. **2** *vt* [amis, invités] to put up. || [suj: hôtel, maison] to accommodate, to take. **O se loger** *vp* [trouver un logement] to find accommodation. || [se placer - ballon, balle]: **se ~ dans** to lodge in, to stick in.

logiciel [lɔʒisjɛl] *nm* software (*U*); ~ **intégré** integrated software.

logique [lɔʒik] **1** *nf* logic. **2** *adj* logical.

logiquement [lɔʒikmɑ̃] *adv* logically.

logis [lɔʒi] *nm* abode.

logistique [lɔʒistik] *nf* logistics (*pl*).

logo [logo] *nm* logo.

loi [lwa] *nf* [gén] law.

loin [lwɛ̃] *adv* [dans l'espace] far; **plus ~** further. || [dans le temps - passé] a long time ago; [- futur] a long way off. **O au loin** *loc adv* in the distance, far off. **O de loin** *loc adv* [depuis une grande distance] from a distance. **O loin de** *loc prép* [gén] far from; ~ **de là!** *fig* far from it! || [dans le temps]: **il n'est pas ~ de 9 h** it's nearly 9 o'clock, it's not far off 9 o'clock.

lointain, -e [lwɛ̃tɛ̃, ɛn] *adj* [pays, avenir, parent] distant.

loir [lwar] *nm* dormouse.

loisir [lwazir] *nm* [temps libre] leisure. || (*gén pl*) [distractions] leisure activities (*pl*).

londonien, -ienne [lɔ̃dɔnjɛ̃, jɛn] *adj* London (*avant n*). **O Londonien, -ienne** *nm, f* Londoner.

Londres [lɔ̃dr] *n* London.

long, longue [lɔ̃, lɔ̃g] *adj* [gén] long. || [lent] slow; **être ~ à faire qqch** to take a long time doing sthg. **O long 1** *nm* [longueur]: **4 mètres de ~** 4 metres long ou in length; **de ~ en large** up and down, to

and fro; **en ~ et en large** in great detail; **(tout) le ~ de** [espace] all along; **tout au ~ de** [année, carrière] throughout. **2** *adv* [beaucoup]: **en savoir ~ sur qqch** to know a lot about sthg. **O à la longue** *loc adv* in the end.

longe [lɔ̃ʒ] *nf* [courroie] halter.

longer [lɔ̃ʒe] *vt* [border] to go along ou alongside. || [marcher le long de] to walk along; [raser] to stay close to, to hug.

longévité [lɔ̃ʒevite] *nf* longevity.

longiligne [lɔ̃ʒiliɲ] *adj* long-limbed.

longitude [lɔ̃ʒityd] *nf* longitude.

longtemps [lɔ̃tɑ̃] *adv* (for) a long time; **depuis ~** (for) a long time; **il y a ~ qu'il est là** he's been here a long time; **mettre ~ à faire qqch** to take a long time to do sthg.

longue → long.

longuement [lɔ̃gmɑ̃] *adv* [longtemps] for a long time. || [en détail] at length.

longueur [lɔ̃gœr] *nf* length; **faire 5 mètres de ~** to be 5 metres long; **à ~ de journée/temps** the entire day/time. **O longueurs** *nfpl* [de film, de livre] boring parts.

longue-vue [lɔ̃gvy] *nf* telescope.

look [luk] *nm* look.

looping [lupiŋ] *nm* loop the loop.

lopin [lɔpɛ̃] *nm*: ~ **(de terre)** patch ou plot of land.

loquace [lɔkas] *adj* loquacious.

loque [lɔk] *nf* [lambeau] rag. || *fig* [personne] wreck.

loquet [lɔkɛ] *nm* latch.

lorgner [lɔrɲe] *vt fam* [observer] to eye. || [guigner] to have one's eye on.

lors [lɔr] *adv*: **depuis ~** since that time; ~ **de** at the time of.

lorsque [lɔrsk(ə)] *conj* when.

losange [lɔzɑ̃ʒ] *nm* lozenge.

lot [lo] *nm* [part] share; [de terre] plot. || [stock] batch. || [prix] prize. || *fig* [destin] fate, lot.

loterie [lɔtri] *nf* lottery.

loti, -e [lɔti] *adj*: **être bien/mal ~** to be well/badly off.

lotion [losjɔ̃] *nf* lotion.

lotir [lɔtir] *vt* to divide up.

lotissement [lɔtismɑ̃] *nm* [terrain] plot.

loto [lɔto] *nm* [jeu de société] lotto. || [loterie] *popular national lottery*.

lotte [lɔt] *nf* monkfish.

lotus [lɔtys] *nm* lotus.

louange [lwɑ̃ʒ] *nf* praise.

louche[1] [luʃ] *nf* ladle.

louche² [luʃ] *adj fam* [personne, histoire] suspicious.

loucher [luʃe] *vi* [être atteint de strabisme] to squint. || *fam fig* [lorgner]: ~ **sur** to have one's eye on.

louer [lwe] *vt* [glorifier] to praise. || [donner en location] to rent (out); **à** ~ for rent. || [prendre en location] to rent. || [réserver] to book. ○ **se louer** *vp sout* [se féliciter]: **se** ~ **de qqch/de faire qqch** to be very pleased about sthg/about doing sthg.

loufoque [lufɔk] *fam adj* nuts, crazy.

loup [lu] *nm* [carnassier] wolf. || [poisson] bass. || [masque] mask.

loupe [lup] *nf* [optique] magnifying glass.

louper [lupe] *vt fam* [travail] to make a mess of; [train] to miss.

loup-garou [lugaru] (*pl* **loups-garous**) *nm* werewolf.

lourd, -e [lur, lurd] *adj* [gén] heavy; ~ **de** *fig* full of. || [tâche] difficult; [faute] serious. || MÉTÉOR close. ○ **lourd** *adv*: **peser** ~ to be heavy, to weigh a lot; **il n'en fait pas** ~ *fam* he doesn't do much.

loutre [lutr] *nf* otter.

louve [luv] *nf* she-wolf.

louveteau, -x [luvto] *nm* ZOOL wolf cub. || [scout] cub.

louvoyer [luvwaje] *vi* NAVIG to tack. || *fig* [tergiverser] to beat about the bush.

Louvre [luvr] *n*: **le** ~ **the** Louvre (museum).

lover [lɔve] ○ **se lover** *vp* [serpent] to coil up.

loyal, -e, -aux [lwajal, o] *adj* [fidèle] loyal. || [honnête] fair.

loyauté [lwajote] *nf* [fidélité] loyalty. || [honnêteté] fairness.

loyer [lwaje] *nm* rent.

LP (*abr de* **lycée professionnel**) *nm* secondary school for vocational training.

lu, -e [ly] *pp* → **lire**.

lubie [lybi] *nf fam* whim.

lubrifier [lybrifje] *vt* to lubricate.

lubrique [lybrik] *adj* lewd.

lucarne [lykarn] *nf* [fenêtre] skylight. || FOOTBALL top corner of the net.

lucide [lysid] *adj* lucid.

lucidité [lysidite] *nf* lucidity.

lucratif, -ive [lykratif, iv] *adj* lucrative.

ludique [lydik] *adj* play (*avant n*).

ludothèque [lydɔtɛk] *nf* toy library.

lueur [lɥœr] *nf* [de bougie, d'étoile] light; **à la** ~ **de** by the light of. || *fig* [de colère]

gleam; [de raison] spark; ~ **d'espoir** glimmer of hope.

luge [lyʒ] *nf* toboggan.

lugubre [lygybr] *adj* lugubrious.

lui¹ [lɥi] *pp inv* → **luire**.

lui² [lɥi] *pron pers* [complément d'objet indirect - homme] (to) him; [- femme] (to) her; [- animal, chose] (to) it; **je** ~ **ai parlé** I've spoken to him/to her; **il** ~ **a serré la main** he shook his/her hand. || [sujet, en renforcement de «il»] he. || [objet, après préposition, comparatif - personne] him; [- animal, chose] it; **elle est plus jeune que** ~ she's younger than him ou than he is. || [remplaçant «soi» en fonction de pronom réfléchi - personne] himself; [- animal, chose] itself; **il est content de** ~ he's pleased with himself. ○ **lui-même** *pron pers* [personne] himself; [animal, chose] itself.

luire [lɥir] *vi* [soleil, métal] to shine; *fig* [espoir] to glow, to glimmer.

luisant, -e [lɥizɑ̃, ɑ̃t] *adj* gleaming.

lumière [lymjɛr] *nf* [éclairage & *fig*] light.

lumineux, -euse [lyminø, øz] *adj* [couleur, cadran] luminous. || *fig* [visage] radiant; [idée] brilliant. || [explication] clear.

luminosité [lyminozite] *nf* [du regard, ciel] radiance. || PHYS & SCIENCE luminosity.

lump [lœp] *nm*: **œufs de** ~ lumpfish roe.

lunaire [lynɛr] *adj* ASTRON lunar. || *fig* [visage] moon (*avant n*); [paysage] lunar.

lunatique [lynatik] *adj* temperamental.

lunch [lœ̃ʃ] *nm* buffet lunch.

lundi [lœ̃di] *nm* Monday; *voir aussi* **samedi**.

lune [lyn] *nf* ASTRON moon; **pleine** ~ full moon; ~ **de miel** *fig* honeymoon.

lunette [lynɛt] *nf* ASTRON telescope. ○ **lunettes** *nfpl* glasses; ~**s de soleil** sunglasses.

lurette [lyrɛt] *nf*: **il y a belle** ~ **que** ... *fam* it's been ages since ....

lustre [lystr] *nm* [luminaire] chandelier. || [éclat] sheen, shine; *fig* reputation.

lustrer [lystre] *vt* [faire briller] to make shine. || [user] to wear.

luth [lyt] *nm* lute.

lutte [lyt] *nf* [combat] fight, struggle; **la** ~ **des classes** the class struggle. || SPORT wrestling.

lutter [lyte] *vi* to fight, to struggle; ~ **contre** to fight (against).

lutteur, -euse [lytœr, øz] *nm, f* SPORT wrestler; *fig* fighter.

luxation [lyksasjɔ̃] *nf* dislocation.

luxe [lyks] *nm* luxury; **de ~** luxury.

Luxembourg [lyksɑ̃bur] *nm* [pays]: **le ~** Luxembourg.

luxueux, -euse [lyksɥø, øz] *adj* luxurious.

luzerne [lyzɛrn] *nf* lucerne, alfalfa.

lycée [lise] *nm* ≃ high school *Am*; **~ technique/professionnel** ≃ technical/ training college.

lycéen, -enne [liseɛ̃, ɛn] *nm, f* high school pupil *Am*.

lymphatique [lɛ̃fatik] *adj* MÉD lymphatic. || *fig* [apathique] sluggish.

lyncher [lɛ̃ʃe] *vt* to lynch.

lynx [lɛ̃ks] *nm* lynx.

Lyon [ljɔ̃] *n* Lyons.

lyre [lir] *nf* lyre.

lyrique [lirik] *adj* [poésie & *fig*] lyrical; [drame, chanteur, poète] lyric.

lys = lis.

m, M [ɛm] 1 *nm inv* m, M. 2 (*abr de* mètre) m. ○ **M** (*abr de* **Monsieur**) Mr. || (*abr de* **million**) M.

ma → mon.

macabre [makabr] *adj* macabre.

macadam [makadam] *nm* [revêtement] macadam; [route] road.

macaron [makarɔ̃] *nm* [pâtisserie] macaroon. || [autocollant] sticker.

macaronis [makarɔni] *nmpl* CULIN macaroni (*U*).

macédoine [masedwan] *nf* CULIN: **~ de fruits** fruit salad.

macérer [masere] 1 *vt* to steep. 2 *vi* [mariner] to steep; **faire ~** to steep. || *fig & péj* [personne] to wallow.

mâche [maʃ] *nf* lamb's lettuce.

mâcher [maʃe] *vt* [mastiquer] to chew.

machiavélique [makjavelik] *adj* Machiavellian.

machin [maʃɛ̃] *nm* [chose] thing, thingamajig.

Machin, -e [maʃɛ̃, in] *nm, f fam* what's his name (*f* what's her name).

machinal, -e, -aux [maʃinal, o] *adj* mechanical.

machination [maʃinasjɔ̃] *nf* machination.

machine [maʃin] *nf* TECHNOL machine; **~ à coudre** sewing machine; **~ à écrire** typewriter; **~ à laver** washing machine. || NAVIG engine.

machine-outil [maʃinuti] *nf* machine tool.

machiniste [maʃinist] *nm* CIN & THÉÂTRE scene shifter. || TRANSPORT driver.

macho [matʃo] *péj nm* macho man.

mâchoire [maʃwar] *nf* jaw.

mâchonner [maʃɔne] *vt* [mâcher, mordiller] to chew.

maçon [masɔ̃] *nm* mason.

maçonnerie [masɔnri] *nf* [travaux] building; [construction] masonry; [franc-maçonnerie] freemasonry.

macramé [makrame] *nm* macramé.

maculer [makyle] *vt* to stain.

madame [madam] (*pl* **mesdames** [medam]) *nf* [titre]: **~ X** Mrs X; **bonjour ~!** good morning!; [dans hôtel, restaurant] good morning, madam!; **bonjour mesdames!** good morning (ladies)!; **Madame le Ministre n'est pas là** the Minister is out.

mademoiselle [madmwazɛl] (*pl* **mesdemoiselles** [medmwazɛl]) *nf* [titre]: **~ X** Miss X; **bonjour ~!** good morning!; [à l'école, dans hôtel] good morning, miss!; **bonjour mesdemoiselles!** good morning (ladies)!

madone [madɔn] *nf* ART & RELIC Madonna.

Madrid [madrid] *n* Madrid.

madrier [madrije] *nm* beam.

maf(f)ia [mafja] *nf* Mafia.

magasin [magazɛ̃] *nm* [boutique] store *Am*; **grand ~** department store; **faire les ~s** *fig* to go round the shops *Br* ou stores *Am*. || [d'arme, d'appareil photo] magazine.

magazine [magazin] *nm* magazine.

mage [maʒ] *nm*: **les trois Rois ~s** the Three Wise Men.

maghrébin, -e [magrebɛ̃, in] *adj* North African. ○ **Maghrébin, -e** *nm, f* North African.

magicien, -ienne [maʒisjɛ̃, jɛn] *nm, f* magician.

magie [maʒi] *nf* magic.

magique [maʒik] *adj* [occulte] magic. ||
[merveilleux] magical.

magistral, -e, -aux [maʒistral, o] *adj*
[œuvre, habileté] masterly. || [dispute, fessée] enormous. || [attitude, ton] authoritative.

magistrat [maʒistra] *nm* magistrate.

magistrature [maʒistratyr] *nf* magistracy, magistrature.

magma [magma] *nm* GÉOL magma. || *fig*
[mélange] muddle.

magnanime [maɲanim] *adj* magnanimous.

magnat [maɲa] *nm* magnate, tycoon.

magnésium [maɲezjɔm] *nm* magnesium.

magnétique [maɲetik] *adj* magnetic.

magnétisme [maɲetism] *nm* [PHYS &
fascination] magnetism.

magnéto(phone) [maɲeto(fɔn)] *nm*
tape recorder.

magnétoscope [maɲetoskɔp] *nm*
videorecorder.

magnifique [maɲifik] *adj* magnificent.

magnum [magnɔm] *nm* magnum.

magot [mago] *nm fam* tidy sum, packet.

mai [mɛ] *nm* May; **le premier ~** May
Day; *voir aussi* **septembre**.

maigre [mɛgr] *adj* [très mince] thin. ||
[aliment] low-fat; [viande] lean. || [peu
important] meagre; [végétation] sparse.

maigreur [mɛgrœr] *nf* thinness.

maigrir [mɛgrir] *vi* to lose weight.

maille [maj] *nf* [de tricot] stitch. || [de
filet] mesh.

maillet [majɛ] *nm* mallet.

maillon [majɔ̃] *nm* link.

maillot [majo] *nm* [de sport] shirt, jersey; **~ de bain** swimsuit; **~ de corps** vest
Br, undershirt *Am*.

main [mɛ̃] *nf* hand; **à la ~** by hand; **attaque à ~ armée** armed attack; **donner
la ~ à qqn** to take sb's hand; **haut les ~s!**
hands up!

main-d'œuvre [mɛ̃dœvr] *nf* labour,
workforce.

mainmise [mɛ̃miz] *nf* seizure.

maint, -e [mɛ̃, mɛ̃t] *adj littéraire* many
a; **~s** many; **~es fois** time and time again.

maintenance [mɛ̃tnɑ̃s] *nf* maintenance.

maintenant [mɛ̃tnɑ̃] *adv* now.
○ **maintenant que** *loc prép* now that.

maintenir [mɛ̃tnir] *vt* [soutenir] to support; **~ qqn à distance** to keep sb away. ||
[garder, conserver] to maintain. || [affirmer]: **~ que** to maintain (that). ○ **se**

maintenir *vp* [durer] to last. || [rester]
to remain.

maintenu, -e [mɛ̃tny] *pp* → **maintenir**.

maintien [mɛ̃tjɛ̃] *nm* [conservation]
maintenance; [de tradition] upholding. ||
[tenue] posture.

maire [mɛr] *nm* mayor.

mairie [meri] *nf* [bâtiment] city hall *Am*.
|| [administration] city hall *Am*.

mais [mɛ] **1** *conj* but; **~ non!** of course
not! **2** *adv* but; **vous êtes prêts? - ~ bien
sûr!** are you ready? - but of course! **3**
nm: **il n'y a pas de ~** (there are) no buts.

maïs [mais] *nm* maize *Br*, corn *Am*.

maison [mɛzɔ̃] *nf* [habitation, lignée &
ASTROL] house; **~ individuelle** detached
house. || [foyer] home; [famille] family; **à
la ~** [au domicile] at home. || COMM company. || [institut]: **~ d'arrêt** prison; **~ de
la culture** arts centre; **~ de retraite** old
people's home. || (*en apposition*) [artisanal] homemade; [dans restaurant - vin]
house (*avant n*).

Maison-Blanche [mɛzɔ̃blɑ̃ʃ] *nf*: **la ~**
the White House.

maisonnée [mɛzɔne] *nf* household.

maisonnette [mɛzɔnɛt] *nf* small house.

maître, -esse [mɛtr, mɛtrɛs] *nm, f* [professeur] teacher; **~ d'école** schoolteacher;
~ nageur swimming instructor. || [modèle, artiste & *fig*] master. || [dirigeant]
ruler; [d'animal] master (*f* mistress) ; **~
d'hôtel** head waiter; **être ~ de soi** to be in
control of oneself, to have self-control. ||
(*en apposition*) [principal] main, principal. ○ **maîtresse** *nf* mistress.

maître-assistant, -e [mɛtrasistɑ̃, ɑ̃t]
nm, f ≃ assistant professor *Am*.

maîtresse → **maître**.

maîtrise [mɛtriz] *nf* [sang-froid, domination] control. || [connaissance] mastery,
command. || UNIV ≃ master's degree.

maîtriser [mɛtrize] *vt* [animal, forcené]
to subdue. || [émotion, réaction] to control, to master. || [incendie] to bring under control. ○ **se maîtriser** *vp* to control o.s.

majesté [maʒeste] *nf* majesty. ○ **Majesté** *nf*: **Sa Majesté** His/Her Majesty.

majestueux, -euse [maʒestɥø, øz] *adj*
majestic.

majeur, -e [maʒœr] *adj* [gén] major. ||
[personne] of age. ○ **majeur** *nm* middle
finger.

major [maʒɔr] *nm* MIL ≃ adjutant.

majordome [maʒɔrdɔm] *nm* majordomo.

majorer [maʒɔre] *vt* to increase.

majorette [maʒɔrɛt] *nf* majorette.

majoritaire [maʒɔritɛr] *adj* majority (*avant n*); **être ~** to be in the majority.

majorité [maʒɔrite] *nf* majority; **en (grande) ~** in the majority; **~ absolue/relative** POLIT absolute/relative majority.

majuscule [maʒyskyl] **1** *nf* capital (letter). **2** *adj* capital (*avant n*).

mal, maux [mal, mo] *nm* [ce qui est contraire à la morale] evil. ‖ [souffrance physique] pain; **avoir ~ au cœur** to feel sick; **avoir ~ au dos** to have backache; **avoir ~ à la gorge** to have a sore throat; **avoir le ~ de mer** to be seasick; **avoir ~ aux dents/à la tête** to have toothache/a headache; **faire ~ à qqn** to hurt sb; **ça fait ~** it hurts; **se faire ~** to hurt o.s. ‖ [difficulté] difficulty. ‖ [douleur morale] pain, suffering (*U*); **faire du ~ (à qqn)** to hurt (sb). ○ **mal** *adv* [malade] ill; **aller ~** not to be well; **se sentir ~** to feel ill. ‖ [respirer] with difficulty. ‖ [informé, se conduire] badly; **~ prendre qqch** to take sthg badly; **~ tourner** to go wrong. ‖ *loc*: **pas ~** not bad (*adj*), not badly (*adv*); **pas ~ de** quite a lot of.

malade [malad] **1** *nmf* invalid, sick person; **~ mental** mentally ill person. **2** *adj* [souffrant - personne] ill, sick; [- organe] bad; **tomber ~** to fall ill ou sick. ‖ *fam* [fou] crazy.

maladie [maladi] *nf* MÉD illness. ‖ [passion, manie] mania.

maladresse [maladrɛs] *nf* [inhabileté] clumsiness. ‖ [bévue] blunder.

maladroit, -e [maladrwa, at] *adj* clumsy.

malaise [malɛz] *nm* [indisposition] discomfort. ‖ [trouble] unease (*U*).

Malaisie [malɛzi] *nf*: **la ~** Malaya.

malaria [malarja] *nf* malaria.

malaxer [malakse] *vt* to knead.

malchance [malʃɑ̃s] *nf* bad luck (*U*).

malchanceux, -euse [malʃɑ̃sø, øz] **1** *adj* unlucky. **2** *nm, f* unlucky person.

mâle [mal] **1** *adj* [enfant, animal, hormone] male. ‖ [voix, assurance] manly. ‖ ÉLECTR male. **2** *nm* male.

malédiction [malediksjɔ̃] *nf* curse.

maléfique [malefik] *adj sout* evil.

malencontreux, -euse [malɑ̃kɔ̃trø, øz] *adj* [hasard, rencontre] unfortunate.

malentendant, -e [malɑ̃tɑ̃dɑ̃, ɑ̃t] *nm, f* person who is hard of hearing.

malentendu [malɑ̃tɑ̃dy] *nm* misunderstanding.

malfaçon [malfasɔ̃] *nf* defect.

malfaiteur [malfɛtœr] *nm* criminal.

malfamé, -e, mal famé, -e [malfame] *adj* disreputable.

malformation [malfɔrmasjɔ̃] *nf* malformation.

malfrat [malfra] *nm fam* crook.

malgré [malgre] *prép* in spite of; **~ tout** [quoi qu'il arrive] in spite of everything; [pourtant] even so, yet.

malhabile [malabil] *adj* clumsy.

malheur [malœr] *nm* misfortune; **par ~** unfortunately; **porter ~ à qqn** to bring sb bad luck.

malheureusement [malœrøzmɑ̃] *adv* unfortunately.

malheureux, -euse [malœrø, øz] **1** *adj* [triste] unhappy. ‖ [désastreux, regrettable] unfortunate. ‖ [malchanceux] unlucky. ‖ (*avant n*) [sans valeur] pathetic, miserable. **2** *nm, f* [infortuné] poor soul.

malhonnête [malɔnɛt] **1** *nmf* dishonest person. **2** *adj* [personne, affaire] dishonest. ‖ *hum* [proposition, propos] indecent.

malhonnêteté [malɔnɛtte] *nf* [de personne] dishonesty.

malice [malis] *nf* mischief.

malicieux, -ieuse [malisjø, jøz] *adj* mischievous.

malin, -igne [malɛ̃, iɲ] **1** *adj* [rusé] crafty, cunning. ‖ [méchant] malicious, spiteful. ‖ MÉD malignant. **2** *nm, f* cunning ou crafty person.

malingre [malɛ̃gr] *adj* sickly.

malle [mal] *nf* [coffre] trunk; [de voiture] boot *Br*, trunk *Am*.

malléable [maleabl] *adj* malleable.

mallette [malɛt] *nf* briefcase.

mal-logé, -e [malɔʒe] (*mpl* **mal-logés**, *fpl* **mal-logées**) *nm, f* person living in poor accommodation.

malmener [malməne] *vt* [brutaliser] to handle roughly, to ill-treat.

malnutrition [malnytrisjɔ̃] *nf* malnutrition.

malodorant, -e [malɔdɔrɑ̃, ɑ̃t] *adj* smelly.

malotru, -e [malɔtry] *nm, f* lout.

malpoli, -e [malpɔli] *nm, f* rude person.

malpropre [malprɔpr] *adj* [sale] dirty.

malsain, -e [malsɛ̃, ɛn] *adj* unhealthy.

malt [malt] *nm* [whisky] malt (whisky).

maltraiter [maltrete] *vt* to ill-treat; [en paroles] to attack, to run down.

malus [malys] *nm increase in car insur-*

ance charges, due to loss of no-claims bonus.

malveillant, -e [malvɛjɑ̃, ɑ̃t] *adj* spiteful.

malversation [malvɛrsasjɔ̃] *nf* embezzlement.

malvoyant, -e [malvwajɑ̃, ɑ̃t] *nm, f* person who is partially sighted.

maman [mamɑ̃] *nf* mummy.

mamelle [mamɛl] *nf* teat; [de vache] udder.

mamelon [mamlɔ̃] *nm* [du sein] nipple.

mamie, mamy [mami] *nf* granny, grandma.

mammifère [mamifɛr] *nm* mammal.

mammouth [mamut] *nm* mammoth.

mamy = **mamie**.

manager [manadʒɛr] *nm* manager.

manche [mɑ̃ʃ] **1** *nf* [de vêtement] sleeve; ~s courtes/longues short/long sleeves. || [de jeu] round, game; TENNIS set. **2** *nm* [d'outil] handle; ~ à balai broomstick. || MUS neck.

Manche [mɑ̃ʃ] *nf* [mer]: la ~ the English Channel.

manchette [mɑ̃ʃɛt] *nf* [de chemise] cuff. || [de journal] headline.

manchon [mɑ̃ʃɔ̃] *nm* [en fourrure] muff.

manchot, -ote [mɑ̃ʃo, ɔt] **1** *adj* one-armed. **2** *nm, f* one-armed person. ○ **manchot** *nm* penguin.

mandarine [mɑ̃darin] *nf* mandarin (orange).

mandat [mɑ̃da] *nm* [pouvoir, fonction] mandate. || JUR warrant; ~ de perquisition search warrant. || [titre postal] money order.

mandataire [mɑ̃datɛr] *nmf* proxy, representative.

mandibule [mɑ̃dibyl] *nf* mandible.

mandoline [mɑ̃dɔlin] *nf* mandolin.

manège [manɛʒ] *nm* [attraction] carousel *Am*. || [de chevaux - lieu] riding school. || [manœuvre] scheme, game.

manette [manɛt] *nf* lever.

mangeable [mɑ̃ʒabl] *adj* edible.

mangeoire [mɑ̃ʒwar] *nf* manger.

manger [mɑ̃ʒe] **1** *vt* [nourriture] to eat. || [fortune] to get through, to squander. **2** *vi* to eat.

mangue [mɑ̃g] *nf* mango.

maniable [manjabl] *adj* [instrument] manageable.

maniaque [manjak] **1** *nmf* [méticuleux] fusspot. || [fou] maniac. **2** *adj* [méticuleux] fussy. || [fou] maniacal.

manie [mani] *nf* [habitude] funny habit; avoir la ~ de qqch/de faire qqch to have a mania for sthg/for doing sthg. || [obsession] mania.

maniement [manimɑ̃] *nm* handling.

manier [manje] *vt* [manipuler, utiliser] to handle; *fig* [ironie, mots] to handle skilfully.

manière [manjɛr] *nf* [méthode] manner, way; de toute ~ at any rate; d'une ~ générale generally speaking. ○ **manières** *nfpl* manners. ○ **de manière à (ce que)** *loc conj* (+ *subjonctif*) so that. ○ **de manière que** *loc conj* (+ *subjonctif*) in such a way that.

maniéré, -e [manjere] *adj* affected.

manif [manif] *nf fam* demo.

manifestant, -e [manifɛstɑ̃, ɑ̃t] *nm, f* demonstrator.

manifestation [manifɛstasjɔ̃] *nf* [témoignage] expression. || [mouvement collectif] demonstration. || [apparition - de maladie] appearance.

manifester [manifɛste] **1** *vt* to show, to express. **2** *vi* to demonstrate. ○ **se manifester** *vp* [apparaître] to show or manifest itself. || [se montrer] to turn up, to appear.

manigancer [manigɑ̃se] *vt fam* to plot.

manioc [manjɔk] *nm* manioc.

manipuler [manipyle] *vt* [colis, appareil] to handle. || [statistiques, résultats] to falsify, to rig. || *péj* [personne] to manipulate.

manivelle [manivɛl] *nf* crank.

mannequin [manfkɛ̃] *nm* [forme humaine] dummy. || [personne] model.

manœuvre [manœvr] *nf* [d'appareil, de véhicule] driving, handling. || MIL manœuvre, exercise. || [machination] ploy, scheme. **2** *nm* labourer.

manœuvrer [manœvre] **1** *vi* to manœuvre. **2** *vt* [faire fonctionner] to operate, to work; [voiture] to manœuvre. || [influencer] to manipulate.

manoir [manwar] *nm* manor, country house.

manquant, -e [mɑ̃kɑ̃, ɑ̃t] *adj* missing.

manque [mɑ̃k] *nm* [pénurie] lack, shortage; par ~ de for want of. || [de toxicomane] withdrawal symptoms (*pl*). || [lacune] gap.

manqué, -e [mɑ̃ke] *adj* [raté] failed; [rendez-vous] missed.

manquer [mɑ̃ke] **1** *vi* [faire défaut] to be lacking, to be missing; l'argent/le temps me manque I don't have enough

margelle

money/time; **tu me manques** I miss you. || [être absent]: ~ **(à)** to be absent (from), to be missing (from). || [échouer] to fail. || [ne pas avoir assez]: ~ **de qqch** to lack sthg, to be short of sthg. || [faillir]: **il a manqué de se noyer** he nearly or almost drowned; **je n'y manquerai pas** I certainly will, I'll definitely do it. || [ne pas respecter]: ~ **à** [devoir] to fail in; ~ **à sa parole** to break one's word. **2** *vt* [gén] to miss. || [échouer à] to bungle, to botch. **3** *v impers*: **il manque quelqu'un** somebody is missing; **il me manque 20 francs** I'm 20 francs short.

mansarde [mɑ̃sard] *nf* attic.

mansardé, -e [mɑ̃sarde] *adj* attic (*avant n*).

manteau, -x [mɑ̃to] *nm* [vêtement] coat.

manucure [manykyr] *nmf* manicurist.

manuel, -elle [manɥɛl] *adj* manual. ○ **manuel** *nm* manual.

manufacture [manyfaktyr] *nf* [fabrique] factory.

manuscrit, -e [manyskri, it] *adj* handwritten. ○ **manuscrit** *nm* manuscript.

manutention [manytɑ̃sjɔ̃] *nf* handling.

manutentionnaire [manytɑ̃sjɔnɛr] *nmf* packer.

mappemonde [mapmɔ̃d] *nf* [carte] map of the world. || [sphère] globe.

maquereau, -elle, -x [makro, ɛl, o] *nm, f fam* pimp (*f* madam). ○ **maquereau** *nm* mackerel.

maquette [makɛt] *nf* [ébauche] paste-up. || [modèle réduit] model.

maquillage [makijaʒ] *nm* [action, produits] make-up.

maquiller [makije] *vt* [farder] to make up. || [fausser] to disguise; [- passeport] to falsify; [- chiffres] to doctor. ○ **se maquiller** *vp* to make up, to put on one's make-up.

maquis [maki] *nm* [végétation] scrub, brush. || HIST Maquis.

maraîcher, -ère [mareʃe, ɛr] **1** *adj* truck farming (*avant n*) *Am*. **2** *nm, f* truck farmer *Am*.

marais [marɛ] *nm* [marécage] marsh, swamp; ~ **salant** saltpan.

marasme [marasm] *nm* [récession] stagnation.

marathon [maratɔ̃] *nm* marathon.

marâtre [maratr] *nf* [mauvaise mère] bad mother. || [belle-mère] stepmother.

maraude [marod] *nf*, **maraudage** [marodaʒ] *nm* pilfering.

marbre [marbr] *nm* [roche, objet] marble.

marc [mar] *nm* [eau-de-vie] *spirit distilled from grape residue*. || [de fruits] residue; [de thé] leaves; ~ **de café** grounds (*pl*).

marcassin [markasɛ̃] *nm* young wild boar.

marchand, -e [marʃɑ̃, ɑ̃d] **1** *adj* [valeur] market (*avant n*). **2** *nm, f* [commerçant] merchant; [détaillant] storekeeper *Am*; ~ **de journaux** newsagent.

marchander [marʃɑ̃de] *vi* to bargain, to haggle.

marchandise [marʃɑ̃diz] *nf* merchandise (*U*), goods (*pl*).

marche [marʃ] *nf* [d'escalier] step. || [de personne] walking; [promenade] walk; ~ **à pied** walking; ~ **à suivre** *fig* correct procedure. || MUS march. || [déplacement - du temps, d'astre] course; **en ~ arrière** in reverse; **faire ~ arrière** to reverse; *fig* to backpedal, to backtrack. || [fonctionnement] running, working; **en ~** running; **se mettre en ~** to start (up).

marché [marʃe] *nm* [gén] market; ~ **noir** black market; ~ **aux puces** flea market. || [contrat] bargain, deal; **(à) bon ~** cheap. ○ **Marché commun** *nm*: **le Marché commun** the Common Market.

marchepied [marʃəpje] *nm* [de train] step.

marcher [marʃe] *vi* [aller à pied] to walk. || [poser le pied] to step. || [fonctionner, tourner] to work; **son affaire marche bien** his business is doing well. || *fam* [accepter] to agree. || *loc*: **faire ~ qqn** *fam* to take sb for a ride.

mardi [mardi] *nm* Tuesday; ~ **gras** Shrove Tuesday; *voir aussi* **samedi**.

mare [mar] *nf* pool.

marécage [marekaʒ] *nm* marsh, bog.

marécageux, -euse [marekaʒø, øz] *adj* [terrain] marshy, boggy.

maréchal, -aux [mareʃal, o] *nm* marshal.

marée [mare] *nf* [de la mer] tide; **(à) ~ haute/basse** (at) high/low tide. || *fig* [de personnes] wave, surge. ○ **marée noire** *nf* oil slick.

marelle [marɛl] *nf* hopscotch.

margarine [margarin] *nf* margarine.

marge [marʒ] *nf* [espace] margin; **vivre en ~ de la société** *fig* to live on the fringes of society. || [latitude] leeway; ~ **d'erreur** margin of error. || COMM margin.

margelle [marʒɛl] *nf* coping.

marginal, -e, -aux [marʒinal, o] **1** *adj* [gén] marginal. ‖ [groupe] dropout (*avant n*). **2** *nm, f* dropout.

marguerite [margərit] *nf* BOT daisy.

mari [mari] *nm* husband.

mariage [marjaʒ] *nm* [union, institution] marriage; **~ civil/religieux** civil/church wedding. ‖ [cérémonie] wedding. ‖ *fig* [de choses] blend.

Marianne [marjan] *n* personification of the French Republic.

marié, -e [marje] **1** *adj* married. **2** *nm, f* groom, bridegroom (*f* bride).

marier [marje] *vt* [personne] to marry. ‖ *fig* [couleurs] to blend. ○ **se marier** *vp* [personnes] to get married; **se ~ avec qqn** to marry sb. ‖ *fig* [couleurs] to blend.

marihuana [marirwana], **marijuana** [mariʒɥana] *nf* marijuana.

marin, -e [marɛ̃, in] *adj* [de la mer] sea (*avant n*); [faune, biologie] marine. ‖ NAVIG [carte, mille] nautical. ○ **marin** *nm* [matelot] sailor; **~ pêcheur** deep-sea fisherman. ○ **marine 1** *nf* [navires] navy; **~e marchande** merchant navy; **~e nationale** navy. **2** *nm* MIL marine. ‖ [couleur] navy (blue). **3** *adj inv* navy.

mariner [marine] *vi* [aliment] to marinate; **faire ~ qqch** to marinate sthg. ‖ *fam fig* [attendre] to hang around; **faire ~ qqn** to let sb stew.

marionnette [marjɔnɛt] *nf* puppet.

marital, -e, -aux [marital, o] *adj*: **autorisation ~e** husband's permission.

maritime [maritim] *adj* [navigation] maritime; [ville] coastal.

mark [mark] *nm* [monnaie] mark.

marketing [marketiŋ] *nm* marketing; **~ téléphonique** telemarketing.

marmaille [marmaj] *nf fam* brood (of kids).

marmelade [marməlad] *nf* stewed fruit.

marmite [marmit] *nf* [casserole] pot.

marmonner [marmɔne] *vt & vi* to mutter, to mumble.

marmot [marmo] *nm fam* kid.

marmotte [marmɔt] *nf* marmot.

Maroc [marɔk] *nm*: **le ~** Morocco.

marocain, -e [marɔkɛ̃, ɛn] *adj* Moroccan. ○ **Marocain, -e** *nm, f* Moroccan.

maroquinerie [marɔkinri] *nf* [magasin] leather-goods shop *BrO* store *Am*.

marotte [marɔt] *nf* [dada] craze.

marquant, -e [markɑ̃, ɑ̃t] *adj* outstanding.

marque [mark] *nf* [signe, trace] mark; *fig* stamp, mark. ‖ [label, fabricant]

make, brand; **de ~** designer (*avant n*); *fig* important; **~ déposée** registered trademark. ‖ SPORT score; **à vos ~s, prêts, partez!** on your marks, get set, go! ‖ [témoignage] sign, token.

marqué, -e [marke] *adj* [net] marked, pronounced. ‖ [personne, visage] marked.

marquer [marke] **1** *vt* [gén] to mark. ‖ *fam* [écrire] to write down, to note down. ‖ [indiquer, manifester] to show. ‖ [SPORT - but, point] to score; [- joueur] to mark. **2** *vi* SPORT to score.

marqueur [markœr] *nm* [crayon] marker (pen).

marquis, -e [marki, iz] *nm, f* marquis (*f* marchioness).

marraine [marɛn] *nf* [de filleul] godmother. ‖ [de navire] christener.

marrant, -e [marɑ̃, ɑ̃t] *adj fam* funny.

marre [mar] *adv*: **en avoir ~ (de)** *fam* to be fed up (with).

marrer [mare] ○ **se marrer** *vp fam* to split one's sides.

marron, -onne [marɔ̃, ɔn] *adj péj* [médecin] quack (*avant n*); [avocat] crooked. ○ **marron 1** *nm* [fruit] chestnut. ‖ [couleur] brown. **2** *adj inv* brown.

marronnier [marɔnje] *nm* chestnut tree.

mars [mars] *nm* March; *voir aussi* **septembre**.

Marseille [marsɛj] *n* Marseilles.

marteau, -x [marto] *nm* [gén] hammer; **~ piqueur, ~ pneumatique** pneumatic drill. ‖ [heurtoir] knocker. ○ **marteau** *adj fam* barmy.

marteler [martəle] *vt* [pieu] to hammer; [table, porte] to hammer on, to pound. ‖ [phrase] to rap out.

martial, -e, -iaux [marsjal, jo] *adj* martial.

martinet [martinɛ] *nm* ZOOL swift. ‖ [fouet] whip.

martingale [martɛ̃gal] *nf* [de vêtement] half-belt. ‖ JEU winning system.

martini [martini] *nm* martini.

martyr, -e [martir] **1** *adj* martyred. **2** *nm, f* martyr. ○ **martyre** *nm* martyrdom.

martyriser [martirize] *vt* to torment.

marxisme [marksism] *nm* Marxism.

mascarade [maskarad] *nf* [mise en scène] masquerade.

mascotte [maskɔt] *nf* mascot.

masculin, -e [maskylɛ̃, in] *adj* [apparence & GRAM] masculine; [métier, popula-

mausolée

tion, sexe] male. ○ **masculin** *nm* GRAM masculine.

maso [mazo] *fam* **1** *nm* masochist. **2** *adj* masochistic.

masochisme [mazɔʃism] *nm* masochism.

masque [mask] *nm* [gén] mask; ~ à gaz gas mask. ‖ *fig* [façade] front, façade.

masquer [maske] *vt* [vérité, crime, problème] to conceal. ‖ [maison, visage] to conceal, to hide.

massacre [masakr] *nm* *litt* & *fig* massacre.

massacrer [masakre] *vt* to massacre.

massage [masaʒ] *nm* massage.

masse [mas] *nf* [de pierre] block; [d'eau] volume. ‖ [grande quantité]: **une ~ de masses** (*pl*) OU **loads** (*pl*) of. ‖ PHYS mass. ‖ ÉLECTR earth *Br*, ground *Am*. ‖ [maillet] sledgehammer. ○ **en masse** *loc adv* [venir] en masse, all together.

masser [mase] *vt* [assembler] to assemble. ‖ [frotter] to massage. ○ **se masser** *vp* [s'assembler] to assemble, to gather. ‖ [se frotter]: **se ~ le bras** to massage one's arm.

masseur, -euse [masœr, øz] *nm, f* [personne] masseur (*f* masseuse).

massif, -ive [masif, iv] *adj* [monument, personne, dose] massive. ‖ [or, chêne] solid. ○ **massif** *nm* [de plantes] clump. ‖ [de montagnes] massif.

massue [masy] *nf* club.

mastic [mastik] *nm* mastic, putty.

mastiquer [mastike] *vt* [mâcher] to chew.

masturber [mastyrbe] ○ **se masturber** *vp* to masturbate.

masure [mazyr] *nf* hovel.

mat, -e [mat] *adj* [peinture, surface] matt. ‖ [peau, personne] dusky. ‖ [bruit, son] dull. ‖ [aux échecs] checkmated. ○ **mat** *nm* checkmate.

mât [ma] *nm* NAVIG mast. ‖ [poteau] pole, post.

match [matʃ] (*pl* **matches** OU **matchs**) *nm* match; (faire) ~ **nul** (to) draw.

matelas [matla] *nm inv* [de lit] mattress; ~ **pneumatique** airbed.

matelot [matlo] *nm* sailor.

mater [mate] *vt* [soumettre, neutraliser] to subdue. ‖ *fam* [regarder] to eye up.

matérialiser [materjalize] ○ **se matérialiser** *vp* [aspirations] to be realized.

matérialiste [materjalist] **1** *nmf* materialist. **2** *adj* materialistic.

matériau, -x [materjo] *nm* material. ○ **matériaux** *nmpl* CONSTR material (*U*), materials.

matériel, -ielle [materjɛl] *adj* [être, substance] material, physical; [confort, avantage, aide] material. ‖ [considération] practical. ○ **matériel** *nm* [gén] equipment (*U*). ‖ INFORM hardware (*U*).

maternel, -elle [matɛrnɛl] *adj* maternal; [langue] mother (*avant n*). ○ **maternelle** *nf* nursery school.

maternité [matɛrnite] *nf* [qualité] maternity, motherhood. ‖ [hôpital] maternity hospital.

mathématicien, -ienne [matematisjɛ̃, jɛn] *nm, f* mathematician.

mathématique [matematik] *adj* mathematical. ○ **mathématiques** *nfpl* mathematics (*U*).

maths [mat] *nfpl fam* math *Am*.

matière [matjɛr] *nf* [substance] matter; ~s **grasses** fats. ‖ [matériau] material; ~s **premières** raw materials. ‖ [discipline, sujet] subject; **en ~ de sport/littérature** as far as sport/literature is concerned.

matin [matɛ̃] *nm* morning; **le ~** in the morning; **ce ~** this morning; **à trois heures du ~** at 3 o'clock in the morning.

matinal, -e, -aux [matinal, o] *adj* [gymnastique, émission] morning (*avant n*). ‖ [personne]: **être ~** to be an early riser.

matinée [matine] *nf* [matin] morning; **faire la grasse ~** *fig* to have a lie in. ‖ [spectacle] matinée, afternoon performance.

matraque [matrak] *nf* truncheon.

matraquer [matrake] *vt* [frapper] to beat, to club.

matrice [matris] *nf* [moule] mould. ‖ MATHS matrix. ‖ ANAT womb.

matricule [matrikyl] *nm*: (**numéro**) ~ number.

matrimonial, -e, -iaux [matrimɔnjal, jo] *adj* matrimonial.

matrone [matron] *nf* *péj* old bag.

mature [matyr] *adj* mature.

mâture [matyr] *nf* masts (*pl*).

maturité [matyrite] *nf* maturity; [de fruit] ripeness.

maudire [modir] *vt* to curse.

maudit, -e [modi, it] **1** *pp* → **maudire**. **2** *adj* [réprouvé] accursed. ‖ (*avant n*) [exécrable] damned.

maugréer [mogree] **1** *vt* to mutter. **2** *vi*: ~ (**contre**) to grumble (about).

mausolée [mozɔle] *nm* mausoleum.

maussade [mosad] *adj* [personne, air] sullen. || [temps] gloomy.

mauvais, -e [move, ɛz] *adj* [gén] bad. || [moment, numéro, réponse] wrong. || [mer] rough. || [personne, regard] nasty. ○ **mauvais** *adv*: **il fait ~** the weather is bad; **sentir ~** to smell bad.

mauve [mov] *nm & adj* mauve.

maux → **mal.**

max [maks] (*abr de* **maximum**) *nm fam*: **un ~ de fric** loads of money.

max. (*abr de* **maximum**) max.

maxillaire [maksiler] *nm* jawbone.

maxime [maksim] *nf* maxim.

maximum [maksimɔm] (*pl* **maxima** [maksima]) **1** *nm* maximum; **le ~ de personnes** the greatest (possible) number of people; **au ~** at the most. **2** *adj* maximum.

mayonnaise [majɔnɛz] *nf* mayonnaise.

mazout [mazut] *nm* fuel oil.

me [mə], **m'** (*devant voyelle ou h muet*) *pron pers* [complément d'objet direct] me. || [complément d'objet indirect] (to) me. || [réfléchi] myself. || [avec un présentatif]: **~ voici** here I am.

méandre [meɑ̃dr] *nm* [de rivière] meander, bend.

mec [mɛk] *nm fam* guy, bloke.

mécanicien, -ienne [mekanisjɛ̃, jɛn] *nm, f* [de garage] mechanic. || [conducteur de train] train driver *Br*, engineer *Am*.

mécanique [mekanik] **1** *nf* TECHNOL mechanical engineering. || [mécanisme] mechanism. **2** *adj* mechanical.

mécanisme [mekanism] *nm* mechanism.

mécène [mesɛn] *nm* patron.

méchamment [meʃamɑ̃] *adv* [cruellement] nastily.

méchanceté [meʃɑ̃ste] *nf* [attitude] nastiness. || *fam* [rosserie] nasty thing.

méchant, -e [meʃɑ̃, ɑ̃t] *adj* [malveillant, cruel] nasty, wicked; [animal] vicious. || [désobéissant] naughty.

mèche [mɛʃ] *nf* [de bougie] wick. || [de cheveux] lock. || [de bombe] fuse.

méchoui [meʃwi] *nm whole roast sheep.*

méconnaissable [mekɔnɛsabl] *adj* unrecognizable.

méconnu, -e [mekɔny] *adj* unrecognized.

mécontent, -e [mekɔ̃tɑ̃, ɑ̃t] **1** *adj* unhappy. **2** *nm, f* malcontent.

mécontenter [mekɔ̃tɑ̃te] *vt* to displease.

Mecque [mɛk] *n*: **La ~** Mecca.

mécréant, -e [mekreɑ̃, ɑ̃t] *nm, f* nonbeliever.

médaille [medaj] *nf* [pièce, décoration] medal. || [bijou] medallion. || [de chien] identification disc, tag.

médaillon [medajɔ̃] *nm* [bijou] locket. || ART & CULIN medallion.

médecin [medsɛ̃] *nm* doctor; **~ de famille** family doctor, GP *Br*; **~ de garde** doctor on duty, duty doctor; **~ légiste** forensic scientist *Br*, medical examiner *Am*; **~ traitant** consulting physician.

médecine [medsin] *nf* medicine.

média [medja] *nm*: **les ~s** the (mass) media.

médian, -e [medjɑ̃, an] *adj* median. ○ **médiane** *nf* median.

médiateur, -trice [medjatœr, tris] *nm, f* mediator; [dans conflit de travail] arbitrator. ○ **médiateur** *nm* ADMIN ombudsman. ○ **médiatrice** *nf* median.

médiathèque [medjatɛk] *nf* media library.

médiatique [medjatik] *adj* media (*avant n*).

médical, -e, -aux [medikal, o] *adj* medical.

médicament [medikamɑ̃] *nm* medicine, drug.

médicinal, -e, -aux [medisinal, o] *adj* medicinal.

médiéval, -e, -aux [medjeval, o] *adj* medieval.

médiocre [medjɔkr] *adj* mediocre.

médiocrité [medjɔkrite] *nf* mediocrity.

médire [medir] *vi* to gossip; **~ de qqn** to speak ill of sb.

médisant, -e [medizɑ̃, ɑ̃t] *adj* slanderous.

méditation [meditasjɔ̃] *nf* meditation.

méditer [medite] **1** *vt* [projeter] to plan; **~ de faire qqch** to plan to do sthg. **2** *vi*: **~ (sur)** to meditate (on).

Méditerranée [mediterane] *nf*: **la ~** the Mediterranean (Sea).

méditerranéen, -enne [mediteraneɛ̃, ɛn] *adj* Mediterranean. ○ **Méditerranéen, -enne** *nm, f* person from the Mediterranean.

médium [medjɔm] *nm* [personne] medium.

médius [medjys] *nm* middle finger.

méduse [medyz] *nf* jellyfish.

méduser [medyze] *vt* to dumbfound.

meeting [mitiŋ] *nm* meeting.

méfait [mefɛ] *nm* misdemeanour, misdeed. ○ **méfaits** *nmpl* [du temps] ravages.

méfiance [mefjɑ̃s] *nf* suspicion, distrust.

méfiant, -e [mefjɑ̃, ɑ̃t] *adj* suspicious, distrustful.

méfier [mefje] ○ **se méfier** *vp* to be wary ou careful; **se ~ de qqn/qqch** to distrust sb/sthg.

mégalo [megalo] *nmf & adj fam* megalomaniac.

mégalomane [megalɔman] *nmf & adj* megalomaniac.

mégalomanie [megalɔmani] *nf* megalomania.

mega-octet [megaɔktɛ] *nm* megabyte.

mégapole [megapɔl] *nf* megalopolis, megacity.

mégarde [megard] ○ **par mégarde** *loc adv* by mistake.

mégère [meʒɛr] *nf péj* shrew.

mégot [mego] *nm fam* butt *Am*.

meilleur, -e [mɛjœr] **1** *adj* (*compar*) better; (*superl*) best. **2** *nm, f* best. ○ **meilleur** *adv* better.

mélancolie [melɑ̃kɔli] *nf* melancholy.

mélancolique [melɑ̃kɔlik] *adj* melancholy.

mélange [melɑ̃ʒ] *nm* [action] mixing. || [mixture] mixture.

mélanger [melɑ̃ʒe] *vt* [mettre ensemble] to mix. || [déranger] to mix up, to muddle up. ○ **se mélanger** *vp* [se mêler] to mix. || [se brouiller] to get mixed up.

mêlée [mele] *nf* RUGBY scrum.

mêler [mele] *vt* [mélanger] to mix. || [déranger] to muddle up, to mix up. || [impliquer]: **~ qqn à qqch** to involve sb in sthg. ○ **se mêler** *vp* [se joindre]: **se ~ à** [groupe] to join. || [s'ingérer]: **se ~ de qqch** to get involved in sthg; **mêlez-vous de ce qui vous regarde!** mind your own business!

mélèze [melɛz] *nm* larch.

mélo [melo] *nm fam* melodrama.

mélodie [melɔdi] *nf* melody.

mélodieux, -ieuse [melɔdjø, jøz] *adj* melodious, tuneful.

mélodrame [melɔdram] *nm* melodrama.

mélomane [melɔman] **1** *nmf* music lover. **2** *adj* music-loving.

melon [məlɔ̃] *nm* [fruit] melon. || [chapeau] bowler (hat).

membrane [mɑ̃bran] *nf* membrane.

membre [mɑ̃br] **1** *nm* [du corps] limb. || [personne, pays, partie] member. **2** *adj* member (*avant n*).

mémé = **mémère**.

même [mɛm] **1** *adj indéf* [indique une identité ou une ressemblance] same; **il a le ~ âge que moi** he's the same age as me. || [sert à souligner]: **ce sont ses paroles ~s** those are his very words; **elle est la bonté ~** she's kindness itself. **2** *pron indéf*: **le/la ~** the same one; **ce sont toujours les ~s qui gagnent** it's always the same people who win. **3** *adv* even. ○ **de même** *loc adv* similarly, likewise; **il en va de ~ pour lui** the same goes for him. ○ **de même que** *loc conj* just as. ○ **tout de même** *loc adv* all the same. ○ **à même** *loc prép*: **s'asseoir à ~ le sol** to sit on the bare ground. ○ **à même de** *loc prép*: **être à ~ de faire qqch** to be able to do sthg, to be in a position to do sthg. ○ **même si** *loc conj* even if.

mémento [memɛ̃to] *nm* [agenda] pocket diary.

mémère [memɛr], **mémé** [meme] *nf fam* [grand-mère] granny. || *péj* [vieille femme] old biddy.

mémoire [memwar] **1** *nf* [gén & INFORM] memory; **de ~** from memory; **avoir bonne/mauvaise ~** to have a good/bad memory; **mettre en ~** INFORM to store; **~ vive** INFORM random access memory; **à la ~ de** in memory of. **2** *nm* UNIV dissertation, paper. ○ **mémoires** *nmpl* memoirs.

mémorable [memɔrabl] *adj* memorable.

mémorial, -iaux [memɔrjal, jo] *nm* [monument] memorial.

menaçant, -e [mənasɑ̃, ɑ̃t] *adj* threatening.

menace [mənas] *nf*: **~ (pour)** threat (to).

menacer [mənase] **1** *vt* to threaten; **~ de faire qqch** to threaten to do sthg; **~ qqn de qqch** to threaten sb with sthg. **2** *vi*: **la pluie menace** it looks like rain.

ménage [menaʒ] *nm* [nettoyage] housework (*U*); **faire le ~** to do the housework. || [couple] couple. || ÉCON household.

ménagement [menaʒmɑ̃] *nm* [égards] consideration; **sans ~** brutally.

ménager[1], -ère [menaʒe, ɛr] *adj* household (*avant n*), domestic. ○ **ménagère** *nf* [femme] housewife. || [de couverts] canteen.

ménager² [menaʒe] *vt* [bien traiter] to treat gently. ‖ [économiser - sucre, réserves] to use sparingly; ~ **ses forces** to conserve one's strength. ‖ [pratiquer - espace] to make. ○ **se ménager** *vp* to take care of o.s., to look after o.s.

ménagerie [menaʒri] *nf* menagerie.

mendiant, -e [mɑ̃djɑ̃, ɑ̃t] *nm, f* beggar.

mendier [mɑ̃dje] **1** *vt* [argent] to beg for. **2** *vi* to beg.

mener [məne] **1** *vt* [emmener] to take. ‖ [diriger - débat, enquête] to conduct; [- affaires] to manage, to run; ~ **qqch à bonne fin** ou **à bien** to see sthg through, to bring sthg to a successful conclusion. ‖ [être en tête de] to lead. **2** *vi* to lead.

meneur, -euse [mənœr, øz] *nm, f* [chef] ringleader; ~ **d'hommes** born leader.

menhir [menir] *nm* standing stone.

méningite [menɛ̃ʒit] *nf* meningitis (*U*).

ménisque [menisk] *nm* meniscus.

ménopause [menɔpoz] *nf* menopause.

menotte [mənɔt] *nf* [main] little hand. ○ **menottes** *nfpl* handcuffs; **passer les** ~**s à qqn** to handcuff sb.

mensonge [mɑ̃sɔ̃ʒ] *nm* [propos] lie.

mensonger, -ère [mɑ̃sɔ̃ʒe, ɛr] *adj* false.

menstruel, -elle [mɑ̃stryɛl] *adj* menstrual.

mensualiser [mɑ̃sɥalize] *vt* to pay monthly.

mensualité [mɑ̃sɥalite] *nf* [traite] monthly instalment.

mensuel, -elle [mɑ̃sɥɛl] *adj* monthly. ○ **mensuel** *nm* monthly (magazine).

mensuration [mɑ̃syrasjɔ̃] *nf* measuring. ○ **mensurations** *nfpl* measurements.

mental, -e, -aux [mɑ̃tal, o] *adj* mental.

mentalité [mɑ̃talite] *nf* mentality.

menteur, -euse [mɑ̃tœr, øz] *nm, f* liar.

menthe [mɑ̃t] *nf* mint.

mention [mɑ̃sjɔ̃] *nf* [citation] mention. ‖ [note] note; «**rayer la ~ inutile**» "delete as appropriate". ‖ UNIV: **avec ~** with distinction.

mentionner [mɑ̃sjɔne] *vt* to mention.

mentir [mɑ̃tir] *vi*: ~ (**à**) to lie (to).

menton [mɑ̃tɔ̃] *nm* chin.

menu, -e [məny] *adj* [très petit] tiny; [mince] thin. ○ **menu** [gén & INFORM] menu; [repas à prix fixe] set menu; ~ **gastronomique/touristique** gourmet/tourist menu.

menuiserie [mənɥizri] *nf* [métier] join-ery, carpentry. ‖ [atelier] joinery (work-shop).

menuisier [mənɥizje] *nm* joiner, carpenter.

méprendre [meprɑ̃dr] ○ **se méprendre** *vp littéraire*: **se ~ sur** to be mistaken about.

mépris, -e [mepri, iz] *pp* → **méprendre**. ○ **mépris** [dédain]: ~ (**pour**) contempt (for), scorn (for). ‖ [indifférence]: ~ **de** disregard for. ○ **au mépris de** *loc prép* regardless of.

méprisable [meprizabl] *adj* contempt-ible, despicable.

méprisant, -e [meprizɑ̃, ɑ̃t] *adj* contemptuous, scornful.

mépriser [meprize] *vt* to despise; [danger, offre] to scorn.

mer [mɛr] *nf* sea; **en ~** at sea; **prendre la ~** to put to sea; **haute** ou **pleine ~** open sea; **la ~ d'Irlande** the Irish Sea; **la ~ Morte** the Dead Sea; **la ~ Noire** the Black Sea; **la ~ du Nord** the North Sea.

mercantile [mɛrkɑ̃til] *adj péj* merce-nary.

mercenaire [mɛrsənɛr] *nm & adj* mer-cenary.

mercerie [mɛrsəri] *nf* [articles] notions (*pl*) *Am*. ‖ [boutique] notions store *Am*.

merci [mɛrsi] **1** *interj* thank you!, thanks!; ~ **beaucoup!** thank you very much! **2** *nm*: ~ (**de** ou **pour**) thank you (for). **3** *nf* mercy; **être à la ~ de** to be at the mercy of.

mercier, -ière [mɛrsje, jɛr] *nm, f* notions dealer *Am*.

mercredi [mɛrkrədi] *nm* Wednesday; *voir aussi* **samedi**.

mercure [mɛrkyr] *nm* mercury.

merde [mɛrd] *tfam nf* shit.

mère [mɛr] *nf* mother; ~ **de famille** mother.

merguez [mɛrgɛz] *nf inv* North African spiced sausage.

méridien, -ienne [meridjɛ̃, jɛn] *adj* [li-gne] meridian. ○ **méridien** *nm* merid-ian.

méridional, -e, -aux [meridjɔnal, o] *adj* southern; [du sud de la France] Southern (French).

meringue [mərɛ̃g] *nf* meringue.

merisier [mərizje] *nm* [arbre] wild cherry (tree). ‖ [bois] cherry.

mérite [merit] *nm* merit; **avoir du ~** [personne] to have talent.

mériter [merite] *vt* [être digne de, encou-

mettre

rir] to deserve. || [valoir] to be worth, to merit.

merlan [mɛrlɑ̃] *nm* whiting.

merle [mɛrl] *nm* blackbird.

merveille [mɛrvɛj] *nf* marvel, wonder; **à ~** marvellously, wonderfully.

merveilleux, -euse [mɛrvɛjø, øz] *adj* [remarquable, prodigieux] marvellous, wonderful. || [magique] magic, magical.

mes → **mon**.

mésange [mezɑ̃ʒ] *nf* ZOOL tit.

mésaventure [mezavɑ̃tyr] *nf* misfortune.

mesdames → **madame**.

mesdemoiselles → **mademoiselle**.

mésentente [mezɑ̃tɑ̃t] *nf* disagreement.

mesquin, -e [mɛskɛ̃, in] *adj* mean, petty.

mesquinerie [mɛskinri] *nf* [étroitesse d'esprit] meanness, pettiness.

mess [mɛs] *nm* mess.

message [mesaʒ] *nm* message; **laisser un ~ à qqn** to leave a message for sb.

messager, -ère [mesaʒe, ɛr] *nm, f* messenger.

messagerie [mesaʒri] *nf* (*gén pl*) [transport de marchandises] freight (*U*). || INFORM: **~ électronique** electronic mail.

messe [mɛs] *nf* mass.

messie [mesi] *nm* Messiah; *fig* saviour.

messieurs → **monsieur**.

mesure [məzyr] *nf* [disposition, acte] measure, step. || [évaluation, dimension] measurement; **prendre les ~s de qqn/qqch** to measure sb/sthg. || [étalon, récipient] measure. || MUS time, tempo. || [modération] moderation. || *loc:* **dans la ~ du possible** as far as possible; **être en ~ de to** be in a position to. ○ **à mesure que** *loc conj* as. ○ **outre mesure** *loc adv* excessively. ○ **sur mesure** *loc adj* custom-made; [costume] made-to-measure.

mesurer [məzyre] *vt* [gén] to measure; **elle mesure 1,50 m** she's 5 feet tall; **la table mesure 1,50 m** the table is 5 feet long. || [risques, portée, ampleur] to weigh up. ○ **se mesurer** *vp:* **se ~ avec** *ou* **à qqn** to pit o.s. against sb.

métabolisme [metabɔlism] *nm* metabolism.

métal, -aux [metal, o] *nm* metal.

métallique [metalik] *adj* [en métal] metal (*avant n*). || [éclat, son] metallic.

métallurgie [metalyrʒi] *nf* [industrie] metallurgical industry.

métamorphose [metamɔrfoz] *nf* metamorphosis.

métaphore [metafɔr] *nf* metaphor.

métaphysique [metafizik] **1** *nf* metaphysics (*U*). **2** *adj* metaphysical.

métayer, -ère [meteje, metejɛr] *nm, f* tenant farmer.

météo [meteo] *nf* [bulletin] weather forecast. || [service] ≃ Met Office *Br*, ≃ National Weather Service *Am*.

météore [meteɔr] *nm* meteor.

météorite [meteɔrit] *nm ou nf* meteorite.

météorologie [meteɔrɔlɔʒi] *nf* SCIENCE meteorology.

météorologique [meteɔrɔlɔʒik] *adj* meteorological, weather (*avant n*).

méthane [metan] *nm* methane.

méthode [metɔd] *nf* [gén] method. || [ouvrage - gén] manual; [- de lecture, de langue] primer.

méthodologie [metɔdɔlɔʒi] *nf* methodology.

méticuleux, -euse [metikylø, øz] *adj* meticulous.

métier [metje] *nm* [profession - manuelle] occupation, trade; [- intellectuelle] occupation, profession.

métis, -isse [metis] *nm, f* half-caste, half-breed. ○ **métis** *nm* [tissu] cotton-linen mix.

métrage [metraʒ] *nm* [mesure] measurement, measuring. || [COUTURE - coupon] length. || CIN footage; **long ~** feature film; **court ~** short (film).

mètre [mɛtr] *nm* LITTÉRATURE & MATHS metre; **~ carré/cube** square/cubic metre. || [instrument] rule.

métro [metro] *nm* subway *Am*.

métronome [metrɔnɔm] *nm* metronome.

métropole [metrɔpɔl] *nf* [ville] metropolis. || [pays] home country.

métropolitain, -e [metrɔpɔlitɛ̃, ɛn] *adj* metropolitan.

mets [mɛ] *nm* CULIN dish.

metteur [metœr] *nm:* **~ en scène** THÉÂTRE producer; CIN director.

mettre [mɛtr] *vt* [placer] to put; **~ de l'eau à bouillir** to put some water on to boil. || [revêtir] to put on; **mets ta robe noire** put your black dress on; **je ne mets plus ma robe noire** I don't wear my black dress any more. || [consacrer - temps] to take; [- argent] to spend. || [allumer - radio, chauffage] to put on, to switch on. || [installer] to put in; **faire ~**

de la moquette to have a carpet put down or fitted. || [inscrire] to put (down). ○ **se mettre** *vp* [se placer]: où est-ce que ça se met? where does this go?; se ~ au lit to get into bed; se ~ à côté de qqn to sit/stand near to sb. || [commencer]: se ~ à qqch/à faire qqch to start sthg/doing sthg. || [revêtir] to put on; **je n'ai rien à me ~** I haven't got a thing to wear.

meuble [mœbl] *nm* piece of furniture; ~s furniture (*U*).

meublé, -e [mœble] *adj* furnished. ○ **meublé** *nm* furnished apartment *Am*.

meubler [mœble] *vt* [pièce, maison] to furnish. || *fig* [occuper]: ~ **qqch (de)** to fill sthg (with).

meugler [møgle] *vi* to moo.

meule [møl] *nf* [à moudre] millstone. || [à aiguiser] grindstone. || [de fromage] round. || AGRIC stack; ~ **de foin** haystack.

meunier, -ière [mønje, jɛr] *nm, f* miller (*f* miller's wife).

meurtre [mœrtr] *nm* murder.

meurtrier, -ière [mœrtrije, jɛr] **1** *adj* [épidémie, arme] deadly; [fureur] murderous; [combat] bloody. **2** *nm, f* murderer.

meurtrir [mœrtrir] *vt* [contusionner] to bruise. || *fig* [blesser] to wound.

meurtrissure [mœrtrisyr] *nf* [marque] bruise.

meute [møt] *nf* pack.

mexicain, -e [mɛksikɛ̃, ɛn] *adj* Mexican. ○ **Mexicain, -e** *nm, f* Mexican.

Mexique [mɛksik] *nm*: **le ~** Mexico.

mezzanine [mɛdzanin] *nf* mezzanine.

mi [mi] *nm inv* E; [chanté] mi.

mi- [mi] **1** *adj inv* half; **à la ~juin** in mid-June. **2** *adv* half-.

miasme [mjasm] *nm* (*gén pl*) putrid or foul smell.

miaulement [mjolmɑ̃] *nm* miaowing.

miauler [mjole] *vi* to miaow.

mi-bas [miba] *nm inv* knee-sock.

mi-carême [mikarɛm] *nf* feast day on third Thursday in Lent.

mi-chemin [miʃmɛ̃] ○ **à mi-chemin** *loc adv* halfway (there).

mi-clos, -e [miklo, oz] *adj* half-closed.

micro [mikro] *nm* [microphone] mike. || [micro-ordinateur] micro.

microbe [mikrɔb] *nm* MÉD microbe, germ. || *péj* [avorton] (little) runt.

microclimat [mikroklima] *nm* microclimate.

microcosme [mikrɔkɔsm] *nm* microcosm.

microfiche [mikrofiʃ] *nf* microfiche.

microfilm [mikrofilm] *nm* microfilm.

micro-ondes [mikrɔ̃d] *nfpl* microwaves; **four à ~** microwave (oven).

micro-ordinateur [mikroɔrdinatœr] (*pl* **micro-ordinateurs**) *nm* micro, microcomputer.

microphone [mikrofɔn] *nm* microphone.

microprocesseur [mikroprosesœr] *nm* microprocessor.

microscope [mikroskɔp] *nm* microscope.

midi [midi] *nm* [période du déjeuner] lunchtime. || [heure] midday, noon. ○ **Midi** *nm*: **le Midi** the South of France.

mie [mi] *nf* [de pain] soft part, inside.

miel [mjɛl] *nm* honey.

mielleux, -euse [mjɛlø, øz] *adj* [personne] unctuous; [paroles, air] honeyed.

mien [mjɛ̃] ○ **le mien** (*f* **la mienne** [lamjɛn], *mpl* **les miens** [lemjɛ̃], *fpl* **les miennes** [lemjɛn]) *pron poss* mine.

miette [mjɛt] *nf* [de pain] crumb, breadcrumb. || (*gén pl*) [débris] shreds (*pl*).

mieux [mjø] **1** *adv* [comparatif]: ~ **(que)** better (than); **il pourrait ~ faire** he could do better; **il va ~** he's better; **vous feriez ~ de vous taire** you would do better to keep quiet, you would be well-advised to keep quiet. || [superlatif] best; **il est le ~ payé du service** he's the best or highest paid member of the department; **le ~ qu'il peut** as best he can. **2** *adj* better. **3** *nm* (*sans déterminant*): **j'espérais ~** I was hoping for something better. || (*avec déterminant*) best; **il y a un ou du ~** there's been an improvement; **faire de son ~** to do one's best. ○ **au mieux** *loc adv* at best. ○ **de mieux en mieux** *loc adv* better and better.

mièvre [mjevr] *adj* insipid.

mignon, -onne [miɲɔ̃, ɔn] *adj* [charmant] sweet, cute. || [gentil] nice.

migraine [migrɛn] *nf* headache; MÉD migraine.

migrant, -e [migrɑ̃, ɑ̃t] *nm, f* migrant.

migrateur, -trice [migratœr, tris] *adj* migratory.

migration [migrasjɔ̃] *nf* migration.

mijoter [miʒɔte] **1** *vt fam* [tramer] to cook up. **2** *vi* CULIN to simmer.

mi-journée [miʒurne] *nf*: **les informations de la ~** the lunchtime news.

milan [milɑ̃] *nm* kite (*bird*).

milice [milis] *nf* militia.

milicien, -ienne [milisjɛ̃, jɛn] *nm, f* militiaman (*f* militiawoman).

milieu, -x [miljø] *nm* [centre] middle; **au ~ de** [au centre de] in the middle of; [parmi] among, surrounded by. || [stade intermédiaire] middle course. || BIOL & SOCIOL environment; **~ familial** family background. || [pègre]: **le ~** the underworld. || FOOTBALL: **~ de terrain** midfielder, midfield player.

militaire [militɛr] **1** *nm* soldier; **~ de carrière** professional soldier. **2** *adj* military.

militant, -e [militɑ̃, ɑ̃t] *adj & nm, f* militant.

militer [milite] *vi* to be active; **~ pour/contre** to militate in favour of/against.

mille [mil] **1** *nm inv* [unité] a ou one thousand. || [de cible]: **dans le ~** on target. || NAVIG: **~ marin** nautical mile. || *Can* [distance] mile. **2** *adj inv* thousand; **je lui ai dit ~ fois** I've told him/her a thousand times.

mille-feuille [milfœj] (*pl* **mille-feuilles**) *nm* ≃ napoleon *Am*.

millénaire [milenɛr] **1** *nm* millennium, thousand years (*pl*). **2** *adj* thousand-year-old (*avant n*).

mille-pattes [milpat] *nm inv* centipede, millipede.

millésime [milezim] *nm* [de pièce] date. || [de vin] vintage, year.

millésimé, -e [milezime] *adj* [vin] vintage (*avant n*).

millet [mijɛ] *nm* millet.

milliard [miljar] *nm* billion *Am*.

milliardaire [miljardɛr] *nmf* billionaire *Am*.

millier [milje] *nm* thousand; **un ~ de francs/personnes** about a thousand francs/people; **par ~s** in (their) thousands.

milligramme [miligram] *nm* milligram, milligramme.

millilitre [mililitr] *nm* millilitre.

millimètre [milimɛtr] *nm* millimetre.

million [miljɔ̃] *nm* million; **un ~ de francs** a million francs.

millionnaire [miljɔnɛr] *nmf* millionaire.

mime [mim] *nm* mime.

mimer [mime] *vt* [exprimer sans parler] to mime. || [imiter] to mimic.

mimétisme [mimetism] *nm* mimicry.

mimique [mimik] *nf* [grimace] face.

mimosa [mimɔza] *nm* mimosa.

min. (*abr de* **minimum**) min.

minable [minabl] *adj fam* [misérable] seedy, shabby. || [médiocre] pathetic.

minaret [minarɛ] *nm* minaret.

minauder [minode] *vi* to simper.

mince [mɛ̃s] *adj* [maigre - gén] thin; [- personne, taille] slender, slim. || *fig* [faible] small, meagre.

minceur [mɛ̃sœr] *nf* [gén] thinness; [de personne] slenderness, slimness. || *fig* [insuffisance] meagreness.

mincir [mɛ̃sir] *vi* to get thinner ou slimmer.

mine [min] *nf* [expression] look; **avoir bonne/mauvaise ~** to look well/ill. || [apparence] appearance. || [gisement & *fig*] mine; **~ de charbon** coalmine. || [explosif] mine. || [de crayon] lead.

miner [mine] *vt* MIL to mine. || [ronger] to undermine, to wear away; *fig* to wear down.

minerai [minrɛ] *nm* ore.

minéral, -e, -aux [mineral, o] *adj* CHIM inorganic. || [eau, source] mineral (*avant n*). ○ **minéral** *nm* mineral.

minéralogie [mineralɔʒi] *nf* mineralogy.

minéralogique [mineralɔʒik] *adj* AUTOM → **plaque**. || GÉOL mineralogical.

minet, -ette [minɛ, ɛt] *nm, f fam* [chat] pussycat, pussy. || [personne] trendy.

mineur, -e [minœr] **1** *adj* minor. **2** *nm, f* JUR minor. ○ **mineur** *nm* [ouvrier] miner; **~ de fond** face worker.

miniature [minjatyr] **1** *nf* miniature. **2** *adj* miniature.

miniaturiser [minjatyrize] *vt* to miniaturize.

minibus [minibys] *nm* minibus.

minichaîne [miniʃɛn] *nf* portable hi-fi.

minier, -ière [minje, jɛr] *adj* mining (*avant n*).

minijupe [miniʒyp] *nf* miniskirt.

minimal, -e, -aux [minimal, o] *adj* minimum.

minimalisme [minimalism] *nm* minimalism.

minime [minim] **1** *nmf* SPORT ≃ junior. **2** *adj* minimal.

minimiser [minimize] *vt* to minimize.

minimum [minimɔm] (*pl* **minimums** OU **minima** [minima]) **1** *nm* [gén & MATHS] minimum; **au ~** at least; **le strict ~** the bare minimum. **2** *adj* minimum.

ministère [ministɛr] *nm* [département] department. || [cabinet] government.

ministériel, -ielle [ministerjɛl] *adj* [du ministère] ministerial *Br*, departmental.

ministre [ministr] *nm* minister *Br*, secretary; ~ **d'État** secretary of state, cabinet minister *Br*; **premier** ~ prime minister.

Minitel® [minitɛl] *nm* teletext system run by the French national telephone company, providing an information and communication network.

minois [minwa] *nm* sweet (little) face.

minoritaire [minɔriter] *adj* minority (*avant n*); **être** ~ to be in the minority.

minorité [minɔrite] *nf* minority; **en** ~ in the minority.

minuit [minɥi] *nm* midnight.

minuscule [minyskyl] **1** *nf* [lettre] small letter. **2** *adj* [lettre] small. || [très petit] tiny, minuscule.

minute [minyt] **1** *nf* minute; **dans une** ~ in a minute; **d'une** ~ **à l'autre** in next to no time, **2** *interj fam* hang on (a minute)!

minuter [minyte] *vt* [chronométrer] to time (precisely).

minuterie [minytri] *nf* [d'éclairage] time switch, timer.

minuteur [minytœr] *nm* timer.

minutie [minysi] *nf* [soin] meticulousness; [précision] attention to detail; **avec** ~ [avec soin] meticulously; [dans le détail] in minute detail.

minutieux, -ieuse [minysjø, jøz] *adj* [méticuleux] meticulous; [détaillé] minutely detailed.

mioche [mjɔʃ] *nmf fam* kiddy.

mirabelle [mirabɛl] *nf* [fruit] mirabelle (plum). || [alcool] plum brandy.

miracle [mirakl] *nm* miracle; **par** ~ by some ou a miracle, miraculously.

miraculeux, -euse [mirakylø, øz] *adj* miraculous.

mirador [miradɔr] *nm* MIL watchtower.

mirage [miraʒ] *nm* mirage.

mire [mir] *nf* TÉLÉ test card. || [visée]: **ligne de** ~ line of sight.

mirifique [mirifik] *adj* fabulous.

mirobolant, -e [mirɔbɔlã, ãt] *adj* fabulous, fantastic.

miroir [mirwar] *nm* mirror.

miroiter [mirwate] *vi* to sparkle, to gleam; **faire** ~ **qqch à qqn** to hold out the prospect of sthg to sb.

mis, mise [mi, miz] *pp* → **mettre**.

misanthrope [mizãtrɔp] **1** *nmf* misanthropist, misanthrope. **2** *adj* misanthropic.

mise [miz] *nf* [action] putting; ~ **à jour** updating; ~ **au point** PHOT focusing; *fig* clarification; ~ **en scène** production. || [d'argent] stake.

miser [mize] **1** *vt* to bet. **2** *vi*: ~ **sur** to bet on; *fig* to count on.

misérable [mizerabl] *adj* [pauvre] poor, wretched. || [sans valeur] paltry, miserable.

misère [mizɛr] *nf* [indigence] poverty. || [infortune] misery. || *fig* [bagatelle] trifle.

miséricorde [mizerikɔrd] *nf* [clémence] mercy.

misogyne [mizɔʒin] *adj* misogynous.

missel [misel] *nm* missal.

missile [misil] *nm* missile.

mission [misjɔ̃] *nf* mission; **en** ~ on a mission.

missionnaire [misjɔner] *nmf* missionary.

missive [misiv] *nf* letter.

mitaine [miten] *nf* fingerless glove.

mite [mit] *nf* [clothes] moth.

mité, -e [mite] *adj* moth-eaten.

mi-temps [mitɑ̃] *nf inv* [SPORT - période] half; [- pause] half-time. ○ **à mi-temps** *loc adj* & *loc adv* part-time.

miteux, -euse [mitø, øz] *fam adj* seedy, dingy.

mitigé, -e [mitiʒe] *adj* [tempéré] lukewarm. || *fam* [mélangé] mixed.

mitonner [mitɔne] *vt* [préparer avec soin] to prepare lovingly.

mitoyen, -enne [mitwajɛ̃, ɛn] *adj* party (*avant n*), common.

mitrailler [mitraje] *vt* MIL to machinegun. || *fam* [photographier] to click away at.

mitraillette [mitrajet] *nf* submachine gun.

mitrailleuse [mitrajøz] *nf* machinegun.

mi-voix [mivwa] ○ **à mi-voix** *loc adv* in a low voice.

mixage [miksaʒ] *nm* CIN & RADIO (sound) mixing.

mixer¹, mixeur [miksœr] *nm* (food) mixer.

mixer² [mikse] *vt* to mix.

mixte [mikst] *adj* mixed.

mixture [mikstyr] *nf* CHIM & CULIN mixture. || *péj* [mélange] concoction.

MJC (*abr de* **maison des jeunes et de la culture**) *nf* youth and cultural centre.

ml (*abr de* **millilitre**) ml.

Mlle (*abr de* **Mademoiselle**) Miss.

mm (*abr de* **millimètre**) mm.

MM (*abr de* **Messieurs**) Messrs.

Mme (*abr de* **Madame**) Mrs.

Mo (*abr de* **méga-octet**) MB.

mobile [mɔbil] **1** *nm* [objet] mobile. ‖ [motivation] motive. **2** *adj* [gén] movable, mobile; [partie, pièce] moving. ‖ [population, main-d'œuvre] mobile.

mobilier, -ière [mɔbilje, jɛr] *adj* JUR movable. ○ **mobilier** *nm* furniture.

mobilisation [mɔbilizasjɔ̃] *nf* mobilization.

mobiliser [mɔbilize] *vt* [gén] to mobilize. ‖ [moralement] to rally. ○ **se mobiliser** *vp* to mobilize, to rally.

mobilité [mɔbilite] *nf* mobility.

Mobylette® [mɔbilɛt] *nf* moped.

mocassin [mɔkasɛ̃] *nm* moccasin.

moche [mɔʃ] *adj fam* [laid] ugly. ‖ [triste, méprisable] lousy, rotten.

modalité [mɔdalite] *nf* [convention] form; **~s de paiement** methods of payment.

mode [mɔd] **1** *nf* [gén] fashion; **à la ~** in fashion, fashionable. ‖ [coutume] custom, style; **à la ~ de** in the style of. **2** *nm* [manière] mode, form; **~ de vie** way of life. ‖ [méthode] method; **~ d'emploi** instructions (for use). ‖ GRAM mood. ‖ MUS mode.

modèle [mɔdɛl] *nm* [gén] model; **~ déposé** registered design. ‖ (*en apposition*) [exemplaire] model (*avant n*).

modeler [mɔdle] *vt* to shape; **~ qqch sur qqch** *fig* to model sthg on sthg.

modélisme [mɔdelism] *nm* modelling (*of scale models*).

modération [mɔderasjɔ̃] *nf* moderation.

modéré, -e [mɔdere] *adj & nm, f* moderate.

modérer [mɔdere] *vt* to moderate. ○ **se modérer** *vp* to restrain o.s., to control o.s.

moderne [mɔdɛrn] *adj* modern.

moderniser [mɔdɛrnize] *vt* to modernize. ○ **se moderniser** *vp* to become (more) modern.

modeste [mɔdɛst] *adj* modest; [origine] humble.

modestie [mɔdɛsti] *nf* modesty; **fausse ~** false modesty.

modification [mɔdifikasjɔ̃] *nf* alteration, modification.

modifier [mɔdifje] *vt* to alter, to modify. ○ **se modifier** *vp* to alter.

modique [mɔdik] *adj* modest.

modiste [mɔdist] *nf* milliner.

modulation [mɔdylasjɔ̃] *nf* modulation.

module [mɔdyl] *nm* module.

moduler [mɔdyle] *vt* [air] to warble. ‖ [structure] to adjust.

moelle [mwal] *nf* ANAT marrow. ○ **moelle épinière** *nf* spinal cord.

moelleux, -euse [mwalø, øz] *adj* [canapé, tapis] soft. ‖ [fromage, vin] mellow.

moellon [mwalɔ̃] *nm* rubble stone.

mœurs [mœr(s)] *nfpl* [morale] morals. ‖ [coutumes] customs, habits. ‖ ZOOL behaviour (*U*).

mohair [mɔɛr] *nm* mohair.

moi [mwa] *pron pers* [objet, après préposition, comparatif] me; **aide-~** help me; **plus âgé que ~** older than me *ou* than I (am). ‖ [sujet] I; **~ non plus, je n'en sais rien** I don't know anything about it either; **qui est là? - (c'est) ~** who's there? - it's me. ○ **moi-même** *pron pers* myself.

moignon [mwaɲɔ̃] *nm* stump.

moindre [mwɛ̃dr] **1** *adj superl*: **le/la ~** the least; (*avec négation*) the least *ou* slightest; **les ~s détails** the smallest details; **sans la ~ difficulté** without the slightest problem; **c'est la ~ des choses** it's the least I/you *etc* could do. **2** *adj compar* less; [prix] lower.

moine [mwan] *nm* monk.

moineau, -x [mwano] *nm* sparrow.

moins [mwɛ̃] **1** *adv* [quantité] less; **~ de lait** less milk; **~ de gens** fewer people; **~ de dix** less than ten. ‖ [comparatif]: **~ (que)** less (than); **bien ~ grand que** much smaller than; **~ il mange, ~ il travaille** the less he eats, the less he works. ‖ [superlatif]: **le ~** (the) least; **le ~ riche des hommes** the poorest man; **c'est lui qui travaille le ~** he works (the) least; **le ~ possible** as little as possible. **2** *prép* [gén] minus; **dix ~ huit font deux** ten minus eight is two; **il est huit heures ~ le quart** it's quarter to eight; **huit ~ deux font six** eight minus two is six; **il fait ~ vingt** it's twenty below, it's minus twenty. ‖ [servant à indiquer l'heure]: **il est trois heures ~ le quart** it's quarter to 3; **il est ~ dix** it's ten to. **3** *nm loc*: **le ~ qu'on puisse dire, c'est que ...** it's an understatement to say .... ○ **à moins de** *loc prép* unless; **à ~ de battre le record** unless I/you *etc* beat the record. ○ **à moins que** *loc adv* (+ *subjonctif*) unless. ○ **au moins** *loc adv* at least. ○ **de moins en moins** *loc adv* less and less. ○ **du moins** *loc adv* at least. ○ **en moins** *adv*: **il a une dent en**

~ he's missing ou minus a tooth. ○ **pour le moins** *loc adv* at (the very) least. ○ **tout au moins** *loc adv* at (the very) least.

moiré, -e [mware] *adj* [tissu] watered.

mois [mwa] *nm* [laps de temps] month.

moisi, -e [mwazi] *adj* mouldy. ○ **moisi** *nm* mould.

moisir [mwazir] *vi* [pourrir] to go mouldy. ‖ *fig* [personne] to rot.

moisissure [mwazisyr] *nf* mould.

moisson [mwasɔ̃] *nf* [récolte] harvest; **faire la ~** ou **les ~s** to harvest, to bring in the harvest. ‖ *fig* [d'idées, de projets] wealth.

moissonner [mwasɔne] *vt* to harvest, to gather (in); *fig* to collect, to gather.

moissonneuse-batteuse [mwasɔnøzbatøz] *nf* combine (harvester).

moite [mwat] *adj* [peau, mains] moist, sweaty; [atmosphère] muggy.

moiteur [mwatœr] *nf* [de peau, mains] moistness; [d'atmosphère] mugginess.

moitié [mwatje] *nf* [gén] half; **à ~ vide** half-empty; **faire qqch à ~** to half-do sthg; **la ~ du temps** half the time; **à la ~ de qqch** halfway through sthg.

moka [mɔka] *nm* [café] mocha (coffee). ‖ [gâteau] coffee cake.

mol → **mou**.

molaire [mɔlɛr] *nf* molar.

molécule [mɔlekyl] *nf* molecule.

molester [mɔlɛste] *vt* to manhandle.

molle → **mou**.

mollement [mɔlmɑ̃] *adv* [faiblement] weakly, feebly.

mollesse [mɔlɛs] *nf* [de chose] softness. ‖ [de personne] lethargy.

mollet [mɔlɛ] **1** *nm* calf. **2** *adj* → **œuf**.

mollir [mɔlir] *vi* [physiquement, moralement] to give way. ‖ [vent] to drop, to die down.

mollusque [mɔlysk] *nm* ZOOL mollusc.

molosse [mɔlɔs] *nm* [chien] *large ferocious dog.* ‖ *fig & péj* [personne] hulking great brute ou fellow.

môme [mom] *fam nmf* [enfant] kid, youngster.

moment [mɔmɑ̃] *nm* [gén] moment; **au ~ de l'accident** at the time of the accident, when the accident happened; **au ~ de partir** just as we/you *etc* were leaving; **au ~ où** just as; **dans un ~** in a moment; **d'un ~ à l'autre, à tout ~** (at) any moment, any moment now; **par ~s** at times, now and then; **en ce ~** at the moment; **pour le ~** for the moment. ‖ [du-

rée] (short) time; **passer un mauvais ~** to have a bad time. ‖ [occasion] time; **ce n'est pas le ~ (de faire qqch)** this is not the time (to do sthg). ○ **du moment que** *loc prép* since, as.

momentané, -e [mɔmɑ̃tane] *adj* temporary.

momie [mɔmi] *nf* mummy.

mon [mɔ̃] (*f* **ma** [ma], *pl* **mes** [me]) *adj poss* my.

Monaco [mɔnako] *n:* (**la principauté de**) **~** (the principality of) Monaco.

monarchie [mɔnarʃi] *nf* monarchy; **~ absolue/constitutionnelle** absolute/constitutional monarchy.

monarque [mɔnark] *nm* monarch.

monastère [mɔnastɛr] *nm* monastery.

monceau, -x [mɔ̃so] *nm* [tas] heap.

mondain, -e [mɔ̃dɛ̃, ɛn] *adj* [chronique, journaliste] society (*avant n*). ‖ *péj* [futile] frivolous, superficial.

mondanités [mɔ̃danite] *nfpl* [événements] society life (*U*). ‖ [paroles] small talk (*U*); [comportements] formalities.

monde [mɔ̃d] *nm* [gén] world; **le/la plus ... au ~, le/la plus ... du ~** the most ... in the world; **pour rien au ~** not for the world, not for all the tea in China; **mettre un enfant au ~** to bring a child into the world. ‖ [gens] people (*pl*); **beaucoup/peu de ~** a lot of/not many people; **tout le ~** everyone, everybody. ‖ *loc:* **c'est un ~!** that's really the limit!; **se faire un ~ de qqch** to make too much of sthg; **noir de ~** packed with people.

mondial, -e, -iaux [mɔ̃djal, jo] *adj* world (*avant n*).

mondialement [mɔ̃djalmɑ̃] *adv* throughout ou all over the world.

monétaire [mɔneter] *adj* monetary.

Mongolie [mɔ̃gɔli] *nf:* **la ~** Mongolia.

mongolien, -ienne [mɔ̃gɔljɛ̃, jɛn] *vieilli nm, f* mongol.

moniteur, -trice [mɔnitœr, tris] *nm, f* [enseignant] instructor, coach; **~ d'auto-école** driving instructor. ‖ [de colonie de vacances] supervisor, leader. ○ **moniteur** *nm* [appareil & INFORM] monitor.

monnaie [mɔnɛ] *nf* [moyen de paiement] money. ‖ [de pays] currency. ‖ [pièces] change; **faire (de) la ~** to get (some) change.

monnayer [mɔneje] *vt* [biens] to convert into cash. ‖ *fig* [silence] to buy.

monochrome [mɔnɔkrom] *adj* monochrome, monochromatic.

monocle [mɔnɔkl] *nm* monocle.

moquer

monocoque [mɔnɔkɔk] *nm & adj* [bateau] monohull.

monocorde [mɔnɔkɔrd] *adj* [monotone] monotonous.

monogramme [mɔnɔgram] *nm* monogram.

monolingue [mɔnɔlɛ̃g] *adj* monolingual.

monologue [mɔnɔlɔg] *nm* THÉÂTRE soliloquy. || [discours individuel] monologue.

monologuer [mɔnɔlɔge] *vi* THÉÂTRE to soliloquize. || *fig & péj* [parler] to talk away.

monoplace [mɔnɔplas] *adj* single-seater (*avant n*).

monopole [mɔnɔpɔl] *nm* monopoly; **avoir le ~ de qqch** *litt & fig* to have a monopoly of ou on sthg.

monopoliser [mɔnɔpɔlize] *vt* to monopolize.

monoski [mɔnɔski] *nm* [objet] monoski. || [sport] monoskiing.

monosyllabe [mɔnɔsilab] **1** *nm* monosyllable. **2** *adj* monosyllabic.

monotone [mɔnɔtɔn] *adj* monotonous.

monotonie [mɔnɔtɔni] *nf* monotony.

monseigneur [mɔ̃sɛɲœr] (*pl* **messeigneurs** [mesɛɲœr]) *nm* [titre - d'évêque, de duc] His Grace; [- de cardinal] His Eminence; [- de prince] His (Royal) Highness.

monsieur [məsjø] (*pl* **messieurs** [mesjø]) *nm* [titre]: **~ X** Mr X; **bonjour ~** good morning; [dans hôtel, restaurant] good morning, sir; **bonjour messieurs** good morning (gentlemen); **Monsieur le Ministre n'est pas là** the Minister is out. || [homme quelconque] gentleman.

monstre [mɔ̃str] *nm* [gén] monster. || (*en apposition*) *fam* [énorme] colossal.

monstrueux, -euse [mɔ̃stryø, øz] *adj* [gén] monstrous. || *fig* [erreur] terrible.

monstruosité [mɔ̃stryozite] *nf* monstrosity.

mont [mɔ̃] *nm* GÉOGR Mount; **le ~ Blanc** Mont Blanc; **le ~ Cervin** the Matterhorn.

montage [mɔ̃taʒ] *nm* [assemblage] assembly; [de bijou] setting. || PHOT photomontage. || CIN editing.

montagnard, -e [mɔ̃taɲar, ard] *nm, f* mountain dweller.

montagne [mɔ̃taɲ] *nf* [gén] mountain; **les ~s Rocheuses** the Rocky Mountains. || [région]; **la ~** the mountains (*pl*); **à la ~** in the mountains; **en haute ~** at high altitudes. ○ **montagnes russes** *nfpl* big dipper (*sg*), roller coaster (*sg*).

montant, -e [mɔ̃tɑ̃, ɑ̃t] *adj* [mouvement] rising. ○ **montant** *nm* [pièce verticale] upright. || [somme] total (amount).

mont-de-piété [mɔ̃dpjete] (*pl* **monts-de-piété**) *nm* pawnshop.

monte-charge [mɔ̃tʃarʒ] *nm inv* goods lift *Br*, service elevator *Am*.

montée [mɔ̃te] *nf* [de montagne] climb, ascent. || [de prix] rise. || [relief] slope, gradient.

monte-plats [mɔ̃tpla] *nm inv* dumbwaiter.

monter [mɔ̃te] **1** *vi* (*aux: être*) [personne] to come/go up; [température, niveau] to rise; [route, avion] to climb; **~ sur qqch** to climb onto sthg. || [passager] to get on; **~ dans un bus** to get on a bus; **~ dans une voiture** to get into a car. || [cavalier] to ride; **~ à cheval** to ride. || [marée] to go/come in. **2** *vt* (*aux: avoir*) [escalier, côte] to climb, to come/go up. || [chauffage, son] to turn up. || [valise] to take/bring up. || [meuble] to assemble; COUTURE to assemble, to put ou sew together; [tente] to put up. || [cheval] to mount. || THÉÂTRE to put on. || [société, club] to set up. || CULIN to beat, to whisk (up). ○ **se monter** *vp* [atteindre]: **se ~ à** to amount to, to add up to.

monteur, -euse [mɔ̃tœr, øz] *nm, f* TECHNOL fitter. || CIN editor.

monticule [mɔ̃tikyl] *nm* mound.

montre [mɔ̃tr] *nf* watch; **~ à quartz** quartz watch; **~ en main** to the minute, exactly; **contre la ~** [sport] time-trialling; [épreuve] time trial.

montre-bracelet [mɔ̃trəbraslɛ] *nf* wristwatch.

montrer [mɔ̃tre] *vt* [gén] to show; **~ qqch à qqn** to show sb sthg, to show sthg to sb. || [désigner] to show, to point out. ○ **se montrer** *vp* [se faire voir] to appear. || *fig* [se présenter] to show o.s. || *fig* [se révéler] to prove (to be).

monture [mɔ̃tyr] *nf* [animal] mount. || [de lunettes] frame.

monument [mɔnymɑ̃] *nm* [gén]: **~ (à)** monument (to); **~ aux morts** war memorial.

monumental, -e, -aux [mɔnymɑ̃tal, o] *adj* monumental.

moquer [mɔke] ○ **se moquer** *vp*: **se ~ de** [plaisanter sur] to make fun of, to laugh at; [ne pas se soucier de] not to give a damn about.

moquerie [mɔkri] *nf* mockery (*U*), jibe.

moquette [mɔkɛt] *nf* (fitted) carpet.

moqueur, -euse [mɔkœr, øz] *adj* mocking.

moral, -e, -aux [mɔral, o] *adj* moral. ○ **moral** *nm* [état d'esprit] morale, spirits (*pl*); **avoir/ne pas avoir le ~** to be in good/bad spirits; **remonter le ~ à qqn** to cheer sb up. ○ **morale** *nf* [science] moral philosophy, morals (*pl*). || [mœurs] morals (*pl*). || [leçon] moral; **faire la ~e à qqn** to preach at ou lecture sb.

moralisateur, -trice [mɔralizatœr, tris] **1** *adj* moralizing. **2** *nm, f* moralizer.

moraliste [mɔralist] *nmf* moralist.

moralité [mɔralite] *nf* [gén] morality. || [enseignement] morals.

moratoire [mɔratwar] *nm* moratorium.

morbide [mɔrbid] *adj* morbid.

morceau, -x [mɔrso] *nm* [gén] piece. || [de poème, de musique] passage.

morceler [mɔrsəle] *vt* to break up, to split up.

mordant, -e [mɔrdɑ̃, ɑ̃t] *adj* biting. ○ **mordant** *nm* [vivacité] keenness, bite.

mordiller [mɔrdije] *vt* to nibble.

mordoré, -e [mɔrdɔre] *adj* bronze.

mordre [mɔrdr] **1** *vt* [blesser] to bite. **2** *vi* [saisir avec les dents]: **~ à** to bite. || [croquer]: **~ dans qqch** to bite into sthg. || SPORT: **~ sur la ligne** to step over the line.

mordu, -e [mɔrdy] **1** *pp* → **mordre**. **2** *adj* [amoureux] hooked. **3** *nm, f*: **~ de foot/ski** *etc* football/ski *etc* addict.

morfondre [mɔrfɔ̃dr] ○ **se morfondre** *vp* to mope.

morgue [mɔrg] *nf* [attitude] pride. || [lieu] morgue.

moribond, -e [mɔribɔ̃, ɔ̃d] **1** *adj* dying. **2** *nm, f* dying person.

morille [mɔrij] *nf* morel.

morne [mɔrn] *adj* [personne, visage] gloomy; [paysage, temps, ville] dismal, dreary.

morose [mɔroz] *adj* gloomy.

morphine [mɔrfin] *nf* morphine.

morphologie [mɔrfɔlɔʒi] *nf* morphology.

mors [mɔr] *nm* bit.

morse [mɔrs] *nm* ZOOL walrus. || [code] Morse (code).

morsure [mɔrsyr] *nf* bite.

mort, -e [mɔr, mɔrt] **1** *pp* → **mourir**. **2** *adj* dead; **~ de fatigue** *fig* dead tired; **~**

de peur *fig* frightened to death. **3** *nm, f* [cadavre] corpse, dead body. || [défunt] dead person. ○ **mort 1** *nm* [victime] fatality. **2** *nf litt & fig* death; **se donner la ~** to take one's own life, to commit suicide.

mortadelle [mɔrtadɛl] *nf* mortadella.

mortalité [mɔrtalite] *nf* mortality, death rate.

mort-aux-rats [mɔrora] *nf inv* rat poison.

mortel, -elle [mɔrtɛl] **1** *adj* [humain] mortal. || [accident, maladie] fatal. || *fig* [ennuyeux] deadly (dull). **2** *nm, f* mortal.

morte-saison [mɔrtəsɛzɔ̃] *nf* slack season, off-season.

mortier [mɔrtje] *nm* mortar.

mortification [mɔrtifikasjɔ̃] *nf* mortification.

mort-né, -e [mɔrne] (*mpl* **mort-nés**, *fpl* **mort-nées**) *adj* [enfant] still-born.

mortuaire [mɔrtɥɛr] *adj* funeral (*avant n*).

morue [mɔry] *nf* ZOOL cod.

mosaïque [mɔzaik] *nf litt & fig* mosaic.

Moscou [mɔsku] *n* Moscow.

mosquée [mɔske] *nf* mosque.

mot [mo] *nm* [gén] word; **gros ~** swearword; **~ de passe** password; **~s croisés** crossword (puzzle) (*sg*). || [message] note, message.

motard [mɔtar] *nm* [motocycliste] motorcyclist. || [policier] motorcycle policeman.

motel [mɔtɛl] *nm* motel.

moteur, -trice [mɔtœr, tris] *adj* [force, énergie] driving (*avant n*); **à quatre roues motrices** AUTOM with four-wheel drive. ○ **moteur** *nm* TECHNOL motor, engine; *fig* driving force.

motif [mɔtif] *nm* [raison] motive, grounds (*pl*). || [dessin, impression] motif.

motion [mɔsjɔ̃] *nf* POLIT motion; **~ de censure** motion of censure.

motiver [mɔtive] *vt* [stimuler] to motivate. || [justifier] to justify.

moto [mɔto] *nf* motorbike.

motocross [mɔtɔkrɔs] *nm* motocross.

motoculteur [mɔtɔkyltœr] *nm* ≃ Rotavator®.

motocyclette [mɔtɔsiklɛt] *nf* motorcycle, motorbike.

motocycliste [mɔtɔsiklist] *nmf* motorcyclist.

motorisé, -e [mɔtɔrize] *adj* motorized; **être ~** *fam* to have a car, to have wheels.

motrice → **moteur**.

motte [mɔt] *nf*: ~ **(de terre)** clod, lump of earth; ~ **de beurre** slab of butter.

mou, molle [mu, mɔl] *adj* (**mol** *devant voyelle ou h muet*) [gén] soft. || [faible] weak. || [résistance, protestation] half-hearted. || *fam* [de caractère] wet, wimpy.

mouchard, -e [muʃar, ard] *nm, f fam* [personne] sneak. ○ **mouchard** *nm fam* [dans camion, train] spy in the cab.

mouche [muʃ] *nf* ZOOL fly. || [accessoire féminin] beauty spot.

moucher [muʃe] *vt* [nez] to wipe; ~ **un enfant** to wipe a child's nose. || [chandelle] to snuff out. || *fam fig* [personne]: ~ **qqn** to put sb in his/her place. ○ **se moucher** *vp* to blow one's nose.

moucheron [muʃrɔ̃] *nm* [insecte] gnat.

moucheté, -e [muʃte] *adj* [laine] flecked. || [animal] spotted, speckled.

mouchoir [muʃwar] *nm* handkerchief.

moudre [mudr] *vt* to grind.

moue [mu] *nf* pout; **faire la** ~ to pull a face.

mouette [mwɛt] *nf* seagull.

moufle [mufl] *nf* mitten.

mouillage [muja ʒ] *nm* [NAVIG - emplacement] anchorage, moorings (*pl*).

mouillé, -e [muje] *adj* wet.

mouiller [muje] *vt* [personne, objet] to wet. || NAVIG: ~ **l'ancre** to drop anchor. || *fam fig* [compromettre] to involve. ○ **se mouiller** *vp* [se tremper] to get wet. || *fam fig* [prendre des risques] to stick one's neck out.

moulage [mula ʒ] *nm* [action] moulding, casting. || [objet] cast.

moule [mul] **1** *nm* mould; ~ **à gâteau** cake tin; ~ **à tarte** flan dish. **2** *nf* ZOOL mussel.

mouler [mule] *vt* [objet] to mould. || [forme] to make a cast of.

moulin [mulɛ̃] *nm* mill; ~ **à café** coffee mill; ~ **à paroles** *fig* chatterbox.

moulinet [muline] *nm* PÊCHE reel. || [mouvement]: **faire des** ~**s** to whirl one's arms around.

Moulinette® [mulinɛt] *nf* food mill.

moulu, -e [muly] *adj* [en poudre] ground.

moulure [mulyr] *nf* moulding.

mourant, -e [murɑ̃, ɑ̃t] **1** *adj* [moribond] dying. || *fig* [voix] faint. **2** *nm, f* dying person.

mourir [murir] *vi* [personne] to die; **s'ennuyer à** ~ to be bored to death.

mousquetaire [muskətɛr] *nm* musketeer.

moussant, -e [musɑ̃, ɑ̃t] *adj* foaming.

mousse [mus] **1** *nf* BOT moss. || [substance] foam; ~ **à raser** shaving foam. || CULIN mousse. || [matière plastique] foam rubber. **2** *nm* NAVIG cabin boy.

mousseline [muslin] *nf* muslin.

mousser [muse] *vi* to foam, to lather.

mousseux, -euse [musø, øz] *adj* [shampooing] foaming, frothy. || [vin, cidre] sparkling. ○ **mousseux** *nm* sparkling wine.

mousson [musɔ̃] *nf* monsoon.

moustache [mustaʃ] *nf* moustache. ○ **moustaches** *nfpl* [d'animal] whiskers.

moustachu, -e [mustaʃy] *adj* with a moustache.

moustiquaire [mustikɛr] *nf* mosquito net.

moustique [mustik] *nm* mosquito.

moutarde [mutard] *nf* mustard.

mouton [mutɔ̃] *nm* ZOOL & *fig* sheep. || [viande] mutton. || *fam* [poussière] piece of fluff, fluff (*U*).

mouture [mutyr] *nf* [de céréales, de café] grinding. || [de thème, d'œuvre] rehash.

mouvant, -e [muvɑ̃, ɑ̃t] *adj* [terrain] unstable. || [situation] uncertain.

mouvement [muvmɑ̃] *nm* [gén] movement; **en** ~ on the move. || [de colère, d'indignation] burst, fit.

mouvementé, -e [muvmɑ̃te] *adj* [terrain] rough. || [réunion, soirée] eventful.

mouvoir [muvwar] *vt* to move. ○ **se mouvoir** *vp* to move.

moyen, -enne [mwajɛ̃, ɛn] *adj* [intermédiaire] medium. || [médiocre, courant] average. ○ **moyen** *nm* means (*sg*), way; ~ **de communication** means of communication; ~ **de locomotion** ou **transport** means of transport. ○ **moyenne** *nf* average; **en moyenne** on average. ○ **moyens** *nmpl* [ressources] means; **avoir les** ~**s** to be comfortably off. || [capacités] powers, ability; **faire qqch par ses propres** ~**s** to do sthg on one's own. ○ **au moyen de** *loc prép* by means of.

Moyen Âge [mwajɛna ʒ] *nm*: **le** ~ the Middle Ages (*pl*).

Moyen-Orient [mwajɛnɔrjɑ̃] *nm*: **le** ~ the Middle East.

mû, mue [my] *pp* → **mouvoir**.

mue [my] *nf* [de pelage] moulting. || [de serpent] skin, slough. || [de voix] breaking.

muer [mɥe] *vi* [mammifère] to moult. || [serpent] to slough its skin. || [voix] to break.

muet, muette [mɥe, ɛt] **1** *adj* MÉD dumb. || [silencieux] silent; ~ **d'admiration/d'étonnement** speechless with admiration/surprise. || LING silent, mute. **2** *nm, f* mute, dumb person. ○ **muet** *nm*: **le** ~ CIN silent films (*pl*).

mufle [myfl] *nm* [d'animal] muzzle, snout. || *fig* [goujat] lout.

mugir [myʒir] *vi* [vache] to moo. || [vent, sirène] to howl.

muguet [mygɛ] *nm* [fleur] lily of the valley. || MÉD thrush.

mule [myl] *nf* mule.

mulet [mylɛ] *nm* [âne] mule. || [poisson] mullet.

mulot [mylo] *nm* field mouse.

multicolore [myltikɔlɔr] *adj* multicoloured.

multifonction [myltifɔ̃ksjɔ̃] *adj inv* multifunction.

multilatéral, -e, -aux [myltilateral, o] *adj* multilateral.

multinational, -e, -aux [myltinasjɔnal, o] *adj* multinational. ○ **multinationale** *nf* multinational (company).

multiple [myltipl] **1** *nm* multiple. **2** *adj* [nombreux] multiple, numerous. || [divers] many, various.

multiplication [myltiplikasjɔ̃] *nf* multiplication.

multiplier [myltiplije] *vt* [accroître] to increase. || MATHS to multiply; **X multiplié par Y égale Z** X multiplied by ou times Y equals Z. ○ **se multiplier** *vp* to multiply.

multiracial, -e, -iaux [myltirasjal, jo] *adj* multiracial.

multirisque [myltirisk] *adj* comprehensive.

multitude [myltityd] *nf*: ~ **(de)** multitude (of).

municipal, -e, -aux [mynisipal, o] *adj* municipal. ○ **municipales** *nfpl*: **les ~es** the local government elections.

municipalité [mynisipalite] *nf* [commune] municipality. || [conseil] town council.

munir [mynir] *vt*: ~ **qqn/qqch de** to equip sb/sthg with. ○ **se munir** *vp*: **se ~ de** to equip o.s. with.

munitions [mynisjɔ̃] *nfpl* ammunition (*U*), munitions.

muqueuse [mykøz] *nf* mucous membrane.

mur [myr] *nm* [gén] wall. || *fig* [obstacle] barrier, brick wall; ~ **du son** AÉRON sound barrier.

mûr, mûre [myr] *adj* ripe; [personne] mature. ○ **mûre** *nf* [de mûrier] mulberry. || [de ronce] blackberry, bramble.

muraille [myraj] *nf* wall.

murène [myren] *nf* moray eel.

murer [myre] *vt* [boucher] to wall up, to block up. || [enfermer] to wall in. ○ **se murer** *vp* to shut o.s. up ou away.

muret [myre] *nm* low wall.

mûrier [myrje] *nm* [arbre] mulberry tree. || [ronce] blackberry bush, bramble bush.

mûrir [myrir] *vi* [fruits, légumes] to ripen. || *fig* [idée, projet] to develop. || [personne] to mature.

murmure [myrmyr] *nm* murmur.

murmurer [myrmyre] *vt & vi* to murmur.

musaraigne [myzareɲ] *nf* shrew.

musarder [myzarde] *vi fam* to dawdle.

muscade [myskad] *nf* nutmeg.

muscat [myska] *nm* [raisin] muscat grape. || [vin] sweet wine.

muscle [myskl] *nm* muscle.

musclé, -e [myskle] *adj* [personne] muscular. || *fig* [mesure, décision] forceful.

muscler [myskle] *vt*: ~ **son corps** to build up one's muscles. ○ **se muscler** *vp* to build up one's muscles.

musculation [myskylasjɔ̃] *nf*: **faire de la** ~ to do muscle-building exercises.

muse [myz] *nf* muse.

museau [myzo] *nm* [d'animal] muzzle, snout. || *fam* [de personne] face.

musée [myze] *nm* museum; [d'art] art gallery.

museler [myzle] *vt litt & fig* to muzzle.

muselière [myzəljer] *nf* muzzle.

musette [myzet] *nf* haversack.

musical, -e, -aux [myzikal, o] *adj* [son] musical. || [émission, critique] music (*avant n*).

music-hall [myzikol] (*pl* **music-halls**) *nm* music-hall.

musicien, -ienne [myzisjɛ̃, jen] **1** *adj* musical. **2** *nm, f* musician.

musique [myzik] *nf* music; ~ **de chambre** chamber music; ~ **de film** film *Br* ou movie *Am* score.

musulman, -e [myzylmɑ̃, an] *adj & nm, f* Muslim.

mutant, -e [mytã, ãt] *adj* mutant.
○ **mutant** *nm* mutant.

mutation [mytasjɔ̃] *nf* BIOL mutation. ||
fig [changement] transformation. || [de
fonctionnaire] transfer.

muter [myte] *vt* to transfer.

mutilation [mytilasjɔ̃] *nf* mutilation.

mutilé, -e [mytile] *nm, f* disabled person.

mutiler [mytile] *vt* to mutilate.

mutinerie [mytinri] *nf* rebellion; MIL &
NAVIG mutiny.

mutisme [mytism] *nm* silence.

mutualité [mytɥalite] *nf* [assurance]
mutual insurance.

mutuel, -elle [mytɥel] *adj* mutual.
○ **mutuelle** *nf* mutual insurance company.

mycose [mikoz] *nf* mycosis, fungal infection.

myocarde [mjɔkard] *nm* myocardium.

myopathie [mjɔpati] *nf* myopathy.

myope [mjɔp] **1** *nmf* shortsighted person. **2** *adj* shortsighted, myopic.

myopie [mjɔpi] *nf* shortsightedness,
myopia.

myosotis [mjozɔtis] *nm* forget-me-not.

myrtille [mirtij] *nf* blueberry *Am*.

mystère [mistɛr] *nm* [gén] mystery.

mystérieux, -ieuse [misterjø, jøz] *adj*
mysterious.

mysticisme [mistisism] *nm* mysticism.

mystification [mistifikasjɔ̃] *nf* [tromperie] hoax, practical joke.

mystifier [mistifje] *vt* [duper] to take in.

mystique [mistik] **1** *nmf* mystic. **2** *adj*
mystic, mystical.

mythe [mit] *nm* myth.

mythique [mitik] *adj* mythical.

mythologie [mitɔlɔʒi] *nf* mythology.

mythomane [mitɔman] *nmf* pathological liar.

n, N [ɛn] *nm inv* [lettre] n, N. ○ **N** (*abr
de nord*) N.

nacelle [nasɛl] *nf* [de montgolfière] basket.

nacre [nakr] *nf* mother-of-pearl.

nage [naʒ] *nf* [natation] swimming; **traverser à la ~** to swim across. || *loc*: **en ~**
bathed in sweat.

nageoire [naʒwar] *nf* fin.

nager [naʒe] *vi* [se baigner] to swim. ||
[flotter] to float. || *fig* [dans vêtement]: **~
dans** to be lost in.

nageur, -euse [naʒœr, øz] *nm, f* swimmer.

naguère [nagɛr] *adv littéraire* a short
time ago.

naïf, naïve [naif, iv] *adj* [ingénu, art]
naive. || *péj* [crédule] gullible.

nain, -e [nɛ̃, nɛn] **1** *adj* dwarf (*avant
n*). **2** *nm, f* dwarf.

naissance [nɛsãs] *nf* [de personne]
birth; **donner ~ à** to give birth to. || [endroit] source; [du cou] nape. || *fig* [de
science, nation] birth; **donner ~ à** to give
rise to.

naissant, -e [nɛsã, ãt] *adj* [brise] rising;
[jour] dawning. || [barbe] incipient.

naître [nɛtr] *vi* [enfant] to be born; **elle
est née en 1965** she was born in 1965. ||
[espoir] to spring up; **~ de** to arise from;
faire ~ qqch to give rise to sthg.

naïveté [naivte] *nf* [candeur] innocence.
|| *péj* [crédulité] gullibility.

nana [nana] *nf fam* [jeune fille] girl.

nanti, -e [nãti] *nm, f* wealthy person.

nappe [nap] *nf* [de table] tablecloth,
cloth. || *fig* [étendue - gén] sheet; [- de
brouillard] blanket. || [couche] layer.

napper [nape] *vt* CULIN to coat.

napperon [naprɔ̃] *nm* tablemat.

narcisse [narsis] *nm* BOT narcissus.

narcissisme [narsisism] *nm* narcissism.

narcotique [narkɔtik] *nm & adj* narcotic.

narguer [narge] *vt* [danger] to flout; [personne] to scorn, to scoff at.

narine [narin] *nf* nostril.

narquois, -e [narkwa, az] *adj* sardonic.

narrateur, -trice [naratœr, tris] *nm, f* narrator.

narrer [nare] *vt littéraire* to narrate.

nasal, -e, -aux [nazal, o] *adj* nasal.

naseau, -x [nazo] *nm* nostril.

nasillard, -e [nazijar, ard] *adj* nasal.

nasse [nas] *nf* keep net.

natal, -e, -als [natal] *adj* [d'origine] native.

natalité [natalite] *nf* birth rate.

natation [natasjɔ̃] *nf* swimming; **faire de la** ~ to swim.

natif, -ive [natif, iv] **1** *adj* [originaire]: ~ **de** native of. **2** *nm, f* native.

nation [nasjɔ̃] *nf* nation. ○ **Nations unies** *nfpl*: **les Nations unies** the United Nations.

national, -e, -aux [nasjɔnal, o] *adj* national. ○ **nationale** *nf*: (route) ~**e** ≃ A road *Br*, ≃ state highway *Am*.

nationaliser [nasjɔnalize] *vt* to nationalize.

nationalisme [nasjɔnalism] *nm* nationalism.

nationalité [nasjɔnalite] *nf* nationality; **de ~ française** of French nationality.

natte [nat] *nf* [tresse] plait. || [tapis] mat.

naturaliser [natyralize] *vt* [personne, plante] to naturalize. || [empailler] to stuff.

nature [natyr] **1** *nf* nature. **2** *adj inv* [simple] plain. || *fam* [spontané] natural.

naturel, -elle [natyrɛl] *adj* natural. ○ **naturel** *nm* [tempérament] nature; **être d'un ~ affable/sensible** *etc* to be affable/sensitive *etc* by nature. || [aisance, spontanéité] naturalness.

naturellement [natyrɛlmɑ̃] *adv* [gén] naturally. || [logiquement] rationally.

naturiste [natyrist] *nmf* naturist.

naufrage [nofraʒ] *nm* [navire] shipwreck; **faire** ~ to be wrecked. || *fig* [effondrement] collapse.

naufragé, -e [nofraʒe] **1** *adj* shipwrecked. **2** *nm, f* shipwrecked person.

nauséabond, -e [nozeabɔ̃, ɔ̃d] *adj* nauseating.

nausée [noze] *nf* MÉD nausea; **avoir la** ~ to feel nauseous OU sick.

nautique [notik] *adj* nautical; [ski, sport] water (*avant n*).

naval, -e, -als [naval] *adj* naval.

navet [navɛ] *nm* BOT turnip. || *fam péj* [œuvre] load of rubbish.

navette [navɛt] *nf* shuttle; ~ **spatiale** AÉRON space shuttle; **faire la** ~ to shuttle.

navigable [navigabl] *adj* navigable.

navigateur, -trice [navigatœr, tris] *nm, f* navigator.

navigation [navigasjɔ̃] *nf* navigation; COMM shipping.

naviguer [navige] *vi* [voguer] to sail. || [piloter] to navigate.

navire [navir] *nm* ship.

navrant, -e [navrɑ̃, ɑ̃t] *adj* [triste] upsetting, distressing. || [regrettable, mauvais] unfortunate.

navrer [navre] *vt* to upset; **être navré de qqch/de faire qqch** to be sorry about sthg/to do sthg.

nazi, -e [nazi] *nm, f* Nazi.

nazisme [nazism] *nm* Nazism.

NB (*abr de* Nota Bene) NB.

NDLR (*abr de* note de la rédaction) editor's note.

NDT (*abr de* note du traducteur) translator's note.

ne [nə], **n'** (*devant voyelle ou h muet*) *adv* [négation] → **pas, plus, rien** *etc*. || [négation implicite]: **il se porte mieux que je** ~ **(le) croyais** he's in better health than I thought (he would be). || [avec verbes ou expressions marquant le doute, la crainte etc]: **je crains qu'il n'oublie** I'm afraid he'll forget.

né, -e [ne] *adj* born; ~ **en 1965** born in 1965; **née X, -e Y** Mrs X née Y.

néanmoins [neɑ̃mwɛ̃] *adv* nevertheless.

néant [neɑ̃] *nm* [absence d'existence] nothingness; **réduire à** ~ to reduce to nothing.

nébuleux, -euse [nebylø, øz] *adj* [ciel] cloudy. || [idée, projet] nebulous. ○ **nébuleuse** *nf* ASTRON nebula.

nécessaire [nesesɛr] **1** *adj* necessary; ~ **à** necessary for; **il est ~ de faire qqch** it is necessary to do sthg; **il est ~ que** (+ *subjonctif*): **il est ~ qu'elle vienne** she must come. **2** *nm* [biens] necessities (*pl*); **le strict** ~ the bare essentials (*pl*). || [mesures]: **faire le** ~ to do the necessary. || [trousse] bag.

nécessité [nesesite] *nf* [obligation, situation] necessity.

nécessiter [nesesite] *vt* to necessitate.

nécrologique [nekrɔlɔʒik] *adj* obituary (*avant n*).

nectar [nɛktar] *nm* nectar.

nectarine [nɛktarin] *nf* nectarine.

néerlandais, -e [neɛrlɑ̃dɛ, ɛz] *adj* Dutch. ○ **néerlandais** *nm* [langue] Dutch. ○ **Néerlandais, -e** *nm, f* Dutchman (*f* Dutchwoman); **les Néerlandais** the Dutch.

nef [nɛf] *nf* [d'église] nave.

néfaste [nefast] *adj* [jour, événement] fateful. || [influence] harmful.

négatif, -ive [negatif, iv] *adj* negative. ○ **négatif** PHOT negative. ○ **négative** *nf*: **répondre par la négative** to reply in the negative.

négation [negasjɔ̃] *nf* [rejet] denial. || GRAM negative.

négligé, -e [negliʒe] *adj* [travail, tenue] untidy. || [ami, jardin] neglected.

négligeable [negliʒabl] *adj* negligible.

négligemment [negliʒamɑ̃] *adv* [avec indifférence] casually.

négligence [negliʒɑ̃s] *nf* [laisser-aller] carelessness. || [omission] negligence.

négligent, e [negliʒɑ̃, ɑ̃t] *adj* [sans soin] careless. || [indifférent] casual.

négliger [negliʒe] *vt* [ami, jardin] to neglect; **~ de faire qqch** to fail to do sthg. || [avertissement] to ignore. ○ **se négliger** *vp* to neglect o.s.

négoce [negɔs] *nm* business.

négociant, -e [negɔsjɑ̃, ɑ̃t] *nm, f* dealer.

négociateur, -trice [negɔsjatœr, tris] *nm, f* negotiator.

négociation [negɔsjasjɔ̃] *nf* negotiation; **~s de paix** peace negotiations.

négocier [negɔsje] *vt* to negotiate.

nègre, négresse [nɛgr, negrɛs] *nm, f* negro (*f* negress) (*beware: the terms 'nègre' and 'négresse' are considered racist*). ○ **nègre** *nm fam* ghost writer.

neige [nɛʒ] *nf* [flocons] snow.

neiger [neʒe] *v impers*: **il neige** it is snowing.

neigeux, -euse [nɛʒø, øz] *adj* snowy.

nénuphar [nenyfar] *nm* water-lily.

néologisme [neɔlɔʒism] *nm* neologism.

néon [neɔ̃] *nm* [gaz] neon. || [enseigne] neon light.

néophyte [neɔfit] *nmf* novice.

néo-zélandais, -e [neɔzelɑ̃dɛ, ɛz] (*mpl inv, fpl* néo-zélandaises) *adj* New Zealand (*avant n*). ○ **Néo-Zélandais, -e** *nm, f* New Zealander.

Népal [nepal] *nm*: **le ~** Nepal.

nerf [nɛr] *nm* ANAT nerve. || *fig* [vigueur] spirit.

nerveux, -euse [nɛrvø, øz] *adj* [gén] nervous. || [voiture] nippy.

nervosité [nɛrvozite] *nf* nervousness.

nervure [nɛrvyr] *nf* [de feuille, d'aile] vein.

n'est-ce pas [nɛspa] *adv*: **vous me croyez, ~?** you believe me, don't you?

net, nette [nɛt] *adj* [écriture, image, idée] clear. || [propre, rangé] clean, neat. ||, COMM & FIN net; **~ d'impôt** tax-free. ○ **net** *adv* [sur le coup] on the spot; **s'arrêter ~** to stop dead; **se casser ~** to break clean off.

nettement [nɛtmɑ̃] *adv* [clairement] clearly. || [incontestablement] definitely; **~ plus/moins** much more/less.

netteté [nɛtte] *nf* clearness.

nettoyage [netwajaʒ] *nm* [de vêtement] cleaning; **~ à sec** dry cleaning.

nettoyer [netwaje] *vt* [gén] to clean. || [grenier] to clear out.

neuf¹, neuve [nœf, nœv] *adj* new. ○ **neuf** *nm*: **quoi de ~?** what's new?

neuf² [nœf] *adj num & nm* nine; *voir aussi* six.

neurasthénique [nørastenik] *nmf & adj* depressive.

neurologie [nørɔlɔʒi] *nf* neurology.

neutraliser [nøtralize] *vt* to neutralize.

neutralité [nøtralite] *nf* neutrality.

neutre [nøtr] **1** *nm* LING neuter. **2** *adj* [gén] neutral. || LING neuter.

neutron [nøtrɔ̃] *nm* neutron.

neuve → neuf.

neuvième [nœvjɛm] *adj num, nm & nmf* ninth; *voir aussi* sixième.

névé [neve] *nm* snowbank.

neveu, -x [nəvø] *nm* nephew.

névralgie [nevralʒi] *nf* MÉD neuralgia.

névrose [nevroz] *nf* neurosis.

névrosé, -e [nevroze] *adj & nm, f* neurotic.

nez [ne] *nm* nose; **saigner du ~** to have a nosebleed; **~ aquilin** aquiline nose; **~ busqué** hooked nose; **~ à ~** face to face.

ni [ni] *conj*: **sans pull ~ écharpe** without a sweater or a scarf. ○ **ni ... ni** *loc corrélative* neither ... nor; **~ lui ~ moi** neither of us; **je ne les aime ~ l'un ~ l'autre** I don't like either of them.

niais, -e [njɛ, njɛz] **1** *adj* silly, foolish. **2** *nm, f* fool.

Nicaragua [nikaragwa] *nm*: **le ~** Nicaragua.

niche [niʃ] *nf* [de chien] kennel. || [de statue] niche.

nicher [niʃe] *vi* [oiseaux] to rest.

nickel [nikɛl] 1 *nm* nickel. 2 *adj inv fam* spotless, spick and span.

nicotine [nikotin] *nf* nicotine.

nid [ni] *nm* nest.

nièce [njɛs] *nf* niece.

nier [nje] *vt* to deny.

nigaud, -e [nigo, od] *nm, f* simpleton.

Niger [niʒɛr] *nm* [fleuve]: le ~ the River Niger. || [État]: le ~ Niger.

Nigeria [niʒɛrja] *nm*: le ~ Nigeria.

Nil [nil] *nm*: le ~ the Nile.

n'importe → importer.

nippon, -one [nipɔ̃, ɔn] *adj* Japanese. ○ **Nippon, -one** *nm, f* Japanese (person); les **Nippons** the Japanese.

nitrate [nitrat] *nm* nitrate.

nitroglycérine [nitrogliserin] *nf* nitroglycerine.

niveau, -x [nivo] *nm* [gén] level; le ~ de la mer sea level; ~ de vie standard of living; au ~ de at the level of; *fig* [en ce qui concerne] as regards.

niveler [nivle] *vt* to level; *fig* to level out.

n° (*abr de* **numéro**) no.

noble [nɔbl] 1 *nmf* nobleman (*f* noblewoman). 2 *adj* noble.

noblesse [nɔblɛs] *nf* nobility.

noce [nɔs] *nf* [mariage] wedding. ○ **noces** *nfpl* wedding (*sg*); ~s d'or/d'argent golden/silver wedding (anniversary).

nocif, -ive [nɔsif, iv] *adj* [produit, gaz] noxious.

noctambule [nɔktɑ̃byl] *nmf* night bird.

nocturne [nɔktyrn] 1 *nm ou nf* [d'un magasin] late opening. 2 *adj* [émission, attaque] night (*avant n*). || [animal] nocturnal.

Noël [nɔɛl] *nm* Christmas; joyeux ~! happy ou merry Christmas!

nœud [nø] *nm* [de fil, de bois] knot; double ~ double knot. || NAVIG knot. || [de l'action, du problème] crux. || [ornement] bow; ~ de cravate knot (*in one's tie*); ~ papillon bow tie. || ANAT, ASTRON, ÉLECTR & RAIL node.

noir, -e [nwar] *adj* [gén] black; ~ de [poussière, suie] black with. || [pièce, couloir] dark. ○ **Noir, -e** *nm, f* black. ○ **noir** *nm* [couleur] black; ~ sur blanc *fig* in black and white. || [obscurité] dark. || *loc*: travail au ~ moonlighting. ○ **noire** *nf* quarter note *Am*.

noirâtre [nwaratr] *adj* blackish.

noirceur [nwarsœr] *nf fig* [méchanceté] wickedness.

noircir [nwarsir] 1 *vi* to darken. 2 *vt litt* & *fig* to blacken.

noisetier [nwaztje] *nm* hazel tree.

noisette [nwazɛt] *nf* [fruit] hazelnut.

noix [nwa] *nf* [fruit] walnut; ~ de cajou cashew (nut); ~ de coco coconut; ~ de muscade nutmeg. || *loc*: à la ~ *fam* dreadful.

nom [nɔ̃] *nm* [gén] name; au ~ de in the name of; ~ déposé trade name; ~ de famille surname; ~ de jeune fille maiden name. || [prénom] (first) name. || GRAM noun; ~ propre/commun proper/common noun.

nomade [nɔmad] 1 *nmf* nomad. 2 *adj* nomadic.

nombre [nɔ̃br] *nm* number; ~ pair/impair even/odd number.

nombreux, -euse [nɔ̃brø, øz] *adj* [famille, foule] large. || [erreurs, occasions] numerous; peu ~ few.

nombril [nɔ̃bril] *nm* navel; il se prend pour le ~ du monde he thinks the world revolves around him.

nominal, -e, -aux [nɔminal, o] *adj* [liste] of names. || [valeur, autorité] nominal. || GRAM noun (*avant n*).

nomination [nɔminasjɔ̃] *nf* nomination, appointment.

nommé, -e [nɔme] *adj* [désigné] named. || [choisi] appointed.

nommément [nɔmemɑ̃] *adv* [citer] by name.

nommer [nɔme] *vt* [appeler] to name, to call. || [qualifier] to call. || [promouvoir] to appoint, to nominate. || [dénoncer, mentionner] to name. ○ **se nommer** *vp* [s'appeler] to be called.

non [nɔ̃] 1 *adv* [réponse négative] no. || [se rapportant à une phrase précédente] not; moi ~ not me; moi ~ plus (and) neither am/do *etc* I. || [sert à demander une confirmation]: c'est une bonne idée, ~? it's a good idea, isn't it? || [modifie un adjectif ou un adverbe] not; ~ loin d'ici not far from here. 2 *nm inv* no. ○ **non (pas) que ... mais** *loc corrélative* not that ... but. ○ **non seulement ... mais (encore)** *loc corrélative* not only ... but also.

nonagénaire [nɔnaʒenɛr] *nmf* & *adj* nonagenarian.

non-agression [nɔnagrɛsjɔ̃] *nf* non-aggression.

nonante [nɔnɑ̃t] *adj num* Belg & Helv ninety.

nonchalance [nɔ̃ʃalɑ̃s] *nf* nonchalance, casualness.

non-fumeur, -euse [nɔ̃fymœr, øz] *nm, f* non-smoker.

non-lieu [nɔ̃ljø] (*pl* **non-lieux**) *nm* JUR dismissal through lack of evidence.

nonne [nɔn] *nf* nun.

non-sens [nɔ̃sɑ̃s] *nm inv* [absurdité] nonsense. || [contresens] meaningless word.

non-violence [nɔ̃vjɔlɑ̃s] *nf* non-violence.

non-voyant, -e [nɔ̃vwajɑ̃, ɑ̃t] *nm, f* visually handicapped.

nord [nɔr] **1** *nm* north; **un vent du ~** a northerly wind; **au ~** in the north; **au ~ (de)** to the north (of); **le grand Nord** the frozen North. **2** *adj inv* north; [province, région] northern.

nord-africain, -e [nɔrafrikɛ̃, ɛn] (*mpl* **nord-africains,** *fpl* **nord-africaines**) *adj* North African. ○ **Nord-Africain, -e** *nm, f* North African.

nord-américain, -e [nɔramerikɛ̃, ɛn] (*mpl* **nord-américains,** *fpl* **nord-américaines**) *adj* North American. ○ **Nord-Américain, -e** *nm, f* North American.

nord-est [nɔrɛst] *nm & adj inv* north-east.

nordique [nɔrdik] *adj* Nordic, Scandinavian. ○ **Nordique** *nmf* [Scandinave] Scandinavian. || *Can* North Canadian.

nord-ouest [nɔrwɛst] *nm & adj inv* north-west.

normal, -e, -aux [nɔrmal, o] *adj* normal. ○ **normale** *nf*: **la ~** the norm.

normalement [nɔrmalmɑ̃] *adv* normally, usually; **~ il devrait déjà être arrivé** he should have arrived by now.

normaliser [nɔrmalize] *vt* [situation] to normalize. || [produit] to standardize.

normand, -e [nɔrmɑ̃, ɑ̃d] *adj* Norman. ○ **Normand, -e** *nm, f* Norman.

Normandie [nɔrmɑ̃di] *nf*: **la ~** Normandy.

norme [nɔrm] *nf* [gén] standard, norm.

Norvège [nɔrvɛʒ] *nf*: **la ~** Norway.

norvégien, -ienne [nɔrveʒjɛ̃, jɛn] *adj* Norwegian. ○ **norvégien** *nm* [langue] Norwegian. ○ **Norvégien, -ienne** *nm, f* Norwegian.

nos → **notre**.

nostalgie [nɔstalʒi] *nf* nostalgia.

nostalgique [nɔstalʒik] *adj* nostalgic.

notable [nɔtabl] **1** *adj* noteworthy, notable. **2** *nm* notable.

notaire [nɔtɛr] *nm* ≃ lawyer.

notamment [nɔtamɑ̃] *adv* in particular.

note [nɔt] *nf* [gén & MUS] note; **prendre des ~s** to take notes. || SCOL & UNIV mark, grade *Am*. || [facture] bill.

noter [nɔte] *vt* [écrire] to note down. || [constater] to note, to notice. || SCOL & UNIV to mark, to grade *Am*.

notice [nɔtis] *nf* instructions (*pl*).

notifier [nɔtifje] *vt*: **~ qqch à qqn** to notify sb of sthg.

notion [nɔsjɔ̃] *nf* [conscience, concept] notion, concept. || (*gén pl*) [rudiment] smattering (*U*).

notoire [nɔtwar] *adj* [fait] well-known; [criminel] notorious.

notre [nɔtr] (*pl* **nos** [no]) *adj poss* our.

nôtre [notr] ○ **le nôtre** (*f* **la nôtre,** *pl* **les nôtres**) *pron poss* ours.

nouer [nwe] *vt* [corde, lacet] to tie; [bouquet] to tie up. ○ **se nouer** *vp* [gorge] to tighten. || [intrigue] to start.

noueux, -euse [nwø, øz] *adj* [bois] knotty; [mains] gnarled.

nougat [nuga] *nm* nougat.

nouille [nuj] *nf fam péj* idiot. ○ **nouilles** *nfpl* [pâtes] pasta (*U*), noodles (*pl*).

nourrice [nuris] *nf* [garde d'enfants] nanny, child-minder; [qui allaite] wet nurse.

nourrir [nurir] *vt* [gén] to feed. || [sentiment, projet] to nurture. ○ **se nourrir** *vp* to eat; **se ~ de qqch** *litt & fig* to live on sthg.

nourrissant, -e [nurisɑ̃, ɑ̃t] *adj* nutritious, nourishing.

nourrisson [nurisɔ̃] *nm* infant.

nourriture [nurityr] *nf* food.

nous [nu] *pron pers* [sujet] we. || [objet] us. ○ **nous-mêmes** *pron pers* ourselves.

nouveau, -elle, -x [nuvo, ɛl, o] (**nouvel** *devant voyelle et h muet*) **1** *adj* new; **-x mariés** newlyweds. **2** *nm, f* new boy (*f* new girl). ○ **nouveau** *nm*: **il y a du ~** there's something new. ○ **nouvelle** *nf* [information] (piece of) news (*U*). || [court récit] short story. ○ **nouvelles** *nfpl* news; **les nouvelles** MÉDIA the news (*sg*); **il a donné de ses nouvelles** I/we *etc* have heard from him. ○ **à nouveau** *loc adv* [encore] again. ○ **de nouveau** *loc adv* again.

nouveau-né, -e [nuvone] (*mpl*

nouveau-nés, *fpl* **nouveau-nées**) *nm*, *f* newborn baby.

nouveauté [nuvote] *nf* [actualité] novelty. || [innovation] something new. || [ouvrage] new book/film *etc.*

nouvel, nouvelle → **nouveau**.

Nouvelle-Calédonie [nuvɛlkaledɔni] *nf*: **la ~** New Caledonia.

Nouvelle-Zélande [nuvɛlzelɑ̃d] *nf*: **la ~** New Zealand.

novateur, -trice [nɔvatœr, trɪs] 1 *adj* innovative. 2 *nm*, *f* innovator.

novembre [nɔvɑ̃br] *nm* November; *voir aussi* **septembre**.

novice [nɔvis] 1 *nmf* novice. 2 *adj* inexperienced.

noyade [nwajad] *nf* drowning.

noyau, -x [nwajo] *nm* [de fruit] stone, pit. || ASTRON, BIOL & PHYS nucleus. || *fig* [d'amis] group, circle; [d'opposants, de résistants] cell; **~ dur** hard core. || *fig* [centre] core.

noyé, -e [nwaje] 1 *adj* [inondé] flooded; **yeux ~s de larmes** eyes swimming with tears. 2 *nm*, *f* drowned person.

noyer [nwaje] *vt* [animal, personne] to drown. || [terre, moteur] to flood. || [estomper, diluer] to swamp; [contours] to blur. ○ **se noyer** *vp* [personne] to drown. || *fig* [se perdre]: **se ~ dans** to become bogged down in.

N/Réf (*abr de* **Notre référence**) O/Ref.

nu, -e [ny] *adj* [personne] naked. || [paysage, fil électrique] bare. || [style, vérité] plain. ○ **nu** *nm* nude; **à ~** stripped, bare; **mettre à ~** to strip bare.

nuage [nɥaʒ] *nm* [gén] cloud. || [petite quantité]: **un ~ de lait** a drop of milk.

nuageux, -euse [nɥaʒø, øz] *adj* [temps, ciel] cloudy. || *fig* [esprit] hazy.

nuance [nɥɑ̃s] *nf* [de couleur] shade; [de son, de sens] nuance.

nubile [nybil] *adj* nubile.

nucléaire [nykleer] 1 *nm* nuclear energy. 2 *adj* nuclear.

nudisme [nydism] *nm* nudism, naturism.

nudité [nydite] *nf* [de personne] nudity, nakedness. || [de lieu, style] bareness.

nuée [nɥe] *nf* [multitude]: **une ~ de** a horde of. || *littéraire* [nuage] cloud.

nues [ny] *nfpl*: **tomber des ~** to be completely taken aback.

nui [nɥi] *pp inv* → **nuire**.

nuire [nɥir] *vi*: **~ à** to harm, to injure.

nuisance [nɥizɑ̃s] *nf* nuisance (*U*), harm (*U*).

nuisible [nɥizibl] *adj* harmful.

nuit [nɥi] *nf* [laps de temps] night; **cette ~** [la nuit dernière] last night; [la nuit prochaine] tonight; **de ~** at night; **bateau/vol de ~** night ferry/flight; **~ blanche** sleepless night. || [obscurité] darkness, night; **il fait ~** it's dark.

nuitée [nɥite] *nf* overnight stay.

nul, nulle [nyl] 1 *adj indéf* (*avant n*) *littéraire* no. 2 *adj* (*après n*) [égal à zéro] nil. || [sans valeur] useless, hopeless; **être ~ en maths** to be hopeless ou useless at maths. 3 *nm*, *f péj* nonentity. 4 *pron indéf sout* no one, nobody. ○ **nulle part** *adv* nowhere.

nullement [nylmɑ̃] *adv* by no means.

nullité [nylite] *nf* [médiocrité] incompetence. || JUR invalidity, nullity.

numéraire [nymerer] *nm* cash.

numérique [nymerik] *adj* [gén] numerical. || INFORM digital.

numéro [nymero] *nm* [gén] number; **faire un faux ~** to dial a wrong number; **~ minéralogique** ou **d'immatriculation** registration *Br* ou license *Am* number; **~ de téléphone** telephone number; **~ vert** ≃ freefone number. || [de spectacle] act, turn. || *fam* [personne]: **quel ~!** what a character!

numéroter [nymerɔte] *vt* to number.

nu-pieds [nypje] *nm inv* [sandale] sandal.

nuptial, -e, -iaux [nypsjal, jo] *adj* nuptial.

nuque [nyk] *nf* nape.

nurse [nœrs] *nf* children's nurse, nanny.

nutritif, -ive [nytritif, iv] *adj* nutritious.

nutritionniste [nytrisjɔnist] *nmf* nutritionist, dietician.

Nylon® [nilɔ̃] *nm* nylon.

nymphomane [nɛ̃fɔman] *nf & adj* nymphomaniac.

o, O [o] *nm inv* [lettre] o, O. ○ **O** (*abr de* Ouest) W.

oasis [ɔazis] *nf* [dans désert] oasis.

obéir [ɔbeir] *vi* [personne]: ~ à qqn/qqch to obey sb/sthg. || [freins] to respond.

obéissant, -e [ɔbeisɑ̃, ɑ̃t] *adj* obedient.

obélisque [ɔbelisk] *nm* obelisk.

obèse [ɔbɛz] *adj* obese.

obésité [ɔbezite] *nf* obesity.

objecteur [ɔbʒɛktœr] *nm* objector; ~ de conscience conscientious objector.

objectif, -ive [ɔbʒɛktif, iv] *adj* objective. ○ **objectif** *nm* PHOT lens. || [but, cible] objective, target.

objection [ɔbʒɛksjɔ̃] *nf* objection.

objectivité [ɔbʒɛktivite] *nf* objectivity.

objet [ɔbʒɛ] *nm* [chose] object; ~ d'art objet d'art; ~ de valeur valuable; ~s trouvés lost property office *Br*, lost and found (office) *Am*. || [sujet] subject.

obligation [ɔbligasjɔ̃] *nf* [gén] obligation; être dans l'~ de faire qqch to be obliged to do sthg. || FIN bond, debenture.

obligatoire [ɔbligatwar] *adj* [imposé] compulsory, obligatory. || *fam* [inéluctable] inevitable.

obligeance [ɔbliʒɑ̃s] *nf sout* obligingness; avoir l'~ de faire qqch to be good ou kind enough to do sthg.

obliger [ɔbliʒe] *vt* [forcer]: ~ qqn à qqch to impose sthg on sb; ~ qqn à faire qqch to force sb to do sthg; être obligé de faire qqch to be obliged to do sthg. || [rendre service à] to oblige. ○ **s'obliger** *vp*: s'~ à qqch to impose sthg on o.s.; s'~ à faire qqch to force o.s. to do sthg.

oblique [ɔblik] *adj* oblique.

obliquer [ɔblike] *vi* to turn off.

oblitérer [ɔblitere] *vt* [tamponner] to cancel. || MÉD to obstruct. || [effacer] to obliterate.

obnubiler [ɔbnybile] *vt* to obsess; être obnubilé par to be obsessed with ou by.

obole [ɔbɔl] *nf* small contribution.

obscène [ɔpsɛn] *adj* obscene.

obscénité [ɔpsenite] *nf* obscenity.

obscur, -e [ɔpskyr] *adj* [sombre] dark. || [inconnu, douteux] obscure.

obscurantisme [ɔpskyrɑ̃tism] *nm* obscurantism.

obscurcir [ɔpskyrsir] *vt* [assombrir] to darken. || [embrouiller] to confuse. ○ **s'obscurcir** *vp* [s'assombrir] to grow dark. || [s'embrouiller] to become confused.

obscurité [ɔpskyrite] *nf* [nuit] darkness.

obsédé, -e [ɔpsede] **1** *adj* obsessed. **2** *nm, f* obsessive.

obséder [ɔpsede] *vt* to obsess, to haunt.

obsèques [ɔpsɛk] *nfpl* funeral (*sg*).

obséquieux, -ieuse [ɔpsekjø, jøz] *adj* obsequious.

observateur, -trice [ɔpsɛrvatœr, tris] **1** *adj* observant. **2** *nm, f* observer.

observation [ɔpsɛrvasjɔ̃] *nf* [gén] observation; être en ~ MÉD to be under observation. || [critique] remark.

observatoire [ɔpsɛrvatwar] *nm* ASTRON observatory.

observer [ɔpsɛrve] *vt* [regarder, remarquer, respecter] to observe. || [épier] to watch. || [constater]: faire ~ qqch à qqn to point sthg out to sb.

obsession [ɔpsesjɔ̃] *nf* obsession.

obsolète [ɔpsɔlɛt] *adj* obsolete.

obstacle [ɔpstakl] *nm* [entrave] obstacle. || *fig* [difficulté] hindrance; faire ~ à qqch/qqn to hinder sthg/sb.

obstination [ɔpstinasjɔ̃] *nf* stubbornness, obstinacy.

obstiné, -e [ɔpstine] *adj* [entêté] stubborn, obstinate. || [acharné] dogged.

obstiner [ɔpstine] ○ **s'obstiner** *vp* to insist; s'~ à faire qqch to persist stubbornly in doing sthg; s'~ dans qqch to cling stubbornly to sthg.

obstruction [ɔpstryksjɔ̃] *nf* MÉD obstruction, blockage. || POLIT & SPORT obstruction.

obstruer [ɔpstrye] *vt* to block, to obstruct. ○ **s'obstruer** *vp* to become blocked.

obtempérer [ɔptɑ̃pere] *vi*: ~ à to comply with.

obtenir [ɔptənir] *vt* to get, to obtain; ~ qqch de qqn to get sthg from sb.

obtention [ɔptɑ̃sjɔ̃] *nf* obtaining.

obtenu, -e [ɔptəny] *pp* → obtenir.

obturer

obturer [ɔptyre] *vt* tò close, to seal; [dent] to fill.

obtus, -e [ɔpty, yz] *adj* obtuse.

obus [ɔby] *nm* shell.

OC (*abr de* **ondes courtes**) SW.

occasion [ɔkazjɔ̃] *nf* [possibilité, chance] opportunity, chance; **saisir l'~ (de faire qqch)** to seize or grab the chance (to do sthg); **à l'~** some time; [de temps en temps] sometimes, on occasion; **à la première ~** at the first opportunity. ‖ [circonstance] occasion; **à l'~ de** on the occasion of. ‖ [bonne affaire] bargain. ○ **d'occasion** *loc adv & loc adj* second-hand.

occasionnel, -elle [ɔkazjɔnɛl] *adj* [irrégulier - visite, problème] occasional; [- travail] casual.

occasionner [ɔkazjɔne] *vt* to cause.

occident [ɔksidɑ̃] *nm* west. ○ **Occident** *nm*: **l'Occident** the West.

occidental, -e, -aux [ɔksidɑtal, o] *adj* western. ○ **Occidental, -e, -aux** *nm, f* Westerner.

occlusion [ɔklyzjɔ̃] *nf* MÉD blockage, obstruction. ‖ LING & CHIM occlusion.

occulte [ɔkylt] *adj* occult.

occulter [ɔkylte] *vt* [sentiments] to conceal.

occupation [ɔkypasjɔ̃] *nf* [activité] occupation, job. ‖ MIL occupation.

occupé, -e [ɔkype] *adj* [personne] busy. ‖ [appartement, zone] occupied. ‖ [place] taken; [toilettes] engaged; **c'est ~** [téléphone] it's engaged *Br* ou busy *Am*.

occuper [ɔkype] *vt* [place] to occupy. ‖ [espace] to take up. ‖ [fonction, poste] to hold. ○ **s'occuper** *vp* [s'activer] to keep o.s. busy; **s'~ à qqch/à faire qqch** to be busy with sthg/doing sthg. ‖ **s'~ de qqch** [se charger de] to take care of sthg, to deal with sthg; [s'intéresser à] to take an interest in, to be interested in; **occupez-vous de vos affaires!** mind your own business! ‖ [prendre soin]: **s'~ de qqn** to take care of sb, to look after sb.

occurrence [ɔkyrɑ̃s] *nf* [circonstance]: **en l'~** in this case. ‖ LING occurrence.

OCDE (*abr de* **Organisation de coopération et de développement économique**) *nf* OECD.

océan [ɔseɑ̃] *nm* ocean; **l'~ Antarctique** the Antarctic Ocean; **l'~ Arctique** the Arctic Ocean; **l'~ Atlantique** the Atlantic Ocean; **l'~ Indien** the Indian Ocean; **l'~ Pacifique** the Pacific Ocean.

Océanie [ɔseani] *nf*: **l'~** Oceania.

océanique [ɔseanik] *adj* ocean (*avant n*).

ocre [ɔkr] *adj inv & nf* ochre.

octante [ɔktɑ̃t] *adj num Belg & Helv* eighty.

octave [ɔktav] *nf* octave.

octet [ɔktɛ] *nm* INFORM byte.

octobre [ɔktɔbr] *nm* October; *voir aussi* **septembre**.

octogénaire [ɔktɔʒenɛr] *nmf & adj* octogenarian.

octroyer [ɔktrwaje] *vt*: **~ qqch à qqn** to grant sb sthg, to grant sthg to sb. ○ **s'octroyer** *vp* to grant o.s., to treat o.s. to.

oculaire [ɔkylɛr] *adj* ocular, eye (*avant n*).

oculiste [ɔkylist] *nmf* ophthalmologist.

ode [ɔd] *nf* ode.

odeur [ɔdœr] *nf* smell.

odieux, -ieuse [ɔdjø, jøz] *adj* [crime] odious, abominable. ‖ [personne, attitude] unbearable, obnoxious.

odorant, -e [ɔdɔrɑ̃, ɑ̃t] *adj* sweet-smelling, fragrant.

odorat [ɔdɔra] *nm* (sense of) smell.

œdème [edɛm] *nm* oedema.

œil [œj] (*pl* **yeux** [jø]) *nm* [gén] eye; **yeux bridés/exorbités/globuleux** slanting/bulging/protruding eyes; **avoir les yeux cernés** to have bags under one's eyes. ‖ *loc*: **avoir qqch/qqn à l'~** to have one's eye on sthg/sb; **n'avoir pas froid aux yeux** not to be afraid of anything, to have plenty of nerve; **mon ~!** *fam* like hell; **cela saute aux yeux** it's obvious.

œillade [œjad] *nf* wink; **lancer une ~ à qqn** to wink at sb.

œillère [œjɛr] *nf* eyebath. ○ **œillères** *nfpl* blinkers *Br*, blinders *Am*.

œillet [œjɛ] *nm* [fleur] carnation. ‖ [de chaussure] eyelet.

œnologue [enɔlɔg] *nmf* wine expert.

œsophage [ezɔfaʒ] *nm* oesophagus.

œstrogène [estrɔʒɛn] *nm* œstrogen.

œuf [œf] *nm* egg; **~ à la coque/au plat/poché** boiled/fried/poached egg; **~ mollet/dur** soft-boiled/hard-boiled egg; **~s brouillés** scrambled eggs.

œuvre [œvr] *nf* [travail] work; **se mettre à l'~** to get down to work; **mettre qqch en ~** [loi, accord, projet] to implement sthg. ‖ [d'artiste] work; [- ensemble de sa production] works (*pl*); **~ d'art** work of art. ‖ [organisation] charity; **~ de bienfaisance** charity, charitable organization.

onde

offense [ɔfɑ̃s] *nf* [insulte] insult.

offenser [ɔfɑ̃se] *vt* [personne] to offend. || [bon goût] to offend against. ○ **s'offenser** *vp*: **s'~ de** to take offence at, to be offended by.

offensif, -ive [ɔfɑ̃sif, iv] *adj* offensive. ○ **offensive** *nf* MIL offensive; **passer à l'offensive** to go on the offensive; **prendre l'offensive** to take the offensive.

offert, -e [ɔfɛr, ɛrt] *pp* → **offrir**.

office [ɔfis] *nm* [bureau] office, agency; **~ du tourisme** tourist office. || [fonction]: **faire ~ de** to act as; **remplir son ~** to do its job, to fulfil its function. || RELIG service. ○ **d'office** *loc adv* automatically, as a matter of course; **commis d'~** officially appointed.

officialiser [ɔfisjalize] *vt* to make official.

officiel, -ielle [ɔfisjɛl] *adj & nm, f* official.

officier¹ [ɔfisje] *vi* to officiate.

officier² [ɔfisje] *nm* officer.

officieux, -ieuse [ɔfisjø, jøz] *adj* unofficial.

offrande [ɔfrɑ̃d] *nf* [don] offering. || RELIG offertory.

offre [ɔfr] *nf* [proposition] offer; [aux enchères] bid; [pour contrat] tender; **«~s d'emploi»** "situations vacant", "vacancies"; **~ d'essai** trial offer; **~ de lancement** introductory offer; **~ publique d'achat** takeover bid. || ÉCON supply.

offrir [ɔfrir] *vt* [faire cadeau]: **~ qqch à qqn** to give sb sthg, to give sthg to sb. || [proposer]: **~ (qqch à qqn)** to offer (sb sthg ou sthg to sb). || [présenter] to offer, to present. ○ **s'offrir** *vp* [croisière, livre] to treat o.s. to. || [se présenter] to present itself. || [se proposer] to offer one's services, to offer o.s.

offusquer [ɔfyske] *vt* to offend. ○ **s'offusquer** *vp*: **s'~ (de)** to take offence (at).

ogive [ɔʒiv] *nf* ARCHIT ogive. || [MIL - d'obus] head; [- de fusée] nosecone; **~ nucléaire** nuclear warhead.

ogre, ogresse [ɔgr, ɔgrɛs] *nm, f* ogre (*f* ogress).

oh [o] *interj* oh!; **~ la la!** dear oh dear!

ohé [ɔe] *interj* hey!

oie [wa] *nf* goose.

oignon [ɔɲɔ̃] *nm* [plante] onion. || [bulbe] bulb. || MÉD bunion.

oiseau, -x [wazo] *nm* ZOOL bird; **~ de proie** bird of prey.

oisif, -ive [wazif, iv] **1** *adj* idle. **2** *nm, f* man of leisure (*f* woman of leisure).

oisillon [wazijɔ̃] *nm* fledgling.

oisiveté [wazivte] *nf* idleness.

O.K. [ɔke] *interj fam* okay.

oléoduc [ɔleɔdyk] *nm* (oil) pipeline.

olfactif, -ive [ɔlfaktif, iv] *adj* olfactory.

olive [ɔliv] *nf* olive.

olivier [ɔlivje] *nm* [arbre] olive tree; [bois] olive wood.

OLP (*abr de* **Organisation de libération de la Palestine**) *nf* PLO.

olympique [ɔlɛ̃pik] *adj* Olympic (*avant n*).

ombilical, -e, -aux [ɔ̃bilikal, o] *adj* umbilical.

ombrage [ɔ̃braʒ] *nm* shade.

ombragé, -e [ɔ̃braʒe] *adj* shady.

ombrageux, -euse [ɔ̃braʒø, øz] *adj* [personne] touchy, prickly. || [cheval] nervous, skittish.

ombre [ɔ̃br] *nf* [zone sombre] shade; **à l'~ de** [arbre] in the shade of; **laisser qqch dans l'~** *fig* to deliberately ignore sthg. || [forme, fantôme] shadow. || [trace] hint.

ombrelle [ɔ̃brɛl] *nf* parasol.

omelette [ɔmlɛt] *nf* omelette.

omettre [ɔmetr] *vt* to omit; **~ de faire qqch** to omit to do sthg.

omis, -e [ɔmi, iz] *pp* → **omettre**.

omission [ɔmisjɔ̃] *nf* omission; **par ~** by omission.

omnibus [ɔmnibys] *nm* stopping ou local train.

omniprésent, -e [ɔmniprezɑ̃, ɑ̃t] *adj* omnipresent.

omnivore [ɔmnivɔr] **1** *nm* omnivore. **2** *adj* omnivorous.

omoplate [ɔmoplat] *nf* [os] shoulder blade; [épaule] shoulder.

OMS (*abr de* **Organisation mondiale de la santé**) *nf* WHO.

on [ɔ̃] *pron pers indéf* [indéterminé] you, one; **~ n'a pas le droit de fumer ici** you're not allowed ou one isn't allowed to smoke here, smoking isn't allowed here. || [les gens, l'espèce humaine] they, people. || [quelqu'un] someone; **~ vous a appelé au téléphone ce matin** there was a telephone call for you this morning. || *fam* [nous] we.

oncle [ɔ̃kl] *nm* uncle.

onctueux, -euse [ɔ̃ktɥø, øz] *adj* smooth.

onde [ɔ̃d] *nf* PHYS wave. ○ **ondes** *nfpl* [radio] air (*sg*).

ondée [ɔ̃de] *nf* shower (of rain).

ondulation [ɔ̃dylasjɔ̃] *nf* [mouvement] rippling; [de sol, terrain] undulation. || [de coiffure] wave.

onduler [ɔ̃dyle] *vi* [drapeau] to ripple, to wave; [cheveux] to be wavy; [route] to undulate.

onéreux, -euse [ɔnerø, øz] *adj* costly.

ongle [ɔ̃gl] *nm* [de personne] fingernail, nail. || [d'animal] claw.

onglet [ɔ̃glɛ] *nm* [de lame] thumbnail groove. || CULIN top skirt.

onguent [ɔ̃gɑ̃] *nm* ointment.

onomatopée [ɔnɔmatɔpe] *nf* onomatopoeia.

ont → **avoir**.

ONU, Onu [ɔny] (*abr de* **Organisation des Nations unies**) *nf* UN, UNO.

onyx [ɔniks] *nm* onyx.

onze [ɔ̃z] *adj num* & *nm* eleven; *voir aussi* **six**.

onzième [ɔ̃zjɛm] *adj num*, *nm* & *nmf* eleventh; *voir aussi* **sixième**.

OPA (*abr de* **offre publique d'achat**) *nf* take-over bid.

opale [ɔpal] *nf* & *adj inv* opal.

opaline [ɔpalin] *nf* opaline.

opaque [ɔpak] *adj*: ~ (à) opaque (to).

OPEP, Opep (*abr de* **Organisation des pays exportateurs de pétrole**) *nf* OPEC.

opéra [ɔpera] *nm* MUS opera. || [théâtre] opera house.

opéra-comique [ɔperakɔmik] *nm* light opera.

opérateur, -trice [ɔperatœr, tris] *nm*, *f* operator.

opération [ɔperasjɔ̃] *nf* [gén] operation. || COMM deal, transaction.

opérationnel, -elle [ɔperasjɔnɛl] *adj* operational.

opérer [ɔpere] **1** *vt* MÉD to operate on. || [exécuter] to carry out, to implement; [choix, tri] to make. **2** *vi* [agir] to take effect; [personne] to operate, to proceed. ○ **s'opérer** *vp* to come about, to take place.

opérette [ɔperɛt] *nf* operetta.

ophtalmologiste [ɔftalmɔlɔʒist] *nmf* ophthalmologist.

opiniâtre [ɔpinjatr] *adj* [caractère, personne] stubborn, obstinate. || [effort] dogged; [travail] unrelenting; [fièvre, toux] persistent.

opinion [ɔpinjɔ̃] *nf* opinion; l'~ publique public opinion.

opium [ɔpjɔm] *nm* opium.

opportun, -e [ɔpɔrtœ̃, yn] *adj* opportune, timely.

opportuniste [ɔpɔrtynist] **1** *nmf* opportunist. **2** *adj* opportunistic.

opportunité [ɔpɔrtynite] *nf* [à-propos] opportuneness, timeliness. || [occasion] opportunity.

opposant, -e [ɔpozɑ̃, ɑ̃t] **1** *adj* opposing. **2** *nm*, *f*: ~ (à) opponent (of).

opposé, -e [ɔpoze] *adj* [direction, côté, angle] opposite. || [intérêts, opinions] conflicting; [forces] opposing. || [hostile]: ~ à opposed to. ○ **opposé** *nm*: l'~ the opposite; à l'~ de in the opposite direction from; *fig* unlike, contrary to.

opposer [ɔpoze] *vt* [mettre en opposition - choses, notions]: ~ **qqch** (à) to contrast sthg (with). || [mettre en présence - personnes, armées] to oppose; ~ **deux équipes** to bring two teams together; ~ **qqn à qqn** to pit oʊ set sb against sb. || [refus, protestation, objection] to put forward. || [diviser] to divide. ○ **s'opposer** *vp* [contraster] to contrast. || [entrer en conflit] to clash. || s'~ à [se dresser contre] to oppose, to be opposed to; s'~ à ce que **qqn fasse qqch** to be opposed to sb's doing sthg.

opposition [ɔpozisjɔ̃] *nf* [gén] opposition; faire ~ à [décision, mariage] to oppose; [chèque] to stop; **entrer en ~ avec** to come into conflict with. || JUR: ~ (à) objection (to). || [contraste] contrast; par ~ à in contrast with, as opposed to.

oppresser [ɔprese] *vt* [étouffer] to suffocate, to stifle. || *fig* [tourmenter] to oppress.

oppresseur [ɔpresœr] *nm* oppressor.

oppressif, -ive [ɔpresif, iv] *adj* oppressive.

oppression [ɔpresjɔ̃] *nf* [asservissement] oppression. || [malaise] tightness of the chest.

opprimé, -e [ɔprime] **1** *adj* oppressed. **2** *nm*, *f* oppressed person.

opprimer [ɔprime] *vt* [asservir] to oppress. || [étouffer] to stifle.

opter [ɔpte] *vi*: ~ **pour** to opt for.

opticien, -ienne [ɔptisjɛ̃, jɛn] *nm*, *f* optician.

optimal, -e, -aux [ɔptimal, o] *adj* optimal.

optimiste [ɔptimist] **1** *nmf* optimist. **2** *adj* optimistic.

option [ɔpsjɔ̃] *nf* [gén] option; **prendre une ~ sur** FIN to take (out) an option on. || [accessoire] optional extra.

optionnel, -elle [ɔpsjɔnɛl] *adj* optional.

optique [ɔptik] **1** *nf* [science, technique] optics (*U*). || [perspective] viewpoint. **2** *adj* [nerf] optic; [verre] optical.

opulence [ɔpylɑ̃s] *nf* [richesse] opulence. || [ampleur] fullness, ampleness.

opulent, -e [ɔpylɑ̃, ɑ̃t] *adj* [riche] rich. || [gros] ample.

or[1] [ɔr] *nm* [métal, couleur] gold; **en ~** [objet] gold (*avant n*); **une occasion en ~** a golden opportunity; **une affaire en ~** [achat] an excellent bargain. || [dorure] gilding.

or[2] [ɔr] *conj* [pour introduire un contraste] well, but.

oracle [ɔrakl] *nm* oracle.

orage [ɔraʒ] *nm* [tempête] storm.

orageux, -euse [ɔraʒø, øz] *adj* stormy.

oraison [ɔrɛzɔ̃] *nf* prayer; **~ funèbre** funeral oration.

oral, -e, -aux [ɔral, o] *adj* oral. ○ **oral** *nm* oral (examination).

oralement [ɔralmɑ̃] *adv* orally.

orange [ɔrɑ̃ʒ] **1** *nf* orange. **2** *nm & adj inv* [couleur] orange.

orangé, -e [ɔrɑ̃ʒe] *adj* orangey.

orangeade [ɔrɑ̃ʒad] *nf* orange squash.

oranger [ɔrɑ̃ʒe] *nm* orange tree.

orang-outan, orang-outang [ɔrɑ̃utɑ̃] *nm* orangutang.

orateur, -trice [ɔratœr, tris] *nm, f* [conférencier] speaker. || [personne éloquente] orator.

orbital, -e, -aux [ɔrbital, o] *adj* [mouvement] orbital; [station] orbiting.

orbite [ɔrbit] *nf* ANAT (eye) socket. || ASTRON & *fig* orbit; **mettre sur ~** AÉRON to put into orbit; *fig* to launch.

orchestre [ɔrkɛstr] *nm* MUS orchestra. || CIN & THÉÂTRE stalls (*pl*) *Br*, orchestra *Am*; **fauteuil d'~** seat in the stalls *Br*, orchestra seat *Am*.

orchestrer [ɔrkɛstre] *vt litt & fig* to orchestrate.

orchidée [ɔrkide] *nf* orchid.

ordinaire [ɔrdinɛr] *adj* [usuel, standard] ordinary, normal. || *péj* [commun] ordinary, common. ○ **d'ordinaire** *loc adv* normally, usually.

ordinal, -e, -aux [ɔrdinal, o] *adj* ordinal. ○ **ordinal, -aux** *nm* ordinal (number).

ordinateur [ɔrdinatœr] *nm* computer; **~ individuel** personal computer, PC.

ordonnance [ɔrdɔnɑ̃s] **1** *nf* MÉD prescription. || [de gouvernement, juge] order. **2** *nm ou nf* MIL orderly.

ordonné, -e [ɔrdɔne] *adj* [maison, élève] tidy.

ordonner [ɔrdɔne] *vt* [ranger] to organize, to put in order. || [enjoindre] to order, to tell; **~ à qqn de faire qqch** to order sb to do sthg.

ordre [ɔrdr] *nm* [gén, MIL & RELIG] order; **par ~ alphabétique/chronologique/décroissant** in alphabetical/chronological/descending order; **donner un ~ à qqn** to give sb an order; **être aux ~s de qqn** to be at sb's disposal; **jusqu'à nouvel ~** until further notice; **l'~ public** law and order. || [bonne organisation] tidiness, orderliness; **en ~** orderly, tidy; **mettre en ~** to put in order, to tidy (up). || [catégorie]: **de premier/second ~** first-/second-rate; **d'~ privé/pratique** of a private/practical nature; **pouvez-vous me donner un ~ de grandeur?** can you give me some idea of the size/amount *etc*? || [corporation] professional association; **l'Ordre des médecins** ≃ the American Medical Association *Am*. || FIN: **à l'~ de** payable to. ○ **ordre du jour** *nm* [de réunion] agenda; **à l'~ du jour** [de réunion] on the agenda.

ordure [ɔrdyr] *nf fig* [grossièreté] filth (*U*). || *péj* [personne] scum (*U*), bastard. ○ **ordures** *nfpl* [déchets] rubbish (*U*) *Br*, garbage (*U*) *Am*.

ordurier, -ière [ɔrdyrje, jɛr] *adj* filthy, obscene.

orée [ɔre] *nf* edge.

oreille [ɔrɛj] *nf* ANAT ear. || [ouïe] hearing. || [de fauteuil, écrou] wing; [de marmite, tasse] handle.

oreiller [ɔrɛje] *nm* pillow.

oreillette [ɔrɛjɛt] *nf* [du cœur] auricle. || [de casquette] earflap.

oreillons [ɔrɛjɔ̃] *nmpl* mumps (*sg*).

ores [ɔr] ○ **d'ores et déjà** *loc adv* from now on.

orfèvre [ɔrfɛvr] *nm* goldsmith; [d'argent] silversmith.

orfèvrerie [ɔrfɛvrəri] *nf* [art] goldsmith's art; [d'argent] silversmith's art.

organe [ɔrgan] *nm* ANAT organ. || [institution] organ, body. || *fig* [porte-parole] representative.

organigramme [ɔrganigram] *nm* [hiérarchique] organization chart. || INFORM flow chart.

organique [ɔrganik] *adj* organic.

organisateur, -trice [ɔrganizatœr, tris] **1** adj organizing (avant n). **2** nm, f organizer.

organisation [ɔrganizasjɔ̃] nf organization.

organisé, -e [ɔrganize] adj organized.

organiser [ɔrganize] vt to organize. ○ **s'organiser** vp [personne] to be ou get organized. || [prendre forme] to take shape.

organisme [ɔrganism] nm BIOL & ZOOL organism. || [institution] body, organization.

organiste [ɔrganist] nmf organist.

orgasme [ɔrgasm] nm orgasm.

orge [ɔrʒ] nf barley.

orgie [ɔrʒi] nf orgy.

orgue [ɔrg] nm organ.

orgueil [ɔrgœj] nm pride.

orgueilleux, -euse [ɔrgœjø, øz] **1** adj proud. **2** nm, f proud person.

orient [ɔrjɑ̃] nm east. ○ **Orient** nm: l'Orient the Orient, the East.

oriental, -e, -aux [ɔrjɑ̃tal, o] adj [région, frontière] eastern; [d'Extrême-Orient] oriental.

orientation [ɔrjɑ̃tasjɔ̃] nf [direction] orientation; **avoir le sens de l'~** to have a good sense of direction. || SCOL career. || [de maison] aspect. || fig [de politique, recherche] direction, trend.

orienter [ɔrjɑ̃te] vt [disposer] to position. || [voyageur, élève, recherches] to guide, to direct. ○ **s'orienter** vp [se repérer] to find ou get one's bearings. || fig [se diriger]: **s'~ vers** to move towards.

orifice [ɔrifis] nm orifice.

originaire [ɔriʒinɛr] adj [natif]: **être ~ de** [personne] to be a native of.

original, -e, -aux [ɔriʒinal, o] **1** adj [premier, inédit] original. || [singulier] eccentric. **2** nm, f [personne] (outlandish) character. ○ **original, -aux** nm [œuvre, document] original.

originalité [ɔriʒinalite] nf [nouveauté] originality. || [excentricité] eccentricity.

origine [ɔriʒin] nf [gén] origin; **d'~** [originel] original; [de départ] of origin; **pays d'~** country of origin; **d'~ anglaise** of English origin; **à l'~** originally. || [souche] origins (pl). || [provenance] source.

ORL nmf (abr de oto-rhino-laryngologiste) ENT specialist.

orme [ɔrm] nm elm.

ornement [ɔrnəmɑ̃] nm [gén & MUS] ornament; **d'~** [plante, arbre] ornamental.

orner [ɔrne] vt [décorer]: **~ (de)** to decorate (with). || [agrémenter] to adorn.

ornière [ɔrnjɛr] nf rut.

ornithologie [ɔrnitɔlɔʒi] nf ornithology.

orphelin, -e [ɔrfəlɛ̃, in] **1** adj orphan (avant n), orphaned. **2** nm, f orphan.

orphelinat [ɔrfəlina] nm orphanage.

orteil [ɔrtɛj] nm toe.

orthodontiste [ɔrtɔdɔ̃tist] nmf orthodontist.

orthodoxe [ɔrtɔdɔks] **1** adj RELIG Orthodox. || [conformiste] orthodox. **2** nmf RELIG Orthodox Christian.

orthographe [ɔrtɔgraf] nf spelling.

orthopédiste [ɔrtɔpedist] nmf orthopaedist.

orthophoniste [ɔrtɔfɔnist] nmf speech therapist.

ortie [ɔrti] nf nettle.

os [ɔs, pl o] nm [gén] bone; **~ à moelle** marrowbone. || fam fig [difficulté] snag, hitch.

oscillation [ɔsilasjɔ̃] nf oscillation; [de navire] rocking.

osciller [ɔsile] vi [se balancer] to swing; [navire] to rock.

osé, -e [oze] adj daring, audacious.

oseille [ozɛj] nf BOT sorrel.

oser [oze] vt to dare; **~ faire qqch** to dare (to) do sthg.

osier [ozje] nm BOT osier. || [fibre] wickerwork.

ossature [ɔsatyr] nf ANAT skeleton. || fig [structure] framework.

ossements [ɔsmɑ̃] nmpl bones.

osseux, -euse [ɔsø, øz] adj ANAT & MÉD bone (avant n). || [maigre] bony.

ossuaire [ɔsɥɛr] nm ossuary.

ostensible [ɔstɑ̃sibl] adj conspicuous.

ostentation [ɔstɑ̃tasjɔ̃] nf ostentation.

ostéopathe [ɔsteɔpat] nmf osteopath.

otage [ɔtaʒ] nm hostage; **prendre qqn en ~** to take sb hostage.

OTAN, Otan [ɔtɑ̃] (abr de Organisation du traité de l'Atlantique Nord) nf NATO.

otarie [ɔtari] nf sea lion.

ôter [ote] vt [enlever] to take off. || [soustraire] to take away. || [retirer, prendre]: **~ qqch à qqn** to take sthg away from sb.

otite [ɔtit] nf ear infection.

oto-rhino-laryngologie [ɔtɔrinɔlarɛ̃gɔlɔʒi] nf ear, nose and throat medicine, ENT.

ou [u] *conj* [indique une alternative, une approximation] or. || [sinon]: ~ **(bien)** or (else). ○ **ou (bien) ... ou (bien)** *loc corrélative* either ... or; ~ **c'est elle, ~ c'est moi!** it's either her or me!

où [u] **1** *pron rel* [spatial] where; **le village ~ j'habite** the village where I live, the village I live in; **partout ~ vous irez** wherever you go. || [temporel] when; **le jour ~ je suis venu** the day (that) I came. **2** *adv* where; **je vais ~ je veux** I go where I please; ~ **que vous alliez** wherever you go. **3** *adv interr* where? ○ **d'où** *loc adv* [conséquence] hence.

ouaté, -e [wate] *adj* [garni d'ouate] cotton (*avant n*) *Am*; [vêtement] quilted. || *fig* [feutré] muffled.

oubli [ubli] *nm* [acte d'oublier] forgetting. || [négligence] omission; [étourderie] oversight. || [général] oblivion; **tomber dans l'~** to sink into oblivion.

oublier [ublije] *vt* to forget; ~ **de faire qqch** to forget to do sthg.

oubliettes [ublijɛt] *nfpl* dungeon (*sg*).

ouest [wɛst] **1** *nm* west; **un vent d'~** a westerly wind; **à l'~** in the west; **à l'~ (de)** to the west (of). **2** *adj inv* [gén] west; [province, région] western.

ouest-allemand, -e [wɛstalmɑ̃, ɑ̃d] *adj* West German.

ouf [uf] *interj* phew!

oui [wi] **1** *adv* yes; **tu viens, ~ ou non?** are you coming or not?, are you coming or aren't you?; **je crois que ~** I think so. **2** *nm inv* yes; **pour un ~ pour un non** for no apparent reason.

ouï-dire [widir] *nm inv*; **par ~** by ou from hearsay.

ouïe [wi] *nf* hearing; **avoir l'~ fine** to have excellent hearing. ○ **ouïes** *nfpl* [de poisson] gills.

ouragan [uragɑ̃] *nm* MÉTÉOR hurricane.

ourlet [urlɛ] *nm* COUTURE hem.

ours [urs] *nm* bear; ~ **(en peluche)** teddy (bear); ~ **polaire** polar bear.

ourse [urs] *nf* she-bear.

oursin [ursɛ̃] *nm* sea urchin.

ourson [ursɔ̃] *nm* bear cub.

outil [uti] *nm* tool.

outillage [utijaʒ] *nm* [équipement] tools (*pl*), equipment.

outrage [utraʒ] *nm* JUR: ~ **à la pudeur** indecent behaviour (*U*).

outrager [utraʒe] *vt* [offenser] to insult.

outrance [utrɑ̃s] *nf* excess; **à ~** excessively.

outrancier, -ière [utrɑ̃sje, jɛr] *adj* extravagant.

outre[1] [utr] *nf* wineskin.

outre[2] [utr] **1** *prép* besides, as well as. **2** *adv*: **passer ~** to go on, to proceed further. ○ **en outre** *loc adv* moreover, besides.

outre-Atlantique [utratlɑ̃tik] *loc adv* across the Atlantic.

outre-Manche [utrəmɑ̃ʃ] *loc adv* across the Channel.

outremer [utrəmer] *adj inv* ultramarine.

outre-mer [utrəmer] *loc adv* overseas.

outrepasser [utrəpase] *vt* to exceed.

outrer [utre] *vt* [personne] to outrage.

outre-Rhin [utrərɛ̃] *loc adv* across the Rhine.

ouvert, -e [uver, ert] **1** *pp* → **ouvrir**. **2** *adj* [gén] open; **grand ~** wide open. || [robinet] on, running.

ouvertement [uvertəmɑ̃] *adv* openly.

ouverture [uvertyr] *nf* [gén] opening; [d'hostilités] outbreak; ~ **d'esprit** open-mindedness. || MUS overture. || PHOT aperture. ○ **ouvertures** *nfpl* [propositions] overtures.

ouvrable [uvrabl] *adj* working.

ouvrage [uvraʒ] *nm* [travail] work (*U*); task; **se mettre à l'~** to start work. || [objet produit] (piece of) work; COUTURE work (*U*). || [livre, écrit] work.

ouvré, -e [uvre] *adj*: **jour ~** working day.

ouvre-boîtes [uvrəbwat] *nm inv* tin opener *Br*, can opener.

ouvre-bouteilles [uvrəbutɛj] *nm inv* bottle opener.

ouvreuse [uvrøz] *nf* usherette.

ouvrier, -ière [uvrije, jɛr] **1** *adj* [quartier, enfance] working-class; [questions, statut] labour (*avant n*); **classe ouvrière** working class. **2** *nm, f* worker; ~ **agricole** farm worker; ~ **qualifié** skilled worker; ~ **spécialisé** semi-skilled worker.

ouvrir [uvrir] **1** *vt* [gén] to open. || [chemin, voie] to open up. || [gaz] to turn on. **2** *vi* to open; ~ **sur qqch** to open onto sthg. ○ **s'ouvrir** *vp* [porte, fleur] to open. || [route, perspectives] to open up. || [personne]: **s'~ (à qqn)** to confide (in sb), to open up (to sb). || [se blesser]: **s'~ le genou** to cut one's knee open; **s'~ les veines** to slash ou cut one's wrists.

ovaire [ɔver] *nm* ovary.

ovale [ɔval] *adj & nm* oval.

ovation [ɔvasjɔ̃] *nf* ovation; **faire une ~ à qqn** to give sb an ovation.

overdose [ɔvœrdoz] *nf* overdose.

ovin, -e [ɔvɛ̃, in] *adj* ovine. ○ **ovin** *nm* sheep.

OVNI, Ovni [ɔvni] (*abr de* **objet volant non identifié**) *nm* UFO.

oxydation [ɔksidasjɔ̃] *nf* oxidation, oxidization.

oxyde [ɔksid] *nm* oxide.

oxyder [ɔkside] *vt* to oxidize.

oxygène [ɔksiʒɛn] *nm* oxygen.

oxygéné, -e [ɔksiʒene] *adj* CHIM oxygenated; → **eau.**

ozone [ozon] *nm* ozone.

p¹, P [pe] *nm inv* p, P.

p² (*abr de* **page**) p. || *abr de* **pièce.**

pachyderme [paʃidɛrm] *nm* elephant.

pacifier [pasifje] *vt* to pacify.

pacifique [pasifik] *adj* peaceful.

Pacifique [pasifik] *nm*: **le ~** the Pacific (Ocean).

pacifiste [pasifist] *nmf & adj* pacifist.

pack [pak] *nm* pack.

pacotille [pakɔtij] *nf* shoddy goods (*pl*), rubbish; **de ~** cheap.

pacte [pakt] *nm* pact.

pactiser [paktize] *vi*: **~ avec** [faire un pacte avec] to make a pact with; [transiger avec] to come to terms with.

pactole [paktɔl] *nm* gold mine *fig.*

pagaie [page] *nf* paddle.

pagaille, pagaye, pagaïe [pagaj] *nf fam* mess.

pagayer [pageje] *vi* to paddle.

page [paʒ] 1 *nf* [feuillet] page; **~ blanche** blank page; **mettre en ~s** TYPO to make up (into pages). || *loc*: **être à la ~** to be up-to-date. 2 *nm* page (boy).

pagne [paɲ] *nm* loincloth.

pagode [pagɔd] *nf* pagoda.

paie, paye [pɛ] *nf* pay (*U*), wages (*pl*).

paiement, payement [pɛmɑ̃] *nm* payment.

païen, -ienne [pajɛ̃, jɛn] *adj & nm, f* pagan, heathen.

paillard, -e [pajar, ard] *adj* bawdy.

paillasse [pajas] *nf* [matelas] straw mattress. || [d'évier] draining board.

paillasson [pajasɔ̃] *nm* [tapis] doormat.

paille [paj] *nf* BOT straw. || [pour boire] straw. ○ **paille de fer** *nf* steel wool.

pailleté, -e [pajte] *adj* sequined.

paillette [pajɛt] *nf* (*gén pl*) [sur vêtements] sequin, spangle. || [de lessive, savon] flake; **savon en ~s** soap flakes (*pl*).

pain [pɛ̃] *nm* [aliment] bread; **un ~** a loaf; **petit ~** (bread) roll; **~ complet** wholemeal bread; **~ d'épice** ≃ gingerbread; **~ de mie** sandwich loaf. || [de savon, cire] bar.

pair, -e [pɛr] *adj* even. ○ **pair** *nm* peer. ○ **paire** *nf* pair; **une ~e de** [lunettes, ciseaux, chaussures] a pair of. ○ **au pair** *loc adv* for board and lodging, for one's keep; **jeune fille au ~** au pair (girl). ○ **de pair** *loc adv*: **aller de ~ avec** to go hand in hand with.

paisible [pezibl] *adj* peaceful.

paître [pɛtr] *vi* to graze.

paix [pɛ] *nm* peace; **avoir la ~** to have peace and quiet.

Pakistan [pakistɑ̃] *nm*: **le ~** Pakistan.

palace [palas] *nm* luxury hotel.

palais [palɛ] *nm* [château] palace. || [grand édifice] centre; **~ de justice** JUR law courts (*pl*). || ANAT palate.

palan [palɑ̃] *nm* block and tackle, hoist.

pale [pal] *nf* [de rame, d'hélice] blade.

pâle [pal] *adj* pale.

Palestine [palestin] *nf*: **la ~** Palestine.

palet [palɛ] *nm* HOCKEY puck.

palette [palɛt] *nf* [de peintre] palette.

pâleur [palœr] *nf* [de visage] pallor.

palier [palje] *nm* [d'escalier] landing. || [étape] level. || TECHNOL bearing.

pâlir [palir] *vi* [couleur, lumière] to fade; [personne] to turn ou go pale.

palissade [palisad] *nf* [clôture] fence.

palliatif, -ive [paljatif, iv] *adj* palliative. ○ **palliatif** *nm* MÉD palliative. || *fig* stopgap measure.

pallier [palje] *vt* to make up for.

palmarès [palmarɛs] *nm* [de lauréats] list of (medal) winners; SCOL list of prizewinners. || [de succès] record (of achievements).

palme [palm] *nf* [de palmier] palm-leaf. || [de nageur] flipper.

palmé, -e [palme] *adj* BOT palmate. || ZOOL web-footed; [patte] webbed.

paquetage

palmier [palmje] *nm* BOT palm tree.

palmipède [palmiped] *nm* web-footed bird.

palombe [palɔ̃b] *nf* woodpigeon.

pâlot, -otte [palo, ɔt] *adj* pale, sickly-looking.

palourde [palurd] *nf* clam.

palper [palpe] *vt* [toucher] to feel, to finger; MÉD to palpate.

palpitant, -e [palpitɑ̃, ɑ̃t] *adj* exciting, thrilling.

palpitation [palpitasjɔ̃] *nf* palpitation.

palpiter [palpite] *vi* [paupières] to flutter; [cœur] to pound.

paludisme [palydism] *nm* malaria.

pamphlet [pɑ̃flɛ] *nm* satirical tract.

pamplemousse [pɑ̃pləmus] *nm* grapefruit.

pan [pɑ̃] **1** *nm* [de vêtement] tail. || [d'affiche] piece, bit; ~ **de mur** section of wall. **2** *interj* bang!

panache [panaʃ] *nm* [de plumes, fumée] plume. || [éclat] panache.

panaché, -e [panaʃe] *adj* [de plusieurs couleurs] multicoloured. || [mélangé] mixed. ○ **panaché** *nm* shandy.

Panama [panama] *nm* [pays]: **le ~** Panama.

panaris [panari] *nm* whitlow.

pancarte [pɑ̃kart] *nf* [de manifestant] placard. || [de signalisation] sign.

pancréas [pɑ̃kreas] *nm* pancreas.

pané, -e [pane] *adj* breaded, in breadcrumbs.

panier [panje] *nm* basket; ~ **à provisions** shopping basket.

panique [panik] **1** *nf* panic. **2** *adj* panicky; **être pris d'une peur ~** to be panic-stricken.

paniquer [panike] *vt & vi* to panic.

panne [pan] *nf* [arrêt] breakdown; **tomber en ~** to break down; ~ **de courant** ou **d'électricité** power failure.

panneau, -x [pano] *nm* [pancarte] sign; ~ **indicateur** signpost; ~ **publicitaire** (advertising) hoarding *Br*, billboard *Am*; ~ **de signalisation** road sign. || [élément] panel.

panoplie [panɔpli] *nf* [jouet] outfit. || *fig* [de mesures] package.

panorama [panɔrama] *nm* [vue] view, panorama; *fig* overview.

panse [pɑ̃s] *nf* [d'estomac] first stomach, rumen. || *fam* [gros ventre] belly, paunch.

pansement [pɑ̃smɑ̃] *nm* dressing, bandage; ~ **(adhésif)** (sticking) plaster *Br*, Bandaid® *Am*.

panser [pɑ̃se] *vt* [plaie] to dress, to bandage; [jambe] to put a dressing on, to bandage; [avec pansement adhésif] to put a plaster *Br* ou Bandaid® *Am* on. || [cheval] to groom.

pantalon [pɑ̃talɔ̃] *nm* pants (*pl*) *Am*.

pantelant, -e [pɑ̃tlɑ̃, ɑ̃t] *adj* panting, gasping.

panthère [pɑ̃tɛr] *nf* panther.

pantin [pɑ̃tɛ̃] *nm* [jouet] jumping jack. || *péj* [personne] puppet.

pantomime [pɑ̃tɔmim] *nf* [art, pièce] mime.

pantoufle [pɑ̃tufl] *nf* slipper.

PAO (*abr de* **publication assistée par ordinateur**) *nf* DTP.

paon [pɑ̃] *nm* peacock.

papa [papa] *nm* dad, daddy.

pape [pap] *nm* RELIG pope.

paperasse [papras] *nf péj* [papier sans importance] bumf (*U*) *Br*, papers (*pl*). || [papiers administratifs] paperwork (*U*).

papeterie [papetri] *nf* [magasin] stationer's; [fabrique] paper mill.

papetier, -ière [paptje, jɛr] *nm, f* [commerçant] stationer; [fabricant] paper manufacturer.

papier [papje] *nm* [matière, écrit] paper; ~ **alu** ou **aluminium** aluminium *Br* ou aluminum *Am* foil, tinfoil; ~ **carbone** carbon paper; ~ **crépon** crêpe paper; ~ **d'emballage** wrapping paper; ~ **à entête** headed notepaper; ~ **hygiénique** toilet paper; ~ **à lettres** writing paper, notepaper; ~ **peint** wallpaper; ~ **de verre** glasspaper, sandpaper. ○ **papiers** *nmpl*: ~**s (d'identité)** (identity) papers.

papier-calque [papjekalk] (*pl* **papiers-calque**) *nm* tracing paper.

papillon [papijɔ̃] *nm* ZOOL butterfly. || [nage] butterfly (stroke).

papillonner [papijɔne] *vi* to flit about ou around.

papillote [papijɔt] *nf* [de bonbon] candy paper *Am*. || [de cheveux] curl paper.

papilloter [papijɔte] *vi* [lumière] to twinkle; [yeux] to blink.

papoter [papɔte] *vi fam* to chatter.

paprika [paprika] *nm* paprika.

paquebot [pakbo] *nm* liner.

pâquerette [pakrɛt] *nf* daisy.

Pâques [pak] *nfpl* Easter (*sg*).

paquet [pakɛ] *nm* [colis] parcel. || [emballage] packet; ~**-cadeau** gift-wrapped parcel.

paquetage [paktaʒ] *nm* MIL kit.

par [par] *prép* [spatial] through, by (way of); **passer ~ la Suède et le Danemark** to go via Sweden and Denmark; **regarder ~ la fenêtre** to look out of the window; **~ endroits** in places; **~ ici/là** this/that way; **mon cousin habite ~ ici** my cousin lives round here. || [temporel] on; **~ un beau jour d'été** on a lovely summer's day; **~ le passé** in the past. || [moyen, manière, cause] by; **~ bateau/train/avion** by boat/train/plane; **~ pitié** out of ou from pity; **~ accident** by accident, by chance. || [introduit le complément d'agent] by; **faire faire qqch ~ qqn** to have sthg done by sb. || [sens distributif] per, a; **une heure ~ jour** one hour a ou per day; **deux ~ deux** two at a time. ○ **par-ci par-là** *loc adv* here and there.

para [para] (*abr de* **parachutiste**) *nm* para.

parabole [parabɔl] *nf* [récit] parable. || MATHS parabola.

parabolique [parabɔlik] *adj* parabolic; **antenne ~** dish ou parabolic aerial.

parachever [paraʃve] *vt* to put the finishing touches to.

parachute [paraʃyt] *nm* parachute; **~ ascensionnel** parachute (*for parascending*).

parachutiste [paraʃytist] *nmf* parachutist; MIL paratrooper.

parade [parad] *nf* [spectacle] parade. || [défense] parry; *fig* riposte.

paradis [paradi] *nm* paradise.

paradoxal, -e, -aux [paradɔksal, o] *adj* paradoxical.

paradoxe [paradɔks] *nm* paradox.

parafer, parapher [parafe] *vt* to initial.

paraffine [parafin] *nf* paraffin *Br*, kerosene *Am*; [solide] paraffin wax.

parages [paraʒ] *nmpl*: **être ou se trouver dans les ~** *fig* to be in the area ou vicinity.

paragraphe [paragraf] *nm* paragraph.

Paraguay [paragwɛ] *nm*: **le ~** Paraguay.

paraître [parɛtr] **1** *v attr* to look, to seem, to appear. **2** *vi* [se montrer] to appear. || [être publié] to come out, to be published. **3** *v impers*: **il paraît/paraîtrait que** it appears/would appear that.

parallèle [paralɛl] **1** *nm* parallel; **établir un ~ entre** *fig* to draw a parallel between. **2** *nf* parallel (line). **3** *adj* [action, en maths] parallel. || [marché] unofficial; [médecine, énergie] alternative.

parallélisme [paralelism] *nm* parallelism; [de roues] alignment.

paralyser [paralize] *vt* to paralyse.

paralysie [paralizi] *nf* paralysis.

paramédical, -e, -aux [paramedikal, o] *adj* paramedical.

paramètre [parametr] *nm* parameter.

paranoïa [paranɔja] *nf* paranoia.

paranoïaque [paranɔjak] **1** *adj* paranoid. **2** *nmf* paranoiac.

parapente [parapɑ̃t] *nm* paragliding.

parapet [parapɛ] *nm* parapet.

paraphe = **parafe**.

parapher = **parafer**.

paraphrase [parafraz] *nf* paraphrase.

paraplégique [parapleʒik] *nmf & adj* paraplegic.

parapluie [paraplɥi] *nm* umbrella.

parasite [parazit] **1** *nm* parasite. **2** *adj* parasitic. ○ **parasites** *nmpl* RADIO & TÉLÉ interference (*U*).

parasol [parasɔl] *nm* parasol, sunshade.

paratonnerre [paratɔnɛr] *nm* lightning conductor.

paravent [paravɑ̃] *nm* screen.

parc [park] *nm* [jardin] park; [de château] grounds (*pl*); **~ d'attractions** amusement park; **~ national** national park. || [pour l'élevage] pen. || [de bébé] playpen.

parcelle [parsɛl] *nf* [petite partie] fragment, particle. || [terrain] parcel of land.

parce que [parsk(ə)] *loc conj* because.

parchemin [parʃəmɛ̃] *nm* parchment.

parcimonieux, -ieuse [parsimɔnjø, jøz] *adj* parsimonious.

parcmètre [parkmɛtr] *nm* parking meter.

parcourir [parkurir] *vt* [région, route] to cover. || [journal, dossier] to skim ou glance through, to scan.

parcours [parkur] *nm* [trajet, voyage] journey; [itinéraire] route. || GOLF [terrain] course; [trajet] round.

parcouru, -e [parkury] *pp* → **parcourir**.

par-delà [pardəla] *prép* beyond.

par-derrière [pardɛrjer] *adv* [par le côté arrière] round the back. || [en cachette] behind one's back.

par-dessous [pardəsu] *prép & adv* under, underneath.

pardessus [pardəsy] *nm inv* overcoat.

par-dessus [pardəsy] *prép* over, over the top of; **~ tout** above all.

par-devant [pardəvɑ̃] **1** *prép* in front of. **2** *adv* in front.

pardi [pardi] *interj fam* of course!

paroi

pardon [pardɔ̃] 1 *nm* forgiveness; demander ~ to say (one is) sorry. 2 *interj*
[excuses] (I'm) sorry!; [pour attirer
l'attention] excuse me!; ~? (I beg your)
pardon? *Br*, pardon me? *Am*.

pardonner [pardɔne] 1 *vt* to forgive; ~
qqch à qqn to forgive sb for sthg; ~ à
qqn d'avoir fait qqch to forgive sb for
doing sthg. 2 *vi*: ce genre d'erreur ne
pardonne pas this kind of mistake is fatal.

paré, -e [pare] *adj* [prêt] ready.

pare-balles [parbal] *adj inv* bullet-
proof.

pare-brise [parbriz] *nm inv* windscreen
Br, windshield *Am*.

pare-chocs [parʃɔk] *nm inv* bumper.

pareil, -eille [parej] *adj* [semblable]: ~
(à) similar (to). || [tel] such; un ~ film
such a film, a film like this. ○ **pareil** *adv*
fam the same (way).

parent, -e [parɑ̃, ɑ̃t] 1 *adj*: ~ (de) related (to). 2 *nm, f* relative, relation.
○ **parents** *nmpl* [père et mère] parents,
mother and father.

parenté [parɑ̃te] *nf* [lien, affinité] rela-
tionship.

parenthèse [parɑ̃tɛz] *nf* [digression] di-
gression, parenthesis. || TYPO bracket,
parenthesis; entre ~s in brackets; *fig* incidentally, by the way.

parer [pare] 1 *vt sout* [orner] to adorn. ||
[vêtir]: ~ qqn de qqch to dress sb up in
sthg, to deck sb out in sthg; *fig* to at-
tribute sthg to sb. || [contrer] to ward off,
to parry. 2 *vi*: ~ à [faire face à] to deal with;
[pourvoir à] to prepare for; ~ au plus
pressé to see to what is most urgent.

pare-soleil [parsɔlɛj] *nm inv* sun visor.

paresse [parɛs] *nf* [fainéantise] laziness,
idleness. || MÉD sluggishness.

paresser [parɛse] *vi* to laze about ou
around.

paresseux, -euse [parɛsø, øz] 1 *adj*
[fainéant] lazy. || MÉD sluggish. 2 *nm, f*
[personne] lazy ou idle person.

parfaire [parfɛr] *vt* to complete, to perfect.

parfait, -e [parfɛ, ɛt] *adj* perfect.
○ **parfait** *nm* GRAM perfect (tense).

parfaitement [parfɛtmɑ̃] *adv* [admira-
blement, très] perfectly. || [marque
l'assentiment] absolutely.

parfois [parfwa] *adv* sometimes.

parfum [parfœ̃] *nm* [de fleur] scent, fra-
grance. || [à base d'essences] perfume,
scent. || [de glace] flavour.

parfumé, -e [parfyme] *adj* [fleur] fra-
grant. || [mouchoir] perfumed. ||
[femme]: elle est trop ~e she's wearing
too much perfume.

parfumer [parfyme] *vt* [suj: fleurs] to
perfume. || [mouchoir] to perfume, to
scent. || CULIN to flavour. ○ **se parfu-
mer** *vp* to put perfume on.

parfumerie [parfymri] *nf* perfumery.

pari [pari] *nm* [entre personnes] bet.

paria [parja] *nm* pariah.

parier [parje] *vt*: ~ (sur) to bet (on).

parieur [parjœr] *nm* punter.

Paris [pari] *n* Paris.

parisien, -ienne [parizjɛ̃, jɛn] *adj* [vie,
société] Parisian; [métro, banlieue, région]
Paris (*avant n*). ○ **Parisien, -ienne**
nm, f Parisian.

parité [parite] *nf* parity.

parjure [parʒyr] 1 *nmf* [personne] per-
jurer. 2 *nm* [faux serment] perjury.

parjurer [parʒyre] ○ **se parjurer** *vp*
to perjure o.s.

parka [parka] *nm ou nf* parka.

parking [parkiŋ] *nm* [parc] car park *Br*,
parking lot *Am*.

parlant, -e [parlɑ̃, ɑ̃t] *adj* [qui parle]: le
cinéma ~ talking pictures; l'horloge ~e
TÉLÉCOM the speaking clock. || *fig* [chif-
fres, données] eloquent; [portrait] vivid.

parlement [parləmɑ̃] *nm* parliament; le
Parlement européen the European Parliament.

parlementaire [parləmɑ̃tɛr] 1 *nmf* [dé-
puté] member of parliament; [négocia-
teur] negotiator. 2 *adj* parliamentary.

parlementer [parləmɑ̃te] *vi* [négocier]
to negotiate, to parley.

parler [parle] 1 *vi* [gén] to talk, to
speak; ~ à/avec qqn to speak to/with sb,
to talk to/with sb; ~ de qqch à qqn to
speak ou talk to sb about sthg; ~ de
qqn/qqch to talk about sb/sthg; ~ de
faire qqch to talk about doing sthg; ~ en
français to speak in French; sans ~ de
apart from, not to mention; à propre-
ment ~ strictly speaking; tu parles! *fam*
you can say that again!; n'en parlons
plus we'll say no more about it. ||
[avouer] to talk. 2 *vt* [langue] to speak; ~
(le) français to speak French.

parloir [parlwar] *nm* parlour.

parmi [parmi] *prép* among.

parodie [parɔdi] *nf* parody.

parodier [parɔdje] *vt* to parody.

paroi [parwa] *nf* [mur] wall; [cloison]

partition; ~ **rocheuse** rock face. || [de récipient] inner side.

paroisse [parwas] *nf* parish.

paroissial, -e, -iaux [parwasjal, jo] *adj* parish (*avant n*).

paroissien, -ienne [parwasjɛ̃, jɛn] *nm, f* parishioner.

parole [parɔl] *nf* [faculté de parler]: **la ~** speech. || [propos, discours]: **adresser la ~ à qqn** to speak to sb; **couper la ~ à qqn** to cut sb off; **prendre la ~** to speak. || [promesse, mot] word; **tenir ~** to keep one's word; **donner sa ~ (d'honneur)** to give one's word (of honour). ○ **paroles** *nfpl* MUS words, lyrics.

paroxysme [parɔksism] *nm* height.

parquer [parke] *vt* [animaux] to pen in ou up. || [prisonniers] to shut up ou in.

parquet [parkɛ] *nm* [plancher] parquet floor. || JUR ≃ District Attorney's Office *Am.*

parqueter [parkəte] *vt* to lay a parquet floor in.

parrain [parɛ̃] *nm* [d'enfant] godfather. || [de festival, sportif] sponsor.

parrainer [parɛne] *vt* to sponsor, to back.

parsemer [parsəme] *vt*: ~ **(de)** to strew (with).

part [par] *nf* [de gâteau] portion; [de bonheur, héritage] share; [partie] part. || [participation]: **prendre ~ à qqch** to take part in sthg. || *loc*: **c'est de la ~ de qui?** [au téléphone] who's speaking ou calling?; **dites-lui de ma ~ que ...** tell him from me that ...; **ce serait bien aimable de votre ~** it would be very kind of you; **pour ma ~** as far as I'm concerned; **faire ~ à qqn de qqch** to inform sb of sthg. ○ **à part 1** *loc adv* aside, separately. **2** *loc adj* exceptional. **3** *loc prép* apart from. ○ **autre part** *loc adv* somewhere else. ○ **d'autre part** *loc adv* besides, moreover. ○ **d'une part ..., d'autre part** *loc corrélative* on the one hand ..., on the other hand. ○ **nulle part** *loc adv* nowhere. ○ **quelque part** *loc adv* somewhere.

part. *abr de* **particulier.**

partage [partaʒ] *nm* [action] sharing (out).

partager [partaʒe] *vt* [morceler] to divide (up). || [mettre en commun]: ~ **qqch avec qqn** to share sthg with sb. ○ **se partager** *vp* [se diviser] to be divided. || [partager son temps] to divide one's time.

|| [se répartir]: **se ~ qqch** to share sthg between themselves/ourselves *etc.*

partance [partɑ̃s] *nf*: **en ~** outward bound; **en ~ pour** bound for.

partant, -e [partɑ̃, ɑ̃t] *adj*: **être ~ pour** to be ready for. ○ **partant** *nm* starter.

partenaire [partənɛr] *nmf* partner.

partenariat [partənarja] *nm* partnership.

parterre [partɛr] *nm* [de fleurs] (flower) bed. || THÉÂTRE orchestra *Am.*

parti, -e [parti] **1** *pp* → **partir.** **2** *adj fam* [ivre] tipsy. ○ **parti** *nm* POLIT party. || [choix, décision] course of action; **prendre ~** to make up one's mind; **en prendre son ~** to be resigned; **être de ~ pris** to be prejudiced ou biased; **tirer ~ de** to make (good) use of. || [personne à marier] match. ○ **partie** *nf* [élément, portion] part; **en grande ~** largely; **en majeure ~** for the most part; **faire ~ (intégrante) de qqch** to be (an integral) part of sthg. || SPORT game. || JUR party; **la ~e adverse** the opposing party. || *loc*: **prendre qqn à ~e** to attack sb. ○ **en partie** *loc adv* partly, in part.

partial, -e, -iaux [parsjal, jo] *adj* biased.

partialité [parsjalite] *nf* partiality, bias.

participant, -e [partisipɑ̃, ɑ̃t] *nm, f* [à réunion] participant. || SPORT competitor. || [à concours] entrant.

participation [partisipasjɔ̃] *nf* [collaboration] participation. || ÉCON interest; ~ **aux bénéfices** profit-sharing.

participe [partisip] *nm* participle; ~ **passé/présent** past/present participle.

participer [partisipe] *vi*: ~ **à** [réunion, concours] to take part in; [frais] to contribute to; [bénéfices] to share in.

particularité [partikylarite] *nf* distinctive feature.

particule [partikyl] *nf* [gén & LING] particle. || [nobiliaire] nobiliary particle.

particulier, -ère [partikylje, jɛr] *adj* [personnel, privé] private. || [spécial] particular, special; [propre] peculiar, characteristic; ~ **à** peculiar to, characteristic of. || [remarquable] unusual, exceptional; **cas ~** special case. || [assez bizarre] peculiar.

particulièrement [partikyljɛrmɑ̃] *adv* particularly; **tout ~** especially.

partie → **parti.**

partiel, -ielle [parsjɛl] *adj* partial. ○ **partiel** *nm* UNIV ≃ end-of-term exam.

partir [partir] *vi* [personne] to go, to leave; **~ à** to go to; **~ pour** to leave for; **~ de** [bureau] to leave; [aéroport, gare] to leave from; [hypothèse, route] to start from; [date] to run from. || [voiture] to start. || [coup de feu] to go off; [bouchon] to pop. || [tache] to come out, to go. ○ **à partir de** *loc prép* from.

partisan, -e [partizã, an] *adj* [partial] partisan; **être ~ de** to be in favour of. ○ **partisan** *nm* [adepte] supporter, advocate.

partition [partisjɔ̃] *nf* [séparation] partition. || MUS score.

partout [partu] *adv* everywhere.

paru, -e [pary] *pp* → **paraître**.

parure [paryr] *nf* (matching) set.

parution [parysjɔ̃] *nf* publication.

parvenir [parvənir] *vi*: **~ à faire qqch** to manage to do sthg; **faire ~ qqch à qqn** to send sthg to sb.

parvenu, -e [parvəny] **1** *pp* → **parvenir**. **2** *péj* upstart.

pas¹ [pa] *nm* [gén] step; **allonger le ~** to quicken one's pace; **revenir sur ses ~** to retrace one's steps; **~ à ~** step by step; **à ~ de loup** *fig* stealthily. || TECHNOL thread. || *loc*: **c'est à deux ~ (d'ici)** it's very near (here); **faire les cent ~** to pace up and down; **faire un faux ~** to slip; *fig* to make a faux pas; **faire le premier ~** to make the first move; **(rouler) au ~** (to move) at a snail's pace; **sur le ~ de la porte** on the doorstep.

pas² [pa] *adv* [avec ne] not; **elle n'a ~ mangé** she hasn't eaten; **je ne le connais ~** I don't know him; **il n'y a ~ de vin** there's no wine, there isn't any wine; **je préférerais ne ~ le rencontrer** I would prefer not to meet him, I would rather not meet him. || [sans ne] not; **l'as-tu vu ou ~?** have you seen him or not?; **il est très satisfait, moi ~** he's very pleased, but I'm not; **~ encore** not yet. || [avec pron indéf]: **~ un** [aucun] none, not one.

pascal, -e [paskal] (*pl* **pascals** OU **pascaux** [pasko]) *adj* Easter (*avant n*).

passable [pasabl] *adj* passable, fair.

passage [pasaʒ] *nm* [action de passer] going past; [- de traverser] crossing; **être de ~** to be passing through. || [endroit] passage, way; **«~ interdit»** "no entry"; **~ clouté** OU **pour piétons** pedestrian crossing; **~ à niveau** level crossing *Br*, grade crossing *Am*; **~ souterrain** underpass *Br*, subway *Am*. || [extrait] passage.

passager, -ère [pasaʒe, ɛr] **1** *adj* [bonheur] fleeting, short-lived. **2** *nm, f* passenger.

passant, -e [pasã, ãt] **1** *adj* busy. **2** *nm, f* passer-by. ○ **passant** *nm* [de ceinture] (belt) loop.

passe [pas] **1** *nm* passkey. **2** *nf* [au sport] pass. || NAVIG channel.

passé, -e [pase] *adj* [qui n'est plus] past; [précédent]: **la semaine ~e** last week; **au cours de la semaine ~e** in the last week; **il est trois heures ~es** it's gone three *Br*, it's after three. || [fané] faded. ○ **passé 1** *nm* past; **~ composé** perfect tense; **~ simple** past historic. **2** *prép* after.

passe-droit [pasdrwa] (*pl* **passe-droits**) *nm* privilege.

passe-montagne [pasmɔ̃taɲ] (*pl* **passe-montagnes**) *nm* Balaclava (helmet).

passe-partout [paspartu] *nm inv* [clé] passkey. || (*en apposition*) [tenue] all-purpose; [phrase] stock (*avant n*).

passeport [paspɔr] *nm* passport.

passer [pase] **1** *vi* [se frayer un chemin] to pass, to get past. || [défiler] to go by OU past. || [aller] to go; **~ chez qqn** to call on sb, to drop in on sb; **~ devant** [bâtiment] to pass; [juge] to come before; **en passant** in passing. || [venir - facteur] to come, to call. || SCOL to pass, to be admitted; **~ dans la classe supérieure** to move up, to be moved up (a class). || [être accepté] to be accepted. || [fermer les yeux]: **~ sur qqch** to pass over sthg. || [temps] to pass, to go by. || [disparaître - souvenir, couleur] to fade; [- douleur] to pass, to go away. || CIN, TÉLÉ & THÉÂTRE to be on; **~ à la radio/télévision** to be on the radio/television. || CARTES to pass. || *loc*: **~ inaperçu** to pass OU go unnoticed; **passons ...** let's move on ...; **~ pour** to be regarded as; **se faire ~ pour qqn** to pass o.s. off as sb. **2** *vt* [franchir - frontière, rivière] to cross; [- douane] to go through. || [soirée, vacances] to spend. || [sauter - ligne, tour] to miss. || [faire aller - bras] to pass, to put. || [filtrer - huile] to strain; [- café] to filter. || [film, disque] to put on. || [vêtement] to slip on. || [vitesses] to change; **~ la** OU **en troisième** to change into third (gear). || [donner]: **~ qqch à qqn** to pass sb sthg; MÉD to give sb sthg. || [accord]: **~ un contrat avec qqn** to have an agreement with sb. || SCOL & UNIV [examen] to sit, to take. || [au téléphone]: **je vous passe Mme Ledoux** [transmettre]

I'll put you through to Mme Ledoux; [donner l'écouteur à] I'll hand you Mme Ledoux. ○ **se passer** *vp* [événement] to happen, to take place; **comment ça s'est passé?** how did it go? || [s'abstenir]: **se ~ de qqch/de faire qqch** to do without sthg/doing sthg.

passerelle [pasʁɛl] *nf* [pont] footbridge. || [passage mobile] gangway.

passe-temps [pastɑ̃] *nm inv* pastime.

passif, -ive [pasif, iv] *adj* passive. ○ **passif** *nm* CRAM passive. || FIN liabilities (*pl*).

passion [pasjɔ̃] *nf* passion; **avoir la ~ de qqch** to have a passion for sthg.

passionnant, -e [pasjɔnɑ̃, ɑ̃t] *adj* exciting, fascinating.

passionné, -e [pasjɔne] **1** *adj* [personne] passionate. || [récit, débat] impassioned. **2** *nm, f* passionate person; **~ de ski/d'échecs** *etc* skiing/chess *etc* fanatic.

passionnel, -elle [pasjɔnɛl] *adj* [crime] of passion.

passionner [pasjɔne] *vt* [personne] to grip, to fascinate. ○ **se passionner** *vp*: **se ~ pour** to have a passion for.

passivité [pasivite] *nf* passivity.

passoire [paswar] *nf* [à liquide] sieve; [à légumes] colander.

pastel [pastɛl] **1** *nm* pastel. **2** *adj inv* [couleur] pastel (*avant n*).

pastèque [pastɛk] *nf* watermelon.

pasteur [pastœr] *nm littéraire* [berger] shepherd. || RELIG pastor, minister.

pasteuriser [pastœrize] *vt* to pasteurize.

pastille [pastij] *nf* [bonbon] pastille, lozenge.

pastis [pastis] *nm aniseed-flavoured aperitif.*

patate [patat] *nf fam* [pomme de terre] spud. || *fam* [imbécile] fathead.

patauger [patoʒe] *vi* [barboter] to splash about.

pâte [pat] *nf* [à tarte] pastry; [à pain] dough; **~ brisée** shortcrust pastry; **~ feuilletée** puff ou flaky pastry; **~ à frire** batter. || [mélange] paste; **~ d'amandes** almond paste; **~ de fruits** *jelly made from fruit paste*; **~ à modeler** modelling clay. ○ **pâtes** *nfpl* pasta (*sg*).

pâté [pate] *nm* CULIN pâté; **~ de campagne** farmhouse pâté; **~ en croûte** *pâté baked in a pastry case*; **~ de foie** liver pâté. || [tache] ink blot. || [bloc]: **~ de maisons** block (of houses).

patelin [patlɛ̃] *nm fam* village, place.

patente [patɑ̃t] *nf* licence fee (*for traders and professionals*).

patère [pater] *nf* [portemanteau] coat hook.

paternalisme [paternalism] *nm* paternalism.

paternel, -elle [paternɛl] *adj* [devoir, autorité] paternal; [amour, ton] fatherly.

paternité [paternite] *nf* paternity, fatherhood; *fig* authorship, paternity.

pâteux, -euse [patø, øz] *adj* [aliment] doughy; [encre] thick.

pathétique [patetik] *adj* moving, pathetic.

pathologie [patɔlɔʒi] *nf* pathology.

patibulaire [patibyler] *adj péj* sinister.

patience [pasjɑ̃s] *nf* [gén] patience. || [jeu de cartes] patience *Br*, solitaire *Am*.

patient, -e [pasjɑ̃, ɑ̃t] **1** *adj* patient. **2** *nm, f* MÉD patient.

patienter [pasjɑ̃te] *vi* to wait.

patin [patɛ̃] *nm* SPORT skate; **~ à glace/à roulettes** ice/roller skate; **faire du ~ à glace/à roulettes** to go ice-/roller-skating.

patinage [patinaʒ] *nm* SPORT skating; **~ artistique/de vitesse** figure/speed skating.

patiner [patine] *vi* SPORT to skate. || [véhicule] to skid. ○ **se patiner** *vp* to take on a patina.

patineur, -euse [patinœr, øz] *nm, f* skater.

patinoire [patinwar] *nf* ice ou skating rink.

pâtisserie [patisri] *nf* [gâteau] pastry. || [commerce] ≃ cake shop.

pâtissier, -ière [patisje, jer] **1** *adj*: **crème pâtissière** confectioner's custard. **2** *nm, f* pastrycook.

patois [patwa] *nm* patois.

patriarche [patrijarʃ] *nm* patriarch.

patrie [patri] *nf* country, homeland.

patrimoine [patrimwan] *nm* [familial] inheritance; [collectif] heritage.

patriote [patrijɔt] *nmf* patriot.

patriotique [patrijɔtik] *adj* patriotic.

patron, -onne [patrɔ̃, ɔn] *nm, f* [d'entreprise] head. || [chef] boss. || RELIG patron saint. ○ **patron** *nm* [modèle] pattern.

patronage [patrɔnaʒ] *nm* [protection] patronage; [de saint] protection.

patronal, -e, -aux [patrɔnal, o] *adj* [organisation, intérêts] employers' (*avant n*).

patronat [patrɔna] *nm* employers.

patronyme [patrɔnim] *nm* patronymic.

patrouille [patruj] *nf* patrol.

patte [pat] *nf* [d'animal] paw; [d'oiseau] foot. || *fam* [jambe] leg; [pied] foot; [main] hand, paw. || [favori] sideburn.

pâturage [patyraʒ] *nm* [lieu] pasture land.

pâture [patyr] *nf* [nourriture] food, fodder; *fig* intellectual nourishment.

paume [pom] *nf* [de main] palm.

paumé, -e [pome] *fam* **1** *adj* lost. **2** *nm, f* down and out.

paumer [pome] *fam vt* to lose. ○ **se paumer** *vp* to get lost.

paupière [popjɛr] *nf* eyelid.

pause [poz] *nf* [arrêt] break; **~-café** coffee-break. || MUS pause.

pauvre [povr] **1** *nmf* poor person. **2** *adj* poor; **~ en** low in.

pauvreté [povrəte] *nf* poverty.

pavaner [pavane] ○ **se pavaner** *vp* to strut.

pavé, -e [pave] *adj* cobbled. ○ **pavé** *nm* [de pierre] cobblestone, paving stone. || *fam* [livre] tome. || INFORM: **~ numérique** keypad.

pavillon [pavijɔ̃] *nm* [bâtiment] detached house. || [drapeau] flag.

pavot [pavo] *nm* poppy.

payant, -e [pɛjɑ̃, ɑ̃t] *adj* [hôte] paying (*avant n*). || [spectacle] with an admission charge. || *fam* [affaire] profitable.

paye = **paie**.

payement = **paiement**.

payer [peje] **1** *vt* [gén] to pay; [achat] to pay for; **~ qqch à qqn** to buy sthg for sb, to buy sb sthg, to treat sb to sthg. || [expier - crime, faute] to pay for. **2** *vi*: **~ (pour)** to pay (for).

pays [pei] *nm* [gén] country. || [région, province] region. ○ **pays de Galles** *nm*: **le ~ de Galles** Wales.

paysage [peizaʒ] *nm* [site, vue] landscape, scenery. || [tableau] landscape.

paysagiste [peizaʒist] *nmf* [peintre] landscape artist. || [concepteur de parcs] landscape gardener.

paysan, -anne [peizɑ̃, an] **1** *adj* [vie, coutume] country (*avant n*), rural; [organisation, revendication] farmers' (*avant n*); *péj* peasant (*avant n*). **2** *nm, f* [agriculteur] (small) farmer. || *péj* [rustre] peasant.

Pays-Bas [peiba] *nmpl*: **les ~** the Netherlands.

PC *nm* (*abr de* **Parti communiste**) Communist Party. || (*abr de* **personal computer**) PC.

PCV (*abr de* **à percevoir**) *nm* reverse charge call.

P-DG (*abr de* **président-directeur général**) *nm* Chairman and President *Am*.

péage [peaʒ] *nm* toll.

peau [po] *nf* [gén] skin. || [cuir] hide, leather (*U*).

péché [peʃe] *nm* sin.

pêche [pɛʃ] *nf* [fruit] peach. || [activité] fishing; [poissons] catch; **aller à la ~** to go fishing.

pécher [peʃe] *vi* to sin.

pêcher[1] [peʃe] *vt* [poisson] to catch. || *fam* [trouver] to dig up.

pêcher[2] [peʃe] *nm* peach tree.

pécheur, -eresse [peʃœr, peʃrɛs] **1** *adj* sinful. **2** *nm, f* sinner.

pêcheur, -euse [pɛʃœr, øz] *nm, f* fisherman (*f* fisherwoman).

pectoral, -e, -aux [pɛktɔral, o] *adj* [sirop] cough (*avant n*). ○ **pectoraux** *nmpl* pectorals.

pécuniaire [pekynjɛr] *adj* financial.

pédagogie [pedagɔʒi] *nf* [science] education, pedagogy. || [qualité] teaching ability.

pédagogue [pedagɔg] **1** *nmf* teacher. **2** *adj*: **être ~** to be a good teacher.

pédale [pedal] *nf* [gén] pedal.

pédaler [pedale] *vi* [à bicyclette] to pedal.

pédalo [pedalo] *nm* pedal boat.

pédant, -e [pedɑ̃, ɑ̃t] *adj* pedantic.

pédéraste [pederast] *nm* homosexual, pederast.

pédiatre [pedjatr] *nmf* pediatrician.

pédicure [pedikyr] *nmf* chiropodist.

peigne [pɛɲ] *nm* [démêloir, barrette] comb.

peigner [peɲe] *vt* [cheveux] to comb. ○ **se peigner** *vp* to comb one's hair.

peignoir [peɲwar] *nm* dressing gown *Br*, robe *Am*, bathrobe *Am*.

peindre [pɛ̃dr] *vt* to paint; *fig* [décrire] to depict.

peine [pɛn] *nf* [châtiment] punishment, penalty; JUR sentence; **sous ~ de qqch** on pain of sthg; **~ capitale** OU **de mort** capital punishment, death sentence. || [chagrin] sorrow, sadness (*U*); **faire de la ~ à qqn** to upset sb, to distress sb. || [effort] trouble; **ça ne vaut pas ou ce n'est pas la ~** it's not worth it. || [difficulté] difficulty; **avoir de la ~ à faire qqch** to have difficulty oı trouble doing sthg; **à grand-~** with great difficulty. ○ **à peine** *loc adv* scarcely, hardly; **à ~ ... que** hardly ... than.

peint, -e [pɛ̃, pɛ̃t] *pp* → **peindre**.

peintre [pɛ̃tr] *nm* painter.

peinture [pɛ̃tyr] *nf* [gén] painting. || [produit] paint; **«~ fraîche»** "wet paint".

péjoratif, -ive [peʒɔratif, iv] *adj* pejorative.

Pékin [pekɛ̃] *n* Peking, Beijing.

pelage [pəlaʒ] *nm* coat, fur.

pêle-mêle [pɛlmɛl] *adv* pell-mell.

peler [pəle] *vt & vi* to peel.

pèlerin [pɛlrɛ̃] *nm* pilgrim.

pèlerinage [pɛlrinaʒ] *nm* [voyage] pilgrimage. || [lieu] place of pilgrimage.

pélican [pelikɑ̃] *nm* pelican.

pelle [pɛl] *nf* [instrument] shovel. || [machine] digger.

pellicule [pelikyl] *nf* film. ○ **pellicules** *nfpl* dandruff (*U*).

pelote [pəlɔt] *nf* [de laine, ficelle] ball.

peloter [pəlɔte] *vt fam* to paw.

peloton [pəlɔtɔ̃] *nm* [de soldats] squad; **~ d'exécution** firing squad. || [de concurrents] pack.

pelotonner [pəlɔtɔne] ○ **se pelotonner** *vp* to curl up.

pelouse [pəluz] *nf* [de jardin] lawn.

peluche [pəlyʃ] *nf* [jouet] soft toy. || [d'étoffe] piece of fluff.

pelure [pəlyr] *nf* [fruit] peel.

pénal, -e, -aux [penal, o] *adj* penal.

pénaliser [penalize] *vt* to penalize.

penalty [penalti] (*pl* **penaltys** OU **penalties**) *nm* penalty.

penaud, -e [pəno, od] *adj* sheepish.

penchant [pɑ̃ʃɑ̃] *nm* [inclination] tendency. || [sympathie]: **~ pour** liking oı fondness for.

pencher [pɑ̃ʃe] **1** *vi* to lean; **~ vers/pour** *fig* to incline towards/in favour of. **2** *vt* to bend. ○ **se pencher** *vp* [s'incliner] to lean over; [se baisser] to bend down.

pendaison [pɑ̃dɛzɔ̃] *nf* hanging.

pendant¹, -e [pɑ̃dɑ̃, ɑ̃t] *adj* [bras] hanging, dangling. ○ **pendant** *nm* [bijou]: **~ d'oreilles** (drop) earring. || [de paire] counterpart.

pendant² [pɑ̃dɑ̃] *prép* during. ○ **pendant que** *loc conj* while, whilst; **~ que j'y suis, ...** while I'm at it, ...

pendentif [pɑ̃dɑ̃tif] *nm* pendant.

penderie [pɑ̃dri] *nf* wardrobe.

pendre [pɑ̃dr] **1** *vi* [être fixé en haut]: **~ (à)** to hang (from). || [descendre trop bas]

to hang down. **2** *vt* [rideaux, tableau] to hang (up), to put up. || [personne] to hang. ○ **se pendre** *vp* [se suicider] to hang o.s.

pendule [pɑ̃dyl] **1** *nm* pendulum. **2** *nf* clock.

pénétrer [penetre] **1** *vi* to enter. **2** *vt* [mur, vêtement] to penetrate.

pénible [penibl] *adj* [travail] laborious. || [nouvelle, maladie] painful. || *fam* [personne] tiresome.

péniche [peniʃ] *nf* barge.

pénicilline [penisilin] *nf* penicillin.

péninsule [penɛ̃syl] *nf* peninsula.

pénis [penis] *nm* penis.

pénitence [penitɑ̃s] *nf* [repentir] penitence. || [peine, punition] penance.

pénitencier [penitɑ̃sje] *nm* prison, penitentiary *Am*.

pénombre [penɔ̃br] *nf* half-light.

pense-bête [pɑ̃sbɛt] (*pl* **pense-bêtes**) *nm* reminder.

pensée [pɑ̃se] *nf* [idée, faculté] thought. || [esprit] mind, thoughts (*pl*). || [doctrine] thought, thinking. || BOT pansy.

penser [pɑ̃se] **1** *vi* to think; **~ à qqn/qqch** [avoir à l'esprit] to think of sb/sthg, to think about sb/sthg; [se rappeler] to remember sb/sthg; **~ à faire qqch** [se rappeler] to remember to do sthg; **qu'est-ce que tu en penses?** what do you think (of it)? **2** *vt* to think; **je pense que oui** I think so; **je pense que non** I don't think so; **~ faire qqch** to be planning to do sthg.

pensif, -ive [pɑ̃sif, iv] *adj* pensive, thoughtful.

pension [pɑ̃sjɔ̃] *nf* [allocation] pension; **~ alimentaire** [dans un divorce] alimony. || [hébergement] board and lodgings; **~ complète** full board; **demi-~** half board. || [hôtel] guesthouse; **~ de famille** guesthouse, boarding house. || [internat] boarding school.

pensionnaire [pɑ̃sjɔnɛr] *nmf* [élève] boarder. || [hôte payant] lodger.

pensionnat [pɑ̃sjɔna] *nm* [internat] boarding school.

pentagone [pɛ̃tagɔn] *nm* pentagon.

pente [pɑ̃t] *nf* slope; **en ~** sloping, inclined.

pentecôte [pɑ̃tkot] *nf* [juive] Pentecost; [chrétienne] Whitsun.

pénurie [penyri] *nf* shortage.

pépin [pepɛ̃] *nm* [graine] pip. || *fam* [ennui] hitch.

pépinière [pepinjɛr] *nf* tree nursery.

pépite [pepit] *nf* nugget.

perçant, -e [pɛrsɑ̃, ɑ̃t] *adj* [regard, son] piercing. || [froid] bitter, biting.

percepteur [pɛrsɛptœr] *nm* tax collector.

perception [pɛrsɛpsjɔ̃] *nf* [bureau] tax office. || [sensation] perception.

percer [pɛrse] 1 *vt* [mur, roche] to make a hole in; [coffre-fort] to crack. || [trou] to make; [avec perceuse] to drill. || [silence, oreille] to pierce. || *fig* [mystère] to penetrate. 2 *vi* [soleil] to break through. || [abcès] to burst; **avoir une dent qui perce** to be cutting a tooth. || [réussir] to make a name for o.s., to break through.

perceuse [pɛrsøz] *nf* drill.

percevoir [pɛrsəvwar] *vt* [intention, nuance] to perceive. || [retraite, indemnité] to receive. || [impôts] to collect.

perche [pɛrʃ] *nf* [poisson] perch. || [de bois, métal] pole.

percher [pɛrʃe] 1 *vi* [oiseau] to perch. 2 *vt* to perch. ○ **se percher** *vp* to perch.

perchoir [pɛrʃwar] *nm* perch.

percolateur [pɛrkɔlatœr] *nm* percolator.

perçu, -e [pɛrsy] *pp* → **percevoir**.

percussion [pɛrkysjɔ̃] *nf* percussion.

percutant, -e [pɛrkytɑ̃, ɑ̃t] *adj* [obus] explosive. || *fig* [argument] forceful.

percuter [pɛrkyte] 1 *vt* to strike, to smash into. 2 *vi* to explode.

perdant, -e [pɛrdɑ̃, ɑ̃t] 1 *adj* losing. 2 *nm, f* loser.

perdre [pɛrdr] 1 *vt* [gén] to lose. || [temps] to waste; [occasion] to miss, to waste. || [suj: bonté, propos] to be the ruin of. 2 *vi* to lose. ○ **se perdre** *vp* [coutume] to die out, to become lost. || [personne] to get lost, to lose one's way.

perdrix [pɛrdri] *nf* partridge.

perdu, -e [pɛrdy] 1 *pp* → **perdre**. 2 *adj* [égaré] lost. || [endroit] out-of-the-way. || [balle] stray. || [temps, occasion] wasted. || [récolte, robe] spoilt, ruined.

père [pɛr] *nm* [gén] father; ~ **de famille** father. ○ **père Noël** *nm*: **le ~ Noël** Father Christmas, Santa Claus.

péremptoire [perɑ̃ptwar] *adj* peremptory.

perfection [pɛrfɛksjɔ̃] *nf* [qualité] perfection.

perfectionner [pɛrfɛksjɔne] *vt* to perfect. ○ **se perfectionner** *vp* to improve.

perfide [pɛrfid] *adj* perfidious.

perforer [pɛrfɔre] *vt* to perforate.

performance [pɛrfɔrmɑ̃s] *nf* performance.

performant, -e [pɛrfɔrmɑ̃, ɑ̃t] *adj* [personne] efficient. || [machine] high-performance (*avant n*).

perfusion [pɛrfyzjɔ̃] *nf* perfusion.

péridurale [peridyral] *nf* epidural.

péril [peril] *nm* peril.

périlleux, -euse [perijø, øz] *adj* perilous, dangerous.

périmé, -e [perime] *adj* out-of-date; *fig* [idées] outdated.

périmètre [perimetr] *nm* [contour] perimeter. || [contenu] area.

période [perjɔd] *nf* period.

périodique [perjɔdik] 1 *nm* periodical. 2 *adj* periodic.

péripétie [peripesi] *nf* event.

périphérie [periferi] *nf* [de ville] outskirts (*pl*). || [bord] periphery; [de cercle] circumference.

périphérique [periferik] 1 *nm* [route] ring road *Br*, beltway *Am*. || INFORM peripheral device. 2 *adj* peripheral.

périphrase [perifraz] *nf* periphrasis.

périple [peripl] *nm* [voyage] trip.

périr [perir] *vi* to perish.

périssable [perisabl] *adj* [denrée] perishable. || [sentiment] transient.

perle [pɛrl] *nf* [de nacre] pearl. || [de bois, verre] bead. || [personne] gem.

permanence [pɛrmanɑ̃s] *nf* [continuité] permanence; **en ~** constantly. || [service]: **être de ~** to be on duty. || SCOL: **(salle de) ~** study room.

permanent, -e [pɛrmanɑ̃, ɑ̃t] *adj* permanent; [cinéma] with continuous showings. ○ **permanente** *nf* perm.

permettre [pɛrmɛtr] *vt* to permit, to allow; ~ **à qqn de faire qqch** to permit ou allow sb to do sthg. ○ **se permettre** *vp*: **se ~ qqch** to allow o.s. sthg; [avoir les moyens de] to be able to afford sthg; **se ~ de faire qqch** to take the liberty of doing sthg.

permis, -e [pɛrmi, iz] *pp* → **permettre**. ○ **permis** *nm* licence, permit; ~ **de conduire** driving licence *Br*, driver's license *Am*; ~ **de construire** planning permission *Br*, building permit *Am*.

permission [pɛrmisjɔ̃] *nf* [autorisation] permission. || MIL leave.

permuter [pɛrmyte] 1 *vt* to change round; [mots, figures] to transpose. 2 *vi* to change, to switch.

pérorer [perɔre] *vi* *péj* to hold forth.

Pérou [peru] *nm*: **le ~** Peru.

perpendiculaire [pɛrpɑ̃dikylɛr] **1** *nf* perpendicular. **2** *adj*: ~ (à) perpendicular (to).

perpétrer [pɛrpetre] *vt* to perpetrate.

perpétuel, -elle [pɛrpetɥɛl] *adj* [fréquent, continu] perpetual.

perpétuer [pɛrpetɥe] *vt* to perpetuate. ○ **se perpétuer** *vp* to continue; [espèce] to perpetuate itself.

perpétuité [pɛrpetɥite] *nf* perpetuity; à ~ for life; **être condamné à ~** to be sentenced to life imprisonment.

perplexe [pɛrplɛks] *adj* perplexed.

perquisition [pɛrkizisjɔ̃] *nf* search.

perron [pɛrɔ̃] *nm* steps (*pl*).

perroquet [pɛrɔkɛ] *nm* [animal] parrot.

perruche [pɛryʃ] *nf* budgerigar.

perruque [pɛryk] *nf* wig.

persan, -e [pɛrsɑ̃, an] *adj* Persian.

persécuter [pɛrsekyte] *vt* [martyriser] to persecute. || [harceler] to harass.

persécution [pɛrsekysjɔ̃] *nf* persecution.

persévérant, -e [pɛrseverɑ̃, ɑ̃t] *adj* persevering.

persévérer [pɛrsevere] *vi*: ~ **(dans)** to persevere (in).

persienne [pɛrsjɛn] *nf* shutter.

persil [pɛrsi] *nm* parsley.

Persique [pɛrsik] → **golfe**.

persistant, -e [pɛrsistɑ̃, ɑ̃t] *adj* persistent; **arbre à feuillage ~** evergreen (tree).

persister [pɛrsiste] *vi* to persist; ~ **à faire qqch** to persist in doing sthg.

personnage [pɛrsɔnaʒ] *nm* THÉÂTRE character; ART figure.

personnalité [pɛrsɔnalite] *nf* [gén] personality. || JUR status.

personne [pɛrsɔn] **1** *nf* person; ~**s** people; **en ~** in person, personally; ~ **âgée** elderly person. **2** *pron indéf* [quelqu'un] anybody, anyone; [aucune personne] nobody, no one; ~ **ne viendra** nobody will come; **il n'y a jamais ~** there's never anybody there.

personnel, -elle [pɛrsɔnɛl] *adj* [gén] personal. || [égoïste] self-centred. ○ **personnel** *nm* staff, personnel.

personnellement [pɛrsɔnɛlmɑ̃] *adv* personally.

personnifier [pɛrsɔnifje] *vt* to personify.

perspective [pɛrspɛktiv] *nf* [ART & point de vue] perspective. || [panorama] view. || [éventualité] prospect.

perspicace [pɛrspikas] *adj* perspicacious.

persuader [pɛrsɥade] *vt*: ~ **qqn de qqch/de faire qqch** to persuade sb of sthg/to do sthg, to convince sb of sthg/to do sthg.

persuasif, -ive [pɛrsɥazif, iv] *adj* persuasive.

persuasion [pɛrsɥazjɔ̃] *nf* persuasion.

perte [pɛrt] *nf* [gén] loss. || [gaspillage - de temps] waste. ○ **pertes** *nfpl* [morts] losses. ○ **à perte de vue** *loc adv* as far as the eye can see.

pertinent, -e [pɛrtinɑ̃, ɑ̃t] *adj* pertinent, relevant.

perturber [pɛrtyrbe] *vt* [gén] to disrupt; ~ **l'ordre public** to disturb the peace. || PSYCHOL to disturb.

pervenche [pɛrvɑ̃ʃ] *nf* BOT periwinkle. || *fam* [contractuelle] meter maid *Am*.

pervers, -e [pɛrver, ɛrs] **1** *adj* [vicieux] perverted. || [effet] unwanted. **2** *nm, f* pervert.

perversion [pɛrvɛrsjɔ̃] *nf* perversion.

perversité [pɛrvɛrsite] *nf* perversity.

pervertir [pɛrvɛrtir] *vt* to pervert.

pesamment [pəzamɑ̃] *adv* heavily.

pesant, -e [pəzɑ̃, ɑ̃t] *adj* [lourd] heavy. || [style, architecture] ponderous.

pesanteur [pəzɑ̃tœr] *nf* PHYS gravity.

pesée [pəze] *nf* [opération] weighing.

pèse-personne [pɛzpɛrsɔn] (*pl inv* OU **pèse-personnes**) *nm* scales (*pl*).

peser [pəze] **1** *vt* to weigh. **2** *vi* [avoir un certain poids] to weigh. || [être lourd] to be heavy. || [appuyer]: ~ **sur qqch** to press (down) on sthg.

peseta [pezeta] *nf* peseta.

pessimisme [pesimism] *nm* pessimism.

pessimiste [pesimist] **1** *nmf* pessimist. **2** *adj* pessimistic.

peste [pɛst] *nf* MÉD plague.

pestilentiel, -ielle [pɛstilɑ̃sjɛl] *adj* pestilential.

pet [pɛ] *nm fam* fart.

pétale [petal] *nm* petal.

pétanque [petɑ̃k] *nf* ≈ bowls (*U*).

pétarader [petarade] *vi* to backfire.

pétard [petar] *nm* [petit explosif] banger *Br*, firecracker. || *fam* [revolver] gun. || *fam* [haschich] joint.

péter [pete] **1** *vi tfam* [personne] to fart. || *fam* [câble, élastique] to snap. **2** *vt fam* to bust.

pétiller [petije] *vi* [vin, eau] to sparkle, to bubble. || *fig* [yeux] to sparkle.

petit, -e [pəti, it] **1** adj [de taille, jeune] small, little; ~ **frère** little ou younger brother. ‖ [voyage, visite] short, little. ‖ [faible, infime - somme d'argent] small; [- bruit] faint, slight. ‖ [de peu d'importance, de peu de valeur] minor. ‖ [médiocre, mesquin] petty. ‖ [de rang modeste - commerçant, propriétaire, pays] small; [- fonctionnaire] minor. **2** nm, f [enfant] little one, child; **pauvre ~!** poor little thing!; **la classe des ~s** SCOL the infant class. **3** nm [jeune animal] young (U); **faire des ~s** to have puppies/kittens etc. ○ **petit à petit** loc adv little by little, gradually.

petit déjeuner [p(ə)tideʒøne] nm breakfast.

petite-fille [p(ə)titfij] nf granddaughter.

petit-fils [p(ə)tifis] nm grandson.

petit-four [p(ə)tifur] nm petit-four.

pétition [petisjɔ̃] nf petition.

petit-lait [p(ə)tilɛ] nm whey.

petit-nègre [p(ə)tinɛgr] nm inv fam pidgin French.

petits-enfants [p(ə)tizɑ̃fɑ̃] nmpl grandchildren.

petit-suisse [p(ə)tisɥis] nm fresh soft cheese, eaten with sugar.

pétrifier [petrifje] vt litt & fig to petrify.

pétrin [petrɛ̃] nm [de boulanger] kneading machine. ‖ fam [embarras] pickle; **se fourrer/être dans le ~** to get into/to be in a pickle.

pétrir [petrir] vt [pâte, muscle] to knead.

pétrole [petrɔl] nm oil, petroleum.

pétrolier, -ière [petrɔlje, jɛr] adj oil (avant n), petroleum (avant n). ○ **pétrolier** nm [navire] oil tanker.

pétrolifère [petrɔlifɛr] adj oil-bearing.

pétulant, -e [petylɑ̃, ɑ̃t] adj exuberant.

peu [pø] **1** adv (avec verbe, adjectif, adverbe): **il a ~ dormi** he didn't sleep much, he slept little. ‖ fam [embarras] pickle; ~ **souvent** not very often, rarely. ‖ ~ **de** (+ nom sg) little, not much; (+ nom pl) few, not many; ~ **de gens le connaissent** few ou not many know him. **2** nm: **un ~ a** little, a bit; **un (tout) petit ~ a** little bit; **elle est un ~ sotte** she's a bit stupid; **un ~ de a** little; **un ~ de vin/patience** a little wine/ patience. ○ **avant peu** loc adv soon, before long. ○ **depuis peu** loc adv recently. ○ **peu à peu** loc adv gradually, little by little. ○ **pour peu que** loc conj (+ subjonctif) if ever, if only. ○ **pour**

un peu loc adv nearly, almost. ○ **sous peu** loc adv soon, shortly.

peuplade [pœplad] nf tribe.

peuple [pœpl] nm [gén] people; **le ~** the (common) people. ‖ fam [multitude]: **quel ~!** what a crowd!

peuplement [pœpləmɑ̃] nm [action] populating. ‖ [population] population.

peupler [pœple] vt [pourvoir d'habitants - région] to populate; [- bois, étang] to stock. ‖ [habiter, occuper] to inhabit. ‖ fig [remplir] to fill. ○ **se peupler** vp [région] to become populated. ‖ [rue, salle] to be filled.

peuplier [pœplije] nm poplar.

peur [pœr] nf fear; **avoir ~ de qqn/qqch** to be afraid of sb/sthg; **avoir ~ de faire qqch** to be afraid of doing sthg; **j'ai ~ qu'il ne vienne pas** I'm afraid he won't come; **faire ~ à qqn** to frighten sb; **par** ou **de ~ de qqch** for fear of sthg; **par** ou **de ~ de faire qqch** for fear of doing sthg.

peureux, -euse [pœrø, øz] **1** adj fearful, timid. **2** nm, f fearful ou timid person.

peut → **pouvoir.**

peut-être [pøtɛtr] adv perhaps, maybe; ~ **qu'ils ne viendront pas, ils ne viendront ~ pas** perhaps ou maybe they won't come.

peux → **pouvoir.**

phalange [falɑ̃ʒ] nf ANAT phalanx.

phallocrate [falɔkrat] nm male chauvinist.

phallus [falys] nm phallus.

pharaon [faraɔ̃] nm pharaoh.

phare [far] **1** nm [tour] lighthouse. ‖ AUTOM headlight; ~ **antibrouillard** fog lamp.

pharmaceutique [farmasøtik] adj pharmaceutical.

pharmacie [farmasi] nf [science] pharmacology. ‖ [magasin] chemist's Br, drugstore Am. ‖ [meuble]: (**armoire à**) ~ medicine cupboard.

pharmacien, -ienne [farmasjɛ̃, jɛn] nm, f chemist Br, druggist Am.

pharynx [farɛ̃ks] nm pharynx.

phase [faz] nf phase.

phénoménal, -e, -aux [fenɔmenal, o] adj phenomenal.

phénomène [fenɔmɛn] nm [fait] phenomenon. ‖ [être anormal] freak. ‖ fam [excentrique] character.

philanthropie [filɑ̃trɔpi] nf philanthropy.

philatélie [filateli] *nf* philately, stamp-collecting.

philharmonique [filarmɔnik] *adj* philharmonic.

Philippines [filipin] *nfpl* : les ~ the Philippines.

philosophe [filɔzɔf] 1 *nmf* philosopher. 2 *adj* philosophical.

philosophie [filɔzɔfi] *nf* philosophy.

phobie [fɔbi] *nf* phobia.

phonétique [fɔnetik] 1 *nf* phonetics (U). 2 *adj* phonetic.

phonographe [fɔnɔgraf] *nm vieilli* gramophone *Br*, phonograph *Am*.

phoque [fɔk] *nm* seal.

phosphate [fɔsfat] *nm* phosphate.

phosphore [fɔsfɔr] *nm* phosphorus.

phosphorescent, -e [fɔsfɔresɑ̃, ɑ̃t] *adj* phosphorescent.

photo [fɔto] *nf* [technique] photography. || [image] photo, picture; **prendre qqn en** ~ to take a photo of sb; ~ **d'identité** passport photo.

photocopie [fɔtɔkɔpi] *nf* [procédé] photocopying. || [document] photocopy.

photocopier [fɔtɔkɔpje] *vt* to photocopy.

photocopieur [fɔtɔkɔpjœr] *nm*, **photocopieuse** [fɔtɔkɔpjøz] *nf* photocopier.

photoélectrique [fɔtɔelektrik] *adj* photoelectric.

photogénique [fɔtɔʒenik] *adj* photogenic.

photographe [fɔtɔgraf] *nmf* [artiste, technicien] photographer. || [commerçant] camera dealer.

photographie [fɔtɔgrafi] *nf* [technique] photography. || [cliché] photograph.

photographier [fɔtɔgrafje] *vt* to photograph.

Photomaton® [fɔtɔmatɔ̃] *nm* photo booth.

phrase [fraz] *nf* LING sentence; ~ **toute faite** stock phrase. || MUS phrase.

physicien, -ienne [fizisjɛ̃, jɛn] *nm, f* physicist.

physiologie [fizjɔlɔʒi] *nf* physiology.

physiologique [fizjɔlɔʒik] *adj* physiological.

physionomie [fizjɔnɔmi] *nf* [faciès] face. || [apparence] physiognomy.

physionomiste [fizjɔnɔmist] *adj*: être ~ to have a good memory for faces.

physique [fizik] 1 *adj* physical. 2 *nf* SCIENCE physics (U). 3 *nm* [constitution] physical well-being. || [apparence] physique.

physiquement [fizikmɑ̃] *adv* physically.

piaffer [pjafe] *vi* [cheval] to paw the ground. || [personne] to fidget.

piailler [pjaje] *vi* [oiseaux] to cheep. || [enfant] to squawk.

pianiste [pjanist] *nmf* pianist.

piano [pjano] *nm* piano.

pianoter [pjanɔte] *vi* [jouer du piano] to plunk away (on the piano). || [sur table] to drum one's fingers.

piaule [pjol] *nf fam* [hébergement] place; [chambre] room.

pic [pik] *nm* [outil] pick, pickaxe. || [montagne] peak. ○ **à pic** *loc adv* [verticalement] vertically; **couler à** ~ to sink like a stone. || *fam fig* [à point nommé] just at the right moment.

pichenette [piʃnet] *nf* flick (of the finger).

pichet [piʃe] *nm* jug.

pickpocket [pikpɔket] *nm* pickpocket.

picorer [pikɔre] *vi & vt* to peck.

picotement [pikɔtmɑ̃] *nm* prickling (U), prickle.

pie [pi] 1 *nf* [oiseau] magpie. || *fig & péj* [bavard] chatterbox. 2 *adj inv* [cheval] piebald.

pièce [pjɛs] *nf* [élément] piece; [de moteur] part; ~ **de collection** collector's item; ~ **détachée** spare part. || [unité] : **quinze francs** ~ fifteen francs each ou apiece; **acheter/vendre qqch à la** ~ to buy/sell sthg singly, to buy/sell sthg separately; **travailler à la** ~ to do piece work. || [document] document, paper; ~ **d'identité** identification papers (pl); ~ **justificative** written proof (U), supporting document. || [œuvre littéraire ou musicale] piece; ~ **(de théâtre)** play. || [argent] : ~ **(de monnaie)** coin. || [de maison] room. || COUTURE patch.

pied [pje] *nm* [gén] foot; **à** ~ on foot; **avoir** ~ to be able to touch the bottom; **perdre** ~ *litt & fig* to be out of one's depth; **être/marcher** ~s **nus** ou **nu-**~s to be/to go barefoot. || [base - de montagne, table] foot; [- de verre] stem; [- de lampe] base. || [plant - de tomate] stalk; [- de vigne] stock. || *loc*: **être sur** ~ to be (back) on one's feet, to be up and about; **faire du** ~ à to play footsie with; **mettre qqch sur** ~ to get sthg on its feet, to get sthg off the ground; **je n'ai jamais mis les** ~s

chez lui I've never set foot in his house; **au ~ de la lettre** literally, to the letter.

pied-de-biche [pjedbiʃ] (*pl* **pieds-de-biche**) *nm* [outil] nail claw.

piédestal, -aux [pjedɛstal, o] *nm* pedestal.

pied-noir [pjenwar] *nmf* French settler *in Algeria*.

piège [pjɛʒ] *nm litt* & *fig* trap.

piéger [pjeʒe] *vt* [animal, personne] to trap. || [colis, véhicule] to boobytrap.

pierraille [pjeraj] *nf* loose stones (*pl*).

pierre [pjɛr] *nf* stone; **~ d'achoppement** *fig* stumbling block; **~ précieuse** precious stone.

pierreries [pjɛrri] *nfpl* precious stones, jewels.

piété [pjete] *nf* piety.

piétiner [pjetine] 1 *vi* [trépigner] to stamp (one's feet). || *fig* [ne pas avancer] to make no progress, to be at a standstill. 2 *vt* [personne, parterre] to trample.

piéton, -onne [pjetɔ̃, ɔn] 1 *nm, f* pedestrian. 2 *adj* pedestrian (*avant n*).

piétonnier, -ière [pjetɔnje, jɛr] *adj* pedestrian (*avant n*).

piètre [pjɛtr] *adj* poor.

pieu, -x [pjø] *nm* [poteau] post, stake. || *fam* [lit] pit *Br*, sack *Am*.

pieuvre [pjœvr] *nf* octopus.

pieux, pieuse [pjø, pjøz] *adj* [personne, livre] pious.

pif [pif] *nm fam* conk; **au ~** *fig* by guess-work.

pigeon [piʒɔ̃] *nm* [oiseau] pigeon. || *fam péj* [personne] sucker.

pigeonnier [piʒɔnje] *nm* [pour pigeons] pigeon loft, dovecote.

pigment [pigmã] *nm* pigment.

pignon [piɲɔ̃] *nm* [de mur] gable. || [d'engrenage] gearwheel. || [de pomme de pin] pine kernel.

pile [pil] 1 *nf* [de livres, journaux] pile. || ÉLECTR battery. || [de pièce]: **~ ou face** heads or tails. 2 *adv fam* on the dot; **tomber/arriver ~** to come/to arrive at just the right time.

piler [pile] 1 *vt* [amandes] to crush, to grind. 2 *vi fam* AUTOM to jam on the brakes.

pilier [pilje] *nm* [de construction] pillar. || *fig* [soutien] mainstay, pillar. || RUGBY prop (forward).

pillard, -e [pijar, ard] *nm, f* looter.

piller [pije] *vt* [ville, biens] to loot.

pilon [pilɔ̃] *nm* [instrument] pestle. || [de poulet] drumstick.

pilonner [pilɔne] *vt* to pound.

pilori [pilɔri] *nm* pillory; **mettre** or **clouer qqn au ~** *fig* to pillory sb.

pilotage [pilɔtaʒ] *nm* piloting.

pilote [pilɔt] 1 *nm* [d'avion] pilot; [de voiture] driver; **~ automatique** autopilot; **~ de chasse** fighter pilot; **~ de course** racing driver; **~ d'essai** test pilot; **~ de ligne** airline pilot. 2 *adj* pilot (*avant n*), experimental.

piloter [pilɔte] *vt* [avion] to pilot; [voiture] to drive. || [personne] to show around.

pilotis [pilɔti] *nm* pile.

pilule [pilyl] *nf* pill; **prendre la ~** to be on the pill.

piment [pimã] *nm* [plante] pepper, capsicum; **~ rouge** chilli pepper, hot red pepper. || *fig* [piquant] spice.

pimpant, -e [pɛ̃pã, ãt] *adj* smart.

pin [pɛ̃] *nm* pine; **~ parasol** umbrella pine; **~ sylvestre** Scots pine.

pince [pɛ̃s] *nf* [grande] pliers (*pl*). || [petite]: **~ (à épiler)** tweezers (*pl*); **~ à linge** clothes peg. || [de crabe] pincer. || COUTURE dart.

pinceau, -x [pɛ̃so] *nm* [pour peindre] brush.

pincée [pɛ̃se] *nf* pinch.

pincer [pɛ̃se] 1 *vt* [serrer] to pinch; MUS to pluck; [lèvres] to purse. || *fam fig* [arrêter] to catch.

pincettes [pɛ̃sɛt] *nfpl* [ustensile] tongs.

pingouin [pɛ̃gwɛ̃] *nm* penguin.

ping-pong [piŋpɔ̃g] *nm* ping pong, table tennis.

pinson [pɛ̃sɔ̃] *nm* chaffinch.

pintade [pɛ̃tad] *nf* guinea fowl.

pin-up [pinœp] *nf inv* pinup (girl).

pioche [pjɔʃ] *nf* [outil] pick. || JEU pile.

piocher [pjɔʃe] 1 *vt* [terre] to dig. || JEU to take. || *fig* [choisir] to pick at random. 2 *vi* [creuser] to dig. || JEU to pick up; **~ dans** [tas] to delve into.

pion, pionne [pjɔ̃, pjɔn] *nm, f fam* SCOL supervisor (often a student who does this as a part-time job). ○ **pion** *nm* [aux échecs] pawn; [aux dames] piece.

pionnier, -ière [pjɔnje, jɛr] *nm, f* pioneer.

pipe [pip] *nf* pipe.

pipeline, pipe-line [pajplajn, piplin] (*pl* **pipe-lines**) *nm* pipeline.

pipi [pipi] *nm fam* wee; **faire ~** to have a wee.

piquant, -e [pikã, ãt] *adj* [barbe, feuille] prickly. || [sauce] spicy, hot. ○ **piquant**

nm [d'animal] spine; [de végétal] thorn, prickle. || *fig* [d'histoire] spice.

pique [pik] **1** *nf* [arme] pike. || *fig* [mot blessant] barbed comment. **2** *nm* [aux cartes] spade.

pique-assiette [pikasjεt] (*pl inv* OU **pique-assiettes**) *nmf péj* sponger.

pique-nique [piknik] (*pl* **pique-niques**) *nm* picnic.

piquer [pike] *vt* [suj: guêpe, méduse] to sting; [suj: serpent, moustique] to bite. || [avec pointe] to prick. || [animal] to put down. || [fleur] : ~ **qqch dans** to stick sthg into. || [suj: tissu, barbe] to prickle. || [suj: fumée, froid] to sting. || COUTURE to sew, to machine. || *fam* [voler] to pinch. || *fam* [voleur, escroc] to catch. **2** *vi* [ronce] to prick; [ortie] to sting. || [guêpe, méduse] to sting; [serpent, moustique] to bite. || [épice] to burn. || [avion] to dive.

piquet [pikε] *nm* [pieu] peg, stake. ○ **piquet de grève** *nm* picket.

piqûre [pikyr] *nf* [de guêpe, méduse] sting; [de serpent, moustique] bite. || [d'ortie] sting. || [injection] jab *Br*, shot.

piratage [pirataʒ] *nm* piracy. INFORM hacking.

pirate [pirat] **1** *nm* [corsaire] pirate; ~ **de l'air** hijacker, skyjacker. **2** *adj* pirate (*avant n*).

pire [pir] **1** *adj* [comparatif relatif] worse. || [superlatif] : **le/la** ~ the worst. **2** *nm* : **le** ~ (**de**) the worst (of).

pirogue [pirɔg] *nf* dugout canoe.

pirouette [pirwεt] *nf* [saut] pirouette. || *fig* [faux-fuyant] prevarication, evasive answer.

pis [pi] **1** *adv* worse; **de mal en** ~ from bad to worse. **2** *nm* udder.

pis-aller [pizale] *nm inv* last resort.

pisciculture [pisikyltyr] *nf* fish farming.

piscine [pisin] *nf* swimming pool; ~ **couverte/découverte** indoor/open-air swimming pool.

pissenlit [pisɑ̃li] *nm* dandelion.

pisser [pise] *fam* **1** *vt* [suj: plaie] : **son genou pissait le sang** blood was gushing from his knee. **2** *vi* to pee, to piss.

pissotière [pisɔtjεr] *nf fam* public urinal.

pistache [pistaʃ] *nf* [fruit] pistachio (nut).

piste [pist] *nf* [trace] trail. || [zone aménagée] : ~ **d'atterrissage** runway; ~ **cyclable** cycle track; ~ **de danse** dance floor; ~ **de ski** ski run. || [chemin] path, track. || [d'enregistrement] track.

pistil [pistil] *nm* pistil.

pistolet [pistɔlε] *nm* [arme] pistol, gun. || [à peinture] spray gun.

piston [pistɔ̃] *nm* [de moteur] piston. || *fig* [appui] string-pulling.

pistonner [pistɔne] *vt* to pull strings for; **se faire** ~ to have strings pulled for one.

pitance [pitɑ̃s] *nf péj & vieilli* sustenance.

piteux, -euse [pitø, øz] *adj* piteous.

pitié [pitje] *nf* pity; **avoir** ~ **de qqn** to have pity on sb, to pity sb.

piton [pitɔ̃] *nm* [clou] piton. || [pic] peak.

pitoyable [pitwajabl] *adj* pitiful.

pitre [pitr] *nm* clown.

pitrerie [pitrəri] *nf* tomfoolery.

pittoresque [pitɔrεsk] *adj* [région] picturesque. || [détail] colourful, vivid.

pivot [pivo] *nm* [de machine, au basket] pivot. || [de dent] post. || [centre] *fig* mainspring.

pivoter [pivɔte] *vi* to pivot; [porte] to revolve.

pizza [pidza] *nf* pizza.

Pl., pl. *abr de* place.

placard [plakar] *nm* [armoire] cupboard. || [affiche] poster, notice.

placarder [plakarde] *vt* [affiche] to put up, to stick up; [mur] to placard, to stick a notice on.

place [plas] *nf* [espace] space, room; **prendre de la** ~ to take up (a lot of) space. || [emplacement, position] position; **changer qqch de** ~ to put sthg in a different place, to move sthg; **prendre la** ~ **de qqn** to take sb's place; **à la** ~ **de qqn** instead of sb, in sb's place. || [siège] seat; ~ **assise** seat. || [rang] place. || [de ville] square. || [emploi] position, job. || MIL [garnison] garrison (town); ~ **forte** fortified town.

placement [plasmɑ̃] *nm* [d'argent] investment. || [d'employé] placing.

placenta [plasɛ̃ta] *nm* ANAT placenta.

placer [plase] *vt* [gén] to place; [invités, spectateurs] to seat. || [mot, anecdote] to put in, to get in. || [argent] to invest. ○ **se placer** *vp* [prendre place - debout] to stand; [- assis] to sit (down). || *fig* [dans situation] to put o.s. || [se classer] to come, to be.

placide [plasid] *adj* placid.

plafond [plafɔ̃] *nm litt* & *fig* ceiling; **faux ~** false ceiling.

plafonner [plafɔne] *vi* [prix, élève] to peak; [avion] to reach its ceiling.

plage [plaʒ] *nf* [de sable] beach. || [d'ombre, de prix] band; *fig* [de temps] slot. || [de disque] track. || [dans voiture]: **~ arrière** back shelf.

plagiat [plaʒja] *nm* plagiarism.

plagier [plaʒje] *vt* to plagiarize.

plaider [plede] JUR **1** *vt* to plead. **2** *vi* to plead; **~ pour qqn** JUR to plead for sb; [justifier] to plead sb's cause.

plaidoirie [pledwari] *nf*, **plaidoyer** [pledwaje] *nm* JUR speech for the defence; *fig* plea.

plaie [plɛ] *nf litt* & *fig* [blessure] wound. || *fam* [personne] pest.

plaindre [plɛ̃dr] *vt* to pity. ○ **se plaindre** *vp* to complain.

plaine [plɛn] *nf* plain.

plain-pied [plɛ̃pje] ○ **de plain-pied** *loc adv* [pièce] on one floor; **de ~ avec** *litt* & *fig* on a level with. || *fig* [directement] straight.

plaint, -e [plɛ̃, plɛ̃t] *pp* → plaindre.

plainte [plɛ̃t] *nf* [gémissement] moan, groan; *fig* & *litt* [du vent] moan. || [doléance & JUR] complaint; **porter ~** to lodge a complaint.

plaintif, -ive [plɛ̃tif, iv] *adj* plaintive.

plaire [plɛr] *vi* to be liked; **il me plaît** I like him; **ça te plairait d'aller au cinéma?** would you like to go to the cinema?; **s'il vous/te plaît** please.

plaisance [plɛzɑ̃s] ○ **de plaisance** *loc adj* sailing (*avant n*); **navigation de ~** sailing; **port de ~** marina.

plaisant, -e [plɛzɑ̃, ɑ̃t] *adj* pleasant.

plaisanter [plɛzɑ̃te] *vi* to joke; **tu plaisantes?** you must be joking!

plaisanterie [plɛzɑ̃tri] *nf* joke; **c'est une ~?** *iron* you must be joking!

plaisantin [plɛzɑ̃tɛ̃] *nm* joker.

plaisir [plezir] *nm* pleasure; **avoir du/prendre ~ à faire qqch** to have/to take pleasure in doing sthg; **faire ~ à qqn** to please sb; **avec ~** with pleasure; **j'ai le ~ de vous annoncer que ...** I have the (great) pleasure of announcing that ....

plan¹, -e [plɑ̃, plan] *adj* level, flat.

plan² [plɑ̃] *nm* [dessin - de ville] map; [- de maison] plan. || [projet] plan; **faire des ~s** to make plans. || [domaine]: **sur tous les ~s** in all respects; **sur le ~ familial** as far as the family is concerned. || [surface]: **~ d'eau** lake; **~ de travail** work surface, worktop. || GÉOM plane. || CIN take; **gros ~** close-up. ○ **au premier plan** *loc adv* [dans l'espace] in the foreground. ○ **en plan** *loc adv*: **laisser qqn en ~** to leave sb stranded, to abandon sb; **il a tout laissé en ~** he dropped everything.

planche [plɑ̃ʃ] *nf* [en bois] plank; **~ à dessin** drawing board; **~ à repasser** ironing board; **~ à voile** [planche] sailboard; [sport] windsurfing; **faire la ~** *fig* to float. || [d'illustration] plate.

plancher [plɑ̃ʃe] *nm* [de maison, de voiture] floor. || *fig* [limite] floor, lower limit.

plancton [plɑ̃ktɔ̃] *nm* plankton.

planer [plane] *vi* [avion, oiseau] to glide. || [nuage, fumée, brouillard] to float. || *fig* [danger]: **~ sur qqn** to hang over sb. || *fam fig* [personne] to be out of touch with reality, to have one's head in the clouds.

planétaire [planeter] *adj* ASTRON planetary. || [mondial] world (*avant n*).

planétarium [planetarjɔm] *nm* planetarium.

planète [planɛt] *nf* planet.

planeur [plancɛr] *nm* glider.

planification [planifikasjɔ̃] *nf* ÉCON planning.

planisphère [planisfer] *nm* map of the world, planisphere.

planning [planiŋ] *nm* [de fabrication] workflow schedule. || [agenda personnel] schedule; **~ familial** [organisme] family planning centre.

planque [plɑ̃k] *nf fam* [cachette] hideout. || *fig* [situation, travail] cushy number.

plant [plɑ̃] *nm* [plante] seedling.

plantaire [plɑ̃ter] *adj* plantar.

plantation [plɑ̃tasjɔ̃] *nf* [exploitation - d'arbres, de coton, de café] plantation; [- de légumes] patch. || [action] planting.

plante [plɑ̃t] *nf* BOT plant; **~ verte** ou **d'appartement** ou **d'intérieur** house ou pot plant. || ANAT sole.

planter [plɑ̃te] *vt* [arbre, terrain] to plant. || [clou] to hammer in, to drive in; [pieu] to drive in; [couteau, griffes] to stick in. || [tente] to pitch. || *fam fig* [laisser tomber] to dump.

plantureux, -euse [plɑ̃tyrø, øz] *adj* [repas] lavish. || [femme] buxom.

plaque [plak] *nf* [de métal, de verre, de verglas] sheet; [de marbre] slab; **~ chauffante** ou **de cuisson** hotplate; **~ de chocolat** bar of chocolate. || [gravée] plaque; **~ d'immatriculation** ou **minéralogique**

number plate *Br*, license plate *Am*. || [insigne] badge. || [sur la peau] patch.

plaqué, -e [plake] *adj* [métal] plated; ~ or/argent gold-/silver-plated. ○ **plaqué** *nm* [métal]: **du ~ or/argent** gold/silver plate.

plaquer [plake] *vt* [bois] to veneer. || [aplatir] to flatten; ~ **qqn contre qqch** to pin sb against sthg. || RUGBY to tackle. || MUS [accord] to play. || *fam* [travail, personne] to chuck.

plaquette [plaket] *nf* [de métal] plaque; [de marbre] tablet. || [de chocolat] bar; [de beurre] pat. || [de comprimés] packet, strip. || [mets] course; ~ **de frein** brake pad.

plasma [plasma] *nm* plasma.

plastique [plastik] *adj & nm* plastic.

plat, -e [pla, plat] *adj* [gén] flat. || [eau] still. ○ **plat** *nm* [partie plate] flat. || [récipient] dish. || [mets] course; ~ **cuisiné** ready-cooked meal ou dish; ~ **du jour** today's special; ~ **de résistance** main course. || [plongeon] belly-flop. ○ **à plat** *loc adv* [horizontalement, dégonflé] flat. || *fam* [épuisé] exhausted.

platane [platan] *nm* plane tree.

plateau, -x [plato] *nm* [de cuisine] tray; ~ **de/à fromages** cheese board. || [de balance] pan. || GÉOGR & *fig* plateau. || THÉÂTRE stage; CIN & TÉLÉ set. || [de vélo] chain wheel.

plateau-repas [platoʀəpa] *nm* tray (of food).

plate-bande [platbɑ̃d] *nf* flower bed.

plate-forme [platfɔʀm] *nf* [gén] platform; ~ **de forage** drilling platform.

platine [platin] 1 *adj inv* platinum. 2 *nm* [métal] platinum. 3 *nf* [de tourne-disque] deck; ~ **laser** compact disc player.

platonique [platɔnik] *adj* [amour, amitié] platonic.

plâtras [platra] *nm* [gravats] rubble.

plâtre [platʀ] *nm* CONSTR & MÉD plaster. || [sculpture] plaster cast.

plâtrer [platʀe] *vt* [mur] to plaster. || MÉD to put in plaster.

plausible [plozibl] *adj* plausible.

play-back [plɛbak] *nm inv* miming; **chanter en ~** to mime.

play-boy [plɛbɔj] (*pl* **play-boys**) *nm* playboy.

plébiscite [plebisit] *nm* plebiscite.

plein, -e [plɛ̃, plɛn] *adj* [rempli, complet] full; **en ~e nuit** in the middle of the night; **en ~ air** in the open air. || [non creux] solid. || [femelle] pregnant.

○ **plein 1** *adv fam*: **il a de l'encre ~ les doigts** he has ink all over his fingers; **en ~ dans/sur qqch** right in/on sthg. 2 *nm* [de réservoir] full tank; **le ~, s'il vous plaît** fill her up please; **faire le ~** to fill up.

plein-temps [plɛ̃tɑ̃] *nm* full-time work (*U*). ○ **à plein temps** *loc adj & loc adv* full-time.

plénitude [plenityd] *nf* fullness.

pléonasme [pleonasm] *nm* pleonasm.

pleurer [plœʀe] **1** *vi* [larmoyer] to cry; ~ **de joie** to weep for joy, to cry with joy; ~ *péj* [se plaindre] to whinge. || [se lamenter]: ~ **sur** to lament. **2** *vt* to mourn.

pleurnicher [plœʀniʃe] *vi* to whine, to whinge.

pleurs [plœʀ] *nmpl*: **être en ~** to be in tears.

pleuvoir [pløvwaʀ] *v impers litt & fig* to rain; **il pleut** it is raining.

Plexiglas® [plɛksiglas] *nm* Plexiglass®.

plexus [plɛksys] *nm* plexus; ~ **solaire** solar plexus.

pli [pli] *nm* [de tissu] pleat; [de pantalon] crease; **faux ~** crease. || [du front] line; [du cou] fold. || [lettre] letter; [enveloppe] envelope; **sous ~ séparé** under separate cover. || CARTES trick. || GÉOL fold.

pliant, -e [plijɑ̃, ɑ̃t] *adj* folding (*avant n*).

plier [plije] **1** *vt* [papier, tissu] to fold. || [vêtement, vélo] to fold (up). || [branche, bras] to bend. **2** *vi* [se courber] to bend. || *fig* [céder] to bow. ○ **se plier** *vp* [être pliable] to fold (up). || *fig* [se soumettre]: **se ~ à qqch** to bow to sthg.

plinthe [plɛ̃t] *nf* plinth.

plissé, -e [plise] *adj* [jupe] pleated. || [peau] wrinkled.

plissement [plismɑ̃] *nm* [de front] creasing; [d'yeux] screwing up.

plisser [plise] **1** *vt* COUTURE to pleat. || [front] to crease; [lèvres] to pucker; [yeux] to screw up. **2** *vi* [étoffe] to crease.

plomb [plɔ̃] *nm* [métal, de vitrail] lead. || [de chasse] shot. || ÉLECTR fuse; **les ~s ont sauté** a fuse has blown ou gone. || [de pêche] sinker.

plombage [plɔ̃baʒ] *nm* [de dent] filling.

plomber [plɔ̃be] *vt* [ligne] to weight (with lead). || [dent] to fill.

plombier [plɔ̃bje] *nm* plumber.

plonge [plɔ̃ʒ] *nf* dishwashing; **faire la ~** to wash dishes.

plongeant, -e [plɔ̃ʒɑ̃, ɑ̃t] *adj* [vue] from above. || [décolleté] plunging.

plongeoir [plɔ̃ʒwar] *nm* diving board.

plongeon [plɔ̃ʒɔ̃] *nm* [dans l'eau, au football] dive.

plonger [plɔ̃ʒe] **1** *vt* [immerger, enfoncer] to plunge; ~ **la tête sous l'eau** to put one's head under the water. || *fig* [précipiter]: ~ **qqn dans qqch** to throw sb into sthg. **2** *vi* [dans l'eau, gardien de but] to dive. ○ **se plonger** *vp* [s'immerger] to submerge. || *fig* [s'absorber]: **se ~ dans qqch** to immerse o.s. in sthg.

plongeur, -euse [plɔ̃ʒœr, øz] *nm, f* [dans l'eau] diver. || [dans restaurant] dishwasher.

ployer [plwaje] *vt & vi litt & fig* to bend.

plu [ply] **1** *pp inv* → **plaire**. **2** *pp inv* → **pleuvoir**.

pluie [plɥi] *nf* [averse] rain (*U*); **sous la ~** in the rain. || *fig* [grande quantité]: **une ~ de** a shower of.

plume [plym] *nf* [d'oiseau] feather. || [pour écrire - d'oiseau] quill pen; [- de stylo] nib.

plumeau, -x [plymo] *nm* feather duster.

plumer [plyme] *vt* [volaille] to pluck. || *fam fig & péj* [personne] to fleece.

plumier [plymje] *nm* pencil box.

plupart [plypar] *nf*: **la ~ de** most of, the majority of; **pour la ~** mostly, for the most part.

pluriel, -ielle [plyrjɛl] *adj* GRAM plural. || [société] pluralist. ○ **pluriel** *nm* plural; **au ~** in the plural.

plus [ply(s)] **1** *adv* [quantité] more; **beaucoup ~ de** (+ *n sg*) a lot more, much more; (+ *n pl*) a lot more, many more; **un peu ~ de** (+ *n sg*) a little more; (+ *n pl*) a few more; ~ **j'y pense, ~ je me dis que ...** the more I think about it, the more I'm sure .... || [comparaison] more; **c'est ~ court par là** it's shorter that way; **viens ~ souvent** come more often; **c'est ~ simple qu'on ne le croit** it's simpler than you think. || [superlatif]: **le ~ the** most; **le ~ souvent** the most often; **le ~ loin** the furthest; **le ~ vite possible** as quickly as possible. || [négation] no more; ~ **un mot!** not another word!; **ne ... ~** no longer, no more; **il ne vient ~ me voir** he doesn't come to see me any more, he no longer comes to see me. **2** *nm* [signe] plus (sign). || *fig* [atout] plus. **3** *prép* plus; **trois ~ trois font six** three plus three is six, three and three are six. ○ **au plus** *loc adv* at the most; **tout au ~** at the very most. ○ **de plus** *loc adv* [en supplément, en

trop] more; **elle a cinq ans de ~ que moi** she's five years older than me. || [en outre] furthermore, what's more. ○ **de plus en plus** *loc adv* more and more. ○ **de plus en plus de** *loc prép* more and more. ○ **en plus** *loc adv* [en supplément] extra. || [d'ailleurs] moreover, what's more. ○ **en plus de** *loc prép* in addition to. ○ **ni plus ni moins** *loc adv* no more no less. ○ **plus ou moins** *loc adv* more or less. ○ **sans plus** *loc adv*: **elle est gentille, sans ~** she's nice, but no more than that.

plusieurs [plyzjœr] *adj indéf pl & pron indéf mfpl* several.

plus-que-parfait [plyskəparfɛ] *nm* GRAM pluperfect.

plus-value [plyvaly] *nf* [d'investissement] appreciation.

plutôt [plyto] *adv* rather; ~ **que de faire qqch** instead of doing sthg, rather than doing ○ do sthg.

pluvieux, -ieuse [plyvjø, jøz] *adj* rainy.

PME (*abr de* petite et moyenne entreprise) *nf* SME.

PMU (*abr de* **Pari mutuel urbain**) *nm* system for betting on horses.

PNB (*abr de* **produit national brut**) *nm* GNP.

pneu, -x [pnø] *nm* [de véhicule] tyre.

pneumatique [pnømatik] **1** *nf* PHYS pneumatics (*U*). **2** *adj* [fonctionnant à l'air] pneumatic. || [gonflé à l'air] inflatable.

pneumonie [pnømɔni] *nf* pneumonia.

PO (*abr de* **petites ondes**) MW.

poche [pɔʃ] *nf* [de vêtement, de sac, d'air] pocket; **de ~** pocket (*avant n*). || [sac, sous les yeux] bag; **faire des ~s** [vêtement] to bag.

pocher [pɔʃe] *vt* CULIN to poach. || [blesser]: ~ **l'œil à qqn** to give sb a black eye.

pochette [pɔʃɛt] *nf* [enveloppe] envelope; [d'allumettes] book; [de photos] packet. || [de disque] sleeve. || [mouchoir] (pocket) handkerchief.

pochoir [pɔʃwar] *nm* stencil.

podium [pɔdjɔm] *nm* podium.

poêle [pwal] **1** *nf* pan; ~ **à frire** frying pan. **2** *nm* stove.

poème [pɔɛm] *nm* poem.

poésie [pɔezi] *nf* [genre littéraire] poetry. || [pièce écrite] poem.

poète [pɔɛt] *nm* [écrivain] poet. || *fig & hum* [rêveur] dreamer.

poids [pwa] *nm* [gén] weight; **quel ~ fait-il?** how heavy is it/he?; **vendre au ~** to sell by weight; **~ lourd** [camion] heavy goods vehicle; **de ~** [argument] weighty. || SPORT [lancer] shot.

poignant, -e [pwaɲɑ̃, ɑ̃t] *adj* poignant.

poignard [pwaɲar] *nm* dagger.

poignée [pwaɲe] *nf* [quantité, petit nombre] handful. || [manche] handle. ○ **poignée de main** *nf* handshake.

poignet [pwaɲɛ] *nm* ANAT wrist. || [de vêtement] cuff.

poil [pwal] *nm* [du corps] hair. || [d'animal] hair, coat. || [de pinceau] bristle; [de tapis] strand. || *fam* [peu]: **il s'en est fallu d'un ~ que je réussisse** I came within a hair's breadth of succeeding.

poilu, -e [pwaly] *adj* hairy.

poinçon [pwɛ̃sɔ̃] *nm* [outil] awl. || [marque] hallmark.

poinçonner [pwɛ̃sɔne] *vt* [bijou] to hallmark. || [billet, tôle] to punch.

poing [pwɛ̃] *nm* fist.

point [pwɛ̃] 1 *nm* COUTURE & TRICOT stitch; **~s de suture** MÉD stitches. || [de ponctuation]: **~ (final)** full stop *Br*, period *Am*; **~ d'interrogation/d'exclamation** question/exclamation mark; **~s de suspension** suspension points. || [petite tache] dot; **~ noir** [sur la peau] blackhead; *fig* [problème] problem. || [endroit] spot, point; *fig* point; **~ culminant** [en montagne] summit; *fig* climax; **~ de repère** [temporel] reference point; [spatial] landmark; **~ de vente** point of sale, sale outlet; **~ de vue** [panorama] viewpoint; *fig* [opinion, aspect] point of view; **avoir un ~ commun avec qqn** to have something in common with sb. || [degré] point; **au ~ que, à tel ~ que** to such an extent that; **je ne pensais pas que cela le vexerait à ce ~** I didn't think it would make him so cross; **être ... au ~ de faire qqch** to be so ... as to do sthg. || *fig* [position] position. || [réglage]: **mettre au ~** [machine] to adjust; [idée, projet] to finalize; **à ~** [cuisson] just right; **à ~ (nommé)** just in time. || [question, détail] point, detail; **~ faible** weak point. || [score] point. || [douleur] pain; **~ de côté** stitch. || [début]: **être sur le ~ de faire qqch** to be on the point of doing sthg, to be about to do sthg. || AUTOM: **au ~ mort** in neutral. || GÉOGR: **~s cardinaux** points of the compass. 2 *adv vieilli*: **ne ~** not (at all).

pointe [pwɛ̃t] *nf* [extrémité] point; [de nez] tip; **se hausser sur la ~ des pieds** to stand on tiptoe; **~ d'asperge** asparagus tip. || [clou] tack. || [sommet] peak, summit; **à la ~ de la technique** at the forefront ou leading edge of technology. || *fig* [trait d'esprit] witticism. || *fig* [petite quantité]: **une ~ de** a touch of. ○ **pointes** *nfpl* DANSE points; **faire des ou les ~s** to dance on one's points. ○ **de pointe** *loc adj* [vitesse] maximum, top. || [industrie, secteur] leading; [technique] latest.

pointer [pwɛ̃te] 1 *vt* [cocher] to tick (off). || [employés - à l'entrée] to check in; [- à la sortie] to check out. || [diriger]: **~ qqch vers/sur** to point sthg towards/at. 2 *vi* [à l'usine - à l'entrée] to clock in; [- à la sortie] to clock out.

pointillé [pwɛ̃tije] *nm* [ligne] dotted line; **en ~** [ligne] dotted. || [perforations] perforations (*pl*).

pointilleux, -euse [pwɛ̃tijø, øz] *adj*: **~ (sur)** particular (about).

pointu, -e [pwɛ̃ty] *adj* [objet] pointed. || [étude, formation] specialized.

pointure [pwɛ̃tyr] *nf* size.

point-virgule [pwɛ̃virgyl] *nm* semicolon.

poire [pwar] *nf* [fruit] pear. || *fam* [visage] face. || *fam* [naïf] dope.

poireau, -x [pwaro] *nm* leek.

poirier [pwarje] *nm* pear tree.

pois [pwa] *nm* BOT pea; **~ chiche** chickpea; **petits ~** garden peas, petits pois; **~ de senteur** sweet pea. || *fig* [motif] dot, spot; **à ~** spotted, polka-dot.

poison [pwazɔ̃] 1 *nm* [substance] poison. 2 *nmf fam fig* [personne] drag, pain.

poisse [pwas] *nf fam* bad luck; **porter la ~** to be bad luck.

poisseux, -euse [pwasø, øz] *adj* sticky.

poisson [pwasɔ̃] *nm* fish; **~ d'avril** [farce] April fool; [en papier] *paper fish pinned to someone's back as a prank on April Fools' Day*; **~ rouge** goldfish. ○ **Poissons** *nmpl* ASTROL Pisces (*sg*).

poissonnerie [pwasɔnri] *nf* [boutique] fish shop, fishmonger's (shop).

poissonnier, -ière [pwasɔnje, jɛr] *nm, f* fishmonger.

poitrine [pwatrin] *nf* [thorax] chest; [de femme] chest, bust.

poivre [pwavr] *nm* pepper; **~ blanc** white pepper; **~ gris, ~ noir** black pepper.

poivrier [pwavrije] *nm*, **poivrière** [pwavrijɛr] *nf* pepper pot.

pondéré

poivron [pwavrɔ̃] *nm* pepper, capsicum; ~ **rouge/vert** red/green pepper.

poker [pɔkɛr] *nm* poker.

polaire [pɔlɛr] *adj* polar.

polar [pɔlar] *nm fam* thriller, whodunnit.

Polaroïd® [pɔlarɔid] *nm* Polaroid®.

pôle [pol] *nm* pole; ~ **Nord/Sud** North/South Pole.

polémique [pɔlemik] *nf* controversy.

poli, -e [pɔli] *adj* [personne] polite. || [surface] polished.

police [pɔlis] *nf* [force de l'ordre] police; ~ **secours** emergency service provided by the police. || [contrat] policy; ~ **d'assurance** insurance policy.

polichinelle [pɔliʃinɛl] *nm* [personnage] Punch; **secret de** ~ *fig* open secret.

policier, -ière [pɔlisje, jɛr] *adj* [de la police] police (*avant n*). || [film, roman] detective (*avant n*). ○ **policier** *nm* police officer.

poliomyélite [pɔljɔmjelit] *nf* poliomyelitis.

polir [pɔlir] *vt* to polish.

polisson, -onne [pɔlisɔ̃, ɔn] **1** *adj* [chanson, propos] lewd, suggestive. || [enfant] naughty. **2** *nm, f* [enfant] naughty child.

politesse [pɔlitɛs] *nf* [courtoisie] politeness. || [action] polite action.

politicien, -ienne [pɔlitisjɛ̃, jɛn] **1** *adj* *péj* politicking, politically unscrupulous. **2** *nm, f* politician, politico.

politique [pɔlitik] **1** *nf* [de gouvernement, de personne] policy. || [affaires publiques] politics (*U*). **2** *adj* [pouvoir, théorie] political.

politiser [pɔlitize] *vt* to politicize.

pollen [pɔlɛn] *nm* pollen.

polluer [pɔlɥe] *vt* to pollute.

pollution [pɔlysjɔ̃] *nf* pollution.

polo [pɔlo] *nm* [sport] polo. || [chemise] polo shirt.

Pologne [pɔlɔɲ] *nf*: **la** ~ Poland.

polonais, -e [pɔlɔnɛ, ɛz] *adj* Polish. ○ **polonais** *nm* [langue] Polish. ○ **Polonais, -e** *nm, f* Pole.

poltron, -onne [pɔltrɔ̃, ɔn] **1** *nm, f* coward. **2** *adj* cowardly.

polychrome [pɔlikrom] *adj* polychrome, polychromatic.

polyclinique [pɔliklinik] *nf* general hospital.

polycopié, -e [pɔlikɔpje] *adj* duplicate (*avant n*). ○ **polycopié** *nm* duplicated lecture notes.

polyester [pɔliɛstɛr] *nm* polyester.

polygame [pɔligam] *adj* polygamous.

polyglotte [pɔliglɔt] *nmf & adj* polyglot.

polygone [pɔligɔn] *nm* MATHS polygon.

Polynésie [pɔlinezi] *nf*: **la** ~ Polynesia.

polystyrène [pɔlistirɛn] *nm* polystyrene.

polytechnicien, -ienne [pɔlitɛknisjɛ̃, jɛn] *nm, f* student or ex-student of the École Polytechnique.

Polytechnique [pɔlitɛknik] *n*: **l'École** ~ *prestigious engineering college*.

polyvalent, -e [pɔlivalɑ̃, ɑ̃t] *adj* [salle] multi-purpose. || [personne] versatile.

pommade [pɔmad] *nf* [médicament] ointment.

pomme [pɔm] *nf* [fruit] apple; ~ **de pin** pine ou fir cone. || [pomme de terre]: ~**s frites** chips *Br*, (French) fries *Am*; ~**s vapeur** steamed potatoes. ○ **pomme d'Adam** *nf* Adam's apple.

pomme de terre [pɔmdətɛr] *nf* potato.

pommette [pɔmɛt] *nf* cheekbone.

pommier [pɔmje] *nm* apple tree.

pompe [pɔ̃p] *nf* [appareil] pump; ~ **à essence** petrol pump *Br*, gas pump *Am*. || [magnificence] pomp, ceremony. || *fam* [chaussure] shoe. ○ **pompes funèbres** *nfpl* undertaker's (*sg*), mortician's (*sg*) *Am*.

pomper [pɔ̃pe] *vt* [eau, air] to pump.

pompeux, -euse [pɔ̃pø, øz] *adj* pompous.

pompier [pɔ̃pje] *nm* fire fighter *Am*.

pompiste [pɔ̃pist] *nmf* petrol *Br* ou gas *Am* pump attendant.

pompon [pɔ̃pɔ̃] *nm* pompom.

pomponner [pɔ̃pɔne] ○ **se pomponner** *vp* to get dressed up.

ponce [pɔ̃s] *adj*: **pierre** ~ pumice (stone).

poncer [pɔ̃se] *vt* [bois] to sand (down).

ponceuse [pɔ̃søz] *nf* sander, sanding machine.

ponction [pɔ̃ksjɔ̃] *nf* [MÉD - lombaire] puncture; [- pulmonaire] tapping.

ponctualité [pɔ̃ktɥalite] *nf* punctuality.

ponctuation [pɔ̃ktɥasjɔ̃] *nf* punctuation.

ponctuel, -elle [pɔ̃ktɥɛl] *adj* [action] specific, selective. || [personne] punctual.

ponctuer [pɔ̃ktɥe] *vt* to punctuate.

pondéré, -e [pɔ̃dere] *adj* [personne] level-headed. || ÉCON weighted.

pondre [pɔ̃dr] *vt* [œufs] to lay. || *fam fig* [projet, texte] to produce.

pondu, -e [pɔ̃dy] *pp* → pondre.

poney [pɔnɛ] *nm* pony.

pont [pɔ̃] *nm* CONSTR bridge; ~s et chaussées ADMIN ≃ highways department. || [lien] link, connection; ~ aérien airlift. || [congé] *day off granted by an employer to fill the gap between a national holiday and a weekend.* || [de navire] deck.

ponte [pɔ̃t] **1** *nf* [action] laying; [œufs] clutch. **2** *nm fam* [autorité] big shot.

pont-levis [pɔ̃ləvi] *nm* drawbridge.

ponton [pɔ̃tɔ̃] *nm* [plate-forme] pontoon.

pop [pɔp] **1** *nm* pop. **2** *adj* pop (*avant n*).

pop-corn [pɔpkɔrn] *nm inv* popcorn (*U*).

populace [pɔpylas] *nf péj* mob.

populaire [pɔpylɛr] *adj* [du peuple - volonté] popular, of the people; [- quartier] working-class; [- art, chanson] folk. || [personne] popular.

populariser [pɔpylarize] *vt* to popularize.

popularité [pɔpylarite] *nf* popularity.

population [pɔpylasjɔ̃] *nf* population; ~ active working population.

porc [pɔr] *nm* [animal] pig, hog *Am.* || *fig & péj* [personne] pig, swine. || [viande] pork. || [peau] pigskin.

porcelaine [pɔrsəlɛn] *nf* [matière] china, porcelain. || [objet] piece of china or porcelain.

porc-épic [pɔrkepik] *nm* porcupine.

porche [pɔrʃ] *nm* porch.

porcherie [pɔrʃəri] *nf litt & fig* pigsty.

porcin, -e [pɔrsɛ̃, in] *adj* [élevage] pig (*avant n*). || *fig & péj* [yeux] piggy.

pore [pɔr] *nm* pore.

poreux, -euse [pɔrø, øz] *adj* porous.

pornographie [pɔrnɔgrafi] *nf* pornography.

port [pɔr] *nm* [lieu] port; ~ de commerce/pêche commercial/fishing port. || [fait de porter sur soi - d'objet] carrying; [- de vêtement, décoration] wearing; ~ d'armes carrying of weapons. || [transport] carriage.

portable [pɔrtabl] **1** *nm* [TV] portable; INFORM laptop, portable. **2** *adj* [vêtement] wearable. || [ordinateur, machine à écrire] portable, laptop.

portail [pɔrtaj] *nm* portal.

portant, -e [pɔrtɑ̃, ɑ̃t] *adj*: être bien/mal ~ to be in good/poor health.

portatif, -ive [pɔrtatif, iv] *adj* portable.

porte [pɔrt] *nf* [de maison, voiture] door; mettre qqn à la ~ to throw sb out; ~ d'entrée front door. || [AÉRON, SKI & de ville] gate.

porte-à-faux [pɔrtafo] *nm inv* [roche] overhang; CONSTR cantilever; en ~ overhanging; CONSTR cantilevered; *fig* in a delicate situation.

porte-à-porte [pɔrtapɔrt] *nm inv*: faire du ~ to sell from door to door.

porte-avions [pɔrtavjɔ̃] *nm inv* aircraft carrier.

porte-bagages [pɔrtbagaʒ] *nm inv* luggage rack; [de voiture] roof rack.

porte-bonheur [pɔrtbɔnœr] *nm inv* lucky charm.

porte-clefs, porte-clés [pɔrtəkle] *nm inv* keyring.

porte-documents [pɔrtdɔkymɑ̃] *nm inv* attaché or document case.

portée [pɔrte] *nf* [de missile] range; à ~ de main within reach; à ~ de voix within earshot; à ~ de vue in sight; à la ~ de qqn *fig* within sb's reach. || [d'événement] impact, significance. || MUS stave, staff. || [de femelle] litter.

porte-fenêtre [pɔrtfənɛtr] *nf* French window or door *Am*.

portefeuille [pɔrtəfœj] *nm* [pour billets] wallet. || FIN & POLIT portfolio.

porte-jarretelles [pɔrtʒartɛl] *nm inv* suspender belt *Br*, garter belt *Am*.

portemanteau, -x [pɔrtmɑ̃to] *nm* [au mur] coat-rack; [sur pied] coat stand.

porte-monnaie [pɔrtmɔnɛ] *nm inv* purse.

porte-parole [pɔrtparɔl] *nm inv* spokesman (*f* spokeswoman).

porter [pɔrte] **1** *vt* [gén] to carry. || [vêtement, lunettes, montre] to wear; [barbe] to have. || [nom, date, inscription] to bear. **2** *vi* [remarque] to strike home. || [voix, tir] to carry. ○ **se porter 1** *vp* [se sentir]: se ~ bien/mal to be well/unwell. **2** *v attr*: se ~ garant de qqch to guarantee sthg, to vouch for sthg; se ~ candidat à to stand for election to *Br*, to run for *Am*.

porte-savon [pɔrtsavɔ̃] (*pl inv* OU **porte-savons**) *nm* soap dish.

porte-serviettes [pɔrtsɛrvjɛt] *nm inv* towel rail.

porteur, -euse [pɔrtœr, øz] **1** *nm, f* [de message, nouvelle] bringer, bearer. || [de bagages] porter. || [détenteur - de papiers, d'actions] holder; [- de chèque] bearer. || [de maladie] carrier.

portier [pɔrtje] *nm* commissionaire.

portière [pɔrtjɛr] *nf* [de voiture, train] door.

portillon [pɔrtijɔ̃] *nm* barrier, gate.

portion [pɔrsjɔ̃] *nf* [de gâteau] portion, helping.

portique [pɔrtik] *nm* ARCHIT portico. || SPORT crossbeam (*for hanging apparatus*).

porto [pɔrto] *nm* port.

Porto Rico [pɔrtoriko], **Puerto Rico** [pwɛrtoriko] *n* Puerto Rico.

portrait [pɔrtrɛ] *nm* portrait; PHOT photograph; **faire le ~ de qqn** *fig* to describe sb.

portraitiste [pɔrtrɛtist] *nmf* portrait painter.

portrait-robot [pɔrtrɛrɔbo] *nm* Photofit® picture, Identikit® picture.

portuaire [pɔrtɥɛr] *adj* port (*avant n*), harbour (*avant n*).

portugais, -e [pɔrtygɛ, ɛz] *adj* Portuguese. ○ **portugais** *nm* [langue] Portuguese. ○ **Portugais, -e** *nm, f* Portuguese (person); **les Portugais** the Portuguese.

Portugal [pɔrtygal] *nm*: **le ~** Portugal.

pose [poz] *nf* [de pierre, moquette] laying; [de papier peint, rideaux] hanging; [position] pose. || PHOT exposure.

posé, -e [poze] *adj* sober, steady.

poser [poze] 1 *vt* [mettre] to put down; **~ qqch sur qqch** to put sthg on sthg. || [installer - rideaux, papier peint] to hang; [- étagère] to put up; [- moquette, carrelage] to lay. || [donner à résoudre - problème, difficulté] to pose; **~ une question** to ask a question; **~ sa candidature** to apply; POLIT to stand for election. 2 *vi* to pose. ○ **se poser** *vp* [oiseau, avion] to land. || [question, problème] to arise, to come up.

positif, -ive [pozitif, iv] *adj* positive.

position [pozisjɔ̃] *nf* position; **prendre ~** *fig* to take up a position, to take a stand.

posologie [pozɔlɔʒi] *nf* dosage.

posséder [pɔsede] *vt* [détenir - voiture, maison] to possess, to own; [- diplôme] to have; [- capacités, connaissances] to possess, to have. || [langue, art] to have mastered. || *fam* [personne] to have.

possesseur [pɔsesœr] *nm* [de bien] pos-

sessor, owner. || [de secret, diplôme] holder.

possessif, -ive [pɔsesif, iv] *adj* possessive. ○ **possessif** *nm* GRAM possessive.

possession [pɔsesjɔ̃] *nf* [gén] possession; **être en ma/ta** *etc* **~** to be in my/your *etc* possession.

possibilité [pɔsibilite] *nf* [gén] possibility. || [moyen] chance, opportunity.

possible [pɔsibl] 1 *adj* possible; **dès que** OU **aussitôt que ~** as soon as possible. 2 *nm*: **faire tout son ~** to do one's utmost, to do everything possible; **dans la mesure du ~** as far as possible.

postal, -e, -aux [pɔstal, o] *adj* postal.

poste [pɔst] 1 *nf* [service] post *Br*, mail *Am*. || [bureau] post office; **~ restante** poste restante *Br*, general delivery *Am*. 2 *nm* [emplacement] post; **~ de police** police station. || [emploi] position, post. || [appareil]: **~ de radio** radio; **~ de télévision** television (set). || TÉLÉCOM extension.

poster¹ [pɔster] *nm* poster.

poster² [pɔste] *vt* [lettre] to post *Br*, to mail *Am*. || [sentinelle] to post. ○ **se poster** *vp* to position o.s., to station o.s.

postérieur, -e [pɔsterjœr] *adj* [date] later, subsequent. || [membre] hind (*avant n*), back (*avant n*). ○ **postérieur** *nm hum* posterior.

posteriori [pɔsterjɔri] ○ **a posteriori** *loc adv* a posteriori.

postérité [pɔsterite] *nf* [générations à venir] posterity.

posthume [pɔstym] *adj* posthumous.

postiche [pɔstiʃ] *adj* false.

postier, -ière [pɔstje, jɛr] *nm, f* post-office worker.

postillonner [pɔstijɔne] *vi* to splutter.

post-scriptum [pɔstskriptɔm] *nm inv* postscript.

postulant, -e [pɔstylɑ̃, ɑ̃t] *nm, f* [pour emploi] applicant.

postuler [pɔstyle] *vt* [emploi] to apply for. || PHILO to postulate.

posture [pɔstyr] *nf* posture; **être** OU **se trouver en mauvaise ~** *fig* to be in a difficult position.

pot [po] *nm* [récipient] pot, jar; [à eau, à lait] jug; **~ de chambre** chamber pot; **~ de fleurs** flowerpot. || AUTOM: **~ catalytique** catalytic convertor; **~ d'échappement** exhaust (pipe). || *fam* [boisson] drink.

potable [pɔtabl] *adj* [liquide] drinkable; **eau ~** drinking water. || *fam* [travail] acceptable.

potage [pɔtaʒ] *nm* soup.

potager, -ère [pɔtaʒe, ɛr] *adj*: **jardin ~** vegetable garden; **plante potagère** vegetable. ○ **potager** *nm* kitchen ou vegetable garden.

potassium [pɔtasjɔm] *nm* potassium.

pot-au-feu [pɔtofø] *nm inv* [plat] boiled beef with vegetables.

pot-de-vin [podvɛ̃] (*pl* **pots-de-vin**) *nm* bribe.

pote [pɔt] *nm fam* mate *Br*, buddy *Am*.

poteau, -x [pɔto] *nm* post; **~ de but** goalpost; **~ indicateur** signpost; **~ télégraphique** telegraph pole.

potelé, -e [pɔtle] *adj* plump, chubby.

potence [pɔtɑ̃s] *nf* CONSTR bracket. || [de pendaison] gallows (*sg*).

potentiel, -ielle [pɔtɑ̃sjɛl] *adj* potential. ○ **potentiel** *nm* potential.

poterie [pɔtri] *nf* [art] pottery. || [objet] piece of pottery.

potiche [pɔtiʃ] *nf* [vase] vase.

potier, -ière [pɔtje, jɛr] *nm, f* potter.

potin [pɔtɛ̃] *nm fam* [bruit] din. ○ **potins** *nmpl fam* [ragots] gossip (*U*).

potion [posjɔ̃] *nf* potion.

potiron [pɔtirɔ̃] *nm* pumpkin.

pot-pourri [popuri] *nm* potpourri.

pou, -x [pu] *nm* louse.

poubelle [pubɛl] *nf* trashcan *Am*.

pouce [pus] *nm* [de main] thumb; [de pied] big toe. || [mesure] inch.

poudre [pudr] *nf* powder.

poudreux, -euse [pudrø, øz] *adj* powdery. ○ **poudreuse** *nf* powder (snow).

poudrier [pudrije] *nm* [boîte] powder compact.

poudrière [pudrijɛr] *nf* powder magazine; *fig* powder keg.

pouf [puf] 1 *nm* pouffe. 2 *interj* thud!

pouffer [pufe] *vi*: **~ (de rire)** to snigger.

pouilleux, -euse [pujø, øz] *adj* [personne, animal] flea-ridden. || [endroit] squalid.

poulailler [pulaje] *nm* [de ferme] henhouse. || *fam* THÉÂTRE gods (*sg*).

poulain [pulɛ̃] *nm* foal; *fig* protégé.

poule [pul] *nf* ZOOL hen. || *fam péj* [femme] broad *Am*. || SPORT [compétition] round robin; RUGBY [groupe] pool.

poulet [pulɛ] *nm* ZOOL chicken. || *fam* [policier] cop.

pouliche [puliʃ] *nf* filly.

poulie [puli] *nf* pulley.

poulpe [pulp] *nm* octopus.

pouls [pu] *nm* pulse.

poumon [pumɔ̃] *nm* lung.

poupe [pup] *nf* stern.

poupée [pupe] *nf* [jouet] doll.

poupon [pupɔ̃] *nm* [jouet] baby doll.

pouponnière [pupɔnjɛr] *nf* nursery.

pour [pur] 1 *prép* [gén] for. || (+ *infinitif*): **~ faire** in order to do, (so as) to do; **~ m'avoir aidé** for having helped me, for helping me. || [indique un rapport] for; **avancé ~ son âge** advanced for his/her age; **~ moi** for my part, as far as I'm concerned; **~ ce qui est de** as regards, with regard to. 2 *adv*: **je suis ~** I'm (all) for it. 3 *nm*: **le ~ et le contre** the pros and cons (*pl*). ○ **pour que** *loc conj* (+ *subjonctif*) so that, in order that.

pourboire [purbwar] *nm* tip.

pourcentage [pursɑ̃taʒ] *nm* percentage.

pourparlers [purparle] *nmpl* talks.

pourpre [purpr] *nm & adj* crimson.

pourquoi [purkwa] 1 *adv* why; **~ pas?** why not?; **c'est ~ ...** that's why .... 2 *nm inv*: **le ~ (de)** the reason (for).

pourri, -e [puri] *adj* [fruit] rotten. || [personne, milieu] corrupt. || [enfant] spoiled rotten, ruined.

pourrir [purir] 1 *vt* [matière, aliment] to rot, to spoil. || [enfant] to ruin, to spoil rotten. 2 *vi* [matière] to rot; [fruit, aliment] to go rotten ou bad.

pourriture [purityr] *nf* [d'aliment] rot. || *fig* [de personne, de milieu] corruption.

poursuite [pursɥit] *nf* [de personne] chase. || [d'argent, de vérité] pursuit. || [de négociations] continuation. ○ **poursuites** *nfpl* JUR (legal) proceedings.

poursuivi, -e [pursɥivi] *pp* → **poursuivre**.

poursuivre [pursɥivr] 1 *vt* [voleur] to pursue, to chase; [gibier] to hunt. || [enquête, travail] to carry on with, to continue. || JUR [criminel] to prosecute; [voisin] to sue. 2 *vi* to go on, to carry on.

pourtant [purtɑ̃] *adv* nevertheless, even so.

pourtour [purtur] *nm* perimeter.

pourvoir [purvwar] 1 *vt*: **~ qqn de** to provide sb with; **~ qqch de** to equip ou fit sthg with. 2 *vi*: **~ à** to provide for.

pourvu, -e [purvy] *pp* → **pourvoir**. ○ **pourvu que** *loc conj* (+*subjonctif*) [condition] providing, provided (that). || [souhait] let's hope (that).

pousse [pus] *nf* [croissance] growth. || [bourgeon] shoot.

poussé, -e [puse] *adj* [travail] meticulous. || [moteur] souped-up.

pousse-café [puskafe] *nm inv fam* liqueur.

poussée [puse] *nf* [pression] pressure. || [coup] push. || [de fièvre, inflation] rise.

pousse-pousse [puspus] *nm inv* [voiture] rickshaw. || *Helv* [poussette] pushchair.

pousser [puse] 1 *vt* [personne, objet] to push. || [moteur, voiture] to drive hard. || [cri, soupir] to give. || [inciter]: ~ **qqn à faire qqch** to urge sb to do sthg. || [au crime, au suicide]: ~ **qqn à** to drive sb to. 2 *vi* [exercer une pression] to push. || [croître] to grow. || *fam* [exagérer] to overdo it. ○ **se pousser** *vp* to move up.

poussette [puset] *nf* pushchair.

poussière [pusjɛr] *nf* [gén] dust.

poussiéreux, -euse [pusjɛrø, øz] *adj* [meuble] dusty.

poussif, -ive [pusif, iv] *adj fam* wheezy.

poussin [pusɛ̃] *nm* ZOOL chick. || SPORT under-11.

poutre [putr] *nf* beam.

poutrelle [putrɛl] *nf* girder.

pouvoir [puvwar] 1 *nm* [gén] power; ~ **d'achat** purchasing power; **les ~s publics** the authorities. 2 *vt* [avoir la possibilité de, parvenir à]: ~ **faire qqch** to be able to do sthg; **je ne peux pas venir ce soir** I can't come tonight; **je n'en peux plus** [exaspéré] I'm at the end of my tether; [fatigué] I'm exhausted; **je/tu n'y peux rien** there's nothing I/you can do about it. || [avoir la permission de]: **je peux prendre la voiture?** can I borrow the car?; **aucun élève ne peut partir** no pupil may leave. || [indiquant l'éventualité]: **vous pourriez rater votre train** you could miss your train. ○ **se pouvoir** *v impers*: **il se peut que je me trompe** I may be mistaken; **cela se peut/pourrait bien** that's quite possible.

pragmatique [pragmatik] *adj* pragmatic.

Prague [prag] *n* Prague.

prairie [preri] *nf* meadow; [aux États-Unis] prairie.

praline [pralin] *nf* [amande] sugared almond. || *Belg* [chocolat] chocolate.

praticable [pratikabl] *adj* [route] passable. || [plan] feasible, practicable.

praticien, -ienne [pratisjɛ̃, jɛn] *nm, f* practitioner; MÉD medical practitioner.

pratiquant, -e [pratikɑ̃, ɑ̃t] *adj* practising.

pratique [pratik] 1 *nf* [expérience] practical experience. || [usage] practice; **mettre qqch en ~** to put sthg into practice. 2 *adj* practical; [gadget, outil] handy.

pratiquement [pratikmɑ̃] *adv* [en fait] in practice. || [quasiment] practically.

pratiquer [pratike] 1 *vt* [métier] to practice *Am*; [méthode] to apply. || [ouverture] to make. 2 *vi* RELIG to be a practising Christian/Jew/Muslim *etc*.

pré [pre] *nm* meadow.

préalable [prealabl] 1 *adj* prior, previous. 2 *nm* precondition. ○ **au préalable** *loc adv* first, beforehand.

préambule [preɑ̃byl] *nm* [introduction, propos] preamble; **sans ~** immediately.

préau, -x [preo] *nm* [d'école] (covered) play area.

préavis [preavi] *nm inv* advance notice ou warning.

précaire [prekɛr] *adj* [incertain] precarious.

précaution [prekosjɔ̃] *nf* [prévoyance] precaution; **prendre des ~** to take precautions. || [prudence] caution.

précédent, -e [presedɑ̃, ɑ̃t] *adj* previous. ○ **précédent** *nm* precedent; **sans ~** unprecedented.

précéder [presede] *vt* [dans le temps - gén] to precede; [- suj: personne] to arrive before. || [marcher devant] to go in front of. || *fig* [devancer] to get ahead of.

précepte [presɛpt] *nm* precept.

précepteur, -trice [preseptœr, tris] *nm, f* (private) tutor.

prêcher [preʃe] *vt & vi* to preach.

précieux, -ieuse [presjø, jøz] *adj* [pierre, métal] precious; [objet] valuable; [collaborateur] invaluable, valued. || *péj* [style] precious, affected.

précipice [presipis] *nm* precipice.

précipitation [presipitasjɔ̃] *nf* [hâte] haste. ○ **précipitations** *nfpl* MÉTÉOR precipitation (*U*).

précipiter [presipite] *vt* [objet, personne] to throw, to hurl; ~ **qqn/qqch du haut de** to throw sb/sthg off, to hurl sb/sthg off. || [départ] to hasten. ○ **se précipiter** *vp* [se jeter] to throw o.s., to hurl o.s. || [s'élancer]: **se ~ (vers qqn)** to rush ou hurry (towards sb). || [s'accélérer - gén] to speed up; [- choses, événements] to move faster.

précis, -e [presi, iz] *adj* [exact] precise,

accurate. || [fixé] definite, precise. ○ **précis** *nm* handbook.

précisément [presizemã] *adv* precisely, exactly.

préciser [presize] *vt* [heure, lieu] to specify. || [pensée] to clarify. ○ **se préciser** *vp* to become clear.

précision [presizjɔ̃] *nf* [de style, d'explication] precision. || [détail] detail.

précoce [prekɔs] *adj* [plante, fruit] early. || [enfant] precocious.

préconçu, -e [prekɔ̃sy] *adj* preconceived.

préconiser [prekɔnize] *vt* to recommend.

précurseur [prekyrsœr] 1 *nm* precursor, forerunner. 2 *adj* precursory.

prédécesseur [predesesœr] *nm* predecessor.

prédestiner [predɛstine] *vt* to predestine.

prédicateur, -trice [predikatœr, tris] *nm, f* preacher.

prédiction [prediksjɔ̃] *nf* prediction.

prédilection [predilɛksjɔ̃] *nf* partiality, liking.

prédire [predir] *vt* to predict.

prédit, -e [predi, it] *pp* → prédire.

prédominer [predɔmine] *vt* to predominate.

préfabriqué, -e [prefabrike] *adj* [maison] prefabricated. ○ **préfabriqué** *nm* prefabricated material.

préface [prefas] *nf* preface.

préfecture [prefɛktyr] *nf* prefecture.

préférable [preferabl] *adj* preferable.

préféré, -e [prefere] *adj & nm, f* favourite.

préférence [preferãs] *nf* preference; **de ~** preferably.

préférentiel, -ielle [preferãsjɛl] *adj* preferential.

préférer [prefere] *vt*: ~ qqn/qqch (à) to prefer sb/sthg (to); **je préfère rentrer** I would rather go home, I would prefer to go home.

préfet [prefɛ] *nm* prefect.

préfixe [prefiks] *nm* prefix.

préhistoire [preistwar] *nf* prehistory.

préjudice [preʒydis] *nm* harm (*U*), detriment (*U*); **porter ~ à qqn** to harm sb.

préjugé [preʒyʒe] *nm*: ~ (**contre**) prejudice (against).

prélasser [prelase] ○ **se prélasser** *vp* to lounge.

prélavage [prelavaʒ] *nm* pre-wash.

prélèvement [prelɛvmã] *nm* MÉD removal; [de sang] sample. || FIN deduction; ~ **automatique** direct debit; ~ **mensuel** monthly standing order; ~s **obligatoires** tax and social security contributions.

prélever [prelɔve] *vt* FIN: ~ **de l'argent** (**sur**) to deduct money (from). || MÉD to remove; ~ **du sang** to take a blood sample.

préliminaire [preliminɛr] *adj* preliminary. ○ **préliminaires** *nmpl* [de paix] preliminary talks. || [de discours] preliminaries.

prématuré, -e [prematyre] 1 *adj* premature. 2 *nm, f* premature baby.

préméditation [premeditasjɔ̃] *nf* premeditation; **avec ~** [meurtre] premeditated; [agir] with premeditation.

premier, -ière [prəmje, jɛr] 1 *adj* [gén] first; [étage] first *Br*, second *Am*. || [qualité] top. || [état] original. 2 *nm, f* first. ○ **première** *nf* CIN première; THÉÂTRE première, first night. || [exploit] first. || [première classe] first class. || SCOL ≃ eleventh grade *Am*. || AUTOM first (gear). ○ **premier de l'an** *nm*: **le ~ de l'an** New Year's Day. ○ **en premier** *loc adv* first, firstly.

premièrement [prəmjɛrmã] *adv* first, firstly.

prémonition [premɔnisjɔ̃] *nf* premonition.

prémunir [premynir] *vt*: ~ qqn (**contre**) to protect sb (against). ○ **se prémunir** *vp* to protect o.s.; **se ~ contre qqch** to guard against sthg.

prénatal, -e [prenatal] (*pl* **prénatals** OU **prénataux** [prenato]) *adj* antenatal.

prendre [prãdr] 1 *vt* [gén] to take. || [enlever] to take (away); ~ **qqch à qqn** to take sthg from sb. || [aller chercher - objet] to get, to fetch; [- personne] to pick up. || [repas, boisson] to have; **vous prendrez quelque chose?** would you like something to eat/drink? || [voleur] to catch; **se faire ~** to get caught. || [responsabilité] to take (on). || [aborder - personne] to handle; [- problème] to tackle. || [poids] to gain, to put on. 2 *vi* [ciment, sauce] to set. || [plante, greffe] to take; [mode] to catch on. || [feu] to catch. || [se diriger]: ~ **à droite** to turn right. ○ **se prendre** *vp* [se considérer]: **pour qui se prend-il?** who does he think he is? || *loc*: **s'en ~ à qqn** [physiquement] to set about sb; [verbalement] to take it out on sb; **je**

sais comment m'y ~ I know how to do it ou do it ou go about it.

prénom [prenɔ̃] *nm* first name.

prénommer [prenɔme] *vt* to name, to call. ○ **se prénommer** *vp* to be called.

prénuptial, -e, -iaux [prenypsjal, jo] *adj* premarital.

préoccupation [preɔkypasjɔ̃] *nf* preoccupation.

préoccuper [preɔkype] *vt* to preoccupy. ○ **se préoccuper** *vp*: **se ~ de qqch** to be worried about sthg.

préparatifs [preparatif] *nmpl* preparations.

préparation [preparasjɔ̃] *nf* preparation.

préparer [prepare] *vt* [gén] to prepare; [plat, repas] to cook, to prepare; **~ qqn à qqch** to prepare sb for sthg. || [réserver]: **~ qqch à qqn** to have sthg in store for sb. || [congrès] to organize. ○ **se préparer** *vp* [personne]: **se ~ à qqch/à faire qqch** to prepare for sthg/to do sthg.

prépondérant, -e [prepɔ̃derɑ̃, ɑ̃t] *adj* dominating.

préposé, -e [prepoze] *nm, f* (minor) official; [de vestiaire] attendant; [facteur] mailman (*f* mailwoman) *Am*; **~ à qqch** person in charge of sthg.

préposition [prepozisjɔ̃] *nf* preposition.

préretraite [preratret] *nf* early retirement.

prérogative [prerɔgativ] *nf* prerogative.

près [pre] *adv* near, close. ○ **de près** *loc adv* closely. ○ **près de** *loc prép* [dans l'espace] near, close to. || [dans le temps] close to. || [presque] nearly, almost. ○ **à peu près** *loc adv* more or less, just about. ○ **à ceci près que, à cela près que** *loc conj* except that, apart from the fact that. ○ **à ... près** *loc adv*: **à dix centimètres ~** to within ten centimetres; **il n'en est pas à un ou deux jours ~** a day or two more or less won't make any difference.

présage [prezaʒ] *nm* omen.

présager [prezaʒe] *vt* [annoncer] to portend. || [prévoir] to predict.

presbytère [presbiter] *nm* presbytery.

presbytie [presbisi] *nf* longsightedness *Br*, farsightedness *Am*.

prescription [preskripsjɔ̃] *nf* MÉD prescription. || JUR limitation.

prescrire [preskrir] *vt* [mesures, condi-

tions] to lay down, to stipulate. || MÉD to prescribe.

prescrit, e [preskri, it] *pp* → **prescrire**.

préséance [preseɑ̃s] *nf* precedence.

présence [prezɑ̃s] *nf* [gén] presence; **en ~** face to face; **en ~ de** in the presence of. || [compagnie] company (*U*). || [assiduité] attendance. ○ **présence d'esprit** *nf* presence of mind.

présent, -e [prezɑ̃, ɑ̃t] *adj* [gén] present; **le ~ ouvrage** this work; **avoir qqch à l'esprit** to remember sthg. ○ **présent** *nm* [gén] present; **à ~** at present; **à ~ que** now that; **jusqu'à ~** up to now, so far. || GRAM: **le ~** the present tense.

présentable [prezɑ̃tabl] *adj* [d'aspect] presentable.

présentateur, -trice [prezɑ̃tatœr, tris] *nm, f* presenter.

présentation [prezɑ̃tasjɔ̃] *nf* [de personne]: **faire les ~s** to make the introductions. || [aspect extérieur] appearance. || [de papiers, de produit, de film] presentation. || [de magazine] layout.

présenter [prezɑ̃te] *vt* [gén] to present; [projet] to present, to submit. || [invité] to introduce. || [condoléances, félicitations, avantages] to offer; [hommages] to pay; **~ qqch à qqn** to offer sb sthg. ○ **se présenter** *vp* [se faire connaître]: **se ~ (à)** to introduce o.s. (to). || [être candidat]: **se ~ à** [élection] to stand in *Br*, to run in *Am*; [examen] to sit *Br*, to take. || [occasion, situation] to arise, to present itself. || [affaire, contrat]: **se ~ bien/mal** to look good/bad.

présentoir [prezɑ̃twar] *nm* display stand.

préservatif [prezervatif] *nm* condom.

préserver [prezerve] *vt* to preserve. ○ **se préserver** *vp*: **se ~ de** to protect o.s. from.

présidence [prezidɑ̃s] *nf* [de groupe] chairmanship. || [d'État] presidency.

président, -e [prezidɑ̃, ɑ̃t] *nm, f* [d'assemblée] chairman (*f* chairwoman). || [d'État] president; **~ de la République** President (of the Republic) of France. || JUR [de tribunal] presiding judge; [de jury] foreman (*f* forewoman).

présider [prezide] *vt* [réunion] to chair. || [banquet, dîner] to preside over.

présomption [prezɔ̃psjɔ̃] *nf* [hypothèse] presumption. || JUR presumption.

présomptueux, -euse [prezɔ̃ptɥø, øz] *adj* presumptuous.

presque [presk] *adv* almost, nearly; ~ **rien** next to nothing, scarcely anything; ~ **jamais** hardly ever.

presqu'île [preskil] *nf* peninsula.

pressant, -e [presɑ̃, ɑ̃t] *adj* pressing.

presse [pres] *nf* press.

pressé, -e [prese] *adj* [travail] urgent. || [personne]: **être ~** to be in a hurry. || [citron, orange] freshly squeezed.

pressentiment [presɑ̃timɑ̃] *nm* premonition.

pressentir [presɑ̃tir] *vt* [événement] to have a premonition of.

presse-papiers [prespapje] *nm inv* paperweight.

presser [prese] *vt* [écraser - olives] to press; [- citron, orange] to squeeze. || [bouton] to press, to push. || [accélérer] to speed up; ~ **le pas** to speed up, to walk faster. ○ **se presser** *vp* [se dépêcher] to hurry (up). || [s'agglutiner]: **se ~ (autour de)** to crowd (around). || [se serrer] to huddle.

pressing [presiŋ] *nm* [établissement] dry cleaner's.

pression [presjɔ̃] *nf* [gén] pressure; **exercer une ~ sur qqch** to exert pressure on sthg; **sous ~** [liquide & *fig*] under pressure. || [sur vêtement] snap fastener *Am*. || [bière] draught beer.

pressoir [preswar] *nm* [machine] press.

prestance [prestɑ̃s] *nf* bearing; **avoir de la ~** to have presence.

prestataire [prestatɛr] *nmf* [bénéficiaire] person in receipt of benefit, claimant. || [fournisseur] provider; ~ **de service** service provider.

prestation [prestasjɔ̃] *nf* [allocation] benefit; ~ **en nature** payment in kind. || [de comédien] performance.

preste [prest] *adj littéraire* nimble.

prestidigitateur, -trice [prestidiʒitatœr, tris] *nm, f* conjurer.

prestige [prestiʒ] *nm* prestige.

prestigieux, -ieuse [prestiʒjø, jøz] *adj* [réputé] prestigious.

présumer [prezyme] **1** *vt* to presume, to assume; **être présumé coupable/innocent** to be presumed guilty/innocent. **2** *vi*: ~ **de qqch** to overestimate sthg.

prêt, -e [prɛ, prɛt] *adj* ready; ~ **à qqch/à faire qqch** ready for sthg/to do sthg; ~**s? partez!** SPORT get set, go! ○ **prêt** *nm* [action] lending (*U*); [somme] loan.

prêt-à-porter [prɛtaporte] *nm* ready-to-wear clothing (*U*).

prétendant [pretɑ̃dɑ̃] *nm* [au trône] pretender. || [amoureux] suitor.

prétendre [pretɑ̃dr] *vt* [affecter]: ~ **faire qqch** to claim to do sthg. || [affirmer]: ~ **que** to claim (that), to maintain (that).

prétendu, -e [pretɑ̃dy] **1** *pp* → prétendre. **2** *adj* (*avant n*) so-called.

prête-nom [prɛtnɔ̃] (*pl* **prête-noms**) *nm* front man.

prétentieux, -ieuse [pretɑ̃sjø, jøz] *adj* pretentious.

prétention [pretɑ̃sjɔ̃] *nf* [suffisance] pretentiousness. || [ambition] pretension, ambition; **avoir la ~ de faire qqch** to claim ou pretend to do sthg.

prêter [prete] *vt* [fournir]: ~ **qqch (à qqn)** [objet, argent] to lend (sb) sthg; *fig* [concours, appui] to lend (sb) sthg, to give (sb) sthg. || [attribuer]: ~ **qqch à qqn** to attribute sthg to sb. ○ **se prêter** *vp*: **se ~ à** [convenir à] to fit, to suit.

prétérit [preterit] *nm* preterite.

prêteur, -euse [pretœr, øz] *nm, f*: ~ **sur gages** pawnbroker.

prétexte [pretɛkst] *nm* pretext, excuse; **sous ~ de faire qqch/que** on the pretext of doing sthg/that, under the pretext of doing sthg/that; **sous aucun ~** on no account.

prétexter [pretɛkste] *vt* to give as an excuse.

prêtre [prɛtr] *nm* priest.

preuve [prœv] *nf* [gén] proof. || JUR evidence. || [témoignage] sign, token; **faire ~ de qqch** to show sthg; **faire ses ~s** to prove o.s./itself.

prévaloir [prevalwar] *vi* [dominer]: ~ **(sur)** to prevail (over). ○ **se prévaloir** *vp*: **se ~ de** to boast about.

prévalu [prevaly] *pp inv* → prévaloir.

prévenance [prevnɑ̃s] *nf* [attitude] thoughtfulness, consideration.

prévenant, -e [prevnɑ̃, ɑ̃t] *adj* considerate, attentive.

prévenir [prevnir] *vt* [employé, élève]: ~ **qqn (de)** to warn sb (about). || [police] to inform. || [désirs] to anticipate. || [maladie] to prevent.

préventif, -ive [prevɑ̃tif, iv] *adj* [mesure, médecine] preventive.

prévention [prevɑ̃sjɔ̃] *nf* [protection]: ~ **(contre)** prevention (of); ~ **routière** road safety (measures). || JUR remand.

prévenu, -e [prevny] **1** *pp* → **prévenir**. **2** *nm, f* accused, defendant.

prévision [previzjɔ̃] *nf* forecast (*U*), prediction; [de coûts] estimate; ÉCON forecast; **les ~s météorologiques** the weather forecast. ○ **en prévision de** *loc prép* in anticipation of.

prévoir [prevwar] *vt* [s'attendre à] to expect. ‖ [prédire] to predict. ‖ [anticiper] to foresee, to anticipate. ‖ [programmer] to plan; **comme prévu** as planned, according to plan.

prévoyant, -e [prevwajɑ̃, ɑ̃t] *adj* provident.

prévu, e [prevy] *pp* → **prévoir**.

prier [prije] **1** *vt* RELIG to pray to. ‖ [implorer] to beg; **(ne pas) se faire ~ (pour faire qqch)** (not) to need to be persuaded (to do sthg); **je vous en prie** [de grâce] please, I beg you; [de rien] don't mention it, not at all. ‖ *sout* [demander]: **~ qqn de faire qqch** to request sb to do sthg. **2** *vi* RELIG to pray.

prière [prijɛr] *nf* [RELIG - recueillement] prayer (*U*), praying (*U*); [- formule] prayer. ‖ *littéraire* [demande] entreaty; **~ de frapper avant d'entrer** please knock before entering.

primaire [primɛr] *adj* [premier]: **études ~s** primary education (*U*). ‖ *péj* [primitif] limited.

prime [prim] *nf* [d'employé] bonus. ‖ [allocation - de déménagement, de transport] allowance; [- à l'exportation] incentive. ‖ [d'assurance] premium.

primer [prime] **1** *vi* to take precedence, to come first. **2** *vt* [être supérieur à] to take precedence over. ‖ [récompenser] to award a prize to.

primeur [primœr] *nf* immediacy; **avoir la ~ de qqch** to be the first to hear sthg. ○ **primeurs** *nfpl* early produce (*U*).

primevère [primver] *nf* primrose.

primitif, -ive [primitif, iv] *adj* [gén] primitive. ‖ [aspect] original.

primordial, -e, -iaux [primɔrdjal, jo] *adj* essential.

prince [prɛ̃s] *nm* prince.

princesse [prɛ̃sɛs] *nf* princess.

princier, -ière [prɛ̃sje, jɛr] *adj* princely.

principal, -e, -aux [prɛ̃sipal, o] **1** *adj* [gén] main, principal. **2** *nm, f* [important]: **le ~** the main thing. ‖ SCOL principal *Am*.

principalement [prɛ̃sipalmɑ̃] *adv* mainly, principally.

principauté [prɛ̃sipote] *nf* principality.

principe [prɛ̃sip] *nm* principle; **par ~** on principle. ○ **en principe** *loc adv* theoretically, in principle.

printanier, -ière [prɛ̃tanje, jɛr] *adj* [temps] spring-like.

printemps [prɛ̃tɑ̃] *nm* [saison] spring.

priori [priɔri] ○ **a priori 1** *loc adv* in principle. **2** *nm inv* initial reaction.

prioritaire [prijɔritɛr] *adj* [industrie, mesure] priority (*avant n*). ‖ AUTOM with right of way.

priorité [prijɔrite] *nf* [importance primordiale] priority; **en ~** first. ‖ AUTOM right of way; **~ à droite** give way to the right.

pris, -e [pri, priz] **1** *pp* → **prendre**. **2** *adj* [place] taken; [personne] busy; [mains] full. ‖ [nez] blocked; [gorge] sore. ○ **prise** *nf* [sur barre, sur branche] grip, hold; **lâcher ~e** to let go; *fig* to give up. ‖ [action de prendre - de ville] seizure, capture; **~e de sang** blood test; **~e de vue** shot. ‖ [à la pêche] haul. ‖ ÉLECTR: **~e (de courant)** [mâle] plug; [femelle] socket. ‖ [de judo] hold.

prisme [prism] *nm* prism.

prison [prizɔ̃] *nf* [établissement] prison. ‖ [réclusion] imprisonment.

prisonnier, -ière [prizɔnje, jɛr] **1** *nm, f* prisoner; **faire qqn ~** to take sb prisoner, to capture sb. **2** *adj* imprisoned; *fig* trapped.

privation [privasjɔ̃] *nf* deprivation. ○ **privations** *nfpl* privations, hardships.

privatisation [privatizasjɔ̃] *nf* privatization.

privatiser [privatize] *vt* to privatize.

privé, -e [prive] *adj* private. ○ **privé** *nm* ÉCON private sector. ‖ [détective] private eye. ‖ [intimité]: **en ~** in private; **dans le ~** in private life.

priver [prive] *vt*: **~ qqn (de)** to deprive sb (of).

privilège [privilɛʒ] *nm* privilege.

privilégié, -e [privileʒje] **1** *adj* [personne] privileged. ‖ [climat, site] favoured. **2** *nm, f* privileged person.

prix [pri] *nm* [coût] price; **~ d'achat** purchase price; **à ~ fixe** set-price (*avant n*); **hors de ~** too expensive; **à tout ~** at all costs; **~ de revient** cost price; **y mettre le ~** to pay a lot. ‖ [importance] value. ‖ [récompense] prize.

probabilité [prɔbabilite] *nf* [chance] probability. ‖ [vraisemblance] probability, likelihood; **selon toute ~** in all probability.

probable [prɔbabl] *adj* probable, likely.

probant, -e [prɔbã, ãt] *adj* convincing, conclusive.

probité [prɔbite] *nf* integrity.

problème [prɔblɛm] *nm* problem; **(il n'y a) pas de ~!** *fam* no problem!

procédé [prɔsede] *nm* [méthode] process. || [conduite] behaviour (*U*).

procéder [prɔsede] *vi* [agir] to proceed. || [exécuter]: **~ à qqch** to set about sthg.

procédure [prɔsedyr] *nf* procedure; [démarche] proceedings (*pl*).

procès [prɔsɛ] *nm* JUR trial; **intenter un ~ à qqn** to sue sb.

processeur [prɔsesœr] *nm* processor.

procession [prɔsesjõ] *nf* procession.

processus [prɔsesys] *nm* process.

procès-verbal [prɔsɛverbal] *nm* [contravention - gén] ticket; [- pour stationnement interdit] parking ticket. || [compte-rendu] minutes.

prochain, -e [prɔʃɛ̃, ɛn] *adj* [suivant] next; **à la ~e!** *fam* see you! || [imminent] impending. ○ **prochain** *nm littéraire* [semblable] fellow man.

prochainement [prɔʃɛnmã] *adv* soon, shortly.

proche [prɔʃ] *adj* [dans l'espace] near; **~ de** near, close to; [semblable à] very similar to, closely related to. || [dans le temps] imminent, near; **dans un ~ avenir** in the immediate future. || [ami, parent] close. ○ **proches** *nmpl*: **les ~s** the close family (*sg*).

Proche-Orient [prɔʃɔrjã] *nm*: **le ~** the Near East.

proclamation [prɔklamasjõ] *nf* proclamation.

proclamer [prɔklame] *vt* to proclaim, to declare.

procréer [prɔkree] *vt littéraire* to procreate.

procuration [prɔkyrasjõ] *nf* proxy; **par ~** by proxy.

procurer [prɔkyre] *vt*: **~ qqch à qqn** [suj: personne] to obtain sthg for sb; [suj: chose] to give or bring sb sthg. ○ **se procurer** *vp*: **se ~ qqch** to obtain sthg.

procureur [prɔkyrœr] *nm*: **Procureur de la République** ≃ Attorney General.

prodige [prɔdiʒ] *nm* [miracle] miracle. || [tour de force] marvel, wonder. || [génie] prodigy.

prodigieux, -ieuse [prɔdiʒjø, jøz] *adj* fantastic, incredible.

prodigue [prɔdig] *adj* [dépensier] extravagant.

prodiguer [prɔdige] *vt littéraire* [soins, amitié]: **~ qqch (à)** to lavish sthg (on).

producteur, -trice [prɔdyktœr, tris] **1** *nm, f* [gén] producer. || AGRIC producer, grower. **2** *adj*: **~ de pétrole** oil-producing (*avant n*).

productif, -ive [prɔdyktif, iv] *adj* productive.

production [prɔdyksjõ] *nf* [gén] production; **la ~ littéraire d'un pays** the literature of a country.

productivité [prɔdyktivite] *nf* productivity.

produire [prɔdɥir] *vt* [gén] to produce. || [provoquer] to cause. ○ **se produire** *vp* [arriver] to occur, to take place. || [acteur, chanteur] to appear.

produit, -e [prɔdɥi, ɥit] *pp* → **produire**. ○ **produit** *nm* [gén] product; **~ de beauté** cosmetic, beauty product; **~s d'entretien** cleaning products.

proéminent, -e [prɔeminã, ãt] *adj* prominent.

profane [prɔfan] *adj* [laïc] secular. || [ignorant] ignorant.

profaner [prɔfane] *vt* [église] to desecrate. || *fig* [mémoire] to defile.

proférer [prɔfere] *vt* to utter.

professeur [prɔfesœr] *nm* [enseignant] teacher. || [titre] professor.

profession [prɔfesjõ] *nf* [métier] occupation; **sans ~** unemployed; **~ libérale** profession. || [corps de métier - libéral] profession; [- manuel] trade.

professionnel, -elle [prɔfesjɔnɛl] **1** *adj* [gén] professional. || [école] technical. **2** *nm, f* professional.

professorat [prɔfesɔra] *nm* teaching.

profil [prɔfil] *nm* [de personne, d'emploi] profile; [de bâtiment] outline; **de ~** [visage, corps] in profile.

profiler [prɔfile] *vt* to shape. ○ **se profiler** *vp* [bâtiment, arbre] to stand out. || [solution] to emerge.

profit [prɔfi] *nm* [avantage] benefit; **au ~ de** in aid of; **tirer ~ de** to profit from, to benefit from. || [gain] profit.

profitable [prɔfitabl] *adj* profitable; **être ~ à qqn** to benefit sb, to be beneficial to sb.

profiter [prɔfite] *vi* [tirer avantage]: **~ de** [vacances] to benefit from; [personne] to take advantage of; **~ de qqch pour**

faire qqch to take advantage of sthg to do sthg; **en ~** to make the most of it.

profond, -e [pʀɔfɔ̃, ɔ̃d] *adj* [gén] deep. || [pensée] deep, profound.

profondément [pʀɔfɔ̃demã] *adv* [enfoui] deep. || [intensément - aimer, intéresser] deeply; [- dormir] soundly; **être ~ endormi** to be fast asleep. || [extrêmement - convaincu, ému] deeply, profoundly; [- différent] profoundly.

profondeur [pʀɔfɔ̃dœʀ] *nf* depth; **en ~** in depth.

profusion [pʀɔfyzjɔ̃] *nf*: **à ~** in abundance, in profusion.

progéniture [pʀɔʒenityʀ] *nf* offspring.

programmable [pʀɔgʀamabl] *adj* programmable.

programmateur, -trice [pʀɔgʀamatœʀ, tʀis] *nm, f* programme planner. ○ **programmateur** *nm* automatic control unit.

programmation [pʀɔgʀamasjɔ̃] *nf* INFORM programming. || RADIO & TÉLÉ programme planning.

programme [pʀɔgʀam] *nm* [gén] program *Am*. || INFORM program. || [planning] schedule. || SCOL syllabus.

programmer [pʀɔgʀame] *vt* [organiser] to plan. || RADIO & TÉLÉ to schedule. || INFORM to program.

programmeur, -euse [pʀɔgʀamœʀ, øz] *nm, f* INFORM (computer) programmer.

progrès [pʀɔgʀɛ] *nm* progress (*U*); **faire des ~** to make progress.

progresser [pʀɔgʀese] *vi* [avancer] to progress, to advance. || [maladie] to spread. || [élève] to make progress.

progressif, -ive [pʀɔgʀesif, iv] *adj* progressive; [difficulté] increasing.

progression [pʀɔgʀesjɔ̃] *nf* [avancée] advance. || [de maladie, du nationalisme] spread.

prohiber [pʀɔibe] *vt* to ban, to prohibit.

proie [pʀwa] *nf* prey; **être la ~ de qqch** *fig* to be the victim of sthg; **être en ~ à** [sentiment] to be prey to.

projecteur [pʀɔʒɛktœʀ] *nm* [de lumière] floodlight; THÉÂTRE spotlight. || [d'images] projector.

projectile [pʀɔʒɛktil] *nm* missile.

projection [pʀɔʒɛksjɔ̃] *nf* [gén] projection. || [jet] throwing.

projectionniste [pʀɔʒɛksjɔnist] *nmf* projectionist.

projet [pʀɔʒɛ] *nm* [perspective] plan. || [étude, ébauche] draft; **~ de loi** bill.

projeter [pʀɔʒte] *vt* [envisager] to plan; **~ de faire qqch** to plan to do sthg. || [missile, pierre] to throw. || [film, diapositives] to show.

prolétaire [pʀɔleteʀ] *nmf* & *adj* proletarian.

prolétariat [pʀɔletaʀja] *nm* proletariat.

proliférer [pʀɔlifeʀe] *vi* to proliferate.

prolifique [pʀɔlifik] *adj* prolific.

prologue [pʀɔlɔg] *nm* prologue.

prolongation [pʀɔlɔ̃gasjɔ̃] *nf* [extension] extension, prolongation. ○ **prolongations** *nfpl* SPORT extra time (*U*).

prolongement [pʀɔlɔ̃ʒmã] *nm* [de mur, quai] extension; **être dans le ~ de** to be a continuation of.

prolonger [pʀɔlɔ̃ʒe] *vt* [dans le temps]: **~ qqch (de)** to prolong sthg (by). || [dans l'espace]: **~ qqch (de)** to extend sthg (by).

promenade [pʀɔmnad] *nf* [balade] walk, stroll; *fig* trip, excursion; **~ en voiture** drive; **~ à vélo** (bike) ride; **faire une ~** to go for a walk. || [lieu] promenade.

promener [pʀɔmne] *vt* [personne] to take out (for a walk); [en voiture] to take for a drive. || *fig* [regard, doigts]: **~ qqch sur** to run sthg over. ○ **se promener** *vp* to go for a walk.

promesse [pʀɔmɛs] *nf* [serment] promise; **tenir sa ~** to keep one's promise. || *fig* [espérance]: **être plein de ~s** to be very promising.

prometteur, -euse [pʀɔmɛtœʀ, øz] *adj* promising.

promettre [pʀɔmɛtʀ] **1** *vt* to promise; **~ qqch à qqn** to promise sb sthg; **~ de faire qqch** to promise to do sthg; **~ à qqn que** to promise sb that. **2** *vi* to be promising; **ça promet!** *iron* that bodes well!

promis, -e [pʀɔmi, iz] **1** *pp* → promettre. **2** *adj* promised. **3** *nm, f hum* intended.

promiscuité [pʀɔmiskyite] *nf* overcrowding.

promontoire [pʀɔmɔ̃twaʀ] *nm* promontory.

promoteur, -trice [pʀɔmɔtœʀ, tʀis] *nm, f* [novateur] instigator. || [constructeur] property developer.

promotion [pʀɔmɔsjɔ̃] *nf* [gén] promotion; **en ~** [produit] on special offer. || MIL & SCOL year.

promouvoir [pʀɔmuvwaʀ] *vt* to promote.

prompt, -e [pʀɔ̃, pʀɔ̃t] *adj sout*: **~ (à faire qqch)** swift (to do sthg).

promu, -e [pʀɔmy] *pp* → promouvoir.

promulguer [prɔmylge] *vt* to promulgate.

prôner [prone] *vt sout* to advocate.

pronom [prɔnɔ̃] *nm* pronoun.

pronominal, -e, -aux [prɔnɔminal, o] *adj* pronominal.

prononcé, -e [prɔnɔ̃se] *adj* marked.

prononcer [prɔnɔ̃se] *vt* JUR & LING to pronounce. || [dire] to utter. ○ **se prononcer** *vp* [se dire] to be pronounced. || [trancher - assemblée] to decide, to reach a decision; [- magistrat] to deliver a verdict; **se ~ sur** to give one's opinion of.

prononciation [prɔnɔ̃sjasjɔ̃] *nf* LING pronunciation. || JUR pronouncement.

pronostic [prɔnɔstik] *nm* (*gén pl*) [prévision] forecast. || MÉD prognosis.

propagande [prɔpagɑ̃d] *nf* [endoctrinement] propaganda.

propager [prɔpaʒe] *vt* to spread. ○ **se propager** *vp* to spread; BIOL to be propagated; PHYS to propagate.

propane [prɔpan] *nm* propane.

prophète [prɔfɛt], **prophétesse** [prɔfetɛs] *nm, f* prophet (*f* prophetess).

prophétie [prɔfesi] *nf* prophecy.

propice [prɔpis] *adj* favourable.

proportion [prɔpɔrsjɔ̃] *nf* proportion; **toutes ~s gardées** relatively speaking.

proportionné, -e [prɔpɔrsjɔne] *adj* : **bien/mal ~** well-/badly-proportioned.

proportionnel, -elle [prɔpɔrsjɔnɛl] *adj* : **~ (à)** proportional (to). ○ **proportionnelle** *nf* : **la ~le** proportional representation.

propos [prɔpo] **1** *nm* [discours] talk. || [but] intention; **c'est à quel ~?** what is it about?; **hors de ~** at the wrong time. **2** *nmpl* [paroles] talk (*U*), words. ○ **à propos** *loc adv* [opportunément] at (just) the right time. || [au fait] by the way. ○ **à propos de** *loc prép* about.

proposer [prɔpoze] *vt* [offrir] to offer, to propose; **~ qqch à qqn** to offer sb sthg, to offer sthg to sb; || [suggérer] to suggest, to propose; **~ de faire qqch** to suggest ou propose doing sthg.

proposition [prɔpozisjɔ̃] *nf* [offre] offer, proposal. || [suggestion] suggestion, proposal. || GRAM clause.

propre [prɔpr] **1** *adj* [nettoyé] clean. || [soigné] neat, tidy. || [personnel] own. || [particulier] : **~ à** peculiar to. **2** *nm* [propreté] cleanness, cleanliness; **recopier qqch au ~** to make a fair copy of sthg, to copy sthg up.

proprement [prɔprəmɑ̃] *adv* [convenablement - habillé] neatly, tidily; [- se tenir] correctly. || [véritablement] completely; **à ~ parler** strictly ou properly speaking; **l'événement ~ dit** the event itself, the actual event.

propreté [prɔprəte] *nf* cleanness, cleanliness.

propriétaire [prɔprijetɛr] *nmf* [possesseur] owner; **~ terrien** landowner. || [dans l'immobilier] landlord.

propriété [prɔprijete] *nf* [gén] property; **~ privée** private property. || [droit] ownership. || [terres] property (*U*).

propulser [prɔpylse] *vt litt & fig* to propel; *fig* to fling. ○ **se propulser** *vp* to move forward, to propel o.s. forward ou along; *fig* to shoot.

prorata [prɔrata] ○ **au prorata de** *loc prép* in proportion to.

prosaïque [prozaik] *adj* prosaic, mundane.

proscrit, -e [prɔskri, it] *adj* [interdit] banned, prohibited.

prose [proz] *nf* prose; **en ~** in prose.

prospecter [prɔspɛkte] *vt* [pays, région] to prospect. || COMM to canvass.

prospection [prɔspɛksjɔ̃] *nf* [de ressources] prospecting. || COMM canvassing.

prospectus [prɔspɛktys] *nm* (advertising) leaflet.

prospérer [prɔspere] *vi* to prosper, to thrive; [plante, insecte] to thrive.

prospérité [prɔsperite] *nf* [richesse] prosperity. || [bien-être] well-being.

prostate [prɔstat] *nf* prostate (gland).

prosterner [prɔstɛrne] ○ **se prosterner** *vp* to bow down.

prostituée [prɔstitɥe] *nf* prostitute.

prostituer [prɔstitɥe] ○ **se prostituer** *vp* to prostitute o.s.

prostitution [prɔstitysjɔ̃] *nf* prostitution.

prostré, -e [prɔstre] *adj* prostrate.

protagoniste [prɔtagɔnist] *nmf* protagonist, hero (*f* heroine).

protecteur, -trice [prɔtɛktœr, tris] **1** *adj* protective. **2** *nm, f* [défenseur] protector. || [des arts] patron.

protection [prɔtɛksjɔ̃] *nf* [défense] protection; **prendre qqn sous sa ~** to take sb under one's wing. || [des arts] patronage.

protectionnisme [prɔtɛksjɔnism] *nm* protectionism.

protégé, -e [prɔteʒe] **1** *adj* protected. **2** *nm, f* protégé.

protège-cahier [prɔtɛʒkaje] (*pl* protège-cahiers*) *nm* exercise book cover.

protéger [prɔteʒe] *vt* [gén] to protect.

protéine [prɔtein] *nf* protein.

protestant, -e [prɔtɛstɑ̃, ɑ̃t] *adj & nm, f* Protestant.

protestation [prɔtɛstasjɔ̃] *nf* [contestation] protest.

protester [prɔtɛste] *vi* to protest; ~ contre qqch to protest against sthg, to protest sthg *Am*.

prothèse [prɔtɛz] *nf* prosthesis; ~ dentaire dentures (*pl*), false teeth (*pl*).

protide [prɔtid] *nm* protein.

protocolaire [prɔtɔkɔlɛr] *adj* [question] of protocol.

protocole [prɔtɔkɔl] *nm* protocol.

proton [prɔtɔ̃] *nm* proton.

prototype [prɔtɔtip] *nm* prototype.

protubérance [prɔtyberɑ̃s] *nf* bulge, protuberance.

proue [pru] *nf* bows (*pl*), prow.

prouesse [prues] *nf* feat.

prouver [pruve] *vt* [établir] to prove. || [montrer] to demonstrate, to show.

provenance [prɔvnɑ̃s] *nf* origin; **en ~ de** from.

provenir [prɔvnir] *vi*: ~ **de** to come from; *fig* to be due to, to be caused by.

proverbe [prɔvɛrb] *nm* proverb.

proverbial, -e, -iaux [prɔvɛrbjal, jo] *adj* proverbial.

providence [prɔvidɑ̃s] *nf* providence.

providentiel, -ielle [prɔvidɑ̃sjɛl] *adj* providential.

province [prɔvɛ̃s] *nf* [gén] province. || [campagne] provinces (*pl*).

provincial, -e, -iaux [prɔvɛ̃sjal, jo] *adj & nm, f* provincial.

proviseur [prɔvizœr] *nm* ≃ principal *Am*.

provision [prɔvizjɔ̃] *nf* [réserve] stock, supply. || FIN retainer; → **chèque**. ○ **provisions** *nfpl* provisions.

provisoire [prɔvizwar] **1** *adj* temporary; JUR provisional. **2** *nm*: **ce n'est que du ~** it's only a temporary arrangement.

provocant, -e [prɔvɔkɑ̃, ɑ̃t] *adj* provocative.

provocation [prɔvɔkasjɔ̃] *nf* provocation.

provoquer [prɔvɔke] *vt* [entraîner] to cause. || [personne] to provoke.

proxénète [prɔksenɛt] *nm* pimp.

proximité [prɔksimite] *nf* [de lieu] proximity, nearness; **à ~ de** near.

prude [pryd] *adj* prudish.

prudence [prydɑ̃s] *nf* care, caution.

prudent, -e [prydɑ̃, ɑ̃t] *adj* careful, cautious.

prune [pryn] *nf* plum.

pruneau, -x [pryno] *nm* [fruit] prune.

prunelle [prynɛl] *nf* ANAT pupil.

prunier [prynje] *nm* plum tree.

PS¹ (*abr de* **Parti socialiste**) *nm French socialist party.*

PS², P-S (*abr de* **post-scriptum**) *nm* PS.

psaume [psom] *nm* psalm.

pseudonyme [psødɔnim] *nm* pseudonym.

psy [psi] *fam nmf* (*abr de* **psychiatre**) psychiatrist, shrink *fam*.

psychanalyse [psikanaliz] *nf* psychoanalysis.

psychanalyste [psikanalist] *nmf* psychoanalyst, analyst.

psychédélique [psikedelik] *adj* psychedelic.

psychiatre [psikjatr] *nmf* psychiatrist.

psychiatrie [psikjatri] *nf* psychiatry.

psychique [psiʃik] *adj* psychic; [maladie] psychosomatic.

psychologie [psikɔlɔʒi] *nf* psychology.

psychologique [psikɔlɔʒik] *adj* psychological.

psychologue [psikɔlɔg] **1** *nmf* psychologist. **2** *adj* psychological.

psychose [psikoz] *nf* MÉD psychosis. || [crainte] obsessive fear.

psychosomatique [psikɔsɔmatik] *adj* psychosomatic.

psychothérapie [psikɔterapi] *nf* psychotherapy.

PTT (*abr de* **Postes, télécommunications et télédiffusion**) *nfpl former French post office and telecommunications network.*

pu [py] *pp* → **pouvoir**.

puant, -e [pyɑ̃, ɑ̃t] *adj* [fétide] smelly, stinking. || *fam fig* [personne] bumptious, full of oneself.

puanteur [pyɑ̃tœr] *nf* stink, stench.

pub¹ [pyb] *nf fam* ad, advert *Br*; [métier] advertising.

pub² [pœb] *nm* pub.

pubère [pybɛr] *adj* pubescent.

puberté [pybɛrte] *nf* puberty.

pubis [pybis] *nm* [zone] pubis.

public, -ique [pyblik] *adj* public. ○ **public** *nm* [auditoire] audience; **en ~** in public. || [population] public.

publication [pyblikasjɔ̃] *nf* publication.

publicitaire [pyblisiter] *adj* [campagne] advertising (*avant n*); [vente, film] promotional.

publicité [pyblisite] *nf* [domaine] advertising; ~ **comparative** comparative advertising; ~ **mensongère** misleading advertising, deceptive advertising. || [réclame] advertisement, advert. || [autour d'une affaire] publicity (*U*).

publier [pyblije] *vt* [livre] to publish; [communiqué] to issue, to release.

puce [pys] *nf* [insecte] flea. || INFORM (silicon) chip.

pudeur [pydœr] *nf* [physique] modesty, decency. || [morale] restraint.

pudibond, -e [pydibɔ̃, ɔ̃d] *adj* prudish, prim and proper.

pudique [pydik] *adj* [physiquement] modest, decent. || [moralement] restrained.

puer [pɥe] **1** *vi* to stink; **ça pue ici!** it stinks in here! **2** *vt* to reek of, to stink of.

puéricultrice [pɥerikyltris] *nf* nursery nurse.

puériculture [pɥerikyltyr] *nf* childcare.

puéril, -e [pɥeril] *adj* childish.

Puerto Rico = **Porto Rico**.

pugilat [pyʒila] *nm* fight.

puis [pɥi] *adv* then; **et ~** [d'ailleurs] and moreover ou besides.

puiser [pɥize] *vt* [liquide] to draw; ~ **qqch dans qqch** *fig* to draw ou take sthg from sthg.

puisque [pɥiskə] *conj* [gén] since.

puissance [pɥisɑ̃s] *nf* power. ○ **en puissance** *loc adj* potential.

puissant, -e [pɥisɑ̃, ɑ̃t] *adj* powerful.

puisse, puisses *etc* → **pouvoir**.

puits [pɥi] *nm* [d'eau] well. || [de gisement] shaft; ~ **de pétrole** oil well.

pull [pyl], **pull-over** [pylɔvɛr] (*pl* **pull-overs**) *nm* jumper *Br*, sweater.

pulluler [pylyle] *vi* to swarm.

pulmonaire [pylmɔnɛr] *adj* lung (*avant n*), pulmonary.

pulpe [pylp] *nf* pulp.

pulsation [pylsasjɔ̃] *nf* beat, beating (*U*).

pulsion [pylsjɔ̃] *nf* impulse.

pulvériser [pylverize] *vt* [projeter] to spray. || [détruire] to pulverize; *fig* to smash.

puma [pyma] *nm* puma.

punaise [pynɛz] *nf* [insecte] bug. || [clou] drawing pin *Br*, thumbtack *Am*.

punch [pɔ̃ʃ] *nm* punch.

puni, -e [pyni] *adj* punished.

punir [pynir] *vt*: ~ **qqn (de)** to punish sb (with).

punition [pynisjɔ̃] *nf* punishment.

pupille [pypij] **1** *nf* ANAT pupil. **2** *nmf* [orphelin] ward; ~ **de l'État** ≃ child in care.

pupitre [pypitr] *nm* [d'orateur] lectern; MUS stand. || TECHNOL console. || [d'écolier] desk.

pur, -e [pyr] *adj* [gén] pure. || *fig* [absolu] pure, sheer; ~ **et simple** pure and simple. || *fig & littéraire* [intention] honourable. || [lignes] pure, clean.

purée [pyre] *nf* purée; ~ **de pommes de terre** mashed potatoes.

purement [pyrmɑ̃] *adv* purely; ~ **et simplement** purely and simply.

pureté [pyrte] *nf* [gén] purity. || [de sculpture, de diamant] perfection. || [d'intention] honourableness.

purgatoire [pyrgatwar] *nm* purgatory.

purge [pyrʒ] *nf* MÉD & POLIT purge.

purger [pyrʒe] *vt* MÉD & POLIT to purge. || [radiateur] to bleed. || [peine] to serve.

purifier [pyrifje] *vt* to purify.

purin [pyrɛ̃] *nm* slurry.

puritain, -e [pyritɛ̃, ɛn] **1** *adj* [pudibond] puritanical. **2** *nm, f* [prude] puritan. || RELIG Puritan.

puritanisme [pyritanism] *nm* puritanism; RELIG Puritanism.

pur-sang [pyrsɑ̃] *nm inv* thoroughbred.

purulent, -e [pyrylɑ̃, ɑ̃t] *adj* purulent.

pus [py] *nm* pus.

putréfier [pytrefje] ○ **se putréfier** *vp* to putrefy, to rot.

putsch [putʃ] *nm* uprising, coup.

puzzle [pœzl] *nm* jigsaw (puzzle).

P-V *nm abr de* **procès-verbal**.

pyjama [piʒama] *nm* pyjamas (*pl*).

pylône [pilon] *nm* pylon.

pyramide [piramid] *nf* pyramid.

Pyrénées [pirene] *nfpl*: **les ~** the Pyrenees.

Pyrex® [pirɛks] *nm* Pyrex®.

pyromane [piroman] *nmf* arsonist; MÉD pyromaniac.

python [pitɔ̃] *nm* python.

q, Q [ky] *nm inv* [lettre] q, Q.

QCM (*abr de* **questionnaire à choix multiple**) *nm* multiple choice questionnaire.

QG (*abr de* **quartier général**) *nm* HQ.

QI (*abr de* **quotient intellectuel**) *nm* IQ.

qqch (*abr de* **quelque chose**) sthg.

qqn (*abr de* **quelqu'un**) s.o., sb.

quadragénaire [kwadraʒenɛr] *nmf* forty year old.

quadrilatère [kwadrilatɛr] *nm* quadrilateral.

quadrillage [kadrijaʒ] *nm* [de papier, de tissu] criss-cross pattern. ‖ [policier] combing.

quadriller [kadrije] *vt* [papier] to mark with squares. ‖ [ville - suj: rues] to criss-cross; [- suj: police] to comb.

quadrimoteur [kwadrimɔtœr] *nm* four-engined plane.

quadrupède [k(w)adrypɛd] *nm & adj* quadruped.

quadruplés, -ées [k(w)adryple] *nm, f pl* quadruplets, quads.

quai [kɛ] *nm* [de gare] platform. ‖ [de port] quay, wharf. ‖ [de rivière] embankment.

qualificatif, -ive [kalifikatif, iv] *adj* qualifying. ○ **qualificatif** *nm* term.

qualification [kalifikasjɔ̃] *nf* [gén] qualification.

qualifier [kalifje] *vt* [gén] to qualify; **être qualifié pour qqch/pour faire qqch** to be qualified for sthg/to do sthg. ‖ [caractériser]: **~ qqn/qqch de qqch** to describe sb/sthg as sthg, to call sb/sthg sthg. ○ **se qualifier** *vp* to qualify.

qualitatif, -ive [kalitatif, iv] *adj* qualitative.

qualité [kalite] *nf* [gén] quality; **de bonne/mauvaise ~** of good/poor quality. ‖ [condition] position, capacity.

quand [kɑ̃] **1** *conj* [lorsque, alors que] when; **~ tu le verras, demande-lui de me téléphoner** when you see him, ask him

to phone me. **2** *adv interr* when; **~ arriveras-tu?** when will you arrive?; **jusqu'à ~ restez-vous?** how long are you staying for? ○ **quand même 1** *loc adv* all the same. **2** *interj*: **~ même, à son âge!** really, at his/her age! ○ **quand bien même** *loc conj sout* even though, even if.

quant [kɑ̃] ○ **quant à** *loc prép* as for.

quantifier [kɑ̃tifje] *vt* to quantify.

quantitatif, -ive [kɑ̃titatif, iv] *adj* quantitative.

quantité [kɑ̃tite] *nf* [mesure] quantity, amount. ‖ [abondance]: **(une) ~ de** a great many, a lot of; **en ~** in large numbers.

quarantaine [karɑ̃tɛn] *nf* [nombre]: **une ~ de** about forty. ‖ [âge]: **avoir la ~** to be in one's forties. ‖ [isolement] quarantine.

quarante [karɑ̃t] *adj num & nm* forty; *voir aussi* **six**.

quarantième [karɑ̃tjɛm] *adj num, nm & nmf* fortieth; *voir aussi* **sixième**.

quart [kar] *nm* [fraction] quarter; **deux heures moins le ~** (a) quarter to two, (a) quarter of two *Am*; **deux heures et ~** (a) quarter past two, (a) quarter after two *Am*; **il est moins le ~** it's (a) quarter to; **un ~ d'heure** a quarter of an hour. ‖ NA-VIG watch. ‖ **~ de finale** quarter final.

quartier [kartje] *nm* [de ville] area, district. ‖ [de fruit] piece; [de viande] quarter. ‖ [héraldique, de lune] quarter. ‖ (*gén pl*) MIL quarters (*pl*); **~ général** headquarters (*pl*).

quartz [kwarts] *nm* quartz; **montre à ~** quartz watch.

quasi [kazi] *adv* almost, nearly.

quasi- [kazi] *préfixe* near.

quasiment [kazimɑ̃] *adv fam* almost, nearly.

quatorze [katɔrz] *adj num & nm* fourteen; *voir aussi* **six**.

quatorzième [katɔrzjɛm] *adj num, nm & nmf* fourteenth; *voir aussi* **sixième**.

quatrain [katrɛ̃] *nm* quatrain.

quatre [katr] **1** *adj num* four; **monter l'escalier ~ à ~** to take the stairs four at a time; **se mettre en ~ pour qqn** to bend over backwards for sb. **2** *nm* four; *voir aussi* **six**.

quatre-vingt = **quatre-vingts**.

quatre-vingt-dix [katrəvɛ̃dis] *adj num & nm* ninety; *voir aussi* **six**.

quatre-vingt-dixième [katrəvědizjɛm] *adj num, nm & nmf* ninetieth; *voir aussi* **sixième**.

quatre-vingtième [katrəvɛ̃tjɛm] *adj num, nm & nmf* eightieth; *voir aussi* **sixième**.

quatre-vingts, quatre-vingt [katrəvɛ̃] *adj num & nm* eighty; *voir aussi* **six**.

quatrième [katrijɛm] **1** *adj num, nm & nmf* fourth; *voir aussi* **sixième**. **2** *nf* SCOL ≃ ninth grade *Am*.

quatuor [kwatɥɔr] *nm* quartet.

que [k(ə)] **1** *conj* [introduit une subordonnée] that; **il a dit qu'il viendrait** he said (that) he'd come. ‖ [introduit une hypothèse] whether; **~ vous le vouliez ou non** whether you like it or not. ‖ [reprend une autre conjonction] **s'il fait beau et ~ nous avons le temps ...** if the weather is good and we have time .... ‖ [indique un ordre, un souhait] **qu'il entre!** let him come in! ‖ [après un présentatif] **voilà/voici ~ ça recommence!** here we go again! ‖ [comparatif - après moins, plus] than; [- après autant, aussi, même] as; **plus jeune ~ moi** younger than I (am). ‖ [seulement] **ne ... ~** only; **je n'ai qu'une sœur** I've only got one sister. **2** *pron rel* [chose, animal] which, that; [personne] whom, that; **le livre qu'il m'a prêté** the book (which ou that) he lent me. **3** *pron interr* what; **~ savez-vous au juste?** what exactly do you know?; **je me demande ~ faire** I wonder what I should do. **4** *adv excl* **qu'elle est belle!** how beautiful she is!; **~ de monde!** what a lot of people! ○ **c'est que** *loc conj* it's because; **si je vais me coucher, c'est ~ j'ai sommeil** if I'm going to bed, it's because I'm tired. ○ **qu'est-ce que** *pron interr* what; **qu'est-ce ~ tu veux encore?** what else do you want? ○ **qu'est-ce qui** *pron interr* what; **qu'est-ce qui se passe?** what's going on?

Québec [kebɛk] *nm* [province] **le ~** Quebec.

québécois, -e [kebekwa, az] *adj* Quebec (*avant n*). ○ **québécois** *nm* [langue] Quebec French. ○ **Québécois, -e** *nm, f* Quebecker, Québecois.

quel [kɛl] (*f* **quelle**, *mpl* **quels**, *fpl* **quelles**) **1** *adj interr* [personne] which; [chose] what, which; **~ livre voulez-vous?** what ou which book do you want?; **je ne sais ~s sont ses projets** I don't know what his plans are; **quelle heure est-il?** what time is it?, what's the time? **2** *adj excl*: **~ idiot!** what an idiot!; **quelle**

honte! the shame of it! **3** *adj indéf*: **~ que** (+ *subjonctif*) [chose, animal] whatever; [personne] whoever; **il se baigne, ~ que soit le temps** he goes swimming whatever the weather. **4** *pron interr* which (one); **de vous trois, ~ est le plus jeune?** which (one) of you three is the youngest?

quelconque [kɛlkɔ̃k] *adj* [n'importe lequel] any; **donner un prétexte ~** to give any old excuse; **si pour une raison ~ ...** if for any reason ...; **une ~ observation** some remark or other. ‖ (*après n*) *péj* [banal] ordinary, mediocre.

quelque [kɛlk(ə)] **1** *adj indéf* some; **à ~ distance de là** some way away (from there); **j'ai ~s lettres à écrire** I have some ou a few letters to write; **les ~s fois où j'étais absent** the few times I wasn't there; **les ~s 200 francs qu'il m'a prêtés** the 200 francs ou so (that) he lent me; **~ route que je prenne** whatever route I take; **~ peu** somewhat, rather. **2** *adv* [environ] about; **200 francs et ~** about 200 francs; **il est midi et ~** *fam* it's just after midday.

quelque chose [kɛlkəʃoz] *pron indéf* something; **~ de différent** something different; **~ d'autre** something else; **tu veux boire ~?** do you want something ou anything to drink?; **apporter un petit ~ à qqn** to give sb a little something; **c'est ~!** [ton admiratif] it's really something!; **cela m'a fait ~** I really felt it.

quelquefois [kɛlkəfwa] *adv* sometimes, occasionally.

quelque part [kɛlkəpar] *adv* somewhere; **l'as-tu vu ~?** did you see him anywhere?, have you seen him anywhere?

quelques-uns, quelques-unes [kɛlkəzœ̃, yn] *pron indéf* some, a few.

quelqu'un [kɛlkœ̃] *pron indéf m* someone, somebody; **c'est ~ d'ouvert/d'intelligent** he's/she's a frank/an intelligent person.

quémander [kemɑ̃de] *vt* to beg for; **~ qqch à qqn** to beg sb for sthg.

qu'en-dira-t-on [kɑ̃diratɔ̃] *nm inv fam* tittle-tattle.

quenelle [kənɛl] *nf very finely chopped mixture of fish or chicken cooked in stock.*

querelle [kərɛl] *nf* quarrel.

quereller [kərele] ○ **se quereller** *vp*: **se ~ (avec)** to quarrel (with).

querelleur, -euse [kərelœr, øz] *adj* quarrelsome.

qu'est-ce que [kɛskə] → que.

qu'est-ce qui [kɛski] → que.

question [kɛstjɔ̃] *nf* question; **poser une ~ à qqn** to ask sb a question; **il est ~ de faire qqch** it's a question or matter of doing sthg; **il n'en est pas ~** there is no question of it; **remettre qqn/qqch en ~** to question sb/sthg, to challenge sb/ sthg; **~ subsidiaire** tiebreaker.

questionnaire [kɛstjɔnɛr] *nm* questionnaire.

questionner [kɛstjɔne] *vt* to question.

quête [kɛt] *nf sout* [d'objet, de personne] quest; **se mettre en ~ de** to go in search of. || [d'aumône]: **faire la ~** to take a collection.

quêter [kete] **1** *vi* to collect. **2** *vt fig* to seek, to look for.

queue [kø] *nf* [d'animal] tail; **faire une ~ de poisson à qqn** *fig* & *AUTOM* to cut sb up. || [de fruit] stalk. || [de poêle] handle. || [de liste, de classe] bottom; [de file, peloton] rear. || [file] queue *Br*, line *Am*; **faire la ~** to queue *Br*, to stand in line *Am*; **à la ~ leu leu** in single file.

queue-de-cheval [kødʃəval] (*pl* **queues-de-cheval**) *nf* ponytail.

queue-de-pie [kødpi] (*pl* **queues-de-pie**) *nf fam* tails (*pl*).

qui [ki] **1** *pron rel* (*sujet*) [personne] who; [chose] which, that; **l'homme ~ parle** the man who's talking; **~ plus est** (and) what's more. || (*complément d'objet direct*) who; **tu vois ~ je veux dire** you see who I mean; **invite ~ tu veux** invite whoever or anyone you like. || (*après une préposition*) who, whom; **la personne à ~ je parle** the person I'm talking to, the person to whom I'm talking. || (*indéfini*): **~ que tu sois** whoever you are. **2** *pron interr* (*sujet*) who; **~ es-tu?** who are you? || (*complément d'objet, après une préposition*) who, whom; **dites-moi ~ vous demandez** tell me who you want to see; **à ~ vas-tu le donner?** who are you going to give it to?, to whom are you going to give it? ○ **qui est-ce qui** *pron interr* who. ○ **qui est-ce que** *pron interr* who, whom.

quiche [kiʃ] *nf* quiche.

quiconque [kikɔ̃k] **1** *pron indéf* anyone, anybody. **2** *pron rel indéf sout* anyone who, whoever.

quiétude [kjetyd] *nf* tranquillity.

quignon [kiɲɔ̃] *nm fam* hunk.

quille [kij] *nf* [de bateau] keel.

○ **quilles** *nfpl* [jeu]: (jeu de) **~s** skittles (*U*).

quincaillerie [kɛ̃kajri] *nf* [magasin] ironmonger's (shop) *Br*, hardware shop.

quinconce [kɛ̃kɔ̃s] *nm*: **en ~** in a staggered arrangement.

quinine [kinin] *nf* quinine.

quinquagénaire [kɛ̃kaʒenɛr] *nmf* fifty year old.

quinquennal, -e, -aux [kɛ̃kenal, o] *adj* [plan] five-year (*avant n*); [élection] five-yearly.

quintal, -aux [kɛ̃tal, o] *nm* quintal.

quinte [kɛ̃t] *nf* *MUS* fifth. ○ **quinte de toux** *nf* coughing fit.

quintuple [kɛ̃typl] *nm* & *adj* quintuple.

quinzaine [kɛ̃zɛn] *nf* [nombre] fifteen (or so); **une ~ de** about fifteen. || [deux semaines] fortnight *Br*, two weeks (*pl*).

quinze [kɛ̃z] **1** *adj num* fifteen; **dans ~ jours** in a fortnight *Br*, in two weeks. **2** *nm* [chiffre] fifteen; *voir aussi* **six**.

quinzième [kɛ̃zjɛm] *adj num*, *nm* & *nmf* fifteenth; *voir aussi* **sixième**.

quiproquo [kiprɔko] *nm* misunderstanding.

quittance [kitɑ̃s] *nf* receipt.

quitte [kit] *adj* quits; **en être ~ pour qqch/pour faire qqch** to get off with sthg/doing sthg; **~ à faire qqch** even if it means doing sthg.

quitter [kite] *vt* [gén] to leave; **ne quittez pas!** [au téléphone] hold the line, please! || [fonctions] to give up. ○ **se quitter** *vp* to part.

qui-vive [kiviv] *nm inv*: **être sur le ~** to be on the alert.

quoi [kwa] **1** *pron rel* (*après prép*): **ce à ~ je me suis intéressé** what I was interested in; **après ~** after which; **avoir de ~ vivre** to have enough to live on; **avez-vous de ~ écrire?** have you got something to write with?; **merci — il n'y a pas de ~** thank you — don't mention it. **2** *pron interr* what; **à ~ penses-tu?** what are you thinking about?; **je ne sais pas dire** I don't know what to say; **décide-toi, ~!** *fam* make your mind up, will you? ○ **quoi que** *loc conj* (+ *subjonctif*) whatever; **~ qu'il arrive** whatever happens; **~ qu'il dise** whatever he says; **~ qu'il en soit** be that as it may.

quoique [kwakə] *conj* although, though.

quolibet [kɔlibɛ] *nm sout* jeer, taunt.

quota [k(w)ɔta] *nm* quota.

quotidien, -ienne [kɔtidjɛ̃, jɛn] *adj* daily. ○ **quotidien** *nm* [routine] daily life; **au ~** on a day-to-day basis. || [journal] daily (newspaper).

quotient [kɔsjɑ̃] *nm* quotient; **~ intellectuel** intelligence quotient.

r¹, R [ɛr] *nm inv* [lettre] r, R.

r² *abr de* rue.

rabâcher [rabaʃe] **1** *vi fam* to harp on. **2** *vt* to go over (and over).

rabais [rabɛ] *nm* reduction, discount.

rabaisser [rabese] *vt* [réduire] to reduce; [orgueil] to humble. || [personne] to belittle. ○ **se rabaisser** *vp* [se déprécier] to belittle o.s. || [s'humilier]: **se ~ à faire qqch** to demean o.s. by doing sthg.

rabat [raba] *nm* [partie rabattue] flap.

rabat-joie [rabaʒwa] **1** *nm inv* killjoy. **2** *adj inv*: **être ~** to be a killjoy.

rabattre [rabatr] *vt* [col] to turn down. || [siège] to tilt back; [couvercle] to shut. || [gibier] to drive. ○ **se rabattre** *vp* [siège] to tilt back; [couvercle] to shut. || [voiture, coureur] to cut in. || [se contenter]: **se ~ sur** to fall back on.

rabattu, -e [rabaty] *pp* → **rabattre**.

rabbin [rabɛ̃] *nm* rabbi.

râblé, -e [rable] *adj* stocky.

rabot [rabo] *nm* plane.

raboter [rabɔte] *vt* to plane.

rabougri, -e [rabugri] *adj* [plante] stunted. || [personne] shrivelled, wizened.

rabrouer [rabrue] *vt* to snub.

raccommodage [rakɔmɔdaʒ] *nm* mending.

raccommoder [rakɔmɔde] *vt* [vêtement] to mend. || *fam fig* [personnes] to reconcile, to get back together.

raccompagner [rakɔ̃paɲe] *vt* to see home, to take home.

raccord [rakɔr] *nm* [liaison] join. || [pièce] connector, coupling. || CIN link.

raccordement [rakɔrdəmɑ̃] *nm* connection, linking.

raccorder [rakɔrde] *vt*: **~ qqch (à)** to connect sthg (to), to join sthg (to). ○ **raccorder** *vp*: **se ~ à** to be connected to.

raccourci [rakursi] *nm* shortcut.

raccourcir [rakursir] **1** *vt* to shorten. **2** *vi* to grow shorter.

raccrocher [rakrɔʃe] **1** *vt* to hang back up. **2** *vi* [au téléphone]: **~ (au nez de qqn)** to hang up (on sb), to put the phone down (on sb). ○ **se raccrocher** *vp*: **se ~ à** to cling to, to hang on to.

race [ras] *nf* [humaine] race; [animale] breed; **de ~** pedigree; [cheval] thoroughbred.

racé, -e [rase] *adj* [animal] purebred. || [voiture] of distinction.

rachat [raʃa] *nm* [transaction] repurchase. || *fig* [de péchés] atonement.

racheter [raʃte] *vt* [acheter en plus - gén] to buy another; [- pain, lait] to buy some more. || [acheter après avoir vendu] to buy back. || *fig* [péché, faute] to atone for; [défaut, lapsus] to make up for. || COMM [société] to buy out. ○ **se racheter** *vp fig* to redeem o.s.

rachitique [raʃitik] *adj* suffering from rickets.

racial, -e, -iaux [rasjal, jo] *adj* racial.

racine [rasin] *nf* root; [de nez] base; **~ carrée/cubique** MATHS square/cube root.

racisme [rasism] *nm* racism.

raciste [rasist] *nmf & adj* racist.

racketter [rakete] *vt*: **~ qqn** to subject sb to a protection racket.

raclée [rakle] *nf* hiding, thrashing.

racler [rakle] *vt* to scrape. ○ **se racler** *vp*: **se ~ la gorge** to clear one's throat.

racoler [rakɔle] *vt fam péj* [suj: prostituée] to solicit.

racoleur, -euse [rakɔlœr, øz] *adj fam péj* [air, sourire] come-hither; [publicité] strident.

racontar [rakɔ̃tar] *nm fam péj* piece of gossip. ○ **racontars** *nmpl fam péj* tittle-tattle (*U*).

raconter [rakɔ̃te] *vt* [histoire] to tell, to relate; [événement] to relate, to tell about; **~ qqch à qqn** to tell sb sthg, to relate sthg to sb. || [ragot, mensonge] to tell.

radar [radar] *nm* radar.

rade [rad] *nf* (natural) harbour.

radeau, -x [rado] *nm* [embarcation] raft.

radiateur [radjatœr] *nm* radiator.

radiation [radjasjɔ̃] *nf* PHYS radiation.

radical, -e, -aux [radikal, o] *adj* radical. ○ **radical** *nm* [gén] radical. || LING stem.

radier [radje] *vt* to strike off.

radieux, -ieuse [radjø, jøz] *adj* radiant; [soleil] dazzling.

radin, -e [radɛ̃, in] *fam péj* **1** *adj* stingy. **2** *nm, f* skinflint.

radio [radjo] *nf* [station, poste] radio; à la ~ on the radio. || MÉD: passer une ~ to have an X-ray, to be X-rayed.

radioactif, -ive [radjoaktif, iv] *adj* radioactive.

radioactivité [radjoaktivite] *nf* radioactivity.

radiodiffuser [radjodifyze] *vt* to broadcast.

radiographie [radjografi] *nf* [technique] radiography. || [image] X-ray.

radiologue [radjolɔg], **radiologiste** [radjolɔʒist] *nmf* radiologist.

radioréveil, radio-réveil [radjorevɛj] *nm* radio alarm, clock radio.

radiotélévisé, -e [radjotelevize] *adj* broadcast on both radio and television.

radis [radi] *nm* radish.

radoter [radote] *vi* to ramble.

radoucir [radusir] *vt* to soften. ○ **se radoucir** *vp* [temps] to become milder; [personne] to calm down.

radoucissement [radusismɑ̃] *nm* [d'attitude] softening. || [de température] rise; **un ~ du temps** a spell of milder weather.

rafale [rafal] *nf* [de vent] gust. || [de coups de feu, d'applaudissements] burst.

raffermir [rafɛrmir] *vt* [muscle] to firm up. || *fig* [pouvoir] to strengthen.

raffinage [rafinaʒ] *nm* refining.

raffiné, -e [rafine] *adj* refined.

raffinement [rafinmɑ̃] *nm* refinement.

raffiner [rafine] *vt* to refine.

raffinerie [rafinri] *nf* refinery.

raffoler [rafole] *vi*: ~ **de qqn/qqch** to adore sb/sthg.

raffut [rafy] *nm fam* row, racket.

rafistoler [rafistole] *vt fam* to patch up.

rafle [rafl] *nf* raid.

rafler [rafle] *vt* to swipe.

rafraîchir [rafreʃir] *vt* [nourriture, vin] to chill, to cool; [air] to cool. || [vêtement, appartement] to smarten up; *fig* [mémoire, idées] to refresh. ○ **se rafraîchir** *vp* [se refroidir] to cool (down). || *fam* [personne] to have a drink.

rafraîchissant, -e [rafreʃisɑ̃, ɑ̃t] *adj* refreshing.

rafraîchissement [rafreʃismɑ̃] *nm* [climat] cooling. || [boisson] cold drink.

raft(ing) [raft(iŋ)] *nm* whitewater rafting.

ragaillardir [ragajardir] *vt fam* to buck up, to perk up.

rage [raʒ] *nf* [fureur] rage; **faire ~** [tempête] to rage. || [maladie] rabies (*U*). ○ **rage de dents** *nf* (raging) toothache.

rager [raʒe] *vi fam* to fume.

rageur, -euse [raʒœr, øz] *adj* bad-tempered.

ragot [rago] *nm* (*gén pl*) *fam* (malicious) rumour, tittle-tattle (*U*).

ragoût [ragu] *nm* stew.

rai [rɛ] *nm littéraire* [de soleil] ray.

raid [rɛd] *nm* AÉRON, BOURSE & MIL raid.

raide [rɛd] **1** *adj* [cheveux] straight. || [tendu - corde] taut; [- membre] stiff. || [pente] steep. || *fam* [histoire] hard to swallow, far-fetched. **2** *adv* [abruptement] steeply. || *loc*: **tomber ~ mort** to fall down dead.

raideur [rɛdœr] *nf* [de membre] stiffness.

raidir [rɛdir] *vt* [muscle] to tense; [corde] to tighten, to tauten. ○ **se raidir** *vp* [se contracter] to grow stiff, to stiffen.

raie [rɛ] *nf* [rayure] stripe. || [dans les cheveux] parting *Br*, part *Am*. || [des fesses] crack. || [poisson] skate.

rail [raj] *nm* rail.

raillerie [rajri] *nf sout* mockery (*U*).

railleur, -euse [rajœr, øz] *sout* **1** *adj* mocking. **2** *nm, f* scoffer.

rainure [renyr] *nf* [longue] groove, channel; [courte] slot.

raisin [rezɛ̃] *nm* [fruit] grapes.

raison [rezɔ̃] *nf* [gén] reason; **à plus forte ~** all the more (so); **se faire une ~** to resign o.s.; **~ de plus pour faire qqch** all the more reason to do sthg. || [justesse, équité]: **avoir ~** to be right; **donner ~ à qqn** to prove sb right. ○ **à raison de** *loc prép* at (the rate of). ○ **en raison de** *loc prép* owing to, because of.

raisonnable [rezɔnabl] *adj* reasonable.

raisonnement [rezɔnmɑ̃] *nm* [faculté] reason, power of reasoning. || [argumentation] reasoning, argument.

raisonner [rezɔne] **1** *vt* [personne] to reason with. **2** *vi* [penser] to reason. || [discuter]: ~ **avec** to reason with.

rajeunir [raʒœnir] **1** *vt* [suj: couleur, vêtement]: ~ **qqn** to make sb look younger. || [suj: personne]: ~ **qqn de trois ans** to take three years off sb's age. || [vêtement, canapé) to renovate, to do up; [meubles] to modernize. **2** *vi* [personne] to look younger; [se sentir plus jeune] to feel younger ou rejuvenated.

rajouter [raʒute] *vt* to add; **en ~** *fam* to exaggerate.

rajuster [raʒyste], **réajuster** [reaʒyste] *vt* to adjust; [cravate] to straighten. ○ **se rajuster** *vp* to straighten one's clothes.

râle [ral] *nm* moan; [de mort] death rattle.

ralenti, -e [ralɑ̃ti] *adj* slow. ○ **ralenti** *nm* AUTOM idling speed; **tourner au ~** AUTOM to idle. ‖ CIN slow motion.

ralentir [ralɑ̃tir] **1** *vt* [allure, expansion] to slow (down). ‖ [rythme] to slacken. **2** *vi* to slow down ou up.

ralentissement [ralɑ̃tismɑ̃] *nm* [d'allure, d'expansion] slowing (down). ‖ [de rythme] slackening. ‖ [embouteillage] hold-up. ‖ PHYS deceleration.

râler [rale] *vi* [malade] to breathe with difficulty. ‖ *fam* [grogner] to moan.

ralliement [ralimɑ̃] *nm* rallying.

rallier [ralje] *vt* [poste, parti] to join. ‖ [suffrages] to win. ‖ [troupes] to rally. ○ **se rallier** *vp* to rally; **se ~ à** [parti] to join; [cause] to rally to; [avis] to come round to.

rallonge [ralɔ̃ʒ] *nf* [de table] leaf, extension. ‖ [électrique] extension (lead).

rallonger [ralɔ̃ʒe] *vt* to lengthen.

rallumer [ralyme] *vt* [feu, cigarette] to relight; *fig* [querelle] to revive. ‖ [appareil, lumière électrique] to switch (back) on again.

rallye [rali] *nm* rally.

ramadan [ramadɑ̃] *nm* Ramadan.

ramassage [ramasaʒ] *nm* collection; **~ scolaire** [service] school bus.

ramasser [ramase] *vt* [récolter, réunir] to gather, to collect. ‖ [prendre] to pick up. ‖ *fam* [claque, rhume] to get. ○ **se ramasser** *vp* [se replier] to crouch.

rambarde [rɑ̃bard] *nf* (guard) rail.

rame [ram] *nf* [aviron] oar. ‖ RAIL train. ‖ [de papier] ream.

rameau, -x [ramo] *nm* branch.

ramener [ramne] *vt* [remmener] to take back. ‖ [rapporter, restaurer] to bring back. ‖ [réduire]: **~ qqch à qqch** to reduce sthg to sthg, to bring sthg down to sthg.

ramer [rame] *vi* [rameur] to row.

rameur, -euse [ramœr, øz] *nm, f* rower.

ramification [ramifikasjɔ̃] *nf* [division] branch.

ramolli, -e [ramɔli] *adj* soft; *fig* soft (in the head).

ramollir [ramɔlir] *vt* [beurre] to soften. ○ **se ramollir** *vp* [beurre] to go soft, to soften.

ramoner [ramɔne] *vt* to sweep.

ramoneur [ramɔnœr] *nm* (chimney) sweep.

rampant, -e [rɑ̃pɑ̃, ɑ̃t] *adj* [animal] crawling. ‖ [plante] creeping.

rampe [rɑ̃p] *nf* [d'escalier] banister, handrail. ‖ [d'accès] ramp; **~ de lancement** launch pad. ‖ THÉÂTRE: **la ~** the footlights (*pl*).

ramper [rɑ̃pe] *vi* [animal, soldat, enfant] to crawl. ‖ [plante] to creep.

rance [rɑ̃s] *adj* [beurre] rancid.

rancir [rɑ̃sir] *vi* to go rancid.

rancœur [rɑ̃kœr] *nf* rancour, resentment.

rançon [rɑ̃sɔ̃] *nf* ransom; *fig* price.

rancune [rɑ̃kyn] *nf* rancour, spite; **garder** ou **tenir ~ à qqn de qqch** to hold a grudge against sb for sthg; **sans ~!** no hard feelings!

rancunier, -ière [rɑ̃kynje, jɛr] *adj* vindictive, spiteful.

randonnée [rɑ̃dɔne] *nf* [à pied] walk. ‖ [à bicyclette] ride; [en voiture] drive.

randonneur, -euse [rɑ̃dɔnœr, øz] *nm, f* walker, rambler.

rang [rɑ̃] *nm* [d'objets, de personnes] row; **se mettre en ~ par deux** to line up in twos. ‖ MIL rank. ‖ [position sociale] station. ‖ *Can* [peuplement rural] rural district. ‖ *Can* [chemin] country road.

rangé, -e [rɑ̃ʒe] *adj* [sérieux] well-ordered, well-behaved.

rangée [rɑ̃ʒe] *nf* row.

rangement [rɑ̃ʒmɑ̃] *nm* tidying up.

ranger [rɑ̃ʒe] *vt* [chambre] to tidy. ‖ [objets] to arrange. ‖ [voiture] to park. ○ **se ranger** *vp* [élèves, soldats] to line up. ‖ [voiture] to pull in. ‖ [piéton] to step aside. ‖ [s'assagir] to settle down.

ranimer [ranime] *vt* [personne] to revive, to bring round. ‖ [feu] to rekindle. ‖ *fig* [sentiment] to reawaken.

rapace [rapas] **1** *nm* bird of prey. **2** *adj* [cupide] rapacious, grasping.

rapatrier [rapatrije] *vt* to repatriate.

râpe [rap] *nf* [de cuisine] grater.

râpé, -e [rape] *adj* CULIN grated. ‖ [manteau] threadbare. ‖ *fam* [raté]: **c'est ~!** we've had it!

rationaliser

râper [rape] *vt* CULIN to grate.

râpeux, -euse [rapø, øz] *adj* [tissu] rough. || [vin] harsh.

rapide [rapid] **1** *adj* [gén] rapid. || [train, coureur] fast. || [musique, intelligence] lively, quick. **2** *nm* [train] express (train). || [de fleuve] rapid.

rapidement [rapidmã] *adv* rapidly.

rapidité [rapidite] *nf* rapidity.

rapiécer [rapjese] *vt* to patch.

rappel [rapɛl] *nm* [de réservistes, d'ambassadeur] recall. || [souvenir] reminder; ~ à l'ordre call to order. || [de paiement] back pay. || [de vaccination] booster. || [au spectacle] curtain call, encore. || SPORT abseiling; **descendre en ~** to abseil (down).

rappeler [raple] *vt* [gén] to call back; ~ qqn à qqch *fig* to bring sb back to sthg. || [faire penser à]: ~ qqch à qqn to remind sb of sthg. ○ **se rappeler** *vp* to remember.

rapport [rapɔr] *nm* [corrélation] link, connection. || [compte-rendu] report. || [profit] return, yield. || MATHS ratio. ○ **rapports** *nmpl* [relations] relations. || [sexuels]: ~s (**sexuels**) intercourse (*sg*). ○ **par rapport à** *loc prép* in comparison to, compared with.

rapporter [rapɔrte] *vt* to bring back. ○ **se rapporter** *vp*: se ~ à to refer ou relate to.

rapporteur, -euse [rapɔrtœr, øz] *nm, f* sneak, telltale. ○ **rapporteur** *nm* [de commission] rapporteur. || GÉOM protractor.

rapprochement [raprɔʃmã] *nm* [d'objets, de personnes] bringing together. || *fig* [entre événements] link, connection. || *fig* [de pays, de parti] rapprochement.

rapprocher [raprɔʃe] *vt* [mettre plus près]: ~ qqn/qqch de qqch to bring sb/ sthg nearer to sthg, to bring sb/sthg closer to sthg. || *fig* [personnes] to bring together. || *fig* [idée, texte]: ~ qqch (de) to compare sthg (with). ○ **se rapprocher** *vp* [approcher]: se ~ (de qqn/qqch) to approach (sb/sthg). || [se ressembler]: se ~ de qqch to be similar to sthg. || [se réconcilier]: se ~ de qqn to become closer to sb.

rapt [rapt] *nm* abduction.

raquette [rakɛt] *nf* [de tennis, de squash] racket; [de ping-pong] bat. || [à neige] snowshoe.

rare [rar] *adj* [peu commun, peu fréquent] rare; **ses ~s amis** his few friends.

raréfier [rarefje] *vt* to rarefy. ○ **se raréfier** *vp* to become rarefied.

rarement [rarmã] *adv* rarely.

rareté [rarte] *nf* [de denrées, de nouvelles] scarcity. || [de visites, de lettres] infrequency. || [objet précieux] rarity.

ras, -e [ra, raz] *adj* [herbe, poil] short. || [mesure] full. ○ **ras** *adv* short; **à ~ de** level with; **en avoir ~ le bol** *fam* to be fed up.

rasade [razad] *nf* glassful.

rasage [razaʒ] *nm* shaving.

rasant, -e [razã, ãt] *adj* [lumière] low-angled. || *fam* [film, discours] boring.

raser [raze] *vt* [barbe, cheveux] to shave off. || [mur, sol] to hug. || [village] to raze. || *fam* [personne] to bore. ○ **se raser** *vp* [avec rasoir] to shave.

ras-le-bol [ralbɔl] *nm inv fam* discontent.

rasoir [razwar] **1** *nm* razor; ~ **électrique** electric shaver. **2** *adj inv fam* boring.

rassasier [rasazje] *vt* to satisfy.

rassemblement [rasãbləmã] *nm* [foule] crowd, gathering. || [union, parti] union. || MIL parade; ~! fall in!

rassembler [rasãble] *vt* [personnes, documents] to collect, to gather. || [courage] to summon up; [idées] to collect. ○ **se rassembler** *vp* [manifestants] to assemble. || [famille] to get together.

rasseoir [raswar] ○ **se rasseoir** *vp* to sit down again.

rassis, -e [rasi, iz] *adj* [pain] stale.

rassurant, -e [rasyrã, ãt] *adj* reassuring.

rassuré, -e [rasyre] *adj* confident, at ease.

rassurer [rasyre] *vt* to reassure.

rat [ra] *nm* rat.

ratatiné, -e [ratatine] *adj* [fruit, personne] shrivelled.

rate [rat] *nf* [animal] female rat. || [organe] spleen.

raté, -e [rate] *nm, f* [personne] failure. ○ **raté** *nm* (*gén pl*) AUTOM misfiring (*U*); **faire des ~s** to misfire.

râteau, -x [rato] *nm* rake.

rater [rate] **1** *vt* [train, occasion] to miss. || [plat, affaire] to make a mess of; [examen] to fail. **2** *vi* to go wrong.

ratification [ratifikasjɔ̃] *nf* ratification.

ratifier [ratifje] *vt* to ratify.

ration [rasjɔ̃] *nf* [quantité] portion; *fig* share.

rationaliser [rasjɔnalize] *vt* to rationalize.

rationnel, -elle [rasjɔnɛl] *adj* rational.

rationnement [rasjɔnmɑ̃] *nm* rationing.

rationner [rasjɔne] *vt* to ration.

ratissage [ratisaʒ] *nm* [de jardin] raking. || [de quartier] search.

ratisser [ratise] *vt* [jardin] to rake. || [quartier] to search, to comb.

raton [ratɔ̃] *nm* ZOOL young rat.
○ **raton laveur** *nm* racoon.

RATP (*abr de* **Régie autonome des transports parisiens**) *nf Paris transport authority.*

rattacher [rataʃe] *vt* [attacher de nouveau] to do up, to fasten again. || [relier] : ~ **qqch à** to join sthg to; *fig* to link sthg with. || [unir] : ~ **qqn à** to bind sb to. ○ **se rattacher** *vp* : ~ **à** to be linked to.

rattrapage [ratrapaʒ] *nm* SCOL : **cours de** ~ remedial class.

rattraper [ratrape] *vt* [animal, prisonnier] to recapture. || [temps] : ~ **le temps perdu** to make up for lost time. || [rejoindre] to catch up with. || [erreur] to correct. || [personne qui tombe] to catch.
○ **se rattraper** *vp* [se retenir] : **se** ~ **à qqn/qqch** to catch hold of sb/sthg. || [se faire pardonner] to make amends.

rature [ratyr] *nf* alteration.

rauque [rok] *adj* hoarse, husky.

ravagé, -e [ravaʒe] *adj fam* [fou] : **être** ~ to be off one's head.

ravager [ravaʒe] *vt* [gén] to devastate, to ravage.

ravages [ravaʒ] *nmpl* [de troupes, d'inondation] devastation (*sg*).

ravaler [ravale] *vt* [façade] to clean, to restore. || [personne] : ~ **qqn au rang de** to lower sb to the level of. || *fig* [larmes, colère] to stifle, to hold back.

ravauder [ravode] *vt* to mend, to repair.

ravi, -e [ravi] *adj* : ~ **(de)** delighted (with); ~ **de vous connaître** pleased to meet you.

ravin [ravɛ̃] *nm* ravine, gully.

raviolis [ravjɔli] *nmpl* ravioli (*U*).

ravir [ravir] *vt* [charmer] to delight; **à** ~ beautifully.

raviser [ravize] ○ **se raviser** *vp* to change one's mind.

ravissant, -e [ravisɑ̃, ɑ̃t] *adj* delightful, beautiful.

ravisseur, -euse [ravisœr, øz] *nm, f* abductor.

ravitaillement [ravitajmɑ̃] *nm* [en denrées] resupplying; [en carburant] refuelling.

ravitailler [ravitaje] *vt* [en denrées] to resupply; [en carburant] to refuel.

raviver [ravive] *vt* [feu] to rekindle. || [couleurs] to brighten up. || *fig* [douleur] to revive. || [plaie] to reopen.

rayer [reje] *vt* [disque, vitre] to scratch. || [nom, mot] to cross out.

rayon [rejɔ̃] *nm* [de lumière] beam, ray. || (*gén pl*) [radiation] radiation (*U*); ~ **laser** laser beam; ~**s X** X-rays. || [de roue] spoke. || GÉOM radius; **dans un** ~ **de** *fig* within a radius of. || [étagère] shelf. || [dans un magasin] department.

rayonnant, -e [rejɔnɑ̃, ɑ̃t] *adj litt & fig* radiant.

rayonnement [rejɔnmɑ̃] *nm* [gén] radiance. || PHYS radiation.

rayonner [rejɔne] *vi* [soleil] to shine; ~ **de joie** *fig* to radiate happiness. || [touriste] to tour around (*from a base*).

rayure [rejyr] *nf* [sur étoffe] stripe. || [sur disque, sur meuble] scratch.

raz [ra] ○ **raz de marée** *nm* tidal wave; POLIT & *fig* landslide.

razzia [razja] *nf fam* raid.

RDA (*abr de* **République démocratique allemande**) *nf* GDR.

RdC *abr de* **rez-de-chaussée**.

ré [re] *nm inv* MUS D; [chanté] re.

réacteur [reaktœr] *nm* [d'avion] jet engine; ~ **nucléaire** nuclear reactor.

réaction [reaksjɔ̃] *nf* : ~ **(à/contre)** reaction (to/against).

réactionnaire [reaksjɔner] *nmf & adj péj* reactionary.

réactiver [reaktive] *vt* to reactivate.

réactualiser [reaktualize] *vt* [moderniser] to update, to bring up to date.

réadapter [readapte] *vt* to readapt.

réagir [reaʒir] *vi* : ~ **(à/contre)** to react (to/against); ~ **sur** to affect.

réajuster = **rajuster**.

réalisable [realizabl] *adj* [projet] feasible. || FIN realizable.

réalisateur, -trice [realizatœr, tris] *nm, f* CIN & TÉLÉ director.

réaliser [realize] *vt* [projet] to carry out; [ambitions, rêves] to achieve, to realize. || CIN & TÉLÉ to produce. || [s'apercevoir de] to realize. ○ **se réaliser** *vp* [ambition] to be realized; [rêve] to come true.

réaliste [realist] **1** *nmf* realist. **2** *adj* [personne, objectif] realistic. || ART & LITTÉRATURE realist.

réalité [realite] *nf* reality; **en ~** in reality.

réaménagement [reamenaʒmã] *nm* [de projet] restructuring.

réamorcer [reamɔrse] *vt* to start up again.

réanimation [reanimasjɔ̃] *nf* resuscitation; **en ~** in intensive care.

réanimer [reanime] *vt* to resuscitate.

réapparaître [reaparɛtr] *vi* to reappear.

rébarbatif, -ive [rebarbatif, iv] *adj* [travail] daunting.

rebâtir [rebɑtir] *vt* to rebuild.

rebattu, -e [rəbaty] *adj* overworked, hackneyed.

rebelle [rəbɛl] *adj* [personne] rebellious; [troupes] rebel (*avant n*). || [mèche, boucle] unruly.

rebeller [rəbele] ○ **se rebeller** *vp*: se ~ (**contre**) to rebel (against).

rébellion [rebeljɔ̃] *nf* rebellion.

rebiffer [rəbife] ○ **se rebiffer** *vp fam*: se ~ (**contre**) to rebel (against).

reboiser [rəbwaze] *vt* to reafforest.

rebond [rəbɔ̃] *nm* bounce.

rebondir [rəbɔ̃dir] *vi* [objet] to bounce; [contre mur] to rebound. || *fig* [affaire] to come to life (again).

rebondissement [rəbɔ̃dismã] *nm* [d'affaire] new development.

rebord [rəbɔr] *nm* [de table] edge; [de fenêtre] sill, ledge.

reboucher [rəbuʃe] *vt* [bouteille] to put the cork back in, to recork; [trou] to fill in.

rebours [rəbur] ○ **à rebours** *loc adv* the wrong way.

rebrousse-poil [rəbruspwal] ○ **à rebrousse-poil** *loc adv* the wrong way; **prendre qqn à ~** *fig* to rub sb up the wrong way.

rebrousser [rəbruse] *vt* to brush back; **~ chemin** *fig* to retrace one's steps.

rébus [rebys] *nm* rebus.

rebut [rəby] *nm* scrap; **mettre qqch au ~** to get rid of sthg, to scrap sthg.

rebuter [rəbyte] *vt* [suj: travail] to dishearten.

récalcitrant, -e [rekalsitrã, ãt] *adj* recalcitrant, stubborn.

recaler [rəkale] *vt fam* to fail.

récapitulatif, -ive [rekapitylatif, iv] *adj* summary (*avant n*). ○ **récapitulatif** *nm* summary.

récapituler [rekapityle] *vt* to recapitulate, to recap.

recel [rəsɛl] *nm* [délit] possession of stolen goods.

receleur, -euse [rəsəlœr, øz] *nm, f* receiver (*of stolen goods*).

récemment [resamã] *adv* recently.

recensement [rəsɑ̃smã] *nm* [de population] census. || [d'objets] inventory.

recenser [rəsɑ̃se] *vt* [population] to take a census of. || [objets] to take an inventory of.

récent, -e [resã, ãt] *adj* recent.

recentrer [rəsɑ̃tre] *vt* to refocus.

récépissé [resepise] *nm* receipt.

récepteur, -trice [resɛptœr, tris] *adj* receiving. ○ **récepteur** *nm* receiver.

réception [resɛpsjɔ̃] *nf* [gén] reception. || [de marchandises] receipt. || [bureau] reception (desk). || SPORT [de sauteur, skieur] landing.

réceptionner [resɛpsjɔne] *vt* [marchandises] to take delivery of.

réceptionniste [resɛpsjɔnist] *nmf* receptionist.

récession [resesjɔ̃] *nf* recession.

recette [rəsɛt] *nf* COMM takings (*pl*). || CULIN recipe.

recevable [rəsəvabl] *adj* [excuse, offre] acceptable. || JUR admissible.

receveur, -euse [rəsəvœr, øz] *nm, f* ADMIN: **~ des impôts** tax collector; **~ des postes** postmaster (*f* postmistress).

recevoir [rəsəvwar] *vt* [gén] to receive. || [coup] to get, to receive. || [invités] to entertain; [client] to see. || SCOL & UNIV: **être reçu à un examen** to pass an exam. ○ **se recevoir** *vp* SPORT to land.

rechange [rəʃɑ̃ʒ] ○ **de rechange** *loc adj* spare; *fig* alternative.

réchapper [reʃape] *vi*: **~ de** to survive.

recharge [rəʃarʒ] *nf* [cartouche] refill.

rechargeable [rəʃarʒabl] *adj* [batterie] rechargeable; [briquet] refillable.

réchaud [reʃo] *nm* [portable] stove.

réchauffé, -e [reʃofe] *adj* [plat] reheated; *fig* rehashed.

réchauffement [reʃofmã] *nm* warming (up).

réchauffer [reʃofe] *vt* [nourriture] to reheat. || [personne] to warm up. ○ **se réchauffer** *vp* to warm up.

rêche [rɛʃ] *adj* rough.

recherche [rəʃɛrʃ] *nf* [quête & INFORM] search; **être à la ~ de** to be in search of; **faire** ou **effectuer des ~s** to make inquiries. || SCIENCE research; **faire de la ~** to do research. || [raffinement] elegance.

recherché, -e [rəʃɛrʃe] adj [ouvrage] sought-after. || [raffiné - vocabulaire] refined; [- mets] exquisite.

rechercher [rəʃɛrʃe] vt [objet, personne] to search for, to hunt for.

rechigner [rəʃiɲe] vi: ~ à to balk at.

rechute [rəʃyt] nf relapse.

récidiver [residive] vi JUR to commit another offence. || MÉD to recur.

récidiviste [residivist] nmf repeat ou persistent offender.

récif [resif] nm reef.

récipient [resipjɑ̃] nm container.

réciproque [resiprɔk] 1 adj reciprocal. 2 nf: la ~ the reverse.

réciproquement [resiprɔkmɑ̃] adv mutually; et ~ and vice versa.

récit [resi] nm story.

récital, -als [resital] nm recital.

récitation [resitasjɔ̃] nf recitation.

réciter [resite] vt to recite.

réclamation [reklamasjɔ̃] nf complaint; **faire/déposer une ~** to make/ lodge a complaint.

réclame [reklam] nf [annonce] advert, advertisement. || [promotion]: **en ~** on special offer.

réclamer [reklame] vt [demander] to ask for, to request; [avec insistance] to demand. || [nécessiter] to require, to demand.

reclasser [rəklase] vt [dossiers] to refile. || ADMIN to regrade.

réclusion [reklyzjɔ̃] nf imprisonment; ~ à perpétuité life imprisonment.

recoiffer [rəkwafe] ○ **se recoiffer** vp to do one's hair again.

recoin [rəkwɛ̃] nm nook.

recoller [rəkɔle] vt [objet brisé] to stick back together.

récolte [rekɔlt] nf [AGRIC - action] harvesting (U), gathering (U); [- produit] harvest, crop. || fig collection.

récolter [rekɔlte] vt to harvest; fig to collect.

recommandable [rəkɔmɑ̃dabl] adj commendable; **peu ~** undesirable.

recommandation [rəkɔmɑ̃dasjɔ̃] nf recommendation.

recommandé, -e [rəkɔmɑ̃de] adj [envoi] registered; **envoyer qqch en ~** to send sthg by registered post Br ou mail Am. || [conseillé] advisable.

recommander [rəkɔmɑ̃de] vt to recommend; ~ à qqn de faire qqch to advise sb to do sthg.

recommencer [rəkɔmɑ̃se] 1 vt [travail] to start ou begin again; ~ à faire qqch to start ou begin doing sthg again. 2 vi to start ou begin again; **ne recommence pas!** don't do that again!

récompense [rekɔ̃pɑ̃s] nf reward.

récompenser [rekɔ̃pɑ̃se] vt to reward.

recompter [rəkɔ̃te] vt to recount.

réconciliation [rekɔ̃siljasjɔ̃] nf reconciliation.

réconcilier [rekɔ̃silje] vt to reconcile.

reconduire [rəkɔ̃dɥir] vt [personne] to accompany, to take. || [politique, bail] to renew.

reconduit, -e [rəkɔ̃dɥi, ɥit] pp → reconduire.

réconfort [rekɔ̃fɔr] nm comfort.

réconfortant, -e [rekɔ̃fɔrtɑ̃, ɑ̃t] adj comforting.

réconforter [rekɔ̃fɔrte] vt to comfort.

reconnaissable [rəkɔnɛsabl] adj recognizable.

reconnaissance [rəkɔnɛsɑ̃s] nf [gén] recognition. || MIL reconnaissance; **aller/ partir en ~** to go out on reconnaissance. || [gratitude] gratitude.

reconnaissant, -e [rəkɔnɛsɑ̃, ɑ̃t] adj grateful.

reconnaître [rəkɔnɛtr] vt [gén] to recognize. || [erreur] to admit, to acknowledge. || MIL to reconnoitre.

reconnu, -e [rəkɔny] 1 pp → reconnaître. 2 adj well-known.

reconquérir [rəkɔ̃kerir] vt to reconquer.

reconquis, -e [rəkɔ̃ki, iz] pp → reconquérir.

reconsidérer [rəkɔ̃sidere] vt to reconsider.

reconstituant, -e [rəkɔ̃stitɥɑ̃, ɑ̃t] adj invigorating. ○ **reconstituant** nm tonic.

reconstituer [rəkɔ̃stitɥe] vt [puzzle] to put together. || [crime, délit] to reconstruct.

reconstitution [rəkɔ̃stitysjɔ̃] nf [de puzzle] putting together. || [de crime, délit] reconstruction.

reconstruction [rəkɔ̃stryksjɔ̃] nf reconstruction, rebuilding.

reconstruire [rəkɔ̃strɥir] vt to reconstruct, to rebuild.

reconstruit, -e [rəkɔ̃strɥi, ɥit] pp → reconstruire.

reconversion [rəkɔ̃vɛrsjɔ̃] nf [d'employé] redeployment. || [d'usine, de société] conversion.

reconvertir [rəkɔ̃vertir] *vt* [employé] to redeploy. ○ **se reconvertir** *vp*: se ~ dans to move into.

recopier [rəkɔpje] *vt* to copy out.

record [rəkɔr] **1** *nm* record; **détenir/ améliorer/battre un ~** to hold/improve/ beat a record. **2** *adj inv* record (*avant n*).

recoucher [rəkuʃe] ○ **se recoucher** *vp* to go back to bed.

recoudre [rəkudr] *vt* to sew (up) again.

recoupement [rəkupmɑ̃] *nm* cross-check; **par ~** by cross-checking.

recouper [rəkupe] ○ **se recouper** *vp* [lignes] to intersect. || [témoignages] to match up.

recourir [rəkurir] *vi*: ~ à [médecin, agence] to turn to; [force, mensonge] to resort to.

recours [rəkur] *nm* [emploi]: **avoir ~ à** [médecin, agence] to turn to; [force, mensonge] to resort to, to have recourse to. || [solution] solution, way out; **en dernier ~** as a last resort. || JUR action.

recouvert, -e [rəkuver, ɛrt] *pp* → recouvrir.

recouvrir [rəkuvrir] *vt* [gén] to cover. ○ **se recouvrir** *vp* [surface]: se ~ (de) to be covered (with).

recracher [rəkraʃe] *vt* to spit out.

récréatif, -ive [rekreatif, iv] *adj* entertaining.

récréation [rekreasjɔ̃] *nf* [détente] relaxation, recreation. || SCOL break.

recréer [rəkree] *vt* to recreate.

récrimination [rekriminasjɔ̃] *nf* complaint.

récrire [rekrir], **réécrire** [reekrir] *vt* to rewrite.

recroqueviller [rəkrɔkvije] ○ **se recroqueviller** *vp* to curl up.

recru, -e [rəkry] *adj*: ~ **de fatigue** *littéraire* exhausted. ○ **recrue** *nf* recruit.

recrudescence [rəkrydesɑ̃s] *nf* renewed outbreak.

recrutement [rəkrytmɑ̃] *nm* recruitment.

recruter [rəkryte] *vt* to recruit.

rectal, -e, -aux [rɛktal, o] *adj* rectal.

rectangle [rɛktɑ̃gl] *nm* rectangle.

rectangulaire [rɛktɑ̃gyler] *adj* rectangular.

recteur [rɛktœr] *nm* SCOL *chief administrative officer of an education authority*.

rectificatif, -ive [rɛktifikatif, iv] *adj*

correcting. ○ **rectificatif** *nm* correction.

rectification [rɛktifikasjɔ̃] *nf* [correction] correction. || [de tir] adjustment.

rectifier [rɛktifje] *vt* [tir] to adjust. || [erreur] to rectify, to correct.

rectiligne [rɛktiliɲ] *adj* rectilinear.

recto [rɛkto] *nm* right side; ~ **verso** on both sides.

rectorat [rɛktɔra] *nm* SCOL *offices of the education authority*.

reçu, -e [rəsy] *pp* → recevoir. ○ **reçu** *nm* receipt.

recueil [rəkœj] *nm* collection.

recueillement [rəkœjmɑ̃] *nm* meditation.

recueillir [rəkœjir] *vt* [fonds] to collect. || [suffrages] to win. || [enfant] to take in. ○ **se recueillir** *vp* to meditate.

recul [rəkyl] *nm* [mouvement arrière] step backwards; MIL retreat. || [d'arme à feu] recoil. || [d'inflation, de chômage]: ~ **(de)** downturn (in). || *fig* [retrait]: **avec du ~** with hindsight.

reculé, -e [rəkyle] *adj* distant.

reculer [rəkyle] **1** *vt* [voiture] to back up. || [date] to put back, to postpone. **2** *vi* [aller en arrière] to move backwards; [voiture] to reverse. || [maladie, pauvreté] to be brought under control.

reculons [rəkylɔ̃] ○ **à reculons** *adv* backwards.

récupération [rekyperasjɔ̃] *nf* salvage.

récupérer [rekypere] **1** *vt* [objet] to get back. || [déchets] to salvage. || [journée] to make up. **2** *vi* to recover.

récurer [rekyre] *vt* to scour.

récuser [rekyze] *vt* JUR to challenge. || *sout* [refuser] to reject.

recyclage [rəsiklaʒ] *nm* [d'employé] retraining. || [de déchets] recycling.

recycler [rəsikle] *vt* [employé] to retrain. || [déchets] to recycle. ○ **se recycler** *vp* [employé] to retrain.

rédacteur, -trice [redaktœr, tris] *nm, f* [de journal] subeditor; [d'ouvrage de référence] editor; ~ **en chef** editor-in-chief.

rédaction [redaksjɔ̃] *nf* [de texte] editing. || SCOL essay. || [personnel] editorial staff.

redécouvrir [rədekuvrir] *vt* to rediscover.

redéfinir [rədefinir] *vt* to redefine.

redemander [rədəmɑ̃de] *vt* to ask again for.

rédemption [redɑ̃psjɔ̃] *nf* redemption.

redescendre [rədesɑ̃dr] **1** *vt* (*aux: avoir*) [escalier] to go/come down again. || [objet - d'une étagère] to take down again. **2** *vi* (*aux: être*) to go/come down again.

redevable [rədəvabl] *adj:* être ~ à qqn de qqch [service] to be indebted to sb for sthg.

redevance [rədəvɑ̃s] *nf* [de radio, télévision] licence fee; [téléphonique] rental (fee).

rédhibitoire [redibitwar] *adj* [défaut] crippling; [prix] prohibitive.

rediffusion [rədifyzjɔ̃] *nf* repeat.

rédiger [rediʒe] *vt* to write.

redire [rədir] *vt* to repeat; **avoir** OU **trouver à** ~ **à qqch** *fig* to find fault with sthg.

redistribuer [rədistribɥe] *vt* to redistribute.

redit, -e [rədi, it] *pp* → **redire**.

redite [rədit] *nf* repetition.

redonner [rədɔne] *vt* to give back; [confiance, forces] to restore.

redoublant, -e [rədublɑ̃, ɑ̃t] *nm, f* pupil who is repeating a year.

redoubler [rəduble] **1** *vt* SCOL to repeat. **2** *vi* to intensify.

redoutable [rədutabl] *adj* formidable.

redouter [rədute] *vt* to fear.

redressement [rədresmɑ̃] *nm* [de pays, d'économie] recovery. || JUR: ~ **fiscal** payment of back taxes.

redresser [rədrese] **1** *vt* [poteau, arbre] to put OU set upright; ~ **la tête** to raise one's head. || [situation] to set right. **2** *vi* AUTOM to straighten up. ○ **se redresser** *vp* [personne] to stand OU sit straight. || [pays] to recover.

réducteur, -trice [redyktœr, tris] *adj* [limitatif] simplistic.

réduction [redyksjɔ̃] *nf* [gén] reduction. || MÉD setting.

réduire [redɥir] **1** *vt* [gén] to reduce; ~ **en** to reduce to. || MÉD to set. || *Helv* [ranger] to put away. **2** *vi* CULIN to reduce.

réduit, -e [redɥi, it] **1** *pp* → **réduire**. **2** *adj* reduced. ○ **réduit** *nm* [local] small room.

rééchelonner [reeʃlɔne] *vt* to reschedule.

réécrire = **récrire**.

réédition [reedisjɔ̃] *nf* new edition.

rééducation [reedykasjɔ̃] *nf* [de délinquant, malade] rehabilitation.

réel, -elle [reɛl] *adj* real.

réélection [reelɛksjɔ̃] *nf* re-election.

réellement [reelmɑ̃] *adv* really.

rééquilibrer [reekilibre] *vt* to balance (again).

réévaluer [reevalɥe] *vt* to revalue.

réexpédier [reɛkspedje] *vt* to send back.

réf. (*abr de* **référence**) ref.

refaire [rəfɛr] *vt* [faire de nouveau - travail, devoir] to do again; [- voyage] to make again. || [mur, toit] to repair.

refait, -e [rəfɛ, ɛt] *pp* → **refaire**.

réfection [refɛksjɔ̃] *nf* repair.

réfectoire [refɛktwar] *nm* refectory.

référence [referɑ̃s] *nf* reference; **faire** ~ **à** to refer to.

référendum [referɛ̃dɔm] *nm* referendum.

référer [refere] *vi:* **en** ~ **à qqn** to refer the matter to sb.

refermer [rəfɛrme] *vt* to close OU shut again.

réfléchi, -e [refleʃi] *adj* [action] considered. || [personne] thoughtful. || GRAM reflexive.

réfléchir [refleʃir] **1** *vt* [refléter] to reflect. **2** *vi* to think, to reflect; ~ **à** OU **sur qqch** to think about sthg.

reflet [rəflɛ] *nm* [image] reflection. || [de lumière] glint.

refléter [rəflete] *vt* to reflect. ○ **se refléter** *vp* [se réfléchir] to be reflected. || [transparaître] to be mirrored.

refleurir [rəflœrir] *vi* [fleurir à nouveau] to flower again.

réflexe [reflɛks] *nm* reflex.

réflexion [reflɛksjɔ̃] *nf* [de lumière, d'ondes] reflection. || [pensée] reflection, thought. || [remarque] remark.

refluer [rəflye] *vi* [liquide] to flow back. || [foule] to flow back.

reflux [rəfly] *nm* [d'eau] ebb.

refonte [rəfɔ̃t] *nf* [de métal] remelting. || [d'ouvrage] recasting. || [d'institution, de système] overhaul, reshaping.

reforestation [rəfɔrestasjɔ̃] *nf* reforestation.

réformateur, -trice [reformatœr, tris] **1** *adj* reforming. **2** *nm, f* [personne] reformer. || RELIG Reformer.

réforme [reform] *nf* reform.

reformer [rəfɔrme] *vt* to re-form.

réformer [reforme] *vt* [améliorer] to reform, to improve. || MIL to invalid out.

réformiste [reformist] *adj* & *nmf* reformist.

refoulé, -e [rəfule] **1** *adj* repressed, frustrated. **2** *nm, f* repressed person.

refouler [rəfule] *vt* [personnes] to repel, to repulse. || PSYCHOL to repress.

réfractaire [refrakter] **1** *adj* [rebelle] insubordinate; ~ à resistant to. || [matière] refractory. **2** *nmf* insubordinate.

refrain [rəfrɛ̃] *nm* MUS refrain, chorus.

refréner [rəfrene] *vt* to check, to hold back.

réfrigérant, -e [refriʒerɑ̃, ɑ̃t] *adj* [liquide] refrigerating, refrigerant.

réfrigérateur [refriʒeratœr] *nm* refrigerator.

refroidir [rəfrwadir] **1** *vt* [plat] to cool. || [décourager] to discourage. **2** *vi* to cool.

refroidissement [rəfrwadismɑ̃] *nm* [de température] drop, cooling. || [grippe] chill.

refuge [rəfyʒ] *nm* [abri] refuge. || [de montagne] hut.

réfugié, -e [refyʒje] *nm, f* refugee.

réfugier [refyʒje] ○ **se réfugier** *vp* to take refuge.

refus [rəfy] *nm inv* refusal; **ce n'est pas de ~** *fam* I wouldn't say no.

refuser [rəfyze] *vt* [repousser] to refuse; ~ **de faire qqch** to refuse to do sthg. || [contester] : **~ qqch à qqn** to deny sb sthg. || [clients, spectateurs] to turn away. || [candidat] : **être refusé** to fail. ○ **se refuser** *vp* : **se ~ à faire qqch** to refuse to do sthg.

réfuter [refyte] *vt* to refute.

regagner [rəgaɲe] *vt* [reprendre] to regain, to win back. || [revenir à] to get back to.

regain [rəgɛ̃] *nm* [retour] : **un ~ de** a revival of, a renewal of.

régal, -als [regal] *nm* treat, delight.

régaler [regale] *vt* to treat; **c'est moi qui régale!** it's my treat! ○ **se régaler** *vp* : **je me régale** [nourriture] I'm thoroughly enjoying it; [activité] I'm having the time of my life.

regard [rəgar] *nm* look.

regardant, -e [rəgardɑ̃, ɑ̃t] *adj fam* [minutieux] : **être très/peu ~ sur qqch** to be very/not very particular about sthg.

regarder [rəgarde] **1** *vt* [observer, examiner, consulter] to look at; [télévision, spectacle] to watch; ~ **qqn faire qqch** to watch sb doing sthg; ~ **les trains passer** to watch the trains go by. || [concerner] to concern; **cela ne te regarde pas** it's none of your business. **2** *vi* [observer, examiner] to look. || [faire attention] : **sans ~ à la dépense** regardless of the expense; **y ~ à deux fois** to think twice about it.

régate [regat] *nf* (*gén pl*) regatta.

régénérer [reʒenere] *vt* to regenerate. ○ **se régénérer** *vp* to regenerate.

régent, -e [reʒɑ̃, ɑ̃t] *nm, f* regent.

régenter [reʒɑ̃te] *vt* : **vouloir tout ~** *péj* to want to be the boss.

reggae [rege] *nm & adj inv* reggae.

régie [reʒi] *nf* [entreprise] state-controlled company. || RADIO & TÉLÉ [pièce] control room.

regimber [rəʒɛ̃be] *vi* to balk.

régime [reʒim] *nm* [politique] regime. || [alimentaire] diet; **se mettre au/suivre un ~** to go on/to be on a diet. || [de moteur] speed. || [de fleuve, des pluies] cycle. || [de bananes, dattes] bunch.

régiment [reʒimɑ̃] *nm* MIL regiment.

région [reʒjɔ̃] *nf* region.

régional, -e, -aux [reʒjɔnal, o] *adj* regional.

régir [reʒir] *vt* to govern.

régisseur [reʒisœr] *nm* [intendant] steward. || [de théâtre] stage manager.

registre [rəʒistr] *nm* [gén] register; ~ **de comptabilité** ledger.

réglable [reglabl] *adj* [adaptable] adjustable. || [payable] payable.

réglage [reglaʒ] *nm* adjustment, setting.

règle [regl] *nf* [instrument] ruler. || [principe, loi] rule; **je suis en ~** my papers are in order. ○ **en règle générale** *loc adv* as a general rule. ○ **règles** *nfpl* [menstruation] period (*sg*).

réglé, -e [regle] *adj* [organisé] regular, well-ordered.

règlement [regləmɑ̃] *nm* [résolution] settling; ~ **de comptes** *fig* settling of scores. || [règle] regulation. || [paiement] settlement.

réglementaire [regləmɑ̃tɛr] *adj* [régulier] statutory. || [imposé] regulation (*avant n*).

réglementation [regləmɑ̃tasjɔ̃] *nf* [action] regulation. || [ensemble de règles] regulations (*pl*), rules (*pl*).

régler [regle] *vt* [affaire, conflit] to settle, to sort out. || [appareil] to adjust. || [payer - note] to settle, to pay; [- commerçant] to pay.

réglisse [reglis] *nf* liquorice.

règne [rɛɲ] *nm* [de souverain] reign; **sous le ~ de** in the reign of. || [pouvoir] rule. || BIOL kingdom.

régner [reɲe] *vi* [souverain] to rule, to reign. || [silence] to reign.

regorger [rəgɔrʒe] *vi* : ~ **de** to be abundant in.

régresser [regrese] *vi* [sentiment, douleur] to diminish. || [personne] to regress.

régression [regresjɔ̃] *nf* [recul] decline. || PSYCHOL regression.

regret [rəgrɛ] *nm*: ~ (de) regret (for); à ~ with regret; sans ~ with no regrets.

regrettable [rəgrɛtabl] *adj* regrettable.

regretter [rəgrɛte] **1** *vt* [époque] to miss, to regret; [personne] to miss. || [faute] to regret; ~ **d'avoir fait qqch** to regret having done sthg. || [déplorer]: ~ **que** (+ *subjonctif*) to be sorry ou to regret that. **2** *vi* to be sorry.

regrouper [rəgrupe] *vt* [réunir] to group together. ○ **se regrouper** *vp* to gather, to assemble.

régulariser [regylarize] *vt* [documents] to sort out, to put in order; [situation] to straighten out.

régularité [regylarite] *nf* [gén] regularity. || [de travail, résultats] consistency.

régulation [regylasjɔ̃] *nf* [contrôle] control, regulation.

régulier, -ière [regylje, jɛr] *adj* [gén] regular. || [uniforme, constant] steady, regular. || [travail, résultats] consistent. || [légal] legal; **être en situation régulière** to have all the legally required documents.

régulièrement [regyljɛrmɑ̃] *adv* [gén] regularly. || [uniformément] steadily, regularly; [étalé, façonné] evenly.

réhabilitation [reabilitasjɔ̃] *nf* rehabilitation.

réhabiliter [reabilite] *vt* [accusé] to rehabilitate, to clear; *fig* [racheter] to restore to favour. || [rénover] to restore.

rehausser [rəose] *vt* [surélever] to heighten. || *fig* [mettre en valeur] to enhance.

rein [rɛ̃] *nm* kidney. ○ **reins** *nmpl* small of the back (*sg*); **avoir mal aux ~s** to have backache.

réincarnation [reɛ̃karnasjɔ̃] *nf* reincarnation.

reine [rɛn] *nf* queen.

réinsertion [reɛ̃sɛrsjɔ̃] *nf* [de délinquant] rehabilitation.

réintégrer [reɛ̃tegre] *vt* [rejoindre] to return to. || JUR to reinstate.

rejaillir [rəʒajir] *vi* to splash up; ~ **sur qqn** *fig* to rebound on sb.

rejet [rəʒɛ] *nm* [gén] rejection. || [pousse] shoot.

rejeter [rəʒte] *vt* [offre, personne] to reject. || [partie du corps]: ~ **la tête/les bras en arrière** to throw back one's head/

one's arms. || [imputer]: ~ **la responsabilité de qqch sur qqn** to lay the responsibility for sthg at sb's door.

rejeton [rəʒtɔ̃] *nm* offspring (*U*).

rejoindre [rəʒwɛ̃dr] *vt* [retrouver] to join. || [regagner] to return to. || [rattraper] to catch up with. ○ **se rejoindre** *vp* [personnes, routes] to meet.

rejoint, -e [rəʒwɛ̃, ɛ̃t] *pp* → **rejoindre**.

réjoui, -e [reʒwi] *adj* joyful.

réjouir [reʒwir] *vt* to delight. ○ **se réjouir** *vp* to be delighted; **se ~ de qqch** to be delighted at ou about sthg.

réjouissance [reʒwisɑ̃s] *nf* rejoicing. ○ **réjouissances** *nfpl* festivities.

relâche [rəlɑʃ] *nf* [pause]: **sans ~** without respite ou a break. || THÉÂTRE: **faire ~** to be closed.

relâchement [rəlɑʃmɑ̃] *nm* relaxation.

relâcher [rəlɑʃe] *vt* [étreinte, cordes] to loosen. || [discipline, effort] to relax, to slacken. || [prisonnier] to release. ○ **se relâcher** *vp* [se desserrer] to loosen. || [faiblir - discipline] to become lax; [- attention] to flag. || [se laisser aller] to slacken off.

relais [rəlɛ] *nm* [auberge] post house. || SPORT & TÉLÉ: **prendre/passer le ~** to take/hand over.

relance [rəlɑ̃s] *nf* [économique] revival, boost; [de projet] relaunch.

relancer [rəlɑ̃se] *vt* [renvoyer] to throw back. || [faire reprendre - économie] to boost; [- projet] to relaunch; [- moteur, machine] to restart.

relater [rəlate] *vt littéraire* to relate.

relatif, -ive [rəlatif, iv] *adj* relative; ~ **à** relating to; **tout est** ~ it's all relative.

relation [rəlasjɔ̃] *nf* relationship; **mettre qqn en ~ avec qqn** to put sb in touch with sb. ○ **relations** *nfpl* [rapport] relationship (*sg*); **~s sexuelles** sexual relations, intercourse (*U*). || [connaissance] acquaintance; **avoir des ~s** to have connections.

relative → **relatif**.

relativement [rəlativmɑ̃] *adv* relatively.

relativiser [rəlativize] *vt* to relativize.

relativité [rəlativite] *nf* relativity.

relax, relaxe [rəlaks] *adj fam* relaxed.

relaxation [rəlaksasjɔ̃] *nf* relaxation.

relaxe = **relax**.

relaxer [rəlakse] *vt* [reposer] to relax. || JUR to discharge. ○ **se relaxer** *vp* to relax.

relayer [rəleje] *vt* to relieve. ○ **se re-layer** *vp* to take over from one another.

relecture [rələktyr] *nf* second reading, rereading.

reléguer [rəlege] *vt* to relegate.

relent [rəlã] *nm* [odeur] stink, stench.

relevé, -e [rəlve] *adj* CULIN spicy. ○ **relevé** *nm* reading; **faire le ~ de** qqch to read sthg; **~ de compte** bank statement; **~ d'identité bancaire** bank account number.

relève [rəlεv] *nf* relief; **prendre la ~** to take over.

relever [rəlve] **1** *vt* [redresser - personne] to help up; [- pays, économie] to rebuild; [- moral, niveau] to raise. || [ramasser] to collect. || [tête, col, store] to raise; [manches] to push up. || [CULIN - mettre en valeur] to bring out; [- pimenter] to season. || [compteur] to read. || [relayer] to take over from, to relieve. || [erreur] to note. **2** *vi* [être du domaine]: **~ de** to come under. ○ **se relever** *vp* [se mettre debout] to stand up; [sortir du lit] to get up.

relief [rəljεf] *nm* relief; **en ~** in relief, raised; **une carte en ~** relief map; **mettre en ~** *fig* to enhance, to bring out.

relier [rəlje] *vt* [livre] to bind. || [joindre] to connect. || *fig* [associer] to link up.

religieux, -ieuse [rəliʒjø, jøz] *adj* [vie, chant] religious; [mariage] religious, church (*avant n*). || [respectueux] reverent. ○ **religieux** *nm* monk. ○ **religieuse** *nf* RELIG nun.

religion [rəliʒjɔ̃] *nf* [culte] religion. || [croyance] religion, faith.

relique [rəlik] *nf* relic.

relire [rəlir] *vt* [lire] to reread. || [vérifier] to read over.

reliure [rəljyr] *nf* binding.

reloger [rələʒe] *vt* to rehouse.

relu, -e [rəly] *pp* → **relire**.

reluire [rəlɥir] *vi* to shine, to gleam.

reluisant, -e [rəlɥizã, ãt] *adj* shining, gleaming; **peu** OU **pas très ~** *fig* [avenir, situation] not all that marvellous.

remaniement [rəmanimã] *nm* restructuring; **~ ministériel** cabinet reshuffle.

remarier [rəmarje] ○ **se remarier** *vp* to remarry.

remarquable [rəmarkabl] *adj* remarkable.

remarque [rəmark] *nf* [observation] remark; [critique] critical remark. || [annotation] note.

remarquer [rəmarke] **1** *vt* [apercevoir] to notice; **faire ~** qqch (à qqn) to point sthg out (to sb); **se faire ~** *péj* to draw attention to o.s. || [noter] to remark, to comment. **2** *vi*: **ce n'est pas l'idéal, remarque!** it's not ideal, mind you!

remblai [rãblε] *nm* embankment.

rembobiner [rãbɔbine] *vt* to rewind.

rembourrer [rãbure] *vt* to stuff, to pad.

remboursement [rãbursəmã] *nm* refund, repayment.

rembourser [rãburse] *vt* [dette] to pay back, to repay. || [personne] to pay back; **~ qqn de** qqch to reimburse sb for sthg.

remède [rəmεd] *nm* litt & fig remedy, cure.

remédier [rəmedje] *vi*: **~ à** qqch to put sthg right, to remedy sthg.

remembrement [rəmãbrəmã] *nm* land regrouping.

remerciement [rəmεrsimã] *nm* thanks (*pl*); **une lettre de ~** a thank-you letter.

remercier [rəmεrsje] *vt* [dire merci à] to thank; **~ qqn de** OU **pour** qqch to thank sb for sthg; **non, je vous remercie** no, thank you. || [congédier] to dismiss.

remettre [rəmεtr] *vt* [replacer] to put back; **~ en question** to call into question; **~ qqn à sa place** to put sb in his place. || [enfiler de nouveau] to put back on. || [rétablir - lumière, son] to put back on; **~ qqch en marche** to restart sthg; **~ une montre à l'heure** to put a watch right. || [donner]: **~ qqch à qqn** to hand sthg over to sb; [médaille, prix] to present sthg to sb. || [ajourner]: **~ qqch (à)** to put sthg off (until). ○ **se remettre** *vp* [recommencer]: **se ~ à** qqch to take up sthg again; **se ~ à fumer** to start smoking again. || [se rétablir] to get better; **se ~ de** qqch to get over sthg. || [redevenir]: **se ~ debout** to stand up again.

réminiscence [reminisãs] *nf* reminiscence.

remis, -e [rəmi, iz] *pp* → **remettre**.

remise [rəmiz] *nf* [action]: **~ en jeu** throw-in; **~ en question** OU **en cause** calling into question. || [de message, colis] handing over; [de médaille, prix] presentation. || [réduction] discount; **~ de peine** JUR remission. || [hangar] shed.

rémission [remisjɔ̃] *nf* remission.

remodeler [rəmɔdle] *vt* [forme] to remodel. || [remanier] to restructure.

remontant, -e [rəmɔ̃tã, ãt] *adj* [tonique] invigorating. ○ **remontant** *nm* tonic.

remonte-pente [rəmɔ̃tpɑ̃t] (*pl* **remonte-pentes**) *nm* ski-tow.

remonter [rəmɔ̃te] **1** *vt* (*aux: avoir*) [escalier, pente] to go/come back up. || [assembler] to put together again. || [manches] to turn up. || [horloge, montre] to wind up. || [ragaillardir] to put new life into, to cheer up. **2** *vi* (*aux: être*) [monter à nouveau - personne] to go/come back up; [- baromètre] to rise again; [- prix, température] to go up again, to rise; [- sur vélo] to get back on; **~ dans une voiture** to get back into a car. || [dater]: **~ à** to date *ou* go back to.

remontoir [rəmɔ̃twar] *nm* winder.

remontrer [rəmɔ̃tre] *vt* to show again; **vouloir en ~ à qqn** to try to show sb up.

remords [rəmɔr] *nm* remorse.

remorque [rəmɔrk] *nf* trailer; **être en ~** to be on tow.

remorquer [rəmɔrke] *vt* [voiture, bateau] to tow.

remorqueur [rəmɔrkœr] *nm* tug, tugboat.

remous [rəmu] **1** *nm* [de bateau] wash, backwash; [de rivière] eddy. **2** *nmpl fig* stir, upheaval.

rempailler [rɑ̃paje] *vt* to re-cane.

rempart [rɑ̃par] *nm* (*gén pl*) rampart.

remplaçant, -e [rɑ̃plasɑ̃, ɑ̃t] *nm, f* [suppléant] stand-in; SPORT substitute.

remplacement [rɑ̃plasmɑ̃] *nm* [changement] replacing, replacement. || [intérim] substitution; **faire des ~s** to stand in; [docteur] to act as a locum.

remplacer [rɑ̃plase] *vt* [gén] to replace. || [prendre la place de] to stand in for; SPORT to substitute.

remplir [rɑ̃plir] *vt* [gén] to fill; **~ de** to fill with; **~ qqn de joie/d'orgueil** to fill sb with happiness/pride. || [questionnaire] to fill in *ou* out. || [mission, fonction] to complete, to fulfil.

remplissage [rɑ̃plisaʒ] *nm* [de récipient] filling up. || *fig & péj* [de texte] padding out.

remporter [rɑ̃pɔrte] *vt* [repartir avec] to take away again. || [gagner] to win.

remuant, -e [rəmɥɑ̃, ɑ̃t] *adj* restless, overactive.

remue-ménage [rəmymenaʒ] *nm inv* commotion, confusion.

remuer [rəmɥe] **1** *vt* [bouger, émouvoir] to move. || [café, thé] to stir; [salade] to toss. **2** *vi* to move, to stir; **arrête de ~ comme ça** stop being so restless. ○ **se**

remuer *vp* [se mouvoir] to move. || *fig* [réagir] to make an effort.

rémunération [remynerasjɔ̃] *nf* remuneration.

rémunérer [remynere] *vt* [personne] to remunerate, to pay. || [activité] to pay for.

renâcler [rənakle] *vi fam* to make a fuss; **~ devant** *ou* **à qqch** to balk at sthg.

renaissance [rənɛsɑ̃s] *nf* rebirth.

renaître [rənɛtr] *vi* [ressusciter] to come back to life, to come to life again; **faire ~** [passé, tradition] to revive. || [revenir - sentiment, printemps] to return; [- économie] to revive, to recover.

renard [rənar] *nm* fox.

renchérir [rɑ̃ʃerir] *vi* [augmenter] to become more expensive; [prix] to go up. || [surenchérir]: **~ sur** to add to.

rencontre [rɑ̃kɔ̃tr] *nf* [gén] meeting; **faire une mauvaise ~** to meet an unpleasant person; **aller/venir à la ~ de qqn** to go/come to meet sb.

rencontrer [rɑ̃kɔ̃tre] *vt* [gén] to meet. || [heurter] to strike. ○ **se rencontrer** *vp* [gén] to meet. || [opinions] to agree.

rendement [rɑ̃dmɑ̃] *nm* [de machine, travailleur] output; [de terre, placement] yield.

rendez-vous [rɑ̃devu] *nm inv* [rencontre] appointment; [amoureux] date; **on a tous ~ au café** we're all meeting at the café; **prendre ~ avec qqn** to make an appointment with sb; **donner ~ à qqn** to arrange to meet sb. || [lieu] meeting place.

rendormir [rɑ̃dɔrmir] ○ **se rendormir** *vp* to go back to sleep.

rendre [rɑ̃dr] **1** *vt* [restituer]: **~ qqch à qqn** to give sthg back to sb, to return sthg to sb. || [donner en retour - invitation, coup] to return. || [JUR - jugement] to pronounce. || [vomir] to vomit, to cough up. || (+ *adj*) [faire devenir] to make; **~ qqn fou** to drive sb mad. || [exprimer] to render. **2** *vi* [produire - champ] to yield. || [vomir] to vomit, to be sick. ○ **se rendre** *vp* [céder, capituler] to give in; **j'ai dû me ~ à l'évidence** I had to face facts. || [aller]: **se ~ à** to go to. || (+ *adj*) [se faire tel]: **se ~ utile/malade** to make o.s. useful/ill.

rêne [rɛn] *nf* rein.

renégat, -e [rənega, at] *nm, f sout* renegade.

renfermé, -e [rɑ̃fɛrme] *adj* introverted,

withdrawn. ○ **renfermé** *nm*: ça sent le ~ it smells stuffy in here.
renfermer [rɑ̃fɛrme] *vt* [contenir] to contain. ○ **se renfermer** *vp* to withdraw.
renflé, -e [rɑ̃fle] *adj* bulging.
renflouer [rɑ̃flue] *vt* [bateau] to refloat. || *fig* [entreprise, personne] to bail out.
renfoncement [rɑ̃fɔ̃smɑ̃] *nm* recess.
renforcer [rɑ̃fɔrse] *vt* [contenir] to reinforce, to strengthen.
renfort [rɑ̃fɔr] *nm* reinforcement; venir en ~ to come as reinforcements.
renfrogné, -e [rɑ̃frɔɲe] *adj* scowling.
renfrogner [rɑ̃frɔɲe] ○ **se renfrogner** *vp* to scowl, to pull a face.
rengaine [rɑ̃gɛn] *nf* [formule répétée] (old) story. || [chanson] (old) song.
rengorger [rɑ̃gɔrʒe] ○ **se rengorger** *vp fig* to puff o.s. up.
renier [rənje] *vt* [famille, ami] to disown. || [foi, opinion] to renounce, to repudiate.
renifler [rənifle] **1** *vi* to sniff. **2** *vt* to sniff.
renne [rɛn] *nm* reindeer (*inv*).
renom [rənɔ̃] *nm* renown, fame.
renommé, -e [rənɔme] *adj* renowned, famous. ○ **renommée** *nf* renown, fame; de ~e internationale world-famous, internationally renowned.
renoncement [rənɔ̃smɑ̃] *nm*: ~ (à) renunciation (of).
renoncer [rənɔ̃se] *vi*: ~ à to give up; ~ à comprendre qqch to give up trying to understand sthg.
renouer [rənwe] **1** *vt* [lacet, corde] to re-tie, to tie up again. || [contact, conversation] to resume. **2** *vi*: ~ avec qqn to take up with sb again.
renouveau, -x [rənuvo] *nm* [transformation] revival.
renouvelable [rənuvlabl] *adj* renewable; [expérience] repeatable.
renouveler [rənuvle] *vt* [gén] to renew. ○ **se renouveler** *vp* [être remplacé] to be renewed. || [se répéter] to be repeated, to recur.
renouvellement [rənuvɛlmɑ̃] *nm* renewal.
rénovation [renɔvasjɔ̃] *nf* renovation, restoration.
rénover [renɔve] *vt* [immeuble] to renovate, to restore.
renseignement [rɑ̃sɛɲmɑ̃] *nm* information (*U*); un ~ a piece of information; prendre des ~s (sur) to make enquiries

(about). ○ **renseignements** *nmpl* [service d'information] enquiries, information.
renseigner [rɑ̃seɲe] *vt*: ~ qqn (sur) to give sb information (about), to inform sb (about). ○ **se renseigner** *vp* [s'enquérir] to make enquiries, to ask for information. || [s'informer] to find out.
rentabiliser [rɑ̃tabilize] *vt* to make profitable.
rentabilité [rɑ̃tabilite] *nf* profitability.
rentable [rɑ̃tabl] *adj* COMM profitable.
rente [rɑ̃t] *nf* [d'un capital] revenue, income. || [pension] pension, annuity.
rentier, -ière [rɑ̃tje, jɛr] *nm, f* person of independent means.
rentrée [rɑ̃tre] *nf* [fait de rentrer] return. || [reprise des activités]: la ~ parlementaire the reopening of parliament; la ~ des classes the start of the new school year. || [recette] income.
rentrer [rɑ̃tre] **1** *vi* (*aux: être*) [entrer de nouveau] to go/come back in; tout a fini par ~ dans l'ordre everything returned to normal. || [entrer] to go/come in. || [revenir chez soi] to go/come back, to go/come home. || [recouvrer, récupérer]: ~ dans ses frais to cover one's costs, to break even. || [se jeter avec violence]: ~ dans to crash into. || [s'emboîter] to go in, to fit. || [être perçu - fonds] to come in. **2** *vt* (*aux: avoir*) [mettre ou remettre à l'intérieur] to bring in. || [ventre] to pull in; [griffes] to retract, to draw in; [chemise] to tuck in. || *fig* [rage, larmes] to hold back.
renversant, -e [rɑ̃vɛrsɑ̃, ɑ̃t] *adj* staggering, astounding.
renverse [rɑ̃vɛrs] *nf*: tomber à la ~ to fall over backwards.
renversement [rɑ̃vɛrsəmɑ̃] *nm* [de situation] reversal.
renverser [rɑ̃vɛrse] *vt* [mettre à l'envers] to turn upside down. || [faire tomber] to knock over; [- piéton] to run over; [- liquide] to spill. || *fig* [régime] to overthrow; [ministre] to throw out of office. || [tête, buste] to tilt back. ○ **se renverser** *vp* [incliner le corps en arrière] to lean back. || [tomber] to overturn.
renvoi [rɑ̃vwa] *nm* [licenciement] dismissal. || [de colis, lettre] return, sending back. || [ajournement] postponement. || [référence] cross-reference. || JUR referral. || [éructation] belch.

renvoyer [rãvwaje] *vt* [faire retourner] to send back. || [congédier] to dismiss. || [colis, lettre] to send back, to return. || [balle] to throw back. || [réfléchir - lumière] to reflect; [- son] to echo. || [référer]: ~ **qqn à** to refer sb to. || [différer] to postpone, to put off.

réorganisation [reɔrganizasjɔ̃] *nf* reorganization.

réorganiser [reɔrganize] *vt* to reorganize.

réouverture [reuvɛrtyr] *nf* reopening.

repaire [rəpɛr] *nm* den.

répandre [repãdr] *vt* [verser, renverser] to spill. || [diffuser, dégager] to give off. || *fig* [effroi, terreur, nouvelle] to spread.

répandu, -e [repãdy] **1** *pp* → **répandre**. **2** *adj* [opinion, maladie] widespread.

réparable [reparabl] *adj* [objet] repairable. || [erreur] that can be put right.

réparateur, -trice [reparatœr, tris] **1** *adj* [sommeil] refreshing. **2** *nm, f* repairer.

réparation [reparasjɔ̃] *nf* [d'objet - action] repairing; [- résultat] repair; **en ~** under repair. || [de faute]: ~ (**de**) atonement (for). || [indemnité] reparation, compensation.

réparer [repare] *vt* [objet] to repair. || [faute, oubli] to make up for.

reparler [rəparle] *vi*: ~ **de qqn/qqch** to talk about sb/sthg again.

repartie [rəparti] *nf* retort; **avoir de la ~** to be good at repartee.

repartir [rəpartir] *vi* [retourner] to go back, to return. || [partir de nouveau] to set off again. || [recommencer] to start again.

répartir [repartir] *vt* [partager] to share out, to divide up. || [dans l'espace] to spread out, to distribute. || [classer] to divide or split up. ○ **se répartir** *vp* to divide up.

répartition [repartisjɔ̃] *nf* [partage] sharing out; [de tâches] allocation. || [dans l'espace] distribution.

repas [rəpa] *nm* meal; **prendre son ~** to eat.

repassage [rəpasaʒ] *nm* ironing.

repasser [rəpase] **1** *vi* (*aux: être*) [passer à nouveau] to go/come back; [film] to be on again. **2** *vt* (*aux: avoir*) [frontière, montagne] to cross again, to recross. || [examen] to resit. || [film] to show again. || [linge] to iron.

repêcher [rəpeʃe] *vt* [noyé, voiture] to fish out. || *fam* [candidat] to let through.

repeindre [rəpɛ̃dr] *vt* to repaint.

repeint, -e [rəpɛ̃, ɛ̃t] *pp* → **repeindre**.

repentir [rəpãtir] *nm* repentance. ○ **se repentir** *vp* to repent; **se ~ de qqch/d'avoir fait qqch** to be sorry for sthg/for having done sthg.

répercussion [repɛrkysjɔ̃] *nf* repercussion.

répercuter [repɛrkyte] *vt* [lumière] to reflect; [son] to throw back. || [ordre, augmentation] to pass on. ○ **se répercuter** *vp* [lumière] to be reflected; [son] to echo. || [influer]: **se ~ sur** to have repercussions on.

repère [rəpɛr] *nm* [marque] mark; [objet concret] landmark.

repérer [rəpere] *vt* [situer] to locate, to pinpoint. || *fam* [remarquer] to spot.

répertoire [repɛrtwar] *nm* [agenda] thumb-indexed notebook. || [de théâtre, d'artiste] repertoire. || INFORM directory.

répertorier [repɛrtɔrje] *vt* to make a list of.

répéter [repete] **1** *vt* [gén] to repeat. || [leçon] to go over, to learn; [rôle] to rehearse. **2** *vi* to rehearse. ○ **se répéter** *vp* [radoter] to repeat o.s. || [se reproduire] to be repeated.

répétitif, -ive [repetitif, iv] *adj* repetitive.

répétition [repetisjɔ̃] *nf* [réitération] repetition. || MUS & THÉÂTRE rehearsal.

repeupler [rəpœple] *vt* [région, ville] to repopulate. || [forêt] to replant; [étang] to restock.

repiquer [rəpike] *vt* [replanter] to plant out. || [disque, cassette] to re-record.

répit [repi] *nm* respite.

replacer [rəplase] *vt* [remettre] to replace, to put back. || [situer] to place, to put.

replanter [rəplãte] *vt* to replant.

replet, -ète [rəplɛ, ɛt] *adj* chubby.

repli [rəpli] *nm* [de tissu] fold; [de rivière] bend; [de troupes] withdrawal.

replier [rəplije] *vt* [plier de nouveau] to fold up again. || [ramener en pliant] to fold back. || [armée] to withdraw. ○ **se replier** *vp* [armée] to withdraw. || [personne]: **se ~ sur soi-même** to withdraw into o.s. || [journal, carte] to fold.

réplique [replik] *nf* [riposte] reply. || [d'acteur] line; **donner la ~ à qqn** to play opposite sb. || [copie] replica.

répliquer [replike] **1** *vt*: ~ **à qqn que** to reply to sb that. **2** *vi* [répondre] to reply;

[avec impertinence] to answer back. || *fig* [riposter] to retaliate.

replonger [rəplɔ̃ʒe] **1** *vt* to plunge back. **2** *vi* to dive back. ○ **se replonger** *vp*: se ~ **dans qqch** to immerse o.s. in sthg again.

répondeur [repɔ̃dœr] *nm*: ~ (**téléphonique** OU **automatique** OU -**enregistreur**) answering machine.

répondre [repɔ̃dr] **1** *vi*: ~ **à qqn** [faire connaître sa pensée] to answer sb, to reply to sb; [riposter] to answer sb back; ~ **à qqch** [en se défendant] to respond to sthg; ~ **au téléphone** to answer the telephone. **2** *vt* to answer, to reply. ○ **répondre à** *vt* [correspondre à - besoin] to answer; [- conditions] to meet. || [ressembler à - description] to match. ○ **répondre de** *vt* to answer for.

réponse [repɔ̃s] *nf* [action de répondre] answer, reply; **en ~ à votre lettre ...** in reply OU in answer OU in response to your letter .... || [solution] answer. || [réaction] response.

report [rəpɔr] *nm* [de réunion, rendezvous] postponement.

reportage [rəpɔrtaʒ] *nm* [article, enquête] report.

reporter¹ [rəpɔrtɛr] *nm* reporter.

reporter² [rəpɔrte] *vt* [rapporter] to take back. || [différer]: ~ **qqch à** to postpone sthg till, to put sthg off till. || [transférer]: ~ **sur** to transfer to. ○ **se reporter** *vp*: se ~ **à** [se référer à] to refer to.

repos [rəpo] *nm* [gén] rest; **prendre un jour de ~** to take a day off. || [tranquillité] peace and quiet.

reposé, -e [rəpoze] *adj* rested; **à tête ~e** with a clear head.

reposer [rəpoze] **1** *vt* [poser à nouveau] to put down again, to put back down. || [remettre] to put back. || [poser de nouveau - question] to ask again. || [appuyer] to rest. || [délasser] to rest, to relax. **2** *vi* [pâte] to sit, to stand; [vin] to stand. || [théorie]: ~ **sur** to rest on. ○ **se reposer** *vp* [se délasser] to rest. || [faire confiance]: se ~ **sur qqn** to rely on sb.

repoussant, -e [rəpusɑ̃, ɑ̃t] *adj* repulsive.

repousser [rəpuse] **1** *vi* to grow again, to grow back. **2** *vt* [écarter] to push away, to push back; [l'ennemi] to repel, to drive back. || [éconduire] to reject. || [proposition] to reject, to turn down. || [différer] to put back, to postpone.

répréhensible [repreɑ̃sibl] *adj* reprehensible.

reprendre [rəprɑ̃dr] **1** *vt* [prendre de nouveau] to take again; ~ **haleine** to get one's breath back. || [récupérer - objet prêté] to take back; [- prisonnier, ville] to recapture. || COMM [entreprise, affaire] to take over. || [se resservir]: ~ **un gâteau/de la viande** to take another cake/some more meat. || [recommencer] to resume. || [corriger] to correct. **2** *vi* [affaires, plante] to pick up. || [recommencer] to start again.

représailles [rəprezaj] *nfpl* reprisals.

représentant, -e [rəprezɑ̃tɑ̃, ɑ̃t] *nm, f* representative.

représentatif, -ive [rəprezɑ̃tatif, iv] *adj* representative.

représentation [rəprezɑ̃tasjɔ̃] *nf* [gén] representation. || [spectacle] performance.

représentativité [rəprezɑ̃tativite] *nf* representativeness.

représenter [rəprezɑ̃te] *vt* to represent. ○ **se représenter** *vp* [s'imaginer]: se ~ **qqch** to visualize sthg. || [se présenter à nouveau]: se ~ **à** [aux élections] to stand again at; [à un examen] to resit, to represent.

répression [represjɔ̃] *nf* [de révolte] repression. || [de criminalité, d'injustices] suppression.

réprimande [reprimɑ̃d] *nf* reprimand.

réprimander [reprimɑ̃de] *vt* to reprimand.

réprimer [reprime] *vt* [émotion, rire] to repress, to check. || [révolte, crimes] to put down, to suppress.

repris, -e [rəpri, iz] *pp* → **reprendre**. ○ **repris** *nm*: ~ **de justice** habitual criminal.

reprise [rəpriz] *nf* [recommencement - des hostilités] resumption, renewal; [- des affaires] revival, recovery; [- de pièce] revival; **à plusieurs ~s** on several occasions, several times. || BOXE round. || [raccommodage] mending.

repriser [rəprize] *vt* to mend.

réprobateur, -trice [reprɔbatœr, tris] *adj* reproachful.

réprobation [reprɔbasjɔ̃] *nf* disapproval.

reproche [rəprɔʃ] *nm* reproach; **faire des ~s à qqn** to reproach sb.

reprocher [rəprɔʃe] *vt*: ~ **qqch à qqn** to reproach sb for sthg. ○ **se reprocher** *vp*: se ~ (**qqch**) to blame o.s. (for sthg).

reproducteur, -trice [rəprɔdyktœr, tris] *adj* reproductive.

reproduction [rəprɔdyksjɔ̃] *nf* reproduction.

reproduire [rəprɔdyir] *vt* to reproduce. ○ **se reproduire** *vp* BIOL to reproduce, to breed. || [se répéter] to recur.

reproduit, -e [rəprɔdyi, yit] *pp* → **reproduire**.

réprouver [repruve] *vt* [blâmer] to reprove.

reptile [rɛptil] *nm* reptile.

repu, -e [rəpy] *adj* full, sated.

républicain, -e [repyblikɛ̃, ɛn] *adj* & *nm, f* republican.

république [repyblik] *nf* republic.

répudier [repydje] *vt* [femme] to repudiate.

répugnance [repyɲɑ̃s] *nf* [horreur] repugnance. || [réticence] reluctance; **avoir** ou **éprouver de la ~ à faire qqch** to be reluctant to do sthg.

répugnant, -e [repyɲɑ̃, ɑ̃t] *adj* repugnant.

répugner [repyɲe] *vi*: **~ à qqn** to disgust sb, to fill sb with repugnance; **~ à faire qqch** to be reluctant to do sthg, to be loath to do sthg.

répulsion [repylsjɔ̃] *nf* repulsion.

réputation [repytasjɔ̃] *nf* reputation; **avoir bonne/mauvaise ~** to have a good/bad reputation.

réputé, -e [repyte] *adj* famous, well-known.

requérir [rəkerir] *vt* [nécessiter] to require, to call for. || [solliciter] to solicit.

requête [rəkɛt] *nf* [prière] petition. || JUR appeal.

requiem [rekɥijɛm] *nm inv* requiem.

requin [rəkɛ̃] *nm* shark.

requis, -e [rəki, iz] **1** *pp* → **requérir**. **2** *adj* required, requisite.

réquisition [rekizisjɔ̃] *nf* MIL requisition.

réquisitionner [rekizisjɔne] *vt* to requisition.

réquisitoire [rekizitwar] *nm* JUR closing speech for the prosecution.

RER (*abr de* **réseau express régional**) *nm train service linking central Paris with its suburbs and airports.*

rescapé, -e [rɛskape] *nm, f* survivor.

rescousse [rɛskus] ○ **à la rescousse** *loc adv*: **venir à la ~ de qqn** to come to sb's rescue; **appeler qqn à la ~** to call on sb for help.

réseau, -x [rezo] *nm* network.

réservation [rezɛrvasjɔ̃] *nf* reservation.

réserve [rezɛrv] *nf* [gén] reserve; **en ~** in reserve. || [restriction] reservation; **faire des ~s (sur)** to have reservations (about); **sous ~ de** subject to; **sans ~** unreservedly. || [territoire] reserve; [- d'Indiens] reservation; **~ naturelle** nature reserve. || [local] storeroom.

réservé, -e [rezɛrve] *adj* reserved.

réserver [rezɛrve] *vt* [destiner]: **~ qqch (à qqn)** [chambre, place] to reserve ou book sthg (for sb); *fig* [surprise, désagrément] to have sthg in store (for sb). || [mettre de côté, garder]: **~ qqch (pour)** to put sthg on one side (for), to keep sthg (for). ○ **se réserver** *vp* [s'accorder]: **~ qqch** to keep sthg for o.s. || [se ménager] to save o.s.

réservoir [rezɛrvwar] *nm* [cuve] tank. || [bassin] reservoir.

résidence [rezidɑ̃s] *nf* [habitation] residence; **~ principale** main residence ou home; **~ secondaire** second home; **~ universitaire** hall of residence. || [immeuble] luxury apartment block *Am*.

résident, -e [rezidɑ̃, ɑ̃t] *nm, f* [de pays]: **les ~s français en Écosse** French nationals resident in Scotland. || [habitant d'une résidence] resident.

résidentiel, -ielle [rezidɑ̃sjɛl] *adj* residential.

résider [rezide] *vi* [habiter]: **~ à/dans/en** to reside in. || [consister]: **~ dans** to lie in.

résidu [rezidy] *nm* [reste] residue; [déchet] waste.

résignation [reziɲasjɔ̃] *nf* resignation.

résigné, -e [reziɲe] *adj* resigned.

résigner [reziɲe] ○ **se résigner** *vp*: **se ~ (à)** to resign o.s. (to).

résilier [rezilje] *vt* to cancel, to terminate.

résille [rezij] *nf* [pour cheveux] hairnet. || **bas ~** fishnet stockings.

résine [rezin] *nf* resin.

résistance [rezistɑ̃s] *nf* [gén, ÉLECTR & PHYS] resistance; **manquer de ~** to lack stamina; **opposer une ~** to put up resistance. || [de radiateur, chaudière] element.

résistant, -e [rezistɑ̃, ɑ̃t] **1** *adj* [personne] tough; [tissu] hard-wearing, tough; **être ~ au froid/aux infections** to be resistant to the cold/to infection. **2** *nm, f* [gén] resistance fighter; [de la Résistance] member of the Resistance.

résister [reziste] *vi* to resist; ~ à [attaque, désir] to resist; [tempête, fatigue] to withstand; [personne] to stand up to, to oppose.

résolu, -e [rezɔly] **1** *pp* → résoudre. **2** *adj* resolute; être bien ~ à faire qqch to be determined to do sthg.

résolument [rezɔlymã] *adv* resolutely.

résolution [rezɔlysjɔ̃] *nf* [décision] resolution; prendre la ~ de faire qqch to make a resolution to do sthg. || [détermination] resolve, determination. || [solution] solving.

résonance [rezɔnãs] *nf* ÉLECTR & PHYS resonance. || *fig* [écho] echo.

résonner [rezɔne] *vi* [retentir] to resound; [renvoyer le son] to echo.

résorber [rezɔrbe] *vt* [déficit] to absorb. || MÉD to resorb. ○ **se résorber** *vp* [déficit] to be absorbed. || MÉD to be resorbed.

résoudre [rezudr] *vt* [problème] to solve, to resolve. ○ **se résoudre** *vp*: se ~ à faire qqch to make up one's mind to do sthg, to decide ou resolve to do sthg.

respect [rεspε] *nm* respect.

respectable [rεspεktabl] *adj* respectable.

respecter [rεspεkte] *vt* to respect; faire ~ la loi to enforce the law.

respectif, -ive [rεspεktif, iv] *adj* respective.

respectivement [rεspεktivmã] *adv* respectively.

respectueux, -euse [rεspεktɥø, øz] *adj* respectful; être ~ de to have respect for.

respiration [rεspirasjɔ̃] *nf* breathing (*U*); retenir sa ~ to hold one's breath.

respiratoire [rεspiratwar] *adj* respiratory.

respirer [rεspire] **1** *vi* [inspirer-expirer] to breathe. || *fig* [être soulagé] to be able to breathe again. **2** *vt* [aspirer] to breathe in. || *fig* [exprimer] to exude.

resplendissant, -e [rεsplãdisã, ãt] *adj* radiant.

responsabilité [rεspɔ̃sabilite] *nf* [morale] responsibility; avoir la ~ de to be responsible for, to have the responsibility of. || JUR liability.

responsable [rεspɔ̃sabl] **1** *adj* [gén]: ~ (de) responsible (for); [légalement] liable (for); [chargé de] in charge of), responsible (for). || [sérieux] responsible. **2** *nmf* [auteur, coupable] person responsible. || [dirigeant] official. || [personne compétente] person in charge.

resquiller [rεskije] *vi* [au théâtre etc] to sneak in without paying. || [dans autobus etc] to dodge paying the fare.

resquilleur, -euse [rεskijœr, øz] *nm, f* [au théâtre etc] person who sneaks in without paying. || [dans autobus etc] fare-dodger.

ressac [rəsak] *nm* undertow.

ressaisir [rəsezir] ○ **se ressaisir** *vp* to pull o.s. together.

ressasser [rəsase] *vt* [répéter] to keep churning out.

ressemblance [rəsãblãs] *nf* [gén] resemblance, likeness; [trait] resemblance.

ressemblant, -e [rəsãblã, ãt] *adj* lifelike.

ressembler [rəsãble] *vi*: ~ à [physiquement] to resemble, to look like; [moralement] to be like, to resemble; cela ne lui ressemble pas that's not like him. ○ **se ressembler** *vp* to look alike, to resemble each other.

ressemeler [rəsəmle] *vt* to resole.

ressentiment [rəsãtimã] *nm* resentment.

ressentir [rəsãtir] *vt* to feel.

resserrer [rəsere] *vt* [ceinture, boulon] to tighten. || *fig* [lien] to strengthen. ○ **se resserrer** *vp* [route] to (become) narrow. || [nœud, étreinte] to tighten. || *fig* [relations] to grow stronger, to strengthen.

resservir [rəservir] **1** *vt* [personne] to give another helping to. **2** *vi* to be used again. ○ **se resservir** *vp*: se ~ de qqch [plat] to take another helping of sthg.

ressort [rəsɔr] *nm* [mécanisme] spring. || *fig* [énergie] spirit. || *fig* [compétence]: être du ~ de qqn to be sb's area of responsibility, to come under sb's jurisdiction. ○ **en dernier ressort** *loc adv* in the last resort, as a last resort.

ressortir [rəsɔrtir] *vi* (*aux: être*) [personne] to go out again. || *fig* [couleur]: ~ (sur) to stand out (against); faire ~ to highlight. || *fig* [résulter de]: ~ de to emerge from. **2** *vt* (*aux: avoir*) to take ou get ou bring out again.

ressortissant, -e [rəsɔrtisã, ãt] *nm, f* national.

ressource [rəsurs] *nf* resort. ○ **ressources** *nfpl* [financières] means. || [énergétiques, de langue] resources; ~s naturelles natural resources.

ressurgir [rəsyrʒir] *vi* to reappear.

ressusciter [resysite] *vi* to rise (from the dead); *fig* to revive.

restant, -e [rɛstɑ̃, ɑ̃t] *adj* remaining, left. ○ **restant** *nm* rest, remainder.

restaurant [rɛstɔrɑ̃] *nm* restaurant; **manger au ~** to eat out; **~ d'entreprise** staff canteen.

restaurateur, -trice [rɛstɔratœr, tris] *nm, f* CULIN restaurant owner. ‖ ART restorer.

restauration [rɛstɔrasjɔ̃] *nf* CULIN restaurant business; **~ rapide** fast food. ‖ ART & POLIT restoration.

restaurer [rɛstɔre] *vt* to restore. ○ **se restaurer** *vp* to have something to eat.

reste [rɛst] *nm* [de lait, temps]: **le ~ (de)** the rest (of). ‖ MATHS remainder. ○ **restes** *nmpl* [de repas] leftovers. ○ **au reste, du reste** *loc adv* besides.

rester [rɛste] **1** *vi* [dans lieu, état] to stay, to remain. ‖ [subsister] to remain, to be left; **le seul bien qui me reste** the only thing I have left. ‖ [s'arrêter]: **en ~ à qqch** to stop at sthg; **en ~ là** to finish there. ‖ *loc*: **y ~** *fam* [mourir] to pop one's clogs. **2** *v impers*: **il en reste un peu** there's still a little left; **il te reste de l'argent?** do you still have some money left?

restituer [rɛstitɥe] *vt* [argent, objet volé] to return, to restore. ‖ [énergie] to release. ‖ [son] to reproduce.

resto [rɛsto] *nm fam* restaurant; **les ~s du cœur** *charity food distribution centres*; **~-U** UNIV refectory.

restreindre [rɛstrɛ̃dr] *vt* to restrict. ○ **se restreindre** *vp* [domaine, champ] to narrow. ‖ [personne] to cut back.

restreint, -e [rɛstrɛ̃, ɛ̃t] *pp* → **restreindre**.

restrictif, -ive [rɛstriktif, iv] *adj* restrictive.

restriction [rɛstriksjɔ̃] *nf* [condition] condition; **sans ~** unconditionally. ‖ [limitation] restriction.

restructurer [rəstryktyre] *vt* to restructure.

résultat [rezylta] *nm* result; [d'action] outcome.

résulter [rezylte] **1** *vi*: **~ de** to be the result of, to result from. **2** *v impers*: **il en résulte que ...** as a result, ...

résumé [rezyme] *nm* summary, résumé; **en ~** [pour conclure] to sum up.

résumer [rezyme] *vt* to summarize. ○ **se résumer** *vp* [se réduire]: **se ~ à qqch/à faire qqch** to come down to sthg/to doing sthg.

résurgence [rezyrʒɑ̃s] *nf* resurgence.

résurrection [rezyrɛksjɔ̃] *nf* resurrection.

rétablir [retablir] *vt* [gén] to restore. ‖ [communications, contact] to re-establish. ○ **se rétablir** *vp* [silence] to return, to be restored. ‖ [malade] to recover. ‖ GYM to pull o.s. up.

rétablissement [retablismɑ̃] *nm* [d'ordre] restoration. ‖ [de communications] re-establishment. ‖ [de malade] recovery. ‖ GYM pull-up.

retard [rətar] *nm* [délai] delay; **être en ~** [sur heure] to be late; [sur échéance] to be behind; **avoir du ~** to be late ou delayed. ‖ [de pays, peuple, personne] backwardness.

retardataire [rətardatɛr] *nmf* [en retard] latecomer.

retardement [rətardəmɑ̃] *nm*: **à ~** belatedly; *voir aussi* **bombe**.

retarder [rətarde] **1** *vt* [personne, train] to delay; [sur échéance] to put back. ‖ [ajourner - rendez-vous] to put back ou off; [- départ] to put back ou off, to delay. **2** *vi* [horloge] to be slow. ‖ *fam* [ne pas être au courant] to be behind the times.

retenir [rətənir] *vt* [physiquement - objet, personne, cri] to hold back; [- souffle] to hold. ‖ [retarder] to keep, to detain. ‖ [chambre] to reserve. ‖ [leçon, cours] to remember. ‖ [projet] to accept, to adopt. ‖ [eau, chaleur] to retain. ‖ MATHS to carry. ‖ [intérêt, attention] to hold. ○ **se retenir** *vp* [s'accrocher]: **se ~ à** to hold onto; **se ~** to hold on; **se ~ de faire qqch** to refrain from doing sthg.

rétention [retɑ̃sjɔ̃] *nf* MÉD retention.

retentir [rətɑ̃tir] *vi* [son] to ring (out). ‖ *fig* [fatigue, blessure]: **~ sur** to have an effect on.

retentissant, -e [rətɑ̃tisɑ̃, ɑ̃t] *adj* resounding.

retentissement [rətɑ̃tismɑ̃] *nm* [de mesure] repercussions (*pl*).

retenu, -e [rətəny] *pp* → **retenir**.

retenue [rətəny] *nf* [prélèvement] deduction. ‖ MATHS amount carried. ‖ SCOL detention. ‖ *fig* [de personne - dans relations] reticence; [- dans comportement] restraint; **sans ~** without restraint.

réticence [retisɑ̃s] *nf* [hésitation] hesitation, reluctance; **avec ~** hesitantly.

réticent, -e [retisɑ̃, ɑ̃t] *adj* hesitant, reluctant.

rétine [retin] *nf* retina.

retiré, -e [rətire] *adj* [lieu] remote, isolated; [vie] quiet.

réunir

retirer [rətire] *vt* [vêtement, emballage] to take off, to remove; [permis, jouet] to take away; ~ qqch à qqn to take sthg away from sb. || [plainte] to withdraw, to take back. || [avantages, bénéfices]: ~ qqch de qqch to get ou derive sthg from sthg. || [bagages, billet] to collect; [argent] to withdraw. ○ **se retirer** *vp* [s'isoler] to withdraw, to retreat. || [refluer] to recede.

retombées [rətɔ̃be] *nfpl* repercussions, fallout (*sg*).

retomber [rətɔ̃be] *vi* [gymnaste, chat] to land. || [redevenir]: ~ malade to relapse. || [cheveux] to hang down. || *fig* [responsabilité]: ~ sur to fall on.

rétorquer [retɔrke] *vt* to retort; ~ à qqn que ... to retort to sb that ....

retors, -e [rətɔr, ɔrs] *adj* wily.

rétorsion [retɔrsjɔ̃] *nf* retaliation; mesures de ~ reprisals.

retouche [rətuʃ] *nf* [de texte, vêtement] alteration. || ART & PHOT touching up.

retoucher [rətuʃe] *vt* [texte, vêtement] to alter. || ART & PHOT to touch up.

retour [rətur] *nm* [gén] return; à mon/ton ~ when I/you get back, on my/your return; être de ~ (de) to be back (from). || [trajet] journey back, return journey.

retourner [rəturne] 1 *vt* (*aux: avoir*) [carte, matelas] to turn over; [terre] to turn over. || [compliment, objet prêté]: ~ qqch (à qqn) to return sthg (to sb). || [lettre, colis] to send back, to return. 2 *vi* (*aux: être*) to come/go back; ~ en arrière ou sur ses pas to retrace one's steps. ○ **se retourner** *vp* [basculer] to turn over. || [pivoter] to turn round. || *fig* [s'opposer]: se ~ contre to turn against.

retracer [rətrase] *vt* [ligne] to redraw. || [événement] to relate.

rétracter [retrakte] *vt* to retract. ○ **se rétracter** *vp* [se contracter] to retract. || [se dédire] to back down.

retrait [rətrɛ] *nm* [gén] withdrawal. || [de bagages] collection. || [des eaux] ebbing. ○ **en retrait** *loc adj* & *loc adv* [maison] set back from the road; rester en ~ *fig* to hang back. || [texte] indented.

retraite [rətrɛt] *nf* [gén] retreat. || [cessation d'activité] retirement; être à la ~ to be retired. || [revenu] (retirement) pension.

retraité, -e [rətrete] 1 *adj* [personne] retired. 2 *nm, f* retired person, pensioner.

retrancher [rətrɑ̃ʃe] *vt* [montant]: ~ qqch (de) to take sthg away (from), to deduct sthg (from). ○ **se retrancher** *vp* to entrench o.s.; se ~ derrière/dans *fig* to take refuge behind/in.

retransmettre [rətrɑ̃smɛtr] *vt* to broadcast.

retransmis, -e [rətrɑ̃smi, iz] *pp* → retransmettre.

retransmission [rətrɑ̃smisjɔ̃] *nf* broadcast.

retravailler [rətravaje] 1 *vt*: ~ qqch to work on sthg again. 2 *vi* to start work again.

rétrécir [retresir] *vi* [tissu] to shrink.

rétrécissement [retresismɑ̃] *nm* [de vêtement] shrinkage. || MÉD stricture.

rétribution [retribysjɔ̃] *nf* remuneration.

rétro [retro] 1 *nm fam* [rétroviseur] rear-view mirror. 2 *adj inv* old-style.

rétroactif, -ive [retroaktif, iv] *adj* retrospective.

rétrograde [retrograd] *adj péj* reactionary.

rétrograder [retrograde] 1 *vt* to demote. 2 *vi* AUTOM to change down.

rétroprojecteur [retroprɔʒɛktœr] *nm* overhead projector.

rétrospectif, -ive [retrospɛktif, iv] *adj* retrospective. ○ **rétrospective** *nf* retrospective.

rétrospectivement [retrospɛktivmɑ̃] *adv* retrospectively.

retrousser [rətruse] *vt* [manches, pantalon] to roll up. || [lèvres] to curl.

retrouvailles [rətruvaj] *nfpl* reunion (*sg*).

retrouver [rətruve] *vt* [gén] to find; [appétit] to recover, to regain. || [ami] to meet, to see. ○ **se retrouver** *vp* [entre amis] to meet (up) again; on se retrouve au café? shall we meet up ou see each other at the cafe? || [être de nouveau] to find o.s. again. || [s'orienter] to find one's way; ne pas s'y ~ [dans papiers] to be completely lost.

rétroviseur [retrovizœr] *nm* rear-view mirror.

réunification [reynifikasjɔ̃] *nf* reunification.

réunion [reynjɔ̃] *nf* [séance] meeting. || [jonction] union, merging. || [d'amis, de famille] reunion.

réunir [reynir] *vt* [fonds] to collect. || [qualités] to combine. || [personnes] to bring together; [- après séparation] to reunite. ○ **se réunir** *vp* [personnes] to meet. || [fleuves, rues] to converge.

réussi, -e [reysi] *adj* successful.

réussir [reysir] **1** *vi* [personne, affaire] to succeed, to be a success; **~ à faire qqch** to succeed in doing sthg. || [climat]: **~ à** to agree with. **2** *vt* [portrait, plat] to make a success of. || [examen] to pass.

réussite [reysit] *nf* [succès] success. || [jeu de cartes] patience *Br*, solitaire *Am*.

réutiliser [reytilize] *vt* to reuse.

revaloriser [rəvalɔrize] *vt* [monnaie] to revalue; [salaires] to raise.

revanche [rəvãʃ] *nf* [vengeance] revenge; **prendre sa ~** to take one's revenge. || SPORT return (match). ○ **en revanche** *loc adv* [par contre] on the other hand.

rêvasser [rɛvase] *vi* to daydream.

rêve [rɛv] *nm* dream.

rêvé, -e [rɛve] *adj* ideal.

revêche [rəvɛʃ] *adj* surly.

réveil [revɛj] *nm* [de personne] waking (up). || [pendule] alarm clock.

réveiller [reveje] *vt* [personne] to wake up. || [courage] to revive. ○ **se réveiller** *vp* [personne] to wake (up).

réveillon [revɛjɔ̃] *nm* [jour - de Noël] Christmas Eve; [- de nouvel an] New Year's Eve.

réveillonner [revɛjɔne] *vi* to have a Christmas Eve/New Year's Eve meal.

révélateur, -trice [revelatœr, tris] *adj* revealing.

révélation [revelasjɔ̃] *nf* [gén] revelation. || [artiste] discovery.

révéler [revele] *vt* [gén] to reveal. || [artiste] to discover. ○ **se révéler** *vp* [s'avérer] to prove to be.

revenant [rəvnã] *nm* [fantôme] spirit, ghost. || *fam* [personne] stranger.

revendeur, -euse [rəvãdœr, øz] *nm, f* retailer.

revendication [rəvãdikasjɔ̃] *nf* claim, demand.

revendiquer [rəvãdike] *vt* [dû, responsabilité] to claim; [avec force] to demand.

revendre [rəvãdr] *vt* [après utilisation] to resell.

revendu, -e [rəvãdy] *pp* → **revendre**.

revenir [rəvnir] *vi* [gén] to come back, to return; **~ sur** [sujet] to go over again; [décision] to go back on; **~ à soi** to come to. || [mot, sujet] to crop up. || [à l'esprit]: **~ à** to come back to. || [impliquer]: **cela revient au même/à dire que ... il** amounts to the same thing/to saying (that) .... || [coûter]: **~ à** to come to, to amount to; **~ cher** to be expensive. ||

[honneur, tâche]: **~ à** to fall to. || CULIN: **faire ~** to brown. || *loc*: **sa tête ne me revient pas** I don't like the look of him/her; **il n'en revenait pas** he couldn't get over it.

revente [rəvãt] *nf* resale.

revenu, -e [rəvny] *pp* → **revenir**. ○ **revenu** *nm* [de pays] revenue; [de personne] income.

rêver [rɛve] **1** *vi* to dream; [rêvasser] to daydream; **~ de/à** to dream of/about. **2** *vt* to dream; **~ que** to dream (that).

réverbération [reverberasjɔ̃] *nf* reverberation.

réverbère [reverber] *nm* street lamp ou light.

révérence [reverãs] *nf* [salut] bow.

révérend, -e [reverã, ãd] *adj* reverend. ○ **révérend** *nm* reverend.

rêverie [rɛvri] *nf* reverie.

revers [rəver] *nm* [de main] back; [de pièce] reverse. || [de veste] lapel; [de pantalon] turn-up *Br*, cuff *Am*. || TENNIS backhand. || *fig* [de fortune] reverse.

réversible [reversibl] *adj* reversible.

revêtement [rəvɛtmã] *nm* surface.

revêtir [rəvɛtir] *vt* [mur, surface]: **~ (de)** to cover (with). || [aspect] to take on, to assume. || [vêtement] to put on.

revêtu, -e [rəvɛty] *pp* → **revêtir**.

rêveur, -euse [rɛvœr, øz] **1** *adj* dreamy. **2** *nm, f* dreamer.

revient [rəvjɛ̃] → **prix**.

revigorer [rəvigɔre] *vt* to invigorate.

revirement [rəvirmã] *nm* change.

réviser [revize] *vt* [réexaminer, modifier] to revise, to review. || SCOL to revise. || [machine] to check.

révision [revizjɔ̃] *nf* [réexamen, modification] revision, review. || SCOL revision. || [de machine] checkup.

revisser [rəvise] *vt* to screw back again.

revivre [rəvivr] **1** *vi* [personne] to come back to life, to revive; *fig* [espoir] to be revived, to revive; **faire ~** to revive. **2** *vt* to relive; **faire ~ qqch à qqn** to bring sthg back to sb.

revoici [rəvwasi] *prép*: **me ~!** it's me again!, I'm back!

revoir [rəvwar] *vt* [renouer avec] to see again. || [corriger, étudier] to review *Am*. ○ **se revoir** *vp* [amis] to see each other again. ○ **au revoir** *interj* & *nm* goodbye.

révoltant, -e [revɔltã, ãt] *adj* revolting.

révolte [revɔlt] *nf* revolt.

révolter [revolte] *vt* to disgust. ○ **se révolter** *vp*: se ~ (**contre**) to revolt (against).

révolu, -e [revoly] *adj* past; avoir 15 ans ~s ADMIN to be over 15.

révolution [revolysjɔ̃] *nf* [gén] revolution. || *fam* [effervescence] uproar.

révolutionnaire [revolysjɔner] *nmf & adj* revolutionary.

révolutionner [revolysjɔne] *vt* [transformer] to revolutionize. || [mettre en émoi] to stir up.

revolver [revolver] *nm* revolver.

révoquer [revoke] *vt* [fonctionnaire] to dismiss. || [loi] to revoke.

revue [rovy] *nf* [gén] review; ~ de presse press review; passer en ~ *fig* to review. || [défilé] march-past. || [magazine] magazine. || [spectacle] revue.

rez-de-chaussée [redʃose] *nm inv* ground floor *Br*, first floor *Am*.

RFA (*abr de* **République fédérale d'Allemagne**) *nf* FRG.

rhabiller [rabije] *vt* to dress again. ○ **se rhabiller** *vp* to get dressed again.

rhésus [rezys] *nm* rhesus (factor); ~ positif/négatif rhesus positive/negative.

rhétorique [retɔrik] *nf* rhetoric.

Rhin [rɛ̃] *nm*: le ~ the Rhine.

rhinocéros [rinɔseros] *nm* rhinoceros.

rhino-pharyngite [rinɔfarɛ̃ʒit] (*pl* rhino-pharyngites) *nf* throat infection.

rhododendron [rɔdɔdɛ̃drɔ̃] *nm* rhododendron.

Rhône [ron] *nm*: le ~ the (River) Rhone.

rhubarbe [rybarb] *nf* rhubarb.

rhum [rɔm] *nm* rum.

rhumatisme [rymatism] *nm* rheumatism.

rhume [rym] *nm* cold; attraper un ~ to catch a cold; ~ des foins hay fever.

ri [ri] *pp inv* → **rire**.

riant, -e [rijɑ̃, ɑ̃t] *adj* smiling; *fig* cheerful.

RIB, Rib [rib] (*abr de* **relevé d'identité bancaire**) *nm* bank account identification slip.

ribambelle [ribɑ̃bɛl] *nf*: ~ de string of.

ricaner [rikane] *vi* to snigger.

riche [riʃ] 1 *adj* [gén] rich; [personne, pays] rich, wealthy; ~ en ou de rich in. 2 *nmf* rich person; les ~s the rich.

richesse [riʃɛs] *nf* [de personne, pays] wealth (*U*). || [de faune, flore] abundance. ○ **richesses** *nfpl* [gén] wealth (*U*).

ricochet [rikɔʃɛ] *nm litt & fig* rebound; [de balle d'arme] ricochet.

rictus [riktys] *nm* rictus.

ride [rid] *nf* wrinkle; [de surface d'eau] ripple.

rideau, -x [rido] *nm* curtain; ~ de fer [frontière] Iron Curtain.

rider [ride] *vt* [peau] to wrinkle. || [surface] to ruffle. ○ **se rider** *vp* to become wrinkled.

ridicule [ridikyl] 1 *adj* ridiculous. 2 *nm*: se couvrir de ~ to make o.s. look ridiculous; tourner qqn/qqch en ~ to ridicule sb/sthg.

ridiculiser [ridikylize] *vt* to ridicule. ○ **se ridiculiser** *vp* to make o.s. look ridiculous.

rien [rjɛ̃] 1 *pron indéf* [en contexte négatif]: ne ... rien nothing, not ... anything; je n'ai ~ fait I've done nothing, I haven't done anything. || [aucune chose] nothing; que fais-tu? — ~ what are you doing? — nothing; ~ de nouveau nothing new; ~ du tout nothing at all; ~ à faire it's no good; de ~! don't mention it!, not at all!; pour ~ for nothing. || [quelque chose] anything; sans ~ dire without saying anything. 2 *nm*: pour un ~ [se fâcher, pleurer] for nothing, at the slightest thing; en un ~ de temps in no time at all. ○ **rien que** *loc adv* only, just; la vérité, ~ que la vérité the truth and nothing but the truth.

rieur, rieuse [rijœr, rijøz] *adj* cheerful.

rigide [riʒid] *adj* rigid; [muscle] tense.

rigidité [riʒidite] *nf* rigidity; [de principes, mœurs] strictness.

rigole [rigɔl] *nf* channel.

rigoler [rigɔle] *vi fam* [rire] to laugh. || [plaisanter]: ~ (de) to joke (about).

rigolo, -ote [rigɔlo, ɔt] *fam* 1 *adj* funny. 2 *nm, f péj* phoney.

rigoureux, -euse [rigurø, øz] *adj* [discipline, hiver] harsh. || [analyse] rigorous.

rigueur [rigœr] *nf* [de punition] severity, harshness. || [de climat] harshness. || [d'analyse] rigour, exactness. ○ **à la rigueur** *loc adv* if necessary, if need be.

rime [rim] *nf* rhyme.

rimer [rime] *vi*: ~ (**avec**) to rhyme (with).

rinçage [rɛ̃saʒ] *nm* rinsing.

rincer [rɛ̃se] *vt* [bouteille] to rinse out; [cheveux, linge] to rinse.

ring [riŋ] *nm* BOXE ring. || *Belg* [route] bypass.

riposte [ripɔst] *nf* [réponse] retort, riposte. ‖ [contre-attaque] counterattack.

riposter [ripɔste] 1 *vt*: ~ que to retort ou riposte that. 2 *vi* [répondre] to riposte. ‖ [contre-attaque] to counter, to retaliate.

rire [rir] 1 *nm* laugh; éclater de ~ to burst out laughing. 2 *vi* [gén] to laugh. ‖ [plaisanter]: **pour ~** *fam* as a joke, for a laugh.

risée [rize] *nf* ridicule; être la ~ de to be the laughing stock of.

risible [rizibl] *adj* [ridicule] ridiculous.

risque [risk] *nm* risk; à tes/vos ~s et périls at your own risk.

risqué, -e [riske] *adj* [entreprise] risky, dangerous.

risquer [riske] *vt* [vie, prison] to risk; ~ **de faire qqch** to be likely to do sthg; **je risque de perdre tout ce que j'ai** I'm running the risk of losing everything I have. ‖ [tenter] to venture. ○ **se risquer** *vp* to venture; **se ~ à faire qqch** to dare to do sthg.

rissoler [risɔle] *vi* to brown.

rite [rit] *nm* RELIG rite. ‖ [cérémonial & *fig*] ritual.

rituel, -elle [rityɛl] *adj* ritual. ○ **rituel** *nm* ritual.

rivage [rivaʒ] *nm* shore.

rival, -e, -aux [rival, o] 1 *adj* rival (*avant n*). 2 *nm, f* rival.

rivaliser [rivalize] *vi*: ~ **avec** to compete with.

rivalité [rivalite] *nf* rivalry.

rive [riv] *nf* [de rivière] bank.

river [rive] *vt* [fixer]: ~ **qqch à qqch** to rivet sthg to sthg. ‖ [clou] to clinch; être rivé à *fig* to be riveted ou glued to.

riverain, -e [rivrɛ̃, ɛn] *nm, f* resident.

rivet [rivɛ] *nm* rivet.

rivière [rivjɛr] *nf* river.

rixe [riks] *nf* fight, brawl.

riz [ri] *nm* rice.

rizière [rizjɛr] *nf* paddy (field).

RMI (*abr de* **revenu minimum d'insertion**) *nm* minimum guaranteed income (for people with no other source of income).

robe [rɔb] *nf* [de femme] dress; ~ **de mariée** wedding dress. ‖ [peignoir]: ~ **de chambre** dressing gown. ‖ [de cheval] coat. ‖ [de vin] colour.

robinet [rɔbinɛ] *nm* tap.

robinetterie [rɔbinɛtri] *nf* [installations] taps (*pl*).

robot [rɔbo] *nm* [gén] robot. ‖ [ménager] food processor.

robotique [rɔbɔtik] *nf* robotics (*U*).

robuste [rɔbyst] *adj* [personne, santé] robust. ‖ [plante] hardy. ‖ [voiture] sturdy.

roc [rɔk] *nm* rock.

rocade [rɔkad] *nf* bypass.

rocaille [rɔkaj] *nf* [cailloux] loose stones (*pl*). ‖ [dans jardin] rock garden, rockery.

rocailleux, -euse [rɔkajø, øz] *adj* [terrain] rocky. ‖ *fig* [voix] harsh.

rocambolesque [rɔkɑ̃bɔlɛsk] *adj* fantastic.

roche [rɔʃ] *nf* rock.

rocher [rɔʃe] *nm* rock.

rocheux, -euse [rɔʃø, øz] *adj* rocky. ○ **Rocheuses** *nfpl*: **les Rocheuses** the Rockies.

rock [rɔk] *nm* rock ('n' roll).

rodage [rɔdaʒ] *nm* [de véhicule] running-in; «**en ~**» "running in".

rodéo [rɔdeo] *nm* rodeo.

roder [rɔde] *vt* [véhicule] to run in. ‖ *fam* [méthode] to run in, to debug; [personne] to break in.

rôdeur, -euse [rɔdœr, øz] *nm, f* prowler.

rogne [rɔɲ] *nf fam* bad temper; être/se mettre en ~ to be in/to get into a bad mood, to be in/to get into a temper.

rogner [rɔɲe] 1 *vt* [ongles] to trim. ‖ [revenus] to eat into. 2 *vi*: ~ **sur qqch** to cut down on sthg.

roi [rwa] *nm* king; tirer les ~s to celebrate Epiphany.

rôle [rol] *nm* role, part.

romain, -e [rɔmɛ̃, ɛn] *adj* Roman. ○ **Romain, -e** *nm, f* Roman.

roman, -e [rɔmɑ̃, an] *adj* [langue] Romance. ‖ ARCHIT Romanesque. ○ **roman** *nm* LITTÉRATURE novel.

romance [rɔmɑ̃s] *nf* [chanson] love song.

romancier, -ière [rɔmɑ̃sje, jɛr] *nm, f* novelist.

romanesque [rɔmanɛsk] *adj* LITTÉRATURE novelistic. ‖ [aventure] fabulous, storybook (*avant n*).

roman-feuilleton [rɔmɑ̃fœjtɔ̃] *nm* serial; *fig* soap opera.

roman-photo [rɔmɑ̃foto] *nm* story told in photographs.

romantique [rɔmɑ̃tik] *nmf & adj* romantic.

romantisme [rɔmɑ̃tism] *nm* ART Romantic movement. ‖ [sensibilité] romanticism.

rouler

romarin [rɔmarɛ̃] *nm* rosemary.

rompre [rɔ̃pr] **1** *vt sout* [objet] to break. || [charme, marché] to break; [fiançailles, relations] to break off. **2** *vi* to break; ~ avec qqn *fig* to break up with sb. ○ **se rompre** *vp* to break; **se ~ le cou/les reins** to break one's neck/back.

ronce [rɔ̃s] *nf* [arbuste] bramble.

ronchonner [rɔ̃ʃɔne] *vi fam*: ~ (après) to grumble (at).

rond, -e [rɔ̃, rɔ̃d] *adj* [forme, chiffre] round. || [joue, ventre] chubby, plump. || *fam* [ivre] tight. ○ **rond** *nm* [cercle] circle; **en ~** in a circle or ring; **tourner en ~** *fig* to go round in circles. || [anneau] ring. || *fam* [argent]: **je n'ai pas un ~** I haven't got a penny or bean.

ronde [rɔ̃d] *nf* [de surveillance] rounds (*pl*); [de policier] beat. || [danse] round. || MUS semibreve *Br*, whole note *Am*. ○ **à la ronde** *loc adv*: **à des kilomètres à la ~** for miles around.

rondelle [rɔ̃dɛl] *nf* [de saucisson] slice. || [de métal] washer.

rondeur [rɔ̃dœr] *nf* [forme] roundness. || [partie charnue] curve.

rond-point [rɔ̃pwɛ̃] *nm* roundabout *Br*, traffic circle *Am*.

ronflant, -e [rɔ̃flɑ̃, ɑ̃t] *adj péj* grandiose.

ronflement [rɔ̃fləmɑ̃] *nm* [de dormeur] snore. || [de poêle, moteur] hum, purr.

ronfler [rɔ̃fle] *vi* [dormeur] to snore. || [poêle, moteur] to hum, to purr.

ronger [rɔ̃ʒe] *vt* [bois, os] to gnaw; [métal, falaise] to eat away at. ○ **se ronger** *vp* [grignoter]: **se ~ les ongles** to bite one's nails. || *fig* [se tourmenter] to worry, to torture o.s.

rongeur, -euse [rɔ̃ʒœr, øz] *adj* gnawing, rodent (*avant n*). ○ **rongeur** *nm* rodent.

ronronner [rɔ̃rɔne] *vi* [chat] to purr; [moteur] to purr, to hum.

rosace [rozas] *nf* [vitrail] rose window. || [figure géométrique] rosette.

rosbif [rɔzbif] *nm* [viande] roast beef.

rose [roz] **1** *nf* rose. **2** *nm* pink. **3** *adj* pink.

rosé, -e [roze] *adj* [teinte] rosy. ○ **rosé** *nm* rosé. ○ **rosée** *nf* dew.

roseau, -x [rozo] *nm* reed.

rosier [rozje] *nm* rose bush.

rosir [rozir] *vt* & *vi* to turn pink.

rosser [rɔse] *vt* to thrash.

rossignol [rɔsiɲɔl] *nm* [oiseau] nightingale.

rot [ro] *nm* burp.

rotatif, -ive [rɔtatif, iv] *adj* rotary.

rotation [rɔtasjɔ̃] *nf* rotation.

roter [rɔte] *vi fam* to burp.

rôti, -e [roti] *adj* roast. ○ **rôti** *nm* roast, joint.

rotin [rɔtɛ̃] *nm* rattan.

rôtir [rotir] *vt* to roast.

rôtisserie [rotisri] *nf* [magasin] *shop selling roast meat*.

rotonde [rɔtɔ̃d] *nf* [bâtiment] rotunda.

rotule [rɔtyl] *nf* kneecap.

rouage [rwaʒ] *nm* cog, gearwheel; **les ~s de l'État** *fig* the wheels of State.

rouble [rubl] *nm* rouble.

roucouler [rukule] *vi* to coo.

roue [ru] *nf* [gén] wheel; ~ **de secours** spare wheel. || [de paon]: **faire la ~** to display. || GYM cartwheel.

rouer [rwe] *vt*: ~ **qqn de coups** to thrash sb, to beat sb.

rouge [ruʒ] **1** *nm* [couleur] red. || *fam* [vin] red (wine). || [fard] rouge, blusher; ~ **à lèvres** lipstick. || AUTOM: **passer au ~** to turn red; [conducteur] to go through a red light. **2** *adj* [gén] red. || [fer, tison] red-hot.

rouge-gorge [ruʒgɔrʒ] *nm* robin.

rougeole [ruʒɔl] *nf* measles (*sg*).

rougeoyer [ruʒwaje] *vi* to turn red.

rougeur [ruʒœr] *nf* [sur peau] red spot or blotch.

rougir [ruʒir] **1** *vt* [colorer] to turn red. || [chauffer] to make red-hot. **2** *vi* [devenir rouge] to turn red. || [d'émotion]: ~ (de) [de plaisir, colère] to flush (with); [de gêne] to blush (with). || *fig* [avoir honte]: ~ **de qqch** to be ashamed of sthg.

rouille [ruj] **1** *nf* [oxyde] rust. || CULIN *spicy garlic sauce for fish soup*. **2** *adj inv* rust.

rouiller [ruje] **1** *vt* to rust, to make rusty. **2** *vi* to rust.

roulade [rulad] *nf* [galipette] roll.

rouleau, -x [rulo] *nm* [gén & TECHNOL] roller; ~ **compresseur** steamroller. || [de papier] roll. || [à pâtisserie] rolling pin.

roulement [rulmɑ̃] *nm* [de personnel] rotation. || [de tambour, tonnerre] roll. || TECHNOL rolling bearing.

rouler [rule] **1** *vt* [déplacer] to wheel. || [enrouler - tapis] to roll up; [- cigarette] to roll. || LING to roll. || *fam fig* [duper] to swindle, to do. **2** *vi* [ballon, bateau] to roll. || [véhicule] to go, to run; [suj: personne] to drive. ○ **se rouler** *vp* to roll about; **se ~ en boule** to roll o.s. into a ball.

roulette [rulɛt] *nf* [petite roue] castor. || [de dentiste] drill. || JEU roulette.

roulis [ruli] *nm* roll.

roulotte [rulɔt] *nf* [de gitan] caravan; [de tourisme] caravan *Br*, trailer *Am*.

roumain, -e [rumɛ̃, ɛn] *adj* Romanian. ○ **roumain** *nm* [langue] Romanian. ○ **Roumain, -e** *nm, f* Romanian.

Roumanie [rumani] *nf:* **la ~** Romania.

rouquin, -e [rukɛ̃, in] *fam* **1** *adj* red-headed. **2** *nm, f* redhead.

rouspéter [ruspete] *vi fam* to grumble, to moan.

rousse → **roux.**

rousseur → **tache.**

roussir [rusir] **1** *vt* [rendre roux] to turn brown. || [brûler légèrement] to singe. **2** *vi* to turn brown; CULIN to brown.

route [rut] *nf* [gén] road; **en ~** on the way; **en ~!** let's go!; **mettre en ~** [démarrer] to start up; *fig* to get under way. || [itinéraire] route.

routier, -ière [rutje, jɛr] *adj* road (*avant n*). ○ **routier** *nm* [chauffeur] long-distance lorry driver *Br* ou trucker *Am*.|| [restaurant] ≃ truck stop *Am*.

routine [rutin] *nf* routine.

rouvert, -e [ruver, ɛrt] *pp* → **rouvrir.**

rouvrir [ruvrir] *vt* to reopen, to open again. ○ **se rouvrir** *vp* to reopen, to open again.

roux, rousse [ru, rus] **1** *adj* [cheveux] red. || [sucre] brown. **2** *nm, f* [personne] redhead.

royal, -e, -aux [rwajal, o] *adj* [de roi] royal. || [magnifique] princely.

royaliste [rwajalist] *nmf & adj* royalist.

royaume [rwajom] *nm* kingdom.

Royaume-Uni [rwajomyni] *nm:* **le ~** the United Kingdom.

royauté [rwajɔte] *nf* [fonction] king-ship. || [régime] monarchy.

RPR (*abr de* **Rassemblement pour la République**) *nm French political party to the right of the political spectrum.*

rte *abr de* **route.**

ruade [rɥad] *nf* kick.

ruban [rybɑ̃] *nm* ribbon; **~ adhésif** adhesive tape.

rubéole [rybeɔl] *nf* German measles (*sg*), rubella.

rubis [rybi] *nm* [pierre précieuse] ruby.

rubrique [rybrik] *nf* [chronique] column. || [dans classement] heading.

ruche [ryʃ] *nf* [abri] hive, beehive.

rude [ryd] *adj* [surface] rough. || [voix] harsh. || [personne, manières] rough, un-couth. || [hiver, épreuve] harsh, severe; [tâche, adversaire] tough.

rudement [rydmɑ̃] *adv* [brutalement - tomber] hard; [- répondre] harshly. || *fam* [très] damn.

rudesse [rydɛs] *nf* harshness, severity.

rudimentaire [rydimɑ̃ter] *adj* rudi-mentary.

rudoyer [rydwaje] *vt* to treat harshly.

rue [ry] *nf* street.

ruée [rɥe] *nf* rush.

ruelle [rɥɛl] *nf* [rue] alley, lane.

ruer [rɥe] *vi* to kick. ○ **se ruer** *vp:* **se ~ sur** to pounce on.

rugby [rygbi] *nm* rugby.

rugir [ryʒir] *vi* to roar; [vent] to howl.

rugissement [ryʒismɑ̃] *nm* roar, roar-ing (*U*); [de vent] howling.

rugosité [rygozite] *nf* [de surface] roughness. || [aspérité] rough patch.

rugueux, -euse [rygø, øz] *adj* rough.

ruine [rɥin] *nf* [gén] ruin. || [effondre-ment] ruin, downfall. || [humaine] wreck.

ruiner [rɥine] *vt* to ruin. ○ **se ruiner** *vp* to ruin o.s., to bankrupt o.s.

ruineux, -euse [rɥinø, øz] *adj* ruinous.

ruisseau, -x [rɥiso] *nm* [cours d'eau] stream. || *fig & péj* [caniveau] gutter.

ruisseler [rɥisle] *vi:* **~ (de)** to stream (with).

rumeur [rymœr] *nf* [bruit] murmur. || [nouvelle] rumour.

ruminer [rymine] *vt* to ruminate; *fig* to mull over.

rupture [ryptyr] *nf* [cassure] breaking. || *fig* [changement] abrupt change. || [de négociations, fiançailles] breaking off; [de contrat] breach. || [amoureuse] breakup.

rural, -e, -aux [ryral, o] *adj* country (*avant n*), rural.

ruse [ryz] *nf* [habileté] cunning, crafti-ness. || [subterfuge] ruse.

rusé, -e [ryze] *adj* cunning, crafty.

russe [rys] **1** *adj* Russian. **2** *nm* [langue] Russian. ○ **Russe** *nmf* Russian.

Russie [rysi] *nf:* **la ~** Russia.

rustine [rystin] *nf small rubber patch for repairing bicycle tyres.*

rustique [rystik] *adj* rustic.

rustre [rystr] *péj nmf* lout.

rutilant, -e [rytilɑ̃, ɑ̃t] *adj* [brillant] gleaming.

rythme [ritm] *nm* MUS rhythm. || [de tra-vail, production] pace, rate.

rythmique [ritmik] *adj* rhythmical.

s, S [ɛs] *nm inv* [lettre] s, S. || [forme] zig-zag. ○ **S** (*abr de* **Sud**) S.

s' → **se**.

s/ *abr de* **sur**.

sa → **son**.

SA (*abr de* **société anonyme**) *nf* ≃ Ltd *Br*, ≃ Inc. *Am*.

sabbatique [sabatik] *adj* RELIG Sab-bath (*avant n*). || [congé] sabbatical.

sable [sabl] *nm* sand; **~s mouvants** quicksand (*sg*), quicksands.

sablé, -e [sable] *adj* [route] sandy. ○ **sablé** *nm* ≃ shortbread (*U*).

sabler [sable] *vt* [route] to sand. || [boire]: **~ le champagne** to crack a bottle of champagne.

sablier [sablije] *nm* hourglass.

sablonneux, -euse [sablɔnø, øz] *adj* sandy.

saborder [saborde] *vt* [navire] to scut-tle; *fig* [entreprise] to wind up.

sabot [sabo] *nm* [chaussure] clog. || [de cheval] hoof. || AUTOM: **~ de Denver** wheel clamp, Denver boot.

sabotage [sabotaʒ] *nm* [volontaire] sabotage. || [bâclage] bungling.

saboter [sabote] *vt* [volontairement] to sabotage. || [bâcler] to bungle.

saboteur, -euse [sabotœr, øz] *nm, f* MIL & POLIT saboteur.

sabre [sabr] *nm* sabre.

sac [sak] *nm* [gén] bag; [pour grains] sack; **~ de couchage** sleeping bag; **~ à dos** rucksack; **~ à main** handbag. || *fam* [10 francs] 10 francs.

saccade [sakad] *nf* jerk.

saccadé, -e [sakade] *adj* jerky.

saccage [sakaʒ] *nm* havoc.

saccager [sakaʒe] *vt* [piller] to sack. || [dévaster] to destroy.

sachant *ppr* → **savoir**.

sache, saches *etc* → **savoir**.

sachet [saʃɛ] *nm* [de bonbons] bag; [de shampooing] sachet; **~ de thé** tea-bag.

sacoche [sakɔʃ] *nf* [de médecin, d'écolier] bag. || [de cycliste] pannier.

sac-poubelle [sakpubel] (*pl* **sacs-poubelle**) *nm* [petit] dustbin liner.

sacre [sakr] *nm* [de roi] coronation.

sacré, -e [sakre] *adj* [gén] sacred. || RE-LIG [ordres, écritures] holy. || (*avant n*) *fam* [maudit] goddam (*avant n*) *Am*.

sacrement [sakrəmã] *nm* sacrament.

sacrément [sakremã] *adv fam vieilli* dashed.

sacrer [sakre] *vt* [roi] to crown. || *fig* [déclarer] to hail.

sacrifice [sakrifis] *nm* sacrifice.

sacrifier [sakrifje] *vt* [gén] to sacrifice; **~ qqn/qqch à** to sacrifice sb/sthg to. ○ **se sacrifier** *vp*: **se ~ à/pour** to sac-rifice o.s. to/for.

sacrilège [sakrilɛʒ] **1** *nm* sacrilege. **2** *adj* sacrilegious.

sacristain [sakristɛ̃] *nm* sacristan.

sacristie [sakristi] *nf* sacristy.

sadique [sadik] **1** *nmf* sadist. **2** *adj* sa-distic.

sadisme [sadism] *nm* sadism.

safari [safari] *nm* safari.

safran [safrã] *nm* [épice] saffron.

saga [saga] *nf* saga.

sage [saʒ] **1** *adj* [personne, conseil] wise, sensible. || [enfant, chien] good. **2** *nm* wise man, sage.

sage-femme [saʒfam] *nf* midwife.

sagement [saʒmã] *adv* [avec bon sens] wisely, sensibly. || [docilement] like a good girl/boy.

sagesse [saʒɛs] *nf* [bon sens] wisdom, good sense. || [docilité] good behaviour.

Sagittaire [saʒitɛr] *nm* ASTROL Sagitta-rius.

Sahara [saara] *nm*: **le ~** the Sahara.

saignant, -e [seɲã, ãt] *adj* [blessure] bleeding. || [viande] rare, underdone.

saignement [seɲmã] *nm* bleeding.

saigner [seɲe] **1** *vt* [malade, animal] to bleed. || [financièrement]: **~ qqn (à blanc)** to bleed sb (white). **2** *vi* to bleed; **je sai-gne du nez** my nose is bleeding, I've got a nosebleed.

saillant, -e [sajã, ãt] *adj* [proéminent] projecting, protruding; [muscles] bulg-ing; [pommettes] prominent.

saillie [saji] *nf* [avancée] projection; **en ~** projecting.

saillir [sajir] *vi* [muscles] to bulge.

sain, -e [sɛ̃, sɛn] *adj* [gén] healthy; **~ et sauf** safe and sound. || [lecture] whole-some. || [fruit] fit to eat.

saint, -e [sɛ̃, sɛt] **1** *adj* [sacré] holy. **2** *nm, f* saint.

saint-bernard [sɛbɛrnar] *nm inv* [chien] St Bernard.

saintement [sɛ̃tmɑ̃] *adv*: **vivre ~** to lead a saintly life.

sainte-nitouche [sɛ̃tnituʃ] *nf péj*: **c'est une ~** butter wouldn't melt in her mouth.

sainteté [sɛ̃tte] *nf* holiness.

sais, sait *etc* → **savoir**.

saisie [sezi] *nf* FISC & JUR distraint, seizure. ‖ INFORM input; **~ de données** data capture.

saisir [sezir] *vt* [empoigner] to take hold of; [avec force] to seize. ‖ FIN & JUR to seize, to distrain. ‖ INFORM to capture. ‖ [comprendre] to grasp. ‖ [suj: sensation, émotion] to grip, to seize. ‖ [surprendre]: **être saisi par** to be struck by. ‖ CULIN to seal. ○ **se saisir** *vp*: **se ~ de qqn/qqch** to seize sb/sthg, to grab sb/sthg.

saisissant, -e [sezisɑ̃, ɑ̃t] *adj* [spectacle] gripping; [ressemblance] striking.

saison [sɛzɔ̃] *nf* season; **en/hors ~** in/out of season; **la haute/basse/morte ~** the high/low/off season.

saisonnier, -ière [sɛzɔnje, jɛr] **1** *adj* seasonal. **2** *nm, f* seasonal worker.

salace [salas] *adj* salacious.

salade [salad] *nf* [plante] lettuce. ‖ [plat] (green) salad.

saladier [saladje] *nm* salad bowl.

salaire [salɛr] *nm* [rémunération] salary, wage. ‖ *fig* [récompense] reward.

salant [salɑ̃] → **marais**.

salarial, -e, -iaux [salarjal, jo] *adj* wage (*avant n*).

salarié, -e [salarje] **1** *adj* [personne] wage-earning. ‖ [travail] paid. **2** *nm, f* salaried employee.

salaud [salo] *vulg* **1** *nm* bastard. **2** *adj m* shitty.

sale [sal] *adj* [linge, mains] dirty; [couleur] dirty, dingy. ‖ (*avant n*) [type, gueule, coup] nasty; [tour, histoire] dirty; [bête, temps] filthy.

salé, -e [sale] *adj* [eau, saveur] salty; [beurre] salted; [viande, poisson] salt (*avant n*), salted. ‖ *fig* [histoire] spicy. ‖ *fam fig* [addition, facture] steep.

saler [sale] *vt* [gén] to salt.

saleté [salte] *nf* [malpropreté] dirtiness, filthiness. ‖ [crasse] dirt (*U*), filth (*U*); **faire des ~s** to make a mess. ‖ *fam* [maladie] bug. ‖ [obscénité] dirty thing, obscenity; **il m'a dit des ~s** he used obscenities to me. ‖ [action] disgusting thing; **faire une ~ à qqn** to play a dirty trick on sb.

salière [saljer] *nf* saltcellar.

salir [salir] *vt* [linge, mains] to (make) dirty, to soil. ‖ *fig* [réputation, personne] to sully.

salissant, -e [salisɑ̃, ɑ̃t] *adj* [tissu] easily soiled. ‖ [travail] dirty, messy.

salive [saliv] *nf* saliva.

saliver [salive] *vi* to salivate.

salle [sal] *nf* [pièce] room; **~ d'attente** waiting room; **~ de bains** bathroom; **~ de classe** classroom; **~ d'embarquement** departure lounge; **~ à manger** dining room; **~ d'opération** operating theatre; **~ de séjour** living room; **~ de spectacle** theatre; **~ des ventes** saleroom. ‖ [de spectacle] auditorium.

salon [salɔ̃] *nm* [de maison] lounge *Br*, living room. ‖ [commerce]: **~ de coiffure** hairdressing salon, hairdresser's; **~ de thé** tearoom. ‖ [foire-exposition] show.

salope [salɔp] *nf vulg* bitch.

saloperie [salɔpri] *nf fam* [pacotille] rubbish (*U*). ‖ [maladie] bug. ‖ [saleté] junk (*U*), rubbish (*U*). ‖ [action] dirty trick; **faire des ~s à qqn** to play dirty tricks on sb. ‖ [propos] dirty comment.

salopette [salɔpet] *nf* [d'ouvrier] overalls (*pl*); [à bretelles] dungarees (*pl*).

saltimbanque [saltɛ̃bɑ̃k] *nmf* acrobat.

salubrité [salybrite] *nf* healthiness.

saluer [salɥe] *vt* [accueillir] to greet. ‖ [dire au revoir à] to take one's leave of. ‖ MIL & *fig* to salute. ○ **se saluer** *vp* to say hello/goodbye (to one another).

salut [saly] **1** *nm* [de la main] wave; [de la tête] nod; [propos] greeting. ‖ MIL salute. ‖ RELIG salvation. **2** *interj fam* [bonjour] hi!; [au revoir] bye!, see you!

salutaire [salyter] *adj* [conseil, expérience] salutary. ‖ [remède, repos] beneficial.

salutation [salytasjɔ̃] *nf littéraire* salutation, greeting. ○ **salutations** *nfpl*: **veuillez agréer, Monsieur, mes ~s distinguées** ou **mes sincères ~s** *sout* yours faithfully, yours sincerely.

salve [salv] *nf* salvo.

samedi [samdi] *nm* Saturday; **nous sommes partis** we left on Saturday; **~ 13 septembre** Saturday 13th September; **~ dernier/prochain** last/next Saturday; **le ~** on Saturdays.

SAMU, Samu [samy] (*abr de* **Service**

d'aide médicale d'urgence) *nm French ambulance and emergency service.*

sanatorium [sanatɔrjɔm] *nm* sanatorium.

sanction [sɑ̃ksjɔ̃] *nf* sanction; *fig* [conséquence] penalty, price; **prendre des ~s contre** to impose sanctions on.

sanctionner [sɑ̃ksjɔne] *vt* to sanction.

sanctuaire [sɑ̃ktɥɛr] *nm* [d'église] sanctuary. ‖ [lieu saint] shrine.

sandale [sɑ̃dal] *nf* sandal.

sandalette [sɑ̃dalɛt] *nf* sandal.

sandwich [sɑ̃dwitʃ] (*pl* **sandwiches** OU **sandwichs**) *nm* sandwich.

sang [sɑ̃] *nm* blood.

sang-froid [sɑ̃frwa] *nm inv* calm; **de ~** in cold blood; **perdre/garder son ~** to lose/to keep one's head.

sanglant, -e [sɑ̃glɑ̃, ɑ̃t] *adj* bloody.

sangle [sɑ̃gl] *nf* strap; [de selle] girth.

sangler [sɑ̃gle] *vt* [attacher] to strap; [cheval] to girth.

sanglier [sɑ̃glije] *nm* boar.

sanglot [sɑ̃glo] *nm* sob; **éclater en ~s** to burst into sobs.

sangloter [sɑ̃glɔte] *vi* to sob.

sangsue [sɑ̃sy] *nf* leech; *fig* [personne] bloodsucker.

sanguin, -e [sɑ̃gɛ̃, in] *adj* ANAT blood (*avant n*). ‖ [rouge - visage] ruddy; [- orange] blood (*avant n*).

sanguinaire [sɑ̃giner] *adj* [tyran] bloodthirsty. ‖ [lutte] bloody.

Sanisette® [sanizɛt] *nf automatic public toilet.*

sanitaire [saniter] *adj* [service, mesure] health (*avant n*). ‖ [installation, appareil] bathroom (*avant n*). ○ **sanitaires** *nmpl* toilets and showers.

sans [sɑ̃] **1** *prép* without; **~ argent** without any money; **~ faire un effort** without making an effort. **2** *adv*: **passe-moi mon manteau, je ne veux pas sortir ~** pass me my coat, I don't want to go out without it. ○ **sans que** *loc conj*: **~ que vous le sachiez** without your knowing.

sans-abri [sɑ̃zabri] *nmf inv* homeless person.

sans-emploi [sɑ̃zɑ̃plwa] *nmf inv* unemployed person.

sans-gêne [sɑ̃ʒɛn] **1** *nm inv* [qualité] rudeness, lack of consideration. **2** *adj inv* rude, inconsiderate.

santé [sɑ̃te] *nf* health; **à ta/votre ~!** cheers!, good health!

santon [sɑ̃tɔ̃] *nm figure placed in Christmas crib.*

saoul = **soûl.**

saouler = **soûler.**

sapeur-pompier [sapœrpɔ̃pje] *nm* fireman, fire fighter.

saphir [safir] *nm* sapphire.

sapin [sapɛ̃] *nm* [arbre] fir, firtree; **~ de Noël** Christmas tree. ‖ [bois] fir, deal *Br*.

sarcasme [sarkasm] *nm* sarcasm.

sarcastique [sarkastik] *adj* sarcastic.

sarcler [sarkle] *vt* to weed.

sarcophage [sarkɔfaʒ] *nm* sarcophagus.

Sardaigne [sardɛɲ] *nf*: **la ~** Sardinia.

sardine [sardin] *nf* sardine.

SARL, Sarl (*abr de société à responsabilité limitée*) *nf* limited liability company; **Leduc, ~** ≃ **Leduc Ltd.**

sarment [sarmɑ̃] *nm* [de vigne] shoot.

sas [sas] *nm* AÉRON & NAVIG airlock. ‖ [d'écluse] lock. ‖ [tamis] sieve.

satanique [satanik] *adj* satanic.

satellite [satelit] *nm* satellite.

satiété [sasjete] *nf*: **à ~** [boire, manger] one's fill; [répéter] ad nauseam.

satin [satɛ̃] *nm* satin.

satiné, -e [satine] *adj* satin (*avant n*); [peau] satiny-smooth.

satire [satir] *nf* satire.

satirique [satirik] *adj* satirical.

satisfaction [satisfaksjɔ̃] *nf* satisfaction.

satisfaire [satisfer] *vt* to satisfy. ○ **se satisfaire** *vp*: **se ~ de** to be satisfied with.

satisfaisant, -e [satisfəzɑ̃, ɑ̃t] *adj* [travail] satisfactory. ‖ [expérience] satisfying.

satisfait, -e [satisfɛ, ɛt] **1** *pp* → **satisfaire. 2** *adj* satisfied; **être ~ de** to be satisfied with.

saturation [satyrasjɔ̃] *nf* saturation.

saturé, -e [satyre] *adj*: **~ (de)** saturated (with).

saturne [satyrn] *nm vieilli* lead. ○ **Saturne** *nf* ASTRON Saturn.

satyre [satir] *nm* satyr; *fig* sex maniac.

sauce [sos] *nf* CULIN sauce.

saucière [sosjer] *nf* sauceboat.

saucisse [sosis] *nf* CULIN sausage.

saucisson [sosisɔ̃] *nm* slicing sausage.

sauf[1], sauve [sof, sov] *adj* [personne] safe, unharmed; *fig* [honneur] saved, intact.

sauf[2] [sof] *prép* [à l'exclusion de] except, apart from. ‖ [sous réserve de] barring; **~ que** except (that).

sauf-conduit [sofkɔ̃dɥi] (*pl* **sauf-conduits**) *nm* safe-conduct.

sauge [soʒ] *nf* CULIN sage.

saugrenu, -e [sogrəny] *adj* ridiculous, nonsensical.

saule [sol] *nm* willow; **~ pleureur** weeping willow.

saumon [somɔ̃] *nm* salmon.

saumoné, -e [somone] *adj* salmon (*avant n*).

saumure [somyr] *nf* brine.

sauna [sona] *nm* sauna.

saupoudrer [sopudre] *vt*: **~ qqch de** to sprinkle sthg with.

saurai, sauras *etc* → **savoir**.

saut [so] *nm* [bond] leap, jump; **~ en hauteur** SPORT high jump; **~ en longueur** SPORT long jump, broad jump *Am*; **faire un ~ chez qqn** *fig* to pop in and see sb.

sauté, -e [sote] *adj* sautéed.

saute-mouton [sotmutɔ̃] *nm inv*: **jouer à ~** to play leapfrog.

sauter [sote] **1** *vi* [bondir] to jump, to leap; **~ à la corde** to skip; **~ d'un sujet à l'autre** *fig* to jump from one subject to another; **~ au cou de qqn** *fig* to throw one's arms around sb. ‖ [exploser] to blow up; [fusible] to blow. ‖ [partir - bouchon] to fly out; [- serrure] to burst off; [- bouton] to fly off; [- chaîne de vélo] to come off. **2** *vt* [fossé, obstacle] to jump ou leap over. ‖ *fig* [page, repas] to skip.

sauterelle [sotrɛl] *nf* ZOOL grasshopper.

sautiller [sotije] *vi* to hop.

sautoir [sotwar] *nm* [bijou] chain.

sauvage [sovaʒ] **1** *adj* [plante, animal] wild. ‖ [farouche - animal familier] shy, timid; [- personne] unsociable. ‖ [conduite, haine] savage. **2** *nmf* [solitaire] recluse. ‖ *péj* [brute, indigène] savage.

sauvagerie [sovaʒri] *nf* [férocité] brutality, savagery. ‖ [insociabilité] unsociableness.

sauve → **sauf**.

sauvegarde [sovgard] *nf* [protection] safeguard. ‖ INFORM saving.

sauvegarder [sovgarde] *vt* [protéger] to safeguard. ‖ INFORM to save; [copier] to back up.

sauve-qui-peut [sovkipø] **1** *nm inv* [débandade] stampede. **2** *interj* every man for himself!

sauver [sove] *vt* [gén] to save; **~ qqn/qqch de** to save sb/sthg from, to rescue sb/sthg from. ‖ [navire, biens] to salvage. ○ **se sauver** *vp*: **se ~ (de)** to run away (from); [prisonnier] to escape (from).

sauvetage [sovtaʒ] *nm* [de personne] rescue. ‖ [de navire, biens] salvage.

sauveteur [sovtœr] *nm* rescuer.

sauvette [sovɛt] ○ **à la sauvette** *loc adv* hurriedly, at great speed.

savamment [savamɑ̃] *adv* [avec habileté] skilfully, cleverly.

savane [savan] *nf* savanna.

savant, -e [savɑ̃, ɑ̃t] *adj* [érudit] scholarly. ‖ [animal] performing (*avant n*). ○ **savant** *nm* scientist.

saveur [savœr] *nf* flavour; *fig* savour.

savoir [savwar] **1** *vt* [gén] to know; **faire ~ qqch à qqn** to tell sb sthg, to inform sb of sthg; **sans le ~** unconsciously, without being aware of it; **tu (ne) peux pas ~** *fam* you have no idea; **pas que je sache** not as far as I know. ‖ [être capable de] to know how to; **sais-tu conduire?** can you drive? **2** *nm* learning. ○ **à savoir** *loc conj* namely, that is.

savoir-faire [savwarfɛr] *nm inv* know-how, expertise.

savoir-vivre [savwarvivr] *nm inv* good manners (*pl*).

savon [savɔ̃] *nm* [matière] soap; [pain] cake ou bar of soap. ‖ *fam* [réprimande] telling-off.

savonner [savone] *vt* [linge] to soap.

savonnette [savonɛt] *nf* guest soap.

savourer [savure] *vt* to savour.

savoureux, -euse [savurø, øz] *adj* [mets] tasty. ‖ *fig* [anecdote] juicy.

saxophone [saksɔfɔn] *nm* saxophone.

scabreux, -euse [skabrø, øz] *adj* [propos] shocking, indecent.

scalpel [skalpɛl] *nm* scalpel.

scalper [skalpe] *vt* to scalp.

scandale [skɑ̃dal] *nm* [fait choquant] scandal. ‖ [indignation] uproar. ‖ [tapage] scene; **faire du ou un ~** to make a scene.

scandaleux, -euse [skɑ̃dalø, øz] *adj* scandalous, outrageous.

scandaliser [skɑ̃dalize] *vt* to shock, to scandalize.

scander [skɑ̃de] *vt* [vers] to scan. ‖ [slogan] to chant.

scandinave [skɑ̃dinav] *adj* Scandinavian. ○ **Scandinave** *nmf* Scandinavian.

Scandinavie [skɑ̃dinavi] *nf*: **la ~** Scandinavia.

scanner¹ [skane] *vt* to scan.

scanner² [skanɛr] *nm* scanner.

scaphandre [skafɑ̃dr] *nm* [de plongeur] diving suit. ‖ [d'astronaute] spacesuit.

scarabée [skarabe] *nm* beetle, scarab.

scatologique [skatɔlɔʒik] *adj* scatological.

sceau, -x [so] *nm* seal; *fig* stamp, hallmark.

scélérat, -e [selera, at] *nm, f* villain.

sceller [sele] *vt* [gén] to seal. || CONSTR [fixer] to embed.

scénario [senarjo] *nm* CIN, LITTÉRATURE & THÉÂTRE [canevas] scenario. || CIN & TÉLÉ [découpage, synopsis] screenplay, script. || *fig* [rituel] pattern.

scénariste [senarist] *nmf* scriptwriter.

scène [sɛn] *nf* [gén] scene. || [estrade] stage; **mettre en ~** THÉÂTRE to stage; CIN to direct.

scepticisme [sɛptisism] *nm* scepticism.

sceptique [sɛptik] **1** *nmf* sceptic. **2** *adj* [incrédule] sceptical. || PHILO sceptic.

sceptre [sɛptr] *nm* sceptre.

schéma [ʃema] *nm* [diagramme] diagram.

schématique [ʃematik] *adj* [dessin] diagrammatic. || [interprétation, exposé] simplified.

schématiser [ʃematize] *vt péj* [généraliser] to oversimplify.

schisme [ʃism] *nm* RELIG schism. || [d'opinion] split.

schizophrène [skizɔfrɛn] *nmf & adj* schizophrenic.

schizophrénie [skizɔfreni] *nf* schizophrenia.

sciatique [sjatik] **1** *nf* sciatica. **2** *adj* sciatic.

scie [si] *nf* [outil] saw.

sciemment [sjamɑ̃] *adv* knowingly.

science [sjɑ̃s] *nf* [connaissances scientifiques] science; **~s humaines** ou **sociales** UNIV social sciences. || [érudition] knowledge. || [art] art.

science-fiction [sjɑ̃sfiksjɔ̃] *nf* science fiction.

scientifique [sjɑ̃tifik] **1** *nmf* scientist. **2** *adj* scientific.

scier [sje] *vt* [branche] to saw.

scierie [siri] *nf* sawmill.

scinder [sɛ̃de] *vt*: **~ (en)** to split (into), to divide (into). ○ **se scinder** *vp*: **se ~ (en)** to split (into), to divide (into).

scintiller [sɛ̃tije] *vi* to sparkle.

scission [sisjɔ̃] *nf* split.

sciure [sjyr] *nf* sawdust.

sclérose [skleroz] *nf* sclerosis; *fig* ossification; **~ en plaques** multiple sclerosis.

sclérosé, -e [skleroze] *adj* sclerotic; *fig* ossified.

scolaire [skɔlɛr] *adj* school (*avant n*); *péj* bookish.

scolarité [skɔlarite] *nf* schooling; **frais de ~** SCOL school fees; UNIV tuition fees.

scooter [skutœr] *nm* scooter.

scorbut [skɔrbyt] *nm* scurvy.

score [skɔr] *nm* SPORT score.

scorpion [skɔrpjɔ̃] *nm* scorpion. ○ **Scorpion** *nm* ASTROL Scorpio.

scotch [skɔtʃ] *nm* [alcool] whisky, Scotch.

Scotch® [skɔtʃ] *nm* [adhésif] ≃ Scotch tape® *Am*.

scotcher [skɔtʃe] *vt* to scotch-tape *Am*.

scout, -e [skut] *adj* scout (*avant n*). ○ **scout** *nm* scout.

scribe [skrib] *nm* HIST scribe.

script [skript] *nm* CIN & TÉLÉ script.

scripte [skript] *nmf* CIN & TÉLÉ continuity person.

scrupule [skrypyl] *nm* scruple; **sans ~s** [être] unscrupulous; [agir] unscrupulously.

scrupuleux, -euse [skrypylø, øz] *adj* scrupulous.

scrutateur, -trice [skrytatœr, tris] *adj* searching.

scruter [skryte] *vt* to scrutinize.

scrutin [skrytɛ̃] *nm* [vote] ballot. || [système] voting system; **~ majoritaire** first-past-the-post system; **~ proportionnel** proportional representation system.

sculpter [skylte] *vt* to sculpt.

sculpteur [skyltœr] *nm* sculptor.

sculpture [skyltyr] *nf* sculpture.

SDF (*abr de* **sans domicile fixe**) *nmf*: **les ~** the homeless.

se [sə], **s'** (*devant voyelle ou h muet*) *pron pers* (*réfléchi*) [personne] oneself, himself (*f* herself), (*pl*) themselves; [chose, animal] itself, (*pl*) themselves; **elle ~ regarde dans le miroir** she looks at herself in the mirror. || (*réciproque*) each other, one another; **ils ~ sont rencontrés hier** they met yesterday. || (*passif*): **ce produit ~ vend bien/est vendu partout** this product is selling well/is sold everywhere. || [remplace l'adjectif possessif]: **~ laver les mains** to wash one's hands.

séance [seɑ̃s] *nf* [réunion] meeting, sitting, session. || [période] session; [de pose] sitting. || CIN & THÉÂTRE performance. || *loc*: **~ tenante** right away, forthwith.

seau, -x [so] *nm* [récipient] bucket. || [contenu] bucketful.

sec, sèche [sɛk, sɛʃ] *adj* [gén] dry. || [fruits] dried. || [personne - maigre] lean; [- austère] austere. || *fig* [cœur] hard; [voix, ton] sharp. ○ **sec 1** *adv* [beaucoup]: **boire ~** to drink heavily. **2** *nm*: **tenir au ~** to keep in a dry place.

sécable [sekabl] *adj* divisible.

sécateur [sekatœr] *nm* secateurs (*pl*).

sécession [sesesjɔ̃] *nf* secession; **faire ~ (de)** to secede (from).

sèche-cheveux [sɛʃʃəvø] *nm inv* hairdryer.

sécher [seʃe] **1** *vt* [linge] to dry. || *arg scol* [cours] to skip. **2** *vi* [linge] to dry. || [peau] to dry out. || *arg scol* [ne pas savoir répondre] to dry up.

sécheresse [sɛʃrɛs] *nf* [de terre, climat, style] dryness. || [absence de pluie] drought. || [de réponse] curtness.

séchoir [seʃwar] *nm* [tringle] airer, clotheshorse. || [électrique] dryer; **~ à cheveux** hairdryer.

second, -e [səgɔ̃, ɔ̃d] **1** *adj num* second; **dans un état ~** dazed. **2** *nm, f* second; *voir aussi* **sixième**. ○ **seconde** *nf* [unité de temps & MUS] second. || SCOL ≃ tenth grade *Am*. || TRANSPORT second class.

secondaire [səgɔ̃dɛr] *adj* [gén & SCOL] secondary; **effets ~s** MÉD side effects.

seconder [səgɔ̃de] *vt* to assist.

secouer [səkwe] *vt* [gén] to shake. ○ **se secouer** *vp fam* to snap out of it.

secourable [səkurabl] *adj* helpful.

secourir [səkurir] *vt* [blessé, miséreux] to help; [personne en danger] to rescue.

secouriste [səkurist] *nmf* first-aid worker.

secours [səkur] *nm* [aide] help; **appeler au ~** to call for help; **au ~!** help! || [dons] aid, relief. || [soins] aid; **les premiers ~** first aid (*U*). ○ **de secours** *loc adj* [trousse, poste] first-aid (*avant n*). || [éclairage, issue] emergency (*avant n*). || [roue] spare.

secouru, -e [səkury] *pp* → **secourir**.

secousse [səkus] *nf* [mouvement] jerk, jolt. || *fig* [psychologique] shock. || [tremblement de terre] tremor.

secret, -ète [səkrɛ, ɛt] *adj* [gén] secret. || [personne] reticent. ○ **secret** *nm* [gén] secret. || [discrétion] secrecy.

secrétaire [səkretɛr] **1** *nmf* [personne] secretary; **~ de direction** executive secretary. **2** *nm* [meuble] writing desk, secretaire.

secrétariat [səkretarja] *nm* [bureau] secretary's office; [d'organisation interna-

tionale] secretariat. || [métier] secretarial work.

sécréter [sekrete] *vt* to secrete.

sécrétion [sekresjɔ̃] *nf* secretion.

sectaire [sɛktɛr] *nmf & adj* sectarian.

secte [sɛkt] *nf* sect.

secteur [sɛktœr] *nm* [zone] area; **se trouver dans le ~** *fam* to be somewhere around. || ADMIN district. || ÉCON, GÉOM & MIL sector. || ÉLECTR mains; **sur ~** off ou from the mains.

section [sɛksjɔ̃] *nf* [gén] section; [de parti] branch. || MIL platoon.

sectionner [sɛksjɔne] *vt fig* [diviser] to divide into sections. || [trancher] to sever.

Sécu [seky] *nf fam abr de* **Sécurité sociale**.

séculaire [sekylɛr] *adj* [ancien] age-old.

sécurisant, -e [sekyrizɑ̃, ɑ̃t] *adj* [milieu] secure; [attitude] reassuring.

sécurité [sekyrite] *nf* [d'esprit] security. || [absence de danger] safety; **la ~ routière** road safety. || [dispositif] safety catch. || [organisme]: **la Sécurité sociale** ≃ the Social Security *Am*.

sédatif, -ive [sedatif, iv] *adj* sedative. ○ **sédatif** *nm* sedative.

sédentaire [sedɑ̃tɛr] *adj* [personne, métier] sedentary; [casanier] stay-at-home.

sédentariser [sedɑ̃tarize] ○ **se sédentariser** *vp* [tribu] to settle, to become settled.

sédiment [sedimɑ̃] *nm* sediment.

sédition [sedisjɔ̃] *nf* sedition.

séducteur, -trice [sedyktœr, tris] **1** *adj* seductive. **2** *nm, f* seducer (*f* seductress).

séduire [seduir] *vt* [plaire à] to attract, to appeal to. || [abuser de] to seduce.

séduisant, -e [sedɥizɑ̃, ɑ̃t] *adj* attractive.

séduit, -e [sedɥi, ɥit] *pp* → **séduire**.

segment [sɛgmɑ̃] *nm* GÉOM segment.

segmenter [sɛgmɑ̃te] *vt* to segment.

ségrégation [segregasjɔ̃] *nf* segregation.

seigle [sɛgl] *nm* rye.

seigneur [sɛɲœr] *nm* lord. ○ **Seigneur** *nm*: **le Seigneur** the Lord.

sein [sɛ̃] *nm* breast; *fig* bosom; **donner le ~ (à un bébé)** to breast-feed (a baby). ○ **au sein de** *loc prép* within.

Seine [sɛn] *nf*: **la ~** the (River) Seine.

séisme [seism] *nm* earthquake.

seize [sɛz] *adj num & nm* sixteen; *voir aussi* **six**.

seizième [sɛzjɛm] *adj num, nm & nmf* sixteenth; *voir aussi* **sixième**.

séjour [seʒur] *nm* [durée] stay; **interdit de ~ ≃** banned; **~ linguistique** stay abroad (*to develop language skills*). ‖ [pièce] living room.

séjourner [seʒurne] *vi* to stay.

sel [sɛl] *nm* salt; *fig* piquancy.

sélection [selɛksjɔ̃] *nf* selection.

sélectionner [selɛksjɔne] *vt* to select, to pick.

self-service [sɛlfsɛrvis] (*pl* **self-services**) *nm* self-service cafeteria.

selle [sɛl] *nf* [gén] saddle.

seller [sele] *vt* to saddle.

selon [səlɔ̃] *prép* [conformément à] in accordance with. ‖ [d'après] according to. ○ **selon que** *loc conj* depending on whether.

semaine [səmɛn] *nf* [période] week.

sémantique [semɑ̃tik] *adj* semantic.

semblable [sɑ̃blabl] **1** *nm* [prochain] fellow man. **2** *adj* [analogue] similar; **~ à** like, similar to. ‖ (*avant n*) [tel] such.

semblant [sɑ̃blɑ̃] *nm*: **un ~ de** a semblance of; **faire ~ (de faire qqch)** to pretend (to do sthg).

sembler [sɑ̃ble] **1** *vi* to seem. **2** *v impers*: **il (me/te) semble que** it seems (to me/you) that.

semelle [səmɛl] *nf* [de chaussure - dessous] sole; [- à l'intérieur] insole.

semence [səmɑ̃s] *nf* [graine] seed. ‖ [sperme] semen (*U*).

semer [səme] *vt* [planter & *fig*] to sow. ‖ [répandre] to scatter. ‖ *fam* [se débarrasser de] to shake off.

semestre [səmɛstr] *nm* half year, six-month period; SCOL semester.

semestriel, -ielle [səmɛstrijɛl] *adj* [qui a lieu tous les six mois] half-yearly, six-monthly.

séminaire [seminɛr] *nm* RELIG seminary. ‖ [UNIV & colloque] seminar.

séminariste [seminarist] *nm* seminarist.

semi-remorque [səmirəmɔrk] (*pl* **semi-remorques**) *nm* semitrailer *Am*.

semis [səmi] *nm* [méthode] sowing broadcast. ‖ [plant] seedling.

semoule [səmul] *nf* semolina.

sempiternel, -elle [sɑ̃pitɛrnɛl] *adj* eternal.

sénat [sena] *nm* senate; **le Sénat** *upper house of the French parliament.*

sénateur [senatœr] *nm* senator.

Sénégal [senegal] *nm*: **le ~** Senegal.

sénile [senil] *adj* senile.

sénilité [senilite] *nf* senility.

sens [sɑ̃s] *nm* [fonction, instinct, raison] sense; **avoir le ~ de l'humour** to have a sense of humour; **bon ~** good sense. ‖ [direction] direction; **dans le ~ de la longueur** lengthways; **dans le ~ des aiguilles d'une montre** clockwise; **dans le ~ contraire des aiguilles d'une montre** anticlockwise; **~ dessus dessous** upside down; **~ interdit** OU **unique** one-way street. ‖ [signification] meaning; **~ propre/figuré** literal/figurative sense.

sensation [sɑ̃sasjɔ̃] *nf* [perception] sensation, feeling. ‖ [impression] feeling.

sensationnel, -elle [sɑ̃sasjɔnɛl] *adj* sensational.

sensé, -e [sɑ̃se] *adj* sensible.

sensibiliser [sɑ̃sibilize] *vt fig* [public]: **~ (à)** to make aware (of).

sensibilité [sɑ̃sibilite] *nf*: **~ (à)** sensitivity (to).

sensible [sɑ̃sibl] *adj* [gén]: **~ (à)** sensitive (to). ‖ [notable] considerable, appreciable.

sensiblement [sɑ̃siblǝmɑ̃] *adv* [à peu près] more or less. ‖ [notablement] appreciably, considerably.

sensoriel, -ielle [sɑ̃sɔrjɛl] *adj* sensory.

sensualité [sɑ̃sɥalite] *nf* [lascivité] sensuousness; [charnelle] sensuality.

sensuel, -elle [sɑ̃sɥɛl] *adj* [charnel] sensual. ‖ [lascif] sensuous.

sentence [sɑ̃tɑ̃s] *nf* [jugement] sentence. ‖ [maxime] adage.

sentencieux, -ieuse [sɑ̃tɑ̃sjø, jøz] *adj péj* sententious.

senteur [sɑ̃tœr] *nf littéraire* perfume.

sentier [sɑ̃tje] *nm* path.

sentiment [sɑ̃timɑ̃] *nm* feeling; **veuillez agréer, Monsieur, l'expression de mes ~s distingués/cordiaux/les meilleurs** yours faithfully/sincerely/truly.

sentimental, -e, -aux [sɑ̃timɑ̃tal, o] *adj* [amoureux] love (*avant n*). ‖ [sensible, romanesque] sentimental.

sentinelle [sɑ̃tinɛl] *nf* sentry.

sentir [sɑ̃tir] *vt* **1** [percevoir - par l'odorat] to smell; [- par le goût] to taste; [- par le toucher] to feel. ‖ [exhaler - odeur] to smell of. ‖ [danger] to sense, to be aware of. **2** *vi*: **~ bon/mauvais** to smell good/bad. ○ **se sentir 1** *v attr*: **se ~ bien/fatigué** to feel well/tired. **2** *vp* [être perceptible]: **ça se sent!** you can really tell!

séparation [separasjɔ̃] *nf* separation.

séparatiste [separatist] *nmf* separatist.

séparé, -e [separe] *adj* [intérêts] separate. || [couple] separated.

séparer [separe] *vt* [gén]: ~ (de) to separate (from). || [suj: divergence] to divide. ○ **se séparer** *vp* [se défaire]: **se ~ de** to part with. || [conjoints] to separate, to split up; **se ~ de** to separate from, to split up with. || [route]: **se ~ (en)** to split (into), to divide (into).

sept [sɛt] *adj num & nm* seven; *voir aussi* **six**.

septembre [sɛptɑ̃br] *nm* September; **en ~, au mois de ~** in September; **début ~, au début du mois de ~** at the beginning of September; **fin ~, à la fin du mois de ~** at the end of September; **d'ici ~** by September; **(à la) mi-~** (in) mid-September; **le premier/deux/ dix ~** the first/second/tenth of September.

septennat [sɛptena] *nm* seven-year term (of office).

septicémie [sɛptisemi] *nf* septicaemia, blood poisoning.

septième [sɛtjɛm] *adj num, nm & nmf* seventh; *voir aussi* **sixième**.

sépulcre [sepylkr] *nm* sepulchre.

sépulture [sepyltyr] *nf* [lieu] burial place. || [inhumation] burial.

séquelle [sekel] *nf (gén pl)* aftermath; MÉD aftereffect.

séquence [sekɑ̃s] *nf* sequence.

séquestrer [sekɛstre] *vt* [personne] to confine. || [biens] to impound.

serai, seras *etc* → **être**.

serbe [sɛrb] *adj* Serbian. ○ **Serbe** *nmf* Serb.

Serbie [sɛrbi] *nf*: **la ~** Serbia.

serein, -e [sərɛ̃, ɛn] *adj* [calme] serene.

sérénade [serenad] *nf* MUS serenade.

sérénité [serenite] *nf* serenity.

serf, serve [sɛrf, sɛrv] *nm, f* serf.

sergent [sɛrʒɑ̃] *nm* sergeant.

série [seri] *nf* [gén] series (*sg*). || SPORT rank; [au tennis] seeding.

sérieusement [serjøzmɑ̃] *adv* seriously.

sérieux, -ieuse [serjø, jøz] *adj* [grave] serious. || [digne de confiance] reliable; [client, offre] genuine. || [consciencieux] responsible; **ce n'est pas ~** it's irresponsible. || [considérable] considerable. ○ **sérieux** *nm* [application] sense of responsibility. || [gravité] seriousness; **garder son ~** to keep a straight face; **prendre qqn/qqch au ~** to take sb/sthg seriously.

serin, -e [sərɛ̃, in] *nm, f* [oiseau] canary.

seringue [sərɛ̃g] *nf* syringe.

serment [sɛrmɑ̃] *nm* [affirmation solennelle] oath; **sous ~** on ou under oath. || [promesse] vow, pledge.

sermon [sɛrmɔ̃] *nm litt & fig* sermon.

séronégatif, -ive [seronegatif, iv] *adj* HIV-negative.

séropositif, -ive [seropozitif, iv] *adj* HIV-positive.

serpe [sɛrp] *nf* billhook.

serpent [sɛrpɑ̃] *nm* ZOOL snake.

serpenter [sɛrpɑ̃te] *vi* to wind.

serpillière [sɛrpijɛr] *nf* floor cloth.

serre [sɛr] *nf* [bâtiment] greenhouse, glasshouse. ○ **serres** *nfpl* ZOOL talons, claws.

serré, -e [sere] *adj* [écriture] cramped; [rangs] serried. || [vêtement, chaussure] tight. || [match] close-fought. || [poing, dents] clenched; **la gorge ~e** with a lump in one's throat. || [café] strong.

serrer [sere] **1** *vt* [saisir] to grip, to hold tight; **~ la main à qqn** to shake sb's hand; **~ qqn dans ses bras** to hug sb. || *fig* [rapprocher] to bring together; **~ les rangs** to close ranks. || [poing, dents] to clench; [lèvres] to purse; *fig* [cœur] to wring. || [suj: vêtement, chaussure] to be too tight for. || [vis, ceinture] to tighten. **2** *vi* AUTOM: **~ à droite/gauche** to keep right/left. ○ **se serrer** *vp* [se blottir]: **se ~ contre** to huddle up to ou against. || [se rapprocher] to squeeze up.

serre-tête [sɛrtɛt] *nm inv* headband.

serrure [sɛryr] *nf* lock.

serrurier [sɛryrje] *nm* locksmith.

sertir [sɛrtir] *vt* [pierre précieuse] to set. || TECHNOL [assujettir] to crimp.

sérum [serɔm] *nm* serum.

servante [sɛrvɑ̃t] *nf* [domestique] maidservant.

serveur, -euse [sɛrvœr, øz] *nm, f* [de restaurant] waiter (*f* waitress); [de bar] barman (*f* barmaid). ○ **serveur** *nm* INFORM server.

serviable [sɛrvjabl] *adj* helpful, obliging.

service [sɛrvis] *nm* [gén] service; **être en ~** to be in use, to be set up; **hors ~** out of order. || [travail] duty; **pendant le ~** while on duty. || [département] department; **~ d'ordre** police and stewards (*at a demonstration*). || MIL: **~ (militaire)** military ou national service. || [aide, assistance] favour; **rendre un ~ à qqn** to do sb a favour; **rendre ~** to be helpful; **~ après-vente** after-sales service. || [à table]: **premier/deuxième** ~ first/second sitting. || [pourboire] service (charge); ~ **compris/non compris** service included/not included. || [assortiment - de porcelaine] service, set; [- de linge] set.

serviette [sɛrvjɛt] nf [de table] serviette, napkin. || [de toilette] towel. || [porte-documents] briefcase. ○ **serviette hygiénique** nf sanitary napkin Am.

serviette-éponge [sɛrvjɛtepɔ̃ʒ] nf terry towel.

servile [sɛrvil] adj [gén] servile. || [traduction, imitation] slavish.

servir [sɛrvir] **1** vt [gén] to serve; ~ **qqch à qqn** to serve sb sthg, to help sb to sthg. || [avantager] to serve (well), to help. **2** vi [avoir un usage] to be useful ou of use. || [être utile]: ~ **à qqch/à faire qqch** to be used for sthg/for doing sthg; **ça ne sert à rien** it's pointless. || [tenir lieu]: ~ **de** [personne] to act as; [chose] to serve as. || MIL & SPORT to serve. || CARTES to deal. ○ **se servir** vp [prendre]: **se** ~ (**de**) to help o.s. (to). || [utiliser]: **se** ~ **de qqn/qqch** to use sb/sthg.

serviteur [sɛrvitœr] nm servant.

servitude [sɛrvityd] nf [esclavage] servitude. || (gén pl) [contrainte] constraint.

ses → **son**.

session [sesjɔ̃] nf [d'assemblée] session, sitting. || UNIV exam session. || INFORM: **fermer** ou **clore une** ~ to log out ou off.

set [sɛt] nm TENNIS set. || [napperon]: ~ (**de table**) set of table ou place mats.

seuil [sœj] nm litt & fig threshold.

seul, -e [sœl] **1** adj [isolé] alone; ~ **à** ~ alone (together), privately. || [unique]: **le** ~ ... the only ...; **un** ~ ... a single ...; **pas un** ~ not one, not a single. || [esseulé] lonely. **2** nm, f: **le** ~ the only one; **un** ~ a single one, only one. ○ **seul** adv [sans compagnie] alone, by o.s.; **parler tout** ~ to talk to o.s. || [sans aide] on one's own, by o.s.

seulement [sœlmɑ̃] adv [gén] only.

sève [sɛv] nf BOT sap.

sévère [sevɛr] adj severe.

sévérité [severite] nf severity.

sévices [sevis] nmpl sout ill treatment (U).

sévir [sevir] vi [épidémie, guerre] to rage. || [punir] to give out a punishment.

sevrer [səvre] vt to wean.

sexe [sɛks] nm [gén] sex. || [organe] genitals (pl).

sexiste [sɛksist] nmf & adj sexist.

sexologue [sɛksɔlɔg] nmf sexologist.

sex-shop [sɛksʃɔp] (pl **sex-shops**) nm sex shop.

sextant [sɛkstɑ̃] nm sextant.

sexualité [sɛksɥalite] nf sexuality.

sexuel, -elle [sɛksɥɛl] adj sexual.

sexy [sɛksi] adj inv fam sexy.

seyant, -e [sɛjɑ̃, ɑ̃t] adj becoming.

shampooing [ʃɑ̃pwɛ̃] nm shampoo.

shérif [ʃerif] nm sheriff.

shopping [ʃɔpiŋ] nm shopping; **faire du** ~ to go (out) shopping.

short [ʃɔrt] nm shorts (pl), pair of shorts.

show-business [ʃobiznɛs] nm inv show business.

si[1] [si] nm inv MUS B; [chanté] ti.

si[2] [si] **1** adv [tellement] so; **il roulait** ~ **vite qu'il a eu un accident** he was driving so fast (that) he had an accident; **ce n'est pas** ~ **facile que ça** it's not as easy as that; ~ **vieux qu'il soit** however old he may be, old as he is. || [oui] yes. **2** conj [gén] if; ~ **tu veux, on y va** we'll go if you want; ~ **seulement** if only. || [dans une question indirecte] if, whether. ○ **si bien que** loc conj so that, with the result that.

SI nm (abr de **syndicat d'initiative**) tourist office.

siamois, -e [sjamwa, az] adj: **frères** ~, **sœurs** ~**es** MÉD Siamese twins.

Sibérie [siberi] nf: **la** ~ Siberia.

sibyllin, -e [sibilɛ̃, in] adj enigmatic.

SICAV, Sicav [sikav] (abr de **société d'investissement à capital variable**) nf [société] unit trust, mutual fund. || [action] share in a unit trust.

Sicile [sisil] nf: **la** ~ Sicily.

SIDA, Sida [sida] (abr de **syndrome immuno-déficitaire acquis**) nm AIDS.

side-car [sidkar] (pl **side-cars**) nm sidecar.

sidérer [sidere] vt fam to stagger.

sidérurgie [sideryrʒi] nf [industrie] iron and steel industry.

siècle [sjɛkl] nm [cent ans] century. || (gén pl) fam [longue durée] ages (pl).

siège [sjɛʒ] nm [meuble & POLIT] seat. || MIL siege. || [d'organisme] headquarters, head office; ~ **social** registered office. || MÉD: **se présenter par le** ~ to be in the breech position.

siéger [sjeʒe] vi [juge, assemblée] to sit.

sien [sjɛ̃] ○ **le sien** (f **la sienne** [lasjɛn], mpl **les siens** [lesjɛ̃], fpl **les siennes** [lesjɛn]) pron poss [d'homme] his; [de femme] hers; [de chose, d'animal] its.

sieste [sjɛst] nf siesta.

sifflement [siflǝmɑ̃] *nm* [son] whistling; [de serpent] hissing.

siffler [sifle] **1** *vi* to whistle; [serpent] to hiss. **2** *vt* [air de musique] to whistle. || [femme] to whistle at. || [chien] to whistle (for). || [acteur] to boo, to hiss. || *fam* [verre] to knock back.

sifflet [sifle] *nm* whistle. ○ **sifflets** *nmpl* hissing (*U*), boos.

siffloter [siflɔte] *vi* & *vt* to whistle.

sigle [sigl] *nm* acronym, (set of) initials.

signal, -aux [siɲal, o] *nm* [geste, son] signal; [d'alarme] alarm (signal); **donner le ~ (de)** to give the signal (for). || [panneau] sign.

signalement [siɲalmɑ̃] *nm* description.

signaler [siɲale] *vt* [fait] to point out; **rien à ~** nothing to report. || [à la police] to denounce.

signalisation [siɲalizasjɔ̃] *nf* [signaux] signs (*pl*); NAVIG signals (*pl*).

signataire [siɲatɛr] *nmf* signatory.

signature [siɲatyr] *nf* [nom, marque] signature. || [acte] signing.

signe [siɲ] *nm* [gén] sign; **être ~ de** to be a sign of; **~ avant-coureur** advance indication. || [trait] mark; **~ particulier** distinguishing mark.

signer [siɲe] *vt* to sign. ○ **se signer** *vp* to cross o.s.

signet [siɲe] *nm* bookmark (*attached to spine of book*).

significatif, -ive [siɲifikatif, iv] *adj* significant.

signification [siɲifikasjɔ̃] *nf* [sens] meaning.

signifier [siɲifje] *vt* [vouloir dire] to mean. || [faire connaître] to make known. || JUR to serve notice of.

silence [silɑ̃s] *nm* [gén] silence; **garder le ~ (sur)** to remain silent (about). || MUS rest.

silencieux, -ieuse [silɑ̃sjø, jøz] *adj* [lieu, appareil] quiet; [personne - taciturne] quiet; [- muet] silent. ○ **silencieux** *nm* silencer.

silex [silɛks] *nm* flint.

silhouette [silwɛt] *nf* [de personne] silhouette; [de femme] figure; [d'objet] outline. || ART silhouette.

silicium [silisjɔm] *nm* silicon.

silicone [silikon] *nf* silicone.

sillage [sijaʒ] *nm* wake.

sillon [sijɔ̃] *nm* [tranchée, ride] furrow. || [de disque] groove.

sillonner [sijɔne] *vt* [champ] to furrow. || [ciel] to crisscross.

silo [silo] *nm* silo.

simagrées [simagre] *nfpl péj*: **faire des ~** to make a fuss.

similaire [similɛr] *adj* similar.

similicuir [similikɥir] *nm* imitation leather.

similitude [similityd] *nf* similarity.

simple [sɛ̃pl] **1** *adj* [gén] simple. || [ordinaire] ordinary. || [billet]: **un aller ~ a** single ticket. **2** *nm* TENNIS singles (*sg*).

simplicité [sɛ̃plisite] *nf* simplicity.

simplifier [sɛ̃plifje] *vt* to simplify.

simpliste [sɛ̃plist] *adj péj* simplistic.

simulacre [simylakr] *nm* [semblant]: **un ~ de** a pretence of, a sham. || [action simulée] enactment.

simulateur, -trice [simylatœr, tris] *nm, f* pretender; [de maladie] malingerer. ○ **simulateur** *nm* TECHNOL simulator.

simulation [simylasjɔ̃] *nf* [gén] simulation. || [comédie] shamming, feigning.

simuler [simyle] *vt* [gén] to simulate. || [feindre] to feign, to sham.

simultané, -e [simyltane] *adj* simultaneous.

sincère [sɛ̃sɛr] *adj* sincere.

sincèrement [sɛ̃sɛrmɑ̃] *adv* [franchement] honestly, sincerely. || [vraiment] really, truly.

sincérité [sɛ̃serite] *nf* sincerity.

sine qua non [sinekwanɔn] *adj*: **condition ~** prerequisite.

Singapour [sɛ̃gapur] *n* Singapore.

singe [sɛ̃ʒ] *nm* ZOOL monkey; [de grande taille] ape.

singer [sɛ̃ʒe] *vt* [personne] to mimic, to ape. || [sentiment] to feign.

singerie [sɛ̃ʒri] *nf* [grimace] face.

singulariser [sɛ̃gylarize] ○ **se singulariser** *vp* to draw ou call attention to o.s.

singularité [sɛ̃gylarite] *nf littéraire* [particularité] peculiarity.

singulier, -ière [sɛ̃gylje, jɛr] *adj sout* [bizarre] strange; [spécial] uncommon. || GRAM singular. || [d'homme à homme]: **combat ~** single combat. ○ **singulier** *nm* GRAM singular.

singulièrement [sɛ̃gyljɛrmɑ̃] *adv littéraire* [bizarrement] strangely. || [beaucoup, très] particularly.

sinistre [sinistr] **1** *nm* [catastrophe] disaster. || JUR damage (*U*). **2** *adj* [personne, regard] sinister; [maison, ambiance] gloomy.

sinistré, -e [sinistre] **1** *adj* [région] disaster (*avant n*), disaster-stricken; [famille] disaster-stricken. **2** *nm, f* disaster victim.

sinon [sinɔ̃] *conj* [autrement] or else, otherwise. || [si ce n'est] if not.

sinueux, -euse [sinɥø, øz] *adj* winding.

sinus [sinys] *nm* ANAT sinus. || MATHS sine.

sinusite [sinyzit] *nf* sinusitis (*U*).

sionisme [sjɔnism] *nm* Zionism.

siphon [sifɔ̃] *nm* [tube] siphon. || [bouteille] soda siphon.

siphonner [sifɔne] *vt* to siphon.

sirène [siʀɛn] *nf* siren.

sirop [siʀo] *nm* syrup; ~ **d'érable** maple syrup; ~ **de menthe** mint cordial.

siroter [siʀɔte] *vt fam* to sip.

sis, -e [si, siz] *adj* JUR located.

sismique [sismik] *adj* seismic.

site [sit] *nm* [emplacement] site; ~ **archéologique/historique** archaeological/historic site. || [paysage] beauty spot.

sitôt [sito] *adv*: **pas de** ~ not for some time, not for a while; ~ **dit, ~ fait** no sooner said than done. ○ **sitôt que** *loc conj* as soon as.

situation [sitɥasjɔ̃] *nf* [position, emplacement] position, location. || [contexte, circonstance] situation; ~ **de famille** marital status. || [emploi] job, position. || FIN financial statement.

situer [sitɥe] *vt* [maison] to site, to situate; **bien/mal situé** well/badly situated. || [sur carte] to locate. ○ **se situer** *vp* [scène] to be set; [dans classement] to be.

six [sis *en fin de phrase, si devant consonne ou h aspiré, siz devant voyelle ou h muet*] **1** *adj num* six; **il a** ~ **ans** he is six (years old); **il est** ~ **heures** it's six (o'clock); **le** ~ **janvier** (on) the sixth of January; **daté du** ~ **septembre** dated the sixth of September; **Charles Six** Charles the Sixth; **page** ~ page six. **2** *nm inv* [gén] six; ~ **de pique** six of spades. || [adresse] (number) six. **3** *pron* six; **ils étaient** ~ there were six of them; ~ **par** ~ six at a time.

sixième [sizjɛm] **1** *adj num* sixth. **2** *nmf* sixth; **arriver/se classer** ~ to come (in)/ to be placed sixth. **3** *nf* SCOL ≃ sixth grade *Am*; **être en** ~ to be in sixth grade *Am*. **4** *nm* [part]: **le/un** ~ **de** one/a sixth of; **cinq** ~**s** five sixths. || [arrondissement] sixth arrondissement. || [étage] seventh floor *Am*.

skateboard [skɛtbɔʀd] *nm* skateboard.

sketch [skɛtʃ] (*pl* **sketches**) *nm* sketch (*in a revue etc*).

ski [ski] *nm* [objet] ski. || [sport] skiing; **faire du** ~ to ski; ~ **acrobatique/alpin/ de fond** freestyle/alpine/cross-country skiing; ~ **nautique** water-skiing.

skier [skje] *vi* to ski.

skieur, -ieuse [skjœʀ, jøz] *nm, f* skier.

skipper [skipœʀ] *nm* [capitaine] skipper. || [barreur] helmsman.

slalom [slalɔm] *nm* SKI slalom.

slave [slav] *adj* Slavonic. ○ **Slave** *nmf* Slav.

slip [slip] *nm* briefs (*pl*); ~ **de bain** [d'homme] swimming trunks (*pl*).

slogan [slɔgã] *nm* slogan.

Slovaquie [slɔvaki] *nf*: **la** ~ Slovakia.

Slovénie [slɔveni] *nf*: **la** ~ Slovenia.

slow [slo] *nm* slow dance.

smasher [smaʃe] *vi* TENNIS to smash (the ball).

SME (*abr de* **Système monétaire européen**) *nm* EMS.

SMIC, Smic [smik] (*abr de* **salaire minimum interprofessionnel de croissance**) *nm* index-linked guaranteed minimum wage.

smoking [smɔkiŋ] *nm* tuxedo *Am*.

SNCF (*abr de* **Société nationale des chemins de fer français**) *nf* French railways board.

snob [snɔb] **1** *nmf* snob. **2** *adj* snobbish.

snober [snɔbe] *vt* to snub, to cold-shoulder.

snobisme [snɔbism] *nm* snobbery, snobbishness.

sobre [sɔbʀ] *adj* [personne] temperate. || [style] sober; [décor, repas] simple.

sobriété [sɔbʀijete] *nf* sobriety.

sobriquet [sɔbʀikɛ] *nm* nickname.

soc [sɔk] *nm* ploughshare.

sociable [sɔsjabl] *adj* sociable.

social, -e, -iaux [sɔsjal, jo] *adj* [rapports, classe, service] social. || COMM: **raison** ~ company name.

socialisme [sɔsjalism] *nm* socialism.

socialiste [sɔsjalist] *nmf & adj* socialist.

sociétaire [sɔsjeteʀ] *nmf* member.

société [sɔsjete] *nf* [communauté, classe sociale, groupe] society; **en** ~ in society. || [présence] company, society. || COMM company, firm.

sociologie [sɔsjɔlɔʒi] *nf* sociology.

sociologue [sɔsjɔlɔg] *nmf* sociologist.

socioprofessionnel, -elle [sɔsjɔprɔfesjɔnɛl] *adj* socioprofessional.

socle [sɔkl] *nm* [de statue] plinth, pedestal. || [de lampe] base.

socquette [sɔkɛt] *nf* ankle ou short sock.

soda [sɔda] *nm* fizzy drink.

sodium [sɔdjɔm] *nm* sodium.

sodomiser [sɔdɔmize] *vt* to sodomize.

sœur [sœr] *nf* [gén] sister; **grande/petite ~** big/little sister. ‖ RELIG nun, sister.

sofa [sɔfa] *nm* sofa.

software [sɔftwɛr] *nm* software.

soi [swa] *pron pers* oneself. ○ **soi-même** *pron pers* oneself.

soi-disant [swadizã] **1** *adj inv* (*avant n*) so-called. **2** *adv fam* supposedly.

soie [swa] *nf* [textile] silk. ‖ [poil] bristle.

soierie [swari] *nf* (*gén pl*) [textile] silk.

soif [swaf] *nf* thirst; **~ (de)** *fig* thirst (for), craving (for); **avoir ~** to be thirsty.

soigné, -e [swaɲe] *adj* [travail] meticulous. ‖ [personne] well-groomed; [jardin, mains] well-cared-for.

soigner [swaɲe] *vt* [suj: médecin] to treat; [suj: infirmière, parent] to nurse. ‖ [invités, jardin, mains] to look after. ‖ [travail, présentation] to take care over. ○ **se soigner** *vp* to take care of o.s., to look after o.s.

soigneusement [swaɲøzmã] *adv* carefully.

soigneux, -euse [swaɲø, øz] *adj* [personne] tidy, neat. ‖ [travail] careful.

soin [swẽ] *nm* [attention] care; **avoir ou prendre ~ de faire qqch** to be sure to do sthg; **avec ~** carefully; **sans ~** [procéder] carelessly; [travail] careless. ○ **soins** *nmpl* care (*U*); **les premiers ~s** first aid (*sg*).

soir [swar] *nm* evening; **demain ~** tomorrow evening ou night; **le ~** in the evening; **à ce ~!** see you tonight!

soirée [sware] *nf* [soir] evening. ‖ [réception] party.

sois → **soir**.

soit¹ [swat] *adv* so be it.

soit² [swa] **1** *vb* → **être**. **2** *conj* [c'est-à-dire] in other words, that is to say. ‖ MATHS [étant donné]: **~ une droite AB** given a straight line AB. ○ **soit ... soit** *loc corrélative* either ... or.

soixante [swasãt] **1** *adj num* sixty. **2** *nm* sixty; *voir aussi* **six**.

soixante-dix [swasãtdis] **1** *adj num* seventy. **2** *nm* seventy; *voir aussi* **six**.

soixante-dixième [swasãtdizjɛm] *adj num, nm & nmf* seventieth; *voir aussi* **sixième**.

soixantième [swasãtjɛm] *adj num, nm & nmf* sixtieth; *voir aussi* **sixième**.

soja [sɔʒa] *nm* soya.

sol [sɔl] *nm* [terre] ground. ‖ [de maison] floor. ‖ [territoire] soil. ‖ MUS G; [chanté] so.

solaire [sɔlɛr] *adj* [énergie, four] solar. ‖ [crème] sun (*avant n*).

solarium [sɔlarjɔm] *nm* solarium.

soldat [sɔlda] *nm* MIL soldier; [grade] private. ‖ [jouet] (toy) soldier.

solde [sɔld] **1** *nm* [de compte, facture] balance; **~ créditeur/débiteur** credit/debit balance. ‖ [rabais]: **en ~** [acheter] in a sale. **2** *nf* MIL pay. ○ **soldes** *nmpl* sales.

solder [sɔlde] *vt* [compte] to close. ‖ [marchandises] to sell off. ○ **se solder** *vp*: **se ~ par** *fig* [aboutir] to end in.

sole [sɔl] *nf* sole.

soleil [sɔlɛj] *nm* [astre, motif] sun; **~ couchant/levant** setting/rising sun. ‖ [lumière, chaleur] sun, sunlight; **au ~** in the sun; **en plein ~** right in the sun.

solennel, -elle [sɔlanɛl] *adj* [cérémonieux] ceremonial. ‖ [grave] solemn.

solennité [sɔlanite] *nf* [gravité] solemnity. ‖ [raideur] stiffness, formality.

solfège [sɔlfɛʒ] *nm*: **apprendre le ~** to learn the rudiments of music.

solidaire [sɔlidɛr] *adj* [lié]: **être ~ de qqn** to be behind sb, to show solidarity with sb. ‖ [relié] interdependent, integral.

solidarité [sɔlidarite] *nf* [entraide] solidarity; **par ~** [se mettre en grève] in sympathy.

solide [sɔlid] **1** *adj* [état, corps] solid. ‖ [construction] solid, sturdy. ‖ [personne] sturdy, robust. ‖ [argument] solid, sound. ‖ [relation] stable, strong. **2** *nm* solid.

solidifier [sɔlidifje] *vt* [ciment, eau] to solidify. ‖ [structure] to reinforce. ○ **se solidifier** *vp* to solidify.

solidité [sɔlidite] *nf* [de matière, construction] solidity. ‖ [de mariage] stability, strength. ‖ [de raisonnement, d'argument] soundness.

soliste [sɔlist] *nmf* soloist.

solitaire [sɔliter] **1** *adj* [de caractère] solitary. ‖ [esseulé, retiré] lonely. **2** *nmf* [personne] loner, recluse. **3** *nm* [jeu, diamant] solitaire.

solitude [sɔlityd] *nf* [isolement] loneliness. ‖ [retraite] solitude.

sollicitation [sɔlisitasjɔ̃] *nf* (*gén pl*) entreaty.

solliciter [sɔlisite] *vt* [demander - entretien, audience] to request; [- attention, intérêt] to seek. || [s'intéresser à]: **être sollicité** to be in demand. || [faire appel à]: **~ qqn pour faire qqch** to appeal to sb to do sthg.

sollicitude [sɔlisityd] *nf* solicitude, concern.

solo [sɔlo] *nm* solo; **en ~** solo.

solstice [sɔlstis] *nm*: **~ d'été/d'hiver** summer/winter solstice.

soluble [sɔlybl] *adj* [matière] soluble; [café] instant. || *fig* [problème] solvable.

solution [sɔlysjɔ̃] *nf* [résolution] solution, answer. || [liquide] solution.

solvable [sɔlvabl] *adj* solvent, creditworthy.

solvant [sɔlvã] *nm* solvent.

Somalie [sɔmali] *nf*: **la ~** Somalia.

sombre [sɔ̃br] *adj* [couleur, costume, pièce] dark. || *fig* [pensées, avenir] dark, gloomy.

sombrer [sɔ̃bre] *vi* to sink.

sommaire [sɔmɛr] **1** *adj* [explication] brief. || [exécution] summary. || [installation] basic. **2** *nm* summary.

sommation [sɔmasjɔ̃] *nf* [assignation] summons (*sg*). || [ordre - de payer] demand; [- de se rendre] warning.

somme [sɔm] **1** *nf* [addition] total, sum. || [d'argent] sum, amount. || [ouvrage] overview. **2** *nm* nap. ○ **en somme** *loc adv* in short. ○ **somme toute** *loc adv* when all's said and done.

sommeil [sɔmɛj] *nm* sleep; **avoir ~** to be sleepy.

sommeiller [sɔmeje] *vi* [personne] to doze. || *fig* [qualité] to be dormant.

sommelier, -ière [sɔmǝlje, jɛr] *nm, f* wine waiter (*f* wine waitress).

sommes → être.

sommet [sɔmɛ] *nm* [de montagne] summit, top. || *fig* [de hiérarchie] top; [de perfection] height. || GÉOM apex.

sommier [sɔmje] *nm* base, bed base.

sommité [sɔmite] *nf* [personne] leading light.

somnambule [sɔmnãbyl] **1** *nmf* sleepwalker. **2** *adj*: **être ~** to be a sleepwalker.

somnifère [sɔmnifɛr] *nm* sleeping pill.

somnolent, -e [sɔmnɔlã, ãt] *adj* [personne] sleepy, drowsy.

somnoler [sɔmnɔle] *vi* to doze.

somptueux, -euse [sɔ̃ptɥø, øz] *adj* sumptuous, lavish.

somptuosité [sɔ̃ptɥozite] *nf* lavishness.

son¹ [sɔ̃] *nm* [bruit] sound; **~ et lumière** son et lumière. || [céréale] bran.

son² [sɔ̃] (*f* **sa** [sa], *pl* **ses** [se]) *adj poss* [possesseur défini - homme] his; [- femme] her; [- chose, animal] its. || [possesseur indéfini] one's; [- après «chacun», «tout le monde» etc] his/her, their.

sonate [sɔnat] *nf* sonata.

sondage [sɔ̃daʒ] *nm* [enquête] poll, survey; **~ d'opinion** opinion poll. || TECHNOL drilling. || MÉD probing.

sonde [sɔ̃d] *nf* MÉTÉOR sonde; [spatiale] probe. || MÉD probe. || NAVIG sounding line. || TECHNOL drill.

sonder [sɔ̃de] *vt* MÉD & NAVIG to sound. || [terrain] to drill. || *fig* [opinion, personne] to sound out.

songe [sɔ̃ʒ] *nm littéraire* dream.

songer [sɔ̃ʒe] **1** *vt*: **~ que** to consider that. **2** *vi*: **~ à** to think about.

songeur, -euse [sɔ̃ʒœr, øz] *adj* pensive, thoughtful.

sonnant, -e [sɔnã, ãt] *adj*: **à six heures ~es** at six o'clock sharp.

sonné, -e [sɔne] *adj* [passé]: **il est trois heures ~es** it's gone three o'clock; **il a quarante ans bien ~s** *fam fig* he's the wrong side of forty. || *fig* [étourdi] groggy.

sonner [sɔne] **1** *vt* [cloche] to ring. || [retraite, alarme] to sound. || [domestique] to ring for. **2** *vi* [gén] to ring; **~ chez qqn** to ring sb's bell.

sonnerie [sɔnri] *nf* [bruit] ringing. || [mécanisme] striking mechanism. || [signal] call.

sonnet [sɔnɛ] *nm* sonnet.

sonnette [sɔnɛt] *nf* bell.

sono [sɔno] *nf fam* [de salle] P.A. (system); [de discothèque] sound system.

sonore [sɔnɔr] *adj* CIN & PHYS sound (*avant n*). || [voix, rire] ringing, resonant. || [salle] resonant.

sonorisation [sɔnɔrizasjɔ̃] *nf* [action - de film] addition of the soundtrack; [- de salle] wiring for sound.

sonoriser [sɔnɔrize] *vt* [film] to add the soundtrack to. || [salle] to wire for sound.

sonorité [sɔnɔrite] *nf* [de piano, voix] tone. || [de salle] acoustics (*pl*).

sont → être.

sophistiqué, -e [sɔfistike] *adj* sophisticated.

soporifique [sɔpɔrifik] *adj* soporific.

soprano [sɔprano] (*pl* **sopranos** OU **soprani** [sɔprani]) *nm* & *nmf* soprano.

sorbet [sɔrbɛ] *nm* sorbet.

sorcellerie [sɔrsɛlri] *nf* witchcraft, sorcery.

sorcier, -ière [sɔrsje, jɛr] *nm, f* sorcerer (*f* witch).

sordide [sɔrdid] *adj* squalid; *fig* sordid.

sornettes [sɔrnɛt] *nfpl* nonsense (*U*).

sort [sɔr] *nm* [maléfice] spell; **jeter un ~** (**à qqn**) to cast a spell (on sb). || [destinée] fate. || [condition] lot. || [hasard]: **le ~** fate; **tirer au ~** to draw lots.

sortant, -e [sɔrtã, ãt] *adj* [numéro] winning. || [président, directeur] outgoing (*avant n*).

sorte [sɔrt] *nf* sort, kind; **une ~ de** a sort of, a kind of; **toutes ~s de** all kinds of, all sorts of.

sortie [sɔrti] *nf* [issue] exit, way out; [d'eau, d'air] outlet; **~ de secours** emergency exit. || [départ]: **à la ~ du travail** when work finishes, after work. || [de produit] launch, launching; [de disque] release; [de livre] publication. || (*gén pl*) [dépense] outgoings (*pl*), expenditure (*U*). || [excursion] outing. || MIL sortie. || INFORM: **~ imprimante** printout.

sortilège [sɔrtilɛʒ] *nm* spell.

sortir [sɔrtir] **1** *vi* (*aux: être*) [de la maison, du bureau etc] to leave, to go/come out; **~ de** to go/come out of, to leave. || [pour se distraire] to go out. || *fig* [de maladie]: **~ de** to get over, to recover from; [coma] to come out of. || [film, livre, produit] to come out; [disque] to be released. || [au jeu - carte, numéro] to come up. || [s'écarter de]: **~ de** [sujet] to get away from. || *loc*: **~ de l'ordinaire** to be out of the ordinary; **d'où il sort, celui-là?** where did HE spring from? **2** *vt* (*aux: avoir*) [gén]: **~ qqch (de)** to take sthg out (of). || [de situation difficile] to get out, to extract. || [produit] to launch; [disque] to bring out, to release; [livre] to bring out, to publish. **○ se sortir** *vp fig* [de pétrin] to get out; **s'en ~** [en réchapper] to come out of it; [y arriver] to get through it.

SOS *nm* SOS; **lancer un ~** to send out an SOS.

sosie [sɔzi] *nm* double.

sot, sotte [so, sɔt] **1** *adj* silly, foolish. **2** *nm, f* fool.

sottise [sɔtiz] *nf* stupidity (*U*), foolishness (*U*); **dire/faire une ~** to say/do something stupid.

sou [su] *nm*: **être sans le ~** to be penniless. **○ sous** *nmpl fam* money (*U*).

soubassement [subasmã] *nm* base.

soubresaut [subrəso] *nm* [de voiture] jolt. || [de personne] start.

souche [suʃ] *nf* [d'arbre] stump. || [de carnet] counterfoil, stub.

souci [susi] *nm* [tracas] worry; **se faire du ~** to worry. || [préoccupation] concern.

soucier [susje] **○ se soucier** *vp*: **se ~ de** to care about.

soucieux, -ieuse [susjø, jøz] *adj* [préoccupé] worried, concerned. || [concerné]: **être ~ de qqch/de faire qqch** to be concerned about sthg/about doing sthg.

soucoupe [sukup] *nf* [assiette] saucer. || [vaisseau]: **~ volante** flying saucer.

soudain, -e [sudɛ̃, ɛn] *adj* sudden. **○ soudain** *adv* suddenly, all of a sudden.

soude [sud] *nf* soda.

souder [sude] *vt* TECHNOL to weld, to solder. || MÉD to knit. || *fig* [unir] to bind together.

soudoyer [sudwaje] *vt* to bribe.

soudure [sudyr] *nf* TECHNOL welding; [résultat] weld.

souffert, -e [sufɛr, ɛrt] *pp* → **souffrir**.

souffle [sufl] *nm* [respiration] breathing; **un ~ d'air** *fig* a breath of air, a puff of wind. || [d'explosion] blast. || MÉD: **~ au cœur** heart murmur. || *loc*: **avoir le ~ coupé** to have one's breath taken away.

souffler [sufle] **1** *vt* [bougie] to blow out. || [vitre] to blow out, to shatter. || [chuchoter]: **~ qqch à qqn** to whisper sthg to sb. **2** *vi* [gén] to blow. || [respirer] to puff, to pant.

soufflet [sufle] *nm* [instrument] bellows (*sg*). || [de train] connecting corridor, concertina vestibule. || COUTURE gusset.

souffleur, -euse [suflœr, øz] *nm, f* THÉÂTRE prompt. **○ souffleur** *nm* [de verre] blower.

souffrance [sufrãs] *nf* suffering.

souffrant, -e [sufrã, ãt] *adj* poorly.

souffre-douleur [sufrədulœr] *nm inv* whipping boy.

souffrir [sufrir] **1** *vi* to suffer; **~ de** to suffer from; **~ du dos/cœur** to have back/heart problems. **2** *vt littéraire* [supporter] to stand, to bear.

soufre [sufr] *nm* sulphur.

souhait [swɛ] *nm* wish; **à tes/vos ~s!** bless you!

souhaiter [swete] *vt*: **~ faire qqch** to hope to do sthg; **~ qqch à qqn** to wish sb sthg; **~ à qqn de faire qqch** to hope that sb does sthg; **souhaiter que ...** (+ *subjonctif*) to hope that ....

souiller [suje] *vt littéraire* [salir] to soil; *fig & sout* to sully.

soûl, -e, saoul, -e [su, sul] *adj* drunk.

soulagement [sulaʒmɑ̃] *nm* relief.

soulager [sulaʒe] *vt* [gén] to relieve.

soûler, saouler [sule] *vt fam* [enivrer]: ~ qqn to get sb drunk; *fig* to intoxicate sb. || *fig & péj* [de plaintes]: ~ qqn to bore sb silly. ○ **se soûler** *vp fam* to get drunk.

soulèvement [sulεvmɑ̃] *nm* uprising.

soulever [sulve] *vt* [fardeau, poids] to lift; [rideau] to raise. || *fig* [question] to raise, to bring up. || *fig* [enthousiasme] to generate, to arouse; [tollé] to stir up. ○ **se soulever** *vp* [s'élever] to raise o.s., to lift o.s. || [se révolter] to rise up.

soulier [sulje] *nm* shoe.

souligner [suliɲe] *vt* [par un trait] to underline. || *fig* [insister sur] to underline, to emphasize. || [mettre en valeur] to emphasize.

soumettre [sumεtr] *vt* [astreindre]: ~ qqn à to subject sb to. || [ennemi, peuple] to subjugate. || [projet, problème]: ~ qqch (à) to submit sthg (to). ○ **se soumettre** *vp*: se ~ (à) to submit (to).

soumis, -e [sumi, iz] 1 *pp* → **soumettre.** 2 *adj* submissive.

soumission [sumisjɔ̃] *nf* submission.

soupape [supap] *nf* valve.

soupçon [supsɔ̃] *nm* [suspicion, intuition] suspicion.

soupçonner [supsɔne] *vt* [suspecter] to suspect; ~ qqn de qqch/de faire qqch to suspect sb of sthg/of doing sthg.

soupçonneux, -euse [supsɔnø, øz] *adj* suspicious.

soupe [sup] *nf* CULIN soup; ~ **populaire** soup kitchen.

souper [supe] 1 *nm* supper. 2 *vi* to have supper.

soupeser [supəze] *vt* [poids] to feel the weight of. || *fig* [évaluer] to weigh up.

soupière [supjεr] *nf* tureen.

soupir [supir] *nm* [souffle] sigh; **pousser un** ~ to let out ou give a sigh. || MUS crotchet rest *Br*, quarter-note rest *Am*.

soupirail, -aux [supiraj, o] *nm* barred basement window.

soupirant [supirɑ̃] *nm* suitor.

soupirer [supire] *vi* [souffler] to sigh.

souple [supl] *adj* [gymnaste] supple. || [paquet, col] soft. || [tissu, cheveux] flowing. || [tuyau, horaire, caractère] flexible.

souplesse [suplεs] *nf* [de gymnaste] suppleness. || [flexibilité - de tuyau] pliability, flexibility; [- de matière] suppleness. || [de personne] flexibility.

source [surs] *nf* [gén] source. || [d'eau] spring; **prendre sa** ~ **à** to rise in.

sourcil [sursi] *nm* eyebrow.

sourcilière [sursiljεr] → **arcade.**

sourciller [sursije] *vi*: **sans** ~ without batting an eyelid.

sourcilleux, -euse [sursijø, øz] *adj* fussy, finicky.

sourd, -e [sur, surd] 1 *adj* [personne] deaf. || [bruit, voix] muffled. || [douleur] dull. || [lutte, hostilité] silent. 2 *nm, f* deaf person.

sourdine [surdin] *nf* mute; **en** ~ [sans bruit] softly; [secrètement] in secret.

sourd-muet, sourde-muette [surmɥε, surdmɥεt] *nm, f* deaf-mute, deaf and dumb person.

souriant, -e [surjɑ̃, ɑ̃t] *adj* smiling, cheerful.

souricière [surisjεr] *nf* mousetrap; *fig* trap.

sourire [surir] 1 *vi* to smile; ~ **à** qqn to smile at sb; *fig* [destin, chance] to smile on sb. 2 *nm* smile.

souris [suri] *nf* INFORM & ZOOL mouse.

sournois, -e [surnwa, az] 1 *adj* [personne] underhand. || *fig* [maladie, phénomène] unpredictable.

sous [su] *prép* [gén] under; **nager** ~ **l'eau** to swim underwater; ~ **la pluie** in the rain; ~ **cet aspect** ou **angle** from that point of view. || [dans un délai de] within.

sous-alimenté, -e [suzalimɑ̃te] *adj* malnourished, underfed.

sous-bois [subwa] *nm inv* undergrowth.

souscription [suskripsjɔ̃] *nf* subscription.

souscrire [suskrir] *vi*: ~ **à** to subscribe to.

sous-développé, -e [sudevlɔpe] *adj* ÉCON underdeveloped; *fig & péj* backward.

sous-directeur, -trice [sudirεktœr, tris] *nm, f* assistant manager (*f* assistant manageress).

sous-ensemble [suzɑ̃sɑ̃bl] *nm* subset.

sous-entendu [suzɑ̃tɑ̃dy] *nm* insinuation.

sous-estimer [suzεstime] *vt* to underestimate, to underrate.

sous-évaluer [suzevalɥe] *vt* to underestimate.

sous-jacent, -e [suʒasɑ̃, ɑ̃t] *adj* underlying.

sous-louer [sulwe] *vt* to sublet.

sous-marin, -e [sumarɛ̃, in] *adj* under-water (*avant n*). ○ **sous-marin** *nm* submarine.

sous-officier [suzɔfisje] *nm* non-commissioned officer.

sous-préfecture [suprefɛktyr] *nf* sub-prefecture.

sous-préfet [suprefɛ] *nm* sub-prefect.

sous-produit [suprɔdɥi] *nm* [objet] by-product.

soussigné, -e [susiɲe] **1** *adj*: je ~ l the undersigned. **2** *nm, f* undersigned.

sous-sol [susɔl] *nm* [de bâtiment] base-ment. || [naturel] subsoil.

sous-tasse [sutas] *nf* saucer.

sous-titre [sutitr] *nm* subtitle.

soustraction [sustraksjɔ̃] *nf* MATHS subtraction.

soustraire [sustrɛr] *vt* [retrancher]: ~ qqch de to subtract sthg from. || *sout* [voler]: ~ qqch à qqn to take sthg away from sb. ○ **se soustraire** *vp*: se ~ à to escape from.

sous-traitant, -e [sutrɛtɑ̃, ɑ̃t] *adj* sub-contracting. ○ **sous-traitant** *nm* subcontractor.

sous-verre [suvɛr] *nm inv* picture or document framed between a sheet of glass and a rigid backing.

sous-vêtement [suvɛtmɑ̃] *nm* under-garment; ~s underwear (*U*), under-clothes.

soutane [sutan] *nf* cassock.

soute [sut] *nf* hold.

soutenance [sutnɑ̃s] *nf* viva.

'souteneur [sutnœr] *nm* procurer.

soutenir [sutnir] *vt* [immeuble, per-sonne] to support, to hold up. || [encoura-ger] to support; POLIT to back, to support. || [affirmer]: ~ **que** to maintain (that).

soutenu, -e [sutny] *adj* [style, langage] elevated. || [attention, rythme] sustained. || [couleur] vivid.

souterrain, -e [sutɛrɛ̃, ɛn] *adj* under-ground. ○ **souterrain** *nm* under-ground passage.

soutien [sutjɛ̃] *nm* support.

soutien-gorge [sutjɛ̃gɔrʒ] (*pl* soutiens-gorge) *nm* bra.

soutirer [sutire] *vt fig* [tirer]: ~ qqch à qqn to extract sthg from sb.

souvenir [suvnir] *nm* [réminiscence, mé-moire] memory. || [objet] souvenir. ○ **se souvenir** *vp* [ne pas oublier]: se ~ de qqch/de qqn to remember sthg/sb.

souvent [suvɑ̃] *adv* often.

souvenu, -e [suvny] *pp* → **souvenir**.

souverain, -e [suvrɛ̃, ɛn] **1** *adj* [remède, état] sovereign. || [indifférence] supreme. **2** *nm, f* [monarque] sovereign, monarch.

souveraineté [suvrɛnte] *nf* sovereign-ty.

soviétique [sɔvjetik] *adj* Soviet. ○ **Soviétique** *nmf* Soviet (citizen).

soyeux, -euse [swajø, øz] *adj* silky.

soyez → **être**.

SPA (*abr de* **Société protectrice des animaux**) *nf* French society for the pro-tection of animals, ≃ SPCA *Am*.

spacieux, -ieuse [spasjø, jøz] *adj* spa-cious.

spaghettis [spageti] *nmpl* spaghetti (*U*).

sparadrap [sparadra] *nm* sticking plas-ter.

spasme [spasm] *nm* spasm.

spasmodique [spasmɔdik] *adj* spas-modic.

spatial, -e, -iaux [spasjal, jo] *adj* space (*avant n*).

spatule [spatyl] *nf* [ustensile] spatula. || [de ski] tip.

speaker, speakerine [spikœr, spikrin] *nm, f* announcer.

spécial, -e, -iaux [spesjal, jo] *adj* [par-ticulier] special. || *fam* [bizarre] peculiar.

spécialiser [spesjalize] *vt* to specialize. ○ **se spécialiser** *vp*: se ~ (**dans**) to spe-cialize (in).

spécialiste [spesjalist] *nmf* specialist.

spécialité [spesjalite] *nf* speciality.

spécifier [spesifje] *vt* to specify.

spécifique [spesifik] *adj* specific.

spécimen [spesimɛn] *nm* [représentant] specimen. || [exemplaire] sample.

spectacle [spɛktakl] *nm* [représenta-tion] show. || [domaine] show business, entertainment. || [tableau] spectacle, sight.

spectaculaire [spɛktakylɛr] *adj* spec-tacular.

spectateur, -trice [spɛktatœr, tris] *nm, f* [témoin] witness. || [de spectacle] spectator.

spectre [spɛktr] *nm* [fantôme] spectre. || PHYS spectrum.

spéculateur, -trice [spekylatœr, tris] *nm, f* speculator.

spéculation [spekylasjɔ̃] *nf* specula-tion.

spéculer [spekyle] *vi*: ~ **sur** FIN to speculate in; *fig* [miser] to count on.

spéléologie [speleɔlɔʒi] *nf* [exploration] potholing; [science] speleology.

spermatozoïde [spɛrmatɔzɔid] *nm* sperm, spermatozoon.

sperme [spɛrm] *nm* sperm, semen.

sphère [sfɛr] *nf* sphere.

sphérique [sferik] *adj* spherical.

spirale [spiral] *nf* spiral.

spirituel, -elle [spirityɛl] *adj* [de l'âme, moral] spiritual. || [vivant, drôle] witty.

splendeur [splɑ̃dœr] *nf* [beauté, prospérité] splendour. || [merveille]: **c'est une ~!** it's magnificent!

splendide [splɑ̃did] *adj* magnificent, splendid.

spongieux, -ieuse [spɔ̃ʒjø, jøz] *adj* spongy.

sponsor [spɔ̃sɔr] *nm* sponsor.

sponsoriser [spɔ̃sɔrize] *vt* to sponsor.

spontané, -e [spɔ̃tane] *adj* spontaneous.

spontanéité [spɔ̃taneite] *nf* spontaneity.

sporadique [spɔradik] *adj* sporadic.

sport [spɔr] *nm* sport; **~s d'hiver** winter sports.

sportif, -ive [spɔrtif, iv] **1** *adj* [association, résultats] sports (*avant n*). || [personne, physique] sporty, athletic. **2** *nm, f* sportsman (*f* sportswoman).

spot [spɔt] *nm* [lampe] spot, spotlight. || [publicité]: **~ (publicitaire)** commercial, advert.

sprint [sprint] *nm* [SPORT - accélération] spurt; [- course] sprint.

square [skwar] *nm* small public garden.

squash [skwaʃ] *nm* squash.

squelette [skəlɛt] *nm* skeleton.

squelettique [skəletik] *adj* [corps] emaciated.

St (*abr de* **saint**) St.

stabiliser [stabilize] *vt* [gén] to stabilize; [meuble] to steady. ○ **se stabiliser** *vp* [véhicule, prix, situation] to stabilize. || [personne] to settle down.

stabilité [stabilite] *nf* stability.

stable [stabl] *adj* [gén] stable. || [meuble] steady, stable.

stade [stad] *nm* [terrain] stadium. || [étape & MÉD] stage.

stage [staʒ] *nm* COMM work placement; [sur le temps de travail] in-service training; **faire un ~** [cours] to go on a training course; [expérience professionnelle] to go on a work placement.

stagiaire [staʒjɛr] *nmf* trainee.

stagnant, -e [stagnɑ̃, ɑ̃t] *adj* stagnant.

stagner [stagne] *vi* to stagnate.

stalactite [stalaktit] *nf* stalactite.

stalagmite [stalagmit] *nf* stalagmite.

stand [stɑ̃d] *nm* [d'exposition] stand. || [de fête] stall.

standard [stɑ̃dar] **1** *adj inv* standard. **2** *nm* [norme] standard. || [téléphonique] switchboard.

standardiste [stɑ̃dardist] *nmf* switchboard operator.

standing [stɑ̃diŋ] *nm* standing; **quartier de grand ~** select district.

star [star] *nf* CIN star.

starter [startɛr] *nm* AUTOM choke; **mettre le ~** to pull the choke out.

starting-block [startiŋblɔk] (*pl* **starting-blocks**) *nm* starting-block.

station [stasjɔ̃] *nf* [arrêt - de bus] stop; [- de métro] station; **~ de taxis** taxi rank. || [installations] station; **~ d'épuration** sewage treatment plant. || [ville] resort; **~ balnéaire** seaside resort; **~ de ski/de sports d'hiver** ski/winter sports resort; **~ thermale** spa (town). || INFORM: **~ de travail** work station.

stationnaire [stasjɔnɛr] *adj* stationary.

stationnement [stasjɔnmɑ̃] *nm* parking; **«~ interdit»** "no parking".

stationner [stasjɔne] *vi* to park.

station-service [stasjɔ̃sɛrvis] (*pl* **stations-service**) *nf* gas station *Am*.

statique [statik] *adj* static.

statisticien, -ienne [statistisjɛ̃, jɛn] *nm, f* statistician.

statistique [statistik] **1** *adj* statistical. **2** *nf* [donnée] statistic.

statue [staty] *nf* statue.

statuer [statye] *vi*: **~ sur** to give a decision on.

statuette [statyɛt] *nf* statuette.

statu quo [statykwo] *nm inv* status quo.

stature [statyr] *nf* stature.

statut [staty] *nm* status. ○ **statuts** *nmpl* statutes.

Ste (*abr de* **sainte**) St.

Sté (*abr de* **société**) Co.

steak [stɛk] *nm* steak; **~ haché** mince.

stèle [stɛl] *nf* stele.

sténo [steno] *nf* shorthand.

sténodactylo [stenɔdaktilo] *nmf* shorthand typist.

sténodactylographie [stenɔdaktilɔgrafi] *nf* shorthand typing.

steppe [stɛp] *nf* steppe.

stéréo [stereo] **1** *adj inv* stereo. **2** *nf* stereo; **en ~** in stereo.

stéréotype [stereɔtip] *nm* stereotype.

stérile [steril] *adj* [personne] sterile, infertile; [terre] barren. || *fig* [inutile - discussion] sterile; [- efforts] futile. || MÉD sterile.

stérilet [sterilɛ] *nm* IUD, intra-uterine device.

stériliser [sterilize] *vt* to sterilize.

stérilité [sterilite] *nf litt & fig* sterility.

sternum [stɛrnɔm] *nm* breastbone, sternum.

stéthoscope [stetɔskɔp] *nm* stethoscope.

steward [stiwart] *nm* steward.

stigmate [stigmat] *nm* (*gén pl*) mark, scar.

stimulant, -e [stimylɑ̃, ɑ̃t] *adj* stimulating. ○ **stimulant** *nm* [remontant] stimulant.

stimulation [stimylasjɔ̃] *nf* stimulation.

stimuler [stimyle] *vt* to stimulate.

stipuler [stipyle] *vt*: ~ que to stipulate (that).

stock [stɔk] *nm* stock; en ~ in stock.

stocker [stɔke] *vt* [marchandises] to stock. || INFORM to store.

stoïque [stɔik] *adj* stoical.

stop [stɔp] 1 *interj* stop! 2 *nm* [panneau] stop sign. || [auto-stop] hitch-hiking, hitching.

stopper [stɔpe] 1 *vt* [arrêter] to stop, to halt. 2 *vi* to stop.

store [stɔr] *nm* [de fenêtre] blind. || [de magasin] awning.

strabisme [strabism] *nm* squint.

strangulation [strɑ̃gylasjɔ̃] *nf* strangulation.

strapontin [strapɔ̃tɛ̃] *nm* [siège] pull-down seat.

strass [stras] *nm* paste.

stratagème [strataʒɛm] *nm* stratagem.

stratégie [strateʒi] *nf* strategy.

stratégique [strateʒik] *adj* strategic.

stress [strɛs] *nm* stress.

stressant, -e [strɛsɑ̃, ɑ̃t] *adj* stressful.

strict, -e [strikt] *adj* [personne, règlement] strict. || [sobre] plain. || [absolu - minimum] bare, absolute; [- vérité] absolute; **dans la plus ~e intimité** strictly in private.

strident, -e [stridɑ̃, ɑ̃t] *adj* strident, shrill.

strié, -e [strije] *adj* [rayé] striped.

strip-tease [striptiz] (*pl* **strip-teases**) *nm* striptease.

strophe [strɔf] *nf* verse.

structure [stryktyr] *nf* structure.

structurer [stryktyre] *vt* to structure.

studieux, -ieuse [stydjø, jøz] *adj* [personne] studious.

studio [stydjo] *nm* CIN, PHOT & TÉLÉ studio. || [appartement] studio apartment *Am*.

stupéfaction [stypefaksjɔ̃] *nf* astonishment, stupefaction.

stupéfait, -e [stypefɛ, ɛt] *adj* astounded, stupefied.

stupéfiant, -e [stypefjɑ̃, ɑ̃t] *adj* astounding, stunning. ○ **stupéfiant** *nm* narcotic, drug.

stupeur [stypœr] *nf* [stupéfaction] astonishment. || MÉD stupor.

stupide [stypid] *adj péj* [abruti] stupid. || [insensé - mort] senseless; [- accident] stupid.

stupidité [stypidite] *nf* stupidity.

style [stil] *nm* [gén] style. || GRAM: ~ direct/indirect direct/indirect speech.

styliste [stilist] *nmf* COUTURE designer.

stylo [stilo] *nm* pen; ~ plume fountain pen.

stylo-feutre [stiloføtr] *nm* felt-tip pen.

su, -e [sy] *pp* → **savoir**.

suave [sɥav] *adj* [voix] smooth.

subalterne [sybaltɛrn] 1 *nmf* subordinate, junior. 2 *adj* [rôle] subordinate; [employé] junior.

subconscient, -e [sybkɔ̃sjɑ̃, ɑ̃t] *adj* subconscious. ○ **subconscient** *nm* subconscious.

subdiviser [sybdivize] *vt* to subdivide.

subir [sybir] *vt* [conséquences, colère] to suffer; [personne] to put up with. || [opération, épreuve, examen] to undergo. || [dommages, pertes] to sustain, to suffer.

subit, -e [sybi, it] *adj* sudden.

subitement [sybitmɑ̃] *adv* suddenly.

subjectif, -ive [sybʒɛktif, iv] *adj* [personnel, partial] subjective.

subjonctif [sybʒɔ̃ktif] *nm* subjunctive.

subjuguer [sybʒyge] *vt* to captivate.

sublime [syblim] *adj* sublime.

submerger [symbɛrʒe] *vt* [inonder] to flood. || [déborder] to overwhelm; **être submergé de travail** to be swamped with work.

subordonné, -e [sybɔrdɔne] 1 *adj* GRAM subordinate, dependent. 2 *nm, f* subordinate.

subornation [sybɔrnasjɔ̃] *nf* bribing, subornation.

subrepticement [sybrɛptismɑ̃] *adv* surreptitiously.

subsidiaire [sybzidjɛr] *adj* subsidiary.

subsistance [sybzistɑ̃s] *nf* subsistence.

subsister [sybziste] *vi* [chose] to remain. || [personne] to live, to subsist.

substance [sypstɑ̃s] *nf* [matière] substance. || [essence] gist.

substantiel, -ielle [sypstɑ̃sjɛl] *adj* substantial.

substantif [sypstɑ̃tif] *nm* noun.

substituer [sypstitɥe] *vt*: ~ qqch à qqch to substitute sthg for sthg. ○ **se substituer** *vp*: se ~ à [personne] to stand in for, to substitute for; [chose] to take the place of.

substitut [sypstity] *nm* [remplacement] substitute.

substitution [sypstitysjɔ̃] *nf* substitution.

subterfuge [sypterfyʒ] *nm* subterfuge.

subtil, -e [syptil] *adj* subtle.

subtiliser [syptilize] *vt* to steal.

subtilité [syptilite] *nf* subtlety.

subvenir [sybvənir] *vi*: ~ à to meet, to cover.

subvention [sybvɑ̃sjɔ̃] *nf* grant, subsidy.

subventionner [sybvɑ̃sjɔne] *vt* to give a grant to, to subsidize.

subversif, -ive [sybversif, iv] *adj* subversive.

succédané [syksedane] *nm* substitute.

succéder [syksede] *vt*: ~ à [suivre] to follow; [remplacer] to succeed, to take over from. ○ **se succéder** *vp* to follow one another.

succès [syksɛ] *nm* [gén] success; **avoir du ~** to be very successful; **sans ~** [essayer] unsuccessfully. || [chanson, pièce] hit.

successeur [syksesœr] *nm* [gén] successor. || JUR successor, heir.

successif, -ive [syksesif, iv] *adj* successive.

succession [syksesjɔ̃] *nf* [gén] succession; **prendre la ~ de qqn** to take over from sb, to succeed sb. || JUR succession, inheritance; **droits de ~** death duties.

succinct, -e [syksɛ̃, ɛ̃t] *adj* [résumé] succinct. || [repas] frugal.

succion [sysjɔ̃] *nf* suction, sucking.

succomber [sykɔ̃be] *vi*: ~ (à) to succumb (to).

succulent, -e [sykylɑ̃, ɑ̃t] *adj* delicious.

succursale [sykyrsal] *nf* branch.

sucer [syse] *vt* to suck.

sucette [sysɛt] *nf* [friandise] lollipop.

sucre [sykr] *nm* sugar; ~ **en morceaux**

lump sugar; ~ **en poudre**, ~ **semoule** caster sugar.

sucré, -e [sykre] *adj* [goût] sweet.

sucrer [sykre] *vt* [café, thé] to sweeten, to sugar.

sucrerie [sykrəri] *nf* [usine] sugar refinery. || [friandise] sweet *Br*, candy *Am*.

sucrette [sykret] *nf* sweetener.

sucrier [sykrije] *nm* sugar bowl.

sud [syd] **1** *nm* south; **un vent du** ~ a southerly wind; **au** ~ in the south; **au** ~ **(de)** to the south (of). **2** *adj inv* [gén] south; [province, région] southern.

sud-africain, -e [sydafrikɛ̃, ɛn] (*mpl* **sud-africains,** *fpl* **sud-africaines**) *adj* South African. ○ **Sud-Africain, -e** *nm*, *f* South African.

sud-américain, -e [sydamerikɛ̃, ɛn] (*mpl* **sud-américains,** *fpl* **sud-américaines**) *adj* South American. ○ **Sud-Américain, -e** *nm*, *f* South American.

sud-est [sydest] *nm* & *adj inv* southeast.

sud-ouest [sydwest] *nm* & *adj inv* southwest.

Suède [sɥed] *nf*: **la** ~ Sweden.

suédois, -e [sɥedwa, az] *adj* Swedish. ○ **suédois** *nm* [langue] Swedish. ○ **Suédois, -e** *nm*, *f* Swede.

suer [sɥe] *vi* [personne] to sweat.

sueur [sɥœr] *nf* sweat; **avoir des ~s froides** *fig* to be in a cold sweat.

Suez [sɥɛz] *n*: **le canal de** ~ the Suez Canal.

suffi [syfi] *pp inv* → **suffire**.

suffire [syfir] **1** *vi* [être assez]: ~ **pour qqch/pour faire qqch** to be enough for sthg/to do sthg, to be sufficient for sthg/to do sthg; **ça suffit!** that's enough! || [satisfaire]: ~ **à** to be enough for. **2** *v impers*: **il suffit de ...** all that is necessary is ..., all that you have to do is ...; **il suffit que vous lui écriviez** all (that) you need do is write to him. ○ **se suffire** *vp*: se ~ **à soi-même** to be self-sufficient.

suffisamment [syfizamɑ̃] *adv* sufficiently.

suffisant, -e [syfizɑ̃, ɑ̃t] *adj* [satisfaisant] sufficient. || [vaniteux] self-important.

suffixe [syfiks] *nm* suffix.

suffoquer [syfɔke] **1** *vt* [suj: chaleur, fumée] to suffocate. || *fig* [suj: colère] to choke; [suj: nouvelle, révélation] to astonish, to stun. **2** *vi* to choke.

suffrage [syfraʒ] *nm* vote.

suggérer [sygʒere] *vt* [proposer] to suggest; ~ à qqn de faire qqch to suggest that sb (should) do sthg. || [faire penser à] to evoke.

suggestif, -ive [sygʒestif, iv] *adj* [pose, photo] suggestive.

suggestion [sygʒestjɔ̃] *nf* suggestion.

suicidaire [sɥisidɛr] *adj* suicidal.

suicide [sɥisid] *nm* suicide.

suicider [sɥiside] ○ **se suicider** *vp* to commit suicide, to kill o.s.

suie [sɥi] *nf* soot.

suinter [sɥɛ̃te] *vi* [eau, sang] to ooze, to seep. || [surface, mur] to sweat; [plaie] to weep.

suis → être.

suisse [sɥis] *adj* Swiss. ○ **Suisse 1** *nf* [pays]: la ~ Switzerland; la ~ allemande/italienne/romande German-/Italian-/French-speaking Switzerland. 2 *nmf* [personne] Swiss (person); les Suisses the Swiss.

suite [sɥit] *nf* [de liste, feuilleton] continuation. || [série - de maisons, de succès] series; [- d'événements] sequence. || [succession]: prendre la ~ de [personne] to succeed, to take over from. à la ~ one after the other; à la ~ de *fig* following. || [escorte] retinue. || [appartement] suite. ○ **suites** *nfpl* consequences. ○ **par suite de** *loc prép* owing to, because of.

suivant, -e [sɥivɑ̃, ɑ̃t] 1 *adj* next, following. 2 *nm, f* next ou following one; au ~! next!

suivi, -e [sɥivi] 1 *pp* → suivre. 2 *adj* [visites] regular; [travail] sustained; [qualité] consistent. ○ **suivi** *nm* follow-up.

suivre [sɥivr] 1 *vt* [gén] to follow; «faire ~» "please forward"; à ~ to be continued. || [suj: médecin] to treat. 2 *vi* SCOL to keep up. || [venir après] to follow. ○ **se suivre** *vp* to follow one another.

sujet, -ette [syʒɛ, ɛt] 1 *adj*: être ~ à qqch to be subject ou prone to sthg. 2 *nm, f* [de souverain] subject. ○ **sujet** *nm* [gén] subject; c'est à quel ~? what is it about?; au ~ de about, concerning.

sulfate [sylfat] *nm* sulphate.

sulfurique [sylfyrik] *adj* sulphuric.

super [sypɛr] *fam* 1 *adj inv* super, great. 2 *nm* premium *Am*.

superbe [sypɛrb] *adj* superb; [enfant, femme] beautiful.

supercherie [sypɛrʃəri] *nf* deception.

superficie [sypɛrfisi] *nf* [surface] area. || *fig* [aspect superficiel] surface.

superficiel, -ielle [sypɛrfisjɛl] *adj* superficial.

superflu, -e [sypɛrfly] *adj* superfluous.

supérieur, -e [syperjœr] 1 *adj* [étage] upper. || [intelligence, qualité] superior; ~ à superior to; [température] higher than, above. || [dominant - équipe] superior; [- cadre] senior. || [SCOL - classe] upper, senior; [- enseignement] higher. || *péj* [air] superior. 2 *nm, f* superior.

supériorité [syperjɔrite] *nf* superiority.

superlatif [sypɛrlatif] *nm* superlative.

supermarché [sypɛrmarʃe] *nm* supermarket.

superposer [sypɛrpoze] *vt* to stack. ○ **se superposer** *vp* to be stacked.

superproduction [sypɛrprɔdyksjɔ̃] *nf* spectacular.

superpuissance [sypɛrpɥisɑ̃s] *nf* superpower.

supersonique [sypɛrsɔnik] *adj* supersonic.

superstitieux, -ieuse [sypɛrstisjø, jøz] *adj* superstitious.

superstition [sypɛrstisjɔ̃] *nf* [croyance] superstition.

superviser [sypɛrvize] *vt* to supervise.

supplanter [syplɑ̃te] *vt* to supplant.

suppléant, -e [sypleɑ̃, ɑ̃t] 1 *adj* acting (*avant n*), temporary. 2 *nm, f* substitute, deputy.

suppléer [syplee] *vt littéraire* [carence] to compensate for. || [personne] to stand in for.

supplément [syplemɑ̃] *nm* [surplus]: un ~ de détails additional details, extra details. || PRESSE supplement. || [de billet] extra charge.

supplémentaire [syplemɑ̃tɛr] *adj* extra, additional.

supplication [syplikasjɔ̃] *nf* plea.

supplice [syplis] *nm* torture; *fig* [souffrance] torture, agony.

supplier [syplije] *vt*: ~ qqn de faire qqch to beg ou implore sb to do sthg.

support [sypɔr] *nm* [socle] support, base. || *fig* [de communication] medium; ~ publicitaire advertising medium.

supportable [sypɔrtabl] *adj* [douleur] bearable.

supporter¹ [sypɔrte] *vt* [soutenir, encourager] to support. || [endurer] to bear, to stand; ~ que (+ *subjonctif*): il ne supporte pas qu'on le contredise he cannot bear being contradicted. || [résister à] to withstand.

supporter² [sypɔrtɛr] *nm* supporter.

supposer [sypoze] *vt* [imaginer] to suppose, to assure; **en supposant que** (+ *subjonctif*), **à ~ que** (+ *subjonctif*) supposing (that). || [impliquer] to imply, to presuppose.

supposition [sypozisjɔ̃] *nf* supposition, assumption.

suppositoire [sypozitwar] *nm* suppository.

suppression [sypresjɔ̃] *nf* [de mot, passage] deletion. || [de loi, poste] abolition.

supprimer [syprime] *vt* [obstacle, difficulté] to remove. || [mot, passage] to delete. || [loi, poste] to abolish. || [témoin] to do away with, to eliminate. || [permis de conduire, revenus] : **~ qqch à qqn** to take sthg away from sb. || [douleur] to take away, to suppress.

suprématie [sypremasi] *nf* supremacy.

suprême [syprɛm] *adj* [gén] supreme.

sur [syr] *prép* [position - dessus] on; [- au-dessus de] above, over; **~ la table** on the table. || [direction] towards; **~ la droite/gauche** on the right/left, to the right/left. || [distance] : **travaux ~ 10 kilomètres** roadworks for 10 kilometres. || [au sujet de] on, about. || [proportion] out of; [mesure] by; **9 ~ 10** 9 out of 10; **un mètre ~ deux** one metre by two; **un jour ~ deux** every other day. ○ **sur ce** *loc adv* whereupon.

sûr, -e [syr] *adj* [sans danger] safe. || [digne de confiance - personne] reliable, trustworthy; [- goût] reliable, sound; [- investissement] sound. || [certain] sure, certain; **~ de** sure of; **~ de soi** self-confident.

surabondance [syrabɔ̃dɑ̃s] *nf* overabundance.

suraigu, -ë [syregy] *adj* high-pitched, shrill.

suranné, -e [syrane] *adj littéraire* old-fashioned, outdated.

surcharge [syrʃarʒ] *nf* [excès de poids] excess load; [- de bagages] excess weight. || *fig* [surcroît] : **une ~ de travail** extra work. || [de document] alteration.

surcharger [syrʃarʒe] *vt* [véhicule, personne] : **~ (de)** to overload (with).

surcroît [syrkrwa] *nm* : **un ~ de travail/d'inquiétude** additional work/anxiety.

surdité [syrdite] *nf* deafness.

surdoué, -e [syrdwe] *adj* exceptionally or highly gifted.

sureffectif [syrefɛktif] *nm* overmanning, overstaffing.

surélever [syrelve] *vt* to raise, to heighten.

sûrement [syrmɑ̃] *adv* [certainement] certainly; **~ pas!** *fam* no way!, definitely not! || [sans doute] certainly, surely.

surenchère [syrɑ̃ʃɛr] *nf* higher bid; *fig* overstatement, exaggeration.

surenchérir [syrɑ̃ʃerir] *vi* to bid higher; *fig* to try to go one better.

surendetté, -e [syrɑ̃dɛte] *adj* overindebted.

surestimer [syrɛstime] *vt* [exagérer] to overestimate. || [surévaluer] to overvalue. ○ **se surestimer** *vp* to overestimate o.s.

sûreté [syrte] *nf* [sécurité] safety; **en ~** safe; **de ~** safety (*avant n*). || [fiabilité] reliability. || JUR surety.

surexposer [syrɛkspoze] *vt* to overexpose.

surf [sœrf] *nm* surfing.

surface [syrfas] *nf* [extérieur, apparence] surface. || [superficie] surface area. ○ **grande surface** *nf* hypermarket.

surfait, -e [syrfɛ, ɛt] *adj* overrated.

surfer [sœrfe] *vi* to go surfing.

surgelé, -e [syrʒəle] *adj* frozen. ○ **surgelé** *nm* frozen food.

surgir [syrʒir] *vi* to appear suddenly; *fig* [difficulté] to arise, to come up.

surhumain, -e [syrymɛ̃, ɛn] *adj* superhuman.

surimpression [syrɛ̃presjɔ̃] *nf* double exposure.

sur-le-champ [syrləʃɑ̃] *loc adv* immediately, straightaway.

surlendemain [syrlɑ̃dmɛ̃] *nm* : **le ~** two days later; **le ~ de mon départ** two days after I left.

surligner [syrliɲe] *vt* to highlight.

surligneur [syrliɲœr] *nm* highlighter (pen).

surmenage [syrmənaʒ] *nm* overwork.

surmener [syrməne] *vt* to overwork. ○ **se surmener** *vp* to overwork.

surmonter [syrmɔ̃te] *vt* [obstacle, peur] to overcome, to surmount. || [suj: statue, croix] to surmount, to top.

surnager [syrnaʒe] *vi* [flotter] to float (on the surface).

surnaturel, -elle [syrnatyrɛl] *adj* supernatural. ○ **surnaturel** *nm* : **le ~** the supernatural.

surnom [syrnɔ̃] *nm* nickname.

surpasser [syrpase] *vt* to surpass, to outdo. ○ **se surpasser** *vp* to surpass or excel o.s.

surpeuplé, -e [syrpœple] *adj* over-populated.

surplomb [syrplɔ̃] ○ **en surplomb** *loc adj* overhanging.

surplomber [syrplɔ̃be] **1** *vt* to overhang. **2** *vi* to be out of plumb.

surplus [syrply] *nm* [excédent] surplus.

surprenant, -e [syrprənɑ̃, ɑ̃t] *adj* surprising, amazing.

surprendre [syrprɑ̃dr] *vt* [voleur] to catch (in the act). || [prendre à l'improviste] to surprise, to catch unawares. || [étonner] to surprise, to amaze.

surpris, -e [syrpri, iz] *pp* → surprendre.

surprise [syrpriz] *nf* surprise; **par ~** by surprise; **faire une ~ à qqn** to give sb a surprise.

surproduction [syrprɔdyksjɔ̃] *nf* overproduction.

surréalisme [syrrealism] *nm* surrealism.

sursaut [syrso] *nm* [de personne] jump, start; **en ~** with a start.

sursauter [syrsote] *vi* to start, to give a start.

sursis [syrsi] *nm* JUR & *fig* reprieve; **six mois avec ~** six months' suspended sentence.

surtaxe [syrtaks] *nf* surcharge.

surtout [syrtu] *adv* [avant tout] above all. || [spécialement] especially, particularly; **~ pas** certainly not. ○ **surtout que** *loc conj fam* especially as.

survécu, -e [syrveky] *pp* → survivre.

surveillance [syrvɛjɑ̃s] *nf* supervision.

surveillant, -e [syrvɛjɑ̃, ɑ̃t] *nm, f* supervisor; [de prison] warder *Br*, guard.

surveiller [syrvɛje] *vt* [enfant] to watch, to keep an eye on. || [travaux] to supervise; [examen] to invigilate. || [ligne, langage] to watch. ○ **se surveiller** *vp* to watch o.s.

survenir [syrvənir] *vi* [incident] to occur.

survenu, -e [syrvəny] *pp* → survenir.

survêtement [syrvɛtmɑ̃] *nm* tracksuit.

survie [syrvi] *nf* [de personne] survival.

survivant, -e [syrvivɑ̃, ɑ̃t] **1** *nm, f* survivor. **2** *adj* surviving.

survivre [syrvivr] *vi* to survive; **~ à** [personne] to outlive, to survive; [accident, malheur] to survive.

survoler [syrvɔle] *vt* [territoire] to fly over. || [texte] to skim (through).

sus [sy(s)] ○ **en sus** *loc adv* moreover,

in addition; **en ~ de** over and above, in addition to.

susceptibilité [sysɛptibilite] *nf* touchiness, sensitivity.

susceptible [sysɛptibl] *adj* [ombrageux] touchy, sensitive. || [en mesure de]: **~ de faire qqch** liable or likely to do sthg.

susciter [sysite] *vt* [admiration, curiosité] to arouse.

suspect, -e [syspɛ, ɛkt] **1** *adj* [personne] suspicious. || [douteux] suspect. **2** *nm, f* suspect.

suspecter [syspɛkte] *vt* to suspect, to have one's suspicions about; **~ qqn de qqch/de faire qqch** to suspect sb of sthg/of doing sthg.

suspendre [syspɑ̃dr] *vt* [lustre, tableau] to hang (up). || [pourparlers] to suspend; [séance] to adjourn. || [fonctionnaire, constitution] to suspend. || [jugement] to postpone, to defer.

suspendu, -e [syspɑ̃dy] **1** *pp* → suspendre. **2** *adj* [fonctionnaire] suspended. || [séance] adjourned. || [lustre, tableau]: **~ au plafond/au mur** hanging from the ceiling/on the wall.

suspens [syspɑ̃] ○ **en suspens** *loc adv* in abeyance.

suspense [syspɛns] *nm* suspense.

suspension [syspɑ̃sjɔ̃] *nf* [gén] suspension. || [de combat] halt; [d'audience] adjournment. || [lustre] light fitting.

suspicion [syspisjɔ̃] *nf* suspicion.

susurrer [sysyre] *vt* & *vi* to murmur.

suture [sytyr] *nf* suture.

svelte [zvɛlt] *adj* slender.

SVP *abr de* s'il vous plaît.

sweat-shirt [switfœrt] (*pl* sweat-shirts) *nm* sweatshirt.

syllabe [silab] *nf* syllable.

symbole [sɛ̃bɔl] *nm* symbol.

symbolique [sɛ̃bɔlik] *adj* [figure] symbolic. || [geste, contribution] token (*avant n*). || [rémunération] nominal.

symboliser [sɛ̃bɔlize] *vt* to symbolize.

symétrie [simetri] *nf* symmetry.

symétrique [simetrik] *adj* symmetrical.

sympa [sɛ̃pa] *adj fam* [personne] likeable, nice; [soirée, maison] pleasant, nice; [ambiance] friendly.

sympathie [sɛ̃pati] *nf* [pour personne, projet] liking. || [condoléances] sympathy.

sympathique [sɛ̃patik] *adj* [personne] likeable, nice; [soirée, maison] pleasant, nice; [ambiance] friendly. || ANAT & MÉD sympathetic.

sympathiser [sɛ̃patize] *vi* to get on well; ~ **avec qqn** to get on well with sb.

symphonie [sɛ̃fɔni] *nf* symphony.

symphonique [sɛ̃fɔnik] *adj* [musique] symphonic; [concert, orchestre] symphony (*avant n*).

symptomatique [sɛ̃ptɔmatik] *adj* symptomatic.

symptôme [sɛ̃ptom] *nm* symptom.

synagogue [sinagɔg] *nf* synagogue.

synchroniser [sɛ̃krɔnize] *vt* to synchronize.

syncope [sɛ̃kɔp] *nf* [évanouissement] blackout. ‖ MUS syncopation.

syndic [sɛ̃dik] *nm* [de copropriété] representative.

syndicaliste [sɛ̃dikalist] **1** *nmf* trade unionist. **2** *adj* (trade) union (*avant n*).

syndicat [sɛ̃dika] *nm* [d'employés, d'agriculteurs] (trade) union; [d'employeurs, de propriétaires] association. ○ **syndicat d'initiative** *nm* tourist office.

syndiqué, -e [sɛ̃dike] *adj* unionized.

syndrome [sɛ̃drom] *nm* syndrome.

synonyme [sinɔnim] **1** *nm* synonym. **2** *adj* synonymous.

syntaxe [sɛ̃taks] *nf* syntax.

synthèse [sɛ̃tɛz] *nf* [opération & CHIM] synthesis. ‖ [exposé] overview.

synthétique [sɛ̃tetik] *adj* [vue] overall. ‖ [produit] synthetic.

synthétiseur [sɛ̃tetizœr] *nm* synthesizer.

syphilis [sifilis] *nf* syphilis.

Syrie [siri] *nf*: **la ~** Syria.

syrien, -ienne [sirjɛ̃, jɛn] *adj* Syrian. ○ **Syrien, -ienne** *nm, f* Syrian.

systématique [sistematik] *adj* systematic.

systématiser [sistematize] *vt* to systematize.

système [sistɛm] *nm* system; ~ **expert** INFORM expert system; ~ **d'exploitation** INFORM operating system; ~ **nerveux** nervous system; ~ **solaire** solar system.

t, T [te] *nm inv* t, T.

ta → **ton**.

tabac [taba] *nm* [plante, produit] tobacco; ~ **blond** mild ou Virginia tobacco; ~ **brun** dark tobacco; ~ **à priser** snuff. ‖ [magasin] tobacconist's.

tabagisme [tabaʒism] *nm* [intoxication] nicotine addiction. ‖ [habitude] smoking.

table [tabl] *nf* [meuble] table; **à ~!** lunch/dinner *etc* is ready!; **se mettre à ~** to sit down to eat; **dresser** ou **mettre la ~** to lay the table; ~ **de chevet** ou **de nuit** bedside table. ○ **table des matières** *nf* contents (*pl*), table of contents. ○ **table de multiplication** *nf* (multiplication) table.

tableau, -x [tablo] *nm* [peinture] painting, picture; *fig* [description] picture. ‖ [panneau] board; ~ **d'affichage** notice board *Br*, bulletin board *Am*; ~ **de bord** AÉRON instrument panel; AUTOM dashboard; ~ **noir** blackboard. ‖ [de données] table.

tabler [table] *vi*: ~ **sur** to count ou bank on.

tablette [tablɛt] *nf* [planchette] shelf. ‖ [de chewing-gum] stick; [de chocolat] bar.

tableur [tablœr] *nm* INFORM spreadsheet.

tablier [tablije] *nm* [de cuisinière] apron; [d'écolier] smock. ‖ [de pont] roadway, deck.

tabloïd(e) [tablɔid] *nm* tabloid.

tabou, -e [tabu] *adj* taboo. ○ **tabou** *nm* taboo.

tabouret [taburɛ] *nm* stool.

tabulateur [tabylatœr] *nm* tabulator, tab.

tac [tak] *nm*: **du ~ au ~** tit for tat.

tache [taʃ] *nf* [de pelage] marking; [de peau] mark; ~ **de rousseur** ou **de son** freckle. ‖ [de couleur, lumière] spot, patch. ‖ [sur nappe, vêtement] stain.

tâche [taʃ] *nf* task.

tacher [taʃe] *vt* [nappe, vêtement] to stain, to mark.

tâcher [taʃe] *vi*: ~ de faire qqch to try to do sthg.

tacheter [taʃte] *vt* to spot, to speckle.

tacite [tasit] *adj* tacit.

taciturne [tasityrn] *adj* taciturn.

tact [takt] *nm* [délicatesse] tact; **manquer de** ~ to be tactless.

tactique [taktik] **1** *adj* tactical. **2** *nf* tactics (*pl*).

tag [tag] *nm* *identifying name written with a spray can on walls, the sides of trains etc.*

taie [tɛ] *nf* [enveloppe]: ~ (d'oreiller) pillowcase, pillow slip.

taille [taj] *nf* [action - de pierre, diamant] cutting; [- d'arbre, haie] pruning. || [stature] height. || [mesure, dimensions] size; **vous faites quelle** ~? what size are you?, what size do you take?; **de** ~ sizeable, considerable. || [milieu du corps] waist.

taille-crayon [tajkrɛjɔ̃] (*pl* **taille-crayons**) *nm* pencil sharpener.

tailler [taje] *vt* [couper - chair, pierre, diamant] to cut; [- arbre, haie] to prune; [- crayon] to sharpen; [- bois] to carve. || [vêtement] to cut out.

tailleur [tajœr] *nm* [couturier] tailor. || [vêtement] (lady's) suit. || [de diamants, pierre] cutter.

taillis [taji] *nm* coppice, copse.

tain [tɛ̃] *nm* silvering; **miroir sans** ~ two-way mirror.

taire [tɛr] *vt* to conceal. ○ **se taire** *vp* [rester silencieux] to be silent ou quiet. || [cesser de s'exprimer] to fall silent; **tais-toi!** shut up!

Taiwan [tajwan] *n* Taiwan.

talc [talk] *nm* talcum powder.

talent [talɑ̃] *nm* talent; **avoir du** ~ to be talented, to have talent.

talentueux, -euse [talɑ̃tɥø, øz] *adj* talented.

talisman [talismɑ̃] *nm* talisman.

talkie-walkie [tɔkiwɔki] *nm* walkie-talkie.

talon [talɔ̃] *nm* [gén] heel; **~s aiguilles/ hauts** stiletto/high heels; **~s plats** low ou flat heels. || [de chèque] counterfoil, stub. || CARTES stock.

talonner [talɔne] *vt* [suj: poursuivant] to be hard on the heels of.

talonnette [talɔnɛt] *nf* [de chaussure] heel cushion, heel-pad.

talquer [talke] *vt* to put talcum powder on.

talus [taly] *nm* embankment.

tambour [tɑ̃bur] *nm* [instrument, cylindre] drum. || [musicien] drummer. || [porte à tourniquet] revolving door.

tambourin [tɑ̃burɛ̃] *nm* [à grelots] tambourine. || [tambour] tambourin.

tambouriner [tɑ̃burine] *vi*: ~ **sur** ou **à** to drum on; ~ **contre** to drum against.

tamis [tami] *nm* [crible] sieve.

Tamise [tamiz] *nf*: **la ~** the Thames.

tamisé, -e [tamize] *adj* [éclairage] subdued.

tamiser [tamize] *vt* [farine] to sieve. || [lumière] to filter.

tampon [tɑ̃pɔ̃] *nm* [bouchon] stopper, plug. || [éponge] pad; ~ **à récurer** scourer. || [de coton, d'ouate] pad; ~ **hygiénique** ou **périodique** tampon. || [cachet] stamp. || *litt & fig* [amortisseur] buffer.

tamponner [tɑ̃pɔne] *vt* [document] to stamp. || [plaie] to dab.

tam-tam [tamtam] (*pl* **tam-tams**) *nm* tom-tom.

tandem [tɑ̃dɛm] *nm* [vélo] tandem. || [duo] pair; **en** ~ together, in tandem.

tandis [tɑ̃di] ○ **tandis que** *loc conj* [pendant que] while. || [alors que] while, whereas.

tangage [tɑ̃gaʒ] *nm* pitching, pitch.

tangent, -e [tɑ̃ʒɑ̃, ɑ̃t] *adj*: c'était ~ *fig* it was close, it was touch and go. ○ **tangente** *nf* tangent.

tangible [tɑ̃ʒibl] *adj* tangible.

tango [tɑ̃go] *nm* tango.

tanguer [tɑ̃ge] *vi* to pitch.

tanière [tanjɛr] *nf* den, lair.

tank [tɑ̃k] *nm* tank.

tanner [tane] *vt* [peau] to tan.

tant [tɑ̃] *adv* [quantité]: ~ **de travail** so much work. || [nombre]: ~ **de livres/ d'élèves** so many books/pupils. || [tellement] such a lot, so much. || [quantité indéfinie] so much; **ça coûte** ~ it costs so much. || [comparatif]: ~ **que** as much as. || [valeur temporelle]: ~ **que** [aussi longtemps que] as long as; [pendant que] while. ○ **en tant que** *loc conj* as. ○ **tant bien que mal** *loc adv* after a fashion, somehow or other. ○ **tant mieux** *loc adv* so much the better; ~ **mieux pour lui** good for him. ○ **tant pis** *loc adv* too bad.

tante [tɑ̃t] *nf* [parente] aunt.

tantinet [tɑ̃tinɛ] *nm*: **un ~ exagéré/ trop long** a bit exaggerated/too long.

tantôt [tɑ̃to] *adv* [parfois] sometimes.

tapage [tapaʒ] *nm* [bruit] row. || *fig* [battage] fuss (*U*).

tapageur, -euse [tapaʒœr, øz] *adj* [style] flashy. || [liaison, publicité] blatant.

tape [tap] *nf* slap.

tape-à-l'œil [tapalœj] *adj inv* flashy.

taper [tape] **1** *vt* [personne, cuisse] to slap; ~ (un coup) à la porte to knock at the door. || [à la machine] to type. **2** *vi* [frapper] to hit; ~ du poing sur to bang one's fist on. || [à la machine] to type. || *fam* [soleil] to beat down.

tapis [tapi] *nm* carpet; [de gymnase] mat; ~ roulant [pour bagages] conveyor belt; [pour personnes] travolator.

tapisser [tapise] *vt*: ~ (de) to cover (with).

tapisserie [tapisri] *nf* tapestry.

tapissier, -ière [tapisje, jɛr] *nm, f* [décorateur] (interior) decorator. || [commerçant] upholsterer.

tapoter [tapɔte] **1** *vt* to tap; [joue] to pat. **2** *vi*: ~ sur to tap on.

taquin, -e [takɛ̃, in] *adj* teasing.

taquiner [takine] *vt* [suj: personne] to tease. || [suj: douleur] to worry.

tarabuster [tarabyste] *vt* [suj: personne] to badger. || [suj: idée] to niggle at.

tard [tar] *adv* late; plus ~ later; au plus ~ at the latest.

tarder [tarde] **1** *vi*: ~ à faire qqch [être lent à] to take a long time to do sthg; elle ne devrait plus ~ maintenant she should be here any time now. **2** *v impers*: il me tarde de te revoir/qu'il vienne I am longing to see you again/for him to come.

tardif, -ive [tardif, iv] *adj* [heure] late.

tare [tar] *nf* [défaut] defect. || [de balance] tare.

tarif [tarif] *nm* [prix - de restaurant, café] price; [- de service] rate, price; [douanier] tariff; demi-~ half rate or price; ~ réduit reduced price; [au cinéma, théâtre] concession. || [tableau] price list.

tarir [tarir] *vi* to dry up; elle ne tarit pas d'éloges sur son professeur she never stops praising her teacher. ○ se tarir *vp* to dry up.

tarot [taro] *nm* tarot. ○ tarots *nmpl* tarot cards.

tartare [tartar] *adj* Tartar; (steak) ~ steak tartare.

tarte [tart] **1** *nf* [gâteau] tart. || *fam fig* [gifle] slap. **2** *adj* (avec ou sans accord) *fam* [idiot] stupid.

tartine [tartin] *nf* [de pain] piece of bread and butter.

tartiner [tartine] *vt* [pain] to spread; chocolat/fromage à ~ chocolate/cheese spread. || *fam fig* [pages] to cover.

tartre [tartr] *nm* [de dents, vin] tartar. || [de chaudière] fur, scale.

tas [ta] *nm* heap; un ~ de a lot of.

tasse [tas] *nf* cup; ~ à café/à thé coffee/tea cup.

tasser [tase] *vt* [neige] to compress, to pack down. || [vêtements, personnes]: ~ qqn/qqch dans to stuff sb/sthg into. ○ se tasser *vp* [fondations] to settle. || *fig* [vieillard] to shrink. || [personnes] to squeeze up. || *fam fig* [situation] to settle down.

tâter [tate] *vt* to feel; *fig* to sound out. ○ se tâter *vp fam fig* [hésiter] to be in two minds.

tatillon, -onne [tatijɔ̃, ɔn] *adj* finicky.

tâtonner [tatɔne] *vi* to grope around.

tâtons [tatɔ̃] ○ à tâtons *loc adv*: marcher/procéder à ~ to feel one's way.

tatouage [tatwaʒ] *nm* [dessin] tattoo.

tatouer [tatwe] *vt* to tattoo.

taudis [todi] *nm* slum.

taupe [top] *nf litt & fig* mole.

taureau, -x [tɔro] *nm* [animal] bull. ○ Taureau *nm* ASTROL Taurus.

tauromachie [tɔrɔmaʃi] *nf* bullfighting.

taux [to] *nm* rate; [de cholestérol, d'alcool] level; ~ de change exchange rate; ~ d'intérêt interest rate.

taverne [tavɛrn] *nf* tavern.

taxe [taks] *nf* tax; hors ~ COMM exclusive of tax, before tax; toutes ~s comprises inclusive of tax; ~ sur la valeur ajoutée value added tax.

taxer [takse] *vt* [imposer] to tax.

taxi [taksi] *nm* [voiture] taxi. || [chauffeur] taxi driver.

TB, tb (*abr de* très bien) VG.

tchécoslovaque [tʃekɔslɔvak] *adj* Czechoslovakian. ○ Tchécoslovaque *nmf* Czechoslovak.

Tchécoslovaquie [tʃekɔslɔvaki] *nf*: la ~ Czechoslovakia.

tchèque [tʃɛk] **1** *adj* Czech. **2** *nm* [langue] Czech. ○ Tchèque *nmf* Czech.

TD (*abr de* travaux dirigés) *nmpl* supervised practical work.

te [tə], **t'** *pron pers* [complément d'objet direct] you. || [complément d'objet indirect] (to) you. || [réfléchi] yourself.

technicien, -ienne [tɛknisjɛ̃, jɛn] *nm, f* [professionnel] technician.

technico-commercial, -e [tɛkniko-kɔmersjal] (*mpl* **technico-commerciaux,** *fpl* **technico-commerciales**) *nm, f* sales engineer.

technique [tɛknik] **1** *adj* technical. **2** *nf* technique.

technocrate [tɛknɔkrat] *nmf* technocrat.

technologie [tɛknɔlɔʒi] *nf* technology.

technologique [tɛknɔlɔʒik] *adj* technological.

teckel [tekɛl] *nm* dachshund.

tee-shirt (*pl* **tee-shirts**), **T-shirt** (*pl* **T-shirts**) [tiʃœrt] *nm* T-shirt.

teigne [tɛɲ] *nf* [mite] moth. || MÉD ringworm. || *fam fig & péj* [femme] cow; [homme] bastard.

teindre [tɛ̃dr] *vt* to dye.

teint, -e [tɛ̃, tɛ̃t] **1** *pp* → teindre. **2** *adj* dyed. ○ **teint** *nm* [carnation] complexion. ○ **teinte** *nf* colour.

teinté, -e [tɛ̃te] *adj* tinted.

teinter [tɛ̃te] *vt* to stain.

teinture [tɛ̃tyr] *nf* [action] dyeing. || [produit] dye. ○ **teinture d'iode** *nf* tincture of iodine.

teinturerie [tɛ̃tyrri] *nf* [pressing] dry cleaner's. || [métier] dyeing.

teinturier, -ière [tɛ̃tyrje, jɛr] *nm, f* [de pressing] dry cleaner.

tel [tɛl] (*f* **telle**, *mpl* **tels**, *fpl* **telles**) *adj* [valeur indéterminée] such-and-such a. || [semblable] such; **un ~ homme** such a man; **je n'ai rien dit de ~** I never said anything of the sort. || [valeur emphatique ou intensive] such; **un ~ génie** such a genius. || [introduit un exemple ou une énumération]: **~ (que)** such as, like. || [introduit une comparaison] like; **il est ~ que je l'avais toujours rêvé** he's just like I always dreamt he would be; **~ quel** as it is/was *etc*. ○ **de telle sorte que** *loc conj* with the result that, so that.

tél. (*abr de* **téléphone**) tel.

télé [tele] *nf fam* TV, telly *Br*.

téléachat [teleaʃa] *nm* teleshopping.

télécommande [telekɔmɑ̃d] *nf* remote control.

télécommunication [telekɔmynikasjɔ̃] *nf* telecommunications (*pl*).

télécopie [telekɔpi] *nf* fax.

télécopieur [telekɔpjœr] *nm* fax (machine).

téléfilm [telefilm] *nm* film made for television.

télégramme [telegram] *nm* telegram.

télégraphe [telegraf] *nm* telegraph.

télégraphier [telegrafje] *vt* to telegraph.

téléguider [telegide] *vt* to operate by remote control; *fig* to mastermind.

télématique [telematik] *nf* telematics (*U*).

téléobjectif [teleɔbʒɛktif] *nm* telephoto lens (*sg*).

télépathie [telepati] *nf* telepathy.

téléphérique [teleferik] *nm* cableway.

téléphone [telefɔn] *nm* telephone; **~ sans fil** cordless telephone.

téléphoner [telefɔne] *vi* to telephone, to phone; **~ à qqn** to telephone sb, to phone sb (up).

téléphonique [telefɔnik] *adj* telephone (*avant n*), phone (*avant n*).

télescope [teleskɔp] *nm* telescope.

télescoper [teleskɔpe] *vt* [véhicule] to crash into. ○ **se télescoper** *vp* [véhicules] to concertina.

télescopique [teleskɔpik] *adj* [antenne] telescopic.

téléscripteur [teleskriptœr] *nm* teleprinter *Br*, teletypewriter *Am*.

télésiège [telesjɛʒ] *nm* chairlift.

téléski [teleski] *nm* ski tow.

téléspectateur, -trice [telespɛktatœr, tris] *nm, f* (television) viewer.

téléviseur [televizœr] *nm* television (set).

télévision [televizjɔ̃] *nf* television; **à la ~** on television.

télex [telɛks] *nm inv* telex.

tellement [tɛlmɑ̃] *adv* [si, à ce point] so; (*+ comparatif*) so much; **~ plus jeune que** so much younger than; **pas ~** not especially, not particularly. || [autant]: **~ de** [personnes, objets] so many; [gentillesse, travail] so much. || [tant] so much; **elle a ~ changé** she's changed so much; **je ne comprends rien ~ il parle vite** he talks so quickly that I can't understand a word.

téméraire [temerer] **1** *adj* [audacieux] bold. || [imprudent] rash. **2** *nmf* hothead.

témérité [temerite] *nf* [audace] boldness. || [imprudence] rashness.

témoignage [temwaɲaʒ] *nm* JUR testimony, evidence (*U*); **faux ~** perjury. || [gage] token, expression; **en ~ de** as a token of. || [récit] account.

témoigner [temwaɲe] **1** *vt* [manifester] to show, to display. **2** *vi* JUR to testify; **~ contre** to testify against.

témoin [temwɛ̃] **1** *nm* [gén] witness; **être ~ de qqch** to be a witness to sthg, to witness sthg; **~ oculaire** eyewitness. || SPORT baton. **2** *adj* [appartement] show (*avant n*).

tempe [tɑ̃p] *nf* temple.

tempérament [tɑ̃peramɑ̃] *nm* temperament; **avoir du ~** to be hot-blooded.

température [tɑ̃peratyr] *nf* temperature; **avoir de la ~** to have a temperature.

tempéré, -e [tɑ̃pere] *adj* [climat] temperate.

tempérer [tɑ̃pere] *vt* [adoucir] to temper; *fig* [enthousiasme, ardeur] to moderate.

tempête [tɑ̃pɛt] *nf* storm.

temple [tɑ̃pl] *nm* HIST temple. || [protestant] church.

tempo [tempo] *nm* tempo.

temporaire [tɑ̃pɔrɛr] *adj* temporary.

temporairement [tɑ̃pɔrɛrmɑ̃] *adv* temporarily.

temporel, -elle [tɑ̃pɔrɛl] *adj* [défini dans le temps] time (*avant n*).

temps [tɑ̃] *nm* [gén] time; **à plein ~** full-time; **à mi-~, à ~ partiel** part-time; **au** ou **du ~ où** (in the days) when; **de mon ~** in my day; **ces --ci, ces derniers ~** these days; **pendant ce ~** meanwhile; **en ~ de guerre/paix** in wartime/peacetime; **il était ~!** *iron* and about time too!; **avoir le ~ de faire qqch** to have time to do sthg; **~ libre** free time; **à ~** in time; **de ~ à autre** now and then ou again; **de ~ en ~** from time to time; **en même ~** at the same time; **tout le ~** all the time, the whole time. || MUS beat. || GRAM tense. || MÉTÉOR weather.

tenable [tənabl] *adj* bearable.

tenace [tənas] *adj* [gén] stubborn. || *fig* [odeur, rhume] lingering.

ténacité [tenasite] *nf* [de préjugé, personne] stubbornness.

tenailler [tənaje] *vt* to torment.

tenailles [tənaj] *nfpl* pincers.

tenancier, -ière [tənɑ̃sje, jɛr] *nm, f* manager (*f* manageress).

tendance [tɑ̃dɑ̃s] *nf* [disposition] tendency; **avoir ~ à qqch/à faire qqch** to have a tendency to sthg/to do sthg, to be inclined to sthg/to do sthg. || [économique, de mode] trend.

tendancieux, -ieuse [tɑ̃dɑ̃sjø, jøz] *adj* tendentious.

tendeur [tɑ̃dœr] *nm* [sangle] elastic strap (*for fastening luggage etc*).

tendinite [tɑ̃dinit] *nf* tendinitis.

tendon [tɑ̃dɔ̃] *nm* tendon.

tendre¹ [tɑ̃dr] *adj* [gén] tender. || [matériau] soft. || [couleur] delicate.

tendre² [tɑ̃dr] *vt* [corde] to tighten. || [muscle] to tense. || [objet, main]: **~ qqch à qqn** to hold out sthg to sb. || [bâche] to hang. || [piège] to set (up). ○ **se tendre** *vp* to tighten; *fig* [relations] to become strained.

tendresse [tɑ̃drɛs] *nf* [affection] tenderness. || [indulgence] sympathy.

tendu, -e [tɑ̃dy] **1** *pp* → **tendre**. **2** *adj* [fil, corde] taut. || [personne] tense. || [atmosphère, rapports] strained. || [main] outstretched.

ténèbres [tenɛbr] *nfpl* darkness (*sg*).

ténébreux, -euse [tenebrø, øz] *adj fig* [dessein, affaire] mysterious. || [personne] serious, solemn.

teneur [tənœr] *nf* content; [de traité] terms (*pl*); **~ en alcool/cuivre** alcohol/copper content.

tenir [tənir] **1** *vt* [objet, personne, solution] to hold. || [garder, conserver, respecter] to keep. || [gérer - boutique] to keep, to run. || [apprendre]: **~ qqch de qqn** to have sthg from sb. || [considérer]: **~ qqn pour** to regard sb as. **2** *vi* [être solide] to stay up, to hold together. || [durer] to last. || [pouvoir être contenu] to fit. || [être attaché]: **~ à** [personne] to care about; [privilèges] to value. || [vouloir absolument]: **~ à faire qqch** to insist on doing sthg. || [ressembler]: **~ de** to take after. || [relever de]: **~ de** to have something of. || *loc*: **~ bon** to stand firm; **tiens!** [en donnant] here!; [surprise] well, well!; [pour attirer attention] look! ○ **se tenir** *vp* [réunion] to be held. || [personnes] to hold one another; **se ~ par la main** to hold hands. || [être présent] to be. || [être cohérent] to make sense. || [se conduire] to behave (o.s.). || [se retenir]: **se ~ (à)** to hold on (to). || [se borner]: **s'en ~ à** to stick to.

tennis [tenis] **1** *nm* [sport] tennis. **2** *nmpl* tennis shoes.

ténor [tenɔr] *nm* [chanteur] tenor.

tension [tɑ̃sjɔ̃] *nf* [contraction, désaccord] tension. || MÉD pressure; **avoir de la ~** to have high blood pressure. || ÉLECTR voltage; **haute/basse ~** high/low voltage.

tentant, -e [tɑ̃tɑ̃, ɑ̃t] *adj* tempting.

tentation [tɑ̃tasjɔ̃] *nf* temptation.

tentative [tɑ̃tativ] *nf* attempt.

tente [tɑ̃t] *nf* tent.

tenter [tɑ̃te] *vt* [entreprendre]: **~ qqch**

de faire qqch to attempt sthg/to do sthg. || [plaire] to tempt.

tenture [tɑ̃tyr] *nf* hanging.

tenu, -e [təny] 1 *pp* → **tenir**. 2 *adj* [obligé]: **être ~ de faire qqch** to be required ou obliged to do sthg. || [en ordre]: **bien/mal ~** [maison] well/badly kept.

ténu, -e [teny] *adj* [fil] fine; *fig* [distinction] tenuous. || [voix] thin.

tenue [təny] *nf* [entretien] running. || [manières] good manners (*pl*). || [costume] dress; **être en petite ~** to be scantily dressed. ○ **tenue de route** *nf* roadholding.

ter [tɛr] 1 *adv* MUS three times. 2 *adj*: 12 ~ 12B.

Tergal® [tɛrgal] *nm* ≃ Terylene®.

tergiverser [tɛrʒivɛrse] *vi* to shilly-shally.

terme [tɛrm] *nm* [fin] end; **mettre un ~ à** to put an end ou a stop to. || [de grossesse] term; **avant ~** prematurely. || [échéance] time limit; [de loyer] rent day; **à court/moyen/long ~** [calculer] in the short/medium/long term; [projet] short-/medium-/long-term. || [mot, élément] term. ○ **termes** *nmpl* [expressions] words. || [de contrat] terms.

terminaison [tɛrminɛzɔ̃] *nf* GRAM ending.

terminal, -e, -aux [tɛrminal, o] *adj* [au bout] final. || MÉD [phase] terminal. ○ **terminal, -aux** *nm* terminal. ○ **terminale** *nf* SCOL ≃ senior year *Am*.

terminer [tɛrmine] *vt* to end, to finish; [travail, repas] to finish. ○ **se terminer** *vp* to end, to finish.

terminologie [tɛrminɔlɔʒi] *nf* terminology.

terminus [tɛrminys] *nm* terminus.

termite [tɛrmit] *nm* termite.

terne [tɛrn] *adj* dull.

ternir [tɛrnir] *vt* to dirty; [métal, réputation] to tarnish.

terrain [tɛrɛ̃] *nm* [sol] soil; **vélo tout ~** mountain bike. || [surface] piece of land. || [emplacement - de football, rugby] pitch; [- de golf] course; **~ d'aviation** airfield; **~ de camping** campsite. || *fig* [domaine] ground.

terrasse [tɛras] *nf* terrace.

terrassement [tɛrasmɑ̃] *nm* [action] excavation.

terrasser [tɛrase] *vt* [suj: personne] to bring down; [suj: émotion] to overwhelm; [suj: maladie] to conquer.

terre [tɛr] *nf* [monde] world. || [sol] ground; **par ~** on the ground; **~ à ~** *fig* down-to-earth. || [matière] earth, soil. || [propriété] land (*U*). || [territoire, continent] land. || ÉLECTR earth *Br*, ground *Am*. ○ **Terre** *nf*: **la Terre** Earth.

terreau [tero] *nm* compost.

terre-plein [tɛrplɛ̃] (*pl* **terre-pleins**) *nm* platform.

terrer [tɛre] ○ **se terrer** *vp* to go to earth.

terrestre [tɛrɛstr] *adj* [croûte, atmosphère] of the earth. || [animal, transport] land (*avant n*).

terreur [tɛrœr] *nf* terror.

terrible [tɛribl] *adj* [gén] terrible. || [appétit, soif] terrific, enormous. || *fam* [excellent] brilliant.

terriblement [tɛribləmɑ̃] *adv* terribly.

terrien, -ienne [tɛrjɛ̃, jɛn] 1 *adj* [foncier]: **propriétaire ~** landowner. 2 *nm, f* [habitant de la Terre] earthling.

terrier [tɛrje] *nm* [tanière] burrow. || [chien] terrier.

terrifier [tɛrifje] *vt* to terrify.

terrine [tɛrin] *nf* terrine.

territoire [tɛritwar] *nm* [pays, zone] territory. ○ **territoire d'outre-mer** *nm* (French) overseas territory.

territorial, -e, -iaux [tɛritɔrjal, jo] *adj* territorial.

terroir [tɛrwar] *nm* [sol] soil. || [région rurale] country.

terroriser [tɛrɔrize] *vt* to terrorize.

terrorisme [tɛrɔrism] *nm* terrorism.

terroriste [tɛrɔrist] *nmf* terrorist.

tertiaire [tɛrsjɛr] *adj* tertiary.

tes → **ton**.

tesson [tesɔ̃] *nm* piece of broken glass.

test [tɛst] *nm* test.

testament [tɛstamɑ̃] *nm* will.

tester [tɛste] *vt* to test.

testicule [tɛstikyl] *nm* testicle.

tétaniser [tetanize] *vt* to cause to go into spasm; *fig* to paralyse.

tétanos [tetanos] *nm* tetanus.

têtard [tɛtar] *nm* tadpole.

tête [tɛt] *nf* [gén] head; **de la ~ aux pieds** from head to foot ou toe; **la ~ la première** head first; **calculer qqch de ~** to calculate sthg in one's head; **~ de lecture** INFORM read head; **~ de liste** POLIT main candidate; **être ~ en l'air** to have one's head in the clouds; **faire la ~** to sulk; **tenir ~ à qqn** to stand up to sb. || [visage] face. || [devant - de cortège, peloton] head, front; **en ~** SPORT in the lead.

tête-à-queue [tɛtakø] *nm inv* spin.

tête-à-tête [tɛtatɛt] *nm inv* tête-à-tête.

tête-bêche [tɛtbɛʃ] *loc adv* head to tail.

tétée [tete] *nf* feed.

tétine [tetin] *nf* [de biberon, mamelle] teat. || [sucette] dummy *Br*, pacifier *Am*.

têtu, -e [tety] *adj* stubborn.

texte [tɛkst] *nm* [écrit] wording. || [imprimé] text. || [extrait] passage.

textile [tɛkstil] **1** *adj* textile (*avant n*). **2** *nm* [matière] textile. || [industrie]: **le ~** textiles (*pl*), the textile industry.

textuel, -elle [tɛkstɥɛl] *adj* [analyse] textual; [citation] exact. || [traduction] literal.

texture [tɛkstyr] *nf* texture.

TF1 (*abr de* Télévision Française 1) *nf* French independent television company.

TGV (*abr de* train à grande vitesse) *nm* French high-speed train linking major cities.

thaïlandais, -e [tajlɑ̃dɛ, ɛz] *adj* Thai. ○ **Thaïlandais, -e** *nm, f* Thai.

Thaïlande [tajlɑ̃d] *nf*: **la ~** Thailand.

thalasso(thérapie) [talaso(terapi)] *nf* seawater therapy.

thé [te] *nm* tea.

théâtral, -e, -aux [teatral, o] *adj* [ton] theatrical.

théâtre [teatr] *nm* [bâtiment, représentation] theatre. || [art]: **faire du ~** to be on the stage; **adapté pour le ~** adapted for the stage. || [lieu] scene; **~ d'opérations** MIL theatre of operations.

théière [tejɛr] *nf* teapot.

thématique [tematik] *adj* thematic.

thème [tɛm] *nm* [sujet & MUS] theme. || SCOL prose.

théologie [teɔlɔʒi] *nf* theology.

théorème [teɔrɛm] *nm* theorem.

théorie [teɔri] *nf* theory; **en ~** in theory.

théorique [teɔrik] *adj* theoretical.

thérapeute [terapøt] *nmf* therapist.

thérapie [terapi] *nf* therapy.

thermal, -e, -aux [tɛrmal, o] *adj* thermal.

thermes [tɛrm] *nmpl* thermal baths.

thermique [tɛrmik] *adj* thermal.

thermomètre [tɛrmɔmɛtr] *nm* [instrument] thermometer.

Thermos® [tɛrmos] *nm ou nf* Thermos® (flask).

thermostat [tɛrmɔsta] *nm* thermostat.

thèse [tɛz] *nf* [opinion] argument. || PHI-LO & UNIV thesis; **~ de doctorat** doctorate. || [théorie] theory.

thon [tɔ̃] *nm* tuna.

thorax [tɔraks] *nm* thorax.

thym [tɛ̃] *nm* thyme.

thyroïde [tirɔid] *nf* thyroid (gland).

Tibet [tibɛ] *nm*: **le ~** Tibet.

tibia [tibja] *nm* tibia.

tic [tik] *nm* tic.

ticket [tikɛ] *nm* ticket; **~ de caisse** (till) receipt; **~-repas** ≃ luncheon voucher.

tic-tac [tiktak] *nm inv* tick-tock.

tiède [tjɛd] *adj* [boisson, eau] tepid, lukewarm. || [vent] mild.

tiédir [tjedir] **1** *vt* to warm. **2** *vi* to become warm; **faire ~ qqch** to warm sthg.

tien [tjɛ̃] ○ **le tien** (*f* la tienne [latjɛn], *mpl* les tiens [letjɛ̃], *fpl* les tiennes [letjɛn]) *pron poss* yours; **à la tienne!** cheers!

tierce [tjɛrs] **1** *nf* MUS third. || CARTES & ESCRIME tierce. **2** *adj* → **tiers**.

tiercé [tjɛrse] *nm* system of betting involving the first three horses in a race.

tiers, tierce [tjɛr, tjɛrs] *adj*: **une tierce personne** a third party. ○ **tiers** *nm* [tierce personne] third party. || [de fraction]: **le ~** the one-third of.

tiers-monde [tjɛrmɔ̃d] *nm*: **le ~** the Third World.

tige [tiʒ] *nf* [de plante] stem, stalk. || [de bois, métal] rod.

tignasse [tiɲas] *nf fam* mop (of hair).

tigre [tigr] *nm* tiger.

tigresse [tigrɛs] *nf* tigress.

tilleul [tijœl] *nm* lime (tree).

timbale [tɛ̃bal] *nf* [gobelet] (metal) cup. || MUS kettledrum.

timbre [tɛ̃br] *nm* [gén] stamp. || [de voix] timbre. || [de bicyclette] bell.

timbrer [tɛ̃bre] *vt* to stamp.

timide [timid] *adj* [personne] shy. || [protestation, essai] timid.

timoré, -e [timɔre] *adj* fearful, timorous.

tintamarre [tɛ̃tamar] *nm fam* racket.

tintement [tɛ̃tmɑ̃] *nm* [de cloche, d'horloge] chiming; [de pièces] jingling.

tinter [tɛ̃te] *vi* [cloche, horloge] to chime. || [pièces] to jingle.

tir [tir] *nm* [SPORT - activité] shooting; [- lieu]: **(centre de) ~** shooting range. || [trajectoire] shot. || [salve] fire (*U*).

tirage [tiraʒ] *nm* [de journal] circulation; [de livre] print run; **à grand ~** mass circulation. || [du loto] draw; **~ au sort** drawing lots. || [de cheminée] draught.

tiraillement [tirajmɑ̃] *nm* (*gén pl*) [crampe] cramp. || *fig* [conflit] conflict.

tirailler [tiraje] **1** *vt* [tirer sur] to tug (at). || *fig* [écarteler]: **être tiraillé par/ entre qqch** to be torn by/between sthg. **2** *vi* to fire wildly.

tiré, -e [tire] *adj* [fatigué]: **avoir les traits ~s** *ou* **le visage ~** to look drawn.

tire-bouchon [tirbuʃɔ̃] (*pl* **tire-bouchons**) *nm* corkscrew. ❍ **en tire-bouchon** *loc adv* corkscrew (*avant n*).

tirelire [tirlir] *nf* moneybox.

tirer [tire] **1** *vt* [gén] to pull; [rideaux] to draw. || [tracer - trait] to draw. || [revue, livre] to print. || [avec arme] to fire. || [faire sortir - vin] to draw off; ~ **qqn de** *litt & fig* to help *ou* get sb out of; ~ **un revolver/un mouchoir de sa poche** to pull a gun/a handkerchief out of one's pocket; ~ **la langue** to stick out one's tongue. || [aux cartes, au loto] to draw. || [plaisir, profit] to derive. || [déduire - conclusion] to draw; [- leçon] to learn. **2** *vi* [tendre]: ~ **sur** to pull on *ou* at. || [couleur]: **bleu tirant sur le vert** greenish blue. || [cheminée] to draw. || [avec arme] to fire, to shoot. || SPORT to shoot. ❍ **se tirer** *vp fam* [s'en aller] to push off. || [se sortir]: **se ~ de** to get o.s. out of; **s'en ~** *fam* to escape.

tiret [tirɛ] *nm* dash.

tireur, -euse [tirœr, øz] *nm, f* [avec arme] gunman.

tiroir [tirwar] *nm* drawer.

tiroir-caisse [tirwarkɛs] *nm* till.

tisane [tizan] *nf* herb tea.

tisonnier [tizɔnje] *nm* poker.

tissage [tisaʒ] *nm* weaving.

tisser [tise] *vt litt & fig* to weave; [suj: araignée] to spin.

tissu [tisy] *nm* [étoffe] cloth, material. || BIOL tissue.

titiller [titije] *vt* to titillate.

titre [titr] *nm* [gén] title. || [de presse] headline; **gros ~** headline. || [universitaire] diploma, qualification. || FIN security. ❍ **titre de transport** *nm* ticket. ❍ **à titre de** *loc prép*: **à ~ d'exemple** by way of example; **à ~ d'information** for information.

tituber [titybe] *vi* to totter.

titulaire [titylɛr] **1** *adj* [employé] permanent; UNIV with tenure. **2** *nmf* [de passeport, permis] holder; [de poste, chaire] occupant.

titulariser [titylarize] *vt* to give tenure to.

toast [tost] *nm* [pain grillé] toast (*U*). || [discours] toast; **porter un ~ à** to drink a toast to.

toboggan [tɔbɔgɑ̃] *nm* [de terrain de jeu] slide; [de piscine] chute.

toc [tɔk] **1** *interj*: **et ~!** so there! **2** *nm fam*: **en ~** fake (*avant n*).

toi [twa] *pron pers* you. ❍ **toi-même** *pron pers* yourself.

toile [twal] *nf* [étoffe] cloth; [de lin] linen; ~ **cirée** oilcloth. || [tableau] canvas, picture. ❍ **toile d'araignée** *nf* spider's web.

toilette [twalɛt] *nf* [de personne, d'animal] washing; **faire sa ~** to (have a) wash. || [parure, vêtements] outfit. ❍ **toilettes** *nfpl* toilet (*sg*), toilets.

toise [twaz] *nf* height gauge.

toison [twazɔ̃] *nf* [pelage] fleece. || [chevelure] mop (of hair).

toit [twa] *nm* roof; ~ **ouvrant** sunroof.

toiture [twatyr] *nf* roof, roofing.

tôle [tol] *nf* [de métal] sheet metal; ~ **ondulée** corrugated iron.

tolérance [tɔlerɑ̃s] *nf* [gén] tolerance. || [liberté] concession.

tolérant, -e [tɔlerɑ̃, ɑ̃t] *adj* [large d'esprit] tolerant. || [indulgent] liberal.

tolérer [tɔlere] *vt* to tolerate.

tollé [tɔle] *nm* protest.

tomate [tɔmat] *nf* tomato.

tombal, -e, -aux [tɔ̃bal, o] *adj*: **pierre ~e** gravestone.

tombant, -e [tɔ̃bɑ̃, ɑ̃t] *adj* [moustaches] drooping; [épaules] sloping.

tombe [tɔ̃b] *nf* [fosse] grave, tomb.

tombeau, -x [tɔ̃bo] *nm* tomb.

tombée [tɔ̃be] *nf* fall; **à la ~ du jour** *ou* **de la nuit** at nightfall.

tomber [tɔ̃be] *vi* [gén] to fall; **faire ~ qqn** to knock sb over *ou* down; ~ **bien** [robe] to hang well; *fig* [visite, personne] to come at a good time. || [cheveux] to fall out. || [diminuer - prix] to drop, to fall; [- fièvre, vent] to drop; [- jour] to come to an end; [- colère] to die down. || [devenir brusquement]: ~ **malade** to fall ill; ~ **amoureux** to fall in love; **être bien/mal tombé** to be lucky/unlucky; [trouver]: ~ **sur** to come across. || [date, événement] to fall on.

tombola [tɔ̃bɔla] *nf* raffle.

tome [tɔm] *nm* volume.

ton¹ [tɔ̃] *nm* [de voix] tone; **hausser/ baisser le ~** to raise/lower one's voice. || MUS key; **donner le ~** to give an "A"; *fig* to set the tone.

ton² [tɔ̃] (*f* **ta** [ta], *pl* **tes** [te]) *adj poss* your.

tonalité [tɔnalite] *nf* MUS tonality. ‖ [au téléphone] dialling tone.

tondeuse [tɔ̃døz] *nf* [à cheveux] clippers (*pl*); ~ (à gazon) mower, lawn-mower.

tondre [tɔ̃dr] *vt* [gazon] to mow; [mouton] to shear; [caniche, cheveux] to clip.

tondu, -e [tɔ̃dy] *adj* [caniche, cheveux] clipped; [pelouse] mown.

tonifier [tɔnifje] *vt* [peau] to tone; [esprit] to stimulate.

tonique [tɔnik] *adj* [boisson] tonic (*avant n*); [froid] bracing; [lotion] toning. ‖ LING & MUS tonic.

tonitruant, -e [tɔnitryɑ̃, ɑ̃t] *adj* booming.

tonnage [tɔnaʒ] *nm* tonnage.

tonne [tɔn] *nf* [1000 kg] tonne.

tonneau, -x [tɔno] *nm* [baril] barrel, cask. ‖ [de voiture] roll. ‖ NAVIG ton.

tonnelle [tɔnɛl] *nf* bower, arbour.

tonner [tɔne] *vi* to thunder.

tonnerre [tɔnɛr] *nm* thunder; **coup de ~** thunderclap; *fig* bombshell.

tonte [tɔ̃t] *nf* [de mouton] shearing; [de gazon] mowing; [de caniche, cheveux] clipping.

tonus [tɔnys] *nm* [dynamisme] energy. ‖ [de muscle] tone.

top [tɔp] *nm* [signal] beep.

topographie [tɔpɔɡrafi] *nf* topography.

toque [tɔk] *nf* [de juge, de jockey] cap; [de cuisinier] hat.

torche [tɔrʃ] *nf* torch.

torcher [tɔrʃe] *vt fam* [assiette, fesses] to wipe. ‖ [travail] to dash off.

torchon [tɔrʃɔ̃] *nm* [serviette] cloth. ‖ *fam* [travail] mess.

tordre [tɔrdr] *vt* [gén] to twist. ○ **se tordre** *vp*: **se ~ la cheville** to twist one's ankle; **se ~ de rire** *fam fig* to double up with laughter.

tordu, -e [tɔrdy] **1** *pp* → tordre. **2** *adj fam* [bizarre, fou] crazy; [esprit] warped.

tornade [tɔrnad] *nf* tornado.

torpeur [tɔrpœr] *nf* torpor.

torpille [tɔrpij] *nf* MIL torpedo.

torréfaction [tɔrefaksjɔ̃] *nf* roasting.

torrent [tɔrɑ̃] *nm* torrent; **un ~ de** *fig* [injures] a stream of.

torrentiel, -ielle [tɔrɑ̃sjɛl] *adj* torrential.

torride [tɔrid] *adj* torrid.

torse [tɔrs] *nm* chest.

torsade [tɔrsad] *nf* [de cheveux] twist, coil. ‖ [de pull] cable.

torsion [tɔrsjɔ̃] *nf* twisting; PHYS torsion.

tort [tɔr] *nm* [erreur] fault; **avoir ~** to be wrong; **être dans son ou en ~** to be in the wrong; **à ~** wrongly. ‖ [préjudice] wrong.

torticolis [tɔrtikɔli] *nm* stiff neck.

tortiller [tɔrtije] *vt* [enrouler] to twist. ○ **se tortiller** *vp* to writhe, to wriggle.

tortionnaire [tɔrsjɔnɛr] *nmf* torturer.

tortue [tɔrty] *nf* tortoise; *fig* slowcoach *Br*, slowpoke *Am*.

tortueux, -euse [tɔrtɥø, øz] *adj* winding, twisting; *fig* tortuous.

torture [tɔrtyr] *nf* torture.

torturer [tɔrtyre] *vt* to torture.

tôt [to] *adv* [de bonne heure] early. ‖ [vite] soon, early. ○ **au plus tôt** *loc adv* at the earliest.

total, -e, -aux [tɔtal, o] *adj* total. ○ **total** *nm* total.

totalement [tɔtalmɑ̃] *adv* totally.

totaliser [tɔtalize] *vt* [additionner] to add up, to total. ‖ [réunir] to have a total of.

totalitaire [tɔtalitɛr] *adj* totalitarian.

totalitarisme [tɔtalitarism] *nm* totalitarianism.

totalité [tɔtalite] *nf* whole; **en ~** entirely.

toubib [tubib] *nmf fam* doc.

touchant, -e [tuʃɑ̃, ɑ̃t] *adj* touching.

touche [tuʃ] *nf* [de clavier] key; **~ de fonction** function key. ‖ [de peinture] stroke. ‖ *fig* [note]: **une ~ de** a touch of. ‖ PÊCHE bite. ‖ [FOOTBALL - ligne] touch line; [- remise en jeu] throw-in; [RUGBY - ligne] touch (line); [- remise en jeu] line-out. ‖ ESCRIME hit.

toucher [tuʃe] **1** *nm*: **le ~** the (sense of) touch; **au ~** to the touch. **2** *vt* [palper, émouvoir] to touch. ‖ [cible] to hit. ‖ [salaire] to get, to be paid; [chèque] to cash. ‖ [concerner] to affect, to concern. **3** *vi*: **à** to touch; [problème] to touch on; **~ à sa fin** to draw to a close. ○ **se toucher** *vp* [maisons] to be adjacent (to each other), to adjoin (each other).

touffe [tuf] *nf* tuft.

touffu, -e [tufy] *adj* [forêt] dense; [barbe] bushy.

toujours [tuʒur] *adv* [continuité, répétition] always; **ils s'aimeront ~** they will always love one another, they will love one another forever; **~ plus** more and more. ‖ [encore] still. ‖ [de toute façon] anyway, anyhow. ○ **pour toujours** *loc adv* forever, for good. ○ **toujours est-il que** *loc conj* the fact remains that.

toupet [tupɛ] *nm* [de cheveux] quiff *Br*, tuft of hair. || *fam fig* [aplomb] cheek; **avoir du ~, ne pas manquer de ~** *fam* to have a cheek.

toupie [tupi] *nf* (spinning) top.

tour [tur] **1** *nm* [périmètre] circumference; **faire le ~ de** to go round; **faire un ~** to go for a walk/drive *etc*; **~ d'horizon** survey; **~ de piste** SPORT lap; **~ de taille** waist measurement. || [rotation] turn; **fermer à double ~** to double-lock. || [plaisanterie] trick. || [succession] turn; **à ~ de rôle** in turn; **à ~** alternately, in turn. || [de potier] wheel. **2** *nf* [monument, de château] tower; [immeuble] high-rise *Am*. || ÉCHECS rook, castle. ○ **tour de contrôle** *nf* control tower.

tourbe [turb] *nf* peat.

tourbillon [turbijɔ̃] *nm* [de vent] whirlwind. || [de poussière, fumée] swirl. || [d'eau] whirlpool.

tourbillonner [turbijɔne] *vi* to whirl, to swirl; *fig* to whirl (round).

tourelle [turɛl] *nf* turret.

tourisme [turism] *nm* tourism.

touriste [turist] *nmf* tourist.

touristique [turistik] *adj* tourist (*avant n*).

tourment [turmɑ̃] *nm sout* torment.

tourmente [turmɑ̃t] *nf littéraire* [tempête] storm, tempest. || *fig* turmoil.

tourmenter [turmɑ̃te] *vt* to torment. ○ **se tourmenter** *vp* to worry o.s., to fret.

tournage [turnaʒ] *nm* CIN shooting.

tournant, -e [turnɑ̃, ɑ̃t] *adj* [porte] revolving; [fauteuil] swivel (*avant n*); [pont] swing (*avant n*). ○ **tournant** *nm* bend; *fig* turning point.

tourne-disque [turnədisk] (*pl* **tourne-disques**) *nm* record player.

tournée [turne] *nf* [voyage] tour. || *fam* [consommations] round.

tourner [turne] **1** *vt* [gén] to turn. || CIN to shoot. **2** *vi* [gén] to turn; [moteur] to turn over; [planète] to revolve; **~ autour de qqn** *fig* to hang around sb; **~ autour du pot** ou **du sujet** *fig* to beat about the bush. || *fam* [entreprise] to tick over. || [lait] to go off. ○ **se tourner** *vp* to turn (right) round; **se ~ vers** to turn towards.

tournesol [turnəsɔl] *nm* [plante] sunflower.

tournevis [turnəvis] *nm* screwdriver.

tourniquet [turnikɛ] *nm* [entrée] turnstile. || MÉD tourniquet.

tournis [turni] *nm fam*: **avoir le ~** to feel dizzy ou giddy.

tournoi [turnwa] *nm* tournament.

tournoyer [turnwaje] *vi* to wheel, to whirl.

tournure [turnyr] *nf* [apparence] turn. || [formulation] form; **~ de phrase** turn of phrase.

tourteau, -x [turto] *nm* [crabe] crab.

tourterelle [turtərɛl] *nf* turtledove.

tous → **tout**.

Toussaint [tusɛ̃] *nf*: **la ~** All Saints' Day.

tousser [tuse] *vi* to cough.

toussoter [tusɔte] *vi* to cough.

tout [tu] (*f* **toute** [tut], *mpl* **tous** [tus], *fpl* **toutes** [tut]) **1** *adj qualificatif* (*avec substantif singulier déterminé*) all; **~ le vin** all the wine; **~ un gâteau** a whole cake; **toute la journée/la nuit** all day/ night, the whole day/night. || (*avec pronom démonstratif*): **~ ceci/cela** all this/ that; **~ ce que je sais** all I know. **2** *adj indéf* [exprime la totalité] all; **tous les gâteaux** all the cakes; **tous les deux** both of us/them *etc*; **tous les trois** all three of us/them *etc*. || [chaque] every; **tous les deux ans** every two years. || [n'importe quel] every. **3** *pron indéf* everything, all; **je t'ai ~ dit** I've told you everything; **ils voulaient tous la voir** they all wanted to see her. ○ **tout 1** *adv* [entièrement, tout à fait] very, quite; **~ jeune/près** very young/near; **~ en haut** right at the top. || [avec un gérondif]: **~ en marchant** while walking. **2** *nm*: **le ~ est de ...** the main thing is to .... ○ **pas du tout** *loc adv* not at all. ○ **tout à fait** *loc adv* [complètement] quite, entirely. || [exactement] exactly. ○ **tout à l'heure** *loc adv* [futur] in a little while, shortly; **à ~ à l'heure!** see you later! || [passé] a little while ago. ○ **tout de suite** *loc adv* immediately, at once.

tout-à-l'égout [tutalegu] *nm inv* mains drainage.

toutefois [tutfwa] *adv* however.

tout-petit [tup(ə)ti] (*pl* **tout-petits**) *nm* toddler, tot.

tout-puissant, toute-puissante [tupɥisɑ̃, tutpɥisɑ̃t] (*mpl* **tout-puissants**, *fpl* **toutes-puissantes**) *adj* omnipotent, all-powerful.

toux [tu] *nf* cough.

toxicomane [tɔksikɔman] *nmf* drug addict.

toxine [tɔksin] *nf* toxin.

toxique [tɔksik] *adj* toxic.

trac [trak] *nm* nerves (*pl*); THÉÂTRE stage fright; **avoir le ~** to get nervous; THÉÂTRE to get stage fright.

tracas [traka] *nm* worry.

tracasser [trakase] *vt* to worry, to bother. ○ **se tracasser** *vp* to worry.

tracasserie [trakasri] *nf* annoyance.

trace [tras] *nf* [d'animal] track. || [de brûlure, fatigue] mark. || (*gén pl*) [vestige] trace. || [très petite quantité]: **une ~ de** a trace of.

tracé [trase] *nm* [lignes] plan, drawing; [de parcours] line.

tracer [trase] *vt* [dessiner, dépeindre] to draw. || [route, piste] to mark out.

trachéite [trakeit] *nf* throat infection.

tract [trakt] *nm* leaflet.

tractations [traktasjɔ̃] *nfpl* negotiations, dealings.

tracter [trakte] *vt* to tow.

tracteur [traktœr] *nm* tractor.

traction [traksjɔ̃] *nf* [action de tirer] towing, pulling; **~ avant/arrière** front-/rear-wheel drive. || [SPORT - au sol] push-up *Am*; [- à la barre] pull-up.

tradition [tradisjɔ̃] *nf* tradition.

traditionnel, -elle [tradisjɔnɛl] *adj* [de tradition] traditional. || [habituel] usual.

traducteur, -trice [tradyktœr, tris] *nm, f* translator.

traduction [tradyksjɔ̃] *nf* [gén] translation.

traduire [tradɥir] *vt* [texte] to translate; **~ qqch en français/anglais** to translate sthg into French/English. || [révéler - crise] to reveal, to betray; [- sentiments, pensée] to render, to express. || JUR: **~ qqn en justice** to bring sb before the courts.

trafic [trafik] *nm* [de marchandises] traffic, trafficking. || [circulation] traffic.

trafiquant, -e [trafikɑ̃, ɑ̃t] *nm, f* trafficker, dealer.

trafiquer [trafike] **1** *vt* [falsifier] to tamper with. || *fam* [manigancer]: **qu'est-ce que tu trafiques?** what are you up to? **2** *vi* to be involved in trafficking.

tragédie [traʒedi] *nf* tragedy.

tragique [traʒik] *adj* tragic.

tragiquement [traʒikmɑ̃] *adv* tragically.

trahir [trair] *vt* [gén] to betray. || [suj: moteur] to let down; [suj: forces] to fail. ○ **se trahir** *vp* to give o.s. away.

trahison [traizɔ̃] *nf* [gén] betrayal. || JUR treason.

train [trɛ̃] *nm* TRANSPORT train. || [allure] pace. ○ **train de vie** *nm* lifestyle. ○ **en train de** *loc prép*: **être en ~ de lire/travailler** to be reading/working.

traînant, -e [trenɑ̃, ɑ̃t] *adj* [voix] drawling; [démarche] dragging.

traîne [trɛn] *nf* [de robe] train. || *loc*: **être à la ~** to lag behind.

traîneau, -x [treno] *nm* sleigh, sledge.

traînée [trene] *nf* [trace] trail. || *tfam péj* [prostituée] tart, whore.

traîner [trene] **1** *vt* [tirer, emmener] to drag. || [trimbaler] to lug around, to cart around. **2** *vi* [personne] to dawdle. || [maladie, affaire] to drag on; **~ en longueur** to drag. || [vêtements, livres] to lie around ou about. ○ **se traîner** *vp* [personne] to drag o.s. along.

train-train [trɛ̃trɛ̃] *nm fam* routine, daily grind.

traire [trer] *vt* [vache] to milk.

trait [tre] *nm* [ligne] line, stroke; **~ d'union** hyphen. || (*gén pl*) [de visage] feature. || [caractéristique] trait, feature. || *loc*: **avoir ~ à** to be to do with, to concern. ○ **d'un trait** *loc adv* [boire, lire] in one go.

traitant, -e [trɛtɑ̃, ɑ̃t] *adj* [shampooing, crème] medicated; → **médecin**.

traite [trɛt] *nf* [de vache] milking. || COMM bill, draft. ○ **d'une seule traite** *loc adv* without stopping, in one go.

traité [trete] *nm* [ouvrage] treatise. || POLIT treaty.

traitement [trɛtmɑ̃] *nm* [gén & MÉD] treatment; **mauvais ~** ill-treatment. || [rémunération] wage. || IND & INFORM processing; **~ de texte** word processing. || [de problème] handling.

traiter [trete] **1** *vt* [gén & MÉD] to treat. || [qualifier]: **~ qqn d'imbécile/de lâche** *etc* to call sb an imbecile/a coward *etc*. || [question, thème] to deal with. || IND & INFORM to process. **2** *vi* [négocier] to negotiate. || [livre]: **~ de** to deal with.

traiteur [trɛtœr] *nm* caterer.

traître, -esse [trɛtr, ɛs] **1** *adj* treacherous. **2** *nm, f* traitor.

traîtrise [tretriz] *nf* [déloyauté] treachery. || [acte] act of treachery.

trajectoire [traʒɛktwar] *nf* trajectory, path; *fig* path.

trajet [traʒɛ] *nm* [distance] distance. || [itinéraire] route. || [voyage] journey.

trame [tram] *nf* weft; *fig* framework.

tramer [trame] *vt sout* to plot. ○ **se tramer** 1 *vp* to be plotted. 2 *v impers*: **il se trame quelque chose** there's something afoot.

trampoline [trɑ̃pɔlin] *nm* trampoline.

tram(way) [tram(wɛ)] *nm* tram *Br*, streetcar *Am*.

tranchant, -e [trɑ̃ʃɑ̃, ɑ̃t] *adj* [instrument] sharp. || [personne] assertive. || [ton] curt. ○ **tranchant** *nm* edge.

tranche [trɑ̃ʃ] *nf* [de gâteau, jambon] slice; **~ d'âge** *fig* age bracket. || [de livre, pièce] edge. || [de revenus] portion; [de paiement] instalment; [fiscale] bracket.

trancher [trɑ̃ʃe] 1 *vt* [couper] to cut; [pain, jambon] to slice; **~ la question** *fig* to settle the question. 2 *vi fig* [décider] to decide. || [contraster]: **~ avec** ou **sur** to contrast with.

tranquille [trɑ̃kil] *adj* [endroit, vie] quiet; **laisser qqn/qqch ~** to leave sb/ sthg alone. || [rassuré] at ease, easy; **soyez ~** don't worry.

tranquillement [trɑ̃kilmɑ̃] *adv* [sans s'agiter] quietly.

tranquillisant, -e [trɑ̃kilizɑ̃, ɑ̃t] *adj* [médicament] tranquillizing. ○ **tranquillisant** *nm* tranquillizer.

tranquilliser [trɑ̃kilize] *vt* to reassure.

tranquillité [trɑ̃kilite] *nf* [calme] peacefulness, quietness. || [sérénité] peace, tranquillity.

transaction [trɑ̃zaksjɔ̃] *nf* transaction.

transat [trɑ̃zat] *nm* deckchair.

transatlantique [trɑ̃zatlɑ̃tik] 1 *adj* transatlantic. 2 *nm* transatlantic liner. 3 *nf* transatlantic race.

transcription [trɑ̃skripsjɔ̃] *nf* [de document & MUS] transcription; [dans un autre alphabet] transliteration.

transcrire [trɑ̃skrir] *vt* [document & MUS] to transcribe; [dans un autre alphabet] to transliterate.

transcrit, -e [trɑ̃skri, it] *pp* → transcrire.

transe [trɑ̃s] *nf*: **être en ~** *fig* to be beside o.s.

transférer [trɑ̃sfere] *vt* to transfer.

transfert [trɑ̃sfɛr] *nm* transfer.

transfigurer [trɑ̃sfigyre] *vt* to transfigure.

transformateur, -trice [trɑ̃sfɔrmatœr, tris] *adj* IND processing (*avant n*). ○ **transformateur** *nm* transformer.

transformation [trɑ̃sfɔrmasjɔ̃] *nf* [de pays, personne] transformation. || IND processing. || RUGBY conversion.

transformer [trɑ̃sfɔrme] *vt* [gén] to transform; [magasin] to convert; **~ qqch en** to turn sthg into. || IND & RUGBY to convert. ○ **se transformer** *vp*: **se ~ en monstre/papillon** to turn into a monster/butterfly.

transfuge [trɑ̃sfyʒ] *nmf* renegade.

transfuser [trɑ̃sfyze] *vt* [sang] to transfuse.

transfusion [trɑ̃sfyzjɔ̃] *nf*: **~ (sanguine)** (blood) transfusion.

transgresser [trɑ̃sgrese] *vt* [loi] to infringe; [ordre] to disobey.

transhumance [trɑ̃zymɑ̃s] *nf* transhumance.

transi, -e [trɑ̃zi] *adj*: **être ~ de froid** to be chilled to the bone.

transiger [trɑ̃ziʒe] *vi*: **~ (sur)** to compromise (on).

transistor [trɑ̃zistɔr] *nm* transistor.

transit [trɑ̃zit] *nm* transit.

transiter [trɑ̃zite] *vi* to pass in transit.

transitif, -ive [trɑ̃zitif, iv] *adj* transitive.

transition [trɑ̃zisjɔ̃] *nf* transition; **sans ~** with no transition, abruptly.

transitoire [trɑ̃zitwar] *adj* [passager] transitory.

translucide [trɑ̃slysid] *adj* translucent.

transmettre [trɑ̃smetr] *vt* [message, salutations]: **~ qqch (à)** to pass sthg on (to). || [tradition, propriété]: **~ qqch (à)** to hand sthg down (to). || [fonction, pouvoir]: **~ qqch (à)** to hand sthg over (to). || [maladie]: **~ qqch (à)** to transmit sthg (to), to pass sthg on (to). || [concert, émission] to broadcast. ○ **se transmettre** *vp* [maladie] to be passed on, to be transmitted. || [courant, onde] to be transmitted. || [tradition] to be handed down.

transmis, -e [trɑ̃smi, iz] *pp* → transmettre.

transmissible [trɑ̃smisibl] *adj* [maladie] transmissible.

transmission [trɑ̃smisjɔ̃] *nf* [de biens] transfer. || [de maladie] transmission. || [de message] passing on. || [de tradition] handing down.

transparaître [trɑ̃sparetr] *vi* to show.

transparence [trɑ̃sparɑ̃s] *nf* transparency.

transparent, -e [trɑ̃sparɑ̃, ɑ̃t] *adj* transparent. ○ **transparent** *nm* transparency.

transpercer [trɑ̃sperse] *vt* to pierce; *fig* [suj: froid, pluie] to go right through.

transpiration [trãspirasjɔ̃] nf [sueur] perspiration.

transpirer [trãspire] vi [suer] to perspire.

transplanter [trãsplãte] vt to transplant.

transport [trãspɔr] nm transport (U); ~s en commun public transport (sg).

transportable [trãspɔrtabl] adj [marchandise] transportable; [blessé] fit to be moved.

transporter [trãspɔrte] vt [marchandises, personnes] to transport.

transporteur [trãspɔrtœr] nm [personne] carrier; ~ routier road haulier.

transposer [trãspoze] vt [déplacer] to transpose. || [adapter]: ~ qqch (à) to adapt sthg (for).

transposition [trãspozisjɔ̃] nf [déplacement] transposition. || [adaptation]: ~ (à) adaptation (for).

transsexuel, -elle [trãssɛksɥɛl] adj & nm, f transsexual.

transvaser [trãsvaze] vt to decant.

transversal, -e, -aux [trãsversal, o] adj [coupe] cross (avant n). || [chemin] cross (avant n) Am.

trapèze [trapɛz] nm GÉOM trapezium. || GYM trapeze.

trapéziste [trapezist] nmf trapeze artist.

trappe [trap] nf [ouverture] trapdoor. || [piège] trap.

trapu, -e [trapy] adj [personne] stocky, solidly built. || [édifice] squat.

traquenard [traknar] nm trap.

traquer [trake] vt [animal] to track; [personne, faute] to track ou hunt down.

traumatiser [tromatize] vt to traumatize.

traumatisme [tromatism] nm traumatism.

travail [travaj] nm [gén] work (U); se mettre au ~ to get down to work. || [tâche, emploi] job. || [du métal, du bois] working. || [phénomène - du bois] warping; [- du temps, fermentation] action. || MÉD: être/entrer en ~ to be in/go into labour. ○ **travaux** nmpl [d'aménagement] work (U); [routiers] roadworks; travaux publics civil engineering (sg). || SCOL: travaux dirigés class work; travaux manuels arts and crafts; travaux pratiques practical work (U).

travaillé, -e [travaje] adj [matériau] wrought, worked. || [style] laboured.

travailler [travaje] 1 vi [gén] to work; ~ à qqch to work on sthg. || [métal, bois] to warp. 2 vt [étudier] to work at ou on; [piano] to practise. || [suj: idée, remords] to torment. || [matière] to work, to fashion.

travailleur, -euse [travajœr, øz] 1 adj hard-working. 2 nm, f worker.

travelling [travliŋ] nm [mouvement] travelling shot.

travers [traver] nm failing, fault. ○ à **travers** loc adv & loc prép through. ○ au **travers** loc adv through. ○ au **travers de** loc prép through. ○ de **travers** loc adv [nez, escalier] crooked. || [obliquement] sideways. || [mal] wrong; comprendre qqch de ~ to misunderstand sthg. ○ en **travers** loc adv crosswise. ○ en **travers de** loc prép across.

traverse [travers] nf [de chemin de fer] sleeper, tie Am. || [chemin] short cut.

traversée [traverse] nf crossing.

traverser [traverse] vt [rue, mer, montagne] to cross; [ville] to go through. || [peau, mur] to go through, to pierce. || [crise, période] to go through.

traversin [traversɛ̃] nm bolster.

travestir [travestir] vt [déguiser] to dress up. || fig [vérité, idée] to distort. ○ se **travestir** vp [pour bal] to wear fancy dress. || [en femme] to put on drag.

trébucher [trebyʃe] vi: ~ (sur/contre) to stumble (over/against).

trèfle [trefl] nm [plante] clover. || [carte] club; [famille] clubs (pl).

treille [trɛj] nf [vigne] climbing vine. || [tonnelle] trellised vines (pl).

treillis [treji] nm [clôture] trellis (fencing). || MIL combat uniform.

treize [trɛz] adj num & nm thirteen; voir aussi six.

treizième [trɛzjɛm] adj num, nm & nmf thirteenth; voir aussi sixième.

trekking [trekiŋ] nm trek.

tréma [trema] nm diaeresis.

tremblant, -e [trãblã, ãt] adj [personne - de froid] shivering; [- d'émotion] trembling, shaking. || [voix] quavering.

tremblement [trãbləmã] nm [de corps] trembling. || [de voix] quavering. || [de feuilles] fluttering. ○ **tremblement de terre** nm earthquake.

trembler [trãble] vi [personne - de froid] to shiver; [- d'émotion] to tremble, to shake. || [voix] to quaver. || [lumière] to flicker. || [terre] to shake.

trembloter [trãblɔte] *vi* [personne] to tremble. || [voix] to quaver.

trémousser [tremuse] ○ **se trémousser** *vp* to jig up and down.

trempe [trãp] *nf* [envergure] calibre; **de sa ~** of his/her calibre. || *fam* [coups] thrashing.

tremper [trãpe] **1** *vt* [mouiller] to soak. || [plonger]: **~ qqch dans** to dip sthg into. || [métal] to harden, to quench. **2** *vi* [linge] to soak.

tremplin [trãplɛ̃] *nm litt & fig* springboard; SKI ski jump.

trentaine [trãtɛn] *nf* [nombre]: **une ~ de** about thirty. || [âge]: **avoir la ~** to be in one's thirties.

trente [trãt] **1** *adj num* thirty. **2** *nm* thirty; *voir aussi* **six**.

trentième [trãtjɛm] *adj num, nm & nmf* thirtieth; *voir aussi* **sixième**.

trépidant, -e [trepidã, ãt] *adj* [vie] hectic.

trépied [trepje] *nm* [support] tripod.

trépigner [trepiɲe] *vi* to stamp one's feet.

très [trɛ] *adv* very; **~ bien** very well; **être ~ aimé** to be much ou greatly liked; **j'ai ~ envie de ...** I'd very much like to .....

trésor [trezɔr] *nm* treasure. ○ **Trésor** *nm*: **le Trésor public** the public revenue department.

trésorerie [trezɔrri] *nf* [service] accounts department. || [gestion] accounts (*pl*). || [fonds] finances (*pl*), funds (*pl*).

trésorier, -ière [trezɔrje, jɛr] *nm, f* treasurer.

tressaillement [tresajmã] *nm* [de joie] thrill; [de douleur] wince.

tressaillir [tresajir] *vi* [de joie] to thrill; [de douleur] to wince. || [sursauter] to start, to jump.

tressauter [tresote] *vi* [sursauter] to jump, to start; [dans véhicule] to be tossed about.

tresse [trɛs] *nf* [de cheveux] plait. || [de rubans] braid.

tresser [trese] *vt* [cheveux] to plait. || [osier] to braid. || [panier, guirlande] to weave.

tréteau, -x [treto] *nm* trestle.

treuil [trœj] *nm* winch, windlass.

trêve [trɛv] *nf* [cessez-le-feu] truce. || *fig* [répit] rest, respite; **~ de plaisanteries/de sottises** that's enough joking/nonsense.

tri [tri] *nm* [de lettres] sorting; [de candidats] selection.

triage [trijaʒ] *nm* [de lettres] sorting.

triangle [trijãgl] *nm* triangle.

triangulaire [trijãgylɛr] *adj* triangular.

triathlon [trijatlɔ̃] *nm* triathlon.

tribal, -e, -aux [tribal, o] *adj* tribal.

tribord [tribɔr] *nm* starboard; **à ~ on** the starboard side, to starboard.

tribu [triby] *nf* tribe.

tribulations [tribylasjɔ̃] *nfpl* tribulations, trials.

tribunal, -aux [tribynal, o] *nm* JUR court; **~ correctionnel** ≃ Magistrates' Court; **~ de grande instance** ≃ Crown Court.

tribune [tribyn] *nf* [d'orateur] platform. || (*gén pl*) [de stade] stand.

tribut [triby] *nm littéraire* tribute.

tributaire [tribytɛr] *adj*: **être ~ de** to depend ou be dependent on.

tricher [triʃe] *vi* [au jeu, à examen] to cheat. || [mentir]: **~ sur** to lie about.

tricherie [triʃri] *nf* cheating.

tricheur, -euse [triʃœr, øz] *nm, f* cheat.

tricolore [trikɔlɔr] *adj* [à trois couleurs] three-coloured. || [français] French.

tricot [triko] *nm* [vêtement] jumper *Br*, sweater. || [ouvrage] knitting; **faire du ~** to knit. || [étoffe] knitted fabric, jersey.

tricoter [trikɔte] *vi & vt* to knit.

tricycle [trisikl] *nm* tricycle.

trier [trije] *vt* [classer] to sort out. || [sélectionner] to select.

trilingue [trilɛ̃g] *adj* trilingual.

trimestre [trimɛstr] *nm* [période] term.

trimestriel, -ielle [trimɛstrijɛl] *adj* [loyer, magazine] quarterly; SCOL end-of-term (*avant n*).

tringle [trɛ̃gl] *nf* rod.

trinquer [trɛ̃ke] *vi* [boire] to toast, to clink glasses; **~ à** to drink to.

trio [trijo] *nm* trio.

triomphal, -e, -aux [trijɔ̃fal, o] *adj* [succès] triumphal; [accueil] triumphant.

triomphant, -e [trijɔ̃fã, ãt] *adj* [équipe] winning; [air] triumphant.

triomphe [trijɔ̃f] *nm* triumph.

triompher [trijɔ̃fe] *vi* [gén] to triumph; **~ de** to triumph over.

tripes [trip] *nfpl* [d'animal, de personne] guts. || CULIN tripe (*sg*).

triple [tripl] **1** *adj* triple. **2** *nm*: **le ~ (de)** three times as much (as).

triplé [triple] *nm* [au turf] *bet on three horses winning in three different races.*
○ **triplés, -ées** *nm, f pl* triplets.

trouver

triste [trist] *adj* [personne, nouvelle] sad; **être ~ de qqch/de faire qqch** to be sad about sthg/about doing sthg. || [paysage, temps] gloomy; [couleur] dull. || (*avant n*) [lamentable] sorry.

tristesse [tristɛs] *nf* [de personne, nouvelle] sadness. || [de paysage, temps] gloominess.

triturer [trityre] *vt fam* [mouchoir] to knead. ○ **se triturer** *vp fam*: **se ~ l'esprit** *ou* **les méninges** to rack one's brains.

trivial, -e, -iaux [trivjal, jo] *adj* [banal] trivial. || *péj* [vulgaire] crude, coarse.

troc [trɔk] *nm* [échange] exchange. || [système économique] barter.

trois [trwa] **1** *nm* three. **2** *adj num* three; *voir aussi* **six**.

troisième [trwazjɛm] **1** *adj num & nmf* third. **2** *nm* third; [étage] third floor *Br*, fourth floor *Am*. **3** *nf* SCOL fourth year. || [vitesse] third (gear); *voir aussi* **sixième**.

trombe [trɔ̃b] *nf* water spout.

trombone [trɔ̃bɔn] *nm* [agrafe] paper clip. || [instrument] trombone.

trompe [trɔ̃p] *nf* [instrument] trumpet. || [d'éléphant] trunk. || [d'insecte] proboscis. || ANAT tube.

trompe-l'œil [trɔ̃plœj] *nm inv* [peinture] trompe-l'oeil.

tromper [trɔ̃pe] *vt* [personne] to deceive. || [vigilance] to elude. ○ **se tromper** *vp* to make a mistake, to be mistaken; **se ~ de jour/maison** to get the wrong day/house.

tromperie [trɔ̃pri] *nf* deception.

trompette [trɔ̃pɛt] *nf* trumpet.

trompettiste [trɔ̃petist] *nmf* trumpeter.

trompeur, -euse [trɔ̃pœr, øz] *adj* [calme, apparence] deceptive.

tronc [trɔ̃] *nm* [d'arbre, de personne] trunk. || [d'église] collection box. ○ **tronc commun** *nm* SCOL core syllabus.

tronçon [trɔ̃sɔ̃] *nm* [morceau] piece, length. || [de route, de chemin de fer] section.

tronçonneuse [trɔ̃sɔnøz] *nf* chain saw.

trône [tron] *nm* throne.

trôner [trone] *vi* [personne] to sit enthroned; [objet] to have pride of place.

trop [tro] *adv* (*devant adj, adv*) too; **avoir ~ chaud/froid/peur** to be too hot/cold/frightened. || (*avec verbe*) too much; **je n'aime pas ~ le chocolat** I don't like chocolate very much. || (*avec complément*): **~ de** [quantité] too much; [nombre] too many. ○ **en trop, de trop** *loc adv* too much/many; **10 francs de** *ou* **en ~** 10 francs too much; **être de ~** [personne] to be in the way, to be unwelcome.

trophée [trɔfe] *nm* trophy.

tropical, -e, -aux [trɔpikal, o] *adj* tropical.

tropique [trɔpik] *nm* tropic.

trop-plein [trɔplɛ̃] (*pl* **trop-pleins**) *nm* [excès] excess; *fig* excess, surplus.

troquer [trɔke] *vt*: **~ qqch (contre)** to barter sthg (for); *fig* to swap sthg (for).

trot [tro] *nm* trot; **au ~** at a trot.

trotter [trɔte] *vi* [cheval] to trot. || [personne] to run around.

trotteur, -euse [trɔtœr, øz] *nm, f* trotter. ○ **trotteuse** *nf* second hand.

trottiner [trɔtine] *vi* to trot.

trottoir [trɔtwar] *nm* sidewalk *Am*.

trou [tru] *nm* [gén] hole; **~ d'air** air pocket. || [manque, espace vide] gap; **~ de mémoire** memory lapse.

troublant, -e [trublɑ̃, ɑ̃t] *adj* disturbing.

trouble [trubl] **1** *adj* [eau] cloudy. || [image, vue] blurred. **2** *nm* [désordre] trouble, discord. || [gêne] confusion. || (*gén pl*) [dérèglement] disorder. ○ **troubles** *nmpl* unrest (*U*).

trouble-fête [trubləfɛt] *nmf inv* spoilsport.

troubler [truble] *vt* [eau] to cloud, to make cloudy. || [image, vue] to blur. || [inquiéter, émouvoir] to disturb. || [rendre perplexe] to trouble. ○ **se troubler** *vp* [eau] to become cloudy. || [personne] to become flustered.

trouée [true] *nf* gap; MIL breach.

trouer [true] *vt* [chaussette] to make a hole in. || *fig* [silence] to disturb.

trouille [truj] *nf fam* fear, terror.

troupe [trup] *nf* MIL troop. || [d'amis] group, band. || THÉÂTRE theatre group.

troupeau, -x [trupo] *nm* [de vaches, d'éléphants] herd; [de moutons, d'oies] flock; *péj* [de personnes] herd.

trousse [trus] *nf* case, bag; **~ de secours** first-aid kit; **~ de toilette** toilet bag.

trousseau, -x [truso] *nm* [de mariée] trousseau. || [de clefs] bunch.

trouvaille [truvaj] *nf* [découverte] find, discovery. || [invention] new idea.

trouver [truve] **1** *vt* to find; **~ que** to feel (that); **~ bon/mauvais que ...** to think (that) it is right/wrong that .... **2** *v* *impers*: **il se trouve que ...** the fact is that .... || **se trouver** *vp* [dans un endroit] to be. || [dans un état] to find o.s. || [se sentir] to feel; **se ~ mal** [s'évanouir] to faint.

truand [tryɑ̃] *nm* crook.

truc [tryk] *nm* [combine] trick. || *fam* [chose] thing, thingamajig.

trucage = **truquage**.

truculent, -e [trykylɑ̃, ɑ̃t] *adj* colourful.

truelle [tryɛl] *nf* trowel.

truffe [tryf] *nf* [champignon] truffle. || [museau] muzzle.

truffer [tryfe] *vt* [volaille] to garnish with truffles. || *fig* [discours]: **~ de** to stuff with.

truie [trɥi] *nf* sow.

truite [trɥit] *nf* trout.

truquage, trucage [trykaʒ] *nm* CIN (special) effect.

truquer [tryke] *vt* [élections] to rig.

trust [trœst] *nm* [groupement] trust. || [entreprise] corporation.

tsar, tzar [tzar] *nm* tsar.

tsigane = **tzigane**.

TSVP (*abr de* **tournez s'il vous plaît**) PTO.

tt *conf. abr de* **tout confort**.

TTX (*abr de* **traitement de texte**) WP.

tu¹, -e [ty] *pp* → **taire**.

tu² [ty] *pron pers* you.

tuba [tyba] *nm* MUS tuba. || [de plongée] snorkel.

tube [tyb] *nm* [gén] tube; **~ cathodique** cathode ray tube. || *fam* [chanson] hit. **tube digestif** *nm* digestive tract.

tubercule [tyberkyl] *nm* BOT tuber.

tuberculose [tyberkyloz] *nf* tuberculosis.

tuer [tɥe] *vt* to kill. **se tuer** *vp* [se suicider] to kill o.s. || [par accident] to die.

tuerie [tyri] *nf* slaughter.

tue-tête [tytɛt] **à tue-tête** *loc adv* at the top of one's voice.

tueur, -euse [tɥœr, øz] *nm, f* [meurtrier] killer.

tuile [tɥil] *nf* [de toit] tile. || *fam* [désagrément] blow.

tulipe [tylip] *nf* tulip.

tulle [tyl] *nm* tulle.

tuméfié, -e [tymefje] *adj* swollen.

tumeur [tymœr] *nf* tumour.

tumulte [tymylt] *nm* [désordre] hubbub. || *littéraire* [trouble] tumult.

tunique [tynik] *nf* tunic.

Tunisie [tynizi] *nf*: **la ~** Tunisia.

tunisien, -ienne [tynizjɛ̃, jɛn] *adj* Tunisian. **Tunisien, -ienne** *nm, f* Tunisian.

tunnel [tynɛl] *nm* tunnel.

turban [tyrbɑ̃] *nm* turban.

turbine [tyrbin] *nf* turbine.

turbo [tyrbo] *nm & nf* turbo.

turbulence [tyrbylɑ̃s] *nf* MÉTÉOR turbulence.

turbulent, -e [tyrbylɑ̃, ɑ̃t] *adj* boisterous.

turc, turque [tyrk] *adj* Turkish. **turc** *nm* [langue] Turkish. **Turc, Turque** *nm, f* Turk.

turf [tœrf] *nm* [activité]: **le ~** racing.

turque → **turc**.

Turquie [tyrki] *nf*: **la ~** Turkey.

turquoise [tyrkwaz] *nf & adj inv* turquoise.

tutelle [tytɛl] *nf* JUR guardianship. || [dépendance] supervision.

tuteur, -trice [tytœr, tris] *nm, f* guardian. **tuteur** *nm* [pour plante] stake.

tutoyer [tytwaje] *vt*: **~ qqn** to use the "tu" form to sb.

tuyau, -x [tɥijo] *nm* [conduit] pipe; **~ d'arrosage** hosepipe. || *fam* [renseignement] tip.

tuyauterie [tɥijotri] *nf* piping (*U*), pipes (*pl*).

TV (*abr de* **télévision**) *nf* TV.

TVA (*abr de* **taxe à la valeur ajoutée**) *nf* ≃ VAT.

tweed [twid] *nm* tweed.

tympan [tɛ̃pɑ̃] *nm* ANAT eardrum.

type [tip] **1** *nm* [genre] type. || *fam* [individu] guy, bloke. **2** *adj inv* [caractéristique] typical.

typhoïde [tifɔid] *nf* typhoid.

typhon [tifɔ̃] *nm* typhoon.

typhus [tifys] *nm* typhus.

typique [tipik] *adj* typical.

typographie [tipɔgrafi] *nf* typography.

tyran [tirɑ̃] *nm* tyrant.

tyrannique [tiranik] *adj* tyrannical.

tyranniser [tiranize] *vt* to tyrannize.

tzar = **tsar**.

tzigane, tsigane [tsigan] *nmf* gipsy.

u, U [y] *nm inv* u, U.

UDF (*abr de* **Union pour la démocratie française**) *nf* French political party to the right of the political spectrum.

Ukraine [ykrɛn] *nf:* l'~ the Ukraine.

ulcère [ylsɛr] *nm* ulcer.

ULM (*abr de* **ultra léger motorisé**) *nm* microlight.

ultérieur, -e [ylterjœr] *adj* later, subsequent.

ultimatum [yltimatɔm] *nm* ultimatum.

ultime [yltim] *adj* ultimate, final.

ultramoderne [yltramɔdɛrn] *adj* ultramodern.

ultrasensible [yltrasɑ̃sibl] *adj* [pellicule] high-speed.

ultrason [yltrasɔ̃] *nm* ultrasound (*U*).

ultraviolet, -ette [yltravjɔlɛ, ɛt] *adj* ultraviolet. ○ **ultraviolet** *nm* ultraviolet.

un [œ̃] (*f* **une** [yn]) **1** *art indéf* a, an (*devant voyelle*); **une pomme** an apple. **2** *pron indéf* one; **l'~ de mes amis** one of my friends; **l'~ l'autre** each other; **les ~s les autres** one another; **les ~s ...**, **les autres** some ..., others. **3** *adj num* one. **4** *nm* one; *voir aussi* **six**. ○ **une** *nf:* **faire la/ être à la une** PRESSE to make the/to be on the front page.

unanime [ynanim] *adj* unanimous.

unanimité [ynanimite] *nf* unanimity; **faire l'~** to be unanimously approved; **à l'~** unanimously.

UNESCO, Unesco [ynɛsko] (*abr de* **United Nations Educational, Scientific and Cultural Organization**) *nf* UNESCO.

uni, -e [yni] *adj* [joint, réuni] united. || [famille, couple] close. || [surface, mer] smooth; [route] even. || [étoffe, robe] self-coloured.

UNICEF, Unicef [ynisɛf] (*abr de* **United Nations International Children's Emergency Fund**) *nm* UNICEF.

unifier [ynifje] *vt* [régions, parti] to unify. || [programmes] to standardize.

uniforme [yniform] **1** *adj* uniform; [régulier] regular. **2** *nm* uniform.

uniformiser [yniformize] *vt* [couleur] to make uniform. || [programmes, lois] to standardize.

unilatéral, -e, -aux [ynilateral, o] *adj* unilateral; **stationnement ~** parking on only one side of the street.

union [ynjɔ̃] *nf* [mariage] union; **~ libre** cohabitation. || [de pays] union; [de syndicats] confederation. || [entente] unity. ○ **Union soviétique** *nf:* l'(ex-)Union soviétique the (former) Soviet Union.

unique [ynik] *adj* [seul - enfant, veston] only; [- préoccupation] sole. || [principe, prix] single. || [exceptionnel] unique.

uniquement [ynikmɑ̃] *adv* [exclusivement] only, solely. || [seulement] only, just.

unir [ynir] *vt* [assembler - mots, qualités] to put together, to combine; [- pays] to unite; **~ qqch à** [pays] to unite sthg with; [mot, qualité] to combine sthg with. || [marier] to unite, to join in marriage. ○ **s'unir** *vp* [s'associer] to unite, to join together. || [se marier] to be joined in marriage.

unitaire [yniter] *adj* [à l'unité]: **prix ~** unit price.

unité [ynite] *nf* [cohésion] unity. || COMM, MATHS & MIL unit. ○ **unité centrale** *nf* INFORM central processing unit.

univers [yniver] *nm* universe; *fig* world.

universel, -elle [yniversɛl] *adj* universal.

universitaire [yniversiter] **1** *adj* university (*avant n*). **2** *nmf* academic.

université [yniversite] *nf* university.

uranium [yranjɔm] *nm* uranium.

urbain, -e [yrbɛ̃, ɛn] *adj* [de la ville] urban. || *littéraire* [affable] urbane.

urbaniser [yrbanize] *vt* to urbanize.

urbanisme [yrbanism] *nm* town planning.

urgence [yrʒɑ̃s] *nf* [de mission] urgency. || MÉD emergency; **les ~s** the casualty department (*sg*). ○ **d'urgence** *loc adv* immediately.

urgent, -e [yrʒɑ̃, ɑ̃t] *adj* urgent.

urine [yrin] *nf* urine.

uriner [yrine] *vi* to urinate.

urinoir [yrinwar] *nm* urinal.

urne [yrn] *nf* [vase] urn. || [de vote] ballot box.

URSS (*abr de* **Union des républiques socialistes soviétiques**) *nf*: **l'(ex-)~** the (former) USSR.

urticaire [yrtikɛr] *nf* urticaria, hives (*pl*).

Uruguay [yrygwɛ] *nm*: **l'~** Uruguay.

USA (*abr de* **United States of America**) *nmpl* USA.

usage [yzaʒ] *nm* [gén] use; **à ~ externe/interne** for external/internal use; **hors d'~** out of action. ‖ [coutume] custom.

usagé, -e [yzaʒe] *adj* worn, old.

usager [yzaʒe] *nm* user.

usé, -e [yze] *adj* [détérioré] worn; **eaux ~es** waste water (*sg*). ‖ [plaisanterie] hackneyed, well-worn.

user [yze] *vt* [consommer] to use. ‖ [vêtement] to wear out. [santé] to ruin; [personne] to wear out. ○ **s'user** *vp* [chaussure] to wear out.

usine [yzin] *nf* factory.

usité, -e [yzite] *adj* in common use.

ustensile [ystɑ̃sil] *nm* implement, tool.

usuel, -elle [yzɥɛl] *adj* common, usual.

usure [yzyr] *nf* [de vêtement, meuble] wear. ‖ [intérêt] usury.

usurier, -ière [yzyrje, jɛr] *nm, f* usurer.

usurpateur, -trice [yzyrpatœr, tris] *nm, f* usurper.

usurper [yzyrpe] *vt* to usurp.

ut [yt] *nm inv* C.

utérus [yterys] *nm* uterus, womb.

utile [ytil] *adj* useful; **être ~ à qqn** to be useful ou of help to sb, to help sb.

utilisateur, -trice [ytilizatœr, tris] *nm, f* user.

utiliser [ytilize] *vt* to use.

utilitaire [ytiliter] **1** *adj* [pratique] utilitarian; [véhicule] commercial. **2** *nm* IN-FORM utility (program).

utilité [ytilite] *nf* [usage] usefulness. ‖ JUR: **organisme d'~ publique** registered charity.

utopie [ytɔpi] *nf* [idéal] utopia. ‖ [projet irréalisable] unrealistic idea.

utopiste [ytɔpist] *nmf* utopian.

UV 1 *nf* (*abr de* **unité de valeur**) ≃ credit *Am*. **2** (*abr de* **ultraviolet**) UV.

v, V [ve] *nm inv* v, V.

v. ‖ (*abr de* **vers**) [environ] approx.

va [va] *interj*: **courage, ~!** come on, cheer up!; **~ pour 50 francs/demain** OK, let's say 50 francs/tomorrow.

vacance [vakɑ̃s] *nf* vacancy. ○ **vacances** *nfpl* vacation (*sg*) *Am*; **être/partir en ~s** to be/go on holiday; **les grandes ~s** the summer holidays.

vacancier, -ière [vakɑ̃sje, jɛr] *nm, f* vacationer *Am*.

vacant, -e [vakɑ̃, ɑ̃t] *adj* [poste] vacant; [logement] vacant, unoccupied.

vacarme [vakarm] *nm* racket, din.

vacataire [vakatɛr] **1** *adj* [employé] temporary. **2** *nmf* temporary worker.

vacation [vakasjɔ̃] *nf* [d'expert] session.

vaccin [vaksɛ̃] *nm* vaccine.

vaccination [vaksinasjɔ̃] *nf* vaccination.

vacciner [vaksine] *vt*: **~ qqn (contre)** MÉD to vaccinate sb (against).

vache [vaʃ] **1** *nf* ZOOL cow. ‖ [cuir] cowhide. ‖ *fam péj* [femme] cow; [homme] pig. **2** *adj fam* rotten.

vachement [vaʃmɑ̃] *adv fam* real *Am*.

vaciller [vasije] *vi* [jambes, fondations] to shake; [lumière] to flicker. ‖ [mémoire, santé] to fail.

va-et-vient [vaevjɛ̃] *nm inv* [de personnes] comings and goings (*pl*), toing and froing. ‖ [de balancier] to-and-fro movement. ‖ ÉLECTR two-way switch.

vagabond, -e [vagabɔ̃, ɔ̃d] *nm, f* [rôdeur] vagrant, tramp.

vagabondage [vagabɔ̃daʒ] *nm* [délit] vagrancy; [errance] wandering, roaming.

vagin [vaʒɛ̃] *nm* vagina.

vagissement [vaʒismɑ̃] *nm* cry, wail.

vague [vag] **1** *adj* [idée, promesse] vague. ‖ [vêtement] loose-fitting. **2** *nf* wave; **une ~ de froid** a cold spell; **~ de chaleur** heatwave.

vaguement [vagmɑ̃] *adv* vaguely.

vautour

vaillant, **-e** [vajɑ̃, ɑ̃t] *adj* [enfant, vieillard] hale and hearty. || *littéraire* [héros] valiant.

vain, **-e** [vɛ̃, vɛn] *adj* [inutile] vain, useless; **en ~** in vain, to no avail. || *littéraire* [vaniteux] vain.

vaincre [vɛ̃kr] *vt* [ennemi] to defeat. || [obstacle, peur] to overcome.

vaincu, **-e** [vɛ̃ky] **1** *pp* → **vaincre**. **2** *adj* defeated. **3** *nm, f* defeated person.

vainement [vɛnmɑ̃] *adv* vainly.

vainqueur [vɛ̃kœr] **1** *nm* [de combat] conqueror, victor. || SPORT winner. **2** *adj m* victorious, conquering.

vais → **aller**.

vaisseau, **-x** [vɛso] *nm* NAVIG vessel, ship; **~ spatial** AÉRON spaceship. || ANAT vessel.

vaisselle [vɛsɛl] *nf* crockery; **faire** ou **laver la ~** to do the dishes, to wash up.

valable [valabl] *adj* [passeport] valid. || [raison, excuse] valid, legitimate.

valet [valɛ] *nm* [serviteur] servant. || CARTES jack, knave.

valeur [valœr] *nf* [gén & MUS] value; **avoir de la ~** to be valuable; **mettre en ~** [talents] to bring out; **~ ajoutée** ÉCON added value; **de (grande) ~** [chose] (very) valuable. || (*gén pl*) BOURSE stocks and shares (*pl*), securities (*pl*). || [mérite] worth, merit. || *fig* [importance] value, importance.

valide [valid] *adj* [personne] spry. || [contrat] valid.

valider [valide] *vt* to validate, to authenticate.

validité [validite] *nf* validity.

valise [valiz] *nf* case, suitcase; **faire sa ~/ses ~s** to pack one's case/cases; *fam fig* [partir] to pack one's bags.

vallée [vale] *nf* valley.

vallon [valɔ̃] *nm* small valley.

vallonné, **-e** [valɔne] *adj* undulating.

valoir [valwar] **1** *vi* [gén] to be worth; **ça vaut combien?** how much is it?; **ne rien ~** not to be any good, to be worthless; **ça vaut mieux** *fam* that's best; **faire ~** [vues] to assert; [talent] to show. || [règle]: **~ pour** to apply to, to hold good for. **2** *vt* [médaille, gloire] to bring, to earn. **3** *v impers*: **il vaudrait mieux que nous partions** it would be better if we left, we'd better leave. ○ **se valoir** *vp* to be equally good/bad.

valoriser [valɔrize] *vt* [immeuble, région] to develop; [individu, société] to improve the image of.

valse [vals] *nf* waltz.

valser [valse] *vi* to waltz; **envoyer ~ qqch** *fam fig* to send sthg flying.

valu [valy] *pp inv* → **valoir**.

valve [valv] *nf* valve.

vampire [vɑ̃pir] *nm* [fantôme] vampire. || ZOOL vampire bat.

vandalisme [vɑ̃dalism] *nm* vandalism.

vanille [vanij] *nf* vanilla.

vanité [vanite] *nf* vanity.

vaniteux, **-euse** [vanitø, øz] *adj* vain, conceited.

vanne [van] *nf* [d'écluse] lockgate. || *fam* [remarque] gibe.

vannerie [vanri] *nf* basketwork, wickerwork.

vantard, **-e** [vɑ̃tar, ard] **1** *adj* bragging, boastful. **2** *nm, f* boaster.

vanter [vɑ̃te] *vt* to vaunt. ○ **se vanter** *vp* to boast, to brag; **se ~ de faire qqch** to boast ou brag about doing sthg.

va-nu-pieds [vanypje] *nmf inv fam* beggar.

vapeur [vapœr] *nf* [d'eau] steam; **à la ~** steamed. || [émanation] vapour.

vapocuiseur [vapokɥizœr] *nm* pressure cooker.

vaporisateur [vaporizatœr] *nm* [atomiseur] spray, atomizer. || IND vaporizer.

vaporiser [vaporize] *vt* [parfum, déodorant] to spray. || PHYS to vaporize.

vaquer [vake] *vi*: **~ à** to see to, to attend to.

varappe [varap] *nf* rock climbing.

variable [varjabl] **1** *adj* [temps] changeable. || [distance, résultats] varied, varying. || [température] variable. **2** *nf* variable.

variante [varjɑ̃t] *nf* variant.

variateur [varjatœr] *nm* ÉLECTR dimmer switch.

variation [varjasjɔ̃] *nf* variation.

varice [varis] *nf* varicose vein.

varicelle [varisɛl] *nf* chickenpox.

varié, **-e** [varje] *adj* [divers] various. || [non monotone] varied, varying.

varier [varje] *vt & vi* to vary.

variété [varjete] *nf* variety. ○ **variétés** *nfpl* variety show (*sg*).

variole [varjɔl] *nf* smallpox.

Varsovie [varsɔvi] *n* Warsaw.

vase [vaz] **1** *nm* vase. **2** *nf* mud, silt.

vaste [vast] *adj* vast, immense.

Vatican [vatikɑ̃] *nm*: **le ~** the Vatican.

vaudrait → **valoir**.

vaut → **valoir**.

vautour [votur] *nm* vulture.

vd *abr de* **vend.**

veau, -x [vo] *nm* [animal] calf. || [viande] veal. || [peau] calfskin.

vecteur [vɛktœr] *nm* GÉOM vector.

vécu, -e [veky] **1** *pp* → **vivre. 2** *adj* real.

vedette [vədɛt] *nf* NAVIG patrol boat. || [star] star.

végétal, -e, -aux [veʒetal, o] *adj* [huile] vegetable (*avant n*); [cellule, fibre] plant (*avant n*).

végétalien, -ienne [veʒetaljɛ̃, jɛn] *adj & nm, f* vegan.

végétarien, -ienne [veʒetarjɛ̃, jɛn] *adj & nm, f* vegetarian.

végétation [veʒetasjɔ̃] *nf* vegetation. ○ **végétations** *nfpl* adenoids.

végéter [veʒete] *vi* to vegetate.

véhémence [veemɑ̃s] *nf* vehemence.

véhicule [veikyl] *nm* vehicle.

veille [vɛj] *nf* [jour précédent] day before, eve; **la ~ de mon anniversaire** the day before my birthday; **la ~ de Noël** Christmas Eve.

veillée [veje] *nf* [soirée] evening. || [de mort] watch.

veiller [veje] **1** *vi* [rester éveillé] to stay up. || [rester vigilant]: **~ à qqch** to look after sthg; **~ à faire qqch** to see that sthg is done; **~ sur** to watch over. **2** *vt* to sit up with.

veilleur [vejœr] *nm*: **~ de nuit** night watchman.

veilleuse [vejøz] *nf* [lampe] nightlight. || AUTOM sidelight. || [de chauffe-eau] pilot light.

veinard, -e [venar, ard] *fam* **1** *adj* lucky. **2** *nm, f* lucky devil.

veine [vɛn] *nf* [gén] vein. || [de bois] grain. || *fam* [chance] luck.

veineux, -euse [venø, øz] *adj* ANAT venous. || [marbre] veined; [bois] grainy.

véliplanchiste [veliplɑ̃ʃist] *nmf* windsurfer.

velléité [veleite] *nf* whim.

vélo [velo] *nm fam* bike; **faire du ~** to go cycling.

vélodrome [velɔdrom] *nm* velodrome.

vélomoteur [velɔmɔtœr] *nm* light motorcycle.

velours [vəlur] *nm* velvet.

velouté, -e [vəlute] *adj* velvety. ○ **velouté** *nm* [potage] cream soup.

velu, -e [vəly] *adj* hairy.

vénal, -e, -aux [venal, o] *adj* venal.

vendange [vɑ̃dɑ̃ʒ] *nf* [récolte] grape harvest, wine harvest. || [période]: **les ~s** (grape) harvest time (*sg*).

vendanger [vɑ̃dɑ̃ʒe] *vi* to harvest the grapes.

vendeur, -euse [vɑ̃dœr, øz] *nm, f* salesman (*f* saleswoman).

vendre [vɑ̃dr] *vt* to sell.

vendredi [vɑ̃drədi] *nm* Friday; **Vendredi Saint** Good Friday; *voir aussi* **samedi.**

vendu, -e [vɑ̃dy] **1** *pp* → **vendre. 2** *nm, f* traitor.

vénéneux, -euse [venenø, øz] *adj* poisonous.

vénérable [venerabl] *adj* venerable.

vénération [venerasjɔ̃] *nf* veneration, reverence.

vénérer [venere] *vt* to venerate, to revere.

vénérien, -ienne [venerjɛ̃, jɛn] *adj* venereal.

Venezuela [venezɥela] *nm*: **le ~** Venezuela.

vengeance [vɑ̃ʒɑ̃s] *nf* vengeance.

venger [vɑ̃ʒe] *vt* to avenge. ○ **se venger** *vp* to get one's revenge; **se ~ de qqn** to take revenge on sb; **se ~ de qqch** to take revenge for sthg; **se ~ sur** to take it out on.

vengeur, vengeresse [vɑ̃ʒœr, vɑ̃ʒrɛs] **1** *adj* vengeful. **2** *nm, f* avenger.

venimeux, -euse [vənimø, øz] *adj* venomous.

venin [vənɛ̃] *nm* venom.

venir [vənir] *vi* to come; **~ de** [personne, mot] to come from; [échec] to be due to; **je viens de la voir** I've just seen her; **où veux-tu en ~?** what are you getting at?

vent [vɑ̃] *nm* wind.

vente [vɑ̃t] *nf* [cession, transaction] sale; **en ~** on sale; **en ~ libre** available over the counter; **~ par correspondance** mail order. || [technique] selling.

venteux, -euse [vɑ̃tø, øz] *adj* windy.

ventilateur [vɑ̃tilatœr] *nm* fan.

ventilation [vɑ̃tilasjɔ̃] *nf* [de pièce] ventilation. || FIN breakdown.

ventouse [vɑ̃tuz] *nf* [de caoutchouc] suction pad; [d'animal] sucker. || MÉD cupping glass. || TECHNOL air vent.

ventre [vɑ̃tr] *nm* [de personne] stomach; **avoir/prendre du ~** to have/be getting (a bit of) a paunch; **à plat ~** flat on one's stomach.

ventriloque [vɑ̃trilɔk] *nmf* ventriloquist.

venu, -e [vəny] **1** *pp* → **venir. 2** *adj*: **il serait mal ~ de faire cela** it would be improper to do that. **3** *nm, f*: **nouveau ~** newcomer. ○ **venue** *nf* coming, arrival.

vêpres [vɛpr] *nfpl* vespers.

ver [vɛr] *nm* worm.

véracité [verasite] *nf* truthfulness.

véranda [verɑ̃da] *nf* veranda.

verbal, -e, -aux [vɛrbal, o] *adj* [promesse, violence] verbal. || GRAM verb (*avant n*).

verbaliser [vɛrbalize] **1** *vt* to verbalize. **2** *vi* to make out a report.

verbe [vɛrb] *nm* GRAM verb.

verdeur [vɛrdœr] *nf* [de personne] vigour, vitality. || [de langage] crudeness.

verdict [vɛrdikt] *nm* verdict.

verdir [vɛrdir] *vt & vi* to turn green.

verdoyant, -e [vɛrdwajɑ̃, ɑ̃t] *adj* green.

verdure [vɛrdyr] *nf* [végétation] greenery.

véreux, -euse [verø, øz] *adj* wormeaten, maggoty; *fig* shady.

verge [vɛrʒ] *nf* ANAT penis. || *littéraire* [baguette] rod, stick.

verger [vɛrʒe] *nm* orchard.

vergeture [vɛrʒətyr] *nf* stretchmark.

verglas [vɛrɡla] *nm* (black) ice.

véridique [veridik] *adj* truthful.

vérification [verifikasjɔ̃] *nf* [contrôle] check, checking.

vérifier [verifje] *vt* [contrôler] to check. || [confirmer] to prove, to confirm.

véritable [veritabl] *adj* real; [ami] true.

vérité [verite] *nf* [chose vraie, réalité, principe] truth (*U*).

vermeil, -eille [vɛrmɛj] *adj* scarlet. ○ **vermeil** *nm* silver-gilt.

vermicelle [vɛrmisɛl] *nm* vermicelli (*U*).

vermine [vɛrmin] *nf* [parasites] vermin.

vermoulu, -e [vɛrmuly] *adj* riddled with woodworm; *fig* moth-eaten.

verni, -e [vɛrni] *adj* [bois] varnished. || [souliers]: **chaussures ~es** patent-leather shoes. || *fam* [chanceux] lucky.

vernir [vɛrnir] *vt* to varnish.

vernis [vɛrni] *nm* varnish; *fig* veneer; ~ **à ongles** nail polish OU varnish.

vernissage [vɛrnisaʒ] *nm* [d'exposition] private viewing.

verre [vɛr] *nm* [matière, récipient] glass; [quantité] glassful, glass. || [optique] lens; ~**s de contact** contact lenses. || [boisson] drink; **boire un ~** to have a drink.

verrière [vɛrjɛr] *nf* [toit] glass roof.

verrou [vɛru] *nm* bolt.

verrouillage [vɛrujaʒ] *nm* AUTOM: ~ **central** central locking.

verrouiller [vɛruje] *vt* [porte] to bolt.

verrue [vɛry] *nf* wart; ~ **plantaire** verruca.

vers¹ [vɛr] **1** *nm* line. **2** *nmpl*: **en ~** in verse; **faire des ~** to write poetry.

vers² [vɛr] *prép* [dans la direction de] towards. || [aux environs de - temporel] around, about; [- spatial] near; ~ **la fin du mois** towards the end of the month.

versant [vɛrsɑ̃] *nm* side.

versatile [vɛrsatil] *adj* changeable, fickle.

verse [vɛrs] ○ **à verse** *loc adv*: **pleuvoir à ~** to pour down.

Verseau [vɛrso] *nm* ASTROL Aquarius.

versement [vɛrsəmɑ̃] *nm* payment.

verser [vɛrse] *vt* [eau] to pour; [larmes, sang] to shed. || [argent] to pay.

verset [vɛrsɛ] *nm* verse.

version [vɛrsjɔ̃] *nf* [gén] version. || [traduction] translation (*into mother tongue*).

verso [vɛrso] *nm* back.

vert, -e [vɛr, vɛrt] *adj* [couleur, fruit, légume, bois] green. || *fig* [vieillard] sprightly. ○ **vert** *nm* [couleur] green. ○ **Verts** *nmpl*: **les Verts** POLIT the Greens.

vertébral, -e, -aux [vɛrtebral, o] *adj* vertebral.

vertèbre [vɛrtɛbr] *nf* vertebra.

vertement [vɛrtəmɑ̃] *adv* sharply.

vertical, -e, -aux [vɛrtikal, o] *adj* vertical. ○ **verticale** *nf* vertical; **à la ~e** [descente] vertical; [descendre] vertically.

vertige [vɛrtiʒ] *nm* [peur du vide] vertigo. || [étourdissement] dizziness; **avoir des ~s** to suffer from OU have dizzy spells.

vertigineux, -euse [vɛrtiʒinø, øz] *adj* *fig* [vue, vitesse] breathtaking. || [hauteur] dizzy.

vertu [vɛrty] *nf* [morale, chasteté] virtue. || [pouvoir] properties (*pl*), power.

vertueux, -euse [vɛrtɥø, øz] *adj* virtuous.

verve [vɛrv] *nf* eloquence.

vésicule [vezikyl] *nf* vesicle.

vessie [vesi] *nf* bladder.

veste [vɛst] *nf* [vêtement] jacket; ~ **croisée/droite** double-/single-breasted jacket.

vestiaire [vɛstjɛr] *nm* [au théâtre] cloakroom. || (*gén pl*) SPORT changing-room, locker-room.

vestibule [vɛstibyl] *nm* [pièce] hall, vestibule.

vestige [vɛstiʒ] *nm* (*gén pl*) [de ville]

remains (*pl*); *fig* [de civilisation, grandeur] vestiges (*pl*), relic.

vestimentaire [vɛstimɑ̃tɛr] *adj* [industrie] clothing (*avant* n); [dépense] on clothes; **détail** ~ accessory.

veston [vɛstɔ̃] *nm* jacket.

vêtement [vɛtmɑ̃] *nm* garment, article of clothing; ~s clothing (*U*), clothes.

vétéran [veterɑ̃] *nm* veteran.

vétérinaire [veteriner] *nmf* vet, veterinary surgeon.

vêtir [vetir] *vt* to dress. ○ **se vêtir** *vp* to dress, to get dressed.

veto [veto] *nm inv* veto; **mettre son** ~ **à qqch** to veto sthg.

vêtu, -e [vety] **1** *pp* → **vêtir**. **2** *adj*: ~ (**de**) dressed (in).

vétuste [vetyst] *adj* dilapidated.

veuf, veuve [vœf, vœv] *nm, f* widower (*f* widow).

veuille *etc* → **vouloir**.

veuve → **veuf**.

vexation [vɛksasjɔ̃] *nf* [humiliation] insult.

vexer [vɛkse] *vt* to offend. ○ **se vexer** *vp* to take offence.

VF (*abr de* **version française**) *nf* indicates that a film has been dubbed into French.

via [vja] *prép* via.

viable [vjabl] *adj* viable.

viaduc [vjadyk] *nm* viaduct.

viager, -ère [vjaʒe, ɛr] *adj* life (*avant* n). ○ **viager** *nm* life annuity.

viande [vjɑ̃d] *nf* meat.

vibration [vibrasjɔ̃] *nf* vibration.

vibrer [vibre] *vi* [trembler] to vibrate.

vice [vis] *nm* [de personne] vice. || [d'objet] fault, defect.

vice-président, -e [visprezidɑ̃, ɑ̃t] (*mpl* **vice-présidents**, *fpl* **vice-présidentes**) *nm, f* POLIT vice-president; [de société] vice-chairman.

vice versa [visvɛrsa] *loc adv* vice versa.

vicié, -e [visje] *adj* [air] polluted.

vicieux, -ieuse [visjø, jøz] *adj* [personne, conduite] perverted, depraved. || [animal] restive. || [attaque] underhand.

victime [viktim] *nf* victim; [blessé] casualty.

victoire [viktwar] *nf* MIL victory; POLIT & SPORT win, victory.

victorieux, -ieuse [viktɔrjø, jøz] *adj* MIL victorious; POLIT & SPORT winning (*avant* n), victorious. || [air] triumphant.

victuailles [viktɥaj] *nfpl* provisions.

vidange [vidɑ̃ʒ] *nf* [action] emptying, draining. || AUTOM oil change. || [mécanisme] waste outlet.

vidanger [vidɑ̃ʒe] *vt* to empty, to drain.

vide [vid] **1** *nm* [espace] void; *fig* [néant, manque] emptiness. || [absence d'air] vacuum; **conditionné sous** ~ vacuum-packed. || [ouverture] gap, space. **2** *adj* empty.

vidéo [video] **1** *nf* video. **2** *adj inv* video (*avant* n).

vidéocassette [videokasɛt] *nf* video cassette.

vidéodisque [videodisk] *nm* videodisc.

vide-ordures [vidɔrdyr] *nm inv* rubbish chute.

vidéothèque [videotɛk] *nf* video library.

vide-poches [vidpɔʃ] *nm inv* [de voiture] glove compartment.

vider [vide] *vt* [rendre vide] to empty. || [évacuer]: ~ **les lieux** to vacate the premises. || [poulet] to clean. || *fam* [personne - épuiser] to drain; [- expulser] to chuck out. ○ **se vider** *vp* [baignoire, salle] to empty.

videur [vidœr] *nm* bouncer.

vie [vi] *nf* [gén] life; **sauver la** ~ **à qqn** to save sb's life; **être en** ~ to be alive; **à** ~ for life. || [subsistance] cost of living; **gagner sa** ~ to earn one's living.

vieil → **vieux**.

vieillard [vjejar] *nm* old man.

vieille → **vieux**.

vieillerie [vjɛjri] *nf* [objet] old thing.

vieillesse [vjɛjɛs] *nf* [fin de la vie] old age.

vieillir [vjejir] **1** *vi* [personne] to grow old, to age. || CULIN to mature, to age. || [tradition, idée] to become dated ou outdated. **2** *vt* [suj: coiffure, vêtement]: ~ **qqn** to make sb look older.

vieillissement [vjejismɑ̃] *nm* [de personne] ageing.

Vienne [vjɛn] *n* [en Autriche] Vienna.

vierge [vjɛrʒ] **1** *nf* virgin; **la (Sainte) Vierge** the Virgin (Mary). **2** *adj* [personne] virgin. || [terre] virgin; [page] blank; [casier judiciaire] clean. ○ **Vierge** *nf* ASTROL Virgo.

Viêt-nam [vjɛtnam] *nm*: **le** ~ Vietnam.

vieux, vieille [vjø, vjɛj] **1** *adj* (**vieil** *devant voyelle ou h muet*) old; ~ **jeu** old-fashioned. **2** *nm, f* [personne âgée] old man (*f* woman); **les** ~ the old. || *fam* [ami]: **mon** ~ old chap ou boy *Br*, old buddy *Am*; **ma vieille** old girl.

visée

vif, vive [vif, viv] *adj* [preste - enfant] lively; [- imagination] vivid. || [couleur, œil] bright. || [reproche] sharp; [discussion] bitter. || [douleur, déception] acute; [intérêt] keen. ○ **à vif** *loc adj* [plaie] open; **j'ai les nerfs à ~** *fig* my nerves are frayed.

vigie [viʒi] *nf* [NAVIG - personne] lookout; [- poste] crow's nest.

vigilant, -e [viʒilɑ̃, ɑ̃t] *adj* vigilant, watchful.

vigile [viʒil] *nm* watchman.

vigne [viɲ] *nf* [plante] vine, grapevine. || [plantation] vineyard.

vigneron, -onne [viɲrɔ̃, ɔn] *nm, f* wine grower.

vignette [viɲɛt] *nf* [timbre] label; [de médicament] price sticker (*for reimbursement by the social security services*); AUTOM tax disc. || [motif] vignette.

vignoble [viɲɔbl] *nm* [plantation] vineyard. || [vignes] vineyards (*pl*).

vigoureux, -euse [vigurø, øz] *adj* [corps, personne] vigorous.

vigueur [vigœr] *nf* vigour. ○ **en vigueur** *loc adj* in force.

vilain, -e [vilɛ̃, ɛn] *adj* [gén] nasty. || [laid] ugly.

vilebrequin [vilbrəkɛ̃] *nm* [outil] brace and bit. || AUTOM crankshaft.

villa [vila] *nf* villa.

village [vilaʒ] *nm* village.

villageois, -e [vilaʒwa, az] *nm, f* villager.

ville [vil] *nf* [petite, moyenne] town; [importante] city.

villégiature [vileʒjatyr] *nf* holiday.

vin [vɛ̃] *nm* wine; **~ blanc/rosé/rouge** white/rosé/red wine. ○ **vin d'honneur** *nm* reception.

vinaigre [vinɛgr] *nm* vinegar.

vinaigrette [vinɛgrɛt] *nf* oil and vinegar dressing.

vindicatif, -ive [vɛ̃dikatif, iv] *adj* vindictive.

vingt [vɛ̃] *adj num & nm* twenty; *voir aussi* **six**.

vingtaine [vɛ̃tɛn] *nf*: **une ~ de** about twenty.

vingtième [vɛ̃tjɛm] *adj num, nm & nmf* twentieth; *voir aussi* **sixième**.

vinicole [vinikɔl] *adj* wine-growing, wine-producing.

viol [vjɔl] *nm* [de femme] rape. || [de sépulture] desecration.

violation [vjɔlasjɔ̃] *nf* violation, breach.

violence [vjɔlɑ̃s] *nf* violence; **se faire ~** to force o.s.

violent, -e [vjɔlɑ̃, ɑ̃t] *adj* [personne, tempête] violent. || *fig* [douleur, angoisse, chagrin] acute; [haine, passion] violent.

violer [vjɔle] *vt* [femme] to rape. || [loi, traité] to break. || [sépulture] to desecrate; [sanctuaire] to violate.

violet, -ette [vjɔlɛ, ɛt] *adj* purple; [pâle] violet. ○ **violet** *nm* purple.

violette [vjɔlɛt] *nf* violet.

violeur [vjɔlœr] *nm* rapist.

violon [vjɔlɔ̃] *nm* [instrument] violin.

violoncelle [vjɔlɔ̃sɛl] *nm* [instrument] cello.

violoniste [vjɔlɔnist] *nmf* violinist.

vipère [vipɛr] *nf* viper.

virage [viraʒ] *nm* [sur route] bend.

viral, -e, -aux [viral, o] *adj* viral.

virement [virmɑ̃] *nm* FIN transfer; **~ bancaire/postal** bank/giro transfer.

virer [vire] **1** *vi* [tourner]: **~ à droite/à gauche** to turn right/left. || [étoffe] to change colour; **~ au blanc/jaune** to go white/yellow. **2** *vt* FIN to transfer. || *fam* [renvoyer] to kick out.

virevolter [virvɔlte] *vi* [tourner] to twirl ou spin round.

virginité [virʒinite] *nf* [de personne] virginity. || [de sentiment] purity.

virgule [virgyl] *nf* [entre mots] comma; [entre chiffres] (decimal) point.

viril, -e [viril] *adj* virile.

virilité [virilite] *nf* virility.

virtuel, -elle [virtɥɛl] *adj* potential.

virtuose [virtɥoz] *nmf* virtuoso.

virulence [virylɑ̃s] *nf* virulence.

virulent, -e [virylɑ̃, ɑ̃t] *adj* virulent.

virus [virys] *nm* INFORM & MÉD virus.

vis [vis] *nf* screw.

visa [viza] *nm* visa.

visage [vizaʒ] *nm* face.

vis-à-vis [vizavi] *nm* [personne] person sitting opposite. || [immeuble]: **avoir un ~** to have a building opposite. ○ **vis-à-vis de** *loc prép* [en face de] opposite. || [à l'égard de] towards.

viscéral, -e, -aux [viseral, o] *adj* ANAT visceral. || *fam* [réaction] gut (*avant n*); [haine, peur] deep-seated.

viscère [visɛr] *nm* (*gén pl*) innards (*pl*).

viscose [viskoz] *nf* viscose.

visé, -e [vize] *adj* [concerné] concerned.

visée [vize] *nf* [avec arme] aiming. || (*gén pl*) *fig* [intention, dessein] aim.

viser [vize] **1** vt [cible] to aim at. ‖ fig [poste] to aspire to, to aim for; [personne] to be directed or aimed at. ‖ [document] to check, to stamp. **2** vi to aim, to take aim; **~ à faire qqch** to aim to do sthg, to be intended to do sthg.

viseur [vizœr] nm [d'arme] sights (pl). ‖ PHOT viewfinder.

visibilité [vizibilite] nf visibility.

visible [vizibl] adj [gén] visible. ‖ [personne]: **il n'est pas ~** he's not seeing visitors.

visiblement [vizibləmɑ̃] adv visibly.

visière [vizjɛr] nf [de casque] visor. ‖ [de casquette] peak. ‖ [de protection] eyeshade.

vision [vizjɔ̃] nf [faculté] eyesight, vision. ‖ [représentation] view, vision. ‖ [mirage] vision.

visionnaire [vizjɔnɛr] nmf & adj visionary.

visionner [vizjɔne] vt to view.

visite [vizit] nf [chez ami, officielle] visit; **rendre ~ à qqn** to pay sb a visit. ‖ MÉD - à l'extérieur] call, visit; [- dans hôpital] rounds (pl); **passer une ~ médicale** to have a medical. ‖ [de monument] tour.

visiter [vizite] vt [en touriste] to tour. ‖ [malade, prisonnier] to visit.

visiteur, -euse [vizitœr, øz] nm, f visitor.

vison [vizɔ̃] nm mink.

visqueux, -euse [viskø, øz] adj [liquide] viscous. ‖ [surface] sticky.

visser [vise] vt [planches] to screw together. ‖ [couvercle] to screw down. ‖ [bouchon] to screw in; [écrou] to screw on.

visualiser [vizɥalize] vt [gén] to visualize. ‖ INFORM to display.

visuel, -elle [vizɥɛl] adj visual.

vital, -e, -aux [vital, o] adj vital.

vitalité [vitalite] nf vitality.

vitamine [vitamin] nf vitamin.

vitaminé, -e [vitamine] adj with added vitamins, vitamin-enriched.

vite [vit] adv [rapidement] quickly, fast; **fais ~!** hurry up! ‖ [tôt] soon.

vitesse [vites] nf [gén] speed; **à toute ~** at top speed. ‖ AUTOM gear.

viticole [vitikɔl] adj wine-growing.

viticulteur, -trice [vitikyltœr, tris] nm, f wine-grower.

vitrail, -aux [vitraj, o] nm stained-glass window.

vitre [vitr] nf [de fenêtre] pane of glass,

window pane. ‖ [de voiture, train] window.

vitré, -e [vitre] adj glass (avant n).

vitreux, -euse [vitrø, øz] adj [roche] vitreous. ‖ [œil, regard] glassy, glazed.

vitrine [vitrin] nf [de boutique] (shop) window. ‖ [meuble] display cabinet.

vivable [vivabl] adj [appartement] livable-in; [situation] bearable, tolerable; [personne]: **il n'est pas ~** he's impossible to live with.

vivace [vivas] adj [plante] perennial; [arbre] hardy. ‖ fig [haine, ressentiment] deep-rooted, entrenched; [souvenir] enduring.

vivacité [vivasite] nf [promptitude - de personne] liveliness, vivacity; **~ d'esprit** quick-wittedness. ‖ [de propos] sharpness.

vivant, -e [vivɑ̃, ɑ̃t] adj [en vie] alive, living. ‖ [enfant, quartier] lively. ‖ [souvenir] still fresh. ○ **vivant** nm [personne]: **les ~s** the living.

vive [viv] interj three cheers for; **~ le roi!** long live the King!

vivement [vivmɑ̃] **1** adv [agir] quickly. ‖ [répondre] sharply. **2** interj: **~ les vacances!** roll on the holidays!; **~ que l'été arrive** I'll be glad when summer comes, summer can't come quick enough.

vivifiant, -e [vivifjɑ̃, ɑ̃t] adj invigorating, bracing.

vivisection [vivisɛksjɔ̃] nf vivisection.

vivre [vivr] **1** vi to live; [être en vie] to be alive; **~ de** to live on; **faire ~ sa famille** to support one's family; **être difficile/facile à ~** to be hard/easy to get on with. **2** vt [passer] to spend. ‖ [éprouver] to experience. ○ **vivres** nmpl provisions.

VO (abr de **version originale**) nf indicates that a film has not been dubbed.

vocable [vɔkabl] nm term.

vocabulaire [vɔkabylɛr] nm [gén] vocabulary. ‖ [livre] lexicon, glossary.

vocal, -e, -aux [vɔkal, o] adj: **ensemble ~** choir; → **corde**.

vocation [vɔkasjɔ̃] nf [gén] vocation. ‖ [d'organisation] mission.

vociférer [vɔsifere] vt to shout, to scream.

vodka [vɔdka] nf vodka.

vœu, -x [vø] nm [RELIG & résolution] vow; **faire ~ de silence** to take a vow of silence. ‖ [souhait, requête] wish. ○ **vœux** nmpl greetings.

vogue [vɔg] nf vogue, fashion; **en ~** fashionable, in vogue.

voguer [vɔge] *vi littéraire* to sail.

voici [vwasi] *prép* [pour désigner, introduire] here is/are; **le ~** here he/it is; **les ~** here they are; **~ ce qui s'est passé** this is what happened. ‖ [il y a]: **~ trois mois** three months ago; **~ quelques années que je ne l'ai pas vu** I haven't seen him for some years (now), it's been some years since I last saw him.

voie [vwa] *nf* [route] road; **route à deux ~s** two-lane road; **la ~ publique** the public highway. ‖ RAIL track, line; **~ ferrée** railway line *Br*, railroad line *Am*. ‖ [mode de transport] route. ‖ ANAT passage, tract; **par ~ buccale** ou **orale** orally, by mouth; **~ respiratoire** respiratory tract. ‖ *fig* [chemin] way. ‖ [filière, moyen] means (*pl*). ○ **Voie lactée** *nf*: **la Voie lactée** the Milky Way. ○ **en voie de** *loc prép* on the way ou road to; **en ~ de développement** developing.

voilà [vwala] *prép* [pour désigner] there is/are; **le ~** there he/it is; **les ~** there they are; **nous ~ arrivés** we've arrived. ‖ [reprend ce dont on a parlé] that is; [introduit ce dont on va parler] this is; **~ ce que j'en pense** this is/that is what I think; **~ tout** that's all; **et ~!** there we are! ‖ [il y a]: **~ dix jours** ten days ago; **~ dix ans que je le connais** I've known him for ten years (now).

voile [vwal] **1** *nf* [de bateau] sail. ‖ [activité] sailing. **2** *nm* [textile] voile. ‖ [coiffure] veil. ‖ [de brume] mist.

voilé, -e [vwale] *adj* [visage, allusion] veiled. ‖ [ciel, regard] dull. ‖ [roue] buckled. ‖ [son, voix] muffled.

voiler [vwale] *vt* [visage] to veil. ‖ [suj: brouillard, nuages] to cover. ○ **se voiler** *vp* [femme] to wear a veil. ‖ [ciel] to cloud over. ‖ [roue] to buckle.

voilier [vwalje] *nm* [bateau] sailing boat, sailboat *Am*.

voilure [vwalyr] *nf* [de bateau] sails (*pl*).

voir [vwar] **1** *vt* [gén] to see; **je l'ai vu tomber** I saw him fall; **faire ~ qqch à qqn** to show sb sthg; **ne rien avoir à ~ avec** *fig* to have nothing to do with; **voyons, ...** [en réfléchissant] let's see, ... **2** *vi* to see. ○ **se voir** *vp* [se rencontrer] to see one another ou each other. ‖ [se remarquer] to be obvious, to show.

voire [vwar] *adv* even.

voirie [vwari] *nf* ADMIN ≃ Department of Transport.

voisin, -e [vwazɛ̃, in] **1** *adj* [pays, ville] neighbouring; [maison] next-door. ‖ [idée] similar. **2** *nm, f* neighbour.

voisinage [vwazinaʒ] *nm* [quartier] neighbourhood. ‖ [environs] vicinity.

voiture [vwatyr] *nf* [automobile] car; **~ de fonction** company car; **~ de location** hire car; **~ d'occasion/de sport** second-hand/sports car. ‖ [de train] carriage.

voix [vwa] *nf* [gén] voice; **à mi-~** in an undertone; **à ~ basse** in a low voice, quietly; **à ~ haute** [parler] in a loud voice; [lire] aloud; **de vive ~** in person. ‖ [suffrage] vote.

vol [vɔl] *nm* [d'oiseau, avion] flight; **à ~ d'oiseau** as the crow flies. ‖ [groupe d'oiseaux] flight, flock. ‖ [délit] theft.

vol. (*abr de* volume) vol.

volage [vɔlaʒ] *adj littéraire* fickle.

volaille [vɔlaj] *nf*: **la ~** poultry, (domestic) fowl.

volant, -e [vɔlɑ̃, ɑ̃t] *adj* [qui vole] flying. ‖ [mobile]: **feuille ~e** loose sheet. ○ **volant** *nm* [de voiture] steering wheel. ‖ [de robe] flounce. ‖ [de badminton] shuttlecock.

volatiliser [vɔlatilize] ○ **se volatiliser** *vp fig* to vanish into thin air.

volcan [vɔlkɑ̃] *nm* volcano; *fig* spitfire.

volcanique [vɔlkanik] *adj* volcanic; *fig* [tempérament] fiery.

volée [vɔle] *nf* [de flèches] volley; **une ~ de coups** a hail of blows. ‖ FOOTBALL & TENNIS volley.

voler [vɔle] **1** *vi* to fly. **2** *vt* [personne] to rob; [chose] to steal.

volet [vɔlɛ] *nm* [de maison] shutter. ‖ [de dépliant] leaf; [d'émission] part.

voleur, -euse [vɔlœr, øz] *nm, f* thief.

volière [vɔljer] *nf* aviary.

volley-ball [vɔlɛbol] (*pl* volley-balls) *nm* volleyball.

volontaire [vɔlɔ̃ter] **1** *nmf* volunteer. **2** *adj* [omission] deliberate; [activité] voluntary. ‖ [enfant] strong-willed.

volonté [vɔlɔ̃te] *nf* [vouloir] will; **à ~** unlimited, as much as you like. ‖ [disposition]: **bonne ~** willingness, good will; **mauvaise ~** unwillingness. ‖ [détermination] willpower.

volontiers [vɔlɔ̃tje] *adv* [avec plaisir] with pleasure, gladly, willingly.

volt [vɔlt] *nm* volt.

voltage [vɔltaʒ] *nm* voltage.

volte-face [vɔltəfas] *nf inv* about-face *Am*.

voltige [vɔltiʒ] *nf* [au trapèze] trapeze work; **haute ~ trapèze act; *fam fig* mental gymnastics (*U*). || [à cheval] circus riding. || [en avion] aerobatics (*U*).

voltiger [vɔltiʒe] *vi* [insecte, oiseau] to flit ou flutter about. || [feuilles] to flutter about.

volubile [vɔlybil] *adj* voluble.

volume [vɔlym] *nm* volume.

volumineux, -euse [vɔlyminø, øz] *adj* voluminous, bulky.

volupté [vɔlypte] *nf* [sensuelle] sensual ou voluptuous pleasure.

voluptueux, -euse [vɔlyptɥø, øz] *adj* voluptuous.

volute [vɔlyt] *nf* [de fumée] wreath. || ARCHIT volute, helix.

vomi [vɔmi] *nm fam* vomit.

vomir [vɔmir] *vt* [aliments] to bring up. || [injures] to spit out.

vorace [vɔras] *adj* voracious.

voracité [vɔrasite] *nf* voracity.

vos → votre.

vote [vɔt] *nm* vote.

voter [vɔte] 1 *vi* to vote. 2 *vt* POLIT to vote for; [crédits] to vote; [loi] to pass.

votre [vɔtr] (*pl* vos [vo]) *adj poss* your.

vôtre [votr] O **le vôtre** (*f* la vôtre, *pl* les vôtres) *pron poss* yours; **à la ~!** your good health!

vouer [vwe] *vt* [promettre, jurer]: **~ qqch à qqn** to swear ou vow sthg to sb. || [consacrer] to devote to. || [condamner]: **être voué à** to be doomed to.

vouloir [vulwar] 1 *vt* [gén] to want; **je voudrais savoir** I would like to know; **~ que** (+ *subjonctif*): **je veux qu'il parte** I want him to leave; **combien voulez-vous de votre maison?** how much do you want for your house?; **ne pas ~ de qqn/qqch** not to want sb/sthg; **je veux bien** I don't mind; **veuillez vous asseoir** please take a seat; **sans le ~** without meaning ou wishing to, unintentionally. || [suj: coutume] to demand. || *loc*: **~ dire** to mean; **si on veut** more or less, if you like; **en ~ à qqn** to have a grudge against sb. 2 *nm*: **le bon ~ de qqn** sb's good will. O **se vouloir** *vp*: **elle se veut différente** she thinks she's different; **s'en ~ de faire qqch** to be cross with o.s. for doing sthg.

voulu, -e [vuly] 1 *pp* → vouloir. 2 *adj* [requis] requisite. || [délibéré] intentional.

vous [vu] *pron pers* [sujet, objet direct] you. || [objet indirect] (to) you. || [après préposition, comparatif] you. || [réfléchi] yourself, (*pl*) yourselves. O **vous-**

même *pron pers* yourself. O **vous-mêmes** *pron pers* yourselves.

voûte [vut] *nf* ARCHIT vault; *fig* arch. || ANAT: **~ du palais** roof of the mouth; **~ plantaire** arch (of the foot).

voûter [vute] O **se voûter** *vp* to be ou become stooped.

vouvoyer [vuvwaje] *vt*: **~ qqn** to use the "vous" form to sb.

voyage [vwajaʒ] *nm* journey, trip; **les ~s** travel (*sg*), travelling (*U*); **partir en ~** to go away, to go on a trip; **~ d'affaires** business trip; **~ organisé** package tour; **~ de noces** honeymoon.

voyager [vwajaʒe] *vi* to travel.

voyageur, -euse [vwajaʒœr, øz] *nm, f* traveller.

voyant, -e [vwajã, ãt] 1 *adj* loud, gaudy. 2 *nm, f* [devin] seer. O **voyant** *nm* [lampe] light; AUTOM indicator (light); **~ d'essence/d'huile** petrol/oil warning light.

voyelle [vwajɛl] *nf* vowel.

voyeur, -euse [vwajœr, øz] *nm, f* voyeur, Peeping Tom.

voyou [vwaju] *nm* [garnement] urchin. || [loubard] lout.

vrac [vrak] O **en vrac** *loc adv* [sans emballage] loose. || [en désordre] higgledy-piggledy. || [au poids] in bulk.

vrai, -e [vrɛ] *adj* [histoire] true. || [or, perle, nom] real. || [personne] natural. || [ami, raison] real, true. O **vrai** *nm*: **à ~ dire, à dire ~** to tell the truth.

vraiment [vremã] *adv* really.

vraisemblable [vrɛsãblabl] *adj* likely, probable. || [excuse] plausible.

vraisemblance [vrɛsãblãs] *nf* likelihood, probability. || [d'excuse] plausibility.

V/Réf (*abr de* Votre référence) your ref.

vrille [vrij] *nf* BOT tendril. || [outil] gimlet. || [spirale] spiral.

vrombir [vrɔ̃bir] *vi* to hum.

VTT (*abr de* vélo tout terrain) *nm* mountain bike.

vu, -e [vy] 1 *pp* → voir. 2 *adj* [perçu]: **être bien/mal ~** to be acceptable/unacceptable. || [compris] clear. O **vu** *prép* given, in view of. O **vue** *nf* [sens, vision] sight, eyesight. || [regard] gaze; **à première ~e** at first sight; **de ~e** by sight; **perdre qqn de ~e** to lose touch with sb. || [panorama, idée] view. || CIN → prise. O **en vue de** *loc prép* with a view to. O **vu que** *loc conj* given that, seeing that.

vulgaire [vylgɛr] *adj* [grossier] vulgar, coarse. || (*avant n*) *péj* [quelconque] common.
vulgarisation [vylgarizasjɔ̃] *nf* popularization.
vulgarité [vylgarite] *nf* vulgarity, coarseness.
vulnérable [vylnerabl] *adj* vulnerable.
vulve [vylv] *nf* vulva.

x, X [iks] *nm inv* x, X.
xénophobie [gzenɔfɔbi] *nf* xenophobia.
xérès [gzerɛs, kserɛs] *nm* sherry.
xylophone [ksilɔfɔn] *nm* xylophone.

w, W [dubləve] *nm inv* w, W.
wagon [vagɔ̃] *nm* carriage.
wagon-lit [vagɔ̃li] *nm* sleeping car, sleeper.
wagon-restaurant [vagɔ̃rɛstɔrɑ̃] *nm* restaurant *ou* dining car.
Walkman® [wɔkman] *nm* personal stereo, Walkman®.
wallon, -onne [walɔ̃, ɔn] *adj* Walloon. ○ **wallon** *nm* [langue] Walloon. ○ **Wallon, -onne** *nm, f* Walloon.
Washington [waʃiɲtɔn] *n* [ville] Washington D.C. || [État] Washington State.
water-polo [watɛrpɔlo] *nm* water polo.
watt [wat] *nm* watt.
W.-C. [vese] (*abr de* water closet) *nmpl* WC (*sg*), toilets.
week-end [wikɛnd] (*pl* week-ends) *nm* weekend.
western [wɛstɛrn] *nm* western.
whisky [wiski] (*pl* whiskies) *nm* whisky.
white-spirit [wajtspirit] (*pl* white-spirits) *nm* white spirit.

y¹, Y [igrɛk] *nm inv* y, Y.
y² [i] **1** *adv* [lieu] there; **j'y vais demain** I'm going there tomorrow; **mets-y du sel** put some salt in it. **2** *pron* (*la traduction varie selon la préposition utilisée avec le verbe*): **pensez-y** think about it; **n'y comptez pas** don't count on it; **j'y suis!** I've got it!; *voir aussi* **aller, avoir** *etc.*
yacht [jot] *nm* yacht.
yaourt [jaurt], **yogourt, yoghourt** [jɔgurt] *nm* yoghurt.
yen [jɛn] *nm* yen.
yeux → **œil.**
yiddish [jidiʃ] *nm inv & adj inv* Yiddish.
yoga [jɔga] *nm* yoga.
yoghourt = yaourt.
yogourt = yaourt.
yougoslave [jugɔslav] *adj* Yugoslav, Yugoslavian. ○ **Yougoslave** *nmf* Yugoslav, Yugoslavian.
Yougoslavie [jugɔslavi] *nf*: **la ~** Yugoslavia.

z, Z [zɛd] *nm inv* z, Z.

zapper [zape] *vi* to zap, to channel-hop.

zapping [zapiŋ] *nm* zapping, channel-hopping.

zèbre [zɛbr] *nm* zebra; **un drôle de ~** *fam fig* an oddball.

zébrure [zebryr] *nf* [de pelage] stripe. || [marque] weal.

zèle [zɛl] *nm* zeal; **faire du ~** *péj* to be over-zealous.

zélé, -e [zele] *adj* zealous.

zénith [zenit] *nm* zenith.

zéro [zero] **1** *nm* [chiffre] zero, nought; [dans numéro de téléphone] O *Br*, zero *Am*. || [nombre] nought, nothing. || [de graduation] freezing point, zero; **au-dessus/au-dessous de ~** above/below (zero); **avoir le moral à ~** *fig* to be or feel down. **2** *adj*: **~ faute** no mistakes.

zeste [zɛst] *nm* peel, zest.

zézayer [zezeje] *vi* to lisp.

zigzag [zigzag] *nm* zigzag; **en ~** winding.

zigzaguer [zigzage] *vi* to zigzag (along).

zinc [zɛ̃g] *nm* [matière] zinc.

zizi [zizi] *nm fam* willy *Br*, peter *Am*.

zodiaque [zɔdjak] *nm* zodiac.

zone [zon] *nf* [région] zone, area; **~ bleue** restricted parking zone; **~ industrielle** industrial estate; **~ piétonne** or **piétonnière** pedestrian precinct *Br* or zone *Am*. || *fam* [faubourg]: **la ~** the slum belt.

zoo [zo(o)] *nm* zoo.

zoologie [zɔɔlɔʒi] *nf* zoology.

zoom [zum] *nm* [objectif] zoom (lens). || [gros plan] zoom.

zut [zyt] *interj fam* damn!

ENGLISH–FRENCH
ANGLAIS–FRANÇAIS

a¹ (*pl* **a's** OR **as**), **A** (*pl* **A's** OR **As**) [eɪ] *n* [letter] a *m inv*, A *m inv*; **to get from A to B** aller d'un point à un autre. ○ **A** *n* MUS la *m inv*. || SCH [mark] A *m inv*.

a² [*stressed* eɪ, *unstressed* ə] (*before vowel or silent 'h'* **an** [*stressed* æn, *unstressed* ən]) *indef art* **1** [gen] un (une); **a boy** un garçon; **a table** une table; **an orange** une orange. || [referring to occupation]: **to be a doctor/lawyer/plumber** être médecin/avocat/plombier. || [instead of the number one] un (une); **a hundred/thousand pounds** cent/mille livres. || [to express prices, ratios etc] **20p a kilo** 20p le kilo; **£10 a person** 10 livres par personne; **twice a week/month** deux fois par semaine/mois; **50 km an hour** 50 km à l'heure.

AA *n* (*abbr of* **Automobile Association**) *automobile club britannique*, ≃ ACF *m*, ≃ TCF *m*.

AAA *n* (*abbr of* **American Automobile Association**) *automobile club américain*, ≃ ACF *m*, ≃ TCF *m*.

AB *n Am abbr of* **Bachelor of Arts**.

aback [ə'bæk] *adv*: **to be taken ~** être décontenancé(e).

abandon [ə'bændən] **1** *vt* abandonner. **2** *n*: **with ~** avec abandon.

abate [ə'beɪt] *vi* [storm, fear] se calmer.

abattoir ['æbətwɑːr] *n* abattoir *m*.

abbey ['æbɪ] *n* abbaye *f*.

abbot ['æbət] *n* abbé *m*.

abbreviate [ə'briːvɪeɪt] *vt* abréger.

abbreviation [ə,briːvɪ'eɪʃn] *n* abréviation *f*.

ABC *n* [alphabet] alphabet *m*.

abdicate ['æbdɪkeɪt] *vt & vi* abdiquer.

abdomen ['æbdəmen] *n* abdomen *m*.

abduct [əb'dʌkt] *vt* enlever.

aberration [,æbə'reɪʃn] *n* aberration *f*.

abet [ə'bet] *vt* → **aid**.

abide [ə'baɪd] *vt* supporter, souffrir. ○ **abide by** *vt fus* respecter, se soumettre à.

ability [ə'bɪlətɪ] *n* [capacity, capability] aptitude *f*. || [skill] talent *m*.

abject ['æbdʒekt] *adj* [poverty] noir(e). || [person] pitoyable; [apology] servile.

ablaze [ə'bleɪz] *adj* [on fire] en feu.

able ['eɪbl] *adj* [capable]: **to be ~ to do sthg** pouvoir faire qqch. || [accomplished] compétent(e).

abnormal [æb'nɔːml] *adj* anormal(e).

aboard [ə'bɔːd] **1** *adv* à bord. **2** *prep* [ship, plane] à bord; [bus, train] dans.

abode [ə'bəʊd] *n fml*: **of no fixed ~** sans domicile fixe.

abolish [ə'bɒlɪʃ] *vt* abolir.

abolition [,æbə'lɪʃn] *n* abolition *f*.

aborigine [,æbə'rɪdʒənɪ] *n* aborigène *mf* d'Australie.

abort [ə'bɔːt] *vt fig* [plan, project] abandonner, faire avorter. || COMPUT abandonner.

abortion [ə'bɔːʃn] *n* avortement *m*, interruption *f* (volontaire) de grossesse; **to have an ~** se faire avorter.

abortive [ə'bɔːtɪv] *adj* manqué(e).

abound [ə'baʊnd] *vi* [be plentiful] abonder. || [be full]: **to ~ with** OR **in** abonder en.

about [ə'baʊt] **1** *adv* [approximately] environ, à peu près; **~ fifty/a hundred/a thousand** environ cinquante/cent/mille; **at ~ five o'clock** vers cinq heures; **I'm just ~ ready** je suis presque prêt. || [referring to place]: **to run ~** courir çà et là; **to leave things lying ~** laisser traîner des affaires; **to walk ~** aller et venir, se promener. || [on the point of]: **to be ~ to do sthg** être sur le point de faire qqch. **2** *prep* [relating to, concerning] au sujet de; **a film ~ Paris** un film sur Paris; **what is it ~?** de quoi s'agit-il?; **to talk ~ sthg** parler de qqch. || [referring to place]: **his belongings were scattered ~ the room** ses affaires étaient éparpillées dans toute la pièce; **to wander ~ the streets** errer de par les rues.

about-turn, about-face *n* MIL demitour *m*; *fig* volte-face *f inv*.

above [ə'bʌv] **1** *adv* [on top, higher up] au-dessus. || [in text] ci-dessus, plus haut. || [more, over] plus; **children aged 5 and ~** les enfants âgés de 5 ans et plus OR de plus de 5 ans. **2** *prep* [on top of, higher up than] au-dessus de. || [more than] plus de. ○ **above all** *adv* avant tout.

aboveboard [ə,bʌv'bɔːd] *adj* honnête.

abrasive [ə'breɪsɪv] *adj* [substance] abrasif(ive); *fig* caustique, acerbe.

abreast [ə'brest] *adv* de front. ○ **abreast of** *prep*: **to keep ~ of** se tenir au courant de.

abridged [ə'brɪdʒd] *adj* abrégé(e).

abroad [ə'brɔːd] *adv* à l'étranger.

abrupt [ə'brʌpt] *adj* [sudden] soudain(e), brusque. || [brusque] abrupt(e).

abscess ['æbsɪs] *n* abcès *m*.

abscond [əb'skɒnd] *vi* s'enfuir.

abseil ['æbseɪl] *vi* descendre en rappel.

absence ['æbsəns] *n* absence *f*.

absent ['æbsənt] *adj*: **~ (from)** absent(e) (de).

absentee [,æbsən'tiː] *n* absent *m*, -e *f*.

absent-minded [-'maɪndɪd] *adj* distrait(e).

absolute ['æbsəluːt] *adj* [complete - fool, disgrace] complet(ète). || [totalitarian - ruler, power] absolu(e).

absolutely ['æbsəluːtlɪ] *adv* absolument.

absolve [əb'zɒlv] *vt*: **to ~ sb (from)** absoudre qqn (de).

absorb [əb'sɔːb] *vt* absorber; [information] retenir, assimiler; **to be ~ed in sthg** être absorbé dans qqch.

absorbent [əb'sɔːbənt] *adj* absorbant(e).

absorption [əb'sɔːpʃn] *n* absorption *f*.

abstain [əb'steɪn] *vi*: **to ~ (from)** s'abstenir (de).

abstention [əb'stenʃn] *n* abstention *f*.

abstract ['æbstrækt] **1** *adj* abstrait(e). **2** *n* [summary] résumé *m*, abrégé *m*.

absurd [əb'sɜːd] *adj* absurde.

abundant [ə'bʌndənt] *adj* abondant(e).

abuse [*n* ə'bjuːs, *vb* ə'bjuːz] **1** *n* (*U*) [offensive remarks] insultes *fpl*, injures *fpl*. || [maltreatment] mauvais traitement *m*; **child ~** mauvais traitements infligés aux enfants. || [of power, drugs etc] abus *m*. **2** *vt* [insult] insulter, injurier. || [maltreat] maltraiter. || [power, drugs etc] abuser de.

abusive [ə'bjuːsɪv] *adj* grossier(ière), injurieux(ieuse).

abysmal [ə'bɪzml] *adj* épouvantable, abominable.

abyss [ə'bɪs] *n* abîme *m*, gouffre *m*.

a/c (*abbr of* **account (current)**) cc.

AC *n* (*abbr of* **alternating current**) courant *m* alternatif.

academic [,ækə'demɪk] **1** *adj* [of college, university] universitaire. || [person] intellectuel(elle). || [question, discussion] théorique. **2** *n* universitaire *mf*.

academy [ə'kædəmɪ] *n* [school, college] école *f*; **~ of music** conservatoire *m*. || [institution, society] académie *f*.

accede [æk'siːd] *vi* [agree]: **to ~ to** agréer, donner suite à. || [monarch]: **to ~ to the throne** monter sur le trône.

accelerate [ək'seləreɪt] *vi* [car, driver] accélérer. || [inflation, growth] s'accélérer.

accelerator [ək'seləreɪtə] *n* accélérateur *m*.

accent ['æksent] *n* accent *m*.

accept [ək'sept] *vt* [gen] accepter; [for job, as member of club] recevoir, admettre. || [agree]: **to ~ that ...** admettre que ....

acceptable [ək'septəbl] *adj* acceptable.

acceptance [ək'septəns] *n* [gen] acceptation *f*. || [for job, as member of club] admission *f*.

access ['ækses] *n* [entry, way in] accès *m*. || [opportunity to use, see]: **to have ~ to sthg** avoir qqch à sa disposition, disposer de qqch.

accessible [ək'sesəbl] *adj* [reachable - place] accessible. || [available] disponible.

accessory [ək'sesərɪ] *n* [of car, vacuum cleaner] accessoire *m*. || JUR complice *mf*.

accident ['æksɪdənt] *n* accident *m*; **by ~** par hasard, par accident.

accidental [,æksɪ'dentl] *adj* accidentel(elle).

accidentally [,æksɪ'dentəlɪ] *adv* [drop, break] par mégarde. || [meet] par hasard.

accident-prone adj prédisposé(e) aux accidents.

acclaim [ə'kleɪm] n (U) éloges mpl.

acclimatize, -ise [ə'klaɪmətaɪz], **acclimate** Am ['ækləmeɪt] vi: **to ~ (to)** s'acclimater (à).

accommodate [ə'kɒmədeɪt] vt [provide room for] loger. || [oblige - person, wishes] satisfaire.

accommodation Br [ə,kɒmə'deɪʃn] n, **accommodations** Am [ə,kɒmə'deɪʃnz] npl logement m.

accompany [ə'kʌmpənɪ] vt [gen] accompagner.

accomplice [ə'kʌmplɪs] n complice mf.

accomplish [ə'kʌmplɪʃ] vt accomplir.

accomplishment [ə'kʌmplɪʃmənt] n [action] accomplissement m. || [achievement] réussite f. ○ **accomplishments** npl talents mpl.

accord [ə'kɔːd] n: **to do sthg of one's own ~** faire qqch de son propre chef OR de soi-même.

accordance [ə'kɔːdəns] n: **in ~ with** conformément à.

according [ə'kɔːdɪŋ] ○ **according to** prep [as stated or shown by] d'après; **to go ~ to plan** se passer comme prévu. || [with regard to] suivant, en fonction de.

accordingly [ə'kɔːdɪŋlɪ] adv [appropriately] en conséquence. || [consequently] par conséquent.

accordion [ə'kɔːdjən] n accordéon m.

accost [ə'kɒst] vt accoster.

account [ə'kaʊnt] n [with bank, shop, company] compte m. || [report] compte-rendu m. || phr: **to take ~ of sthg, to take sthg into ~** prendre qqch en compte; **on no ~** sous aucun prétexte, en aucun cas. ○ **accounts** npl [of business] comptabilité f, comptes mpl. ○ **by all accounts** adv d'après ce que l'on dit, au dire de tous. ○ **on account of** prep à cause de. ○ **account for** vt fus [explain] justifier, expliquer. || [represent] représenter.

accountable [ə'kaʊntəbl] adj [responsible]: **~ (for)** responsable (de).

accountant [ə'kaʊntənt] n comptable mf.

accumulate [ə'kjuːmjʊleɪt] **1** vt accumuler, amasser. **2** vi s'accumuler.

accuracy ['ækjʊrəsɪ] n [of description, report] exactitude f. || [of weapon, typist, figures] précision f.

accurate ['ækjʊrət] adj [description, re-

port] exact(e). || [weapon, typist, figures] précis(e).

accurately ['ækjʊrətlɪ] adv [truthfully - describe, report] fidèlement. || [precisely - aim] avec précision; [- type] sans faute.

accusation [,ækjuː'zeɪʃn] n accusation f.

accuse [ə'kjuːz] vt: **to ~ sb of sthg/of doing sthg** accuser qqn de qqch/de faire qqch.

accused [ə'kjuːzd] (pl inv) n JUR: **the ~** l'accusé m, -e f.

accustomed [ə'kʌstəmd] adj: **to be ~ to sthg/to doing sthg** avoir l'habitude de qqch/de faire qqch.

ace [eɪs] n as m.

ache [eɪk] **1** n douleur f. **2** vi [back, limb] faire mal; **my head ~s** j'ai mal à la tête.

achieve [ə'tʃiːv] vt [success, victory] obtenir, remporter; [goal] atteindre; [ambition] réaliser; [fame] parvenir à.

achievement [ə'tʃiːvmənt] n [success] réussite f.

Achilles' tendon [ə'kɪliːz-] n tendon m d'Achille.

acid ['æsɪd] **1** adj lit & fig acide. **2** n acide m.

acid rain n (U) pluies fpl acides.

acknowledge [ək'nɒlɪdʒ] vt [fact, situation, person] reconnaître. || [letter]: **to ~ (receipt of)** accuser réception de.

acknowledg(e)ment [ək'nɒlɪdʒmənt] n [gen] reconnaissance f. || [letter] accusé m de réception. ○ **acknowledg(e)ments** npl [in book] remerciements mpl.

acne ['æknɪ] n acné f.

acorn ['eɪkɔːn] n gland m.

acoustic [ə'kuːstɪk] adj acoustique. ○ **acoustics** npl [of room] acoustique f.

acquaint [ə'kweɪnt] vt: **to ~ sb with sthg** mettre qqn au courant de qqch; **to be ~ed with sb** connaître qqn.

acquaintance [ə'kweɪntəns] n [person] connaissance f.

acquire [ə'kwaɪər] vt acquérir.

acquit [ə'kwɪt] vt JUR acquitter. || [perform]: **to ~ o.s. well/badly** bien/mal se comporter.

acquittal [ə'kwɪtl] n acquittement m.

acre ['eɪkər] n = 4046,9 m², ≃ demi-hectare m.

acrid ['ækrɪd] adj [taste, smell] âcre.

acrobat ['ækrəbæt] n acrobate mf.

across [ə'krɒs] **1** adv [from one side to the other] en travers. || [in measurements]: **the river is 2 km ~** la rivière mesure 2 km de large. || [in crossword]: **21 ~** 21 horizontalement. 2 *prep* [from one side to the other] d'un côté à l'autre de, en travers de; **to walk ~ the road** traverser la route. ‖ [on the other side of] de l'autre côté de; **the house ~ the road** la maison d'en face. ○ **across from** *prep* en face de.

acrylic [ə'krɪlɪk] 1 *adj* acrylique. 2 *n* acrylique *m*.

act [ækt] 1 *n* [action, deed] acte *m*; **to catch sb in the ~ of doing sthg** surprendre qqn en train de faire qqch. ‖ JUR loi *f*. ‖ [of play, opera] acte *m*; [in cabaret etc] numéro *m*; *fig* [pretence]: **to put on an ~** jouer la comédie. ‖ *phr*: **to get one's ~ together** se reprendre en main. 2 *vi* [gen] agir. ‖ [behave] se comporter; **to ~ as if** se conduire comme si, se comporter comme si; **to ~ like** se conduire comme, se comporter comme. ‖ [in play, film] jouer; *fig* [pretend] jouer la comédie. ‖ [function]: **to ~ as** [person] être; [object] servir de. 3 *vt* [part] jouer.

ACT (*abbr of* **American College Test**) *n examen américain de fin d'études secondaires*.

acting ['æktɪŋ] 1 *adj* par intérim, provisoire. 2 *n* [in play, film] interprétation *f*.

action ['ækʃn] *n* [gen] action *f*; **to take ~** agir, prendre des mesures; **to put sthg into ~** mettre qqch à exécution; **in ~** [person] en action; [machine] en marche; **out of ~** [person] hors de combat; [machine] hors service, hors d'usage. ‖ JUR procès *m*, action *f*.

action replay *n* répétition *f* immédiate (au ralenti).

activate ['æktɪveɪt] *vt* mettre en marche.

active ['æktɪv] *adj* [gen] actif(ive); [encouragement] vif (vive). ‖ [volcano] en activité.

actively ['æktɪvlɪ] *adv* activement.

activity [æk'tɪvətɪ] *n* activité *f*.

actor ['æktər] *n* acteur *m*.

actress ['æktrɪs] *n* actrice *f*.

actual ['æktʃʊəl] *adj* réel(elle).

actually ['æktʃʊəlɪ] *adv* [really, in truth] vraiment. ‖ [by the way] au fait.

acumen ['ækjʊmen] *n* flair *m*.

acupuncture ['ækjʊpʌŋktʃər] *n* acupuncture *f*.

acute [ə'kjuːt] *adj* [severe - pain, illness] aigu(ë); [- danger] sérieux(ieuse), grave. ‖ [perceptive - person, mind] perspicace. ‖ [keen - eyesight] perçant(e); [- hearing] fin(e); [- sense of smell] développé(e). ‖

MATH: **~ angle** angle *m* aigu. ‖ LING: **e ~ e** accent aigu.

ad [æd] (*abbr of* **advertisement**) *n inf* [in newspaper] annonce *f*; [on TV] pub *f*.

AD (*abbr of* **Anno Domini**) ap. J.-C.

adamant ['ædəmənt] *adj*: **to be ~** être inflexible.

Adam's apple ['ædəmz-] *n* pomme *f* d'Adam.

adapt [ə'dæpt] 1 *vt* adapter. 2 *vi*: **to ~ (to)** s'adapter (à).

adaptable [ə'dæptəbl] *adj* [person] souple.

adapter, adaptor [ə'dæptər] *n* [ELEC - for several devices] prise *f* multiple; [- for foreign plug] adaptateur *m*.

add [æd] *vt* [gen]: **to ~ sthg (to)** ajouter qqch (à). ‖ [numbers] additionner. ○ **add on** *vt sep*: **to ~ sthg on (to)** ajouter qqch (à); [charge, tax] rajouter qqch (à). ○ **add to** *vt fus* ajouter à, augmenter. ○ **add up** *vt sep* additionner. ○ **add up to** *vt fus* se monter à.

adder ['ædər] *n* vipère *f*.

addict ['ædɪkt] *n lit & fig* drogué *m*, -e *f*; **drug ~** drogué.

addicted [ə'dɪktɪd] *adj*: **~ (to)** drogué(e) (à); *fig* passionné(e) (de).

addictive [ə'dɪktɪv] *adj* qui rend dépendant(e).

addition [ə'dɪʃn] *n* addition *f*; **in ~ (to)** en plus (de).

additional [ə'dɪʃənl] *adj* supplémentaire.

additive ['ædɪtɪv] *n* additif *m*.

address [ə'dres] 1 *n* [place] adresse *f*. ‖ [speech] discours *m*. 2 *vt* [gen] adresser. ‖ [meeting, conference] prendre la parole à. ‖ [problem, issue] aborder, examiner.

address book *n* carnet *m* d'adresses.

adept ['ædept] *adj*: **~ (at)** doué(e) (pour).

adequate ['ædɪkwət] *adj* adéquat(e).

adhere [əd'hɪər] *vi* [stick]: **to ~ (to)** adhérer (à). ‖ [observe]: **to ~ to** obéir à. ‖ [keep]: **to ~ to** adhérer à.

adhesive [əd'hiːsɪv] *n* adhésif *m*.

adhesive tape *n* ruban *m* adhésif.

adjacent [ə'dʒeɪsənt] *adj*: **~ (to)** adjacent(e) (à), contigu(ë) (à).

adjective ['ædʒɪktɪv] *n* adjectif *m*.

adjoining [ə'dʒɔɪnɪŋ] 1 *adj* voisin(e). 2 *prep* attenant à.

adjourn [ə'dʒɜːn] 1 *vt* ajourner. 2 *vi* suspendre la séance.

adjust [ə'dʒʌst] 1 *vt* ajuster, régler. 2 *vi*: **to ~ (to)** s'adapter (à).

adjustable [ə'dʒʌstəbl] *adj* réglable.

adjustment [ə'dʒʌstmənt] *n* [modification] ajustement *m*; TECH réglage *m*. || [change in attitude]: ~ (**to**) adaptation *f* (à).

ad lib [,æd'lɪb] *adv* à volonté. ○ **ad-lib** *vi* improviser.

administer [əd'mɪnɪstə'] *vt* [company, business] administrer, gérer. || [justice, punishment] dispenser. || [drug, medication] administrer.

administration [əd,mɪnɪ'streɪʃn] *n* administration *f*.

administrative [əd'mɪnɪstrətɪv] *adj* administratif(ive).

admiral ['ædmərəl] *n* amiral *m*.

admiration [,ædmə'reɪʃn] *n* admiration *f*.

admire [əd'maɪə'] *vt* admirer.

admirer [əd'maɪərə'] *n* admirateur *m*, -trice *f*.

admission [əd'mɪʃn] *n* [permission to enter] admission *f*. || [to museum etc] entrée *f*. || [confession] confession *f*, aveu *m*.

admit [əd'mɪt] **1** *vt* [confess] reconnaître; **to ~ (that)** ... reconnaître que ...; **to ~ doing sthg** reconnaître avoir fait qqch; **to ~ defeat** *fig* s'avouer vaincu(e). || [allow to enter, join] admettre; **to be admitted to hospital** *Br* OR **to the hospital** *Am* être admis(e) à l'hôpital. **2** *vi*: **to ~ to** admettre, reconnaître.

admittance [əd'mɪtəns] *n* admission *f*; "**no ~**" «entrée interdite».

admittedly [əd'mɪtɪdlɪ] *adv* de l'aveu général.

ad nauseam [,æd'nɔːzɪæm] *adv* [talk] à n'en plus finir.

ado [ə'duː] *n*: **without further** OR **more ~** sans plus de cérémonie.

adolescence [,ædə'lesns] *n* adolescence *f*.

adolescent [,ædə'lesnt] **1** *adj* adolescent(e); *pej* puéril(e). **2** *n* adolescent *m*, -e *f*.

adopt [ə'dɒpt] *vt* adopter.

adoption [ə'dɒpʃn] *n* adoption *f*.

adore [ə'dɔːr] *vt* adorer.

adorn [ə'dɔːn] *vt* orner.

adrenalin [ə'drenəlɪn] *n* adrénaline *f*.

Adriatic [,eɪdrɪ'ætɪk] *n*: **the ~ (Sea)** l'Adriatique *f*, la mer Adriatique.

adrift [ə'drɪft] **1** *adj* à la dérive. **2** *adv*: **to go ~** *fig* aller à la dérive.

adult ['ædʌlt] **1** *adj* [gen] adulte. || [films, literature] pour adultes. **2** *n* adulte *mf*.

adultery [ə'dʌltərɪ] *n* adultère *m*.

advance [əd'vɑːns] **1** *n* [gen] avance *f*. || [progress] progrès *m*. **2** *comp* à l'avance. **3** *vt* [gen] avancer. || [improve] faire progresser OR avancer. **4** *vi* [gen] avancer. || [improve] progresser. ○ **advances** *npl*: **to make ~s to sb** [sexual] faire des avances à qqn; [business] faire des propositions à qqn. ○ **in advance** *adv* à l'avance.

advanced [əd'vɑːnst] *adj* avancé(e).

advantage [əd'vɑːntɪdʒ] *n*: ~ (**over**) avantage *m* (sur); **to be to one's ~** être à son avantage; **to take ~ of sthg** profiter de qqch; **to take ~ of sb** exploiter qqn.

advent ['ædvənt] *n* avènement *m*. ○ **Advent** *n* RELIG Avent *m*.

adventure [əd'ventʃə'] *n* aventure *f*.

adventure playground *n* terrain *m* d'aventures.

adventurous [əd'ventʃərəs] *adj* aventureux(euse).

adverb ['ædvɜːb] *n* adverbe *m*.

adverse ['ædvɜːs] *adj* défavorable.

advert ['ædvɜːt] *Br* = **advertisement**.

advertise ['ædvətaɪz] **1** *vt* COMM faire de la publicité pour; [event] annoncer. **2** *vi* faire de la publicité; **to ~ for sb/sthg** chercher qqn/qqch par voie d'annonce.

advertisement [əd'vɜːtɪsmənt] *n* [in newspaper] annonce *f*, COMM & *fig* publicité *f*.

advertiser ['ædvətaɪzə'] *n* annonceur *m*.

advertising ['ædvətaɪzɪŋ] *n* (*U*) publicité *f*.

advice [əd'vaɪs] *n* (*U*) conseils *mpl*; **a piece of ~** un conseil; **to take sb's ~** suivre les conseils de qqn.

advisable [əd'vaɪzəbl] *adj* conseillé(e), recommandé(e).

advise [əd'vaɪz] **1** *vt* [give advice to]: **to ~ sb to do sthg** conseiller à qqn de faire qqch; **to ~ sb against sthg** déconseiller qqch à qqn; [professionally]: **to ~ sb on sthg** conseiller qqn sur qqch. || [inform]: **to ~ sb (of sthg)** aviser qqn (de qqch). **2** *vi* [give advice]: **to ~ against sthg/against doing sthg** déconseiller qqch/de faire qqch. || [professionally]: **to ~ on sthg** conseiller sur qqch.

adviser *Br*, **advisor** *Am* [əd'vaɪzə'] *n* conseiller *m*, -ère *f*.

advisory [əd'vaɪzərɪ] *adj* consultatif(ive).

advocate [*n* 'ædvəkət, *vb* 'ædvəkeɪt] **1**

n JUR avocat *m*, -e *f*. ‖ [supporter] partisan *m*. **2** *vt* préconiser, recommander.

Aegean [iː'dʒiːən] *n*: the ~ (Sea) la mer Égée.

aerial ['eərɪəl] **1** *adj* aérien(ienne). **2** *n Br* antenne *f*.

aerobics [eə'rəʊbɪks] *n* (U) aérobic *m*.

aerodynamic [,eərəʊdaɪ'næmɪk] *adj* aérodynamique.

aerosol ['eərəsɒl] *n* aérosol *m*.

aesthetic, esthetic *Am* [iːs'θetɪk] *adj* esthétique.

afar [ə'fɑːr] *adv*: **from ~** de loin.

affable ['æfəbl] *adj* affable.

affair [ə'feər] *n* [gen] affaire *f*. ‖ [extramarital relationship] liaison *f*.

affect [ə'fekt] *vt* [influence] avoir un effet OR des conséquences sur. ‖ [emotionally] affecter, émouvoir.

affection [ə'fekʃn] *n* affection *f*.

affectionate [ə'fekʃnət] *adj* affectueux(euse).

affirm [ə'fɜːm] *vt* [declare] affirmer. ‖ [confirm] confirmer.

affix [ə'fɪks] *vt* [stamp] coller.

afflict [ə'flɪkt] *vt* affliger; **to be ~ed with** souffrir de.

affluence ['æfluəns] *n* prospérité *f*.

affluent ['æfluənt] *adj* riche.

afford [ə'fɔːd] *vt* [buy, pay for]: **to be able to ~ sthg** avoir les moyens d'acheter qqch. ‖ [spare]: **to be able to ~ the time (to do sthg)** avoir le temps (de faire qqch). ‖ [harmful, embarrassing thing]: **to be able to ~ sthg** pouvoir se permettre qqch. ‖ [provide, give] procurer.

Afghanistan [æf'gænɪstæn] *n* Afghanistan *m*.

afield [ə'fiːld] *adv*: **far ~** loin.

afloat [ə'fləʊt] *adj lit & fig* à flot.

afoot [ə'fʊt] *adj* en préparation.

afraid [ə'freɪd] *adj* [frightened]: **to be ~ (of)** avoir peur (de); **to be ~ of doing** OR **to do sthg** avoir peur de faire qqch. ‖ [reluctant, apprehensive]: **to be ~ of** craindre. ‖ [in apologies]: **to be ~ (that) ...** regretter que ...; **I'm ~ so/not** j'ai bien peur que oui/non.

afresh [ə'freʃ] *adv* de nouveau.

Africa ['æfrɪkə] *n* Afrique *f*.

African ['æfrɪkən] **1** *adj* africain(e). **2** *n* Africain *m*, -e *f*.

aft [ɑːft] *adv* sur OR à l'arrière.

after ['ɑːftər] **1** *prep* [gen] après; **~ you!** après vous!; **to be ~ sb/sthg** *inf* [in search of] chercher qqn/qqch. ‖ *Am* [telling the time]: **it's twenty ~ three** il est trois heu-

res vingt. **2** *adv* après. **3** *conj* après que.

○ **after all** *adv* après tout.

aftereffects ['ɑːftərɪ,fekts] *npl* suites *fpl*, répercussions *fpl*.

aftermath ['ɑːftəmæθ] *n* conséquences *fpl*, suites *fpl*.

afternoon [,ɑːftə'nuːn] *n* après-midi *m inv*; **in the ~** l'après-midi; **good ~** bonjour.

aftershave ['ɑːftəʃeɪv] *n* après-rasage *m*.

aftertaste ['ɑːftəteɪst] *n lit & fig* arrière-goût *m*.

afterthought ['ɑːftəθɔːt] *n* pensée *f* OR réflexion *f* après coup.

afterward(s) ['ɑːftəwəd(z)] *adv* après.

again [ə'gen] *adv* encore une fois, de nouveau; **to do ~** refaire; **to say ~** répéter; **to start ~** recommencer; **~ and ~** à plusieurs reprises; **all over ~** une fois de plus; **time and ~** maintes et maintes fois; **half as much ~** à moitié autant; **(twice) as much ~** deux fois autant; **then** OR **there ~** d'autre part.

against [ə'genst] *prep & adv* contre; **(as) ~** contre.

age [eɪdʒ] (*cont* **ageing** OR **aging**) **1** *n* [gen] âge *m*; **she's 20 years of ~** elle a 20 ans; **what ~ are you?** quel âge avez-vous?; **to be under ~** être mineur; **to come of ~** atteindre sa majorité. ‖ [old age] vieillesse *f*. ‖ [in history] époque *f*. **2** *vt & vi* vieillir. ○ **ages** *npl*: **~s ago** il y a une éternité; **I haven't seen him for ~s** je ne l'ai pas vu depuis une éternité.

aged [*adj sense 1* eɪdʒd, *adj sense 2* æ *npl* 'eɪdʒɪd] **1** *adj* [of stated age]: **~ 15** âgé(e) de 15 ans. ‖ [very old] âgé(e), vieux (vieille). **2** *npl*: **the ~** les personnes *fpl* âgées.

age group *n* tranche *f* d'âge.

agency ['eɪdʒənsɪ] *n* [business] agence *f*. ‖ [organization] organisme *m*.

agenda [ə'dʒendə] (*pl* **-s**) *n* ordre *m* du jour.

agent ['eɪdʒənt] *n* agent *m*.

aggravate ['ægrəveɪt] *vt* [make worse] aggraver. ‖ [annoy] agacer.

aggregate ['ægrɪgət] **1** *adj* total(e). **2** *n* [total] total *m*.

aggressive [ə'gresɪv] *adj* agressif(ive).

aghast [ə'gɑːst] *adj*: ~ (at sthg) atterré(e) (par qqch).

agile [*Br* 'ædʒaɪl, *Am* 'ædʒəl] *adj* agile.

agitate ['ædʒɪteɪt] *vt* [disturb] inquiéter.

AGM (*abbr of* **annual general meeting**) *n Br* AGA *f*.

agnostic [æg'nɒstɪk] **1** *adj* agnostique. **2** *n* agnostique *mf*.

ago [ə'gəʊ] *adv*: **a long time ~** il y a longtemps; **three days ~** il y a trois jours.

agonizing ['ægənaɪzɪŋ] *adj* déchirant(e).

agony ['ægənɪ] *n* [physical pain] douleur *f* atroce; **to be in ~** souffrir le martyre. ‖ [mental pain] angoisse *f*; **to be in ~** être angoissé.

agony aunt *n Br inf* personne qui tient la rubrique du courrier du cœur.

agree [ə'griː] **1** *vi* [concur]: **to ~ (with/about)** être d'accord (avec/au sujet de); **to ~ on** [price, terms] convenir de. ‖ [consent]: **to ~ (to sthg)** donner son consentement (à qqch). ‖ [be consistent] concorder. ‖ [food]: **to ~ with** être bon (bonne) pour, réussir à. ‖ GRAMM: **to ~ (with)** s'accorder (avec). **2** *vt* [price, conditions] accepter, convenir de. ‖ [concur, concede]: **to ~ (that)** ... admettre que .... ‖ [arrange]: **to ~ to do sthg** se mettre d'accord pour faire qqch.

agreeable [ə'griːəbl] *adj* [pleasant] agréable. ‖ [willing]: **to be ~** consentir à.

agreed [ə'griːd] *adj*: **to be ~ (on sthg)** être d'accord (à propos de qqch).

agreement [ə'griːmənt] *n* [gen] accord *m*; **to be in ~ (with)** être d'accord (avec). ‖ [consistency] concordance *f*.

agricultural [,ægrɪ'kʌltʃərəl] *adj* agricole.

agriculture ['ægrɪkʌltʃər] *n* agriculture *f*.

aground [ə'graʊnd] *adv*: **to run ~** s'échouer.

ahead [ə'hed] *adv* [in front] devant, en avant; **right ~, straight ~** droit devant. ‖ [in better position] en avance; **Scotland are ~ by two goals to one** l'Écosse mène par deux à un; **to get ~** [be successful] réussir. ‖ [in time] à l'avance; **the months ~** les mois à venir. ○ **ahead of** *prep* [in front of] devant. ‖ [in time] avant; **~ of schedule** [work] en avance sur le planning.

aid [eɪd] **1** *n* aide *f*; **with the ~ of** [person] avec l'aide de; [thing] à l'aide de; **in ~ of** au profit de. **2** *vt* [help] aider. ‖ JUR: **to ~ and abet** être complice de.

AIDS, Aids [eɪdz] (*abbr of* **acquired immune deficiency syndrome**) *n* SIDA *m*, Sida *m*.

ailing ['eɪlɪŋ] *adj* [ill] souffrant(e). ‖ *fig* [economy, industry] dans une mauvaise passe.

ailment ['eɪlmənt] *n* maladie *f*.

aim [eɪm] **1** *n* [objective] but *m*, objectif *m*. ‖ [in firing gun, arrow]: **to take ~** viser. **2** *vt* [gun, camera]: **to ~ sthg at** braquer qqch sur. ‖ *fig*: **to be ~ed at** [plan, campaign etc] être destiné(e) à, viser; [criticism] être dirigé(e) contre. **3** *vi*: **to ~ (at)** viser; **to ~ at** OR **for** *fig* viser; **to ~ to do sthg** viser à faire qqch.

aimless ['eɪmlɪs] *adj* [person] désœuvré(e); [life] sans but.

ain't [eɪnt] *inf* = **am not, are not, is not, have not, has not**.

air [eər] **1** *n* [gen] air *m*; **to throw sthg into the ~** jeter qqch en l'air; **by ~** [travel] par avion; **to be (up) in the ~** *fig* [plans] être vague. ‖ RADIO & TV: **on the ~** à l'antenne. **2** *comp* [transport] aérien(ienne). **3** *vt* [gas] aérer. ‖ [make publicly known] faire connaître OR communiquer. **4** *vi* sécher.

airbag ['eəbæg] *n* AUT coussin *m* pneumatique (de sécurité).

airbase ['eəbeɪs] *n* base *f* aérienne.

airbed ['eəbed] *n Br* matelas *m* pneumatique.

airborne ['eəbɔːn] *adj* [plane] qui a décollé.

air-conditioned [-kən'dɪʃnd] *adj* climatisé(e), à air conditionné.

air-conditioning [-kən'dɪʃnɪŋ] *n* climatisation *f*.

aircraft ['eəkrɑːft] (*pl inv*) *n* avion *m*.

aircraft carrier *n* porte-avions *m inv*.

airfield ['eəfiːld] *n* terrain *m* d'aviation.

airforce ['eəfɔːs] *n* armée *f* de l'air.

airgun ['eəgʌn] *n* carabine *f* OR fusil *m* à air comprimé.

airhostess ['eə,həʊstɪs] *n* hôtesse *f* de l'air.

airlift ['eəlɪft] **1** *n* pont *m* aérien. **2** *vt* transporter par pont aérien.

airline ['eəlaɪn] *n* compagnie *f* aérienne.

airliner ['eəlaɪnər] *n* [short-distance] (avion *m*) moyen-courrier *m*; [long-distance] (avion) long-courrier *m*.

airlock ['eəlɒk] *n* [in tube, pipe] poche *f* d'air. ‖ [airtight chamber] sas *m*.

airmail ['eəmeɪl] *n* poste *f* aérienne; **by ~** par avion.

airplane ['eəpleɪn] *n Am* avion *m*.

airport ['eəpɔːt] *n* aéroport *m*.

air raid *n* attaque *f* aérienne.

air rifle n carabine f à air comprimé.

airsick ['eəsɪk] adj: **to be ~** avoir le mal de l'air.

airspace ['eəspeɪs] n espace m aérien.

air steward n steward m.

airstrip ['eəstrɪp] n piste f.

air terminal n aérogare f.

airtight ['eətaɪt] adj hermétique.

air-traffic controller n aiguilleur m (du ciel).

airy ['eərɪ] adj [room] aéré(e). || [notions, promises] chimérique, vain(e). || [nonchalant] nonchalant(e).

aisle [aɪl] n allée f; [in plane] couloir m.

ajar [ə'dʒɑːr] adj entrouvert(e).

aka (abbr of also known as) alias.

alarm [ə'lɑːm] **1** n [fear] alarme f, inquiétude f. || [device] alarme f; **to raise** OR **sound the ~** donner OR sonner l'alarme. **2** vt alarmer, alerter.

alarm clock n réveil m, réveille-matin m inv.

alarming [ə'lɑːmɪŋ] adj alarmant(e), inquiétant(e).

alas [ə'læs] excl hélas!

albeit [ɔːl'biːɪt] conj bien que (+ subjunctive).

albino [æl'biːnəʊ] (pl -s) n albinos mf.

album ['ælbəm] n album m.

alcohol ['ælkəhɒl] n alcool m.

alcoholic [,ælkə'hɒlɪk] **1** adj [drink] alcoolisé(e). **2** n alcoolique mf.

alcove ['ælkəʊv] n alcôve f.

alderman ['ɔːldəmən] (pl -men [-mən]) n conseiller m municipal.

ale [eɪl] n bière f.

alert [ə'lɜːt] **1** adj [vigilant] vigilant(e). || [perceptive] vif (vive), éveillé(e). || [aware]: **to be ~ to** être conscient(e) de. **2** n [warning] alerte f; **on the ~** [watchful] sur le qui-vive; MIL en état d'alerte. **3** vt alerter; **to ~ sb to** sthg avertir qqn de qqch.

A-level (abbr of Advanced level) n ≃ baccalauréat m.

algebra ['ældʒɪbrə] n algèbre f.

Algeria [æl'dʒɪərɪə] n Algérie f.

alias ['eɪlɪəs] (pl -es) **1** adv alias. **2** n faux nom m, nom d'emprunt.

alibi ['ælɪbaɪ] n alibi m.

alien ['eɪlɪən] **1** adj [gen] étranger(ère). || [from outer space] extraterrestre. **2** n [from outer space] extraterrestre mf. || JUR [foreigner] étranger m, -ère f.

alienate ['eɪlɪəneɪt] vt aliéner.

alight [ə'laɪt] **1** adj allumé(e), en feu. **2**

vi [bird etc] se poser. || [from bus, train]: **to ~ from** descendre de.

align [ə'laɪn] vt [line up] aligner.

alike [ə'laɪk] **1** adj semblable. **2** adv de la même façon; **to look ~** se ressembler.

alimony ['ælɪmənɪ] n pension f alimentaire.

alive [ə'laɪv] adj [living] vivant(e), en vie. || [practice, tradition] vivace; **to keep ~** préserver. || [lively] plein(e) de vitalité; **to come ~** [story, description] prendre vie; [person, place] s'animer.

alkali ['ælkəlaɪ] (pl -s OR -es) n alcali m.

all [ɔːl] **1** adj (with sg noun) tout (toute); **~ day/night/evening** toute la journée/la nuit/la soirée; **~ the drink** toute la boisson; **~ the time** tout le temps. || (with pl noun) tous (toutes); **~ the boxes** toutes les boîtes; **~ men** tous les hommes; **~ three died** ils sont morts tous les trois, tous les trois sont morts. **2** pron (sg) [the whole amount] tout m; **she drank it ~, she drank ~ of it** elle a tout bu. || (pl) [everybody, everything] tous (toutes), **~ of them came, they ~ came** ils sont tous venus. || (with superl): **... of ~** ... de tous (toutes); **I like this one best of ~** je préfère celui-ci entre tous. || above **~** → above; **after ~** → after; **at ~** → at. **3** adv [entirely] complètement; **~ alone** tout seul (toute seule). || [in sport, competitions]: **the score is five ~** le score est cinq partout. || (with compar): **to run ~ the faster** courir d'autant plus vite; **~ the better** d'autant mieux. ○ **all but** adv presque, pratiquement. ○ **all in all** adv dans l'ensemble. ○ **in all** adv en tout.

Allah ['ælə] n Allah m.

all-around Am = all-round.

allay [ə'leɪ] vt [fears, anger] apaiser, calmer; [doubts] dissiper.

all clear n signal m de fin d'alerte; fig feu m vert.

allegation [,ælɪ'geɪʃn] n allégation f.

allege [ə'ledʒ] vt prétendre, alléguer; **she is ~d to have done it** on prétend qu'elle l'a fait.

allegedly [ə'ledʒɪdlɪ] adv prétendument.

allegiance [ə'liːdʒəns] n allégeance f.

allergic [ə'lɜːdʒɪk] adj: **~ (to)** allergique (à).

allergy ['ælədʒɪ] n allergie f; **to have an ~ to** sthg être allergique à qqch.

alleviate [ə'liːvɪeɪt] vt apaiser, soulager.

alto

alley(way) ['ælɪ(weɪ)] n [street] ruelle f.
alliance [ə'laɪəns] n alliance f.
allied ['ælaɪd] adj MIL allié(e). || [related] connexe.
alligator ['ælɪgeɪtə'] (pl inv OR -s) n alligator m.
all-important adj capital(e), crucial(e).
all-night adj [party etc] qui dure toute la nuit; [bar etc] ouvert(e) toute la nuit.
allocate ['æləkeɪt] vt [money, resources]: to ~ sthg (to sb) attribuer qqch (à qqn).
allot [ə'lɒt] vt [job] assigner; [money, resources] attribuer; [time] allouer.
all-out adj [effort] maximum (inv); [war] total(e).
allow [ə'laʊ] vt [permit - activity, behaviour] autoriser, permettre; to ~ sb to do sthg permettre à qqn de faire qqch, autoriser qqn à faire qqch. || [set aside - money, time] prévoir. || [officially accept] accepter. || [concede]: to ~ that ... admettre que .... ○ **allow for** vt fus tenir compte de.
allowance [ə'laʊəns] n [money received] indemnité f. || Am [pocket money] argent m de poche. || [excuse]: to make ~s for sb faire preuve d'indulgence envers qqn; to make ~s for sthg prendre qqch en considération.
alloy ['ælɔɪ] n alliage m.
all right [adv] bien; [in answer - yes] d'accord. 2 adj [healthy] en bonne santé; [unharmed] sain et sauf (saine et sauve). || inf [acceptable, satisfactory]: it was ~ c'était pas mal; that's ~ [never mind] ce n'est pas grave.
all-round Br, **all-around** Am adj [multi-skilled] doué(e) dans tous les domaines.
all-time adj [record] sans précédent.
allude [ə'lu:d] vi: to ~ to faire allusion à.
alluring [ə'ljʊərɪŋ] adj séduisant(e).
allusion [ə'lu:ʒn] n allusion f.
ally [n 'ælaɪ, vb ə'laɪ] 1 n allié m, -e f. 2 vt: to ~ o.s. with s'allier à.
almond ['ɑːmənd] n [nut] amande f.
almost ['ɔːlməʊst] adv presque; I ~ missed the bus j'ai failli rater le bus.
aloft [ə'lɒft] adv [in the air] en l'air.
alone [ə'ləʊn] 1 adj seul(e). 2 adv seul; to leave sthg ~ ne pas toucher à qqch; leave me ~! laisse-moi tranquille! ○ **let alone** conj encore moins.
along [ə'lɒŋ] 1 adv: to walk ~ se promener; to move ~ avancer; can I come ~ (with you)? est-ce que je peux venir

(avec vous)? 2 prep le long de; to run/walk ~ the street courir/marcher le long de la rue. ○ **all along** adv depuis le début. ○ **along with** prep ainsi que.
alongside [ə,lɒŋ'saɪd] 1 prep le long de, à côté de; [person] à côté de. 2 adv bord à bord.
aloof [ə'lu:f] 1 adj distant(e). 2 adv: to remain ~ (from) garder ses distances (vis-à-vis de).
aloud [ə'laʊd] adv à voix haute, tout haut.
alphabet ['ælfəbet] n alphabet m.
alphabetical [,ælfə'betɪkl] adj alphabétique.
Alps [ælps] npl: the ~ les Alpes fpl.
already [ɔːl'redɪ] adv déjà.
alright [,ɔːl'raɪt] = all right.
Alsatian [æl'seɪʃn] n [dog] berger m allemand.
also ['ɔːlsəʊ] adv aussi.
altar ['ɔːltə'] n autel m.
alter ['ɔːltə'] 1 vt changer, modifier. 2 vi changer.
alteration [,ɔːltə'reɪʃn] n modification f, changement m.
alternate [adj Br ɔːl'tɜːnət, Am 'ɔːltərnət, vb 'ɔːltərneɪt] 1 adj alterné(e), alternatif(ive); ~ days tous les deux jours, un jour sur deux. 2 vt faire alterner. 3 vi: to ~ (with) alterner (avec); to ~ between sthg and sthg passer de qqch à qqch.
alternately [ɔːl'tɜːnətlɪ] adv alternativement.
alternating current ['ɔːltəneɪtɪŋ-] n courant m alternatif.
alternative [ɔːl'tɜːnətɪv] 1 adj [different] autre. || [non-traditional - society] parallèle; [- art, energy] alternatif(ive). 2 n [between two solutions] alternative f. || [other possibility]: ~ (to) solution f de remplacement (à); to have no ~ but to do sthg ne pas avoir d'autre choix que de faire qqch.
alternatively [ɔːl'tɜːnətɪvlɪ] adv ou bien.
alternative medicine n médecine f parallèle OR douce.
alternator ['ɔːltəneɪtə'] n ELEC alternateur m.
although [ɔːl'ðəʊ] conj bien que (+ subjunctive).
altitude ['æltɪtjuːd] n altitude f.
alto ['æltəʊ] (pl -s) n [male voice] haute-contre f. || [female voice] contralto m.

altogether [ˌɔːltə'geðər] *adv* [completely] entièrement, tout à fait. ‖ [considering all things] tout compte fait. ‖ [in all] en tout.

aluminium *Br* [ˌæljʊ'mɪnɪəm], **aluminum** *Am* [ə'luːmɪnəm] *n* aluminium *m*.

always ['ɔːlweɪz] *adv* toujours.

am [æm] → be.

a.m. (*abbr of* **ante meridiem**): **at 3 ~** à 3h (du matin).

AM (*abbr of* **amplitude modulation**) *n* AM *f*.

amalgamate [ə'mælgəmeɪt] *vt & vi* [unite] fusionner.

amass [ə'mæs] *vt* amasser.

amateur ['æmətər] **1** *adj* amateur (*inv*); *pej* d'amateur. **2** *n* amateur *m*.

amaze [ə'meɪz] *vt* étonner, stupéfier.

amazed [ə'meɪzd] *adj* stupéfait(e).

amazement [ə'meɪzmənt] *n* stupéfaction *f*.

amazing [ə'meɪzɪŋ] *adj* [surprising] étonnant(e), ahurissant(e). ‖ [wonderful] excellent(e).

Amazon ['æməzn] *n* [river]: **the ~** l'Amazone *f*. ‖ [region]: **the ~ (Basin)** l'Amazonie *f*; **the ~ rainforest** la forêt amazonienne.

ambassador [æm'bæsədər] *n* ambassadeur *m*, -drice *f*.

amber ['æmbər] **1** *adj* [amber-coloured] ambré(e). ‖ *Br* [traffic light] orange (*inv*). **2** *n* [substance] ambre *m*.

ambiguous [æm'bɪgjʊəs] *adj* ambigu(ë).

ambition [æm'bɪʃn] *n* ambition *f*.

ambitious [æm'bɪʃəs] *adj* ambitieux(ieuse).

amble ['æmbl] *vi* déambuler.

ambulance ['æmbjʊləns] *n* ambulance *f*.

ambush ['æmbʊʃ] **1** *n* embuscade *f*. **2** *vt* tendre une embuscade à.

amenable [ə'miːnəbl] *adj*: **~ (to)** ouvert(e) (à).

amend [ə'mend] *vt* modifier; [law] amender. ○ **amends** *npl*: **to make ~s (for)** se racheter (pour).

amendment [ə'mendmənt] *n* modification *f*; [to law] amendement *m*.

amenities [ə'miːnətɪz] *npl* aménagements *mpl*, équipements *mpl*.

America [ə'merɪkə] *n* Amérique *f*; **in ~** en Amérique.

American [ə'merɪkn] **1** *adj* américain(e). **2** *n* Américain *m*, -e *f*.

American Indian *n* Indien *m*, -ienne *f* d'Amérique, Amérindien *m*, -ienne *f*.

amicable ['æmɪkəbl] *adj* amical(e).

amid(st) [ə'mɪd(st)] *prep* au milieu de, parmi.

ammonia [ə'məʊnjə] *n* [liquid] ammoniaque *f*.

ammunition [ˌæmjʊ'nɪʃn] *n* (*U*) MIL munitions *fpl*. ‖ *fig* [argument] argument *m*.

amnesia [æm'niːzjə] *n* amnésie *f*.

amnesty ['æmnəstɪ] *n* amnistie *f*.

among(st) [ə'mʌŋ(st)] *prep* parmi, entre; **~ other things** entre autres (choses).

amoral [ˌeɪ'mɒrəl] *adj* amoral(e).

amorous ['æmərəs] *adj* amoureux (euse).

amount [ə'maʊnt] *n* [quantity] quantité *f*; **a great ~ of** beaucoup de. ‖ [sum of money] somme *f*, montant *m*. ○ **amount to** *vt fus* [total] se monter à, s'élever à. ‖ [be equivalent to] revenir à, équivaloir à.

amp [æmp] *n abbr of* **ampere**.

ampere ['æmpeər] *n* ampère *m*.

amphibious [æm'fɪbɪəs] *adj* amphibie.

ample ['æmpl] *adj* [enough] suffisamment de, assez de. ‖ [large] ample.

amplifier ['æmplɪfaɪər] *n* amplificateur *m*.

amputate ['æmpjʊteɪt] *vt & vi* amputer.

Amsterdam [ˌæmstə'dæm] *n* Amsterdam.

Amtrak ['æmtræk] *n société nationale de chemins de fer aux États-Unis.*

amuse [ə'mjuːz] *vt* [make laugh] amuser, faire rire. ‖ [entertain] divertir, distraire; **to ~ o.s. (by doing sthg)** s'occuper (à faire qqch).

amused [ə'mjuːzd] *adj* [laughing] amusé(e); **to be ~ at** OR **by sthg** trouver qqch amusant. ‖ [entertained]: **to keep o.s. ~** s'occuper.

amusement [ə'mjuːzmənt] *n* [laughter] amusement *m*. ‖ [diversion, game] distraction *f*.

amusement arcade *n* galerie *f* de jeux.

amusement park *n* parc *m* d'attractions.

amusing [ə'mjuːzɪŋ] *adj* amusant(e).

an [*stressed* æn, *unstressed* ən] → **a**.

anabolic steroid [ˌænə'bɒlɪk-] *n* (stéroïde *m*) anabolisant *m*.

anaemic *Br*, **anemic** *Am* [ə'niːmɪk] *adj* anémique; *fig & pej* fade, plat(e).

anaesthetic *Br*, **anesthetic** *Am* [ˌænɪs'θetɪk] *n* anesthésique *m*; **under ~** sous anesthésie; **local/general ~** anesthésie *f* locale/générale.

analogy [ə'nælədʒɪ] *n* analogie *f*.

analyse *Br*, **analyze** *Am* ['ænəlaɪz] *vt* analyser.

analysis [ə'næləsɪs] (*pl* **analyses** [ə'næləsiːz]) *n* analyse *f*.

analyst ['ænəlɪst] *n* analyste *mf*.

analytic(al) [ˌænə'lɪtɪk(l)] *adj* analytique.

analyze *Am* = **analyse**.

anarchist ['ænəkɪst] *n* anarchiste *mf*.

anarchy ['ænəkɪ] *n* anarchie *f*.

anathema [ə'næθəmə] *n* anathème *m*.

anatomy [ə'nætəmɪ] *n* anatomie *f*.

ANC (*abbr of* **African National Congress**) *n* ANC *m*.

ancestor ['ænsestər] *n lit & fig* ancêtre *m*.

anchor ['æŋkər] **1** *n* ancre *f*; **to drop/weigh ~** jeter/lever l'ancre. **2** *vt* [secure] ancrer. ‖ TV présenter. **3** *vi* NAUT jeter l'ancre.

anchovy ['æntʃəvɪ] (*pl inv* OR **-ies**) *n* anchois *m*.

ancient ['eɪnʃənt] *adj* [monument etc] historique; [custom] ancien(ienne). ‖ *hum* [car etc] antique; [person] vieux (vieille).

ancillary [æn'sɪlərɪ] *adj* auxiliaire.

and [strong form ænd, weak form ənd, ən] *conj* [as well as, plus] et. ‖ [in numbers]: **one hundred ~ eighty** cent quatre-vingts; **six ~ a half** six et demi. ‖ [to]: **come ~ see!** venez voir!; **try ~ come** essayez de venir; **wait ~ see** vous verrez bien. ○ **and so on, and so forth** *adv* et ainsi de suite.

Andes ['ændiːz] *npl*: **the ~** les Andes *fpl*.

Andorra [æn'dɔːrə] *n* Andorre *f*.

anecdote ['ænɪkdəʊt] *n* anecdote *f*.

anemic *Am* = **anaemic**.

anesthetic *etc Am* = **anaesthetic** *etc*.

anew [ə'njuː] *adv*: **to start ~** recommencer (à zéro).

angel ['eɪndʒəl] *n* ange *m*.

anger ['æŋgər] **1** *n* colère *f*. **2** *vt* fâcher, irriter.

angina [æn'dʒaɪnə] *n* angine *f* de poitrine.

angle ['æŋgl] *n* [gen] angle *m*; **at an ~ de** travers, en biais. ‖ [point of view] point *m* de vue, angle *m*.

angler ['æŋglər] *n* pêcheur *m* (à la ligne).

Anglican ['æŋglɪkən] *adj* anglican(e).

angling ['æŋglɪŋ] *n* pêche *f* à la ligne.

angry ['æŋgrɪ] *adj* [person] en colère, fâché(e); [words, quarrel] violent(e); **to be ~ with** OR **at sb** être en colère OR fâché contre qqn; **to get ~** se mettre en colère, se fâcher.

anguish ['æŋgwɪʃ] *n* angoisse *f*.

animal ['ænɪml] *n* animal *m*; *pej* brute *f*.

animate ['ænɪmət] *adj* animé(e), vivant(e).

animated ['ænɪmeɪtɪd] *adj* animé(e).

aniseed ['ænɪsiːd] *n* anis *m*.

ankle ['æŋkl] **1** *n* cheville *f*. **2** *comp*: **~ socks** socquettes *fpl*; **~ boots** bottines *fpl*.

annex(e) ['æneks] **1** *n* [building] annexe *f*. **2** *vt* annexer.

annihilate [ə'naɪəleɪt] *vt* anéantir, annihiler.

anniversary [ˌænɪ'vɜːsərɪ] *n* anniversaire *m*.

announce [ə'naʊns] *vt* annoncer.

announcement [ə'naʊnsmənt] *n* [statement] déclaration *f*; [in newspaper] avis *m*. ‖ (*U*) [act of stating] annonce *f*.

announcer [ə'naʊnsər] *n* RADIO & TV speaker *m*, speakerine *f*.

annoy [ə'nɔɪ] *vt* agacer, contrarier.

annoyance [ə'nɔɪəns] *n* contrariété *f*.

annoyed [ə'nɔɪd] *adj* mécontent(e), agacé(e); **to get ~** se fâcher; **to be ~ at sthg** être contrarié par qqch; **to be ~ with sb** être fâché contre qqn.

annoying [ə'nɔɪɪŋ] *adj* agaçant(e).

annual ['ænjʊəl] **1** *adj* annuel(elle). **2** *n* [plant] plante *f* annuelle. ‖ [book - gen] publication *f* annuelle; [- for children] album *m*.

annual general meeting *n* assemblée *f* générale annuelle.

annul [ə'nʌl] *vt* annuler; [law] abroger.

annum ['ænəm] → **per annum**.

anomaly [ə'nɒməlɪ] *n* anomalie *f*.

anonymous [ə'nɒnɪməs] *adj* anonyme.

anorak ['ænəræk] *n* anorak *m*.

anorexia (nervosa) [ˌænə'reksɪə (nɜː'vəʊsə)] *n* anorexie *f* mentale.

anorexic [ˌænə'reksɪk] *adj* anorexique.

another [ə'nʌðər] **1** *adj* [additional]: **~ apple** encore une pomme, une pomme de plus, une autre pomme; **(would you like) ~ drink?** encore un verre? ‖ [different]: **~ job** un autre travail. **2** *pron* [additional one] un autre (une autre), encore un (encore une); **one after ~** l'un après l'autre (l'une après l'autre). || [different one] un autre (une autre); **one ~** l'un l'autre (l'une l'autre).

answer ['ɑːnsər] **1** n [gen] réponse f; **in ~ to** en réponse à. || [to problem] solution f. **2** vt répondre à; **to ~ the door** aller ouvrir la porte; **to ~ the phone** répondre au téléphone. **3** vi [reply] répondre. ○ **answer back** vi répondre. ○ **answer for** vt fus être responsable de, répondre de.

answerable ['ɑːnsərəbl] adj: **~ to sb/for sthg** responsable devant qqn/de qqch.

answering machine ['ɑːnsərɪŋ-] n répondeur m.

ant [ænt] n fourmi f.

antagonism [æn'tægənɪzm] n antagonisme m, hostilité f.

antagonize, **-ise** [æn'tægənaɪz] vt éveiller l'hostilité de.

Antarctic [æn'tɑːktɪk] **1** n: **the ~** l'Antarctique m. **2** adj antarctique.

antelope ['æntɪləʊp] (pl inv OR **-s**) n antilope f.

antenatal [,æntɪ'neɪtl] adj prénatal(e).

antenatal clinic n service m de consultation prénatale.

antenna [æn'tenə] (pl sense 1 **-nae** [-niː], pl sense 2 **-s**) n [of insect] antenne f. || Am [for TV, radio] antenne f.

anthem ['ænθəm] n hymne m.

anthology [æn'θɒlədʒɪ] n anthologie f.

antibiotic [,æntɪbaɪ'ɒtɪk] n antibiotique m.

antibody ['æntɪ,bɒdɪ] n anticorps m.

anticipate [æn'tɪsɪpeɪt] vt [expect] s'attendre à, prévoir. || [request, movement] anticiper; [competitor] prendre de l'avance sur. || [look forward to] savourer à l'avance.

anticipation [æn,tɪsɪ'peɪʃn] n [expectation] attente f; [eagerness] impatience f; **in ~ of** en prévision de.

anticlimax [,æntɪ'klaɪmæks] n déception f.

anticlockwise [,æntɪ'klɒkwaɪz] adj & adv Br dans le sens inverse des aiguilles d'une montre.

antics ['æntɪks] npl [of children, animals] gambades fpl. || pej [of politicians etc] bouffonneries fpl.

anticyclone [,æntɪ'saɪkləʊn] n anticyclone m.

antidepressant [,æntɪdɪ'presnt] n antidépresseur m.

antidote ['æntɪdəʊt] n lit & fig: **~ (to)** antidote m (contre).

antifreeze ['æntɪfriːz] n antigel m.

antihistamine [,æntɪ'hɪstəmɪn] n antihistaminique m.

antiperspirant [,æntɪ'pɜːspərənt] n déodorant m.

antiquated ['æntɪkweɪtɪd] adj dépassé(e).

antique [æn'tiːk] **1** adj ancien(ienne). **2** n [object] objet m ancien; [piece of furniture] meuble m ancien.

antique shop n magasin m d'antiquités.

anti-Semitism [,æntɪ'semɪtɪzm] n antisémitisme m.

antiseptic [,æntɪ'septɪk] n désinfectant m.

antisocial [,æntɪ'səʊʃl] adj [against society] antisocial(e). || [unsociable] peu sociable, sauvage.

antlers [,æntləz] npl bois mpl.

anus ['eɪnəs] n anus m.

anvil ['ænvɪl] n enclume f.

anxiety [æŋ'zaɪətɪ] n [worry] anxiété f. || [cause of worry] souci m.

anxious ['æŋkʃəs] adj [worried] anxieux(ieuse), très inquiet(iète); **to be ~ about** se faire du souci au sujet de. || [keen]: **to be ~ to do sthg** tenir à faire qqch; **to be ~ that** tenir à ce que (+ subjunctive).

any ['enɪ] **1** adj (with negative) de, d'; **I haven't got ~ money/tickets** je n'ai pas d'argent/de billets; **he never does ~ work** il ne travaille jamais. || [some - with sg noun] du, de l', de la; [- with pl noun] des; **have you got ~ money/milk/cousins?** est-ce que vous avez de l'argent/du lait/des cousins? || [no matter which] n'importe quel (n'importe quelle); **~ box will do** n'importe quelle boîte fera l'affaire; see also **case, day, moment, rate**. **2** pron (with negative) en; **I didn't buy ~ (of them)** je n'en ai pas acheté; **I didn't know ~ of the guests** je ne connaissais aucun des invités. || [some] en; **do you have ~?** est-ce que vous en avez? || [no matter which one or ones] n'importe lequel (n'importe laquelle); **take ~ you like** prenez n'importe lequel/laquelle, prenez celui/celle que vous voulez. **3** adv (with negative): **I can't stand it ~ longer** je ne peux plus le supporter. || [some, a little] un peu; **do you want ~ more potatoes?** voulez-vous encore des pommes de terre?; **is that ~ better/different?** est-ce que c'est mieux/différent comme ça?

anybody ['enɪ,bɒdɪ] = **anyone**.

anyhow ['enɪhaʊ] *adv* [in spite of that] quand même, néanmoins. ‖ [carelessly] n'importe comment. ‖ [in any case] de toute façon.

anyone ['enɪwʌn] *pron* (*in negative sentences*): **I didn't see ~** je n'ai vu personne. ‖ (*in questions*) quelqu'un. ‖ [any person] n'importe qui.

anyplace *Am* = **anywhere.**

anything ['enɪθɪŋ] *pron* (*in negative sentences*): **I didn't see ~** je n'ai rien vu. ‖ (*in questions*) quelque chose. ‖ [any object, event] n'importe quoi; **if ~ happens ...** s'il arrive quoi que ce soit ...

anyway ['enɪweɪ] *adv* [in any case] de toute façon.

anywhere ['enɪweəʳ], **anyplace** *Am* ['enɪpleɪs] *adv* (*in negative sentences*): **I haven't seen him ~** je ne l'ai vu nulle part. ‖ (*in questions*) quelque part. ‖ [any place] n'importe où.

apart [ə'pɑːt] *adv* [separated] séparé(e), éloigné(e). ‖ [to one side] à l'écart. ‖ [aside]: **joking ~** sans plaisanter, plaisanterie à part. ○ **apart from** *prep* [except for] à part, sauf. ‖ [as well as] en plus de, outre.

apartheid [ə'pɑːtheɪt] *n* apartheid *m.*

apartment [ə'pɑːtmənt] *n* appartement *m.*

apartment building *n Am* immeuble *m* (*d'habitation*).

apathy ['æpəθɪ] *n* apathie *f.*

ape [eɪp] **1** *n* singe *m.* **2** *vt* singer.

aperitif [əperə'tiːf] *n* apéritif *m.*

aperture ['æpə,tjʊəʳ] *n* [hole, opening] orifice *m*, ouverture *f.* ‖ PHOT ouverture *f.*

apex ['eɪpeks] (*pl* **-es** OR **apices**) *n* sommet *m.*

apices ['eɪpɪsiːz] *pl* → **apex.**

apiece [ə'piːs] *adv* [for each person] chacun(e), par personne; [for each thing] chacun(e), pièce (*inv*).

apologetic [ə,pɒlə'dʒetɪk] *adj* [letter etc] d'excuse; **to be ~ about sthg** s'excuser de qqch.

apologize, **-ise** [ə'pɒlədʒaɪz] *vi* s'excuser; **to ~ to sb (for sthg)** faire des excuses à qqn (pour qqch).

apology [ə'pɒlədʒɪ] *n* excuses *fpl.*

apostle [ə'pɒsl] *n* RELIG apôtre *m.*

apostrophe [ə'pɒstrəfɪ] *n* apostrophe *f.*

appal *Br*, **appall** *Am* [ə'pɔːl] *vt* horrifier.

appalling [ə'pɔːlɪŋ] *adj* épouvantable.

apparatus [,æpə'reɪtəs] (*pl inv* OR **-es**) *n* [device] appareil *m*, dispositif *m.* ‖ (*U*) [in gym] agrès *mpl.*

apparel [ə'pærəl] *n Am* habillement *m.*

apparent [ə'pærənt] *adj* [evident] évident(e). ‖ [seeming] apparent(e).

apparently [ə'pærəntlɪ] *adv* [it seems] à ce qu'il paraît. ‖ [seemingly] apparemment, en apparence.

appeal [ə'piːl] **1** *vi* [request]: **to ~ (to sb for sthg)** lancer un appel (à qqn pour obtenir qqch). ‖ [make a plea]: **to ~ to** faire appel à. ‖ JUR: **to ~ (against)** faire appel (de). ‖ [attract, interest]: **to ~ to sb** plaire à qqn. **2** *n* [request] appel *m.* ‖ JUR appel *m.* ‖ [charm, interest] intérêt *m*, attrait *m.*

appealing [ə'piːlɪŋ] *adj* [attractive] attirant(e), sympathique.

appear [ə'pɪəʳ] *vi* [gen] apparaître; [book] sortir, paraître. ‖ [seem] sembler, paraître; **to ~ to be/do** sembler être/faire; **it would ~ (that)** ... il semblerait que .... ‖ [in play, film etc] jouer. ‖ JUR comparaître.

appearance [ə'pɪərəns] *n* [gen] apparition *f*; **to make an ~** se montrer. ‖ [look] apparence *f*, aspect *m.*

appease [ə'piːz] *vt* apaiser.

append [ə'pend] *vt* ajouter; [signature] apposer.

appendices [ə'pendɪsiːz] *pl* → **appendix.**

appendicitis [ə,pendɪ'saɪtɪs] *n* (*U*) appendicite *f.*

appendix [ə'pendɪks] (*pl* **-dixes** OR **-dices**) *n* appendice *m*; **to have one's ~ out** OR **removed** se faire opérer de l'appendicite.

appetite ['æpɪtaɪt] *n* [for food]: **~ (for)** appétit *m* (pour). ‖ *fig* [enthusiasm]: **~ (for)** goût *m* (de OR pour).

appetizer, **-iser** ['æpɪtaɪzəʳ] *n* [food] amuse-gueule *m inv*; [drink] apéritif *m.*

appetizing, **-ising** ['æpɪtaɪzɪŋ] *adj* [food] appétissant(e).

applaud [ə'plɔːd] **1** *vt* [clap] applaudir. ‖ [approve] approuver, applaudir à. **2** *vi* applaudir.

applause [ə'plɔːz] *n* (*U*) applaudissements *mpl.*

apple ['æpl] *n* pomme *f.*

apple tree *n* pommier *m.*

appliance [ə'plaɪəns] *n* [device] appareil *m.*

applicable [ə'plɪkəbl] *adj*: **~ (to)** applicable (à).

applicant ['æplɪkənt] *n*: **~ (for)** [job]

candidat *m*, -e *f* (à); [state benefit] demandeur *m*, -euse *f* (de).

application [ˌæplɪ'keɪʃn] *n* [gen] application *f*. || [for job etc]: ~ **(for)** demande *f* (de).

application form *n* formulaire *m* de demande.

apply [ə'plaɪ] 1 *vt* appliquer. 2 *vi* [for work, grant]: **to ~ (for)** faire une demande (de); **to ~ for a job** faire une demande d'emploi; **to ~ to sb (for sthg)** s'adresser à qqn (pour obtenir qqch). || [be relevant]: **to ~ (to)** s'appliquer (à), concerner.

appoint [ə'pɔɪnt] *vt* [to job, position]: **to ~ sb (as sthg)** nommer qqn (qqch); **to ~ sb to sthg** nommer qqn à qqch. || [time, place] fixer.

appointment [ə'pɔɪntmənt] *n* [to job, position] nomination *f*, désignation *f*. || [job, position] poste *m*, emploi *m*. || [arrangement to meet] rendez-vous *m*; **to make an ~** prendre un rendez-vous.

appraisal [ə'preɪzl] *n* évaluation *f*.

appreciable [ə'priːʃəbl] *adj* [difference] sensible; [amount] appréciable.

appreciate [ə'priːʃɪeɪt] 1 *vt* [value, like] apprécier, aimer. || [recognize, understand] comprendre, se rendre compte de. || [be grateful for] être reconnaissant(e) de. 2 *vi* FIN prendre de la valeur.

appreciation [əˌpriːʃɪ'eɪʃn] *n* [liking] contentement *m*. || [understanding] compréhension *f*. || [gratitude] reconnaissance *f*.

apprehensive [ˌæprɪ'hensɪv] *adj* inquiet(iète); **to be ~ about sthg** appréhender OR craindre qqch.

apprentice [ə'prentɪs] *n* apprenti *m*, -e *f*.

apprenticeship [ə'prentɪʃɪp] *n* apprentissage *m*.

approach [ə'prəʊtʃ] 1 *n* [gen] approche *f*. || [method] démarche *f*, approche *f*. || [to person]: **to make an ~ to sb** faire une proposition à qqn. 2 *vt* [come near to - place, person, thing] s'approcher de. || [ask]: **to ~ sb about sthg** aborder qqch avec qqn; COMM entrer en contact avec qqn au sujet de qqch. || [tackle - problem] aborder. 3 *vi* s'approcher.

approachable [ə'prəʊtʃəbl] *adj* accessible.

appropriate [ə'prəʊprɪət] *adj* [clothing] convenable; [action] approprié(e); [moment] opportun(e).

approval [ə'pruːvl] *n* approbation *f*; **on ~** COMM à condition, à l'essai.

approve [ə'pruːv] 1 *vi*: **to ~ (of sthg)** approuver (qqch). 2 *vt* [ratify] approuver, ratifier.

approx. [ə'prɒks] (*abbr of* **approximately**) approx., env.

approximate [ə'prɒksɪmət] *adj* approximatif(ive).

approximately [ə'prɒksɪmətlɪ] *adv* à peu près, environ.

apricot ['eɪprɪkɒt] *n* abricot *m*.

April ['eɪprəl] *n* avril *m*; *see also* **September**.

April Fools' Day *n* le premier avril.

apron ['eɪprən] *n* [clothing] tablier *m*.

apt [æpt] *adj* [pertinent] pertinent(e), approprié(e). || [likely]: **to be ~ to do sthg** avoir tendance à faire qqch.

aptitude ['æptɪtjuːd] *n* aptitude *f*, disposition *f*; **to have an ~ for** avoir des dispositions pour.

aptly ['æptlɪ] *adv* avec justesse, à propos.

aqualung ['ækwəlʌŋ] *n* scaphandre *m* autonome.

aquarium [ə'kweərɪəm] (*pl* -**riums** OR -**ria** [-rɪə]) *n* aquarium *m*.

Aquarius [ə'kweərɪəs] *n* Verseau *m*.

aqueduct ['ækwɪdʌkt] *n* aqueduc *m*.

Arab ['ærəb] 1 *adj* arabe. 2 *n* [person] Arabe *mf*.

Arabian [ə'reɪbjən] *adj* d'Arabie, arabe.

Arabic ['ærəbɪk] 1 *adj* arabe. 2 *n* arabe *m*.

Arabic numeral *n* chiffre *m* arabe.

arable ['ærəbl] *adj* arable.

arbitrary ['ɑːbɪtrərɪ] *adj* arbitraire.

arbitration [ˌɑːbɪ'treɪʃn] *n* arbitrage *m*; **to go to ~** recourir à l'arbitrage.

arcade [ɑː'keɪd] *n* [for shopping] galerie *f* marchande. || [covered passage] arcades *fpl*.

arch [ɑːtʃ] 1 *adj* malicieux(ieuse), espiègle. 2 *n* ARCHIT arc *m*, voûte *f*. || [of foot] voûte *f* plantaire, cambrure *f*. 3 *vt* cambrer, arquer.

archaeologist [ˌɑːkɪ'ɒlədʒɪst] *n* archéologue *mf*.

archaeology [ˌɑːkɪ'ɒlədʒɪ] *n* archéologie *f*.

archaic [ɑː'keɪɪk] *adj* archaïque.

archbishop [ˌɑːtʃ'bɪʃəp] *n* archevêque *m*.

archenemy [ˌɑːtʃ'enɪmɪ] *n* ennemi *m* numéro un.

archeology *etc* [,ɑːkɪ'ɒlədʒɪ] = **ar-chaeology** *etc.*

archer ['ɑːtʃər] *n* archer *m*.

archery ['ɑːtʃərɪ] *n* tir *m* à l'arc.

archetypal [,ɑːkɪ'taɪpl] *adj* typique.

architect ['ɑːkɪtekt] *n lit & fig* architecte *m*.

architecture ['ɑːkɪtektʃər] *n* [gen & COMPUT] architecture *f*.

archives ['ɑːkaɪvz] *npl* archives *fpl*.

archway ['ɑːtʃweɪ] *n* passage *m* voûté.

Arctic ['ɑːktɪk] **1** *adj* GEOGR arctique. || *inf* [very cold] glacial(e). **2** *n*: **the ~** l'Arctique *m*.

ardent ['ɑːdənt] *adj* fervent(e), passionné(e).

arduous ['ɑːdjʊəs] *adj* ardu(e).

are [*weak form* ər, *strong form* ɑːr] → be.

area ['eərɪə] *n* [region] région *f*; **parking ~** aire de stationnement; **in the ~ of** [approximately] environ, à peu près. || [surface size] aire *f*, superficie *f*. || [of knowledge, interest etc] domaine *m*.

area code *n* indicatif *m* de zone.

aren't [ɑːnt] = **are not.**

Argentina [,ɑːdʒən'tiːnə] *n* Argentine *f*.

Argentine ['ɑːdʒəntaɪn], **Argentinian** [,ɑːdʒən'tɪnɪən] **1** *adj* argentin(ine). **2** *n* Argentin *m*, -ine *f*.

argue ['ɑːgjuː] **1** *vi* [quarrel]: **to ~ (with sb about sthg)** se disputer (avec qqn à propos de qqch). || [reason]: **to ~ (for/against)** argumenter (pour/contre). **2** *vt* [debate]: **to ~ that** soutenir OR maintenir que.

argument ['ɑːgjʊmənt] *n* [quarrel] dispute *f*; **to have an ~ (with sb)** se disputer (avec qqn). || [reason] argument *m*.

argumentative [,ɑːgjʊ'mentətɪv] *adj* querelleur(euse), batailleur(euse).

arid ['ærɪd] *adj lit & fig* aride.

Aries ['eəriːz] *n* Bélier *m*.

arise [ə'raɪz] (*pt* **arose**, *pp* **arisen** [ə'rɪzn]) *vi* [appear] surgir, survenir; **to ~ from** résulter de, provenir de; **if the need ~s** si le besoin se fait sentir.

aristocrat [*Br* 'ærɪstəkræt, *Am* ə'rɪstəkræt] *n* aristocrate *mf*.

arithmetic [ə'rɪθmətɪk] *n* arithmétique *f*.

ark [ɑːk] *n* arche *f*.

arm [ɑːm] **1** *n* [of person, chair] bras *m*; **~ in ~** bras dessus bras dessous; **to twist sb's ~** *fig* forcer la main à qqn. || [of garment] manche *f*. **2** *vt* armer. ○ **arms** *npl* armes *fpl*; **to be up in ~s about sthg** s'élever contre qqch.

armaments ['ɑːməmənts] *npl* [weapons] matériel *m* de guerre, armements *mpl*.

armchair ['ɑːmtʃeər] *n* fauteuil *m*.

armed [ɑːmd] *adj lit & fig*: **~ (with)** armé(e) (de).

armed forces *npl* forces *fpl* armées.

armhole ['ɑːmhəʊl] *n* emmanchure *f*.

armour *Br*, **armor** *Am* ['ɑːmər] *n* [for person] armure *f*.

armoured car [,ɑːməd-] *n* voiture *f* blindée.

armpit ['ɑːmpɪt] *n* aisselle *f*.

armrest ['ɑːmrest] *n* accoudoir *m*.

arms control ['ɑːmz-] *n* contrôle *m* des armements.

army ['ɑːmɪ] *n lit & fig* armée *f*.

A road *n Br* route *f* nationale.

aroma [ə'rəʊmə] *n* arôme *m*.

arose [ə'rəʊz] *pt* → arise.

around [ə'raʊnd] **1** *adv* [about, round]: **to walk ~** marcher par-ci par-là, errer; **to lie ~** [clothes etc] traîner. || [on all sides] (tout) autour. || [near] dans les parages. || [in circular movement]: **to turn ~** se retourner. || *phr*: **he has been ~** *inf* il n'est pas né d'hier, il a de l'expérience. **2** *prep* [gen] autour de; **to walk ~ a garden/ town** faire le tour d'un jardin/ d'une ville; **all ~ the country** dans tout le pays. || [near]: **~ here** par ici. || [approximately] environ, à peu près.

arouse [ə'raʊz] *vt* [excite - feeling] éveiller, susciter; [- person] exciter.

arrange [ə'reɪndʒ] *vt* [flowers, books, furniture] arranger, disposer. || [event, meeting etc] organiser, fixer; **to ~ to do sthg** convenir de faire qqch. || MUS arranger.

arrangement [ə'reɪndʒmənt] *n* [agreement] accord *m*, arrangement *m*; **to come to an ~** s'entendre, s'arranger. || [of furniture, books] arrangement *m*. || MUS arrangement *m*. ○ **arrangements** *npl* dispositions *fpl*, préparatifs *mpl*.

array [ə'reɪ] *n* [of objects] étalage *m*.

arrears [ə'rɪəz] *npl* [money owed] arriéré *m*; **to be in ~** [late] être en retard; [owing money] avoir des arriérés.

arrest [ə'rest] **1** *n* [by police] arrestation *f*; **under ~** en état d'arrestation. **2** *vt* [gen] arrêter.

arrival [ə'raɪvl] *n* [gen] arrivée *f*; **late ~** [of train etc] retard *m*. || [person - at airport, hotel] arrivant *m*, -e *f*; **new ~** [person] nouveau venu *m*, nouvelle venue *f*; [baby] nouveau-né *m*, nouveau-née *f*.

arrive [ə'raɪv] vi arriver; [baby] être né(e); **to ~ at** [conclusion, decision] arriver à.

arrogant ['ærəgənt] adj arrogant(e).

arrow ['ærəʊ] n flèche f.

arse Br [ɑːs], **ass** Am [æs] n v inf cul m.

arsenic ['ɑːsnɪk] n arsenic m.

arson ['ɑːsn] n incendie m criminel OR volontaire.

art [ɑːt] **1** n art m. **2** comp [exhibition] d'art; [college] des beaux-arts; **~ student** étudiant m, -e f d'une école des beaux-arts. ○ **arts** npl SCH & UNIV lettres fpl. ‖ [fine arts] the ~s les arts mpl.

artefact ['ɑːtɪfækt] = **artifact**.

artery ['ɑːtərɪ] n artère f.

art gallery n [public] musée m d'art; [for selling paintings] galerie f d'art.

arthritis [ɑː'θraɪtɪs] n arthrite f.

artichoke ['ɑːtɪtʃəʊk] n artichaut m.

article ['ɑːtɪkl] n article m.

articulate [ɑː'tɪkjʊlət] adj [person] qui sait s'exprimer; [speech] net (nette), distinct(e).

articulated lorry [ɑː'tɪkjʊleɪtɪd-] n Br semi-remorque m.

artifact ['ɑːtɪfækt] n objet m fabriqué.

artificial [,ɑːtɪ'fɪʃl] adj [not natural] artificiel(ielle). ‖ [insincere] affecté(e).

artillery [ɑː'tɪlərɪ] n artillerie f.

artist ['ɑːtɪst] n artiste mf.

artiste [ɑː'tiːst] n artiste mf.

artistic [ɑː'tɪstɪk] adj [person] artiste; [style etc] artistique.

as [unstressed əz, stressed æz] **1** conj [referring to time] comme, alors que; **she rang (just) ~ I was leaving** elle m'a téléphoné au moment même où OR juste comme je partais; **~ time goes by** à mesure que le temps passe, avec le temps. ‖ [referring to manner, way] comme; **do ~ I say** fais ce que je (te) dis. ‖ [introducing a statement] comme; **~ you know, ...** comme tu le sais, ... ‖ [because] comme. **2** prep [referring to function, characteristic] en, comme, en tant que; **I'm speaking ~ your friend** je te parle en ami; **she works ~ a nurse** elle est infirmière. ‖ [referring to attitude, reaction]: **it came ~ a shock** cela nous a fait un choc. **3** adv (in comparisons): **~ rich ~** aussi riche que; **~ red ~ a tomato** rouge comme une tomate; **he's ~ tall ~ I am** il est aussi grand que moi; **twice ~ big ~** deux fois plus gros que; **~ much/many ~** autant que; **much wine/many chocolates ~** autant de vin/de chocolats que. ○ **as for** prep

quant à. ○ **as from, as of** prep dès, à partir de. ○ **as if, as though** conj comme si; **it looks ~ if** OR **~ though it will rain** on dirait qu'il va pleuvoir.

a.s.a.p. (abbr of **as soon as possible**) d'urgence, dans les meilleurs délais.

asbestos [æs'bestəs] n asbeste m, amiante m.

ascend [ə'send] vt & vi monter.

ascent [ə'sent] n lit & fig ascension f.

ascertain [,æsə'teɪn] vt établir.

ascribe [ə'skraɪb] vt: **to ~ sthg to** attribuer qqch à; [blame] imputer qqch à.

ash [æʃ] n [from cigarette, fire] cendre f. ‖ [tree] frêne m.

ashamed [ə'ʃeɪmd] adj honteux(euse), confus(e); **to be ~ of** avoir honte de; **to be ~ to do sthg** avoir honte de faire qqch.

ashore [ə'ʃɔːr] adv à terre.

ashtray ['æʃtreɪ] n cendrier m.

Ash Wednesday n le mercredi des Cendres.

Asia [Br 'eɪʃə, Am 'eɪʒə] n Asie f.

Asian [Br 'eɪʃn, Am 'eɪʒn] **1** adj asiatique. **2** n [person] Asiatique mf.

aside [ə'saɪd] **1** adv [to one side] de côté; **to move ~** s'écarter; **to take sb ~** prendre qqn à part. ‖ [apart] à part; **~ from** à l'exception de. **2** n [in play] aparté m. ‖ [remark] réflexion f, commentaire m.

ask [ɑːsk] **1** vt [gen] demander; **to ~ sb sthg** demander qqch à qqn; **he ~ed me my name** il m'a demandé mon nom; **to ~ sb for sthg** demander qqch à qqn; **to ~ sb to do sthg** demander à qqn de faire qqch. ‖ [put - question] poser. ‖ [invite] inviter. **2** vi demander. ○ **ask after** vt fus demander des nouvelles de. ○ **ask for** vt fus [person] demander à voir. ‖ [thing] demander.

askew [ə'skjuː] adj [not straight] de travers.

asking price ['ɑːskɪŋ-] n prix m demandé.

asleep [ə'sliːp] adj endormi(e); **to fall ~** s'endormir.

asparagus [ə'spærəgəs] n (U) asperges fpl.

aspect ['æspekt] n [gen] aspect m. ‖ [of building] orientation f.

aspersions [ə'spɜːʃnz] npl: **to cast ~ on** jeter le discrédit sur.

asphalt ['æsfælt] n asphalte m.

asphyxiate [əs'fɪksɪeɪt] vt asphyxier.

aspiration [,æspə'reɪʃn] n aspiration f.

aspire [ə'spaɪər] vi: **to ~ to sthg/to do sthg** aspirer à qqch/à faire qqch.

at

aspirin ['æsprɪn] n aspirine f.

ass [æs] n [donkey] âne m. || Br inf [idiot] imbécile mf, idiot m, -e f. || Am v inf = **arse**.

assailant [ə'seɪlənt] n assaillant m, -e f.

assassin [ə'sæsɪn] n assassin m.

assassinate [ə'sæsɪneɪt] vt assassiner.

assassination [ə,sæsɪ'neɪʃn] n assassinat m.

assault [ə'sɔːlt] 1 n MIL: ~ (on) assaut m (de), attaque f (de). || [physical attack]: ~ (on sb) agression f (contre qqn). 2 vt [attack - physically] agresser; [- sexually] violenter.

assemble [ə'sembl] 1 vt [gather] réunir. || [fit together] assembler, monter. 2 vi se réunir, s'assembler.

assembly [ə'semblɪ] n [gen] assemblée f. || [fitting together] assemblage m.

assembly line n chaîne f de montage.

assent [ə'sent] 1 n consentement m, assentiment m. 2 vi: to ~ (to) donner son consentement OR assentiment (à).

assert [ə'sɜːt] vt [fact, belief] affirmer, soutenir. || [authority] imposer.

assertive [ə'sɜːtɪv] adj assuré(e).

assess [ə'ses] vt évaluer, estimer.

assessment [ə'sesmənt] n [opinion] opinion f. || [calculation] évaluation f, estimation f.

assessor [ə'sesər] n [of tax] contrôleur m (des impôts).

asset ['æset] n avantage m, atout m. ○ **assets** npl COMM actif m.

assign [ə'saɪn] vt [allot]: to ~ sthg (to) assigner qqch (à). || [give task to]: to ~ sb (to sthg/to do sthg) nommer qqn (à qqch/pour faire qqch).

assignment [ə'saɪnmənt] n [task] mission f; SCH devoir m. || [act of assigning] attribution f.

assimilate [ə'sɪmɪleɪt] vt assimiler.

assist [ə'sɪst] vt: to ~ sb (with sthg/in doing sthg) aider qqn (dans qqch/à faire qqch); [professionally] assister qqn (dans qqch/pour faire qqch).

assistance [ə'sɪstəns] n aide f; to be of ~ (to) être utile (à).

assistant [ə'sɪstənt] 1 n assistant m, -e f; (shop) ~ vendeur m, -euse f. 2 comp: ~ editor rédacteur en chef adjoint m, rédactrice en chef adjointe f; ~ manager sous-directeur m, -trice f.

associate [adj & n ə'səʊʃɪət, vb ə'səʊʃɪeɪt] 1 adj associé(e). 2 n associé m, -e f. 3 vt: to ~ sb/sthg (with) associer qqn/qqch (à); to be ~d with être asso-

cié(e) à. 4 vi: to ~ with sb fréquenter qqn.

association [ə,səʊsɪ'eɪʃn] n association f; in ~ with avec la collaboration de.

assorted [ə'sɔːtɪd] adj varié(e).

assortment [ə'sɔːtmənt] n mélange m.

assume [ə'sjuːm] vt [suppose] supposer, présumer. || [power, responsibility] assumer. || [appearance, attitude] adopter.

assumed name [ə'sjuːmd-] n nom m d'emprunt.

assuming [ə'sjuːmɪŋ] conj en supposant que.

assumption [ə'sʌmpʃn] n [supposition] supposition f.

assurance [ə'ʃʊərəns] n [gen] assurance f. || [promise] garantie f, promesse f.

assure [ə'ʃʊər] vt: to ~ sb (of) assurer qqn (de).

asterisk ['æstərɪsk] n astérisque m.

asthma ['æsmə] n asthme m.

astonish [ə'stɒnɪʃ] vt étonner.

astonishment [ə'stɒnɪʃmənt] n étonnement m.

astound [ə'staʊnd] vt stupéfier.

astray [ə'streɪ] adv: to go ~ [become lost] s'égarer; to lead sb ~ détourner qqn du droit chemin.

astride [ə'straɪd] prep à cheval OR califourchon sur.

astrology [ə'strɒlədʒɪ] n astrologie f.

astronaut ['æstrənɔːt] n astronaute mf.

astronomical [,æstrə'nɒmɪkl] adj astronomique.

astronomy [ə'strɒnəmɪ] n astronomie f.

astute [ə'stjuːt] adj malin(igne).

asylum [ə'saɪləm] n asile m.

at [unstressed ət, stressed æt] prep [indicating place, position] à; ~ my father's chez mon père; ~ home à la maison, chez soi; ~ school à l'école; ~ work au travail. || [indicating direction] vers; to look ~ sb regarder qqn; to smile ~ sb sourire à qqn. || [indicating a particular time] à; ~ midnight/noon/eleven o'clock à minuit/midi/onze heures; ~ night la nuit. || [indicating age, speed, rate] à; ~ 52 (years of age) à 52 ans; ~ 100 mph à 160 km/h. || [indicating price]: ~ £50 a pair 50 livres la paire. || [indicating particular state, condition] en; ~ peace/war en paix/guerre; to be ~ lunch/dinner être en train de déjeuner/dîner. || (after adjectives): amused/appalled/puzzled ~ sthg diverti/effaré/intrigué par qqch; delighted ~ sthg ravi de qqch; to be bad/good ~ sthg être mauvais/bon en qqch. ○ **at all** adv (with *negative*): **not ~ all** [when thanked] je vous en prie; [when answering a question] pas du tout; **she's not ~ all happy** elle n'est pas du tout contente. || [in the slightest]: **anything ~ all will do** n'importe quoi fera l'affaire; **do you know her ~ all?** est-ce que vous la connaissez?

ate [*Br* et, *Am* eɪt] *pt* → eat.

atheist [ˈeɪθɪɪst] *n* athée *mf*.

Athens [ˈæθɪnz] *n* Athènes.

athlete [ˈæθliːt] *n* athlète *mf*.

athletic [æθˈletɪk] *adj* athlétique. ○ **athletics** *npl* athlétisme *m*.

Atlantic [ətˈlæntɪk] -*n*: **the ~** (Ocean) l'océan *m* Atlantique, l'Atlantique *m*.

atlas [ˈætləs] *n* atlas *m*.

atmosphere [ˈætmə,sfɪə*r*] *n* atmosphère *f*.

atmospheric [,ætməsˈferɪk] *adj* [pressure, pollution etc] atmosphérique. || [film, music etc] d'ambiance.

atom [ˈætəm] *n* TECH atome *m*.

atom bomb *n* bombe *f* atomique.

atomic [əˈtɒmɪk] *adj* atomique.

atomic bomb = atom bomb.

atomizer, **-iser** [ˈætəmaɪzə*r*] *n* atomiseur *m*, vaporisateur *m*.

atone [əˈtəʊn] *vi*: **to ~ for** racheter.

A to Z *n* plan *m* de ville.

atrocious [əˈtrəʊʃəs] *adj* [very bad] atroce, affreux(euse).

atrocity [əˈtrɒsətɪ] *n* [terrible act] atrocité *f*.

attach [əˈtætʃ] *vt* [gen]: **to ~ sthg (to)** attacher qqch (à). || [letter etc] joindre.

attaché case [əˈtæʃeɪ-] *n* attaché-case *m*.

attached [əˈtætʃt] *adj* [fond]: **~ to** attaché(e) à.

attachment [əˈtætʃmənt] *n* [device] accessoire *m*. || [fondness]: **~ (to)** attachement *m* (à).

attack [əˈtæk] **1** *n* [physical, verbal]: **~ (on)** attaque *f* (contre). || [of illness] crise *f*. **2** *vt* [gen] attaquer. || [job, problem] s'attaquer à. **3** *vi* attaquer.

attacker [əˈtækə*r*] *n* [assailant] agresseur *m*. || SPORT attaquant *m*, -*e f*.

attain [əˈteɪn] *vt* atteindre, parvenir à.

attempt [əˈtempt] **1** *n*: **~ (at)** tentative *f* (de); **~ on sb's life** tentative d'assassinat. **2** *vt* tenter, essayer; **to ~ to do sthg** essayer OR tenter de faire qqch.

attend [əˈtend] **1** *vt* [meeting, party] assister à. || [school, church] aller à. || [be present] être présent(e). || [pay attention]: **to ~ (to)** prêter attention (à). ○ **attend**

to *vt fus* [deal with] s'occuper de, régler. || [look after - customer] s'occuper de; [- patient] soigner.

attendance [əˈtendəns] *n* [number present] assistance *f*, public *m*. || [presence] présence *f*.

attendant [əˈtendənt] *n* [at museum, car park] gardien *m*, -ienne *f*; [at petrol station] pompiste *mf*.

attention [əˈtenʃn] **1** *n* (*U*) [gen] attention *f*; **to bring sthg to sb's ~**, **to draw sb's ~ to sthg** attirer l'attention de qqn sur qqch; **to attract** OR **catch sb's ~** attirer l'attention de qqn; **to pay ~ to** prêter attention à; **for the ~ of** COMM à l'attention de. || [care] soins *mpl*, attentions *fpl*. **2** *excl* MIL garde-à-vous!

attentive [əˈtentɪv] *adj* attentif(ive).

attic [ˈætɪk] *n* grenier *m*.

attitude [ˈætɪtjuːd] *n* [gen]: **~ (to** OR **towards)** attitude *f* (envers). || [posture] pose *f*.

attn. (*abbr of* **for the attention of**) à l'attention de.

attorney [əˈtɜːnɪ] *n Am* avocat *m*, -*e f*.

attorney general (*pl* **attorneys general**) *n* ministre *m* de la Justice.

attract [əˈtrækt] *vt* attirer.

attraction [əˈtrækʃn] *n* [gen] attraction *f*; **~ to sb** attirance *f* envers qqn. || [of thing] attrait *m*.

attractive [əˈtræktɪv] *adj* [person] attirant(e), séduisant(e); [thing, idea] attrayant(e), séduisant.

attribute [*vb* əˈtrɪbjuːt, *n* ˈætrɪbjuːt] **1** *vt*: **to ~ sthg to** attribuer qqch à. **2** *n* attribut *m*.

auburn [ˈɔːbən] *adj* auburn (*inv*).

auction [ˈɔːkʃn] **1** *n* vente *f* aux enchères; **at** OR **by ~** vente *f* aux enchères, aux enchères. ○ **auction off** *vt sep* vendre aux enchères.

auctioneer [,ɔːkʃəˈnɪə*r*] *n* commissaire-priseur *m*.

audacious [ɔːˈdeɪʃəs] *adj* audacieux(ieuse).

audible [ˈɔːdəbl] *adj* audible.

audience [ˈɔːdjəns] *n* [of play, film] public *m*, spectateurs *mpl*; [of TV programme] téléspectateurs *mpl*. || [formal meeting] audience *f*.

audio-visual [,ɔːdɪəʊ-] *adj* audiovisuel(elle).

audit [ˈɔːdɪt] **1** *n* audit *m*, vérification *f* des comptes. **2** *vt* vérifier, apurer.

audition [ɔːˈdɪʃn] *n* THEATRE audition *f*; CINEMA bout *m* d'essai.

auditor ['ɔːdɪtər] *n* auditeur *m*, -trice *f*.

auditorium [,ɔːdɪ'tɔːrɪəm] (*pl* -riums OR -ria [-rɪə]) *n* salle *f*.

augur ['ɔːgər] *vi*: **to ~ well/badly** être de bon/mauvais augure.

August ['ɔːgəst] *n* août *m*; *see also* September.

Auld Lang Syne [,ɔːldlæŋ'saɪn] *n* chant traditionnel britannique correspondant à «ce n'est qu'un au revoir, mes frères».

aunt [ɑːnt] *n* tante *f*.

auntie, aunty ['ɑːntɪ] *n inf* tata *f*, tantine *f*.

au pair [,əʊ'peər] *n* jeune fille *f* au pair.

aura ['ɔːrə] *n* atmosphère *f*.

aural ['ɔːrəl] *adj* auditif(ive).

auspices ['ɔːspɪsɪz] *npl*: **under the ~ of** sous les auspices de.

auspicious [ɔː'spɪʃəs] *adj* prometteur(euse).

austere [ɒ'stɪər] *adj* austère.

austerity [ɒ'sterətɪ] *n* austérité *f*.

Australia [ɒ'streɪljə] *n* Australie *f*.

Australian [ɒ'streɪljən] **1** *adj* australien(ienne). **2** *n* Australien *m*, -ienne *f*.

Austria ['ɒstrɪə] *n* Autriche *f*.

Austrian ['ɒstrɪən] **1** *adj* autrichien(ienne). **2** *n* Autrichien *m*, -ienne *f*.

authentic [ɔː'θentɪk] *adj* authentique.

author ['ɔːθər] *n* auteur *m*.

authoritarian [ɔː,θɒrɪ'teərɪən] *adj* autoritaire.

authoritative [ɔː'θɒrɪtətɪv] *adj* [person, voice] autoritaire. || [study] qui fait autorité.

authority [ɔː'θɒrətɪ] *n* [organization, power] autorité *f*; **to be in ~** être le/la responsable. || [permission] autorisation *f*. || [expert]: **~ (on sthg)** expert *m*, -e *f* (en qqch). ○ **authorities** *npl*: **the authorities** les autorités *fpl*.

authorize, -ise ['ɔːθəraɪz] *vt*: **to ~ sb (to do sthg)** autoriser qqn (à faire qqch).

autistic [ɔː'tɪstɪk] *adj* [child] autiste; [behaviour] autistique.

auto ['ɔːtəʊ] (*pl* -s) *n Am* auto *f*, voiture *f*.

autobiography [,ɔːtəbaɪ'ɒgrəfɪ] *n* autobiographie *f*.

autograph ['ɔːtəɡrɑːf] **1** *n* autographe *m*. **2** *vt* signer.

automatic [,ɔːtə'mætɪk] **1** *adj* [gen] automatique. **2** *n* [car] voiture *f* à transmission automatique. || [gun] automatique *m*. || [washing machine] lave-linge *m* automatique.

automatically [,ɔːtə'mætɪklɪ] *adv* [gen] automatiquement.

automation [,ɔːtə'meɪʃn] *n* automatisation *f*, automation *f*.

automobile ['ɔːtəməbiːl] *n Am* automobile *f*.

autonomy [ɔː'tɒnəmɪ] *n* autonomie *f*.

autopsy ['ɔːtɒpsɪ] *n* autopsie *f*.

autumn ['ɔːtəm] *n* automne *m*.

auxiliary [ɔːg'zɪljərɪ] **1** *adj* auxiliaire. **2** *n* auxiliaire *mf*.

Av. (*abbr of* avenue) av.

available [ə'veɪləbl] *adj* disponible.

avalanche ['ævəlɑːnʃ] *n lit & fig* avalanche *f*.

avarice ['ævərɪs] *n* avarice *f*.

Ave. (*abbr of* avenue) av.

avenge [ə'vendʒ] *vt* venger.

avenue ['ævənjuː] *n* avenue *f*.

average ['ævərɪdʒ] **1** *adj* moyen(enne). **2** *n* moyenne *f*; **on ~** en moyenne. **3** *vt*: the cars were averaging 90 mph = les voitures roulaient en moyenne à 150 km/h.

aversion [ə'vɜːʃn] *n*: **~ (to)** aversion *f* (pour).

avert [ə'vɜːt] *vt* [avoid] écarter; [accident] empêcher. || [eyes, glance] détourner.

avid ['ævɪd] *adj*: **~ (for)** avide (de).

avocado [,ævə'kɑːdəʊ] (*pl* -s OR -es) *n*: **~ (pear)** avocat *m*.

avoid [ə'vɔɪd] *vt* éviter; **to ~ doing sthg** éviter de faire qqch.

avoidance [ə'vɔɪdəns] *n* → **tax avoidance**.

await [ə'weɪt] *vt* attendre.

awake [ə'weɪk] (*pt* **awoke** OR **awaked**, *pp* **awoken**) **1** *adj* [not sleeping] réveillé(e); **are you ~?** tu dors? **2** *vt* [wake up] réveiller. || *fig* [feeling] éveiller. **3** *vi* [wake up] se réveiller. || *fig* [feeling] s'éveiller.

awakening [ə'weɪknɪŋ] *n* [from sleep] réveil *m*. || *fig* [of feeling] éveil *m*.

award [ə'wɔːd] **1** *n* [prize] prix *m*. **2** *vt*: **to ~ sb sthg, to ~ sthg to sb** [prize] décerner qqch à qqn; [compensation, free kick] accorder qqch à qqn.

aware [ə'weər] *adj*: **to be ~ of sthg** se rendre compte de qqch, être conscient(e) de qqch; **to be ~ that** se rendre compte que, être conscient que.

awareness [ə'weənɪs] *n* (*U*) conscience *f*.

away [ə'weɪ] **1** *adv* [in opposite direction]: **to move** OR **walk ~ (from)** s'éloigner (de); **to look ~** détourner le regard; **to turn ~** se détourner. || [in distance]: **we**

live 4 miles ~ (from here) nous habitons à 6 kilomètres (d'ici). ‖ [in time]: **the elections are a month ~** les élections se dérouleront dans un mois. ‖ [absent] absent(e); **she's ~ on holiday** elle est partie en vacances. ‖ [in safe place]: **to put sthg ~** ranger qqch. ‖ [so as to be gone or used up]: **to fade ~** disparaître; **to give sthg ~** donner qqch, faire don de qqch; **to take sthg ~** emporter qqch. ‖ [continuously]: **to be working ~** travailler sans arrêt. **2** *adj* SPORT [team, fans] de l'équipe des visiteurs; **~ game** match *m* à l'extérieur.

awe [ɔ:] *n* respect *m* mêlé de crainte; **to be in ~ of sb** être impressionné par qqn.

awesome ['ɔ:səm] *adj* impressionnant(e).

awful ['ɔ:ful] *adj* [terrible] affreux (euse). ‖ *inf* [very great]: **an ~ lot (of)** énormément (de).

awfully ['ɔ:flɪ] *adv inf* [bad, difficult] affreusement; [nice, good] extrêmement.

awkward ['ɔ:kwəd] *adj* [clumsy] gauche, maladroit(e). ‖ [embarrassed] mal à l'aise, gêné(e). ‖ [difficult - person, problem, task] difficile. ‖ [inconvenient] incommode. ‖ [embarrassing] embarrassant(e), gênant(e).

awning ['ɔ:nɪŋ] *n* [of tent] auvent *m*. ‖ [of shop] banne *f*.

awoke [ə'wəuk] *pt* → awake.

awoken [ə'wəukn] *pp* → awake.

axe *Br*, **ax** *Am* [æks] **1** *n* hache *f*. **2** *vt* [project] abandonner; [jobs] supprimer.

axes ['æksi:z] *pl* → axis.

axis ['æksɪs] (*pl* **axes**) *n* axe *m*.

axle ['æksl] *n* essieu *m*.

B

b (*pl* **b's** OR **bs**), **B** (*pl* **B's** OR **Bs**) [bi:] *n* [letter] b *m inv*, B *m inv*. ○ **B** *n* MUS si *m*. ‖ SCH [mark] B *m inv*.

BA *n abbr of* **Bachelor of Arts**.

babble ['bæbl] **1** *n* [of voices] murmure *m*, rumeur *f*. **2** *vi* [person] babiller.

baboon [bə'bu:n] *n* babouin *m*.

baby ['beɪbɪ] *n* [child] bébé *m*. ‖ *inf* [darling] chéri *m*, -e *f*.

baby buggy *n* *Br* [foldable pushchair] poussette *f*. ‖ *Am* = **baby carriage**.

baby carriage *n* *Am* landau *m*.

baby-sit *vi* faire du baby-sitting.

baby-sitter [-,sɪtər] *n* baby-sitter *mf*.

bachelor ['bætʃələr] *n* célibataire *m*.

Bachelor of Arts *n* licencié *m*, -e *f* en OR ès Lettres.

Bachelor of Science *n* licencié *m*, -e *f* en OR ès Sciences.

back [bæk] **1** *adv* [backwards] en arrière; **to step/move ~** reculer; **to push ~** repousser. ‖ [to former position or state]: **I'd like my money ~** [in shop] je voudrais me faire rembourser; **to go ~** retourner; **to come ~** revenir, rentrer; **to go ~ to sleep** se rendormir; **to be ~ (in fashion)** revenir à la mode. ‖ [in time]: **to think ~ (to)** se souvenir (de). ‖ [in return]: **to phone** OR **call ~** rappeler. **2** *n* [of person, animal] dos *m*; **behind sb's ~** *fig* derrière le dos de qqn. ‖ [of door, book, hand] dos *m*; [of head] derrière *m*; [of envelope, cheque] revers *m*; [of page] verso *m*; [of chair] dossier *m*. ‖ [of room, fridge] fond *m*; [of car] arrière *m*. ‖ SPORT arrière *m*. **3** *adj* (*in compounds*) [at the back] de derrière; [seat, wheel] arrière (*inv*); [page] dernier(ière). ‖ [overdue]: **~ rent** arriéré *m* de loyer. **4** *vt* [reverse] reculer. ‖ [support] appuyer, soutenir. ‖ [bet on] parier sur, miser sur. **5** *vi* reculer. ○ **back to back** *adv* [stand] dos à dos. ‖ [happen] l'un après l'autre. ○ **back to front** *adv* à l'envers. ○ **back down** *vi* céder. ○ **back out** *vi* [of promise etc] se dédire.

bail

○ **back up 1** *vt sep* [support - claim] appuyer, soutenir; [- person] épauler, soutenir. || [reverse] reculer. || COMPUT sauvegarder, faire une copie de sauvegarde de. **2** *vi* [reverse] reculer.

backache ['bækeɪk] *n*: **to have ~** avoir mal aux reins OR au dos.

backbone ['bækbəʊn] *n* épine *f* dorsale, colonne *f* vertébrale; *fig* [main support] pivot *m*.

backdate [,bæk'deɪt] *vt* antidater.

back door *n* porte *f* de derrière.

backdrop ['bækdrɒp] *n* *lit* & *fig* toile *f* de fond.

backfire [,bæk'faɪər] *vi* AUT pétarader. || [plan]: **to ~ (on sb)** se retourner (contre qqn).

backgammon ['bæk,gæmən] *n* backgammon *m*, ≃ jacquet *m*.

background ['bækgraʊnd] *n* [in picture, view] arrière-plan *m*; **in the ~** dans le fond, à l'arrière-plan; *fig* au second plan. || [of event, situation] contexte *m*. || [upbringing] milieu *m*.

backhand ['bækhænd] *n* revers *m*.

backing ['bækɪŋ] *n* [support] soutien *m*. || [lining] doublage *m*.

backlash ['bæklæʃ] *n* contrecoup *m*, choc *m* en retour.

backlog ['bæklɒg] *n*: **~ (of work)** arriéré *m* de travail, travail *m* en retard.

back number *n* vieux numéro *m*.

backpack ['bækpæk] *n* sac *m* à dos.

back pay *n* rappel *m* de salaire.

back seat *n* [in car] siège *m* OR banquette *f* arrière; **to take a ~** *fig* jouer un rôle secondaire.

backside [,bæk'saɪd] *n* *inf* postérieur *m*, derrière *m*.

backstage [,bæk'steɪdʒ] *adv* dans les coulisses.

back street *n* petite rue *f*.

backstroke ['bækstrəʊk] *n* dos *m* crawlé.

backup ['bækʌp] **1** *adj* [plan, team] de secours, de remplacement. **2** *n* [gen] aide *f*, soutien *m*. || COMPUT (copie *f* de) sauvegarde *f*.

backward ['bækwəd] **1** *adj* [movement, look] en arrière. || [country] arriéré(e); [person] arriéré, attardé(e). **2** *adv* *Am* = **backwards**.

backwards ['bækwədz], **backward** *Am adv* [move, go] en arrière, à reculons; [read list] à rebours, à l'envers; **~ and forwards** [movement] de va-et-vient,

d'avant en arrière et d'arrière en avant; **to walk ~ and forwards** aller et venir.

backwater ['bæk,wɔːtər] *n* *fig* désert *m*.

backyard [,bæk'jɑːd] *n* *Br* [yard] arrière-cour *f*. || *Am* [garden] jardin *m* de derrière.

bacon ['beɪkən] *n* bacon *m*.

bacteria [bæk'tɪərɪə] *npl* bactéries *fpl*.

bad [bæd] (*compar* **worse**, *superl* **worst**) **1** *adj* [not good] mauvais(e); **to be ~ at sthg** être mauvais en qqch; **too ~!** dommage!; **not ~** pas mal. || [unhealthy] malade; **smoking is ~ for you** fumer est mauvais pour la santé; **I'm feeling ~** je ne suis pas dans mon assiette. || [serious]: **a ~ cold** un gros rhume. || [rotten] pourri(e), gâté(e); **to go ~** se gâter, s'avarier. || [guilty]: **to feel ~ about sthg** se sentir coupable de qqch. || [naughty] méchant(e). **2** *adv* *Am* = **badly**.

badge [bædʒ] *n* [metal, plastic] badge *m*. || [sewn-on] écusson *m*.

badger ['bædʒər] **1** *n* blaireau *m*. **2** *vt*: **to ~ sb (to do sthg)** harceler qqn (pour qu'il fasse qqch).

badly ['bædlɪ] (*compar* **worse**, *superl* **worst**) *adv* [not well] mal. || [seriously - wounded] grièvement; [- affected] gravement, sérieusement; **to be ~ in need of sthg** avoir vraiment OR absolument besoin de qqch.

badly-off *adj* [poor] pauvre, dans le besoin.

bad-mannered [-'mænəd] *adj* [child] mal élevé(e); [shop assistant] impoli(e).

badminton ['bædmɪntən] *n* badminton *m*.

bad-tempered [-'tempəd] *adj* [by nature] qui a mauvais caractère. || [in a bad mood] de mauvaise humeur.

baffle ['bæfl] *vt* déconcerter, confondre.

bag [bæg] *n* [gen] sac *m*; **to pack one's ~s** *fig* plier bagage. || [handbag] sac *m* à main. ○ **bags** *npl* [under eyes] poches *fpl*. || *inf* [lots]: **~s of** plein OR beaucoup de.

bagel ['beɪgəl] *n* petit pain *m* en couronne.

baggage ['bægɪdʒ] *n* (*U*) bagages *mpl*.

baggage reclaim *n* retrait *m* des bagages.

baggy ['bægɪ] *adj* ample.

bagpipes ['bægpaɪps] *npl* cornemuse *f*.

Bahamas [bə'hɑːməz] *npl*: **the ~** les Bahamas *fpl*.

bail [beɪl] *n* (*U*) caution *f*; **on ~** sous caution. ○ **bail out 1** *vt sep* [pay bail for] se porter garant de. || *fig* [rescue] tirer d'affaire. **2** *vi* [from plane] sauter (en parachute).

bailiff ['beɪlɪf] *n* huissier *m*.

bait [beɪt] **1** *n* appât *m*. **2** *vt* [put bait on] appâter. ‖ [tease] tourmenter.

bake [beɪk] **1** *vt* CULIN faire cuire au four. ‖ [clay, bricks] cuire. **2** *vi* [food] cuire au four.

baked beans [beɪkt-] *npl* haricots *mpl* blancs à la tomate.

baked potato [beɪkt-] *n* pomme *f* de terre en robe de chambre.

baker ['beɪkə*r*] *n* boulanger *m*, -ère *f*; ~'s (**shop**) boulangerie *f*.

bakery ['beɪkərɪ] *n* boulangerie *f*.

baking ['beɪkɪŋ] *n* cuisson *f*.

balance ['bæləns] **1** *n* [equilibrium] équilibre *m*; **to keep/lose one's** ~ garder/perdre l'équilibre; **off** ~ déséquilibré(e). ‖ *fig* [counterweight] contrepoids *m*; [of evidence] poids *m*, force *f*. ‖ FIN solde *m*. **2** *vt* [keep in balance] maintenir en équilibre. ‖ [compare]: **to** ~ **sthg against sthg** mettre qqch et qqch en balance. ‖ [in accounting]: **to** ~ **a budget** équilibrer un budget; **to** ~ **the books** clôturer les comptes, dresser le bilan. **3** *vi* [maintain equilibrium] se tenir en équilibre. ‖ [budget, accounts] s'équilibrer. ○ **on balance** *adv* tout bien considéré.

balance of payments *n* balance *f* des paiements.

balance of trade *n* balance *f* commerciale.

balance sheet *n* bilan *m*.

balcony ['bælkənɪ] *n* balcon *m*.

bald [bɔːld] *adj* [head, man] chauve. ‖ [tyre] lisse. ‖ *fig* [blunt] direct(e).

bale [beɪl] *n* balle *f*. ○ **bale out** *Br* **1** *vt sep* [boat] écoper, vider. **2** *vi* [from plane] sauter en parachute.

Balearic Islands [ˌbælɪˈærɪk-], **Balearics** [ˌbælɪˈærɪks] *npl*: **the** ~ les Baléares *fpl*.

balk [bɔːk] *vi*: **to** ~ (**at**) hésiter OR reculer (devant).

Balkans ['bɔːlkənz], **Balkan States** ['bɔːlkən-] *npl*: **the** ~ les Balkans *mpl*, les États *mpl* balkaniques.

ball [bɔːl] *n* [round shape] boule *f*; [in game] balle *f*; [football] ballon *m*; **to be on the** ~ *fig* connaître son affaire, s'y connaître. ‖ [of foot] plante *f*. ‖ [dance] bal *m*. ○ **balls** *v inf* **1** *npl* [testicles] couilles *fpl*. **2** *n* (*U*) [nonsense] conneries *fpl*.

ballad ['bæləd] *n* ballade *f*.

ballast ['bæləst] *n* lest *m*.

ball bearing *n* roulement *m* à billes.

ball boy *n* ramasseur *m* de balles.

ballerina [ˌbæləˈriːnə] *n* ballerine *f*.

ballet ['bæleɪ] *n* (*U*) [art of dance] danse *f*. ‖ [work] ballet *m*.

ballet dancer *n* danseur *m*, -euse *f* de ballet.

ball game *n Am* [baseball match] match *m* de base-ball. ‖ *inf* [situation]: **it's a whole new** ~ c'est une autre paire de manches.

balloon [bəˈluːn] *n* [gen] ballon *m*. ‖ [in cartoon] bulle *f*.

ballot ['bælət] **1** *n* [voting paper] bulletin *m* de vote. ‖ [voting process] scrutin *m*. **2** *vt* appeler à voter.

ballot box *n* [container] urne *f*. ‖ [voting process] scrutin *m*.

ballot paper *n* bulletin *m* de vote.

ball park *n Am* terrain *m* de base-ball.

ballpoint (pen) ['bɔːlpɔɪnt-] *n* stylo *m* à bille.

ballroom ['bɔːlrʊm] *n* salle *f* de bal.

ballroom dancing *n* (*U*) danse *f* de salon.

balmy ['bɑːmɪ] *adj* doux (douce).

balsa(wood) ['bɒlsə(wʊd)] *n* balsa *m*.

Baltic ['bɔːltɪk] **1** *adj* [port, coast] de la Baltique. **2** *n*: **the** ~ (**Sea**) la Baltique.

Baltic Republic *n*: **the** ~s les républiques *fpl* baltes.

bamboo [bæmˈbuː] *n* bambou *m*.

bamboozle [bæmˈbuːzl] *vt inf* embobiner.

ban [bæn] **1** *n* interdiction *f*. **2** *vt* interdire; **to** ~ **sb from doing sthg** interdire à qqn de faire qqch.

banal [bəˈnɑːl] *adj pej* banal(e), ordinaire.

banana [bəˈnɑːnə] *n* banane *f*.

band [bænd] *n* [MUS - rock] groupe *m*; [- military] fanfare *f*; [- jazz] orchestre *m*. ‖ [group, strip] bande *f*. ‖ [stripe] rayure *f*. ‖ [range] tranche *f*. ○ **band together** *vi* s'unir.

bandage ['bændɪdʒ] **1** *n* bandage *m*, bande *f*. **2** *vt* mettre un pansement OR un bandage sur.

Band-Aid® *n* pansement *m* adhésif.

b and b, B and B *n abbr of* **bed and breakfast**.

bandit ['bændɪt] *n* bandit *m*.

bandstand ['bændstænd] *n* kiosque *m* à musique.

bandwagon ['bændwægən] *n*: **to jump on the** ~ suivre le mouvement.

bandy ['bændɪ] *adj* qui a les jambes arquées. ○ **bandy about**, **bandy around** *vt sep* répandre, faire circuler.

bandy-legged [-,legd] *adj* = **bandy**.

bang [bæŋ] **1** *adv* [exactly]: ~ **in the middle** en plein milieu; **to be ~ on time** être pile à l'heure. **2** *n* [blow] coup *m* violent. || [of gun etc] détonation *f*; [of door] claquement *m*. **3** *vt* frapper violemment; [door] claquer; **to ~ one's head/knee** se cogner la tête/le genou. **4** *vi* [knock]: **to ~ on** frapper à. || [make a loud noise - gun etc] détoner; [- door] claquer. || [crash]: **to ~ into** se cogner contre. **5** *excl* boum! ○ **bangs** *npl Am* frange *f*.

bangle ['bæŋgl] *n* bracelet *m*.

banish ['bænɪʃ] *vt* bannir.

banister ['bænɪstər] *n*, **banisters** ['bænɪstəz] *npl* rampe *f*.

bank [bæŋk] **1** *n* FIN & *fig* banque *f*. || [of river, lake] rive *f*, bord *m*. || [of earth] talus *m*. **2** *vt* FIN mettre OR déposer à la banque. **3** *vi* FIN: **to ~ with** avoir un compte à. || [plane] tourner. ○ **bank on** *vt fus* compter sur.

bank account *n* compte *m* en banque.

bank balance *n* solde *m* bancaire.

bank charges *npl* frais *mpl* bancaires.

bank draft *n* traite *f* bancaire.

banker ['bæŋkər] *n* banquier *m*.

bank holiday *n Br* jour *m* férié.

bank manager *n* directeur *m* de banque.

bank note *n* billet *m* de banque.

bank rate *n* taux *m* d'escompte.

bankrupt ['bæŋkrʌpt] *adj* failli(e); **to go ~** faire faillite.

bankruptcy ['bæŋkrəptsɪ] *n* [gen] faillite *f*.

bank statement *n* relevé *m* de compte.

banner ['bænər] *n* banderole *f*.

bannister(s) ['bænɪstə(z)] = **banister(s)**.

banquet ['bæŋkwɪt] *n* banquet *m*.

banter ['bæntər] *n* (U) plaisanterie *f*, badinage *m*.

baptism ['bæptɪzm] *n* baptême *m*.

Baptist ['bæptɪst] *n* baptiste *mf*.

baptize, -ise [*Br* bæp'taɪz, *Am* 'bæptaɪz] *vt* baptiser.

bar [baːr] **1** *n* [piece - of gold] lingot *m*; [- of chocolate] tablette *f*; **a ~ of soap** une savonnette. || [length of wood, metal] barre *f*; **to be behind ~s** être derrière les barreaux OR sous les verrous. || *fig* [obstacle] obstacle *m*. || [pub] bar *m*. || [counter of pub] comptoir *m*, zinc *m*. || MUS mesure *f*. **2** *vt* [door, road] barrer; [window] mettre des barreaux à; **to ~ sb's way** barrer la route OR le passage à qqn. || [ban] interdire, défendre; **to ~ sb (from)** interdire à qqn (de). **3** *prep* sauf, excepté; **~ none** sans exception. ○ **Bar** *n* JUR: **the Bar** *Br* le barreau; *Am* les avocats *mpl*.

barbaric [baː'bærɪk] *adj* barbare.

barbecue ['baːbɪkjuː] *n* barbecue *m*.

barbed wire [baːbd-] *n* (U) fil *m* de fer barbelé.

barber ['baːbər] *n* coiffeur *m* (pour hommes); **~'s (shop)** salon *m* de coiffure (pour hommes); **to go to the ~'s** aller chez le coiffeur.

barbiturate [baː'bɪtjʊrət] *n* barbiturique *m*.

bar code *n* code *m* (à) barres.

bare [beər] **1** *adj* [feet, arms etc] nu(e); [trees, hills etc] dénudé(e). || [absolute, minimum]: **the ~ facts** les simples faits; **the ~ minimum** le strict minimum. || [empty] vide. **2** *vt* découvrir; **to ~ one's teeth** montrer les dents.

bareback ['beəbæk] *adv* à cru, à nu.

barefoot(ed) [,beə'fʊt(ɪd)] **1** *adj* aux pieds nus. **2** *adv* nu-pieds, pieds nus.

barely ['beəlɪ] *adv* [scarcely] à peine, tout juste.

bargain ['baːgɪn] **1** *n* [agreement] marché *m*; **into the ~** en plus, par-dessus le marché. || [good buy] affaire *f*, occasion *f*. **2** *vi* négocier; **to ~ with sb for sthg** négocier qqch avec qqn. ○ **bargain for**, **bargain on** *vt fus* compter sur, prévoir.

barge [baːdʒ] **1** *n* péniche *f*. **2** *vi inf*: **to ~ past sb** bousculer qqn. ○ **barge in** *vi inf*: **to ~ in (on)** interrompre.

baritone ['bærɪtəʊn] *n* baryton *m*.

bark [baːk] **1** *n* [of dog] aboiement *m*. || [on tree] écorce *f*. **2** *vi* [dog]: **to ~ (at)** aboyer (après).

barley ['baːlɪ] *n* orge *f*.

barmaid ['baːmeɪd] *n* barmaid *f*, serveuse *f* de bar.

barman ['baːmən] (*pl* -men [-mən]) *n* barman *m*, serveur *m* de bar.

barn [baːn] *n* grange *f*.

barometer [bə'rɒmɪtər] *n lit* & *fig* baromètre *m*.

baron ['bærən] *n* baron *m*.

baroness ['bærənɪs] *n* baronne *f*.

barrack ['bærək] *vt Br* huer, conspuer. ○ **barracks** *npl* caserne *f*.

barrage ['bæraːʒ] *n* [of firing] barrage

m. || [of questions etc] avalanche *f,* déluge *m.*

barrel ['bærəl] *n* [for beer, wine] tonneau *m,* fût *m.* || [for oil] baril *m.* || [of gun] canon *m.*

barren ['bærən] *adj* stérile.

barricade [,bærɪ'keɪd] *n* barricade *f.*

barrier ['bærɪə'] *n lit & fig* barrière *f.*

barring ['bɑːrɪŋ] *prep* sauf.

barrister ['bærɪstə'] *n Br* avocat *m,* -e *f.*

barrow ['bærəʊ] *n* brouette *f.*

bartender ['bɑːtendə'] *n Am* barman *m.*

barter ['bɑːtə'] **1** *n* troc *m.* **2** *vt:* **to ~ sthg (for)** troquer OR échanger qqch (contre). **3** *vi* faire du troc.

base [beɪs] **1** *n* base *f.* **2** *vt* baser; **to ~ sthg on** OR **upon** baser OR fonder qqch sur. **3** *adj* indigne, ignoble.

baseball ['beɪsbɔːl] *n* base-ball *m.*

baseball cap *n* casquette *f* de base-ball.

basement ['beɪsmənt] *n* sous-sol *m.*

base rate *n* taux *m* de base.

bases ['beɪsiːz] *pl →* **basis.**

bash [bæʃ] *inf* **1** *n* [painful blow] coup *m.* || [attempt]: **to have a ~** tenter le coup. **2** *vt* [hit - gen] frapper, cogner; [- car] percuter.

bashful ['bæʃfʊl] *adj* timide.

basic ['beɪsɪk] *adj* fondamental(e); [vocabulary, salary]. de base. ○ **basics** *npl* [rudiments] éléments *mpl,* bases *fpl.*

BASIC ['beɪsɪk] *(abbr of* **Beginner's All-purpose Symbolic Instruction Code)** *n* basic *m.*

basically ['beɪsɪklɪ] *adv* [essentially] au fond, fondamentalement. || [really] en fait.

basil ['bæzl] *n* basilic *m.*

basin ['beɪsn] *n Br* [bowl - for cooking] terrine *f;* [- for washing] cuvette *f.* || [in bathroom] lavabo *m.* || GEOGR bassin *m.*

basis ['beɪsɪs] *(pl* -ses*) n* base *f;* **on the ~ of** sur la base de; **on a regular ~** de façon régulière.

bask [bɑːsk] *vi:* **to ~ in the sun** se chauffer au soleil.

basket ['bɑːskɪt] *n* corbeille *f;* [with handle] panier *m.*

basketball ['bɑːskɪtbɔːl] *n* basket-ball *m,* basket *m.*

bass [beɪs] **1** *adj* bas (basse). **2** *n* [singer] basse *f.* || [double bass] contrebasse *f.* || = **bass guitar.**

bass drum [beɪs-] *n* grosse caisse *f.*

bass guitar [beɪs-] *n* basse *f.*

bassoon [bə'suːn] *n* basson *m.*

bastard ['bɑːstəd] *n* [illegitimate child] bâtard *m,* -e *f,* enfant naturel *m,* enfant naturelle *f.* || *v inf* [unpleasant person] salaud *m,* saligaud *m.*

bat [bæt] *n* [animal] chauve-souris *f.* || [for cricket, baseball] batte *f;* [for table-tennis] raquette *f.* || *phr:* **to do sthg off one's own ~** faire qqch de son propre chef.

batch [bætʃ] *n* [of papers] tas *m,* liasse *f;* [of letters, applicants] série *f.* || [of products] lot *m.*

bath [bɑːθ] **1** *n* [bathtub] baignoire *f.* || [act of washing] bain *m;* **to have** OR **take a bath** prendre un bain. **2** *vt* baigner, donner un bain à. ○ **baths** *npl Br* piscine *f.*

bathe [beɪð] **1** *vt* [wound] laver. || [subj: light, sunshine]: **to be ~d in** OR **with** être baigné(e) de. **2** *vi* [swim] se baigner. || *Am* [take a bath] prendre un bain.

bathing ['beɪðɪŋ] *n (U)* baignade *f.*

bathing cap *n* bonnet *m* de bain.

bathing costume, bathing suit *n* maillot *m* de bain.

bathrobe ['bɑːθrəʊb] *n* [made of towelling] sortie *f* de bain; [dressing gown] peignoir *m.*

bathroom ['bɑːθrʊm] *n Br* [room with bath] salle *f* de bains. || *Am* [toilet] toilettes *fpl.*

bath towel *n* serviette *f* de bain.

bathtub ['bɑːθtʌb] *n* baignoire *f.*

baton ['bætən] *n* [of conductor] baguette *f.* || [in relay race] témoin *m.*

batsman ['bætsmən] *(pl* -men [-mən]*) n* batteur *m.*

battalion [bə'tæljən] *n* bataillon *m.*

batten ['bætn] *n* planche *f,* latte *f.*

batter ['bætə'] **1** *n (U)* pâte *f.* **2** *vt* battre.

battered ['bætəd] *adj* [child, woman] battu(e). || [car, hat] cabossé(e).

battery ['bætərɪ] *n* batterie *f;* [of calculator, toy] pile *f.*

battle ['bætl] **1** *n* [in war] bataille *f.* || [struggle]: **~ (for/against/with)** lutte *f* (pour/contre/avec), combat *m* (pour/contre/avec). **2** *vi:* **to ~ (for/against/with)** se battre (pour/contre/avec), lutter (pour/contre/avec).

battlefield ['bætlfiːld], **battleground** ['bætlgraʊnd] *n* MIL champ *m* de bataille.

battlements ['bætlmənts] *npl* remparts *mpl.*

battleship ['bætlʃɪp] *n* cuirassé *m.*

bauble ['bɔːbl] *n* babiole *f,* colifichet *m.*

baulk [bɔːk] = **balk.**

bawdy ['bɔːdɪ] *adj* grivois(e), salé(e).

bawl [bɔːl] *vt* & *vi* brailler.

bay [beɪ] 1 *n* GEOGR baie *f*. || [for loading] aire *f* (de chargement). || [for parking] place *f* (de stationnement). || *phr*: to keep sb/sthg at ~ tenir qqn/qqch à distance, tenir qqn/qqch en échec.

bay leaf *n* feuille *f* de laurier.

bay window *n* fenêtre *f* en saillie.

bazaar [bə'zɑːr] *n* [market] bazar *m*.

B & B *n abbr of* bed and breakfast.

BBC (*abbr of* British Broadcasting Corporation) *n* office national britannique de radiodiffusion.

BC (*abbr of* before Christ) *av.* J.-C.

be [biː] (*pt* was OR were, *pp* been) 1 *aux vb* (*in combination with pp: to form cont tense*): what is he doing? qu'est-ce qu'il fait?; it's snowing il neige. || (*in combination with pp: to form passive*) être; to ~ loved être aimé(e); there was no one to ~ seen il n'y avait personne. || (*in question tags*): she's pretty, isn't she? elle est jolie, n'est-ce pas?; the meal was delicious, wasn't it? le repas était délicieux, non? OR vous n'avez pas trouvé? || (*followed by "to" + infin*): the firm is to ~ sold on va vendre la société; you're not to tell anyone ne le dis à personne. 2 *copulative vb* (*with adj, n*) être; to ~ a doctor/lawyer/plumber être médecin/avocat/plombier; she's intelligent/attractive elle est intelligente/jolie; I'm hot/cold j'ai chaud/froid; 1 and 1 are 2 1 et 1 font 2. || [referring to health] aller, se porter; to ~ seriously ill être gravement malade; she's better now elle va mieux maintenant; how are you? comment allez-vous? || [referring to age]: how old are you? quel âge avez-vous?; I'm 20 (years old) j'ai 20 ans. || [cost] coûter, faire; how much was it? combien cela a-t-il coûté?, combien ça faisait? 3 *vi* [exist] être, exister; ~ that as it may quoi qu'il en soit. || [referring to place] être; Toulouse is in France Toulouse se trouve OR est en France; he will ~ here tomorrow il sera là demain. || [referring to movement] aller, être; I've been to the cinema j'ai été OR je suis allé au cinéma. 4 *v impers* [referring to time, dates, distance] être; it's two o'clock il est deux heures; it's 3 km to the next town la ville voisine est à 3 km. || [referring to the weather] faire; it's hot/cold il fait chaud/froid. || [for emphasis]: it's me/ Paul/the milkman c'est moi/Paul/le laitier.

beach [biːtʃ] 1 *n* plage *f*. 2 *vt* échouer.

beacon ['biːkən] *n* [warning fire] feu *m*, fanal *m*. || [lighthouse] phare *m*. || [radio beacon] radiophare *m*.

bead [biːd] *n* [of wood, glass] perle *f*. || [of sweat] goutte *f*.

beagle ['biːgl] *n* beagle *m*.

beak [biːk] *n* bec *m*.

beaker ['biːkər] *n* gobelet *m*.

beam [biːm] 1 *n* [of wood, concrete] poutre *f*. || [of light] rayon *m*. 2 *vt* [signal, news] transmettre. 3 *vi* [smile] faire un sourire radieux.

bean [biːn] *n* [gen] haricot *m*; [of coffee] grain *m*; to be full of ~s *inf* péter le feu; to spill the ~s *inf* manger le morceau.

beanbag ['biːnbæg] *n* [chair] sacco *m*.

beanshoot ['biːnʃuːt], **beansprout** ['biːnspraʊt] *n* germe *m* OR pousse *f* de soja.

bear [beər] (*pt* bore, *pp* borne) 1 *n* [animal] ours *m*. 2 *vt* [carry] porter. || [support, tolerate] supporter. || [feeling]: to ~ sb a grudge garder rancune à qqn. 3 *vi*: to ~ left/right se diriger vers la gauche/la droite; to bring pressure/influence to ~ on sb exercer une pression/une influence sur qqn. ○ **bear down** *vi*: to ~ down on sb/sthg s'approcher de qqn/qqch de façon menaçante. ○ **bear out** *vt sep* confirmer, corroborer. ○ **bear up** *vi* tenir le coup. ○ **bear with** *vt fus* être patient(e) avec.

beard [bɪəd] *n* barbe *f*.

bearer ['beərər] *n* [gen] porteur *m*, -euse *f*. || [of passport] titulaire *mf*.

bearing ['beərɪŋ] *n* [connection]: ~ (on) rapport *m* (avec). || [deportment] allure *f*, maintien *m*. || TECH [for shaft] palier *m*. || [on compass] orientation *f*; to get one's ~s s'orienter, se repérer.

beast [biːst] *n* [animal] bête *f*. || *inf pej* [person] brute *f*.

beat [biːt] (*pt* beat, *pp* beaten ['biːtn]) 1 *n* [of heart, drum, wings] battement *m*. || MUS [rhythm] mesure *f*, temps *m*. || [of policeman] ronde *f*. 2 *vt* [gen] battre; it ~s me *inf* ça me dépasse. || [be better than] être bien mieux que, valoir mieux que. || *phr*: ~ it! *inf* décampe!, fiche le camp! 3 *vi* battre. ○ **beat off** *vt sep* [resist] repousser. ○ **beat up** *vt sep inf* tabasser.

beating ['biːtɪŋ] *n* [blows] raclée *f*, rossée *f*. || [defeat] défaite *f*.

beautiful ['bju:tɪfʊl] *adj* [gen] beau (belle). || *inf* [very good] joli(e).

beautifully ['bju:təflɪ] *adv* [attractively - dressed] élégamment; [- decorated] avec goût. || *inf* [very well] parfaitement, à la perfection.

beauty ['bju:tɪ] *n* [gen] beauté *f*.

beauty parlour *n* institut *m* de beauté.

beauty salon = beauty parlour.

beauty spot *n* [picturesque place] site *m* pittoresque. || [on skin] grain *m* de beauté.

beaver ['bi:vər] *n* castor *m*.

became [bɪ'keɪm] *pt* → become.

because [bɪ'kɒz] *conj* parce que. ○ **because of** *prep* à cause de.

beck [bek] *n*: **to be at sb's ~ and call** être aux ordres OR à la disposition de qqn.

beckon ['bekən] **1** *vt* [signal to] faire signe à. **2** *vi* [signal]: **to ~ to sb** faire signe à qqn.

become [bɪ'kʌm] (*pt* **became**, *pp* **become**) *vi* devenir; **to ~ quieter** se calmer; **to ~ irritated** s'énerver.

bed [bed] *n* [to sleep on] lit *m*; **to go to ~** se coucher; **to go to ~ with sb** *euphemism* coucher avec qqn. || [flowerbed] parterre *m*. || [of sea, river] lit *m*, fond *m*.

bed and breakfast *n* ≃ chambre *f* d'hôte.

bedclothes ['bedkləʊðz] *npl* draps *mpl* et couvertures *fpl*.

bedlam ['bedləm] *n* pagaille *f*.

bed linen *n* (*U*) draps *mpl* et taies *fpl*.

bedraggled [bɪ'drægld] *adj* [person] débraillé(e); [hair] embroussaillé(e).

bedridden ['bed,rɪdn] *adj* grabataire.

bedroom ['bedrʊm] *n* chambre *f* (à coucher).

bedside ['bedsaɪd] *n* chevet *m*.

bedsore ['bedsɔːr] *n* escarre *f*.

bedspread ['bedspred] *n* couvre-lit *m*, dessus-de-lit *m inv*.

bedtime ['bedtaɪm] *n* heure *f* du coucher.

bee [bi:] *n* abeille *f*.

beech [bi:tʃ] *n* hêtre *m*.

beef [bi:f] *n* bœuf *m*.

beefburger ['bi:f,bɜːgər] *n* hamburger *m*.

beefsteak ['bi:f,steɪk] *n* bifteck *m*.

beehive ['bi:haɪv] *n* [for bees] ruche *f*.

beeline ['bi:laɪn] *n*: **to make a ~ for** *inf* aller tout droit OR directement vers.

been [bi:n] *pp* → be.

beer [bɪər] *n* bière *f*.

beet [bi:t] *n* betterave *f*.

beetle ['bi:tl] *n* scarabée *m*.

beetroot ['bi:tru:t] *n* betterave *f*.

before [bɪ'fɔːr] **1** *adv* auparavant, avant; **I've never been there ~** je n'y suis jamais allé; **I've seen it ~** je l'ai déjà vu; **the year ~** l'année d'avant OR précédente. **2** *prep* [in time] avant. || [in space] devant. **3** *conj* avant de (+ *infin*), avant que (+ *subjunctive*); **~ leaving** avant de partir; **~ you leave** avant que vous ne partiez.

beforehand [bɪ'fɔːhænd] *adv* à l'avance.

befriend [bɪ'frend] *vt* prendre en amitié.

beg [beg] **1** *vt* [money, food] mendier. || [favour] solliciter, quémander; [forgiveness] demander; **to ~ sb to do sthg** prier OR supplier qqn de faire qqch. **2** *vi* [for money, food]: **to ~ (for sthg)** mendier (qqch). || [plead] supplier; **to ~ for** [forgiveness etc] demander.

began [bɪ'gæn] *pt* → begin.

beggar ['begər] *n* mendiant *m*, -e *f*.

begin [bɪ'gɪn] (*pt* **began**, *pp* **begun**) **1** *vt* commencer; **to ~ doing** OR **to do sthg** commencer OR se mettre à faire qqch. **2** *vi* commencer; **to ~ with** pour commencer, premièrement.

beginner [bɪ'gɪnər] *n* débutant *m*, -e *f*.

beginning [bɪ'gɪnɪŋ] *n* début *m*, commencement *m*.

begrudge [bɪ'grʌdʒ] *vt* [envy]: **to ~ sb sthg** envier qqch à qqn. || [do unwillingly]: **to ~ doing sthg** rechigner à faire qqch.

begun [bɪ'gʌn] *pp* → begin.

behalf [bɪ'hɑːf] *n*: **on ~ of** *Br*, **in ~ of** *Am* de la part de, au nom de.

behave [bɪ'heɪv] **1** *vt*: **to ~ o.s.** se conduire OR se comporter bien. **2** *vi* [in a particular way] se conduire, se comporter. || [acceptably] se tenir bien.

behaviour *Br*, **behavior** *Am* [bɪ'heɪvjər] *n* conduite *f*, comportement *m*.

behead [bɪ'hed] *vt* décapiter.

behind [bɪ'haɪnd] **1** *prep* [gen] derrière. || [in time] en retard sur. **2** *adv* [gen] derrière. || [in time] en retard; **to leave sthg ~** oublier qqch; **to stay ~** rester; **to be ~ with sthg** être en retard dans qqch. **3** *n* *inf* derrière *m*, postérieur *m*.

beige [beɪʒ] **1** *adj* beige. **2** *n* beige *m*.

Beijing [,beɪ'dʒɪŋ] *n* Beijing.

being ['bi:ɪŋ] *n* [creature] être *m*. || [existence]: **in ~** existant(e); **to come into ~** voir le jour, prendre naissance.

Beirut [,beɪ'ruːt] n Beyrouth.

belch [beltʃ] **1** n renvoi m, rot m. **2** vt [smoke, fire] vomir, cracher. **3** vi [person] éructer, roter.

Belgian ['beldʒən] **1** adj belge. **2** n Belge mf.

Belgium ['beldʒəm] n Belgique f; **in ~** en Belgique.

Belgrade [,bel'greɪd] n Belgrade.

belie [bɪ'laɪ] (cont **belying**) vt [disprove] démentir. || [give false idea of] donner une fausse idée de.

belief [bɪ'liːf] n [faith, certainty]: **~ (in)** croyance f (en). || [principle, opinion] opinion f, conviction f.

believe [bɪ'liːv] **1** vt croire; **~ it or not** tu ne me croiras peut-être pas. **2** vi croire; **to ~ in sb** croire en qqn; **to ~ in sthg** croire à qqch.

believer [bɪ'liːvər] n RELIG croyant m, -e f. || [in idea, action]: **~ in** partisan m, -e f de.

belittle [bɪ'lɪtl] vt dénigrer, rabaisser.

bell [bel] n [of church] cloche f; [handbell] clochette f; [on door] sonnette f; [on bike] timbre m.

bellow ['beləʊ] vi [person] brailler, beugler. || [bull] beugler.

bellows ['beləʊz] npl soufflet m.

belly ['belɪ] n [of person] ventre m; [of animal] panse f.

bellyache ['belɪeɪk] n mal m de ventre.

belly button n inf nombril m.

belong [bɪ'lɒŋ] vi [be property]: **to ~ to sb** appartenir OR être à qqn. || [be member]: **to ~ to sthg** être membre de qqch. || [be in right place] être à sa place; **that chair ~s here** ce fauteuil va ici.

belongings [bɪ'lɒŋɪŋz] npl affaires fpl.

beloved [bɪ'lʌvd] adj bien-aimé(e).

below [bɪ'ləʊ] **1** adv [lower] en dessous, en bas. || [in text] ci-dessous. || NAUT en bas. **2** prep sous, au-dessous de.

belt [belt] **1** n [for clothing] ceinture f. || TECH courroie f. **2** vt inf flanquer une raclée à.

beltway ['belt,weɪ] n Am route f périphérique.

bemused [bɪ'mjuːzd] adj perplexe.

bench [bentʃ] n [gen & POL] banc m. || [in lab, workshop] établi m.

bend [bend] (pt & pp **bent**) **1** n [in road] courbe f, virage m. || [in pipe, river] coude m. || phr: **round the ~** inf dingue, fou (folle). **2** vt [arm, leg] plier. || [wire,

fork etc] tordre, courber. **3** vi [person] se baisser, se courber; [tree, rod] plier; **to ~ over backwards for sb** se mettre en quatre pour qqn.

beneath [bɪ'niːθ] **1** adv dessous, en bas. **2** prep [under] sous. || [unworthy of] indigne de.

benefactor ['benɪfæktər] n bienfaiteur m.

beneficial [,benɪ'fɪʃl] adj: **~ (to sb)** salutaire (à qqn); **~ (to sthg)** utile (à qqch).

beneficiary [,benɪ'fɪʃərɪ] n bénéficiaire mf.

benefit ['benɪfɪt] **1** n [advantage] avantage m; **for the ~ of** dans l'intérêt de; **to be to sb's ~**, **to be of ~ to sb** être dans l'intérêt de qqn. || ADMIN [allowance of money] allocation f, prestation f. **2** vt profiter à. **3** vi: **to ~ from** tirer avantage de, profiter de.

Benelux ['benɪlʌks] n Bénélux m.

benevolent [bɪ'nevələnt] adj bienveillant(e).

benign [bɪ'naɪn] adj [person] gentil(ille), bienveillant(e). || MED bénin(igne).

bent [bent] **1** pt & pp → **bend**. **2** adj [wire, bar] tordu(e). || [person, body] courbé(e), voûté(e). || [determined]: **to be ~ on doing sthg** vouloir absolument faire qqch, être décidé(e) à faire qqch. **3** n: **~ (for)** penchant m (pour).

bequeath [bɪ'kwiːð] vt lit & fig léguer.

bequest [bɪ'kwest] n legs m.

bereaved [bɪ'riːvd] (pl inv) **1** adj endeuillé(e), affligé(e). **2** n: **the ~** la famille du défunt.

beret ['bereɪ] n béret m.

Berlin [bɜː'lɪn] n Berlin.

berm [bɜːm] n Am bas-côté m.

Bermuda [bə'mjuːdə] n Bermudes fpl.

Bern [bɜːn] n Berne.

berry ['berɪ] n baie f.

berserk [bə'zɜːk] adj: **to go ~** devenir fou furieux (folle furieuse).

berth [bɜːθ] **1** n [in harbour] poste m d'amarrage, mouillage m. || [in ship, train] couchette f. **2** vi [ship] accoster, se ranger à quai.

beset [bɪ'set] (pt & pp **beset**) **1** adj: **~ with** OR **by** [doubts etc] assailli(e) de. **2** vt assaillir.

beside [bɪ'saɪd] prep [next to] à côté de, auprès de. || [compared with] comparé(e) à, à côté de. || phr: **to be ~ o.s. with anger** être hors de soi; **to be ~ o.s. with joy** être fou (folle) de joie.

besides [bɪ'saɪdz] **1** *adv* en outre, en plus. **2** *prep* en plus de.

besiege [bɪ'si:dʒ] *vt* [town, fortress] assiéger.

besotted [bɪ'sɒtɪd] *adj*: ~ **(with sb)** entiché(e) (de qqn).

best [best] **1** *adj* le meilleur (la meilleure). **2** *adv* le mieux. **3** *n* le mieux; **to do one's** ~ faire de son mieux; **all the** ~! meilleurs souhaits!; **to be for the** ~ être pour le mieux; **to make the** ~ **of sthg** s'accommoder de qqch, prendre son parti de qqch. ○ **at best** *adv* au mieux.

best man *n* garçon *m* d'honneur.

bestow [bɪ'stəʊ] *vt fml*: **to** ~ **sthg on sb** conférer qqch à qqn.

best-seller *n* [book] best-seller *m*.

bet [bet] (*pt & pp* **bet** OR **-ted**) **1** *n* pari *m*. **2** *vt* parier. **3** *vi* parier; **I wouldn't** ~ **on it** *fig* je n'en suis pas si sûr.

betray [bɪ'treɪ] *vt* trahir.

betrayal [bɪ'treɪəl] *n* [of person] trahison *f*.

better ['betər] **1** *adj (compar of* **good)** meilleur(e); **to get** ~ s'améliorer; [after illness] se remettre, se rétablir. **2** *adv (compar of* **well)** mieux; **I'd** ~ **leave** il faut que je parte, je dois partir. **3** *n* meilleur *m*, -e *f*; **to get the** ~ **of sb** avoir raison de qqn. **4** *vt* améliorer; **to** ~ **o.s.** s'élever.

better off *adj* [financially] plus à son aise. ‖ [in better situation] mieux.

betting ['betɪŋ] *n (U)* paris *mpl*.

between [bɪ'twi:n] **1** *prep* entre. **2** *adv*: **(in)** ~ [in space] au milieu; [in time] dans l'intervalle.

beverage ['bevərɪdʒ] *n fml* boisson *f*.

beware [bɪ'weər] *vi*: **to** ~ **(of)** prendre garde (à), se méfier (de); ~ **of ...** attention à ....

bewildered [bɪ'wɪldəd] *adj* déconcerté(e), perplexe.

beyond [bɪ'jɒnd] **1** *prep* [in space] au-delà de. ‖ [in time] après, plus tard que. ‖ [exceeding] au-dessus de; **it's** ~ **my control** je n'y peux rien; **it's** ~ **my responsibility** cela n'entre pas dans le cadre de mes responsabilités. **2** *adv* au-delà.

bias ['baɪəs] *n* [prejudice] préjugé *m*, parti *m* pris. ‖ [tendency] tendance *f*.

biased ['baɪəst] *adj* partial(e); **to be** ~ **towards sb/sthg** favoriser qqn/qqch; **to be** ~ **against sb/sthg** défavoriser qqn/qqch.

bib [bɪb] *n* [for baby] bavoir *m*, bavette *f*.

Bible ['baɪbl] *n*: **the** ~ la Bible.

bicarbonate of soda [baɪ'kɑ:bənət-] *n* bicarbonate *m* de soude.

biceps ['baɪseps] (*pl inv*) *n* biceps *m*.

bicker ['bɪkər] *vi* se chamailler.

bicycle ['baɪsɪkl] **1** *n* bicyclette *f*, vélo *m*. **2** *vi* aller en bicyclette OR vélo.

bicycle path *n* piste *f* cyclable.

bicycle pump *n* pompe *f* à vélo.

bid [bɪd] (*pt & pp* **bid**) **1** *n* [attempt] tentative *f*. ‖ [at auction] enchère *f*. ‖ COMM offre *f*. **2** *vt* [at auction] faire une enchère de. **3** *vi* [at auction]: **to** ~ **(for)** faire une enchère (pour). ‖ [attempt]: **to** ~ **for sthg** briguer.

bidder ['bɪdər] *n* enchérisseur *m*, -euse *f*.

bidding ['bɪdɪŋ] *n (U)* enchères *fpl*.

bide [baɪd] *vt*: **to** ~ **one's time** attendre son heure OR le bon moment.

bifocals [,baɪ'fəʊklz] *npl* lunettes *fpl* bifocales.

big [bɪg] *adj* [gen] grand(e). ‖ [in amount, bulk - box, problem, book] gros (grosse).

bigamy ['bɪgəmɪ] *n* bigamie *f*.

big deal *inf* **1** *n*: **it's no** ~ ce n'est pas dramatique; **what's the** ~? où est le problème? **2** *excl* tu parles!, et alors?

Big Dipper [-'dɪpər] *n Am* ASTRON: **the** ~ la Grande Ourse.

bigheaded [,bɪg'hedɪd] *adj inf* crâneur(euse).

bigot ['bɪgət] *n* sectaire *mf*.

bigoted ['bɪgətɪd] *adj* sectaire.

big toe *n* gros orteil *m*.

big top *n* chapiteau *m*.

bike [baɪk] *n inf* [bicycle] vélo *m*. ‖ [motorcycle] bécane *f*, moto *f*.

bikeway ['baɪkweɪ] *n Am* piste *f* cyclable.

bikini [bɪ'ki:nɪ] *n* Bikini® *m*.

bile [baɪl] *n* [fluid] bile *f*. ‖ [anger] mauvaise humeur *f*.

bilingual [baɪ'lɪŋgwəl] *adj* bilingue.

bill [bɪl] **1** *n* [statement of cost]: ~ **(for)** note *f* OR facture *f* (de); [in restaurant] addition *f* (de). ‖ [in parliament] projet *m* de loi. ‖ [of show, concert] programme *m*. ‖ *Am* [banknote] billet *m* de banque. ‖ [poster]: **"post OR stick no ~s"** «défense d'afficher». ‖ [beak] bec *m*. **2** *vt* [invoice]: **to** ~ **sb (for)** envoyer une facture à qqn (pour).

billboard ['bɪlbɔ:d] *n* panneau *m* d'affichage.

billet ['bɪlɪt] *n* logement *m* (chez l'habitant).

billfold ['bɪlfəʊld] *n Am* portefeuille *m*.

billiards ['bɪljədz] *n* billard *m*.

billion ['bɪljən] *num Am* [thousand million] milliard *m*. || *Br* [million million] billion *m*.

Bill of Rights *n*: the ~ les dix premiers amendements à la Constitution américaine.

bin [bɪn] *n Br* [for rubbish] poubelle *f*. || [for grain, coal] coffre *m*.

bind [baɪnd] (*pt & pp* **bound**) *vt* [tie up] attacher, lier. || [unite - people] lier. || [bandage] panser. || [book] relier. || [constrain] contraindre, forcer.

binder ['baɪndər] *n* [cover] classeur *m*.

binding ['baɪndɪŋ] **1** *adj* qui lie OR engage; [agreement] irrévocable. **2** *n* [on book] reliure *f*.

binge [bɪndʒ] *inf* **1** *n*: to go on a ~ prendre une cuite. **2** *vi*: to ~ on sthg se gaver OR se bourrer de qqch.

bingo ['bɪŋgəʊ] *n* bingo *m*, ≃ loto *m*.

binoculars [bɪ'nɒkjʊləz] *npl* jumelles *fpl*.

biochemistry [,baɪəʊ'kemɪstrɪ] *n* biochimie *f*.

biodegradable [,baɪəʊdɪ'greɪdəbl] *adj* biodégradable.

biography [baɪ'ɒgrəfɪ] *n* biographie *f*.

biological [,baɪə'lɒdʒɪkl] *adj* biologique; [washing powder] aux enzymes.

biology [baɪ'ɒlədʒɪ] *n* biologie *f*.

birch [bɜːtʃ] *n* [tree] bouleau *m*.

bird [bɜːd] *n* [creature] oiseau *m*. || *inf* [woman] gonzesse *f*.

birdie ['bɜːdɪ] *n* GOLF birdie *m*.

bird's-eye view *n* vue *f* aérienne.

bird-watcher [-,wɒtʃər] *n* observateur *m*, -trice *f* d'oiseaux.

Biro® ['baɪərəʊ] *n* stylo *m* à bille.

birth [bɜːθ] *n lit & fig* naissance *f*; to give ~ (to) donner naissance (à).

birth certificate *n* acte *m* OR extrait *m* de naissance.

birth control *n* (*U*) régulation *f* OR contrôle *m* des naissances.

birthday ['bɜːθdeɪ] *n* anniversaire *m*.

birthmark ['bɜːθmɑːk] *n* tache *f* de vin.

birthrate ['bɜːθreɪt] *n* (taux *m* de) natalité *f*.

Biscay ['bɪskeɪ] *n*: the Bay of ~ le golfe de Gascogne.

biscuit ['bɪskɪt] *n Am* scone *m*.

bisect [baɪ'sekt] *vt* couper OR diviser en deux.

bishop ['bɪʃəp] *n* RELIG évêque *m*. || [in chess] fou *m*.

bison ['baɪsn] (*pl inv* OR **-s**) *n* bison *m*.

bit [bɪt] **1** *pt* → **bite**. **2** *n* [small piece - of paper, cheese etc] morceau *m*, bout *m*; [- of book, film] passage *m*; to take sthg to ~s démonter qqch. || [amount]: a ~ of un peu de; a ~ of **shopping** quelques courses; it's a ~ of a **nuisance** c'est un peu embêtant; a ~ of **trouble** un petit problème; quite a ~ of pas mal de, beaucoup de. || [short time]: for a ~ pendant quelque temps. || [of drill] mèche *f*. || [of bridle] mors *m*. || COMPUT bit *m*. ○ **a bit** *adv* un peu. ○ **bit by bit** *adv* petit à petit.

bitch [bɪtʃ] *n* [female dog] chienne *f*. || *inf pej* [woman] salope *f*, garce *f*.

bitchy [bɪtʃɪ] *adj inf* vache, rosse.

bite [baɪt] (*pt* bit, *pp* bitten) **1** *n* [act of biting] morsure *f*, coup *m* de dent. || *inf* [food]: to have a ~ (to eat) manger un morceau. || [wound] piqûre *f*. **2** *vt* [subj: person, animal] mordre. || [subj: insect, snake] piquer, mordre. **3** *vi* [animal, person]: to ~ (into) mordre (dans); to ~ off sthg arracher qqch d'un coup de dents. || [insect, snake] mordre, piquer.

biting ['baɪtɪŋ] *adj* [very cold] cinglant(e), piquant(e). || [humour, comment] mordant(e), caustique.

bitten ['bɪtn] *pp* → **bite**.

bitter ['bɪtər] *adj* [gen] amer(ère). || [icy] glacial(e). || [argument] violent(e).

bitter lemon *n* Schweppes® *m* au citron.

bitterness ['bɪtənɪs] *n* [gen] amertume *f*. || [of wind, weather] âpreté *f*.

bizarre [bɪ'zɑːr] *adj* bizarre.

blab [blæb] *vi inf* lâcher le morceau.

black [blæk] **1** *adj* [colour] noir(e). || [person] noir(e), -e *f*. || *phr*: in ~ and white [in writing] noir sur blanc, par écrit; in the ~ [financially solvent] solvable, sans dettes. ○ **black out** *vi* [faint] s'évanouir.

blackberry ['blækbərɪ] *n* mûre *f*.

blackbird ['blækbɜːd] *n* merle *m*.

blackboard ['blækbɔːd] *n* tableau *m* (noir).

blackcurrant [,blæk'kʌrənt] *n* cassis *m*.

blacken ['blækn] **1** *vt* [make dark] noircir. **2** *vi* s'assombrir.

black eye *n* œil *m* poché OR au beurre noir.

blackhead ['blækhed] *n* point *m* noir.

black ice *n* verglas *m*.

blackleg ['blækleg] *n pej* jaune *m*.

blacklist ['blæklɪst] **1** n liste f noire. **2** vt mettre sur la liste noire.

blackmail ['blækmeɪl] **1** n lit & fig chantage m. **2** vt [for money] faire chanter. || fig [emotionally] faire du chantage à.

black market n marché m noir.

blackout ['blækaut] n MIL & PRESS black-out m. || [power cut] panne f d'électricité. || [fainting fit] évanouissement m.

Black Sea n: the ~ la mer Noire.

black sheep n brebis f galeuse.

blacksmith ['blæksmɪθ] n forgeron m; [for horses] maréchal-ferrant m.

black spot n AUT point m noir.

bladder ['blædər] n vessie f.

blade [bleɪd] n [of knife, saw] lame f. || [of propeller] pale f. || [of grass] brin m.

blame [bleɪm] **1** n responsabilité f, faute f; to take the ~ for sthg endosser la responsabilité de qqch. **2** vt blâmer, condamner; to ~ sthg on rejeter la responsabilité de qqch sur, imputer qqch à; to ~ sb/sthg for sthg reprocher qqch à qqn/qqch; to be to ~ for sthg être responsable de qqch.

bland [blænd] adj [person] terne. || [food] fade, insipide. || [music, style] insipide.

blank [blæŋk] **1** adj [sheet of paper] blanc (blanche); [wall] nu(e). || fig [look] vide, sans expression. **2** n [empty space] blanc m. || [cartridge] cartouche f à blanc.

blank cheque n chèque m en blanc.

blanket ['blæŋkɪt] n [for bed] couverture f. || [of snow] couche f, manteau m; [of fog] nappe f.

blare [bleər] vi hurler; [radio] beugler.

blasphemy ['blæsfəmɪ] n blasphème m.

blast [blɑːst] **1** n [explosion] explosion f. || [of air, from bomb] souffle m. **2** vt [hole, tunnel] creuser à la dynamite. ○ **(at) full blast** adv [play music etc] à pleins gaz OR tubes.

blasted ['blɑːstɪd] adj inf fichu(e), maudit(e).

blast-off n SPACE lancement m.

blatant ['bleɪtənt] adj criant(e), flagrant(e).

blaze [bleɪz] **1** n [fire] incendie m. || fig [of colour, light] éclat m, flamboiement m. **2** vi [fire] flamber. || fig [with colour] flamboyer.

blazer ['bleɪzər] n blazer m.

bleach [bliːtʃ] **1** n eau f de Javel. **2** vt [hair] décolorer; [clothes] blanchir.

bleached [bliːtʃt] adj décoloré(e).

bleachers ['bliːtʃəz] npl Am SPORT gradins mpl.

bleak [bliːk] adj [future] sombre. || [place, weather, face] lugubre, triste.

bleary-eyed [,blɪərɪ'aɪd] adj aux yeux troubles OR voilés.

bleat [bliːt] **1** n bêlement m. **2** vi bêler.

bleed [bliːd] (pt & pp **bled** [bled]) **1** vt [radiator etc] purger. **2** vi saigner.

bleeper ['bliːpər] n bip m, bip-bip m.

blemish ['blemɪʃ] n lit & fig défaut m.

blend [blend] **1** n mélange m. **2** vt: to ~ sthg (with) mélanger qqch (avec OR à). **3** vi: to ~ (with) se mêler (à OR avec).

blender ['blendər] n mixer m.

bless [bles] (pt & pp **-ed** OR **blest**) vt bénir; ~ you! [after sneezing] à vos souhaits!; [thank you] merci mille fois!

blessing ['blesɪŋ] n lit & fig bénédiction f.

blest [blest] pt & pp > **bless**.

blew [bluː] pt > **blow**.

blind [blaɪnd] **1** adj lit & fig aveugle; to be ~ to sthg ne pas voir qqch. **2** n [for window] store m. **3** npl: the ~ les aveugles mpl. **4** vt aveugler; to ~ sb to sthg fig cacher qqch à qqn.

blind alley n lit & fig impasse f.

blind corner n virage m sans visibilité.

blind date n rendez-vous avec quelqu'un qu'on ne connaît pas.

blinders ['blaɪndəz] npl Am œillères fpl.

blindfold ['blaɪndfəʊld] **1** adv les yeux bandés. **2** n bandeau m. **3** vt bander les yeux à.

blindly ['blaɪndlɪ] adv lit & fig à l'aveuglette, aveuglément.

blindness ['blaɪndnɪs] n cécité f; ~ (to) fig aveuglement m (devant).

blind spot n AUT angle m mort. || fig [inability to understand] blocage m.

blink [blɪŋk] **1** n phr: on the ~ [machine] détraqué(e). **2** vt [eyes] cligner. **3** vi [person] cligner des yeux. || [light] clignoter.

blinkered ['blɪŋkəd] adj: to be ~ lit & fig avoir des œillères.

bliss [blɪs] n bonheur m suprême, félicité f.

blissful ['blɪsfʊl] adj [day, silence] merveilleux(euse); [ignorance] total(e).

blister ['blɪstər] **1** n [on skin] ampoule f, cloque f. **2** vi [skin] se couvrir d'ampoules. || [paint] cloquer, se boursoufler.

blithely ['blaɪðlɪ] *adv* gaiement, joyeusement.

blitz [blɪts] *n* MIL bombardement *m* aérien.

blizzard ['blɪzəd] *n* tempête *f* de neige.

bloated ['bləʊtɪd] *adj* [face] bouffi(e). || [with food] ballonné(e).

blob [blɒb] *n* [drop] goutte *f*. || [indistinct shape] forme *f*; **a ~ of colour** une tache de couleur.

block [blɒk] **1** *n* [building]: **office ~** immeuble *m* de bureaux. || *Am* [of buildings] pâté *m* de maisons. || [of stone, ice] bloc *m*. || [obstruction] blocage *m*. **2** *vt* [road, pipe, view] boucher. || [prevent] bloquer, empêcher.

blockade [blɒ'keɪd] **1** *n* blocus *m*. **2** *vt* faire le blocus de.

blockage ['blɒkɪdʒ] *n* obstruction *f*.

blockbuster ['blɒkbʌstər] *n inf* [book] best-seller *m*; [film] film *m* à succès.

block capitals *npl* majuscules *fpl* d'imprimerie.

block letters *npl* majuscules *fpl* d'imprimerie.

blond [blɒnd] *adj* blond(e).

blonde [blɒnd] **1** *adj* blond(e). **2** *n* [woman] blonde *f*.

blood [blʌd] *n* sang *m*; **in cold ~** de sang-froid.

blood cell *n* globule *m*.

blood donor *n* donneur *m*, -euse *f* de sang.

blood group *n* groupe *m* sanguin.

bloodhound ['blʌdhaʊnd] *n* limier *m*.

blood poisoning *n* septicémie *f*.

blood pressure *n* tension *f* artérielle; **to have high ~** faire de l'hypertension.

bloodshed ['blʌdʃed] *n* carnage *m*.

bloodshot ['blʌdʃɒt] *adj* [eyes] injecté(e) de sang.

bloodstream ['blʌdstriːm] *n* sang *m*.

blood test *n* prise *f* de sang.

bloodthirsty ['blʌd,θɜːstɪ] *adj* sanguinaire.

blood transfusion *n* transfusion *f* sanguine.

bloody ['blʌdɪ] *adj* [gen] sanglant(e).

bloom [bluːm] **1** *n* fleur *f*. **2** *vi* fleurir.

blossom ['blɒsəm] **1** *n* [of tree] fleurs *fpl*; **in ~** en fleur OR fleurs. **2** *vi* [tree] fleurir. || *fig* [person] s'épanouir.

blot [blɒt] **1** *n lit & fig* tache *f*. **2** *vt* [paper] faire des pâtés sur. || [ink] sécher. ○ **blot out** *vt sep* voiler, cacher; [memories] effacer.

blotchy ['blɒtʃɪ] *adj* couvert(e) de marbrures OR taches.

blotting paper ['blɒtɪŋ-] *n* (*U*) (papier *m*) buvard *m*.

blouse [blaʊz] *n* chemisier *m*.

blow [bləʊ] (*pt* **blew**, *pp* **blown**) **1** *vi* [gen] souffler. || [in wind]: **to ~ off** s'envoler. || [fuse] sauter. **2** *vt* [subj: wind] faire voler, chasser. || [clear]: **to ~ one's nose** se moucher. || [trumpet] jouer de, souffler dans; **to ~ a whistle** donner un coup de sifflet, siffler. **3** *n* [hit] coup *m*. ○ **blow out 1** *vt sep* souffler. **2** *vi* [candle] s'éteindre. || [tyre] éclater. ○ **blow over** *vi* se calmer. ○ **blow up 1** *vt sep* [inflate] gonfler. || [with bomb] faire sauter. || [photograph] agrandir. **2** *vi* exploser.

blow-dry 1 *n* brushing *m*. **2** *vt* faire un brushing à.

blowlamp *Br* ['bləʊlæmp], **blowtorch** ['bləʊtɔːtʃ] *n* chalumeau *m*, lampe *f* à souder.

blown [bləʊn] *pp* → **blow**.

blowout ['bləʊaʊt] *n* [of tyre] éclatement *m*.

blowtorch = **blowlamp**.

blubber ['blʌbər] **1** *n* graisse *f* de baleine. **2** *vi pej* chialer.

blue [bluː] **1** *adj* [colour] bleu(e). || *inf* [sad] triste, cafardeux(euse). || [pornographic] porno (*inv*). **2** *n* bleu *m*; **out of the ~** [happen] subitement; [arrive] à l'improviste. ○ **blues** *npl*: **the ~s** MUS le blues; *inf* [sad feeling] le blues, le cafard.

bluebell ['bluːbel] *n* jacinthe *f* des bois.

blueberry ['bluːbərɪ] *n* myrtille *f*.

bluebottle ['bluː,bɒtl] *n* mouche *f* bleue, mouche de la viande.

blue cheese *n* (fromage *m*) bleu *m*.

blue-collar *adj* manuel(elle).

blue jeans *npl Am* blue-jean *m*, jean *m*.

blueprint ['bluːprɪnt] *n* photocalque *m*; *fig* plan *m*, projet *m*.

bluff [blʌf] **1** *adj* franc (franche). **2** *n* [deception] bluff *m*; **to call sb's ~** prendre qqn au mot. **3** *vt* bluffer, donner le change à. **4** *vi* faire du bluff, bluffer.

blunder ['blʌndər] **1** *n* gaffe *f*, bévue *f*. **2** *vi* [make mistake] faire une gaffe, commettre une bévue.

blunt [blʌnt] **1** *adj* [knife] émoussé(e); [pencil] épointé(e); [object, instrument] contondant(e). || [person, manner] direct(e). **2** *vt lit & fig* émousser.

blur [blɜːr] **1** *n* forme *f* confuse, tache *f* floue. **2** *vt* [vision] troubler, brouiller.

blurb [blɜːb] *n* texte *m* publicitaire.

blurt [blɜːt] ○ **blurt out** *vt sep* laisser échapper.

blush [blʌʃ] **1** *n* rougeur *f*. **2** *vi* rougir.

blusher ['blʌʃər] *n* fard *m* à joues, blush *m*.

blustery ['blʌstərɪ] *adj* venteux(euse).

BMX (*abbr of* **bicycle motorcross**) *n* bicross *m*.

BO *abbr of* **body odour**.

boar [bɔːr] *n* [male pig] verrat *m*. ‖ [wild pig] sanglier *m*.

board [bɔːd] **1** *n* [plank] planche *f*. ‖ [for notices] panneau *m* d'affichage. ‖ [for games - gen] tableau *m*; [- for chess] échiquier *m*. ‖ [blackboard] tableau *m* (noir). ‖ [of company]: ~ **(of directors)** conseil *m* d'administration. ‖ [committee] comité *m*, conseil *m*. ‖ **on** ~ [on ship, plane, bus, train] à bord. ‖ *phr*: **to take sthg on** ~ [knowledge] assimiler qqch; [advice] accepter qqch; **above** ~ régulier(ière), dans les règles. **2** *vt* [ship, aeroplane] monter à bord de; [train, bus] monter dans.

boarder ['bɔːdər] *n* [lodger] pensionnaire *mf*. ‖ [at school] interne *mf*, pensionnaire *mf*.

boarding card ['bɔːdɪŋ-] *n* carte *f* d'embarquement.

boardinghouse ['bɔːdɪŋhaʊs, *pl* -haʊzɪz] *n* pension *f* de famille.

boarding school ['bɔːdɪŋ-] *n* pensionnat *m*, internat *m*.

boardroom ['bɔːdrʊm] *n* salle *f* du conseil (d'administration).

boast [bəʊst] **1** *n* vantardise *f*, fanfaronnade *f*. **2** *vi*: **to** ~ **(about)** se vanter (de).

boastful ['bəʊstfʊl] *adj* vantard(e), fanfaron(onne).

boat [bəʊt] *n* [large] bateau *m*; [small] canot *m*, embarcation *f*; **by** ~ en bateau.

boater ['bəʊtər] *n* [hat] canotier *m*.

boatswain ['bəʊsn] *n* maître *m* d'équipage.

bob [bɒb] **1** *n* [hairstyle] coupe *f* au carré. ‖ *Br inf dated* [shilling] shilling *m*. ‖ = **bobsleigh**. **2** *vi* [boat, ship] tanguer.

bobbin ['bɒbɪn] *n* bobine *f*.

bobsleigh ['bɒbsleɪ] *n* bobsleigh *m*.

bode [bəʊd] *vi literary*: **to** ~ **ill/well (for)** être de mauvais/bon augure (pour).

bodily ['bɒdɪlɪ] **1** *adj* [needs] matériel(ielle). **2** *adv* [lift, move] à bras-le-corps.

body ['bɒdɪ] *n* [of person] corps *m*. ‖ [corpse] corps *m*, cadavre *m*. ‖ [organization] organisme *m*, organisation *f*. ‖ [of

car] carrosserie *f*; [of plane] fuselage *m*. ‖ (*U*) [of wine] corps *m*. ‖ (*U*) [of hair] volume *m*. ‖ [garment] body *m*.

body building *n* culturisme *m*.

bodyguard ['bɒdɪgɑːd] *n* garde *m* du corps.

body odour *n* odeur *f* corporelle.

bodywork ['bɒdɪwɜːk] *n* carrosserie *f*.

bog [bɒg] *n* [marsh] marécage *m*.

bogged down [,bɒgd-] *adj fig* [in work]: ~ **(in)** submergé(e) (de). ‖ [car etc]: ~ **(in)** enlisé(e) (dans).

boggle ['bɒgl] *vi*: **the mind** ~**s!** ce n'est pas croyable!, on croit rêver!

bogus ['bəʊgəs] *adj* faux (fausse), bidon (*inv*).

boil [bɔɪl] **1** *n* MED furoncle *m*. ‖ [boiling point]: **to bring sthg to the** ~ porter qqch à ébullition; **to come to the** ~ venir à ébullition. **2** *vt* [water, food] faire bouillir. ‖ [kettle] mettre sur le feu. **3** *vi* [water] bouillir. ○ **boil down to** *vt fus fig* revenir à, se résumer à. ○ **boil over** *vi* [liquid] déborder. ‖ *fig* [feelings] exploser.

boiled ['bɔɪld] *adj*: ~ **egg** œuf *m* à la coque; ~ **sweet** *Br* bonbon *m* (dur).

boiler ['bɔɪlər] *n* chaudière *f*.

boiling ['bɔɪlɪŋ] *adj* [liquid] bouillant(e). ‖ *inf* [weather] très chaud(e), torride; [person]: **I'm** ~ **(hot)!** je crève de chaleur!

boiling point *n* point *m* d'ébullition.

boisterous ['bɔɪstərəs] *adj* turbulent(e), remuant(e).

bold [bəʊld] *adj* [confident] hardi(e), audacieux(ieuse). ‖ [lines, design] hardi(e); [colour] vif (vive), éclatant(e). ‖ TYPO: ~ **type** OR **print** caractères *mpl* gras.

bollard ['bɒlɑːd] *n* [on road] borne *f*.

bolster ['bəʊlstər] **1** *n* [pillow] traversin *m*. **2** *vt* renforcer, affirmer. ○ **bolster up** *vt fus* soutenir, appuyer.

bolt [bəʊlt] **1** *n* [on door, window] verrou *m*. ‖ [type of screw] boulon *m*. **2** *adv*: ~ **upright** droit(e) comme un piquet. **3** *vt* [fasten together] boulonner. ‖ [close - door, window] verrouiller. ‖ [food] engouffrer, engloutir. **4** *vi* [run] détaler.

bomb [bɒm] **1** *n* bombe *f*. **2** *vt* bombarder.

bombard [bɒm'bɑːd] *vt* MIL & *fig*: **to** ~ **(with)** bombarder (de).

bombastic [bɒm'bæstɪk] *adj* pompeux(euse).

bomb disposal squad *n* équipe *f* de déminage.

borough

bomber ['bɒmə'] n [plane] bombardier m. ‖ [person] plastiqueur m.

bombing ['bɒmɪŋ] n bombardement m.

bombshell ['bɒmʃel] n fig bombe f.

bona fide [,bəʊnə'faɪdɪ] adj véritable, authentique; [offer] sérieux(ieuse).

bond [bɒnd] 1 n [between people] lien m. ‖ [promise] engagement m. ‖ FIN bon m, titre m. 2 vt [glue]: **to ~ sthg to sthg** coller qqch sur qqch. ‖ fig [people] unir.

bondage ['bɒndɪdʒ] n servitude f, esclavage m.

bone [bəʊn] 1 n os m; [of fish] arête f. 2 vt [meat] désosser; [fish] enlever les arêtes de.

bone-dry adj tout à fait sec (sèche).

bone-idle adj paresseux(euse) comme une couleuvre OR un lézard.

bonfire ['bɒn,faɪə'] n [for fun] feu m de joie; [to burn rubbish] feu m.

Bonn [bɒn] n Bonn.

bonnet ['bɒnɪt] n [hat] bonnet m.

bonus ['bəʊnəs] (pl -es) n [extra money] prime f, gratification f. ‖ fig [added advantage] plus m.

bony ['bəʊnɪ] adj [person, hand, face] maigre, osseux(euse). ‖ [meat] plein(e) d'os; [fish] plein d'arêtes.

boo [buː] (pl -s) 1 excl hou! 2 n huée f. 3 vt & vi huer.

boob [buːb] n inf [mistake] gaffe f, bourde f. ○ **boobs** npl Br v inf nichons mpl.

booby trap ['buːbɪ-] n [bomb] objet m piégé. ‖ [practical joke] farce f.

book [bʊk] 1 n [for reading] livre m. ‖ [of stamps, tickets, cheques] carnet m; [of matches] pochette f. 2 vt [reserve - gen] réserver; [- performer] engager; **to be fully ~ed** être complet. ‖ inf [subj: police] coller un PV à. 3 vi réserver. ○ **books** npl COMM livres mpl de comptes. ○ **book up** vt sep réserver, retenir.

bookcase ['bʊkkeɪs] n bibliothèque f.

bookie ['bʊkɪ] n inf bookmaker m.

booking ['bʊkɪŋ] n [reservation] réservation f.

booking office n bureau m de réservation OR location.

bookkeeping ['bʊk,kiːpɪŋ] n comptabilité f.

booklet ['bʊklɪt] n brochure f.

bookmaker ['bʊk,meɪkə'] n bookmaker m.

bookmark ['bʊkmɑːk] n signet m.

bookseller ['bʊk,selə'] n libraire mf.

bookshelf ['bʊkʃelf] (pl -shelves [-ʃelvz]) n rayon m OR étagère f à livres.

bookshop Br ['bʊkʃɒp], **bookstore** Am ['bʊkstɔːr] n librairie f.

book token n chèque-livre m.

boom [buːm] 1 n [loud noise] grondement m. ‖ [in business, trade] boom m. ‖ NAUT bôme f. ‖ [for TV camera, microphone] girafe f, perche f. 2 vi [make noise] gronder. ‖ [business, trade] être en plein essor OR en hausse.

boon [buːn] n avantage m, bénédiction f.

boost [buːst] 1 n [to production, sales] augmentation f; [to economy] croissance f. 2 vt [production, sales] stimuler. ‖ [popularity] accroître, renforcer.

booster ['buːstə'] n MED rappel m.

boot [buːt] 1 n [for walking, sport] chaussure f. ‖ [fashion item] botte f. ‖ Br [of car] coffre m. 2 vt inf flanquer des coups de pied à. ○ **to boot** adv pardessus le marché.

booth [buːð] n [at fair] baraque f foraine. ‖ [telephone booth] cabine f. ‖ [voting booth] isoloir m.

booty ['buːtɪ] n butin m.

booze [buːz] inf 1 n (U) alcool m, boisson f alcoolisée. 2 vi picoler.

bop [bɒp] inf 1 n [hit] coup m. ‖ [disco, dance] boum f. 2 vi [dance] danser.

border ['bɔːdə'] 1 n [between countries] frontière f. ‖ [edge] bord m. ‖ [in garden] bordure f. 2 vt [country] être limitrophe de. ‖ [edge] border. ○ **border on** vt fus friser, être voisin(e) de.

borderline ['bɔːdəlaɪn] 1 adj: **~ case** cas m limite. 2 n fig limite f, ligne f de démarcation.

bore [bɔːr] 1 pt → **bear**. 2 n [person] raseur m, -euse f; [situation, event] corvée f. ‖ [of gun] calibre m. 3 vt [not interest] ennuyer, raser; **to ~ sb stiff** OR **to tears** OR **to death** ennuyer qqn à mourir. ‖ [drill] forer, percer.

bored [bɔːd] adj [person] qui s'ennuie; [look] d'ennui; **to be ~ with** en avoir assez de.

boredom ['bɔːdəm] n (U) ennui m.

boring ['bɔːrɪŋ] adj ennuyeux(euse).

born [bɔːn] adj né(e); **to be ~** naître; **I was ~ in 1965** je suis né en 1965; **when were you ~?** quelle est ta date de naissance?

borne [bɔːn] pp → **bear**.

borough ['bʌrə] n municipalité f.

borrow ['bɒrəʊ] *vt* emprunter; **to ~ sthg (from sb)** emprunter qqch (à qqn).

Bosnia ['bɒznɪə] *n* Bosnie *f*.

Bosnia-Herzegovina [-,hɜːtsəgə-'viːnə] *n* Bosnie-Herzégovine *f*.

Bosnian ['bɒznɪən] **1** *adj* bosniaque. **2** *n* Bosniaque *mf*.

bosom ['bʊzəm] *n* poitrine *f*, seins *mpl*; *fig* sein *m*; **~ friend** ami *m* intime.

boss [bɒs] *n* patron *m*, -onne *f*, chef *m*. ○ **boss about, boss around** *vt sep pej* donner des ordres à, régenter.

bossy ['bɒsɪ] *adj* autoritaire.

bosun ['bəʊsn] = **boatswain.**

botany ['bɒtənɪ] *n* botanique *f*.

botch [bɒtʃ] ○ **botch up** *vt sep inf* bousiller, saboter.

both [bəʊθ] **1** *adj* les deux. **2** *pron*: **~ of them**) (tous) les deux ((toutes) les deux); **~ of us are coming** on vient tous les deux. **3** *adv*: **she is ~ intelligent and amusing** elle est à la fois intelligente et drôle.

bother ['bɒðər] **1** *vt* [worry] ennuyer, inquiéter; **to ~ o.s. (about)** se tracasser (au sujet de); **I can't be ~ed to do it** je n'ai vraiment pas envie de le faire. || [pester, annoy] embêter; **I'm sorry to ~ you** excusez-moi de vous déranger. **2** *vi*: **to ~ about sthg** s'inquiéter de qqch; **don't ~ (to do it)** ce n'est pas la peine (de le faire). **3** *n* (*U*) embêtement *m*; **it's no ~ at all** cela ne me dérange OR m'ennuie pas du tout.

bothered ['bɒðəd] *adj* inquiet(iète).

bottle ['bɒtl] **1** *n* [gen] bouteille *f*; [for medicine, perfume] flacon *m*; [for baby] biberon *m*. **2** *vt* [wine etc] mettre en bouteilles; [fruit] mettre en bocal. ○ **bottle up** *vt sep* [feelings] refouler, contenir.

bottle bank *n* container *m* pour verre usagé.

bottleneck ['bɒtlnek] *n* [in traffic] bouchon *m*, embouteillage *m*. || [in production] goulet *m* d'étranglement.

bottle-opener *n* ouvre-bouteilles *m inv*, décapsuleur *m*.

bottom ['bɒtəm] **1** *adj* [lowest] du bas. || [in class] dernier(ière). **2** *n* [of bottle, lake, garden] fond *m*; [of page, ladder, street] bas *m*; [of hill] pied *m*. || [of scale] bas *m*; [of class] dernier *m*, -ière *f*. || [buttocks] derrière *m*. || [cause]: **to get to the ~ of sthg** aller au fond de qqch, découvrir la cause de qqch. ○ **bottom out** *vi* atteindre son niveau le plus bas.

bottom line *n fig*: **the ~** l'essentiel *m*.

bought [bɔːt] *pt & pp* → **buy.**

boulder ['bəʊldər] *n* rocher *m*.

bounce [baʊns] **1** *vi* [ball] rebondir; [person] sauter. || *inf* [cheque] être sans provision. **2** *vt* [ball] faire rebondir. **3** *n* rebond *m*.

bouncer ['baʊnsər] *n inf* videur *m*.

bound [baʊnd] **1** *pt & pp* → **bind. 2** *adj* [certain]: **he's ~ to win** il va sûrement gagner; **she's ~ to see it** elle ne peut pas manquer de le voir. || [obliged]: **to be ~ to do sthg** être obligé(e) OR tenu(e) de faire qqch; **I'm ~ to say/admit** je dois dire/reconnaître. || [for place]: **to be ~ for** [subj: person] être en route pour; [subj: plane, train] être à destination de. **3** *n* [leap] bond *m*, saut *m*. **4** *vt*: **to be ~ed by** [subj: field] être limité(e) OR délimité(e) par; [subj: country] être limitrophe de. ○ **bounds** *npl* limites *fpl*; **out of ~s** interdit, défendu.

boundary ['baʊndərɪ] *n* [gen] frontière *f*; [of property] limite *f*, borne *f*.

bourbon ['bɜːbən] *n* bourbon *m*.

bout [baʊt] *n* [of illness] accès *m*; **a ~ of flu** une grippe. || [session] période *f*. || [boxing match] combat *m*.

bow¹ [baʊ] **1** *n* [in greeting] révérence *f*. || [of ship] proue *f*, avant *m*. **2** *vt* [head] baisser, incliner. **3** *vi* [make a bow] saluer. || [defer]: **to ~ to** s'incliner devant.

bow² [bəʊ] *n* [weapon] arc *m*. || MUS archet *m*. || [knot] nœud *m*.

bowels ['baʊəlz] *npl* intestins *mpl*; *fig* entrailles *fpl*.

bowl [bəʊl] *n* [container - gen] jatte *f*, saladier *m*; [- small] bol *m*; [- for washing up] cuvette *f*. || [of toilet, sink] cuvette *f*; [of pipe] fourneau *m*. ○ **bowls** *n* (*U*) boules *fpl* (*sur herbe*). ○ **bowl over** *vt sep lit & fig* renverser.

bow-legged [,bəʊ'legɪd] *adj* aux jambes arquées.

bowler ['bəʊlər]: **~ (hat)** chapeau *m* melon.

bowling ['bəʊlɪŋ] *n* (*U*) bowling *m*.

bowling alley *n* [building] bowling *m*; [alley] piste *f* de bowling.

bowling green *n* terrain *m* de boules (*sur herbe*).

bow tie [bəʊ-] *n* nœud *m* papillon.

box [bɒks] **1** *n* [gen] boîte *f*. || THEATRE loge *f*. **2** *vi* boxer, faire de la boxe.

boxer ['bɒksər] *n* [fighter] boxeur *m*. || [dog] boxer *m*.

boxer shorts *npl* caleçon *m*.

boxing ['bɒksɪŋ] *n* boxe *f*.

Boxing Day *n jour des étrennes en Grande-Bretagne (le 26 décembre).*

boxing glove *n gant m de boxe.*

box office *n bureau m de location.*

boy [bɔɪ] **1** *n* [male child] garçon *m.* **2** *excl inf:* (**oh**) ~! ben, mon vieux!, ben, dis-donc!

boycott ['bɔɪkɒt] **1** *n* boycott *m,* boycottage *m.* **2** *vt* boycotter.

boyfriend ['bɔɪfrend] *n* copain *m,* petit ami *m.*

boyish ['bɔɪɪʃ] *adj* [appearance - of man] gamin(e); [- of woman] de garçon; [behaviour] garçonnier(ière).

BR (*abbr of* **British Rail**) *n* ≃ SNCF *f.*

bra [brɑː] *n soutien-gorge m.*

brace [breɪs] **1** *n* [on teeth] appareil *m* (dentaire). || [on leg] appareil *m* orthopédique. **2** *vt* [steady] soutenir, consolider; **to ~ o.s.** s'accrocher, se cramponner. || *fig* [prepare]: **to ~ o.s. (for sthg)** se préparer (à qqch). ○ **braces** *npl Br* bretelles *fpl.*

bracelet ['breɪslɪt] *n* bracelet *m.*

bracing ['breɪsɪŋ] *adj* vivifiant(e).

bracken ['brækn] *n* fougère *f.*

bracket ['brækɪt] *n* [support] support *m.* || [parenthesis - round] parenthèse *f;* [- square] crochet *m;* **in ~s** entre parenthèses/crochets. || [group]: **age/income ~** tranche *f* d'âge/de revenus.

brag [bræg] *vi* se vanter.

braid [breɪd] **1** *n* [on uniform] galon *m.* || [of hair] tresse *f,* natte *f.* **2** *vt* [hair] tresser, natter.

brain [breɪn] *n* cerveau *m.* ○ **brains** *npl* [intelligence] intelligence *f.*

brainchild ['breɪntʃaɪld] *n inf* idée *f* personnelle, invention *f* personnelle.

brainwash ['breɪnwɒʃ] *vt* faire un lavage de cerveau à.

brainwave ['breɪnweɪv] *n* idée *f* géniale ᴏʀ de génie.

brainy ['breɪnɪ] *adj inf* intelligent(e).

brake [breɪk] **1** *n lit & fig* frein *m.* **2** *vi* freiner.

brake light *n* stop *m,* feu *m* arrière.

bramble ['bræmbl] *n* [bush] ronce *f;* [fruit] mûre *f.*

bran [bræn] *n* son *m.*

branch [brɑːntʃ] **1** *n* [of tree, subject] branche *f.* || [of railway] bifurcation *f,* embranchement *m.* || [of company] filiale *f,* succursale *f;* [of bank] agence *f.* **2** *vi* bifurquer. ○ **branch out** *vi* [person, company] étendre ses activités, se diversifier.

brand [brænd] **1** *n* ᴄᴏᴍᴍ marque *f.* || *fig* [type, style] type *m,* genre *m.* **2** *vt* [cattle] marquer au fer rouge. || *fig* [classify]: **to ~ sb (as) sthg** étiqueter qqn comme qqch, coller à qqn l'étiquette de qqch.

brandish ['brændɪʃ] *vt* brandir.

brand name *n* marque *f.*

brand-new *adj* flambant neuf (flambant neuve), tout neuf (toute neuve).

brandy ['brændɪ] *n* cognac *m.*

brash [bræʃ] *adj* effronté(e).

brass [brɑːs] *n* [metal] laiton *m,* cuivre *m* jaune. || ᴍᴜs: **the ~** les cuivres *mpl.*

brass band *n* fanfare *f.*

brassiere [*Br* 'bræsɪə, *Am* brə'zɪr] *n* soutien-gorge *m.*

brat [bræt] *n inf pej* sale gosse *m.*

bravado [brə'vɑːdəʊ] *n* bravade *f.*

brave [breɪv] **1** *adj* courageux(euse), brave. **2** *n* guerrier *m* indien, brave *m.* **3** *vt* braver, affronter.

bravery ['breɪvərɪ] *n* courage *m,* bravoure *f.*

brawl [brɔːl] *n* bagarre *f,* rixe *f.*

brawn [brɔːn] *n* (*U*) [muscle] muscle *m.*

brazen ['breɪzn] *adj* [person] effronté(e), impudent(e); [lie] éhonté(e). ○ **brazen out** *vt sep:* **to ~ it out** crâner.

brazier ['breɪzjər] *n* brasero *m.*

Brazil [brə'zɪl] *n* Brésil *m.*

Brazilian [brə'zɪljən] **1** *adj* brésilien(ienne). **2** *n* Brésilien *m,* -ienne *f.*

brazil nut *n* noix *f* du Brésil.

breach [briːtʃ] **1** *n* [of law, agreement] infraction *f,* violation *f;* [of promise] rupture *f;* **to be in ~ of sthg** enfreindre ᴏʀ violer qqch; **~ of contract** rupture *f* de contrat. || [opening, gap] trou *m,* brèche *f.* **2** *vt* [agreement, contract] rompre. || [make hole in] faire une brèche dans.

breach of the peace *n* atteinte *f* à l'ordre public.

bread [bred] *n* pain *m;* **~ and butter** tartine *f* beurrée, pain beurré; *fig* gagne-pain *m.*

bread bin *Br,* **bread box** *Am n* boîte *f* à pain.

breadcrumbs ['bredkrʌmz] *npl* chapelure *f.*

breadline ['bredlaɪn] *n:* **to be on the ~** être sans ressources ᴏʀ sans le sou.

breadth [bretθ] *n* [width] largeur *f.* || *fig* [scope] ampleur *f,* étendue *f.*

breadwinner ['bred,wɪnər] *n* soutien *m* de famille.

break [breɪk] (*pt* **broke**, *pp* **broken**) **1** *n* [gap]: **~ (in)** trouée *f* (dans). || [fracture]

breakage

fracture f. ‖ [pause - gen] pause f; [- at school] récréation f; **to take a ~** [short] faire une pause; [longer] prendre des jours de congé; **without a ~** sans interruption. ‖ *inf* [luck]: **(lucky)** ~ chance f, veine f. 2 *vt* [gen] casser, briser; **to ~ one's arm/leg** se casser le bras/la jambe; **to ~ a record** battre un record. ‖ [interrupt - journey] interrompre; [- contact, silence] rompre. ‖ [not keep - law, rule] enfreindre, violer; [- promise] manquer à. ‖ [tell]: **to ~ the news (of sth to sb)** annoncer la nouvelle (de qqch à qqn). 3 *vi* [gen] se casser, se briser; **to ~ loose** OR **free** se dégager, s'échapper. ‖ [pause] s'arrêter, faire une pause. ‖ [weather] se gâter. ‖ [voice - with emotion] se briser; [- at puberty] muer. ‖ [news] se répandre, éclater. ‖ *phr*: **to ~ even** rentrer dans ses frais. ○ **break down** 1 *vt sep* [destroy - barrier] démolir; [- door] enfoncer. ‖ [analyse] analyser. 2 *vi* [car, machine] tomber en panne; [resistance] céder; [negotiations] échouer. ‖ [emotionally] fondre en larmes, éclater en sanglots. ○ **break in** 1 *vi* [burglar] entrer par effraction. ‖ [interrupt]: **to ~ in (on sb/sthg)** interrompre (qqn/qqch). 2 *vt sep* [horse] dresser; [person] rompre, accoutumer. ○ **break into** *vt fus* [subj: burglar] entrer par effraction dans. ‖ [begin]: **to ~ into song/applause** se mettre à chanter/applaudir. ○ **break off** 1 *vt sep* [detach] détacher. ‖ [talks, relationship] rompre; [holiday] interrompre. 2 *vi* [become detached] se casser, se détacher. ‖ [stop talking] s'interrompre, se taire. ○ **break out** *vi* [begin - fire] se déclarer; [- fighting] éclater. ‖ [escape]: **to ~ out (of)** s'échapper (de), s'évader (de). ○ **break up** 1 *vt sep* [into smaller pieces] mettre en morceaux. ‖ [end - marriage, relationship] détruire; [- fight, party] mettre fin à. 2 *vi* [into smaller pieces - gen] se casser en morceaux; [- ship] se briser. ‖ [end - marriage, relationship] se briser; [- talks, party] prendre fin; [- school] finir, fermer; **to ~ up (with sb)** rompre (avec qqn). ‖ [crowd] se disperser.

breakage ['breɪkɪdʒ] *n* bris *m*.

breakdown ['breɪkdaʊn] *n* [of vehicle, machine] panne f; [of negotiations] échec *m*; [in communications] rupture f. ‖ [analysis] détail *m*.

breakfast ['brekfəst] *n* petit déjeuner *m*.

break-in *n* cambriolage *m*.

breaking ['breɪkɪŋ] *n*: **~ and entering** JUR entrée f par effraction.

breakthrough ['breɪkθruː] *n* percée f.

breakup ['breɪkʌp] *n* [of marriage, relationship] rupture f.

breast [brest] *n* [of woman] sein *m*; [of man] poitrine f. ‖ [meat of bird] blanc *m*.

breast-feed *vt* & *vi* allaiter.

breaststroke ['breststrəʊk] *n* brasse f.

breath [breθ] *n* souffle *m*, haleine f; **out of ~** hors d'haleine, à bout de souffle; **to get one's ~ back** reprendre haleine OR son souffle.

breathalyse *Br*, **-yze** *Am* ['breθəlaɪz] *vt* ≃ faire subir l'Alcootest® à.

breathe [briːð] 1 *vi* respirer. 2 *vt* [inhale] respirer. ‖ [exhale - smell] souffler des relents de. ○ **breathe in** 1 *vi* inspirer. 2 *vt sep* aspirer. ○ **breathe out** *vi* expirer.

breather ['briːðər] *n inf* moment *m* de repos OR répit.

breathing ['briːðɪŋ] *n* respiration f.

breathless ['breθlɪs] *adj* [out of breath] hors d'haleine, essoufflé(e). ‖ [with excitement] fébrile, fiévreux(euse).

breathtaking ['breθ,teɪkɪŋ] *adj* à vous couper le souffle.

breed [briːd] (*pt* & *pp* **bred** [bred]) 1 *n lit* & *fig* race f, espèce f. 2 *vt* [animals, plants] élever. ‖ *fig* [suspicion, contempt] faire naître, engendrer. 3 *vi* se reproduire.

breeding ['briːdɪŋ] *n* (*U*) [of animals, plants] élevage *m*. ‖ [manners] bonnes manières *fpl*, savoir-vivre *m*.

breeze [briːz] *n* brise f.

breezy ['briːzɪ] *adj* [windy] venteux(euse). ‖ [cheerful] jovial(e), enjoué(e).

brevity ['brevɪtɪ] *n* brièveté f.

brew [bruː] 1 *vt* [beer] brasser; [tea] faire infuser; [coffee] préparer, faire. 2 *vi* [tea] infuser; [coffee] se faire. ‖ *fig* [trouble, storm] se préparer, couver.

brewery ['brʊərɪ] *n* brasserie f.

bribe [braɪb] 1 *n* pot-de-vin *m*. 2 *vt*: **to ~ sb (to do sthg)** soudoyer qqn (pour qu'il fasse qqch).

bribery ['braɪbərɪ] *n* corruption f.

brick [brɪk] *n* brique f.

bricklayer ['brɪk,leɪər] *n* maçon *m*.

bridal ['braɪdl] *adj* [dress] de mariée; [suite etc] nuptial(e).

bride [braɪd] *n* mariée f.

bridegroom ['braɪdgrʊm] *n* marié *m*.

bridesmaid ['braɪdzmeɪd] *n* demoiselle *f* d'honneur.

bridge [brɪdʒ] **1** *n* [gen] pont *m*. || [on ship] passerelle *f*. || [of nose] arête *f*. || [card game, for teeth] bridge *m*. **2** *vt fig* [gap] réduire.

bridle ['braɪdl] *n* bride *f*.

bridle path *n* piste *f* cavalière.

brief [briːf] **1** *adj* [short] bref (brève), court(e); **in ~** en bref, en deux mots. || [revealing] très court(e). **2** *n* JUR affaire *f*, dossier *m*. **3** *vt*: **to ~ sb (on)** [bring up to date] mettre qqn au courant (de); [instruct] briefer qqn (sur). **○ briefs** *npl* slip *m*.

briefcase ['briːfkeɪs] *n* serviette *f*.

briefing ['briːfɪŋ] *n* instructions *fpl*, briefing *m*.

briefly ['briːflɪ] *adv* [for a short time] un instant. || [concisely] brièvement.

brigade [brɪ'geɪd] *n* brigade *f*.

brigadier [,brɪgə'dɪər] *n* général *m* de brigade.

bright [braɪt] *adj* [room] clair(e); [light, colour] vif (vive); [sunlight] éclatant(e); [eyes, future] brillant(e). || [intelligent] intelligent(e).

brighten ['braɪtn] *vi* [become lighter] s'éclaircir. **○ brighten up 1** *vt sep* égayer. **2** *vi* [person] s'égayer, s'animer. || [weather] se dégager, s'éclaircir.

brilliance ['brɪljəns] *n* [cleverness] intelligence *f*. || [of colour, light] éclat *m*.

brilliant ['brɪljənt] *adj* [gen] brillant(e). || [colour] éclatant(e). || *inf* [wonderful] super (*inv*), génial(e).

Brillo pad® ['brɪləʊ-] *n* ≃ tampon *m* Jex®.

brim [brɪm] **1** *n* bord *m*. **2** *vi*: **to ~ with** *lit & fig* être plein(e) de.

brine [braɪn] *n* saumure *f*.

bring [brɪŋ] (*pt & pp* **brought**) *vt* [person] amener; [object] apporter. || [cause - happiness, shame] entraîner, causer; **to ~ sthg to an end** mettre fin à qqch. **○ bring about** *vt sep* causer, provoquer. **○ bring around** *vt sep* [make conscious] ranimer. **○ bring back** *vt sep* [object] rapporter; [person] ramener. || [memories] rappeler. || [reinstate] rétablir. || [of colour, light] introduire. **○ bring down** *vt sep* [plane] abattre; [government] renverser. || [prices] faire baisser. **○ bring forward** *vt sep* [gen] avancer. || [in bookkeeping] reporter. **○ bring in** *vt sep* [law] introduire. || [money - subj: person] gagner; [- subj: deal] rapporter. **○ bring off** *vt sep* [plan] réaliser, réussir; [deal] conclure,

mener à bien. **○ bring out** *vt sep* [product] lancer; [book] publier, faire paraître. || [cause to appear] faire ressortir. **○ bring round, bring to = bring around. ○ bring up** *vt sep* [raise - children] élever. || [mention] mentionner. || [vomit] rendre, vomir.

brink [brɪŋk] *n*: **on the ~ of** au bord de, à la veille de.

brisk [brɪsk] *adj* [quick] vif (vive), rapide. || [manner, tone] déterminé(e).

bristle ['brɪsl] **1** *n* poil *m*. **2** *vi lit & fig* se hérisser.

Britain ['brɪtn] *n* Grande-Bretagne *f*; **in ~** en Grande-Bretagne.

British ['brɪtɪʃ] **1** *adj* britannique. **2** *npl*: **the ~** les Britanniques *mpl*.

British Isles *npl*: **the ~** les îles *fpl* Britanniques.

Briton ['brɪtn] *n* Britannique *mf*.

Brittany ['brɪtənɪ] *n* Bretagne *f*.

brittle ['brɪtl] *adj* fragile.

broach [brəʊtʃ] *vt* [subject] aborder.

broad [brɔːd] *adj* [wide] large; [- range, interests] divers(e), varié(e). || [description] général(e). || [hint] transparent(e); [accent] prononcé(e). **○ in broad daylight** *adv* en plein jour.

broad bean *n* fève *f*.

broadcast ['brɔːdkɑːst] (*pt & pp* **broadcast**) **1** *n* RADIO & TV émission *f*. **2** *vt* RADIO radiodiffuser; TV téléviser.

broaden ['brɔːdn] **1** *vt* élargir. **2** *vi* s'élargir.

broadly ['brɔːdlɪ] *adv* [generally] généralement.

broadminded [,brɔːd'maɪndɪd] *adj* large d'esprit.

broccoli ['brɒkəlɪ] *n* brocoli *m*.

brochure ['brəʊʃər] *n* brochure *f*, prospectus *m*.

broil [brɔɪl] *vt Am* griller.

broke [brəʊk] **1** *pt* → **break**. **2** *adj inf* fauché(e).

broken ['brəʊkn] **1** *pp* → **break**. **2** *adj* [gen] cassé(e); **to have a ~ leg** avoir la jambe cassée. || [interrupted - journey, sleep] interrompu(e); [- line] brisé(e). || [marriage] brisé(e), détruit(e); [home] désuni(e). || [hesitant]: **to speak in ~ English** parler un anglais hésitant.

broker ['brəʊkər] *n* courtier *m*; **(insurance) ~** assureur *m*, courtier *m* d'assurances.

bronchitis [brɒŋ'kaɪtɪs] *n* (*U*) bronchite *f*.

bronze [brɒnz] **1** *adj* [colour] (couleur) bronze (*inv*). **2** *n* [gen] bronze *m*.

brooch [brəʊtʃ] *n* broche *f*.

brood [bruːd] *vi*: **to ~ (over** OR **about** sthg) ressasser (qqch), remâcher (qqch).

brook [brʊk] *n* ruisseau *m*.

broom [bruːm] *n* balai *m*.

broomstick ['bruːmstɪk] *n* manche *m* à balai.

Bros, bros (*abbr of* **brothers**) Frères.

broth [brɒθ] *n* bouillon *m*.

brothel ['brɒθl] *n* bordel *m*.

brother ['brʌðər] *n* frère *m*.

brother-in-law (*pl* **brothers-in-law**) *n* beau-frère *m*.

brought [brɔːt] *pt & pp* → **bring**.

brow [braʊ] *n* [forehead] front *m*. || [eyebrow] sourcil *m*. || [of hill] sommet *m*.

brown [braʊn] **1** *adj* [colour] brun(e), marron (*inv*). || [tanned] bronzé(e), hâlé(e). **2** *n* [colour] marron *m*, brun *m*. **3** *vt* [food] faire dorer.

Brownie (Guide) ['braʊnɪ-] *n* ≃ jeannette *f*.

Brownie point ['braʊnɪ-] *n* bon point *m*.

brown paper *n* papier *m* d'emballage, papier kraft.

brown rice *n* riz *m* complet.

brown sugar *n* sucre *m* roux.

browse [braʊz] *vi* [look]: **I'm just browsing** [in shop] je ne fais que regarder; **to ~ through** [magazines etc] feuilleter. || [animal] brouter.

bruise [bruːz] **1** *n* bleu *m*. **2** *vt* [skin, arm] se faire un bleu à; [fruit] taler.

brunch [brʌntʃ] *n* brunch *m*.

brunette [bruːˈnet] *n* brunette *f*.

brunt [brʌnt] *n*: **to bear** OR **take the ~ of** subir le plus gros de.

brush [brʌʃ] **1** *n* [gen] brosse *f*; [of painter] pinceau *m*. || [encounter]: **to have a ~ with the police** avoir des ennuis avec la police. **2** *vt* [clean with brush] brosser. || [touch lightly] effleurer. ○ **brush aside** *vt sep fig* écarter, repousser. ○ **brush off** *vt sep* [dismiss] envoyer promener. ○ **brush up** *vi*: **to ~ up on sthg** réviser qqch.

brush-off *n inf*: **to give sb the ~** envoyer promener qqn.

brusque [bruːsk] *adj* brusque.

Brussels ['brʌslz] *n* Bruxelles.

brussels sprout *n* chou *m* de Bruxelles.

brutal ['bruːtl] *adj* brutal(e).

brute [bruːt] **1** *adj* [force] brutal(e). **2** *n* brute *f*.

BSc (*abbr of* **Bachelor of Science**) *n* (*titulaire d'une*) *licence de sciences*.

bubble ['bʌbl] **1** *n* bulle *f*. **2** *vi* [liquid] faire des bulles, bouillonner.

bubble bath *n* bain *m* moussant.

bubble gum *n* bubble-gum *m*.

bubblejet printer ['bʌbldʒet-] *n* imprimante *f* à bulle d'encre.

Bucharest [,bjuːkəˈrest] *n* Bucarest.

buck [bʌk] *n* [male animal] mâle *m*. || *inf* [dollar] dollar *m*. || *inf* [responsibility]: **to pass the ~** refiler la responsabilité. **1** *vi* [horse] ruer. ○ **buck up** *inf vi* [hurry up] se remuer, se dépêcher. || [cheer up] ne pas se laisser abattre.

bucket ['bʌkɪt] *n* [gen] seau *m*.

Buckingham Palace ['bʌkɪŋəm-] *n* le palais de Buckingham (*résidence officielle du souverain britannique*).

buckle ['bʌkl] **1** *n* boucle *f*. **2** *vt* [fasten] boucler. || [bend] tordre. **3** *vi* [wheel] se voiler; [knees, legs] se plier.

bud [bʌd] **1** *n* bourgeon *m*. **2** *vi* bourgeonner.

Budapest [,bjuːdəˈpest] *n* Budapest.

Buddha ['bʊdə] *n* Bouddha *m*.

Buddhism ['bʊdɪzm] *n* bouddhisme *m*.

buddy ['bʌdɪ] *n inf* pote *m*.

budge [bʌdʒ] **1** *vt* faire bouger. **2** *vi* bouger.

budgerigar ['bʌdʒərɪgɑːr] *n* perruche *f*.

budget ['bʌdʒɪt] **1** *adj* [holiday, price] pour petits budgets. **2** *n* budget *m*. ○ **budget for** *vt fus* prévoir.

budgie ['bʌdʒɪ] *n inf* perruche *f*.

buff [bʌf] **1** *adj* [brown] chamois (*inv*). **2** *n inf* [expert] mordu *m*, -e *f*.

buffalo ['bʌfələʊ] (*pl inv* OR **-es** OR **-s**) *n* buffle *m*.

buffer ['bʌfər] *n* [gen] tampon *m*. || COMPUT mémoire *f* tampon.

buffet [*Br* 'bʊfeɪ, *Am* bəˈfeɪ] *n* [food, cafeteria] buffet *m*.

buffet car ['bʊfeɪ-] *n* wagon-restaurant *m*.

bug [bʌg] **1** *n* [insect] punaise *f*. || *inf* [germ] microbe *m*. || *inf* [listening device] micro *m*. || COMPUT défaut *m*, bug *m*. **2** *vt inf* [telephone] mettre sur table d'écoute; [room] cacher des micros dans. || *inf* [annoy] embêter.

buggy ['bʌgɪ] *n* [carriage] boghei *m*. || [pushchair] poussette *f*; *Am* [pram] landau *m*.

bugle ['bju:gl] n clairon m.

build [bɪld] (pt & pp **built**) 1 vt lit & fig construire, bâtir. 2 n carrure f. ○ **build on, build upon** 1 vt fus [success] tirer avantage de. 2 vt sep [base on] baser sur. ○ **build up** 1 vt sep [business] développer; [reputation] bâtir. 2 vi [clouds] s'amonceler; [traffic] augmenter.

builder ['bɪldə'] n entrepreneur m.

building ['bɪldɪŋ] n bâtiment m.

building and loan association n Am société d'épargne et de financement immobilier.

building site n chantier m.

building society n Br ≃ société f d'épargne et de financement immobilier.

buildup ['bɪldʌp] n [increase] accroissement m.

built [bɪlt] pt & pp → build.

built-in adj CONSTR encastré(e). || [inherent] inné(e).

built-up adj: ~ area agglomération f.

bulb [bʌlb] n ELEC ampoule f. || BOT oignon m.

Bulgaria [bʌl'geərɪə] n Bulgarie f.

Bulgarian [bʌl'geərɪən] 1 adj bulgare. 2 n [person] Bulgare mf. || [language] bulgare m.

bulge [bʌldʒ] 1 n [lump] bosse f. 2 vi: to ~ (with) être gonflé (de).

bulk [bʌlk] 1 n [mass] volume m. || [of person] corpulence f. || COMM: in ~ en gros. || [majority]: **the ~ of** le plus gros de. 2 adj en gros.

bulky ['bʌlkɪ] adj volumineux(euse).

bull [bʊl] n [male cow] taureau m; [male elephant, seal] mâle m.

bulldog ['bʊldɒg] n bouledogue m.

bulldozer ['bʊldəʊzə'] n bulldozer m.

bullet ['bʊlɪt] n [for gun] balle f.

bulletin ['bʊlətɪn] n bulletin m.

bullet-proof adj pare-balles (inv).

bullfight ['bʊlfaɪt] n corrida f.

bullfighter ['bʊl,faɪtə'] n toréador m.

bullfighting ['bʊl,faɪtɪŋ] n (U) courses fpl de taureaux; [art] tauromachie f.

bullion ['bʊljən] n (U): gold ~ or m en barres.

bullock ['bʊlək] n bœuf m.

bullring ['bʊlrɪŋ] n arène f.

bull's-eye n centre m.

bully ['bʊlɪ] 1 n tyran m. 2 vt tyranniser, brutaliser.

bum [bʌm] n v inf [bottom] derrière m. || inf pej [tramp] clochard m.

bumblebee ['bʌmblbi:] n bourdon m.

bump [bʌmp] 1 n [lump] bosse f. || [knock, blow] choc m. || [noise] bruit m sourd. 2 vt [head etc] cogner; [car] heurter. ○ **bump into** vt fus [meet by chance] rencontrer par hasard.

bumper ['bʌmpə'] 1 adj [harvest, edition] exceptionnel(elle). 2 n AUT pare-chocs m inv. || Am RAIL tampon m.

bumpy ['bʌmpɪ] adj [surface] défoncé(e). || [ride] cahoteux(euse); [sea crossing] agité(e).

bun [bʌn] n [cake] petit pain m aux raisins; [bread roll] petit pain au lait. || [hairstyle] chignon m.

bunch [bʌntʃ] n [of people] groupe m; [of flowers] bouquet m; [of grapes] grappe f; [of bananas] régime m; [of keys] trousseau m. ○ **bunches** npl [hairstyle] couettes fpl.

bundle ['bʌndl] 1 n [of clothes] paquet m; [of notes, newspapers] liasse f; [of wood] fagot m. 2 vt [put roughly - person] entasser; [- clothes] fourrer, entasser.

bungalow ['bʌŋgələʊ] n bungalow m.

bungle ['bʌŋgl] vt gâcher, bâcler.

bunion ['bʌnjən] n oignon m.

bunk [bʌŋk] n [bed] couchette f.

bunk bed n lit m superposé.

bunker ['bʌŋkə'] n GOLF & MIL bunker m. || [for coal] coffre m.

bunny ['bʌnɪ] n: ~ (rabbit) lapin m.

bunting ['bʌntɪŋ] n (U) guirlandes fpl (de drapeaux).

buoy [Br bɔɪ, Am 'bu:ɪ] n bouée f.

buoyant ['bɔɪənt] adj [able to float] qui flotte. || fig [person] enjoué(e); [economy] florissant(e); [market] ferme.

burden ['bɜ:dn] 1 n lit & fig: ~ (on) charge f (pour), fardeau m (pour). 2 vt: to ~ sb with [responsibilities, worries] accabler qqn de.

bureau ['bjʊərəʊ] (pl -x) n Br [desk] bureau m; Am [chest of drawers] commode f. || [office] bureau m.

bureaucracy [bjʊə'rɒkrəsɪ] n bureaucratie f.

bureaux ['bjʊərəʊz] pl → bureau.

burger ['bɜ:gə'] n hamburger m.

burglar ['bɜ:glə'] n cambrioleur m, -euse f.

burglar alarm n système m d'alarme.

burglarize Am = burgle.

burglary ['bɜ:glərɪ] n cambriolage m.

burgle ['bɜ:gl], **burglarize** Am ['bɜ:gləraɪz] vt cambrioler.

Burgundy ['bɜ:gəndɪ] n Bourgogne f.

burial ['berɪəl] n enterrement m.

Burma ['bɜːmə] *n* Birmanie *f*.

burn [bɜːn] (*pt & pp* burnt OR -ed) 1 *vt* brûler. 2 *vi* brûler. 3 *n* brûlure *f*. ❍ **burn down** 1 *vt sep* [building, town] incendier. 2 *vi* [building] brûler complètement.

burner ['bɜːnər] *n* brûleur *m*.

burnt [bɜːnt] *pt & pp* → burn.

burp [bɜːp] *inf* 1 *n* rot *m*. 2 *vi* roter.

burrow ['bʌrəʊ] 1 *n* terrier *m*. 2 *vi* [dig] creuser un terrier. || *fig* [search] fouiller.

bursar ['bɜːsər] *n* intendant *m*, -e *f*.

burst [bɜːst] (*pt & pp* burst) 1 *vi* [gen] éclater. 2 *vt* faire éclater. 3 *n* [of gunfire] rafale *f*; [of enthusiasm] élan *m*. ❍ **burst into** *vt fus* [room] faire irruption dans. || [begin suddenly]: **to ~ into tears** fondre en larmes; **to ~ into flames** prendre feu. ❍ **burst out** *vt fus* [say suddenly] s'exclamer; **to ~ out laughing** éclater de rire.

bury ['berɪ] *vt* [in ground] enterrer. || [hide] cacher, enfouir.

bus [bʌs] *n* autobus *m*, bus *m*; [long-distance] car *m*; **by ~** en autobus/car.

bush [bʊʃ] *n* [plant] buisson *m*. || [open country]: **the ~** la brousse. || *phr:* **she doesn't beat about the ~** elle n'y va pas par quatre chemins.

bushy ['bʊʃɪ] *adj* touffu(e).

business ['bɪznɪs] *n* (*U*) [commerce] affaires *fpl*; **on ~** pour affaires; **to mean ~** *inf* ne pas plaisanter; **to go out of ~** fermer, faire faillite. || [company, duty] affaire *f*; **mind your own ~!** *inf* occupe-toi de tes oignons! || [affair, matter] histoire *f*, affaire *f*.

business class *n* classe *f* affaires.

businesslike ['bɪznɪslaɪk] *adj* efficace.

businessman ['bɪznɪsmæn] (*pl* -men [-men]) *n* homme *m* d'affaires.

business trip *n* voyage *m* d'affaires.

businesswoman ['bɪznɪs,wʊmən] (*pl* -women [-,wɪmɪn]) *n* femme *f* d'affaires.

bus shelter *n* Abribus® *m*.

bus station *n* gare *f* routière.

bus stop *n* arrêt *m* de bus.

bust [bʌst] (*pt & pp* bust OR -ed) 1 *adj* *inf* [broken] foutu(e). || [bankrupt]: **to go ~** faire faillite. 2 *n* [bosom] poitrine *f*. || [statue] buste *m*. 3 *vt inf* [break] péter.

bustle ['bʌsl] 1 *n* (*U*) [activity] remue-ménage *m*. 2 *vi* s'affairer.

busy ['bɪzɪ] *adj* [gen] occupé(e); **to be ~ doing sthg** être occupé à faire qqch. || [life, week] chargé(e); [town, office] animé(e).

busybody ['bɪzɪ,bɒdɪ] *n pej* mouche *f* du coche.

busy signal *n Am* TELEC tonalité *f* «occupé».

but [bʌt] 1 *conj* mais. 2 *prep* sauf, excepté; **he has no one ~ himself to blame** il ne peut s'en prendre qu'à lui-même. 3 *adv fml* seulement, ne ... que; **we can ~ try** on peut toujours essayer. ❍ **but for** *prep* sans.

butcher ['bʊtʃər] 1 *n* boucher *m*; **~'s (shop)** boucherie *f*. 2 *vt fig* [massacre] massacrer.

butler ['bʌtlər] *n* maître *m* d'hôtel (*chez un particulier*).

butt [bʌt] 1 *n* [of cigarette, cigar] mégot *m*. || [of rifle] crosse *f*. || [for water] tonneau *m*. || [of joke, criticism] cible *f*. 2 *vt* donner un coup de tête à. ❍ **butt in** *vi* [interrupt]: **to ~ in on sb** interrompre qqn; **to ~ in on sthg** s'immiscer OR s'imposer dans qqch.

butter ['bʌtər] 1 *n* beurre *m*. 2 *vt* beurrer.

buttercup ['bʌtəkʌp] *n* bouton *m* d'or.

butter dish *n* beurrier *m*.

butterfly ['bʌtəflaɪ] *n* SWIMMING & ZOOL papillon *m*.

buttocks ['bʌtəks] *npl* fesses *fpl*.

button ['bʌtn] 1 *n* [gen] bouton *m*. || *Am* [badge] badge *m*. 2 *vt* = button up. ❍ **button up** *vt sep* boutonner.

button mushroom *n* champignon *m* de Paris.

buttress ['bʌtrɪs] *n* contrefort *m*.

buy [baɪ] (*pt & pp* bought) 1 *vt* acheter; **to ~ sthg from sb** acheter qqch à qqn. 2 *n*: **a good ~** une bonne affaire. ❍ **buy up** *vt sep* acheter en masse.

buyer ['baɪər] *n* acheteur *m*, -euse *f*.

buyout ['baɪaʊt] *n* rachat *m*.

buzz [bʌz] 1 *n* [of insect] bourdonnement *m*. || *inf* [telephone call]: **to give sb a ~** passer un coup de fil à qqn. 2 *vi*: **to ~ (with)** bourdonner (de). 3 *vt* [on intercom] appeler.

buzzer ['bʌzər] *n* sonnerie *f*.

buzzword ['bʌzwɜːd] *n inf* mot *m* à la mode.

by [baɪ] 1 *prep* [indicating cause, agent] par. || [indicating means, method, manner]: **to pay ~ cheque** payer par chèque; **to travel ~ bus/train/plane/ship** voyager en bus/par le train/en avion/en bateau; **he's a lawyer ~ profession** il est avocat de son métier; **~ doing sthg** en faisant qqch. || [beside, close to] près de; **~ the sea** au bord de la mer; **I sat ~ her bed** j'étais assis à son chevet. || [past]: **to pass**

~ sb/sthg passer devant qqn/qqch. ||
[via, through] par. || [at or before a
particular time] avant, pas plus tard que;
I'll be there ~ eight j'y serai avant huit
heures; **~ now** déjà. || [during]: **~ day** le OR
de jour; **~ night** la OR de nuit. || [according
to] selon, suivant; **~ law** conformément à
la loi. || [in arithmetic] par; **divide/
multiply 20 ~ 3** divisez/multipliez 20 par
2. || [in measurements]: **2 metres ~ 4** 2
mètres sur 4. || [in quantities, amounts] à;
~ the yard au mètre; **~ the thousand** par
milliers; **paid ~ the day/week/month**
payé à la journée/à la semaine/au mois;
to cut prices ~ 50% réduire les prix de
50%. || [indicating gradual change]: **day ~
day** jour après jour, de jour en jour; **one
~ one** un à un, un par un. || *phr:* **(all) ~
oneself** (tout) seul ((toute) seule). **2** *adv*
→ **go, pass** *etc.*

bye(-bye) [baɪ(baɪ)] *excl inf* au revoir!,
salut!

bye-election = by-election.

byelaw ['baɪlɔː] = bylaw.

by-election *n* élection *f* partielle.

bylaw ['baɪlɔː] *n* arrêté *m*.

bypass ['baɪpɑːs] **1** *n* [road] route *f* de
contournement. || MED: **~ (operation)**
pontage *m*. **2** *vt* [town, difficulty] contourner; [subject] éviter.

by-product *n* [product] dérivé *m*.

bystander ['baɪˌstændər] *n* spectateur
m, -trice *f*.

byte [baɪt] *n* COMPUT octet *m*.

byword ['baɪwɜːd] *n* [symbol]: **to be a ~
for** être synonyme de.

C

c (*pl* **c's** OR **cs**), **C** (*pl* **C's** OR **Cs**) [siː] *n*
[letter] c *m inv*, C *m inv*. ○ **C** *n* MUS do *m*.
|| SCH [mark] C *m inv*. || (*abbr of* **Celsius,
centigrade**) C.

c., ca. *abbr of* **circa**.

cab [kæb] *n* [taxi] taxi *m*. || [of lorry] ca-
bine *f*.

cabaret ['kæbəreɪ] *n* cabaret *m*.

cabbage ['kæbɪdʒ] *n* [vegetable] chou *m*.

cabin ['kæbɪn] *n* [on ship, plane] cabine
f. || [house] cabane *f*.

cabin class *n* seconde classe *f*.

cabinet ['kæbɪnɪt] *n* [cupboard] meuble
m. || POL cabinet *m*.

cable ['keɪbl] **1** *n* câble *m*. **2** *vt* [news] câbler; [person] câbler à.

cable car *n* téléphérique *m*.

cable television, cable TV *n* télévision *f* par câble.

cackle ['kækl] *vi* [hen] caqueter. || [per-
son] jacasser.

cactus ['kæktəs] (*pl* **-tuses** OR **-ti** [-taɪ])
n cactus *m*.

cadet [kə'det] *n* élève *m* officier.

caesarean (section) *Br*, **cesarean
(section)** *Am* [sɪ'zeərɪən-] *n* césarienne
f.

cafe, café ['kæfeɪ] *n* café *m*.

cafeteria [ˌkæfɪ'tɪərɪə] *n* cafétéria *f*.

caffeine ['kæfiːn] *n* caféine *f*.

cage [keɪdʒ] *n* [for animal] cage *f*.

cajole [kə'dʒəʊl] *vt*: **to ~ sb (into doing
sthg)** enjôler qqn (pour qu'il fasse qqch).

cake [keɪk] *n* CULIN gâteau *m*; [of fish,
potato] croquette *f*; **it's a piece of ~** *inf fig*
c'est du gâteau. || [of soap] pain *m*.

calcium ['kælsɪəm] *n* calcium *m*.

calculate ['kælkjʊleɪt] *vt* [result, num-
ber] calculer; [consequences] évaluer. ||
[plan]: **to be ~d to do sthg** être calculé(e)
pour faire qqch.

calculating ['kælkjʊleɪtɪŋ] *adj pej* cal-
culateur(trice).

calculation [ˌkælkjʊ'leɪʃn] *n* calcul *m*.

calculator ['kælkjʊleɪtə] *n* calculatrice *f*.

calendar ['kælɪndə] *n* calendrier *m*.

calendar year *n* année *f* civile.

calf [kɑːf] (*pl* **calves**) *n* [of cow, leather] veau *m*; [of elephant] éléphanteau *m*; [of seal] bébé *m* phoque. ‖ ANAT mollet *m*.

calibre, caliber *Am* ['kælɪbə] *n* calibre *m*.

California [,kælɪ'fɔːnjə] *n* Californie *f*.

calipers *Am* = **callipers**.

call [kɔːl] **1** *n* [cry] appel *m*, cri *m*. ‖ TELEC appel *m* (téléphonique). ‖ [summons, invitation] appel *m*; **to be on ~** [doctor etc] être de garde. ‖ [visit] visite *f*; **to pay a ~ on sb** rendre visite à qqn. ‖ [demand]: **~ (for)** demande *f* (de). **2** *vt* [name, summon, phone] appeler; **she's ~ed Joan** elle s'appelle Joan; **let's ~ it £10** disons 10 livres. ‖ [label]: **he ~ed me a liar** il m'a traité de menteur. ‖ [shout] appeler, crier. ‖ [announce - meeting] convoquer; [- strike] lancer; [- flight] appeler; [- election] annoncer. **3** *vi* [shout - person] crier; [- animal, bird] pousser un cri/des cris. ‖ TELEC appeler; **who's ~ing?** qui est à l'appareil? ‖ [visit] passer. ○ **call back 1** *vt sep* rappeler. **2** *vi* TELEC rappeler. ‖ [visit again] repasser. ○ **call for** *vt fus* [collect - person] passer prendre; [- package, goods] passer chercher. ‖ [demand] demander. ○ **call in 1** *vt sep* [expert, police etc] faire venir. **2** *vi* passer. ○ **call off** *vt sep* [cancel] annuler. ‖ [dog] rappeler. ○ **call on** *vt fus* [visit] passer voir. ‖ [ask]: **to ~ on sb to do sthg** demander à qqn de faire qqch. ○ **call out 1** *vt sep* [police, doctor] appeler; [cry out] crier. **2** *vi* [cry out] crier. ○ **call round** *vi* passer. ○ **call up** *vt sep* MIL & TELEC appeler. ‖ COMPUT rappeler.

caller ['kɔːlə] *n* [visitor] visiteur *m*, -euse *f*. ‖ TELEC demandeur *m*.

call-in *n* *Am* RADIO & TV programme *m* à ligne ouverte.

calling ['kɔːlɪŋ] *n* [profession] métier *m*. ‖ [vocation] vocation *f*.

calling card *n* *Am* carte *f* de visite.

callipers *Br*, **calipers** *Am* ['kælɪpəz] *npl* MATH compas *m*. ‖ MED appareil *m* orthopédique.

callous ['kæləs] *adj* dur(e).

callus ['kæləs] (*pl* **-es**) *n* cal *m*, durillon *m*.

calm [kɑːm] **1** *adj* calme. **2** *n* calme *m*. **3** *vt* calmer. ○ **calm down 1** *vt sep* calmer. **2** *vi* se calmer.

calorie ['kælərɪ] *n* calorie *f*.

calves [kɑːvz] *pl* → **calf**.

camber ['kæmbə] *n* [of road] bombement *m*.

Cambodia [kæm'bəʊdjə] *n* Cambodge *m*.

camcorder ['kæm,kɔːdə] *n* Camé-scope® *m*.

came [keɪm] *pt* → **come**.

camel ['kæml] *n* chameau *m*.

cameo ['kæmɪəʊ] (*pl* **-s**) *n* [jewellery] camée *m*. ‖ CINEMA & THEATRE courte apparition *f* (d'une grande vedette).

camera ['kæmərə] *n* PHOT appareil-photo *m*; CINEMA & TV caméra *f*.

cameraman ['kæmərəmæn] (*pl* **-men** [-men]) *n* cameraman *m*.

Cameroon [,kæmə'ruːn] *n* Cameroun *m*.

camouflage ['kæməflɑːʒ] **1** *n* camouflage *m*. **2** *vt* camoufler.

camp [kæmp] **1** *n* camp *m*. **2** *vi* camper. ○ **camp out** *vi* camper.

campaign [kæm'peɪn] **1** *n* campagne *f*. **2** *vi*: **to ~ (for/against)** mener une campagne (pour/contre).

camp bed *n* lit *m* de camp.

camper ['kæmpə] *n* [person] campeur *m*, -euse *f*. ‖ [vehicle]: **~ (van)** camping-car *m*.

campground ['kæmpgraʊnd] *n* *Am* terrain *m* de camping.

camping ['kæmpɪŋ] *n* camping *m*; **to go ~** faire du camping.

camping site, campsite ['kæmpsaɪt] *n* (terrain *m* de) camping *m*.

campus ['kæmpəs] (*pl* **-es**) *n* campus *m*.

can¹ [kæn] (*pt* & *pp* **-ned**, *cont* **-ning**) **1** *n* [of drink, food] boîte *f*; [of oil] bidon *m*; [of paint] pot *m*. **2** *vt* mettre en boîte.

can² [*weak form* kən, *strong form* kæn] (*pt* & *conditional* **could**, *negative* **cannot** OR **can't**) *modal vb* [be able to] pouvoir; **~ you come to lunch?** tu peux venir déjeuner?; **~ you see/hear/smell something?** tu vois/entends/sens quelque chose? ‖ [know how to] savoir; **~ you drive/cook?** tu sais conduire/cuisiner?; **I ~ speak French** je parle le français. ‖ [indicating permission, in polite requests] pouvoir; **~ I speak to John, please?** est-ce que je pourrais parler à John, s'il vous plaît? ‖ [indicating disbelief, puzzlement] pouvoir; **what ~ she have done with it?** qu'est-ce qu'elle a bien pu en faire? ‖ [indicating possibility]: **I could see**

capsize

you tomorrow je pourrais vous voir demain; **the train could have been cancelled** peut-être que le train a été annulé.

Canada ['kænədə] *n* Canada *m*; **in ~** au Canada.

Canadian [kə'neɪdʒən] **1** *adj* canadien(ienne). **2** *n* Canadien *m*, -ienne *f*.

canal [kə'næl] *n* canal *m*.

Canaries [kə'neərɪz] *npl*: **the ~** les Canaries *fpl*.

canary [kə'neərɪ] *n* canari *m*.

cancel ['kænsl] *vt* [gen] annuler; [appointment, delivery] décommander. || [stamp] oblitérer; [cheque] faire opposition à. ○ **cancel out** *vt sep* annuler; **to ~ each other out** s'annuler.

cancellation [ˌkænsə'leɪʃn] *n* annulation *f*.

cancer ['kænsər] *n* cancer *m*. ○ **Cancer** *n* Cancer *m*.

candid ['kændɪd] *adj* franc (franche).

candidate ['kændɪdət] *n*: **~ (for)** candidat *m*, -e *f* (pour).

candle ['kændl] *n* bougie *f*, chandelle *f*.

candlelight ['kændllaɪt] *n* lueur *f* d'une bougie OR d'une chandelle.

candlelit ['kændllɪt] *adj* aux chandelles.

candlestick ['kændlstɪk] *n* bougeoir *m*.

candour *Br*, **candor** *Am* ['kændər] *n* franchise *f*.

candy ['kændɪ] *n* (*U*) [confectionery] confiserie *f*. || [sweet] bonbon *m*.

cane [keɪn] **1** *n* (*U*) [for furniture] rotin *m*. || [walking stick] canne *f*. || [for.punishment]: **the ~** la verge. || [for supporting plant] tuteur *m*. **2** *vt* fouetter.

canine ['keɪnaɪn] **1** *adj* canin(e). **2** *n*: **~ (tooth)** canine *f*.

canister ['kænɪstər] *n* [for film, tea] boîte *f*; [for gas, smoke] bombe *f*.

cannabis ['kænəbɪs] *n* cannabis *m*.

canned [kænd] *adj* [food, drink] en boîte.

cannibal ['kænɪbl] *n* cannibale *mf*.

cannon ['kænən] (*pl inv* OR **-s**) *n* canon *m*.

cannonball ['kænənbɔːl] *n* boulet *m* de canon.

cannot ['kænɒt] *fml* → **can²**.

canoe [kə'nuː] *n* canoë *m*, kayak *m*.

canoeing [kə'nuːɪŋ] *n* (*U*) canoë-kayak *m*.

canon ['kænən] *n* canon *m*.

can opener *n* ouvre-boîtes *m inv*.

canopy ['kænəpɪ] *n* [over bed] baldaquin *m*; [over seat] dais *m*. || [of trees, branches] voûte *f*.

can't [kɑːnt] = **cannot**.

cantankerous [kæn'tæŋkərəs] *adj* hargneux(euse).

canteen [kæn'tiːn] *n* [restaurant] cantine *f*. || [box of cutlery] ménagère *f*.

canter ['kæntər] **1** *n* petit galop *m*. **2** *vi* aller au petit galop.

cantilever ['kæntɪliːvər] *n* cantilever *m*.

canvas ['kænvəs] *n* toile *f*.

canvass ['kænvəs] *vt* POL [person] solliciter la voix de. || [opinion] sonder.

canyon ['kænjən] *n* cañon *m*.

cap [kæp] **1** *n* [hat - gen] casquette *f*. || [of pen] capuchon *m*; [of bottle] capsule *f*; [of lipstick] bouchon *m*. **2** *vt* [top]: **to be capped** with être coiffé(e) de. || [outdo]: **to ~ it all** pour couronner le tout.

capability [ˌkeɪpə'bɪlətɪ] *n* capacité *f*.

capable ['keɪpəbl] *adj*: **~ (of)** capable (de).

capacity [kə'pæsɪtɪ] *n* (*U*) [limit] capacité *f*, contenance *f*. || [ability]: **~ (for)** aptitude *f* (à). || [role] qualité *f*; **in an advisory ~** en tant que conseiller.

cape [keɪp] *n* GEOGR cap *m*. || [cloak] cape *f*.

caper ['keɪpər] *n* CULIN câpre *f*. || *inf* [dishonest activity] coup *m*, combine *f*.

capita → **per capita**.

capital ['kæpɪtl] **1** *adj* [letter] majuscule. || [offence] capital(e). **2** *n* [of country]: **~ (city)** capitale *f*. || TYPO: **~ (letter)** majuscule *f*. || (*U*) [money] capital *m*.

capital expenditure *n* (*U*) dépenses *fpl* d'investissement.

capital gains tax *n* impôt *m* sur les plus-values.

capital goods *npl* biens *mpl* d'équipement.

capitalism ['kæpɪtəlɪzm] *n* capitalisme *m*.

capitalist ['kæpɪtəlɪst] **1** *adj* capitaliste. **2** *n* capitaliste *mf*.

capitalize, -ise ['kæpɪtəlaɪz] *vi*: **to ~ on** tirer parti de.

capital punishment *n* peine *f* capitale OR de mort.

Capitol Hill ['kæpɪtl-] *n* siège du *Congrès à Washington*.

capitulate [kə'pɪtjʊleɪt] *vi* capituler.

Capricorn ['kæprɪkɔːn] *n* Capricorne *m*.

capsize [kæp'saɪz] **1** *vt* faire chavirer. **2** *vi* chavirer.

capsule ['kæpsju:l] *n* [gen] capsule *f*. ||
MED gélule *f*.

captain ['kæptɪn] *n* capitaine *m*.

caption ['kæpʃn] *n* légende *f*.

captive ['kæptɪv] **1** *adj* captif(ive). **2** *n*
captif *m*, -ive *f*.

captor ['kæptər] *n* ravisseur *m*, -euse *f*.

capture ['kæptʃər] **1** *vt* [person, animal]
capturer; [city] prendre. || [attention,
imagination] captiver. || COMPUT saisir. **2** *n*
[of person, animal] capture *f*; [of city]
prise *f*.

car [kɑ:r] **1** *n* AUT voiture *f*. || RAIL wagon
m, voiture *f*. **2** *comp* [door, accident] de
voiture; [industry] automobile.

carafe [kə'ræf] *n* carafe *f*.

caramel ['kærəmel] *n* caramel *m*.

caravan ['kærəvæn] *n* [gen] caravane *f*;
[towed by horse] roulotte *f*.

carbohydrate [,kɑ:bəʊ'haɪdreɪt] *n*
CHEM hydrate *m* de carbone. ○ **carbo-
hydrates** *npl* [in food] glucides *mpl*.

carbon ['kɑ:bən] *n* [element] carbone *m*.

carbonated ['kɑ:bəneɪtɪd] *adj* [mineral
water] gazeux(euse).

carbon copy *n* [document] carbone *m*.
|| *fig* [exact copy] réplique *f*.

carbon dioxide [-daɪ'ɒksaɪd] *n* gaz *m*
carbonique.

carbon monoxide [-mɒ'nɒksaɪd] *n*
oxyde *m* de carbone.

carbon paper *n* (*U*) (papier *m*) carbone *m*.

carburettor *Br*, **carburetor** *Am*
[,kɑ:bə'retər] *n* carburateur *m*.

carcass ['kɑ:kəs] *n* [of animal] carcasse
f.

card [kɑ:d] *n* [gen] carte *f*. || (*U*) [card-
board] carton *m*. ○ **cards** *npl*: **to play ~s**
jouer aux cartes.

cardboard ['kɑ:dbɔ:d] *n* (*U*) carton *m*.

cardboard box *n* boîte *f* en carton.

cardiac ['kɑ:dɪæk] *adj* cardiaque.

cardigan ['kɑ:dɪɡən] *n* cardigan *m*.

cardinal ['kɑ:dɪnl] **1** *adj* cardinal(e). **2** *n*
RELIG cardinal *m*.

care [keər] **1** *n* (*U*) [protection, attention]
soin *m*, attention *f*; **to take ~ of** [look
after] s'occuper de; **to take ~ (to do sthg)**
prendre soin (de faire qqch); **take ~!** fai-
tes bien attention à vous! || [cause of wor-
ry] souci *m*. **2** *vi* [be concerned]: **to ~
about** se soucier de. || [mind]: **I don't ~** ça
m'est égal; **who ~s?** qu'est-ce que ça
peut faire? ○ **care of** *prep* chez.

career [kə'rɪər] *n* carrière *f*.

careers adviser [kə'rɪəz-] *n* conseiller
m, -ère *f* d'orientation.

carefree ['keəfri:] *adj* insouciant(e).

careful ['keəfʊl] *adj* [cautious] pru-
dent(e); **to be ~ to do sthg** prendre soin
de faire qqch, faire attention à faire
qqch; **be ~!** fais attention!; **to be ~ with
one's money** regarder à la dépense. ||
[work] soigné(e); [worker] conscien-
cieux(ieuse).

carefully ['keəflɪ] *adv* [cautiously] pru-
demment. || [thoroughly] soigneusement.

careless ['keəlɪs] *adj* [work] peu soi-
gné(e); [driver] négligent(e). || [uncon-
cerned] insouciant(e).

caress [kə'res] **1** *n* caresse *f*. **2** *vt* caresser.

caretaker ['keə,teɪkər] *n* *Br* gardien *m*,
-ienne *f*.

car ferry *n* ferry *m*.

cargo ['kɑ:ɡəʊ] (*pl* -es OR -s) *n* cargaison *f*.

car hire *n* *Br* location *f* de voitures.

Caribbean [*Br* kærɪ'bɪən, *Am* kə'rɪbɪən]
n: **the ~ (Sea)** la mer des Caraïbes OR des
Antilles.

caring ['keərɪŋ] *adj* bienveillant(e).

carnage ['kɑ:nɪdʒ] *n* carnage *m*.

carnation [kɑ:'neɪʃn] *n* œillet *m*.

carnival ['kɑ:nɪvl] *n* carnaval *m*.

carnivorous [kɑ:'nɪvərəs] *adj* carnivore.

carol ['kærəl] *n*: **(Christmas) ~** chant *m*
de Noël.

carousel [,kærə'sel] *n* [at fair] manège
m. || [at airport] carrousel *m*.

carp [kɑ:p] (*pl inv* OR -s) **1** *n* carpe *f*. **2**
vi: **to ~ (about sthg)** critiquer (qqch).

carpenter ['kɑ:pəntər] *n* [on building site, in shipyard] charpentier *m*;
[furniture-maker] menuisier *m*.

carpentry ['kɑ:pəntrɪ] *n* [on building site, in shipyard] charpenterie *f*;
[furniture-making] menuiserie *f*.

carpet ['kɑ:pɪt] *n* *lit* & *fig* tapis *m*;
(fitted) ~ moquette *f*.

carpet sweeper [-,swi:pər] *n* balai *m*
mécanique.

car phone *n* téléphone *m* pour automobile.

car rental *n* *Am* location *f* de voitures.

carriage ['kærɪdʒ] *n* [of train, horse-
drawn] voiture *f*. || (*U*) [transport of
goods] transport *m*; **~ paid** OR **free** *Br*
franco de port.

carriage return *n* retour *m* chariot.

carrier ['kærɪə'] n COMM transporteur m. || [of disease] porteur m, -euse f. || = **carrier bag**.

carrier bag n sac m (en plastique).

carrot ['kærət] n carotte f.

carry ['kærɪ] 1 vt [subj: person, wind, water] porter; [subj: vehicle] transporter. || [disease] transmettre. || [responsibility] impliquer; [consequences] entraîner. || [motion, proposal] voter. || [baby] attendre. || MATH retenir. 2 vi [sound] porter. ○ **carry away** vt fus: to get carried away s'enthousiasmer. ○ **carry forward** vt sep FIN reporter. ○ **carry off** vt sep [plan] mener à bien. || [prize] remporter. ○ **carry on** 1 vt fus continuer; to ~ on doing sthg continuer à OR de faire qqch. 2 vi [continue] continuer; to ~ on with sthg continuer qqch. ○ **carry out** vt fus [task] remplir; [plan, order] exécuter; [experiment] effectuer; [investigation] mener. ○ **carry through** vt sep [accomplish] réaliser.

carryall ['kærɪɔːl] n Am fourre-tout m inv.

carrycot ['kærɪkɒt] n couffin m.

carry-out n plat m à emporter.

carsick ['kɑː,sɪk] adj: to be ~ être malade en voiture.

cart [kɑːt] 1 n charrette f. 2 vt inf traîner.

carton ['kɑːtn] n [box] boîte f en carton. || [of cream, yoghurt] pot m; [of milk] carton m.

cartoon [kɑːˈtuːn] n [satirical drawing] dessin m humoristique. || [comic strip] bande f dessinée. || [film] dessin m animé.

cartridge ['kɑːtrɪdʒ] n [for gun, pen] cartouche f. || [for camera] chargeur m.

cartwheel ['kɑːtwiːl] n [movement] roue f.

carve [kɑːv] 1 vt [wood, stone] sculpter; [design, name] graver. || [slice - meat] découper. 2 vi découper. ○ **carve out** vt sep fig se tailler. ○ **carve up** vt sep fig diviser.

carving ['kɑːvɪŋ] n [of wood] sculpture f; [of stone] ciselure f.

carving knife n couteau m à découper.

car wash n [process] lavage m de voitures; [place] station f de lavage de voitures.

case [keɪs] n [gen] cas m; to be the ~ être le cas; in ~ of en cas de; in that ~ dans ce cas; in which ~ auquel cas; as OR whatever the ~ may be selon le cas. || [argu-

ment]: ~ (for/against) arguments mpl (pour/contre). || JUR affaire f, procès m. || [container - gen] caisse f; [- for glasses etc] étui m. ○ **in any case** adv quoi qu'il en soit, de toute façon. ○ **in case 1** conj au cas où. 2 adv: (just) in ~ à tout hasard.

cash [kæʃ] 1 n (U) [notes and coins] liquide m; to pay (in) ~ payer comptant OR en espèces. || inf [money] sous mpl, fric m. || [payment]: ~ in advance paiement m à l'avance; ~ on delivery paiement à la livraison. 2 vt encaisser.

cash and carry n libre-service m de gros, cash-and-carry m.

cashbook ['kæʃbuk] n livre m de caisse.

cash box n caisse f.

cash card n carte f de retrait.

cash dispenser [-dɪ,spensə'] n distributeur m automatique de billets.

cashew (nut) ['kæʃuː-] n noix f de cajou.

cashier [kæˈʃɪə'] n caissier m, -ière f.

cash machine n distributeur m de billets.

cashmere [kæʃˈmɪə'] n cachemire m.

cash register n caisse f enregistreuse.

casing ['keɪsɪŋ] n revêtement m; TECH boîtier m.

casino [kəˈsiːnəʊ] (pl -s) n casino m.

cask [kɑːsk] n tonneau m.

casket ['kɑːskɪt] n [for jewels] coffret m. || Am [coffin] cercueil m.

casserole ['kæsərəʊl] n [stew] ragoût m. || [pan] cocotte f.

cassette [kæˈset] n [of magnetic tape] cassette f; PHOT recharge f.

cassette player n lecteur m de cassettes.

cassette recorder n magnétophone m à cassettes.

cast [kɑːst] (pt & pp cast) 1 n CINEMA & THEATRE - actors] acteurs mpl; [- list of actors] distribution f. 2 vt [throw] jeter; to ~ doubt on sthg jeter le doute sur qqch. || CINEMA & THEATRE donner un rôle à. || [vote]: to ~ one's vote voter. || [metal] couler; [statue] mouler. ○ **cast aside** vt sep fig écarter, rejeter. ○ **cast off** vi NAUT larguer les amarres.

castaway ['kɑːstəweɪ] n naufragé m, -e f.

caster ['kɑːstə'] n [wheel] roulette f.

casting vote ['kɑːstɪŋ-] n voix f prépondérante.

cast iron n fonte f.

castle ['kɑːsl] n [building] château m. || CHESS tour f.

castor ['kɑ:stər] = caster.

castor oil n huile f de ricin.

castor sugar = caster sugar.

castrate [kæ'streɪt] vt châtrer.

casual ['kæʒʊəl] adj [relaxed, indifferent] désinvolte. || [offhand] sans-gêne. || [chance] fortuit(e). || [clothes] décontracté(e), sport (inv). || [work, worker] temporaire.

casually ['kæʒʊəlɪ] adv [in a relaxed manner] avec désinvolture; **~ dressed** habillé simplement.

casualty ['kæʒʊəltɪ] n [dead person] mort m, -e f, victime f; [injured person] blessé m, -e f; [of road accident] accidenté m, -e f. || = casualty department.

casualty department n service m des urgences.

cat [kæt] n [domestic] chat m. || [wild] fauve m.

catalogue Br, **catalog** Am ['kætəlɒg] 1 n [gen] catalogue m; [in library] fichier m. 2 vt cataloguer.

catalyst ['kætəlɪst] n lit & fig catalyseur m.

catalytic convertor [,kætə'lɪtɪkkən'vɜ:tər] n pot m catalytique.

cataract ['kætərækt] n cataracte f.

catarrh [kə'tɑ:r] n catarrhe m.

catastrophe [kə'tæstrəfɪ] n catastrophe f.

catch [kætʃ] (pt & pp caught) 1 vt [gen] attraper; **to ~ sight OR a glimpse of** apercevoir; **to ~ sb's attention** attirer l'attention de qqn. || [discover, surprise] prendre, surprendre; **to ~ sb doing sthg** surprendre qqn à faire qqch. || [hear clearly] saisir, comprendre. || [trap]: **I caught my finger in the door** je me suis pris le doigt dans la porte. || [strike] frapper. 2 vi [become hooked, get stuck] se prendre. || [fire] prendre, partir. 3 n [of ball, thing caught] prise f. || [fastener - of box] fermoir m; [- of window] loqueteau m; [- of door] loquet m. || [snag] hic m, entourloupette f. ○ **catch on** vi [become popular] prendre. || inf [understand]: **to ~ on (to sthg)** piger (qqch). ○ **catch out** vt sep [trick] prendre en défaut, coincer. ○ **catch up** 1 vt sep rattraper. 2 vi: **to ~ up on sthg** rattraper. ○ **catch up with** vt fus rattraper.

catching ['kætʃɪŋ] adj contagieux (ieuse).

catchphrase ['kætʃfreɪz] n rengaine f, scie f.

catchy ['kætʃɪ] adj facile à retenir, entraînant(e).

categorically [,kætə'gɒrɪklɪ] adv catégoriquement.

category ['kætəgərɪ] n catégorie f.

cater ['keɪtər] vi [provide food] s'occuper de la nourriture, prévoir les repas.

caterer ['keɪtərər] n traiteur m.

catering ['keɪtərɪŋ] n [trade] restauration f.

caterpillar ['kætəpɪlər] n chenille f.

caterpillar tracks npl chenille f.

cathedral [kə'θi:drəl] n cathédrale f.

Catholic ['kæθlɪk] 1 adj catholique. 2 n catholique mf.

cattle ['kætl] npl bétail m.

catwalk ['kætwɔ:k] n passerelle f.

caucus ['kɔ:kəs] n Am POL comité m électoral (d'un parti).

caught [kɔ:t] pt & pp → catch.

cauliflower ['kɒlɪ,flaʊər] n chou-fleur m.

cause [kɔ:z] 1 n cause f; **to have ~ to do sthg** avoir lieu OR des raisons de faire qqch. 2 vt causer; **to ~ sb to do sthg** faire faire qqch à qqn; **to ~ sthg to be done** faire faire qqch.

caustic ['kɔ:stɪk] adj caustique.

caution ['kɔ:ʃn] 1 n (U) [care] précaution f, prudence f. || [warning] avertissement m. 2 vt [warn]: **to ~ sb against doing sthg** déconseiller à qqn de faire qqch.

cautious ['kɔ:ʃəs] adj prudent(e).

cavalry ['kævlrɪ] n cavalerie f.

cave [keɪv] n caverne f, grotte f. ○ **cave in** vi [roof, ceiling] s'affaisser.

caveman ['keɪvmæn] (pl -men [-men]) n homme m des cavernes.

cavernous ['kævənəs] adj [room, building] immense.

caviar(e) ['kævɪɑ:r] n caviar m.

cavity ['kævətɪ] n cavité f.

cavort [kə'vɔ:t] vi gambader.

CB n (abbr of citizens' band) CB f.

cc 1 n (abbr of cubic centimetre) cm³. 2 (abbr of carbon copy) pcc.

CD n (abbr of compact disc) CD m.

CD player n lecteur m de CD.

CD-ROM [,si:di:'rɒm] (abbr of compact disc read only memory) n CD-ROM m, CD-Rom m.

cease [si:s] fml 1 vt cesser; **to ~ doing OR to do sthg** cesser de faire qqch. 2 vi cesser.

cease-fire *n* cessez-le-feu *m inv*.

cedar (tree) ['si:dəʳ] *n* cèdre *m*.

cedilla [sɪ'dɪlə] *n* cédille *f*.

ceiling ['si:lɪŋ] *n* lit & fig plafond *m*.

celebrate ['selɪbreɪt] **1** *rt* [gen] célébrer, fêter. **2** *vi* faire la fête.

celebrated ['selɪbreɪtɪd] *adj* célèbre.

celebration [,selɪ'breɪʃn] *n* (*U*) [activity, feeling] fête *f*, festivités *fpl*. || [event] festivités *fpl*.

celebrity [sɪ'lebrətɪ] *n* célébrité *f*.

celery ['selərɪ] *n* céleri *m* (en branches).

celibate ['selɪbət] *adj* célibataire.

cell [sel] *n* [gen & COMPUT] cellule *f*.

cellar ['seləʳ] *n* cave *f*.

cello ['tʃeləʊ] (*pl* -s) *n* violoncelle *m*.

Cellophane® ['seləfeɪn] *n* Cellophane® *f*.

Celsius ['selsɪəs] *adj* Celsius (*inv*).

Celt [kelt] *n* Celte *mf*.

Celtic ['keltɪk] **1** *adj* celte. **2** *n* [language] celte *m*.

cement [sɪ'ment] **1** *n* ciment *m*. **2** *rt* lit & fig cimenter.

cement mixer *n* bétonnière *f*.

cemetery ['semɪtrɪ] *n* cimetière *m*.

censor ['sensəʳ] **1** *n* censeur *m*. **2** *rt* censurer.

censorship ['sensəʃɪp] *n* censure *f*.

censure ['senʃəʳ] **1** *n* blâme *m*, critique *f*. **2** *rt* blâmer, critiquer.

census ['sensəs] (*pl* censuses) *n* recensement *m*.

cent [sent] *n* cent *m*.

centenary *Br* [sen'ti:nərɪ], **centennial** *Am* [sen'tenjəl] *n* centenaire *m*.

center *Am* = centre.

centigrade ['sentɪgreɪd] *adj* centigrade.

centilitre *Br*, **centiliter** *Am* ['sentɪ,li:təʳ] *n* centilitre *m*.

centimetre *Br*, **centimeter** *Am* ['sentɪ,mi:təʳ] *n* centimètre *m*.

centipede ['sentɪpi:d] *n* mille-pattes *m inv*.

central ['sentrəl] *adj* central(e).

Central America *n* Amérique *f* centrale.

central heating *n* chauffage *m* central.

centralize, -ise ['sentrəlaɪz] *rt* centraliser.

central locking [-'lɒkɪŋ] *n* AUT verrouillage *m* centralisé.

centre *Br*, **center** *Am* ['sentəʳ] **1** *n* centre *m*. **2** *adj* [middle] central(e); **a ~ parting** une raie au milieu. || POL du centre, centriste. **3** *rt* centrer.

centre back *n* FTBL arrière *m* central.

centre forward *n* FTBL avant-centre *m inv*.

centre half *n* FTBL arrière *m* central.

century ['sentʃʊrɪ] *n* siècle *m*.

ceramic [sɪ'ræmɪk] *adj* en céramique. ○ **ceramics** *npl* [objects] objets *mpl* en céramique.

cereal ['sɪərɪəl] *n* céréale *f*.

ceremonial [,serɪ'məʊnjəl] **1** *adj* [dress] de cérémonie; [duties] honorifique. **2** *n* cérémonial *m*.

ceremony ['serɪmənɪ] *n* [event] cérémonie *f*. || (*U*) [pomp, formality] cérémonies *fpl*; **to stand on ~** faire des cérémonies.

certain ['sɜ:tn] *adj* [gen] certain(e); **he is ~ to be late** il est certain qu'il sera en retard, il sera certainement en retard; **to be ~ of sthg/of doing sthg** être assuré de qqch/de faire qqch, être sûr de qqch/de faire qqch; **to make ~** vérifier; **to make ~ of** s'assurer de; **to a ~ extent** jusqu'à un certain point, dans une certaine mesure.

certainly ['sɜ:tnlɪ] *adv* certainement.

certainty ['sɜ:tntɪ] *n* certitude *f*.

certificate [sə'tɪfɪkət] *n* certificat *m*.

certified ['sɜ:tɪfaɪd] *adj* [teacher] diplômé(e); [document] certifié(e).

certified mail *n Am* envoi *m* recommandé.

certified public accountant *n Am* expert-comptable *m*.

certify ['sɜ:tɪfaɪ] *rt* [declare true]: **to ~ (that)** certifier OR attester que. || [declare insane] déclarer mentalement aliéné(e).

cervical smear [sə'vaɪkl] *n* frottis *m* vaginal.

cervix ['sɜ:vɪks] (*pl* -ices [-ɪsi:z]) *n* col *m* de l'utérus.

cesarean (section) = caesarean (section).

cesspit ['sespɪt], **cesspool** ['sespu:l] *n* fosse *f* d'aisance.

cf. (*abbr of* confer) cf.

CFC (*abbr of* chlorofluorocarbon) *n* CFC *m*.

ch. (*abbr of* chapter) chap.

chafe [tʃeɪf] *rt* [rub] irriter.

chaffinch ['tʃæfɪntʃ] *n* pinson *m*.

chain [tʃeɪn] **1** *n* chaîne *f*; **~ of events** suite *f* OR série *f* d'événements. **2** *rt* [person, animal] enchaîner; [object] attacher avec une chaîne.

chain reaction *n* réaction *f* en chaîne.

chain saw *n* tronçonneuse *f*.

chain-smoke *vi* fumer cigarette sur cigarette.

chain store n grand magasin m (*à succursales multiples*).

chair [tʃeəʳ] **1** n [gen] chaise f; [armchair] fauteuil m. ‖ [university post] chaire f. ‖ [of meeting] présidence f. **2** vt [meeting] présider; [discussion] diriger.

chair lift n télésiège m.

chairman ['tʃeəmən] (pl -men [-mən]) n président m.

chairperson ['tʃeə,pɜːsn] (pl -s) n président m, -e f.

chalet ['ʃæleɪ] n chalet m.

chalk [tʃɔːk] n craie f.

chalkboard ['tʃɔːkbɔːd] n Am tableau m (noir).

challenge ['tʃælɪndʒ] **1** n défi m. **2** vt [to fight, competition]: **she ~d me to a race/a game of chess** elle m'a défié à la course/aux échecs; **to ~ sb to do sthg** défier qqn de faire qqch. ‖ [question] mettre en question OR en doute.

challenging ['tʃælɪndʒɪŋ] adj [task, job] stimulant(e). ‖ [look, tone of voice] provocateur(trice).

chambermaid ['tʃeɪmbəmeɪd] n femme f de chambre.

chamber music n musique f de chambre.

chamber of commerce n chambre f de commerce.

chameleon [kə'miːljən] n caméléon m.

champagne [,ʃæm'peɪn] n champagne m.

champion ['tʃæmpjən] n champion m, -ionne f.

championship ['tʃæmpjənʃɪp] n championnat m.

chance [tʃɑːns] **1** n (U) [luck] hasard m; **by ~** par hasard. ‖ [likelihood] chance f; **she didn't stand a ~ (of doing sthg)** elle n'avait aucune chance (de faire qqch); **on the off ~** à tout hasard. ‖ [opportunity] occasion f. ‖ [risk] risque m; **to take a ~** risquer le coup. **2** adj fortuit(e), accidentel(elle). **3** vt [risk] risquer; **to ~ it** tenter sa chance.

chancellor ['tʃɑːnsələʳ] n [chief minister] chancelier m. ‖ UNIV président m, -e f honoraire.

Chancellor of the Exchequer n Br Chancelier m de l'Échiquier, ≃ ministre m des Finances.

chandelier [,ʃændə'lɪəʳ] n lustre m.

change [tʃeɪndʒ] **1** n [gen]: **~ (in sb/in sthg)** changement m (en qqn/de qqch); **for a ~** pour changer (un peu). ‖ [money] monnaie f. **2** vt [gen] changer; **to ~ sthg**

into sthg changer OR transformer qqch en qqch; **to ~ one's mind** changer d'avis. ‖ [jobs, trains, sides] changer de. ‖ [money into smaller units] faire la monnaie de; [~ into different currency] changer. **3** vi [gen] changer. ‖ [change clothes] se changer. ‖ [be transformed]: **to ~ into** se changer en. ○ **change over** vi [convert]: **to ~ over from/to** passer de/à.

changeable ['tʃeɪndʒəbl] adj [mood] changeable; [weather] variable.

change machine n distributeur m de monnaie.

changeover ['tʃeɪndʒ,əʊvəʳ] n: **~ (to)** passage m (à), changement m (pour).

changing ['tʃeɪndʒɪŋ] adj changeant(e).

changing room n SPORT vestiaire m; [in shop] cabine f d'essayage.

channel ['tʃænl] **1** n TV chaîne f; RADIO station f. ‖ [for irrigation] canal m; [duct] conduit m. ‖ [on river, sea] chenal m. **2** vt lit & fig canaliser. ○ **Channel** n: **the (English) Channel** la Manche. ○ **channels** npl: **to go through the proper ~s** suivre OR passer la filière.

Channel Islands npl: **the ~** les îles fpl Anglo-Normandes.

Channel tunnel n: **the ~** le tunnel sous la Manche.

chant [tʃɑːnt] **1** n chant m. **2** vt RELIG chanter. ‖ [words, slogan] scander.

chaos ['keɪɒs] n chaos m.

chaotic [keɪ'ɒtɪk] adj chaotique.

chapel ['tʃæpl] n chapelle f.

chaplain ['tʃæplɪn] n aumônier m.

chapped [tʃæpt] adj [skin, lips] gercé(e).

chapter ['tʃæptəʳ] n chapitre m.

char [tʃɑːʳ] vt [burn] calciner.

character ['kærəktəʳ] n [gen] caractère m. ‖ [in film, book, play] personnage m. ‖ inf [eccentric] phénomène m, original m.

characteristic [,kærəktə'rɪstɪk] **1** adj caractéristique. **2** n caractéristique f.

characterize, -ise ['kærəktəraɪz] vt caractériser.

charade [ʃə'rɑːd] n farce f.

charcoal ['tʃɑːkəʊl] n [for drawing] charbon m; [for burning] charbon de bois.

charge [tʃɑːdʒ] **1** n [cost] prix m; **free of ~** gratuit. ‖ JUR accusation f, inculpation f. ‖ [responsibility]: **to take ~ of** se charger de; **to be in ~ of, to have ~ of** être responsable de, s'occuper de; **in ~** responsable. ‖ ELEC & MIL charge f. **2** vt [customer, sum] faire payer; **how much do**

you ~? vous prenez combien?; **to ~ sthg to sb** mettre qqch sur le compte de qqn. || [suspect, criminal]: **to ~ sb (with)** accuser qqn (de). || ELEC & MIL charger. **3** *vi* [rush] se précipiter, foncer.

charge card *n* carte *f* de compte crédit (*auprès d'un magasin*).

charger ['tʃɑːdʒər] *n* [for batteries] chargeur *m*.

charisma [kə'rɪzmə] *n* charisme *m*.

charity ['tʃærətɪ] *n* charité *f*.

charm [tʃɑːm] **1** *n* charme *m*. **2** *vt* charmer.

charming ['tʃɑːmɪŋ] *adj* charmant(e).

chart [tʃɑːt] **1** *n* [diagram] graphique *m*, diagramme *m*. || [map] carte *f*. **2** *vt* [plot, map] porter sur une carte. || *fig* [record] retracer. ○ **charts** *npl*: **the ~s** le hit-parade.

charter ['tʃɑːtər] **1** *n* [document] charte *f*. **2** *vt* [plane, boat] affréter.

charter flight *n* vol *m* charter.

chase [tʃeɪs] **1** *n* [pursuit] poursuite *f*, chasse *f*. **2** *vt* [pursue] poursuivre. || [drive away] chasser. **to ~ after sb/sthg** courir après qqn/qqch.

chassis ['ʃæsɪ] (*pl inv*) châssis *m*.

chat [tʃæt] **1** *n* causerie *f*, bavardage *m*; **to have a ~** causer, bavarder. **2** *vi* causer, bavarder.

chatter ['tʃætər] **1** *n* [of person] bavardage *m*. || [of animal, bird] caquetage *m*. **2** *vi* [person] bavarder. || [animal, bird] jacasser, caqueter. || [teeth]: **his teeth were ~ing** il claquait des dents.

chatterbox ['tʃætəbɒks] *n* inf moulin *m* à paroles.

chauffeur ['ʃəʊfər] *n* chauffeur *m*.

chauvinist ['ʃəʊvɪnɪst] *n* [sexist] macho *m*. || [nationalist] chauvin *m*, -e *f*.

cheap [tʃiːp] **1** *adj* [inexpensive] pas cher (chère), bon marché (*inv*). || [at a reduced price - fare, rate] réduit(e); [- ticket] à prix réduit. || [low-quality] de mauvaise qualité. || [joke, comment] facile. **2** *adv* (à) bon marché.

cheapen ['tʃiːpn] *vt* [degrade] rabaisser.

cheaply ['tʃiːplɪ] *adv* à bon marché, pour pas cher.

cheat [tʃiːt] **1** *n* tricheur *m*, -euse *f*. **2** *vt* tromper; **to ~ sb out of sthg** escroquer qqch à qqn. **3** *vi* [in game, exam] tricher. || *inf* [be unfaithful]: **to ~ on sb** tromper qqn.

check [tʃek] **1** *n* [inspection, test]: **~ (on)** contrôle *m* (de). || [restraint]: **~ (on)** frein *m* (à), restriction *f* (sur). || *Am* [bill] note

f. || [pattern] carreaux *mpl*. || *Am* = **cheque**. **2** *vt* [test, verify] vérifier; [passport, ticket] contrôler. || [restrain, stop] enrayer, arrêter. **3** *vi*: **to ~ (for sthg)** vérifier (qqch); **to ~ on sthg** vérifier OR contrôler qqch. ○ **check in 1** *vt sep* [luggage, coat] enregistrer. **2** *vi* [at hotel] signer le registre. || [at airport] se présenter à l'enregistrement. ○ **check out 1** *vt sep* [luggage, coat] retirer. || [investigate] vérifier. **2** *vi* [from hotel] régler sa note. ○ **check up** *vi*: **to ~ up on sb** prendre des renseignements sur qqn; **to ~ up (on sthg)** vérifier (qqch).

checkbook *Am* = **chequebook**.

checked [tʃekt] *adj* à carreaux.

checkered *Am* = **chequered**.

checkers ['tʃekəz] *n* (U) *Am* jeu *m* de dames.

check-in *n* enregistrement *m*.

checking account ['tʃekɪŋ-] *n Am* compte *m* courant.

checkmate ['tʃekmeɪt] *n* échec et mat *m*.

checkout ['tʃekaʊt] *n* [in supermarket] caisse *f*.

checkpoint ['tʃekpɔɪnt] *n* [place] (poste *m* de) contrôle *m*.

checkup ['tʃekʌp] *n* MED bilan *m* de santé, check-up *m*.

Cheddar (cheese) ['tʃedər-] *n* (fromage *m* de) cheddar *m*.

cheek [tʃiːk] *n* [of face] joue *f*. || *inf* [impudence] culot *m*.

cheekbone ['tʃiːkbəʊn] *n* pommette *f*.

cheeky ['tʃiːkɪ] *adj* insolent(e), effronté(e).

cheer [tʃɪər] **1** *n* [shout] acclamation *f*. **2** *vt* [shout for] acclamer. || [gladden] réjouir. **3** *vi* applaudir. ○ **cheers** *excl* [said before drinking] santé! || *inf* [goodbye] salut!, ciao!, tchao! || *inf* [thank you] merci. ○ **cheer up 1** *vt sep* remonter le moral à. **2** *vi* s'égayer.

cheerful ['tʃɪəfʊl] *adj* joyeux(euse), gai(e).

cheerio [,tʃɪərɪ'əʊ] *excl inf* au revoir!, salut!

cheese [tʃiːz] *n* fromage *m*.

cheeseboard ['tʃiːzbɔːd] *n* plateau *m* à fromage.

cheeseburger ['tʃiːz,bɜːgər] *n* cheeseburger *m*, hamburger *m* au fromage.

cheesecake ['tʃiːzkeɪk] *n* CULIN gâteau *m* au fromage blanc, cheesecake *m*.

cheetah ['tʃiːtə] *n* guépard *m*.

chef [ʃef] *n* chef *m*.

chemical ['kemɪkl] **1** *adj* chimique. **2** *n* produit *m* chimique.

chemist ['kemɪst] *n* [scientist] chimiste *mf*.

chemistry ['kemɪstrɪ] *n* chimie *f*.

cheque *Br*, **check** *Am* [tʃek] *n* chèque *m*.

chequebook *Br*, **checkbook** *Am* ['tʃekbʊk] *n* chéquier *m*, carnet *m* de chèques.

cheque card *n Br* carte *f* bancaire.

cherish ['tʃerɪʃ] *vt* chérir; [hope] nourrir, caresser.

cherry ['tʃerɪ] *n* [fruit] cerise *f*; ~ **(tree)** cerisier *m*.

chess [tʃes] *n* échecs *mpl*.

chessboard ['tʃesbɔ:d] *n* échiquier *m*.

chessman ['tʃesmæn] (*pl* **-men** [-men]) *n* pièce *f*.

chest [tʃest] *n* ANAT poitrine *f*. || [box] coffre *m*.

chestnut ['tʃesnʌt] **1** *adj* [colour] châtain (*inv*). **2** *n* [nut] châtaigne *f*; ~ **(tree)** châtaignier *m*.

chest of drawers (*pl* **chests of drawers**) *n* commode *f*.

chew [tʃu:] **1** *n* [sweet] bonbon *m* (à mâcher). **2** *vt* mâcher. ○ **chew up** *vt sep* mâchouiller.

chewing gum ['tʃu:ɪŋ-] *n* chewing-gum *m*.

chic [ʃi:k] *adj* chic (*inv*).

chick [tʃɪk] *n* [baby bird] oisillon *m*.

chicken ['tʃɪkɪn] *n* [bird, food] poulet *m*. || *inf* [coward] froussard *m*, -e *f*. ○ **chicken out** *vi inf* se dégonfler.

chickenpox ['tʃɪkɪnpɒks] *n* (*U*) varicelle *f*.

chickpea ['tʃɪkpi:] *n* pois *m* chiche.

chicory ['tʃɪkərɪ] *n* [vegetable] endive *f*.

chief [tʃi:f] **1** *adj* [main - aim, problem] principal(e). || [head] en chef. **2** *n* chef *m*.

chief executive *n* directeur général *m*, directrice générale *f*.

chiefly ['tʃi:flɪ] *adv* [mainly] principalement. || [above all] surtout.

chiffon ['ʃɪfɒn] *n* mousseline *f*.

chilblain ['tʃɪlbleɪn] *n* engelure *f*.

child [tʃaɪld] (*pl* **children**) *n* enfant *mf*.

childbirth ['tʃaɪldbɜ:θ] *n* (*U*) accouchement *m*.

childhood ['tʃaɪldhʊd] *n* enfance *f*.

childish ['tʃaɪldɪʃ] *adj pej* puéril(e), enfantin(e).

children ['tʃɪldrən] *pl* → **child**.

children's home *n* maison *f* d'enfants.

Chile ['tʃɪlɪ] *n* Chili *m*.

Chilean ['tʃɪlɪən] **1** *adj* chilien(ienne). **2** *n* Chilien *m*, -ienne *f*.

chili ['tʃɪlɪ] = **chilli**.

chill [tʃɪl] **1** *adj* frais (fraîche). **2** *n* [illness] coup *m* de froid. || [in temperature]: there's a ~ **in the air** le fond de l'air est frais. || [feeling of fear] frisson *m*. **3** *vt* [drink, food] mettre au frais. || [person] faire frissonner. **4** *vi* [drink, food] rafraîchir.

chilli ['tʃɪlɪ] (*pl* **-ies**) *n* [vegetable] piment *m*.

chilling ['tʃɪlɪŋ] *adj* [very cold] glacial(e). || [frightening] qui glace le sang.

chilly ['tʃɪlɪ] *adj* froid(e); **to feel ~** avoir froid; **it's ~** il fait froid.

chime [tʃaɪm] **1** *n* [of bell, clock] carillon *m*. **2** *vt* [time] sonner. **3** *vi* [bell, clock] carillonner.

chimney ['tʃɪmnɪ] *n* cheminée *f*.

chimneypot ['tʃɪmnɪpɒt] *n* mitre *f* de cheminée.

chimneysweep ['tʃɪmnɪswi:p] *n* ramoneur *m*.

chimp(anzee) [tʃɪmp(ən'zi:)] *n* chimpanzé *m*.

chin [tʃɪn] *n* menton *m*.

china ['tʃaɪnə] *n* porcelaine *f*.

China ['tʃaɪnə] *n* Chine *f*.

Chinese [,tʃaɪ'ni:z] **1** *adj* chinois(e). **2** *n* [language] chinois *m*. **3** *npl*: **the ~** les Chinois *mpl*.

Chinese cabbage *n* chou *m* chinois.

chink [tʃɪŋk] *n* [narrow opening] fente *f*. || [sound] tintement *m*.

chip [tʃɪp] **1** *n Br* [fried potato] frite *f*; *Am* [potato crisp] chip *m*. || [of glass, metal] éclat *m*; [of wood] copeau *m*. || [flaw] ébréchure *f*. || [microchip] puce *f*. || [for gambling] jeton *m*. **2** *vt* [cup, glass] ébrécher. ○ **chip in** *inf vi* [contribute] contribuer. || [interrupt] mettre son grain de sel. ○ **chip off** *vt sep* enlever petit morceau par petit morceau.

chipboard ['tʃɪpbɔ:d] *n* aggloméré *m*.

chiropodist [kɪ'rɒpədɪst] *n* pédicure *mf*.

chirp [tʃɜ:p] *vi* [bird] pépier; [cricket] chanter.

chirpy ['tʃɜ:pɪ] *adj* gai(e).

chisel ['tʃɪzl] **1** *n* [for wood] ciseau *m*; [for metal, rock] burin *m*. **2** *vt* ciseler.

chit [tʃɪt] *n* [note] note *f*, reçu *m*.

chitchat ['tʃɪttʃæt] *n* (*U*) *inf* bavardage *m*.

chivalry ['ʃɪvlrɪ] *n* (*U*) *literary* [of

knights] chevalerie *f.* || [good manners] galanterie *f.*

chives [tʃaɪvz] *npl* ciboulette *f.*

chlorine ['klɔ:ri:n] *n* chlore *m.*

chock [tʃɒk] *n* cale *f.*

chock-a-block, chock-full *adj inf:* ~ (with) plein(e) à craquer (de).

chocolate ['tʃɒkələt] 1 *n* chocolat *m.* 2 *comp* au chocolat.

choice [tʃɔɪs] 1 *n* choix *m.* 2 *adj* de choix.

choir ['kwaɪər] *n* chœur *m.*

choirboy ['kwaɪəbɔɪ] *n* jeune choriste *m.*

choke [tʃəʊk] 1 *n* AUT starter *m.* 2 *vt* [strangle] étrangler, étouffer. || [block] obstruer, boucher. 3 *vi* s'étrangler.

cholera ['kɒlərə] *n* choléra *m.*

choose [tʃu:z] (*pt* chose, *pp* chosen) 1 *vt* [select] choisir. || [decide]: **to ~ to do** sthg décider OR choisir de faire qqch. 2 *vi* [select]: **to ~ (from)** choisir (parmi OR entre).

choos(e)y ['tʃu:zɪ] (*compar* -ier, *superl* -iest) *adj* difficile.

chop [tʃɒp] 1 *n* CULIN côtelette *f.* 2 *vt* [wood] couper; [vegetables] hacher. || *inf fig* [funding, budget] réduire. ○ **chop down** *vt sep* [tree] abattre. ○ **chop up** *vt sep* couper en morceaux.

chopper ['tʃɒpər] *n* [axe] couperet *m.* || *inf* [helicopter] hélico *m.*

choppy ['tʃɒpɪ] *adj* [sea] agité(e).

chopsticks ['tʃɒpstɪks] *npl* baguettes *fpl.*

chord [kɔ:d] *n* MUS accord *m.*

chore [tʃɔ:r] *n* corvée *f;* **household ~s** travaux *mpl* ménagers.

chortle ['tʃɔ:tl] *vi* glousser.

chorus ['kɔ:rəs] *n* [part of song] refrain *m.* || [singers] chœur *m.* || *fig* [of praise, complaints] concert *m.*

chose [tʃəʊz] *pt* → **choose**.

chosen ['tʃəʊzn] *pp* → **choose**.

Christ [kraɪst] 1 *n* Christ *m.* 2 *excl* Seigneur!, bon Dieu!

christen ['krɪsn] *vt* [baby] baptiser. || [name] nommer.

christening ['krɪsnɪŋ] *n* baptême *m.*

Christian ['krɪstʃən] 1 *adj* RELIG chrétien(ienne). 2 *n* chrétien *m.*, -ienne *f.*

Christianity [,krɪstɪ'ænətɪ] *n* christianisme *m.*

Christian name *n* prénom *m.*

Christmas ['krɪsməs] *n* Noël *m;* **happy OR merry ~!** joyeux Noël!

Christmas card *n* carte *f* de Noël.

Christmas Day *n* jour *m* de Noël.

Christmas Eve *n* veille *f* de Noël.

Christmas tree *n* arbre *m* de Noël.

chrome [krəʊm], **chromium** ['krəʊmɪəm] 1 *n* chrome *m.* 2 *comp* chromé(e).

chronic ['krɒnɪk] *adj* [illness, unemployment] chronique; [liar, alcoholic] invétéré(e).

chronicle ['krɒnɪkl] *n* chronique *f.*

chronological [,krɒnə'lɒdʒɪkl] *adj* chronologique.

chrysanthemum [krɪ'sænθəməm] (*pl* -s) *n* chrysanthème *m.*

chubby ['tʃʌbɪ] *adj* [cheeks, face] joufflu(e); [person, hands] potelé(e).

chuck [tʃʌk] *vt inf* [throw] lancer, envoyer. || [job, boyfriend] laisser tomber. ○ **chuck away, chuck out** *vt sep inf* jeter, balancer.

chuckle ['tʃʌkl] *vi* glousser.

chug [tʃʌg] *vi* [train] faire teuf-teuf.

chum [tʃʌm] *n inf* copain *m,* copine *f.*

chunk [tʃʌŋk] *n* gros morceau *m.*

church [tʃɜ:tʃ] *n* [building] église *f;* **to go to ~** aller à l'église; [Catholics] aller à la messe.

Church of England *n:* **the ~** l'Église d'Angleterre.

churchyard ['tʃɜ:tʃjɑ:d] *n* cimetière *m.*

churn [tʃɜ:n] 1 *n* [for making butter] baratte *f.* || [for milk] bidon *m.* 2 *vt* [stir up] battre. ○ **churn out** *vt sep inf* produire en série.

chute [ʃu:t] *n* glissière *f;* **rubbish ~** vide-ordures *m inv.*

chutney ['tʃʌtnɪ] *n* chutney *m.*

CIA (*abbr of* **Central Intelligence Agency**) *n* CIA *f.*

cider ['saɪdər] *n* cidre *m.*

cigar [sɪ'gɑ:r] *n* cigare *m.*

cigarette [,sɪgə'ret] *n* cigarette *f.*

cinder ['sɪndər] *n* cendre *f.*

Cinderella [,sɪndə'relə] *n* Cendrillon *f.*

cine-camera ['sɪnɪ-] *n* caméra *f.*

cine-film ['sɪnɪ-] *n* film *m.*

cinema ['sɪnəmə] *n* cinéma *m.*

cinnamon ['sɪnəmən] *n* cannelle *f.*

circa ['sɜ:kə] *prep* environ.

circle ['sɜ:kl] 1 *n* [gen] cercle *m;* **to go round in ~s** *fig* tourner en rond. || [in theatre, cinema] balcon *m.* 2 *vt* [draw a circle round] entourer (d'un cercle). || [move round] faire le tour de. 3 *vi* [plane] tourner en rond.

circuit ['sɜ:kɪt] *n* [gen & ELEC] circuit *m.*

|| [lap] tour *m*; [movement round] révolution *f*.

circular ['sɜːkjʊləʳ] **1** *adj* [gen] circulaire. **2** *n* [letter] circulaire *f*; [advertisement] prospectus *m*.

circulate ['sɜːkjʊleɪt] **1** *vi* [gen] circuler. || [socialize] se mêler aux invités. **2** *vt* [rumour] propager; [document] faire circuler.

circulation [,sɜːkjʊ'leɪʃn] *n* [gen] circulation *f*. || PRESS tirage *m*.

circumcision [,sɜːkəm'sɪʒn] *n* circoncision *f*.

circumference [sə'kʌmfərəns] *n* circonférence *f*.

circumflex ['sɜːkəmfleks] *n*: ~ (accent) accent *m* circonflexe.

circumspect ['sɜːkəmspekt] *adj* circonspect(e).

circumstances ['sɜːkəmstənsɪz] *npl* circonstances *fpl*; **under** OR **in no** ~ en aucun cas; **under** OR **in the** ~ en de telles circonstances.

circumvent [,sɜːkəm'vent] *vt fml* [law, rule] tourner.

circus ['sɜːkəs] *n* cirque *m*.

CIS (*abbr of* **Commonwealth of Independent States**) *n* CEI *f*.

cistern ['sɪstən] *n* [in toilet] réservoir *m* de chasse d'eau.

cite [saɪt] *vt* citer.

citizen ['sɪtɪzn] *n* [of country] citoyen *m*, -enne *f*. || [of town] habitant *m*, -e *f*.

Citizens' Band *n* fréquence radio réservée au public, citizen band *f*.

citizenship ['sɪtɪznʃɪp] *n* citoyenneté *f*.

citrus fruit ['sɪtrəs-] *n* agrume *m*.

city ['sɪtɪ] *n* ville *f*, cité *f*. ○ **City** *n* Br: **the City** la City (*quartier financier de Londres*).

city centre *n* centre-ville *m*.

city hall *n* Am ≃ mairie *f*, ≃ hôtel *m* de ville.

civic ['sɪvɪk] *adj* [leader, event] municipal(e); [duty, pride] civique.

civil ['sɪvl] *adj* [public] civil(e). || [polite] courtois(e), poli(e).

civil engineering *n* génie *m* civil.

civilian [sɪ'vɪljən] **1** *n* civil *m*, -e *f*. **2** *comp* civil(e).

civilization [,sɪvɪlaɪ'zeɪʃn] *n* civilisation *f*.

civilized ['sɪvɪlaɪzd] *adj* civilisé(e).

civil law *n* droit *m* civil.

civil liberties *npl* libertés *fpl* civiques.

civil rights *npl* droits *mpl* civils.

civil servant *n* fonctionnaire *mf*.

civil service *n* fonction *f* publique.

civil war *n* guerre *f* civile.

cl (*abbr of* **centilitre**) cl.

claim [kleɪm] **1** *n* [for pay etc] revendication *f*; [for expenses, insurance] demande *f*. || [right] droit *m*; **to lay** ~ **to sthg** revendiquer qqch. || [assertion] affirmation *f*. **2** *vt* [ask for] réclamer. || [responsibility, credit] revendiquer. || [maintain] prétendre. **3** *vi*: **to** ~ **for sthg** faire une demande d'indemnité pour qqch; **to** ~ **(on one's insurance)** faire une déclaration de sinistre.

claimant ['kleɪmənt] *n* [to throne] prétendant *m*, -e *f*; [of state benefit] demandeur *m*, -euse *f*, requérant *m*, -e *f*.

clairvoyant [kleə'vɔɪənt] *n* voyant *m*, -e *f*.

clam [klæm] *n* palourde *f*.

clamber ['klæmbəʳ] *vi* grimper.

clamp [klæmp] **1** *n* [gen] pince *f*, agrafe *f*; [for carpentry] serre-joint *m*; MED clamp *m*. **2** *vt* [gen] serrer. || AUT poser un sabot de Denver à. ○ **clamp down** *vi*: **to** ~ **down (on)** sévir (contre).

clan [klæn] *n* clan *m*.

clandestine [klæn'destɪn] *adj* clandestin(e).

clang [klæŋ] *n* bruit *m* métallique.

clap [klæp] **1** *vt* [hands]: **to** ~ **one's hands** applaudir, taper des mains. **2** *vi* applaudir, taper des mains.

clapping ['klæpɪŋ] *n* (*U*) applaudissements *mpl*.

claret ['klærət] *n* [wine] bordeaux *m* rouge. || [colour] bordeaux *m inv*.

clarify ['klærɪfaɪ] *vt* [explain] éclaircir, clarifier.

clarinet [,klærə'net] *n* clarinette *f*.

clarity ['klærətɪ] *n* clarté *f*.

clash [klæʃ] **1** *n* [of interests, personalities] conflit *m*. || [fight, disagreement] heurt *m*, affrontement *m*. || [noise] fracas *m*. **2** *vi* [fight, disagree] se heurter. || [differ, conflict] entrer en conflit. || [coincide]: **to** ~ **(with sthg)** tomber en même temps (que qqch). || [colours] jurer.

clasp [klɑːsp] **1** *n* [on necklace etc] fermoir *m*; [on belt] boucle *f*. **2** *vt* [hold tight] serrer.

class [klɑːs] **1** *n* [gen] classe *f*. || [lesson] cours *m*, classe *f*. || [category] catégorie *f*. **2** *vt* classer.

classic ['klæsɪk] **1** *adj* classique. **2** *n* classique *m*.

classical ['klæsɪkl] *adj* classique.

classified ['klæsıfaıd] *adj* [information, document] classé secret (classée secrète).

classified ad *n* petite annonce *f*.

classify ['klæsıfaı] *vt* classifier, classer.

classmate ['klɑːsmeıt] *n* camarade *mf* de classe.

classroom ['klɑːsrom] *n* (salle *f* de) classe *f*.

clatter ['klætər] *n* cliquetis *m*; [louder] fracas *m*.

clause [klɔːz] *n* [in document] clause *f*. || GRAMM proposition *f*.

claw [klɔː] **1** *n* [of cat, bird] griffe *f*. || [of crab, lobster] pince *f*. **2** *vt* griffer. **3** *vi* [person]: **to ~ at** s'agripper à.

clay [kleı] *n* argile *f*.

clean [kliːn] **1** *adj* [not dirty] propre. || [sheet of paper, driving licence] vierge; [reputation] sans tache. || [joke] de bon goût. || [smooth] net (nette). **2** *vt* nettoyer; **to ~ one's teeth** se brosser OR laver les dents. **3** *vi* faire le ménage. ○ **clean out** *vt sep* [room, drawer] nettoyer à fond. ○ **clean up** *vt sep* [clear up] nettoyer.

cleaner ['kliːnər] *n* [person] personne *f* qui fait le ménage. || [substance] produit *m* d'entretien.

cleaning ['kliːnıŋ] *n* nettoyage *m*.

cleanliness ['klenlınıs] *n* propreté *f*.

cleanse [klenz] *vt* [skin, wound] nettoyer. || *fig* [make pure] purifier.

cleanser ['klenzər] *n* [detergent] détergent *m*; [for skin] démaquillant *m*.

clean-shaven [-'ʃeıvn] *adj* rasé(e) de près.

clear [klıər] **1** *adj* [gen] clair(e); [glass, plastic] transparent(e); [difference] net (nette). || **to make sthg ~ (to sb)** expliquer qqch clairement (à qqn); **to make it ~ that** préciser que; **to make o.s. ~** bien se faire comprendre. || [voice, sound] qui s'entend nettement. || [road, space] libre, dégagé(e). **2** *adv*: **to stand ~** s'écarter; **to stay ~ of sb/sthg, to steer ~ of sb/sthg** éviter qqn/qqch. **3** *vt* [road, path] dégager; [table] débarrasser. || [obstacle, fallen tree] enlever. || [jump] sauter, franchir. || [debt] s'acquitter de. || [authorize] donner le feu vert à. || JUR innocenter. **4** *vi* [fog, smoke] se dissiper; [weather, sky] s'éclaircir. ○ **clear away** *vt sep* [plates] débarrasser; [books] enlever. ○ **clear out 1** *vt sep* [cupboard] vider; [room] ranger. **2** *vi inf* [leave] dégager. ○ **clear up 1** *vt sep* [tidy] ranger. || [mystery, mis-

understanding] éclaircir. **2** *vi* [weather] s'éclaircir. || [tidy up] tout ranger.

clearance ['klıərəns] *n* [of rubbish] enlèvement *m*; [of land] déblaiement *m*. || [permission] autorisation *f*.

clear-cut *adj* net (nette).

clearing ['klıərıŋ] *n* [in wood] clairière *f*.

clearly ['klıəlı] *adv* [distinctly, lucidly] clairement. || [obviously] manifestement.

cleavage ['kliːvıdʒ] *n* [between breasts] décolleté *m*.

cleaver ['kliːvər] *n* couperet *m*.

clef [klef] *n* clef *f*.

cleft [kleft] *n* fente *f*.

clench [klentʃ] *vt* serrer.

clergy ['klɜːdʒı] *npl*: **the ~** le clergé.

clergyman ['klɜːdʒımən] (*pl* -men [-mən]) *n* membre *m* du clergé.

clerical ['klerıkl] *adj* ADMIN de bureau. || RELIG clérical(e).

clerk [*Br* klɑːk, *Am* klɜːrk] *n* [in office] employé *m*, -e *f* de bureau. || JUR clerc *m*. || *Am* [shop assistant] vendeur *m*, -euse *f*.

clever ['klevər] *adj* [intelligent - person] intelligent(e); [- idea] ingénieux(ieuse). || [skilful] habile, adroit(e).

click [klık] **1** *n* [of lock] déclic *m*; [of tongue, heels] claquement *m*. **2** *vt* faire claquer. **3** *vi* [heels] claquer; [camera] faire un déclic.

client ['klaıənt] *n* client *m*, -e *f*.

cliff [klıf] *n* falaise *f*.

climate ['klaımıt] *n* climat *m*.

climax ['klaımæks] *n* [culmination] apogée *m*.

climb [klaım] **1** *n* ascension *f*, montée *f*. **2** *vt* [tree, rope] monter à; [stairs] monter; [wall, hill] escalader. **3** *vi* [person] monter, grimper. || [plant] grimper; [road] monter; [plane] prendre de l'altitude. || [increase] augmenter.

climb-down *n* reculade *f*.

climber ['klaımər] *n* [person] alpiniste *mf*, grimpeur *m*, -euse *f*.

climbing ['klaımıŋ] *n* [rock climbing] varappe *f*; [mountain climbing] alpinisme *m*.

cling [klıŋ] (*pt & pp* **clung**) *vi* [hold tightly]: **to ~ (to)** s'accrocher (à), se cramponner (à). || [clothes]: **to ~ (to)** coller (à).

clinic ['klınık] *n* [building] centre *m* médical, clinique *f*.

clinical ['klınıkl] *adj* MED clinique. || *fig* [attitude] froid(e).

clink [klıŋk] *vi* tinter.

clip

clip [klɪp] **1** *n* [for paper] trombone *m*; [for hair] pince *f*; [of earring] clip *m*; TECH collier *m*. || [excerpt] extrait *m*. **2** *vt* [fasten] attacher. || [nails] couper; [hedge] tailler; [newspaper cutting] découper.

clipboard ['klɪpbɔːd] *n* écritoire *f* à pince, clipboard *m*.

clippers ['klɪpəz] *npl* [for hair] tondeuse *f*; [for nails] pince *f* à ongles; [for hedge] cisaille *f* à haie; [for pruning] sécateur *m*.

clipping ['klɪpɪŋ] *n* [from newspaper] coupure *f*.

cloak [kləʊk] *n* [garment] cape *f*.

cloakroom ['kləʊkrʊm] *n* [for clothes] vestiaire *m*. || *Br* [toilets] toilettes *fpl*.

clock [klɒk] *n* [large] horloge *f*; [small] pendule *f*; **round the ~** [work, be open] 24 heures sur 24. || AUT [mileometer] compteur *m*.

clockwise ['klɒkwaɪz] *adj & adv* dans le sens des aiguilles d'une montre.

clockwork ['klɒkwɜːk] **1** *n*: **to go like ~** *fig* aller OR marcher comme sur des roulettes. **2** *comp* [toy] mécanique.

clog [klɒg] *vt* boucher. ○ **clogs** *npl* sabots *mpl*. ○ **clog up 1** *vt sep* boucher. **2** *vi* se boucher.

close¹ [kləʊs] **1** *adj* [near]: **~ (to)** proche (de), près (de); **a ~ friend** un ami intime (une amie intime); **~ up, ~ to** de près; **~ by, ~ at hand** tout près; **that was a ~ shave** OR **thing** OR **call** on l'a échappé belle. || [link, resemblance] fort(e); [cooperation, connection] étroit(e). || [questioning] serré(e); [examination] minutieux(ieuse); **to keep a ~ watch on sb/sthg** surveiller qqn/qqch de près; **to pay ~ attention** faire très attention. || [weather] lourd(e); [air in room] renfermé(e). || [result, contest, race] serré(e). **2** *adv*: **~ (to)** près (de); **to come ~r (together)** se rapprocher. ○ **close on, close to** *prep* [almost] près de.

close² [kləʊz] **1** *vt* [gen] fermer. || [end] clore. **2** *vi* [shop, bank] fermer; [door, lid] (se) fermer. || [end] se terminer, finir. **3** *n* fin *f*. ○ **close down** *vt sep & vi* fermer.

closed [kləʊzd] *adj* fermé(e).

close-knit [ˌkləʊs-] *adj* (très) uni(e).

closely ['kləʊslɪ] *adv* [listen, examine, watch] de près; [resemble] beaucoup; **to be ~ related to** OR **with** être proche parent de.

closet ['klɒzɪt] **1** *n Am* [cupboard] placard *m*. **2** *adj inf* non avoué(e).

close-up ['kləʊs-] *n* gros plan *m*.

closing time ['kləʊzɪŋ-] *n* heure *f* de fermeture.

closure ['kləʊʒər] *n* fermeture *f*.

clot [klɒt] **1** *n* [of blood, milk] caillot *m*. **2** *vi* [blood] coaguler.

cloth [klɒθ] *n* (*U*) [fabric] tissu *m*. || [duster] chiffon *m*; [for drying] torchon *m*.

clothes [kləʊðz] *npl* vêtements *mpl*, habits *mpl*; **to put one's ~ on** s'habiller; **to take one's ~ off** se déshabiller.

clothes brush *n* brosse *f* à habits.

clothesline ['kləʊðzlaɪn] *n* corde *f* à linge.

clothes peg *Br*, **clothespin** *Am* ['kləʊðzpɪn] *n* pince *f* à linge.

clothing ['kləʊðɪŋ] *n* (*U*) vêtements *mpl*, habits *mpl*.

cloud [klaʊd] *n* nuage *m*. ○ **cloud over** *vi* [sky] se couvrir.

cloudy ['klaʊdɪ] *adj* [sky, day] nuageux(euse). || [liquid] trouble.

clove [kləʊv] *n*: **a ~ of garlic** une gousse d'ail. ○ **cloves** *npl* [spice] clous *mpl* de girofle.

clover ['kləʊvər] *n* trèfle *m*.

clown [klaʊn] **1** *n* [performer] clown *m*. || [fool] pitre *m*. **2** *vi* faire le pitre.

cloying ['klɔɪɪŋ] *adj* [smell] écœurant(e). || [sentimentality] à l'eau de rose.

club [klʌb] **1** *n* [organization, place] club *m*. || [weapon] massue *f*. || [golf] ~ club *m*. **2** *vt* matraquer. ○ **clubs** *npl* CARDS trèfle *m*. ○ **club together** *vi* se cotiser.

club car *n Am* RAIL wagon-restaurant *m*.

clubhouse ['klʌbhaʊs, *pl* -haʊzɪz] *n* club *m*, pavillon *m*.

cluck [klʌk] *vi* glousser.

clue [kluː] *n* [in crime] indice *m*; **I haven't (got) a ~ (about)** je n'ai aucune idée (sur). || [in crossword] définition *f*.

clump [klʌmp] *n* [of trees, bushes] massif *m*, bouquet *m*.

clumsy ['klʌmzɪ] *adj* [ungraceful] gauche, maladroit(e). || [tactless] sans tact.

clung [klʌŋ] *pt & pp* → **cling**.

cluster ['klʌstər] **1** *n* [group] groupe *m*. **2** *vi* [people] se rassembler; [buildings etc] être regroupé(e).

clutch [klʌtʃ] **1** *n* AUT embrayage *m*. **2** *vt* agripper. **3** *vi*: **to ~ at** s'agripper à.

clutter ['klʌtər] **1** *n* désordre *m*. **2** *vt* mettre en désordre.

cm (*abbr of* **centimetre**) *n* cm.

CND (*abbr of* **Campaign for Nuclear**

Disarmament) *n* *mouvement pour le désarmement nucléaire.*

c/o (*abbr of* **care of**) a/s.

Co. (*abbr of* **Company**) Cie. || *abbr of* County.

coach [kəʊtʃ] **1** *n* [bus] car *m*, autocar *m*. || RAIL voiture *f*. || [horsedrawn] carrosse *m*. || SPORT entraîneur *m*. || [tutor] répétiteur *m*, -trice *f*. **2** *vt* SPORT entraîner. || [tutor] donner des leçons (particulières) à.

coal [kəʊl] *n* charbon *m*.

coalfield ['kəʊlfiːld] *n* bassin *m* houiller.

coalition [,kəʊə'lɪʃn] *n* coalition *f*.

coalmine ['kəʊlmaɪn] *n* mine *f* de charbon.

coarse [kɔːs] *adj* [rough - cloth] grossier(ière); [- hair] épais(aisse); [- skin] granuleux(euse). || [vulgar] grossier(ière).

coast [kəʊst] **1** *n* côte *f*. **2** *vi* [in car, on bike] avancer en roue libre.

coastal ['kəʊstl] *adj* côtier(ière).

coaster ['kəʊstər] *n* [small mat] dessous *m* de verre.

coastguard ['kəʊstɡɑːd] *n* [person] garde-côte *m*. || [organization]: **the ~** la gendarmerie maritime.

coastline ['kəʊstlaɪn] *n* côte *f*.

coat [kəʊt] **1** *n* [garment] manteau *m*. || [of animal] pelage *m*. || [layer] couche *f*. **2** *vt*: **to ~ sthg (with)** recouvrir qqch (de); [with paint etc] enduire qqch (de).

coat hanger *n* cintre *m*.

coating ['kəʊtɪŋ] *n* couche *f*; CULIN glaçage *m*.

coat of arms (*pl* **coats of arms**) *n* blason *m*.

coax [kəʊks] *vt*: **to ~ sb (to do** OR **into doing sthg)** persuader qqn (de faire qqch) à force de cajoleries.

cob [kɒb] *n* → **corn**.

cobbled ['kɒbld] *adj* pavé(e).

cobbler ['kɒblər] *n* cordonnier *m*.

cobbles ['kɒblz], **cobblestones** ['kɒblstəʊnz] *npl* pavés *mpl*.

cobweb ['kɒbweb] *n* toile *f* d'araignée.

Coca-Cola® [,kəʊkə'kəʊlə] *n* Coca-Cola® *m*.

cocaine [kəʊ'keɪn] *n* cocaïne *f*.

cock [kɒk] **1** *n* [male chicken] coq *m*. || [male bird] mâle *m*. **2** *vt* [gun] armer. || [head] incliner.

cockerel ['kɒkrəl] *n* jeune coq *m*.

cockle ['kɒkl] *n* [shellfish] coque *f*.

cockpit ['kɒkpɪt] *n* [in plane] cockpit *m*.

cockroach ['kɒkrəʊtʃ] *n* cafard *m*.

cocksure [,kɒk'ʃɔːr] *adj* trop sûr(e) de soi.

cocktail ['kɒkteɪl] *n* cocktail *m*.

cocky ['kɒkɪ] *adj inf* suffisant(e).

cocoa ['kəʊkəʊ] *n* cacao *m*.

coconut ['kəʊkənʌt] *n* noix *f* de coco.

cod [kɒd] (*pl inv*) *n* morue *f*.

COD *abbr of* **cash on delivery**.

code [kəʊd] **1** *n* code *m*. **2** *vt* coder.

cod-liver oil *n* huile *f* de foie de morue.

coerce [kəʊ'ɜːs] *vt*: **to ~ sb (into doing sthg)** contraindre qqn (à faire qqch).

C of E *abbr of* **Church of England**.

coffee ['kɒfɪ] *n* café *m*.

coffee break *n* pause-café *f*.

coffeepot ['kɒfɪpɒt] *n* cafetière *f*.

coffee shop *n* Br [shop] café *m*. || Am [restaurant] ≃ café-restaurant *m*.

coffee table *n* table *f* basse.

coffin ['kɒfɪn] *n* cercueil *m*.

cog [kɒg] *n* [tooth on wheel] dent *f*; [wheel] roue *f* dentée.

coherent [kəʊ'hɪərənt] *adj* cohérent(e).

coil [kɔɪl] **1** *n* [of rope etc] rouleau *m*; [one loop] boucle *f*. || ELEC bobine *f*. **2** *vt* enrouler. **3** *vi* s'enrouler. ○ **coil up** *vt sep* enrouler.

coin [kɔɪn] *n* pièce *f* (de monnaie).

coinage ['kɔɪnɪdʒ] *n* (U) [currency] monnaie *f*.

coincide [,kəʊɪn'saɪd] *vi* coïncider.

coincidence [kəʊ'ɪnsɪdəns] *n* coïncidence *f*.

coincidental [kəʊ,ɪnsɪ'dentl] *adj* de coïncidence.

coke [kəʊk] *n* [fuel] coke *m*. || *drugs sl* coco *f*.

Coke® [kəʊk] *n* Coca® *m*.

cola ['kəʊlə] *n* cola *m*.

colander ['kʌləndər] *n* passoire *f*.

cold [kəʊld] **1** *adj* froid(e); **it's ~** il fait froid; **to be ~** avoir froid; **to get ~** [person] avoir froid; [hot food] refroidir. **2** *n* [ill-ness] rhume *m*; **to catch (a) ~** attraper un rhume, s'enrhumer. || [low temperature] froid *m*.

cold-blooded [-'blʌdɪd] *adj fig* [killer] sans pitié; [murder] de sang-froid.

cold sore *n* bouton *m* de fièvre.

cold war *n*: **the ~** la guerre froide.

coleslaw ['kəʊlslɔː] *n* chou *m* cru mayonnaise.

colic ['kɒlɪk] *n* colique *f*.

collaborate [kə'læbəreɪt] *vi* collaborer.

collapse [kə'læps] **1** *n* [gen] écroulement *m*, effondrement *m*; [of marriage] échec *m*. **2** *vi* [building, person] s'effondrer, s'écrouler; [marriage] échouer. || [fold up] être pliant(e).

collapsible [kə'læpsəbl] *adj* pliant(e).

collar ['kɒlər] *n* [on clothes] col *m*. || [for dog] collier *m*.

collarbone ['kɒləbəun] *n* clavicule *f*.

collate [kə'leɪt] *vt* collationner.

collateral [kɒ'lætərəl] *n* (*U*) nantissement *m*.

colleague ['kɒliːg] *n* collègue *mf*.

collect [kə'lekt] **1** *vt* [gather together - gen] rassembler, recueillir; [- wood etc] ramasser; **to ~ o.s.** se reprendre. || [as a hobby] collectionner. || [go to get] aller chercher, passer prendre. || [money] recueillir; [taxes] percevoir. **2** *vi* [crowd, people] se rassembler. || [dust, leaves, dirt] s'amasser, s'accumuler. || [for charity, gift] faire la quête. **3** *adv Am* TELEC: **to call (sb) ~** téléphoner (à qqn) en PCV.

collection [kə'lekʃn] *n* [of objects] collection *f*. || LITERATURE recueil *m*. || [of money] quête *f*. || [of mail] levée *f*.

collective [kə'lektɪv] **1** *adj* collectif(ive). **2** *n* coopérative *f*.

collector [kə'lektər] *n* [as a hobby] collectionneur *m*, -euse *f*. || [of debts, rent] encaisseur *m*; **~ of taxes** percepteur *m*.

college ['kɒlɪdʒ] *n* [gen] ≃ école *f* d'enseignement (technique) supérieur. || [of university] maison communautaire d'étudiants sur un campus universitaire.

college of education *n* ≃ institut *m* de formation de maîtres.

collide [kə'laɪd] *vi*: **to ~ (with)** entrer en collision (avec).

collie ['kɒlɪ] *n* colley *m*.

colliery ['kɒljərɪ] *n* mine *f*.

collision [kə'lɪʒn] *n* [crash]: **~ (with/between)** collision *f* (avec/entre); **to be on a ~ course (with)** *fig* aller au-devant de l'affrontement (avec).

colloquial [kə'ləukwɪəl] *adj* familier(ière).

collude [kə'luːd] *vi*: **to ~ with sb** comploter avec qqn.

Colombia [kə'lɒmbɪə] *n* Colombie *f*.

colon ['kəulən] *n* ANAT côlon *m*. || [punctuation mark] deux-points *m inv*.

colonel ['kɜːnl] *n* colonel *m*.

colonial [kə'ləunjəl] *adj* colonial(e).

colonize, -ise ['kɒlənaɪz] *vt* coloniser.

colony ['kɒlənɪ] *n* colonie *f*.

color *etc Am* = **colour** *etc*.

colour *Br*, **color** *Am* ['kʌlər] **1** *n* couleur *f*; **in ~** en couleur. **2** *adj* en couleur. **3** *vt* [food, liquid etc] colorer; [with pen, crayon] colorier. || [dye] teindre. || *fig* [judgment] fausser. **4** *vi* rougir.

colour bar *n* discrimination *f* raciale.

colour-blind *adj* daltonien(ienne).

coloured *Br*, **colored** *Am* ['kʌləd] *adj* de couleur; **brightly ~** couleur vive.

colourful *Br*, **colorful** *Am* ['kʌləful] *adj* [gen] coloré(e). || [person, area] haut(e) en couleur (*inv*).

colouring *Br*, **coloring** *Am* ['kʌlərɪŋ] *n* [dye] colorant *m*. || (*U*) [complexion] teint *m*.

colour scheme *n* combinaison *f* de couleurs.

colt [kəult] *n* [young horse] poulain *m*.

column ['kɒləm] *n* [gen] colonne *f*. || PRESS [article] rubrique *f*.

columnist ['kɒləmnɪst] *n* chroniqueur *m*.

coma ['kəumə] *n* coma *m*.

comb [kəum] **1** *n* [for hair] peigne *m*. **2** *vt* [hair] peigner. || [search] ratisser.

combat ['kɒmbæt] **1** *n* combat *m*. **2** *vt* combattre.

combination [ˌkɒmbɪ'neɪʃn] *n* combinaison *f*.

combine [kəm'baɪn] **1** *vt* [gen] rassembler; [pieces] combiner; **to ~ sthg with sthg** [two substances] mélanger qqch avec OR à qqch; *fig* allier qqch à qqch. **2** *vi* COMM & POL: **to ~ (with)** fusionner (avec).

combine harvester [-'hɑːvɪstər] *n* moissonneuse-batteuse *f*.

come [kʌm] (*pt* **came**, *pp* **come**) *vi* [move] venir; [arrive] arriver, venir; **coming!** j'arrive! || [reach]: **to ~ up to** arriver à, monter jusqu'à; **to ~ down to** descendre OR tomber jusqu'à. || [happen] arriver se produire; **~ what may** quoi qu'il arrive. || [become]: **to ~ true** se réaliser; **to ~ undone** se défaire. || [begin gradually]: **to ~ to do sthg** en arriver à OR en venir à faire qqch. || [be placed in order] venir, être placé(e); **she came second in the exam** elle a été deuxième à l'examen. || *phr*: **~ to think of it** maintenant que j'y pense, réflexion faite. ○ **to come** *adv* à venir. ○ **come about** *vi* [happen] arriver, se produire. ○ **come across** *vt fus* tomber sur, trouver par hasard. ○ **come along** *vi* [arrive by chance] arriver. || [improve - work] avancer; [- student] faire des progrès. ○ **come apart** *vi* [fall to pieces] tomber en morceaux. || [come off] se détacher.

○ **come back** *vi* [in talk, writing]: **to ~ back to sthg** revenir à qqch. || [memory]: **to ~ back (to sb)** revenir (à qqn). ○ **come down** *vi* [decrease] baisser. || [descend] descendre. ○ **come down to** *vt fus* se résumer à, se réduire à. ○ **come down with** *vt fus* [cold, flu] attraper. ○ **come forward** *vi* se présenter. ○ **come from** *vt fus* venir de. ○ **come in** *vi* [enter] entrer. ○ **come in for** *vt fus* [criticism] être l'objet de. ○ **come into** *vt fus* [inherit] hériter de. || [begin to be]: **to ~ into being** prendre naissance, voir le jour. ○ **come off** *vi* [button, label] se détacher; [stain] s'enlever. || [joke, attempt] réussir. || *phr*: **~ off it!** *inf* et puis quoi encore!, non mais sans blague! ○ **come on** *vi* [start] commencer, apparaître. || [start working - light, heating] s'allumer. || [progress, improve] avancer, faire des progrès. || *phr*: **~ on!** [expressing encouragement] allez!; [hurry up] allez, dépêche-toi!; [expressing disbelief] allons donc! ○ **come out** *vi* [become known] être découvert(e). || [appear - product, book, film] sortir, paraître; [- sun, moon, stars] paraître. || [go on strike] faire grève. || [declare publicly]: **to ~ out for/against sthg** se déclarer pour/contre qqch. ○ **come round** *vi* [regain consciousness] reprendre connaissance, revenir à soi. ○ **come through** *vt fus* survivre à. ○ **come to** 1 *vt fus* [reach]: **to ~ to an end** se terminer, prendre fin; **to ~ to a decision** arriver à OR prendre une décision. || [amount to] s'élever à. 2 *vi* [regain consciousness] revenir à soi, reprendre connaissance. ○ **come under** *vt fus* [be governed by] être soumis(e) à. || [suffer]: **to ~ under attack (from)** être en butte aux attaques (de). ○ **come up** *vi* [be mentioned] survenir. || [be imminent] approcher. || [happen unexpectedly] se présenter. || [sun, moon] se lever. ○ **come up against** *vt fus* se heurter à. ○ **come up to** *vt fus* [approach - in space] s'approcher de. ○ **come up with** *vt fus* [answer, idea] proposer.

comeback ['kʌmbæk] *n* come-back *m*; **to make a ~** [actor etc] revenir à la scène.

comedian [kə'mi:djən] *n* [comic] comique *m*; THEATRE comédien *m*.

comedown ['kʌmdaʊn] *n inf*: **it was a ~ for her** elle est tombée bien bas pour faire ça.

comedy ['kɒmədɪ] *n* comédie *f*.

comet ['kɒmɪt] *n* comète *f*.

come-uppance [,kʌm'ʌpəns] *n*: **to get one's ~** *inf* recevoir ce qu'on mérite.

comfort ['kʌmfət] 1 *n* (U) [ease] confort *m*. || [luxury] commodité *f*. || [solace] réconfort *m*, consolation *f*. 2 *vt* réconforter, consoler.

comfortable ['kʌmftəbl] *adj* [gen] confortable. || *fig* [person - at ease, financially] à l'aise. || [after operation, accident]: **he's ~** son état est stationnaire.

comfortably ['kʌmftəblɪ] *adv* [sit, sleep] confortablement. || [without financial difficulty] à l'aise. || [win] aisément.

comfort station *n Am* toilettes *fpl* publiques.

comic ['kɒmɪk] 1 *adj* comique, amusant(e). 2 *n* [comedian] comique *m*, actrice *f* comique. || [magazine] bande *f* dessinée.

comical ['kɒmɪkl] *adj* comique, drôle.

comic strip *n* bande *f* dessinée.

coming ['kʌmɪŋ] 1 *adj* [future] à venir, futur(e). 2 *n*: **~s and goings** allées et venues *fpl*.

comma ['kɒmə] *n* virgule *f*.

command [kə'mɑːnd] 1 *n* [order] ordre *m*. || (U) [control] commandement *m*. || [of language, subject] maîtrise *f*; **to have at one's ~** [language] maîtriser; [resources] avoir à sa disposition. || COMPUT commande *f*. 2 *vt* [order]: **to ~ sb to do sthg** ordonner OR commander à qqn de faire qqch. || MIL [control] commander. || [deserve - respect] inspirer; [- attention, high price] mériter.

commandeer [,kɒmən'dɪər] *vt* réquisitionner.

commander [kə'mɑːndər] *n* [in army] commandant *m*. || [in navy] capitaine *m* de frégate.

commando [kə'mɑːndəʊ] (*pl* -s OR -es) *n* commando *m*.

commemorate [kə'meməreɪt] *vt* commémorer.

commemoration [kə,memə'reɪʃn] *n* commémoration *f*.

commence [kə'mens] *fml* 1 *vt* commencer, entamer; **to ~ doing sthg** commencer à faire qqch. 2 *vi* commencer.

commend [kə'mend] *vt* [praise]: **to ~ sb (on OR for)** féliciter qqn (de). || [recommend]: **to ~ sthg (to sb)** recommander qqch (à qqn).

comment ['kɒment] 1 *n* commentaire *m*, remarque *f*; **no ~!** sans commentaire! 2 *vt*: **to ~ that** remarquer que. 3 *vi*: **to ~**

(on) faire des commentaires OR remarques (sur).

commentary ['kɒməntrɪ] *n* commentaire *m*.

commentator ['kɒmənteɪtər] *n* commentateur *m*, -trice *f*.

commerce ['kɒmɜːs] *n* (*U*) commerce *m*, affaires *fpl*.

commercial [kə'mɜːʃl] **1** *adj* commercial(e). **2** *n* publicité *f*, spot *m* publicitaire.

commercial break *n* publicités *fpl*.

commission [kə'mɪʃn] **1** *n* [money, investigative body] commission *f*. ‖ [order for work] commande *f*. **2** *vt* [work] commander; **to ~ sb to do sthg** charger qqn de faire qqch.

commissioner [kə'mɪʃnər] *n* [in police] commissaire *m*.

commit [kə'mɪt] *vt* [crime, sin etc] commettre; **to ~ suicide** se suicider. ‖ [promise - money, resources] allouer; **to ~ o.s. (to sthg/to doing sthg)** s'engager (à qqch/à faire qqch). ‖ [consign]: **to ~ sb to prison** faire incarcérer qqn; **to ~ sthg to memory** apprendre qqch par cœur.

commitment [kə'mɪtmənt] *n* (*U*) [dedication] engagement *m*. ‖ [responsibility] obligation *f*.

committee [kə'mɪtɪ] *n* commission *f*, comité *m*.

commodity [kə'mɒdətɪ] *n* marchandise *f*.

common ['kɒmən] **1** *adj* [frequent] courant(e). ‖ [shared]: **~ (to)** commun(e) (à). ‖ [ordinary] banal(e). **2** *n* [land] terrain *m* communal. ○ **in common** *adv* en commun.

common law *n* droit *m* coutumier. ○ **common-law** *adj*: **common-law wife** concubine *f*.

commonly ['kɒmənlɪ] *adv* [generally] d'une manière générale, généralement.

Common Market *n*: **the ~** le Marché commun.

commonplace ['kɒmənpleɪs] *adj* banal(e), ordinaire.

common room *n* [staffroom] salle *f* des professeurs; [for students] salle commune.

Commons ['kɒmənz] *npl Br*: **the ~** les Communes *fpl*, la Chambre des Communes.

common sense *n* (*U*) bon sens *m*.

Commonwealth ['kɒmənwelθ] *n*: **the ~** le Commonwealth.

Commonwealth of Independent States *n*: **the ~** la Communauté des États Indépendants.

commotion [kə'məʊʃn] *n* remue-ménage *m*.

communal ['kɒmjʊnl] *adj* [kitchen, garden] commun(e); [life etc] communautaire, collectif(ive).

commune [*n* 'kɒmjuːn, *vb* kə'mjuːn] **1** *n* communauté *f*. **2** *vi*: **to ~ with** communier avec.

communicate [kə'mjuːnɪkeɪt] *vt & vi* communiquer.

communication [kə,mjuːnɪ'keɪʃn] *n* contact *m*; TELEC communication *f*.

communion [kə'mjuːnjən] *n* communion *f*.

Communism ['kɒmjʊnɪzm] *n* communisme *m*.

Communist ['kɒmjʊnɪst] **1** *adj* communiste. **2** *n* communiste *mf*.

community [kə'mjuːnətɪ] *n* communauté *f*.

community centre *n* foyer *m* municipal.

commutation ticket *n Am* carte *f* de transport.

commute [kə'mjuːt] **1** *vt* JUR commuer. **2** *vi* [to work] *faire la navette pour se rendre à son travail*.

commuter [kə'mjuːtər] *n personne qui fait tous les jours la navette de banlieue en ville pour se rendre à son travail*.

compact [*adj & vb* kəm'pækt, *n* 'kɒmpækt] **1** *adj* compact(e). **2** *n* [for face powder] poudrier *m*. ‖ *Am* AUT: **~ (car)** petite voiture *f*.

compact disc *n* compact *m* (disc *m*), disque *m* compact.

compact disc player *n* lecteur *m* de disques compacts.

companion [kəm'pænjən] *n* [person] camarade *mf*.

companionship [kəm'pænjənʃɪp] *n* compagnie *f*.

company ['kʌmpənɪ] *n* [COMM - gen] société *f*; [- insurance, airline, shipping company] compagnie *f*. ‖ [companionship] compagnie *f*; **to keep sb ~** tenir compagnie à qqn. ‖ [of actors] troupe *f*.

company secretary *n* secrétaire général *m*, secrétaire générale *f*.

comparable ['kɒmprəbl] *adj*: **~ (to** OR **with)** comparable (à).

comparative [kəm'pærətɪv] *adj* [relative] relatif(ive). ‖ [study, in grammar] comparatif(ive).

comparatively [kəm'pærətɪvlɪ] *adv* [relatively] relativement.

compare [kəm'peəʳ] **1** *vt*: to ~ sb/sthg **(with),** to ~ sb/sthg **(to)** comparer qqn/qqch (avec), comparer qqn/qqch (à); ~d **with** OR **to** par rapport à. **2** *vi*: to ~ **(with)** être comparable (à).

comparison [kəm'pærɪsn] *n* comparaison *f*; **in ~ with** OR **to** en comparaison de, par rapport à.

compartment [kəm'pɑːtmənt] *n* compartiment *m*.

compass ['kʌmpəs] *n* [magnetic] boussole *f*. ○ **compasses** *npl*: **(a pair of)** ~es un compas.

compassion [kəm'pæʃn] *n* compassion *f*.

compassionate [kəm'pæʃənət] *adj* compatissant(e).

compatible [kəm'pætəbl] *adj* [gen & COMPUT]: ~ **(with)** compatible (avec).

compel [kəm'pel] *vt* [force]: to ~ sb **(to do sthg)** contraindre OR obliger qqn (à faire qqch).

compelling [kəm'pelɪŋ] *adj* [forceful] irrésistible.

compensate ['kɒmpenseɪt] **1** *vt*: to ~ sb **for sthg** [financially] dédommager OR indemniser qqn de qqch. **2** *vi*: to ~ **for sthg** compenser qqch.

compensation [,kɒmpen'seɪʃn] *n* [money]: ~ **(for)** dédommagement *m* (pour). || [way of compensating]: ~ **(for)** compensation *f* (pour).

compete [kəm'piːt] *vi* [vie - people]: to ~ **with sb for sthg** disputer qqch à qqn; to ~ **for sthg** se disputer qqch. || COMM: to ~ **(with)** être en concurrence (avec); to ~ **for sthg** se faire concurrence pour qqch. || [take part] être en compétition.

competence ['kɒmpɪtəns] *n* (*U*) [proficiency] compétence *f*, capacité *f*.

competent ['kɒmpɪtənt] *adj* compétent(e).

competition [,kɒmpɪ'tɪʃn] *n* (*U*) [rivalry] rivalité *f*, concurrence *f*. || (*U*) COMM concurrence *f*. || [race, contest] concours *m*, compétition *f*.

competitive [kəm'petətɪv] *adj* [person] qui a l'esprit de compétition; [match, sport] de compétition. || [COMM - goods] compétitif(ive); [- manufacturer] concurrentiel(ielle).

competitor [kəm'petɪtəʳ] *n* concurrent *m*, -e *f*.

compile [kəm'paɪl] *vt* rédiger.

complacency [kəm'pleɪsnsɪ] *n* autosatisfaction *f*.

complain [kəm'pleɪn] *vi* [moan]: to ~ **(about)** se plaindre (de). || MED: to ~ **of** se plaindre de.

complaint [kəm'pleɪnt] *n* [gen] plainte *f*; [in shop] réclamation *f*. || MED affection *f*, maladie *f*.

complement [*n* 'kɒmplɪmənt, *vb* 'kɒmplɪ,ment] **1** *n* [accompaniment] accompagnement *m*. || [number] effectif *m*. || GRAMM complément *m*. **2** *vt* aller bien avec.

complementary [,kɒmplɪ'mentərɪ] *adj* complémentaire.

complete [kəm'pliːt] **1** *adj* [gen] complet(ète); ~ **with** doté(e) de, muni(e) de. || [finished] achevé(e). **2** *vt* [make whole] compléter. || [finish] achever, terminer. || [questionnaire, form] remplir.

completely [kəm'pliːtlɪ] *adv* complètement.

completion [kəm'pliːʃn] *n* achèvement *m*.

complex ['kɒmpleks] **1** *adj* complexe. **2** *n* [mental, of buildings] complexe *m*.

complexion [kəm'plekʃn] *n* teint *m*.

complicate ['kɒmplɪkeɪt] *vt* compliquer.

complicated ['kɒmplɪkeɪtɪd] *adj* compliqué(e).

complication [,kɒmplɪ'keɪʃn] *n* complication *f*.

compliment [*n* 'kɒmplɪmənt, *vb* 'kɒmplɪment] **1** *n* compliment *m*. **2** *vt*: to ~ sb **(on)** féliciter qqn (de).

complimentary [,kɒmplɪ'mentərɪ] *adj* [admiring] flatteur(euse). || [free] gratuit(e).

comply [kəm'plaɪ] *vi*: to ~ **with** se conformer à.

component [kəm'pəʊnənt] *n* composant *m*.

compose [kəm'pəʊz] *vt* [gen] composer; **to be ~d of** se composer de, être composé de. || [calm]: to ~ **o.s.** se calmer.

composed [kəm'pəʊzd] *adj* [calm] calme.

composer [kəm'pəʊzəʳ] *n* compositeur *m*, -trice *f*.

composition [,kɒmpə'zɪʃn] *n* composition *f*.

compost [*Br* 'kɒmpɒst, *Am* 'kɒmpəʊst] *n* compost *m*.

composure [kəm'pəʊʒəʳ] *n* sang-froid *m*, calme *m*.

compound ['kɒmpaʊnd] n CHEM & LING composé m. || [enclosed area] enceinte f.

comprehend [,kɒmprɪ'hend] vt [understand] comprendre.

comprehension [,kɒmprɪ'henʃn] n compréhension f.

comprehensive [,kɒmprɪ'hensɪv] adj [account, report] exhaustif(ive), détaillé(e). || [insurance] tous-risques (inv).

compress [kəm'pres] vt [squeeze, press] comprimer. || [shorten - text] condenser.

comprise [kəm'praɪz] vt comprendre; **to be ~d of** consister en, comprendre.

compromise ['kɒmprəmaɪz] 1 n compromis m. 2 vt compromettre. 3 vi transiger.

compulsive [kəm'pʌlsɪv] adj [smoker, liar etc] invétéré(e). || [book, TV programme] captivant(e).

compulsory [kəm'pʌlsərɪ] adj obligatoire.

computer [kəm'pjuːtə'] 1 n ordinateur m. 2 comp: ~ **graphics** infographie f; ~ **program** programme m informatique.

computer game n jeu m électronique.

computing [kəm'pjuːtɪŋ], **computer science** n informatique f.

comrade ['kɒmreɪd] n camarade mf.

con [kɒn] inf 1 n [trick] escroquerie f. 2 vt [trick]: **to ~ sb (out of)** escroquer qqn (de).

concave [,kɒn'keɪv] adj concave.

conceal [kən'siːl] vt cacher, dissimuler; **to ~ sthg from sb** cacher qqch à qqn.

concede [kən'siːd] 1 vt concéder. 2 vi céder.

conceit [kən'siːt] n [arrogance] vanité f.

conceited [kən'siːtɪd] adj vaniteux(euse).

conceive [kən'siːv] vi MED concevoir. || [imagine]: **to ~ of** concevoir.

concentrate ['kɒnsəntreɪt] 1 vt concentrer. 2 vi: **to ~ (on)** se concentrer (sur).

concentration [,kɒnsən'treɪʃn] n concentration f.

concentration camp n camp m de concentration.

concept ['kɒnsept] n concept m.

concern [kən'sɜːn] 1 n [worry, anxiety] souci m, inquiétude f. || COMM [company] affaire f. 2 vt [worry] inquiéter; **to be ~ed (about)** s'inquiéter (de). || [involve] concerner, intéresser; **as far as I'm ~ed** en ce qui me concerne; **to be ~ed with** [subj: person] s'intéresser à. || [subj: book, film] traiter de.

concerning [kən'sɜːnɪŋ] prep en ce qui concerne.

concert ['kɒnsət] n concert m.

concerted [kən'sɜːtɪd] adj [effort] concerté(e).

concert hall n salle f de concert.

concertina [,kɒnsə'tiːnə] n concertina m.

concerto [kən'tʃeətəʊ] (pl -s) n concerto m.

concession [kən'seʃn] n [gen] concession f. || [special price] réduction f.

conciliatory [kən'sɪliətrɪ] adj conciliant(e).

concise [kən'saɪs] adj concis(e).

conclude [kən'kluːd] 1 vt conclure. 2 vi [meeting] prendre fin; [speaker] conclure.

conclusion [kən'kluːʒn] n conclusion f.

conclusive [kən'kluːsɪv] adj concluant(e).

concoct [kən'kɒkt] vt préparer; fig concocter.

concourse ['kɒŋkɔːs] n [hall] hall m.

concrete ['kɒŋkriːt] 1 adj [definite] concret(ète). 2 n (U) béton m.

concur [kən'kɜː'] vi [agree]: **to ~ (with)** être d'accord (avec).

concurrently [kən'kʌrəntlɪ] adv simultanément.

concussion [kən'kʌʃn] n commotion f.

condemn [kən'dem] vt condamner.

condensation [,kɒnden'seɪʃn] n condensation f.

condense [kən'dens] 1 vt condenser. 2 vi se condenser.

condensed milk [kən'denst-] n lait m condensé.

condescending [,kɒndɪ'sendɪŋ] adj condescendant(e).

condition [kən'dɪʃn] 1 n [gen] condition f; **in (a) good/bad ~** en bon/mauvais état; **out of ~** pas en forme. || MED maladie f. 2 vt [gen] conditionner.

conditional [kən'dɪʃənl] adj conditionnel(elle).

conditioner [kən'dɪʃnə'] n [for hair] après-shampooing m. || [for clothes] assouplissant m.

condolences [kən'dəʊlənsɪz] npl condoléances fpl.

condom ['kɒndəm] n préservatif m.

condominium [,kɒndə'mɪnɪəm] n Am [apartment] appartement m dans un immeuble en copropriété. || [apartment block] immeuble m en copropriété.

condone [kən'dəʊn] vt excuser.

conducive [kən'djuːsɪv] *adj*: **to be ~ to sthg/to doing sthg** inciter à qqch/à faire qqch.

conduct [*n* 'kɒndʌkt, *vb* kən'dʌkt] **1** *n* conduite *f*. **2** *vt* [carry out, transmit] conduire. ‖ MUS diriger.

conducted tour [kən'dʌktɪd-] *n* visite *f* guidée.

conductor [kən'dʌktər] *n* MUS chef *m* d'orchestre. ‖ [on bus] receveur *m*. ‖ *Am* [on train] chef *m* de train.

conductress [kən'dʌktrɪs] *n* [on bus] receveuse *f*.

cone [kəʊn] *n* [shape] cône *m*. ‖ [for ice cream] cornet *m*. ‖ [from tree] pomme *f* de pin.

confectioner [kən'fekʃnər] *n* confiseur *m*; **~'s (shop)** confiserie *f*.

confectionery [kən'fekʃnərɪ] *n* confiserie *f*.

confederation [kən,fedə'reɪʃn] *n* confédération *f*.

confer [kən'fɜːr] **1** *vt*: **to ~ sthg (on sb)** conférer qqch (à qqn). **2** *vi*: **to ~ (with sb on OR about sthg)** s'entretenir (avec qqn de qqch).

conference ['kɒnfərəns] *n* conférence *f*.

confess [kən'fes] **1** *vt* [admit] avouer, confesser. ‖ RELIG confesser. **2** *vi*: **to ~ (to sthg)** avouer (qqch).

confession [kən'feʃn] *n* confession *f*.

confetti [kən'fetɪ] *n* (*U*) confettis *mpl*.

confide [kən'faɪd] *vi*: **to ~ in sb** se confier à qqn.

confidence ['kɒnfɪdəns] *n* [self-assurance] confiance *f* en soi, assurance *f*. ‖ [trust] confiance *f*; **to have ~ in** avoir confiance en. ‖ [secrecy]: **in ~** en confidence. ‖ [secret] confidence *f*.

confidence trick *n* abus *m* de confiance.

confident ['kɒnfɪdənt] *adj* [self-assured]: **to be ~** avoir confiance en soi. ‖ [sure] sûr(e).

confidential [,kɒnfɪ'denʃl] *adj* confidentiel(ielle).

confine [kən'faɪn] *vt* [limit] limiter; **to ~ o.s. to** se limiter à. ‖ [shut up] enfermer, confiner.

confined [kən'faɪnd] *adj* [space, area] restreint(e).

confinement [kən'faɪnmənt] *n* [imprisonment] emprisonnement *m*.

confirm [kən'fɜːm] *vt* confirmer.

confirmation [,kɒnfə'meɪʃn] *n* confirmation *f*.

confirmed [kən'fɜːmd] *adj* [habitual] invétéré(e); [bachelor, spinster] endurci(e).

confiscate ['kɒnfɪskeɪt] *vt* confisquer.

conflict [*n* 'kɒnflɪkt, *vb* kən'flɪkt] **1** *n* conflit *m*. **2** *vi*: **to ~ (with)** s'opposer (à), être en conflit (avec).

conflicting [kən'flɪktɪŋ] *adj* contradictoire.

conform [kən'fɔːm] *vi*: **to ~ (to OR with)** se conformer (à).

confront [kən'frʌnt] *vt* [problem, enemy] affronter. ‖ [challenge]: **to ~ sb (with)** confronter qqn (avec).

confrontation [,kɒnfrʌn'teɪʃn] *n* affrontement *m*.

confuse [kən'fjuːz] *vt* [disconcert] troubler. ‖ [mix up] confondre.

confused [kən'fjuːzd] *adj* [not clear] compliqué(e). ‖ [disconcerted] troublé(e), désorienté(e); **I'm ~** je n'y comprends rien.

confusing [kən'fjuːzɪŋ] *adj* pas clair(e).

confusion [kən'fjuːʒn] *n* confusion *f*.

congeal [kən'dʒiːl] *vi* [blood] se coaguler.

congested [kən'dʒestɪd] *adj* [street, area] encombré(e). ‖ MED congestionné(e).

congestion [kən'dʒestʃn] *n* [of traffic] encombrement *m*. ‖ MED congestion *f*.

conglomerate [,kən'glɒmərət] *n* COMM conglomérat *m*.

congratulate [kən'grætʃʊleɪt] *vt*: **to ~ sb (on sthg/on doing sthg)** féliciter qqn (de qqch/d'avoir fait qqch).

congratulations [kən,grætʃʊ'leɪʃənz] *npl* félicitations *fpl*.

congregate ['kɒŋgrɪgeɪt] *vi* se rassembler.

congregation [,kɒŋgrɪ'geɪʃn] *n* assemblée *f* des fidèles.

congress ['kɒŋgres] *n* [meeting] congrès *m*. ○ **Congress** *n* *Am* POL le Congrès.

congressman ['kɒŋgresmən] (*pl* -men [-mən]) *n* *Am* POL membre *m* du Congrès.

conifer ['kɒnɪfər] *n* conifère *m*.

conjugation [,kɒndʒʊ'geɪʃn] *n* GRAMM conjugaison *f*.

conjunction [kən'dʒʌŋkʃn] *n* GRAMM conjonction *f*.

conjunctivitis [kən,dʒʌŋktɪ'vaɪtɪs] *n* conjonctivite *f*.

conjure ['kʌndʒər] *vi* [by magic] faire des tours de prestidigitation. ○ **conjure up** *vt sep* évoquer.

conjurer ['kʌndʒərər] *n* prestidigitateur *m*, -trice *f*.

conjuror ['kʌndʒərər] = conjurer.

conman ['kɒnmæn] (*pl* -men [-men]) *n* escroc *m*.

connect [kə'nekt] 1 *vt* [join]: to ~ sthg (to) relier qqch (à). || [on telephone] mettre en communication. || [associate] associer; to ~ sb/sthg to, to ~ sb/sthg with associer qqn/qqch à. || ELEC [to power supply]: to ~ sthg to brancher qqch à. 2 *vi* [train, plane, bus]: to ~ (with) assurer la correspondance (avec).

connected [kə'nektɪd] *adj* [related]: to be ~ with avoir un rapport avec.

connection [kə'nekʃn] *n* [relationship]: ~ (between/with) rapport *m* (entre/avec); in ~ with à propos de. || ELEC branchement *m*, connexion *f*. || [on telephone] communication *f*. || [plane, train, bus] correspondance *f*. || [professional acquaintance] relation *f*.

connive [kə'naɪv] *vi* [plot] comploter. || [allow to happen]: to ~ at sthg fermer les yeux sur qqch.

connoisseur [,kɒnə'sɜːr] *n* connaisseur *m*, -euse *f*.

conquer ['kɒŋkər] *vt* [country, people etc] conquérir. || [fears, inflation etc] vaincre.

conqueror ['kɒŋkərər] *n* conquérant *m*, -e *f*.

conquest ['kɒŋkwest] *n* conquête *f*.

conscience ['kɒnʃəns] *n* conscience *f*.

conscientious [,kɒnʃɪ'enʃəs] *adj* consciencieux(ieuse).

conscious ['kɒnʃəs] *adj* [not unconscious] conscient(e). || [aware]: ~ of sthg conscient(e) de qqch. || [intentional - insult] délibéré(e), intentionnel(elle); [- effort] conscient(e).

consciousness ['kɒnʃəsnɪs] *n* conscience *f*.

conscript ['kɒnskrɪpt] MIL *n* conscrit *m*.

conscription [kən'skrɪpʃn] *n* conscription *f*.

consecutive [kən'sekjutɪv] *adj* consécutif(ive).

consent [kən'sent] 1 *n* (*U*) [permission] consentement *m*. || [agreement] accord *m*. 2 *vi*: to ~ (to) consentir (à).

consequence ['kɒnsɪkwəns] *n* [result] conséquence *f*; in ~ par conséquent. || [importance] importance *f*.

consequently ['kɒnsɪkwəntlɪ] *adv* par conséquent.

conservation [,kɒnsə'veɪʃn] *n* [of nature] protection *f*; [of buildings] conservation *f*; [of energy, water] économie *f*.

conservative [kən'sɜːvətɪv] 1 *adj* [not modern] traditionnel(elle). || [cautious] prudent(e). 2 *n* traditionaliste *mf*. ○ **Conservative** POL 1 *adj* conservateur(trice). 2 *n* conservateur *m*, -trice *f*.

conservatory [kən'sɜːvətrɪ] *n* [of house] véranda *f*.

conserve [*n* 'kɒnsɜːv, *vb* kən'sɜːv] 1 *n* confiture *f*. 2 *vt* [energy, supplies] économiser; [nature, wildlife] protéger.

consider [kən'sɪdər] *vt* [think about] examiner. || [take into account] prendre en compte; all things ~ed tout compte fait. || [judge] considérer.

considerable [kən'sɪdrəbl] *adj* considérable.

considerably [kən'sɪdrəblɪ] *adv* considérablement.

considerate [kən'sɪdərət] *adj* prévenant(e).

consideration [kən,sɪdə'reɪʃn] *n* (*U*) [careful thought] réflexion *f*; to take sthg into ~ tenir compte de qqch, prendre qqch en considération; under ~ à l'étude. || (*U*) [care] attention *f*. || [factor] facteur *m*.

considering [kən'sɪdərɪŋ] 1 *prep* étant donné. 2 *conj* étant donné que.

consign [kən'saɪn] *vt*: to ~ sb/sthg to reléguer qqn/qqch à.

consignment [kən'saɪnmənt] *n* [load] expédition *f*.

consist [kən'sɪst] ○ **consist of** *vt fus* consister en.

consistency [kən'sɪstənsɪ] *n* [coherence] cohérence *f*. || [texture] consistance *f*.

consistent [kən'sɪstənt] *adj* [regular - behaviour] conséquent(e); [- improvement] régulier(ière); [- supporter] constant(e). || [coherent] cohérent(e); to be ~ with [with one's position] être compatible avec; [with the facts] correspondre avec.

consolation [,kɒnsə'leɪʃn] *n* réconfort *m*.

console [*n* 'kɒnsəul, *vt* kən'səul] 1 *n* tableau *m* de commande. 2 *vt* consoler.

consonant ['kɒnsənənt] *n* consonne *f*.

consortium [kən'sɔːtjəm] (*pl* -tiums OR -tia [-tjə]) *n* consortium *m*.

conspicuous [kən'spɪkjuəs] *adj* voyant(e), qui se remarque.

conspiracy [kən'spɪrəsɪ] *n* conspiration *f*, complot *m*.

conspire [kən'spaɪəʳ] *vt*: **to ~ to do sthg** comploter de faire qqch; [subj: events] contribuer à faire qqch.

constabulary [kən'stæbjʊlərɪ] *n* police *f*.

constant ['kɒnstənt] *adj* [unvarying] constant(e). || [recurring] continuel(elle).

constantly ['kɒnstəntlɪ] *adv* constamment.

consternation [ˌkɒnstə'neɪʃn] *n* consternation *f*.

constipated ['kɒnstɪpeɪtɪd] *adj* constipé(e).

constipation [ˌkɒnstɪ'peɪʃn] *n* constipation *f*.

constituency [kən'stɪtjuənsɪ] *n* [area] circonscription *f* électorale.

constituent [kən'stɪtjuənt] *n* [voter] électeur *m*, -trice *f*. || [element] composant *m*.

constitute ['kɒnstɪtjuːt] *vt* [form, represent] représenter, constituer. || [establish, set up] constituer.

constitution [ˌkɒnstɪ'tjuːʃn] *n* constitution *f*.

constraint [kən'streɪnt] *n* [restriction]: **~ (on)** limitation *f* (à). || (U) [self-control] retenue *f*, réserve *f*. || [coercion] contrainte *f*.

construct [kən'strʌkt] *vt* construire.

construction [kən'strʌkʃn] *n* construction *f*.

constructive [kən'strʌktɪv] *adj* constructif(ive).

construe [kən'struː] *vt fml* [interpret]: **to ~ sthg as** interpréter qqch comme.

consul ['kɒnsəl] *n* consul *m*.

consulate ['kɒnsjʊlət] *n* consulat *m*.

consult [kən'sʌlt] **1** *vt* consulter. **2** *vi*: **to ~ with sb** s'entretenir avec qqn.

consultant [kən'sʌltənt] *n* [expert] expert-conseil *m*.

consultation [ˌkɒnsəl'teɪʃn] *n* [meeting, discussion] entretien *m*.

consulting room [kən'sʌltɪŋ-] *n* cabinet *m* de consultation.

consume [kən'sjuːm] *vt* [food, fuel etc] consommer.

consumer [kən'sjuːməʳ] *n* consommateur *m*, -trice *f*.

consumer goods *npl* biens *mpl* de consommation.

consummate ['kɒnsəmeɪt] *vt* consommer.

consumption [kən'sʌmpʃn] *n* [use] consommation *f*.

cont. *abbr of* **continued**.

contact ['kɒntækt] **1** *n* (U) [touch, communication] contact *m*; **in ~ (with sb)** en rapport OR contact (avec qqn); **to lose ~ with sb** perdre le contact avec qqn; **to make ~ with sb** prendre contact OR entrer en contact avec qqn. || [person] relation *f*, contact *m*. **2** *vt* contacter, prendre contact avec; [by phone] joindre, contacter.

contact lens *n* verre *m* de contact, lentille *f* (cornéenne).

contagious [kən'teɪdʒəs] *adj* contagieux(ieuse).

contain [kən'teɪn] *vt* [hold, include] contenir, renfermer.

container [kən'teɪnəʳ] *n* [box, bottle etc] récipient *m*. || [for transporting goods] conteneur *m*, container *m*.

contaminate [kən'tæmɪneɪt] *vt* contaminer.

cont'd *abbr of* **continued**.

contemplate ['kɒntempleɪt] **1** *vt* [consider] envisager. || *fml* [look at] contempler. **2** *vi* [consider] méditer.

contemporary [kən'tempərərɪ] **1** *adj* contemporain(e). **2** *n* contemporain *m*, -e *f*.

contempt [kən'tempt] *n* [scorn]: **~ (for)** mépris *m* (pour). || JUR: **~ (of court)** outrage *m* à la cour.

contemptuous [kən'temptʃuəs] *adj* méprisant(e).

contend [kən'tend] **1** *vi* [deal]: **to ~ with sthg** faire face à qqch. || [compete]: **to ~ for** [subj: several people] se disputer; [subj: one person] se battre pour; **to ~ against** lutter contre. **2** *vt fml* [claim]: **to ~ that ...** soutenir OR prétendre que ....

contender [kən'tendəʳ] *n* [in election] candidat *m*, -e *f*; [in competition] concurrent *m*, -e *f*; [in boxing etc] prétendant *m*, -e *f*.

content [*n* 'kɒntent, *adj & vb* kən'tent] **1** *adj*: **~ (with)** satisfait(e) (de), content(e) (de); **to be ~ to do sthg** ne pas demander mieux que de faire qqch. **2** *n* [amount] teneur *f*. || [subject matter] contenu *m*. **3** *vt*: **to ~ o.s. with sthg/doing sthg** se contenter de qqch/de faire qqch. ○ **contents** *npl* [of container, document] contenu *m*. || [at front of book] table *f* des matières.

contented [kən'tentɪd] *adj* satisfait(e).

contention [kən'tenʃn] *n fml* [argument, assertion] assertion *f*, affirmation *f*. || (U) [disagreement] dispute *f*, contestation *f*.

contest [n 'kɒntest, vb kən'test] 1 n [competition] concours m. ‖ [for power, control] combat m, lutte f. 2 vt [compete for] disputer. ‖ [dispute] contester.

contestant [kən'testənt] n concurrent m, -e f.

context ['kɒntekst] n contexte m.

continent ['kɒntɪnənt] n continent m.

continental [ˌkɒntɪ'nentl] adj GEOGR continental(e).

continental breakfast n petit déjeuner m (par opposition à 'English breakfast').

contingency [kən'tɪndʒənsɪ] n éventualité f.

contingency plan n plan m d'urgence.

continual [kən'tɪnjʊəl] adj continuel(elle).

continually [kən'tɪnjʊəlɪ] adv continuellement.

continuation [kən,tɪnjʊ'eɪʃn] n (U) [act] continuation f. ‖ [sequel] suite f.

continue [kən'tɪnju:] 1 vt [carry on] continuer, poursuivre; to ~ doing or to do sthg continuer à or de faire qqch. ‖ [after an interruption] reprendre. 2 vi [carry on] continuer; to ~ with sthg poursuivre qqch, continuer qqch. ‖ [after an interruption] reprendre, se poursuivre.

continuous [kən'tɪnjʊəs] adj continu(e).

continuously [kən'tɪnjʊəslɪ] adv sans arrêt, continuellement.

contort [kən'tɔ:t] vt tordre.

contortion [kən'tɔ:ʃn] n (U) [twisting] torsion f. ‖ [position] contorsion f.

contour ['kɒn,tʊər] n [outline] contour m. ‖ [on map] courbe f de niveau.

contraband ['kɒntrəbænd] 1 adj de contrebande. 2 n contrebande f.

contraception [ˌkɒntrə'sepʃn] n contraception f.

contraceptive [ˌkɒntrə'septɪv] n contraceptif m.

contract [n 'kɒntrækt, vb kən'trækt] 1 n contrat m. 2 vt [gen] COMM: to ~ sb (to do sthg) passer un contrat avec qqn (pour faire qqch); to ~ to do sthg s'engager par contrat à faire qqch. 3 vi [decrease in size, length] se contracter.

contraction [kən'trækʃn] n contraction f.

contractor [kən'træktər] n entrepreneur m.

contradict [ˌkɒntrə'dɪkt] vt contredire.

contradiction [ˌkɒntrə'dɪkʃn] n contradiction f.

contraflow ['kɒntrəfləʊ] n circulation f à contre-sens.

contraption [kən'træpʃn] n machin m, truc m.

contrary ['kɒntrərɪ, adj sense 2 kən'treərɪ] 1 adj [opposite]: ~ (to) contraire (à), opposé(e) (à). ‖ [awkward] contrariant(e). 2 n contraire m; on the ~ au contraire. ○ **contrary to** prep contrairement à.

contrast [n 'kɒntrɑ:st, vb kən'trɑ:st] 1 n contraste m; by or in ~ par contraste. 2 vt contraster. 3 vi: to ~ (with) faire contraste (avec).

contravene [ˌkɒntrə'vi:n] vt enfreindre, transgresser.

contribute [kən'trɪbju:t] 1 vt [money] apporter; [help, advice, ideas] apporter. 2 vi [gen]: to ~ (to) contribuer (à). ‖ [write material]: to ~ to collaborer à.

contribution [ˌkɒntrɪ'bju:ʃn] n [money]: ~ (to) cotisation f (à), contribution f (à). ‖ [article] article m.

contributor [kən'trɪbjʊtər] n [of money] donateur m, -trice f. ‖ [to magazine, newspaper] collaborateur m, -trice f.

contrive [kən'traɪv] vt fml [engineer] combiner. ‖ [manage]: to ~ to do sthg se débrouiller pour faire qqch, trouver moyen de faire qqch.

contrived [kən'traɪvd] adj tiré(e) par les cheveux.

control [kən'trəʊl] 1 n [gen] contrôle m; [of traffic] régulation f; to get sb/sthg under ~ maîtriser qqn/qqch; to be in ~ of sthg [subj: boss, government] diriger qqch; [subj: army] avoir le contrôle de qqch; [of emotions, situation] maîtriser qqch; to lose ~ [of emotions] perdre le contrôle. 2 vt [company, country] être à la tête de, diriger. ‖ [operate] commander, faire fonctionner. ‖ [restrict, restrain - disease] enrayer, juguler; [- inflation] mettre un frein à, contenir; [- children] tenir; [- crowd] contenir; [- emotions] maîtriser, contenir; to ~ o.s. se maîtriser, se contrôler. ○ **controls** npl [of machine, vehicle] commandes fpl.

controller [kən'trəʊlər] n [person] contrôleur m.

control panel n tableau m de bord.

control tower n tour f de contrôle.

controversial [ˌkɒntrə'vɜ:ʃl] adj [writer, theory etc] controversé(e); to be ~ donner matière à controverse.

controversy ['kɒntrəvɜːsɪ, *Br* kən-'trɒvəsɪ] *n* controverse *f*, polémique *f*.

convalesce [,kɒnvə'les] *vi* se remettre d'une maladie, relever de maladie.

convene [kən'viːn] 1 *vt* convoquer, réunir. 2 *vi* se réunir, s'assembler.

convenience [kən'viːnjəns] *n* [usefulness] commodité *f*. || [personal comfort, advantage] agrément *m*, confort *m*; **at your earliest ~** *fml* dès que possible.

convenience store *n Am* petit supermarché de quartier.

convenient [kən'viːnjənt] *adj* [suitable] qui convient. || [handy] pratique, commode.

convent ['kɒnvənt] *n* couvent *m*.

convention [kən'venʃn] *n* [agreement, assembly] convention *f*. || [practice] usage *m*, convention *f*.

conventional [kən'venʃənl] *adj* conventionnel(elle).

converge [kən'vɜːdʒ] *vi*: **to ~ (on)** converger (sur).

conversation [,kɒnvə'seɪʃn] *n* conversation *f*.

converse [*n* & *adj* 'kɒnvɜːs, *vb* kən'vɜːs] 1 *n* [opposite]: **the ~** le contraire, l'inverse *m*. 2 *vi fml* converser.

conversely [kən'vɜːslɪ] *adv fml* inversement.

conversion [kən'vɜːʃn] *n* [changing, in religious beliefs] conversion *f*. || [in building] aménagement *m*, transformation *f*. || RUGBY transformation *f*.

convert [*vb* kən'vɜːt, *n* 'kɒnvɜːt] 1 *vt* [change]: **to ~ sthg to** OR **into** convertir qqch en; **to ~ sb (to)** RELIG convertir qqn (à). || [building, ship]: **to ~ sthg to** OR **into** transformer qqch en, aménager qqch en. 2 *vi*: **to ~ from sthg to sthg** passer de qqch à qqch. 3 *n* converti *m*, -e *f*.

convertible [kən'vɜːtəbl] *n* (voiture) décapotable *f*.

convex [kɒn'veks] *adj* convexe.

convey [kən'veɪ] *vt* [express]: **to ~ sthg (to sb)** communiquer qqch (à qqn).

conveyer belt [kən'veɪər-] *n* convoyeur *m*, tapis *m* roulant.

convict [*n* 'kɒnvɪkt, *vb* kən'vɪkt] 1 *n* détenu *m*. 2 *vt*: **to ~ sb of sthg** reconnaître qqn coupable de qqch.

conviction [kən'vɪkʃn] *n* [belief, fervour] conviction *f*. || JUR [of criminal] condamnation *f*.

convince [kən'vɪns] *vt* convaincre, persuader; **to ~ sb of sthg/to do sthg** convaincre qqn de qqch/de faire qqch, persuader qqn de qqch/de faire qqch.

convincing [kən'vɪnsɪŋ] *adj* [persuasive] convaincant(e).

convoluted ['kɒnvəluːtɪd] *adj* [tortuous] compliqué(e).

convoy ['kɒnvɔɪ] *n* convoi *m*.

convulsion [kən'vʌlʃn] *n* MED convulsion *f*.

coo [kuː] *vi* roucouler.

cook [kʊk] 1 *n* cuisinier *m*, -ière *f*. 2 *vt* [food] faire cuire; [meal] préparer. 3 *vi* [person] cuisiner, faire la cuisine; [food] cuire.

cookbook ['kʊkbʊk] = **cookery book**.

cooker ['kʊkər] *n* [stove] cuisinière *f*.

cookery ['kʊkərɪ] *n* cuisine *f*.

cookery book *n* livre *m* de cuisine.

cookie ['kʊkɪ] *n Am* [biscuit] biscuit *m*, gâteau *m* sec.

cooking ['kʊkɪŋ] *n* cuisine *f*.

cool [kuːl] 1 *adj* [not warm] frais (fraîche); [dress] léger(ère). || [calm] calme. || [unfriendly] froid(e). || *inf* [excellent] génial(e); [trendy] branché(e). 2 *vt* faire refroidir. 3 *vi* [become less warm] refroidir. 4 *n* [calm]: **to keep/lose one's ~** garder/perdre son sang-froid, garder/perdre son calme. ○ **cool down** *vi* [become less warm - food, engine] refroidir; [- person] se rafraîchir.

cool box *n* glacière *f*.

coop [kuːp] *n* poulailler *m*. ○ **coop up** *vt sep inf* confiner.

Co-op ['kəʊˌɒp] (*abbr of* **co-operative society**) *n* Coop *f*.

cooperate [kəʊ'ɒpəreɪt] *vi*: **to ~ (with sb/sthg)** coopérer (avec qqn/à qqch), collaborer (avec qqn/à qqch).

cooperation [kəʊˌɒpə'reɪʃn] *n* (*U*) [collaboration] coopération *f*, collaboration *f*. || [assistance] aide *f*, concours *m*.

cooperative [kəʊ'ɒpərətɪv] 1 *adj* coopératif(ive). 2 *n* coopérative *f*.

coordinate [*n* kəʊ'ɔːdɪnət, *vt* kəʊ'ɔːdɪneɪt] 1 *n* [on map, graph] coordonnée *f*. 2 *vt* coordonner. ○ **coordinates** *npl* [clothes] coordonnés *mpl*.

coordination [kəʊˌɔːdɪ'neɪʃn] *n* coordination *f*.

cop [kɒp] *n inf* flic *m*.

cope [kəʊp] *vi* se débrouiller; **to ~ with** faire face à.

Copenhagen [,kəʊpən'heɪɡən] *n* Copenhague *f*.

copier ['kɒpɪəʳ] n copieur m, photocopieur m.

copper ['kɒpəʳ] n [metal] cuivre m.

copy ['kɒpɪ] 1 n [imitation] copie f, reproduction f. || [duplicate] copie f. || [of book] exemplaire m; [of magazine] numéro m. 2 vt [imitate] copier, imiter. || [photocopy] photocopier.

copyright ['kɒpɪraɪt] n copyright m, droit m d'auteur.

coral ['kɒrəl] n corail m.

cord [kɔːd] n [string] ficelle f; [rope] corde f. || [electric] fil m, cordon m. || [fabric] velours m côtelé. ○ **cords** npl pantalon m en velours côtelé.

cordial ['kɔːdjəl] 1 adj cordial(e), chaleureux(euse). 2 n cordial m.

cordon ['kɔːdn] n cordon m. ○ **cordon off** vt sep barrer (par un cordon de police).

corduroy ['kɔːdərɔɪ] n velours m côtelé.

core [kɔːʳ] 1 n [of apple etc] trognon m, cœur m. || [of cable, Earth] noyau m; [of nuclear reactor] cœur m. || fig [of people] noyau m; [of problem, policy] essentiel m. 2 vt enlever le cœur de.

corgi ['kɔːgɪ] (pl -s) n corgi m.

coriander [,kɒrɪ'ændəʳ] n coriandre f.

cork [kɔːk] n [material] liège m. || [stopper] bouchon m.

corkscrew ['kɔːkskruː] n tire-bouchon m.

corn [kɔːn] n Am [maize] maïs m; ~ **on the cob** épi m de maïs cuit. || [on foot] cor m.

cornea ['kɔːnɪə] (pl -s) n cornée f.

corned beef [kɔːnd-] n corned-beef m inv.

corner ['kɔːnəʳ] 1 n [angle] coin m, angle m; **to cut ~s** fig brûler les étapes. || [bend in road] virage m, tournant m. 2 vt [person, animal] acculer.

corner shop n magasin m du coin OR du quartier.

cornet ['kɔːnɪt] n [instrument] cornet m à pistons.

cornflakes ['kɔːnfleɪks] npl corn-flakes mpl.

cornflour Br ['kɔːnflauəʳ], **cornstarch** Am ['kɔːnstɑːtʃ] n ≃ Maïzena® f, fécule f de maïs.

Cornwall ['kɔːnwɔːl] n Cornouailles f.

corny ['kɔːnɪ] adj inf [joke] peu original(e); [story, film] à l'eau de rose.

coronary ['kɒrənrɪ], **coronary**

thrombosis [-θrɒm'bəʊsɪs] n infarctus m du myocarde.

coronation [,kɒrə'neɪʃn] n couronnement m.

coroner ['kɒrənəʳ] n coroner m.

corporal ['kɔːpərəl] n [gen] caporal m; [in artillery] brigadier m.

corporal punishment n châtiment m corporel.

corporate ['kɔːpərət] adj [business] corporatif(ive), de société. || [collective] collectif(ive).

corporation [,kɔːpə'reɪʃn] n [town council] conseil m municipal. || [large company] compagnie f, société f enregistrée.

corps [kɔːʳ] (pl inv) n corps m.

corpse [kɔːps] n cadavre m.

correct [kə'rekt] 1 adj [accurate] correct(e), exact(e); **you're quite ~** tu as parfaitement raison. || [proper, socially acceptable] correct(e), convenable. 2 vt corriger.

correction [kə'rekʃn] n correction f.

correspond [,kɒrɪ'spɒnd] vi [gen]: **to ~ (with OR to)** correspondre (à). || [write letters]: **to ~ (with sb)** correspondre (avec qqn).

correspondence [,kɒrɪ'spɒndəns] n: ~ **(with)** correspondance f (avec).

correspondence course n cours m par correspondance.

correspondent [,kɒrɪ'spɒndənt] n correspondant m, -e f.

corridor ['kɒrɪdɔːʳ] n [in building] couloir m, corridor m.

corrode [kə'rəʊd] 1 vt corroder, attaquer. 2 vi se corroder.

corrosion [kə'rəʊʒn] n corrosion f.

corrugated ['kɒrəgeɪtɪd] adj ondulé(e).

corrugated iron n tôle f ondulée.

corrupt [kə'rʌpt] 1 adj [gen & COMPUT] corrompu(e). 2 vt corrompre, dépraver.

corruption [kə'rʌpʃn] n corruption f.

corset ['kɔːsɪt] n corset m.

Corsica ['kɔːsɪkə] n Corse f.

cosh [kɒʃ] n matraque f, gourdin m.

cosmetic [kɒz'metɪk] 1 n cosmétique m, produit m de beauté. 2 adj fig superficiel(ielle).

cosmopolitan [kɒzmə'pɒlɪtn] adj cosmopolite.

cost [kɒst] (pt & pp cost OR -ed) 1 n lit & fig coût m; **at all ~s** à tout prix, coûte que coûte. 2 vt lit & fig coûter. || COMM [estimate] évaluer le coût de. 3 vi coûter;

how much does it ~? combien ça coûte?, combien cela coûte-t-il? ○ **costs** *npl* JUR dépens *mpl*.

co-star ['kəʊ-] *n* partenaire *mf*.

Costa Rica [,kɒstə'ri:kə] *n* Costa Rica *m*.

cost-effective *adj* rentable.

costing ['kɒstɪŋ] *n* évaluation *f* du coût.

costly ['kɒstlɪ] *adj* lit & fig coûteux(euse).

cost of living *n*: **the ~** le coût de la vie.

cost price *n* prix *m* coûtant.

costume ['kɒstju:m] *n* [gen] costume *m*. || [swimming costume] maillot *m* (de bain).

costume jewellery *n* (U) bijoux *mpl* fantaisie.

cosy *Br*, **cozy** *Am* ['kəʊzɪ] *adj* [house, room] douillet(ette); [atmosphere] chaleureux(euse).

cot [kɒt] *n Am* [folding bed] lit *m* de camp.

cottage ['kɒtɪdʒ] *n* cottage *m*, petite maison *f* (de campagne).

cottage cheese *n* fromage *m* blanc.

cotton ['kɒtn] *n* [gen] coton *m*.

cotton candy *n Am* barbe *f* à papa.

cotton wool *n* ouate *f*, coton *m* hydrophile.

couch [kaʊtʃ] *n* [sofa] canapé *m*. || [in doctor's surgery] lit *m*.

cough [kɒf] **1** *n* toux *f*. **2** *vi* tousser.

could [kʊd] *pt* → **can²**.

couldn't ['kʊdnt] = **could not**.

could've ['kʊdəv] = **could have**.

council ['kaʊnsl] *n* conseil *m* municipal.

council estate *n* quartier *m* de logements sociaux.

councillor ['kaʊnsələr] *n* conseiller municipal *m*, conseillère municipale *f*.

counsel ['kaʊnsəl] *n* (U) *fml* [advice] conseil *m*. || [lawyer] avocat *m*, -e *f*.

counsellor *Br*, **counselor** *Am* ['kaʊnsələr] *n* [gen] conseiller *m*, -ère *f*. || *Am* [lawyer] avocat *m*.

count [kaʊnt] **1** *n* [total] total *m*; **to keep ~** of tenir le compte de; **to lose ~ of** sthg ne plus savoir qqch, ne pas se rappeler qqch. || [aristocrat] comte *m*. **2** *vt* [gen] compter. || [consider]: **to ~ sb as** sthg considérer qqn comme qqch. **3** *vi* [gen] compter. ○ **count against** *vt fus* jouer contre. ○ **count (up)on** *vt fus* [rely on] compter sur. || [expect] s'attendre à, prévoir. ○ **count up** *vt fus* compter.

countdown ['kaʊntdaʊn] *n* compte *m* à rebours.

counter ['kaʊntər] **1** *n* [in shop, bank] comptoir *m*. || [in board game] pion *m*. **2** *vt*: **to ~** sthg **(with)** [criticism etc] riposter à qqch (par). **3** *vi*: **to ~ with** sthg/**by doing** sthg riposter par qqch/en faisant qqch. ○ **counter to** *adv* contrairement à; **to run ~ to** aller à l'encontre de.

counteract [,kaʊntə'rækt] *vt* contrebalancer, compenser.

counterattack [,kaʊntərə'tæk] *vt & vi* contre-attaquer.

counterclockwise [,kaʊntə'klɒkwaɪz] *adj & adv Am* dans le sens inverse des aiguilles d'une montre.

counterfeit ['kaʊntəfɪt] **1** *adj* faux (fausse). **2** *vt* contrefaire.

counterfoil ['kaʊntəfɔɪl] *n* talon *m*, souche *f*.

counterpart ['kaʊntəpɑ:t] *n* [person] homologue *mf*; [thing] équivalent *m*, -e *f*.

counterproductive [,kaʊntəprə-'dʌktɪv] *adj* qui a l'effet inverse.

countess ['kaʊntɪs] *n* comtesse *f*.

countless ['kaʊntlɪs] *adj* innombrable.

country ['kʌntrɪ] *n* [nation] pays *m*. || [countryside]: **the ~** la campagne; **in the ~** à la campagne.

country dancing *n* (U) danse *f* folklorique.

country house *n* manoir *m*.

countryman ['kʌntrɪmən] (*pl* **-men** [-mən]) *n* [from same country] compatriote *m*.

countryside ['kʌntrɪsaɪd] *n* campagne *f*.

county ['kaʊntɪ] *n* comté *m*.

coup [ku:] *n* [rebellion]: **~ (d'état)** coup *m* d'État. || [success] coup *m* (de maître), beau coup *m*.

couple ['kʌpl] **1** *n* [in relationship] couple *m*. || [small number]: **a ~ (of)** [two] deux; [a few] quelques, deux ou trois. **2** *vt* [join]: **to ~** sthg **(to)** atteler qqch (à).

coupon ['ku:pɒn] *n* [voucher] bon *m*. || [form] coupon *m*.

courage ['kʌrɪdʒ] *n* courage *m*.

courier ['kʊrɪər] *n* [on holiday] guide *m*, accompagnateur *m*, -trice *f*. || [to deliver letters, packages] courrier *m*, messager *m*.

course [kɔ:s] *n* [gen & SCH] cours *m*; **~ of action** ligne *f* de conduite; **in the ~ of** au cours de. || MED [of injections] série *f*; **~ of treatment** traitement *m*. || [of ship, plane] route *f*; **to be on ~** suivre le cap fixé; *fig* [on target] être dans la bonne voie; **to be off ~** faire fausse route. || [of meal] plat *m.* || SPORT terrain *m.* ○ **of course** *adv* [inevitably, not surprisingly] évidemment, naturellement. || [certainly] bien sûr; **of ~ not** bien sûr que non.

coursebook ['kɔːsbʊk] *n* livre *m* de cours.

coursework ['kɔːswɜːk] *n* (*U*) travail *m* personnel.

court [kɔːt] **1** *n* [JUR - building, room] cour *f*, tribunal *m*; [- judge, jury etc]: **the ~** la justice; **to take sb to ~** faire un procès à qqn. || [SPORT - gen] court *m*; [- for basketball, volleyball] terrain *m.* || [courtyard, of monarch] cour *f*.

courtesy ['kɜːtɪsɪ] *n* courtoisie *f*, politesse *f*. ○ **(by) courtesy of** *prep* avec la permission de.

courthouse ['kɔːthaʊs, *pl* -haʊzɪz] *n* *Am* palais *m* de justice, tribunal *m*.

courtier ['kɔːtjər] *n* courtisan *m*.

court-martial (*pl* **court-martials** OR **courts-martial**) *n* cour *f* martiale.

courtroom ['kɔːtrʊm] *n* salle *f* de tribunal.

courtyard ['kɔːtjɑːd] *n* cour *f*.

cousin ['kʌzn] *n* cousin *m*, -e *f*.

cove [kəʊv] *n* [bay] crique *f*.

covenant ['kʌvənənt] *n* [of money] engagement *m* contractuel.

cover ['kʌvər] **1** *n* [covering - of furniture] housse *f*; [- of pan] couvercle *m*; [- of book, magazine] couverture *f.* || [blanket] couverture *f.* || [protection, shelter] abri *m*; **to take ~** s'abriter, se mettre à l'abri; **under ~** à l'abri, à couvert. || [concealment] couverture *f.* || [insurance] couverture *f*, garantie *f.* **2** *vt* [gen]: **to ~ sthg (with)** couvrir qqch (de). || [insure]: **to ~ sb against** couvrir qqn en cas de. || [include] englober, comprendre. ○ **cover up** *vt sep fig* [scandal etc] dissimuler, cacher.

coverage ['kʌvərɪdʒ] *n* [of news] reportage *m*.

cover charge *n* couvert *m.*

covering ['kʌvərɪŋ] *n* [of floor etc] revêtement *m*; [of snow, dust] couche *f.*

covering letter *Br*, **cover letter** *Am* *n* lettre *f* explicative OR d'accompagnement.

cover-up *n* étouffement *m.*

covet ['kʌvɪt] *vt* convoiter.

cow [kaʊ] **1** *n* [female type of cattle] vache *f.* || [female elephant etc] femelle *f.* **2** *vt* intimider, effrayer.

coward ['kaʊəd] *n* lâche *mf.*

cowardly ['kaʊədlɪ] *adj* lâche.

cowboy ['kaʊbɔɪ] *n* [cattlehand] cowboy *m.*

cower ['kaʊər] *vi* se recroqueviller.

cox [kɒks], **coxswain** ['kɒksən] *n* barreur *m.*

coy [kɔɪ] *adj* qui fait le/la timide.

cozy *Am* = **cosy.**

CPA *n abbr of* **certified public accountant.**

crab [kræb] *n* crabe *m.*

crab apple *n* pomme *f* sauvage.

crack [kræk] **1** *n* [in glass, pottery] fêlure *f*; [in wall, wood, ground] fissure *f*; [in skin] gerçure *f.* || [gap - in door] entrebâillement *m*; [- in curtains] interstice *m.* || [noise - of whip] claquement *m*; [- of twigs] craquement *m.* || *inf* [attempt]: **to have a ~ at sthg** tenter qqch, essayer de faire qqch. || *drugs sl* crack *m.* **2** *vt* [glass, plate] fêler; [wood, wall] fissurer. || [egg, nut] casser. || [whip] faire claquer. || [bang, hit sharply]: **to ~ one's head** se cogner la tête. || [solve - problem] résoudre; [- code] déchiffrer. **3** *vi* [glass, pottery] se fêler; [ground, wood, wall] se fissurer; [skin] se crevasser, se gercer. || [break down - person] craquer, s'effondrer; [- resistance] se briser. ○ **crack down** *vi*: **to ~ down (on)** sévir (contre). ○ **crack up** *vi* craquer.

cracker ['krækər] *n* [biscuit] cracker *m*, craquelin *m.*

crackle ['krækl] *vi* [frying food] grésiller; [fire] crépiter; [radio etc] crachoter.

cradle ['kreɪdl] **1** *n* berceau *m.* **2** *vt* [baby] bercer; [object] tenir délicatement.

craft [krɑːft] (*pl sense 2 inv*) *n* [trade, skill] métier *m.* || [boat] embarcation *f.*

craftsman ['krɑːftsmən] (*pl* -men [-mən]) *n* artisan *m*, homme *m* de métier.

craftsmanship ['krɑːftsmənʃɪp] *n* (*U*) [skill] dextérité *f*, art *m.* || [skilled work] travail *m*, exécution *f.*

craftsmen *pl* → **craftsman.**

crafty ['krɑːftɪ] *adj* rusé(e).

crag [kræg] *n* rocher *m* escarpé.

cram [kræm] **1** *vt* [stuff] fourrer. || [overfill]: **to ~ sthg with** bourrer qqch de. **2** *vi* bachoter.

cramp [kræmp] *n* crampe *f.*

cranberry ['krænbərɪ] *n* canneberge *f.*

crane [kreɪn] *n* grue *f.*

crank [kræŋk] **1** *n* TECH manivelle *f.* || *inf* [person] excentrique *mf.* **2** *vt* [wind -

handle] tourner; [- mechanism] remonter (à la manivelle).

crankshaft ['kræŋkʃɑ:ft] n vilebrequin m.

cranny ['krænɪ] n → nook.

crap [kræp] n (U) v inf merde f; it's a load of ~ tout ça, c'est des conneries.

crash [kræʃ] 1 n [accident] accident m. || [noise] fracas m. 2 vt: I ~ed the car j'ai eu un accident avec la voiture. 3 vi [cars, trains] se percuter, se rentrer dedans; [car, train] avoir un accident; [plane] s'écraser; to ~ into [wall] rentrer dans, embouter. || [FIN - business, company] faire faillite; [- stock market] s'effondrer.

crash course n cours m intensif.

crash helmet n casque m de protection.

crash-land vi atterrir en catastrophe.

crass [kræs] adj grossier(ière).

crate [kreɪt] n cageot m, caisse f.

crater ['kreɪtər] n cratère m.

cravat [krə'væt] n cravate f.

crave [kreɪv] 1 vt [affection, luxury] avoir soif de; [cigarette, chocolate] avoir un besoin fou OR maladif de. 2 vi: to ~ for [affection, luxury] avoir soif de; [cigarette, chocolate] avoir un besoin fou OR maladif de.

crawl [krɔːl] 1 vi [baby] marcher à quatre pattes; [person] se traîner. || [insect] ramper. || [vehicle, traffic] avancer au pas. || inf [place, floor]: to be ~ing with grouiller de. 2 n [swimming stroke]: the ~ le crawl.

crayfish ['kreɪfɪʃ] (pl inv OR -es) n écrevisse f.

crayon ['kreɪɒn] n crayon m de couleur.

craze [kreɪz] n engouement m.

crazy ['kreɪzɪ] adj inf [mad] fou (folle). || [enthusiastic]: to be ~ about sb/sthg être fou (folle) de qqn/qqch.

creak [kriːk] vi [door, handle] craquer; [floorboard, bed] grincer.

cream [kriːm] 1 adj [in colour] crème (inv). 2 n [gen] crème f.

cream cheese n fromage m frais.

crease [kriːs] 1 n [in fabric - deliberate] pli m; [- accidental] (faux) pli. 2 vt froisser. 3 vi [fabric] se froisser.

create [kriː'eɪt] vt créer.

creation [kriː'eɪʃn] n création f.

creative [kriː'eɪtɪv] adj créatif(ive).

creature ['kriːtʃər] n créature f.

credentials [krɪ'denʃlz] npl [papers] pièce f d'identité; fig [qualifications] capacités fpl. || [references] références fpl.

credibility [,kredə'bɪlətɪ] n crédibilité f.

credit ['kredɪt] 1 n FIN crédit m; to be in ~ [person] avoir un compte approvisionné; [account] être approvisionné; on ~ à crédit. || (U) [praise] honneur m, mérite m; to give sb ~ for sthg reconnaître que qqn a fait qqch. || UNIV unité f de valeur. 2 vt FIN: to ~ £10 to an account, to ~ an account with £10 créditer un compte de 10 livres. || inf [believe] croire. || [give the credit to]: to ~ sb with sthg accorder OR attribuer qqch à qqn. ○ **credits** npl CINEMA générique m.

credit card n carte f de crédit.

credit note n avoir m; FIN note f de crédit.

creditor ['kredɪtər] n créancier m, -ière f.

creed [kriːd] n RELIG croyance f.

creek [kriːk] n [inlet] crique f. || Am [stream] ruisseau m.

creep [kriːp] (pt & pp **crept**) 1 vi [insect] ramper; [traffic] avancer au pas. || [move stealthily] se glisser. 2 n inf [nasty person] sale type m. ○ **creeps** npl: to give sb the ~s inf donner la chair de poule à qqn.

creeper ['kriːpər] n [plant] plante f grimpante.

creepy ['kriːpɪ] adj inf qui donne la chair de poule.

cremate [krɪ'meɪt] vt incinérer.

cremation [krɪ'meɪʃn] n incinération f.

crematorium Br [,kremə'tɔːrɪəm] (pl -riums OR -ria [-rɪə]), **crematory** Am ['kremətrɪ] n crématorium m.

crepe [kreɪp] n [cloth, rubber] crêpe m. || [pancake] crêpe f.

crepe paper n (U) papier m crépon.

crept [krept] pt & pp → creep.

crescent ['kresnt] n [shape] croissant m. || [street] rue f en demi-cercle.

cress [kres] n cresson m.

crest [krest] n [of bird, hill] crête f. || [on coat of arms] timbre m.

crevice ['krevɪs] n fissure f.

crew [kruː] n [of ship, plane] équipage m. || [team] équipe f.

crew cut n coupe f en brosse.

crew-neck(ed) [-nek(t)] adj ras du cou.

crib [krɪb] 1 n [cot] lit m d'enfant. 2 vt inf [copy]: to ~ sthg off OR from sb copier qqch sur qqn.

crick [krɪk] n [in neck] torticolis m.

cricket ['krɪkɪt] n [game] cricket m. || [insect] grillon m.

crime

crime [kraim] *n* crime *m*.

criminal ['krımınl] **1** *adj* criminel(elle). **2** *n* criminel *m*, -elle *f*.

crimson ['krımzn] **1** *adj* [in colour] rouge foncé (*inv*); [with embarrassment] cramoisi(e). **2** *n* cramoisi *m*.

cringe [krındʒ] *vi* [in fear] avoir un mouvement de recul (par peur). || *inf* [with embarrassment]: **to ~ (at sthg)** ne plus savoir où se mettre (devant qqch).

cripple ['krıpl] **1** *n* *dated & offensive* infirme *mf*. **2** *vt* MED [disable] estropier. || [country] paralyser; [ship, plane] endommager.

crisis ['kraısıs] (*pl* **crises** ['kraısi:z]) *n* crise *f*.

crisp [krısp] *adj* [pastry] croustillant(e); [apple, vegetables] croquant(e). || [weather, manner] vif (vive).

crisscross ['krıskrɒs] **1** *adj* entrecroisé(e). **2** *vt* entrecroiser.

criterion [kraı'tıərıən] (*pl* **-rions** OR **-ria** [-rıə]) *n* critère *m*.

critic ['krıtık] *n* [reviewer] critique *m*. || [detractor] détracteur *m*, -trice *f*.

critical ['krıtıkl] *adj* critique; **to be ~ of** sb/sthg critiquer qqn/qqch.

critically ['krıtıklı] *adv* [ill] gravement; **~ important** d'une importance capitale. || [analytically] de façon critique.

criticism ['krıtısızm] *n* critique *f*.

criticize, -ise ['krıtısaız] *vt & vi* critiquer.

croak [krəʊk] *vi* [frog] coasser; [raven] croasser. || [person] parler d'une voix rauque.

Croat ['krəʊæt], **Croatian** [krəʊ'eıʃn] **1** *adj* croate. **2** *n* [person] Croate *mf*. || [language] croate *m*.

Croatia [krəʊ'eıʃə] *n* Croatie *f*.

Croatian = **Croat**.

crochet ['krəʊʃeı] *n* crochet *m*.

crockery ['krɒkərı] *n* vaisselle *f*.

crocodile ['krɒkədaıl] (*pl inv* OR **-s**) *n* crocodile *m*.

crocus ['krəʊkəs] (*pl* **-cuses**) *n* crocus *m*.

crook [krʊk] *n* [criminal] escroc *m*. || [of arm, elbow] pliure *f*. || [shepherd's staff] houlette *f*.

crooked ['krʊkıd] *adj* [bent] courbé(e). || [teeth, tie] de travers. || *inf* [dishonest] malhonnête.

crop [krɒp] *n* [kind of plant] culture *f*; [harvested produce] récolte *f*. || [whip] cravache *f*. ○ **crop up** *vi* survenir.

croquette [krɒ'ket] *n* croquette *f*.

cross [krɒs] **1** *adj* [person] fâché(e); [look] méchant(e). **to get ~ (with sb)** se fâcher (contre qqn). **2** *n* [gen] croix *f*. || [hybrid] croisement *m*. **3** *vt* [gen] traverser. || [arms, legs] croiser. || *Br* [cheque] barrer. **4** *vi* [intersect] se croiser. ○ **cross off, cross out** *vt sep* rayer.

crossbar ['krɒsbɑːr] *n* SPORT barre *f* transversale. || [on bicycle] barre *f*.

cross-Channel *adj* transmanche.

cross-country 1 *adj*: **~ running** cross *m*; **~ skiing** ski *m* de fond. **2** *n* cross-country *m*, cross *m*.

cross-examine *vt* JUR faire subir un contre-interrogatoire à; *fig* questionner de près.

cross-eyed [-aıd] *adj* qui louche.

crossfire ['krɒsˌfaıər] *n* (*U*) feu *m* croisé.

crossing ['krɒsıŋ] *n* [on road] passage *m* clouté; [on railway line] passage à niveau. || [sea journey] traversée *f*.

cross-legged [-legd] *adv* en tailleur.

cross-purposes *npl*: **to talk at ~** ne pas parler de la même chose; **to be at ~** ne pas être sur la même longueur d'ondes.

cross-reference *n* renvoi *m*.

crossroads ['krɒsrəʊdz] (*pl inv*) *n* croisement *m*.

cross-section *n* [drawing] coupe *f* transversale. || [sample] échantillon *m*.

crosswalk ['krɒswɔːk] *n* *Am* passage *m* clouté, passage pour piétons.

crossways ['krɒsweız] = **crosswise**.

crosswind ['krɒswınd] *n* vent *m* de travers.

crosswise ['krɒswaız] *adv* en travers.

crossword (puzzle) ['krɒswɜːd-] *n* mots croisés *mpl*.

crotch [krɒtʃ] *n* entrejambe *m*.

crotchety ['krɒtʃıtı] *adj* *Br inf* grognon(onne).

crouch [kraʊtʃ] *vi* s'accroupir.

crow [krəʊ] **1** *n* corbeau *m*; **as the ~ flies** à vol d'oiseau. **2** *vi* [cock] chanter. || *inf* [person] frimer.

crowbar ['krəʊbɑːr] *n* pied-de-biche *m*.

crowd [kraʊd] **1** *n* [mass of people] foule *f*. **2** *vi* s'amasser. **3** *vt* [streets, town] remplir. || [force into small space] entasser.

crowded ['kraʊdıd] *adj*: **~ (with)** bondé(e) (de), plein(e) (de).

crown [kraʊn] **1** *n* [of king, on tooth] couronne *f*. || [of head, hill] sommet *m*; [of hat] fond *m*. **2** *vt* couronner. ○ **Crown** *n*: **the Crown** [monarchy] la Couronne.

crown jewels *npl* joyaux *mpl* de la Couronne.

crown prince *n* prince *m* héritier.

crow's feet *npl* pattes *fpl* d'oie.

crucial ['kru:ʃl] *adj* crucial(e).

crucifix ['kru:sɪfɪks] *n* crucifix *m*.

Crucifixion [,kru:sɪ'fɪkʃn] *n*: **the ~** la Crucifixion.

crude [kru:d] *adj* [material] brut(e). || [joke, drawing] grossier(ière).

crude oil *n* (U) brut *m*.

cruel [kruəl] *adj* cruel(elle).

cruelty ['kruəltɪ] *n* (U) cruauté *f*.

cruet ['kru:ɪt] *n* service *m* à condiments.

cruise [kru:z] 1 *n* croisière *f*. 2 *vi* [sail] croiser. || [car] rouler; [plane] voler.

cruiser ['kru:zə'] *n* [warship] croiseur *m*. || [cabin cruiser] yacht *m* de croisière.

crumb [krʌm] *n* [of food] miette *f*.

crumble ['krʌmbl] 1 *n* crumble *m* (aux fruits). 2 *vt* émietter. 3 *vi* [bread, cheese] s'émietter; [building, wall] s'écrouler; [cliff] s'ébouler; [plaster] s'effriter. || *fig* [society, relationship] s'effondrer.

crumbly ['krʌmblɪ] *adj* friable.

crumpet ['krʌmpɪt] *n* CULIN petite crêpe *f* épaisse.

crumple ['krʌmpl] *vt* [crease] froisser.

crunch [krʌntʃ] 1 *n* crissement *m*; **if it comes to the ~** *inf* s'il le faut. 2 *vt* [with teeth] croquer. || [underfoot] crisser.

crunchy ['krʌntʃɪ] *adj* [food] croquant(e).

crusade [kru:'seɪd] *n* lit & fig croisade *f*.

crush [krʌʃ] 1 *n* [crowd] foule *f*. || *inf* [infatuation]: **to have a ~ on sb** avoir le béguin pour qqn. 2 *vt* [gen] écraser; [ice] piler. || *fig* [hopes] anéantir.

crust [krʌst] *n* croûte *f*.

crutch [krʌtʃ] *n* [stick] béquille *f*.

crux [krʌks] *n* nœud *m*.

cry [kraɪ] 1 *n* [of person, bird] cri *m*. 2 *vi* [weep] pleurer. || [shout] crier. ○ **cry off** *vi* se dédire. ○ **cry out** 1 *vt* crier. 2 *vi* crier; [in pain, dismay] pousser un cri.

cryptic ['krɪptɪk] *adj* mystérieux(ieuse), énigmatique.

crystal ['krɪstl] *n* cristal *m*.

crystal clear *adj* [obvious] clair(e) comme de l'eau de roche.

cub [kʌb] *n* [young animal] petit *m*. || [boy scout] louveteau *m*.

Cuba ['kju:bə] *n* Cuba.

Cuban ['kju:bən] 1 *adj* cubain(e). 2 *n* Cubain *m*, -e *f*.

cubbyhole ['kʌbɪhəʊl] *n* cagibi *m*.

cube [kju:b] 1 *n* cube *m*. 2 *vt* MATH élever au cube.

cubic ['kju:bɪk] *adj* cubique.

cubicle ['kju:bɪkl] *n* cabine *f*.

Cub Scout *n* louveteau *m*.

cuckoo ['kʊku:] *n* coucou *m*.

cuckoo clock *n* coucou *m*.

cucumber ['kju:kʌmbə'] *n* concombre *m*.

cuddle ['kʌdl] 1 *n* caresse *f*, câlin *m*. 2 *vt* caresser, câliner. 3 *vi* s'enlacer.

cuddly toy ['kʌdlɪ-] *n* jouet *m* en peluche.

cue [kju:] *n* RADIO, THEATRE & TV signal *m*; **on ~** au bon moment. || [in snooker, pool] queue *f* (de billard).

cuff [kʌf] *n* [of sleeve] poignet *m*; **off the ~** au pied levé. || Am [of trousers] revers *m inv*. || [blow] gifle *f*.

cuff link *n* bouton *m* de manchette.

cul-de-sac ['kʌldəsæk] *n* cul-de-sac *m*.

cull [kʌl] 1 *n* massacre *m*. 2 *vt* [kill] massacrer. || [gather] recueillir.

culminate ['kʌlmɪneɪt] *vi*: **to ~ in sthg** se terminer par qqch, aboutir à qqch.

culmination [,kʌlmɪ'neɪʃn] *n* apogée *m*.

culottes [kju:'lɒts] *npl* jupe-culotte *f*.

culprit ['kʌlprɪt] *n* coupable *mf*.

cult [kʌlt] 1 *n* culte *m*. 2 *comp* culte.

cultivate ['kʌltɪveɪt] *vt* cultiver.

cultivation [,kʌltɪ'veɪʃn] *n* (U) [farming] culture *f*.

cultural ['kʌltʃərəl] *adj* culturel(elle).

culture ['kʌltʃə'] *n* culture *f*.

cultured ['kʌltʃəd] *adj* [educated] cultivé(e).

cumbersome ['kʌmbəsəm] *adj* [object] encombrant(e).

cunning ['kʌnɪŋ] *adj* [person] rusé(e); [plan, method, device] astucieux(ieuse).

cup [kʌp] *n* [container, unit of measurement] tasse *f*. || [prize, competition] coupe *f*. || [of bra] bonnet *m*.

cupboard ['kʌbəd] *n* placard *m*.

curate ['kjʊərət] *n* vicaire *m*.

curator [,kjʊə'reɪtə'] *n* conservateur *m*.

curb [kɜ:b] 1 *n* [control]: **~ (on)** frein *m* (à). || Am [of road] bord *m* du trottoir. 2 *vt* mettre un frein à.

curdle ['kɜ:dl] *vi* cailler.

cure [kjʊə'] 1 *n*: **~ (for)** MED remède *m* (contre); *fig* remède (à). 2 *vt* MED guérir. || [solve - problem] éliminer. || [rid]: **to ~ sb of sthg** guérir qqn de qqch, faire perdre l'habitude de qqch à qqn. || [preserve - by smoking] fumer; [- by salting] saler.

curfew ['kɜ:fju:] *n* couvre-feu *m*.

curiosity [ˌkjʊərɪ'ɒsətɪ] *n* curiosité *f.*

curious ['kjʊərɪəs] *adj:* ~ **(about)** curieux(ieuse) (à propos de).

curl [kɜːl] **1** *n* [of hair] boucle *f.* **2** *vt* [hair] boucler. || [roll up] enrouler. **3** *vi* [hair] boucler. || [roll up] s'enrouler. ○ **curl up** *vi* [person, animal] se mettre en boule, se pelotonner.

curler ['kɜːlər] *n* bigoudi *m.*

curling tongs ['kɜːlɪŋ-] *npl* fer *m* à friser.

curly ['kɜːlɪ] *adj* [hair] bouclé(e).

currant ['kʌrənt] *n* [dried grape] raisin *m* de Corinthe, raisin sec.

currency ['kʌrənsɪ] *n* [type of money] monnaie *f.* || (*U*) [money] devise *f.* || *fml* [acceptability]: **to gain** ~ s'accréditer.

current ['kʌrənt] **1** *adj* [price, method] actuel(elle); [year, week] en cours; [boyfriend, girlfriend] du moment; ~ **issue** dernier numéro. **2** *n* [of water, air, electricity] courant *m.*

current affairs *npl* actualité *f*, questions *fpl* d'actualité.

currently ['kʌrəntlɪ] *adv* actuellement.

curriculum [kə'rɪkjələm] (*pl* -**lums** OR -**la** [-lə]) *n* programme *m* d'études.

curriculum vitae [-'viːtaɪ] (*pl* **curricula vitae**) *n* curriculum vitae *m.*

curry ['kʌrɪ] *n* curry *m.*

curse [kɜːs] **1** *n* [evil spell] malédiction *f*; *fig* fléau *m.* || [swearword] juron *m.* **2** *vt* maudire. **3** *vi* jurer.

cursor ['kɜːsər] *n* COMPUT curseur *m.*

curt [kɜːt] *adj* brusque.

curtain ['kɜːtn] *n* rideau *m.*

curts(e)y ['kɜːtsɪ] (*pt & pp* **curtsied**) **1** *n* révérence *f.* **2** *vi* faire une révérence.

curve [kɜːv] **1** *n* courbe *f.* **2** *vi* faire une courbe.

cushion ['kʊʃn] **1** *n* coussin *m.* **2** *vt* [fall, blow, effects] amortir.

custard ['kʌstəd] *n* crème *f* anglaise.

custodian [kʌ'stəʊdjən] *n* [of building] gardien *m*, -ienne *f*; [of museum] conservateur *m.*

custody ['kʌstədɪ] *n* [of child] garde *f.* || JUR: **in** ~ en garde à vue.

custom ['kʌstəm] *n* [tradition, habit] coutume *f.* || COMM clientèle *f.* ○ **customs** *n* [place] douane *f.*

customary ['kʌstəmrɪ] *adj* [behaviour] coutumier(ière); [way, time] habituel(elle).

customer ['kʌstəmər] *n* [client] client *m*, -e *f.* || *inf* [person] type *m.*

customize, -ise ['kʌstəmaɪz] *vt* [make] fabriquer OR assembler sur commande; [modify] modifier sur commande.

customs duty *n* droit *m* de douane.

customs officer *n* douanier *m*, -ière *f.*

cut [kʌt] (*pt & pp* **cut**) **1** *n* [in wood etc] entaille *f*; [in skin] coupure *f.* || [of meat] morceau *m.* || [reduction]: ~ **(in)** [taxes, salary, personnel] réduction *f* (de); [film, article] coupure *f* (dans). || [of suit, hair] coupe *f.* **2** *vt* [gen] couper; [taxes, costs, workforce] réduire; **to** ~ **one's finger** se couper le doigt. **3** *vi* [gen] couper. || [intersect] se couper. ○ **cut back 1** *vt sep* [prune] tailler. || [reduce] réduire. **2** *vi:* **to** ~ **back on** réduire, diminuer. ○ **cut down 1** *vt sep* [chop down] couper. || [reduce] réduire, diminuer. **2** *vi:* **to** ~ **down on smoking/eating/spending** fumer/manger/dépenser moins. ○ **cut in** *vi* [interrupt]: **to** ~ **in (on sb)** interrompre (qqn). || AUT & SPORT se rabattre. ○ **cut off** *vt sep* [piece, crust] couper; [finger, leg - subj: surgeon] amputer. || [power, telephone, funding] couper. || [separate]: **to be** ~ **off (from)** [person] être coupé(e) (de); [village] être isolé(e) (de). ○ **cut out** *vt sep* [photo, article] découper; [sewing pattern] couper; [dress] tailler. || [stop]: **to** ~ **out smoking/ chocolates** arrêter de fumer/de manger des chocolats; ~ **it out!** *inf* ça suffit! || [exclude] exclure. ○ **cut up** *vt sep* [chop up] couper, hacher.

cutback ['kʌtbæk] *n:* ~ **(in)** réduction *f* (de).

cute [kjuːt] *adj* [appealing] mignon(onne).

cuticle ['kjuːtɪkl] *n* envie *f.*

cutlery ['kʌtlərɪ] *n* (*U*) couverts *mpl.*

cutlet ['kʌtlɪt] *n* côtelette *f.*

cutout ['kʌtaʊt] *n* [on machine] disjoncteur *m.* || [shape] découpage *m.*

cut-price, cut-rate *Am adj* à prix réduit.

cutthroat ['kʌtθrəʊt] *adj* [ruthless] acharné(e).

cutting ['kʌtɪŋ] **1** *adj* [sarcastic - remark] cinglant(e); [- wit] acerbe. **2** *n* [of plant] bouture *f.* || [from newspaper] coupure *f.* || *Br* [for road, railway] tranchée *f.*

CV (*abbr of* **curriculum vitae**) *n* CV *m.*

cwt. *abbr of* **hundredweight.**

cyanide ['saɪənaɪd] *n* cyanure *m.*

cycle ['saɪkl] **1** *n* [of events, songs] cycle *m.* || [bicycle] bicyclette *f.* **2** *comp* [path,

dapper

track] cyclable; [race] cycliste; [shop] de cycles. **3** *vi* faire de la bicyclette.

cycling ['saɪklɪŋ] *n* cyclisme *m*.

cyclist ['saɪklɪst] *n* cycliste *mf*.

cygnet ['sɪgnɪt] *n* jeune cygne *m*.

cylinder ['sɪlɪndər] *n* cylindre *m*.

cymbals ['sɪmblz] *npl* cymbales *fpl*.

cynic ['sɪnɪk] *n* cynique *mf*.

cynical ['sɪnɪkl] *adj* cynique.

cynicism ['sɪnɪsɪzm] *n* cynisme *m*.

cypress ['saɪprəs] *n* cyprès *m*.

Cyprus ['saɪprəs] *n* Chypre *f*.

cyst [sɪst] *n* kyste *m*.

cystitis [sɪs'taɪtɪs] *n* cystite *f*.

czar [zɑːr] *n* tsar *m*.

Czech [tʃek] **1** *adj* tchèque. **2** *n* [person] Tchèque *mf*. ‖ [language] tchèque *m*.

Czechoslovak [,tʃekə'sləʊvæk] = **Czechoslovakian.**

Czechoslovakia [,tʃekəslə'vækɪə] *n* Tchécoslovaquie *f*.

Czechoslovakian [,tʃekəslə'vækɪən] **1** *adj* tchécoslovaque. **2** *n* Tchécoslovaque *mf*.

d (*pl* d's OR ds), **D** (*pl* D's OR Ds) [diː] *n* [letter] d *m inv*, D *m inv*. ○ **D** *n* MUS ré *m*. ‖ SCH [mark] D *m inv*.

DA *abbr of* **district attorney.**

dab [dæb] **1** *n* [of cream, powder, ointment] petit peu *m*; [of paint] touche *f*. **2** *vt* [skin, wound] tamponner. ‖ [apply - cream, ointment] : **to ~ sthg on** OR **onto** appliquer qqch sur.

dabble ['dæbl] *vi* : **to ~ in** toucher un peu à.

dachshund ['dækshʊnd] *n* teckel *m*.

dad [dæd], **daddy** ['dædɪ] *n inf* papa *m*.

daddy longlegs [-'lɒŋlegz] (*pl inv*) *n* faucheur *m*.

daffodil ['dæfədɪl] *n* jonquille *f*.

daft [dɑːft] *adj inf* stupide, idiot(e).

dagger ['dægər] *n* poignard *m*.

daily ['deɪlɪ] **1** *adj* [newspaper, occurrence] quotidien(ienne). ‖ [rate, output] journalier(ière). **2** *adv* [happen, write] quotidiennement; **twice ~** deux fois par jour. **3** *n* [newspaper] quotidien *m*.

dainty ['deɪntɪ] *adj* délicat(e).

dairy ['deərɪ] *n* [on farm] laiterie *f*. ‖ [shop] crémerie *f*.

dairy products *npl* produits *mpl* laitiers.

dais ['deɪɪs] *n* estrade *f*.

daisy ['deɪzɪ] *n* [weed] pâquerette *f*; [cultivated] marguerite *f*.

daisy-wheel printer *n* imprimante *f* à marguerite.

dam [dæm] **1** *n* [across river] barrage *m*. **2** *vt* construire un barrage sur.

damage ['dæmɪdʒ] **1** *n* [physical harm] dommage *m*, dégât *m*. ‖ [harmful effect] tort *m*. **2** *vt* [harm physically] endommager, abîmer. ‖ [have harmful effect on] nuire à. ○ **damages** *npl* JUR dommages et intérêts *mpl*.

damn [dæm] **1** *adj inf* fichu(e), sacré(e). **2** *adv inf* sacrément. **3** *n inf* : **not to give OR care a ~ (about sthg)** se ficher pas mal (de qqch). **4** *vt* RELIG [condemn] damner. **5** *excl inf* zut!

damned [dæmd] *inf adj* fichu(e), sacré(e); **well I'll be** OR **I'm ~!** c'est trop fort!, elle est bien bonne celle-là!

damp [dæmp] **1** *adj* humide. **2** *n* humidité *f*. **3** *vt* [make wet] humecter.

dampen ['dæmpən] *vt* [make wet] humecter. ‖ *fig* [emotion] abattre.

damson ['dæmzn] *n* prune *f* de Damas.

dance [dɑːns] **1** *n* [gen] danse *f*. ‖ [social event] bal *m*. **2** *vi* danser.

dancer ['dɑːnsər] *n* danseur *m*, -euse *f*.

dancing ['dɑːnsɪŋ] *n* (*U*) danse *f*.

dandelion ['dændɪlaɪən] *n* pissenlit *m*.

dandruff ['dændrʌf] *n* (*U*) pellicules *fpl*.

Dane [deɪn] *n* Danois *m*, -e *f*.

danger ['deɪndʒər] *n* [possibility of harm] danger *m*; **in ~** en danger; **out of ~** hors de danger. ‖ [hazard, risk] : **~ (to)** risque *m* (pour); **to be in ~ of doing sthg** risquer de faire qqch.

dangerous ['deɪndʒərəs] *adj* dangereux(euse).

dangle ['dæŋgl] **1** *vt* laisser pendre. **2** *vi* pendre.

Danish ['deɪnɪʃ] **1** *adj* danois(e). **2** *n* [language] danois *m*. ‖ *Am* = **Danish pastry. 3** *npl* : **the ~** les Danois *mpl*.

Danish pastry *n* gâteau feuilleté fourré *aux fruits*.

dapper ['dæpər] *adj* pimpant(e).

dappled ['dæpld] *adj* [light] tacheté(e).
|| [horse] pommelé(e).

dare [deə⁽ʳ⁾] **1** *vt* [be brave enough]: **to ~ to do sthg** oser faire qqch. || [challenge]: **to ~ sb to do sthg** défier qqn de faire qqch. || *phr*: **I ~ say** je suppose, sans doute. **2** *vi* oser; **how ~ you!** comment osez-vous! **3** *n* défi *m*.

daredevil ['deə,devl] *n* casse-cou *mf inv*.

daring ['deərɪŋ] **1** *adj* audacieux(ieuse). **2** *n* audace *f*.

dark [dɑːk] **1** *adj* [room, night] sombre; **it's getting ~** il commence à faire nuit. || [in colour] foncé(e). || [dark-haired] brun(e); [dark-skinned] basané(e). **2** *n* [darkness]: **the ~** l'obscurité *f*; **to be in the ~ about sthg** ignorer tout de qqch. || [night]: **before/after ~** avant/après la tombée de la nuit.

darken ['dɑːkn] **1** *vt* assombrir. **2** *vi* s'assombrir.

dark glasses *npl* lunettes *fpl* noires.

darkness ['dɑːknɪs] *n* obscurité *f*.

darkroom ['dɑːkrum] *n* chambre *f* noire.

darling ['dɑːlɪŋ] *n* [loved person, term of address] chéri *m*, -e *f*. || [idol] chouchou *m*, idole *f*.

darn [dɑːn] **1** *vt* repriser. **2** *adj inf* sacré(e), satané(e). **3** *adv inf* sacrément.

dart [dɑːt] **1** *n* [arrow] fléchette *f*. **2** *vi* se précipiter. ○ **darts** *n* [game] jeu *m* de fléchettes.

dartboard ['dɑːtbɔːd] *n* cible *f* de jeu de fléchettes.

dash [dæʃ] **1** *n* [of milk, wine] goutte *f*; [of cream] soupçon *m*; [of salt] pincée *f*; [of colour, paint] touche *f*. || [in punctuation] tiret *m*. || [rush]: **to make a ~ for** se ruer vers. **2** *vt* [throw] jeter avec violence. || [hopes] anéantir. **3** *vi* se précipiter.

dashboard ['dæʃbɔːd] *n* tableau *m* de bord.

dashing ['dæʃɪŋ] *adj* fringant(e).

data ['deɪtə] *n* (*U*) données *fpl*.

database ['deɪtəbeɪs] *n* base *f* de données.

data processing *n* traitement *m* de données.

date [deɪt] **1** *n* [in time] date *f*; **to ~** à ce jour. || [appointment] rendez-vous *m*. || [person] petit ami *m*, petite amie *f*. || [fruit] datte *f*. **2** *vt* [gen] dater. || [go out with] sortir avec. **3** *vi* [go out of fashion] dater.

dated ['deɪtɪd] *adj* qui date.

date of birth *n* date *f* de naissance.

daub [dɔːb] *vt*: **to ~ sthg with sthg** barbouiller qqch de qqch.

daughter ['dɔːtə⁽ʳ⁾] *n* fille *f*.

daughter-in-law (*pl* **daughters-in-law**) *n* belle-fille *f*.

daunting ['dɔːntɪŋ] *adj* intimidant(e).

dawdle ['dɔːdl] *vi* flâner.

dawn [dɔːn] **1** *n lit & fig* aube *f*. **2** *vi* [day] poindre. ○ **dawn (up)on** *vt fus* venir à l'esprit de.

day [deɪ] *n* jour *m*; [duration] journée *f*; **the ~ before** la veille; **the ~ after** le lendemain; **the ~ before yesterday** avant-hier; **the ~ after tomorrow** après-demain; **any ~ now** d'un jour à l'autre; **one ~, some ~, one of these ~s** un jour (ou l'autre), un de ces jours; **in my ~** de mon temps; **to make sb's ~** réchauffer le cœur de qqn. ○ **days** *adv* le jour.

daybreak ['deɪbreɪk] *n* aube *f*; **at ~** à l'aube.

daydream ['deɪdriːm] *vi* rêvasser.

daylight ['deɪlaɪt] *n* [light] lumière *f* du jour. || [dawn] aube *f*.

day off (*pl* **days off**) *n* jour *m* de congé.

daytime ['deɪtaɪm] **1** *n* jour *m*, journée *f*. **2** *comp* [television] pendant la journée; [job, flight] de jour.

day-to-day *adj* [routine, life] journalier(ière); **on a ~ basis** au jour le jour.

day trip *n* excursion *f* d'une journée.

daze [deɪz] **1** *n*: **in a ~** hébété(e), ahuri(e). **2** *vt* [subj: blow] étourdir. || *fig* [subj: shock, event] abasourdir, sidérer.

dazzle ['dæzl] *vt* éblouir.

DC *n* (*abbr of* **direct current**) courant *m* continu.

D-day ['diːdeɪ] *n* le jour J.

DEA (*abbr of* **Drug Enforcement Administration**) *n* agence américaine de lutte contre la drogue.

deacon ['diːkn] *n* diacre *m*.

deactivate [,diːˈæktɪveɪt] *vt* désamorcer.

dead [ded] **1** *adj* [not alive, not lively] mort(e). || [numb] engourdi(e). || [not operating - battery] à plat. || [complete - silence] de mort. **2** *adv* [directly, precisely]: **~ ahead** droit devant soi; **~ on time** pile à l'heure. || *inf* [completely] tout à fait. || [suddenly]: **to stop ~** s'arrêter net. **3** *npl*: **the ~** les morts *mpl*.

deaden ['dedn] *vt* [sound] assourdir; [pain] calmer.

dead end *n* impasse *f*.

dead heat *n* arrivée *f* ex-aequo.

deadline ['dedlaɪn] n dernière limite f.

deadlock ['dedlɒk] n impasse f.

dead loss n inf: **to be a ~** [person] être bon (bonne) à rien; [object] ne rien valoir.

deadly ['dedlɪ] 1 adj [poison, enemy] mortel(elle). || [accuracy] imparable. 2 adv [boring, serious] tout à fait.

deadpan ['dedpæn] 1 adj pince-sans-rire (inv). 2 adv impassiblement.

deaf [def] 1 adj sourd(e); **to be ~ to sthg** être sourd à qqch. 2 npl: **the ~** les sourds mpl.

deaf-and-dumb adj sourd-muet (sourde-muette).

deafen ['defn] vt assourdir.

deaf-mute 1 adj sourd-muet (sourde-muette). 2 n sourd-muet m, sourde-muette f.

deafness ['defnɪs] n surdité f.

deal [di:l] (pt & pp **dealt**) 1 n [quantity]: **a good** OR **great ~** beaucoup; **a good** OR **great ~ of** beaucoup de, bien de/des. || [business agreement] marché m, affaire f; **to do** OR **strike a ~ with sb** conclure un marché avec qqn. || inf [treatment]: **to get a bad ~** ne pas faire une affaire. 2 vt [strike]: **to ~ sb/sthg a blow**, **to ~ a blow to sb/sthg** porter un coup à qqn/qqch. || [cards] donner, distribuer. 3 vi [at cards] donner, distribuer. || [in drugs] faire le trafic (de drogues). ○ **deal in** vt fus COMM faire le commerce de. ○ **deal out** vt sep distribuer. ○ **deal with** vt fus [handle] s'occuper de. || [be about] traiter de. || [be faced with] avoir affaire à.

dealer ['di:lər] n [trader] négociant m; [in drugs] trafiquant m. || [cards] donneur m.

dealing ['di:lɪŋ] n commerce m. ○ **dealings** npl relations fpl, rapports mpl.

dealt [delt] pt & pp → **deal**.

dean [di:n] n doyen m.

dear [dɪər] 1 adj: **~ (to)** cher (chère) (à); **Dear Sir** [in letter] Cher Monsieur; **Dear Madam** Chère Madame. 2 n chéri m, -e f. 3 excl: **oh ~!** mon Dieu!

dearly ['dɪəlɪ] adv [love, wish] de tout son cœur.

death [deθ] n mort f; **to frighten sb to ~** faire une peur bleue à qqn; **to be sick to ~ of sthg/of doing sthg** en avoir marre de qqch/de faire qqch.

death certificate n acte m de décès.

death duty Br, **death tax** Am n droits mpl de succession.

death penalty n peine f de mort.

death rate n taux m de mortalité.

death tax Am = **death duty**.

death trap n inf véhicule m/bâtiment m dangereux.

debar [di:'bɑ:r] vt: **to ~ sb (from)** [place] exclure qqn (de); **to ~ sb from doing sthg** interdire à qqn de faire qqch.

debate [dɪ'beɪt] 1 n débat m; **open to ~** discutable. 2 vt débattre, discuter; **to ~ whether** s'interroger pour savoir si.

debating society [dɪ'beɪtɪŋ-] n club m de débats.

debauchery [dɪ'bɔ:tʃərɪ] n débauche f.

debit ['debɪt] 1 n débit m. 2 vt débiter.

debit note n note f de débit.

debris ['deɪbri:] n (U) débris mpl.

debt [det] n dette f; **to be in ~** avoir des dettes, être endetté(e); **to be in sb's ~** être redevable à qqn.

debt collector n agent m de recouvrements.

debtor ['detər] n débiteur m, -trice f.

debug [,di:'bʌg] vt COMPUT [program] mettre au point, déboguer.

debut ['deɪbju:] n débuts mpl.

decade ['dekeɪd] n décennie f.

decadence ['dekədəns] n décadence f.

decadent ['dekədənt] adj décadent(e).

decaffeinated [dɪ'kæfɪneɪtɪd] adj décaféiné(e).

decanter [dɪ'kæntər] n carafe f.

decathlon [dɪ'kæθlɒn] n décathlon m.

decay [dɪ'keɪ] 1 n [of body, plant] pourriture f, putréfaction f; [of tooth] carie f. || fig [of building] délabrement m; [of society] décadence f. 2 vi [rot] pourrir; [tooth] se carier.

deceased [dɪ'si:st] (pl inv) 1 adj décédé(e). 2 n: **the ~** le défunt, la défunte.

deceit [dɪ'si:t] n tromperie f, supercherie f.

deceitful [dɪ'si:tfʊl] adj trompeur(euse).

deceive [dɪ'si:v] vt [person] tromper, duper; [subj: memory, eyes] jouer des tours à; **to ~ o.s.** se tromper, s'abuser.

December [dɪ'sembər] n décembre m; see also **September**.

decency ['di:snsɪ] n décence f, bienséance f.

decent ['di:snt] adj [behaviour, dress] décent(e). || [wage, meal] correct(e), décent(e). || [person] gentil(ille), brave.

deception [dɪ'sepʃn] n [lie, pretence] tromperie f, duperie f. || (U) [act of lying] supercherie f.

deceptive [dɪ'septɪv] *adj* trompeur(euse).

decide [dɪ'saɪd] 1 *vt* décider; **to ~ to do sthg** décider de faire qqch. 2 *vi* se décider. ○ **decide (up)on** *vt fus* se décider pour, choisir.

decided [dɪ'saɪdɪd] *adj* [definite] certain(e), incontestable. || [resolute] décidé(e), résolu(e).

decidedly [dɪ'saɪdɪdlɪ] *adv* [clearly] manifestement, incontestablement. || [resolutely] résolument.

deciduous [dɪ'sɪdjʊəs] *adj* à feuilles caduques.

decimal ['desɪml] 1 *adj* décimal(e). 2 *n* décimale *f*.

decimal point *n* virgule *f*.

decipher [dɪ'saɪfər] *vt* déchiffrer.

decision [dɪ'sɪʒn] *n* décision *f*.

decisive [dɪ'saɪsɪv] *adj* [person] déterminé(e), résolu(e). || [factor, event] décisif(ive).

deck [dek] *n* [of ship] pont *m*. || [of bus] impériale *f*. || [of cards] jeu *m*. || *Am* [of house] véranda *f*.

deckchair ['dektʃeər] *n* chaise longue *f*, transat *m*.

declaration [,deklə'reɪʃn] *n* déclaration *f*.

Declaration of Independence *n*: the ~ la *Déclaration d'Indépendance des États-Unis d'Amérique (1776)*.

declare [dɪ'kleər] *vt* déclarer.

decline [dɪ'klaɪn] 1 *n* déclin *m*; **to be in ~** être en déclin; **on the ~** en baisse. 2 *vt* décliner; **to ~ to do sthg** refuser de faire qqch. 3 *vi* [deteriorate] décliner. || [refuse] refuser.

decode [,di:'kəʊd] *vt* décoder.

decompose [,di:kəm'pəʊz] *vi* se décomposer.

decongestant [,di:kən'dʒestənt] *n* décongestionnant *m*.

decorate ['dekəreɪt] *vt* décorer.

decoration [,dekə'reɪʃn] *n* décoration *f*.

decorator ['dekəreɪtər] *n* décorateur *m*, -trice *f*.

decoy [*n* 'di:kɔɪ, *vt* dɪ'kɔɪ] 1 *n* [for hunting] appât *m*, leurre *m*; [person] compère *m*. 2 *vt* attirer dans un piège.

decrease [*n* 'di:kri:s, *vb* dɪ'kri:s] 1 *n*: ~ **(in)** diminution *f* (de), baisse *f* (de). 2 *vt* diminuer, réduire. 3 *vi* diminuer, décroître.

decree [dɪ'kri:] 1 *n* [order, decision] décret *m*. || *Am* JUR arrêt *m*, jugement *m*. 2 *vt* décréter, ordonner.

decrepit [dɪ'krepɪt] *adj* [person] décrépit(e); [house] délabré(e).

dedicate ['dedɪkeɪt] *vt* [book etc] dédier. || [life, career] consacrer.

dedication [,dedɪ'keɪʃn] *n* [commitment] dévouement *m*. || [in book] dédicace *f*.

deduce [dɪ'dju:s] *vt* déduire, conclure.

deduct [dɪ'dʌkt] *vt* déduire, retrancher.

deduction [dɪ'dʌkʃn] *n* déduction *f*.

deed [di:d] *n* [action] action *f*, acte *m*. || JUR acte *m* notarié.

deem [di:m] *vt* juger, considérer; **to ~ it wise to do sthg** juger prudent de faire qqch.

deep [di:p] 1 *adj* profond(e). 2 *adv* profondément; **~ down** [fundamentally] au fond.

deepen ['di:pn] *vi* [river, sea] devenir profond(e). || [crisis, recession, feeling] s'aggraver.

deep freeze *n* congélateur *m*.

deep fry *vt* faire frire.

deeply ['di:plɪ] *adv* profondément.

deep-sea *adj*: ~ **diving** plongée *f* sousmarine; ~ **fishing** pêche *f* hauturière.

deer [dɪər] (*pl inv*) *n* cerf *m*.

deface [dɪ'feɪs] *vt* barbouiller.

default [dɪ'fɔ:lt] 1 *n* [failure] défaillance *f*; **by ~** par défaut. || COMPUT valeur *f* par défaut. 2 *vi* manquer à ses engagements.

defeat [dɪ'fi:t] 1 *n* défaite *f*; **to admit ~** s'avouer battu(e) ou vaincu(e). 2 *vt* [team, opponent] vaincre, battre. || [motion, proposal] rejeter.

defeatist [dɪ'fi:tɪst] *adj* défaitiste.

defect [*n* 'di:fekt, *vi* dɪ'fekt] 1 *n* défaut *m*. 2 *vi*: **to ~ to** passer à.

defective [dɪ'fektɪv] *adj* défectueux(euse).

defence *Br*, **defense** *Am* [dɪ'fens] *n* [gen] défense *f*. || [protective device, system] protection *f*. || JUR: **the ~** la défense.

defenceless *Br*, **defenseless** *Am* [dɪ'fenslɪs] *adj* sans défense.

defend [dɪ'fend] *vt* défendre.

defendant [dɪ'fendənt] *n* défendeur *m*, -eresse *f*.

defender [dɪ'fendər] *n* défenseur *m*.

defense *Am* = **defence**.

defenseless *Am* = **defenceless**.

defensive [dɪ'fensɪv] 1 *adj* défensif(ive). 2 *n*: **on the ~** sur la défensive.

defer [dɪ'fɜ:r] 1 *vt* différer. 2 *vi*: **to ~ to sb** s'en remettre à (l'opinion de) qqn.

defiance [dɪ'faɪəns] n défi m; **in ~ of** au mépris de.

defiant [dɪ'faɪənt] adj [person] intraitable, intransigeant(e); [action] de défi.

deficiency [dɪ'fɪʃnsɪ] n [lack] manque m; [of vitamins etc] carence f. ‖ [inadequacy] imperfection f.

deficient [dɪ'fɪʃnt] adj [lacking]: **to be ~ in** manquer de. ‖ [inadequate] insuffisant(e), médiocre.

deficit ['defɪsɪt] n déficit m.

defile [dɪ'faɪl] vt souiller, salir.

define [dɪ'faɪn] vt définir.

definite ['defɪnɪt] adj [plan] bien déterminé(e); [date] certain(e). ‖ [improvement, difference] net (nette), marqué(e). ‖ [answer] précis(e), catégorique.

definitely ['defɪnɪtlɪ] adv [without doubt] sans aucun doute, certainement. ‖ [for emphasis] catégoriquement.

definition [defɪ'nɪʃn] n [gen] définition f. ‖ [clarity] clarté f, précision f.

deflate [dɪ'fleɪt] 1 vt [balloon, tyre] dégonfler. 2 vi [balloon, tyre] se dégonfler.

deflation [dɪ'fleɪʃn] n ECON déflation f.

deflect [dɪ'flekt] vt [ball, bullet] dévier; [criticism] détourner.

defogger [,di:'fɒgər] n Am AUT dispositif m antibuée.

deformed [dɪ'fɔ:md] adj difforme.

defraud [dɪ'frɔ:d] vt [person] escroquer; [Inland Revenue etc] frauder.

defrost [,di:'frɒst] 1 vt [fridge] dégivrer; [frozen food] décongeler. ‖ Am [AUT - de-ice] dégivrer; [- demist] désembuer. 2 vi [fridge] dégivrer; [frozen food] se décongeler.

deft [deft] adj adroit(e).

defunct [dɪ'fʌŋkt] adj qui n'existe plus.

defy [dɪ'faɪ] vt [gen] défier; **to ~ sb to do sthg** mettre qqn au défi de faire qqch. ‖ [efforts] résister à, faire échouer.

degenerate [adj & n dɪ'dʒenərət, vb dɪ'dʒenəreɪt] 1 adj dégénéré(e). 2 vi: **to ~ (into)** dégénérer (en).

degrading [dɪ'greɪdɪŋ] adj dégradant(e), avilissant(e).

degree [dɪ'gri:] n [measurement] degré m. ‖ UNIV diplôme m universitaire; **to have/take a ~ (in)** avoir/faire une licence (de). ‖ [amount]: **to a certain ~** jusqu'à un certain point, dans une certaine mesure; **a ~ of truth** une certaine part de vérité; **by ~s** progressivement, petit à petit.

dehydrated [,di:haɪ'dreɪtɪd] adj déshydraté(e).

de-ice [di:'aɪs] vt dégivrer.

deign [deɪn] vt: **to ~ to do sthg** daigner faire qqch.

deity ['di:ɪtɪ] n dieu m, déesse f, divinité f.

dejected [dɪ'dʒektɪd] adj abattu(e), découragé(e).

delay [dɪ'leɪ] 1 n retard m, délai m. 2 vt [cause to be late] retarder. ‖ [defer] différer; **to ~ doing sthg** tarder à faire qqch. 3 vi: **to ~ (in doing sthg)** tarder (à faire qqch).

delayed [dɪ'leɪd] adj: **to be ~** [person, train] être retardé(e).

delegate [n 'delɪgət, vb 'delɪgeɪt] 1 n délégué m, -e f. 2 vt déléguer; **to ~ sb to do sthg** déléguer qqn pour faire qqch; **to ~ sthg to sb** déléguer qqch à qqn.

delegation [,delɪ'geɪʃn] n délégation f.

delete [dɪ'li:t] vt supprimer, effacer.

deli ['delɪ] n inf abbr of **delicatessen**.

deliberate [adj dɪ'lɪbərət, vb dɪ'lɪbəreɪt] 1 adj [intentional] voulu(e), délibéré(e). ‖ [slow] lent(e), sans hâte. 2 vi délibérer.

deliberately [dɪ'lɪbərətlɪ] adv [on purpose] exprès, à dessein.

delicacy ['delɪkəsɪ] n [gen] délicatesse f. ‖ [food] mets m délicat.

delicate ['delɪkət] adj délicat(e); [movement] gracieux(ieuse).

delicatessen [,delɪkə'tesn] n épicerie f fine.

delicious [dɪ'lɪʃəs] adj délicieux(ieuse).

delight [dɪ'laɪt] 1 n [great pleasure] délice m; **to take ~ in doing sthg** prendre grand plaisir à faire qqch. 2 vt enchanter, charmer. 3 vi: **to ~ in sthg/in doing sthg** prendre grand plaisir à qqch/à faire qqch.

delighted [dɪ'laɪtɪd] adj: **~ (by OR with)** enchanté(e) (de), ravi(e) (de); **to be ~ to do sthg** être enchanté OR ravi de faire qqch.

delightful [dɪ'laɪtfʊl] adj ravissant(e), charmant(e); [meal] délicieux(ieuse).

delinquent [dɪ'lɪŋkwənt] 1 adj délinquant(e). 2 n délinquant m, -e f.

delirious [dɪ'lɪrɪəs] adj lit & fig délirant(e).

deliver [dɪ'lɪvər] vt [distribute]: **to ~ sthg (to sb)** [mail, newspaper] distribuer qqch (à qqn); COMM livrer qqch (à qqn). ‖ [speech] faire; [message] remettre; [blow, kick] donner, porter. ‖ [baby] mettre au monde. ‖ Am POL [votes] obtenir.

delivery [dɪ'lɪvərɪ] n COMM livraison f. ‖

[way of speaking] élocution f. || [birth] accouchement m.

delude [dɪ'lu:d] vt tromper, induire en erreur; **to ~ o.s.** se faire des illusions.

delusion [dɪ'lu:ʒn] n illusion f.

delve [delv] vi: **to ~ into** [past] fouiller; [bag etc] fouiller dans.

demand [dɪ'mɑ:nd] **1** n [claim, firm request] revendication f, exigence f; **on ~** sur demande. || [need]: **~ (for)** demande f (de); **in ~** demandé(e), recherché(e). **2** vt [ask for - justice, money] réclamer; [- explanation, apology] exiger; **to ~ to do sthg** exiger de faire qqch. || [require] demander, exiger.

demanding [dɪ'mɑ:ndɪŋ] adj [exhausting] astreignant(e). || [not easily satisfied] exigeant(e).

demean [dɪ'mi:n] vt: **to ~ o.s.** s'abaisser.

demeaning [dɪ'mi:nɪŋ] adj avilissant(e), dégradant(e).

demented [dɪ'mentɪd] adj fou (folle), dément(e).

demise [dɪ'maɪz] n (U) décès m; fig mort f, fin f.

demo ['deməʊ] (abbr of **demonstration**) n inf manif f.

democracy [dɪ'mɒkrəsɪ] n démocratie f.

democrat ['deməkræt] n démocrate mf. ○ **Democrat** n Am démocrate mf.

democratic [demə'krætɪk] adj démocratique. ○ **Democratic** adj Am démocrate.

Democratic Party n Am: **the ~** le Parti démocrate.

demolish [dɪ'mɒlɪʃ] vt [destroy] démolir.

demonstrate ['demənstreɪt] **1** vt [prove] démontrer, prouver. || [machine, computer] faire une démonstration de. **2** vi: **to ~ (for/against)** manifester (pour/contre).

demonstration [demən'streɪʃn] n [of machine, emotions] démonstration f. || [public meeting] manifestation f.

demonstrator ['demənstreɪtər] n [in march] manifestant m, -e f. || [of machine, product] démonstrateur m, -trice f.

demoralized [dɪ'mɒrəlaɪzd] adj démoralisé(e).

demote [,di:'məʊt] vt rétrograder.

den [den] n [of animal] antre m, tanière f.

denial [dɪ'naɪəl] n [of rights, facts, truth] dénégation f; [of accusation] démenti m.

denier ['denɪə] n denier m.

denim ['denɪm] n jean m. ○ **denims** npl: **a pair of ~s** un jean.

Denmark ['denmɑ:k] n Danemark m.

denomination [dɪ,nɒmɪ'neɪʃn] n RELIG confession f. || [money] valeur f.

denounce [dɪ'naʊns] vt dénoncer.

dense [dens] adj [crowd, forest] dense; [fog] dense, épais(aisse). || inf [stupid] bouché(e).

density ['densətɪ] n densité f.

dent [dent] **1** n bosse f. **2** vt cabosser.

dental ['dentl] adj dentaire; **~ appointment** rendez-vous m chez le dentiste.

dental floss n fil m dentaire.

dental surgeon n chirurgien-dentiste m.

dentist ['dentɪst] n dentiste mf.

dentures [dentʃəz] npl dentier m.

deny [dɪ'naɪ] vt [refute] nier. || fml [refuse] nier, refuser; **to ~ sb sthg** refuser qqch à qqn.

deodorant [di:'əʊdərənt] n déodorant m.

depart [dɪ'pɑ:t] vi fml [leave]: **to ~ (from)** partir de. || [differ]: **to ~ from sthg** s'écarter de qqch.

department [dɪ'pɑ:tmənt] n [in organization] service m. || [in shop] rayon m. || SCH & UNIV département m. || [in government] département m, ministère m.

department store n grand magasin m.

departure [dɪ'pɑ:tʃər] n [leaving] départ m. || [change] nouveau départ m.

departure lounge n salle f d'embarquement.

depend [dɪ'pend] vi: **to ~ on** [be dependent on] dépendre de; [rely on] compter sur; [emotionally] se reposer sur; **it ~s** cela dépend; **~ing on** selon.

dependable [dɪ'pendəbl] adj [person] sur qui on peut compter; [car] fiable.

dependant [dɪ'pendənt] n personne f à charge.

dependent [dɪ'pendənt] adj [reliant]: **~ (on)** dépendant(e) (de); **to be ~ on sb/sthg** dépendre de qqn/qqch. || [addicted] dépendant(e), accro. || [contingent]: **to be ~ on** dépendre de.

depict [dɪ'pɪkt] vt [show in picture] représenter. || [describe]: **to ~ sb/sthg as** dépeindre qqn/qqch comme.

deplete [dɪ'pli:t] vt épuiser.

deplorable [dɪ'plɔ:rəbl] adj déplorable.

deplore [dɪ'plɔ:r] vt déplorer.

deploy [dɪ'plɔɪ] vt déployer.

depopulation [diː,pɒpjuˈleɪʃn] n dépeuplement m.

deport [dɪˈpɔːt] vt expulser.

depose [dɪˈpəʊz] vt déposer.

deposit [dɪˈpɒzɪt] **1** n [gen] dépôt m; **to make a ~** [into bank account] déposer de l'argent. ‖ [payment - as guarantee] caution f; [- as instalment] acompte m; [- on bottle] consigne f. **2** vt déposer.

depot ['depəʊ] n [gen] dépôt m. ‖ Am [station] gare.

depreciate [dɪˈpriːʃɪeɪt] vi se déprécier.

depress [dɪˈpres] vt [sadden, discourage] déprimer. ‖ [weaken - economy] affaiblir; [- prices] faire baisser.

depressed [dɪˈprest] adj [sad] déprimé(e). ‖ [run-down - area] en déclin.

depressing [dɪˈpresɪŋ] adj déprimant(e).

depression [dɪˈpreʃn] n [gen] dépression f. ‖ [sadness] tristesse f.

deprivation [,deprɪˈveɪʃn] n privation f.

deprive [dɪˈpraɪv] vt: **to ~ sb of sthg** priver qqn de qqch.

depth [depθ] n profondeur f; **in ~** [study, analyse] en profondeur; **to be out of one's ~** [in water] ne pas avoir pied; fig avoir perdu pied, être dépassé. ○ **depths** npl: **in the ~s of winter** au cœur de l'hiver; **to be in the ~s of despair** toucher le fond du désespoir.

deputation [,depjʊˈteɪʃn] n délégation f.

deputize, -ise ['depjʊtaɪz] vi: **to ~ for sb** assurer les fonctions de qqn, remplacer qqn.

deputy ['depjʊtɪ] **1** adj adjoint(e); **~ chairman** vice-président m; **~ head** SCH directeur m adjoint; **~ leader** POL vice-président m. **2** n [second-in-command] adjoint m, -e f. ‖ Am [deputy sheriff] shérif m adjoint.

derail [dɪˈreɪl] vt [train] faire dérailler.

derby [Br 'dɑːbɪ, Am 'dɜːbɪ] n SPORT derby m. ‖ Am [hat] chapeau m melon.

derelict ['derəlɪkt] adj en ruines.

deride [dɪˈraɪd] vt railler.

derivative [dɪˈrɪvətɪv] n dérivé m.

derive [dɪˈraɪv] **1** vt [draw, gain]: **to ~ sthg from sthg** tirer qqch de qqch. ‖ [originate]: **to be ~d from** venir de. **2** vi: **to ~ from** venir de.

derogatory [dɪˈrɒgətrɪ] adj désobligeant(e).

descend [dɪˈsend] **1** vt fml [go down] descendre. **2** vi fml [go down] descendre.

‖ [fall]: **to ~ (on)** [enemy] s'abattre (sur); [subj: silence, gloom] tomber (sur). ‖ [stoop]: **to ~ to sthg/to doing sthg** s'abaisser à qqch/à faire qqch.

descendant [dɪˈsendənt] n descendant m, -e f.

descended [dɪˈsendɪd] adj: **to be ~ from sb** descendre de qqn.

descent [dɪˈsent] n [downwards movement] descente f. ‖ (U) [origin] origine f.

describe [dɪˈskraɪb] vt décrire.

description [dɪˈskrɪpʃn] n [account] description f. ‖ [type] sorte f, genre m.

desecrate ['desɪkreɪt] vt profaner.

desert [n 'dezət, vb & npl dɪˈzɜːt] **1** n désert m. **2** vt [place] déserter. ‖ [person, group] déserter, abandonner. **3** vi MIL déserter. ○ **deserts** npl: **to get one's just ~s** recevoir ce que l'on mérite.

deserted [dɪˈzɜːtɪd] adj désert(e).

deserter [dɪˈzɜːtər] n déserteur m.

desert island ['dezət-] n île f déserte.

deserve [dɪˈzɜːv] vt mériter; **to ~ to do sthg** mériter de faire qqch.

design [dɪˈzaɪn] **1** n [plan, drawing] plan m, étude f. ‖ (U) [art] design m. ‖ [pattern] motif m, dessin m. ‖ [shape] ligne f; [of dress] style m. ‖ fml [intention] dessein m; **by ~** à dessein. **2** vt [draw plans for - building, car] faire les plans de, dessiner; [- dress] créer. ‖ [plan] concevoir, mettre au point; **to be ~ed for sthg/to do sthg** être conçu pour qqch/pour faire qqch.

designate [adj 'dezɪgnət, vb 'dezɪgneɪt] **1** adj désigné(e). **2** vt désigner.

designer [dɪˈzaɪnər] **1** adj de marque. **2** n INDUSTRY concepteur m, -trice f; ARCHIT dessinateur m, -trice f; [of dresses etc] styliste mf; THEATRE décorateur m, -trice f.

desirable [dɪˈzaɪərəbl] adj [enviable, attractive] désirable. ‖ fml [appropriate] désirable, souhaitable.

desire [dɪˈzaɪər] **1** n désir m; **~ for sthg/to do sthg** désir de qqch/de faire qqch. **2** vt désirer.

desist [dɪˈzɪst] vi fml: **to ~ (from doing sthg)** cesser (de faire qqch).

desk [desk] n bureau m; **reception ~** réception f; **information ~** bureau m de renseignements.

desktop publishing ['desk,tɒp-] n publication f assistée par ordinateur, PAO f.

desolate ['desələt] adj [place] abandonné(e). ‖ [person] désespéré(e), désolé(e).

despair [dɪ'speəʳ] **1** *n* (*U*) désespoir *m*. **2** *vi* désespérer; **to ~ of** désespérer de.

despatch [dɪ'spætʃ] = **dispatch**.

desperate ['desprət] *adj* désespéré(e); **to be ~ for sthg** avoir absolument besoin de qqch.

desperately ['desprətlɪ] *adv* désespérément; **~ ill** gravement malade.

desperation [ˌdespə'reɪʃn] *n* désespoir *m*; **in ~** de désespoir.

despicable [dɪ'spɪkəbl] *adj* ignoble.

despise [dɪ'spaɪz] *vt* [person] mépriser; [racism] exécrer.

despite [dɪ'spaɪt] *prep* malgré.

despondent [dɪ'spɒndənt] *adj* découragé(e).

dessert [dɪ'zɜːt] *n* dessert *m*.

dessertspoon [dɪ'zɜːtspuːn] *n* [spoon] cuillère *f* à dessert.

destination [ˌdestɪ'neɪʃn] *n* destination *f*.

destined ['destɪnd] *adj* [intended]: **~ for** destiné(e) à; **~ to do sthg** destiné à faire qqch. || [bound]: **~ for** à destination de.

destiny ['destɪnɪ] *n* destinée *f*.

destroy [dɪ'strɔɪ] *vt* [ruin] détruire.

destruction [dɪ'strʌkʃn] *n* destruction *f*.

detach [dɪ'tætʃ] *vt* [pull off] détacher; **to ~ sthg from sthg** détacher qqch de qqch. || [dissociate]: **to ~ o.s. from sthg** [from reality] se détacher de qqch; [from proceedings, discussions] s'écarter de qqch.

detached house *n* maison *f* individuelle.

detachment [dɪ'tætʃmənt] *n* détachement *m*.

detail ['diːteɪl] **1** *n* [small point] détail *m*; **in ~** en détail. **2** *vt* [list] détailler. ○ **details** *npl* [personal information] coordonnées *fpl*.

detailed ['diːteɪld] *adj* détaillé(e).

detain [dɪ'teɪn] *vt* [in police station] détenir. || [delay] retenir.

detect [dɪ'tekt] *vt* [subj: person] déceler. || [subj: machine] détecter.

detection [dɪ'tekʃn] *n* (*U*) [of crime] dépistage *m*. || [of aircraft, submarine] détection *f*.

detective [dɪ'tektɪv] *n* détective *m*.

detective novel *n* roman *m* policier.

detention [dɪ'tenʃn] *n* [of suspect, criminal] détention *f*. || SCH retenue *f*.

deter [dɪ'tɜːʳ] *vt* dissuader; **to ~ sb from doing sthg** dissuader qqn de faire qqch.

detergent [dɪ'tɜːdʒənt] *n* détergent *m*.

deteriorate [dɪ'tɪərɪəreɪt] *vi* se détériorer.

determination [dɪˌtɜːmɪ'neɪʃn] *n* détermination *f*.

determine [dɪ'tɜːmɪn] *vt* [establish, control] déterminer. || *fml* [decide]: **to ~ to do sthg** décider de faire qqch.

determined [dɪ'tɜːmɪnd] *adj* [person] déterminé(e); **~ to do sthg** déterminé à faire qqch. || [effort] obstiné(e).

deterrent [dɪ'terənt] *n* moyen *m* de dissuasion.

detest [dɪ'test] *vt* détester.

detonate ['detəneɪt] *vt* faire détoner.

detour ['diːˌtʊəʳ] *n* détour *m*.

detract [dɪ'trækt] *vi*: **to ~ from** diminuer.

detriment ['detrɪmənt] *n*: **to the ~ of** au détriment de.

detrimental [ˌdetrɪ'mentl] *adj* préjudiciable.

deuce [djuːs] *n* TENNIS égalité *f*.

devaluation [ˌdiːvæljʊ'eɪʃn] *n* dévaluation *f*.

devastated ['devəsteɪtɪd] *adj* [area, city] dévasté(e). || *fig* [person] accablé(e).

devastating ['devəsteɪtɪŋ] *adj* [hurricane, remark] dévastateur(trice). || [upsetting] accablant(e).

develop [dɪ'veləp] **1** *vt* [gen] développer. || [land, area] aménager, développer. || [illness, fault, habit] contracter. || [resources] développer, exploiter. **2** *vi* [grow, advance] se développer. || [appear - problem, trouble] se déclarer.

developing country [dɪ'veləpɪŋ-] *n* pays *m* en voie de développement.

development [dɪ'veləpmənt] *n* [gen] développement *m*. || (*U*) [of land, area] exploitation *f*. || [land being developed] zone *f* d'aménagement; [developed area] zone aménagée. || (*U*) [of illness, fault] évolution *f*.

deviate ['diːvɪeɪt] *vi*: **to ~ (from)** dévier (de), s'écarter (de).

device [dɪ'vaɪs] *n* [apparatus] appareil *m*, dispositif *m*. || [plan, method] moyen *m*.

devil ['devl] *n* [evil spirit] diable *m*. || *inf* [person] type *m*; **poor ~!** pauvre diable! || [for emphasis]: **who/where/why the ~ ...?** qui/où/pourquoi diable ...? ○ **Devil** *n* [Satan]: **the Devil** le Diable.

devious ['diːvjəs] *adj* [dishonest - person] retors(e), à l'esprit tortueux; [- scheme, means] détourné(e). || [tortuous] tortueux(euse).

dike

devise [dɪ'vaɪz] *vt* concevoir.

devolution [,diːvə'luːʃn] *n* POL décentralisation *f.*

devote [dɪ'vəʊt] *vt*: to ~ sthg to sthg consacrer qqch à qqch.

devoted [dɪ'vəʊtɪd] *adj* dévoué(e).

devotee [,devə'tiː] *n* [fan] passionné *m*, -e *f.*

devotion [dɪ'vəʊʃn] *n* [commitment]: ~ (to) dévouement *m* (à).

devour [dɪ'vaʊə] *vt lit & fig* dévorer.

devout [dɪ'vaʊt] *adj* dévot(e).

dew [djuː] *n* rosée *f.*

diabetes [,daɪə'biːtiːz] *n* diabète *m.*

diabetic [,daɪə'betɪk] 1 *adj* [person] diabétique. 2 *n* diabétique *mf.*

diabolic(al) [,daɪə'bɒlɪk(l)] *adj* [evil] diabolique. || *inf* [very bad] atroce.

diagnose ['daɪəgnəʊz] *vt* diagnostiquer.

diagnosis [,daɪəg'nəʊsɪs] (*pl* -oses [-əʊsiːz]) *n* diagnostic *m.*

diagonal [daɪ'ægənl] 1 *adj* [line] diagonal(e). 2 *n* diagonale *f.*

diagram ['daɪəgræm] *n* diagramme *m.*

dial ['daɪəl] 1 *n* cadran *m*; [of radio] cadran de fréquences. 2 *vt* [number] composer.

dialect ['daɪəlekt] *n* dialecte *m.*

dialling tone *Br* ['daɪəlɪŋ-], **dial tone** *Am n* tonalité *f.*

dialogue *Br*, **dialog** *Am* ['daɪəlɒg] *n* dialogue *m.*

dial tone *Am* = **dialling tone.**

dialysis [daɪ'ælɪsɪs] *n* dialyse *f.*

diameter [daɪ'æmɪtə] *n* diamètre *m.*

diamond ['daɪəmənd] *n* [gem] diamant *m.* || [shape] losange *m.* ○ **diamonds** *npl* carreau *m.*

diaper ['daɪpə] *n Am* couche *f.*

diaphragm ['daɪəfræm] *n* diaphragme *m.*

diarrh(o)ea [,daɪə'rɪə] *n* diarrhée *f.*

diary ['daɪərɪ] *n* [appointment book] agenda *m.* || [journal] journal *m.*

dice [daɪs] (*pl inv*) 1 *n* [for games] dé *m.* 2 *vt* couper en dés.

dictate [*vb* dɪk'teɪt, *n* 'dɪkteɪt] 1 *vt* dicter. 2 *n* ordre *m.*

dictation [dɪk'teɪʃn] *n* dictée *f.*

dictator [dɪk'teɪtə] *n* dictateur *m.*

dictatorship [dɪk'teɪtəʃɪp] *n* dictature *f.*

dictionary ['dɪkʃənrɪ] *n* dictionnaire *m.*

did [dɪd] *pt* → do.

didn't ['dɪdnt] = did not.

die [daɪ] (*pl* dice, *pt & pp* died, *cont* dying) 1 *vi* mourir; to be dying se mourir; to be dying to do sthg mourir d'envie de faire qqch. 2 *n* [dice] dé *m.* ○ **die away** *vi* [sound] s'éteindre; [wind] tomber. ○ **die down** *vi* [sound] s'affaiblir; [wind] tomber; [fire] baisser. ○ **die out** *vi* s'éteindre, disparaître.

diehard ['daɪhɑːd] *n*: to be a ~ être coriace; [reactionary] être réactionnaire.

diesel ['diːzl] *n* diesel *m.*

diesel engine *n* AUT moteur *m* diesel; RAIL locomotive *f* diesel.

diesel fuel, diesel oil *n* diesel *m.*

diet ['daɪət] 1 *n* [eating pattern] alimentation *f.* || [to lose weight] régime *m*; to be on a ~ être au régime, faire un régime. 2 *comp* [low-calorie] de régime. 3 *vi* suivre un régime.

differ ['dɪfə] *vi* [be different] être différent(e), différer; [people] être différent; to ~ from être différent de. || [disagree]: to ~ with sb (about sthg) ne pas être d'accord avec qqn (à propos de qqch).

difference ['dɪfrəns] *n* différence *f.*

different ['dɪfrənt] *adj*: ~ (from) différent(e) (de).

differentiate [,dɪfə'renʃɪeɪt] *vi*: to ~ (between) faire la différence (entre).

difficult ['dɪfɪkəlt] *adj* difficile.

difficulty ['dɪfɪkəltɪ] *n* difficulté *f*; to have ~ in doing sthg avoir de la difficulté OR du mal à faire qqch.

diffident ['dɪfɪdənt] *adj* [person] qui manque d'assurance; [manner, voice, approach] hésitant(e).

diffuse [dɪ'fjuːz] *vt* diffuser, répandre.

dig [dɪg] (*pt & pp* dug) 1 *vi* [in ground] creuser. || [subj: belt, strap]: to ~ into sb couper qqn. 2 *n fig* [unkind remark] pique *f.* || ARCHEOL fouilles *fpl.* 3 *vt* [hole] creuser. || [garden] bêcher. ○ **dig out** *vt sep inf* [find] dénicher. ○ **dig up** *vt sep* [from ground] déterrer; [potatoes] arracher. || *inf* [information] dénicher.

digest [*n* 'daɪdʒest, *vb* dɪ'dʒest] 1 *n* résumé *m*, digest *m.* 2 *vt lit & fig* digérer.

digestion [dɪ'dʒestʃn] *n* digestion *f.*

digit ['dɪdʒɪt] *n* [figure] chiffre *m.* || [finger] doigt *m*; [toe] orteil *m.*

digital ['dɪdʒɪtl] *adj* numérique, digital(e).

dignified ['dɪgnɪfaɪd] *adj* digne, plein(e) de dignité.

dignity ['dɪgnətɪ] *n* dignité *f.*

digress [daɪ'gres] *vi*: to ~ (from) s'écarter de.

dike [daɪk] *n* [wall, bank] digue *f.* || *inf pej* [lesbian] gouine *f.*

dilapidated [dɪ'læpɪdeɪtɪd] *adj* délabré(e).

dilate [daɪ'leɪt] *vi* se dilater.

dilemma [dɪ'lemə] *n* dilemme *m*.

diligent ['dɪlɪdʒənt] *adj* appliqué(e).

dilute [daɪ'luːt] 1 *adj* dilué(e). 2 *vt*: to ~ sthg (with) diluer qqch (avec).

dim [dɪm] 1 *adj* [dark - light] faible; [- room] sombre. || [indistinct - memory, outline] vague. || [weak - eyesight] faible. || *inf* [stupid] borné(e). 2 *vt & vi* baisser.

dime [daɪm] *n Am* (pièce *f* de) dix cents *mpl*.

dimension [dɪ'menʃn] *n* dimension *f*.

diminish [dɪ'mɪnɪʃ] *vt & vi* diminuer.

diminutive [dɪ'mɪnjʊtɪv] *fml* 1 *adj* minuscule. 2 *n* GRAMM diminutif *m*.

dimmers ['dɪməz] *npl Am* [dipped headlights] phares *mpl* code (*inv*); [parking lights] feux *mpl* de position.

dimmer (switch) ['dɪmər-] *n* variateur *m* de lumière.

dimple ['dɪmpl] *n* fossette *f*.

din [dɪn] *n inf* barouf *m*.

dine [daɪn] *vi fml* dîner.

diner ['daɪnər] *n* [person] dîneur *m*, -euse *f*. || *Am* [café] ≃ resto *m* routier.

dinghy ['dɪŋgɪ] *n* [for sailing] dériveur *m*; [for rowing] (petit) canot *m*.

dingy ['dɪndʒɪ] *adj* miteux(euse), crasseux(euse).

dining car ['daɪnɪŋ-] *n* wagonrestaurant *m*.

dining room ['daɪnɪŋ-] *n* [in house] salle *f* à manger. || [in hotel] restaurant *m*.

dinner ['dɪnər] *n* dîner *m*.

dinner jacket *n* smoking *m*.

dinner party *n* dîner *m*.

dinnertime ['dɪnətaɪm] *n* heure *f* du dîner.

dinosaur ['daɪnəsɔːr] *n* dinosaure *m*.

dint [dɪnt] *n fml*: by ~ of à force de.

dip [dɪp] 1 *n* [in road, ground] déclivité *f*. || [sauce] sauce *f*, dip *m*. || [swim] baignade *f* (rapide); to go for a ~ aller se baigner en vitesse, aller faire trempette. 2 *vt* [into liquid]: to ~ sthg in OR into tremper OR plonger qqch dans. 3 *vi* [sun] baisser, descendre à l'horizon; [wing] plonger. || [road, ground] descendre.

diploma [dɪ'pləʊmə] (*pl* -s) *n* diplôme *m*.

diplomacy [dɪ'pləʊməsɪ] *n* diplomatie *f*.

diplomat ['dɪpləmæt] *n* diplomate *m*.

diplomatic [ˌdɪplə'mætɪk] *adj* [service, corps] diplomatique. || [tactful] diplomate.

dipstick ['dɪpstɪk] *n* AUT jauge *f* (*de niveau d'huile*).

dire ['daɪər] *adj* [need, consequences] extrême; [warning] funeste.

direct [dɪ'rekt] 1 *adj* direct(e); [challenge] manifeste. 2 *vt* [gen] diriger. || [aim]: to ~ sthg at sb [question, remark] adresser qqch à qqn; the campaign is ~ed at teenagers cette campagne vise les adolescents. || [order]: to ~ sb to do sthg ordonner à qqn de faire qqch. 3 *adv* directement.

direct current *n* courant *m* continu.

direction [dɪ'rekʃn] *n* direction *f*. ○ **directions** *npl* [to find a place] indications *fpl*. || [for use] instructions *fpl*.

directly [dɪ'rektlɪ] *adv* [in straight line] directement. || [honestly, clearly] sans détours. || [exactly - behind, above] exactement. || [immediately] immédiatement. || [very soon] tout de suite.

director [dɪ'rektər] *n* [of company] directeur *m*, -trice *f*. || THEATRE metteur *m* en scène; CINEMA & TV réalisateur *m*, -trice *f*.

directory [dɪ'rektərɪ] *n* [annual publication] annuaire *m*. || COMPUT répertoire *m*.

dire straits *npl*: in ~ dans une situation désespérée.

dirt [dɜːt] *n* (*U*) [mud, dust] saleté *f*. || [earth] terre *f*.

dirt cheap *inf* 1 *adj* très bon marché, donné(e). 2 *adv* pour trois fois rien.

dirty ['dɜːtɪ] 1 *adj* [not clean, not fair] sale. || [smutty - language, person] grossier(ière); [- book, joke] cochon(onne). 2 *vt* salir.

disability [ˌdɪsə'bɪlətɪ] *n* infirmité *f*.

disabled [dɪs'eɪbld] 1 *adj* [person] handicapé(e), infirme. 2 *npl*: the ~ les handicapés, les infirmes.

disadvantage [ˌdɪsəd'vɑːntɪdʒ] *n* désavantage *m*, inconvénient *m*.

disagree [ˌdɪsə'griː] *vi* [have different opinions]: to ~ (with) ne pas être d'accord (avec). || [differ] ne pas concorder. || [subj: food, drink]: to ~ with sb ne pas réussir à qqn.

disagreeable [ˌdɪsə'griːəbl] *adj* désagréable.

disagreement [ˌdɪsə'griːmənt] *n* [in opinion] désaccord *m*. || [argument] différend *m*.

disappear [ˌdɪsə'pɪər] *vi* disparaître.

disappearance [ˌdɪsə'pɪərəns] *n* disparition *f*.

disappoint [ˌdɪsə'pɔɪnt] *vt* décevoir.

disappointed [ˌdɪsəˈpɔɪntɪd] *adj*: ~ (in OR with) déçu(e) (par).

disappointing [ˌdɪsəˈpɔɪntɪŋ] *adj* décevant(e).

disappointment [ˌdɪsəˈpɔɪntmənt] *n* déception *f*.

disapproval [ˌdɪsəˈpruːvl] *n* désapprobation *f*.

disapprove [ˌdɪsəˈpruːv] *vi*: **to ~ of sb/sthg** désapprouver qqn/qqch; **do you ~?** est-ce que tu as quelque chose contre?

disarm [dɪsˈɑːm] *vt & vi lit & fig* désarmer.

disarmament [dɪsˈɑːməmənt] *n* désarmement *m*.

disarray [ˌdɪsəˈreɪ] *n*: **in ~** en désordre; [government] en pleine confusion.

disaster [dɪˈzɑːstə⁽ʳ⁾] *n* [damaging event] catastrophe *f*. || (U) [misfortune] échec *m*, désastre *m*. || *inf* [failure] désastre *m*.

disastrous [dɪˈzɑːstrəs] *adj* désastreux(euse).

disband [dɪsˈbænd] **1** *vt* dissoudre. **2** *vi* se dissoudre.

disbelief [ˌdɪsbɪˈliːf] *n*: **in** OR **with ~** avec incrédulité.

disc *Br*, **disk** *Am* [dɪsk] *n* disque *m*.

discard [dɪsˈkɑːd] *vt* mettre au rebut.

discern [dɪˈsɜːn] *vt* discerner, distinguer.

discerning [dɪˈsɜːnɪŋ] *adj* judicieux(ieuse).

discharge [*n* ˈdɪstʃɑːdʒ, *vt* dɪsˈtʃɑːdʒ] **1** *n* [of patient] autorisation *f* de sortie, décharge *f*; JUR relaxe *f*; **to get one's ~** MIL être rendu à la vie civile. || [emission - of smoke] émission *f*; [- of sewage] déversement *m*; MED écoulement *m*. **2** *vt* [allow to leave - patient] signer la décharge de; [- prisoner, defendant] relaxer; [- soldier] rendre à la vie civile. || [emit - smoke] émettre; [- sewage, chemicals] déverser.

disciple [dɪˈsaɪpl] *n* disciple *m*.

discipline [ˈdɪsɪplɪn] **1** *n* discipline *f*. **2** *vt* [control] discipliner. || [punish] punir.

disc jockey *n* disc-jockey *m*.

disclaim [dɪsˈkleɪm] *vt fml* nier.

disclose [dɪsˈkləʊz] *vt* révéler, divulguer.

disclosure [dɪsˈkləʊʒə⁽ʳ⁾] *n* révélation *f*, divulgation *f*.

disco [ˈdɪskəʊ] (*pl* -**s**) (*abbr of* **discotheque**) *n* discothèque *f*.

discomfort [dɪsˈkʌmfət] *n* (U) [physical pain] douleur *f*. || (U) [anxiety, embarrassment] malaise *m*.

disconcert [ˌdɪskənˈsɜːt] *vt* déconcerter.

disconnect [ˌdɪskəˈnekt] *vt* [detach] détacher. || [from gas, electricity - appliance] débrancher; [- house] couper. || TELEC couper.

discontent [ˌdɪskənˈtent] *n*: ~ (**with**) mécontentement *m* (à propos de).

discontented [ˌdɪskənˈtentɪd] *adj* mécontent(e).

discontinue [ˌdɪskənˈtɪnjuː] *vt* cesser, interrompre.

discord [ˈdɪskɔːd] *n* (U) [disagreement] discorde *f*, désaccord *m*. || MUS dissonance *f*.

discotheque [ˈdɪskəʊtek] *n* discothèque *f*.

discount [*n* ˈdɪskaʊnt, *vb Br* dɪsˈkaʊnt, *Am* ˈdɪskaʊnt] **1** *n* remise *f*. **2** *vt* [report, claim] ne pas tenir compte de.

discourage [dɪsˈkʌrɪdʒ] *vt* décourager; **to ~ sb from doing sthg** dissuader qqn de faire qqch.

discover [dɪsˈkʌvə⁽ʳ⁾] *vt* découvrir.

discovery [dɪsˈkʌvərɪ] *n* découverte *f*.

discredit [dɪsˈkredɪt] **1** *n* discrédit *m*. **2** *vt* discréditer.

discreet [dɪsˈkriːt] *adj* discret(ète).

discrepancy [dɪsˈkrepənsɪ] *n*: ~ (**in/between**) divergence *f* (entre).

discretion [dɪsˈkreʃn] *n* (U) [tact] discrétion *f*. || [judgment] jugement *m*, discernement *m*; **at the ~ of** avec l'autorisation de.

discriminate [dɪsˈkrɪmɪneɪt] *vi* [distinguish] différencier, distinguer; **to ~ between** faire la distinction entre. || [be prejudiced]: **to ~ against sb** faire de la discrimination envers qqn.

discrimination [dɪˌskrɪmɪˈneɪʃn] *n* [prejudice] discrimination *f*. || [judgment] discernement *m*, jugement *m*.

discus [ˈdɪskəs] (*pl* -**es**) *n* disque *m*.

discuss [dɪsˈkʌs] *vt* discuter (de); **to ~ sthg with sb** discuter de qqch avec qqn.

discussion [dɪsˈkʌʃn] *n* discussion *f*; **under ~** en discussion.

disdain [dɪsˈdeɪn] *n*: ~ (**for**) dédain *m* (pour).

disease [dɪˈziːz] *n* [illness] maladie *f*.

disembark [ˌdɪsɪmˈbɑːk] *vi* débarquer.

disenchanted [ˌdɪsɪnˈtʃɑːntɪd] *adj*: ~ (**with**) désenchanté(e) (de).

disengage [ˌdɪsɪnˈɡeɪdʒ] *vt* [release]: **to ~ sthg (from)** libérer OR dégager qqch (de). || TECH déclencher; **to ~ the gears** débrayer.

disfavour Br, **disfavor** Am [dɪs'feɪvər] n [dislike, disapproval] désapprobation f.

disfigure [dɪs'fɪgər] vt défigurer.

disgrace [dɪs'greɪs] 1 n [shame] honte f; in ~ en défaveur. || [cause of shame - thing] honte f, scandale m; [- person] honte f. 2 vt faire honte à; to ~ o.s. se couvrir de honte.

disgraceful [dɪs'greɪsful] adj honteux(euse), scandaleux(euse).

disgruntled [dɪs'grʌntld] adj mécontent(e).

disguise [dɪs'gaɪz] 1 n déguisement m; in ~ déguisé(e). 2 vt [person, voice] déguiser. || [hide - fact, feelings] dissimuler.

disgust [dɪs'gʌst] 1 n: ~ (at) [behaviour, violence etc] dégoût m (pour); [decision] dégoût (devant). 2 vt dégoûter, écœurer.

disgusting [dɪs'gʌstɪŋ] adj dégoûtant(e).

dish [dɪʃ] n plat m; Am [plate] assiette f. ○ **dishes** npl vaisselle f; to do OR wash the ~es faire la vaisselle.

dish aerial Br, **dish antenna** Am n antenne f parabolique.

dishcloth ['dɪʃklɒθ] n lavette f.

disheartened [dɪs'hɑːtnd] adj découragé(e).

dishevelled Br, **disheveled** Am [dɪ'ʃevəld] adj [person] échevelé(e); [hair] en désordre.

dishonest [dɪs'ɒnɪst] adj malhonnête.

dishonor etc Am = **dishonour** etc.

dishonour Br, **dishonor** Am [dɪs'ɒnər] 1 n déshonneur m. 2 vt déshonorer.

dishonourable Br, **dishonorable** Am [dɪs'ɒnərəbl] adj [person] peu honorable; [behaviour] déshonorant(e).

dish soap n Am liquide m pour la vaisselle.

dish towel n Am torchon m.

dishwasher ['dɪʃˌwɒʃər] n [machine] lave-vaisselle m inv.

disillusioned [ˌdɪsɪ'luːʒnd] adj désillusionné(e), désenchanté(e); to be ~ with ne plus avoir d'illusions sur.

disinclined [ˌdɪsɪn'klaɪnd] adj: to be ~ to do sthg être peu disposé(e) à faire qqch.

disinfect [ˌdɪsɪn'fekt] vt désinfecter.

disinfectant [ˌdɪsɪn'fektənt] n désinfectant m.

disintegrate [dɪs'ɪntɪgreɪt] vi [object] se désintégrer, se désagréger.

disinterested [ˌdɪs'ɪntrəstɪd] adj [objective] désintéressé(e). || inf [uninterested]: ~ (in) indifférent(e) (à).

disjointed [dɪs'dʒɔɪntɪd] adj décousu(e).

disk [dɪsk] n COMPUT disque m, disquette f. || Am = disc.

disk drive Br, **diskette drive** Am n COMPUT lecteur m de disques OR de disquettes.

diskette [dɪsk'et] n COMPUT disquette f.

diskette drive n Am = **disk drive**.

dislike [dɪs'laɪk] 1 n: ~ (of) aversion f (pour); to take a ~ to sb/sthg prendre qqn/qqch en grippe. 2 vt ne pas aimer.

dislocate ['dɪsləkeɪt] vt MED se démettre. || [disrupt] désorganiser.

dislodge [dɪs'lɒdʒ] vt: to ~ sthg (from) déplacer qqch (de); [free] décoincer qqch (de).

disloyal [ˌdɪs'lɔɪəl] adj: ~ (to) déloyal(e) (envers).

dismal ['dɪzml] adj [gloomy, depressing] lugubre. || [unsuccessful - attempt] infructueux(euse); [- failure] lamentable.

dismantle [dɪs'mæntl] vt démanteler.

dismay [dɪs'meɪ] 1 n consternation f. 2 vt consterner.

dismiss [dɪs'mɪs] vt [from job]: to ~ sb (from) congédier qqn (de). || [refuse to take seriously - idea, person] écarter; [- plan, challenge] rejeter. || [allow to leave - class] laisser sortir; [- troops] faire rompre les rangs à.

dismissal [dɪs'mɪsl] n [from job] licenciement m, renvoi m.

dismount [ˌdɪs'maʊnt] vi: to ~ (from) descendre (de).

disobedience [ˌdɪsə'biːdjəns] n désobéissance f.

disobedient [ˌdɪsə'biːdjənt] adj désobéissant(e).

disobey [ˌdɪsə'beɪ] vt désobéir à.

disorder [dɪs'ɔːdər] n [disarray]: in ~ en désordre. || (U) [rioting] troubles mpl. || MED trouble m.

disorganized, **-ised** [dɪs'ɔːgənaɪzd] adj [person] désordonné(e), brouillon(onne); [system] mal conçu(e).

disorientated Br [dɪs'ɔːrɪənteɪtɪd], **disoriented** Am [dɪs'ɔːrɪəntɪd] adj désorienté(e).

disown [dɪs'əʊn] vt désavouer.

disparaging [dɪ'spærɪdʒɪŋ] adj désobligeant(e).

dispatch [dɪ'spætʃ] 1 n [message] dépêche f. 2 vt [send] envoyer, expédier.

dispel [dɪ'spel] *vt* [feeling] dissiper, chasser.

dispensary [dɪ'spensərɪ] *n* officine *f.*

dispense [dɪ'spens] *vt* [justice, medicine] administrer. ○ **dispense with** *vt fus* [do without] se passer de. || [make unnecessary] rendre superflu(e).

dispensing chemist *Br,* **dispensing pharmacist** *Am* [dɪ'spensɪŋ-] *n* pharmacien *m,* -ienne *f.*

disperse [dɪ'spɜːs] **1** *vt* [crowd] disperser. || [knowledge, news] répandre, propager. **2** *vi* se disperser.

dispirited [dɪ'spɪrɪtɪd] *adj* découragé(e), abattu(e).

displace [dɪs'pleɪs] *vt* [cause to move] déplacer. || [supplant] supplanter.

display [dɪ'spleɪ] **1** *n* [arrangement] exposition *f.* || [demonstration] manifestation *f.* || [public event] spectacle *m.* || [COMPUT - device] écran *m;* [- information displayed] affichage *m,* visualisation *f.* **2** *vt* [arrange] exposer. || [show] faire preuve de, montrer.

displease [dɪs'pliːz] *vt* déplaire à, mécontenter; **to be ~d with** être mécontent(e) de.

displeasure [dɪs'pleʒər] *n* mécontentement *m.*

disposable [dɪ'spəuzəbl] *adj* [throw away] jetable. || [income] disponible.

disposal [dɪ'spəuzl] *n* [removal] enlèvement *m.* || [availability]: **at sb's ~** à la disposition de qqn.

dispose [dɪ'spəuz] ○ **dispose of** *vt fus* [get rid of] se débarrasser de; [problem] résoudre.

disposed [dɪ'spəuzd] *adj* [willing]: **to be ~ to do sthg** être disposé(e) à faire qqch. || [friendly]: **to be well ~ to** OR **towards sb** être bien disposé(e) envers qqn.

disposition [,dɪspə'zɪʃn] *n* [temperament] caractère *m,* tempérament *m.* || [tendency]: **~ to do sthg** tendance *f* à faire qqch.

disprove [,dɪs'pruːv] *vt* réfuter.

dispute [dɪ'spjuːt] **1** *n* [quarrel] dispute *f.* || (U) [disagreement] désaccord *m.* || INDUSTRY conflit *m.* **2** *vt* contester.

disqualify [,dɪs'kwɒlɪfaɪ] *vt* [subj: authority]: **to ~ sb (from doing sthg)** interdire à qqn (de faire qqch). || SPORT disqualifier.

disquiet [dɪs'kwaɪət] *n* inquiétude *f.*

disregard [,dɪsrɪ'gɑːd] **1** *n* (U): **~ (for)** [money, danger] mépris *m* (pour); [feelings] indifférence *f* (à). **2** *vt* [fact] igno-

rer; [danger] mépriser; [warning] ne pas tenir compte de.

disrepair [,dɪsrɪ'peər] *n* délabrement *m;* **to fall into ~** tomber en ruines.

disreputable [dɪs'repjutəbl] *adj* peu respectable.

disrepute [,dɪsrɪ'pjuːt] *n:* **to bring sthg into ~** discréditer qqch; **to fall into ~** acquérir une mauvaise réputation.

disrupt [dɪs'rʌpt] *vt* perturber.

dissatisfaction ['dɪs,sætɪs'fækʃn] *n* mécontentement *m.*

dissatisfied [,dɪs'sætɪsfaɪd] *adj:* **~ (with)** mécontent(e) (de), pas satisfait(e) (de).

dissect [dɪ'sekt] *vt lit & fig* disséquer.

dissent [dɪ'sent] *n* dissentiment *m.*

dissertation [,dɪsə'teɪʃn] *n* dissertation *f.*

disservice [,dɪs'sɜːvɪs] *n:* **to do sb a ~** rendre un mauvais service à qqn.

dissimilar [,dɪ'sɪmɪlər] *adj:* **~ (to)** différent(e) (de).

dissociate [dɪ'səuʃɪeɪt] *vt* dissocier; **to ~ o.s. from** se désolidariser de.

dissolve [dɪ'zɒlv] **1** *vt* dissoudre. **2** *vi* [substance] se dissoudre.

dissuade [dɪ'sweɪd] *vt:* **to ~ sb (from)** dissuader qqn (de).

distance ['dɪstəns] *n* distance *f;* **at a ~** assez loin; **from a ~** de loin; **in the ~** au loin.

distant ['dɪstənt] *adj* [gen]: **~ (from)** éloigné(e) (de). || [reserved - person, manner] distant(e).

distaste [dɪs'teɪst] *n:* **~ (for)** dégoût *m* (pour).

distasteful [dɪs'teɪstful] *adj* répugnant(e), déplaisant(e).

distil *Br,* **distill** *Am* [dɪ'stɪl] *vt* [liquid] distiller. || *fig* [information] tirer.

distillery [dɪ'stɪlərɪ] *n* distillerie *f.*

distinct [dɪ'stɪŋkt] *adj* [different]: **~ (from)** distinct(e) (de), différent(e) (de); **as ~ from** par opposition à. || [definite - improvement] net (nette).

distinction [dɪ'stɪŋkʃn] *n* [difference] distinction *f,* différence *f;* **to draw** OR **make a ~ between** faire une distinction entre. || (U) [excellence] distinction *f.* || [exam result] mention *f* très bien.

distinctive [dɪ'stɪŋktɪv] *adj* caractéristique.

distinguish [dɪ'stɪŋgwɪʃ] *vt* [tell apart]: **to ~ sthg from sthg** distinguer qqch de qqch, faire la différence entre qqch et qqch. ‖ [perceive] distinguer. ‖ [characterize] caractériser.

distinguished [dɪ'stɪŋgwɪʃt] *adj* distingué(e).

distinguishing [dɪ'stɪŋgwɪʃɪŋ] *adj* [feature, mark] caractéristique.

distort [dɪ'stɔːt] *vt* déformer.

distract [dɪ'strækt] *vt*: **to ~ sb (from)** distraire qqn (de).

distracted [dɪ'stræktɪd] *adj* [preoccupied] soucieux(ieuse).

distraction [dɪ'strækʃn] *n* [interruption, diversion] distraction *f*.

distraught [dɪ'strɔːt] *adj* éperdu(e).

distress [dɪ'stres] **1** *n* [anxiety] détresse *f*. **2** *vt* affliger.

distressing [dɪ'stresɪŋ] *adj* [news, image] pénible.

distribute [dɪ'strɪbjuːt] *vt* [gen] distribuer. ‖ [spread out] répartir.

distribution [ˌdɪstrɪ'bjuːʃn] *n* [gen] distribution *f*. ‖ [spreading out] répartition *f*.

distributor [dɪ'strɪbjʊtər] *n* AUT & COMM distributeur *m*.

district ['dɪstrɪkt] *n* [area - of country] région *f*; [- of town] quartier *m*. ‖ ADMIN district *m*.

district attorney *n Am* ≃ procureur *m* de la République.

distrust [dɪs'trʌst] **1** *n* méfiance *f*. **2** *vt* se méfier de.

disturb [dɪ'stɜːb] *vt* [interrupt] déranger. ‖ [upset, worry] inquiéter. ‖ [sleep, surface] troubler.

disturbance [dɪ'stɜːbəns] *n* POL troubles *mpl*; [fight] tapage *m*. ‖ [interruption] dérangement *m*. ‖ [of mind, emotions] trouble *m*.

disturbed [dɪ'stɜːbd] *adj* [emotionally, mentally] perturbé(e). ‖ [worried] inquiet(iète).

disturbing [dɪ'stɜːbɪŋ] *adj* [image] bouleversant(e); [news] inquiétant(e).

disuse [ˌdɪs'juːs] *n*: **to fall into ~** [factory] être à l'abandon; [regulation] tomber en désuétude.

disused [ˌdɪs'juːzd] *adj* désaffecté(e).

ditch [dɪtʃ] *n* fossé *m*.

dither ['dɪðər] *vi* hésiter.

ditto ['dɪtəʊ] *adv* idem.

dive [daɪv] (*Br pt & pp* **-d**, *Am pt & pp* **-d** OR **dove**) **1** *vi* plonger; [bird, plane] piquer. **2** *n* [gen] plongeon *m*. ‖ [of plane] piqué *m*.

diver ['daɪvər] *n* plongeur *m*, -euse *f*.

diverge [daɪ'vɜːdʒ] *vi*: **to ~ (from)** diverger (de).

diversify [daɪ'vɜːsɪfaɪ] **1** *vt* diversifier. **2** *vi* se diversifier.

diversion [daɪ'vɜːʃn] *n* [amusement] distraction *f*; [tactical] diversion *f*. ‖ [of traffic] déviation *f*. ‖ [of river, funds] détournement *m*.

diversity [daɪ'vɜːsətɪ] *n* diversité *f*.

divert [daɪ'vɜːt] *vt* [traffic] dévier. ‖ [river, funds] détourner. ‖ [person - amuse] distraire; [- tactically] détourner.

divide [dɪ'vaɪd] **1** *vt* [separate] séparer. ‖ [share out] diviser, partager. ‖ [split up]: **to ~ sthg (into)** diviser qqch (en). ‖ MATH: **89 ~d by 3** 89 divisé par 3. ‖ [people - in disagreement] diviser. **2** *vi* se diviser.

dividend ['dɪvɪdend] *n* dividende *m*.

divine [dɪ'vaɪn] *adj* divin(e).

diving ['daɪvɪŋ] *n* (*U*) plongeon *m*; [with breathing apparatus] plongée *f* (sousmarine).

divingboard ['daɪvɪŋbɔːd] *n* plongeoir *m*.

divinity [dɪ'vɪnətɪ] *n* [godliness, god] divinité *f*. ‖ [study] théologie *f*.

division [dɪ'vɪʒn] *n* [gen] division *f*. ‖ [separation] séparation *f*.

divorce [dɪ'vɔːs] **1** *n* divorce *m*. **2** *vt* [husband, wife] divorcer.

divorced [dɪ'vɔːst] *adj* divorcé(e).

divorcee [dɪvɔː'siː] *n* divorcé *m*, -e *f*.

divulge [daɪ'vʌldʒ] *vt* divulguer.

dizzy ['dɪzɪ] *adj* [giddy]: **to feel ~** avoir la tête qui tourne.

DJ *n* (*abbr of* **disc jockey**) disc-jockey *m*.

DNA (*abbr of* **deoxyribonucleic acid**) *n* ADN *m*.

do [duː] (*pt* **did**, *pp* **done**, *pl* **dos** OR **do's**) **1** *aux vb* (*in negatives*): **don't leave it there** ne le laisse pas là. ‖ (*in questions*): **what did he want?** qu'est-ce qu'il voulait?; **~ you think she'll come?** tu crois qu'elle viendra? ‖ (*referring back to previous verb*): **she reads more than I ~** elle lit plus que moi; **I like reading — so ~ I** j'aime lire — moi aussi. ‖ (*in question tags*): **so you think you can dance, ~ you?** alors tu t'imagines que tu sais danser, c'est ça? ‖ [for emphasis]: **I did tell you but you've forgotten** je te l'avais bien dit, mais tu l'as oublié; **~ come in** entrez donc. **2** *vt* [perform an activity, a service] faire; **to ~ aerobics/gymnastics** faire de l'aérobic/de la gymnastique; **to ~ one's hair** se coiffer. ‖

doorman

[take action] faire; **to ~ something about sthg** trouver une solution pour qqch. || [referring to job]: **what do you ~?** qu'est-ce que vous faites dans la vie? || [study] faire; **I did physics at school** j'ai fait de la physique à l'école. || [travel at a particular speed] faire, rouler; **the car can ~ 110 mph** ≃ la voiture peut faire du 180 à l'heure. **3** vi [act] faire; **as I tell you** je fais comme je te dis. || [perform in a particular way]: **they're ~ing really well** leurs affaires marchent bien; **he could ~ better** il pourrait mieux faire. || [be good enough, be sufficient] suffire, aller; **that will ~** ça suffit. **4** n [party] fête f, soirée f. ○ **dos** npl: **~s and don'ts** ce qu'il faut faire et ne pas faire. ○ **do away with** vt fus supprimer. ○ **do out of** vt sep inf: **to ~ sb out of sthg** escroquer OR carotter qqch à qqn. ○ **do up** vt sep [fasten - shoelaces, shoes] attacher; [- buttons, coat] boutonner. || [decorate - room, house] refaire. || [wrap up] emballer. ○ **do with** vt fus [need] avoir besoin de. || [have connection with]: **that has nothing to ~ with it** ça n'a rien à voir, ça n'a aucun rapport. ○ **do without 1** vt fus se passer de. **2** vi s'en passer.

docile [Br 'dəʊsaɪl, Am 'dɒsəl] adj docile.

dock [dɒk] **1** n [in harbour] docks mpl. || JUR banc m des accusés. **2** vi [ship] arriver à quai.

docker ['dɒkər] n docker m.

dockworker ['dɒkwɜːkər] = docker.

dockyard ['dɒkjɑːd] n chantier m naval.

doctor ['dɒktər] **1** n MED docteur m, médecin m; **to go to the ~'s** aller chez le docteur. || UNIV docteur m. **2** vt [results, report] falsifier; [text, food] altérer.

doctorate ['dɒktərət], **doctor's degree** n doctorat m.

doctrine ['dɒktrɪn] n doctrine f.

document ['dɒkjʊmənt] n document m.

documentary [ˌdɒkjʊ'mentərɪ] **1** adj documentaire. **2** n documentaire m.

dodge [dɒdʒ] vt éviter, esquiver.

doe [dəʊ] n [deer] biche f.

does [weak form dəz, strong form dʌz] → do.

doesn't ['dʌznt] = does not.

dog [dɒg] **1** n [animal] chien m, chienne f. **2** vt [subj: person - follow] suivre de près. || [subj: problems, bad luck] poursuivre.

dog collar n [of dog] collier m de chien. || [of priest] col m d'ecclésiastique.

dog-eared [-ɪəd] adj écorné(e).

dog food n nourriture f pour chiens.

dogged ['dɒgɪd] adj opiniâtre.

doing ['duːɪŋ] n: **is this your ~?** c'est toi qui es cause de tout cela?

do-it-yourself n (U) bricolage m.

doldrums ['dɒldrəmz] npl: **to be in the ~** fig être dans le marasme.

dole [dəʊl] ○ **dole out** vt sep [food, money] distribuer au compte-gouttes.

doll [dɒl] n poupée f.

dollar ['dɒlər] n dollar m.

dollop ['dɒləp] n inf bonne cuillerée f.

dolphin ['dɒlfɪn] n dauphin m.

domain [də'meɪn] n lit & fig domaine m.

dome [dəʊm] n dôme m.

domestic [də'mestɪk] **1** adj [policy, politics, flight] intérieur(e). || [chores, animal] domestique. **2** n domestique mf.

domestic appliance n appareil m ménager.

dominant ['dɒmɪnənt] adj dominant(e); [personality, group] dominateur(trice).

dominate ['dɒmɪneɪt] vt dominer.

domineering [ˌdɒmɪ'nɪərɪŋ] adj autoritaire.

dominion [də'mɪnjən] n (U) [power] domination f. || [land] territoire m.

domino ['dɒmɪnəʊ] (pl -es) n domino m. ○ **dominoes** npl dominos mpl.

donate [də'neɪt] vt faire don de.

done [dʌn] **1** pp → do. **2** adj [job, work] achevé(e). || [cooked] cuit(e). **3** excl [to conclude deal] tope!

donkey ['dɒŋkɪ] (pl donkeys) n âne m, ânesse f.

donor ['dəʊnər] n MED donneur m, -euse f. || [to charity] donateur m, -trice f.

donor card n carte f de donneur.

don't [dəʊnt] = do not.

doodle ['duːdl] **1** n griffonnage m. **2** vi griffonner.

doom [duːm] n [fate] destin m.

doomed [duːmd] adj condamné(e); **the plan was ~ to failure** le plan était voué à l'échec.

door [dɔːr] n porte f; [of vehicle] portière f.

doorbell ['dɔːbel] n sonnette f.

doorknob ['dɔːnɒb] n bouton m de porte.

doorman ['dɔːmən] (pl -men [-mən]) n portier m.

doormat ['dɔːmæt] *n lit & fig* paillasson *m*.

doorstep ['dɔːstep] *n* pas *m* de la porte.

doorway ['dɔːweɪ] *n* embrasure *f* de la porte.

dope [dəup] **1** *n inf drugs sl* dope *f*. || [for athlete, horse] dopant *m*. || *inf* [fool] imbécile *mf*. **2** *vt* [horse] doper.

dormant ['dɔːmənt] *adj* [volcano] endormi(e). || [law] inappliqué(e).

dormitory ['dɔːmətrɪ] *n* [gen] dortoir *m*. || *Am* [in university] ≃ cité *f* universitaire.

DOS [dɒs] (*abbr of* **disk operating system**) *n* DOS *m*.

dose [dəus] *n* MED dose *f*. || *fig* [amount]: a ~ **of the measles** la rougeole.

dot [dɒt] **1** *n* point *m*; **on the** ~ à l'heure pile. **2** *vt*: **dotted with** parsemé(e) de.

dote [dəut] ○ **dote (up)on** *vt fus* adorer.

dot-matrix printer *n* imprimante *f* matricielle.

dotted line ['dɒtɪd-] *n* ligne *f* pointillée.

double ['dʌbl] **1** *adj* double. **2** *adv* [twice]: ~ **the amount** deux fois plus; **to see** ~ voir double. || [in two] en deux; **to bend** ~ se plier en deux. **3** *n* [twice as much]: **I earn** ~ **what I used to** je gagne le double de ce que je gagnais auparavant. || [drink, look-alike] double *m*. || CINEMA doublure *f*. **4** *vt* doubler. **5** *vi* [increase twofold] doubler. ○ **doubles** *npl* TENNIS double *m*.

double-barrelled *Br*, **double-barreled** *Am* [-'bærəld] *adj* [shotgun] à deux coups. || [name] à rallonge.

double bass [-'beɪs] *n* contrebasse *f*.

double bed *n* lit *m* pour deux personnes, grand lit.

double-breasted [-'brestɪd] *adj* [jacket] croisé(e).

double-check *vt & vi* revérifier.

double chin *n* double menton *m*.

double-cross *vt* trahir.

double-decker [-'dekər] *n* [bus] autobus *m* à impériale.

double-glazing [-'gleɪzɪŋ] *n* double vitrage *m*.

double room *n* chambre *f* pour deux personnes.

double vision *n* vue *f* double.

doubly ['dʌblɪ] *adv* doublement.

doubt [daut] **1** *n* doute *m*; **there is no** ~ **that** il n'y a aucun doute que; **without (a)** ~ sans aucun doute; **to be in** ~ [outcome] être incertain(e); **no** ~ sans aucun doute.

2 *vt* douter; **to** ~ **whether** OR **if** douter que.

doubtful ['dautful] *adj* [decision, future] incertain(e). || [person, value] douteux(euse).

doubtless ['dautlɪs] *adv* sans aucun doute.

dough [dəu] *n* (*U*) CULIN pâte *f*.

doughnut ['dəunʌt] *n* beignet *m*.

douse [daus] *vt* [fire, flames] éteindre. || [drench] tremper.

dove¹ [dʌv] *n* [bird] colombe *f*.

dove² [dəuv] *Am pt* → **dive**.

Dover ['dəuvər] *n* Douvres.

dovetail ['dʌvteɪl] *fig vi* coïncider.

dowdy ['daudɪ] *adj* sans chic.

down [daun] **1** *adv* [downwards] en bas, vers le bas; **to bend** ~ se pencher; **to climb** ~ descendre; **to fall** ~ tomber (par terre). || [along]: **we went** ~ **to have a look** on est allé jeter un coup d'œil; **I'm going** ~ **to the shop** je vais au magasin. || [southwards]: **we travelled** ~ **to London** on est descendu à Londres. || [lower in amount]: **prices are coming** ~ les prix baissent; ~ **to the last detail** jusqu'au moindre détail. **2** *prep* [downwards]: **they ran** ~ **the hill/stairs** ils ont descendu la colline/l'escalier en courant. || [along]: **to walk** ~ **the street** descendre la rue. **3** *adj inf* [depressed]: **to feel** ~ avoir le cafard. || [computer, telephones] en panne. **4** *n* (*U*) duvet *m*.

down-and-out **1** *adj* indigent(e). **2** *n* personne dans le besoin.

down-at-heel *adj* déguenillé(e).

downbeat ['daunbiːt] *adj inf* pessimiste.

downcast ['daunkɑːst] *adj* [sad] démoralisé(e).

downfall ['daunfɔːl] *n* (*U*) ruine *f*.

downhearted [ˌdaun'hɑːtɪd] *adj* découragé(e).

downhill [ˌdaun'hɪl] **1** *adj* [downward] en pente. **2** *n* SKIING [race] descente *f*. **3** *adv*: **to walk** ~ descendre la côte; **her career is going** ~ *fig* sa carrière est sur le déclin.

down payment *n* acompte *m*.

downpour ['daunpɔːr] *n* pluie *f* torrentielle.

downright ['daunraɪt] **1** *adj* franc (franche); [lie] effronté(e). **2** *adv* franchement.

downstairs [ˌdaun'steəz] **1** *adj* du bas; [on floor below] à l'étage en-dessous. **2**

adv en bas; [on floor below] à l'étage en-dessous; **to come** OR **go** ~ descendre.

downstream [,daʊn'striːm] *adv* en aval.

down-to-earth *adj* pragmatique, terre-à-terre (*inv*).

downtown [,daʊn'taʊn] **1** *adj*: ~ **New York** le centre de New York. **2** *adv* en ville.

downturn ['daʊntɜːn] *n*: ~ **(in)** baisse *f* (de).

down under *adv* en Australie/Nouvelle-Zélande.

downward ['daʊnwəd] **1** *adj* [towards ground] vers le bas. || [trend] à la baisse. **2** *adv Am* = **downwards**.

downwards ['daʊnwədz] *adv* [look, move] vers le bas.

dowry ['daʊərɪ] *n* dot *f*.

doz. (*abbr of* **dozen**) douz.

doze [dəʊz] **1** *n* somme *m*. **2** *vi* sommeiller. ○ **doze off** *vi* s'assoupir.

dozen ['dʌzn] **1** *num adj*: **a ~ eggs** une douzaine d'œufs. **2** *n* douzaine *f*; **~s of** *inf* des centaines de.

Dr. (*abbr of* **Drive**) av. || (*abbr of* **Doctor**) Dr.

drab [dræb] *adj* terne.

draft [drɑːft] **1** *n* [early version] premier jet *m*, ébauche *f*; [of letter] brouillon *m*. || [money order] traite *f*. || *Am* MIL: **the ~** la conscription *f*. || *Am* = **draught**. **2** *vt* [speech] ébaucher, faire le plan de; [letter] faire le brouillon de. || *Am* MIL appeler. || [staff] muter.

draftsman *Am* = **draughtsman**.

drafty *Am* = **draughty**.

drag [dræg] **1** *vt* [gen] traîner. || [lake, river] draguer. **2** *vi* [dress, coat] traîner. || *fig* [time, action] traîner en longueur. **3** *n* *inf* [bore] plaie *f*. || *inf* [on cigarette] bouffée *f*. || [cross-dressing]: **in ~** en travesti. ○ **drag on** *vi* [meeting, time] s'éterniser, traîner en longueur.

dragon ['drægən] *n* *lit* & *fig* dragon *m*.

dragonfly ['drægnflaɪ] *n* libellule *f*.

drain [dreɪn] **1** *n* [pipe] égout *m*. || [depletion - of resources, funds]: ~ **on** épuisement *m* de. **2** *vt* [vegetables] égoutter; [land] assécher, drainer. || [strength, resources] épuiser. || [drink, glass] boire. **3** *vi* [dishes] égoutter.

drainage ['dreɪnɪdʒ] *n* [pipes, ditches] (système *m* du) tout-à-l'égout *m*. || [draining - of land] drainage *m*.

draining board *Br* ['dreɪnɪŋ-], **drainboard** *Am* ['dreɪnbɔːrd] *n* égouttoir *m*.

drainpipe ['dreɪnpaɪp] *n* tuyau *m* d'écoulement.

drama ['drɑːmə] *n* [play, excitement] drame *m*. || (*U*) [art] théâtre *m*.

dramatic [drə'mætɪk] *adj* [gen] dramatique. || [sudden, noticeable] spectaculaire.

dramatist ['dræmətɪst] *n* dramaturge *mf*.

dramatize, -ise ['dræmətaɪz] *vt* [rewrite as play, film] adapter pour la télévision/la scène/l'écran. || *pej* [make exciting] dramatiser.

drank [dræŋk] *pt* → **drink**.

drape [dreɪp] *vt* draper; **to be ~d with** OR **in** être drapé(e) de. ○ **drapes** *npl Am* rideaux *mpl*.

drastic ['dræstɪk] *adj* [measures] drastique, radical(e). || [improvement, decline] spectaculaire.

draught *Br*, **draft** *Am* [drɑːft] *n* [air current] courant *m* d'air. || [from barrel]: **on ~** [beer] à la pression.

draughtsman *Br* (*pl* **-men** [-mən]), **draftsman** *Am* (*pl* **-men** [-mən]) ['drɑːftsmən] *n* dessinateur *m*, -trice *f*.

draughty *Br*, **drafty** *Am* ['drɑːftɪ] *adj* plein(e) de courants d'air.

draw [drɔː] (*pt* **drew**, *pp* **drawn**) **1** *vt* [gen] tirer. || [sketch] dessiner. || [comparison, distinction] établir, faire. || [attract] attirer, entraîner; **to ~ sb's attention to** attirer l'attention de qqn sur. **2** *vi* [sketch] dessiner. || [move]: **to ~ near** [person] s'approcher; [time] approcher; **to ~ away** reculer. || SPORT faire match nul; **to be ~ing** être à égalité. **3** *n* SPORT [result] match *m* nul. || [lottery] tirage *m*. || [attraction] attraction *f*. ○ **draw out** *vt sep* [encourage - person] faire sortir de sa coquille. || [prolong] prolonger. || [money] faire un retrait de, retirer. ○ **draw up** **1** *vt sep* [contract, plan] établir, dresser. **2** *vi* [vehicle] s'arrêter.

drawback ['drɔːbæk] *n* inconvénient *m*, désavantage *m*.

drawbridge ['drɔːbrɪdʒ] *n* pont-levis *m*.

drawer [drɔːr] *n* [in desk, chest] tiroir *m*.

drawing ['drɔːɪŋ] *n* dessin *m*.

drawing board *n* planche *f* à dessin.

drawing room *n* salon *m*.

drawl [drɔːl] *n* voix *f* traînante.

drawn [drɔːn] *pp* → **draw**.

dread [dred] **1** *n* (*U*) épouvante *f.* **2** *vt* appréhender; **to ~ doing sthg** appréhender de faire qqch.

dreadful ['dredful] *adj* affreux(euse), épouvantable.

dreadfully ['dredful] *adv* [badly] terriblement. || [extremely] extrêmement; **I'm ~ sorry** je regrette infiniment.

dream [dri:m] (*pt* & *pp* -ed OR **dreamt**) **1** *n* rêve *m.* **2** *adj* de rêve. **3** *vt*: **to ~ (that)** ... rêver que .... **4** *vi*: **to ~ (of** OR **about)** rêver (de); **I wouldn't ~ of it** cela ne me viendrait même pas à l'idée. ○ **dream up** *vt sep* inventer.

dreamt [dremt] *pp* → **dream.**

dreamy ['dri:mi] *adj* [distracted] rêveur(euse). || [dreamlike] de rêve.

dreary ['drɪərɪ] *adj* [weather] morne. || [dull, boring] ennuyeux(euse).

dredge [dredʒ] *vt* draguer. ○ **dredge up** *vt sep* [with dredger] draguer. || *fig* [from past] déterrer.

dregs [dregz] *npl lit* & *fig* lie *f.*

drench [drentʃ] *vt* tremper; **to be ~ed in** OR **with** être inondé(e) de.

dress [dres] **1** *n* [woman's garment] robe *f.* || (*U*) [clothing] costume *m*, tenue *f.* **2** *vt* [clothe] habiller; **to be ~ed** être habillé(e); **to be ~ed in** être vêtu(e) de; **to get ~ed** s'habiller. || [bandage] panser. || CULIN [salad] assaisonner. **3** *vi* s'habiller. ○ **dress up** *vi* [in costume] se déguiser. || [in best clothes] s'habiller (élégamment).

dresser ['dresər] *n* [for dishes] vaisselier *m.* || *Am* [chest of drawers] commode *f.*

dressing ['dresɪŋ] *n* [bandage] pansement *m.* || [for salad] assaisonnement *m.* || *Am* [for turkey etc] farce *f.*

dressing gown *n* robe *f* de chambre.

dressing room *n* THEATRE loge *f.* || SPORT vestiaire *m.*

dressing table *n* coiffeuse *f.*

dressmaker ['dres,meɪkər] *n* couturier *m*, -ière *f.*

dressmaking ['dres,meɪkɪŋ] *n* couture *f.*

dress rehearsal *n* générale *f.*

drew [dru:] *pt* → **draw.**

dribble ['drɪbl] **1** *n* [saliva] bave *f.* || [trickle] traînée *f.* **2** *vt* SPORT dribbler. **3** *vi* [drool] baver. || [liquid] tomber goutte à goutte, couler.

dried [draɪd] *adj* [milk, eggs] en poudre; [fruit] sec (sèche); [flowers] séché(e).

drier ['draɪər] = **dryer.**

drift [drɪft] **1** *n* [movement] mouvement *m*; [direction] direction *f*, sens *m.* || [meaning] sens *m* général. || [of snow] congère *f*; [of sand, leaves] amoncellement *m*, entassement *m.* **2** *vi* [boat] dériver. || [snow, sand, leaves] s'amasser, s'amonceler.

driftwood ['drɪftwud] *n* bois *m* flottant.

drill [drɪl] **1** *n* [tool] perceuse *f*; [dentist's] fraise *f*; [in mine etc] perforatrice *f.* || [exercise, training] exercice *m.* **2** *vt* [wood, hole] percer; [tooth] fraiser; [well] forer. || [soldiers] entraîner. **3** *vi* [excavate]: **to ~ for oil** forer à la recherche de pétrole.

drink [drɪŋk] (*pt* **drank**, *pp* **drunk**) **1** *n* [gen] boisson *f*; **to have a ~** boire un verre. || (*U*) [alcohol] alcool *m.* **2** *vt* boire. **3** *vi* boire.

drink-driving *Br*, **drunk-driving** *Am* *n* conduite *f* en état d'ivresse.

drinker ['drɪŋkər] *n* buveur *m*, -euse *f.*

drinking water ['drɪŋkɪŋ-] *n* eau *f* potable.

drip [drɪp] **1** *n* [drop] goutte *f.* || MED goutte-à-goutte *m inv.* **2** *vi* [gen] goutter, tomber goutte à goutte.

drip-dry *adj* qui ne se repasse pas.

drive [draɪv] (*pt* **drove**, *pp* **driven**) **1** *n* [in car] trajet *m* (en voiture); **to go for a ~** faire une promenade (en voiture). || [urge] désir *m*, besoin *m.* || [campaign] campagne *f.* || (*U*) [energy] dynamisme *m*, énergie *f.* || [road to house] allée *f.* || SPORT drive *m.* **2** *vt* [vehicle, passenger] conduire. || TECH entraîner, actionner. || [animals, people] pousser. || [motivate] pousser. || [force]: **to ~ sb to sthg/to do sthg** pousser qqn à qqch/à faire qqch, conduire qqn à qqch/à faire qqch; **to ~ sb mad** OR **crazy** rendre qqn fou. || [nail, stake] enfoncer. **3** *vi* [driver] conduire; [travel by car] aller en voiture.

drivel ['drɪvl] *n* (*U*) *inf* foutaises *fpl*, idioties *fpl.*

driven ['drɪvn] *pp* → **drive.**

driver ['draɪvər] *n* [of vehicle - gen] conducteur *m*, -trice *f*; [- of taxi] chauffeur *m.*

driver's license *Am* = **driving licence.**

drive shaft *n* arbre *m* de transmission.

driveway ['draɪvweɪ] *n* allée *f.*

driving ['draɪvɪŋ] *n* (*U*) conduite *f.*

driving instructor *n* moniteur *m*, -trice *f* d'auto-école.

driving lesson *n* leçon *f* de conduite.

driving licence *Br*, **driver's license** *Am* *n* permis *m* de conduire.

driving mirror *n* rétroviseur *m.*

driving school n auto-école f.

driving test n (examen m du) permis m de conduire.

drizzle ['drɪzl] 1 n bruine f. 2 v impers bruiner.

droll [drəʊl] adj drôle.

drone [drəʊn] n [of traffic, voices] ronronnement m; [of insect] bourdonnement m.

drool [druːl] vi baver; **to ~ over** fig baver (d'admiration) devant.

droop [druːp] vi [head] pencher; [shoulders, eyelids] tomber.

drop [drɒp] 1 n [of liquid] goutte f. || [sweet] pastille f. || [decrease]: ~ (in) baisse f (de). || [distance down] dénivellation f; **sheer ~** à-pic m inv. 2 vt [let fall] laisser tomber. || [voice, speed, price] baisser. || [abandon] abandonner; [player] exclure. || [let out of car] déposer. || [write]: **to ~ sb a note** OR **line** écrire un petit mot à qqn. 3 vi [fall] tomber. || [temperature, demand] baisser; [voice, wind] tomber. ○ **drops** npl MED gouttes fpl. ○ **drop in** vi inf: **to ~ in (on sb)** passer (chez qqn). ○ **drop off** 1 vt sep déposer. 2 vi [fall asleep] s'endormir. || [interest, sales] baisser. ○ **drop out** vi: **to ~ out (of** OR **from sthg)** abandonner (qqch); **to ~ out of society** vivre en marge de la société.

dropout ['drɒpaʊt] n [from society] marginal m, -e f; [from college] étudiant m, -e f qui abandonne ses études.

droppings ['drɒpɪŋz] npl [of bird] fiente f; [of animal] crottes fpl.

drought [draʊt] n sécheresse f.

drove [drəʊv] pt → drive.

drown [draʊn] 1 vt [in water] noyer. 2 vi se noyer.

drowsy ['draʊzɪ] adj assoupi(e), somnolent(e).

drug [drʌg] 1 n [medicine] médicament m. || [narcotic] drogue f. 2 vt droguer.

drug abuse n usage m de stupéfiants.

drug addict n drogué m, -e f.

druggist ['drʌgɪst] n Am pharmacien m, -ienne f.

drugstore ['drʌgstɔːr] n Am drugstore m.

drum [drʌm] 1 n MUS tambour m. || [container] bidon m. 2 vt & vi tambouriner. ○ **drums** npl batterie f. ○ **drum up** vt sep [support, business] rechercher, solliciter.

drummer ['drʌmər] n [gen] (joueur m,

-euse f de) tambour m; [in pop group] batteur m, -euse f.

drumstick ['drʌmstɪk] n [for drum] baguette f de tambour. || [of chicken] pilon m.

drunk [drʌŋk] 1 pp → drink. 2 adj [on alcohol] ivre, soûl(e); **to get ~** se soûler, s'enivrer. 3 n soûlard m, -e f.

drunkard ['drʌŋkəd] n alcoolique mf.

drunk-driving Am = drink-driving.

drunken ['drʌŋkn] adj [person] ivre; [quarrel] d'ivrognes.

drunken driving = drink-driving.

dry [draɪ] 1 adj [gen] sec (sèche); [day] sans pluie. || [river, earth] asséché(e). || [wry] pince-sans-rire (inv). 2 vt [gen] sécher; [with cloth] essuyer. 3 vi sécher. ○ **dry up** 1 vt sep [dishes] essuyer. 2 vi [river, lake] s'assécher. || [supply] se tarir.

dry cleaner n: **~'s** pressing m.

dryer ['draɪər] n [for clothes] séchoir m.

dry land n terre f ferme.

dry rot n pourriture f sèche.

dry ski slope n piste f de ski artificielle.

DTP (abbr of **desktop publishing**) n PAO f.

dual ['djuːəl] adj double.

dubbed [dʌbd] adj CINEMA doublé(e). || [nicknamed] surnommé(e).

dubious ['djuːbjəs] adj [suspect] douteux(euse). || [uncertain] hésitant(e), incertain(e); **to be ~ about doing sthg** hésiter à faire qqch.

Dublin ['dʌblɪn] n Dublin.

duchess ['dʌtʃɪs] n duchesse f.

duck [dʌk] 1 n canard m. 2 vt [head] baisser. || [responsibility] esquiver, se dérober à. 3 vi [lower head] se baisser.

duckling ['dʌklɪŋ] n caneton m.

duct [dʌkt] n [pipe] canalisation f. || ANAT canal m.

dud [dʌd] 1 adj [bomb] non éclaté(e); [cheque] sans provision, en bois. 2 n obus m non éclaté.

dude [djuːd] n Am inf [man] gars m, type m.

due [djuː] 1 adj [expected]: **she's ~ back shortly** elle devrait rentrer sous peu; **when is the train ~?** à quelle heure le train doit-il arriver? || [appropriate] dû (due), qui convient; **in ~ course** au moment voulu; [eventually] à la longue. || [owed, owing] dû (due). 2 adv: **~ west** droit vers l'ouest. 3 n dû m. ○ **dues** npl cotisation f. ○ **due to** prep [owing to] dû à; [because of] provoqué par, à cause de.

duel ['dju:əl] **1** *n* duel *m*. **2** *vi* se battre en duel.

duet [dju:'et] *n* duo *m*.

duffel bag ['dʌfl-] *n* sac *m* marin.

duffel coat ['dʌfl-] *n* duffel-coat *m*.

duffle bag ['dʌfl-] = **duffel bag**.

duffle coat ['dʌfl-] = **duffel coat**.

dug [dʌg] *pt* & *pp* → **dig**.

duke [dju:k] *n* duc *m*.

dull [dʌl] **1** *adj* [boring - book, conversation] ennuyeux(euse); [- person] terne. || [colour, light] terne. || [weather] maussade. || [sound, ache] sourd(e). **2** *vt* [pain] atténuer; [senses] émousser. || [make less bright] ternir.

duly ['dju:lɪ] *adv* [properly] dûment. || [as expected] comme prévu.

dumb [dʌm] *adj* [unable to speak] muet(ette). || *inf* [stupid] idiot(e).

dumbfound [dʌm'faʊnd] *vt* stupéfier, abasourdir; **to be ~ed** ne pas en revenir.

dummy ['dʌmɪ] **1** *adj* faux (fausse). **2** *n* [of tailor] mannequin *m*. || [copy] maquette *f*. || SPORT feinte *f*.

dump [dʌmp] **1** *n* [for rubbish] décharge *f*. || MIL dépôt *m*. **2** *vt* [put down] déposer. || [dispose of] jeter. || *inf* [boyfriend, girlfriend] laisser tomber, plaquer.

dumper (truck) *Br* ['dʌmpə-], **dump truck** *Am n* tombereau *m*, dumper *m*.

dumping ['dʌmpɪŋ] *n* décharge *f*; "no ~" «décharge interdite».

dumpling ['dʌmplɪŋ] *n* boulette *f* de pâte.

dump truck *Am* = **dumper (truck)**.

dumpy ['dʌmpɪ] *adj inf* boulot(otte).

dunce [dʌns] *n* cancre *m*.

dune [dju:n] *n* dune *f*.

dung [dʌŋ] *n* fumier *m*.

dungarees [,dʌŋgə'ri:z] *npl Br* [for work] bleu *m* de travail; [fashion garment] salopette *f*.

dungeon ['dʌndʒən] *n* cachot *m*.

Dunkirk [dʌn'kɜːk] *n* Dunkerque.

duo ['dju:əʊ] *n* duo *m*.

duplex ['dju:pleks] *n Am* [apartment] duplex *m*. || [house] maison *f* jumelée.

duplicate [*adj* & *n* 'dju:plɪkət, *vb* 'dju:plɪkeɪt] **1** *adj* [key, document] en double. **2** *n* double *m*; **in ~** en double. **3** *vt* [copy - gen] faire un double de; [- on photocopier] photocopier.

durable ['djʊərəbl] *adj* solide, résistant(e).

duration [djʊ'reɪʃn] *n* durée *f*; **for the ~ of** jusqu'à la fin de.

duress [djʊ'res] *n*: **under ~** sous la contrainte.

Durex® ['djʊəreks] *n* préservatif *m*.

during ['djʊərɪŋ] *prep* pendant, au cours de.

dusk [dʌsk] *n* crépuscule *m*.

dust [dʌst] **1** *n* (*U*) poussière *f*. **2** *vt* [clean] épousseter. || [cover with powder]: **to ~ sthg (with)** saupoudrer qqch (de).

duster ['dʌstər] *n* [cloth] chiffon *m* (à poussière).

dust jacket *n* [on book] jaquette *f*.

dustpan ['dʌstpæn] *n* pelle *f* à poussière.

dusty ['dʌstɪ] *adj* poussiéreux(euse).

Dutch [dʌtʃ] **1** *adj* néerlandais(e), hollandais(e). **2** *n* [language] néerlandais *m*, hollandais *m*. **3** *npl*: **the ~** les Néerlandais, les Hollandais. **4** *adv*: **to go ~** partager les frais.

dutiful ['dju:tɪfʊl] *adj* obéissant(e).

duty ['dju:tɪ] *n* (*U*) [responsibility] devoir *m*; **to do one's ~** faire son devoir. || [work]: **to be on/off ~** être/ne pas être de service. || [tax] droit *m*. ○ **duties** *npl* fonctions *fpl*.

duty-free *adj* hors taxe.

dwarf [dwɔːf] (*pl* **-s** OR **dwarves** [dwɔːvz]) **1** *n* nain *m*, -e *f*. **2** *vt* [tower over] écraser.

dwell [dwel] (*pt* & *pp* **dwelt** OR **-ed**) *vi literary* habiter. ○ **dwell on** *vt fus* s'étendre sur.

dwelt [dwelt] *pt* & *pp* → **dwell**.

dye [daɪ] **1** *n* teinture *f*. **2** *vt* teindre.

dying ['daɪɪŋ] **1** *cont* → **die**. **2** *adj* [person] mourant(e), moribond(e); [plant, language, industry] moribond.

dyke [daɪk] = **dike**.

dynamic [daɪ'næmɪk] *adj* dynamique.

dynamite ['daɪnəmaɪt] *n* (*U*) *lit* & *fig* dynamite *f*.

dynamo ['daɪnəməʊ] (*pl* **-s**) *n* dynamo *f*.

dynasty [*Br* 'dɪnəstɪ, *Am* 'daɪnəstɪ] *n* dynastie *f*.

dyslexia [dɪs'leksɪə] *n* dyslexie *f*.

dyslexic [dɪs'leksɪk] *adj* dyslexique.

E

e (*pl* **e's** OR **es**), **E** (*pl* **E's** OR **Es**) [i:] *n* [letter] e *m inv*, E *m inv*. ○ **E** *n* MUS mi *m*. || (*abbr of* **east**) E.

each [i:tʃ] **1** *adj* chaque. **2** *pron* chacun(e); **the books cost £10.99** ~ les livres coûtent 10,99 livres (la) pièce; ~ **other** l'un l'autre (l'une l'autre), les uns les autres (les unes les autres); **they love** ~ **other** ils s'aiment.

eager ['i:gər] *adj* passionné(e), avide; **to be** ~ **for** être avide de; **to be** ~ **to do sthg** être impatient de faire qqch.

eagle ['i:gl] *n* [bird] aigle *m*.

ear [ɪər] *n* [gen] oreille *f*. || [of corn] épi *m*.

earache ['ɪəreɪk] *n*: **to have** ~ avoir mal à l'oreille.

eardrum ['ɪədrʌm] *n* tympan *m*.

earl [ɜːl] *n* comte *m*.

earlier ['ɜːlɪər] **1** *adj* [previous] précédent(e); [more early] plus tôt. **2** *adv* plus tôt; ~ **on** plus tôt.

earliest ['ɜːlɪəst] **1** *adj* [first] premier(ière); [most early] le plus tôt. **2** *n*: **at the** ~ au plus tôt.

earlobe ['ɪələʊb] *n* lobe *m* de l'oreille.

early ['ɜːlɪ] **1** *adj* [before expected time] en avance. || [in day] de bonne heure; **the** ~ **train** le premier train; **to make an** ~ **start** partir de bonne heure. || [at beginning]: **in the** ~ **sixties** au début des années soixante. **2** *adv* [before expected time] en avance; **I was ten minutes** ~ j'étais en avance de dix minutes. || [in day] tôt, de bonne heure; **as** ~ **as** dès; ~ **on** tôt. || [at beginning]: ~ **in her life** dans sa jeunesse.

early retirement *n* retraite *f* anticipée.

earmark ['ɪəmɑːk] *vt*: **to be** ~**ed for** être réservé(e) à.

earn [ɜːn] *vt* [as salary] gagner. || COMM rapporter. || *fig* [respect, praise] gagner, mériter.

earnest ['ɜːnɪst] *adj* sérieux(ieuse). ○ **in earnest 1** *adj* sérieux(ieuse). **2** *adv* pour de bon, sérieusement.

earnings ['ɜːnɪŋz] *npl* [of person] salaire *m*, gains *mpl*; [of company] bénéfices *mpl*.

earphones ['ɪəfəʊnz] *npl* casque *m*.

earplugs ['ɪəplʌgz] *npl* boules *fpl* Quiès®.

earring ['ɪərɪŋ] *n* boucle *f* d'oreille.

earshot ['ɪəʃɒt] *n*: **within** ~ à portée de voix; **out of** ~ hors de portée de voix.

earth [ɜːθ] *n* [gen & ELEC] terre *f*; **how/what/where/why on** ~ ...? mais comment/que/où/pourquoi donc ...?

earthquake ['ɜːθkweɪk] *n* tremblement *m* de terre.

earthworm ['ɜːθwɜːm] *n* ver *m* de terre.

earthy ['ɜːθɪ] *adj fig* [humour, person] truculent(e). || [taste, smell] de terre, terreux(euse).

earwig ['ɪəwɪg] *n* perce-oreille *m*.

ease [i:z] **1** *n* (*U*) [lack of difficulty] facilité *f*; **to do sthg with** ~ faire qqch sans difficulté OR facilement. || [comfort]: **at** ~ à l'aise; **ill at** ~ mal à l'aise. **2** *vt* [pain] calmer; [restrictions] modérer. || [move carefully]: **to** ~ **sthg in/out** faire entrer/sortir qqch délicatement. ○ **ease off** *vi* [pain] s'atténuer; [rain] diminuer. ○ **ease up** *vi* [rain] diminuer. || [relax] se détendre.

easel ['i:zl] *n* chevalet *m*.

easily ['i:zɪlɪ] *adv* [without difficulty] facilement. || [without doubt] de loin. || [in a relaxed manner] tranquillement.

east [i:st] **1** *n* [direction] est *m*. || [region]: **the** ~ l'est *m*. **2** *adj* est (*inv*); [wind] d'est. **3** *adv* à l'est, vers l'est; ~ **of** à l'est de. ○ **East** *n*: **the East** [gen & POL] l'Est *m*; [Asia] l'Orient *m*.

Easter ['i:stər] *n* Pâques *m*.

Easter egg *n* œuf *m* de Pâques.

easterly ['i:stəlɪ] *adj* à l'est, de l'est; [wind] de l'est.

eastern ['i:stən] *adj* de l'est. ○ **Eastern** *adj* [gen & POL] de l'Est; [from Asia] oriental(e).

East German 1 *adj* d'Allemagne de l'Est. **2** *n* Allemand *m*, -e *f* de l'Est.

East Germany *n*: (**former**) ~ (l'ex-) Allemagne *f* de l'Est.

eastward ['i:stwəd] **1** *adj* à l'est, vers l'est. **2** *adv* = **eastwards**.

eastwards ['i:stwədz] *adv* vers l'est.

easy ['iːzɪ] **1** *adj* [not difficult, comfortable] facile. || [relaxed - manner] naturel(elle). **2** *adv*: **to take it** OR **things ~** *inf* ne pas se fatiguer.

easy chair *n* fauteuil *m*.

easygoing ['iːzɪ'gəʊɪŋ] *adj* [person] facile à vivre; [manner] complaisant(e).

eat [iːt] (*pt* **ate**, *pp* **eaten**) *vt & vi* manger. ○ **eat away**, **eat into** *vt fus* [subj: acid, rust] ronger. || [deplete] grignoter.

eaten ['iːtn] *pp* → **eat**.

eaves ['iːvz] *npl* avant-toit *m*.

eavesdrop ['iːvzdrɒp] *vi*: **to ~ (on sb)** écouter (qqn) de façon indiscrète.

ebb [eb] **1** *n* reflux *m*. **2** *vi* [tide, sea] se retirer, refluer.

ebony ['ebənɪ] **1** *adj* [colour] noir(e) d'ébène. **2** *n* ébène *f*.

EC (*abbr of* **European Community**) *n* CE *f*.

eccentric [ɪk'sentrɪk] **1** *adj* [odd] excentrique, bizarre. **2** *n* [person] excentrique *mf*.

echo ['ekəʊ] (*pl* -es) **1** *n* lit & fig écho *m*. **2** *vt* [words] répéter; [opinion] faire écho à. **3** *vi* retentir, résonner.

eclipse [ɪ'klɪps] **1** *n* lit & fig éclipse *f*. **2** *vt fig* éclipser.

ecological [,iːkə'lɒdʒɪkl] *adj* écologique.

ecology [ɪ'kɒlədʒɪ] *n* écologie *f*.

economic [,iːkə'nɒmɪk] *adj* ECON économique. || [profitable] rentable.

economical [,iːkə'nɒmɪkl] *adj* [cheap] économique. || [person] économe.

economics [,iːkə'nɒmɪks] **1** *n* (*U*) économie *f* politique, économique *f*. **2** *npl* [of plan, business] aspect *m* financier.

economize, **-ise** [ɪ'kɒnəmaɪz] *vi* économiser.

economy [ɪ'kɒnəmɪ] *n* économie *f*.

economy class *n* classe *f* touriste.

ecstasy ['ekstəsɪ] *n* extase *f*, ravissement *m*.

ecstatic [ek'stætɪk] *adj* [person] en extase; [feeling] extatique.

ECU, **Ecu** ['ekjuː] (*abbr of* **European Currency Unit**) *n* ECU *m*, écu *m*.

eczema ['eksɪmə] *n* eczéma *m*.

Eden ['iːdn] *n*: (**the Garden of**) **~** le jardin *m* d'Éden, l'Éden *m*.

edge [edʒ] **1** *n* [gen] bord *m*; [of coin, book] tranche *f*; [of knife] tranchant *m*; **to be on the ~ of** *fig* être à deux doigts de. || [advantage]: **to have an ~ over** OR **the ~ on** avoir un léger avantage sur. **2** *vi*: **to ~**

forward avancer tout doucement. ○ **on edge** *adj* contracté(e), tendu(e).

edgeways ['edʒweɪz], **edgewise** ['edʒwaɪz] *adv* latéralement, de côté.

edgy ['edʒɪ] *adj* contracté(e), tendu(e).

edible ['edɪbl] *adj* [safe to eat] comestible.

edict ['iːdɪkt] *n* décret *m*.

Edinburgh ['edɪnbrə] *n* Édimbourg.

edit ['edɪt] *vt* [correct - text] corriger. || CINEMA monter; RADIO & TV réaliser. || [magazine] diriger; [newspaper] être le rédacteur en chef de.

edition [ɪ'dɪʃn] *n* édition *f*.

editor ['edɪtər] *n* [of magazine] directeur *m*, -trice *f*; [of newspaper] rédacteur *m*, -trice *f* en chef. || [of text] correcteur *m*, -trice *f*. || CINEMA monteur *m*, -euse *f*; RADIO & TV réalisateur *m*, -trice *f*.

editorial [,edɪ'tɔːrɪəl] **1** *adj* [department, staff] de la rédaction; [style, policy] éditorial(e). **2** *n* éditorial *m*.

educate ['edʒʊkeɪt] *vt* SCH & UNIV instruire. || [inform] informer, éduquer.

education [,edʒʊ'keɪʃn] *n* [gen] éducation *f*. || [teaching] enseignement *m*, instruction *f*.

educational [,edʒʊ'keɪʃənl] *adj* [establishment, policy] pédagogique. || [toy, experience] éducatif(ive).

EEC (*abbr of* **European Economic Community**) *n* ancien nom de la Communauté Européenne.

eel [iːl] *n* anguille *f*.

eerie ['ɪərɪ] *adj* inquiétant(e), sinistre.

efface [ɪ'feɪs] *vt* effacer.

effect [ɪ'fekt] **1** *n* [gen] effet *m*; **to have an ~ on** avoir OR produire un effet sur; **to take ~** [law] prendre effet, entrer en vigueur; **to put sthg into ~** [policy, law] mettre qqch en application. **2** *vt* [repairs, change] effectuer; [reconciliation] amener. ○ **effects** *npl*: (**special**) **~s** effets *mpl* spéciaux.

effective [ɪ'fektɪv] *adj* [successful] efficace. || [actual, real] effectif(ive).

effectively [ɪ'fektɪvlɪ] *adv* [successfully] efficacement. || [in fact] effectivement.

effectiveness [ɪ'fektɪvnɪs] *n* efficacité *f*.

efficiency [ɪ'fɪʃənsɪ] *n* [of person, method] efficacité *f*; [of factory, system] rendement *m*.

efficient [ɪ'fɪʃənt] *adj* efficace.

effluent ['efluənt] *n* effluent *m*.

effort ['efət] *n* effort *m*; **to be worth the ~** valoir la peine; **with ~** avec peine; **to make an/no ~ to do sthg** faire un effort/ne faire aucun effort pour faire qqch.

effortless ['efətlɪs] *adj* [easy] facile; [natural] aisé(e).

e.g. (*abbr of* **exempli gratia**) *adv* par exemple.

egg [eg] *n* œuf *m*. ○ **egg on** *vt sep* pousser, inciter.

eggcup ['egkʌp] *n* coquetier *m*.

eggplant ['egplɑ:nt] *n Am* aubergine *f*.

eggshell ['egʃel] *n* coquille *f* d'œuf.

egg white *n* blanc *m* d'œuf.

egg yolk [-jəʊk] *n* jaune *m* d'œuf.

ego ['i:gəʊ] (*pl* -s) *n* moi *m*.

egotistic(al) [,i:gə'tɪstɪk(l)] *adj* égotiste.

Egypt ['i:dʒɪpt] *n* Égypte *f*.

Egyptian [ɪ'dʒɪpʃn] **1** *adj* égyptien(ienne). **2** *n* Égyptien *m*, -ienne *f*.

eiderdown ['aɪdədaʊn] *n* [bed cover] édredon *m*.

eight [eɪt] *num* huit; *see also* **six**.

eighteen [,eɪ'ti:n] *num* dix-huit; *see also* **six**.

eighth [eɪtθ] *num* huitième; *see also* **sixth**.

eighty ['eɪtɪ] *num* quatre-vingts; *see also* **sixty**.

Eire ['eərə] *n* République *f* d'Irlande.

either ['aɪðər, 'i:ðər] **1** *adj* [one or the other] l'un ou l'autre (l'une ou l'autre) (des deux); **she couldn't find ~ jumper** elle ne trouva ni l'un ni l'autre des pulls; **~ way** de toute façon. || [each] chaque; **on ~ side** de chaque côté. **2** *pron*: **~ (of them)** l'un ou l'autre *m* (l'une ou l'autre *f*); **I don't like ~ (of them)** je n'aime aucun des deux, je n'aime ni l'un ni l'autre. **3** *adv* (*in negatives*) non plus; **I don't ~** moi non plus. **4** *conj*: **~ ... or** soit ... soit, ou ... ou; **I'm not fond of ~ him or his wife** je ne les aime ni lui ni sa femme.

eject [ɪ'dʒekt] *vt* [object] éjecter, émettre. || [person] éjecter, expulser.

eke [i:k] ○ **eke out** *vt sep* [money, food] économiser, faire durer.

elaborate [*adj* ɪ'læbrət, *vb* ɪ'læbəreɪt] **1** *adj* [ceremony, procedure] complexe; [explanation, plan] détaillé(e), minutieux(ieuse). **2** *vi*: **to ~ (on)** donner des précisions (sur).

elapse [ɪ'læps] *vi* s'écouler.

elastic [ɪ'læstɪk] **1** *adj* lit & fig élastique. **2** *n* (*U*) élastique *m*.

elasticated [ɪ'læstɪkeɪtɪd] *adj* élastique.

elbow ['elbəʊ] *n* coude *m*.

elder ['eldər] **1** *adj* aîné(e). **2** *n* [older person] aîné *m*, -e *f*. || [of tribe, church] ancien *m*. || [tree] sureau *m*.

elderly ['eldəlɪ] **1** *adj* âgé(e). **2** *npl*: **the ~** les personnes *fpl* âgées.

eldest ['eldɪst] *adj* aîné(e).

elect [ɪ'lekt] **1** *adj* élu(e). **2** *vt* [by voting] élire.

election [ɪ'lekʃn] *n* élection *f*; **to have OR hold an ~** procéder à une élection.

elector [ɪ'lektər] *n* électeur *m*, -trice *f*.

electorate [ɪ'lektərət] *n*: **the ~** l'électorat *m*.

electric [ɪ'lektrɪk] *adj* lit & fig électrique.

electrical [ɪ'lektrɪkl] *adj* électrique.

electrical shock *Am* = **electric shock**.

electric blanket *n* couverture *f* chauffante.

electric cooker *n* cuisinière *f* électrique.

electric fire *n* radiateur *m* électrique.

electrician [,ɪlek'trɪʃn] *n* électricien *m*, -ienne *f*.

electricity [,ɪlek'trɪsətɪ] *n* électricité *f*.

electric shock *Br*, **electrical shock** *Am n* décharge *f* électrique.

electrify [ɪ'lektrɪfaɪ] *vt* TECH électrifier. || *fig* [excite] galvaniser, électriser.

electrocute [ɪ'lektrəkju:t] *vt* électrocuter.

electrolysis [,ɪlek'trɒləsɪs] *n* électrolyse *f*.

electron [ɪ'lektrɒn] *n* électron *m*.

electronic [,ɪlek'trɒnɪk] *adj* électronique. ○ **electronics 1** *n* (*U*) [technology, science] électronique *f*. **2** *npl* [equipment] (équipement *m*) électronique *f*.

electronic data processing *n* traitement *m* électronique de données.

electronic mail *n* courrier *m* électronique.

elegant ['elɪgənt] *adj* élégant(e).

element ['elɪmənt] *n* [gen] élément *m*; **an ~ of truth** une part de vérité. || [in heater, kettle] résistance *f*. ○ **elements** *npl* [basics] rudiments *mpl*. || [weather]: **the ~s** les éléments *mpl*.

elementary [,elɪ'mentərɪ] *adj* élémentaire.

elementary school *n Am* école *f* primaire.

elephant ['elɪfənt] (*pl inv* OR -s) *n* éléphant *m*.

elevate ['elɪveɪt] *vt* [give importance to]: **to ~ sb/sthg (to)** élever qqn/qqch (à). || [raise] soulever.

elevator ['elɪveɪtə*r*] *n Am* ascenseur *m*.

eleven [ɪ'levn] *num* onze; *see also* **six**.

eleventh [ɪ'levnθ] *num* onzième; *see also* **sixth**.

elicit [ɪ'lɪsɪt] *vt fml*: **to ~ sthg (from sb)** arracher qqch (à qqn).

eligible ['elɪdʒəbl] *adj* [suitable, qualified] admissible; **to be ~ for sthg** avoir droit à qqch.

eliminate [ɪ'lɪmɪneɪt] *vt*: **to ~ sb/sthg (from)** éliminer qqn/qqch (de).

elite [ɪ'liːt] **1** *adj* d'élite. **2** *n* élite *f*.

elitist [ɪ'liːtɪst] **1** *adj* élitiste. **2** *n* élitiste *mf*.

elk [elk] (*pl inv* OR **-s**) *n* élan *m*.

elm [elm] *n*: **~ (tree)** orme *m*.

elocution [,elə'kjuːʃn] *n* élocution *f*, diction *f*.

elongated ['iːlɒŋgeɪtɪd] *adj* allongé(e); [fingers] long (longue).

elope [ɪ'ləʊp] *vi*: **to ~ (with)** s'enfuir (avec).

eloquent ['eləkwənt] *adj* éloquent(e).

El Salvador [,el'sælvədɔː*r*] *n* Salvador *m*.

else [els] *adv*: **anything ~** n'importe quoi d'autre; **anything ~?** [in shop] et avec ça?, il vous faudra autre chose?; **everyone ~** tous les autres; **nothing ~** rien d'autre; **someone ~** quelqu'un d'autre; **something ~** quelque chose d'autre; **somewhere ~** autre part; **who/ what ~?** qui/quoi d'autre?; **where ~?** (à) quel autre endroit? ○ **or else** *conj* [or if not] sinon, sans quoi.

elsewhere [els'weə*r*] *adv* ailleurs, autre part.

elude [ɪ'luːd] *vt* échapper à.

elusive [ɪ'luːsɪv] *adj* insaisissable; [success] qui échappe.

emaciated [ɪ'meɪʃɪeɪtɪd] *adj* [face] émacié(e); [person, limb] décharné(e).

E-mail (*abbr of* **electronic mail**) *n* BAL *f*.

emancipate [ɪ'mænsɪpeɪt] *vt*: **to ~ sb (from)** affranchir OR émanciper qqn (de).

embankment [ɪm'bæŋkmənt] *n* [of river] berge *f*; [of railway] remblai *m*; [of road] banquette *f*.

embark [ɪm'bɑːk] *vi* [board ship]: **to ~ (on)** embarquer (sur). || [start]: **to ~ on** OR **upon sthg** s'embarquer dans qqch.

embarkation [,embɑː'keɪʃn] *n* embarquement *m*.

embarrass [ɪm'bærəs] *vt* embarrasser.

embarrassed [ɪm'bærəst] *adj* embarrassé(e).

embarrassing [ɪm'bærəsɪŋ] *adj* embarrassant(e).

embarrassment [ɪm'bærəsmənt] *n* embarras *m*.

embassy ['embəsɪ] *n* ambassade *f*.

embedded [ɪm'bedɪd] *adj* [buried]: **~ in** [in rock, wood] incrusté(e) dans; [in mud] noyé(e) dans. || [ingrained] enraciné(e).

embellish [ɪm'belɪʃ] *vt* [decorate]: **to ~ sthg (with)** [room, house] décorer qqch (de). || [story] enjoliver.

embers ['embəz] *npl* braises *fpl*.

embezzle [ɪm'bezl] *vt* détourner.

emblem ['embləm] *n* emblème *m*.

embody [ɪm'bɒdɪ] *vt* incarner; **to be embodied in sthg** être exprimé dans qqch.

embossed [ɪm'bɒst] *adj* [heading, design]: **~ (on)** inscrit(e) (sur), gravé(e) en relief (sur). || [wallpaper] gaufré(e); [leather] frappé(e).

embrace [ɪm'breɪs] **1** *n* étreinte *f*. **2** *vt* embrasser. **3** *vi* s'embrasser, s'étreindre.

embroider [ɪm'brɔɪdə*r*] **1** *vt* SEWING broder. || *pej* [embellish] enjoliver. **2** *vi* SEWING broder.

embroidery [ɪm'brɔɪdərɪ] *n* (*U*) broderie *f*.

embroil [ɪm'brɔɪl] *vt*: **to be ~ed (in)** être mêlé(e) (à).

embryo ['embrɪəʊ] (*pl* **-s**) *n* embryon *m*.

emerald ['emərəld] **1** *adj* [colour] émeraude (*inv*). **2** *n* [stone] émeraude *f*.

emerge [ɪ'mɜːdʒ] **1** *vi* [come out]: **to ~ (from)** émerger (de). || [from experience, situation]: **to ~ from** sortir de. || [become known] apparaître. **2** *vt*: **it ~s that ...** il ressort OR il apparaît que ....

emergence [ɪ'mɜːdʒəns] *n* émergence *f*.

emergency [ɪ'mɜːdʒənsɪ] **1** *adj* d'urgence. **2** *n* urgence *f*; **in an ~, in emergencies** en cas d'urgence.

emergency exit *n* sortie *f* de secours.

emergency landing *n* atterrissage *m* forcé.

emergency services *npl* ≃ police-secours *f*.

emery board ['emərɪ-] *n* lime *f* à ongles.

emigrant ['emɪgrənt] *n* émigré *m*, -e *f*.

emigrate ['emɪgreɪt] *vi*: **to ~ (to)** émigrer (en/à).

eminent ['emɪnənt] *adj* éminent(e).

emission [ɪ'mɪʃn] *n* émission *f*.

emit [ɪ'mɪt] *vt* émettre.

emotion [ɪ'məʊʃn] *n* (*U*) [strength of feeling] émotion *f*. || [particular feeling] sentiment *m*.

emotional [ɪ'məʊʃənl] *adj* [sensitive, demonstrative] émotif(ive). || [moving] émouvant(e). || [psychological] émotionnel(elle).

emperor ['empərər] *n* empereur *m*.

emphasis ['emfəsɪs] (*pl* -ases [-əsiːz]) *n*: ~ (on) accent *m* (sur); **to lay** OR **place ~ on sthg** insister sur OR souligner qqch.

emphasize, -ise ['emfəsaɪz] *vt* insister sur.

emphatic [ɪm'fætɪk] *adj* [forceful] catégorique.

emphatically [ɪm'fætɪklɪ] *adv* [with emphasis] catégoriquement. || [certainly] absolument.

empire ['empaɪər] *n* empire *m*.

employ [ɪm'plɔɪ] *vt* employer; **to be ~ed as** être employé comme.

employee [ɪm'plɔɪiː] *n* employé *m*, -e *f*.

employer [ɪm'plɔɪər] *n* employeur *m*, -euse *f*.

employment [ɪm'plɔɪmənt] *n* emploi *m*, travail *m*.

employment agency *n* bureau *m* OR agence *f* de placement.

empress ['emprɪs] *n* impératrice *f*.

empty ['emptɪ] **1** *adj* [containing nothing] vide. || *pej* [meaningless] vain(e). **2** *vt* vider; **to ~ sthg into/out of** vider qqch dans/de. **3** *vi* se vider.

empty-handed [-'hændɪd] *adv* les mains vides.

EMS (*abbr of* **European Monetary System**) *n* SME *m*.

emulate ['emjʊleɪt] *vt* imiter.

emulsion [ɪ'mʌlʃn] *n*: ~ (**paint**) peinture *f* mate OR à émulsion.

enable [ɪ'neɪbl] *vt*: **to ~ sb to do sthg** permettre à qqn de faire qqch.

enact [ɪ'nækt] *vt* JUR promulguer.

enamel [ɪ'næml] *n* [material] émail *m*. || [paint] peinture *f* laquée.

encampment [ɪn'kæmpmənt] *n* campement *m*.

encase [ɪn'keɪs] *vt*: **to be ~d in** [armour] être enfermé(e) dans; [leather] être bardé(e) de.

enchanted [ɪn'tʃɑːntɪd] *adj*: ~ (**by/with**) enchanté(e) (par/de).

enchanting [ɪn'tʃɑːntɪŋ] *adj* enchanteur(eresse).

encircle [ɪn'sɜːkl] *vt* entourer; [subj: troops] encercler.

enclose [ɪn'kləʊz] *vt* [surround, contain] entourer. || [put in envelope] joindre; **please find ~d ...** veuillez trouver ci-joint ....

enclosure [ɪn'kləʊʒər] *n* [place] enceinte *f*. || [in letter] pièce *f* jointe.

encompass [ɪn'kʌmpəs] *vt fml* [include] contenir. || [surround] entourer; [subj: troops] encercler.

encore ['ɒŋkɔːr] **1** *n* rappel *m*. **2** *excl* bis!

encounter [ɪn'kaʊntər] **1** *n* rencontre *f*. **2** *vt fml* rencontrer.

encourage [ɪn'kʌrɪdʒ] *vt* [give confidence to]: **to ~ sb (to do sthg)** encourager qqn (à faire qqch). || [promote] encourager, favoriser.

encouragement [ɪn'kʌrɪdʒmənt] *n* encouragement *m*.

encroach [ɪn'krəʊtʃ] *vi*: **to ~ on** OR **upon** empiéter sur.

encyclop(a)edia [ɪnˌsaɪklə'piːdjə] *n* encyclopédie *f*.

end [end] **1** *n* [gen] fin *f*; **at an ~** terminé, fini; **to come to an ~** se terminer, s'arrêter; **to put an ~ to sthg** mettre fin à qqch; **at the ~ of the day** *fig* en fin de compte; **in the ~** [finally] finalement. || [of rope, path, garden, table etc] bout *m*, extrémité *f*; [of box] côté *m*. || [leftover part - of cigarette] mégot *m*; [- of pencil] bout *m*. **2** *vt* mettre fin à; [day] finir; **to ~ sthg with** terminer OR finir qqch par. **3** *vi* se terminer; **to ~ in** se terminer par; **to ~ with** se terminer par OR avec. ○ **on end** *adv* [upright] debout. || [continuously] d'affilée. ○ **end up** *vi* finir; **to ~ up doing sthg** finir par faire qqch.

endanger [ɪn'deɪndʒər] *vt* mettre en danger.

endearing [ɪn'dɪərɪŋ] *adj* engageant(e).

endeavour *Br*, **endeavor** *Am* [ɪn'devər] *fml* **1** *n* effort *m*, tentative *f*. **2** *vt*: **to ~ to do sthg** s'efforcer OR tenter de faire qqch.

ending ['endɪŋ] *n* fin *f*, dénouement *m*.

endive ['endaɪv] *n* [salad vegetable] endive *f*. || [chicory] chicorée *f*.

endless ['endlɪs] *adj* [unending] interminable; [patience, possibilities] infini(e); [resources] inépuisable. || [vast] infini(e).

endorse [ɪn'dɔːs] *vt* [approve] approuver. || [cheque] endosser.

endorsement [ɪn'dɔːsmənt] *n* [approval] approbation *f*.

endow [ɪn'daʊ] *vt* [equip]: **to be ~ed with sthg** être doté(e) de qqch. || [donate money to] faire des dons à.

endurance [ɪn'djʊərəns] *n* endurance *f*.

endure [ɪn'djʊəʳ] **1** *vt* supporter, endurer. **2** *vi* perdurer.

endways *Br* ['endweɪz], **endwise** *Am* ['endwaɪz] *adv* [not sideways] en long. || [with ends touching] bout à bout.

enemy ['enɪmɪ] *n* ennemi *m*, -e *f*.

energetic [,enə'dʒetɪk] *adj* énergique; [person] plein(e) d'entrain.

energy ['enədʒɪ] *n* énergie *f*.

enforce [ɪn'fɔ:s] *vt* appliquer, faire respecter.

enforced [ɪn'fɔ:st] *adj* forcé(e).

engage [ɪn'geɪdʒ] **1** *vt* [attention, interest] susciter, éveiller. || TECH engager. || *fml* [employ] engager; **to be ~d in** OR **on sthg** prendre part à qqch. **2** *vi* [be involved]: **to ~ in** s'occuper de.

engaged [ɪn'geɪdʒd] *adj* [to be married]: **~ (to sb)** fiancé(e) (à qqn); **to get ~** se fiancer. || [busy] occupé(e); **~ in sthg** engagé dans qqch. || [telephone, toilet] occupé(e).

engagement [ɪn'geɪdʒmənt] *n* [to be married] fiançailles *fpl*. || [appointment] rendez-vous *m inv*.

engagement ring *n* bague *f* de fiançailles.

engaging [ɪn'geɪdʒɪŋ] *adj* engageant(e); [personality] attirant(e).

engine ['endʒɪn] *n* [of vehicle] moteur *m*. || RAIL locomotive *f*.

engineer [,endʒɪ'nɪəʳ] *n* [of roads] ingénieur *m*; [of machinery, on ship] mécanicien *m*; [of electrical equipment] technicien *m*. || *Am* [engine driver] mécanicien *m*.

engineering [,endʒɪ'nɪərɪŋ] *n* ingénierie *f*.

England ['ɪŋglənd] *n* Angleterre *f*; **in ~** en Angleterre.

English ['ɪŋglɪʃ] **1** *adj* anglais(e). **2** *n* [language] anglais *m*. **3** *npl*: **the ~** les Anglais.

English breakfast *n* petit déjeuner anglais traditionnel.

English Channel *n*: **the ~** la Manche.

Englishman ['ɪŋglɪʃmən] (*pl* -men [-mən]) *n* Anglais *m*.

Englishwoman ['ɪŋglɪʃ,wʊmən] (*pl* -women [-wɪmɪn]) *n* Anglaise *f*.

engrave [ɪn'greɪv] *vt*: **to ~ sthg (on stone/in one's memory)** graver qqch (sur la pierre/dans sa mémoire).

engraving [ɪn'greɪvɪŋ] *n* gravure *f*.

engrossed [ɪn'grəʊst] *adj*: **to be ~ (in sthg)** être absorbé(e) (par qqch).

engulf [ɪn'gʌlf] *vt* engloutir.

enhance [ɪn'hɑ:ns] *vt* accroître.

enjoy [ɪn'dʒɔɪ] *vt* [like] aimer; **to ~ doing sthg** avoir plaisir à OR aimer faire qqch; **to ~ o.s.** s'amuser. || *fml* [possess] jouir de.

enjoyable [ɪn'dʒɔɪəbl] *adj* agréable.

enjoyment [ɪn'dʒɔɪmənt] *n* [gen] plaisir *m*.

enlarge [ɪn'lɑ:dʒ] *vt* agrandir. ○ **enlarge (up)on** *vt fus* développer.

enlargement [ɪn'lɑ:dʒmənt] *n* [expansion] extension *f*. || PHOT agrandissement *m*.

enlighten [ɪn'laɪtn] *vt* éclairer.

enlightened [ɪn'laɪtnd] *adj* éclairé(e).

enlist [ɪn'lɪst] **1** *vt* MIL enrôler. || [recruit] recruter. || [obtain] s'assurer. **2** *vi* MIL: **to ~ (in)** s'enrôler (dans).

enmity ['enmɪtɪ] *n* hostilité *f*.

enormity [ɪ'nɔ:mətɪ] *n* [extent] étendue *f*.

enormous [ɪ'nɔ:məs] *adj* énorme; [patience, success] immense.

enough [ɪ'nʌf] **1** *adj* assez de; **~ money/time** assez d'argent/de temps. **2** *pron* assez; **more than ~** largement, bien assez; **to have had ~ (of sthg)** en avoir assez (de qqch). **3** *adv* [sufficiently] assez; **to be good ~ to do sthg** *fml* être assez gentil pour OR de faire qqch, être assez aimable pour OR de faire qqch. || [rather] plutôt; **strangely ~** bizarrement, c'est bizarre.

enquire [ɪn'kwaɪəʳ] **1** *vt*: **to ~ when/whether/how ...** demander quand/si/comment .... **2** *vi*: **to ~ (about)** se renseigner (sur).

enquiry [ɪn'kwaɪərɪ] *n* [question] demande *f* de renseignements; **"Enquiries"** «renseignements». || [investigation] enquête *f*.

enraged [ɪn'reɪdʒd] *adj* déchaîné(e); [animal] enragé(e).

enrol, enroll *Am* [ɪn'rəʊl] **1** *vt* inscrire. **2** *vi*: **to ~ (in)** s'inscrire (à).

ensue [ɪn'sju:] *vi* s'ensuivre.

ensure [ɪn'ʃʊəʳ] *vt* assurer; **to ~ (that) ...** s'assurer que ....

ENT (*abbr of* **Ear, Nose & Throat**) *n* ORL *f*.

entail [ɪn'teɪl] *vt* entraîner; **what does the work ~?** en quoi consiste le travail?

enter ['entər] **1** vt [room, vehicle] entrer dans. || [university, army] entrer à; [school] s'inscrire à, s'inscrire dans. || [competition, race] s'inscrire à; [politics] se lancer dans. || [register]: **to ~ sb/sthg for sthg** inscrire qqn/qqch à qqch. || [write down] inscrire. || COMPUT entrer. **2** vi [come or go in] entrer. || [register]: **to ~ (for)** s'inscrire (à). ○ **enter into** vt fus [negotiations, correspondence] entamer.

enter key n COMPUT (touche f) entrée f.

enterprise ['entəpraɪz] n entreprise f.

enterprising ['entəpraɪzɪŋ] adj qui fait preuve d'initiative.

entertain [,entə'teɪn] vt [amuse] divertir. || [invite - guests] recevoir. || fml [thought, proposal] considérer.

entertainer [,entə'teɪnər] n fantaisiste mf.

entertaining [,entə'teɪnɪŋ] adj divertissant(e).

entertainment [,entə'teɪnmənt] n (U) [amusement] divertissement m. || [show] spectacle m.

enthral, enthrall Am [ɪn'θrɔːl] vt captiver.

enthusiasm [ɪn'θjuːzɪæzm] n [passion, eagerness]: ~ **(for)** enthousiasme m (pour). || [interest] passion f.

enthusiast [ɪn'θjuːzɪæst] n amateur m, -trice f.

enthusiastic [ɪn,θjuːzɪ'æstɪk] adj enthousiaste.

entice [ɪn'taɪs] vt entraîner.

entire [ɪn'taɪər] adj entier(ière).

entirely [ɪn'taɪəlɪ] adv totalement.

entirety [ɪn'taɪrətɪ] n: **in its** ~ en entier.

entitle [ɪn'taɪtl] vt [allow]: **to ~ sb to sthg** donner droit à qqch à qqn; **to ~ sb to do sthg** autoriser qqn à faire qqch.

entitled [ɪn'taɪtld] adj [allowed] autorisé(e); **to be ~ to sthg** avoir droit à qqch; **to be ~ to do sthg** avoir le droit de faire qqch. || [called] intitulé(e).

entrance [n 'entrəns, vt ɪn'trɑːns] **1** n [way in]: ~ **(to)** entrée f (de). || [arrival] entrée f. || [entry]: **to gain ~ to** [building] obtenir l'accès à. **2** vt ravir, enivrer.

entrance examination n examen m d'entrée.

entrance fee n [to cinema, museum] droit m d'entrée. || [for club] droit m d'inscription.

entrant ['entrənt] n [in race, competition] concurrent m, -e f.

entreat [ɪn'triːt] vt: **to ~ sb (to do sthg)** supplier qqn (de faire qqch).

entrepreneur [,ɒntrəprə'nɜːr] n entrepreneur m.

entrust [ɪn'trʌst] vt: **to ~ sthg to sb, to ~ sb with sthg** confier qqch à qqn.

entry ['entrɪ] n [gen] entrée f; **to gain ~ to** avoir accès à; **"no ~"** «défense d'entrer»; AUT «sens interdit». || [in competition] inscription f. || [in dictionary] entrée f; [in diary, ledger] inscription f.

entry form n formulaire m OR feuille f d'inscription.

entry phone n portier m électronique.

envelop [ɪn'veləp] vt envelopper.

envelope ['envələʊp] n enveloppe f.

envious ['envɪəs] adj envieux(ieuse).

environment [ɪn'vaɪərənmənt] n [surroundings] milieu m, cadre m. || [natural world]: **the** ~ l'environnement m.

environmental [ɪn,vaɪərən'mentl] adj [pollution, awareness] de l'environnement; [impact] sur l'environnement.

environmentally [ɪn,vaɪərən'mentəlɪ] adv [damaging] pour l'environnement; ~ **friendly** qui préserve l'environnement.

envisage [ɪn'vɪzɪdʒ], **envision** Am [ɪn'vɪʒn] vt envisager.

envoy ['envɔɪ] n émissaire m.

envy ['envɪ] **1** n envie f, jalousie f. **2** vt envier; **to ~ sb sthg** envier qqch à qqn.

epic ['epɪk] **1** adj épique. **2** n épopée f.

epidemic [,epɪ'demɪk] n épidémie f.

epileptic [,epɪ'leptɪk] **1** adj épileptique. **2** n épileptique mf.

episode ['epɪsəʊd] n épisode m.

epistle [ɪ'pɪsl] n épître f.

epitaph ['epɪtɑːf] n épitaphe f.

epitome [ɪ'pɪtəmɪ] n: **the** ~ **of** le modèle de.

epitomize, -ise [ɪ'pɪtəmaɪz] vt incarner.

epoch ['iːpɒk] n époque f.

equal ['iːkwəl] **1** adj [gen]: ~ **(to)** égal(e) (à). || [capable]: ~ **to sthg** à la hauteur de qqch. **2** n égal m, -e f. **3** vt égaler.

equality [iː'kwɒlətɪ] n égalité f.

equalize, -ise ['iːkwəlaɪz] **1** vt niveler. **2** vi SPORT égaliser.

equalizer ['iːkwəlaɪzər] n SPORT but m égalisateur.

equally ['iːkwəlɪ] adv [important, stupid etc] tout aussi. || [in amount] en parts égales. || [also] en même temps.

equal opportunities npl égalité f des chances.

equate [ɪ'kweɪt] vt: **to ~ sthg with** assimiler qqch à.

equation [ɪ'kweɪʒn] n équation f.

equator [ɪ'kweɪtər] *n*: the ~ l'équateur *m*.

equilibrium [,i:kwɪ'lɪbrɪəm] *n* équilibre *m*.

equip [ɪ'kwɪp] *vt* équiper; **to ~ sb/sthg with** équiper qqn/qqch de, munir qqn/qqch de; **he's well equipped for the job** il est bien préparé pour ce travail.

equipment [ɪ'kwɪpmənt] *n* (U) équipement *m*, matériel *m*.

equities ['ekwətɪz] *npl* ST EX actions *fpl* ordinaires.

equivalent [ɪ'kwɪvələnt] **1** *adj* équivalent(e); **to be ~ to** être équivalent à, équivaloir à. **2** *n* équivalent *m*.

er [ɜ:r] *excl* euh!

era ['ɪərə] (*pl* -**s**) *n* ère *f*, période *f*.

eradicate [ɪ'rædɪkeɪt] *vt* éradiquer.

erase [ɪ'reɪz] *vt* [rub out] gommer. || *fig* [memory] effacer; [hunger, poverty] éliminer.

eraser [ɪ'reɪzər] *n* gomme *f*.

erect [ɪ'rekt] **1** *adj* [person, posture] droit(e). || [penis] en érection. **2** *vt* [statue] ériger; [building] construire. || [tent] dresser.

erection [ɪ'rekʃn] *n* (U) [of statue] érection *f*; [of building] construction *f*. || [erect penis] érection *f*.

ERM (*abbr of* **Exchange Rate Mechanism**) *n* mécanisme *m* des changes (du SME).

erode [ɪ'rəʊd] **1** *vt* [rock, soil] éroder. || *fig* [confidence, rights] réduire. **2** *vi* [rock, soil] s'éroder. || *fig* [confidence] diminuer; [rights] se réduire.

erosion [ɪ'rəʊʒn] *n* [of rock, soil] érosion *f*. || *fig* [of confidence] baisse *f*; [of rights] diminution *f*.

erotic [ɪ'rɒtɪk] *adj* érotique.

err [ɜ:r] *vi* se tromper.

errand ['erənd] *n* course *f*, commission *f*; **to go on** OR **run an ~** faire une course.

erratic [ɪ'rætɪk] *adj* irrégulier(ière).

error ['erər] *n* erreur *f*; **a spelling/ typing ~** une faute d'orthographe/de frappe.

erupt [ɪ'rʌpt] *vi* [volcano] entrer en éruption.

eruption [ɪ'rʌpʃn] *n* [of volcano] éruption *f*.

escalate ['eskəleɪt] *vi* [conflict] s'intensifier. || [costs] monter en flèche.

escalator ['eskəleɪtər] *n* escalier *m* roulant.

escapade [,eskə'peɪd] *n* aventure *f*, exploit *m*.

escape [ɪ'skeɪp] **1** *n* [gen] fuite *f*, évasion *f*; **to make one's ~** s'échapper; **to have a lucky ~** l'échapper belle. || [leakage - of gas, water] fuite *f*. **2** *vt* échapper à. **3** *vi* [gen] s'échapper, fuir; [from prison] s'évader; **to ~ from** [place] s'échapper de; [danger, person] échapper à. || [survive] s'en tirer.

escapism [ɪ'skeɪpɪzm] *n* (U) évasion *f* (de la réalité).

escort [*n* 'eskɔ:t, *vb* ɪ'skɔ:t] **1** *n* [guard] escorte *f*; **under ~** sous escorte. || [companion - male] cavalier *m*; [- female] hôtesse *f*. **2** *vt* escorter, accompagner.

Eskimo ['eskɪməʊ] (*pl* -**s**) *n* [person] Esquimau *m*, -aude *f*.

espadrille [,espə'drɪl] *n* espadrille *f*.

especially [ɪ'speʃəlɪ] *adv* [in particular] surtout. || [more than usually] particulièrement. || [specifically] spécialement.

espionage ['espɪə,nɑ:ʒ] *n* espionnage *m*.

esplanade [,esplə'neɪd] *n* esplanade *f*.

Esquire [ɪ'skwaɪər] *n*: **G. Curry ~** Monsieur G. Curry.

essay ['eseɪ] *n* SCH & UNIV dissertation *f*. || LITERATURE essai *m*.

essence ['esns] *n* [nature] essence *f*, nature *f*; **in ~** par essence. || CULIN extrait *m*.

essential [ɪ'senʃl] *adj* [absolutely necessary]: **~ (to** OR **for)** indispensable (à). || [basic] essentiel(ielle), de base. ○ **essentials** *npl* [basic commodities] produits *mpl* de première nécessité. || [most important elements] essentiel *m*.

essentially [ɪ'senʃəlɪ] *adv* fondamentalement, avant tout.

establish [ɪ'stæblɪʃ] *vt* [gen] établir. || [organization, business] fonder, créer.

establishment [ɪ'stæblɪʃmənt] *n* [gen] établissement *m*. || [of organization, business] fondation *f*, création *f*. ○ **Establishment** *n* [status quo]: **the Establishment** l'ordre *m* établi, l'Establishment *m*.

estate [ɪ'steɪt] *n* [land, property] propriété *f*, domaine *m*. || (**housing**) **~** lotissement *m*. || (**industrial**) **~** zone *f* industrielle. || JUR [inheritance] biens *mpl*.

esteem [ɪ'sti:m] **1** *n* estime *f*. **2** *vt* estimer.

esthetic *etc Am* = **aesthetic** *etc*.

estimate [*n* 'estɪmət, *vb* 'estɪmeɪt] **1** *n* [calculation, judgment] estimation *f*, évaluation *f*. || COMM devis *m*. **2** *vt* estimer, évaluer.

estimation [,estɪ'meɪʃn] n [opinion] opinion f. || [calculation] estimation f, évaluation f.

Estonia [e'stəʊnɪə] n Estonie f.

estranged [ɪ'streɪndʒd] adj [couple] séparé(e); [husband, wife] dont on s'est séparé.

estuary ['estjʊərɪ] n estuaire m.

etc. (abbr of et cetera) etc.

etching ['etʃɪŋ] n gravure f à l'eau forte.

eternal [ɪ'tɜːnl] adj [life] éternel(elle); fig [complaints, whining] sempiternel(elle). || [truth, value] immuable.

eternity [ɪ'tɜːnətɪ] n éternité f.

ethic ['eθɪk] n éthique f, morale f. ○ **ethics** 1 n (U) [study] éthique f, morale f. 2 npl [morals] morale f.

ethical ['eθɪkl] adj moral(e).

Ethiopia [,iːθɪ'əʊpɪə] n Éthiopie f.

ethnic ['eθnɪk] adj [traditions, groups] ethnique. || [clothes] folklorique.

etiquette ['etɪket] n convenances fpl, étiquette f.

eulogy ['juːlədʒɪ] n panégyrique m.

euphemism ['juːfəmɪzm] n euphémisme m.

euphoria [juː'fɔːrɪə] n euphorie f.

Euro MP n député m européen.

Europe ['jʊərəp] n Europe f.

European [,jʊərə'piːən] 1 adj européen(enne). 2 n Européen m, -enne f.

European Community n: the ~ la Communauté européenne.

European Monetary System n: the ~ le Système monétaire européen.

European Parliament n: the ~ le Parlement européen.

euthanasia [,juːθə'neɪzjə] n euthanasie f.

evacuate [ɪ'vækjʊeɪt] vt évacuer.

evade [ɪ'veɪd] vt [gen] échapper à. || [issue, question] esquiver, éluder.

evaluate [ɪ'væljʊeɪt] vt évaluer.

evaporate [ɪ'væpəreɪt] vi [liquid] s'évaporer. || fig [hopes, fears] s'envoler; [confidence] disparaître.

evaporated milk [ɪ'væpəreɪtɪd-] n lait m condensé (non sucré).

evasion [ɪ'veɪʒn] n [of responsibility] dérobade f. || [lie] faux-fuyant m.

evasive [ɪ'veɪsɪv] adj évasif(ive); **to take ~ action** faire une manœuvre d'évitement.

eve [iːv] n veille f.

even ['iːvn] 1 adj [speed, rate] régulier(ière); [temperature, temperament] égal(e). || [flat, level] plat(e), régu-

lier(ière). || [equal - contest] équilibré(e); [- teams, players] de la même force; [- scores] à égalité; **to get ~ with sb** se venger de qqn. || [not odd - number] pair(e). 2 adv [gen] même; **~ now** encore maintenant; **~ then** même alors. || [in comparisons]: **~ bigger/better/more stupid** encore plus grand/mieux/plus bête. ○ **even if** conj même si. ○ **even so** adv quand même. ○ **even though** conj bien que (+ subjunctive). ○ **even out** 1 vt sep égaliser. 2 vi s'égaliser.

evening ['iːvnɪŋ] n soir m; [duration, entertainment] soirée f; **in the ~** le soir. ○ **evenings** adv Am le soir.

evening class n cours m du soir.

evening dress n [worn by man] habit m de soirée; [worn by woman] robe f du soir.

event [ɪ'vent] n [happening] événement m. || SPORT épreuve f. || [case]: **in the ~ of** en cas de; **in the ~ that** au cas où. ○ **in any event** adv en tout cas, de toute façon.

eventful [ɪ'ventfʊl] adj mouvementé(e).

eventual [ɪ'ventʃʊəl] adj final(e).

eventuality [ɪ,ventʃʊ'ælətɪ] n éventualité f.

eventually [ɪ'ventʃʊəlɪ] adv finalement, en fin de compte.

ever ['evər] adv [at any time] jamais; **have you ~ been to Paris?** êtes-vous déjà allé à Paris?; **I hardly ~ see him** je ne le vois presque jamais. || [all the time] toujours; **as ~** comme toujours; **for ~** pour toujours. || [for emphasis]: **~ so** tellement; **~ such** vraiment; **why/how ~?** pourquoi/comment donc? ○ **ever since** 1 adv depuis (ce moment-là). 2 conj depuis que. 3 prep depuis.

evergreen ['evəgriːn] n arbre m à feuilles persistantes.

everlasting [,evə'lɑːstɪŋ] adj éternel(elle).

every ['evrɪ] adj chaque; **~ morning** chaque matin, tous les matins. ○ **every now and then, every so often** adv de temps en temps, de temps à autre. ○ **every other** adj: **~ other day** tous les deux jours, un jour sur deux; **~ other street** une rue sur deux. ○ **every which way** adv Am partout, de tous côtés.

everybody ['evrɪ,bɒdɪ] = everyone.

everyday ['evrɪdeɪ] adj quotidien(ienne).

everyone ['evrɪwʌn] pron chacun, tout le monde.

everyplace *Am* = everywhere.

everything ['evrɪθɪŋ] *pron* tout.

everywhere ['evrɪweəʳ], **everyplace** *Am* ['evrɪ,pleɪs] *adv* partout.

evict [ɪ'vɪkt] *vt* expulser.

evidence ['evɪdəns] *n* (*U*) [proof] preuve *f*. || JUR [of witness] témoignage *m*; **to give ~** témoigner.

evident ['evɪdənt] *adj* évident(e), manifeste.

evidently ['evɪdəntlɪ] *adv* [seemingly] apparemment. || [obviously] de toute évidence, manifestement.

evil ['iːvl] 1 *adj* [person] mauvais(e), malveillant(e). 2 *n* mal *m*.

evoke [ɪ'vəʊk] *vt* [memory] évoquer; [emotion, response] susciter.

evolution [ˌiːvə'luːʃn] *n* évolution *f*.

evolve [ɪ'vɒlv] *vi*: **to ~ (into/from)** se développer (en/à partir de).

ewe [juː] *n* brebis *f*.

ex- [eks] *prefix* ex-.

exacerbate [ɪg'zæsəbeɪt] *vt* [feeling] exacerber; [problems] aggraver.

exact [ɪg'zækt] 1 *adj* exact(e), précis(e). 2 *vt*: **to ~ sthg (from)** exiger qqch (de).

exacting [ɪg'zæktɪŋ] *adj* [job, standards] astreignant(e); [person] exigeant(e).

exactly [ɪg'zæktlɪ] 1 *adv* exactement. 2 *excl* exactement!, parfaitement!

exaggerate [ɪg'zædʒəreɪt] *vt* & *vi* exagérer.

exaggeration [ɪg,zædʒə'reɪʃn] *n* exagération *f*.

exam [ɪg'zæm] *n* examen *m*; **to take** OR **sit an ~** passer un examen.

examination [ɪg,zæmɪ'neɪʃn] *n* examen *m*.

examine [ɪg'zæmɪn] *vt* [gen] examiner; [passport] contrôler. || JUR, SCH & UNIV interroger.

examiner [ɪg'zæmɪnəʳ] *n* examinateur *m*, -trice *f*.

example [ɪg'zɑːmpl] *n* exemple *m*; **for ~** par exemple.

exasperate [ɪg'zæspəreɪt] *vt* exaspérer.

exasperation [ɪg,zæspə'reɪʃn] *n* exaspération *f*.

excavate ['ekskəveɪt] *vt* [land] creuser. || [object] déterrer.

exceed [ɪk'siːd] *vt* [amount, number] excéder. || [limit, expectations] dépasser.

exceedingly [ɪk'siːdɪŋlɪ] *adv* extrêmement.

excel [ɪk'sel] *vi*: **to ~ (in** OR **at)** exceller (dans); **to ~ o.s.** *Br* se surpasser.

excellence ['eksələns] *n* excellence *f*, supériorité *f*.

excellent ['eksələnt] *adj* excellent(e).

except [ɪk'sept] 1 *prep* & *conj*: **~ (for)** à part, sauf. 2 *vt*: **to ~ sb (from)** exclure qqn (de).

excepting [ɪk'septɪŋ] *prep* & *conj* = **except**.

exception [ɪk'sepʃn] *n* [exclusion]: **~ (to)** exception *f* (à); **with the ~ of** à l'exception de. || [offence]: **to take ~ to** s'offenser de, se froisser de.

exceptional [ɪk'sepʃənl] *adj* exceptionnel(elle).

excerpt ['eksɜːpt] *n*: **~ (from)** extrait *m* (de), passage *m* (de).

excess [ɪk'ses, *before nouns* 'ekses] 1 *adj* excédentaire. 2 *n* excès *m*.

excess baggage *n* excédent *m* de bagages.

excessive [ɪk'sesɪv] *adj* excessif(ive).

exchange [ɪks'tʃeɪndʒ] 1 *n* [gen] échange *m*; **in ~ (for)** en échange (de). || TELEC: **(telephone) ~** central *m* (téléphonique). 2 *vt* [swap] échanger; **to ~ sthg for sthg** échanger qqch contre qqch.

exchange rate *n* FIN taux *m* de change.

excise ['eksaɪz] *n* (*U*) contributions *fpl* indirectes.

excite [ɪk'saɪt] *vt* exciter.

excited [ɪk'saɪtɪd] *adj* excité(e).

excitement [ɪk'saɪtmənt] *n* [state] excitation *f*.

exciting [ɪk'saɪtɪŋ] *adj* passionnant(e); [prospect] excitant(e).

exclaim [ɪk'skleɪm] 1 *vt* s'écrier. 2 *vi* s'exclamer.

exclamation [ˌeksklə'meɪʃn] *n* exclamation *f*.

exclamation mark *Br*, **exclamation point** *Am* *n* point *m* d'exclamation.

exclude [ɪk'skluːd] *vt*: **to ~ sb/sthg (from)** exclure qqn/qqch (de).

excluding [ɪk'skluːdɪŋ] *prep* sans compter, à l'exclusion de.

exclusive [ɪk'skluːsɪv] 1 *adj* [high-class] fermé(e). || [unique - use, news story] exclusif(ive). 2 *n* PRESS exclusivité *f*. ○ **exclusive of** *prep*: **~ of interest** intérêts non compris.

excrement ['ekskrɪmənt] *n* excrément *m*.

excruciating [ɪk'skruːʃɪeɪtɪŋ] *adj* atroce.

excursion [ɪk'skɜːʃn] n [trip] excursion f.

excuse [n ɪk'skjuːs, vb ɪk'skjuːz] 1 n excuse f. 2 vt [gen] excuser; **to ~ sb for sthg/for doing sthg** excuser qqn de qqch/de faire qqch; **~ me** [to attract attention] excusez-moi; [forgive me] pardon, excusez-moi; Am [sorry] pardon. || [let off]: **to ~ sb (from)** dispenser qqn (de).

execute ['eksɪkjuːt] vt exécuter.

execution [ˌeksɪ'kjuːʃn] n exécution f.

executioner [ˌeksɪ'kjuːʃnər] n bourreau m.

executive [ɪg'zekjʊtɪv] 1 adj [power, board] exécutif(ive). 2 n COMM cadre m. || [of government] exécutif m.

executive director n cadre m supérieur.

executor [ɪg'zekjʊtər] n exécuteur m testamentaire.

exemplify [ɪg'zemplɪfaɪ] vt [typify] exemplifier. || [give example of] exemplifier, illustrer.

exempt [ɪg'zempt] 1 adj: **~ (from)** exempt(e) (de). 2 vt: **to ~ sb (from)** exempter qqn (de).

exercise ['eksəsaɪz] 1 n exercice m. 2 vt [gen] exercer. 3 vi prendre de l'exercice.

exercise book n [notebook] cahier m d'exercices; [published book] livre m d'exercices.

exert [ɪg'zɜːt] vt exercer; [strength] employer; **to ~ o.s.** se donner du mal.

exertion [ɪg'zɜːʃn] n effort m.

exhale [eks'heɪl] vi expirer.

exhaust [ɪg'zɔːst] 1 n (U) [fumes] gaz mpl d'échappement. || **~ (pipe)** pot m d'échappement. 2 vt épuiser.

exhausted [ɪg'zɔːstɪd] adj épuisé(e).

exhausting [ɪg'zɔːstɪŋ] adj épuisant(e).

exhaustion [ɪg'zɔːstʃn] n épuisement m.

exhaustive [ɪg'zɔːstɪv] adj complet(ète), exhaustif(ive).

exhibit [ɪg'zɪbɪt] 1 n ART objet m exposé. || JUR pièce f à conviction. 2 vt [demonstrate - feeling] montrer; [- skill] faire preuve de. || ART exposer.

exhibition [ˌeksɪ'bɪʃn] n ART exposition f. || [of feeling] démonstration f.

exhilarating [ɪg'zɪləreɪtɪŋ] adj [experience] grisant(e); [walk] vivifiant(e).

exile ['eksaɪl] 1 n [condition] exil m; **in ~** en exil. || [person] exilé m, -e f. 2 vt: **to ~ sb (from/to)** exiler qqn (de/vers).

exist [ɪg'zɪst] vi exister.

existence [ɪg'zɪstəns] n existence f; **in ~** qui existe, existant(e); **to come into ~** naître.

existing [ɪg'zɪstɪŋ] adj existant(e).

exit ['eksɪt] 1 n sortie f. 2 vi sortir.

exodus ['eksədəs] n exode m.

exonerate [ɪg'zɒnəreɪt] vt: **to ~ sb (from)** disculper qqn (de).

exorbitant [ɪg'zɔːbɪtənt] adj exorbitant(e).

exotic [ɪg'zɒtɪk] adj exotique.

expand [ɪk'spænd] 1 vt [production, influence] accroître; [business, department, area] développer. 2 vi [population, influence] s'accroître; [business, department, market] se développer; [metal] se dilater. ○ **expand (up)on** vt fus développer.

expanse [ɪk'spæns] n étendue f.

expansion [ɪk'spænʃn] n [of production, population] accroissement m; [of business, department, area] développement m; [of metal] dilatation f.

expect [ɪk'spekt] 1 vt [anticipate] s'attendre à; [event, letter, baby] attendre; **to ~ sb to do sthg** s'attendre à ce que qqn fasse qqch. || [count on] compter sur. || [demand] exiger, demander; **to ~ sb to do sthg** attendre de qqn qu'il fasse qqch. || [suppose] supposer; **I ~ so** je crois que oui. 2 vi [anticipate]: **to ~ to do sthg** compter faire qqch. || [be pregnant]: **to be ~ing** être enceinte, attendre un bébé.

expectant [ɪk'spektənt] adj qui est dans l'expectative.

expectant mother n femme f enceinte.

expectation [ˌekspek'teɪʃn] n [hope] espoir m, attente f. || [belief]: **it's my ~ that ...** à mon avis, ...; **against all ~** OR **~s, contrary to all ~** OR **~s** contre toute attente.

expedient [ɪk'spiːdjənt] fml 1 adj indiqué(e). 2 n expédient m.

expedition [ˌekspɪ'dɪʃn] n expédition f.

expel [ɪk'spel] vt [gen] expulser. || SCH renvoyer.

expend [ɪk'spend] vt: **to ~ time/money (on)** consacrer du temps/de l'argent (à).

expendable [ɪk'spendəbl] adj dont on peut se passer, qui n'est pas indispensable.

expenditure [ɪk'spendɪtʃər] n (U) dépense f.

expense [ɪk'spens] n [amount spent] dépense f. || (U) [cost] frais mpl; **at the ~ of**

au prix de; **at sb's ~** [financial] aux frais de qqn; *fig* aux dépens de qqn. ○ **expenses** *npl* COMM frais *mpl*.

expense account *n* frais *mpl* de représentation.

expensive [ɪk'spensɪv] *adj* [financially - gen] cher (chère), coûteux(euse); [- tastes] dispendieux(ieuse). || [mistake] qui coûte cher.

experience [ɪk'spɪərɪəns] **1** *n* expérience *f*. **2** *vt* [difficulty] connaître; [loss, change] subir.

experienced [ɪk'spɪərɪənst] *adj* expérimenté(e).

experiment [ɪk'sperɪmənt] **1** *n* expérience *f*. **2** *vi*: **to ~ (with sthg)** expérimenter (qqch).

expert ['eksp3ːt] **1** *adj* expert(e); [advice] d'expert. **2** *n* expert *m*, -e *f*.

expertise [,eksp3ː'tiːz] *n* (*U*) compétence *f*.

expire [ɪk'spaɪər] *vi* expirer.

expiry [ɪk'spaɪərɪ] *n* expiration *f*.

explain [ɪk'spleɪn] **1** *vt* expliquer; **to ~ sthg to sb** expliquer qqch à qqn. **2** *vi* s'expliquer; **to ~ to sb (about sthg)** expliquer (qqch) à qqn.

explanation [,eksplə'neɪʃn] *n*: **~ (for)** explication *f* (de).

explicit [ɪk'splɪsɪt] *adj* explicite.

explode [ɪk'spləʊd] **1** *vt* [bomb] faire exploser. **2** *vi lit* & *fig* exploser.

exploit [*n* 'eksplɔɪt, *vb* ɪk'splɔɪt] **1** *n* exploit *m*. **2** *vt* exploiter.

exploitation [,eksplɔɪ'teɪʃn] *n* (*U*) exploitation *f*.

exploration [,eksplə'reɪʃn] *n* exploration *f*.

explore [ɪk'splɔːr] *vt* & *vi* explorer.

explorer [ɪk'splɔːrər] *n* explorateur *m*, -trice *f*.

explosion [ɪk'spləʊʒn] *n* explosion *f*.

explosive [ɪk'spləʊsɪv] **1** *adj lit* & *fig* explosif(ive). **2** *n* explosif *m*.

exponent [ɪk'spəʊnənt] *n* [of theory] défenseur *m*.

export [*n* & *comp* 'ekspɔːt, *vb* ɪk'spɔːt] **1** *n* exportation *f*. **2** *vt* exporter.

exporter [ek'spɔːtər] *n* exportateur *m*, -trice *f*.

expose [ɪk'spəʊz] *vt* [uncover] exposer, découvrir; **to be ~d to sthg** être exposé à qqch. || [unmask - corruption] révéler; [- person] démasquer.

exposed [ɪk'spəʊzd] *adj* [land, house, position] exposé(e).

exposure [ɪk'spəʊʒər] *n* [to light, radiation] exposition *f*. || MED: **to die of ~** mourir de froid. || [PHOT - time] temps *m* de pose; [- photograph] pose *f*. || (*U*) [publicity] publicité *f*; [coverage] couverture *f*.

exposure meter *n* posemètre *m*.

express [ɪk'spres] **1** *adj* [train, coach] express (*inv*). || *fml* [specific] exprès(esse). **2** *n* [train] rapide *m*, express *m*. **3** *vt* exprimer.

expression [ɪk'spreʃn] *n* expression *f*.

expressive [ɪk'spresɪv] *adj* expressif(ive).

expressly [ɪk'spreslɪ] *adv* expressément.

expressway [ɪk'spresweɪ] *n* Am voie *f* express.

exquisite [ɪk'skwɪzɪt] *adj* exquis(e).

ext., extn. (*abbr of* extension): **~ 4174** p. 4174.

extend [ɪk'stend] **1** *vt* [enlarge - building] agrandir. || [make longer - gen] prolonger; [- visa] proroger; [- deadline] repousser. || [expand - rules, law] étendre (la portée de); [- power] accroître. || [offer - help] apporter, offrir; [- credit] accorder. **2** *vi* [stretch - in space] s'étendre; [- in time] continuer.

extension [ɪk'stenʃn] *n* [to building] agrandissement *m*. || [lengthening - gen] prolongement *m*; [- of visit] prolongation *f*; [- of visa] prorogation *f*; [- of deadline] report *m*. || [of power] accroissement *m*; [of law] élargissement *m*. || TELEC poste *m*. || ELEC prolongateur *m*.

extension cable *n* rallonge *f*.

extensive [ɪk'stensɪv] *adj* [in amount] considérable. || [in area] vaste. || [in range - discussions] approfondi(e); [- changes, use] considérable.

extensively [ɪk'stensɪvlɪ] *adv* [in amount] considérablement. || [in range] abondamment, largement.

extent [ɪk'stent] *n* [of land, area] étendue *f*, superficie *f*; [of problem, damage] étendue *f*. || [degree]: **to what ~ ...?** dans quelle mesure ...?; **to the ~ that** [in so far as] dans la mesure où; [to the point where] au point que; **to a large** OR **great ~** en grande partie, pour une large part; **to some ~** en partie.

extenuating circumstances [ɪk'stenjʊeɪtɪŋ-] *npl* circonstances *fpl* atténuantes.

exterior [ɪk'stɪərɪər] **1** *adj* extérieur(e). **2** *n* [of house, car] extérieur *m*.

exterminate [ɪk'st3ːmɪneɪt] *vt* exterminer.

external [ɪk'stɜːnl] *adj* externe.

extinct [ɪk'stɪŋkt] *adj* [species] disparu(e). || [volcano] éteint(e).

extinguish [ɪk'stɪŋgwɪʃ] *vt* [fire, cigarette] éteindre.

extinguisher [ɪk'stɪŋgwɪʃəʳ] *n* extincteur *m*.

extn. = ext.

extol, extoll *Am* [ɪk'stəʊl] *vt* louer.

extort [ɪk'stɔːt] *vt*: **to ~ sthg from sb** extorquer qqch à qqn.

extortionate [ɪk'stɔːʃnət] *adj* exorbitant(e).

extra ['ekstrə] **1** *adj* supplémentaire. **2** *n* [addition] supplément *m*; **optional ~** option *f*. || CINEMA & THEATRE figurant *m*, -e *f*. **3** *adv* [hard, big etc] extra; [pay, charge etc] en plus.

extra- ['ekstrə] *prefix* extra-.

extract [*n* 'ekstrækt, *vb* ɪk'strækt] **1** *n* extrait *m*. **2** *vt* [take out - tooth] arracher; **to ~ sthg from** tirer qqch de. || [confession, information]: **to ~ sthg (from sb)** arracher qqch (à qqn), tirer qqch (de qqn). || [coal, oil] extraire.

extradite ['ekstrədaɪt] *vt*: **to ~ sb (from/to)** extrader qqn (de/vers).

extramarital [ˌekstrə'mærɪtl] *adj* extraconjugal(e).

extramural [ˌekstrə'mjʊərəl] *adj* UNIV hors faculté.

extraordinary [ɪk'strɔːdnrɪ] *adj* extraordinaire.

extravagance [ɪk'strævəgəns] *n* (*U*) [excessive spending] gaspillage *m*, prodigalités *fpl*. || [luxury] extravagance *f*, folie *f*.

extravagant [ɪk'strævəgənt] *adj* [wasteful - person] dépensier(ière); [- use, tastes] dispendieux(ieuse). || [elaborate, exaggerated] extravagant(e).

extreme [ɪk'striːm] **1** *adj* extrême. **2** *n* extrême *m*.

extremely [ɪk'striːmlɪ] *adv* extrêmement.

extremist [ɪk'striːmɪst] *n* extrémiste *mf*.

extricate ['ekstrɪkeɪt] *vt*: **to ~ sthg (from)** dégager qqch (de); **to ~ o.s. (from)** [from seat belt etc] s'extirper (de); [from difficult situation] se tirer (de).

extrovert ['ekstrəvɜːt] **1** *adj* extraverti(e). **2** *n* extraverti *m*, -e *f*.

exuberance [ɪg'zjuːbərəns] *n* exubérance *f*.

eye [aɪ] (*cont* eyeing OR eying) **1** *n* [gen] œil *m*; **to catch sb's ~** attirer l'attention

de qqn; **to have one's ~ on sb** avoir qqn à l'œil; **to have one's ~ on sthg** avoir repéré qqch; **to keep one's ~s open for sthg** [try to find] essayer de repérer qqch; **to keep an ~ on sthg** surveiller qqch, garder l'œil sur qqch. || [of needle] chas *m*. **2** *vt* regarder, reluquer.

eyeball ['aɪbɔːl] *n* globe *m* oculaire.

eyebrow ['aɪbraʊ] *n* sourcil *m*.

eyebrow pencil *n* crayon *m* à sourcils.

eyedrops ['aɪdrɒps] *npl* gouttes *fpl* pour les yeux.

eyelash ['aɪlæʃ] *n* cil *m*.

eyelid ['aɪlɪd] *n* paupière *f*.

eyeliner ['aɪˌlaɪnəʳ] *n* eye-liner *m*.

eye-opener *n inf* révélation *f*.

eye shadow *n* fard *m* à paupières.

eyesight ['aɪsaɪt] *n* vue *f*.

eyesore ['aɪsɔːʳ] *n* horreur *f*.

eyestrain ['aɪstreɪn] *n* fatigue *f* des yeux.

eyewitness [ˌaɪ'wɪtnɪs] *n* témoin *m* oculaire.

f (*pl* **f's** OR **fs**), **F** (*pl* **F's** OR **Fs**) [ef] *n* [letter] f *m inv*, F *m inv*. ○ **F** *n* MUS fa *m*. || (*abbr of* **Fahrenheit**) F.

fable ['feɪbl] *n* fable *f*.

fabric ['fæbrɪk] *n* [cloth] tissu *m*. || [of building, society] structure *f*.

fabrication [ˌfæbrɪ'keɪʃn] *n* [lie, lying] fabrication *f*, invention *f*.

fabulous ['fæbjʊləs] *adj* [gen] fabuleux(euse). || *inf* [excellent] sensationnel(elle), fabuleux(euse).

facade [fə'sɑːd] *n* façade *f*.

face [feɪs] **1** *n* [of person] visage *m*, figure *f*; **~ to ~** face à face. || [expression] visage *m*, mine *f*; **to make** OR **pull a ~** faire la grimace. || [of cliff, mountain] face *f*, paroi *f*; [of clock, watch] cadran *m*; [of coin, shape] face. || [surface - of planet] surface *f*; **on the ~ of it** à première vue. || [respect]: **to save/lose ~** sauver/perdre la face. **2** *vt* [look towards - subj: person] faire face à; **the house ~s the sea/south**

la maison donne sur la mer/est orientée vers le sud. || [decision, crisis] être confronté(e) à; [problem, danger] faire face à. || [facts, truth] faire face à, admettre. || *inf* [cope with] affronter. ○ **face down** *adv* [person] face contre terre; [object] à l'envers; [card] face en dessous. ○ **face up** *adv* [person] sur le dos; [object] à l'endroit; [card] face en dessus. ○ **in the face of** *prep* devant. ○ **face up to** *vt fus* faire face à.

face cream *n* crème *f* pour le visage.

face-lift *n* lifting *m*; *fig* restauration *f*, rénovation *f*.

face powder *n* poudre *f* de riz, poudre pour le visage.

face-saving [-ˌseɪvɪŋ] *adj* qui sauve la face.

facet ['fæsɪt] *n* facette *f*.

facetious [fəˈsiːʃəs] *adj* facétieux(ieuse).

face value *n* [of coin, stamp] valeur *f* nominale; **to take sthg at ~** prendre qqch au pied de la lettre.

facility [fəˈsɪlətɪ] *n* [feature] fonction *f*. ○ **facilities** *npl* [amenities] équipement *m*, aménagement *m*.

facing ['feɪsɪŋ] *adj* d'en face; [sides] opposé(e).

facsimile [fækˈsɪmɪlɪ] *n* [fax] télécopie *f*, fax *m*. || [copy] fac-similé *m*.

fact [fækt] *n* [true piece of information] fait *m*. || (*U*) [truth] faits *mpl*, réalité *f*. ○ **in fact 1** *adv* de fait, effectivement. **2** *conj* en fait.

fact of life *n* fait *m*, réalité *f*; **the facts of life** *euphemism* les choses *fpl* de la vie.

factor ['fæktər] *n* facteur *m*.

factory ['fæktərɪ] *n* fabrique *f*, usine *f*.

factual ['fæktʃʊəl] *adj* factuel(elle), basé(e) sur les faits.

faculty ['fækltɪ] *n* [gen] faculté *f*. || *Am* [in college]: **the ~** le corps enseignant.

fad [fæd] *n* engouement *m*, mode *f*; [personal] marotte *f*.

fade [feɪd] **1** *vt* [jeans, curtains, paint] décolorer. **2** *vi* [jeans, curtains, paint] se décolorer; [colour] passer; [flower] se flétrir. || [light] baisser, diminuer. || [sound] diminuer, s'affaiblir. || [memory] s'effacer; [feeling, interest] diminuer.

faeces *Br*, **feces** *Am* ['fiːsiːz] *npl* fèces *fpl*.

fag [fæg] *n inf Am pej* [homosexual] pédé *m*.

Fahrenheit ['færənhaɪt] *adj* Fahrenheit (*inv*).

fail [feɪl] **1** *vt* [exam, test] rater, échouer à. || [not succeed]: **to ~ to do sthg** ne pas arriver à faire qqch. || [neglect]: **to ~ to do sthg** manquer OR omettre de faire qqch. || [candidate] refuser. **2** *vi* [not succeed] ne pas réussir OR y arriver. || [not pass exam] échouer. || [weaken - health, daylight] décliner; [- eyesight] baisser.

failing ['feɪlɪŋ] **1** *n* [weakness] défaut *m*, point *m* faible. **2** *prep* à moins de; **~ that** à défaut.

failure ['feɪljər] *n* [lack of success, unsuccessful thing] échec *m*. || [person] raté *m*, -e *f*. || [of engine, brake etc] défaillance *f*.

faint [feɪnt] **1** *adj* [smell] léger(ère); [memory] vague; [sound, hope] faible. || [slight - chance] petit(e), faible. || [dizzy]: **I'm feeling a bit ~** je ne me sens pas bien. **2** *vi* s'évanouir.

fair [feər] **1** *adj* [just] juste, équitable. || [quite large] grand(e), important(e). || [quite good] assez bon (assez bonne). || [hair] blond(e). || [skin, complexion] clair(e). || [weather] beau (belle). **2** *n* [trade fair] foire *f*. **3** *adv* [fairly] loyalement.

fair-haired [-'heəd] *adj* [person] blond(e).

fairly ['feəlɪ] *adv* [rather] assez; **~ certain** presque sûr. || [justly] équitablement; [describe] avec impartialité; [fight, play] loyalement.

fairness ['feənɪs] *n* [justness] équité *f*.

fairy ['feərɪ] *n* [imaginary creature] fée *f*.

fairy tale *n* conte *m* de fées.

faith [feɪθ] *n* [belief] foi *f*, confiance *f*. || RELIG foi *f*.

faithful ['feɪθfʊl] *adj* fidèle.

faithfully ['feɪθfʊlɪ] *adv* [loyally] fidèlement.

fake [feɪk] **1** *adj* faux (fausse). **2** *n* [object, painting] faux *m*. || [person] imposteur *m*. **3** *vt* [results] falsifier; [signature] imiter. || [illness, emotions] simuler. **4** *vi* [pretend] simuler, faire semblant.

falcon ['fɔːlkən] *n* faucon *m*.

Falkland Islands ['fɔːklənd-], **Falklands** ['fɔːkləndz] *npl*: **the ~** les îles *fpl* Falkland, les Malouines *fpl*.

fall [fɔːl] (*pt* fell, *pp* fallen) **1** *vi* [gen] tomber; **to ~ flat** [joke] tomber à plat. || [decrease] baisser. || [become]: **to ~ asleep** s'endormir; **to ~ in love** tomber amoureux(euse). **2** *n* [gen]: **~ (in)** chute (de). || *Am* [autumn] automne *m*. ○ **falls** *npl* chutes *fpl*. ○ **fall apart** *vi* [disintegrate - book, chair] tomber en morceaux. || *fig* [country] tomber en ruine; [person] s'effondrer. ○ **fall back on** *vt fus* [resort to] se rabattre sur. ○ **fall behind** *vi* [in race] se faire distancer. || [with rent] être en retard; **to ~ behind with one's work** avoir du retard dans son travail. ○ **fall for** *vt fus inf* [fall in love with] tomber amoureux(euse) de. || [trick, lie] se laisser prendre à. ○ **fall in** *vi* [roof, ceiling] s'écrouler, s'affaisser. ○ **fall off** *vi* [branch, handle] se détacher, tomber. || [demand, numbers] baisser, diminuer. ○ **fall out** *vi* [hair, tooth] tomber. || [friends] se brouiller. ○ **fall over 1** *vt fus*: **to ~ over sthg** trébucher sur qqch et tomber. **2** *vi* [person, chair etc] tomber. ○ **fall through** *vi* [plan, deal] échouer.

fallacy ['fæləsı] *n* erreur *f*, idée *f* fausse.

fallen ['fɔːln] *pp* → **fall**.

fallible ['fæləbl] *adj* faillible.

fallout ['fɔːlaʊt] *n* (U) [radiation] retombées *fpl*.

fallout shelter *n* abri *m* antiatomique.

fallow ['fæləʊ] *adj*: **to lie ~** être en jachère.

false [fɔːls] *adj* faux (fausse).

false alarm *n* fausse alerte *f*.

falsely ['fɔːlslı] *adv* à tort; [smile, laugh] faussement.

false teeth *npl* dentier *m*.

falsify ['fɔːlsıfaı] *vt* falsifier.

falter ['fɔːltər] *vi* [move unsteadily] chanceler. || [steps, voice] devenir hésitant(e). || [hesitate, lose confidence] hésiter.

fame [feım] *n* gloire *f*, renommée *f*.

familiar [fə'mıljər] *adj* familier(ière); **~ with sthg** familiarisé(e) avec qqch.

familiarity [fə,mılı'ærətı] *n* (U) [knowledge]: **~ with sthg** connaissance *f* de qqch, familiarité *f* avec qqch.

familiarize, -ise [fə'mıljəraız] *vt*: **to ~ o.s. with sthg** se familiariser avec qqch.

family ['fæmlı] *n* famille *f*.

family doctor *n* médecin *m* de famille.

family planning *n* planning *m* familial; **~ clinic** centre *m* de planning familial.

famine ['fæmın] *n* famine *f*.

famished ['fæmıʃt] *adj inf* [very hungry] affamé(e); **I'm ~!** je meurs de faim!

famous ['feıməs] *adj*: **~ (for)** célèbre (pour).

famously ['feıməslı] *adv dated*: **to get on** OR **along ~** s'entendre comme larrons en foire.

fan [fæn] **1** *n* [of paper, silk] éventail *m*. || [electric or mechanical] ventilateur *m*. || [enthusiast] fan *mf*. **2** *vt* [face] éventer. ○ **fan out** *vi* se déployer.

fanatic [fə'nætık] *n* fanatique *mf*.

fan belt *n* courroie *f* de ventilateur.

fancy ['fænsı] **1** *adj* [elaborate - hat, clothes] extravagant(e); [- food, cakes] raffiné(e). || [expensive - restaurant, hotel] de luxe; [- prices] fantaisiste. **2** *n* [desire, liking] envie *f*, lubie *f*; **to take a ~ to sb** se prendre d'affection pour qqn; **to take a ~ to sthg** se mettre à aimer qqch; **to take sb's ~** faire envie à qqn, plaire à qqn. **3** *vt inf* [want] avoir envie de; **to ~ doing sthg** avoir envie de faire qqch. || *inf* [like]: **I ~ her** elle me plaît. || [imagine]: **~ that!** ça alors!

fancy dress *n* (U) déguisement *m*.

fancy-dress party *n* bal *m* costumé.

fanfare ['fænfeər] *n* fanfare *f*.

fang [fæŋ] *n* [of wolf] croc *m*; [of snake] crochet *m*.

fan heater *n* radiateur *m* soufflant.

fanny ['fænı] *n Am inf* [buttocks] fesses *fpl*.

fantasize, -ise ['fæntəsaız] *vi*: **to ~ (about sthg/about doing sthg)** fantasmer (sur qqch/sur le fait de faire qqch).

fantastic [fæn'tæstık] *adj inf* [wonderful] fantastique, formidable. || [incredible] extraordinaire, incroyable.

fantasy ['fæntəsı] *n* [dream, imaginary event] rêve *m*, fantasme *m*. || (U) [fiction] fiction *f*. || [imagination] fantaisie *f*.

fao (*abbr of* **for the attention of**) à l'attention de.

far [fɑːr] (*compar* **farther** OR **further**, *superl* **farthest** OR **furthest**) **1** *adv* [in distance] loin; **how ~ is it?** c'est à quelle distance?, (est-ce que) c'est loin?; **~ away** OR **off** loin; **as ~ as** jusqu'à. || [in time]: **~ away** OR **off** loin; **so ~** jusqu'à maintenant, jusqu'ici. || [in degree or extent] bien; **as ~ as** autant que; **as ~ as I'm concerned** en ce qui me concerne; **as ~ as possible** autant que possible, dans la mesure du possible; **~ and away, by ~** de loin; **~ from it** loin de là, au contraire. **2** *adj* [extreme]: **the ~ end of the street** l'autre bout de la rue; **the ~ right of the party** l'extrême droite du parti.

faraway ['fɑːrəweı] *adj* lointain(e).

farce [fɑːs] *n* THEATRE farce *f*. || *fig* [disaster] pagaille *f*, vaste rigolade *f*.

farcical ['fɑːsıkl] *adj* grotesque.

fare [feə[r]] *n* [payment] prix *m*, tarif *m*. ‖ *dated* [food] nourriture *f*.

Far East *n*: **the ~** l'Extrême-Orient *m*.

farewell [,feə'wel] **1** *n* adieu *m*. **2** *excl literary* adieu !

farm [fɑːm] **1** *n* ferme *f*. **2** *vt* cultiver.

farmer ['fɑːmə[r]] *n* fermier *m*.

farmhand ['fɑːmhænd] *n* ouvrier *m*, -ière *f* agricole.

farmhouse ['fɑːmhaʊs, *pl* -haʊzɪz] *n* ferme *f*.

farming ['fɑːmɪŋ] *n* (*U*) agriculture *f*; [of animals] élevage *m*.

farm labourer = farmhand.

farmland ['fɑːmlænd] *n* (*U*) terres *fpl* cultivées ou arables.

farmstead ['fɑːmsted] *n Am* ferme *f*.

farm worker = farmhand.

farmyard ['fɑːmjɑːd] *n* cour *f* de ferme.

far-reaching [-'riːtʃɪŋ] *adj* d'une grande portée.

farsighted [,fɑː'saɪtɪd] *adj* [person] prévoyant(e); [plan] élaboré(e) avec clairvoyance. ‖ *Am* [longsighted] hypermétrope.

fart [fɑːt] *v inf* **1** *n* [air] pet *m*. **2** *vi* péter.

farther ['fɑːðə[r]] *compar* → far.

farthest ['fɑːðəst] *superl* → far.

fascinate ['fæsɪneɪt] *vt* fasciner.

fascinating ['fæsɪneɪtɪŋ] *adj* [person, country] fascinant(e); [job] passionnant(e); [idea, thought] très intéressant(e).

fascination [,fæsɪ'neɪʃn] *n* fascination *f*.

fascism ['fæʃɪzm] *n* fascisme *m*.

fashion ['fæʃn] *n* [clothing, style] mode *f*; **to be in/out of ~** être/ne plus être à la mode. ‖ [manner] manière *f*.

fashionable ['fæʃnəbl] *adj* à la mode.

fashion show *n* défilé *m* de mode.

fast [fɑːst] **1** *adj* [rapid] rapide. ‖ [clock, watch] qui avance. **2** *adv* [rapidly] vite. ‖ [firmly] solidement; **to hold ~ to sthg** *lit* & *fig* s'accrocher à qqch; **~ asleep** profondément endormi. **3** *n* jeûne *m*. **4** *vi* jeûner.

fasten ['fɑːsn] **1** *vt* [jacket, bag] fermer; [seat belt] attacher; **to ~ sthg to sthg** attacher qqch à qqch. **2** *vi*: **to ~ on to sb/sthg** se cramponner à qqn/qqch.

fastener ['fɑːsnə[r]] *n* [of bag, necklace] fermoir *m*; [of dress] fermeture *f*.

fastening ['fɑːsnɪŋ] *n* fermeture *f*.

fast food *n* fast food *m*.

fat [fæt] **1** *adj* [overweight] gros (grosse), gras (grasse); **to get ~** grossir. ‖ [not lean - meat] gras (grasse). **2** *n* [flesh, on meat, in food] graisse *f*. ‖ (*U*) [for cooking] matière *f* grasse.

fatal ['feɪtl] *adj* [serious - mistake] fatal(e); [- decision, words] fatidique. ‖ [accident, illness] mortel(elle).

fatality [fə'tælətɪ] *n* [accident victim] mort *m*.

fate [feɪt] *n* [destiny] destin *m*; **to tempt ~** tenter le diable. ‖ [result, end] sort *m*.

fateful ['feɪtfʊl] *adj* fatidique.

father ['fɑːðə[r]] *n* père *m*.

father-in-law (*pl* father-in-laws OR fathers-in-law) *n* beau-père *m*.

fatherly ['fɑːðəlɪ] *adj* paternel(elle).

fathom ['fæðəm] **1** *n* brasse *f*. **2** *vt*: **~ sb/sthg (out)** comprendre qqn/qqch.

fatigue [fə'tiːg] *n* [exhaustion] épuisement *m*. ‖ [in metal] fatigue *f*.

fatten ['fætn] *vt* engraisser.

fattening ['fætnɪŋ] *adj* qui fait grossir.

fatty ['fætɪ] **1** *adj* gras (grasse). **2** *n inf pej* gros *m*, grosse *f*.

faucet ['fɔːsɪt] *n Am* robinet *m*.

fault ['fɔːlt] **1** *n* [responsibility, in tennis] faute *f*; **it's my ~** c'est de ma faute. ‖ [mistake, imperfection] défaut *m*; **to find ~ with sb/sthg** critiquer qqn/qqch; **at ~** fautif(ive). ‖ GEOL faille *f*. **2** *vt*: **to ~ sb (on sthg)** prendre qqn en défaut (sur qqch).

faultless ['fɔːltlɪs] *adj* impeccable.

faulty ['fɔːltɪ] *adj* défectueux(euse).

fauna ['fɔːnə] *n* faune *f*.

favour *Br*, **favor** *Am* ['feɪvə[r]] **1** *n* [approval] faveur *f*, approbation *f*; **in sb's ~** en faveur de qqn; **to be in/out of ~ with sb** avoir/ne pas avoir les faveurs de qqn, avoir/ne pas avoir la cote avec qqn. ‖ [kind act] service *m*; **to do sb a ~** rendre (un) service à qqn. **2** *vt* [prefer] préférer, privilégier. ‖ [treat better, help] favoriser. ○ **in favour** *adv* [in agreement] pour, d'accord. ○ **in favour of** *prep* [in preference to] au profit de. ‖ [in agreement with]: **to be in ~ of sthg/of doing sthg** être partisan(e) de qqch/de faire qqch.

favourable *Br*, **favorable** *Am* ['feɪvrəbl] *adj* [positive] favorable.

favourite *Br*, **favorite** *Am* ['feɪvrɪt] **1** *adj* favori(ite). **2** *n* favori *m*, -ite *f*.

favouritism *Br*, **favoritism** *Am* ['feɪvrɪtɪzm] *n* favoritisme *m*.

fawn [fɔːn] **1** *adj* fauve (*inv*). **2** *n* [animal] faon *m*.

fax [fæks] **1** *n* fax *m*, télécopie *f*. **2** *vt* [person] envoyer un fax à. ‖ [document] envoyer en fax.

ferris wheel

fax machine n fax m, télécopieur m.

FBI (abbr of **Federal Bureau of Investigation**) n FBI m.

fear [fɪər] **1** n (U) [feeling] peur f. || [object of fear] crainte f. || [risk] risque m; **for ~ of** de peur de (+ infin), de peur que (+ subjunctive). **2** vt [be afraid of] craindre, avoir peur de. || [anticipate] craindre; **to ~ (that)** ... craindre que ..., avoir peur que ....

fearful ['fɪəful] adj fml [frightened] peureux(euse); **to be ~ of sthg** avoir peur de qqch. || [frightening] effrayant(e).

fearless ['fɪəlɪs] adj intrépide.

feasible ['fiːzəbl] adj faisable, possible.

feast [fiːst] **1** n [meal] festin m, banquet m. **2** vi: **to ~ on** OR **off sthg** se régaler de qqch.

feat [fiːt] n exploit m, prouesse f.

feather ['feðər] n plume f.

feature ['fiːtʃər] **1** n [characteristic] caractéristique f. || GEOGR particularité f. || [article] article m de fond. || RADIO & TV émission f spéciale, spécial m. || CINEMA long métrage m. **2** vt [subj: film, exhibition] mettre en vedette. || [comprise] présenter, comporter. **3** vi: **to ~ (in)** figurer en vedette (dans). ○ **features** npl [of face] traits mpl.

feature film n long métrage m.

February ['februərɪ] n février m; see also **September**.

feces Am = **faeces**.

fed [fed] pt & pp → **feed**.

federal ['fedrəl] adj fédéral(e).

federation [,fedə'reɪʃn] n fédération f.

fed up adj: **to be ~ (with)** en avoir marre (de).

fee [fiː] n [of school] frais mpl; [of doctor] honoraires mpl; [for membership] cotisation f; [for entrance] tarif m, prix m.

feeble ['fiːbl] adj faible.

feed [fiːd] (pt & pp **fed**) **1** vt [give food to] nourrir. || [fire, fears etc] alimenter. || [put, insert]: **to ~ sthg into sthg** mettre OR insérer qqch dans qqch. **2** vi [take food]: **to ~ (on** OR **off)** se nourrir (de). **3** n [for baby] repas m. || [animal food] nourriture f.

feedback ['fiːdbæk] n (U) [reaction] réactions fpl.

feel [fiːl] (pt & pp **felt**) **1** vt [touch] toucher. || [sense, experience, notice] sentir; [emotion] ressentir; **to ~ sthg doing sthg** sentir faire qqch. || [believe]: **to ~ (that)** ... croire que ..., penser que .... **2** vi [have sensation]: **to ~ cold/hot/sleepy** avoir froid/chaud/sommeil; **to ~ like sthg/like doing sthg** [be in mood for] avoir envie de qqch/de faire qqch. || [have emotion] se sentir; **to ~ angry** être en colère. || [seem] sembler; **it ~s strange** ça fait drôle. || [by touch]: **to ~ for sthg** chercher qqch. **3** n [sensation, touch] toucher m, sensation f. || [atmosphere] atmosphère f.

feeler ['fiːlər] n antenne f.

feeling ['fiːlɪŋ] n [emotion] sentiment m. || [physical sensation] sensation f. || [intuition, sense] sentiment m, impression f. || [understanding] sensibilité f. ○ **feelings** npl sentiments mpl; **to hurt sb's ~s** blesser (la sensibilité de) qqn.

feet [fiːt] pl → **foot**.

fell [fel] **1** pt → **fall**. **2** vt [tree, person] abattre. ○ **fells** npl GEOGR lande f.

fellow ['feləu] **1** n dated [man] homme m. || [comrade, peer] camarade m, compagnon m. || [of society, college] membre m, associé m. **2** adj: **one's ~ men** ses semblables; **~ student** camarade mf (d'études).

fellowship ['feləuʃɪp] n [comradeship] amitié f, camaraderie f. || [society] association f, corporation f. || [of society, college] titre m de membre OR d'associé.

felony ['felənɪ] n JUR crime m, forfait m.

felt [felt] **1** pt & pp → **feel**. **2** n (U) feutre m.

felt-tip pen n stylo-feutre m.

female ['fiːmeɪl] **1** adj [person] de sexe féminin; [animal, plant] femelle; [sex, figure] féminin(e); **~ student** étudiante f. **2** n femelle f.

feminine ['femɪnɪn] **1** adj féminin(e). **2** n GRAMM féminin m.

feminist ['femɪnɪst] n féministe mf.

fence [fens] **1** n [barrier] clôture f. **2** vt clôturer, entourer d'une clôture.

fencing ['fensɪŋ] n SPORT escrime f.

fend [fend] vi: **to ~ for o.s.** se débrouiller tout seul. ○ **fend off** vt sep [blows] parer; [questions, reporters] écarter.

fender ['fendər] n [round fireplace] pare-feu m inv. || Am [on car] aile f.

ferment [n 'fɜːment, vb fə'ment] **1** n (U) [unrest] agitation f, effervescence f. **2** vi [wine, beer] fermenter.

fern [fɜːn] n fougère f.

ferocious [fə'rəuʃəs] adj féroce.

ferret ['ferɪt] n furet m. ○ **ferret about**, **ferret around** vi inf fureter un peu partout.

ferris wheel ['ferɪs-] n grande roue f.

ferry ['ferɪ] **1** *n* ferry *m*, ferry-boat *m*; [smaller] bac *m*. **2** *vt* transporter.

ferryboat ['ferɪbəʊt] *n* = ferry.

fertile ['fɜːtaɪl] *adj* [land, imagination] fertile, fécond(e). || [woman] féconde.

fertilizer ['fɜːtɪlaɪzər] *n* engrais *m*.

fervent ['fɜːvənt] *adj* fervent(e).

fester ['festər] *vi* [wound, sore] suppurer.

festival ['festəvl] *n* [event, celebration] festival *m*. || [holiday] fête *f*.

festive ['festɪv] *adj* de fête.

festive season *n*: the ~ la période des fêtes.

festivities [fes'tɪvətɪz] *npl* réjouissances *fpl*.

fetch [fetʃ] *vt* [go and get] aller chercher. || [raise - money] rapporter.

fete, fête [feɪt] *n* fête *f*, kermesse *f*.

fetish ['fetɪʃ] *n* [sexual obsession] objet *m* de fétichisme. || [mania] manie *f*, obsession *f*.

fetus ['fiːtəs] = foetus.

feud [fjuːd] **1** *n* querelle *f*. **2** *vi* se quereller.

feudal ['fjuːdl] *adj* féodal(e).

fever ['fiːvər] *n* fièvre *f*.

feverish ['fiːvərɪʃ] *adj* fiévreux(euse).

few [fjuː] **1** *adj* peu de; **the first ~ pages** les toutes premières pages; **quite a ~, a good ~** pas mal de, un bon nombre de. **2** *pron* peu; **a ~** quelques-uns *mpl*, quelques-unes *fpl*.

fewer ['fjuːər] **1** *adj* moins (de). **2** *pron* moins.

fewest ['fjuːəst] *adj* le moins (de).

fiancé [fɪ'ɒnseɪ] *n* fiancé *m*.

fiancée [fɪ'ɒnseɪ] *n* fiancée *f*.

fiasco [fɪ'æskəʊ] (*Br pl* -s, *Am pl* -es) *n* fiasco *m*.

fib [fɪb] *inf* **1** *n* bobard *m*, blague *f*. **2** *vi* raconter des bobards ou des blagues.

fibre *Br*, **fiber** *Am* ['faɪbər] *n* fibre *f*.

fibreglass *Br*, **fiberglass** *Am* ['faɪbəɡlɑːs] *n* (*U*) fibre *f* de verre.

fickle ['fɪkl] *adj* versatile.

fiction ['fɪkʃn] *n* fiction *f*.

fictional ['fɪkʃənl] *adj* fictif(ive).

fictitious [fɪk'tɪʃəs] *adj* [false] fictif(ive).

fiddle ['fɪdl] **1** *vi* [play around]: **to ~ with sthg** tripoter qqch. **2** *n* [violin] violon *m*.

fidget ['fɪdʒɪt] *vi* remuer.

field [fiːld] *n* [gen & COMPUT] champ *m*. || [for sports] terrain *m*. || [of knowledge] domaine *m*.

field day *n*: **to have a ~** s'en donner à cœur joie.

field glasses *npl* jumelles *fpl*.

field marshal *n* ≃ maréchal *m* (de France).

field trip *n* voyage *m* d'étude.

fieldwork ['fiːldwɜːk] *n* (*U*) recherches *fpl* sur le terrain.

fiend [fiːnd] *n* [cruel person] monstre *m*. || *inf* [fanatic] fou *m*, folle *f*, mordu *m*, -e *f*.

fierce [fɪəs] *adj* féroce; [heat] torride; [storm, temper] violent(e).

fiery ['faɪərɪ] *adj* [burning] ardent(e). || [volatile - speech] enflammé(e); [- temper, person] fougueux(euse).

fifteen [fɪf'tiːn] *num* quinze; *see also* **six**.

fifth [fɪfθ] *num* cinquième; *see also* **sixth**.

fifty ['fɪftɪ] *num* cinquante; *see also* **sixty**.

fifty-fifty **1** *adj* moitié-moitié, fifty-fifty; **to have a ~ chance** avoir cinquante pour cent de chances. **2** *adv* moitié-moitié, fifty-fifty.

fig [fɪɡ] *n* figue *f*.

fight [faɪt] (*pt* & *pp* **fought**) **1** *n* [physical] bagarre *f*; **to have a ~ (with sb)** se battre (avec qqn), se bagarrer (avec qqn). || *fig* [battle, struggle] lutte *f*, combat *m*. || [argument] dispute *f*; **to have a ~ (with sb)** se disputer (avec qqn). **2** *vt* [physically] se battre contre ou avec. || [conduct - war] mener. || [enemy, racism] combattre. **3** *vi* [in war, punch-up] se battre. || *fig* [struggle]: **to ~ for/against sthg** lutter pour/contre qqch. || [argue]: **to ~ (about ou over)** se battre ou se disputer (à propos de). ○ **fight back 1** *vt fus* refouler. **2** *vi* riposter.

fighter ['faɪtər] *n* [plane] avion *m* de chasse, chasseur *m*. || [soldier] combattant *m*.

fighting ['faɪtɪŋ] *n* (*U*) [punch-up] bagarres *fpl*; [in war] conflits *mpl*.

figment ['fɪɡmənt] *n*: **a ~ of sb's imagination** le fruit de l'imagination de qqn.

figurative ['fɪɡərətɪv] *adj* [meaning] figuré(e).

figure [*Br* 'fɪɡər, *Am* 'fɪɡjər] **1** *n* [statistic, number] chiffre *m*. || [human shape, outline] silhouette *f*, forme *f*. || [personality, diagram] figure *f*. || [shape of body] ligne *f*. **2** *vt* [suppose] penser, supposer. **3** *vi* [feature] figurer, apparaître. ○ **figure**

out *vt sep* [understand] comprendre; [find] trouver.

figurehead ['fɪgəhed] *n* [on ship] figure *f* de proue. || *fig & pej* [leader] homme *m* de paille.

figure of speech *n* figure *f* de rhétorique.

file [faɪl] **1** *n* [folder, report] dossier *m*. || COMPUT fichier *m*. || [tool] lime *f*. || [line]: **in single ∼** en file indienne. **2** *vt* [document] classer. || [JUR - accusation, complaint] porter, déposer; [- lawsuit] intenter. || [fingernails, wood] limer. **3** *vi* [walk in single file] marcher en file indienne. || JUR: **to ∼ for divorce** demander le divorce.

filet *Am* = fillet.

filing cabinet ['faɪlɪŋ-] *n* classeur *m*, fichier *m*.

Filipino [,fɪlɪ'piːnəʊ] (*pl* -s) **1** *adj* philippin(e). **2** *n* Philippin *m*, -e *f*.

fill [fɪl] **1** *vt* [gen] remplir; **to ∼ sthg with sthg** remplir qqch de qqch. || [gap, hole] boucher. || [vacancy - subj: employer] pourvoir à; [- subj: employee] prendre. **2** *n*: **to eat one's ∼** manger à sa faim. ○ **fill in 1** *vt sep* [form] remplir. || [inform]: **to ∼ sb in (on)** mettre qqn au courant (de). **2** *vi* [substitute]: **to ∼ in for sb** remplacer qqn. ○ **fill out 1** *vt sep* [form] remplir. **2** *vi* [get fatter] prendre de l'embonpoint. ○ **fill up 1** *vt sep* remplir. **2** *vi* se remplir.

fillet *Br*, **filet** *Am* ['fɪlɪt] *n* filet *m*.

fillet steak *n* filet *m* de bœuf.

filling ['fɪlɪŋ] **1** *adj* qui rassasie, très nourrissant(e). **2** *n* [in tooth] plombage *m*. || [in cake, sandwich] garniture *f*.

filling station *n* station-service *f*.

film [fɪlm] **1** *n* [movie] film *m*. || [layer, for camera] pellicule *f*. || [footage] images *fpl*. **2** *vt & vi* filmer.

film star *n* vedette *f* de cinéma.

filter ['fɪltər] **1** *n* filtre *m*. **2** *vt* [coffee] passer; [water, oil, air] filtrer.

filter coffee *n* café *m* filtre.

filter-tipped [-'tɪpt] *adj* à bout filtre.

filth [fɪlθ] *n* (*U*) [dirt] saleté *f*, crasse *f*. || [obscenity] obscénités *fpl*.

filthy ['fɪlθɪ] *adj* [very dirty] dégoûtant(e), répugnant(e). || [obscene] obscène.

fin [fɪn] *n* [of fish] nageoire *f*.

final ['faɪnl] **1** *adj* [last] dernier(ière). || [at end] final(e). || [definitive] définitif(ive). **2** *n* finale *f*. ○ **finals** *npl* UNIV examens *mpl* de dernière année.

finale [fɪ'nɑːlɪ] *n* finale *m*.

finalize, -ise ['faɪnəlaɪz] *vt* mettre au point.

finally ['faɪnəlɪ] *adv* enfin.

finance [*n* 'faɪnæns, *vb* faɪ'næns] **1** (*U*) finance *f*. **2** *vt* financer. ○ **finances** *npl* finances *fpl*.

financial [fɪ'nænʃl] *adj* financier(ière).

find [faɪnd] (*pt & pp* found) **1** *vt* [gen] trouver. || [realize]: **to ∼ (that) ...** s'apercevoir que .... || JUR: **to be found guilty/not guilty (of)** être déclaré(e) coupable/non coupable (de). **2** *n* trouvaille *f*. ○ **find out 1** *vi* se renseigner. **2** *vt fus* [information] se renseigner sur. || [truth] découvrir, apprendre. **3** *vt sep* démasquer.

findings ['faɪndɪŋz] *npl* conclusions *fpl*.

fine [faɪn] **1** *adj* [good - work] excellent(e); [- building, weather] beau (belle). || [perfectly satisfactory] très bien; **I'm ∼** ça va bien. || [thin, smooth] fin(e). || [minute - detail, distinction] subtil(e); [- adjustment, tuning] délicat(e). **2** *adv* [very well] très bien. **3** *n* amende *f*. **4** *vt* condamner à une amende.

fine arts *npl* beaux-arts *mpl*.

fine-tune *vt* [mechanism] régler au quart de tour; *fig* régler minutieusement.

finger ['fɪŋgər] **1** *n* doigt *m*. **2** *vt* [feel] palper.

fingernail ['fɪŋgəneɪl] *n* ongle *m* (*de la main*).

fingerprint ['fɪŋgəprɪnt] *n* empreinte *f* (digitale).

fingertip ['fɪŋgətɪp] *n* bout *m* du doigt; **at one's ∼s** sur le bout des doigts.

finish ['fɪnɪʃ] **1** *n* [end] fin *f*; [of race] arrivée *f*. || [texture] finition *f*. **2** *vt* finir, terminer; **to ∼ doing sthg** finir OU terminer de faire qqch. **3** *vi* finir, terminer; [school, film] se terminer. ○ **finish off** *vt sep* finir, terminer. ○ **finish up** *vi* finir.

finishing line ['fɪnɪʃɪŋ-] *n* ligne *f* d'arrivée.

finishing school ['fɪnɪʃɪŋ-] *n* école privée pour jeunes filles surtout axée sur l'enseignement de bonnes manières.

finite ['faɪnaɪt] *adj* fini(e).

Finland ['fɪnlənd] *n* Finlande *f*.

Finn [fɪn] *n* Finlandais *m*, -e *f*.

Finnish ['fɪnɪʃ] **1** *adj* finlandais(e), finnois(e). **2** *n* [language] finnois *m*.

fir [fɜːr] *n* sapin *m*.

fire ['faɪər] **1** *n* [gen] feu *m*; **on ∼** en feu; **to catch ∼** prendre feu; **to set ∼ to sthg** mettre le feu à qqch. || [out of control] incendie *m*. || (*U*) [shooting] coups *mpl* de feu; **to open ~ (on)** ouvrir le feu (sur). **2** *vt* [shoot] tirer. ‖ [dismiss] renvoyer. **3** *vi*: **to ~ (on** OR **at)** faire feu (sur), tirer (sur).

fire alarm *n* avertisseur *m* d'incendie.

firearm ['faɪrɑːm] *n* arme *f* à feu.

firebomb ['faɪəbɒm] **1** *n* bombe *f* incendiaire. **2** *vt* lancer des bombes incendiaires à.

fire brigade *Br*, **fire department** *Am n* sapeurs-pompiers *mpl*.

fire door *n* porte *f* coupe-feu.

fire engine *n* voiture *f* de pompiers.

fire escape *n* escalier *m* de secours.

fire extinguisher *n* extincteur *m* d'incendie.

fireguard ['faɪəgɑːd] *n* garde-feu *m inv*.

firelighter ['faɪəlaɪtə*r*] *n* allume-feu *m inv*.

fireman ['faɪəmən] (*pl* **-men** [-mən]) *n* pompier *m*.

fireplace ['faɪəpleɪs] *n* cheminée *f*.

fireproof ['faɪəpruːf] *adj* ignifugé(e).

fireside ['faɪəsaɪd] *n*: **by the ~** au coin du feu.

fire station *n* caserne *f* des pompiers.

firewood ['faɪəwʊd] *n* bois *m* de chauffage.

firework ['faɪəwɜːk] *n* fusée *f* de feu d'artifice.

firing ['faɪərɪŋ] *n* (*U*) MIL tir *m*, fusillade *f*.

firing squad *n* peloton *m* d'exécution.

firm [fɜːm] **1** *adj* [gen] ferme; **to stand ~** tenir bon. ‖ [support, structure] solide. ‖ [evidence, news] certain(e). **2** *n* firme *f*, société *f*.

first [fɜːst] **1** *adj* premier(ière); **for the ~ time** pour la première fois; **~ thing in the morning** tôt le matin. **2** *adv* [before anyone else] en premier. ‖ [before anything else] d'abord; **~ of all** tout d'abord. ‖ [for the first time] (pour) la première fois. **3** *n* [person] premier *m*, -ière *f*. ‖ [unprecedented event] première *f*. ○ **at first** *adv* d'abord. ○ **at first hand** *adv* de première main.

first aid *n* (*U*) premiers secours *mpl*.

first-aid kit *n* trousse *f* de premiers secours.

first-class *adj* [excellent] excellent(e). ‖ [ticket, compartment] de première classe; [stamp, letter] tarif normal.

first floor *n Br* premier étage *m*; *Am* rez-de-chaussée *m inv*.

firsthand [fɜːst'hænd] *adj* & *adv* de première main.

first lady *n* première dame *f* du pays.

firstly ['fɜːstlɪ] *adv* premièrement.

first name *n* prénom *m*.

first-rate *adj* excellent(e).

firtree ['fɜːtriː] = **fir**.

fish [fɪʃ] (*pl inv*) **1** *n* poisson *m*. **2** *vi* [fisherman]: **to ~ (for sthg)** pêcher (qqch).

fishbowl ['fɪʃbəʊl] *n* bocal *m* (à poissons).

fishcake ['fɪʃkeɪk] *n* croquette *f* de poisson.

fisherman ['fɪʃəmən] (*pl* **-men** [-mən]) *n* pêcheur *m*.

fish fingers *Br*, **fish sticks** *Am npl* bâtonnets *mpl* de poisson panés.

fishing ['fɪʃɪŋ] *n* pêche *f*; **to go ~** aller à la pêche.

fishing boat *n* bateau *m* de pêche.

fishing line *n* ligne *f*.

fishing rod *n* canne *f* à pêche.

fishmonger ['fɪʃmʌŋgə*r*] *n* poissonnier *m*, -ière *f*; **~'s (shop)** poissonnerie *f*.

fish sticks *Am* = **fish fingers**.

fishy ['fɪʃɪ] *adj* [smell, taste] de poisson. ‖ [suspicious] louche.

fist [fɪst] *n* poing *m*.

fit [fɪt] **1** *adj* [suitable] convenable; **to be ~ for sthg** être bon (bonne) à qqch. ‖ [healthy] en forme; **to keep ~** se maintenir en forme. **2** *n* [of clothes, shoes etc] ajustement *m*; **it's a tight ~** c'est un peu juste; **it's a good ~** c'est la bonne taille. ‖ [epileptic seizure] crise *f*; **to have a ~** avoir une crise; *fig* piquer une crise. ‖ [bout - of crying] crise *f*; [- of rage] accès *m*; [- of sneezing] suite *f*; **in ~s and starts** par à-coups. **3** *vt* [be correct size for] aller à. ‖ [place]: **to ~ sthg into sthg** insérer qqch dans qqch. ‖ [provide]: **to ~ sthg with sthg** équiper OR munir qqch de qqch. ‖ [be suitable for] correspondre à. **4** *vi* [be correct size, go] aller; [into container] entrer. ○ **fit in 1** *vt sep* [accommodate] prendre. **2** *vi* s'intégrer; **to ~ in with sthg** correspondre à qqch; **to ~ in with sb** s'accorder à qqn.

fitful ['fɪtfʊl] *adj* [sleep] agité(e); [wind, showers] intermittent(e).

fitness ['fɪtnɪs] *n* (*U*) [health] forme *f*. ‖ [suitability]: **~ (for)** aptitude *f* (pour).

fitted carpet [,fɪtəd-] *n* moquette *f*.

fitter ['fɪtə*r*] *n* [mechanic] monteur *m*.

fitting ['fɪtɪŋ] **1** *adj fml* approprié(e). **2** *n* [part] appareil *m*. ‖ [for clothing] essayage *m*. ○ **fittings** *npl* installations *fpl*.

fitting room *n* cabine *f* d'essayage.

flavour

five [faɪv] *num* cinq; *see also* **six**.

fiver ['faɪvər] *n inf Am* [amount] cinq dollars *mpl*; [note] billet *m* de cinq dollars.

fix [fɪks] **1** *vt* [gen] fixer; **to ~ sthg to sthg** fixer qqch à qqch. || [in memory] graver. || [repair] réparer. || *inf* [rig] truquer. || [food, drink] préparer. **2** *n inf* [difficult situation]: **to be in a ~** être dans le pétrin. || [drugs *sl*] piqûre *f*. ○ **fix up** *vt sep* [provide]: **to ~ sb up with sthg** obtenir qqch pour qqn. || [arrange] arranger.

fixation [fɪk'seɪʃn] *n*: ~ **(on** OR **about)** obsession *f* (de).

fixed [fɪkst] *adj* [attached] fixé(e). || [set, unchanging] fixe; [smile] figé(e).

fixture ['fɪkstʃər] *n* [furniture] installation *f*. || [permanent feature] tradition *f* bien établie. || SPORT rencontre *f* (sportive).

fizz [fɪz] *vi* [lemonade, champagne] pétiller; [fireworks] crépiter.

fizzle ['fɪzl] ○ **fizzle out** *vi* [fire] s'éteindre; [firework] se terminer; [interest, enthusiasm] se dissiper.

fizzy ['fɪzɪ] *adj* pétillant(e).

flabbergasted ['flæbəgɑːstɪd] *adj* sidéré(e).

flabby ['flæbɪ] *adj* mou (molle).

flag [flæg] **1** *n* drapeau *m*. **2** *vi* [person, enthusiasm, energy] faiblir; [conversation] traîner. ○ **flag down** *vt sep* [taxi] héler; **to ~ sb down** faire signe à qqn de s'arrêter.

flagpole ['flægpəʊl] *n* mât *m*.

flagrant ['fleɪgrənt] *adj* flagrant(e).

flagstone ['flægstəʊn] *n* dalle *f*.

flair [fleər] *n* [talent] don *m*. || (*U*) [stylishness] style *m*.

flak [flæk] *n* (*U*) [gunfire] tir *m* antiaérien. || *inf* [criticism] critiques *fpl* sévères.

flake [fleɪk] **1** *n* [of paint, plaster] écaille *f*; [of snow] flocon *m*. **2** *vi* [paint, plaster] s'écailler; [skin] peler.

flamboyant [flæm'bɔɪənt] *adj* [showy, confident] extravagant(e). || [brightly coloured] flamboyant(e).

flame [fleɪm] *n* flamme *f*; **in ~s** en flammes; **to burst into ~s** s'enflammer.

flamingo [flə'mɪŋgəʊ] (*pl* -s OR -es) *n* flamant *m* rose.

flammable ['flæməbl] *adj* inflammable.

flan [flæn] *n* tarte *f*.

flank [flæŋk] **1** *n* flanc *m*. **2** *vt*: **to be ~ed by** être flanqué(e) de.

flannel ['flænl] *n* [fabric] flanelle *f*.

flap [flæp] **1** *n* [of envelope, pocket] rabat *m*; [of skin] lambeau *m*. || *inf* [panic]: **in a ~** paniqué(e). **2** *vt & vi* battre.

flapjack ['flæpdʒæk] *n Am* [pancake] crêpe *f* épaisse.

flare [fleər] **1** *n* [distress signal] fusée *f* éclairante. **2** *vi* [burn brightly]: **to ~ (up)** s'embraser. || [intensify]: **to ~ (up)** [war, revolution] s'intensifier soudainement; [person] s'emporter. || [widen - trousers, skirt] s'évaser; [- nostrils] se dilater.

flash [flæʃ] **1** *n* [of light, colour] éclat *m*; **~ of lightning** éclair *m*. || PHOT flash *m*. || [sudden moment] éclair *m*; **in a ~** en un rien de temps. **2** *vt* [shine] projeter; **to ~ one's headlights** faire un appel de phares. || [send out - signal, smile] envoyer; [- look] jeter. || [show] montrer. **3** *vi* [torch] briller. || [light - on and off] clignoter; [eyes] jeter des éclairs. || [rush]: **to ~ by** OR **past** passer comme un éclair.

flashback ['flæʃbæk] *n* flashback *m*, retour *m* en arrière.

flashbulb ['flæʃbʌlb] *n* ampoule *f* de flash.

flashgun ['flæʃgʌn] *n* flash *m*.

flashlight ['flæʃlaɪt] *n* [torch] lampe *f* électrique.

flashy ['flæʃɪ] *adj inf* tape-à-l'œil (*inv*).

flask [flɑːsk] *n* [thermos flask] thermos® *m* or *f*.

flat [flæt] **1** *adj* [gen] plat(e). || [tyre] crevé(e). || [refusal, denial] catégorique. || [dull - voice, tone] monotone; [- performance, writing] terne. || MUS - person] qui chante trop grave; [- note] bémol. || [beer, lemonade] éventé(e), || [battery] à plat. **2** *adv* [level] à plat. || [exactly]: **two hours ~** deux heures pile. **3** *n* MUS bémol *m*. ○ **flat out** *adv* [work] d'arrache-pied; [travel - subj: vehicle] le plus vite possible.

flatly ['flætlɪ] *adv* [absolutely] catégoriquement. || [dully - say] avec monotonie; [- perform] de façon terne.

flat rate *n* tarif *m* forfaitaire.

flatten ['flætn] *vt* [make flat - steel, paper] aplatir; [- wrinkles, bumps] aplanir. || [destroy] raser. ○ **flatten out 1** *vi* s'aplanir. **2** *vt sep* aplanir.

flatter ['flætər] *vt* flatter.

flattering ['flætərɪŋ] *adj* [complimentary] flatteur(euse). || [clothes] seyant(e).

flattery ['flætərɪ] *n* flatterie *f*.

flaunt [flɔːnt] *vt* faire étalage de.

flavour *Br*, **flavor** *Am* ['fleɪvər] **1** *n* [of food] goût *m*; [of ice cream, yoghurt] parfum *m*. || *fig* [atmosphere] atmosphère *f*. 2 *vt* parfumer.

flavouring *Br*, **flavoring** *Am* ['fleɪvərɪŋ] *n* (*U*) parfum *m*.

flaw [flɔː] *n* [in material, character] défaut *m*; [in plan, argument] faille *f*.

flawless ['flɔːlɪs] *adj* parfait(e).

flea [fliː] *n* puce *f*.

flea market *n* marché *m* aux puces.

fleck [flek] 1 *n* moucheture *f*, petite tache *f*. 2 *vt*: **~ed with** moucheté(e) de.

fled [fled] *pt & pp* → **flee**.

flee [fliː] (*pt & pp* **fled**) *vt & vi* fuir.

fleece [fliːs] 1 *n* toison *f*. 2 *vt inf* escroquer.

fleet [fliːt] *n* [of ships] flotte *f*. || [of cars, buses] parc *m*.

fleeting ['fliːtɪŋ] *adj* [moment] bref (brève); [look] fugitif(ive); [visit] éclair (*inv*).

Flemish ['flemɪʃ] 1 *adj* flamand(e). 2 *n* [language] flamand *m*. 3 *npl*: **the ~** les Flamands *mpl*.

flesh [fleʃ] *n* chair *f*; **his/her ~ and blood** [family] les siens.

flew [fluː] *pt* → **fly**.

flex [fleks] 1 *n* ELEC fil *m*. 2 *vt* [bend] fléchir.

flexible ['fleksəbl] *adj* flexible.

flexitime ['fleksɪtaɪm] *n* (*U*) horaire *m* à la carte OR flexible.

flick [flɪk] 1 *n* [of whip, towel] petit coup *m*. || [with finger] chiquenaude *f*. 2 *vt* [switch] appuyer sur. ○ **flick through** *vt fus* feuilleter.

flicker ['flɪkər] *vi* [candle, light] vaciller. || [shadow] trembler; [eyelids] ciller.

flight [flaɪt] *n* [gen] vol *m*. || [of steps, stairs] volée *f*. || [escape] fuite *f*.

flight attendant *n* steward *m*, hôtesse *f* de l'air.

flight crew *n* équipage *m*.

flight deck *n* [of aircraft carrier] pont *m* d'envol. || [of plane] cabine *f* de pilotage.

flight recorder *n* enregistreur *m* de vol.

flimsy ['flɪmzɪ] *adj* [dress, material] léger(ère); [building, bookcase] peu solide.

flinch [flɪntʃ] *vi* tressaillir; **to ~ from sthg/from doing sthg** reculer devant qqch/à l'idée de faire qqch.

fling [flɪŋ] (*pt & pp* **flung**) 1 *n* [affair] aventure *f*, affaire *f*. 2 *vt* lancer.

flint [flɪnt] *n* [in lighter] pierre *f*.

flip [flɪp] 1 *vt* [turn - pancake] faire sauter; [- record] tourner. || [switch] appuyer sur. 2 *vi inf* [become angry] piquer une

colère. 3 *n* [flick] chiquenaude *f*. || [somersault] saut *m* périlleux. ○ **flip through** *vt fus* feuilleter.

flip-flop *n* [shoe] tong *f*.

flippant ['flɪpənt] *adj* désinvolte.

flipper ['flɪpər] *n* [of animal] nageoire *f*. || [for swimmer, diver] palme *f*.

flirt [flɜːt] 1 *n* flirt *m*. 2 *vi* [with person]: **to ~ (with sb)** flirter (avec qqn).

flirtatious [flɜːˈteɪʃəs] *adj* flirteur(euse).

flit [flɪt] *vi* [bird] voleter.

float [fləʊt] 1 *n* [for buoyancy] flotteur *m*. || [in procession] char *m*. || [money] petite caisse *f*. 2 *vt* [on water] faire flotter. 3 *vi* [on water] flotter; [through air] glisser.

flock [flɒk] *n* [of birds] vol *m*; [of sheep] troupeau *m*. || *fig* [of people] foule *f*.

flog [flɒg] *vt* [whip] flageller.

flood [flʌd] 1 *n* [of water] inondation *f*. || [great amount] déluge *m*, avalanche *f*. 2 *vt* [with water, light] inonder. || [overwhelm]: **to ~ sthg (with)** inonder qqch (de).

flooding ['flʌdɪŋ] *n* (*U*) inondations *fpl*.

floodlight ['flʌdlaɪt] *n* projecteur *m*.

floor [flɔːr] 1 *n* [of room] sol *m*; [of club, disco] piste *f*. || [of valley, sea, forest] fond *m*. || [storey] étage *m*. 2 *vt* [knock down] terrasser. || [baffle] dérouter.

floorboard ['flɔːbɔːd] *n* plancher *m*.

floor show *n* spectacle *m* de cabaret.

flop [flɒp] *inf n* [failure] fiasco *m*.

floppy ['flɒpɪ] *adj* [flower] flasque; [collar] lâche.

floppy (disk) *n* disquette *f*, disque *m* souple.

flora ['flɔːrə] *n* flore *f*.

florid ['flɒrɪd] *adj* [red] rougeaud(e). || [extravagant] fleuri(e).

florist ['flɒrɪst] *n* fleuriste *mf*; **~'s (shop)** magasin *m* de fleuriste.

flotsam ['flɒtsəm] *n* (*U*): **~ and jetsam** débris *mpl*; *fig* épaves *fpl*.

flounder ['flaʊndər] *vi* [in water, mud, snow] patauger. || [in conversation] bredouiller.

flour ['flaʊər] *n* farine *f*.

flourish ['flʌrɪʃ] 1 *vi* [plant, flower] bien pousser; [company, business] prospérer; [arts] s'épanouir. 2 *vt* brandir. 3 *n* grand geste *m*.

flout [flaʊt] *vt* bafouer.

flow [fləʊ] 1 *n* [movement - of water, information] circulation *f*; [- of funds] mouvement *m*; [- of words] flot *m*. || [of tide]

flux *m.* 2 *vi* [gen] couler. || [traffic, days, weeks] s'écouler. || [hair, clothes] flotter.

flow chart, flow diagram *n* organigramme *m.*

flower ['flauə'] 1 *n* fleur *f.* 2 *vi* [bloom] fleurir.

flowerbed ['flauəbed] *n* parterre *m.*

flowerpot ['flauəppt] *n* pot *m* de fleurs.

flowery ['flauərı] *adj* [dress, material] à fleurs. || *pej* [style] fleuri(e).

flown [fləun] *pp* → **fly.**

flu [flu:] *n* (*U*) grippe *f.*

fluctuate ['flʌktʃueɪt] *vi* fluctuer.

fluency ['flu:ənsı] *n* aisance *f.*

fluent ['flu:ənt] *adj* [in foreign language]: **to speak ~ French** parler couramment le français.

fluff [flʌf] *n* (*U*) [down] duvet *m.* || [dust] moutons *mpl.*

fluffy ['flʌfı] *adj* duveteux(euse); [toy] en peluche.

fluid ['flu:ɪd] 1 *n* fluide *m*; [in diet, for cleaning] liquide *m.* 2 *adj* [flowing] fluide.

fluid ounce *n = 0,03 litre.*

fluke [flu:k] *n inf* [chance] coup *m* de bol.

flung [flʌŋ] *pt & pp* → **fling.**

flunk [flʌŋk] *inf vt* [exam, test] rater. || [student] recaler.

fluorescent [fluə'resənt] *adj* fluorescent(e).

fluoride ['fluəraɪd] *n* fluorure *m.*

flurry ['flʌrı] *n* [of rain, snow] rafale *f.* || [of activity, excitement] débordement *m.*

flush [flʌʃ] 1 *adj* [level]: **~ with** de niveau avec. 2 *n* [in lavatory] chasse *f* d'eau. || [blush] rougeur *f.* || [sudden feeling] accès *m.* 3 *vt* [toilet]: **to ~ the toilet** tirer la chasse d'eau. 4 *vi* [blush] rougir.

flushed [flʌʃt] *adj* [red-faced] rouge. || [excited]: **~ with** exalté(e) par.

flustered ['flʌstəd] *adj* troublé(e).

flute [flu:t] *n* MUS flûte *f.*

flutter ['flʌtə'] 1 *n* [of wings] battement *m.* || *inf* [of excitement] émoi *m.* 2 *vi* [bird, insect] voleter; [wings] battre. || [flag, dress] flotter.

flux [flʌks] *n* [change]: **to be in a state of ~** être en proie à des changements permanents.

fly [flaı] (*pt* flew, *pp* flown) 1 *n* [insect] mouche *f.* || [of trousers] braguette *f.* 2 *vt* [kite, plane] faire voler. || [passengers, supplies] transporter par avion. || [flag] faire flotter. 3 *vi* [bird, insect, plane] voler. || [pilot] faire voler un avion. || [passenger] voyager en avion. || [move fast,

pass quickly] filer. || [flag] flotter. O **fly away** *vi* s'envoler.

flying ['flaıŋ] *n*: **to like ~** aimer prendre l'avion.

flying colours *npl*: **to pass (sthg) with ~** réussir (qqch) haut la main.

flying picket *n* piquet *m* de grève volant.

flying saucer *n* soucoupe *f* volante.

flying start *n*: **to get off to a ~** prendre un départ sur les chapeaux de roue.

flying visit *n* visite *f* éclair.

flysheet ['flaıʃi:t] *n* auvent *m.*

fly spray *n* insecticide *m.*

FM (*abbr of* **frequency modulation**) *n* FM *f.*

foal [fəul] *n* poulain *m.*

foam [fəum] 1 *n* (*U*) [bubbles] mousse *f.* || **~ (rubber)** caoutchouc *m* mousse. 2 *vi* [water, champagne] mousser.

fob [fɒb] O **fob off** *vt sep* repousser; **to ~ sthg off on sb** refiler qqch à qqn; **to ~ sb off with sthg** se débarrasser de qqn à l'aide de qqch.

focal point ['fəukl-] *n* foyer *m*; *fig* point *m* central.

focus ['fəukəs] (*pl* -cuses OR -ci [-kaı]) 1 *n* PHOT mise *f* au point; **in ~** net; **out of ~** flou. || [centre - of rays] foyer *m*; [- of earthquake] centre *m.* 2 *vt* [lens, camera] mettre au point. 3 *vi* [with camera, lens] se fixer; [eyes] accommoder; **to ~ on sthg** [with camera, lens] se fixer sur qqch; [with eyes] fixer qqch. || [attention]: **to ~ on sthg** se concentrer sur qqch.

fodder ['fɒdə'] *n* (*U*) fourrage *m.*

foe [fəu] *n literary* ennemi *m.*

foetus ['fi:təs] *n* fœtus *m.*

fog [fɒg] *n* (*U*) brouillard *m.*

foggy ['fɒgı] *adj* [misty] brumeux(euse).

foghorn ['fɒghɔ:n] *n* sirène *f* de brume.

fog lamp *n* feu *m* de brouillard.

foible ['fɔıbl] *n* marotte *f.*

foil [fɔıl] 1 *n* (*U*) [metal sheet - of tin, silver] feuille *f*; [- CULIN] papier *m* d'aluminium. 2 *vt* déjouer.

fold [fəuld] 1 *vt* [bend, close up] plier; **to ~ one's arms** croiser les bras. || [wrap] envelopper. 2 *vi* [close up - table, chair] se plier; [- petals, leaves] se refermer. || *inf* [company, project] échouer; THEATRE quitter l'affiche. 3 *n* [in material, paper] pli *m.* || [for animals] parc *m.* || *fig* [spiritual home]: **the ~** le bercail. O **fold up** *vt sep* plier. 2 *vi* [close up - table, map] se plier; [- petals, leaves] se refermer. || [company, project] échouer.

folder ['fəʊldər] *n* [for papers - wallet] chemise *f*; [- binder] classeur *m*.

folding ['fəʊldɪŋ] *adj* [table, umbrella] pliant(e); [doors] en accordéon.

foliage ['fəʊlɪdʒ] *n* feuillage *m*.

folk [fəʊk] **1** *adj* [art, dancing] folklorique; [medicine] populaire. **2** *npl* [people] gens *mpl*. ○ **folks** *npl inf* [relatives] famille *f*.

folklore ['fəʊklɔːr] *n* folklore *m*.

folk music *n* musique *f* folk.

folk song *n* chanson *f* folk.

follow ['fɒləʊ] **1** *vt* suivre. **2** *vi* [gen] suivre. || [be logical] tenir debout; **it ~s that** ... il s'ensuit que .... ○ **follow up** *vt sep* [pursue - idea, suggestion] prendre en considération; [- advertisement] donner suite à. || [complete]: **to ~ sthg up with** faire suivre qqch de.

follower ['fɒləʊər] *n* [believer] disciple *mf*.

following ['fɒləʊɪŋ] **1** *adj* suivant(e). **2** *n* groupe *m* d'admirateurs. **3** *prep* après.

folly ['fɒlɪ] *n* (*U*) [foolishness] folie *f*.

fond [fɒnd] *adj* [affectionate] affectueux(euse); **to be ~ of** aimer beaucoup.

fondle ['fɒndl] *vt* caresser.

font [fɒnt] *n* [in church] fonts *mpl* baptismaux. || COMPUT & TYPO police *f* (de caractères).

food [fuːd] *n* nourriture *f*.

food mixer *n* mixer *m*.

food poisoning [-,pɔɪznɪŋ] *n* intoxication *f* alimentaire.

food processor [-,prəʊsesər] *n* robot *m* ménager.

foodstuffs ['fuːdstʌfs] *npl* denrées *fpl* alimentaires.

fool [fuːl] **1** *n* [idiot] idiot *m*, -e *f*. **2** *vt* duper; **to ~ sb into doing sthg** amener qqn à faire qqch en le dupant. ○ **fool about**, **fool around** *vi* [behave foolishly] faire l'imbécile. || [be unfaithful] être infidèle.

foolhardy ['fuːl,hɑːdɪ] *adj* téméraire.

foolish ['fuːlɪʃ] *adj* idiot(e), stupide.

foolproof ['fuːlpruːf] *adj* infaillible.

foot [fʊt] (*pl sense 1* feet, *pl sense 2 inv* OR feet) **1** *n* [gen] pied *m*; [of animal] patte *f*; [of page, stairs] bas *m*; **to get to one's feet** se mettre debout, se lever; **on ~** à pied; **to put one's ~ in it** mettre les pieds dans le plat; **to put one's feet up** se reposer. || [unit of measurement] = *30,48 cm*, ≈ pied *m*. **2** *vt inf*: **to ~ the bill** payer la note.

footage ['fʊtɪdʒ] *n* (*U*) séquences *fpl*.

football ['fʊtbɔːl] *n* [game - soccer] football *m*, foot *m*; [- American football] football américain. || [ball] ballon *m* de football OR foot.

footbrake ['fʊtbreɪk] *n* frein *m* (à pied).

footbridge ['fʊtbrɪdʒ] *n* passerelle *f*.

foothills ['fʊthɪlz] *npl* contreforts *mpl*.

foothold ['fʊthəʊld] *n* prise *f* (de pied).

footing ['fʊtɪŋ] *n* [foothold] prise *f*; **to lose one's ~** trébucher. || *fig* [basis] position *f*.

footlights ['fʊtlaɪts] *npl* rampe *f*.

footnote ['fʊtnəʊt] *n* note *f* en bas de page.

footpath ['fʊtpɑːθ, *pl* -pɑːðz] *n* sentier *m*.

footprint ['fʊtprɪnt] *n* empreinte *f* (de pied), trace *f* (de pas).

footstep ['fʊtstep] *n* [sound] bruit *m* de pas. || [footprint] empreinte *f* (de pied).

footwear ['fʊtweər] *n* (*U*) chaussures *fpl*.

for [fɔːr] **1** *prep* [referring to intention, destination, purpose] pour; **this is ~ you** c'est pour vous; **the plane ~ Paris** l'avion à destination de Paris; **what's it ~?** ça sert à quoi? || [representing, on behalf of] pour; **the MP ~ Barnsley** le député de Barnsley; **let me do that ~ you** laissez-moi faire, je vais vous le faire. || [because of] pour, en raison de; **~ various reasons** pour plusieurs raisons; **a prize ~ swimming** un prix de natation. || [with regard to] pour; **to be ready ~ sthg** être prêt à OR pour qqch; **it's not ~ me to say** ce n'est pas à moi de le dire; **to feel sorry ~ sb** plaindre qqn. || [indicating amount of time, space]: **there's no time ~ that now** on n'a pas le temps de faire cela OR de s'occuper de cela maintenant; **there's room ~ another person** il y a de la place pour encore une personne. || [indicating period of time]: **she'll be away ~ a month** elle sera absente (pendant) un mois; **I've lived here ~ 3 years** j'habite ici depuis 3 ans, cela fait 3 ans que j'habite ici; **I can do it for you ~ tomorrow** je peux vous le faire pour demain. || [indicating distance] pendant, sur; **I walked ~ miles** j'ai marché (pendant) des kilomètres. || [indicating particular occasion] pour; **~ Christmas** pour Noël. || [indicating amount of money, price]: **they're 50p ~ ten** cela coûte 50p les dix; **I bought/sold it ~ £10** je l'ai acheté/vendu 10 livres. || [in favour of, in

forger

support of] pour; **to be all ~ sthg** être tout à fait pour OR en faveur de qqch. || [in ratios] pour. || [indicating meaning]: **P ~ Peter** P comme Peter; **what's the Greek ~ "mother"?** comment dit-on «mère» en grec? **2** *conj fml* [as, since] car. ○ **for all 1** *prep* malgré. **2** *conj* bien que (+ *subjunctive*); **~ all I know** pour ce que j'en sais.

foray ['fɔreɪ] *n*: **~ (into)** *lit* & *fig* incursion *f* (dans).

forbad [fə'bæd], **forbade** [fə'beɪd] *pt* → forbid.

forbid [fə'bɪd] (*pt* **-bade** OR **-bad**, *pp* **forbid** OR **-bidden**) *vt* interdire, défendre; **to ~ sb to do sthg** interdire OR défendre à qqn de faire qqch.

forbidden [fə'bɪdn] **1** *pp* → forbid. **2** *adj* interdit(e), défendu(e).

forbidding [fə'bɪdɪŋ] *adj* [severe, unfriendly] austère; [threatening] sinistre.

force [fɔːs] **1** *n* [gen] force *f*; **by ~ de force.** || [effect]: **to be in/to come into ~** être/entrer en vigueur. **2** *vt* [gen] forcer; **to ~ sb to do sthg** forcer qqn à faire qqch. || [press]: **to ~ sthg on sb** imposer qqch à qqn. ○ **forces** *npl*: **the ~s** les forces *fpl* armées; **to join ~s** joindre ses efforts.

force-feed *vt* nourrir de force.

forceful ['fɔːsful] *adj* [person] énergique; [speech] vigoureux(euse).

forceps ['fɔːseps] *npl* forceps *m*.

forcibly ['fɔːsəblɪ] *adv* [using physical force] de force. || [powerfully] avec vigueur.

ford [fɔːd] *n* gué *m*.

fore [fɔːʳ] **1** *adj* NAUT à l'avant. **2** *n*: **to come to the ~** s'imposer.

forearm ['fɔːrɑːm] *n* avant-bras *m inv*.

foreboding [fɔː'bəʊdɪŋ] *n* pressentiment *m*.

forecast ['fɔːkɑːst] (*pt* & *pp* **forecast** OR **-ed**) **1** *n* prévision *f*; (weather) **~** prévisions météorologiques. **2** *vt* prévoir.

foreclose [fɔː'kləʊz] **1** *vt* saisir. **2** *vi*: **to ~ on sb** saisir qqn.

forecourt ['fɔːkɔːt] *n* [of petrol station] devant *m*; [of building] avant-cour *f*.

forefinger ['fɔːˌfɪŋgəʳ] *n* index *m*.

forefront ['fɔːfrʌnt] *n*: **in** OR **at the ~ of** au premier plan de.

forego [fɔː'gəʊ] = forgo.

foregone conclusion ['fɔːgɒn-] *n*: **it's a ~** c'est couru.

foreground ['fɔːgraʊnd] *n* premier plan *m*.

forehand ['fɔːhænd] *n* TENNIS coup *m* droit.

forehead ['fɔːhed] *n* front *m*.

foreign ['fɒrən] *adj* [gen] étranger(ère); [correspondent] à l'étranger. || [policy, trade] extérieur(e).

foreign affairs *npl* affaires *fpl* étrangères.

foreign currency *n* (U) devises *fpl* étrangères.

foreigner ['fɒrənəʳ] *n* étranger *m*, -ère *f*.

foreign minister *n* ministre *m* des Affaires étrangères.

Foreign Office *n Br*: **the ~** ≃ le ministère des Affaires étrangères.

Foreign Secretary *n Br* ≃ ministre *m* des Affaires étrangères.

foreleg ['fɔːleg] *n* [of horse] membre *m* antérieur; [of other animals] patte *f* de devant.

foreman ['fɔːmən] (*pl* **-men** [-mən]) *n* [of workers] contremaître *m*.

foremost ['fɔːməʊst] **1** *adj* principal(e). **2** *adv*: **first and ~** tout d'abord.

forensic medicine, forensic science *n* médecine *f* légale.

forerunner ['fɔːˌrʌnəʳ] *n* précurseur *m*.

foresee [fɔː'siː] (*pt* **-saw** [-'sɔː], *pp* **-seen**) *vt* prévoir.

foreseeable [fɔː'siːəbl] *adj* prévisible; **for the ~ future** pour tous les jours/mois *etc* à venir.

foreseen [fɔː'siːn] *pp* → foresee.

foreshadow [fɔː'ʃædəʊ] *vt* présager.

foresight ['fɔːsaɪt] *n* (U) prévoyance *f*.

forest ['fɒrɪst] *n* forêt *f*.

forestall [fɔː'stɔːl] *vt* [attempt, discussion] prévenir; [person] devancer.

forestry ['fɒrɪstrɪ] *n* sylviculture *f*.

foretaste ['fɔːteɪst] *n* avant-goût *m*.

foretell [fɔː'tel] (*pt* & *pp* **-told**) *vt* prédire.

foretold [fɔː'təʊld] *pt* & *pp* → foretell.

forever [fə'revəʳ] *adv* [eternally] (pour) toujours.

forewarn [fɔː'wɔːn] *vt* avertir.

foreword ['fɔːwɜːd] *n* avant-propos *m inv*.

forfeit ['fɔːfɪt] **1** *n* amende *f*; [in game] gage *m*. **2** *vt* perdre.

forgave [fə'geɪv] *pt* → forgive.

forge [fɔːdʒ] **1** *n* forge *f*. **2** *vt* INDUSTRY & *fig* forger. || [signature, money] contrefaire; [passport] falsifier. ○ **forge ahead** *vi* prendre de l'avance.

forger ['fɔːdʒəʳ] *n* faussaire *mf*.

forgery ['fɔ:dʒərɪ] *n* (*U*) [crime] contre-façon *f*. || [forged article] faux *m*.

forget [fə'get] (*pt* -got, *pp* -gotten) **1** *vt* oublier; **to ~ to do sthg** oublier de faire qqch; **~ it!** laisse tomber! **2** *vi*: **to ~ (about sthg)** oublier (qqch).

forgetful [fə'getful] *adj* distrait(e), étourdi(e).

forget-me-not *n* myosotis *m*.

forgive [fə'gɪv] (*pt* -gave, *pp* -given [-'gɪvən]) *vt* pardonner; **to ~ sb for sthg/for doing sthg** pardonner qqch à qqn/à qqn d'avoir fait qqch.

forgiveness [fə'gɪvnɪs] *n* (*U*) pardon *m*.

forgo [fɔ:'gəʊ] (*pt* -went, *pp* -gone [-'gɒn]) *vt* renoncer à.

forgot [fə'gɒt] *pt* → forget.

forgotten [fə'gɒtn] *pp* → forget.

fork [fɔ:k] **1** *n* [for eating] fourchette *f*. || [for gardening] fourche *f*. || [in road] bifurcation *f*; [of river] embranchement *m*. **2** *vi* bifurquer. ○ **fork out** *inf* **1** *vt fus* allonger, débourser. **2** *vi*: **to ~ out (for)** casquer (pour).

forklift truck ['fɔ:klɪft-] *n* chariot *m* élévateur.

forlorn [fə'lɔ:n] *adj* [person, face] malheureux(euse), triste. || [place, landscape] désolé(e). || [hope, attempt] désespéré(e).

form [fɔ:m] **1** *n* [shape, fitness, type] forme *f*; **on ~** *Br*, **in ~** *Am* en forme; **off ~** pas en forme; **in the ~ of** sous forme de. || [questionnaire] formulaire *m*. **2** *vt* former. **3** *vi* se former.

formal ['fɔ:ml] *adj* [person] formaliste; [language] soutenu(e). || [dinner party, announcement] officiel(ielle); [dress] de cérémonie.

formality [fɔ:'mælətɪ] *n* formalité *f*.

format ['fɔ:mæt] **1** *n* [gen & COMPUT] format *m*. **2** *vt* COMPUT formater.

formation [fɔ:'meɪʃn] *n* [gen] formation *f*. || [of idea, plan] élaboration *f*.

former ['fɔ:mə*r*] **1** *adj* [previous] ancien(ienne); **~ husband** ex-mari *m*; **~ pupil** ancien élève *m*, ancienne élève *f*. || [first of two] premier(ière). **2** *n*: **the ~** le premier (la première), celui-là (celle-là).

formerly ['fɔ:məlɪ] *adv* autrefois.

formidable ['fɔ:mɪdəbl] *adj* impressionnant(e).

formula ['fɔ:mjʊlə] (*pl* -as OR -ae [-i:]) *n* formule *f*.

formulate ['fɔ:mjʊleɪt] *vt* formuler.

forsaken [fə'seɪkn] *adj* abandonné(e).

fort [fɔ:t] *n* fort *m*.

forte ['fɔ:tɪ] *n* point *m* fort.

forthcoming [fɔ:θ'kʌmɪŋ] *adj* [imminent] à venir. || [helpful] communicatif(ive).

forthright ['fɔ:θraɪt] *adj* franc (franche), direct(e).

fortified wine ['fɔ:tɪfaɪd-] *n* vin *m* de liqueur.

fortify ['fɔ:tɪfaɪ] *vt* MIL fortifier. || *fig* [resolve etc] renforcer.

fortnight ['fɔ:tnaɪt] *n Br* quinze jours *mpl*, quinzaine *f*.

fortnightly ['fɔ:t,naɪtlɪ] *Br* **1** *adj* bimensuel(elle). **2** *adv* tous les quinze jours.

fortress ['fɔ:trɪs] *n* forteresse *f*.

fortunate ['fɔ:tʃnət] *adj* heureux(euse); **to be ~** avoir de la chance.

fortunately ['fɔ:tʃnətlɪ] *adv* heureusement.

fortune ['fɔ:tʃu:n] *n* [wealth] fortune *f*. || [luck] fortune *f*, chance *f*. || [future]: **to tell sb's ~** dire la bonne aventure à qqn.

fortune-teller [-,telə*r*] *n* diseuse *f* de bonne aventure.

forty ['fɔ:tɪ] *num* quarante; *see also* **sixty**.

forward ['fɔ:wəd] **1** *adj* [movement] en avant. || [planning] à long terme. || [impudent] effronté(e). **2** *adv* [ahead] en avant; **to go** OR **move ~** avancer. || [in time]: **to bring a meeting ~** avancer la date d'une réunion. **3** *n* SPORT avant *m*. **4** *vt* [letter] faire suivre; [goods] expédier.

forwarding address ['fɔ:wədɪŋ-] *n* adresse *f* où faire suivre le courrier.

forwards ['fɔ:wədz] *adv* = forward.

forwent [fɔ:'went] *pt* → forgo.

fossil ['fɒsl] *n* fossile *m*.

foster ['fɒstə*r*] **1** *adj* [family] d'accueil. **2** *vt* [child] accueillir. || *fig* [nurture] nourrir, entretenir.

foster child *n* enfant *m* placé en famille d'accueil.

foster parent *n* parent *m* nourricier.

fought [fɔ:t] *pt & pp* → fight.

foul [faul] **1** *adj* [gen] infect(e); [water] croupi(e). || [language] ordurier(ière). **2** *n* SPORT faute *f*. **3** *vt* [make dirty] souiller, salir. || SPORT commettre une faute contre.

found [faund] **1** *pt & pp* → find. **2** *vt* [hospital, town] fonder. || [base]: **to ~ sthg on** fonder OR baser qqch sur.

foundation [faun'deɪʃn] *n* [creation, organization] fondation *f*. || [basis] fondement *m*, base *f*. || **~ (cream)** fond *m* de

freewheel

teint. ○ **foundations** *npl* CONSTR fondations *fpl*.

founder ['faʊndər] **1** *n* fondateur *m*, -trice *f*. **2** *vi* [ship] sombrer.

foundry ['faʊndrɪ] *n* fonderie *f*.

fountain ['faʊntɪn] *n* fontaine *f*.

fountain pen *n* stylo *m* à encre.

four [fɔːr] *num* quatre; **on all ~s** à quatre pattes; *see also* **six**.

four-letter word *n* mot *m* grossier.

four-poster (bed) *n* lit *m* à baldaquin.

foursome ['fɔːsəm] *n* groupe *m* de quatre.

fourteen [ˌfɔːˈtiːn] *num* quatorze; *see also* **six**.

fourth [fɔːθ] *num* quatrième; *see also* **sixth**.

Fourth of July *n*: **the ~** Fête de l'Indépendance américaine.

four-wheel drive *n*: **with ~** à quatre roues motrices.

fowl [faʊl] (*pl inv* OR **-s**) *n* volaille *f*.

fox [fɒks] **1** *n* renard *m*. **2** *vt* laisser perplexe.

foxglove ['fɒksɡlʌv] *n* digitale *f*.

foyer ['fɔɪeɪ] *n* [of hotel, theatre] foyer *m*. || *Am* [of house] hall *m* d'entrée.

fracas ['frækɑː, *Am* 'freɪkəs] (*Br pl inv*, *Am pl* **-cases**) *n* bagarre *f*.

fraction ['frækʃn] *n* fraction *f*.

fractionally ['frækʃnəlɪ] *adv* un tout petit peu.

fracture ['fræktʃər] **1** *n* fracture *f*. **2** *vt* fracturer.

fragile ['frædʒaɪl] *adj* fragile.

fragment ['fræɡmənt] *n* fragment *m*.

fragrance ['freɪɡrəns] *n* parfum *m*.

fragrant ['freɪɡrənt] *adj* parfumé(e).

frail [freɪl] *adj* fragile.

frame [freɪm] **1** *n* [gen] cadre *m*; [of glasses] monture *f*; [of door, window] encadrement *m*. || [physique] charpente *f*. **2** *vt* [gen] encadrer. || [express] formuler. || *inf* [set up] monter un coup contre.

frame of mind *n* état *m* d'esprit.

framework ['freɪmwɜːk] *n* [structure] armature *f*, carcasse *f*. || *fig* [basis] structure *f*, cadre *m*.

France [frɑːns] *n* France *f*; **in ~** en France.

franchise ['fræntʃaɪz] *n* POL droit *m* de vote. || COMM franchise *f*.

frank [fræŋk] **1** *adj* franc (franche). **2** *vt* affranchir.

frankly ['fræŋklɪ] *adv* franchement.

frantic ['fræntɪk] *adj* frénétique.

fraternity [frəˈtɜːnətɪ] *n* [community] confrérie *f*. || (*U*) [friendship] fraternité *f*. || *Am* [of students] club *m* d'étudiants.

fraternize, -ise ['frætənaɪz] *vi* fraterniser.

fraud [frɔːd] *n* (*U*) [crime] fraude *f*. || *pej* [impostor] imposteur *m*.

fraught [frɔːt] *adj* [full]: **~ with** plein(e) de. || *Br* [person] tendu(e); [time, situation] difficile.

fray [freɪ] **1** *vt fig*: **my nerves were ~ed** j'étais extrêmement tendu(e), j'étais à bout de nerfs. **2** *vi* [material, sleeves] s'user; **tempers ~ed** *fig* l'atmosphère était tendue OR électrique.

frayed [freɪd] *adj* [jeans, collar] élimé(e).

freak [friːk] **1** *adj* bizarre, insolite. **2** *n* [strange creature] monstre *m*, phénomène *m*. || [unusual event] accident *m* bizarre. || *inf* [fanatic] fana *mf*.

freckle ['frekl] *n* tache *f* de rousseur.

free [friː] (*compar* **freer**, *superl* **freest**, *pt & pp* **freed**) **1** *adj* [gen] libre; **to be ~ to do sthg** être libre de faire qqch; **feel ~!** je t'en prie!; **to set ~** libérer. || [not paid for] gratuit(e); **~ of charge** gratuitement. **2** *adv* [without payment] gratuitement; **for ~** gratuitement. || [run, live] librement. **3** *vt* [gen] libérer. || [trapped person, object] dégager.

freedom ['friːdəm] *n* [gen] liberté *f*; **~ of speech** liberté d'expression. || [exception]: **~ (from)** exemption *f* (de).

free-for-all *n* mêlée *f* générale.

free gift *n* prime *f*.

freehand ['friːhænd] *adj & adv* à main levée.

freehold ['friːhəʊld] *n* propriété *f* foncière inaliénable.

free kick *n* coup *m* franc.

freelance ['friːlɑːns] **1** *adj* indépendant(e), free-lance (*inv*). **2** *n* indépendant *m*, -e *f*, free-lance *mf*.

freely ['friːlɪ] *adv* [gen] librement. || [generously] sans compter.

Freemason ['friːˌmeɪsn] *n* franc-maçon *m*.

freepost ['friːpəʊst] *n* port *m* payé.

free-range *adj* de ferme.

freestyle ['friːstaɪl] *n* SWIMMING nage *f* libre.

free trade *n* (*U*) libre-échange *m*.

freeway ['friːweɪ] *n Am* autoroute *f*.

freewheel [ˌfriːˈwiːl] *vi* [on bicycle] rouler en roue libre; [in car] rouler au point mort.

free will n (U) libre arbitre m; **to do sthg of one's own ~** faire qqch de son propre gré.

freeze [fri:z] (pt **froze**, pp **frozen**) 1 vt [gen] geler; [food] congeler. || [wages, prices] bloquer. 2 vi [gen] geler. || [stop moving] s'arrêter. 3 n [cold weather] gel m. || [of wages, prices] blocage m.

freeze-dried [-'draɪd] adj lyophilisé(e).

freezer ['fri:zər] n congélateur m.

freezing ['fri:zɪŋ] 1 adj glacé(e); **I'm ~** je gèle. 2 n = **freezing point**.

freezing point n point m de congélation.

freight [freɪt] n [goods] fret m.

freight train n train m de marchandises.

French [frentʃ] 1 adj français(e). 2 n [language] français m. 3 npl: **the ~** les Français mpl.

French bean n haricot m vert.

French bread n (U) baguette f.

French Canadian 1 adj canadien français (canadienne française). 2 n Canadien français m, Canadienne française f.

French doors = **French windows**.

French dressing n [in UK] vinaigrette f; [in US] sauce-salade à base de mayonnaise et de ketchup.

French fries npl frites fpl.

Frenchman ['frentʃmən] (pl **-men** [-mən]) n Français m.

French windows npl porte-fenêtre f.

Frenchwoman ['frentʃˌwumən] (pl **-women** [-ˌwɪmɪn]) n Française f.

frenetic [frə'netɪk] adj frénétique.

frenzy ['frenzɪ] n frénésie f.

frequency ['fri:kwənsɪ] n fréquence f.

frequent [adj 'fri:kwənt, vb frɪ'kwent] 1 adj fréquent(e). 2 vt fréquenter.

frequently ['fri:kwəntlɪ] adv fréquemment.

fresh [freʃ] adj [gen] frais (fraîche). || [not salty] doux (douce). || [new - drink, piece of paper] autre; [- look, approach] nouveau(elle).

freshen ['freʃn] vt rafraîchir. ○ **freshen up** vi faire un brin de toilette.

freshly ['freʃlɪ] adv [squeezed, ironed] fraîchement.

freshman ['freʃmən] (pl **-men** [-mən]) n étudiant m, -e f de première année.

freshness ['freʃnɪs] n (U) [gen] fraîcheur f. || [originality] nouveauté f.

freshwater ['freʃˌwɔːtər] adj d'eau douce.

fret [fret] vi [worry] s'inquiéter.

friar ['fraɪər] n frère m.

friction ['frɪkʃn] n (U) friction f.

Friday ['fraɪdɪ] n vendredi m; see also **Saturday**.

fridge [frɪdʒ] n frigo m.

fried [fraɪd] adj frit(e); **~ egg** œuf m au plat.

friend [frend] n ami m, -e f; **to be ~s with sb** être ami avec qqn; **to make ~s (with sb)** se lier d'amitié (avec qqn).

friendly ['frendlɪ] adj [person, manner, match] amical(e); [nation] ami(e); **to be ~ with sb** être ami avec qqn.

friendship ['frendʃɪp] n amitié f.

fries [fraɪz] = **French fries**.

frieze [fri:z] n frise f.

fright [fraɪt] n peur f; **to give sb a ~** faire peur à qqn; **to take ~** prendre peur.

frighten ['fraɪtn] vt faire peur à, effrayer.

frightened ['fraɪtnd] adj apeuré(e); **to be ~ of sthg/of doing sthg** avoir peur de qqch/de faire qqch.

frightening ['fraɪtnɪŋ] adj effrayant(e).

frigid ['frɪdʒɪd] adj [sexually] frigide.

frill [frɪl] n [decoration] volant m. || inf [extra] supplément m.

fringe [frɪndʒ] n [gen] frange f. || [edge - of village] bordure f; [- of wood, forest] lisière f.

fringe benefit n avantage m extrasalarial.

frisk [frɪsk] vt fouiller.

frisky ['frɪskɪ] adj inf vif (vive).

fritter ['frɪtər] n beignet m. ○ **fritter away** vt sep gaspiller.

frivolous ['frɪvələs] adj frivole.

frizzy ['frɪzɪ] adj crépu(e).

fro [frəʊ] → **to**.

frock [frɒk] n dated robe f.

frog [frɒg] n [animal] grenouille f; **to have a ~ in one's throat** avoir un chat dans la gorge.

frogman ['frɒgmən] (pl **-men**) n homme-grenouille m.

frogmen ['frɒgmən] pl → **frogman**.

frolic ['frɒlɪk] (pt & pp **-ked**, cont **-king**) vi folâtrer.

from [weak form frəm, strong form frɒm] prep [indicating source, origin, removal] de; **where are you ~?**, d'où venez-vous?, d'où êtes-vous?; **a flight ~ Paris** un vol en provenance de Paris; **to translate ~ Spanish into English** traduire d'espagnol en anglais; **to take sthg (away) ~ sb** prendre qqch à qqn. || [indicating a deduction] de; **to deduct sthg ~ sthg** retrancher qqch de qqch. || [indicating escape, separation] de; **he ran away ~ home** il a fait une fugue, il s'est sauvé de chez lui. || [indicating position] de; **seen ~ above/below** vu d'en haut/d'en bas. || [indicating distance] de; **it's 60 km ~ here** c'est à 60 km d'ici. || [indicating material object is made out of] en; **it's made ~ wood/plastic** c'est en bois/plastique. || [starting at a particular time] de; **~ 2 pm to OR till 6 pm** de 14 h à 18 h. || [indicating difference] de; **to be different ~ sb/sthg** être différent de qqn/qqch. || [indicating change] **~ ... to de ... à**; **the price went up ~ £100 to £150** le prix est passé OR monté de 100 livres à 150 livres. || [because of, as a result of] de; **to suffer ~ cold/hunger** souffrir du froid/de la faim. || [on the evidence of] d'après, à. || [indicating lowest amount] depuis, à partir de; **prices start ~ £50** le premier prix est de 50 livres.

front [frʌnt] **1** n [most forward part - gen] avant m; [- of dress, envelope, house] devant m; [- of class] premier rang m. || METEOR & MIL front m. || (**sea**) **~** front m de mer. || [outward appearance - of person] contenance f; pej [- of business] façade f. **2** adj [tooth, garden] de devant; [row, page] premier(ière). ○ **in front** adv [further forward - walk, push] devant; [- people] à l'avant; [- winning]: **to be in ~** mener. ○ **in front of** prep devant.

front door n porte f d'entrée.

frontier ['frʌn,tɪər, Am frʌn'tɪər] n [border] frontière f, fig limite f.

front man n [of company, organization] porte-parole m inv. || TV présentateur m.

front room n salon m.

front-runner n favori m, -ite f.

front-wheel drive n traction f avant.

frost [frɒst] n gel m.

frostbite ['frɒstbaɪt] n (U) gelure f.

frosted ['frɒstɪd] adj [glass] dépoli(e). || Am CULIN glacé(e).

frosty ['frɒstɪ] adj [weather, welcome] glacial(e). || [field, window] gelé(e).

froth [frɒθ] n [on beer] mousse f; [on sea] écume f.

frown [fraʊn] vi froncer les sourcils. ○ **frown (up)on** vt fus désapprouver.

froze [frəʊz] pt → freeze.

frozen ['frəʊzn] **1** pp → freeze. **2** adj gelé(e); [food] congelé(e).

frugal ['fru:gl] adj [meal] frugal(e). || [person, life] économe.

fruit [fru:t] (pl inv OR **fruits**) n fruit m.

fruitcake ['fru:tkeɪk] n cake m.

fruitful ['fru:tfʊl] adj [successful] fructueux(euse).

fruition [fru:'ɪʃn] n: **to come to ~** se réaliser.

fruit juice n jus m de fruits.

fruitless ['fru:tlɪs] adj vain(e).

fruit salad n salade f de fruits.

frumpy ['frʌmpɪ] adj mal attifé(e), mal fagoté(e).

frustrate [frʌ'streɪt] vt [annoy, disappoint] frustrer. || [prevent] faire échouer.

frustrated [frʌ'streɪtɪd] adj [person, artist] frustré(e). || [effort, love] vain(e).

frustration [frʌ'streɪʃn] n frustration f.

fry [fraɪ] (pt & pp **-ied**) vt & vi frire.

frying pan ['fraɪŋ-] n poêle f à frire.

ft. abbr of **foot, feet**.

fuck [fʌk] vulg vt & vi baiser. ○ **fuck off** vi vulg: **~ off!** fous le camp!

fudge [fʌdʒ] n (U) [sweet] caramel m (mou).

fuel [fjʊəl] **1** n combustible m; [for engine] carburant m. **2** vt [supply with fuel] alimenter (en combustible/carburant). || fig [speculation] nourrir.

fuel pump n pompe f d'alimentation.

fuel tank n réservoir m à carburant.

fugitive ['fju:dʒətɪv] n fugitif m, -ive f.

fulfil, fulfill Am [fʊl'fɪl] vt [duty, role] remplir; [hope] répondre à; [ambition, prophecy] réaliser. || [satisfy - need] satisfaire.

fulfilment, fulfillment Am [fʊl'fɪlmənt] n (U) [satisfaction] grande satisfaction f. || [of ambition, dream] réalisation f; [of role, promise] exécution f; [of need] satisfaction f.

full [fʊl] **1** adj [gen] plein(e); [bus, car park] complet(ète); [with food] gavé(e), repu(e). || [complete - recovery, control] total(e); [- explanation, day] entier(ière); [- volume] maximum. || [busy - life] rempli(e); [- timetable, day] chargé(e). || [flavour] riche. || [plump - figure] rondelet(ette); [- mouth] charnu(e). || [skirt, sleeve] ample. **2** adv [very]: **you know ~ well that ...** tu sais très bien que .... **3** n: **in ~** complètement, entièrement.

full board n pension f complète.

full-fledged Am = **fully-fledged**.

full moon n pleine lune f.

full-scale adj [life-size] grandeur na-

ture (*inv*). || [complete] de grande enver-
gure.

full stop *n* point *m*.

full time *n* Br SPORT fin *f* de match.
○ **full-time** *adj* & *adv* [work, worker] à
temps plein.

full up *adj* [bus, train] complet(ète);
[with food] gavé(e), repu(e).

fully ['fʊlɪ] *adv* [understand, satisfy] tout
à fait; [trained, describe] entièrement.

fully-fledged *Br*, **full-fledged** *Am*
[-'fledʒd] *adj* diplômé(e).

fumble ['fʌmbl] *vi* fouiller, tâtonner; **to
~ for** fouiller pour trouver.

fume [fju:m] *vi* [with anger] rager.
○ **fumes** *npl* [from paint] émanations
fpl; [from smoke] fumées *fpl*; [from car]
gaz *mpl* d'échappement.

fumigate ['fju:mɪgeɪt] *vt* fumiger.

fun [fʌn] *n* (*U*) [pleasure, amusement]: **to
have ~** s'amuser. || [playfulness]: **to be
full of ~** être plein(e) d'entrain. || [ri-
dicule]: **to make ~ of** OR **poke ~ at sb** se
moquer de qqn.

function ['fʌŋkʃn] **1** *n* [gen] fonction *f*.
|| [formal social event] réception *f* offi-
cielle. **2** *vi* fonctionner; **to ~ as** servir de.

functional ['fʌŋkʃnəl] *adj* [practical]
fonctionnel(elle). || [operational] en état
de marche.

fund [fʌnd] **1** *n* fonds *m*. **2** *vt* financer.
○ **funds** *npl* fonds *mpl*.

fundamental [,fʌndə'mentl] *adj*: **~ (to)**
fondamental(e) (à).

funding ['fʌndɪŋ] *n* (*U*) financement *m*.

funeral ['fju:nərəl] *n* obsèques *fpl*.

funeral parlour *n* entreprise *f* de pompes funèbres.

funfair ['fʌnfeər] *n* fête *f* foraine.

fungus ['fʌŋgəs] (*pl* -**gi** [-gaɪ] OR
-**guses**) *n* champignon *m*.

funnel ['fʌnl] *n* [tube] entonnoir *m*. || [of
ship] cheminée *f*.

funny ['fʌnɪ] *adj* [amusing, odd] drôle. ||
[ill] tout drôle (toute drôle).

fur [fɜ:r] *n* fourrure *f*.

fur coat *n* (manteau *m* de) fourrure *f*.

furious ['fjʊərɪəs] *adj* [very angry] fu-
rieux(ieuse).

furlong ['fɜ:lɒŋ] *n* = 201,17 mètres.

furnace ['fɜ:nɪs] *n* [fire] fournaise *f*.

furnish ['fɜ:nɪʃ] *vt* [fit out] meubler. ||
fml [provide] fournir; **to ~ sb with sthg**
fournir qqch à qqn.

furnished ['fɜ:nɪʃt] *adj* meublé(e).

furnishings ['fɜ:nɪʃɪŋz] *npl* mobilier *m*.

furniture ['fɜ:nɪtʃər] *n* (*U*) meubles
mpl; **a piece of ~** un meuble.

furry ['fɜ:rɪ] *adj* [animal] à fourrure. ||
[material] recouvert(e) de fourrure.

further ['fɜ:ðər] **1** *compar* → **far. 2** *adv*
[gen] plus loin; **how much ~ is it?**
combien de kilomètres y a-t-il?; **~ on**
plus loin. || [more - complicate, develop]
davantage; [- enquire] plus avant. || [in
addition] de plus. **3** *adj* nouveau(elle),
supplémentaire; **until ~ notice** jusqu'à
nouvel ordre. **4** *vt* [career, aims] faire
avancer; [cause] encourager.

furthermore [,fɜ:ðə'mɔ:r] *adv* de plus.

furthest ['fɜ:ðɪst] **1** *superl* → **far. 2** *adj*
le plus éloigné (la plus éloignée). **3** *adv* le
plus loin.

furtive ['fɜ:tɪv] *adj* [person] sour-
nois(e); [glance] furtif(ive).

fury ['fjʊərɪ] *n* fureur *f*.

fuse *esp Br*, **fuze** *Am* [fju:z] **1** *n* ELEC fu-
sible *m*, plomb *m*. || [of bomb] détonateur
m. **2** *vt* [join by heat] réunir par la fusion.
|| [combine] fusionner. **3** *vi* ELEC: **the
lights have ~d** les plombs ont sauté. ||
[join by heat] fondre. || [combine] fusion-
ner.

fuse-box *n* boîte *f* à fusibles.

fused [fju:zd] *adj* [plug] avec fusible incorporé.

fuss [fʌs] **1** *n* [excitement, anxiety] agita-
tion *f*; **to make a ~** faire des histoires. ||
(*U*) [complaints] protestations *fpl*. **2** *vi*
faire des histoires.

fussy ['fʌsɪ] *adj* [fastidious - person] ta-
tillon(onne); [- eater] difficile. || [over-
decorated] tarabiscoté(e).

futile ['fju:taɪl] *adj* vain(e).

futon ['fu:tɒn] *n* futon *m*.

future ['fju:tʃər] **1** *n* [gen] avenir *m*; **in
~** à l'avenir; **in the ~** dans le futur, à
l'avenir. || GRAMM: **~ (tense)** futur *m*. **2** *adj*
futur(e).

fuze *Am* = **fuse**.

fuzzy ['fʌzɪ] *adj* [photo, image] flou(e).

g¹ (*pl* **g's** OR **gs**), **G** (*pl* **G's** OR **Gs**) [dʒiː] *n* [letter] g *m inv*, G *m inv*. ○ **G** *n* MUS sol *m*. || (*abbr of* **good**) B.

g² (*abbr of* **gram**) g.

gabble ['gæbl] *vt & vi* baragouiner.

gable ['geɪbl] *n* pignon *m*.

gadget ['gædʒɪt] *n* gadget *m*.

Gaelic ['geɪlɪk] **1** *adj* gaélique. **2** *n* gaélique *m*.

gag [gæg] **1** *n* [for mouth] bâillon *m*. || *inf* [joke] blague *f*, gag *m*. **2** *vt* [put gag on] bâillonner.

gage *Am* = **gauge**.

gaiety ['geɪətɪ] *n* gaieté *f*.

gaily ['geɪlɪ] *adv* [cheerfully] gaiement. || [thoughtlessly] allègrement.

gain [geɪn] **1** *n* [gen] profit *m*. || [improvement] augmentation *f*. **2** *vt* [acquire] gagner. || [increase in - speed, weight] prendre; [- confidence] gagner en. **3** *vi* [advance]: **to ~ in sthg** gagner en qqch. || [benefit]: **to ~ from** OR **by sthg** tirer un avantage de qqch. || [watch, clock] avancer. ○ **gain on** *vt fus* rattraper.

gal. *abbr of* **gallon**.

gala ['gɑːlə] *n* [celebration] gala *m*.

galaxy ['gæləksɪ] *n* galaxie *f*.

gale [geɪl] *n* [wind] grand vent *m*.

gall [gɔːl] *n* [nerve]: **to have the ~ to do sthg** avoir le toupet de faire qqch.

gallant [*sense 1* 'gælənt, *sense 2* gə'lænt, 'gælənt] *adj* [courageous] courageux(euse). || [polite to women] galant.

gall bladder *n* vésicule *f* biliaire.

gallery ['gælərɪ] *n* [gen] galerie *f*. || [for displaying art] musée *m*.

galley ['gælɪ] (*pl* **galleys**) *n* [ship] galère *f*. || [kitchen] coquerie *f*.

Gallic ['gælɪk] *adj* français(e).

galling ['gɔːlɪŋ] *adj* humiliant(e).

gallon ['gælən] *n* = 4,546 litres, gallon *m*.

gallop ['gæləp] **1** *n* galop *m*. **2** *vi* galoper.

gallows ['gæləʊz] (*pl inv*) *n* gibet *m*.

gallstone ['gɔːlstəʊn] *n* calcul *m* biliaire.

galore [gə'lɔːr] *adj* en abondance.

galvanize, -ise ['gælvənaɪz] *vt* [impel]: **to ~ sb into action** pousser qqn à agir.

gambit ['gæmbɪt] *n* entrée *f* en matière.

gamble ['gæmbl] **1** *n* [calculated risk] risque *m*. **2** *vi* [bet] jouer; **to ~ on** jouer de l'argent sur. || [take risk]: **to ~ on** miser sur.

gambler ['gæmblər] *n* joueur *m*, -euse *f*.

gambling ['gæmblɪŋ] *n* (*U*) jeu *m*.

game [geɪm] **1** *n* [gen] jeu *m*. || [match] match *m*. || (*U*) [hunted animals] gibier *m*. **2** *adj* [brave] courageux(euse). || [willing]: **~ (for sthg/to do sthg)** partant(e) (pour qqch/pour faire qqch). ○ **games 1** *n* SCH éducation *f* physique. **2** *npl* [sporting contest] jeux *mpl*.

gamekeeper ['geɪmˌkiːpər] *n* garde-chasse *m*.

game reserve *n* réserve *f* (de chasse).

gammon ['gæmən] *n* jambon *m* fumé.

gamut ['gæmət] *n* gamme *f*.

gang [gæŋ] *n* [of criminals] gang *m*. || [of young people] bande *f*. ○ **gang up** *vi inf*: **to ~ up (on)** se liguer (contre).

gangland ['gæŋlænd] *n* (*U*) milieu *m*.

gangrene ['gæŋgriːn] *n* gangrène *f*.

gangster ['gæŋstər] *n* gangster *m*.

gantry ['gæntrɪ] *n* portique *m*.

gap [gæp] *n* [empty space] trou *m*; [in text] blanc *m*; *fig* [in knowledge, report] lacune *f*. || [interval of time] période *f*. || *fig* [great difference] fossé *m*.

gape [geɪp] *vi* [person] rester bouche bée. || [hole, shirt] bâiller.

gaping ['geɪpɪŋ] *adj* [open-mouthed] bouche bée (*inv*). || [wide-open] béant(e).

garage [*Br* 'gærɑːʒ, 'gærɪdʒ, *Am* gə'rɑːʒ] *n* [gen] garage *m*.

garbage ['gɑːbɪdʒ] *n* (*U*) [refuse] détritus *mpl*. || *inf* [nonsense] idioties *fpl*.

garbage can *n Am* poubelle *f*.

garbage truck *n Am* camion-poubelle *m*.

garbled ['gɑːbld] *adj* confus(e).

garden ['gɑːdn] **1** *n* jardin *m*. **2** *vi* jardiner.

garden centre *n* jardinerie *f*, garden centre *m*.

gardener ['gɑːdnər] *n* [professional] jardinier *m*, -ière *f*.

gardening ['gɑːdnɪŋ] *n* jardinage *m*.

gargle ['gɑːgl] *vi* se gargariser.

gargoyle ['gɑːgɔɪl] *n* gargouille *f*.

garish ['geərɪʃ] *adj* criard(e).

garland ['gɑːlənd] *n* guirlande *f* de fleurs.

garlic ['gɑːlɪk] *n* ail *m*.

garlic bread *n* pain *m* à l'ail.

garment ['gɑːmənt] *n* vêtement *m*.

garnish ['gɑːnɪʃ] 1 *n* garniture *f*. 2 *vt* garnir.

garrison ['gærɪsn] *n* [soldiers] garnison *f*.

garrulous ['gærələs] *adj* volubile.

garter ['gɑːtər] *n* [for socks] support-chaussette *m*; [for stockings] jarretière *f*. || *Am* [suspender] jarretelle *f*.

gas [gæs] (*pl* **-es** OR **-ses**) 1 *n* [gen] gaz *m inv*. || *Am* [for vehicle] essence *f*. 2 *vt* gazer.

gas cylinder *n* bouteille *f* de gaz.

gas gauge *n Am* jauge *f* d'essence.

gash [gæʃ] 1 *n* entaille *f*. 2 *vt* entailler.

gasket ['gæskɪt] *n* joint *m* d'étanchéité.

gasman ['gæsmæn] (*pl* **-men** [-men]) *n* [who reads meter] employé *m* du gaz; [for repairs] installateur *m* de gaz.

gas mask *n* masque *m* à gaz.

gas meter *n* compteur *m* à gaz.

gasoline ['gæsəliːn] *n Am* essence *f*.

gasp [gɑːsp] 1 *n* halètement *m*. 2 *vi* [breathe quickly] haleter. || [in shock, surprise] avoir le souffle coupé.

gas pedal *n Am* accélérateur *m*.

gas station *n Am* station-service *f*.

gas tank *n Am* réservoir *m*.

gas tap *n* [for mains supply] robinet *m* de gaz; [on gas fire] prise *f* de gaz.

gastroenteritis ['gæstrəʊ,entə'raɪtɪs] *n* gastro-entérite *f*.

gastronomy [gæs'trɒnəmɪ] *n* gastronomie *f*.

gasworks ['gæswɜːks] (*pl inv*) *n* usine *f* à gaz.

gate [geɪt] *n* [of garden, farm] barrière *f*; [of town, at airport] porte *f*; [of park] grille *f*.

gatecrash ['geɪtkræʃ] *vt & vi inf* prendre part à une réunion, une réception sans y avoir été convié.

gateway ['geɪtweɪ] *n* [entrance] entrée *f*. || [means of access]: **to ~** porte *f* de.

gather ['gæðər] 1 *vt* [collect] ramasser; [flowers] cueillir; [information] recueillir; [courage, strength] rassembler; **to ~ together** rassembler. || [increase - speed, force] prendre. || [understand]: **to ~ (that)** ... croire comprendre que .... || [cloth - into folds] plisser. 2 *vi* [come together] se rassembler; [clouds] s'amonceler.

gathering ['gæðərɪŋ] *n* [meeting] rassemblement *m*.

gaudy ['gɔːdɪ] *adj* voyant(e).

gauge, gage *Am* [geɪdʒ] 1 *n* [for rain] pluviomètre *m*; [for fuel] jauge *f* (d'essence); [for tyre pressure] manomètre *m*. || [of gun, wire] calibre *m*. || RAIL écartement *m*. 2 *vt* [measure] mesurer. || [evaluate] jauger.

Gaul [gɔːl] *n* [country] Gaule *f*. || [person] Gaulois *m*, -e *f*.

gaunt [gɔːnt] *adj* [thin] hâve. || [bare, grim] désolé(e).

gauntlet ['gɔːntlɪt] *n* gant *m* (de protection); **to run the ~ of sthg** endurer qqch. || **to throw down the ~ (to sb)** jeter le gant (à qqn).

gauze [gɔːz] *n* gaze *f*.

gave [geɪv] *pt → **give**.

gawky ['gɔːkɪ] *adj* [person] dégingandé(e); [movement] désordonné(e).

gawp [gɔːp] *vi*: **to ~ (at)** rester bouche bée (devant).

gay [geɪ] 1 *adj* [gen] gai(e). || [homosexual] homo (*inv*), gay (*inv*). 2 *n* homo *mf*, gay *mf*.

gaze [geɪz] 1 *n* regard *m* (fixe). 2 *vi*: **to ~ at sb/sthg** regarder qqn/qqch (fixement).

gazelle [gə'zel] (*pl inv* OR **-s**) *n* gazelle *f*.

gazetteer [,gæzɪ'tɪər] *n* index *m* géographique.

GB (*abbr of* **Great Britain**) *n* G-B *f*.

GDP (*abbr of* **gross domestic product**) *n* PIB *m*.

gear [gɪər] 1 *n* TECH [mechanism] embrayage *m*. || [speed - of car, bicycle] vitesse *f*; **to be in/out of ~** être en prise/au point mort. || (*U*) [equipment, clothes] équipement *m*. 2 *vt*: **to ~ sthg to sb/sthg** destiner qqch à qqn/qqch. ○ **gear up** *vi*: **to ~ up for sthg/to do sthg** se préparer pour qqch/à faire qqch.

gearbox ['gɪəbɒks] *n* boîte *f* de vitesses.

gear lever, gear stick *Br*, **gear shift** *Am n* levier *m* de changement de vitesse.

gear wheel *n* pignon *m*, roue *f* d'engrenage.

geese [giːs] *pl → **goose**.

gel [dʒel] 1 *n* [for hair] gel *m*. 2 *vi* [thicken] prendre. || *fig* [take shape] prendre tournure.

gelatin ['dʒelətɪn], **gelatine** [,dʒelə'tiːn] *n* gélatine *f*.

gelignite ['dʒelɪgnaɪt] *n* gélignite *f*.

gem [dʒem] n [jewel] pierre f précieuse, gemme f. || fig [person, thing] perle f.

Gemini ['dʒemɪnaɪ] n Gémeaux mpl.

gender ['dʒendər] n [sex] sexe m. || GRAMM genre m.

gene [dʒiːn] n gène m.

general ['dʒenərəl] 1 adj général(e). 2 n général m. ○ **in general** adv en général.

general anaesthetic n anesthésie f générale.

general delivery n Am poste f restante.

general election n élection f générale.

generalization [,dʒenərəlaɪ'zeɪʃn] n généralisation f.

general knowledge n culture f générale.

generally ['dʒenərəlɪ] adv [usually, in most cases] généralement. || [unspecifically] en général; [describe] en gros.

general practitioner n (médecin m) généraliste m.

general public n: **the ~** le grand public.

general strike n grève f générale.

generate ['dʒenəreɪt] vt [energy, jobs] générer; [electricity, heat] produire; [interest, excitement] susciter.

generation [,dʒenə'reɪʃn] n [gen] génération f. || [creation - of jobs] création f; [- of interest, excitement] induction f; [- of electricity] production f.

generator ['dʒenəreɪtər] n générateur m; ELEC génératrice f, générateur.

generosity [,dʒenə'rɒsətɪ] n générosité f.

generous ['dʒenərəs] adj généreux (euse).

genetic [dʒɪ'netɪk] adj génétique. ○ **genetics** n (U) génétique f.

Geneva [dʒɪ'niːvə] n Genève.

genial ['dʒiːnjəl] adj affable.

genitals ['dʒenɪtlz] npl organes mpl génitaux.

genius ['dʒiːnjəs] (pl -es) n génie m.

genteel [dʒen'tiːl] adj raffiné(e).

gentle ['dʒentl] adj doux (douce); [hint] discret(ète); [telling-off] léger(ère).

gentleman ['dʒentlmən] (pl -men [-mən]) n [well-behaved man] gentleman m. || [man] monsieur m.

gently ['dʒentlɪ] adv [gen] doucement; [speak, smile] avec douceur.

gentry ['dʒentrɪ] n petite noblesse f.

genuine ['dʒenjʊɪn] adj authentique; [interest, customer] sérieux(ieuse); [person, concern] sincère.

geography [dʒɪ'ɒgrəfɪ] n géographie f.

geology [dʒɪ'ɒlədʒɪ] n géologie f.

geometric(al) [,dʒɪə'metrɪk(l)] adj géométrique.

geometry [dʒɪ'ɒmətrɪ] n géométrie f.

geranium [dʒɪ'reɪnjəm] (pl -s) n géranium m.

gerbil ['dʒɜːbɪl] n gerbille f.

geriatric [,dʒerɪ'ætrɪk] adj MED gériatrique.

germ [dʒɜːm] n [bacterium] germe m.

German ['dʒɜːmən] 1 adj allemand(e). 2 n [person] Allemand m, -e f. || [language] allemand m.

German measles n (U) rubéole f.

Germany ['dʒɜːmənɪ] n Allemagne f.

germinate ['dʒɜːmɪneɪt] vi lit & fig germer.

gerund ['dʒerənd] n gérondif m.

gesticulate [dʒes'tɪkjʊleɪt] vi gesticuler.

gesture ['dʒestʃər] 1 n geste m. 2 vi: **to ~ to** OR **towards sb** faire signe à qqn.

get [get] (Br pt & pp **got**, Am pt **got**, pp **gotten**) 1 vt [cause to do]: **to ~ sb to do sthg** faire faire qqch à qqn; **I'll ~ my sister to help** je vais demander à ma sœur de nous aider. || [cause to be done]: **to ~ sthg done** faire faire qqch. || [cause to become]: **to ~ sb pregnant** rendre qqn enceinte; **I can't ~ the car started** je n'arrive pas à mettre la voiture en marche. || [cause to move]: **to ~ sb/sthg through sthg** faire passer qqn/qqch par qqch; **to ~ sb/sthg out of sthg** faire sortir qqn/qqch de qqch. || [bring, fetch] aller chercher; **can I ~ you something to eat/drink?** est-ce que je peux vous offrir quelque chose à manger/boire? || [obtain - gen] obtenir; [- job, house] trouver. || [receive] recevoir, avoir; **she ~s a good salary** elle touche un bon traitement. || [experience a sensation] avoir; **do you ~ the feeling he doesn't like us?** tu n'as pas l'impression qu'il ne nous aime pas? || [be infected with, suffer from] avoir, attraper; **to ~ a cold** attraper un rhume. || [understand] comprendre, saisir. || [catch - bus, train, plane] prendre. || [capture] prendre, attraper. || [find]: **you ~ a lot of artists here** on trouve OR il y a beaucoup d'artistes ici; see also **have**. 2 vi [become] devenir; **to ~ suspicious** devenir méfiant; **I'm getting cold/bored** je commence à avoir froid/à m'ennuyer; **it's getting late** il se fait tard. || [arrive] arriver; **I only got back yesterday** je suis rentré hier seulement. || [eventually succeed in]: **to ~ to do sthg** parvenir à OR finir par faire qqch; **did you ~ to see him?** est-ce que tu as réussi à le voir? || [progress]: **how far have you got?** où en es-tu?; **now we're getting somewhere** enfin on avance. **3** aux vb: **to ~ excited** s'exciter; **to ~ hurt** se faire mal; **to ~ beaten up** se faire tabasser; **let's ~ going** OR **moving** allons-y; see also **have**. ○ **get about, get around** vi [move from place to place] se déplacer. || [circulate - news, rumour] circuler, se répandre; see also **get around**. ○ **get along** vi [manage] se débrouiller. || [progress] avancer, faire des progrès. || [have a good relationship] s'entendre. ○ **get around, get round 1** vt fus [overcome] venir à bout de, surmonter. **2** vi [circulate] circuler, se répandre. || [eventually do]: **to ~ around to (doing) sthg** trouver le temps de faire qqch; see also **get about**. ○ **get at** vt fus [reach] parvenir à. || [imply] vouloir dire; **what are you getting at?** où veux-tu en venir? || inf [criticize] critiquer, dénigrer. ○ **get away** vi [leave] partir, s'en aller. || [go on holiday] partir en vacances. || [escape] s'échapper, s'évader. ○ **get away with** vt fus: **to let sb ~ away with sthg** passer qqch à qqn. ○ **get back 1** vt sep [recover, regain] retrouver, récupérer. **2** vi [move away] s'écarter. ○ **get back to** vt fus [return to previous state, activity] revenir à; **to ~ back to sleep** se rendormir; **to ~ back to work** [after pause] se remettre au travail; [after illness] reprendre son travail. || inf [phone back] rappeler. ○ **get by** vi se débrouiller, s'en sortir. ○ **get down** vt sep [depress] déprimer. || [fetch from higher level] descendre. ○ **get down to** vt fus: **to ~ down to doing sthg** se mettre à faire qqch. ○ **get in** vi [enter - gen] entrer; [- referring to vehicle] monter. || [arrive] arriver; [arrive home] rentrer. ○ **get into** vt fus [car] monter dans. || [become involved in] se lancer dans; **to ~ into an argument with sb** se disputer avec qqn. || [enter into a particular situation, state]: **to ~ into a panic** s'affoler; **to ~ into trouble** s'attirer des ennuis. ○ **get off 1** vt sep [remove] enlever. **2** vt fus [go away from] partir de. || [train, bus etc] descendre de. **3** vi [leave bus, train] descendre. || [escape punishment] s'en tirer. || [depart] partir. ○ **get on 1** vt fus [bus, train, plane] monter dans. || [horse] monter sur. **2** vi [enter bus, train] monter. || [have good relation-

ship] s'entendre, s'accorder. || [progress] avancer, progresser; **how are you getting on?** comment ça va? || [proceed]: **to ~ on (with sthg)** continuer (qqch), poursuivre (qqch). || [be successful professionally] réussir. ○ **get out 1** vt sep [take out] sortir. || [remove] enlever. **2** vi [from car, bus, train] descendre. || [news] s'ébruiter. ○ **get out of** vt fus [car etc] descendre de. || [escape from] s'évader de, s'échapper de. || [avoid] éviter, se dérober à; **to ~ out of doing sthg** se dispenser de faire qqch. ○ **get over** vt fus [recover from] se remettre de. || [overcome] surmonter, venir à bout de. || [communicate] communiquer. ○ **get round** = **get around**. ○ **get through 1** vt fus [job, task] arriver au bout de. || [exam] réussir à. || [food, drink] consommer. || [unpleasant situation] endurer, supporter. **2** vi [make o.s. understood]: **to ~ through (to sb)** se faire comprendre (de qqn). || TELEC obtenir la communication. ○ **get together 1** vt sep [organize - team, belongings] rassembler; [- project, report] préparer. **2** vi se réunir. ○ **get up 1** vi se lever. **2** vt fus [petition, demonstration] organiser. ○ **get up to** vt fus inf faire.

getaway ['getəweɪ] n fuite f.

get-together n inf réunion f.

geyser ['giːzə'] n [hot spring] geyser m.

ghastly ['gɑːstlɪ] adj inf [very bad, unpleasant] épouvantable. || [horrifying, macabre] effroyable.

gherkin ['gɜːkɪn] n cornichon m.

ghetto ['getəʊ] (pl -s OR -es) n ghetto m.

ghetto blaster [-,blɑːstə'] n inf grand radiocassette m portatif.

ghost [gəʊst] n [spirit] spectre m.

giant ['dʒaɪənt] **1** adj géant(e). **2** n géant m.

gibberish ['dʒɪbərɪʃ] n (U) charabia m, inepties fpl.

gibe [dʒaɪb] n insulte f.

giblets ['dʒɪblɪts] npl abats mpl.

Gibraltar [dʒɪ'brɔːltə'] n Gibraltar m.

giddy ['gɪdɪ] adj [dizzy]: **to feel ~** avoir la tête qui tourne.

gift [gɪft] n [present] cadeau m. || [talent] don m.

gifted ['gɪftɪd] adj doué(e).

gig [gɪg] n inf [concert] concert m.

gigabyte ['gaɪgəbaɪt] n COMPUT giga-octet m.

gigantic [dʒaɪ'gæntɪk] adj énorme, gigantesque.

glassware

giggle ['gɪgl] 1 n [laugh] gloussement m.
2 vi [laugh] glousser.

gilded ['gɪldɪd] adj = gilt.

gill [dʒɪl] n [unit of measurement] =
0,142 litre, quart m de pinte.

gills [gɪlz] npl [of fish] branchies fpl.

gilt [gɪlt] 1 adj [covered in gold] doré(e).
2 n (U) [gold layer] dorure f.

gimmick ['gɪmɪk] n pej artifice m.

gin [dʒɪn] n gin m; ~ and tonic gin tonic.

ginger ['dʒɪndʒər] n [root] gingembre
m. || [powder] gingembre m en poudre.

ginger ale n boisson gazeuse au gingembre.

ginger beer n boisson non-alcoolisée
au gingembre.

gingerbread ['dʒɪndʒəbred] n pain m
d'épice.

ginger-haired [-'heəd] adj roux
(rousse).

gingerly ['dʒɪndʒəlɪ] adv avec précaution.

gipsy ['dʒɪpsɪ] 1 adj gitan(e). 2 n gitan
m, -e f; Br pej bohémien m, -ienne f.

giraffe [dʒɪ'rɑːf] (pl inv OR -s) n girafe
f.

girder ['gɜːdər] n poutrelle f.

girdle ['gɜːdl] n [corset] gaine f.

girl [gɜːl] n [gen] fille f. || [girlfriend] pe-
tite amie f.

girlfriend ['gɜːlfrend] n [female lover]
petite amie f. || [female friend] amie f.

girl guide Br, **girl scout** Am n éclai-
reuse f, guide f.

girth [gɜːθ] n [circumference - of tree]
circonférence f; [- of person] tour m de
taille. || [of horse] sangle f.

gist [dʒɪst] n substance f; to get the ~ of
sthg comprendre OR saisir l'essentiel de
qqch.

give [gɪv] (pt gave, pp given) 1 vt [gen]
donner; [message] transmettre; [atten-
tion, time] consacrer; to ~ sb/sthg sthg
donner qqch à qqn/qqch; to ~ sb
pleasure/a fright/a smile faire plaisir/
peur/un sourire à qqn. || [as present]: to ~
sb sthg, to ~ sthg to sb donner qqch à
qqn, offrir qqch à qqn. 2 vi [collapse,
break] céder, s'affaisser. 3 n [elasticity]
élasticité f, souplesse f. ○ **give or take**
prep: ~ or take a day/£10 à un jour/10
livres près. ○ **give away** vt sep [get rid
of] donner. || [reveal] révéler. ○ **give
back** vt sep [return] rendre. ○ **give in** vi
[admit defeat] abandonner, se rendre. ||
[agree unwillingly]: to ~ in to sthg céder à
qqch. ○ **give off** vt fus [smell] exhaler;

[smoke] faire; [heat] produire. ○ **give
out** 1 vt sep [distribute] distribuer. 2 vi
[supplies] s'épuiser; [car] lâcher. ○ **give
up** 1 vt sep [stop] renoncer à; to ~ up
drinking/smoking arrêter de boire/de
fumer. || [surrender]: to ~ o.s. up (to sb)
se rendre (à qqn). 2 vi abandonner, se
rendre.

given ['gɪvn] 1 adj [set, fixed] conve-
nu(e), fixé(e). || [prone]: to be ~ to sthg/
to doing sthg être enclin(e) à qqch/à
faire qqch. 2 prep étant donné; ~ that
étant donné que.

given name n Am prénom m.

glacier ['glæsjər] n glacier m.

glad [glæd] adj [happy, pleased]
content(e); to be ~ about sthg être
content de qqch. || [willing]: to be ~ to do
sthg faire volontiers OR avec plaisir.
|| [grateful]: to be ~ of sthg être
content(e) de qqch.

gladly ['glædlɪ] adv [happily, eagerly]
avec joie. || [willingly] avec plaisir.

glamor Am = glamour.

glamorous ['glæmərəs] adj [person] sé-
duisant(e); [appearance] élégant(e); [job,
place] prestigieux(ieuse).

glamour Br, **glamor** Am ['glæmər] n
[of person] charme m; [of appearance]
élégance f, chic m; [of job, place] prestige
m.

glance [glɑːns] 1 n [quick look] regard
m, coup d'œil m; at a ~ d'un coup d'œil;
at first ~ au premier coup d'œil. 2 vi
[look quickly]: to ~ at sb/sthg jeter un
coup d'œil à qqn/qqch. ○ **glance off**
fus [subj: ball, bullet] ricocher sur.

gland [glænd] n glande f.

glandular fever [,glændjulər-] n mono-
nucléose f infectieuse.

glare [gleər] 1 n [scowl] regard m mau-
vais. || (U) [of headlights, publicity] lu-
mière f aveuglante. 2 vi [scowl]: to ~ at
sb/sthg regarder qqn/qqch d'un œil
mauvais. || [sun, lamp] briller d'une lu-
mière éblouissante.

glaring ['gleərɪŋ] adj [very obvious] fla-
grant(e). || [blazing, dazzling] aveu-
glant(e).

glasnost ['glæznɒst] n glasnost f, transparence f.

glass [glɑːs] 1 n [gen] verre m. || (U)
[glassware] verrerie f. 2 comp [bottle, jar]
en or de verre; [door, partition] vitré(e).
○ **glasses** npl [spectacles] lunettes fpl.

glassware ['glɑːsweər] n (U) verrerie f.

glassy ['glɑːsɪ] *adj* [smooth, shiny] lisse comme un miroir. ‖ [blank, lifeless] vitreux(euse).

glaze [gleɪz] **1** *n* [on pottery] vernis *m*; [on pastry, flan] glaçage *m*. **2** *vt* [pottery, tiles, bricks] vernisser; [pastry, flan] glacer.

glazier ['gleɪzjər] *n* vitrier *m*.

gleam [gliːm] **1** *n* [of gold] reflet *m*; [of fire, sunset, disapproval] lueur *f*. **2** *vi* [surface, object] luire. ‖ [light, eyes] briller.

gleaming ['gliːmɪŋ] *adj* brillant(e).

glee [gliː] *n* (*U*) [joy] joie *f*, jubilation *f*.

glib [glɪb] *adj pej* [salesman, politician] qui a du bagout; [promise, excuse] facile.

glide [glaɪd] *vi* [move smoothly - dancer, boat] glisser sans effort; [- person] se mouvoir sans effort. ‖ [fly] planer.

glider ['glaɪdər] *n* [plane] planeur *m*.

gliding ['glaɪdɪŋ] *n* [sport] vol *m* à voile.

glimmer ['glɪmər] *n* [faint light] faible lueur *f*; *fig* signe *m*, lueur.

glimpse [glɪmps] **1** *n* [look, sight] aperçu *m*. ‖ [idea, perception] idée *f*. **2** *vt* [catch sight of] apercevoir, entrevoir. ‖ [perceive] pressentir.

glint [glɪnt] **1** *n* [flash] reflet *m*. ‖ [in eyes] éclair *m*. **2** *vi* étinceler.

glisten ['glɪsn] *vi* briller.

glitter ['glɪtər] **1** *n* (*U*) scintillement *m*. **2** *vi* [object, light] scintiller. ‖ [eyes] briller.

gloat [gləʊt] *vi*: to ~ (over sthg) se réjouir (de qqch).

global ['gləʊbl] *adj* [worldwide] mondial(e).

global warming [-'wɔːmɪŋ] *n* réchauffement *m* de la planète.

globe [gləʊb] *n* [Earth]: the ~ la terre. ‖ [spherical map] globe *m* terrestre. ‖ [spherical object] globe *m*.

gloom [gluːm] *n* (*U*) [darkness] obscurité *f*. ‖ [unhappiness] tristesse *f*.

gloomy ['gluːmɪ] *adj* [room, sky, prospects] sombre. ‖ [person, atmosphere, mood] triste, lugubre.

glorious ['glɔːrɪəs] *adj* [beautiful, splendid] splendide. ‖ [very enjoyable] formidable. ‖ [successful, impressive] magnifique.

glory ['glɔːrɪ] *n* (*U*) [fame, admiration] gloire *f*. ‖ (*U*) [beauty] splendeur *f*. ○ **glory in** *vt fus* [relish] savourer.

gloss [glɒs] *n* (*U*) [shine] brillant *m*, lustre *m*. ‖ ~ (paint) peinture *f* brillante. ○ **gloss over** *vt fus* passer sur.

glossary ['glɒsərɪ] *n* glossaire *m*.

glossy ['glɒsɪ] *adj* [hair, surface] brillant(e). ‖ [book, photo] sur papier glacé.

glove [glʌv] *n* gant *m*.

glove compartment *n* boîte *f* à gants.

glow [gləʊ] **1** *n* (*U*) [of fire, light, sunset] lueur *f*. **2** *vi* [shine out - fire] rougeoyer; [light, stars, eyes] flamboyer. ‖ [shine in light] briller.

glower ['glaʊər] *vi*: to ~ (at) lancer des regards noirs (à).

glucose ['gluːkəʊs] *n* glucose *m*.

glue [gluː] (*cont* glueing OR gluing). **1** *n* (*U*) colle *f*. **2** *vt* [stick with glue] coller; to ~ sthg to sthg coller qqch à OR avec qqch.

glum [glʌm] *adj* [unhappy] morne.

glut [glʌt] *n* surplus *m*.

glutton ['glʌtn] *n* [greedy person] glouton *m*, -onne *f*; to be a ~ for punishment être maso, être masochiste.

gnarled [nɑːld] *adj* [tree, hands] noueux(euse).

gnat [næt] *n* moucheron *m*.

gnaw [nɔː] **1** *vt* [chew] ronger. **2** *vi* [worry]: to ~ (away) at sb ronger qqn.

gnome [nəʊm] *n* gnome *m*, lutin *m*.

GNP (*abbr of* **gross national product**) *n* PNB *m*.

go [gəʊ] (*pt* went, *pp* gone, *pl* goes) **1** *vi* [move, travel] aller; **he's gone to Portugal** il est allé au Portugal; **where does this path ~?** où mène ce chemin?; **to ~ and do sthg** aller faire qqch; **to ~ for a walk** aller se promener, faire une promenade. ‖ [depart] partir, s'en aller; **what time does the bus ~?** à quelle heure part le bus?; **let's ~!** allons-y! ‖ [become] devenir; **to ~ grey** grisonner, devenir gris. ‖ [pass - time] passer. ‖ [progress] marcher, se dérouler; **to ~ well/badly** aller bien/mal; **how's it ~ing?** *inf* comment ça va? ‖ [function, work] marcher; **the car won't ~** la voiture ne veut pas démarrer. ‖ [indicating intention, expectation]: **to be ~ing to do sthg** aller faire qqch; **we're ~ing (to ~) to America in June** on va (aller) en Amérique en juin; **she's ~ing to have a baby** elle attend un bébé. ‖ [bell, alarm] sonner. ‖ [stop working, break - light bulb, fuse] sauter. ‖ [deteriorate - hearing, sight etc] baisser. ‖ [match, be compatible]: to ~ (with) aller (avec); **those colours don't really ~** ces couleurs ne vont pas bien ensemble. ‖ [fit] aller. ‖ [belong] aller, se mettre. ‖ [in division]: **three into two won't ~** deux divisé par trois n'y va pas. ‖ *inf* [expressing irritation, surprise]: **now**

what's he gone and done? qu'est-ce qu'il a fait encore? **2** *n* [turn] tour *m*; **it's my ~** c'est à moi (de jouer). || *inf* [attempt]: **to have a ~ (at sthg)** essayer (de faire qqch). || *phr*: **to be on the ~** *inf* être sur la brèche. ○ **to go** *adv* [remaining]: **there are only three days to ~** il ne reste que trois jours. ○ **go about 1** *vt fus* [perform]: **to ~ about one's business** vaquer à ses occupations. **2** *vi* = **go around.** ○ **go ahead** *vi* [begin]: **to ~ ahead with sthg** mettre qqch à exécution; **~ ahead!** allez-y! || [take place] avoir lieu. ○ **go along** *vi* [proceed] avancer; **as you ~ along** au fur et à mesure. ○ **go along with** *vt fus* [suggestion, idea] appuyer, soutenir; [person] suivre. ○ **go around** *vi* [frequent]: **to ~ around with sb** fréquenter qqn. || [spread] circuler, courir. ○ **go back on** *vt fus* [one's word, promise] revenir sur. ○ **go back to** *vt fus* [return to activity] reprendre, se remettre à; **to ~ back to sleep** se rendormir. || [date from] remonter à, dater de. ○ **go by 1** *vi* [time] s'écouler, passer. **2** *vt fus* [be guided by] suivre. || [judge from] juger d'après. ○ **go down 1** *vi* [get lower - prices etc] baisser. || [be accepted]: **to ~ down well/badly** être bien/mal accueilli. || [sun] se coucher. || [tyre, balloon] se dégonfler. **2** *vt fus* descendre. ○ **go for** *vt fus* [choose] choisir. || [be attracted to] être attiré(e) par. || [attack] tomber sur, attaquer. || [try to obtain - job, record] essayer d'obtenir. ○ **go in** *vi* entrer. ○ **go in for** *vt fus* [competition] prendre part à; [exam] se présenter à. || [activity - enjoy] aimer; [- participate in] faire, s'adonner à. ○ **go into** *vt fus* [investigate] étudier, examiner. || [take up as a profession] entrer dans. ○ **go off 1** *vi* [explode] exploser. || [alarm] sonner. || [go bad - food] se gâter. || [lights, heating] s'éteindre. **2** *vt fus* [lose interest in] ne plus aimer. ○ **go on 1** *vi* [take place, happen] se passer. || [heating etc] se mettre en marche. || [continue]: **to ~ on (doing)** continuer (à faire). || [proceed to further activity]: **to ~ on to sthg** passer à qqch; **to ~ on to do sthg** faire qqch après. || [talk for too long] parler n'en plus finir; **to ~ on about sthg** ne pas arrêter de parler de qqch. **2** *vt fus* [be guided by] se fonder sur. ○ **go out** *vi* [leave] sortir. || [for amusement]: **to ~ out (with sb)** sortir (avec qqn). || [light, fire, cigarette] s'éteindre. ○ **go over** *vt fus* [examine] examiner, vérifier. || [repeat, review] re-

passer. ○ **go round** *vi* [revolve] tourner; *see also* **go around.** ○ **go through** *vt fus* [experience] subir, souffrir. || [study, search through] examiner; **she went through his pockets** elle lui a fait les poches, elle a fouillé dans ses poches. ○ **go through with** *vt fus* [action, threat] aller jusqu'au bout de. ○ **go towards** *vt fus* contribuer à. ○ **go under** *vi lit & fig* couler. ○ **go up 1** *vi* [gen] monter. || [prices] augmenter. **2** *vt fus* monter. ○ **go without 1** *vt fus* se passer de. **2** *vi* s'en passer.

goad [gəʊd] *vt* [provoke] talonner.

go-ahead 1 *adj* [dynamic] dynamique. **2** *n* (U) [permission] feu *m* vert.

goal [gəʊl] *n* but *m*.

goalkeeper ['gəʊl,kiːpər] *n* gardien *m* de but.

goalmouth ['gəʊlmaʊθ, *pl* -maʊðz] *n* but *m*.

goalpost ['gəʊlpəʊst] *n* poteau *m* de but.

goat [gəʊt] *n* chèvre *f*.

gobble ['gɒbl] *vt* engloutir. ○ **gobble down, gobble up** *vt sep* engloutir.

go-between *n* intermédiaire *mf*.

go-cart = **go-kart.**

god [gɒd] *n* dieu *m*, divinité *f*. ○ **God** *n* Dieu *m*; **God knows** Dieu seul le sait; **for God's sake** pour l'amour de Dieu; **thank God** Dieu merci. **2** *excl*: **(my) God!** mon Dieu!

godchild ['gɒdtʃaɪld] (*pl* **-children** [-,tʃɪldrən]) *n* filleul *m*, -e *f*.

goddaughter ['gɒd,dɔːtər] *n* filleule *f*.

goddess ['gɒdɪs] *n* déesse *f*.

godfather ['gɒd,fɑːðər] *n* parrain *m*.

godforsaken ['gɒdfə,seɪkn] *adj* morne, désolé(e).

godmother ['gɒd,mʌðər] *n* marraine *f*.

godsend ['gɒdsend] *n* aubaine *f*.

godson ['gɒdsʌn] *n* filleul *m*.

goes [gəʊz] → **go.**

goggles ['gɒglz] *npl* lunettes *fpl*.

going ['gəʊɪŋ] *n* (U) [rate of advance] allure *f*. || [travel conditions] conditions *fpl*.

go-kart [-kɑːt] *n* kart *m*.

gold [gəʊld] **1** *n* (U) [metal, jewellery] or *m*. **2** *comp* [made of gold] en or. **3** *adj* [gold-coloured] doré(e).

golden ['gəʊldən] *adj* [made of gold] en or. || [gold-coloured] doré(e).

goldfish ['gəʊldfɪʃ] (*pl inv*) *n* poisson *m* rouge.

gold leaf *n* (U) feuille *f* d'or.

gold medal *n* médaille *f* d'or.

goldmine ['gəʊldmaɪn] *n lit & fig* mine *f* d'or.

gold-plated [-'pleɪtɪd] *adj* plaqué(e) or.

goldsmith ['gəʊldsmɪθ] *n* orfèvre *m*.

golf [gɒlf] *n* golf *m*.

golf ball *n* [for golf] balle *f* de golf. || [for typewriter] boule *f*.

golf club *n* [stick, place] club *m* de golf.

golf course *n* terrain *m* de golf.

golfer ['gɒlfər] *n* golfeur *m*, -euse *f*.

gone [gɒn] 1 *pp* → **go**. 2 *adj* [no longer here] parti(e). 3 *prep*: it's ~ ten (o'clock) il est dix heures passées.

gong [gɒŋ] *n* gong *m*.

good [gʊd] (*compar* **better**, *superl* **best**) 1 *adj* [gen] bon (bonne); it's ~ to see you again ça fait plaisir de te revoir; to be ~ at sthg être bon en qqch; it's ~ for you c'est bon pour toi OR pour la santé; to feel ~ [person] se sentir bien; it's ~ that ... c'est bien que ...; ~! très bien! || [kind-person] gentil(ille); to be ~ to sb être très attentionné envers qqn; to be ~ enough to do sthg avoir l'amabilité de faire qqch. || [well-behaved - child] sage; [- behaviour] correct(e); be ~! sois sage!, tiens-toi tranquille! 2 *n* (*U*) [benefit] bien *m*; it will do him ~ ça lui fera du bien. || [use] utilité *f*; what's the ~ of doing that? à quoi bon faire ça?; it's no ~ ça ne sert à rien. || (*U*) [morally correct behaviour] bien *m*; to be up to no ~ préparer un sale coup. ○ **goods** *npl* [merchandise] marchandises *fpl*, articles *mpl*. ○ **as good as** *adv* pratiquement, pour ainsi dire. ○ **for good** *adv* [forever] pour de bon, définitivement. ○ **good afternoon** *excl* bonjour! ○ **good evening** *excl* bonsoir! ○ **good morning** *excl* bonjour! ○ **good night** *excl* bonsoir!; [at bedtime] bonne nuit!

goodbye [,gʊd'baɪ] 1 *excl* au revoir! 2 *n* au revoir *m*.

Good Friday *n* Vendredi *m* saint.

good-humoured [-'hjuːməd] *adj* [person] de bonne humeur; [smile, remark, rivalry] bon enfant.

good-looking [-'lʊkɪŋ] *adj* [person] beau (belle).

good-natured [-'neɪtʃəd] *adj* [person] d'un naturel aimable; [rivalry, argument] bon enfant.

goodness ['gʊdnɪs] 1 *n* (*U*) [kindness] bonté *f*. || [nutritive quality] valeur *f* nutritive. 2 *excl*: (my) ~! mon Dieu!, Sei-

gneur!; for ~' sake! par pitié!, pour l'amour de Dieu!; thank ~! grâce à Dieu!

goodwill [,gʊd'wɪl] *n* bienveillance *f*.

goody ['gʊdɪ] *inf* 1 *n* [person] bon *m*. 2 *excl* chouette! ○ **goodies** *npl inf* [delicious food] friandises *fpl*. || [desirable objects] merveilles *fpl*, trésors *mpl*.

goose [guːs] (*pl* **geese**) *n* [bird] oie *f*.

gooseberry ['gʊzbərɪ] *n* [fruit] groseille *f* à maquereau.

gooseflesh ['guːsfleʃ] *n*, **goose pimples** *Br*, **goosebumps** *Am* ['guːsbʌmps] *npl* chair *f* de poule.

gore [gɔːr] 1 *n* (*U*) *literary* [blood] sang *m*. 2 *vt* encorner.

gorge [gɔːdʒ] 1 *n* gorge *f*, défilé *m*. 2 *vt*: to ~ o.s. on OR with sthg se bourrer OR se goinfrer de qqch.

gorgeous ['gɔːdʒəs] *adj* divin(e); *inf* [good-looking] magnifique, splendide.

gorilla [gə'rɪlə] *n* gorille *m*.

gorse [gɔːs] *n* (*U*) ajonc *m*.

gory ['gɔːrɪ] *adj* sanglant(e).

gosh [gɒʃ] *excl inf* ça alors!

gospel ['gɒspl] *n* [doctrine] évangile *m*. ○ **Gospel** *n* Évangile *m*.

gossip ['gɒsɪp] 1 *n* [conversation] bavardage *m*; *pej* commérage *m*. || [person] commère *f*. 2 *vi* [talk] bavarder, papoter; *pej* cancaner.

gossip column *n* échos *mpl*.

got [gɒt] *pt & pp* → **get**.

gotten ['gɒtn] *Am pp* → **get**.

goulash ['guːlæʃ] *n* goulache *m*.

gourmet ['gʊəmeɪ] 1 *n* gourmet *m*. 2 *comp* [food, restaurant] gastronomique; [cook] gastronome.

gout [gaʊt] *n* (*U*) goutte *f*.

govern ['gʌvən] 1 *vt* [gen] gouverner. || [control] régir. 2 *vi* POL gouverner.

governess ['gʌvənɪs] *n* gouvernante *f*.

government ['gʌvnmənt] *n* gouvernement *m*.

governor ['gʌvənər] *n* POL gouverneur *m*. || [of school] ≃ membre *m* du conseil d'établissement; [of bank] gouverneur *m*. || [of prison] directeur *m*.

gown [gaʊn] *n* [for woman] robe *f*. || [for surgeon] blouse *f*; [for judge, academic] robe *f*, toge *f*.

GP *n abbr of* **general practitioner**.

grab [græb] 1 *vt* [seize] saisir. || *inf* [sandwich] avaler en vitesse; to ~ a few hours' sleep dormir quelques heures. || *inf* [appeal to] emballer. 2 *vi*: to ~ at sthg faire un geste pour attraper qqch.

grace [greɪs] **1** n [elegance] grâce f. || (U) [extra time] répit m. || [prayer] grâces fpl.

graceful ['greɪsfʊl] adj gracieux(ieuse), élégant(e).

gracious ['greɪʃəs] **1** adj [polite] courtois(e). **2** excl: (good) ~! juste ciel!

grade [greɪd] **1** n [quality - of worker] catégorie f; [- of wool, paper] qualité f; [- of petrol] type m; [- of eggs] calibre m. || Am [class] classe f. || [mark] note f. **2** vt [classify] classer. || [mark, assess] noter.

grade crossing n Am passage m à niveau.

grade school n Am école f primaire.

gradient ['greɪdjənt] n pente f, inclinaison f.

gradual ['grædʒʊəl] adj graduel(elle), progressif(ive).

gradually ['grædʒʊəlɪ] adv graduellement, petit à petit.

graduate [n 'grædʒʊət, vb 'grædʒʊeɪt] **1** n [from university] diplômé m, -e f. || Am [of high school] ≃ titulaire mf du baccalauréat. **2** vi [from university]: **to ~ (from)** ≃ obtenir son diplôme (à). || Am [from high school]: **to ~ (from)** ≃ obtenir son baccalauréat (à).

graduation [,grædʒʊ'eɪʃn] n (U) [ceremony] remise f des diplômes.

graffiti [grə'fiːtɪ] n (U) graffiti mpl.

graft [grɑːft] **1** n [from plant] greffe f, greffon m. || MED greffe f. || Am inf [corruption] graissage m de patte. **2** vt [plant, skin] greffer.

grain [greɪn] n [gen] grain m. || (U) [crops] céréales fpl. || (U) [pattern - in wood] fil m; [- in material] grain m; [- in stone, marble] veines fpl.

gram [græm] n gramme m.

grammar ['græmər] n grammaire f.

grammar school n [in UK] ≃ lycée m; [in US] école f primaire.

grammatical [grə'mætɪkl] adj grammatical(e).

grand [grænd] **1** adj [impressive] grandiose, imposant(e). || [ambitious] grand(e). || [important] important(e); [socially] distingué(e). || inf dated [excellent] sensationnel(elle), formidable. **2** n inf [thousand dollars] mille dollars mpl.

grandad ['grændæd] n inf papi m, pépé m.

grandchild ['græntʃaɪld] (pl -children [-,tʃɪldrən]) n [boy] petit-fils m; [girl] petite-fille f. ○ **grandchildren** npl petits-enfants mpl.

granddad = grandad.

granddaughter ['græn,dɔːtər] n petite-fille f.

grandeur ['grændʒər] n [splendour] splendeur f, magnificence f.

grandfather ['grænd,fɑːðər] n grand-père m.

grandma ['grænmɑː] n inf mamie f, mémé f.

grandmother ['græn,mʌðər] n grand-mère f.

grandpa ['grænpɑː] n inf papi m, pépé m.

grandparents ['græn,peərənts] npl grands-parents mpl.

grand piano n piano m à queue.

grand slam n SPORT grand chelem m.

grandson ['grænsʌn] n petit-fils m.

grandstand ['grændstænd] n tribune f.

grand total n somme f globale, total m général.

granite ['grænɪt] n granit m.

granny ['grænɪ] n inf mamie f, mémé f.

grant [grɑːnt] **1** n subvention f; [for study] bourse f. **2** vt [wish, appeal] accorder; [request] accéder à. || [admit] admettre, reconnaître. || [give] accorder; **to take sb for ~ed** [not appreciate sb's help] penser que tout ce que qqn fait va de soi; [not value sb's presence] penser que qqn fait partie des meubles; **to take sthg for ~ed** [result, sb's agreement] considérer qqch comme acquis.

granulated sugar ['grænjʊleɪtɪd-] n sucre m cristallisé.

granule ['grænjuːl] n granule m; [of sugar] grain m.

grape [greɪp] n (grain m de) raisin m; **a bunch of ~s** une grappe de raisin.

grapefruit ['greɪpfruːt] (pl inv OR -s) n pamplemousse m.

grapevine ['greɪpvaɪn] n vigne f; **on the ~** fig par le téléphone arabe.

graph [grɑːf] n graphique m.

graphic ['græfɪk] adj [vivid] vivant(e). || ART graphique. ○ **graphics** npl graphique f.

graph paper n (U) papier m millimétré.

grapple ['græpl] ○ **grapple with** vt fus [person, animal] lutter avec. || [problem] se débattre avec, se colleter avec.

grasp [grɑːsp] **1** n [grip] prise f. || [understanding] compréhension f; **to have a good ~ of sthg** avoir une bonne connaissance de qqch. **2** vt [grip, seize] saisir, empoigner. ‖ [understand] saisir, comprendre. ‖ [opportunity] saisir.

grass [grɑːs] n BOT & drugs sl herbe f.

grasshopper ['grɑːs,hɒpə'] n sauterelle f.

grass roots 1 npl fig base f. 2 comp du peuple.

grass snake n couleuvre f.

grate [greɪt] 1 n grille f de foyer. 2 vt râper. 3 vi grincer, crisser.

grateful ['greɪtful] adj: **to be ~ to sb (for sthg)** être reconnaissant(e) à qqn (de qqch).

grater ['greɪtə'] n râpe f.

gratify ['grætɪfaɪ] vt [please - person]: **to be gratified** être content(e), être satisfait(e). ‖ [satisfy - wish] satisfaire, assouvir.

grating ['greɪtɪŋ] 1 adj grinçant(e); [voix] de crécelle. 2 n [grille] grille f.

gratitude ['grætɪtjuːd] n (U): **~ (to sb for sthg)** gratitude f OR reconnaissance f (envers qqn de qqch).

gratuitous [grə'tjuːɪtəs] adj fml gratuit(e).

grave¹ [greɪv] 1 adj grave; [concern] sérieux(ieuse). 2 n tombe f.

grave² [grɑːv] adj LING: **e ~** e m accent grave.

gravel ['grævl] n (U) gravier m.

gravestone ['greɪvstəʊn] n pierre f tombale.

graveyard ['greɪvjɑːd] n cimetière m.

gravity ['grævətɪ] n [force] gravité f, pesanteur f. ‖ [seriousness] gravité f.

gravy ['greɪvɪ] n (U) [meat juice] jus m de viande.

gray Am = grey.

graze [greɪz] 1 vt [subj: cows, sheep] brouter, paître. ‖ [subj: farmer] faire paître. ‖ [skin] écorcher, égratigner. ‖ [touch lightly] frôler, effleurer. 2 vi brouter, paître. 3 n écorchure f, égratignure f.

grease [griːs] 1 n graisse f. 2 vt graisser.

greasy ['griːzɪ] adj [covered in grease] graisseux(euse); [clothes] taché(e) de graisse. ‖ [food, skin, hair] gras (grasse).

great [greɪt] adj [gen] grand(e); **~ big** énorme. ‖ inf [splendid] génial(e), formidable; **to feel ~** se sentir en pleine forme; **~! super!, génial!**

Great Britain n Grande-Bretagne f; **in ~** en Grande-Bretagne.

greatcoat ['greɪtkəʊt] n pardessus m.

Great Dane n danois m.

great-grandchild n [boy] arrière-petit-fils m; [girl] arrière-petite-fille f.

○ **great-grandchildren** npl arrière-petits-enfants mpl.

great-grandfather n arrière-grand-père m.

great-grandmother n arrière-grand-mère f.

greatly ['greɪtlɪ] adv beaucoup; [different] très.

greatness ['greɪtnɪs] n grandeur f.

Greece [griːs] n Grèce f.

greed [griːd] n (U) [for food] gloutonnerie f. ‖ fig [for money, power]: **~ (for)** avidité f (de).

greedy ['griːdɪ] adj [for food] glouton(onne). ‖ [for money, power]: **~ for sthg** avide de qqch.

Greek [griːk] 1 adj grec (grecque). 2 n [person] Grec m, Grecque f. ‖ [language] grec m.

green [griːn] 1 adj [in colour, unripe] vert(e). ‖ [ecological - issue, politics] écologique; [- person] vert(e). ‖ inf [inexperienced] inexpérimenté(e), jeune. 2 n [colour] vert m. ‖ GOLF vert m. ‖ **village ~** pelouse f communale. ○ **Green** n POL vert m, -e f, écologiste mf; **the Greens** les Verts, les Écologistes. ○ **greens** npl [vegetables] légumes mpl verts.

greenback ['griːnbæk] n Am inf billet m vert.

green card n Am [residence permit] carte f de séjour.

greenery ['griːnərɪ] n verdure f.

greenfly ['griːnflaɪ] (pl inv OR -ies) n puceron m.

greengage ['griːngeɪdʒ] n reine-claude f.

greengrocer ['griːn,grəʊsə'] n marchand m, -e f de légumes; **~'s (shop)** magasin m de fruits et légumes.

greenhouse ['griːnhaʊs, pl -haʊzɪz] n serre f.

greenhouse effect n: **the ~** l'effet m de serre.

Greenland ['griːnlənd] n Groenland m.

green salad n salade f verte.

greet [griːt] vt [say hello to] saluer. ‖ [receive] accueillir.

greeting ['griːtɪŋ] n salutation f, salut m. ○ **greetings** npl: **Christmas/birthday ~s** vœux mpl de Noël/d'anniversaire.

greetings card Br, **greeting card** Am n carte f de vœux.

grenade [grə'neɪd] n: **(hand) ~** grenade f (à main).

grew [gruː] pt → grow.

grey *Br*, **gray** *Am* [greɪ] **1** *adj* [in colour] gris(e). ‖ [grey-haired]: **to go ~** grisonner. ‖ [dull, gloomy] morne, triste. **2** *n* gris *m*.

grey-haired [-'heəd] *adj* aux cheveux gris.

greyhound ['greɪhaʊnd] *n* lévrier *m*.

grid [grɪd] *n* [grating] grille *f*. ‖ [system of squares] quadrillage *m*.

griddle ['grɪdl] *n* plaque *f* à cuire.

gridlock ['grɪdlɒk] *n* *Am* embouteillage *m*.

grief [griːf] *n* (U) [sorrow] chagrin *m*, peine *f*. ‖ *inf* [trouble] ennuis *mpl*. ‖ *phr*: **to come to ~** échouer; **good ~!** Dieu du ciel!, mon Dieu!

grievance ['griːvns] *n* grief *m*, doléance *f*.

grieve [griːv] *vi* [at death] être en deuil; **to ~ for sb/sthg** pleurer qqn/qqch.

grievous bodily harm *n* (U) coups *mpl* et blessures *fpl*.

grill [grɪl] **1** *n* [on cooker, fire] gril *m*. **2** *vt* [cook on grill] griller, faire griller. ‖ *inf* [interrogate] cuisiner.

grille [grɪl] *n* grille *f*.

grim [grɪm] *adj* [stern - face, expression] sévère; [- determination] inflexible. ‖ [cheerless - truth, news] sinistre; [- room, walls] lugubre; [- day] morne, triste.

grimace [grɪ'meɪs] **1** *n* grimace *f*. **2** *vi* grimacer, faire la grimace.

grime [graɪm] *n* (U) crasse *f*, saleté *f*.

grimy ['graɪmɪ] *adj* sale, encrassé(e).

grin [grɪn] **1** *n* (large) sourire *m*. **2** *vi*: **to ~ (at sb/sthg)** adresser un large sourire (à qqn/qqch).

grind [graɪnd] (*pt & pp* **ground**) **1** *vt* [crush] moudre. **2** *vi* [scrape] grincer. **3** *n* [hard, boring work] corvée *f*. ◆ **grind down** *vt sep* [oppress] opprimer. ○ **grind up** *vt sep* pulvériser.

grinder ['graɪndə^r] *n* moulin *m*.

grip [grɪp] **1** *n* [grasp, hold] prise *f*. ‖ [control] contrôle *m*; **he's got a good ~ on the situation** il a la situation bien en main; **to get to ~s with sthg** s'attaquer à qqch; **to get a ~ on o.s.** se ressaisir. ‖ [adhesion] adhérence *f*. ‖ [handle] poignée *f*. **2** *vt* [grasp] saisir; [subj: tyres] adhérer à. ‖ *fig* [imagination, country] captiver.

gripping ['grɪpɪŋ] *adj* passionnant(e).

grisly ['grɪzlɪ] *adj* [horrible, macabre] macabre.

gristle ['grɪsl] *n* (U) nerfs *mpl*.

grit [grɪt] **1** *n* (U) [stones] gravillon *m*; [in eye] poussière *f*. **2** *vt* sabler.

gritty ['grɪtɪ] *adj* [stony] couvert(e) de gravillon.

groan [grəʊn] **1** *n* gémissement *m*. **2** *vi* [moan] gémir. ‖ [creak] grincer, gémir.

grocer ['grəʊsə^r] *n* épicier *m*, -ière *f*; **~'s (shop)** épicerie *f*.

groceries ['grəʊsərɪz] *npl* [foods] provisions *fpl*.

grocery ['grəʊsərɪ] *n* [shop] épicerie *f*.

groggy ['grɒgɪ] *adj* groggy (*inv*).

groin [grɔɪn] *n* aine *f*.

groom [gruːm] **1** *n* [of horses] palefrenier *m*, garçon *m* d'écurie. ‖ [bridegroom] marié *m*. **2** *vt* [brush] panser. ‖ *fig* [prepare]: **to ~ sb (for sthg)** préparer OR former qqn (pour qqch).

groove [gruːv] *n* [in metal, wood] rainure *f*; [in record] sillon *m*.

grope [grəʊp] *vi*: **to ~ (about) for sthg** chercher qqch à tâtons.

gross [grəʊs] (*pl inv* OR **-es**) **1** *adj* [total] brut(e). ‖ *fml* [serious - negligence] coupable; [- misconduct] choquant(e); [- inequality] flagrant(e). ‖ [coarse, vulgar] grossier(ière). ‖ *inf* [obese] obèse, énorme. **2** *n* grosse *f*, douze douzaines *fpl*.

grossly ['grəʊslɪ] *adv* [seriously] extrêmement, énormément.

grotesque [grəʊ'tesk] *adj* grotesque.

grotto ['grɒtəʊ] (*pl* **-es** OR **-s**) *n* grotte *f*.

ground [graʊnd] **1** *pt & pp* → **grind**. **2** *n* (U) [surface of earth] sol *m*, terre *f*; **above ~** en surface; **below ~** sous terre; **on the ~** par terre, au sol. ‖ (U) [area of land] terrain *m*. ‖ [for sport etc] terrain *m*. ‖ [advantage]: **to gain/lose ~** gagner/perdre du terrain. **3** *vt* [base]: **to be ~ed on** OR **in sthg** être fondé(e) sur qqch. ‖ [child] priver de sortie. ‖ *Am* ELEC: **to be ~ed** être à la masse. ○ **grounds** *npl* [reason] motif *m*, raison *f*; **~s for sthg** motifs de qqch. ‖ [land round building] parc *m*. ‖ [of coffee] marc *m*.

ground crew *n* personnel *m* au sol.

ground floor *n* rez-de-chaussée *m*.

grounding ['graʊndɪŋ] *n*: **~ (in)** connaissances *fpl* de base (en).

groundless ['graʊndlɪs] *adj* sans fondement.

groundsheet ['graʊndʃiːt] *n* tapis *m* de sol.

ground staff *n* [at sports ground] personnel *m* d'entretien (*d'un terrain de sport*). ‖ *Br* = **ground crew**.

groundwork ['graʊndwɜːk] n (U) travail m préparatoire.

group [gruːp] 1 n groupe m. 2 vt grouper, réunir. 3 vi: to ~ (together) se grouper.

groupie ['gruːpɪ] n inf groupie f.

grouse [graʊs] (pl inv OR -s) n [bird] grouse f, coq m de bruyère.

grove [grəʊv] n [group of trees] bosquet m.

grovel ['grɒvl] vi: to ~ (to sb) ramper (devant qqn).

grow [grəʊ] (pt grew, pp grown) 1 vi [gen] pousser; [person, animal] grandir; [company, city] s'agrandir; [fears, influence, traffic] augmenter, s'accroître; [problem, idea, plan] prendre de l'ampleur; [economy] se développer. || [become] devenir; to ~ old vieillir; to ~ tired of sthg se fatiguer de qqch. 2 vt [plants] faire pousser. || [hair, beard] laisser pousser. ○ **grow on** vt fus inf: **it'll ~ on you** cela finira par te plaire. ○ **grow out of** vt fus [clothes, shoes] devenir trop grand pour. || [habit] perdre. ○ **grow up** vi [become adult] grandir, devenir adulte; ~ up! ne fais pas l'enfant! || [develop] se développer.

grower ['grəʊər] n cultivateur m, -trice f.

growl [graʊl] vi [animal] grogner, gronder; [person] grogner.

grown [grəʊn] 1 pp → grow. 2 adj adulte.

grown-up 1 adj [fully grown] adulte, grand(e). || [mature] mûr(e). 2 n adulte mf, grande personne f.

growth [grəʊθ] n [increase - gen] croissance f; [- of opposition, company] développement m; [- of population] augmentation f, accroissement m. || MED [lump] tumeur f, excroissance f.

grub [grʌb] n [insect] larve f. || inf [food] bouffe f.

grubby ['grʌbɪ] adj sale, malpropre.

grudge [grʌdʒ] 1 n rancune f; to bear sb a ~, to bear a ~ against sb garder rancune à qqn. 2 vt: to ~ sb sthg donner qqch à qqn à contrecœur; [success] en vouloir à qqn à cause de qqch.

gruelling Br, **grueling** Am ['groəlɪŋ] adj épuisant(e), exténuant(e).

gruesome ['gruːsəm] adj horrible.

gruff [grʌf] adj [hoarse] gros (grosse). || [rough, unfriendly] brusque, bourru(e).

grumble ['grʌmbl] vi [complain]: to ~

about sthg rouspéter OR grommeler contre qqch.

grumpy ['grʌmpɪ] adj inf renfrogné(e).

grunt [grʌnt] 1 n grognement m. 2 vi grogner.

guarantee [,gærən'tiː] 1 n garantie f. 2 vt garantir.

guard [gaːd] 1 n [person] garde m; [in prison] gardien m. || [group of guards] garde f. || [defensive operation] garde f. || to be on ~ être de garde OR de faction; to catch sb off ~ prendre qqn au dépourvu. || [protective device - for body] protection f; [- for fire] garde-feu m inv. 2 vt [protect - building] protéger, garder; [- person] protéger. || [prisoner] garder, surveiller. || [hide - secret] garder.

guard dog n chien m de garde.

guarded ['gaːdɪd] adj prudent(e).

guardian ['gaːdjən] n [of child] tuteur m, -trice f. || [protector] gardien m, -ienne f, protecteur m, -trice f.

guardrail ['gaːdreɪl] n Am [on road] barrière f de sécurité.

guerilla [gə'rɪlə] = guerrilla.

guerrilla [gə'rɪlə] n guérillero m.

guerrilla warfare n (U) guérilla f.

guess [ges] 1 n conjecture f. 2 vt deviner; ~ what? tu sais quoi? 3 vi [conjecture] deviner; to ~ at sthg deviner qqch. || [suppose]: I ~ (so) je suppose (que oui).

guesswork ['geswɜːk] n (U) conjectures fpl, hypothèses fpl.

guest [gest] n [gen] invité m, -e f. || [at hotel] client m, -e f.

guesthouse ['gesthaʊs, pl -haʊzɪz] n pension f de famille.

guestroom ['gestrʊm] n chambre f d'amis.

guffaw [gʌ'fɔː] 1 n gros rire m. 2 vi rire bruyamment.

guidance ['gaɪdəns] n (U) [help] conseils mpl. || [leadership] direction f.

guide [gaɪd] 1 n [person, book] guide m. || [indication] indication f. 2 vt [show by leading] guider. || [control] diriger. || [influence]: to be ~d by sb/sthg se laisser guider par qqn/qqch. ○ **Guide** n = girl guide.

guide book n guide m.

guide dog n chien m d'aveugle.

guidelines ['gaɪdlaɪnz] npl directives fpl, lignes fpl directrices.

guild [gɪld] n [association] association f.

guillotine ['gɪlə,tiːn] 1 n [for executions] guillotine f. || [for paper] massicot m. 2 vt [execute] guillotiner.

guilt [gɪlt] *n* culpabilité *f*.

guilty ['gɪltɪ] *adj* coupable; **to be ~ of** sthg être coupable de qqch; **to be found ~/not ~** JUR être reconnu coupable/non coupable.

guinea pig ['gɪnɪ-] *n* cobaye *m*.

guitar [gɪ'tɑːʳ] *n* guitare *f*.

guitarist [gɪ'tɑːrɪst] *n* guitariste *mf*.

gulf [gʌlf] *n* [sea] golfe *m*. ‖ [breach, chasm]: ~ (between) abîme *m* (entre). ○ **Gulf** *n*: the Gulf le Golfe.

gull [gʌl] *n* mouette *f*.

gullet ['gʌlɪt] *n* œsophage *m*; [of bird] gosier *m*.

gullible ['gʌləbl] *adj* crédule.

gully ['gʌlɪ] *n* [valley] ravine *f*. ‖ [ditch] rigole *f*.

gulp [gʌlp] **1** *n* [of drink] grande gorgée *f*; [of food] grosse bouchée *f*. **2** *vt* avaler. **3** *vi* avoir la gorge nouée. ○ **gulp down** *vt sep* avaler.

gum [gʌm] **1** *n* [chewing gum] chewing-gum *m*. ‖ [adhesive] colle *f*, gomme *f*. ‖ ANAT gencive *f*. **2** *vt* coller.

gun [gʌn] *n* [weapon - small] revolver *m*; [- rifle] fusil *m*; [- large] canon *m*. ‖ [starting pistol] pistolet *m*. ‖ [tool] pistolet *m*; [for staples] agrafeuse *f*. ○ **gun down** *vt sep* abattre.

gunboat ['gʌnbəʊt] *n* canonnière *f*.

gunfire ['gʌnfaɪəʳ] *n* (U) coups *mpl* de feu.

gunman ['gʌnmən] (*pl* **-men** [-mən]) *n* personne *f* armée.

gunpoint ['gʌnpɔɪnt] *n*: **at ~** sous la menace d'un fusil *ou* pistolet.

gunpowder ['gʌn,paʊdəʳ] *n* poudre *f* à canon.

gunshot ['gʌnʃɒt] *n* [firing of gun] coup *m* de feu.

gunsmith ['gʌnsmɪθ] *n* armurier *m*.

gurgle ['gɜːgl] *vi* [water] glouglouter. ‖ [baby] gazouiller.

guru ['gʊruː] *n* gourou *m*, guru *m*.

gush [gʌʃ] **1** *n* jaillissement *m*. **2** *vi* [flow out] jaillir. ‖ *pej* [enthuse] s'exprimer de façon exubérante.

gusset ['gʌsɪt] *n* gousset *m*.

gust [gʌst] *n* rafale *f*, coup *m* de vent.

gusto ['gʌstəʊ] *n*: **with ~** avec enthousiasme.

gut [gʌt] **1** *n* MED intestin *m*. **2** *vt* [remove organs from] vider. ‖ [destroy] réduire à rien. ○ **guts** *npl inf* [intestines] intestins *mpl*. ‖ to hate sb's **~s** ne pas pouvoir piffer qqn, ne pas pouvoir voir qqn en peinture. ‖ [courage] cran *m*.

gutter ['gʌtəʳ] *n* [ditch] rigole *f*. ‖ [on roof] gouttière *f*.

gutter press *n* presse *f* à sensation.

guy [gaɪ] *n inf* [man] type *m*. ‖ [person] copain *m*, copine *f*.

guy rope *n* corde *f* de tente.

guzzle ['gʌzl] **1** *vt* bâfrer; [drink] lamper. **2** *vi* s'empiffrer.

gym [dʒɪm] *n inf* [gymnasium] gymnase *m*. ‖ [exercises] gym *f*.

gymnasium [dʒɪm'neɪzjəm] (*pl* **-iums** OR **-ia** [-jə]) *n* gymnase *m*.

gymnast ['dʒɪmnæst] *n* gymnaste *mf*.

gymnastics [dʒɪm'næstɪks] *n* (U) gymnastique *f*.

gym shoes *npl* (chaussures *fpl* de) tennis *mpl*.

gynaecologist Br, **gynecologist** Am [,gaɪnə'kɒlədʒɪst] *n* gynécologue *mf*.

gynaecology Br, **gynecology** Am [,gaɪnə'kɒlədʒɪ] *n* gynécologie *f*.

gypsy ['dʒɪpsɪ] = **gipsy**.

gyrate [dʒaɪ'reɪt] *vi* tournoyer.

h (*pl* **h's** OR **hs**), **H** (*pl* **H's** OR **Hs**) [eɪtʃ] *n* [letter] h *m inv*, H *m inv*.

haberdashery ['hæbədæʃərɪ] *n* mercerie *f*.

habit ['hæbɪt] *n* [customary practice] habitude *f*; **out of ~** par habitude; **to make a ~ of doing sthg** avoir l'habitude de faire qqch. ‖ [garment] habit *m*.

habitat ['hæbɪtæt] *n* habitat *m*.

habitual [hə'bɪtʃʊəl] *adj* [usual, characteristic] habituel(elle). ‖ [regular] invétéré(e).

hack [hæk] **1** *n* [writer] écrivailleur *m*, -euse *f*. **2** *vt* [cut] tailler. ○ **hack into** *vt fus* COMPUT pirater.

hacker ['hækəʳ] *n*: **(computer) ~** pirate *m* informatique.

hackneyed ['hæknɪd] *adj* rebattu(e).

hacksaw ['hæksɔː] *n* scie *f* à métaux.

had [*weak form* həd, *strong form* hæd] *pt & pp* → **have**.

haddock ['hædək] (pl inv) n églefin m, aiglefin m.

hadn't ['hædnt] = had not.

haemophiliac [,hi:mə'fılı,æk] = hemophiliac.

haemorrhage ['hemərıdʒ] = hemorrhage.

haemorrhoids ['hemərɔıdz] = hemorrhoids.

haggard ['hægəd] adj [face] défait(e); [person] abattu(e).

haggle ['hægl] vi marchander; **to ~ over** OR **about** sthg marchander qqch.

Hague [heıg] n: **The ~** La Haye.

hail [heıl] **1** n grêle f; fig pluie f. **2** vt [call] héler. || [acclaim]: **to ~ sb/sthg as** sthg acclamer qqn/qqch comme qqch. **3** v impers grêler.

hailstone ['heılstəʊn] n grêlon m.

hair [heə^r] n (U) [on human head] cheveux mpl; **to do one's ~** se coiffer. || (U) [on animal, human skin] poils mpl. || [individual hair - on head] cheveu m; [- on skin] poil m.

hairbrush ['heəbrʌʃ] n brosse f à cheveux.

haircut ['heəkʌt] n coupe f de cheveux.

hairdresser ['heə,dresə^r] n coiffeur m, -euse f; **~'s** (salon) salon m de coiffure.

hairdryer ['heə,draıə^r] n [handheld] sèche-cheveux m inv; [with hood] casque m.

hair gel n gel m coiffant.

hairpin ['heəpın] n épingle f à cheveux.

hairpin bend n virage m en épingle à cheveux.

hair-raising [-,reızıŋ] adj à faire dresser les cheveux sur la tête; [journey] effrayant(e).

hair remover [-rı,mu:və^r] n (crème f) dépilatoire m.

hairspray ['heəspreı] n laque f.

hairstyle ['heəstaıl] n coiffure f.

hairy ['heərı] adj [covered in hair] velu(e), poilu(e). || inf [dangerous] à faire dresser les cheveux sur la tête.

Haiti ['heıtı] n Haïti m.

hake [heık] (pl inv OR -s) n colin m, merluche f.

half [Br hɑ:f, Am hæf] (pl senses 1 and 2 halves, pl senses 3, 4 and 5 halves OR halfs) **1** adj demi(e); **~ a dozen** une demi-douzaine; **~ an hour** une demi-heure; **~ a pound** une demi-livre; **~ English** à moitié anglais. **2** adv [gen] à moitié; **~-and-~** moitié-moitié. || [by half] de moitié. || [in telling the time]: **~ past ten**

Br, **~ after ten** Am dix heures et demie; **it's ~ past** il est la demie. **3** n [gen] moitié f; **in ~** en deux; **to go halves (with sb)** partager (avec qqn). || SPORT [of match] mi-temps f. || SPORT [halfback] demi m. || [of beer] demi m. || [child's ticket] demi-tarif m, tarif m enfant. **4** pron la moitié; **~ of them** la moitié d'entre eux.

halfback ['hɑ:fbæk] n demi m.

half board n demi-pension f.

half-breed 1 adj métis(isse). **2** n métis m, -isse f (attention: le terme 'half-breed' est considéré raciste).

half-caste [-kɑ:st] **1** adj métis(isse). **2** n métis m, -isse f (attention: le terme 'half-caste' est considéré raciste).

half-hearted [-'hɑ:tıd] adj sans enthousiasme.

half hour n demi-heure f.

half-mast n: **at ~** [flag] en berne.

half moon n demi-lune f.

half note n Am MUS blanche f.

half-price adj à moitié prix.

half time n (U) mi-temps f.

halfway [hɑ:f'weı] **1** adj à mi-chemin. **2** adv [in space] à mi-chemin. || [in time] à la moitié.

halibut ['hælıbət] (pl inv OR -s) n flétan m.

hall [hɔ:l] n [in house] vestibule m, entrée f. || [meeting room, building] salle f. || [country house] manoir m.

hallmark ['hɔ:lmɑ:k] n [typical feature] marque f. || [on metal] poinçon m.

hallo [hə'ləʊ] = hello.

Hallowe'en [,hæləʊ'i:n] n Halloween f (fête des sorcières et des fantômes).

hallucinate [hə'lu:sıneıt] vi avoir des hallucinations.

hallway ['hɔ:lweı] n vestibule m.

halo ['heıləʊ] (pl -es OR -s) n nimbe m; ASTRON halo m.

halt [hɔ:lt] **1** n [stop]: **to come to a ~** [vehicle] s'arrêter, s'immobiliser; [activity] s'interrompre; **to call a ~ to sthg** mettre fin à qqch. **2** vt arrêter. **3** vi s'arrêter.

halterneck ['hɔ:ltənek] adj dos nu (inv).

halve [Br hɑ:v, Am hæv] vt [reduce by half] réduire de moitié. || [divide] couper en deux.

halves [Br hɑ:vz, Am hævz] pl → half.

ham [hæm] **1** n [meat] jambon m. **2** comp au jambon.

hamburger ['hæmbɜ:gə^r] n [burger] hamburger m. || (U) Am [mince] viande f hachée.

hamlet ['hæmlɪt] *n* hameau *m*.

hammer ['hæmər] **1** *n* marteau *m*. **2** *vt* [with tool] marteler; [nail] enfoncer à coups de marteau. || [with fist] marteler du poing. || *fig* [fact]: **to ~ sthg into sb** faire entrer qqch dans la tête de qqn. || *inf* [defeat] battre à plates coutures. **3** *vi* [with fist]: **to ~ (on)** cogner du poing (à). ○ **hammer out** *vt fus* [agreement, solution] parvenir finalement à.

hammock ['hæmək] *n* hamac *m*.

hamper ['hæmpər] **1** *n* [for food] panier *m* d'osier. || *Am* [for laundry] coffre *m* à linge. **2** *vt* gêner.

hamster ['hæmstər] *n* hamster *m*.

hamstring ['hæmstrɪŋ] *n* tendon *m* du jarret.

hand [hænd] **1** *n* [part of body] main *f*; **to hold ~s** se tenir la main; **by ~** à la main; **to get out of ~** échapper à tout contrôle; **to have one's ~s full** avoir du pain sur la planche; **to try one's ~ at sthg** s'essayer à qqch. || [help] coup *m* de main; **to give** OR **lend sb a ~ (with sthg)** donner un coup de main à qqn (pour faire qqch). || [worker] ouvrier *m*, -ière *f*. || [of clock, watch] aiguille *f*. || [handwriting] écriture *f*. || [of cards] jeu *m*, main *f*. **2** *vt*: **to ~ sthg to sb, to ~ sb sthg** passer qqch à qqn. ○ **(close) at hand** *adv* proche. ○ **on hand** *adv* disponible. ○ **on the other hand** *conj* d'autre part. ○ **out of hand** *adv* [completely] d'emblée. ○ **to hand** *adv* à portée de la main, sous la main. ○ **hand down** *vt sep* transmettre. ○ **hand in** *vt sep* remettre. ○ **hand out** *vt sep* distribuer. ○ **hand over 1** *vt sep* [baton, money] remettre. || [responsibility, power] transmettre. **2** *vi*: **to ~ over (to)** passer le relais (à).

handbag ['hændbæg] *n* sac *m* à main.

handbook ['hændbʊk] *n* manuel *m*; [for tourist] guide *m*.

handbrake ['hændbreɪk] *n* frein *m* à main.

handcuffs ['hændkʌfs] *npl* menottes *fpl*.

handful ['hændfʊl] *n* [of sand, grass, people] poignée *f*.

handgun ['hændgʌn] *n* revolver *m*, pistolet *m*.

handicap ['hændɪkæp] **1** *n* handicap *m*. **2** *vt* handicaper; [progress, work] entraver.

handicapped ['hændɪkæpt] **1** *adj* handicapé(e). **2** *npl*: **the ~** les handicapés *mpl*.

handicraft ['hændɪkrɑːft] *n* activité *f* artisanale.

handiwork ['hændɪwɜːk] *n* (*U*) ouvrage *m*.

handkerchief ['hæŋkətʃɪf] (*pl* **-chiefs** OR **-chieves** [-tʃiːvz]) *n* mouchoir *m*.

handle ['hændl] **1** *n* poignée *f*; [of jug, cup] anse *f*; [of knife, pan] manche *m*. **2** *vt* [with hands] manipuler; [without permission] toucher à. || [deal with, be responsible for] s'occuper de; [difficult situation] faire face à. || [treat] traiter, s'y prendre avec.

handlebars ['hændlbɑːz] *npl* guidon *m*.

handler ['hændlər] *n* [of dog] maître-chien *m*. || [at airport]: (**baggage**) **~** bagagiste *m*.

handmade [ˌhænd'meɪd] *adj* fait(e) (à la) main.

handout ['hændaʊt] *n* [gift] don *m*. || [leaflet] prospectus *m*.

handrail ['hændreɪl] *n* rampe *f*.

handset ['hændset] *n* combiné *m*.

handshake ['hændʃeɪk] *n* serrement *m* OR poignée *f* de main.

handsome ['hænsəm] *adj* [good-looking] beau (belle). || [reward, profit] beau (belle); [gift] généreux(euse).

handstand ['hændstænd] *n* équilibre *m* (*sur les mains*).

handwriting ['hændˌraɪtɪŋ] *n* écriture *f*.

handy ['hændɪ] *adj inf* [useful] pratique; **to come in ~** être utile. || [skilful] adroit(e). || [near] tout près, à deux pas.

handyman ['hændɪmæn] (*pl* **-men** [-men]) *n* bricoleur *m*.

hang [hæŋ] (*pt & pp* sense 1 **hung**, *pt & pp* sense 2 **hung** OR **hanged**) **1** *vt* [fasten] suspendre. || [execute] pendre. **2** *vi* [be fastened] pendre, être accroché(e). || [be executed] être pendu(e). **3** *n*: **to get the ~ of sthg** *inf* saisir le truc OR attraper le coup pour faire qqch. ○ **hang about, hang around** *vi* traîner. ○ **hang on** *vi* [keep hold]: **to ~ on (to)** s'accrocher OR se cramponner (à). || *inf* [continue waiting] attendre. || [persevere] tenir bon. ○ **hang out** *vi inf* [spend time] traîner. ○ **hang round** = hang about. ○ **hang up 1** *vt sep* pendre. **2** *vi* [on telephone] raccrocher. ○ **hang up on** *vt fus* TELEC raccrocher au nez de.

hangar ['hæŋər] *n* hangar *m*.

hanger ['hæŋər] *n* cintre *m*.

hanger-on (*pl* **hangers-on**) *n* parasite *m*.

hang gliding *n* deltaplane *m*, vol *m* libre.

hangover ['hæŋ,əʊvəʳ] *n* [from drinking] gueule *f* de bois.

hang-up *n inf* complexe *m*.

hanker ('hæŋkəʳ **after, hanker for** *vt fus* convoiter.

hankie, hanky ['hæŋkɪ] (*abbr of* **handkerchief**) *n inf* mouchoir *m*.

haphazard [,hæp'hæzəd] *adj* fait(e) au hasard.

happen ['hæpən] *vi* [occur] arriver, se passer; **to ~ to sb** arriver à qqn. || [chance]: **I just ~ed to meet him** je l'ai rencontré par hasard; **as it ~s** en fait.

happening ['hæpənɪŋ] *n* événement *m*.

happily ['hæpɪlɪ] *adv* [with pleasure] de bon cœur. || [contentedly]: **to be ~ doing sthg** être bien tranquillement en train de faire qqch. || [fortunately] heureusement.

happiness ['hæpɪnɪs] *n* bonheur *m*.

happy ['hæpɪ] *adj* [gen] heureux(euse); **to be ~ to do sthg** être heureux de faire qqch; **~ Christmas/birthday!** joyeux Noël/anniversaire!; **~ New Year!** bonne année! || [satisfied] heureux(euse), content(e); **to be ~ with** OR **about sthg** être heureux de qqch.

happy-go-lucky *adj* décontracté(e).

happy medium *n* juste milieu *m*.

harangue [hə'ræŋ] **1** *n* harangue *f*. **2** *vt* haranguer.

harass ['hærəs] *vt* harceler.

harbour *Br*, **harbor** *Am* ['hɑ:bəʳ] **1** *n* port *m*. **2** *vt* [feeling] entretenir; [doubt, grudge] garder. || [person] héberger.

hard [hɑ:d] **1** *adj* [gen] dur(e); **to be on sb/sthg** être dur avec qqn/pour qqch. || [winter, frost] rude. || [water] calcaire. || [fact] concret(ète); [news] sûr(e), vérifié(e). **2** *adv* [strenuously - work] dur; [- listen, concentrate] avec effort; **to try ~ (to do sthg)** faire de son mieux (pour faire qqch). || [forcefully] fort. || [heavily - rain] à verse; [- snow] dru. || *phr*: **to be ~ pushed** OR **put** OR **pressed to do sthg** avoir bien de la peine à faire qqch.

hardback ['hɑ:dbæk] *n* livre *m* relié.

hardboard ['hɑ:dbɔ:d] *n* panneau *m* de fibres.

hard-boiled *adj* CULIN: **~ egg** œuf *m* dur.

hard cash *n* (*U*) espèces *fpl*.

hard copy *n* COMPUT sortie *f* papier.

hard disk *n* COMPUT disque *m* dur.

harden ['hɑ:dn] **1** *vt* durcir; [steel] trem-per. **2** *vi* [glue, concrete] durcir. || [attitude, opposition] se durcir.

hard-headed [-'hedɪd] *adj* [decision] pragmatique; **to be ~** [person] avoir la tête froide.

hard-hearted [-'hɑ:tɪd] *adj* insensible, impitoyable.

hard labour *n* (*U*) travaux *mpl* forcés.

hard-liner *n* partisan *m* de la manière forte.

hardly ['hɑ:dlɪ] *adv* [scarcely] à peine, ne ... guère; **~ ever/anything** presque jamais/rien. || [only just] à peine.

hardness ['hɑ:dnɪs] *n* [firmness] dureté *f*. || [difficulty] difficulté *f*.

hardship ['hɑ:dʃɪp] *n* (*U*) [difficult conditions] épreuves *fpl*. || [difficult circumstance] épreuve *f*.

hard up *adj inf* fauché(e); **~ for sthg** à court de qqch.

hardware ['hɑ:dweəʳ] *n* (*U*) [tools, equipment] quincaillerie *f*. || COMPUT hardware *m*, matériel *m*.

hardware shop *n* quincaillerie *f*.

hardworking [,hɑ:d'wɜ:kɪŋ] *adj* travailleur(euse).

hardy ['hɑ:dɪ] *adj* [person, animal] vigoureux(euse), robuste. || [plant] résistant(e), vivace.

hare [heəʳ] *n* lièvre *m*.

harebrained ['heə,breɪnd] *adj inf* [person] écervelé(e); [scheme, idea] insensé(e).

harelip [,heə'lɪp] *n* bec-de-lièvre *m*.

haricot (bean) ['hærɪkəʊ-] *n* haricot *m* blanc.

harm [hɑ:m] **1** *n* [injury] mal *m*. || [damage - to clothes, plant] dommage *m*; [- to reputation] tort *m*; **to do ~ to sb, to do sb ~** faire du tort à qqn; **to do ~ to sthg, to do sthg ~** endommager qqch; **to be out of ~'s way** [person] être en sûreté OR lieu sûr; [thing] être en lieu sûr. **2** *vt* [injure] faire du mal à. || [damage - clothes, plant] endommager; [- reputation] faire du tort à.

harmful ['hɑ:mfʊl] *adj* nuisible, nocif(ive).

harmless ['hɑ:mlɪs] *adj* [not dangerous] inoffensif(ive). || [inoffensive] innocent(e).

harmonica [hɑ:'mɒnɪkə] *n* harmonica *m*.

harmonize, -ise ['hɑ:mənaɪz] **1** *vt* harmoniser. **2** *vi* s'harmoniser.

harmony ['hɑ:mənɪ] *n* harmonie *f*.

harness ['hɑːnɪs] **1** n [for horse, child] harnais m. **2** vt [horse] harnacher. || [energy, resources] exploiter.

harp [hɑːp] n harpe f. ○ **harp on** vi: to ~ **on** (**about sthg**) rabâcher (qqch).

harpoon [hɑːˈpuːn] n harpon m.

harrowing ['hærəʊɪŋ] adj [experience] éprouvant(e); [report, film] déchirant(e).

harsh [hɑːʃ] adj [life, conditions] rude; [criticism, treatment] sévère. || [to senses - sound] discordant(e); [- light, voice] criard(e).

harvest ['hɑːvɪst] **1** n [of cereal crops] moisson f; [of fruit] récolte f; [of grapes] vendange f, vendanges fpl. **2** vt [cereals] moissonner; [fruit] récolter; [grapes] vendanger.

has [weak form həz, strong form hæz] → **have**.

has-been n inf pej ringard m, -e f.

hash [hæʃ] n [meat] hachis m. || inf [mess]: **to make a ~ of sthg** faire un beau gâchis de qqch.

hashish ['hæʃiʃ] n haschich m.

hasn't ['hæznt] = **has not**.

hassle ['hæsl] inf **1** n [annoyance] tracas m, embêtement m. **2** vt tracasser.

haste [heɪst] n hâte f; **to do sthg in** ~ faire qqch à la hâte.

hasten ['heɪsn] fml **1** vt hâter, accélérer. **2** vi se hâter, se dépêcher; **to ~ to do sthg** s'empresser de faire qqch.

hastily ['heɪstɪlɪ] adv [quickly] à la hâte. || [rashly] sans réfléchir.

hasty ['heɪstɪ] adj [quick] hâtif(ive). || [rash] irréfléchi(e).

hat [hæt] n chapeau m.

hatch [hætʃ] **1** vt [chick] faire éclore; [egg] couver. || fig [scheme, plot] tramer. **2** vi [chick, egg] éclore. **3** n [for serving food] passe-plats m inv.

hatchback ['hætʃ,bæk] n voiture f avec hayon.

hatchet ['hætʃɪt] n hachette f.

hatchway ['hætʃ,weɪ] n passe-plats m inv, guichet m.

hate [heɪt] **1** n (U) haine f. **2** vt [detest] haïr. || [dislike] détester; **to ~ doing sthg** avoir horreur de faire qqch.

hateful ['heɪtfʊl] adj odieux(ieuse).

hatred ['heɪtrɪd] n (U) haine f.

hat trick n SPORT: **to score a ~** marquer trois buts.

haughty ['hɔːtɪ] adj hautain(e).

haul [hɔːl] **1** n [of drugs, stolen goods] prise f, butin m. || [distance]: **long ~ long**

voyage m OR trajet m. **2** vt [pull] traîner, tirer.

haulage ['hɔːlɪdʒ] n transport m routier, camionnage m.

haulier Br ['hɔːlɪər], **hauler** Am ['hɔːlər] n entrepreneur m de transports routiers.

haunch [hɔːntʃ] n [of person] hanche f; [of animal] derrière m, arrière-train m.

haunt [hɔːnt] **1** n repaire m. **2** vt hanter.

have [hæv] (pt & pp had) **1** aux vb (to form perfect tenses - gen) avoir; (- with many intransitive verbs) être; **to ~ eaten** avoir mangé; **to ~ left** être parti(e); **she hasn't gone yet, has she?** elle n'est pas encore partie, si?; **I was out of breath, having run all the way** j'étais essoufflé d'avoir couru tout le long du chemin. **2** vt [possess, receive]: **to ~ (got)** avoir; **I ~ no money, I haven't got any money** je n'ai pas d'argent. || [experience illness] avoir; **to ~ flu** avoir la grippe. || (referring to an action, instead of another verb): **to ~ a read** lire; **to ~ a bath/shower** prendre un bain/une douche; **to ~ a meeting** tenir une réunion. || [give birth to]: **to ~ a baby** avoir un bébé. || [cause to be done]: **to ~ sb do sthg** faire faire qqch à qqn; **to ~ sthg done** faire faire qqch; **to ~ one's hair cut** se faire couper les cheveux. || [be treated in a certain way]: **I had my car stolen** je me suis fait voler ma voiture, on m'a volé ma voiture. || inf [cheat]: **to be had** se faire avoir. || phr: **to ~ it in for sb** en avoir après qqn, en vouloir à qqn; **to ~ had it** [car, machine, clothes] avoir fait son temps. **3** modal vb [be obliged]: **to ~ (got) to do sthg** devoir faire qqch, être obligé(e) de faire qqch; **do you ~ to go?**, **you got to go?** est-ce que tu dois partir?, est-ce que tu es obligé de partir?; **I've got to go to work** il faut que je aille travailler. ○ **have on** vt sep [be wearing] porter. || [tease] faire marcher. ○ **have out** vt sep [have removed]: **to ~ one's appendix/tonsils out** se faire opérer de l'appendicite/des amygdales. || [discuss frankly]: **to ~ it out with sb** s'expliquer avec qqn.

haven ['heɪvn] n havre m.

haven't ['hævnt] = **have not**.

haversack ['hævəsæk] n sac m à dos.

havoc ['hævək] n (U) dégâts mpl; **to play ~ with** [gen] abîmer; [with health] détraquer; [with plans] ruiner.

Hawaii [həˈwaɪiː] n Hawaii m.

hawk [hɔːk] *n* faucon *m*.

hawker ['hɔːkər] *n* colporteur *m*.

hay [heɪ] *n* foin *m*.

hay fever *n* (*U*) rhume *m* des foins.

haystack ['heɪˌstæk] *n* meule *f* de foin.

haywire ['heɪwaɪər] *adj inf*: **to go ~** [person] perdre la tête; [machine] se détraquer.

hazard ['hæzəd] *n* hasard *m*.

hazardous ['hæzədəs] *adj* hasardeux(euse).

haze [heɪz] *n* brume *f*.

hazel ['heɪzl] *adj* noisette (*inv*).

hazelnut ['heɪzlˌnʌt] *n* noisette *f*.

hazy ['heɪzɪ] *adj* [misty] brumeux(euse). || [memory, ideas] flou(e), vague.

he [hiː] *pers pron* (*unstressed*) il; **~'s tall** il est grand; **there ~ is** le voilà. || (*stressed*) lui; **HE can't do it** lui ne peut pas le faire.

head [hed] **1** *n* [of person, animal] tête *f*; **a** OR **per ~** par tête, par personne; **to be off one's ~** *Br*, **to be out of one's ~** *Am* être dingue; **to be soft in the ~** être débile; **to go to one's ~** [alcohol, praise] monter à la tête; **to keep one's ~** garder son sang-froid; **to lose one's ~** perdre la tête. || [of table, bed, hammer] tête *f*; [of stairs, page] haut *m*. || [of flower] tête *f*; [of cabbage] pomme *f*. || [leader] chef *m*. || [head teacher] directeur *m*, -trice *f*. **2** *vt* [procession, list] être en tête de. || [be in charge of] être à la tête de. **3** *vi*: **where are you ~ing?** où allez-vous? ○ **heads** *npl* [on coin] face *f*; **~s or tails?** pile ou face? ○ **head for** *vt fus* [place] se diriger vers. || *fig* [trouble, disaster] aller au devant de.

headache ['hedeɪk] *n* mal *m* de tête; **to have a ~** avoir mal à la tête.

headband ['hedbænd] *n* bandeau *m*.

headdress ['hedˌdres] *n* coiffe *f*.

headfirst [ˌhed'fɜːst] *adv* (la) tête la première.

heading ['hedɪŋ] *n* titre *m*, intitulé *m*.

headland ['hedlənd] *n* cap *m*.

headlight ['hedlaɪt] *n* phare *m*.

headline ['hedlaɪn] *n* [in newspaper] gros titre *m*; TV & RADIO grand titre *m*.

headlong ['hedlɒŋ] *adv* [quickly] à toute allure. || [unthinkingly] tête baissée. || [headfirst] (la) tête la première.

headmaster [ˌhed'mɑːstər] *n* directeur *m* (d'une école).

headmistress [ˌhed'mɪstrɪs] *n* directrice *f* (d'une école).

head office *n* siège *m* social.

head-on 1 *adj* [collision] de plein fouet; [confrontation] de front. **2** *adv* de plein fouet.

headphones ['hedfəʊnz] *npl* casque *m*.

headquarters [ˌhed'kwɔːtəz] *npl* [of business, organization] siège *m*; [of armed forces] quartier *m* général.

headrest ['hedrest] *n* appui-tête *m*.

headroom ['hedrʊm] *n* (*U*) hauteur *f*.

headscarf ['hedskɑːf] (*pl* **-scarves** [-skɑːvz] OR **-scarfs**) *n* foulard *m*.

headset ['hedset] *n* casque *m*.

head start *n* avantage *m* au départ; **~ on** OR **over** avantage sur.

headstrong ['hedstrɒŋ] *adj* volontaire, têtu(e).

head waiter *n* maître *m* d'hôtel.

headway ['hedweɪ] *n*: **to make ~** faire des progrès.

heady ['hedɪ] *adj* [exciting] grisant(e). || [causing giddiness] capiteux(euse).

heal [hiːl] **1** *vt* [cure] guérir. || *fig* [troubles, discord] apaiser. **2** *vi* se guérir.

healing ['hiːlɪŋ] **1** *adj* curatif(ive). **2** *n* (*U*) guérison *f*.

health [helθ] *n* santé *f*.

health centre *n* ≃ centre *m* médico-social.

health food *n* produits *mpl* diététiques.

health food shop *n* magasin *m* de produits diététiques.

health service *n* ≃ sécurité *f* sociale.

healthy ['helθɪ] *adj* [gen] sain(e). || [well] en bonne santé, bien portant(e). || *fig* [economy, company] qui se porte bien. || [profit] bon (bonne).

heap [hiːp] **1** *n* tas *m*. **2** *vt* [pile up] entasser. ○ **heaps** *npl inf*: **~s of** [people, objects] des tas de; [time, money] énormément de.

hear [hɪər] (*pt & pp* **heard** [hɜːd]) **1** *vt* [gen & JUR] entendre. || [learn of] apprendre; **to ~ (that)** ... apprendre que .... **2** *vi* [perceive sound] entendre. || [receive news]: **to ~ about** entendre parler de. || **to ~ about** avoir des nouvelles de; **to ~ from sb** recevoir des nouvelles de qqn. || *phr*: **to have heard of** avoir entendu parler de; **I won't ~ of it!** je ne veux pas en entendre parler!

hearing ['hɪərɪŋ] *n* [sense] ouïe *f*; **hard of ~** dur(e) d'oreille. || [trial] audience *f*.

hearing aid *n* audiophone *m*.

hearsay ['hɪəseɪ] *n* ouï-dire *m*.

hearse [hɜːs] *n* corbillard *m*.

heart [hɑːt] *n lit & fig* cœur *m*; **to lose ~** perdre courage; **to break sb's ~** briser le cœur à qqn. ○ **hearts** *npl* cœur *m*. ○ **at heart** *adv* au fond (de soi). ○ **by heart** *adv* par cœur.

heartache ['hɑːteɪk] *n* peine *f* de cœur.

heart attack *n* crise *f* cardiaque.

heartbeat ['hɑːtbiːt] *n* battement *m* de cœur.

heartbroken ['hɑːt,brəʊkn] *adj* qui a le cœur brisé.

heartburn ['hɑːtbɜːn] *n* (U) brûlures *fpl* d'estomac.

heart failure *n* arrêt *m* cardiaque.

heartfelt ['hɑːtfelt] *adj* sincère.

hearth [hɑːθ] *n* foyer *m*.

heartless ['hɑːtlɪs] *adj* sans cœur.

heartwarming ['hɑːt,wɔːmɪŋ] *adj* réconfortant(e).

hearty ['hɑːtɪ] *adj* [greeting, person] cordial(e). || [substantial - meal] copieux(ieuse); [- appetite] gros (grosse).

heat [hiːt] 1 *n* (U) [warmth] chaleur *f*. || (U) *fig* [pressure] pression *f*. || [eliminating round] éliminatoire *f*. || ZOOL: **on Br** OR **in ~** en chaleur. 2 *vt* chauffer. ○ **heat up** 1 *vt sep* réchauffer. 2 *vi* chauffer.

heated ['hiːtɪd] *adj* [argument, discussion, person] animé(e); [issue] chaud(e).

heater ['hiːtər] *n* appareil *m* de chauffage.

heath [hiːθ] *n* lande *f*.

heathen ['hiːðn] 1 *adj* païen(enne). 2 *n* païen *m*, -enne *f*.

heather ['heðər] *n* bruyère *f*.

heating ['hiːtɪŋ] *n* chauffage *m*.

heatstroke ['hiːtstrəʊk] *n* (U) coup *m* de chaleur.

heat wave *n* canicule *f*, vague *f* de chaleur.

heave [hiːv] 1 *vt* [pull] tirer (avec effort); [push] pousser (avec effort). 2 *vi* [pull] tirer. || [rise and fall] se soulever. || [retch] avoir des haut-le-cœur.

heaven ['hevn] *n* paradis *m*. ○ **heavens** 1 *npl*: **the ~s** *literary* les cieux *mpl*. 2 *excl*: **(good) ~s!** juste ciel!

heavenly ['hevnlɪ] *adj inf* [delightful] délicieux(ieuse), merveilleux(euse).

heavily ['hevɪlɪ] *adv* [booked, in debt] lourdement. || [rain, smoke, drink] énormément. || [solidly - built] solidement. || [breathe, sigh] péniblement, bruyamment. || [fall, sit down] lourdement.

heavy ['hevɪ] *adj* [gen] lourd(e); **how ~ is it?** ça pèse combien? || [traffic] dense; [rain] battant(e); [fighting] acharné(e); [casualties, corrections] nombreux(euses); [smoker, drinker] gros (grosse). || [noisy - breathing] bruyant(e). || [schedule] chargé(e). || [physically exacting - work, job] pénible.

heavy cream *n Am* crème *f* fraîche épaisse.

heavyweight ['hevɪweɪt] SPORT 1 *adj* poids lourd. 2 *n* poids lourd *m*.

Hebrew ['hiːbruː] 1 *adj* hébreu, hébraïque. 2 *n* [person] Hébreu *m*, Israélite *mf*. || [language] hébreu *m*.

heck [hek] *excl inf*: **what/where/why the ~ ...?** que/où/pourquoi diable ...?; **~ of a nice guy** un type vachement sympa; **a ~ of a lot of people** un tas de gens.

heckle ['hekl] *vt* interrompre bruyamment.

hectic ['hektɪk] *adj* [meeting, day] agité(e), mouvementé(e).

he'd [hiːd] = he had, he would.

hedge [hedʒ] 1 *n* haie *f*. 2 *vi* [prevaricate] répondre de façon détournée.

hedgehog ['hedʒhɒg] *n* hérisson *m*.

heed [hiːd] 1 *n*: **to take ~ of sthg** tenir compte de qqch. 2 *vt fml* tenir compte de.

heedless ['hiːdlɪs] *adj*: **~ of sthg** qui ne tient pas compte de qqch.

heel [hiːl] *n* talon *m*.

hefty ['heftɪ] *adj* [well-built] costaud(e). || [large] gros (grosse).

heifer ['hefər] *n* génisse *f*.

height [haɪt] *n* [of building, mountain] hauteur *f*; [of person] taille *f*; **5 metres in ~** 5 mètres de haut; **what ~ is it?** ça fait quelle hauteur?; **what ~ are you?** combien mesurez-vous? || [above ground - of aircraft] altitude *f*. || [zenith]: **at the ~ of the summer/season** au cœur de l'été/de la saison; **at the ~ of his fame** au sommet de sa gloire.

heighten ['haɪtn] *vt & vi* augmenter.

heir [eər] *n* héritier *m*.

heiress ['eərɪs] *n* héritière *f*.

heirloom ['eəluːm] *n* meuble *m*/bijou *m* de famille.

heist [haɪst] *n inf* casse *m*.

held [held] *pt & pp* → hold.

helicopter ['helɪkɒptər] *n* hélicoptère *m*.

helium ['hiːlɪəm] *n* hélium *m*.

hell [hel] 1 *n lit & fig* enfer *m*. || *inf* [for emphasis]: **he's a ~ of a nice guy** un type vachement sympa; **what/where/why the ~ ...?** que/où/pourquoi .... bon sang? || *phr*: **to do sthg for the ~ of it** *inf* faire qqch pour le plaisir, faire qqch juste comme ça; **go to ~!** *v inf* va te faire foutre! **2** *excl inf* merde!, zut!

he'll [hi:l] = **he will.**

hello [hə'ləu] *excl* [as greeting] bonjour!; [on phone] allô! || [to attract attention] hé!

helm [helm] *n lit & fig* barre *f*.

helmet ['helmɪt] *n* casque *m*.

help [help] **1** *n* (*U*) [assistance] aide *f*; **he gave me a lot of ~** il m'a beaucoup aidé; **with the ~ of sthg** à l'aide de qqch; **with sb's ~** avec l'aide de qqn; **to be of ~** rendre service. || (*U*) [emergency aid] secours *m*. || [useful person or object]: **to be a ~** aider, rendre service. **2** *vi* aider. **3** *vt* [assist] aider; **to ~ sb (to) do sthg** aider qqn à faire qqch; **to ~ sb with sthg** aider qqn à faire qqch. || [avoid]: **I can't ~ it** je n'y peux rien; **I couldn't ~ laughing** je ne pouvais pas m'empêcher de rire. || *phr*: **to ~ o.s. (to sthg)** se servir (de qqch). **4** *excl* au secours!, à l'aide! ○ **help out** *vt sep & vi* aider.

helper ['helpər] *n* [gen] aide *mf*. || *Am* [to do housework] femme *f* de ménage.

helpful ['helpful] *adj* [person] serviable. || [advice, suggestion] utile.

helping ['helpɪŋ] *n* portion *f*; [of cake, tart] part *f*.

helpless ['helplɪs] *adj* impuissant(e); [look, gesture] d'impuissance.

helpline ['helplaɪn] *n* ligne *f* d'assistance téléphonique.

hem [hem] **1** *n* ourlet *m*. **2** *vt* ourler. ○ **hem in** *vt sep* encercler.

hemisphere ['hemɪˌsfɪər] *n* hémisphère *m*.

hemline ['hemlaɪn] *n* ourlet *m*.

hemophiliac [ˌhi:mə'fɪlɪæk] *n* hémophile *mf*.

hemorrhage ['hemərɪdʒ] *n* hémorragie *f*.

hemorrhoids ['hemərɔɪdz] *npl* hémorroïdes *fpl*.

hen [hen] *n* [female chicken] poule *f*.

hence [hens] *adv fml* [therefore] d'où. || [from now] d'ici.

henceforth [ˌhens'fɔ:θ] *adv fml* dorénavant.

henchman ['hentʃmən] (*pl* -men [-mən]) *n pej* acolyte *m*.

henna ['henə] *n* henné *m*.

henpecked ['henpekt] *adj pej* dominé par sa femme.

her [hɜ:r] **1** *pers pron* (direct - unstressed) la, l' (+ vowel or silent 'h');

(- stressed) elle; **I know/like ~** je la connais/l'aime; **it's ~** c'est elle. || (referring to animal, car, ship etc) follow the gender of your translation. || (indirect) lui; **we spoke to ~** nous lui avons parlé; **he sent ~ a letter** il lui a envoyé une lettre. || (after prep, in comparisons etc) elle; **I'm shorter than ~** je suis plus petit que elle. **2** *poss adj* son (sa), ses (*pl*); **~ coat** son manteau; **~ bedroom** sa chambre; **~ children** ses enfants; **it was HER fault** c'était de sa faute à elle.

herald ['herəld] **1** *vt fml* annoncer. **2** *n* [messenger] héraut *m*.

herb [hɜ:b] *n* herbe *f*.

herd [hɜ:d] **1** *n* troupeau *m*. **2** *vt* [cattle, sheep] mener. || *fig* [people] conduire, mener; [into confined space] parquer.

here [hɪər] *adv* [in this place] ici; **~ he is/they are** le/les voici; **~ is/are voici; **~ and there** çà et là. || [present] là.

hereabouts *Br* [ˌhɪərə'bauts], **hereabout** *Am* [ˌhɪərə'baut] *adv* par ici.

hereafter [ˌhɪər'ɑ:ftər] **1** *adv fml* ci-après. **2** *n*: **the ~** l'au-delà *m*.

hereby [ˌhɪə'baɪ] *adv fml* par la présente.

hereditary [hɪ'redɪtrɪ] *adj* héréditaire.

heresy ['herəsɪ] *n* hérésie *f*.

herewith [ˌhɪə'wɪð] *adv fml* [with letter] ci-joint, ci-inclus.

heritage ['herɪtɪdʒ] *n* héritage *m*, patrimoine *m*.

hermetically [hɜ:'metɪklɪ] *adv*: **~ sealed** fermé(e) hermétiquement.

hermit ['hɜ:mɪt] *n* ermite *m*.

hernia ['hɜ:njə] *n* hernie *f*.

hero ['hɪərəu] (*pl* -es) *n* héros *m*.

heroic [hɪ'rəuɪk] *adj* héroïque.

heroin ['herəuɪn] *n* héroïne *f*.

heroine ['herəuɪn] *n* héroïne *f*.

heron ['herən] (*pl inv* OR -s) *n* héron *m*.

herring ['herɪŋ] (*pl inv* OR -s) *n* hareng *m*.

hers [hɜ:z] *poss pron* le sien (la sienne), les siens (les siennes) (*pl*); **that money is ~** cet argent est à elle OR est le sien; **a friend of ~** un ami à elle, un de ses amis.

herself [hɜ:'self] *pron* (reflexive) se; (after prep) elle. || (for emphasis) elle-même.

he's [hi:z] = **he is, he has.**

hesitant ['hezɪtənt] *adj* hésitant(e).

hesitate ['hezɪteɪt] *vi* hésiter; **to ~ to do sthg** hésiter à faire qqch.

hesitation [ˌhezɪ'teɪʃn] *n* hésitation *f*.

heterosexual [ˌhetərəʊ'sekʃʊəl] **1** *adj* hétérosexuel(elle). **2** *n* hétérosexuel *m*, -elle *f*.

het up [het-] *adj inf* excité(e), énervé(e).

hexagon ['heksəgən] *n* hexagone *m*.

hey [heɪ] *excl* hé!

heyday ['heɪdeɪ] *n* âge *m* d'or.

hi [haɪ] *excl inf* salut!

hiatus [haɪ'eɪtəs] (*pl* -es) *n fml* pause *f*.

hibernate ['haɪbəneɪt] *vi* hiberner.

hiccough, hiccup ['hɪkʌp] **1** *n* hoquet *m*; *fig* [difficulty] accroc *m*; **to have ~s** avoir le hoquet. **2** *vi* hoqueter.

hid [hɪd] *pt* → **hide**.

hidden ['hɪdn] **1** *pp* → **hide**. **2** *adj* caché(e).

hide [haɪd] (*pt* **hid**, *pp* **hidden**) **1** *vt*: **to ~ sthg (from sb)** cacher qqch (à qqn); [information] taire qqch (à qqn). **2** *vi* se cacher. **3** *n* [animal skin] peau *f*. || [for watching birds, animals] cachette *f*.

hide-and-seek *n* ~~cache-cache~~ *m*.

hideaway ['haɪdəweɪ] *n* cachette *f*.

hideous ['hɪdɪəs] *adj* hideux(euse).

hiding ['haɪdɪŋ] *n* [concealment]: **to be in ~** se tenir caché(e). || *inf* [beating]: **to give sb a (good) ~** donner une (bonne) raclée OR correction à qqn.

hiding place *n* cachette *f*.

hierarchy ['haɪərɑːkɪ] *n* hiérarchie *f*.

hi-fi ['haɪfaɪ] *n* hi-fi *f inv*.

high [haɪ] **1** *adj* [gen] haut(e); **it's 3 feet/6 metres ~** cela fait 3 pieds/6 mètres de haut; **how ~ is it?** cela fait combien de haut? || [speed, figure, altitude, office] élevé(e). || [high-pitched] aigu(uë). || *drugs sl* qui plane, défoncé(e). **2** *adv* haut. **3** *n* [highest point] maximum *m*.

highbrow ['haɪbraʊ] *adj* intellectuel(elle).

high chair *n* chaise *f* haute (*d'enfant*).

high-class *adj* de premier ordre; [hotel, restaurant] de grande classe.

higher ['haɪər] *adj* [exam, qualification] supérieur(e).

higher education *n* (*U*) études *fpl* supérieures.

high-handed [-'hændɪd] *adj* despotique.

high jump *n* saut *m* en hauteur.

Highland Games ['haɪlənd-] *npl* jeux *mpl* écossais.

Highlands ['haɪləndz] *npl*: **the ~** les Highlands *fpl* (*région montagneuse du nord de l'Écosse*).

highlight ['haɪlaɪt] **1** *n* [of event, occasion] moment *m* OR point *m* fort. **2** *vt* souligner; [with highlighter] surligner. ○ **highlights** *npl* [in hair] reflets *mpl*, mèches *fpl*.

highlighter (pen) ['haɪlaɪtər-] *n* surligneur *m*.

highly ['haɪlɪ] *adv* [very] extrêmement, très. || [in important position]: **~ placed** haut placé(e). || [favourably]: **to think ~ of sb/sthg** penser du bien de qqn/qqch.

highly-strung *adj* nerveux(euse).

Highness ['haɪnɪs] *n*: **His/Her/Your (Royal) ~** Son/Votre Altesse (Royale); **their (Royal) ~es** leurs Altesses (Royales).

high-pitched [-'pɪtʃt] *adj* aigu(uë).

high point *n* [of occasion] point *m* fort.

high-powered [-'paʊəd] *adj* [powerful] de forte puissance. || [prestigious - activity, place] de haut niveau; [- job, person] important(e).

high-ranking [-'ræŋkɪŋ] *adj* de haut rang.

high-rise *adj*: **~ block of flats** tour *f*.

high school *n Br* lycée *m*; *Am* établissement *m* d'enseignement supérieur.

high season *n* haute saison *f*.

high spot *n* point *m* fort.

high-tech [-'tek] *adj* [method, industry] de pointe.

high tide *n* marée *f* haute.

highway ['haɪweɪ] *n Am* [motorway] autoroute *f*. || [main road] grande route *f*.

hijack ['haɪdʒæk] **1** *n* détournement *m*. **2** *vt* détourner.

hijacker ['haɪdʒækər] *n* [of aircraft] pirate *m* de l'air; [of vehicle] pirate *m* de la route.

hike [haɪk] **1** *n* [long walk] randonnée *f*. **2** *vi* faire une randonnée.

hiker ['haɪkər] *n* randonneur *m*, -euse *f*.

hiking ['haɪkɪŋ] *n* marche *f*.

hilarious [hɪ'leərɪəs] *adj* hilarant(e).

hill [hɪl] *n* [mound] colline *f*. || [slope] côte *f*.

hillside ['hɪlsaɪd] *n* coteau *m*.

hilly ['hɪlɪ] *adj* vallonné(e).

hilt [hɪlt] *n* garde *f*; **to support/defend sb to the ~** soutenir/défendre qqn à fond.

him [hɪm] *pers pron* (*direct - unstressed*) le, l' (*+ vowel or silent 'h'*); (*- stressed*) lui; **I know/like ~** je le connais/l'aime; **it's ~** c'est lui. || (*indirect*) lui; **we spoke to ~** nous lui avons parlé; **she sent ~ a letter** elle lui a envoyé une lettre. || (*after prep, in comparisons*) lui; **I'm shorter than ~** je suis plus petit que lui.

Himalayas [ˌhɪməˈleɪəz] *npl*: **the ~** l'Himalaya *m*.

himself [hɪmˈself] *pron* (*reflexive*) se; (*after prep*) lui. ‖ (*for emphasis*) lui-même.

hind [haɪnd] (*pl inv* OR **-s**) **1** *adj* de derrière. **2** *n* biche *f*.

hinder [ˈhɪndər] *vt* gêner, entraver.

Hindi [ˈhɪndɪ] *n* hindi *m*.

hindrance [ˈhɪndrəns] *n* obstacle *m*.

hindsight [ˈhaɪndsaɪt] *n*: **with the benefit of ~** avec du recul.

Hindu [ˈhɪnduː] (*pl* -s) **1** *adj* hindou(e). **2** *n* Hindou *m*, -e *f*.

hinge [hɪndʒ] *n* [whole fitting] charnière *f*; [pin] gond *m*. ○ **hinge (up)on** *vt fus* [depend on] dépendre de.

hint [hɪnt] **1** *n* [indication] allusion *f*; **to drop a ~** faire une allusion. ‖ [piece of advice] conseil *m*, indication *f*. ‖ [small amount] soupçon *m*. **2** *vi*: **to ~ at sthg** faire allusion à qqch. **3** *vt*: **to ~ that ...** insinuer que ....

hip [hɪp] *n* hanche *f*.

hippie [ˈhɪpɪ] = **hippy**.

hippo [ˈhɪpəʊ] (*pl* -s) *n* hippopotame *m*.

hippopotamus [ˌhɪpəˈpɒtəməs] (*pl* -muses OR -mi [-maɪ]) *n* hippopotame *m*.

hippy [ˈhɪpɪ] *n* hippie *mf*.

hire [ˈhaɪər] **1** *n* (*U*) [of car, equipment] location *f*; **for ~** [bicycles etc] à louer; [taxi] libre. **2** *vt* [rent] louer. ‖ [employ] employer les services de. ○ **hire out** *vt sep* louer.

his [hɪz] **1** *poss adj* son (sa), ses (*pl*); **~ house** sa maison; **~ money** son argent; **~ children** ses enfants; **~ name is Joe** il s'appelle Joe. **2** *poss pron* le sien (la sienne), les siens (les siennes) (*pl*); **that money is ~** cet argent est à lui OR est le sien; **it wasn't her fault, it was HIS** ce n'était pas de sa faute à elle, c'était de sa faute à lui; **a friend of ~** un ami à lui, un de ses amis.

hiss [hɪs] **1** *n* [of animal, gas etc] sifflement *m*; [of crowd] sifflet *m*. **2** *vi* [animal, gas etc] siffler.

historic [hɪˈstɒrɪk] *adj* historique.

historical [hɪˈstɒrɪkəl] *adj* historique.

history [ˈhɪstərɪ] *n* [gen] histoire *f*. ‖ [past record] antécédents *mpl*; **medical ~** passé *m* médical.

hit [hɪt] (*pt & pp* hit) **1** *n* [blow] coup *m*. ‖ [successful strike] coup *m* OR tir *m* réussi; [in fencing] touche *f*. ‖ [success] succès *m*; **to be a ~ with** plaire à. **2** *comp* à succès. **3** *vt* [strike] frapper; [nail] taper sur. ‖ [crash into] heurter, percuter. ‖ [reach] atteindre. ‖ [affect badly] toucher, affecter. ‖ *phr*: **to ~ it off (with sb)** bien s'entendre (avec qqn).

hit-and-miss = **hit-or-miss**.

hit-and-run *adj* [accident] avec délit de fuite; **~ driver** chauffard *m* (*qui a commis un délit de fuite*).

hitch [hɪtʃ] **1** *n* [problem, snag] ennui *m*. **2** *vt* [catch]: **to ~ a lift** faire du stop. ‖ [fasten]: **to ~ sthg on** OR **onto** accrocher OR attacher qqch à. **3** *vi* [hitchhike] faire du stop. ○ **hitch up** *vt sep* [pull up] remonter.

hitchhike [ˈhɪtʃhaɪk] *vi* faire de l'auto-stop.

hitchhiker [ˈhɪtʃhaɪkər] *n* auto-stoppeur *m*, -euse *f*.

hi-tech [ˌhaɪˈtek] = **high-tech**.

hit-or-miss *adj* aléatoire.

HIV (*abbr of* human immunodeficiency virus) *n* VIH *m*, HIV *m*; **to be ~-positive** être séropositif.

hive [haɪv] *n* ruche *f*; **a ~ of activity** une véritable ruche. ○ **hive off** *vt sep* [assets] séparer.

hoard [hɔːd] **1** *n* [store] réserves *fpl*; [of useless items] tas *m*. **2** *vt* amasser; [food, petrol] faire des provisions de.

hoarse [hɔːs] *adj* [person, voice] enroué(e); [shout, whisper] rauque.

hoax [həʊks] *n* canular *m*.

hobble [ˈhɒbl] *vi* [limp] boitiller.

hobby [ˈhɒbɪ] *n* passe-temps *m inv*, hobby *m*.

hobbyhorse [ˈhɒbɪhɔːs] *n* [toy] cheval *m* à bascule. ‖ *fig* [favourite topic] dada *m*.

hobo [ˈhəʊbəʊ] (*pl* -es OR -s) *n Am* clochard *m*, -e *f*.

hockey [ˈhɒkɪ] *n* [on grass] hockey *m*. ‖ *Am* [ice hockey] hockey *m* sur glace.

hoe [həʊ] **1** *n* houe *f*. **2** *vt* biner.

hog [hɒg] **1** *n Am* [pig] cochon *m*. ‖ *inf* [greedy person] goinfre *m*. ‖ *phr*: **to go the whole ~** aller jusqu'au bout. **2** *vt inf* [monopolize] accaparer, monopoliser.

hoist [hɔɪst] **1** *n* [device] treuil *m*. **2** *vt* hisser.

hold [həʊld] (*pt & pp* held) **1** *vt* [gen] tenir. ‖ [keep in position] maintenir. ‖ [as prisoner] détenir; **to ~ sb prisoner/**

hostage détenir qqn prisonnier/comme otage. || [have, possess] avoir. || *fml* [consider] considérer, estimer; **to ~ sb responsible for sthg** rendre qqn responsable de qqch, tenir qqn pour responsable de qqch. || [on telephone]: **please ~ the line** ne quittez pas, je vous prie. || [keep, maintain] retenir. || [sustain, support] supporter. || [contain] contenir. || *phr*: **~ it!, ~ everything!** attendez!, arrêtez!; **to ~ one's own** se défendre. **2** *vi* [remain unchanged - gen] tenir; [- luck] persister; [- weather] se maintenir; **to ~ still** OR **steady** ne pas bouger, rester tranquille. || [on phone] attendre. **3** *n* [grasp, grip] prise *f*, étreinte *f*; **to take** OR **lay ~ of sthg** saisir qqch; **to get ~ of sthg** [obtain] se procurer qqch; **to get ~ of sb** [find] joindre. || [of ship, aircraft] cale *f*. || [control, influence] prise *f*. ○ **hold back** *vt sep* [restrain, prevent] retenir; [anger] réprimer. || [keep secret] cacher. ○ **hold down** *vt sep* [job] garder. ○ **hold off** *vt sep* [fend off] tenir à distance. ○ **hold on** *vi* [wait] attendre; [on phone] ne pas quitter. || [grip]: **to ~ on (to sthg)** se tenir (à qqch). ○ **hold out 1** *vt sep* [hand, arms] tendre. **2** *vi* [last] durer. || [resist]: **to ~ out (against sb/sthg)** résister (à qqn/qqch). ○ **hold up** *vt sep* [raise] lever. || [delay] retarder.

holder ['həʊldər] *n* [for cigarette] porte-cigarettes *m inv*. || [owner] détenteur *m*, -trice *f*; [of position, title] titulaire *mf*.

holding ['həʊldɪŋ] *n* [investment] effets *mpl* en portefeuille. || [farm] ferme *f*.

holdup ['həʊldʌp] *n* [robbery] hold-up *m*. || [delay] retard *m*.

hole [həʊl] *n* [gen] trou *m*. || *inf* [predicament] pétrin *m*.

holiday ['hɒlɪdeɪ] *n* [vacation] vacances *fpl*; **to be/go on ~** être/partir en vacances. || [public holiday] jour *m* férié.

holistic [həʊ'lɪstɪk] *adj* holistique.

Holland ['hɒlənd] *n* Hollande *f*.

holler ['hɒlər] *vi & vt inf* gueuler, brailler.

hollow ['hɒləʊ] **1** *adj* creux (creuse); [eyes] cave; [promise, victory] faux (fausse); [laugh] qui sonne faux. **2** *n* creux *m*. ○ **hollow out** *vt sep* creuser, évider.

holly ['hɒlɪ] *n* houx *m*.

holocaust ['hɒləkɔːst] *n* [destruction] destruction *f*, holocauste *m*. ○ **Holocaust** *n*: **the Holocaust** l'holocauste *m*.

holster ['həʊlstər] *n* étui *m*.

holy ['həʊlɪ] *adj* saint(e); [ground] sacré(e).

Holy Ghost *n*: **the ~** le Saint-Esprit.

Holy Land *n*: **the ~** la Terre sainte.

Holy Spirit *n*: **the ~** le Saint-Esprit.

home [həʊm] **1** *n* [house, institution] maison *f*; **to make one's ~** s'installer. || [own country] patrie *f*; [city] ville *f* natale. || [one's family] foyer *m*; **to leave ~** quitter la maison. || *fig* [place of origin] berceau *m*. **2** *adj* [not foreign] intérieur(e); [- product] national(e). || [in one's own home - cooking] familial(e); [- life] de famille; [- improvements] domestique. || [SPORT - game] sur son propre terrain; [- team] qui reçoit. **3** *adv* [to or at one's house] chez soi, à la maison. ○ **at home** *adv* [in one's house, flat] chez soi, à la maison. || [comfortable] à l'aise; **at ~ with sthg** à l'aise dans qqch; **to make o.s. at ~** faire comme chez soi. || [in one's own country] chez soi.

home address *n* adresse *f* du domicile.

home brew *n* (*U*) [beer] bière *f* faite à la maison.

home computer *n* ordinateur *m* domestique.

home economics *n* (*U*) économie *f* domestique.

homeland ['həʊmlænd] *n* [country of birth] patrie *f*. || [in South Africa] homeland *m*, bantoustan *m*.

homeless ['həʊmlɪs] **1** *adj* sans abri. **2** *npl*: **the ~** les sans-abri *mpl*.

homely ['həʊmlɪ] *adj* [simple] simple. || [unattractive] ordinaire.

homemade [,həʊm'meɪd] *adj* fait(e) (à la) maison.

Home Office *n Br*: **the ~** ≃ le ministère de l'Intérieur.

homeopathy [,həʊmɪ'ɒpəθɪ] *n* homéopathie *f*.

Home Secretary *n Br* ≃ ministre *m* de l'Intérieur.

homesick ['həʊmsɪk] *adj* qui a le mal du pays.

hometown ['həʊmtaʊn] *n* ville *f* natale.

homeward ['həʊmwəd] **1** *adj* de retour. **2** *adv* = **homewards**.

homewards ['həʊmwədz] *adv* vers la maison.

homework ['həʊmwɜːk] *n* (*U*) SCH devoirs *mpl*. || *inf* [preparation] boulot *m*.

homey, homy ['həʊmɪ] *adj Am* confortable, agréable.

homicide ['hɒmɪsaɪd] *n* homicide *m*.

homoeopathy *etc* [ˌhəʊmɪˈɒpəθɪ] = homeopathy *etc*.

homosexual [ˌhɒməˈsekʃʊəl] 1 *adj* homosexuel(elle). 2 *n* homosexuel *m*, -elle *f*.

homy = homey.

hone [həʊn] *vt* aiguiser.

honest [ˈɒnɪst] 1 *adj* [trustworthy] honnête, probe. || [frank] franc (franche), sincère; **to be ~,** ... pour dire la vérité, ...; à dire vrai, ... || [legal] légitime. 2 *adv inf* = honestly 2.

honestly [ˈɒnɪstlɪ] 1 *adv* [truthfully] honnêtement. || [expressing sincerity] je vous assure. 2 *excl* [expressing impatience, disapproval] franchement!

honesty [ˈɒnɪstɪ] *n* honnêteté *f*, probité *f*.

honey [ˈhʌnɪ] *n* [food] miel *m*. || [dear] chéri *m*, -e *f*.

honeycomb [ˈhʌnɪkəʊm] *n* gâteau *m* de miel.

honeymoon [ˈhʌnɪmuːn] *n lit & fig* lune *f* de miel.

honeysuckle [ˈhʌnɪˌsʌkl] *n* chèvrefeuille *m*.

Hong Kong [ˌhɒŋˈkɒŋ] *n* Hong Kong, Hongkong.

honk [hɒŋk] 1 *vi* [motorist] klaxonner. || [goose] cacarder. 2 *vt*: **to ~ the horn** klaxonner.

honor *etc Am* = honour *etc*.

honorary [*Br* ˈɒnərərɪ, *Am* ɒnəˈreərɪ] *adj* honoraire.

honour *Br*, **honor** *Am* [ˈɒnər] 1 *n* honneur *m*; **in ~ of sb/sthg** en l'honneur de qqn/qqch. 2 *vt* honorer. ○ **honours** *npl* [tokens of respect] honneurs *mpl*. || [of university degree] ≃ licence *f*.

honourable *Br*, **honorable** *Am* [ˈɒnrəbl] *adj* honorable.

hood [hʊd] *n* [on cloak, jacket] capuchon *m*. || [of cooker] hotte *f*. || [of pram, convertible car] capote *f*. || *Am* [car bonnet] capot *m*.

hoodlum [ˈhuːdləm] *n Am inf* gangster *m*, truand *m*.

hoof [huːf, hʊf] (*pl* -s OR **hooves**) *n* sabot *m*.

hook [hʊk] 1 *n* [for hanging things on] crochet *m*. || [for catching fish] hameçon *m*. || [fastener] agrafe *f*. || [of telephone]: **off the ~** décroché. 2 *vt* [attach with hook] accrocher. || [catch with hook] prendre. ○ **hook up** *vt sep*: **to ~ sthg up to sthg** connecter qqch à qqch.

hooked [hʊkt] *adj* [shaped like a hook] crochu(e). || *inf* [addicted]: **to be ~ (on)** être accro (à); [music, art] être mordu(e) (de).

hook(e)y [ˈhʊkɪ] *n Am inf*: **to play ~** faire l'école buissonnière.

hooligan [ˈhuːlɪgən] *n* hooligan *m*, vandale *m*.

hoop [huːp] *n* [circular band] cercle *m*. || [toy] cerceau *m*.

hooray [hʊˈreɪ] = hurray.

hoot [huːt] 1 *n* [of owl] hululement *m*. || [of horn] coup *m* de Klaxon.® 2 *vi* [owl] hululer. || [horn] klaxonner. 3 *vt*: **to ~ the horn** klaxonner.

hooter [ˈhuːtər] *n* [horn] Klaxon® *m*.

hooves [huːvz] *pl* → hoof.

hop [hɒp] 1 *n* saut *m*; [on one leg] saut à cloche-pied. 2 *vi* sauter; [on one leg] sauter à cloche-pied; [bird] sautiller. ○ **hops** *npl* houblon *m*.

hope [həʊp] 1 *vi* espérer; **to ~ for sthg** espérer qqch; **I ~ so** j'espère bien; **I ~ not** j'espère bien que non. 2 *vt*: **to ~ (that)** espérer que; **to ~ to do sthg** espérer faire qqch. 3 *n* espoir *m*; **in the ~ of** dans l'espoir de.

hopeful [ˈhəʊpfʊl] *adj* [optimistic] plein(e) d'espoir; **to be ~ of doing sthg** avoir l'espoir de faire qqch; **to be ~ of sthg** espérer qqch. || [promising] encourageant(e), qui promet.

hopefully [ˈhəʊpfəlɪ] *adv* [in a hopeful way] avec bon espoir, avec optimisme. || [with luck]: ~, ... espérons que ....

hopeless [ˈhəʊplɪs] *adj* [gen] désespéré(e); [tears] de désespoir. || *inf* [useless] nul (nulle).

hopelessly [ˈhəʊplɪslɪ] *adv* [despairingly] avec désespoir. || [completely] complètement.

horizon [həˈraɪzn] *n* horizon *m*.

horizontal [ˌhɒrɪˈzɒntl] 1 *adj* horizontal(e). 2 *n*: **the ~** l'horizontale *f*.

hormone [ˈhɔːməʊn] *n* hormone *f*.

horn [hɔːn] *n* [of animal] corne *f*. || MUS [instrument] cor *m*. || [on car] Klaxon® *m*; [on ship] sirène *f*.

hornet [ˈhɔːnɪt] *n* frelon *m*.

horny [ˈhɔːnɪ] *adj* [hard] corné(e); [hand] calleux(euse). || *v inf* [sexually excited] excité(e) (sexuellement).

horoscope [ˈhɒrəskəʊp] *n* horoscope *m*.

horrendous [hɒˈrendəs] *adj* horrible.

horrible [ˈhɒrəbl] *adj* horrible.

horrid ['hɒrɪd] *adj* [unpleasant] horrible.

horrific [hɒ'rɪfɪk] *adj* horrible.

horrify ['hɒrɪfaɪ] *vt* horrifier.

horror ['hɒrər] *n* horreur *f*.

horror film *n* film *m* d'épouvante.

horse [hɔːs] *n* [animal] cheval *m*.

horseback ['hɔːsbæk] **1** *adj* à cheval; **riding** *Am* équitation *f*. **2** *n*: **on ~** à cheval.

horse chestnut *n* [nut] marron *m* d'Inde; **~ (tree)** marronnier *m* d'Inde.

horseman ['hɔːsmən] (*pl* **-men** [-mən]) *n* cavalier *m*.

horsepower ['hɔːs,pauər] *n* puissance *f* en chevaux.

horse racing *n* (*U*) courses *fpl* de chevaux.

horseradish ['hɔːs,rædɪʃ] *n* [plant] raifort *m*.

horse riding *n* équitation *f*.

horseshoe ['hɔːsʃuː] *n* fer *m* à cheval.

horsewoman ['hɔːs,wumən] (*pl* **-women** [-,wɪmɪn]) *n* cavalière *f*.

horticulture ['hɔːtɪkʌltʃər] *n* horticulture *f*.

hose [həuz] **1** *n* [hosepipe] tuyau *m*. **2** *vt* arroser au jet.

hosepipe ['həuzpaɪp] *n* = hose.

hosiery ['həuzɪərɪ] *n* bonneterie *f*.

hospitable [hɒ'spɪtəbl] *adj* hospitalier(ière), accueillant(e).

hospital ['hɒspɪtl] *n* hôpital *m*.

hospitality [,hɒspɪ'tælətɪ] *n* hospitalité *f*.

host [həust] **1** *n* [gen] hôte *m*. || [compere] animateur *m*, -trice *f*. || [large number]: **a ~ of** une foule de. **2** *vt* présenter, animer.

hostage ['hɒstɪdʒ] *n* otage *m*.

hostel ['hɒstl] *n* [basic accommodation] foyer *m*. || [youth hostel] auberge *f* de jeunesse.

hostess ['həustes] *n* hôtesse *f*.

hostile [*Br* 'hɒstaɪl, *Am* 'hɒstl] *adj*: **~ (to)** hostile (à).

hostility [hɒ'stɪlətɪ] *n* [antagonism, unfriendliness] hostilité *f*. ○ **hostilities** *npl* hostilités *fpl*.

hot [hɒt] *adj* [gen] chaud(e); **I'm ~** = j'ai chaud; **it's ~** = il fait chaud. || [spicy] épicé(e). || *inf* [expert] fort(e), calé(e); **to be ~ on OR at sthg** être fort OR calé en qqch. || [recent] de dernière heure OR minute. || [temper] colérique.

hot-air balloon *n* montgolfière *f*.

hotbed ['hɒtbed] *n* foyer *m*.

hot-cross bun *n* petit pain sucré que l'on mange le vendredi saint.

hot dog *n* hot dog *m*.

hotel [həu'tel] *n* hôtel *m*.

hot flush *Br*, **hot flash** *Am* *n* bouffée *f* de chaleur.

hotfoot ['hɒt,fut] *adv* à toute vitesse.

hotheaded [,hɒt'hedɪd] *adj* impulsif(ive).

hothouse ['hɒthaus, *pl* -hauzɪz] *n* [greenhouse] serre *f*.

hot line *n* [between government heads] téléphone *m* rouge. || [special line] ligne ouverte 24 heures sur 24.

hotly ['hɒtlɪ] *adv* [passionately] avec véhémence. || [closely] de près.

hotplate ['hɒtpleɪt] *n* plaque *f* chauffante.

hot-tempered [-'tempəd] *adj* colérique.

hot-water bottle *n* bouillotte *f*.

hound [haund] **1** *n* [dog] chien *m*. **2** *vt* [persecute] poursuivre, pourchasser. || [drive]: **to ~ sb out (of)** chasser qqn (de).

hour ['auər] *n* heure *f*; **half an ~** une demi-heure; **70 miles per OR an ~** 110 km à l'heure; **on the ~** à l'heure juste. ○ **hours** *npl* [of business] heures *fpl* d'ouverture.

hourly ['auəlɪ] **1** *adj* [happening every hour] toutes les heures. || [per hour] à l'heure. **2** *adv* [every hour] toutes les heures. || [per hour] à l'heure.

house [*n & adj* haus, *pl* 'hauzɪz, *vb* hauz] **1** *n* [gen] maison *f*; **on the ~** aux frais de la maison. || POL chambre *f*. || [in debates] assistance *f*. || THEATRE [audience] auditoire *m*, salle *f*; **to bring the house down** *inf* faire crouler la salle sous les applaudissements. **2** *vt* [accommodate] loger, héberger; [department, store] abriter. **3** *adj* [within business] d'entreprise. || [wine] maison (*inv*).

house arrest *n*: **under ~** en résidence surveillée.

houseboat ['hausbəut] *n* péniche *f* aménagée.

housebreaking ['haus,breɪkɪŋ] *n* (*U*) cambriolage *m*.

housecoat ['hauskəut] *n* peignoir *m*.

household ['haushəuld] **1** *adj* [domestic] ménager(ère). || [word, name] connu(e) de tous. **2** *n* maison *f*, ménage *m*.

housekeeper ['haus,kiːpər] *n* gouvernante *f*.

housekeeping ['haʊs,ki:pɪŋ] *n* (*U*) [work] ménage *m*. || ~ (**money**) argent *m* du ménage.

house music *n* house music *f*.

House of Representatives *n* Am: the ~ la Chambre des représentants.

houseplant ['haʊsplɑ:nt] *n* plante *f* d'appartement.

Houses of Parliament *npl*: the ~ le Parlement britannique (*où se réunissent la Chambre des communes et la Chambre des lords*).

housewarming (party) ['haʊs-,wɔ:mɪŋ-] *n* pendaison *f* de crémaillère.

housewife ['haʊswaɪf] (*pl* -**wives** [-waɪvz]) *n* femme *f* au foyer.

housework ['haʊswɜ:k] *n* (*U*) ménage *m*.

housing ['haʊzɪŋ] *n* (*U*) [accommodation] logement *m*.

housing estate *Br*, **housing project** *Am n* cité *f*.

hovel ['hɒvl] *n* masure *f*, taudis *m*.

hover ['hɒvə^r] *vi* [fly] planer.

hovercraft ['hɒvəkrɑ:ft] (*pl inv* OR -**s**) *n* aéroglisseur *m*, hovercraft *m*.

how [haʊ] *adv* [gen] comment; ~ **are you?** comment allez-vous?; ~ **do you do?** enchanté(e) (de faire votre connaissance). || [referring to degree, amount]: ~ **high is it?** combien cela fait-il de haut?, quelle en est la hauteur?; ~ **long have you been waiting?** cela fait combien de temps que vous attendez?; ~ **many people came?** combien de personnes sont venues?; ~ **old are you?** quel âge as-tu? || [in exclamations]: ~ **nice!** que c'est bien!; ~ **awful!** quelle horreur! ○ **how about** *adv*: ~ **about a drink?** si on prenait un verre?; ~ **about you?** et toi? ○ **how much 1** *pron* combien; ~ **much does it cost?** combien ça coûte? **2** *adj* combien de; ~ **much bread?** combien de pain?

however [haʊ'evə^r] **1** *adv* [nevertheless] cependant, toutefois. || [no matter how] quelque ... que (+ *subjunctive*), si ... que (+ *subjunctive*); ~ **many/much** peu importe la quantité de. || [how] comment. **2** *conj* [in whatever way] de quelque manière que (+ *subjunctive*).

howl [haʊl] **1** *n* hurlement *m*; [of laughter] éclat *m*. **2** *vi* hurler; [with laughter] rire aux éclats.

hp (*abbr of* **horsepower**) *n* CV *m*.

HQ (*abbr of* **headquarters**) *n* QG *m*.

hr (*abbr of* **hour**) h.

hub [hʌb] *n* [of wheel] moyeu *m*. || [of activity] centre *m*.

hubbub ['hʌbʌb] *n* vacarme *m*, brouhaha *m*.

hubcap ['hʌbkæp] *n* enjoliveur *m*.

huddle ['hʌdl] **1** *vi* se blottir. **2** *n* petit groupe *m*.

hue [hju:] *n* [colour] teinte *f*, nuance *f*.

huff [hʌf] *n*: **in a** ~ froissé(e).

hug [hʌg] **1** *n* étreinte *f*; **to give sb a** ~ serrer qqn dans ses bras. **2** *vt* [embrace] étreindre, serrer dans ses bras. || [hold] tenir. || [stay close to] serrer.

huge [hju:dʒ] *adj* [subject] énorme; vaste; [success] fou (folle).

hulk [hʌlk] *n* [of ship] carcasse *f*. || [person] malabar *m*, mastodonte *m*.

hull [hʌl] *n* coque *f*.

hullo [hə'ləʊ] *excl* = hello.

hum [hʌm] **1** *vi* [buzz] bourdonner; [machine] vrombir, ronfler. || [sing] fredonner, chantonner. || [be busy] être en pleine activité. **2** *vt* fredonner, chantonner.

human ['hju:mən] **1** *adj* humain(e). **2** *n*: ~ (**being**) être *m* humain.

humane [hju:'meɪn] *adj* humain(e).

humanitarian [hju:,mænɪ'teərɪən] *adj* humanitaire.

humanity [hju:'mænətɪ] *n* humanité *f*. ○ **humanities** *npl*: **the humanities** les humanités *fpl*, les sciences *fpl* humaines.

human race *n*: **the** ~ la race humaine.

human rights *npl* droits *mpl* de l'homme.

humble ['hʌmbl] **1** *adj* humble; [origins, employee] modeste. **2** *vt* humilier.

humbug ['hʌmbʌg] *n* dated [hypocrisy] hypocrisie *f*.

humdrum ['hʌmdrʌm] *adj* monotone.

humid ['hju:mɪd] *adj* humide.

humidity [hju:'mɪdətɪ] *n* humidité *f*.

humiliate [hju:'mɪlɪeɪt] *vt* humilier.

humiliation [hju:,mɪlɪ'eɪʃn] *n* humiliation *f*.

humility [hju:'mɪlətɪ] *n* humilité *f*.

humor *Am* = humour.

humorous ['hju:mərəs] *adj* humoristique; [person] plein(e) d'humour.

humour *Br*, **humor** *Am* ['hju:mə^r] **1** *n* [sense of fun] humour *m*. || [of situation, remark] côté *m* comique. **2** *vt* se montrer conciliant(e) envers.

hump [hʌmp] *n* bosse *f*.

humpbacked bridge ['hʌmpbækt-] *n* pont *m* en dos d'âne.

hunch [hʌntʃ] *n inf* pressentiment *m*, intuition *f*.

hunchback ['hʌntʃbæk] *n* bossu *m*, -e *f*.

hunched [hʌntʃt] *adj* voûté(e).

hundred ['hʌndrəd] *num* cent; **a** OR **one** ~ cent; *see also* **six**. ○ **hundreds** *npl* des centaines.

hundredth ['hʌndrətθ] *num* centième; *see also* **sixth**.

hundredweight ['hʌndrədweɪt] *n* [in US] poids *m* de 100 livres, = *45,3 kg*.

hung [hʌŋ] *pt & pp* → **hang**.

Hungarian [hʌŋ'geərɪən] 1 *adj* hongrois(e). 2 *n* [person] Hongrois *m*, -e *f*. || [language] hongrois *m*.

Hungary ['hʌŋgərɪ] *n* Hongrie *f*.

hunger ['hʌŋgər] *n* [gen] faim *f*. || [strong desire] soif *f*.

hunger strike *n* grève *f* de la faim.

hung over *adj inf*: **to be** ~ avoir la gueule de bois.

hungry ['hʌŋgrɪ] *adj* [for food]: **to be** ~ avoir faim; [starving] être affamé(e). || [eager]: **to be** ~ **for** être avide de.

hung up *adj inf*: **to be** ~ (**on** OR **about**) être obsédé(e) (par).

hunk [hʌŋk] *n* [large piece] gros morceau *m*. || *inf* [man] beau mec *m*.

hunt [hʌnt] 1 *n* chasse *f*; [for missing person] recherches *fpl*. 2 *vi* [chase animals, birds] chasser. || [search]: **to** ~ (**for sthg**) chercher partout (qqch). 3 *vt* [animals, birds] chasser. || [person] poursuivre, pourchasser.

hunter ['hʌntər] *n* [of animals, birds] chasseur *m*.

hunting ['hʌntɪŋ] *n* [of animals] chasse *f*.

hurdle ['hɜːdl] *n* [in race] haie *f*. || [obstacle] obstacle *m*.

hurl [hɜːl] *vt* [throw] lancer avec violence. || [shout] lancer.

hurray [hʊ'reɪ] *excl* hourra!

hurricane ['hʌrɪkən] *n* ouragan *m*.

hurried ['hʌrɪd] *adj* [hasty] précipité(e).

hurriedly ['hʌrɪdlɪ] *adv* précipitamment; [eat, write] vite, en toute hâte.

hurry ['hʌrɪ] 1 *vt* [person] faire se dépêcher; [process] hâter; **to** ~ **to do sthg** se dépêcher OR se presser de faire qqch. 2 *vi* se dépêcher, se presser. 3 *n* hâte *f*, précipitation *f*; **to be in a** ~ être pressé; **to do sthg in a** ~ faire qqch à la hâte. ○ **hurry up** *vi* se dépêcher.

hurt [hɜːt] (*pt & pp* **hurt**) 1 *vt* [physically, emotionally] blesser; [one's leg, arm] se faire mal à; **to** ~ **o.s.** se faire mal. || *fig* [harm] faire du mal à. 2 *vi* [gen] faire mal; **my leg** ~**s** ma jambe me fait mal. || *fig* [do harm] faire du mal. 3 *adj* blessé(e); [voice] offensé(e).

hurtful ['hɜːtful] *adj* blessant(e).

hurtle ['hɜːtl] *vi* aller à toute allure.

husband ['hʌzbənd] *n* mari *m*.

hush [hʌʃ] *excl* silence!, chut!

husk [hʌsk] *n* [of seed, grain] enveloppe *f*.

husky ['hʌskɪ] 1 *adj* [hoarse] rauque. 2 *n* chien *m* esquimau.

hustle ['hʌsl] 1 *vt* [hurry] pousser, bousculer. 2 *n* agitation *f*.

hut [hʌt] *n* [rough house] hutte *f*. || [shed] cabane *f*.

hutch [hʌtʃ] *n* clapier *m*.

hyacinth ['haɪəsɪnθ] *n* jacinthe *f*.

hydrant ['haɪdrənt] *n* bouche *f* d'incendie.

hydraulic [haɪ'drɔːlɪk] *adj* hydraulique.

hydroelectric [,haɪdrəʊɪ'lektrɪk] *adj* hydro-électrique.

hydrofoil ['haɪdrəfɔɪl] *n* hydrofoil *m*.

hydrogen ['haɪdrədʒən] *n* hydrogène *m*.

hyena [haɪ'iːnə] *n* hyène *f*.

hygiene ['haɪdʒiːn] *n* hygiène *f*.

hygienic [haɪ'dʒiːnɪk] *adj* hygiénique.

hymn [hɪm] *n* hymne *m*, cantique *m*.

hype [haɪp] *inf* 1 *n* (*U*) battage *m* publicitaire. 2 *vt* faire un battage publicitaire autour de.

hyperactive [,haɪpər'æktɪv] *adj* hyperactif(ive).

hypermarket ['haɪpə,mɑːkɪt] *n* hypermarché *m*.

hyphen ['haɪfn] *n* trait *m* d'union.

hypnosis [hɪp'nəʊsɪs] *n* hypnose *f*.

hypnotic [hɪp'nɒtɪk] *adj* hypnotique.

hypnotize, -ise ['hɪpnətaɪz] *vt* hypnotiser.

hypocrisy [hɪ'pɒkrəsɪ] *n* hypocrisie *f*.

hypocrite ['hɪpəkrɪt] *n* hypocrite *mf*.

hypocritical [,hɪpə'krɪtɪkl] *adj* hypocrite.

hypothesis [haɪ'pɒθɪsɪs] (*pl* **-theses** [-θɪsiːz]) *n* hypothèse *f*.

hypothetical [,haɪpə'θetɪkl] *adj* hypothétique.

hysteria [hɪs'tɪərɪə] *n* hystérie *f*.

hysterical [hɪs'terɪkl] *adj* [gen] hystérique. || *inf* [very funny] désopilant(e).

hysterics [hɪs'terɪks] *npl* [panic, excitement] crise *f* de nerfs. || *inf* [laughter] fou rire *m*.

i (*pl* **i's** OR **is**), **I** (*pl* **I's** OR **Is**) [aɪ] *n* [letter] i *m inv*, I *m inv*.

I [aɪ] *pers pron* (*unstressed*) je, j' (*before vowel or silent 'h'*); **he and I are leaving for Paris** lui et moi (nous) partons pour Paris. || (*stressed*) moi; **I can't do it** moi je ne peux pas le faire.

ice [aɪs] *n* [frozen water, ice cream] glace *f*. || [on road] verglas *m*. || (*U*) [ice cubes] glaçons *mpl*. ○ **ice over, ice up** *vi* [lake, pond] geler; [window, windscreen] givrer; [road] se couvrir de verglas.

iceberg ['aɪsbɜːg] *n* iceberg *m*.

icebox ['aɪsbɒks] *n* *Am* [refrigerator] réfrigérateur *m*.

ice cream *n* glace *f*.

ice cube *n* glaçon *m*.

ice hockey *n* hockey *m* sur glace.

Iceland ['aɪslənd] *n* Islande *f*.

ice pick *n* pic *m* à glace.

ice rink *n* patinoire *f*.

ice skate *n* patin *m* à glace. ○ **ice-skate** *vi* faire du patin (à glace).

ice-skating *n* patinage *m* (sur glace).

icicle ['aɪsɪkl] *n* glaçon *m* (naturel).

icing ['aɪsɪŋ] *n* (*U*) glaçage *m*, glace *f*.

icon ['aɪkɒn] *n* [gen & COMPLT] icône *f*.

icy ['aɪsɪ] *adj* [weather, manner] glacial(e). || [covered in ice] verglacé(e).

I'd [aɪd] = **I would, I had**.

ID *n* (*abbr of* **identification**) (*U*) papiers *mpl*.

idea [aɪ'dɪə] *n* idée *f*; [intention] intention *f*; **to have an ~ (that) ...** avoir idée que ...; **to have no ~** n'avoir aucune idée; **to get the ~** *inf* piger.

ideal [aɪ'dɪəl] **1** *adj* idéal(e). **2** *n* idéal *m*.

ideally [aɪ'dɪəlɪ] *adv* idéalement; [suited] parfaitement.

identical [aɪ'dentɪkl] *adj* identique.

identification [aɪˌdentɪfɪ'keɪʃn] *n* (*U*) [gen]: **~ (with)** identification *f* (à). || [documentation] pièce *f* d'identité.

identify [aɪ'dentɪfaɪ] **1** *vt* [recognize] identifier. || [subj: document, card] permettre de reconnaître. || [associate]: **to ~ sb with sthg** associer qqn à qqch. **2** *vi* [empathize]: **to ~ with** s'identifier à.

Identikit picture® [aɪ'dentɪkɪt-] *n* portrait-robot *m*.

identity [aɪ'dentətɪ] *n* identité *f*.

identity card *n* carte *f* d'identité.

identity parade *n* séance d'identification d'un suspect dans un échantillon de plusieurs personnes.

idiom ['ɪdɪəm] *n*. [phrase] expression *f* idiomatique. || *fml* [style] langue *f*.

idiomatic [ˌɪdɪə'mætɪk] *adj* idiomatique.

idiosyncrasy [ˌɪdɪə'sɪŋkrəsɪ] *n* particularité *f*, caractéristique *f*.

idiot ['ɪdɪət] *n* idiot *m*, -e *f*, imbécile *mf*.

idiotic [ˌɪdɪ'ɒtɪk] *adj* idiot(e).

idle ['aɪdl] **1** *adj* [lazy] oisif(ive), désœuvré(e). || [not working - machine, factory] arrêté(e); [- worker] qui chôme, en chômage. || [threat] vain(e). || [curiosity] simple, pur(e). **2** *vi* tourner au ralenti. ○ **idle away** *vt sep* [time] perdre à ne rien faire.

idol ['aɪdl] *n* idole *f*.

idolize, -ise ['aɪdəlaɪz] *vt* idolâtrer, adorer.

idyllic [ɪ'dɪlɪk] *adj* idyllique.

i.e. (*abbr of* **id est**) c-à-d.

if [ɪf] *conj* [gen] si; **~ I were you** à ta place, si j'étais toi. || [though] bien que. || [that] que. ○ **if not** *conj* sinon. ○ **if only** *conj* [naming a reason] ne serait-ce que. || [expressing regret] si seulement.

igloo ['ɪɡluː] *n* (*pl* -s) *n* igloo *m*, iglou *m*.

ignite [ɪɡ'naɪt] *vi* prendre feu, s'enflammer.

ignition [ɪɡ'nɪʃn] *n* [act of igniting] ignition *f*. || AUT allumage *m*; **to switch on the ~** mettre le contact.

ignition key *n* clef *f* de contact.

ignorance ['ɪɡnərəns] *n* ignorance *f*.

ignorant ['ɪɡnərənt] *adj* [uneducated, unaware] ignorant(e); **to be ~ of sthg** être ignorant de qqch. || [rude] mal élevé(e).

ignore [ɪɡ'nɔːr] *vt* [advice, facts] ne pas tenir compte de; [person] faire semblant de ne pas voir.

ill [ɪl] **1** *adj* [unwell] malade; **to feel ~** se sentir malade OR souffrant; **to be taken ~, to fall ~** tomber malade. || [bad] mauvais(e); **~ luck** malchance *f*. **2** *adv* mal; **to speak/think ~ of sb** dire/penser du mal de qqn.

I'll [aɪl] = **I will, I shall**.

ill-advised [-əd'vaɪzd] *adj* [remark, action] peu judicieux(ieuse); [person] malavisé(e).

ill at ease *adj* mal à l'aise.

illegal [ɪ'li:gl] *adj* illégal(e); [immigrant] en situation irrégulière.

illegible [ɪ'ledʒəbl] *adj* illisible.

illegitimate [,ɪlɪ'dʒɪtɪmət] *adj* illégitime.

ill-equipped [-ɪ'kwɪpt] *adj*: to be ~ to do sthg être mal placé(e) pour faire qqch.

ill-fated [-'feɪtɪd] *adj* fatal(e), funeste.

ill feeling *n* animosité *f*.

ill health *n* mauvaise santé *f*.

illicit [ɪ'lɪsɪt] *adj* illicite.

illiteracy [ɪ'lɪtərəsɪ] *n* analphabétisme *m*, illettrisme *m*.

illiterate [ɪ'lɪtərət] *adj* analphabète, illettré(e).

illness ['ɪlnɪs] *n* maladie *f*.

illogical [ɪ'lɒdʒɪkl] *adj* illogique.

ill-suited *adj* mal assorti(e); to be ~ for sthg être inapte à qqch.

ill-timed [-'taɪmd] *adj* déplacé(e), mal à propos.

ill-treat *vt* maltraiter.

illuminate [ɪ'lu:mɪneɪt] *vt* éclairer.

illumination [ɪ,lu:mɪ'neɪʃn] *n* [lighting] éclairage *m*.

illusion [ɪ'lu:ʒn] *n* illusion *f*; to have no ~s about ne se faire OR n'avoir aucune illusion sur; to be under the ~ that croire OR s'imaginer que, avoir l'illusion que.

illustrate ['ɪləstreɪt] *vt* illustrer.

illustration [,ɪlə'streɪʃn] *n* illustration *f*.

illustrious [ɪ'lʌstrɪəs] *adj* illustre, célèbre.

ill will *n* animosité *f*.

I'm [aɪm] = I am.

image ['ɪmɪdʒ] *n* [gen] image *f*. || [of company, politician] image *f* de marque.

imagery ['ɪmɪdʒrɪ] *n* (*U*) images *fpl*.

imaginary [ɪ'mædʒɪnrɪ] *adj* imaginaire.

imagination [ɪ,mædʒɪ'neɪʃn] *n* [ability] imagination *f*. || [fantasy] invention *f*.

imaginative [ɪ'mædʒɪnətɪv] *adj* imaginatif(ive); [solution] plein(e) d'imagination.

imagine [ɪ'mædʒɪn] *vt* imaginer; to ~ doing sthg s'imaginer OR se voir faisant qqch; ~ (that)! tu t'imagines!

imbalance [,ɪm'bæləns] *n* déséquilibre *m*.

imbecile ['ɪmbɪsi:l] *n* imbécile *mf*, idiot *m*, -e *f*.

IMF (*abbr of* **International Monetary Fund**) *n* FMI *m*.

imitate ['ɪmɪteɪt] *vt* imiter.

imitation [,ɪmɪ'teɪʃn] **1** *n* imitation *f*. **2** *adj* [leather] imitation (*before* n); [jewellery] en toc.

immaculate [ɪ'mækjʊlət] *adj* impeccable.

immaterial [,ɪmə'tɪərɪəl] *adj* [unimportant] sans importance.

immature [,ɪmə'tjʊər] *adj* [lacking judgment] qui manque de maturité. || [not fully grown] jeune, immature.

immediate [ɪ'mi:djət] *adj* [urgent] immédiat(e); [problem, meeting] urgent(e). || [very near] immédiat(e); [family] le plus proche.

immediately [ɪ'mi:djətlɪ] **1** *adv* [at once] immédiatement. || [directly] directement. **2** *conj* dès que.

immense [ɪ'mens] *adj* immense; [improvement, change] énorme.

immerse [ɪ'mɜ:s] *vt*: to ~ sthg in sthg immerger OR plonger qqch dans qqch; to ~ o.s. in sthg *fig* se plonger dans qqch.

immersion heater [ɪ'mɜ:ʃn-] *n* chauffe-eau *m inv* électrique.

immigrant ['ɪmɪgrənt] *n* immigré *m*, -e *f*.

immigration [,ɪmɪ'greɪʃn] *n* immigration *f*.

imminent ['ɪmɪnənt] *adj* imminent(e).

immobilize, -ise [ɪ'məʊbɪlaɪz] *vt* immobiliser.

immoral [ɪ'mɒrəl] *adj* immoral(e).

immortal [ɪ'mɔ:tl] **1** *adj* immortel(elle). **2** *n* immortel *m*, -elle *f*.

immune [ɪ'mju:n] *adj* MED: ~ (to) immunisé(e) (contre).

immunity [ɪ'mju:nətɪ] *n* MED: ~ (to) immunité *f* (contre).

immunize, -ise ['ɪmjuːnaɪz] *vt*: to ~ sb (against) immuniser qqn (contre).

imp [ɪmp] *n* [creature] lutin *m*. || [naughty child] petit diable *m*, coquin *m*, -e *f*.

impact ['ɪmpækt] *n* impact *m*; to make an ~ on OR upon sb faire une forte impression sur qqn; to make an ~ on OR upon sthg avoir un impact sur qqch.

impair [ɪm'peər] *vt* affaiblir, abîmer; [efficiency] réduire.

impart [ɪm'pɑ:t] *vt fml* [information]: to ~ sthg (to sb) communiquer OR transmettre qqch (à qqn). || [feeling, quality]: to ~ sthg (to) donner qqch (à).

impartial [ɪm'pɑ:ʃl] *adj* impartial(e).

impassive [ɪm'pæsɪv] *adj* impassible.

impatience [ɪm'peɪʃns] *n* [gen] impatience *f*. || [irritability] irritation *f*.

impatient [ɪm'peɪʃnt] *adj* [gen] impatient(e); **to be ~ to do sthg** être impatient de faire qqch; **to be ~ for sthg** attendre qqch avec impatience. || [irritable]: **to become OR get ~** s'impatienter.

impeccable [ɪm'pekəbl] *adj* impeccable.

impede [ɪm'piːd] *vt* entraver, empêcher; [person] gêner.

impediment [ɪm'pedɪmənt] *n* [obstacle] obstacle *m*. || [disability] défaut *m*.

impel [ɪm'pel] *vt*: **to ~ sb to do sthg** inciter qqn à faire qqch.

impending [ɪm'pendɪŋ] *adj* imminent(e).

imperative [ɪm'perətɪv] **1** *adj* [essential] impératif(ive), essentiel(ielle). **2** *n* impératif *m*.

imperfect [ɪm'pɜːfɪkt] **1** *adj* imparfait(e). **2** *n* GRAMM: **~ (tense)** imparfait *m*.

imperial [ɪm'pɪərɪəl] *adj* [of empire] impérial(e).

impersonal [ɪm'pɜːsnl] *adj* impersonnel(elle).

impersonate [ɪm'pɜːsəneɪt] *vt* se faire passer pour.

impersonation [ɪm,pɜːsə'neɪʃn] *n* usurpation *f* d'identité; [by mimic] imitation *f*.

impertinent [ɪm'pɜːtɪnənt] *adj* impertinent(e).

impervious [ɪm'pɜːvjəs] *adj* [not influenced]: **~ to** indifférent(e) à.

impetuous [ɪm'petʃʊəs] *adj* impétueux(euse).

impetus ['ɪmpɪtəs] *n* (*U*) [momentum] élan *m*. || [stimulus] impulsion *f*.

impinge [ɪm'pɪndʒ] *vi*: **to ~ on sb/sthg** affecter qqn/qqch.

implant [*n* 'ɪmplɑːnt, *vb* ɪm'plɑːnt] **1** *n* implant *m*. **2** *vt*: **to ~ sthg in OR into sb** implanter qqch dans qqn.

implausible [ɪm'plɔːzəbl] *adj* peu plausible.

implement [*n* 'ɪmplɪmənt, *vb* 'ɪmplɪment] **1** *n* outil *m*, instrument *m*. **2** *vt* exécuter, appliquer.

implication [,ɪmplɪ'keɪʃn] *n* implication *f*; **by ~** par voie de conséquence.

implicit [ɪm'plɪsɪt] *adj* [inferred] implicite. || [belief, faith] absolu(e).

implore [ɪm'plɔː] *vt*: **to ~ sb (to do sthg)** implorer qqn (de faire qqch).

imply [ɪm'plaɪ] *vt* [suggest] sous-

entendre, laisser supposer OR entendre. || [involve] impliquer.

impolite [,ɪmpə'laɪt] *adj* impoli(e).

import [*n* 'ɪmpɔːt, *vb* ɪm'pɔːt] **1** *n* [product, action] importation *f*. **2** *vt* [gen & COMPUT] importer.

importance [ɪm'pɔːtns] *n* importance *f*.

important [ɪm'pɔːtnt] *adj* important(e); **to be ~ to sb** importer à qqn.

importer [ɪm'pɔːtə] *n* importateur *m*, -trice *f*.

impose [ɪm'pəʊz] **1** *vt* [force]: **to ~ sthg (on)** imposer qqch (à). **2** *vi* [cause trouble]: **to ~ (on sb)** abuser (de la gentillesse de qqn).

imposing [ɪm'pəʊzɪŋ] *adj* imposant(e).

imposition [,ɪmpə'zɪʃn] *n* [of tax, limitations etc] imposition *f*. || [cause of trouble]: **it's an ~** c'est abuser de ma/notre gentillesse.

impossible [ɪm'pɒsəbl] *adj* impossible.

impostor, imposter *Am* [ɪm'pɒstə] *n* imposteur *m*.

impotent ['ɪmpətənt] *adj* impuissant(e).

impound [ɪm'paʊnd] *vt* confisquer.

impoverished [ɪm'pɒvərɪʃt] *adj* appauvri(e).

impractical [ɪm'præktɪkl] *adj* pas pratique.

impregnable [ɪm'pregnəbl] *adj* [fortress, defences] imprenable.

impregnate ['ɪmpregneɪt] *vt* [introduce substance into]: **to ~ sthg with** imprégner qqch de. || *fml* [fertilize] féconder.

impress [ɪm'pres] *vt* [person] impressionner. || [stress]: **to ~ sthg on sb** faire bien comprendre qqch à qqn.

impression [ɪm'preʃn] *n* [gen] impression *f*; **to be under the ~ (that) ...** avoir l'impression que ...; **to make an ~** faire impression. || [by mimic] imitation *f*.

impressive [ɪm'presɪv] *adj* impressionnant(e).

imprint ['ɪmprɪnt] *n* [mark] empreinte *f*.

imprison [ɪm'prɪzn] *vt* emprisonner.

improbable [ɪm'prɒbəbl] *adj* [story, excuse] improbable.

impromptu [ɪm'prɒmptjuː] *adj* impromptu(e).

improper [ɪm'prɒpə] *adj* [unsuitable] impropre. || [incorrect, illegal] incorrect(e). || [rude] indécent(e).

improve [ɪm'pruːv] **1** *vi* s'améliorer; [patient] aller mieux; **to ~ on OR upon sthg** améliorer qqch. **2** *vt* améliorer.

improvement [ɪm'pruːvmənt] *n*: ~ **(in/on)** amélioration *f* (de/par rapport à).

improvise ['ɪmprəvaɪz] *vt* & *vi* improviser.

impudent ['ɪmpjʊdənt] *adj* impudent(e).

impulse ['ɪmpʌls] *n* impulsion *f*; **on** ~ par impulsion.

impulsive [ɪm'pʌlsɪv] *adj* impulsif(ive).

impunity [ɪm'pjuːnətɪ] *n*: **with** ~ avec impunité.

impurity [ɪm'pjʊərətɪ] *n* impureté *f*.

in [ɪn] **1** *prep* [indicating place, position] dans; ~ **Paris** à Paris; ~ **Belgium** en Belgique; ~ **the United States** aux États-Unis; ~ **the country** à la campagne; ~ **here** ici; ~ **there** là. || [wearing] en; **dressed** ~ **a suit** vêtu d'un costume. || [at a particular time, season]: ~ **1994** en 1994; ~ **April** en avril; ~ **(the) spring** au printemps; ~ **(the) winter** en hiver. || [period of time - within] en; [- after] dans; **he learned to type** ~ **two weeks** il a appris à taper à la machine en deux semaines; **I'll be ready** ~ **five minutes** je serai prêt dans 5 minutes. || [during]: **it's my first decent meal** ~ **weeks** c'est mon premier repas correct depuis des semaines. || [indicating situation, circumstances]: ~ **the sun** au soleil; ~ **the rain** sous la pluie; ~ **danger/difficulty** en danger/difficulté. || [indicating manner, condition]: ~ **a loud/soft voice** d'une voix forte/douce; **to write** ~ **pencil/ink** écrire au crayon/à l'encre; **to speak** ~ **English/French** parler (en) anglais/français. || [indicating emotional state]: ~ **anger** sous le coup de la colère; ~ **joy/delight** avec joie/plaisir. || [specifying area of activity] dans; **he's** ~ **computers** il est dans l'informatique. || [referring to quantity, numbers, age]: ~ **large/small quantities** en grande/petite quantité; ~ **(their) thousands** par milliers; **she's** ~ **her sixties** elle a la soixantaine. || [describing arrangement]: ~ **twos** par deux; ~ **a line/row/circle** en ligne/rang/cercle. || [as regards]: **to be three metres** ~ **length/width** faire trois mètres de long/large; **a change** ~ **direction** un changement de direction. || [in ratios]: **one** ~ **ten** un sur dix. || (*after superl*) de; **the longest river** ~ **the world** le fleuve le plus long du monde. || (+ *present participle*): ~ **doing sthg** en faisant qqch. **2** *adv* [inside] dedans, à l'intérieur. || [at home, work] là; **I'm staying** ~ **tonight** je reste à la maison OR chez moi ce soir; **is Judith** ~? est-ce que Judith est là? || [of train, boat, plane]: **to be** ~ être arrivé(e). || [of tide]: **the tide's** ~ c'est la marée haute. || *phr*: **you're** ~ **for a shock** tu vas avoir un choc. **3** *adj inf* à la mode. ○ **ins** *npl*: **the** ~**s and outs** les tenants et les aboutissants *mpl*.

in. *abbr of* **inch.**

inability [ˌɪnə'bɪlətɪ] *n*: ~ **(to do sthg)** incapacité *f* (à faire qqch).

inaccessible [ˌɪnək'sesəbl] *adj* inaccessible.

inaccurate [ɪn'ækjʊrət] *adj* inexact(e).

inadequate [ɪn'ædɪkwət] *adj* insuffisant(e).

inadvertently [ˌɪnəd'vɜːtəntlɪ] *adv* par inadvertance.

inadvisable [ˌɪnəd'vaɪzəbl] *adj* déconseillé(e).

inane [ɪ'neɪn] *adj* inepte; [person] stupide.

inanimate [ɪn'ænɪmət] *adj* inanimé(e).

inappropriate [ˌɪnə'prəʊprɪət] *adj* inopportun(e); [expression, word] impropre; [clothing] peu approprié(e).

inarticulate [ˌɪnɑː'tɪkjʊlət] *adj* inarticulé(e), indistinct(e); [person] qui s'exprime avec difficulté; [explanation] mal exprimé(e).

inasmuch [ˌɪnəz'mʌtʃ] ○ **inasmuch as** *conj fml* attendu que.

inaudible [ɪ'nɔːdɪbl] *adj* inaudible.

inaugural [ɪ'nɔːgjʊrəl] *adj* inaugural(e).

inauguration [ɪˌnɔːgjʊ'reɪʃn] *n* [of leader, president] investiture *f*; [of building, system] inauguration *f*.

in-between *adj* intermédiaire.

inborn [ˌɪn'bɔːn] *adj* inné(e).

inbound ['ɪnbaʊnd] *adj Am* qui arrive.

inbred [ˌɪn'bred] *adj* [closely related] consanguin(e); [animal] croisé(e). || [inborn] inné(e).

inbuilt [ˌɪn'bɪlt] *adj* [inborn] inné(e).

inc. (*abbr of* **inclusive**): **12-15 April** ~ du 12 au 15 avril inclus.

Inc. [ɪŋk] (*abbr of* **incorporated**) ≃ SARL.

incapable [ɪn'keɪpəbl] *adj* incapable; **to be** ~ **of sthg/of doing sthg** être incapable de qqch/de faire qqch.

incapacitated [ˌɪnkə'pæsɪteɪtɪd] *adj* inapte physiquement.

incarcerate [ɪn'kɑːsəreɪt] *vt* incarcérer.

incendiary device [ɪn'sendjərɪ-] *n* dispositif *m* incendiaire.

incense [*n* 'ɪnsens, *vb* ɪn'sens] **1** *n* encens *m*. **2** *vt* [anger] mettre en colère.

incentive [ɪn'sentɪv] *n* [encouragement] motivation *f*. || COMM récompense *f*, prime *f*.

incentive scheme *n* programme *m* d'encouragement.

inception [ɪn'sepʃn] *n fml* commencement *m*.

incessant [ɪn'sesnt] *adj* incessant(e).

incessantly [ɪn'sesntlɪ] *adv* sans cesse.

incest ['ɪnsest] *n* inceste *m*.

inch [ɪntʃ] **1** *n* = 2,5 cm, ≃ pouce *m*. **2** *vi*: to ~ **forward** avancer petit à petit.

incidence ['ɪnsɪdəns] *n* [of disease, theft] fréquence *f*.

incident ['ɪnsɪdənt] *n* incident *m*.

incidental [,ɪnsɪ'dentl] *adj* accessoire.

incidentally [,ɪnsɪ'dentəlɪ] *adv* à propos.

incinerate [ɪn'sɪnəreɪt] *vt* incinérer.

incisive [ɪn'saɪsɪv] *adj* incisif(ive).

incite [ɪn'saɪt] *vt* inciter; to ~ **sb to do sthg** inciter qqn à faire qqch.

inclination [,ɪnklɪ'neɪʃn] *n* (U) [liking, preference] inclination *f*, goût *m*. || [tendency]: ~ **to do sthg** inclination *f* à faire qqch.

incline [*n* 'ɪnklaɪn, *vb* ɪn'klaɪn] **1** *n* inclinaison *f*. **2** *vt* [head] incliner.

inclined [ɪn'klaɪnd] *adj* [tending]: **to be ~ to/to do sthg** avoir tendance à qqch/à faire qqch. || [wanting]: **to be ~ to do sthg** être enclin(e) à faire qqch.

include [ɪn'kluːd] *vt* inclure.

included [ɪn'kluːdɪd] *adj* inclus(e).

including [ɪn'kluːdɪŋ] *prep* y compris.

inclusive [ɪn'kluːsɪv] *adj* inclus(e); [including all costs] tout compris; ~ **of VAT** TVA incluse OR comprise.

incoherent [,ɪnkəʊ'hɪərənt] *adj* incohérent(e).

income ['ɪŋkʌm] *n* revenu *m*.

income tax *n* impôt *m* sur le revenu.

incompatible [,ɪnkəm'pætɪbl] *adj*: ~ **(with)** incompatible (avec).

incompetent [ɪn'kɒmpɪtənt] *adj* incompétent(e).

incomplete [,ɪnkəm'pliːt] *adj* incomplet(ète).

incomprehensible [ɪn,kɒmprɪ'hensəbl] *adj* incompréhensible.

inconceivable [,ɪnkən'siːvəbl] *adj* inconcevable.

inconclusive [,ɪnkən'kluːsɪv] *adj* peu concluant(e).

incongruous [ɪn'kɒŋgruəs] *adj* incongru(e).

inconsiderable [,ɪnkən'sɪdərəbl] *adj*: **not ~** non négligeable.

inconsiderate [,ɪnkən'sɪdərət] *adj* inconsidéré(e); [person] qui manque de considération.

inconsistency [,ɪnkən'sɪstənsɪ] *n* inconsistance *f*.

inconsistent [,ɪnkən'sɪstənt] *adj* [not agreeing, contradictory] contradictoire; [person] inconséquent(e); ~ **with sthg** en contradiction avec qqch. || [erratic] inconsistant(e).

inconspicuous [,ɪnkən'spɪkjuəs] *adj* qui passe inaperçu(e).

inconvenience [,ɪnkən'viːnjəns] **1** *n* désagrément *m*. **2** *vt* déranger.

inconvenient [,ɪnkən'viːnjənt] *adj* inopportun(e).

incorporate [ɪn'kɔːpəreɪt] *vt* [integrate]: **to ~ sb/sthg (into)** incorporer qqn/qqch (dans). || [comprise] contenir, comprendre.

incorporated [ɪn'kɔːpəreɪtɪd] *adj* COMM constitué(e) en société commerciale.

incorrect [,ɪnkə'rekt] *adj* incorrect(e).

increase [*n* 'ɪnkriːs, *vb* ɪn'kriːs] **1** *n*: ~ **(in)** augmentation *f* (de); **to be on the ~** aller en augmentant. **2** *vt & vi* augmenter.

increasing [ɪn'kriːsɪŋ] *adj* croissant(e).

increasingly [ɪn'kriːsɪŋlɪ] *adv* de plus en plus.

incredible [ɪn'kredəbl] *adj* incroyable.

increment ['ɪnkrɪmənt] *n* augmentation *f*.

incriminating [ɪn'krɪmɪneɪtɪŋ] *adj* compromettant(e).

incubator ['ɪnkjubeɪtə'] *n* [for baby] incubateur *m*, couveuse *f*.

incumbent [ɪn'kʌmbənt] *fml n* [of post] titulaire *m*.

incur [ɪn'kɜːr] *vt* encourir.

indebted [ɪn'detɪd] *adj* [grateful]: ~ **to sb** redevable à qqn.

indecent [ɪn'diːsnt] *adj* [improper] indécent(e). || [unreasonable] malséant(e).

indecent assault *n* attentat *m* à la pudeur.

indecent exposure *n* outrage *m* public à la pudeur.

indecisive [,ɪndɪ'saɪsɪv] *adj* indécis(e).

indeed [ɪn'diːd] *adv* [certainly, to express surprise] vraiment; ~ **I am, yes ~** certainement. || [in fact] en effet. || [for emphasis]: **very big/bad** ~ extrêmement grand/mauvais, vraiment grand/mauvais.

indefinite [ɪn'defɪnɪt] *adj* [not fixed] indéfini(e). || [imprecise] vague.

indefinitely [ɪn'defɪnətlɪ] *adv* [for unfixed period] indéfiniment. || [imprecisely] vaguement.

indemnity [ɪn'demnətɪ] *n* indemnité *f*.

indent [ɪn'dent] *vt* [dent] entailler. || [text] mettre en retrait.

independence [,ɪndɪ'pendəns] *n* indépendance *f*.

Independence Day *n* fête de l'indépendance américaine, le 4 juillet.

independent [,ɪndɪ'pendənt] *adj*: ~ **(of)** indépendant(e) (de).

in-depth *adj* approfondi(e).

indescribable [,ɪndɪ'skraɪbəbl] *adj* indescriptible.

indestructible [,ɪndɪ'strʌktəbl] *adj* indestructible.

index ['ɪndeks] (*pl senses 1 and 2* -es, *sense 3* -es OR **indices**) *n* [of book] index *m*. || [in library] répertoire *m*, fichier *m*. || ECON indice *m*.

index card *n* fiche *f*.

index finger *n* index *m*.

index-linked [-,lɪŋkt] *adj* indexé(e).

India ['ɪndjə] *n* Inde *f*.

Indian ['ɪndjən] **1** *adj* indien(ienne). **2** *n* Indien *m*, -ienne *f*.

Indian Ocean *n*: **the** ~ l'océan *m* Indien.

indicate ['ɪndɪkeɪt] **1** *vt* indiquer. **2** *vi* AUT mettre son clignotant.

indication [,ɪndɪ'keɪʃn] *n* [suggestion] indication *f*. || [sign] signe *m*.

indicative [ɪn'dɪkətɪv] **1** *adj*: ~ **of** indicatif(ive) de. **2** *n* GRAMM indicatif *m*.

indicator ['ɪndɪkeɪtər] *n* [sign] indicateur *m*. || AUT clignotant *m*.

indices ['ɪndɪsiːz] *pl* → index.

indict [ɪn'daɪt] *vt*: **to** ~ **sb (for)** accuser qqn (de).

indictment [ɪn'daɪtmənt] *n* JUR acte *m* d'accusation. || [criticism] mise *f* en accusation.

indifference [ɪn'dɪfrəns] *n* indifférence *f*.

indifferent [ɪn'dɪfrənt] *adj* [uninterested]: ~ **(to)** indifférent(e) (à). || [mediocre] médiocre.

indigenous [ɪn'dɪdʒɪnəs] *adj* indigène.

indigestion [,ɪndɪ'dʒestʃn] *n* (*U*) indigestion *f*.

indignant [ɪn'dɪgnənt] *adj*: ~ **(at)** indigné(e) (de).

indignity [ɪn'dɪgnətɪ] *n* indignité *f*.

indigo ['ɪndɪgəʊ] *adj* indigo (*inv*).

indirect [,ɪndɪ'rekt] *adj* indirect(e).

indiscreet [,ɪndɪ'skriːt] *adj* indiscret(ète).

indiscriminate [,ɪndɪ'skrɪmɪnət] *adj* [person] qui manque de discernement; [treatment] sans distinction; [killing] commis au hasard.

indispensable [,ɪndɪ'spensəbl] *adj* indispensable.

indisputable [,ɪndɪ'spjuːtəbl] *adj* indiscutable.

indistinguishable [,ɪndɪ'stɪŋgwɪʃəbl] *adj*: ~ **(from)** que l'on ne peut distinguer (de).

individual [,ɪndɪ'vɪdʒʊəl] **1** *adj* [separate, for one person] individuel(elle). || [distinctive] personnel(elle). **2** *n* individu *m*.

individually [,ɪndɪ'vɪdʒʊəlɪ] *adv* individuellement.

indoctrination [ɪn,dɒktrɪ'neɪʃn] *n* endoctrinement *m*.

Indonesia [,ɪndə'niːzjə] *n* Indonésie *f*.

indoor ['ɪndɔːr] *adj* d'intérieur; [swimming pool] couvert(e); [sports] en salle.

indoors [,ɪn'dɔːz] *adv* à l'intérieur.

induce [ɪn'djuːs] *vt* [persuade]: **to** ~ **sb to do sthg** inciter OR pousser qqn à faire qqch. || [bring about] provoquer.

inducement [ɪn'djuːsmənt] *n* [incentive] incitation *f*, encouragement *m*.

induction [ɪn'dʌkʃn] *n* [into official position]: ~ **(into)** installation *f* (à).

induction course *n* stage *m* d'initiation.

indulge [ɪn'dʌldʒ] **1** *vt* [whim, passion] céder à. || [child, person] gâter. **2** *vi*: **to** ~ **in sthg** se permettre qqch.

indulgence [ɪn'dʌldʒəns] *n* [act of indulging] indulgence *f*. || [special treat] gâterie *f*.

indulgent [ɪn'dʌldʒənt] *adj* indulgent(e).

industrial [ɪn'dʌstrɪəl] *adj* industriel(ielle).

industrial action *n*: **to take** ~ se mettre en grève.

industrial estate *Br*, **industrial park** *Am n* zone *f* industrielle.

industrialist [ɪn'dʌstrɪəlɪst] *n* industriel *m*.

industrial park *Am* = **industrial estate**.

industrial relations *npl* relations *fpl* patronat-syndicats.

industrial revolution *n* révolution *f* industrielle.

industrious [ɪn'dʌstrɪəs] *adj* industrieux(ieuse).

industry ['ɪndəstrɪ] *n* [gen] industrie *f*.

inebriated [ɪ'niːbrɪeɪtɪd] *adj fml* ivre.

inedible [ɪn'edɪbl] *adj* [meal, food] immangeable. || [plant, mushroom] non comestible.

ineffective [,ɪnɪ'fektɪv] *adj* inefficace.

ineffectual [,ɪnɪ'fektʃʊəl] *adj* inefficace; [person] incapable, incompétent(e).

inefficiency [,ɪnɪ'fɪʃnsɪ] *n* inefficacité *f*; [of person] incapacité *f*, incompétence *f*.

inefficient [,ɪnɪ'fɪʃnt] *adj* inefficace; [person] incapable, incompétent(e).

ineligible [ɪn'elɪdʒəbl] *adj* inéligible; **to be ~ for sthg** ne pas avoir droit à qqch.

inept [ɪ'nept] *adj* inepte; [person] stupide.

inequality [,ɪnɪ'kwɒlətɪ] *n* inégalité *f*.

inert [ɪ'nɜːt] *adj* inerte.

inertia [ɪ'nɜːʃə] *n* inertie *f*.

inescapable [,ɪnɪ'skeɪpəbl] *adj* inéluctable.

inevitable [ɪn'evɪtəbl] *adj* inévitable.

inevitably [ɪn'evɪtəblɪ] *adv* inévitablement.

inexcusable [,ɪnɪk'skjuːzəbl] *adj* inexcusable, impardonnable.

inexpensive [,ɪnɪk'spensɪv] *adj* bon marché (*inv*), pas cher (chère).

inexperienced [,ɪnɪk'spɪərɪənst] *adj* inexpérimenté(e), qui manque d'expérience.

inexplicable [,ɪnɪk'splɪkəbl] *adj* inexplicable.

infallible [ɪn'fæləbl] *adj* infaillible.

infamous ['ɪnfəməs] *adj* infâme.

infancy ['ɪnfənsɪ] *n* petite enfance *f*.

infant ['ɪnfənt] *n* [baby] nouveau-né *m*, nouveau-née *f*, nourrisson *m*. || [young child] enfant *mf* en bas âge.

infantry ['ɪnfəntrɪ] *n* infanterie *f*.

infatuated [ɪn'fætjʊeɪtɪd] *adj*: ~ **(with)** entiché(e) (de).

infatuation [ɪn,fætjʊ'eɪʃn] *n*: ~ **(with)** béguin *m* (pour).

infect [ɪn'fekt] *vt* MED infecter.

infection [ɪn'fekʃn] *n* infection *f*.

infectious [ɪn'fekʃəs] *adj* [disease] infectieux(ieuse). || *fig* [feeling, laugh] contagieux(ieuse).

infer [ɪn'fɜːr] *vt* [deduce]: **to ~ sthg (from)** déduire qqch (de).

inferior [ɪn'fɪərɪər] **1** *adj* [in status] inférieur(e). || [product] de qualité inférieure; [work] médiocre. **2** *n* [in status] subalterne *mf*.

inferiority [ɪn,fɪərɪ'ɒrətɪ] *n* infériorité *f*.

inferiority complex *n* complexe *m* d'infériorité.

inferno [ɪn'fɜːnəʊ] (*pl* -s) *n* brasier *m*.

infertile [ɪn'fɜːtaɪl] *adj* [woman] stérile. || [soil] infertile.

infested [ɪn'festɪd] *adj*: ~ **with** infesté(e) de.

infighting ['ɪn,faɪtɪŋ] *n* (*U*) querelles *fpl* intestines.

infiltrate ['ɪnfɪltreɪt] *vt* infiltrer.

infinite ['ɪnfɪnət] *adj* infini(e).

infinitive [ɪn'fɪnɪtɪv] *n* infinitif *m*.

infinity [ɪn'fɪnətɪ] *n* infini *m*.

infirm [ɪn'fɜːm] *adj* infirme.

infirmary [ɪn'fɜːmərɪ] *n* [hospital] hôpital *m*.

inflamed [ɪn'fleɪmd] *adj* MED enflammé(e).

inflammable [ɪn'flæməbl] *adj* inflammable.

inflammation [,ɪnflə'meɪʃn] *n* MED inflammation *f*.

inflatable [ɪn'fleɪtəbl] *adj* gonflable.

inflate [ɪn'fleɪt] *vt* [tyre, life jacket etc] gonfler.

inflation [ɪn'fleɪʃn] *n* ECON inflation *f*.

inflationary [ɪn'fleɪʃnrɪ] *adj* ECON inflationniste.

inflict [ɪn'flɪkt] *vt*: **to ~ sthg on sb** infliger qqch à qqn.

influence ['ɪnflʊəns] **1** *n* influence *f*; **under the ~ of** [person, group] sous l'influence de; [alcohol, drugs] sous l'effet OR l'empire de. **2** *vt* influencer.

influential [,ɪnflʊ'enʃl] *adj* influent(e).

influenza [,ɪnflʊ'enzə] *n* (*U*) grippe *f*.

influx ['ɪnflʌks] *n* afflux *m*.

inform [ɪn'fɔːm] *vt*: **to ~ sb (of)** informer qqn de; **to ~ sb about** renseigner qqn sur. ○ **inform on** *vt fus* dénoncer.

informal [ɪn'fɔːml] *adj* [party, person] simple; [clothes] de tous les jours. || [negotiations, visit] officieux(ieuse); [meeting] informel(elle).

informant [ɪn'fɔːmənt] *n* informateur *m*, -trice *f*.

information [,ɪnfə'meɪʃn] *n* (*U*): ~ **(on** OR **about)** renseignements *mpl* OR informations *fpl* (sur); **a piece of ~** un renseignement; **for your** ~ *fml* à titre d'information.

information desk *n* bureau *m* de renseignements.

information technology *n* informatique *f.*

informative [ɪnˈfɔːmətɪv] *adj* informatif(ive).

informer [ɪnˈfɔːmər] *n* indicateur *m*, -trice *f.*

infrared [ˌɪnfrəˈred] *adj* infrarouge.

infrastructure [ˈɪnfrəˌstrʌktʃər] *n* infrastructure *f.*

infringe [ɪnˈfrɪndʒ] **1** *vt* [right] empiéter sur. || [law, agreement] enfreindre. **2** *vi* [on right]: **to ~ on** empiéter sur. || [on law, agreement]: **to ~ on** enfreindre.

infringement [ɪnˈfrɪndʒmənt] *n* [of right]: ~ **(of)** atteinte *f* (à). || [of law, agreement] transgression *f.*

infuriating [ɪnˈfjʊərɪeɪtɪŋ] *adj* exaspérant(e).

ingenious [ɪnˈdʒiːnjəs] *adj* ingénieux(ieuse).

ingenuity [ˌɪndʒɪˈnjuːətɪ] *n* ingéniosité *f.*

ingot [ˈɪŋgət] *n* lingot *m.*

ingrained [ˌɪnˈgreɪnd] *adj* [dirt] incrusté(e). || *fig* [belief, hatred] enraciné(e).

ingratiating [ɪnˈgreɪʃɪeɪtɪŋ] *adj* doucereux(euse), mielleux(euse).

ingredient [ɪnˈgriːdjənt] *n* ingrédient *m*; *fig* élément *m.*

inhabit [ɪnˈhæbɪt] *vt* habiter.

inhabitant [ɪnˈhæbɪtənt] *n* habitant *m*, -e *f.*

inhale [ɪnˈheɪl] **1** *vt* inhaler, respirer. **2** *vi* [breathe in] respirer.

inhaler [ɪnˈheɪlər] *n* MED inhalateur *m.*

inherent [ɪnˈhɪərənt, ɪnˈherənt] *adj*: ~ **(in)** inhérent(e) (à).

inherit [ɪnˈherɪt] **1** *vt*: **to ~ sthg (from sb)** hériter qqch (de qqn). **2** *vi* hériter.

inheritance [ɪnˈherɪtəns] *n* héritage *m.*

inhibit [ɪnˈhɪbɪt] *vt* [prevent] empêcher. || PSYCH inhiber.

inhibition [ˌɪnhɪˈbɪʃn] *n* inhibition *f.*

inhospitable [ˌɪnhɒˈspɪtəbl] *adj* inhospitalier(ière).

in-house 1 *adj* interne; [staff] de la maison. **2** *adv* [produce, work] sur place.

inhuman [ɪnˈhjuːmən] *adj* inhumain(e).

initial [ɪˈnɪʃl] **1** *adj* initial(e), premier(ière); ~ **letter** initiale *f.* **2** *vt* parapher. ○ **initials** *npl* initiales *fpl.*

initially [ɪˈnɪʃəlɪ] *adv* initialement, au début.

initiate [ɪˈnɪʃɪeɪt] *vt* [talks] engager; [scheme] ébaucher, inaugurer. || [teach]: **to ~ sb into sthg** initier qqn à qqch.

initiative [ɪˈnɪʃətɪv] *n* [gen] initiative *f.* || [advantage]: **to have the ~** avoir l'avantage *m.*

inject [ɪnˈdʒekt] *vt* MED: **to ~ sb with sthg, to ~ sthg into sb** injecter qqch à qqn. || *fig* [excitement] insuffler; [money] injecter.

injection [ɪnˈdʒekʃn] *n* *lit* & *fig* injection *f.*

injure [ˈɪndʒər] *vt* [limb, person] blesser. || *fig* [reputation, chances] compromettre.

injured [ˈɪndʒəd] **1** *adj* [limb, person] blessé(e). **2** *npl*: **the ~** les blessés *mpl.*

injury [ˈɪndʒərɪ] *n* [to limb, person] blessure *f*; **to do o.s. an ~** se blesser. || *fig* [to reputation] coup *m*, atteinte *f.*

injury time *n* (*U*) arrêts *mpl* de jeu.

injustice [ɪnˈdʒʌstɪs] *n* injustice *f.*

ink [ɪŋk] *n* encre *f.*

ink-jet printer *n* COMPUT imprimante *f* à jet d'encre.

inkling [ˈɪŋklɪŋ] *n*: **to have an ~ of** avoir une petite idée de.

inlaid [ˌɪnˈleɪd] *adj*: ~ **(with)** incrusté(e) (de).

inland [*adj* ˈɪnlənd, *adv* ɪnˈlænd] **1** *adj* intérieur(e). **2** *adv* à l'intérieur.

inlet [ˈɪnlet] *n* [of lake, sea] avancée *f.* || TECH arrivée *f.*

inmate [ˈɪnmeɪt] *n* [of prison] détenu *m*, -e *f*; [of mental hospital] interné *m*, -e *f.*

inn [ɪn] *n* auberge *f.*

innate [ˌɪˈneɪt] *adj* inné(e).

inner [ˈɪnər] *adj* [on inside] interne, intérieur(e). || [feelings] intime.

inner city *n*: **the ~** les quartiers *mpl* pauvres.

inner tube *n* chambre *f* à air.

innocence [ˈɪnəsəns] *n* innocence *f.*

innocent [ˈɪnəsənt] *adj* innocent(e); ~ **of** [crime] non coupable de.

innocuous [ɪˈnɒkjuəs] *adj* inoffensif(ive).

innovation [ˌɪnəˈveɪʃn] *n* innovation *f.*

innovative [ˈɪnəvətɪv] *adj* [idea, design] innovateur(trice). || [person, company] novateur(trice).

innuendo [ˌɪnjuːˈendəʊ] (*pl* -es OR -s) *n* insinuation *f.*

innumerable [ɪˈnjuːmərəbl] *adj* innombrable.

inoculate [ɪˈnɒkjuleɪt] *vt*: **to ~ sb (with sthg)** inoculer (qqch à) qqn.

in-patient *n* malade hospitalisé *m*, malade hospitalisée *f*.

input ['ɪnpʊt] (*pt & pp* **input** OR **-ted**) **1** *n* [contribution] contribution *f*, concours *m*. || COMPUT & ELEC entrée *f*. **2** *vt* COMPUT entrer.

inquest ['ɪnkwest] *n* enquête *f*.

inquire [ɪn'kwaɪə'] **1** *vt*: **to ~ when/whether/how ...** demander quand/si/comment .... **2** *vi*: **to ~ (about)** se renseigner (sur). ○ **inquire after** *vt fus* s'enquérir de. ○ **inquire into** *vt fus* enquêter sur.

inquiry [ɪn'kwaɪərɪ] *n* [question] demande *f* de renseignements; **"Inquiries"** «renseignements». || [investigation] enquête *f*.

inquiry desk *n* bureau *m* de renseignements.

inquisitive [ɪn'kwɪzətɪv] *adj* inquisiteur(trice).

inroads ['ɪnrəʊdz] *npl*: **to make ~ into** [savings] entamer.

insane [ɪn'seɪn] *adj* fou (folle).

insanity [ɪn'sænətɪ] *n* folie *f*.

insatiable [ɪn'seɪʃəbl] *adj* insatiable.

inscription [ɪn'skrɪpʃn] *n* [engraved] inscription *f*. || [written] dédicace *f*.

inscrutable [ɪn'skruːtəbl] *adj* impénétrable.

insect ['ɪnsekt] *n* insecte *m*.

insecticide [ɪn'sektɪsaɪd] *n* insecticide *m*.

insect repellent *n* crème *f* anti-insectes.

insecure [ˌɪnsɪ'kjʊə'] *adj* [person] anxieux(ieuse). || [job, investment] incertain(e).

insensitive [ɪn'sensətɪv] *adj*: **~ (to)** insensible (à).

inseparable [ɪn'seprəbl] *adj* inséparable.

insert [*vb* ɪn'sɜːt, *n* 'ɪnsɜːt] *vt*: **to ~ sthg (in** OR **into)** insérer qqch (dans). **2** *n* [in newspaper] encart *m*.

insertion [ɪn'sɜːʃn] *n* insertion *f*.

inshore [*adj* 'ɪnʃɔː', *adv* ɪn'ʃɔː'] **1** *adj* côtier(ière). **2** *adv* [be situated] près de la côte; [move] vers la côte.

inside [ɪn'saɪd] **1** *prep* [building, object] à l'intérieur de, dans; [group, organization] au sein de. || [time]: **~ three weeks** en moins de trois semaines. **2** *adv* [gen] dedans, à l'intérieur; **to go ~** entrer. || *prison sl* en taule. **3** *adj* intérieur(e). **4** *n* [interior]: **the ~** l'intérieur *m*; **~ out** [clothes] à l'envers; **to know sthg ~ out**

connaître qqch à fond. || AUT: **the ~** [in Europe, US etc] la droite. ○ **inside of** *prep Am* [building, object] à l'intérieur de, dans.

inside lane *n* AUT [in Europe, US etc] voie *f* de droite.

insight ['ɪnsaɪt] *n* [wisdom] sagacité *f*, perspicacité *f*. || [glimpse]: **~ (into)** aperçu *m* (de).

insignificant [ˌɪnsɪg'nɪfɪkənt] *adj* insignifiant(e).

insincere [ˌɪnsɪn'sɪə'] *adj* pas sincère.

insinuate [ɪn'sɪnjʊeɪt] *vt* insinuer, laisser entendre.

insipid [ɪn'sɪpɪd] *adj* insipide.

insist [ɪn'sɪst] **1** *vt* [claim]: **to ~ (that) ...** insister sur le fait que .... || [demand]: **to ~ (that) ...** insister pour que (+ *subjunctive*) .... **2** *vi*: **to ~ (on sthg)** exiger (qqch); **to ~ on doing sthg** tenir à faire qqch, vouloir absolument faire qqch.

insistent [ɪn'sɪstənt] *adj* [determined] insistant(e); **to be ~ on** insister sur. || [continual] incessant(e).

insole ['ɪnsəʊl] *n* semelle *f* intérieure.

insolent ['ɪnsələnt] *adj* insolent(e).

insolvent [ɪn'sɒlvənt] *adj* insolvable.

insomnia [ɪn'sɒmnɪə] *n* insomnie *f*.

inspect [ɪn'spekt] *vt* [letter, person] examiner. || [factory, troops etc] inspecter.

inspection [ɪn'spekʃn] *n* [investigation] examen *m*. || [official check] inspection *f*.

inspector [ɪn'spektə'] *n* inspecteur *m*, -trice *f*.

inspiration [ˌɪnspə'reɪʃn] *n* inspiration *f*.

inspire [ɪn'spaɪə'] *vt*: **to ~ sb to do sthg** pousser OR encourager qqn à faire qqch; **to ~ sb with sthg, to ~ sthg in sb** inspirer qqch à qqn.

install *Br*, **instal** *Am* [ɪn'stɔːl] *vt* [fit] installer.

installation [ˌɪnstə'leɪʃn] *n* installation *f*.

instalment *Br*, **installment** *Am* [ɪn'stɔːlmənt] *n* [payment] acompte *m*; **in ~s** par acomptes. || [episode] épisode *m*.

instance ['ɪnstəns] *n* exemple *m*; **for ~** par exemple.

instant ['ɪnstənt] **1** *adj* [immediate] instantané(e), immédiat(e). || [coffee] soluble; [food] à préparation rapide. **2** *n* instant *m*; **this ~** tout de suite, immédiatement.

instantly ['ɪnstəntlɪ] *adv* immédiatement.

instead [ɪn'sted] *adv* au lieu de cela.
○ **instead of** *prep* au lieu de; ~ **of him** à sa place.

instep ['ɪnstep] *n* cou-de-pied *m*.

instigate ['ɪnstɪgeɪt] *vt* être à l'origine de, entreprendre.

instil *Br*, **instill** *Am* [ɪn'stɪl] *vt*: **to ~ sthg in** OR **into sb** instiller qqch à qqn.

instinct ['ɪnstɪŋkt] *n* [intuition] instinct *m*. || [impulse] réaction *f*, mouvement *m*.

instinctive [ɪn'stɪŋktɪv] *adj* instinctif(ive).

institute ['ɪnstɪtjuːt] 1 *n* institut *m*. 2 *vt* instituer.

institution [,ɪnstɪ'tjuːʃn] *n* institution *f*.

instruct [ɪn'strʌkt] *vt* [tell, order]: **to ~ sb to do sthg** charger qqn de faire qqch. || [teach] instruire; **to ~ sb in sthg** enseigner qqch à qqn.

instruction [ɪn'strʌkʃn] *n* instruction *f*.
○ **instructions** *npl* mode *m* d'emploi, instructions *fpl*.

instructor [ɪn'strʌktər] *n* [gen] instructeur *m*, -trice *f*, moniteur *m*, -trice *f*. || *Am* SCH enseignant *m*, -e *f*.

instrument ['ɪnstrəmənt] *n lit & fig* instrument *m*.

instrumental [,ɪnstrʊ'mentl] *adj* [important, helpful]: **to be ~ in** contribuer à.

instrument panel *n* tableau *m* de bord.

insubstantial [,ɪnsəb'stænʃl] *adj* [structure] peu solide.

insufficient [,ɪnsə'fɪʃnt] *adj fml* insuffisant(e).

insular ['ɪnsjʊlər] *adj* [outlook] borné(e); [person] à l'esprit étroit.

insulate ['ɪnsjʊleɪt] *vt* [loft, cable] isoler; [hot water tank] calorifuger.

insulation [,ɪnsjʊ'leɪʃn] *n* isolation *f*.

insulin ['ɪnsjʊlɪn] *n* insuline *f*.

insult [*vt* ɪn'sʌlt, *n* 'ɪnsʌlt] 1 *vt* insulter, injurier. 2 *n* insulte *f*, injure *f*.

insuperable [ɪn'suːprəbl] *adj fml* insurmontable.

insurance [ɪn'ʃʊərəns] *n* [against fire, accident, theft] assurance *f*. || *fig* [safeguard, protection] protection *f*, garantie *f*.

insurance policy *n* police *f* d'assurance.

insure [ɪn'ʃʊər] 1 *vt* [against fire, accident, theft]: **to ~ sb/sthg against sthg** assurer qqn/qqch contre qqch. || *Am* [make certain] s'assurer. 2 *vi* [prevent]: **to ~ against** se protéger de.

insurer [ɪn'ʃʊərər] *n* assureur *m*.

insurmountable [,ɪnsə'maʊntəbl] *adj fml* insurmontable.

intact [ɪn'tækt] *adj* intact(e).

intake ['ɪnteɪk] *n* [amount consumed] consommation *f*. || [people recruited] admission *f*. || [inlet] prise *f*, arrivée *f*.

integral ['ɪntɪgrəl] *adj* intégral(e); **to be ~ to sthg** faire partie intégrante de qqch.

integrate ['ɪntɪgreɪt] 1 *vi* s'intégrer. 2 *vt* intégrer.

integrity [ɪn'tegrətɪ] *n* [honour] intégrité *f*, honnêteté *f*.

intellect ['ɪntəlekt] *n* [ability to think] intellect *m*. || [cleverness] intelligence *f*.

intellectual [,ɪntə'lektjʊəl] 1 *adj* intellectuel(elle). 2 *n* intellectuel *m*, -elle *f*.

intelligence [ɪn'telɪdʒəns] *n* (*U*) [ability to think] intelligence *f*. || [information service] service *m* de renseignements.

intelligent [ɪn'telɪdʒənt] *adj* intelligent(e).

intelligent card *n* carte *f* à puce OR à mémoire.

intend [ɪn'tend] *vt* [mean] avoir l'intention de; **to be ~ed for** être destiné à; **to ~ doing** OR **to do sthg** avoir l'intention de faire qqch.

intended [ɪn'tendɪd] *adj* [result] voulu(e); [victim] visé(e).

intense [ɪn'tens] *adj* [gen] intense. || [serious - person] sérieux(ieuse).

intensely [ɪn'tenslɪ] *adv* [irritating, boring] extrêmement; [suffer] énormément. || [look] intensément.

intensify [ɪn'tensɪfaɪ] 1 *vt* intensifier, augmenter. 2 *vi* s'intensifier.

intensity [ɪn'tensətɪ] *n* intensité *f*.

intensive [ɪn'tensɪv] *adj* intensif(ive).

intensive care *n* réanimation *f*.

intent [ɪn'tent] 1 *adj* [absorbed] absorbé(e). || [determined]: **to be ~ on** OR **upon doing sthg** être résolu(e) OR décidé(e) à faire qqch. 2 *n fml* intention *f*, dessein *m*; **to all ~s and purposes** pratiquement, virtuellement.

intention [ɪn'tenʃn] *n* intention *f*.

intentional [ɪn'tenʃənl] *adj* intentionnel(elle), voulu(e).

intently [ɪn'tentlɪ] *adv* avec attention, attentivement.

interact [,ɪntər'ækt] *vi* [communicate, work together]: **to ~ (with sb)** communiquer (avec qqn). || [react]: **to ~ (with sthg)** interagir (avec qqch).

intercede [,ɪntə'siːd] *vi fml*: **to ~ (with sb)** intercéder (auprès de qqn).

intercept [,ɪntə'sept] *vt* intercepter.

interchange [n 'ɪntətʃeɪndʒ, vb ˌɪntə'tʃeɪndʒ] **1** n [exchange] échange m. ‖ [road junction] échangeur m. **2** vt échanger.

interchangeable [ˌɪntə'tʃeɪndʒəbl] adj: ~ (with) interchangeable (avec).

intercom ['ɪntəkɒm] n Interphone® m.

intercourse ['ɪntəkɔːs] n (U) [sexual] rapports mpl (sexuels).

interest ['ɪntrəst] **1** n [gen] intérêt m; to lose ~ se désintéresser. ‖ [hobby] centre m d'intérêt. ‖ (U) FIN intérêt m, intérêts mpl. **2** vt intéresser.

interested ['ɪntrəstɪd] adj intéressé(e); to be ~ in s'intéresser à; I'm not ~ in that cela ne m'intéresse pas; to be ~ in doing sthg avoir envie de faire qqch.

interesting ['ɪntrəstɪŋ] adj intéressant(e).

interest rate n taux m d'intérêt.

interface ['ɪntəfeɪs] n COMPUT interface f. ‖ fig [junction] rapports mpl, relations fpl.

interfere [ˌɪntə'fɪər] vi [meddle]: to ~ in sthg s'immiscer dans qqch, se mêler de qqch. ‖ [damage]: to ~ with sthg gêner OR contrarier qqch; [routine] déranger qqch.

interference [ˌɪntə'fɪərəns] n (U) [meddling]: ~ (with OR in) ingérence f (dans), intrusion f (dans). ‖ TELEC parasites mpl.

interim ['ɪntərɪm] **1** adj provisoire. **2** n: in the ~ dans l'intérim, entre-temps.

interior [ɪn'tɪərɪər] **1** adj [inner] intérieur(e). ‖ POL de l'Intérieur. **2** n intérieur m.

interlock [ˌɪntə'lɒk] vi [gears] s'enclencher, s'engrener; [fingers] s'entrelacer.

interloper ['ɪntələupər] n intrus m, -e f.

interlude ['ɪntəluːd] n [pause] intervalle m. ‖ [interval] interlude m.

intermediary [ˌɪntə'miːdjərɪ] n intermédiaire mf.

intermediate [ˌɪntə'miːdjət] adj [transitional] intermédiaire. ‖ [post-beginner - level] moyen(enne); [- student, group] de niveau moyen.

interminable [ɪn'tɜːmɪnəbl] adj interminable, sans fin.

intermission [ˌɪntə'mɪʃn] n entracte m.

intermittent [ˌɪntə'mɪtənt] adj intermittent(e).

intern [vb ɪn'tɜːn, n 'ɪntɜːn] **1** vt interner. **2** n Am [gen] stagiaire mf; MED interne mf.

internal [ɪn'tɜːnl] adj [gen] interne. ‖ [within country] intérieur(e).

internally [ɪn'tɜːnəlɪ] adv [within the body]: to bleed ~ faire une hémorragie interne. ‖ [within country] à l'intérieur. ‖ [within organization] intérieurement.

Internal Revenue n Am: the ~ ≃ le fisc.

international [ˌɪntə'næʃənl] adj international(e).

interpret [ɪn'tɜːprɪt] **1** vt: to ~ sthg (as) interpréter qqch (comme). **2** vi [translate] faire l'interprète.

interpreter [ɪn'tɜːprɪtər] n interprète mf.

interracial [ˌɪntə'reɪʃl] adj entre des races différentes, racial(e).

interrelate [ˌɪntərɪ'leɪt] vi: to ~ (with) être lié(e) (à), être en corrélation (avec).

interrogate [ɪn'terəgeɪt] vt interroger.

interrogation [ɪnˌterə'geɪʃn] n interrogatoire m.

interrogation mark n Am point m d'interrogation.

interrogative [ˌɪntə'rɒgətɪv] GRAMM **1** adj interrogatif(ive). **2** n interrogatif m.

interrupt [ˌɪntə'rʌpt] **1** vt interrompre; [calm] rompre. **2** vi interrompre.

interruption [ˌɪntə'rʌpʃn] n interruption f.

intersect [ˌɪntə'sekt] **1** vi s'entrecroiser, s'entrecouper. **2** vt croiser, couper.

intersection [ˌɪntə'sekʃn] n [in road] croisement m, carrefour m.

intersperse [ˌɪntə'spɜːs] vt: to be ~d with être émaillé(e) de, être entremêlé(e) de.

interstate (highway) ['ɪntəsteɪt-] n Am autoroute f.

interval ['ɪntəvl] n [gen] intervalle m; at ~s par intervalles; at monthly/yearly ~s tous les mois/ans.

intervene [ˌɪntə'viːn] vi [person, police]: to ~ (in) intervenir (dans), s'interposer (dans). ‖ [event, war, strike] survenir. ‖ [time] s'écouler.

intervention [ˌɪntə'venʃn] n intervention f.

interview ['ɪntəvjuː] **1** n [for job] entrevue f, entretien m. ‖ PRESS interview f. **2** vt [for job] faire passer une entrevue OR un entretien à. ‖ PRESS interviewer.

intestine [ɪn'testɪn] n intestin m.

intimacy ['ɪntɪməsɪ] n [closeness]: ~ (between/with) intimité f (entre/avec).

intimate [adj & n 'ɪntɪmət, vb 'ɪntɪmeɪt] **1** adj [gen] intime. ‖ [detailed -

knowledge] approfondi(e). **2** *vt fml* faire savoir, faire connaître.

intimately ['ɪntɪmətlɪ] *adv* [very closely] étroitement. || [as close friends] intimement. || [in detail] à fond.

intimidate [ɪn'tɪmɪdeɪt] *vt* intimider.

into ['ɪntʊ] *prep* [inside] dans. || [against]: **to bump ~ sthg** se cogner contre qqch; **to crash ~** rentrer dans. || [referring to change in state] en; **to translate sthg ~ Spanish** traduire qqch en espagnol. || [concerning]: **research/investigation ~** recherche/enquête sur. || MATH: **3 ~ 2** 2 divisé par 3. || *inf* [interested in]: **to be ~ sthg** être passionné(e) par qqch.

intolerable [ɪn'tɒlrəbl] *adj* intolérable, insupportable.

intolerance [ɪn'tɒlərəns] *n* intolérance *f*.

intolerant [ɪn'tɒlərənt] *adj* intolérant(e).

intoxicated [ɪn'tɒksɪkeɪtɪd] *adj* [drunk] ivre. || *fig* [excited]: **to be ~ by** OR **with sthg** être grisé(e) OR enivré(e) par qqch.

intransitive [ɪn'trænzətɪv] *adj* intransitif(ive).

intravenous [ˌɪntrə'viːnəs] *adj* intraveineux(euse).

in-tray *n* casier *m* des affaires à traiter.

intricate ['ɪntrɪkət] *adj* compliqué(e).

intrigue [ɪn'triːg] **1** *n* intrigue *f*. **2** *vt* intriguer, exciter la curiosité de.

intriguing [ɪn'triːgɪŋ] *adj* fascinant(e).

intrinsic [ɪn'trɪnsɪk] *adj* intrinsèque.

introduce [ˌɪntrə'djuːs] *vt* [present] présenter; **to ~ sb to sb** présenter qqn à qqn. || [bring in]: **to ~ sthg (to** OR **into)** introduire qqch (dans). || [allow to experience]: **to ~ sb to sthg** initier qqn à qqch, faire découvrir qqch à qqn. || [signal beginning of] annoncer.

introduction [ˌɪntrə'dʌkʃn] *n* [in book, of new method etc] introduction *f*. || [of people]: **~ (to sb)** présentation *f* (à qqn).

introductory [ˌɪntrə'dʌktrɪ] *adj* d'introduction, préliminaire.

introvert ['ɪntrəvɜːt] *n* introverti *m*, -e *f*.

introverted ['ɪntrəvɜːtɪd] *adj* introverti(e).

intrude [ɪn'truːd] *vi* faire intrusion; **to ~ on sb** déranger qqn.

intruder [ɪn'truːdər] *n* intrus *m*, -e *f*.

intrusive [ɪn'truːsɪv] *adj* gênant(e), importun(e).

intuition [ˌɪntjuː'ɪʃn] *n* intuition *f*.

inundate ['ɪnʌndeɪt] *vt* [overwhelm]: **to be ~d with** être submergé(e) de.

invade [ɪn'veɪd] *vt* MIL & *fig* envahir. || [disturb - privacy etc] violer.

invalid [*adj* ɪn'vælɪd, *n* & *vb* 'ɪnvəlɪd] **1** *adj* [illegal, unacceptable] non valide, non valable. || [not reasonable] non valable. **2** *n* invalide *mf*.

invaluable [ɪn'væljʊəbl] *adj*: **~ (to)** [help, advice, person] précieux(ieuse) (pour); [experience, information] inestimable (pour).

invariably [ɪn'veərɪəblɪ] *adv* invariablement, toujours.

invasion [ɪn'veɪʒn] *n lit* & *fig* invasion *f*.

invent [ɪn'vent] *vt* inventer.

invention [ɪn'venʃn] *n* invention *f*.

inventive [ɪn'ventɪv] *adj* inventif(ive).

inventor [ɪn'ventər] *n* inventeur *m*, -trice *f*.

inventory ['ɪnvəntrɪ] *n* [list] inventaire *m*. || *Am* [goods] stock *m*.

invert [ɪn'vɜːt] *vt* retourner.

invest [ɪn'vest] **1** *vt* [money]: **to ~ sthg (in)** investir qqch (dans). || [time, energy]: **to ~ sthg in sthg/in doing sthg** consacrer qqch à qqch/à faire qqch, employer qqch à qqch/à faire qqch. **2** *vi* FIN: **to ~ (in sthg)** investir (dans qqch). || *fig* [buy]: **to ~ in sthg** se payer qqch, s'acheter qqch.

investigate [ɪn'vestɪgeɪt] *vt* enquêter sur, faire une enquête sur; [subj: scientist] faire des recherches sur.

investigation [ɪn,vestɪ'geɪʃn] *n* [enquiry]: **~ (into)** enquête *f* (sur); [scientific] recherches *fpl* (sur). || (U) [investigating] investigation *f*.

investment [ɪn'vestmənt] *n* FIN investissement *m*, placement *m*.

investor [ɪn'vestər] *n* investisseur *m*.

inveterate [ɪn'vetərət] *adj* invétéré(e).

invigorating [ɪn'vɪgəreɪtɪŋ] *adj* tonifiant(e), vivifiant(e).

invincible [ɪn'vɪnsɪbl] *adj* [army, champion] invincible; [record] imbattable.

invisible [ɪn'vɪzɪbl] *adj* invisible.

invitation [ˌɪnvɪ'teɪʃn] *n* [request] invitation *f*.

invite [ɪn'vaɪt] *vt* [ask to come]: **to ~ sb (to)** inviter qqn (à). || [ask politely]: **to ~ sb to do sthg** inviter qqn à faire qqch. || [encourage]: **to ~ trouble** aller au devant des ennuis; **to ~ gossip** faire causer.

inviting [ɪn'vaɪtɪŋ] *adj* attrayant(e), agréable; [food] appétissant(e).

invoice ['ɪnvɔɪs] **1** *n* facture *f*. **2** *vt* [client] envoyer la facture à. || [goods] facturer.

invoke [ɪn'vəʊk] *vt fml* [law, act] invoquer. || [help] demander, implorer.

involuntary [ɪn'vɒləntrɪ] *adj* involontaire.

involve [ɪn'vɒlv] *vt* [entail] nécessiter; **what's ~d?** de quoi s'agit-il?; **to ~ doing sthg** nécessiter de faire qqch. || [concern, affect] toucher. || [person]: **to ~ sb in sthg** impliquer qqn dans qqch.

involved [ɪn'vɒlvd] *adj* [complex] complexe, compliqué(e). || [participating]: **to be ~ in sthg** participer OR prendre part à qqch. || [in relationship]: **to be ~ with sb** avoir des relations intimes avec qqn.

involvement [ɪn'vɒlvmənt] *n* [participation]: **~ (in)** participation *f* (à). || [concern, enthusiasm]: **~ (in)** engagement *m* (dans).

inward ['ɪnwəd] **1** *adj* [inner] intérieur(e). || [towards the inside] vers l'intérieur. **2** *adv Am* = **inwards.**

inwards ['ɪnwədz] *adv* vers l'intérieur.

iodine [*Am* 'aɪədaɪn] *n* iode *m*.

iota [aɪ'əʊtə] *n* brin *m*, grain *m*.

IOU (*abbr of* **I owe you**) *n* reconnaissance *f* de dette.

IQ (*abbr of* **intelligence quotient**) *n* QI *m*.

IRA *n* (*abbr of* **Irish Republican Army**) IRA *f*.

Iran [ɪ'rɑːn] *n* Iran *m*.

Iranian [ɪ'reɪnjən] **1** *adj* iranien(ienne). **2** *n* Iranien *m*, -ienne *f*.

Iraq [ɪ'rɑːk] *n* Iraq *m*, Irak *m*.

Iraqi [ɪ'rɑːkɪ] **1** *adj* iraquien(ienne), irakien(ienne). **2** *n* Iraquien *m*, -ienne *f*, Irakien *m*, -ienne *f*.

irate [aɪ'reɪt] *adj* furieux(ieuse).

Ireland ['aɪələnd] *n* Irlande *f*.

iris ['aɪərɪs] (*pl* -es) *n* iris *m*.

Irish ['aɪrɪʃ] **1** *adj* irlandais(e). **2** *n* [language] irlandais *m*. **3** *npl*: **the ~** les Irlandais.

Irishman ['aɪrɪʃmən] (*pl* -men [-mən]) *n* Irlandais *m*.

Irish Sea *n*: **the ~** la mer d'Irlande.

Irishwoman ['aɪrɪʃ,wʊmən] (*pl* -women [-,wɪmɪn]) *n* Irlandaise *f*.

irksome ['ɜːksəm] *adj* ennuyeux(euse), assommant(e).

iron ['aɪən] **1** *adj* [made of iron] de OR en fer. || *fig* [very strict] de fer. **2** *n* [metal, golf club] fer *m*. || [for clothes] fer *m* à re-

passer. **3** *vt* repasser. ○ **iron out** *vt sep fig* [difficulties] aplanir; [problems] résoudre.

Iron Curtain *n*: **the ~** le rideau de fer.

ironic(al) [aɪ'rɒnɪk(l)] *adj* ironique.

ironing ['aɪənɪŋ] *n* repassage *m*.

ironing board *n* planche *f* OR table *f* à repasser.

irony ['aɪrənɪ] *n* ironie *f*.

irrational [ɪ'ræʃənl] *adj* irrationnel(elle), déraisonnable; [person] non rationnel(elle).

irreconcilable [ɪ,rekən'saɪləbl] *adj* inconciliable.

irregular [ɪ'regjʊlər] *adj* irrégulier(ière).

irrelevant [ɪ'reləvənt] *adj* sans rapport.

irreparable [ɪ'repərəbl] *adj* irréparable.

irreplaceable [,ɪrɪ'pleɪsəbl] *adj* irremplaçable.

irrepressible [,ɪrɪ'presəbl] *adj* [enthusiasm] que rien ne peut entamer; **he's ~** il est d'une bonne humeur à toute épreuve.

irresistible [,ɪrɪ'zɪstəbl] *adj* irrésistible.

irrespective [,ɪrɪ'spektɪv] ○ **irrespective of** *prep* sans tenir compte de.

irresponsible [,ɪrɪ'spɒnsəbl] *adj* irresponsable.

irrigate ['ɪrɪgeɪt] *vt* irriguer.

irrigation [,ɪrɪ'geɪʃn] *n* irrigation *f*.

irritable ['ɪrɪtəbl] *adj* irritable.

irritate ['ɪrɪteɪt] *vt* irriter.

irritating ['ɪrɪteɪtɪŋ] *adj* irritant(e).

irritation [ɪrɪ'teɪʃn] *n* [anger, soreness] irritation *f*. || [cause of anger] source *f* d'irritation.

IRS (*abbr of* **Internal Revenue Service**) *n Am*: **the ~** ≃ le fisc.

is [ɪz] → **be.**

Islam ['ɪzlɑːm] *n* islam *m*.

island ['aɪlənd] *n* [isle] île *f*. || AUT refuge *m* pour piétons.

islander ['aɪləndər] *n* habitant *m*, -e *f* d'une île.

isle [aɪl] *n* île *f*.

isn't ['ɪznt] = **is not.**

isobar ['aɪsəbɑːr] *n* isobare *f*.

isolate ['aɪsəleɪt] *vt*: **to ~ sb/sthg (from)** isoler qqn/qqch (de).

isolated ['aɪsəleɪtɪd] *adj* isolé(e).

Israel ['ɪzreɪəl] *n* Israël *m*.

Israeli [ɪz'reɪlɪ] **1** *adj* israélien(ienne). **2** *n* Israélien *m*, -ienne *f*.

issue ['ɪʃuː] **1** *n* [important subject] question *f*, problème *m*; **to make an ~ of sthg**

faire toute une affaire de qqch; **at ~** en question, en cause. || [edition] numéro *m*. || [bringing out - of banknotes, shares] émission *f*. **2** *vt* [make public - decree, statement] faire; [- warning] lancer. || [bring out - banknotes, shares] émettre; [- book] publier. || [passport etc] délivrer.

isthmus ['ɪsməs] *n* isthme *m*.

it [ɪt] *pron* [referring to specific person or thing - subj] il (elle); [- direct object] le (la), l' (*+ vowel or silent 'h'*); [- indirect object] lui; **did you find ~?** tu l'as trouvé(e)?; **give ~ to me at once** donne-moi ça tout de suite. || [with prepositions]: **in/to/at ~** y; **on ~** dessus; **about ~** en; **under ~** dessous; **beside ~** à côté; **from/of ~** en; **he's very proud of ~** il en est très fier. || [impersonal use] il, ce; **~ is cold today** il fait froid aujourd'hui; **~'s two o'clock** il est deux heures; **who is ~?** — **~'s Mary/me** qui est-ce? — c'est Mary/moi.

IT *n abbr of* **information technology**.

Italian [ɪ'tæljən] **1** *adj* italien(ienne). **2** *n* [person] Italien *m*, -ienne *f*. || [language] italien *m*.

italic [ɪ'tælɪk] *adj* italique. ○ **italics** *npl* italiques *fpl*.

Italy ['ɪtəlɪ] *n* Italie *f*.

itch [ɪtʃ] **1** *n* démangeaison *f*. **2** *vi* [be itchy]: **my arm ~es** mon bras me démange. || *fig* [be impatient]: **to be ~ing to do sthg** mourir d'envie de faire qqch.

it'd ['ɪtəd] = **it would, it had**.

item ['aɪtəm] *n* [gen] chose *f*, article *m*; [on agenda] question *f*, point *m*. || PRESS article *m*.

itemize, -ise ['aɪtəmaɪz] *vt* détailler.

itinerary [aɪ'tɪnərərɪ] *n* itinéraire *m*.

it'll [ɪtl] = **it will**.

its [ɪts] *poss adj* son (sa), ses (*pl*).

it's [ɪts] = **it is, it has**.

itself [ɪt'self] *pron* (*reflexive*) se; (*after prep*) soi. || (*for emphasis*) lui-même (elle-même); **in ~** en soi.

I've [aɪv] = **I have**.

ivory ['aɪvərɪ] *n* ivoire *m*.

ivy ['aɪvɪ] *n* lierre *m*.

Ivy League *n Am* les huit grandes universités de l'est des États-Unis.

j (*pl* **j's** OR **js**), **J** (*pl* **J's** OR **Js**) [dʒeɪ] *n* [letter] j *m inv*, J *m inv*.

jab [dʒæb] *vt*: **to ~ sthg into** planter OR enfoncer qqch dans.

jabber ['dʒæbər] *vt & vi* baragouiner.

jack [dʒæk] *n* [device] cric *m*. || [playing card] valet *m*. ○ **jack up** *vt sep* [car] soulever avec un cric. || *fig* [prices] faire grimper.

jackal ['dʒækəl] *n* chacal *m*.

jackdaw ['dʒækdɔː] *n* choucas *m*.

jacket ['dʒækɪt] *n* [garment] veste *f*. || [of potato] peau *f*, pelure *f*. || [of book] jaquette *f*. || *Am* [of record] pochette *f*.

jacket potato *n* pomme de terre *f* en robe de chambre.

jackhammer ['dʒæk,hæmər] *n Am* marteau-piqueur *m*.

jack knife *n* canif *m*. ○ **jack-knife** *vi* [lorry] se mettre en travers de la route.

jack plug *n* jack *m*.

jackpot ['dʒækpɒt] *n* gros lot *m*.

jaded ['dʒeɪdɪd] *adj* blasé(e).

jagged ['dʒægɪd] *adj* déchiqueté(e), dentelé(e).

jail [dʒeɪl] **1** *n* prison *f*. **2** *vt* emprisonner, mettre en prison.

jailer ['dʒeɪlər] *n* geôlier *m*, -ière *f*.

jam [dʒæm] **1** *n* [preserve] confiture *f*. || [of traffic] embouteillage *m*, bouchon *m*. || *inf* [difficult situation]: **to get into/be in a ~** se mettre/être dans le pétrin. **2** *vt* [mechanism, door] bloquer, coincer. || [push tightly]: **to ~ sthg into** entasser OR tasser qqch dans; **to ~ sthg onto** enfoncer qqch sur. || [block - streets] embouteiller; [- switchboard] surcharger. || RADIO brouiller. **3** *vi* [lever, door] se coincer; [brakes] se bloquer.

Jamaica [dʒə'meɪkə] *n* la Jamaïque.

jam-packed [-'pækt] *adj inf* plein(e) à craquer.

jangle ['dʒæŋgl] **1** *vt* [keys] faire cliqueter; [bells] faire retentir. **2** *vi* [keys] cliqueter; [bells] retentir.

janitor ['dʒænɪtər] *n Am & Scot* concierge *mf*.

January ['dʒænjʊərɪ] *n* janvier *m; see also* **September**.

Japan [dʒə'pæn] *n* Japon *m*.

Japanese [,dʒæpə'niːz] (*pl inv*) **1** *adj* japonais(e). **2** *n* [language] japonais *m*. **3** *npl* [people]: **the ~** les Japonais *mpl*.

jar [dʒɑːr] **1** *n* pot *m*. **2** *vt* [shake] secouer. **3** *vi* [noise, voice]: **to ~ (on sb)** irriter (qqn), agacer (qqn). ‖ [colours] jurer.

jargon ['dʒɑːgən] *n* jargon *m*.

jaundice ['dʒɔːndɪs] *n* jaunisse *f*.

jaunt [dʒɔːnt] *n* balade *f*.

jaunty ['dʒɔːntɪ] *adj* désinvolte, insouciant(e).

javelin ['dʒævlɪn] *n* javelot *m*.

jaw [dʒɔː] *n* mâchoire *f*.

jay [dʒeɪ] *n* geai *m*.

jaywalker ['dʒeɪwɔːkər] *n* piéton *m* qui traverse en dehors des clous.

jazz [dʒæz] *n* MUS jazz *m*.

jazzy ['dʒæzɪ] *adj* [bright] voyant(e).

jealous ['dʒeləs] *adj* jaloux(ouse).

jealousy ['dʒeləsɪ] *n* jalousie *f*.

jeans [dʒiːnz] *npl* jean *m*, blue-jean *m*.

Jeep® [dʒiːp] *n* Jeep® *f*.

jeer [dʒɪər] **1** *vt* huer, conspuer. **2** *vi*: **to ~ (at sb)** huer (qqn), conspuer (qqn).

Jehovah's Witness [dʒɪ,həʊvəz-] *n* témoin *m* de Jéhovah.

Jello® ['dʒeləʊ] *n Am* gelée *f*.

jelly ['dʒelɪ] *n* gelée *f*.

jellyfish ['dʒelɪfɪʃ] (*pl inv* OR **-es**) *n* méduse *f*.

jeopardize, -ise ['dʒepədaɪz] *vt* compromettre, mettre en danger.

jerk [dʒɜːk] **1** *n* [movement] secousse *f*, saccade *f*. ‖ *v inf* [fool] abruti *m*, -e *f*. **2** *vi* [person] sursauter; [vehicle] cahoter.

jersey ['dʒɜːzɪ] (*pl* **jerseys**) *n* [sweater] pull *m*. ‖ [cloth] jersey *m*.

jest [dʒest] *n* plaisanterie *f*; **in ~** pour rire.

Jesus (Christ) ['dʒiːzəs-] *n* Jésus *m*, Jésus-Christ *m*.

jet [dʒet] *n* [plane] jet *m*, avion *m* à réaction. ‖ [of fluid] jet *m*. ‖ [nozzle, outlet] ajutage *m*.

jet-black *adj* noir(e) comme (du) jais.

jet engine *n* moteur *m* à réaction.

jetfoil ['dʒetfɔɪl] *n* hydroglisseur *m*.

jet lag *n* fatigue *f* due au décalage horaire.

jetsam ['dʒetsəm] → **flotsam**.

jettison ['dʒetɪsən] *vt* [cargo] jeter, larguer.

jetty ['dʒetɪ] *n* jetée *f*.

Jew [dʒuː] *n* Juif *m*, -ive *f*.

jewel ['dʒuːəl] *n* bijou *m*.

jeweller *Br*, **jeweler** *Am* ['dʒuːələr] *n* bijoutier *m*; **~'s (shop)** bijouterie *f*.

jewellery *Br*, **jewelry** *Am* ['dʒuːəlrɪ] *n* (*U*) bijoux *mpl*.

Jewess ['dʒuːɪs] *n* juive *f*.

Jewish ['dʒuːɪʃ] *adj* juif(ive).

jib [dʒɪb] *n* [of crane] flèche *f*. ‖ [sail] foc *m*.

jibe [dʒaɪb] *n* sarcasme *m*, moquerie *f*.

jiffy ['dʒɪfɪ] *n inf*: **in a ~** en un clin d'œil.

jiffy bag® *n* enveloppe *f* matelassée.

jig [dʒɪg] *n* gigue *f*.

jigsaw (puzzle) ['dʒɪgsɔː-] *n* puzzle *m*.

jilt [dʒɪlt] *vt* laisser tomber.

jingle ['dʒɪŋgl] **1** *n* [sound] cliquetis *m*. ‖ [song] jingle *m*, indicatif *m*. **2** *vi* [bell] tinter; [coins, bracelets] cliqueter.

jinx [dʒɪŋks] *n* poisse *f*.

jitters ['dʒɪtəz] *npl inf*: **the ~** le trac.

job [dʒɒb] *n* [employment] emploi *m*, boulot *m inf*. ‖ [task] travail *m*, tâche *f*. ‖ [difficult task]: **to have a ~ doing sthg** avoir du mal à faire qqch.

jobless ['dʒɒblɪs] *adj* au chômage.

jobsharing ['dʒɒbʃeərɪŋ] *n* partage *m* de l'emploi.

jockey ['dʒɒkɪ] (*pl* **jockeys**) **1** *n* jockey *m*. **2** *vi*: **to ~ for position** manœuvrer pour devancer ses concurrents.

jocular ['dʒɒkjʊlər] *adj* [cheerful] enjoué(e), jovial(e). ‖ [funny] amusant(e).

jodhpurs ['dʒɒdpəz] *npl* jodhpurs *mpl*, culotte *f* de cheval.

jog [dʒɒg] **1** *n*: **to go for a ~** faire du jogging. **2** *vt* pousser; **to ~ sb's memory** rafraîchir la mémoire de qqn. **3** *vi* faire du jogging, jogger.

jogging ['dʒɒgɪŋ] *n* jogging *m*.

john [dʒɒn] *n Am inf* petit coin *m*, cabinets *mpl*.

join [dʒɔɪn] **1** *n* raccord *m*, joint *m*. **2** *vt* [connect - gen] unir, joindre; [- towns etc] relier. ‖ [get together with] rejoindre, retrouver. ‖ [political party] devenir membre de; [club] s'inscrire à; **to ~ a queue** *Br*, **to ~ a line** *Am* prendre la queue. **3** *vi* [connect] se joindre. ‖ [become a member - gen] devenir membre; [- of club] s'inscrire. ○ **join in** *vt fus* prendre part à, participer à. **2** *vi* participer. ○ **join up** *vi* MIL s'engager dans l'armée.

joiner ['dʒɔɪnər] *n* menuisier *m*.

joinery ['dʒɔɪnərɪ] *n* menuiserie *f*.

joint [dʒɔɪnt] **1** *adj* [effort] conjugué(e); [responsibility] collectif(ive). **2** *n* [gen & TECH] joint *m*. || ANAT articulation *f*. || *inf* [place] bouge *m*. || *drugs sl* joint *m*.

joint account *n* compte *m* joint.

jointly ['dʒɔɪntlɪ] *adv* conjointement.

joke [dʒəʊk] **1** *n* blague *f*, plaisanterie *f*; **to play a ~ on sb** faire une blague à qqn, jouer un tour à qqn. **2** *vi* plaisanter, blaguer; **to ~ about sthg** plaisanter sur qqch, se moquer de qqch.

joker ['dʒəʊkər] *n* [person] blagueur *m*, -euse *f*. || [playing card] joker *m*.

jolly ['dʒɒlɪ] *adj* [person] jovial(e), enjoué(e); [time, party] agréable.

jolt [dʒəʊlt] **1** *n* [jerk] secousse *f*, soubresaut *m*. || [shock] choc *m*. **2** *vt* secouer.

Jordan ['dʒɔːdn] *n* Jordanie *f*.

jostle ['dʒɒsl] **1** *vt* bousculer. **2** *vi* se bousculer.

jot [dʒɒt] *n* [of truth] grain *m*, brin *m*. ○ **jot down** *vt sep* noter, prendre note de.

jotter ['dʒɒtər] *n* [notepad] bloc-notes *m*.

journal ['dʒɜːnl] *n* [magazine] revue *f*. || [diary] journal *m*.

journalism ['dʒɜːnəlɪzm] *n* journalisme *m*.

journalist ['dʒɜːnəlɪst] *n* journaliste *mf*.

journey ['dʒɜːnɪ] (*pl* **journeys**) *n* voyage *m*.

jovial ['dʒəʊvjəl] *adj* jovial(e).

joy [dʒɔɪ] *n* joie *f*.

joyful ['dʒɔɪfʊl] *adj* joyeux(euse).

joyride ['dʒɔɪraɪd] (*pt* **-rode**, *pp* **-ridden**) *vi* faire une virée dans une voiture volée.

joystick ['dʒɔɪstɪk] *n* AERON manche *m* (à balai); COMPUT manette *f*.

Jr. (*abbr of* **Junior**) Jr.

jubilant ['dʒuːbɪlənt] *adj* [person] débordant(e) de joie, qui jubile.

jubilee ['dʒuːbɪliː] *n* jubilé *m*.

judge [dʒʌdʒ] **1** *n* juge *m*. **2** *vt* [gen] juger. || [estimate] évaluer, juger. **3** *vi* juger; **to ~ from** OR **by, judging from** OR **by** à en juger par.

judg(e)ment ['dʒʌdʒmənt] *n* jugement *m*.

judicial [dʒuːˈdɪʃl] *adj* judiciaire.

judiciary [dʒuːˈdɪʃərɪ] *n*: **the ~** la magistrature.

judicious [dʒuːˈdɪʃəs] *adj* judicieux(ieuse).

judo ['dʒuːdəʊ] *n* judo *m*.

jug [dʒʌg] *n* pot *m*, pichet *m*.

juggernaut ['dʒʌgənɔːt] *n* poids *m* lourd.

juggle ['dʒʌgl] **1** *vt* lit & fig jongler avec. **2** *vi* jongler.

juggler ['dʒʌglər] *n* jongleur *m*, -euse *f*.

juice [dʒuːs] *n* jus *m*.

juicy ['dʒuːsɪ] *adj* [fruit] juteux(euse).

jukebox ['dʒuːkbɒks] *n* juke-box *m*.

July [dʒuːˈlaɪ] *n* juillet *m*; *see also* **September**.

jumble ['dʒʌmbl] **1** *n* [mixture] mélange *m*, fatras *m*. **2** *vt*: **to ~ (up)** mélanger, embrouiller.

jumbo jet ['dʒʌmbəʊ-] *n* jumbo-jet *m*.

jumbo-sized [-saɪzd] *adj* géant(e).

jump [dʒʌmp] **1** *n* [leap] saut *m*, bond *m*. || [rapid increase] flambée *f*, hausse *f* brutale. **2** *vt* [fence, stream etc] sauter, franchir d'un bond. || *inf* [attack] sauter sur, tomber sur. **3** *vi* [gen] sauter, bondir; [in surprise] sursauter. || [increase rapidly] grimper en flèche, faire un bond. ○ **jump at** *vt fus fig* sauter sur.

jumper ['dʒʌmpər] *n* Am [dress] robe *f* chasuble.

jump leads *npl* câbles *mpl* de démarrage.

jump-start *vt*: **to ~ a car** faire démarrer une voiture en la poussant.

jumpy ['dʒʌmpɪ] *adj* nerveux(euse).

Jun. = **Junr**.

junction ['dʒʌŋkʃn] *n* [of roads] carrefour *m*; RAIL embranchement *m*.

June [dʒuːn] *n* juin *m*; *see also* **September**.

jungle ['dʒʌŋgl] *n* lit & fig jungle *f*.

junior ['dʒuːnjər] **1** *adj* [gen] jeune. || Am [after name] junior. **2** *n* [in rank] subalterne *mf*. || [in age] cadet *m*, -ette *f*. || Am SCH ≃ élève *mf* de première; UNIV ≃ étudiant *m*, -e *f* de deuxième année.

junior high school *n* Am ≃ collège *m* d'enseignement secondaire.

junk [dʒʌŋk] *n* [unwanted objects] bricà-brac *m*.

junk food *n* (*U*) *pej* cochonneries *fpl*.

junkie ['dʒʌŋkɪ] *n* drugs sl drogué *m*, -e *f*.

junk mail *n* (*U*) *pej* prospectus *mpl* publicitaires envoyés par la poste.

junk shop *n* boutique *f* de brocanteur.

Junr (*abbr of* **Junior**) Jr.

Jupiter ['dʒuːpɪtər] *n* [planet] Jupiter *f*.

jurisdiction [ˌdʒʊərɪsˈdɪkʃn] *n* juridiction *f*.

juror ['dʒʊərər] *n* juré *m*, -e *f*.

jury ['dʒʊərɪ] *n* jury *m*.

just [dʒʌst] **1** *adv* [recently]: **he's ~ left** il vient de partir. || [at that moment]: **I was ~ about to go** j'allais juste partir, j'étais sur le point de partir; **I'm ~ going to do it now** je vais le faire tout de suite OR à l'instant; **she arrived ~ as I was leaving** elle est arrivée au moment même où je partais OR juste comme je partais. || [only, simply]: **it's ~ a rumour** ce n'est qu'une rumeur; **~ add water** vous n'avez plus qu'à ajouter de l'eau; **~ a minute** OR **moment** OR **second!** un (petit) instant! || [almost not] tout juste, à peine; **I only ~ missed the train** j'ai manqué le train de peu; **we have ~ enough time** on a juste assez de temps. || [for emphasis]: **~ look at this mess!** non, mais regarde un peu ce désordre! || [exactly, precisely] tout à fait, exactement. || [in requests]: **could you ~ move over please?** pourriez-vous vous pousser un peu s'il vous plaît? **2** *adj* juste, équitable. ○ **just about** *adv* à peu près, plus ou moins. ○ **just as** *adv* [in comparison] tout aussi. ○ **just now** *adv* [a short time ago] tout à l'heure. || [at this moment] en ce moment.

justice ['dʒʌstɪs] *n* [gen] justice *f*. || [of claim, cause] bien-fondé *m*.

justify ['dʒʌstɪfaɪ] *vt* [give reasons for] justifier.

jut [dʒʌt] *vi*: **to ~ (out)** faire saillie, avancer.

juvenile ['dʒuːvənaɪl] **1** *adj* JUR mineur(e), juvénile. || [childish] puéril(e). **2** *n* JUR mineur *m*, -e *f*.

juxtapose [,dʒʌkstə'pəʊz] *vt* juxtaposer.

k (*pl* **k's** OR **ks**), **K** (*pl* **K's** OR **Ks**) [keɪ] *n* [letter] k *m inv*, K *m inv*. ○ **K** (*abbr of* **kilobyte**) Ko. || (*abbr of* **thousand**) K.

kaleidoscope [kə'laɪdəskəʊp] *n* kaléidoscope *m*.

kangaroo [,kæŋgə'ruː] *n* kangourou *m*.

karat ['kærət] *n Am* carat *m*.

karate [kə'rɑːtɪ] *n* karaté *m*.

kayak ['kaɪæk] *n* kayak *m*.

KB (*abbr of* **kilobyte(s)**) *n* COMPUT Ko *m*.

kcal (*abbr of* **kilocalorie**) Kcal.

kebab [kɪ'bæb] *n* brochette *f*.

keel [kiːl] *n* quille *f*; **on an even ~** stable. ○ **keel over** *vi* [ship] chavirer; [person] tomber dans les pommes.

keen [kiːn] *adj* [enthusiastic] enthousiaste, passionné(e); **to be ~ on sthg** avoir la passion de qqch; **he's ~ on her** elle lui plaît; **to be ~ to do** OR **on doing sthg** tenir à faire qqch. || [interest, desire, mind] vif (vive); [competition] âpre, acharné(e). || [sense of smell] fin(e); [eyesight] perçant(e).

keep [kiːp] (*pt & pp* **kept**) **1** *vt* [retain, store] garder; **to ~ sthg warm** garder OR tenir qqch au chaud. || [prevent]: **to keep sb/sthg from doing sthg** empêcher qqn/qqch de faire qqch. || [detain] retenir; [prisoner] détenir; **to ~ sb waiting** faire attendre qqn. || [promise] tenir; [appointment] aller à; [vow] être fidèle à. || [not disclose]: **to ~ sthg from sb** cacher qqch à qqn; **to ~ sthg to o.s.** garder qqch pour soi. || [diary, record, notes] tenir. || [own - sheep, pigs etc] élever; [- shop] tenir. **2** *vi* [remain]: **to ~ warm** se tenir au chaud; **to ~ quiet** garder le silence. || [continue]: **he ~s interrupting me** il n'arrête pas de m'interrompre; **to ~ talking/walking** continuer à parler/à marcher. || [continue moving]: **to ~ left/right** garder sa gauche/sa droite. || [food] se conserver. **3** *n*: **to earn one's ~** gagner sa vie. ○ **keeps** *n*: **for ~s** pour toujours. ○ **keep back** *vt sep* [information] ca-

kindly

cher, ne pas divulguer; [money] retenir.
○ **keep off** vt fus: "~ **off the grass**" «(il
est) interdit de marcher sur la pelouse».
○ **keep on** vi [continue]: **to ~ on (doing
sthg)** [without stopping] continuer (de OR
à faire qqch); [repeatedly] ne pas arrêter
(de faire qqch). || [talk incessantly]: **to ~
on (about sthg)** ne pas arrêter de parler
(de qqch). ○ **keep out 1** vt sep empêcher d'entrer. **2** vi: "~ **out**" «défense
d'entrer». ○ **keep to** vt fus [rules, dead-
line] respecter, observer. ○ **keep up 1** vt
sep [continue to do] continuer; [maintain]
maintenir. **2** vi [maintain pace, level etc]:
to ~ up (with sb) aller aussi vite (que
qqn).

keeper ['ki:pə'] n gardien m, -ienne f.
keeping ['ki:pıŋ] n [care] garde f. ||
[conformity, harmony]: **to be in/out of ~
with** [rules etc] être/ne pas être conforme
à; [subj: clothes, furniture] aller/ne pas aller avec.
keepsake ['ki:pseık] n souvenir m.
keg [keg] n tonnelet m, baril m.
kennel ['kenl] n [shelter for dog] niche f.
|| Am = **kennels**. ○ **kennels** npl Br che-
nil m.
Kenya ['kenjə] n Kenya m.
kept [kept] pt & pp → **keep**.
kernel ['kɜ:nl] n amande f.
kerosene ['kerəsi:n] n kérosène m.
ketchup ['ketʃəp] n ketchup m.
kettle ['ketl] n bouilloire f.
key [ki:] **1** n [gen & MUS] clef f, clé f; **the
~ (to sthg)** fig la clé (de qqch). || [of type-
writer, computer, piano] touche f. || [of
map] légende f. **2** adj clé (after n).
keyboard ['ki:bɔ:d] n [gen & COMPUT]
clavier m.
keyed up [,ki:d-] adj tendu(e), éner-
vé(e).
keyhole ['ki:həʊl] n trou m de serrure.
keynote ['ki:nəʊt] **1** n note f domi-
nante. **2** comp: ~ **speech** discours-
programme m.
keypad ['ki:pæd] n COMPUT pavé m numérique.
key ring n porte-clés m inv.
kg (abbr of **kilogram**) kg.
khaki ['kɑːkı] **1** adj kaki (inv). **2** n
[colour] kaki m.
kick [kık] **1** n [with foot] coup m de pied.
|| inf [excitement]: **to get a ~ from sthg**
trouver qqch excitant. **2** vt [with foot]
donner un coup de pied à; **to ~ o.s.** fig se
donner des gifles OR des claques. || inf
[give up]: **to ~ the habit** arrêter. **3** vi [per-

son - repeatedly] donner des coups de
pied; [- once] donner un coup de pied;
[baby] gigoter; [animal] ruer. ○ **kick
out** vt sep inf vider, jeter dehors.
kid [kıd] **1** n inf [child] gosse mf, gamin
m, -e f. || inf [young person] petit jeune m,
petite jeune f. || [goat, leather] chevreau
m. **2** comp inf [brother, sister] petit(e). **3**
vt inf [tease] faire marcher. || [delude]: **to
~ o.s.** se faire des illusions. **4** vi inf: **to be
kidding** plaisanter.
kidnap ['kıdnæp] vt kidnapper, enlever.
kidnapper Br, **kidnaper** Am ['kıd-
næpə'] n kidnappeur m, -euse f, ravisseur m, -euse f.
kidnapping Br, **kidnaping** Am
['kıdnæpıŋ] n enlèvement m.
kidney ['kıdnı] (pl **kidneys**) n ANAT rein
m. || CULIN rognon m.
kidney bean n haricot m rouge.
kill [kıl] **1** vt [cause death of] tuer. || fig
[hope, chances] mettre fin à; [pain] supprimer. **2** vi tuer. **3** n mise f à mort.
killer ['kılə'] n [person] meurtrier m,
-ière f; [animal] tueur m, -euse f.
killing ['kılıŋ] n meurtre m.
killjoy ['kıldʒɔı] n rabat-joie m inv.
kiln [kıln] n four m.
kilo ['ki:ləʊ] (pl **-s**) (abbr of **kilogram**)
n kilo m.
kilobyte ['kıləbaıt] n COMPUT kilo-octet
m.
kilogram(me) ['kıləgræm] n kilogramme m.
kilohertz ['kıləhɜ:tz] (pl inv) n kilohertz m.
kilometre Br ['kılə,mi:tə'], **kilometer**
Am [kı'lɒmıtə'] n kilomètre m.
kilowatt ['kıləwɒt] n kilowatt m.
kilt [kılt] n kilt m.
kin [kın] n → **kith**.
kind [kaınd] **1** adj gentil(ille), aimable.
2 n genre m, sorte f; **they're two of a ~** ils
se ressemblent; **in ~** [payment] en nature;
a ~ of une espèce de, une sorte de; **~ of**
Am inf un peu.
kindergarten ['kındə,gɑ:tn] n jardin m
d'enfants.
kind-hearted [-'hɑ:tıd] adj qui a bon
cœur, bon (bonne).
kindle ['kındl] vt [fire] allumer. || fig
[feeling] susciter.
kindly ['kaındlı] **1** adj [person] plein(e)
de bonté, bienveillant(e). || [gesture]
plein(e) de gentillesse. **2** adv [speak,
smile etc] avec gentillesse. || [please]: ~
leave the room! veuillez sortir, s'il vous

plaît!; **will you ~ ...?** veuillez .... je vous prie de ....

kindness ['kaındnıs] *n* gentillesse *f*.

kindred ['kındrıd] *adj* [similar] semblable, similaire; **~ spirit** âme *f* sœur.

king [kıŋ] *n* roi *m*.

kingdom ['kıŋdəm] *n* [country] royaume *m*. || [of animals, plants] règne *m*.

kingfisher ['kıŋ‚fıʃər] *n* martin-pêcheur *m*.

king-size(d) [-saız(d)] *adj* [cigarette] long (longue); [pack] géant(e); **a ~ bed** un grand lit *(de 195 cm)*.

kinky ['kıŋkı] *adj inf* vicieux(ieuse).

kiosk ['ki:ɒsk] *n* [small shop] kiosque *m*.

kipper ['kıpər] *n* hareng *m* fumé OR saur.

kiss [kıs] **1** *n* baiser *m*; **to give sb a ~** embrasser qqn, donner un baiser à qqn. **2** *vt* embrasser. **3** *vi* s'embrasser.

kiss of life *n*: **the ~** le bouche-à-bouche.

kit [kıt] *n* [set] trousse *f*. || [to be assembled] kit *m*.

kit bag *n* sac *m* de marin.

kitchen ['kıtʃın] *n* cuisine *f*.

kitchen sink *n* évier *m*.

kitchen unit *n* élément *m* de cuisine.

kite [kaıt] *n* [toy] cerf-volant *m*.

kith [kıθ] *n*: **~ and kin** parents et amis *mpl*.

kitten ['kıtn] *n* chaton *m*.

kitty ['kıtı] *n* [shared fund] cagnotte *f*.

kiwi ['ki:wi:] *n* [bird] kiwi *m*, aptéryx *m*.

kiwi fruit *n* kiwi *m*.

km *(abbr of* **kilometre)** km.

km/h *(abbr of* **kilometres per hour)** km/h.

knack [næk] *n*: **to have a** OR **the ~ (for doing sthg)** avoir le coup (pour faire qqch).

knapsack ['næpsæk] *n* sac *m* à dos.

knead [ni:d] *vt* pétrir.

knee [ni:] *n* genou *m*.

kneecap ['ni:kæp] *n* rotule *f*.

kneel [ni:l] (*Br pt & pp* **knelt**, *Am pt & pp* **knelt** OR **-ed**) *vi* se mettre à genoux, s'agenouiller. ○ **kneel down** *vi* se mettre à genoux, s'agenouiller.

knelt [nelt] *pt & pp* → **kneel**.

knew [nju:] *pt* → **know**.

knickers ['nıkəz] *npl Am* [knickerbockers] pantalon *m* de golf.

knick-knack ['nıknæk] *n* babiole *f*, bibelot *m*.

knife [naıf] (*pl* **knives**) **1** *n* couteau *m*. **2** *vt* donner un coup de couteau à, poignarder.

knight [naıt] **1** *n* [in history, member of nobility] chevalier *m*. || [in chess] cavalier *m*. **2** *vt* faire chevalier.

knighthood ['naıthʊd] *n* titre *m* de chevalier.

knit [nıt] (*pt & pp* **knit** OR **-ted**) **1** *adj*: **closely** OR **tightly ~** *fig* très uni(e). **2** *vt* tricoter. **3** *vi* [with wool] tricoter. || [broken bones] se souder.

knitting ['nıtıŋ] *n (U)* tricot *m*.

knitting needle *n* aiguille *f* à tricoter.

knitwear ['nıtweər] *n (U)* tricots *mpl*.

knives [naıvz] *pl* → **knife**.

knob [nɒb] *n* [on door] poignée *f*, bouton *m*; [on drawer] poignée; [on bedstead] pomme *f*. || [on TV, radio etc] bouton *m*.

knock [nɒk] **1** *n* [hit] coup *m*. || [piece of bad luck] coup *m* dur. **2** *vt* [hit] frapper, cogner; **to ~ sb/sthg over** renverser qqn/qqch. || *inf* [criticize] critiquer, dire du mal de. **3** *vi* [on door]; **to ~ (at** OR **on)** frapper (à). || [car engine] cogner, avoir des ratés. ○ **knock down** *vt sep* [subj: car, driver] renverser. || [building] démolir. ○ **knock off** *vi inf* [stop working] finir son travail OR sa journée. ○ **knock out** *vt sep* [make unconscious] assommer. || [from competition] éliminer.

knocker ['nɒkər] *n* [on door] heurtoir *m*.

knock-kneed [-'ni:d] *adj* cagneux(euse), qui a les genoux cagneux.

knockout ['nɒkaʊt] *n* knock-out *m*, K.-O. *m*.

knot [nɒt] **1** *n* [gen] nœud *m*; **to tie/untie a ~** nouer/défaire un nœud. **2** *vt* nouer, faire un nœud à.

knotty ['nɒtı] *adj fig* épineux(euse).

know [nəʊ] (*pt* **knew**, *pp* **known**) **1** *vt* [gen] savoir; [language] savoir parler; **to ~ (that) ...** savoir que ...; **to let sb ~ (about sthg)** faire savoir (qqch) à qqn, informer qqn (de qqch); **to ~ how to do sthg** savoir faire qqch; **to get to ~ sthg** apprendre qqch. || [person, place] connaître; **to get to ~ sb** apprendre à mieux connaître qqn. **2** *vi* savoir; **to ~ of sthg** connaître qqch; **to ~ about** [be aware of] être au courant de; [be expert in] s'y connaître en. **3** *n*: **to be in the ~** être au courant.

know-how *n* savoir-faire *m*, technique *f*.

knowing ['nəʊıŋ] *adj* [smile, look] entendu(e).

knowingly ['nəʊıŋlı] *adv* [smile, look] d'un air entendu. || [intentionally] sciemment.

knowledge ['nɒlɪdʒ] n (U) [gen] connaissance f; **without my ~** à mon insu; **to the best of my ~** à ma connaissance, autant que je sache. || [learning, understanding] savoir m, connaissances fpl.

knowledgeable ['nɒlɪdʒəbl] adj bien informé(e).

known [nəʊn] pp → know.

knuckle ['nʌkl] n ANAT articulation f OR jointure f du doigt. || [of meat] jarret m.

knuckle-duster n coup-de-poing m américain.

koala (bear) [kəʊ'ɑːlə-] n koala m.

Koran [kɒ'rɑːn] n: **the ~** le Coran.

Korea [kə'rɪə] n Corée f.

Korean [kə'rɪən] 1 adj coréen(enne). 2 n [person] Coréen m, -enne f. || [language] coréen m.

kosher ['kəʊʃər] adj [meat] kasher (inv).

Koweit = Kuwait.

kung fu [,kʌŋ'fuː] n kung-fu m.

Kurd [kɜːd] n Kurde mf.

Kuwait [ku'weɪt], **Koweit** [kəʊ'weɪt] n [country] Koweït m. || [city] Koweït City.

l¹ (pl **l's** OR **ls**), **L** (pl **L's** OR **Ls**) [el] n [letter] l m inv, L m inv.

l² (abbr of litre) l.

lab [læb] n inf labo m.

label ['leɪbl] 1 n [identification] étiquette f. || [of record] label m, maison f de disques. 2 vt [fix label to] étiqueter. || [describe]: **to ~ sb (as)** cataloguer OR étiqueter qqn (comme).

labor etc Am = labour etc.

laboratory [Br lə'bɒrətrɪ, Am 'læbrə-,tɔːrɪ] n laboratoire m.

laborious [lə'bɔːrɪəs] adj laborieux (ieuse).

labor union n Am syndicat m.

labour Br, **labor** Am ['leɪbər] 1 n [gen & MED] travail m. || [workers, work carried out] main d'œuvre f. 2 vi travailler dur; **to ~ at** OR **over** peiner sur.

laboured Br, **labored** Am ['leɪbəd] adj [breathing] pénible; [style] lourd(e), laborieux(ieuse).

labourer Br, **laborer** Am ['leɪbərər] n travailleur manuel m, travailleuse manuelle f; [agricultural] ouvrier agricole m, ouvrière agricole f.

Labrador ['læbrədɔːr] n [dog] labrador m.

labyrinth ['læbərɪnθ] n labyrinthe m.

lace [leɪs] 1 n [fabric] dentelle f. || [of shoe etc] lacet m. 2 vt [shoe etc] lacer. || [drink] verser de l'alcool dans. ○ **lace up** vt sep lacer.

lack [læk] 1 n manque m; **for** OR **through ~ of** par manque de; **no ~ of** bien assez de. 2 vt manquer de. 3 vi: **to be ~ing in** sthg manquer de qqch; **to be ~ing** manquer, faire défaut.

lackadaisical [,lækə'deɪzɪkl] adj pej nonchalant(e).

lacklustre Br, **lackluster** Am ['læk-,lʌstər] adj terne.

laconic [lə'kɒnɪk] adj laconique.

lacquer ['lækər] 1 n [for wood] vernis m, laque f; [for hair] laque f. 2 vt laquer.

lad [læd] n inf [boy] garçon m, gars m.

ladder ['lædər] n [for climbing] échelle f.

laden ['leɪdn] adj: **~ (with)** chargé(e) (de).

ladies Br ['leɪdɪz], **ladies' room** Am n toilettes fpl (pour dames).

ladle ['leɪdl] 1 n louche f. 2 vt servir (à la louche).

lady ['leɪdɪ] 1 n [gen] dame f. 2 comp: **a ~ doctor** une femme docteur. ○ **Lady** n Lady f.

ladybird Br ['leɪdɪbɜːd], **ladybug** Am ['leɪdɪbʌg] n coccinelle f.

lady-in-waiting [-'weɪtɪŋ] (pl ladies-in-waiting) n dame f d'honneur.

ladylike ['leɪdɪlaɪk] adj distingué(e).

Ladyship ['leɪdɪʃɪp] n: **her/your ~** Madame la baronne/la duchesse etc.

lag [læg] 1 vi: **to ~ (behind)** [person, runner] traîner; [economy, development] être en retard, avoir du retard. 2 vt [roof, pipe] calorifuger. 3 n [timelag] décalage m.

lager ['lɑːgər] n (bière f) blonde f.

lagoon [lə'guːn] n lagune f.

laid [leɪd] pt & pp → lay.

laid-back adj inf relaxe, décontracté(e).

lain [leɪn] pp → lie.

lair [leər] n repaire m, antre m.

lake [leɪk] n lac m.

Lake Geneva *n* le lac Léman OR de Genève.

lamb [læm] *n* agneau *m*.

lambswool ['læmzwol] **1** *n* lambswool *m*. **2** *comp* en lambswool, en laine d'agneau.

lame [leɪm] *adj* lit & fig boiteux(euse).

lament [lə'ment] **1** *n* lamentation *f*. **2** *vt* [lack, loss, fate] se lamenter sur.

lamentable ['læməntəbl] *adj* lamentable.

laminated ['læmɪneɪtɪd] *adj* [wood] stratifié(e); [glass] feuilleté(e); [steel] laminé(e).

lamp [læmp] *n* lampe *f*.

lampoon [læm'puːn] **1** *n* satire *f*. **2** *vt* faire la satire de.

lamppost ['læmppəʊst] *n* réverbère *m*.

lampshade ['læmpʃeɪd] *n* abat-jour *m* inv.

lance [lɑːns] **1** *n* lance *f*. **2** *vt* [boil] percer.

land [lænd] **1** *n* [solid ground] terre *f* (ferme); [farming ground] terre, terrain *m*. || [property] terres *fpl*, propriété *f*. || [nation] pays *m*. **2** *vt* [from ship, plane] débarquer. || [catch - fish] prendre. || [plane] atterrir. || *inf* [obtain] décrocher. || *inf* [place]: **to ~ sb in trouble** attirer des ennuis à qqn; **to be ~ed with sthg** se coltiner qqch. **3** *vi* [plane] atterrir. || [fall] tomber. ○ **land up** *vi inf* atterrir.

landing ['lændɪŋ] *n* [of stairs] palier *m*. || AERON atterrissage *m*. || [of goods from ship] débarquement *m*.

landing card *n* carte *f* de débarquement.

landing gear *n* (U) train *m* d'atterrissage.

landing stage *n* débarcadère *m*.

landing strip *n* piste *f* d'atterrissage.

landlady ['lænd,leɪdɪ] *n* [living in] logeuse *f*; [owner] propriétaire *f*.

landlord ['lændlɔːd] *n* [of rented property] propriétaire *m*. || [of pub] patron *m*.

landmark ['lændmɑːk] *n* point *m* de repère; fig événement *m* marquant.

landowner ['lænd,əʊnər] *n* propriétaire foncier *m*, propriétaire foncière *f*.

landscape ['lændskeɪp] *n* paysage *m*.

landslide ['lændslaɪd] *n* [of earth] glissement *m* de terrain; [of rocks] éboulement *m*. || fig [election victory] victoire *f* écrasante.

lane [leɪn] *n* [in country] petite route *f*, chemin *m*. || [in town] ruelle *f*. || [for

traffic] voie *f*; "**keep in ~**" «ne changez pas de file». || AERON & SPORT couloir *m*.

language ['læŋgwɪdʒ] *n* [of people, country] langue *f*. || [terminology, ability to speak] langage *m*.

language laboratory *n* laboratoire *m* de langues.

languish ['læŋgwɪʃ] *vi* languir.

lank [læŋk] *adj* terne.

lanky ['læŋkɪ] *adj* dégingandé(e).

lantern ['læntən] *n* lanterne *f*.

lap [læp] **1** *n* [of person]: **on sb's ~** sur les genoux de qqn. || [of race] tour *m* de piste. **2** *vt* [subj: animal] laper. || [in race] prendre un tour d'avance sur. **3** *vi* [water, waves] clapoter.

lapel [lə'pel] *n* revers *m*.

lapse [læps] **1** *n* [failing] défaillance *f*. || [in behaviour] écart *m* de conduite. || [of time] intervalle *m*, laps *m* de temps. **2** *vi* [passport] être périmé(e); [membership] prendre fin; [tradition] se perdre. || [person]: **to ~ into bad habits** prendre de mauvaises habitudes.

lap-top (computer) *n* (ordinateur *m*) portable *m*.

larceny ['lɑːsənɪ] *n* (U) vol *m* (simple).

lard [lɑːd] *n* saindoux *m*.

larder ['lɑːdər] *n* garde-manger *m* inv.

large [lɑːdʒ] *adj* grand(e); [person, animal, book] gros (grosse). ○ **at large** *adv* [as a whole] dans son ensemble. || [prisoner, animal] en liberté. ○ **by and large** *adv* dans l'ensemble.

largely ['lɑːdʒlɪ] *adv* en grande partie.

lark [lɑːk] *n* [bird] alouette *f*. || *inf* [joke] blague *f*. ○ **lark about** *vi* s'amuser.

laryngitis [,lærɪn'dʒaɪtɪs] *n* (U) laryngite *f*.

larynx ['lærɪŋks] *n* larynx *m*.

lasagna, lasagne [lə'zænjə] *n* (U) lasagnes *fpl*.

laser ['leɪzər] *n* laser *m*.

laser printer *n* imprimante *f* (à) laser.

lash [læʃ] **1** *n* [eyelash] cil *m*. || [with whip] coup *m* de fouet. **2** *vt* [gen] fouetter. || [tie] attacher. ○ **lash out** *vi* [physically]: **to ~ out (at OR against)** envoyer un coup (à).

lass [læs] *n* jeune fille *f*.

lasso [læ'suː] (*pl* -s) **1** *n* lasso *m*. **2** *vt* attraper au lasso.

last [lɑːst] **1** *adj* dernier(ière); **~ night** hier soir; **~ but one** avant-dernier (avant-dernière). **2** *adv* [most recently] la dernière fois. || [finally] en dernier, le dernier (la dernière). **3** *pron*: **the Satur-**

day before ~ pas samedi dernier. mais le samedi d'avant; **the year before** ~ il y a deux ans; **the ~ but one** l'avant-dernier *m*, l'avant-dernière *f*; **to leave sthg till** ~ faire qqch en dernier. **4** *n*: **the ~ I saw of him** la dernière fois que je l'ai vu. **5** *vi* durer; [food] se garder, se conserver; [feeling] persister. ○ **at (long) last** *adv* enfin.

lasting ['lɑːstɪŋ] *adj* durable.

lastly ['lɑːstlɪ] *adv* pour terminer, finalement.

last-minute *adj* de dernière minute.

last name *n* nom *m* de famille.

latch [lætʃ] *n* loquet *m*.

late [leɪt] **1** *adj* [not on time]: **to be** ~ (for sthg) être en retard (pour qqch). ‖ [near end of]: **in** ~ **December** vers la fin décembre. ‖ [later than normal] tardif(ive). ‖ [former] ancien(ienne). ‖ [dead] feu(e). **2** *adv* [not on time] en retard; **to arrive 20 minutes** ~ arriver avec 20 minutes de retard. ‖ [later than normal] tard. ○ **of late** *adv* récemment, dernièrement.

latecomer ['leɪt,kʌmər] *n* retardataire *mf*.

lately ['leɪtlɪ] *adv* ces derniers temps, dernièrement.

latent ['leɪtənt] *adj* latent(e).

later ['leɪtər] **1** *adj* [date] ultérieur(e); [edition] postérieur(e). **2** *adv*: ~ **(on)** plus tard.

lateral ['lætərəl] *adj* latéral(e).

latest ['leɪtɪst] **1** *adj* dernier(ière). **2** *n*: **at the** ~ au plus tard.

lathe [leɪð] *n* tour *m*.

lather ['lɑːðər] **1** *n* mousse *f* (de savon). **2** *vt* savonner.

Latin ['lætɪn] **1** *adj* latin(e). **2** *n* [language] latin *m*.

Latin America *n* Amérique *f* latine.

Latin American 1 *adj* latino-américain(e). **2** *n* [person] Latino-Américain *m*, -e *f*.

latitude ['lætɪtjuːd] *n* latitude *f*.

latter ['lætər] **1** *adj* [later] dernier(ière). ‖ [second] deuxième. **2** *n*: **the** ~ celui-ci (celle-ci), ce dernier (cette dernière).

lattice ['lætɪs] *n* treillis *m*, treillage *m*.

Latvia ['lætvɪə] *n* Lettonie *f*.

laudable ['lɔːdəbl] *adj* louable.

laugh [lɑːf] **1** *n* rire *m*; **we had a good** ~ *inf* on a bien rigolé. on s'est bien amusé. **2** *vi* rire. ○ **laugh at** *vt fus* [mock] se moquer de, rire de. ○ **laugh off** *vt sep* tourner en plaisanterie.

laughable ['lɑːfəbl] *adj* ridicule, risible.

laughingstock ['lɑːfɪŋstɒk] *n* risée *f*.

laughter ['lɑːftər] *n* (*U*) rire *m*, rires *mpl*.

launch [lɔːntʃ] **1** *n* [gen] lancement *m*. ‖ [boat] chaloupe *f*. **2** *vt* lancer.

launch(ing) pad ['lɔːntʃ(ɪŋ)-] *n* pas *m* de tir.

launder ['lɔːndər] *vt* lit & *fig* blanchir.

laund(e)rette [lɔːn'dret], **Laundromat**® *Am* ['lɔːndrəmæt] *n* laverie *f* automatique.

laundry ['lɔːndrɪ] *n* (*U*) [clothes] lessive *f*. ‖ [business] blanchisserie *f*.

laurel ['lɒrəl] *n* laurier *m*.

lava ['lɑːvə] *n* lave *f*.

lavatory ['lævətrɪ] *n* toilettes *fpl*.

lavender ['lævəndər] *n* [plant] lavande *f*.

lavish ['lævɪʃ] **1** *adj* [generous] généreux(euse); **to be** ~ **with** être prodigue de. ‖ [sumptuous] somptueux(euse). **2** *vt*: **to** ~ **sthg on sb** prodiguer qqch à qqn.

law [lɔː] *n* [gen] loi *f*; **against the** ~ contraire à la loi, illégal(e); **to break the** ~ enfreindre OR transgresser la loi; ~ **and order** ordre *m* public. ‖ JUR droit *m*.

law-abiding [-ə,baɪdɪŋ] *adj* respectueux(euse) des lois.

law court *n* tribunal *m*, cour *f* de justice.

lawful ['lɔːful] *adj* légal(e), licite.

lawn [lɔːn] *n* pelouse *f*, gazon *m*.

lawnmower ['lɔːn,məʊər] *n* tondeuse *f* à gazon.

lawn tennis *n* tennis *m*.

law school *n* faculté *f* de droit.

lawsuit ['lɔːsuːt] *n* procès *m*.

lawyer ['lɔːjər] *n* [in court] avocat *m*; [of company] conseiller *m* juridique; [for wills, sales] notaire *m*.

lax [læks] *adj* relâché(e).

laxative ['læksətɪv] *n* laxatif *m*.

lay [leɪ] (*pt* & *pp* **laid**) **1** *pt* → **lie**. **2** *vt* [gen] poser, mettre; *fig*: **to** ~ **the blame for sthg on sb** rejeter la responsabilité de qqch sur qqn. ‖ [trap, snare] tendre, dresser; [plans] faire; **to** ~ **the table** mettre la table OR le couvert. ‖ [egg] pondre. **3** *adj* RELIG laïque. ‖ [untrained] profane. ○ **lay aside** *vt sep* mettre de côté. ○ **lay down** *vt sep* [guidelines, rules] imposer, stipuler. ‖ [put down] déposer. ○ **lay off 1** *vt sep* [make redundant] licencier. **2** *vt fus inf* [leave alone] ficher la paix à. ‖ [give up] arrêter. ○ **lay out** *vt sep* [arrange] arranger, disposer. ‖ [design] concevoir.

layer ['leɪə'] n couche f; fig [level] niveau m.

layman ['leɪmən] (pl -men [-mən]) n [untrained person] profane m. || RELIG laïc m.

layout ['leɪaʊt] n [of office, building] agencement m; [of garden] plan m; [of page] mise f en page.

laze [leɪz] vi: to ~ (about OR around) paresser.

lazy ['leɪzɪ] adj [person] paresseux(euse), fainéant(e); [action] nonchalant(e).

lazybones ['leɪzɪbəʊnz] (pl inv) n paresseux m, -euse f, fainéant m, -e f.

lb (abbr of pound) livre (unité de poids).

LCD (abbr of liquid crystal display) n affichage à cristaux liquides.

lead¹ [liːd] (pt & pp led) 1 n [winning position]: **to be in** OR **have the ~** mener, être en tête. || [amount ahead]: **to have a ~ of ...** devancer de .... || [initiative, example] initiative f, exemple m; **to take the ~** montrer l'exemple. || THEATRE: **the ~** le rôle principal. || [clue] indice m. || [for dog] laisse f. || [wire, cable] câble m, fil m. 2 adj [role etc] principal(e). 3 vt [be at front of] mener, être à la tête de. || [guide] guider, conduire. || [be in charge of] être à la tête de, diriger. || [organize - protest etc] mener, organiser. || [life] mener. || [cause]: **to ~ sb to do sthg** inciter OR pousser qqn à faire qqch. 4 vi [path, cable etc] mener, conduire. || [give access]: **to ~ to/into** donner sur, donner accès à. || [in race, match] mener. || [result in]: **to ~ to sthg** aboutir à qqch, causer qqch. ○ **lead up to** vt fus [precede] conduire à, aboutir à. || [build up to] amener.

lead² [led] 1 n plomb m; [in pencil] mine f. 2 comp en OR de plomb.

leaded ['ledɪd] adj [petrol] au plomb.

leader ['liːdə'] n [head, chief] chef m; POL leader m. || [in race, competition] premier m, -ière f. || Br PRESS éditorial m.

leadership ['liːdəʃɪp] n [people in charge]: **the ~** les dirigeants mpl. || [position of leader] direction f. || [qualities of leader] qualités fpl de chef.

lead-free [led-] adj sans plomb.

leading ['liːdɪŋ] adj [most important] principal(e). || [at front] de tête.

leaf [liːf] (pl **leaves**) n [of tree, plant] feuille f. || [of table - hinged] abattant m; [- pull-out] rallonge f. || [of book] feuille f, page f. ○ **leaf through** vt fus [magazine etc] parcourir, feuilleter.

leaflet ['liːflɪt] n prospectus m.

league [liːg] n ligue f; SPORT championnat m; **to be in ~ with** être de connivence avec.

leak [liːk] 1 n lit & fig fuite f. 2 vt fig [secret, information] divulguer. 3 vi fuir. ○ **leak out** vi [liquid] fuir. || fig [secret, information] transpirer, être divulgué(e).

lean [liːn] (pt & pp **leant** OR -**ed**) 1 adj [slim] mince. || [meat] maigre. || fig [month, time] mauvais(e). 2 vt [rest]: **to ~ sthg against** appuyer qqch contre, adosser qqch à. 3 vi [bend, slope] se pencher. || [rest]: **to ~ on/against** s'appuyer sur/contre.

leaning ['liːnɪŋ] n: ~ (**towards**) penchant m (pour).

leant [lent] pt & pp → **lean**.

lean-to (pl **lean-tos**) n appentis m.

leap [liːp] (pt & pp **leapt** OR -**ed**) 1 n lit & fig bond m. 2 vi [gen] bondir. || fig [increase] faire un bond.

leapfrog ['liːpfrɒg] 1 n saute-mouton m. 2 vi: **to ~ over** sauter par-dessus.

leapt [lept] pt & pp → **leap**.

leap year n année f bissextile.

learn [lɜːn] (pt & pp -**ed** OR **learnt**) 1 vt: **to ~ (that) ...** apprendre que ...; **to ~ (how) to do sthg** apprendre à faire qqch. 2 vi: **to ~ (of** OR **about sthg)** apprendre (qqch).

learned ['lɜːnɪd] adj savant(e).

learner ['lɜːnə'] n débutant m, -e f.

learner (driver) n conducteur débutant m, conductrice débutante f (qui n'a pas encore son permis).

learning ['lɜːnɪŋ] n savoir m, érudition f.

learnt [lɜːnt] pt & pp → **learn**.

lease [liːs] 1 n bail m. 2 vt louer; **to ~ sthg from sb** louer qqch à qqn; **to ~ sthg to sb** louer qqch à qqn.

leasehold ['liːshəʊld] 1 adj loué(e) à bail, tenu(e) à bail. 2 adv à bail.

leash [liːʃ] n laisse f.

least [liːst] (superl of little) 1 adj: **the ~** le moindre (la moindre), le plus petit (la plus petite). 2 pron [smallest amount]: **the ~** le moins; **it's the ~ (that) he can do** c'est la moindre des choses qu'il puisse faire; **not in the ~** pas du tout, pas le moins du monde; **to say the ~** c'est le moins qu'on puisse dire. 3 adv: **(the) ~** le moins (la moins). ○ **at least** adv au moins; [to correct] du moins. ○ **least of all** adv surtout pas, encore moins. ○ **not least** adv fml notamment.

leather ['leðəʳ] *n* cuir *m*.

leave [li:v] (*pt & pp* **left**) **1** *rt* [gen] laisser. || [go away from] quitter; **to ~ sb alone** laisser qqn tranquille. || [bequeath]: **to ~ sb sthg, to ~ sthg to sb** léguer ou laisser qqch à qqn; *see also* **left. 2** *vi* partir. **3** *n* congé *m*; **to be on ~** [from work] être en congé; [from army] être en permission. ❍ **leave behind** *rt sep* [abandon] abandonner, laisser. || [forget] oublier, laisser. ❍ **leave out** *rt sep* omettre, exclure.

leave of absence *n* congé *m*.

leaves [li:vz] *pl* → **leaf**.

Lebanon ['lebənən] *n* Liban *m*.

lecherous ['letʃərəs] *adj* lubrique, libidineux(euse).

lecture ['lektʃəʳ] **1** *n* [talk - gen] conférence *f*; [- UNIV] cours *m* magistral. || [scolding]: **to give sb a ~** réprimander qqn, sermonner qqn. **2** *rt* [scold] réprimander, sermonner. **3** *ri*: **to ~ on sthg** faire un cours sur qqch; **to ~ in sthg** être professeur de qqch.

lecturer ['lektʃərəʳ] *n* [speaker] conférencier *m*, -ière *f*; UNIV maître assistant *m*.

led [led] *pt & pp* → **lead¹**.

ledge [ledʒ] *n* [of window] rebord *m*. || [of mountain] corniche *f*.

ledger ['ledʒəʳ] *n* grand livre *m*.

leech [li:tʃ] *n lit & fig* sangsue *f*.

leek [li:k] *n* poireau *m*.

leer [lɪəʳ] **1** *ri*: **to ~ at** reluquer.

leeway ['li:weɪ] *n* [room to manoeuvre] marge *f* de manœuvre.

left [left] **1** *pt & pp* → **leave. 2** *adj* [remaining]: **to be ~** rester; **have you any money ~?** il te reste de l'argent? || [not right] gauche. **3** *adv* à gauche. **4** *n*: **on** ou **to the ~** à gauche. ❍ **Left** *n* POL: **the Left** la Gauche.

left-hand *adj* de gauche; **~ side** gauche *f*, côté *m* gauche.

left-hand drive *adj* [car] avec la conduite à gauche.

left-handed [-'hændɪd] *adj* [person] gaucher(ère). || [implement] pour gaucher.

leftover ['leftəʊvəʳ] *adj* qui reste, en surplus. ❍ **leftovers** *npl* restes *mpl*.

left wing POL *n* gauche *f*. ❍ **left-wing** *adj* de gauche.

leg [leg] *n* [of person, trousers] jambe *f*; [of animal] patte *f*; **to pull sb's ~** faire marcher qqn. || CULIN [of lamb] gigot *m*;

[of pork, chicken] cuisse *f*. || [of furniture] pied *m*. || [of journey, match] étape *f*.

legacy ['legəsɪ] *n lit & fig* legs *m*, héritage *m*.

legal ['li:gl] *adj* [concerning the law] juridique. || [lawful] légal(e).

legalize, -ise ['li:gəlaɪz] *rt* légaliser, rendre légal.

legal tender *n* monnaie *f* légale.

legend ['ledʒənd] *n lit & fig* légende *f*.

leggings ['legɪŋz] *npl* jambières *fpl*, leggings *mpl* or *fpl*.

legible ['ledʒəbl] *adj* lisible.

legislation [,ledʒɪs'leɪʃn] *n* législation *f*.

legislature ['ledʒɪsleɪtʃəʳ] *n* corps *m* législatif.

legitimate [lɪ'dʒɪtɪmət] *adj* légitime.

legroom ['legrum] *n* (U) place *f* pour les jambes.

leg-warmers [-,wɔ:məz] *npl* jambières *fpl*.

leisure [Br 'leʒəʳ, Am 'li:ʒər] *n* loisir *m*, temps *m* libre.

leisure centre *n* centre *m* de loisirs.

leisurely [Br 'leʒəlɪ, Am 'li:ʒərlɪ] *adj* [pace] lent(e), tranquille.

leisure time *n* (U) temps *m* libre, loisirs *mpl*.

lemon ['lemən] *n* [fruit] citron *m*.

lemonade [,lemə'neɪd] *n* [still] citronnade *f*.

lemon juice *n* jus *m* de citron.

lemon squeezer [-'skwi:zəʳ] *n* presse-citron *m inv*.

lemon tea *n* thé *m* (au) citron.

lend [lend] (*pt & pp* **lent**) *rt* [loan] prêter; **to ~ sb sthg, to ~ sthg to sb** prêter qqch à qqn. || [offer]: **to ~ support** (**to sb**) offrir son soutien (à qqn); **to ~ assistance** (**to sb**) prêter assistance (à qqn). || [add]: **to ~ sthg to sthg** [quality etc] ajouter qqch à qqch.

lending rate ['lendɪŋ-] *n* taux *m* de crédit.

length [leŋθ] *n* [gen] longueur *f*; **what ~ is it?** ça fait quelle longueur? || [piece - of string, wood] morceau *m*, bout *m*; [- of cloth] coupon *m*. || [duration] durée *f*. || *phr*: **to go to great ~s to do sthg** tout faire pour faire qqch. ❍ **at length** *adv* [eventually] enfin. || [in detail] à fond.

lengthen ['leŋθən] **1** *rt* [dress etc] rallonger; [life] prolonger. **2** *vi* allonger.

lengthways ['leŋθweɪz] *adv* dans le sens de la longueur.

lengthy ['leŋθɪ] *adj* très long (longue).

lenient ['li:njənt] *adj* [person] indulgent(e); [laws] clément(e).

lens [lenz] *n* [of camera] objectif *m*; [of glasses] verre *m*. || [contact lens] verre *m* de contact, lentille *f* (cornéenne).

lent [lent] *pt & pp* → **lend**.

Lent [lent] *n* Carême *m*.

lentil ['lentɪl] *n* lentille *f*.

Leo ['li:əʊ] *n* le Lion.

leopard ['lepəd] *n* léopard *m*.

leotard ['li:ətɑ:d] *n* collant *m*.

leper ['lepər] *n* lépreux *m*, -euse *f*.

leprosy ['leprəsɪ] *n* lèpre *f*.

lesbian ['lezbɪən] *n* lesbienne *f*.

less [les] (*compar of* little) **1** *adj* moins de; ~ **money/time than me** moins d'argent/de temps que moi. **2** *pron* moins; **it costs ~ than you think** ça coûte moins cher que tu ne le crois; **no ~ than £50** pas moins de 50 livres; **the ~ ... the ~ ...** moins ... moins ... . **3** *adv* moins; ~ **than five** moins de cinq; ~ **and ~** de moins en moins. **4** *prep* [minus] moins.

lessen ['lesn] **1** *vt* [risk, chance] diminuer, réduire; [pain] atténuer. **2** *vi* [gen] diminuer; [pain] s'atténuer.

lesser ['lesər] *adj* moindre; **to a ~ extent** OR **degree** à un degré moindre.

lesson ['lesn] *n* leçon *f*, cours *m*; **to teach sb a ~** *fig* donner une (bonne) leçon à qqn.

let [let] (*pt & pp* let) *vt* [allow]: **to ~ sb do sthg** laisser qqn faire qqch; **to ~ sb know sthg** dire qqch à qqn; **to ~ go of sb/sthg** lâcher qqn/qqch; **to ~ sb go** [gen] laisser (partir) qqn; [prisoner] libérer qqn. || [in verb forms]: ~ **them wait** qu'ils attendent; ~'**s go!** allons-y! || [rent out] louer; **"to ~"** «à louer». ○ **let alone** *adv* encore moins, sans parler de. ○ **let down** *vt sep* [deflate] dégonfler. || [disappoint] décevoir. ○ **let in** *vt sep* [admit] laisser OR faire entrer. ○ **let off** *vt sep* [excuse]: **to ~ sb off sthg** dispenser qqn de qqch. || [not punish] ne pas punir. || [bomb] faire éclater; [gun, firework] faire partir. ○ **let on** *vi*: **don't ~ on!** ne dis rien (à personne)! ○ **let out** *vt sep* [allow to go out] laisser sortir; **to ~ air out of sthg** dégonfler qqch. ○ **let up** *vi* [rain] diminuer. || [person] s'arrêter.

letdown ['letdaʊn] *n inf* déception *f*.

lethal ['li:θl] *adj* mortel(elle), fatal(e).

lethargic [lə'θɑ:dʒɪk] *adj* léthargique.

let's [lets] = **let us**.

letter ['letər] *n* lettre *f*.

letter bomb *n* lettre *f* piégée.

letter of credit *n* lettre *f* de crédit.

lettuce ['letɪs] *n* laitue *f*, salade *f*.

letup ['letʌp] *n* [in fighting] répit *m*; [in work] relâchement *m*.

leuk(a)emia [lu:'ki:mɪə] *n* leucémie *f*.

level ['levl] **1** *adj* [equal in height] à la même hauteur; [horizontal] horizontal(e); **to be ~ with** être au niveau de. || [equal in standard] à égalité. || [flat] plat(e), plan(e). **2** *n* [gen] niveau *m*. || *Am* [spirit level] niveau *m* à bulle. **3** *vt* [make flat] niveler, aplanir. || [demolish] raser. ○ **level off, level out** *vi* [inflation etc] se stabiliser. || [aeroplane] se mettre en palier. ○ **level with** *vt fus inf* être franc (franche) OR honnête avec.

level-headed [-'hedɪd] *adj* raisonnable.

lever [*Br* 'li:vər, *Am* 'levər] *n* levier *m*.

levy ['levɪ] **1** *n* prélèvement *m*, impôt *m*. **2** *vt* prélever, percevoir.

lewd [lju:d] *adj* obscène.

liability [,laɪə'bɪlətɪ] *n* responsabilité *f*; *fig* [person] danger *m* public. ○ **liabilities** *npl* FIN dettes *fpl*.

liable ['laɪəbl] *adj* [likely]: **to be ~ to do sthg** risquer de faire qqch, être susceptible de faire qqch. || [prone]: **to be ~ to sthg** être sujet(ette) à qqch. || JUR: **to be ~ (for)** être responsable (de).

liaise [lɪ'eɪz] *vi*: **to ~ with** assurer la liaison avec.

liar ['laɪər] *n* menteur *m*, -euse *f*.

libel ['laɪbl] **1** *n* diffamation *f*. **2** *vt* diffamer.

liberal ['lɪbərəl] **1** *adj* [tolerant] libéral(e). || [generous] généreux(euse). **2** *n* libéral *m*, -e *f*. ○ **Liberal** POL **1** *adj* libéral(e). **2** *n* libéral *m*, -e *f*.

liberate ['lɪbəreɪt] *vt* libérer.

liberation [,lɪbə'reɪʃn] *n* libération *f*.

liberty ['lɪbətɪ] *n* liberté *f*; **at ~** en liberté; **to be at ~ to do sthg** être libre de faire qqch; **to take liberties (with sb)** prendre des libertés (avec qqn).

Libra ['li:brə] *n* Balance *f*.

librarian [laɪ'breərɪən] *n* bibliothécaire *mf*.

library ['laɪbrərɪ] *n* bibliothèque *f*.

library book *n* livre *m* de bibliothèque.

libretto [lɪ'bretəʊ] (*pl* -s) *n* livret *m*.

Libya ['lɪbɪə] *n* Libye *f*.

lice [laɪs] *pl* → **louse**.

licence ['laɪsəns] **1** *n* [gen] permis *m*, autorisation *f*; **driving ~** permis *m* de conduire; TV ~ redevance *f* télé. || COMM licence *f*. 2 *vt Am* = **license**.

license ['laɪsns] 1 *vt* autoriser. 2 *n Am* = **licence**.

licensed ['laɪsənst] *adj* [person]: to be ~ to do sthg avoir un permis pour OR l'autorisation de faire qqch.

license plate *n Am* plaque *f* d'immatriculation.

lick [lɪk] *vt* [gen] lécher. || *inf* [defeat] écraser.

licorice ['lɪkərɪs] = **liquorice**.

lid [lɪd] *n* [cover] couvercle *m*. || [eyelid] paupière *f*.

lie [laɪ] (*pt sense 1* lied, *pt senses 2-6* lay, *pp sense 1* lied, *pp senses 2-6* lain, *cont all senses* lying) 1 *n* mensonge *m*; to tell ~s mentir, dire des mensonges. 2 *vi* [tell lie]: to ~ (to sb) mentir (à qqn). || [be horizontal] être allongé(e), être couché(e). || [lie down] s'allonger, se coucher. || [be situated] se trouver, être. || [difficulty, solution etc] résider. || *phr*: to ~ low se planquer, se tapir. ○ **lie about**, **lie around** *vi* traîner. ○ **lie down** *vi* s'allonger, se coucher.

lieutenant [*Br* lef'tenənt, *Am* luː'tenənt] *n* lieutenant *m*.

life [laɪf] (*pl* lives) *n* [gen] vie *f*; that's ~! c'est la vie!; for ~ à vie; to come to ~ s'éveiller, s'animer; to come to ~ of sb faire une peur bleue à qqn. || (*U*) *inf* [life imprisonment] emprisonnement *m* perpétuel.

life assurance = **life insurance**.

life belt *n* bouée *f* de sauvetage.

lifeboat ['laɪfbəʊt] *n* canot *m* de sauvetage.

life buoy *n* bouée *f* de sauvetage.

life expectancy [-ɪk'spektənsɪ] *n* espérance *f* de vie.

lifeguard ['laɪfɡɑːd] *n* [at swimming pool] maître-nageur sauveteur *m*; [at beach] gardien *m* de plage.

life imprisonment [-ɪm'prɪznmənt] *n* emprisonnement *m* à perpétuité.

life insurance *n* assurance-vie *f*.

life jacket *n* gilet *m* de sauvetage.

lifeless ['laɪflɪs] *adj* [dead] sans vie, inanimé(e). || [listless - performance] qui manque de vie; [- voice] monotone.

lifelike ['laɪflaɪk] *adj* [statue, doll] qui semble vivant(e). || [portrait] ressemblant(e).

lifeline ['laɪflaɪn] *n* corde *f* (de sauvetage); *fig* lien *m* vital (avec l'extérieur).

lifelong ['laɪflɒŋ] *adj* de toujours.

life preserver [-prɪˌzɜːvəʳ] *n Am* [life belt] bouée *f* de sauvetage; [life jacket] gilet *m* de sauvetage.

life raft *n* canot *m* pneumatique (de sauvetage).

lifesaver ['laɪfˌseɪvəʳ] *n* [person] maître-nageur sauveteur *m*.

life sentence *n* condamnation *f* à perpétuité.

life-size(d) [-saɪz(d)] *adj* grandeur nature (*inv*).

lifespan ['laɪfspæn] *n* [of person, animal] espérance *f* de vie.

lifestyle ['laɪfstaɪl] *n* style *m* de vie.

life-support system *n* respirateur *m* artificiel.

lifetime ['laɪftaɪm] *n* vie *f*; in my ~ de mon vivant.

lift [lɪft] 1 *n* [in car]: to give sb a ~ emmener OR prendre qqn en voiture. 2 *vt* [gen] lever; [weight] soulever. || [plagiarize] plagier. || *inf* [steal] voler. 3 *vi* [lid etc] s'ouvrir. || [fog etc] se lever.

lift-off *n* décollage *m*.

light [laɪt] (*pt & pp* lit OR -ed) 1 *adj* [not dark] clair(e). || [not heavy] léger(ère). || [traffic] fluide; [corrections] peu nombreux(euses). || [work] facile. 2 *n* (*U*) [brightness] lumière *f*. || [device] lampe *f*; [AUT - gen] feu *m*; [- headlamp] phare *m*. || [for cigarette etc] feu *m*; have you got a ~? vous avez du feu?; to set ~ to sthg mettre le feu à qqch. || [perspective]: in the ~ of *Br*, in ~ of *Am* à la lumière de. || *phr*: to come to ~ être découvert(e) OR dévoilé(e). 3 *vt* [fire, cigarette] allumer. || [room, stage] éclairer. 4 *adv*: to travel ~ voyager léger. ○ **light up** 1 *vt sep* [illuminate] éclairer; [cigarette etc] allumer. 2 *vi* [face] s'éclairer. || *inf* [start smoking] allumer une cigarette.

light bulb *n* ampoule *f*.

lighten ['laɪtn] 1 *vt* [in colour] éclaircir. || [make less heavy] alléger. 2 *vi* [brighten] s'éclaircir.

lighter ['laɪtəʳ] *n* [cigarette lighter] briquet *m*.

light-headed [-'hedɪd] *adj*: to feel ~ avoir la tête qui tourne.

light-hearted [-'hɑːtɪd] *adj* [cheerful] joyeux(euse), gai(e). || [amusing] amusant(e).

lighthouse ['laɪthaʊs, *pl* -haʊzɪz] *n* phare *m*.

lighting ['laɪtɪŋ] *n* éclairage *m*.

light meter *n* posemètre *m*, cellule *f* photoélectrique.

lightning ['laɪtnɪŋ] n (U) éclair m, foudre f.

lightweight ['laɪtweɪt] **1** adj [object] léger(ère). **2** n [boxer] poids m léger.

likable ['laɪkəbl] adj sympathique.

like [laɪk] **1** prep [gen] comme; **to look ~ sb/sthg** ressembler à qqn/qqch; **to taste ~ sthg** avoir un goût de qqch; **~ this/that** comme ci/ça. || [such as] tel que, comme. **2** vt [gen] aimer; **I ~ her** elle me plaît; **to ~ doing** OR **to do sthg** aimer faire qqch. || [expressing a wish]: **would you ~ some more cake?** vous prendrez encore un peu de gâteau?; **I'd ~ to go** je voudrais bien OR j'aimerais y aller; **I'd ~ you to come** je voudrais bien OR j'aimerais que vous veniez; **if you ~** si vous voulez. **3** n: **the ~** une chose pareille. ○ **likes** npl: **~s and dislikes** goûts mpl.

likeable ['laɪkəbl] = likable.

likelihood ['laɪklɪhʊd] n (U) chances fpl, probabilité f.

likely ['laɪklɪ] adj [probable] probable; **he's ~ to get angry** il risque de se fâcher; **a ~ story!** iro à d'autres! || [candidate] prometteur(euse).

liken ['laɪkn] vt: **to ~ sb/sthg to** assimiler qqn/qqch à.

likewise ['laɪkwaɪz] adv [similarly] de même; **to do ~** faire pareil OR de même.

liking ['laɪkɪŋ] n [for person] affection f, sympathie f; [for food. music] goût m, penchant m; **to be to sb's ~** être du goût de qqn, plaire à qqn.

lilac ['laɪlək] **1** adj [colour] lilas (inv). **2** n lilas m.

lily ['lɪlɪ] n lis m.

lily of the valley (pl **lilies of the valley**) n muguet m.

limb [lɪm] n [of body] membre m.

limber ['lɪmbər] ○ **limber up** vi s'échauffer.

limbo ['lɪmbəʊ] (pl -s) n (U) [uncertain state]: **to be in ~** être dans les limbes.

lime [laɪm] n [fruit] citron m vert. || [drink]: **~ (juice)** jus m de citron vert. || [linden tree] tilleul m. || [substance] chaux f.

limelight ['laɪmlaɪt] n: **to be in the ~** être au premier plan.

limerick ['lɪmərɪk] n poème humoristique en cinq vers.

limestone ['laɪmstəʊn] n (U) pierre f à chaux, calcaire m.

limey ['laɪmɪ] (pl **limeys**) n Am inf terme péjoratif désignant un Anglais.

limit ['lɪmɪt] **1** n limite f; **off ~s** d'accès interdit; **within ~s** [to an extent] dans une certaine mesure. **2** vt limiter, restreindre.

limitation [,lɪmɪ'teɪʃn] n limitation f, restriction f.

limited ['lɪmɪtɪd] adj limité(e), restreint(e).

limited (liability) company n société f anonyme.

limousine ['lɪməzi:n] n limousine f.

limp [lɪmp] **1** adj mou (molle). **2** n: **to have a ~** boiter. **3** vi boiter.

limpet ['lɪmpɪt] n patelle f, bernique f.

line [laɪn] **1** n [gen] ligne f. || [row] rangée f. || [queue] file f, queue f; **to stand** OR **wait in ~** faire la queue. || [RAIL - track] voie f; [- route] ligne f. || [of poem, song] vers m. || [wrinkle] ride f. || [string, wire etc] corde f; **a fishing ~** une ligne. || TELEC ligne f; **hold the ~!** ne quittez pas! || inf [short letter]: **to drop sb a ~** écrire un (petit) mot à qqn. || COMM gamme f. || phr: **to draw the ~ at sthg** refuser de faire OR d'aller jusqu'à faire qqch; **to step out of ~** faire cavalier seul. **2** vt [drawer, box] tapisser; [clothes] doubler. ○ **out of line** adj [remark, behaviour] déplacé(e). ○ **line up 1** vt sep [in rows] aligner. || [organize] prévoir. **2** vi [in row] s'aligner; [in queue] faire la queue.

lined [laɪnd] adj [paper] réglé(e). || [wrinkled] ridé(e).

linen ['lɪnɪn] n (U) [cloth] lin m. || [tablecloths, sheets] linge m (de maison).

liner ['laɪnər] n [ship] paquebot m.

linesman ['laɪnzmən] (pl **-men** [-mən]) n TENNIS juge m de ligne.

lineup ['laɪnʌp] n SPORT équipe f. || Am [identification parade] rangée f de suspects (pour identification par un témoin).

linger ['lɪŋgər] vi [person] s'attarder. || [doubt, pain] persister.

linguist ['lɪŋgwɪst] n linguiste mf.

linguistics [lɪŋ'gwɪstɪks] n (U) linguistique f.

lining ['laɪnɪŋ] n [of coat, curtains, box] doublure f. || [of stomach] muqueuse f. || AUT [of brakes] garniture f.

link [lɪŋk] **1** n [of chain] maillon m. || [connection]: **~ (between/with)** lien m (entre/avec). **2** vt [cities, parts] relier; [events etc] lier; **to ~ arms** se donner le bras. ○ **link up** vt sep relier; **to ~ sthg up with sthg** relier qqch avec OR à qqch.

links [lɪŋks] (*pl inv*) *n* terrain *m* de golf (*au bord de la mer*).

lino ['laɪnəʊ], **linoleum** [lɪ'nəʊlɪəm] *n* lino *m*, linoléum *m*.

lion ['laɪən] *n* lion *m*.

lioness ['laɪənes] *n* lionne *f*.

lip [lɪp] *n* [of mouth] lèvre *f*. || [of container] bord *m*.

lip-read *vi* lire sur les lèvres.

lip service *n*: **to pay ~ to sthg** approuver qqch pour la forme.

lipstick ['lɪpstɪk] *n* rouge *m* à lèvres.

liqueur [lɪ'kjʊər] *n* liqueur *f*.

liquid ['lɪkwɪd] **1** *adj* liquide. **2** *n* liquide *m*.

liquidation [ˌlɪkwɪ'deɪʃn] *n* liquidation *f*.

liquor ['lɪkər] *n* (*U*) alcool *m*, spiritueux *mpl*.

liquorice ['lɪkərɪs, 'lɪkərɪʃ] *n* réglisse *f*.

liquor store *n Am* magasin *m* de vins et d'alcools.

Lisbon ['lɪzbən] *n* Lisbonne.

lisp [lɪsp] **1** *n* zézaiement *m*. **2** *vi* zézayer.

list [lɪst] **1** *n* liste *f*. **2** *vt* [in writing] faire la liste de; [in speech] énumérer.

listen ['lɪsn] *vi*: **to ~ to (sb/sthg)** écouter (qqn/qqch); **to ~ for sthg** guetter qqch.

listener ['lɪsnər] *n* auditeur *m*, -trice *f*.

listless ['lɪstlɪs] *adj* apathique, mou (molle).

lit [lɪt] *pt & pp* → **light**.

liter *Am* = **litre**.

literacy ['lɪtərəsɪ] *n* fait *m* de savoir lire et écrire.

literal ['lɪtərəl] *adj* littéral(e).

literally ['lɪtərəlɪ] *adv* littéralement; **to take sthg ~** prendre qqch au pied de la lettre.

literary ['lɪtərərɪ] *adj* littéraire.

literate ['lɪtərət] *adj* [able to read and write] qui sait lire et écrire. || [well-read] cultivé(e).

literature ['lɪtrətʃər] *n* littérature *f*; [printed information] documentation *f*.

lithe [laɪð] *adj* souple, agile.

Lithuania [ˌlɪθjʊ'eɪnɪə] *n* Lituanie *f*.

litigation [ˌlɪtɪ'geɪʃn] *n* litige *m*; **to go to ~** aller en justice.

litre *Br*, **liter** *Am* ['liːtər] *n* litre *m*.

litter ['lɪtər] **1** *n* (*U*) [rubbish] ordures *fpl*, détritus *mpl*. || [of animals] portée *f*. **2** *vt*: **to be ~ed with** être couvert(e) de.

little ['lɪtl] (*compar sense 2* **less**, *superl sense 2* **least**) **1** *adj* [not big] petit(e). **||** [not much] peu de; **~ money** peu d'argent; **a ~ money** un **||** [short – distance, time]: **a ~ while** un petit moment. || [not much] peu de; **~ money** peu d'argent; **a ~ money** un peu d'argent. **2** *pron*: **~ of the money was left** il ne restait pas beaucoup d'argent, il restait peu d'argent; **a ~** un peu. **3** *adv* peu, pas beaucoup; **~ by ~** peu à peu.

little finger *n* petit doigt *m*, auriculaire *m*.

live¹ [lɪv] **1** *vi* [gen] vivre. **||** [have one's home] habiter, vivre; **to ~ in Paris** habiter (à) Paris. **2** *vt*: **to ~ a quiet life** mener une vie tranquille; **to ~ it up** *inf* faire la noce. **○ live down** *vt sep* faire oublier. **○ live off** *vt fus* [savings, the land] vivre de; [family] vivre aux dépens de. **○ live on 1** *vt fus* vivre de. **2** *vi* [memory, feeling] rester, survivre. **○ live together** *vi* vivre ensemble. **○ live up to** *vt fus*: **to ~ up to sb's expectations** répondre à l'attente de qqn; **to ~ up to one's reputation** faire honneur à sa réputation. **○ live with** *vt fus* [cohabit with] vivre avec. **||** *inf* [accept] se faire à, accepter.

live² [laɪv] *adj* [living] vivant(e). **||** [coal] ardent(e). **||** [bullet, bomb] non explosé(e). **||** ELEC sous tension. **||** RADIO & TV en direct; [performance] en public.

livelihood ['laɪvlɪhʊd] *n* gagne-pain *m*.

lively ['laɪvlɪ] *adj* [person] plein(e) d'entrain. **||** [debate, meeting] animé(e).

liven ['laɪvn] **○ liven up** **1** *vt sep* [person] égayer; [place] animer. **2** *vi* s'animer.

liver ['lɪvər] *n* foie *m*.

livery ['lɪvərɪ] *n* livrée *f*.

lives [laɪvz] *pl* → **life**.

livestock ['laɪvstɒk] *n* (*U*) bétail *m*.

livid ['lɪvɪd] *adj* [angry] furieux (ieuse).

living ['lɪvɪŋ] **1** *adj* vivant(e), en vie. **2** *n*: **to earn** OR **make a ~** gagner sa vie; **what do you do for a ~?** qu'est-ce que vous faites dans la vie?

living conditions *npl* conditions *fpl* de vie.

living room *n* salle *f* de séjour, living *m*.

living standards *npl* niveau *m* de vie.

living wage *n* minimum *m* vital.

lizard ['lɪzəd] *n* lézard *m*.

llama ['lɑːmə] (*pl inv* OR **-s**) *n* lama *m*.

load [ləʊd] **1** *n* [something carried] chargement *m*, charge *f*. **||** [large amount]: **~s of, a ~ of** *inf* des tas de, plein de; **a ~ of rubbish** *inf* de la foutaise. **2** *vt* [gen & COMPUT] charger; [video recorder] mettre une vidéo-cassette dans; **to ~ sb/sthg with** charger qqn/qqch de. **○ load up** *vt sep & vi* charger.

loaded ['ləʊdɪd] *adj* [question] insidieux(ieuse). **||** *inf* [rich] plein(e) aux as.

loading bay ['ləʊdɪŋ-] *n* aire *f* de chargement.

loaf [ləʊf] (*pl* **loaves**) *n*: **a ~ (of bread)** un pain.

loafer ['ləʊfər] *n* [shoe] mocassin *m*.

loan [ləʊn] **1** *n* prêt *m*; **on ~** prêté(e). **2** *vt* prêter; **to ~ sthg to sb, to ~ sb sthg** prêter qqch à qqn.

loath [ləʊθ] *adj*: **to be ~ to do sthg** ne pas vouloir faire qqch, hésiter à faire qqch.

loathe [ləʊð] *vt* détester; **to ~ doing sthg** avoir horreur de OR détester faire qqch.

loaves [ləʊvz] *pl* → **loaf**.

lob [lɒb] **1** *n* TENNIS lob *m*. **2** *vt* [throw] lancer. || TENNIS: **to ~ a ball** lober, faire un lob.

lobby ['lɒbɪ] **1** *n* [of hotel] hall *m*. || [pressure group] lobby *m*, groupe *m* de pression. **2** *vt* faire pression sur.

lobe [ləʊb] *n* lobe *m*.

lobster ['lɒbstər] *n* homard *m*.

local ['ləʊkl] **1** *adj* local(e). **2** *n inf* [person]: **the ~s** les gens *mpl* du coin OR du pays.

local call *n* communication *f* urbaine.

local government *n* administration *f* municipale.

locality [ləʊ'kælətɪ] *n* endroit *m*.

locally ['ləʊkəlɪ] *adv* [on local basis] localement. || [nearby] dans les environs, à proximité.

locate [*Br* ləʊ'keɪt, *Am* 'ləʊkeɪt] *vt* [find - position] trouver, repérer; [- source, problem] localiser. || [situate - business, factory] implanter, établir; **to be ~d** être situé.

location [ləʊ'keɪʃn] *n* [place] emplacement *m*. || CINEMA: **on ~** en extérieur.

lock [lɒk] **1** *n* [of door etc] serrure *f*. || [on canal] écluse *f*. || [of hair] mèche *f*. **2** *vt* [door, car, drawer] fermer à clef; [bicycle] cadenasser. || [immobilize] bloquer. **3** *vi* [door, suitcase] fermer à clef. || [become immobilized] se bloquer. ○ **lock in** *vt sep* enfermer (à clef). ○ **lock out** *vt sep* [accidentally] enfermer dehors, laisser dehors; **to ~ o.s. out** s'enfermer dehors. || [deliberately] empêcher d'entrer, mettre à la porte. ○ **lock up** *vt sep* [person - in prison] mettre en prison OR sous les verrous; [- in asylum] enfermer; [house] fermer à clef; [valuables] enfermer, mettre sous clef.

locker ['lɒkər] *n* casier *m*.

locker room *n Am* vestiaire *m*.

locket ['lɒkɪt] *n* médaillon *m*.

locksmith ['lɒksmɪθ] *n* serrurier *m*.

locomotive [,ləʊkə'məʊtɪv] *n* locomotive *f*.

locust ['ləʊkəst] *n* sauterelle *f*, locuste *f*.

lodge [lɒdʒ] **1** *n* [of caretaker, freemasons] loge *f*. || [of manor house] pavillon *m* (de gardien). || [for hunting] pavillon *m* de chasse. **2** *vi* [stay]: **to ~ with sb** loger chez qqn. || [become stuck] se loger, se coincer. || *fig* [in mind] s'enraciner, s'ancrer. **3** *vt* [complaint] déposer; **to ~ an appeal** interjeter OR faire appel.

lodger ['lɒdʒər] *n* locataire *mf*.

lodgings *npl* chambre *f* meublée.

loft [lɒft] *n* grenier *m*.

log [lɒg] **1** *n* [of wood] bûche *f*. || [of ship] journal *m* de bord; [of plane] carnet *m* de vol. **2** *vt* consigner, enregistrer.

logbook ['lɒgbʊk] *n* [of ship] journal *m* de bord; [of plane] carnet *m* de vol. || [of car] ≃ carte *f* grise.

loggerheads ['lɒgəhedz] *n*: **at ~** en désaccord.

logic ['lɒdʒɪk] *n* logique *f*.

logical ['lɒdʒɪkl] *adj* logique.

logistics [lə'dʒɪstɪks] **1** *n* (*U*) MIL. logistique *f*. **2** *npl fig* organisation *f*.

logo ['ləʊgəʊ] (*pl* **-s**) *n* logo *m*.

loin [lɔɪn] *n* filet *m*.

loiter ['lɔɪtər] *vi* traîner.

loll [lɒl] *vi* [sit, lie about] se prélasser. || [hang down - head, tongue] pendre.

lollipop ['lɒlɪpɒp] *n* sucette *f*.

lolly ['lɒlɪ] *n inf* [lollipop] sucette *f*.

London ['lʌndən] *n* Londres.

Londoner ['lʌndənər] *n* Londonien *m*, -ienne *f*.

lone [ləʊn] *adj* solitaire.

loneliness ['ləʊnlɪnɪs] *n* [of person] solitude *f*; [of place] isolement *m*.

lonely ['ləʊnlɪ] *adj* [person] solitaire, seul(e). || [childhood] solitaire. || [place] isolé(e).

loner ['ləʊnər] *n* solitaire *mf*.

lonesome ['ləʊnsəm] *adj Am inf* [person] solitaire, seul(e). || [place] isolé(e).

long [lɒŋ] **1** *adj* long (longue); **two days/years ~** de deux jours/ans, qui dure deux jours/ans; **10 metres/miles ~** long de 10 mètres/miles, de 10 mètres/miles (de long). **2** *adv* longtemps; **how ~ will it take?** combien de temps cela va-t-il prendre?; **how ~ will you be?** tu en as pour combien de temps?; **I can't wait any ~er** je ne peux pas attendre plus longtemps; **so ~!** *inf* au revoir!, salut!;

before ~ sous peu. **3** *vt*: **to ~ to do sthg** avoir très envie de faire qqch. ○ **as long as, so long as** *conj* tant que. ○ **long for** *vt fus* [peace and quiet] désirer ardemment; [holidays] attendre avec impatience.

long-distance call *n* communication *f* interurbaine.

longhand ['lɒŋhænd] *n* écriture *f* normale.

long-haul *adj* long-courrier.

longing ['lɒŋɪŋ] *n* [desire] envie *f*, convoitise *f*; **a ~ for** un grand désir OR une grande envie de. || [nostalgia] nostalgie *f*, regret *m*.

longitude ['lɒndʒɪtjuːd] *n* longitude *f*.

long jump *n* saut *m* en longueur.

long-life *adj* [milk] longue conservation (*inv*); [battery] longue durée (*inv*).

long-range *adj* [missile, bomber] à longue portée. || [plan, forecast] à long terme.

long shot *n* [guess] coup *m* à tenter (*sans grand espoir de succès*).

longsighted [,lɒŋ'saɪtɪd] *adj* presbyte.

long-standing *adj* de longue date.

longsuffering [,lɒŋ'sʌfərɪŋ] *adj* [person] à la patience infinie.

long term *n*: **in the ~** à long terme.

long wave *n* (*U*) grandes ondes *fpl*.

longwinded [,lɒŋ'wɪndɪd] *adj* [person] prolixe, verbeux(euse); [speech] interminable, qui n'en finit pas.

look [lʊk] **1** *n* [with eyes] regard *m*; **to take** OR **have a ~ (at sthg)** regarder (qqch), jeter un coup d'œil (à qqch); **to give sb a ~** jeter un regard à qqn, regarder qqn de travers. || [search]: **to have a ~ (for sthg)** chercher (qqch). || [appearance] aspect *m*, air *m*; **by the ~** OR **~s of it, by the ~** OR **~s of things** vraisemblablement, selon toute probabilité. **2** *vi* [with eyes] regarder. || [search] chercher. || [building, window]: **to ~ (out) onto** donner sur. || [seem] avoir l'air, sembler; **it ~s like rain** OR **as if it will rain** on dirait qu'il va pleuvoir; **she ~s like her mother** elle ressemble à sa mère. ○ **looks** *npl* [attractiveness] beauté *f*. ○ **look after** *vt fus* s'occuper de. ○ **look at** *vt fus* [see, glance at] regarder; [examine] examiner. || [judge] considérer. ○ **look down on** *vt fus* [condescend to] mépriser. ○ **look for** *vt fus* chercher. ○ **look forward to** *vt fus* attendre avec impatience. ○ **look into** *vt fus* examiner, étudier. ○ **look out** *vi* prendre garde, faire at-

tention; **~ out!** attention! ○ **look out for** *vt fus* [person] guetter; [new book] être à l'affût de, essayer de repérer. ○ **look round 1** *vt fus* [house, shop, town] faire le tour de. **2** *vi* [turn] se retourner. || [browse] regarder. ○ **look up 1** *vt sep* [in book] chercher. || [visit - person] aller or passer voir. **2** *vi* [improve - business] reprendre; **things are ~ing up** ça va mieux, la situation s'améliore. ○ **look up to** *vt fus* admirer.

lookout ['lʊkaʊt] *n* [place] poste *m* de guet. || [person] guetteur *m*. || [search]: **to be on the ~ for** être à la recherche de.

loom [luːm] **1** *n* métier *m* à tisser. **2** *vi* [building, person] se dresser; *fig* [date, threat] être imminent(e). ○ **loom up** *vi* surgir.

loony ['luːnɪ] *inf* **1** *adj* cinglé(e), timbré(e). **2** *n* cinglé *m*, -e *f*, fou *m*, folle *f*.

loop [luːp] *n* [gen & COMPUT] boucle *f*. || [contraceptive] stérilet *m*.

loophole ['luːphəʊl] *n* faille *f*, échappatoire *f*.

loose [luːs] *adj* [not firm - joint] desserré(e); [- handle, post] branlant(e); [- tooth] qui bouge OR branle; [- knot] défait(e). || [unpackaged - sweets, nails] en vrac, au poids. || [clothes] ample, large. || [not restrained - hair] dénoué(e); [- animal] en liberté, détaché(e). || *pej* & *dated* [woman] facile; [living] dissolu(e). || [inexact - translation] approximatif(ive).

loose change *n* petite OR menue monnaie *f*.

loose end *n*: **to be at a ~** *Br*, **to be at ~s** *Am* être désœuvré, n'avoir rien à faire.

loosely ['luːslɪ] *adv* [not firmly] sans serrer. || [inexactly] approximativement.

loosen ['luːsn] *vt* desserrer, défaire. ○ **loosen up** *vi* [before game, race] s'échauffer. || *inf* [relax] se détendre.

loot [luːt] **1** *n* butin *m*. **2** *vt* piller.

looting ['luːtɪŋ] *n* pillage *m*.

lop [lɒp] *vt* élaguer, émonder. ○ **lop off** *vt sep* couper.

lop-sided [-'saɪdɪd] *adj* [table] bancal(e), boiteux(euse); [picture] de travers.

lord [lɔːd] *n* seigneur *m*. ○ **Lord** *n* RELIG: **the Lord** [God] le Seigneur. || [in titles] Lord *m*; [as form of address]: **my Lord** Monsieur le duc/comte *etc*.

Lordship ['lɔːdʃɪp] *n*: **your/his ~** Monsieur le duc/comte *etc*.

lore [lɔːr] *n* (*U*) traditions *fpl*.

lose [luːz] (*pt & pp* **lost**) **1** *vt* [gen] perdre; **to ~ sight of** *lit & fig* perdre de vue; **to ~ one's way** se perdre, perdre son chemin. || [subj: clock, watch] retarder de; **to ~ time** retarder. || [pursuers] semer. **2** *vi* perdre. ○ **lose out** *vi* être perdant(e).

loser ['luːzər] *n* [gen] perdant *m*, -e *f*. || *inf pej* [unsuccessful person] raté *m*, -e *f*.

loss [lɒs] *n* [gen] perte *f*. || *phr:* **to be at a ~** être perplexe, être embarrassé(e).

lost [lɒst] **1** *pt & pp* → **lose**. **2** *adj* [gen] perdu(e); **to get ~** se perdre; **get ~!** *inf* fous/foutez le camp!

lost-and-found office *n Am* bureau *m* des objets trouvés.

lot [lɒt] *n* [large amount]: **a ~ (of)**, **~s (of)** beaucoup (de); [entire amount]: **the ~** le tout. || [at auction] lot *m*. || [destiny] sort *m*. || *Am* [of land] terrain *m*; [car park] parking *m*. || *phr:* **to draw ~s** tirer au sort. ○ **a lot** *adv* beaucoup.

lotion ['ləʊʃn] *n* lotion *f*.

lottery ['lɒtərɪ] *n lit & fig* loterie *f*.

loud [laʊd] **1** *adj* [not quiet, noisy - gen] fort(e); [- person] bruyant(e). || [colour, clothes] voyant(e). **2** *adv* fort; **out ~** tout haut.

loudly ['laʊdlɪ] *adv* [noisily] fort. || [gaudily] de façon voyante.

loudspeaker [,laʊd'spiːkər] *n* haut-parleur *m*.

lounge [laʊndʒ] **1** *n* [in house] salon *m*. || [in airport] hall *m*, salle *f*. **2** *vi* se prélasser.

louse [laʊs] (*pl sense 1* **lice**, *pl sense 2* **-s**) *n* [insect] pou *m*. || *inf pej* [person] salaud *m*.

lousy ['laʊzɪ] *adj inf* minable, nul(le); [weather] pourri(e).

lout [laʊt] *n* rustre *m*.

louvre *Br*, **louver** *Am* ['luːvər] *n* persienne *f*.

lovable ['lʌvəbl] *adj* adorable.

love [lʌv] **1** *n* [gen] amour *m*; **to be in ~** être amoureux(euse); **to fall in ~** tomber amoureux(euse); **to make ~** faire l'amour; **give her my ~** embrasse-la pour moi; **~ from** [at end of letter] affectueusement, grosses bises. || *inf* [form of address] mon chéri (ma chérie). || TENNIS zéro *m*. **2** *vt* aimer; **to ~ to do sthg** OR **doing sthg** aimer OR adorer faire qqch.

love affair *n* liaison *f*.

love life *n* vie *f* amoureuse.

lovely ['lʌvlɪ] *adj* [beautiful] très joli(e). || [pleasant] très agréable, excellent(e).

lover ['lʌvər] *n* [sexual partner] amant *m*, -e *f*. || [enthusiast] passionné *m*, -e *f*, amoureux *m*, -euse *f*.

loving ['lʌvɪŋ] *adj* [person, relationship] affectueux(euse); [care] tendre.

low [ləʊ] **1** *adj* [not high - gen] bas (basse); [- wall, building] peu élevé(e); [- standard, quality] mauvais(e); [- intelligence] faible; [- neckline] décolleté(e). || [little remaining] presque épuisé(e). || [not loud - voice] bas (basse); [- whisper, moan] faible. || [depressed] déprimé(e). **2** *adv* [not high] bas. || [not loudly - speak] à voix basse; [- whisper] faiblement. **3** *n* [low point] niveau *m* OR point *m* bas. || METEOR dépression *f*.

low-calorie *adj* à basses calories.

low-cut *adj* décolleté(e).

lower ['ləʊər] **1** *adj* inférieur(e). **2** *vt* [gen] baisser; [flag] abaisser. || [reduce - price, level] baisser; [- age of consent] abaisser; [- resistance] diminuer.

low-fat *adj* [yoghurt, crisps] allégé(e); [milk] demi-écrémé(e).

low-key *adj* discret(ète).

lowly ['ləʊlɪ] *adj* modeste, humble.

low-lying *adj* bas (basse).

loyal ['lɔɪəl] *adj* loyal(e).

loyalty ['lɔɪəltɪ] *n* loyauté *f*.

lozenge ['lɒzɪndʒ] *n* [tablet] pastille *f*. || [shape] losange *m*.

LP (*abbr of* **long-playing record**) *n* 33 tours *m*.

Ltd, ltd (*abbr of* **limited**) ≃ SARL; **Smith and Sons, ~** ≃ Smith & Fils, SARL.

lubricant ['luːbrɪkənt] *n* lubrifiant *m*.

lubricate ['luːbrɪkeɪt] *vt* lubrifier.

lucid ['luːsɪd] *adj* lucide.

luck [lʌk] *n* chance *f*; **good ~ chance**; **good ~!** bonne chance!; **bad ~** malchance *f*; **bad** OR **hard ~!** pas de chance!; **to be in ~** avoir de la chance; **with (any) ~** avec un peu de chance.

luckily ['lʌkɪlɪ] *adv* heureusement.

lucky ['lʌkɪ] *adj* [fortunate - person] qui a de la chance; [- event] heureux(euse). || [bringing good luck] porte-bonheur (*inv*).

lucrative ['luːkrətɪv] *adj* lucratif(ive).

ludicrous ['luːdɪkrəs] *adj* ridicule.

lug [lʌg] *vt inf* traîner.

lukewarm ['luːkwɔːm] *adj lit & fig* tiède.

lull [lʌl] **1** *n:* **~ (in)** [storm] accalmie *f* (de); [fighting, conversation] arrêt *m* (de). **2** *vt:* **to ~ sb to sleep** endormir qqn en le berçant; **to ~ sb into a false sense of security** endormir les soupçons de qqn.

lullaby ['lʌləbaɪ] *n* berceuse *f*.

lumber ['lʌmbər] *n* (*U*) *Am* [timber] bois *m* de charpente.

lumberjack ['lʌmbədʒæk] *n* bûcheron *m*, -onne *f*.

luminous ['luːmɪnəs] *adj* [dial] lumineux(euse); [paint, armband] phosphorescent(e).

lump [lʌmp] **1** *n* [gen] morceau *m*; [of earth, clay] motte *f*; [in sauce] grumeau *m*. ‖ [on body] grosseur *f*. **2** *vt*: **to ~ sthg together** réunir qqch; **to ~ it** *inf* faire avec, s'en accommoder.

lump sum *n* somme *f* globale.

lunacy ['luːnəsɪ] *n* folie *f*.

lunar ['luːnər] *adj* lunaire.

lunatic ['luːnətɪk] **1** *adj pej* dément(e), démentiel(ielle). **2** *n pej* [fool] fou *m*, folle *f*. ‖ [insane person] fou *m*, folle *f*, aliéné *m*, -e *f*.

lunch [lʌntʃ] **1** *n* déjeuner *m*, **2** *vi* déjeuner.

luncheon meat *n* sorte de saucisson.

lunch hour *n* pause *f* de midi.

lunchtime ['lʌntʃtaɪm] *n* heure *f* du déjeuner.

lung [lʌŋ] *n* poumon *m*.

lunge [lʌndʒ] *vi* faire un brusque mouvement (du bras) en avant; **to ~ at sb** s'élancer sur qqn.

lurch [lɜːtʃ] **1** *n* [of person] écart *m* brusque; [of car] embardée *f*; **to leave sb in the ~** laisser qqn dans le pétrin. **2** *vi* [person] tituber; [car] faire une embardée.

lure [ljʊər] **1** *n* charme *m* trompeur. **2** *vt* attirer OR persuader par la ruse.

lurid ['ljʊərɪd] *adj* [outfit] aux couleurs criardes. ‖ [story, details] affreux(euse).

lurk [lɜːk] *vi* [person] se cacher, se dissimuler. ‖ [memory, danger, fear] subsister.

luscious ['lʌʃəs] *adj* [delicious] succulent(e). ‖ *fig* [woman] appétissant(e).

lush [lʌʃ] *adj* [luxuriant] luxuriant(e). ‖ [rich] luxueux(euse).

lust [lʌst] *n* [sexual desire] désir *m*. ‖ *fig*: **~ for sthg** soif *f* de qqch. ○ **lust after, lust for** *vt fus* [wealth, power etc] être assoiffé(e) de. ‖ [person] désirer.

Luxembourg ['lʌksəmbɜːg] *n* [country] Luxembourg *m*. ‖ [city] Luxembourg.

luxurious [lʌg'ʒʊərɪəs] *adj* [expensive] luxueux(euse). ‖ [pleasurable] voluptueux(euse).

luxury ['lʌkʃərɪ] **1** *n* luxe *m*. **2** *comp* de luxe.

LW (*abbr of* **long wave**) GO.

Lycra® ['laɪkrə] *n* Lycra® *m*.

lying ['laɪɪŋ] **1** *adj* [person] menteur(euse). **2** *n* (*U*) mensonges *mpl*.

lynch [lɪntʃ] *vt* lyncher.

lyrical ['lɪrɪkl] *adj* lyrique.

lyrics ['lɪrɪks] *npl* paroles *fpl*.

m[1] (*pl* **m's** OR **ms**), **M** (*pl* **M's** OR **Ms**) [em] *n* [letter] m *m inv*, M *m inv*.

m[2] (*abbr of* **metre**) m. ‖ (*abbr of* **million**) M. ‖ *abbr of* **mile**.

MA *n abbr of* **Master of Arts**.

macaroni [,mækə'rəʊnɪ] *n* (*U*) macaronis *mpl*.

mace [meɪs] *n* [ornamental rod] masse *f*. ‖ [spice] macis *m*.

machine [mə'ʃiːn] **1** *n lit & fig* machine *f*. **2** *vt* SEWING coudre à la machine. ‖ TECH usiner.

machinegun [mə'ʃiːngʌn] *n* mitrailleuse *f*.

machine language *n* COMPUT langage *m* machine.

machinery [mə'ʃiːnərɪ] *n* (*U*) machines *fpl*; *fig* mécanisme *m*.

macho ['mætʃəʊ] *adj* macho (*inv*).

mackerel ['mækrəl] (*pl inv* OR **-s**) *n* maquereau *m*.

mad [mæd] *adj* [insane] fou (folle); **to go ~** devenir fou. ‖ [foolish] insensé(e). ‖ [furious] furieux(ieuse). ‖ [hectic - rush, pace] fou (folle). ‖ [very enthusiastic]: **to be ~ about sb/sthg** être fou (folle) de qqn/qqch.

Madagascar [,mædə'gæskər] *n* Madagascar *m*.

madam ['mædəm] *n* madame *f*.

madcap ['mædkæp] *adj* risqué(e), insensé(e).

madden ['mædn] *vt* exaspérer.

made [meɪd] *pt & pp* → **make**.

made-to-measure *adj* fait(e) sur mesure.

made-up *adj* [with make-up] maquillé(e). || [invented] fabriqué(e).

madly ['mædlɪ] *adv* [frantically] comme un fou; ~ **in love** follement amoureux.

madman ['mædmən] (*pl* **-men** [-mən]) *n* fou *m*.

madness ['mædnɪs] *n lit* & *fig* folie *f*, démence *f*.

Madrid [mə'drɪd] *n* Madrid.

Mafia ['mæfɪə] *n*: **the ~** la Mafia.

magazine [,mægə'ziːn] *n* PRESS revue *f*, magazine *m*; RADIO & TV magazine. || [of gun] magasin *m*.

maggot ['mægət] *n* ver *m*, asticot *m*.

magic ['mædʒɪk] **1** *adj* magique. **2** *n* magie *f*.

magical ['mædʒɪkl] *adj* magique.

magician [mə'dʒɪʃn] *n* magicien *m*.

magistrate ['mædʒɪstreɪt] *n* magistrat *m*, juge *m*.

magnanimous [mæg'nænɪməs] *adj* magnanime.

magnate ['mægneɪt] *n* magnat *m*.

magnesium [mæg'niːzɪəm] *n* magnésium *m*.

magnet ['mægnɪt] *n* aimant *m*.

magnetic [mæg'netɪk] *adj lit* & *fig* magnétique.

magnetic tape *n* bande *f* magnétique.

magnificent [mæg'nɪfɪsənt] *adj* magnifique, superbe.

magnify ['mægnɪfaɪ] *vt* [in vision] grossir; [sound] amplifier; *fig* exagérer.

magnifying glass ['mægnɪfaɪɪŋ-] *n* loupe *f*.

magnitude ['mægnɪtjuːd] *n* envergure *f*, ampleur *f*.

magpie ['mægpaɪ] *n* pie *f*.

mahogany [mə'hɒgənɪ] *n* acajou *m*.

maid [meɪd] *n* [servant] domestique *f*.

maiden ['meɪdn] **1** *adj* [flight, voyage] premier(ière). **2** *n literary* jeune fille *f*.

maiden aunt *n* tante *f* célibataire.

maiden name *n* nom *m* de jeune fille.

mail [meɪl] **1** *n* [letters, parcels] courrier *m*. || [system] poste *f*. **2** *vt* poster.

mailbox ['meɪlbɒks] *n Am* boîte *f* à OR aux lettres.

mailing list ['meɪlɪŋ-] *n* liste *f* d'adresses.

mailman ['meɪlmən] (*pl* **-men** [-mən]) *n Am* facteur *m*.

mail order *n* vente *f* par correspondance.

mailshot ['meɪlʃɒt] *n* publipostage *m*.

maim [meɪm] *vt* estropier.

main [meɪn] **1** *adj* principal(e). **2** *n* [pipe] conduite *f*. ○ **mains** *npl*: **the ~s** le secteur. ○ **in the main** *adv* dans l'ensemble.

main course *n* plat *m* principal.

mainframe (computer) ['meɪnfreɪm-] *n* ordinateur *m* central.

mainland ['meɪnlənd] **1** *adj* continental(e). **2** *n*: **the ~** le continent.

mainly ['meɪnlɪ] *adv* principalement.

main road *n* route *f* à grande circulation.

mainstay ['meɪnsteɪ] *n* pilier *m*, élément *m* principal.

mainstream ['meɪnstriːm] **1** *adj* dominant(e). **2** *n*: **the ~** la tendance générale.

maintain [meɪn'teɪn] *vt* [preserve, keep constant] maintenir. || [provide for, look after] entretenir. || [assert]: **to ~ (that)** ... maintenir que ..., soutenir que ....

maintenance ['meɪntənəns] *n* [of public order] maintien *m*. || [care] entretien *m*, maintenance *f*. || JUR pension *f* alimentaire.

maize [meɪz] *n* maïs *m*.

majestic [mə'dʒestɪk] *adj* majestueux(euse).

majesty ['mædʒəstɪ] *n* [grandeur] majesté *f*. ○ **Majesty** *n*: **His/Her Majesty** Sa Majesté le roi/la reine.

major ['meɪdʒə'] **1** *adj* [important] majeur(e). || [main] principal(e). || MUS majeur(e). **2** *n* [in army] ≃ chef *m* de bataillon; [in air force] commandant *m*. || UNIV [subject] matière *f*.

Majorca [mə'dʒɔːkə, mə'jɔːkə] *n* Majorque *f*.

majority [mə'dʒɒrətɪ] *n* majorité *f*; **in a** OR **the ~** dans la majorité.

make [meɪk] (*pt* & *pp* **made**) **1** *vt* [generally - produce] faire; [- manufacture] faire, fabriquer; **to ~ a meal** préparer un repas; **to ~ a film** tourner OR réaliser un film. || [perform an action] faire; **to ~ a decision** prendre une décision; **to ~ a mistake** faire une erreur, se tromper. || [cause to be] rendre; **to ~ sb happy/sad** rendre qqn heureux/triste. || [force, cause to do]: **to ~ sb do sthg** faire faire qqch à qqn, obliger qqn à faire qqch; **to ~ sb laugh** faire rire qqn. || [be constructed]: **to be made of** être en. || [add up to] faire; **2 and 2 ~ 4** 2 et 2 font 4. || [calculate]: **I ~ it 50** d'après moi il y en a 50, j'en ai compté 50; **what time do you ~ it?** quelle heure as-tu? || [earn] gagner, se faire; **to ~ a profit** faire des bénéfices; **to ~ a loss** essuyer des pertes. || [reach] arriver à. || [gain - friend, enemy] se faire; **to ~ friends (with sb)** se lier d'amitié (avec qqn). || *phr:* **to ~ it** [reach in time] arriver à temps; [be a success] réussir, arriver; [be able to attend] se libérer, pouvoir venir; **to ~ do with** se contenter de. **2** *n* [brand] marque *f*. ○ **make for** *vt fus* [move towards] se diriger vers. || [contribute to, be conducive to] rendre probable, favoriser. ○ **make of** *vt sep* [understand] comprendre. || [have opinion of] penser de. ○ **make out** **1** *vt sep* [see, hear] discerner; [understand] comprendre. || [fill out - cheque] libeller; [- bill, receipt] faire. **2** *vt fus* [pretend, claim]: **to ~ out (that)** .... prétendre que .... ○ **make up** **1** *vt sep* [compose, constitute] composer, constituer. || [story, excuse] inventer. || [apply cosmetics to] maquiller. || [prepare - gen] faire; [- prescription] préparer, exécuter. || [make complete] compléter. **2** *vi* [become friends again] se réconcilier. ○ **make up for** *vt fus* compenser. ○ **make up to** *vt sep:* **to ~ it up to sb (for sthg)** se racheter auprès de qqn (pour qqch).

make-believe *n:* **it's all ~** c'est (de la) pure fantaisie.

maker ['meɪkəʳ] *n* [of product] fabricant *m*, -e *f*; [of film] réalisateur *m*, -trice *f*.

makeshift ['meɪkʃɪft] *adj* de fortune.

make-up *n* [cosmetics] maquillage *m*; **~ remover** démaquillant *m*. || [person's character] caractère *m*. || [of team, group, object] constitution *f*.

making ['meɪkɪŋ] *n* fabrication *f*; **his problems are of his own ~** ses problèmes sont de sa faute; **in the ~** en formation; **to have the ~s of** avoir l'étoffe de.

malaria [mə'leərɪə] *n* malaria *f*.

Malaysia [mə'leɪzɪə] *n* Malaysia *f*.

male [meɪl] **1** *adj* [gen] mâle; [sex] masculin(e). **2** *n* mâle *m*.

male nurse *n* infirmier *m*.

malevolent [mə'levələnt] *adj* malveillant(e).

malfunction [mæl'fʌŋkʃn] **1** *n* mauvais fonctionnement *m*. **2** *vi* mal fonctionner.

malice ['mælɪs] *n* méchanceté *f*.

malicious [mə'lɪʃəs] *adj* malveillant(e).

malign [mə'laɪn] **1** *adj* pernicieux (ieuse). **2** *vt* calomnier.

malignant [mə'lɪgnənt] *adj* MED malin(igne).

mall [mɔːl] *n:* **(shopping) ~** centre *m* commercial.

mallet ['mælɪt] *n* maillet *m*.

malnutrition [ˌmælnjuːˈtrɪʃn] *n* malnutrition *f*.

malpractice [ˌmælˈpræktɪs] *n* (U) JUR faute *f* professionnelle.

malt [mɔːlt] *n* malt *m*.

mammal ['mæml] *n* mammifère *m*.

mammoth ['mæməθ] **1** *adj* gigantesque. **2** *n* mammouth *m*.

man [mæn] (*pl* **men** [men]) **1** *n* homme *m*; **the ~ in the street** l'homme de la rue. || [as form of address] mon vieux. **2** *vt* [ship, spaceship] fournir du personnel pour; [telephone] répondre au; [switchboard] assurer le service de.

manage ['mænɪdʒ] **1** *vi* [cope] se débrouiller, y arriver. || [survive, get by] s'en sortir. **2** *vt* [succeed]: **to ~ to do sthg** arriver à faire qqch. || [be responsible for, control] gérer.

manageable ['mænɪdʒəbl] *adj* maniable.

management ['mænɪdʒmənt] *n* [control, running] gestion *f*. || [people in control] direction *f*.

manager ['mænɪdʒəʳ] *n* [of organization] directeur *m*, -trice *f*; [of shop, restaurant, hotel] gérant *m*, -e *f*; [of football team, pop star] manager *m*.

managerial [ˌmænɪˈdʒɪərɪəl] *adj* directorial(e).

managing director ['mænɪdʒɪŋ-] *n* directeur général *m*, directrice générale *f*.

mandarin ['mændərɪn] *n* [fruit] mandarine *f*.

mandate ['mændeɪt] *n* mandat *m*.

mandatory ['mændətrɪ] *adj* obligatoire.

mane [meɪn] *n* crinière *f*.

maneuver *Am* = **manoeuvre**.

manfully ['mænfʊlɪ] *adv* courageusement, vaillamment.

mangle ['mæŋgl] *vt* mutiler, déchirer.

mango ['mæŋgəʊ] (*pl* **-es** OR **-s**) *n* mangue *f*.

mangy ['meɪndʒɪ] *adj* galeux(euse).

manhandle ['mæn,hændl] *vt* malmener.

manhole ['mænhəʊl] *n* regard *m*, trou *m* d'homme.

manhood ['mænhʊd] *n:* **to reach ~** devenir un homme.

mania ['meɪnjə] *n:* **~ (for)** manie *f* (de).

maniac ['meɪnɪæk] *n* fou *m*, folle *f*; **a sex ~** un obsédé sexuel (une obsédée sexuelle).

manic ['mænɪk] *adj fig* [person] surexcité(e); [behaviour] de fou.

manicure ['mænɪ,kjʊər] n manucure f.

manifesto [,mænɪ'festəʊ] (pl -s OR -es) n manifeste m.

manipulate [mə'nɪpjʊleɪt] vt lit & fig manipuler.

manipulative [mə'nɪpjʊlətɪv] adj [person] rusé(e); [behaviour] habile, subtil(e).

mankind [mæn'kaɪnd] n humanité f, genre m humain.

manly ['mænlɪ] adj viril(e).

man-made adj [fabric, fibre] synthétique; [environment] artificiel(ielle); [problem] causé (causée) par l'homme.

manner ['mænər] n [method] manière f, façon f. || [attitude] attitude f, comportement m. ○ **manners** npl manières fpl.

mannerism ['mænərɪzm] n tic m, manie f.

manoeuvre Br, **maneuver** Am [mə'nuːvər] 1 n manœuvre f. 2 vt & vi manœuvrer.

manor ['mænər] n manoir m.

manpower ['mæn,paʊər] n main-d'œuvre f.

mansion ['mænʃn] n château m.

manslaughter ['mæn,slɔːtər] n homicide m involontaire.

mantelpiece ['mæntlpiːs] n (dessus m de) cheminée f.

manual ['mænjʊəl] 1 adj manuel(elle). 2 n manuel m.

manual worker n travailleur manuel m, travailleuse manuelle f.

manufacture [,mænjʊ'fæktʃər] 1 n fabrication f; [of cars] construction f. 2 vt fabriquer; [cars] construire.

manufacturer [,mænjʊ'fæktʃərər] n fabricant m; [of cars] constructeur m.

manure [mə'njʊər] n fumier m.

manuscript ['mænjʊskrɪpt] n manuscrit m.

many ['menɪ] (compar **more**, superl **most**) 1 adj beaucoup de; **how ~ ...?** combien de ...?; **too ~** trop de; **as ~ ... as** autant de ... que; **so ~** autant de; **a good** OR **great ~** un grand nombre de. 2 pron [a lot, plenty] beaucoup.

map [mæp] n carte f. ○ **map out** vt sep [plan] élaborer; [timetable] établir; [task] définir.

maple ['meɪpl] n érable m.

mar [mɑːr] vt gâter, gâcher.

marathon ['mærəθn] n marathon m.

marble ['mɑːbl] n [stone] marbre m. || [for game] bille f.

march [mɑːtʃ] 1 n marche f. 2 vi [soldiers etc] marcher au pas. || [demonstrators] manifester, faire une marche de protestation. || [quickly]: **to ~ up to sb** s'approcher de qqn d'un pas décidé.

March [mɑːtʃ] n mars m; see also **September**.

marcher ['mɑːtʃər] n [protester] marcheur m, -euse f.

mare [meər] n jument f.

margarine [,mɑːdʒə'riːn] n margarine f.

margin ['mɑːdʒɪn] n [gen] marge f; **to win by a narrow ~** gagner de peu OR de justesse. || [edge - of an area] bord m.

marginal ['mɑːdʒɪnl] adj [unimportant] marginal(e), secondaire.

marginally ['mɑːdʒɪnəlɪ] adv très peu.

marigold ['mærɪgəʊld] n souci m.

marihuana, marijuana [,mærɪ'wɑːnə] n marihuana f.

marine [mə'riːn] 1 adj marin(e). 2 n marine m.

marital ['mærɪtl] adj [sex, happiness] conjugal(e); [problems] matrimonial(e).

marital status n situation f de famille.

maritime ['mærɪtaɪm] adj maritime.

mark [mɑːk] 1 n [stain] tache f, marque f. || [sign, written symbol] marque f. || [in exam] note f, point m. || [stage, level] barre f. || [currency] mark m. 2 vt [gen] marquer. || [stain] marquer, tacher. || [exam, essay] noter, corriger. ○ **mark off** vt sep [cross off] cocher.

marked [mɑːkt] adj [change, difference] marqué(e); [improvement, deterioration] sensible.

marker ['mɑːkər] n [sign] repère m.

marker pen n marqueur m.

market ['mɑːkɪt] 1 n marché m. 2 vt commercialiser.

market garden n jardin m maraîcher.

marketing ['mɑːkɪtɪŋ] n marketing m.

marketplace ['mɑːkɪtpleɪs] n [in a town] place f du marché. || COMM marché m.

market research n étude f de marché.

market value n valeur f marchande.

marking ['mɑːkɪŋ] n SCH correction f. ○ **markings** npl [on animal, flower] taches fpl, marques fpl; [on road] signalisation f horizontale.

marksman ['mɑːksmən] (pl -men [-mən]) n tireur m d'élite.

marmalade ['mɑːməleɪd] n confiture f d'oranges amères.

maroon [mə'ruːn] adj bordeaux (inv).

marooned [mə'ru:nd] *adj* abandonné(e).

marquee [mɑː'kiː] *n* grande tente *f*.

marriage ['mærɪdʒ] *n* mariage *m*.

marriage certificate *n* acte *m* de mariage.

marriage guidance *n* conseil *m* conjugal.

married ['mærɪd] *adj* [person] marié(e); **to get ~** se marier. || [life] conjugal(e).

marrow ['mærəʊ] *n* [in bones] moelle *f*.

marry ['mærɪ] **1** *vt* [become spouse of] épouser, se marier avec. || [subj: priest, registrar] marier. **2** *vi* se marier.

Mars [mɑːz] *n* [planet] Mars *f*.

marsh [mɑːʃ] *n* marais *m*, marécage *m*.

marshal ['mɑːʃl] **1** *n* MIL maréchal *m*. || [steward] membre *m* du service d'ordre. || *Am* [law officer] officier *m* de police fédérale. **2** *vt lit & fig* rassembler.

martial arts [,mɑː'ʃl-] *npl* arts *mpl* martiaux.

martial law [,mɑː'ʃl-] *n* loi *f* martiale.

martyr ['mɑːtər] *n* martyr *m*, -e *f*.

martyrdom ['mɑːtədəm] *n* martyre *m*.

marvel ['mɑːvl] **1** *n* merveille *f*. **2** *vi*: **to ~ (at)** s'émerveiller (de), s'étonner (de).

marvellous *Br*, **marvelous** *Am* ['mɑːvələs] *adj* merveilleux(euse).

Marxism ['mɑːksɪzm] *n* marxisme *m*.

Marxist ['mɑːksɪst] **1** *adj* marxiste. **2** *n* marxiste *mf*.

marzipan ['mɑːzɪpæn] *n* (*U*) pâte *f* d'amandes.

mascara [mæs'kɑːrə] *n* mascara *m*.

masculine ['mæskjʊlɪn] *adj* masculin(e).

mash [mæʃ] *vt* faire une purée de.

mashed potatoes [mæʃt-] *npl* purée *f* de pommes de terre.

mask [mɑːsk] *lit & fig* **1** *n* masque *m*. **2** *vt* masquer.

masochist ['mæsəkɪst] *n* masochiste *mf*.

mason ['meɪsn] *n* [stonemason] maçon *m*. || [freemason] franc-maçon *m*.

masonry ['meɪsnrɪ] *n* [stones] maçonnerie *f*.

masquerade [,mæskə'reɪd] *vi*: **to ~ as** se faire passer pour.

mass [mæs] **1** *n* [gen & PHYSICS] masse *f*. **2** *adj* [protest, meeting] en masse, en nombre; [unemployment, support] massif(ive). **3** *vi* se masser. ○ **Mass** *n* RELIG messe *f*. ○ **masses** *npl inf* [lots]: **~es (of)** des masses (de); [food] des tonnes (de). || [workers]: **the ~es** les masses *fpl*.

massacre ['mæsəkər] **1** *n* massacre *m*. **2** *vt* massacrer.

massage [*Br* 'mæsɑːʒ, *Am* mə'sɑːʒ] **1** *n* massage *m*. **2** *vt* masser.

massive ['mæsɪv] *adj* massif(ive), énorme.

mass media *n or npl*: **the ~** les (mass) media *mpl*.

mast [mɑːst] *n* [on boat] mât *m*. || RADIO & TV pylône *m*.

master ['mɑːstər] **1** *n* [gen] maître *m*. **2** *adj* maître. **3** *vt* maîtriser; [difficulty] surmonter, vaincre; [situation] se rendre maître de.

master key *n* passe *m*, passe-partout *m inv*.

masterly ['mɑːstəlɪ] *adj* magistral(e).

mastermind ['mɑːstəmaɪnd] **1** *n* cerveau *m*. **2** *vt* organiser, diriger.

Master of Arts (*pl* **Masters of Arts**) *n* [degree] maîtrise *f* ès lettres. || [person] titulaire *mf* d'une maîtrise ès lettres.

Master of Science (*pl* **Masters of Science**) *n* [degree] maîtrise *f* ès sciences. || [person] titulaire *mf* d'une maîtrise ès sciences.

masterpiece ['mɑːstəpiːs] *n* chef-d'œuvre *m*.

master's degree *n* ≃ maîtrise *f*.

mastery ['mɑːstərɪ] *n* maîtrise *f*.

mat [mæt] *n* [on floor] petit tapis *m*; [at door] paillasson *m*. || [on table] set *m* de table; [coaster] dessous *m* de verre.

match [mætʃ] **1** *n* [game] match *m*. || [for lighting] allumette *f*. || [equal]: **to be no ~ for sb** ne pas être de taille à lutter contre qqn. **2** *vt* [be the same as] correspondre à, s'accorder avec. || [pair off] faire correspondre. || [be equal with] égaler, rivaliser avec. **3** *vi* [be the same] correspondre. || [go together well] être assorti(e).

matchbox ['mætʃbɒks] *n* boîte *f* à allumettes.

matching ['mætʃɪŋ] *adj* assorti(e).

mate [meɪt] **1** *n inf* [friend] copain *m*, copine *f*, pote *m*. || [of female animal] mâle *m*; [of male animal] femelle *f*. || NAUT: (first) ~ second *m*. **2** *vi* s'accoupler.

material [mə'tɪərɪəl] **1** *adj* [goods, benefits, world] matériel(ielle). || [important] important(e), essentiel(ielle). **2** *n* [substance] matière *f*, substance *f*; [type of substance] matériau *m*, matière. || [fabric] tissu *m*, étoffe *f*; [type of fabric] tissu. || (*U*) [information - for book, article etc] matériaux *mpl*. ○ **materials** *npl* matériaux *mpl*.

materialistic [mə,tɪərɪə'lɪstɪk] *adj* matérialiste.

materialize, -ise [mə'tɪərɪəlaɪz] *vi* [offer, threat] se concrétiser, se réaliser. ‖ [person, object] apparaître.

maternal [mə'tɜːnl] *adj* maternel(elle).

maternity [mə'tɜːnətɪ] *n* maternité *f*.

maternity hospital *n* maternité *f*.

math *Am* = **maths**.

mathematical [,mæθə'mætɪkl] *adj* mathématique.

mathematics [,mæθə'mætɪks] *n* (*U*) mathématiques *fpl*.

maths *Br* [mæθs], **math** *Am* [mæθ] (*abbr of* **mathematics**) *inf n* (*U*) maths *fpl*.

matinée ['mætɪneɪ] *n* matinée *f*.

mating season ['meɪtɪŋ-] *n* saison *f* des amours.

matrices ['meɪtrɪsiːz] *pl* → **matrix**.

matriculation [mə,trɪkjʊ'leɪʃn] *n* inscription *f*.

matrimony ['mætrɪmənɪ] *n* (*U*) mariage *m*.

matrix ['meɪtrɪks] (*pl* **matrices** OR **-es**) *n* [context, framework] contexte *m*, structure *f*. ‖ MATH & TECH matrice *f*.

matron ['meɪtrən] *n* [in school] infirmière *f*.

matt *Br*, **matte** *Am* [mæt] *adj* mat(e).

matted ['mætɪd] *adj* emmêlé(e).

matter ['mætər] **1** *n* [question, situation] question *f*, affaire *f*; **that's another** OR **a different ~** c'est tout autre chose, c'est une autre histoire; **as a ~ of course** automatiquement; **to make ~s worse** aggraver la situation; **and to make ~ worse ...** pour tout arranger ...; **that's a ~ of opinion** c'est (une) affaire OR question d'opinion. ‖ [trouble, cause of pain] **there's something the ~ with my radio** il y a quelque chose qui cloche OR ne va pas dans ma radio; **what's the ~?** qu'est-ce qu'il y a?; **what's the ~ with him?** qu'est-ce qu'il a? ‖ PHYSICS matière *f*. ‖ (*U*) [material] matière *f*; **reading ~** choses *fpl* à lire. **2** *vi* [be important] importer, avoir de l'importance; **it doesn't ~** cela n'a pas d'importance. ○ **as a matter of fact** *adv* en fait, à vrai dire. ○ **for that matter** *adv* d'ailleurs. ○ **no matter** *adv*: **no ~ what** coûte que coûte, à tout prix; **no ~ how hard I try to explain ...** j'ai beau essayer de lui expliquer ....

Matterhorn ['mætəhɔːn] *n*: **the ~** le mont Cervin.

matter-of-fact *adj* terre-à-terre, neutre.

mattress ['mætrɪs] *n* matelas *m*.

mature [mə'tjʊər] **1** *adj* [person, attitude] mûr(e). ‖ [cheese] fait(e); [wine] arrivé(e) à maturité. **2** *vi* [person] mûrir. ‖ [cheese, wine] se faire.

maul [mɔːl] *vt* mutiler.

mauve [məʊv] **1** *adj* mauve. **2** *n* mauve *m*.

max. [mæks] (*abbr of* **maximum**) max.

maxim ['mæksɪm] (*pl* **-s**) *n* maxime *f*.

maximum ['mæksɪməm] (*pl* **maxima** ['mæksɪmə] OR **-s**) **1** *adj* maximum (*inv*). **2** *n* maximum *m*.

may [meɪ] *modal vb* [expressing possibility]: **it ~ rain** il se peut qu'il pleuve, il va peut-être pleuvoir; **be that as it ~** quoi qu'il en soit. ‖ [can] pouvoir; **on a clear day the coast ~ be seen** on peut voir la côte par temps clair. ‖ [asking permission]: **~ I come in?** puis-je entrer? ‖ [as contrast]: **it ~ be expensive, but ...** c'est peut-être cher, mais .... ‖ *fml* [expressing wish, hope]: **~ they be happy!** qu'ils soient heureux!; *see also* **might**.

May [meɪ] *n* mai *m*; *see also* **September**.

maybe ['meɪbiː] *adv* peut-être.

May Day *n* le Premier mai.

mayhem ['meɪhem] *n* pagaille *f*.

mayonnaise [,meɪə'neɪz] *n* mayonnaise *f*.

mayor [meər] *n* maire *m*.

mayoress ['meərɪs] *n* [female mayor] femme *f* maire. ‖ [mayor's wife] femme *f* du maire.

maze [meɪz] *n lit & fig* labyrinthe *m*, dédale *m*.

MB (*abbr of* **megabyte**) Mo.

MD *n abbr of* **managing director**.

me [miː] *pers pron* [direct, indirect] me, m' (*+ vowel or silent "h"*); **can you see/hear ~?** tu me vois/m'entends?; **it's ~** c'est moi; **they spoke to ~** ils m'ont parlé; **she gave it to ~** elle me l'a donné. ‖ [stressed, after prep, in comparisons etc] moi; **you can't expect ME to do it** tu ne peux pas exiger que ce soit moi qui le fasse; **she's shorter than ~** elle est plus petite que moi.

meadow ['medəʊ] *n* prairie *f*, pré *m*.

meagre *Br*, **meager** *Am* ['miːgər] *adj* maigre.

meal [miːl] *n* repas *m*.

meet

mealtime ['mi:ltaɪm] *n* heure *f* du repas.

mean [mi:n] (*pt & pp* meant) **1** *rt* [signify] signifier, vouloir dire; **money ~s nothing to him** l'argent ne compte pas pour lui. || [intend]: **to ~ to do sthg** vouloir faire qqch, avoir l'intention de faire qqch; **I didn't ~ to drop it** je n'ai pas fait exprès de le laisser tomber; **to be meant for sb/sthg** être destiné(e) à qqn/qqch; **to be meant to do sthg** être censé(e) faire qqch; **to ~ well** agir dans une bonne intention. || [be serious about]: **I ~ it** je suis sérieux(ieuse). || [entail] occasionner, entraîner. || *phr*: **I ~** [as explanation] c'est vrai; [as correction] je veux dire. **2** *adj* [miserly] radin(e), chiche; **to be ~ with sthg** être avare de qqch. || [unkind] mesquin(e), méchant(e); **to be ~ to sb** être mesquin envers qqn. || [average] moyen(enne). **3** *n* [average] moyenne *f*; *see also* **means**.

meander [mɪ'ændər] *ri* [river, road] serpenter; [person] errer.

meaning ['mi:nɪŋ] *n* sens *m*, signification *f*.

meaningful ['mi:nɪŋful] *adj* [look] significatif(ive); [relationship, discussion] important(e).

meaningless ['mi:nɪŋlɪs] *adj* [gesture, word] dénué(e) OR vide de sens; [proposal, discussion] sans importance.

means [mi:nz] **1** *n* [method, way] moyen *m*; **by ~ of** au moyen de. **2** *npl* [money] moyens *mpl*, ressources *fpl*. ○ **by all means** *adr* mais certainement, bien sûr. ○ **by no means** *adr fml* nullement, en aucune façon.

meant [ment] *pt & pp* → **mean**.

meantime ['mi:n,taɪm] *n*: **in the ~** en attendant.

meanwhile ['mi:n,waɪl] *adr* [at the same time] pendant ce temps. || [between two events] en attendant.

measles ['mi:zlz] *n*: **(the) ~** la rougeole.

measly ['mi:zlɪ] *adj inf* misérable, minable.

measure ['meʒər] **1** *n* [gen] mesure *f*. || [indication]: **it is a ~ of her success that ...** la preuve de son succès, c'est que .... **2** *rt & ri* mesurer.

measurement ['meʒəmənt] *n* mesure *f*.

meat [mi:t] *n* viande *f*.

meatball ['mi:tbɔ:l] *n* boulette *f* de viande.

meaty ['mi:tɪ] *adj fig* important(e).

Mecca ['mekə] *n* La Mecque.

mechanic [mɪ'kænɪk] *n* mécanicien *m*, -ienne *f*.

mechanical [mɪ'kænɪkl] *adj* [device] mécanique. || [routine, automatic] machinal(e).

mechanism ['mekənɪzm] *n lit & fig* mécanisme *m*.

medal ['medl] *n* médaille *f*.

medallion [mɪ'dæljən] *n* médaillon *m*.

meddle ['medl] *ri*: **to ~ in** se mêler de.

media ['mi:djə] **1** *pl* → **medium**. **2** *n or npl*: **the ~** les médias *mpl*.

mediaeval [,medɪ'i:vl] = **medieval**.

median ['mi:djən] *n Am* [of road] bande *f* médiane (*qui sépare les deux côtés d'une grande route*).

mediate ['mi:dɪeɪt] *ri*: **to ~ (for/between)** servir de médiateur (pour/entre).

mediator ['mi:dɪeɪtər] *n* médiateur *m*, -trice *f*.

Medicaid ['medɪkeɪd] *n Am assistance médicale aux personnes sans ressources*.

medical ['medɪkl] **1** *adj* médical(e). **2** *n* examen *m* médical.

Medicare ['medɪkeər] *n Am programme fédéral d'assistance médicale pour personnes âgées*.

medicated ['medɪkeɪtɪd] *adj* traitant(e).

medicine ['medsɪn] *n* [subject, treatment] médecine *f*. || [substance] médicament *m*.

medieval [,medɪ'i:vl] *adj* médiéval(e).

mediocre [,mi:dɪ'əʊkər] *adj* médiocre.

meditate ['medɪteɪt] *ri*: **to ~ (on OR upon)** méditer (sur).

Mediterranean [,medɪtə'reɪnjən] **1** *n* [sea]: **the ~ (Sea)** la (mer) Méditerranée. **2** *adj* méditerranéen(enne).

medium ['mi:djəm] (*pl sense 1* media, *pl sense 2* mediums) **1** *adj* moyen (enne). **2** *n* [way of communicating] moyen *m*. || [spiritualist] médium *m*.

medium-size(d) [-saɪz(d)] *adj* de taille moyenne.

medium wave *n* onde *f* moyenne.

medley ['medlɪ] (*pl* medleys) *n* [mixture] mélange *m*. || MUS pot-pourri *m*.

meek [mi:k] *adj* docile.

meet [mi:t] (*pt & pp* met) **1** *rt* [gen] rencontrer; [by arrangement] retrouver. || [go to meet - person] aller/venir attendre, aller/venir chercher; [- train, plane] aller attendre. || [need, requirement] satisfaire, répondre à. || [problem] résoudre; [challenge] répondre à. || [costs] payer. || [join]

rejoindre. 2 *vi* [gen] se rencontrer; [by arrangement] se retrouver; [for a purpose] se réunir. ‖ [join] se joindre. 3 *n Am* [meeting] meeting *m*. ○ **meet up** *vi* se retrouver; **to ~ up with sb** rencontrer qqn, retrouver qqn. ○ **meet with** *vt fus* [encounter - disapproval] être accueilli(e) par; [- success] remporter; [- failure] essuyer. ‖ *Am* [by arrangement] retrouver.

meeting ['mi:tɪŋ] *n* [for discussions, business] réunion *f*. ‖ [by chance] rencontre *f*; [by arrangement] entrevue *f*.

megabyte ['megəbaɪt] *n* COMPUT mégaoctet *m*.

megaphone ['megəfəun] *n* mégaphone *m*, porte-voix *m inv*.

melancholy ['melənkəlɪ] 1 *adj* [person] mélancolique; [news, facts] triste. 2 *n* mélancolie *f*.

mellow ['meləu] 1 *adj* [light, voice] doux (douce); [taste, wine] moelleux(euse). 2 *vi* s'adoucir.

melody ['melədɪ] *n* mélodie *f*.

melon ['melən] *n* melon *m*.

melt [melt] 1 *vt* faire fondre. 2 *vi* [become liquid] fondre. ‖ *fig*: **his heart ~ed at the sight** il fut tout attendri devant ce spectacle. ○ **melt down** *vt sep* fondre.

melting pot ['meltɪŋ-] *n fig* creuset *m*.

member ['membər] *n* membre *m*; [of club] adhérent *m*, -e *f*.

Member of Congress (*pl* **Members of Congress**) *n Am* membre *m* du Congrès.

Member of Parliament (*pl* **Members of Parliament**) *n Br* ≃ député *m*.

membership ['membəʃɪp] *n* [of organization] adhésion *f*. ‖ [number of members] nombre *m* d'adhérents. ‖ [members]: **the ~** les membres *mpl*.

membership card *n* carte *f* d'adhésion.

memento [mɪ'mentəu] (*pl* -s) *n* souvenir *m*.

memo ['meməu] (*pl* -s) *n* note *f* de service.

memoirs ['memwɑ:z] *npl* mémoires *mpl*.

memorial [mɪ'mɔ:rɪəl] 1 *adj* commémoratif(ive). 2 *n* monument *m*.

memorize, -ise ['meməraɪz] *vt* [phone number, list] retenir; [poem] apprendre par cœur.

memory ['memərɪ] *n* [gen & COMPUT] mémoire *f*; **from ~** de mémoire. ‖ [event, experience] souvenir *m*.

men [men] *pl* → **man.**

menace ['menəs] 1 *n* [gen] menace *f*. ‖ *inf* [nuisance] plaie *f*. 2 *vt* menacer.

menacing ['menəsɪŋ] *adj* menaçant(e).

mend [mend] *vt* réparer; [clothes] raccommoder; [sock, pullover] repriser.

menial ['mi:njəl] *adj* avilissant(e).

meningitis [,menɪn'dʒaɪtɪs] *n* (*U*) méningite *f*.

menopause ['menəpɔ:z] *n*: **the ~** la ménopause.

men's room *n Am*: **the ~** les toilettes *fpl* pour hommes.

menstruation [,menstru'eɪʃn] *n* menstruation *f*.

menswear ['menzweər] *n* (*U*) vêtements *mpl* pour hommes.

mental ['mentl] *adj* mental(e); [image, picture] dans la tête.

mental hospital *n* hôpital *m* psychiatrique.

mentality [men'tælətɪ] *n* mentalité *f*.

mentally handicapped ['mentlɪ-] *npl*: **the ~** les handicapés *mpl* mentaux.

mention ['menʃn] 1 *vt* mentionner, signaler; **not to ~** sans parler de; **don't ~ it!** je vous en prie! 2 *n* mention *f*.

menu ['menju:] *n* [gen & COMPUT] menu *m*.

meow *Am* = **miaow.**

MEP (*abbr of* **Member of the European Parliament**) *n* parlementaire *m* européen.

mercenary ['mɜ:sɪnrɪ] 1 *adj* mercenaire. 2 *n* mercenaire *m*.

merchandise ['mɜ:tʃəndaɪz] *n* (*U*) marchandises *fpl*.

merchant ['mɜ:tʃənt] *n* marchand *m*, -e *f*, commerçant *m*, -e *f*.

merchant navy *Br*, **merchant marine** *Am n* marine *f* marchande.

merciful ['mɜ:sɪful] *adj* [person] clément(e). ‖ [death, release] qui est une délivrance.

merciless ['mɜ:sɪlɪs] *adj* impitoyable.

mercury ['mɜ:kjurɪ] *n* mercure *m*.

Mercury ['mɜ:kjurɪ] *n* [planet] Mercure *f*.

mercy ['mɜ:sɪ] *n* [kindness, pity] pitié *f*; **at the ~ of** *fig* à la merci de.

mere [mɪər] *adj* seul(e); **she's a ~ child** ce n'est qu'une enfant.

merely ['mɪəlɪ] *adv* seulement, simplement.

merge [mɜ:dʒ] 1 *vt* COMM & COMPUT fusionner. 2 *vi* COMM: **to ~ (with)** fusionner (avec). ‖ [roads, lines]: **to ~ (with)** se joindre (à). ‖ [colours] se fondre.

midge

merger ['mɜːdʒər] n fusion f.

meringue [mə'ræŋ] n meringue f.

merit ['merɪt] 1 n [value] mérite m, valeur f. 2 vt mériter. ○ **merits** npl [advantages] qualités fpl.

mermaid ['mɜːmeɪd] n sirène f.

merry ['merɪ] adj literary [happy] joyeux(euse); **Merry Christmas!** joyeux Noël! ‖ inf [tipsy] gai(e), éméché(e).

merry-go-round n manège m.

mesh [meʃ] 1 n [net] maille f (du filet); **wire ~** grillage m. 2 vi [gears] s'engrener.

mesmerize, -ise ['mezməraɪz] vt: **to be ~d by** être fasciné(e) par.

mess [mes] n [untidy state] désordre m; fig gâchis m. ‖ MIL mess m. ○ **mess about, mess around** inf 1 vt sep: **to ~ sb about** traiter qqn par-dessus OR par-dessous la jambe. 2 vi [fool around] perdre OR gaspiller son temps. ‖ [interfere]: **to ~ about with sthg** s'immiscer dans qqch. ○ **mess up** vt sep inf [room] mettre en désordre; [clothes] salir. ‖ fig [spoil] gâcher.

message ['mesɪdʒ] n message m.

messenger ['mesɪndʒər] n messager m, -ère f.

messy ['mesɪ] adj [dirty] sale; [untidy] désordonné(e); **a ~ job** un travail salissant. ‖ inf [divorce] difficile; [situation] embrouillé(e).

met [met] pt & pp → **meet**.

metal ['metl] n métal m.

metallic [mɪ'tælɪk] adj [sound, ore] métallique. ‖ [paint, finish] métallisé(e).

metalwork ['metəlwɜːk] n [craft] ferronnerie f.

metaphor ['metəfər] n métaphore f.

mete [miːt] ○ **mete out** vt sep [punishment] infliger.

meteor ['miːtɪər] n météore m.

meteorology [miːtjə'rɒlədʒɪ] n météorologie f.

meter ['miːtər] 1 n [device] compteur m. ‖ Am = metre. 2 vt [gas, electricity] établir la consommation de.

method ['meθəd] n méthode f.

methodical [mɪ'θɒdɪkl] adj méthodique.

Methodist ['meθədɪst] 1 adj méthodiste. 2 n méthodiste mf.

methylated spirits ['meθɪleɪtɪd-] n alcool m à brûler.

meticulous [mɪ'tɪkjʊləs] adj méticuleux(euse).

metre Br, **meter** Am ['miːtər] n mètre m.

metric ['metrɪk] adj métrique.

metronome ['metrənəʊm] n métronome m.

metropolitan [,metrə'pɒlɪtn] adj métropolitain(e).

mettle ['metl] n: **to be on one's ~** être d'attaque; **to show** OR **prove one's ~** montrer ce dont on est capable.

mew [mjuː] = miaow.

Mexican ['meksɪkn] 1 adj mexicain(e). 2 n Mexicain m, -e f.

Mexico ['meksɪkəʊ] n Mexique m.

miaow Br [miː'aʊ], **meow** Am [mɪ'aʊ] 1 n miaulement m, miaou m. 2 vi miauler.

mice [maɪs] pl → **mouse**.

microchip ['maɪkrəʊtʃɪp] n COMPUT puce f.

microcomputer [,maɪkrəʊkəm'pjuːtər] n micro-ordinateur m.

microfilm ['maɪkrəʊfɪlm] n microfilm m.

microphone ['maɪkrəfəʊn] n microphone m, micro m.

microscope ['maɪkrəskəʊp] n microscope m.

microscopic [,maɪkrə'skɒpɪk] adj microscopique.

microwave (oven) ['maɪkrəweɪv-] n (four m à) micro-ondes m.

mid- [mɪd] prefix: **~height** mi-hauteur; **~morning** milieu de la matinée; **~winter** plein hiver.

midair [mɪd'eər] 1 adj en plein ciel. 2 n: **in ~** en plein ciel.

midday [,mɪd'deɪ] n midi m.

middle ['mɪdl] 1 adj [centre] du milieu, du centre. 2 n [centre] milieu m, centre m; **in the ~ (of)** au milieu (de). ‖ [in time] milieu m; **to be in the ~ of doing sthg** être en train de faire qqch; **to be in the ~ of a meeting** être en pleine réunion; **in the ~ of the night** au milieu de la nuit, en pleine nuit. ‖ [waist] taille f.

middle-aged adj d'une cinquantaine d'années.

Middle Ages npl: **the ~** le Moyen Âge.

middle-class adj bourgeois(e).

middle classes npl: **the ~** la bourgeoisie.

Middle East n: **the ~** le Moyen-Orient.

middleman ['mɪdlmæn] (pl -men [-mən]) n intermédiaire mf.

middle name n second prénom m.

middling ['mɪdlɪŋ] adj moyen(enne).

Mideast [,mɪd'iːst] n Am: **the ~** le Moyen-Orient.

midge [mɪdʒ] n moucheron m.

midget ['mɪdʒɪt] *n* nain *m*, -e *f*.

midi system ['mɪdɪ-] *n* chaîne *f* midi.

midnight ['mɪdnaɪt] *n* minuit *m*.

midriff ['mɪdrɪf] *n* diaphragme *m*.

midst [mɪdst] *n* [in space]: **in the ~ of** au milieu de. || [in time]: **to be in the ~ of doing sthg** être en train de faire qqch.

midsummer ['mɪd'sʌmər] *n* cœur *m* de l'été.

Midsummer Day *n* la Saint-Jean.

midway [,mɪd'weɪ] *adv* [in space]: **~ (between)** à mi-chemin (entre). || [in time]: **~ through the meeting** en pleine réunion.

midweek [*adj* 'mɪdwi:k, *adv* mɪd'wi:k] **1** *adj* du milieu de la semaine. **2** *adv* en milieu de semaine.

midwife ['mɪdwaɪf] (*pl* **-wives** [-waɪvz]) *n* sage-femme *f*.

might [maɪt] **1** *modal vb* [expressing possibility]: **the criminal ~ be armed** il est possible que le criminel soit armé. || [expressing suggestion]: **it ~ be better to wait** il vaut peut-être mieux attendre. || *fml* [asking permission]: **he asked if he ~ leave the room** il demanda s'il pouvait sortir de la pièce. || [expressing concession]: **you ~ well be right** vous avez peut-être raison. || *phr*: **I ~ have known** OR **guessed** j'aurais dû m'en douter. **2** *n* (*U*) force *f*.

mighty ['maɪtɪ] **1** *adj* [powerful] puissant(e). **2** *adv Am inf* drôlement, vachement.

migraine ['mi:greɪn, 'maɪgreɪn] *n* migraine *f*.

migrant ['maɪgrənt] **1** *adj* [bird, animal] migrateur(trice). || [workers] émigré(e). **2** *n* [bird, animal] migrateur *m*. || [person] émigré *m*, -e *f*.

migrate [*Br* maɪ'greɪt, *Am* 'maɪgreɪt] *vi* [bird, animal] migrer. || [person] émigrer.

mike [maɪk] (*abbr of* **microphone**) *n inf* micro *m*.

mild [maɪld] *adj* [disinfectant, reproach] léger(ère). || [tone, weather]. doux (douce). || [illness] bénin(igne).

mildew ['mɪldju:] *n* (*U*) moisissure *f*.

mildly ['maɪldlɪ] *adv* [gently] doucement; **to put it ~** le moins qu'on puisse dire. || [not strongly] légèrement. || [slightly] un peu.

mile [maɪl] *n* mile *m*; NAUT mille *m*; **to be ~s away** *fig* être très loin.

mileage ['maɪlɪdʒ] *n* distance *f* en miles, ≃ kilométrage *m*.

mileometer [maɪ'lɒmɪtər] *n* compteur *m* de miles, ≃ compteur kilométrique.

milestone ['maɪlstəʊn] *n* [marker stone] borne *f*; *fig* événement *m* marquant OR important.

militant ['mɪlɪtənt] **1** *adj* militant(e). **2** *n* militant *m*, -e *f*.

military ['mɪlɪtrɪ] **1** *adj* militaire. **2** *n*: **the ~** les militaires *mpl*, l'armée *f*.

militia [mɪ'lɪʃə] *n* milice *f*.

milk [mɪlk] **1** *n* lait *m*. **2** *vt* [cow] traire.

milk chocolate *n* chocolat *m* au lait.

milkman ['mɪlkmən] (*pl* **-men** [-mən]) *n* laitier *m*.

milk shake *n* milk-shake *m*.

milky ['mɪlkɪ] *adj* [pale white] laiteux(euse).

Milky Way *n*: **the ~** la Voie lactée.

mill [mɪl] **1** *n* [flour-mill, grinder] moulin *m*. || [factory] usine *f*. **2** *vt* moudre. ○ **mill about, mill around** *vi* grouiller.

millennium [mɪ'lenɪəm] (*pl* **-nnia** [-nɪə]) *n* millénaire *m*.

miller ['mɪlər] *n* meunier *m*.

milligram(me) ['mɪlɪgræm] *n* milligramme *m*.

millimetre *Br*, **millimeter** *Am* ['mɪlɪ,mi:tər] *n* millimètre *m*.

millinery ['mɪlɪnrɪ] *n* chapellerie *f* féminine.

million ['mɪljən] *n* million *m*; **a ~, ~s** *fig* des milliers de, un million de.

millionaire [,mɪljə'neər] *n* millionnaire *mf*.

millstone ['mɪlstəʊn] *n* meule *f*.

milometer [maɪ'lɒmɪtər] = **mileometer**.

mime [maɪm] **1** *n* mime *m*. **2** *vt & vi* mimer.

mimic ['mɪmɪk] (*pt & pp* **-ked**, *cont* **-king**) **1** *n* imitateur *m*, -trice *f*. **2** *vt* imiter.

mimicry ['mɪmɪkrɪ] *n* imitation *f*.

min. [mɪn] (*abbr of* **minute**) mn, min. || (*abbr of* **minimum**) min.

mince [mɪns] **1** *n* [meat] hacher. **2** *vi* marcher à petits pas maniérés.

mincemeat ['mɪnsmi:t] *n* [fruit] mélange de pommes, raisins secs et épices utilisé en pâtisserie. || *Am* [meat] viande *f* hachée.

mince pie *n* tartelette *f* de Noël.

mincer ['mɪnsər] *n* hachoir *m*.

mind [maɪnd] **1** *n* [gen] esprit *m*; **to bear sthg in ~** ne pas oublier qqch; **to come into/cross sb's ~** venir à/traverser l'esprit de qqn; **to have sthg on one's ~** avoir l'esprit préoccupé, être préoccupé par qqch; **to keep an open ~** réserver son jugement; **to have a ~ to do sthg** avoir bien envie de faire qqch; **to have sthg in ~** avoir qqch dans l'idée; **to make one's ~ up** se décider. ‖ [attention]: **to put one's ~ to sthg** s'appliquer à qqch; **to keep one's ~ on sthg** se concentrer sur qqch. ‖ [opinion]: **to change one's ~** changer d'avis; **to my ~** à mon avis; **to speak one's ~** parler franchement; **to be in two ~s (about sthg)** se tâter OR être indécis (à propos de qqch). ‖ [person] cerveau m. 2 vi [be bothered]: **I don't ~** ça m'est égal; **I hope you don't ~** j'espère que vous n'y voyez pas d'inconvénient; **never ~** [don't worry] ne t'en fais pas; [it's not important] ça ne fait rien. 3 vt [be bothered about, dislike]: **I don't ~ waiting** ça ne me gêne OR dérange pas d'attendre; **do you ~ if ...?** cela ne vous ennuie pas si ...?; **I wouldn't ~ a beer** je prendrais bien une bière. ‖ [pay attention to] faire attention à, prendre garde à. ‖ [take care of - luggage] garder, surveiller; [- shop] tenir. ○ **mind you** adv remarquez.

mindful ['maɪndfʊl] adj: **~ of** [risks] attentif(ive) à; [responsibility] soucieux (ieuse) de.

mindless ['maɪndlɪs] adj stupide, idiot(e).

mine[1] [maɪn] poss pron le mien (la mienne), les miens (les miennes) (pl); **that money is ~** cet argent est à moi; **it wasn't your fault, it was MINE** ce n'était pas de votre faute, c'était de la mienne OR de ma faute à moi; **a friend of ~** un ami à moi, un de mes amis.

mine[2] [maɪn] 1 n mine f. 2 vt [coal, gold] extraire. ‖ [road, beach, sea] miner.

minefield ['maɪnfiːld] n champ m de mines; fig situation f explosive.

miner ['maɪnər] n mineur m.

mineral ['mɪnərəl] 1 adj minéral(e). 2 n minéral m.

mineral water n eau f minérale.

mingle ['mɪŋgl] vi: **to ~ (with)** [sounds, fragrances] se mélanger (à); [people] se mêler (à).

miniature ['mɪnətʃər] 1 adj miniature. 2 n [painting] miniature f. ‖ [of alcohol] bouteille f miniature. ‖ [small scale]: **in ~** en miniature.

minibus ['mɪnɪbʌs] (pl -es) n minibus m.

minima ['mɪnɪmə] pl → minimum.

minimal ['mɪnɪml] adj [cost] insignifiant(e); [damage] minime.

minimum ['mɪnɪməm] (pl -mums OR -ma) 1 adj minimum (inv). 2 n minimum m.

mining ['maɪnɪŋ] 1 n exploitation f minière. 2 adj minier(ière).

miniskirt ['mɪnɪskɜːt] n minijupe f.

minister ['mɪnɪstər] n POL ministre m. ‖ RELIG pasteur m.

ministerial [ˌmɪnɪ'stɪərɪəl] adj ministériel(ielle).

minister of state n secrétaire mf d'État.

ministry ['mɪnɪstrɪ] n POL ministère m. ‖ RELIG: **the ~** le saint ministère.

mink [mɪŋk] (pl inv) n vison m.

minor ['maɪnər] 1 adj [gen & MUS] mineur(e); [detail] petit(e); [role] secondaire. 2 n mineur m, -e f.

minority [maɪ'nɒrətɪ] n minorité f.

mint [mɪnt] 1 n [herb] menthe f. ‖ [sweet] bonbon m à la menthe. ‖ [for coins]: **the Mint** l'hôtel de la Monnaie; **in ~ condition** en parfait état. 2 vt [coins] battre.

minus ['maɪnəs] (pl -es) 1 prep moins. 2 adj [answer, quantity] négatif(ive). 3 n [disadvantage] handicap m.

minus sign n signe m moins.

minute[1] ['mɪnɪt] n minute f; **at any ~** à tout moment, d'une minute à l'autre; **stop that this ~!** arrête tout de suite OR immédiatement! ○ **minutes** npl procès-verbal m, compte m rendu.

minute[2] [maɪ'njuːt] adj minuscule.

miracle ['mɪrəkl] n miracle m.

miraculous [mɪ'rækjʊləs] adj miraculeux(euse).

mirage [mɪ'rɑːʒ] n lit & fig mirage m.

mirror ['mɪrər] 1 n miroir m, glace f. 2 vt refléter.

mirth [mɜːθ] n hilarité f, gaieté f.

misadventure [ˌmɪsəd'ventʃər] n: **death by ~** JUR mort f accidentelle.

misapprehension ['mɪsˌæprɪ'henʃn] n idée f fausse.

misappropriation ['mɪsəˌprəʊprɪ'eɪʃn] n détournement m.

misbehave [ˌmɪsbɪ'heɪv] vi se conduire mal.

miscalculate [ˌmɪs'kælkjʊleɪt] 1 vt mal calculer. 2 vi se tromper.

miscarriage [ˌmɪs'kærɪdʒ] n MED fausse couche f; **to have a ~** faire une fausse couche.

miscellaneous [,mɪsə'leɪnjəs] *adj* varié(e), divers(e).

mischief ['mɪstʃɪf] *n* (U) [playfulness] malice *f*, espièglerie *f*. || [naughty behaviour] sottises *fpl*, bêtises *fpl*. || [harm] dégât *m*.

mischievous ['mɪstʃɪvəs] *adj* [playful] malicieux(ieuse). || [naughty] espiègle, coquin(e).

misconduct [,mɪs'kɒndʌkt] *n* inconduite *f*.

misconstrue [,mɪskən'struː] *vt fml* mal interpréter.

miscount [,mɪs'kaʊnt] *vt* & *vi* mal compter.

misdeed [,mɪs'diːd] *n* méfait *m*.

misdemeanour *Br*, **misdemeanor** *Am* [,mɪsdɪ'miːnəʳ] *n* JUR délit *m*.

miser ['maɪzəʳ] *n* avare *mf*.

miserable ['mɪzrəbl] *adj* [person] malheureux(euse), triste. || [conditions, life] misérable. || [pay] dérisoire. || [weather] maussade. || [failure] pitoyable, lamentable.

miserly ['maɪzəlɪ] *adj* avare.

misery ['mɪzərɪ] *n* [of person] tristesse *f*. || [of conditions, life] misère *f*.

misfire [,mɪs'faɪəʳ] *vi* [gun, plan] rater.

misfit ['mɪsfɪt] *n* inadapté *m*, -e *f*.

misfortune [mɪs'fɔːtʃuːn] *n* [bad luck] malchance *f*. || [piece of bad luck] malheur *m*.

misgivings [mɪs'gɪvɪŋz] *npl* craintes *fpl*, doutes *mpl*.

misguided [,mɪs'gaɪdɪd] *adj* [person] malavisé(e); [attempt] malencontreux (euse); [opinion] peu judicieux(ieuse).

mishandle [,mɪs'hændl] *vt* [person, animal] manier sans précaution. || [negotiations] mal mener; [business] mal gérer.

mishap ['mɪshæp] *n* mésaventure *f*.

misinterpret [,mɪsɪn'tɜːprɪt] *vt* mal interpréter.

misjudge [,mɪs'dʒʌdʒ] *vt* [distance, time] mal évaluer. || [person, mood] méjuger, se méprendre sur.

mislay [,mɪs'leɪ] (*pt* & *pp* **-laid** [-'leɪd]) *vt* égarer.

mislead [,mɪs'liːd] (*pt* & *pp* **-led**) *vt* induire en erreur.

misleading [,mɪs'liːdɪŋ] *adj* trompeur(euse).

misled [,mɪs'led] *pt* & *pp* → **mislead**.

misnomer [,mɪs'nəʊməʳ] *n* nom *m* mal approprié.

misplace [,mɪs'pleɪs] *vt* égarer.

misprint ['mɪsprɪnt] *n* faute *f* d'impression.

miss [mɪs] **1** *vt* [gen] rater, manquer. || [home, person]: **I ~ my family/her** ma famille/elle me manque. || [avoid, escape] échapper à; **I just ~ed being run over** j'ai failli me faire écraser. **2** *vi* rater. **3** *n*: **to give sthg a ~ inf** ne pas aller à qqch. ○ **miss out 1** *vt sep* [- by mistake] oublier; [- deliberately] omettre. **2** *vi*: **to ~ out on sthg** ne pas pouvoir profiter de qqch.

Miss [mɪs] *n* Mademoiselle *f*.

misshapen [,mɪs'ʃeɪpn] *adj* difforme.

missile [*Br* 'mɪsaɪl, *Am* 'mɪsəl] *n* [weapon] missile *m*.

missing ['mɪsɪŋ] *adj* [lost] perdu(e), égaré(e). || [not present] manquant(e), qui manque.

mission ['mɪʃn] *n* mission *f*.

missionary ['mɪʃənrɪ] *n* missionnaire *mf*.

mist [mɪst] *n* brume *f*. ○ **mist over**, **mist up** *vi* s'embuer.

mistake [mɪ'steɪk] (*pt* **-took**, *pp* **-taken**) **1** *n* erreur *f*; **by ~** par erreur; **to make a ~** faire une erreur, se tromper. **2** *vt* [misunderstand - meaning] mal comprendre; [- intention] se méprendre sur. || [fail to recognize]: **to ~ sb/sthg for** prendre qqn/qqch pour, confondre qqn/qqch avec.

mistaken [mɪ'steɪkn] **1** *pp* → **mistake**. **2** *adj* [person]: **to be ~ (about)** se tromper (en ce qui concerne OR sur). || [belief, idea] erroné(e), faux (fausse).

mister ['mɪstəʳ] *n inf* monsieur *m*. ○ **Mister** *n* Monsieur *m*.

mistletoe ['mɪsltəʊ] *n* gui *m*.

mistook [mɪ'stʊk] *pt* → **mistake**.

mistreat [,mɪs'triːt] *vt* maltraiter.

mistress ['mɪstrɪs] *n* maîtresse *f*.

mistrust [,mɪs'trʌst] **1** *n* méfiance *f*. **2** *vt* se méfier de.

misty ['mɪstɪ] *adj* brumeux(euse).

misunderstand [,mɪsʌndə'stænd] (*pt* & *pp* **-stood**) *vt* & *vi* mal comprendre.

misunderstanding [,mɪsʌndə'stænd-ɪŋ] *n* malentendu *m*.

misunderstood [,mɪsʌndə'stʊd] *pt* & *pp* → **misunderstand**.

misuse [*n* ,mɪs'juːs, *vb* ,mɪs'juːz] **1** *n* [of one's time, resources] mauvais emploi *m*. || [of power] abus *m*; [of funds] détournement *m*. **2** *vt* [one's time, resources] mal employer. || [power] abuser de; [funds] détourner.

miter *Am* = mitre.

mitigate ['mɪtɪɡeɪt] *vt* atténuer, mitiger.

mitre *Br*, **miter** *Am* ['maɪtər] *n* [hat] mitre *f*. ‖ [joint] onglet *m*.

mitt [mɪt] *n* = **mitten**. ‖ [in baseball] gant *m*.

mitten ['mɪtn] *n* moufle *f*.

mix [mɪks] 1 *vt* [gen] mélanger. ‖ [activities]: **to ~ sthg with sthg** combiner OR associer qqch et qqch. ‖ [drink] préparer. 2 *vi* [gen] se mélanger. ‖ [socially]: **to ~ with** fréquenter. 3 *n* [gen] mélange *m*. ○ **mix up** *vt sep* [confuse] confondre. ‖ [disorganize] mélanger.

mixed [mɪkst] *adj* [assorted] assortis(ies). ‖ [education] mixte.

mixed grill *n* assortiment *m* de grillades.

mixed up *adj* [confused - person] qui ne sait plus où il en est, paumé(e); [- mind] embrouillé(e). ‖ [involved]: **to be ~ in sthg** être mêlé(e) à qqch.

mixer ['mɪksər] *n* [for food] mixer *m*.

mixture ['mɪkstʃər] *n* [gen] mélange *m*. ‖ MED préparation *f*.

mix-up *n inf* confusion *f*.

mm (*abbr of* **millimetre**) mm.

moan [məʊn] 1 *n* [of pain, sadness] gémissement *m*. 2 *vi* [in pain, sadness] gémir. ‖ *inf* [complain]: **to ~ (about)** rouspéter OR râler (à propos de).

moat [məʊt] *n* douves *fpl*.

mob [mɒb] 1 *n* foule *f*. 2 *vt* assaillir.

mobile ['məʊbaɪl] 1 *adj* [gen] mobile. ‖ [able to travel] motorisé(e). 2 *n* mobile *m*.

mobile home *n* auto-caravane *f*.

mobile phone *n* téléphone *m* portatif.

mobilize, -ise ['məʊbɪlaɪz] *vt & vi* mobiliser.

mock [mɒk] 1 *adj* faux (fausse); **~ exam** examen blanc. 2 *vt* se moquer de.

mockery ['mɒkərɪ] *n* moquerie *f*.

mode [məʊd] *n* mode *m*.

model ['mɒdl] 1 *n* [gen] modèle *m*. ‖ [fashion model] mannequin *m*. 2 *adj* [perfect] modèle. ‖ [reduced-scale] (en) modèle réduit. 3 *vt* [clay] modeler. ‖ [clothes]: **to ~ a dress** présenter un modèle de robe. ‖ [copy]: **to ~ o.s. on sb** prendre modèle OR exemple sur qqn, se modeler sur qqn. 4 *vi* être mannequin.

modem ['məʊdem] *n* COMPUT modem *m*.

moderate [*adj & n* 'mɒdərət, *vb* 'mɒdəreɪt] 1 *adj* modéré(e). 2 *vt* modérer.

moderation [ˌmɒdə'reɪʃn] *n* modération *f*; **in ~** avec modération.

modern ['mɒdən] *adj* moderne.

modernize, -ise ['mɒdənaɪz] 1 *vt* moderniser. 2 *vi* se moderniser.

modern languages *npl* langues *fpl* vivantes.

modest ['mɒdɪst] *adj* modeste.

modesty ['mɒdɪstɪ] *n* modestie *f*.

modify ['mɒdɪfaɪ] *vt* modifier.

module ['mɒdjuːl] *n* module *m*.

mogul ['məʊgl] *n fig* magnat *m*.

mohair ['məʊheər] *n* mohair *m*.

moist [mɔɪst] *adj* [soil, climate] humide; [cake] moelleux(euse).

moisten ['mɔɪsn] *vt* humecter.

moisture ['mɔɪstʃər] *n* humidité *f*.

moisturizer ['mɔɪstʃəraɪzər] *n* crème *f* hydratante, lait *m* hydratant.

molar ['məʊlər] *n* molaire *f*.

molasses [mə'læsɪz] *n* (*U*) mélasse *f*.

mold *etc Am* = **mould**.

mole [məʊl] *n* [animal, spy] taupe *f*. ‖ [on skin] grain *m* de beauté.

molecule ['mɒlɪkjuːl] *n* molécule *f*.

molest [mə'lest] *vt* [attack sexually] attenter à la pudeur de. ‖ [attack] molester.

molt *etc Am* = **moult**.

molten ['məʊltn] *adj* en fusion.

mom [mɒm] *n Am inf* maman *f*.

moment ['məʊmənt] *n* moment *m*, instant *m*; **at any ~** d'un moment à l'autre; **at the ~** en ce moment; **for the ~** pour le moment.

momentarily ['məʊməntərɪlɪ] *adv* [for a short time] momentanément. ‖ *Am* [soon] très bientôt.

momentary ['məʊməntrɪ] *adj* momentané(e), passager(ère).

momentous [mə'mentəs] *adj* capital(e), très important(e).

momentum [mə'mentəm] *n* (*U*) PHYSICS moment *m*. ‖ *fig* [speed, force] vitesse *f*; **to gather ~** prendre de la vitesse.

momma ['mɒmə], **mommy** ['mɒmɪ] *n Am* maman *f*.

Monaco ['mɒnəkəʊ] *n* Monaco.

monarch ['mɒnək] *n* monarque *m*.

monarchy ['mɒnəkɪ] *n* monarchie *f*.

monastery ['mɒnəstrɪ] *n* monastère *m*.

Monday ['mʌndɪ] *n* lundi *m*; *see also* **Saturday**.

monetary ['mʌnɪtrɪ] *adj* monétaire.

money ['mʌnɪ] *n* argent *m*; **to make ~** gagner de l'argent.

moneybox ['mʌnɪbɒks] *n* tirelire *f*.

moneylender ['mʌnɪ,lendər] *n* prêteur *m*, -euse *f* sur gages.

money order *n* mandat *m* postal.

money-spinner [-,spɪnər] *n inf* mine *f* d'or.

Mongolia [mɒŋ'gəʊlɪə] *n* Mongolie *f*.

mongrel ['mʌŋgrəl] *n* [dog] bâtard *m*.

monitor ['mɒnɪtər] **1** *n* COMPUT, MED & TV moniteur *m*. **2** *vt* [check] contrôler, suivre de près. ‖ [broadcasts, messages] être à l'écoute de.

monk [mʌŋk] *n* moine *m*.

monkey ['mʌŋkɪ] (*pl* **monkeys**) *n* singe *m*.

monkey wrench *n* clef *f* à molette.

mono ['mɒnəʊ] **1** *adj* mono (*inv*). **2** *n* [sound] monophonie *f*.

monochrome ['mɒnəkrəʊm] *adj* monochrome.

monocle ['mɒnəkl] *n* monocle *m*.

monologue, monolog *Am* ['mɒnəlɒg] *n* monologue *m*.

monopolize, -ise [mə'nɒpəlaɪz] *vt* monopoliser.

monopoly [mə'nɒpəlɪ] *n*: ~ **(on** OR **of)** monopole *m* (de).

monotone ['mɒnətəʊn] *n* ton *m* monocorde.

monotonous [mə'nɒtənəs] *adj* monotone.

monotony [mə'nɒtənɪ] *n* monotonie *f*.

monsoon [mɒn'suːn] *n* mousson *f*.

monster ['mɒnstər] *n* [creature, cruel person] monstre *m*. ‖ [huge thing, person] colosse *m*.

monstrosity [mɒn'strɒsətɪ] *n* monstruosité *f*.

monstrous ['mɒnstrəs] *adj* monstrueux(euse).

Mont Blanc [,mɔ̃'blɑ̃] *n* le mont Blanc.

month [mʌnθ] *n* mois *m*.

monthly ['mʌnθlɪ] **1** *adj* mensuel(elle). **2** *adv* mensuellement. **3** *n* [publication] mensuel *m*.

Montreal [,mɒntrɪ'ɔːl] *n* Montréal.

monument ['mɒnjʊmənt] *n* monument *m*.

monumental [,mɒnjʊ'mentl] *adj* monumental(e).

moo [muː] (*pl* **-s**) **1** *n* meuglement *m*, beuglement *m*. **2** *vi* meugler, beugler.

mood [muːd] *n* humeur *f*; **in a (bad)** ~ de mauvaise humeur; **in a good** ~ de bonne humeur.

moody ['muːdɪ] *adj pej* [changeable] lunatique. ‖ [bad-tempered] de mauvaise humeur, mal luné(e).

moon [muːn] *n* lune *f*.

moonlight ['muːnlaɪt] (*pt* & *pp* **-ed**) **1** *n* clair *m* de lune. **2** *vi* travailler au noir.

moonlighting ['muːnlaɪtɪŋ] *n* (*U*) travail *m* (au) noir.

moonlit ['muːnlɪt] *adj* [countryside] éclairé(e) par la lune; [night] de lune.

moor [mɔːr] **1** *n* lande *f*. **2** *vt* amarrer. **3** *vi* mouiller.

moorland ['mɔːlənd] *n* lande *f*.

moose [muːs] (*pl inv*) *n* [North American] orignal *m*.

mop [mɒp] **1** *n* [for cleaning] balai *m* à laver. ‖ *inf* [hair] tignasse *f*. **2** *vt* [floor] laver. ‖ [sweat] essuyer; **to** ~ **one's face** s'essuyer le visage. ○ **mop up** *vt sep* [clean up] éponger.

mope [məʊp] *vi* broyer du noir.

moped ['məʊped] *n* vélomoteur *m*.

moral ['mɒrəl] **1** *adj* moral(e). **2** *n* [lesson] morale *f*. ○ **morals** *npl* moralité *f*.

morale [mə'rɑːl] *n* (*U*) moral *m*.

morality [mə'rælətɪ] *n* moralité *f*.

morbid ['mɔːbɪd] *adj* morbide.

more [mɔːr] **1** *adv* (*with adjectives and adverbs*) plus; ~ **often/quickly (than)** plus souvent/rapidement (que). ‖ [to a greater degree] plus, davantage. ‖ [another time]: **once/twice** ~ une fois/deux fois de plus, encore une fois/deux fois. **2** *adj* [larger number, amount of] plus de, davantage de; **there are** ~ **trains in the morning** il y a plus de trains le matin; ~ **than 70 people died** plus de 70 personnes ont péri. ‖ [an extra amount of] encore (de); *I* **finished two** ~ **chapters today** j'ai fini deux autres OR encore deux chapitres aujourd'hui; **we need** ~ **money/time** il nous faut plus d'argent/ de temps, il nous faut davantage d'argent/de temps. **3** *pron* plus, davantage; ~ **than five** plus de cinq; **he's got** ~ **than I have** il en a plus que moi; **there's no** ~ **(left)** il n'y en a plus, il n'en reste plus; **(and) what's** ~ de plus, qui plus est. ○ **any more** *adv*: **not ... any** ~ ne ... plus. ○ **more and more 1** *adv* & *pron* de plus en plus. **2** *adj* de plus en plus de. ○ **more or less** *adv* [almost] plus ou moins. ‖ [approximately] environ, à peu près.

moreover [mɔː'rəʊvər] *adv* de plus.

morgue [mɔːg] *n* morgue *f*.

Mormon ['mɔːmən] *n* mormon *m*, -e *f*.

morning ['mɔːnɪŋ] *n* matin *m*; [duration] matinée *f*; **I'll do it tomorrow** ~ OR in the ~ je le ferai demain. ○ **mornings** *adv Am* le matin.

Moroccan [mə'rɒkən] **1** *adj* marocain(e). **2** *n* Marocain *m*, -e *f*.

Morocco [mə'rɒkəʊ] *n* Maroc *m*.

moron ['mɔːrɒn] *n inf* idiot *m*, -e *f*, crétin *m*, -e *f*.

morphine ['mɔːfiːn] *n* morphine *f*.

Morse (code) [mɔːs-] *n* morse *m*.

morsel ['mɔːsl] *n* bout *m*, morceau *m*.

mortal ['mɔːtl] **1** *adj* mortel(elle). **2** *n* mortel *m*, -elle *f*.

mortality [mɔː'tælətɪ] *n* mortalité *f*.

mortar ['mɔːtər] *n* mortier *m*.

mortgage ['mɔːgɪdʒ] **1** *n* emprunt-logement *m*. **2** *vt* hypothéquer.

mortified ['mɔːtɪfaɪd] *adj* mortifié(e).

mortuary ['mɔːtʃʊərɪ] *n* morgue *f*.

mosaic [mə'zeɪɪk] *n* mosaïque *f*.

Moscow ['mɒskəʊ] *n* Moscou *m*.

Moslem ['mɒzləm] = **Muslim**.

mosque [mɒsk] *n* mosquée *f*.

mosquito [mə'skiːtəʊ] (*pl* **-es** OR **-s**) *n* moustique *m*.

moss [mɒs] *n* mousse *f*.

most [məʊst] (*superl of* **many**) **1** *adj* [the majority of] la plupart de; **~ tourists here are German** la plupart des touristes ici sont allemands. ‖ [largest amount of]: **(the)** ~ le plus de; **she's got (the) ~ money/sweets** c'est elle qui a le plus d'argent/de bonbons. **2** *pron* [the majority] la plupart; **~ of the tourists here are German** la plupart des touristes ici sont allemands; **~ of them** la plupart d'entre eux. ‖ [largest amount]: **(the)** ~ le plus; **at ~ au** maximum, tout au plus. ‖ *phr*: **to make the ~ of sthg** profiter de qqch au maximum. **3** *adv* [to greatest extent]: **(the)** ~ le plus. ‖ *Am* [almost] presque.

mostly ['məʊstlɪ] *adv* principalement, surtout.

motel [məʊ'tel] *n* motel *m*.

moth [mɒθ] *n* papillon *m* de nuit; [in clothes] mite *f*.

mothball ['mɒθbɔːl] *n* boule *f* de naphtaline.

mother ['mʌðər] **1** *n* mère *f*. **2** *vt* [child] materner, dorloter.

motherhood ['mʌðəhʊd] *n* maternité *f*.

mother-in-law (*pl* **mothers-in-law** OR **mother-in-laws**) *n* belle-mère *f*.

motherly ['mʌðəlɪ] *adj* maternel(elle).

mother-of-pearl *n* nacre *f*.

mother-to-be (*pl* **mothers-to-be**) *n* future maman *f*.

mother tongue *n* langue *f* maternelle.

motif [məʊ'tiːf] *n* motif *m*.

motion ['məʊʃn] **1** *n* [gen] mouvement *m*; **to set sthg in** ~ mettre qqch en branle. ‖ [in debate] motion *f*. **2** *vt*: **to ~ sb to do sthg** faire signe à qqn de faire qqch. **3** *vi*: **to ~ to sb** faire signe à qqn.

motionless ['məʊʃənlɪs] *adj* immobile.

motion picture *n Am* film *m*.

motivated ['məʊtɪveɪtɪd] *adj* motivé(e).

motivation [,məʊtɪ'veɪʃn] *n* motivation *f*.

motive ['məʊtɪv] *n* motif *m*.

motor ['məʊtər] *n* [engine] moteur *m*.

motorbike ['məʊtəbaɪk] *n inf* moto *f*.

motorboat ['məʊtəbəʊt] *n* canot *m* automobile.

motorcycle ['məʊtə,saɪkl] *n* moto *f*.

motorcyclist ['məʊtə,saɪklɪst] *n* motocycliste *mf*.

motoring ['məʊtərɪŋ] *n* tourisme *m* automobile.

motorist ['məʊtərɪst] *n* automobiliste *mf*.

motor racing *n* (*U*) course *f* automobile.

motor scooter *n* scooter *m*.

motor vehicle *n* véhicule *m* automobile.

mottled ['mɒtld] *adj* [leaf] tacheté(e); [skin] marbré(e).

motto ['mɒtəʊ] (*pl* **-s** OR **-es**) *n* devise *f*.

mould, mold *Am* [məʊld] **1** *n* [growth] moisissure *f*. ‖ [shape] moule *m*. **2** *vt* [shape] mouler, modeler. ‖ *fig* [influence] former, façonner.

moulding, molding *Am* ['məʊldɪŋ] *n* [decoration] moulure *f*.

mouldy, moldy *Am* ['məʊldɪ] *adj* moisi(e).

moult, molt *Am* [məʊlt] *vi* muer.

mound [maʊnd] *n* [small hill] tertre *m*, butte *f*. ‖ [pile] tas *m*, monceau *m*.

mount [maʊnt] **1** *n* [support - for jewel] monture *f*; [- for photograph] carton *m* de montage; [- for machine] support *m*. ‖ [horse] monture *f*. ‖ [mountain] mont *m*. **2** *vt* monter; **to ~ a horse** monter sur un cheval; **to ~ a bike** monter sur OR enfourcher un vélo. **3** *vi* [increase] monter, augmenter. ‖ [climb on horse] se mettre en selle.

mountain ['maʊntɪn] *n lit & fig* montagne *f*.

mountain bike *n* VTT *m*.

mountaineer [,maʊntɪ'nɪəʳ] n alpiniste mf.

mountaineering [,maʊntɪ'nɪərɪŋ] n alpinisme m.

mountainous ['maʊntɪnəs] adj [region] montagneux(euse).

mourn [mɔ:n] 1 vt pleurer. 2 vi: to ~ (for sb) pleurer (qqn).

mourner ['mɔ:nəʳ] n [related] parent m du défunt; [unrelated] ami m, -e f du défunt.

mournful ['mɔ:nfʊl] adj [face] triste; [sound] lugubre.

mourning ['mɔ:nɪŋ] n deuil m; in ~ en deuil.

mouse [maʊs] (pl mice) n COMPUT & ZOOL souris f.

mousetrap ['maʊstræp] n souricière f.

mousse [mu:s] n mousse f.

moustache Br [mə'stɑ:ʃ], **mustache** Am ['mʌstæʃ] n moustache f.

mouth [maʊθ] n [of person, animal] bouche f; [of dog, cat, lion] gueule f. || [of cave] entrée f; [of river] embouchure f.

mouthful ['maʊθfʊl] n [of food] bouchée f; [of drink] gorgée f.

mouthorgan ['maʊθ,ɔ:gən] n harmonica m.

mouthpiece ['maʊθpi:s] n [of telephone] microphone m; [of musical instrument] bec m. || [spokesperson] porte-parole m inv.

mouthwash ['maʊθwɒʃ] n eau f dentifrice.

mouth-watering [-,wɔ:tərɪŋ] adj alléchant(e).

movable ['mu:vəbl] adj mobile.

move [mu:v] 1 n [movement] mouvement m; to get a ~ on inf se remuer, se grouiller. || [change - of house] déménagement m; [- of job] changement m d'emploi. || [in game - action] coup m; [- turn to play] tour m; fig démarche f. 2 vt [shift] déplacer, bouger. || [change - job, office] changer de; to ~ house déménager. || [cause]: to ~ sb to do sthg inciter qqn à faire qqch. || [emotionally] émouvoir. || [propose]: to ~ sthg/that ... proposer qqch/que .... 3 vi [shift] bouger. || [act] agir. || [to new house] déménager; [to new job] changer d'emploi. ○ **move about** vi [fidget] remuer. || [travel] voyager. ○ **move along** vi se déplacer; the police asked him to ~ along la police lui a demandé de circuler. ○ **move around** = move about. ○ **move away** vi [leave] partir. ○ **move in** vi [to house]

emménager. ○ **move on** vi [after stopping] se remettre en route. || [in discussion] changer de sujet. ○ **move out** vi [from house] déménager. ○ **move over** vi s'écarter, se pousser. ○ **move up** vi [on bench etc] se déplacer.

moveable ['mu:vəbl] = movable.

movement ['mu:vmənt] n mouvement m.

movie ['mu:vɪ] n film m.

movie camera n caméra f.

moving ['mu:vɪŋ] adj [emotionally] émouvant(e), touchant(e). || [not fixed] mobile.

mow [məʊ] (pt -ed, pp -ed OR mown) vt faucher; [lawn] tondre. ○ **mow down** vt sep faucher.

mower ['məʊəʳ] n tondeuse f à gazon.

mown [məʊn] pp → mow.

MP n (abbr of Military Police) PM. || Br (abbr of Member of Parliament) ≃ député m.

mpg (abbr of miles per gallon) n miles au gallon.

mph (abbr of miles per hour) n miles à l'heure.

Mr ['mɪstəʳ] n Monsieur m; [on letter] M.

Mrs ['mɪsɪz] n Madame f; [on letter] Mme.

Ms [mɪz] n titre que les femmes peuvent utiliser au lieu de madame ou mademoiselle pour éviter la distinction entre les femmes mariées et les célibataires.

MS n (abbr of multiple sclerosis) SEP f.

MSc (abbr of Master of Science) n (titulaire d'une) maîtrise de sciences.

much [mʌtʃ] (compar more, superl most) 1 adj beaucoup de; there isn't ~ rice left il ne reste pas beaucoup de riz; as ~ money as ... autant d'argent que ...; too ~ trop de; how ~ ...? combien de ...? 2 pron beaucoup; I don't think ~ of his new house sa nouvelle maison ne me plaît pas trop; as ~ as autant que; too ~ trop; how ~? combien?; I'm not ~ of a cook je suis un piètre cuisinier; so ~ for all my hard work tout ce travail pour rien; I thought as ~ c'est bien ce que je pensais. 3 adv beaucoup; as ~ as autant que; thank you very ~ merci beaucoup; without so ~ as ... sans même .... ○ **much as** conj bien que (+ subjunctive).

muck [mʌk] n (U) inf [dirt] saletés fpl. || [manure] fumier m.

mucky ['mʌkɪ] adj sale.

mucus ['mju:kəs] n mucus m.

mud [mʌd] *n* boue *f.*

muddle ['mʌdl] **1** *n* désordre *m*, fouillis *m*. **2** *vt* [papers] mélanger. || [person] embrouiller. ○ **muddle through** *vi* se tirer d'affaire, s'en sortir tant bien que mal. ○ **muddle up** *vt sep* mélanger.

muddy ['mʌdɪ] **1** *adj* boueux(euse). **2** *vt fig* embrouiller.

mudguard ['mʌdgɑːd] *n* garde-boue *m inv.*

mudslinging ['mʌd,slɪŋɪŋ] *n* (*U*) *fig* attaques *fpl.*

muff [mʌf] **1** *n* manchon *m*. **2** *vt inf* louper.

muffin ['mʌfɪn] *n* muffin *m.*

muffle ['mʌfl] *vt* étouffer.

muffler ['mʌflər] *n Am* [for car] silencieux *m.*

mug [mʌg] **1** *n* [cup] (grande) tasse *f.* || *inf* [fool] andouille *f.* **2** *vt* [attack] agresser.

mugging ['mʌgɪŋ] *n* agression *f.*

muggy ['mʌgɪ] *adj* lourd(e), moite.

mule [mjuːl] *n* mule *f.*

mull [mʌl] ○ **mull over** *vt sep* ruminer, réfléchir à.

mulled [mʌld] *adj*: ~ **wine** vin *m* chaud.

multicoloured *Br*, **multicolored** *Am* ['mʌltɪ,kʌləd] *adj* multicolore.

multilateral [,mʌltɪ'lætərəl] *adj* multilatéral(e).

multinational [,mʌltɪ'næʃənl] *n* multinationale *f.*

multiple ['mʌltɪpl] **1** *adj* multiple. **2** *n* multiple *m.*

multiple sclerosis [-sklɪ'rəusɪs] *n* sclérose *f* en plaques.

multiplex cinema ['mʌltɪpleks-] *n* grand cinéma *m* à plusieurs salles.

multiplication [,mʌltɪplɪ'keɪʃn] *n* multiplication *f.*

multiply ['mʌltɪplaɪ] **1** *vt* multiplier. **2** *vi* se multiplier.

multistorey *Br*, **multistory** *Am* [,mʌltɪ'stɔːrɪ] *adj* à étages.

multitude ['mʌltɪtjuːd] *n* multitude *f.*

mumble ['mʌmbl] *vt & vi* marmotter.

mummy ['mʌmɪ] *n* [preserved body] momie *f.*

mumps [mʌmps] *n* (*U*) oreillons *mpl.*

munch [mʌntʃ] *vt & vi* croquer.

mundane [mʌn'deɪn] *adj* banal(e), ordinaire.

municipal [mjuː'nɪsɪpl] *adj* municipal(e).

municipality [mjuː,nɪsɪ'pælətɪ] *n* municipalité *f.*

mural ['mjuːərəl] *n* peinture *f* murale.

murder ['mɜːdər] **1** *n* meurtre *m*. **2** *vt* assassiner.

murderer ['mɜːdərər] *n* meurtrier *m*, assassin *m.*

murky ['mɜːkɪ] *adj* [place] sombre. || [water, past] trouble.

murmur ['mɜːmər] **1** *n* murmure *m*; MED souffle *m* au cœur. **2** *vt & vi* murmurer.

muscle ['mʌsl] *n* muscle *m*. ○ **muscle in** *vi* intervenir, s'immiscer.

muscular ['mʌskjʊlər] *adj* [spasm, pain] musculaire. || [person] musclé(e).

muse [mjuːz] **1** *n* muse *f.* **2** *vi* méditer, réfléchir.

museum [mjuː'ziːəm] *n* musée *m.*

mushroom ['mʌʃrʊm] **1** *n* champignon *m*. **2** *vi* [organization, party] se développer, grandir; [houses] proliférer.

music ['mjuːzɪk] *n* musique *f.*

musical ['mjuːzɪkl] **1** *adj* [event, voice] musical(e). || [child] doué(e) pour la musique, musicien(ienne). **2** *n* comédie *f* musicale.

musical instrument *n* instrument *m* de musique.

music centre *n* chaîne *f* compacte.

musician [mjuː'zɪʃn] *n* musicien *m*, -ienne *f.*

Muslim ['mʊzlɪm] **1** *adj* musulman(e). **2** *n* musulman *m*, -e *f.*

muslin ['mʌzlɪn] *n* mousseline *f.*

mussel ['mʌsl] *n* moule *f.*

must [mʌst] **1** *modal vb* [expressing obligation] devoir; **I ~ go** il faut que je m'en aille, je dois partir. || [expressing likelihood]: **they ~ have known** ils devaient le savoir. **2** *n inf*: **a ~** un must, un impératif.

mustache *Am* = **moustache**.

mustard ['mʌstəd] *n* moutarde *f.*

muster ['mʌstər] *vt* rassembler.

mustn't [mʌsnt] = **must not**.

must've ['mʌstəv] = **must have**.

musty ['mʌstɪ] *adj* [smell] de moisi; [room] qui sent le renfermé OR le moisi.

mute [mjuːt] **1** *adj* muet(ette). **2** *n* muet *m*, -ette *f.*

muted ['mjuːtɪd] *adj* [colour] sourd(e). || [reaction] peu marqué(e); [protest] voilé(e).

mutilate ['mjuːtɪleɪt] *vt* mutiler.

mutiny ['mjuːtɪnɪ] **1** *n* mutinerie *f.* **2** *vi* se mutiner.

mutter ['mʌtər] **1** *vt* [threat, curse] marmonner. **2** *vi* marmotter, marmonner.

mutton ['mʌtn] *n* mouton *m.*

mutual ['mju:tʃʊəl] *adj* [feeling, help] réciproque, mutuel(elle). || [friend, interest] commun(e).

mutually ['mju:tʃʊəli] *adv* mutuellement, réciproquement.

muzzle ['mʌzl] **1** *n* [of dog - mouth] museau *m*; [- guard] muselière *f*. || [of gun] gueule *f*. **2** *vt* *lit & fig* museler.

MW (*abbr of* medium wave) PO.

my [mai] *poss adj* [referring to oneself] mon (ma), mes (*pl*); ~ **dog** mon chien; ~ **house** ma maison; ~ **children** mes enfants; ~ **name is** Joe/Sarah je m'appelle Joe/Sarah; **it wasn't MY fault** ce n'était pas de ma faute à moi. || [in titles]: **yes**, ~ **Lord** oui, monsieur le comte/duc *etc*.

myself [mai'self] *pron* (*reflexive*) me; (*after prep*) moi. || (*for emphasis*) moi-même; **I did it** ~ je l'ai fait tout seul.

mysterious [mi'stiəriəs] *adj* mystérieux(ieuse).

mystery ['mistəri] *n* mystère *m*.

mystical ['mistikl] *adj* mystique.

mystified ['mistifaid] *adj* perplexe.

mystifying ['mistifaiiŋ] *adj* inexplicable, déconcertant(e).

mystique [mi'sti:k] *n* mystique *f*.

myth [miθ] *n* mythe *m*.

mythical ['miθikl] *adj* mythique.

mythology [mi'θɒlədʒi] *n* mythologie *f*.

n (*pl* n's OR ns), **N** (*pl* N's OR Ns) [en] *n* [letter] n *m inv*, N *m inv*. ○ **N** (*abbr of* north) N.

n/a, N/A (*abbr of* not applicable) s.o.

nab [næb] *vt inf* [arrest] pincer. || [get quickly] attraper, accaparer.

nag [næg] **1** *vt* harceler. **2** *n inf* [horse] canasson *m*.

nagging ['nægiŋ] *adj* [doubt] persistant(e), tenace. || [husband, wife] enquiquineur(euse).

nail [neil] **1** *n* [for fastening] clou *m*. || [of finger, toe] ongle *m*. **2** *vt* clouer. ○ **nail down** *vt sep* [lid] clouer. || *fig* [person]:

to ~ **sb down to sthg** faire préciser qqch à qqn.

nailbrush ['neilbrʌʃ] *n* brosse *f* à ongles.

nail file *n* lime *f* à ongles.

nail polish *n* vernis *m* à ongles.

nail scissors *npl* ciseaux *mpl* à ongles.

nail varnish *n* vernis *m* à ongles.

nail varnish remover [-ri'mu:vər] *n* dissolvant *m*.

naive, naïve [nai'i:v] *adj* naïf(ïve).

naked ['neikid] *adj* [body, flame] nu(e); **with the** ~ **eye** à l'œil nu. || [emotions] manifeste, évident(e); [aggression] non déguisé(e).

name [neim] **1** *n* [identification] nom *m*; **what's your** ~? comment vous appelez-vous?; **in my/his** ~ à mon/son nom; **in the** ~ **of peace** au nom de la paix; **to call sb** ~**s** traiter qqn de tous les noms, injurier qqn. || [reputation] réputation *f*. || [famous person] grand nom *m*, célébrité *f*. **2** *vt* [gen] nommer; **to** ~ **sb/sthg after** *Br*, **to** ~ **sb/sthg for** *Am* donner à qqn/à qqch le nom de. || [date, price] fixer.

nameless ['neimlis] *adj* inconnu(e), sans nom; [author] anonyme.

namely ['neimli] *adv* à savoir, c'est-à-dire.

namesake ['neimseik] *n* homonyme *m*.

nanny ['næni] *n* nurse *f*, bonne *f* d'enfants.

nap [næp] *n*: **to have** OR **take a** ~ faire un petit somme.

nape [neip] *n* nuque *f*.

napkin ['næpkin] *n* serviette *f*.

narcotic [nɑ:'kɒtik] *n* stupéfiant *m*.

narrative ['nærətiv] **1** *adj* narratif (ive). **2** *n* [story] récit *m*, narration *f*. || [skill] art *m* de la narration.

narrator [*Br* nə'reitər, *Am* 'næreitər] *n* narrateur *m*, -trice *f*.

narrow ['nærəu] **1** *adj* [gen] étroit(e); **to have a** ~ **escape** l'échapper belle. || [victory, majority] de justesse. **2** *vt* [reduce] réduire, limiter. || [eyes] fermer à demi, plisser. **3** *vi* *lit & fig* se rétrécir. ○ **narrow down** *vt sep* réduire, limiter.

narrowly ['nærəuli] *adv* [win, lose] de justesse. || [miss] de peu.

narrow-minded [-'maindid] *adj* [person] à l'esprit étroit, borné(e); [attitude] étroit(e), borné(e).

nasal ['neizl] *adj* nasal(e).

nasty ['nɑ:sti] *adj* [unpleasant - smell, feeling] mauvais(e); [- weather] vilain(e), mauvais(e). || [unkind] méchant(e).

[problem] difficile, délicat(e). || [injury] vilain(e); [accident] grave; [fall] mauvais(e).

nation ['neɪʃn] n nation f.

national ['næʃənl] 1 adj national(e); [campaign, strike] à l'échelon national; [custom] du pays, de la nation. 2 n ressortissant m, -e f.

national anthem n hymne m national.

national dress n costume m national.

nationalism ['næʃnəlɪzm] n nationalisme m.

nationalist ['næʃnəlɪst] 1 adj nationaliste. 2 n nationaliste mf.

nationality [,næʃə'nælətɪ] n nationalité f.

nationalize, -ise ['næʃnəlaɪz] vt nationaliser.

national park n parc m national.

nationwide ['neɪʃənwaɪd] 1 adj dans tout le pays; [campaign, strike] à l'échelon national. 2 adv à travers tout le pays.

native ['neɪtɪv] 1 adj [country, area] natal(e). || [language] maternel(elle); **an English ~ speaker** une personne de langue maternelle anglaise. || [plant, animal] indigène; **~ to** originaire de. 2 n autochtone mf; [of colony] indigène mf.

Native American n Indien m, -ienne f d'Amérique, Amérindien m, -ienne f.

Nativity [nə'tɪvətɪ] n: **the ~** la Nativité.

NATO ['neɪtəʊ] (abbr of North Atlantic Treaty Organization) n OTAN f.

natural ['nætʃrəl] adj [gen] naturel(elle). || [instinct, talent] inné(e). || [footballer, musician] né(e).

natural gas n gaz m naturel.

naturalize, -ise ['nætʃrəlaɪz] vt naturaliser; **to be ~d** se faire naturaliser.

naturally ['nætʃrəlɪ] adv [gen] naturellement. || [unaffectedly] sans affectation, avec naturel.

natural wastage n (U) départs mpl volontaires.

nature ['neɪtʃər] n nature f; **by ~** [basically] par essence; [by disposition] de nature, naturellement.

nature reserve n réserve f naturelle.

naughty ['nɔːtɪ] adj [badly behaved] vilain(e), méchant(e). || [rude] grivois(e).

nausea ['nɔːsjə] n nausée f.

nauseam ['nɔːzɪæm] → ad nauseam.

nauseating ['nɔːsɪeɪtɪŋ] adj lit & fig écœurant(e).

nautical ['nɔːtɪkl] adj nautique.

naval ['neɪvl] adj naval(e).

nave [neɪv] n nef f.

navel ['neɪvl] n nombril m.

navigate ['nævɪgeɪt] 1 vt [plane] piloter; [ship] gouverner. || [seas, river] naviguer sur. 2 vi AERON & NAUT naviguer; AUT lire la carte.

navigation [,nævɪ'geɪʃn] n navigation f.

navigator ['nævɪgeɪtər] n navigateur m.

navy ['neɪvɪ] 1 n marine f. 2 adj [in colour] bleu marine (inv).

navy blue 1 adj bleu marine (inv). 2 n bleu m marine.

Nazareth ['næzərɪθ] n Nazareth.

Nazi ['nɑːtsɪ] (pl -s) 1 adj nazi(e). 2 n Nazi m, -e f.

NB (abbr of nota bene) NB.

near [nɪər] 1 adj proche; **a ~ disaster** une catastrophe évitée de justesse or de peu; **in the ~ future** dans un proche avenir, dans un avenir prochain; **it was a ~ thing** il était moins cinq. 2 adv [close] près. || [almost]: **~ impossible** presque impossible; **nowhere ~ ready/enough** loin d'être prêt/assez. 3 prep: **~ (to)** [in space] près de; [in time] près de, vers; **~ to tears** au bord des larmes; **~ (to) death** sur le point de mourir; **~ (to) the truth** proche de la vérité. 4 vt approcher de. 5 vi approcher.

nearby [nɪə'baɪ] 1 adj proche. 2 adv tout près, à proximité.

nearly ['nɪəlɪ] adv presque; **I ~ fell** j'ai failli tomber; **not ~ enough/as good** loin d'être suffisant/aussi bon.

near miss n SPORT coup m qui a raté de peu. || [between planes, vehicles] quasi-collision f.

nearside ['nɪəsaɪd] n [right-hand drive] côté m gauche; [left-hand drive] côté droit.

nearsighted [,nɪə'saɪtɪd] adj Am myope.

neat [niːt] adj [room, house] bien tenu(e), en ordre; [work] soigné(e); [handwriting] net (nette); [appearance] soigné(e), net (nette). || [solution, manœuvre] habile, ingénieux(ieuse). || [alcohol] pur(e), sans eau. || Am inf [very good] chouette, super (inv).

neatly ['niːtlɪ] adv [arrange] avec ordre; [write] soigneusement; [dress] avec soin. || [skilfully] habilement, adroitement.

necessarily [Br 'nesəsrəlɪ, ,nesə'serɪlɪ] adv forcément, nécessairement.

necessary ['nesəsrɪ] *adj* [required] nécessaire, indispensable; **to make the ~ arrangements** faire le nécessaire. || [inevitable] inévitable, inéluctable.

necessity [nɪ'sesətɪ] *n* nécessité *f*.

neck [nek] **1** *n* ANAT cou *m*. || [of shirt, dress] encolure *f*. || [of bottle] col *m*, goulot *m*. **2** *ri inf* se bécoter.

necklace ['neklɪs] *n* collier *m*.

neckline ['neklaɪn] *n* encolure *f*.

necktie ['nektaɪ] *n Am* cravate *f*.

nectarine ['nektərɪn] *n* brugnon *m*, nectarine *f*.

need [ni:d] **1** *n* besoin *m*; **~ for sthg/to do sthg** besoin de qqch/de faire qqch; **to be in** OR **have ~ of sthg** avoir besoin de qqch; **if ~ be** si besoin est, si nécessaire; **in ~** dans le besoin; **there's no ~ to get up** ce n'est pas la peine de te lever. **2** *rt* [require]: **to ~ sthg/to do sthg** avoir besoin de qqch/de faire qqch; **I ~ to go to the doctor** il faut que j'aille chez le médecin. || [be obliged]: **to ~ to do sthg** être obligé(e) de faire qqch. **3** *modal vb*: **~ we go?** faut-il qu'on y aille?; **it ~ not happen** cela ne doit pas forcément se produire.

needle ['ni:dl] **1** *n* [gen] aiguille *f*. || [stylus] saphir *m*. **2** *rt inf* [annoy] asticoter, lancer des piques à.

needless ['ni:dlɪs] *adj* [risk, waste] inutile; [remark] déplacé(e); **~ to say ...** bien entendu ...

needlework ['ni:dlwɜːk] *n* [embroidery] travail *m* d'aiguille. || (*U*) [activity] couture *f*.

needn't ['ni:dnt] = need not.

needy ['ni:dɪ] *adj* nécessiteux(euse), indigent(e).

negative ['negətɪv] **1** *adj* négatif(ive). **2** *n* PHOT négatif *m*. || LING négation *f*.

neglect [nɪ'glekt] **1** *n* [of garden] mauvais entretien *m*; [of children] manque *m* de soins; [of duty] manquement *m*. **2** *rt* négliger; [garden] laisser à l'abandon; **to ~ to do sthg** négliger OR omettre de faire qqch.

negligee ['neglɪʒeɪ] *n* déshabillé *m*, négligé *m*.

negligence ['neglɪdʒəns] *n* négligence *f*.

negligible ['neglɪdʒəbl] *adj* négligeable.

negotiate [nɪ'gəʊʃɪeɪt] **1** *rt* COMM & POL négocier. || [obstacle] franchir; [bend] prendre, négocier. **2** *ri* négocier; **to ~ with sb (for sthg)** engager des négociations avec qqn (pour obtenir qqch).

negotiation [nɪ,gəʊʃɪ'eɪʃn] *n* négociation *f*.

Negress ['ni:grɪs] *n* négresse *f*.

Negro ['ni:grəʊ] (*pl* -es) **1** *adj* noir(e). **2** *n* Noir *m*.

neigh [neɪ] *ri* [horse] hennir.

neighbour *Br*, **neighbor** *Am* ['neɪbər] *n* voisin *m*, -e *f*.

neighbourhood *Br*, **neighborhood** *Am* ['neɪbəhʊd] *n* [of town] voisinage *m*, quartier *m*. || [approximate figure]: **in the ~ of £300** environ 300 livres, dans les 300 livres.

neighbouring *Br*, **neighboring** *Am* ['neɪbərɪŋ] *adj* avoisinant(e).

neighbourly *Br*, **neighborly** *Am* ['neɪbəlɪ] *adj* bon voisin (bonne voisine).

neither ['naɪðər, 'ni:ðər] **1** *adv*: **~ good nor bad** ni bon ni mauvais; **that's ~ here nor there** cela n'a rien à voir. **2** *pron & adj* ni l'un ni l'autre (ni l'une ni l'autre). **3** *conj*: **~ do I** moi non plus.

neon ['ni:ɒn] *n* néon *m*.

neon light *n* néon *m*, lumière *f* au néon.

nephew ['nefju:] *n* neveu *m*.

Neptune ['neptju:n] *n* [planet] Neptune *f*.

nerve [nɜːv] *n* ANAT nerf *m*. || [courage] courage *m*, sang-froid *m*; **to lose one's ~** se dégonfler, flancher. || [cheek] culot *m*, toupet *m*. ◊ **nerves** *npl* nerfs *mpl*; **to get on sb's ~s** taper sur les nerfs OR le système de qqn.

nerve-racking [-,rækɪŋ] *adj* angoissant(e), éprouvant(e).

nervous ['nɜːvəs] *adj* [gen] nerveux(euse). || [apprehensive - smile, person etc] inquiet(iète); [- performer] qui a le trac; **to be ~ about sthg** appréhender qqch.

nervous breakdown *n* dépression *f* nerveuse.

nest [nest] **1** *n* nid *m*; **~ of tables** table *f* gigogne. **2** *ri* [bird] faire son nid, nicher.

nest egg *n* pécule *m*, bas *m* de laine.

nestle ['nesl] *ri* se blottir.

net [net] **1** *adj* net (nette); **~ result** résultat final. **2** *n* [gen] filet *m*. || [fabric] voile *m*, tulle *m*. **3** *rt* [fish] prendre au filet. || [money - subj: person] toucher net, gagner net; [- subj: deal] rapporter net.

netball ['netbɔːl] *n* netball *m*.

net curtains *npl* voilage *m*.

Netherlands ['neðələndz] *npl*: **the ~** les Pays-Bas *mpl*.

net profit *n* bénéfice *m* net.

net revenue *n Am* chiffre *m* d'affaires.

nett [net] *adj* = net.

netting ['netɪŋ] *n* [metal, plastic] grillage *m*. || [fabric] voile *m*, tulle *m*.

nettle ['netl] *n* ortie *f*.

network ['netwɜːk] *n* réseau *m*.

neurosis [,njuə'rəusɪs] (*pl* -**ses**) *n* névrose *f*.

neurotic [,njuə'rɒtɪk] *adj* névrosé(e).

neuter ['njuːtər] **1** *adj* neutre. **2** *vt* [cat] châtrer.

neutral ['njuːtrəl] **1** *adj* [gen] neutre. **2** *n* AUT point *m* mort.

neutrality [njuː'trælətɪ] *n* neutralité *f*.

neutralize, -ise ['njuːtrəlaɪz] *vt* neutraliser.

never ['nevər] *adv* jamais ... ne, ne ... jamais; ~ **ever** jamais, au grand jamais; **well I** ~! ça par exemple!

never-ending *adj* interminable.

nevertheless [,nevəðə'les] *adv* néanmoins, pourtant.

new [*adj* njuː, *n* njuːz] *adj* [gen] nouveau(elle). || [not used] neuf (neuve); **as good as** ~ comme neuf. ○ **news** *n* (*U*) [information] nouvelle *f*; **a piece of** ~**s** une nouvelle. || RADIO informations *fpl*. || TV journal *m* télévisé, actualités *fpl*.

newborn ['njuːbɔːn] *adj* nouveau-né(e).

newcomer ['njuː,kʌmər] *n*: ~ (**to sthg**) nouveau-venu *m*, nouvelle-venue *f* (dans qqch).

newfangled [,njuː'fæŋgld] *adj inf pej* ultramoderne, trop moderne.

new-found *adj* récent(e), de fraîche date.

newly ['njuːlɪ] *adv* récemment, fraîchement.

newlyweds ['njuːlɪwedz] *npl* nouveaux OR jeunes mariés *mpl*.

new moon *n* nouvelle lune *f*.

news agency *n* agence *f* de presse.

newsagent *Br* ['njuːzeɪdʒənt], **newsdealer** *Am* ['njuːzdiːlər] *n* marchand *m* de journaux.

newscaster ['njuːzkaːstər] *n* présentateur *m*, -trice *f*.

newsdealer *Am* = newsagent.

newsflash ['njuːzflæʃ] *n* flash *m* d'information.

newsletter ['njuːz,letər] *n* bulletin *m*.

newspaper ['njuːz,peɪpər] *n* journal *m*.

newsprint ['njuːzprɪnt] *n* papier *m* journal.

newsreader ['njuːz,riːdər] *n* présentateur *m*, -trice *f*.

newsreel ['njuːzriːl] *n* actualités *fpl* filmées.

newsstand ['njuːzstænd] *n* kiosque *m* à journaux.

newt [njuːt] *n* triton *m*.

New Year *n* nouvel an *m*, nouvelle année *f*; **Happy** ~! bonne année!

New Year's Day *n* jour *m* de l'an, premier *m* de l'an.

New Year's Eve *n* la Saint-Sylvestre.

New York [-'jɔːk] *n* [city]: ~ (**City**) New York. || [state]: ~ (**State**) l'État *m* de New York.

New Zealand [-'ziːlənd] *n* Nouvelle-Zélande *f*.

New Zealander [-'ziːləndər] *n* Néo-Zélandais *m*, -e *f*.

next [nekst] **1** *adj* prochain(e); [room] d'à côté; [page] suivant(e); ~ **Tuesday** mardi prochain; ~ **time** la prochaine fois; ~ **week** la semaine prochaine; **the** ~ **week** la semaine suivante OR d'après; ~ **year** l'année prochaine; ~, **please!** au suivant!; **the day after** ~ le surlendemain; **the week after** ~ dans deux semaines. **2** *adv* [afterwards] ensuite, après. || [again] la prochaine fois. || (*with superlatives*): **he's the** ~ **biggest after Dan** c'est le plus grand après OR à part Dan. **3** *prep Am* à côté de. ○ **next to** *prep* à côté de; **it cost** ~ **to nothing** cela a coûté une bagatelle OR trois fois rien; **I know** ~ **to nothing** je ne sais presque OR pratiquement rien.

next door *adv* à côté. ○ **next-door** *adj*: **next-door neighbour** voisin *m*, -e *f* d'à côté.

next of kin *n* plus proche parent *m*.

nib [nɪb] *n* plume *f*.

nibble ['nɪbl] *vt* grignoter, mordiller.

Nicaragua [,nɪkə'rægjuə] *n* Nicaragua *m*.

nice [naɪs] *adj* [holiday, food] bon (bonne); [day, picture] beau (belle); [dress] joli(e). || [person] gentil(ille), sympathique; **to be** ~ **to sb** être gentil OR aimable avec qqn.

nice-looking [-'lukɪŋ] *adj* joli(e), beau (belle).

nicely ['naɪslɪ] *adv* [made, manage etc] bien; [dressed] joliment; **that will do** ~ cela fera très bien l'affaire. || [politely - ask] poliment, gentiment; [- behave] bien.

niche [niːʃ] *n* [in wall] niche *f*; *fig* bonne situation *f*, voie *f*.

nick [nɪk] **1** *n* [cut] entaille *f*, coupure *f*. || *phr*: **in the** ~ **of time** juste à temps. **2** *vt* [cut] couper, entailler.

nickel ['nɪkl] n [metal] nickel m. || Am [coin] pièce f de cinq cents.

nickname ['nɪkneɪm] 1 n sobriquet m, surnom m. 2 vt surnommer.

nicotine ['nɪkətiːn] n nicotine f.

niece [niːs] n nièce f.

Nigeria [naɪ'dʒɪərɪə] n Nigeria m.

Nigerian [naɪ'dʒɪərɪən] 1 adj nigérian(e). 2 n Nigérian m, -e f.

night [naɪt] n [not day] nuit f; at ~ la nuit. || [evening] soir m; at ~ le soir. || phr: to have an early ~ se coucher de bonne heure; to have a late ~ veiller. se coucher tard. ○ **nights** adv Am [at night] la nuit.

nightcap ['naɪtkæp] n [drink] boisson alcoolisée prise avant de se coucher.

nightclub ['naɪtklʌb] n boîte f de nuit, night-club m.

nightdress ['naɪtdres] n chemise f de nuit.

nightfall ['naɪtfɔːl] n tombée f de la nuit OR du jour.

nightgown ['naɪtgaʊn] n chemise f de nuit.

nightie ['naɪtɪ] n inf chemise f de nuit.

nightingale ['naɪtɪŋgeɪl] n rossignol m.

nightlife ['naɪtlaɪf] n vie f nocturne, activités fpl nocturnes.

nightly ['naɪtlɪ] 1 adj (de) toutes les nuits OR tous les soirs. 2 adv toutes les nuits, tous les soirs.

nightmare ['naɪtmeər] n lit & fig cauchemar m.

night porter n veilleur m de nuit.

night school n (U) cours mpl du soir.

night shift n [period] poste m de nuit.

nightshirt ['naɪtʃɜːt] n chemise f de nuit d'homme.

nighttime ['naɪttaɪm] n nuit f.

nil [nɪl] n néant m; Br SPORT zéro m.

Nile [naɪl] n: the ~ le Nil.

nimble ['nɪmbl] adj agile, leste; fig [mind] vif (vive).

nine [naɪn] num neuf; see also **six**.

nineteen [ˌnaɪn'tiːn] num dix-neuf; see also **six**.

ninety ['naɪntɪ] num quatre-vingt-dix; see also **sixty**.

ninth [naɪnθ] num neuvième; see also **sixth**.

nip [nɪp] 1 n [pinch] pinçon m; [bite] morsure f. || [of drink] goutte f, doigt m. 2 vt [pinch] pincer; [bite] mordre.

nipple ['nɪpl] n ANAT bout m de sein, mamelon m. || [of bottle] tétine f.

nit [nɪt] n [in hair] lente f.

nitpicking ['nɪtpɪkɪŋ] n inf ergotage m, pinaillage m.

nitrogen ['naɪtrədʒən] n azote m.

nitty-gritty [ˌnɪtɪ'grɪtɪ] n inf: to get down to the ~ en venir à l'essentiel OR aux choses sérieuses.

no [nəʊ] (pl -es) 1 adv [gen] non; [expressing disagreement] mais non. || [not any]: ~ bigger/smaller pas plus grand/petit; ~ better pas mieux. 2 adj aucun(e), pas de; there's ~ telling what will happen impossible de dire ce qui va se passer; he's ~ friend of mine je ne le compte pas parmi mes amis. 3 n non m; she won't take ~ for an answer elle n'accepte pas de refus OR qu'on lui dise non.

No., no. (abbr of number) No, no.

nobility [nə'bɪlətɪ] n noblesse f.

noble ['nəʊbl] 1 adj noble. 2 n noble m.

nobody ['nəʊbədɪ] 1 pron personne, aucun(e). 2 n pej rien-du-tout mf, moins que rien mf.

nocturnal [nɒk'tɜːnl] adj nocturne.

nod [nɒd] 1 vt: to ~ one's head incliner la tête. faire un signe de tête. 2 vi [in agreement] faire un signe de tête affirmatif, faire signe que oui. || [to indicate sthg] faire un signe de tête. || [as greeting]: to ~ to sb saluer qqn d'un signe de tête. ○ **nod off** vi somnoler, s'assoupir.

noise [nɔɪz] n bruit m.

noisy ['nɔɪzɪ] adj bruyant(e).

no-man's-land n no man's land m.

nominal ['nɒmɪnl] adj [in name only] de nom seulement, nominal(e). || [very small] nominal(e), insignifiant(e).

nominate ['nɒmɪneɪt] vt [propose]: to ~ sb (for/as sthg) proposer qqn (pour/comme qqch). || [appoint]: to ~ sb (as sthg) nommer qqn (qqch).

nominee [ˌnɒmɪ'niː] n personne f nommée OR désignée.

nonalcoholic [ˌnɒnælkə'hɒlɪk] adj non-alcoolisé(e).

nonchalant [Br 'nɒnʃələnt, Am ˌnɒnʃə'lɑːnt] adj nonchalant(e).

noncommittal [ˌnɒnkə'mɪtl] adj évasif(ive).

nonconformist [ˌnɒnkən'fɔːmɪst] adj non-conformiste.

nondescript [Br 'nɒndɪskrɪpt, Am ˌnɒndɪ'skrɪpt] adj quelconque, terne.

none [nʌn] 1 pron [gen] aucun(e); there was ~ left il n'y en avait plus. il n'en restait plus. || [nobody] personne, nul (nulle). 2 adv: ~ the worse/wiser pas plus mal/avancé; **~ the better** pas mieux. ○ **none too** *adv* pas tellement OR trop.

nonentity [nɒˈnentətɪ] *n* nullité *f*, zéro *m*.

nonetheless [ˌnʌnðəˈles] *adv* néanmoins, pourtant.

nonexistent [ˌnɒnɪgˈzɪstənt] *adj* inexistant(e).

nonfiction [ˌnɒnˈfɪkʃn] *n* (*U*) ouvrages *mpl* généraux.

no-nonsense *adj* direct(e), sérieux(ieuse).

nonpayment [ˌnɒnˈpeɪmənt] *n* nonpaiement *m*.

nonplussed, **nonplused** *Am* [ˌnɒnˈplʌst] *adj* déconcerté(e), perplexe.

nonreturnable [ˌnɒnrɪˈtɜːnəbl] *adj* [bottle] non consigné(e).

nonsense [ˈnɒnsəns] **1** *n* (*U*) [meaningless words] charabia *m*. ‖ [foolish idea]: **it was ~ to suggest** ... il était absurde de suggérer .... ‖ [foolish behaviour] bêtises *fpl*, idioties *fpl*; **to make (a) ~ of sthg** gâcher OR saboter qqch. **2** *excl* quelles bêtises OR foutaises!

nonsmoker [ˌnɒnˈsmoʊkər] *n* nonfumeur *m*, -euse *f*, personne *f* qui ne fume pas.

nonstick [ˌnɒnˈstɪk] *adj* qui n'attache pas, téflonisé(e).

nonstop [ˌnɒnˈstɒp] **1** *adj* [flight] direct(e), sans escale; [activity] continu(e); [rain] continuel(elle). **2** *adv* [talk, work] sans arrêt; [rain] sans discontinuer.

noodles [ˈnuːdlz] *npl* nouilles *fpl*.

nook [nʊk] *n* [of room] coin *m*, recoin *m*; **every ~ and cranny** tous les coins, les coins et les recoins.

noon [nuːn] *n* midi *m*.

no one *pron* = **nobody**.

noose [nuːs] *n* nœud *m* coulant.

no-place *Am* = **nowhere**.

nor [nɔːr] *conj*: **~ do I** moi non plus; → **neither**.

norm [nɔːm] *n* norme *f*.

normal [ˈnɔːml] *adj* normal(e).

normality [nɔːˈmælɪtɪ], **normalcy** *Am* [ˈnɔːmlsɪ] *n* normalité *f*.

normally [ˈnɔːməlɪ] *adv* normalement.

Normandy [ˈnɔːməndɪ] *n* Normandie *f*.

north [nɔːθ] **1** *n* [direction] nord *m*. ‖ [region]: **the ~** le nord. **2** *adj* nord (*inv*); [wind] du nord. **3** *adv* au nord, vers le nord; **~ of** au nord de.

North Africa *n* Afrique *f* du Nord.

North America *n* Amérique *f* du Nord.

North American 1 *adj* nordaméricain(aine). **2** *n* Nord-Américain *m*, -aine *f*.

northeast [ˌnɔːθˈiːst] **1** *n* [direction] nord-est *m*. ‖ [region]: **the ~** le nord-est. **2** *adj* nord-est (*inv*); [wind] du nord-est. **3** *adv* au nord-est, vers le nord-est; **~ of** au nord-est de.

northerly [ˈnɔːðəlɪ] *adj* du nord; **in a ~ direction** vers le nord, en direction du nord.

northern [ˈnɔːðən] *adj* du nord, nord (*inv*).

Northern Ireland *n* Irlande *f* du Nord.

northernmost [ˈnɔːðənməʊst] *adj* le plus au nord (la plus au nord), à l'extrême nord.

North Korea *n* Corée *f* du Nord.

North Pole *n*: **the ~** le pôle Nord.

North Sea *n*: **the ~** la mer du Nord.

northward [ˈnɔːθwəd] **1** *adj* au nord. **2** *adv* = **northwards**.

northwards [ˈnɔːθwədz] *adv* au nord, vers le nord.

northwest [ˌnɔːθˈwest] **1** *n* [direction] nord-ouest *m*. ‖ [region]: **the ~** le nord-ouest. **2** *adj* nord-ouest (*inv*); [wind] du nord-ouest. **3** *adv* au nord-ouest, vers le nord-ouest; **~ of** au nord-ouest de.

Norway [ˈnɔːweɪ] *n* Norvège *f*.

Norwegian [nɔːˈwiːdʒən] **1** *adj* norvégien(ienne). **2** *n* [person] Norvégien *m*, -ienne *f*. ‖ [language] norvégien *m*.

nose [nəʊz] *n* nez *m*; **to look down one's ~ at sb** *fig* traiter qqn de haut (en bas); **to poke** OR **stick one's ~ into sthg** mettre OR fourrer son nez dans qqch; **to turn up one's ~ at sthg** dédaigner qqch. ○ **nose about**, **nose around** *vi* fouiner, fureter.

nosebleed [ˈnəʊzbliːd] *n*: **to have a ~** saigner du nez.

nosedive [ˈnəʊzdaɪv] **1** *n* [of plane] piqué *m*. **2** *vi* [plane] descendre en piqué, piquer du nez. ‖ *fig* [prices] dégringoler; [hopes] s'écrouler.

nosey [ˈnəʊzɪ] = **nosy**.

nostalgia [nɒˈstældʒə] *n*: **~ (for sthg)** nostalgie *f* (de qqch).

nostril [ˈnɒstrəl] *n* narine *f*.

nosy [ˈnəʊzɪ] *adj* curieux(ieuse), fouinard(e).

not [nɒt] *adv* ne pas, pas; **I think ~** je ne crois pas; **I'm afraid ~** je crains que non; **~ always** pas toujours; **~ that ...** ce n'est pas que ..., non pas que ...; **~ at all** [no] pas du tout; [to acknowledge thanks] de rien, je vous en prie.

notable ['nəʊtəbl] *adj* notable, remarquable; **to be ~ for sthg** être célèbre pour qqch.

notably ['nəʊtəbli] *adv* [in particular] notamment, particulièrement. || [noticeably] sensiblement, nettement.

notary ['nəʊtəri] *n*: ~ **(public)** notaire *m*.

notch [nɒtʃ] *n* [cut] entaille *f*, encoche *f*. || *fig* [on scale] cran *m*.

note [nəʊt] **1** *n* [gen & MUS] note *f*; [short letter] mot *m*; **to take ~ of sthg** prendre note de qqch. || [money] billet *m* (de banque). **2** *vt* [notice] remarquer, constater. ○ **notes** *npl* [in book] notes *fpl*. ○ **note down** *vt sep* noter, inscrire.

notebook ['nəʊtbʊk] *n* [for notes] carnet *m*, calepin *m*. || COMPUT ordinateur *m* portable compact.

noted ['nəʊtɪd] *adj* célèbre, éminent(e).

notepad ['nəʊtpæd] *n* bloc-notes *m*.

notepaper ['nəʊtpeɪpə'] *n* papier *m* à lettres.

noteworthy ['nəʊt‚wɜːðɪ] *adj* remarquable, notable.

nothing ['nʌθɪŋ] **1** *pron* rien; **I've got ~ to do** je n'ai rien à faire; **~ but** ne ... que, rien que. **2** *adv*: **you're ~ like your brother** tu ne ressembles pas du tout *or* en rien à ton frère; **I'm ~ like finished** je suis loin d'avoir fini.

notice ['nəʊtɪs] **1** *n* [written announcement] affiche *f*, placard *m*. || [attention]: **to take ~ (of sb/sthg)** faire *or* prêter attention (à qqn/qqch). || [warning] avis *m*, avertissement *m*; **at short ~** dans un bref délai; **until further ~** jusqu'en nouvel ordre. || [at work]: **to be given one's ~** recevoir son congé, être renvoyé(e); **to hand in one's ~** donner sa démission, demander son congé. **2** *vt* remarquer, s'apercevoir de.

noticeable ['nəʊtɪsəbl] *adj* sensible, perceptible.

notice board *n* panneau *m* d'affichage.

notify ['nəʊtɪfaɪ] *vt*: **to ~ sb (of sthg)** avertir *or* aviser qqn (de qqch).

notion ['nəʊʃn] *n* idée *f*, notion *f*. ○ **notions** *npl Am* mercerie *f*.

notorious [nəʊ'tɔːrɪəs] *adj* [criminal] notoire; [place] mal famé(e).

nought [nɔːt] *num* zéro *m*; **~s and crosses** morpion *m*.

noun [naʊn] *n* nom *m*.

nourish ['nʌrɪʃ] *vt* nourrir.

nourishing ['nʌrɪʃɪŋ] *adj* nourrissant(e).

nourishment ['nʌrɪʃmənt] *n* (U) nourriture *f*, aliments *mpl*.

novel ['nɒvl] **1** *adj* nouveau(nouvelle), original(e). **2** *n* roman *m*.

novelist ['nɒvəlɪst] *n* romancier *m*, -ière *f*.

novelty ['nɒvltɪ] *n* [gen] nouveauté *f*. || [cheap object] gadget *m*.

November [nə'vembə'] *n* novembre *m*; *see also* **September**.

novice ['nɒvɪs] *n* novice *mf*.

now [naʊ] **1** *adv* [at this time, at once] maintenant; **any day/time ~** d'un jour/ moment à l'autre; **~ and then** *or* **again** de temps en temps, de temps à autre. || [in past] à ce moment-là, alors. || [to introduce statement]: **~ let's just calm down** bon, on se calme maintenant. **2** *conj*: **~ (that)** maintenant que. **3** *n*: **for ~** pour le présent; **from ~ on** à partir de maintenant, désormais; **up until ~** jusqu'à présent; **by ~** déjà.

nowadays ['naʊədeɪz] *adv* actuellement, aujourd'hui.

nowhere *Br* ['nəʊweə'], **no-place** *Am adv* nulle part; **~ near** loin de; **we're getting ~** on n'avance pas, on n'arrive à rien.

nozzle ['nɒzl] *n* ajutage *m*, buse *f*.

nuance ['njuːɑːns] *n* nuance *f*.

nuclear bomb *n* bombe *f* nucléaire.

nuclear disarmament *n* désarmement *m* nucléaire.

nuclear energy *n* énergie *f* nucléaire.

nuclear power *n* énergie *f* nucléaire.

nuclear reactor *n* réacteur *m* nucléaire.

nucleus ['njuːklɪəs] (*pl* **-lei** [-lɪaɪ]) *n lit & fig* noyau *m*.

nude [njuːd] **1** *adj* nu(e). **2** *n* nu *m*; **in the ~** nu(e).

nudge [nʌdʒ] *vt* pousser du coude.

nudist ['njuːdɪst] **1** *adj* nudiste. **2** *n* nudiste *mf*.

nugget ['nʌgɪt] *n* pépite *f*.

nuisance ['njuːsns] *n* ennui *m*, embêtement *m*; **to make a ~ of o.s.** embêter le monde; **what a ~!** quelle plaie!

null [nʌl] *adj*: **~ and void** nul et non avenu.

numb [nʌm] **1** *adj* engourdi(e); **to be ~ with** [fear] être paralysé par; [cold] être transi de. **2** *vt* engourdir.

number ['nʌmbəʳ] **1** *n* [numeral] chiffre *m*. || [of telephone, house, car] numéro *m*. || [quantity] nombre *m*; **a ~ of** un certain nombre de. plusieurs; **any ~ of** un grand nombre de. bon nombre de. || [song] chanson *f*. **2** *vt* [amount to. include] compter. || [give number to] numéroter.

number one 1 *adj* premier(ière), principal(e). **2** *n inf* [oneself] soi, sa pomme.

numberplate ['nʌmbəpleɪt] *n* plaque *f* d'immatriculation.

numeral ['nju:mərəl] *n* chiffre *m*.

numerical [nju:'merɪkl] *adj* numérique.

numerous ['nju:mərəs] *adj* nombreux(euse).

nun [nʌn] *n* religieuse *f*, sœur *f*.

nurse [nɜ:s] **1** *n* infirmière *f*; **(male) ~** infirmier *m*. **2** *vt* [patient. cold] soigner. || *fig* [desires. hopes] nourrir. || [subj: mother] allaiter.

nursery ['nɜ:sərɪ] *n* [for children] garderie *f*. || [for plants] pépinière *f*.

nursery rhyme *n* comptine *f*.

nursery school *n* (école *f*) maternelle *f*.

nursery slopes *npl* pistes *fpl* pour débutants.

nursing ['nɜ:sɪŋ] *n* métier *m* d'infirmière.

nursing home *n* [for old people] maison *f* de retraite privée; [for childbirth] maternité *f* privée.

nurture ['nɜ:tʃəʳ] *vt* [children] élever; [plants] soigner. || *fig* [hopes etc] nourrir.

nut [nʌt] *n* [to eat] *terme générique désignant les fruits tels que les noix, noisettes etc.* || [of metal] écrou *m*. || *inf* [mad person] cinglé *m*, -e *f*. ○ **nuts 1** *adj inf*: **to be ~s** être dingue. **2** *excl Am inf* zut!

nutcrackers ['nʌt,krækəz] *npl* casse-noix *m inr*, casse-noisettes *m inr*.

nutmeg ['nʌtmeg] *n* noix *f* (de) muscade.

nutritious [nju:'trɪʃəs] *adj* nourrissant(e).

nutshell ['nʌtʃel] *n*: **in a ~** en un mot.

nuzzle ['nʌzl] *vi*: **to ~ (up) against** se frotter contre. frotter son nez contre.

nylon ['naɪlɒn] **1** *n* Nylon® *m*. **2** *comp* en Nylon®.

o (*pl* **o's** OR **os**), **O** (*pl* **O's** OR **Os**) [əʊ] *n* [letter] o *m inr*, O *m inr*. || [zero] zéro *m*.

oak [əʊk] *n* chêne *m*.

oar [ɔːʳ] *n* rame *f*, aviron *m*.

oasis [əʊ'eɪsɪs] (*pl* **oases** [əʊ'eɪsiːz]) *n* oasis *f*.

oath [əʊθ] *n* [promise] serment *m*; **on** OR **under ~** sous serment. || [swearword] juron *m*.

oatmeal ['əʊtmiːl] *n* (*U*) flocons *mpl* d'avoine.

oats [əʊts] *npl* [grain] avoine *f*.

obedience [ə'biːdjəns] *n* obéissance *f*.

obedient [ə'biːdjənt] *adj* obéissant(e), docile.

obese [əʊ'biːs] *adj fml* obèse.

obey [ə'beɪ] **1** *vt* obéir à. **2** *ri* obéir.

obituary [ə'bɪtjʊərɪ] *n* nécrologie *f*.

object [*n* 'ɒbdʒɪkt, *vb* ɒb'dʒekt] **1** *n* [gen] objet *m*. || [aim] objectif *m*, but *m*. || GRAMM complément *m* d'objet. **2** *vt* objecter. **3** *ri* protester; **tô ~ to sthg** faire objection à qqch. s'opposer à qqch; **to ~ to doing sthg** se refuser à faire qqch.

objection [əb'dʒekʃn] *n* objection *f*; **to have no ~ to sthg/to doing sthg** ne voir aucune objection à qqch/à faire qqch.

objectionable [əb'dʒekʃənəbl] *adj* [person, behaviour] désagréable.

objective [əb'dʒektɪv] **1** *adj* objectif(ive). **2** *n* objectif *m*.

obligation [,ɒblɪ'geɪʃn] *n* obligation *f*.

obligatory [ə'blɪgətrɪ] *adj* obligatoire.

oblige [ə'blaɪdʒ] *vt* [force]: **to ~ sb to do sthg** forcer OR obliger qqn à faire qqch.

obliging [ə'blaɪdʒɪŋ] *adj* obligeant(e).

oblique [ə'bliːk] **1** *adj* oblique; [reference. hint] indirect(e). **2** *n* TYPO barre *f* oblique.

obliterate [ə'blɪtəreɪt] *vt* [destroy] détruire, raser.

oblivion [ə'blɪvɪən] *n* oubli *m*.

oblivious [ə'blɪvɪəs] *adj*: **to be ~ to** OR **of** être inconscient(e) de.

oblong ['ɒblɒŋ] **1** *adj* rectangulaire. **2** *n* rectangle *m*.

obnoxious [əb'nɒkʃəs] *adj* [person] odieux(ieuse); [comment] désobligeant(e).

oboe ['əubəu] *n* hautbois *m*.

obscene [əb'si:n] *adj* obscène.

obscure [əb'skjuəʳ] **1** *adj* obscur(e). **2** *vt* [gen] obscurcir. || [view] masquer.

observance [əb'zɜ:vəns] *n* observation *f*.

observant [əb'zɜ:vnt] *adj* observateur(trice).

observation [,ɒbzə'veɪʃn] *n* observation *f*.

observatory [əb'zɜ:vətrɪ] *n* observatoire *m*.

observe [əb'zɜ:v] *vt* [gen] observer. || [remark] remarquer, faire observer.

observer [əb'zɜ:vəʳ] *n* observateur *m*, -trice *f*.

obsess [əb'ses] *vt*: **to be ~ed by** OR **with sb/sthg** être obsédé par qqn/qqch.

obsessive [əb'sesɪv] *adj* [person] obsessionnel(elle).

obsolescent [,ɒbsə'lesnt] *adj* [system] qui tombe en désuétude; [machine] obsolescent(e).

obsolete ['ɒbsəli:t] *adj* obsolète.

obstacle ['ɒbstəkl] *n* obstacle *m*.

obstetrics [ɒb'stetrɪks] *n* obstétrique *f*.

obstinate ['ɒbstənət] *adj* [stubborn] obstiné(e). || [cough] persistant(e); [stain, resistance] tenace.

obstruct [əb'strʌkt] *vt* [block] obstruer. || [hinder] entraver, gêner.

obstruction [əb'strʌkʃn] *n* [in road] encombrement *m*; [in pipe] engorgement *m*. || SPORT obstruction *f*.

obtain [əb'teɪn] *vt* obtenir.

obtainable [əb'teɪnəbl] *adj* que l'on peut obtenir.

obtrusive [əb'tru:sɪv] *adj* [behaviour] qui attire l'attention; [smell] fort(e).

obtuse [əb'tju:s] *adj* obtus(e).

obvious ['ɒbvɪəs] *adj* évident(e).

obviously ['ɒbvɪəslɪ] *adv* [of course] bien sûr. || [clearly] manifestement.

occasion [ə'keɪʒn] *n* [gen] occasion *f*. || [important event] événement *m*; **to rise to the ~** se montrer à la hauteur de la situation.

occasional [ə'keɪʒənl] *adj* [showers] passager(ère); [visit] occasionnel(elle); **I have the ~ drink/cigarette** je bois un verre/je fume une cigarette de temps à autre.

occasionally [ə'keɪʒnəlɪ] *adv* de temps en temps, quelquefois.

occult [ɒ'kʌlt] *adj* occulte.

occupant ['ɒkjupənt] *n* occupant *m*, -e *f*; [of vehicle] passager *m*.

occupation [,ɒkju'peɪʃn] *n* [job] profession *f*. || [pastime, by army] occupation *f*.

occupational hazard [ɒkju,peɪʃənl-] *n* risque *m* du métier.

occupational therapy [ɒkju,peɪʃənl-] *n* thérapeutique *f* occupationnelle, ergothérapie *f*.

occupier ['ɒkjupaɪəʳ] *n* occupant *m*, -e *f*.

occupy ['ɒkjupaɪ] *vt* occuper; **to ~ o.s.** s'occuper.

occur [ə'kɜ:ʳ] *vi* [happen - gen] avoir lieu, se produire; [- difficulty] se présenter. || [be present] se trouver, être présent(e). || [thought, idea]: **to ~ to sb** venir à l'esprit de qqn.

occurrence [ə'kʌrəns] *n* [event] événement *m*, circonstance *f*.

ocean ['əuʃn] *n* océan *m*; *Am* [sea] mer *f*.

oceangoing ['əuʃn,gəuɪŋ] *adj* au long cours.

o'clock [ə'klɒk] *adv*: **two ~** deux heures.

octave ['ɒktɪv] *n* octave *f*.

October [ɒk'təubəʳ] *n* octobre *m*; *see also* **September**.

octopus ['ɒktəpəs] (*pl* **-puses** OR **-pi** [-paɪ]) *n* pieuvre *f*.

OD *abbr of* **overdose**. || *abbr of* **overdrawn**.

odd [ɒd] *adj* [strange] bizarre, étrange. || [leftover] qui reste. || [occasional]: **I play the ~ game of tennis** je joue au tennis de temps en temps. || [not part of pair] dépareillé(e). || [number] impair(e). || *phr*: **twenty ~ years** une vingtaine d'années. ○ **odds** *npl*: **the ~s** les chances *fpl*; **the ~s are that ...** il y a des chances pour que ... (+ *subjunctive*), il est probable que ...; **against the ~s** envers et contre tout; **~s and ends** petites choses *fpl*, petits bouts *mpl*.

oddity ['ɒdɪtɪ] (*pl* **-ies**) *n* [person] personne *f* bizarre; [thing] chose *f* bizarre.

odd jobs *npl* petits travaux *mpl*.

oddly ['ɒdlɪ] *adv* curieusement; **~ enough** chose curieuse.

oddments ['ɒdmənts] *npl* fins *fpl* de série.

odds-on ['ɒdz-] *adj inf*: **~ favourite** grand favori.

odour *Br*, **odor** *Am* ['əudəʳ] *n* odeur *f*.

often

of [*unstressed* əv, *stressed* ɒv] *prep* [gen] de; **the cover ~ a book** la couverture d'un livre; **to die ~ cancer** mourir d'un cancer. ‖ [expressing quantity, amount, age etc] de; **thousands ~ people** des milliers de gens; **a piece ~ cake** un morceau de gâteau. ‖ [made from] en. ‖ [with dates, periods of time]: **the 12th ~ February** le 12 février.

off [ɒf] **1** *adv* [at a distance, away]: **10 miles ~** à 16 kilomètres; **two days ~** dans deux jours; **far ~** au loin; **to be ~** partir, s'en aller. ‖ [so as to remove]: **to take ~** enlever; **to cut sthg ~** couper qqch. ‖ [so as to complete]: **to finish ~** terminer; **to kill ~** achever. ‖ [not at work etc]: **a day/week ~** un jour/une semaine de congé. ‖ [discounted]: **£10 ~** 10 livres de remise OR réduction. **2** *prep* [at a distance from, away from] de; **to take a book ~ a shelf** prendre un livre sur une étagère; **~ the coast** près de la côte. ‖ [not attending]: **to be ~ work** ne pas travailler; **~ school** absent de l'école. ‖ [no longer liking]: **she's ~ her food** elle n'a pas d'appétit. ‖ [deducted from] sur. ‖ *inf* [from]: **to buy sthg ~ sb** acheter qqch à qqn. **3** *adj* [food] avarié(e), gâté(e); [milk] tourné(e). ‖ [TV, light] éteint(e); [engine] coupé(e). ‖ [cancelled] annulé(e). ‖ [not at work etc] absent(e). ‖ *inf* [offhand]: **he was a bit ~ with me** il n'a pas été sympa avec moi.

offal [ˈɒfl] *n* (*U*) abats *mpl*.

off-chance *n*: **on the ~ that ...** au cas où ....

off colour *adj* [ill] patraque.

off duty *adj* qui n'est pas de service; [doctor, nurse] qui n'est pas de garde.

offence *Br*, **offense** *Am* [əˈfens] *n* [crime] délit *m*. ‖ [upset]: **to cause sb ~** vexer qqn; **to take ~** se vexer.

offend [əˈfend] *vt* offenser.

offender [əˈfendər] *n* [criminal] criminel *m*, -elle *f*. ‖ [culprit] coupable *mf*.

offense [*sense 2* ˈɒfens] *n Am* = offence. ‖ SPORT attaque *f*.

offensive [əˈfensɪv] **1** *adj* [behaviour, comment] blessant(e). ‖ [weapon, action] offensif(ive). **2** *n* offensive *f*.

offer [ˈɒfər] **1** *n* [gen] offre *f*, proposition *f*. ‖ [price, bid] offre *f*. ‖ [in shop] promotion *f*; **on ~** [available] en vente; [at a special price] en réclame, en promotion. **2** *vt* [gen] offrir; **to ~ sthg to sb, to ~ sb sthg** offrir qqch à qqn; **to ~ to do sthg** proposer OR offrir de faire qqch. ‖ [provide -

services etc] proposer; [- hope] donner. **3** *vi* s'offrir.

offering [ˈɒfərɪŋ] *n* RELIG offrande *f*.

off-guard *adj* au dépourvu.

offhand [ˌɒfˈhænd] **1** *adj* cavalier(ière). **2** *adv* tout de suite.

office [ˈɒfɪs] *n* [place, staff] bureau *m*. ‖ [department] département *m*, service *m*. ‖ [position] fonction *f*, poste *m*; **in ~** en fonction; **to take ~** entrer en fonction.

office block *n* immeuble *m* de bureaux.

office hours *npl* heures *fpl* de bureau.

officer [ˈɒfɪsər] *n* [in armed forces] officier *m*. ‖ [in organization] agent *m*, fonctionnaire *mf*. ‖ [in police force] officier *m* (de police).

office worker *n* employé *m*, -e *f* de bureau.

official [əˈfɪʃl] **1** *adj* officiel(ielle). **2** *n* fonctionnaire *mf*.

offing [ˈɒfɪŋ] *n*: **in the ~** en vue, en perspective.

off-line *adj* COMPUT non connecté(e).

off-peak *adj* [electricity] utilisé(e) aux heures creuses; [fare] réduit(e) aux heures creuses.

off-putting [-ˌpʊtɪŋ] *adj* désagréable, rébarbatif(ive).

off season *n*: **the ~** la morte-saison.

offset [ˈɒfset] (*pt & pp* **offset**) *vt* [losses] compenser.

offshoot [ˈɒfʃuːt] *n*: **to be an ~ of sthg** être né(e) OR provenir de qqch.

offshore [ˈɒfʃɔːr] **1** *adj* [oil rig] offshore (*inv*); [island] proche de la côte; [fishing] côtier(ière). **2** *adv* au large.

offside [*adj & adv* ˌɒfˈsaɪd, *n* ˈɒfsaɪd] **1** *adj* [right-hand drive] de droite; [left-hand drive] de gauche. ‖ SPORT hors-jeu (*inv*). **2** *adv* SPORT hors-jeu. **3** *n* [right-hand drive] côté *m* droit; [left-hand drive] côté gauche.

offspring [ˈɒfsprɪŋ] (*pl inv*) *n* rejeton *m*.

offstage [ˌɒfˈsteɪdʒ] *adj & adv* dans les coulisses.

off-the-cuff **1** *adj* impromptu(e). **2** *adv* impromptu.

off-the-record *adv* confidentiellement.

off-white *adj* blanc cassé (*inv*).

often [ˈɒfn, ˈɒftn] *adv* souvent, fréquemment; **how ~ do you visit her?** vous la voyez tous les combien?; **as ~ as not** assez souvent; **every so ~** de temps en temps; **more ~ than not** le plus souvent. la plupart du temps.

ogle ['əʊgl] *vt* reluquer.

oh [əʊ] *excl* oh!; [expressing hesitation] euh!

oil [ɔɪl] **1** *n* [gen] huile *f*. || [for heating] mazout *m*. || [petroleum] pétrole *m*. **2** *vt* graisser, lubrifier.

oilcan ['ɔɪlkæn] *n* burette *f* d'huile.

oilfield ['ɔɪfi:ld] *n* gisement *m* pétrolifère.

oil filter *n* filtre *m* à huile.

oil-fired [-,faɪəd] *adj* au mazout.

oil painting *n* peinture *f* à l'huile.

oilrig ['ɔɪlrɪg] *n* [at sea] plate-forme *f* de forage OR pétrolière; [on land] derrick *m*.

oilskins ['ɔɪlskɪnz] *npl* ciré *m*.

oil slick *n* marée *f* noire.

oil tanker *n* [ship] pétrolier *m*, tanker *m*. || [lorry] camion-citerne *m*.

oil well *n* puits *m* de pétrole.

oily ['ɔɪlɪ] *adj* [rag etc] graisseux(euse); [food] gras (grasse).

ointment ['ɔɪntmənt] *n* pommade *f*.

OK (*pt & pp* **OKed**, *cont* **OKing**), **okay** [,əʊ'keɪ] *inf* **1** *adj*: **is it ~ with** OR **by you?** ça vous va?, vous êtes d'accord?; **are you ~?** ça va? **2** *excl* [expressing agreement] d'accord, O.K. || [to introduce new topic]: **~, can we start now?** bon, on commence? **3** *vt* approuver, donner le feu vert à.

old [əʊld] **1** *adj* [gen] vieux (vieille), âgé(e); **I'm 20 years ~** j'ai 20 ans; **how ~ are you?** quel âge as-tu? || [former] ancien(ienne). || *inf* [as intensifier]: **any ~** n'importe quel (n'importe quelle). **2** *npl*: **the ~** les personnes *fpl* âgées.

old age *n* vieillesse *f*.

old-fashioned [-'fæʃnd] *adj* [outmoded] démodé(e), passé(e) de mode. || [traditional] vieux jeu (*inv*).

old people's home *n* hospice *m* de vieillards.

olive ['ɒlɪv] **1** *adj* olive (*inv*). **2** *n* olive *f*.

olive green *adj* vert olive (*inv*).

olive oil *n* huile *f* d'olive.

Olympic [ə'lɪmpɪk] *adj* olympique.

Olympic Games *npl*: **the ~** les Jeux *mpl* Olympiques.

ombudsman ['ɒmbʊdzmən] (*pl* **-men** [-mən]) *n* ombudsman *m*.

omelet(te) ['ɒmlɪt] *n* omelette *f*.

omen ['əʊmen] *n* augure *m*, présage *m*.

ominous ['ɒmɪnəs] *adj* [event, situation] de mauvais augure; [sign] inquiétant(e); [look, silence] menaçant(e).

omission [ə'mɪʃn] *n* omission *f*.

omit [ə'mɪt] *vt* omettre; **to ~ to do sthg** oublier de faire qqch.

on [ɒn] **1** *prep* [indicating position, location] sur; **~ a chair/the wall** sur une chaise/le mur; **~ the ceiling** au plafond; **~ the left/right** à gauche/droite. || [indicating means]: **the car runs ~ petrol** la voiture marche à l'essence; **~ the radio** à la radio; **~ the telephone** au téléphone; **to hurt o.s. ~ sthg** se faire mal avec qqch. || [indicating mode of transport]: **to travel ~ a bus/train/ship** voyager en bus/par le train/en bateau; **I was ~ the bus** j'étais dans le bus; **~ foot** à pied. || [concerning] sur; **a book ~ astronomy** un livre sur l'astronomie. || [indicating time, activity]: **~ Thursday** jeudi; **~ the 10th of February** le 10 février; **~ my return**, **returning** à mon retour; **~ holiday** en vacances. || [indicating influence] sur; **the impact ~ the environment** l'impact sur l'environnement. || [using, supported by]: **he's ~ tranquillizers** il prend des tranquillisants; **to be ~ drugs** se droguer. || [earning]: **to be ~ £25,000 a year** gagner 25 000 livres par an; **to be ~ a low income** avoir un faible revenu. || [referring to musical instrument]: **to play sthg ~ the violin/flute/guitar** jouer qqch au violon/à la flûte/à la guitare. || *inf* [paid by]: **the drinks are ~ me** c'est moi qui régale, c'est ma tournée. **2** *adv* [indicating covering, clothing]: **put the lid ~** mettez le couvercle; **to put a sweater ~** mettre un pull; **what did she have ~?** qu'est-ce qu'elle portait?; **he had nothing ~** il était tout nu. || [being shown]: **what's ~ at the Ritz?** qu'est-ce qu'on joue OR donne au Ritz? || [working - radio, TV, light] allumé(e); [- machine] en marche; [- tap] ouvert(e); **turn ~ the power** mets le courant. || [indicating continuing action]: **to work ~** continuer à travailler; **he kept ~ walking** il continua à marcher. || [forward]: **send my mail ~ (to me)** faites suivre mon courrier; **later ~** plus tard; **earlier ~** plus tôt. || *inf* [referring to behaviour]: **it's just not ~!** cela ne se fait pas! ○ **from ... on** *adv*: **from now ~** dorénavant. désormais; **from then ~** à partir de ce moment-là. ○ **on and off** *adv* de temps en temps. ○ **on to, onto** *prep* (*only written as* **onto** *for senses 4 and 5*) [to a position on top of] sur; **she jumped ~ to the chair** elle a sauté sur la chaise. || [to a position on a vehicle] dans; **she got ~**

to the bus elle est montée dans le bus. ||
[to a position attached to]: **stick the photo
~ to the page with glue** colle la photo sur
la page. || [aware of wrongdoing]: **to be
onto sb** être sur la piste de qqn. || [into
contact with]: **get onto - the factory**
contactez l'usine.

once [wʌns] **1** *adv* [on one occasion] une
fois; **~ a day** une fois par jour; **~ again** OR
more encore une fois; **~ and for all** une
fois pour toutes; **~ in a while** de temps en
temps; **~ or twice** une ou deux fois; **for ~**
pour une fois. || [previously] autrefois, ja-
dis; **~ upon a time** il était une fois. **2** *conj*
dès que. ○ **at once** *adv* [immediately]
immédiatement. || [at the same time] en
même temps; **all at ~** tout d'un coup.

one [wʌn] **1** *num* [the number 1] un
(une); **~ of my friends** l'un de mes amis,
un ami à moi; **~ fifth** un cinquième. **2**
adj [only] seul(e), unique; **it's her ~
ambition/love** c'est son unique am-
bition/son seul amour. || [indefinite]: **~ of
these days** un de ces jours. **3** *pron* [refer-
ring to a particular thing or person]: **which
~ do you want?** lequel voulez-vous?; **this
~** celui-ci; **that ~** celui-là; **she's the ~ I
told you about** c'est celle dont je vous ai
parlé. || *fml* [you, anyone] on; **to do ~'s
duty** faire son devoir. ○ **for one** *adv*: **I
for ~ remain unconvinced** pour ma part
je ne suis pas convaincu.

one-armed bandit *n* machine *f* à sous.

one-man *adj* [business] dirigé(e) par un
seul homme.

one-man band *n* [musician] homme-
orchestre *m*.

one-off *inf adj* [offer, event, product]
unique.

one-on-one *Am* = one-to-one.

one-parent family *n* famille *f* mono-
parentale.

oneself [wʌn'self] *pron* (*reflexive*) se;
(*after prep*) soi. || (*emphatic*) soi-
même.

one-sided [-'saɪdɪd] *adj* [unequal] iné-
gal(e). || [biased] partial(e).

one-to-one *Br*, **one-on-one** *Am adj*
[discussion] en tête-à-tête; **~ tuition**
cours *mpl* particuliers.

one-upmanship [,wʌn'ʌpmənʃɪp] *n* art
m de faire toujours mieux que les autres.

one-way *adj* [street] à sens unique. ||
[ticket] simple.

ongoing ['ɒn,gəʊɪŋ] *adj* en cours, conti-
nu(e).

onion ['ʌnjən] *n* oignon *m*.

online ['ɒnlaɪn] *adj & adv* COMPUT en ligne, connecté(e).

onlooker ['ɒn,lʊkər] *n* spectateur *m*,
-trice *f*.

only ['əʊnlɪ] **1** *adj* seul(e), unique; **an ~
child** un enfant unique. **2** *adv* [gen] ne ...
que, seulement; **he ~ reads science
fiction** il ne lit que de la science fiction;
it's ~ a scratch c'est juste une égratignure; **he left ~ a few minutes ago** il est
parti il n'y a pas deux minutes. || [for em-
phasis]: **I ~ wish I could** je voudrais bien;
it's ~ natural (that) ... c'est tout à fait
normal que ...; **not ~ ... but also** non seulement ... mais encore; **I ~ just caught
the train** j'ai eu le train de justesse. **3**
conj seulement, mais.

onset ['ɒnset] *n* début *m*, commencement *m*.

onshore ['ɒnʃɔːr] *adj & adv* [from sea]
du large; [on land] à terre.

onslaught ['ɒnslɔːt] *n* attaque *f*.

onto [unstressed before consonant
'ɒntə, unstressed before vowel 'ɒntʊ,
stressed 'ɒntuː] = on to.

onus ['əʊnəs] *n* responsabilité *f*, charge
f.

onward ['ɒnwəd] *adj & adv* en avant.

onwards ['ɒnwədz] *adv* en avant; **from
now ~** dorénavant, désormais; **from then
~** à partir de ce moment-là.

ooze [uːz] **1** *vt fig* [charm, confidence]
respirer. **2** *vi*: **to ~ from** OR **out of sthg**
suinter de qqch.

opaque [əʊ'peɪk] *adj* opaque.

OPEC ['əʊpek] (*abbr of* **Organization
of Petroleum Exporting Countries**) *n*
OPEP *f*.

open ['əʊpn] **1** *adj* [gen] ouvert(e). || [re-
ceptive]: **to be ~ (to)** être réceptif(ive) (à).
|| [view, road, space] dégagé(e). || [uncov-
ered - car] découvert(e). || [meeting] pu-
blic(ique); [competition] ouvert(e) à
tous. || [disbelief, honesty] manifeste, évi-
dent(e). || [unresolved] non résolu(e). **2**
n: **in the ~** [sleep] à la belle étoile; [eat]
au grand air; **to bring sthg out into the ~**
divulguer qqch, exposer qqch au grand
jour. **3** *vt* [gen] ouvrir. || [inaugurate]
inaugurer. **4** *vi* [door, flower] s'ouvrir. ||
[shop, library etc] ouvrir. || [meeting, play
etc] commencer. ○ **open on to** *vt fus*
[subj: room, door] donner sur. ○ **open
up 1** *vt sep* [develop] exploiter, développer. **2** *vi* [possibilities etc] s'offrir, se pré-
senter. || [unlock door] ouvrir.

opener ['əʊpnər] *n* [for cans] ouvre-boîtes *m inv*; [for bottles] ouvre-bouteilles *m inv*, décapsuleur *m*.

opening ['əʊpnɪŋ] **1** *adj* [first] premier(ière); [remarks] préliminaire. **2** *n* [beginning] commencement *m*, début *m*. ‖ [in fence] trou *m*, percée *f*; [in clouds] trouée *f*, déchirure *f*. ‖ [opportunity - gen] occasion *f*; [- COMM] débouché *m*. ‖ [job vacancy] poste *m*.

opening hours *npl* heures *fpl* d'ouverture.

openly ['əʊpənlɪ] *adv* ouvertement, franchement.

open-minded [-'maɪndɪd] *adj* [person] qui a l'esprit large; [attitude] large.

open-plan *adj* non cloisonné(e).

opera ['ɒpərə] *n* opéra *m*.

opera house *n* opéra *m*.

operate ['ɒpəreɪt] **1** *vt* [machine] faire marcher, faire fonctionner. **2** *vi* [rule, law, system] jouer, être appliqué(e); [machine] fonctionner, marcher. ‖ COMM opérer, travailler. ‖ MED opérer; **to ~ on sb/sthg** opérer qqn/de qqch.

operating theatre *Br*, **operating room** *Am* ['ɒpəreɪtɪŋ-] *n* salle *f* d'opération.

operation [ˌɒpə'reɪʃn] *n* [gen & MED] opération *f*; **to have an ~ (for)** se faire opérer (de). ‖ [of machine] marche *f*, fonctionnement *m*; **to be in ~** [machine] être en marche OR en service; [law, system] être en vigueur. ‖ [COMM - company] exploitation *f*; [- management] administration *f*, gestion *f*.

operational [ˌɒpə'reɪʃənl] *adj* [machine] en état de marche.

operative ['ɒprətɪv] **1** *adj* en vigueur. **2** *n* ouvrier *m*, -ière *f*.

operator ['ɒpəreɪtər] *n* TELEC standardiste *mf*. ‖ [of machine] opérateur *m*, -trice *f*. ‖ COMM directeur *m*, -trice *f*.

opinion [ə'pɪnjən] *n* opinion *f*, avis *m*; **in my ~** à mon avis.

opinionated [ə'pɪnjəneɪtɪd] *adj pej* dogmatique.

opinion poll *n* sondage *m* d'opinion.

opponent [ə'pəʊnənt] *n* adversaire *mf*.

opportune ['ɒpətjuːn] *adj* opportun(e).

opportunist [ˌɒpə'tjuːnɪst] *n* opportuniste *mf*.

opportunity [ˌɒpə'tjuːnətɪ] *n* occasion *f*; **to take the ~ to do** OR **of doing sthg** profiter de l'occasion pour faire qqch.

oppose [ə'pəʊz] *vt* s'opposer à.

opposed [ə'pəʊzd] *adj*: **to be ~ to** être contre. être opposé à; **as ~ to** par opposition à.

opposing [ə'pəʊzɪŋ] *adj* opposé(e).

opposite ['ɒpəzɪt] **1** *adj* opposé(e); [house] d'en face. **2** *adv* en face. **3** *prep* en face de. **4** *n* contraire *m*.

opposite number *n* homologue *mf*.

opposition [ˌɒpə'zɪʃn] *n* [gen] opposition *f*. ‖ [opposing team] adversaire *mf*.

oppress [ə'pres] *vt* [persecute] opprimer. ‖ [depress] oppresser.

oppressive [ə'presɪv] *adj* [unjust] oppressif(ive). ‖ [weather, heat] étouffant(e), lourd(e). ‖ [silence] oppressant(e).

opt [ɒpt] **1** *vt*: **to ~ to do sthg** choisir de faire qqch. **2** *vi*: **to ~ for** opter pour.
○ **opt out** *vi*: **to ~ out (of)** [gen] choisir de ne pas participer (à); [of responsibility] se dérober (à).

optical ['ɒptɪkl] *adj* optique.

optician [ɒp'tɪʃn] *n* [who sells glasses] opticien *m*, -ienne *f*. ‖ [ophthalmologist] ophtalmologiste *mf*.

optimist ['ɒptɪmɪst] *n* optimiste *mf*.

optimistic [ˌɒptɪ'mɪstɪk] *adj* optimiste.

optimum ['ɒptɪməm] *adj* optimum.

option ['ɒpʃn] *n* option *f*, choix *m*.

optional ['ɒpʃənl] *adj* facultatif(ive); **an ~ extra** un accessoire.

or [ɔːr] *conj* [gen] ou. ‖ [after negative]: **he can't read ~ write** il ne sait ni lire ni écrire. ‖ [otherwise] sinon. ‖ [as correction] ou plutôt.

oral ['ɔːrəl] **1** *adj* [spoken] oral(e). **2** *n* oral *m*, épreuve *f* orale.

orally ['ɔːrəlɪ] *adv* [in spoken form] oralement. ‖ MED par voie orale.

orange ['ɒrɪndʒ] **1** *adj* orange (*inv*). **2** *n* [fruit] orange *f*. ‖ [colour] orange *m*.

orbit ['ɔːbɪt] **1** *n* orbite *f*. **2** *vt* décrire une orbite autour de.

orchard ['ɔːtʃəd] *n* verger *m*.

orchestra ['ɔːkɪstrə] *n* orchestre *m*.

orchestral [ɔː'kestrəl] *adj* orchestral(e).

orchid ['ɔːkɪd] *n* orchidée *f*.

ordain [ɔː'deɪn] *vt* [decree] ordonner, décréter. ‖ RELIG: **to be ~ed** être ordonné prêtre.

ordeal [ɔː'diːl] *n* épreuve *f*.

order ['ɔːdər] **1** *n* [gen] ordre *m*; **to be under ~s to do sthg** avoir (reçu) l'ordre de faire qqch. ‖ COMM commande *f*; **to place an ~ with sb for sthg** passer une commande de qqch à qqn; **to ~ sur**

commande. || [sequence] ordre *m*; **in ~** dans l'ordre. || [fitness for use]: **in working ~** en état de marche; **out of ~** [machine] en panne; [behaviour] déplacé(e); **in ~** [correct] en ordre. || (*U*) [discipline - gen] ordre *m*; [- in classroom] discipline *f*. || *Am* [portion] part *f*. 2 *vt* [command] ordonner; **to ~ sb to do sthg** ordonner à qqn de faire qqch. || COMM commander. ○ **in the order of** *Br*, **on the order of** *Am prep* environ, de l'ordre de. ○ **in order that** *conj* pour que, afin que. ○ **in order to** *conj* pour, afin de. ○ **order about**, **order around** *vt sep* commander.

order form *n* bulletin *m* de commande.

orderly ['ɔːdəlɪ] 1 *adj* [person] ordonné(e); [crowd] discipliné(e). 2 *n* [in hospital] garçon *m* de salle.

ordinarily ['ɔːdənrəlɪ] *adv* d'habitude, d'ordinaire.

ordinary ['ɔːdənrɪ] 1 *adj* [normal] ordinaire. || *pej* [unexceptional] ordinaire, quelconque. 2 *n*: **out of the ~** qui sort de l'ordinaire, exceptionnel(elle).

ordnance ['ɔːdnəns] *n* (*U*) [supplies] matériel *m* militaire. || [artillery] artillerie *f*.

ore [ɔːr] *n* minerai *m*.

oregano [,ɒrɪ'gɑːnəʊ] *n* origan *m*.

organ ['ɔːgən] *n* [gen] organe *m*. || MUS orgue *m*.

organic [ɔː'gænɪk] *adj* [of animals, plants] organique. || [farming, food] biologique.

organization [,ɔːgənaɪ'zeɪʃn] *n* organisation *f*.

organize, -ise ['ɔːgənaɪz] *vt* organiser.

organizer ['ɔːgənaɪzər] *n* organisateur *m*, -trice *f*.

orgasm ['ɔːgæzm] *n* orgasme *m*.

orgy ['ɔːdʒɪ] *n* lit & fig orgie *f*.

Orient ['ɔːrɪənt] *n*: **the ~** l'Orient *m*.

oriental [,ɔːrɪ'entl] *adj* oriental(e).

orienteering [,ɔːrɪən'tɪərɪŋ] *n* (*U*) course *f* d'orientation.

origami [,ɒrɪ'gɑːmɪ] *n* origami *m*.

origin ['ɒrɪdʒɪn] *n* [of river] source *f*; [of word, conflict] origine *f*. || [birth]: **country of ~** pays *m* d'origine.

original [ə'rɪdʒənl] 1 *adj* original(e); [owner] premier(ière). 2 *n* original *m*.

originally [ə'rɪdʒənəlɪ] *adv* à l'origine, au départ.

originate [ə'rɪdʒəneɪt] *vi* [belief, custom]: **to ~ (in)** prendre naissance (dans); **to ~ from** provenir de.

ornament ['ɔːnəmənt] *n* [object] bibelot *m*. || (*U*) [decoration] ornement *m*.

ornamental [,ɔːnə'mentl] *adj* [garden, pond] d'agrément; [design] décoratif (ive).

ornate [ɔː'neɪt] *adj* orné(e).

ornithology [,ɔːnɪ'θɒlədʒɪ] *n* ornithologie *f*.

orphan ['ɔːfn] 1 *n* orphelin *m*, -e *f*. 2 *vt*: **to be ~ed** devenir orphelin(e).

orphanage ['ɔːfənɪdʒ] *n* orphelinat *m*.

orthodox ['ɔːθədɒks] *adj* [conventional] orthodoxe. || RELIG [traditional] traditionaliste.

orthopaedic [,ɔːθə'piːdɪk] *adj* orthopédique.

orthopedic *etc* [,ɔːθə'piːdɪk] = **orthopaedic** *etc*.

oscillate ['ɒsɪleɪt] *vi* lit & fig osciller.

ostensible [ɒ'stensəbl] *adj* prétendu(e).

ostentatious [,ɒstən'teɪʃəs] *adj* ostentatoire.

osteopath ['ɒstɪəpæθ] *n* ostéopathe *mf*.

ostracize, -ise ['ɒstrəsaɪz] *vt* frapper d'ostracisme, mettre au ban.

ostrich ['ɒstrɪtʃ] *n* autruche *f*.

other ['ʌðər] 1 *adj* autre; **the ~ one** l'autre; **the ~ day/week** l'autre jour/ semaine. 2 *adv*: **there was nothing to do ~ than confess** il ne pouvait faire autrement que d'avouer; **~ than John** John à part. 3 *pron* **~ s** d'autres; **the ~** l'autre; **the ~s** les autres; **one after the ~** l'un après l'autre (l'une après l'autre); **one or ~ of you** l'un (l'une) de vous deux; **none ~ than** nul (nulle) autre que. ○ **something or other** *pron* quelque chose, je ne sais quoi. ○ **somehow or other** *adv* d'une manière ou d'une autre.

otherwise ['ʌðəwaɪz] 1 *adv* autrement; **or ~** [or not] ou non. 2 *conj* sinon.

otter ['ɒtər] *n* loutre *f*.

ouch [aʊtʃ] *excl* aïe!, ouïe!

ought [ɔːt] *aux vb* [sensibly]: **I really ~ to go** il faut absolument que je m'en aille; **you ~ to see a doctor** tu devrais aller chez le docteur. || [morally]: **you ~ not to have done that** tu n'aurais pas dû faire cela. || [expressing probability]: **she ~ to pass her exam** elle devrait réussir à son examen.

ounce [aʊns] *n* = 28,35 g, once *f*.

our ['auər] *poss adj* notre, nos (*pl*); ~ **money/house** notre argent/maison; ~ **children** nos enfants; **it wasn't OUR fault** ce n'était pas de notre faute à nous.

ours ['auəz] *poss pron* le nôtre (la nôtre), les nôtres (*pl*); **that money is** ~ cet argent est à nous OR est le nôtre; **it wasn't their fault, it was OURS** ce n'était pas de leur faute. c'était de notre faute à nous OR de la nôtre; **a friend of** ~ un ami à nous, un de nos amis.

ourselves [auə'selvz] *pron pl* (*reflexive*) nous. || (*for emphasis*) nous-mêmes; **we did it by** ~ nous l'avons fait tout seuls.

oust [aust] *vt*: **to** ~ **sb (from)** évincer qqn (de).

out [aut] *adv* [not inside. out of doors] dehors; **I'm going** ~ **for a walk** je sors me promener; **to run** ~ sortir en courant; ~ **here** ici; ~ **there** là-bas. || [away from home, office, published] sorti(e); **John's** ~ **at the moment** John est sorti. John n'est pas là en ce moment. || [extinguished] éteint(e); **the lights went** ~ les lumières se sont éteintes. || [of tides]: **the tide is** ~ la marée est basse. || [out of fashion] démodé(e), passé(e) de mode. || [in flower] en fleur. || *inf* [on strike] en grève. || [determined]: **to be** ~ **to do sthg** être résolu(e) OR décidé(e) à faire qqch. ○ **out of** *prep* [outside] en dehors de; **to go** ~ **of the room** sortir de la pièce; **to be** ~ **of the country** être à l'étranger. || [indicating cause] par; ~ **of spite/love/boredom** par dépit/amour/ennui. || [indicating origin. source] de, dans; **a page** ~ **of a book** une page d'un livre; **it's made** ~ **of plastic** c'est en plastique. || [without] sans; ~ **of petrol/money** à court d'essence/d'argent. || [sheltered from] à l'abri de. || [to indicate proportion] sur; **one** ~ **of ten people** une personne sur dix; **ten** ~ **of ten** dix sur dix.

out-and-out *adj* [liar] fieffé(e); [disgrace] complet(ète).

outboard (motor) ['autbɔ:d-] *n* (moteur *m*) hors-bord *m inv*.

outbreak ['autbreik] *n* [of war, crime] début *m*, déclenchement *m*; [of spots etc] éruption *f*.

outburst ['autbɜ:st] *n* explosion *f*.

outcast ['autkɑ:st] *n* paria *m*.

outcome ['autkʌm] *n* issue *f*, résultat *m*.

outcrop ['autkrɒp] *n* affleurement *m*.

outcry ['autkrai] *n* tollé *m*.

outdated [,aut'deitid] *adj* démodé(e), vieilli(e).

outdid [,aut'did] *pt* → **outdo.**

outdo [,aut'du:] (*pt* **-did,** *pp* **-done** [-'dʌn]) *vt* surpasser.

outdoor ['autdɔ:r] *adj* [life, swimming pool] en plein air; [activities] de plein air.

outdoors [aut'dɔ:z] *adv* dehors.

outer ['autər] *adj* extérieur(e).

outer space *n* cosmos *m*.

outfit ['autfit] *n* [clothes] tenue *f*.

outgoing ['aut,gəuiŋ] *adj* [chairman etc] sortant(e); [mail] à expédier; [train] en partance. || [friendly, sociable] ouvert(e).

outgrow [,aut'grəu] (*pt* **-grew,** *pp* **-grown**) *vt* [clothes] devenir trop grand(e) pour. || [habit] se défaire de.

outhouse ['authaus, *pl* -hauziz] *n* appentis *m*.

outing ['autiŋ] *n* [trip] sortie *f*.

outlandish [aut'lændiʃ] *adj* bizarre.

outlaw ['autlɔ:] **1** *n* hors-la-loi *m inv*. **2** *vt* [practice] proscrire.

outlay ['autlei] *n* dépenses *fpl*.

outlet ['autlet] *n* [for emotion] exutoire *m*. || [hole, pipe] sortie *f*. || [shop]: **retail** ~ point *m* de vente. || *Am* ELEC prise *f* (de courant).

outline ['autlain] **1** *n* [brief description] grandes lignes *fpl*; **in** ~ en gros. || [silhouette] silhouette *f*. **2** *vt* [describe briefly] exposer les grandes lignes de.

outlive [,aut'liv] *vt* [subj: person] survivre à.

outlook ['autluk] *n* [disposition] attitude *f*, conception *f*. || [prospect] perspective *f*.

outlying ['aut,laiiŋ] *adj* [village] reculé(e); [suburbs] écarté(e).

outnumber [,aut'nʌmbər] *vt* surpasser en nombre.

out-of-date *adj* [passport] périmé(e); [clothes] démodé(e); [belief] dépassé(e).

out of doors *adv* dehors.

outpatient ['aut,peiʃnt] *n* malade *mf* en consultation externe.

outpost ['autpəust] *n* avant-poste *m*.

output ['autput] *n* [production] production *f*. || COMPUT sortie *f*.

outrage ['autreidʒ] **1** *n* [emotion] indignation *f*. || [act] atrocité *f*. **2** *vt* outrager.

outrageous [aut'reidʒəs] *adj* [offensive, shocking] scandaleux(euse), monstrueux(euse). || [very unusual] choquant(e).

outright [*adj* 'aʊtraɪt, *adv* ˌaʊt'raɪt] **1** *adj* absolu(e), total(e). **2** *adv* [*deny*] carrément, franchement. || [*win, fail*] complètement, totalement.

outset ['aʊtset] *n*: **at the ~** au commencement, au début.

outside [*adv* ˌaʊt'saɪd, *adj, prep & n* 'aʊtsaɪd] **1** *adj* [*gen*] extérieur(e); **an ~ opinion** une opinion indépendante. || [*unlikely - chance, possibility*] faible. **2** *adv* à l'extérieur; **to go/run/look ~** aller/courir/regarder dehors. **3** *prep* [*not inside*] à l'extérieur de, en dehors de. || [*beyond*]: **~ office hours** en dehors des heures de bureau. **4** *n* extérieur *m*. ○ **outside of** *prep Am* [*apart from*] à part.

outside lane *n* AUT [*in Europe, US*] voie *f* de gauche.

outside line *n* TELEC ligne *f* extérieure.

outsider [ˌaʊt'saɪdər] *n* [*in race*] outsider *m*. || [*from society*] étranger *m*, -ère *f*.

outsize ['aʊtsaɪz] *adj* [*bigger than usual*] énorme, colossal(e). || [*clothes*] grande taille (*inv*).

outskirts ['aʊtskɜːts] *npl*: **the ~** la banlieue.

outspoken [ˌaʊt'spəʊkn] *adj* franc (franche).

outstanding [ˌaʊt'stændɪŋ] *adj* [*excellent*] exceptionnel(elle), remarquable. || [*example*] marquant(e). || [*not paid*] impayé(e). || [*unfinished - work, problem*] en suspens.

outstretched [ˌaʊt'stretʃt] *adj* [*arms, hands*] tendu(e); [*wings*] déployé(e).

outstrip [ˌaʊt'strɪp] *vt* devancer.

out-tray *n* corbeille *f* pour le courrier à expédier.

outward ['aʊtwəd] **1** *adj* [*going away*]: **~ journey** aller *m*. || [*apparent, visible*] extérieur(e). **2** *adv Am* = **outwards**.

outwardly ['aʊtwədlɪ] *adv* [*apparently*] en apparence.

outwards *Br* ['aʊtwədz], **outward** *Am adv* vers l'extérieur.

outweigh [ˌaʊt'weɪ] *vt fig* primer sur.

outwit [ˌaʊt'wɪt] *vt* se montrer plus malin(igne) que.

oval ['əʊvl] **1** *adj* ovale. **2** *n* ovale *m*.

Oval Office *n*: **the ~** *bureau du président des États-Unis à la Maison-Blanche.*

ovary ['əʊvərɪ] *n* ovaire *m*.

ovation [əʊ'veɪʃn] *n* ovation *f*; **the audience gave her a standing ~** le public l'a ovationnée.

oven ['ʌvn] *n* [*for cooking*] four *m*.

ovenproof ['ʌvnpruːf] *adj* qui va au four.

over ['əʊvər] **1** *prep* [*above*] au-dessus de. || [*on top of*] sur. || [*on other side of*] de l'autre côté de; **they live ~ the road** ils habitent en face. || [*to other side of*] pardessus; **to go ~ the border** franchir la frontière. || [*more than*] plus de; **~ and above** en plus de. || [*concerning*] à propos de, au sujet de. || [*during*] pendant. **2** *adv* [*distance away*]: **~ here** ici; **~ there** là-bas. || [*across*]: **they flew ~ to America** ils se sont envolés pour les États-Unis; **we invited them ~** nous les avons invités chez nous. || [*more*] plus. || [*remaining*]: **there's nothing left** ~ il ne reste rien. || RADIO: **~ and out!** à vous! || [*involving repetitions*]: **(all) ~ again** (tout) au début; **~ and ~ again** à maintes reprises, maintes fois. **3** *adj* [*finished*] fini(e), terminé(e). ○ **all over 1** *prep* [*throughout*] partout, dans tout; **all ~ the world** dans le monde entier. **2** *adv* [*everywhere*] partout. **3** *adj* [*finished*] fini(e).

overall [*adj & n* 'əʊvərɔːl, *adv* ˌəʊvər'ɔːl] **1** *adj* [*general*] d'ensemble. **2** *adv* en général. **3** *n* [*gen*] tablier *m*. || *Am* [*for work*] bleu *m* de travail. ○ **overalls** *npl Am* [*dungarees*] salopette *f*.

overawe [ˌəʊvər'ɔː] *vt* impressionner.

overbalance [ˌəʊvə'bæləns] *vi* basculer.

overbearing [ˌəʊvə'beərɪŋ] *adj* autoritaire.

overboard ['əʊvəbɔːd] *adv*: **to fall ~** tomber par-dessus bord.

overbook [ˌəʊvə'bʊk] *vi* surréserver.

overcame [ˌəʊvə'keɪm] *pt* → **overcome**.

overcast [ˌəʊvə'kɑːst] *adj* couvert(e).

overcharge [ˌəʊvə'tʃɑːdʒ] *vt*: **to ~ sb (for sthg)** faire payer (qqch) trop cher à qqn.

overcoat ['əʊvəkəʊt] *n* pardessus *m*.

overcome [ˌəʊvə'kʌm] (*pt* **-came**, *pp* **-come**) *vt* [*fears, difficulties*] surmonter. || [*overwhelm*]: **to be ~ (by** OR **with)** [*emotion*] être submergé(e) (de); [*grief*] être accablé(e) (de).

overcrowded [ˌəʊvə'kraʊdɪd] *adj* bondé(e).

overcrowding [ˌəʊvə'kraʊdɪŋ] *n* surpeuplement *m*.

overdo [ˌəʊvə'duː] (*pt* **-did** [-'dɪd], *pp* **-done**) *vt* [*exaggerate*] exagérer. || [*do too*

much] trop faire; **to ~ it** se surmener. ||
[overcook] trop cuire.

overdone [,əʊvə'dʌn] **1** *pp* → **overdo. 2**
adj [food] trop cuit(e).

overdose ['əʊvədəʊs] *n* overdose *f*.

overdraft ['əʊvədrɑːft] *n* découvert *m*.

overdrawn [,əʊvə'drɔːn] *adj* à découvert.

overdue [,əʊvə'djuː] *adj* [late]: **~ (for)**
en retard (pour). || [change, reform]:
(long) ~ attendu(e) (depuis longtemps).
|| [unpaid] arriéré(e), impayé(e).

overestimate [,əʊvər'estɪmeɪt] *vt* sur-
estimer.

overflow [*vb* ,əʊvə'fləʊ, *n* 'əʊvəfləʊ] **1**
vi [gen] déborder. **2** *n* [pipe, hole] trop-
plein *m*.

overgrown [,əʊvə'grəʊn] *adj* [garden]
envahi(e) par les mauvaises herbes.

overhaul [*n* 'əʊvəhɔːl, *vb* ,əʊvə'hɔːl] **1** *n*
[of car, machine] révision *f*. || *fig* [of sys-
tem] refonte *f*, remaniement *m*. **2** *vt* [car,
machine] réviser. || *fig* [system] refondre,
remanier.

overhead [*adv* ,əʊvə'hed, *adj* & *n*
'əʊvəhed] **1** *adj* aérien(ienne). **2** *adv* au-
dessus. **3** *n Am* (U) frais *mpl* généraux.

overhead projector *n* rétroprojecteur *m*.

overhear [,əʊvə'hɪər] (*pt* & *pp* **-heard**
[-'hɜːd]) *vt* entendre par hasard.

overheat [,əʊvə'hiːt] **1** *vt* surchauffer.
2 *vi* [engine] chauffer.

overjoyed [,əʊvə'dʒɔɪd] *adj*: **~ (at)**
transporté(e) de joie (à).

overladen [,əʊvə'leɪdn] **1** *pp* → **overload. 2** *adj* surchargé(e).

overland ['əʊvəlænd] *adj* & *adv* par
voie de terre.

overlap [,əʊvə'læp] *vi lit* & *fig* se chevaucher.

overleaf [,əʊvə'liːf] *adv* au verso, au
dos.

overload [,əʊvə'ləʊd] (*pp* **-loaded** OR
-laden) *vt* surcharger.

overlook [,əʊvə'lʊk] *vt* [subj: building,
room] donner sur. || [disregard, miss] ou-
blier, négliger. || [excuse] passer sur, fer-
mer les yeux sur.

overnight [*adj* 'əʊvənaɪt, *adv*
,əʊvə'naɪt] **1** *adj* [journey, parking] de
nuit; [stay] d'une nuit. || *fig* [sudden]: **~**
success succès *m* immédiat. **2** *adv* [stay,
leave] la nuit. || [suddenly] du jour au len-
demain.

overpass ['əʊvəpɑːs] *n Am* ≃ Tobog-
gan® *m*.

overpower [,əʊvə'paʊər] *vt* [in fight]
vaincre. || *fig* [overwhelm] accabler, ter-
rasser.

overpowering [,əʊvə'paʊərɪŋ] *adj* [de-
sire] irrésistible; [smell] entêtant(e).

overran [,əʊvə'ræn] *pt* → **overrun**.

overrated [,əʊvə'reɪtɪd] *adj* surfait(e).

override [,əʊvə'raɪd] (*pt* **-rode,** *pp*
-ridden) *vt* [be more important than]
l'emporter sur, prévaloir sur. || [overrule
- decision] annuler.

overriding [,əʊvə'raɪdɪŋ] *adj* [need, im-
portance] primordial(e).

overrode [,əʊvə'rəʊd] *pt* → **override**.

overrule [,əʊvə'ruːl] *vt* [person] prévaloir contre; [decision] annuler; [objection]
rejeter.

overrun [,əʊvə'rʌn] (*pt* **-ran,** *pp* **-run**
) **1** *vt fig* [cover, fill]: **to be ~ with** [weeds]
être envahi(e) de; [rats] être infesté(e)
de. **2** *vi* dépasser (le temps alloué).

oversaw [,əʊvə'sɔː] *pt* → **oversee**.

overseas [*adj* 'əʊvəsiːz, *adv* ,əʊvə'siːz]
1 *adj* [sales, company] à l'étranger; [mar-
ket] extérieur(e); [visitor, student] étran-
ger(ère); **~ aid** aide *f* aux pays étrangers.
2 *adv* à l'étranger.

oversee [,əʊvə'siː] (*pt* **-saw,** *pp* **-seen**
[-'siːn]) *vt* surveiller.

overseer ['əʊvə,siːər] *n* contremaître *m*.

overshadow [,əʊvə'ʃædəʊ] *vt* [subj:
building, tree] dominer; *fig* éclipser.

overshoot [,əʊvə'ʃuːt] (*pt* & *pp* **-shot**)
vt dépasser, rater.

oversight ['əʊvəsaɪt] *n* oubli *m*.

oversleep [,əʊvə'sliːp] (*pt* & *pp* **-slept**
[-'slept]) *vi* ne pas se réveiller à temps.

overspill ['əʊvəspɪl] *n* [of population]
excédent *m*.

overstep [,əʊvə'step] *vt* dépasser; **to ~**
the mark dépasser la mesure.

overt ['əʊvɜːt] *adj* déclaré(e), non dé-
guisé(e).

overtake [,əʊvə'teɪk] (*pt* **-took,** *pp*
-taken [-'teɪkn]) **1** *vt* AUT doubler, dépasser. **2** *vi* AUT doubler.

overthrow [*n* 'əʊvəθrəʊ, *vb* ,əʊvə'θrəʊ]
(*pt* **-threw** [-'θruː], *pp* **-thrown**
[-'θrəʊn]) **1** *n* [of government] coup *m*
d'État. **2** *vt* [government] renverser.

overtime ['əʊvətaɪm] **1** *n* (U) [extra
work] heures *fpl* supplémentaires. || *Am*
SPORT prolongations *fpl*. **2** *adv*: **to work ~**
faire des heures supplémentaires.

overtones ['əʊvətəʊnz] *npl* notes *fpl*,
accents *mpl*.

overtook [,əʊvə'tʊk] *pt* → **overtake**.

overture ['əʊvə,tjʊə^r] n MUS ouverture f.

overturn [,əʊvə'tɜːn] 1 vt [gen] renverser. || [decision] annuler. 2 vi [vehicle] se renverser; [boat] chavirer.

overweight [,əʊvə'weɪt] adj trop gros (grosse).

overwhelm [,əʊvə'welm] vt [subj: grief, despair] accabler; **to be ~ed with joy** être au comble de la joie. || MIL [gain control of] écraser.

overwhelming [,əʊvə'welmɪŋ] adj [overpowering] irrésistible, irrépressible. || [defeat, majority] écrasant(e).

overwork [,əʊvə'wɜːk] 1 n surmenage m. 2 vt [person, staff] surmener.

overwrought [,əʊvə'rɔːt] adj excédé(e), à bout.

owe [əʊ] vt: **to ~ sthg to sb, to ~ sb sthg** devoir qqch à qqn.

owing ['əʊɪŋ] adj dû (due). ○ **owing to** prep à cause de, en raison de.

owl [aʊl] n hibou m.

own [əʊn] 1 adj propre; **she has her ~ style** elle a son style à elle. 2 pron: **I've got my ~** j'ai le mien; **he has a house of his ~** il a une maison à lui, il a sa propre maison; **on one's ~** tout seul (toute seule); **to get one's ~ back** inf prendre sa revanche. 3 vt posséder. ○ **own up** vi: **to ~ up (to sthg)** avouer OR confesser (qqch).

owner ['əʊnə^r] n propriétaire mf.

ownership ['əʊnəʃɪp] n propriété f.

ox [ɒks] (pl **oxen**) n bœuf m.

oxen ['ɒksn] pl → **ox**.

oxtail soup ['ɒksteɪl-] n soupe f à la queue de bœuf.

oxygen ['ɒksɪdʒən] n oxygène m.

oxygen mask n masque m à oxygène.

oxygen tent n tente f à oxygène.

oyster ['ɔɪstə^r] n huître f.

oz. abbr of **ounce**.

ozone-friendly adj qui préserve la couche d'ozone.

ozone layer n couche f d'ozone.

p¹ (pl **p's** OR **ps**), **P** (pl **P's** OR **Ps**) [piː] n [letter] p m inv, P m inv.

p² (abbr of **page**) p.

pa [pɑː] n inf papa m.

p.a. (abbr of **per annum**) p.a.

PA n (abbr of **public address system**) sono f.

pace [peɪs] 1 n [speed, rate] vitesse f, allure f; **to keep ~ (with sthg)** se maintenir au même niveau (que qqch). || [step] pas m. 2 vi: **to ~ (up and down)** faire les cent pas.

pacemaker ['peɪs,meɪkə^r] n MED stimulateur m cardiaque, pacemaker m.

Pacific [pə'sɪfɪk] 1 adj du Pacifique. 2 n: **the ~ (Ocean)** l'océan m Pacifique, le Pacifique.

pacifier ['pæsɪfaɪə^r] n Am [for child] tétine f, sucette f.

pacifist ['pæsɪfɪst] n pacifiste mf.

pacify ['pæsɪfaɪ] vt [person, baby] apaiser. || [country] pacifier.

pack [pæk] 1 n [bag] sac m. || [packet] paquet m. || [of cards] jeu m. || [of dogs] meute f; [of wolves, thieves] bande f. 2 vt [clothes, belongings] emballer; **to ~ one's bags** faire ses bagages. || [fill] remplir; **to be ~ed into** être entassé dans. 3 vi [for journey] faire ses bagages OR sa valise. ○ **pack off** vt sep inf [send away] expédier.

package ['pækɪdʒ] 1 n [of books, goods] paquet m. || COMPUT progiciel m. 2 vt [wrap up] conditionner.

package deal n contrat m global.

package tour n vacances fpl organisées.

packaging ['pækɪdʒɪŋ] n conditionnement m.

packed [pækt] adj: **~ (with)** bourré(e) (de).

packet ['pækɪt] n [gen] paquet m.

packing ['pækɪŋ] n [material] emballage m.

packing case n caisse f d'emballage.

pact [pækt] *n* pacte *m*.

pad [pæd] **1** *n* [of cotton wool etc] morceau *m*. || [of paper] bloc *m*. || [of cat, dog] coussinet *m*. **2** *vt* [furniture, jacket] rembourrer; [wound] tamponner. **3** *vi* [walk softly] marcher à pas feutrés.

padding ['pædɪŋ] *n* [material] rembourrage *m*. || *fig* [in speech, letter] délayage *m*.

paddle ['pædl] **1** *n* [for canoe etc] pagaie *f*. || [in sea]: **to have a ~** faire trempette. **2** *vi* [in canoe etc] avancer en pagayant. || [in sea] faire trempette.

paddle boat, paddle steamer *n* bateau *m* à aubes.

paddock ['pædək] *n* [small field] enclos *m*. || [at racecourse] paddock *m*.

paddy field ['pædɪ-] *n* rizière *f*.

padlock ['pædlɒk] **1** *n* cadenas *m*. **2** *vt* cadenasser.

paediatrics [,piːdɪ'ætrɪks] = **pediatrics**.

pagan ['peɪgən] **1** *adj* païen(ïenne). **2** *n* païen *m*, -ïenne *f*.

page [peɪdʒ] **1** *n* [of book] page *f*. || [sheet of paper] feuille *f*. **2** *vt* [in airport] appeler au micro.

pageant ['pædʒənt] *n* [show] spectacle *m* historique.

pageantry ['pædʒəntrɪ] *n* apparat *m*.

paid [peɪd] **1** *pt* & *pp* → **pay**. **2** *adj* [work, holiday, staff] rémunéré(e), payé(e).

pail [peɪl] *n* seau *m*.

pain [peɪn] *n* [hurt] douleur *f*; **to be in ~** souffrir. || *inf* [annoyance]: **it's/he is such a ~** c'est/il est vraiment assommant. ○ **pains** *npl* [effort, care]: **to be at ~s to do sthg** vouloir absolument faire qqch; **to take ~s to do sthg** se donner beaucoup de mal ou peine pour faire qqch.

pained [peɪnd] *adj* peiné(e).

painful ['peɪnfʊl] *adj* [physically] douloureux(euse). || [emotionally] pénible.

painfully ['peɪnfʊlɪ] *adv* [fall, hit] douloureusement. || [remember, feel] péniblement.

painkiller ['peɪn,kɪlər] *n* calmant *m*, analgésique *m*.

painless ['peɪnlɪs] *adj* [without hurt] indolore, sans douleur. || *fig* [changeover] sans heurt.

painstaking ['peɪnz,teɪkɪŋ] *adj* [worker] assidu(e); [detail, work] soigné(e).

paint [peɪnt] **1** *n* peinture *f*. **2** *vt* [gen] peindre.

paintbrush ['peɪntbrʌʃ] *n* pinceau *m*.

painter ['peɪntər] *n* peintre *m*.

painting ['peɪntɪŋ] *n* (U) [gen] peinture *f*. || [picture] toile *f*, tableau *m*.

paint stripper *n* décapant *m*.

paintwork ['peɪntwɜːk] *n* (U) surfaces *fpl* peintes.

pair [peər] *n* [of shoes, wings etc] paire *f*; **a ~ of trousers** un pantalon. || [couple] couple *m*.

pajamas [pə'dʒɑːməz] = **pyjamas**.

Pakistan [*Br* ,pɑːkɪ'stɑːn, *Am* ,pækɪ'stæn] *n* Pakistan *m*.

Pakistani [*Br* ,pɑːkɪ'stɑːnɪ, *Am* ,pækɪ'stænɪ] **1** *adj* pakistanais(e). **2** *n* Pakistanais *m*, -e *f*.

pal [pæl] *n inf* [friend] copain *m*, copine *f*. || [as term of address] mon vieux *m*.

palace ['pælɪs] *n* palais *m*.

palatable ['pælətəbl] *adj* [food] agréable au goût.

palate ['pælət] *n* palais *m*.

palaver [pə'lɑːvər] *n* (U) *inf* [talk] palabres *fpl*. || [fuss] histoire *f*, affaire *f*.

pale [peɪl] *adj* pâle.

Palestine ['pælə,staɪn] *n* Palestine *f*.

Palestinian [,pælə'stɪnɪən] **1** *adj* palestinien(ïenne). **2** *n* Palestinien *m*, -ïenne *f*.

palette ['pælət] *n* palette *f*.

pall [pɔːl] **1** *n* [of smoke] voile *m*. || *Am* [coffin] cercueil *m*. **2** *vi* perdre de son charme.

pallet ['pælɪt] *n* palette *f*.

pallor ['pælər] *n literary* pâleur *f*.

palm [pɑːm] *n* [tree] palmier *m*. || [of hand] paume *f*. ○ **palm off** *vt sep inf*: **to ~ sthg off on sb** refiler qqch à qqn; **to ~ sb off with sthg** se débarrasser de qqn avec qqch.

Palm Sunday *n* dimanche *m* des Rameaux.

palm tree *n* palmier *m*.

palpable ['pælpəbl] *adj* évident(e), manifeste.

paltry ['pɔːltrɪ] *adj* dérisoire.

pamper ['pæmpər] *vt* choyer, dorloter.

pamphlet ['pæmflɪt] *n* brochure *f*.

pan [pæn] **1** *n* [gen] casserole *f*. || *Am* [for bread, cakes etc] moule *m*. **2** *vt inf* [criticize] démolir. **3** *vi* CINEMA faire un panoramique.

panacea [,pænə'sɪə] *n* panacée *f*.

Panama ['pænə'mɑː] *n* Panama *m*.

Panama Canal *n*: **the ~** le canal de Panama.

pancake ['pænkeɪk] *n* crêpe *f*.

Pancake Tuesday *n* mardi gras *m*.

panda ['pændə] (*pl inv* OR **-s**) *n* panda *m*.

pandemonium [,pændɪ'məʊnjəm] *n* tohu-bohu *m inv*.

pander ['pændər] *vi*: **to ~ to sb** se prêter aux exigences de qqn; **to ~ to sthg** se plier à qqch.

pane [peɪn] *n* vitre *f*, carreau *m*.

panel ['pænl] *n* TV & RADIO invités *mpl*; [of experts] comité *m*. || [of wood] panneau *m*. || [of machine] tableau *m* de bord.

panelling *Br*, **paneling** *Am* ['pænəlɪŋ] *n* (*U*) lambris *m*.

pang [pæŋ] *n* tiraillement *m*.

panic ['pænɪk] (*pt* & *pp* **-ked**, *cont* **-king**) **1** *n* panique *f*. **2** *vi* paniquer.

panicky ['pænɪkɪ] *adj* [person] paniqué(e); [feeling] de panique.

panic-stricken *adj* affolé(e), pris(e) de panique.

panorama [,pænə'rɑːmə] *n* panorama *m*.

pansy ['pænzɪ] *n* [flower] pensée *f*.

pant [pænt] *vi* haleter.

panther ['pænθər] (*pl inv* OR **-s**) *n* panthère *f*.

panties ['pæntɪz] *npl inf* culotte *f*.

pantihose ['pæntɪhəʊz] = **panty hose**.

pantry ['pæntrɪ] *n* garde-manger *m inv*.

pants [pænts] *npl Am* [trousers] pantalon *m*.

panty hose ['pæntɪhəʊz] *npl Am* collant *m*.

papa [*Br* pə'pɑː, *Am* 'pæpə] *n* papa *m*.

paper ['peɪpər] **1** *n* (*U*) [for writing on] papier *m*; **a piece of ~** [sheet] une feuille de papier; [scrap] un bout de papier. || [newspaper] journal *m*. || [in exam - test] épreuve *f*; [- answers] copie *f*. || [essay]: **~ (on)** essai *m* (sur). **2** *adj* [hat, bag etc] en papier. **3** *vt* tapisser. ○ **papers** *npl* [official documents] papiers *mpl*.

paperback ['peɪpəbæk] *n*: **~ (book)** livre *m* de poche.

paper clip *n* trombone *m*.

paper handkerchief *n* mouchoir *m* en papier.

paper knife *n* coupe-papier *m inv*.

paperweight ['peɪpəweɪt] *n* presse-papiers *m inv*.

paperwork ['peɪpəwɜːk] *n* paperasserie *f*.

paprika ['pæprɪkə] *n* paprika *m*.

par [pɑːr] *n* [parity]: **on a ~ with** à égalité avec. || GOLF par *m*. || [good health]: **below** OR **under ~** pas en forme.

parable ['pærəbl] *n* parabole *f*.

parachute ['pærəʃuːt] **1** *n* parachute *m*. **2** *vi* sauter en parachute.

parade [pə'reɪd] **1** *n* [celebratory] parade *f*, revue *f*. || MIL défilé *m*. **2** *vt* [people] faire défiler. || [object] montrer. || *fig* [flaunt] afficher. **3** *vi* défiler.

paradise ['pærədaɪs] *n* paradis *m*.

paradox ['pærədɒks] *n* paradoxe *m*.

paraffin ['pærəfɪn] *n* paraffine *f*.

paragon ['pærəgən] *n* modèle *m*, parangon *m*.

paragraph ['pærəgrɑːf] *n* paragraphe *m*.

Paraguay ['pærəgwaɪ] *n* Paraguay *m*.

parallel ['pærəlel] **1** *adj lit* & *fig*: **~ (to** OR **with)** parallèle (à). **2** *n* GEOM parallèle *f*. || [similarity & GEOGR] parallèle *m*. || *fig* [similar person, object] équivalent *m*.

paralyse *Br*, **-yze** *Am* ['pærəlaɪz] *vt lit* & *fig* paralyser.

paralysis [pə'rælɪsɪs] (*pl* **-lyses** [-lɪsiːz]) *n* paralysie *f*.

paramedic [,pærə'medɪk] *n* auxiliaire médical *m*, auxiliaire médicale *f*.

parameter [pə'ræmɪtər] *n* paramètre *m*.

paramount ['pærəmaʊnt] *adj* primordial(e); **of ~ importance** d'une importance suprême.

paranoid ['pærənɔɪd] *adj* paranoïaque.

paraphernalia [,pærəfə'neɪljə] *n* (*U*) attirail *m*, bazar *m*.

parasite ['pærəsaɪt] *n lit* & *fig* parasite *m*.

parasol ['pærəsɒl] *n* [above table] parasol *m*; [hand-held] ombrelle *f*.

paratrooper ['pærətruːpər] *n* parachutiste *mf*.

parcel ['pɑːsl] *n* paquet *m*. ○ **parcel up** *vt sep* empaqueter.

parched [pɑːtʃt] *adj* [gen] desséché(e). || *inf* [very thirsty] assoiffé(e), mort(e) de soif.

parchment ['pɑːtʃmənt] *n* parchemin *m*.

pardon ['pɑːdn] **1** *n* JUR grâce *f*. || (*U*) [forgiveness] pardon *m*; **I beg your ~?** [showing surprise, asking for repetition] comment?, pardon?; **I beg your ~!** [to apologize] je vous demande pardon! **2** *vt* [forgive] pardonner; **to ~ sb for sthg** pardonner qqch à qqn; **~ me!** pardon!, excusez-moi! || JUR gracier. **3** *excl* comment?

parent ['peərənt] *n* père *m*, mère *f*. ○ **parents** *npl* parents *mpl*.

parental [pə'rentl] *adj* parental(e).

Paris ['pærɪs] *n* Paris.

parish ['pærɪʃ] *n* RELIG paroisse *f*.

Parisian [pə'rɪzjən] **1** *adj* parisien (ienne). **2** *n* Parisien *m*, -ienne *f*.

parity ['pærətɪ] *n* égalité *f*.

park [pɑːk] **1** *n* parc *m*, jardin *m* public. **2** *vt* garer. **3** *vi* se garer, stationner.

parking ['pɑːkɪŋ] *n* stationnement *m*; "no ~" «défense de stationner», «stationnement interdit».

parking lot *n Am* parking *m*.

parking meter *n* parcmètre *m*.

parking ticket *n* contravention *f*, PV *m*.

parlance ['pɑːləns] *n*: **in common/legal** *etc* ~ en langage courant/juridique *etc*.

parliament ['pɑːləmənt] *n* parlement *m*.

parliamentary [,pɑːlə'mentərɪ] *adj* parlementaire.

parochial [pə'rəʊkjəl] *adj pej* de clocher.

parody ['pærədɪ] **1** *n* parodie *f*. **2** *vt* parodier.

parole [pə'rəʊl] *n* (*U*) parole *f*; **on** ~ en liberté conditionnelle.

parrot ['pærət] *n* perroquet *m*.

parry ['pærɪ] *vt* [blow] parer. || [question] éluder.

parsley ['pɑːslɪ] *n* persil *m*.

parsnip ['pɑːsnɪp] *n* panais *m*.

parson ['pɑːsn] *n* pasteur *m*.

part [pɑːt] **1** *n* [gen] partie *f*; **for the most** ~ dans l'ensemble. || [of TV serial *etc*] épisode *m*. || [component] pièce *f*. || [in proportions] mesure *f*. || THEATRE rôle *m*. || [involvement]: ~ **in** participation *f* à; **to play an important** ~ **in** jouer un rôle important dans; **to take** ~ **in** participer à; **for my** ~ en ce qui me concerne. || *Am* [hair parting] raie *f*. **2** *adv* en partie. **3** *vt*: **to** ~ **one's hair** se faire une raie. **4** *vi* [couple] se séparer. || [curtains] s'écarter, s'ouvrir. ○ **parts** *npl*: **in these** ~**s** dans cette région. ○ **part with** *vt fus* [money] débourser; [possession] se défaire de.

part exchange *n* reprise *f*; **in** ~ comme reprise en compte.

partial ['pɑːʃl] *adj* [incomplete] partiel(ielle). || [biased] partial(e). || [fond]: **to be** ~ **to** avoir un penchant pour.

participant [pɑː'tɪsɪpənt] *n* participant *m*, -e *f*.

participate [pɑː'tɪsɪpeɪt] *vi*: **to** ~ **(in)** participer (à).

participation [pɑː,tɪsɪ'peɪʃn] *n* participation *f*.

participle ['pɑːtɪsɪpl] *n* participe *m*.

particle ['pɑːtɪkl] *n* particule *f*.

particular [pə'tɪkjʊləʳ] *adj* [gen] particulier(ière). || [fussy] pointilleux(euse); ~ **about** exigeant(e) à propos de. ○ **particulars** *npl* renseignements *mpl*. ○ **in particular** *adv* en particulier.

particularly [pə'tɪkjʊləlɪ] *adv* particulièrement.

parting ['pɑːtɪŋ] *n* [separation] séparation *f*. || *Br* [in hair] raie *f*.

partisan [,pɑːtɪ'zæn] *n* partisan *m*, -e *f*.

partition [pɑː'tɪʃn] **1** *n* [wall, screen] cloison *f*. **2** *vt* [room] cloisonner. || [country] partager.

partly ['pɑːtlɪ] *adv* partiellement, en partie.

partner ['pɑːtnəʳ] **1** *n* [gen] partenaire *mf*. || [in a business, crime] associé *m*, -e *f*. **2** *vt* être le partenaire de.

partnership ['pɑːtnəʃɪp] *n* association *f*.

partridge ['pɑːtrɪdʒ] *n* perdrix *f*.

part-time *adj & adv* à temps partiel.

party ['pɑːtɪ] *n* POL parti *m*. || [social gathering] fête *f*, réception *f*. || [group] groupe *m*. || JUR partie *f*.

party line *n* POL ligne *f* du parti. || TELEC ligne *f* commune à deux abonnés.

pass [pɑːs] **1** *n* SPORT passe *f*. || [document - for security] laissez-passer *m inv*; [- for travel] carte *f* d'abonnement. || [between mountains] col *m*. || *phr*: **to make a** ~ **at sb** faire du plat à qqn. **2** *vt* [object, time] passer; **to** ~ **sthg to sb**, **to** ~ **sb sthg** passer qqch à qqn. || [person in street *etc*] croiser. || [place] passer devant. || AUT dépasser, doubler. || [exceed] dépasser. || [exam] réussir (à); [driving test] passer. || [law, motion] voter. || [judgment] rendre, prononcer. **3** *vi* [gen] passer. || AUT doubler, dépasser. || SPORT faire une passe. || [in exam] réussir, être reçu(e). ○ **pass as** *vt fus* passer pour. ○ **pass away** *vi* s'éteindre. ○ **pass by 1** *vt sep*: **the news** ~**ed him by** la nouvelle ne l'a pas affecté. **2** *vi* passer à côté. ○ **pass for** = **pass as**. ○ **pass on 1** *vt sep*: **to** ~ **sthg on (to)** [object] faire passer qqch (à); [tradition, information] transmettre qqch (à). **2** *vi* [move on] continuer son chemin. || = **pass away**. ○ **pass out** *vi* [faint] s'évanouir. ○ **pass over** *vt fus* [problem, topic] passer sous silence. ○ **pass up** *vt* *sep* [opportunity. invitation] laisser passer.

passable ['pɑːsəbl] *adj* [satisfactory] passable. ‖ [road] praticable; [river] franchissable.

passage ['pæsɪdʒ] *n* [gen] passage *m*. ‖ [between rooms] couloir *m*. ‖ [sea journey] traversée *f*.

passageway ['pæsɪdʒweɪ] *n* [between houses] passage *m*; [between rooms] couloir *m*.

passbook ['pɑːsbuk] *n* livret *m* de banque.

passenger ['pæsɪndʒər] *n* passager *m*, -ère *f*.

passerby [,pɑːsə'baɪ] (*pl* **passersby** [,pɑːsəz'baɪ]) *n* passant *m*, -e *f*.

passing ['pɑːsɪŋ] *adj* [remark] en passant; [trend] passager(ère). ○ **in passing** *adv* en passant.

passion ['pæʃn] *n* passion *f*.

passionate ['pæʃənət] *adj* passionné(e).

passive ['pæsɪv] *adj* passif(ive).

Passover ['pɑːs,əʊvər] *n*: **(the) ~** la Pâque juive.

passport ['pɑːspɔːt] *n* [document] passeport *m*.

passport control *n* contrôle *m* des passeports.

password ['pɑːswɜːd] *n* mot *m* de passe.

past [pɑːst] **1** *adj* [former] passé(e); **for the ~ five years** ces cinq dernières années; **the ~ week** la semaine passée OR dernière. ‖ [finished] fini(e). **2** *adv* [in times]: **it's ten ~** il est dix. ‖ [in front]: **to drive ~** passer (devant) en voiture; **to run ~** passer (devant) en courant. **3** *n* passé *m*; **in the ~** dans le temps. **4** *prep* [in times]: **it's half ~ eight** il est huit heures et demie; **it's five ~ nine** il est neuf heures cinq. ‖ [in front of] devant; **we drove ~ them** nous les avons dépassés en voiture. ‖ [beyond] après, au-delà de.

pasta ['pæstə] *n* (*U*) pâtes *fpl*.

paste [peɪst] **1** *n* [gen] pâte *f*. ‖ CULIN pâté *m*. ‖ (*U*) [glue] colle *f*. **2** *vt* coller.

pastel ['pæstl] *adj* pastel (*inv*).

pasteurize, -ise ['pɑːstʃəraɪz] *vt* pasteuriser.

pastille ['pæstɪl] *n* pastille *f*.

pastime ['pɑːstaɪm] *n* passe-temps *m inv*.

pastor ['pɑːstər] *n* pasteur *m*.

past participle *n* participe *m* passé.

pastry ['peɪstrɪ] *n* [mixture] pâte *f*. ‖ [cake] pâtisserie *f*.

past tense *n* passé *m*.

pasture ['pɑːstʃər] *n* pâturage *m*, pré *m*.

pasty ['peɪstɪ] *adj* blafard(e), terreux(euse).

pat [pæt] **1** *n* [light stroke] petite tape *f*; [to animal] caresse *f*. ‖ [of butter] noix *f*, noisette *f*. **2** *vt* [person] tapoter, donner une tape à; [animal] caresser.

patch [pætʃ] **1** *n* [piece of material] pièce *f*; [to cover eye] bandeau *m*. ‖ [small area of snow. ice] plaque *f*. ‖ [of land] parcelle *f*, lopin *m*. ‖ [period of time]: **a difficult ~** une mauvaise passe. **2** *vt* rapiécer. ○ **patch up** *vt sep* [mend] rafistoler, bricoler. ‖ *fig* [quarrel] régler, arranger.

patchwork ['pætʃwɜːk] *n* patchwork *m*.

patchy ['pætʃɪ] *adj* [gen] inégal(e); [knowledge] insuffisant(e), imparfait(e).

pâté ['pæteɪ] *n* pâté *m*.

patent [*Br* 'peɪtənt, *Am* 'pætənt] **1** *n* brevet *m* (d'invention). **2** *vt* faire breveter.

patent leather *n* cuir *m* verni.

paternal [pə'tɜːnl] *adj* paternel(elle).

path [pɑːθ, *pl* pɑːðz] *n* [track] chemin *m*, sentier *m*. ‖ [way ahead. course of action] voie *f*, chemin *m*. ‖ [trajectory] trajectoire *f*.

pathetic [pə'θetɪk] *adj* [causing pity] pitoyable, attendrissant(e). ‖ [useless - efforts. person] pitoyable, minable.

pathology [pə'θɒlədʒɪ] *n* pathologie *f*.

pathos ['peɪθɒs] *n* pathétique *m*.

pathway ['pɑːθweɪ] *n* chemin *m*, sentier *m*.

patience ['peɪʃns] *n* [of person] patience *f*. ‖ [card game] réussite *f*.

patient ['peɪʃnt] **1** *adj* patient(e). **2** *n* [in hospital] patient *m*, -e *f*, malade *mf*; [of doctor] patient.

patio ['pætɪəʊ] (*pl* -s) *n* patio *m*.

patriotic [*Br* ,pætrɪ'ɒtɪk, *Am* ,peɪtrɪ'ɒtɪk] *adj* [gen] patriotique; [person] patriote.

patrol [pə'trəʊl] **1** *n* patrouille *f*. **2** *vt* patrouiller dans, faire une patrouille dans.

patrol car *n* voiture *f* de police.

patrolman [pə'trəʊlmən] (*pl* -men [-mən]) *n* *Am* agent *m* de police.

patron ['peɪtrən] *n* [of arts] mécène *m*, protecteur *m*, -trice *f*. ‖ *fml* [customer] client *m*, -e *f*.

patronize, -ise ['pætrənaız] *vt* [talk down to] traiter avec condescendance. || *fml* [back financially] patronner, protéger.

patronizing ['pætrənaızıŋ] *adj* condescendant(e).

patter ['pætər] **1** *n* [sound - of rain] crépitement *m*. || [talk] baratin *m*, bavardage *m*. **2** *vi* [feet, paws] trottiner; [rain] frapper, fouetter.

pattern ['pætən] *n* [design] motif *m*, dessin *m*. || [of distribution, population] schéma *m*; [of life, behaviour] mode *m*. || [diagram]: (**sewing**) ~ patron *m*. || [model] modèle *m*.

paunch [pɔ:ntʃ] *n* bedaine *f*.

pauper ['pɔ:pər] *n* indigent *m*, -e *f*, nécessiteux *m*, -euse *f*.

pause [pɔ:z] **1** *n* [short silence] pause *f*, silence *m*. || [break] pause *f*, arrêt *m*. **2** *vi* [stop speaking] marquer un temps. || [stop moving, doing] faire une pause, s'arrêter.

pave [peıv] *vt* paver; **to ~ the way for sb/sthg** ouvrir la voie à qqn/qqch.

pavement ['peıvmənt] *n Am* [roadway] chaussée *f*.

pavilion [pə'vıljən] *n* pavillon *m*.

paving ['peıvıŋ] *n* (*U*) pavé *m*.

paving stone *n* pavé *m*.

paw [pɔ:] *n* patte *f*.

pawn [pɔ:n] **1** *n lit & fig* pion *m*. **2** *vt* mettre en gage.

pawnbroker ['pɔ:n,brəʊkər] *n* prêteur *m*, -euse *f* sur gages.

pawnshop ['pɔ:nʃɒp] *n* mont-de-piété *m*.

pay [peı] (*pt & pp* **paid**) **1** *vt* [gen] payer; **to ~ sb for sthg** payer qqn pour qqch, payer qqch à qqn; **to ~ a cheque into an account** déposer un chèque sur un compte. || [be profitable to] rapporter à. || [give, make]: **to ~ attention (to sb/sthg)** prêter attention (à qqn/qqch); **to ~ sb a compliment** faire un compliment à qqn; **to ~ sb a visit** rendre visite à qqn. **2** *vi* payer; **to ~ dearly for sthg** *fig* payer qqch cher. **3** *n* salaire *m*, traitement *m*. ○ **pay back** *vt sep* [return loan of money] rembourser. || [revenge oneself on]: **I'll ~ you back for that** tu me le paieras, je te le revaudrai. ○ **pay off 1** *vt sep* [repay - debt] s'acquitter de, régler; [- loan] rembourser. || [dismiss] licencier, congédier. || [bribe] soudoyer, acheter. **2** *vi* [course of action] être payant(e). ○ **pay up** *vi* payer.

payable ['peıəbl] *adj* [gen] payable. || [on cheque]: ~ **to** à l'ordre de.

paycheck ['peıtʃek] *n Am* paie *f*.

payday ['peıdeı] *n* jour *m* de paie.

payee [peı'i:] *n* bénéficiaire *mf*.

pay envelope *n Am* salaire *m*.

payment ['peımənt] *n* paiement *m*.

pay phone, pay station *Am n* téléphone *m* public, cabine *f* téléphonique.

payroll ['peırəʊl] *n* registre *m* du personnel.

pay station *Am* = **pay phone**.

pc (*abbr of* **per cent**) p. cent.

PC *n* (*abbr of* **personal computer**) PC *m*, micro *m*.

PE (*abbr of* **physical education**) *n* EPS *f*.

pea [pi:] *n* pois *m*.

peace [pi:s] *n* (*U*) paix *f*; [quiet, calm] calme *m*, tranquillité *f*.

peaceable ['pi:səbl] *adj* paisible, pacifique.

peaceful ['pi:sful] *adj* [quiet, calm] paisible, calme. || [not aggressive - person] pacifique; [- demonstration] non-violent(e).

peacetime ['pi:staım] *n* temps *m* de paix.

peach [pi:tʃ] **1** *adj* couleur pêche (*inv*). **2** *n* pêche *f*.

peacock ['pi:kɒk] *n* paon *m*.

peak [pi:k] **1** *n* [mountain top] sommet *m*, cime *f*. || *fig* [of career, success] apogée *m*, sommet *m*. || [of cap] visière *f*. **2** *adj* [condition] optimum. **3** *vi* atteindre un niveau maximum.

peaked [pi:kt] *adj* [cap] à visière.

peak hours *npl* heures *fpl* d'affluence OR de pointe.

peak period *n* période *f* de pointe.

peak rate *n* tarif *m* normal.

peal [pi:l] **1** *n* [of bells] carillonnement *m*; [of laughter] éclat *m*; [of thunder] coup *m*. **2** *vi* [bells] carillonner.

peanut ['pi:nʌt] *n* cacahuète *f*.

peanut butter *n* beurre *m* de cacahuètes.

pear [peər] *n* poire *f*.

pearl [pɜ:l] *n* perle *f*.

peasant ['peznt] *n* [in countryside] paysan *m*, -anne *f*.

peat [pi:t] *n* tourbe *f*.

pebble ['pebl] *n* galet *m*, caillou *m*.

peck [pek] **1** *n* [with beak] coup *m* de bec. || [kiss] bise *f*. **2** *vt* [with beak] picoter, becqueter. || [kiss]: **to ~ sb on the cheek** faire une bise à qqn.

pen name

pecking order ['pekɪŋ-] n hiérarchie f.

peculiar [pɪ'kjuːljər] adj [odd] bizarre, curieux(ieuse). || [slightly ill]: **to feel ~** se sentir tout drôle (toute drôle) OR tout chose (toute chose). || [characteristic]: **~ to** propre à, particulier(ière) à.

peculiarity [pɪˌkjuːlɪ'ærətɪ] n [oddness] bizarrerie f, singularité f. || [characteristic] particularité f, caractéristique f.

pedal ['pedl] 1 n pédale f. 2 vi pédaler.

pedal bin n poubelle f à pédale.

pedantic [pɪ'dæntɪk] adj pej pédant(e).

peddle ['pedl] vt [drugs] faire le trafic de.

pedestal ['pedɪstl] n piédestal m.

pedestrian [pɪ'destrɪən] 1 adj pej médiocre, dépourvu(e) d'intérêt. 2 n piéton m.

pedestrian precinct Br, **pedestrian zone** Am n zone f piétonne.

pediatrics [ˌpiːdɪ'ætrɪks] n pédiatrie f.

pedigree ['pedɪgriː] 1 adj [animal] de race. 2 n [of animal] pedigree m. || [of person] ascendance f, généalogie f.

pedlar Br, **peddler** Am ['pedlər] n colporteur m.

pee [piː] inf 1 n pipi m, pisse f. 2 vi faire pipi, pisser.

peek [piːk] inf 1 n coup m d'œil furtif. 2 vi jeter un coup d'œil furtif.

peel [piːl] 1 n [of apple, potato] peau f; [of orange, lemon] écorce f. 2 vt éplucher, peler. 3 vi [paint] s'écailler. || [wallpaper] se décoller. || [skin] peler.

peelings ['piːlɪŋz] npl épluchures fpl.

peep [piːp] 1 n [look] coup m d'œil OR regard m furtif. || inf [sound] bruit m. 2 vi jeter un coup d'œil furtif. ○ **peep out** vi apparaître, se montrer.

peephole ['piːphəʊl] n judas m.

peer [pɪər] 1 n pair m. 2 vi scruter, regarder attentivement.

peerage ['pɪərɪdʒ] n [rank] pairie f; **the ~ les** pairs mpl.

peer group n pairs mpl.

peeved [piːvd] adj inf fâché(e), irrité(e).

peevish ['piːvɪʃ] adj grincheux(euse).

peg [peg] 1 n [hook] cheville f. || [for clothes] pince f à linge. || [on tent] piquet m. 2 vt fig [prices] bloquer.

pejorative [pɪ'dʒɒrətɪv] adj péjoratif(ive).

pekinese [ˌpiːkə'niːz], **pekingese** [ˌpiːkɪŋ'iːz] (pl inv OR -s) n [dog] pékinois m.

Peking [piː'kɪŋ] n Pékin.

pekingese = **pekinese**.

pelican ['pelɪkən] (pl inv OR -s) n pélican m.

pellet ['pelɪt] n [small ball] boulette f. || [for gun] plomb m.

pelt [pelt] 1 n [animal skin] peau f, fourrure f. 2 vt: **to ~ sb (with sthg)** bombarder qqn (de qqch). 3 vi [rain] tomber à verse. || [run fast]: **to ~ along** courir ventre à terre; **to ~ down the stairs** dévaler l'escalier.

pelvis ['pelvɪs] (pl -vises OR -ves [-viːz]) n pelvis m, bassin m.

pen [pen] 1 n [for writing] stylo m. || [enclosure] parc m, enclos m. 2 vt [enclose] parquer.

penal ['piːnl] adj pénal(e).

penalize, -ise ['piːnəlaɪz] vt [gen] pénaliser. || [put at a disadvantage] désavantager.

penalty ['penltɪ] n [punishment] pénalité f; **to pay the ~ (for sthg)** fig supporter OR subir les conséquences (de qqch). || [fine] amende f. || HOCKEY pénalité f.

penance ['penəns] n RELIG pénitence f. || fig [punishment] corvée f, pensum m.

penchant [Br pãʃã, Am 'pentʃənt] n: **to have a ~ for sthg** avoir un faible pour qqch; **to have a ~ for doing sthg** avoir tendance à OR bien aimer faire qqch.

pencil ['pensl] 1 n crayon m; **in ~** au crayon. 2 vt griffonner au crayon, crayonner.

pencil case n trousse f (d'écolier).

pencil sharpener n taille-crayon m.

pendant ['pendənt] n [jewel on chain] pendentif m.

pending ['pendɪŋ] fml 1 adj [imminent] imminent(e). || [court case] en instance. 2 prep en attendant.

pendulum ['pendjʊləm] (pl -s) n balancier m.

penetrate ['penɪtreɪt] vt [gen] pénétrer dans; [subj: light] percer; [subj: rain] s'infiltrer dans. || [subj: spy] infiltrer.

pen friend n correspondant m, -e f.

penguin ['peŋgwɪn] n manchot m.

penicillin [ˌpenɪ'sɪlɪn] n pénicilline f.

peninsula [pə'nɪnsjʊlə] (pl -s) n péninsule f.

penis ['piːnɪs] (pl penises ['piːnɪsɪz]) n pénis m.

penitentiary [ˌpenɪ'tenʃərɪ] n Am prison f.

penknife ['pennaɪf] (pl -knives [-naɪvz]) n canif m.

pen name n pseudonyme m.

pennant ['penənt] *n* fanion *m*, flamme *f*.

penniless ['penɪlɪs] *adj* sans le sou.

penny ['penɪ] *n* [coin] *Am* cent *m*.

pen pal *n inf* correspondant *m*, -e *f*.

pension ['penʃn] *n* [from disability] pension *f*.

pensive ['pensɪv] *adj* songeur(euse).

pentagon ['pentəgən] *n* pentagone *m*.
○ **Pentagon** *n Am*: **the Pentagon** le Pentagone (*siège du ministère américain de la Défense*).

Pentecost ['pentɪkɒst] *n* Pentecôte *f*.

penthouse ['penthaʊs, *pl* -haʊzɪz] *n* appartement *m* de luxe (en attique).

pent up ['pent-] *adj* [emotions] refoulé(e); [energy] contenu(e).

penultimate [pe'nʌltɪmət] *adj* avant-dernier(ière).

people ['piːpl] **1** *n* [nation, race] nation *f*, peuple *m*. **2** *npl* [persons] personnes *fpl*; **few/a lot of ~** peu/beaucoup de monde, peu/beaucoup de gens. ‖ [in general] gens *mpl*; **~ say that ... on** dit que .... ‖ [inhabitants] habitants *mpl*. ‖ POL: **the ~** le peuple. **3** *vt*: **to be ~d by** OR **with** être peuplé(e) de.

pep [pep] *n inf* (U) entrain *m*, pep *m*.
○ **pep up** *vt sep inf* [person] remonter, requinquer. ‖ [party, event] animer.

pepper ['pepər] *n* [spice] poivre *m*. ‖ [vegetable] poivron *m*.

pepperbox *n Am* = pepper pot.

peppermint ['pepəmɪnt] *n* [sweet] bonbon *m* à la menthe. ‖ [herb] menthe *f* poivrée.

pepper pot *Br*, **pepperbox** *Am* ['pepəbɒks] *n* poivrier *m*.

pep talk *n inf* paroles *fpl* OR discours *m* d'encouragement.

per [pɜːr] *prep*: **~ person** par personne; **to be paid £10 ~ hour** être payé 10 livres de l'heure; **~ kilo** le kilo.

per annum *adv* par an.

per capita [pə'kæpɪtə] *adj & adv* par habitant OR tête.

perceive [pə'siːv] *vt* [notice] percevoir. ‖ [understand, realize] remarquer, s'apercevoir de. ‖ [consider]: **to ~ sb/sthg as** considérer qqn/qqch comme.

per cent *adv* pour cent.

percentage [pə'sentɪdʒ] *n* pourcentage *m*.

perception [pə'sepʃn] *n* [aural, visual] perception *f*. ‖ [insight] perspicacité *f*, intuition *f*.

perceptive [pə'septɪv] *adj* perspicace.

perch [pɜːtʃ] **1** *n lit & fig* [position] perchoir *m*. **2** *vi* se percher.

percolator ['pɜːkəleɪtər] *n* cafetière *f* à pression.

percussion [pə'kʌʃn] *n* MUS percussion *f*.

perennial [pə'renjəl] **1** *adj* permanent(e), perpétuel(elle); BOT vivace. **2** *n* BOT plante *f* vivace.

perfect [*adj & n* 'pɜːfɪkt, *vb* pə'fekt] **1** *adj* parfait(e); **he's a ~ nuisance** il est absolument insupportable. **2** *n* GRAMM: **~ (tense)** parfait *m*. **3** *vt* parfaire, mettre au point.

perfection [pə'fekʃn] *n* perfection *f*.

perfectionist [pə'fekʃənɪst] *n* perfectionniste *mf*.

perfectly ['pɜːfɪktlɪ] *adv* parfaitement; **you know ~ well** tu sais très bien.

perforate ['pɜːfəreɪt] *vt* perforer.

perforations [,pɜːfə'reɪʃnz] *npl* [in paper] pointillés *mpl*.

perform [pə'fɔːm] **1** *vt* [carry out] exécuter; [- function] remplir. ‖ [play, concert] jouer. **2** *vi* [machine] marcher, fonctionner; [team, person]: **to ~ well/badly** avoir de bons/mauvais résultats. ‖ [actor] jouer; [singer] chanter.

performance [pə'fɔːməns] *n* [carrying out] exécution *f*. ‖ [show] représentation *f*. ‖ [by actor, singer etc] interprétation *f*. ‖ [of car, engine] performance *f*.

performer [pə'fɔːmər] *n* artiste *mf*, interprète *mf*.

perfume ['pɜːfjuːm] *n* parfum *m*.

perfunctory [pə'fʌŋktərɪ] *adj* rapide, superficiel(ielle).

perhaps [pə'hæps] *adv* peut-être; **~ so/not** peut-être que oui/non.

peril ['perɪl] *n* danger *m*, péril *m*.

perimeter [pə'rɪmɪtər] *n* périmètre *m*.

period ['pɪərɪəd] **1** *n* [gen] période *f*. ‖ SCH ≃ heure *f*. ‖ [menstruation] règles *fpl*. ‖ *Am* [full stop] point *m*. **2** *comp* [dress, house] d'époque.

periodic [,pɪərɪ'ɒdɪk] *adj* périodique.

periodical [,pɪərɪ'ɒdɪkl] **1** *adj* = **periodic**. **2** *n* [magazine] périodique *m*.

peripheral [pə'rɪfərəl] **1** *adj* [unimportant] secondaire. ‖ [at edge] périphérique. **2** *n* COMPUT périphérique *m*.

perish ['perɪʃ] *vi* [die] périr, mourir. ‖ [food] pourrir, se gâter; [rubber] se détériorer.

perishable ['perɪʃəbl] *adj* périssable.

perjury ['pɜːdʒərɪ] *n* (U) JUR parjure *m*, faux serment *m*.

perk [pɜːk] *n inf* à-côté *m*, avantage *m*.
○ **perk up** *vi* se ragaillardir.

perky ['pɜːkɪ] *adj inf* [cheerful] guilleret(ette); [lively] plein(e) d'entrain.

perm [pɜːm] *n* permanente *f*.

permanent ['pɜːmənənt] **1** *adj* permanent(e). **2** *n Am* [perm] permanente *f*.

permeate ['pɜːmɪeɪt] *vt* [subj: liquid, smell] s'infiltrer dans, pénétrer. || [subj: feeling, idea] se répandre dans.

permissible [pəˈmɪsəbl] *adj* acceptable, admissible.

permission [pəˈmɪʃn] *n* permission *f*, autorisation *f*.

permissive [pəˈmɪsɪv] *adj* permissif(ive).

permit [*vb* pəˈmɪt, *n* ˈpɜːmɪt] **1** *vt* permettre; **to ~ sb to do sthg** permettre à qqn de faire qqch, autoriser qqn à faire qqch; **to ~ sb sthg** permettre qqch à qqn. **2** *n* permis *m*.

perpendicular [ˌpɜːpənˈdɪkjʊləʳ] **1** *adj* perpendiculaire. **2** *n* perpendiculaire *f*.

perpetrate ['pɜːpɪtreɪt] *vt* perpétrer, commettre.

perpetual [pəˈpetʃʊəl] *adj pej* [continuous] continuel(elle), incessant(e). || [long-lasting] perpétuel(elle).

perplex [pəˈpleks] *vt* rendre perplexe.

perplexing [pəˈpleksɪŋ] *adj* déroutant(e), déconcertant(e).

persecute ['pɜːsɪkjuːt] *vt* persécuter, tourmenter.

perseverance [ˌpɜːsɪˈvɪərəns] *n* persévérance *f*, ténacité *f*.

persevere [ˌpɜːsɪˈvɪəʳ] *vi* [with difficulty] persévérer, persister; **to ~ with** persévérer ou persister dans. || [with determination]: **to ~ in doing sthg** persister à faire qqch.

Persian ['pɜːʃn] *adj* persan(e); HISTORY perse.

persist [pəˈsɪst] *vi*: **to ~ (in doing sthg)** persister ou s'obstiner (à faire qqch).

persistence [pəˈsɪstəns] *n* persistance *f*.

persistent [pəˈsɪstənt] *adj* [noise, rain] continuel(elle); [problem] constant(e). || [determined] tenace, obstiné(e).

person ['pɜːsn] (*pl* **people** OR **persons** *fml*) *n* [man or woman] personne *f*; **in ~** en personne. || *fml* [body]: **about one's ~** sur soi.

personal ['pɜːsənl] *adj* [gen] personnel(elle). || *pej* [rude] désobligeant(e).

personal assistant *n* secrétaire *mf* de direction.

personal column *n* petites annonces *fpl*.

personal computer *n* ordinateur *m* personnel OR individuel.

personality [ˌpɜːsəˈnælətɪ] *n* personnalité *f*.

personally ['pɜːsnəlɪ] *adv* personnellement; **to take sthg ~** se sentir visé par qqch.

personal organizer *n* agenda *m* modulaire multifonction.

personal property *n* (*U*) JUR biens *mpl* personnels.

personal stereo *n* baladeur *m*, Walkman® *m*.

personify [pəˈsɒnɪfaɪ] *vt* personnifier.

personnel [ˌpɜːsəˈnel] **1** *n* (*U*) [department] service *m* du personnel. **2** *npl* [staff] personnel *m*.

perspective [pəˈspektɪv] *n* ART perspective *f*. || [view, judgment] point *m* de vue, optique *f*.

perspiration [ˌpɜːspəˈreɪʃn] *n* [sweat] sueur *f*. || [act of perspiring] transpiration *f*.

persuade [pəˈsweɪd] *vt*: **to ~ sb to do sthg** persuader OR convaincre qqn de faire qqch; **to ~ sb that** convaincre qqn que; **to ~ sb of** convaincre qqn de.

persuasion [pəˈsweɪʒn] *n* [act of persuading] persuasion *f*. || [belief - religious] confession *f*; [- political] opinion *f*, conviction *f*.

persuasive [pəˈsweɪsɪv] *adj* [person] persuasif(ive); [argument] convaincant (e).

pert [pɜːt] *adj* mutin(e), coquin(e).

pertain [pəˈteɪn] *vi fml*: **~ing to** concernant, relatif(ive) à.

pertinent ['pɜːtɪnənt] *adj* pertinent(e), approprié(e).

perturb [pəˈtɜːb] *vt* inquiéter, troubler.

Peru [pəˈruː] *n* Pérou *m*.

peruse [pəˈruːz] *vt* lire attentivement.

pervade [pəˈveɪd] *vt* [subj: smell] se répandre dans; [subj: feeling, influence] envahir.

perverse [pəˈvɜːs] *adj* [contrary - person] contrariant(e); [- enjoyment] malin (igne).

perversion [*Br* pəˈvɜːʃn, *Am* pəˈvɜːrʒn] *n* [sexual] perversion *f*. || [of truth] travestissement *m*.

pervert [*n* ˈpɜːvɜːt, *vb* pəˈvɜːt] **1** *n* pervers *m*, -e *f*. **2** *vt* [truth, meaning] travestir, déformer; [course of justice] entraver. || [sexually] pervertir.

pessimist ['pesɪmɪst] *n* pessimiste *mf*.

pessimistic [,pesɪ'mɪstɪk] *adj* pessimiste.

pest [pest] *n* [insect] insecte *m* nuisible; [animal] animal *m* nuisible. ‖ *inf* [nuisance] casse-pieds *mf inv*.

pester ['pestər] *vt* harceler, importuner.

pet [pet] **1** *adj* [favourite]: ~ **subject** dada *m*; ~ **hate** bête *f* noire. **2** *n* [animal] animal *m* (familier). ‖ [favourite person] chouchou *m*, -oute *f*. **3** *vt* caresser, câliner. **4** *vi* se peloter, se caresser.

petal ['petl] *n* pétale *m*.

peter ['pi:tər] ○ **peter out** *vi* [path] s'arrêter, se perdre; [interest] diminuer, décliner.

petite [pə'ti:t] *adj* menu(e).

petition [pɪ'tɪʃn] **1** *n* pétition *f*. **2** *vt* adresser une pétition à.

petrified ['petrɪfaɪd] *adj* [terrified] paralysé(e) ou pétrifié(e) de peur.

petroleum [pɪ'trəʊljəm] *n* pétrole *m*.

petticoat ['petɪkəʊt] *n* jupon *m*.

petty ['petɪ] *adj* [small-minded] mesquin(e). ‖ [trivial] insignifiant(e), sans importance.

petty cash *n* (*U*) caisse *f* des dépenses courantes.

petulant ['petjʊlənt] *adj* irritable.

pew [pju:] *n* banc *m* d'église.

pewter ['pju:tər] *n* étain *m*.

phantom ['fæntəm] **1** *adj* fantomatique, spectral(e). **2** *n* [ghost] fantôme *m*.

pharmaceutical [,fɑ:mə'sju:tɪkl] *adj* pharmaceutique.

pharmacist ['fɑ:məsɪst] *n* pharmacien *m*, -ienne *f*.

pharmacy ['fɑ:məsɪ] *n* pharmacie *f*.

phase [feɪz] *n* phase *f*. ○ **phase in** *vt sep* introduire progressivement. ○ **phase out** *vt sep* supprimer progressivement.

PhD (*abbr of* **Doctor of Philosophy**) *n* (*titulaire d'un*) doctorat de 3ᵉ cycle.

pheasant ['feznt] (*pl inv* OR **-s**) *n* faisan *m*.

phenomena [fɪ'nɒmɪnə] *pl* → **phenomenon**.

phenomenal [fɪ'nɒmɪnl] *adj* phénoménal(e), extraordinaire.

phenomenon [fɪ'nɒmɪnən] (*pl* **-mena**) *n* phénomène *m*.

phial ['faɪəl] *n* fiole *f*.

philanthropist [fɪ'lænθrəpɪst] *n* philanthrope *mf*.

philately [fɪ'lætəlɪ] *n* philatélie *f*.

Philippine ['fɪlɪpi:n] *adj* philippin(e). ○ **Philippines** *npl*: **the ~s** les Philippines *fpl*.

philosopher [fɪ'lɒsəfər] *n* philosophe *mf*.

philosophical [,fɪlə'sɒfɪkl] *adj* philosophique. ‖ [stoical] philosophe.

philosophy [fɪ'lɒsəfɪ] *n* philosophie *f*.

phlegm [flem] *n* flegme *m*.

phobia ['fəʊbjə] *n* phobie *f*.

phone [fəʊn] **1** *n* téléphone *m*; **to be on the ~** [speaking] être au téléphone. **2** *comp* téléphonique. **3** *vt* téléphoner à, appeler. **4** *vi* téléphoner. ○ **phone up 1** *vt sep* téléphoner à. **2** *vi* téléphoner.

phone book *n* annuaire *m* (du téléphone).

phone booth *n* cabine *f* téléphonique.

phone call *n* coup *m* de téléphone OR fil; **to make a ~** passer OR donner un coup de fil.

phonecard ['fəʊnkɑ:d] *n* ≈ Télécarte® *f*.

phone-in *n* RADIO & TV programme *m* à ligne ouverte.

phone number *n* numéro *m* de téléphone.

phonetics [fə'netɪks] *n* (*U*) phonétique *f*.

phoney *Br*, **phony** *Am* ['fəʊnɪ] *inf* **1** *adj* [passport, address] bidon (*inv*). ‖ [person] hypocrite, pas franc (pas franche). **2** *n* poseur *m*, -euse *f*.

photo ['fəʊtəʊ] *n* photo *f*; **to take a ~ of sb/sthg** photographier qqn/qqch, prendre qqn/qqch en photo.

photocopier [,fəʊtəʊ'kɒpɪər] *n* photocopieur *m*, copieur *m*.

photocopy ['fəʊtəʊ,kɒpɪ] **1** *n* photocopie *f*. **2** *vt* photocopier.

photograph ['fəʊtəgrɑ:f] **1** *n* photographie *f*; **to take a ~ (of sb/sthg)** prendre (qqn/qqch) en photo, photographier (qqn/qqch). **2** *vt* photographier, prendre en photo.

photographer [fə'tɒgrəfər] *n* photographe *mf*.

photography [fə'tɒgrəfɪ] *n* photographie *f*.

phrasal verb ['freɪzl-] *n* verbe *m* à postposition.

phrase [freɪz] *n* expression *f*.

phrasebook ['freɪzbʊk] *n* guide *m* de conversation (*pour touristes*).

physical ['fɪzɪkl] **1** *adj* [gen] physique. ‖ [world, objects] matériel(ielle). **2** *n* [examination] visite *f* médicale.

pilfer

physical education n éducation f physique.

physically ['fızıklı] adv physiquement.

physically handicapped npl: the ~ les handicapés mpl physiques.

physician [fı'zıʃn] n médecin m.

physicist ['fızısıst] n physicien m, -ienne f.

physics ['fızıks] n (U) physique f.

physiotherapy [,fızıəʊ'θerəpı] n kinésithérapie f.

physique [fı'zi:k] n physique m.

pianist ['pıənıst] n pianiste mf.

piano [pı'ænəʊ] (pl -s) n piano m.

pick [pık] 1 n [tool] pioche f, pic m. || [selection]: **to take one's** ~ choisir, faire son choix. || [best]: **the** ~ **of** le meilleur (la meilleure) de. 2 vt [select, choose] choisir, sélectionner. || [gather] cueillir. || [remove] enlever. || [nose]: **to** ~ **one's nose** se décrotter le nez. || [fight, quarrel]: **to** ~ **a fight (with sb)** chercher la bagarre (à qqn). || [lock] crocheter. **○ pick on** vt fus s'en prendre à, être sur le dos de. **○ pick out** vt sep [recognize] repérer, reconnaître. || [select, choose] choisir, désigner. **○ pick up 1** vt sep [lift up] ramasser. || [collect] aller chercher, passer prendre. || [collect in car] prendre, chercher. || [skill, language] apprendre; [habit] prendre; [bargain] découvrir. || inf [sexually - woman, man] draguer. || RADIO & TELEC [detect, receive] capter, recevoir. || [conversation, work] reprendre, continuer. 2 vi [improve, start again] reprendre.

pickaxe Br, **pickax** Am ['pıkæks] n pioche f, pic m.

picket ['pıkıt] 1 n piquet m de grève. 2 vt mettre un piquet de grève devant.

picket line n piquet m de grève.

pickle ['pıkl] 1 n pickles mpl; **to be in a** ~ être dans le pétrin. 2 vt conserver dans du vinaigre/de la saumure etc.

pickpocket ['pık,pɒkıt] n pickpocket m, voleur m à la tire.

pick-up n [of record player] pick-up m inv. || [truck] camionnette f.

picnic ['pıknık] (pt & pp -ked, cont -king) n pique-nique m.

pictorial [pık'tɔ:rıəl] adj illustré(e).

picture ['pıktʃər] 1 n [in painting] tableau m, peinture f; [drawing] dessin m. || [photograph] photo f, photographie f. || TV image f. || CINEMA film m. || [in mind] tableau m, image f. || phr: **to get the** ~ inf piger; **to put sb in the** ~ mettre qqn au courant. 2 vt [in mind] imaginer, s'imaginer, se représenter. || [in photo] photographier. || [in painting] représenter, peindre.

picture book n livre m d'images.

picturesque [,pıktʃə'resk] adj pittoresque.

pie [paı] n tourte f.

piece [pi:s] n [gen] morceau m; [of string] bout m; **a** ~ **of furniture** un meuble; **a** ~ **of clothing** un vêtement; **a** ~ **of advice** un conseil; **a** ~ **of information** un renseignement; **to fall to** ~**s** tomber en morceaux; **to take sthg to** ~**s** démonter qqch; **in** ~**s** en morceaux; **in one** ~ [intact] intact(e); [unharmed] sain et sauf (saine et sauve). || [coin, item, in chess] pièce f; [in draughts] pion m. || PRESS article m. **○ piece together** vt sep [facts] coordonner.

piecemeal ['pi:smi:l] 1 adj fait(e) petit à petit. 2 adv petit à petit, peu à peu.

piecework ['pi:swɜ:k] n (U) travail m à la pièce or aux pièces.

pie chart n camembert m, graphique m rond.

pier [pıər] n [at seaside] jetée f.

pierce [pıəs] vt percer, transpercer; **to have one's ears** ~**d** se faire percer les oreilles.

piercing ['pıəsıŋ] adj [sound, look] perçant(e). || [wind] pénétrant(e).

pig [pıg] n [animal] porc m, cochon m. || inf pej [greedy eater] goinfre m, glouton m. || inf pej [unkind person] sale type m.

pigeon ['pıdʒın] (pl inv or -s) n pigeon m.

pigeonhole ['pıdʒınhəʊl] 1 n [compartment] casier m. 2 vt [classify] étiqueter, cataloguer.

piggybank ['pıgıbæŋk] n tirelire f.

pigheaded [,pıg'hedıd] adj têtu(e).

pigment ['pıgmənt] n pigment m.

pigpen Am = pigsty.

pigskin ['pıgskın] n (peau f de) porc m.

pigsty ['pıgstaı], **pigpen** Am ['pıgpen] n lit & fig porcherie f.

pigtail ['pıgteıl] n natte f.

pilchard ['pıltʃəd] n pilchard m.

pile [paıl] n [heap] tas m; **a** ~ **of**, ~**s of** un tas or des tas de. || [neat stack] pile f. || [of carpet] poil m. **○ piles** npl MED hémorroïdes fpl. **○ pile up 1** vt sep empiler, entasser. 2 vi [form a heap] s'entasser. || fig [work, debts] s'accumuler.

pileup ['paılʌp] n AUT carambolage m.

pilfer ['pılfər] vt chaparder.

pilgrim ['pɪlgrɪm] n pèlerin m.

pilgrimage ['pɪlgrɪmɪdʒ] n pèlerinage m.

pill [pɪl] n [gen] pilule f. || [contraceptive]: **the ~** la pilule.

pillage ['pɪlɪdʒ] vt piller.

pillar ['pɪlər] n lit & fig pilier m.

pillion ['pɪljən] n siège m arrière; **to ride ~** monter derrière.

pillow ['pɪləʊ] n [for bed] oreiller m. || Am [on sofa, chair] coussin m.

pillowcase ['pɪləʊkeɪs], **pillowslip** ['pɪləʊslɪp] n taie f d'oreiller.

pilot ['paɪlət] 1 n AERON & NAUT pilote m. || TV émission f pilote. 2 vt piloter.

pilot burner, **pilot light** n veilleuse f.

pilot study n étude f pilote OR expérimentale.

pimp [pɪmp] n inf maquereau m, souteneur m.

pimple ['pɪmpl] n bouton m.

pin [pɪn] 1 n [for sewing] épingle f; **to have ~s and needles** avoir des fourmis. || [drawing pin] punaise f. || [safety pin] épingle f de nourrice OR de sûreté. || [of plug] fiche f. 2 vt: **to ~ sthg to/on sthg** épingler qqch à/sur qqch; **to ~ sb against** OR **to clouer qqn contre; to ~ sthg on sb** [blame] mettre OR coller qqch sur le dos de qqn; **to ~ one's hopes on sb/sthg** mettre tous ses espoirs en qqn/dans qqch. ○ **pin down** vt sep [identify] définir, identifier. || [force to make a decision]: **to ~ sb down** obliger qqn à prendre une décision.

pinafore ['pɪnəfɔːr] n [apron] tablier m.

pinball ['pɪnbɔːl] n flipper m.

pincers ['pɪnsəz] npl [tool] tenailles fpl. || [of crab] pinces fpl.

pinch [pɪntʃ] 1 n [nip] pincement m. || [of salt] pincée f. 2 vt [nip] pincer. || [subj: shoes] serrer. || inf [steal] piquer, faucher. ○ **at a pinch** Br, **in a pinch** Am adv à la rigueur.

pincushion ['pɪn,kʊʃn] n pelote f à épingles.

pine [paɪn] 1 n pin m. 2 vi: **to ~ for** désirer ardemment.

pineapple ['paɪnæpl] n ananas m.

pinetree ['paɪntriː] n pin m.

ping [pɪŋ] n [of bell] tintement m; [of metal] bruit m métallique.

Ping-Pong® [-pɒŋ] n ping-pong m.

pink [pɪŋk] 1 n rose; **to go** OR **turn ~** rosir, rougir. 2 n [colour] rose m.

pinnacle ['pɪnəkl] n [mountain peak, spire] pic m, cime f. || fig [high point] apogée m.

pinpoint ['pɪnpɔɪnt] vt [cause. problem] définir, mettre le doigt sur. || [position] localiser.

pin-striped [-,straɪpt] adj à très fines rayures.

pint [paɪnt] n Am [unit of measurement] = 0,473 litre, ≃ demi-litre m.

pioneer [,paɪə'nɪər] 1 n lit & fig pionnier m. 2 vt: **to ~ sthg** être un des premiers (une des premières) à faire qqch.

pious ['paɪəs] adj RELIG pieux (pieuse). || pej [sanctimonious] moralisateur(trice).

pip [pɪp] n [seed] pépin m.

pipe [paɪp] 1 n [for gas, water] tuyau m. || [for smoking] pipe f. 2 vt acheminer par tuyau. ○ **pipes** npl MUS cornemuse f. ○ **pipe down** vi inf se taire, la fermer. ○ **pipe up** vi inf se faire entendre.

pipe cleaner n cure-pipe m.

pipe dream n projet m chimérique.

pipeline ['paɪplaɪn] n [for gas] gazoduc m; [for oil] oléoduc m, pipeline m.

piping hot ['paɪpɪŋ-] adj bouillant(e).

pique [piːk] n dépit m.

pirate ['paɪrət] 1 adj [video. program] pirate. 2 n pirate m.

pirouette [,pɪruː'et] 1 n pirouette f. 2 vi pirouetter.

Pisces ['paɪsiːz] n Poissons mpl.

piss [pɪs] vulg 1 n [urine] pisse f. 2 vi pisser.

pissed [pɪst] adj vulg Am [annoyed] en boule.

pissed off adj vulg qui en a plein le cul.

pistol ['pɪstl] n pistolet m.

piston ['pɪstən] n piston m.

pit [pɪt] 1 n [hole] trou m; [in road] petit trou; [on face] marque f. || [for orchestra] fosse f. || [mine] mine f. || Am [of fruit] noyau m. 2 vt: **to ~ sb against sb** opposer qqn à qqn. ○ **pits** npl [in motor racing]: **the ~s** les stands mpl.

pitch [pɪtʃ] 1 n SPORT terrain m. || MUS ton m. || [level. degree] degré m. || [selling place] place f. || inf [sales talk] baratin m. 2 vt [throw] lancer. || [set - price] fixer; [- speech] adapter. || [tent] dresser; [camp] établir. 3 vi [ball] rebondir. || [fall]: **to ~ forward** être projeté(e) en avant. || AERON & NAUT tanguer.

pitch-black adj noir(e) comme dans un four.

pitched battle [,pɪtʃt-] n bataille f rangée.

pitcher ['pɪtʃər] n Am [jug] cruche f. || [in baseball] lanceur m.

pitchfork ['pɪtʃfɔːk] n fourche f.

pitfall ['pɪtfɔːl] n piège m.

pith [pɪθ] n [of fruit] peau f blanche.

pithy ['pɪθɪ] adj [brief] concis(e); [terse] piquant(e).

pitiful ['pɪtɪfʊl] adj [condition] pitoyable; [excuse, effort] lamentable.

pitiless ['pɪtɪlɪs] adj sans pitié, impitoyable.

pit stop n [in motor racing] arrêt m aux stands.

pittance ['pɪtəns] n [wage] salaire m de misère.

pity ['pɪtɪ] 1 n pitié f; what a ~! quel dommage!; it's a ~ c'est dommage; to take OR have ~ on sb prendre qqn en pitié, avoir pitié de qqn. 2 vt plaindre.

pivot ['pɪvət] n lit & fig pivot m.

pizza ['piːtsə] n pizza f.

placard ['plækɑːd] n placard m, affiche f.

placate [pləˈkeɪt] vt calmer, apaiser.

place [pleɪs] 1 n [location] endroit m, lieu m; ~ of birth lieu de naissance. || [proper position, seat, vacancy, rank] place f. || [home]: at/to my ~ chez moi. || [in book]: to lose one's ~ perdre sa page. || MATH: decimal ~ décimale f. || [instance]: in the first ~ tout de suite; in the first ~ ... and in the second ~ ... premièrement ... et deuxièmement .... || phr: to take ~ avoir lieu; to take the ~ of prendre la place de, remplacer. 2 vt [position, put] placer, mettre. || [apportion]: to ~ the responsibility for sthg on sb tenir qqn pour responsable de qqch. || [identify] remettre. || [an order] passer; to ~ a bet parier. ○ all over the place adv [everywhere] partout. ○ in place adv [in proper position] à sa place. || [established] mis en place. ○ in place of prep à la place de. ○ out of place adv pas à sa place; fig déplacé(e).

place mat n set m (de table).

placement ['pleɪsmənt] n placement m.

placid ['plæsɪd] adj [person] placide.

plagiarize, -ise ['pleɪdʒəraɪz] vt plagier.

plague [pleɪg] 1 n MED peste f. 2 vt: to be ~d by [bad luck] être poursuivi(e) par; [doubt] être rongé(e) par; to ~ sb with questions harceler qqn de questions.

plaice [pleɪs] (pl inv) n carrelet m.

plaid [plæd] n plaid m.

plain [pleɪn] 1 adj [not patterned] uni(e). || [simple] simple. || [clear] clair(e), évident(e). || [blunt] carré(e), franc (franche). || [absolute] pur(e) (et simple). || [not pretty] quelconque, ordinaire. 2 adv inf complètement. 3 n GEOGR plaine f.

plain-clothes adj en civil.

plainly ['pleɪnlɪ] adv [obviously] manifestement. || [distinctly] clairement. || [frankly] carrément, sans détours. || [simply] simplement.

plaintiff ['pleɪntɪf] n demandeur m, -eresse f.

plait [plæt] 1 n natte f. 2 vt natter, tresser.

plan [plæn] 1 n plan m, projet m; to go according to ~ se passer OR aller comme prévu. 2 vt [organize] préparer. || [propose]: to ~ to do sthg projeter de faire qqch, avoir l'intention de faire qqch. || [design] concevoir. 3 vi: to ~ (for sthg) faire des projets (pour qqch). ○ plans npl plans mpl, projets mpl; have you any ~s for tonight? avez-vous prévu quelque chose pour ce soir? ○ plan on vt fus: to ~ on doing sthg prévoir de faire qqch.

plane [pleɪn] 1 adj plan(e). 2 n [aircraft] avion m. || GEOM plan m. || fig [level] niveau m. || [tool] rabot m. || [tree] platane m.

planet ['plænɪt] n planète f.

plank [plæŋk] n [of wood] planche f.

planning ['plænɪŋ] n [designing] planification f. || [preparation] préparation f, organisation f.

planning permission n permis m de construire.

plant [plɑːnt] 1 n BOT plante f. || [factory] usine f. || (U) [heavy machinery] matériel m. 2 vt [gen] planter. || [bomb] poser.

plantation [plænˈteɪʃn] n plantation f.

plaque [plɑːk] n [commemorative sign] plaque f. || (U) [on teeth] plaque f dentaire.

plaster ['plɑːstər] 1 n [material] plâtre m. 2 vt [wall, ceiling] plâtrer. || [cover]: to ~ sthg (with) couvrir qqch (de).

plaster cast n [for broken bones] plâtre m. || [model, statue] moule m.

plastered ['plɑːstəd] adj inf [drunk] bourré(e).

plasterer ['plɑːstərər] n plâtrier m.

plaster of Paris n plâtre m de moulage.

plastic ['plæstɪk] 1 adj plastique. 2 n plastique m.

Plasticine® *Br* ['plæstɪsiːn], **play dough** *Am n* pâte *f* à modeler.

plastic surgery *n* chirurgie *f* esthétique OR plastique.

plate [pleɪt] **1** *n* [dish] assiette *f*. || [sheet of metal, plaque] tôle *f*. || (U) [metal covering]: gold/silver ~ plaqué *m* or/argent. || [in book] planche *f*. || [in dentistry] dentier *m*. **2** *vt*: to be ~d (with) être plaqué(e) (de).

plateau ['plætəʊ] (*pl* **-s** OR **-x** [-z]) *n* plateau *m*; *fig* phase *f* OR période *f* de stabilité.

plate-glass *adj* vitré(e).

platform ['plætfɔːm] *n* [stage] estrade *f*; [for speaker] tribune *f*. || [raised structure, of bus, of political party] plate-forme *f*. || RAIL quai *m*.

platinum ['plætɪnəm] *n* platine *m*.

platoon [plə'tuːn] *n* section *f*.

platter ['plætər] *n* [dish] plat *m*.

plausible ['plɔːzəbl] *adj* plausible.

play [pleɪ] **1** *n* (U) [amusement] jeu *m*, amusement *m*. || THEATRE pièce *f* (de théâtre). || [game]: ~ on words jeu *m* de mots. || TECH jeu *m*. **2** *vt* [gen] jouer; to ~ a part OR role in *fig* jouer un rôle dans. || [game, sport] jouer à. || [team, opponent] jouer contre. || MUS [instrument] jouer de. || *phr*: to ~ it safe ne pas prendre de risques. **3** *vi* jouer. ○ **play along** *vi*: to ~ along (with sb) entrer dans le jeu (de qqn). ○ **play down** *vt sep* minimiser. ○ **play up 1** *vt sep* [emphasize] insister sur. **2** *vi* [machine] faire des siennes. || [child] ne pas être sage.

play-act *vi* jouer la comédie.

playboy ['pleɪbɔɪ] *n* playboy *m*.

play dough *Am* = Plasticine®.

player ['pleɪər] *n* [gen] joueur *m*, -euse *f*. || THEATRE acteur *m*, -trice *f*.

playful ['pleɪfʊl] *adj* [person, mood] taquin(e). || [kitten, puppy] joueur(euse).

playground ['pleɪgraʊnd] *n* cour *f* de récréation.

playgroup ['pleɪgruːp] *n* jardin *m* d'enfants.

playing card ['pleɪɪŋ-] *n* carte *f* à jouer.

playing field ['pleɪɪŋ-] *n* terrain *m* de sport.

playmate ['pleɪmeɪt] *n* camarade *mf*.

play-off *n* SPORT belle *f*.

playpen ['pleɪpen] *n* parc *m*.

playschool ['pleɪskuːl] *n* jardin *m* d'enfants.

plaything ['pleɪθɪŋ] *n lit & fig* jouet *m*.

playtime ['pleɪtaɪm] *n* récréation *f*.

playwright ['pleɪraɪt] *n* dramaturge *m*.

plea [pliː] *n* [for forgiveness, mercy] supplication *f*; [for help, quiet] appel *m*. || JUR: to enter a ~ of not guilty plaider non coupable.

plead [pliːd] (*pt & pp* **-ed** OR **pled**) **1** *vt* JUR plaider. || [give as excuse] invoquer. **2** *vi* [beg]: to ~ with sb (to do sthg) supplier qqn (de faire qqch); to ~ for sthg implorer qqch. || JUR plaider.

pleasant ['pleznt] *adj* agréable.

pleasantry ['plezntrɪ] *n*: to exchange pleasantries échanger des propos aimables.

please [pliːz] **1** *vt* plaire à, faire plaisir à; ~ yourself! comme vous voulez! **2** *vi* plaire, faire plaisir; to do as one ~s faire comme on veut. **3** *adv* s'il vous plaît.

pleased [pliːzd] *adj* [satisfied]: to be ~ (with) être content(e) (de). || [happy]: to be ~ (about) être heureux(euse) (de); ~ to meet you! enchanté(e)!

pleasing ['pliːzɪŋ] *adj* plaisant(e).

pleasure ['pleʒər] *n* plaisir *m*; it's a ~, my ~ je vous en prie.

pleat [pliːt] **1** *n* pli *m*. **2** *vt* plisser.

pled [pled] *pt & pp* → plead.

pledge [pledʒ] **1** *n* [promise] promesse *f*. || [token] gage *m*. **2** *vt* [promise] promettre. || [make promise]: to ~ o.s. to s'engager à; to ~ sb to secrecy faire promettre le secret à qqn.

plentiful ['plentɪfʊl] *adj* abondant(e).

plenty ['plentɪ] **1** *n* (U) abondance *f*. **2** *pron*: ~ of beaucoup de; we've got ~ of time nous avons largement le temps. **3** *adv Am* [very] très.

pliable ['plaɪəbl], **pliant** ['plaɪənt] *adj* [material] pliable, souple.

pliers ['plaɪəz] *npl* tenailles *fpl*, pinces *fpl*.

plight [plaɪt] *n* condition *f* critique.

plinth [plɪnθ] *n* socle *m*.

PLO (*abbr of* **Palestine Liberation Organization**) *n* OLP *f*.

plod [plɒd] *vi* [walk slowly] marcher lentement OR péniblement. || [work slowly] peiner.

plodder ['plɒdər] *n pej* bûcheur *m*, -euse *f*.

plot [plɒt] **1** *n* [plan] complot *m*, conspiration *f*. || [story] intrigue *f*. || [of land] (parcelle *f* de) terrain *m*, lopin *m*. **2** *vt* [plan] comploter; to ~ to do sthg comploter de faire qqch. || [chart] déterminer, marquer. || MATH tracer, marquer.

plotter ['plɒtər] *n* [schemer] conspirateur *m*, -trice *f*.

plough *Br*, **plow** *Am* [plaʊ] **1** *n* charrue *f*. **2** *vt* [field] labourer. ○ **plough into 1** *vt sep* [money] investir. **2** *vt fus* [subj: car] rentrer dans.

plow *etc Am* = **plough** *etc*.

ploy [plɔɪ] *n* stratagème *m*, ruse *f*.

pluck [plʌk] *vt* [flower, fruit] cueillir. || [pull sharply] arracher. || [chicken, turkey] plumer. || [eyebrows] épiler. || MUS pincer. ○ **pluck up** *vt fus*: **to ~ up the courage to do sthg** rassembler son courage pour faire qqch.

plucky ['plʌkɪ] *adj dated* qui a du cran, courageux(euse).

plug [plʌg] **1** *n* ELEC prise *f* de courant. || [for bath, sink] bonde *f*. **2** *vt* [hole] boucher, obturer. || *inf* [new book, film etc] faire de la publicité pour. ○ **plug in** *vt sep* brancher.

plughole ['plʌghəʊl] *n* bonde *f*, trou *m* d'écoulement.

plum [plʌm] **1** *adj* [colour] prune (*inv*). || [very good]: **a ~ job** un boulot en or. **2** *n* [fruit] prune *f*.

plumber ['plʌmər] *n* plombier *m*.

plumbing ['plʌmɪŋ] *n* (*U*) [fittings] plomberie *f*, tuyauterie *f*. || [work] plomberie *f*.

plume [plu:m] *n* [feather] plume *f*. || [on hat] panache *m*. || [column]: **a ~ of smoke** un panache de fumée.

plummet ['plʌmɪt] *vi* [bird, plane] plonger. || *fig* [decrease] dégringoler.

plump [plʌmp] *adj* bien en chair, grassouillet(ette). ○ **plump for** *vt fus* opter pour, choisir. ○ **plump up** *vt sep* [cushion] secouer.

plum pudding *n* pudding *m* de Noël.

plunder ['plʌndər] **1** *n* (*U*) [stealing, raiding] pillage *m*. || [stolen goods] butin *m*. **2** *vt* piller.

plunge [plʌndʒ] **1** *n* [dive] plongeon *m*; **to take the ~** se jeter à l'eau. || *fig* [decrease] dégringolade *f*, chute *f*. **2** *vt*: **to ~ sthg into** plonger qqch dans. **3** *vi* [dive] plonger, tomber. || *fig* [decrease] dégringoler.

plunger ['plʌndʒər] *n* débouchoir *m* à ventouse.

pluperfect [,plu:'pɜ:fɪkt] *n*: **~ (tense)** plus-que-parfait *m*.

plural ['plʊərəl] **1** *adj* GRAMM pluriel(ielle). || [not individual] collectif(ive). || [multicultural] multiculturel(elle). **2** *n* pluriel *m*.

plus [plʌs] (*pl* **-es** OR **-ses**) **1** *adj*: **30 ~ 30** ou plus. **2** *n* [inf] [bonus] plus *m*, atout *m*. **3** *prep* et. **4** *conj* [moreover] de plus.

plush [plʌʃ] *adj* luxueux(euse), somptueux(euse).

plus sign *n* signe *m* plus.

Pluto ['plu:təʊ] *n* [planet] Pluton *f*.

plutonium [plu:'təʊnɪəm] *n* plutonium *m*.

ply [plaɪ] **1** *n* [of wool] fil *m*; [of wood] pli *m*. **2** *vt* [trade] exercer. || [supply]: **to ~ sb with drink** ne pas arrêter de remplir le verre de qqn. **3** *vi* [ship etc] faire la navette.

plywood ['plaɪwʊd] *n* contreplaqué *m*.

p.m., pm (*abbr of* **post meridiem**) **at 3 ~** à 15 h.

PM *abbr of* **prime minister**.

PMT *abbr of* **premenstrual tension**.

pneumatic drill *n* marteau piqueur *m*.

pneumonia [nju:'məʊnjə] *n* (*U*) pneumonie *f*.

poach [pəʊtʃ] **1** *vt* [fish] pêcher sans permis; [deer etc] chasser sans permis. || *fig* [idea] voler. || CULIN pocher. **2** *vi* braconner.

poacher ['pəʊtʃər] *n* braconnier *m*.

poaching ['pəʊtʃɪŋ] *n* braconnage *m*.

PO Box (*abbr of* **Post Office Box**) *n* BP *f*.

pocket ['pɒkɪt] **1** *n* lit & fig poche *f*; **to be out of ~** en être de sa poche; **to pick sb's ~** faire les poches à qqn. **2** *adj* de poche. **3** *vt* empocher.

pocketbook ['pɒkɪtbʊk] *n* [notebook] carnet *m*. || *Am* [handbag] sac *m* à main.

pocketknife ['pɒkɪtnaɪf] (*pl* **-knives** [-naɪvz]) *n* canif *m*.

pocket money *n* argent *m* de poche.

pod [pɒd] *n* [of plants] cosse *f*.

podiatrist [pə'daɪətrɪst] *n Am* pédicure *mf*.

podium ['pəʊdɪəm] (*pl* **-diums** OR **-dia** [-dɪə]) *n* podium *m*.

poem ['pəʊɪm] *n* poème *m*.

poet ['pəʊɪt] *n* poète *m*.

poetic [pəʊ'etɪk] *adj* poétique.

poetry ['pəʊɪtrɪ] *n* poésie *f*.

poignant ['pɔɪnjənt] *adj* poignant(e).

point [pɔɪnt] **1** *n* [tip] pointe *f*. || [place] endroit *m*, point *m*. || [time] stade *m*, moment *m*. || [detail, argument] question *f*, détail *m*; **you have a ~** il y a du vrai dans ce que vous dites; **to make a ~** faire une remarque; **to make one's ~** dire ce qu'on a à dire, dire son mot. || [main idea] point *m* essentiel; **to get** OR **come to the ~** en venir au fait; **to miss the ~** ne pas comprendre; **beside the ~** à côté de la question. || [feature]: **good ~** qualité *f*; **bad ~** défaut *m*. || [purpose]: **what's the ~ in buying a new car?** à quoi bon acheter une nouvelle voiture?; **there's no ~ in having a meeting** cela ne sert à rien d'avoir une réunion. || [on scale, in scores] point *m*. || MATH: **two ~ six** deux virgule six. || [of compass] aire *f* du vent. || *Am* [full stop] point *m* (final). || *phr*: **to make a ~ of doing sthg** ne pas manquer de faire qqch. **2** *vt*: **to ~ sthg (at)** [gun, camera] braquer qqch (sur); [finger, hose] pointer qqch (sur). **3** *vi* [indicate with finger]: **to ~ (at sb/sthg), to ~ (to sb/sthg)** montrer (qqn/qqch) du doigt, indiquer (qqn/ qqch) du doigt. || *fig* [suggest]: **to ~ to sthg** suggérer qqch, laisser supposer qqch. ○ **up to a point** *adv* jusqu'à un certain point, dans une certaine mesure. ○ **on the point of** *prep* sur le point de. ○ **point out** *vt sep* [person, place] montrer, indiquer; [fact, mistake] signaler.

point-blank *adv* [refuse] catégoriquement; [ask] de but en blanc. || [shoot] à bout portant.

pointed ['pɔɪntɪd] *adj* [sharp] pointu(e). || *fig* [remark] mordant(e), incisif(ive).

pointer ['pɔɪntər] *n* [piece of advice] tuyau *m*, conseil *m*. || [needle] aiguille *f*. || [stick] baguette *f*. || COMPUT pointeur *m*.

pointless ['pɔɪntlɪs] *adj* inutile, vain(e).

point of view (*pl* **points of view**) *n* point *m* de vue.

poise [pɔɪz] *n fig* calme *m*, sang-froid *m*.

poised [pɔɪzd] *adj* [ready]: **~ (for)** prêt(e) (pour). || *fig* [calm] calme, posé(e).

poison ['pɔɪzn] **1** *n* poison *m*. **2** *vt* [gen] empoisonner. || [pollute] polluer.

poisoning ['pɔɪznɪŋ] *n* empoisonnement *m*.

poisonous ['pɔɪznəs] *adj* [fumes] toxique; [plant] vénéneux(euse). || [snake] venimeux(euse).

poke [pəʊk] **1** *vt* [prod] pousser, donner un coup de coude à. || [put] fourrer. || [fire] attiser, tisonner. **2** *vi* [protrude] sortir, dépasser. ○ **poke about**, **poke around** *vi inf* fouiller, fourrager.

poker ['pəʊkər] *n* [game] poker *m*. || [for fire] tisonnier *m*.

poky ['pəʊkɪ] *adj pej* [room] exigu(ë), minuscule.

Poland ['pəʊlənd] *n* Pologne *f*.

polar ['pəʊlər] *adj* polaire.

Polaroid® ['pəʊlərɔɪd] *n* [camera] Polaroid® *m*. || [photograph] photo *f* polaroid.

pole [pəʊl] *n* [rod, post] perche *f*, mât *m*. || ELEC & GEOGR pôle *m*.

Pole [pəʊl] *n* Polonais *m*, -e *f*.

pole vault *n*: **the ~** le saut à la perche.

police [pə'liːs] **1** *npl* [police force]: **the ~** la police. || [policemen] agents *mpl* de police. **2** *vt* maintenir l'ordre dans.

police car *n* voiture *f* de police.

police force *n* police *f*.

policeman [pə'liːsmən] (*pl* -men [-mən]) *n* agent *m* de police.

police officer *n* policier *m*.

police record *n* casier *m* judiciaire.

police station *n* commissariat *m* (de police).

policewoman [pə'liːsˌwʊmən] (*pl* -women [-ˌwɪmɪn]) *n* femme *f* agent de police.

policy ['pɒləsɪ] *n* [plan] politique *f*. || [document] police *f*.

polio ['pəʊlɪəʊ] *n* polio *f*.

polish ['pɒlɪʃ] **1** *n* [for shoes] cirage *m*; [for floor] cire *f*, encaustique *f*. || [shine] brillant *m*, lustre *m*. || *fig* [refinement] raffinement *m*. **2** *vt* [shoes, floor] cirer; [car] astiquer; [cutlery, glasses] faire briller. ○ **polish off** *vt sep inf* expédier.

Polish ['pəʊlɪʃ] **1** *adj* polonais(e). **2** *n* [language] polonais *m*. **3** *npl*: **the ~** les Polonais *mpl*.

polished ['pɒlɪʃt] *adj* [refined] raffiné(e). || [accomplished] accompli(e), parfait(e).

polite [pə'laɪt] *adj* [courteous] poli(e).

political [pə'lɪtɪkl] *adj* politique.

politically correct [pə,lɪtɪklɪ-] *adj* conforme au mouvement qui préconise le remplacement de termes jugés discriminants par d'autres "politiquement corrects".

politician [,pɒlɪ'tɪʃn] *n* homme *m*, femme *f* politique.

politics ['pɒlɪtɪks] *n* (*U*) politique *f*.

polka ['pɒlkə] *n* polka *f*.

polka dot *n* pois *m*.

poll [pəʊl] **1** *n* vote *m*, scrutin *m*. **2** *vt* [people] interroger, sonder. || [votes] obtenir. ○ **polls** *npl*: **to go to the ~s** aller aux urnes.

pollen ['pɒlən] *n* pollen *m*.

polling booth ['pəʊlɪŋ-] *n* isoloir *m*.

polling station ['pəʊlɪŋ-] *n* bureau *m* de vote.

pollute [pə'luːt] *vt* polluer.

pollution [pə'luːʃn] *n* pollution *f*.

polo ['pəʊləʊ] *n* polo *m*.

polyethylene *Am* = polythene.

Polynesia [,pɒlɪ'niːzjə] *n* Polynésie *f*.

polystyrene [,pɒlɪ'staɪriːn] *n* polysty-rène *m*.

polythene *Br* ['pɒlɪθiːn], **polyethylene** *Am* [,pɒlɪ'eθɪliːn] *n* polyéthylène *m*.

pomegranate ['pɒmɪ,grænɪt] *n* grenade *f*.

pomp [pɒmp] *n* pompe *f*, faste *m*.

pompom ['pɒmpɒm] *n* pompon *m*.

pompous ['pɒmpəs] *adj* [person] fat, suffisant(e). || [style, speech] pompeux(euse).

pond [pɒnd] *n* étang *m*, mare *f*.

ponder ['pɒndər] *vt* considérer, peser.

ponderous ['pɒndərəs] *adj* [dull] lourd(e). || [large, heavy] pesant(e).

pontoon [pɒn'tuːn] *n* [bridge] ponton *m*. || *Br* [game] vingt-et-un *m*.

pony ['pəʊnɪ] *n* poney *m*.

ponytail ['pəʊnɪteɪl] *n* queue-de-cheval *f*.

pony-trekking [-,trekɪŋ] *n* randonnée *f* à cheval OR en poney.

poodle ['puːdl] *n* caniche *m*.

pool [puːl] **1** *n* [pond, of blood] mare *f*; [of rain, light] flaque *f*. || [swimming pool] piscine *f*. || SPORT billard *m* américain. **2** *vt* [resources etc] mettre en commun.

poor [pɔːr] **1** *adj* [gen] pauvre. || [not very good] médiocre, mauvais(e). **2** *npl*: **the ~** les pauvres *mpl*.

poorly ['pɔːlɪ] *adv* mal, médiocrement.

pop [pɒp] **1** *n* (*U*) [music] pop *m*. || (*U*) *inf* [fizzy drink] boisson *f* gazeuse. || *inf* [father] papa *m*. || [sound] pan *m*. **2** *vt* [burst] faire éclater, crever. || [put quickly] mettre, fourrer. **3** *vi* [balloon] éclater, crever; [cork, button] sauter. || [eyes]: **his eyes popped** il a écarquillé les yeux. ○ **pop in** *vi* faire une petite visite. ○ **pop up** *vi* surgir.

pop concert *n* concert *m* pop.

popcorn ['pɒpkɔːn] *n* pop-corn *m*.

pope [pəʊp] *n* pape *m*.

pop group *n* groupe *m* pop.

poplar ['pɒplər] *n* peuplier *m*.

poppy ['pɒpɪ] *n* coquelicot *m*, pavot *m*.

Popsicle® ['pɒpsɪkl] *n Am* sucette *f* glacée.

populace ['pɒpjʊləs] *n*: **the ~** le peuple.

popular ['pɒpjʊlər] *adj* [gen] populaire. || [name, holiday resort] à la mode.

popularize, -ise ['pɒpjʊləraɪz] *vt* [make popular] populariser. || [simplify] vulgariser.

population [,pɒpjʊ'leɪʃn] *n* population *f*.

porcelain ['pɔːsəlɪn] *n* porcelaine *f*.

porch [pɔːtʃ] *n* [entrance] porche *m*. || *Am* [verandah] véranda *f*.

porcupine ['pɔːkjʊpaɪn] *n* porc-épic *m*.

pore [pɔːr] *n* pore *m*. ○ **pore over** *vt fus* examiner de près.

pork [pɔːk] *n* porc *m*.

pork pie *n* pâté *m* de porc en croûte.

pornography [pɔː'nɒgrəfɪ] *n* pornographie *f*.

porous ['pɔːrəs] *adj* poreux(euse).

porridge ['pɒrɪdʒ] *n* porridge *m*.

port [pɔːt] *n* [town, harbour] port *m*. NAUT [left-hand side] bâbord *m*. || [drink] porto *m*. || COMPUT port *m*.

portable ['pɔːtəbl] *adj* portatif(ive).

portent ['pɔːtənt] *n* présage *m*.

porter ['pɔːtər] *n* [for luggage] porteur *m*. || *Am* [on train] employé *m*, -e *f* des wagons-lits.

portfolio [,pɔːt'fəʊljəʊ] (*pl* **-s**) *n* [case] serviette *f*. || [sample of work] portfolio *m*. || FIN portefeuille *m*.

porthole ['pɔːthəʊl] *n* hublot *m*.

portion ['pɔːʃn] *n* [section] portion *f*, part *f*. || [of food] portion *f*.

portly ['pɔːtlɪ] *adj* corpulent(e).

portrait ['pɔːtreɪt] *n* portrait *m*.

portray [pɔː'treɪ] *vt* CINEMA & THEATRE jouer, interpréter. || [describe] dépeindre. || [paint] faire le portrait de.

Portugal ['pɔːtʃʊgl] *n* Portugal *m*.

Portuguese [,pɔːtʃʊ'giːz] **1** *adj* portugais(e). **2** *n* [language] portugais *m*. **3** *npl*: **the ~** les Portugais *mpl*.

pose [pəʊz] **1** *n* [stance] pose *f*. || *pej* [affectation] pose *f*, affectation *f*. **2** *vt* [danger] présenter. || [problem, question] poser. **3** *vi* ART & *pej* poser. || [pretend to be]: **to ~ as** se faire passer pour.

posh [pɒʃ] *adj inf* [hotel, clothes etc] chic (*inv*). || *Br* [accent, person] de la haute.

position [pə'zɪʃn] **1** *n* [gen] position *f*. || [job] poste *m*, emploi *m*. || [state] situation *f*. **2** *vt* placer, mettre en position.

positive ['pɒzətɪv] *adj* [gen] positif(ive). || [sure] sûr(e), certain(e); **to be ~ about sthg** être sûr de qqch. || [optimistic] positif(ive), optimiste. || [definite] formel(elle), précis(e). || [evidence] irréfutable, indéniable. || [downright] véritable.

posse ['pɒsɪ] *n* *Am* détachement *m*, troupe *f*.

possess [pə'zes] *vt* posséder.

possession [pə'zeʃn] *n* possession *f*. ○ **possessions** *npl* possessions *fpl*, biens *mpl*.

possessive [pə'zesɪv] **1** *adj* possessif(ive). **2** *n* GRAMM possessif *m*.

possibility [,pɒsə'bɪlətɪ] *n* [chance, likelihood] possibilité *f*, chances *fpl*; **there is a ~ that** ... il se peut que ... (+ *subjunctive*). || [option] possibilité *f*, option *f*.

possible ['pɒsəbl] **1** *adj* possible; **as much as ~** autant que possible; **as soon as ~** dès que possible. **2** *n* possible *m*.

possibly ['pɒsəblɪ] *adv* [perhaps] peut-être. || [expressing surprise]: **how could he ~ have known?** mais comment a-t-il pu le savoir? || [for emphasis]: **I can't ~ accept your money** je ne peux vraiment pas accepter cet argent.

post [pəʊst] **1** *n* [service]: **the ~** la poste; **by ~** par la poste. || [letters, delivery] courrier *m*. || [pole] poteau *m*. || [position, job] poste *m*, emploi *m*. || MIL poste *m*. **2** *vt* [by mail] poster, mettre à la poste. || [employee] muter.

postage ['pəʊstɪdʒ] *n* affranchissement *m*; **~ and packing** frais *mpl* de port et d'emballage.

postal ['pəʊstl] *adj* postal(e).

postal order *n* mandat *m* postal.

postcard ['pəʊstkɑːd] *n* carte *f* postale.

postdate [,pəʊst'deɪt] *vt* postdater.

poster ['pəʊstər] *n* [for advertising] affiche *f*; [for decoration] poster *m*.

poste restante [,pəʊst'restɑːnt] *n* poste *f* restante.

posterior [pɒ'stɪərɪər] *adj* postérieur(e).

postgraduate [,pəʊst'grædʒʊət] **1** *adj* de troisième cycle. **2** *n* étudiant *m*, -e *f* de troisième cycle.

posthumous ['pɒstjʊməs] *adj* posthume.

postman ['pəʊstmən] (*pl* **-men** [-mən]) *n* facteur *m*.

postmark ['pəʊstmɑːk] **1** *n* cachet *m* de la poste. **2** *vt* timbrer, tamponner.

postmaster ['pəʊst,mɑːstər] *n* receveur *m* des postes.

postmortem [,pəʊst'mɔːtəm] *n* *lit & fig* autopsie *f*.

post office *n* [organization]: **the Post Office** les Postes et Télécommunications *fpl*. || [building] (bureau *m* de) poste *f*.

post office box *n* boîte *f* postale.

postpone [,pəʊst'pəʊn] *vt* reporter, remettre.

postscript ['pəʊstskrɪpt] *n* postscriptum *m inv*.

posture ['pɒstʃər] *n* (U) [pose] position *f*, posture *f*. || *fig* [attitude] attitude *f*.

postwar [,pəʊst'wɔːr] *adj* d'après-guerre.

posy ['pəʊzɪ] *n* petit bouquet *m* de fleurs.

pot [pɒt] **1** *n* [for cooking] marmite *f*, casserole *f*. || [for tea] théière *f*; [for coffee] cafetière *f*. || [for paint, jam, plant] pot *m*. || (U) inf [cannabis] herbe *f*. **2** *vt* [plant] mettre en pot.

potassium [pə'tæsɪəm] *n* potassium *m*.

potato [pə'teɪtəʊ] (*pl* **-es**) *n* pomme *f* de terre.

potato peeler [-,piːlər] *n* (couteau *m*) éplucheur *m*.

potent ['pəʊtənt] *adj* [powerful, influential] puissant(e). || [drink] fort(e). || [man] viril.

potential [pə'tenʃl] **1** *adj* [energy, success] potentiel(ielle); [uses, danger] possible; [enemy] en puissance. **2** *n* (U) [of person] capacités *fpl* latentes; **to have ~** [person] promettre; [company] avoir de l'avenir; [scheme] offrir des possibilités.

pothole ['pɒthəʊl] *n* [in road] nid-de-poule *m*. || [underground] caverne *f*, grotte *f*.

potion ['pəʊʃn] *n* [magic] breuvage *m*; **love ~** philtre *m*.

potluck [,pɒt'lʌk] *n*: **to take ~** [gen] choisir au hasard; [at meal] manger à la fortune du pot.

potshot ['pɒt,ʃɒt] *n*: **to take a ~ (at sthg)** tirer (sur qqch) sans viser.

potted ['pɒtɪd] *adj* [plant]: **~ plant** plante *f* d'appartement. || [food] conservé(e) en pot.

potter ['pɒtər] *n* potier *m*.

pottery ['pɒtərɪ] *n* poterie *f*; **a piece of ~** une poterie.

pouch [paʊtʃ] *n* [small bag] petit sac *m*; **tobacco ~** blague *f* à tabac. || [of kangaroo] poche *f* ventrale.

precarious

poultry ['pəʊltrɪ] **1** *n* (*U*) [meat] volaille *f*. **2** *npl* [birds] volailles *fpl*.

pounce [paʊns] *vi*: to ~ (on) [bird] fondre (sur); [person] se jeter (sur).

pound [paʊnd] **1** *n* [money] livre *f*. || [weight] = 453,6 *grammes*, ≃ livre *f*. || [for cars, dogs] fourrière *f*. **2** *vt* [strike loudly] marteler. || [crush] piler, broyer. **3** *vi* [strike loudly]: to ~ on donner de grands coups à. || [heart] battre fort.

pound sterling *n* livre *f* sterling.

pour [pɔːr] **1** *vt* verser; shall I ~ you a drink? je te sers quelque chose à boire? **2** *vi* [liquid] couler à flots. || *fig* [rush]: to ~ in/out entrer/sortir en foule. **3** *v impers* [rain hard] pleuvoir à verse. ○ **pour in** *vi* [letters, news] affluer. ○ **pour out** *vt sep* [empty] vider. || [serve - drink] verser, servir.

pouring ['pɔːrɪŋ] *adj* [rain] torrentiel(ielle).

pout [paʊt] *vi* faire la moue.

poverty ['pɒvətɪ] *n* pauvreté *f*.

poverty-stricken *adj* [person] dans la misère; [area] misérable, très pauvre.

powder ['paʊdər] **1** *n* poudre *f*. **2** *vt* [face, body] poudrer.

powder compact *n* poudrier *m*.

powdered ['paʊdəd] *adj* [milk, eggs] en poudre. || [face] poudré(e).

powder puff *n* houppette *f*.

powder room *n* toilettes *fpl* pour dames.

power ['paʊər] **1** *n* (*U*) [authority, ability] pouvoir *m*; to take ~ prendre le pouvoir; to come to ~ parvenir au pouvoir; to be in ~ être au pouvoir; to be in OR within one's ~ to do sthg être en son pouvoir de faire qqch. || [strength, powerful person] puissance *f*, force *f*. || (*U*) [energy] énergie *f*. || [electricity] courant *m*, électricité *f*. **2** *vt* faire marcher, actionner.

powerboat ['paʊəbəʊt] *n* hors-bord *m inv*.

power cut *n* coupure *f* de courant.

power failure *n* panne *f* de courant.

powerful ['paʊəfʊl] *adj* [gen] puissant(e). || [smell, voice] fort(e). || [speech, novel] émouvant(e).

powerless ['paʊəlɪs] *adj* impuissant(e); to be ~ to do sthg être dans l'impossibilité de faire qqch, ne pas pouvoir faire qqch.

power station *n* centrale *f* électrique.

power steering *n* direction *f* assistée.

pp (*abbr of* per procurationem) pp.

p & p *abbr of* postage and packing.

PR *n abbr of* proportional representation. || *abbr of* public relations.

practicable ['præktɪkəbl] *adj* réalisable, faisable.

practical ['præktɪkl] *adj* [gen] pratique. || [plan, solution] réalisable.

practicality [,præktɪ'kælətɪ] *n* (*U*) aspect *m* pratique.

practical joke *n* farce *f*.

practically ['præktɪklɪ] *adv* [in a practical way] d'une manière pratique. || [almost] presque, pratiquement.

practice, practise *Am* ['præktɪs] *n* (*U*) [at sport] entraînement *m*; [at music etc] répétition *f*; to be out of ~ être rouillé(e). || [training session - at sport] séance *f* d'entraînement; [- at music etc] répétition *f*. || [act of doing]: to put sthg into ~ mettre qqch en pratique; in ~ [in fact] en réalité, en fait. || [habit] pratique *f*, coutume *f*. || (*U*) [of profession] exercice *m*. || [of doctor] cabinet *m*; [of lawyer] étude *f*.

practicing *Am* = **practising**.

practise, practice *Am* ['præktɪs] **1** *vt* [sport] s'entraîner à; [piano etc] s'exercer à. || [custom] suivre, pratiquer; [religion] pratiquer. || [profession] exercer. **2** *vi* SPORT s'entraîner; MUS s'exercer. || [doctor, lawyer] exercer.

practising, practicing *Am* ['præktɪsɪŋ] *adj* [doctor, lawyer] en exercice; [Christian etc] pratiquant(e).

practitioner [præk'tɪʃnər] *n* praticien *m*, -ienne *f*.

Prague [prɑːg] *n* Prague.

prairie ['preərɪ] *n* prairie *f*.

praise [preɪz] **1** *n* (*U*) louange *f*, louanges *fpl*, éloge *m*, éloges *mpl*. **2** *vt* louer, faire l'éloge de.

praiseworthy ['preɪz,wɜːðɪ] *adj* louable, méritoire.

pram [præm] *n* landau *m*.

prance [prɑːns] *vi* [person] se pavaner. || [horse] caracoler.

prank [præŋk] *n* tour *m*, niche *f*.

prawn [prɔːn] *n* crevette *f* rose.

pray [preɪ] *vi*: to ~ (to sb) prier (qqn).

prayer [preər] *n lit & fig* prière *f*.

prayer book *n* livre *m* de messe.

preach [priːtʃ] **1** *vt* [gen] prêcher; [sermon] prononcer. **2** *vi* RELIG: to ~ (to sb) prêcher (qqn). || *pej* [pontificate]: to ~ (at sb) sermonner (qqn).

preacher ['priːtʃər] *n* prédicateur *m*, pasteur *m*.

precarious [prɪ'keərɪəs] *adj* précaire.

precaution [prɪ'kɔːʃn] n précaution f.

precede [prɪ'siːd] vt précéder.

precedence ['presɪdəns] n: **to take ~ over sthg** avoir la priorité sur qqch; **to have** OR **take ~ over sb** avoir la préséance sur qqn.

precedent ['presɪdənt] n précédent m.

precinct ['priːsɪŋkt] n Am [district] circonscription f (administrative). ○ **precincts** npl [of institution] enceinte f.

precious ['preʃəs] adj [gen] précieux(ieuse). ‖ inf iro [damned] sacré(e). ‖ [affected] affecté(e).

precipice ['presɪpɪs] n précipice m, paroi f à pic.

precipitate [prɪ'sɪpɪteɪt] fml vt [hasten] hâter, précipiter.

precise [prɪ'saɪs] adj précis(e); [measurement, date] exact(e).

precisely [prɪ'saɪslɪ] adv précisément, exactement.

precision [prɪ'sɪʒn] n précision f, exactitude f.

preclude [prɪ'kluːd] vt fml empêcher; [possibility] écarter; **to ~ sb from doing sthg** empêcher qqn de faire qqch.

precocious [prɪ'kəʊʃəs] adj précoce.

preconceived [,priːkən'siːvd] adj préconçu(e).

predator ['predətər] n [animal, bird] prédateur m, rapace m.

predecessor ['priːdɪsesər] n [person] prédécesseur m. ‖ [thing] précédent m, -e f.

predicament [prɪ'dɪkəmənt] n situation f difficile; **to be in a ~** être dans de beaux draps.

predict [prɪ'dɪkt] vt prédire.

predictable [prɪ'dɪktəbl] adj prévisible.

prediction [prɪ'dɪkʃn] n prédiction f.

predispose [,priːdɪs'pəʊz] vt: **to be ~d to sthg/to do sthg** être prédisposé(e) à qqch/à faire qqch.

predominant [prɪ'dɒmɪnənt] adj prédominant(e).

preempt [,priː'empt] vt [action, decision] devancer, prévenir.

preemptive [,priː'emptɪv] adj préventif(ive).

preen [priːn] vt [subj: bird] lisser, nettoyer. ‖ fig [subj: person]: **to ~ o.s.** se faire beau (belle).

prefab ['priːfæb] n inf maison f préfabriquée.

preface ['prefɪs] n: **~ (to)** préface f (de), préambule m (de).

prefer [prɪ'fɜːr] vt préférer; **to ~ sthg to sthg** préférer qqch à qqch, aimer mieux qqch que qqch; **to ~ to do sthg** préférer faire qqch, aimer mieux faire qqch.

preferable ['prefrəbl] adj: **~ (to)** préférable (à).

preferably ['prefrəblɪ] adv de préférence.

preference ['prefərəns] n préférence f.

preferential [,prefə'renʃl] adj préférentiel(ielle).

prefix ['priːfɪks] n préfixe m.

pregnancy ['pregnənsɪ] n grossesse f.

pregnant ['pregnənt] adj [woman] enceinte; [animal] pleine, gravide.

prehistoric [,priːhɪ'stɒrɪk] adj préhistorique.

prejudice ['predʒʊdɪs] **1** n [biased view]: **~ (in favour of/against)** préjugé m (en faveur de/contre), préjugés mpl (en faveur de/contre). ‖ (U) [harm] préjudice m, tort m. **2** vt [bias]: **to ~ sb (in favour of/against)** prévenir qqn (en faveur de/contre), influencer qqn (en faveur de/contre). ‖ [harm] porter préjudice à.

prejudiced ['predʒʊdɪst] adj [person] qui a des préjugés; [opinion] préconçu(e); **to be ~ in favour of/against** avoir des préjugés en faveur de/contre.

prejudicial [,predʒʊ'dɪʃl] adj: **~ (to)** préjudiciable (à), nuisible (à).

preliminary [prɪ'lɪmɪnərɪ] adj préliminaire.

prelude ['preljuːd] n [event]: **~ to sthg** prélude m de qqch.

premarital [,priː'mærɪtl] adj avant le mariage.

premature ['premə,tjʊər] adj prématuré(e).

premeditated [,priː'medɪteɪtɪd] adj prémédité(e).

premenstrual syndrome, premenstrual tension [priː'menstrʊəl-] n syndrome m prémenstruel.

premier ['premjər] **1** adj primordial(e), premier(ière). **2** n premier ministre m.

premiere ['premɪeər] n première f.

premise ['premɪs] n prémisse f. ○ **premises** npl local m, locaux mpl; **on the ~s** sur place, sur les lieux.

premium ['priːmjəm] n prime f; **at a ~** [above usual value] à prix d'or; [in great demand] très recherché OR demandé.

premonition [,premə'nɪʃn] n prémonition f, pressentiment m.

preoccupied [priː'ɒkjʊpaɪd] adj: **~ (with)** préoccupé(e) (de).

prepaid ['pri:peɪd] *adj* payé(e) d'avance; [envelope] affranchi(e).

preparation [,prepə'reɪʃn] *n* préparation *f*. ○ **preparations** *npl* préparatifs *mpl*.

preparatory [prɪ'pærətrɪ] *adj* [work, classes] préparatoire; [actions, measures] préliminaire.

preparatory school *n* [in US] *école privée qui prépare à l'enseignement supérieur*.

prepare [prɪ'peər] **1** *vt* préparer. **2** *vi*: to ~ for sthg/to do sthg se préparer à qqch/à faire qqch.

prepared [prɪ'peəd] *adj* [done beforehand] préparé(e) d'avance. ‖ [willing]: to be ~ to do sthg être prêt(e) OR disposé(e) à faire qqch. ‖ [ready]: to be ~ for sthg être prêt(e) pour qqch.

preposition [,prepə'zɪʃn] *n* préposition *f*.

preposterous [prɪ'pɒstərəs] *adj* ridicule, absurde.

prep school *abbr of* **preparatory school**.

prerequisite [,pri:'rekwɪzɪt] *n* condition *f* préalable.

prerogative [prɪ'rɒgətɪv] *n* prérogative *f*, privilège *m*.

Presbyterian [,prezbɪ'tɪərɪən] *adj* presbytérien(ienne).

preschool [,pri:'sku:l] **1** *adj* préscolaire. **2** *n Am* école *f* maternelle.

prescribe [prɪ'skraɪb] *vt* MED prescrire. ‖ [order] ordonner, imposer.

prescription [prɪ'skrɪpʃn] *n* [MED - written form] ordonnance *f*; [- medicine] médicament *m*.

presence ['prezns] *n* présence *f*; to be in sb's ~ OR in the ~ of sb être en présence de qqn.

presence of mind *n* présence *f* d'esprit.

present [*adj & n* 'preznt, *vb* prɪ'zent] **1** *adj* [current] actuel(elle). ‖ [in attendance] présent(e); to be ~ at assister à. **2** *n* [current time]: the ~ le présent; at ~ actuellement, en ce moment. ‖ [gift] cadeau *m*. ‖ GRAMM: ~ (tense) présent *m*. **3** *vt* [gen] présenter; [opportunity] donner. ‖ [give]: to ~ sb with sthg, to ~ sthg to sb donner OR remettre qqch à qqn. ‖ [portray] représenter, décrire. ‖ [arrive]: to ~ o.s. se présenter.

presentable [prɪ'zentəbl] *adj* présentable.

presentation [,prezn'teɪʃn] *n* [gen] présentation *f*. ‖ [ceremony] remise *f* (de récompense/prix). ‖ [talk] exposé *m*.

present day *n*: the ~ aujourd'hui. ○ **present-day** *adj* d'aujourd'hui, contemporain(e).

presently ['prezntlɪ] *adv* [soon] bientôt, tout à l'heure. ‖ [at present] actuellement, en ce moment.

preservation [,prezə'veɪʃn] *n* (U) [maintenance] maintien *m*. ‖ [protection] protection *f*, conservation *f*.

preservative [prɪ'zɜ:vətɪv] *n* conservateur *m*.

preserve [prɪ'zɜ:v] *vt* [maintain] maintenir. ‖ [protect] conserver. ‖ [food] conserver, mettre en conserve. ○ **preserves** *npl* [jam] confiture *f*; [vegetables] pickles *mpl*, condiments *mpl*.

preset [,pri:'set] (*pt & pp* **preset**) *vt* prérégler.

president ['prezɪdənt] *n* [gen] président *m*. ‖ *Am* [company chairman] P-DG *m*.

presidential [,prezɪ'denʃl] *adj* présidentiel(ielle).

press [pres] **1** *n* [push] pression *f*. ‖ [journalism]: the ~ [newspapers] la presse, les journaux *mpl*; [reporters] les journalistes *mpl*. ‖ [printing machine] presse *f*; [for wine] pressoir *m*. **2** *vt* [push] appuyer sur; to ~ sthg against sthg appuyer qqch sur qqch. ‖ [squeeze] serrer. ‖ [iron] repasser, donner un coup de fer à. ‖ [urge]: to ~ sb (to do sthg OR into doing sthg) presser qqn (de faire qqch). ‖ [pursue - claim] insister sur. **3** *vi* [push]: to ~ (on) appuyer (sur). ‖ [squeeze]: to ~ (on sthg) serrer (qqch). ‖ [crowd] se presser. ○ **press for** *vt fus* demander avec insistance. ○ **press on** *vi* [continue]: to ~ on (with sthg) continuer (qqch), ne pas abandonner (qqch).

press agency *n* agence *f* de presse.

press conference *n* conférence *f* de presse.

pressed [prest] *adj*: to be ~ for time/money être à court de temps/d'argent.

pressing ['presɪŋ] *adj* urgent(e).

press officer *n* attaché *m* de presse.

press release *n* communiqué *m* de presse.

pressure ['preʃər] *n* (U) [gen] pression *f*; to put ~ on sb (to do sthg) faire pression sur qqn (pour qu'il fasse qqch). ‖ [stress] tension *f*.

pressure cooker n Cocotte-Minute® f, autocuiseur m.

pressure gauge n manomètre m.

pressure group n groupe m de pression.

prestige [pre'sti:ʒ] n prestige m.

presumably [prɪ'zju:məblɪ] adv vraisemblablement.

presume [prɪ'zju:m] vt présumer; **to ~ (that)** ... supposer que ....

presumption [prɪ'zʌmpʃn] n [assumption] supposition f, présomption f. || (U) [audacity] présomption f.

presumptuous [prɪ'zʌmptʃʊəs] adj présomptueux(euse).

pretence, pretense Am [prɪ'tens] n prétention f; **to make a ~ of doing sthg** faire semblant de faire qqch; **under false ~s** sous des prétextes fallacieux.

pretend [prɪ'tend] 1 vt: **to ~ to do sthg** faire semblant de faire qqch. 2 vi faire semblant.

pretense Am = pretence.

pretension [prɪ'tenʃn] n prétention f.

pretentious [prɪ'tenʃəs] adj prétentieux(ieuse).

pretext ['pri:tekst] n prétexte m; **on OR under the ~ that** ... sous prétexte que ....

pretty ['prɪtɪ] 1 adj joli(e). 2 adv [quite] plutôt; **~ much OR well** pratiquement, presque.

prevail [prɪ'veɪl] vi [be widespread] avoir cours, régner. || [triumph]: **to ~ (over)** prévaloir (sur), l'emporter (sur). || [persuade]: **to ~ on OR upon sb to do sthg** persuader qqn de faire qqch.

prevailing [prɪ'veɪlɪŋ] adj [current] actuel(elle). || [wind] dominant(e).

prevalent ['prevələnt] adj courant(e), répandu(e).

prevent [prɪ'vent] vt: **to ~ sb/sthg (from doing sthg)** empêcher qqn/qqch (de faire qqch).

preventive [prɪ'ventɪv] adj préventif(ive).

preview ['pri:vju:] n avant-première f.

previous ['pri:vjəs] adj [earlier] antérieur(e). || [preceding] précédent(e).

previously ['pri:vjəslɪ] adv avant, auparavant.

prewar [,pri:'wɔːr] adj d'avant-guerre.

prey [preɪ] n proie f. O **prey on** vt fus [live off] faire sa proie de. || [trouble]: **to ~ on sb's mind** ronger qqn, tracasser qqn.

price [praɪs] 1 n [cost] prix m; **at any ~** à tout prix. 2 vt fixer le prix de.

priceless ['praɪslɪs] adj sans prix, inestimable.

price list n tarif m.

price tag n [label] étiquette f.

prick [prɪk] 1 n [scratch, wound] piqûre f. || vulg [stupid person] con m, conne f. 2 vt piquer. O **prick up** vt fus: **to ~ up one's ears** [animal] dresser les oreilles; [person] dresser OR tendre l'oreille.

prickle ['prɪkl] 1 n [thorn] épine f. || [sensation on skin] picotement m. 2 vi picoter.

prickly ['prɪklɪ] adj [plant, bush] épineux(euse). || fig [person] irritable.

prickly heat n (U) boutons mpl de chaleur.

pride [praɪd] 1 n (U) [satisfaction] fierté f. || [self-esteem] orgueil m, amour-propre m. || pej [arrogance] orgueil m. 2 vt: **to ~ o.s. on sthg** être fier (fière) de qqch.

priest [pri:st] n prêtre m.

priestess [pri:'stɪs] n prêtresse f.

priesthood ['pri:sthʊd] n [position, office]: **the ~** le sacerdoce. || [priests]: **the ~** le clergé.

prig [prɪg] n petit saint m, petite sainte f.

prim [prɪm] adj guindé(e).

primarily ['praɪmərɪlɪ] adv principalement.

primary ['praɪmərɪ] 1 adj [main] premier(ière), principal(e). || SCH primaire. 2 n Am POL primaire f.

primary school n école f primaire.

primate ['praɪmeɪt] n ZOOL primate m. || RELIG primat m.

prime [praɪm] 1 adj [main] principal(e), primordial(e). || [excellent] excellent(e); **~ quality** première qualité. 2 n: **to be in one's ~** être dans la fleur de l'âge. 3 vt [paint] apprêter. || [inform]: **to ~ sb about sthg** mettre qqn au courant de qqch.

prime minister n premier ministre m.

primer ['praɪmər] n [paint] apprêt m. || [textbook] introduction f.

primeval [praɪ'mi:vl] adj [ancient] primitif(ive).

primitive ['prɪmɪtɪv] adj primitif(ive).

primrose ['prɪmrəʊz] n primevère f.

Primus stove® ['praɪməs-] n réchaud m de camping.

prince [prɪns] n prince m.

princess [prɪn'ses] n princesse f.

principal ['prɪnsəpl] 1 adj principal(e). 2 n SCH directeur m, -trice f; UNIV doyen m, -enne f.

principle ['prɪnsəpl] n principe m; **on ~, as a matter of ~** par principe. ○ **in principle** adv en principe.

print [prɪnt] **1** n (U) [type] caractères mpl; **to be out of ~** être épuisé. ‖ ART gravure f. ‖ [photograph] épreuve f. ‖ [fabric] imprimé m. ‖ [mark] empreinte f. **2** vt [produce by printing] imprimer. ‖ [publish] publier. ‖ [write in block letters] écrire en caractères d'imprimerie. ○ **print out** vt sep COMPUT imprimer.

printed matter ['prɪntɪd-] n (U) imprimés mpl.

printer ['prɪntər] n [person, firm] imprimeur m. ‖ COMPUT imprimante f.

printing ['prɪntɪŋ] n (U) [act of printing] impression f. ‖ [trade] imprimerie f.

printout ['prɪntaʊt] n COMPUT sortie f d'imprimante, listing m.

prior ['praɪər] **1** adj antérieur(e), précédent(e). **2** n [monk] prieur m. ○ **prior to** prep avant; **~ to doing sthg** avant de faire qqch.

priority [praɪ'ɒrətɪ] n priorité f.

prise [praɪz] vt: **to ~ sthg away from sb** arracher qqch à qqn; **to ~ sthg open** forcer qqch.

prison ['prɪzn] n prison f.

prisoner ['prɪznər] n prisonnier m, -ière f.

prisoner of war (pl **prisoners of war**) n prisonnier m, -ière f de guerre.

privacy [Br 'prɪvəsɪ, Am 'praɪvəsɪ] n intimité f.

private ['praɪvɪt] **1** adj [not public] privé(e). ‖ [confidential] confidentiel(ielle). ‖ [personal] personnel(elle). ‖ [unsociable - person] secret(ète). **2** n [soldier] (simple) soldat m. ‖ [secrecy]: **in ~** en privé.

private enterprise n (U) entreprise f privée.

private eye n détective m privé.

privately ['praɪvɪtlɪ] adv [not by the state]: **~ owned** du secteur privé. ‖ [confidentially] en privé. ‖ [personally] intérieurement, dans son for intérieur.

private property n propriété f privée.

private school n école f privée.

privatize, -ise ['praɪvɪtaɪz] vt privatiser.

privet ['prɪvɪt] n troène m.

privilege ['prɪvɪlɪdʒ] n privilège m.

privy ['prɪvɪ] adj: **to be ~ to sthg** être dans le secret de qqch.

prize [praɪz] **1** adj [possession] très précieux(ieuse); [animal] primé(e); [idiot,

example] parfait(e). **2** n prix m. **3** vt priser.

prizewinner ['praɪz,wɪnər] n gagnant m, -e f.

pro [prəʊ] (pl **-s**) n inf [professional] pro mf. ‖ [advantage]: **the ~s and cons** le pour et le contre.

probability [,prɒbə'bɪlətɪ] n probabilité f.

probable ['prɒbəbl] adj probable.

probably ['prɒbəblɪ] adv probablement.

probation [prə'beɪʃn] n (U) JUR mise à l'épreuve; **to put sb on ~** mettre qqn en sursis avec mise à l'épreuve. ‖ [trial period] essai m; **to be on ~** être à l'essai.

probe [prəʊb] **1** n [investigation]: **~ (into)** enquête f (sur). ‖ MED & TECH sonde f. **2** vt sonder.

problem ['prɒbləm] n problème m.

procedure [prə'siːdʒər] n procédure f.

proceed [vb prə'siːd, npl 'prəʊsiːdz] vt [do subsequently]: **to ~ to do sthg** se mettre à faire qqch. **2** vi [continue]: **to ~ (with sthg)** continuer (qqch), poursuivre (qqch). ‖ fml [advance] avancer. ○ **proceeds** npl recette f.

proceedings [prə'siːdɪŋz] npl [of meeting] débats mpl. ‖ JUR poursuites fpl.

process ['prəʊsess] **1** n [series of actions] processus m; **in the ~** ce faisant; **to be in the ~ of doing sthg** être en train de faire qqch. ‖ [method] procédé m. **2** vt [raw materials, food, data] traiter, transformer; [application] s'occuper de.

processing ['prəʊsesɪŋ] n traitement m, transformation f.

procession [prə'seʃn] n cortège m, procession f.

proclaim [prə'kleɪm] vt [declare] proclamer.

procrastinate [prə'kræstɪneɪt] vi faire traîner les choses.

procure [prə'kjʊər] vt [for oneself] se procurer; [for someone else] procurer; [release] obtenir.

prod [prɒd] vt [push, poke] pousser doucement.

prodigy ['prɒdɪdʒɪ] n prodige m.

produce [n 'prɒdjuːs, vb prə'djuːs] **1** n (U) produits mpl. **2** vt [gen] produire. ‖ [cause] provoquer, causer. ‖ [show] présenter. ‖ THEATRE mettre en scène.

producer [prə'djuːsər] n [of film, manufacturer] producteur m, -trice f. ‖ THEATRE metteur m en scène.

product ['prɒdʌkt] n produit m.

production [prə'dʌkʃn] *n* (*U*) [manufacture, of film] production *f*. || (*U*) [output] rendement *m*. || (*U*) THEATRE [of play] mise *f* en scène. || [show - gen] production *f*; [- THEATRE] pièce *f*.

production line *n* chaîne *f* de fabrication.

productive [prə'dʌktɪv] *adj* [land, business, workers] productif(ive). || [meeting, experience] fructueux(euse).

productivity [,prɒdʌk'tɪvətɪ] *n* productivité *f*.

profane [prə'feɪn] *adj* impie.

profession [prə'feʃn] *n* profession *f*.

professional [prə'feʃənl] **1** *adj* [gen] professionnel(elle). || [of high standard] de (haute) qualité. **2** *n* professionnel *m*, - elle *f*.

professor [prə'fesər] *n* Am & Can [teacher] professeur *m*.

proficiency [prə'fɪʃənsɪ] *n*: ~ (in) compétence *f* (en).

profile ['prəʊfaɪl] *n* profil *m*.

profit ['prɒfɪt] **1** *n* [financial] bénéfice *m*, profit *m*; **to make a ~** faire un bénéfice. || [advantage] profit *m*. **2** *vi* [financially] être le bénéficiaire; [gain advantage] tirer avantage OR profit.

profitability [,prɒfɪtə'bɪlətɪ] *n* rentabilité *f*.

profitable ['prɒfɪtəbl] *adj* [financially] rentable, lucratif(ive). || [beneficial] fructueux(euse), profitable.

profiteering [,prɒfɪ'tɪərɪŋ] *n* affairisme *m*, mercantilisme *m*.

profound [prə'faʊnd] *adj* profond(e).

profusely [prə'fjuːslɪ] *adv* [sweat, bleed] abondamment; **to apologize ~** se confondre en excuses.

profusion [prə'fjuːʒn] *n* profusion *f*.

prognosis [prɒg'nəʊsɪs] (*pl* -noses [-'nəʊsiːz]) *n* pronostic *m*.

program ['prəʊgræm] (*pt & pp* -med OR -ed, *cont* -ming OR -ing) **1** *n* COMPUT programme *m*. || *Am* = **programme**. **2** *vt* COMPUT programmer. || *Am* = **programme**.

programer *Am* = **programmer**.

programme *Br*, **program** *Am* ['prəʊgræm] **1** *n* [schedule, booklet] programme *m*. || RADIO & TV émission *f*. **2** *vt* programmer.

programmer *Br*, **programer** *Am* ['prəʊgræmər] *n* COMPUT programmeur *m*, -euse *f*.

programming ['prəʊgræmɪŋ] *n* programmation *f*.

progress [*n* 'prəʊgres, *vb* prə'gres] **1** *n* progrès *m*; **to make ~** [improve] faire des progrès; **to make ~ in sthg** avancer dans qqch; **in ~** en cours. **2** *vi* [improve - gen] progresser, avancer; [- person] faire des progrès. || [continue] avancer.

progressive [prə'gresɪv] *adj* [enlightened] progressiste. || [gradual] progressif(ive).

prohibit [prə'hɪbɪt] *vt* prohiber; **to ~ sb from doing sthg** interdire OR défendre à qqn de faire qqch.

project [*n* 'prɒdʒekt, *vb* prə'dʒekt] **1** *n* [plan, idea] projet *m*, plan *m*. || SCH [study]: ~ (**on**) dossier *m* (sur), projet *m* (sur). **2** *vt* [gen] projeter. || [estimate] prévoir. **3** *vi* [jut out] faire saillie.

projectile [prə'dʒektaɪl] *n* projectile *m*.

projection [prə'dʒekʃn] *n* [estimate] prévision *f*. || [protrusion] saillie *f*. || (*U*) [display, showing] projection *f*.

projector [prə'dʒektər] *n* projecteur *m*.

proletariat [,prəʊlɪ'teərɪət] *n* prolétariat *m*.

prolific [prə'lɪfɪk] *adj* prolifique.

prologue, prolog *Am* ['prəʊlɒg] *n lit & fig* prologue *m*.

prolong [prə'lɒŋ] *vt* prolonger.

prom [prɒm] *n* Am [ball] bal *m* d'étudiants.

prominent ['prɒmɪnənt] *adj* [important] important(e). || [noticeable] proéminent(e).

promiscuous [prɒ'mɪskjʊəs] *adj* [person] aux mœurs légères.

promise ['prɒmɪs] **1** *n* promesse *f*. **2** *vt*: **to ~ (sb) to do sthg** promettre (à qqn) de faire qqch; **to ~ sb sthg** promettre qqch à qqn. **3** *vi* promettre.

promising ['prɒmɪsɪŋ] *adj* prometteur(euse).

promontory ['prɒməntrɪ] *n* promontoire *m*.

promote [prə'məʊt] *vt* [foster] promouvoir. || [push, advertise] promouvoir, lancer. || [in job] promouvoir.

promoter [prə'məʊtər] *n* [organizer] organisateur *m*, -trice *f*. || [supporter] promoteur *m*, -trice *f*.

promotion [prə'məʊʃn] *n* promotion *f*, avancement *m*.

prompt [prɒmpt] **1** *adj* rapide, prompt(e). **2** *adv*: **at nine o'clock ~** à neuf heures précises OR tapantes. **3** *vt* [motivate, encourage]: **to ~ sb (to do sthg)** pousser OR inciter qqn (à faire qqch). || THEATRE souffler sa réplique à.

promptly ['promptlɪ] *adv* [immediately] rapidement, promptement. || [punctually] ponctuellement.

prone [prəʊn] *adj* [susceptible]: **to be ~ to sthg** être sujet(ette) à qqch; **to be ~ to do sthg** avoir tendance à faire qqch. || [lying flat] étendu(e) face contre terre.

prong [prɒŋ] *n* [of fork] dent *f*.

pronoun ['prəʊnaʊn] *n* pronom *m*.

pronounce [prə'naʊns] **1** *vt* prononcer. **2** *vi*: **to ~ on** se prononcer sur.

pronounced [prə'naʊnst] *adj* prononcé(e).

pronouncement [prə'naʊnsmənt] *n* déclaration *f*.

pronunciation [prə,nʌnsɪ'eɪʃn] *n* prononciation *f*.

proof [pruːf] *n* [evidence] preuve *f*. || [of book etc] épreuve *f*. || [of alcohol] teneur *f* en alcool.

prop [prɒp] **1** *n* [physical support] support *m*, étai *m*. || *fig* [supporting thing, person] soutien *m*. **2** *vt*: **to ~ sthg against** appuyer qqch contre OR à. ○ **props** *npl* accessoires *mpl*. ○ **prop up** *vt sep* [physically support] soutenir, étayer. || *fig* [sustain] soutenir.

propaganda [,prɒpə'gændə] *n* propagande *f*.

propel [prə'pel] *vt* propulser; *fig* pousser.

propeller [prə'pelər] *n* hélice *f*.

proper ['prɒpər] *adj* [real] vrai(e). || [correct] correct(e), bon (bonne). || [decent - behaviour etc] convenable.

properly ['prɒpəlɪ] *adv* [satisfactorily, correctly] correctement, comme il faut. || [decently] convenablement, comme il faut.

proper noun *n* nom *m* propre.

property ['prɒpətɪ] *n* (U) [possessions] biens *mpl*, propriété *f*. || [building] bien *m* immobilier; [land] terres *fpl*. || [quality] propriété *f*.

prophecy ['prɒfɪsɪ] *n* prophétie *f*.

prophesy ['prɒfɪsaɪ] *vt* prédire.

prophet ['prɒfɪt] *n* prophète *m*.

proportion [prə'pɔːʃn] *n* [part] part *f*, partie *f*. || [ratio] rapport *m*, proportion *f*. || ART: **in ~** proportionné(e); **out of ~** mal proportionné(e); **a sense of ~** *fig* le sens de la mesure.

proportional [prə'pɔːʃənl] *adj* proportionnel(elle).

proportional representation *n* représentation *f* proportionnelle.

proportionate [prə'pɔːʃnət] *adj* proportionné(elle).

proposal [prə'pəʊzl] *n* [suggestion] proposition *f*, offre *f*. || [offer of marriage] demande *f* en mariage.

propose [prə'pəʊz] **1** *vt* [suggest] proposer. || [intend]: **to ~ to do** OR **doing sthg** avoir l'intention de faire qqch, se proposer de faire qqch. || [toast] porter. **2** *vi*: **to ~ to sb** demander qqn en mariage.

proposition [,prɒpə'zɪʃn] *n* proposition *f*.

proprietor [prə'praɪətər] *n* propriétaire *mf*.

propriety [prə'praɪətɪ] *n* (U) *fml* [moral correctness] bienséance *f*.

pro rata [-'rɑːtə] *adv* au prorata.

prose [prəʊz] *n* (U) prose *f*.

prosecute ['prɒsɪkjuːt] **1** *vt* poursuivre (en justice). **2** *vi* [police] engager des poursuites judiciaires; [lawyer] représenter la partie plaignante.

prosecution [,prɒsɪ'kjuːʃn] *n* poursuites *fpl* judiciaires, accusation *f*; **the ~** la partie plaignante; [in Crown case] ≃ le ministère public.

prosecutor ['prɒsɪkjuːtər] *n* plaignant *m*, -e *f*.

prospect [*n* 'prɒspekt, *vb* prə'spekt] **1** *n* [hope] possibilité *f*, chances *fpl*. || [probability] perspective *f*. **2** *vi*: **to ~ (for sthg)** prospecter (pour chercher qqch). ○ **prospects** *npl*: **~s (for)** chances *fpl* (de), perspectives *fpl* (de).

prospecting [prə'spektɪŋ] *n* prospection *f*.

prospective [prə'spektɪv] *adj* éventuel(elle).

prospector [prə'spektər] *n* prospecteur *m*, -trice *f*.

prospectus [prə'spektəs] (*pl* **-es**) *n* prospectus *m*.

prosper ['prɒspər] *vi* prospérer.

prosperity [prɒ'sperətɪ] *n* prospérité *f*.

prosperous ['prɒspərəs] *adj* prospère.

prostitute ['prɒstɪtjuːt] *n* prostituée *f*.

prostrate ['prɒstreɪt] *adj* [lying down] à plat ventre. || [with grief etc] prostré(e).

protagonist [prə'tægənɪst] *n* protagoniste *mf*.

protect [prə'tekt] *vt*: **to ~ sb/sthg (against)**, **to ~ sb/sthg (from)** protéger qqn/qqch (contre), protéger qqn/qqch (de).

protection [prə'tekʃn] *n*: **~ (from** OR **against)** protection *f* (contre), défense *f* (contre).

protective [prə'tektɪv] *adj* [layer. clothing] de protection. || [person, feelings] protecteur(trice).

protein ['prəʊtiːn] *n* protéine *f*.

protest [*n* 'prəʊtest, *vb* prə'test] **1** *n* protestation *f*. **2** *rt* [state] protester de. || *Am* [protest against] protester contre. **3** *vi*: **to ~ (about/against)** protester (à propos de/contre).

Protestant ['prɒtɪstənt] **1** *adj* protestant(e). **2** *n* protestant *m*, -e *f*.

protester [prə'testər] *n* [on march, at demonstration] manifestant *m*, -e *f*.

protest march *n* manifestation *f*, marche *f* de protestation.

protocol ['prəʊtəkɒl] *n* protocole *m*.

prototype ['prəʊtətaɪp] *n* prototype *m*.

protracted [prə'træktɪd] *adj* prolongé(e).

protrude [prə'truːd] *vi* avancer, dépasser.

proud [praʊd] *adj* [satisfied, dignified] fier (fière). || *pej* [arrogant] orgueilleux(euse), fier (fière).

prove [pruːv] (*pp* **-d** OR **proven**) *vt* [show to be true] prouver. || [turn out]: **to ~ (to be) false/useful** s'avérer faux/utile; **to ~ o.s. to be sthg** se révéler être qqch.

proven ['pruːvn, 'prəʊvn] **1** *pp* → **prove**. **2** *adj* [fact] avéré(e), établi(e); [liar] fieffé(e).

proverb ['prɒvɜːb] *n* proverbe *m*.

provide [prə'vaɪd] *vt* fournir; **to ~ sb with sthg** fournir qqch à qqn. ○ **provide for** *vt fus* [support] subvenir aux besoins de. || *fml* [make arrangements for] prévoir.

providing [prə'vaɪdɪŋ] ○ **providing (that)** *conj* à condition que (+ *subjunctive*), pourvu que (+ *subjunctive*).

province ['prɒvɪns] *n* [part of country] province *f*. || [speciality] domaine *m*, compétence *f*.

provincial [prə'vɪnʃl] *adj* [town, newspaper] de province. || *pej* [narrowminded] provincial(e).

provision [prə'vɪʒn] *n* (*U*) [act of supplying]: **~ (of)** approvisionnement *m* (en), fourniture *f* (de). || [supply] provision *f*, réserve *f*. || (*U*) [arrangements]: **to make ~ for** [the future] prendre des mesures pour. || [in agreement, law] clause *f*, disposition *f*. ○ **provisions** *npl* [supplies] provisions *fpl*.

provisional [prə'vɪʒənl] *adj* provisoire.

proviso [prə'vaɪzəʊ] (*pl* **-s**) *n* condi-

tion *f*, stipulation *f*; **with the ~ that** à (la) condition que (+ *subjunctive*).

provocative [prə'vɒkətɪv] *adj* provocant(e).

provoke [prə'vəʊk] *vt* [annoy] agacer, contrarier. || [cause - fight, argument] provoquer; [- reaction] susciter.

prow [praʊ] *n* proue *f*.

prowess ['praʊɪs] *n* prouesse *f*.

prowl [praʊl] **1** *vt* [streets etc] rôder dans. **2** *vi* rôder.

prowler ['praʊlər] *n* rôdeur *m*, -euse *f*.

proxy ['prɒksɪ] *n*: **by ~** par procuration.

prudent ['pruːdnt] *adj* prudent(e).

prudish ['pruːdɪʃ] *adj* prude, pudibond(e).

prune [pruːn] **1** *n* [fruit] pruneau *m*. **2** *vt* [tree, bush] tailler.

pry [praɪ] *vi* se mêler de ce qui ne vous regarde pas.

PS (*abbr of* **postscript**) *n* PS *m*.

psalm [sɑːm] *n* psaume *m*.

pseudonym ['sjuːdənɪm] *n* pseudonyme *m*.

psyche ['saɪkɪ] *n* psyché *f*.

psychiatric [,saɪkɪ'ætrɪk] *adj* psychiatrique.

psychiatrist [saɪ'kaɪətrɪst] *n* psychiatre *mf*.

psychiatry [saɪ'kaɪətrɪ] *n* psychiatrie *f*.

psychic ['saɪkɪk] **1** *adj* [clairvoyant - person] doué(e) de seconde vue; [- powers] parapsychique. || MED psychique. **2** *n* médium *m*.

psychoanalysis [,saɪkəʊə'næləsɪs] *n* psychanalyse *f*.

psychoanalyst [,saɪkəʊ'ænəlɪst] *n* psychanalyste *mf*.

psychological [,saɪkə'lɒdʒɪkl] *adj* psychologique.

psychologist [saɪ'kɒlədʒɪst] *n* psychologue *mf*.

psychology [saɪ'kɒlədʒɪ] *n* psychologie *f*.

psychopath ['saɪkəpæθ] *n* psychopathe *mf*.

psychotic [saɪ'kɒtɪk] **1** *adj* psychotique. **2** *n* psychotique *mf*.

pt *abbr of* **pint**. || *abbr of* **point**.

PT (*abbr of* **physical training**) *n* EPS *f*.

PTO (*abbr of* **please turn over**) TSVP.

pub [pʌb] *n* pub *m*.

puberty ['pjuːbətɪ] *n* puberté *f*.

pubic ['pjuːbɪk] *adj* du pubis.

public ['pʌblɪk] **1** *adj* public(ique); [library] municipal(e). **2** *n*: **the ~** le public; **in ~** en public.

public-address system n système m de sonorisation.

publication [ˌpʌblɪˈkeɪʃn] n publication f.

public company n société f anonyme (cotée en Bourse).

public holiday n jour m férié.

publicity [pʌbˈlɪsɪtɪ] n (U) publicité f.

publicize, -ise [ˈpʌblɪsaɪz] vt faire connaître au public.

public limited company n société f anonyme (cotée en Bourse).

public opinion n (U) opinion f publique.

public prosecutor n ≃ procureur m de la République.

public relations 1 n (U) relations fpl publiques. **2** npl relations fpl publiques.

public school n Am [state school] école f publique.

public-spirited adj qui fait preuve de civisme.

public transport n (U) transports mpl en commun.

publish [ˈpʌblɪʃ] vt publier.

publisher [ˈpʌblɪʃə'] n éditeur m, -trice f.

publishing [ˈpʌblɪʃɪŋ] n (U) [industry] édition f.

pucker [ˈpʌkə'] vt plisser.

pudding [ˈpʊdɪŋ] n [food - sweet] entremets m; [- savoury] pudding m.

puddle [ˈpʌdl] n flaque f.

puff [pʌf] 1 n [of cigarette, smoke] bouffée f. || [gasp] souffle m. 2 vt [cigarette etc] tirer sur. 3 vi [smoke]: **to ~ at** OR **on sthg** fumer qqch. || [pant] haleter. O **puff out** vt sep [cheeks, chest] gonfler.

puffed [pʌft] adj [swollen]: **~ (up)** gonflé(e).

puffin [ˈpʌfɪn] n macareux m.

puff pastry, puff paste Am n (U) pâte f feuilletée.

puffy [ˈpʌfɪ] adj gonflé(e), bouffi(e).

pull [pʊl] 1 vt [gen] tirer. || [strain - muscle, hamstring] se froisser. || [attract] attirer. 2 vi tirer. 3 n [tug with hand]: **to give sthg a ~** tirer sur qqch. || (U) [influence] influence f. O **pull apart** vt sep [separate] séparer. O **pull at** vt fus tirer sur. O **pull away** vi AUT démarrer. || [in race] prendre de l'avance. O **pull down** vt sep [building] démolir. O **pull in** vi AUT se ranger. O **pull off** vt sep [take off] enlever, ôter. || [succeed in] réussir. O **pull out 1** vt sep [troops etc] retirer; **2** vi RAIL partir, démarrer. || AUT déboîter. || [with-

draw] se retirer. O **pull over** vi AUT se ranger. O **pull through** vi s'en sortir, s'en tirer. O **pull together** vt sep: **to ~ o.s. together** se ressaisir, se reprendre. O **pull up 1** vt sep [raise] remonter. || [chair] avancer. 2 vi s'arrêter.

pulley [ˈpʊlɪ] (pl **pulleys**) n poulie f.

pullover [ˈpʊlˌəʊvə'] n pull m.

pulp [pʌlp] 1 adj [fiction, novel] de quatre sous. 2 n [for paper] pâte f à papier. || [of fruit] pulpe f.

pulpit [ˈpʊlpɪt] n chaire f.

pulsate [pʌlˈseɪt] vi [heart] battre fort; [air, music] vibrer.

pulse [pʌls] 1 n MED pouls m. O **pulses** npl [food] légumes mpl secs.

puma [ˈpjuːmə] (pl inv OR **-s**) n puma m.

pumice (stone) [ˈpʌmɪs-] n pierre f ponce.

pummel [ˈpʌml] vt bourrer de coups.

pump [pʌmp] 1 n pompe f. 2 vt [water, gas etc] pomper. || inf [interrogate] essayer de tirer les vers du nez à. 3 vi [heart] battre fort. O **pumps** npl [shoes] escarpins mpl.

pumpkin [ˈpʌmpkɪn] n potiron m.

pun [pʌn] n jeu m de mots, calembour m.

punch [pʌntʃ] 1 n [blow] coup m de poing. || [tool] poinçonneuse f. || [drink] punch m. 2 vt [hit - once] donner un coup de poing à; [- repeatedly] donner des coups de poing à. || [ticket] poinçonner; [paper] perforer.

Punch-and-Judy show [-ˈdʒuːdɪ-] n guignol m.

punch line n trait m final (d'une blague).

punctual [ˈpʌŋktʃʊəl] adj ponctuel(elle).

punctuation [ˌpʌŋktʃʊˈeɪʃn] n ponctuation f.

punctuation mark n signe m de ponctuation.

puncture [ˈpʌŋktʃə'] 1 n crevaison f. 2 vt [tyre, ball] crever; [skin] piquer.

pundit [ˈpʌndɪt] n pontife m.

pungent [ˈpʌndʒənt] adj [smell] âcre; [taste] piquant(e).

punish [ˈpʌnɪʃ] vt punir; **to ~ sb for sthg/for doing sthg** punir qqn pour qqch/pour avoir fait qqch.

punishing [ˈpʌnɪʃɪŋ] adj [schedule, work] épuisant(e), éreintant(e); [defeat] cuisant(e).

punishment ['pʌnɪʃmənt] *n* punition *f*, châtiment *m*.

punk [pʌŋk] 1 *adj* punk (*inv*). 2 *n* (U) [music]: ~ (**rock**) punk *m*. || ~ (**rocker**) punk *mf*. || *Am inf* [lout] loubard *m*.

punt [pʌnt] *n* [boat] bateau *m* à fond plat.

puny ['pju:nɪ] *adj* chétif(ive).

pup [pʌp] *n* [young dog] chiot *m*.

pupil ['pju:pl] *n* [student] élève *mf*. || [of eye] pupille *f*.

puppet ['pʌpɪt] *n* [toy] marionnette *f*. || *pej* [person, country] fantoche *m*, pantin *m*.

puppy ['pʌpɪ] *n* chiot *m*.

purchase ['pɜ:tʃəs] 1 *n* achat *m*. 2 *vt* acheter.

purchaser ['pɜ:tʃəsər] *n* acheteur *m*, -euse *f*.

pure [pjʊər] *adj* pur(e).

puree ['pjʊəreɪ] *n* purée *f*.

purge [pɜ:dʒ] 1 *n* POL purge *f*. 2 *vt* POL purger. || [rid] débarrasser, purger.

purify ['pjʊərɪfaɪ] *vt* purifier, épurer.

purist ['pjʊərɪst] *n* puriste *mf*.

puritan ['pjʊərɪtən] *n* puritain *m*, -e *f*.

purity ['pjʊərətɪ] *n* pureté *f*.

purl [pɜ:l] 1 *n* (U) maille *f* à l'envers. 2 *vt* tricoter à l'envers.

purple ['pɜ:pl] 1 *adj* violet(ette). 2 *n* violet *m*.

purpose ['pɜ:pəs] *n* [reason] raison *f*, motif *m*. || [aim] but *m*, objet *m*; **to no** ~ en vain, pour rien. || [determination] détermination *f*. ○ **on purpose** *adv* exprès.

purposeful ['pɜ:pəsfʊl] *adj* résolu(e), déterminé(e).

purr [pɜ:r] *vi* ronronner.

purse [pɜ:s] 1 *n* [for money] porte-monnaie *m inv*, bourse *f*. || *Am* [handbag] sac *m* à main. 2 *vt* [lips] pincer.

purser ['pɜ:sər] *n* commissaire *m* de bord.

pursue [pə'sju:] *vt* [follow] poursuivre, pourchasser. || [policy, aim] poursuivre; [question] continuer à débattre; [matter] approfondir; [project] donner suite à; **to ~ an interest in sthg** se livrer à qqch.

pursuer [pə'sju:ər] *n* poursuivant *m*, -e *f*.

pursuit [pə'sju:t] *n* (U) *fml* [attempt to obtain] recherche *f*, poursuite *f*. || [chase, in sport] poursuite *f*. || [occupation] occupation *f*, activité *f*.

pus [pʌs] *n* pus *m*.

push [pʊʃ] 1 *vt* [press, move - gen] pousser; [- button] appuyer sur. || [encourage]: **to ~ sb (to do sthg)** inciter ou pousser qqn (à faire qqch). || [force]: **to ~ sb (into doing sthg)** forcer ou obliger qqn (à faire qqch). || *inf* [promote] faire de la réclame pour. 2 *vi* [gen] pousser; [on button] appuyer. || [campaign]: **to ~ for sthg** faire pression pour obtenir qqch. 3 *n* [with hand] poussée *f*. || [forceful effort] effort *m*. ○ **push around** *vt sep inf fig* marcher sur les pieds de. ○ **push in** *vi* [in queue] resquiller. ○ **push off** *vi inf* filer, se sauver. ○ **push on** *vi* continuer. ○ **push through** *vt sep* [law, reform] faire accepter.

pushed [pʊʃt] *adj inf*: **to be ~ for sthg** être à court de qqch; **to be hard ~ to do sthg** avoir du mal ou de la peine à faire qqch.

pusher ['pʊʃər] *n drugs sl* dealer *m*.

push-up *n* pompe *f*, traction *f*.

pushy ['pʊʃɪ] *adj pej* qui se met toujours en avant.

puss [pʊs], **pussy (cat)** ['pʊsɪ-] *n inf* minet *m*, minou *m*.

put [pʊt] (*pt* & *pp* **put**) *vt* [gen] mettre. || [place] mettre, poser, placer; **to ~ the children to bed** coucher les enfants. || [express] dire, exprimer. || [question] poser. || [estimate] estimer, évaluer. || [invest]: **to ~ money into** investir de l'argent dans. ○ **put across** *vt sep* [ideas] faire comprendre. ○ **put away** *vt sep* [tidy away] ranger. ○ **put back** *vt sep* [replace] remettre (à sa place ou en place). || [postpone] remettre. || [clock, watch] retarder. ○ **put by** *vt sep* [money] mettre de côté. ○ **put down** *vt sep* [lay down] poser, déposer. || [quell - rebellion] réprimer. || [write down] inscrire, noter. ○ **put down to** *vt sep* attribuer à. ○ **put forward** *vt sep* [propose] proposer, avancer. || [meeting, clock, watch] avancer. ○ **put in** *vt sep* [spend - time] passer. || [submit] présenter. ○ **put off** *vt sep* [postpone] remettre (à plus tard). || [cause to wait] décommander. || [discourage] dissuader. || [disturb] déconcerter, troubler. || [cause to dislike] dégoûter. || [switch off - radio, TV] éteindre. ○ **put on** *vt sep* [clothes] mettre, enfiler. || [arrange - exhibition etc] organiser; [- play] monter. || [gain]: **to ~ on weight** prendre du poids, grossir. || [switch on - radio, TV] allumer, mettre; **to ~ the light on** allumer (la lumière). || [record, CD, tape] passer, mettre. || [start cooking] mettre à cuire. || [pretend - gen] feindre; [- accent etc] prendre. || [bet] parier, miser. || [add] ajouter. ○ **put out** *rt sep* [place outside] mettre dehors. || [book, statement] publier; [record] sortir. || [fire, cigarette] éteindre; **to ~ the light out** éteindre (la lumière). || [extend - hand] tendre. || [annoy, upset]: **to be ~ out** être contrarié(e). || [inconvenience] déranger. ○ **put through** *rt sep* TELEC passer. ○ **put up 1** *rt sep* [build - gen] ériger; [- tent] dresser. || [umbrella] ouvrir; [flag] hisser. || [fix to wall] accrocher. || [provide - money] fournir. || [increase] augmenter. || [provide accommodation for] loger, héberger. **2** *rt fus*: **to ~ up a fight** se défendre. ○ **put up with** *rt fus* supporter.

putrid ['pju:trɪd] *adj* putride.

putt [pʌt] **1** *n* putt *m*. **2** *rt & vi* putter.

putting green ['pʌtɪŋ-] *n* green *m*.

putty ['pʌtɪ] *n* mastic *m*.

puzzle ['pʌzl] **1** *n* [toy] casse-tête *m inv*; [mental] devinette *f*. || [mystery] mystère *m*, énigme *f*. **2** *rt* rendre perplexe. **3** *vi*: **to ~ over sthg** essayer de comprendre qqch. ○ **puzzle out** *rt sep* comprendre.

puzzling ['pʌzlɪŋ] *adj* curieux(ieuse).

pyjamas [pə'dʒɑ:məz] *npl* pyjama *m*.

pylon ['paɪlən] *n* pylône *m*.

pyramid ['pɪrəmɪd] *n* pyramide *f*.

Pyrenees [ˌpɪrə'niːz] *npl*: **the ~** les Pyrénées *fpl*.

Pyrex® ['paɪreks] *n* Pyrex® *m*.

python ['paɪθn] (*pl inv* OR **-s**) *n* python *m*.

q (*pl* **q's** OR **qs**), **Q** (*pl* **Q's** OR **Qs**) [kju:] *n* [letter] q *m inv*, Q *m inv*.

quack [kwæk] *n* [noise] coin-coin *m inv*. || *inf pej* [doctor] charlatan *m*.

quadrangle ['kwɒdræŋgl] *n* [figure] quadrilatère *m*. || [courtyard] cour *f*.

quadruple [kwɒ'dru:pl] **1** *adj* quadruple. **2** *rt & vi* quadrupler.

quadruplets ['kwɒdruplɪts] *npl* quadruplés *mpl*.

quail [kweɪl] (*pl inv* OR **-s**) **1** *n* caille *f*. **2** *vi literary* reculer.

quaint [kweɪnt] *adj* pittoresque.

quake [kweɪk] *vi* trembler.

Quaker ['kweɪkər] *n* quaker *m*, -eresse *f*.

qualification [ˌkwɒlɪfɪ'keɪʃn] *n* [certificate] diplôme *m*. || [quality, skill] compétence *f*. || [qualifying statement] réserve *f*.

qualified ['kwɒlɪfaɪd] *adj* [trained] diplômé(e). || [able]: **to be ~ to do sthg** avoir la compétence nécessaire pour faire qqch. || [limited] restreint(e), modéré(e).

qualify ['kwɒlɪfaɪ] **1** *rt* [modify] apporter des réserves à. || [entitle]: **to ~ sb to do sthg** qualifier qqn pour faire qqch. **2** *vi* [pass exams] obtenir un diplôme. || [be entitled]: **to ~ (for sthg)** avoir droit (à qqch), remplir les conditions requises (pour qqch). || SPORT se qualifier.

quality ['kwɒlətɪ] *n* qualité *f*.

qualms [kwɑ:mz] *npl* doutes *mpl*.

quandary ['kwɒndərɪ] *n* embarras *m*; **to be in a ~ about** OR **over sthg** être bien embarrassé à propos de qqch.

quantify ['kwɒntɪfaɪ] *rt* quantifier.

quantity ['kwɒntətɪ] *n* quantité *f*.

quantity surveyor *n* métreur *m*, -euse *f*.

quarantine ['kwɒrəntiːn] **1** *n* quarantaine *f*. **2** *rt* mettre en quarantaine.

quarrel ['kwɒrəl] **1** *n* querelle *f*, dispute *f*. **2** *vi*: **to ~ (with)** se quereller (avec), se disputer (avec).

quarrelsome ['kwɒrəlsəm] *adj* querel-
leur(euse).

quarry ['kwɒrɪ] *n* [place] carrière *f*. ||
[prey] proie *f*.

quart [kwɔ:t] *n* = 1,136 litre *Br*, =
0,946 litre Am, ≃ litre *f*.

quarter ['kwɔ:tər] *n* [fraction, weight]
quart *m*; **a ~ past two** *Br*, **a ~ after two**
Am deux heures et quart; **a ~ to two** *Br*, **a
~ of two** *Am* deux heures moins le quart.
|| [of year] trimestre *m*. || *Am* [coin] pièce
f de 25 cents. || [area in town] quartier *m*.
|| [direction]: **from all ~s** de tous côtés.
○ **quarters** *npl* [rooms] quartiers *mpl*.
○ **at close quarters** *adv* de près.

quarterfinal [,kwɔ:tə'faɪnl] *n* quart *m*
de finale.

quarterly ['kwɔ:təlɪ] **1** *adj* trimes-
triel(ielle). **2** *adv* trimestriellement. **3** *n*
publication *f* trimestrielle.

quartet [kwɔ:'tet] *n* quatuor *m*.

quartz [kwɔ:ts] *n* quartz *m*.

quash [kwɒʃ] *vt* [sentence] annuler, cas-
ser. || [rebellion] réprimer.

quaver ['kweɪvər] **1** *n* MUS croche *f*. || [in
voice] tremblement *m*, chevrotement *m*.
2 *vi* trembler, chevroter.

quay [ki:] *n* quai *m*.

quayside ['ki:saɪd] *n* bord *m* du quai.

queasy ['kwi:zɪ] *adj*: **to feel ~** avoir mal
au cœur.

Quebec [kwɪ'bek] *n* [province] Québec
m.

queen [kwi:n] *n* [gen] reine *f*. || [playing
card] dame *f*.

Queen Mother *n*: **the ~** la reine mère.

queer [kwɪər] **1** *adj* [odd] étrange, bizarre. **2** *n inf pej* pédé *m*, homosexuel *m*.

quell [kwel] *vt* réprimer, étouffer.

quench [kwentʃ] *vt*: **to ~ one's thirst** se
désaltérer.

query ['kwɪərɪ] **1** *n* question *f*. **2** *vt* mettre en doute, douter de.

quest [kwest] *n literary*: **~ (for)** quête *f*
(de).

question ['kwestʃn] **1** *n* [gen] question
f; **to ask (sb) a ~** poser une question (à
qqn). || [doubt] doute *m*; **to call** OR **bring
sthg into ~** mettre qqch en doute; **without ~** incontestablement, sans aucun
doute. || *phr*: **there's no ~ of ...** il n'est
pas question de .... **2** *vt* [interrogate]
questionner. || [express doubt about] met-
tre en question OR en doute. ○ **in question**
adv: **the ... in ~** le/la/les ... en question.
○ **out of the question** *adv* hors de
question.

questionable ['kwestʃənəbl] *adj* [un-
certain] discutable. || [not right, not hon-
est] douteux(euse).

question mark *n* point *m* d'interrogation.

questionnaire [,kwestʃə'neər] *n* questionnaire *m*.

quibble ['kwɪbl] *pej vi*: **to ~ (over** OR
about) chicaner (à propos de).

quiche [ki:ʃ] *n* quiche *f*.

quick [kwɪk] **1** *adj* [gen] rapide. || [re-
sponse, decision] prompt(e), rapide. **2**
adv vite, rapidement.

quicken ['kwɪkn] **1** *vt* accélérer, presser.
2 *vi* s'accélérer.

quickly ['kwɪklɪ] *adv* [rapidly] vite, ra-
pidement. || [without delay] prompte-
ment, immédiatement.

quicksand ['kwɪksænd] *n* sables *mpl*
mouvants.

quick-witted [-'wɪtɪd] *adj* [person] à
l'esprit vif.

quiet ['kwaɪət] **1** *adj* [not noisy] tranquille; [voice] bas (basse); [engine] silen-
cieux(ieuse); **be ~!** taisez-vous! || [not
busy] calme. || [silent] silencieux(ieuse);
to keep ~ about sthg ne rien dire à pro-
pos de qqch, garder qqch secret. || [inti-
mate] intime. **2** *n* tranquillité *f*; **on the ~
*inf** en douce. **3** *vt Am* calmer, apaiser.

quieten ['kwaɪətn] *vt* calmer, apaiser.
○ **quieten down 1** *vt sep* calmer, apaiser. **2** *vi* se calmer.

quietly ['kwaɪətlɪ] *adv* [without noise]
sans faire de bruit, silencieusement;
[say] doucement. || [without excitement]
tranquillement, calmement. || [without
fuss - leave] discrètement.

quilt [kwɪlt] *n* [padded] édredon *m*;
(continental) ~ couette *f*.

quinine [kwɪ'ni:n] *n* quinine *f*.

quins *Br* [kwɪnz], **quints** *Am* [kwɪnts]
npl inf quintuplés *mpl*.

quintet [kwɪn'tet] *n* quintette *m*.

quints *Am* = **quins**.

quintuplets [kwɪn'tju:plɪts] *npl* quintuplés *mpl*.

quip [kwɪp] **1** *n* raillerie *f*. **2** *vi* railler.

quirk [kwɜ:k] *n* bizarrerie *f*.

quit [kwɪt] (*Br pt & pp* quit OR **-ted**,
Am pt & pp quit) **1** *vt* [resign from] quit-
ter. || [stop]: **to ~ smoking** arrêter de fu-
mer. **2** *vi* [resign] démissionner. || [give
up] abandonner.

quite [kwaɪt] *adv* [completely] tout à
fait, complètement; **not ~** pas tout à fait;
I don't ~ understand je ne comprends

pas bien. ‖ [fairly] assez, plutôt. ‖ [for emphasis]: **she's ~ a singer** c'est une chanteuse formidable. ‖ [to express agreement]: **~ (so)**! exactement!

quits [kwɪts] *adj inf*: **to be ~ (with sb)** être quitte (envers qqn); **to call it ~** en rester là.

quiver ['kwɪvər] **1** *n* [shiver] frisson *m*. ‖ [for arrows] carquois *m*. **2** *vi* frissonner.

quiz [kwɪz] (*pl* **-zes**) *n* [gen] quiz *m*, jeu-concours *m*. ‖ *Am* SCH interrogation *f*.

quizzical ['kwɪzɪkl] *adj* narquois(e), moqueur(euse).

quota ['kwəʊtə] *n* quota *m*.

quotation [kwəʊ'teɪʃn] *n* [citation] citation *f*. ‖ COMM devis *m*.

quotation marks *npl* guillemets *mpl*; **in ~** entre guillemets.

quote [kwəʊt] **1** *n* [citation] citation *f*. ‖ COMM devis *m*. **2** *vt* [cite] citer. ‖ COMM indiquer, spécifier. **3** *vi* [cite]: **to ~ (from sthg)** citer (qqch). ‖ COMM: **to ~ for sthg** établir un devis pour qqch.

quotient ['kwəʊʃnt] *n* quotient *m*.

r (*pl* **r's** OR **rs**), **R** (*pl* **R's** OR **Rs**) [ɑːr] *n* [letter] r *m inv*, R *m inv*.

rabbi ['ræbaɪ] *n* rabbin *m*.

rabbit ['ræbɪt] *n* lapin *m*.

rabbit hutch *n* clapier *m*.

rabble ['ræbl] *n* cohue *f*.

rabies ['reɪbiːz] *n* rage *f*.

race [reɪs] **1** *n* [competition] course *f*. ‖ [people, ethnic background] race *f*. **2** *vt* [compete against] faire la course avec. ‖ [horse] faire courir. **3** *vi* [compete] courir. ‖ [rush]: **to ~ in/out** entrer/sortir à toute allure. ‖ [pulse] être très rapide. ‖ [engine] s'emballer.

race car *Am* = **racing car**.

racecourse ['reɪskɔːs] *n* champ *m* de courses.

race driver *Am* = **racing driver**.

racehorse ['reɪshɔːs] *n* cheval *m* de course.

racetrack ['reɪstræk] *n* piste *f*.

racial discrimination ['reɪʃl-] *n* discrimination *f* raciale.

racing ['reɪsɪŋ] *n* (*U*): **(horse) ~** les courses *fpl*.

racing car *Br*, **race car** *Am* *n* voiture *f* de course.

racing driver *Br*, **race driver** *Am* *n* coureur *m* automobile, pilote *m* de course.

racism ['reɪsɪzm] *n* racisme *m*.

racist ['reɪsɪst] **1** *adj* raciste. **2** *n* raciste *mf*.

rack [ræk] *n* [for bottles] casier *m*; [for luggage] porte-bagages *m inr*; [for plates] égouttoir *m*; **toast ~** porte-toasts *m inr*.

racket ['rækɪt] *n* [noise] boucan *m*. ‖ [illegal activity] racket *m*. ‖ SPORT raquette *f*.

racquet ['rækɪt] *n* raquette *f*.

racy ['reɪsɪ] *adj* [novel, style] osé(e).

radar ['reɪdɑːr] *n* radar *m*.

radial (tyre) ['reɪdjəl-] *n* pneu *m* à carcasse radiale.

radiant ['reɪdjənt] *adj* [happy] radieux(ieuse).

radiate ['reɪdɪeɪt] **1** *vt* [heat, light] émettre, dégager. ‖ *fig* [confidence, health] respirer. **2** *vi* [heat, light] irradier.

radiation [,reɪdɪ'eɪʃn] *n* [radioactive] radiation *f*.

radiator ['reɪdɪeɪtər] *n* radiateur *m*.

radical ['rædɪkl] *adj* radical(e).

radii ['reɪdɪaɪ] *pl* → **radius**.

radio ['reɪdɪəʊ] (*pl* **-s**) **1** *n* radio *f*; **on the ~** à la radio. **2** *comp* de radio. **3** *vt* [person] appeler par radio; [information] envoyer par radio.

radioactive [,reɪdɪəʊ'æktɪv] *adj* radioactif(ive).

radio alarm *n* radio-réveil *m*.

radio-controlled [-kən'trəʊld] *adj* téléguidé(e).

radiography [,reɪdɪ'ɒɡrəfɪ] *n* radiographie *f*.

radiology [,reɪdɪ'ɒlədʒɪ] *n* radiologie *f*.

radiotherapy [,reɪdɪəʊ'θerəpɪ] *n* radiothérapie *f*.

radish ['rædɪʃ] *n* radis *m*.

radius ['reɪdɪəs] (*pl* **radii**) *n* MATH rayon *m*. ‖ ANAT radius *m*.

raffle ['ræfl] **1** *n* tombola *f*. **2** *vt* mettre en tombola.

raft [rɑːft] *n* [of wood] radeau *m*.

rafter ['rɑːftər] *n* chevron *m*.

rag [ræɡ] *n* [piece of cloth] chiffon *m*. ○ **rags** *npl* [clothes] guenilles *fpl*.

rag-and-bone man *n* chiffonnier *m*.

rag doll n poupée f de chiffon.

rage [reɪdʒ] **1** n [fury] rage f, fureur f. ||
inf [fashion]: **to be (all) the ~** faire fureur.
2 vi [person] être furieux(ieuse). || [storm,
argument] faire rage.

ragged ['rægɪd] adj [person] en haillons;
[clothes] en lambeaux. || [line, edge, per-
formance] inégal(e).

raid [reɪd] **1** n MIL raid m. || [by crimi-
nals] hold-up m inv; [by police] descente
f. **2** vt MIL faire un raid sur. || [subj: crimi-
nals] faire un hold-up dans; [subj: police]
faire une descente dans.

rail [reɪl] **1** n [on ship] bastingage m; [on
staircase] rampe f; [on walkway] garde-
fou m. || [bar] barre f. || RAIL rail m; **by ~**
en train. **2** comp [transport, travel] par le
train; [strike] des cheminots.

railing ['reɪlɪŋ] n [fence] grille f; [on
ship] bastingage m; [on staircase] rampe
f; [on walkway] garde-fou m.

railway Br ['reɪlweɪ], **railroad** Am
['reɪlrəʊd] n [system, company] chemin m
de fer; [track] voie f ferrée.

railway line n [route] ligne f de chemin
de fer; [track] voie f ferrée.

railway station n gare f.

railway track n voie f ferrée.

rain [reɪn] **1** n pluie f. **2** v impers METEOR
pleuvoir; **it's ~ing** il pleut.

rainbow ['reɪnbəʊ] n arc-en-ciel m.

rain check n Am: **I'll take a ~ (on that)**
une autre fois peut-être.

raincoat ['reɪnkəʊt] n imperméable m.

raindrop ['reɪndrɒp] n goutte f de pluie.

rainfall ['reɪnfɔːl] n [shower] chute f de
pluie; [amount] précipitations fpl.

rain forest n forêt f tropicale humide.

rainy ['reɪnɪ] adj pluvieux(ieuse).

raise [reɪz] **1** vt [lift up] lever. || [increase
- gen] augmenter; [- standards] élever; **to
~ one's voice** élever la voix. || [obtain]: **to
~ money** [from donations] collecter des
fonds; [by selling, borrowing] se procurer
de l'argent. || [subject, doubt] soulever;
[memories] évoquer. || [children, cattle]
élever. || [crops] cultiver. **2** n Am augmen-
tation f (de salaire).

raisin ['reɪzn] n raisin m sec.

rake [reɪk] **1** n [implement] râteau m. **2**
vt [path, lawn] ratisser; [leaves] râteler.

rally ['rælɪ] **1** n [meeting] rassemble-
ment m. || [car race] rallye m. || SPORT [ex-
change of shots] échange m. **2** vt rallier.
3 vi [supporters] se rallier. || [patient]
aller mieux; [prices] remonter. **○ rally**

round 1 vt fus apporter son soutien à. **2**
vi inf venir en aide.

ram [ræm] **1** n bélier m. **2** vt [crash into]
percuter contre, emboutir. || [force] tas-
ser.

RAM [ræm] (abbr of **random access
memory**) n RAM f.

ramble ['ræmbl] **1** n randonnée f, promenade f à pied. **2** vi [walk] faire une
promenade à pied. || pej [talk] radoter.
○ ramble on vi pej radoter.

rambler ['ræmblər] n [walker] randonneur m, -euse f.

rambling ['ræmblɪŋ] adj [house]
plein(e) de coins et recoins. || [speech]
décousu(e).

ramp [ræmp] n [slope] rampe f. || AUT [to
slow traffic down] ralentisseur m.

rampage [ræm'peɪdʒ] n: **to go on the ~**
tout saccager.

rampant ['ræmpənt] adj qui sévit.

ramparts ['ræmpɑːts] npl rempart m.

ramshackle ['ræm,ʃækl] adj bran-
lant(e).

ran [ræn] pt → **run**.

ranch [rɑːntʃ] n ranch m.

rancher ['rɑːntʃər] n propriétaire mf de
ranch.

rancid ['rænsɪd] adj rance.

rancour Br, **rancor** Am ['ræŋkər] n
rancœur f.

random ['rændəm] **1** adj fait(e) au hasard; [number] aléatoire. **2** n: **at ~** au hasard.

random access memory n COMPUT
mémoire f vive.

R and R (abbr of **rest and recreation**) n
Am permission f.

randy ['rændɪ] adj inf excité(e).

rang [ræŋ] pt → **ring**.

range [reɪndʒ] **1** n [of plane, telescope
etc] portée f; **at close ~** à bout portant. ||
[of vehicles, goods] gamme f; **price ~**
éventail m des prix. || [of mountains]
chaîne f. || [shooting area] champ m de
tir. || MUS [of voice] tessiture f. **2** vt [place
in row] mettre en rang. **3** vi [vary]: **to ~
between ... and ...** varier entre ... et ...; **to
~ from ... to ...** varier de ... à .... || [in-
clude]: **to ~ over sthg** couvrir qqch.

ranger ['reɪndʒər] n garde m forestier.

rank [ræŋk] **1** adj [absolute - disgrace,
stupidity] complet(ète); [- injustice] fla-
grant(e); **he's a ~ outsider** il n'a aucune
chance. || [smell] fétide. **2** n [in army, po-
lice etc] grade m. || [social class] rang m. ||
[row] rangée f. || phr: **the ~ and file** la

masse; [of union] la base. **3** vt [classify] classer. **4** vi: **to ~ among** compter parmi. ○ **ranks** npl MIL: **the ~s** le rang. || fig [members] rangs mpl.

rankle ['ræŋkl] vi: it ~d **with him** ça lui est resté sur l'estomac OR le cœur.

ransack ['rænsæk] vt [search through] mettre tout sens dessus dessous dans; [damage] saccager.

ransom ['rænsəm] n rançon f.

rant [rænt] vi déblatérer.

rap [ræp] **1** n [knock] coup m sec. || MUS rap m. **2** vt [table] frapper sur; [knuckles] taper sur.

rape [reɪp] **1** n [crime, attack] viol m. || [plant] colza m. **2** vt violer.

rapid ['ræpɪd] adj rapide. ○ **rapids** npl rapides mpl.

rapidly ['ræpɪdlɪ] adv rapidement.

rapist ['reɪpɪst] n violeur m.

rapport [ræ'pɔːr] n rapport m.

rapture ['ræptʃər] n ravissement m.

rapturous ['ræptʃərəs] adj [applause, welcome] enthousiaste.

rare [reər] adj [gen] rare. || [meat] saignant(e).

rarely ['reəlɪ] adv rarement.

raring ['reərɪŋ] adj: **to be ~ to go** être impatient(e) de commencer.

rarity ['reərətɪ] n rareté f.

rascal ['rɑːskl] n polisson m, -onne f.

rash [ræʃ] **1** adj irréfléchi(e), imprudent(e). **2** n MED éruption f. || [spate] succession f, série f.

rasher ['ræʃər] n tranche f.

rasp [rɑːsp] n [harsh sound] grincement m.

raspberry ['rɑːzbərɪ] n [fruit] framboise f. || [rude sound]: **to blow a ~** faire pfft.

rat [ræt] n [animal] rat m. || inf pej [person] ordure f, salaud m.

rate [reɪt] **1** n [speed] vitesse f; [of pulse] fréquence f; **at this ~** à ce train-là. || [ratio, proportion] taux m. || [price] tarif m. **2** vt [consider]: **to ~ sb/sthg as** considérer qqn/qqch comme; **to ~ sb/sthg among** classer qqn/qqch parmi. || [deserve] mériter. ○ **at any rate** adv en tout cas.

rather ['rɑːðər] adv [somewhat, more exactly] plutôt. || [to small extent] un peu. || [preferably]: **I'd ~ wait** je préférerais attendre. || [on the contrary]: **(but) ~ ...** au contraire .... ○ **rather than** conj plutôt que.

ratify ['rætɪfaɪ] vt ratifier, approuver.

rating ['reɪtɪŋ] n [of popularity etc] cote f.

ratio ['reɪʃɪəʊ] (pl -s) n rapport m.

ration ['ræʃn] **1** n ration f. **2** vt rationner. ○ **rations** npl vivres mpl.

rational ['ræʃənl] adj rationnel(elle).

rationalize, -ise ['ræʃənəlaɪz] vt rationaliser.

rat race n jungle f.

rattle ['rætl] **1** n [of bottles, typewriter keys] cliquetis m; [of engine] bruit m de ferraille. || [toy] hochet m. **2** vt [bottles] faire s'entrechoquer; [keys] faire cliqueter. || [unsettle] secouer. **3** vi [bottles] s'entrechoquer; [keys, machine] cliqueter; [engine] faire un bruit de ferraille.

rattlesnake ['rætlsneɪk], **rattler** Am ['rætlər] n serpent m à sonnettes.

raucous ['rɔːkəs] adj [voice, laughter] rauque; [behaviour] bruyant(e).

ravage ['rævɪdʒ] vt ravager. ○ **ravages** npl ravages mpl.

rave [reɪv] **1** adj [review] élogieux(ieuse). **2** vi [talk angrily]: **to ~ at** OR **against** tempêter OR fulminer contre. || [talk enthusiastically]: **to ~ about** parler avec enthousiasme de.

raven ['reɪvn] n corbeau m.

ravenous ['rævənəs] adj [person] affamé(e); [animal, appetite] vorace.

ravine [rə'viːn] n ravin m.

raving ['reɪvɪŋ] adj: **~ lunatic** fou furieux (folle furieuse).

ravioli [,rævɪ'əʊlɪ] n (U) raviolis mpl.

ravishing ['rævɪʃɪŋ] adj ravissant(e), enchanteur(eresse).

raw [rɔː] adj [uncooked] cru(e). || [untreated] brut(e). || [painful] à vif. || [inexperienced] novice; **~ recruit** bleu m.

raw deal n: **to get a ~** être défavorisé(e).

raw material n matière f première.

ray [reɪ] n [beam] rayon m; fig [of hope] lueur f.

rayon ['reɪɒn] n rayonne f.

raze [reɪz] vt raser.

razor ['reɪzər] n rasoir m.

razor blade n lame f de rasoir.

RC abbr of **Roman Catholic**.

Rd abbr of **Road**.

R & D (abbr of **research and development**) n R-D f.

re [riː] prep concernant.

RE n (abbr of **religious education**) instruction f religieuse.

reach [riːtʃ] **1** vt [gen] atteindre; [place, destination] arriver à; [agreement, decision] parvenir à. || [contact] joindre, contacter. **2** *vi* [land] s'étendre; **to ~ out** tendre le bras; **to ~ down to pick sthg up** se pencher pour ramasser qqch. **3** *n* [of arm, boxer] allonge *f*; **within ~** [object] à portée; [place] à proximité; **out of** OR **beyond sb's ~** [object] hors de portée; [place] d'accès difficile, difficilement accessible.

react [rɪˈækt] *vi* [gen] réagir.

reaction [rɪˈækʃn] *n* réaction *f*.

reactionary [rɪˈækʃənrɪ] **1** *adj* réactionnaire. **2** *n* réactionnaire *mf*.

reactor [rɪˈæktər] *n* réacteur *m*.

read [riːd] (*pt* & *pp* **read** [red]) **1** *vt* [gen] lire. ‖ [subj: sign, letter] dire. ‖ [interpret, judge] interpréter. ‖ [subj: meter, thermometer etc] indiquer. **2** *vi* lire; **the book ~s well** le livre se lit bien. ○ **read out** *vt sep* lire à haute voix. ○ **read up on** *vt fus* étudier.

reader [ˈriːdər] *n* [of book, newspaper] lecteur *m*, -trice *f*.

readership [ˈriːdəʃɪp] *n* [of newspaper] nombre *m* de lecteurs.

readily [ˈredɪlɪ] *adv* [willingly] volontiers. ‖ [easily] facilement.

reading [ˈriːdɪŋ] *n* (*U*) [gen] lecture *f*. ‖ [interpretation] interprétation *f*. ‖ [on thermometer, meter etc] indications *fpl*.

readjust [ˌriːəˈdʒʌst] **1** *vt* [instrument] régler (de nouveau); [mirror] rajuster; [policy] rectifier. **2** *vi* [person]: **to ~ (to)** se réadapter (à).

readout [ˈriːdaʊt] *n* COMPUT affichage *m*.

ready [ˈredɪ] **1** *adj* [prepared] prêt(e); **to get ~** se préparer; **to get sthg ~** préparer qqch. ‖ [willing]: **to be ~ to do sthg** être prêt(e) OR disposé(e) à faire qqch. **2** *vt* préparer.

ready-made *adj* lit & *fig* tout fait (toute faite).

ready money *n* liquide *m*.

ready-to-wear *adj* prêt-à-porter.

reafforestation [ˈriːəˌfɒrɪˈsteɪʃn] *n* reboisement *m*.

real [rɪəl] **1** *adj* [gen] vrai(e), véritable; **~ life** réalité *f*; **for ~** pour de vrai. ‖ [actual] réel(elle); **in ~ terms** dans la pratique. **2** *adv* Am très.

real estate *n* (*U*) biens *mpl* immobiliers.

realism [ˈrɪəlɪzm] *n* réalisme *m*.

realistic [ˌrɪəˈlɪstɪk] *adj* réaliste.

reality [rɪˈælətɪ] *n* réalité *f*.

realization [ˌrɪəlaɪˈzeɪʃn] *n* réalisation *f*.

realize, -ise [ˈrɪəlaɪz] *vt* [understand] se rendre compte de, réaliser. ‖ [sum of money, idea, ambition] réaliser.

really [ˈrɪəlɪ] **1** *adv* [gen] vraiment. ‖ [in fact] en réalité. **2** *excl* [expressing doubt] vraiment? ‖ [expressing surprise] pas possible! ‖ [expressing disapproval] franchement!, ça alors!

realm [relm] *n fig* [subject area] domaine *m*. ‖ [kingdom] royaume *m*.

realtor [ˈrɪəltər] *n Am* agent *m* immobilier.

reap [riːp] *vt* [harvest] moissonner.

reappear [ˌriːəˈpɪər] *vi* réapparaître, reparaître.

rear [rɪər] **1** *adj* arrière (*inv*), de derrière. **2** *n* [back] arrière *m*; **to bring up the ~** fermer la marche. ‖ *inf* [bottom] derrière *m*. **3** *vt* [children, animals] élever. **4** *vi* [horse]: **to ~ (up)** se cabrer.

rearm [riːˈɑːm] *vt* & *vi* réarmer.

rearrange [ˌriːəˈreɪndʒ] *vt* [furniture, room] réarranger; [plans] changer. ‖ [meeting - to new time] changer l'heure de; [- to new date] changer la date de.

rearview mirror [ˈrɪəvjuː-] *n* rétroviseur *m*.

reason [ˈriːzn] **1** *n* [cause]: **~ (for)** raison *f* (de); **for some ~** pour une raison ou pour une autre. ‖ (*U*) [justification]: **to have ~ to do sthg** avoir de bonnes raisons de faire qqch. ‖ [common sense] bon sens *m*; **he won't listen to ~** on ne peut pas lui faire entendre raison; **it stands to ~** c'est logique. **2** *vt* déduire. **3** *vi* raisonner. ○ **reason with** *vt fus* raisonner (avec).

reasonable [ˈriːznəbl] *adj* raisonnable.

reasonably [ˈriːznəblɪ] *adv* [quite] assez. ‖ [sensibly] raisonnablement.

reasoning [ˈriːznɪŋ] *n* raisonnement *m*.

reassess [ˌriːəˈses] *vt* réexaminer.

reassurance [ˌriːəˈʃɔːrəns] *n* [comfort] réconfort *m*. ‖ [promise] assurance *f*.

reassure [ˌriːəˈʃɔːr] *vt* rassurer.

reassuring [ˌriːəˈʃɔːrɪŋ] *adj* rassurant(e).

rebate [ˈriːbeɪt] *n* [on product] rabais *m*; **tax ~** ≃ dégrèvement *m* fiscal.

rebel [*n* ˈrebl, *vb* rɪˈbel] **1** *n* rebelle *mf*. **2** *vi*: **to ~ (against)** se rebeller (contre).

rebellion [rɪˈbeljən] *n* rébellion *f*.

rebellious [rɪˈbeljəs] *adj* rebelle.

rebound [*n* ˈriːbaʊnd, *vb* rɪˈbaʊnd] **1** *n* [of ball] rebond *m*. **2** *vi* [ball] rebondir.

rebuff [rɪˈbʌf] *n* rebuffade *f*.

rebuild [ˌriːˈbɪld] *vt* reconstruire.

rebuke [rɪ'bjuːk] 1 *n* réprimande *f*. 2 *vt* réprimander.

recalcitrant [rɪ'kælsɪtrənt] *adj* récalcitrant(e).

recall [rɪ'kɔːl] 1 *n* [memory] rappel *m*. 2 *vt* [remember] se rappeler, se souvenir de. || [summon back] rappeler.

recant [rɪ'kænt] *vi* se rétracter; RELIG abjurer.

recap ['riːkæp] *vi* récapituler.

recapitulate [,riːkə'pɪtjʊleɪt] *vt* & *vi* récapituler.

recd, rec'd *abbr of* **received**.

recede [rɪ'siːd] *vi* [person, car etc] s'éloigner; [hopes] s'envoler.

receding [rɪ'siːdɪŋ] *adj* [hairline] dégarni(e); [chin, forehead] fuyant(e).

receipt [rɪ'siːt] *n* [piece of paper] reçu *m*. || (*U*) [act of receiving] réception *f*. ○ **receipts** *npl* recettes *fpl*.

receive [rɪ'siːv] *vt* [gen] recevoir; [news] apprendre. || [welcome] accueillir, recevoir; **to be well/badly ~d** [film, speech etc] être bien/mal accueilli.

receiver [rɪ'siːvə'] *n* [of telephone] récepteur *m*, combiné *m*. || [criminal] receleur *m*, -euse *f*. || FIN [official] administrateur *m*, -trice *f* judiciaire.

recent ['riːsnt] *adj* récent(e).

recently ['riːsntlɪ] *adv* récemment; **until ~** jusqu'à ces derniers temps.

receptacle [rɪ'septəkl] *n* récipient *m*.

reception [rɪ'sepʃn] *n* [gen] réception *f*. || [welcome] accueil *m*, réception *f*.

reception desk *n* réception *f*.

receptionist [rɪ'sepʃənɪst] *n* réceptionniste *mf*.

recess ['riːses, *Br* rɪ'ses] *n* [alcove] niche *f*. || [secret place] recoin *m*. || POL: **to be in ~** être en vacances. || *Am* SCH récréation *f*.

recession [rɪ'seʃn] *n* récession *f*.

recharge [,riː'tʃɑːdʒ] *vt* recharger.

recipe ['resɪpɪ] *n lit* & *fig* recette *f*.

recipient [rɪ'sɪpɪənt] *n* [of letter] destinataire *mf*; [of cheque] bénéficiaire *mf*; [of award] récipiendaire *mf*.

reciprocal [rɪ'sɪprəkl] *adj* réciproque.

recital [rɪ'saɪtl] *n* récital *m*.

recite [rɪ'saɪt] *vt* [say aloud] réciter. || [list] énumérer.

reckless ['reklɪs] *adj* imprudent(e).

reckon ['rekn] *vt inf* [think] penser. || [consider, judge] considérer. || [calculate] calculer. ○ **reckon on** *vt fus* compter sur. ○ **reckon with** *vt fus* [expect] s'attendre à.

reckoning ['rekənɪŋ] (*U*) *n* [calculation] calculs *mpl*.

reclaim [rɪ'kleɪm] *vt* [claim back] réclamer. || [land] assécher.

recline [rɪ'klaɪn] *vi* [person] être allongé(e).

reclining [rɪ'klaɪnɪŋ] *adj* [chair] à dossier réglable.

recluse [rɪ'kluːs] *n* reclus *m*, -e *f*.

recognition [,rekəg'nɪʃn] *n* reconnaissance *f*; **in ~ of** en reconnaissance de.

recognizable ['rekəgnaɪzəbl] *adj* reconnaissable.

recognize, -ise ['rekəgnaɪz] *vt* reconnaître.

recoil [rɪ'kɔɪl] *vi*: **to ~ (from)** reculer (devant).

recollect [,rekə'lekt] *vt* se rappeler.

recollection [,rekə'lekʃn] *n* souvenir *m*.

recommend [,rekə'mend] *vt* [commend]: **to ~ sb/sthg (to sb)** recommander qqn/qqch (à qqn). || [advise] conseiller, recommander.

recompense ['rekəmpens] 1 *n* dédommagement *m*. 2 *vt* dédommager.

reconcile ['rekənsaɪl] *vt* [beliefs, ideas] concilier. || [people] réconcilier. || [accept]: **to ~ o.s. to sthg** se faire à l'idée de qqch.

reconditioned [,riːkən'dɪʃnd] *adj* remis(e) en état.

reconnaissance [rɪ'kɒnɪsəns] *n* reconnaissance *f*.

reconnoitre *Br*, **reconnoiter** *Am* [,rekə'nɔɪtə'] *vi* aller en reconnaissance.

reconsider [,riːkən'sɪdə'] 1 *vt* reconsidérer. 2 *vi* reconsidérer la question.

reconstruct [,riːkən'strʌkt] *vt* [gen] reconstruire. || [crime, event] reconstituer.

record [*n* & *adj* 'rekɔːd, *vb* rɪ'kɔːd] 1 *n* [written account] rapport *m*; [file] dossier *m*; **to keep sthg on ~** archiver qqch; (**police**) **~** casier *m* judiciaire; **off the ~** non officiel. || [vinyl disc] disque *m*. || [best achievement] record *m*. 2 *adj* record (*inv*). 3 *vt* [write down] noter. || [put on tape] enregistrer.

recorded delivery [rɪ'kɔːdɪd-] *n*: **to send sthg by ~** envoyer qqch en recommandé.

recorder [rɪ'kɔːdə'] *n* [musical instrument] flûte *f* à bec.

recording [rɪ'kɔːdɪŋ] *n* enregistrement *m*.

record player *n* tourne-disque *m*.

recount [*n* 'ri:kaʊnt, *vt sense 1* rɪ'kaʊnt, *sense 2* ˌri:'kaʊnt] **1** *n* [of vote] deuxième dépouillement *m* du scrutin. **2** *vt* [narrate] raconter. || [count again] recompter.

recoup [rɪ'ku:p] *vt* récupérer.

recourse [rɪ'kɔ:s] *n*: **to have ~ to** avoir recours à.

recover [rɪ'kʌvər] **1** *vt* [retrieve] récupérer; **to ~ sthg from sb** reprendre qqch à qqn. || [one's balance] retrouver; [consciousness] reprendre. **2** *vi* [from illness] se rétablir; [from shock, divorce] se remettre. || *fig* [economy] se redresser; [trade] reprendre.

recovery [rɪ'kʌvərɪ] *n* [from illness] guérison *f*, rétablissement *m*. || *fig* [of economy] redressement *m*, reprise *f*. || [retrieval] récupération *f*.

recreation [ˌrekrɪ'eɪʃn] *n* (*U*) [leisure] récréation *f*, loisirs *mpl*.

recrimination [rɪˌkrɪmɪ'neɪʃn] *n* récrimination *f*.

recruit [rɪ'kru:t] **1** *n* recrue *f*. **2** *vt* recruter.

recruitment [rɪ'kru:tmənt] *n* recrutement *m*.

rectangle ['rek,tæŋgl] *n* rectangle *m*.

rectangular [rek'tæŋgjʊlər] *adj* rectangulaire.

rectify ['rektɪfaɪ] *vt* [mistake] rectifier.

rector ['rektər] *n* [priest] pasteur *m*.

rectory ['rektərɪ] *n* presbytère *m*.

recuperate [rɪ'ku:pəreɪt] *vi* se rétablir.

recur [rɪ'kɜ:r] *vi* [error, problem] se reproduire; [dream] revenir; [pain] réapparaître.

recurrent [rɪ'kʌrənt] *adj* [error, problem] qui se reproduit souvent; [dream] qui revient souvent.

recycle [ˌri:'saɪkl] *vt* recycler.

red [red] **1** *adj* rouge; [hair] roux (rousse). **2** *n* rouge *m*; **to be in the ~** *inf* être à découvert.

red carpet *n*: **to roll out the ~ for sb** dérouler le tapis rouge pour qqn.
○ **red-carpet** *adj*: **to give sb the red-carpet treatment** recevoir qqn en grande pompe.

Red Cross *n*: **the ~** la Croix-Rouge.

redcurrant [ˌred'kʌrənt] *n* [fruit] groseille *f*; [bush] groseillier *m*.

redden ['redn] *vt & vi* rougir.

redecorate [ˌri:'dekəreɪt] **1** *vt* repeindre et retapisser. **2** *vi* refaire la peinture et les papiers peints.

redeem [rɪ'di:m] *vt* [save, rescue] racheter. || [from pawnbroker] dégager.

redeeming [rɪ'di:mɪŋ] *adj* qui rachète (les défauts).

redeploy [ˌri:dɪ'plɔɪ] *vt* MIL redéployer; [staff] réorganiser, réaffecter.

red-faced [-'feɪst] *adj* rougeaud(e), rubicond(e); [with embarrassment] rouge de confusion.

red-haired [-'heəd] *adj* roux (rousse).

red-handed [-'hændɪd] *adj*: **to catch sb ~** prendre qqn en flagrant délit OR la main dans le sac.

redhead ['redhed] *n* roux *m*, rousse *f*.

red herring *n fig* fausse piste *f*.

red-hot *adj* [extremely hot] brûlant(e); [metal] chauffé(e) au rouge.

redid [ˌri:'dɪd] *pt* → redo.

redirect [ˌri:dɪ'rekt] *vt* [energy, money] réorienter. || [traffic] détourner. || [letters] faire suivre.

rediscover [ˌri:dɪ'skʌvər] *vt* redécouvrir.

red light *n* [traffic signal] feu *m* rouge.

red-light district *n* quartier *m* chaud.

redo [ˌri:'du:] (*pt* -did, *pp* -done) *vt* refaire.

redolent ['redələnt] *adj literary* [reminiscent]: **~ of** qui rappelle, évocateur(trice) de. || [smelling]: **~ of** qui sent.

redone [ˌri:'dʌn] *pp* → redo.

redouble [ˌri:'dʌbl] *vt*: **to ~ one's efforts (to do sthg)** redoubler d'efforts (pour faire qqch).

redraft [ˌri:'drɑ:ft] *vt* rédiger à nouveau.

redress [rɪ'dres] **1** *n* (*U*) *fml* réparation *f*. **2** *vt*: **to ~ the balance** rétablir l'équilibre.

Red Sea *n*: **the ~** la mer Rouge.

red tape *n fig* paperasserie *f* administrative.

reduce [rɪ'dju:s] **1** *vt* réduire; **to be ~d to doing sthg** en être réduit à faire qqch; **to ~ sb to tears** faire pleurer qqn. **2** *vi* *Am* [diet] suivre un régime amaigrissant.

reduction [rɪ'dʌkʃn] *n* [decrease]: **~ (in)** réduction *f* (de), baisse *f* (de). || [discount] rabais *m*, réduction *f*.

redundant [rɪ'dʌndənt] *adj* [not required] superflu(e).

reed [ri:d] *n* [plant] roseau *m*.

reef [ri:f] *n* récif *m*, écueil *m*.

reek [ri:k] **1** *n* relent *m*. **2** *vi*: **to ~ (of sthg)** puer (qqch), empester (qqch).

reel [ri:l] **1** *n* [roll] bobine *f*. || [on fishing rod] moulinet *m*. **2** *vi* [stagger] chanceler.
○ **reel off** *vt sep* [list] débiter.

reenact [,ri:ɪ'nækt] *vt* [play] reproduire; [event] reconstituer.

ref [ref] *n inf* (*abbr of* **referee**) arbitre *m*. || (*abbr of* **reference**) ADMIN réf. *f*.

refectory [rɪ'fektərɪ] *n* réfectoire *m*.

refer [rɪ'fɜːr] *vt* [person]: **to ~ sb to** [hospital] envoyer qqn à; [specialist] adresser qqn à; ADMIN renvoyer qqn à. || [report, case, decision]: **to ~ sthg to** soumettre qqch à. ○ **refer to** *vt fus* [speak about] parler de, faire allusion à OR mention de. || [apply to] s'appliquer à, concerner. || [consult] se référer à, se reporter à.

referee [,refə'riː] **1** *n* SPORT arbitre *m*. **2** *vt* SPORT arbitrer. **3** *vi* SPORT être arbitre.

reference ['refrəns] *n* [mention]: **~ (to)** allusion *f* (à), mention *f* (de); **with ~ to** comme suite à. || (*U*) [for advice, information]: **~ (to)** consultation *f* (de), référence *f* (à). || COMM référence *f*. || [in book] renvoi *m*; **map ~** coordonnées *fpl*. || [for job application - letter] référence *f*; [- person] répondant *m*, -e *f*.

reference book *n* ouvrage *m* de référence.

reference number *n* numéro *m* de référence.

referendum [,refə'rendəm] (*pl* **-s** OR **-da** [-də]) *n* référendum *m*.

refill [*n* 'riː.fɪl, *vb* ,riː'fɪl] **1** *n* [for pen] recharge *f*. **2** *vt* remplir à nouveau.

refine [rɪ'faɪn] *vt* raffiner; *fig* peaufiner.

refined [rɪ'faɪnd] *adj* raffiné(e); [system, theory] perfectionné(e).

refinement [rɪ'faɪnmənt] *n* [improvement] perfectionnement *m*. || (*U*) [gentility] raffinement *m*.

reflect [rɪ'flekt] **1** *vt* [be a sign of] refléter. || [light, image] réfléchir, refléter; [heat] réverbérer. **2** *vi* [think]: **to ~ (on** OR **upon)** réfléchir (sur). penser à.

reflection [rɪ'flekʃn] *n* [sign] indication *f*, signe *m*. || [criticism]: **~ on** critique *f* de. || [image] reflet *m*. || (*U*) [of light, heat] réflexion *f*. || [thought] réflexion *f*; **on ~** réflexion faite.

reflector [rɪ'flektər] *n* réflecteur *m*.

reflex ['riː.fleks] *n*: **~ (action)** réflexe *m*.

reflexive [rɪ'fleksɪv] *adj* GRAMM [pronoun] réfléchi(e); **~ verb** verbe *m* pronominal réfléchi.

reforestation [riː,fɒrɪ'steɪʃn] = **reafforestation**

reform [rɪ'fɔːm] **1** *n* réforme *f*. **2** *vt* [gen] réformer; [person] corriger. **3** *vi* [behave better] se corriger, s'amender.

reformatory [rɪ'fɔːmətrɪ] *n Am* centre *m* d'éducation surveillée (pour jeunes délinquants).

reformer [rɪ'fɔːmər] *n* réformateur *m*, -trice *f*.

refrain [rɪ'freɪn] **1** *n* refrain *m*. **2** *vi*: **to ~ from doing sthg** s'abstenir de faire qqch.

refresh [rɪ'freʃ] *vt* rafraîchir, revigorer.

refreshed [rɪ'freʃt] *adj* reposé(e).

refresher course [rɪ'freʃər-] *n* cours *m* de recyclage OR remise à niveau.

refreshing [rɪ'freʃɪŋ] *adj* [pleasantly different] agréable, réconfortant(e). || [drink, swim] rafraîchissant(e).

refreshments [rɪ'freʃmənts] *npl* rafraîchissements *mpl*.

refrigerator [rɪ'frɪdʒəreɪtər] *n* réfrigérateur *m*, Frigidaire® *m*.

refuel [,riː'fjʊəl] **1** *vt* ravitailler. **2** *vi* se ravitailler en carburant.

refuge ['refjuːdʒ] *n lit & fig* refuge *m*, abri *m*; **to take ~ in** se réfugier dans.

refugee [,refjʊ'dʒiː] *n* réfugié *m*, -e *f*.

refund [*n* 'riːfʌnd, *vb* rɪ'fʌnd] **1** *n* remboursement *m*. **2** *vt*: **to ~ sthg to sb, to ~ sb sthg** rembourser qqch à qqn.

refurbish [,riː'fɜːbɪʃ] *vt* remettre à neuf, rénover.

refusal [rɪ'fjuːzl] *n*: **~ (to do sthg)** refus *m* (de faire qqch).

refuse[1] [rɪ'fjuːz] **1** *vt* refuser; **to ~ to do sthg** refuser de faire qqch. **2** *vi* refuser.

refuse[2] ['refjuːs] *n* (*U*) [rubbish] ordures *fpl*, détritus *mpl*.

refuse collection ['refjuːs-] *n* enlèvement *m* des ordures ménagères.

refute [rɪ'fjuːt] *vt* réfuter.

regain [rɪ'geɪn] *vt* [composure, health] retrouver; [leadership] reprendre.

regal ['riːgl] *adj* majestueux(euse), royal(e).

regalia [rɪ'geɪljə] *n* (*U*) insignes *mpl*.

regard [rɪ'gɑːd] **1** *n* (*U*) [respect] estime *f*, respect *m*. || [aspect]: **in this/that ~** à cet égard. **2** *vt* considérer; **to be highly ~ed** être tenu(e) en haute estime. ○ **regards** *npl*: **(with best) ~s** bien amicalement; **give her my ~s** faites-lui mes amitiés. ○ **as regards** *prep* en ce qui concerne. ○ **in regard to, with regard to** *prep* en ce qui concerne, relativement à.

regarding [rɪ'gɑːdɪŋ] *prep* concernant, en ce qui concerne.

regardless [rɪ'gɑːdlɪs] *adv* quand même. ○ **regardless of** *prep* sans tenir compte de, sans se soucier de.

regime [reɪˈʒiːm] *n* régime *m*.

regiment [ˈredʒɪmənt] *n* régiment *m*.

region [ˈriːdʒən] *n* région *f*; **in the ~ of** environ.

regional [ˈriːdʒənl] *adj* régional(e).

register [ˈredʒɪstər] **1** *n* [record] registre *m*. **2** *vt* [record officially] déclarer. || [show, measure] indiquer, montrer. || [express] exprimer. **3** *vi* [on official list] s'inscrire, se faire inscrire. || [at hotel] signer le registre.

registered [ˈredʒɪstəd] *adj* [person] inscrit(e); [car] immatriculé(e). || [letter, parcel] recommandé(e).

registered trademark *n* marque *f* déposée.

registrar [ˌredʒɪˈstrɑːr] *n* [keeper of records] officier *m* de l'état civil. || UNIV secrétaire *m* général.

registration [ˌredʒɪˈstreɪʃn] *n* [gen] enregistrement *m*, inscription *f*.

registration number *n* AUT numéro *m* d'immatriculation.

registry [ˈredʒɪstrɪ] *n* bureau *m* de l'enregistrement.

registry office *n* bureau *m* de l'état civil.

regret [rɪˈgret] **1** *n* regret *m*. **2** *vt* [be sorry about]: **to ~ sthg/doing sthg** regretter qqch/d'avoir fait qqch.

regretfully [rɪˈgretfʊlɪ] *adv* à regret.

regrettable [rɪˈgretəbl] *adj* regrettable, fâcheux(euse).

regroup [ˌriːˈgruːp] *vi* se regrouper.

regular [ˈregjʊlər] **1** *adj* [gen] régulier(ière); [customer] fidèle. || [usual] habituel(elle). || *Am* [normal - size] standard (*inv*). || *Am* [pleasant] sympa (*inv*). **2** *n* [at pub] habitué *m*, -e *f*; [at shop] client *m*, -e *f* fidèle.

regularly [ˈregjʊləlɪ] *adv* régulièrement.

regulate [ˈregjʊleɪt] *vt* régler.

regulation [ˌregjʊˈleɪʃn] **1** *adj* [standard] réglementaire. **2** *n* [rule] règlement *m*. || (*U*) [control] réglementation *f*.

rehearsal [rɪˈhɜːsl] *n* répétition *f*.

rehearse [rɪˈhɜːs] *vt* & *vi* répéter.

reign [reɪn] **1** *n* règne *m*. **2** *vi*: **to ~ (over)** *lit* & *fig* régner (sur).

reimburse [ˌriːɪmˈbɜːs] *vt*: **to ~ sb (for)** rembourser qqn (de).

rein [reɪn] *n* *fig*: **to give (a) free ~ to sb, to give sb free ~** laisser la bride sur le cou à qqn. ○ **reins** *npl* [for horse] rênes *fpl*.

reindeer [ˈreɪndɪər] (*pl inv*) *n* renne *m*.

reinforce [ˌriːɪnˈfɔːs] *vt* [strengthen] renforcer. || [back up, confirm] appuyer, étayer.

reinforced concrete [ˌriːɪnˈfɔːst-] *n* béton *m* armé.

reinforcement [ˌriːɪnˈfɔːsmənt] *n* (*U*) [strengthening] renforcement *m*. || [strengthener] renfort *m*. ○ **reinforcements** *npl* renforts *mpl*.

reinstate [ˌriːɪnˈsteɪt] *vt* [employee] rétablir dans ses fonctions, réintégrer; [policy, method] rétablir.

reiterate [riːˈɪtəreɪt] *vt* réitérer, répéter.

reject [*n* ˈriːdʒekt, *vb* rɪˈdʒekt] **1** *n* [product] article *m* de rebut. **2** *vt* [not accept] rejeter. || [candidate, coin] refuser.

rejection [rɪˈdʒekʃn] *n* [non-acceptance] rejet *m*. || [of candidate] refus *m*.

rejoice [rɪˈdʒɔɪs] *vi*: **to ~ (at OR in)** se réjouir (de).

rejuvenate [rɪˈdʒuːvəneɪt] *vt* rajeunir.

rekindle [ˌriːˈkɪndl] *vt* *fig* ranimer, raviver.

relapse [rɪˈlæps] **1** *n* rechute *f*. **2** *vi*: **to ~ into** retomber dans.

relate [rɪˈleɪt] **1** *vt* [connect]: **to ~ sthg to sthg** établir un lien OR rapport entre qqch et qqch. || [tell] raconter. **2** *vi* [be connected]: **to ~ to** avoir un rapport avec. || [concern]: **to ~ to** se rapporter à. || [empathize]: **to ~ (to sb)** s'entendre (avec qqn). ○ **relating to** *prep* concernant.

related [rɪˈleɪtɪd] *adj* [people] apparenté(e). || [issues, problems etc] lié(e).

relation [rɪˈleɪʃn] *n* [connection]: **~ (to/between)** rapport *m* (avec/entre). || [person] parent *m*, -e *f*. ○ **relations** *npl* [relationship] relations *fpl*, rapports *mpl*.

relationship [rɪˈleɪʃnʃɪp] *n* [between people, countries] relations *fpl*, rapports *mpl*; [romantic] liaison *f*. || [connection] rapport *m*, lien *m*.

relative [ˈrelətɪv] *adj* relatif(ive). **2** *n* parent *m*, -e *f*.

relatively [ˈrelətɪvlɪ] *adv* relativement.

relax [rɪˈlæks] **1** *vt* [person] détendre, relaxer. || [muscle, body] décontracter, relâcher; [one's grip] desserrer. || [rule] relâcher. **2** *vi* [person] se détendre, se décontracter. || [muscle, body] se relâcher, se décontracter. || [one's grip] se desserrer.

relaxation [ˌriːlækˈseɪʃn] *n* [of person] relaxation *f*, détente *f*.

relaxed [rɪˈlækst] *adj* détendu(e), décontracté(e).

relaxing [rɪ'læksɪŋ] *adj* relaxant(e), qui détend.

relay ['riːleɪ] **1** *n* SPORT: ~ **(race)** course *f* de relais. || RADIO & TV [broadcast] retransmission *f*. **2** *rt* RADIO & TV [broadcast] relayer. || [message, information] transmettre, communiquer.

release [rɪ'liːs] **1** *n* [from prison, cage] libération *f*. || [from pain, misery] délivrance *f*. || [statement] communiqué *m*. || [of gas, heat] échappement *m*. || (*U*) [of film, record] sortie *f*. || [film] nouveau film *m*; [record] nouveau disque *m*. **2** *rt* [set free] libérer. || [lift restriction on]: **to ~ sb from** dégager qqn de. || [make available - supplies] libérer; [- funds] débloquer. || [let go of] lâcher. || TECH [brake, handle] desserrer; [mechanism] déclencher. || [gas, heat]: **to be ~d (from/into)** se dégager (de/dans), s'échapper (de/dans). || [film, record] sortir; [statement, report] publier.

relegate ['relɪgeɪt] *rt* reléguer.

relent [rɪ'lent] *vi* [person] se laisser fléchir; [wind, storm] se calmer.

relentless [rɪ'lentlɪs] *adj* implacable.

relevant ['reləvənt] *adj* [connected]: ~ **(to)** qui a un rapport (avec). || [significant]: ~ **(to)** important(e) (pour). || [appropriate - information] utile; [- document] justificatif(ive).

reliable [rɪ'laɪəbl] *adj* [person] sur qui on peut compter, fiable; [device] fiable; [company, information] sérieux(ieuse).

reliant [rɪ'laɪənt] *adj*: **to be ~ on** être dépendant(e) de.

relic ['relɪk] *n* relique *f*; [of past] vestige *m*.

relief [rɪ'liːf] *n* [comfort] soulagement *m*. || [for poor, refugees] aide *f*, assistance *f*. || *Am* [social security] aide *f* sociale.

relieve [rɪ'liːv] *rt* [pain, anxiety] soulager; **to ~ sb of sthg** [take away from] délivrer qqn de qqch. || [take over from] relayer. || [give help to] secourir, venir en aide à.

religion [rɪ'lɪdʒn] *n* religion *f*.

religious [rɪ'lɪdʒəs] *adj* religieux(ieuse); [book] de piété.

relinquish [rɪ'lɪŋkwɪʃ] *rt* [power] abandonner; [claim, plan] renoncer à; [post] quitter.

relish ['relɪʃ] **1** *n* [enjoyment]: **with (great) ~** avec délectation. || [pickle] condiment *m*. **2** *rt* [enjoy] prendre plaisir à.

relocate [ˌriːləʊ'keɪt] **1** *rt* installer ailleurs, transférer. **2** *vi* s'installer ailleurs, déménager.

reluctance [rɪ'lʌktəns] *n* répugnance *f*.

reluctant [rɪ'lʌktənt] *adj* peu enthousiaste; **to be ~ to do sthg** rechigner à faire qqch, être peu disposé à faire qqch.

reluctantly [rɪ'lʌktəntlɪ] *adv* à contrecœur, avec répugnance.

rely [rɪ'laɪ] ○ **rely on** *vt fus* [count on] compter sur. || [be dependent on] dépendre de.

remain [rɪ'meɪn] **1** *rt* rester; **to ~ to be done** rester à faire. **2** *vi* rester. ○ **remains** *npl* [remnants] restes *mpl*. || [antiquities] ruines *fpl*, vestiges *mpl*.

remainder [rɪ'meɪndər] *n* reste *m*.

remaining [rɪ'meɪnɪŋ] *adj* qui reste.

remand [rɪ'mɑːnd] JUR **1** *n*: **on ~** en détention préventive. **2** *rt*: **to ~ sb (in custody)** placer qqn en détention préventive.

remark [rɪ'mɑːk] **1** *n* [comment] remarque *f*, observation *f*. **2** *rt* [comment]: **to ~ that ...** faire remarquer que ....

remarkable [rɪ'mɑːkəbl] *adj* remarquable.

remarry [ˌriː'mærɪ] *vi* se remarier.

remedial [rɪ'miːdjəl] *adj* [pupil, class] de rattrapage. || [action] de rectification.

remedy ['remɪdɪ] **1** *n*: ~ **(for)** MED remède *m* (pour OR contre); *fig* remède (à OR contre). **2** *rt* remédier à.

remember [rɪ'membər] **1** *rt* [gen] se souvenir de, se rappeler; **to ~ to do sthg** ne pas oublier de faire qqch, penser à faire qqch; **to ~ doing sthg** se souvenir d'avoir fait qqch, se rappeler avoir fait qqch. **2** *vi* se souvenir, se rappeler.

remembrance [rɪ'membrəns] *n*: **in ~ of** en souvenir OR mémoire de.

Remembrance Day *n* l'Armistice *m*.

remind [rɪ'maɪnd] *rt*: **to ~ sb of** OR **about sthg** rappeler qqch à qqn; **to ~ sb to do sthg** rappeler à qqn de faire qqch, faire penser à qqn à faire qqch.

reminder [rɪ'maɪndər] *n* [to jog memory]: **to give sb a ~ (to do sthg)** faire penser à qqn (à faire qqch). || [letter, note] rappel *m*.

reminisce [ˌremɪ'nɪs] *vi* évoquer des souvenirs; **to ~ about sthg** évoquer qqch.

reminiscent [ˌremɪ'nɪsnt] *adj*: ~ **of** qui rappelle, qui fait penser à.

remiss [rɪ'mɪs] *adj* négligent(e).

remit [rɪ'mɪt] *rt* [money] envoyer, verser.

remittance [rɪ'mɪtns] n [amount of money] versement m. || COMM règlement m, paiement m.

remnant ['remnənt] n [remaining part] reste m, restant m. || [of cloth] coupon m.

remorse [rɪ'mɔːs] n (U) remords m.

remorseful [rɪ'mɔːsfʊl] adj plein(e) de remords.

remorseless [rɪ'mɔːslɪs] adj implacable.

remote [rɪ'məʊt] adj [far-off - place] éloigné(e); [- time] lointain(e). || [person] distant(e). || [possibility, chance] vague.

remote control n télécommande f.

remotely [rɪ'məʊtlɪ] adv [in the slightest]: **not ~** pas le moins du monde, absolument pas. || [far off] au loin.

removable [rɪ'muːvəbl] adj [detachable] détachable, amovible.

removal [rɪ'muːvl] n (U) [act of removing] enlèvement m.

remove [rɪ'muːv] vt [take away - gen] enlever; [- stain] faire partir, enlever; [- suspicion] dissiper. || [clothes] ôter, enlever. || [employee] renvoyer.

remuneration [rɪ,mjuːnə'reɪʃn] n rémunération f.

Renaissance [rə'neɪsəns] n: **the ~** la Renaissance.

render ['rendər] vt rendre; [assistance] porter; FIN [account] présenter.

rendezvous ['rɒndɪvuː] (pl inv) n rendez-vous m inv.

renegade ['renɪgeɪd] n renégat m, -e f.

renew [rɪ'njuː] vt [gen] renouveler; [negotiations, strength] reprendre; [interest] faire renaître. || [replace] remplacer.

renewable [rɪ'njuːəbl] adj renouvelable.

renewal [rɪ'njuːəl] n [of activity] reprise f. || [of contract, licence etc] renouvellement m.

renounce [rɪ'naʊns] vt [reject] renoncer à.

renovate ['renəveɪt] vt rénover.

renown [rɪ'naʊn] n renommée f, renom m.

renowned [rɪ'naʊnd] adj: **~ (for)** renommé(e) (pour).

rent [rent] 1 n [for house] loyer m. 2 vt louer.

rental ['rentl] 1 adj de location. 2 n [for car, television, video] prix m de location; [for house] loyer m.

renunciation [rɪ,nʌnsɪ'eɪʃn] n renonciation f.

reorganize, -ise [,riː'ɔːgənaɪz] vt réorganiser.

rep [rep] n (abbr of representative) VRP m. || abbr of repertory.

repaid [riː'peɪd] pt & pp → repay.

repair [rɪ'peər] 1 n réparation f; **in good/bad ~** en bon/mauvais état. 2 vt réparer.

repair kit n trousse f à outils.

repartee [,repɑː'tiː] n repartie f.

repatriate [,riː'pætrɪeɪt] vt rapatrier.

repay [riː'peɪ] (pt & pp repaid) vt [money]: **to ~ sb sthg, to ~ sthg to sb** rembourser qqch à qqn. || [favour] payer de retour, récompenser.

repayment [riː'peɪmənt] n remboursement m.

repeal [rɪ'piːl] 1 n abrogation f. 2 vt abroger.

repeat [rɪ'piːt] 1 vt [gen] répéter. 2 n RADIO & TV reprise f, rediffusion f.

repeatedly [rɪ'piːtɪdlɪ] adv à maintes reprises, très souvent.

repel [rɪ'pel] vt repousser.

repellent [rɪ'pelənt] 1 adj répugnant(e), repoussant(e). 2 n: **insect ~** crème f anti-insecte.

repent [rɪ'pent] 1 vt se repentir de. 2 vi: **to ~ (of)** se repentir (de).

repentance [rɪ'pentəns] n (U) repentir m.

repercussions [,riːpə'kʌʃnz] npl répercussions fpl.

repertoire ['repətwɑːr] n répertoire m.

repertory ['repətrɪ] n répertoire m.

repetition [,repɪ'tɪʃn] n répétition f.

repetitious [,repɪ'tɪʃəs], **repetitive** [rɪ'petɪtɪv] adj [action, job] répétitif(ive); [article, speech] qui a des redites.

replace [rɪ'pleɪs] vt [gen] remplacer. || [put back] remettre (à sa place).

replacement [rɪ'pleɪsmənt] n [substituting] remplacement m; [putting back] replacement m. || [new person]: **~ (for sb)** remplaçant m, -e f (de qqn).

replay [n 'riːpleɪ, vb ,riː'pleɪ] 1 n match m rejoué. 2 vt [match, game] rejouer.

replenish [rɪ'plenɪʃ] vt: **to ~ one's supply of sthg** se réapprovisionner en qqch.

replica ['replɪkə] n copie f exacte, réplique f.

reply [rɪ'plaɪ] 1 n: **~ (to)** réponse f (à). 2 vt & vi répondre.

report [rɪ'pɔːt] 1 n [account] rapport m, compte rendu m; PRESS reportage m. 2 vt [news, crime] rapporter, signaler. || [make known]: **to ~ that ...** annoncer que

.... || [complain about]: **to ~ sb (to)** dénoncer qqn (à). **3** vi [give account]: **tò ~ (on)** faire un rapport (sur); PRESS faire un reportage (sur). || [present oneself]: **to ~ (to sb/for sthg)** se présenter (à qqn/pour qqch).

report card n bulletin m scolaire.

reportedly [rɪˈpɔːtɪdlɪ] adv à ce qu'il paraît.

reporter [rɪˈpɔːtər] n reporter m.

repose [rɪˈpəʊz] n literary repos m.

repossess [ˌriːpəˈzes] vt saisir.

reprehensible [ˌreprɪˈhensəbl] adj répréhensible.

represent [ˌreprɪˈzent] vt [gen] représenter.

representation [ˌreprɪzenˈteɪʃn] n [gen] représentation f.

representative [ˌreprɪˈzentətɪv] **1** adj représentatif(ive). **2** n représentant m, -e f.

repress [rɪˈpres] vt réprimer.

repression [rɪˈpreʃn] n répression f; [sexual] refoulement m.

reprieve [rɪˈpriːv] **1** n fig [delay] sursis m, répit m. || JUR sursis m. **2** vt accorder un sursis à.

reprimand [ˈreprɪmɑːnd] **1** n réprimande f. **2** vt réprimander.

reprisal [rɪˈpraɪzl] n représailles fpl.

reproach [rɪˈprəʊtʃ] **1** n reproche m. **2** vt: **to ~ sb for** OR **with sthg** reprocher qqch à qqn.

reproachful [rɪˈprəʊtʃfʊl] adj [look, words] de reproche.

reproduce [ˌriːprəˈdjuːs] **1** vt reproduire. **2** vi se reproduire.

reproduction [ˌriːprəˈdʌkʃn] n reproduction f.

reproof [rɪˈpruːf] n reproche m, blâme m.

reprove [rɪˈpruːv] vt: **to ~ sb (for)** blâmer qqn (pour OR de), réprimander qqn (pour).

reptile [ˈreptaɪl] n reptile m.

republic [rɪˈpʌblɪk] n république f.

republican [rɪˈpʌblɪkən] **1** adj républicain(e). **2** n républicain m, -e f. ○ **Republican 1** adj républicain(e); **the Republican Party** Am le parti républicain. **2** n républicain m, -e f.

repulse [rɪˈpʌls] vt repousser.

repulsive [rɪˈpʌlsɪv] adj repoussant(e).

reputable [ˈrepjʊtəbl] adj de bonne réputation.

reputation [ˌrepjʊˈteɪʃn] n réputation f.

reputed [rɪˈpjuːtɪd] adj réputé(e); **to be ~ to be sthg** être réputé pour être qqch, avoir la réputation d'être qqch.

reputedly [rɪˈpjuːtɪdlɪ] adv à OR d'après ce qu'on dit.

request [rɪˈkwest] **1** n: **~ (for)** demande f (de); **on ~** sur demande. **2** vt demander.

require [rɪˈkwaɪər] vt [subj: person] avoir besoin de; [subj: situation] nécessiter; **to ~ sb to do sthg** exiger de qqn qu'il fasse qqch.

requirement [rɪˈkwaɪəmənt] n besoin m.

requisition [ˌrekwɪˈzɪʃn] vt réquisitionner.

reran [ˌriːˈræn] pt → rerun.

rerun [n ˈriːrʌn, vb ˌriːˈrʌn] (pt -ran, pp -run) **1** n [of TV programme] rediffusion f, reprise f; fig répétition f. **2** vt [race] réorganiser. || [TV programme] rediffuser; [tape] passer à nouveau, repasser.

rescind [rɪˈsɪnd] vt [contract] annuler; [law] abroger.

rescue [ˈreskjuː] **1** n (U) [help] secours mpl. || [successful attempt] sauvetage m. **2** vt sauver, secourir.

rescuer [ˈreskjuər] n sauveteur m.

research [ˌrɪˈsɜːtʃ] **1** n (U): **~ (on** OR **into)** recherche f (sur), recherches fpl (sur). **2** vt faire des recherches sur.

researcher [rɪˈsɜːtʃər] n chercheur m, -euse f.

resemblance [rɪˈzembləns] n: **~ (to)** ressemblance f (avec).

resemble [rɪˈzembl] vt ressembler à.

resent [rɪˈzent] vt être indigné(e) par.

resentful [rɪˈzentfʊl] adj plein(e) de ressentiment.

resentment [rɪˈzentmənt] n ressentiment m.

reservation [ˌrezəˈveɪʃn] n [booking] réservation f. || [uncertainty]: **without ~** sans réserve. || Am [for Native Americans] réserve f indienne. ○ **reservations** npl [doubts] réserves fpl.

reserve [rɪˈzɜːv] **1** n [gen] réserve f; **in ~** en réserve. || SPORT remplaçant m, -e f. **2** vt [save] garder, réserver. || [book] réserver. || [retain]: **to ~ the right to do sthg** se réserver le droit de faire qqch.

reserved [rɪˈzɜːvd] adj réservé(e).

reservoir [ˈrezəvwɑːr] n réservoir m.

reset [ˌriːˈset] (pt & pp reset) vt [clock, watch] remettre à l'heure; [meter, controls] remettre à zéro.

reshape [ˌriːˈʃeɪp] vt [policy, thinking] réorganiser.

reshuffle [ˌriːˈʃʌfl] **1** *n* remaniement *m*; **cabinet ~** remaniement ministériel. **2** *vt* remanier.

reside [rɪˈzaɪd] *vi fml* résider.

residence [ˈrezɪdəns] *n* résidence *f*.

residence permit *n* permis *m* de séjour.

resident [ˈrezɪdənt] **1** *adj* résidant(e); [chaplain, doctor] à demeure. **2** *n* résident *m*, -e *f*.

residential area *n* quartier *m* résidentiel.

residue [ˈrezɪdjuː] *n* reste *m*; CHEM résidu *m*.

resign [rɪˈzaɪn] **1** *vt* [job] démissionner de. ‖ [accept calmly]: **to ~ o.s. to** se résigner à. **2** *vi*: **to ~ (from)** démissionner (de).

resignation [ˌrezɪgˈneɪʃn] *n* [from job] démission *f*. ‖ [calm acceptance] résignation *f*.

resigned [rɪˈzaɪnd] *adj*: **~ (to)** résigné(e) (à).

resilient [rɪˈzɪlɪənt] *adj* [material] élastique; [person] qui a du ressort.

resin [ˈrezɪn] *n* résine *f*.

resist [rɪˈzɪst] *vt* résister à.

resistance [rɪˈzɪstəns] *n* résistance *f*.

resolute [ˈrezəluːt] *adj* résolu(e).

resolution [ˌrezəˈluːʃn] *n* résolution *f*.

resolve [rɪˈzɒlv] **1** *n* (*U*) [determination] résolution *f*. **2** *vt* [decide]: **to ~ (that)** ... décider que ...; **to ~ to do sthg** résoudre OR décider de faire qqch. ‖ [solve] résoudre.

resort [rɪˈzɔːt] *n* [for holidays] lieu *m* de vacances. ‖ [recourse] recours *m*; **as a last ~, in the last ~** en dernier ressort OR recours. ○ **resort to** *vt fus* recourir à. avoir recours à.

resound [rɪˈzaʊnd] *vi* [noise] résonner. ‖ [place]: **to ~ with** retentir de.

resounding [rɪˈzaʊndɪŋ] *adj* retentissant(e).

resource [rɪˈsɔːs] *n* ressource *f*.

resourceful [rɪˈsɔːsful] *adj* plein(e) de ressources, débrouillard(e).

respect [rɪˈspekt] **1** *n* [gen]: **~ (for)** respect *m* (pour); **with ~, ...** sauf votre respect. .... ‖ [aspect]: **in this** OR **that ~** à cet égard; **in some ~s** à certains égards. **2** *vt* respecter. ○ **respects** *npl* respects *mpl*, hommages *mpl*. ○ **with respect to** *prep* en ce qui concerne, quant à.

respectable [rɪˈspektəbl] *adj* [morally correct] respectable. ‖ [adequate] raisonnable, honorable.

respectful [rɪˈspektful] *adj* respectueux(euse).

respective [rɪˈspektɪv] *adj* respectif(ive).

respectively [rɪˈspektɪvlɪ] *adv* respectivement.

respite [ˈrespaɪt] *n* répit *m*.

resplendent [rɪˈsplendənt] *adj* resplendissant(e).

respond [rɪˈspɒnd] *vi*: **to ~ (to)** répondre (à).

response [rɪˈspɒns] *n* réponse *f*.

responsibility [rɪˌspɒnsəˈbɪlətɪ] *n*: **~ (for)** responsabilité *f* (de).

responsible [rɪˈspɒnsəbl] *adj* [gen]: **~ (for sthg)** responsable (de qqch). ‖ [job, position] qui comporte des responsabilités.

responsibly [rɪˈspɒnsəblɪ] *adv* de façon responsable.

responsive [rɪˈspɒnsɪv] *adj* [quick to react] qui réagit bien. ‖ [aware]: **~ (to)** attentif(ive) (à).

rest [rest] **1** *n* [remainder]: **the ~ (of)** le reste (de); **the ~ (of them)** les autres *mfpl*. ‖ [relaxation, break] repos *m*; **to have a ~** se reposer. ‖ [support] support *m*, appui *m*. **2** *vt* [relax] laisser OR laisser reposer. ‖ [support]: **to ~ sthg on/against** appuyer qqch sur/contre. ‖ *phr*: **~ assured** soyez certain(e). **3** *vi* [relax] se reposer. ‖ [be supported]: **to ~ on/against** s'appuyer sur/contre.

restaurant [ˈrestərɒnt] *n* restaurant *m*.

restful [ˈrestful] *adj* reposant(e).

rest home *n* maison *f* de repos.

restive [ˈrestɪv] *adj* agité(e).

restless [ˈrestlɪs] *adj* agité(e).

restoration [ˌrestəˈreɪʃn] *n* [of law and order, monarchy] rétablissement *m*. ‖ [renovation] restauration *f*.

restore [rɪˈstɔːr] *vt* [law and order, monarchy] rétablir; [confidence] redonner. ‖ [renovate] restaurer. ‖ [give back] rendre, restituer.

restrain [rɪˈstreɪn] *vt* [person, crowd] contenir, retenir; **to ~ o.s. from doing sthg** se retenir de faire qqch.

restrained [rɪˈstreɪnd] *adj* [tone] mesuré(e); [person] qui se domine.

restraint [rɪˈstreɪnt] *n* [restriction] restriction *f*, entrave *f*. ‖ (*U*) [self-control] mesure *f*, retenue *f*.

restrict [rɪˈstrɪkt] *vt* restreindre, limiter.

restriction [rɪˈstrɪkʃn] *n* restriction *f*, limitation *f*.

restrictive [rɪ'strɪktɪv] *adj* restrictif(ive).

rest room *n Am* toilettes *fpl*.

result [rɪ'zʌlt] 1 *n* résultat *m*; **as a ~** en conséquence. 2 *vi* [cause]: **to ~ in** aboutir à. ‖ [be caused]: **to ~ (from)** résulter (de).

resume [rɪ'zju:m] *vt & vi* reprendre.

résumé ['rezju:meɪ] *n* [summary] résumé *m*. ‖ *Am* [curriculum vitae] curriculum vitae *m inv*, CV *m*.

resumption [rɪ'zʌmpʃn] *n* reprise *f*.

resurgence [rɪ'sɜ:dʒəns] *n* réapparition *f*.

resurrection [,rezə'rekʃn] *n fig* résurrection *f*.

resuscitation [rɪ,sʌsɪ'teɪʃn] *n* réanimation *f*.

retail ['ri:teɪl] *n* (*U*) détail *m*.

retailer ['ri:teɪlər] *n* détaillant *m*, -e *f*.

retail price *n* prix *m* de détail.

retain [rɪ'teɪn] *vt* conserver.

retainer [rɪ'teɪnər] *n* [fee] provision *f*.

retaliate [rɪ'tælɪeɪt] *vi* rendre la pareille, se venger.

retaliation [rɪ,tælɪ'eɪʃn] *n* (*U*) vengeance *f*, représailles *fpl*.

retarded [rɪ'tɑ:dɪd] *adj* retardé(e).

retch [retʃ] *vi* avoir des haut-le-cœur.

retentive [rɪ'tentɪv] *adj* [memory] fidèle.

reticent ['retɪsənt] *adj* peu communicatif(ive).

retina ['retɪnə] (*pl* -nas OR -nae [-ni:]) *n* rétine *f*.

retinue ['retɪnju:] *n* suite *f*.

retire [rɪ'taɪər] *vi* [from work] prendre sa retraite. ‖ [withdraw] se retirer. ‖ [to bed] (aller) se coucher.

retired [rɪ'taɪəd] *adj* à la retraite, retraité(e).

retirement [rɪ'taɪəmənt] *n* retraite *f*.

retiring [rɪ'taɪərɪŋ] *adj* [shy] réservé(e).

retort [rɪ'tɔ:t] 1 *n* [sharp reply] riposte *f*. 2 *vt* riposter.

retrace [rɪ'treɪs] *vt*: **to ~ one's steps** revenir sur ses pas.

retract [rɪ'trækt] 1 *vt* [statement] rétracter. ‖ [undercarriage] rentrer, escamoter; [claws] rentrer. 2 *vi* [undercarriage] rentrer, s'escamoter.

retrain [,ri:'treɪn] *vt* recycler.

retreat [rɪ'tri:t] 1 *n* retraite *f*. 2 *vi* [move away] se retirer; MIL battre en retraite.

retribution [,retrɪ'bju:ʃn] *n* châtiment *m*.

retrieval [rɪ'tri:vl] *n* (*U*) COMPUT recherche *f* et extraction *f*.

retrieve [rɪ'tri:v] *vt* [get back] récupérer. ‖ COMPUT rechercher et extraire.

retriever [rɪ'tri:vər] *n* [dog] retriever *m*.

retrograde ['retrəgreɪd] *adj* rétrograde.

retrospect ['retrəspekt] *n*: **in ~** après coup.

retrospective [,retrə'spektɪv] *adj* [mood, look] rétrospectif(ive). ‖ JUR [law, pay rise] rétroactif(ive).

return [rɪ'tɜ:n] 1 *n* (*U*) [arrival back, giving back] retour *m*. ‖ TENNIS renvoi *m*. ‖ [profit] rapport *m*, rendement *m*. 2 *vt* [gen] rendre; [a loan] rembourser; [library book] rapporter. ‖ [send back] renvoyer. ‖ [replace] remettre. ‖ POL élire. 3 *vi* [come back] revenir; [go back] retourner. ○ **returns** *npl* COMM recettes *fpl*; **many happy ~s (of the day)!** bon anniversaire! ○ **in return** *adv* en retour, en échange. ○ **in return for** *prep* en échange de.

reunification [,ri:ju:nɪfɪ'keɪʃn] *n* réunification *f*.

reunion [,ri:'ju:njən] *n* réunion *f*.

reunite [,ri:ju:'naɪt] *vt*: **to be ~d with sb** retrouver qqn.

rev [rev] *inf* 1 *n* (*abbr of* revolution) tour *m*. 2 *vt*: **to ~ the engine (up)** emballer le moteur. 3 *vi*: **to ~ (up)** s'emballer.

revamp [,ri:'væmp] *vt inf* [system, department] réorganiser; [house] retaper.

reveal [rɪ'vi:l] *vt* révéler.

revealing [rɪ'vi:lɪŋ] *adj* [clothes - low-cut] décolleté(e); [- transparent] qui laisse deviner le corps. ‖ [comment] révélateur(trice).

reveille [*Br* rɪ'væli, *Am* 'revəli] *n* réveil *m*.

revel ['revl] *vi*: **to ~ in sthg** se délecter de qqch.

revelation [,revə'leɪʃn] *n* révélation *f*.

revenge [rɪ'vendʒ] 1 *n* vengeance *f*. 2 *vt* venger; **to ~ o.s. on sb** se venger de qqn.

revenue ['revənju:] *n* revenu *m*.

reverberate [rɪ'vɜ:bəreɪt] *vi* retentir, se réverbérer.

reverberations [rɪ,vɜ:bə'reɪʃnz] *npl* réverbérations *fpl*; *fig* répercussions *fpl*.

revere [rɪ'vɪər] *vt* révérer, vénérer.

reverence ['revərəns] *n* révérence *f*, vénération *f*.

Reverend ['revərənd] *n* révérend *m*.

reverie ['revəri] *n* rêverie *f*.

reversal [rɪ'vɜ:sl] *n* [of policy, decision] revirement *m*. ‖ [ill fortune] revers *m* de fortune.

reverse [rɪ'vɜːs] **1** *adj* [order, process] inverse. **2** *n* AUT: ~ **(gear)** marche *f* arrière. || [opposite]: **the** ~ le contraire. || [back]: **the** ~ [of paper] le verso, le dos; [of coin] le revers. **3** *vt* [order, positions] inverser; [decision, trend] renverser. || [turn over] retourner. **4** *vi* AUT faire marche arrière.

revert [rɪ'vɜːt] *vi*: **to** ~ **to** retourner à.

review [rɪ'vjuː] **1** *n* [of salary, spending] révision *f*; [of situation] examen *m*. || [of book, play etc] critique *f*, compte rendu *m*. **2** *vt* [salary] réviser; [situation] examiner. || [book, play etc] faire la critique de. || *Am* [study again] réviser.

reviewer [rɪ'vjuːər] *n* critique *mf*.

revile [rɪ'vaɪl] *vt* injurier.

revise [rɪ'vaɪz] *vt* [reconsider] modifier. || [rewrite] corriger.

revision [rɪ'vɪʒn] *n* révision *f*.

revitalize, -ise [,riː'vaɪtəlaɪz] *vt* revitaliser.

revival [rɪ'vaɪvl] *n* [of economy, trade] reprise *f*; [of interest] regain *m*.

revive [rɪ'vaɪv] **1** *vt* [person] ranimer. || *fig* [economy] relancer; [interest] faire renaître; [tradition] rétablir; [musical, play] reprendre; [memories] ranimer, raviver. **2** *vi* [person] reprendre connaissance. || *fig* [economy] repartir, reprendre; [hopes] renaître.

revolt [rɪ'vəʊlt] **1** *n* révolte *f*. **2** *vt* révolter, dégoûter. **3** *vi* se révolter.

revolting [rɪ'vəʊltɪŋ] *adj* dégoûtant(e); [smell] infect(e).

revolution [,revə'luːʃn] *n* [gen] révolution *f*. || TECH tour *m*, révolution *f*.

revolutionary [,revə'luːʃnərɪ] **1** *adj* révolutionnaire. **2** *n* révolutionnaire *mf*.

revolve [rɪ'vɒlv] *vi*: **to** ~ **(around)** tourner (autour de).

revolver [rɪ'vɒlvər] *n* revolver *m*.

revolving door *n* tambour *m*.

revue [rɪ'vjuː] *n* revue *f*.

revulsion [rɪ'vʌlʃn] *n* répugnance *f*.

reward [rɪ'wɔːd] **1** *n* récompense *f*. **2** *vt*: **to** ~ **sb (for/with sthg)** récompenser qqn (de/par qqch).

rewarding [rɪ'wɔːdɪŋ] *adj* [job] qui donne de grandes satisfactions.

rewind [,riː'waɪnd] (*pt* & *pp* **rewound**) *vt* [tape] rembobiner.

rewire [,riː'waɪər] *vt* [house] refaire l'installation électrique de.

reword [,riː'wɜːd] *vt* reformuler.

rewound [,riː'waʊnd] *pt* & *pp* → **rewind**.

rewrite [,riː'raɪt] (*pt* **rewrote** [,riː'rəʊt], *pp* **rewritten** [,riː'rɪtn]) *vt* récrire.

rhapsody ['ræpsədɪ] *n* rhapsodie *f*; **to go into rhapsodies about sthg** s'extasier sur qqch.

rhetoric ['retərɪk] *n* rhétorique *f*.

rhetorical question [rɪ'tɒrɪkl-] *n* question *f* pour la forme.

rheumatism ['ruːmətɪzm] *n* (*U*) rhumatisme *m*.

Rhine [raɪn] *n*: **the** ~ le Rhin.

rhino ['raɪnəʊ] (*pl inv* OR **-s**), **rhinoceros** [raɪ'nɒsərəs] (*pl inv* OR **-es**) *n* rhinocéros *m*.

rhododendron [,rəʊdə'dendrən] *n* rhododendron *m*.

Rhône [rəʊn] *n*: **the (River)** ~ le Rhône.

rhubarb ['ruːbɑːb] *n* rhubarbe *f*.

rhyme [raɪm] **1** *n* [word, technique] rime *f*. || [poem] poème *m*. **2** *vi*: **to** ~ **(with)** rimer (avec).

rhythm ['rɪðm] *n* rythme *m*.

rib [rɪb] *n* ANAT côte *f*.

ribbed [rɪbd] *adj* [jumper, fabric] à côtes.

ribbon ['rɪbən] *n* ruban *m*.

rice [raɪs] *n* riz *m*.

rice pudding *n* riz *m* au lait.

rich [rɪtʃ] **1** *adj* riche; [clothes, fabrics] somptueux(euse). **2** *npl*: **the** ~ les riches *mpl*. ○ **riches** *npl* richesses *fpl*, richesse *f*.

richly ['rɪtʃlɪ] *adv* [rewarded] largement; [provided] très bien. || [sumptuously] richement.

richness ['rɪtʃnɪs] *n* (*U*) richesse *f*.

rickety ['rɪkətɪ] *adj* branlant(e).

rickshaw ['rɪkʃɔː] *n* pousse-pousse *m inv*.

ricochet ['rɪkəʃeɪ] (*pt* & *pp* **-ed** OR **-ted**, *cont* **-ing** OR **-ting**) **1** *n* ricochet *m*. **2** *vi*: **to** ~ **(off)** ricocher (sur).

rid [rɪd] (*pt* **rid** OR **-ded**, *pp* **rid**) *vt*: **to** ~ **sb/sthg of** débarrasser qqn/qqch de; **to get** ~ **of** se débarrasser de.

ridden ['rɪdn] *pp* → **ride**.

riddle ['rɪdl] *n* énigme *f*.

riddled ['rɪdld] *adj*: **to be** ~ **with** être criblé(e) de.

ride [raɪd] (*pt* **rode**, *pp* **ridden**) **1** *n* promenade *f*, tour *m*; **to take sb for a** ~ *inf fig* faire marcher qqn. **2** *vt* [travel on]: **to** ~ **a horse/a bicycle** monter à cheval/à bicyclette. || *Am* [travel in - bus, train, elevator] prendre. || [distance] parcourir, faire. **3** *vi* [on horseback] monter à cheval, faire du cheval; [on bicycle] faire de

ripple

la bicyclette OR du vélo; **to ~ in a car/bus** aller en voiture/bus.

rider ['raɪdər] n [of horse] cavalier m, -ière f; [of bicycle] cycliste mf; [of motorbike] motocycliste mf.

ridge [rɪdʒ] n [of mountain, roof] crête f, arête f. || [on surface] strie f.

ridicule ['rɪdɪkjuːl] **1** n ridicule m. **2** vt ridiculiser.

ridiculous [rɪ'dɪkjʊləs] adj ridicule.

riding ['raɪdɪŋ] n équitation f.

riding school n école f d'équitation.

rife [raɪf] adj répandu(e).

riffraff ['rɪfræf] n racaille f.

rifle ['raɪfl] **1** n fusil m. **2** vt [drawer, bag] vider.

rifle range n [indoor] stand m de tir; [outdoor] champ m de tir.

rift [rɪft] n GEOL fissure f. || [quarrel] désaccord m.

rig [rɪg] **1** n: (oil) ~ [on land] derrick m; [at sea] plate-forme f de forage. **2** vt [match, election] truquer. ○ **rig up** vt sep installer avec les moyens du bord.

rigging ['rɪgɪŋ] n [of ship] gréement m.

right [raɪt] **1** adj [correct - answer, time] juste, exact(e); [- decision, direction, idea] bon (bonne); **to be ~ (about)** avoir raison (au sujet de). || [morally correct] bien (inv); **to be ~ to do sthg** avoir raison de faire qqch. || [appropriate] qui convient. || [not left] droit(e). **2** n (U) [moral correctness] bien m; **to be in the ~** avoir raison. || [entitlement, claim] droit m; **by ~s** en toute justice. || [not left] droite f. **3** adv [correctly] correctement. || [not left] à droite. || [emphatic use]: ~ **down/up** tout en bas/en haut; ~ **here** ici (même); ~ **in the middle** en plein milieu; ~ **now** tout de suite; ~ **away** immédiatement. **4** vt [injustice, wrong] réparer. **5** excl bon! ○ **Right** n POL: **the Right** la droite.

right angle n angle m droit.

righteous ['raɪtʃəs] adj [person] droit(e); [indignation] justifié(e).

rightful ['raɪtful] adj légitime.

right-hand adj de droite; ~ **side** droite f, côté m droit.

right-hand drive adj avec conduite à droite.

right-handed [-'hændɪd] adj [person] droitier(ière).

right-hand man n bras m droit.

rightly ['raɪtlɪ] adv [answer, believe] correctement. || [behave] bien. || [angry, worried etc] à juste titre.

right of way n AUT priorité f. || [access] droit m de passage.

right wing n: **the ~** la droite. ○ **right-wing** adj de droite.

rigid ['rɪdʒɪd] adj [gen] rigide. || [harsh] strict(e).

rigmarole ['rɪgmərəʊl] n pej [process] comédie f. || [story] galimatias m.

rigor Am = rigour.

rigorous ['rɪgərəs] adj rigoureux(euse).

rigour Br, **rigor** Am ['rɪgər] n rigueur f.

rile [raɪl] vt agacer.

rim [rɪm] n [of container] bord m; [of wheel] jante f; [of spectacles] monture f.

rind [raɪnd] n [of fruit] peau f; [of cheese] croûte f; [of bacon] couenne f.

ring [rɪŋ] (pt **rang**, pp vt sense 1 & vi **rung**, pt & pp vt sense 2 only **ringed**) **1** n [telephone call]: **to give sb a ~** donner OR passer un coup de téléphone à qqn. || [sound of bell] sonnerie f. || [circular object] anneau m; [on finger] bague f; [for napkin] rond m. || [of people, trees etc] cercle m. || [for boxing] ring m. || [of criminals, spies] réseau m. **2** vt [bell] (faire) sonner; **to ~ the doorbell** sonner à la porte. || [draw a circle round, surround] entourer. **3** vi [bell, telephone, person] sonner; **to ~ for sb** sonner qqn. || [resound]: **to ~ with** résonner de.

ring binder n classeur m à anneaux.

ringing ['rɪŋɪŋ] n [of bell] sonnerie f; [in ears] tintement m.

ringleader ['rɪŋ,liːdər] n chef m.

ringlet ['rɪŋlɪt] n anglaise f.

rink [rɪŋk] n [for ice-skating] patinoire f; [for roller-skating] skating m.

rinse [rɪns] vt rincer.

riot ['raɪət] **1** n émeute f; **to run ~** se déchaîner. **2** vi participer à une émeute.

rioter ['raɪətər] n émeutier m, -ière f.

riotous ['raɪətəs] adj [crowd] tapageur(euse); [behaviour] séditieux(ieuse); [party] bruyant(e).

riot police npl ≃ CRS mpl.

rip [rɪp] **1** n déchirure f, accroc m. **2** vt [tear] déchirer. || [remove violently] arracher. **3** vi se déchirer.

RIP (abbr of **rest in peace**) qu'il/elle repose en paix.

ripe [raɪp] adj mûr(e).

ripen ['raɪpn] vt & vi mûrir.

rip-off n inf: **that's a ~!** c'est de l'escroquerie OR de l'arnaque!

ripple ['rɪpl] **1** n ondulation f, ride f; **a ~ of applause** des applaudissements discrets. **2** vt rider.

rise [raɪz] (*pt* **rose**, *pp* **risen** ['rɪzn]) **1** *n* [to power, fame] ascension *f*. ‖ [slope] côte *f*, pente *f*. ‖ *phr*: **to give ~ to** donner lieu à. **2** *vi* [move upwards] s'élever, monter; **to ~ to power** arriver au pouvoir; **to ~ to fame** devenir célèbre; **to ~ to a challenge/to the occasion** se montrer à la hauteur d'un défi/de la situation. ‖ [from chair, bed] se lever. ‖ [increase - gen] monter, augmenter; [- voice, level] s'élever. ‖ [rebel] se soulever.

rising ['raɪzɪŋ] **1** *adj* [ground, tide] montant(e). ‖ [prices, inflation, temperature] en hausse. ‖ [star, politician etc] à l'avenir prometteur. **2** *n* [revolt] soulèvement *m*.

risk [rɪsk] **1** *n* risque *m*, danger *m*; **at one's own ~** à ses risques et périls; **to take a ~** prendre un risque; **at ~** en danger. **2** *vt* [health, life etc] risquer; **to ~ doing sthg** courir le risque de faire qqch.

risky ['rɪskɪ] *adj* risqué(e).

risqué ['riːskeɪ] *adj* risqué(e), osé(e).

rite [raɪt] *n* rite *m*.

ritual ['rɪtʃʊəl] **1** *adj* rituel(elle). **2** *n* rituel *m*.

rival ['raɪvl] **1** *adj* rival(e), concurrent(e). **2** *n* rival *m*, -e *f*. **3** *vt* rivaliser avec.

rivalry ['raɪvlrɪ] *n* rivalité *f*.

river ['rɪvə*r*] *n* rivière *f*, fleuve *m*.

river bank *n* berge *f*, rive *f*.

riverbed ['rɪvəbed] *n* lit *m* (de rivière OR de fleuve).

riverside ['rɪvəsaɪd] *n*: **the ~** le bord de la rivière OR du fleuve.

rivet ['rɪvɪt] **1** *n* rivet *m*. **2** *vt* [fasten with rivets] river, riveter. ‖ *fig* [fascinate]: **to be ~ed by** être fasciné(e) par.

Riviera [ˌrɪvɪ'eərə] *n*: **the French ~** la Côte d'Azur; **the Italian ~** la Riviera italienne.

road [rəʊd] *n* route *f*; [small] chemin *m*; [in town] rue *f*; **by ~** par la route; **on the ~ to** *fig* sur le chemin de.

roadblock ['rəʊdblɒk] *n* barrage *m* routier.

road hog *n inf pej* chauffard *m*.

road map *n* carte *f* routière.

road safety *n* sécurité *f* routière.

roadside ['rəʊdsaɪd] *n*: **the ~** le bord de la route.

road sign *n* panneau *m* routier OR de signalisation.

road tax *n* ≃ vignette *f*.

roadway ['rəʊdweɪ] *n* chaussée *f*.

road works [-wɜːks] *npl* travaux *mpl* (de réfection des routes).

roadworthy ['rəʊdˌwɜːðɪ] *adj* en bon état de marche.

roam [rəʊm] **1** *vt* errer dans. **2** *vi* errer.

roar [rɔː*r*] **1** *vi* [person, lion] rugir; [wind] hurler; [car] gronder; [plane] vrombir; **to ~ with laughter** se tordre de rire. **2** *vt* hurler. **3** *n* [of person, lion] rugissement *m*; [of traffic] grondement *m*; [of plane, engine] vrombissement *m*.

roaring ['rɔːrɪŋ] *adj*: **a ~ fire** une belle flambée; **~ drunk** complètement saoul(e); **to do a ~ trade** faire des affaires en or.

roast [rəʊst] **1** *adj* rôti(e). **2** *n* rôti *m*. **3** *vt* [meat, potatoes] rôtir. ‖ [coffee, nuts etc] griller.

roast beef *n* rôti *m* de bœuf, rosbif *m*.

rob [rɒb] *vt* [person] voler; [bank] dévaliser; **to ~ sb of sthg** [money, goods] voler OR dérober qqch à qqn; [opportunity, glory] enlever qqch à qqn.

robber ['rɒbə*r*] *n* voleur *m*, -euse *f*.

robbery ['rɒbərɪ] *n* vol *m*.

robe [rəʊb] *n* [gen] robe *f*. ‖ *Am* [dressing gown] peignoir *m*.

robin ['rɒbɪn] *n* rouge-gorge *m*.

robot ['rəʊbɒt] *n* robot *m*.

robust [rəʊ'bʌst] *adj* robuste.

rock [rɒk] **1** *n* (*U*) [substance] roche *f*. ‖ [boulder] rocher *m*. ‖ *Am* [pebble] caillou *m*. ‖ [music] rock *m*. **2** *comp* [music, band] de rock. **3** *vt* [baby] bercer; [cradle, boat] balancer. ‖ [shock] secouer. **4** *vi* (se) balancer. ○ **on the rocks** *adv* [drink] avec de la glace OR des glaçons. ‖ [marriage, relationship] près de la rupture.

rock and roll *n* rock *m*, rock and roll *m*.

rock bottom *n*: **to hit ~** toucher le fond. ○ **rock-bottom** *adj* [price] sacrifié(e).

rockery ['rɒkərɪ] *n* rocaille *f*.

rocket ['rɒkɪt] **1** *n* [gen] fusée *f*. ‖ MIL fusée *f*, roquette *f*. **2** *vi* monter en flèche.

rocket launcher [-ˌlɔːntʃə*r*] *n* lance-fusées *m inv*, lance-roquettes *m inv*.

rocking chair ['rɒkɪŋ-] *n* fauteuil *m* à bascule, rocking-chair *m*.

rocking horse ['rɒkɪŋ-] *n* cheval *m* à bascule.

rock'n'roll [ˌrɒkən'rəʊl] = **rock and roll**.

rocky ['rɒkɪ] *adj* [ground, road] rocailleux(euse), caillouteux(euse). ‖ *fig* [economy, marriage] précaire.

Rocky Mountains *npl*: **the ~** les montagnes *fpl* Rocheuses.

rod [rɒd] *n* [metal] tige *f*; [wooden] baguette *f*; **(fishing) ~** canne *f* à pêche.

rode [rəʊd] *pt* → ride.

rodent ['rəʊdənt] *n* rongeur *m*.

roe [rəʊ] *n* (*U*) œufs *mpl* de poisson.

roe deer *n* chevreuil *m*.

rogue [rəʊg] *n* [likeable rascal] coquin *m*. || *dated* [dishonest person] filou *m*, crapule *f*.

role [rəʊl] *n* rôle *m*.

roll [rəʊl] **1** *n* [of material, paper etc] rouleau *m*. || [of bread] petit pain *m*. || [list] liste *f*. || [of drums, thunder] roulement *m*. **2** *vt* rouler; [log, ball etc] faire rouler. **3** *vi* rouler. ○ **roll about**, **roll around** *vi* [person] se rouler; [object] rouler çà et là. ○ **roll over** *vi* se retourner. ○ **roll up 1** *vt sep* [carpet, paper etc] rouler. || [sleeves] retrousser. **2** *vi inf* [arrive] s'amener, se pointer.

roll call *n* appel *m*.

roller ['rəʊlər] *n* rouleau *m*.

roller coaster *n* montagnes *fpl* russes.

roller skate *n* patin *m* à roulettes.

rolling pin *n* rouleau *m* à pâtisserie.

rolling stock *n* matériel *m* roulant.

ROM [rɒm] (*abbr of* read only memory) *n* ROM *f*.

Roman ['rəʊmən] **1** *adj* romain(e). **2** *n* Romain *m*, -e *f*.

Roman Catholic 1 *adj* catholique. **2** *n* catholique *mf*.

romance [rəʊ'mæns] *n* (*U*) [romantic quality] charme *m*. || [love affair] idylle *f*.

Romania [ruː'meɪnjə] *n* Roumanie *f*.

Romanian [ruː'meɪnjən] **1** *adj* roumain(e). **2** *n* [person] Roumain *m*, -e *f*. || [language] roumain *m*.

Roman numerals *npl* chiffres *mpl* romains.

romantic [rəʊ'mæntɪk] *adj* romantique.

Rome [rəʊm] *n* Rome.

romp [rɒmp] **1** *n* ébats *mpl*. **2** *vi* s'ébattre.

roof [ruːf] *n* toit *m*; [of cave, tunnel] plafond *m*; **the ~ of the mouth** la voûte du palais; **to go through** OR **hit the ~** *fig* exploser.

roofing ['ruːfɪŋ] *n* toiture *f*.

roof rack *n* galerie *f*.

rooftop ['ruːftɒp] *n* toit *m*.

rook [rʊk] *n* [bird] freux *m*. || [chess piece] tour *f*.

rookie ['rʊkɪ] *n Am inf* bleu *m*.

room [ruːm, rʊm] *n* [in building] pièce *f*. || [bedroom] chambre *f*. || (*U*) [space] place *f*.

rooming house ['ruːmɪŋ-] *n Am* maison *f* de rapport.

roommate ['ruːmmeɪt] *n* camarade *mf* de chambre.

room service *n* service *m* dans les chambres.

roomy ['ruːmɪ] *adj* spacieux(ieuse).

roost [ruːst] **1** *n* perchoir *m*, juchoir *m*. **2** *vi* se percher, se jucher.

rooster ['ruːstər] *n* coq *m*.

root [ruːt] **1** *n* racine *f*; *fig* [of problem] origine *f*; **to take ~** *lit & fig* prendre racine. **2** *vi*: **to ~ through** fouiller dans. ○ **roots** *npl* racines *fpl*. ○ **root for** *vt fus Am inf* encourager. ○ **root out** *vt sep* [eradicate] extirper.

rope [rəʊp] **1** *n* corde *f*; **to know the ~s** connaître son affaire, être au courant. **2** *vt* corder; [climbers] encorder. ○ **rope in** *vt sep inf fig* enrôler.

rosary ['rəʊzərɪ] *n* rosaire *m*.

rose [rəʊz] **1** *pt* → **rise**. **2** *adj* [pink] rose. **3** *n* [flower] rose *f*.

rosé ['rəʊzeɪ] *n* rosé *m*.

rosebud ['rəʊzbʌd] *n* bouton *m* de rose.

rose bush *n* rosier *m*.

rosemary ['rəʊzmərɪ] *n* romarin *m*.

rosette [rəʊ'zet] *n* rosette *f*.

roster ['rɒstər] *n* liste *f*, tableau *m*.

rostrum ['rɒstrəm] (*pl* -trums OR -tra [-trə]) *n* tribune *f*.

rosy ['rəʊzɪ] *adj* rose.

rot [rɒt] **1** *n* (*U*) [decay] pourriture *f*. **2** *vt & vi* pourrir.

rota ['rəʊtə] *n* liste *f*, tableau *m*.

rotary ['rəʊtərɪ] **1** *adj* rotatif(ive). **2** *n Am* [roundabout] rond-point *m*.

rotate [rəʊ'teɪt] **1** *vt* [turn] faire tourner. **2** *vi* [turn] tourner.

rotation [rəʊ'teɪʃn] *n* [turning movement] rotation *f*.

rote [rəʊt] *n*: **by ~** de façon machinale, par cœur.

rotten ['rɒtn] *adj* [decayed] pourri(e). || *inf* [bad] moche. || *inf* [unwell]: **to feel ~** se sentir mal fichu(e).

rouge [ruːʒ] *n* rouge *m* à joues.

rough [rʌf] **1** *adj* [not smooth - surface] rugueux(euse), rêche; [- road] accidenté(e); [- sea] agité(e), houleux(euse); [- crossing] mauvais(e). || [person, treatment] brutal(e); [manners, conditions] rude; [area] mal fréquenté(e). || [guess] approximatif(ive); **~ copy**, **~ draft**

brouillon *m*; ~ **sketch** ébauche *f.* || [harsh - voice, wine] âpre; [- life] dur(e); **to have a ~ time** en baver. **2** *adv*: **to sleep ~** coucher à la dure. **3** *n* GOLF rough *m.* || [undetailed form]: **in ~** au brouillon. **4** *vt phr*: **to ~ it** vivre à la dure.

roughage ['rʌfɪdʒ] *n* (U) fibres *fpl* alimentaires.

rough and ready *adj* rudimentaire.

roughen ['rʌfn] *vt* rendre rugueux(euse) OR rêche.

roughly ['rʌflɪ] *adv* [approximately] approximativement. || [handle, treat] brutalement. || [built, made] grossièrement.

roulette [ru:'let] *n* roulette *f.*

round [raund] **1** *adj* rond(e). **2** *prep* autour de; ~ **here** par ici; **all ~ the country** dans tout le pays; **just ~ the corner** au coin de la rue; *fig* tout près; **to go ~ sthg** [obstacle] contourner qqch; **to go ~ a museum** visiter un musée. **3** *adv* [surrounding]: **all ~** tout autour. || [near]: ~ **about** dans le coin. || [in measurements]: **10 metres ~** 10 mètres de diamètre. || [to other side]: **to go ~** faire le tour; **to turn ~** se retourner; **to look ~** se retourner (pour regarder). || [at or to nearby place]: **come ~ and see us** venez OR passez nous voir; **he's ~ at her house** il est chez elle. || [approximately]: ~ **(about)** vers, environ. **4** *n* [of talks etc] série *f*; **a ~ of applause** une salve d'applaudissements. || [of competition] manche *f.* || [of doctor] visites *fpl*; [of postman, milkman] tournée *f.* || [of ammunition] cartouche *f.* || [of drinks] tournée *f.* || BOXING reprise *f*, round *m.* || GOLF partie *f.* **5** *vt* [corner] tourner; [bend] prendre. ○ **rounds** *npl* [of doctor] visites *fpl.* ○ **round off** *vt sep* terminer, conclure. ○ **round up** *vt sep* [gather together] rassembler. || MATH arrondir.

roundly ['raundlɪ] *adv* [beaten] complètement; [condemned etc] franchement, carrément.

round-shouldered [-'ʃəuldəd] *adj* voûté(e).

round trip *n* aller et retour *m.*

roundup ['raundʌp] *n* [summary] résumé *m.*

rouse [rauz] *vt* [wake up] réveiller. || [impel]: **to ~ o.s. to do sthg** se forcer à faire qqch; **to ~ sb to action** pousser OR inciter qqn à agir. || [emotions] susciter, provoquer.

rousing ['rauzɪŋ] *adj* [speech] vibrant(e), passionné(e); [welcome] enthousiaste.

rout [raut] **1** *n* déroute *f.* **2** *vt* mettre en déroute.

route [ru:t] **1** *n* [gen] itinéraire *m.* || *fig* [way] chemin *m*, voie *f.* **2** *vt* [goods] acheminer.

route map *n* [for journey] croquis *m* d'itinéraire; [for buses, trains] carte *f* du réseau.

routine [ru:'ti:n] **1** *adj* [normal] habituel(elle), de routine. || *pej* [uninteresting] de routine. **2** *n* routine *f.*

roving ['rəuvɪŋ] *adj* itinérant(e).

row[1] [rəu] **1** *n* [line] rangée *f*; [of seats] rang *m.* || *fig* [of defeats, victories] série *f*; **in a ~** d'affilée, de suite. **2** *vt* [boat] faire aller à la rame; [person] transporter en canot OR bateau. **3** *vi* ramer.

row[2] [rau] **1** *n* [quarrel] dispute *f*, querelle *f.* || *inf* [noise] vacarme *m*, raffut *m.* **2** *vi* [quarrel] se disputer, se quereller.

rowboat ['rəubəut] *n Am* canot *m.*

rowdy ['raudɪ] *adj* chahuteur(euse), tapageur(euse).

row house [rəu-] *n Am* maison attenante aux maisons voisines.

rowing ['rəuɪŋ] *n* SPORT aviron *m.*

royal ['rɔɪəl] *adj* royal(e).

Royal Air Force *n*: **the ~** l'armée *f* de l'air britannique.

royal family *n* famille *f* royale.

Royal Navy *n*: **the ~** la marine de guerre britannique.

royalty ['rɔɪəltɪ] *n* royauté *f.* ○ **royalties** *npl* droits *mpl* d'auteur.

RSVP (*abbr of* **répondez s'il vous plaît**) RSVP.

rub [rʌb] **1** *vt* frotter; **to ~ sthg in** [cream etc] faire pénétrer qqch (en frottant); **to ~ sb up the wrong way** Br, **to ~ sb the wrong way** Am *fig* prendre qqn à rebrousse-poil. **2** *vi* frotter. ○ **rub off on** *vt fus* [subj: quality] déteindre sur. ○ **rub out** *vt sep* [erase] effacer.

rubber ['rʌbə[r]] **1** *adj* en caoutchouc. **2** *n* [substance] caoutchouc *m.* || *Am inf* [condom] préservatif *m.* || [in bridge] robre *m*, rob *m.*

rubber band *n* élastique *m.*

rubber stamp *n* tampon *m.* ○ **rubber-stamp** *vt fig* approuver sans discussion.

rubbish ['rʌbɪʃ] **1** *n* (U) [refuse] détritus *mpl*, ordures *fpl.* || *inf fig* [worthless objects] camelote *f*; **the play was ~** la pièce était nulle. || *inf* [nonsense] bêtises *fpl*, inepties *fpl.* **2** *vt inf* débiner.

rubble ['rʌbl] *n* (U) décombres *mpl.*

ruby ['ru:bɪ] n rubis m.

rucksack ['rʌksæk] n sac m à dos.

rudder ['rʌdər] n gouvernail m.

ruddy ['rʌdɪ] adj [complexion, face] coloré(e). || Br inf dated [damned] sacré(e).

rude [ru:d] adj [impolite - gen] impoli(e); [- word] grossier(ière); [- noise] incongru(e). || [sudden]: **it was a ~ awakening** le réveil fut pénible.

rudimentary [,ru:dɪ'mentərɪ] adj rudimentaire.

rueful ['ru:fʊl] adj triste.

ruffian ['rʌfjən] n voyou m.

ruffle ['rʌfl] vt [hair] ébouriffer; [water] troubler. || [person] froisser; [composure] faire perdre.

rug [rʌg] n [carpet] tapis m. || [blanket] couverture f.

rugby ['rʌgbɪ] n rugby m.

rugged ['rʌgɪd] adj [landscape] accidenté(e); [features] rude.

ruin ['ru:ɪn] 1 n ruine f. 2 vt ruiner; [clothes, shoes] abîmer. ○ **in ruin(s)** adv lit & fig en ruine.

rule [ru:l] 1 n [gen] règle f; **as a ~** en règle générale. || [regulation] règlement m. || (U) [control] autorité f. 2 vt [control] dominer. || [govern] gouverner. || [decide]: **to ~ (that)** ... décider que ... 3 vi [give decision - gen] décider; [- JUR] statuer. || fml [be paramount] prévaloir. || [king, queen] régner; POL gouverner. ○ **rule out** vt sep exclure, écarter.

ruled [ru:ld] adj [paper] réglé(e).

ruler ['ru:lər] n [for measurement] règle f. || [leader] chef m d'État.

ruling ['ru:lɪŋ] 1 adj au pouvoir. 2 n décision f.

rum [rʌm] n rhum m.

Rumania [ru:'meɪnjə] = Romania.

Rumanian [ru:'meɪnjən] = Romanian.

rumble ['rʌmbl] 1 n [of thunder, traffic] grondement m; [in stomach] gargouillement m. 2 vi [thunder, traffic] gronder; [stomach] gargouiller.

rummage ['rʌmɪdʒ] vi fouiller.

rumour Br, **rumor** Am ['ru:mər] n rumeur f.

rumoured Br, **rumored** Am ['ru:məd] adj: **he is ~ to be very wealthy** le bruit court OR on dit qu'il est très riche.

rump [rʌmp] n [of animal] croupe f. || inf [of person] derrière m.

rump steak n romsteck m.

rumpus ['rʌmpəs] n inf chahut m.

run [rʌn] (pt ran, pp run) 1 n [on foot] course f; **to go for a ~** faire un petit peu de course à pied; **on the ~** en fuite, en cavale. || [in car - for pleasure] tour m; [- journey] trajet m. || [series] suite f, série f; **a ~ of bad luck** une période de déveine; **in the short/long ~** à court/long terme. || THEATRE: **to have a long ~** tenir longtemps l'affiche. || [great demand]: **~ on** ruée f sur. || [in tights] échelle f. || [in cricket, baseball] point m. || [track - for skiing, bobsleigh] piste f. 2 vt [race, distance] courir. || [manage - business] diriger; [- shop, hotel] tenir; [- course] organiser. || [operate] faire marcher. || [car] avoir, entretenir. || [water, bath] faire couler. || [publish] publier. || inf [drive]: **can you ~ me to the station?** tu peux m'amener OR me conduire à la gare? || [move]: **to ~ sthg along/over sthg** passer qqch le long de/sur qqch. 3 vi [on foot] courir. || [pass - road, river, pipe] passer; **to ~ through sthg** traverser qqch. || Am [in election]: **to ~ (for)** être candidat (à). || [operate - machine, factory] marcher; [- engine] tourner; **everything is running smoothly** tout va comme sur des roulettes, tout va bien; **to ~ on sthg** marcher à qqch; **to ~ off sthg** marcher sur qqch. || [bus, train] faire le service; **trains ~ every hour** il y a un train toutes les heures. || [flow] couler; **my nose is running** j'ai le nez qui coule. || [colour] déteindre; [ink] baver. || [continue - contract, insurance policy] être valide; [- THEATRE] se jouer. ○ **run across** vt fus [meet] tomber sur. ○ **run away** vi [flee]: **to ~ away (from)** s'enfuir (de); **to ~ away from home** faire une fugue. ○ **run down** 1 vt sep [in vehicle] renverser. || [criticize] dénigrer. || [production] restreindre; [industry] réduire l'activité de. 2 vi [clock] s'arrêter; [battery] se décharger. ○ **run into** vt fus [encounter - problem] se heurter à; [- person] tomber sur. || [in vehicle] rentrer dans. ○ **run off** 1 vt sep [a copy] tirer. 2 vi: **to ~ off (with)** s'enfuir (avec). ○ **run out** vi [food, supplies] s'épuiser; **time is running out** il ne reste plus beaucoup de temps. || [licence, contract] expirer. ○ **run out of** vt fus manquer de; **to ~ out of petrol** tomber en panne d'essence, tomber en panne sèche. ○ **run over** vt sep renverser. ○ **run through** vt fus [practise] répéter. || [read through] parcourir. ○ **run to** vt fus [amount to] monter à, s'élever à. ○ **run up** vt fus [bill, debt] laisser accumuler. ○ **run up against** vt fus se heurter à. ○

runaway ['rʌnəweɪ] **1** *adj* [train, lorry] fou (folle); [horse] emballé(e); [victory] haut la main; [inflation] galopant(e). **2** *n* fuyard *m*, fugitif *m*, -ive *f*.

rundown ['rʌndaʊn] *n* [report] bref résumé *m*. ○ **run-down** *adj* [building] délabré(e). || [person] épuisé(e).

rung [rʌŋ] **1** *pp* → **ring**. **2** *n* échelon *m*, barreau *m*.

runner ['rʌnə'] *n* [athlete] coureur *m*, -euse *f*. || [of guns, drugs] contrebandier *m*. || [of sledge] patin *m*; [for car seat] glissière *f*; [for drawer] coulisseau *m*.

runner-up (*pl* **runners-up**) *n* second *m*, -e *f*.

running ['rʌnɪŋ] **1** *adj* [argument, battle] continu(e). || [consecutive]: **three weeks ~** trois semaines de suite. || [water] courant(e). **2** *n* (*U*) SPORT course *f*; **to go ~** faire de la course. || [management] direction *f*, administration *f*. || [of machine] marche *f*, fonctionnement *m*. || *phr*: **to be in the ~ (for)** avoir des chances de réussir (dans); **to be out of the ~ (for)** n'avoir aucune chance de réussir (dans).

runny ['rʌnɪ] *adj* [food] liquide. || [nose] qui coule.

run-of-the-mill *adj* banal(e), ordinaire.

runt [rʌnt] *n* avorton *m*.

run-up *n* [preceding time]: **in the ~ to sthg** dans la période qui précède qqch. || SPORT course *f* d'élan.

runway ['rʌnweɪ] *n* piste *f*.

rupture ['rʌptʃə'] *n* rupture *f*.

rural ['rʊərəl] *adj* rural(e).

ruse [ruːz] *n* ruse *f*.

rush [rʌʃ] **1** *n* [hurry] hâte *f*. || [surge] ruée *f*, bousculade *f*; **to make a ~ for sthg** se ruer OR se précipiter vers qqch. || [demand]: **~ (on** OR **for)** ruée *f* (sur). **2** *vt* [hurry - work] faire à la hâte; [- person] bousculer. || [send quickly] transporter OR envoyer d'urgence. || [attack suddenly] prendre d'assaut. **3** *vi* [hurry] se dépêcher; **to ~ into sthg** faire qqch sans réfléchir. || [move quickly, suddenly] se précipiter, se ruer. ○ **rushes** *npl* BOT joncs *mpl*.

rush hour *n* heures *fpl* de pointe OR d'affluence.

rusk [rʌsk] *n* biscotte *f*.

Russia ['rʌʃə] *n* Russie *f*.

Russian ['rʌʃn] **1** *adj* russe. **2** *n* [person] Russe *mf*. || [language] russe *m*.

rust [rʌst] **1** *n* rouille *f*. **2** *vi* se rouiller.

rustic ['rʌstɪk] *adj* rustique.

rustle ['rʌsl] **1** *vt* [paper] froisser. || *Am* [cattle] voler. **2** *vi* [leaves] bruire; [papers] produire un froissement.

rusty ['rʌstɪ] *adj lit & fig* rouillé(e).

rut [rʌt] *n* ornière *f*; **to be in a ~** être prisonnier de la routine.

ruthless ['ruːθlɪs] *adj* impitoyable.

RV *n* *Am* (*abbr of* **recreational vehicle**) camping-car *m*.

rye [raɪ] *n* [grain] seigle *m*.

rye bread *n* pain *m* de seigle.

s (*pl* **ss** OR **s's**), **S** (*pl* **Ss** OR **S's**) [es] *n* [letter] s *m inv*, S *m inv*. ○ **S** (*abbr of* **south**) S.

Sabbath ['sæbəθ] *n*: **the ~** le sabbat.

sabbatical [sə'bætɪkl] *n* année *f* sabbatique.

sabotage ['sæbətɑːʒ] **1** *n* sabotage *m*. **2** *vt* saboter.

saccharin(e) ['sækərɪn] *n* saccharine *f*.

sachet ['sæʃeɪ] *n* sachet *m*.

sack [sæk] **1** *n* [bag] sac *m*.

sacking ['sækɪŋ] *n* [fabric] toile *f* à sac.

sacred ['seɪkrɪd] *adj* sacré(e).

sacrifice ['sækrɪfaɪs] *lit & fig* **1** *n* sacrifice *m*. **2** *vt* sacrifier.

sacrilege ['sækrɪlɪdʒ] *n lit & fig* sacrilège *m*.

sacrosanct ['sækrəʊsæŋkt] *adj* sacrosaint(e).

sad [sæd] *adj* triste.

sadden ['sædn] *vt* attrister, affliger.

saddle ['sædl] **1** *n* selle *f*. **2** *vt* [horse] seller. || *fig* [burden]: **to ~ sb with sthg** coller qqch à qqn.

saddlebag ['sædlbæg] *n* sacoche *f*.

sadistic [sə'dɪstɪk] *adj* sadique.

sadly ['sædlɪ] *adv* [unhappily] tristement. || [unfortunately] malheureusement.

sadness ['sædnɪs] *n* tristesse *f*.

safari [sə'fɑːrɪ] *n* safari *m*.

safe [seɪf] **1** *adj* [not dangerous - gen] sans danger; [- driver, play, guess] prudent(e); **it's ~ to say (that) ...** on peut dire à coup sûr que .... || [not in danger] hors de danger, en sécurité; **~ and sound** sain et sauf (saine et sauve). || [not risky - bet, method] sans risque; [- investment] sûr(e); **to be on the ~ side** par précaution. **2** n coffre-fort m.

safe-conduct n sauf-conduit m.

safe-deposit box n coffre-fort m.

safeguard ['seɪfgɑːd] **1** n: ~ **(against)** sauvegarde f (contre). **2** vt: **to ~ sb/sthg (against)** sauvegarder qqn/qqch (contre), protéger qqn/qqch (contre).

safekeeping [,seɪf'kiːpɪŋ] n bonne garde f.

safely ['seɪflɪ] adv [not dangerously] sans danger. || [not in danger] en toute sécurité, à l'abri du danger. || [arrive - person] à bon port, sain et sauf (saine et sauve); [- parcel] à bon port. || [for certain]: **I can ~ say (that)** ... je peux dire à coup sûr que ....

safe sex n sexe m sans risque, S.S.R. m.

safety ['seɪftɪ] n sécurité f.

safety belt n ceinture f de sécurité.

safety pin n épingle f de sûreté OR de nourrice.

saffron ['sæfrən] n safran m.

sag [sæg] vi [sink downwards] s'affaisser, fléchir.

sage [seɪdʒ] **1** adj sage. **2** n (U) [herb] sauge f. || [wise man] sage m.

Sagittarius [,sædʒɪ'teərɪəs] n Sagittaire m.

Sahara [sə'hɑːrə] n: **the ~ (Desert)** le (désert du) Sahara.

said [sed] pt & pp → say.

sail [seɪl] **1** n [of boat] voile f; **to set ~** faire voile, prendre la mer. || [journey] tour m en bateau. **2** vt [boat] piloter, manœuvrer. || [sea] parcourir. **3** vi [person - gen] aller en bateau; [- SPORT] faire de la voile. || [boat - move] naviguer; [- leave] partir, prendre la mer. || fig [through air] voler. ○ **sail through** vt fus fig réussir les doigts dans le nez.

sailboat Am = sailing boat.

sailing ['seɪlɪŋ] n (U) SPORT voile f; **to go ~** faire de la voile. || [departure] départ m.

sailing boat Br, **sailboat** Am ['seɪlbəʊt] n bateau m à voiles, voilier m.

sailing ship n voilier m.

sailor ['seɪlər] n marin m, matelot m.

saint [seɪnt] n saint m, -e f.

saintly ['seɪntlɪ] adj [person] saint(e); [life] de saint.

sake [seɪk] n: **for the ~ of sb** par égard pour qqn, pour (l'amour de) qqn; **for the ~ of argument** à titre d'exemple; **for God's** OR **heaven's ~** pour l'amour de Dieu OR du ciel.

salad ['sæləd] n salade f.

salad bowl n saladier m.

salad dressing n vinaigrette f.

salami [sə'lɑːmɪ] n salami m.

salary ['sælərɪ] n salaire m, traitement m.

sale [seɪl] n [gen] vente f; **on ~** en vente; **(up) for ~** à vendre. || [at reduced prices] soldes mpl. ○ **sales** npl [quantity sold] ventes fpl. || [at reduced prices]: **the ~s** les soldes mpl.

saleroom Br ['seɪlrʊm], **salesroom** Am ['seɪlzrʊm] n salle f des ventes.

sales assistant ['seɪlz-], **salesclerk** ['seɪlzklɜːrk] Am n vendeur m, -euse f.

salesman ['seɪlzmən] (pl -men [-mən]) n [in shop] vendeur m; [travelling] représentant m de commerce.

salesroom Am = saleroom.

saleswoman ['seɪlz,wʊmən] (pl -women [-,wɪmɪn]) n [in shop] vendeuse f; [travelling] représentante f de commerce.

salient ['seɪljənt] adj fml qui ressort.

saliva [sə'laɪvə] n salive f.

sallow ['sæləʊ] adj cireux(euse).

salmon ['sæmən] (pl inv OR -s) n saumon m.

salmonella [,sælmə'nelə] n salmonelle f.

salon ['sælɒn] n salon m.

saloon [sə'luːn] n Am [bar] saloon m. || [in ship] salon m.

salt [sɔːlt, sɒlt] **1** n sel m. **2** vt [food] saler; [roads] mettre du sel sur.

salt cellar Br, **salt shaker** Am [-,ʃeɪkər] n salière f.

saltwater ['sɔːlt,wɔːtər] **1** n eau f de mer. **2** adj de mer.

salty ['sɔːltɪ] adj [food] salé(e); [water] saumâtre.

salutary ['sæljʊtrɪ] adj salutaire.

salute [sə'luːt] **1** n salut m. **2** vt saluer. **3** vi faire un salut.

salvage ['sælvɪdʒ] **1** n (U) [rescue of ship] sauvetage m. || [property rescued] biens mpl sauvés. **2** vt sauver.

salvation [sæl'veɪʃn] n salut m.

Salvation Army n: **the ~** l'Armée f du Salut.

same [seɪm] **1** adj même; **at the ~ time** en même temps; **one and the ~** un seul et même (une seule et même). **2** *pron*: **the ~** le même (la même), les mêmes (*pl*); **I'll have the ~ as you** je prendrai la même chose que toi; **she earns the ~ as I do** elle gagne autant que moi; **to do the ~** faire de même, en faire autant; **all** OR **just the ~** [anyway] quand même, tout de même; **it's all the ~ to me** ça m'est égal; **it's not the ~** ce n'est pas pareil. **3** *adv*: **the ~** [treat, spelled] de la même manière.

sample ['sɑːmpl] **1** *n* échantillon *m*. **2** *vt* [taste] goûter.

sanatorium (*pl* **-riums** OR **-ria** [-rɪə]), **sanitorium** *Am* (*pl* **-riums** OR **-ria** [-rɪə]) [ˌsænəˈtɔːrɪəm] *n* sanatorium *m*.

sanctimonious [ˌsæŋktɪˈməʊnjəs] *adj* moralisateur(trice).

sanction ['sæŋkʃn] **1** *n* sanction *f*. **2** *vt* sanctionner.

sanctity ['sæŋktətɪ] *n* sainteté *f*.

sanctuary ['sæŋktʃʊərɪ] *n* [for birds, wildlife] réserve *f*. ‖ [refuge] asile *m*.

sand [sænd] **1** *n* sable *m*. **2** *vt* [wood] poncer.

sandal ['sændl] *n* sandale *f*.

sandbox *Am* = **sandpit**.

sandcastle ['sænd,kɑːsl] *n* château *m* de sable.

sand dune *n* dune *f*.

sandpaper ['sænd,peɪpəʳ] **1** *n* (*U*) papier *m* de verre. **2** *vt* poncer (au papier de verre).

sandpit *Br* ['sændpɪt], **sandbox** *Am* ['sændbɒks] *n* bac *m* à sable.

sandstone ['sændstəʊn] *n* grès *m*.

sandwich ['sænwɪdʒ] **1** *n* sandwich *m*. **2** *vt fig*: **to be ~ed between** être (pris(e)) en sandwich entre.

sandwich board *n* panneau *m* publicitaire (*d'homme sandwich ou posé comme un tréteau*).

sandy ['sændɪ] *adj* [beach] de sable; [earth] sableux(euse). ‖ [sand-coloured] sable (*inv*).

sane [seɪn] *adj* [not mad] sain(e) d'esprit. ‖ [sensible] raisonnable, sensé(e).

sang [sæŋ] *pt* → **sing**.

sanitary ['sænɪtrɪ] *adj* [method, system] sanitaire. ‖ [clean] hygiénique, salubre.

sanitary towel, sanitary napkin *Am* *n* serviette *f* hygiénique.

sanitation [ˌsænɪˈteɪʃn] *n* (*U*) [in house] installations *fpl* sanitaires.

sanitorium *Am* = **sanatorium**.

sanity ['sænətɪ] *n* (*U*) [saneness] santé *f* mentale, raison *f*. ‖ [good sense] bon sens *m*.

sank [sæŋk] *pt* → **sink**.

Santa (Claus) ['sæntə,(klɔːz)] *n* le père Noël.

sap [sæp] **1** *n* [of plant] sève *f*. **2** *vt* [weaken] saper.

sapling ['sæplɪŋ] *n* jeune arbre *m*.

sapphire ['sæfaɪəʳ] *n* saphir *m*.

sarcastic [sɑːˈkæstɪk] *adj* sarcastique.

sardine [sɑːˈdiːn] *n* sardine *f*.

Sardinia [sɑːˈdɪnjə] *n* Sardaigne *f*.

sardonic [sɑːˈdɒnɪk] *adj* sardonique.

SASE *abbr of* **self-addressed stamped envelope**.

sash [sæʃ] *n* [of cloth] écharpe *f*.

sat [sæt] *pt & pp* → **sit**.

SAT [sæt] *n* (*abbr of* **Scholastic Aptitude Test**) *examen d'entrée à l'université aux États-Unis*.

Satan ['seɪtn] *n* Satan *m*.

satchel ['sætʃəl] *n* cartable *m*.

satellite ['sætəlaɪt] **1** *n* satellite *m*. **2** *comp* [link] par satellite; **~ dish** antenne *f* parabolique.

satellite TV *n* télévision *f* par satellite.

satin ['sætɪn] **1** *n* satin *m*. **2** *comp* [sheets, pyjamas] de OR en satin; [wallpaper, finish] satiné(e).

satire ['sætaɪəʳ] *n* satire *f*.

satisfaction [ˌsætɪsˈfækʃn] *n* satisfaction *f*.

satisfactory [ˌsætɪsˈfæktərɪ] *adj* satisfaisant(e).

satisfied ['sætɪsfaɪd] *adj* [happy]: **~ (with)** satisfait(e) (de).

satisfy ['sætɪsfaɪ] *vt* [gen] satisfaire. ‖ [convince] convaincre, persuader.

satisfying ['sætɪsfaɪɪŋ] *adj* satisfaisant(e).

satsuma [ˌsætˈsuːmə] *n* satsuma *f*.

saturate ['sætʃəreɪt] *vt*: **to ~ sthg (with)** saturer qqch (de).

Saturday ['sætədɪ] **1** *n* samedi *m*; **it's ~** on est samedi; **on ~** samedi; **on ~s** le samedi; **last ~** samedi dernier; **this ~** ce samedi; **next ~** samedi prochain; **every ~** tous les samedis; **every other ~** un samedi sur deux; **the ~ before** l'autre samedi; **the ~ before last** pas samedi dernier, mais le samedi d'avant; **the ~ after next, ~ week, a week on ~** samedi en huit. **2** *comp* [paper] du OR de samedi; **~ morning/afternoon/evening** samedi matin/après-midi/soir.

sauce [sɔːs] *n* CULIN sauce *f*.

saucepan ['sɔːspən] *n* casserole *f*.

saucer ['sɔːsəʳ] *n* sous-tasse *f*, soucoupe *f*.

saucy ['sɔːsɪ] *adj inf* coquin(e).

Saudi Arabia [,saʊdɪə'reɪbjə] *n* Arabie Saoudite *f*.

Saudi (Arabian) ['saʊdɪ-] **1** *adj* saoudien(ienne). **2** *n* [person] Saoudien *m*, -ienne *f*.

sauna ['sɔːnə] *n* sauna *m*.

saunter ['sɔːntəʳ] *vi* flâner.

sausage ['sɒsɪdʒ] *n* saucisse *f*.

sauté [*Br* 'səʊteɪ, *Am* səʊ'teɪ] (*pt & pp* **sautéed** OR **sautéd**) **1** *adj* sauté(e). **2** *vt* [potatoes] faire sauter; [onions] faire revenir.

savage ['sævɪdʒ] **1** *adj* [fierce] féroce. **2** *n* sauvage *mf*. **3** *vt* attaquer avec férocité.

save [seɪv] **1** *vt* [rescue] sauver; **to ~ sb's life** sauver la vie à OR de qqn. || [time] gagner; [strength] économiser; [food] garder; [money - set aside] mettre de côté; [- spend less] économiser. || [avoid] éviter, épargner; **to ~ sb sthg** épargner qqch à qqn; **to ~ sb from doing sthg** éviter à qqn de faire qqch. || SPORT arrêter. || COMPUT sauvegarder. **2** *vi* [save money] mettre de l'argent de côté. **3** *n* SPORT arrêt *m*. **4** *prep fml*: **~ (for)** sauf, à l'exception de. ○ **save up** *vi* mettre de l'argent de côté.

saving grace ['seɪvɪŋ-] *n*: **it's ~ was ...** ce qui le rachetait, c'était ....

savings ['seɪvɪŋz] *npl* économies *fpl*.

savings account *n Am* compte *m* d'épargne.

savings and loan association *n Am* société *f* de crédit immobilier.

savings bank *n* caisse *f* d'épargne.

saviour *Br*, **savior** *Am* ['seɪvjəʳ] *n* sauveur *m*.

savour *Br*, **savor** *Am* ['seɪvəʳ] *vt lit & fig* savourer.

savoury *Br*, **savory** *Am* ['seɪvərɪ] **1** *adj* [food] salé(e). **2** *n* petit plat *m* salé.

saw [sɔː] (*Br pt* -**ed**, *pp* **sawn**, *Am pt &* *pp* -**ed**) **1** *pt* → **see**. **2** *n* scie *f*. **3** *vt* scier.

sawdust ['sɔːdʌst] *n* sciure *f* (de bois).

sawed-off shotgun *Am* = **sawn-off shotgun**.

sawmill ['sɔːmɪl] *n* scierie *f*.

sawn [sɔːn] *pp Br* → **saw**.

sawn-off shotgun *Br*, **sawed-off shotgun** ['sɔːd-] *Am n* carabine *f* à canon scié.

saxophone ['sæksəfəʊn] *n* saxophone *m*.

say [seɪ] (*pt & pp* **said**) **1** *vt* [gen] dire; **could you ~ that again?** vous pouvez répéter ce que vous venez de dire?; **(let's) ~ you won a lottery ...** supposons que tu gagnes le gros lot ...; **it ~s a lot about him** cela en dit long sur lui; **she's said to be ...** on dit qu'elle est ...; **that goes without ~ing** cela va sans dire; **it has a lot to be said for it** cela a beaucoup d'avantages. || [subj: clock, watch] indiquer. **2** *n*: **to have a/no ~** avoir/ne pas avoir voix au chapitre; **to have a ~ in sthg** avoir son mot à dire sur qqch; **to have one's ~** dire ce que l'on a à dire, dire son mot. ○ **that is to say** *adv* c'est-à-dire.

saying ['seɪɪŋ] *n* dicton *m*.

scab [skæb] *n* [of wound] croûte *f*. || *inf pej* [non-striker] jaune *m*.

scaffold ['skæfəʊld] *n* échafaud *m*.

scaffolding ['skæfəldɪŋ] *n* échafaudage *m*.

scald [skɔːld] **1** *n* brûlure *f*. **2** *vt* ébouillanter.

scale [skeɪl] **1** *n* [gen] échelle *f*; **to ~** [map, drawing] à l'échelle. || [of ruler, thermometer] graduation *f*. || MUS gamme *f*. || [of fish, snake] écaille *f*. || *Am* = **scales**. **2** *vt* [cliff, fence] escalader. || [fish] écailler. ○ **scales** *npl* balance *f*. ○ **scale down** *vt fus* réduire.

scale model *n* modèle *m* réduit.

scallop ['skɒləp] **1** *n* [shellfish] coquille *f* Saint-Jacques. **2** *vt* [edge, garment] festonner.

scalp [skælp] **1** *n* ANAT cuir *m* chevelu. || [trophy] scalp *m*. **2** *vt* scalper.

scalpel ['skælpəl] *n* scalpel *m*.

scamper ['skæmpəʳ] *vi* trottiner.

scampi ['skæmpɪ] *n* (*U*) scampi *mpl*.

scan [skæn] **1** *n* MED scanographie *f*; [during pregnancy] échographie *f*. **2** *vt* [examine carefully] scruter. || [glance at] parcourir. || TECH balayer. || COMPUT faire un scannage de.

scandal ['skændl] *n* [gen] scandale *m*. || [gossip] médisance *f*.

scandalize, -ise ['skændəlaɪz] *vt* scandaliser.

Scandinavia [,skændɪ'neɪvjə] *n* Scandinavie *f*.

Scandinavian [,skændɪ'neɪvjən] **1** *adj* scandinave. **2** *n* [person] Scandinave *mf*.

scant [skænt] *adj* insuffisant(e).

scanty ['skæntɪ] *adj* [amount, resources] insuffisant(e); [income] maigre; [dress] minuscule.

scapegoat ['skeɪpgəʊt] *n* bouc *m* émissaire.

scar [skɑːr] *n* cicatrice *f*.

scarce ['skeəs] *adj* rare, peu abondant(e).

scarcely ['skeəslɪ] *adv* à peine; ~ **anyone** presque personne; **I ~ ever go there now** je n'y vais presque OR pratiquement plus jamais.

scare [skeər] **1** *n* [sudden fear]: **to give sb a ~** faire peur à qqn. || [public fear] panique *f*; **bomb ~** alerte *f* à la bombe. **2** *vt* faire peur à, effrayer. ○ **scare away**, **scare off** *vt sep* faire fuir.

scarecrow ['skeəkrəʊ] *n* épouvantail *m*.

scared ['skeəd] *adj* apeuré(e); **to be ~** avoir peur; **to be ~ stiff** OR **to death** être mort de peur.

scarf [skɑːf] (*pl* -**s** OR **scarves**) *n* [wool] écharpe *f*; [silk etc] foulard *m*.

scarlet ['skɑːlət] **1** *adj* écarlate. **2** *n* écarlate *f*.

scarves [skɑːvz] *pl* → **scarf**.

scathing ['skeɪðɪŋ] *adj* [criticism] acerbe; [reply] cinglant(e).

scatter ['skætər] **1** *vt* [clothes, paper etc] éparpiller; [seeds] semer à la volée. **2** *vi* se disperser.

scatterbrained ['skætəbreɪnd] *adj inf* écervelé(e).

scavenger ['skævɪndʒər] *n* [animal] animal *m* nécrophage. || [person] personne *f* qui fait les poubelles.

scenario [sɪ'nɑːrɪəʊ] (*pl* -**s**) *n* [possible situation] hypothèse *f*, scénario *m*. || [of film, play] scénario *m*.

scene [siːn] *n* [in play, film, book] scène *f*; **behind the ~s** dans les coulisses. || [sight] spectacle *m*, vue *f*; [picture] tableau *m*. || [location] lieu *m*, endroit *m*. || [area of activity]: **the political ~** la scène politique; **the music ~** le monde de la musique. || *phr*: **to set the ~ for sthg** préparer la voie à qqch.

scenery ['siːnərɪ] *n* (*U*) [of countryside] paysage *m*. || THEATRE décor *m*, décors *mpl*.

scenic ['siːnɪk] *adj* [tour] touristique; **a ~ view** un beau panorama.

scent [sent] *n* [smell - of flowers] senteur *f*, parfum *m*; [- of animal] odeur *f*, fumet *m*. || (*U*) [perfume] parfum *m*.

scepter *Am* = **sceptre**.

sceptic *Br*, **skeptic** *Am* ['skeptɪk] *n* sceptique *mf*.

sceptical *Br*, **skeptical** *Am* ['skeptɪkl] *adj*: ~ **(about)** sceptique (sur).

sceptre *Br*, **scepter** *Am* ['septər] *n* sceptre *m*.

schedule [*Br* 'ʃedjuːl, *Am* 'skedʒʊl] **1** *n* [plan] programme *m*, plan *m*; **on ~** [at expected time] à l'heure (prévue); [on expected day] à la date prévue; **ahead of/behind ~** en avance/en retard (sur le programme). || [list - of times] horaire *m*; [- of prices] tarif *m*. **2** *vt*: **to ~ sthg (for)** prévoir qqch (pour).

scheduled flight [*Br* 'ʃedjuːld-, *Am* 'skedʒʊld-] *n* vol *m* régulier.

scheme [skiːm] **1** *n* [plan] plan *m*, projet *m*. || *pej* [dishonest plan] combine *f*. || [arrangement] arrangement *m*; **colour ~** combinaison *f* de couleurs. **2** *vi pej* conspirer.

scheming ['skiːmɪŋ] *adj* intrigant(e).

schism ['sɪzm, 'skɪzm] *n* schisme *m*.

schizophrenic [,skɪtsə'frenɪk] **1** *adj* schizophrène. **2** *n* schizophrène *mf*.

scholar ['skɒlər] *n* [expert] érudit *m*, -e *f*, savant *m*, -e *f*.

scholarship ['skɒləʃɪp] *n* [grant] bourse *f* (d'études). || [learning] érudition *f*.

school [skuːl] *n* [gen] école *f*; [secondary school] lycée *m*, collège *m*. || [university department] faculté *f*. || *Am* [university] université *f*.

school age *n* âge *m* scolaire.

schoolbook ['skuːlbʊk] *n* livre *m* scolaire OR de classe.

schoolboy ['skuːlbɔɪ] *n* écolier *m*, élève *m*.

schoolchild ['skuːltʃaɪld] (*pl* -**children** [-tʃɪldrən]) *n* écolier *m*, -ière *f*, élève *mf*.

schooldays ['skuːldeɪz] *npl* années *fpl* d'école.

schoolgirl ['skuːlgɜːl] *n* écolière *f*, élève *f*.

schooling ['skuːlɪŋ] *n* instruction *f*.

schoolmaster ['skuːl,mɑːstər] *n* [primary] instituteur *m*, maître *m* d'école; [secondary] professeur *m*.

schoolmistress ['skuːl,mɪstrɪs] *n* [primary] institutrice *f*, maîtresse *f* d'école; [secondary] professeur *m*.

schoolteacher ['skuːl,tiːtʃər] *n* [primary] instituteur *m*, -trice *f*; [secondary] professeur *m*.

school year *n* année *f* scolaire.

schooner ['skuːnər] *n* [ship] schooner *m*, goélette *f*.

sciatica [saɪ'ætɪkə] *n* sciatique *f*.

science ['saɪəns] *n* science *f*.

science fiction n science-fiction f.

scientific [ˌsaɪən'tɪfɪk] adj scientifique.

scientist ['saɪəntɪst] n scientifique mf.

scintillating ['sɪntɪleɪtɪŋ] adj brillant(e).

scissors ['sɪzəz] npl ciseaux mpl.

sclerosis [sklɪ'rəʊsɪs] → **multiple sclerosis.**

scoff [skɒf] vi: to ~ (at) se moquer (de).

scold [skəʊld] vt gronder, réprimander.

scone [skɒn] n scone m.

scoop [skuːp] **1** n [for sugar] pelle f à main; [for ice cream] cuiller f à glace. || [of ice cream] boule f. || [news report] exclusivité f, scoop m. **2** vt [with hands] prendre avec les mains; [with scoop] prendre avec une pelle à main. ○ **scoop out** vt sep évider.

scooter ['skuːtə^r] n [toy] trottinette f. || [motorcycle] scooter m.

scope [skəʊp] n (U) [opportunity] occasion f, possibilité f. || [of report, inquiry] étendue f, portée f.

scorch [skɔːtʃ] vt [clothes] brûler légèrement, roussir; [land, grass] dessécher.

scorching ['skɔːtʃɪŋ] adj inf [day] torride; [sun] brûlant(e).

score [skɔː^r] **1** n SPORT score m. || [in test] note f. || dated [twenty] vingt. || MUS partition f. || [subject]: **on that ~** à ce sujet, sur ce point. **2** vt [goal, point etc] marquer; **to ~ 100%** avoir 100 sur 100. || [success, victory] remporter. || [cut] entailler. **3** vi SPORT marquer (un but/point etc).

scoreboard ['skɔːbɔːd] n tableau m.

scorer ['skɔːrə^r] n marqueur m.

scorn [skɔːn] **1** n (U) mépris m, dédain m. **2** vt [person, attitude] mépriser. || [help, offer] rejeter, dédaigner.

scornful ['skɔːnfʊl] adj méprisant(e); **to be ~ of sthg** mépriser qqch, dédaigner qqch.

Scorpio ['skɔːpɪəʊ] (pl -s) n Scorpion m.

scorpion ['skɔːpjən] n scorpion m.

Scot [skɒt] n Écossais m, -e f.

scotch [skɒtʃ] vt [rumour] étouffer; [plan] faire échouer.

Scotch [skɒtʃ] **1** adj écossais(e). **2** n scotch m, whisky m.

Scotch (tape)® n Am Scotch® m.

scot-free adj inf: **to get off ~** s'en tirer sans être puni(e).

Scotland ['skɒtlənd] n Écosse f.

Scots [skɒts] **1** adj écossais(e). **2** n [dialect] écossais m.

Scotsman ['skɒtsmən] (pl -men [-mən]) n Écossais m.

Scotswoman ['skɒtswʊmən] (pl -women [-ˌwɪmɪn]) n Écossaise f.

Scottish ['skɒtɪʃ] adj écossais(e).

scoundrel ['skaʊndrəl] n dated gredin m.

scour [skaʊə^r] vt [clean] récurer. || [search - town etc] parcourir; [- countryside] battre.

scout [skaʊt] n MIL éclaireur m. ○ **Scout** n [boy scout] Scout m. ○ **scout around** vi: to ~ around (for) aller à la recherche (de).

scowl [skaʊl] **1** n regard m noir. **2** vi se renfrogner, froncer les sourcils; **to ~ at sb** jeter des regards noirs à qqn.

scrabble ['skræbl] vi [scrape]: **to ~ at sthg** gratter qqch. || [feel around]: **to ~ around for sthg** tâtonner pour trouver qqch.

scramble ['skræmbl] **1** n [rush] bousculade f, ruée f. **2** vi [climb]: **to ~ up a hill** grimper une colline en s'aidant des mains OR à quatre pattes. || [compete]: **to ~ for sthg** se disputer qqch.

scrambled eggs ['skræmbld-] npl œufs mpl brouillés.

scrap [skræp] **1** n [of paper, material] bout m; [of information] fragment m. || [metal] ferraille f. || inf [fight, quarrel] bagarre f. **2** vt [car] mettre à la ferraille; [plan, system] abandonner, laisser tomber. ○ **scraps** npl [food] restes mpl.

scrapbook ['skræpbʊk] n album m (de coupures de journaux etc).

scrap dealer n ferrailleur m, marchand m de ferraille.

scrape [skreɪp] **1** n [scraping noise] raclement m, grattement m. || dated [difficult situation]: **to get into a ~** se fourrer dans le pétrin. **2** vt [clean, rub] gratter, racler; **to ~ sthg off sthg** enlever qqch de qqch en grattant OR raclant. || [surface, car, skin] érafler. **3** vi gratter. ○ **scrape through** vt fus réussir de justesse.

scraper ['skreɪpə^r] n grattoir m, racloir m.

scrap paper Br, **scratch paper** Am n (papier m) brouillon m.

scrapyard ['skræpjɑːd] n parc m à ferraille.

scratch [skrætʃ] **1** n [wound] égratignure f, éraflure f. || [on glass, paint etc] éraflure f. || phr: **to be up to ~** être à la hauteur; **to do sthg from ~** faire qqch à partir de rien. **2** vt [wound] écorcher, égratigner. || [mark - paint, glass etc] rayer, érafler. || [rub] gratter. 3 *vi* gratter; [person] se gratter.

scratch paper *Am* = scrap paper.

scrawl [skrɔːl] 1 *n* griffonnage *m*, gribouillage *m*. 2 *vt* griffonner, gribouiller.

scrawny ['skrɔːnɪ] *adj* [person] efflanqué(e); [body, animal] décharné(e).

scream [skriːm] 1 *n* [cry] cri *m* perçant, hurlement *m*; [of laughter] éclat *m*. 2 *vt* hurler. 3 *vi* [cry out] crier, hurler.

screech [skriːtʃ] 1 *n* [cry] cri *m* perçant. || [of tyres] crissement *m*. 2 *vt* hurler. 3 *vi* [cry out] pousser des cris perçants. || [tyres] crisser.

screen [skriːn] 1 *n* [gen] écran *m*. || [panel] paravent *m*. 2 *vt* CINEMA projeter, passer; TV téléviser, passer. || [hide] cacher, masquer. || [shield] protéger. || [candidate, employee] passer au crible, filtrer.

screening ['skriːnɪŋ] *n* CINEMA projection *f*; TV passage *m* à la télévision. || [for security] sélection *f*, tri *m*. || MED dépistage *m*.

screenplay ['skriːnpleɪ] *n* scénario *m*.

screw [skruː] 1 *n* [for fastening] vis *f*. 2 *vt* [fix with screws]: **to ~ sthg to sthg** visser qqch à OR sur qqch. || [twist] visser. 3 *vi* se visser. ○ **screw up** *vt sep* [crumple up] froisser, chiffonner. || [eyes] plisser; [face] tordre. || *v inf* [ruin] gâcher, bousiller.

screwdriver ['skruː,draɪvər] *n* [tool] tournevis *m*.

scribble ['skrɪbl] 1 *n* gribouillage *m*, griffonnage *m*. 2 *vt & vi* gribouiller, griffonner.

script [skrɪpt] *n* [of play, film etc] scénario *m*, script *m*.

Scriptures ['skrɪptʃəz] *npl*: **the ~** les (Saintes) Écritures *fpl*.

scriptwriter ['skrɪpt,raɪtər] *n* scénariste *mf*.

scroll [skrəʊl] 1 *n* rouleau *m*. 2 *vt* COMPUT faire défiler.

scrounge [skraʊndʒ] *inf vt*: **to ~ money off sb** taper qqn; **can I ~ a cigarette off you?** je peux te piquer une cigarette?

scrounger ['skraʊndʒər] *n inf* parasite *m*.

scrub [skrʌb] 1 *n* [rub]: **to give sthg a ~** nettoyer qqch à la brosse. || (*U*) [undergrowth] broussailles *fpl*. 2 *vt* [floor, clothes etc] laver OR nettoyer à la brosse; [hands, back] frotter; [saucepan] récurer.

scruff [skrʌf] *n*: **by the ~ of the neck** par la peau du cou.

scruffy ['skrʌfɪ] *adj* mal soigné(e), débraillé(e).

scruples ['skruːplz] *npl* scrupules *mpl*.

scrutinize, -ise ['skruːtɪnaɪz] *vt* scruter, examiner attentivement.

scrutiny ['skruːtɪnɪ] *n* (*U*) examen *m* attentif.

scuff [skʌf] *vt* [damage] érafler. || [drag]: **to ~ one's feet** traîner les pieds.

scuffle ['skʌfl] *n* bagarre *f*, échauffourée *f*.

sculptor ['skʌlptər] *n* sculpteur *m*.

sculpture ['skʌlptʃər] 1 *n* sculpture *f*. 2 *vt* sculpter.

scum [skʌm] *n* (*U*) [froth] écume *f*, mousse *f*. || *v inf pej* [person] salaud *m*. || (*U*) *v inf pej* [people] déchets *mpl*.

scupper ['skʌpər] *vt* NAUT couler.

scurrilous ['skʌrələs] *adj* calomnieux(ieuse).

scurry ['skʌrɪ] *vi* se précipiter; **to ~ away** OR **off** se sauver, détaler.

scuttle ['skʌtl] 1 *n* seau *m* à charbon. 2 *vi* courir précipitamment OR à pas précipités.

scythe [saɪð] *n* faux *f*.

sea [siː] 1 *n* [gen] mer *f*; **at ~** en mer; **by the ~** par mer; **by the ~** au bord de la mer; **out to ~** au large. || *phr*: **to be all at ~** nager complètement. 2 *comp* [voyage] en mer; [animal] marin(e), de mer.

seabed ['siːbed] *n*: **the ~** le fond de la mer.

sea breeze *n* brise *f* de mer.

seafood ['siːfuːd] *n* (*U*) fruits *mpl* de mer.

seafront ['siːfrʌnt] *n* front *m* de mer.

seagull ['siːgʌl] *n* mouette *f*.

seal [siːl] (*pl inv* OR **-s**) 1 *n* [animal] phoque *m*. || [official mark] cachet *m*, sceau *m*. || [official fastening] cachet *m*. 2 *vt* [envelope] coller, fermer. || [document, letter] sceller, cacheter. || [block off] obturer, boucher. ○ **seal off** *vt sep* [area, entrance] interdire l'accès de.

sea level *n* niveau *m* de la mer.

sea lion (*pl inv* OR **-s**) *n* otarie *f*.

seam [siːm] *n* SEWING couture *f*. || [of coal] couche *f*, veine *f*.

seaman ['siːmən] (*pl* **-men** [-mən]) *n* marin *m*.

seamy ['siːmɪ] *adj* sordide.

séance ['seɪɒns] *n* séance *f* de spiritisme.

seaplane ['siːpleɪn] *n* hydravion *m*.

seaport ['si:pɔ:t] *n* port *m* de mer.

search [sɜ:tʃ] **1** *n* [of person, luggage, house] fouille *f*; [for lost person, thing] recherche *f*, recherches *fpl*; **in ~ of** à la recherche de. **2** *vt* [house, area, person] fouiller; [memory, mind, drawer] fouiller dans. **3** *vi*: **to ~ (for sb/sthg)** chercher (qqn/qqch).

searching ['sɜ:tʃɪŋ] *adj* [question] poussé(e), approfondi(e); [review, examination] minutieux(ieuse).

searchlight ['sɜ:tʃlaɪt] *n* projecteur *m*.

search party *n* équipe *f* de secours.

search warrant *n* mandat *m* de perquisition.

seashell ['si:ʃel] *n* coquillage *m*.

seashore ['si:ʃɔ:r] *n*: **the ~** le rivage, la plage.

seasick ['si:sɪk] *adj*: **to be** OR **feel ~** avoir le mal de mer.

seaside ['si:saɪd] *n*: **the ~** le bord de la mer.

seaside resort *n* station *f* balnéaire.

season ['si:zn] **1** *n* [gen] saison *f*; **in ~** [food] de saison; **out of ~** [holiday] hors saison; [food] hors de saison. || [of films] cycle *m*. **2** *vt* assaisonner, relever.

seasonal ['si:zənl] *adj* saisonnier(ière).

seasoned ['si:znd] *adj* [traveller, campaigner] chevronné(e), expérimenté(e).

seasoning ['si:zniŋ] *n* assaisonnement *m*.

season ticket *n* carte *f* d'abonnement.

seat [si:t] **1** *n* [gen] siège *m*; [in theatre] fauteuil *m*; **take a ~!** asseyez-vous! || [place to sit - in bus, train] place *f*. || [of trousers] fond *m*. **2** *vt* [sit down] faire asseoir, placer; **please be ~ed** veuillez vous asseoir.

seat belt *n* ceinture *f* de sécurité.

seating ['si:tɪŋ] *n* (*U*) [capacity] sièges *mpl*, places *fpl* (assises).

seawater ['si:,wɔ:tər] *n* eau *f* de mer.

seaweed ['si:wi:d] *n* (*U*) algue *f*.

seaworthy ['si:,wɜ:ðɪ] *adj* en bon état de navigabilité.

sec. *abbr* **of second.**

secede [sɪ'si:d] *vi fml*: **to ~ (from)** se séparer (de), faire sécession (de).

secluded [sɪ'klu:dɪd] *adj* retiré(e), écarté(e).

seclusion [sɪ'klu:ʒn] *n* solitude *f*, retraite *f*.

second ['sekənd] **1** *n* [gen] seconde *f*; **~ (gear)** seconde. **2** *num* deuxième, second(e); **his score was ~ only to hers** il n'y a qu'elle qui a fait mieux que lui OR

qui l'a surpassé; *see also* **sixth. 3** *vt* [proposal, motion] appuyer. ○ **seconds** *npl* COMM articles *mpl* de second choix. || [of food] rabiot *m*.

secondary ['sekəndrɪ] *adj* secondaire.

secondary school *n* école *f* secondaire, lycée *m*.

second-class ['sekənd-] *adj pej* [citizen] de deuxième zone; [product] de second choix. || [ticket] de seconde OR deuxième classe. || [stamp] à tarif réduit.

second-hand ['sekənd-] **1** *adj* [goods, shop] d'occasion. **2** *adv* [not new] d'occasion.

second hand ['sekənd-] *n* [of clock] trotteuse *f*.

secondly ['sekəndlɪ] *adv* deuxièmement, en second lieu.

second-rate ['sekənd-] *adj pej* de deuxième ordre, médiocre.

second thought ['sekənd-] *n*: **to have ~s about sthg** avoir des doutes sur qqch; **on ~s** *Br*, **on ~** *Am* réflexion faite, tout bien réfléchi.

secrecy ['si:krəsɪ] *n* (*U*) secret *m*.

secret ['si:krɪt] **1** *adj* secret(ète). **2** *n* secret *m*; **in ~** en secret.

secretarial [,sekrə'teərɪəl] *adj* [course, training] de secrétariat, de secrétaire; **~ staff** secrétaires *mpl*.

secretary [*Br* 'sekrətrɪ, *Am* 'sekrə,terɪ] *n* [gen] secrétaire *mf*. || POL [minister] ministre *m*.

Secretary of State *n Br*: **~ (for)** ministre *m* (de). || *Am* ≃ ministre *m* des Affaires étrangères.

secretive ['si:krətɪv] *adj* secret(ète), dissimulé(e).

secretly ['si:krɪtlɪ] *adv* secrètement.

sect [sekt] *n* secte *f*.

sectarian [sek'teərɪən] *adj* [killing, violence] d'ordre religieux.

section ['sekʃn] **1** *n* [portion - gen] section *f*, partie *f*; [- of road, pipe] tronçon *m*; [- of document, law] article *m*. || GEOM coupe *f*, section *f*. **2** *vt* sectionner.

sector ['sektər] *n* secteur *m*.

secular ['sekjulər] *adj* [life] séculier(ière); [education] laïque; [music] profane.

secure [sɪ'kjuər] **1** *adj* [fixed - gen] fixe; [- windows, building] bien fermé(e). || [safe - job, future] sûr(e); [- valuable object] en sécurité, en lieu sûr. || [free of anxiety - childhood] sécurisant(e); [- marriage] solide. **2** *vt* [obtain] obtenir. || [fasten - gen] attacher; [- door, window]

bien fermer. || [make safe] assurer la sé-
curité de.

security [sɪˈkjʊərətɪ] n sécurité f.
○ **securities** npl FIN titres mpl, valeurs
fpl.

security guard n garde m de sécurité.

sedan [sɪˈdæn] n Am berline f.

sedate [sɪˈdeɪt] 1 adj posé(e), calme. 2
vt donner un sédatif à.

sedation [sɪˈdeɪʃn] n (U) sédation f;
under ~ sous calmants.

sedative [ˈsedətɪv] n sédatif m, calmant
m.

sediment [ˈsedɪmənt] n sédiment m,
dépôt m.

seduce [sɪˈdjuːs] vt séduire.

seductive [sɪˈdʌktɪv] adj séduisant(e).

see [siː] (pt saw, pp seen) 1 vt [gen]
voir; **~ you!** au revoir! || [accompany]: **I
saw her to the door** je l'ai accompagnée
OR reconduite jusqu'à la porte. || [make
sure]: **to ~ (that)** ... s'assurer que .... 2 vi
voir; **you ~, ...** voyez-vous. ...; **I ~** je vois,
je comprends; **let's ~, let me ~** voyons.
voyons voir. ○ **seeing as, seeing that**
conj inf vu que, étant donné que. ○ **see
about** vt fus [arrange] s'occuper de.
○ **see off** vt sep [say goodbye to] accompagner (pour dire au revoir). ○ **see
through** 1 vt fus [scheme] voir clair
dans; **to ~ through sb** voir dans le jeu de
qqn. 2 vt sep [deal, project] mener à
terme, mener à bien. ○ **see to** vt fus
s'occuper de, se charger de.

seed [siːd] n [of plant] graine f. || SPORT:
fifth ~ joueur classé cinquième m,
joueuse classée cinquième f. ○ **seeds**
npl fig germes mpl, semences fpl.

seedling [ˈsiːdlɪŋ] n jeune plant m, semis m.

seedy [ˈsiːdɪ] adj miteux(euse).

seek [siːk] (pt & pp sought) vt [gen]
chercher; [peace, happiness] rechercher;
to ~ to do sthg chercher à faire qqch. ||
[advice, help] demander.

seem [siːm] 1 vi sembler, paraître; **to ~
sad/tired** avoir l'air triste/fatigué. 2 v
impers: **it ~s (that)** ... il semble OR paraît
que ....

seemingly [ˈsiːmɪŋlɪ] adv apparemment.

seen [siːn] pp → see.

seep [siːp] vi suinter.

seesaw [ˈsiːsɔː] n bascule f.

seethe [siːð] vi [person] bouillir, être fu-
rieux(ieuse). || [place]: **to be seething
with** grouiller de.

see-through adj transparent(e).

segment [ˈsegmənt] n [section] partie f,
section f. || [of fruit] quartier m.

segregate [ˈsegrɪgeɪt] vt séparer.

Seine [seɪn] n: **the (River) ~** la Seine.

seize [siːz] vt [grab] saisir, attraper. ||
[capture] s'emparer de, prendre. || [ar-
rest] arrêter. || fig [opportunity, chance]
saisir, sauter sur. ○ **seize (up)on** vt fus
saisir, sauter sur. ○ **seize up** vi [body]
s'ankyloser. || [engine, part] se gripper.

seizure [ˈsiːʒə^r] n MED crise f, attaque f.
|| (U) [of town] capture f; [of power] prise
f.

seldom [ˈseldəm] adv peu souvent, rarement.

select [sɪˈlekt] 1 adj [carefully chosen]
choisi(e). || [exclusive] de premier ordre,
d'élite. 2 vt sélectionner, choisir.

selection [sɪˈlekʃn] n sélection f, choix
m.

selective [sɪˈlektɪv] adj sélectif(ive);
[person] difficile.

self [self] (pl selves) n moi m; **she's her
old ~ again** elle est redevenue elle-
même.

self-addressed stamped envelope
[-əˌdrestˈstæmpt-] n Am enveloppe f af-
franchie pour la réponse.

self-assured adj sûr(e) de soi, plein(e)
d'assurance.

self-catering adj [holiday - in house] en
maison louée; [- in flat] en appartement
loué.

self-centred [-ˈsentəd] adj égocentrique.

self-confessed [-kənˈfest] adj de son
propre aveu.

self-confident adj sûr(e) de soi,
plein(e) d'assurance.

self-conscious adj timide.

self-contained [-kənˈteɪnd] adj [flat]
indépendant(e), avec entrée particulière;
[person] qui se suffit à soi-même.

self-control n maîtrise f de soi.

self-defence n autodéfense f.

self-discipline n autodiscipline f.

self-employed [-ɪmˈplɔɪd] adj qui travaille à son propre compte.

self-esteem n respect m de soi, estime f
de soi.

self-evident adj qui va de soi, évi-
dent(e).

self-explanatory adj évident(e), qui
ne nécessite pas d'explication.

self-government n autonomie f.

self-important adj suffisant(e).

self-indulgent *adj pej* [person] qui ne se refuse rien; [film, book, writer] nombriliste.

self-interest *n* (*U*) *pej* intérêt *m* personnel.

selfish ['selfɪʃ] *adj* égoïste.

selfishness ['selfɪʃnɪs] *n* égoïsme *m*.

selfless ['selflɪs] *adj* désintéressé(e).

self-made *adj*: ~ **man** self-made-man *m*.

self-pity *n* apitoiement *m* sur soi-même.

self-portrait *n* autoportrait *m*.

self-possessed [-pə'zest] *adj* maître (maîtresse) de soi.

self-raising flour *Br* [-,reɪzɪŋ-], **self-rising flour** *Am* *n* farine *f* avec levure incorporée.

self-reliant *adj* indépendant(e), qui ne compte que sur soi.

self-respect *n* respect *m* de soi.

self-restraint *n* (*U*) retenue *f*, mesure *f*.

self-righteous *adj* satisfait(e) de soi.

self-rising flour *Am* = self-raising flour.

self-sacrifice *n* abnégation *f*.

self-satisfied *adj* suffisant(e), content(e) de soi.

self-service *n* libre-service *m*, self-service *m*.

self-sufficient *adj* autosuffisant(e); to be ~ **in** satisfaire à ses besoins en.

self-taught *adj* autodidacte.

sell [sel] (*pt & pp* **sold**) **1** *vt* [gen] vendre; **to ~ sthg for £100** vendre qqch 100 livres; **to ~ sthg to sb, to ~ sb sthg** vendre qqch à qqn. ‖ *fig* [make acceptable]: **to ~ sthg to sb, to ~ sb sthg** faire accepter qqch à qqn. **2** *vi* [person] vendre. ‖ [product] se vendre; **it ~s for** OR **at £10** il se vend 10 livres. ○ **sell off** *vt sep* vendre, liquider. ○ **sell out 1** *vt sep*: **the performance is sold out** il ne reste plus de places, tous les billets ont été vendus. **2** *vi* [shop]: **we have sold out** on n'en a plus. ‖ [betray one's principles] être infidèle à ses principes.

seller ['selər] *n* vendeur *m*, -euse *f*.

selling price ['selɪŋ-] *n* prix *m* de vente.

sell-out *n*: **the match was a ~** on a joué à guichets fermés.

selves [selvz] *pl* → self.

semaphore ['seməfɔːr] *n* (*U*) signaux *mpl* à bras.

semblance ['sembləns] *n* semblant *m*.

semen ['siːmen] *n* (*U*) sperme *m*, semence *f*.

semester [sɪ'mestər] *n* semestre *m*.

semicircle ['semɪ,sɜːkl] *n* demi-cercle *m*.

semicolon [,semɪ'kəulən] *n* point-virgule *m*.

semidetached [,semɪdɪ'tætʃt] **1** *adj* jumelé(e). **2** *n* *Br* maison *f* jumelée.

semifinal [,semɪ'faɪnl] *n* demi-finale *f*.

seminar ['semɪnɑːr] *n* séminaire *m*.

seminary ['semɪnərɪ] *n* RELIG séminaire *m*.

semiskilled [,semɪ'skɪld] *adj* spécialisé(e).

semolina [,semə'liːnə] *n* semoule *f*.

Senate ['senɪt] *n* POL: **the ~** le sénat; **the United States ~** le Sénat américain.

senator ['senətər] *n* sénateur *m*.

send [send] (*pt & pp* **sent**) *vt* [gen] envoyer; [letter] expédier, envoyer; **to ~ sb sthg, to ~ sthg to sb** envoyer qqch à qqn; **~ her my love** embrasse-la pour moi. ○ **send for** *vt fus* [person] appeler, faire venir. ‖ [by post] commander par correspondance. ○ **send in** *vt sep* [report, application] envoyer, soumettre. ○ **send off** *vt sep* [by post] expédier. ‖ SPORT expulser. ○ **send off for** *vt fus* commander par correspondance.

sender ['sendər] *n* expéditeur *m*, -trice *f*.

send-off *n* fête *f* d'adieu.

senile ['siːnaɪl] *adj* sénile.

senior ['siːnjər] **1** *adj* [highest-ranking] plus haut placé(e). ‖ [higher-ranking]: **~ to sb** d'un rang plus élevé que qqn. ‖ SCH [pupils, classes] grand(e). **2** *n* [older person] aîné *m*, -e *f*. ‖ SCH grand *m*, -e *f*.

senior citizen *n* personne *f* âgée OR du troisième âge.

sensation [sen'seɪʃn] *n* sensation *f*.

sensational [sen'seɪʃənl] *adj* [gen] sensationnel(elle).

sensationalist [sen'seɪʃnəlɪst] *adj pej* à sensation.

sense [sens] **1** *n* [ability, meaning] sens *m*; **to make ~** [have meaning] avoir un sens; **~ of humour** sens de l'humour; **~ of smell** odorat *m*. ‖ [feeling] sentiment *m*. ‖ [wisdom] bon sens *m*, intelligence *f*; **to make ~** [be sensible] être logique. **2** *vt* [feel] sentir. ○ **in a sense** *adv* dans un sens.

senseless ['senslɪs] *adj* [stupid] stupide. ‖ [unconscious] sans connaissance.

sensibilities [,sensɪ'bɪlətɪz] *npl* susceptibilité *f*.

sensible ['sensǝbl] *adj* [reasonable] raisonnable, judicieux(ieuse).

sensitive ['sensɪtɪv] *adj* [gen]: ~ **(to)** sensible (à). || [subject] délicat(e). || [easily offended]: ~ **(about)** susceptible (en ce qui concerne).

sensual ['sensjʊǝl] *adj* sensuel(elle).

sensuous ['sensjʊǝs] *adj* qui affecte les sens.

sent [sent] *pt & pp* → send.

sentence ['sentǝns] **1** *n* GRAMM phrase *f*. || JUR condamnation *f*, sentence *f*. **2** *vt*: to ~ **sb (to)** condamner qqn (à).

sentiment ['sentɪmǝnt] *n* [feeling] sentiment *m*. || [opinion] opinion *f*, avis *m*.

sentimental [ˌsentɪ'mentl] *adj* sentimental(e).

sentry ['sentrɪ] *n* sentinelle *f*.

separate [*adj & n* 'seprǝt, *vb* 'sepǝreɪt] **1** *adj* [not joined]: ~ **(from)** séparé(e) (de). || [individual, distinct] distinct(e). **2** *vt* [gen]: to ~ **sb/sthg (from)** séparer qqn/qqch (de). || [distinguish]: to ~ **sb/ sthg (from)** distinguer qqn/qqch (de). **3** *vi* se séparer; to ~ **into** se diviser OR se séparer en.

separately ['seprǝtlɪ] *adv* séparément.

separation [ˌsepǝ'reɪʃn] *n* séparation *f*.

September [sep'tembǝr] *n* septembre *m*; **in** ~ en septembre; **last** ~ en septembre dernier; **this** ~ en septembre de cette année; **next** ~ en septembre prochain; **by** ~ en septembre, d'ici septembre; **every** ~ tous les ans en septembre; **during** ~ pendant le mois de septembre; **at the beginning of** ~ au début du mois de septembre, début septembre; **at the end of** ~ à la fin du mois de septembre, fin septembre; **in the middle of** ~ au milieu du mois de septembre, à la mi-septembre.

septic ['septɪk] *adj* infecté(e).

septic tank *n* fosse *f* septique.

sequel ['siːkwǝl] *n* [book, film]: ~ **(to)** suite *f* (de). || [consequence]: ~ **(to)** conséquence *f* (de).

sequence ['siːkwǝns] *n* [series] suite *f*, succession *f*. || [order] ordre *m*. || [of film] séquence *f*.

Serb = Serbian.

Serbia ['sɜːbjǝ] *n* Serbie *f*.

Serbian ['sɜːbjǝn], **Serb** [sɜːb] **1** *adj* serbe. **2** *n* [person] Serbe *mf*. || [dialect] serbe *m*.

serene [sɪ'riːn] *adj* [calm] serein(e), tranquille.

sergeant ['sɑːdʒǝnt] *n* MIL sergent *m*. || [in police] brigadier *m*.

sergeant major *n* sergent-major *m*.

serial ['sɪǝrɪǝl] *n* feuilleton *m*.

serial number *n* numéro *m* de série.

series ['sɪǝriːz] (*pl inv*) *n* série *f*.

serious ['sɪǝrɪǝs] *adj* sérieux(ieuse); [illness, accident, trouble] grave.

seriously ['sɪǝrɪǝslɪ] *adv* sérieusement; [ill] gravement; [wounded] grièvement, gravement; **to take sb/sthg** ~ prendre qqn/qqch au sérieux.

seriousness ['sɪǝrɪǝsnɪs] *n* [of mistake, illness] gravité *f*. || [of person, speech] sérieux *m*.

sermon ['sɜːmǝn] *n* sermon *m*.

serrated [sɪ'reɪtɪd] *adj* en dents de scie.

servant ['sɜːvǝnt] *n* domestique *mf*.

serve [sɜːv] **1** *vt* [work for] servir. || [have effect]: to ~ **to do sthg** servir à faire qqch; to ~ **a purpose** [subj: device etc] servir à un usage. || [provide for] desservir. || [meal, drink, customer] servir. || JUR: to ~ **sb with a summons/writ**, to ~ **a summons/writ on sb** signifier une assignation, une citation à qqn. || [prison sentence] purger, faire; [apprenticeship] faire. || SPORT servir. || *phr*: **it ~s him/you right** c'est bien fait pour lui/toi. **2** *vi* servir; to ~ **as** servir de. **3** *n* SPORT service *m*. ○ **serve out, serve up** *vt sep* [food] servir.

service ['sɜːvɪs] **1** *n* [gen] service *m*; **in/out of** ~ en/hors service; **to be of** ~ **(to sb)** être utile (à qqn), rendre service (à qqn). || [of car] révision *f*; [of machine] entretien *m*. **2** *vt* [car] réviser; [machine] assurer l'entretien de. ○ **services** *npl* [on motorway] aire *f* de services. || [armed forces]: **the** ~**s** les forces *fpl* armées.

serviceable ['sɜːvɪsǝbl] *adj* pratique.

service area *n* aire *f* de services.

service charge *n* service *m*.

serviceman ['sɜːvɪsmǝn] (*pl* -**men** [-mǝn]) *n* soldat *m*, militaire *m*.

service station *n* station-service *f*.

serviette [ˌsɜːvɪ'et] *n* serviette *f* (de table).

sesame ['sesǝmɪ] *n* sésame *m*.

session ['seʃn] *n* [gen] séance *f*. || *Am* [school term] trimestre *m*.

set [set] (*pt & pp* **set**) **1** *adj* [fixed - gen] fixe; [- phrase] figé(e). || [ready]: ~ **(for sthg/to do sthg)** prêt(e) (à qqch/à faire qqch). || [determined]: **to be** ~ **on sthg** vouloir absolument qqch; **to be** ~ **on doing sthg** être résolu(e) à faire qqch; **to be dead** ~ **against sthg** s'opposer formellement à qqch. **2** *n* [of keys, tools, golf clubs etc] jeu *m*; [of tyres] train *m*; **a ~ of teeth** [natural] une dentition, une denture; [false] un dentier. || [television, radio] poste *m*. || CINEMA plateau *m*; THEATRE scène *f*. || TENNIS manche *f*, set *m*. **3** *vt* [place] placer, poser, mettre. || [cause to be]: **to ~ sb free** libérer qqn, mettre qqn en liberté; **to ~ sthg on fire** mettre le feu à qqch. || [prepare - trap] tendre; [- table] mettre. || [adjust] régler. || [fix - date, deadline, target] fixer. || [establish - example] donner; [- trend] lancer; [- record] établir. || [homework, task] donner; [problem] poser. || MED [bone, leg] remettre. || [story]: **to be ~** se passer, se dérouler. **4** *vi* [sun] se coucher. || [jelly] prendre; [glue, cement] durcir. ○ **set about** *vt fus* [start] entreprendre, se mettre à; **to ~ about doing sthg** se mettre à faire qqch. ○ **set aside** *vt sep* [save] mettre de côté. || [not consider] rejeter, écarter. ○ **set back** *vt sep* [delay] retarder. ○ **set off 1** *vt sep* [cause] déclencher, provoquer. || [bomb] faire exploser; [firework] faire partir. **2** *vi* se mettre en route, partir. ○ **set out 1** *vt sep* [arrange] disposer. || [explain] présenter, exposer. **2** *vt fus* [intend]: **to ~ out to do sthg** entreprendre OR tenter de faire qqch. **3** *vi* [on journey] se mettre en route, partir. ○ **set up** *vt sep* [organization] créer, fonder; [committee, procedure] constituer, mettre en place; [meeting] arranger, organiser. || [roadblock] placer, installer. || [equipment] préparer, installer. || *inf* [make appear guilty] monter un coup contre.

setback ['setbæk] *n* contretemps *m*, revers *m*.

set menu *n* menu *m* fixe.

settee [se'tiː] *n* canapé *m*.

setting ['setɪŋ] *n* [surroundings] décor *m*, cadre *m*. || [of dial, machine] réglage *m*.

settle ['setl] **1** *vt* [argument] régler; **that's ~d then** (c'est) entendu. || [bill, account] régler, payer. || [calm - nerves] calmer; **to ~ one's stomach** calmer les douleurs d'estomac. **2** *vi* [make one's home] s'installer, se fixer. || [make oneself comfortable] s'installer. || [dust] retomber; [sediment] se déposer; [bird, insect] se poser. ○ **settle down** *vi* [give one's attention]: **to ~ down to sthg/to doing sthg** se mettre à qqch/à faire qqch. || [make oneself comfortable] s'installer. || [become respectable] se ranger. || [become calm] se

calmer. ○ **settle for** *vt fus* accepter, se contenter de. ○ **settle in** *vi* s'adapter. ○ **settle on** *vt fus* [choose] fixer son choix sur, se décider pour. ○ **settle up** *vi*: **to ~ up (with sb)** régler (qqn).

settlement ['setlmənt] *n* [agreement] accord *m*. || [colony] colonie *f*. || [payment] règlement *m*.

settler ['setlər] *n* colon *m*.

seven ['sevn] *num* sept; *see also* **six**.

seventeen [,sevn'tiːn] *num* dix-sept; *see also* **six**.

seventh ['sevnθ] *num* septième; *see also* **sixth**.

seventy ['sevntɪ] *num* soixante-dix; *see also* **sixty**.

sever ['sevər] *vt* [cut through] couper. || *fig* [relationship, ties] rompre.

several ['sevrəl] **1** *adj* plusieurs. **2** *pron* plusieurs *mfpl*.

severance pay *n* indemnité *f* de licenciement.

severe [sɪ'vɪər] *adj* [shock] gros (grosse), dur(e); [pain] violent(e); [illness, injury] grave. || [person, criticism] sévère.

severity [sɪ'verətɪ] *n* [of storm] violence *f*; [of problem, illness] gravité *f*. || [sternness] sévérité *f*.

sew [səʊ] (*Br pp* sewn, *Am pp* sewed OR sewn) *vt* & *vi* coudre. ○ **sew up** *vt sep* [join] recoudre.

sewage ['suːɪdʒ] *n* (*U*) eaux *fpl* d'égout, eaux usées.

sewer ['sʊər] *n* égout *m*.

sewing ['səʊɪŋ] *n* (*U*) [activity] couture *f*. || [work] ouvrage *m*.

sewing machine *n* machine *f* à coudre.

sewn [səʊn] *pp* → **sew**.

sex [seks] *n* [gender] sexe *m*. || (*U*) [sexual intercourse] rapports *mpl* (sexuels); **to have ~ with** avoir des rapports (sexuels) avec.

sexist ['seksɪst] *adj* sexiste.

sexual ['sekʃʊəl] *adj* sexuel(elle).

sexual harassment *n* harcèlement *m* sexuel.

sexual intercourse *n* (*U*) rapports *mpl* (sexuels).

sexy ['seksɪ] *adj inf* sexy (*inv*).

shabby ['ʃæbɪ] *adj* [clothes] élimé(e), râpé(e); [furniture] minable. || [behaviour] moche, méprisable.

shack [ʃæk] *n* cabane *f*, hutte *f*.

shackle ['ʃækl] *vt* enchaîner; *fig* 'entraver. ○ **shackles** *npl* fers *mpl*; *fig* entraves *fpl*.

shade [ʃeɪd] **1** *n* (U) [shadow] ombre *f*. || [lampshade] abat-jour *m* *inv*. || [colour] nuance *f*, ton *m*. || [of meaning, opinion] nuance *f*. **2** *vt* [from light] abriter.

shadow ['ʃædəʊ] *n* ombre *f*.

shadow cabinet *n* cabinet *m* fantôme.

shadowy ['ʃædəʊɪ] *adj* [dark] ombreux(euse). || [sinister] mystérieux (ieuse).

shady ['ʃeɪdɪ] *adj* [garden, street etc] ombragé(e); [tree] qui donne de l'ombre. || *inf* [dishonest] louche.

shaft [ʃɑ:ft] *n* [vertical passage] puits *m*; [of lift] cage *f*. || TECH arbre *m*. || [of light] rayon *m*. || [of tool, golf club] manche *m*.

shaggy ['ʃægɪ] *adj* hirsute.

shake [ʃeɪk] (*pt* **shook**, *pp* **shaken**) **1** *vt* [move vigorously - gen] secouer; [- bottle] agiter; **to ~ hands** se serrer la main; **to ~ one's head** secouer la tête; [to say no] faire non de la tête. || [shock] ébranler, secouer. **2** *vi* trembler. **3** *n* [tremble] tremblement *m*; **to give sthg a ~** secouer qqch. ○ **shake off** *vt sep* [police, pursuers] semer; [illness] se débarrasser de.

shaken ['ʃeɪkn] *pp* → **shake**.

shaky ['ʃeɪkɪ] *adj* [building, table] branlant(e); [hand] tremblant(e); [person] faible; [argument, start] incertain(e).

shall [weak form ʃəl, strong form ʃæl] *aux vb* (*1st person sg & 1st person pl*) (*to express future tense*): **I ~ be ...** je serai .... || (*esp 1st person sg & 1st person pl*) (*in questions*): **~ we have lunch now?** tu veux qu'on déjeune maintenant?; **where ~ I put this?** où est-ce qu'il faut mettre ça? || (*in orders*): **you ~ tell me!** tu vas OR dois me le dire!

shallow ['ʃæləʊ] *adj* [water, dish, hole] peu profond(e). || *pej* [superficial] superficiel(ielle).

sham [ʃæm] **1** *adj* feint(e), simulé(e). **2** *n* comédie *f*.

shambles ['ʃæmblz] *n* désordre *m*, pagaille *f*.

shame [ʃeɪm] **1** *n* (U) [remorse, humiliation] honte *f*. || [pity]: **it's a ~ (that ...)** c'est dommage (que ... (+ *subjunctive*)); **what a ~!** quel dommage! **2** *vt* [make ashamed] faire honte à, mortifier; **to ~ sb into doing sthg** obliger qqn à faire qqch en lui faisant honte.

shamefaced [,ʃeɪm'feɪst] *adj* honteux(euse), penaud(e).

shameful ['ʃeɪmfʊl] *adj* honteux(euse), scandaleux(euse).

shameless ['ʃeɪmlɪs] *adj* effronté(e), éhonté(e).

shampoo [ʃæm'pu:] (*pl* **-s**, *pt & pp* **-ed**, *cont* **-ing**) **1** *n* shampooing *m*. **2** *vt*: **to ~ sb** OR **sb's hair** faire un shampooing à qqn.

shamrock ['ʃæmrɒk] *n* trèfle *m*.

shandy ['ʃændɪ] *n* panaché *m*.

shan't [ʃɑ:nt] = **shall not**.

shantytown ['ʃæntɪtaʊn] *n* bidonville *m*.

shape [ʃeɪp] **1** *n* [gen] forme *f*; **to take ~** prendre forme OR tournure. || [health]: **to be in good/bad ~** être en bonne/mauvaise forme. **2** *vt* [pastry, clay etc] **to ~ sthg (into)** façonner OR modeler qqch (en). || [ideas, project, character] former. ○ **shape up** *vi* [person, plans] se développer, progresser.

-shaped ['ʃeɪpt] *suffix*: **egg~** en forme d'œuf; **L~** en forme de L.

shapeless ['ʃeɪplɪs] *adj* informe.

shapely ['ʃeɪplɪ] *adj* bien fait(e).

share [ʃeər] **1** *n* [portion, contribution] part *f*. **2** *vt* partager. ○ **shares** *npl* actions *fpl*. ○ **share out** *vt sep* partager, répartir.

shareholder ['ʃeə,həʊldər] *n* actionnaire *mf*.

shark [ʃɑ:k] (*pl inv* OR **-s**) *n* [fish] requin *m*.

sharp [ʃɑ:p] **1** *adj* [knife, razor] tranchant(e), affilé(e); [needle, pencil, teeth] pointu(e). || [image, outline, contrast] net (nette). || [person, mind] vif (vive); [eyesight] perçant(e). || [sudden - change, rise] brusque, soudain(e); [- hit, tap] sec (sèche). || [words, order, voice] cinglant(e). || [cry, sound] perçant(e); [pain, cold] vif (vive). || MUS: **C/D ~** do/ré dièse. **2** *adv* [punctually]: **at 8 o'clock ~** à 8 heures pile OR tapantes. || [immediately]: **~ left/right** tout à fait à gauche/droite.

sharpen ['ʃɑ:pn] *vt* [knife, tool] aiguiser; [pencil] tailler.

sharpener ['ʃɑ:pnər] *n* [for pencil] taille-crayon *m*; [for knife] aiguisoir *m* (pour couteaux).

sharp-eyed [-'aɪd] *adj*: **she's very ~** elle remarque tout, rien ne lui échappe.

sharply ['ʃɑ:plɪ] *adv* [distinctly] nettement. || [suddenly] brusquement. || [harshly] sévèrement, durement.

shat [ʃæt] *pt & pp* → **shit**.

shatter ['ʃætər] **1** *vt* [window, glass] briser, fracasser. || *fig* [hopes, dreams] détruire. **2** *vi* se fracasser, voler en éclats.

shattered ['ʃætəd] *adj* [upset] boule-versé(e). || *Br inf* [very tired] flapi(e).

shave [ʃeɪv] **1** *n*: to have a ~ se raser. **2** *vt* [remove hair from] raser. || [wood] planer, raboter. **3** *vi* se raser.

shaver ['ʃeɪvəʳ] *n* rasoir *m* électrique.

shaving brush ['ʃeɪvɪŋ-] *n* blaireau *m*.

shaving cream ['ʃeɪvɪŋ-] *n* crème *f* à raser.

shaving foam ['ʃeɪvɪŋ-] *n* mousse *f* à raser.

shavings ['ʃeɪvɪŋz] *npl* [of wood, metal] copeaux *mpl*.

shawl [ʃɔːl] *n* châle *m*.

she [ʃiː] **1** *pers pron* [referring to woman, girl, animal] elle; ~'s tall elle est grande; SHE **can't do it** elle, elle ne peut pas le faire; **there** ~ **is** la voilà; **if I were** OR **was** ~ *fml* si j'étais elle, à sa place. || [referring to boat, car, country] *follow the gender of your translation.* **2** *comp*: ~-**elephant** éléphant *m* femelle; ~-**wolf** louve *f*.

sheaf [ʃiːf] (*pl* **sheaves**) *n* [of papers, letters] liasse *f*. || [of corn, grain] gerbe *f*.

shear [ʃɪəʳ] (*pt* -ed, *pp* -ed OR **shorn**) *vt* [sheep] tondre. ○ **shears** *npl* [for garden] sécateur *m*, cisaille *f*. || [for dressmaking] ciseaux *mpl*. ○ **shear off** *vi* se détacher.

sheath [ʃiːθ] (*pl* -s [ʃiːðz]) *n* [for knife, cable] gaine *f*.

sheaves [ʃiːvz] *pl* → **sheaf**.

shed [ʃed] (*pt* & *pp* **shed**) **1** *n* [small] remise *f*, cabane *f*; [larger] hangar *m*. **2** *vt* [hair, skin, leaves] perdre. || [tears] verser, répandre.

she'd [weak form ʃɪd, strong form ʃiːd] = **she had, she would**.

sheen [ʃiːn] *n* lustre *m*, éclat *m*.

sheep [ʃiːp] (*pl inv*) *n* mouton *m*.

sheepdog ['ʃiːpdɒg] *n* chien *m* de berger.

sheepish ['ʃiːpɪʃ] *adj* penaud(e).

sheepskin ['ʃiːpskɪn] *n* peau *f* de mouton.

sheer [ʃɪəʳ] *adj* [absolute] pur(e). || [very steep] à pic, abrupt(e). || [material] fin(e).

sheet [ʃiːt] *n* [for bed] drap *m*. || [of paper, glass, wood] feuille *f*; [of metal] plaque *f*.

sheik(h) [ʃeɪk] *n* cheik *m*.

shelf [ʃelf] (*pl* **shelves**) *n* [for storage] rayon *m*, étagère *f*.

shell [ʃel] **1** *n* [of egg, nut, snail] coquille *f*. || [of tortoise, crab] carapace *f*. || [on beach] coquillage *m*. || MIL obus *m*. **2** *vt* [peas] écosser; [nuts, prawns] décortiquer; [eggs] enlever la coquille de, écaler. || MIL bombarder.

she'll [ʃiːl] = **she will, she shall**.

shellfish ['ʃelfɪʃ] (*pl inv*) *n* [creature] crustacé *m*, coquillage *m*. || (*U*) [food] fruits *mpl* de mer.

shelter ['ʃeltəʳ] **1** *n* abri *m*. **2** *vt* [protect] abriter, protéger. || [refugee, homeless person] offrir un asile à; [criminal, fugitive] cacher. **3** *vi* s'abriter, se mettre à l'abri.

sheltered ['ʃeltəd] *adj* [from weather] abrité(e). || [life, childhood] protégé(e), sans soucis.

shelve [ʃelv] *vt fig* mettre au frigidaire, mettre en sommeil.

shelves [ʃelvz] *pl* → **shelf**.

shepherd ['ʃepəd] **1** *n* berger *m*. **2** *vt fig* conduire.

shepherd's pie ['ʃepədz-] *n* ≃ hachis *m* Parmentier.

sheriff ['ʃerɪf] *n Am* shérif *m*.

sherry ['ʃerɪ] *n* xérès *m*, sherry *m*.

she's [ʃiːz] = **she is, she has**.

sh(h) [ʃ] *excl* chut!

shield [ʃiːld] **1** *n* [armour] bouclier *m*. **2** *vt*: to ~ sb (from) protéger qqn (de OR contre).

shift [ʃɪft] **1** *n* [change] changement *m*, modification *f*. || [period of work] poste *m*; [workers] équipe *f*. **2** *vt* [move] déplacer, changer de place. || [change] changer, modifier. **3** *vi* [move - gen] changer de place; [- wind] tourner, changer. || [change] changer, se modifier. || *Am* AUT changer de vitesse.

shifty ['ʃɪftɪ] *adj inf* sournois(e), louche.

shimmer ['ʃɪməʳ] **1** *n* reflet *m*, miroitement *m*. **2** *vi* miroiter.

shin [ʃɪn] *n* tibia *m*.

shinbone ['ʃɪnbəʊn] *n* tibia *m*.

shine [ʃaɪn] (*pt* & *pp* **shone**) **1** *n* brillant *m*. **2** *vt* [direct]: to ~ a torch on sthg éclairer qqch. || [polish] faire briller, astiquer. **3** *vi* briller.

shingle ['ʃɪŋgl] *n* (*U*) [on beach] galets *mpl*. ○ **shingles** *n* (*U*) zona *m*.

shiny ['ʃaɪnɪ] *adj* brillant(e).

ship [ʃɪp] **1** *n* bateau *m*; [larger] navire *m*. **2** *vt* [goods] expédier; [troops, passengers] transporter.

shipbuilding ['ʃɪp,bɪldɪŋ] *n* construction *f* navale.

shipment ['ʃɪpmənt] *n* [cargo] cargaison *f*, chargement *m*.

shipper ['ʃɪpəʳ] n affréteur m, chargeur m.

shipping ['ʃɪpɪŋ] n (U) [transport] transport m maritime. ‖ [ships] navires mpl.

shipshape ['ʃɪpʃeɪp] adj bien rangé(e), en ordre.

shipwreck ['ʃɪprek] 1 n [destruction of ship] naufrage m. ‖ [wrecked ship] épave f. 2 vt: to be ~ed faire naufrage.

shipyard ['ʃɪpjɑːd] n chantier m naval.

shirk [ʃɜːk] vt se dérober à.

shirt [ʃɜːt] n chemise f.

shirtsleeves ['ʃɜːtsliːvz] npl: to be in (one's) ~ être en manches OR en bras de chemise.

shit [ʃɪt] (pt & pp **shit** OR **-ted** OR **shat**) vulg 1 n [excrement] merde f. ‖ (U) [nonsense] conneries fpl. 2 excl merde!

shiver ['ʃɪvəʳ] 1 n frisson m. 2 vi: to ~ (with) trembler (de), frissonner (de).

shoal [ʃəʊl] n [of fish] banc m.

shock [ʃɒk] 1 n [surprise] choc m, coup m. ‖ (U) MED: to be suffering from ~, to be in (a state of) ~ être en état de choc. ‖ [impact] choc m, heurt m. ‖ ELEC décharge f électrique. 2 vt [upset] bouleverser. ‖ [offend] choquer, scandaliser.

shock absorber [-əb,zɔːbəʳ] n amortisseur m.

shocking ['ʃɒkɪŋ] adj [very bad] épouvantable, terrible. ‖ [outrageous] scandaleux(euse).

shod [ʃɒd] pt & pp → **shoe**.

shoddy ['ʃɒdɪ] adj [goods, work] de mauvaise qualité; [treatment] indigne, méprisable.

shoe [ʃuː] (pt & pp **-ed** OR **shod**) 1 n chaussure f, soulier m. 2 vt [horse] ferrer.

shoebrush ['ʃuːbrʌʃ] n brosse f à chaussures.

shoehorn ['ʃuːhɔːn] n chausse-pied m.

shoelace ['ʃuːleɪs] n lacet m de soulier.

shoe polish n cirage m.

shoe shop n magasin m de chaussures.

shoestring ['ʃuːstrɪŋ] n fig: on a ~ à peu de frais.

shone [ʃɒn] pt & pp → **shine**.

shoo [ʃuː] 1 vt chasser. 2 excl ouste!

shook [ʃʊk] pt → **shake**.

shoot [ʃuːt] (pt & pp **shot**) 1 vt [kill with gun] tuer d'un coup de feu; [wound with gun] blesser d'un coup de feu; to ~ o.s. [kill o.s.] se tuer avec une arme à feu. ‖ [arrow] décocher, tirer. ‖ CINEMA tourner. 2 vi [fire gun]: to ~ (at) tirer (sur). ‖ [move quickly]: to ~ in/out/past entrer/

sortir/passer en trombe, entrer/sortir/passer comme un bolide. ‖ CINEMA tourner. ‖ SPORT tirer, shooter. 3 n [of plant] pousse f. ○ **shoot down** vt sep [aeroplane] descendre, abattre. ‖ [person] abattre. ○ **shoot up** vi [child, plant] pousser vite. ‖ [price, inflation] monter en flèche.

shooting ['ʃuːtɪŋ] n [killing] meurtre m.

shooting star n étoile f filante.

shop [ʃɒp] 1 n [store] magasin m, boutique f. ‖ [workshop] atelier m. 2 vi faire ses courses; to go shopping aller faire les courses OR commissions.

shop floor n: the ~ fig les ouvriers mpl.

shopkeeper ['ʃɒp,kiːpəʳ] n commerçant m, -e f.

shoplifting ['ʃɒp,lɪftɪŋ] n (U) vol m à l'étalage.

shopper ['ʃɒpəʳ] n personne f qui fait ses courses.

shopping ['ʃɒpɪŋ] n (U) [purchases] achats mpl.

shopping bag n sac m à provisions.

shopping centre Br, **shopping mall** Am, **shopping plaza** Am [-,plɑːzə] n centre m commercial.

shopsoiled Br ['ʃɒpsɔɪld], **shopworn** Am ['ʃɒpwɔːn] adj qui a fait l'étalage, abîmé(e) (en magasin).

shop steward n délégué syndical m, déléguée syndicale f.

shopwindow [,ʃɒp'wɪndəʊ] n vitrine f.

shopworn Am = **shopsoiled**.

shore [ʃɔːʳ] n rivage m, bord m; on ~ à terre. ○ **shore up** vt sep étayer, étançonner; fig consolider.

shorn [ʃɔːn] 1 pp → **shear**. 2 adj tondu(e).

short [ʃɔːt] 1 adj [not long - in time] court(e), bref (brève); [- in space] court. ‖ [not tall] petit(e). ‖ [curt] brusque, sec (sèche). ‖ [lacking]: to be ~ of manquer de. ‖ [abbreviated]: to be ~ for être le diminutif de. 2 adv: to be running ~ of [running out of] commencer à manquer de, commencer à être à court de; to cut sthg ~ [visit, speech] écourter qqch; [discussion] couper court à qqch; to stop ~ s'arrêter net. 3 n [film] court métrage m. ○ **shorts** npl [gen] short m. ‖ Am [underwear] caleçon m. ○ **for short** adv: he's called Bob for ~ Bob est son diminutif. ○ **in short** adv (enfin) bref. ○ **short of** prep [unless, without]: ~ of doing sthg à moins de faire qqch, à part faire qqch.

shortage ['ʃɔːtɪdʒ] *n* manque *m*, insuffisance *f*.

shortbread ['ʃɔːtbred] *n* sablé *m*.

short-change *vt* [subj: shopkeeper]: **to ~ sb** ne pas rendre assez à qqn.

short circuit *n* court-circuit *m*.

shortcomings ['ʃɔːt,kʌmɪŋz] *npl* défauts *mpl*.

shortcrust pastry ['ʃɔːtkrʌst-] *n* pâte *f* brisée.

short cut *n* [quick route] raccourci *m*. || [quick method] solution *f* miracle.

shorten ['ʃɔːtn] **1** *vt* [holiday, time] écourter. || [skirt, rope etc] raccourcir. **2** *vi* [days] raccourcir.

shortfall ['ʃɔːtfɔːl] *n* déficit *m*.

shorthand ['ʃɔːthænd] *n* (U) [writing system] sténographie *f*.

shortly ['ʃɔːtlɪ] *adv* [soon] bientôt.

shortsighted [,ʃɔːt'saɪtɪd] *adj* myope; *fig* imprévoyant(e).

short-staffed [-'stɑːft] *adj*: **to be ~** manquer de personnel.

short story *n* nouvelle *f*.

short-tempered [-'tempəd] *adj* emporté(e), irascible.

short-term *adj* [effects, solution] à court terme; [problem] de courte durée.

short wave *n* (U) ondes *fpl* courtes.

shot [ʃɒt] **1** *pt* & *pp* → **shoot**. **2** *n* [gunshot] coup *m* de feu; **like a ~** sans tarder, sans hésiter. || [marksman] tireur *m*. || SPORT coup *m*. || [photograph] photo *f*; CINEMA plan *m*. || *inf* [attempt]: **to have a ~ at sthg** essayer de faire qqch. || [injection] piqûre *f*.

shotgun ['ʃɒtgʌn] *n* fusil *m* de chasse.

should [ʃʊd] *aux vb* [indicating duty]: **we ~ leave now** il faudrait partir maintenant. || [seeking advice, permission]: **~ I go too?** est-ce que je devrais y aller aussi? || [as suggestion]: **I ~ deny everything** moi, je nierais tout. || [indicating probability]: **she ~ be home soon** elle devrait être de retour bientôt, elle va bientôt rentrer. || [was or were expected]: **they ~ have won the match** ils auraient dû gagner le match. || [indicating intention, wish]: **I ~ like to come with you** j'aimerais bien venir avec vous. || (*as conditional*): **you ~ go if you're invited** tu devrais y aller si tu es invité. || (*in subordinate clauses*): **we decided that you ~ meet him** nous avons décidé que ce serait toi qui irais le chercher. || [expressing uncertain opinion]: **I ~ think he's about 50 (years old)** je pense qu'il doit avoir dans les 50 ans.

shoulder ['ʃəʊldər] **1** *n* épaule *f*. **2** *vt* [carry] porter. || [responsibility] endosser.

shoulder blade *n* omoplate *f*.

shoulder strap *n* [on dress] bretelle *f*. || [on bag] bandoulière *f*.

shouldn't ['ʃʊdnt] = **should not**.

should've ['ʃʊdəv] = **should have**.

shout [ʃaʊt] **1** *n* [cry] cri *m*. **2** *vt* & *vi* crier. ○ **shout down** *vt sep* huer, conspuer.

shouting ['ʃaʊtɪŋ] *n* (U) cris *mpl*.

shove [ʃʌv] **1** *n*: **to give sb/sthg a ~** pousser qqn/qqch. **2** *vt* pousser; **to ~ clothes into a bag** fourrer des vêtements dans un sac.

shovel ['ʃʌvl] **1** *n* [tool] pelle *f*. **2** *vt* enlever à la pelle, pelleter.

show [ʃəʊ] (*pt* **-ed**, *pp* **shown** OR **-ed**) **1** *n* [display] démonstration *f*, manifestation *f*. || [at theatre] spectacle *m*; [on radio, TV] émission *f*. || CINEMA séance *f*. || [exhibition] exposition *f*. **2** *vt* [gen] montrer; [profit, loss] indiquer; [respect] témoigner; [courage, mercy] faire preuve de; **to ~ sb sthg, to ~ sthg to sb** montrer qqch à qqn. || [escort]: **to ~ sb to his seat/table** conduire qqn à sa place/sa table. || [film] projeter, passer; [TV programme] donner, passer. **3** *vi* [indicate] indiquer, montrer. || [be visible] se voir, être visible. || CINEMA: **what's ~ing tonight?** qu'est-ce qu'on joue comme film ce soir? ○ **show off** *vt sep* exhiber. **2** *vi* faire l'intéressant(e). ○ **show up 1** *vt sep* [embarrass] embarrasser, faire honte à. **2** *vi* [stand out] se voir, ressortir. || [arrive] s'amener, rappliquer.

show business *n* (U) monde *m* du spectacle, show-business *m*.

showdown ['ʃəʊdaʊn] *n*: **to have a ~ with sb** s'expliquer avec qqn, mettre les choses au point avec qqn.

shower ['ʃaʊər] **1** *n* [device, act] douche *f*; **to have** OR **take a ~** prendre une douche, se doucher. || [of rain] averse *f*. **2** *vt*: **to ~ sb with** couvrir qqn de. **3** *vi* [wash] prendre une douche, se doucher.

shower cap *n* bonnet *m* de douche.

showing ['ʃəʊɪŋ] *n* CINEMA projection *f*.

show jumping [-,dʒʌmpɪŋ] *n* jumping *m*.

shown [ʃəʊn] *pp* → **show**.

show-off *n inf* m'as-tu-vu *m*, -e *f*.

showpiece ['ʃəʊpiːs] *n* [main attraction] joyau *m*, trésor *m*.

showroom ['ʃəʊrʊm] *n* salle *f* OR magasin *m* d'exposition; [for cars] salle de démonstration.

shrank [ʃræŋk] *pt* → **shrink**.

shrapnel ['ʃræpnl] *n* (*U*) éclats *mpl* d'obus.

shred [ʃred] 1 *n* [of material, paper] lambeau *m*, brin *m*. ‖ *fig* [of evidence] parcelle *f*; [of truth] once *f*, grain *m*. 2 *vt* [food] râper; [paper] déchirer en lambeaux.

shredder ['ʃredər] *n* [machine] destructeur *m* de documents.

shrewd [ʃruːd] *adj* fin(e), astucieux(ieuse).

shriek [ʃriːk] 1 *n* cri *m* perçant, hurlement *m*; [of laughter] éclat *m*. 2 *vi* pousser un cri perçant.

shrill [ʃrɪl] *adj* [sound, voice] aigu(ë).

shrimp [ʃrɪmp] *n* crevette *f*.

shrine [ʃraɪn] *n* [place of worship] lieu *m* saint.

shrink [ʃrɪŋk] (*pt* **shrank**, *pp* **shrunk**) 1 *vt* rétrécir. 2 *vi* [cloth, garment] rétrécir; [person] rapetisser; *fig* [popularity etc] baisser, diminuer. ‖ [recoil]: **to ~ away from sthg** reculer devant qqch; **to ~ from doing sthg** rechigner OR répugner à faire qqch.

shrinkage ['ʃrɪŋkɪdʒ] *n* rétrécissement *m*; *fig* diminution *f*, baisse *f*.

shrink-wrap *vt* emballer sous film plastique.

shrivel ['ʃrɪvl] 1 *vt*: **to ~ (up)** rider, flétrir. 2 *vi*: **to ~ (up)** se rider, se flétrir.

shroud [ʃraʊd] 1 *n* [cloth] linceul *m*. 2 *vt*: **to be ~ed in** [darkness, fog] être enseveli(e) sous; [mystery] être enveloppé(e) de.

Shrove Tuesday ['ʃrəʊv-] *n* Mardi *m* gras.

shrub [ʃrʌb] *n* arbuste *m*.

shrug [ʃrʌg] 1 *vt*: **to ~ one's shoulders** hausser les épaules. 2 *vi* hausser les épaules. ○ **shrug off** *vt sep* ignorer.

shrunk [ʃrʌŋk] *pp* → **shrink**.

shudder ['ʃʌdər] *vi* [tremble]: **to ~ (with)** frémir (de), frissonner (de). ‖ [shake] vibrer, trembler.

shuffle ['ʃʌfl] *vt* [drag]: **to ~ one's feet** traîner les pieds. ‖ [cards] mélanger, battre.

shun [ʃʌn] *vt* fuir, éviter.

shunt [ʃʌnt] *vt* RAIL aiguiller.

shut [ʃʌt] (*pt & pp* **shut**) 1 *adj* [closed] fermé(e). 2 *vt* fermer. 3 *vi* [door, window] se fermer. ‖ [shop] fermer. ○ **shut away** *vt sep* [valuables, papers] mettre

sous clef. ○ **shut down** *vt sep & vi* fermer. ○ **shut out** *vt sep* [noise] supprimer; [light] ne pas laisser entrer; **to ~ sb out** laisser qqn à la porte. ○ **shut up** *inf* 1 *vt sep* [silence] faire taire. 2 *vi* se taire.

shutter ['ʃʌtər] *n* [on window] volet *m*. ‖ [in camera] obturateur *m*.

shuttle ['ʃʌtl] 1 *adj*: **~ service** (service *m* de) navette *f*. 2 *n* [train, bus, plane] navette *f*.

shuttlecock ['ʃʌtlkɒk] *n* volant *m*.

shy [ʃaɪ] 1 *adj* [timid] timide. 2 *vi* [horse] s'effaroucher.

Siberia [saɪˈbɪərɪə] *n* Sibérie *f*.

sibling ['sɪblɪŋ] *n* [brother] frère *m*; [sister] sœur *f*.

Sicily ['sɪsɪlɪ] *n* Sicile *f*.

sick [sɪk] *adj* [ill] malade. ‖ [nauseous]: **to feel ~** avoir envie de vomir, avoir mal au cœur. ‖ [fed up]: **to be ~ of** en avoir assez OR marre de. ‖ [joke, humour] macabre.

sickbay ['sɪkbeɪ] *n* infirmerie *f*.

sicken ['sɪkn] *vt* écœurer, dégoûter.

sickening ['sɪknɪŋ] *adj* [disgusting] écœurant(e), dégoûtant(e).

sickle ['sɪkl] *n* faucille *f*.

sick leave *n* (*U*) congé *m* de maladie.

sickly ['sɪklɪ] *adj* [unhealthy] maladif(ive), souffreteux(euse). ‖ [smell, taste] écœurant(e).

sickness ['sɪknɪs] *n* [illness] maladie *f*.

sick pay *n* (*U*) indemnité *f* OR allocation *f* de maladie.

side [saɪd] 1 *n* [gen] côté *m*; **at** OR **by my/her** *etc* **~** à mes/ses *etc* côtés; **from ~ to ~** d'un côté à l'autre; **~ by ~** côte à côte. ‖ [of table, river] bord *m*. ‖ [of hill, valley] versant *m*, flanc *m*. ‖ [in war, debate] camp *m*, côté *m*; SPORT équipe *f*, camp; [of argument] point *m* de vue; **to take sb's ~** prendre le parti de qqn. ‖ [aspect - gen] aspect *m*; [- of character] facette *f*; **to be on the safe ~** pour plus de sûreté, par précaution. 2 *adj* [situated on side] latéral(e).

sideboard ['saɪdbɔːd] *n* [cupboard] buffet *m*.

sideboards *Br* ['saɪdbɔːdz], **sideburns** *Am* ['saɪdbɜːnz] *npl* favoris *mpl*, rouflaquettes *fpl*.

side effect *n* MED effet *m* secondaire OR indésirable.

sidelight ['saɪdlaɪt] *n* AUT feu *m* de position.

sideline ['saɪdlaɪn] *n* [extra business] activité *f* secondaire. ‖ SPORT ligne *f* de touche.

sidelong ['saɪdlɒŋ] *adj* & *adv* de côté.

sidesaddle ['saɪd,sædl] *adv*: **to ride ~** monter en amazone.

sideshow ['saɪdʃəʊ] *n* spectacle *m* forain.

sidestep ['saɪdstep] *vt* faire un pas de côté pour éviter OR esquiver; *fig* éviter.

side street *n* [not main street] petite rue *f*; [off main street] rue transversale.

sidetrack ['saɪdtræk] *vt*: **to be ~ed** se laisser distraire.

sidewalk ['saɪdwɔːk] *n* *Am* trottoir *m*.

sideways ['saɪdweɪz] *adj* & *adv* de côté.

siding ['saɪdɪŋ] *n* voie *f* de garage.

sidle ['saɪdl] ○ **sidle up** *vi*: **to ~ up to sb** se glisser vers qqn.

siege [siːdʒ] *n* siège *m*.

sieve [sɪv] **1** *n* [for flour, sand etc] tamis *m*; [for liquids] passoire *f*. **2** *vt* [flour etc] tamiser; [liquid] passer.

sift [sɪft] **1** *vt* [flour, sand] tamiser. **2** *vi*: **to ~ through** examiner, éplucher.

sigh [saɪ] **1** *n* soupir *m*. **2** *vi* [person] soupirer, pousser un soupir.

sight [saɪt] **1** *n* [seeing] vue *f*; **in/out of ~** en/hors de vue; **at first ~** à première vue, au premier abord. ‖ [spectacle] spectacle *m*. ‖ [on gun] mire *f*. **2** *vt* apercevoir. ○ **sights** *npl* [of city] attractions *fpl* touristiques.

sightseeing ['saɪt,siːɪŋ] *n* tourisme *m*; **to go ~** faire du tourisme.

sightseer ['saɪt,siːər] *n* touriste *mf*.

sign [saɪn] **1** *n* [gen] signe *m*; **no ~ of** aucune trace de. ‖ [notice] enseigne *f*; AUT panneau *m*. **2** *vt* signer. ○ **sign up 1** *vt sep* [worker] embaucher; [soldier] engager. **2** *vi* MIL s'engager; [for course] s'inscrire.

signal ['sɪgnl] **1** *n* signal *m*. **2** *vt* [indicate] indiquer. ‖ [gesture to]: **to ~ sb (to do sthg)** faire signe à qqn (de faire qqch). **3** *vi* AUT clignoter, mettre son clignotant. ‖ [gesture]: **to ~ to sb (to do sthg)** faire signe à qqn (de faire qqch).

signalman ['sɪgnlmən] (*pl* **-men** [-mən]) *n* RAIL aiguilleur *m*.

signature ['sɪgnətʃər] *n* [name] signature *f*.

signature tune *n* indicatif *m*.

signet ring ['sɪgnɪt-] *n* chevalière *f*.

significance [sɪg'nɪfɪkəns] *n* [importance] importance *f*, portée *f*. ‖ [meaning] signification *f*.

significant [sɪg'nɪfɪkənt] *adj* [considerable] considérable. ‖ [important] important(e). ‖ [meaningful] significatif(ive).

signify ['sɪgnɪfaɪ] *vt* signifier, indiquer.

signpost ['saɪnpəʊst] *n* poteau *m* indicateur.

Sikh [siːk] **1** *adj* sikh (*inv*). **2** *n* [person] Sikh *mf*.

silence ['saɪləns] **1** *n* silence *m*. **2** *vt* réduire au silence, faire taire.

silencer ['saɪlənsər] *n* silencieux *m*.

silent ['saɪlənt] *adj* [person, place] silencieux(ieuse). ‖ CINEMA & LING muet(ette).

silhouette [,sɪluː'et] *n* silhouette *f*.

silicon chip [,sɪlɪkən-] *n* puce *f*, pastille *f* de silicium.

silk [sɪlk] **1** *n* soie *f*. **2** *comp* en OR de soie.

silky ['sɪlkɪ] *adj* soyeux(euse).

sill [sɪl] *n* [of window] rebord *m*.

silly ['sɪlɪ] *adj* stupide, bête.

silo ['saɪləʊ] (*pl* **-s**) *n* silo *m*.

silt [sɪlt] *n* vase *f*, limon *m*.

silver ['sɪlvər] **1** *adj* [colour] argenté(e). **2** *n* (*U*) [metal] argent *m*. ‖ [coins] pièces *fpl* d'argent. ‖ [silverware] argenterie *f*. **3** *comp* en argent, d'argent.

silver foil, silver paper *n* (*U*) papier *m* d'argent OR d'étain.

silver-plated [-'pleɪtɪd] *adj* plaqué(e) argent.

silversmith ['sɪlvəsmɪθ] *n* orfèvre *mf*.

silverware ['sɪlvəweər] *n* (*U*) [dishes, spoons etc] argenterie *f*. ‖ *Am* [cutlery] couverts *mpl*.

similar ['sɪmɪlər] *adj*: **~ (to)** semblable (à), similaire (à).

similarly ['sɪmɪləlɪ] *adv* de la même manière, pareillement.

simmer ['sɪmər] *vt* faire cuire à feu doux, mijoter.

simple ['sɪmpl] *adj* [gen] simple.

simple-minded [-'maɪndɪd] *adj* simplet(ette), simple d'esprit.

simplicity [sɪm'plɪsətɪ] *n* simplicité *f*.

simplify ['sɪmplɪfaɪ] *vt* simplifier.

simply ['sɪmplɪ] *adv* [gen] simplement. ‖ [for emphasis] absolument.

simulate ['sɪmjʊleɪt] *vt* simuler.

simultaneous [*Br* ,sɪmʊl'teɪnjəs, *Am* ,saɪməl'teɪnjəs] *adj* simultané(e).

sin [sɪn] **1** *n* péché *m*. **2** *vi*: **to ~ (against)** pécher (contre).

since [sɪns] **1** *adv* depuis. **2** *prep* depuis. **3** *conj* [in time] depuis que. ‖ [because] comme, puisque.

sincere [sɪn'sɪər] *adj* sincère.

sincerely [sɪnˈsɪəlɪ] *adv* sincèrement;
Yours ~ [at end of letter] veuillez agréer,
Monsieur/Madame, l'expression de mes
sentiments les meilleurs.

sincerity [sɪnˈserətɪ] *n* sincérité *f*.

sinful [ˈsɪnful] *adj* [thought] mauvais(e);
[desire, act] coupable.

sing [sɪŋ] (*pt* **sang**, *pp* **sung**) *vt & vi*
chanter.

Singapore [ˌsɪŋəˈpɔːr] *n* Singapour *m*.

singe [sɪndʒ] *vt* brûler légèrement;
[cloth] roussir.

singer [ˈsɪŋər] *n* chanteur *m*, -euse *f*.

singing [ˈsɪŋɪŋ] *n* (*U*) chant *m*.

single [ˈsɪŋgl] **1** *adj* [only one] seul(e),
unique; **every ~** chaque. || [unmarried]
célibataire. **2** *n* MUS (disque *m*) 45 tours
m. ○ **singles** *npl* TENNIS simples *mpl*.
○ **single out** *vt sep*: **to ~ sb out (for)**
choisir qqn (pour).

single bed *n* lit *m* à une place.

single-breasted [-ˈbrestɪd] *adj* [jacket]
droit(e).

single file *n*: **in ~** en file indienne, à la
file.

single-handed [-ˈhændɪd] *adv* tout seul
(toute seule).

single-minded [-ˈmaɪndɪd] *adj* réso-
lu(e).

single-parent family *n* famille *f* mo-
noparentale.

single room *n* chambre *f* pour une personne OR à un lit.

singular [ˈsɪŋgjʊlər] **1** *adj* singu-
lier(ière). **2** *n* singulier *m*.

sinister [ˈsɪnɪstər] *adj* sinistre.

sink [sɪŋk] (*pt* **sank**, *pp* **sunk**) **1** *n* [in
kitchen] évier *m*; [in bathroom] lavabo *m*.
2 *vt* [ship] couler. || [teeth, claws]: **to ~**
sthg into enfoncer qqch dans. **3** *vi* [in water - ship] couler, sombrer; [- person, ob-
ject] couler. || [ground] s'affaisser; [sun]
baisser; **to ~ into poverty/despair** som-
brer dans la misère/le désespoir. ||
[value, amount] baisser, diminuer; [voice]
faiblir. ○ **sink in** *vi*: **it hasn't sunk in yet**
je n'ai pas encore réalisé.

sink unit *n* bloc-évier *m*.

sinner [ˈsɪnər] *n* pécheur *m*, -eresse *f*.

sinus [ˈsaɪnəs] (*pl* -es) *n* sinus *m inv*.

sip [sɪp] **1** *n* petite gorgée *f*. **2** *vt* siroter,
boire à petits coups.

siphon [ˈsaɪfn] *n* siphon *m*. ○ **siphon**
off *vt sep* [liquid] siphonner. || *fig*
[money] canaliser.

sir [sɜːr] *n* [form of address] monsieur *m*.

|| [in titles]: **Sir Phillip Holden** sir Phillip
Holden.

siren [ˈsaɪərən] *n* sirène *f*.

sirloin (steak) [ˈsɜːlɔɪn-] *n* bifteck *m*
dans l'aloyau OR d'aloyau.

sissy [ˈsɪsɪ] *n inf* poule *f* mouillée, dé-
gonflé *m*, -e *f*.

sister [ˈsɪstər] *n* [sibling] sœur *f*. || [nun]
sœur *f*, religieuse *f*.

sister-in-law (*pl* **sisters-in-law** OR
sister-in-laws) *n* belle-sœur *f*.

sit [sɪt] (*pt & pp* **sat**) *vi* [person]
s'asseoir; **to be sitting** être assis(e); **to ~**
on a committee faire partie OR être mem-
bre d'un comité. || [court, parliament] sié-
ger, être en séance. ○ **sit down** *vi*
s'asseoir. ○ **sit in on** *vt fus* assister à.
○ **sit through** *vt fus* rester jusqu'à la
fin de. ○ **sit up** *vi* [sit upright] se redres-
ser, s'asseoir. || [stay up] veiller.

sitcom [ˈsɪtkɒm] *n inf* sitcom *f*.

site [saɪt] **1** *n* [of town, building] emplacement *m*; [archaeological] site *m*; CONSTR
chantier *m*. **2** *vt* situer, placer.

sit-in *n* sit-in *m*, occupation *f* des locaux.

sitting [ˈsɪtɪŋ] *n* [of meal] service *m*. ||
[of court, parliament] séance *f*.

sitting room *n* salon *m*.

situated [ˈsɪtjʊeɪtɪd] *adj*: **to be ~** être
situé(e), se trouver.

situation [ˌsɪtjʊˈeɪʃn] *n* [gen] situation
f. || [job] situation *f*, emploi *m*.

six [sɪks] **1** *num adj* six (*inv*); **she's ~**
(years old) elle a six ans. **2** *num pron* six
mfpl; **I want ~** j'en veux six; **there were ~**
of us nous étions six. **3** *num n* [gen] six *m*
inv; **two hundred and ~** deux cent six. ||
[six o'clock]: **it's ~** il est six heures; **we ar-**
rived at ~ nous sommes arrivés à six
heures.

sixteen [sɪksˈtiːn] *num* seize; *see also*
six.

sixth [sɪksθ] **1** *num adj* sixième. **2** *num*
adv [in race, competition] sixième, en
sixième place. || [in list] sixièmement. **3**
num pron sixième *mf*. **4** *n* [fraction]
sixième *m*. || [in dates]: **the ~ (of Septem-**
ber) le six (septembre).

sixty [ˈsɪkstɪ] *num* soixante; *see also*
six. ○ **sixties** *npl* [decade]: **the sixties**
les années *fpl* soixante. || [in ages]: **to be**
in one's sixties être sexagénaire.

size [saɪz] *n* [of person, clothes, company]
taille *f*; [of building] grandeur *f*, dimen-
sions *fpl*; [of problem] ampleur *f*, taille;
[of shoes] pointure *f*. ○ **size up** *vt sep*

[person] jauger; [situation] apprécier, peser.

sizeable ['saɪzəbl] *adj* assez important(e).

sizzle ['sɪzl] *vi* grésiller.

skate [skeɪt] (*pl sense 2 only inv* OR **-s**) **1** *n* [ice skate, roller skate] patin *m*. ‖ [fish] raie *f*. **2** *vi* [on ice skates] faire du patin sur glace, patiner; [on roller skates] faire du patin à roulettes.

skateboard ['skeɪtbɔːd] *n* planche *f* à roulettes, skateboard *m*, skate *m*.

skater ['skeɪtə*r*] *n* [on ice] patineur *m*, -euse *f*; [on roller skates] patineur à roulettes.

skating ['skeɪtɪŋ] *n* [on ice] patinage *m*; [on roller skates] patinage à roulettes.

skating rink *n* patinoire *f*.

skeleton ['skelɪtn] *n* squelette *m*.

skeleton key *n* passe *m*, passe-partout *m inv*.

skeleton staff *n* personnel *m* réduit.

skeptic *etc Am* = **sceptic** *etc*.

sketch [sketʃ] **1** *n* [drawing] croquis *m*, esquisse *f*. ‖ [description] aperçu *m*, résumé *m*. ‖ [by comedian] sketch *m*. **2** *vt* [draw] dessiner, faire un croquis de. ‖ [describe] donner un aperçu de, décrire à grands traits.

sketchbook ['sketʃbʊk] *n* carnet *m* à dessins.

sketchpad ['sketʃpæd] *n* bloc *m* à dessins.

sketchy ['sketʃɪ] *adj* incomplet(ète).

skewer ['skjʊə*r*] *n* brochette *f*, broche *f*.

ski [skiː] (*pt & pp* **skied**, *cont* **skiing**) **1** *n* ski *m*. **2** *vi* skier, faire du ski.

ski boots *npl* chaussures *fpl* de ski.

skid [skɪd] **1** *n* dérapage *m*; **to go into a ~** déraper. **2** *vi* déraper.

skier ['skiːə*r*] *n* skieur *m*, -ieuse *f*.

skies [skaɪz] *pl* → **sky**.

skiing ['skiːɪŋ] *n* (*U*) ski *m*; **to go ~** faire du ski.

skilful, skillful *Am* ['skɪlfʊl] *adj* habile, adroit(e).

ski lift *n* remonte-pente *m*.

skill [skɪl] *n* (*U*) [ability] habileté *f*, adresse *f*. ‖ [technique] technique *f*, art *m*.

skilled [skɪld] *adj* [skilful]: **~ (in** OR **at doing sthg)** habile OR adroit(e) (pour faire qqch). ‖ [trained] qualifié(e).

skillful *etc Am* = **skilful** *etc*.

skim [skɪm] **1** *vt* [cream] écrémer; [soup] écumer. ‖ [move above] effleurer, raser. **2**

vi: **to ~ through sthg** [newspaper, book] parcourir qqch.

skim(med) milk [skɪm(d)-] *n* lait *m* écrémé.

skimp [skɪmp] *vi*: **to ~ on** lésiner sur.

skimpy ['skɪmpɪ] *adj* [meal] maigre; [clothes] étriqué(e); [facts] insuffisant(e).

skin [skɪn] **1** *n* peau *f*. **2** *vt* [dead animal] écorcher, dépouiller; [fruit] éplucher, peler. ‖ [graze]: **to ~ one's knee** s'érafler OR s'écorcher le genou.

skin-deep *adj* superficiel(ielle).

skin diving *n* plongée *f* sous-marine.

skinny ['skɪnɪ] *adj* maigre.

skin-tight *adj* moulant(e), collant(e).

skip [skɪp] **1** *n* [jump] petit saut *m*. **2** *vt* [page, class, meal] sauter. **3** *vi* [gen] sauter, sautiller.

ski pole *n* bâton *m* de ski.

skipper ['skɪpə*r*] *n* NAUT & SPORT capitaine *m*.

skirmish ['skɜːmɪʃ] *n* escarmouche *f*.

skirt [skɜːt] *n* [garment] jupe *f*. ○ **skirt round** *vt fus* [town, obstacle] contourner. ‖ [problem] éviter.

skit [skɪt] *n* sketch *m*.

skittle ['skɪtl] *n Br* quille *f*. ○ **skittles** *n* (*U*) [game] quilles *fpl*.

skulk [skʌlk] *vi* [hide] se cacher; [prowl] rôder.

skull [skʌl] *n* crâne *m*.

skunk [skʌŋk] *n* [animal] mouffette *f*.

sky [skaɪ] *n* ciel *m*.

skylight ['skaɪlaɪt] *n* lucarne *f*.

skyscraper ['skaɪˌskreɪpə*r*] *n* gratte-ciel *m inv*.

slab [slæb] *n* [of concrete] dalle *f*; [of stone] bloc *m*; [of cake] pavé *m*.

slack [slæk] **1** *adj* [not tight] lâche. ‖ [not busy] calme. ‖ [person] négligent(e), pas sérieux(ieuse). **2** *n* [in rope] mou *m*.

slacken ['slækn] **1** *vt* [speed, pace] ralentir; [rope] relâcher. **2** *vi* [speed, pace] ralentir.

slag [slæg] *n* (*U*) [waste material] scories *fpl*.

slagheap ['slæghiːp] *n* terril *m*.

slam [slæm] **1** *vt* [shut] claquer. ‖ [place with force]: **to ~ sthg on** OR **onto** jeter qqch brutalement sur, flanquer qqch sur. **2** *vi* claquer.

slander ['slɑːndə*r*] **1** *n* calomnie *f*; JUR diffamation *f*. **2** *vt* calomnier; JUR diffamer.

slang [slæŋ] *n* (*U*) argot *m*.

slant [slɑːnt] **1** *n* [angle] inclinaison *f*. ‖ [perspective] point *m* de vue, perspective *f.* **2** *vt* [bias] présenter d'une manière tendancieuse. **3** *vi* [slope] être incliné(e), pencher.

slanting ['slɑ:ntɪŋ] *adj* [roof] en pente.

slap [slæp] **1** *n* claque *f*, tape *f*; [on face] gifle *f*. **2** *vt* [person, face] gifler; [back] donner une claque OR une tape à. || [place with force]: **to ~ sthg on** OR **onto** jeter qqch brutalement sur, flanquer qqch sur. **3** *adv inf* [directly] en plein.

slapdash ['slæpdæʃ], **slaphappy** ['slæp,hæpɪ] *adj inf* [work] bâclé(e); [person, attitude] insouciant(e).

slapstick ['slæpstɪk] *n* (*U*) grosse farce *f*.

slash [slæʃ] **1** *n* [long cut] entaille *f*. || [oblique stroke] barre *f* oblique. **2** *vt* [cut] entailler. || *inf* [prices] casser; [budget, unemployment] réduire considérablement.

slat [slæt] *n* lame *f*; [wooden] latte *f*.

slate [sleɪt] **1** *n* ardoise *f*. **2** *vt inf* [criticize] descendre en flammes.

slaughter ['slɔ:tər] **1** *n* [of animals] abattage *m*. || [of people] massacre *m*, carnage *m*. **2** *vt* [animals] abattre. || [people] massacrer.

slaughterhouse ['slɔ:təhaʊs, *pl* -haʊzɪz] *n* abattoir *m*.

slave [sleɪv] **1** *n* esclave *mf*. **2** *vi*: **to ~ over sthg** peiner sur qqch.

slavery ['sleɪvərɪ] *n* esclavage *m*.

sleazy ['sli:zɪ] *adj* [disreputable] mal famé(e).

sledge [sledʒ], **sled** *Am* [sled] *n* luge *f*; [larger] traîneau *m*.

sledgehammer ['sledʒ,hæmər] *n* masse *f*.

sleek [sli:k] *adj* [hair, fur] lisse, luisant(e). || [shape] aux lignes pures.

sleep [sli:p] (*pt & pp* **slept**) **1** *n* sommeil *m*; **to go to ~** s'endormir. **2** *vi* [be asleep] dormir. || [spend night] coucher. ○ **sleep in** *vi* faire la grasse matinée. ○ **sleep with** *vt fus euphemism* coucher avec.

sleeper ['sli:pər] *n* [person]: **to be a heavy/light ~** avoir le sommeil lourd/léger. || [RAIL - berth] couchette *f*; [- carriage] wagon-lit *m*; [- train] train-couchettes *m*.

sleeping bag ['sli:pɪŋ-] *n* sac *m* de couchage.

sleeping car ['sli:pɪŋ-] *n* wagon-lit *m*.

sleeping pill ['sli:pɪŋ-] *n* somnifère *m*.

sleepless ['sli:plɪs] *adj*: **to have a ~ night** passer une nuit blanche.

sleepwalk ['sli:pwɔ:k] *vi* être somnambule.

sleepy ['sli:pɪ] *adj* [person] qui a envie de dormir.

sleet [sli:t] **1** *n* neige *f* fondue. **2** *v impers*: **it's ~ing** il tombe de la neige fondue.

sleeve [sli:v] *n* [of garment] manche *f*. || [for record] pochette *f*.

sleigh [sleɪ] *n* traîneau *m*.

sleight of hand [,slaɪt-] *n* (*U*) [skill] habileté *f*. || [trick] tour *m* de passe-passe.

slender ['slendər] *adj* [thin] mince. || *fig* [resources, income] modeste, maigre; [hope, chance] faible.

slept [slept] *pt & pp → **sleep**.

slice [slaɪs] **1** *n* [thin piece] tranche *f*. || *fig* [of profits, glory] part *f*. **2** *vt* [cut into slices] couper en tranches. || [cut cleanly] trancher.

slick [slɪk] **1** *adj* [skilful] bien mené(e), habile. || *pej* [superficial - talk] facile; [- person] rusé(e). **2** *n* nappe *f* de pétrole, marée *f* noire.

slide [slaɪd] (*pt & pp* **slid** [slɪd]) **1** *n* [in playground] toboggan *m*. || PHOT diapositive *f*, diapo *f*. || [decline] déclin *m*; [in prices] baisse *f*. **2** *vt* faire glisser. **3** *vi* glisser.

sliding door [,slaɪdɪŋ-] *n* porte *f* coulissante.

slight [slaɪt] **1** *adj* [minor] léger(ère); **the ~est** le moindre (la moindre); **not in the ~est** pas du tout. || [thin] mince. **2** *n* affront *m*. **3** *vt* offenser.

slightly ['slaɪtlɪ] *adv* [to small extent] légèrement.

slim [slɪm] **1** *adj* [person, object] mince. || [chance, possibility] faible. **2** *vi* maigrir; [diet] suivre un régime amaigrissant.

slime [slaɪm] *n* (*U*) substance *f* visqueuse; [of snail] bave *f*.

slimming ['slɪmɪŋ] **1** *n* amaigrissement *m*. **2** *adj* [product] amaigrissant(e).

sling [slɪŋ] (*pt & pp* **slung** [slʌŋ]) **1** *n* [for arm] écharpe *f*. **2** *vt* [hammock etc] suspendre. || *inf* [throw] lancer.

slip [slɪp] **1** *n* [mistake] erreur *f*; **a ~ of the tongue** un lapsus. || [of paper - gen] morceau *m*; [- strip] bande *f*. || [underwear] combinaison *f*. || *phr*: **to give sb the ~** *inf* fausser compagnie à qqn. **2** *vt* glisser; **to ~ sthg on** enfiler qqch. **3** *vi* [slide] glisser; **to ~ into sthg** se glisser dans qqch. || [decline] décliner. ○ **slip up** *vi fig* faire une erreur.

slipped disc [,slɪpt-] n hernie f discale.

slipper ['slɪpər] n pantoufle f, chausson m.

slippery ['slɪpərɪ] adj glissant(e).

slipshod ['slɪpʃɒd] adj peu soigné(e).

slip-up n inf gaffe f.

slipway ['slɪpweɪ] n cale f de lancement.

slit [slɪt] (pt & pp **slit**) 1 n [opening] fente f; [cut] incision f. 2 rt [make opening in] faire une fente dans, fendre; [cut] inciser.

slither ['slɪðər] vi [person] glisser; [snake] onduler.

sliver ['slɪvər] n [of glass, wood] éclat m; [of meat, cheese] lamelle f.

slob [slɒb] n inf [in habits] saligaud m; [in appearance] gros lard m.

slog [slɒg] inf 1 n [tiring work] corvée f. 2 vi [work] travailler comme un bœuf OR un nègre.

slogan ['slǝʊgǝn] n slogan m.

slop [slɒp] 1 rt renverser. 2 ri déborder.

slope [slǝʊp] 1 n pente f. 2 vi [land] être en pente; [handwriting, table] pencher.

sloping ['slǝʊpɪŋ] adj [land, shelf] en pente; [handwriting] penché(e).

sloppy ['slɒpɪ] adj [careless] peu soigné(e).

slot [slɒt] n [opening] fente f. || [groove] rainure f. || [in schedule] créneau m.

slot machine n [vending machine] distributeur m automatique. || [for gambling] machine f à sous.

slouch [slaʊtʃ] vi être avachi(e).

Slovakia [slǝ'vækɪǝ] n Slovaquie f.

slovenly ['slʌvnlɪ] adj négligé(e).

slow [slǝʊ] 1 adj [gen] lent(e). || [clock, watch]: **to be ~** retarder. 2 adv lentement; **to go ~** [driver] aller lentement; [workers] faire la grève perlée. ○ **slow down**, **slow up** rt sep & ri ralentir.

slowdown ['slǝʊdaʊn] n ralentissement m.

slowly ['slǝʊlɪ] adv lentement.

slow motion n: **in ~** au ralenti m.

sludge [slʌdʒ] n boue f.

slug [slʌg] n [animal] limace f. || inf [of alcohol] rasade f. || Am inf [bullet] balle f.

sluggish ['slʌgɪʃ] adj [person] apathique; [movement, growth] lent(e).

sluice [slu:s] n écluse f.

slum [slʌm] n [area] quartier m pauvre.

slumber ['slʌmbər] literary n sommeil m.

slump [slʌmp] 1 n [decline]: **~ (in)** baisse f (de). || [period of poverty] crise f (économique). 2 vi lit & fig s'effondrer.

slung [slʌŋ] pt & pp → **sling**.

slur [slɜːr] 1 n [slight]: **~ (on)** atteinte f (à). || [insult] affront m, insulte f. 2 rt mal articuler.

slush [slʌʃ] n [snow] neige f fondue.

slush fund, **slush money** Am n fonds mpl secrets, caisse f noire.

slut [slʌt] n inf [dirty, untidy] souillon f. || r inf [sexually immoral] salope f.

sly [slaɪ] (compar **slyer** OR **slier**, superl **slyest** OR **sliest**) adj [look, smile] entendu(e). || [person] rusé(e), sournois(e).

smack [smæk] 1 n [slap] claque f; [on face] gifle f. || [impact] claquement m. 2 rt [slap] donner une claque à; [face] gifler. || [place violently] poser violemment.

small [smɔːl] adj [gen] petit(e). || [trivial] petit, insignifiant(e).

small change n petite monnaie f.

small hours npl: **in the ~** au petit jour OR matin.

smallpox ['smɔːlpɒks] n variole f, petite vérole f.

small print n: **the ~** les clauses fpl écrites en petits caractères.

small talk n (U) papotage m, bavardage m.

smarmy ['smɑːmɪ] adj mielleux(euse).

smart [smɑːt] 1 adj [stylish - person, clothes, car] élégant(e). || [clever] intelligent(e). || [fashionable - club, society, hotel] à la mode, in (inv). || [quick - answer, tap] vif (vive), rapide. 2 vi [eyes, skin] brûler, piquer. || [person] être blessé(e).

smarten ['smɑːtn] ○ **smarten up** rt sep [room] arranger; **to ~ o.s. up** se faire beau (belle).

smash [smæʃ] 1 n [sound] fracas m. || SPORT smash m. 2 rt [glass, plate etc] casser, briser. || fig [defeat] détruire. 3 vi [glass, plate etc] se briser. || [crash]: **to ~ into sthg** s'écraser contre qqch.

smashing ['smæʃɪŋ] adj inf super (inv).

smattering ['smætǝrɪŋ] n: **to have a ~ of German** savoir quelques mots d'allemand.

smear [smɪǝr] 1 n [dirty mark] tache f. || MED frottis m. || [slander] diffamation f. 2 rt [smudge] barbouiller, maculer. || [spread]: **to ~ sthg with sthg** enduire qqch de qqch. || [slander] calomnier.

smell [smel] (pt & pp **-ed** OR **smelt**) 1 n [odour] odeur f. || [sense of smell] odorat m. 2 rt sentir. 3 vi [flower, food] sentir; **to ~ of sthg** sentir qqch. || [smell unpleasantly] sentir (mauvais), puer.

smelly ['smelɪ] *adj* qui sent mauvais, qui pue.

smelt [smelt] **1** *pt & pp* → **smell**. **2** *vt* [metal] extraire par fusion; [ore] fondre.

smile [smaɪl] **1** *n* sourire *m*. **2** *vi* sourire.

smirk [smɜːk] *n* sourire *m* narquois.

smock [smɒk] *n* blouse *f*.

smog [smɒg] *n* smog *m*.

smoke [sməʊk] **1** *n* (*U*) [from fire] fumée *f*. **2** *vt & vi* fumer.

smoked [sməʊkt] *adj* [food] fumé(e).

smoker ['sməʊkər] *n* [person] fumeur *m*, -euse *f*. || RAIL compartiment *m* fumeurs.

smoke shop *n Am* bureau *m* de tabac.

smoking ['sməʊkɪŋ] *n* tabagisme *m*; "no ~" «défense de fumer».

smoky ['sməʊkɪ] *adj* [room, air] enfumé(e). || [taste] fumé(e).

smolder *Am* = **smoulder**.

smooth [smuːð] **1** *adj* [surface] lisse. || [sauce] homogène, onctueux(euse). || [movement] régulier(ère). || [taste] moelleux(euse). || [flight, ride] confortable; [landing, take-off] en douceur. || *pej* [person, manner] doucereux(euse), mielleux(euse). || [operation, progress] sans problèmes. **2** *vt* [hair] lisser; [clothes, tablecloth] défroisser.

smother ['smʌðər] *vt* [cover thickly]: to ~ sb/sthg with couvrir qqn/qqch de. || [person, fire] étouffer. || *fig* [emotions] cacher, étouffer.

smoulder *Br*, **smolder** *Am* ['sməʊldər] *vi lit & fig* couver.

smudge [smʌdʒ] **1** *n* tache *f*; [of ink] bavure *f*. **2** *vt* [drawing, painting] maculer; [paper] faire une marque OR trace sur; [face] salir.

smug [smʌg] *adj* suffisant(e).

smuggle ['smʌgl] *vt* [across frontiers] faire passer en contrebande.

smuggler ['smʌglər] *n* contrebandier *m*, -ière *f*.

smuggling ['smʌglɪŋ] *n* (*U*) contrebande *f*.

snack [snæk] *n* casse-croûte *m inv*.

snack bar *n* snack *m*, snack-bar *m*.

snag [snæg] **1** *n* [problem] inconvénient *m*, écueil *m*. **2** *vi*: to ~ (on) s'accrocher (à).

snail [sneɪl] *n* escargot *m*.

snake [sneɪk] *n* serpent *m*.

snap [snæp] **1** *adj* [decision, election] subit(e); [judgment] irréfléchi(e). **2** *n* [of branch] craquement *m*; [of fingers] claquement *m*. || [photograph] photo *f*. || [card game] ≃ bataille *f*. **3** *vt* [break] casser net. || [speak sharply] dire d'un ton sec. **4** *vi* [break] se casser net. || [dog]: to ~ at essayer de mordre. || [speak sharply]: to ~ (at sb) parler (à qqn) d'un ton sec.

snap fastener *n* pression *f*.

snappy ['snæpɪ] *adj inf* [stylish] chic. || [quick] prompt(e); **make it ~!** dépêche-toi!, et que ça saute!

snapshot ['snæpʃɒt] *n* photo *f*.

snare [sneər] **1** *n* piège *m*, collet *m*. **2** *vt* prendre au piège, attraper.

snarl [snɑːl] **1** *n* grondement *m*. **2** *vi* gronder.

snatch [snætʃ] **1** *n* [of conversation] bribe *f*; [of song] extrait *m*. **2** *vt* [grab] saisir.

sneak [sniːk] (*Am pt* **snuck**) **1** *vt*: to ~ a look at sb/sthg regarder qqn/qqch à la dérobée. **2** *vi* [move quietly] se glisser.

sneakers ['sniːkəz] *npl Am* tennis *mpl*, baskets *fpl*.

sneaky ['sniːkɪ] *adj inf* sournois(e).

sneer [snɪər] **1** *n* [smile] sourire *m* dédaigneux; [laugh] ricanement *m*. **2** *vi* [smile] sourire dédaigneusement.

sneeze [sniːz] **1** *n* éternuement *m*. **2** *vi* éternuer.

snide [snaɪd] *adj* sournois(e).

sniff [snɪf] **1** *vt* [smell] renifler. **2** *vi* [to clear nose] renifler.

snigger ['snɪgər] **1** *n* rire *m* en dessous. **2** *vi* ricaner.

snip [snɪp] *vt* couper.

sniper ['snaɪpər] *n* tireur *m* isolé.

snippet ['snɪpɪt] *n* fragment *m*.

snivel ['snɪvl] *vi* geindre.

snob [snɒb] *n* snob *mf*.

snobbish ['snɒbɪʃ], **snobby** ['snɒbɪ] *adj* snob (*inv*).

snoop [snuːp] *vi inf* fureter.

snooty ['snuːtɪ] *adj inf* prétentieux (ieuse).

snooze [snuːz] **1** *n* petit somme *m*. **2** *vi* faire un petit somme.

snore [snɔːr] **1** *n* ronflement *m*. **2** *vi* ronfler.

snoring ['snɔːrɪŋ] *n* (*U*) ronflement *m*, ronflements *mpl*.

snorkel ['snɔːkl] *n* tuba *m*.

snort [snɔːt] **1** *n* [of person] grognement *m*; [of horse, bull] ébrouement *m*. **2** *vi* [person] grogner; [horse] s'ébrouer.

snout [snaʊt] *n* groin *m*.

snow [snəʊ] **1** *n* neige *f*. **2** *v impers* neiger.

snowball ['snəʊbɔːl] **1** *n* boule *f* de neige. **2** *vi fig* faire boule de neige.

snowbound ['snəʊbaʊnd] *adj* bloqué(e) par la neige.

snowdrift ['snəʊdrɪft] *n* congère *f*.

snowdrop ['snəʊdrɒp] *n* perce-neige *m inv*.

snowfall ['snəʊfɔːl] *n* chute *f* de neige.

snowflake ['snəʊfleɪk] *n* flocon *m* de neige.

snowman ['snəʊmæn] (*pl* **-men** [-men]) *n* bonhomme *m* de neige.

snowplough *Br*, **snowplow** *Am* ['snəʊplaʊ] *n* chasse-neige *m inv*.

snowshoe ['snəʊʃuː] *n* raquette *f*.

snowstorm ['snəʊstɔːm] *n* tempête *f* de neige.

Snr, snr *abbr of* **senior**.

snub [snʌb] **1** *n* rebuffade *f*. **2** *vt* snober, ignorer.

snuck [snʌk] *pt* → **sneak**.

snuff [snʌf] *n* tabac *m* à priser.

snug [snʌg] *adj* [person] à l'aise, confortable; [in bed] bien au chaud. || [place] douillet(ette). || [close-fitting] bien ajusté(e).

snuggle ['snʌgl] *vi* se blottir.

so [səʊ] **1** *adv* [to such a degree] si, tellement; ~ **difficult (that)** ... si OR tellement difficile que ...; **we had ~ much work!** nous avions tant de travail!; **I've never seen ~ much money/many cars** je n'ai jamais vu autant d'argent/de voitures. || [in referring back to previous statement, event etc]: ~ **you knew already?** alors tu le savais déjà?; **I don't think ~** je ne crois pas; **I'm afraid ~** je crains bien que oui; **if ~** si oui; **is that ~?** vraiment? || [also] aussi; ~ **can/do/would** *etc* **I** moi aussi. || [in this way]: **(like) ~** comme cela OR ça, de cette façon. || [in expressing agreement]: ~ **there is** en effet, c'est vrai; ~ **I see** c'est ce que je vois. || [unspecified amount, limit]: **they pay us** ~ **much a week** ils nous payent tant par semaine; **or** ~ environ, à peu près. **2** *conj* alors; **I'm away next week** ~ **I won't be there** je suis en voyage la semaine prochaine donc OR par conséquent je ne serai pas là; ~ **what?** *inf* et alors?, et après?; ~ **there!** *inf* là!, et voilà! ○ **and so on, and so forth** *adv* et ainsi de suite. ○ **so as** *conj* afin de, pour. ○ **so that** *conj* [for the purpose that] pour que (+ *subjunctive*).

soak [səʊk] **1** *vt* laisser OR faire tremper. **2** *vi* [become thoroughly wet]: **to leave sthg to ~, to let sthg ~** laisser OR faire tremper qqch. || [spread]: **to ~ into sthg** tremper dans qqch; **to ~ through (sthg)** traverser (qqch). ○ **soak up** *vt sep* absorber.

soaking ['səʊkɪŋ] *adj* trempé(e).

so-and-so *n inf* [to replace a name]: **Mr ~** Monsieur un tel. || [annoying person] enquiquineur *m*, -euse *f*.

soap [səʊp] *n* (*U*) [for washing] savon *m*.

soap flakes *npl* savon *m* en paillettes.

soap opera *n* soap opera *m*.

soap powder *n* lessive *f*.

soar [sɔːr] *vi* [bird] planer. || [balloon, kite] monter. || [prices, temperature] monter en flèche.

sob [sɒb] **1** *n* sanglot *m*. **2** *vi* sangloter.

sober ['səʊbər] *adj* [not drunk] qui n'est pas ivre. || [serious] sérieux(ieuse). || [plain - clothes, colours] sobre. ○ **sober up** *vi* dessoûler.

sobering ['səʊbərɪŋ] *adj* qui donne à réfléchir.

so-called [-kɔːld] *adj* [misleadingly named] soi-disant (*inv*). || [widely known as] ainsi appelé(e).

soccer ['sɒkər] *n* football *m*.

sociable ['səʊʃəbl] *adj* sociable.

social ['səʊʃl] *adj* social(e).

social club *n* club *m*.

socialism ['səʊʃəlɪzm] *n* socialisme *m*.

socialist ['səʊʃəlɪst] **1** *adj* socialiste. **2** *n* socialiste *mf*.

socialize, -ise ['səʊʃəlaɪz] *vi* fréquenter des gens.

social security *n* aide *f* sociale.

social services *npl* services *mpl* sociaux.

social worker *n* assistant social *m*, assistante sociale *f*.

society [sə'saɪətɪ] *n* [gen] société *f*. || [club] association *f*, club *m*.

sociology [,səʊsɪ'ɒlədʒɪ] *n* sociologie *f*.

sock [sɒk] *n* chaussette *f*.

socket ['sɒkɪt] *n* [for light bulb] douille *f*; [for plug] prise *f* de courant. || [of eye] orbite *f*; [for bone] cavité *f* articulaire.

sod [sɒd] *n* [of turf] motte *f* de gazon.

soda ['səʊdə] *n* CHEM soude *f*. || *Am* [fizzy drink] soda *m*.

soda water *n* eau *f* de Seltz.

sodden ['sɒdn] *adj* trempé(e), détrempé(e).

sodium ['səʊdɪəm] *n* sodium *m*.

sofa ['səʊfə] *n* canapé *m*.

Sofia ['səʊfjə] *n* Sofia.

soft [sɒft] *adj* [not hard] doux (douce), mou (molle). || [smooth, not loud, not bright] doux (douce). || [without force] léger(ère). || [caring] tendre. || [lenient] faible, indulgent(e).

soft drink n boisson f non alcoolisée.

soften ['sɒfn] 1 vt [fabric] assouplir; [substance] ramollir; [skin] adoucir. || [shock, blow] atténuer, adoucir. || [attitude] modérer, adoucir. 2 vi [substance] se ramollir. || [attitude, person] s'adoucir, se radoucir.

softhearted [,sɒft'hɑ:tɪd] adj au cœur tendre.

softly ['sɒftlɪ] adv [gently, quietly] doucement. || [not brightly] faiblement. || [leniently] avec indulgence.

soft-spoken adj à la voix douce.

software ['sɒftweəʳ] n (U) COMPUT logiciel m.

soggy ['sɒgɪ] adj trempé(e), détrempé(e).

soil [sɔɪl] 1 n (U) [earth] sol m, terre f. || fig [territory] sol m, territoire m. 2 vt souiller, salir.

soiled [sɔɪld] adj sale.

solace ['sɒləs] n literary consolation f, réconfort m.

solar ['səʊləʳ] adj solaire.

sold [səʊld] pt & pp → sell.

solder ['səʊldəʳ] 1 n (U) soudure f. 2 vt souder.

soldier ['səʊldʒəʳ] n soldat m.

sold-out adj [tickets] qui ont tous été vendus; [play, concert] qui joue à guichets fermés.

sole [səʊl] (pl sense 2 only inv OR -s) 1 adj [only] seul(e), unique. || [exclusive] exclusif(ive). 2 n [of foot] semelle f. || [fish] sole f.

solemn ['sɒləm] adj solennel(elle); [person] sérieux(ieuse).

solicit [sə'lɪsɪt] 1 vt [request] solliciter. 2 vi [prostitute] racoler.

solid ['sɒlɪd] 1 adj [not fluid, sturdy, reliable] solide. || [not hollow - tyres] plein(e); [- wood, rock, gold] massif(ive). || [without interruption]: **two hours ~** deux heures d'affilée. 2 n solide m.

solidarity [,sɒlɪ'dærətɪ] n solidarité f.

solitaire [,sɒlɪ'teəʳ] n [jewel, board game] solitaire m. || Am [card game] réussite f, patience f.

solitary ['sɒlɪtrɪ] adj [lonely, alone] solitaire. || [just one] seul(e).

solitary confinement n isolement m cellulaire.

solitude ['sɒlɪtju:d] n solitude f.

solo ['səʊləʊ] (pl -s) 1 adj solo (inv). 2 n solo m. 3 adv en solo.

soloist ['səʊləʊɪst] n soliste mf.

soluble ['sɒljʊbl] adj soluble.

solution [sə'lu:ʃn] n [to problem]: ~ (to) solution f. || [liquid] solution f.

solve [sɒlv] vt résoudre.

solvent ['sɒlvənt] 1 adj FIN solvable. 2 n dissolvant m, solvant m.

Somalia [sə'mɑ:lɪə] n Somalie f.

sombre Br, **somber** Am ['sɒmbəʳ] adj sombre.

some [sʌm] 1 adj [a certain amount, number of]: ~ **meat** de la viande; ~ **money** de l'argent; ~ **coffee** du café; ~ **sweets** des bonbons. || [fairly large number or quantity of] quelque; **I've known him for ~ years** je le connais depuis plusieurs années OR pas mal d'années. || (contrastive use) [certain]: ~ **jobs are better paid than others** certains boulots sont mieux rémunérés que d'autres; ~ **people like his music** il y en a qui aiment sa musique. || [in imprecise statements] quelque, quelconque; **there must be ~ mistake** il doit y avoir erreur. || inf [very good]: **that was ~ party!** c'était une soirée formidable!, quelle soirée! 2 pron [a certain amount]: **can I have ~?** [money, milk, coffee etc] est-ce que je peux en prendre?; ~ **of it is mine** une partie est à moi. || [a certain number] quelques-uns (quelques-unes), certains (certaines); **can I have ~?** [books, pens, potatoes etc] est-ce que je peux en prendre (quelques-uns)? 3 adv quelque, environ; **there were ~ 7,000 people there** il y avait quelque OR environ 7 000 personnes.

somebody ['sʌmbədɪ] pron quelqu'un.

someday ['sʌmdeɪ] adv un jour, un de ces jours.

somehow ['sʌmhaʊ], **someway** Am ['sʌmweɪ] adv [by some action] d'une manière ou d'une autre. || [for some reason] pour une raison ou pour une autre.

someone ['sʌmwʌn] pron quelqu'un.

someplace Am = **somewhere**.

somersault ['sʌməsɔ:lt] 1 n cabriole f, culbute f. 2 vi faire une cabriole OR culbute.

something ['sʌmθɪŋ] 1 pron [unknown thing] quelque chose; ~ **odd/interesting** quelque chose de bizarre/d'intéressant; **or ~** inf ou quelque chose comme ça. 2 adv: ~ **like**, ~ **in the region of** environ, à peu près.

source

sometime ['sʌmtaɪm] *adv* un de ces jours; ~ **last week** la semaine dernière.

sometimes ['sʌmtaɪmz] *adv* quelquefois, parfois.

someway *Am* = **somehow**.

somewhat ['sʌmwɒt] *adv* quelque peu.

somewhere *Br* ['sʌmweəʳ], **someplace** *Am* ['sʌmpleɪs] *adv* [unknown place] quelque part; ~ **else** ailleurs; ~ **near here** près d'ici. || [used in approximations] environ, à peu près.

son [sʌn] *n* fils *m*.

song [sɒŋ] *n* chanson *f*; [of bird] chant *m*, ramage *m*.

sonic ['sɒnɪk] *adj* sonique.

son-in-law (*pl* **sons-in-law** OR **son-in-laws**) *n* gendre *m*, beau-fils *m*.

sonnet ['sɒnɪt] *n* sonnet *m*.

soon [suːn] *adv* [before long] bientôt; ~ **after** peu après. || [early] tôt; **write back ~** réponds-moi vite; **how ~ will it be ready?** ce sera prêt quand?; dans combien de temps est-ce que ce sera prêt?; **as ~ as** dès que, aussitôt que.

sooner ['suːnəʳ] *adv* [in time] plus tôt; **no ~ ... than ...** à peine ... que ...; ~ **or later** tôt ou tard; **the ~ the better** le plus tôt sera le mieux. || [expressing preference]: **I would ~ ...** je préférerais ..., j'aimerais mieux ....

soot [sʊt] *n* suie *f*.

soothe [suːð] *vt* calmer, apaiser.

sophisticated [sə'fɪstɪkeɪtɪd] *adj* [stylish] raffiné(e), sophistiqué(e). || [intelligent] averti(e). || [complicated] sophistiqué(e), très perfectionné(e).

sophomore ['sɒfəmɔːʳ] *n* *Am* étudiant *m*, -e *f* de seconde année.

sopping ['sɒpɪŋ] *adj*: ~ **(wet)** tout trempé (toute trempée).

soppy ['sɒpɪ] *adj inf* [sentimental - book, film] à l'eau de rose; [- person] sentimental(e). || [silly] bêta(asse), bête.

soprano [sə'prɑːnəʊ] (*pl* -**s**) *n* [person] soprano *mf*; [voice] soprano *m*.

sorbet ['sɔːbeɪ] *n* sorbet *m*.

sorcerer ['sɔːsərəʳ] *n* sorcier *m*.

sordid ['sɔːdɪd] *adj* sordide.

sore [sɔːʳ] 1 *adj* [painful] douloureux(euse); **to have a ~ throat** avoir mal à la gorge. || *Am* [upset] fâché(e), contrarié(e). 2 *n* plaie *f*.

sorely ['sɔːlɪ] *adv literary* [needed] grandement.

sorrow ['sɒrəʊ] *n* peine *f*, chagrin *m*.

sorry ['sɒrɪ] 1 *adj* [expressing apology, disappointment, sympathy] désolé(e); **to**

be ~ about sthg s'excuser pour qqch; **to be ~ for sthg** regretter qqch; **to be** OR **feel ~ for sb** plaindre qqn. || [poor]: **in a ~ state** en piteux état, dans un triste état. 2 *excl* [expressing apology] pardon!, excusez-moi!; ~, **we're sold out** désolé, on n'en a plus. || [asking for repetition] pardon?, comment? || [to correct oneself] non, pardon OR je veux dire.

sort [sɔːt] 1 *n* genre *m*, sorte *f*, espèce *f*; ~ **of** [rather] plutôt, quelque peu. 2 *vt* trier, classer. ○ **sort out** *vt sep* [classify] ranger, classer. || [solve] résoudre.

sorting office ['sɔːtɪŋ-] *n* centre *m* de tri.

SOS (*abbr of* save our souls) *n* SOS *m*.

so-so *inf* 1 *adj* quelconque. 2 *adv* comme ci comme ça.

sought [sɔːt] *pt* & *pp* → **seek**.

soul [səʊl] *n* [gen] âme *f*. || [music] soul *m*.

soul-destroying [-dɪ,strɔɪɪŋ] *adj* abrutissant(e).

soulful ['səʊlfʊl] *adj* [look] expressif(ive); [song etc] sentimental(e).

sound [saʊnd] 1 *adj* [healthy - body] sain(e), en bonne santé; [- mind] sain. || [sturdy] solide. || [reliable - advice] judicieux(ieuse), sage; [- investment] sûr(e). 2 *adv*: **to be ~ asleep** dormir à poings fermés, dormir d'un sommeil profond. 3 *n* son *m*; [particular sound] bruit *m*, son *m*; **by the ~ of it ...** d'après ce que j'ai compris .... 4 *vt* [alarm, bell] sonner. 5 *vi* [make a noise] sonner, retentir; **to ~ like sthg** ressembler à qqch. || [seem] sembler, avoir l'air. ○ **sound out** *vt sep*: **to ~ sb out (on** OR **about)** sonder qqn (sur).

sound barrier *n* mur *m* du son.

sound effects *npl* bruitage *m*, effets *mpl* sonores.

soundly ['saʊndlɪ] *adv* [beaten] à plates coutures. || [sleep] profondément.

soundproof ['saʊndpruːf] *adj* insonorisé(e).

soundtrack ['saʊndtræk] *n* bande-son *f*.

soup [suːp] *n* soupe *f*, potage *m*.

soup plate *n* assiette *f* creuse OR à soupe.

soup spoon *n* cuiller *f* à soupe.

sour ['saʊəʳ] *adj* [taste, fruit] acide, aigre. || [milk] aigre. || [ill-tempered] aigre, acerbe.

source [sɔːs] *n* [gen] source *f*. || [cause] origine *f*, cause *f*.

sour grapes *n* (*U*) *inf*: what he said was just ~ il a dit ça par dépit.

south [saʊθ] **1** *n* [direction] sud *m*. ‖ [region]: **the ~** le sud; **the South of France** le Sud de la France. le Midi (de la France). **2** *adj* sud (*inv*); [wind] du sud. **3** *adr* au sud, vers le sud; **~ of** au sud de.

South Africa *n* Afrique *f* du Sud.

South African 1 *adj* sud-africain(e). **2** *n* [person] Sud-Africain *m*, -e *f*.

South America *n* Amérique *f* du Sud.

South American 1 *adj* sud-américain(e). **2** *n* [person] Sud-Américain *m*, -e *f*.

southeast [,saʊθ'iːst] **1** *n* [direction] sud-est *m*. ‖ [region]: **the ~** le sud-est. **2** *adj* au sud-est, du sud-est; [wind] du sud-est. **3** *adr* au sud-est, vers le sud-est; **~ of** au sud-est de.

southerly ['sʌðəlɪ] *adj* au sud, du sud; [wind] du sud.

southern ['sʌðən] *adj* du sud; [France] du Midi.

South Korea *n* Corée *f* du Sud.

South Pole *n*: **the ~** le pôle Sud.

southward ['saʊθwəd] **1** *adj* au sud, du sud. **2** *adr* = **southwards**.

southwards ['saʊθwədz] *adr* vers le sud.

southwest [,saʊθ'west] **1** *n* [direction] sud-ouest *m*. ‖ [region]: **the ~** le sud-ouest. **2** *adj* au sud-ouest, du sud-ouest; [wind] du sud-ouest. **3** *adr* au sud-ouest, vers le sud-ouest; **~ of** au sud-ouest de.

souvenir [,suːvə'nɪər] *n* souvenir *m*.

sovereign ['sɒvrɪn] *n* [ruler] souverain *m*, -e *f*. ‖ [coin] souverain *m*.

soviet ['səʊvɪət] *n* soviet *m*. ○ **Soviet 1** *adj* soviétique. **2** *n* [person] Soviétique *mf*.

Soviet Union *n*: **the (former) ~** l'(ex-)Union *f* soviétique.

sow¹ [səʊ] (*pt* -ed, *pp* sown OR -ed) *vt lit & fig* semer.

sow² [saʊ] *n* truie *f*.

sown [səʊn] *pp* → **sow¹**.

soya ['sɔɪə] *n* soja *m*.

soy(a) bean ['sɔɪ(ə)-] *n* graine *f* de soja.

spa [spɑː] *n* station *f* thermale.

space [speɪs] **1** *n* [gap, roominess, outer space] espace *m*; [on form] blanc *m*, espace. ‖ [room] place *f*. ‖ [of time]: **within** OR **in the ~ of ten minutes** en l'espace de dix minutes. **2** *comp* spatial(e). **3** *vt* espacer. ○ **space out** *vt sep* espacer.

spacecraft ['speɪskrɑːft] (*pl inv*) *n* vaisseau *m* spatial.

spaceman ['speɪsmæn] (*pl* -men [-men]) *n* astronaute *m*, cosmonaute *m*.

spaceship ['speɪsʃɪp] *n* vaisseau *m* spatial.

space shuttle *n* navette *f* spatiale.

spacesuit ['speɪssuːt] *n* combinaison *f* spatiale.

spacing ['speɪsɪŋ] *n* TYPO espacement *m*.

spacious ['speɪʃəs] *adj* spacieux(ieuse).

spade [speɪd] *n* [tool] pelle *f*. ‖ [playing card] pique *m*. ○ **spades** *npl* pique *m*.

spaghetti [spə'getɪ] *n* (*U*) spaghettis *mpl*.

Spain [speɪn] *n* Espagne *f*.

span [spæn] **1** *pt* → **spin**. **2** *n* [in time] espace *m* de temps, durée *f*. ‖ [range] éventail *m*, gamme *f*. ‖ [of bird. plane] envergure *f*. **3** *vt* [in time] embrasser, couvrir. ‖ [subj: bridge] franchir.

Spaniard ['spænjəd] *n* Espagnol *m*, -e *f*.

spaniel ['spænjəl] *n* épagneul *m*.

Spanish ['spænɪʃ] **1** *adj* espagnol(e). **2** *n* [language] espagnol *m*. **3** *npl*: **the ~** les Espagnols.

spank [spæŋk] *vt* donner une fessée à, fesser.

spanner ['spænər] *n* clé *f* à écrous.

spar [spɑːr] **1** *n* espar *m*. **2** *vi* BOXING s'entraîner à la boxe.

spare [speər] **1** *adj* [surplus] de trop; [component. clothing etc] de réserve, de rechange. ‖ [available - seat. time, tickets] disponible. **2** *n* [part] pièce *f* détachée OR de rechange. **3** *vt* [make available - staff. money] se passer de; [- time] disposer de; **to have an hour to ~** avoir une heure de battement OR de libre; **with a minute to ~** avec une minute d'avance. ‖ [not harm] épargner. ‖ [not use] épargner, ménager. ‖ [save from]: **to ~ sb sthg** épargner qqch à qqn. éviter qqch à qqn.

spare part *n* pièce *f* détachée OR de rechange.

spare time *n* (*U*) temps *m* libre, loisirs *mpl*.

spare wheel *n* roue *f* de secours.

sparing ['speərɪŋ] *adj*: **to be ~ with** OR **of sthg** être économe de qqch, ménager qqch.

sparingly ['speərɪŋlɪ] *adr* [use] avec modération; [spend] avec parcimonie.

spark [spɑːk] *n lit & fig* étincelle *f*.

sparkle ['spɑːkl] **1** *n* (*U*) [of eyes, jewel] éclat *m*; [of stars] scintillement *m*. **2** *vi* étinceler, scintiller.

sparkling wine ['spɑːklɪŋ-] *n* vin *m* mousseux.

spark plug n bougie f.

sparrow ['spærəʊ] n moineau m.

sparse ['spɑːs] adj clairsemé(e), épars(e).

spasm ['spæzm] n MED spasme m; [of coughing] quinte f.

spastic ['spæstik] MED n handicapé m, -e f moteur.

spat [spæt] pt & pp → spit.

spate [speit] n [of attacks etc] série f.

spatter ['spætər] vt éclabousser.

spawn [spɔːn] 1 n (U) frai m, œufs mpl. 2 vt fig donner naissance à, engendrer.

speak [spiːk] (pt spoke, pp spoken) 1 vt [say] dire. || [language] parler. 2 vi parler; to ~ to OR with sb parler à qqn; to ~ about sb/sthg parler de qqn/qqch. ○ **so to speak** adv pour ainsi dire. ○ **speak for** vt fus [represent] parler pour, parler au nom de. ○ **speak up** vi [support]: to ~ up for sb/sthg parler en faveur de qqn/qqch, soutenir qqn/qqch. || [speak louder] parler plus fort.

speaker ['spiːkər] n [person talking] personne f qui parle. || [person making speech] orateur m. || [of language]: a German ~ une personne qui parle allemand. || [loudspeaker] haut-parleur m.

spear [spiər] 1 n lance f. 2 vt transpercer d'un coup de lance.

spearhead ['spiəhed] 1 n fer m de lance. 2 vt [campaign] mener; [attack] être le fer de lance de.

special ['speʃl] adj [gen] spécial(e). || [needs, effort, attention] particulier(ère).

special delivery n (U) [service] exprès m, envoi m par exprès; by ~ en exprès.

specialist ['speʃəlist] 1 adj spécialisé(e). 2 n spécialiste mf.

speciality [ˌspeʃiˈæləti], **specialty** Am ['speʃlti] n spécialité f.

specialize, -ise ['speʃəlaiz] vi: to ~ (in) se spécialiser (dans).

specially ['speʃəli] adv [specifically] spécialement; [on purpose] exprès. || [particularly] particulièrement.

specialty n Am = speciality.

species ['spiːʃiːz] (pl inv) n espèce f.

specific [spəˈsifik] adj [particular] particulier(ère), précis(e). || [precise] précis(e). || [unique]: ~ to propre à.

specifically [spəˈsifikli] adv [particularly] particulièrement, spécialement. || [precisely] précisément.

specify ['spesifai] vt préciser, spécifier.

specimen ['spesimən] n [example]

exemple m, spécimen m. || [of blood] prélèvement m; [of urine] échantillon m.

speck [spek] n [small stain] toute petite tache f. || [of dust] grain m.

speckled ['spekld] adj: ~ (with) tacheté(e) de.

spectacle ['spektəkl] n spectacle m.

spectacular [spekˈtækjʊlər] adj spectaculaire.

spectator [spekˈteitər] n spectateur m, -trice f.

spectre Br, **specter** Am ['spektər] n spectre m.

spectrum ['spektrəm] (pl -tra [-trə]) n PHYSICS spectre m. || fig [variety] gamme f.

speculation [ˌspekjʊˈleiʃn] n [gen] spéculation f. || [conjecture] conjectures fpl.

sped [sped] pt & pp → speed.

speech [spiːtʃ] n (U) [ability] parole f. || [formal talk] discours m. || THEATRE texte m. || [manner of speaking] façon f de parler. || [dialect] parler m.

speechless ['spiːtʃlis] adj: ~ (with) muet(ette) (de).

speed [spiːd] (pt & pp -ed OR sped) 1 n vitesse f; [of reply, action] vitesse, rapidité f. 2 vi [move fast]: to ~ away démarrer à toute allure. || AUT [go too fast] rouler trop vite, faire un excès de vitesse. ○ **speed up** 1 vt sep [person] faire aller plus vite; [work, production] accélérer. 2 vi aller plus vite; [car] accélérer.

speedboat ['spiːdbəʊt] n hors-bord m inv.

speeding ['spiːdiŋ] n (U) excès m de vitesse.

speed limit n limitation f de vitesse.

speedometer [spiˈdɒmitər] n compteur m (de vitesse).

speedway ['spiːdwei] n (U) SPORT course f de motos. || Am [road] voie f express.

speedy ['spiːdi] adj rapide.

spell [spel] (Br pt & pp spelt OR -ed, Am pt & pp -ed) 1 n [period of time] période f. || [enchantment] charme m; [words] formule f magique; to cast OR put a ~ on sb jeter un sort à qqn, envoûter qqn. 2 vt [word, name] écrire. || fig [signify] signifier. 3 vi épeler. ○ **spell out** vt sep [read aloud] épeler. || [explain]: to ~ sthg out (for OR to sb) expliquer qqch clairement (à qqn).

spellbound ['spelbaʊnd] adj subjugué(e).

spelling ['speliŋ] n orthographe f.

spelt [spelt] Br pt & pp → spell.

spend [spend] (*pt* & *pp* **spent**) *vt* [pay out]: **to ~ money (on)** dépenser de l'argent (pour). || [time, life] passer.

spendthrift ['spendθrɪft] *n* dépensier *m*, -ière *f*.

spent [spent] **1** *pt* & *pp* → **spend**. **2** *adj* [fuel, match, ammunition] utilisé(e); [patience, energy] épuisé(e).

sperm [spɜːm] (*pl inv* OR **-s**) *n* sperme *m*.

spew [spjuː] *vt* & *vi* vomir.

sphere [sfɪər] *n* sphère *f*.

spice [spaɪs] *n* CULIN épice *f*. || (*U*) *fig* [excitement] piment *m*.

spick-and-span ['spɪkən,spæn] *adj* impeccable, nickel (*inv*).

spicy ['spaɪsɪ] *adj* CULIN épicé(e). || *fig* [story] pimenté(e), piquant(e).

spider ['spaɪdər] *n* araignée *f*.

spike [spaɪk] *n* [metal] pointe *f*, lance *f*; [of plant] piquant *m*; [of hair] épi *m*.

spill [spɪl] (*Br pt* & *pp* **spilt** OR **-ed**, *Am pt* & *pp* **-ed**) **1** *vt* renverser. **2** *vi* [liquid] se répandre.

spilt [spɪlt] *Br pt* & *pp* → **spill**.

spin [spɪn] (*pt* **span** OR **spun**, *pp* **spun**) **1** *n* [turn]: **to give sthg a ~** faire tourner qqch. || AERON vrille *f*. || *inf* [in car] tour *m*. || SPORT effet *m*. **2** *vt* [wheel] faire tourner; **to ~ a coin** jouer à pile ou face. || [washing] essorer. || [thread, wool, cloth] filer. || SPORT [ball] donner de l'effet à. **3** *vi* tourner, tournoyer. **◯ spin out** *vt sep* [money, story] faire durer.

spinach ['spɪnɪdʒ] *n* (*U*) épinards *mpl*.

spinal column ['spaɪnl-] *n* colonne *f* vertébrale.

spinal cord ['spaɪnl-] *n* moelle *f* épinière.

spindly ['spɪndlɪ] *adj* grêle, chétif(ive).

spine [spaɪn] *n* ANAT colonne *f* vertébrale. || [of book] dos *m*. || [of plant, hedgehog] piquant *m*.

spinning ['spɪnɪŋ] *n* [of thread] filage *m*.

spinning top *n* toupie *f*.

spin-off *n* [by-product] dérivé *m*.

spinster ['spɪnstər] *n* célibataire *f*; *pej* vieille fille *f*.

spiral ['spaɪərəl] **1** *adj* spiral(e). **2** *n* spirale *f*.

spiral staircase *n* escalier *m* en colimaçon.

spire [spaɪər] *n* flèche *f*.

spirit ['spɪrɪt] *n* [gen] esprit *m*. || (*U*) [determination] caractère *m*, courage *m*. **◯ spirits** *npl* [mood] humeur *f*; **to be in**

high **~s** être gai(e); **to be in low ~s** être déprimé(e). || [alcohol] spiritueux *mpl*.

spirited ['spɪrɪtɪd] *adj* fougueux(euse); [performance] interprété(e) avec brio.

spirit level *n* niveau *m* à bulle d'air.

spiritual ['spɪrɪtʃʊəl] *adj* spirituel(elle).

spit [spɪt] (*Br pt* & *pp* **spat**, *Am pt* & *pp* **spit**) **1** *n* (*U*) [spittle] crachat *m*; [saliva] salive *f*. || [skewer] broche *f*. **2** *vi* cracher.

spite [spaɪt] **1** *n* rancune *f*. **2** *vt* contrarier. **◯ in spite of** *prep* en dépit de, malgré.

spiteful ['spaɪtfʊl] *adj* malveillant(e).

spittle ['spɪtl] *n* (*U*) crachat *m*.

splash [splæʃ] **1** *n* [sound] plouf *m*. || [of colour, light] tache *f*. **2** *vt* éclabousser. **3** *vi* [person]: **to ~ about** OR **around** barboter. || [liquid] jaillir. **◯ splash out** *inf vi*: **to ~ out (on)** dépenser une fortune (pour).

spleen [spliːn] *n* ANAT rate *f*.

splendid ['splendɪd] *adj* splendide; [work, holiday, idea] excellent(e).

splint [splɪnt] *n* attelle *f*.

splinter ['splɪntər] **1** *n* éclat *m*. **2** *vi* [wood] se fendre en éclats; [glass] se briser en éclats.

split [splɪt] (*pt* & *pp* **split**, *cont* **-ting**) **1** *n* [in wood] fente *f*; [in garment - tear] déchirure *f*; [- by design] échancrure *f*. || POL: **~ (in)** division *f* OR scission *f* (au sein de). || [difference]: **~ between** écart *m* entre. **2** *vt* [wood] fendre; [clothes] déchirer. || POL diviser. || [share] partager. **3** *vi* [wood] se fendre; [clothes] se déchirer. || POL se diviser; [road, path] se séparer. **◯ split up** *vi* [group, couple] se séparer.

split second *n* fraction *f* de seconde.

splutter ['splʌtər] *vi* [person] bredouiller, bafouiller; [engine] tousser.

spoil [spɔɪl] (*pt* & *pp* **-ed** OR **spoilt**) *vt* [ruin - holiday] gâcher, gâter; [- view] gâter; [- food] gâter, abîmer. || [overindulge, treat well] gâter. **◯ spoils** *npl* butin *m*.

spoiled [spɔɪld] *adj* = **spoilt**.

spoilsport ['spɔɪlspɔːt] *n* trouble-fête *mf inv*.

spoilt [spɔɪlt] **1** *pt* & *pp* → **spoil**. **2** *adj* [child] gâté(e).

spoke [spəʊk] **1** *pt* → **speak**. **2** *n* rayon *m*.

spoken ['spəʊkn] *pp* → **speak**.

spokesman ['spəʊksmən] (*pl* **-men** [-mən]) *n* porte-parole *m inv*.

spokeswoman ['spəʊks,wʊmən] (*pl* **-women** [-,wɪmɪn]) *n* porte-parole *m inv*.

sponge [spʌndʒ] (*Br cont* **spongeing**, *Am cont* **sponging**) **1** *n* [for cleaning, washing] éponge *f.* || [cake] gâteau *m* OR biscuit *m* de Savoie. **2** *vt* éponger. **3** *vi* *inf:* **to ~ off sb** taper qqn.

sponge cake *n* gâteau *m* OR biscuit *m* de Savoie.

sponsor ['spɒnsər] **1** *n* sponsor *m.* **2** *vt* [finance, for charity] sponsoriser, parrainer. || [support] soutenir.

sponsored walk [,spɒnsəd-] *n marche organisée pour recueillir des fonds.*

sponsorship ['spɒnsəʃɪp] *n* sponsoring *m,* parrainage *m.*

spontaneous [spɒn'teɪnjəs] *adj* spontané(e).

spool [spuːl] *n* [gen & COMPUT] bobine *f.*

spoon [spuːn] *n* cuillère *f,* cuiller *f.*

spoon-feed *vt* nourrir à la cuillère; **to ~ sb** *fig* mâcher le travail à qqn.

spoonful ['spuːnful] (*pl* **-s** OR **spoonsful**) *n* cuillerée *f.*

sporadic [spə'rædɪk] *adj* sporadique.

sport [spɔːt] *n* [game] sport *m.*

sporting ['spɔːtɪŋ] *adj* [relating to sport] sportif(ive). || [generous, fair] chic (*inv*); **to have a ~ chance of doing sthg** avoir des chances de faire qqch.

sports car ['spɔːts-] *n* voiture *f* de sport.

sports jacket ['spɔːts-] *n* veste *f* sport.

sportsman ['spɔːtsmən] (*pl* **-men** [-mən]) *n* sportif *m.*

sportsmanship ['spɔːtsmənʃɪp] *n* sportivité *f,* esprit *m* sportif.

sportswear ['spɔːtsweər] *n* (*U*) vêtements *mpl* de sport.

sportswoman ['spɔːts,wumən] (*pl* **-women** [-,wɪmɪn]) *n* sportive *f.*

sporty ['spɔːtɪ] *adj inf* [person] sportif(ive).

spot [spɒt] **1** *n* [mark, dot] tache *f.* || [pimple] bouton *m.* || [drop] goutte *f.* || *inf* [small amount]: **to have a ~ of** **bother** avoir quelques ennuis. || [place] endroit *m;* **on the ~** sur place. || RADIO & TV numéro *m.* **2** *vt* [notice] apercevoir.

spot check *n* contrôle *m* au hasard OR intermittent.

spotless ['spɒtlɪs] *adj* [clean] impeccable.

spotlight ['spɒtlaɪt] *n* [in theatre] projecteur *m,* spot *m;* [in home] spot *m;* **to be in the ~** *fig* être en vedette.

spotted ['spɒtɪd] *adj* [pattern, material] à pois.

spouse [spaus] *n* époux *m,* épouse *f.*

spout [spaut] **1** *n* bec *m.* **2** *vi:* **to ~ from** OR **out of** jaillir de.

sprain [spreɪn] **1** *n* entorse *f.* **2** *vt:* **to ~ one's ankle/wrist** se faire une entorse à la cheville/au poignet, se fouler la cheville/le poignet.

sprang [spræŋ] *pt* → **spring.**

sprawl [sprɔːl] *vi* [person] être affalé(e). || [city] s'étaler.

spray [spreɪ] **1** *n* (*U*) [of water] gouttelettes *fpl;* [from sea] embruns *mpl.* || [container] bombe *f,* pulvérisateur *m.* || [of flowers] gerbe *f.* **2** *vt* [product] pulvériser; [plants, crops] pulvériser de l'insecticide sur.

spread [spred] (*pt & pp* **spread**) **1** (*U*) [food] pâte *f* à tartiner. || [of fire, disease] propagation *f.* || [of opinions] gamme *f.* **2** *vt* [map, rug] étaler, étendre; [fingers, arms, legs] écarter. || [butter, jam etc]: **to ~ sthg (over)** étaler qqch (sur). || [disease, rumour, germs] répandre, propager. **3** *vi* [disease, rumour] se propager, se répandre. || [water, cloud] s'étaler.
○ **spread out** *vi* se disperser.

spread-eagled [-,iːgld] *adj* affalé(e).

spreadsheet ['spredʃiːt] *n* COMPUT tableur *m.*

spree [spriː] *n:* **to go on a spending** OR **shopping ~** faire des folies.

sprightly ['spraɪtlɪ] *adj* alerte, fringant(e).

spring [sprɪŋ] (*pt* **sprang**, *pp* **sprung**) **1** *n* [season] printemps *m;* **in ~** au printemps. || [coil] ressort *m.* || [water source] source *f.* **2** *vi* [jump] sauter, bondir. || [originate]: **to ~ from** provenir de.
○ **spring up** *vi* [problem] surgir, se présenter; [friendship] naître; [wind] se lever.

springboard ['sprɪŋbɔːd] *n lit & fig* tremplin *m.*

spring-clean *vt* nettoyer de fond en comble.

springtime ['sprɪŋtaɪm] *n:* **in (the) ~** au printemps.

sprinkle ['sprɪŋkl] *vt:* **to ~ water over** OR **on sthg, to ~ sthg with water** asperger qqch d'eau; **to ~ salt** *etc* **over** OR **on sthg,** **to ~ sthg with salt** *etc* saupoudrer qqch de sel *etc.*

sprinkler ['sprɪŋklər] *n* [for water] arroseur *m.*

sprint [sprɪnt] **1** *n* sprint *m.* **2** *vi* sprinter.

sprout [spraut] **1** *n* [vegetable]: **(Brussels) ~s** choux *mpl* de Bruxelles. || [shoot]

pousse *f*. **2** *vt* [leaves] produire; **to ~ shoots** germer. **3** *vi* [grow] pousser.

spruce [spru:s] **1** *adj* net (nette), pimpant(e). **2** *n* épicéa *m*. ○ **spruce up** *vt sep* astiquer, briquer.

sprung [sprʌŋ] *pp* → **spring**.

spun [spʌn] *pt* & *pp* → **spin**.

spur [spɜːr] **1** *n* [incentive] incitation *f*. ‖ [on rider's boot] éperon *m*. **2** *vt* [encourage]: **to ~ sb to do sthg** encourager OR inciter qqn à faire qqch. ○ **on the spur of the moment** *adv* sur un coup de tête, sous l'impulsion du moment. ○ **spur on** *vt sep* encourager.

spurious ['spʊərɪəs] *adj* [affection, interest] feint(e). ‖ [argument, logic] faux (fausse).

spurn [spɜːn] *vt* repousser.

spurt [spɜːt] **1** *n* [gush] jaillissement *m*. ‖ [of activity, energy] sursaut *m*. ‖ [burst of speed] accélération *f*. **2** *vi* [gush]: **to ~ (out OR from)** jaillir (de).

spy [spaɪ] **1** *n* espion *m*. **2** *vi* espionner, faire de l'espionnage; **to ~ on sb** espionner qqn.

spying ['spaɪɪŋ] *n* (*U*) espionnage *m*.

Sq., sq. *abbr of* **square**.

squabble ['skwɒbl] **1** *n* querelle *f*. **2** *vi*: **to ~ (about OR over)** se quereller (à propos de).

squad [skwɒd] *n* [of police] brigade *f*. ‖ MIL peloton *m*. ‖ SPORT [group of players] équipe *f* (*parmi laquelle la sélection sera faite*).

squadron ['skwɒdrən] *n* escadron *m*.

squalid ['skwɒlɪd] *adj* sordide, ignoble.

squalor ['skwɒlər] *n* (*U*) conditions *fpl* sordides.

squander ['skwɒndər] *vt* gaspiller.

square [skweər] **1** *adj* [in shape] carré(e); **three metres ~** trois mètres sur trois. ‖ [not owing money]: **to be ~** être quitte. **2** *n* [shape] carré *m*. ‖ [in town] place *f*. ‖ *inf* [unfashionable person]: **he's a ~** il est vieux jeu. **3** *vt* MATH élever au carré. ○ **square up** *vi* [settle up]: **to ~ up with sb** régler ses comptes avec qqn.

squarely ['skweəlɪ] *adv* [directly] carrément. ‖ [honestly] honnêtement.

square meal *n* bon repas *m*.

squash [skwɒʃ] **1** *n* SPORT squash *m*. ‖ *Am* [vegetable] courge *f*. **2** *vt* écraser.

squat [skwɒt] **1** *adj* courtaud(e), ramassé(e). **2** *vi* [crouch]: **to ~ (down)** s'accroupir.

squawk [skwɔːk] *n* cri *m* strident OR perçant.

squeak [skwiːk] *n* [of animal] petit cri *m* aigu. ‖ [of door, hinge] grincement *m*.

squeal [skwiːl] *vi* [person, animal] pousser des cris aigus.

squeamish ['skwiːmɪʃ] *adj* facilement dégoûté(e).

squeeze [skwiːz] **1** *n* [pressure] pression *f*. **2** *vt* [press firmly] presser. ‖ [liquid, toothpaste] exprimer. ‖ [cram]: **to ~ sthg into sthg** entasser qqch dans qqch.

squelch [skwɛltʃ] *vi*: **to ~ through mud** patauger dans la boue.

squid [skwɪd] (*pl inv* OR **-s**) *n* calmar *m*.

squiggle ['skwɪgl] *n* gribouillis *m*.

squint [skwɪnt] **1** *n*: **to have a ~** loucher, être atteint(e) de strabisme. **2** *vi*: **to ~ at sthg** regarder qqch en plissant les yeux.

squirm [skwɜːm] *vi* [wriggle] se tortiller.

squirrel [*Br* 'skwɪrəl, *Am* 'skwɜːrəl] *n* écureuil *m*.

squirt [skwɜːt] **1** *vt* [water, oil] faire jaillir, faire gicler. **2** *vi*: **to ~ (out of)** jaillir (de), gicler (de).

Sr *abbr of* **senior**.

Sri Lanka [ˌsriː'læŋkə] *n* Sri Lanka *m*.

St (*abbr of* **saint**) St, Ste. ‖ *abbr of* **Street**.

stab [stæb] **1** *n* [with knife] coup *m* de couteau. ‖ *inf* [attempt]: **to have a ~ (at sthg)** essayer (qqch), tenter (qqch). ‖ [twinge]: **~ of pain** élancement *m*; **~ of guilt** remords *m*. **2** *vt* [person] poignarder. ‖ [food] piquer.

stable ['steɪbl] **1** *adj* stable. **2** *n* écurie *f*.

stack [stæk] **1** *n* [pile] pile *f*. **2** *vt* [pile up] empiler.

stadium ['steɪdjəm] (*pl* **-diums** OR **-dia** [-djə]) *n* stade *m*.

staff [stɑːf] **1** *n* [employees] personnel *m*; [of school] personnel enseignant, professeurs *mpl*. **2** *vt* pourvoir en personnel.

stag [stæg] (*pl inv* OR **-s**) *n* cerf *m*.

stage [steɪdʒ] **1** *n* [phase] étape *f*, phase *f*, stade *m*. ‖ [platform] scène *f*. ‖ [acting profession]: **the ~** le théâtre. **2** *vt* THEATRE monter, mettre en scène. ‖ [organize] organiser.

stagecoach ['steɪdʒkəʊtʃ] *n* diligence *f*.

stage fright *n* trac *m*.

stage-manage *vt lit* & *fig* mettre en scène.

stagger ['stægər] **1** *vt* [astound] stupéfier. ‖ [working hours] échelonner; [holidays] étaler. **2** *vi* tituber.

stagnant ['stægnənt] *adj* stagnant(e).

stagnate [stæg'neɪt] *vi* stagner.

stag party n soirée f entre hommes; [before wedding] soirée où un futur marié enterre sa vie de garçon avec ses amis.

staid [steɪd] adj guindé(e), collet monté.

stain [steɪn] 1 n [mark] tache f. 2 vt [discolour] tacher.

stained glass [,steɪnd-] n (U) [windows] vitraux mpl.

stainless steel ['steɪnlɪs-] n acier m inoxydable, Inox® m.

stain remover [-rɪ,muːvəʳ] n détachant m.

stair [steəʳ] n marche f. ○ **stairs** npl escalier m.

staircase ['steəkeɪs] n escalier m.

stairway ['steəweɪ] n escalier m.

stairwell ['steəwel] n cage f d'escalier.

stake [steɪk] 1 n [share]: **to have a ~ in** sthg avoir des intérêts dans qqch. || [wooden post] poteau m. || [in gambling] enjeu m. 2 vt: **to ~ money (on OR upon)** jouer OR miser de l'argent (sur); **to ~ one's reputation (on)** jouer OR risquer sa réputation (sur). ○ **at stake** adv en jeu.

stale [steɪl] adj [food, water] pas frais (fraîche); [bread] rassis(e); [air] qui sent le renfermé.

stalemate ['steɪlmeɪt] n [deadlock] impasse f. || CHESS pat m.

stalk [stɔːk] 1 n [of flower, plant] tige f. || [of leaf, fruit] queue f. 2 vt [hunt] traquer. 3 vi: **to ~ in/out** entrer/sortir d'un air hautain.

stall [stɔːl] 1 n [in street, market] éventaire m, étal m; [at exhibition] stand m. || [in stable] stalle f. 2 vi AUT caler. || [delay] essayer de gagner du temps.

stallion ['stæljən] n étalon m.

stalwart ['stɔːlwət] n pilier m.

stamina ['stæmɪnə] n (U) résistance f.

stammer ['stæməʳ] 1 n bégaiement m. 2 vi bégayer.

stamp [stæmp] 1 n [for letter] timbre m. || [tool] tampon m. || fig [of authority etc] marque f. 2 vt [mark by stamping] tamponner. 3 vi [stomp] taper du pied. || [tread heavily]: **to ~ on sthg** marcher sur qqch.

stamp album n album m de timbres.

stamp-collecting [-kə,lektɪŋ] n philatélie f.

stampede [stæm'piːd] n débandade f.

stance [stæns] n lit & fig position f.

stand [stænd] (pt & pp **stood**) 1 n [stall] stand m; [selling newspapers] kiosque m. || [supporting object]: **umbrel-**la ~ porte-parapluies m inv; **hat ~** porte-chapeaux m inv. || SPORT tribune f. || MIL résistance f; **to make a ~** résister. || [public position] position f. || Am JUR barre f. 2 vt [place] mettre (debout), poser (debout). || [withstand, tolerate] supporter. 3 vi [be upright - person] être OR se tenir debout; [- object] se trouver; [- building] se dresser; ~ **still!** ne bouge pas!, reste tranquille! || [stand up] se lever. || [liquid] reposer. || [offer] tenir toujours; [decision] demeurer valable. || [be in particular state]: **as things ~ ...** vu l'état actuel des choses .... || Am [park car]: **"no ~ing"** «stationnement interdit». ○ **stand back** vi reculer. ○ **stand by** 1 vt fus [person] soutenir. || [statement, decision] s'en tenir à. 2 vi [in readiness]: **to ~ by (for sthg/to do sthg)** être prêt(e) (pour qqch/pour faire qqch). || [remain inactive] rester là. ○ **stand down** vi [resign] démissionner. ○ **stand for** vt fus [signify] représenter. || [tolerate] supporter, tolérer. ○ **stand in** vi: **to ~ in for sb** remplacer qqn. ○ **stand out** vi ressortir. ○ **stand up** 1 vt sep inf [boyfriend, girlfriend] poser un lapin à. 2 vi [rise from seat] se lever; ~ **up!** debout! ○ **stand up for** vt fus défendre. ○ **stand up to** vt fus [person, boss] tenir tête à.

standard ['stændəd] 1 adj [normal - gen] normal(e); [- size] standard (inv). || [accepted] correct(e). 2 n [level] niveau m. || [point of reference] critère m; TECH norme f. ○ **standards** npl [principles] valeurs fpl.

standard of living (pl **standards of living**) n niveau m de vie.

standby ['stændbaɪ] (pl **standbys**) 1 n [person] remplaçant m, -e f; **on ~** prêt à intervenir. 2 comp [ticket, flight] standby (inv).

stand-in n remplaçant m, -e f.

standing ['stændɪŋ] 1 adj [invitation, army] permanent(e); [joke] continuel(elle). 2 n [reputation] importance f, réputation f. || [duration]: **of long ~** de longue date.

standing order n prélèvement m automatique.

standpoint ['stændpɔɪnt] n point m de vue.

standstill ['stændstɪl] n: **at a ~** [traffic, train] à l'arrêt; [negotiations, work] paralysé(e); **to come to a ~** [traffic, train] s'immobiliser; [negotiations, work] cesser.

stank [stæŋk] *pt* → **stink**.

staple ['steɪpl] **1** *adj* [principal] principal(e), de base. **2** *n* [for paper] agrafe *f*. ‖ [principal commodity] produit *m* de base. **3** *vt* agrafer.

stapler ['steɪplər] *n* agrafeuse *f*.

star [stɑːr] **1** *n* [gen] étoile *f*. ‖ [celebrity] vedette *f*, star *f*. **2** *vi*: **to ~ (in)** être la vedette (de). **○ stars** *npl* horoscope *m*.

starboard ['stɑːbəd] **1** *adj* de tribord. **2** *n*: **to ~** à tribord.

starch [stɑːtʃ] *n* amidon *m*.

stardom ['stɑːdəm] *n* (*U*) célébrité *f*.

stare [steər] **1** *n* regard *m* fixe. **2** *vi*: **to ~ at sb/sthg** fixer qqn/qqch du regard.

stark [stɑːk] **1** *adj* [room, decoration] austère; [landscape] désolé(e). ‖ [reality, fact] à l'état brut; [contrast] dur(e). **2** *adv*: **~ naked** tout nu (toute nue), à poil.

starling ['stɑːlɪŋ] *n* étourneau *m*.

starry ['stɑːrɪ] *adj* étoilé(e).

starry-eyed [-'aɪd] *adj* innocent(e).

Stars and Stripes *n*: **the ~** le drapeau des États-Unis, la bannière étoilée.

start [stɑːt] **1** *n* [beginning] début *m*. ‖ [jump] sursaut *m*. ‖ [starting place] départ *m*. ‖ [time advantage] avance *f*. **2** *vt* [begin] commencer; **to ~ doing** OR **to do sthg** commencer à faire qqch. ‖ [turn on - machine] mettre en marche; [- engine, vehicle] démarrer, mettre en marche. ‖ [set up - business, band] créer. **3** *vi* [begin] commencer, débuter; **to ~ with** pour commencer, d'abord. ‖ [function - machine] se mettre en marche; [- car] démarrer. ‖ [begin journey] partir. ‖ [jump] sursauter. **○ start off 1** *vt sep* [meeting] ouvrir, commencer; [discussion] entamer, commencer. **2** *vi* [begin] commencer; [begin job] débuter. ‖ [leave on journey] partir. **○ start out** *vi* [in job] débuter. ‖ [leave on journey] partir. **○ start up 1** *vt sep* [business] créer; [shop] ouvrir. ‖ [car, engine] mettre en marche. **2** *vi* [begin] commencer. ‖ [machine] se mettre en route; [car, engine] démarrer.

starter ['stɑːtər] *n* AUT démarreur *m*. ‖ [to begin race] starter *m*.

starting point ['stɑːtɪŋ-] *n* point *m* de départ.

startle ['stɑːtl] *vt* faire sursauter.

startling ['stɑːtlɪŋ] *adj* surprenant(e).

starvation [stɑː'veɪʃn] *n* faim *f*.

starve [stɑːv] **1** *vt* [deprive of food] affamer. **2** *vi* [have no food] être affamé(e); **to ~ to death** mourir de faim. ‖ *inf* [be hungry] avoir très faim, crever OR mourir de faim.

state [steɪt] **1** *n* état *m*; **to be in a ~** être dans tous ses états. **2** *comp* d'État. **3** *vt* [express - reason] donner; [- name and address] décliner; **to ~ that ...** déclarer que .... ‖ [specify] préciser. **○ States** *npl*: **the States** les États-Unis *mpl*.

State Department *n Am* ≃ ministère *m* des Affaires étrangères.

stately ['steɪtlɪ] *adj* majestueux(euse).

statement ['steɪtmənt] *n* [declaration] déclaration *f*. ‖ JUR déposition *f*. ‖ [from bank] relevé *m* de compte.

state of mind (*pl* states of mind) *n* humeur *f*.

statesman ['steɪtsmən] (*pl* **-men** [-mən]) *n* homme *m* d'État.

static ['stætɪk] *n* (*U*) parasites *mpl*.

static electricity *n* électricité *f* statique.

station ['steɪʃn] **1** *n* RAIL gare *f*; [for buses, coaches] gare routière. ‖ RADIO station *f*. ‖ [building] poste *m*. ‖ *fml* [rank] rang *m*. **2** *vt* [position] placer, poster. ‖ MIL poster.

stationary ['steɪʃnərɪ] *adj* immobile.

stationer ['steɪʃnər] *n* papetier *m*, -ière *f*; **~'s (shop)** papeterie *f*.

stationery ['steɪʃnərɪ] *n* (*U*) [equipment] fournitures *fpl* de bureau; [paper] papier *m* à lettres.

stationmaster ['steɪʃn,mɑːstər] *n* chef *m* de gare.

station wagon *n Am* break *m*.

statistic [stə'tɪstɪk] *n* statistique *f*.

statistical [stə'tɪstɪkl] *adj* statistique; [expert] en statistiques; [report] de statistiques.

statue ['stætʃuː] *n* statue *f*.

stature ['stætʃər] *n* [height, size] stature *f*, taille *f*. ‖ [importance] envergure *f*.

status ['steɪtəs] *n* (*U*) [legal or social position] statut *m*. ‖ [prestige] prestige *m*.

status symbol *n* signe *m* extérieur de richesse.

statute ['stætjuːt] *n* loi *f*.

statutory ['stætjʊtrɪ] *adj* statutaire.

staunch [stɔːntʃ] **1** *adj* loyal(e). **2** *vt* [flow] arrêter; [blood] étancher.

stave [steɪv] (*pt & pp* **-d** OR **stove**) *n* MUS portée *f*. **○ stave off** *vt sep* [disaster, defeat] éviter; [hunger] tromper.

stay [steɪ] **1** *vi* [not move away] rester. ‖ [as visitor - with friends] passer quelques jours; [- in town, country] séjourner; **to ~ in a hotel** descendre à l'hôtel. ‖ [con-

stick

tinue, remain] rester, demeurer; **to ~ out of sthg** ne pas se mêler de qqch. **2** *n* [visit] séjour *m*. ○ **stay in** *vi* rester chez soi, ne pas sortir. ○ **stay on** *vi* rester (plus longtemps). ○ **stay out** *vi* [from home] ne pas rentrer. ○ **stay up** *vi* ne pas se coucher, veiller.

staying power ['steɪŋ-] *n* endurance *f*.

stead [sted] *n*: **to stand sb in good ~** être utile à qqn.

steadfast ['stedfɑːst] *adj* ferme, résolu(e); [supporter] loyal(e).

steadily ['stedɪlɪ] *adv* [gradually] progressivement. || [regularly - breathe] régulièrement; [- move] sans arrêt. || [calmly] de manière imperturbable.

steady ['stedɪ] **1** *adj* [gradual] progressif(ive). || [regular] régulier(ière). || [not shaking] ferme. || [calm - voice] calme; [- stare] imperturbable. || [stable - job, relationship] stable. || [sensible] sérieux(ieuse). **2** *vt* [stop from shaking] empêcher de bouger; **to ~ o.s.** se remettre d'aplomb. || [control - nerves] calmer.

steak [steɪk] *n* steak *m*, bifteck *m*; [of fish] darne *f*.

steal [stiːl] (*pt* stole, *pp* stolen) **1** *vt* voler, dérober. **2** *vi* [move secretly] se glisser.

stealthy ['stelθɪ] *adj* furtif(ive).

steam [stiːm] **1** *n* (*U*) vapeur *f*. **2** *vt* CULIN cuire à la vapeur. **3** *vi* [give off steam] fumer. ○ **steam up 1** *vt sep* [mist up] embuer. **2** *vi* se couvrir de buée.

steamboat ['stiːmbəʊt] *n* (bateau *m* à) vapeur *m*.

steam engine *n* locomotive *f* à vapeur.

steamer ['stiːmər] *n* [ship] (bateau *m* à) vapeur *m*.

steamroller ['stiːm,rəʊlər] *n* rouleau *m* compresseur.

steamy ['stiːmɪ] *adj* [full of steam] embué(e). || *inf* [erotic] érotique.

steel [stiːl] *n* (*U*) acier *m*.

steelworks ['stiːlwɜːks] (*pl inv*) *n* aciérie *f*.

steep [stiːp] *adj* [hill, road] raide, abrupt(e). || [increase, decline] énorme.

steeple ['stiːpl] *n* clocher *m*, flèche *f*.

steeplechase ['stiːpltʃeɪs] *n* [horse race] steeple-chase *m*. || [athletics race] steeple *m*.

steer ['stɪər] **1** *n* bœuf *m*. **2** *vt* [ship] gouverner; [car, aeroplane] conduire, diriger. || [person] diriger, guider. **3** *vi*: **to ~ clear of sb/sthg** éviter qqn/qqch.

steering ['stɪərɪŋ] *n* (*U*) direction *f*.

steering wheel *n* volant *m*.

stem [stem] **1** *n* [of plant] tige *f*. || [of glass] pied *m*. || [of pipe] tuyau *m*. || GRAMM radical *m*. **2** *vt* [stop] arrêter. ○ **stem from** *vt fus* provenir de.

stench [stentʃ] *n* puanteur *f*.

stencil ['stensl] **1** *n* pochoir *m*. **2** *vt* faire au pochoir.

stenographer [stə'nɒgrəfər] *n Am* sténographe *mf*.

step [step] **1** *n* [pace] pas *m*; **in/out of ~ with** *fig* en accord/désaccord avec. || [action] mesure *f*. || [stage] étape *f*; **~ by ~** petit à petit, progressivement. || [stair] marche *f*. || [of ladder] barreau *m*, échelon *m*. **2** *vi* [move foot]: **to ~ forward** avancer; **to ~ back** reculer. || [tread]: **to ~ on/in sthg** marcher sur/dans qqch. ○ **steps** *npl* [stairs] marches *fpl*. ○ **step down** *vi* [leave job] démissionner. ○ **step in** *vi* intervenir. ○ **step up** *vt sep* intensifier.

stepbrother ['step,brʌðər] *n* demi-frère *m*.

stepdaughter ['step,dɔːtər] *n* belle-fille *f*.

stepfather ['step,fɑːðər] *n* beau-père *m*.

stepladder ['step,lædər] *n* escabeau *m*.

stepmother ['step,mʌðər] *n* belle-mère *f*.

stepping-stone ['stepɪŋ-] *n* pierre *f* de gué; *fig* tremplin *m*.

stepsister ['step,sɪstər] *n* demi-sœur *f*.

stepson ['stepsʌn] *n* beau-fils *m*.

stereo ['sterɪəʊ] (*pl* -s) *n* [appliance] chaîne *f* stéréo. || [sound]: **in ~** en stéréo.

stereotype ['sterɪətaɪp] *n* stéréotype *m*.

sterile ['steraɪl] *adj* stérile.

sterilize, -ise ['sterəlaɪz] *vt* stériliser.

sterling ['stɜːlɪŋ] **1** *adj* [of British money] sterling (*inv*). || [excellent] exceptionnel(elle). **2** *n* (*U*) livre *f* sterling.

sterling silver *n* argent *m* fin.

stern [stɜːn] **1** *adj* sévère. **2** *n* NAUT arrière *m*.

steroid ['stɪərɔɪd] *n* stéroïde *m*.

stethoscope ['steθəskəʊp] *n* stéthoscope *m*.

stew [stjuː] **1** *n* ragoût *m*. **2** *vt* [meat] cuire en ragoût; [fruit] faire cuire.

steward ['stjʊəd] *n* [on plane, ship, train] steward *m*.

stewardess ['stjʊədɪs] *n* hôtesse *f*.

stick [stɪk] (*pt & pp* stuck) **1** *n* [of wood, dynamite, candy] bâton *m*. || [walking stick] canne f. || SPORT crosse f. 2 vt [push]: to ~ sthg in OR into planter qqch dans. || [with glue, Sellotape®]: to ~ sthg (on OR to) coller qqch (sur). || inf [put] mettre. 3 vi [adhere]: to ~ (to) coller (à). || [jam] se coincer. ○ **stick out** 1 vt sep [head] sortir; [hand] lever; [tongue] tirer. || inf [endure]: to ~ it out tenir le coup. 2 vi [protrude] dépasser. || inf [be noticeable] se remarquer. ○ **stick to** vt fus [follow closely] suivre. || [principles] rester fidèle à; [decision] s'en tenir à; [promise] tenir. ○ **stick up** vi dépasser. ○ **stick up for** vt fus défendre.

sticker ['stɪkər] n [label] autocollant m.

sticking plaster ['stɪkɪŋ-] n sparadrap m.

stickler ['stɪklər] n: to be a ~ for être à cheval sur.

stick shift n Am levier m de vitesses.

stick-up n inf vol m à main armée.

sticky ['stɪkɪ] adj [hands, sweets] poisseux(euse); [label, tape] adhésif(ive). || inf [awkward] délicat(e).

stiff [stɪf] 1 adj [rod, paper, material] rigide; [shoes, brush] dur(e); [fabric] raide. || [door, drawer, window] dur(e) (à ouvrir/fermer); [joint] ankylosé(e); to have a ~ neck avoir le torticolis. || [severe - penalty] sévère; [- competition] serré(e). || [difficult - task] difficile. 2 adv inf: to be bored ~ s'ennuyer à mourir; to be frozen/scared ~ mourir de froid/peur.

stiffen ['stɪfn] 1 vt [material] raidir; [with starch] empeser. || [resolve] renforcer. 2 vi [body] se raidir; [joints] s'ankyloser. || [competition, resistance] s'intensifier.

stifle ['staɪfl] vt & vi étouffer.

stifling ['staɪflɪŋ] adj étouffant(e).

stigma ['stɪgmə] n [disgrace] honte f, stigmate m. || BOT stigmate m.

stile [staɪl] n échalier m.

still [stɪl] 1 adv [up to now, up to then] encore, toujours; I've ~ got £5 left il me reste encore 5 livres. || [even now] encore. || [nevertheless] tout de même. || (with comparatives): ~ bigger/more important encore plus grand/plus important. 2 adj [not moving] immobile. || [calm] calme, tranquille. || [not windy] sans vent. || [not fizzy - gen] non gazeux(euse); [- mineral water] plat(e). 3 n PHOT photo f. || [for making alcohol] alambic m.

stillborn ['stɪlbɔːn] adj mort-né(e).

still life (pl -s) n nature f morte.

stilted ['stɪltɪd] adj emprunté(e), qui manque de naturel.

stilts ['stɪlts] npl [for person] échasses fpl. || [for building] pilotis mpl.

stimulate ['stɪmjʊleɪt] vt stimuler.

stimulating ['stɪmjʊleɪtɪŋ] adj stimulant(e).

stimulus ['stɪmjʊləs] (pl -li [-laɪ]) n [encouragement] stimulant m. || BIOL & PSYCH stimulus m.

sting [stɪŋ] (pt & pp stung) 1 n [by bee] piqûre f; [of bee] dard m. || [sharp pain] brûlure f. 2 vt [gen] piquer. 3 vi piquer.

stingy ['stɪndʒɪ] adj inf radin(e).

stink [stɪŋk] (pt stank OR stunk, pp stunk) 1 n puanteur f. 2 vi [smell] puer, empester.

stint [stɪnt] 1 n [period of work] part f de travail. 2 vi: to ~ on lésiner sur.

stipulate ['stɪpjʊleɪt] vt stipuler.

stir [stɜːr] 1 n [public excitement] sensation f. 2 vt [mix] remuer. || [move gently] agiter. || [move emotionally] émouvoir. 3 vi bouger, remuer. ○ **stir up** vt sep [dust] soulever. || [trouble] provoquer; [resentment, dissatisfaction] susciter.

stirrup ['stɪrəp] n étrier m.

stitch [stɪtʃ] 1 n SEWING point m; [in knitting] maille f. || MED point m de suture. || [stomach pain]: to have a ~ avoir un point de côté. 2 vt SEWING coudre; MED suturer.

stoat [stəʊt] n hermine f.

stock [stɒk] 1 n [supply] réserve f. || (U) COMM stock m, réserve f; in ~ en stock; out of ~ épuisé(e). || FIN valeurs fpl; ~s and shares titres mpl. || [ancestry] souche f. || CULIN bouillon m. || [livestock] cheptel m. || phr: to take ~ (of) faire le point (de). 2 vt COMM vendre, avoir en stock. || [fill - shelves] garnir. ○ **stock up** vi: to ~ up (with) faire des provisions (de).

stockbroker ['stɒk,brəʊkər] n agent m de change.

stock exchange n Bourse f.

stockholder ['stɒk,həʊldər] n Am actionnaire mf.

stocking ['stɒkɪŋ] n [for woman] bas m.

stock market n Bourse f.

stock phrase n cliché m.

stockpile ['stɒkpaɪl] 1 n stock m. 2 vt [weapons] amasser; [food] stocker.

stocktaking ['stɒk,teɪkɪŋ] n (U) inventaire m.

stocky ['stɒkɪ] adj trapu(e).

stodgy ['stɒdʒɪ] *adj* [food] lourd(e) (à digérer).

stoical ['stəʊɪkl] *adj* stoïque.

stoke [stəʊk] *vt* [fire] entretenir.

stole [stəʊl] 1 *pt* → **steal.** 2 *n* étole *f*.

stolen ['stəʊln] *pp* → **steal.**

stolid ['stɒlɪd] *adj* impassible.

stomach ['stʌmək] 1 *n* [organ] estomac *m*; [abdomen] ventre *m*. 2 *vt* [tolerate] encaisser, supporter.

stomachache ['stʌməkeɪk] *n* mal *m* de ventre, douleurs *fpl* d'estomac.

stomach upset *n* embarras *m* gastrique.

stone [stəʊn] (*pl sense 3 only inv* OR **-s**) 1 *n* [rock] pierre *f*; [smaller] caillou *m*. || [seed] noyau *m*. || *Br* [unit of measurement] = 6,348 kg. 2 *comp* de OR en pierre. 3 *vt* [person, car etc] jeter des pierres sur.

stone-cold *adj* complètement froid(e) OR glacé(e).

stonewashed ['stəʊnwɒʃt] *adj* délavé(e).

stonework ['stəʊnwɜːk] *n* maçonnerie *f*.

stood [stʊd] *pt & pp* → **stand.**

stool [stuːl] *n* [seat] tabouret *m*.

stoop [stuːp] *ri* [bend down] se pencher. || [hunch shoulders] être voûté(e).

stop [stɒp] 1 *n* [gen] arrêt *m*; **to put a ~ to sthg** mettre un terme à qqch. || [full stop] point *m*. 2 *vt* [gen] arrêter; [end] mettre fin à; **to ~ doing sthg** arrêter de faire qqch. || [prevent]: **to ~ sb/sthg (from doing sthg)** empêcher qqn/qqch (de faire qqch). 3 *ri* s'arrêter, cesser. ○ **stop off** *ri* s'arrêter, faire halte. ○ **stop up** *vt sep* [block] boucher.

stopgap ['stɒpgæp] *n* bouche-trou *m*.

stopover ['stɒp,əʊvə'] *n* halte *f*.

stoppage ['stɒpɪdʒ] *n* [strike] grève *f*.

stopper ['stɒpə'] *n* bouchon *m*.

stop press *n* nouvelles *fpl* de dernière heure.

stopwatch ['stɒpwɒtʃ] *n* chronomètre *m*.

storage ['stɔːrɪdʒ] *n* [of goods] entreposage *m*, emmagasinage *m*; [of household objects] rangement *m*.

store [stɔːr] 1 *n* [shop] magasin *m*. || [supply] provision *f*. || [place of storage] réserve *f*. 2 *vt* [save] mettre en réserve; [goods] entreposer, emmagasiner. || COMPUT stocker, mémoriser. ○ **store up** *vt sep* [provisions] mettre en réserve; [goods] emmagasiner; [information] mettre en mémoire, noter.

storekeeper ['stɔː,kiːpə'] *n Am* commerçant *m*, -e *f*.

storeroom ['stɔːrʊm] *n* magasin *m*.

storey *Br* (*pl* **storeys**), **story** *Am* (*pl* **-ies**) ['stɔːrɪ] *n* étage *m*.

stork [stɔːk] *n* cigogne *f*.

storm [stɔːm] 1 *n* [bad weather] orage *m*. || *fig* [of abuse] torrent *m*. 2 *vt* MIL prendre d'assaut. 3 *ri* [go angrily]: **to ~ in/out** entrer/sortir comme un ouragan. || [speak angrily] fulminer.

stormy ['stɔːmɪ] *adj lit & fig* orageux(euse).

story ['stɔːrɪ] *n* [gen] histoire *f*. || PRESS article *m*; RADIO & TV nouvelle *f*. || *Am* = **storey.**

storyteller ['stɔːrɪ,telə'] *n* [narrator] conteur *m*, -euse *f*. || *euphemism* [liar] menteur *m*, -euse *f*.

stout [staʊt] 1 *adj* [rather fat] corpulent(e). || [strong] solide. || [resolute] ferme, résolu(e). 2 *n* (*U*) stout *m*, bière *f* brune.

stove [stəʊv] 1 *pt & pp* → **stave.** 2 *n* [for cooking] cuisinière *f*; [for heating] poêle *m*.

stow [stəʊ] *vt*: **to ~ sthg (away)** ranger qqch.

stowaway ['stəʊəweɪ] *n* passager *m* clandestin.

straddle ['strædl] *vt* enjamber; [chair] s'asseoir à califourchon sur.

straggle ['strægl] *ri* [buildings] s'étendre, s'étaler; [hair] être en désordre. || [person] traîner, lambiner.

straggler ['stræglə'] *n* traînard *m*, -e *f*.

straight [streɪt] 1 *adj* [not bent] droit(e); [hair] raide. || [frank] franc (franche), honnête. || [tidy] en ordre. || [choice, exchange] simple. || [alcoholic drink] sec, sans eau. || *phr*: **let's get this ~** entendons-nous bien. 2 *adv* [in a straight line] droit. || [directly, immediately] droit, tout de suite. || [frankly] carrément, franchement. ○ **straight off** *adv* tout de suite, sur-le-champ. ○ **straight out** *adv* sans mâcher ses mots.

straightaway [,streɪtə'weɪ] *adv* tout de suite, immédiatement.

straighten ['streɪtn] *vt* [tidy - hair, dress] arranger; [- room] mettre de l'ordre dans. || [make straight - horizontally] rendre droit(e); [- vertically] redresser. ○ **straighten out** *vt sep* [problem] résoudre.

straight face *n*: **to keep a ~** garder son sérieux.

straightforward [,streɪt'fɔ:wəd] *adj* [easy] simple. ‖ [frank] honnête, franc (franche).

strain [streɪn] **1** *n* [mental] tension *f*, stress *m*. ‖ MED foulure *f*. ‖ TECH contrainte *f*, effort *m*. **2** *vt* [work hard - eyes] plisser fort. ‖ [MED - muscle] se froisser; [- eyes] se fatiguer; **to ~ one's back** se faire un tour de reins. ‖ [patience] mettre à rude épreuve; [budget] grever. ‖ [drain] passer. **3** *vi* [try very hard]: **to ~ to do sthg** faire un gros effort pour faire qqch, se donner du mal pour faire qqch. ○ **strains** *npl* [of music] accords *mpl*, airs *mpl*.

strained [streɪnd] *adj* [worried] contracté(e), tendu(e). ‖ [relations, relationship] tendu(e). ‖ [unnatural] forcé(e).

strainer ['streɪnər] *n* passoire *f*.

strait [streɪt] *n* détroit *m*. ○ **straits** *npl*: **in dire** OR **desperate ~s** dans une situation désespérée.

straitjacket ['streɪt,dʒækɪt] *n* camisole *f* de force.

straitlaced [,streɪt'leɪst] *adj* collet monté (*inv*).

strand [strænd] *n* [of cotton, wool] brin *m*, fil *m*; [of hair] mèche *f*. ‖ [theme] fil *m*.

stranded ['strændɪd] *adj* [boat] échoué(e); [people] abandonné(e), en rade.

strange [streɪndʒ] *adj* [odd] étrange, bizarre. ‖ [unfamiliar] inconnu(e).

stranger ['streɪndʒər] *n* [unfamiliar person] inconnu *m*, -e *f*. ‖ [from another place] étranger *m*, -ère *f*.

strangle ['stræŋgl] *vt* étrangler.

stranglehold ['stræŋglhəʊld] *n* [round neck] étranglement *m*. ‖ *fig* [control]: **(on)** domination *f* (de).

strap [stræp] **1** *n* [for fastening] sangle *f*, courroie *f*; [of bag] bandoulière *f*; [of rifle, dress, bra] bretelle *f*; [of watch] bracelet *m*. **2** *vt* [fasten] attacher.

strapping ['stræpɪŋ] *adj* bien bâti(e), robuste.

Strasbourg ['stræzbɜ:g] *n* Strasbourg.

strategic [strə'ti:dʒɪk] *adj* stratégique.

strategy ['strætɪdʒɪ] *n* stratégie *f*.

straw [strɔ:] *n* paille *f*; **that's the last ~!** ça c'est le comble!

strawberry ['strɔ:bərɪ] **1** *n* [fruit] fraise *f*. **2** *comp* [tart, yoghurt] aux fraises; [jam] de fraises.

stray [streɪ] **1** *adj* [animal] errant(e), perdu(e). ‖ [bullet] perdu(e); [example]

isolé(e). **2** *vi* [person, animal] errer, s'égarer. ‖ [thoughts] vagabonder, errer.

streak [stri:k] **1** *n* [line] bande *f*, marque *f*. ‖ [in character] côté *m*. **2** *vi* [move quickly] se déplacer comme un éclair.

stream [stri:m] **1** *n* [small river] ruisseau *m*. ‖ [of liquid, light] flot *m*, jet *m*. ‖ [of people, cars] flot *m*; [of complaints, abuse] torrent *m*. **2** *vi* [liquid] couler à flots, ruisseler; [light] entrer à flots. ‖ [people, cars] affluer; **to ~ past** passer à flots.

streamer ['stri:mər] *n* [for party] serpentin *m*.

streamlined ['stri:mlaɪnd] *adj* [aerodynamic] au profil aérodynamique. ‖ [efficient] rationalisé(e).

street [stri:t] *n* rue *f*.

streetcar ['stri:tkɑ:r] *n* Am tramway *m*.

street lamp, street light *n* réverbère *m*.

street plan *n* plan *m*.

strength [streŋθ] *n* [gen] force *f*. ‖ [power, influence] puissance *f*. ‖ [solidity, of currency] solidité *f*.

strengthen ['streŋθn] *vt* [structure, team, argument] renforcer. ‖ [economy, currency, friendship] consolider. ‖ [resolve, dislike] fortifier, affermir. ‖ [person] enhardir.

strenuous ['strenjʊəs] *adj* [exercise, activity] fatigant(e), dur(e); [effort] vigoureux(euse), acharné(e).

stress [stres] **1** *n* [emphasis]: **~ (on)** accent *m* (sur). ‖ [mental] stress *m*, tension *f*. ‖ TECH: **~ (on)** contrainte *f* (sur), effort *m* (sur). ‖ LING accent *m*. **2** *vt* [emphasize] souligner, insister sur. ‖ LING accentuer.

stressful ['stresfʊl] *adj* stressant(e).

stretch [stretʃ] **1** *n* [of land, water] étendue *f*; [of road, river] partie *f*, section *f*. ‖ [of time] période *f*. **2** *vt* [arms] allonger; [legs] se dégourdir; [muscles] distendre. ‖ [pull taut] tendre, étirer. ‖ [overwork - person] surmener; [- resources, budget] grever. ‖ [challenge]: **to ~ sb** pousser qqn à la limite de ses capacités. **3** *vi* [area]: **to ~ from ... to** s'étendre de ... à. ‖ [person, animal] s'étirer; [material, elastic] se tendre, s'étirer. ○ **stretch out 1** *vt sep* [arm, leg, hand] tendre. **2** *vi* [lie down] s'étendre, s'allonger.

stretcher ['stretʃər] *n* brancard *m*, civière *f*.

strew [stru:] (*pt* **-ed**, *pp* **strewn** [stru:n]

stubble

OR **-ed**) *rt*: **to be strewn with** être jonché(e) de.

strict [strikt] *adj* [gen] strict(e).

strictly ['striktli] *adr* [gen] strictement; **~ speaking** à proprement parler. || [severely] d'une manière stricte, sévèrement.

stride [straid] (*pt* **strode**, *pp* **stridden** ['stridn]) **1** *n* [long step] grand pas *m*, enjambée *f*. **2** *ri* marcher à grandes enjambées OR à grands pas.

strident ['straidnt] *adj* [voice, sound] strident(e). || [demand, attack] véhément(e), bruyant(e).

strife [straif] *n* (*U*) conflit *m*, lutte *f*.

strike [straik] (*pt & pp* **struck**) **1** *n* [by workers] grève *f*; **to go on ~** faire grève, se mettre en grève. || MIL raid *m*. || [of oil, gold] découverte *f*. **2** *rt* [hit - deliberately] frapper; [- accidentally] heurter. || [subj: thought] venir à l'esprit de. || [conclude - deal, bargain] conclure. || [light - match] frotter. **3** *ri* [workers] faire grève. || [hit] frapper. || [attack] attaquer. || [chime] sonner. ○ **strike down** *rt sep* terrasser. ○ **strike out** **1** *rt sep* rayer, barrer. **2** *ri* [head out] se mettre en route, partir. ○ **strike up** *rt fus* [conversation] commencer, engager; **to ~ up a friendship (with)** se lier d'amitié (avec). || [music] commencer à jouer.

striker ['straikər] *n* [person on strike] gréviste *mf*. || FTBL buteur *m*.

striking ['straikiŋ] *adj* [noticeable] frappant(e), saisissant(e). || [attractive] d'une beauté frappante.

string [striŋ] (*pt & pp* **strung**) *n* (*U*) [thin rope] ficelle *f*. || [piece of thin rope] bout *m* de ficelle; **to pull ~s** faire jouer le piston. || [of beads, pearls] rang *m*. || [series] série *f*, suite *f*. || [of musical instrument] corde *f*. ○ **strings** *npl* MUS: **the ~s** les cordes *fpl*.

string bean *n* haricot *m* vert.

stringent ['strindʒənt] *adj* strict(e), rigoureux(euse).

strip [strip] **1** *n* [narrow piece] bande *f*. **2** *rt* [undress] déshabiller, dévêtir. || [paint, wallpaper] enlever. **3** *ri* [undress] se déshabiller, se dévêtir. ○ **strip off** *ri* se déshabiller, se dévêtir.

stripe [straip] *n* [band of colour] rayure *f*. || [sign of rank] galon *m*.

striped [straipt] *adj* à rayures, rayé(e).

strip lighting *n* éclairage *m* au néon.

stripper ['stripər] *n* [performer of strip-tease] strip-teaseuse *f*, effeuilleuse *f*. || [for paint] décapant *m*.

striptease ['striptiːz] *n* strip-tease *m*.

strive [straiv] (*pt* **strove**, *pp* **striven** ['strivn]) *ri*: **to ~ to do sthg** s'efforcer de faire qqch.

strode [strəud] *pt* → **stride**.

stroke [strəuk] **1** *n* MED attaque *f* cérébrale. || [of pen, brush] trait *m*. || [in swimming - movement] mouvement *m* des bras; [in rowing] coup *m* d'aviron; [in golf, tennis etc] coup *m*. || [of clock]: **on the third ~** ≃ au quatrième top. || [piece]: **a ~ of genius** un trait de génie; **a ~ of luck** un coup de chance OR de veine; **at a ~** d'un seul coup. **2** *rt* caresser.

stroll [strəul] **1** *n* petite promenade *f*, petit tour *m*. **2** *ri* se promener, flâner.

stroller ['strəulər] *n* Am [for baby] poussette *f*.

strong [strɒŋ] *adj* [gen] fort(e); **~ point** point *m* fort. || [structure, argument, friendship] solide. || [healthy] robuste, vigoureux(euse). || [in numbers]: **the crowd was 2,000 ~** il y avait une foule de 2 000 personnes. || [team, candidate] sérieux(ieuse), qui a des chances de gagner.

strongbox ['strɒŋbɒks] *n* coffre-fort *m*.

stronghold ['strɒŋhəuld] *n* fig bastion *m*.

strongly ['strɒŋli] *adr* [gen] fortement. || [solidly] solidement.

strong room *n* chambre *f* forte.

strove [strəuv] *pt* → **strive**.

struck [strʌk] *pt & pp* → **strike**.

structure ['strʌktʃər] *n* [organization] structure *f*. || [building] construction *f*.

struggle ['strʌgl] **1** *n* [great effort]: **~ (for sthg/to do sthg)** lutte *f* (pour qqch/pour faire qqch). || [fight] bagarre *f*. **2** *ri* [make great effort]: **to ~ (for)** lutter (pour); **to ~ to do sthg** s'efforcer de faire qqch. || [to free oneself] se débattre; [fight] se battre.

strum [strʌm] *rt* [guitar] gratter de.

strung [strʌŋ] *pt & pp* → **string**.

strut [strʌt] **1** *n* CONSTR étai *m*, support *m*. **2** *ri* se pavaner.

stub [stʌb] **1** *n* [of cigarette] mégot *m*; [of pencil] morceau *m*. || [of ticket, cheque] talon *m*. **2** *rt*: **to ~ one's toe** se cogner le doigt de pied. ○ **stub out** *rt sep* écraser.

stubble ['stʌbl] *n* (*U*) [in field] chaume *m*. || [on chin] barbe *f* de plusieurs jours.

stubborn ['stʌbən] *adj* [person] têtu(e), obstiné(e). || [stain] qui ne veut pas partir, rebelle.

stuck [stʌk] 1 *pt & pp* → **stick**. 2 *adj* [jammed, trapped] coincé(e). || [stumped]: **to be ~** sécher. || [stranded] bloqué(e), en rade.

stuck-up *adj inf pej* bêcheur(euse).

stud [stʌd] *n* [metal decoration] clou *m* décoratif. || [earring] clou *m* d'oreille. || [of horses] haras *m*.

studded ['stʌdɪd] *adj*: **~ (with)** parsemé(e) (de), constellé(e) (de).

student ['stju:dnt] 1 *n* étudiant *m*, -e *f*. 2 *comp* [life] estudiantin(e); [politics] des étudiants; [disco] pour étudiants.

studio ['stju:dɪəʊ] (*pl* -**s**) *n* studio *m*; [of artist] atelier *m*.

studio flat *Br*, **studio apartment** *Am n* studio *m*.

studious ['stju:djəs] *adj* studieux(ieuse).

study ['stʌdɪ] 1 *n* [gen] étude *f*. || [room] bureau *m*. 2 *vt* [learn] étudier, faire des études de. || [examine] examiner, étudier. 3 *vi* étudier, faire ses études.

stuff [stʌf] 1 *n* (*U*) *inf* [things] choses *fpl*. || [substance] substance *f*. || *inf* [belongings] affaires *fpl*. 2 *vt* [push] fourrer. || [fill]: **to ~ sthg (with)** remplir OR bourrer qqch (de). || CULIN farcir.

stuffed [stʌft] *adj* [filled]: **~ with** bourré(e) de. || *inf* [with food] gavé(e) de. || CULIN farci(e). || [preserved - animal] empaillé(e).

stuffing ['stʌfɪŋ] *n* (*U*) [filling] bourre *f*, rembourrage *m*. || CULIN farce *f*.

stuffy ['stʌfɪ] *adj* [room] mal aéré(e), qui manque d'air. || [person, club] vieux jeu (*inv*).

stumble ['stʌmbl] *vi* trébucher.
○ **stumble across, stumble on** *vt fus* tomber sur.

stumbling block ['stʌmblɪŋ-] *n* pierre *f* d'achoppement.

stump [stʌmp] 1 *n* [of tree] souche *f*; [of arm, leg] moignon *m*. 2 *vt* [subj: question, problem] dérouter, rendre perplexe.

stun [stʌn] *vt* [knock unconscious] étourdir, assommer. || [surprise] stupéfier, renverser.

stung [stʌŋ] *pt & pp* → **sting**.

stunk [stʌŋk] *pt & pp* → **stink**.

stunning ['stʌnɪŋ] *adj* [very beautiful] ravissant(e); [scenery] merveilleux(euse). || [surprising] stupéfiant(e), renversant(e).

stunt [stʌnt] 1 *n* [for publicity] coup *m*. || CINEMA cascade *f*. 2 *vt* retarder, arrêter.

stunted ['stʌntɪd] *adj* rabougri(e).

stunt man *n* cascadeur *m*.

stupefy ['stju:pɪfaɪ] *vt* [tire] abrutir. || [surprise] stupéfier, abasourdir.

stupid ['stju:pɪd] *adj* [foolish] stupide, bête. || *inf* [annoying] fichu(e).

stupidity [stju:'pɪdətɪ] *n* (*U*) bêtise *f*, stupidité *f*.

sturdy ['stɜ:dɪ] *adj* [person] robuste; [furniture, structure] solide.

stutter ['stʌtər] *vi* bégayer.

sty [staɪ] *n* [pigsty] porcherie *f*.

stye [staɪ] *n* orgelet *m*, compère-loriot *m*.

style [staɪl] 1 *n* [characteristic manner] style *m*. || (*U*) [elegance] chic *m*, élégance *f*. || [design] genre *m*, modèle *m*. 2 *vt* [hair] coiffer.

stylish ['staɪlɪʃ] *adj* chic (*inv*), élégant(e).

stylist ['staɪlɪst] *n* [hairdresser] coiffeur *m*, -euse *f*.

stylus ['staɪləs] (*pl* -**es**) *n* [on record player] pointe *f* de lecture, saphir *m*.

suave [swɑ:v] *adj* doucereux(euse).

subconscious [,sʌb'kɒnʃəs] 1 *adj* inconscient(e). 2 *n*: **the ~** l'inconscient *m*.

subcontract [,sʌbkən'trækt] *vt* sous-traiter.

subdivide [,sʌbdɪ'vaɪd] *vt* subdiviser.

subdue [səb'dju:] *vt* [control - rioters, enemy] soumettre, subjuguer; [- temper, anger] maîtriser, réprimer.

subdued [səb'dju:d] *adj* [person] abattu(e). || [anger, emotion] contenu(e). || [colour] doux (douce); [light] tamisé(e).

subject [*adj, n & prep* 'sʌbdʒekt, *vt* səb'dʒekt] 1 *adj* soumis(e); **to be ~ to** [tax, law] être soumis à; [disease, headaches] être sujet (sujette) à. 2 *n* [gen] sujet *m*. || SCH & UNIV matière *f*. 3 *vt* [control] soumettre, assujettir. || [force to experience]: **to ~ sb to sthg** exposer OR soumettre qqn à qqch. ○ **subject to** *prep* sous réserve de.

subjective [səb'dʒektɪv] *adj* subjectif(ive).

subject matter *n* (*U*) sujet *m*.

subjunctive [səb'dʒʌŋktɪv] *n* GRAMM: **~ (mood)** (mode *m*) subjonctif *m*.

sublet [,sʌb'let] (*pt & pp* **sublet**) *vt* sous-louer.

sublime [sə'blaɪm] *adj* sublime.

submachine gun [,sʌbmə'ʃi:n-] *n* mitraillette *f*.

submarine [ˌsʌbməˈriːn] *n* sous-marin *m*.

submerge [səbˈmɜːdʒ] **1** *vt* immerger, plonger. **2** *vi* s'immerger, plonger.

submission [səbˈmɪʃn] *n* [obedience] soumission *f.* ‖ [presentation] présentation *f*, soumission *f*.

submissive [səbˈmɪsɪv] *adj* soumis(e), docile.

submit [səbˈmɪt] **1** *vt* soumettre. **2** *vi*: to ~ (to) se soumettre (à).

subnormal [ˌsʌbˈnɔːml] *adj* arriéré(e), attardé(e).

subordinate [səˈbɔːdɪnət] **1** *adj fml* [less important]: ~ (to) subordonné(e) (à), moins important(e) (que). **2** *n* subordonné *m*, -e *f*.

subpoena [səˈpiːnə] (*pt* & *pp* **-ed**) JUR **1** *n* citation *f*, assignation *f*. **2** *vt* citer OR assigner à comparaître.

subscribe [səbˈskraɪb] *vi* [to magazine, newspaper] s'abonner, être abonné(e).

subscriber [səbˈskraɪbər] *n* [to magazine, service] abonné *m*, -e *f*.

subscription [səbˈskrɪpʃn] *n* [to magazine] abonnement *m*. ‖ [to club] cotisation *f*.

subsequent [ˈsʌbsɪkwənt] *adj* ultérieur(e), suivant(e).

subsequently [ˈsʌbsɪkwəntlɪ] *adv* par la suite, plus tard.

subservient [səbˈsɜːvjənt] *adj* [servile]: ~ (to) servile (vis-à-vis de), obséquieux(ieuse) (envers).

subside [səbˈsaɪd] *vi* [pain, anger] se calmer, s'atténuer; [noise] diminuer. ‖ [CONSTR - building] s'affaisser; [- ground] se tasser.

subsidence [səbˈsaɪdns, ˈsʌbsɪdns] *n* [CONSTR - of building] affaissement *m*; [- of ground] tassement *m*.

subsidiary [səbˈsɪdjərɪ] **1** *adj* subsidiaire. **2** *n*: ~ (**company**) filiale *f*.

subsidize, -ise [ˈsʌbsɪdaɪz] *vt* subventionner.

subsidy [ˈsʌbsɪdɪ] *n* subvention *f*, subside *m*.

substance [ˈsʌbstəns] *n* [gen] substance *f*. ‖ [importance] importance *f*.

substantial [səbˈstænʃl] *adj* [considerable] considérable, important(e); [meal] substantiel(ielle). ‖ [solid, well-built] solide.

substantially [səbˈstænʃəlɪ] *adv* [considerably] considérablement. ‖ [mainly] en grande partie.

substitute [ˈsʌbstɪtjuːt] **1** *n* [replacement]: ~ (**for**) [person] remplaçant *m*, -e *f* (de); [thing] succédané *m* (de). ‖ SPORT remplaçant *m*, -e *f*. **2** *vt*: to ~ **A for B** substituer A à B, remplacer B par A.

subtitle [ˈsʌb̩taɪtl] *n* sous-titre *m*.

subtle [ˈsʌtl] *adj* subtil(e).

subtlety [ˈsʌtltɪ] *n* subtilité *f*.

subtract [səbˈtrækt] *vt*: to ~ sthg (**from**) soustraire qqch (de).

subtraction [səbˈtrækʃn] *n* soustraction *f*.

suburb [ˈsʌbɜːb] *n* faubourg *m*. ○ **suburbs** *npl*: **the ~s** la banlieue.

suburban [səˈbɜːbn] *adj* [of suburbs] de banlieue. ‖ *pej* [life] étriqué(e).

suburbia [səˈbɜːbɪə] *n* (*U*) la banlieue.

subversive [səbˈvɜːsɪv] *adj* subversif(ive).

subway [ˈsʌbweɪ] *n Am* [underground railway] métro *m*.

succeed [səkˈsiːd] **1** *vt* succéder à. **2** *vi* réussir; **to ~ in doing sthg** réussir à faire qqch.

succeeding [səkˈsiːdɪŋ] *adj fml* [in future] à venir; [in past] suivant(e).

success [səkˈses] *n* succès *m*, réussite *f*.

successful [səkˈsesful] *adj* [attempt] couronné(e) de succès. ‖ [film, book etc] à succès; [person] qui a du succès.

succession [səkˈseʃn] *n* succession *f*.

successive [səkˈsesɪv] *adj* successif(ive).

succinct [səkˈsɪŋkt] *adj* succinct(e).

succumb [səˈkʌm] *vi*: **to ~ (to)** succomber (à).

such [sʌtʃ] **1** *adj* tel (telle), pareil(eille); ~ **nonsense** de telles inepties; **do you have ~ a thing as a tin-opener?** est-ce que tu aurais un ouvre-boîtes par hasard?; ~ ... **that** tel ... que. **2** *adv* [for emphasis] si, tellement; **it's ~ a horrible day!** quelle journée épouvantable!; ~ **a lot of books** tellement de livres; ~ **a long time** si OR tellement longtemps. ‖ [in comparisons] aussi. **3** *pron*: **and ~ (like)** et autres choses de ce genre. ○ **as such** *adv* en tant que tel (telle), en soi. ○ **such and such** *adj* tel et tel (telle et telle).

suck [sʌk] *vt* [with mouth] sucer. ‖ [draw in] aspirer.

sucker [ˈsʌkər] *n* [suction pad] ventouse *f*. ‖ *inf* [gullible person] poire *f*.

suction [ˈsʌkʃn] *n* succion *f*.

sudden [ˈsʌdn] *adj* soudain(e), brusque; **all of a ~** tout d'un coup, soudain.

suddenly ['sʌdnlɪ] *adv* soudainement, tout d'un coup.

suds [sʌdz] *npl* mousse *f* de savon.

sue [su:] *vt*: **to ~ sb (for)** poursuivre qqn (pour).

suede [sweɪd] *n* daim *m*.

suet ['suɪt] *n* graisse *f* de rognon.

suffer ['sʌfər] **1** *vt* [pain, injury] souffrir de. || [consequences, setback, loss] subir. **2** *vi* souffrir; **to ~ from** MED souffrir de.

suffering ['sʌfrɪŋ] *n* souffrance *f*.

suffice [sə'faɪs] *vi fml* suffire.

sufficient [sə'fɪʃnt] *adj* suffisant(e).

sufficiently [sə'fɪʃntlɪ] *adv* suffisamment.

suffocate ['sʌfəkeɪt] *vt & vi* suffoquer.

suffrage ['sʌfrɪdʒ] *n* suffrage *m*.

sugar ['ʃʊɡər] **1** *n* sucre *m*. **2** *vt* sucrer.

sugar beet *n* betterave *f* à sucre.

sugarcane ['ʃʊɡəkeɪn] *n* (*U*) canne *f* à sucre.

suggest [sə'dʒest] *vt* [propose] proposer, suggérer. || [imply] suggérer.

suggestion [sə'dʒestʃn] *n* [proposal] proposition *f*, suggestion *f*. || (*U*) [implication] suggestion *f*.

suggestive [sə'dʒestɪv] *adj* suggestif(ive); **to be ~ of sthg** suggérer qqch.

suicide ['suɪsaɪd] *n* suicide *m*; **to commit ~** se suicider.

suit [su:t] **1** *n* [for man] costume *m*, complet *m*; [for woman] tailleur *m*. || [in cards] couleur *f*. || JUR procès *m*, action *f*. **2** *vt* [subj: clothes, hairstyle] aller à. || [be convenient, appropriate to] convenir à.

suitable ['su:təbl] *adj* qui convient, qui va.

suitably ['su:təblɪ] *adv* convenablement.

suitcase ['su:tkeɪs] *n* valise *f*.

suite [swi:t] *n* [of rooms] suite *f*. || [of furniture] ensemble *m*.

suited ['su:tɪd] *adj* [suitable]: **to be ~ to/for** convenir à/pour, aller à/pour. || [couple]: **well ~** très bien assortis.

suitor ['su:tər] *n dated* soupirant *m*.

sulfur *Am* = **sulphur**.

sulk [sʌlk] *vi* bouder.

sulky ['sʌlkɪ] *adj* boudeur(euse).

sullen ['sʌlən] *adj* maussade.

sulphur *Br*, **sulfur** *Am* ['sʌlfər] *n* soufre *m*.

sultry ['sʌltrɪ] *adj* [weather] lourd(e). || [sexual] sensuel(elle).

sum [sʌm] *n* [amount of money] somme *f*. || [calculation] calcul *m*. ○ **sum up 1** *vt*

sep [summarize] résumer. **2** *vi* récapituler.

summarize, -ise ['sʌməraɪz] **1** *vt* résumer. **2** *vi* récapituler.

summary ['sʌmərɪ] *n* résumé *m*.

summer ['sʌmər] **1** *n* été *m*; **in ~** en été. **2** *comp* d'été; **the ~ holidays** les grandes vacances *fpl*.

summerhouse ['sʌməhaus, *pl* -hauzɪz] *n* pavillon *m* (de verdure).

summer school *n* université *f* d'été.

summertime ['sʌmətaɪm] *n* été *m*.

summit ['sʌmɪt] *n* sommet *m*.

summon ['sʌmən] *vt* appeler, convoquer. ○ **summon up** *vt sep* rassembler.

summons ['sʌmənz] (*pl* **summonses**) JUR **1** *n* assignation *f*. **2** *vt* assigner.

sump [sʌmp] *n* carter *m*.

sumptuous ['sʌmptʃʊəs] *adj* somptueux(euse).

sun [sʌn] *n* soleil *m*; **in the ~** au soleil.

sunbathe ['sʌnbeɪð] *vi* prendre un bain de soleil.

sunbed ['sʌnbed] *n* lit *m* à ultra-violets.

sunburn ['sʌnbɜ:n] *n* (*U*) coup *m* de soleil.

sunburned ['sʌnbɜ:nd], **sunburnt** ['sʌnbɜ:nt] *adj* brûlé(e) par le soleil, qui a attrapé un coup de soleil.

Sunday ['sʌndɪ] *n* dimanche *m*; *see also* **Saturday**.

Sunday school *n* catéchisme *m*.

sundial ['sʌndaɪəl] *n* cadran *m* solaire.

sundown ['sʌndaun] *n* coucher *m* du soleil.

sundries ['sʌndrɪz] *npl fml* articles *mpl* divers, objets *mpl* divers.

sunflower ['sʌn,flaʊər] *n* tournesol *m*.

sung [sʌŋ] *pp* → **sing**.

sunglasses ['sʌn,ɡlɑ:sɪz] *npl* lunettes *fpl* de soleil.

sunk [sʌŋk] *pp* → **sink**.

sunlight ['sʌnlaɪt] *n* lumière *f* du soleil.

sunny ['sʌnɪ] *adj* [day, place] ensoleillé(e).

sunrise ['sʌnraɪz] *n* lever *m* du soleil.

sunroof ['sʌnru:f] *n* toit *m* ouvrant.

sunset ['sʌnset] *n* coucher *m* du soleil.

sunshade ['sʌnʃeɪd] *n* parasol *m*.

sunshine ['sʌnʃaɪn] *n* lumière *f* du soleil.

sunstroke ['sʌnstrəuk] *n* (*U*) insolation *f*.

suntan ['sʌntæn] **1** *n* bronzage *m*. **2** *comp* [lotion, cream] solaire.

suntrap ['sʌntræp] *n* endroit très ensoleillé.

super ['su:pər] *adj inf* génial(e), super (*inv*).

superannuation ['su:pə,rænju'eɪʃn] *n* (*U*) pension *f* de retraite.

superb [su:'pɜ:b] *adj* superbe.

supercilious [,su:pə'sɪliəs] *adj* hautain(e).

superficial [,su:pə'fɪʃl] *adj* superficiel(ielle).

superfluous [su:'pɜ:fluəs] *adj* superflu(e).

superhuman [,su:pə'hju:mən] *adj* surhumain(e).

superimpose [,su:pərɪm'pəuz] *vt*: **to ~ sthg (on)** superposer qqch (à).

superintendent [,su:pərɪn'tendənt] *n* [of department] directeur *m*, -trice *f*.

superior [su:'pɪəriər] **1** *adj* [gen]: **~ (to)** supérieur(e) (à). || [goods, craftsmanship] de qualité supérieure. **2** *n* supérieur *m*, -e *f*.

superlative [su:'pɜ:lətɪv] **1** *adj* exceptionnel(elle), sans pareil(eille). **2** *n* GRAMM superlatif *m*.

supermarket ['su:pə,ma:kɪt] *n* supermarché *m*.

supernatural [,su:pə'nætʃrəl] *adj* surnaturel(elle).

superpower ['su:pə,pauər] *n* superpuissance *f*.

supersede [,su:pə'si:d] *vt* remplacer.

supersonic [,su:pə'sɒnɪk] *adj* supersonique.

superstitious [,su:pə'stɪʃəs] *adj* superstitieux(ieuse).

superstore ['su:pəstɔ:r] *n* hypermarché *m*.

supervise ['su:pəvaɪz] *vt* surveiller; [work] superviser.

supervisor ['su:pəvaɪzər] *n* surveillant *m*, -e *f*.

supper ['sʌpər] *n* [evening meal] dîner *m*. || [before bedtime] collation *f*.

supple ['sʌpl] *adj* souple.

supplement [*n* 'sʌplɪmənt, *vb* 'sʌplɪment] **1** *n* supplément *m*. **2** *vt* compléter.

supplementary [,sʌplɪ'mentərɪ] *adj* supplémentaire.

supplier [sə'plaɪər] *n* fournisseur *m*.

supply [sə'plaɪ] **1** *n* [store] réserve *f*, provision *f*. || [system] alimentation *f*. **2** *vt* [provide]: **to ~ sthg (to sb)** fournir qqch (à qqn). || [provide to]: **to ~ sb (with)** fournir qqn (en), approvisionner qqn (en); **to ~ sthg with sthg** alimenter qqch

en qqch. ○ **supplies** *npl* [food] vivres *mpl*; MIL approvisionnements *mpl*.

support [sə'pɔ:t] **1** *n* (*U*) [physical help] appui *m*. || (*U*) [emotional, financial help] soutien *m*. || [object] support *m*, appui *m*. **2** *vt* [physically] soutenir, supporter; [weight] supporter. || [emotionally] soutenir. || [financially] subvenir aux besoins de. || [political party, candidate] appuyer; SPORT être un supporter de.

supporter [sə'pɔ:tər] *n* [of person, plan] partisan *m*, -e *f*. || SPORT supporter *m*.

suppose [sə'pəuz] **1** *vt* supposer. **2** *vi* supposer; **I ~ (so)** je suppose que oui; **I ~ not** je suppose que non.

supposed [sə'pəuzd] *adj* [doubtful] supposé(e). || [reputed, intended]: **to be ~ to be** être censé(e) être.

supposedly [sə'pəuzɪdlɪ] *adv* soidisant.

supposing [sə'pəuzɪŋ] *conj* et si, à supposer que (+ *subjunctive*).

suppress [sə'pres] *vt* [uprising] réprimer. || [information] supprimer. || [emotions] réprimer, étouffer.

supreme [su'pri:m] *adj* suprême.

Supreme Court *n* [in US]: **the ~** la Cour Suprême.

surcharge ['sɜ:tʃa:dʒ] *n* [extra payment] surcharge *f*; [extra tax] surtaxe *f*.

sure [ʃuər] **1** *adj* [gen] sûr(e); **to be ~ of o.s.** être sûr de soi. || [certain]: **to be ~ (of sthg/of doing sthg)** être sûr(e) (de qqch/de faire qqch), être certain(e) (de qqch/de faire qqch); **to make ~ (that)** ... s'assurer OR vérifier que .... **2** *adv inf* [yes] bien sûr. || *Am* [really] vraiment. ○ **for sure** *adv* sans aucun doute. ○ **sure enough** *adv* en effet, effectivement.

surely ['ʃuəlɪ] *adv* sûrement.

surf [sɜ:f] *n* ressac *m*.

surface ['sɜ:fɪs] **1** *n* surface *f*; **on the ~** *fig* à première vue, vu de l'extérieur. **2** *vi* [diver] remonter à la surface; [submarine] faire surface. || [problem, rumour] apparaître OR s'étaler au grand jour.

surface mail *n* courrier *m* par voie de terre/de mer.

surfboard ['sɜ:fbɔ:d] *n* planche *f* de surf.

surfeit ['sɜ:fɪt] *n fml* excès *m*.

surfing ['sɜ:fɪŋ] *n* surf *m*.

surge [sɜ:dʒ] **1** *n* [of people, vehicles] déferlement *m*; ELEC surtension *f*. || [of emotion, interest] vague *f*, montée *f*; [of anger] bouffée *f*. **2** *vi* [people, vehicles] déferler.

surgeon ['sɜ:dʒən] *n* chirurgien *m*.

surgery ['sɜːdʒərɪ] *n* (*U*) MED [performing operations] chirurgie *f*.

surgical ['sɜːdʒɪkl] *adj* chirurgical(e); ~ **stocking** bas *m* orthopédique.

surly ['sɜːlɪ] *adj* revêche, renfrogné(e).

surmount [sɜːˈmaʊnt] *vt* surmonter.

surname ['sɜːneɪm] *n* nom *m* de famille.

surpass [səˈpɑːs] *vt fml* dépasser.

surplus ['sɜːpləs] **1** *adj* en surplus. **2** *n* surplus *m*.

surprise [səˈpraɪz] **1** *n* surprise *f*. **2** *vt* surprendre.

surprised [səˈpraɪzd] *adj* surpris(e).

surprising [səˈpraɪzɪŋ] *adj* surprenant(e).

surprisingly [səˈpraɪzɪŋlɪ] *adv* étonnamment.

surrender [səˈrendər] **1** *n* reddition *f*, capitulation *f*. **2** *vi* [stop fighting]: **to ~ (to)** se rendre (à). || *fig* [give in]: **to ~ (to)** se laisser aller (à). se livrer (à).

surreptitious [ˌsʌrəpˈtɪʃəs] *adj* subreptice.

surrogate ['sʌrəgeɪt] *n* substitut *m*.

surrogate mother *n* mère *f* porteuse.

surround [səˈraʊnd] *vt* entourer; [subj: police. army] cerner.

surrounding [səˈraʊndɪŋ] *adj* environnant(e).

surroundings [səˈraʊndɪŋz] *npl* environnement *m*.

surveillance [sɜːˈveɪləns] *n* surveillance *f*.

survey [*n* 'sɜːveɪ, *vb* səˈveɪ] **1** *n* [investigation] étude *f*; [of public opinion] sondage *m*. || [of building] inspection *f*. **2** *vt* [contemplate] passer en revue. || [investigate] faire une étude de, enquêter sur. || [building] inspecter.

surveyor [səˈveɪər] *n* [of building] expert *m*; [of land] géomètre *m*.

survival [səˈvaɪvl] *n* [continuing to live] survie *f*.

survive [səˈvaɪv] **1** *vt* survivre à. **2** *vi* survivre.

survivor [səˈvaɪvər] *n* survivant *m*, -e *f*; *fig* battant *m*, -e *f*.

susceptible [səˈseptəbl] *adj*: ~ **(to)** sensible (à).

suspect [*adj* & *n* 'sʌspekt, *vb* səˈspekt] **1** *adj* suspect(e). **2** *n* suspect *m*, -e *f*. **3** *vt* [distrust] douter de. || [think likely, consider guilty] soupçonner.

suspend [səˈspend] *vt* [gen] suspendre. || [from school] renvoyer temporairement.

suspended sentence [səˈspendɪd-] *n* condamnation *f* avec sursis.

suspenders [səˈspendəz] *npl Am* [for trousers] bretelles *fpl*.

suspense [səˈspens] *n* suspense *m*.

suspension [səˈspenʃn] *n* [gen & AUT] suspension *f*. || [from school] renvoi *m* temporaire.

suspension bridge *n* pont *m* suspendu.

suspicion [səˈspɪʃn] *n* soupçon *m*.

suspicious [səˈspɪʃəs] *adj* [having suspicions] soupçonneux(euse). || [causing suspicion] suspect(e), louche.

sustain [səˈsteɪn] *vt* [maintain] soutenir. || *fml* [suffer - damage] subir; [- injury] recevoir. || *fml* [weight] supporter.

sustenance ['sʌstɪnəns] *n* (*U*) *fml* nourriture *f*.

SW (*abbr of* **short wave**) OC.

swab [swɒb] *n* MED tampon *m*.

swagger ['swægər] *vi* parader.

swallow ['swɒləʊ] **1** *n* [bird] hirondelle *f*. **2** *vt* avaler; *fig* [anger, tears] ravaler.

swam [swæm] *pt* → **swim**.

swamp [swɒmp] **1** *n* marais *m*. **2** *vt* [flood] submerger. || [overwhelm] déborder, submerger.

swan [swɒn] *n* cygne *m*.

swap [swɒp] *vt*: **to ~ sthg (with sb/for sthg)** échanger qqch (avec qqn/contre qqch).

swarm [swɔːm] **1** *n* essaim *m*. **2** *vi fig* [people] grouiller; **to be ~ing (with)** [place] grouiller (de).

swarthy ['swɔːðɪ] *adj* basané(e).

swastika ['swɒstɪkə] *n* croix *f* gammée.

swat [swɒt] *vt* écraser.

sway [sweɪ] **1** *vt* [influence] influencer. **2** *vi* se balancer.

swear [sweər] (*pt* **swore**, *pp* **sworn**) **1** *vt* jurer; **to ~ to do sthg** jurer de faire qqch. **2** *vi* jurer.

swearword ['sweəwɜːd] *n* juron *m*, gros mot *m*.

sweat [swet] **1** *n* [perspiration] transpiration *f*, sueur *f*. **2** *vi* [perspire] transpirer, suer. || *inf* [worry] se faire du mouron.

sweater ['swetər] *n* pullover *m*.

sweatshirt ['swetʃɜːt] *n* sweat-shirt *m*.

sweaty ['swetɪ] *adj* [skin, clothes] mouillé(e) de sueur.

Swede [swiːd] *n* Suédois *m*, -e *f*.

Sweden ['swiːdn] *n* Suède *f*.

Swedish ['swiːdɪʃ] **1** *adj* suédois(e). **2** *n* [language] suédois *m*. **3** *npl*: **the ~** les Suédois *mpl*.

sweep [swi:p] (*pt & pp* **swept**) **1** *n* [sweeping movement] grand geste *m*. ‖ [with brush]: **to give sthg a ~** donner un coup de balai à qqch, balayer qqch. **2** *vt* [gen] balayer; [scan with eyes] parcourir des yeux. ○ **sweep away** *vt sep* [destroy] emporter, entraîner. ○ **sweep up 1** *vt sep* [with brush] balayer. **2** *vi* balayer.

sweeping ['swi:pɪŋ] *adj* [effect, change] radical(e). ‖ [statement] hâtif(ive).

sweet [swi:t] *adj* [gen] doux (douce); [cake, flavour, pudding] sucré(e). ‖ [kind] gentil(ille). ‖ [attractive] adorable, mignon(onne).

sweet corn *n* maïs *m*.

sweeten ['swi:tn] *vt* sucrer.

sweetheart ['swi:thɑ:t] *n* [term of endearment] chéri *m*, -e *f*, mon cœur *m*.

sweetness ['swi:tnɪs] *n* [gen] douceur *f*; [of taste] goût *m* sucré, douceur. ‖ [attractiveness] charme *m*.

sweet pea *n* pois *m* de senteur.

swell [swel] (*pt* **-ed**, *pp* **swollen** OR **-ed**) **1** *vi* [leg, face etc] enfler; [lungs, balloon] se gonfler. ‖ [crowd, population etc] grossir, augmenter; [sound] grossir, s'enfler. **2** *vt* grossir, augmenter. **3** *n* [of sea] houle *f*. **4** *adj Am inf* chouette, épatant(e).

swelling ['swelɪŋ] *n* enflure *f*.

sweltering ['sweltərɪŋ] *adj* étouffant(e), suffocant(e).

swept [swept] *pt & pp* → **sweep**.

swerve [swɜ:v] *ri* faire une embardée.

swift [swɪft] **1** *adj* [fast] rapide. ‖ [prompt] prompt(e). **2** *n* [bird] martinet *m*.

swig [swɪg] *inf n* lampée *f*.

swill [swɪl] *n* (*U*) [pig food] pâtée *f*.

swim [swɪm] (*pt* **swam**, *pp* **swum**) **1** *n*: **to have a ~** nager; **to go for a ~** aller se baigner, aller nager. **2** *vi* [person, fish, animal] nager. ‖ [room] tourner; **my head was swimming** j'avais la tête qui tournait.

swimmer ['swɪmər] *n* nageur *m*, -euse *f*.

swimming ['swɪmɪŋ] *n* natation *f*; **to go ~** aller nager.

swimming cap *n* bonnet *m* de bain.

swimming pool *n* piscine *f*.

swimming trunks *npl* maillot *m* OR slip *m* de bain.

swimsuit ['swɪmsu:t] *n* maillot *m* de bain.

swindle ['swɪndl] **1** *n* escroquerie *f*. **2** *vt* escroquer, rouler; **to ~ sb out of sthg** escroquer qqch à qqn.

swine [swaɪn] *n inf* [person] salaud *m*.

swing [swɪŋ] (*pt & pp* **swung**) **1** *n* [child's toy] balançoire *f*. ‖ [change - of opinion] revirement *m*; [- of mood] changement *m*, saute *f*. ‖ [sway] balancement *m*. ‖ *phr*: **to be in full ~** battre son plein. **2** *vt* [move back and forth] balancer. ‖ [move in a curve] faire virer. **3** *ri* [move back and forth] se balancer. ‖ [turn - vehicle] virer, tourner; **to ~ round** [person] se retourner. ‖ [change] changer.

swing door *n* porte *f* battante.

swingeing ['swɪndʒɪŋ] *adj* très sévère.

swipe [swaɪp] **1** *vt inf* [steal] faucher, piquer. **2** *vi*: **to ~ at** envoyer OR donner un coup à.

swirl [swɜ:l] **1** *n* tourbillon *m*. **2** *ri* tourbillonner, tournoyer.

swish [swɪʃ] *vt* [tail] battre l'air de.

Swiss [swɪs] **1** *adj* suisse. **2** *n* [person] Suisse *mf*. **3** *npl*: **the ~** les Suisses *mpl*.

switch [swɪtʃ] **1** *n* [control device] interrupteur *m*, commutateur *m*; [on radio, stereo etc] bouton *m*. ‖ [change] changement *m*. **2** *vt* [swap] échanger; [jobs] changer de. ○ **switch off** *vt sep* éteindre. ○ **switch on** *vt sep* allumer.

switchboard ['swɪtʃbɔ:d] *n* standard *m*.

Switzerland ['swɪtsələnd] *n* Suisse *f*; **in ~** en Suisse.

swivel ['swɪvl] **1** *vt* [chair] faire pivoter; [head, eyes] faire tourner. **2** *ri* [chair] pivoter; [head, eyes] tourner.

swivel chair *n* fauteuil *m* pivotant OR tournant.

swollen ['swəʊln] **1** *pp* → **swell**. **2** *adj* [ankle, face] enflé(e); [river] en crue.

swoop [swu:p] *ri* [bird, plane] piquer. ‖ [police, army] faire une descente.

swop [swɒp] = **swap**.

sword [sɔ:d] *n* épée *f*.

swordfish ['sɔ:dfɪʃ] (*pl inv* OR **-es**) *n* espadon *m*.

swore [swɔ:r] *pt* → **swear**.

sworn [swɔ:n] **1** *pp* → **swear**. **2** *adj* JUR sous serment.

swum [swʌm] *pp* → **swim**.

swung [swʌŋ] *pt & pp* → **swing**.

sycamore ['sɪkəmɔ:r] *n* sycomore *m*.

syllable ['sɪləbl] *n* syllabe *f*.

syllabus ['sɪləbəs] (*pl* **-buses** OR **-bi** [-baɪ]) *n* programme *m*.

symbol ['sɪmbl] *n* symbole *m*.

symbolize, -ise ['sɪmbəlaɪz] *vt* symboliser.

symmetry ['sɪmətrɪ] *n* symétrie *f*.

sympathetic [,sɪmpə'θetɪk] *adj* [understanding] compatissant(e), compréhensif(ive). ‖ [willing to support]: ~ **(to)** bien disposé(e) (à l'égard de).

sympathize, -ise ['sɪmpəθaɪz] *vi* [feel sorry] compatir; **to ~ with sb** plaindre qqn; [in grief] compatir à la douleur de qqn. ‖ [understand]: **to ~ with sthg** comprendre qqch. ‖ [support]: **to ~ with sthg** approuver qqch, soutenir qqch.

sympathizer, -iser ['sɪmpəθaɪzər] *n* sympathisant *m*, -e *f*.

sympathy ['sɪmpəθɪ] *n* (*U*) [understanding]: ~ **(for)** compassion *f* (pour), sympathie *f* (pour). ‖ [agreement] approbation *f*, sympathie *f*. ○ **sympathies** *npl* [to bereaved person] condoléances *fpl*.

symphony ['sɪmfənɪ] *n* symphonie *f*.

symposium [sɪm'pəʊzjəm] (*pl* **-siums** OR **-sia** [-zjə]) *n* symposium *m*.

symptom ['sɪmptəm] *n* symptôme *m*.

synagogue ['sɪnəgɒg] *n* synagogue *f*.

syndicate ['sɪndɪkət] *n* syndicat *m*, consortium *m*.

syndrome ['sɪndrəʊm] *n* syndrome *m*.

synonym ['sɪnənɪm] *n*: ~ **(for** OR **of)** synonyme *m* (de).

synopsis [sɪ'nɒpsɪs] (*pl* **-ses** [-siːz]) *n* résumé *m*.

syntax ['sɪntæks] *n* syntaxe *f*.

synthesis ['sɪnθəsɪs] (*pl* **-ses** [-siːz]) *n* synthèse *f*.

synthetic [sɪn'θetɪk] *adj* [man-made] synthétique.

syphilis ['sɪfɪlɪs] *n* syphilis *f*.

syphon ['saɪfn] = **siphon**.

Syria ['sɪrɪə] *n* Syrie *f*.

syringe [sɪ'rɪndʒ] *n* seringue *f*.

syrup ['sɪrəp] *n* (*U*) [sugar and water] sirop *m*.

system ['sɪstəm] *n* [gen] système *m*; **road/railway ~** réseau *m* routier/de chemins de fer. ‖ [equipment - gen] installation *f*; [- electric, electronic] appareil *m*. ‖ (*U*) [methodical approach] système *m*, méthode *f*.

systematic [,sɪstə'mætɪk] *adj* systématique.

system disk *n* COMPUT disque *m* système.

systems analyst ['sɪstəmz-] *n* COMPUT analyste fonctionnel *m*, analyste fonctionnelle *f*.

t (*pl* **t's** OR **ts**), **T** (*pl* **T's** OR **Ts**) [tiː] *n* [letter] t *m inv*, T *m inv*.

tab [tæb] *n* [of cloth] étiquette *f*. ‖ [of metal] languette *f*. ‖ *Am* [bill] addition *f*. ‖ *phr*: **to keep ~s on sb** tenir OR avoir qqn à l'œil, surveiller qqn.

tabby ['tæbɪ] *n*: ~ **(cat)** chat tigré *m*, chatte tigrée *f*.

table ['teɪbl] *n* table *f*.

tablecloth ['teɪblklɒθ] *n* nappe *f*.

table lamp *n* lampe *f*.

tablemat ['teɪblmæt] *n* dessous-de-plat *m inv*.

tablespoon ['teɪblspuːn] *n* [spoon] cuiller *f* de service. ‖ [spoonful] cuillerée *f* à soupe.

tablet ['tæblɪt] *n* [pill] comprimé *m*, cachet *m*.

table tennis *n* ping-pong *m*, tennis *m* de table.

table wine *n* vin *m* de table.

tabloid ['tæblɔɪd] *n*: ~ **(newspaper)** tabloïd *m*, tabloïde *m*.

tabulate ['tæbjʊleɪt] *vt* présenter sous forme de tableau.

tacit ['tæsɪt] *adj* tacite.

taciturn ['tæsɪtɜːn] *adj* taciturne.

tack [tæk] **1** *n* [nail] clou *m*. ‖ *fig* [course of action] tactique *f*, méthode *f*. **2** *vt* [fasten with nail - gen] clouer; [- notice] punaiser. ‖ SEWING faufiler. **3** *vi* NAUT tirer une bordée.

tackle ['tækl] **1** *n* FTBL tacle *m*. ‖ [equipment] équipement *m*, matériel *m*. ‖ [for lifting] palan *m*, appareil *m* de levage. **2** *vt* [deal with] s'attaquer à. ‖ FTBL tacler. ‖ [attack] empoigner.

tacky ['tækɪ] *adj inf* [film, remark] d'un goût douteux; [jewellery] de pacotille. ‖ [sticky] collant(e), pas encore sec (sèche).

tact [tækt] *n* (*U*) tact *m*, délicatesse *f*.

tactful ['tæktfʊl] *adj* [remark] plein(e) de tact; [person] qui a du tact OR de la délicatesse.

tactic ['tæktɪk] *n* tactique *f.*

tactical ['tæktɪkl] *adj* tactique.

tactless ['tæktlɪs] *adj* qui manque de tact OR délicatesse.

tadpole ['tædpəʊl] *n* têtard *m.*

tag [tæg] *n* [of cloth] marque *f.* ‖ [of paper] étiquette *f.* ○ **tag along** *vi inf* suivre.

tail [teɪl] **1** *n* [gen] queue *f.* ‖ [of coat] basque *f*, pan *m*; [of shirt] pan. **2** *vt inf* [follow] filer. ○ **tails** *npl* [formal dress] queue-de-pie *f*, habit *m.* ‖ [side of coin] pile *f.* ○ **tail off** *vi* [voice] s'affaiblir; [noise] diminuer.

tailcoat [,teɪl'kəʊt] *n* habit *m*, queue-de-pie *f.*

tail end *n* fin *f.*

tailor ['teɪlər] **1** *n* tailleur *m.* **2** *vt fig* adapter.

tailor-made *adj fig* sur mesure.

tailwind ['teɪlwɪnd] *n* vent *m* arrière.

tainted ['teɪntɪd] *adj* [reputation] souillé(e), entaché(e). ‖ *Am* [food] avarié(e).

Taiwan [,taɪ'wɑːn] *n* Taiwan.

take [teɪk] (*pt* **took**, *pp* **taken**) **1** *vt* [gen] prendre; **to ~ an exam** passer un examen; **to ~ a walk** se promener, faire une promenade; **to ~ a bath/photo** prendre un bain/une photo. ‖ [lead, drive] emmener. ‖ [accept] accepter. ‖ [contain] contenir, avoir une capacité de. ‖ [tolerate] supporter. ‖ [require] demander; **how long will it ~?** combien de temps cela va-t-il prendre? ‖ [wear]: **what size do you ~?** [clothes] quelle taille faites-vous?; [shoes] vous chaussez du combien? ‖ [assume]: **I ~ it (that)** ... je suppose que .... je pense que .... ‖ [rent] prendre, louer. **2** *n* CINEMA prise *f* de vues. ○ **take after** *vt fus* tenir de, ressembler à. ○ **take apart** *vt sep* [dismantle] démonter. ○ **take away** *vt sep* [remove] enlever. ‖ [deduct] retrancher, soustraire. ○ **take back** *vt sep* [return] rendre, rapporter. ‖ [accept] reprendre. ‖ [statement, accusation] retirer. ○ **take down** *vt sep* [dismantle] démonter. ‖ [write down] prendre. ‖ [lower] baisser. ○ **take in** *vt sep* [deceive] rouler, tromper. ‖ [understand] comprendre. ○ **take off 1** *vt sep* [remove] enlever, ôter. ‖ [have as holiday]: **to ~ a week/day off** prendre une semaine/un jour de congé. **2** *vi* [plane] décoller. ‖ [go away suddenly] partir. ○ **take on** *vt sep* [accept] accepter, prendre. ‖ [employ] embaucher, prendre. ‖ [confront] s'attaquer à; [competitor] faire concurrence à; SPORT jouer contre. ○ **take out** *vt sep* [from container] sortir; [from pocket] prendre. ‖ [go out with] emmener, sortir avec. ○ **take over 1** *vt sep* [take control of] reprendre, prendre la direction de. ‖ [job]: **to ~ over sb's job** remplacer qqn, prendre la suite de qqn. **2** *vi* [take control] prendre le pouvoir. ‖ [in job] prendre la relève. ○ **take to** *vt fus* [person] éprouver de la sympathie pour, sympathiser avec; [activity] prendre goût à. ‖ [begin]: **to ~ to doing sthg** se mettre à faire qqch. ○ **take up** *vt sep* [begin - job] prendre; **to ~ up singing** se mettre au chant. ‖ [use up] prendre, occuper. ○ **take up on** *vt sep* [accept]: **to ~ sb up on an offer** accepter l'offre de qqn.

takeaway *Br* ['teɪkə,weɪ], **takeout** *Am* ['teɪkaʊt] *n* [food] plat *m* à emporter.

taken ['teɪkn] *pp* → take.

takeoff ['teɪkɒf] *n* [of plane] décollage *m.*

takeout *Am* = takeaway.

takeover ['teɪk,əʊvər] *n* [of company] prise *f* de contrôle, rachat *m.* ‖ [of government] prise *f* de pouvoir.

takings ['teɪkɪŋz] *npl* recette *f.*

talc [tælk], **talcum (powder)** ['tælkəm-] *n* talc *m.*

tale [teɪl] *n* [fictional story] histoire *f*, conte *m.* ‖ [anecdote] récit *m*, histoire *f.*

talent ['tælənt] *n*: **~ (for)** talent *m* (pour).

talented ['tæləntɪd] *adj* qui a du talent, talentueux(euse).

talk [tɔːk] **1** *n* [conversation] discussion *f*, conversation *f.* ‖ (*U*) [gossip] bavardages *mpl*, racontars *mpl.* ‖ [lecture] conférence *f*, causerie *f.* **2** *vi* [speak]: **to ~ (to sb)** parler (à qqn); **to ~ about** parler de. ‖ [gossip] bavarder, jaser. ‖ [make a speech] faire un discours, parler; **to ~ on** OR **about** parler de. **3** *vt* parler. ○ **talks** *npl* entretiens *mpl*, pourparlers *mpl.* ○ **talk into** *vt sep*: **to ~ sb into doing sthg** persuader qqn de faire qqch. ○ **talk out of** *vt sep*: **to ~ sb out of doing sthg** dissuader qqn de faire qqch. ○ **talk over** *vt sep* discuter de.

talkative ['tɔːkətɪv] *adj* bavard(e), loquace.

talk show *Am n* talk-show *m*, causerie *f.*

tall [tɔːl] *adj* grand(e); **how ~ are you?** combien mesurez-vous?

tall story *n* histoire *f* à dormir debout.

tally 310

tally ['tælɪ] **1** *n* compte *m*. **2** *vi* correspondre, concorder.

talon ['tælən] *n* serre *f*, griffe *f*.

tambourine [,tæmbə'riːn] *n* tambourin *m*.

tame [teɪm] **1** *adj* [animal, bird] apprivoisé(e). ‖ *pej* [person] docile; [party, story, life] terne, morne. **2** *vt* [animal, bird] apprivoiser.

tamper ['tæmpə'] ○ **tamper with** *vt fus* [machine] toucher à; [records, file] altérer, falsifier; [lock] essayer de crocheter.

tampon ['tæmpɒn] *n* tampon *m*.

tan [tæn] **1** *adj* brun clair (*inv*). **2** *n* bronzage *m*, hâle *m*. **3** *vi* bronzer.

tang [tæŋ] *n* [taste] saveur *f* forte OR piquante; [smell] odeur *f* forte OR piquante.

tangent ['tændʒənt] *n*: **to go off at a ~** *fig* changer de sujet, faire une digression.

tangerine [,tændʒə'riːn] *n* mandarine *f*.

tangible ['tændʒəbl] *adj* tangible.

Tangier [tæn'dʒɪə'] *n* Tanger *m*.

tangle ['tæŋgl] *n* [mass] enchevêtrement *m*, emmêlement *m*. ‖ *fig* [confusion]: **to get into a ~** s'empêtrer, s'embrouiller.

tank [tæŋk] *n* [container] réservoir *m*; **fish ~** aquarium *m*. ‖ MIL tank *m*, char *m* (d'assaut).

tanker ['tæŋkə'] *n* [ship - for oil] pétrolier *m*. ‖ [truck] camion-citerne *m*. ‖ [train] wagon-citerne *m*.

tanned [tænd] *adj* bronzé(e), hâlé(e).

Tannoy® ['tænɔɪ] *n* système *m* de haut-parleurs.

tantalizing ['tæntəlaɪzɪŋ] *adj* [smell] très appétissant(e); [possibility, thought] très tentant(e).

tantamount ['tæntəmaʊnt] *adj*: **~ to** équivalent(e) à.

tantrum ['tæntrəm] (*pl* -s) *n* crise *f* de colère; **to have** OR **throw a ~** faire OR piquer une colère.

tap [tæp] **1** *n* [device] robinet *m*. ‖ [light blow] petite tape *f*, petit coup *m*. **2** *vt* [hit] tapoter, taper. ‖ [resources, energy] exploiter, utiliser. ‖ [telephone, wire] mettre sur écoute.

tap dance *n* claquettes *fpl*.

tape [teɪp] **1** *n* [magnetic tape] bande *f* magnétique; [cassette] cassette *f*. ‖ [strip of cloth, adhesive material] ruban *m*. **2** *vt* [record] enregistrer; [on video] magnétoscoper, enregistrer au magnétoscope. ‖ [stick] scotcher.

tape measure *n* centimètre *m*, mètre *m*.

taper ['teɪpə'] *vi* s'effiler.

tape recorder *n* magnétophone *m*.

tapestry ['tæpɪstrɪ] *n* tapisserie *f*.

tar [tɑː'] *n* (*U*) goudron *m*.

target ['tɑːgɪt] **1** *n* [of missile, bomb] objectif *m*; [for archery, shooting] cible *f*. ‖ *fig* [for criticism] cible *f*. ‖ *fig* [goal] objectif *m*. **2** *vt* [city, building] viser. ‖ *fig* [subj: policy] s'adresser à, viser; [subj: advertising] cibler.

tariff ['tærɪf] *n* [tax] tarif *m* douanier. ‖ [list] tableau *m* OR liste *f* des prix.

Tarmac® ['tɑːmæk] *n* [material] macadam *m*. ○ **tarmac** *n* AERON: **the tarmac** la piste.

tarnish ['tɑːnɪʃ] *vt lit & fig* ternir.

tarpaulin [tɑː'pɔːlɪn] *n* [material] toile *f* goudronnée; [sheet] bâche *f*.

tart [tɑːt] **1** *adj* [bitter] acide. ‖ [sarcastic] acide, acerbe. **2** *n* CULIN tarte *f*. ‖ *v inf* [prostitute] pute *f*.

tartan ['tɑːtn] **1** *n* tartan *m*. **2** *comp* écossais(e).

tartar(e) sauce ['tɑːtə'-] *n* sauce *f* tartare.

task [tɑːsk] *n* tâche *f*, besogne *f*.

task force *n* MIL corps *m* expéditionnaire.

tassel ['tæsl] *n* pompon *m*, gland *m*.

taste [teɪst] **1** *n* [gen] goût *m*; **have a ~!** goûte!; **in good/bad ~** de bon/mauvais goût. ‖ *fig* [liking]: **~ (for)** penchant *m* (pour), goût *m* (pour). ‖ *fig* [experience] aperçu *m*. **2** *vt* [sense - food] sentir. ‖ [test, try] déguster, goûter. ‖ *fig* [experience] tâter de, goûter de. **3** *vi*: **to ~ of/like** avoir le goût de; **to ~ good/odd** *etc* avoir bon goût/un drôle de goût *etc*.

tasteful ['teɪstfʊl] *adj* de bon goût.

tasteless ['teɪstlɪs] *adj* [object, decor, remark] de mauvais goût. ‖ [food] qui n'a aucun goût, fade.

tasty ['teɪstɪ] *adj* [delicious] délicieux(ieuse), succulent(e).

tatters ['tætəz] *npl*: **in ~** [clothes] en lambeaux; [reputation] ruiné(e).

tattoo [tə'tuː] (*pl* -s) **1** *n* [design] tatouage *m*. **2** *vt* tatouer.

taught [tɔːt] *pt & pp* → **teach**.

taunt [tɔːnt] **1** *vt* railler, se moquer de. **2** *n* raillerie *f*, moquerie *f*.

Taurus ['tɔːrəs] *n* Taureau *m*.

taut [tɔːt] *adj* tendu(e).

tawdry ['tɔːdrɪ] *adj pej* [jewellery] clinquant(e); [clothes] voyant(e), criard(e).

tax [tæks] **1** *n* taxe *f*, impôt *m*. **2** *vt* [goods] taxer. ‖ [profits, business, person] imposer. ‖ [strain] mettre à l'épreuve.

taxable ['tæksəbl] *adj* imposable.

tax allowance *n* abattement *m* fiscal.

taxation [tæk'seɪʃn] *n* (U) [system] imposition *f*. ‖ [amount] impôts *mpl*.

tax avoidance [-ə'vɔɪdəns] *n* évasion *f* fiscale.

tax collector *n* percepteur *m*.

tax evasion *n* fraude *f* fiscale.

tax-free *Br*, **tax-exempt** *Am adj* exonéré(e) (d'impôt).

taxi ['tæksɪ] **1** *n* taxi *m*. **2** *vi* [plane] rouler au sol.

taxi driver *n* chauffeur *m* de taxi.

tax inspector *n* inspecteur *m* des impôts.

taxi rank *Br*, **taxi stand** *n* station *f* de taxis.

taxpayer ['tæks,peɪər] *n* contribuable *mf*.

tax relief *n* allègement *m* OR dégrèvement *m* fiscal.

tax return *n* déclaration *f* d'impôts.

TB *n abbr of* **tuberculosis**.

tea [tiː] *n* [drink, leaves] thé *m*.

teabag ['tiːbæg] *n* sachet *m* de thé.

teach [tiːtʃ] (*pt & pp* taught) **1** *vt* [instruct] apprendre; **to ~ sb sthg**, **to ~ sthg to sb** apprendre qqch à qqn; **to ~ sb to do sthg** apprendre à qqn à faire qqch. ‖ [subj: teacher] enseigner; **to ~ sb sthg**, **to ~ sthg to sb** enseigner qqch à qqn. **2** *vi* enseigner.

teacher ['tiːtʃər] *n* [in primary school] instituteur *m*, -trice *f*, maître *m*, maîtresse *f*; [in secondary school] professeur *m*.

teacher training college *Br*, **teachers college** *Am n* ≃ institut *m* universitaire de formation de maîtres, ≃ IUFM *m*.

teaching ['tiːtʃɪŋ] *n* enseignement *m*.

tea cosy *Br*, **tea cozy** *Am n* couvre-théière *m*, cosy *m*.

teacup ['tiːkʌp] *n* tasse *f* à thé.

teak [tiːk] *n* teck *m*.

team [tiːm] *n* équipe *f*.

teammate ['tiːmmeɪt] *n* co-équipier *m*, -ière *f*.

teamwork ['tiːmwɜːk] *n* (U) travail *m* d'équipe, collaboration *f*.

teapot ['tiːpɒt] *n* théière *f*.

tear¹ [tɪər] *n* larme *f*.

tear² [teər] (*pt* tore, *pp* torn) **1** *vt* [rip] déchirer. ‖ [remove roughly] arracher. **2** *vi* [rip] se déchirer. ‖ [move quickly] foncer, aller à toute allure. **3** *n* déchirure *f*, accroc *m*. ○ **tear apart** *vt sep* [rip up] déchirer, mettre en morceaux. ‖ *fig* [country, company] diviser; [person] déchirer. ○ **tear down** *vt sep* [building] démolir; [poster] arracher. ○ **tear up** *vt sep* déchirer.

teardrop ['tɪədrɒp] *n* larme *f*.

tearful ['tɪəful] *adj* [person] en larmes.

tear gas [tɪər-] *n* (U) gaz *m* lacrymogène.

tearoom ['tiːrʊm] *n* salon *m* de thé.

tease [tiːz] **1** *n* taquin *m*, -e *f*. **2** *vt* [mock]: **to ~ sb (about sthg)** taquiner qqn (à propos de qqch).

tea service, **tea set** *n* service *m* à thé.

teaspoon ['tiːspuːn] *n* [utensil] petite cuillère *f*, cuillère *f* à café. ‖ [amount] cuillerée *f* à café.

teat [tiːt] *n* tétine *f*.

tea towel *n* torchon *m*.

technical ['teknɪkl] *adj* technique.

technicality [,teknɪ'kælətɪ] *n* [detail] détail *m* technique.

technically ['teknɪklɪ] *adv* [gen] techniquement. ‖ [theoretically] en théorie.

technician [tek'nɪʃn] *n* technicien *m*, -ienne *f*.

technique [tek'niːk] *n* technique *f*.

technological [,teknə'lɒdʒɪkl] *adj* technologique.

technology [tek'nɒlədʒɪ] *n* technologie *f*.

teddy ['tedɪ] *n*: **~ (bear)** ours *m* en peluche, nounours *m*.

tedious ['tiːdjəs] *adj* ennuyeux(euse).

tee [tiː] *n* GOLF tee *m*.

teem [tiːm] *vi* [rain] pleuvoir à verse. ‖ [place]: **to be ~ing with** grouiller de.

teenage ['tiːneɪdʒ] *adj* adolescent(e).

teenager ['tiːn,eɪdʒər] *n* adolescent *m*, -e *f*.

teens [tiːnz] *npl* adolescence *f*.

tee shirt *n* tee-shirt *m*.

teeter ['tiːtər] *vi* vaciller; **to ~ on the brink of** *fig* être au bord de.

teeth [tiːθ] *pl* → **tooth**.

teethe [tiːð] *vi* [baby] percer ses dents.

teething troubles ['tiːðɪŋ-] *npl* *fig* difficultés *fpl* initiales.

teetotaler *Br*, **teetotaler** *Am* [tiː'təʊtlər] *n* personne *f* qui ne boit jamais d'alcool.

TEFL ['tefl] (*abbr of* teaching of English as a foreign language) *n* enseignement de l'anglais langue étrangère.

tel. (*abbr of* telephone) tél.

telecommunications ['telɪkə,mjuːnɪ-'keɪʃnz] *npl* télécommunications *fpl*.

telegram ['telɪgræm] *n* télégramme *m*.

telegraph ['telɪgrɑːf] **1** *n* télégraphe *m*. **2** *rt* télégraphier.

telegraph pole, **telegraph post** *Br n* poteau *m* télégraphique.

telepathy [tɪ'lepəθɪ] *n* télépathie *f*.

telephone ['telɪfəʊn] **1** *n* téléphone *m*. **2** *rt* téléphoner à. **3** *ri* téléphoner.

telephone book *n* annuaire *m*.

telephone booth *n* cabine *f* téléphonique.

telephone call *n* appel *m* téléphonique, coup *m* de téléphone.

telephone directory *n* annuaire *m*.

telephone number *n* numéro *m* de téléphone.

telephoto lens [,telɪ'fəʊtəʊ-] *n* téléobjectif *m*.

telescope ['telɪskəʊp] *n* télescope *m*.

teletext ['telɪtekst] *n* télétexte *m*.

televise ['telɪvaɪz] *rt* téléviser.

television ['telɪ,vɪʒn] *n* (*U*) [medium, industry] télévision *f*; **on** ~ à la télévision. ‖ [apparatus] (poste *m* de) télévision *f*, téléviseur *m*.

television set *n* poste *m* de télévision, téléviseur *m*.

telex ['teleks] **1** *n* télex *m*. **2** *vt* [message] envoyer par télex, télexer; [person] envoyer un télex à.

tell [tel] (*pt & pp* **told**) **1** *rt* [gen] dire; [story] raconter; **to** ~ **sb (that)** ... dire à qqn que ...; **to** ~ **sb sthg**, **to** ~ **sthg to sb** dire qqch à qqn; **to** ~ **sb to do sthg** dire OR ordonner à qqn de faire qqch. ‖ [judge, recognize] savoir, voir. **2** *ri* [speak] parler. ‖ [judge] savoir. ‖ [have effect] se faire sentir. ○ **tell apart** *vt sep* distinguer. ○ **tell off** *rt sep* gronder.

telling ['telɪŋ] *adj* [remark] révélateur(trice).

telltale ['telteɪl] **1** *adj* révélateur(trice). **2** *n* rapporteur *m*, -euse *f*, mouchard *m*, -e *f*.

temp [temp] *inf* **1** *n* (*abbr of* **temporary (employee)**) intérimaire *mf*. **2** *ri* travailler comme intérimaire.

temper ['tempər] **1** *n* [angry state]: **to be in a** ~ être en colère; **to lose one's** ~ se mettre en colère. ‖ [mood] humeur *f*. ‖ [temperament] tempérament *m*. **2** *rt* [moderate] tempérer.

temperament ['temprəmənt] *n* tempérament *m*.

temperamental [,temprə'mentl] *adj* [volatile, unreliable] capricieux(ieuse).

temperate ['temprət] *adj* tempéré(e).

temperature ['temprətʃər] *n* température *f*; **to have a** ~ avoir de la température OR de la fièvre.

template ['templɪt] *n* gabarit *m*.

temple ['templ] *n* RELIG temple *m*. ‖ ANAT tempe *f*.

temporarily [,tempə'rerəlɪ] *adv* temporairement, provisoirement.

temporary ['tempərərɪ] *adj* temporaire, provisoire.

tempt [tempt] *rt* tenter; **to** ~ **sb to do sthg** donner à qqn l'envie de faire qqch.

temptation [temp'teɪʃn] *n* tentation *f*.

tempting ['temptɪŋ] *adj* tentant(e).

ten [ten] *num* dix; *see also* **six**.

tenable ['tenəbl] *adj* [argument, position] défendable.

tenacious [tɪ'neɪʃəs] *adj* tenace.

tenancy ['tenənsɪ] *n* location *f*.

tenant ['tenənt] *n* locataire *mf*.

tend [tend] *rt* [have tendency]: **to** ~ **to do sthg** avoir tendance à faire qqch. ‖ [look after] s'occuper de, garder.

tendency ['tendənsɪ] *n*: ~ **(to do sthg)** tendance *f* (à faire qqch).

tender ['tendər] **1** *adj* tendre; [bruise, part of body] sensible, douloureux(euse). **2** *n* COMM soumission *f*. **3** *rt fml* [apology, money] offrir; [resignation] donner.

tendon ['tendən] *n* tendon *m*.

tenement ['tenəmənt] *n* immeuble *m*.

tenet ['tenɪt] *n fml* principe *m*.

tennis ['tenɪs] *n* (*U*) tennis *m*.

tennis ball *n* balle *f* de tennis.

tennis court *n* court *m* de tennis.

tennis racket *n* raquette *f* de tennis.

tenor ['tenər] *n* [singer] ténor *m*.

tense [tens] **1** *adj* tendu(e). **2** *n* temps *m*. **3** *rt* tendre.

tension ['tenʃn] *n* tension *f*.

tent [tent] *n* tente *f*.

tentacle ['tentəkl] *n* tentacule *m*.

tentative ['tentətɪv] *adj* [hesitant] hésitant(e). ‖ [not final] provisoire.

tenterhooks ['tentəhʊks] *npl*: **to be on** ~ être sur des charbons ardents.

tenth [tenθ] *num* dixième; *see also* **sixth**.

tent peg *n* piquet *m* de tente.

tent pole *n* montant *m* OR mât *m* de tente.

tenuous ['tenjʊəs] *adj* ténu(e).

tenure ['tenjər] *n* (*U*) *fml* [of property] bail *m*. ‖ [of job]: **to have** ~ être titulaire.

that

tepid ['tepɪd] *adj* tiède.

term [tɜ:m] **1** *n* [word, expression] terme *m*. || SCH & UNIV trimestre *m*. || [period of time] durée *f*, période *f*; **in the long/short ~** à long/court terme. **2** *vt* appeler. ○ **terms** *npl* [of contract, agreement] conditions *fpl*. || [basis]: **in international/real ~s** en termes internationaux/réels; **to be on good ~s (with sb)** être en bons termes (avec qqn); **to come to ~s with sthg** accepter qqch. ○ **in terms of** *prep* sur le plan de, en termes de.

terminal ['tɜ:mɪnl] **1** *adj* MED en phase terminale. **2** *n* AERON, COMPUT & RAIL terminal *m*. || ELEC borne *f*.

terminate ['tɜ:mɪneɪt] **1** *vt fml* [end - gen] terminer, mettre fin à; [- contract] résilier. || [pregnancy] interrompre. **2** *vi* [bus, train] s'arrêter. || [contract] se terminer.

termini ['tɜ:mɪnaɪ] *pl* → terminus.

terminus ['tɜ:mɪnəs] (*pl* **-ni** OR **-nuses**) terminus *m*.

terrace ['terəs] *n* [patio, on hillside] terrasse *f*.

terraced ['terəst] *adj* [hillside] en terrasses.

terrain [te'reɪn] *n* terrain *m*.

terrible ['terəbl] *adj* terrible; [holiday, headache, weather] affreux(euse), épouvantable.

terribly ['terəbli] *adv* terriblement; [sing, write, organized] affreusement mal; [injured] affreusement.

terrier ['terɪər] *n* terrier *m*.

terrific [tə'rɪfɪk] *adj* [wonderful] fantastique, formidable. || [enormous] énorme, fantastique.

terrified ['terɪfaɪd] *adj* terrifié(e); **to be ~ of** avoir une terreur folle OR peur folle de.

terrifying ['terɪfaɪɪŋ] *adj* terrifiant(e).

territory ['terətrɪ] *n* territoire *m*.

terror ['terər] *n* terreur *f*.

terrorism ['terərɪzm] *n* terrorisme *m*.

terrorist ['terərɪst] *n* terroriste *mf*.

terrorize, -ise ['terəraɪz] *vt* terroriser.

terse [tɜ:s] *adj* brusque.

Terylene® ['terəli:n] *n* Térylène® *m*.

test [test] **1** *n* [trial] essai *m*; [of friendship, courage] épreuve *f*. || [examination - of aptitude, psychological] test *m*; [- SCH & UNIV] interrogation *f* écrite/orale; [- of driving] (examen *m* du) permis *m* de conduire. || [MED - of blood, urine] analyse *f*; [- of eyes] examen *m*. **2** *vt* [try] essayer;

[determination, friendship] mettre à l'épreuve. || SCH & UNIV faire faire une interrogation écrite/orale à; **to ~ sb on sthg** interroger qqn sur qqch. || [MED - blood, urine] analyser; [- eyes, reflexes] faire un examen de.

testament ['testəmənt] *n* [will] testament *m*.

test-drive *vt* essayer.

testicles ['testɪklz] *npl* testicules *mpl*.

testify ['testɪfaɪ] **1** *vt*: **to ~ that ...** témoigner que .... **2** *vi* JUR témoigner. || [be proof]: **to ~ to sthg** témoigner de qqch.

testimony [*Br* 'testɪmənɪ, *Am* 'testəmounɪ] *n* témoignage *m*.

testing ['testɪŋ] *adj* éprouvant(e).

test pilot *n* pilote *m* d'essai.

test tube *n* éprouvette *f*.

test-tube baby *n* bébé-éprouvette *m*.

tetanus ['tetənəs] *n* tétanos *m*.

tether ['teðər] **1** *vt* attacher. **2** *n*: **to be at the end of one's ~** être au bout du rouleau.

text [tekst] *n* texte *m*.

textbook ['tekstbuk] *n* livre *m* OR manuel *m* scolaire.

textile ['tekstaɪl] *n* textile *m*.

texture ['tekstʃər] *n* texture *f*; [of paper, wood] grain *m*.

Thai [taɪ] **1** *adj* thaïlandais(e). **2** *n* [person] Thaïlandais *m*, -e *f*. || [language] thaï *m*.

Thailand ['taɪlænd] *n* Thaïlande *f*.

Thames [temz] *n*: **the ~** la Tamise.

than [weak form ðən, strong form ðæn] *conj* que; **Sarah is younger ~ her sister** Sarah est plus jeune que sa sœur; **more ~ three days/50 people** plus de trois jours/50 personnes.

thank [θæŋk] *vt*: **to ~ sb (for)** remercier qqn (pour OR de); **~ God OR goodness OR heavens!** Dieu merci! ○ **thanks 1** *npl* remerciements *mpl*. **2** *excl* merci! ○ **thanks to** *prep* grâce à.

thankful ['θæŋkful] *adj* [grateful]: **~ (for)** reconnaissant(e) (de). || [relieved] soulagé(e).

thankless ['θæŋklɪs] *adj* ingrat(e).

thanksgiving ['θæŋks,gɪvɪŋ] *n* action *f* de grâce. ○ **Thanksgiving (Day)** *n* fête nationale américaine commémorant, le 4e jeudi de novembre, l'installation des premiers colons en Amérique.

thank you *excl*: **~ (for)** merci (pour OR de).

that [ðæt, *weak form of pron sense 2 & conj* ðət] (*pl* **those**) **1** *pron* (*demon-*

strative use: pl 'those') ce, cela, ça; (*as opposed to 'this'*) celui-là (celle-là); **who's ~?** qui est-ce?; **what's ~?** qu'est-ce que c'est que ça?; **which shoes are you going to wear, these or those?** quelles chaussures vas-tu mettre, celles-ci ou celles-là?; **those who** ceux (celles) qui. || (*to introduce relative clauses - subject*) qui; (- *object*) que; (- *with prep*) lequel (laquelle), lesquels (lesquelles) (*pl*); **we came to a path ~ led into the woods** nous arrivâmes à un sentier qui menait dans les bois; **show me the book ~ you bought** montre-moi le livre que tu as acheté; **on the day ~ we left** le jour où nous sommes partis. **2** *adj* (*demonstrative: pl 'those'*) ce (cette), cet (*before vowel or silent "h"*), ces (*pl*); (*as opposed to 'this'*) ce (cette) ... -là, ces ... -là (*pl*); **those chocolates are delicious** ces chocolats sont délicieux; **I prefer ~ book** je préfère ce livre-là; **I'll have ~ one** je prendrai celui-là. **3** *adv* aussi, si; **it wasn't ~ bad/good** ce n'était pas si mal/bien que ça. **4** *conj* que; **tell him ~ the children aren't coming** dites-lui que les enfants ne viennent pas; **he recommended ~ I phone you** il m'a conseillé de vous appeler. ○ **that is (to say)** *adv* c'est-à-dire.

thatched [θæt∫t] *adj* de chaume.

that's [ðæts] = **that is.**

thaw [θɔː] **1** *vt* [ice] faire fondre OR dégeler; [frozen food] décongeler. **2** *vi* [ice] dégeler, fondre; [frozen food] décongeler. **3** *n* dégel *m*.

the [*weak form* ðə, *before vowel* ði, *strong form* ðiː] *def art* [gen] le (la), l' (+ *vowel or silent "h"*), les (*pl*); **~ book** le livre; **~ sea** la mer; **~ man** l'homme; **~ boys/girls** les garçons/filles; **to play ~ piano** jouer du piano. || (*with an adjective to form a noun*): **~ old/young** les vieux/jeunes; **~ impossible** l'impossible. || [in dates]: **~ twelfth of May** le douze mai; **~ forties** les années quarante. || [in comparisons]: **~ more ... ~ less** plus ... moins; **~ sooner ~ better** le plus tôt sera le mieux. || [in titles]: **Alexander ~ Great** Alexandre le Grand; **George ~ First** Georges Premier.

theatre *Br* , **theater** *Am* ['θɪətə'] *n* [plays, building] théâtre *m*. || *Am* [cinema] cinéma *m*.

theatregoer, **theatergoer** *Am* ['θɪətə,gəʊə'] *n* habitué *m*, -e *f* du théâtre.

theatrical [θɪ'ætrɪkl] *adj* théâtral(e); [company] de théâtre.

theft [θeft] *n* vol *m*.

their [ðeə'] *poss adj* leur, leurs (*pl*); **~ house** leur maison; **~ children** leurs enfants; **it wasn't THEIR fault** ce n'était pas de leur faute à eux.

theirs [ðeəz] *poss pron* le leur (la leur), les leurs (*pl*); **that house is ~** cette maison est la leur. cette maison est à eux/elles; **it wasn't our fault, it was THEIRS** ce n'était pas de notre faute. c'était de la leur; **a friend of ~** un de leurs amis. un ami à eux/elles.

them [*weak form* ðəm, *strong form* ðem] *pers pron pl* (*direct*) les; **I know ~** je les connais; **if I were ~** si j'étais eux/elles. à leur place. || (*indirect*) leur; **we spoke to ~** nous leur avons parlé; **she sent ~ a letter** elle leur a envoyé une lettre; **I gave it to ~** je le leur ai donné. || (*stressed, after prep, in comparisons etc*) eux (elles); **you can't expect THEM to do it** tu ne peux pas exiger que ce soit eux qui le fassent; **with ~** avec eux/elles; **without ~** sans eux/elles; **we're not as wealthy as ~** nous ne sommes pas aussi riches qu'eux/qu'elles.

theme [θiːm] *n* [topic, motif] thème *m*, sujet *m*. || MUS thème *m*; [signature tune] indicatif *m*.

theme tune *n* chanson *f* principale.

themselves [ðem'selvz] *pron* (*reflexive*) se; (*after prep*) eux (elles). || (*for emphasis*) eux-mêmes *mpl*, elles-mêmes *fpl*; **they did it ~** ils l'ont fait tout seuls.

then [ðen] *adv* [not now] alors, à cette époque. || [next] puis, ensuite. || [in that case] alors, dans ce cas. || [therefore] donc. || [also] d'ailleurs, et puis.

theology [θɪ'ɒlədʒɪ] *n* théologie *f*.

theoretical [θɪə'retɪkl] *adj* théorique.

theory ['θɪərɪ] *n* théorie *f*; **in ~** en théorie.

therapist ['θerəpɪst] *n* thérapeute *mf*, psychothérapeute *mf*.

therapy ['θerəpɪ] *n* (*U*) thérapie *f*.

there [ðeə'] **1** *pron* [indicating existence of sthg]: **~ is/are** il y a; **~ must be some mistake** il doit y avoir erreur. **2** *adv* [in existence, available] y, là; **is anybody ~?** il y a quelqu'un?; **is John ~, please?** [when telephoning] est-ce que John est là. s'il vous plaît? || [referring to place] y, là; **I'm going ~ next week** j'y vais la semaine prochaine; **~ it is** c'est là; **~ he is!** le voi-

this

là!; over ~ là-bas. **3** *excl:* **~, I knew he'd turn up** tiens OR voilà, je savais bien qu'il s'amènerait; **~, ~** allons, allons. ○ **there and then, then and there** *adv* immédiatement, sur-le-champ.

thereabouts [ðɛərəˈbauts], **thereabout** *Am* [ðɛərəˈbaut] *adv:* **or ~** [nearby] par là; [approximately] environ.

thereby [,ðɛərˈbaɪ] *adv fml* ainsi, de cette façon.

therefore [ˈðɛəfɔːr] *adv* donc, par conséquent.

there's [ðɛəz] = there is.

thermal [ˈθɜːml] *adj* thermique; [clothes] en thermolactyl.

thermometer [θəˈmɒmɪtər] *n* thermomètre *m*.

Thermos (flask)® [ˈθɜːməs-] *n* bouteille *f* Thermos®, Thermos® *m* or *f*.

thermostat [ˈθɜːməstæt] *n* thermostat *m*.

thesaurus [θɪˈsɔːrəs] (*pl* **-es**) *n* dictionnaire *m* de synonymes.

these [ðiːz] *pl* → **this**.

thesis [ˈθiːsɪs] (*pl* **theses** [ˈθiːsiːz]) *n* thèse *f*.

they [ðeɪ] *pers pron pl* [people, things, animals - unstressed] ils (elles); [- stressed] eux (elles); **~'re pleased** ils sont contents (elles sont contentes); **~'re pretty earrings** ce sont de jolies boucles d'oreille; **THEY can't do it** eux (elles), ils (elles) ne peuvent pas le faire; **there ~ are** les voilà. || [unspecified people] on, ils; **~ say it's going to snow** on dit qu'il va neiger.

they'd [ðeɪd] = they had, they would.

they'll [ðeɪl] = they shall, they will.

they're [ðeər] = they are.

they've [ðeɪv] = they have.

thick [θɪk] **1** *adj* [gen] épais (épaisse); [forest, hedge, fog] dense; **to be 6 inches ~** avoir 15 cm d'épaisseur. || *inf* [stupid] bouché(e). **2** *n*: **in the ~ of** au plus fort de, en plein OR au beau milieu de.

thicken [ˈθɪkn] **1** *rt* épaissir. **2** *ri* s'épaissir.

thickness [ˈθɪknɪs] *n* épaisseur *f*.

thickset [,θɪkˈset] *adj* trapu(e).

thick-skinned [-ˈskɪnd] *adj* qui a la peau dure.

thief [θiːf] (*pl* **thieves**) *n* voleur *m*, -euse *f*.

thieve [θiːv] *rt & vi* voler.

thieves [θiːvz] *pl* → **thief**.

thigh [θaɪ] *n* cuisse *f*.

thimble [ˈθɪmbl] *n* dé *m* (à coudre).

thin [θɪn] *adj* [slice, layer, paper] mince; [cloth] léger(ère); [person] maigre. || [liquid, sauce] clair(e), peu épais (peu épaisse). || [sparse - crowd] épars(e); [- vegetation, hair] clairsemé(e). ○ **thin down** *rt sep* [liquid, paint] délayer, diluer; [sauce] éclaircir.

thing [θɪŋ] *n* [gen] chose *f*; **the (best) ~ to do would be ...** le mieux serait de ...; **the ~ is ...** le problème, c'est que .... || [anything]: **I don't know a ~** je n'y connais absolument rien. || [object] chose *f*, objet *m*. || [person]: **you poor ~!** mon pauvre! ○ **things** *npl* [clothes, possessions] affaires *fpl*. || *inf* [life]: **how are ~s?** comment ça va?

think [θɪŋk] (*pt & pp* **thought**) **1** *rt* [believe]: **to ~ (that)** croire que, penser que; **I ~ so/not** je crois que oui/non, je pense que oui/non. || [have in mind] penser à. || [imagine] s'imaginer. || [in polite requests]: **do you ~ you could help me?** tu pourrais m'aider? **2** *ri* [use mind] réfléchir, penser. || [have stated opinion]: **what do you ~ or about his new film?** que pensez-vous de son dernier film? || *phr:* **to ~ twice** y réfléchir à deux fois. ○ **think about** *rt fus*: **to ~ about sb/sthg** songer à OR penser à qqn/qqch; **to ~ about doing sthg** songer à faire qqch; **I'll ~ about it** je vais y réfléchir. ○ **think of** *rt fus* [consider] = think about. || [remember] se rappeler. || [conceive] penser à, avoir l'idée de; **to ~ of doing sthg** avoir l'idée de faire qqch. ○ **think over** *rt sep* réfléchir à. ○ **think up** *rt sep* imaginer.

think tank *n* comité *m* d'experts.

third [θɜːd] **1** *num* troisième; *see also* **sixth**. **2** *n* UNIV ≃ licence *f* mention passable.

thirdly [ˈθɜːdlɪ] *adv* troisièmement, tertio.

third party insurance *n* assurance *f* de responsabilité civile.

third-rate *adj pej* de dernier OR troisième ordre.

Third World *n*: **the ~** le tiers-monde.

thirst [θɜːst] *n* soif *f*; **~ for** *fig* soif de.

thirsty [ˈθɜːstɪ] *adj* [person]: **to be OR feel ~** avoir soif; [work] qui donne soif.

thirteen [,θɜːˈtiːn] *num* treize; *see also* **six**.

thirty [ˈθɜːtɪ] *num* trente; *see also* **sixty**.

this [ðɪs] (*pl* **these**) **1** *pron (demonstrative use)* ce, ceci; (*as opposed to 'that'*) celui-ci (celle-ci); **who's**

~? qui est-ce?; what's ~? qu'est-ce que
c'est?; **which sweets does she prefer,
these or those?** quels bonbons préfère-
t-elle, ceux-ci ou ceux-là?; **~ is Daphne
Logan** [introducing another person] je
vous présente Daphne Logan; [intro-
ducing oneself on phone] ici Daphne Logan, Daphne Logan à l'appareil. **2** *adj*
(*demonstrative use*) ce (cette), cet
(*before vowel or silent "h"*), ces (*pl*);
(*as opposed to 'that'*) ce (cette) ...-ci,
ces ...-ci (*pl*); **these chocolates are delicious** ces chocolats sont délicieux; **I
prefer ~ book** je préfère ce livre-ci; **I'll
have ~ one** je prendrai celui-ci; **~ after-
noon** cet après-midi. || *inf* [a certain] un
certain (une certaine). **3** *adv* aussi; **it
was ~ big** c'était aussi grand que ça;
you'll need about ~ much il vous en faudra à peu près comme ceci.

thistle ['θɪsl] *n* chardon *m*.

thong [θɒŋ] *n* [of leather] lanière *f*.

thorn [θɔːn] *n* épine *f*.

thorough ['θʌrə] *adj* [exhaustive -
search, inspection] minutieux(ieuse);
[- investigation, knowledge] approfon-
di(e). || [meticulous] méticuleux(euse). ||
[complete, utter] complet(ète), absolu(e).

thoroughbred ['θʌrəbred] *n* pur-sang
m inv.

thoroughfare ['θʌrəfeəʳ] *n fml* rue *f*,
voie *f* publique.

thoroughly ['θʌrəlɪ] *adv* [fully, in de-
tail] à fond. || [completely, utterly] absolu-
ment, complètement.

those [ðəʊz] *pl* → **that**.

though [ðəʊ] **1** *conj* bien que (+ *subjunctive*), quoique (+ *subjunctive*). **2**
adv pourtant, cependant.

thought [θɔːt] **1** *pt* & *pp* → **think**. **2** *n*
[gen] pensée *f*; [idea] idée *f*, pensée. || [in-
tention] intention *f*. ○ **thoughts** *npl* [re-
flections] pensées *fpl*, réflexions *fpl*. ||
[views] opinions *fpl*, idées *fpl*.

thoughtful ['θɔːtfʊl] *adj* [pensive] pen-
sif(ive). || [considerate - person] préve-
nant(e), attentionné(e); [- remark, act]
plein(e) de gentillesse.

thoughtless ['θɔːtlɪs] *adj* [person] qui
manque d'égards (pour les autres); [re-
mark, behaviour] irréfléchi(e).

thousand ['θaʊznd] *num* mille; **a** OR **one
~** mille; **~s of** des milliers de; *see also* **six**.

thousandth ['θaʊzntθ] *num* millième;
see also **sixth**.

thrash [θræʃ] *vt* [hit] battre, rosser. || *inf*
[defeat] écraser, battre à plates coutures.

○ **thrash about, thrash around** *vi*
s'agiter. ○ **thrash out** *vt sep* [problem]
débrouiller, démêler.

thread [θred] **1** *n* [gen] fil *m*. || [of screw]
filet *m*, pas *m*. **2** *vt* [needle] enfiler.

threadbare ['θredbeəʳ] *adj* usé(e) jusqu'à la corde.

threat [θret] *n:* **~ (to)** menace *f* (pour).

threaten ['θretn] **1** *vt:* **to ~ sb (with)**
menacer qqn (de); **to ~ to do sthg** menacer de faire qqch. **2** *vi* menacer.

three [θriː] *num* trois; *see also* **six**.

three-dimensional [-dɪ'menʃənl] *adj*
[film, picture] en relief; [object] à trois di-
mensions.

threefold ['θriːfəʊld] **1** *adj* triple. **2**
adv: **to increase ~** tripler.

three-piece *adj:* **~ suit** (costume *m*)
trois pièces *m*; **~ suite** canapé *m* et deux
fauteuils assortis.

thresh [θreʃ] *vt* battre.

threshold ['θreʃhəʊld] *n* seuil *m*.

threw [θruː] *pt* → **throw**.

thrifty ['θrɪftɪ] *adj* économe.

thrill [θrɪl] **1** *n* [sudden feeling] frisson
m, sensation *f*. || [enjoyable experience]
plaisir *m*. **2** *vt* transporter, exciter.

thrilled [θrɪld] *adj:* **~ (with sthg/to do
sthg)** ravi(e) (de qqch/de faire qqch),
enchanté(e) (de qqch/de faire qqch).

thriller ['θrɪləʳ] *n* thriller *m*.

thrilling ['θrɪlɪŋ] *adj* saisissant(e), pal-
pitant(e).

thrive [θraɪv] (*pt* **-d** OR **throve**, *pp* **-d**)
vi [person] bien se porter; [plant] pousser
bien; [business] prospérer.

throat [θrəʊt] *n* gorge *f*.

throb [θrɒb] *vi* [heart] palpiter, battre
fort; [engine] vibrer; [music] taper; **my
head is throbbing** j'ai des élancements
dans la tête.

throes [θrəʊz] *npl:* **to be in the ~ of**
[war, disease] être en proie à.

throne [θrəʊn] *n* trône *m*.

throng [θrɒŋ] **1** *n* foule *f*, multitude *f*. **2**
vt remplir, encombrer.

throttle ['θrɒtl] **1** *n* [valve] papillon *m*
des gaz; [lever] commande *f* des gaz. **2** *vt*
[strangle] étrangler.

through [θruː] **1** *adj* [finished]: **to be ~
with sthg** avoir fini qqch. **2** *adv:* **to let sb
~** laisser passer qqn; **to read sthg ~** lire
qqch jusqu'au bout; **to sleep ~ till ten**
dormir jusqu'à dix heures. **3** *prep* [re-
lating to place, position] à travers; **to travel ~ sthg** traverser qqch; **to cut ~ sthg**
couper qqch. || [during] pendant. || [be-

cause of] à cause de. || [by means of] par l'intermédiaire de, par l'entremise de. || *Am* [up till and including]: Monday ~ Friday du lundi au vendredi. ○ **through and through** *adv* [completely] jusqu'au bout des ongles; [thoroughly] par cœur, à fond.

throughout [θru:'aʊt] **1** *prep* [during] pendant, durant; ~ **the meeting** pendant toute la réunion. || [everywhere in] partout dans. **2** *adv* [all the time] tout le temps. || [everywhere] partout.

throve [θrəʊv] *pt* → **thrive**.

throw [θrəʊ] (*pt* **threw**, *pp* **thrown**) **1** *vt* [gen] jeter; [ball, javelin] lancer. || [rider] désarçonner. || *fig* [confuse] déconcerter, décontenancer. **2** *n* lancement *m*, jet *m*. ○ **throw away** *vt sep* [discard] jeter. || *fig* [money] gaspiller; [opportunity] perdre. ○ **throw out** *vt sep* [discard] jeter. || *fig* [reject] rejeter. || [from house] mettre à la porte; [from army, school] expulser, renvoyer. ○ **throw up** *vi inf* [vomit] dégobiller, vomir.

throwaway ['θrəʊə,weɪ] *adj* [disposable] jetable, à jeter.

thrown [θrəʊn] *pp* → **throw**.

thru [θru:] *Am inf* = **through**.

thrush [θrʌʃ] *n* [bird] grive *f*. || MED muguet *m*.

thrust [θrʌst] **1** *n* [forward movement] poussée *f*; [of knife] coup *m*. || [main aspect] idée *f* principale, aspect *m* principal. **2** *vt* [shove] enfoncer, fourrer.

thud [θʌd] **1** *n* bruit *m* sourd. **2** *vi* tomber en faisant un bruit sourd.

thug [θʌg] *n* brute *f*, voyou *m*.

thumb [θʌm] **1** *n* pouce *m*. **2** *vt inf* [hitch]: **to ~ a lift** faire du stop OR de l'auto-stop.

thumbs down [,θʌmz-] *n*: **to get** OR **be given the ~** être rejeté(e).

thumbs up [,θʌmz-] *n* [go-ahead]: **to give sb the ~** donner le feu vert à qqn.

thumbtack ['θʌmtæk] *n Am* punaise *f*.

thump [θʌmp] **1** *n* [blow] grand coup *m*. || [thud] bruit *m* sourd. **2** *vt* [hit] cogner, taper sur. **3** *vi* [heart] battre fort.

thunder ['θʌndər] **1** *n* (*U*) METEOR tonnerre *m*. || *fig* [of applause] tonnerre *m*. **2** *v impers* METEOR tonner.

thunderbolt ['θʌndəbəʊlt] *n* coup *m* de foudre.

thunderclap ['θʌndəklæp] *n* coup *m* de tonnerre.

thunderstorm ['θʌndəstɔ:m] *n* orage *m*.

thundery ['θʌndərɪ] *adj* orageux(euse).

Thursday ['θɜ:zdɪ] *n* jeudi *m*; *see also* **Saturday**.

thus [ðʌs] *adv fml* [therefore] par conséquent, donc, ainsi. || [in this way] ainsi, de cette façon, comme ceci.

thwart [θwɔ:t] *vt* contrecarrer, contrarier.

thyme [taɪm] *n* thym *m*.

thyroid ['θaɪrɔɪd] *n* thyroïde *f*.

tiara [tɪ'ɑ:rə] *n* [worn by woman] diadème *m*.

Tibet [tɪ'bet] *n* Tibet *m*.

tic [tɪk] *n* tic *m*.

tick [tɪk] **1** *n* [written mark] coche *f*. || [sound] tic-tac *m*. || [insect] tique *f*. **2** *vt* cocher. **3** *vi* faire tic-tac. ○ **tick off** *vt sep* [mark off] cocher. || [tell off] enguirlander. ○ **tick over** *vi* [engine, business] tourner au ralenti.

ticket ['tɪkɪt] *n* [for access, train, plane] billet *m*; [for bus] ticket *m*; [for library] carte *f*; [label on product] étiquette *f*. || [for traffic offence] P.-V. *m*, papillon *m*.

ticket machine *n* distributeur *m* de billets.

ticket office *n* bureau *m* de vente des billets.

tickle ['tɪkl] **1** *vt* [touch lightly] chatouiller. || *fig* [amuse] amuser. **2** *vi* chatouiller.

ticklish ['tɪklɪʃ] *adj* [person] qui craint les chatouilles, chatouilleux(euse).

tidal ['taɪdl] *adj* [river] à marées.

tidal wave *n* raz-de-marée *m inv*.

tidbit *Am* = **titbit**.

tiddlywinks ['tɪdlɪwɪŋks], **tiddledywinks** *Am* ['tɪdldɪwɪŋks] *n* jeu *m* de puce.

tide [taɪd] *n* [of sea] marée *f*. || *fig* [of opinion, fashion] courant *m*, tendance *f*; [of protest] vague *f*.

tidy ['taɪdɪ] **1** *adj* [room, desk] en ordre, bien rangé(e); [hair, dress] soigné(e). || [person - in habits] ordonné(e); [- in appearance] soigné(e). **2** *vt* ranger, mettre de l'ordre dans. ○ **tidy up** *vt sep* ranger, mettre de l'ordre dans. **2** *vi* ranger.

tie [taɪ] (*pt & pp* **tied**, *cont* **tying**) **1** *n* [necktie] cravate *f*. || [in game, competition] égalité *f* de points, match *m* nul. **2** *vt* [attach] attacher. || [shoelaces] nouer, attacher; **to ~ a knot** faire un nœud. || *fig* [link]: **to be ~d to** être lié(e) à. **3** *vi* [draw] être à égalité. ○ **tie down** *vt sep fig* [restrict] restreindre la liberté de. ○ **tie in with** *vt fus* concorder avec, coïncider avec. ○ **tie up** *vt sep* [with string, rope] attacher. || *fig* [money, resources] immobiliser. || *fig* [link]: **to be ~d up with** être lié(e) à.

tiebreak(er) ['taɪbreɪk(ər)] *n* TENNIS tie-break *m*. || [in game, competition] question *f* subsidiaire.

tier [tɪər] *n* [of seats] gradin *m*; [of cake] étage *m*.

tiff [tɪf] *n* bisbille *f*, petite querelle *f*.

tiger ['taɪgər] *n* tigre *m*.

tight [taɪt] **1** *adj* [clothes, group, competition, knot] serré(e). || [taut] tendu(e). || [schedule] serré(e), minuté(e). || [strict] strict(e), sévère. || [corner, bend] raide. || *inf* [miserly] radin(e), avare. **2** *adv* [firmly, securely] bien, fort; **hold ~!** tiens bon!; **to shut** OR **close sthg ~** bien fermer qqch. || [tautly] à fond. ○ **tights** *npl* collant *m*, collants *mpl*.

tighten ['taɪtn] **1** *vt* [belt, knot, screw] resserrer; **to ~ one's hold** OR **grip on** resserrer sa prise sur. || [pull tauter] tendre. || [make stricter] renforcer. **2** *vi* [rope] se tendre. || [grip, hold] se resserrer.

tightfisted [,taɪt'fɪstɪd] *adj pej* radin(e), pingre.

tightly ['taɪtlɪ] *adv* [firmly] bien, fort.

tightrope ['taɪtrəʊp] *n* corde *f* raide.

tile [taɪl] *n* [on roof] tuile *f*; [on floor, wall] carreau *m*.

tiled [taɪld] *adj* [floor, wall] carrelé(e); [roof] couvert de tuiles.

till [tɪl] **1** *prep* jusqu'à; **from six ~ ten o'clock** de six heures à dix heures. **2** *conj* jusqu'à ce que (+ *subjunctive*); **wait ~ I come back** attends que je revienne; (*after negative*) avant que (+ *subjunctive*); **it won't be ready ~ tomorrow** ça ne sera pas prêt avant demain. **3** *n* tiroir-caisse *m*.

tiller ['tɪlər] *n* NAUT barre *f*.

tilt [tɪlt] **1** *vt* incliner, pencher. **2** *vi* s'incliner, pencher.

timber ['tɪmbər] *n* (*U*) [wood] bois *m* de charpente OR de construction. || [beam] poutre *f*, madrier *m*.

time [taɪm] **1** *n* [gen] temps *m*; **a long ~** longtemps; **in a short ~** dans peu de temps, sous peu; **to take ~** prendre du temps; **to be ~ for sthg** être l'heure de qqch; **to have a good ~** s'amuser bien; **in good ~** de bonne heure; **ahead of ~** en avance, avant l'heure; **on ~** à l'heure. || [as measured by clock] heure *f*; **what's the ~?** quelle heure est-il?; **in a week's/year's ~** dans une semaine/un an. ||

[point in time in past] époque *f*; **before my ~** avant que j'arrive ici. || [occasion] fois *f*; **from ~ to ~** de temps en temps, de temps à autre; **~ after ~, ~ and again** à maintes reprises, maintes et maintes fois. || MUS mesure *f*. **2** *vt* [schedule] fixer, prévoir. || [race, runner] chronométrer. || [arrival, remark] choisir le moment de. ○ **times 1** *npl* fois *fpl*; **four ~s as much as me** quatre fois plus que moi. **2** *prep* MATH fois. ○ **at a time** *adv* d'affilée; **one at a ~** un par un, un seul à la fois. ○ **at times** *adv* quelquefois, parfois. ○ **at the same time** *adv* en même temps. ○ **about time** *adv*: **it's about ~ (that)** ... il est grand temps que ...; **about ~ too!** ce n'est pas trop tôt! ○ **for the time being** *adv* pour le moment. ○ **in time** *adv* [not late]: **in ~ (for)** à l'heure (pour). || [eventually] à la fin, à la longue; [after a while] avec le temps, à la longue.

time bomb *n lit & fig* bombe *f* à retardement.

time lag *n* décalage *m*.

timeless ['taɪmlɪs] *adj* éternel(elle).

time limit *n* délai *m*.

timely ['taɪmlɪ] *adj* opportun(e).

time off *n* temps *m* libre.

time out *n* SPORT temps *m* mort.

timer ['taɪmər] *n* minuteur *m*.

time scale *n* période *f*; [of project] délai *m*.

time switch *n* minuterie *f*.

timetable ['taɪm,teɪbl] *n* SCH emploi *m* du temps. || [of buses, trains] horaire *m*. || [schedule] calendrier *m*.

time zone *n* fuseau *m* horaire.

timid ['tɪmɪd] *adj* timide.

timing ['taɪmɪŋ] *n* (*U*) [of remark] à-propos *m*. || [scheduling]: **the ~ of the election** le moment choisi pour l'élection. || [measuring] chronométrage *m*.

tin [tɪn] *n* (*U*) [metal] étain *m*; [in sheets] fer-blanc *m*. || [small container] boîte *f*.

tin can *n* boîte *f* de conserve.

tinfoil ['tɪnfɔɪl] *n* (*U*) papier *m* (d')aluminium.

tinge [tɪndʒ] *n* [of colour] teinte *f*, nuance *f*. || [of feeling] nuance *f*.

tinged [tɪndʒd] *adj*: **~ with** teinté(e) de.

tingle ['tɪŋgl] *vi* picoter.

tinker ['tɪŋkər] *vi*: **to ~ (with sthg)** bricoler (qqch).

tinkle ['tɪŋkl] *vi* [ring] tinter.

tinsel ['tɪnsl] *n* (*U*) guirlandes *fpl* de Noël.

tint [tɪnt] *n* teinte *f*, nuance *f*; [in hair] rinçage *m*.

tinted ['tɪntɪd] *adj* [glasses, windows] teinté(e).

tiny ['taɪnɪ] *adj* minuscule.

tip [tɪp] **1** *n* [end] bout *m*. || [to waiter etc] pourboire *m*. || [piece of advice] tuyau *m*. **2** *vt* [tilt] faire basculer. || [spill] renverser. || [waiter etc] donner un pourboire à. **3** *vi* [tilt] basculer. || [spill] se renverser. ○ **tip over 1** *vt sep* renverser. **2** *vi* se renverser.

tip-off *n* tuyau *m*; [to police] dénonciation *f*.

tipped ['tɪpt] *adj* [cigarette] à bout filtre.

tipsy ['tɪpsɪ] *adj inf* gai(e).

tiptoe ['tɪptəʊ] **1** *n*: on ~ sur la pointe des pieds. **2** *vi* marcher sur la pointe des pieds.

tire ['taɪər] **1** *n Am* = **tyre**. **2** *vt* fatiguer. **3** *vi* [get tired] se fatiguer. || [get fed up]: **to ~ of** se lasser de.

tired ['taɪəd] *adj* [sleepy] fatigué(e), las (lasse). || [fed up]: **to be ~ of sthg/of doing sthg** en avoir assez de qqch/de faire qqch.

tiresome ['taɪəsəm] *adj* ennuyeux(euse).

tiring ['taɪərɪŋ] *adj* fatigant(e).

tissue ['tɪʃuː] *n* [paper handkerchief] mouchoir *m* en papier. || (*U*) BIOL tissu *m*.

tissue paper *n* (*U*) papier *m* de soie.

tit [tɪt] *n* [bird] mésange *f*. || *vulg* [breast] nichon *m*, néné *m*.

titbit *Br* ['tɪtbɪt], **tidbit** *Am* ['tɪdbɪt] *n* [of food] bon morceau *m*. || *fig* [of news] petite nouvelle *f*.

tit for tat [-'tæt] *n* un prêté pour un rendu.

titillate ['tɪtɪleɪt] *vt* titiller.

title ['taɪtl] *n* titre *m*.

title deed *n* titre *m* de propriété.

title role *n* rôle *m* principal.

titter ['tɪtər] *vi* rire bêtement.

TM *abbr of* **trademark**.

to [*unstressed before consonant* tə, *unstressed before vowel* tʊ, *stressed* tuː] **1** *prep* [indicating place, direction] à; **to go ~ Liverpool/Spain/school** aller à Liverpool/en Espagne/à l'école; **to go ~ the butcher's** aller chez le boucher; **~ the left/right** à gauche/droite. || (*to express indirect object*) à; **to give sthg ~ sb** donner qqch à qqn; **we were listening ~ the radio** nous écoutions la radio. || [indi-

cating reaction, effect] à; **~ my delight/ surprise** à ma grande joie/surprise. || [in stating opinion]: **~ me, ...** à mon avis, ...; **it seemed quite unnecessary ~ me/him** *etc* cela me/lui *etc* semblait tout à fait inutile. || [indicating state, process]: **to drive sb ~ drink** pousser qqn à boire; **it could lead ~ trouble** cela pourrait causer des ennuis. || [as far as] à, jusqu'à; **we work from 9 ~ 5** nous travaillons de 9 heures à 17 heures. || [in expressions of time] moins; **it's ten ~ three/quarter ~ one** il est trois heures moins dix/une heure moins le quart. || [per] à; **40 miles ~ the gallon** ≃ 7 litres aux cent (km). || [of, for] de; **the key ~ the car** la clef de la voiture; **a letter ~ my daughter** une lettre à ma fille. **2** *adv* [shut]: **push the door ~** fermez la porte. **3** *with infinitive* (*forming simple infinitive*): **~ walk** marcher; **~ laugh** rire. || (*following another verb*): **to begin ~ do sthg** commencer à faire qqch; **to try ~ do sthg** essayer de faire qqch; **to want ~ do sthg** vouloir faire qqch. || (*following an adjective*): **difficult ~ do** difficile à faire; **ready ~ go** prêt à partir. || (*indicating purpose*) pour; **he worked hard ~ pass his exam** il a travaillé dur pour réussir son examen. || (*substituting for a relative clause*): **I have a lot ~ do** j'ai beaucoup à faire; **he told me ~ leave** il m'a dit de partir. || (*to avoid repetition of infinitive*): **I meant to call him but I forgot ~** je voulais l'appeler, mais j'ai oublié. || [in comments]: **~ be honest ...** en toute franchise ...; **~ sum up, ...** en résumé, ..., pour récapituler, ... ○ **to and fro** *adv*: **to go ~ and fro** aller et venir; **to walk ~ and fro** marcher de long en large.

toad [təʊd] *n* crapaud *m*.

toadstool ['təʊdstuːl] *n* champignon *m* vénéneux.

toast [təʊst] **1** *n* (*U*) [bread] pain *m* grillé, toast *m*. || [drink] toast *m*. **2** *vt* [bread] (faire) griller. || [person] porter un toast à.

toaster ['təʊstər] *n* grille-pain *m inv*.

tobacco [tə'bækəʊ] *n* (*U*) tabac *m*.

tobacconist [tə'bækənɪst] *n* buraliste *mf*; **~'s (shop)** bureau *m* de tabac.

toboggan [tə'bɒgən] *n* luge *f*.

today [tə'deɪ] *adv* aujourd'hui.

toddler ['tɒdlər] *n* tout-petit *m* (*qui commence à marcher*).

toddy ['tɒdɪ] *n* grog *m*.

toe [təʊ] **1** *n* [of foot] orteil *m*, doigt *m* de pied; [of sock, shoe] bout *m*. **2** *vt*: **to ~ the line** se plier.

toenail ['təʊneɪl] *n* ongle *m* d'orteil.

toffee ['tɒfɪ] *n* caramel *m*.

toga ['təʊɡə] *n* toge *f*.

together [tə'ɡeðər] *adv* [gen] ensemble. || [at the same time] en même temps. ○ **together with** *prep* ainsi que.

toil [tɔɪl] *literary* **1** *n* labeur *m*. **2** *vi* travailler dur.

toilet ['tɔɪlɪt] *n* [lavatory] toilettes *fpl*, cabinets *mpl*; **to go to the ~** aller aux toilettes OR aux cabinets.

toilet bag *n* trousse *f* de toilette.

toilet paper *n* (*U*) papier *m* hygiénique.

toiletries ['tɔɪlɪtrɪz] *npl* articles *mpl* de toilette.

toilet roll *n* rouleau *m* de papier hygiénique.

token ['təʊkn] **1** *adj* symbolique. **2** *n* [voucher] bon *m*. || [symbol] marque *f*. ○ **by the same token** *adv* de même.

told [təʊld] *pt & pp* → **tell**.

tolerable ['tɒlərəbl] *adj* passable.

tolerance ['tɒlərəns] *n* tolérance *f*.

tolerant ['tɒlərənt] *adj* tolérant(e).

tolerate ['tɒləreɪt] *vt* [put up with] supporter. || [permit] tolérer.

toll [təʊl] **1** *n* [number] nombre *m*. || [fee] péage *m*. || *phr*: **to take its ~** se faire sentir. **2** *vt & vi* sonner.

toll-free *Am adv*: **to call ~** appeler un numéro vert.

tomato [*Br* tə'mɑːtəʊ, *Am* tə'meɪtəʊ] (*pl* **-es**) *n* tomate *f*.

tomb [tuːm] *n* tombe *f*.

tomboy ['tɒmbɔɪ] *n* garçon *m* manqué.

tombstone ['tuːmstəʊn] *n* pierre *f* tombale.

tomcat ['tɒmkæt] *n* matou *m*.

tomorrow [tə'mɒrəʊ] *adv* demain.

ton [tʌn] (*pl inv* OR **-s**) *n* [imperial] = *1016 kg Br,* = *907,2 kg Am,* ≃ tonne *f*. || [metric] = *1000 kg,* tonne *f*. ○ **tons** *npl inf*: **~s (of)** des tas (de), plein (de).

tone [təʊn] *n* [gen] ton *m*. || [on phone] tonalité *f*. ○ **tone down** *vt sep* modérer. ○ **tone up** *vt sep* tonifier.

tone-deaf *adj* qui n'a aucune oreille.

tongs [tɒŋz] *npl* pinces *fpl*.

tongue [tʌŋ] *n* [gen] langue *f*. || [of shoe] languette *f*.

tongue-in-cheek *adj* ironique.

tongue-tied [-ˌtaɪd] *adj* muet(ette).

tongue twister [-ˌtwɪstər] *n* phrase *f* difficile à dire.

tonic ['tɒnɪk] *n* [medicine] tonique *m*.

tonic water *n* Schweppes® *m*.

tonight [tə'naɪt] *adv* ce soir; [late] cette nuit.

tonnage ['tʌnɪdʒ] *n* tonnage *m*.

tonne [tʌn] (*pl inv* OR **-s**) *n* tonne *f*.

tonsil ['tɒnsl] *n* amygdale *f*.

tonsil(l)itis [ˌtɒnsɪ'laɪtɪs] *n* (*U*) amygdalite *f*.

too [tuː] *adv* [also] aussi. || [excessively] trop; **~ many people** trop de gens; **it was over all ~ soon** ça s'était terminé bien trop tôt; **I wasn't ~ impressed** ça ne m'a pas impressionné outre mesure.

took [tʊk] *pt* → **take**.

tool [tuːl] *n lit & fig* outil *m*.

tool box *n* boîte *f* à outils.

tool kit *n* trousse *f* à outils.

toot [tuːt] **1** *n* coup *m* de klaxon. **2** *vi* klaxonner.

tooth [tuːθ] (*pl* **teeth**) *n* dent *f*.

toothache ['tuːθeɪk] *n* mal *m* OR rage *f* de dents; **to have ~** avoir mal aux dents.

toothbrush ['tuːθbrʌʃ] *n* brosse *f* à dents.

toothpaste ['tuːθpeɪst] *n* (pâte *f*) dentifrice *m*.

toothpick ['tuːθpɪk] *n* cure-dents *m inv*.

top [tɒp] **1** *adj* [highest] du haut. || [most important, successful - officials] important, - officials] important(e); [- executives] supérieur(e); [- sportsman, sportswoman] meilleur(e); [- in exam] premier(ière). || [maximum] maximum. **2** *n* [highest point - of hill] sommet *m*; [- of page, pile] haut *m*; [- of tree] cime *f*; [- of list] début *m*, tête *f*; **on ~** dessus; **at the ~ of one's voice** à tue-tête. || [lid - of bottle, tube] bouchon *m*; [- of pen] capuchon *m*; [- of jar] couvercle *m*. || [of table, box] dessus *m*. || [clothing] haut *m*. || [toy] toupie *f*. || [highest rank - in league] tête *f*; [- in scale] haut *m*; [- SCH] premier *m*, -ière *f*. **3** *vt* [be first in] être en tête de. || [better] surpasser. || [exceed] dépasser. ○ **on top of** *prep* [in space] sur. || [in addition to] en plus de. ○ **top up** *Br*, **top off** *Am vt sep* remplir.

top floor *n* dernier étage *m*.

top hat *n* haut-de-forme *m*.

top-heavy *adj* mal équilibré(e).

topic ['tɒpɪk] *n* sujet *m*.

topical ['tɒpɪkl] *adj* d'actualité.

topless ['tɒplɪs] *adj* [woman] aux seins nus.

top-level *adj* au plus haut niveau.

topping ['tɒpɪŋ] *n* garniture *f.*

topple ['tɒpl] **1** *vt* renverser. **2** *vi* basculer.

top-secret *adj* top secret (top secrète).

topspin ['tɒpspɪn] *n* lift *m.*

topsy-turvy [,tɒpsɪ'tɜːvɪ] *adj* [messy] sens dessus dessous. ‖ [confused]: **to be ~** ne pas tourner rond.

tore [tɔːr] *pt* → tear.

torment [*n* 'tɔːment, *vb* tɔː'ment] **1** *n* tourment *m.* **2** *vt* tourmenter.

torn [tɔːn] *pp* → tear.

tornado [tɔː'neɪdəʊ] (*pl* **-es** OR **-s**) *n* tornade *f.*

torpedo [tɔː'piːdəʊ] (*pl* **-es**) *n* torpille *f.*

torrent ['tɒrənt] *n* torrent *m.*

torrid ['tɒrɪd] *adj* [hot] torride. ‖ *fig* [passionate] ardent(e).

tortoise ['tɔːtəs] *n* tortue *f.*

tortoiseshell ['tɔːtəʃel] **1** *adj*: **~ cat** chat *m* roux tigré. **2** *n* (*U*) [material] écaille *f.*

torture ['tɔːtʃər] **1** *n* torture *f.* **2** *vt* torturer.

toss [tɒs] **1** *vt* [throw] jeter; **to ~ a coin** jouer à pile ou face; **to ~ one's head** rejeter la tête en arrière. ‖ [salad] remuer; [pancake] faire sauter. ‖ [throw about] ballotter. **2** *vi* [move about]: **to ~ and turn** se tourner et se retourner.

tot [tɒt] *n inf* [small child] tout-petit *m.* ‖ [of drink] larme *f,* goutte *f.*

total ['təʊtl] **1** *adj* total(e); [disgrace, failure] complet(ète). **2** *n* total *m.* **3** *vt* [add up] additionner. ‖ [amount to] s'élever à.

totalitarian [,təʊtælɪ'teərɪən] *adj* totalitaire.

totally ['təʊtəlɪ] *adv* totalement; **I ~ agree** je suis entièrement d'accord.

totter ['tɒtər] *vi lit & fig* chanceler.

touch [tʌtʃ] **1** *n* (*U*) [sense] toucher *m.* ‖ [detail] touche *f.* ‖ (*U*) [skill] marque *f,* note *f.* ‖ [contact]: **to keep in ~ (with sb)** rester en contact (avec qqn); **to get in ~ with sb** entrer en contact avec qqn; **to lose ~ with sb** perdre qqn de vue; **to be out of ~ with** ne plus être au courant de. ‖ [small amount]: **a ~** un petit peu. **2** *vt* toucher. **3** *vi* [be in contact] se toucher. ○ **touch down** *vi* [plane] atterrir. ○ **touch on** *vt fus* effleurer.

touch-and-go *adj* incertain(e).

touchdown ['tʌtʃdaʊn] *n* [of plane] atterrissage *m.* ‖ [in American football] but *m.*

touched [tʌtʃt] *adj* [grateful] touché(e).

touching ['tʌtʃɪŋ] *adj* touchant(e).

touchline ['tʌtʃlaɪn] *n* ligne *f* de touche.

touchy ['tʌtʃɪ] *adj* [person] susceptible. ‖ [subject, question] délicat(e).

tough [tʌf] *adj* [material, vehicle, person] solide; [character, life] dur(e). ‖ [meat] dur(e). ‖ [decision, problem, task] difficile. ‖ [rough - area of town] dangereux(euse). ‖ [strict] sévère.

toughen ['tʌfn] *vt* [character] endurcir. ‖ [material] renforcer.

toupee ['tuːpeɪ] *n* postiche *m.*

tour [tʊər] **1** *n* [journey] voyage *m*; [by pop group etc] tournée *f.* ‖ [of town, museum] visite *f,* tour *m.* **2** *vt* visiter.

touring ['tʊərɪŋ] *n* tourisme *m.*

tourism ['tʊərɪzm] *n* tourisme *m.*

tourist ['tʊərɪst] *n* touriste *mf.*

tourist (information) office *n* office *m* de tourisme.

tournament ['tɔːnəmənt] *n* tournoi *m.*

tour operator *n* voyagiste *m.*

tousle ['taʊzl] *vt* ébouriffer.

tout [taʊt] **1** *n* revendeur *m* de billets. **2** *vt* [tickets] revendre; [goods] vendre. **3** *vi*: **to ~ for trade** racoler les clients.

tow [təʊ] *vt* remorquer.

towards *Br* [tə'wɔːdz], **toward** *Am* [tə'wɔːd] *prep* [gen] vers; [movement] vers, en direction de. ‖ [in attitude] envers. ‖ [for the purpose of] pour.

towel ['taʊəl] *n* serviette *f*; [tea towel] torchon *m.*

towelling *Br*, **toweling** *Am* ['taʊəlɪŋ] *n* (*U*) tissu *m* éponge.

towel rail *n* porte-serviettes *m inv.*

tower ['taʊər] **1** *n* tour *f.* **2** *vi* s'élever; **to ~ over sb/sthg** dominer qqn/qqch.

towering ['taʊərɪŋ] *adj* imposant(e).

town [taʊn] *n* ville *f*; **to go to ~ on sthg** *fig* ne pas lésiner sur qqch.

town centre *n* centre-ville *m.*

town council *n* conseil *m* municipal.

town hall *n* mairie *f.*

town plan *n* plan *m* de ville.

town planning *n* urbanisme *m.*

township ['taʊnʃɪp] *n* [in South Africa] township *f.* ‖ [in US] ≃ canton *m.*

towpath ['təʊpɑːθ, *pl* -pɑːðz] *n* chemin *m* de halage.

towrope ['təʊrəʊp] *n* câble *m* de remorquage.

tow truck *n Am* dépanneuse *f.*

toxic ['tɒksɪk] *adj* toxique.

toy [tɔɪ] **1** *n* jouet *m*. ○ **toy with** *rt fus* [idea] caresser. || [coin etc] jouer avec; **to ~ with one's food** manger du bout des dents.

toy shop *n* magasin *m* de jouets.

trace [treɪs] **1** *n* trace *f*. **2** *rt* [relatives, criminal] retrouver; [development, progress] suivre; [history, life] retracer. || [on paper] tracer.

tracing paper ['treɪsɪŋ-] *n* (*U*) papier-calque *m*.

track [træk] **1** *n* [path] chemin *m*. || SPORT piste *f*. || RAIL voie *f* ferrée. || [of animal, person] trace *f*. || [on record, tape] piste *f*. || *phr*: **to keep ~ of sb** rester en contact avec qqn; **to lose ~ of sb** perdre contact avec qqn; **to be on the right ~** être sur la bonne voie; **to be on the wrong ~** être sur la mauvaise piste. **2** *rt* suivre la trace de. ○ **track down** *rt sep* [criminal, animal] dépister; [object, address etc] retrouver.

track record *n* palmarès *m*.

tracksuit ['træksu:t] *n* survêtement *m*.

tract [trækt] *n* [pamphlet] tract *m*. || [of land, forest] étendue *f*.

traction ['trækʃn] *n* (*U*) PHYSICS traction *f*. || MED: **in ~** en extension.

tractor ['træktər] *n* tracteur *m*.

trade [treɪd] **1** *n* (*U*) [commerce] commerce *m*. || [job] métier *m*; **by ~** de son état. **2** *rt* [exchange]: **to ~ sthg (for)** échanger qqch (contre). **3** *ri* COMM: **to ~ (with sb)** commercer (avec qqn). ○ **trade in** *rt sep* [exchange] échanger, faire reprendre.

trade fair *n* exposition *f* commerciale.

trade-in *n* reprise *f*.

trademark ['treɪdmɑ:k] *n* COMM marque *f* de fabrique.

trade name *n* nom *m* de marque.

trader ['treɪdər] *n* marchand *m*, -e *f*, commerçant *m*, -e *f*.

tradesman ['treɪdzmən] (*pl* -men [-mən]) *n* commerçant *m*.

trading ['treɪdɪŋ] *n* (*U*) commerce *m*.

tradition [trə'dɪʃn] *n* tradition *f*.

traditional [trə'dɪʃənl] *adj* traditionnel(elle).

traffic ['træfɪk] (*pt & pp* -ked, *cont* -king) **1** *n* (*U*) [vehicles] circulation *f*. || [illegal trade]: **~ (in)** trafic *m* (de). **2** *ri*: **to ~ in** faire le trafic de.

traffic circle *n Am* rond-point *m*.

traffic jam *n* embouteillage *m*.

trafficker ['træfɪkər] *n*: **~ (in)** trafiquant *m*, -e *f* (de).

traffic lights *npl* feux *mpl* de signalisation.

tragedy ['trædʒədɪ] *n* tragédie *f*.

tragic ['trædʒɪk] *adj* tragique.

trail [treɪl] **1** *n* [path] sentier *m*. || [trace] piste *f*. **2** *rt* [drag] traîner. || [follow] suivre. **3** *ri* [drag, move slowly] traîner. ○ **trail away, trail off** *ri* s'estomper.

trailer ['treɪlər] *n* [vehicle - for luggage] remorque *f*; [- for living in] caravane *f*. || CINEMA bande-annonce *f*.

train [treɪn] **1** *n* RAIL train *m*. || [of dress] traîne *f*. **2** *rt* [teach]: **to ~ sb to do sthg** apprendre à qqn à faire qqch. || [for job] former; **to ~ sb as/in** former qqn comme/dans. || [gun, camera] braquer. **3** *ri* [for job]: **to ~ (as)** recevoir OR faire une formation (de). || SPORT: **to ~ (for)** s'entraîner (pour).

trained [treɪnd] *adj* formé(e).

trainee [treɪ'niː] *n* stagiaire *mf*.

trainer ['treɪnər] *n* [of animals] dresseur *m*, -euse *f*. || SPORT entraîneur *m*.

training ['treɪnɪŋ] *n* (*U*) [for job]: **~ (in)** formation *f* (de). || SPORT entraînement *m*.

train of thought *n*: **my/his ~** le fil de mes/ses pensées.

traipse [treɪps] *ri* traîner.

trait [treɪt] *n* trait *m*.

traitor ['treɪtər] *n* traître *m*.

trajectory [trə'dʒektərɪ] *n* trajectoire *f*.

tramp [træmp] **1** *n* [homeless person] clochard *m*, -e *f*. **2** *ri* marcher d'un pas lourd.

trample ['træmpl] *rt* piétiner.

trampoline ['træmpəliːn] *n* trampoline *m*.

trance [trɑːns] *n* transe *f*.

tranquil ['træŋkwɪl] *adj* tranquille.

tranquillizer *Br*, **tranquilizer** *Am* ['træŋkwɪlaɪzər] *n* tranquillisant *m*, calmant *m*.

transaction [træn'zækʃn] *n* transaction *f*.

transcend [træn'send] *rt* transcender.

transcript ['trænskrɪpt] *n* transcription *f*.

transfer [*n* 'trænsfɜːr, *vb* træns'fɜːr] **1** *n* [gen] transfert *m*; [of power] passation *f*; [of money] virement *m*. || [design] décalcomanie *f*. **2** *rt* [gen] transférer; [power, control] faire passer; [money] virer. || [employee] transférer, muter. **3** *ri* être transféré.

transfix [træns'fɪks] *rt*: **to be ~ed with fear** être paralysé(e) par la peur.

transform [træns'fɔ:m] *vt*: **to ~ sb/sthg (into)** transformer qqn/qqch (en).

transfusion [træns'fju:ʒn] *n* transfusion *f*.

transient ['trænzɪənt] *adj* passager (ère).

transistor radio *n* transistor *m*.

transit ['trænsɪt] *n*: **in ~** en transit.

transition [træn'zɪʃn] *n* transition *f*.

transitive ['trænzɪtɪv] *adj* GRAMM transitif(ive).

transitory ['trænzɪtrɪ] *adj* transitoire.

translate [træns'leɪt] *vt* traduire.

translation [træns'leɪʃn] *n* traduction *f*.

translator [træns'leɪtər] *n* traducteur *m*, -trice *f*.

transmission [trænz'mɪʃn] *n* [gen] transmission *f*. || RADIO & TV [programme] émission *f*.

transmit [trænz'mɪt] *vt* transmettre.

transmitter [trænz'mɪtər] *n* émetteur *m*.

transparency [trans'pærənsɪ] *n* PHOT diapositive *f*; [for overhead projector] transparent *m*.

transparent [træns'pærənt] *adj* transparent(e).

transpire [træn'spaɪər] *fml vt*: **it ~s that ... on a appris que ...**

transplant [*n* 'trænsplɑ:nt, *vb* træns'plɑ:nt] 1 *n* MED greffe *f*, transplantation *f*. 2 *vt* MED greffer, transplanter. || [seedlings] repiquer.

transport [*n* 'trænspɔ:t, *vb* træn'spɔ:t] 1 *n* transport *m*. 2 *vt* transporter.

transportation [ˌtrænspɔ:'teɪʃn] *n* transport *m*.

transpose [træns'pəʊz] *vt* transposer.

trap [træp] 1 *n* piège *m*. 2 *vt* prendre au piège; **to be trapped** être coincé.

trapdoor [ˌtræp'dɔ:r] *n* trappe *f*.

trapeze [trə'pi:z] *n* trapèze *m*.

trash [træʃ] *n* (*U*) *Am* [refuse] ordures *fpl*. || *inf pej* [poor-quality thing] camelote *f*.

trashcan ['træʃkæn] *n Am* poubelle *f*.

traumatic [trɔ:'mætɪk] *adj* traumatisant(e).

travel ['trævl] 1 *n* (*U*) voyage *m*, voyages *mpl*. 2 *vt* parcourir. 3 *vi* [make journey] voyager. || [move - current, signal] aller, passer; [- news] se répandre, circuler.

travel agency *n* agence *f* de voyages.

travel agent *n* agent *m* de voyages.

traveller *Br*, **traveler** *Am* ['trævlər] *n* [person on journey] voyageur *m*, -euse *f*.

traveller's cheque *n* chèque *m* de voyage.

travelling *Br*, **traveling** *Am* ['trævlɪŋ] *adj* [theatre, circus] ambulant(e). || [clock, bag etc] de voyage; [allowance] de déplacement.

travelsick ['trævlsɪk] *adj*: **to be ~** avoir le mal de la route/de l'air/de mer.

travesty ['trævəstɪ] *n* parodie *f*.

trawler ['trɔ:lər] *n* chalutier *m*.

tray [treɪ] *n* plateau *m*.

treacherous ['tretʃərəs] *adj* traître (traîtresse).

treachery ['tretʃərɪ] *n* traîtrise *f*.

tread [tred] (*pt* trod, *pp* trodden) 1 *n* [on tyre] bande *f* de roulement; [of shoe] semelle *f*. || [way of walking] pas *m*; [sound] bruit *m* de pas. 2 *vi*: **to ~ (on)** marcher (sur).

treason ['tri:zn] *n* trahison *f*.

treasure ['treʒər] 1 *n* trésor *m*. 2 *vt* [object] garder précieusement; [memory] chérir.

treasurer ['treʒərər] *n* trésorier *m*, -ière *f*.

treasury ['treʒərɪ] *n* [room] trésorerie *f*. ○ **Treasury** *n*: **the Treasury** le ministère des Finances.

treat [tri:t] 1 *vt* [gen] traiter. || [on special occasion]: **to ~ sb to sthg** offrir OR payer qqch à qqn. 2 *n* [gift] cadeau *m*. || [delight] plaisir *m*.

treatise ['tri:tɪs] *n*: **~ (on)** traité *m* (de).

treatment ['tri:tmənt] *n* traitement *m*.

treaty ['tri:tɪ] *n* traité *m*.

treble ['trebl] 1 *adj* [MUS - voice] de soprano; [- recorder] aigu (aiguë). || [triple] triple. 2 *n* [on stereo control] aigu *m*; [boy singer] soprano *m*. 3 *vt & vi* tripler.

treble clef *n* clef *f* de sol.

tree [tri:] *n* [gen] arbre *m*.

treetop ['tri:top] *n* cime *f*.

tree-trunk *n* tronc *m* d'arbre.

trek [trek] *n* randonnée *f*.

trellis ['trelɪs] *n* treillis *m*.

tremble ['trembl] *vi* trembler.

tremendous [trɪ'mendəs] *adj* [size, success, difference] énorme; [noise] terrible. || *inf* [really good] formidable.

tremor ['tremər] *n* tremblement *m*.

trench [trentʃ] *n* tranchée *f*.

trend [trend] *n* [tendency] tendance *f*.

trendy [trendɪ] *inf adj* branché(e), à la mode.

trepidation [ˌtrepɪ'deɪʃn] *n fml*: **in** OR **with ~** avec inquiétude.

trespass ['trespəs] vi [on land] entrer sans permission; "no ~ing" «défense d'entrer».

trespasser ['trespəsər] n intrus m, -e f.

trestle table ['tresl-] n table f à tréteaux.

trial ['traɪəl] n JUR procès m; **to be on ~ (for)** passer en justice (pour). || [test, experiment] essai m; **on ~** à l'essai; **by ~ and error** en tâtonnant. || [unpleasant experience] épreuve f.

triangle ['traɪæŋgl] n [gen] triangle m.

tribe [traɪb] n tribu f.

tribunal [traɪ'bjuːnl] n tribunal m.

tributary ['trɪbjʊtrɪ] n affluent m.

tribute ['trɪbjuːt] n tribut m, hommage m; **to pay ~ to** payer tribut à, rendre hommage à; **to be a ~ to sthg** témoigner de qqch.

trice [traɪs] n: **in a ~** en un clin d'œil.

trick [trɪk] 1 n [to deceive] tour m, farce f; **to play a ~ on sb** jouer un tour à qqn. || [to entertain] tour m. || [knack] truc m; **that will do the ~** inf ça fera l'affaire. 2 vt attraper, rouler; **to ~ sb into doing sthg** amener qqn à faire qqch (par la ruse).

trickery ['trɪkərɪ] n (U) ruse f.

trickle ['trɪkl] 1 n [of liquid] filet m. 2 vi [liquid] dégouliner; **to ~ in/out** [people] entrer/sortir par petits groupes.

tricky ['trɪkɪ] adj [difficult] difficile.

tricycle ['traɪsɪkl] n tricycle m.

trifle ['traɪfl] n [unimportant thing] bagatelle f. O **a trifle** adv un peu, un tantinet.

trifling ['traɪflɪŋ] adj insignifiant(e).

trigger ['trɪgər] n [on gun] détente f, gâchette f. O **trigger off** vt sep déclencher, provoquer.

trim [trɪm] 1 adj [neat and tidy] net (nette). || [slim] svelte. 2 n [of hair] coupe f. 3 vt [cut - gen] couper; [- hedge] tailler. || [decorate]: **to ~ sthg (with)** garnir OR orner qqch (de).

trimming ['trɪmɪŋ] n [on clothing] parement m. || CULIN garniture f.

trinket ['trɪŋkɪt] n bibelot m.

trio ['triːəʊ] (pl -s) n trio m.

trip [trɪp] 1 n [journey] voyage m. || drugs sl trip m. 2 vt [make stumble] faire un croche-pied à. 3 vi [stumble]: **to ~ (over)** trébucher (sur). O **trip up** vt sep [make stumble] faire un croche-pied à.

tripe [traɪp] n (U) CULIN tripe f. || inf [nonsense] bêtises fpl, idioties fpl.

triple ['trɪpl] 1 adj triple. 2 vt & vi tripler.

triple jump n: **the ~** le triple saut.

triplets ['trɪplɪts] npl triplés mpl, triplées fpl.

triplicate ['trɪplɪkət] n: **in ~** en trois exemplaires.

tripod ['traɪpɒd] n trépied m.

trite [traɪt] adj pej banal(e).

triumph ['traɪəmf] 1 n triomphe m. 2 vi: **to ~ (over)** triompher (de).

trivia ['trɪvɪə] n (U) [trifles] vétilles fpl, riens mpl.

trivial ['trɪvɪəl] adj insignifiant(e).

trod [trɒd] pt → tread.

trodden ['trɒdn] pp → tread.

trolley ['trɒlɪ] (pl trolleys) n Am [tram] tramway m, tram m.

trombone [trɒm'bəʊn] n MUS trombone m.

troop [truːp] 1 n bande f, troupe f. 2 vi: **to ~ in/out/off** entrer/sortir/partir en groupe. O **troops** npl troupes fpl.

trophy ['trəʊfɪ] n trophée m.

tropical ['trɒpɪkl] adj tropical(e).

tropics ['trɒpɪks] npl: **the ~** les tropiques mpl.

trot [trɒt] 1 n [of horse] trot m. 2 vi trotter. O **on the trot** adv inf de suite, d'affilée.

trouble ['trʌbl] 1 n (U) [difficulty] problème m, difficulté f; **to be in ~** avoir des ennuis. || [bother] peine f, mal m; **to take the ~ to do sthg** se donner la peine de faire qqch; **it's no ~!** ça ne me dérange pas! || [fighting] bagarre f; POL troubles mpl, conflits mpl. 2 vt [worry, upset] peiner, troubler. || [bother] déranger. || [give pain to] faire mal à. O **troubles** npl [worries] ennuis mpl. || POL troubles mpl, conflits mpl.

troubled ['trʌbld] adj [worried] inquiet(iète). || [disturbed - period] de troubles, agité(e); [- country] qui connaît une période de troubles.

troublemaker ['trʌbl,meɪkər] n fauteur m, -trice f de troubles.

troubleshooter ['trʌbl,ʃuːtər] n expert m, spécialiste mf.

troublesome ['trʌblsəm] adj [job] pénible; [back, knee] qui fait souffrir.

trough [trɒf] n [for animals - with water] abreuvoir m; [- with food] auge f. || [low point - of wave] creux m; fig point m bas.

troupe [truːp] n troupe f.

trousers ['traʊzəz] npl pantalon m.

trout [traʊt] (pl inv OR -s) n truite f.

trowel ['traʊəl] n [for gardening] déplantoir m; [for cement, plaster] truelle f.

tune

truant ['truːənt] *n*: **to play ~** faire l'école buissonnière.

truce [truːs] *n* trêve *f*.

truck [trʌk] *n* [lorry] camion *m*. || RAIL wagon *m* à plate-forme.

truck driver *n* routier *m*.

trucker ['trʌkər] *n Am* routier *m*.

truck farm *n Am* jardin *m* maraîcher.

truculent ['trʌkjolənt] *adj* agressif(ive).

trudge [trʌdʒ] *vi* marcher péniblement.

true [truː] *adj* [factual] vrai(e); **to come ~** se réaliser. || [genuine] vrai(e), authentique; **~ love** le grand amour. || [exact] exact(e). || [faithful] fidèle, loyal(e).

truffle ['trʌfl] *n* truffe *f*.

truly ['truːlɪ] *adv* [gen] vraiment. || [sincerely] vraiment, sincèrement. || *phr*: **yours ~** [at end of letter] croyez à l'expression de mes sentiments distingués.

trump [trʌmp] *n* atout *m*.

trumped-up ['trʌmpt-] *adj pej* inventé(e) de toutes pièces.

trumpet ['trʌmpɪt] *n* trompette *f*.

truncheon ['trʌntʃən] *n* matraque *f*.

trunk [trʌŋk] *n* [of tree, person] tronc *m*. || [of elephant] trompe *f*. || [box] malle *f*. || *Am* [of car] coffre *m*. ○ **trunks** *npl* maillot *m* de bain.

trunk road *n* (route *f*) nationale *f*.

truss [trʌs] *n* MED bandage *m* herniaire.

trust [trʌst] **1** *vt* [have confidence in] avoir confiance en, se fier à; **to ~ sb to do sthg** compter sur qqn pour faire qqch. || [entrust]: **to ~ sb with sthg** confier qqch à qqn. **2** *n* (*U*) [faith]: **~ (in sb/sthg)** confiance *f* (en qqn/dans qqch). || (*U*) [responsibility] responsabilité *f*. || FIN: **in ~** en dépôt. || COMM trust *m*.

trusted ['trʌstɪd] *adj* [person] de confiance; [method] qui a fait ses preuves.

trustee [trʌsˈtiː] *n* FIN & JUR fidéicommissaire *mf*; [of institution] administrateur *m*, -trice *f*.

trust fund *n* fonds *m* en fidéicommis.

trusting ['trʌstɪŋ] *adj* confiant(e).

trustworthy ['trʌst,wɜːðɪ] *adj* digne de confiance.

truth [truːθ] *n* vérité *f*.

truthful ['truːθfol] *adj* [person, reply] honnête; [story] véridique.

try [traɪ] **1** *vt* [attempt, test] essayer; [food, drink] goûter; **to ~ to do sthg** essayer de faire qqch. || JUR juger. || [put to the test] éprouver, mettre à l'épreuve. **2**

vi essayer; **to ~ for sthg** essayer d'obtenir qqch. **3** *n* [attempt]: **to give sthg a ~** essayer qqch. ○ **try on** *vt sep* [clothes] essayer. ○ **try out** *vt sep* essayer.

trying ['traɪɪŋ] *adj* pénible, éprouvant(e).

T-shirt *n* tee-shirt *m*.

T-square *n* té *m*.

tub [tʌb] *n* [of ice cream - large] boîte *f*; [- small] petit pot *m*; [of margarine] barquette *f*. || [bath] baignoire *f*.

tubby ['tʌbɪ] *adj inf* rondouillard(e), boulot(otte).

tube [tjuːb] *n* [cylinder, container] tube *m*.

tuberculosis [tjuːˌbɜːkjʊˈləʊsɪs] *n* tuberculose *f*.

tubing ['tjuːbɪŋ] *n* (*U*) tubes *mpl*, tuyaux *mpl*.

tubular ['tjuːbjolər] *adj* tubulaire.

tuck [tʌk] *vt* [place neatly] ranger. ○ **tuck away** *vt sep* [store] mettre de côté OR en lieu sûr. ○ **tuck in** *vt* [child, patient] border. || [clothes] rentrer. **2** *vi inf* boulotter. ○ **tuck up** *vt sep* [child, patient] border.

Tuesday ['tjuːzdɪ] *n* mardi *m*; *see also* **Saturday**.

tuft [tʌft] *n* touffe *f*.

tug [tʌg] **1** *n* [pull]: **to give sthg a ~** tirer sur qqch. || [boat] remorqueur *m*. **2** *vt* tirer. **3** *vi*: **to ~ (at)** tirer (sur).

tug-of-war *n* lutte *f* de traction à la corde; *fig* lutte acharnée.

tuition [tjuːˈɪʃn] *n* (*U*) cours *mpl*.

tulip ['tjuːlɪp] *n* tulipe *f*.

tumble ['tʌmbl] **1** *vi* [person] tomber, faire une chute; [water] tomber en cascades. || *fig* [prices] tomber, chuter. **2** *n* chute *f*, culbute *f*.

tumbledown ['tʌmbldaon] *adj* délabré(e), qui tombe en ruines.

tumble-dryer [-,draɪər] *n* sèche-linge *m inv*.

tumbler ['tʌmblər] *n* [glass] verre *m* (droit).

tummy ['tʌmɪ] *n inf* ventre *m*.

tumour *Br*, **tumor** *Am* ['tjuːmər] *n* tumeur *f*.

tuna [*Br* 'tjuːnə, *Am* 'tuːnə] (*pl inv* OR **-s**) *n* thon *m*.

tune [tjuːn] **1** *n* [song, melody] air *m*. || [harmony]: **in ~** [instrument] accordé(e), juste; [play, sing] juste; **out of ~** [instrument] mal accordé(e); [play, sing] faux; **to be in/out of ~ (with)** *fig* être en accord/désaccord (avec). **2** *vt* MUS accorder. || RADIO & TV régler. || [engine] régler. ○ **tune in** *vi* RADIO & TV être à l'écoute; **to ~ in to** se mettre sur. ○ **tune up** *vi* MUS accorder son instrument.

tuneful ['tjuːnful] *adj* mélodieux(ieuse).

tuner ['tjuːnər] *n* RADIO & TV syntoniseur *m*, tuner *m*. || MUS [person] accordeur *m*.

tunic ['tjuːnɪk] *n* tunique *f*.

tuning fork ['tjuːnɪŋ-] *n* diapason *m*.

Tunisia [tjuː'nɪzɪə] *n* Tunisie *f*.

tunnel ['tʌnl] **1** *n* tunnel *m*. **2** *vi* faire OR creuser un tunnel.

turban ['tɜːbən] *n* turban *m*.

turbine ['tɜːbaɪn] *n* turbine *f*.

turbocharged ['tɜːbəʊtʃɑːdʒd] *adj* turbo (*inv*).

turbulence ['tɜːbjʊləns] *n* (*U*) [in air, water] turbulence *f*.

turbulent ['tɜːbjʊlənt] *adj* [air, water] agité(e).

tureen [tə'riːn] *n* soupière *f*.

turf [tɜːf] (*pl* **-s** OR **turves**) *n* [grass surface] gazon *m*; [clod] motte *f* de gazon.

turgid ['tɜːdʒɪd] *adj fml* [style, writing] pompeux(euse), ampoulé(e).

Turk [tɜːk] *n* Turc *m*, Turque *f*.

turkey ['tɜːkɪ] (*pl* **turkeys**) *n* dinde *f*.

Turkey ['tɜːkɪ] *n* Turquie *f*.

Turkish ['tɜːkɪʃ] **1** *adj* turc (turque). **2** *n* [language] turc *m*. **3** *npl*: **the ~** les Turcs *mpl*.

Turkish delight *n* loukoum *m*.

turmoil ['tɜːmɔɪl] *n* agitation *f*, trouble *m*.

turn [tɜːn] **1** *n* [in road] virage *m*, tournant *m*; [in river] méandre *m*. || [revolution, twist] tour *m*. || [change] tournure *f*, tour *m*. || [in game] tour *m*; **in ~** tour à tour, chacun (à) son tour. || [performance] numéro *m*. || MED crise *f*, attaque *f*. || *phr*: **to do sb a good ~** rendre (un) service à qqn. **2** *vt* [gen] tourner; [omelette, steak etc] retourner; **to ~ sthg inside out** retourner qqch; **to ~ one's thoughts/ attention to sthg** tourner ses pensées/son attention vers qqch. || [change]: **to ~ sthg into** changer qqch en. || [become]: **to ~ red** rougir. **3** *vi* [gen] tourner; [person] se tourner, se retourner. || [in book]: **to ~ to a page** se reporter OR aller à une page. || [for consolation]: **to ~ to sb/sthg** se tourner vers qqn/qqch. || [change]: **to ~ into** se changer en, se transformer en. ○ **turn around** = **turn round**. ○ **turn away 1** *vt sep* [refuse entry to] refuser. **2** *vi* se détourner. ○ **turn back 1** *vt sep*

[sheets] replier; [person, vehicle] refouler. **2** *vi* rebrousser chemin. ○ **turn down** *vt sep* [reject] rejeter, refuser. || [radio, volume, gas] baisser. ○ **turn in** *vi inf* [go to bed] se pieuter. ○ **turn off 1** *vt fus* [road, path] quitter. **2** *vt sep* [radio, engine, gas] éteindre; [tap] fermer. **3** *vi* [leave path, road] tourner. ○ **turn on 1** *vt sep* [radio, TV, engine, gas] allumer; [tap] ouvrir; **to ~ the light on** allumer la lumière. || *inf* [excite sexually] exciter. **2** *vt fus* [attack] attaquer. ○ **turn out 1** *vt sep* [light, gas fire] éteindre. || [empty - pocket, bag] retourner, vider. **2** *vt fus*: **to ~ out to be** s'avérer. **3** *vi* [end up] finir. ○ **turn over 1** *vt sep* [playing card, stone] retourner; [page] tourner. || [consider] retourner dans sa tête. || [hand over] rendre, remettre. **2** *vi* [roll over] se retourner. ○ **turn round 1** *vt sep* [reverse] retourner. || [wheel, words] tourner. **2** *vi* [person] se retourner. ○ **turn up 1** *vt sep* [TV, radio] mettre plus fort; [gas] monter. **2** *vi* [arrive - person] se pointer. || [be found - person, object] être retrouvé; [- opportunity] se présenter.

turning ['tɜːnɪŋ] *n* [off road] route *f* latérale.

turning point *n* tournant *m*, moment *m* décisif.

turnip ['tɜːnɪp] *n* navet *m*.

turnout ['tɜːnaʊt] *n* [at election] taux *m* de participation; [at meeting] assistance *f*.

turnover ['tɜːn,əʊvər] *n* (*U*) [of personnel] renouvellement *m*. || FIN chiffre *m* d'affaires.

turnpike ['tɜːnpaɪk] *n Am* autoroute *f* à péage.

turnstile ['tɜːnstaɪl] *n* tourniquet *m*.

turntable ['tɜːn,teɪbl] *n* platine *f*.

turpentine ['tɜːpəntaɪn] *n* térébenthine *f*.

turquoise ['tɜːkwɔɪz] **1** *adj* turquoise (*inv*). **2** *n* [colour] turquoise *m*.

turret ['tʌrɪt] *n* tourelle *f*.

turtle ['tɜːtl] (*pl inv* OR **-s**) *n* tortue *f* de mer.

turtleneck ['tɜːtlnek] *n* [garment] pull *m* à col montant; [neck] col *m* montant.

turves [tɜːvz] *Br pl* → **turf**.

tusk [tʌsk] *n* défense *f*.

tussle ['tʌsl] **1** *n* lutte *f*. **2** *vi* se battre; **to ~ over sthg** se disputer qqch.

tutor ['tjuːtər] *n* [private] professeur *m* particulier. || UNIV directeur *m*, -trice *f* d'études.

tutorial [tjuː'tɔːrɪəl] n travaux mpl dirigés.

tuxedo [tʌk'siːdəʊ] (pl -s) n smoking m.

TV (abbr of television) n (U) [medium, industry] télé f. || [apparatus] (poste m de) télé f.

twang [twæŋ] n [sound] bruit m de pincement. || [accent] nasillement m.

tweed [twiːd] n tweed m.

tweezers ['twiːzəz] npl pince f à épiler.

twelfth [twelfθ] num douzième; see also sixth.

twelve [twelv] num douze; see also six.

twentieth ['twentɪəθ] num vingtième; see also sixth.

twenty ['twentɪ] num vingt; see also six.

twice [twaɪs] adv deux fois; he earns ~ as much as me il gagne deux fois plus que moi OR le double de moi; ~ as big deux fois plus grand; ~ my size/age le double de ma taille/mon âge.

twiddle ['twɪdl] 1 vt jouer avec. 2 vi: to ~ with sthg jouer avec qqch.

twig [twɪg] n brindille f, petite branche f.

twilight ['twaɪlaɪt] n crépuscule m.

twin [twɪn] 1 adj jumeau (jumelle); [town] jumelé(e); ~ beds lits mpl jumeaux. 2 n jumeau m, jumelle f.

twin-bedded [-'bedɪd] adj à deux lits.

twine [twaɪn] 1 n (U) ficelle f. 2 vt: to ~ sthg round sthg enrouler qqch autour de qqch.

twinge [twɪndʒ] n [of pain] élancement m; a ~ of guilt un remords.

twinkle ['twɪŋkl] vi [star, lights] scintiller; [eyes] briller, pétiller.

twin room n chambre f à deux lits.

twin town n ville f jumelée.

twirl [twɜːl] 1 vt faire tourner. 2 vi tournoyer.

twist [twɪst] 1 n [in road] zigzag m, tournant m; [in river] méandre m, coude m; [in rope] entortillement m. || fig [in plot] tour m. 2 vt [wind, curl] entortiller. || [contort] tordre. || [turn] tourner; [lid - to open] dévisser; [- to close] visser. || [sprain]: to ~ one's ankle se tordre OR se fouler la cheville. || [words, meaning] déformer. 3 vi [river, path] zigzaguer. || [be contorted] se tordre. || [turn]: to ~ round se retourner.

twitch [twɪtʃ] 1 n tic m. 2 vi [muscle, eye, face] se contracter.

two [tuː] num deux; see also six.

twofaced [ˌtuːˈfeɪst] adj pej fourbe.

twofold ['tuːfəʊld] adv: to increase ~ doubler.

twosome ['tuːsəm] n inf couple m.

two-way adj [traffic, trade] dans les deux sens.

tycoon [taɪ'kuːn] n magnat m.

type [taɪp] 1 n [sort, kind] genre m, sorte f; [model] modèle m; [in classification] type m. || (U) TYPO caractères mpl. 2 vt [letter, reply] taper (à la machine). 3 vi taper (à la machine).

typecast ['taɪpkɑːst] (pt & pp typecast) vt: to be ~ être cantonné aux mêmes rôles.

typeface ['taɪpfeɪs] n TYPO œil m de caractère.

typescript ['taɪpskrɪpt] n texte m dactylographié.

typeset ['taɪpset] (pt & pp typeset) vt composer.

typewriter ['taɪpˌraɪtər] n machine f à écrire.

typhoid (fever) ['taɪfɔɪd-] n typhoïde f.

typhoon [taɪ'fuːn] n typhon m.

typical ['tɪpɪkl] adj: ~ (of) typique (de), caractéristique (de); that's ~ (of him/her)! c'est bien de lui/d'elle!

typing ['taɪpɪŋ] n dactylo f, dactylographie f.

typist ['taɪpɪst] n dactylo mf, dactylographe mf.

tyranny ['tɪrənɪ] n tyrannie f.

tyrant ['taɪrənt] n tyran m.

tyre Br, **tire** Am ['taɪər] n pneu m.

tyre pressure n pression f (de gonflage).

u (*pl* **u's** OR **us**), **U** (*pl* **U's** OR **Us**) [ju:] *n* [letter] u *m* inv, U *m* inv.

U-bend *n* siphon *m*.

udder ['ʌdər] *n* mamelle *f*.

UFO (*abbr of* **unidentified flying object**) *n* OVNI *m*, ovni *m*.

ugh [ʌg] *excl* pouah!, beurk!

ugly ['ʌglɪ] *adj* [unattractive] laid(e). || *fig* [unpleasant] pénible, désagréable.

UHF (*abbr of* **ultra-high frequency**) *n* UHF.

UK (*abbr of* **United Kingdom**) *n* Royaume-Uni *m*, R.U. *m*.

Ukraine [ju:'kreɪn] *n*: **the ~** l'Ukraine *f*.

ulcer ['ʌlsər] *n* ulcère *m*.

Ulster ['ʌlstər] *n* Ulster *m*.

ulterior [ʌl'tɪərɪər] *adj*: **~ motive** arrière-pensée *f*.

ultimata [ʌltɪ'meɪtə] *pl* → **ultimatum**.

ultimate ['ʌltɪmət] **1** *adj* [final] final(e), ultime. || [most powerful] ultime, suprême. **2** *n*: **the ~ in** le fin du fin dans.

ultimately ['ʌltɪmətlɪ] *adv* [finally] finalement.

ultimatum [ʌltɪ'meɪtəm] (*pl* **-tums** OR **-ta** [-tə]) *n* ultimatum *m*.

ultrasound ['ʌltrəsaʊnd] *n* (*U*) ultrasons *mpl*.

ultraviolet [ʌltrə'vaɪələt] *adj* ultraviolet(ette).

umbilical cord [ʌm'bɪlɪkl-] *n* cordon *m* ombilical.

umbrella [ʌm'brelə] *n* [portable] parapluie *m*; [fixed] parasol *m*.

umpire ['ʌmpaɪər] **1** *n* arbitre *m*. **2** *vt* arbitrer.

umpteen [ʌmp'ti:n] *num adj inf* je ne sais combien de.

umpteenth [ʌmp'ti:nθ] *num adj inf* énième.

UN (*abbr of* **United Nations**) *n*: **the ~** l'ONU *f*, l'Onu *f*.

unable [ʌn'eɪbl] *adj*: **to be ~ to do sthg** ne pas pouvoir faire qqch, être incapable de faire qqch.

unacceptable [ʌnək'septəbl] *adj* inacceptable.

unaccompanied [ʌnə'kʌmpənɪd] *adj* [child] non accompagné(e); [luggage] sans surveillance.

unaccountably [ʌnə'kaʊntəblɪ] *adv* [inexplicably] de façon inexplicable, inexplicablement.

unaccounted [ʌnə'kaʊntɪd] *adj*: **to be ~ for** manquer.

unaccustomed [ʌnə'kʌstəmd] *adj* [unused]: **to be ~ to sthg/to doing sthg** ne pas être habitué(e) à qqch/à faire qqch.

unadulterated [ʌnə'dʌltəreɪtɪd] *adj* [unspoilt - wine] non frelaté(e); [- food] naturel(elle). || [absolute - joy] sans mélange; [- nonsense, truth] pur et simple (pure et simple).

unanimous [ju:'nænɪməs] *adj* unanime.

unanimously [ju:'nænɪməslɪ] *adv* à l'unanimité.

unappetizing, -ising [ʌn'æpɪtaɪzɪŋ] *adj* peu appétissant(e).

unarmed [ʌn'ɑ:md] *adj* non armé(e).

unarmed combat *n* combat *m* sans armes.

unashamed [ʌnə'ʃeɪmd] *adj* [luxury] insolent(e); [liar, lie] effronté(e), éhonté(e).

unassuming [ʌnə'sju:mɪŋ] *adj* modeste, effacé(e).

unattached [ʌnə'tætʃt] *adj* [not fastened, linked]: **~ (to)** indépendant(e) (de). || [without partner] libre, sans attaches.

unattended [ʌnə'tendɪd] *adj* [luggage, shop] sans surveillance; [child] seul(e).

unattractive [ʌnə'træktɪv] *adj* [not beautiful] peu attrayant(e), peu séduisant(e). || [not pleasant] déplaisant(e).

unauthorized, -ised [ʌn'ɔ:θəraɪzd] *adj* non autorisé(e).

unavailable [ʌnə'veɪləbl] *adj* qui n'est pas disponible, indisponible.

unavoidable [ʌnə'vɔɪdəbl] *adj* inévitable.

unaware [ʌnə'weər] *adj* ignorant(e), inconscient(e); **to be ~ of sthg** ne pas avoir conscience de qqch, ignorer qqch.

unawares [ʌnə'weəz] *adv*: **to catch OR take sb ~** prendre qqn au dépourvu.

unbalanced [ʌn'bælənst] *adj* [biased] tendancieux(ieuse), partial(e). || [deranged] déséquilibré(e).

unbearable [ʌn'beərəbl] *adj* insupportable.

unbeatable [ˌʌn'biːtəbl] *adj* imbattable.

unbeknown(st) [ˌʌnbɪ'nəʊn(st)] *adv*: ~ **to** à l'insu de.

unbelievable [ˌʌnbɪ'liːvəbl] *adj* incroyable.

unbending [ˌʌn'bendɪŋ] *adj* inflexible, intransigeant(e).

unbia(s)sed [ˌʌn'baɪəst] *adj* impartial(e).

unborn [ˌʌn'bɔːn] *adj* [child] qui n'est pas encore né(e).

unbreakable [ˌʌn'breɪkəbl] *adj* incassable.

unbutton [ˌʌn'bʌtn] *vt* déboutonner.

uncalled-for [ˌʌn'kɔːld-] *adj* [remark] déplacé(e); [criticism] injustifié(e).

uncanny [ʌn'kænɪ] *adj* étrange, mystérieux(ieuse); [resemblance] troublant(e).

uncertain [ʌn'sɜːtn] *adj* incertain(e); **in no ~ terms** sans mâcher ses mots.

unchanged [ˌʌn'tʃeɪndʒd] *adj* inchangé(e).

unchecked [ˌʌn'tʃekt] *adj* non maîtrisé(e), sans frein.

uncivilized, -ised [ˌʌn'sɪvɪlaɪzd] *adj* non civilisé(e), barbare.

uncle [ˈʌŋkl] *n* oncle *m*.

unclear [ˌʌn'klɪər] *adj* [message, meaning, motive] qui n'est pas clair(e). || [uncertain - person, future] incertain(e).

uncomfortable [ˌʌn'kʌmftəbl] *adj* [shoes, chair, clothes etc] inconfortable; *fig* [fact, truth] désagréable. || [person - physically] qui n'est pas à l'aise; [- ill at ease] mal à l'aise.

uncommon [ʌn'kɒmən] *adj* [rare] rare.

uncompromising [ʌn'kɒmprəmaɪzɪŋ] *adj* intransigeant(e).

unconditional [ˌʌnkən'dɪʃənl] *adj* inconditionnel(elle).

unconscious [ʌn'kɒnʃəs] **1** *adj* [having lost consciousness] sans connaissance. || *fig* [unaware]: **to be ~ of** ne pas avoir conscience de, ne pas se rendre compte de. || [unnoticed - desires, feelings] inconscient(e). **2** *n* PSYCH inconscient *m*.

unconsciously [ʌn'kɒnʃəslɪ] *adv* inconsciemment.

uncontrollable [ˌʌnkən'trəʊləbl] *adj* [unrestrainable - emotion, urge] irrépressible, irrésistible; [- increase, epidemic] qui ne peut être enrayé(e). || [unmanageable - person] impossible, difficile.

unconventional [ˌʌnkən'venʃənl] *adj* peu conventionnel(elle), original(e).

uncouth [ʌn'kuːθ] *adj* grossier(ière).

uncover [ʌn'kʌvər] *vt* découvrir.

undecided [ˌʌndɪ'saɪdɪd] *adj* [person] indécis(e), irrésolu(e); [issue] indécis(e).

undeniable [ˌʌndɪ'naɪəbl] *adj* indéniable, incontestable.

under ['ʌndər] **1** *prep* [gen] sous. || [less than] moins de; **children ~ five** les enfants de moins de cinq ans. || [subject to - effect, influence] sous; **~ the circumstances** dans ces circonstances, étant donné les circonstances; **to be ~ the impression that ...** avoir l'impression que .... || [undergoing]: **~ consideration** à l'étude, à l'examen. || [according to] selon, conformément à. **2** *adv* [beneath] dessous; [underwater] sous l'eau; **to go ~** [company] couler, faire faillite. || [less] au-dessous.

underage [ˌʌndər'eɪdʒ] *adj* mineur(e).

undercarriage ['ʌndəˌkærɪdʒ] *n* train *m* d'atterrissage.

undercharge [ˌʌndə'tʃɑːdʒ] *vt* ne pas faire assez payer à.

underclothes ['ʌndəkləʊðz] *npl* sous-vêtements *mpl*.

undercoat ['ʌndəkəʊt] *n* [of paint] couche *f* de fond.

undercover ['ʌndəˌkʌvər] *adj* secret(ète).

undercurrent ['ʌndəˌkʌrənt] *n fig* [tendency] courant *m* sous-jacent.

undercut [ˌʌndə'kʌt] (*pt & pp* **undercut**) *vt* [in price] vendre moins cher que.

underdeveloped [ˌʌndədɪ'veləpt] *adj* [country] sous-développé(e); [person] qui n'est pas complètement développé(e) OR formé(e).

underdog ['ʌndədɒg] *n*: **the ~** l'opprimé *m*; SPORT celui (celle) que l'on donne perdant(e).

underdone [ˌʌndə'dʌn] *adj* [food] pas assez cuit(e); [steak] saignant(e).

underestimate [ˌʌndər'estɪmeɪt] *vt* sous-estimer.

underexposed [ˌʌndərɪk'spəʊzd] *adj* PHOT sous-exposé(e).

underfoot [ˌʌndə'fʊt] *adv* sous les pieds.

undergo [ˌʌndə'gəʊ] (*pt* -**went**, *pp* -**gone** [-'gɒn]) *vt* subir; [pain, difficulties] éprouver.

undergraduate [ˌʌndə'grædjʊət] *n* étudiant *m*, -e *f* qui prépare la licence.

underground [*adj & n* 'ʌndəgraʊnd, *adv* ˌʌndə'graʊnd] **1** *adj* [below the ground] souterrain(e). || *fig* [secret] clandestin(e). **2** *adv*: **to go/be forced ~** entrer dans la clandestinité. **3** *n* [activist movement] résistance *f*.

undergrowth ['ʌndəgrəʊθ] *n* (*U*) sous-bois *m inv*.

underhand [,ʌndə'hænd] *adj* sournois(e), en dessous.

underline [,ʌndə'laɪn] *vt* souligner.

underlying [,ʌndə'laɪɪŋ] *adj* sous-jacent(e).

undermine [,ʌndə'maɪn] *vt fig* [weaken] saper, ébranler.

underneath [,ʌndə'ni:θ] **1** *prep* [beneath] sous, au-dessous de. || [in movements] sous. **2** *adv* [beneath] en dessous, dessous. || *fig* [fundamentally] au fond. **3** *n* [underside]: **the ~** le dessous.

underpaid ['ʌndəpeɪd] *adj* sous-payé(e).

underpants ['ʌndəpænts] *npl* slip *m*.

underpass ['ʌndəpɑːs] *n* [for cars] passage *m* inférieur; [for pedestrians] passage *m* souterrain.

underprivileged [,ʌndə'prɪvɪlɪdʒd] *adj* défavorisé(e), déshérité(e).

underrated [,ʌndə'reɪtɪd] *adj* sous-estimé(e).

undershirt ['ʌndəʃɜːt] *n Am* maillot *m* de corps.

underside ['ʌndəsaɪd] *n*: **the ~** le dessous.

underskirt ['ʌndəskɜːt] *n* jupon *m*.

understand [,ʌndə'stænd] (*pt & pp* -**stood**) **1** *vt* [gen] comprendre. || *fml* [be informed] **I ~ (that)** ... je crois comprendre que ..., il paraît que .... **2** *vi* comprendre.

understandable [,ʌndə'stændəbl] *adj* compréhensible.

understanding [,ʌndə'stændɪŋ] **1** *n* [knowledge, sympathy] compréhension *f*. || [agreement] accord *m*, arrangement *m*. **2** *adj* [sympathetic] compréhensif(ive).

understatement [,ʌndə'steɪtmənt] *n* [inadequate statement] affirmation *f* en dessous de la vérité. || (*U*) [quality of understating] euphémisme *m*.

understood [,ʌndə'stʊd] *pt & pp* → understand.

understudy ['ʌndə,stʌdɪ] *n* doublure *f*.

undertake [,ʌndə'teɪk] (*pt* -**took**, *pp* -**taken** [-'teɪkn]) *vt* [take on - gen] entreprendre; [- responsibility] assumer. || [promise]: **to ~ to do sthg** promettre de faire qqch, s'engager à faire qqch.

undertaker ['ʌndə,teɪkər] *n* entrepreneur *m* des pompes funèbres.

undertaking [,ʌndə'teɪkɪŋ] *n* [task] entreprise *f*. || [promise] promesse *f*.

undertone ['ʌndətəʊn] *n* [quiet voice] voix *f* basse. || [vague feeling] courant *m*.

undertook [,ʌndə'tʊk] *pt* → undertake.

underwater [,ʌndə'wɔːtər] **1** *adj* sous-marin(e). **2** *adv* sous l'eau.

underwear ['ʌndəweər] *n* (*U*) sous-vêtements *mpl*.

underwent [,ʌndə'went] *pt* → undergo.

underworld ['ʌndə,wɜːld] *n* [criminal society]: **the ~** le milieu, la pègre.

underwriter ['ʌndə,raɪtər] *n* assureur *m*.

undid [,ʌn'dɪd] *pt* → undo.

undisputed [,ʌndɪ'spjuːtɪd] *adj* incontesté(e).

undo [,ʌn'duː] (*pt* -**did**, *pp* -**done**) *vt* [unfasten] défaire. || [nullify] annuler, détruire.

undone [,ʌn'dʌn] **1** *pp* → undo. **2** *adj* [unfastened] défait(e). || [task] non accompli(e).

undoubtedly [ʌn'daʊtɪdlɪ] *adv* sans aucun doute.

undress [,ʌn'dres] **1** *vt* déshabiller. **2** *vi* se déshabiller.

undue [,ʌn'djuː] *adj fml* excessif(ive).

undulate ['ʌndjʊleɪt] *vi* onduler.

unduly [,ʌn'djuːlɪ] *adv fml* trop, excessivement.

unearth [,ʌn'ɜːθ] *vt* [dig up] déterrer. || *fig* [discover] découvrir, exhumer.

unearthly [ʌn'ɜːθlɪ] *adj inf* [uncivilized - time of day] indu(e), impossible.

unease [ʌn'iːz] *n* (*U*) malaise *m*.

uneasy [ʌn'iːzɪ] *adj* [person, feeling] mal à l'aise, gêné(e); [silence] gêné(e).

uneducated [,ʌn'edjʊkeɪtɪd] *adj* [person] sans instruction.

unemployed [,ʌnɪm'plɔɪd] **1** *adj* au chômage, sans travail. **2** *npl*: **the ~** les sans-travail *mpl*, les chômeurs *mpl*.

unemployment [,ʌnɪm'plɔɪmənt] *n* chômage *m*.

unemployment benefit *Br*, **unemployment compensation** *Am n* allocation *f* de chômage.

unerring [,ʌn'ɜːrɪŋ] *adj* sûr(e), infaillible.

uneven [,ʌn'iːvn] *adj* [not flat - surface] inégal(e); [- ground] accidenté(e). || [inconsistent] inégal(e). || [unfair] injuste.

unexpected [,ʌnɪk'spektɪd] *adj* inattendu(e), imprévu(e).

unexpectedly [,ʌnɪk'spektɪdlɪ] adv subitement, d'une manière imprévue.

unfailing [ʌn'feɪlɪŋ] adj qui ne se dément pas, constant(e).

unfair [,ʌn'feəʳ] adj injuste.

unfaithful [,ʌn'feɪθfʊl] adj infidèle.

unfamiliar [,ʌnfə'mɪljəʳ] adj [not well-known] peu familier(ière), peu connu(e). || [not acquainted]: **to be ~ with sthg/sb** mal connaître qqch/qqn, ne pas connaître qqch/qqn.

unfashionable [,ʌn'fæʃnəbl] adj démodé(e), passé(e) de mode; [person] qui n'est plus à la mode.

unfasten [,ʌn'fɑːsn] vt défaire.

unfavourable Br, **unfavorable** Am [,ʌn'feɪvrəbl] adj défavorable.

unfeeling [ʌn'fiːlɪŋ] adj impitoyable, insensible.

unfinished [,ʌn'fɪnɪʃt] adj inachevé(e).

unfit [,ʌn'fɪt] adj [not in good health] qui n'est pas en forme. || [not suitable]: ~ **(for)** impropre (à); [person] inapte (à).

unfold [ʌn'fəʊld] 1 vt [map, newspaper] déplier. 2 vi [become clear] se dérouler.

unforeseen [,ʌnfɔː'siːn] adj imprévu(e).

unforgettable [,ʌnfə'getəbl] adj inoubliable.

unforgivable [,ʌnfə'gɪvəbl] adj impardonnable.

unfortunate [ʌn'fɔːtʃnət] adj [unlucky] malheureux(euse), malchanceux(euse). || [regrettable] regrettable, fâcheux(euse).

unfortunately [ʌn'fɔːtʃnətlɪ] adv malheureusement.

unfounded [,ʌn'faʊndɪd] adj sans fondement, dénué(e) de tout fondement.

unfriendly [,ʌn'frendlɪ] adj hostile, malveillant(e).

unfurnished [,ʌn'fɜːnɪʃt] adj non meublé(e).

ungainly [ʌn'geɪnlɪ] adj gauche.

ungrateful [ʌn'greɪtfʊl] adj ingrat(e), peu reconnaissant(e).

unhappy [ʌn'hæpɪ] adj [sad] triste, malheureux(euse). || [uneasy]: **to be ~ (with OR about)** être inquiet(iète) (au sujet de). || [unfortunate] malheureux(euse), regrettable.

unharmed [,ʌn'hɑːmd] adj indemne, sain et sauf (saine et sauve).

unhealthy [ʌn'helθɪ] adj [person, skin] maladif(ive); [conditions, place] insalubre, malsain(e); [habit] malsain.

unheard-of [ʌn'hɜːd-] adj [unknown] inconnu(e). || [unprecedented] sans précédent, inouï(e).

unhook [,ʌn'hʊk] vt [dress, bra] dégrafer. || [coat, picture, trailer] décrocher.

unhurt [,ʌn'hɜːt] adj indemne, sain et sauf (saine et sauve).

unidentified flying object [,ʌnaɪ'dentɪfaɪd-] n objet m volant non identifié.

unification [,juːnɪfɪ'keɪʃn] n unification f.

uniform ['juːnɪfɔːm] 1 adj [rate, colour] uniforme; [size] même. 2 n uniforme m.

unify ['juːnɪfaɪ] vt unifier.

unilateral [,juːnɪ'lætərəl] adj unilatéral(e).

unimportant [,ʌnɪm'pɔːtənt] adj sans importance, peu important(e).

uninhabited [,ʌnɪn'hæbɪtɪd] adj inhabité(e).

uninjured [,ʌn'ɪndʒəd] adj qui n'est pas blessé(e), indemne.

unintentional [,ʌnɪn'tenʃənl] adj involontaire, non intentionnel(elle).

union ['juːnjən] 1 n [trade union] syndicat m. || [alliance] union f. 2 comp syndical(e).

Union Jack n: **the ~** l'Union Jack m, le drapeau britannique.

unique [juː'niːk] adj [exceptional] unique, exceptionnel(elle). || [exclusive]: ~ **to** propre à. || [very special] unique.

unison ['juːnɪzn] n unisson m; **in ~** à l'unisson; [say] en chœur, en même temps.

unit ['juːnɪt] n [gen] unité f. || [of furniture] élément m. || [department] service m.

unite [juː'naɪt] 1 vt unifier. 2 vi s'unir.

united [juː'naɪtɪd] adj [in harmony] uni(e). || [unified] unifié(e).

United Kingdom n: **the ~** le Royaume-Uni.

United Nations n: **the ~** les Nations fpl Unies.

United States n: **the ~ (of America)** les États-Unis mpl (d'Amérique); **in the ~** aux États-Unis.

unity ['juːnətɪ] n (U) unité f.

universal [,juːnɪ'vɜːsl] adj universel(elle).

universe ['juːnɪvɜːs] n univers m.

university [,juːnɪ'vɜːsətɪ] 1 n université f. 2 comp universitaire.

unjust [,ʌn'dʒʌst] adj injuste.

unkempt [ˌʌnˈkempt] *adj* [clothes, person] négligé(e), débraillé(e).

unkind [ʌnˈkaɪnd] *adj* [uncharitable] méchant(e), pas gentil(ille).

unknown [ˌʌnˈnəʊn] *adj* inconnu(e).

unlawful [ˌʌnˈlɔːfʊl] *adj* illégal(e).

unleaded [ˌʌnˈledɪd] *adj* sans plomb.

unless [ən'les] *conj* à moins que (+ *subjunctive*); ~ **I'm mistaken** à moins que je (ne) me trompe.

unlike [ˌʌnˈlaɪk] *prep* [different from] différent(e) de. ‖ [in contrast to] contrairement à, à la différence de. ‖ [not typical of]: **it's ~ you to complain** cela ne te ressemble pas de te plaindre.

unlikely [ʌnˈlaɪklɪ] [event, result] peu probable, improbable; [story] invraisemblable.

unlisted [ʌnˈlɪstɪd] *adj* Am [phone number] qui est sur la liste rouge.

unload [ˌʌnˈləʊd] *vt* décharger.

unlock [ˌʌnˈlɒk] *vt* ouvrir.

unlucky [ʌnˈlʌkɪ] *adj* [unfortunate - person] malchanceux(euse), qui n'a pas de chance; [- experience, choice] malheureux(euse). ‖ [object, number etc] qui porte malheur.

unmarried [ˌʌnˈmærɪd] *adj* célibataire, qui n'est pas marié(e).

unmistakable [ˌʌnmɪˈsteɪkəbl] *adj* qu'on ne peut pas ne pas reconnaître.

unmitigated [ʌnˈmɪtɪgeɪtɪd] *adj* [disaster] total(e); [evil] non mitigé(e).

unnatural [ʌnˈnætʃrəl] *adj* [unusual] anormal(e), qui n'est pas naturel(elle). ‖ [affected] peu naturel(elle); [smile] forcé(e).

unnecessary [ʌnˈnesəsərɪ] *adj* [remark, expense, delay] inutile.

unnerving [ˌʌnˈnɜːvɪŋ] *adj* troublant(e).

unnoticed [ˌʌnˈnəʊtɪst] *adj* inaperçu(e).

unobtainable [ˌʌnəbˈteɪnəbl] *adj* impossible à obtenir.

unobtrusive [ˌʌnəbˈtruːsɪv] *adj* [person] effacé(e); [object] discret(ète).

unofficial [ˌʌnəˈfɪʃl] *adj* non officiel(ielle).

unorthodox [ˌʌnˈɔːθədɒks] *adj* peu orthodoxe.

unpack [ˌʌnˈpæk] **1** *vt* [suitcase] défaire; [box] vider; [clothes] déballer. **2** *vi* défaire ses bagages.

unparalleled [ʌnˈpærəleld] *adj* [success, crisis] sans précédent; [beauty] sans égal.

unpleasant [ʌnˈpleznt] *adj* désagréable.

unplug [ʌnˈplʌg] *vt* débrancher.

unpopular [ˌʌnˈpɒpjʊləʳ] *adj* impopulaire.

unprecedented [ʌnˈpresɪdəntɪd] *adj* sans précédent.

unpredictable [ˌʌnprɪˈdɪktəbl] *adj* imprévisible.

unqualified [ˌʌnˈkwɒlɪfaɪd] *adj* [person] non qualifié(e); [teacher, doctor] non diplômé(e). ‖ [success] formidable; [support] inconditionnel(elle).

unquestionable [ʌnˈkwestʃənəbl] *adj* [fact] incontestable; [honesty] certain(e).

unquestioning [ʌnˈkwestʃənɪŋ] *adj* aveugle, absolu(e).

unravel [ʌnˈrævl] *vt* [undo - knitting] défaire; [- fabric] effiler; [- threads] démêler. ‖ *fig* [solve] éclaircir.

unreal [ˌʌnˈrɪəl] *adj* [strange] irréel(elle).

unrealistic [ˌʌnrɪəˈlɪstɪk] *adj* irréaliste.

unreasonable [ʌnˈriːznəbl] *adj* qui n'est pas raisonnable, déraisonnable.

unrelated [ˌʌnrɪˈleɪtɪd] *adj*: **to be ~ (to)** n'avoir aucun rapport (avec).

unreliable [ˌʌnrɪˈlaɪəbl] *adj* [machine, method] peu fiable; [person] sur qui on ne peut pas compter.

unrequited [ˌʌnrɪˈkwaɪtɪd] *adj* non partagé(e).

unreserved [ˌʌnrɪˈzɜːvd] *adj* [support, admiration] sans réserve.

unresolved [ˌʌnrɪˈzɒlvd] *adj* non résolu(e).

unrest [ˌʌnˈrest] *n* (*U*) troubles *mpl*.

unrivalled *Br*, **unrivaled** *Am* [ʌnˈraɪvld] *adj* sans égal(e).

unroll [ˌʌnˈrəʊl] *vt* dérouler.

unruly [ʌnˈruːlɪ] *adj* [crowd, child] turbulent(e); [hair] indisciplinés.

unsafe [ˌʌnˈseɪf] *adj* [dangerous] dangereux(euse). ‖ [in danger]: **to feel ~** ne pas se sentir en sécurité.

unsaid [ˌʌnˈsed] *adj*: **to leave sthg ~** passer qqch sous silence.

unsatisfactory ['ʌnˌsætɪsˈfæktərɪ] *adj* qui laisse à désirer, peu satisfaisant(e).

unsavoury, **unsavory** *Am* [ʌnˈseɪvərɪ] *adj* [person] peu recommandable; [district] mal famé(e).

unscathed [ʌnˈskeɪðd] *adj* indemne.

unscrew [ˌʌnˈskruː] *vt* dévisser.

unscrupulous [ʌnˈskruːpjʊləs] *adj* sans scrupules.

unseemly [ʌnˈsiːmlɪ] *adj* inconvenant(e).

unselfish [ˌʌnˈselfɪʃ] *adj* désintéressé(e).

unsettled [ˌʌnˈsetld] *adj* [person] perturbé(e), troublé(e). ǁ [weather] variable, incertain(e). ǁ [argument] qui n'a pas été résolu(e); [situation] incertain(e).

unshak(e)able [ʌnˈʃeɪkəbl] *adj* inébranlable.

unshaven [ˌʌnˈʃeɪvn] *adj* non rasé(e).

unsightly [ʌnˈsaɪtlɪ] *adj* laid(e).

unskilled [ˌʌnˈskɪld] *adj* non qualifié(e).

unsociable [ʌnˈsəʊʃəbl] *adj* sauvage.

unsocial [ˌʌnˈsəʊʃl] *adj*: **to work ~ hours** travailler en dehors des heures normales.

unsound [ˌʌnˈsaʊnd] *adj* [theory] mal fondé(e); [decision] peu judicieux(ieuse). ǁ [building, structure] en mauvais état.

unspeakable [ʌnˈspiːkəbl] *adj* indescriptible.

unstable [ˌʌnˈsteɪbl] *adj* instable.

unsteady [ˌʌnˈstedɪ] *adj* [hand] tremblant(e); [table, ladder] instable.

unstuck [ˌʌnˈstʌk] *adj*: **to come ~** [notice, stamp, label] se décoller; *fig* [plan, system] s'effondrer; *fig* [person] essuyer un échec.

unsuccessful [ˌʌnsəkˈsesfʊl] *adj* [attempt] vain(e); [meeting] infructueux(euse); [candidate] refusé(e).

unsuccessfully [ˌʌnsəkˈsesfʊlɪ] *adv* en vain, sans succès.

unsuitable [ˌʌnˈsuːtəbl] *adj* qui ne convient pas; [clothes] peu approprié(e).

unsure [ˌʌnˈʃɔːr] *adj* [not certain]: **to be ~ (about/of)** ne pas être sûr(e) (de). ǁ [not confident]: **to be ~ (of o.s.)** ne pas être sûr(e) de soi.

unsuspecting [ˌʌnsəˈspektɪŋ] *adj* qui ne se doute de rien.

unsympathetic [ˈʌnˌsɪmpəˈθetɪk] *adj* [unfeeling] indifférent(e).

untangle [ˌʌnˈtæŋgl] *rt* [string, hair] démêler.

untapped [ˌʌnˈtæpt] *adj* inexploité(e).

untenable [ˌʌnˈtenəbl] *adj* indéfendable.

unthinkable [ʌnˈθɪŋkəbl] *adj* impensable.

untidy [ʌnˈtaɪdɪ] *adj* [room, desk] en désordre; [work, handwriting] brouillon (*inv*); [person, appearance] négligé(e).

untie [ˌʌnˈtaɪ] (*cont* **untying**) *rt* [knot, parcel, shoelaces] défaire; [prisoner] détacher.

until [ənˈtɪl] **1** *prep* [gen] jusqu'à; **~ now** jusqu'ici. ǁ (*after negative*) avant; **not ~ tomorrow** pas avant demain. **2** *conj* [gen] jusqu'à ce que (+ *subjunctive*). ǁ (*after negative*) avant que (+ *subjunctive*).

untimely [ʌnˈtaɪmlɪ] *adj* [death] prématuré(e); [remark] mal à propos; [moment] mal choisi(e).

untold [ˌʌnˈtəʊld] *adj* [amount, wealth] incalculable; [suffering, joy] indescriptible.

untrue [ˌʌnˈtruː] *adj* [not accurate] faux (fausse), qui n'est pas vrai(e).

unused [*sense 1* ˌʌnˈjuːzd, *sense 2* ˌʌnˈjuːst] *adj* [clothes] neuf (neuve); [machine] qui n'a jamais servi. ǁ [unaccustomed]: **to be ~ to sthg/to doing sthg** ne pas avoir l'habitude de qqch/de faire qqch.

unusual [ʌnˈjuːʒl] *adj* rare, inhabituel(elle).

unusually [ʌnˈjuːʒəlɪ] *adv* exceptionnellement.

unveil [ˌʌnˈveɪl] *rt lit & fig* dévoiler.

unwanted [ˌʌnˈwɒntɪd] *adj* [object] dont on ne se sert pas; [child] non désiré(e); **to feel ~** se sentir mal-aimé(e).

unwavering [ʌnˈweɪvərɪŋ] *adj* [determination] inébranlable.

unwelcome [ʌnˈwelkəm] *adj* [news, situation] fâcheux(euse); [visitor] importun(e).

unwell [ˌʌnˈwel] *adj*: **to be/feel ~** ne être/se sentir bien.

unwieldy [ʌnˈwiːldɪ] *adj* [cumbersome] peu maniable. ǁ *fig* [system] lourd(e).

unwilling [ˌʌnˈwɪlɪŋ] *adj*: **to be ~ to do sthg** ne pas vouloir faire qqch.

unwind [ˌʌnˈwaɪnd] (*pt & pp* **-wound**) **1** *vt* dérouler. **2** *vi fig* [person] se détendre.

unwise [ˌʌnˈwaɪz] *adj* imprudent(e), peu sage.

unworkable [ˌʌnˈwɜːkəbl] *adj* impraticable.

unworthy [ʌnˈwɜːðɪ] *adj* [undeserving]: **~ (of)** indigne (de).

unwound [ˌʌnˈwaʊnd] *pt & pp* → **unwind**.

unwrap [ˌʌnˈræp] *rt* défaire.

unwritten law [ˌʌnˈrɪtn-] *n* droit *m* coutumier.

up [ʌp] **1** *adv* [towards or in a higher position] en haut; **she's ~ in her bedroom** elle est en haut dans sa chambre; **prices are going** ~ les prix augmentent; ~ **there là-haut.** ‖ [into an upright position]: **to stand** ~ se lever; **to sit** ~ s'asseoir (bien droit). ‖ [northwards]: **I'm coming** ~ **to York next week** je viens à York la semaine prochaine; ~ **north** dans le nord. ‖ [along a road, river]: **their house is a little further** ~ leur maison est un peu plus loin. **2** *prep* [towards or in a higher position] en haut de; ~ **a ladder** sur une échelle; **I went** ~ **the stairs** j'ai monté l'escalier. ‖ [at far end of]: **they live** ~ **the road from us** ils habitent un peu plus haut OR loin que nous (dans la même rue). ‖ [against current of river]: **to sail** ~ **the Amazon** remonter l'Amazone en bateau. **3** *adj* [out of bed] levé(e); **I was** ~ **at six today** je me suis levé à six heures aujourd'hui. ‖ [at an end]: **time's** ~ c'est l'heure. ‖ *inf* [wrong]: **what's** ~? qu'est-ce qui ne va pas?, qu'est-ce qu'il y a? **4** *n*: ~**s and downs** hauts et bas *mpl*. ○ **up and down 1** *adv*: **to jump** ~ **and down** sauter; **to walk** ~ **and down** faire les cent pas. **2** *prep*: **we walked** ~ **and down the avenue** nous avons arpenté l'avenue. ○ **up to** *prep* [indicating level] jusqu'à; **it's not** ~ **to standard** ce n'est pas de la qualité voulue, ceci n'a pas le niveau requis. ‖ [well or able enough for]: **to be** ~ **to doing sthg** [able to] être capable de faire qqch; [well enough for] être en état de faire qqch; **my French isn't** ~ **to much** mon français ne vaut pas grand-chose OR n'est pas fameux. ‖ *inf* [secretly doing something]: **what are you** ~ **to?** qu'est-ce que tu fabriques?; **they're** ~ **to something** ils mijotent quelque chose, ils préparent un coup. ‖ [indicating responsibility]: **it's not** ~ **to me to decide** ce n'est pas moi qui décide, il ne m'appartient pas de décider; **it's** ~ **to you** c'est à vous de voir. ○ **up to, up until** *prep* jusqu'à.

up-and-coming *adj* à l'avenir prometteur.

upbringing ['ʌp,brɪŋɪŋ] *n* éducation *f*.

update [,ʌp'deɪt] *vt* mettre à jour.

upheaval [ʌp'hiːvl] *n* bouleversement *m*.

upheld [ʌp'held] *pt & pp* → **uphold**.

uphill [,ʌp'hɪl] **1** *adj* [slope, path] qui monte. ‖ *fig* [task] ardu(e). **2** *adv*: **to go** ~ monter.

uphold [ʌp'həʊld] (*pt & pp* ´**-held**) *vt* [law] maintenir; [decision, system] soutenir.

upholstery [ʌp'həʊlstərɪ] *n* rembourrage *m*; [of car] garniture *f* intérieure.

upkeep ['ʌpkiːp] *n* entretien *m*.

up-market *adj* haut de gamme (*inv*).

upon [ə'pɒn] *prep fml* sur; ~ **hearing the news ...** à ces nouvelles ....

upper ['ʌpər] **1** *adj* supérieur(e). **2** *n* [of shoe] empeigne *f*.

upper class *n*: **the** ~ la haute société. ○ **upper-class** *adj* [accent, person] aristocratique.

upper hand *n*: **to have the** ~ avoir le dessus.

uppermost ['ʌpəməʊst] *adj* le plus haut (la plus haute); **it was** ~ **in his mind** c'était sa préoccupation majeure.

upright [*adj sense 1 & adv* ,ʌp'raɪt, *adj sense 2 & n* 'ʌpraɪt] **1** *adj* [person] droit(e); [structure] vertical(e); [chair] à dossier droit. ‖ *fig* [honest] droit(e). **2** *adv* [stand, sit] droit. **3** *n* montant *m*.

uprising ['ʌp,raɪzɪŋ] *n* soulèvement *m*.

uproar ['ʌprɔːr] *n* (*U*) [commotion] tumulte *m*. ‖ [protest] protestations *fpl*.

uproot [ʌp'ruːt] *vt* & *fig* déraciner.

upset [ʌp'set] (*pt & pp* **upset**) **1** *adj* [distressed] peiné(e), triste; [offended] vexé(e). ‖ MED: **to have an** ~ **stomach** avoir l'estomac dérangé. **2** *vt* [distress] faire de la peine à. ‖ [plan, operation] déranger. ‖ [over-turn] renverser.

upshot ['ʌpʃɒt] *n* résultat *m*.

upside down [,ʌpsaɪd-] **1** *adj* à l'envers. **2** *adv* à l'envers; **to turn sthg** ~ *fig* mettre qqch sens dessus dessous.

upstairs [,ʌp'steəz] **1** *adj* d'en haut, du dessus. **2** *adv* en haut. **3** *n* étage *m*.

upstart ['ʌpstɑːt] *n* parvenu *m*, -e *f*.

upstream [,ʌp'striːm] **1** *adj* d'amont; **to be** ~ **(from)** être en amont (de). **2** *adv* vers l'amont; [swim] contre le courant.

upsurge ['ʌpsɜːdʒ] *n*: ~ **(of/in)** recrudescence *f* (de).

uptake ['ʌpteɪk] *n*: **to be quick on the** ~ saisir vite.

uptight [ʌp'taɪt] *adj inf* tendu(e).

up-to-date *adj* [modern] moderne. ‖ [most recent - news] tout dernier (toute dernière). ‖ [informed]: **to keep** ~ **with** se tenir au courant de.

upturn ['ʌptɜːn] *n*: ~ **(in)** reprise *f* (de).

upward ['ʌpwəd] **1** *adj* [movement] ascendant(e); [look, rise] vers le haut. **2** *adv Am* = **upwards**.

upwards ['ʌpwədz] *adv* vers le haut.

uranium [jʊ'reɪnjəm] *n* uranium *m*.

urban ['ɜːbən] *adj* urbain(e).

urbane [ɜː'beɪn] *adj* courtois(e).

urchin ['ɜːtʃɪn] *n dated* gamin *m*, -e *f*.

Urdu ['ʊəduː] *n* ourdou *m*.

urge [ɜːdʒ] **1** *n* forte envie *f*. **2** *vt* [try to persuade]: **to ~ sb to do sthg** pousser qqn à faire qqch, presser qqn de faire qqch. ‖ [advocate] conseiller.

urgency ['ɜːdʒənsɪ] *n* (*U*) urgence *f*.

urgent ['ɜːdʒənt] *adj* [letter, case, request] urgent(e); [plea, voice, need] pressant(e).

urinal [ˌjʊə'raɪnl] *n* urinoir *m*.

urinate ['jʊərɪneɪt] *vi* uriner.

urine ['jʊərɪn] *n* urine *f*.

urn [ɜːn] *n* [for ashes] urne *f*. ‖ [for tea]: **tea ~** fontaine *f* à thé.

Uruguay ['jʊərəgwaɪ] *n* Uruguay *m*.

us [ʌs] *pers pron* nous; **can you see/hear ~?** vous nous voyez/entendez?; **it's ~** c'est nous; **you can't expect US to do it** vous ne pouvez pas exiger que ce soit nous qui le fassions; **she gave it to ~** elle nous l'a donné; **with/without ~** avec/sans nous; **they are more wealthy than ~** ils sont plus riches que nous; **some of ~** quelques-uns d'entre nous.

US *n abbr of* United States.

USA *n abbr of* United States of America.

usage ['juːzɪdʒ] *n* LING usage *m*. ‖ (*U*) [handling, treatment] traitement *m*.

use [*n & aux vb* juːs, *vt* juːz] **1** *n* [act of using] utilisation *f*, emploi *m*; **to be in ~** être utilisé; **to be out of ~** être hors d'usage; **to make ~ of sthg** utiliser qqch. ‖ [ability to use] usage *m*. ‖ [usefulness]: **to be of ~** être utile; **it's no ~** ça ne sert à rien; **what's the ~ (of doing sthg)?** à quoi bon (faire qqch)? **2** *aux vb*: **I ~d to live in London** avant j'habitais à Londres; **there ~d to be a tree here** (autrefois) il y avait un arbre ici. **3** *vt* [gen] utiliser, se servir de, employer. ‖ *pej* [exploit] se servir de. ○ **use up** *vt sep* [supply] épuiser; [food] finir; [money] dépenser.

used [*senses 1 and 2* juːzd, *sense 3* juːst] *adj* [handkerchief, towel] sale. ‖ [car] d'occasion. ‖ [accustomed]: **to be ~ to sthg/to doing sthg** avoir l'habitude de qqch/de faire qqch; **to get ~ to sthg** s'habituer à qqch.

useful ['juːsfʊl] *adj* utile.

useless ['juːslɪs] *adj* [gen] inutile.

user ['juːzər] *n* [of product, machine] utilisateur *m*, -trice *f*; [of service] usager *m*.

user-friendly *adj* convivial(e), facile à utiliser.

usher ['ʌʃər] **1** *n* placeur *m*. **2** *vt*: **to ~ sb in/out** faire entrer/sortir qqn.

usherette [ˌʌʃə'ret] *n* ouvreuse *f*.

USSR (*abbr of* **Union of Soviet Socialist Republics**) *n*: **the (former) ~** l'(ex-)URSS *f*.

usual ['juːʒəl] *adj* habituel(elle); **as ~** comme d'habitude.

usually ['juːʒəlɪ] *adv* d'habitude, d'ordinaire.

usurp [juː'zɜːp] *vt* usurper.

utensil [juː'tensl] *n* ustensile *m*.

uterus ['juːtərəs] (*pl* **-ri** [-raɪ] OR **-ruses**) *n* utérus *m*.

utility [juː'tɪlətɪ] *n* (*U*) [usefulness] utilité *f*. ‖ [public service] service *m* public. ‖ COMPUT utilitaire *m*.

utility room *n* buanderie *f*.

utilize, -ise ['juːtɪlaɪz] *vt* utiliser; [resources] exploiter, utiliser.

utmost ['ʌtməʊst] **1** *adj* le plus grand (la plus grande). **2** *n*: **to do one's ~** faire tout son possible, faire l'impossible; **to the ~** au plus haut point.

utter ['ʌtər] **1** *adj* total(e), complet(ète). **2** *vt* prononcer; [cry] pousser.

utterly ['ʌtəlɪ] *adv* complètement.

U-turn *n* demi-tour *m*; *fig* revirement *m*.

v¹ (*pl* **v's** OR **vs**), **V** (*pl* **V's** OR **Vs**) [viː] *n* [letter] v *m inv*, V *m inv*.

v² (*abbr of* **vide**) [cross-reference] v. ‖ *abbr of* **versus**. ‖ (*abbr of* **volt**) v.

vacancy ['veɪkənsɪ] *n* [job] poste *m* vacant. ‖ [room available] chambre *f* à louer; **"no vacancies"** «complet».

vacant ['veɪkənt] *adj* [room] inoccupé(e); [chair, toilet] libre. ‖ [job, post] vacant(e). ‖ [look, expression] distrait(e).

vacant lot *n* terrain *m* inoccupé; [for sale] terrain *m* à vendre.

vacate [və'keɪt] *vt* quitter.

vacation [və'keɪʃn] *n Am* vacances *fpl*.

vacationer [və'keɪʃənər] *n Am* vacancier *m*, -ière *f*.

vaccinate ['væksɪneɪt] *vt* vacciner.

vaccine [*Br* 'væksiːn, *Am* væk'siːn] *n* vaccin *m*.

vacuum ['vækjʊəm] **1** *n* TECH & *fig* vide *m*. ‖ [cleaner] aspirateur *m*. **2** *vt* [room] passer l'aspirateur dans; [carpet] passer à l'aspirateur.

vacuum cleaner *n* aspirateur *m*.

vacuum-packed *adj* emballé(e) sous vide.

vagina [və'dʒaɪnə] *n* vagin *m*.

vagrant ['veɪgrənt] *n* vagabond *m*, -e *f*.

vague [veɪg] *adj* [gen] vague, imprécis(e). ‖ [absent-minded] distrait(e).

vaguely ['veɪglɪ] *adr* vaguement.

vain [veɪn] *adj* [futile, worthless] vain(e). ‖ *pej* [conceited] vaniteux(euse). ○ **in vain** *adv* en vain, vainement.

valentine card ['væləntaɪn-] *n* carte *f* de la Saint-Valentin.

Valentine's Day ['væləntaɪnz-] *n*: (St) ~ la Saint-Valentin.

valet ['væleɪ, 'vælɪt] *n* valet *m* de chambre.

valiant ['væljənt] *adj* vaillant(e).

valid ['vælɪd] *adj* [reasonable] valable. ‖ [legally usable] valide.

valley ['vælɪ] (*pl* **valleys**) *n* vallée *f*.

valour *Br*, **valor** *Am* ['vælər] *n* (*U*) *fml* & *literary* bravoure *f*.

valuable ['væljʊəbl] *adj* [advice, time, information] précieux(ieuse). ‖ [object, jewel] de valeur. ○ **valuables** *npl* objets *mpl* de valeur.

valuation [,væljʊ'eɪʃn] *n* (*U*) [pricing] estimation *f*, expertise *f*. ‖ [estimated price] valeur *f* estimée.

value ['væljuː] **1** *n* valeur *f*; **to be good ~** être d'un bon rapport qualité-prix. **2** *vt* [estimate price of] expertiser. ‖ [cherish] apprécier. ○ **values** *npl* [morals] valeurs *fpl*.

value-added tax [-ædɪd-] *n* taxe *f* sur la valeur ajoutée.

valued ['væljuːd] *adj* précieux(ieuse).

valve [vælv] *n* [on tyre] valve *f*; TECH soupape *f*.

van [væn] *n* AUT camionnette *f*.

vandal ['vændl] *n* vandale *mf*.

vandalism ['vændəlɪzm] *n* vandalisme *m*.

vandalize, -ise ['vændəlaɪz] *rt* saccager.

vanguard ['vængɑːd] *n* avant-garde *f*.

vanilla [və'nɪlə] *n* vanille *f*.

vanish ['vænɪʃ] *vi* disparaître.

vanity ['vænətɪ] *n* (*U*) *pej* vanité *f*.

vantagepoint ['vɑːntɪdʒ,pɔɪnt] *n* [for view] bon endroit *m*; *fig* position *f* avantageuse.

vapour *Br*, **vapor** *Am* ['veɪpər] *n* (*U*) vapeur *f*; [condensation] buée *f*.

variable ['veərɪəbl] *adj* variable.

variance ['veərɪəns] *n fml*: **at ~ (with)** en désaccord (avec).

variation [,veərɪ'eɪʃn] *n*: ~ **(in)** variation *f* (de).

varicose veins ['værɪkəʊs-] *npl* varices *fpl*.

varied ['veərɪd] *adj* varié(e).

variety [və'raɪətɪ] *n* [gen] variété *f*. ‖ [type] variété *f*, sorte *f*.

variety show *n* spectacle *m* de variétés.

various ['veərɪəs] *adj* [several] plusieurs. ‖ [different] divers.

varnish ['vɑːnɪʃ] **1** *n* vernis *m*. **2** *vt* vernir.

vary ['veərɪ] **1** *vt* varier. **2** *vi*: **to ~ (in/with)** varier (en/selon), changer (en/selon).

vase [*Br* vɑːz, *Am* veɪz] *n* vase *m*.

Vaseline® ['væsəliːn] *n* vaseline® *f*.

vast [vɑːst] *adj* vaste, immense.

vat [væt] *n* cuve *f*.

VAT [væt, viːeɪ'tiː] (*abbr of* **value added tax**) *n* TVA *f*.

Vatican ['vætɪkən] *n*: **the ~** le Vatican.

vault [vɔːlt] **1** *n* [in bank] chambre *f* forte. ‖ [in church] caveau *m*. **2** *vi*: **to ~ over sthg** sauter (par-dessus) qqch.

VCR (*abbr of* **video cassette recorder**) *n* magnétoscope *m*.

VD *n abbr of* **venereal disease**.

VDU (*abbr of* **visual display unit**) *n* moniteur *m*.

veal [viːl] *n* (*U*) veau *m*.

veer [vɪər] *vi* virer.

vegan ['viːgən] *adj* végétalien(ienne).

vegetable ['vedʒtəbl] **1** *n* légume *m*. **2** *adj* [matter, protein] végétal(e); [soup, casserole] de ou aux légumes.

vegetarian [,vedʒɪ'teərɪən] *adj* végétarien(ienne).

vegetation [,vedʒɪ'teɪʃn] *n* (*U*) végétation *f*.

vehement ['viːəmənt] *adj* véhément(e).

vehicle ['viːəkl] *n lit & fig* véhicule *m*.

veil [veɪl] *n lit & fig* voile *m*.

vein [veɪn] *n* ANAT veine *f*. ‖ [of leaf] nervure *f*. ‖ [of mineral] filon *m*.

velocity [vɪ'lɒsətɪ] *n* vélocité *f*.

velvet ['velvɪt] *n* velours *m*.

vendetta [ven'detə] *n* vendetta *f*.

vending machine ['vendɪŋ-] *n* distributeur *m* automatique.

vendor ['vendɔːʳ] *n* *fml* [salesperson] marchand *m*, -e *f*. || JUR vendeur *m*, -eresse *f*.

veneer [və'nɪəʳ] *n* placage *m*; *fig* apparence *f*.

venereal disease [vɪ'nɪərɪəl-] *n* maladie *f* vénérienne.

venetian blind [vɪ,niːʃn-] *n* store *m* vénitien.

Venezuela [,venɪz'weɪlə] *n* Venezuela *m*.

vengeance ['vendʒəns] *n* vengeance *f*.

venison ['venɪzn] *n* venaison *f*.

venom ['venəm] *n* *lit* & *fig* venin *m*.

vent [vent] **1** *n* [pipe] tuyau *m*; [opening] orifice *m*. **2** *vt* [anger, feelings] donner libre cours à; **to ~ sthg on sb** décharger qqch sur qqn.

ventilate ['ventɪleɪt] *vt* ventiler.

ventilator ['ventɪleɪtəʳ] *n* ventilateur *m*.

ventriloquist [ven'trɪləkwɪst] *n* ventriloque *mf*.

venture ['ventʃəʳ] **1** *n* entreprise *f*. **2** *vt* risquer; **to ~ to do sthg** se permettre de faire qqch. **3** *vi* s'aventurer.

venue ['venjuː] *n* lieu *m*.

veranda(h) [və'rændə] *n* véranda *f*.

verb [vɜːb] *n* verbe *m*.

verbal ['vɜːbl] *adj* verbal(e).

verbatim [vɜː'beɪtɪm] *adj* & *adv* mot pour mot.

verbose [vɜː'bəʊs] *adj* verbeux(euse).

verdict ['vɜːdɪkt] *n* JUR verdict *m*. || [opinion]: **~ (on)** avis *m* (sur).

verge [vɜːdʒ] *n* [of lawn] bordure *f*; [of road] bas-côté *m*, accotement *m*. || [brink]: **on the ~ of sthg** au bord de qqch; **on the ~ of doing sthg** sur le point de faire qqch. ○ **verge (up)on** *vt fus* friser, approcher de.

verify ['verɪfaɪ] *vt* vérifier.

vermin ['vɜːmɪn] *npl* vermine *f*.

vermouth ['vɜːməθ] *n* vermouth *m*.

versa ['vɜːsə] → **vice versa**.

versatile ['vɜːsətaɪl] *adj* [person, player] aux talents multiples; [machine, tool, food] souple d'emploi.

verse [vɜːs] *n* (*U*) [poetry] vers *mpl*. || [stanza] strophe *f*. || [in Bible] verset *m*.

versed [vɜːst] *adj*: **to be well ~ in sthg** être versé(e) dans qqch.

version ['vɜːʃn] *n* version *f*.

versus ['vɜːsəs] *prep* SPORT contre. || [as opposed to] par opposition à.

vertebra ['vɜːtɪbrə] (*pl* **-brae** [-briː]) *n* vertèbre *f*.

vertical ['vɜːtɪkl] *adj* vertical(e).

vertigo ['vɜːtɪgəʊ] *n* (*U*) vertige *m*.

verve [vɜːv] *n* verve *f*.

very ['verɪ] **1** *adv* [as intensifier] très; **~ much** beaucoup. **2** *adj*: **the ~ room/book** la pièce/le livre même; **the ~ man/thing I've been looking for** juste l'homme/la chose que je cherchais; **at the ~ least** tout au moins; **~ last/first** tout dernier/premier; **of one's ~ own** bien à soi. ○ **very well** *adv* très bien; **I can't ~ well tell him ...** je ne peux tout de même pas lui dire que ....

vessel ['vesl] *n* *fml* [boat] vaisseau *m*. || [container] récipient *m*.

vest [vest] *n* *Am* [waistcoat] gilet *m*.

vested interest ['vestɪd-] *n*: **~ (in)** intérêt *m* particulier (à).

vestibule ['vestɪbjuːl] *n* *fml* [entrance hall] vestibule *m*.

vestige ['vestɪdʒ] *n* vestige *m*.

vestry ['vestrɪ] *n* sacristie *f*.

vet [vet] *vt* [candidates] examiner avec soin.

veteran ['vetrən] **1** *adj* [experienced] chevronné(e). **2** *n* MIL ancien combattant *m*, vétéran *m*. || [experienced person] vétéran *m*.

veterinarian [,vetrɪ'neərɪən] *n* *Am* vétérinaire *mf*.

veto ['viːtəʊ] (*pl* **-es**, *pt* & *pp* **-ed**, *cont* **-ing**) **1** *n* veto *m*. **2** *vt* opposer son veto à.

vex [veks] *vt* contrarier.

vexed question [,vekst-] *n* question *f* controversée.

vg (*abbr of* **very good**) tb.

VHF (*abbr of* **very high frequency**) VHF.

VHS (*abbr of* **video home system**) *n* VHS *m*.

via ['vaɪə] *prep* [travelling through] via, par. || [by means of] au moyen de.

viable ['vaɪəbl] *adj* viable.

vibrate [vaɪ'breɪt] *vi* vibrer.

vicar ['vɪkəʳ] *n* [in Church of England] pasteur *m*.

vicarage ['vɪkərɪdʒ] *n* presbytère *m*.

vicarious [vɪ'keərɪəs] *adj*: **to take a ~ pleasure in sthg** retirer du plaisir indirectement de qqch.

vice [vaɪs] *n* [immorality, fault] vice *m*. || [tool] étau *m*.

vice-chairman *n* vice-président *m*, -e *f*.

vice-chancellor *n* UNIV président *m*, -e *f*.

vice-president *n* vice-président *m*, -e *f*.

vice versa [,vaɪs-] *adv* vice versa.

vicinity [vɪ'sɪnɪtɪ] *n*: **in the ~ (of)** aux alentours (de), dans les environs (de).

vicious ['vɪʃəs] *adj* violent(e), brutal(e).

vicious circle *n* cercle *m* vicieux.

victim ['vɪktɪm] *n* victime *f*.

victimize, -ise ['vɪktɪmaɪz] *rt* faire une victime de.

victor ['vɪktər] *n* vainqueur *m*.

victorious [vɪk'tɔ:rɪəs] *adj* victorieux(ieuse).

victory ['vɪktərɪ] *n*: **~ (over)** victoire *f* (sur).

video ['vɪdɪəʊ] (*pl* -s, *pt & pp* -ed, *cont* -ing) **1** *n* [medium, recording] vidéo *f*. || [machine] magnétoscope *m*. **2** *rt* [using video recorder] magnétoscoper. || [using camera] faire une vidéo de, filmer.

video camera *n* caméra *f* vidéo.

video cassette *n* vidéocassette *f*.

video game *n* jeu *m* vidéo.

videorecorder ['vɪdɪəʊrɪ,kɔ:dər] *n* magnétoscope *m*.

video shop *n* vidéoclub *m*.

videotape ['vɪdɪəʊteɪp] *n* [cassette] vidéocassette *f*. || (*U*) [ribbon] bande *f* vidéo.

vie [vaɪ] (*pt & pp* vied, *cont* vying) *ri*: **to ~ for sthg** lutter pour qqch; **to ~ with sb (for sthg/to do sthg)** rivaliser avec qqn (pour qqch/pour faire qqch).

Vienna [vɪ'enə] *n* Vienne.

Vietnam [*Br* ,vjet'næm, *Am* ,vjet'nɑ:m] *n* Viêt-nam *m*.

Vietnamese [,vjetnə'mi:z] **1** *adj* vietnamien(ienne). **2** *n* [language] vietnamien *m*. **3** *npl*: **the ~** les Vietnamiens.

view [vju:] **1** *n* [opinion] opinion *f*, avis *m*; **in my ~** à mon avis. || [scene, ability to see] vue *f*; **to come into ~** apparaître. **2** *rt* [consider] considérer. || [examine - gen] examiner; [- house] visiter. ○ **in view of** *prep* vu, étant donné.

viewer ['vju:ər] *n* TV téléspectateur *m*, - trice *f*. || [for slides] visionneuse *f*.

viewfinder ['vju:,faɪndər] *n* viseur *m*.

viewpoint ['vju:pɔɪnt] *n* point *m* de vue.

vigil ['vɪdʒɪl] *n* veille *f*; RELIG vigile *f*.

vigilante [,vɪdʒɪ'læntɪ] *n* membre *m* d'un groupe d'autodéfense.

vigorous ['vɪgərəs] *adj* vigoureux(euse).

vile [vaɪl] *adj* [mood] massacrant(e), exécrable; [person, act] vil(e), ignoble; [food] infect(e), exécrable.

villa ['vɪlə] *n* villa *f*; [bungalow] pavillon *m*.

village ['vɪlɪdʒ] *n* village *m*.

villager ['vɪlɪdʒər] *n* villageois *m*, -e *f*.

villain ['vɪlən] *n* [of film, book] méchant *m*, -e *f*; [of play] traître *m*. || [criminal] bandit *m*.

vindicate ['vɪndɪkeɪt] *rt* justifier.

vindictive [vɪn'dɪktɪv] *adj* vindicatif(ive).

vine [vaɪn] *n* vigne *f*.

vinegar ['vɪnɪgər] *n* vinaigre *m*.

vineyard ['vɪnjəd] *n* vignoble *m*.

vintage ['vɪntɪdʒ] **1** *adj* [classic] typique. **2** *n* année *f*, millésime *m*.

vintage wine *n* vin *m* de grand cru.

vinyl ['vaɪnɪl] *n* vinyle *m*.

viola [vɪ'əʊlə] *n* alto *m*.

violate ['vaɪəleɪt] *rt* violer.

violence ['vaɪələns] *n* violence *f*.

violent ['vaɪələnt] *adj* [gen] violent(e).

violet ['vaɪələt] **1** *adj* violet(ette). **2** *n* [flower] violette *f*. || [colour] violet *m*.

violin [,vaɪə'lɪn] *n* violon *m*.

violinist [,vaɪə'lɪnɪst] *n* violoniste *mf*.

VIP (*abbr of* **very important person**) *n* VIP *mf*.

viper ['vaɪpər] *n* vipère *f*.

virgin ['vɜ:dʒɪn] **1** *adj literary* [land, forest, soil] vierge. **2** *n* [woman] vierge *f*.

Virgo ['vɜ:gəʊ] (*pl* -s) *n* Vierge *f*.

virile ['vɪraɪl] *adj* viril(e).

virtually ['vɜ:tʃʊəlɪ] *adv* virtuellement, pratiquement.

virtual reality *n* réalité *f* virtuelle.

virtue ['vɜ:tju:] *n* [good quality] vertu *f*. || [benefit]: **~ (in doing sthg)** mérite *m* (à faire qqch).

virtuous ['vɜ:tʃʊəs] *adj* vertueux(euse).

virus ['vaɪrəs] *n* COMPUT & MED virus *m*.

visa ['vi:zə] *n* visa *m*.

vis-à-vis [,vi:za:'vi:] *prep fml* par rapport à.

viscose ['vɪskəʊs] *n* viscose *f*.

visibility [,vɪzɪ'bɪlɪtɪ] *n* visibilité *f*.

visible ['vɪzəbl] *adj* visible.

vision ['vɪʒn] *n* (*U*) [ability to see] vue *f*. || [foresight, dream] vision *f*.

visit ['vɪzɪt] **1** *n* visite *f*. **2** *rt* [person] rendre visite à; [place] visiter.

visiting hours ['vɪzɪtɪŋ-] *npl* heures *fpl* de visite.

visitor ['vɪzɪtər] *n* [to person] invité *m*, -e *f*; [to place] visiteur *m*, -euse *f*.

visitors' book *n* livre *m* d'or; [in hotel] registre *m*.

visor ['vaɪzər] *n* visière *f*.

vista ['vɪstə] *n* [view] vue *f*.

visual ['vɪʒʊəl] *adj* visuel(elle).

visual aids *npl* supports *mpl* visuels.

visual display unit *n* écran *m* de visualisation.

visualize, -ise ['vɪʒʊəlaɪz] *vt* se représenter, s'imaginer.

vital ['vaɪtl] *adj* [essential] essentiel(ielle).

vitally ['vaɪtlɪ] *adv* absolument.

vital statistics *npl* *inf* [of woman] mensurations *fpl*.

vitamin [*Br* 'vɪtəmɪn, *Am* 'vaɪtəmɪn] *n* vitamine *f*.

vivacious [vɪ'veɪʃəs] *adj* enjoué(e).

vivid ['vɪvɪd] *adj* [bright] vif (vive), || [clear - description] vivant(e); [- memory] net (nette), précis(e).

vividly ['vɪvɪdlɪ] *adv* [describe] d'une manière vivante; [remember] clairement.

vixen ['vɪksn] *n* [fox] renarde *f*.

V-neck *n* [neck] décolleté *m* en V; [sweater] pull *m* à décolleté en V.

vocabulary [və'kæbjʊlərɪ] *n* vocabulaire *m*.

vocal ['vəʊkl] *adj* [outspoken] qui se fait entendre. || [of the voice] vocal(e).

vocal cords *npl* cordes *fpl* vocales.

vocation [vəʊ'keɪʃn] *n* vocation *f*.

vocational [vəʊ'keɪʃənl] *adj* professionnel(elle).

vociferous [və'sɪfərəs] *adj* bruyant(e).

vodka ['vɒdkə] *n* vodka *f*.

vogue [vəʊg] *n* vogue *f*, mode *f*; **in ~** en vogue, à la mode.

voice [vɔɪs] **1** *n* [gen] voix *f*. **2** *vt* [opinion, emotion] exprimer.

void [vɔɪd] **1** *adj* [invalid] nul (nulle); → **null**. || *fml* [empty]: **~ of** dépourvu(e) de, dénué(e) de. **2** *n* vide *m*.

volatile [*Br* 'vɒlətaɪl, *Am* 'vɒlətl] *adj* [situation] explosif(ive); [person] lunatique, versatile; [market] instable.

volcano [vɒl'keɪnəʊ] (*pl* **-es** OR **-s**) *n* volcan *m*.

volley ['vɒlɪ] (*pl* **volleys**) **1** *n* [of gunfire] salve *f*. || *fig* [of questions, curses] torrent *m*; [of blows] volée *f*, pluie *f*. || SPORT volée *f*. **2** *vt* frapper à la volée, reprendre de volée.

volleyball ['vɒlɪbɔːl] *n* volley-ball *m*.

volt [vəʊlt] *n* volt *m*.

voltage ['vəʊltɪdʒ] *n* voltage *m*, tension *f*.

volume ['vɒljuːm] *n* [gen] volume *m*. || [of work, letters] quantité *f*; [of traffic] densité *f*.

voluntarily [*Br* 'vɒləntrɪlɪ, *Am* ˌvɒlən'terəlɪ] *adv* volontairement.

voluntary ['vɒləntrɪ] *adj* [not obligatory] volontaire. || [unpaid] bénévole.

volunteer [ˌvɒlən'tɪər] **1** *n* [gen & MIL] volontaire *mf*. || [unpaid worker] bénévole *mf*. **2** *vt* [offer]: **to ~ to do sthg** se proposer OR se porter volontaire pour faire qqch. || [information, advice] donner spontanément. **3** *vi* [offer one's services]: **to ~ (for)** se porter volontaire (pour), proposer ses services (pour). || MIL s'engager comme volontaire.

vomit ['vɒmɪt] **1** *n* vomi *m*. **2** *vi* vomir.

vote [vəʊt] **1** *n* [individual decision]: **~ (for/against)** vote *m* (pour/contre), voix *f* (pour/contre). || [ballot] vote *m*. || [right to vote] droit *m* de vote. **2** *vt* [elect] élire. || [choose]: **to ~ to do sthg** voter OR se prononcer pour faire; **they ~d to return to work** ils ont voté le retour au travail. **3** *vi*: **to ~ (for/against)** voter (pour/contre).

vote of thanks (*pl* **votes of thanks**) *n* discours *m* de remerciement.

voter ['vəʊtər] *n* électeur *m*, -trice *f*.

voting ['vəʊtɪŋ] *n* scrutin *m*.

vouch [vaʊtʃ] ○ **vouch for** *vt fus* répondre de, se porter garant de.

voucher ['vaʊtʃər] *n* bon *m*, coupon *m*.

vow [vaʊ] **1** *n* vœu *m*, serment *m*. **2** *vt*: **to ~ to do sthg** jurer de faire qqch.

vowel ['vaʊəl] *n* voyelle *f*.

voyage ['vɔɪɪdʒ] *n* voyage *m* en mer; [in space] vol *m*.

vs *abbr of* versus.

vulgar ['vʌlgər] *adj* [in bad taste] vulgaire. || [offensive] grossier(ière).

vulnerable ['vʌlnərəbl] *adj* vulnérable; **~ to** [attack] exposé(e) à; [colds] sensible à.

vulture ['vʌltʃər] *n lit & fig* vautour *m*.

w (*pl* **w's** OR **ws**), **W** (*pl* **W's** OR **Ws**) ['dʌblju:] *n* [letter] w *m inv*, W *m inv*. ○ **W** (*abbr of* **west**) O, W. ‖ (*abbr of* **watt**) w.

wad [wɒd] *n* [of cotton wool, paper] tampon *m*. ‖ [of banknotes, documents] liasse *f*.

waddle ['wɒdl] *vi* se dandiner.

wade [weɪd] *vi* patauger. ○ **wade through** *vt fus fig* se taper.

wading pool ['weɪdɪŋ-] *n Am* pataugeoire *f*.

wafer ['weɪfər] *n* [thin biscuit] gaufrette *f*.

waffle ['wɒfl] *n* CULIN gaufre *f*.

waft [wɑːft, wɒft] *vi* flotter.

wag [wæg] **1** *vt* remuer, agiter. **2** *vi* [tail] remuer.

wage [weɪdʒ] **1** *n* salaire *m*, paie *f*, paye *f*. **2** *vt*: **to ~ war against** faire la guerre à. ○ **wages** *npl* salaire *m*.

wage earner [-,ɜːnər] *n* salarié *m*, -e *f*.

wager ['weɪdʒər] *n* pari *m*.

waggle ['wægl] *inf vt* agiter, remuer; [ears] remuer.

wagon ['wægən] *n* [horse-drawn] chariot *m*, charrette *f*. ‖ *Br* RAIL wagon *m*.

wail [weɪl] **1** *n* gémissement *m*. **2** *vi* gémir.

waist [weɪst] *n* taille *f*.

waistcoat ['weɪskəʊt] *n* gilet *m*.

waistline ['weɪstlaɪn] *n* taille *f*.

wait [weɪt] **1** *n* attente *f*. **2** *vi* attendre; **I can't ~ to do sthg** je brûle d'impatience de faire qqch.; **~ and see!** tu vas le voir! ○ **wait for** *vt fus* attendre; **to ~ for sb to do sthg** attendre que qqn fasse qqch. ○ **wait up** *vi* veiller, ne pas se coucher.

waiter ['weɪtər] *n* garçon *m*, serveur *m*.

waiting list ['weɪtɪŋ-] *n* liste *f* d'attente.

waiting room ['weɪtɪŋ-] *n* salle *f* d'attente.

waitress ['weɪtrɪs] *n* serveuse *f*.

waive [weɪv] *vt* [fee] renoncer à; [rule] prévoir une dérogation à.

wake [weɪk] (*pt* **woke** OR **-d**, *pp* **woken** OR **-d**) **1** *n* [of ship] sillage *m*. **2** *vt* réveiller. **3** *vi* se réveiller. ○ **wake up 1** *vt sep* réveiller. **2** *vi* [wake] se réveiller.

waken ['weɪkən] *fml* **1** *vt* réveiller. **2** *vi* se réveiller.

Wales [weɪlz] *n* pays *m* de Galles.

walk [wɔːk] **1** *n* [way of walking] démarche *f*, façon *f* de marcher. ‖ [journey - for pleasure] promenade *f*; [- long distance] marche *f*; **to go for a ~** aller se promener, aller faire une promenade. **2** *vt* [accompany - person] accompagner; [- dog] promener. ‖ [distance] faire à pied. **3** *vi* [gen] marcher. ‖ [for pleasure] se promener. ○ **walk out** *vi* [leave suddenly] partir. ○ **walk out on** *vt fus* quitter.

walker ['wɔːkər] *n* [for pleasure] promeneur *m*, -euse *f*; [long-distance] marcheur *m*, -euse *f*.

walkie-talkie [,wɔːkɪ'tɔːkɪ] *n* talkie-walkie *m*.

walking ['wɔːkɪŋ] *n* (*U*) marche *f* à pied, promenade *f*.

walking shoes *npl* chaussures *fpl* de marche.

walking stick *n* canne *f*.

Walkman® ['wɔːkmən] *n* baladeur *m*, Walkman® *m*.

walkout ['wɔːkaʊt] *n* [strike] grève *f*, débrayage *m*.

walkover ['wɔːk,əʊvər] *n* victoire *f* facile.

walkway ['wɔːkweɪ] *n* passage *m*; [between buildings] passerelle *f*.

wall [wɔːl] *n* [of room, building] mur *m*; [of rock, cave] paroi *f*. ‖ ANAT paroi *f*.

wallchart ['wɔːltʃɑːt] *n* planche *f* murale.

walled [wɔːld] *adj* fortifié(e).

wallet ['wɒlɪt] *n* portefeuille *m*.

wallflower ['wɔːl,flaʊər] *n* [plant] giroflée *f*. ‖ *inf fig* [person]: **to be a ~** faire tapisserie.

wallow ['wɒləʊ] *vi* [in liquid] se vautrer.

wallpaper ['wɔːl,peɪpər] **1** *n* papier *m* peint. **2** *vt* tapisser.

Wall Street *n* Wall Street *m* (*quartier financier de New York*).

walnut ['wɔːlnʌt] *n* [nut] noix *f*. ‖ [tree, wood] noyer *m*.

walrus ['wɔːlrəs] (*pl inv* OR **-es**) *n* morse *m*.

waltz [wɔːls] **1** *n* valse *f*. **2** *vi* [dance] valser, danser la valse.

wand [wɒnd] *n* baguette *f*.

wander ['wɒndə*r*] *vi* [person] errer. || [mind] divaguer; [thoughts] vagabonder.

wane [weɪn] *vi* [influence, interest] diminuer, faiblir. || [moon] décroître.

wangle ['wæŋgl] *vt inf* se débrouiller pour obtenir.

want [wɒnt] **1** *n* [need] besoin *m*. || [lack] manque *m*; **for ~ of** faute de, par manque de. || [deprivation] pauvreté *f*, besoin *m*. **2** *vt* [desire] vouloir; **to ~ to do sthg** vouloir faire qqch; **to ~ sb to do sthg** vouloir que qqn fasse qqch. || *inf* [need] avoir besoin de.

wanted ['wɒntɪd] *adj*: **to be ~ (by the police)** être recherché(e) (par la police).

wanton ['wɒntən] *adj* [destruction, neglect] gratuit(e).

war [wɔː*r*] *n* guerre *f*.

ward [wɔːd] *n* [in hospital] salle *f*. || JUR pupille *mf*. ○ **ward off** *vt fus* [danger] écarter; [disease, blow] éviter; [evil spirits] éloigner.

warden ['wɔːdn] *n* [of park etc] gardien *m*, -ienne *f*. || *Am* [of prison] directeur *m*, -trice *f*.

warder ['wɔːdə*r*] *n* [in prison] gardien *m*, -ienne *f*.

wardrobe ['wɔːdrəub] *n* garde-robe *f*.

warehouse ['weəhaus, *pl* -hauzɪz] *n* entrepôt *m*, magasin *m*.

wares [weəz] *npl* marchandises *fpl*.

warfare ['wɔːfeə*r*] *n* (*U*) guerre *f*.

warhead ['wɔːhed] *n* ogive *f*, tête *f*.

warily ['weərɪlɪ] *adv* avec précaution OR circonspection.

warm [wɔːm] **1** *adj* [gen] chaud(e); **it's ~ today** il fait chaud aujourd'hui. || [friendly] chaleureux(euse). **2** *vt* chauffer. ○ **warm to** *vt fus* [person] se prendre de sympathie pour; [idea, place] se mettre à aimer. ○ **warm up 1** *vt sep* réchauffer. **2** *vi* [person, room] se réchauffer. || [machine, engine] chauffer. || SPORT. s'échauffer.

warm-hearted [-'hɑːtɪd] *adj* chaleureux(euse), affectueux(euse).

warmly ['wɔːmlɪ] *adv* [in warm clothes]: **to dress ~** s'habiller chaudement. || [in a friendly way] chaleureusement.

warmth [wɔːmθ] *n* chaleur *f*.

warn [wɔːn] *vt* avertir, prévenir; **to ~ sb of sthg** avertir qqn de qqch; **to ~ sb not to do sthg** conseiller à qqn de ne pas faire qqch, déconseiller à qqn de faire qqch.

warning ['wɔːnɪŋ] *n* avertissement *m*.

warning light *n* voyant *m*, avertisseur *m* lumineux.

warp [wɔːp] **1** *vt* [wood] gauchir, voiler. || [personality] fausser, pervertir. **2** *vi* [wood] gauchir, se voiler.

warrant ['wɒrənt] **1** *n* JUR mandat *m*. **2** *vt* [justify] justifier. || [guarantee] garantir.

warranty ['wɒrəntɪ] *n* garantie *f*.

warren ['wɒrən] *n* terrier *m*.

warrior ['wɒrɪə*r*] *n* guerrier *m*, -ière *f*.

Warsaw ['wɔːsɔː] *n* Varsovie; **the ~ Pact** le pacte de Varsovie.

warship ['wɔːʃɪp] *n* navire *m* de guerre.

wart [wɔːt] *n* verrue *f*.

wartime ['wɔːtaɪm] *n*: **in ~** en temps de guerre.

wary ['weərɪ] *adj* prudent(e), circonspect(e); **to be ~ of** se méfier de; **to be ~ of doing sthg** hésiter à faire qqch.

was [weak form wəz, strong form wɒz] *pt* → **be**.

wash [wɒʃ] **1** *n* [act] lavage *m*; **to have a ~** se laver. || [from boat] remous *m*. **2** *vt* [clean] laver; **to ~ one's hands** se laver les mains. **3** *vi* se laver. ○ **wash away** *vt sep* emporter. ○ **wash up** *Am* [wash oneself] se laver.

washable ['wɒʃəbl] *adj* lavable.

washbasin *Br* ['wɒʃ,beɪsn], **washbowl** *Am* ['wɒʃbəul] *n* lavabo *m*.

washcloth ['wɒʃ,klɒθ] *n Am* gant *m* de toilette.

washer ['wɒʃə*r*] *n* TECH rondelle *f*. || [washing machine] machine *f* à laver.

washing ['wɒʃɪŋ] *n* (*U*) [action] lessive *f*. || [clothes] linge *m*, lessive *f*.

washing line *n* corde *f* à linge.

washing machine *n* machine *f* à laver.

Washington ['wɒʃɪŋtən] *n* [city]: **~ D.C.** Washington.

washout ['wɒʃaut] *n inf* fiasco *m*.

washroom ['wɒʃrum] *n Am* toilettes *fpl*.

wasn't [wɒznt] = **was not**.

wasp [wɒsp] *n* guêpe *f*.

wastage ['weɪstɪdʒ] *n* gaspillage *m*.

waste [weɪst] **1** *adj* [material] de rebut; [fuel] perdu(e); [area of land] en friche. **2** *n* [misuse] gaspillage *m*; **a ~ of time** une perte de temps. || (*U*) [refuse] déchets *mpl*, ordures *fpl*. **3** *vt* [money, food, energy] gaspiller; [time, opportunity] perdre.

wastebasket *Am* = **wastepaper basket**.

waste disposal unit *n* broyeur *m* d'ordures.

wasteful ['weɪstful] *adj* [person] gaspilleur(euse); [activity] peu économique.

waste ground *n* (*U*) terrain *m* vague.

wastepaper basket [ˌweɪst'peɪpər-], **wastepaper bin** [ˌweɪst'peɪpər-], **wastebasket** *Am* ['weɪstˌbɑːskɪt] *n* corbeille *f* à papier.

watch [wɒtʃ] **1** *n* [timepiece] montre *f*. || [act of watching]: **to keep ~** faire le guet, monter la garde; **to keep ~ on sb/sthg** surveiller qqn/qqch. || [guard] garde *f*; NAUT [shift] quart *m*. **2** *vt* [look at] regarder. || [spy on, guard] surveiller. || [be careful about] faire attention à. **3** *vi* regarder. ○ **watch out** *vi* faire attention, prendre garde.

watchdog ['wɒtʃdɒg] *n* [dog] chien *m* de garde. || *fig* [organization] organisation *f* de contrôle.

watchful ['wɒtʃful] *adj* vigilant(e).

watchmaker ['wɒtʃˌmeɪkər] *n* horloger *m*.

watchman ['wɒtʃmən] (*pl* -men [-mən]) *n* gardien *m*.

water ['wɔːtər] **1** *n* [liquid] eau *f*. **2** *vt* arroser. **3** *vi* [eyes] pleurer, larmoyer. || [mouth]: **my mouth was ~ing** j'en avais l'eau à la bouche. ○ **waters** *npl* [sea] eaux *fpl*. ○ **water down** *vt sep* [dilute] diluer; [alcohol] couper d'eau. || *usu pej* [plan, demand] atténuer, modérer; [play, novel] édulcorer.

water bottle *n* gourde *f*, bidon *m* (à eau).

watercolour ['wɔːtəˌkʌlər] *n* [picture] aquarelle *f*. || [paint] peinture *f* à l'eau, couleur *f* pour aquarelle.

watercress ['wɔːtəkres] *n* cresson *m*.

waterfall ['wɔːtəfɔːl] *n* chute *f* d'eau, cascade *f*.

water heater *n* chauffe-eau *m inv*.

waterhole ['wɔːtəhəul] *n* mare *f*, point *m* d'eau.

watering can ['wɔːtərɪŋ-] *n* arrosoir *m*.

water level *n* niveau *m* de l'eau.

water lily *n* nénuphar *m*.

waterline ['wɔːtəlaɪn] *n* NAUT ligne *f* de flottaison.

waterlogged ['wɔːtəlɒgd] *adj* [land] détrempé(e). || [vessel] plein(e) d'eau.

water main *n* conduite *f* principale d'eau.

watermark ['wɔːtəmɑːk] *n* [in paper] filigrane *m*. || [showing water level] laisse *f*.

watermelon ['wɔːtəˌmelən] *n* pastèque *f*.

water polo *n* water-polo *m*.

waterproof ['wɔːtəpruːf] **1** *adj* imperméable. **2** *n* imperméable *m*.

watershed ['wɔːtəʃed] *n* *fig* [turning point] tournant *m*, moment *m* critique.

water skiing *n* ski *m* nautique.

water tank *n* réservoir *m* d'eau, citerne *f*.

watertight ['wɔːtətaɪt] *adj* [waterproof] étanche. || *fig* [excuse, contract] parfait(e); [plan] infaillible.

waterway ['wɔːtəweɪ] *n* voie *f* navigable.

waterworks ['wɔːtəwɜːks] (*pl inv*) *n* [building] installation *f* hydraulique, usine *f* de distribution d'eau.

watt [wɒt] *n* watt *m*.

wave [weɪv] **1** *n* [of hand] geste *m*, signe *m*. || [of water, emotion, nausea] vague *f*. || [of light, sound] onde *f*; [of heat] bouffée *f*. || [in hair] cran *m*, ondulation *f*. **2** *vt* [arm, handkerchief] agiter; [flag, stick] brandir. **3** *vi* [with hand] faire signe de la main; **to ~ at** OR **to sb** faire signe à qqn, saluer qqn de la main. || [flags, trees] flotter.

wavelength ['weɪvleŋθ] *n* longueur *f* d'ondes; **to be on the same ~** *fig* être sur la même longueur d'ondes.

waver ['weɪvər] *vi* [falter] vaciller, chanceler. || [hesitate] hésiter, vaciller. || [fluctuate] fluctuer, varier.

wavy ['weɪvɪ] *adj* [hair] ondulé(e); [line] onduleux(euse).

wax [wæks] **1** *n* (*U*) [in candles, polish] cire *f*. || [in ears] cérumen *m*. **2** *vt* cirer. **3** *vi* [moon] croître.

wax paper *n Am* papier *m* sulfurisé.

waxworks ['wæksˌwɜːks] (*pl inv*) *n* [museum] musée *m* de cire.

way [weɪ] **1** *n* [means, method] façon *f*; **to get** OR **have one's ~** obtenir ce qu'on veut. || [manner, style] façon *f*, manière *f*; **in the same ~** de la même manière OR façon; **this/that ~** comme ça, de cette façon; **in a ~** d'une certaine manière, en quelque sorte. || [route, path] chemin *m*; **~ in** entrée *f*; **~ out** sortie *f*; **on the** OR **one's ~** sur le OR son chemin; **to get under ~** [ship] se mettre en route; *fig* [meeting] démarrer; **to be in the ~** gêner; **to go out of one's ~** to do sthg se donner du mal pour faire qqch; **to keep out of sb's ~** éviter qqn; **keep out of the ~!** restez à l'écart!; **to make ~ for** faire place à. || [direction]: **to go/look/come this ~** aller/regarder/venir par ici; **the right/wrong ~ round** [in sequence] dans le bon/mauvais ordre; **she had her hat on the wrong ~ round** elle avait mis son chapeau à l'envers; **the right/wrong ~ up** dans le bon/mauvais sens. || [distance]: **all the ~** tout le trajet; *fig* [support etc] jusqu'au bout; **a long ~** loin. || *phr*: **to give ~** [under weight, pressure] céder; **no ~! pas question!** 2 *adv inf* [a lot] largement; **~ better** bien mieux. ○ **ways** *npl* [customs, habits] coutumes *fpl*. ○ **by the way** *adv* au fait.

waylay [ˌweɪˈleɪ] (*pt & pp* **-laid** [-ˈleɪd]) *vt* arrêter (au passage).

wayward [ˈweɪwəd] *adj* qui n'en fait qu'à sa tête; [behaviour] capricieux(ieuse).

WC (*abbr of* water closet) *n* W.-C. *mpl*.

we [wiː] *pers pron* nous; WE **can't do it** nous, nous ne pouvons pas le faire; **as ~ say in France** comme on dit en France; **~ British** nous autres Britanniques.

weak [wiːk] *adj* [gen] faible. || [delicate] fragile. || [unconvincing] peu convaincant(e). || [drink] léger(ère).

weaken [ˈwiːkn] 1 *vt* [undermine] affaiblir. || [reduce] diminuer. || [physically - person] affaiblir; [- structure] fragiliser. 2 *vi* faiblir.

weakling [ˈwiːklɪŋ] *n pej* mauviette *f*.

weakness [ˈwiːknɪs] *n* (U) [physical - of person] faiblesse *f*; [- of structure] fragilité *f*. || [imperfect point] point *m* faible, faiblesse *f*.

wealth [welθ] *n* (U) [riches] richesse *f*. || [abundance]: **a ~ of** une profusion de.

wealthy [ˈwelθɪ] *adj* riche.

wean [wiːn] *vt* [baby, lamb] sevrer.

weapon [ˈwepən] *n* arme *f*.

wear [weəʳ] (*pt* wore, *pp* worn) 1 *n* (U) [type of clothes] tenue *f*. || [damage] usure *f*; **~ and tear** usure. || [use]: **these shoes have had a lot of ~** ces chaussures ont fait beaucoup d'usage. 2 *vt* [clothes, hair] porter. || [damage] user. 3 *vi* [deteriorate] s'user. || [last]: **to ~ well** durer longtemps, faire de l'usage. ○ **wear away** 1 *vt sep* [rock, wood] user; [grass] abîmer. 2 *vi* [rock, wood] s'user; [grass] s'abîmer. ○ **wear down** *vt sep* [material] user. || [person, resistance] épuiser. ○ **wear off** *vi* disparaître. ○ **wear out** 1 *vt sep* [shoes, clothes] user. || [person] épuiser. 2 *vi* s'user.

weary [ˈwɪərɪ] *adj* [exhausted] las (lasse); [sigh] de lassitude. || [fed up]: **to be ~ of sthg/of doing sthg** être las de qqch/de faire qqch.

weasel [ˈwiːzl] *n* belette *f*.

weather [ˈweðəʳ] 1 *n* temps *m*; **to be under the ~** être patraque. 2 *vt* [crisis, problem] surmonter.

weather-beaten [-ˌbiːtn] *adj* [face, skin] tanné(e).

weathercock [ˈweðəkɒk] *n* girouette *f*.

weather forecast *n* météo *f*, prévisions *fpl* météorologiques.

weatherman [ˈweðəmæn] (*pl* -men [-men]) *n* météorologue *m*.

weather vane [-veɪn] *n* girouette *f*.

weave [wiːv] (*pt* wove, *pp* woven) 1 *vt* [using loom] tisser. 2 *vi* [move] se faufiler.

weaver [ˈwiːvəʳ] *n* tisserand *m*, -e *f*.

web [web] *n* [cobweb] toile *f* (d'araignée). || *fig* [of lies] tissu *m*.

wed [wed] (*pt & pp* wed OR -ded) *literary* 1 *vt* épouser. 2 *vi* se marier.

we'd [wiːd] = we had, we would.

wedding [ˈwedɪŋ] *n* mariage *m*.

wedding anniversary *n* anniversaire *m* de mariage.

wedding cake *n* pièce *f* montée.

wedding dress *n* robe *f* de mariée.

wedding ring *n* alliance *f*.

wedge [wedʒ] 1 *n* [for steadying] cale *f*. || [for splitting] coin *m*. || [of cake, cheese] morceau *m*. 2 *vt* caler.

Wednesday [ˈwenzdɪ] *n* mercredi *m*; *see also* Saturday.

wee [wiː] 1 *adj* Scot petit(e). 2 *n v inf* pipi *m*. 3 *vi v inf* faire pipi.

weed [wiːd] 1 *n* [plant] mauvaise herbe *f*. 2 *vt* désherber.

weedkiller [ˈwiːdˌkɪləʳ] *n* désherbant *m*.

week [wiːk] *n* semaine *f*.

weekday [ˈwiːkdeɪ] *n* jour *m* de semaine.

weekend [ˌwiːkˈend] *n* week-end *m*; **on** OR **at the ~** le week-end.

weekly [ˈwiːklɪ] 1 *adj* hebdomadaire. 2 *adv* chaque semaine. 3 *n* hebdomadaire *m*.

weep [wiːp] (*pt & pp* wept) *vt & vi* pleurer.

weeping willow [ˌwiːpɪŋ-] *n* saule *m* pleureur.

weigh [weɪ] *vt* [gen] peser. || NAUT: **to ~ anchor** lever l'ancre. ○ **weigh down** *vt sep* [physically]: **to be ~ed down with sthg** plier sous le poids de qqch. || [mentally]: **to be ~ed down by** OR **with sthg** être accablé par qqch. ○ **weigh up** *vt sep* [consider carefully] examiner. || [size up] juger, évaluer.

weight [weɪt] *n lit & fig* poids *m*; **to put on** OR **gain ~** prendre du poids. grossir; **to lose ~** perdre du poids. maigrir; **to pull one's ~** faire sa part du travail. participer à la tâche.

weighted ['weɪtɪd] *adj*: **to be ~ in favour of/against** être favorable/défavorable à.

weighting ['weɪtɪŋ] *n* indemnité *f*.

weightlifting ['weɪt,lɪftɪŋ] *n* haltérophilie *f*.

weighty ['weɪtɪ] *adj* [serious] important(e), de poids.

weir [wɪər] *n* barrage *m*.

weird [wɪəd] *adj* bizarre.

welcome ['welkəm] 1 *adj* [guest, help etc] bienvenu(e). || [free]: **you're ~ to ...** n'hésitez pas à .... || [in reply to thanks]: **you're ~** il n'y a pas de quoi. de rien. 2 *n* accueil *m*. 3 *vt* [receive] accueillir. || [approve of] se réjouir de. 4 *excl* bienvenue!

weld [weld] 1 *n* soudure *f*. 2 *vt* souder.

welfare ['welfeər] 1 *adj* social(e). 2 *n* [well-being] bien-être *m*. || *Am* [income support] assistance *f* publique.

welfare state *n* État-providence *m*.

well [wel] (*compar* **better**, *superl* **best**) 1 *adj* bien; **I'm very ~, thanks** je vais très bien. merci; **just as ~** aussi bien. 2 *adv* bien; **to go ~** aller bien; **~ done!** bravo!; **~ and truly** bel et bien. 3 *n* [for water, oil] puits *m*. 4 *excl* [in hesitation] heu!, eh bien! || [to correct oneself] bon!, enfin! || [to express resignation]: **oh ~!** eh bien! || [in surprise] tiens! ○ **as well** *adv* [in addition] aussi, également. || [with same result]: **I/you** *etc* **may** OR **might as ~ (do sthg)** je/tu *etc* ferais aussi bien (de faire qqch). ○ **as well as** *conj* en plus de, aussi bien que. ○ **well up** *vi*: **tears ~ed up in her eyes** les larmes lui montaient aux yeux.

we'll [wiːl] = **we shall**, **we will**.

well-advised [-əd'vaɪzd] *adj* sage; **you would be ~ to do sthg** tu ferais bien de faire qqch.

well-behaved [-bɪ'heɪvd] *adj* sage.

wellbeing [,wel'biːɪŋ] *n* bien-être *m*.

well-built *adj* bien bâti(e).

well-done *adj* CULIN bien cuit(e).

well-dressed [-'drest] *adj* bien habillé(e).

well-earned [-ɜːnd] *adj* bien mérité(e).

well-heeled [-hiːld] *adj inf* nanti(e).

wellington boots ['welɪŋtən-], **wellingtons** ['welɪŋtənz] *npl* bottes *fpl* de caoutchouc.

well-kept *adj* [building, garden] bien tenu(e). || [secret] bien gardé(e).

well-known *adj* bien connu(e).

well-mannered [-'mænəd] *adj* bien élevé(e).

well-meaning *adj* bien intentionné(e).

well-nigh [-naɪ] *adv* presque, pratiquement.

well-off *adj* [rich] riche. || [well-provided]: **to be ~ for sthg** être bien pourvu(e) en qqch.

well-read [-'red] *adj* cultivé(e).

well-rounded [-'raundɪd] *adj* [education, background] complet(ète).

well-timed [-'taɪmd] *adj* bien calculé(e), qui vient à point nommé.

well-to-do *adj* riche.

wellwisher ['wel,wɪʃər] *n* admirateur *m*, -trice *f*.

Welsh [welʃ] 1 *adj* gallois(e). 2 *n* [language] gallois *m*. 3 *npl*: **the ~** les Gallois *mpl*.

Welshman ['welʃmən] (*pl* **-men** [-mən]) *n* Gallois *m*.

Welshwoman ['welʃ,wumən] (*pl* **-women** [-,wɪmɪn]) *n* Galloise *f*.

went [went] *pt* → **go**.

wept [wept] *pt & pp* → **weep**.

were [wɜːr] → **be**.

we're [wɪər] = **we are**.

weren't [wɜːnt] = **were not**.

west [west] 1 *n* [direction] ouest *m*. || [region]: **the ~** l'ouest *m*. 2 *adj* ouest (*inv*); [wind] d'ouest. 3 *adv* de l'ouest, vers l'ouest; **~ of** à l'ouest de. ○ **West** POL: **the West** l'Occident *m*.

West Bank *n*: **the ~** la Cisjordanie.

westerly ['westəlɪ] *adj* à l'ouest; [wind] de l'ouest; **in a ~ direction** vers l'ouest.

western ['westən] 1 *adj* [gen] de l'ouest. || POL occidental(e). 2 *n* [book, film] western *m*.

West German 1 *adj* ouest-allemand(e). 2 *n* Allemand *m*, -e *f* de l'Ouest.

West Germany *n*: **(former) ~** (ex-)Allemagne *f* de l'Ouest.

West Indian 1 *adj* antillais(e). 2 *n* Antillais *m*, -e *f*.

West Indies [-'ɪndiːz] *npl*: **the ~** les Antilles *fpl*.

westward ['westwəd] *adj & adv* vers l'ouest.

westwards ['westwədz] *adv* vers l'ouest.

wet [wet] (*pt & pp* **wet** OR **-ted**) 1 *adj* [damp, soaked] mouillé(e). || [rainy] pluvieux(ieuse). || [not dry - paint, cement] frais (fraîche). 2 *n* *inf* POL modéré *m*, -e *f*. 3 *vt* mouiller.

wet blanket *n* *inf* *pej* rabat-joie *m* *inv*.

wet suit *n* combinaison *f* de plongée.

we've [wiːv] = **we have**.

whack [wæk] *inf* *vt* donner un grand coup à, frapper fort.

whale [weɪl] *n* baleine *f*.

wharf [wɔːf] (*pl* **-s** OR **wharves** [wɔːvz]) *n* quai *m*.

what [wɒt] 1 *adj* (*in direct, indirect questions*) quel (quelle), quels (quelles) (*pl*); **~ colour is it?** c'est de quelle couleur? || (*in exclamations*) quel (quelle), quels (quelles) (*pl*); **~ a surprise!** quelle surprise!; **~ an idiot I am!** ce que je peux être bête! 2 *pron* (*interrogative - subject*) qu'est-ce qui; (- *object*) qu'est-ce que, que; (- *after prep*) quoi; **~ are they doing?** qu'est-ce qu'ils font?, que font-ils?; **~ is going on?** qu'est-ce qui se passe?; **~ are they talking about?** de quoi parlent-ils?; **~ about the rest of us?** et nous alors?; **~ if ...?** et si ...? || (*relative - subject*) ce qui; (- *object*) ce que; **I saw ~ happened/fell** j'ai vu ce qui s'était passé/était tombé; **you can't have ~ you want** tu ne peux pas avoir ce que tu veux. 3 *excl* [expressing disbelief] comment!, quoi!

whatever [wɒt'evər] 1 *adj* quel (quelle) que soit; **any book ~** n'importe quel livre; **no chance ~** pas la moindre chance; **nothing ~** rien du tout. 2 *pron* quoi que (+ *subjunctive*); **I'll do ~ I can** je ferai tout ce que je peux; **~ can this be?** qu'est-ce que cela peut-il bien être?; **~ that may mean** quoi que cela puisse bien vouloir dire; **or ~** ou n'importe quoi d'autre.

whatsoever [ˌwɒtsəu'evər] *adj*: **I had no interest ~** je n'éprouvais pas le moindre intérêt; **nothing ~** rien du tout.

wheat [wiːt] *n* blé *m*.

wheedle ['wiːdl] *vt*: **to ~ sb into doing sthg** enjôler qqn pour qu'il fasse qqch; **to ~ sthg out of sb** enjôler qqn pour obtenir qqch.

wheel [wiːl] 1 *n* [gen] roue *f*. || [steering wheel] volant *m*. 2 *vt* pousser. 3 *vi*: **to ~ (round)** se retourner brusquement.

wheelbarrow ['wiːlˌbærəu] *n* brouette *f*.

wheelchair ['wiːlˌtʃeər] *n* fauteuil *m* roulant.

wheelclamp ['wiːlˌklæmp] 1 *n* sabot *m* de Denver. 2 *vt*: **my car was ~ed** on a mis un sabot à ma voiture.

wheeze [wiːz] 1 *n* [sound] respiration *f* sifflante. 2 *vi* respirer avec un bruit sifflant.

whelk [welk] *n* bulot *m*, buccin *m*.

when [wen] 1 *adv* (*in direct, indirect questions*) quand; **~ does the plane arrive?** quand OR à quelle heure arrive l'avion? 2 *conj* [referring to time] quand, lorsque; **he came to see me ~ I was abroad** il est venu me voir quand j'étais à l'étranger; **one day ~ I was on my own** un jour que OR où j'étais tout seul. || [whereas, considering that] alors que.

whenever [wen'evər] 1 *conj* quand; [each time that] chaque fois que. 2 *adv* n'importe quand.

where [weər] 1 *adv* (*in direct, indirect questions*) où; **do you know ~ he lives?** est-ce que vous savez où il habite? 2 *conj* [referring to place, situation] où; **this is ~ ...** c'est là que .... || [whereas] alors que.

whereabouts [*adv* ˌweərə'bauts, *n* 'weərəbauts] 1 *adv* où. 2 *npl*: **their ~ are still unknown** on ne sait toujours pas où ils se trouvent.

whereas [weər'æz] *conj* alors que.

whereby [weə'baɪ] *conj* *fml* par lequel (laquelle), au moyen duquel (de laquelle).

whereupon [ˌweərə'pɒn] *conj* *fml* après quoi, sur quoi.

wherever [weər'evər] 1 *conj* où que (+ *subjunctive*). 2 *adv* [no matter where] n'importe où. || [where] où donc.

wherewithal ['weəwɪðɔːl] *n* *fml*: **to have the ~ to do sthg** avoir les moyens de faire qqch.

whet [wet] *vt*: **to ~ sb's appetite for sthg** donner à qqn envie de qqch.

whether ['weðər] *conj* [indicating choice, doubt] si. || [no matter if]: **~ I want to or not** que je le veuille ou non.

which [wɪtʃ] 1 *adj* (*in direct, indirect questions*) quel (quelle), quels (quelles) (*pl*); **~ house is yours?** quelle maison est la tienne?; **~ one?** lequel (laquelle)? || [to refer back to sthg]: **in ~ case** auquel cas. 2 *pron* (*in direct, indirect questions*) lequel (laquelle), lesquels (lesquelles) (*pl*); **~ do you prefer?** lequel préférez-vous? || (*in relative clauses - subject*) qui; (- *object*) que; (- *after prep*) lequel (laquelle), lesquels (lesquelles) (*pl*); **take the slice ~ is nearer to you** prends la tranche qui est le plus près de toi; **the television ~ we bought** le téléviseur que nous avons acheté; **the settee on ~ I am sitting** le canapé sur lequel je suis assis; **the film of ~ you spoke** le film dont vous avez parlé. ‖ (*referring back - subject*) ce qui; (*- object*) ce que; **why did you say you were ill, ~ nobody believed?** pourquoi as-tu dit que tu étais malade, ce que personne n'a cru?

whichever [wɪtʃ'evər] **1** *adj* quel (quelle) que soit; **choose ~ colour you prefer** choisissez la couleur que vous préférez, n'importe laquelle. **2** *pron* n'importe lequel (laquelle).

whiff [wɪf] *n* [of perfume, smoke] bouffée *f*; [of food] odeur *f*.

while [waɪl] **1** *n* moment *m*; **let's stay here for a ~** restons ici un moment; **for a long ~** longtemps; **after a ~** après quelque temps. **2** *conj* [during the time that] pendant que. ‖ [as long as] tant que. ‖ [whereas] alors que. ○ **while away** *vt sep* passer.

whilst [waɪlst] *conj* = while.

whim [wɪm] *n* lubie *f*.

whimper ['wɪmpər] *vt & vi* gémir.

whimsical ['wɪmzɪkl] *adj* saugrenu(e).

whine [waɪn] *vi* [make sound] gémir.

whip [wɪp] **1** *n* [for hitting] fouet *m*. **2** *vt* [gen] fouetter. ‖ [take quickly]: **to ~ sthg out** sortir qqch brusquement; **to ~ sthg off** ôter OR enlever qqch brusquement.

whipped cream [wɪpt-] *n* crème *f* fouettée.

whirl [wɜːl] **1** *n lit & fig* tourbillon *m*. **2** *vt*: **to ~ sb/sthg round** [spin round] faire tourbillonner qqn/qqch. **3** *vi* tourbillonner; *fig* [head, mind] tourner.

whirlpool ['wɜːlpuːl] *n* tourbillon *m*.

whirlwind ['wɜːlwɪnd] *n* tornade *f*.

whirr [wɜːr] *vi* [engine] ronronner.

whisk [wɪsk] **1** *n* CULIN fouet *m*, batteur *m* (à œufs). **2** *vt* [move quickly] emmener OR emporter rapidement. ‖ CULIN battre.

whisker ['wɪskər] *n* moustache *f*. ○ **whiskers** *npl* favoris *mpl*.

whisky *Br*, **whiskey** *Am & Irish* (*pl* whiskeys) ['wɪskɪ] *n* whisky *m*.

whisper ['wɪspər] **1** *vt* murmurer, chuchoter. **2** *vi* chuchoter.

whistle ['wɪsl] **1** *n* [sound] sifflement *m*. ‖ [device] sifflet *m*. **2** *vt & vi* siffler.

white [waɪt] **1** *adj* [in colour] blanc (blanche). ‖ [coffee, tea] au lait. **2** *n* [colour, of egg, eye] blanc *m*. ‖ [person] Blanc *m*, Blanche *f*.

white-collar *adj* de bureau.

white elephant *n fig* objet *m* coûteux et inutile.

white-hot *adj* chauffé(e) à blanc.

White House *n*: **the ~** la Maison-Blanche.

white lie *n* pieux mensonge *m*.

whiteness ['waɪtnɪs] *n* blancheur *f*.

white paper *n* POL livre *m* blanc.

white sauce *n* sauce *f* blanche.

whitewash ['waɪtwɒʃ] **1** *n* (U) [paint] chaux *f*. ‖ *pej* [cover-up]: **a government ~** une opération du gouvernement pour étouffer l'affaire. **2** *vt* [paint] blanchir à la chaux.

whiting ['waɪtɪŋ] (*pl inv* OR **-s**) *n* merlan *m*.

Whitsun ['wɪtsn] *n* Pentecôte *f*.

whittle ['wɪtl] *vt* [reduce]: **to ~ away** OR **down** réduire qqch.

whiz, whizz [wɪz] *vi* [go fast] aller à toute allure.

whiz(z) kid *n inf* petit prodige *m*.

who [huː] *pron* (*in direct, indirect questions*) qui; **~ are you?** qui êtes-vous?; **I didn't know ~ she was** je ne savais pas qui c'était. ‖ (*in relative clauses*) qui; **he's the doctor ~ treated me** c'est le médecin qui m'a soigné.

who'd [huːd] = who had, who would.

whodu(n)nit [ˌhuːˈdʌnɪt] *n inf* polar *m*.

whoever [huːˈevər] *pron* [unknown person] quiconque. ‖ [indicating surprise, astonishment] qui donc. ‖ [no matter who] qui que (+ *subjunctive*); **~ you are** qui que vous soyez; **~ wins** qui que ce soit qui gagne.

whole [həʊl] **1** *adj* [entire, complete] entier(ière). ‖ [for emphasis]: **a ~ lot bigger** bien plus gros; **a ~ new idea** une idée tout à fait nouvelle. **2** *n* [all]: **the ~ of the school** toute l'école; **the ~ of the summer** tout l'été. ‖ [unit, complete thing] tout *m*. ○ **as a whole** *adv* dans son ensemble. ○ **on the whole** *adv* dans l'ensemble.

whole-hearted [-ˈhɑːtɪd] *adj* sans réserve, total(e).

wholemeal ['həʊlmiːl] *Br*, **whole wheat** *Am adj* complet(ète).

wholesale ['həʊlseɪl] **1** *adj* [buying, selling] en gros; [price] de gros. ‖ *pej* [excessive] en masse. **2** *adv* [in bulk] en gros. ‖ *pej* [excessively] en masse.

wholesaler ['həʊlˌseɪlər] *n* marchand *m* de gros, grossiste *mf*.

wholesome ['həʊlsəm] *adj* sain(e).

whole wheat *Am* = wholemeal.

who'll [hu:l] = who will.

wholly ['həʊlɪ] *adv* totalement.

whom [hu:m] *pron fml* (*in direct, indirect questions*) qui; ~ **did you phone?** qui avez-vous appelé au téléphone?; **for/of/to** ~ pour/de/à qui. || (*in relative clauses*) que; **the girl** ~ **he married** la jeune fille qu'il a épousée; **the man of** ~ **you speak** l'homme dont vous parlez; **the man to** ~ **you were speaking** l'homme à qui vous parliez.

whooping cough ['hu:pɪŋ-] *n* coqueluche *f*.

whopping ['wɒpɪŋ] *inf* **1** *adj* énorme. **2** *adv*: **a** ~ **great lorry/lie** un camion/mensonge absolument énorme.

whore [hɔ:r] *n offensive* putain *f*.

who're ['hu:ər] = who are.

whose [hu:z] **1** *pron* (*in direct, indirect questions*) à qui; ~ **is this?** à qui est ceci? || (*in relative clauses*) dont; **that's the boy** ~ **father's an MP** c'est le garçon dont le père est député; **the girl** ~ **mother you phoned yesterday** la fille à la mère de qui oʀ de laquelle tu as téléphoné hier. **2** *adj* à qui; ~ **car is that?** à qui est cette voiture?; ~ **son is he?** de qui est-il le fils?

who's who [hu:z-] *n* [book] bottin *m* mondain.

who've [hu:v] = who have.

why [waɪ] **1** *adv* (*in direct questions*) pourquoi; ~ **did you lie to me?** pourquoi m'as-tu menti?; ~ **not?** pourquoi pas? **2** *conj* pourquoi; **I don't know** ~ **he said that** je ne sais pas pourquoi il a dit cela. **3** *pron*: **there are several reasons** ~ **he left** il est parti pour plusieurs raisons, les raisons pour lesquelles il est parti sont nombreuses; **I don't know the reason** ~ je ne sais pas pourquoi. **4** *excl* tiens! ○ **why ever** *adv* pourquoi donc.

wick [wɪk] *n* [of candle, lighter] mèche *f*.

wicked ['wɪkɪd] *adj* [evil] mauvais(e). || [mischievous, devilish] malicieux(ieuse).

wicker ['wɪkər] *adj* en osier.

wickerwork ['wɪkəwɜ:k] *n* vannerie *f*.

wide [waɪd] **1** *adj* [gen] large; **how** ~ **is the room?** quelle est la largeur de la pièce?; **to be six metres** ~ faire six mètres de large oʀ de largeur. || [gap, difference] grand(e). || [experience, knowledge, issue] vaste. **2** *adv* [broadly] largement; **open** ~! ouvrez grand! || [off-target]: **the shot went** ~ le coup est passé loin du but oʀ à côté.

wide-angle lens *n* PHOT objectif *m* grand angle.

wide-awake *adj* tout à fait réveillé(e).

widely ['waɪdlɪ] *adv* [smile, vary] largement. || [extensively] beaucoup; **it is** ~ **believed that ...** beaucoup pensent que ..., nombreux sont ceux qui pensent que ....

widen ['waɪdn] *vt* [make broader] élargir. || [gap, difference] agrandir, élargir.

wide open *adj* grand ouvert (grande ouverte).

wide-ranging [-'reɪndʒɪŋ] *adj* varié(e); [consequences] de grande envergure.

widespread ['waɪdspred] *adj* très répandu(e).

widow ['wɪdəʊ] *n* veuve *f*.

widowed ['wɪdəʊd] *adj* veuf (veuve).

widower ['wɪdəʊər] *n* veuf *m*.

width [wɪdθ] *n* largeur *f*; **in** ~ de large.

wield [wi:ld] *vt* [weapon] manier. || [power] exercer.

wife [waɪf] (*pl* **wives**) *n* femme *f*, épouse *f*.

wig [wɪg] *n* perruque *f*.

wiggle ['wɪgl] *inf vt* remuer.

wild [waɪld] *adj* [animal, attack, scenery, flower] sauvage. || [weather, sea] déchaîné(e). || [laughter, hope, plan] fou (folle). || [random - estimate] fantaisiste; **I made a** ~ **guess** j'ai dit ça au hasard. ○ **wilds** *npl*: **the** ~**s** of le fin fond de; **to live in the** ~**s** habiter en pleine nature.

wilderness ['wɪldənɪs] *n* étendue *f* sauvage.

wild-goose chase *n inf*: **it turned out to be a** ~ ça s'est révélé être totalement inutile.

wildlife ['waɪldlaɪf] *n* (*U*) faune *f* et flore *f*.

wildly ['waɪldlɪ] *adv* [enthusiastically, fanatically] frénétiquement. || [guess, suggest] au hasard. || [very - different, impractical] tout à fait.

wilful *Br*, **willful** *Am* ['wɪlfʊl] *adj* [determined] obstiné(e). || [deliberate] délibéré(e).

will[1] [wɪl] **1** *n* [mental] volonté *f*; **against one's** ~ contre son gré. || [document] testament *m*. **2** *vt*: **to** ~ **sthg to happen** prier de toutes ses forces pour que qqch se passe; **to** ~ **sb to do sthg** concentrer toute sa volonté sur qqn pour qu'il fasse qqch.

will[2] [wɪl] *modal vb* (*to express future tense*): **I** ~ **see you next week** je te verrai la semaine prochaine; **when** ~ **you have finished it?** quand est-ce que vous l'aurez fini?; ~ **you be here next week?** — **yes I** ~/**no I won't** est-ce que tu seras là la semaine prochaine? — oui/non. ‖ [indicating willingness]: **~ you have some more tea?** voulez-vous encore du thé?; **I won't do it** je refuse de le faire, je ne veux pas le faire. ‖ [in commands, requests]: **you ~ leave this house at once** tu vas quitter cette maison tout de suite; **close that window, ~ you?** ferme cette fenêtre, veux-tu?! ‖ **~ you be quiet!** veux-tu te taire!, tu vas te taire! ‖ [indicating possibility, what usually happens]: **the hall ~ hold up to 1000 people** la salle peut abriter jusqu'à 1000 personnes. ‖ [expressing an assumption]: **that'll be your father** cela doit être ton père. ‖ [indicating irritation]: **she ~ keep phoning me** elle n'arrête pas de me téléphoner.

willful Am = **wilful**.

willing ['wılıŋ] adj [prepared]: **to be ~ to do sthg** être disposé(e) or prêt(e) à faire qqch. ‖ [eager] enthousiaste.

willingly ['wılıŋlı] adv volontiers.

willow (tree) ['wıləʊ-] n saule m.

willpower ['wıl,paʊər] n volonté f.

willy-nilly [,wılı'nılı] adv [at random] n'importe comment. ‖ [wanting to or not] bon gré mal gré.

wilt [wılt] vi [plant] se faner; fig [person] dépérir.

wily ['waılı] adj rusé(e).

wimp [wımp] n pej inf mauviette f.

win [wın] (pt & pp **won**) **1** n victoire f. **2** vt [game, prize, competition] gagner. ‖ [support, approval] obtenir; [love, friendship] gagner. **3** vi gagner. ○ **win over**, **win round** vt sep convaincre, gagner à sa cause.

wince [wıns] vi: **to ~ (at/with)** [with body] tressaillir (à/de); [with face] grimacer (à/de).

winch [wıntʃ] n treuil m.

wind¹ [wınd] **1** n METEOR vent m. ‖ [breath] souffle m. ‖ (U) [in stomach] gaz mpl. **2** vt [knock breath out of] couper le souffle à.

wind² [waınd] (pt & pp **wound**) **1** vt [string, thread] enrouler. ‖ [clock] remonter. **2** vi [river, road] serpenter. ○ **wind down 1** vt sep [car window] baisser. ‖ [business] cesser graduellement. **2** vi [relax] se détendre. ○ **wind up** vt sep [finish - meeting] clôturer; [- business] liquider. ‖ [clock, car window] remonter. ‖ inf [end up]: **to ~ up doing sthg** finir par faire qqch.

windfall ['wındfɔ:l] n [unexpected gift] aubaine f.

winding ['waındıŋ] adj sinueux(euse).

wind instrument [wınd-] n instrument m à vent.

windmill ['wındmıl] n moulin m à vent.

window ['wındəʊ] n [gen & COMPUT] fenêtre f. ‖ [pane of glass, in car] vitre f. ‖ [of shop] vitrine f.

window box n jardinière f.

window cleaner n laveur m, -euse f de vitres.

window ledge n rebord m de fenêtre.

window pane n vitre f.

windowsill ['wındəʊsıl] n [outside] rebord m de fenêtre; [inside] appui m de fenêtre.

windpipe ['wındpaıp] n trachée f.

windscreen Br ['wındskri:n], **windshield** Am ['wındʃi:ld] n pare-brise m inv.

windscreen washer n lave-glace m.

windscreen wiper [-,waıpər] n essuie-glace m.

windshield Am = **windscreen**.

windsurfing ['wınd,sɜ:fıŋ] n: **to go ~** faire de la planche à voile.

windswept ['wındswept] adj [scenery] balayé(e) par les vents.

windy ['wındı] adj venteux(euse); **it's ~** il fait du vent.

wine [waın] n vin m.

wine cellar n cave f (à vin).

wineglass ['waınglɑ:s] n verre m à vin.

wine list n carte f des vins.

wine tasting [-,teıstıŋ] n dégustation f (de vins).

wine waiter n sommelier m.

wing [wıŋ] n aile f. ○ **wings** npl THEATRE: **the ~s** les coulisses fpl.

wink [wıŋk] **1** n clin m d'œil. **2** vi [with eyes]: **to ~ (at sb)** faire un clin d'œil (à qqn).

winkle ['wıŋkl] n bigorneau m. ○ **winkle out** vt sep extirper; **to ~ sthg out of sb** arracher qqch à qqn.

winner ['wınər] n [person] gagnant m, -e f.

winning ['wınıŋ] adj [victorious, successful] gagnant(e). ○ **winnings** npl gains mpl.

winning post n poteau m d'arrivée.

winter ['wıntər] **1** n hiver m; **in ~** en hiver. **2** comp d'hiver.

winter sports npl sports mpl d'hiver.

wintertime ['wıntətaım] n (U) hiver m.

wint(e)ry ['wıntrı] adj d'hiver.

wobble

wipe [waip] **1** *n*: to give sthg a ~ essuyer qqch, donner un coup de torchon à qqch. **2** *vt* essuyer. ○ **wipe out** *vt sep* [erase] effacer. || [eradicate] anéantir. ○ **wipe up** *vt sep & vi* essuyer.

wire ['waiə^r] **1** *n* (*U*) [metal] fil *m* de fer. || [cable etc] fil *m*. || [telegram] télégramme *m*. **2** *vt* [ELEC - plug] installer; [- house] faire l'installation électrique de. || [send telegram to] télégraphier à.

wireless ['waiəlis] *n dated* T.S.F. *f*.

wiring ['waiəriŋ] *n* (*U*) installation *f* électrique.

wiry ['waiəri] *adj* [hair] crépu(e). || [body, man] noueux(euse).

wisdom ['wizdəm] *n* sagesse *f*.

wisdom tooth *n* dent *f* de sagesse.

wise [waiz] *adj* sage.

wisecrack ['waizkræk] *n pej* vanne *f*.

wish [wiʃ] **1** *n* [desire] souhait *m*, désir *m*. || [magic request] vœu *m*. **2** *vt* [want]: to ~ to do sthg souhaiter faire qqch; I ~ (that) he'd come j'aimerais bien qu'il vienne; I ~ I could si seulement je pouvais. || [expressing hope]: to ~ sb sthg souhaiter qqch à qqn. **3** *vi* [by magic]: to ~ for sthg souhaiter qqch. ○ **wishes** *npl*: best ~es meilleurs vœux; (with) best ~es [at end of letter] bien amicalement.

wishful thinking [,wiʃful-] *n*: that's just ~ c'est prendre mes/ses *etc* désirs pour des réalités.

wisp [wisp] *n* [tuft] mèche *f*. || [small cloud] mince filet *m* OR volute *f*.

wistful ['wistful] *adj* nostalgique.

wit [wit] *n* [humour] esprit *m*. || [intelligence]: to have the ~ to do sthg avoir l'intelligence de faire qqch. ○ **wits** *npl*: to have OR keep one's ~s about one être attentif(ive) OR sur ses gardes.

witch [witʃ] *n* sorcière *f*.

with [wið] *prep* [in company of] avec; we stayed ~ them for a week nous avons passé une semaine chez eux. || [indicating opposition] avec; the war ~ Germany la guerre avec OR contre l'Allemagne. || [indicating means, manner, feelings] avec; I washed it ~ detergent je l'ai lavé avec un détergent; she was trembling ~ fright elle tremblait de peur. || [having] avec; a man ~ a beard un homme avec une barbe, un barbu; the man ~ the moustache l'homme à la moustache. || [regarding]: he's very mean ~ money il est très près de ses sous, il est très avare; the trouble ~ her is that ... l'ennui avec elle OR ce qu'il y a avec elle c'est que .... ||

[indicating simultaneity]: I can't do it ~ you watching me je ne peux pas le faire quand OR pendant que tu me regardes. || [because of]: ~ my luck, I'll probably lose avec ma chance habituelle, je suis sûr de perdre. || *phr*: I'm ~ you [I understand] je vous suis; [I'm on your side] je suis des vôtres; [I agree] je suis d'accord avec vous.

withdraw [wið'drɔː] (*pt* -drew, *pp* -drawn) **1** *vt fml* [remove]: to ~ sthg (from) enlever qqch (de). || [money, troops, remark] retirer. **2** *vi fml* [leave]: to ~ (from) se retirer (de). || MIL se replier; to ~ from évacuer. || [quit, give up]: to ~ (from) se retirer (de).

withdrawal [wið'drɔːəl] *n* [gen]: ~ (from) retrait *m* (de). || MIL repli *m*.

withdrawal symptoms *npl* crise *f* de manque.

withdrawn [wið'drɔːn] **1** *pp* → withdraw. **2** *adj* [shy, quiet] renfermé(e).

withdrew [wið'druː] *pt* → withdraw.

wither ['wiðə^r] *vi* [dry up] se flétrir. || [weaken] mourir.

withhold [wið'həʊld] (*pt & pp* -held [-'held]) *vt* [services] refuser; [information] cacher; [salary] retenir.

within [wi'ðin] **1** *prep* [inside] à l'intérieur de, dans; ~ her en elle, à l'intérieur d'elle-même. || [budget, comprehension] dans les limites de; [limits] dans. || [less than - distance] à moins de; [- time] d'ici, en moins de; ~ the week avant la fin de la semaine. **2** *adv* à l'intérieur.

without [wið'aut] **1** *prep* sans; I left ~ seeing him je suis parti sans l'avoir vu; I left ~ him seeing me je suis parti sans qu'il m'ait vu; to go ~ sthg se passer de qqch. **2** *adv*: to go OR do ~ s'en passer.

withstand [wið'stænd] (*pt & pp* -stood [-'stud]) *vt* résister à.

witness ['witnis] **1** *n* [gen] témoin *m*. || [testimony]: to bear ~ to sthg témoigner de qqch. **2** *vt* [accident, crime] être témoin de. || *fig* [changes, rise in birth rate] assister à. || [countersign] contresigner.

witness box *Br*, **witness stand** *Am n* barre *f* des témoins.

witticism ['witisizm] *n* mot *m* d'esprit.

witty ['witi] *adj* plein(e) d'esprit, spirituel(elle).

wives [waivz] *pl* → wife.

wizard ['wizəd] *n* magicien *m*.

wobble ['wɒbl] *vi* [hand, wings] trembler; [chair, table] branler.

woe [wəʊ] *n literary* malheur *m*.

woke [wəʊk] *pt* → **wake**.

woken [ˈwəʊkn] *pp* → **wake**.

wolf [wʊlf] (*pl* **wolves**) *n* [animal] loup *m*.

woman [ˈwʊmən] (*pl* **women**) **1** *n* femme *f*. **2** *comp*: **~ doctor** femme *f* médecin; **~ teacher** professeur *m* femme.

womanly [ˈwʊmənlɪ] *adj* féminin(e).

womb [wuːm] *n* utérus *m*.

women [ˈwɪmɪn] *pl* → **woman**.

women's liberation *n* libération *f* de la femme.

won [wʌn] *pt & pp* → **win**.

wonder [ˈwʌndər] **1** *n* (*U*) [amazement] étonnement *m*. || [cause for surprise]: **it's a ~ (that) ...** c'est un miracle que ...; **it's no OR little OR small ~ (that) ...** il n'est pas étonnant que .... || [amazing thing, person] merveille *f*. **2** *vt* [speculate]: **to ~ (if OR whether)** se demander (si). || [in polite requests]: **I ~ whether you would mind shutting the window?** est-ce que cela ne vous ennuierait pas de fermer la fenêtre? **3** *vi* [speculate] se demander; **to ~ about sthg** s'interroger sur qqch.

wonderful [ˈwʌndəful] *adj* merveilleux(euse).

wonderfully [ˈwʌndəfulɪ] *adv* [very well] merveilleusement, à merveille. || [for emphasis] extrêmement.

won't [wəʊnt] = **will not**.

woo [wuː] *vt literary* [court] courtiser. || [try to win over] chercher à rallier (à soi OR à sa cause).

wood [wʊd] **1** *n* bois *m*. **2** *comp* en bois. ○ **woods** *npl* bois *mpl*.

wooden [ˈwʊdn] *adj* [of wood] en bois. || *pej* [actor] gauche.

woodpecker [ˈwʊd.pekər] *n* pivert *m*.

woodwind [ˈwʊdwɪnd] *n*: **the ~** les bois *mpl*.

woodwork [ˈwʊdwɜːk] *n* menuiserie *f*.

woodworm [ˈwʊdwɜːm] *n* ver *m* du bois.

wool [wʊl] *n* laine *f*.

woollen *Br*, **woolen** *Am* [ˈwʊlən] *adj* en laine, de laine. ○ **woollens** *npl* lainages *mpl*.

woolly [ˈwʊlɪ] *adj* [woollen] en laine, de laine. || *inf* [idea, thinking] confus(e).

word [wɜːd] **1** *n* LING mot *m*; **too stupid for ~s** vraiment trop bête; **~ for ~** [repeat, copy] mot pour mot; [translate] mot à mot; **in other ~s** en d'autres OR termes; **to have a ~ (with sb)** parler (à qqn). || (*U*) [news] nouvelles *fpl*. || [promise] parole *f*; **to give sb one's ~** donner sa parole à qqn. **2** *vt* [letter, reply] rédiger.

wording [ˈwɜːdɪŋ] *n* (*U*) termes *mpl*.

word processing *n* (*U*) COMPUT traitement *m* de texte.

word processor [-ˌprəʊsesər] *n* COMPUT machine *f* à traitement de texte.

wore [wɔːr] *pt* → **wear**.

work [wɜːk] **1** *n* (*U*) [employment] travail *m*, emploi *m*; **out of ~** sans emploi, au chômage; **at ~** au travail. || [activity, tasks] travail *m*. || ART & LITERATURE œuvre *f*. **2** *vt* [person, staff] faire travailler. || [machine] faire marcher. || [wood, metal, land] travailler. **3** *vi* [do a job] travailler; **to ~ on sthg** travailler à qqch. || [function] marcher, fonctionner. || [succeed] marcher. || [become]: **to ~ loose** se desserrer. ○ **works 1** *n* [factory] usine *f*. **2** *npl* [mechanism] mécanisme *m*. || [digging, building] travaux *mpl*. ○ **work on** *vt fus* [pay attention to] travailler à. || [take as basis] se baser sur. ○ **work out 1** *vt sep* [plan, schedule] mettre au point. || [total, answer] trouver. **2** *vi* [figure, total]: **to ~ out at** se monter à. || [turn out] se dérouler. || [be successful] (bien) marcher. || [train, exercise] s'entraîner. ○ **work up** *vt sep* [generate]: **to ~ up an appetite** s'ouvrir l'appétit; **to ~ up enthusiasm** s'enthousiasmer.

workable [ˈwɜːkəbl] *adj* [plan] réalisable; [system] fonctionnel(elle).

workaholic [ˌwɜːkəˈhɒlɪk] *n* bourreau *m* de travail.

workday [ˈwɜːkdeɪ] *n* [not weekend] jour *m* ouvrable.

worked up [ˌwɜːkt-] *adj* dans tous ses états.

worker [ˈwɜːkər] *n* travailleur *m*, -euse *f*, ouvrier *m*, -ière *f*.

workforce [ˈwɜːkfɔːs] *n* main *f* d'œuvre.

working [ˈwɜːkɪŋ] *adj* [in operation] qui marche. || [having employment] qui travaille. || [conditions, clothes, hours] de travail. ○ **workings** *npl* [of system, machine] mécanisme *m*.

working class *n*: **the ~** la classe ouvrière. ○ **working-class** *adj* ouvrier(ière).

working order *n*: **in ~** en état de marche.

workload [ˈwɜːkləʊd] *n* quantité *f* de travail.

workman [ˈwɜːkmən] (*pl* **-men** [-mən]) *n* ouvrier *m*.

wrap

workmanship ['wɜːkmənʃɪp] n (U) travail m.

workmate ['wɜːkmeɪt] n camarade mf OR collègue mf de travail.

work permit [-ˌpɜːmɪt] n permis m de travail.

workplace ['wɜːkpleɪs] n lieu m de travail.

workshop ['wɜːkʃɒp] n atelier m.

workstation ['wɜːkˌsteɪʃn] n COMPUT poste m de travail.

world [wɜːld] 1 n [gen] monde m. || loc: to think the ~ of sb admirer qqn énormément, ne jurer que par qqn; a ~ of difference une énorme différence. 2 comp [power] mondial(e); [language] universel(elle); [tour] du monde.

world-class adj de niveau international.

world-famous adj de renommée mondiale.

worldly ['wɜːldlɪ] adj de ce monde, matériel(ielle).

World War I n la Première Guerre mondiale.

World War II n la Deuxième Guerre mondiale.

worldwide ['wɜːldwaɪd] 1 adj mondial(e). 2 adv dans le monde entier.

worm [wɜːm] n [animal] ver m.

worn [wɔːn] 1 pp → wear. 2 adj [threadbare] usé(e). || [tired] las (lasse).

worn-out adj [old, threadbare] usé(e). || [tired] épuisé(e).

worried ['wʌrɪd] adj soucieux(ieuse), inquiet(iète).

worry ['wʌrɪ] 1 n [feeling] souci m. || [problem] souci m, ennui m. 2 vt inquiéter, tracasser. 3 vi s'inquiéter; to ~ about se faire du souci au sujet de.

worrying ['wʌrɪɪŋ] adj inquiétant(e).

worse [wɜːs] 1 adj [not as good] pire; to get ~ [situation] empirer. || [more ill]: he's ~ today il va plus mal aujourd'hui. 2 adv plus mal; they're even ~ off c'est encore pire pour eux; ~ off [financially] plus pauvre. 3 n pire m; for the ~ pour le pire.

worsen ['wɜːsn] vt & vi empirer.

worship ['wɜːʃɪp] 1 vt adorer. 2 n (U) RELIG culte m. || [adoration] adoration f. ○ **Worship** n: Your/Her/His Worship Votre/Son Honneur m.

worst [wɜːst] 1 adj: the ~ le pire (la pire), le plus mauvais (la plus mauvaise). 2 adv le plus mal; the ~ affected area la zone la plus touchée. 3 n: the ~ le

pire; if the ~ comes to the ~ au pire. ○ **at (the) worst** adv au pire.

worth [wɜːθ] 1 prep [in value]: to be ~ sthg valoir qqch; how much is it ~? combien cela vaut-il? || [deserving of]: it's ~ a visit cela vaut une visite; to be ~ doing sthg valoir la peine de faire qqch. 2 n valeur f; a week's/£20 ~ of groceries pour une semaine/20 livres d'épicerie.

worthless ['wɜːθlɪs] adj [object] sans valeur, qui ne vaut rien. || [person] qui n'est bon à rien.

worthwhile [ˌwɜːθ'waɪl] adj [job, visit] qui en vaut la peine; [charity] louable.

worthy ['wɜːðɪ] adj [deserving of respect] digne. || [deserving]: to be ~ of sthg mériter qqch. || pej [good but unexciting] méritant(e).

would [wʊd] modal vb (in reported speech): she said she ~ come elle a dit qu'elle viendrait. || [indicating likelihood]: what ~ you do? que ferais-tu?; what ~ you have done? qu'aurais-tu fait? || [indicating willingness]: she ~n't go elle ne voulait pas y aller; he ~ do anything for her il ferait n'importe quoi pour elle. || (in polite questions): ~ you like a drink? voulez-vous OR voudriez-vous à boire?; ~ you mind closing the window? cela vous ennuierait de fermer la fenêtre? || [indicating inevitability]: he ~ say that j'étais sûr qu'il allait dire ça, ça ne m'étonne pas de lui. || [giving advice]: I ~ report it if I were you si j'étais vous je préviendrais les autorités. || [expressing opinions]: I ~ prefer je préférerais; I ~ have thought (that) ... j'aurais pensé que .... || [indicating habit]: he ~ smoke a cigar after dinner il fumait un cigare après le dîner.

would-be adj prétendu(e).

wouldn't ['wʊdnt] = would not.

would've ['wʊdəv] = would have.

wound¹ [wuːnd] 1 n blessure f. 2 vt blesser.

wound² [waʊnd] pt & pp → wind².

wove [wəʊv] pt → weave.

woven ['wəʊvn] pp → weave.

WP n (abbr of word processing, word processor) TTX m.

wrangle ['ræŋgl] 1 n dispute f. 2 vi: to ~ (with sb over sthg) se disputer (avec qqn à propos de qqch).

wrap [ræp] 1 vt [cover in paper, cloth]: to ~ sthg (in) envelopper OR emballer qqch (dans); to ~ sthg around OR round sthg enrouler qqch autour de qqch. 2 n [garment] châle *m*. ○ **wrap up 1** *vt sep* [cover in paper or cloth] envelopper, emballer. **2** *vi* [put warm clothes on]: **~ up well** OR **warmly! couvrez-vous bien!**

wrapper ['ræpər] *n* papier *m*.

wrapping ['ræpɪŋ] *n* emballage *m*.

wrapping paper *n* (*U*) papier *m* d'emballage.

wrath [rɒθ] *n* (*U*) *literary* courroux *m*.

wreak [riːk] *vt* [destruction, havoc] entraîner.

wreath [riːθ] *n* couronne *f*.

wreck [rek] **1** *n* [car, plane, ship] épave *f*. || *inf* [person] loque *f*. **2** *vt* [destroy] détruire. || NAUT: **to be ~ed** s'échouer. || [spoil - holiday] gâcher; [- health, hopes, plan] ruiner.

wreckage ['rekɪdʒ] *n* (*U*) débris *mpl*.

wren [ren] *n* roitelet *m*.

wrench [rentʃ] **1** *n* [tool] clef *f* anglaise. **2** *vt* [pull violently] tirer violemment; **to ~ sthg off** arracher qqch. || [arm, leg, knee] se tordre.

wrestle ['resl] *vi* [fight]: **to ~ (with sb)** lutter (contre qqn). || *fig* [struggle]: **to ~ with sthg** se débattre OR lutter contre qqch.

wrestler ['reslər] *n* lutteur *m*, -euse *f*.

wrestling ['reslɪŋ] *n* lutte *f*.

wretched ['retʃɪd] *adj* [miserable] misérable. || *inf* [damned] fichu(e).

wriggle ['rɪgl] *vi* remuer, se tortiller.

wring [rɪŋ] (*pt* & *pp* **wrung**) *vt* [washing] essorer, tordre.

wrinkle ['rɪŋkl] **1** *n* [on skin] ride *f*. || [in cloth] pli *m*. **2** *vt* plisser. **3** *vi* se plisser, faire des plis.

wrist [rɪst] *n* poignet *m*.

wristwatch ['rɪstwɒtʃ] *n* montre-bracelet *f*.

writ [rɪt] *n* acte *m* judiciaire.

write [raɪt] (*pt* **wrote**, *pp* **written**) **1** *vt* [gen & COMPUT] écrire. || *Am* [person] écrire à. || [cheque, prescription] faire. **2** *vi* [gen & COMPUT] écrire. ○ **write back** *vi* répondre. ○ **write down** *vt sep* écrire, noter. ○ **write off** *vt sep* [project] considérer comme fichu. || [debt, investment] passer aux profits et pertes. || [person] considérer comme fini. ○ **write up** *vt sep* [notes] mettre au propre.

write-off *n* [vehicle]: **to be a ~** être complètement démoli(e).

writer ['raɪtər] *n* [as profession] écrivain *m*. || [of letter, article, story] auteur *m*.

writhe [raɪð] *vi* se tordre.

writing ['raɪtɪŋ] *n* (*U*) [handwriting, activity] écriture *f*; **in ~** par écrit. || [something written] écrit *m*.

writing paper *n* (*U*) papier *m* à lettres.

written ['rɪtn] **1** *pp* → **write**. **2** *adj* écrit(e).

wrong [rɒŋ] **1** *adj* [not normal, not satisfactory] qui ne va pas; **what's ~?** qu'est-ce qui ne va pas?; **there's something ~ with the switch** l'interrupteur ne marche pas bien. || [not suitable] qui ne convient pas. || [not correct - answer, address] faux (fausse), mauvais(e); [- decision] mauvais; **to be ~** [person] avoir tort; **to be ~ to do sthg** avoir tort de faire qqch. || [morally bad]: **it's ~ to ...** c'est mal de .... **2** *adv* [incorrectly] mal; **to get sthg ~** se tromper à propos de qqch; **to go ~** [make a mistake] se tromper, faire une erreur; [stop functioning] se détraquer. **3** *n* mal *m*; **to be in the ~** être dans son tort. **4** *vt* faire du tort à.

wrongful ['rɒŋful] *adj* [unfair] injuste; [arrest, dismissal] injustifié(e).

wrongly ['rɒŋlɪ] *adv* [unsuitably] mal. || [mistakenly] à tort.

wrong number *n* faux numéro *m*.

wrote [rəʊt] *pt* → **write**.

wrought iron [rɔːt-] *n* fer *m* forgé.

wrung [rʌŋ] *pt* & *pp* → **wring**.

wry [raɪ] *adj* [amused - smile, look] amusé(e); [- humour] ironique. || [displeased] désabusé(e).

x (*pl* **x's** OR **xs**), **X** (*pl* **X's** OR **Xs**) [eks] *n* [letter] x *m inv*, X *m inv*. || [unknown thing] x *m inv*. || [to mark place] croix *f*. || [at end of letter]: **XXX** grosses bises.

xenophobia [ˌzenə'fəʊbjə] *n* xénophobie *f*.

Xmas ['eksməs] *n* Noël *m*.

X-ray 1 *n* [ray] rayon *m* X. || [picture] radiographie *f*, radio *f*. **2** *vt* radiographier.

xylophone ['zaɪləfəʊn] *n* xylophone *m*.

y (*pl* y's OR ys), **Y** (*pl* Y's OR Ys) [waɪ] *n* [letter] y *m inv*, Y *m inv*.

yacht [jɒt] *n* yacht *m*.

yachting ['jɒtɪŋ] *n* yachting *m*.

yachtsman ['jɒtsmən] (*pl* -men [-mən]) *n* yachtman *m*.

Yank [jæŋk] *n Br inf terme péjoratif désignant un Américain*, Amerloque *mf*.

yap [jæp] *vi* [dog] japper.

yard [jɑːd] *n* [unit of measurement] = 91,44 cm, yard *m*. ‖ [walled area] cour *f*. ‖ [area of work] chantier *m*. ‖ *Am* [attached to house] jardin *m*.

yardstick ['jɑːdstɪk] *n* mesure *f*.

yarn [jɑːn] *n* [thread] fil *m*.

yawn [jɔːn] **1** *n* [when tired] bâillement *m*. **2** *vi* [when tired] bâiller.

yd *abbr of* **yard**.

yeah [jeə] *adv inf* ouais.

year [jɪər] *n* [calendar year] année *f*; **all (the) ~ round** toute l'année. ‖ [period of 12 months] année *f*, an *m*; **to be 21 ~s old** avoir 21 ans. ‖ [financial year] année *f*; **the ~ 1992-93** l'exercice 1992-93. ○ **years** *npl* [long time] années *fpl*.

yearly ['jɪəlɪ] **1** *adj* annuel(elle). **2** *adv* [once a year] annuellement. ‖ [every year] chaque année; **twice ~** deux fois par an.

yearn [jɜːn] *vi*: **to ~ for sthg/to do sthg** aspirer à qqch/à faire qqch.

yearning ['jɜːnɪŋ] *n*: **~ (for sb/sthg)** désir *m* ardent (pour qqn/de qqch).

yeast [jiːst] *n* levure *f*.

yell [jel] **1** *n* hurlement *m*. **2** *vi* & *vt* hurler.

yellow ['jeləʊ] **1** *adj* [colour] jaune. **2** *n* jaune *m*.

yes [jes] **1** *adv* [gen] oui. ‖ [expressing disagreement] si. **2** *n* oui *m inv*.

yesterday ['jestədɪ] **1** *n* hier *m*; **the day before ~** avant-hier. **2** *adv* hier.

yet [jet] **1** *adv* [gen] encore; **~ faster** encore plus vite; **not ~** pas encore; **~ again** encore une fois; **as ~** jusqu'ici. ‖ déjà;

have they finished ~? est-ce qu'ils ont déjà fini? **2** *conj* et cependant, mais.

yew [juː] *n* if *m*.

yield [jiːld] **1** *n* rendement *m*. **2** *vt* [produce] produire. ‖ [give up] céder. **3** *vi* [gen]: **to ~ (to)** céder (à). ‖ *Am* AUT [give way]: "**~**" «cédez le passage».

YMCA (*abbr of* **Young Men's Christian Association**) *n* union chrétienne de jeunes gens (*proposant notamment des services d'hébergement*).

yoga ['jəʊgə] *n* yoga *m*.

yoghourt, **yoghurt**, **yogurt** [*Br* 'jɒgət, *Am* 'jəʊgərt] *n* yaourt *m*.

yoke [jəʊk] *n lit & fig* joug *m*.

yolk [jəʊk] *n* jaune *m* (d'œuf).

you [juː] *pers pron* (*subject - sg*) tu; (*- polite form, pl*) vous; **~'re a good cook** tu es/vous êtes bonne cuisinière; **are ~ French?** tu es/vous êtes français?; **~ French?** tu es/vous êtes français?; **~ French** vous autres Français; **~ idiot!** espèce d'idiot!; **if I were** OR **was ~** si j'étais toi/vous, à ta/votre place; **there ~ are** [you've appeared] te/vous voilà; [have this] voilà, tiens/tenez; **that jacket really isn't ~** cette veste n'est pas vraiment ton/votre style. ‖ (*object - unstressed, sg*) te; (*- polite form, pl*) vous; **I can see ~** je te/vous vois; **I gave it to ~** je te/vous l'ai donné. ‖ (*object - stressed, sg*) toi; (*- polite form, pl*) vous; **I don't expect YOU to do it** je n'exige pas que ce soit toi qui le fasses/vous qui le fassiez. ‖ (*after prep, in comparisons etc, sg*) toi; (*- polite form, pl*) vous; **we shall go without ~** nous irons sans toi/vous; **I'm shorter than ~** je suis plus petit que toi/vous. ‖ [anyone, one] on; **~ have to be careful** on doit faire attention; **exercise is good for ~** l'exercice est bon pour la santé.

you'd [juːd] = **you had**, **you would**.

you'll [juːl] = **you will**.

young [jʌŋ] **1** *adj* jeune. **2** *npl* [young people]: **the ~** les jeunes *mpl*. ‖ [baby animals] les petits *mpl*.

younger ['jʌŋgər] *adj* plus jeune.

youngster ['jʌŋstər] *n* jeune *m*.

your [jɔːr] *poss adj* (*referring to one person*) ton (ta), tes (*pl*); (*polite form, pl*) votre, vos (*pl*); **~ dog** ton/votre chien; **~ house** ta/votre maison; **~ children** tes/vos enfants; **what's ~ name?** comment t'appelles-tu/vous appelez-vous?; **it wasn't YOUR fault** ce n'était pas de ta faute à toi/de votre faute à vous. ‖ (*impersonal - one's*) son (sa), ses (*pl*); **~ attitude changes as you get older** on

attitude changes as you get older on change sa manière de voir en vieillissant; **it's good for ~ teeth/hair** c'est bon pour les dents/les cheveux; **~ average Englishman** l'Anglais moyen.

you're [jɔːr] = you are.

yours [jɔːz] *poss pron* (*referring to one person*) le tien (la tienne), les tiens (les tiennes) (*pl*); (*polite form, pl*) le vôtre (la vôtre), les vôtres (*pl*); **that desk is ~** ce bureau est à toi/à vous, ce bureau est le tien/le vôtre; **it wasn't her fault, it was** YOURS ce n'était pas de sa faute, c'était de ta faute à toi/de votre faute à vous; **a friend of ~** un ami à toi/vous, un de tes/vos amis. ○ **Yours** *adv* (in-letter) → **sincerely**.

yourself [jɔːˈself] (*pl* -selves [-ˈselvz]) *pron* (*reflexive - sg*) te; (- *polite form, pl*) vous; (*after preposition - sg*) toi; (- *polite form, pl*) vous. || (*for emphasis - sg*) toi-même; (- *polite form*) vous-même; (- *pl*) vous-mêmes; **did you do it ~?** tu l'as/vous l'avez fait tout seul?

youth [juːθ] *n* (*U*) [period, quality] jeunesse *f*. || [young man] jeune homme *m*. || (*U*) [young people] jeunesse *f*, jeunes *mpl*.

youth club *n* centre *m* de jeunes.

youthful [ˈjuːθfʊl] *adj* [eager, innocent] de jeunesse, juvénile. || [young] jeune.

youth hostel *n* auberge *f* de jeunesse.

you've [juːv] = you have.

Yugoslav = Yugoslavian.

Yugoslavia [ˌjuːgəˈslɑːvɪə] *n* Yougoslavie *f*.

Yugoslavian [ˌjuːgəˈslɑːvɪən], **Yugoslav** [ˌjuːgəˈslɑːv] **1** *adj* yougoslave. **2** *n* Yougoslave *mf*.

yuppie, yuppy [ˈjʌpɪ] *n inf* yuppie *mf*.

YWCA (*abbr of* **Young Women's Christian Association**) *n* union chrétienne de jeunes filles (*proposant notamment des services d'hébergement*).

z (*pl* z's OR zs), **Z** (*pl* Z's OR Zs) [*Br* zed, *Am* ziː] *n* [letter] z *m inv*, Z *m inv*.

zany [ˈzeɪnɪ] *adj inf* dingue.

zeal [ziːl] *n* zèle *m*.

zealous [ˈzeləs] *adj* zélé(e).

zebra [*Br* ˈzebrə, *Am* ˈziːbrə] (*pl inv* OR -s) *n* zèbre *m*.

zenith [*Br* ˈzenɪθ, *Am* ˈziːnəθ] *n lit & fig* zénith *m*.

zero [*Br* ˈzɪərəʊ, *Am* ˈziːrəʊ] (*pl inv* OR -es) **1** *adj* zéro, aucun(e). **2** *n* zéro *m*.

zest [zest] *n* (*U*) [excitement] piquant *m*. || [eagerness] entrain *m*. || [of orange, lemon] zeste *m*.

zigzag [ˈzɪgzæg] *vi* zigzaguer.

zinc [zɪŋk] *n* zinc *m*.

zip [zɪp] *n Br* [fastener] fermeture *f* éclair®. ○ **zip up** *vt sep* [jacket] remonter la fermeture éclair de; [bag] fermer la fermeture éclair de.

zip code *n Am* code *m* postal.

zipper [ˈzɪpər] *n Am* = zip.

zodiac [ˈzəʊdɪæk] *n*: **the ~** le zodiaque.

zone [zəʊn] *n* zone *f*.

zoo [zuː] *n* zoo *m*.

zoology [zəʊˈɒlədʒɪ] *n* zoologie *f*.

zoom [zuːm] **1** *vi inf* [move quickly] aller en trombe. **2** *n* PHOT zoom *m*.

zoom lens *n* zoom *m*.

zucchini [zuːˈkiːnɪ] (*pl inv*) *n Am* courgette *f*.